*The Old
and the New Testaments of*

The

Holy Bible

REVISED STANDARD VERSION

TRANSLATED FROM THE ORIGINAL LANGUAGES
BEING THE VERSION SET FORTH A.D. 1611
REVISED A.D. 1881–1885 AND A.D. 1901
COMPARED WITH THE MOST ANCIENT AUTHORITIES
AND REVISED A.D. 1946–1952
SECOND EDITION OF THE NEW TESTAMENT A.D. 1971

NELSON

THOMAS NELSON AND SONS LTD
36 Park Street, London W1Y 4DE
P.O. Box 18123, Nairobi, Kenya

THOMAS NELSON (AUSTRALIA) LTD
597 Little Collins Street, Melbourne 3000

THOMAS NELSON AND SONS (CANADA) LTD
81 Curlew Drive, Don Mills, Ontario

THOMAS NELSON (NIGERIA) LTD
P.O. Box 336, Apapa, Lagos

THOMAS NELSON AND SONS (SOUTH AFRICA) (PROPRIETARY) LTD
51 Commissioner Street, Johannesburg

ISBN 0 17 111006 4
0 17 437056 3 (School ed.)

Printed in the U.S.A.
for Thomas Nelson & Sons Ltd, 36 Park Street, London W1Y 4DE

PREFACE

T he Revised Standard Version of the Bible is an authorized revision of the American Standard Version, published in 1901, which was a revision of the King James Version, published in 1611.

The first English version of the Scriptures made by direct translation from the original Hebrew and Greek, and the first to be printed, was the work of William Tyndale. He met bitter opposition. He was accused of willfully perverting the meaning of the Scriptures, and his New Testaments were ordered to be burned as "untrue translations." He was finally betrayed into the hands of his enemies, and in October 1536, was publicly executed and burned at the stake.

Yet Tyndale's work became the foundation of subsequent English versions, notably those of Coverdale, 1535; Thomas Matthew (probably a pseudonym for John Rogers), 1537; the Great Bible, 1539; the Geneva Bible, 1560; and the Bishops' Bible, 1568. In 1582 a translation of the New Testament, made from the Latin Vulgate by Roman Catholic scholars, was published at Rheims.

The translators who made the King James Version took into account all of these preceding versions; and comparison shows that it owes something to each of them. It kept felicitous phrases and apt expressions, from whatever source, which had stood the test of public usage. It owed most, especially in the New Testament, to Tyndale.

The King James Version had to compete with the Geneva Bible in popular use; but in the end it prevailed, and for more than two and a half centuries no other authorized translation of the Bible into English was made. The King James Version became the "Authorized Version" of the English-speaking peoples.

The King James Version has with good reason been termed "the noblest monument of English prose." Its revisers in 1881 expressed admiration for "its simplicity, its dignity, its power, its happy turns of expression . . . the music of its cadences, and the felicities of its rhythm." It entered, as no other book has, into the making of the personal character and the public institutions of the English-speaking peoples. We owe to it an incalculable debt.

Yet the King James Version has grave defects. By the middle of the nineteenth century, the development of Biblical studies and the discovery of many manuscripts more ancient than those upon which the King James Version was based, made it manifest that these defects are so many and so serious as to call for revision of the English translation. The task was undertaken, by authority of the Church of England, in 1870. The English Revised Version of the Bible was published in 1881–1885; and the American Standard Version, its variant embodying the preferences of the American scholars associated in the work, was published in 1901.

PREFACE

Because of unhappy experience with unauthorized publications in the two decades between 1881 and 1901, which tampered with the text of the English Revised Version in the supposed interest of the American public, the American Standard Version was copyrighted, to protect the text from unauthorized changes. In 1928 this copyright was acquired by the International Council of Religious Education, and thus passed into the ownership of the churches of the United States and Canada which were associated in this Council through their boards of education and publication.

The Council appointed a committee of scholars to have charge of the text of the American Standard Version and to undertake inquiry as to whether further revision was necessary. For more than two years the Committee worked upon the problem of whether or not revision sh_juld be undertaken; and if so, what should be its nature and extent. In the end the decision was reached that there is need for a thorough revision of the version of 1901, which will stay as close to the Tyndale-King James tradition as it can in the light of our present knowledge of the Hebrew and Greek texts and their meaning on the one hand, and our present understanding of English on the other.

In 1937 the revision was authorized by vote of the Council, which directed that the resulting version should "embody the best results of modern scholarship as to the meaning of the Scriptures, and express this meaning in English diction which is designed for use in public and private worship and preserves those qualities which have given to the King James Version a supreme place in English literature."

Thirty-two scholars have served as members of the Committee charged with making the revision, and they have secured the review and counsel of an Advisory Board of fifty representatives of the co-operating denominations. The Committee has worked in two sections, one dealing with the Old Testament and one with the New Testament. Each section has submitted its work to the scrutiny of the members of the other section; and the charter of the Committee requires that all changes be agreed upon by a two-thirds vote of the total membership of the Committee. The Revised Standard Version of the New Testament was published in 1946. The publication of the Revised Standard Version of the Bible, containing the Old and New Testaments, was authorized by vote of the National Council of the Churches of Christ in the U.S.A. in 1951.

The problem of establishing the correct Hebrew and Aramaic text of the Old Testament is very different from the corresponding problem in the New Testament. For the New Testament we have a large number of Greek manuscripts, preserving many variant forms of the text. Some of them were made only two or three centuries later than the original composition of the books. For the Old Testament only late manuscripts survive, all (with the exception of the Dead Sea texts of Isaiah and Habakkuk and some fragments of other books) based on a standardized form of the text established many centuries after the books were written.

The present revision is based on the consonantal Hebrew and Aramaic text as fixed early in the Christian era and revised by·Jewish scholars (the "Masoretes") of the sixth to ninth centuries. The vowel signs, which were added by the Masoretes, are accepted also in the main, but where a more probable and convincing reading can be obtained by assuming different vowels, this has been done. No notes are given in such cases, because the vowel points are less ancient and reliable than the consonants.

Departures from the consonantal text of the best manuscripts have been made only where it seems clear that errors in copying had been made before the text was standardized. Most of the corrections adopted are based on the ancient versions (translations into Greek, Aramaic, Syriac, and Latin), which were made before the time of the Masoretic revision and therefore reflect earlier forms of the text. In every such instance a footnote specifies the version or versions from which the correction has been derived, and also gives a translation of the Masoretic Text.

Sometimes it is evident that the text has suffered in transmission, but none of the versions provides a satisfactory restoration. Here we can only follow the best judgment of competent scholars as to the most probable reconstruction of the original text. Such corrections are indicated in the footnotes by the abbreviation Cn, and a translation of the Masoretic Text is added.

The discovery of the meaning of the text, once the best readings have been established, is aided by many new resources for understanding the original languages. Much progress has been made in the historical and comparative study of these languages. A vast quantity of writings in related Semitic languages, some of them only recently discovered, has greatly enlarged our knowledge of the vocabulary and grammar of Biblical Hebrew and Aramaic. Sometimes the present translation will be found to render a Hebrew word in a sense quite different from that of the traditional interpretation. It has not been felt necessary in such cases to attach a footnote, because no change in the text is involved and it may be assumed that the new rendering was not adopted without convincing evidence. The analysis of religious texts from the ancient Near East has made clearer the significance of ideas and practices recorded in the Old Testament. Many difficulties and obscurities, of course, remain. Where the choice between two meanings is particularly difficult or doubtful, we have given an alternative rendering in a footnote. If in the judgment of the Committee the meaning of a passage is quite uncertain or obscure, either because of corruption in the text or because of the inadequacy of our present knowledge of the language, that fact is indicated by a note. It should not be assumed, however, that the Committee was entirely sure or unanimous concerning every rendering not so indicated. To record all minority views was obviously out of the question.

A major departure from the practice of the American Standard Version is the rendering of the Divine Name, the "Tetragrammaton." The American Standard Version used the term "Jehovah"; the King James Version had employed this in four places, but everywhere else, except in three cases where it was employed as part of a proper name, used the English word LORD (or in certain cases GOD) printed in capitals. The present revision returns to the procedure of the King James Version, which follows the precedent of the ancient Greek and Latin translators and the long established practice in the reading of the Hebrew scriptures in the synagogue. While it is almost if not quite certain that the Name was originally pronounced "Yahweh," this pronunciation was not indicated when the Masoretes added vowel signs to the consonantal Hebrew text. To the four consonants YHWH of the Name, which had come to be regarded as too sacred to be pronounced, they attached vowel signs indicating that in its place should be read the Hebrew word *Adonai* meaning "Lord" (or *Elohim* meaning "God"). The ancient Greek translators substituted the word *Kyrios* (Lord) for the Name. The Vulgate likewise used the Latin word *Dominus*. The form "Jehovah" is of late medieval origin; it is a combination of the consonants of the Divine Name and the vowels attached to it by the Masoretes but belonging to an entirely different word. The sound of Y is represented by J and the sound of W by V, as in Latin. For two reasons the Committee has returned to the more familiar usage of the King James Version: (1) the word "Jehovah" does not accurately represent any form of the Name ever used in Hebrew; and (2) the use of any proper name for the one and only God, as though there were other gods from whom He had to be distinguished, was discontinued in Judaism before the Christian era and is entirely inappropriate for the universal faith of the Christian Church.

The King James Version of the New Testament was based upon a Greek text that was marred by mistakes, containing the accumulated errors of fourteen centuries of manuscript copying. It was essentially the Greek text of the New Testament as edited by Beza, 1589, who closely followed that published by Erasmus, 1516–1535, which was based upon a few medieval manuscripts. The earliest and best of the eight manuscripts which Erasmus consulted was from the tenth century, and he made the least use of it because it differed most from the commonly received text; Beza had access to two manuscripts of great value, dating from the fifth and sixth centuries, but he made very little use of them because they differed from the text published by Erasmus.

We now possess many more ancient manuscripts of the New Testament, and are far better equipped to seek to recover the original wording of the Greek text. The evidence for the text of the books of the New Testament is better than for any other ancient book, both in the number of extant manuscripts and in the nearness of the date of some of these manuscripts to the date when the book was originally written.

The revisers in the 1870's had most of the evidence that we now have for the Greek text, though the most ancient of all extant manuscripts of the Greek New Testament were not discovered until 1931. But they lacked the resources which discoveries within the past eighty years have afforded for understanding the vocabulary, grammar and idioms of the Greek New Testament. An amazing body of Greek papyri has been unearthed in Egypt since the 1870's — private letters, official reports, wills, business accounts, petitions, and other such trivial, everyday recordings of the activities of human beings. In 1895 appeared the first of Adolf Deissmann's studies of these ordinary materials. He proved that many words which had hitherto been assumed to belong to what was called "Biblical Greek" were current in the spoken vernacular of the first century A.D. The New Testament was written in the Koiné, the common Greek which was spoken and understood practically everywhere throughout the Roman Empire in the early centuries of the Christian era. This development in the study of New Testament Greek has come since the work on the English Revised Version and the American Standard Version was done, and at many points sheds new light upon the meaning of the Greek text.

A major reason for revision of the King James Version, which is valid for both the Old Testament and the New Testament, is the change since 1611 in English usage. Many forms of expression have become archaic, while still generally intelligible — the use of thou, thee, thy, thine and the verb endings -est and -edst, the verb endings -eth and -th, it came to pass that, whosoever, whatsoever, insomuch that, because that, for that, unto, howbeit, peradventure, holden, aforetime, must needs, would fain, behooved, to you-ward, etc. Other words are obsolete and no longer understood by the common reader. The greatest problem, however, is presented by the English words which are still in constant use but now convey a different meaning from that which they had in 1611 and in the King James Version. These words were once accurate translations of the Hebrew and Greek Scriptures; but now, having changed in meaning, they have become misleading. They no longer say what the King James translators meant them to say. Thus, the King James Version uses the word "let" in the sense of "hinder," "prevent" to mean "precede," "allow" in the sense of "approve," "communicate" for "share," "conversation" for "conduct," "comprehend" for "overcome," "ghost" for "spirit," "wealth" for "well-being," "allege" for "prove," "demand" for "ask," "take no thought" for "be not anxious," etc.

The Revised Standard Version of the Bible, containing the Old and New Testaments, was published on September 30, 1952, and has met with wide acceptance. This preface does not undertake to set forth in detail the lines along which the revision proceeded. That is done in pamphlets entitled *An Introduction to the Revised Standard Version of the Old Testament* and *An Introduction to the Revised Standard Version of the New Testament*, written by members of the Committee and designed to help the general public to understand the main principles which have guided this comprehensive revision of the King James and American Standard versions.

These principles were reaffirmed by the Committee in 1959, in connection with a study of criticisms and suggestions from various readers. As a result, a few changes were authorized for subsequent editions, most of them corrections of punctuation, capitalization, or footnotes. Some of them are changes of words or phrases made in the interest of consistency, clarity, or accuracy of translation.

The Revised Standard Version Bible Committee is a continuing body, holding its meetings at regular intervals. It has become both ecumenical and international, with Protestant and Catholic active members, who come from Great Britain, Canada, and the United States.

PREFACE

The Second Edition of the translation of the New Testament (1971) profits from textual and linguistic studies published since the Revised Standard Version New Testament was first issued in 1946. Many proposals for modification were submitted to the Committee by individuals and by two denominational committees. All of these were given careful attention by the Committee.

Two passages, the longer ending of Mark (16.9–20) and the account of the woman taken in adultery (Jn 7.53 – 8.11), are restored to the text, separated from it by a blank space and accompanied by informative notes describing the various arrangements of the text in the ancient authorities. With new manuscript support two passages, Lk 22.19b–20 and 24.51b, are restored to the text, and one passage, Lk 22.43–44, is placed in the note, as is a phrase in Lk 12.39. Notes are added which indicate significant variations, additions, or omissions in the ancient authorities (Mt 9.34; Mk 3.16; 7.4; Lk 24.32, 51; etc.). Among the new notes are those giving the equivalence of ancient coinage with the contemporary day's or year's wages of a laborer (Mt 18.24, 28; 20.2; etc.). Some of the revisions clarify the meaning through rephrasing or reordering the text (see Mk 5.42; Lk 22.28–30; Jn 10.33; 1 Cor 3.9; 2 Cor 5.19; Heb 13.13). Even when the changes appear to be largely matters of English style, they have the purpose of presenting to the reader more adequately the meaning of the text (see Mt 10.8; 12.1; 15.29; 17.20; Lk 7.36; 11.17; 12.40; Jn 16.9; Rom 10.16; 1 Cor 12.24; 2 Cor 2.3; 3.5, 6; etc.).

The Revised Standard Version seeks to preserve all that is best in the English Bible as it has been known and used through the years. It is intended for use in public and private worship, not merely for reading and instruction. We have resisted the temptation to use phrases that are merely current usage, and have sought to put the message of the Bible in simple, enduring words that are worthy to stand in the great Tyndale-King James tradition. We are glad to say, with the King James translators: "Truly (good Christian Reader) we never thought from the beginning, that we should need to make a new Translation, nor yet to make of a bad one a good one . . . but to make a good one better."

The Bible is more than a historical document to be preserved. And it is more than a classic of English literature to be cherished and admired. It is a record of God's dealing with men, of God's revelation of Himself and His will. It records the life and work of Him in whom the Word of God became flesh and dwelt among men. The Bible carries its full message, not to those who regard it simply as a heritage of the past or praise its literary style, but to those who read it that they may discern and understand God's Word to men. That Word must not be disguised in phrases that are no longer clear, or hidden under words that have changed or lost their meaning. It must stand forth in language that is direct and plain and meaningful to people today. It is our hope and our earnest prayer that this Revised Standard Version of the Bible may be used by God to speak to men in these momentous times, and to help them to understand and believe and obey His Word.

The Names and Order of the
BOOKS OF THE OLD TESTAMENT

Abbreviations

In the notes to the books of the Old Testament, the following abbreviations are used: Ms for manuscript; Mss for manuscripts; Heb denotes the Hebrew of the consonantal Masoretic Text of the Old Testament; and MT denotes the Hebrew of the pointed Masoretic Text of the Old Testament.

The ancient versions of the Old Testament are indicated by:

Gk   Septuagint, Greek Version of Old Testament
Sam   Samaritan Hebrew text of Old Testament
Syr   Syriac Version of Old Testament
Tg   Targum
Vg   Vulgate, Latin Version of Old Testament

Cn indicates a correction made where the text has suffered in transmission and the versions provide no satisfactory restoration but the Committee agrees with the judgment of competent scholars as to the most probable reconstruction of the original text. The reader is referred to the Preface for a statement of policy concerning text and notes.

Abbreviations

References to quoted and parallel passages are given following the notes on pages where these are relevant. The following abbreviations are used for the books of the Bible:

THE OLD TESTAMENT

Gen	Genesis	Eccles	Ecclesiastes
Ex	Exodus	Song	Song of Solomon
Lev	Leviticus	Is	Isaiah
Num	Numbers	Jer	Jeremiah
Deut	Deuteronomy	Lam	Lamentations
Josh	Joshua	Ezek	Ezekiel
Judg	Judges	Dan	Daniel
Ruth	Ruth	Hos	Hosea
1 Sam	1 Samuel	Joel	Joel
2 Sam	2 Samuel	Amos	Amos
1 Kings	1 Kings	Obad	Obadiah
2 Kings	2 Kings	Jon	Jonah
1 Chron	1 Chronicles	Mic	Micah
2 Chron	2 Chronicles	Nahum	Nahum
Ezra	Ezra	Hab	Habakkuk
Neh	Nehemiah	Zeph	Zephaniah
Esther	Esther	Hag	Haggai
Job	Job	Zech	Zechariah
Ps	Psalms	Mal	Malachi
Prov	Proverbs		

THE NEW TESTAMENT

Mt	Matthew	1 Tim	1 Timothy
Mk	Mark	2 Tim	2 Timothy
Lk	Luke	Tit	Titus
Jn	John	Philem	Philemon
Acts	Acts of the Apostles	Heb	Hebrews
Rom	Romans	Jas	James
1 Cor	1 Corinthians	1 Pet	1 Peter
2 Cor	2 Corinthians	2 Pet	2 Peter
Gal	Galatians	1 Jn	1 John
Eph	Ephesians	2 Jn	2 John
Phil	Philippians	3 Jn	3 John
Col	Colossians	Jude	Jude
1 Thess	1 Thessalonians	Rev	Revelation
2 Thess	2 Thessalonians		

Key to Pronunciation
of Proper Names

The reader will find that the pronunciation scheme presented in this edition of the Revised Standard Version of the Holy Bible is a practical help in reading and pronouncing the more unfamiliar personal and geographic names. Retaining the text spelling, an easily used system of diacritical marks indicates to the reader the pronunciation, the syllabic division, and the word stress of all except a small number of such names. This latter group includes personal and place names which have become familiar through everyday modern English usage. Such personal names as Adam, Daniel, and Martha, and place names as Bethlehem, Euphrates, and Nile, are typical examples of such anglicized words and are to be pronounced as they are used in current English speech. The key to the symbols used:

VOWELS AND DIPHTHONGS

à	as in watch	ē	as in herd	ŏ	as in odd
ä	" " calm	ĕ	" " get	ô	" " order
ã	" " dart	ē	" " key	ō	" " cope
ă	" " sat	ę	" " sicken	ǫ	" " melon
â	" " dare	ēi	" " receive	oi	" " toil
ā	" " gate	ī	" " ice	ŭ	" " fuss
ą	" " above	ĭ	" " third	ū	" " curd
aă	" " ram	ĭ	" " hit	ü	" " rule
āi	" " pail	į	" " charity	ū	" " use
aī	" " aisle	iă	" " yam	ȳ	" " type
au	" " author	iŏ	" " yonder	y̆	" " lynch

CONSONANTS

c as in clean
ç " " ceiling
g " " game
ġ " " gentle
s " " sail
ş " " rose (z)
x " " x-ray (eks)
x̱ " " xylophone (z)

The following letters are unmarked and are to be pronounced with their normal English sounds:

b, d, f, h, j, k, l, m, n, p, r, t, v, w, z.

ch as in ache (k)
ph " " phone (f)
th " " thick

For some widely used names, as the reader undoubtedly is aware, more than one acceptable pronunciation may be heard; however, in this edition of the Holy Bible but one such standard pronunciation is recorded.

KEY TO PRONUNCIATION

It can also be noted that certain Biblical names have become generic terms in English with a secondary or derived meaning which becomes reflected in its pronunciation. Philistine is a good example; Phĭ·lĭs′tĭnes, Phĭ′lĭs·tĭnes, Phĭ′lĭs·tĭnes, phĭ′lĭs·tĭ(ĭ=ē)nes; the first, the name of the ancient people of Philistia; the second, a widely used variant; the third, originally British in origin; and the last the generic modern term.

It will also be observed that the letter sounds represented by ạ, ẹ, ị, ọ, and ụ are the unstressed vowels of normal English speech. When these same sounds are influenced by a following letter "r" they are marked as ä, ë, ï, ö, and ü, as shown in the familiar illustrative key words.

The word accent or stress in English follows a pattern different from that of other languages both classical and modern. By noting the stressed syllable, indicated by (′) for primary stress and (″) for secondary stress, most of the names are pronounced without any difficulty in reading running text.

When pronunciation for proper names is indicated in the text, the first time a given word is used in a verse the pronunciation is shown, but on its subsequent appearance in the same verse, the pronunciation is not repeated.

The
Old Testament

The First Book of Moses
Commonly Called
Genesis

1 In the beginning God created*a* the heavens and the earth. ²The earth was without form and void, and darkness was upon the face of the deep; and the Spirit*b* of God was moving over the face of the waters.

3 And God said, "Let there be light"; and there was light. ⁴And God saw that the light was good; and God separated the light from the darkness. ⁵God called the light Day, and the darkness he called Night. And there was evening and there was morning, one day.

6 And God said, "Let there be a firmament in the midst of the waters, and let it separate the waters from the waters." ⁷And God made the firmament and separated the waters which were under the firmament from the waters which were above the firmament. And it was so. ⁸And God called the firmament Heaven. And there was evening and there was morning, a second day.

9 And God said, "Let the waters under the heavens be gathered together into one place, and let the dry land appear." And it was so. ¹⁰God called the dry land Earth, and the waters that were gathered together he called Seas. And God saw that it was good. ¹¹And God said, "Let the earth put forth vegetation, plants yielding seed, and fruit trees bearing fruit in which is their seed, each according to its kind, upon the earth." And it was so. ¹²The earth brought forth vegetation, plants yielding seed according to their own kinds, and trees bearing fruit in which is their seed, each according to its kind. And God saw that it was good. ¹³And there was evening and there was morning, a third day.

14 And God said, "Let there be lights in the firmament of the heavens to separate the day from the night; and let them be for signs and for seasons and for days and years, ¹⁵and let them be lights in the firmament of the heavens to give light upon the earth." And it was so. ¹⁶And God made the two great lights, the greater light to rule the day, and the lesser light to rule the night; he made the stars also. ¹⁷And God set them in the firmament of the heavens to give light upon the earth, ¹⁸to rule over the day and over the night, and to separate the light from the darkness. And God saw that it was good. ¹⁹And there was evening and there was morning, a fourth day.

20 And God said, "Let the waters bring forth swarms of living creatures, and let birds fly above the earth across the firmament of the heavens." ²¹So God created the great sea monsters and every living creature that moves, with which the waters swarm, according to their kinds, and every winged bird according to its kind. And God saw that it was good. ²²And God blessed them, saying, "Be fruitful and multiply and fill the waters in the seas, and let birds multiply on the earth." ²³And there was evening and there was morning, a fifth day.

24 And God said, "Let the earth bring forth living creatures according to their kinds: cattle and creeping things and beasts of the earth according to their kinds." And it was so. ²⁵And God made the beasts of the earth according to their kinds and the cattle according to their kinds, and everything that creeps upon the ground according to its kind. And God saw that it was good.

26 Then God said, "Let us make man in our image, after our likeness; and let them have dominion over the fish of the sea, and over the birds of the air, and over the cattle, and over all the earth, and over every creeping thing that creeps upon the earth." ²⁷So God created man in his own image, in the image of God he created him; male and female he created

*a*Or *When God began to create*   *b*Or *wind*
1.1: Jn 1.1.
1.26, 27: Gen 5.1; Mt 19.4; Mk 10.6; Col 3.10; Jas 3.9.

them. ²⁸And God blessed them, and God said to them, "Be fruitful and multiply, and fill the earth and subdue it; and have dominion over the fish of the sea and over the birds of the air and over every living thing that moves upon the earth." ²⁹And God said, "Behold, I have given you every plant yielding seed which is upon the face of all the earth, and every tree with seed in its fruit; you shall have them for food. ³⁰And to every beast of the earth, and to every bird of the air, and to everything that creeps on the earth, everything that has the breath of life, I have given every green plant for food." And it was so. ³¹And God saw everything that he had made, and behold, it was very good. And there was evening and there was morning, a sixth day.

2 Thus the heavens and the earth were finished, and all the host of them. ²And on the seventh day God finished his work which he had done, and he rested on the seventh day from all his work which he had done. ³So God blessed the seventh day and hallowed it, because on it God rested from all his work which he had done in creation.

4 These are the generations of the heavens and the earth when they were created.

In the day that the Lord God made the earth and the heavens, ⁵when no plant of the field was yet in the earth and no herb of the field had yet sprung up—for the Lord God had not caused it to rain upon the earth, and there was no man to till the ground; ⁶but a mist^c went up from the earth and watered the whole face of the ground—⁷then the Lord God formed man of dust from the ground, and breathed into his nostrils the breath of life; and man became a living being. ⁸And the Lord God planted a garden in Eden, in the east; and there he put the man whom he had formed. ⁹And out of the ground the Lord God made to grow every tree that is pleasant to the sight and good for food, the tree of life also in the midst of the garden, and the tree of the knowledge of good and evil.

10 A river flowed out of Eden to water the garden, and there it divided and became four rivers. ¹¹The name of the first is Pī'shŏn; it is the one which flows around the whole land of Hăv'-

ĭ-lah, where there is gold; ¹²and the gold of that land is good; bdellium and onyx stone are there. ¹³The name of the second river is Gī'hŏn; it is the one which flows around the whole land of Cüsh. ¹⁴And the name of the third river is Tigris, which flows east of Assyria. And the fourth river is the Euphrates.

15 The Lord God took the man and put him in the garden of Eden to till it and keep it. ¹⁶And the Lord God commanded the man, saying, "You may freely eat of every tree of the garden; ¹⁷but of the tree of the knowledge of good and evil you shall not eat, for in the day that you eat of it you shall die."

18 Then the Lord God said, "It is not good that the man should be alone; I will make him a helper fit for him." ¹⁹So out of the ground the Lord God formed every beast of the field and every bird of the air, and brought them to the man to see what he would call them; and whatever the man called every living creature, that was its name. ²⁰The man gave names to all cattle, and to the birds of the air, and to every beast of the field; but for the man there was not found a helper fit for him. ²¹So the Lord God caused a deep sleep to fall upon the man, and while he slept took one of his ribs and closed up its place with flesh; ²²and the rib which the Lord God had taken from the man he made into a woman and brought her to the man. ²³Then the man said,

"This at last is bone of my bones
    and flesh of my flesh;
she shall be called Woman,^d
    because she was taken out of
    Man."^e

²⁴Therefore a man leaves his father and his mother and cleaves to his wife, and they become one flesh. ²⁵And the man and his wife were both naked, and were not ashamed.

3 Now the serpent was more subtle than any other wild creature that the Lord God had made. He said to the woman, "Did God say, 'You shall not eat of any tree of the garden'?" ²And the woman said to the serpent, "We may eat of the fruit of the trees of the garden; ³but God said, 'You shall

^cOr *flood* ^dHeb *ishshah* ^eHeb *ish*
2.1-3: Ex 20.11.   2.2: Heb 4.4, 10.   2.7: 1 Cor 15.45, 47.
2.9: Rev 2.7; 22.2, 14, 19.
2.24: Mt 19.5; Mk 10.7; 1 Cor 6.16; Eph 5.31.
3.1: Rev 12.9; 20.2.

not eat of the fruit of the tree which is in the midst of the garden, neither shall you touch it, lest you die.' " ⁴But the serpent said to the woman, "You will not die. ⁵For God knows that when you eat of it your eyes will be opened, - and you will be like God, knowing good and evil." ⁶So when the woman saw that the tree was good for food, and that it was a delight to the eyes, and that the tree was to be desired to make one wise, she took of its fruit and ate; and she also gave some to her husband, and he ate. ⁷Then the eyes of both were opened, and they knew that they were naked; and they sewed fig leaves together and made themselves aprons.

8 And they heard the sound of the LORD God walking in the garden in the cool of the day, and the man and his wife hid themselves from the presence of the LORD God among the trees of the garden. ⁹But the LORD God called to the man, and said to him, "Where are you?" ¹⁰And he said, "I heard the sound of thee in the garden, and I was afraid, because I was naked; and I hid myself." ¹¹He said, "Who told you that you were naked? Have you eaten of the tree of which I commanded you not to eat?" ¹²The man said, "The woman whom thou gavest to be with me, she gave me fruit of the tree, and I ate." ¹³Then the LORD God said to the woman, "What is this that you have done?" The woman said, "The serpent beguiled me, and I ate." ¹⁴The LORD God said to the serpent,
"Because you have done this,
　cursed are you above all cattle,
　and above all wild animals;
upon your belly you shall go,
　and dust you shall eat
　all the days of your life.
¹⁵I will put enmity between you and the woman,
　and between your seed and her seed;
he shall bruise your head,
　and you shall bruise his heel."
¹⁶To the woman he said,
"I will greatly multiply your pain in childbearing;
　in pain you shall bring forth children,
yet your desire shall be for your husband,
　and he shall rule over you."
¹⁷And to Adam he said,

"Because you have listened to the voice of your wife,
　and have eaten of the tree
of which I commanded you,
　'You shall not eat of it,'
cursed is the ground because of you;
　in toil you shall eat of it all the days of your life;
¹⁸thorns and thistles it shall bring forth to you;
　and you shall eat the plants of the field.
¹⁹In the sweat of your face
　you shall eat bread
till you return to the ground,
　for out of it you were taken;
you are dust,
　and to dust you shall return."
20 The man called his wife's name Eve,ᶠ because she was the mother of all living. ²¹And the LORD God made for Adam and for his wife garments of skins, and clothed them.

22 Then the LORD God said, "Behold, the man has become like one of us, knowing good and evil; and now, lest he put forth his hand and take also of the tree of life, and eat, and live for ever"—²³therefore the LORD God sent him forth from the garden of Eden, to till the ground from which he was taken. ²⁴He drove out the man; and at the east of the garden of Eden he placed the cherubim, and a flaming sword which turned every way, to guard the way to the tree of life.

4 Now Adam knew Eve his wife, and she conceived and bore Cain, saying, "I have gottenᵍ a man with the help of the LORD." ²And again, she bore his brother Abel. Now Abel was a keeper of sheep, and Cain a tiller of the ground. ³In the course of time Cain brought to the LORD an offering of the fruit of the ground, ⁴and Abel brought of the firstlings of his flock and of their fat portions. And the LORD had regard for Abel and his offering, ⁵but for Cain and his offering he had no regard. So Cain was very angry, and his countenance fell. ⁶The LORD said to Cain, "Why are you angry, and why has your countenance fallen? ⁷If you do well, will you not be accepted? And if you do not do well, sin is couching at the door; its desire is for you, but you must master it."

ᶠThe name in Hebrew resembles the word for *living*
ᵍHeb *qanah*, get　**3.4:** 2 Cor 11.3.　**3.13:** 2 Cor 11.3.
3.14, 15: Rev 12.9; 20.2.　**3.17, 18:** Heb 6.8.
3.22, 24: Rev 2.7; 22.2, 14, 19.　**4.4:** Heb 11.4.

8 Cain said to Abel his brother, "Let us go out to the field."[h] And when they were in the field, Cain rose up against his brother Abel, and killed him. ⁹Then the LORD said to Cain, "Where is Abel your brother?" He said, "I do not know; am I my brother's keeper?" ¹⁰And the LORD said, "What have you done? The voice of your brother's blood is crying to me from the ground. ¹¹And now you are cursed from the ground, which has opened its mouth to receive your brother's blood from your hand. ¹²When you till the ground, it shall no longer yield to you its strength; you shall be a fugitive and a wanderer on the earth." ¹³Cain said to the LORD, "My punishment is greater than I can bear. ¹⁴Behold, thou hast driven me this day away from the ground; and from thy face I shall be hidden; and I shall be a fugitive and a wanderer on the earth, and whoever finds me will slay me." ¹⁵Then the LORD said to him, "Not so![i] If any one slays Cain, vengeance shall be taken on him sevenfold." And the LORD put a mark on Cain, lest any who came upon him should kill him. ¹⁶Then Cain went away from the presence of the LORD, and dwelt in the land of Nŏd,[j] east of Eden.

17 Cain knew his wife, and she conceived and bore Ē'nŏch; and he built a city, and called the name of the city after the name of his son, Enoch. ¹⁸To Ē'nŏch was born Ī'răd; and Irad was the father of Mĕ·hū'ja–ĕl, and Mehuja–el the father of Mĕ·thü'sha–ĕl, and Methusha–el the father of Lā'mĕch. ¹⁹And Lā'mĕch took two wives; the name of the one was Ā'dah, and the name of the other Zĭl'lah. ²⁰Ā'dah bore Jā'bal; he was the father of those who dwell in tents and have cattle. ²¹His brother's name was Jü'bal; he was the father of all those who play the lyre and pipe. ²²Zĭl'lah bore Tü'bal–cāin; he was the forger of all instruments of bronze and iron. The sister of Tubal–cain was Nā'a·mah.

23 Lā'mĕch said to his wives:
"Ā'dah and Zĭl'lah, hear my voice;
    you wives of Lamech, hearken
        to what I say:
I have slain a man for wounding me,
    a young man for striking me.
²⁴If Cain is avenged sevenfold,
    truly Lā'mĕch seventy-seven-
        fold."

25 And Adam knew his wife again, and she bore a son and called his name Seth, for she said, "God has appointed for me another child instead of Abel, for Cain slew him." ²⁶To Seth also a son was born, and he called his name Ē'nŏsh. At that time men began to call upon the name of the LORD.

5 This is the book of the generations of Adam. When God created man, he made him in the likeness of God. ²Male and female he created them, and he blessed them and named them Man when they were created. ³When Adam had lived a hundred and thirty years, he became the father of a son in his own likeness, after his image, and named him Seth. ⁴The days of Adam after he became the father of Seth were eight hundred years; and he had other sons and daughters. ⁵Thus all the days that Adam lived were nine hundred and thirty years; and he died.

6 When Seth had lived a hundred and five years, he became the father of Ē'nŏsh. ⁷Seth lived after the birth of Ē'nŏsh eight hundred and seven years, and had other sons and daughters. ⁸Thus all the days of Seth were nine hundred and twelve years; and he died.

9 When Ē'nŏsh had lived ninety years, he became the father of Kē'nan. ¹⁰Ē'nŏsh lived after the birth of Kē'nan eight hundred and fifteen years, and had other sons and daughters. ¹¹Thus all the days of Ē'nŏsh were nine hundred and five years; and he died.

12 When Kē'nan had lived seventy years, he became the father of Mă–hăl'a·lĕl. ¹³Kē'nan lived after the birth of Mă–hăl'a·lĕl eight hundred and forty years, and had other sons and daughters. ¹⁴Thus all the days of Kē'nan were nine hundred and ten years; and he died.

15 When Mă–hăl'a·lĕl had lived sixty-five years, he became the father of Jăr'ĕd. ¹⁶Mă–hăl'a·lĕl lived after the birth of Jăr'ĕd eight hundred and thirty years, and had other sons and daughters. ¹⁷Thus all the days of Mă–hăl'a·lĕl were eight hundred and ninety-five years; and he died.

18 When Jăr'ĕd had lived a hundred

*Sam Gk Syr Compare Vg: Heb lacks *Let us go out to the field* *Gk Syr Vg: Heb *Therefore* *That is *Wandering*
4.8: 1 Jn 3.12. **5.1:** Gen 1.27.

and sixty-two years he became the father of Ē'nŏch. ¹⁹Jăr'ĕd lived after the birth of Ē'nŏch eight hundred years, and had other sons and daughters. ²⁰Thus all the days of Jăr'ĕd were nine hundred and sixty-two years; and he died.

21 When Ē'nŏch had lived sixty-five years, he became the father of Mĕ·thü'sĕ·lah. ²²Ē'nŏch walked with God after the birth of Mĕ·thü'sĕ·lah three hundred years, and had other sons and daughters. ²³Thus all the days of Ē'nŏch were three hundred and sixty-five years. ²⁴Ē'nŏch walked with God; and he was not, for God took him.

25 When Mĕ·thü'sĕ·lah had lived a hundred and eighty-seven years, he became the father of Lā'mĕch. ²⁶Mĕ·thü'sĕ·lah lived after the birth of Lā'mĕch seven hundred and eighty-two years, and had other sons and daughters. ²⁷Thus all the days of Mĕ·thü'sĕ·lah were nine hundred and sixty-nine years; and he died.

28 When Lā'mĕch had lived a hundred and eighty-two years, he became the father of a son, ²⁹and called his name Noah, saying, "Out of the ground which the LORD has cursed this one shall bring us relief from our work and from the toil of our hands." ³⁰Lā'mĕch lived after the birth of Noah five hundred and ninety-five years, and had other sons and daughters. ³¹Thus all the days of Lā'mĕch were seven hundred and seventy-seven years; and he died.

32 After Noah was five hundred years old, Noah became the father of Shĕm, Ham, and Jā'phĕth.

6 When men began to multiply on the face of the ground, and daughters were born to them, ²the sons of God saw that the daughters of men were fair; and they took to wife such of them as they chose. ³Then the LORD said, "My spirit shall not abide in man for ever, for he is flesh, but his days shall be a hundred and twenty years." ⁴The Nĕph'ĭ·lĭm were on the earth in those days, and also afterward, when the sons of God came in to the daughters of men, and they bore children to them. These were the mighty men that were of old, the men of renown.

5 The LORD saw that the wickedness of man was great in the earth, and that every imagination of the thoughts of his heart was only evil continually. ⁶And the LORD was sorry that he had made man on the earth, and it grieved him to his heart. ⁷So the LORD said, "I will blot out man whom I have created from the face of the ground, man and beast and creeping things and birds of the air, for I am sorry that I have made them." ⁸But Noah found favor in the eyes of the LORD.

9 These are the generations of Noah. Noah was a righteous man, blameless in his generation; Noah walked with God. ¹⁰And Noah had three sons, Shĕm, Ham, and Jā'phĕth.

11 Now the earth was corrupt in God's sight, and the earth was filled with violence. ¹²And God saw the earth, and behold, it was corrupt; for all flesh had corrupted their way upon the earth. ¹³And God said to Noah, "I have determined to make an end of all flesh; for the earth is filled with violence through them; behold, I will destroy them with the earth. ¹⁴Make yourself an ark of gopher wood; make rooms in the ark, and cover it inside and out with pitch. ¹⁵This is how you are to make it: the length of the ark three hundred cubits, its breadth fifty cubits, and its height thirty cubits. ¹⁶Make a roof*ᵏ* for the ark, and finish it to a cubit above; and set the door of the ark in its side; make it with lower, second, and third decks. ¹⁷For behold, I will bring a flood of waters upon the earth, to destroy all flesh in which is the breath of life from under heaven; everything that is on the earth shall die. ¹⁸But I will establish my covenant with you; and you shall come into the ark, you, your sons, your wife, and your sons' wives with you. ¹⁹And of every living thing of all flesh, you shall bring two of every sort into the ark, to keep them alive with you; they shall be male and female. ²⁰Of the birds according to their kinds, and of the animals according to their kinds, of every creeping thing of the ground according to its kind, two of every sort shall come in to you, to keep them alive. ²¹Also take with you every sort of food that is eaten, and store it up; and it shall serve as food for you and for them." ²²Noah did this; he did all that God commanded him.

ᵏOr *window*
5.24: Heb 11.5.   6.4: Num 13.33.

7 Then the LORD said to Noah, "Go into the ark, you and all your household, for I have seen that you are righteous before me in this generation. ²Take with you seven pairs of all clean animals, the male and his mate; and a pair of the animals that are not clean, the male and his mate; ³and seven pairs of the birds of the air also, male and female, to keep their kind alive upon the face of all the earth. ⁴For in seven days I will send rain upon the earth forty days and forty nights; and every living thing that I have made I will blot out from the face of the ground." ⁵And Noah did all that the LORD had commanded him.

6 Noah was six hundred years old when the flood of waters came upon the earth. ⁷And Noah and his sons and his wife and his sons' wives with him went into the ark, to escape the waters of the flood. ⁸Of clean animals, and of animals that are not clean, and of birds, and of everything that creeps on the ground, ⁹two and two, male and female, went into the ark with Noah, as God had commanded Noah. ¹⁰And after seven days the waters of the flood came upon the earth.

11 In the six hundredth year of Noah's life, in the second month, on the seventeenth day of the month, on that day all the fountains of the great deep burst forth, and the windows of the heavens were opened. ¹²And rain fell upon the earth forty days and forty nights. ¹³On the very same day Noah and his sons, Shĕm and Ham and Jā'phĕth, and Noah's wife and the three wives of his sons with them entered the ark, ¹⁴they and every beast according to its kind, and all the cattle according to their kinds, and every creeping thing that creeps on the earth according to its kind, and every bird according to its kind, every bird of every sort. ¹⁵They went into the ark with Noah, two and two of all flesh in which there was the breath of life. ¹⁶And they that entered, male and female of all flesh, went in as God had commanded him; and the LORD shut him in.

17 The flood continued forty days upon the earth; and the waters increased, and bore up the ark, and it rose high above the earth. ¹⁸The waters prevailed and increased greatly upon the earth; and the ark floated on the face of the waters. ¹⁹And the waters prevailed so mightily upon the earth that all the high mountains under the whole heaven were covered; ²⁰the waters prevailed above the mountains, covering them fifteen cubits deep. ²¹And all flesh died that moved upon the earth, birds, cattle, beasts, all swarming creatures that swarm upon the earth, and every man; ²²everything on the dry land in whose nostrils was the breath of life died. ²³He blotted out every living thing that was upon the face of the ground, man and animals and creeping things and birds of the air; they were blotted out from the earth. Only Noah was left, and those that were with him in the ark. ²⁴And the waters prevailed upon the earth a hundred and fifty days.

8 But God remembered Noah and all the beasts and all the cattle that were with him in the ark. And God made a wind blow over the earth, and the waters subsided; ²the fountains of the deep and the windows of the heavens were closed, the rain from the heavens was restrained, ³and the waters receded from the earth continually. At the end of a hundred and fifty days the waters had abated; ⁴and in the seventh month, on the seventeenth day of the month, the ark came to rest upon the mountains of Ăr'a̧·răt. ⁵And the waters continued to abate until the tenth month; in the tenth month, on the first day of the month, the tops of the mountains were seen.

6 At the end of forty days Noah opened the window of the ark which he had made, ⁷and sent forth a raven; and it went to and fro until the waters were dried up from the earth. ⁸Then he sent forth a dove from him, to see if the waters had subsided from the face of the ground; ⁹but the dove found no place to set her foot, and she returned to him to the ark, for the waters were still on the face of the whole earth. So he put forth his hand and took her and brought her into the ark with him. ¹⁰He waited another seven days, and again he sent forth the dove out of the ark; ¹¹and the dove came back to him in the evening, and lo, in her mouth a freshly plucked olive leaf; so Noah knew that the waters had subsided from the earth. ¹²Then he

7.7: Mt 24.38; Lk 17.27.

waited another seven days, and sent forth the dove; and she did not return to him any more.

13 In the six hundred and first year, in the first month, the first day of the month, the waters were dried from off the earth; and Noah removed the covering of the ark, and looked, and behold, the face of the ground was dry. ¹⁴ In the second month, on the twenty-seventh day of the month, the earth was dry. ¹⁵ Then God said to Noah, ¹⁶ "Go forth from the ark, you and your wife, and your sons and your sons' wives with you. ¹⁷ Bring forth with you every living thing that is with you of all flesh — birds and animals and every creeping thing that creeps on the earth — that they may breed abundantly on the earth, and be fruitful and multiply upon the earth." ¹⁸ So Noah went forth, and his sons and his wife and his sons' wives with him. ¹⁹ And every beast, every creeping thing, and every bird, everything that moves upon the earth, went forth by families out of the ark.

20 Then Noah built an altar to the LORD, and took of every clean animal and of every clean bird, and offered burnt offerings on the altar. ²¹ And when the LORD smelled the pleasing odor, the LORD said in his heart, "I will never again curse the ground because of man, for the imagination of man's heart is evil from his youth; neither will I ever again destroy every living creature as I have done. ²² While the earth remains, seedtime and harvest, cold and heat, summer and winter, day and night, shall not cease."

9 And God blessed Noah and his sons, and said to them, "Be fruitful and multiply, and fill the earth. ²The fear of you and the dread of you shall be upon every beast of the earth, and upon every bird of the air, upon everything that creeps on the ground and all the fish of the sea; into your hand they are delivered. ³Every moving thing that lives shall be food for you; and as I gave you the green plants, I give you everything. ⁴Only you shall not eat flesh with its life, that is, its blood. ⁵For your lifeblood I will surely require a reckoning; of every beast I will require it and of man; of every man's brother I will require the life of man. ⁶Whoever sheds the blood of man, by man shall his blood be shed; for God made man in his own image.

⁷And you, be fruitful and multiply, bring forth abundantly on the earth and multiply in it."

8 Then God said to Noah and to his sons with him, ⁹ "Behold, I establish my covenant with you and your descendants after you, ¹⁰ and with every living creature that is with you, the birds, the cattle, and every beast of the earth with you, as many as came out of the ark.ⁱ ¹¹ I establish my covenant with you, that never again shall all flesh be cut off by the waters of a flood, and never again shall there be a flood to destroy the earth." ¹²And God said, "This is the sign of the covenant which I make between me and you and every living creature that is with you, for all future generations: ¹³ I set my bow in the cloud, and it shall be a sign of the covenant between me and the earth. ¹⁴When I bring clouds over the earth and the bow is seen in the clouds, ¹⁵ I will remember my covenant which is between me and you and every living creature of all flesh; and the waters shall never again become a flood to destroy all flesh. ¹⁶When the bow is in the clouds, I will look upon it and remember the everlasting covenant between God and every living creature of all flesh that is upon the earth." ¹⁷God said to Noah, "This is the sign of the covenant which I have established between me and all flesh that is upon the earth."

18 The sons of Noah who went forth from the ark were Shĕm, Ham, and Jā′phĕth. Ham was the father of Canaan. ¹⁹These three were the sons of Noah; and from these the whole earth was peopled.

20 Noah was the first tiller of the soil. He planted a vineyard; ²¹ and he drank of the wine, and became drunk, and lay uncovered in his tent. ²²And Ham, the father of Canaan, saw the nakedness of his father, and told his two brothers outside. ²³Then Shĕm and Jā′phĕth took a garment, laid it upon both their shoulders, and walked backward and covered the nakedness of their father; their faces were turned away, and they did not see their father's nakedness. ²⁴When Noah awoke from his wine and knew what his youngest son had done to him, ²⁵ he said,

---

ⁱGk: Heb repeats *every beast of the earth*
9.4: Lev 7.26, 27; 17.10-14; Deut 12.16, 23.

"Cursed be Canaan;
a slave of slaves shall he be to his
brothers."
26 He also said,
"Blessed by the LORD my God be
Shĕm;[m]
and let Canaan be his slave.
27 God enlarge Jā'phĕth,
and let him dwell in the tents of
Shĕm;
and let Canaan be his slave."
28 After the flood Noah lived three
hundred and fifty years. 29 All the days
of Noah were nine hundred and fifty
years; and he died.

10 These are the generations of
the sons of Noah, Shĕm, Ham,
and Jā'phĕth; sons were born to them
after the flood.
2 The sons of Jā'phĕth: Gō'mẹr,
Mā'gŏg, Mā'daī, Jā'van, Tü'bạl, Mĕ'-
shĕch, and Tī'ras. 3 The sons of Gō'mẹr:
Ăsh'kẹ·năz, Rī'phạth, and Tō·gär'-
mạh. 4 The sons of Jā'van: Ĕ·lī'shạh,
Tär·shĭsh, Kĭt'tĭm, and Dō'dạ·nĭm.
5 From these the coastland peoples
spread. These are the sons of Jā'phĕth[n]
in their lands, each with his own language, by their families, in their
nations.
6 The sons of Ham: Cŭsh, Egypt,
Püt, and Canaan. 7 The sons of Cŭsh:
Sē'bạ, Hăv'ĭ·lạh, Săb'tạh, Rā'ạ·mạh,
and Săb'tẹ·cạ. The sons of Raamah:
Shē'bạ and Dē'dăn. 8 Cŭsh became the
father of Nĭm'rŏd; he was the first on
earth to be a mighty man. 9 He was a
mighty hunter before the LORD; therefore it is said, "Like Nĭm'rŏd a mighty
hunter before the LORD." 10 The beginning of his kingdom was Bā'bẹl,
Ĕ'rĕch, and Ăc'căd, all of them in the
land of Shī'när. 11 From that land he
went into Assyria, and built Nĭn'-
ẹ·vĕh, Rĕ·hō'bŏth–Ĭr, Cā'lạh, and
12 Rē'sẹn between Nĭn'ẹ·vĕh and Cā'-
lạh; that is the great city. 13 Egypt became the father of Lü'dĭm, Ăn'ạ·mĭm,
Lĕ·hā'bĭm, Năph'tü·hĭm, 14 Păth·rü'-
sĭm, Căs·lü'hĭm (whence came the
Phĭ·lĭs'tīnes), and Căph'tọ·rĭm.
15 Canaan became the father of
Sī'dŏn his first-born, and Hĕth, 16 and
the Jĕb'ū·sītes, the Ăm'ọ·rītes, the
Gĭr'gạ·shītes, 17 the Hī'vītes, the
Ärk'ītes, the Sī'nītes, 18 the Är'vạ·dītes,
the Zĕm'ạ·rītes, and the Hā'mạ·thītes.
Afterward the families of the Canaanites spread abroad. 19 And the territory
of the Canaanites extended from

Sī'dŏn, in the direction of Gē'rär, as
far as Gā'zạ, and in the direction of
Sŏd'ọm, Gọ·môr'rạh, Ăd'mạh, and
Zĕ·boi'ĭm, as far as Lā'shạ. 20 These
are the sons of Ham, by their families,
their languages, their lands, and their
nations.
21 To Shĕm also, the father of all
the children of Ē'bẹr, the elder brother
of Jā'phĕth, children were born. 22 The
sons of Shĕm: Ē'lăm, Ăṣ'shŭr, Är-
păch'shăd, Lüd, and Ăr'ăm. 23 The
sons of Är'ăm: Ŭz, Hül, Gē'thẹr, and
Măsh. 24 Är·păch'shăd became the
father of Shē'lạh; and Shelah became
the father of Ē'bẹr. 25 To Ē'bẹr were
born two sons: the name of the one
was Pē'lẹg,[o] for in his days the earth
was divided, and his brother's name
was Jŏk'tăn. 26 Jŏk'tăn became the
father of Ăl·mō'dăd, Shē'lĕph, Hā'-
zär·mā'vĕth, Jē'rạh, 27 Hạ·dôr'ạm,
Ū'zạl, Dĭk'lạh, 28 Ō'bạl, A·bĭm'ạ–ĕl,
Shē'bạ, 29 Ō'phĭr, Hăv'ĭ·lạh, and Jō'-
băb; all these were the sons of Jŏk'tăn.
30 The territory in which they lived
extended from Mē'shạ in the direction
of Sē'phär to the hill country of the east.
31 These are the sons of Shĕm, by their
families, their languages, their lands,
and their nations.
32 These are the families of the sons
of Noah, according to their genealogies, in their nations; and from these
the nations spread abroad on the earth
after the flood.

11 Now the whole earth had one
language and few words. 2 And
as men migrated from the east, they
found a plain in the land of Shī'när,
and settled there. 3 And they said to
one another, "Come, let us make
bricks, and burn them thoroughly."
And they had brick for stone, and
bitumen for mortar. 4 Then they said,
"Come, let us build ourselves a city,
and a tower with its top in the heavens,
and let us make a name for ourselves,
lest we be scattered abroad upon the
face of the whole earth." 5 And the
LORD came down to see the city and
the tower, which the sons of men had
built. 6 And the LORD said, "Behold,
they are one people, and they have all
one language; and this is only the beginning of what they will do; and nothing that they propose to do will now

[m] Or *Blessed be the* LORD, *the God of Shem*
[n] Compare verses 20, 31. Heb lacks *These are the sons of
Japheth* [o] *That is Division*

be impossible for them. ⁷Come, let us go down, and there confuse their language, that they may not understand one another's speech." ⁸So the LORD scattered them abroad from there over the face of all the earth, and they left off building the city. ⁹Therefore its name was called Ba'bel, because there the LORD confused*ᵖ* the language of all the earth; and from there the LORD scattered them abroad over the face of all the earth.

10 These are the descendants of Shĕm. When Shem was a hundred years old, he became the father of Är·pӑch'shӑd two years after the flood; ¹¹and Shĕm lived after the birth of Är·pӑch'shӑd five hundred years, and had other sons and daughters.

12 When Är·pӑch'shӑd had lived thirty-five years, he became the father of Shē'lah; ¹³and Är·pӑch'shӑd lived after the birth of Shē'lah four hundred and three years, and had other sons and daughters.

14 When Shē'lah had lived thirty years, he became the father of Ē'ber; ¹⁵and Shē'lah lived after the birth of Ē'ber four hundred and three years, and had other sons and daughters.

16 When Ē'ber had lived thirty-four years, he became the father of Pē'leg; ¹⁷and Ē'ber lived after the birth of Pē'leg four hundred and thirty years, and had other sons and daughters.

18 When Pē'leg had lived thirty years, he became the father of Rē'ū; ¹⁹and Pē'leg lived after the birth of Rē'ū two hundred and nine years, and had other sons and daughters.

20 When Rē'ū had lived thirty-two years, he became the father of Sē'rug; ²¹and Rē'ū lived after the birth of Sē'rug two hundred and seven years, and had other sons and daughters.

22 When Sē'rug had lived thirty years, he became the father of Nä'hôr; ²³and Sē'rug lived after the birth of Nä'hôr two hundred years, and had other sons and daughters.

24 When Nä'hôr had lived twenty-nine years, he became the father of Tē'rah; ²⁵and Nä'hôr lived after the birth of Tē'rah a hundred and nineteen years, and had other sons and daughters.

26 When Tē'rah had lived seventy years, he became the father of Abram, Nä'hôr, and Hār'an.

27 Now these are the descendants of Tē'rah. Terah was the father of Abram, Nä'hôr, and Hār'an; and Haran was the father of Lot. ²⁸Hār'an died before his father Tē'rah in the land of his birth, in Ūr of the Chӑl-dē'ans. ²⁹And Abram and Nä'hôr took wives; the name of Abram's wife was Sär'aī, and the name of Nahor's wife, Mĭl'cah, the daughter of Hār'an the father of Milcah and Iş'cah. ³⁰Now Sär'aī was barren; she had no child.

31 Tē'rah took Abram his son and Lot the son of Hār'an, his grandson, and Sär'aī his daughter-in-law, his son Abram's wife, and they went forth together from Ūr of the Chӑl-dē'ans to go into the land of Canaan; but when they came to Haran, they settled there. ³²The days of Tē'rah were two hundred and five years; and Terah died in Hār'an.

12 Now the LORD said to Abram, "Go from your country and your kindred and your father's house to the land that I will show you. ²And I will make of you a great nation, and I will bless you, and make your name great, so that you will be a blessing. ³I will bless those who bless you, and him who curses you I will curse; and by you all the families of the earth shall bless themselves."*q*

4 So Abram went, as the LORD had told him; and Lot went with him. Abram was seventy-five years old when he departed from Hār'an. ⁵And Abram took Sär'aī his wife, and Lot his brother's son, and all their possessions which they had gathered, and the persons that they had gotten in Hār'an; and they set forth to go to the land of Canaan. When they had come to the land of Canaan, ⁶Abram passed through the land to the place at Shē'-chĕm, to the oak*ʳ* of Mō'rĕh. At that time the Canaanites were in the land. ⁷Then the LORD appeared to Abram, and said, "To your descendants I will give this land." So he built there an altar to the LORD, who had appeared to him. ⁸Thence he removed to the mountain on the east of Bĕth·el, and pitched his tent, with Bethel on

*ᵖ*Compare Heb *balal*, confuse
*q*Or *in you all the families of the earth shall be blessed*
*ʳ*Or *terebinth*

12.1: Acts 7.3; Heb 11.8.
12.2: Gen 15.5; 17.4, 5; 18.18; 22.17; 28.14; 32.12; 35.11; 46.3.   **12.3:** Gen 18.18; 22.17, 18; 26.4; 28.14; Gal 3.8.
12.7: Gen 13.15; 15.18; 17.8; 24.7; 26.3; 28.4, 13; 35.12; 48.4; Acts 7.5; Gal 3.16.

the west and Aī on the east; and there he built an altar to the LORD and called on the name of the LORD. ⁹And Abram journeyed on, still going toward the Něg'ěb.

10 Now there was a famine in the land. So Abram went down to Egypt to sojourn there, for the famine was severe in the land. ¹¹When he was about to enter Egypt, he said to Sār'aī his wife, "I know that you are a woman beautiful to behold; ¹²and when the Egyptians see you, they will say, 'This is his wife'; then they will kill me, but they will let you live. ¹³Say you are my sister, that it may go well with me because of you, and that my life may be spared on your account." ¹⁴When Abram entered Egypt the Egyptians saw that the woman was very beautiful. ¹⁵And when the princes of Pharaoh saw her, they praised her to Pharaoh. And the woman was taken into Pharaoh's house. ¹⁶And for her sake he dealt well with Abram; and he had sheep, oxen, he-asses, menservants, maidservants, she-asses, and camels. 17 But the LORD afflicted Pharaoh and his house with great plagues because of Sār'aī, Abram's wife. ¹⁸So Pharaoh called Abram, and said, "What is this you have done to me? Why did you not tell me that she was your wife? ¹⁹Why did you say, 'She is my sister,' so that I took her for my wife? Now then, here is your wife, take her, and be gone." ²⁰And Pharaoh gave men orders concerning him; and they set him on the way, with his wife and all that he had.

13 So Abram went up from Egypt, he and his wife, and all that he had, and Lot with him, into the Něg'ěb. 2 Now Abram was very rich in cattle, in silver, and in gold. ³And he journeyed on from the Něg'ěb as far as Běth'ęl, to the place where his tent had been at the beginning, between Bethel and Aī, ⁴to the place where he had made an altar at the first; and there Abram called on the name of the LORD. ⁵And Lot, who went with Abram, also had flocks and herds and tents, ⁶so that the land could not support both of them dwelling together; for their possessions were so great that they could not dwell together, ⁷and there was strife between the herdsmen of Abram's cattle and the herdsmen of Lot's cattle. At that time the

Canaanites and the Pěr'ĭz·zītes dwelt in the land.

8 Then Abram said to Lot, "Let there be no strife between you and me, and between your herdsmen and my herdsmen; for we are kinsmen. ⁹Is not the whole land before you? Separate yourself from me. If you take the left hand, then I will go to the right; of if you take the right hand, then I will go to the left." ¹⁰And Lot lifted up his eyes, and saw that the Jordan valley was well watered everywhere like the garden of the LORD, like the land of Egypt, in the direction of Zō'ar; this was before the LORD destroyed Sŏd'ǫm and Gǫ·môr'rah. ¹¹So Lot chose for himself all the Jordan valley, and Lot journeyed east; thus they separated from each other. ¹²Abram dwelt in the land of Canaan, while Lot dwelt among the cities of the valley and moved his tent as far as Sŏd'ǫm. ¹³Now the men of Sŏd'ǫm were wicked, great sinners against the LORD.

14 The LORD said to Abram, after Lot had separated from him, "Lift up your eyes, and look from the place where you are, northward and southward and eastward and westward; ¹⁵for all the land which you see I will give to you and to your descendants for ever. ¹⁶I will make your descendants as the dust of the earth; so that if one can count the dust of the earth, your descendants also can be counted. ¹⁷Arise, walk through the length and the breadth of the land, for I will give it to you." ¹⁸So Abram moved his tent, and came and dwelt by the oaksˢ of Măm'rě, which are at Hē'brǫn; and there he built an altar to the LORD.

14 In the days of Ăm'ra·phěl king of Shī'nār, Ăr'ī·ŏch king of Ěl·lä'sar, Chěd"–ôr-la·ō'mer king of Ē'lăm, and Tī'dăl king of Goi'ĭm, ²these kings made war with Bē'ra king of Sŏd'ǫm, Bīr'shạ king of Gǫ·môr'rah, Shī'nạb king of Ăd'mah, Shěm·ē'ber king of Zě·boi'ĭm, and the king of Bē'la (that is, Zō'ar). ³And all these joined forces in the Valley of Sĭd'dĭm (that is, the Salt Sea). ⁴Twelve years they had served Chěd"–ôr-la·ō'mer, but in the thirteenth year they rebelled. ⁵In the fourteenth year Chěd"–ôr-la·ō'mer and the kings who were with him came and subdued the

---

ˢOr *terebinths*
12.10-20: Gen 20.1-18; 26.7-11. **13.15:** Acts 7.5; Gal 3.16.

Rĕph′ạ·ĭm in Ăsh′tĕ·rŏth–kär·nā′ĭm, the Zū′zĭm in Ham, the Ē′mĭm in Shā′-vĕh–kĭr″ĭ·ạ·thā′ĭm, ⁶and the Hôr′ītes in their Mount Sē′ĭr as far as Ēl–pär′ạn on the border of the wilderness; ⁷then they turned back and came to Ĕn-mĭsh′păt (that is, Kā′dĕsh), and sub-dued all the country of the Ạ·măl′-ẹ·kītes, and also the Ăm′ọ·rītes who dwelt in Hăz′ạ·zŏn–tā′mạr. ⁸Then the king of Sŏd′ọm, the king of Gọ·môr′-rạh, the king of Ād′mạh, the king of Zĕ·boi′ĭm, and the king of Bē′lạ (that is, Zō′är) went out, and they joined battle in the Valley of Sĭd′dĭm ⁹with Chĕd″–ôr–lạ·ō′mẹr king of Ē′lăm, Tī′dăl king of Goi′ĭm, Ăm′rạ·phĕl king of Shī′när, and Är′ĭ·ŏch king of Ēl·lä′sạr, four kings against five. ¹⁰Now the Valley of Sĭd′dĭm was full of bitumen pits; and as the kings of Sŏd′ọm and Gọ·môr′rạh fled, some fell into them, and the rest fled to the mountain. ¹¹So the enemy took all the goods of Sŏd′ọm and Gọ·môr′rạh, and all their provisions, and went their way; ¹²they also took Lot, the son of Abram's brother, who dwelt in Sŏd′ọm, and his goods, and departed.

13 Then one who had escaped came, and told Abram the Hebrew, who was living by the oaks⁵ of Măm′rĕ the Ăm′-ọ·rīte, brother of Ĕsh′cọl and of Ā′nẹr; these were allies of Abram. ¹⁴When Abram heard that his kinsman had been taken captive, he led forth his trained men, born in his house, three hundred and eighteen of them, and went in pursuit as far as Dan. ¹⁵And he divided his forces against them by night, he and his servants, and routed them and pursued them to Hō′bạh, north of Damascus. ¹⁶Then he brought back all the goods, and also brought back his kinsman Lot with his goods, and the women and the people.

17 After his return from the defeat of Chĕd″–ôr–lạ·ō′mẹr and the kings who were with him, the king of Sŏd′ọm went out to meet him at the Valley of Shā′vĕh (that is, the King's Valley). ¹⁸And Mĕl·chĭz′ẹ·dĕk king of Salem brought out bread and wine; he was priest of God Most High. ¹⁹And he blessed him and said,

"Blessed be Abram by God Most High,
   maker of heaven and earth;
²⁰and blessed be God Most High,
   who has delivered your enemies
     into your hand!"

And Abram gave him a tenth of every-thing. ²¹And the king of Sŏd′ọm said to Abram, "Give me the persons, but take the goods for yourself." ²²But Abram said to the king of Sŏd′ọm, "I have sworn to the LORD God Most High, maker of heaven and earth, ²³that I would not take a thread or a sandal-thong or anything that is yours, lest you should say, 'I have made Abram rich.' ²⁴I will take nothing but what the young men have eaten, and the share of the men who went with me; let Ā′nẹr, Ĕsh′cọl, and Măm′rĕ take their share."

15 After these things the word of the LORD came to Abram in a vision, "Fear not, Abram, I am your shield; your reward shall be very great." ²But Abram said, "O Lord GOD, what wilt thou give me, for I continue childless, and the heir of my house is Ē·lĭ·ē′zẹr of Damascus?" ³And Abram said, "Behold, thou hast given me no offspring; and a slave born in my house will be my heir." ⁴And behold, the word of the LORD came to him, "This man shall not be your heir; your own son shall be your heir." ⁵And he brought him outside and said, "Look toward heaven, and number the stars, if you are able to number them." Then he said to him, "So shall your descendants be." ⁶And he believed the LORD; and he reckoned it to him as righteousness.

7 And he said to him, "I am the LORD who brought you from Ur of the Chăl·dē′ạns, to give you this land to possess." ⁸But he said, "O Lord GOD, how am I to know that I shall possess it?" ⁹He said to him, "Bring me a heifer three years old, a she-goat three years old, a ram three years old, a turtledove, and a young pigeon." ¹⁰And he brought him all these, cut them in two, and laid each half over against the other; but he did not cut the birds in two. ¹¹And when birds of prey came down upon the carcasses, Abram drove them away.

12 As the sun was going down, a deep sleep fell on Abram; and lo, a dread and great darkness fell upon him. ¹³Then the LORD said to Abram, "Know of a surety that your descend-ants will be sojourners in a land that

---

⁵Or *terebinths*
14.17-20: Heb 7.1-10.   **15.4:** Gen 17.16, 21; 18.10; 21.2.
15.5: Rom 4.18; Heb 11.12.
15.6: Rom 4.3, 9, 22, 23; Gal 3.6.   **15.13, 14:** Acts 7.6, 7.

is not theirs, and will be slaves there, and they will be oppressed for four hundred years; ¹⁴but I will bring judgment on the nation which they serve, and afterward they shall come out with great possessions. ¹⁵As for yourself, you shall go to your fathers in peace; you shall be buried in a good old age. ¹⁶And they shall come back here in the fourth generation; for the iniquity of the Ăm′ọ·rītes is not yet complete."

17 When the sun had gone down and it was dark, behold, a smoking fire pot and a flaming torch passed between these pieces. ¹⁸On that day the LORD made a covenant with Abram, saying, "To your descendants I give this land, from the river of Egypt to the great river, the river Euphrates, ¹⁹the land of the Kĕn′ītes, the Kĕn′ĭz-zītes, the Kăd′mọ·nītes, ²⁰the Hĭt′tītes, the Pĕr′ĭz·zītes, the Rĕph′ạ·ĭm, ²¹the Ăm′ọ·rītes, the Canaanites, the Gīr′gạ·shītes and the Jĕb′ū·sītes."

16 Now Sār′aī, Abram's wife, bore him no children. She had an Egyptian maid whose name was Hā′gạr; ²and Sār′aī said to Abram, "Behold now, the LORD has prevented me from bearing children; go in to my maid; it may be that I shall obtain children by her." And Abram hearkened to the voice of Sār′aī. ³So, after Abram had dwelt ten years in the land of Canaan, Sār′aī, Abram's wife, took Hā′gạr the Egyptian, her maid, and gave her to Abram her husband as a wife. ⁴And he went in to Hā′gạr, and she conceived; and when she saw that she had conceived, she looked with contempt on her mistress. ⁵And Sār′aī said to Abram, "May the wrong done to me be on you! I gave my maid to your embrace, and when she saw that she had conceived, she looked on me with contempt. May the LORD judge between you and me!" ⁶But Abram said to Sār′aī, "Behold, your maid is in your power; do to her as you please." Then Sarai dealt harshly with her, and she fled from her.

7 The angel of the LORD found her by a spring of water in the wilderness, the spring on the way to Shūr. ⁸And he said, "Hā′gạr, maid of Sār′aī, where have you come from and where are you going?" She said, "I am fleeing from my mistress Sarai." ⁹The angel of the LORD said to her, "Return to your mistress, and submit to her."

¹⁰The angel of the LORD also said to her, "I will so greatly multiply your descendants that they cannot be numbered for multitude." ¹¹And the angel of the LORD said to her, "Behold, you are with child, and shall bear a son; you shall call his name Ĭsh′mạ-ĕl;ᵗ because the LORD has given heed to your affliction. ¹²He shall be a wild ass of a man, his hand against every man and every man's hand against him; and he shall dwell over against all his kinsmen." ¹³So she called the name of the LORD who spoke to her, "Thou art a God of seeing"; for she said, "Have I really seen God and remained alive after seeing him?"ᵘ ¹⁴Therefore the well was called Bē′ẹr–lä′haī–roī;ᵛ it lies between Kā′dĕsh and Bē′rĕd.

15 And Hā′gạr bore Abram a son; and Abram called the name of his son, whom Hagar bore, Ĭsh′mạ·ĕl. ¹⁶Abram was eighty-six years old when Hā′gạr bore Ĭsh′mạ·ĕl to Abram.

17 When Abram was ninety-nine years old the LORD appeared to Abram, and said to him, "I am God Almighty;ʷ walk before me, and be blameless. ²And I will make my covenant between me and you, and will multiply you exceedingly." ³Then Abram fell on his face; and God said to him, ⁴"Behold, my covenant is with you, and you shall be the father of a multitude of nations. ⁵No longer shall your name be Abram,ˣ but your name shall be Abraham;ʸ for I have made you the father of a multitude of nations. ⁶I will make you exceedingly fruitful; and I will make nations of you, and kings shall come forth from you. ⁷And I will establish my covenant between me and you and your descendants after you throughout their generations for an everlasting covenant, to be God to you and to your descendants after you. ⁸And I will give to you, and to your descendants after you, the land of your sojournings, all the land of Canaan, for an everlasting possession; and I will be their God."

9 And God said to Abraham, "As for you, you shall keep my covenant, you and your descendants after you

ᵗThat is *God hears*
ᵘCn: Heb *have I even here seen after him who sees me?*
ᵛThat is *the well of one who sees and lives*
ʷHeb *El Shaddai*   ˣThat is *exalted father*
ʸHere taken to mean *father of a multitude*
15.18: Gen 17.2, 7, 9-14, 21.
17.5: Rom 4.17.   **17.7:** Lk 1.55; Gal 3.16.   **17.8:** Acts 7.5.

throughout their generations. ¹⁰This is my covenant, which you shall keep, between me and you and your descendants after you: Every male among you shall be circumcised. ¹¹You shall be circumcised in the flesh of your foreskins, and it shall be a sign of the covenant between me and you. ¹²He that is eight days old among you shall be circumcised; every male throughout your generations, whether born in your house, or bought with your money from any foreigner who is not of your offspring, ¹³both he that is born in your house and he that is bought with your money, shall be circumcised. So shall my covenant be in your flesh an everlasting covenant. ¹⁴Any uncircumcised male who is not circumcised in the flesh of his foreskin shall be cut off from his people; he has broken my covenant."

15 And God said to Abraham, "As for Sār′aī your wife, you shall not call her name Sarai, but Sarah shall be her name. ¹⁶I will bless her, and moreover I will give you a son by her; I will bless her, and she shall be a mother of nations; kings of peoples shall come from her." ¹⁷Then Abraham fell on his face and laughed, and said to himself, "Shall a child be born to a man who is a hundred years old? Shall Sarah, who is ninety years old, bear a child?" ¹⁸And Abraham said to God, "O that Ĭsh′mȧ-ĕl might live in thy sight!" ¹⁹God said, "No, but Sarah your wife shall bear you a son, and you shall call his name Isaac.ᶻ I will establish my covenant with him as an everlasting covenant for his descendants after him. ²⁰As for Ĭsh′mȧ-ĕl, I have heard you; behold, I will bless him and make him fruitful and multiply him exceedingly; he shall be the father of twelve princes, and I will make him a great nation. ²¹But I will establish my covenant with Isaac, whom Sarah shall bear to you at this season next year."

22 When he had finished talking with him, God went up from Abraham. ²³Then Abraham took Ĭsh′mȧ-ĕl his son and all the slaves born in his house or bought with his money, every male among the men of Abraham's house, and he circumcised the flesh of their foreskins that very day, as God had said to him. ²⁴Abraham was ninety-nine years old when he was circumcised in the flesh of his foreskin. ²⁵And

Ĭsh′mȧ-ĕl his son was thirteen years old when he was circumcised in the flesh of his foreskin. ²⁶That very day Abraham and his son Ĭsh′mȧ-ĕl were circumcised; ²⁷and all the men of his house, those born in the house and those bought with money from a foreigner, were circumcised with him.

18 And the LORD appeared to him by the oaksᵃ of Măm′rĕ, as he sat at the door of his tent in the heat of the day. ²He lifted up his eyes and looked, and behold, three men stood in front of him. When he saw them, he ran from the tent door to meet them, and bowed himself to the earth, ³and said, "My lord, if I have found favor in your sight, do not pass by your servant. ⁴Let a little water be brought, and wash your feet, and rest yourselves under the tree, ⁵while I fetch a morsel of bread, that you may refresh yourselves, and after that you may pass on—since you have come to your servant." So they said, "Do as you have said." ⁶And Abraham hastened into the tent to Sarah, and said, "Make ready quickly three measuresᵇ of fine meal, knead it, and make cakes." ⁷And Abraham ran to the herd, and took a calf, tender and good, and gave it to the servant, who hastened to prepare it. ⁸Then he took curds, and milk, and the calf which he had prepared, and set it before them; and he stood by them under the tree while they ate.

9 They said to him, "Where is Sarah your wife?" And he said, "She is in the tent." ¹⁰The LORD said, "I will surely return to you in the spring, and Sarah your wife shall have a son." And Sarah was listening at the tent door behind him. ¹¹Now Abraham and Sarah were old, advanced in age; it had ceased to be with Sarah after the manner of women. ¹²So Sarah laughed to herself, saying, "After I have grown old, and my husband is old, shall I have pleasure?" ¹³The LORD said to Abraham, "Why did Sarah laugh, and say, 'Shall I indeed bear a child, now that I am old?' ¹⁴Is anything too hardᶜ for the LORD? At the appointed time I will return to you, in the spring, and Sarah shall have a son." ¹⁵But Sarah denied,

ᶻThat is *he laughs*   ᵃOr *terebinths*   ᵇHeb *seahs*
ᶜOr *wonderful*
17.10: Acts 7.8.   17.11-14: Gen 17.24; 21.4.
18.10: Rom 9.9.   18.12: 1 Pet 3.6.
18.14: Mt 19.26; Mk 10.27; Lk 1.37; Rom 9.9.

saying, "I did not laugh"; for she was afraid. He said, "No, but you did laugh."

16 Then the men set out from there, and they looked toward Sŏd′ọm; and Abraham went with them to set them on their way. ¹⁷ The LORD said, "Shall I hide from Abraham what I am about to do, ¹⁸ seeing that Abraham shall become a great and mighty nation, and all the nations of the earth shall bless themselves by him?*ᵈ* ¹⁹ No, for I have chosen*ᵉ* him, that he may charge his children and his household after him to keep the way of the LORD by doing righteousness and justice; so that the LORD may bring to Abraham what he has promised him." ²⁰ Then the LORD said, "Because the outcry against Sŏd′ọm and Gọ-môr′rạh is great and their sin is very grave, ²¹ I will go down to see whether they have done altogether according to the outcry which has come to me; and if not, I will know."

22 So the men turned from there, and went toward Sŏd′ọm; but Abraham still stood before the LORD. ²³ Then Abraham drew near, and said, "Wilt thou indeed destroy the righteous with the wicked? ²⁴ Suppose there are fifty righteous within the city; wilt thou then destroy the place and not spare it for the fifty righteous who are in it? ²⁵ Far be it from thee to do such a thing, to slay the righteous with the wicked, so that the righteous fare as the wicked! Far be that from thee! Shall not the Judge of all the earth do right?" ²⁶ And the LORD said, "If I find at Sŏd′ọm fifty righteous in the city, I will spare the whole place for their sake." ²⁷ Abraham answered, "Behold, I have taken upon myself to speak to the Lord, I who am but dust and ashes. ²⁸ Suppose five of the fifty righteous are lacking? Wilt thou destroy the whole city for lack of five?" And he said, "I will not destroy it if I find forty-five there." ²⁹ Again he spoke to him, and said, "Suppose forty are found there." He answered, "For the sake of forty I will not do it." ³⁰ Then he said, "Oh let not the Lord be angry, and I will speak. Suppose thirty are found there." He answered, "I will not do it, if I find thirty there." ³¹ He said, "Behold, I have taken upon myself to speak to the Lord. Suppose twenty are found there." He answered, "For the sake of

twenty I will not destroy it." ³² Then he said, "Oh let not the Lord be angry, and I will speak again but this once. Suppose ten are found there." He answered, "For the sake of ten I will not destroy it." ³³ And the LORD went his way, when he had finished speaking to Abraham; and Abraham returned to his place.

19 The two angels came to Sŏd′ọm in the evening; and Lot was sitting in the gate of Sodom. When Lot saw them, he rose to meet them, and bowed himself with his face to the earth, ² and said, "My lords, turn aside, I pray you, to your servant's house and spend the night, and wash your feet; then you may rise up early and go on your way." They said, "No; we will spend the night in the street." ³ But he urged them strongly; so they turned aside to him and entered his house; and he made them a feast, and baked unleavened bread, and they ate. ⁴ But before they lay down, the men of the city, the men of Sŏd′ọm, both young and old, all the people to the last man, surrounded the house; ⁵ and they called to Lot, "Where are the men who came to you tonight? Bring them out to us, that we may know them." ⁶ Lot went out of the door to the men, shut the door after him, ⁷ and said, "I beg you, my brothers, do not act so wickedly. ⁸ Behold, I have two daughters who have not known man; let me bring them out to you, and do to them as you please; only do nothing to these men, for they have come under the shelter of my roof." ⁹ But they said, "Stand back!" And they said, "This fellow came to sojourn, and he would play the judge! Now we will deal worse with you than with them." Then they pressed hard against the man Lot, and drew near to break the door. ¹⁰ But the men put forth their hands and brought Lot into the house to them, and shut the door. ¹¹ And they struck with blindness the men who were at the door of the house, both small and great, so that they wearied themselves groping for the door.

12 Then the men said to Lot, "Have you any one else here? Sons-in-law, sons, daughters, or any one you have in the city, bring them out of the place;

ᵈOr *in him all the nations of the earth shall be blessed*
ᵉHeb *known*
18.18: Gen 12.3; Acts 3.25; Gal 3.8.

¹³ for we are about to destroy this place, because the outcry against its people has become great before the LORD, and the LORD has sent us to destroy it." ¹⁴ So Lot went out and said to his sons-in-law, who were to marry his daughters, "Up, get out of this place; for the LORD is about to destroy the city." But he seemed to his sons-in-law to be jesting.

15 When morning dawned, the angels urged Lot, saying, "Arise, take your wife and your two daughters who are here, lest you be consumed in the punishment of the city." ¹⁶ But he lingered; so the men seized him and his wife and his two daughters by the hand, the LORD being merciful to him, and they brought him forth and set him outside the city. ¹⁷ And when they had brought them forth, they' said, "Flee for your life; do not look back or stop anywhere in the valley; flee to the hills, lest you be consumed." ¹⁸ And Lot said to them, "Oh, no, my lords; ¹⁹ behold, your servant has found favor in your sight, and you have shown me great kindness in saving my life; but I cannot flee to the hills, lest the disaster overtake me, and I die. ²⁰ Behold, yonder city is near enough to flee to, and it is a little one. Let me escape there—is it not a little one?—and my life will be saved!" ²¹ He said to him, "Behold, I grant you this favor also, that I will not overthrow the city of which you have spoken. ²² Make haste, escape there; for I can do nothing till you arrive there." Therefore the name of the city was called Zō'ăr.ᵍ ²³ The sun had risen on the earth when Lot came to Zō'ăr.

24 Then the LORD rained on Sŏd'ŏm and Gŏ·môr'ṛah brimstone and fire from the LORD out of heaven; ²⁵ and he overthrew those cities, and all the valley, and all the inhabitants of the cities, and what grew on the ground. ²⁶ But Lot's wife behind him looked back, and she became a pillar of salt. ²⁷ And Abraham went early in the morning to the place where he had stood before the LORD; ²⁸ and he looked down toward Sŏd'ŏm and Gŏ·môr'ṛah and toward all the land of the valley, and beheld, and lo, the smoke of the land went up like the smoke of a furnace.

29 So it was that, when God destroyed the cities of the valley, God remembered Abraham, and sent Lot out of the midst of the overthrow, when he overthrew the cities in which Lot dwelt.

30 Now Lot went up out of Zō'ăr, and dwelt in the hills with his two daughters, for he was afraid to dwell in Zoar; so he dwelt in a cave with his two daughters. ³¹ And the first-born said to the younger, "Our father is old, and there is not a man on earth to come in to us after the manner of all the earth. ³² Come, let us make our father drink wine, and we will lie with him, that we may preserve offspring through our father." ³³ So they made their father drink wine that night; and the first-born went in, and lay with her father; he did not know when she lay down or when she arose. ³⁴ And on the next day, the first-born said to the younger, "Behold, I lay last night with my father; let us make him drink wine tonight also; then you go in and lie with him, that we may preserve offspring through our father." ³⁵ So they made their father drink wine that night also; and the younger arose, and lay with him; and he did not know when she lay down or when she arose. ³⁶ Thus both the daughters of Lot were with child by their father. ³⁷ The first-born bore a son, and called his name Mō'ăb; he is the father of the Mō'ăb-ītes to this day. ³⁸ The younger also bore a son, and called his name Bĕn–ăm'mī; he is the father of the Ăm'mo̧-nītes to this day.

20 From there Abraham journeyed toward the territory of the Nĕg'ĕb, and dwelt between Kā'dĕsh and Shŭr; and he sojourned in Gē'rär. ²And Abraham said of Sarah his wife, "She is my sister." And A̧·bĭm'ȩ·lĕch king of Gē'rär sent and took Sarah. ³ But God came to A̧·bĭm'ȩ·lĕch in a dream by night, and said to him, "Behold, you are a dead man, because of the woman whom you have taken; for she is a man's wife." ⁴ Now A̧·bĭm'-ȩ·lĕch had not approched her; so he said, "Lord, wilt thou slay an innocent people? ⁵ Did he not himself say to me, 'She is my sister'? And she herself said, 'He is my brother.' In the integrity of my heart and the innocence of my hands I have done this." ⁶ Then God said to him in the dream, "Yes, I know

ᶠGk Syr Vg: Heb *he*   ᵍThat is *Little*
19.24, 25: Lk 17.29.   19.26: Lk 17.32.   19.28: Rev 9.2.

that you have done this in the integrity of your heart, and it was I who kept you from sinning against me; therefore I did not let you touch her. ⁷Now then restore the man's wife; for he is a prophet, and he will pray for you, and you shall live. But if you do not restore her, know that you shall surely die, you, and all that are yours."

8 So A·bǐm′e·lĕch rose early in the morning, and called all his servants, and told them all these things; and the men were very much afraid. ⁹Then A·bǐm′e·lĕch called Abraham, and said to him, "What have you done to us? And how have I sinned against you, that you have brought on me and my kingdom a great sin? You have done to me things that ought not to be done." ¹⁰And A·bǐm′e·lĕch said to Abraham, "What were you thinking of, that you did this thing?" ¹¹Abraham said, "I did it because I thought, There is no fear of God at all in this place, and they will kill me because of my wife. ¹²Besides she is indeed my sister, the daughter of my father but not the daughter of my mother; and she became my wife. ¹³And when God caused me to wander from my father's house, I said to her, 'This is the kindness you must do me: at every place to which we come, say of me, He is my brother.'" ¹⁴Then A·bǐm′e·lĕch took sheep and oxen, and male and female slaves, and gave them to Abraham, and restored Sarah his wife to him. ¹⁵And A·bǐm′e·lĕch said, "Behold, my land is before you; dwell where it pleases you." ¹⁶To Sarah he said, "Behold, I have given your brother a thousand pieces of silver; it is your vindication in the eyes of all who are with you; and before every one you are righted." ¹⁷Then Abraham prayed to God; and God healed A·bǐm′e·lĕch, and also healed his wife and female slaves so that they bore children. ¹⁸For the LORD had closed all the wombs of the house of A·bǐm′e·lĕch because of Sarah, Abraham's wife.

21 The LORD visited Sarah as he had said, and the LORD did to Sarah as he had promised. ²And Sarah conceived, and bore Abraham a son in his old age at the time of which God had spoken to him. ³Abraham called the name of his son who was born to him, whom Sarah bore him, Isaac. ⁴And Abraham circumcised his son

Isaac when he was eight days old, as God had commanded him. ⁵Abraham was a hundred years old when his son Isaac was born to him. ⁶And Sarah said, "God has made laughter for me; every one who hears will laugh over me." ⁷And she said, "Who would have said to Abraham that Sarah would suckle children? Yet I have borne him a son in his old age."

8 And the child grew, and was weaned; and Abraham made a great feast on the day that Isaac was weaned. ⁹But Sarah saw the son of Hā′gär the Egyptian, whom she had borne to Abraham, playing with her son Isaac.ʰ ¹⁰So she said to Abraham, "Cast out this slave woman with her son; for the son of this slave woman shall not be heir with my son Isaac." ¹¹And the thing was very displeasing to Abraham on account of his son. ¹²But God said to Abraham, "Be not displeased because of the lad and because of your slave woman; whatever Sarah says to you, do as she tells you, for through Isaac shall your descendants be named. ¹³And I will make a nation of the son of the slave woman also, because he is your offspring." ¹⁴So Abraham rose early in the morning, and took bread and a skin of water, and gave it to Hā′gär, putting it on her shoulder, along with the child, and sent her away. And she departed, and wandered in the wilderness of Bē′er-shē′ba.

15 When the water in the skin was gone, she cast the child under one of the bushes. ¹⁶Then she went, and sat down over against him a good way off, about the distance of a bowshot; for she said, "Let me not look upon the death of the child." And as she sat over against him, the child lifted up his voiceⁱ and wept. ¹⁷And God heard the voice of the lad; and the angel of God called to Hā′gär from heaven, and said to her, "What troubles you, Hagar? Fear not; for God has heard the voice of the lad where he is. ¹⁸Arise, lift up the lad, and hold him fast with your hand; for I will make him a great nation." ¹⁹Then God opened her eyes, and she saw a well of water; and she went, and filled the skin with water,

ʰGk Vg: Heb lacks *with her son Isaac*
ⁱGk: Heb *she lifted up her voice*
21.4: Acts 7.8.   **21.10:** Gal 4.30.
21.12: Rom 9.7; Heb 11.18.

and gave the lad a drink. ²⁰And God was with the lad, and he grew up; he lived in the wilderness, and became an expert with the bow. ²¹He lived in the wilderness of Pār′an; and his mother took a wife for him from the land of Egypt.

22 At that time Ạ·bĭm′ẹ·lĕch and Phī′cŏl the commander of his army said to Abraham, "God is with you in all that you do; ²³now therefore swear to me here by God that you will not deal falsely with me or with my offspring or with my posterity, but as I have dealt loyally with you, you will deal with me and with the land where you have sojourned." ²⁴And Abraham said, "I will swear."

25 When Abraham complained to Ạ·bĭm′ẹ·lĕch about a well of water which Abimelech's servants had seized, ²⁶Ạ·bĭm′ẹ·lĕch said, "I do not know who has done this thing; you did not tell me, and I have not heard of it until today." ²⁷So Abraham took sheep and oxen and gave them to Ạ·bĭm′ẹ·lĕch, and the two men made a covenant. ²⁸Abraham set seven ewe lambs of the flock apart. ²⁹And Ạ·bĭm′ẹ·lĕch said to Abraham, "What is the meaning of these seven ewe lambs which you have set apart?" ³⁰He said, "These seven ewe lambs you will take from my hand, that you may be a witness for me that I dug this well." ³¹Therefore that place was called Bē′ẹr-shē′bạ;ʲ because there both of them swore an oath. ³²So they made a covenant at Bē′ẹr-shē′bạ. Then Ạ·bĭm′ẹ·lĕch and Phī′cŏl the commander of his army rose up and returned to the land of the Phĭ·lĭs′tīnes. ³³Abraham planted a tamarisk tree in Bē′ẹr-shē′bạ, and called there on the name of the LORD, the Everlasting God. ³⁴And Abraham sojourned many days in the land of the Phĭ·lĭs′tīnes.

22 After these things God tested Abraham, and said to him, "Abraham!" And he said, "Here am I." ²He said, "Take your son, your only son Isaac, whom you love, and go to the land of Mō·rī′ah, and offer him there as a burnt offering upon one of the mountains of which I shall tell you." ³So Abraham rose early in the morning, saddled his ass, and took two of his young men with him, and his son Isaac; and he cut the wood for the burnt offering, and arose and went to the place of which God had told him. ⁴On the third day Abraham lifted up his eyes and saw the place afar off. ⁵Then Abraham said to his young men, "Stay here with the ass; I and the lad will go yonder and worship, and come again to you." ⁶And Abraham took the wood of the burnt offering, and laid it on Isaac his son; and he took in his hand the fire and the knife. So they went both of them together. ⁷And Isaac said to his father Abraham, "My father!" And he said, "Here am I, my son." He said, "Behold, the fire and the wood; but where is the lamb for a burnt offering?" ⁸Abraham said, "God will provide himself the lamb for a burnt offering, my son." So they went both of them together.

9 When they came to the place of which God had told him, Abraham built an altar there, and laid the wood in order, and bound Isaac his son, and laid him on the altar, upon the wood. ¹⁰Then Abraham put forth his hand, and took the knife to slay his son. ¹¹But the angel of the LORD called to him from heaven, and said, "Abraham, Abraham!" And he said, "Here am I." ¹²He said, "Do not lay your hand on the lad or do anything to him; for now I know that you fear God, seeing you have not withheld your son, your only son, from me." ¹³And Abraham lifted up his eyes and looked, and behold, behind him was a ram, caught in a thicket by his horns; and Abraham went and took the ram, and offered it up as a burnt offering instead of his son. ¹⁴So Abraham called the name of that place The LORD will provide;ᵏ as it is said to this day, "On the mount of the LORD it shall be provided."ˡ

15 And the angel of the LORD called to Abraham a second time from heaven, ¹⁶and said, "By myself I have sworn, says the LORD, because you have done this, and have not withheld your son, your only son, ¹⁷I will indeed bless you, and I will multiply your descendants as the stars of heaven and as the sand which is on the seashore. And your descendants shall possess the gate of their enemies, ¹⁸and by your descendants shall all

ʲThat is *Well of seven* or *Well of the oath*   ᵏOr *see*
ˡOr *he will be seen*
21.31: Gen 26.33.
22.1-18: Heb 11.17-19.   22.9, 10, 12: Jas 2.21.
22.16, 17: Lk 1.73; Heb 6.13, 14; 11.12.
22.18: Acts 3.25; Gal 3.16.

the nations of the earth bless themselves, because you have obeyed my voice." ¹⁹So Abraham returned to his young men, and they arose and went together to Bē′er–shĕ′bạ; and Abraham dwelt at Beer–sheba.

20 Now after these things it was told Abraham, "Behold, Mĭl′cạh also has borne children to your brother Nā′hôr: ²¹Ŭz the first-born, Bŭz his brother, Kĕ′mū·ẹl the father of Är′am, ²²Chē′sĕd, Hā′zō, Pĭl′dăsh, Jĭd′lăph, and Bĕ·thū′ẹl." ²³Bĕ·thū′ẹl became the father of Rebekah. These eight Mĭl′-cạh bore to Nā′hôr, Abraham's brother. ²⁴Moreover, his concubine, whose name was Rĕ·ü′mạh, bore Tē′bạh, Gā′ham, Tā′hăsh, and Mā′ạ·cạh.

23 Sarah lived a hundred and twenty-seven years; these were the years of the life of Sarah. ²And Sarah died at Kĭr′ĭ·ăth–är′bạ (that is, Hē′brọn) in the land of Canaan; and Abraham went in to mourn for Sarah and to weep for her. ³And Abraham rose up from before his dead, and said to the Hĭt′tītes, ⁴"I am a stranger and a sojourner among you; give me property among you for a burying place, that I may bury my dead out of my sight." ⁵The Hĭt′tītes answered Abraham, ⁶"Hear us, my lord; you are a mighty prince among us. Bury your dead in the choicest of our sepulchres; none of us will withhold from you his sepulchre, or hinder you from burying your dead." ⁷Abraham rose and bowed to the Hĭt′tītes, the people of the land. ⁸And he said to them, "If you are willing that I should bury my dead out of my sight, hear me, and entreat for me Ē′phrọn the son of Zō′-hăr, ⁹that he may give me the cave of Măch·pē′lah, which he owns; it is at the end of his field. For the full price let him give it to me in your presence as a possession for a burying place." ¹⁰Now Ē′phrọn was sitting among the Hĭt′tītes; and Ephron the Hittite answered Abraham in the hearing of the Hittites, of all who went in at the gate of his city, ¹¹"No, my lord, hear me; I give you the field, and I give you the cave that is in it; in the presence of the sons of my people I give it to you; bury your dead." ¹²Then Abraham bowed down before the people of the land. ¹³And he said to Ē′phrọn in the hearing of the people of the land, "But if you will, hear me; I will give the

price of the field; accept it from me, that I may bury my dead there." ¹⁴Ē′phrọn answered Abraham, ¹⁵"My lord, listen to me; a piece of land worth four hundred shekels of silver, what is that between you and me? Bury your dead." ¹⁶Abraham agreed with Ē′phrọn; and Abraham weighed out for Ephron the silver which he had named in the hearing of the Hĭt′tītes, four hundred shekels of silver, according to the weights current among the merchants.

17 So the field of Ē′phrọn in Măch-pē′lah, which was to the east of Măm′rĕ, the field with the cave which was in it and all the trees that were in the field, throughout its whole area, was made over ¹⁸to Abraham as a possession in the presence of the Hĭt′-tītes, before all who went in at the gate of his city. ¹⁹After this, Abraham buried Sarah his wife in the cave of the field of Măch·pē′lah east of Măm′rĕ (that is, Hē′brọn) in the land of Canaan. ²⁰The field and the cave that is in it were made over to Abraham as a possession for a burying place by the Hĭt′tītes.

24 Now Abraham was old, well advanced in years; and the LORD had blessed Abraham in all things. ²And Abraham said to his servant, the oldest of his house, who had charge of all that he had, "Put your hand under my thigh, ³and I will make you swear by the LORD, the God of heaven and of the earth, that you will not take a wife for my son from the daughters of the Canaanites, among whom I dwell, ⁴but will go to my country and to my kindred, and take a wife for my son Isaac." ⁵The servant said to him, "Perhaps the woman may not be willing to follow me to this land; must I then take your son back to the land from which you came?" ⁶Abraham said to him, "See to it that you do not take my son back there. ⁷The LORD, the God of heaven, who took me from my father's house and from the land of my birth, and who spoke to me and swore to me, 'To your descendants I will give this land,' he will send his angel before you, and you shall take a wife for my son from there. ⁸But if the woman is not willing to follow you, then you will be free from this oath of mine; only you must not

23.4: Heb 11.9, 13.   23.16, 17: Acts 7.16.

take my son back there." ⁹So the servant put his hand under the thigh of Abraham his master, and swore to him concerning this matter.

10 Then the servant took ten of his master's camels and departed, taking all sorts of choice gifts from his master; and he arose; and went to Mĕs·o·po·tā′mǐ·a, to the city of Nā′hôr. ¹¹And he made the camels kneel down outside the city by the well of water at the time of evening, the time when women go out to draw water. ¹²And he said, "O LORD, God of my master Abraham, grant me success today, I pray thee, and show steadfast love to my master Abraham. ¹³Behold, I am standing by the spring of water, and the daughters of the men of the city are coming out to draw water. ¹⁴Let the maiden to whom I shall say, 'Pray let down your jar that I may drink,' and who shall say, 'Drink, and I will water your camels'—let her be the one whom thou hast appointed for thy servant Isaac. By this I shall know that thou hast shown steadfast love to my master."

15 Before he had done speaking, behold, Rebekah, who was born to Bĕ·thü′el the son of Mĭl′cah, the wife of Nā′hôr, Abraham's brother, came out with her water jar upon her shoulder. ¹⁶The maiden was very fair to look upon, a virgin, whom no man had known. She went down to the spring, and filled her jar, and came up. ¹⁷Then the servant ran to meet her, and said, "Pray give me a little water to drink from your jar." ¹⁸She said, "Drink, my lord"; and she quickly let down her jar upon her hand, and gave him a drink. ¹⁹When she had finished giving him a drink, she said, "I will draw for your camels also, until they have done drinking." ²⁰So she quickly emptied her jar into the trough and ran again to the well to draw, and she drew for all his camels. ²¹The man gazed at her in silence to learn whether the LORD had prospered his journey or not.

22 When the camels had done drinking, the man took a gold ring weighing a half shekel, and two bracelets for her arms weighing ten gold shekels, ²³and said, "Tell me whose daughter you are. Is there room in your father's house for us to lodge in?" ²⁴She said to him, "I am the daughter of Bĕ·thü′el

the son of Mĭl′cah, whom she bore to Nā′hôr." ²⁵She added, "We have both straw and provender enough, and room to lodge in." ²⁶The man bowed his head and worshiped the LORD, ²⁷and said, "Blessed be the LORD, the God of my master Abraham, who has not forsaken his steadfast love and his faithfulness toward my master. As for me, the LORD has led me in the way to the house of my master's kinsmen."

28 Then the maiden ran and told her mother's household about these things. ²⁹Rebekah had a brother whose name was Lā′ban; and Laban ran out to the man, to the spring. ³⁰When he saw the ring, and the bracelets on his sister's arms, and when he heard the words of Rebekah his sister, "Thus the man spoke to me," he went to the man; and behold, he was standing by the camels at the spring. ³¹He said, "Come in, O blessed of the LORD; why do you stand outside? For I have prepared the house and a place for the camels." ³²So the man came into the house; and Lā′ban ungirded the camels, and gave him straw and provender for the camels, and water to wash his feet and the feet of the men who were with him. ³³Then food was set before him to eat; but he said, "I will not eat until I have told my errand." He said, "Speak on."

34 So he said, "I am Abraham's servant. ³⁵The LORD has greatly blessed my master, and he has become great; he has given him flocks and herds, silver and gold, menservants and maidservants, camels and asses. ³⁶And Sarah my master's wife bore a son to my master when she was old; and to him he has given all that he has. ³⁷My master made me swear, saying, 'You shall not take a wife for my son from the daughters of the Canaanites, in whose land I dwell; ³⁸but you shall go to my father's house and to my kindred, and take a wife for my son.' ³⁹I said to my master, 'Perhaps the woman will not follow me.' ⁴⁰But he said to me, 'The LORD, before whom I walk, will send his angel with you and prosper your way; and you shall take a wife for my son from my kindred and from my father's house; ⁴¹then you will be free from my oath, when you come to my kindred; and if they will not give her to you, you will be free from my oath.'

42 "I came today to the spring, and said, 'O Lord, the God of my master Abraham, if now thou wilt prosper the way which I go, ⁴³behold, I am standing by the spring of water; let the young woman who comes out to draw, to whom I shall say, "Pray give me a little water from your jar to drink," ⁴⁴and who will say to me, "Drink, and I will draw for your camels also," let her be the woman whom the Lord has appointed for my master's son.'

45 "Before I had done speaking in my heart, behold, Rebekah came out with her water jar on her shoulder; and she went down to the spring, and drew. I said to her, 'Pray let me drink.' ⁴⁶She quickly let down her jar from her shoulder, and said, 'Drink, and I will give your camels drink also.' So I drank, and she gave the camels drink also. ⁴⁷Then I asked her, 'Whose daughter are you?' She said, 'The daughter of Bĕ·thü'ĕl, Nā'hôr's son, whom Mĭl'cah bore to him.' So I put the ring on her nose, and the bracelets on her arms. ⁴⁸Then I bowed my head and worshiped the Lord, and blessed the Lord, the God of my master Abraham, who had led me by the right way to take the daughter of my master's kinsman for his son. ⁴⁹Now then, if you will deal loyally and truly with my master, tell me; and if not, tell me; that I may turn to the right hand or to the left."

50 Then Lā'ban and Bĕ·thü'ĕl answered, "The thing comes from the Lord; we cannot speak to you bad or good. ⁵¹Behold, Rebekah is before you, take her and go, and let her be the wife of your master's son, as the Lord has spoken."

52 When Abraham's servant heard their words, he bowed himself to the earth before the Lord. ⁵³And the servant brought forth jewelry of silver and of gold, and raiment, and gave them to Rebekah; he also gave to her brother and to her mother costly ornaments. ⁵⁴And he and the men who were with him ate and drank, and they spent the night there. When they arose in the morning, he said, "Send me back to my master." ⁵⁵Her brother and her mother said, "Let the maiden remain with us a while, at least ten days; after that she may go." ⁵⁶But he said to them, "Do not delay me, since the Lord has prospered my way; let me go

that I may go to my master." ⁵⁷They said, "We will call the maiden, and ask her." ⁵⁸And they called Rebekah, and said to her, "Will you go with this man?" She said, "I will go." ⁵⁹So they sent away Rebekah their sister and her nurse, and Abraham's servant and his men. ⁶⁰And they blessed Rebekah, and said to her, "Our sister, be the mother of thousands of ten thousands; and may your descendants possess the gate of those who hate them!" ⁶¹Then Rebekah and her maids arose, and rode upon the camels and followed the man; thus the servant took Rebekah, and went his way.

62 Now Isaac had come fromⁿ Bē'-er–lä'haī–roi, and was dwelling in the Nĕg'ĕb. ⁶³And Isaac went out to meditate in the field in the evening; and he lifted up his eyes and looked, and behold, there were camels coming. ⁶⁴And Rebekah lifted up her eyes, and when she saw Isaac, she alighted from the camel, ⁶⁵and said to the servant, "Who is the man yonder, walking in the field to meet us?" The servant said, "It is my master." So she took her veil and covered herself. ⁶⁶And the servant told Isaac all the things that he had done. ⁶⁷Then Isaac brought her into the tent,ᵒ and took Rebekah, and she became his wife; and he loved her. So Isaac was comforted after his mother's death.

25 Abraham took another wife, whose name was Kĕ·tü'rah. ²She bore him Zĭm'răn, Jŏk'shan, Mē'dăn, Mĭd'ĭ·an, Ĭsh'băk, and Shü'ah. ³Jŏk'shan was the father of Shē'ba and Dē'dăn. The sons of Dedan were As·shü'rĭm, Lĕ·tü'shĭm, and Lĕ·ŭm'-mĭm. ⁴The sons of Mĭd'ĭ·an were Ē'phah, Ē'pher, Hā'noch, A·bī'da, and Ĕl·dā'ah. All these were the children of Kĕ·tü'rah. ⁵Abraham gave all he had to Isaac. ⁶But to the sons of his concubines Abraham gave gifts, and while he was still living he sent them away from his son Isaac, eastward to the east country.

7 These are the days of the years of Abraham's life, a hundred and seventy-five years. ⁸Abraham breathed his last and died in a good old age, an old man and full of years, and was gathered to his people. ⁹Isaac and Ĭsh'-mā·ĕl his sons buried him in the cave

ⁿSyr Tg: Heb *from coming to*
ᵒHeb adds *Sarah his mother*

of Măch·pē'lạh, in the field of Ē'phrọn
the son of Zō'hār the Hĭt'tīte, east of
Măm'rē, 10 the field which Abraham
purchased from the Hĭt'tītes. There
Abraham was buried, with Sarah his
wife. 11 After the death of Abraham
God blessed Isaac his son. And Isaac
dwelt at Bē'ẹr–lă'haī–roi.

12 These are the descendants of
Ĭsh'mạ·ĕl, Abraham's son, whom Hā'-
gạr the Egyptian, Sarah's maid,
bore to Abraham. 13 These are the
names of the sons of Ĭsh'mạ·ĕl, named
in the order of their birth: Nĕ·bā'ĭ·ọth,
the first-born of Ishmael; and Kē'dār,
Ăd'bē·ĕl, Mĭb'sạm, 14 Mĭsh'mạ, Dū'mạh,
Măs'sạ, 15 Hā'dăd, Tē'mạ, Jē'tūr,
Nā'phĭsh, and Kĕd'ĕ·mạh. 16 These are
the sons of Ĭsh'mạ·ĕl and these are
their names, by their villages and by
their encampments, twelve princes
according to their tribes. 17 (These are
the years of the life of Ĭsh'mạ·ĕl, a
hundred and thirty-seven years; he
breathed his last and died, and was
gathered to his kindred.) 18 They
dwelt from Hăv'ĭ·lạh to Shūr, which
is opposite Egypt in the direction of
Assyria; he settled[p] over against all
his people.

19 These are the descendants of
Isaac, Abraham's son: Abraham was
the father of Isaac, 20 and Isaac was
forty years old when he took to wife
Rebekah, the daughter of Bĕ·thū'ẹl
the Ăr·ạ·mē'ạn of Păd'dạn–ăr'ạm, the
sister of Lā'bạn the Aramean. 21 And
Isaac prayed to the LORD for his wife,
because she was barren; and the LORD
granted his prayer, and Rebekah his
wife conceived. 22 The children strug-
gled together within her; and she said,
"If it is thus, why do I live?"[q] So she
went to inquire of the LORD. 23 And the
LORD said to her,

"Two nations are in your womb,
and two peoples, born of you, shall be divided;
the one shall be stronger than the other,
the elder shall serve the younger."

24 When her days to be delivered were
fulfilled, behold, there were twins in
her womb. 25 The first came forth red,
all his body like a hairy mantle; so
they called his name Esau. 26 Afterward his brother came forth, and his
hand had taken hold of Esau's heel; so
his name was called Jacob.[r] Isaac was
sixty years old when she bore them.

27 When the boys grew up, Esau
was a skilful hunter, a man of the field,
while Jacob was a quiet man, dwelling
in tents. 28 Isaac loved Esau, because
he ate of his game; but Rebekah loved
Jacob.

29 Once when Jacob was boiling
pottage, Esau came in from the field,
and he was famished. 30 And Esau said
to Jacob, "Let me eat some of that red
pottage, for I am famished!" (Therefore his name was called Ē'dọm.[s])
31 Jacob said, "First sell me your birthright." 32 Esau said, "I am about to die;
of what use is a birthright to me?"
33 Jacob said, "Swear to me first."[t]
So he swore to him, and sold his birthright to Jacob. 34 Then Jacob gave Esau
bread and pottage of lentils, and he
ate and drank, and rose and went his
way. Thus Esau despised his birthright.

26

Now there was a famine in the
land, besides the former famine
that was in the days of Abraham. And
Isaac went to Gē'rār, to Ạ·bĭm'ẹ·lĕch
king of the Phĭ·lĭs'tīnes. 2 And the LORD
appeared to him, and said, "Do not go
down to Egypt; dwell in the land of
which I shall tell you. 3 Sojourn in this
land, and I will be with you, and will
bless you; for to you and to your
descendants I will give all these lands,
and I will fulfil the oath which I
swore to Abraham your father. 4 I will
multiply your descendants as the stars
of heaven, and will give to your descendants all these lands; and by
your descendants all the nations of
the earth shall bless themselves:
5 because Abraham obeyed my voice
and kept my charge, my commandments, my statutes, and my laws."

6 So Isaac dwelt in Gē'rār. 7 When the
men of the place asked him about his
wife, he said, "She is my sister"; for
he feared to say, "My wife," thinking,
"lest the men of the place should kill
me for the sake of Rebekah"; because
she was fair to look upon. 8 When he
had been there a long time, Ạ·bĭm'-
ẹ·lĕch king of the Phĭ·lĭs'tīnes looked
out of a window and saw Isaac fond-
ling Rebekah his wife. 9 So Ạ·bĭm'-
ẹ·lĕch called Isaac, and said, "Behold,
she is your wife; how then could you
say, 'She is my sister'?" Isaac said to

[p] Heb *fell* [q] Syr: Heb obscure
[r] That is *He takes by the heel* or *He supplants*
[s] That is *Red* [t] Heb *today* **25.13-16:** 1 Chron 1.29-31.

him, "Because I thought, 'Lest I die because of her.'" [10]Ạ·bĭm'ẹ·lĕch said, "What is this you have done to us? One of the people might easily have lain with your wife, and you would have brought guilt upon us." [11]So Ạ·bĭm'ẹ·lĕch warned all the people, saying, "Whoever touches this man or his wife shall be put to death."

12 And Isaac sowed in that land, and reaped in the same year a hundredfold. The LORD blessed him, [13]and the man became rich, and gained more and more until he became very wealthy. [14]He had possessions of flocks and herds, and a great household, so that the Phĭ·lĭs'tĭnes envied him. [15](Now the Phĭ·lĭs'tĭnes had stopped and filled with earth all the wells which his father's servants had dug in the days of Abraham his father.) [16]And Ạ·bĭm'ẹ·lĕch said to Isaac, "Go away from us; for you are much mightier than we."

17 So Isaac departed from there, and encamped in the valley of Gē'rär and dwelt there. [18]And Isaac dug again the wells of water which had been dug in the days of Abraham his father; for the Phĭ·lĭs'tĭnes had stopped them after the death of Abraham; and he gave them the names which his father had given them. [19]But when Isaac's servants dug in the valley and found there a well of springing water, [20]the herdsmen of Gē'rär quarreled with Isaac's herdsmen, saying, "The water is ours." So he called the name of the well Ē'sĕk,ᵘ because they contended with him. [21]Then they dug another well, and they quarreled over that also; so he called its name Sĭt'nạh.ᵛ [22]And he moved from there and dug another well, and over that they did not quarrel; so he called its name Rĕ·hō'bŏth,ʷ saying, "For now the LORD has made room for us, and we shall be fruitful in the land."

23 From there he went up to Bē'ẹr-shē'bạ. [24]And the LORD appeared to him the same night and said, "I am the God of Abraham your father; fear not, for I am with you and will bless you and multiply your descendants for my servant Abraham's sake." [25]So he built an altar there and called upon the name of the LORD, and pitched his tent there. And there Isaac's servants dug a well.

26 Then Ạ·bĭm'ẹ·lĕch went to him

from Gē'rär with Ạ·hŭz'zạth his adviser and Phĭ'cŏl the commander of his army. [27]Isaac said to them, "Why have you come to me, seeing that you hate me and have sent me away from you?" [28]They said, "We see plainly that the LORD is with you; so we say, let there be an oath between you and us, and let us make a covenant with you, [29]that you will do us no harm, just as we have not touched you and have done to you nothing but good and have sent you away in peace. You are now the blessed of the LORD." [30]So he made them a feast, and they ate and drank. [31]In the morning they rose early and took oath with one another; and Isaac set them on their way, and they departed from him in peace. [32]That same day Isaac's servants came and told him about the well which they had dug, and said to him, "We have found water." [33]He called it Shĭ'bạh; therefore the name of the city is Bē'ẹr-shē'bạ to this day.

34 When Esau was forty years old, he took to wife Judith the daughter of Bĕ·ē'rī the Hĭt'tīte, and Bäs'ẹ·mäth the daughter of Ē'lŏn the Hittite; [35]and they made life bitter for Isaac and Rebekah.

27 When Isaac was old and his eyes were dim so that he could not see, he called Esau his older son, and said to him, "My son"; and he answered, "Here I am." [2]He said, "Behold, I am old; I do not know the day of my death. [3]Now then, take your weapons, your quiver and your bow, and go out to the field, and hunt game for me, [4]and prepare for me savory food, such as I love, and bring it to me that I may eat; that I may bless you before I die."

5 Now Rebekah was listening when Isaac spoke to his son Esau. So when Esau went to the field to hunt for game and bring it, [6]Rebekah said to her son Jacob, "I heard your father speak to your brother Esau, [7]'Bring me game, and prepare for me savory food, that I may eat it, and bless you before the LORD before I die.' [8]Now therefore, my son, obey my word as I command you. [9]Go to the flock, and fetch me two good kids, that I may prepare from them savory food for your father, such as

---

ᵘThat is Contention   ʷThat is Enmity
ʷThat is Broad places or Room
26.33: Gen 21.31.   27.5: Gen 12.3; Num 24.9.

he loves; ¹⁰and you shall bring it to your father to eat, so that he may bless you before he dies." ¹¹But Jacob said to Rebekah his mother, "Behold, my brother Esau is a hairy man, and I am a smooth man. ¹²Perhaps my father will feel me, and I shall seem to be mocking him, and bring a curse upon myself and not a blessing." ¹³His mother said to him, "Upon me be your curse, my son; only obey my word, and go, fetch them to me." ¹⁴So he went and took them and brought them to his mother; and his mother prepared savory food, such as his father loved. ¹⁵Then Rebekah took the best garments of Esau her older son, which were with her in the house, and put them on Jacob her younger son; ¹⁶and the skins of the kids she put upon his hands and upon the smooth part of his neck; ¹⁷and she gave the savory food and the bread, which she had prepared, into the hand of her son Jacob.

18 So he went in to his father, and said, "My father"; and he said, "Here I am; who are you, my son?" ¹⁹Jacob said to his father, "I am Esau your first-born. I have done as you told me; now sit up and eat of my game, that you may bless me." ²⁰But Isaac said to his son, "How is it that you have found it so quickly, my son?" He answered, "Because the LORD your God granted me success." ²¹Then Isaac said to Jacob, "Come near, that I may feel you, my son, to know whether you are really my son Esau or not." ²²So Jacob went near to Isaac his father, who felt him and said, "The voice is Jacob's voice, but the hands are the hands of Esau." ²³And he did not recognize him, because his hands were hairy like his brother Esau's hands; so he blessed him. ²⁴He said, "Are you really my son Esau?" He answered, "I am." ²⁵Then he said, "Bring it to me, that I may eat of my son's game and bless you." So he brought it to him, and he ate; and he brought him wine, and he drank. ²⁶Then his father Isaac said to him, "Come near and kiss me, my son." ²⁷So he came near and kissed him; and he smelled the smell of his garments, and blessed him, and said, "See, the smell of my son
is as the smell of a field which the LORD has blessed!
²⁸May God give you of the dew of heaven,
and of the fatness of the earth,
and plenty of grain and wine.
²⁹Let peoples serve you,
and nations bow down to you.
Be lord over your brothers,
and may your mother's sons bow down to you.
Cursed be every one who curses you,
and blessed be every one who blesses you!"

30 As soon as Isaac had finished blessing Jacob, when Jacob had scarcely gone out from the presence of Isaac his father, Esau his brother came in from his hunting. ³¹He also prepared savory food, and brought it to his father. And he said to his father, "Let my father arise, and eat of his son's game, that you may bless me." ³²His father Isaac said to him, "Who are you?" He answered, "I am your son, your first-born, Esau." ³³Then Isaac trembled violently, and said, "Who was it then that hunted game and brought it to me, and I ate it all*ˣ* before you came, and I have blessed him?—yes, and he shall be blessed." ³⁴When Esau heard the words of his father, he cried out with an exceedingly great and bitter cry, and said to his father, "Bless me, even me also, O my father!" ³⁵But he said, "Your brother came with guile, and he has taken away your blessing." ³⁶Esau said, "Is he not rightly named Jacob? For he has supplanted me these two times. He took away my birthright; and behold, now he has taken away my blessing." Then he said, "Have you not reserved a blessing for me?" ³⁷Isaac answered Esau, "Behold, I have made him your lord, and all his brothers I have given to him for servants, and with grain and wine I have sustained him. What then can I do for you, my son?" ³⁸Esau said to his father, "Have you but one blessing, my father? Bless me, even me also, O my father." And Esau lifted up his voice and wept.

39 Then Isaac his father answered him:
"Behold, away from*ʸ* the fatness of the earth shall your dwelling be,
and away from*ʸ* the dew of heaven on high.
⁴⁰By your sword you shall live,
and you shall serve your brother;
but when you break loose

*ˣCn: Heb *of all* *ʸOr *of*

you shall break his yoke from your neck."

41 Now Esau hated Jacob because of the blessing with which his father had blessed him, and Esau said to himself, "The days of mourning for my father are approaching; then I will kill my brother Jacob." ⁴² But the words of Esau her older son were told to Rebekah; so she sent and called Jacob her younger son, and said to him, "Behold, your brother Esau comforts himself by planning to kill you. ⁴³ Now therefore, my son, obey my voice; arise, flee to Lā′ban my brother in Hār′an, ⁴⁴ and stay with him a while, until your brother's fury turns away; ⁴⁵ until your brother's anger turns away, and he forgets what you have done to him; then I will send, and fetch you from there. Why should I be bereft of you both in one day?"

46 Then Rebekah said to Isaac, "I am weary of my life because of the Hĭt′tīte women. If Jacob marries one of the Hittite women such as these, one of the women of the land, what good will my life be to me?" 28 ¹ Then Isaac called Jacob and blessed him, and charged him, "You shall not marry one of the Canaanite women. ² Arise, go to Pӑd′dan–ār′am to the house of Bĕ·thü′ĕl your mother's father; and take as wife from there one of the daughters of Lā′ban your mother's brother. ³ God Almighty^z bless you and make you fruitful and multiply you, that you may become a company of peoples. ⁴ May he give the blessing of Abraham to you and to your descendants with you, that you may take possession of the land of your sojournings which God gave to Abraham!" ⁵ Thus Isaac sent Jacob away; and he went to Pӑd′dan–ār′am to Lā′-ban, the son of Bĕ·thü′ĕl the Ӑr·a-mē′an, the brother of Rebekah, Jacob's and Esau's mother.

6 Now Esau saw that Isaac had blessed Jacob and sent him away to Pӑd′dan–ār′am to take a wife from there, and that as he blessed him he charged him, "You shall not marry one of the Canaanite women," ⁷ and that Jacob had obeyed his father and his mother and gone to Pӑd′dan–ār′am. ⁸ So when Esau saw that the Canaanite women did not please Isaac his father, ⁹ Esau went to Ĭsh′ma·ĕl and took to wife, besides the wives he had, Mă·hā′lăth the daughter of Ishmael Abraham's son, the sister of Nĕ·bā′ĭ·ŏth.

10 Jacob left Bē′er–shē′ba, and went toward Hār′an. ¹¹ And he come to a certain place, and stayed there that night, because the sun had set. Taking one of the stones of the place, he put it under his head and lay down in that place to sleep. ¹² And he dreamed that there was a ladder set up on the earth, and the top of it reached to heaven; and behold, the angels of God were ascending and descending on it! ¹³ And behold, the LORD stood above it^a and said, "I am the LORD, the God of Abraham your father and the God of Isaac; the land on which you lie I will give to you and to your descendants; ¹⁴ and your descendants shall be like the dust of the earth, and you shall spread abroad to the west and to the east and to the north and to the south; and by you and your descendants shall all the families of the earth bless themselves.^b ¹⁵ Behold, I am with you and will keep you wherever you go, and will bring you back to this land; for I will not leave you until I have done that of which I have spoken to you." ¹⁶ Then Jacob awoke from his sleep and said, "Surely the LORD is in this place; and I did not know it." ¹⁷ And he was afraid, and said, "How awesome is this place! This is none other than the house of God, and this is the gate of heaven."

18 So Jacob rose early in the morning, and he took the stone which he had put under his head and set it up for a pillar and poured oil on the top of it. ¹⁹ He called the name of that place Bĕth′el;^c but the name of the city was Lŭz at the first. ²⁰ Then Jacob made a vow, saying, "If God will be with me, and will keep me in this way that I go, and will give me bread to eat and clothing to wear, ²¹ so that I come again to my father's house in peace, then the LORD shall be my God, ²² and this stone, which I have set up for a pillar, shall be God's house; and of all that thou givest me I will give the tenth to thee."

29 Then Jacob went on his journey, and came to the land of the people of the east. ² As he looked, he saw a well in the field, and lo, three

^zHeb El Shaddai   ^aOr beside him   ^bOr be blessed
^cThat is The house of God

flocks of sheep lying beside it; for out of that well the flocks were watered. The stone on the well's mouth was large, ³ and when all the flocks were gathered there, the shepherds would roll the stone from the mouth of the well, and water the sheep, and put the stone back in its place upon the mouth of the well. 4 Jacob said to them, "My brothers, where do you come from?" They said, "We are from Hăr′ạn." ⁵ He said to them, "Do you know Lā′bạn the son of Nā′hôr?" They said, "We know him." ⁶ He said to them, "Is it well with him?" They said, "It is well; and see, Rachel his daughter is coming with the sheep!" ⁷ He said, "Behold, it is still high day, it is not time for the animals to be gathered together; water the sheep, and go, pasture them." ⁸ But they said, "We cannot until all the flocks are gathered together, and the stone is rolled from the mouth of the well; then we water the sheep."

9 While he was still speaking with them, Rachel came with her father's sheep; for she kept them. ¹⁰ Now when Jacob saw Rachel the daughter of Lā′bạn his mother's brother, and the sheep of Laban his mother's brother, Jacob went up and rolled the stone from the well's mouth, and watered the flock of Laban his mother's brother. ¹¹ Then Jacob kissed Rachel, and wept aloud. ¹² And Jacob told Rachel that he was her father's kinsman, and that he was Rebekah's son; and she ran and told her father.

13 When Lā′bạn heard the tidings of Jacob his sister's son, he ran to meet him, and embraced him and kissed him, and brought him to his house. Jacob told Laban all these things, ¹⁴ and Lā′bạn said to him, "Surely you are my bone and my flesh!" And he stayed with him a month.

15 Then Lā′bạn said to Jacob, "Because you are my kinsman, should you therefore serve me for nothing? Tell me, what shall your wages be?" ¹⁶ Now Lā′bạn had two daughters; the name of the older was Leah, and the name of the younger was Rachel. ¹⁷ Leah's eyes were weak, but Rachel was beautiful and lovely. ¹⁸ Jacob loved Rachel; and he said, "I will serve you seven years for your younger daughter Rachel." ¹⁹ Lā′bạn said, "It is better that I give her to you than that I should give her

to any other man; stay with me." ²⁰ So Jacob served seven years for Rachel, and they seemed to him but a few days because of the love he had for her.

21 Then Jacob said to Lā′bạn, "Give me my wife that I may go in to her, for my time is completed." ²² So Lā′bạn gathered together all the men of the place, and made a feast. ²³ But in the evening he took his daughter Leah and brought her to Jacob; and he went in to her. ²⁴ (Lā′bạn gave his maid Zĭl′pạh to his daughter Leah to be her maid.) ²⁵ And in the morning, behold, it was Leah; and Jacob said to Lā′bạn, "What is this you have done to me? Did I not serve with you for Rachel? Why then have you deceived me?" ²⁶ Lā′bạn said, "It is not so done in our country, to give the younger before the first-born. ²⁷ Complete the week of this one, and we will give you the other also in return for serving me another seven years." ²⁸ Jacob did so, and completed her week; then Lā′bạn gave him his daughter Rachel to wife. ²⁹ (Lā′bạn gave his maid Bĭl′hạh to his daughter Rachel to be her maid.) ³⁰ So Jacob went in to Rachel also, and he loved Rachel more than Leah, and served Lā′bạn for another seven years.

31 When the LORD saw that Leah was hated, he opened her womb; but Rachel was barren. ³² And Leah conceived and bore a son, and she called his name Reuben;ᵈ for she said, "Because the LORD has looked upon my affliction; surely now my husband will love me." ³³ She conceived again and bore a son, and said, "Because the LORD has heardᵉ that I am hated, he has given me this son also"; and she called his name Sĭm′ē·ọn. ³⁴ Again she conceived and bore a son, and said, "Now this time my husband will be joinedᶠ to me, because I have borne him three sons"; therefore his name was called Levi. ³⁵ And she conceived again and bore a son, and said, "This time I will praiseᵍ the LORD"; therefore she called his name Judah; then she ceased bearing.

30 When Rachel saw that she bore Jacob no children, she envied her sister; and she said to Jacob, "Give me children, or I shall die!" ² Jacob's anger was kindled against Rachel,

ᵈThat is *See, a son* ᵉHeb *shama* ᶠHeb *lawah* ᵍHeb *hodah*

and he said, "Am I in the place of God, who has withheld from you the fruit of the womb?" [3] Then she said, "Here is my maid Bĭl'hăh; go in to her, that she may bear upon my knees, and even I may have children through her." [4] So she gave him her maid Bĭl'hăh as a wife; and Jacob went in to her. [5] And Bĭl'hăh conceived and bore Jacob a son. [6] Then Rachel said, "God has judged me, and has also heard my voice and given me a son"; therefore she called his name Dan.[h] [7] Rachel's maid Bĭl'hăh conceived again and bore Jacob a second son. [8] Then Rachel said, "With mighty wrestlings I have wrestled[i] with my sister, and have prevailed"; so she called his name Năph'tă-lī.

9 When Leah saw that she had ceased bearing children, she took her maid Zĭl'păh and gave her to Jacob as a wife. [10] Then Leah's maid Zĭl'păh bore Jacob a son. [11] And Leah said, "Good fortune!" so she called his name Găd.[j] [12] Leah's maid Zĭl'păh bore Jacob a second son. [13] And Leah said, "Happy am I! For the women will call me happy"; so she called his name Ăsh'ĕr.[k]

14 In the days of wheat harvest Reuben went and found mandrakes in the field, and brought them to his mother Leah. Then Rachel said to Leah, "Give me, I pray, some of your son's mandrakes." [15] But she said to her, "Is it a small matter that you have taken away my husband? Would you take away my son's mandrakes also?" Rachel said, "Then he may lie with you tonight for your son's mandrakes." [16] When Jacob came from the field in the evening, Leah went out to meet him, and said, "You must come in to me; for I have hired you with my son's mandrakes." So he lay with her that night. [17] And God hearkened to Leah, and she conceived and bore Jacob a fifth son. [18] Leah said, "God has given me my hire[l] because I gave my maid to my husband"; so she called his name Ĭs'să-chăr. [19] And Leah conceived again, and she bore Jacob a sixth son. [20] Then Leah said, "God has endowed me with a good dowry; now my husband will honor[m] me, because I have borne him six sons"; so she called his name Zĕb'ū-lŭn. [21] Afterwards she bore a daughter, and called her name Dinah. [22] Then God remembered Ra-

chel, and God hearkened to her and opened her womb. [23] She conceived and bore a son, and said, "God has taken away my reproach"; [24] and she called his name Joseph,[n] saying, "May the LORD add to me another son!"

25 When Rachel had borne Joseph, Jacob said to Lā'băn, "Send me away, that I may go to my own home and country. [26] Give me my wives and my children for whom I have served you, and let me go; for you know the service which I have given you." [27] But Lā'băn said to him, "If you will allow me to say so, I have learned by divination that the LORD has blessed me because of you; [28] name your wages, and I will give it." [29] Jacob said to him, "You yourself know how I have served you, and how your cattle have fared with me. [30] For you had little before I came, and it has increased abundantly; and the LORD has blessed you wherever I turned. But now when shall I provide for my own household also?" [31] He said, "What shall I give you?" Jacob said, "You shall not give me anything; if you will do this for me, I will again feed your flock and keep it: [32] let me pass through all your flock today, removing from it every speckled and spotted sheep and every black lamb, and the spotted and speckled among the goats; and such shall be my wages. [33] So my honesty will answer for me later, when you come to look into my wages with you. Every one that is not speckled and spotted among the goats and black among the lambs, if found with me, shall be counted stolen." [34] Lā'băn said, "Good! Let it be as you have said." [35] But that day Lā'băn removed the he-goats that were striped and spotted, and all the she-goats that were speckled and spotted, every one that had white on it, and every lamb that was black, and put them in charge of his sons; [36] and he set a distance of three days' journey between himself and Jacob; and Jacob fed the rest of Lā'băn's flock.

37 Then Jacob took fresh rods of poplar and almond and plane, and peeled white streaks in them, exposing the white of the rods. [38] He set the rods which he had peeled in front of the flocks in the runnels, that is, the

---

[h]That is *He judged* [i]Heb *niphtal*
[j]That is *Fortune* [k]That is *Happy* [l]Heb *sakar*
[m]Heb *zabal* [n]That is *He adds*

watering troughs, where the flocks came to drink. And since they bred when they came to drink, ³⁹the flocks bred in front of the rods and so the flocks brought forth striped, speckled, and spotted. ⁴⁰And Jacob separated the lambs, and set the faces of the flocks toward the striped and all the black in the flock of Lā′ban; and he put his own droves apart, and did not put them with Laban's flock. ⁴¹Whenever the stronger of the flock were breeding Jacob laid the rods in the runnels before the eyes of the flock, that they might breed among the rods, ⁴²but for the feebler of the flock he did not lay them there; so the feebler were Lā′ban′s, and the stronger Jacob's. ⁴³Thus the man grew exceedingly rich, and had large flocks, maidservants and menservants, and camels and asses.

31 Now Jacob heard that the sons of Lā′ban were saying, "Jacob has taken all that was our father's; and from what was our father's he has gained all this wealth." ²And Jacob saw that Lā′ban did not regard him with favor as before. ³Then the Lᴏʀᴅ said to Jacob, "Return to the land of your fathers and to your kindred, and I will be with you." ⁴So Jacob sent and called Rachel and Leah into the field where his flock was, ⁵and said to them, "I see that your father does not regard me with favor as he did before. But the God of my father has been with me. ⁶You know that I have served your father with all my strength; ⁷yet your father has cheated me and changed my wages ten times, but God did not permit him to harm me. ⁸If he said, 'The spotted shall be your wages,' then all the flock bore spotted; and if he said, 'The striped shall be your wages,' then all the flock bore striped. ⁹Thus God has taken away the cattle of your father, and given them to me. ¹⁰In the mating season of the flock I lifted up my eyes, and saw in a dream that the he-goats which leaped upon the flock were striped, spotted, and mottled. ¹¹Then the angel of God said to me in the dream, 'Jacob,' and I said, 'Here I am!' ¹²And he said, 'Lift up your eyes and see, all the goats that leap upon the flock are striped, spotted, and mottled; for I have seen all that Lā′ban is doing to you. ¹³I am the God of Bĕth′el, where you

anointed a pillar and made a vow to me. Now arise, go forth from this land, and return to the land of your birth.' " ¹⁴Then Rachel and Leah answered him, "Is there any portion or inheritance left to us in our father's house? ¹⁵Are we not regarded by him as foreigners? For he has sold us, and he has been using up the money given for us. ¹⁶All the property which God has taken away from our father belongs to us and to our children; now then, whatever God has said to you, do."

17 So Jacob arose, and set his sons and his wives on camels; ¹⁸and he drove away all his cattle, all his livestock which he had gained, the cattle in his possession which he had acquired in Păd′dạn-ār′ạm, to go to the land of Canaan to his father Isaac. ¹⁹Lā′ban had gone to shear his sheep, and Rachel stole her father's household gods. ²⁰And Jacob outwitted Lā′-ban the Ä̇r·a·mē′an, in that he did not tell him that he intended to flee. ²¹He fled with all that he had, and arose and crossed the Euphrates, and set his face toward the hill country of Gilead.

22 When it was told Lā′ban on the third day that Jacob had fled, ²³he took his kinsmen with him and pursued him for seven days and followed close after him into the hill country of Gilead. ²⁴But God came to Lā′ban the Ä̇r·a·mē′an in a dream by night, and said to him, "Take heed that you say not a word to Jacob, either good or bad."

25 And Lā′ban overtook Jacob. Now Jacob had pitched his tent in the hill country, and Laban with his kinsmen encamped in the hill country of Gilead. ²⁶And Lā′ban said to Jacob, "What have you done, that you have cheated me, and carried away my daughters like captives of the sword? ²⁷Why did you flee secretly, and cheat me, and did not tell me, so that I might have sent you away with mirth and songs, with tambourine and lyre? ²⁸And why did you not permit me to kiss my sons and my daughters farewell? Now you have done foolishly. ²⁹It is in my power to do you harm; but the God of your father spoke to me last night, saying, 'Take heed that you speak to Jacob neither good nor bad.' ³⁰And now you have gone away because you longed

greatly for your father's house, but why did you steal my gods?" [31] Jacob answered Lā'ban, "Because I was afraid, for I thought that you would take your daughters from me by force. [32] Any one with whom you find your gods shall not live. In the presence of our kinsmen point out what I have that is yours, and take it." Now Jacob did not know that Rachel had stolen them.

33 So Lā'ban went into Jacob's tent, and into Leah's tent, and into the tent of the two maidservants, but he did not find them. And he went out of Leah's tent, and entered Rachel's. [34] Now Rachel had taken the household gods and put them in the camel's saddle, and sat upon them. Lā'ban felt all about the tent, but did not find them. [35] And she said to her father, "Let not my lord be angry that I cannot rise before you, for the way of women is upon me." So he searched, but did not find the household gods.

36 Then Jacob became angry, and upbraided Lā'ban; Jacob said to Laban, "What is my offense? What is my sin, that you have hotly pursued me? [37] Although you have felt through all my goods, what have you found of all your household goods? Set it here before my kinsmen and your kinsmen, that they may decide between us two. [38] These twenty years I have been with you; your ewes and your she-goats have not miscarried, and I have not eaten the rams of your flocks. [39] That which was torn by wild beasts I did not bring to you; I bore the loss of it myself; of my hand you required it, whether stolen by day or stolen by night. [40] Thus I was; by day the heat consumed me, and the cold by night, and my sleep fled from my eyes. [41] These twenty years I have been in your house; I served you fourteen years for your two daughters, and six years for your flock, and you have changed my wages ten times. [42] If the God of my father, the God of Abraham and the Fear of Isaac, had not been on my side, surely now you would have sent me away empty-handed. God saw my affliction and the labor of my hands, and rebuked you last night."

43 Then Lā'ban answered and said to Jacob, "The daughters are my daughters, the children are my children, the flocks are my flocks, and all

that you see is mine. But what can I do this day to these my daughters, or to their children whom they have borne? [44] Come now, let us make a covenant, you and I; and let it be a witness between you and me." [45] So Jacob took a stone, and set it up as a pillar. [46] And Jacob said to his kinsmen, "Gather stones," and they took stones, and made a heap; and they ate there by the heap. [47] Lā'ban called it Jē-gar-sā·hǎ·dū'tha:[o] but Jacob called it Gǎl·ē'ĕd.[p] [48] Lā'ban said, "This heap is a witness between you and me to-day." Therefore he named it Gǎl-ē'ĕd, [49] and the pillar[q] Mīz'pah,[r] for he said, "The LORD watch between you and me, when we are absent one from the other. [50] If you ill-treat my daughters, or if you take wives besides my daughters, although no man is with us, remember, God is witness between you and me."

51 Then Lā'ban said to Jacob, "See this heap and the pillar, which I have set between you and me. [52] This heap is a witness, and the pillar is a witness, that I will not pass over this heap to you, and you will not pass over this heap and this pillar to me, for harm. [53] The God of Abraham and the God of Nā'hôr, the God of their father, judge between us." So Jacob swore by the Fear of his father Isaac, [54] and Jacob offered a sacrifice on the mountain and called his kinsmen to eat bread; and they ate bread and tarried all night on the mountain.

55[s] Early in the morning Lā'ban arose, and kissed his grandchildren and his daughters and blessed them; then he departed and returned home.

32 Jacob went on his way and the angels of God met him; [2] and when Jacob saw them he said, "This is God's army!" So he called the name of that place Mā"ha·nā'ĭm.[t]

3 And Jacob sent messengers before him to Esau his brother in the land of Sē'ĭr, the country of Ē'dom, [4] instructing them, "Thus you shall say to my lord Esau: Thus says your servant Jacob, 'I have sojourned with Lā'ban, and stayed until now; [5] and I have oxen, asses, flocks, menservants, and maidservants; and I have sent to

[o] In Aramaic *The heap of witness*
[p] In Hebrew *The heap of witness*
[q] Compare Sam: Heb lacks *the pillar* [r] That is *Watchpost*
[s] Ch 32.1 in Heb [t] Here taken to mean *Two armies*

tell my lord, in order that I may find favor in your sight.' "

6 And the messengers returned to Jacob, saying, "We came to your brother Esau, and he is coming to meet you, and four hundred men with him." ⁷Then Jacob was greatly afraid and distressed; and he divided the people that were with him, and the flocks and herds and camels, into two companies, ⁸thinking, "If Esau comes to the one company and destroys it, then the company which is left will escape."

9 And Jacob said, "O God of my father Abraham and God of my father Isaac, O LORD who didst say to me, 'Return to your country and to your kindred, and I will do you good,' ¹⁰I am not worthy of the least of all the steadfast love and all the faithfulness which thou hast shown to thy servant, for with only my staff I crossed this Jordan; and now I have become two companies. ¹¹Deliver me, I pray thee, from the hand of my brother, from the hand of Esau, for I fear him, lest he come and slay us all, the mothers with the children. ¹²But thou didst say, 'I will do you good, and make your descendants as the sand of the sea, which cannot be numbered for multitude.' "

13 So he lodged there that night, and took from what he had with him a present for his brother Esau, ¹⁴two hundred she-goats and twenty he-goats, two hundred ewes and twenty rams, ¹⁵thirty milch camels and their colts, forty cows and ten bulls, twenty she-asses and ten he-asses. ¹⁶These he delivered into the hand of his servants, every drove by itself, and said to his servants, "Pass on before me, and put a space between drove and drove." ¹⁷He instructed the foremost, "When Esau my brother meets you, and asks you, 'To whom do you belong? Where are you going? And whose are these before you?' ¹⁸then you shall say, 'They belong to your servant Jacob; they are a present sent to my lord Esau; and moreover he is behind us.' " ¹⁹He likewise instructed the second and the third and all who followed the droves, "You shall say the same thing to Esau when you meet him, ²⁰and you shall say, 'Moreover your servant Jacob is behind us.' " For he thought, "I may appease him with the present that goes before me, and afterwards

I shall see his face; perhaps he will accept me." ²¹So the present passed on before him; and he himself lodged that night in the camp.

22 The same night he arose and took his two wives, his two maids, and his eleven children, and crossed the ford of the Jăb′bŏk. ²³He took them and sent them across the stream, and likewise everything that he had. ²⁴And Jacob was left alone; and a man wrestled with him until the breaking of the day. ²⁵When the man saw that he did not prevail against Jacob, he touched the hollow of his thigh; and Jacob's thigh was put out of joint as he wrestled with him. ²⁶Then he said, "Let me go, for the day is breaking." But Jacob said, "I will not let you go, unless you bless me." ²⁷And he said to him, "What is your name?" And he said, "Jacob." ²⁸Then he said, "Your name shall no more be called Jacob, but Israel,ᵘ for you have striven with God and with men, and have prevailed." ²⁹Then Jacob asked him, "Tell me, I pray, your name." But he said, "Why is it that you ask my name?" And there he blessed him. ³⁰So Jacob called the name of the place Pĕ·nī′ĕl,ᵛ saying, "For I have seen God face to face, and yet my life is preserved." ³¹The sun rose upon him as he passed Pĕ·nū′ĕl, limping because of his thigh. ³²Therefore to this day the Israelites do not eat the sinew of the hip which is upon the hollow of the thigh, because he touched the hollow of Jacob's thigh on the sinew of the hip.

33 And Jacob lifted up his eyes and looked, and behold, Esau was coming, and four hundred men with him. So he divided the children among Leah and Rachel and the two maids. ²And he put the maids with their children in front, then Leah with her children, and Rachel and Joseph last of all. ³He himself went on before them, bowing himself to the ground seven times, until he came near to his brother.

4 But Esau ran to meet him, and embraced him, and fell on his neck and kissed him, and they wept. ⁵And when Esau raised his eyes and saw the women and children, he said, "Who are these with you?" Jacob said, "The children whom God has graciously

ᵘThat is *He who strives with God* or *God strives*
ᵛThat is *The face of God*

given your servant." ⁶Then the maids drew near, they and their children, and bowed down; ⁷Leah likewise and her children drew near and bowed down; and last Joseph and Rachel drew near, and they bowed down. ⁸Esau said, "What do you mean by all this company which I met?" Jacob answered, "To find favor in the sight of my lord." ⁹But Esau said, "I have enough, my brother; keep what you have for yourself." ¹⁰Jacob said, "No, I pray you, if I have found favor in your sight, then accept my present from my hand; for truly to see your face is like seeing the face of God, with such favor have you received me. ¹¹Accept, I pray you, my gift that is brought to you, because God has dealt graciously with me, and because I have enough." Thus he urged him, and he took it.

12 Then Esau said, "Let us journey on our way, and I will go before you." ¹³But Jacob said to him, "My lord knows that the children are frail, and that the flocks and herds giving suck are a care to me; and if they are overdriven for one day, all the flocks will die. ¹⁴Let my lord pass on before his servant, and I will lead on slowly, according to the pace of the cattle which are before me and according to the pace of the children, until I come to my lord in Sē'ïr."

15 So Esau said, "Let me leave with you some of the men who are with me." But he said, "What need is there? Let me find favor in the sight of my lord." ¹⁶So Esau returned that day on his way to Sē'ïr. ¹⁷But Jacob journeyed to Sŭc'cŏth,ᵂ and built himself a house, and made booths for his cattle; therefore the name of the place is called Succoth.

18 And Jacob came safely to the city of Shē'chĕm, which is in the land of Canaan, on his way from Păd'dạn-ăr'ạm; and he camped before the city. ¹⁹And from the sons of Hā'môr, Shē'-chĕm'ş father, he bought for a hundred pieces of moneyˣ the piece of land on which he had pitched his tent. ²⁰There he erected an altar and called it Ĕl–Ĕl'ō-hē-Ĭş'rạ.ĕl.ᵞ

34 Now Dinah the daughter of Leah, whom she had borne to Jacob, went out to visit the women of the land; ²and when Shē'chĕm the son of Hā'môr the Hī'vīte, the prince of the land, saw her, he seized her and lay with her and humbled her. ³And his soul was drawn to Dinah daughter of Jacob; he loved the maiden and spoke tenderly to her. ⁴So Shē'chĕm spoke to his father Hā'-môr, saying, "Get me this maiden for my wife." ⁵Now Jacob heard that he had defiled his daughter Dinah; but his sons were with his cattle in the field, so Jacob held his peace until they came. ⁶And Hā'môr the father of Shē'chĕm went out to Jacob to speak with him. ⁷The sons of Jacob came in from the field when they heard of it; and the men were indignant and very angry, because he had wrought folly in Israel by lying with Jacob's daughter, for such a thing ought not to be done.

8 But Hā'môr spoke with them, saying, "The soul of my son Shē'chĕm longs for your daughter; I pray you, give her to him in marriage. ⁹Make marriages with us; give your daughters to us, and take our daughters for yourselves. ¹⁰You shall dwell with us; and the land shall be open to you; dwell and trade in it, and get property in it." ¹¹Shē'chĕm also said to her father and to her brothers, "Let me find favor in your eyes, and whatever you say to me I will give. ¹²Ask of me ever so much as marriage present and gift, and I will give according as you say to me; only give me the maiden to be my wife."

13 The sons of Jacob answered Shē'chĕm and his father Hā'môr deceitfully, because he had defiled their sister Dinah. ¹⁴They said to them, "We cannot do this thing, to give our sister to one who is uncircumcised, for that would be a disgrace to us. ¹⁵Only on this condition will we consent to you: that you will become as we are and every male of you be circumcised. ¹⁶Then we will give our daughters to you, and we will take your daughters to ourselves, and we will dwell with you and become one people. ¹⁷But if you will not listen to us and be circumcised, then we will take our daughter, and we will be gone."

18 Their words pleased Hā'môr and Hamor's son Shē'chĕm. ¹⁹And the young man did not delay to do the thing, because he had delight in

ᵂ*That is Booths*   ˣ*Heb a hundred qesitah*
ᵞ*That is God, the God of Israel*

Jacob's daughter. Now he was the most honored of all his family. ²⁰ So Hā'môr and his son Shē'chĕm came to the gate of their city and spoke to the men of their city, saying, ²¹ "These men are friendly with us; let them dwell in the land and trade in it, for behold, the land is large enough for them; let us take their daughters in marriage, and let us give them our daughters. ²² Only on this condition will the men agree to dwell with us, to become one people: that every male among us be circumcised as they are circumcised. ²³ Will not their cattle, their property and all their beasts be ours? Only let us agree with them, and they will dwell with us." ²⁴ And all who went out of the gate of his city hearkened to Hā'môr and his son Shē'chĕm; and every male was circumcised, all who went out of the gate of his city.

25 On the third day, when they were sore, two of the sons of Jacob, Sĭm'ē·ọn and Lē'vī, Dinah's brothers, took their swords and came upon the city unawares, and killed all the males. ²⁶ They slew Hā'môr and his son Shē'chĕm with the sword, and took Dinah out of Shechem's house, and went away. ²⁷ And the sons of Jacob came upon the slain, and plundered the city, because their sister had been defiled; ²⁸ they took their flocks and their herds, their asses, and whatever was in the city and in the field; ²⁹ all their wealth, all their little ones and their wives, all that was in the houses, they captured and made their prey. ³⁰ Then Jacob said to Sĭm'ē·ọn and Levi, "You have brought trouble on me by making me odious to the inhabitants of the land, the Canaanites and the Pĕr'ĭz·zītes; my numbers are few, and if they gather themselves against me and attack me, I shall be destroyed, both I and my household." ³¹ But they said, "Should he treat our sister as a harlot?"

35 God said to Jacob, "Arise, go up to Bĕth'ẹl, and dwell there; and make there an altar to the God who appeared to you when you fled from your brother Esau." ² So Jacob said to his household and to all who were with him, "Put away the foreign gods that are among you, and purify yourselves, and change your garments; ³ then let us arise and go up to Bĕth'ẹl, that I may make there an altar to the God who answered me in the day of my distress and has been with me wherever I have gone." ⁴ So they gave to Jacob all the foreign gods that they had, and the rings that were in their ears; and Jacob hid them under the oak which was near Shē'-chĕm.

5 And as they journeyed, a terror from God fell upon the cities that were round about them, so that they did not pursue the sons of Jacob. ⁶ And Jacob came to Lŭz (that is, Bĕth'ẹl), which is in the land of Canaan, he and all the people who were with him, ⁷ and there he built an altar, and called the place Ĕl–bĕth'ẹl,ᶻ because there God had revealed himself to him when he fled from his brother. ⁸ And Dĕb'ọ·rạh, Rebekah's nurse, died, and she was buried under an oak below Bĕth'ẹl; so the name of it was called Ăl'lọn–băc'ụth.ᵃ

9 God appeared to Jacob again, when he came from Păd'dạn–ār'ạm, and blessed him. ¹⁰ And God said to him, "Your name is Jacob; no longer shall your name be called Jacob, but Israel shall be your name." So his name was called Israel. ¹¹ And God said to him, "I am God Almighty:ᵇ be fruitful and multiply; a nation and a company of nations shall come from you, and kings shall spring from you. ¹² The land which I gave to Abraham and Isaac I will give to you, and I will give the land to your descendants after you." ¹³ Then God went up from him in the place where he had spoken with him. ¹⁴ And Jacob set up a pillar in the place where he had spoken with him, a pillar of stone; and he poured out a drink offering on it, and poured oil on it. ¹⁵ So Jacob called the name of the place where God had spoken with him, Bĕth'ẹl.

16 Then they journeyed from Bĕth'ẹl; and when they were still some distance from Ĕph'răth, Rachel travailed, and she had hard labor. ¹⁷ And when she was in her hard labor, the midwife said to her, "Fear not; for now you will have another son." ¹⁸ And as her soul was departing (for she died), she called his name Bĕn–ō'nĭ;ᶜ but his father called his name Benjamin.ᵈ ¹⁹ So Rachel died, and she was buried

---

ᶻ That is God of Bethel ᵃ That is Oak of weeping
ᵇ Heb El Shaddai ᶜ That is Son of my sorrow
ᵈ That is Son of the right hand or Son of the South

on the way to Ĕph'răth (that is, Beth-lehem), ²⁰ and Jacob set up a pillar upon her grave; it is the pillar of Rachel's tomb, which is there to this day. ²¹ Israel journeyed on, and pitched his tent beyond the tower of Ē'dẹr.

22 While Israel dwelt in that land Reuben went and lay with Bĭl'hah his father's concubine; and Israel heard of it.

Now the sons of Jacob were twelve. ²³ The sons of Leah: Reuben (Jacob's first-born), Sĭm'ē·ọn, Lē'vī, Judah, Ĭs'sạ·chär, and Zĕb'ū·lụn. ²⁴ The sons of Rachel: Joseph and Benjamin. ²⁵ The sons of Bĭl'hah, Rachel's maid: Dan and Năph'tạ·lī. ²⁶ The sons of Zĭl'pạh, Leah's maid: Găd and Ăsh'ẹr. These were the sons of Jacob who were born to him in Păd'dạn–är'ạm.

27 And Jacob came to his father Isaac at Măm'rĕ, or Kĭr'ĭ·ăth–är'bạ (that is, Hē'brọn), where Abraham and Isaac had sojourned. ²⁸ Now the days of Isaac were a hundred and eighty years. ²⁹ And Isaac breathed his last; and he died and was gathered to his people, old and full of days; and his sons Esau and Jacob buried him.

36 These are the descendants of Esau (that is, Ē'dọm). ² Esau took his wives from the Canaanites: Ā'dạh the daughter of Ē'lŏn the Hĭt'-tīte, Ō·hŏl·ĭ·bā'mạh the daughter of Ăn'ạh the son[e] of Zĭb'ē·ọn the Hī'vīte, ³ and Băs'ẹ·măth, Ĭsh'mạ·ĕl's daughter, the sister of Nĕ·bā'ĭ·ŏth. ⁴ And Ā'dạh bore to Esau, Ĕ·lī'phăz; Băs'ẹ·măth bore Reü'ĕl; ⁵ and Ō·hŏl·ĭ·bā'mạh bore Jē'ŭsh, Jā'lạm, and Kō'rạh. These are the sons of Esau who were born to him in the land of Canaan.

6 Then Esau took his wives, his sons, his daughters, and all the members of his household, his cattle, all his beasts, and all his property which he had acquired in the land of Canaan; and he went into a land away from his brother Jacob. ⁷ For their possessions were too great for them to dwell to-gether; the land of their sojournings could not support them because of their cattle. ⁸ So Esau dwelt in the hill country of Sē'ĭr; Esau is Ē'dọm.

9 These are the descendants of Esau the father of the Ē'dọm·ītes in the hill country of Sē'ĭr. ¹⁰ These are the names of Esau's sons: Ĕ·lī'phăz the son of Ā'dạh the wifc of Esau, Rcü'ĕl the son of Băs'ẹ·măth the wife of Esau. ¹¹ The

sons of Ĕ·lī'phăz were Tē'mạn, Ō'mär, Zē'phō, Gā'tăm, and Kē'năz. ¹²(Tĭm'nạ was a concubine of Ĕ·lī'phăz, Esau's son; she bore Ăm'ạ·lĕk to Eliphaz.) These are the sons of Ā'dạh, Esau's wife. ¹³ These are the sons of Reü'ĕl: Nā'hăth, Zē'rạh, Shăm'mạh, and Mĭz'zạh. These are the sons of Băs'-ẹ·măth, Esau's wife. ¹⁴ These are the sons of Ō·hŏl·ĭ·bā'mạh the daughter of Ăn'ạh the son[f] of Zĭb'ē·ọn, Esau's wife: she bore to Esau Jē'ŭsh, Jā'lạm, and Kō'rạh.

15 These are the chiefs of the sons of Esau. The sons of Ĕ·lī'phăz the first-born of Esau: the chiefs Tē'mạn, Ō'mär, Zē'phō, Kē'năz, ¹⁶ Kō'rạh, Gā'tăm, and Ăm'ạ·lĕk; these are the chiefs of Ĕ'lī'phăz in the land of Ē'dọm; they are the sons of Ā'dạh. ¹⁷ These are the sons of Reü'ĕl, Esau's son: the chiefs Nā'hăth, Zē'rạh, Shăm'mạh, and Mĭz'zạh; these are the chiefs of Reuel in the land of Ē'dọm; they are the sons of Băs'ẹ·măth, Esau's wife. ¹⁸ These are the sons of Ō·hŏl·ĭ·bā'mạh, Esau's wife: the chiefs Jē'ŭsh, Jā'lạm, and Kō'rạh; these are the chiefs born of Oholi-bamah the daughter of Ăn'ạh, Esau's wife. ¹⁹ These are the sons of Esau (that is, Ē'dọm), and these are their chiefs.

20 These are the sons of Sē'ĭr the Hôr'īte, the inhabitants of the land: Lō'tăn, Shō'bạl, Zĭb'ē·ọn, Ăn'ạh, ²¹ Dī'-shŏn, Ē'zẹr, and Dī'shăn; these are the chiefs of the Hôr'ītes, the sons of Sē'ĭr in the land of Ē'dọm. ²² The sons of Lō'tăn were Hō'rī and Hē'mạn; and Lotan's sister was Tĭm'nạ. ²³ These are the sons of Shō'bạl: Ăl'van, Măn'-ạ·hăth, Ē'bạl, Shē'phō, and Ō'nạm. ²⁴ These are the sons of Zĭb'ē·ọn: Ā'ĭ·ạh and Ăn'ạh; he is the Anah who found the hot springs in the wilderness, as he pastured the asses of Zibeon his father. ²⁵ These are the children of Ăn'ạh: Dī'shŏn and Ō·hŏl·ĭ·bā'mạh the daughter of Anah. ²⁶ These are the sons of Dī'shŏn: Hĕm'dạn, Ĕsh'bạn, Ĭth'-rạn, and Chē'rạn. ²⁷ These are the sons of Ē'zẹr: Bĭl'hạn, Zā'ạ·văn, and Ā'kạn. ²⁸ These are the sons of Dī'shăn: Ŭz and Är'ạn. ²⁹ These are the chiefs of the Hôr'ītes: the chiefs Lō'tăn, Shō'-bạl, Zĭb'ē·ọn, Ăn'ạh, ³⁰ Dī'shŏn, Ē'zẹr, and Dī'shăn; these are the chiefs of

ᵉSam Gk Syr: Heb *daughter*
ᶠGk Syr: Heb *daughter*
36.2: Gen 26.34; 28.9. **36.20-28:** 1 Chron 1.38-42.

the Hôr′ītes, according to their clans in the land of Sē′īr.

31 These are the kings who reigned in the land of Ē′dom, before any king reigned over the Israelites. ³²Bē′la the son of Bē′ôr reigned in Ē′dom, the name of his city being Dĭn′ha·bah. ³³Bē′la died, and Jō′băb the son of Zē′rah of Bŏz′rah reigned in his stead. ³⁴Jō′băb died, and Hū′sham of the land of the Tē′man-ītes reigned in his stead. ³⁵Hū′sham died, and Hā′dăd the son of Bē′dăd, who defeated Mĭd′-ĭ·an in the country of Mō′ăb, reigned in his stead, the name of his city being Ā′vĭth. ³⁶Hā′dăd died, and Săm′lah of Măs·rē′kah reigned in his stead. ³⁷Săm′lah died, and Shā′ül of Rĕ·hō′-bŏth on the Euphrates reigned in his stead. ³⁸Shā′ül died, and Bā′al-hā′nan the son of Ăch′bôr reigned in his stead. ³⁹Bā′al-hā′nan the son of Ăch′bôr died, and Hā′dăr reigned in his stead, the name of his city being Pā′u; his wife's name was Mĕ·hĕt′a·bel, the daughter of Mā′trĕd, daughter of Mē′za·hăb.

40 These are the names of the chiefs of Esau, according to their families and their dwelling places, by their names: the chiefs Tĭm′na, Ăl′vah, Jē′thĕth, ⁴¹Ō·hŏl·ĭ·bā′mah, Ē′lah, Pī′nŏn, ⁴²Kē′năz, Tē′man, Mĭb′zăr, ⁴³Măg′dĭ·el, and Ī′ram; these are the chiefs of Ē′dom (that is, Esau, the father of Edom), according to their dwelling places in the land of their possession.

37 Jacob dwelt in the land of his father's sojournings, in the land of Canaan. ²This is the history of the family of Jacob.

Joseph, being seventeen years old, was shepherding the flock with his brothers; he was a lad with the sons of Bĭl′hah and Zĭl′pah, his father's wives; and Joseph brought an ill report of them to their father. ³Now Israel loved Joseph more than any other of his children, because he was the son of his old age; and he made him a long robe with sleeves. ⁴But when his brothers saw that their father loved him more than all his brothers, they hated him, and could not speak peaceably to him.

5 Now Joseph had a dream, and when he told it to his brothers they only hated him the more. ⁶He said to them, "Hear this dream which I have dreamed: ⁷behold, we were binding sheaves in the field, and lo, my sheaf arose and stood upright; and behold, your sheaves gathered round it, and bowed down to my sheaf." ⁸His brothers said to him, "Are you indeed to reign over us? Or are you indeed to have dominion over us?" So they hated him yet more for his dreams and for his words. ⁹Then he dreamed another dream, and told it to his brothers, and said, "Behold, I have dreamed another dream; and behold, the sun, the moon, and eleven stars were bowing down to me." ¹⁰But when he told it to his father and to his brothers, his father rebuked him, and said to him, "What is this dream that you have dreamed? Shall I and your mother and your brothers indeed come to bow ourselves to the ground before you?" ¹¹And his brothers were jealous of him, but his father kept the saying in mind.

12 Now his brothers went to pasture their father's flock near Shē′chem. ¹³And Israel said to Joseph, "Are not your brothers pasturing the flock at Shē′chem? Come, I will send you to them." And he said to him, "Here I am." ¹⁴So he said to him, "Go now, see if it is well with your brothers, and with the flock; and bring me word again." So he sent him from the valley of Hē′-bron, and he came to Shē′chem. ¹⁵And a man found him wandering in the fields; and the man asked him, "What are you seeking?" ¹⁶"I am seeking my brothers," he said, "tell me, I pray you, where they are pasturing the flock." ¹⁷And the man said, "They have gone away, for I heard them say, 'Let us go to Dō′than.'" So Joseph went after his brothers, and found them at Do′than. ¹⁸They saw him afar off, and before he came near to them they conspired against him to kill him. ¹⁹They said to one another, "Here comes this dreamer. ²⁰Come now, let us kill him and throw him into one of the pits; then we shall say that a wild beast has devoured him, and we shall see what will become of his dreams." ²¹But when Reuben heard it, he delivered him out of their hands, saying, "Let us not take his life." ²²And Reuben said to them, "Shed no blood; cast him into this pit here in the wilderness, but lay no hand upon him"—that he might rescue him out of their hand, to re-

36.31-43: 1 Chron 1.43-53. 37.11, 28: Acts 7.9.

store him to his father. ²³So when Joseph came to his brothers, they stripped him of his robe, the long robe with sleeves that he wore; ²⁴and they took him and cast him into a pit. The pit was empty, there was no water in it.

25 Then they sat down to eat; and looking up they saw a caravan of Ish′ma·el′ites coming from Gilead, with their camels bearing gum, balm, and myrrh, on their way to carry it down to Egypt. ²⁶Then Judah said to his brothers, "What profit is it if we slay our brother and conceal his blood? ²⁷Come, let us sell him to the Ish′ma·el·ites, and let not our hand be upon him, for he is our brother, our own flesh." And his brothers heeded him. ²⁸Then Mid′i·a·nite traders passed by; and they drew Joseph up and lifted him out of the pit, and sold him to the Ish′ma·el·ites for twenty shekels of silver; and they took Joseph to Egypt.

29 When Reuben returned to the pit and saw that Joseph was not in the pit, he rent his clothes ³⁰and returned to his brothers, and said, "The lad is gone; and I, where shall I go?" ³¹Then they took Joseph's robe, and killed a goat, and dipped the robe in the blood; ³²and they sent the long robe with sleeves and brought it to their father, and said, "This we have found; see now whether it is your son's robe or not." ³³And he recognized it, and said, "It is my son's robe; a wild beast has devoured him; Joseph is without doubt torn to pieces." ³⁴Then Jacob rent his garments, and put sackcloth upon his loins, and mourned for his son many days. ³⁵All his sons and all his daughters rose up to comfort him; but he refused to be comforted, and said, "No, I shall go down to She′ol to my son, mourning." Thus his father wept for him. ³⁶Meanwhile the Mid′i·a·nites had sold him in Egypt to Pot′i·phar, an officer of Pharaoh, the captain of the guard.

38 It happened at that time that Judah went down from his brothers, and turned in to a certain A·dul′la·mite, whose name was Hi′rah. ²There Judah saw the daughter of a certain Canaanite whose name was Shu′a; he married her and went in to her, ³and she conceived and bore a son, and he called his name Er. ⁴Again she conceived and bore a son, and she called his name O′nan. ⁵Yet again she

bore a son, and she called his name She′lah. She*ᵍ* was in Che′zib when she bore him. ⁶And Judah took a wife for Er his first-born, and her name was Ta′mar. ⁷But Er, Judah's first-born, was wicked in the sight of the LORD; and the LORD slew him. ⁸Then Judah said to O′nan, "Go in to your brother's wife, and perform the duty of a brother-in-law to her, and raise up offspring for your brother." ⁹But O′nan knew that the offspring would not be his; so when he went in to his brother's wife he spilled the semen on the ground, lest he should give offspring to his brother. ¹⁰And what he did was displeasing in the sight of the LORD, and he slew him also. ¹¹Then Judah said to Ta′mar his daughter-in-law, "Remain a widow in your father's house, till She′lah my son grows up"—for he feared that he would die, like his brothers. So Tamar went and dwelt in her father's house.

12 In course of time the wife of Judah, Shu′a′s daughter, died; and when Judah was comforted, he went up to Tim′nah to his sheepshearers, he and his friend Hi′rah the A·dul′-la·mite. ¹³And when Ta′mar was told, "Your father-in-law is going up to Tim′nah to shear his sheep," ¹⁴she put off her widow's garments, and put on a veil, wrapping herself up, and sat at the entrance to E·na′im, which is on the road to Tim′nah; for she saw that She′lah was grown up, and she had not been given to him in marriage. ¹⁵When Judah saw her, he thought her to be a harlot, for she had covered her face. ¹⁶He went over to her at the road side, and said, "Come, let me come in to you," for he did not know that she was his daughter-in-law. She said, "What will you give me, that you may come in to me?" ¹⁷He answered, "I will send you a kid from the flock." And she said, "Will you give me a pledge, till you send it?" ¹⁸He said, "What pledge shall I give you?" She replied, "Your signet and your cord, and your staff that is in your hand." So he gave them to her, and went in to her, and she conceived by him. ¹⁹Then she arose and went away, and taking off her veil she put on the garments of her widowhood.

20 When Judah sent the kid by his friend the A·dul′la·mite, to receive the

ᵍGk: Heb He

pledge from the woman's hand, he could not find her. ²¹And he asked the men of the place, "Where is the harlot* who was at E·na'im by the wayside?" And they said, "No harlot* has been here." ²²So he returned to Judah, and said, "I have not found her; and also the men of the place said, 'No harlot* has been here.' " ²³And Judah replied, "Let her keep the things as her own, lest we be laughed at; you see, I sent this kid, and you could not find her."

24 About three months later Judah was told, "Tā'mār your daughter-in-law has played the harlot; and moreover she is with child by harlotry." And Judah said, "Bring her out, and let her be burned." ²⁵As she was being brought out, she sent word to her father-in-law, "By the man to whom these belong, I am with child." And she said, "Mark, I pray you, whose these are, the signet and the cord and the staff." ²⁶Then Judah acknowledged them and said, "She is more righteous than I, inasmuch as I did not give her to my son Shē'lah." And he did not lie with her again.

27 When the time of her delivery came, there were twins in her womb. ²⁸And when she was in labor, one put out a hand; and the midwife took and bound on his hand a scarlet thread, saying, "This came out first." ²⁹But as he drew back his hand, behold, his brother came out; and she said, "What a breach you have made for yourself!" Therefore his name was called Pĕr'ĕz.* ³⁰Afterward his brother came out with the scarlet thread upon his hand; and his name was called Zē'rah.

39 Now Joseph was taken down to Egypt, and Pŏt'ĭ·phạr, an officer of Pharaoh, the captain of the guard, an Egyptian, bought him from the Ĭsh'mạ·ĕl·ites who had brought him down there. ²The Lord was with Joseph, and he became a successful man; and he was in the house of his master the Egyptian, ³and his master saw that the Lord was with him, and that the Lord caused all that he did to prosper in his hands. ⁴So Joseph found favor in his sight and attended him, and he made him overseer of his house and put him in charge of all that he had. ⁵From the time that he made him overseer in his house and over all that he had the Lord blessed

the Egyptian's house for Joseph's sake; the blessing of the Lord was upon all that he had, in house and field. ⁶So he left all that he had in Joseph's charge; and having him he had no concern for anything but the food which he ate.

Now Joseph was handsome and good-looking. ⁷And after a time his master's wife cast her eyes upon Joseph, and said, "Lie with me." ⁸But he refused and said to his master's wife, "Lo, having me my master has no concern about anything in the house, and he has put everything that he has in my hand; ⁹he is not greater in this house than I am; nor has he kept back anything from me except yourself, because you are his wife; how then can I do this great wickedness, and sin against God?" ¹⁰And although she spoke to Joseph day after day, he would not listen to her, to lie with her or to be with her. ¹¹But one day, when he went into the house to do his work and none of the men of the house was there in the house, ¹²she caught him by his garment, saying, "Lie with me." But he left his garment in her hand, and fled and got out of the house. ¹³And when she saw that he had left his garment in her hand, and had fled out of the house, ¹⁴she called to the men of her household and said to them, "See, he has brought among us a Hebrew to insult us; he came in to me to lie with me, and I cried out with a loud voice; ¹⁵and when he heard that I lifted up my voice and cried, he left his garment with me, and fled and got out of the house." ¹⁶Then she laid up his garment by her until his master came home, ¹⁷and she told him the same story, saying, "The Hebrew servant, whom you have brought among us, came in to me to insult me; ¹⁸but as soon as I lifted up my voice and cried, he left his garment with me, and fled out of the house."

19 When his master heard the words which his wife spoke to him, "This is the way your servant treated me," his anger was kindled. ²⁰And Joseph's master took him and put him into prison, the place where the king's prisoners were confined, and he was there in prison. ²¹But the Lord was with Joseph and showed him steadfast love,

*Or *cult prostitute*   ʲThat is *A breach*
39.1, 2, 21: Acts 7.9.

and gave him favor in the sight of the keeper of the prison. [22]And the keeper of the prison committed to Joseph's care all the prisoners who were in the prison; and whatever was done there, he was the doer of it; [23]the keeper of the prison paid no heed to anything that was in Joseph's care, because the LORD was with him; and whatever he did, the LORD made it prosper.

40 Some time after this, the butler of the king of Egypt and his baker offended their lord the king of Egypt. [2]And Pharaoh was angry with his two officers, the chief butler and the chief baker, [3]and he put them in custody in the house of the captain of the guard, in the prison where Joseph was confined. [4]The captain of the guard charged Joseph with them, and he waited on them; and they continued for some time in custody. [5]And one night they both dreamed — the butler and the baker of the king of Egypt, who were confined in the prison — each his own dream, and each dream with its own meaning. [6]When Joseph came to them in the morning and saw them, they were troubled. [7]So he asked Pharaoh's officers who were with him in custody in his master's house, "Why are your faces downcast today?" [8]They said to him, "We have had dreams, and there is no one to interpret them." And Joseph said to them, "Do not interpretations belong to God? Tell them to me, I pray you."

9 So the chief butler told his dream to Joseph, and said to him, "In my dream there was a vine before me, [10]and on the vine there were three branches; as soon as it budded, its blossoms shot forth, and the clusters ripened into grapes. [11]Pharaoh's cup was in my hand; and I took the grapes and pressed them into Pharaoh's cup, and placed the cup in Pharaoh's hand." [12]Then Joseph said to him, "This is its interpretation: the three branches are three days; [13]within three days Pharaoh will lift up your head and restore you to your office; and you shall place Pharaoh's cup in his hand as formerly, when you were his butler. [14]But remember me, when it is well with you, and do me the kindness, I pray you, to make mention of me to Pharaoh, and so get me out of this house. [15]For I was indeed stolen out of the land of the Hebrews; and here also I have

done nothing that they should put me into the dungeon."

16 When the chief baker saw that the interpretation was favorable, he said to Joseph, "I also had a dream: there were three cake baskets on my head, [17]and in the uppermost basket there were all sorts of baked food for Pharaoh, but the birds were eating it out of the basket on my head." [18]And Joseph answered, "This is its interpretation: the three baskets are three days; [19]within three days Pharaoh will lift up your head—from you!— and hang you on a tree; and the birds will eat the flesh from you."

20 On the third day, which was Pharaoh's birthday, he made a feast for all his servants, and lifted up the head of the chief butler and the head of the chief baker among his servants. [21]He restored the chief butler to his butlership, and he placed the cup in Pharaoh's hand; [22]but he hanged the chief baker, as Joseph had interpreted to them. [23]Yet the chief butler did not remember Joseph, but forgot him.

41 After two whole years, Pharaoh dreamed that he was standing by the Nile, [2]and behold, there came up out of the Nile seven cows sleek and fat, and they fed in the reed grass. [3]And behold, seven other cows, gaunt and thin, came up out of the Nile after them, and stood by the other cows on the bank of the Nile. [4]And the gaunt and thin cows ate up the seven sleek and fat cows. And Pharaoh awoke. [5]And he fell asleep and dreamed a second time; and behold, seven ears of grain, plump and good, were growing on one stalk. [6]And behold, after them sprouted seven ears, thin and blighted by the east wind. [7]And the thin ears swallowed up the seven plump and full ears. And Pharaoh awoke, and behold, it was a dream. [8]So in the morning his spirit was troubled; and he sent and called for all the magicians of Egypt and all its wise men; and Pharaoh told them his dream, but there was none who could interpret it[j] to Pharaoh.

9 Then the chief butler said to Pharaoh, "I remember my faults today. [10]When Pharaoh was angry with his servants, and put me and the chief baker in custody in the house of the captain of the guard, [11]we dreamed on

[j]Gk: Heb *them*

the same night, he and I, each having a dream with its own meaning. ¹²A young Hebrew was there with us, a servant of the captain of the guard; and when we told him, he interpreted our dreams to us, giving an interpretation to each man according to his dream. ¹³And as he interpreted to us, so it came to pass; I was restored to my office, and the baker was hanged."

14 Then Pharaoh sent and called Joseph, and they brought him hastily out of the dungeon; and when he had shaved himself and changed his clothes, he came in before Pharaoh. ¹⁵And Pharaoh said to Joseph, "I have had a dream, and there is no one who can interpret it; and I have heard it said of you that when you hear a dream you can interpret it." ¹⁶Joseph answered Pharaoh, "It is not in me; God will give Pharaoh a favorable answer." ¹⁷Then Pharaoh said to Joseph, "Behold, in my dream I was standing on the banks of the Nile; ¹⁸and seven cows, fat and sleek, came up out of the Nile and fed in the reed grass; ¹⁹and seven other cows came up after them, poor and very gaunt and thin, such as I had never seen in all the land of Egypt. ²⁰And the thin and gaunt cows ate up the first seven fat cows, ²¹but when they had eaten them no one would have known that they had eaten them, for they were still as gaunt as at the beginning. Then I awoke. ²²I also saw in my dream seven ears growing on one stalk, full and good; ²³and seven ears, withered, thin, and blighted by the east wind, sprouted after them, ²⁴and the thin ears swallowed up the seven good ears. And I told it to the magicians, but there was no one who could explain it to me."

25 Then Joseph said to Pharaoh, "The dream of Pharaoh is one; God has revealed to Pharaoh what he is about to do. ²⁶The seven good cows are seven years, and the seven good ears are seven years; the dream is one. ²⁷The seven lean and gaunt cows that came up after them are seven years, and the seven empty ears blighted by the east wind are also seven years of famine. ²⁸It is as I told Pharaoh, God has shown to Pharaoh what he is about to do. ²⁹There will come seven years of great plenty throughout all the land of Egypt, ³⁰but after them there will arise seven years of famine, and all the plenty will be forgotten in the land of Egypt; the famine will consume the land, ³¹and the plenty will be unknown in the land by reason of that famine which will follow, for it will be very grievous. ³²And the doubling of Pharaoh's dream means that the thing is fixed by God, and God will shortly bring it to pass. ³³Now therefore let Pharaoh select a man discreet and wise, and set him over the land of Egypt. ³⁴Let Pharaoh proceed to appoint overseers over the land, and take the fifth part of the produce of the land of Egypt during the seven plenteous years. ³⁵And let them gather all the food of these good years that are coming, and lay up grain under the authority of Pharaoh for food in the cities, and let them keep it. ³⁶That food shall be a reserve for the land against the seven years of famine which are to befall the land of Egypt, so that the land may not perish through the famine."

37 This proposal seemed good to Pharaoh and to all his servants. ³⁸And Pharaoh said to his servants, "Can we find such a man as this, in whom is the Spirit of God?" ³⁹So Pharaoh said to Joseph, "Since God has shown you all this, there is none so discreet and wise as you are; ⁴⁰you shall be over my house, and all my people shall order themselves as you command; only as regards the throne will I be greater than you." ⁴¹And Pharaoh said to Joseph, "Behold, I have set you over all the land of Egypt." ⁴²Then Pharaoh took his signet ring from his hand and put it on Joseph's hand, and arrayed him in garments of fine linen, and put a gold chain about his neck; ⁴³and he made him to ride in his second chariot; and they cried before him, "Bow the knee!"*ᵏ* Thus he set him over all the land of Egypt. ⁴⁴Moreover Pharaoh said to Joseph, "I am Pharaoh, and without your consent no man shall lift up hand or foot in all the land of Egypt." ⁴⁵And Pharaoh called Joseph's name Zăph′ẹ-năth–pạ·nē′ah; and he gave him in marriage Ăs′ẹ·năth, the daughter of Pō·tī′phẹ·rạ priest of Ŏn. So Joseph went out over the land of Egypt.

46 Joseph was thirty years old when he entered the service of Pharaoh king

---

ᵏAbrek, probably an Egyptian word similar in sound to the Hebrew word meaning *to kneel*
41.38–45: Acts 7.10.

of Egypt. And Joseph went out from the presence of Pharaoh, and went through all the land of Egypt. [47] During the seven plenteous years the earth brought forth abundantly, [48] and he gathered up all the food of the seven years when there was plenty[l] in the land of Egypt, and stored up food in the cities; he stored up in every city the food from the fields around it. [49] And Joseph stored up grain in great abundance, like the sand of the sea, until he ceased to measure it, for it could not be measured.

50 Before the year of famine came, Joseph had two sons, whom Ăs′ẹ·năth, the daughter of Pō·tĭ′phẹ·rạ priest of Ŏn, bore to him. [51] Joseph called the name of the first-born Mạ·năs′sẹh,[m] "For," he said, "God has made me forget all my hardship and all my father's house." [52] The name of the second he called Ē′phrạ·ĭm,[n] "For God has made me fruitful in the land of my affliction."

53 The seven years of plenty that prevailed in the land of Egypt came to an end; [54] and the seven years of famine began to come, as Joseph had said. There was famine in all lands; but in all the land of Egypt there was bread. [55] When all the land of Egypt was famished, the people cried to Pharaoh for bread; and Pharaoh said to all the Egyptians, "Go to Joseph; what he says to you, do." [56] So when the famine had spread over all the land, Joseph opened all the storehouses,[o] and sold to the Egyptians, for the famine was severe in the land of Egypt. [57] Moreover, all the earth came to Egypt to Joseph to buy grain, because the famine was severe over all the earth.

42 When Jacob learned that there was grain in Egypt, he said to his sons, "Why do you look at one another?" [2] And he said, "Behold, I have heard that there is grain in Egypt; go down and buy grain for us there, that we may live, and not die." [3] So ten of Joseph's brothers went down to buy grain in Egypt. [4] But Jacob did not send Benjamin, Joseph's brother, with his brothers, for he feared that harm might befall him. [5] Thus the sons of Israel came to buy among the others who came, for the famine was in the land of Canaan.

6 Now Joseph was governor over the land; he it was who sold to all the people of the land. And Joseph's brothers came, and bowed themselves before him with their faces to the ground. [7] Joseph saw his brothers, and knew them, but he treated them like strangers and spoke roughly to them. "Where do you come from?" he said. They said, "From the land of Canaan, to buy food." [8] Thus Joseph knew his brothers, but they did not know him. [9] And Joseph remembered the dreams which he had dreamed of them; and he said to them, "You are spies, you have come to see the weakness of the land." [10] They said to him, "No, my lord, but to buy food have your servants come. [11] We are all sons of one man, we are honest men, your servants are not spies." [12] He said to them, "No, it is the weakness of the land that you have come to see." [13] And they said, "We, your servants, are twelve brothers, the sons of one man in the land of Canaan; and behold, the youngest is this day with our father, and one is no more." [14] But Joseph said to them, "It is as I said to you, you are spies. [15] By this you shall be tested: by the life of Pharaoh, you shall not go from this place unless your youngest brother comes here. [16] Send one of you, and let him bring your brother, while you remain in prison, that your words may be tested, whether there is truth in you; or else, by the life of Pharaoh, surely you are spies." [17] And he put them all together in prison for three days.

18 On the third day Joseph said to them, "Do this and you will live, for I fear God: [19] if you are honest men, let one of your brothers remain confined in your prison, and let the rest go and carry grain for the famine of your households, [20] and bring your youngest brother to me; so your words will be verified, and you shall not die." And they did so. [21] Then they said to one another, "In truth we are guilty concerning our brother, in that we saw the distress of his soul, when he besought us and we would not listen; therefore is this distress come upon us." [22] And Reuben answered them, "Did I not tell you not

to sin against the lad? But you would not listen. So now there comes a reckoning for his blood." ²³They did not know that Joseph understood them, for there was an interpreter between them. ²⁴Then he turned away from them and wept; and he returned to them and spoke to them. And he took Sĭm'ē·on from them and bound him before their eyes. ²⁵And Joseph gave orders to fill their bags with grain, and to replace every man's money in his sack, and to give them provisions for the journey. This was done for them.

26 Then they loaded their asses with their grain, and departed. ²⁷And as one of them opened his sack to give his ass provender at the lodging place, he saw his money in the mouth of his sack; ²⁸and he said to his brothers, "My money has been put back; here it is in the mouth of my sack!" At this their hearts failed them, and they turned trembling to one another, saying, "What is this that God has done to us?"

29 When they came to Jacob their father in the land of Canaan, they told him all that had befallen them, saying, ³⁰"The man, the lord of the land, spoke roughly to us, and took us to be spies of the land. ³¹But we said to him, 'We are honest men, we are not spies; ³²we are twelve brothers, sons of our father; one is no more, and the youngest is this day with our father in the land of Canaan.' ³³Then the man, the lord of the land, said to us, 'By this I shall know that you are honest men: leave one of your brothers with me, and take grain for the famine of your households, and go your way. ³⁴Bring your youngest brother to me; then I shall know that you are not spies but honest men, and I will deliver to you your brother, and you shall trade in the land.' "

35 As they emptied their sacks, behold, every man's bundle of money was in his sack; and when they and their father saw their bundles of money, they were dismayed. ³⁶And Jacob their father said to them, "You have bereaved me of my children: Joseph is no more, and Sĭm'ē·on is no more, and now you would take Benjamin; all this has come upon me." ³⁷Then Reuben said to his father, "Slay my two sons if I do not bring him back

to you; put him in my hands, and I will bring him back to you." ³⁸But he said, "My son shall not go down with you, for his brother is dead, and he only is left. If harm should befall him on the journey that you are to make, you would bring down my gray hairs with sorrow to Shē'ōl."

43 Now the famine was severe in the land. ²And when they had eaten the grain which they had brought from Egypt, their father said to them, "Go again, buy us a little food." ³But Judah said to him, "The man solemnly warned us, saying, 'You shall not see my face, unless your brother is with you.' ⁴If you will send our brother with us, we will go down and buy you food; ⁵but if you will not send him, we will not go down, for the man said to us, 'You shall not see my face, unless your brother is with you.' " ⁶Israel said, "Why did you treat me so ill as to tell the man that you had another brother?" ⁷They replied, "The man questioned us carefully about ourselves and our kindred, saying, 'Is your father still alive? Have you another brother?' What we told him was in answer to these questions; could we in any way know that he would say, 'Bring your brother down'?" ⁸And Judah said to Israel his father, "Send the lad with me, and we will arise and go, that we may live and not die, both we and you and also our little ones. ⁹I will be surety for him; of my hand you shall require him. If I do not bring him back to you and set him before you, then let me bear the blame for ever; ¹⁰for if we had not delayed, we would now have returned twice."

11 Then their father Israel said to them, "If it must be so, then do this: take some of the choice fruits of the land in your bags, and carry down to the man a present, a little balm and a little honey, gum, myrrh, pistachio nuts, and almonds. ¹²Take double the money with you; carry back with you the money that was returned in the mouth of your sacks; perhaps it was an oversight. ¹³Take also your brother, and arise, go again to the man; ¹⁴may God Almighty*ᵖ* grant you mercy before the man, that he may send back your other brother and Benjamin. If I am bereaved of my children, I am bereaved." ¹⁵So the men took the present,

ᵖ Heb El Shaddai

and they took double the money with them, and Benjamin; and they arose and went down to Egypt, and stood before Joseph.

16 When Joseph saw Benjamin with them, he said to the steward of his house, "Bring the men into the house, and slaughter an animal and make ready, for the men are to dine with me at noon." 17 The man did as Joseph bade him, and brought the men to Joseph's house. 18 And the men were afraid because they were brought to Joseph's house, and they said, "It is because of the money, which was replaced in our sacks the first time, that we are brought in, so that he may seek occasion against us and fall upon us, to make slaves of us and seize our asses." 19 So they went up to the steward of Joseph's house, and spoke with him at the door of the house, 20 and said, "Oh, my lord, we came down the first time to buy food; 21 and when we came to the lodging place we opened our sacks, and there was every man's money in the mouth of his sack, our money in full weight; so we have brought it again with us, 22 and we have brought other money down in our hand to buy food. We do not know who put our money in our sacks." 23 He replied, "Rest assured, do not be afraid; your God and the God of your father must have put treasure in your sacks for you; I received your money." Then he brought Sĭm'ē-on out to them. 24 And when the man had brought the men into Joseph's house, and given them water, and they had washed their feet, and when he had given their asses provender, 25 they made ready the present for Joseph's coming at noon, for they heard that they should eat bread there.

26 When Joseph came home, they brought into the house to him the present which they had with them, and bowed down to him to the ground. 27 And he inquired about their welfare, and said, "Is your father well, the old man of whom you spoke? Is he still alive?" 28 They said, "Your servant our father is well, he is still alive." And they bowed their heads and made obeisance. 29 And he lifted up his eyes, and saw his brother Benjamin, his mother's son, and said, "Is this your youngest brother, of whom you spoke to me? God be gracious to you, my son!"

30 Then Joseph made haste, for his heart yearned for his brother, and he sought a place to weep. And he entered his chamber and wept there. 31 Then he washed his face and came out; and controlling himself he said, "Let food be served." 32 They served him by himself, and them by themselves, and the Egyptians who ate with him by themselves, because the Egyptians might not eat bread with the Hebrews, for that is an abomination to the Egyptians. 33 And they sat before him, the first-born according to his birthright and the youngest according to his youth; and the men looked at one another in amazement. 34 Portions were taken to them from Joseph's table, but Benjamin's portion was five times as much as any of theirs. So they drank and were merry with him.

44 Then he commanded the steward of his house, "Fill the men's sacks with food, as much as they can carry, and put each man's money in the mouth of his sack, 2 and put my cup, the silver cup, in the mouth of the sack of the youngest, with his money for the grain." And he did as Joseph told him. 3 As soon as the morning was light, the men were sent away with their asses. 4 When they had gone but a short distance from the city, Joseph said to his steward, "Up, follow after the men; and when you overtake them, say to them, 'Why have you returned evil for good? Why have you stolen my silver cup?*q* 5 Is it not from this that my lord drinks, and by this that he divines? You have done wrong in so doing.' "

6 When he overtook them, he spoke to them these words. 7 They said to him, "Why does my lord speak such words as these? Far be it from your servants that they should do such a thing! 8 Behold, the money which we found in the mouth of our sacks, we brought back to you from the land of Canaan; how then should we steal silver or gold from your lord's house? 9 With whomever of your servants it be found, let him die, and we also will be my lord's slaves." 10 He said, "Let it be as you say: he with whom it is found shall be my slave, and the rest of you shall be blameless." 11 Then every man quickly lowered his sack to the

q Gk Compare Vg: Heb lacks *Why have you stolen my silver cup?*

ground, and every man opened his sack. [12]And he searched, beginning with the eldest and ending with the youngest; and the cup was found in Benjamin's sack. [13]Then they rent their clothes, and every man loaded his ass, and they returned to the city.

14 When Judah and his brothers came to Joseph's house, he was still there; and they fell before him to the ground. [15]Joseph said to them, "What deed is this that you have done? Do you not know that such a man as I can indeed divine?" [16]And Judah said, "What shall we say to my lord? What shall we speak? Or how can we clear ourselves? God has found out the guilt of your servants; behold, we are my lord's slaves, both we and he also in whose hand the cup has been found." [17]But he said, "Far be it from me that I should do so! Only the man in whose hand the cup was found shall be my slave; but as for you, go up in peace to your father."

18 Then Judah went up to him and said, "O my lord, let your servant, I pray you, speak a word in my lord's ears, and let not your anger burn against your servant; for you are like Pharaoh himself. [19]My lord asked his servants, saying, 'Have you a father, or a brother?' [20]And we said to my lord, 'We have a father, an old man, and a young brother, the child of his old age; and his brother is dead, and he alone is left of his mother's children; and his father loves him.' [21]Then you said to your servants, 'Bring him down to me, that I may set my eyes upon him.' [22]We said to my lord, 'The lad cannot leave his father, for if he should leave his father, his father would die.' [23]Then you said to your servants, 'Unless your youngest brother comes down with you, you shall see my face no more.' [24]When we went back to your servant my father we told him the words of my lord. [25]And when our father said, 'Go again, buy us a little food,' [26]we said, 'We cannot go down. If our youngest brother goes with us, then we will go down; for we cannot see the man's face unless our youngest brother is with us.' [27]Then your servant my father said to us, 'You know that my wife bore me two sons; [28]one left me, and I said, Surely he has been torn to pieces; and I have never seen him since. [29]If you take this one also from

me, and harm befalls him, you will bring down my gray hairs in sorrow to Shē′ōl.' [30]Now therefore, when I come to your servant my father, and the lad is not with us, then, as his life is bound up in the lad's life, [31]when he sees that the lad is not with us, he will die; and your servants will bring down the gray hairs of your servant our father with sorrow to Shē′ōl. [32]For your servant became surety for the lad to my father, saying, 'If I do not bring him back to you, then I shall bear the blame in the sight of my father all my life.' [33]Now therefore, let your servant, I pray you, remain instead of the lad as a slave to my lord; and let the lad go back with his brothers. [34]For how can I go back to my father if the lad is not with me? I fear to see the evil that would come upon my father."

45 Then Joseph could not control himself before all those who stood by him; and he cried, "Make every one go out from me." So no one stayed with him when Joseph made himself known to his brothers. [2]And he wept aloud, so that the Egyptians heard it, and the household of Pharaoh heard it. [3]And Joseph said to his brothers, "I am Joseph; is my father still alive?" But his brothers could not answer him, for they were dismayed at his presence.

4 So Joseph said to his brothers, "Come near to me, I pray you." And they came near. And he said, "I am your brother, Joseph, whom you sold into Egypt. [5]And now do not be distressed, or angry with yourselves, because you sold me here; for God sent me before you to preserve life. [6]For the famine has been in the land these two years; and there are yet five years in which there will be neither plowing nor harvest. [7]And God sent me before you to preserve for you a remnant on earth, and to keep alive for you many survivors. [8]So it was not you who sent me here, but God; and he has made me a father to Pharaoh, and lord of all his house and ruler over all the land of Egypt. [9]Make haste and go up to my father and say to him, 'Thus says your son Joseph, God has made me lord of all Egypt; come down to me, do not tarry; [10]you shall dwell in the land of Gō′shen, and you shall be near me, you and your children and your chil-

45.1: Acts 7.13.

dren's children, and your flocks, your herds, and all that you have; ¹¹and there I will provide for you, for there are yet five years of famine to come; lest you and your household, and all that you have, come to poverty.' ¹²And now your eyes see, and the eyes of my brother Benjamin see, that it is my mouth that speaks to you. ¹³You must tell my father of all my splendor in Egypt, and of all that you have seen. Make haste and bring my father down here." ¹⁴Then he fell upon his brother Benjamin's neck and wept; and Benjamin wept upon his neck. ¹⁵And he kissed all his brothers and wept upon them; and after that his brothers talked with him.

16 When the report was heard in Pharaoh's house, "Joseph's brothers have come," it pleased Pharaoh and his servants well. ¹⁷And Pharaoh said to Joseph, "Say to your brothers, 'Do this: load your beasts and go back to the land of Canaan; ¹⁸and take your father and your households, and come to me, and I will give you the best of the land of Egypt, and you shall eat the fat of the land.' ¹⁹Command themʳ also, 'Do this: take wagons from the land of Egypt for your little ones and for your wives, and bring your father, and come. ²⁰Give no thought to your goods, for the best of all the land of Egypt is yours.' "

21 The sons of Israel did so; and Joseph gave them wagons, according to the command of Pharaoh, and gave them provisions for the journey. ²²To each and all of them he gave festal garments; but to Benjamin he gave three hundred shekels of silver and five festal garments. ²³To his father he sent as follows: ten asses loaded with the good things of Egypt, and ten she-asses loaded with grain, bread, and provision for his father on the journey. ²⁴Then he sent his brothers away, and as they departed, he said to them, "Do not quarrel on the way." ²⁵So they went up out of Egypt, and came to the land of Canaan to their father Jacob. ²⁶And they told him, "Joseph is still alive, and he is ruler over all the land of Egypt." And his heart fainted, for he did not believe them. ²⁷But when they told him all the words of Joseph, which he had said to them, and when he saw the wagons which Joseph had sent to carry him, the spirit of their father Jacob revived; ²⁸and Israel said, "It is enough; Joseph my son is still alive; I will go and see him before I die."

46 So Israel took his journey with all that he had, and came to Bē'er-shē'ba, and offered sacrifices to the God of his father Isaac. ²And God spoke to Israel in visions of the night, and said, "Jacob, Jacob." And he said, "Here am I." ³Then he said, "I am God, the God of your father; do not be afraid to go down to Egypt; for I will there make of you a great nation. ⁴I will go down with you to Egypt, and I will also bring you up again; and Joseph's hand shall close your eyes." ⁵Then Jacob set out from Bē'er-shē'ba; and the sons of Israel carried Jacob their father, their little ones, and their wives, in the wagons which Pharaoh had sent to carry him. ⁶They also took their cattle and their goods, which they had gained in the land of Canaan, and came into Egypt, Jacob and all his offspring with him, ⁷his sons, and his sons' sons with him, his daughters, and his sons' daughters; all his offspring he brought with him into Egypt.

8 Now these are the names of the descendants of Israel, who came into Egypt, Jacob and his sons. Reuben, Jacob's first-born, ⁹and the sons of Reuben: Hā'noch, Păl'lü, Hĕz'ron, and Cär'mī. ¹⁰The sons of Sĭm'ē-on: Je̱mū'e̱l, Jā'mĭn, Ō'hăd, Jā'chĭn, Zō'här, and Shā'ül, the son of a Canaanitish woman. ¹¹The sons of Lē'vī: Gēr'shon, Kō'hăth, and Me̱-râr'ī. ¹²The sons of Judah: Ēr, Ō'nan, Shē'lah, Pĕr'ĕz, and Zē'rah (but Er and Onan died in the land of Canaan); and the sons of Perez were Hĕz'ron and Hā'mul. ¹³The sons of Ĭs'sa̱-chär: Tō'la̱, Pū'vah, Ī'ŏb, and Shĭm'ron. ¹⁴The sons of Zĕb'ū-lun: Sē'red, Ē'lŏn, and Jäh'-lē-e̱l ¹⁵(these are the sons of Leah, whom she bore to Jacob in Păd'dan-är'am, together with his daughter Dinah; altogether his sons and his daughters numbered thirty-three). ¹⁶The sons of Gäd: Zĭph'ĭ-on, Hăg'gī, Shü'nī, Ĕz'bon, Ē'rī, A̱-rō'dī, and A̱-rē'lī. ¹⁷The sons of Ash'er: Ĭm'nah, Ĭsh'vah, Ĭsh'vī, Bē-rī'ah, with Sē'rah their sister. And the sons of Beriah: Hē'ber and Măl'chĭ-ĕl ¹⁸(these are the sons of Zĭl'pah, whom Lā'ban gave to

ʳCompare Gk Vg: Heb *you are commanded*
46.6: Acts 7.14, 15. 46.8-27: Ex 1.1-4; Num 26.4-50.

Leah his daughter; and these she bore to Jacob—sixteen persons). ¹⁹The sons of Rachel, Jacob's wife: Joseph and Benjamin. ²⁰And to Joseph in the land of Egypt were born Mạ·năs'sẹh and Ē'phrạ·ĭm, whom Ăs'ẹ·năth, the daughter of Pō·tī'phẹ·rạ the priest of Ŏn, bore to him. ²¹And the sons of Benjamin: Bē'lạ, Bē'chẹr, Ăsh'bĕl, Gē'rạ, Nā'ạ·măn, Ē'hī, Rŏsh, Mŭp'pĭm, Hŭp'pĭm, and Ărd ²²(these are the sons of Rachel, who were born to Jacob —fourteen persons in all). ²³The sons of Dan: Hū'shĭm. ²⁴The sons of Năph'tạ·lī: Jäh'zē·ẹl, Gū'nī, Jē'zẹr, and Shĭl'lĕm ²⁵(these are the sons of Bĭl'hạh, whom Lā'bạn gave to Rachel his daughter, and these she bore to Jacob —seven persons in all). ²⁶All the persons belonging to Jacob who came into Egypt, who were his own offspring, not including Jacob's sons' wives, were sixty-six persons in all; ²⁷and the sons of Joseph, who were born to him in Egypt, were two; all the persons of the house of Jacob, that came into Egypt, were seventy.

28 He sent Judah before him to Joseph, to appear* before him in Gō'shẹn; and they came into the land of Goshen. ²⁹Then Joseph made ready his chariot and went up to meet Israel his father in Gō'shẹn; and he presented himself to him, and fell on his neck, and wept on his neck a good while. ³⁰Israel said to Joseph, "Now let me die, since I have seen your face and know that you are still alive." ³¹Joseph said to his brothers and to his father's household, "I will go up and tell Pharaoh, and will say to him, 'My brothers and my father's household, who were in the land of Canaan, have come to me; ³²and the men are shepherds, for they have been keepers of cattle; and they have brought their flocks, and their herds, and all that they have.' ³³When Pharaoh calls you, and says, 'What is your occupation?' ³⁴you shall say, 'Your servants have been keepers of cattle from our youth even until now, both we and our fathers,' in order that you may dwell in the land of Gō'shẹn; for every shepherd is an abomination to the Egyptians."

47 So Joseph went in and told Pharaoh, "My father and my brothers, with their flocks and herds and all that they possess, have come from the land of Canaan; they are now in the land of Gō'shẹn." ²And from among his brothers he took five men and presented them to Pharaoh. ³Pharaoh said to his brothers, "What is your occupation?" And they said to Pharaoh, "Your servants are shepherds, as our fathers were." ⁴They said to Pharaoh, "We have come to sojourn in the land; for there is no pasture for your servants' flocks, for the famine is severe in the land of Canaan; and now, we pray you, let your servants dwell in the land of Gō'shẹn." ⁵Then Pharaoh said to Joseph, "Your father and your brothers have come to you. ⁶The land of Egypt is before you; settle your father and your brothers in the best of the land; let them dwell in the land of Gō'shẹn; and if you know any able men among them, put them in charge of my cattle."

7 Then Joseph brought in Jacob his father, and set him before Pharaoh, and Jacob blessed Pharaoh. ⁸And Pharaoh said to Jacob, "How many are the days of the years of your life?" ⁹And Jacob said to Pharaoh, "The days of the years of my sojourning are a hundred and thirty years; few and evil have been the days of the years of my life, and they have not attained to the days of the years of the life of my fathers in the days of their sojourning." ¹⁰And Jacob blessed Pharaoh, and went out from the presence of Pharaoh. ¹¹Then Joseph settled his father and his brothers, and gave them a possession in the land of Egypt, in the best of the land, in the land of Răm'ē·sēṣ, as Pharaoh had commanded. ¹²And Joseph provided his father, his brothers, and all his father's household with food, according to the number of their dependents.

13 Now there was no food in all the land; for the famine was very severe, so that the land of Egypt and the land of Canaan languished by reason of the famine. ¹⁴And Joseph gathered up all the money that was found in the land of Egypt and in the land of Canaan, for the grain which they bought; and Joseph brought the money into Pharaoh's house. ¹⁵And when the money was all spent in the land of Egypt and in the land of Canaan, all the Egyptians came to Joseph, and said, "Give us food; why should we die before your

*Sam Syr Compare Gk Vg: Heb *to show the way*
46.27: Acts 7.14.

eyes? For our money is gone." ¹⁶And Joseph answered, "Give your cattle, and I will give you food in exchange for your cattle, if your money is gone." ¹⁷So they brought their cattle to Joseph; and Joseph gave them food in exchange for the horses, the flocks, the herds, and the asses: and he supplied them with food in exchange for all their cattle that year. ¹⁸And when that year was ended, they came to him the following year, and said to him, "We will not hide from my lord that our money is all spent; and the herds of cattle are my lord's; there is nothing left in the sight of my lord but our bodies and our lands. ¹⁹Why should we die before your eyes, both we and our land? Buy us and our land for food, and we with our land will be slaves to Pharaoh; and give us seed, that we may live, and not die, and that the land may not be desolate."

20 So Joseph bought all the land of Egypt for Pharaoh; for all the Egyptians sold their fields, because the famine was severe upon them. The land became Pharaoh's; ²¹and as for the people, he made slaves of themᶠ from one end of Egypt to the other. ²²Only the land of the priests he did not buy; for the priests had a fixed allowance from Pharaoh, and lived on the allowance which Pharaoh gave them; therefore they did not sell their land. ²³Then Joseph said to the people, "Behold, I have this day bought you and your land for Pharaoh. Now here is seed for you, and you shall sow the land. ²⁴And at the harvests you shall give a fifth to Pharaoh, and four fifths shall be your own, as seed for the field and as food for yourselves and your households, and as food for your little ones." ²⁵And they said, "You have saved our lives; may it please my lord, we will be slaves to Pharaoh." ²⁶So Joseph made it a statute concerning the land of Egypt, and it stands to this day, that Pharaoh should have the fifth; the land of the priests alone did not become Pharaoh's.

27 Thus Israel dwelt in the land of Egypt, in the land of Gō'shen; and they gained possessions in it, and were fruitful and multiplied exceedingly. ²⁸And Jacob lived in the land of Egypt seventeen years; so the days of Jacob, the years of his life, were a hundred and forty-seven years.

29 And when the time drew near that Israel must die, he called his son Joseph and said to him, "If now I have found favor in your sight, put your hand under my thigh, and promise to deal loyally and truly with me. Do not bury me in Egypt, ³⁰but let me lie with my fathers; carry me out of Egypt and bury me in their burying place." He answered, "I will do as you have said." ³¹And he said, "Swear to me"; and he swore to him. Then Israel bowed himself upon the head of his bed.

48 After this Joseph was told, "Behold, your father is ill"; so he took with him his two sons, Mạ·năs'sẹh and Ē'phra·ĭm. ²And it was told to Jacob, "Your son Joseph has come to you"; then Israel summoned his strength, and sat up in bed. ³And Jacob said to Joseph, "God Almightyᵘ appeared to me at Lŭz in the land of Canaan and blessed me, ⁴and said to me, 'Behold, I will make you fruitful, and multiply you, and I will make of you a company of peoples, and will give this land to your descendants after you for an everlasting possession.' ⁵And now your two sons, who were born to you in the land of Egypt before I came to you in Egypt, are mine; Ē'phra·im and Mạ·năs'sẹh shall be mine, as Reuben and Sĭm'ē·ọn are. ⁶And the offspring born to you after them shall be yours; they shall be called by the name of their brothers in their inheritance. ⁷For when I came from Păd'dạn, Rachel to my sorrow died in the land of Canaan on the way, when there was still some distance to go to Ĕph'răth; and I buried her there on the way to Ephrath (that is, Bethlehem)."

8 When Israel saw Joseph's sons, he said, "Who are these?" ⁹Joseph said to his father, "They are my sons, whom God has given me here." And he said, "Bring them to me, I pray you, that I may bless them." ¹⁰Now the eyes of Israel were dim with age, so that he could not see. So Joseph brought them near him; and he kissed them and embraced them. ¹¹And Israel said to Joseph, "I had not thought to see your face; and lo, God has let me see your children also." ¹²Then Joseph removed them from his knees,

ᶠSam Gk Compare Vg: Heb *he removed them to the cities*
ᵘHeb El Shaddai

and he bowed himself with his face to the earth. [13]And Joseph took them both, E'phra·ïm in his right hand toward Israel's left hand, and Ma·näs'seh in his left hand toward Israel's right hand, and brought them near him. [14]And Israel stretched out his right hand and laid it upon the head of E'phra·ïm, who was the younger, and his left hand upon the head of Ma·näs'seh, crossing his hands, for Manasseh was the first-born. [15]And he blessed Joseph, and said,
"The God before whom my fathers Abraham and Isaac walked,
the God who has led me all my life long to this day,
[16]the angel who has redeemed me from all evil, bless the lads;
and in them let my name be perpetuated, and the name of my fathers Abraham and Isaac;
and let them grow into a multitude in the midst of the earth."
17 When Joseph saw that his father laid his right hand upon the head of E'phra·ïm, it displeased him; and he took his father's hand, to remove it from Ephraim's head to Ma·näs'seh's head. [18]And Joseph said to his father, "Not so, my father; for this one is the first-born; put your right hand upon his head." [19]But his father refused, and said, "I know, my son, I know; he also shall become a people, and he also shall be great; nevertheless his younger brother shall be greater than he, and his descendants shall become a multitude of nations." [20]So he blessed them that day, saying,
"By you Israel will pronounce blessings, saying,
'God make you as E'phra·ïm and as Ma·näs'seh' ";
and thus he put Ephraim before Manasseh. [21]Then Israel said to Joseph, "Behold, I am about to die, but God will be with you, and will bring you again to the land of your fathers. [22]Moreover I have given to you rather than to your brothers one mountain slope[v] which I took from the hand of the Äm'o·rītes with my sword and with my bow."

49 Then Jacob called his sons, and said, "Gather yourselves together, that I may tell you what shall befall you in days to come.
[2]Assemble and hear, O sons of Jacob, and hearken to Israel your father.

[3]Reuben, you are my first-born,
my might, and the first fruits of my strength,
pre-eminent in pride and pre-eminent in power.
[4]Unstable as water, you shall not have pre-eminence
because you went up to your father's bed;
then you defiled it—you[w] went up to my couch!

[5]Sïm'e·on and Lē'vī are brothers;
weapons of violence are their swords.
[6]O my soul, come not into their council;
O my spirit,[x] be not joined to their company;
for in their anger they slay men,
and in their wantonness they hamstring oxen.
[7]Cursed be their anger, for it is fierce;
and their wrath, for it is cruel!
I will divide them in Jacob
and scatter them in Israel.

[8]Judah, your brothers shall praise you;
your hand shall be on the neck of your enemies;
your father's sons shall bow down before you.
[9]Judah is a lion's whelp;
from the prey, my son, you have gone up.
He stooped down, he couched as a lion,
and as a lioness; who dares rouse him up?
[10]The scepter shall not depart from Judah,
nor the ruler's staff from between his feet,
until he comes to whom it belongs;[y]
and to him shall be the obedience of the peoples.
[11]Binding his foal to the vine
and his ass's colt to the choice vine,
he washes his garments in wine
and his vesture in the blood of grapes;
[12]his eyes shall be red with wine,
and his teeth white with milk.

[v]Heb *shekem,* shoulder [w]Gk Syr Tg: Heb *he* [x]Or *glory*
[y]Syr Compare Tg: Heb *until Shiloh comes* or *until he comes to Shiloh*
49.9, 10: Num 24.9; Rev 5.5.

¹³Zĕb′ū·lŭn shall dwell at the shore of
the sea;
he shall become a haven for ships,
and his border shall be at Sī′dŏn.

¹⁴Ĭs′sạ·chär is a strong ass,
crouching between the sheepfolds;
¹⁵he saw that a resting place was good,
and that the land was pleasant;
so he bowed his shoulder to bear,
and became a slave at forced labor.

¹⁶Dan shall judge his people
as one of the tribes of Israel.
¹⁷Dan shall be a serpent in the way,
a viper by the path,
that bites the horse's heels
so that his rider falls backward.
¹⁸I wait for thy salvation, O LORD.

¹⁹Raiders*z* shall raid Gȧd,
but he shall raid at their heels.

²⁰Ăsh·ẹr′ṣ food shall be rich,
and he shall yield royal dainties.

²¹Năph′tạ·lī is a hind let loose,
that bears comely fawns.*a*

²²Joseph is a fruitful bough,
a fruitful bough by a spring;
his branches run over the wall.
²³The archers fiercely attacked him,
shot at him, and harassed him
sorely;
²⁴yet his bow remained unmoved,
his arms*b* were made agile
by the hands of the Mighty One of
Jacob
(by the name of the Shepherd,
the Rock of Israel),
²⁵by the God of your father who will
help you,
by God Almighty*u* who will bless
you
with blessings of heaven above,
blessings of the deep that couches
beneath,
blessings of the breasts and of the
womb.
²⁶The blessings of your father
are mighty beyond the blessings
of the eternal mountains,*c*
the bounties of the everlasting
hills;
may they be on the head of Joseph,
and on the brow of him who was
separate from his brothers.

²⁷Benjamin is a ravenous wolf,
in the morning devouring the prey,
and at even dividing the spoil."

28 All these are the twelve tribes of
Israel; and this is what their father
said to them as he blessed them,
blessing each with the blessing suitable to him. ²⁹Then he charged them,
and said to them, "I am to be gathered
to my people; bury me with my fathers
in the cave that is in the field of
Ē′phrọn the Hĭt′tīte, ³⁰in the cave that
is in the field at Măch–pē′lạh, to the
east of Măm′rĕ, in the land of Canaan,
which Abraham bought with the field
from Ē′phrọn the Hĭt′tīte to possess
as a burying place. ³¹There they buried
Abraham and Sarah his wife; there
they buried Isaac and Rebekah his
wife; and there I buried Leah – ³²the
field and the cave that is in it were
purchased from the Hĭt′tītes." ³³When
Jacob finished charging his sons, he
drew up his feet into the bed, and
breathed his last, and was gathered
to his people.

50 Then Joseph fell on his father's
face, and wept over him, and
kissed him. ²And Joseph commanded
his servants the physicians to embalm
his father. So the physicians embalmed Israel; ³forty days were required for it, for so many are required
for embalming. And the Egyptians
wept for him seventy days.
4 And when the days of weeping for
him were past, Joseph spoke to the
household of Pharaoh, saying, "If
now I have found favor in your eyes,
speak, I pray you, in the ears of Pharaoh, saying, ⁵My father made me
swear, saying, 'I am about to die: in
my tomb which I hewed out for myself
in the land of Canaan, there shall you
bury me.' Now therefore let me go
up, I pray you, and bury my father;
then I will return." ⁶And Pharaoh answered, "Go up, and bury your father,
as he made you swear." ⁷So Joseph
went up to bury his father; and with
him went up all the servants of Pharaoh, the elders of his household, and
all the elders of the land of Egypt, ⁸as
well as all the household of Joseph, his
brothers, and his father's household;
only their children, their flocks, and
their herds were left in the land of
Gō′shẹn. ⁹And there went up with him
both chariots and horsemen; it was a

---

*z*Heb *gedud*, a raiding troop
*a*Or *who gives beautiful words*
*b*Heb *the arms of his hands*   *u*Heb El Shaddai
*c*Compare Gk: Heb *of my progenitors to*

very great company. [10]When they came to the threshing floor of Ā'tăd, which is beyond the Jordan, they lamented there with a very great and sorrowful lamentation; and he made a mourning for his father seven days. [11]When the inhabitants of the land, the Canaanites, saw the mourning on the threshing floor of Ā'tăd, they said, "This is a grievous mourning to the Egyptians." Therefore the place was named Ā'bĕl-mĭz'ra·ĭm;[d] it is beyond the Jordan. [12]Thus his sons did for him as he had commanded them; [13]for his sons carried him to the land of Canaan, and buried him in the cave of the field at Măch-pē'lah, to the east of Măm're, which Abraham bought with the field from Ē'phron the Hĭt'tīte, to possess as a burying place. [14]After he had buried his father, Joseph returned to Egypt with his brothers and all who had gone up with him to bury his father.

15 When Joseph's brothers saw that their father was dead, they said, "It may be that Joseph will hate us and pay us back for all the evil which we did to him." [16]So they sent a message to Joseph, saying, "Your father gave this command before he died, [17]'Say to Joseph, Forgive, I pray you, the transgression of your brothers and their sin, because they did evil to you.' And now,

we pray you, forgive the transgression of the servants of the God of your father." Joseph wept when they spoke to him. [18]His brothers also came and fell down before him, and said, "Behold, we are your servants." [19]But Joseph said to them, "Fear not, for am I in the place of God? [20]As for you, you meant evil against me; but God meant it for good, to bring it about that many people should be kept alive, as they are today. [21]So do not fear; I will provide for you and your little ones." Thus he reassured them and comforted them.

22 So Joseph dwelt in Egypt, he and his father's house; and Joseph lived a hundred and ten years. [23]And Joseph saw Ē'phra·ĭm'ş children of the third generation; the children also of Mā'chĭr the son of Ma·năs'şeh were born upon Joseph's knees. [24]And Joseph said to his brothers, "I am about to die; but God will visit you, and bring you up out of this land to the land which he swore to Abraham, to Isaac, and to Jacob." [25]Then Joseph took an oath of the sons of Israel, saying, "God will visit you, and you shall carry up my bones from here." [26]So Joseph died, being a hundred and ten years old; and they embalmed him, and he was put in a coffin in Egypt.

The Second Book of Moses

Commonly Called

Exodus

1 These are the names of the sons of Israel who came to Egypt with Jacob, each with his household: [2]Reuben, Sĭm'e·on, Lē'vī, and Judah, [3]Ĭs'sa·chär, Zĕb'ū·lun, and Benjamin, [4]Dan and Năph'ta·lī, Găd and Ash'er. [5]All the offspring of Jacob were seventy persons; Joseph was already in Egypt. [6]Then Joseph died, and all his brothers, and all that generation. [7]But the descendants of Israel were fruitful and increased greatly; they multi-

plied and grew exceedingly strong; so that the land was filled with them.

8 Now there arose a new king over Egypt, who did not know Joseph. [9]And he said to his people, "Behold, the people of Israel are too many and too mighty for us. [10]Come, let us deal shrewdly with them, lest they mul-

[d]That is *meadow* (or *mourning*) *of Egypt*
50.13: Acts 7.16.
1.1–4: Gen 46.8-27; Num 26.4-50.   **1.5–8:** Acts 7.14-18.
1.10, 11, 22: Acts 7.19.

tiply, and, if war befall us, they join our enemies and fight against us and escape from the land." ¹¹Therefore they set taskmasters over them to afflict them with heavy burdens; and they built for Pharaoh store-cities, Pī'thŏm and Rạ–ăm'sēṣ. ¹²But the more they were oppressed, the more they multiplied and the more they spread abroad. And the Egyptians were in dread of the people of Israel. ¹³So they made the people of Israel serve with rigor, ¹⁴and made their lives bitter with hard service, in mortar and brick, and in all kinds of work in the field; in all their work they made them serve with rigor.

15 Then the king of Egypt said to the Hebrew midwives, one of whom was named Shĭph'rạh and the other Pü'ah, ¹⁶"When you serve as midwife to the Hebrew women, and see them upon the birthstool, if it is a son, you shall kill him; but if it is a daughter, she shall live." ¹⁷But the midwives feared God, and did not do as the king of Egypt commanded them, but let the male children live. ¹⁸So the king of Egypt called the midwives, and said to them, "Why have you done this, and let the male children live?" ¹⁹The midwives said to Pharaoh, "Because the Hebrew women are not like the Egyptian women; for they are vigorous and are delivered before the midwife comes to them." ²⁰So God dealt well with the midwives; and the people multiplied and grew very strong. ²¹And because the midwives feared God he gave them families. ²²Then Pharaoh commanded all his people, "Every son that is born to the Hebrews*a* you shall cast into the Nile, but you shall let every daughter live."

2 Now a man from the house of Lē'vī went and took to wife a daughter of Levi. ²The woman conceived and bore a son; and when she saw that he was a goodly child, she hid him three months. ³And when she could hide him no longer she took for him a basket made of bulrushes, and daubed it with bitumen and pitch; and she put the child in it and placed it among the reeds at the river's brink. ⁴And his sister stood at a distance, to know what would be done to him. ⁵Now the daughter of Pharaoh came down to bathe at the river, and her maidens walked beside the river; she saw the basket among the reeds and sent her maid to fetch it. ⁶When she opened it she saw the child; and lo, the babe was crying. She took pity on him and said, "This is one of the Hebrews' children." ⁷Then his sister said to Pharaoh's daughter, "Shall I go and call you a nurse from the Hebrew women to nurse the child for you?" ⁸And Pharaoh's daughter said to her, "Go." So the girl went and called the child's mother. ⁹And Pharaoh's daughter said to her, "Take this child away, and nurse him for me, and I will give you your wages." So the woman took the child and nursed him. ¹⁰And the child grew, and she brought him to Pharaoh's daughter, and he became her son; and she named him Moses,*b* for she said, "Because I drew him out*c* of the water."

11 One day, when Moses had grown up, he went out to his people and looked on their burdens; and he saw an Egyptian beating a Hebrew, one of his people. ¹²He looked this way and that, and seeing no one he killed the Egyptian and hid him in the sand. ¹³When he went out the next day, behold, two Hebrews were struggling together; and he said to the man that did the wrong, "Why do you strike your fellow?" ¹⁴He answered, "Who made you a prince and a judge over us? Do you mean to kill me as you killed the Egyptian?" Then Moses was afraid, and thought, "Surely the thing is known." ¹⁵When Pharaoh heard of it, he sought to kill Moses.

But Moses fled from Pharaoh, and stayed in the land of Mĭd'ĭ·ạn; and he sat down by a well. ¹⁶Now the priest of Mĭd'ĭ·ạn had seven daughters; and they came and drew water, and filled the troughs to water their father's flock. ¹⁷The shepherds came and drove them away; but Moses stood up and helped them, and watered their flock. ¹⁸When they came to their father Reü'ĕl, he said, "How is it that you have come so soon today?" ¹⁹They said, "An Egyptian delivered us out of the hand of the shepherds, and even drew water for us and watered the flock." ²⁰He said to his daughters, "And where is he? Why have you left

*a*Sam Gk Tg: Heb lacks *to the Hebrews*
*b*Heb *Mosheh* *c*Heb *mashah*
2.2: Acts 7.20; Heb 11.23. **2.5, 10:** Acts 7.21.
2.11: Acts 7.23; Heb 11.24. **2.12:** Acts 7.24.
2.14: Acts 7.27, 28. **2.15, 22:** Acts 7.29.

the man? Call him, that he may eat bread." ²¹And Moses was content to dwell with the man, and he gave Moses his daughter Zĭp·pō'rah. ²²She bore a son, and he called his name Gēr'shŏm; for he said, "I have been a sojourner*ᵈ* in a foreign land."

23 In the course of those many days the king of Egypt died. And the people of Israel groaned under their bondage, and cried out for help, and their cry under bondage came up to God. ²⁴And God heard their groaning, and God remembered his covenant with Abraham, with Isaac, and with Jacob. ²⁵And God saw the people of Israel, and God knew their condition.

3 Now Moses was keeping the flock of his father-in-law, Jĕth'rō, the priest of Mĭd'ĭ·an; and he led his flock to the west side of the wilderness, and came to Hō'rĕb, the mountain of God. ²And the angel of the LORD appeared to him in a flame of fire out of the midst of a bush; and he looked, and lo, the bush was burning, yet it was not consumed. ³And Moses said, "I will turn aside and see this great sight, why the bush is not burnt." ⁴When the LORD saw that he turned aside to see, God called to him out of the bush, "Moses, Moses!" And he said, "Here am I." ⁵Then he said, "Do not come near; put off your shoes from your feet, for the place on which you are standing is holy ground." ⁶And he said, "I am the God of your father, the God of Abraham, the God of Isaac, and the God of Jacob." And Moses hid his face, for he was afraid to look at God.

7 Then the LORD said, "I have seen the affliction of my people who are in Egypt, and have heard their cry because of their taskmasters; I know their sufferings, ⁸and I have come down to deliver them out of the hand of the Egyptians, and to bring them up out of that land to a good and broad land, a land flowing with milk and honey, to the place of the Canaanites, the Hĭt'tītes, the Ăm'ọ·rītes, the Pĕr'ĭz·zītes, the Hī'vītes, and the Jĕb'ū·sītes. ⁹And now, behold, the cry of the people of Israel has come to me, and I have seen the oppression with which the Egyptians oppress them. ¹⁰Come, I will send you to Pharaoh that you may bring forth my people, the sons of Israel, out of Egypt." ¹¹But Moses said to God, "Who am I that I should go to Pharaoh, and bring the sons of Israel out of Egypt?" ¹²He said, "But I will be with you; and this shall be the sign for you, that I have sent you: when you have brought forth the people out of Egypt, you shall serve God upon this mountain."

13 Then Moses said to God, "If I come to the people of Israel and say to them, 'The God of your fathers has sent me to you,' and they ask me, 'What is his name?' what shall I say to them?" ¹⁴God said to Moses, "I AM WHO I AM."*ᵉ* And he said, "Say this to the people of Israel, 'I AM has sent me to you.' " ¹⁵God also said to Moses, "Say this to the people of Israel, 'The LORD,*ᶠ* the God of your fathers, the God of Abraham, the God of Isaac, and the God of Jacob, has sent me to you': this is my name for ever, and thus I am to be remembered throughout all generations. ¹⁶Go and gather the elders of Israel together, and say to them, 'The LORD, the God of your fathers, the God of Abraham, of Isaac, and of Jacob, has appeared to me, saying, "I have observed you and what has been done to you in Egypt; ¹⁷and I promise that I will bring you up out of the affliction of Egypt, to the land of the Canaanites, the Hĭt'tītes, the Ăm'ọ·rītes, the Pĕr'ĭz·zītes, the Hī'-vītes, and the Jĕb'ū·sītes, a land flowing with milk and honey." ' ¹⁸And they will hearken to your voice; and you and the elders of Israel shall go to the king of Egypt and say to him, 'The LORD, the God of the Hebrews, has met with us; and now, we pray you, let us go a three days' journey into the wilderness, that we may sacrifice to the LORD our God.' ¹⁹I know that the king of Egypt will not let you go unless compelled by a mighty hand.*ᵍ* ²⁰So I will stretch out my hand and smite Egypt with all the wonders which I will do in it; after that he will let you go. ²¹And I will give this people favor in the sight of the Egyptians; and when you go, you shall not go empty, ²²but each woman shall ask of her neighbor, and of her who sojourns

*ᵈ*Heb *ger*
*ᵉ*Or I AM WHAT I AM or I WILL BE WHAT I WILL BE
*ᶠ*The word LORD when spelled with capital letters, stands for the divine name, YHWH, which is here connected with the verb *hayah*, to be
*ᵍ*Gk Vg: Heb *no, not by a mighty hand*
2.24: Acts 7.34   **3.2:** Acts 7.30   **3.1-4.17:** Ex 6.2-13.
3.5: Acts 7.33.
3.6: Mt 22, 32; Mk 12.26; Lk 20.37; Acts 3-13; 7.32.

in her house, jewelry of silver and of gold, and clothing, and you shall put them on your sons and on your daughters; thus you shall despoil the Egyptians."

4 Then Moses answered, "But behold, they will not believe me or listen to my voice, for they will say, 'The LORD did not appear to you.'" ²The LORD said to him, "What is that in your hand?" He said, "A rod." ³And he said, "Cast it on the ground." So he cast it on the ground, and it became a serpent; and Moses fled from it. ⁴But the LORD said to Moses, "Put out your hand, and take it by the tail"—so he put out his hand and caught it, and it became a rod in his hand—⁵"that they may believe that the LORD, the God of their fathers, the God of Abraham, the God of Isaac, and the God of Jacob, has appeared to you." ⁶Again, the LORD said to him, "Put your hand into your bosom." And he put his hand into his bosom; and when he took it out, behold, his hand was leprous, as white as snow. ⁷Then God said, "Put your hand back into your bosom." So he put his hand back into his bosom; and when he took it out, behold, it was restored like the rest of his flesh. ⁸"If they will not believe you," God said, "or heed the first sign, they may believe the latter sign. ⁹If they will not believe even these two signs or heed your voice, you shall take some water from the Nile and pour it upon the dry ground; and the water which you shall take from the Nile will become blood upon the dry ground."

10 But Moses said to the LORD, "Oh, my Lord, I am not eloquent, either heretofore or since thou hast spoken to thy servant; but I am slow of speech and of tongue." ¹¹Then the LORD said to him, "Who has made man's mouth? Who makes him dumb, or deaf, or seeing, or blind? Is it not I, the LORD? ¹²Now therefore go, and I will be with your mouth and teach you what you shall speak." ¹³But he said, "Oh, my Lord, send, I pray, some other person." ¹⁴Then the anger of the LORD was kindled against Moses and he said, "Is there not Aaron, your brother, the Lē'vīte? I know that he can speak well; and behold, he is coming out to meet you, and when he sees you he will be glad in his heart. ¹⁵And you shall speak to him and put the words in his mouth;

and I will be with your mouth and with his mouth, and will teach you what you shall do. ¹⁶He shall speak for you to the people; and he shall be a mouth for you, and you shall be to him as God. ¹⁷And you shall take in your hand this rod, with which you shall do the signs."

18 Moses went back to Jĕth'rō his father-in-law and said to him, "Let me go back, I pray, to my kinsmen in Egypt and see whether they are still alive." And Jethro said to Moses, "Go in peace." ¹⁹And the LORD said to Moses in Mĭd'ī·an, "Go back to Egypt; for all the men who were seeking your life are dead." ²⁰So Moses took his wife and his sons and set them on an ass, and went back to the land of Egypt; and in his hand Moses took the rod of God.

21 And the LORD said to Moses, "When you go back to Egypt, see that you do before Pharaoh all the miracles which I have put in your power; but I will harden his heart, so that he will not let the people go. ²²And you shall say to Pharaoh, 'Thus says the LORD, Israel is my first-born son, ²³and I say to you, "Let my son go that he may serve me"; if you refuse to let him go, behold, I will slay your first-born son.'"

24 At a lodging place on the way the LORD met him and sought to kill him. ²⁵Then Zĭp·pō'rah took a flint and cut off her son's foreskin, and touched Moses' feet with it, and said, "Surely you are a bridegroom of blood to me!" ²⁶So he let him alone. Then it was that she said, "You are a bridegroom of blood," because of the circumcision.

27 The LORD said to Aaron, "Go into the wilderness to meet Moses." So he went, and met him at the mountain of God and kissed him. ²⁸And Moses told Aaron all the words of the LORD with which he had sent him, and all the signs which he had charged him to do. ²⁹Then Moses and Aaron went and gathered together all the elders of the people of Israel. ³⁰And Aaron spoke all the words which the LORD had spoken to Moses, and did the signs in the sight of the people. ³¹And the people believed; and when they heard that the LORD had visited the people of Israel and that he had seen their

4.19: Acts 7.34.

affliction, they bowed their heads and worshiped.

5 Afterward Moses and Aaron went to Pharaoh and said, "Thus says the LORD, the God of Israel, 'Let my people go, that they may hold a feast to me in the wilderness.' " ²But Pharaoh said, "Who is the LORD, that I should heed his voice and let Israel go? I do not know the LORD, and moreover I will not let Israel go." ³Then they said, "The God of the Hebrews has met with us; let us go, we pray, a three days' journey into the wilderness, and sacrifice to the LORD our God, lest he fall upon us with pestilence or with the sword." ⁴But the king of Egypt said to them, "Moses and Aaron, why do you take the people away from their work? Get to your burdens." ⁵And Pharaoh said, "Behold, the people of the land are now many and you make them rest from their burdens!" ⁶The same day Pharaoh commanded the taskmasters of the people and their foremen, ⁷"You shall no longer give the people straw to make bricks, as heretofore; let them go and gather straw for themselves. ⁸But the number of bricks which they made heretofore you shall lay upon them, you shall by no means lessen it; for they are idle; therefore they cry, 'Let us go and offer sacrifice to our God.' ⁹Let heavier work be laid upon the men that they may labor at it and pay no regard to lying words."

10 So the taskmasters and the foremen of the people went out and said to the people, "Thus says Pharaoh, 'I will not give you straw. ¹¹Go yourselves, get your straw wherever you can find it; but your work will not be lessened in the least.' " ¹²So the people were scattered abroad throughout all the land of Egypt, to gather stubble for straw. ¹³The taskmasters were urgent, saying, "Complete your work, your daily task, as when there was straw." ¹⁴And the foremen of the people of Israel, whom Pharaoh's taskmasters had set over them, were beaten, and were asked, "Why have you not done all your task of making bricks today, as hitherto?"

15 Then the foremen of the people of Israel came and cried to Pharaoh, "Why do you deal thus with your servants? ¹⁶No straw is given to your servants, yet they say to us, 'Make bricks!' And behold, your servants are beaten; but the fault is in your own people." ¹⁷But he said, "You are idle, you are idle; therefore you say, 'Let us go and sacrifice to the LORD.' ¹⁸Go now, and work; for no straw shall be given you, yet you shall deliver the same number of bricks." ¹⁹The foremen of the people of Israel saw that they were in evil plight, when they said, "You shall by no means lessen your daily number of bricks." ²⁰They met Moses and Aaron, who were waiting for them, as they came forth from Pharaoh; ²¹and they said to them, "The LORD look upon you and judge, because you have made us offensive in the sight of Pharaoh and his servants, and have put a sword in their hand to kill us."

22 Then Moses turned again to the LORD and said, "O LORD, why hast thou done evil to this people? Why didst thou ever send me? ²³For since I came to Pharaoh to speak in thy name, he has done evil to this people, and thou hast not delivered thy people 6 at all." ¹But the LORD said to Moses, "Now you shall see what I will do to Pharaoh; for with a strong hand he will send them out, yea, with a strong hand he will drive them out of his land."

2 And God said to Moses, "I am the LORD. ³I appeared to Abraham, to Isaac, and to Jacob, as God Almighty,ʰ but by my name the LORD I did not make myself known to them. ⁴I also established my covenant with them, to give them the land of Canaan, the land in which they dwelt as sojourners. ⁵Moreover I have heard the groaning of the people of Israel whom the Egyptians hold in bondage and I have remembered my covenant. ⁶Say therefore to the people of Israel, 'I am the LORD, and I will bring you out from under the burdens of the Egyptians, and I will deliver you from their bondage, and I will redeem you with an outstretched arm and with great acts of judgment, ⁷and I will take you for my people, and I will be your God; and you shall know that I am the LORD your God, who has brought you out from under the burdens of the Egyptians. ⁸And I will bring you into the land which I swore to give to Abraham, to Isaac, and to Jacob; I will

ʰHeb El Shaddai
6.1, 6: Acts 13.17.

give it to you for a possession. I am the LORD.' " ⁹Moses spoke thus to the people of Israel; but they did not listen to Moses, because of their broken spirit and their cruel bondage.

10 And the LORD said to Moses, ¹¹"Go in, tell Pharaoh king of Egypt to let the people of Israel go out of his land." ¹²But Moses said to the LORD, "Behold, the people of Israel have not listened to me; how then shall Pharaoh listen to me, who am a man of uncircumcised lips?" ¹³But the LORD spoke to Moses and Aaron, and gave them a charge to the people of Israel and to Pharaoh king of Egypt to bring the people of Israel out of the land of Egypt.

14 These are the heads of their fathers' houses: the sons of Reuben, the first-born of Israel: Hā'noch, Păl'lü, Hĕz'ron, and Cār'mĭ; these are the families of Reuben. ¹⁵The sons of Sĭm'ē·on: Jĕ·mū'ĕl, Jā'mĭn, Ō'hăd, Jā'chĭn, Zō'hār, and Shā'ŭl, the son of a Canaanite woman; these are the families of Simeon. ¹⁶These are the names of the sons of Lē'vī according to their generations: Gēr'shon, Kō'hăth, and Me·rār'ī, the years of the life of Levi being a hundred and thirty-seven years. ¹⁷The sons of Gēr'shon: Lĭb'nī and Shĭm'ē-ī, by their families. ¹⁸The sons of Kō'hăth: Ăm'răm, Ĭz'-hār, Hē'bron, and Ŭz'zĭ-ĕl, the years of the life of Kohath being a hundred and thirty-three years. ¹⁹The sons of Me·rār'ī: Măh'lī and Mū'shī. These are the families of the Lē'vītes according to their generations. ²⁰Ăm'răm took to wife Jŏch'e·bĕd his father's sister and she bore him Aaron and Moses, the years of the life of Amram being one hundred and thirty-seven years. ²¹The sons of Ĭz'hār: Kō'rah, Nē'phĕg, and Zĭch'rī. ²²And the sons of Ŭz'zĭ-ĕl: Mīsh'a-ĕl, Ĕl'za-phăn, and Sĭth'rī. ²³Aaron took to wife Ĕ·lī'-she·ba, the daughter of Ăm·mĭn'-a·dăb and the sister of Näh'shon; and she bore him Nā'dăb, A·bī'hū, Ĕl-ē-ā'zar, and Ĭth'a·mār. ²⁴The sons of Kō'rah: Ăs'sīr, Ĕl·kā'nah, and A·bī'-a·săph; these are the families of the Kō'ra·hītes. ²⁵Ĕl-ē-ā'zar, Aaron's son, took to wife one of the daughters of Pū'tĭ-ĕl; and she bore him Phĭn'e-has. These are the heads of the fathers' houses of the Lē'vītes by their families.

26 These are the Aaron and Moses to whom the LORD said: "Bring out the people of Israel from the land of Egypt by their hosts." ²⁷It was they who spoke to Pharaoh king of Egypt about bringing out the people of Israel from Egypt, this Moses and this Aaron. 28 On the day when the LORD spoke to Moses in the land of Egypt, ²⁹the LORD said to Moses, "I am the LORD; tell Pharaoh king of Egypt all that I say to you." ³⁰But Moses said to the LORD, "Behold, I am of uncircumcised lips; how then shall Pharaoh listen to 7 me?" ¹And the LORD said to Moses, "See, I make you as God to Pharaoh; and Aaron your brother shall be your prophet. ²You shall speak all that I command you; and Aaron your brother shall tell Pharaoh to let the people of Israel go out of his land. ³But I will harden Pharaoh's heart, and though I multiply my signs and wonders in the land of Egypt, ⁴Pharaoh will not listen to you; then I will lay my hand upon Egypt and bring forth my hosts, my people the sons of Israel, out of the land of Egypt by great acts of judgment. ⁵And the Egyptians shall know that I am the LORD, when I stretch forth my hand upon Egypt and bring out the people of Israel from among them." ⁶And Moses and Aaron did so; they did as the LORD commanded them. ⁷Now Moses was eighty years old, and Aaron eighty-three years old, when they spoke to Pharaoh.

8 And the LORD said to Moses and Aaron, ⁹"When Pharaoh says to you, 'Prove yourselves by working a miracle,' then you shall say to Aaron, 'Take your rod and cast it down before Pharaoh, that it may become a serpent.' " ¹⁰So Moses and Aaron went to Pharaoh and did as the LORD commanded; Aaron cast down his rod before Pharaoh and his servants, and it became a serpent. ¹¹Then Pharaoh summoned the wise men and the sorcerers; and they also, the magicians of Egypt, did the same by their secret arts. ¹²For every man cast down his rod, and they became serpents. But Aaron's rod swallowed up their rods. ¹³Still Pharaoh's heart was hardened, and he would not listen to them; as the LORD had said.

6.14-16: Gen 46.8-11; Num 26.5-14.
6.16-19: Num 3.15-20; 26.57-58; 1 Chron 6.1, 16-19.
6.20-23: Num 26.58-60. **7.3:** Acts 7.36.

14 Then the LORD said to Moses, "Pharaoh's heart is hardened, he refuses to let the people go. ¹⁵ Go to Pharaoh in the morning, as he is going out to the water; wait for him by the river's brink, and take in your hand the rod which was turned into a serpent. ¹⁶And you shall say to him, 'The LORD, the God of the Hebrews, sent me to you, saying, "Let my people go, that they may serve me in the wilderness; and behold, you have not yet obeyed." ¹⁷Thus says the LORD, "By this you shall know that I am the LORD: behold, I will strike the water that is in the Nile with the rod that is in my hand, and it shall be turned to blood, ¹⁸ and the fish in the Nile shall die, and the Nile shall become foul, and the Egyptians will loathe to drink water from the Nile." ' " ¹⁹And the LORD said to Moses, "Say to Aaron, 'Take your rod and stretch out your hand over the waters of Egypt, over their rivers, their canals, and their ponds, and all their pools of water, that they may become blood; and there shall be blood throughout all the land of Egypt, both in vessels of wood and in vessels of stone.' "

20 Moses and Aaron did as the LORD commanded; in the sight of Pharaoh and in the sight of his servants, he lifted up the rod and struck the water that was in the Nile, and all the water that was in the Nile turned to blood. ²¹And the fish in the Nile died; and the Nile became foul, so that the Egyptians could not drink water from the Nile; and there was blood throughout all the land of Egypt. ²² But the magicians of Egypt did the same by their secret arts; so Pharaoh's heart remained hardened, and he would not listen to them; as the LORD had said. ²³Pharaoh turned and went into his house, and he did not lay even this to heart. ²⁴And all the Egyptians dug round about the Nile for water to drink, for they could not drink the water of the Nile.

25 Seven days passed after the LORD **8** ⁱ had struck the Nile. ¹Then the LORD said to Moses, "Go in to Pharaoh and say to him, 'Thus says the LORD, "Let my people go, that they may serve me. ²But if you refuse to let them go, behold, I will plague all your country with frogs; ³the Nile shall swarm with frogs which shall

come up into your house, and into your bedchamber and on your bed, and into the houses of your servants and of your people,ʲ and into your ovens and your kneading bowls; ⁴the frogs shall come up on you and on your people and on all your servants." ' " ⁵ᵏAnd the LORD said to Moses, "Say to Aaron, 'Stretch out your hand with your rod over the rivers, over the canals, and over the pools, and cause frogs to come upon the land of Egypt!' " ⁶So Aaron stretched out his hand over the waters of Egypt; and the frogs came up and covered the land of Egypt. ⁷But the magicians did the same by their secret arts, and brought frogs upon the land of Egypt.

8 Then Pharaoh called Moses and Aaron, and said, "Entreat the LORD to take away the frogs from me and from my people; and I will let the people go to sacrifice to the LORD." ⁹Moses said to Pharaoh, "Be pleased to command me when I am to entreat, for you and for your servants and for your people, that the frogs be destroyed from you and your houses and be left only in the Nile." ¹⁰And he said, "Tomorrow." Moses said, "Be it as you say, that you may know that there is no one like the LORD our God. ¹¹The frogs shall depart from you and your houses and your servants and your people; they shall be left only in the Nile." ¹²So Moses and Aaron went out from Pharaoh; and Moses cried to the LORD concerning the frogs, as he had agreed with Pharaoh.ˡ ¹³And the LORD did according to the word of Moses; the frogs died out of the houses and courtyards and out of the fields. ¹⁴And they gathered them together in heaps, and the land stank. ¹⁵But when Pharaoh saw that there was a respite, he hardened his heart, and would not listen to them; as the LORD had said.

16 Then the LORD said to Moses, "Say to Aaron, 'Stretch out your rod and strike the dust of the earth, that it may become gnats throughout all the land of Egypt.' " ¹⁷And they did so; Aaron stretched out his hand with his rod, and struck the dust of the earth, and there came gnats on man and beast; all the dust of the earth became gnats throughout all the land

---

ⁱCh 7.26 in Heb   ʲGk: Heb *upon your people*
ᵏCh 8.1 in Heb
ˡOr *which he had brought upon Pharaoh*

of Egypt. [18]The magicians tried by their secret arts to bring forth gnats, but they could not. So there were gnats on man and beast. [19]And the magicians said to Pharaoh, "This is the finger of God." But Pharaoh's heart was hardened, and he would not listen to them; as the LORD had said.

20 Then the LORD said to Moses, "Rise up early in the morning and wait for Pharaoh, as he goes out to the water, and say to him, 'Thus says the LORD, "Let my people go, that they may serve me. [21]Else, if you will not let my people go, behold, I will send swarms of flies on you and your servants and your people, and into your houses; and the houses of the Egyptians shall be filled with swarms of flies, and also the ground on which they stand. [22]But on that day I will set apart the land of Gō'shĕn, where my people dwell, so that no swarms of flies shall be there; that you may know that I am the LORD in the midst of the earth. [23]Thus I will put a division[m] between my people and your people. By tomorrow shall this sign be."'" [24]And the LORD did so; there came great swarms of flies into the house of Pharaoh and into his servants' houses, and in all the land of Egypt the land was ruined by reason of the flies.

25 Then Pharaoh called Moses and Aaron, and said, "Go, sacrifice to your God within the land." [26]But Moses said, "It would not be right to do so; for we shall sacrifice to the LORD our God offerings abominable to the Egyptians. If we sacrifice offerings abominable to the Egyptians before their eyes, will they not stone us? [27]We must go three days' journey into the wilderness and sacrifice to the LORD our God as he will command us." [28]So Pharaoh said, "I will let you go, to sacrifice to the LORD your God in the wilderness; only you shall not go very far away. Make entreaty for me." [29]Then Moses said, "Behold, I am going out from you and I will pray to the LORD that the swarms of flies may depart from Pharaoh, from his servants, and from his people, tomorrow; only let not Pharaoh deal falsely again by not letting the people go to sacrifice to the LORD." [30]So Moses went out from Pharaoh and prayed to the LORD. [31]And the LORD did as Moses asked, and removed the swarms of flies from Pharaoh,

from his servants, and from his people; not one remained. [32]But Pharaoh hardened his heart this time also, and did not let the people go.

9 Then the LORD said to Moses, "Go in to Pharaoh, and say to him, 'Thus says the LORD, the God of the Hebrews, "Let my people go, that they may serve me. [2]For if you refuse to let them go and still hold them, [3]behold, the hand of the LORD will fall with a very severe plague upon your cattle which are in the field, the horses, the asses, the camels, the herds, and the flocks. [4]But the LORD will make a distinction between the cattle of Israel and the cattle of Egypt, so that nothing shall die of all that belongs to the people of Israel."'" [5]And the LORD set a time, saying, "Tomorrow the LORD will do this thing in the land." [6]And on the morrow the LORD did this thing; all the cattle of the Egyptians died, but of the cattle of the people of Israel not one died. [7]And Pharaoh sent, and behold, not one of the cattle of the Israelites was dead. But the heart of Pharaoh was hardened, and he did not let the people go.

8 And the LORD said to Moses and Aaron, "Take handfuls of ashes from the kiln, and let Moses throw them toward heaven in the sight of Pharaoh. [9]And it shall become fine dust over all the land of Egypt, and become boils breaking out in sores on man and beast throughout all the land of Egypt." [10]So they took ashes from the kiln, and stood before Pharaoh, and Moses threw them toward heaven, and it became boils breaking out in sores on man and beast. [11]And the magicians could not stand before Moses because of the boils, for the boils were upon the magicians and upon all the Egyptians. [12]But the LORD hardened the heart of Pharaoh, and he did not listen to them; as the LORD had spoken to Moses.

13 Then the LORD said to Moses, "Rise up early in the morning and stand before Pharaoh, and say to him, 'Thus says the LORD, the God of the Hebrews, "Let my people go, that they may serve me. [14]For this time I will send all my plagues upon your heart, and upon your servants and your people, that you may know that there is none like me in all the earth. [15]For

by now I could have put forth my hand and struck you and your people with pestilence, and you would have been cut off from the earth; ¹⁶but for this purpose have I let you live, to show you my power, so that my name may be declared throughout all the earth. ¹⁷You are still exalting yourself against my people, and will not let them go. ¹⁸Behold, tomorrow about this time I will cause very heavy hail to fall, such as never has been in Egypt from the day it was founded until now. ¹⁹Now therefore send, get your cattle and all that you have in the field into safe shelter; for the hail shall come down upon every man and beast that is in the field and is not brought home, and they shall die." ' " ²⁰Then he who feared the word of the LORD among the servants of Pharaoh made his slaves and his cattle flee into the houses; ²¹but he who did not regard the word of the LORD left his slaves and his cattle in the field.

22 And the LORD said to Moses, "Stretch forth your hand toward heaven, that there may be hail in all the land of Egypt, upon man and beast and every plant of the field, throughout the land of Egypt." ²³Then Moses stretched forth his rod toward heaven; and the LORD sent thunder and hail, and fire ran down to the earth. And the LORD rained hail upon the land of Egypt; ²⁴there was hail, and fire flashing continually in the midst of the hail, very heavy hail, such as had never been in all the land of Egypt since it became a nation. ²⁵The hail struck down everything that was in the field throughout all the land of Egypt, both man and beast; and the hail struck down every plant of the field, and shattered every tree of the field. ²⁶Only in the land of Gō′shen, where the people of Israel were, there was no hail.

27 Then Pharaoh sent, and called Moses and Aaron, and said to them, "I have sinned this time; the LORD is in the right, and I and my people are in the wrong. ²⁸Entreat the LORD; for there has been enough of this thunder and hail; I will let you go, and you shall stay no longer." ²⁹Moses said to him, "As soon as I have gone out of the city, I will stretch out my hands to the LORD; the thunder will cease, and there will be no more hail, that you may know that the earth is the LORD's. ³⁰But as for you and your servants, I know that you do not yet fear the LORD God." ³¹(The flax and the barley were ruined, for the barley was in the ear and the flax was in bud. ³²But the wheat and the spelt were not ruined, for they are late in coming up.) ³³So Moses went out of the city from Pharaoh, and stretched out his hands to the LORD; and the thunder and the hail ceased, and the rain no longer poured upon the earth. ³⁴But when Pharaoh saw that the rain and the hail and the thunder had ceased, he sinned yet again, and hardened his heart, he and his servants. ³⁵So the heart of Pharaoh was hardened, and he did not let the people of Israel go; as the LORD had spoken through Moses.

10 Then the LORD said to Moses, "Go in to Pharaoh; for I have hardened his heart and the heart of his servants, that I may show these signs of mine among them, ²and that you may tell in the hearing of your son and of your son's son how I have made sport of the Egyptians and what signs I have done among them; that you may know that I am the LORD."

3 So Moses and Aaron went in to Pharaoh, and said to him, "Thus says the LORD, the God of the Hebrews, 'How long will you refuse to humble yourself before me? Let my people go, that they may serve me. ⁴For if you refuse to let my people go, behold, tomorrow I will bring locusts into your country, ⁵and they shall cover the face of the land, so that no one can see the land; and they shall eat what is left to you after the hail, and they shall eat every tree of yours which grows in the field, ⁶and they shall fill your houses, and the houses of all your servants and of all the Egyptians; as neither your fathers nor your grandfathers have seen, from the day they came on earth to this day.' " Then he turned and went out from Pharaoh.

7 And Pharaoh's servants said to him, "How long shall this man be a snare to us? Let the men go, that they may serve the LORD their God; do you not yet understand that Egypt is ruined?" ⁸So Moses and Aaron were brought back to Pharaoh; and he said to them, "Go, serve the LORD your God; but who are to go?" ⁹And Moses said,

9.16: Rom 9.17.

"We will go with our young and our old; we will go with our sons and daughters and with our flocks and herds, for we must hold a feast to the LORD." ¹⁰And he said to them, "The LORD be with you, if ever I let you and your little ones go! Look, you have some evil purpose in mind.[n] ¹¹No! Go, the men among you, and serve the LORD, for that is what you desire." And they were driven out from Pharaoh's presence.

12 Then the LORD said to Moses, "Stretch out your hand over the land of Egypt for the locusts, that they may come upon the land of Egypt, and eat every plant in the land, all that the hail has left." ¹³So Moses stretched forth his rod over the land of Egypt, and the LORD brought an east wind upon the land all that day and all that night; and when it was morning the east wind had brought the locusts. ¹⁴And the locusts came up over all the land of Egypt, and settled on the whole country of Egypt, such a dense swarm of locusts as had never been before, nor ever shall be again. ¹⁵For they covered the face of the whole land, so that the land was darkened, and they ate all the plants in the land and all the fruit of the trees which the hail had left; not a green thing remained, neither tree nor plant of the field, through all the land of Egypt. ¹⁶Then Pharaoh called Moses and Aaron in haste, and said, "I have sinned against the LORD your God, and against you. ¹⁷Now therefore, forgive my sin, I pray you, only this once, and entreat the LORD your God only to remove this death from me." ¹⁸So he went out from Pharaoh, and entreated the LORD. ¹⁹And the LORD turned a very strong west wind, which lifted the locusts and drove them into the Red Sea; not a single locust was left in all the country of Egypt. ²⁰But the LORD hardened Pharaoh's heart, and he did not let the children of Israel go.

21 Then the LORD said to Moses, "Stretch out your hand toward heaven that there may be darkness over the land of Egypt, a darkness to be felt." ²²So Moses stretched out his hand toward heaven, and there was thick darkness in all the land of Egypt three days; ²³they did not see one another, nor did any rise from his place for three days; but all the people of Israel had light where they dwelt. ²⁴Then Pharaoh called Moses, and said, "Go, serve the LORD; your children also may go with you; only let your flocks and your herds remain behind." ²⁵But Moses said, "You must also let us have sacrifices and burnt offerings, that we may sacrifice to the LORD our God. ²⁶Our cattle also must go with us; not a hoof shall be left behind, for we must take of them to serve the LORD our God, and we do not know with what we must serve the LORD until we arrive there." ²⁷But the LORD hardened Pharaoh's heart, and he would not let them go. ²⁸Then Pharaoh said to him, "Get away from me; take heed to yourself; never see my face again; for in the day you see my face you shall die." ²⁹Moses said, "As you say! I will not see your face again."

11 The LORD said to Moses, "Yet one plague more I will bring upon Pharaoh and upon Egypt; afterwards he will let you go hence; when he lets you go, he will drive you away completely. ²Speak now in the hearing of the people, that they ask, every man of his neighbor and every woman of her neighbor, jewelry of silver and of gold." ³And the LORD gave the people favor in the sight of the Egyptians. Moreover, the man Moses was very great in the land of Egypt, in the sight of Pharaoh's servants and in the sight of the people.

4 And Moses said, "Thus says the LORD: About midnight I will go forth in the midst of Egypt; ⁵and all the first-born in the land of Egypt shall die, from the first-born of Pharaoh who sits upon his throne, even to the first-born of the maidservant who is behind the mill; and all the first-born of the cattle. ⁶And there shall be a great cry throughout all the land of Egypt, such as there has never been, nor ever shall be again. ⁷But against any of the people of Israel, either man or beast, not a dog shall growl; that you may know that the LORD makes a distinction between the Egyptians and Israel. ⁸And all these your servants shall come down to me, and bow down to me, saying, 'Get you out, and all the people who follow you.' And after that I will go out." And he went out from Pharaoh in hot anger. ⁹Then the LORD said

[n] Heb *before your face*

to Moses, "Pharaoh will not listen to you; that my wonders may be multiplied in the land of Egypt."

10 Moses and Aaron did all these wonders before Pharaoh; and the Lord hardened Pharaoh's heart, and he did not let the people of Israel go out of his land.

12 The Lord said to Moses and Aaron in the land of Egypt, ² "This month shall be for you the beginning of months; it shall be the first month of the year for you. ³ Tell all the congregation of Israel that on the tenth day of this month they shall take every man a lamb according to their fathers' houses, a lamb for a household; ⁴ and if the household is too small for a lamb, then a man and his neighbor next to his house shall take according to the number of persons; according to what each can eat you shall make your count for the lamb. ⁵ Your lamb shall be without blemish, a male a year old; you shall take it from the sheep or from the goats; ⁶ and you shall keep it until the fourteenth day of this month, when the whole assembly of the congregation of Israel shall kill their lambs in the evening.ᵒ ⁷ Then they shall take some of the blood, and put it on the two doorposts and the lintel of the houses in which they eat them. ⁸ They shall eat the flesh that night, roasted; with unleavened bread and bitter herbs they shall eat it. ⁹ Do not eat any of it raw or boiled with water, but roasted, its head with its legs and its inner parts. ¹⁰ And you shall let none of it remain until the morning, anything that remains until the morning you shall burn. ¹¹ In this manner you shall eat it: your loins girded, your sandals on your feet, and your staff in your hand; and you shall eat it in haste. It is the Lord's passover. ¹² For I will pass through the land of Egypt that night, and I will smite all the firstborn in the land of Egypt, both man and beast; and on all the gods of Egypt I will execute judgments: I am the Lord. ¹³ The blood shall be a sign for you, upon the houses where you are; and when I see the blood, I will pass over you, and no plague shall fall upon you to destroy you, when I smite the land of Egypt.

14 "This day shall be for you a memorial day, and you shall keep it as a feast to the Lord; throughout your generations you shall observe it as an ordinance for ever. ¹⁵ Seven days you shall eat unleavened bread; on the first day you shall put away leaven out of your houses, for if any one eats what is leavened, from the first day until the seventh day, that person shall be cut off from Israel. ¹⁶ On the first day you shall hold a holy assembly, and on the seventh day a holy assembly; no work shall be done on those days; but what every one must eat, that only may be prepared by you. ¹⁷ And you shall observe the feast of unleavened bread, for on this very day I brought your hosts out of the land of Egypt: therefore you shall observe this day, throughout your generations, as an ordinance for ever. ¹⁸ In the first month, on the fourteenth day of the month at evening, you shall eat unleavened bread, and so until the twenty-first day of the month at evening. ¹⁹ For seven days no leaven shall be found in your houses; for if any one eats what is leavened, that person shall be cut off from the congregation of Israel, whether he is a sojourner or a native of the land. ²⁰ You shall eat nothing leavened; in all your dwellings you shall eat unleavened bread."

21 Then Moses called all the elders of Israel, and said to them, "Select lambs for yourselves according to your families, and kill the passover lamb. ²² Take a bunch of hyssop and dip it in the blood which is in the basin, and touch the lintel and the two doorposts with the blood which is in the basin; and none of you shall go out of the door of his house until the morning. ²³ For the Lord will pass through to slay the Egyptians; and when he sees the blood on the lintel and on the two doorposts, the Lord will pass over the door, and will not allow the destroyer to enter your houses to slay you. ²⁴ You shall observe this rite as an ordinance for you and for your sons for ever. ²⁵ And when you come to the land which the Lord will give you, as he has promised, you shall keep this service. ²⁶ And when your children say to you, 'What do you mean by this service?' ²⁷ you shall say, 'It is the sacrifice of the Lord's passover, for he passed over the houses of the people of Israel in Egypt, when he slew the Egyptians but spared our

ᵒHeb *between the two evenings*
12.13: Heb 11.28.

houses.'" And the people bowed their heads and worshiped.

28 Then the people of Israel went and did so; as the Lord had commanded Moses and Aaron, so they did.

29 At midnight the Lord smote all the first-born in the land of Egypt, from the first-born of Pharaoh who sat on his throne to the first-born of the captive who was in the dungeon, and all the first-born of the cattle. ³⁰And Pharaoh rose up in the night, he, and all his servants, and all the Egyptians; and there was a great cry in Egypt, for there was not a house where one was not dead. ³¹And he summoned Moses and Aaron by night, and said, "Rise up, go forth from among my people, both you and the people of Israel; and go, serve the Lord, as you have said. ³²Take your flocks and your herds, as you have said, and be gone; and bless me also!"

33 And the Egyptians were urgent with the people, to send them out of the land in haste; for they said, "We are all dead men." ³⁴So the people took their dough before it was leavened, their kneading bowls being bound up in their mantles on their shoulders. ³⁵The people of Israel had also done as Moses told them, for they had asked of the Egyptians jewelry of silver and of gold, and clothing; ³⁶and the Lord had given the people favor in the sight of the Egyptians, so that they let them have what they asked. Thus they despoiled the Egyptians.

37 And the people of Israel journeyed from Răm′ĕ·sēṣ to Sŭc′cŏth, about six hundred thousand men on foot, besides women and children. ³⁸A mixed multitude also went up with them, and very many cattle, both flocks and herds. ³⁹And they baked unleavened cakes of the dough which they had brought out of Egypt, for it was not leavened, because they were thrust out of Egypt and could not tarry, neither had they prepared for themselves any provisions.

40 The time that the people of Israel dwelt in Egypt was four hundred and thirty years. ⁴¹And at the end of four hundred and thirty years, on that very day, all the hosts of the Lord went out from the land of Egypt. ⁴²It was a night of watching by the Lord, to bring them out of the land of Egypt; so this same night is a night of watching kept to the Lord by all the people of Israel throughout their generations.

43 And the Lord said to Moses and Aaron, "This is the ordinance of the passover: no foreigner shall eat of it; ⁴⁴but every slave that is bought for money may eat of it after you have circumcised him. ⁴⁵No sojourner or hired servant may eat of it. ⁴⁶In one house shall it be eaten; you shall not carry forth any of the flesh outside the house; and you shall not break a bone of it. ⁴⁷All the congregation of Israel shall keep it. ⁴⁸And when a stranger shall sojourn with you and would keep the passover to the Lord, let all his males be circumcised, then he may come near and keep it; he shall be as a native of the land. But no uncircumcised person shall eat of it. ⁴⁹There shall be one law for the native and for the stranger who sojourns among you."

50 Thus did all the people of Israel; as the Lord commanded Moses and Aaron, so they did. ⁵¹And on that very day the Lord brought the people of Israel out of the land of Egypt by their hosts.

13 The Lord said to Moses, ² "Consecrate to me all the first-born; whatever is the first to open the womb among the people of Israel, both of man and of beast, is mine."

3 And Moses said to the people, "Remember this day, in which you came out from Egypt, out of the house of bondage, for by strength of hand the Lord brought you out from this place; no leavened bread shall be eaten. ⁴This day you are to go forth, in the month of Ā′bĭb. ⁵And when the Lord brings you into the land of the Canaanites, the Hĭt′tītes, the Ăm′o·rītes, the Hī′vītes, and the Jĕb′ū·sītes, which he swore to your fathers to give you, a land flowing with milk and honey, you shall keep this service in this month. ⁶Seven days you shall eat unleavened bread, and on the seventh day there shall be a feast to the Lord. ⁷Unleavened bread shall be eaten for seven days; no leavened bread shall be seen with you, and no leaven shall be seen with you in all your territory. ⁸And you shall tell your son

12.40: Acts 7.6.   12.46: Num 9.12; Jn 19.36.
12.49: Lev 24.22; Num 9.14; 15.15, 16, 29.
13.2, 12, 15: Lk 2.23.

on that day, 'It is because of what the Lord did for me when I came out of Egypt.' ⁹And it shall be to you as a sign on your hand and as a memorial between your eyes, that the law of the Lord may be in your mouth; for with a strong hand the Lord has brought you out of Egypt. ¹⁰You shall therefore keep this ordinance at its appointed time from year to year.

11 "And when the Lord brings you into the land of the Canaanites, as he swore to you and your fathers, and shall give it to you, ¹²you shall set apart to the Lord all that first opens the womb. All the firstlings of your cattle that are males shall be the Lord's. ¹³Every firstling of an ass you shall redeem with a lamb, or if you will not redeem it you shall break its neck. Every first-born of man among your sons you shall redeem. ¹⁴And when in time to come your son asks you, 'What does this mean?' you shall say to him, 'By strength of hand the Lord brought us out of Egypt, from the house of bondage. ¹⁵For when Pharaoh stubbornly refused to let us go, the Lord slew all the first-born in the land of Egypt, both the first-born of man and the first-born of cattle. Therefore I sacrifice to the Lord all the males that first open the womb; but all the first-born of my sons I redeem.' ¹⁶It shall be as a mark on your hand or frontlets between your eyes; for by a strong hand the Lord brought us out of Egypt."

17 When Pharaoh let the people go, God did not lead them by way of the land of the Phĭ·lĭs′tĭnes, although that was near; for God said, "Lest the people repent when they see war, and return to Egypt." ¹⁸But God led the people round by the way of the wilderness toward the Red Sea. And the people of Israel went up out of the land of Egypt equipped for battle. ¹⁹And Moses took the bones of Joseph with him; for Joseph had solemnly sworn the people of Israel, saying, "God will visit you; then you must carry my bones with you from here." ²⁰And they moved on from Sŭc′cŏth, and encamped at Ē′thạm, on the edge of the wilderness. ²¹And the Lord went before them by day in a pillar of cloud to lead them along the way, and by night in a pillar of fire to give them light, that they might travel by day and by

night; ²²the pillar of cloud by day and the pillar of fire by night did not depart from before the people.

14 Then the Lord said to Moses, ²"Tell the people of Israel to turn back and encamp in front of Pī·hạ-hī′rŏth, between Mĭg′dŏl and the sea, in front of Bā′ạl–zē′phŏn; you shall encamp over against it, by the sea. ³For Pharaoh will say of the people of Israel, 'They are entangled in the land; the wilderness has shut them in.' ⁴And I will harden Pharaoh's heart, and he will pursue them and I will get glory over Pharaoh and all his host; and the Egyptians shall know that I am the Lord." And they did so.

5 When the king of Egypt was told that the people had fled, the mind of Pharaoh and his servants was changed toward the people, and they said, "What is this we have done, that we have let Israel go from serving us?" ⁶So he made ready his chariot and took his army with him, ⁷and took six hundred picked chariots and all the other chariots of Egypt with officers over all of them. ⁸And the Lord hardened the heart of Pharaoh king of Egypt and he pursued the people of Israel as they went forth defiantly. ⁹The Egyptians pursued them, all Pharaoh's horses and chariots and his horsemen and his army, and overtook them encamped at the sea, by Pī·hạ-hī′rŏth, in front of Bā′ạl–zē′phŏn.

10 When Pharaoh drew near, the people of Israel lifted up their eyes, and behold, the Egyptians were marching after them; and they were in great fear. And the people of Israel cried out to the Lord; ¹¹and they said to Moses, "Is it because there are no graves in Egypt that you have taken us away to die in the wilderness? What have you done to us, in bringing us out of Egypt? ¹²Is not this what we said to you in Egypt, 'Let us alone and let us serve the Egyptians'? For it would have been better for us to serve the Egyptians than to die in the wilderness." ¹³And Moses said to the people, "Fear not, stand firm, and see the salvation of the Lord, which he will work for you today; for the Egyptians whom you see today, you shall never see again. ¹⁴The Lord will fight for you, and you have only to be still." ¹⁵The Lord said to Moses, "Why do you cry to me? Tell

13.19: Gen 50.25.   14.8: Acts 13.17.   14.12: Ex 16.3; 17.3.

the people of Israel to go forward. [16] Lift up your rod, and stretch out your hand over the sea and divide it, that the people of Israel may go on dry ground through the sea. [17] And I will harden the hearts of the Egyptians so that they shall go in after them, and I will get glory over Pharaoh and all his host, his chariots, and his horsemen. [18] And the Egyptians shall know that I am the LORD, when I have gotten glory over Pharaoh, his chariots, and his horsemen."

19 Then the angel of God who went before the host of Israel moved and went behind them; and the pillar of cloud moved from before them and stood behind them, [20] coming between the host of Egypt and the host of Israel. And there was the cloud and the darkness; and the night passed[p] without one coming near the other all night.

21 Then Moses stretched out his hand over the sea; and the LORD drove the sea back by a strong east wind all night, and made the sea dry land, and the waters were divided. [22] And the people of Israel went into the midst of the sea on dry ground, the waters being a wall to them on their right hand and on their left. [23] The Egyptians pursued, and went in after them into the midst of the sea, all Pharaoh's horses, his chariots, and his horsemen. [24] And in the morning watch the LORD in the pillar of fire and of cloud looked down upon the host of the Egyptians, and discomfited the host of the Egyptians, [25] clogging[q] their chariot wheels so that they drove heavily; and the Egyptians said, "Let us flee from before Israel; for the LORD fights for them against the Egyptians."

26 Then the LORD said to Moses, "Stretch out your hand over the sea, that the water may come back upon the Egyptians, upon their chariots, and upon their horsemen." [27] So Moses stretched forth his hand over the sea, and the sea returned to its wonted flow when the morning appeared; and the Egyptians fled into it, and the LORD routed[r] the Egyptians in the midst of the sea. [28] The waters returned and covered the chariots and the horsemen and all the host[s] of Pharaoh that had followed them into the sea; not so much as one of them remained. [29] But the people of Israel walked on dry ground through the sea, the waters being a wall to them on their right hand and on their left.

30 Thus the LORD saved Israel that day from the hand of the Egyptians; and Israel saw the Egyptians dead upon the seashore. [31] And Israel saw the great work which the LORD did against the Egyptians, and the people feared the LORD; and they believed in the LORD and in his servant Moses.

15 Then Moses and the people of Israel sang this song to the LORD, saying,

"I will sing to the LORD, for he has
   triumphed gloriously;
   the horse and his rider[t] he has
   thrown into the sea.
[2] The LORD is my strength and my
   song,
   and he has become my salvation;
this is my God, and I will praise him,
   my father's God, and I will exalt
   him.
[3] The LORD is a man of war;
   the LORD is his name.

[4] "Pharaoh's chariots and his host
   he cast into the sea;
   and his picked officers are sunk in
   the Red Sea.
[5] The floods cover them;
   they went down into the depths
   like a stone.
[6] Thy right hand, O LORD, glorious in
   power,
   thy right hand, O LORD, shatters
   the enemy.
[7] In the greatness of thy majesty
   thou overthrowest thy adversaries;
   thou sendest forth thy fury, it
   consumes them like stubble.
[8] At the blast of thy nostrils the waters
   piled up,
   the floods stood up in a heap;
   the deeps congealed in the heart
   of the sea.
[9] The enemy said, 'I will pursue, I
   will overtake,
   I will divide the spoil, my desire
   shall have its fill of them.
   I will draw my sword, my hand
   shall destroy them.'
[10] Thou didst blow with thy wind,
   the sea covered them;
   they sank as lead in the mighty
   waters.

---

[p] Gk: Heb *and it lit up the night*
[q] Or *binding*. Sam Gk Syr: Heb *removing*
[r] Heb *shook off*   [s] Gk Syr: Heb *to all the host*
[t] Or *its chariot*

¹¹ "Who is like thee, O LORD, among
the gods?
Who is like thee, majestic in
holiness,
terrible in glorious deeds, doing
wonders?
¹² Thou didst stretch out thy right hand,
the earth swallowed them.

¹³ "Thou hast led in thy steadfast love
the people whom thou hast redeemed,
thou hast guided them by thy
strength to thy holy abode.
¹⁴ The peoples have heard, they tremble;
pangs have seized on the inhabitants of Phĭ·lĭs′tĭ·ạ.
¹⁵ Now are the chiefs of Ē′dọm dismayed;
the leaders of Mō′ăb, trembling
seizes them;
all the inhabitants of Canaan have
melted away.
¹⁶ Terror and dread fall upon them;
because of the greatness of thy
arm, they are as still as a stone,
till thy people, O LORD, pass by,
till the people pass by whom thou
hast purchased.
¹⁷ Thou wilt bring them in, and plant
them on thy own mountain,
the place, O LORD, which thou hast
made for thy abode,
the sanctuary, O LORD, which
thy hands have established.
¹⁸ The LORD will reign for ever and
ever."

19 For when the horses of Pharaoh
with his chariots and his horsemen
went into the sea, the LORD brought
back the waters of the sea upon them;
but the people of Israel walked on dry
ground in the midst of the sea. ²⁰ Then
Miriam, the prophetess, the sister of
Aaron, took a timbrel in her hand; and
all the women went out after her with
timbrels and dancing. ²¹ And Miriam
sang to them:
"Sing to the LORD, for he has triumphed gloriously;
the horse and his rider he has thrown
into the sea."

22 Then Moses led Israel onward
from the Red Sea, and they went into
the wilderness of Shŭr; they went
three days in the wilderness and
found no water. ²³ When they came to
Mâr′ạh, they could not drink the water
of Marah because it was bitter; therefore it was named Marah.ᵘ ²⁴ And the
people murmured against Moses, saying, "What shall we drink?" ²⁵ And he
cried to the LORD; and the LORD
showed him a tree, and he threw it
into the water, and the water became
sweet.

There the LORDᵛ made for them a
statute and an ordinance and there
he proved them, ²⁶ saying, "If you will
diligently hearken to the voice of the
LORD your God, and do that which is
right in his eyes, and give heed to his
commandments and keep all his
statutes, I will put none of the diseases
upon you which I put upon the Egyptians; for I am the LORD, your healer."

27 Then they came to Ē′lĭm, where
there were twelve springs of water
and seventy palm trees; and they encamped there by the water.

16 They set out from Ē′lĭm, and
all the congregation of the people of Israel came to the wilderness of
Sĭn, which is between Elim and Sinai,
on the fifteenth day of the second
month after they had departed from
the land of Egypt. ²And the whole congregation of the people of Israel murmured against Moses and Aaron in
the wilderness, ³ and said to them,
"Would that we had died by the hand of
the LORD in the land of Egypt, when we
sat by the fleshpots and ate bread to
the full; for you have brought us out
into this wilderness to kill this whole
assembly with hunger."

4 Then the LORD said to Moses, "Behold, I will rain bread from heaven
for you; and the people shall go out
and gather a day's portion every day,
that I may prove them, whether they
will walk in my law or not. ⁵On the
sixth day, when they prepare what
they bring in, it will be twice as much
as they gather daily." ⁶So Moses and
Aaron said to all the people of Israel,
"At evening you shall know that it
was the LORD who brought you out of
the land of Egypt, ⁷ and in the morning
you shall see the glory of the LORD,
because he has heard your murmurings against the LORD. For what are
we, that you murmur against us?"
⁸ And Moses said, "When the LORD
gives you in the evening flesh to eat
and in the morning bread to the full,
because the LORD has heard your mur-

ᵘ That is *Bitterness*   ᵛ Heb *he*
16.3: Ex 14.12; 17.3.   **16.4, 13:** Jn 6.31.

murings which you murmur against him—what are we? Your murmurings are not against us but against the LORD."

9 And Moses said to Aaron, "Say to the whole congregation of the people of Israel, 'Come near before the LORD, for he has heard your murmurings.'" ¹⁰And as Aaron spoke to the whole congregation of the people of Israel, they looked toward the wilderness, and behold, the glory of the LORD appeared in the cloud. ¹¹And the LORD said to Moses, ¹²"I have heard the murmurings of the people of Israel; say to them, 'At twilight you shall eat flesh, and in the morning you shall be filled with bread; then you shall know that I am the LORD your God.'"

13 In the evening quails came up and covered the camp; and in the morning dew lay round about the camp. ¹⁴And when the dew had gone up, there was on the face of the wilderness a fine, flake-like thing, fine as hoarfrost on the ground. ¹⁵When the people of Israel saw it, they said to one another, "What is it?"ʷ For they did not know what it was. And Moses said to them, "It is the bread which the LORD has given you to eat. ¹⁶This is what the LORD has commanded: 'Gather of it, every man of you, as much as he can eat; you shall take an omer apiece, according to the number of the persons whom each of you has in his tent.'" ¹⁷And the people of Israel did so; they gathered, some more, some less. ¹⁸But when they measured it with an omer, he that gathered much had nothing over, and he that gathered little had no lack; each gathered according to what he could eat. ¹⁹And Moses said to them, "Let no man leave any of it till the morning." ²⁰But they did not listen to Moses; some left part of it till the morning, and it bred worms and became foul; and Moses was angry with them. ²¹Morning by morning they gathered it, each as much as he could eat; but when the sun grew hot, it melted.

22 On the sixth day they gathered twice as much bread, two omers apiece; and when all the leaders of the congregation came and told Moses, ²³he said to them, "This is what the LORD has commanded: 'Tomorrow is a day of solemn rest, a holy sabbath to the LORD; bake what you will bake and boil what you will boil, and all that is left over lay by to be kept till the morning.'" ²⁴So they laid it by till the morning, as Moses bade them; and it did not become foul, and there were no worms in it. ²⁵Moses said, "Eat it today, for today is a sabbath to the LORD; today you will not find it in the field. ²⁶Six days you shall gather it; but on the seventh day, which is a sabbath, there will be none." ²⁷On the seventh day some of the people went out to gather, and they found none. ²⁸And the LORD said to Moses, "How long do you refuse to keep my commandments and my laws? ²⁹See! The LORD has given you the sabbath, therefore on the sixth day he gives you bread for two days; remain every man of you in his place, let no man go out of his place on the seventh day." ³⁰So the people rested on the seventh day.

31 Now the house of Israel called its name manna; it was like coriander seed, white, and the taste of it was like wafers made with honey. ³²And Moses said, "This is what the LORD has commanded: 'Let an omer of it be kept throughout your generations, that they may see the bread with which I fed you in the wilderness, when I brought you out of the land of Egypt.'" ³³And Moses said to Aaron, "Take a jar, and put an omer of manna in it, and place it before the LORD, to be kept throughout your generations." ³⁴As the LORD commanded Moses, so Aaron placed it before the testimony, to be kept. ³⁵And the people of Israel ate the manna forty years, till they came to a habitable land; they ate the manna, till they came to the border of the land of Canaan. ³⁶(An omer is the tenth part of an ephah.)

17 All the congregation of the people of Israel moved on from the wilderness of Sĭn by stages, according to the commandment of the LORD, and camped at Rĕph′ĭ·dĭm; but there was no water for the people to drink. ²Therefore the people found fault with Moses, and said, "Give us water to drink." And Moses said to them, "Why do you find fault with me? Why do you put the LORD to the proof?" ³But the people thirsted there for water, and the people murmured against Moses, and said, "Why did you

ʷOr *"It is manna."* Heb *man hu*
16.18: 2 Cor 8.15.   **17.3:** 14.12; 16.3.

bring us up out of Egypt, to kill us and our children and our cattle with thirst?" ⁴So Moses cried to the LORD, "What shall I do with this people? They are almost ready to stone me." ⁵And the LORD said to Moses, "Pass on before the people, taking with you some of the elders of Israel; and take in your hand the rod with which you struck the Nile, and go. ⁶Behold, I will stand before you there on the rock at Hō'rĕb; and you shall strike the rock, and water shall come out of it, that the people may drink." And Moses did so, in the sight of the elders of Israel. ⁷And he called the name of the place Măs'sah˟ and Mĕr'ĭ·bah,ʸ because of the fault-finding of the children of Israel, and because they put the LORD to the proof by saying, "Is the LORD among us or not?"

8 Then came Ăm'a·lĕk and fought with Israel at Rĕph'ĭ·dĭm. ⁹And Moses said to Joshua, "Choose for us men, and go out, fight with Ăm'a·lĕk; tomorrow I will stand on the top of the hill with the rod of God in my hand." ¹⁰So Joshua did as Moses told him, and fought with Ăm'a·lĕk; and Moses, Aaron, and Hūr went up to the top of the hill. ¹¹Whenever Moses held up his hand, Israel prevailed; and whenever he lowered his hand, Ăm'a·lĕk prevailed. ¹²But Moses' hands grew weary; so they took a stone and put it under him, and he sat upon it, and Aaron and Hūr held up his hands, one on one side, and the other on the other side; so his hands were steady until the going down of the sun. ¹³And Joshua mowed down Ăm'a·lĕk and his people with the edge of the sword.

14 And the LORD said to Moses, "Write this as a memorial in a book and recite it in the ears of Joshua, that I will utterly blot out the remembrance of Ăm'a·lĕk from under heaven." ¹⁵And Moses built an altar and called the name of it, The LORD is my banner, ¹⁶saying, "A hand upon the banner of the LORD!ᶻ The LORD will have war with Ăm'a·lĕk from generation to generation."

18 Jĕth'rō, the priest of Mĭd'ĭ·an, Moses' father-in-law, heard of all that God had done for Moses and for Israel his people, how the LORD had brought Israel out of Egypt. ²Now Jĕth'rō, Moses' father-in-law, had taken Zĭp·pō'rah, Moses' wife, after

he had sent her away, ³and her two sons, of whom the name of the one was Gēr'shom (for he said, "I have been a sojournerᵃ in a foreign land"), ⁴and the name of the other, Ē·lĭ·ē'zerᵇ (for he said, "The God of my father was my help, and delivered me from the sword of Pharaoh"). ⁵And Jĕth'rō, Moses' father-in-law, came with his sons and his wife to Moses in the wilderness where he was encamped at the mountain of God. ⁶And when one told Moses, "Lo,ᶜ your father-in-law Jĕth'rō is coming to you with your wife and her two sons with her," ⁷Moses went out to meet his father-in-law, and did obeisance and kissed him; and they asked each other of their welfare, and went into the tent. ⁸Then Moses told his father-in-law all that the LORD had done to Pharaoh and to the Egyptians for Israel's sake, all the hardship that had come upon them in the way, and how the LORD had delivered them. ⁹And Jĕth'rō rejoiced for all the good which the LORD had done to Israel, in that he had delivered them out of the hand of the Egyptians.

10 And Jĕth'rō said, "Blessed be the LORD, who has delivered you out of the hands of the Egyptians and out of the hand of Pharaoh. ¹¹Now I know that the LORD is greater than all gods, because he delivered the people from under the hand of the Egyptians,ᵈ when they dealt arrogantly with them." ¹²And Jĕth'rō, Moses' father-in-law, offeredᵉ a burnt offering and sacrifices to God; and Aaron came with all the elders of Israel to eat bread with Moses' father-in-law before God.

13 On the morrow Moses sat to judge the people, and the people stood about Moses from morning till evening. ¹⁴When Moses' father-in-law saw all that he was doing for the people, he said, "What is this that you are doing for the people? Why do you sit alone, and all the people stand about you from morning till evening?" ¹⁵And Moses said to his father-in-law, "Because the people come to me to inquire of God; ¹⁶when they have a dispute, they come to me and I decide between a man and his neighbor, and I make

---

ˣThat is *Proof* ʸThat is *Contention* ᶻCn: Heb obscure
ᵃHeb *ger* ᵇHeb *Eli*, my God, *ezer*, help
ᶜSam Gk Syr: Heb *I*
ᵈTransposing the last clause of v. 10 to v. 11
ᵉSyr Tg Vg: Heb *took*
17.14: Deut 25.17-19; 1 Sam 15.2-9. **18.3, 4:** Acts 7.29.

them know the statutes of God and his decisions." [17]Moses' father-in-law said to him, "What you are doing is not good. [18]You and the people with you will wear yourselves out, for the thing is too heavy for you; you are not able to perform it alone. [19]Listen now to my voice; I will give you counsel, and God be with you! You shall represent the people before God, and bring their cases to God; [20]and you shall teach them the statutes and the decisions, and make them know the way in which they must walk and what they must do. [21]Moreover choose able men from all the people, such as fear God, men who are trustworthy and who hate a bribe; and place such men over the people as rulers of thousands, of hundreds, of fifties, and of tens. [22]And let them judge the people at all times; every great matter they shall bring to you, but any small matter they shall decide themselves; so it will be easier for you, and they will bear the burden with you. [23]If you do this, and God so commands you, then you will be able to endure, and all this people also will go to their place in peace."

24 So Moses gave heed to the voice of his father-in-law and did all that he had said. [25]Moses chose able men out of all Israel, and made them heads over the people, rulers of thousands, of hundreds, of fifties, and of tens. [26]And they judged the people at all times; hard cases they brought to Moses, but any small matter they decided themselves. [27]Then Moses let his father-in-law depart, and he went his way to his own country.

19 On the third new moon after the people of Israel had gone forth out of the land of Egypt, on that day they came into the wilderness of Sinai. [2]And when they set out from Rĕph'ĭ·dĭm and came into the wilderness of Sinai, they encamped in the wilderness; and there Israel encamped before the mountain. [3]And Moses went up to God, and the LORD called to him out of the mountain, saying, "Thus you shall say to the house of Jacob, and tell the people of Israel: [4]You have seen what I did to the Egyptians, and how I bore you on eagles' wings and brought you to myself. [5]Now therefore, if you will obey my voice and keep my covenant, you shall be my own possession among all peoples; for all the earth is

mine, [6]and you shall be to me a kingdom of priests and a holy nation. These are the words which you shall speak to the children of Israel."

7 So Moses came and called the elders of the people, and set before them all these words which the LORD had commanded him. [8]And all the people answered together and said, "All that the LORD has spoken we will do." And Moses reported the words of the people to the LORD. [9]And the LORD said to Moses, "Lo, I am coming to you in a thick cloud, that the people may hear when I speak with you, and may also believe you for ever."

Then Moses told the words of the people to the LORD. [10]And the LORD said to Moses, "Go to the people and consecrate them today and tomorrow, and let them wash their garments, [11]and be ready by the third day; for on the third day the LORD will come down upon Mount Sinai in the sight of all the people. [12]And you shall set bounds for the people round about, saying, 'Take heed that you do not go up into the mountain or touch the border of it; whoever touches the mountain shall be put to death; [13]no hand shall touch him, but he shall be stoned or shot; whether beast or man, he shall not live.' When the trumpet sounds a long blast, they shall come up to the mountain." [14]So Moses went down from the mountain to the people, and consecrated the people; and they washed their garments. [15]And he said to the people, "Be ready by the third day; do not go near a woman."

16 On the morning of the third day there were thunders and lightnings, and a thick cloud upon the mountain, and a very loud trumpet blast, so that all the people who were in the camp trembled. [17]Then Moses brought the people out of the camp to meet God; and they took their stand at the foot of the mountain. [18]And Mount Sinai was wrapped in smoke, because the LORD descended upon it in fire; and the smoke of it went up like the smoke of a kiln, and the whole mountain quaked greatly. [19]And as the sound of the trumpet grew louder and louder, Moses spoke, and God answered him in thunder. [20]And the LORD came down

19.5, 6: Deut 7.6; 14.2, 21; 26.19; Tit 2.14; 1 Pe. 2.9; Rev 1.6; 5.10.   19.12-19: Heb 12.18-20.

upon Mount Sinai, to the top of the mountain; and the LORD called Moses to the top of the mountain, and Moses went up. ²¹And the LORD said to Moses, "Go down and warn the people, lest they break through to the LORD to gaze and many of them perish. ²²And also let the priests who come near to the LORD consecrate themselves, lest the LORD break out upon them." ²³And Moses said to the LORD, "The people cannot come up to Mount Sinai; for thou thyself didst charge us, saying, 'Set bounds about the mountain, and consecrate it.'" ²⁴And the LORD said to him, "Go down, and come up bringing Aaron with you; but do not let the priests and the people break through to come up to the LORD, lest he break out against them." ²⁵So Moses went down to the people and told them.

20 And God spoke all these words, saying,

2 "I am the LORD your God, who brought you out of the land of Egypt, out of the house of bondage.

3 "You shall have no other gods before ⸠ me.

4 "You shall not make for yourself a graven image, or any likeness of anything that is in heaven above, or that is in the earth beneath, or that is in the water under the earth; ⁵you shall not bow down to them or serve them; for I the LORD your God am a jealous God, visiting the iniquity of the fathers upon the children to the third and the fourth generation of those who hate me, ⁶but showing steadfast love to thousands of those who love me and keep my commandments.

7 "You shall not take the name of the LORD your God in vain; for the LORD will not hold him guiltless who takes his name in vain.

8 "Remember the sabbath day, to keep it holy. ⁹Six days you shall labor, and do all your work; ¹⁰but the seventh day is a sabbath to the LORD your God; in it you shall not do any work, you, or your son, or your daughter, your manservant, or your maidservant, or your cattle, or the sojourner who is within your gates; ¹¹for in six days the LORD made heaven and earth, the sea, and all that is in them, and rested the seventh day; therefore the LORD blessed the sabbath day and hallowed it.

12 "Honor your father and your mother, that your days may be long in the land which the LORD your God gives you.

13 "You shall not kill.

14 "You shall not commit adultery.

15 "You shall not steal.

16 "You shall not bear false witness against your neighbor.

17 "You shall not covet your neighbor's house; you shall not covet your neighbor's wife, or his manservant, or his maidservant, or his ox, or his ass, or anything that is your neighbor's."

18 Now when all the people perceived the thunderings and the lightnings and the sound of the trumpet and the mountain smoking, the people were afraid and trembled; and they stood afar off, ¹⁹and said to Moses, "You speak to us, and we will hear; but let not God speak to us, lest we die." ²⁰And Moses said to the people, "Do not fear; for God has come to prove you, and that the fear of him may be before your eyes, that you may not sin."

21 And the people stood afar off, while Moses drew near to the thick darkness where God was. ²²And the LORD said to Moses, "Thus you shall say to the people of Israel: 'You have seen for yourselves that I have talked with you from heaven. ²³You shall not make gods of silver to be with me, nor shall you make for yourselves gods of gold. ²⁴An altar of earth you shall make for me and sacrifice on it your burnt offerings and your peace offerings, your sheep and your oxen; in every place where I cause my name to be remembered I will come to you and bless you. ²⁵And if you make me an altar of stone, you shall not build it of hewn stones; for if you wield your tool upon it you profane it. ²⁶And you shall not go up by steps to my altar, that your nakedness be not exposed on it.'

ᶠOr besides
20.2-17: Deut 5.6-21. **20.3:** Ex 20.23; Deut 5.7.
20.4: Ex 20.23; 34.17; Lev 19.4; 26.1; Deut 4.15-19; 5.8; 27.15.
20.5,6: Ex 23.24; 34.6, 7, 14; Deut 4.24; 5.9, 10; 7.9.
20.7: Lev 19.12; Deut 5.11.
20.8: Ex 23.12; 31.12-17; 34.21; 35.2, 3; Lev 19.3; Deut 5.12-15. **20.12-16:** Mt 19.18, 19; Mk 10.19; Lk 18.20.
20.12: Lev 19.3; Deut 5.16; Mt 15.4; Mk 7.10; Eph 6.2.
20.13: Gen 9.6; Ex 21.12; Lev 24.17; Deut 5.17; Mt 5.21; Jas 2.11. **20.13-17:** Rom 13.9.
20.14: Lev 20.10; Deut 5.18; Mt 5.27; Rom 7.7.
20.15: Lev 19.11; Deut 5.19. **20.16:** Ex 23.1; Deut 5.20.
20.17: Deut 5.21; Rom 7.7.
20.23: Ex 20.3, 4; 34.17; Deut 27.15.
20.24: Ex 27.1-8; Deut 12.5; 26.2. **20.25:** Deut 27.5, 6.

21 "Now these are the ordinances which you shall set before them. ²When you buy a Hebrew slave, he shall serve six years, and in the seventh he shall go out free, for nothing. ³If he comes in single, he shall go out single; if he comes in married, then his wife shall go out with him. ⁴If his master gives him a wife and she bears him sons or daughters, the wife and her children shall be her master's and he shall go out alone. ⁵But if the slave plainly says, 'I love my master, my wife, and my children; I will not go out free,' ⁶then his master shall bring him to God, and he shall bring him to the door or the doorpost; and his master shall bore his ear through with an awl; and he shall serve him for life.

7 "When a man sells his daughter as a slave, she shall not go out as the male slaves do. ⁸If she does not please her master, who has designated her*ᵍ* for himself, then he shall let her be redeemed; he shall have no right to sell her to a foreign people, since he has dealt faithlessly with her. ⁹If he designates her for his son, he shall deal with her as with a daughter. ¹⁰If he takes another wife to himself, he shall not diminish her food, her clothing, or her marital rights. ¹¹And if he does not do these three things for her, she shall go out for nothing, without payment of money.

12 "Whoever strikes a man so that he dies shall be put to death. ¹³But if he did not lie in wait for him, but God let him fall into his hand, then I will appoint for you a place to which he may flee. ¹⁴But if a man willfully attacks another to kill him treacherously, you shall take him from my altar, that he may die.

15 "Whoever strikes his father or his mother shall be put to death.

16 "Whoever steals a man, whether he sells him or is found in possession of him, shall be put to death.

17 "Whoever curses his father or his mother shall be put to death.

18 "When men quarrel and one strikes the other with a stone or with his fist and the man does not die but keeps his bed, ¹⁹then if the man rises again and walks abroad with his staff, he that struck him shall be clear; only he shall pay for the loss of his time, and shall have him thoroughly healed.

20 "When a man strikes his slave, male or female, with a rod and the slave dies under his hand, he shall be punished. ²¹But if the slave survives a day or two, he is not to be punished; for the slave is his money.

22 "When men strive together, and hurt a woman with child, so that there is a miscarriage, and yet no harm follows, the one who hurt her shall*ʰ* be fined, according as the woman's husband shall lay upon him; and he shall pay as the judges determine. ²³If any harm follows, then you shall give life for life, ²⁴eye for eye, tooth for tooth, hand for hand, foot for foot, ²⁵burn for burn, wound for wound, stripe for stripe.

26 "When a man strikes the eye of his slave, male or female, and destroys it, he shall let the slave go free for the eye's sake. ²⁷If he knocks out the tooth of his slave, male or female, he shall let the slave go free for the tooth's sake.

28 "When an ox gores a man or a woman to death, the ox shall be stoned, and its flesh shall not be eaten; but the owner of the ox shall be clear. ²⁹But if the ox has been accustomed to gore in the past, and its owner has been warned but has not kept it in, and it kills a man or a woman, the ox shall be stoned, and its owner also shall be put to death. ³⁰If a ransom is laid on him, then he shall give for the redemption of his life whatever is laid upon him. ³¹If it gores a man's son or daughter, he shall be dealt with according to this same rule. ³²If the ox gores a slave, male or female, the owner shall give to their master thirty shekels of silver, and the ox shall be stoned.

33 "When a man leaves a pit open, or when a man digs a pit and does not cover it, and an ox or an ass falls into it, ³⁴the owner of the pit shall make it good; he shall give money to its owner, and the dead beast shall be his.

35 "When one man's ox hurts another's, so that it dies, then they shall sell the live ox and divide the price of it; and the dead beast also they shall divide. ³⁶Or if it is known that the ox has been accustomed to gore in the

ᵍAnother reading is so that he has not designated her
ʰHeb he shall
21.2-11: Lev 25.39-46; Deut 15.12-18.
21.12: Ex 20.13; Lev 24.17; Mt 5.21.
21.13: Num 35.10-34; Deut 19.1-13; Josh 20.1-9.
21.16: Deut 24.7. **21.17:** Lev 20.9; Mt 15.4; Mk 7.10.
21.23-25: Lev 24.19-20; Deut 19.21; Mt 5.38.

past, and its owner has not kept it in, he shall pay ox for ox, and the dead beast shall be his.

22 [i] "If a man steals an ox or a sheep, and kills it or sells it, he shall pay five oxen for an ox, and four sheep for a sheep. [j] He shall make restitution; if he has nothing, then he shall be sold for his theft. [4] If the stolen beast is found alive in his possession, whether it is an ox or an ass or a sheep, he shall pay double.

2[k] "If a thief is found breaking in, and is struck so that he dies, there shall be no bloodguilt for him; [3] but if the sun has risen upon him, there shall be bloodguilt for him.

5 "When a man causes a field or vineyard to be grazed over, or lets his beast loose and it feeds in another man's field, he shall make restitution from the best in his own field and in his own vineyard.

6 "When fire breaks out and catches in thorns so that the stacked grain or the standing grain or the field is consumed, he that kindled the fire shall make full restitution.

7 "If a man delivers to his neighbor money or goods to keep, and it is stolen out of the man's house, then, if the thief is found, he shall pay double. [8] If the thief is not found, the owner of the house shall come near to God, to show whether or not he has put his hand to his neighbor's goods.

9 "For every breach of trust, whether it is for ox, for ass, for sheep, for clothing, or for any kind of lost thing, of which one says, 'This is it,' the case of both parties shall come before God; he whom God shall condemn shall pay double to his neighbor.

10 "If a man delivers to his neighbor an ass or an ox or a sheep or any beast to keep, and it dies or is hurt or is driven away, without any one seeing it, [11] an oath by the LORD shall be between them both to see whether he has not put his hand to his neighbor's property; and the owner shall accept the oath, and he shall not make restitution. [12] But if it is stolen from him, he shall make restitution to its owner. [13] If it is torn by beasts, let him bring it as evidence; he shall not make restitution for what has been torn.

14 "If a man borrows anything of his neighbor, and it is hurt or dies, the owner not being with it, he shall make

full restitution. [15] If the owner was with it, he shall not make restitution; if it was hired, it came for its hire.[l]

16 "If a man seduces a virgin who is not betrothed, and lies with her, he shall give the marriage present for her, and make her his wife. [17] If her father utterly refuses to give her to him, he shall pay money equivalent to the marriage present for virgins.

18 "You shall not permit a sorceress to live.

19 "Whoever lies with a beast shall be put to death.

20 "Whoever sacrifices to any god, save to the LORD only, shall be utterly destroyed.

21 "You shall not wrong a stranger or oppress him, for you were strangers in the land of Egypt. [22] You shall not afflict any widow or orphan. [23] If you do afflict them, and they cry out to me, I will surely hear their cry; [24] and my wrath will burn, and I will kill you with the sword, and your wives shall become widows and your children fatherless.

25 "If you lend money to any of my people with you who is poor, you shall not be to him as a creditor, and you shall not exact interest from him. [26] If ever you take your neighbor's garment in pledge, you shall restore it to him before the sun goes down; [27] for that is his only covering, it is his mantle for his body; in what else shall he sleep? And if he cries to me, I will hear, for I am compassionate.

28 "You shall not revile God, nor curse a ruler of your people.

29 "You shall not delay to offer from the fulness of your harvest and from the outflow of your presses.

"The first-born of your sons you shall give to me. [30] You shall do likewise with your oxen and with your sheep: seven days it shall be with its dam; on the eighth day you shall give it to me.

31 "You shall be men consecrated to me; therefore you shall not eat any

[i] Ch. 21.37 in Heb
[j] Restoring the second half of verse 3 and the whole of verse 4 to their place immediately following verse 1
[k] Ch 22.1 in Heb
[l] Or *it is reckoned in* (Heb *comes into*) *its hire*

22.7-15: Lev 5.14-6.7; Num 5.5-8.
22.16-17: Deut 22.28, 29.   22.18: Lev 20.27; Deut 18.10.
22.19: Lev 18.23; 20.15, 16; Deut 27.21.
22.21: Ex 23.9; Lev 19.33, 34; Deut 27.19.
22.22: Deut 24.17.
22.25-27: Lev 25.36, 37; Deut 23.19, 20.
22.28: Acts 23.5.
22.29: Ex 23.16, 19; Deut 26.2-11; Ex 13.2, 11-16.
22.31: Ex 19.6; Lev 11.44; 19.1; 7.24; 17.15.

flesh that is torn by beasts in the field; you shall cast it to the dogs.

23 "You shall not utter a false report. You shall not join hands with a wicked man, to be a malicious witness. ² You shall not follow a multitude to do evil; nor shall you bear witness in a suit, turning aside after a multitude, so as to pervert justice; ³ nor shall you be partial to a poor man in his suit.

4 "If you meet your enemy's ox or his ass going astray, you shall bring it back to him. ⁵ If you see the ass of one who hates you lying under its burden, you shall refrain from leaving him with it, you shall help him to lift it up.^m

6 "You shall not pervert the justice due to your poor in his suit. ⁷ Keep far from a false charge, and do not slay the innocent and righteous, for I will not acquit the wicked. ⁸ And you shall take no bribe, for a bribe blinds the officials, and subverts the cause of those who are in the right.

9 "You shall not oppress a stranger; you know the heart of a stranger, for you were strangers in the land of Egypt.

10 "For six years you shall sow your land and gather in its yield; ¹¹ but the seventh year you shall let it rest and lie fallow, that the poor of your people may eat; and what they leave the wild beasts may eat. You shall do likewise with your vineyard, and with your olive orchard.

12 "Six days you shall do your work, but on the seventh day you shall rest; that your ox and your ass may have rest, and the son of your bondmaid, and the alien, may be refreshed. ¹³ Take heed to all that I have said to you; and make no mention of the names of other gods, nor let such be heard out of your mouth.

14 "Three times in the year you shall keep a feast to me. ¹⁵ You shall keep the feast of unleavened bread; as I commanded you, you shall eat unleavened bread for seven days at the appointed time in the month of Āʹbĭb, for in it you came out of Egypt. None shall appear before me empty-handed. ¹⁶ You shall keep the feast of harvest, of the first fruits of your labor, of what you sow in the field. You shall keep the feast of ingathering at the end of the year, when you gather in from the field the

fruit of your labor. ¹⁷ Three times in the year shall all your males appear before the Lord GOD.

18 "You shall not offer the blood of my sacrifice with leavened bread, or let the fat of my feast remain until the morning.

19 "The first of the first fruits of your ground you shall bring into the house of the LORD your God.

"You shall not boil a kid in its mother's milk.

20 "Behold, I send an angel before you, to guard you on the way and to bring you to the place which I have prepared. ²¹ Give heed to him and hearken to his voice, do not rebel against him, for he will not pardon your transgression; for my name is in him.

22 "But if you hearken attentively to his voice and do all that I say, then I will be an enemy to your enemies and an adversary to your adversaries.

23 "When my angel goes before you, and brings you in to the Ămʹo·rītes, and the Hĭtʹtītes, and the Pĕrʹĭz·zītes, and the Canaanites, the Hīʹvītes, and the Jĕbʹū·sītes, and I blot them out, ²⁴ you shall not bow down to their gods, nor serve them, nor do according to their works, but you shall utterly overthrow them and break their pillars in pieces. ²⁵ You shall serve the LORD your God, and I^n will bless your bread and your water; and I will take sickness away from the midst of you. ²⁶ None shall cast her young or be barren in your land; I will fulfil the number of your days. ²⁷ I will send my terror before you, and will throw into confusion all the people against whom you shall come, and I will make all your enemies turn their backs to you. ²⁸ And I will send hornets before you, which shall drive out Hīʹvīte, Canaanite, and Hĭtʹtīte from before you. ²⁹ I will not drive them out from before you in one year, lest the land become desolate and the wild beasts multiply against you. ³⁰ Little by little I will drive them out from before you, until you are increased and

ᵐGk: Heb obscure   ⁿGk Vg: Heb *he*
23.1: Ex 20.16; 23.7; Deut 5.20; 19.15-21.
23.3, 6: Lev 19.15.
23.7: Ex 20.16; 23.1.   **23.8:** Deut 16.19.
23.9: Ex 22.21; Lev 19.33, 34; Deut 27.19.
23.10, 11: Lev 25.1-7.
23.12: Ex 20.8-11; 31.15-17; 34.21; 35.2; Deut 5.12-15.
23.14-17: Ex 34.22-24; Lev 23.1-44; Deut 16.1-17.
23.18: Ex 12.10; 34.25; Lev 2.11; 7.15.
23.19: Ex 22.29; 34.26; Deut 26.2-11; 14.21.

possess the land. ³¹And I will set your bounds from the Red Sea to the sea of the Phĭ·lĭs′tĭnes, and from the wilderness to the Euphrates; for I will deliver the inhabitants of the land into your hand, and you shall drive them out before you. ³²You shall make no covenant with them or with their gods. ³³They shall not dwell in your land, lest they make you sin against me; for if you serve their gods, it will surely be a snare to you."

24 And he said to Moses, "Come up to the Lord, you and Aaron, Nā′dăb, and A·bī′hū, and seventy of the elders of Israel, and worship afar off. ²Moses alone shall come near to the Lord; but the others shall not come near, and the people shall not come up with him."

3 Moses came and told the people all the words of the Lord and all the ordinances; and all the people answered with one voice, and said, "All the words which the Lord has spoken we will do." ⁴And Moses wrote all the words of the Lord. And he rose early in the morning, and built an altar at the foot of the mountain, and twelve pillars, according to the twelve tribes of Israel. ⁵And he sent young men of the people of Israel, who offered burnt offerings and sacrificed peace offerings of oxen to the Lord. ⁶And Moses took half of the blood and put it in basins, and half of the blood he threw against the altar. ⁷Then he took the book of the covenant, and read it in the hearing of the people; and they said, "All that the Lord has spoken we will do, and we will be obedient." ⁸And Moses took the blood and threw it upon the people, and said, "Behold the blood of the covenant which the Lord has made with you in accordance with all these words."

9 Then Moses and Aaron, Nā′dăb, and A·bī′hū, and seventy of the elders of Israel went up, ¹⁰and they saw the God of Israel; and there was under his feet as it were a pavement of sapphire stone, like the very heaven for clearness. ¹¹And he did not lay his hand on the chief men of the people of Israel; they beheld God, and ate and drank.

12 The Lord said to Moses, "Come up to me on the mountain, and wait there; and I will give you the tables of stone, with the law and the commandment, which I have written for their instruction." ¹³So Moses rose with his servant Joshua, and Moses went up into the mountain of God. ¹⁴And he said to the elders, "Tarry here for us, until we come to you again; and, behold, Aaron and Hūr are with you; whoever has a cause, let him go to them."

15 Then Moses went up on the mountain, and the cloud covered the mountain. ¹⁶The glory of the Lord settled on Mount Sinai, and the cloud covered it six days; and on the seventh day he called to Moses out of the midst of the cloud. ¹⁷Now the appearance of the glory of the Lord was like a devouring fire on the top of the mountain in the sight of the people of Israel. ¹⁸And Moses entered the cloud, and went up on the mountain. And Moses was on the mountain forty days and forty nights.

25 The Lord said to Moses, ²"Speak to the people of Israel, that they take for me an offering; from every man whose heart makes him willing you shall receive the offering for me. ³And this is the offering which you shall receive from them: gold, silver, and bronze, ⁴blue and purple and scarlet stuff and fine twined linen, goats' hair, ⁵tanned rams' skins, goatskins, acacia wood, ⁶oil for the lamps, spices for the anointing oil and for the fragrant incense, ⁷onyx stones, and stones for setting, for the ephod and for the breastpiece. ⁸And let them make me a sanctuary, that I may dwell in their midst. ⁹According to all that I show you concerning the pattern of the tabernacle, and of all its furniture, so you shall make it.

10 "They shall make an ark of acacia wood; two cubits and a half shall be its length, a cubit and a half its breadth, and a cubit and a half its height. ¹¹And you shall overlay it with pure gold, within and without shall you overlay it, and you shall make upon it a molding of gold round about. ¹²And you shall cast four rings of gold for it and put them on its four feet, two rings on the one side of it, and two rings on the other side of it. ¹³You shall make poles of acacia wood, and overlay them with gold. ¹⁴And you

24.8: Mt 26.28; Mk 14.24; Lk 22.20; 1 Cor 11.25; Heb 9.20; 10.29. 24.12: 2 Cor 3.3. 25-31: Ex 35.40.
25.2-8: Ex 35.4-9. 25.10-22: Ex 37.1-9.

shall put the poles into the rings on the sides of the ark, to carry the ark by them. [15] The poles shall remain in the rings of the ark; they shall not be taken from it. [16] And you shall put into the ark the testimony which I shall give you. [17] Then you shall make a mercy seat[o] of pure gold; two cubits and a half shall be its length, and a cubit and a half its breadth. [18] And you shall make two cherubim of gold; of hammered work shall you make them, on the two ends of the mercy seat. [19] Make one cherub on the one end, and one cherub on the other end; of one piece with the mercy seat shall you make the cherubim on its two ends. [20] The cherubim shall spread out their wings above, overshadowing the mercy seat with their wings, their faces one to another; toward the mercy seat shall the faces of the cherubim be. [21] And you shall put the mercy seat on the top of the ark; and in the ark you shall put the testimony that I shall give you. [22] There I will meet with you, and from above the mercy seat, from between the two cherubim that are upon the ark of the testimony, I will speak with you of all that I will give you in commandment for the people of Israel.

23 "And you shall make a table of acacia wood; two cubits shall be its length, a cubit its breadth, and a cubit and a half its height. [24] You shall overlay it with pure gold, and make a molding of gold around it. [25] And you shall make around it a frame a handbreadth wide, and a molding of gold around the frame. [26] And you shall make for it four rings of gold, and fasten the rings to the four corners at its four legs. [27] Close to the frame the rings shall lie, as holders for the poles to carry the table. [28] You shall make the poles of acacia wood, and overlay them with gold, and the table shall be carried with these. [29] And you shall make its plates and dishes for incense, and its flagons and bowls with which to pour libations; of pure gold you shall make them. [30] And you shall set the bread of the Presence on the table before me always.

31 "And you shall make a lampstand of pure gold. The base and the shaft of the lampstand shall be made of hammered work; its cups, its capitals, and its flowers shall be of one piece with it; [32] and there shall be six branches going out of its sides, three branches of the lampstand out of one side of it and three branches of the lampstand out of the other side of it; [33] three cups made like almonds, each with capital and flower, on one branch, and three cups made like almonds, each with capital and flower, on the other branch—so for the six branches going out of the lampstand; [34] and on the lampstand itself four cups made like almonds, with their capitals and flowers, [35] and a capital of one piece with it under each pair of the six branches going out from the lampstand. [36] Their capitals and their branches shall be of one piece with it, the whole of it one piece of hammered work of pure gold. [37] And you shall make the seven lamps for it; and the lamps shall be set up so as to give light upon the space in front of it. [38] Its snuffers and their trays shall be of pure gold. [39] Of a talent of pure gold shall it be made, with all these utensils. [40] And see that you make them after the pattern for them, which is being shown you on the mountain.

26 "Moreover you shall make the tabernacle with ten curtains of fine twined linen and blue and purple and scarlet stuff; with cherubim skilfully worked shall you make them. [2] The length of each curtain shall be twenty-eight cubits, and the breadth of each curtain four cubits; all the curtains shall have one measure. [3] Five curtains shall be coupled to one another; and the other five curtains shall be coupled to one another. [4] And you shall make loops of blue on the edge of the outmost curtain in the first set; and likewise you shall make loops on the edge of the outmost curtain in the second set. [5] Fifty loops you shall make on the one curtain, and fifty loops you shall make on the edge of the curtain that is in the second set; the loops shall be opposite one another. [6] And you shall make fifty clasps of gold, and couple the curtains one to the other with the clasps, that the tabernacle may be one whole.

7 "You shall also make curtains of goats' hair for a tent over the tabernacle; eleven curtains shall you make.

⁸The length of each curtain shall be thirty cubits, and the breadth of each curtain four cubits; the eleven curtains shall have the same measure. ⁹And you shall couple five curtains by themselves, and six curtains by themselves, and the sixth curtain you shall double over at the front of the tent. ¹⁰And you shall make fifty loops on the edge of the curtain that is outmost in one set, and fifty loops on the edge of the curtain which is outmost in the second set.

11 "And you shall make fifty clasps of bronze, and put the clasps into the loops, and couple the tent together that it may be one whole. ¹²And the part that remains of the curtains of the tent, the half curtain that remains, shall hang over the back of the tabernacle. ¹³And the cubit on the one side, and the cubit on the other side, of what remains in the length of the curtains of the tent shall hang over the sides of the tabernacle, on this side and that side, to cover it. ¹⁴And you shall make for the tent a covering of tanned rams' skins and goatskins.

15 "And you shall make upright frames for the tabernacle of acacia wood. ¹⁶Ten cubits shall be the length of a frame, and a cubit and a half the breadth of each frame. ¹⁷There shall be two tenons in each frame, for fitting together; so shall you do for all the frames of the tabernacle. ¹⁸You shall make the frames for the tabernacle: twenty frames for the south side; ¹⁹and forty bases of silver you shall make under the twenty frames, two bases under one frame for its two tenons, and two bases under another frame for its two tenons; ²⁰and for the second side of the tabernacle, on the north side twenty frames, ²¹and their forty bases of silver, two bases under one frame, and two bases under another frame; ²²and for the rear of the tabernacle westward you shall make six frames. ²³And you shall make two frames for corners of the tabernacle in the rear; ²⁴they shall be separate beneath, but joined at the top, at the first ring; thus shall it be with both of them; they shall form the two corners. ²⁵And there shall be eight frames, with their bases of silver, sixteen bases; two bases under one frame, and two bases under another frame.

26 "And you shall make bars of acacia wood, five for the frames of the one side of the tabernacle, ²⁷and five bars for the frames of the other side of the tabernacle, and five bars for the frames of the side of the tabernacle at the rear westward. ²⁸The middle bar, halfway up the frames, shall pass through from end to end. ²⁹You shall overlay the frames with gold, and shall make their rings of gold for holders for the bars; and you shall overlay the bars with gold. ³⁰And you shall erect the tabernacle according to the plan for it which has been shown you on the mountain.

31 "And you shall make a veil of blue and purple and scarlet stuff and fine twined linen; in skilled work shall it be made, with cherubim; ³²and you shall hang it upon four pillars of acacia overlaid with gold, with hooks of gold, upon four bases of silver. ³³And you shall hang the veil from the clasps, and bring the ark of the testimony in thither within the veil; and the veil shall separate for you the holy place from the most holy. ³⁴You shall put the mercy seat upon the ark of the testimony in the most holy place. ³⁵And you shall set the table outside the veil, and the lampstand on the south side of the tabernacle opposite the table; and you shall put the table on the north side.

36 "And you shall make a screen for the door of the tent, of blue and purple and scarlet stuff and fine twined linen, embroidered with needlework. ³⁷And you shall make for the screen five pillars of acacia, and overlay them with gold; their hooks shall be of gold, and you shall cast five bases of bronze for them.

27 "You shall make the altar of acacia wood, five cubits long and five cubits broad; the altar shall be square, and its height shall be three cubits. ²And you shall make horns for it on its four corners; its horns shall be of one piece with it, and you shall overlay it with bronze. ³You shall make pots for it to receive its ashes, and shovels and basins and forks and firepans; all its utensils you shall make of bronze. ⁴You shall also make for it a grating, a network of bronze; and upon the net you shall make four bronze rings at its four corners. ⁵And you shall

26.15-29: Ex 36.20-34.
26.31-37: Ex 36.35-38. 27.1-8: Ex 38.1-7.

set it under the ledge of the altar so that the net shall extend half way down the altar. ⁶And you shall make poles for the altar, poles of acacia wood, and overlay them with bronze; ⁷and the poles shall be put through the rings, so that the poles shall be upon the two sides of the altar, when it is carried. ⁸You shall make it hollow, with boards; as it has been shown you on the mountain, so shall it be made.

9 "You shall make the court of the tabernacle. On the south side the court shall have hangings of fine twined linen a hundred cubits long for one side; ¹⁰their pillars shall be twenty and their bases twenty, of bronze, but the hooks of the pillars and their fillets shall be of silver. ¹¹And likewise for its length on the north side there shall be hangings a hundred cubits long, their pillars twenty and their bases twenty, of bronze, but the hooks of the pillars and their fillets shall be of silver. ¹²And for the breadth of the court on the west side there shall be hangings for fifty cubits, with ten pillars and ten bases. ¹³The breadth of the court on the front to the east shall be fifty cubits. ¹⁴The hangings for the one side of the gate shall be fifteen cubits, with three pillars and three bases. ¹⁵On the other side the hangings shall be fifteen cubits, with three pillars and three bases. ¹⁶For the gate of the court there shall be a screen twenty cubits long, of blue and purple and scarlet stuff and fine twined linen, embroidered with needlework; it shall have four pillars and with them four bases. ¹⁷All the pillars around the court shall be filleted with silver; their hooks shall be of silver, and their bases of bronze. ¹⁸The length of the court shall be a hundred cubits, the breadth fifty, and the height five cubits, with hangings of fine twined linen and bases of bronze. ¹⁹All the utensils of the tabernacle for every use, and all its pegs and all the pegs of the court, shall be of bronze.

20 "And you shall command the people of Israel that they bring to you pure beaten olive oil for the light, that a lamp may be set up to burn continually. ²¹In the tent of meeting, outside the veil which is before the testimony, Aaron and his sons shall tend it from evening to morning before the LORD. It shall be a statute for ever to be ob-

served throughout their generations by the people of Israel.

28 "Then bring near to you Aaron your brother, and his sons with him, from among the people of Israel, to serve me as priests—Aaron and Aaron's sons, Nā′dăb and A·bī′hū, Ĕl·ē·ā′zar and Ĭth′a·mâr. ²And you shall make holy garments for Aaron your brother, for glory and for beauty. ³And you shall speak to all who have ability, whom I have endowed with an able mind, that they make Aaron's garments to consecrate him for my priesthood. ⁴These are the garments which they shall make: a breastpiece, an ephod, a robe, a coat of checker work, a turban, and a girdle; they shall make holy garments for Aaron your brother and his sons to serve me as priests.

5 "They shall receive gold, blue and purple and scarlet stuff, and fine twined linen. ⁶And they shall make the ephod of gold, of blue and purple and scarlet stuff, and of fine twined linen, skilfully worked. ⁷It shall have two shoulder-pieces attached to its two edges, that it may be joined together. ⁸And the skilfully woven band upon it, to gird it on, shall be of the same workmanship and materials, of gold, blue and purple and scarlet stuff, and fine twined linen. ⁹And you shall take two onyx stones, and engrave on them the names of the sons of Israel, ¹⁰six of their names on the one stone, and the names of the remaining six on the other stone, in the order of their birth. ¹¹As a jeweler engraves signets, so shall you engrave the two stones with the names of the sons of Israel; you shall enclose them in settings of gold filigree. ¹²And you shall set the two stones upon the shoulder-pieces of the ephod, as stones of remembrance for the sons of Israel; and Aaron shall bear their names before the LORD upon his two shoulders for remembrance. ¹³And you shall make settings of gold filigree, ¹⁴and two chains of pure gold, twisted like cords; and you shall attach the corded chains to the settings.

15 "And you shall make a breastpiece of judgment, in skilled work; like the work of the ephod you shall make it; of gold, blue and purple and

27.9-19: Ex 38.9-20.
27.20-21: Lev 24.1-4.   28.6-12: Ex 39.2-7.
28.15-28: Ex 39.8-21.

scarlet stuff, and fine twined linen shall you make it. ¹⁶It shall be square and double, a span its length and a span its breadth. ¹⁷And you shall set in it four rows of stones. A row of sardius, topaz, and carbuncle shall be the first row; ¹⁸and the second row an emerald, a sapphire, and a diamond; ¹⁹and the third row a jacinth, an agate, and an amethyst; ²⁰and the fourth row a beryl, an onyx, and a jasper; they shall be set in gold filigree. ²¹There shall be twelve stones with their names according to the names of the sons of Israel; they shall be like signets, each engraved with its name, for the twelve tribes. ²²And you shall make for the breastpiece twisted chains like cords, of pure gold; ²³and you shall make for the breastpiece two rings of gold, and put the two rings on the two edges of the breastpiece. ²⁴And you shall put the two cords of gold in the two rings at the edges of the breastpiece; ²⁵the two ends of the two cords you shall attach to the two settings of filigree, and so attach it in front to the shoulder-pieces of the ephod. ²⁶And you shall make two rings of gold, and put them at the two ends of the breastpiece, on its inside edge next to the ephod. ²⁷And you shall make two rings of gold, and attach them in front to the lower part of the two shoulder-pieces of the ephod, at its joining above the skilfully woven band of the ephod. ²⁸And they shall bind the breastpiece by its rings to the rings of the ephod with a lace of blue, that it may lie upon the skilfully woven band of the ephod, and that the breastpiece shall not come loose from the ephod. ²⁹So Aaron shall bear the names of the sons of Israel in the breastpiece of judgment upon his heart, when he goes into the holy place, to bring them to continual remembrance before the LORD. ³⁰And in the breastpiece of judgment you shall put the Ū′rīm and the Thŭm′mĭm, and they shall be upon Aaron's heart, when he goes in before the LORD; thus Aaron shall bear the judgment of the people of Israel upon his heart before the LORD continually.

31 "And you shall make the robe of the ephod all of blue. ³²It shall have in it an opening for the head, with a woven binding around the opening, like the opening in a garment,ᵖ that it may not be torn. ³³On its skirts you shall make pomegranates of blue and purple and scarlet stuff, around its skirts, with bells of gold between them, ³⁴a golden bell and a pomegranate, a golden bell and a pomegranate, round about on the skirts of the robe. ³⁵And it shall be upon Aaron when he ministers, and its sound shall be heard when he goes into the holy place before the LORD, and when he comes out, lest he die.

36 "And you shall make a plate of pure gold, and engrave on it, like the engraving of a signet, 'Holy to the LORD.' ³⁷And you shall fasten it on the turban by a lace of blue; it shall be on the front of the turban. ³⁸It shall be upon Aaron's forehead, and Aaron shall take upon himself any guilt incurred in the holy offering which the people of Israel hallow as their holy gifts; it shall always be upon his forehead, that they may be accepted before the LORD.

39 "And you shall weave the coat in checker work of fine linen, and you shall make a turban of fine linen, and you shall make a girdle embroidered with needlework.

40 "And for Aaron's sons you shall make coats and girdles and caps; you shall make them for glory and beauty. ⁴¹And you shall put them upon Aaron your brother, and upon his sons with him, and shall anoint them and ordain them and consecrate them, that they may serve me as priests. ⁴²And you shall make for them linen breeches to cover their naked flesh; from the loins to the thighs they shall reach; ⁴³and they shall be upon Aaron, and upon his sons, when they go into the tent of meeting, or when they come near the altar to minister in the holy place; lest they bring guilt upon themselves and die. This shall be a perpetual statute for him and for his descendants after him.

29 "Now this is what you shall do to them to consecrate them, that they may serve me as priests. Take one young bull and two rams without blemish, ²and unleavened bread, unleavened cakes mixed with oil, and unleavened wafers spread with oil. You shall make them of fine wheat flour. ³And you shall put them in one basket and

ᵖThe Hebrew word is of uncertain meaning
28.31-34: Ex 39.22-26.   28.36, 37: Ex 39.30, 31.
28.39, 40, 42: Ex 39.27-29.   29.1-37: Lev 8.1-34.

bring them in the basket, and bring the bull and the two rams. ⁴You shall bring Aaron and his sons to the door of the tent of meeting, and wash them with water. ⁵And you shall take the garments, and put on Aaron the coat and the robe of the ephod, and the ephod, and the breastpiece, and gird him with the skilfully woven band of the ephod; ⁶and you shall set the turban on his head, and put the holy crown upon the turban. ⁷And you shall take the anointing oil, and pour it on his head and anoint him. ⁸Then you shall bring his sons, and put coats on them, ⁹and you shall gird them with girdles*q* and bind caps on them; and the priesthood shall be theirs by a perpetual statute. Thus you shall ordain Aaron and his sons.

10 "Then you shall bring the bull before the tent of meeting. Aaron and his sons shall lay their hands upon the head of the bull, ¹¹and you shall kill the bull before the LORD, at the door of the tent of meeting, ¹²and shall take part of the blood of the bull and put it upon the horns of the altar with your finger, and the rest of*r* the blood you shall pour out at the base of the altar. ¹³And you shall take all the fat that covers the entrails, and the appendage of the liver, and the two kidneys with the fat that is on them, and burn them upon the altar. ¹⁴But the flesh of the bull, and its skin, and its dung, you shall burn with fire outside the camp; it is a sin offering.

15 "Then you shall take one of the rams, and Aaron and his sons shall lay their hands upon the head of the ram, ¹⁶and you shall slaughter the ram, and shall take its blood and throw it against the altar round about. ¹⁷Then you shall cut the ram into pieces, and wash its entrails and its legs, and put them with its pieces and its head, ¹⁸and burn the whole ram upon the altar; it is a burnt offering to the LORD; it is a pleasing odor, an offering by fire to the LORD.

19 "You shall take the other ram; and Aaron and his sons shall lay their hands upon the head of the ram, ²⁰and you shall kill the ram, and take part of its blood and put it upon the tip of the right ear of Aaron and upon the tips of the right ears of his sons, and upon the thumbs of their right hands, and upon the great toes of their right feet, and throw the rest of the blood against

the altar round about. ²¹Then you shall take part of the blood that is on the altar, and of the anointing oil, and sprinkle it upon Aaron and his garments, and upon his sons and his sons' garments with him; and he and his garments shall be holy, and his sons and his sons' garments with him.

22 "You shall also take the fat of the ram, and the fat tail, and the fat that covers the entrails, and the appendage of the liver, and the two kidneys with the fat that is on them, and the right thigh (for it is a ram of ordination), ²³and one loaf of bread, and one cake of bread with oil, and one wafer, out of the basket of unleavened bread that is before the LORD; ²⁴and you shall put all these in the hands of Aaron and in the hands of his sons, and wave them for a wave offering before the LORD. ²⁵Then you shall take them from their hands, and burn them on the altar in addition to the burnt offering, as a pleasing odor before the LORD; it is an offering by fire to the LORD.

26 "And you shall take the breast of the ram of Aaron's ordination and wave it for a wave offering before the LORD; and it shall be your portion. ²⁷And you shall consecrate the breast of the wave offering, and the thigh of the priests' portion, which is waved, and which is offered from the ram of ordination, since it is for Aaron and for his sons. ²⁸It shall be for Aaron and his sons as a perpetual due from the people of Israel, for it is the priests' portion to be offered by the people of Israel from their peace offerings; it is their offering to the LORD.

29 "The holy garments of Aaron shall be for his sons after him, to be anointed in them and ordained in them. ³⁰The son who is priest in his place shall wear them seven days, when he comes into the tent of meeting to minister in the holy place.

31 "You shall take the ram of ordination, and boil its flesh in a holy place; ³²and Aaron and his sons shall eat the flesh of the ram and the bread that is in the basket, at the door of the tent of meeting. ³³They shall eat those things with which atonement was made, to ordain and consecrate them, but an outsider shall not eat of them, because they are holy. ³⁴And if any of

*q*Gk: Heb *girdles, Aaron and his sons*   *r*Heb *all*
29.18: Eph 5.2; Phil 4.18.

the flesh for the ordination, or of the bread, remain until the morning, then you shall burn the remainder with fire; it shall not be eaten, because it is holy.

35 "Thus you shall do to Aaron and to his sons, according to all that I have commanded you; through seven days shall you ordain them, ³⁶ and every day you shall offer a bull as a sin offering for atonement. Also you shall offer a sin offering for the altar, when you make atonement for it, and shall anoint it, to consecrate it. ³⁷ Seven days you shall make atonement for the altar, and consecrate it, and the altar shall be most holy; whatever touches the altar shall become holy.

38 "Now this is what you shall offer upon the altar: two lambs a year old day by day continually. ³⁹ One lamb you shall offer in the morning, and the other lamb you shall offer in the evening; ⁴⁰ and with the first lamb a tenth measure of fine flour mingled with a fourth of a hin of beaten oil, and a fourth of a hin of wine for a libation. ⁴¹ And the other lamb you shall offer in the evening, and shall offer with it a cereal offering and its libation, as in the morning, for a pleasing odor, an offering by fire to the LORD. ⁴² It shall be a continual burnt offering throughout your generations at the door of the tent of meeting before the LORD, where I will meet with you, to speak there to you. ⁴³ There I will meet with the people of Israel, and it shall be sanctified by my glory; ⁴⁴ I will consecrate the tent of meeting and the altar; Aaron also and his sons I will consecrate, to serve me as priests. ⁴⁵ And I will dwell among the people of Israel, and will be their God. ⁴⁶ And they shall know that I am the LORD their God, who brought them forth out of the land of Egypt that I might dwell among them; I am the LORD their God.

30 "You shall make an altar to burn incense upon; of acacia wood shall you make it. ²A cubit shall be its length, and a cubit its breadth; it shall be square, and two cubits shall be its height; its horns shall be of one piece with it. ³And you shall overlay it with pure gold, its top and its sides round about and its horns; and you shall make for it a molding of gold round about. ⁴And two golden rings shall you make for it; under its mold-

ing on two opposite sides of it shall you make them, and they shall be holders for poles with which to carry it. ⁵ You shall make the poles of acacia wood, and overlay them with gold. ⁶ And you shall put it before the veil that is by the ark of the testimony, before the mercy seat that is over the testimony, where I will meet with you. ⁷ And Aaron shall burn fragrant incense on it; every morning when he dresses the lamps he shall burn it, ⁸ and when Aaron sets up the lamps in the evening, he shall burn it, a perpetual incense before the LORD throughout your generations. ⁹ You shall offer no unholy incense thereon, nor burnt offering, nor cereal offering; and you shall pour no libation thereon. ¹⁰ Aaron shall make atonement upon its horns once a year; with the blood of the sin offering of atonement he shall make atonement for it once in the year throughout your generations; it is most holy to the LORD."

11 The LORD said to Moses, ¹² "When you take the census of the people of Israel, then each shall give a ransom for himself to the LORD when you number them, that there be no plague among them when you number them. ¹³ Each who is numbered in the census shall give this: half a shekel according to the shekel of the sanctuary (the shekel is twenty gerahs), half a shekel as an offering to the LORD. ¹⁴ Every one who is numbered in the census, from twenty years old and upward, shall give the LORD's offering. ¹⁵ The rich shall not give more, and the poor shall not give less, than the half shekel, when you give the LORD's offering to make atonement for yourselves. ¹⁶ And you shall take the atonement money from the people of Israel, and shall appoint it for the service of the tent of meeting; that it may bring the people of Israel to remembrance before the LORD, so as to make atonement for yourselves."

17 The LORD said to Moses, ¹⁸ "You shall also make a laver of bronze, with its base of bronze, for washing. And you shall put it between the tent of meeting and the altar, and you shall put water in it, ¹⁹ with which Aaron and his sons shall wash their hands and their feet. ²⁰ When they go into the tent of meeting, or when they come near

29.38-42: Num 28.3-10.   30.1-5: Ex 37.25-29.
30.11-16: Ex 38.25, 26.   30.18: Ex 38.8.

the altar to minister, to burn an offering by fire to the LORD, they shall wash with water, lest they die. ²¹They shall wash their hands and their feet, lest they die: it shall be a statute for ever to them, even to him and to his descendants throughout their generations."

22 Moreover, the LORD said to Moses, ²³"Take the finest spices: of liquid myrrh five hundred shekels, and of sweet-smelling cinnamon half as much, that is, two hundred and fifty, and of aromatic cane two hundred and fifty, ²⁴and of cassia five hundred, according to the shekel of the sanctuary, and of olive oil a hin; ²⁵and you shall make of these a sacred anointing oil blended as by the perfumer; a holy anointing oil it shall be. ²⁶And you shall anoint with it the tent of meeting and the ark of the testimony, ²⁷and the table and all its utensils, and the lampstand and its utensils, and the altar of incense, ²⁸and the altar of burnt offering with all its utensils and the laver and its base; ²⁹you shall consecrate them, that they may be most holy; whatever touches them will become holy. ³⁰And you shall anoint Aaron and his sons, and consecrate them, that they may serve me as priests. ³¹And you shall say to the people of Israel, 'This shall be my holy anointing oil throughout your generations. ³²It shall not be poured upon the bodies of ordinary men, and you shall make no other like it in composition; it is holy, and it shall be holy to you. ³³Whoever compounds any like it or whoever puts any of it on an outsider shall be cut off from his people.'"

34 And the LORD said to Moses, "Take sweet spices, stacte, and onycha, and galbanum, sweet spices with pure frankincense (of each shall there be an equal part), ³⁵and make an incense blended as by the perfumer, seasoned with salt, pure and holy; ³⁶and you shall beat some of it very small, and put part of it before the testimony in the tent of meeting where I shall meet with you; it shall be for you most holy. ³⁷And the incense which you shall make according to its composition, you shall not make for yourselves; it shall be for you holy to the LORD. ³⁸Whoever makes any like it to use as perfume shall be cut off from his people."

31 The LORD said to Moses, ²"See, I have called by name Běz'-a·lěl the son of Ū'rī, son of Hūr, of the tribe of Judah: ³and I have filled him with the Spirit of God, with ability and intelligence, with knowledge and all craftsmanship, ⁴to devise artistic designs, to work in gold, silver, and bronze, ⁵in cutting stones for setting, and in carving wood, for work in every craft. ⁶And behold, I have appointed with him Ō·hō'lǐ·ăb, the son of A·hǐs'-a·măch, of the tribe of Dan; and I have given to all able men ability, that they may make all that I have commanded you: ⁷the tent of meeting, and the ark of the testimony, and the mercy seat that is thereon, and all the furnishings of the tent, ⁸the table and its utensils, and the pure lampstand with all its utensils, and the altar of incense, ⁹and the altar of burnt offering with all its utensils, and the laver and its base, ¹⁰and the finely worked garments, the holy garments for Aaron the priest and the garments of his sons, for their service as priests, ¹¹and the anointing oil and the fragrant incense for the holy place. According to all that I have commanded you they shall do."

12 And the LORD said to Moses, ¹³"Say to the people of Israel, 'You shall keep my sabbaths, for this is a sign between me and you throughout your generations, that you may know that I, the LORD, sanctify you. ¹⁴You shall keep the sabbath, because it is holy for you; every one who profanes it shall be put to death; whoever does any work on it, that soul shall be cut off from among his people. ¹⁵Six days shall work be done, but the seventh day is a sabbath of solemn rest, holy to the LORD; whoever does any work on the sabbath day shall be put to death. ¹⁶Therefore the people of Israel shall keep the sabbath, observing the sabbath throughout their generations, as a perpetual covenant. ¹⁷It is a sign for ever between me and the people of Israel that in six days the LORD made heaven and earth, and on the seventh day he rested, and was refreshed.'"

18 And he gave to Moses, when he had made an end of speaking with him upon Mount Sinai, the two tables of the testimony, tables of stone, written with the finger of God.

30.22-33: Ex 37.29. 31.1-6: Ex 35.30-36.1.
31.12-17: Ex 20.8; 23.12; 35.2; Deut 5.12-15.

32 When the people saw that Moses delayed to come down from the mountain, the people gathered themselves together to Aaron, and said to him, "Up, make us gods, who shall go before us; as for this Moses, the man who brought us up out of the land of Egypt, we do not know what has become of him." ²And Aaron said to them, "Take off the rings of gold which are in the ears of your wives, your sons, and your daughters, and bring them to me." ³So all the people took off the rings of gold which were in their ears, and brought them to Aaron. ⁴And he received the gold at their hand, and fashioned it with a graving tool, and made a molten calf; and they said, "These are your gods, O Israel, who brought you up out of the land of Egypt!" ⁵When Aaron saw this, he built an altar before it; and Aaron made proclamation and said, "Tomorrow shall be a feast to the LORD." ⁶And they rose up early on the morrow, and offered burnt offerings and brought peace offerings; and the people sat down to eat and drink, and rose up to play.

7 And the LORD said to Moses, "Go down; for your people, whom you brought up out of the land of Egypt, have corrupted themselves; ⁸they have turned aside quickly out of the way which I commanded them; they have made for themselves a molten calf, and have worshiped it and sacrificed to it, and said, 'These are your gods, O Israel, who brought you up out of the land of Egypt!'" ⁹And the LORD said to Moses, "I have seen this people, and behold, it is a stiff-necked people; ¹⁰now therefore let me alone, that my wrath may burn hot against them and I may consume them; but of you I will make a great nation."

11 But Moses besought the LORD his God, and said, "O LORD, why does thy wrath burn hot against thy people, whom thou hast brought forth out of the land of Egypt with great power and with a mighty hand? ¹²Why should the Egyptians say, 'With evil intent did he bring them forth, to slay them in the mountains, and to consume them from the face of the earth'? Turn from thy fierce wrath, and repent of this evil against thy people. ¹³Remember Abraham, Isaac, and Israel, thy servants, to whom thou didst swear by thine own self, and didst say to them, 'I will multiply your descendants as the stars of heaven, and all this land that I have promised I will give to your descendants, and they shall inherit it for ever.' " ¹⁴And the LORD repented of the evil which he thought to do to his people.

15 And Moses turned, and went down from the mountain with the two tables of the testimony in his hands, tables that were written on both sides; on the one side and on the other were they written. ¹⁶And the tables were the work of God, and the writing was the writing of God, graven upon the tables. ¹⁷When Joshua heard the noise of the people as they shouted, he said to Moses, "There is a noise of war in the camp." ¹⁸But he said, "It is not the sound of shouting for victory, or the sound of the cry of defeat, but the sound of singing that I hear." ¹⁹And as soon as he came near the camp and saw the calf and the dancing, Moses' anger burned hot, and he threw the tables out of his hands and broke them at the foot of the mountain. ²⁰And he took the calf which they had made, and burnt it with fire, and ground it to powder, and scattered it upon the water, and made the people of Israel drink it.

21 And Moses said to Aaron, "What did this people do to you that you have brought a great sin upon them?" ²²And Aaron said, "Let not the anger of my lord burn hot; you know the people, that they are set on evil. ²³For they said to me, 'Make us gods, who shall go before us; as for this Moses, the man who brought us up out of the land of Egypt, we do not know what has become of him.' ²⁴And I said to them, 'Let any who have gold take it off'; so they gave it to me, and I threw it into the fire, and there came out this calf."

25 And when Moses saw that the people had broken loose (for Aaron had let them break loose, to their shame among their enemies), ²⁶then Moses stood in the gate of the camp, and said, "Who is on the LORD's side? Come to me." And all the sons of Lē'vī gathered themselves together to him. ²⁷And he said to them, "Thus says the LORD God of Israel, 'Put every man his sword on his side, and go to and fro from gate to gate throughout the camp,

32.1-6: Acts 7.40, 41. 32.6: 1 Cor 10.7.
32.9-14: Ex 32.31-35; Num 14.11-25. 32.23: Acts 7.40.

and slay every man his brother, and every man his companion, and every man his neighbor.'" [28]And the sons of Lē'vī did according to the word of Moses; and there fell of the people that day about three thousand men. [29]And Moses said, "Today you have ordained yourselves[g] for the service of the LORD, each one at the cost of his son and of his brother, that he may bestow a blessing upon you this day."

30 On the morrow Moses said to the people, "You have sinned a great sin. And now I will go up to the LORD; perhaps I can make atonement for your sin." [31]So Moses returned to the LORD and said, "Alas, this people have sinned a great sin; they have made for themselves gods of gold. [32]But now, if thou wilt forgive their sin — and if not, blot me, I pray thee, out of thy book which thou hast written." [33]But the LORD said to Moses, "Whoever has sinned against me, him will I blot out of my book. [34]But now go, lead the people to the place of which I have spoken to you; behold, my angel shall go before you. Nevertheless, in the day when I visit, I will visit their sin upon them."

35 And the LORD sent a plague upon the people, because they made the calf which Aaron made.

33 The LORD said to Moses, "Depart, go up hence, you and the people whom you have brought up out of the land of Egypt, to the land of which I swore to Abraham, Isaac, and Jacob, saying, 'To your descendants I will give it.' [2]And I will send an angel before you, and I will drive out the Cānaanites, the Ām'ọ·rītes, the Hīt'-tītes, the Pĕr'ĭz·zītes, the Hī'vītes, and the Jĕb'ū·sītes. [3]Go up to a land flowing with milk and honey; but I will not go up among you, lest I consume you in the way, for you are a stiff-necked people."

4 When the people heard these evil tidings, they mourned; and no man put on his ornaments. [5]For the LORD had said to Moses, "Say to the people of Israel, 'You are a stiff-necked people; if for a single moment I should go up among you, I would consume you. So now put off your ornaments from you, that I may know what to do with you.' " [6]Therefore the people of Israel stripped themselves of their ornaments, from Mount Hō'rĕb onward.

7 Now Moses used to take the tent and pitch it outside the camp, far off from the camp; and he called it the tent of meeting. And every one who sought the LORD would go out to the tent of meeting, which was outside the camp. [8]Whenever Moses went out to the tent, all the people rose up, and every man stood at his tent door, and looked after Moses, until he had gone into the tent. [9]When Moses entered the tent, the pillar of cloud would descend and stand at the door of the tent, and the LORD would speak with Moses. [10]And when all the people saw the pillar of cloud standing at the door of the tent, all the people would rise up and worship, every man at his tent door. [11]Thus the LORD used to speak to Moses face to face, as a man speaks to his friend. When Moses turned again into the camp, his servant Joshua the son of Nŭn, a young man, did not depart from the tent.

12 Moses said to the LORD, "See, thou sayest to me, 'Bring up this people'; but thou hast not let me know whom thou wilt send with me. Yet thou hast said, 'I know you by name, and you have also found favor in my sight.' [13]Now therefore, I pray thee, if I have found favor in thy sight, show me now thy ways, that I may know thee and find favor in thy sight. Consider too that this nation is thy people." [14]And he said, "My presence will go with you, and I will give you rest." [15]And he said to him, "If thy presence will not go with me, do not carry us up from here. [16]For how shall it be known that I have found favor in thy sight, I and thy people? Is it not in thy going with us, so that we are distinct, I and thy people, from all other people that are upon the face of the earth?"

17 And the LORD said to Moses, "This very thing that you have spoken I will do; for you have found favor in my sight, and I know you by name." [18]Moses said, "I pray thee, show me thy glory." [19]And he said, "I will make all my goodness pass before you, and will proclaim before you my name 'The LORD'; and I will be gracious to whom I will be gracious, and will show mercy on whom I will show mercy. [20]But," he said, "you cannot see my face;

[g]Gk Vg See Tg: Heb *ordain yourselves*
32.32, 33: Rev 3.5.   **33.3:** Acts 7.51.
33.11: Num 12.8; Deut 34.10.   **33.19:** Rom 9.15.

for man shall not see me and live." [21]And the LORD said, "Behold, there is a place by me where you shall stand upon the rock; [22]and while my glory passes by I will put you in a cleft of the rock, and I will cover you with my hand until I have passed by; [23]then I will take away my hand, and you shall see my back; but my face shall not be seen."

34 The LORD said to Moses, "Cut two tables of stone like the first; and I will write upon the tables the words that were on the first tables, which you broke. [2]Be ready in the morning, and come up in the morning to Mount Sinai, and present yourself there to me on the top of the mountain. [3]No man shall come up with you, and let no man be seen throughout all the mountain; let no flocks or herds feed before that mountain." [4]So Moses cut two tables of stone like the first; and he rose early in the morning and went up on Mount Sinai, as the LORD had commanded him, and took in his hand two tables of stone. [5]And the LORD descended in the cloud and stood with him there, and proclaimed the name of the LORD. [6]The LORD passed before him, and proclaimed, "The LORD, the LORD, a God merciful and gracious, slow to anger, and abounding in steadfast love and faithfulness, [7]keeping steadfast love for thousands, forgiving iniquity and transgression and sin, but who will by no means clear the guilty, visiting the iniquity of the fathers upon the children and the children's children, to the third and the fourth generation." [8]And Moses made haste to bow his head toward the earth, and worshiped. [9]And he said, "If now I have found favor in thy sight, O Lord, let the Lord, I pray thee, go in the midst of us, although it is a stiff-necked people; and pardon our iniquity and our sin, and take us for thy inheritance."

10 And he said, "Behold, I make a covenant. Before all your people I will do marvels, such as have not been wrought in all the earth or in any nation; and all the people among whom you are shall see the work of the LORD; for it is a terrible thing that I will do with you.

11 "Observe what I command you this day. Behold, I will drive out before you the Ăm'ọ·rītes, the Canaanites, the Hĭt'tītes, the Pĕr'ĭz·zītes, the Hī'vītes, and the Jĕb'ū·sītes. [12]Take heed to yourself, lest you make a covenant with the inhabitants of the land whither you go, lest it become a snare in the midst of you. [13]You shall tear down their altars, and break their pillars, and cut down their A·shē'rĭm [14](for you shall worship no other god, for the LORD, whose name is Jealous, is a jealous God), [15]lest you make a covenant with the inhabitants of the land, and when they play the harlot after their gods and sacrifice to their gods and one invites you, you eat of his sacrifice, [16]and you take of their daughters for your sons, and their daughters play the harlot after their gods and make your sons play the harlot after their gods.

17 "You shall make for yourself no molten gods.

18 "The feast of unleavened bread you shall keep. Seven days you shall eat unleavened bread, as I commanded you, at the time appointed in the month Ā'bĭb; for in the month of Abib you came out from Egypt. [19]All that opens the womb is mine, all your male[x] cattle, the firstlings of cow and sheep. [20]The firstling of an ass you shall redeem with a lamb, or if you will not redeem it you shall break its neck. All the firstborn of your sons you shall redeem. And none shall appear before me empty.

21 "Six days you shall work, but on the seventh day you shall rest; in plowing time and in harvest you shall rest. [22]And you shall observe the feast of weeks, the first fruits of wheat harvest, and the feast of ingathering at the year's end. [23]Three times in the year shall all your males appear before the LORD God, the God of Israel. [24]For I will cast out nations before you, and enlarge your borders; neither shall any man desire your land, when you go up to appear before the LORD your God three times in the year.

25 "You shall not offer the blood of my sacrifice with leaven; neither shall the sacrifice of the feast of the passover be left until the morning. [26]The

[x]Gk Theodotion Vg Tg: Heb uncertain
34.6: Num 14.18; Neh 9.17; Ps 86.15; 103.8; 145.8; Jon 4.2. **34.14:** Ex 20.5; 34.7; Deut 4.24; 5.9. **34.17:** Ex 20.4. **34.18:** Ex 12.15-20. **34.19-20:** Ex 13.2, 11-16. **34.21:** Ex 20.8-10; 23.12; 31.12-17; 35.2; Deut 5.12-15. **34.22-24:** Ex 23.14-17; Lev 23.1-44; Deut 16.1-17. **34.25:** Ex 23.18; Lev 2.11; Ex 12.10. **34.26:** Ex 23.19; Deut 14.21; 26.2-11.

first of the first fruits of your ground you shall bring to the house of the Lord your God. You shall not boil a kid in its mother's milk."

27 And the Lord said to Moses, "Write these words; in accordance with these words I have made a covenant with you and with Israel." 28 And he was there with the Lord forty days and forty nights; he neither ate bread nor drank water. And he wrote upon the tables the words of the covenant, the ten commandments.[1]

29 When Moses came down from Mount Sinai, with the two tables of the testimony in his hand as he came down from the mountain, Moses did not know that the skin of his face shone because he had been talking with God. 30 And when Aaron and all the people of Israel saw Moses, behold, the skin of his face shone, and they were afraid to come near him. 31 But Moses called to them; and Aaron and all the leaders of the congregation returned to him, and Moses talked with them. 32 And afterward all the people of Israel came near, and he gave them in commandment all that the Lord had spoken with him in Mount Sinai. 33 And when Moses had finished speaking with them, he put a veil on his face; 34 but whenever Moses went in before the Lord to speak with him, he took the veil off, until he came out; and when he came out, and told the people of Israel what he was commanded, 35 the people of Israel saw the face of Moses, that the skin of Moses' face shone; and Moses would put the veil upon his face again, until he went in to speak with him.

35 Moses assembled all the congregation of the people of Israel, and said to them, "These are the things which the Lord has commanded you to do. 2 Six days shall work be done, but on the seventh day you shall have a holy sabbath of solemn rest to the Lord; whoever does any work on it shall be put to death; 3 you shall kindle no fire in all your habitations on the sabbath day."

4 Moses said to all the congregation of the people of Israel, "This is the thing which the Lord has commanded. 5 Take from among you an offering to the Lord; whoever is of a generous heart, let him bring the Lord's offering: gold, silver, and bronze; 6 blue and purple and scarlet stuff and fine twined linen; goats' hair, 7 tanned rams' skins, and goatskins; acacia wood, 8 oil for the light, spices for the anointing oil and for the fragrant incense, 9 and onyx stones and stones for setting, for the ephod and for the breastpiece.

10 "And let every able man among you come and make all that the Lord has commanded: the tabernacle, 11 its tent and its covering, its hooks and its frames, its bars, its pillars, and its bases; 12 the ark with its poles, the mercy seat, and the veil of the screen; 13 the table with its poles and all its utensils, and the bread of the Presence; 14 the lampstand also for the light, with its utensils and its lamps, and the oil for the light; 15 and the altar of incense, with its poles, and the anointing oil and the fragrant incense, and the screen for the door, at the door of the tabernacle; 16 the altar of burnt offering, with its grating of bronze, its poles, and all its utensils, the laver and its base; 17 the hangings of the court, its pillars and its bases, and the screen for the gate of the court; 18 the pegs of the tabernacle and the pegs of the court, and their cords; 19 the finely wrought garments for ministering in the holy place, the holy garments for Aaron the priest, and the garments of his sons, for their service as priests."

20 Then all the congregation of the people of Israel departed from the presence of Moses. 21 And they came, every one whose heart stirred him, and every one whose spirit moved him, and brought the Lord's offering to be used for the tent of meeting, and for all its service, and for the holy garments. 22 So they came, both men and women; all who were of a willing heart brought brooches and earrings and signet rings and armlets, all sorts of gold objects, every man dedicating an offering of gold to the Lord. 23 And every man with whom was found blue or purple or scarlet stuff or fine linen or goats' hair or tanned rams' skins or goatskins, brought them. 24 Every one who could make an offering of silver or bronze brought it as the Lord's

[1] Heb *words*

34.29-35: 2 Cor 3.7-16.

35.2, 3: Ex 23.12; 31.12-17; 34.21; Deut 5.12-15.

35.4-9: Ex 25.1-9.

offering; and every man with whom was found acacia wood of any use in the work, brought it. ²⁵And all women who had ability spun with their hands, and brought what they had spun in blue and purple and scarlet stuff and fine twined linen; ²⁶ all the women whose hearts were moved with ability spun the goats' hair. ²⁷And the leaders brought onyx stones and stones to be set, for the ephod and for the breastpiece, ²⁸ and spices and oil for the light, and for the anointing oil, and for the fragrant incense. ²⁹All the men and women, the people of Israel, whose heart moved them to bring anything for the work which the LORD had commanded by Moses to be done, brought it as their freewill offering to the LORD.

30 And Moses said to the people of Israel, "See, the LORD has called by name Bĕz'a·lĕl the son of Ū'rī, son of Hŭr, of the tribe of Judah; ³¹ and he has filled him with the Spirit of God, with ability, with intelligence, with knowledge, and with all craftsmanship, ³² to devise artistic designs, to work in gold and silver and bronze, ³³ in cutting stones for setting, and in carving wood, for work in every skilled craft. ³⁴And he has inspired him to teach, both him and Ō·hō'lĭ·ăb the son of A·hĭs'a·mäch of the tribe of Dan. ³⁵ He has filled them with ability to do every sort of work done by a craftsman or by a designer or by an embroiderer in blue and purple and scarlet stuff and fine twined linen, or by a weaver—by any sort of workman or

36 skilled designer. ¹Bĕz'a·lĕl and Ō·hō'lĭ·ăb and every able man in whom the LORD has put ability and intelligence to know how to do any work in the construction of the sanctuary shall work in accordance with all that the LORD has commanded."

2 And Moses called Bĕz'a·lĕl and Ō·hō'lĭ·ăb and every able man in whose mind the LORD had put ability, every one whose heart stirred him up to come to do the work; ³ and they received from Moses all the freewill offering which the people of Israel had brought for doing the work on the sanctuary. They still kept bringing him freewill offerings every morning, ⁴ so that all the able men who were doing every sort of task on the sanctuary came, each from the task that he was doing, ⁵ and said to Moses, "The people bring much more

than enough for doing the work which the LORD has commanded us to do." ⁶So Moses gave command, and word was proclaimed throughout the camp, "Let neither man nor woman do anything more for the offering for the sanctuary." So the people were restrained from bringing; ⁷ for the stuff they had was sufficient to do all the work, and more.

8 And all the able men among the workmen made the tabernacle with ten curtains; they were made of fine twined linen and blue and purple and scarlet stuff, with cherubim skilfully worked. ⁹The length of each curtain was twenty-eight cubits, and the breadth of each curtain four cubits; all the curtains had the same measure. 10 And he coupled five curtains to one another, and the other five curtains he coupled to one another. ¹¹And he made loops of blue on the edge of the outmost curtain of the first set; likewise he made them on the edge of the outmost curtain of the second set; ¹² he made fifty loops on the one curtain, and he made fifty loops on the edge of the curtain that was in the second set; the loops were opposite one another. ¹³And he made fifty clasps of gold, and coupled the curtains one to the other with clasps; so the tabernacle was one whole.

14 He also made curtains of goats' hair for a tent over the tabernacle; he made eleven curtains. ¹⁵The length of each curtain was thirty cubits, and the breadth of each curtain four cubits; the eleven curtains had the same measure. ¹⁶He coupled five curtains by themselves, and six curtains by themselves. ¹⁷And he made fifty loops on the edge of the outmost curtain of the one set, and fifty loops on the edge of the other connecting curtain. ¹⁸And he made fifty clasps of bronze to couple the tent together that it might be one whole. ¹⁹And he made for the tent a covering of tanned rams' skins and goatskins.

20 Then he made the upright frames for the tabernacle of acacia wood. ²¹Ten cubits was the length of a frame, and a cubit and a half the breadth of each frame. ²²Each frame had two tenons, for fitting together; he did this for all the frames of the tabernacle.

35.30-36.1: Ex 31.1-6.
36.8-19: Ex 26.1-14. **36.20-34:** Ex 26.15-29.

²³The frames for the tabernacle he made thus: twenty frames for the south side; ²⁴and he made forty bases of silver under the twenty frames, two bases under one frame for its two tenons, and two bases under another frame for its two tenons. ²⁵And for the second side of the tabernacle, on the north side, he made twenty frames ²⁶and their forty bases of silver, two bases under one frame and two bases under another frame. ²⁷And for the rear of the tabernacle westward he made six frames. ²⁸And he made two frames for corners of the tabernacle in the rear. ²⁹And they were separate beneath, but joined at the top, at the first ring; he made two of them thus, for the two corners. ³⁰There were eight frames with their bases of silver: sixteen bases, under every frame two bases.

31 And he made bars of acacia wood, five for the frames of the one side of the tabernacle, ³²and five bars for the frames of the other side of the tabernacle, and five bars for the frames of the tabernacle at the rear westward. ³³And he made the middle bar to pass through from end to end halfway up the frames. ³⁴And he overlaid the frames with gold, and made their rings of gold for holders for the bars, and overlaid the bars with gold.

35 And he made the veil of blue and purple and scarlet stuff and fine twined linen; with cherubim skilfully worked he made it. ³⁶And for it he made four pillars of acacia, and overlaid them with gold; their hooks were of gold, and he cast for them four bases of silver. ³⁷He also made a screen for the door of the tent, of blue and purple and scarlet stuff and fine twined linen, embroidered with needlework; ³⁸and its five pillars with their hooks. He overlaid their capitals and their fillets were of gold, but their five bases were of bronze.

37 Bĕz'a·lĕl made the ark of acacia wood; two cubits and a half was its length, a cubit and a half its breadth, and a cubit and a half its height. ²And he overlaid it with pure gold within and without, and made a molding of gold around it. ³And he cast for it four rings of gold for its four corners, two rings on its one side and two rings on its other side. ⁴And he made poles of acacia wood, and over-

laid them with gold, ⁵and put the poles into the rings on the sides of the ark, to carry the ark. ⁶And he made a mercy seat of pure gold; two cubits and a half was its length, and a cubit and a half its breadth. ⁷And he made two cherubim of hammered gold; on the two ends of the mercy seat he made them, ⁸one cherub on the one end, and one cherub on the other end; of one piece with the mercy seat he made the cherubim on its two ends. ⁹The cherubim spread out their wings above, overshadowing the mercy seat with their wings, with their faces one to another; toward the mercy seat were the faces of the cherubim.

10 He also made the table of acacia wood; two cubits was its length, a cubit its breadth, and a cubit and a half its height; ¹¹and he overlaid it with pure gold, and made a molding of gold around it. ¹²And he made around it a frame a handbreadth wide, and made a molding of gold around the frame. ¹³He cast for it four rings of gold, and fastened the rings to the four corners at its four legs. ¹⁴Close to the frame were the rings, as holders for the poles to carry the table. ¹⁵He made the poles of acacia wood to carry the table, and overlaid them with gold. ¹⁶And he made the vessels of pure gold which were to be upon the table, its plates and dishes for incense, and its bowls and flagons with which to pour libations.

17 He also made the lampstand of pure gold. The base and the shaft of the lampstand were made of hammered work; its cups, its capitals, and its flowers were of one piece with it. ¹⁸And there were six branches going out of its sides, three branches of the lampstand out of one side of it and three branches of the lampstand out of the other side of it; ¹⁹three cups made like almonds, each with capital and flower, on one branch, and three cups made like almonds, each with capital and flower, on the other branch — so for the six branches going out of the lampstand. ²⁰And on the lampstand itself were four cups made like almonds, with their capitals and flowers, ²¹and a capital of one piece with it under each pair of the six branches going out of it. ²²Their capitals and

36.35-38: Ex 26.31-37.   37.1-9: Ex 25.10-22.
37.10-16: Ex 25.23-29.   37.17-24: Ex 25.31-39.

their branches were of one piece with it; the whole of it was one piece of hammered work of pure gold. ²³And he made its seven lamps and its snuffers and its trays of pure gold. ²⁴He made it and all its utensils of a talent of pure gold.

25 He made the altar of incense of acacia wood; its length was a cubit, and its breadth was a cubit; it was square, and two cubits was its height; its horns were of one piece with it. ²⁶He overlaid it with pure gold, its top, and its sides round about, and its horns; and he made a molding of gold round about it, ²⁷and made two rings of gold on it under its molding, on two opposite sides of it, as holders for the poles with which to carry it. ²⁸And he made the poles of acacia wood, and overlaid them with gold.

29 He made the holy anointing oil also, and the pure fragrant incense, blended as by the perfumer.

38 He made the altar of burnt offering also of acacia wood; five cubits was its length, and five cubits its breadth; it was square, and three cubits was its height. ²He made horns for it on its four corners; its horns were of one piece with it, and he overlaid it with bronze. ³And he made all the utensils of the altar, the pots, the shovels, the basins, the forks, and the firepans; all its utensils he made of bronze. ⁴And he made for the altar a grating, a network of bronze, under its ledge, extending halfway down. ⁵He cast four rings on the four corners of the bronze grating as holders for the poles; ⁶he made the poles of acacia wood, and overlaid them with bronze. ⁷And he put the poles through the rings on the sides of the altar, to carry it with them; he made it hollow, with boards.

8 And he made the laver of bronze and its base of bronze, from the mirrors of the ministering women who ministered at the door of the tent of meeting.

9 And he made the court; for the south side the hangings of the court were of fine twined linen, a hundred cubits; ¹⁰their pillars were twenty and their bases twenty, of bronze, but the hooks of the pillars and their fillets were of silver. ¹¹And for the north side a hundred cubits, their pillars twenty, their bases twenty, of bronze, but the

hooks of the pillars and their fillets were of silver. ¹²And for the west side were hangings of fifty cubits, their pillars ten, and their sockets ten; the hooks of the pillars and their fillets were of silver. ¹³And for the front to the east, fifty cubits. ¹⁴The hangings for one side of the gate were fifteen cubits, with three pillars and three bases. ¹⁵And so for the other side; on this hand and that hand by the gate of the court were hangings of fifteen cubits, with three pillars and three bases. ¹⁶All the hangings round about the court were of fine twined linen. ¹⁷And the bases for the pillars were of bronze, but the hooks of the pillars and their fillets were of silver; the overlaying of their capitals was also of silver, and all the pillars of the court were filleted with silver. ¹⁸And the screen for the gate of the court was embroidered with needlework in blue and purple and scarlet stuff and fine twined linen; it was twenty cubits long and five cubits high in its breadth, corresponding to the hangings of the court. ¹⁹And their pillars were four; their four bases were of bronze, their hooks of silver, and the overlaying of their capitals and their fillets of silver. ²⁰And all the pegs for the tabernacle and for the court round about were of bronze.

21 This is the sum of the things for the tabernacle, the tabernacle of the testimony, as they were counted at the commandment of Moses, for the work of the Le′vites under the direction of Ith′a·mär the son of Aaron the priest. ²²Bĕz′a·lĕl the son of Ū′rī, son of Hūr, of the tribe of Judah, made all that the LORD commanded Moses; ²³and with him was Ō·hō′lī·ăb the son of A·hĭs′-a·măch, of the tribe of Dan, a craftsman and designer and embroiderer in blue and purple and scarlet stuff and fine twined linen.

24 All the gold that was used for the work, in all the construction of the sanctuary, the gold from the offering, was twenty-nine talents and seven hundred and thirty shekels, by the shekel of the sanctuary. ²⁵And the silver from those of the congregation who were numbered was a hundred talents and a thousand seven hundred and seventy-five shekels, by the shekel

37.25-29: Ex 30.1-5. 38.1-7: Ex 27.1-8.
38.8: Ex 30.18. 38.9-20: Ex 27.9-19.
38.25, 26: 30.11-16.

of the sanctuary: ²⁶a beka a head (that is, half a shekel, by the the shekel of the sanctuary), for every one who was numbered in the census, from twenty years old and upward, for six hundred and three thousand, five hundred and fifty men. ²⁷The hundred talents of silver were for casting the bases of the sanctuary, and the bases of the veil; a hundred bases for the hundred talents, a talent for a base. ²⁸And of the thousand seven hundred and seventy-five shekels he made hooks for the pillars, and overlaid their capitals and made fillets for them. ²⁹And the bronze that was contributed was seventy talents, and two thousand and four hundred shekels; ³⁰with it he made the bases for the door of the tent of meeting, the bronze altar and the bronze grating for it and all the utensils of the altar, ³¹the bases round about the court, and the bases of the gate of the court, all the pegs of the tabernacle, and all the pegs round about the court.

39 And of the blue and purple and scarlet stuff they made finely wrought garments, for ministering in the holy place; they made the holy garments for Aaron; as the Lord had commanded Moses.

2 And he made the ephod of gold, blue and purple and scarlet stuff, and fine twined linen. ³And gold leaf was hammered out and cut into threads to work into the blue and purple and the scarlet stuff, and into the fine twined linen, in skilled design. ⁴They made for the ephod shoulder-pieces, joined to it at its two edges. ⁵And the skilfully woven band upon it, to gird it on, was of the same materials and workmanship, of gold, blue and purple and scarlet stuff, and fine twined linen; as the Lord had commanded Moses.

6 The onyx stones were prepared, enclosed in settings of gold filigree and engraved like the engravings of a signet, according to the names of the sons of Israel. ⁷And he set them on the shoulder-pieces of the ephod, to be stones of remembrance for the sons of Israel; as the Lord had commanded Moses.

8 He made the breastpiece, in skilled work, like the work of the ephod, of gold, blue and purple and scarlet stuff, and fine twined linen. ⁹It was square; the breastpiece was made double, a span its length and a span its breadth

when doubled. ¹⁰And they set in it four rows of stones. A row of sardius, topaz, and carbuncle was the first row; ¹¹and the second row, an emerald, a sapphire, and a diamond; ¹²and the third row, a jacinth, an agate, and an amethyst; ¹³and the fourth row, a beryl, an onyx, and a jasper; they were enclosed in settings of gold filigree. ¹⁴There were twelve stones with their names according to the names of the sons of Israel; they were like signets, each engraved with its name, for the twelve tribes. ¹⁵And they made on the breastpiece twisted chains like cords, of pure gold; ¹⁶and they made two settings of gold filigree and two gold rings, and put the two rings on the two edges of the breastpiece; ¹⁷and they put the two cords of gold in the two rings at the edges of the breastpiece. ¹⁸Two ends of the two cords they had attached to the two settings of filigree; thus they attached it in front to the shoulder-pieces of the ephod. ¹⁹Then they made two rings of gold, and put them at the two ends of the breastpiece, on its inside edge next to the ephod. ²⁰And they made two rings of gold, and attached them in front to the lower part of the two shoulder-pieces of the ephod, at its joining above the skilfully woven band of the ephod. ²¹And they bound the breastpiece by its rings to the rings of the ephod with a lace of blue, so that it should lie upon the skilfully woven band of the ephod, and that the breastpiece should not come loose from the ephod; as the Lord had commanded Moses.

22 He also made the robe of the ephod woven all of blue; ²³and the opening of the robe in it was like the opening in a garment, with a binding around the opening, that it might not be torn. ²⁴On the skirts of the robe they made pomegranates of blue and purple and scarlet stuff and fine twined linen. ²⁵They also made bells of pure gold, and put the bells between the pomegranates upon the skirts of the robe round about, between the pomegranates; ²⁶a bell and a pomegranate, a bell and a pomegranate round about upon the skirts of the robe for ministering; as the Lord had commanded Moses.

27 They also made the coats, woven of fine linen, for Aaron and his sons,

39.2-7: 28.6-12.   39.8-21: Ex 28.15-28.
39.22-26: Ex 28.31-34.   39.27-29: Ex 28.39, 40, 42.

²⁸ and the turban of fine linen, and the caps of fine linen, and the linen breeches of fine twined linen, ²⁹ and the girdle of fine twined linen and of blue and purple and scarlet stuff, embroidered with needlework; as the LORD had commanded Moses.

30 And they made the plate of the holy crown of pure gold, and wrote upon it an inscription, like the engraving of a signet, "Holy to the LORD." ³¹ And they tied to it a lace of blue, to fasten it on the turban above; as the LORD had commanded Moses.

32 Thus all the work of the tabernacle of the tent of meeting was finished; and the people of Israel had done according to all that the LORD had commanded Moses; so had they done. ³³ And they brought the tabernacle to Moses, the tent and all its utensils, its hooks, its frames, its bars, its pillars, and its bases; ³⁴ the covering of tanned rams' skins and goatskins, and the veil of the screen; ³⁵ the ark of the testimony with its poles and the mercy seat; ³⁶ the table with all its utensils, and the bread of the Presence; ³⁷ the lampstand of pure gold and its lamps with the lamps set and all its utensils, and the oil for the light; ³⁸ the golden altar, the anointing oil and the fragrant incense, and the screen for the door of the tent; ³⁹ the bronze altar, and its grating of bronze, its poles, and all its utensils; the laver and its base; ⁴⁰ the hangings of the court, its pillars, and its bases, and the screen for the gate of the court, its cords, and its pegs; and all the utensils for the service of the tabernacle, for the tent of meeting; ⁴¹ the finely worked garments for ministering in the holy place, the holy garments for Aaron the priest, and the garments of his sons to serve as priests. ⁴² According to all that the LORD had commanded Moses, so the people of Israel had done all the work. ⁴³ And Moses saw all the work, and behold, they had done it; as the LORD had commanded, so had they done it. And Moses blessed them.

40 The LORD said to Moses, ² "On the first day of the first month you shall erect the tabernacle of the tent of meeting. ³ And you shall put in it the ark of the testimony, and you shall screen the ark with the veil. ⁴ And you shall bring in the table, and set its arrangements in order; and you shall

bring in the lampstand, and set up its lamps. ⁵ And you shall put the golden altar for incense before the ark of the testimony, and set up the screen for the door of the tabernacle. ⁶ You shall set the altar of burnt offering before the door of the tabernacle of the tent of meeting, ⁷ and place the laver between the tent of meeting and the altar, and put water in it. ⁸ And you shall set up the court round about, and hang up the screen for the gate of the court. ⁹ Then you shall take the anointing oil, and anoint the tabernacle and all that is in it, and consecrate it and all its furniture; and it shall become holy. ¹⁰ You shall also anoint the altar of burnt offering and all its utensils, and consecrate the altar; and the altar shall be most holy. ¹¹ You shall also anoint the laver and its base, and consecrate it. ¹² Then you shall bring Aaron and his sons to the door of the tent of meeting, and shall wash them with water, ¹³ and put upon Aaron the holy garments, and you shall anoint him and consecrate him, that he may serve me as priest. ¹⁴ You shall bring his sons also and put coats on them, ¹⁵ and anoint them, as you anointed their father, that they may serve me as priests: and their anointing shall admit them to a perpetual priesthood throughout their generations."

16 Thus did Moses; according to all that the LORD commanded him, so he did. ¹⁷ And in the first month in the second year, on the first day of the month, the tabernacle was erected. ¹⁸ Moses erected the tabernacle; he laid its bases, and set up its frames, and put in its poles, and raised up its pillars; ¹⁹ and he spread the tent over the tabernacle, and put the covering of the tent over it, as the LORD had commanded Moses. ²⁰ And he took the testimony and put it into the ark, and put the poles on the ark, and set the mercy seat above on the ark; ²¹ and he brought the ark into the tabernacle, and set up the veil of the screen, and screened the ark of the testimony; as the LORD had commanded Moses. ²² And he put the table in the tent of meeting, on the north side of the tabernacle, outside the veil, ²³ and set the bread in order on it before the LORD;

39.30-31: Ex 28.36, 37.
39.36: Ex 25.30; 40.23; Lev 24.5-9.
40.23: Ex 25.30; 39.36; Lev 24.5-9.

as the LORD had commanded Moses. ²⁴And he put the lampstand in the tent of meeting, opposite the table on the south side of the tabernacle, ²⁵ and set up the lamps before the LORD; as the LORD had commanded Moses. ²⁶And he put the golden altar in the tent of meeting before the veil, ²⁷ and burnt fragrant incense upon it; as the LORD had commanded Moses. ²⁸And he put in place the screen for the door of the tabernacle. ²⁹And he set the altar of burnt offering at the door of the tabernacle of the tent of meeting, and offered upon it the burnt offering and the cereal offering; as the LORD had commanded Moses. ³⁰And he set the laver between the tent of meeting and the altar, and put water in it for washing, ³¹ with which Moses and Aaron and his sons washed their hands and their feet; ³² when they went into the tent of meeting, and when they approached the altar, they washed; as the LORD commanded Moses. ³³ And he erected the court round the tabernacle and the altar, and set up the screen of the gate of the court. So Moses finished the work.

34 Then the cloud covered the tent of meeting, and the glory of the LORD filled the tabernacle. ³⁵ And Moses was not able to enter the tent of meeting, because the cloud abode upon it, and the glory of the LORD filled the tabernacle. ³⁶ Throughout all their journeys, whenever the cloud was taken up from over the tabernacle, the people of Israel would go onward; ³⁷ but if the cloud was not taken up, then they did not go onward till the day that it was taken up. ³⁸ For throughout all their journeys the cloud of the LORD was upon the tabernacle by day, and fire was in it by night, in the sight of all the house of Israel.

The Third Book of Moses
Commonly Called

Leviticus

1 The LORD called Moses, and spoke to him from the tent of meeting, saying, ² "Speak to the people of Israel, and say to them, When any man of you brings an offering to the LORD, you shall bring your offering of cattle from the herd or from the flock.

3 "If his offering is a burnt offering from the herd, he shall offer a male without blemish; he shall offer it at the door of the tent of meeting, that he may be accepted before the LORD; ⁴ he shall lay his hand upon the head of the burnt offering, and it shall be accepted for him to make atonement for him. ⁵ Then he shall kill the bull before the LORD; and Aaron's sons the priests shall present the blood, and throw the blood round about against the altar that is at the door of the tent of meeting. ⁶ And he shall flay the burnt offering and cut it into pieces; ⁷ and the sons of Aaron the priest shall put fire on the altar, and lay wood in order upon the fire; ⁸ and Aaron's sons the priests shall lay the pieces, the head, and the fat, in order upon the wood that is on the fire upon the altar; ⁹ but its entrails and its legs he shall wash with water. And the priest shall burn the whole on the altar, as a burnt offering, an offering by fire, a pleasing odor to the LORD.

10 "If his gift for a burnt offering is from the flock, from the sheep or goats, he shall offer a male without blemish; ¹¹ and he shall kill it on the north side of the altar before the LORD, and Aaron's sons the priests shall throw its blood against the altar round about. ¹² And he shall cut it into pieces, with its head and its fat, and the priest shall lay them in order upon the wood that is on the fire upon the altar; ¹³ but the entrails and the legs he shall wash with water. And the priest shall offer

40.30-32: Ex 30.18-21. **40.34:** Rev 15.8.

the whole, and burn it on the altar; it is a burnt offering, an offering by fire, a pleasing odor to the LORD.

14 "If his offering to the LORD is a burnt offering of birds, then he shall bring his offering of turtledoves or of young pigeons. ¹⁵ And the priest shall bring it to the altar and wring off its head, and burn it on the altar; and its blood shall be drained out on the side of the altar; ¹⁶ and he shall take away its crop with the feathers, and cast it beside the altar on the east side, in the place for ashes; ¹⁷ he shall tear it by its wings, but shall not divide it asunder. And the priest shall burn it on the altar, upon the wood that is on the fire; it is a burnt offering, an offering by fire, a pleasing odor to the LORD.

2 "When any one brings a cereal offering as an offering to the LORD, his offering shall be of fine flour; he shall pour oil upon it, and put frankincense on it, ² and bring it to Aaron's sons the priests. And he shall take from it a handful of the fine flour and oil, with all of its frankincense; and the priest shall burn this as its memorial portion upon the altar, an offering by fire, a pleasing odor to the LORD. ³ And what is left of the cereal offering shall be for Aaron and his sons; it is a most holy part of the offerings by fire to the LORD.

4 "When you bring a cereal offering baked in the oven as an offering, it shall be unleavened cakes of fine flour mixed with oil, or unleavened wafers spread with oil. ⁵ And if your offering is a cereal offering baked on a griddle, it shall be of fine flour unleavened, mixed with oil; ⁶ you shall break it in pieces, and pour oil on it; it is a cereal offering. ⁷ And if your offering is a cereal offering cooked in a pan, it shall be made of fine flour with oil. ⁸ And you shall bring the cereal offering that is made of these things to the LORD; and when it is presented to the priest, he shall bring it to the altar. ⁹ And the priest shall take from the cereal offering its memorial portion and burn this on the altar, an offering by fire, a pleasing odor to the LORD. ¹⁰ And what is left of the cereal offering shall be for Aaron and his sons; it is a most holy part of the offerings by fire to the LORD.

11 "No cereal offering which you bring to the LORD shall be made with leaven; for you shall burn no leaven nor any honey as an offering by fire to the LORD. ¹² As an offering of first fruits you may bring them to the LORD, but they shall not be offered on the altar for a pleasing odor. ¹³ You shall season all your cereal offerings with salt; you shall not let the salt of the covenant with your God be lacking from your cereal offering; with all your offerings you shall offer salt.

14 "If you offer a cereal offering of first fruits to the LORD, you shall offer for the cereal offering of your first fruits crushed new grain from fresh ears, parched with fire. ¹⁵ And you shall put oil upon it, and lay frankincense on it; it is a cereal offering. ¹⁶ And the priest shall burn as its memorial portion part of the crushed grain and of the oil with all of its frankincense; it is an offering by fire to the LORD.

3 "If a man's offering is a sacrifice of peace offering, if he offers an animal from the herd, male or female, he shall offer it without blemish before the LORD. ² And he shall lay his hand upon the head of his offering and kill it at the door of the tent of meeting; and Aaron's sons the priests shall throw the blood against the altar round about. ³ And from the sacrifice of the peace offering, as an offering by fire to the LORD, he shall offer the fat covering the entrails and all the fat that is on the entrails, ⁴ and the two kidneys with the fat that is on them at the loins, and the appendage of the liver which he shall take away with the kidneys. ⁵ Then Aaron's sons shall burn it on the altar upon the burnt offering, which is upon the wood on the fire; it is an offering by fire, a pleasing odor to the LORD.

6 "If his offering for a sacrifice of peace offering to the LORD is an animal from the flock, male or female, he shall offer it without blemish. ⁷ If he offers a lamb for his offering, then he shall offer it before the LORD, ⁸ laying his hand upon the head of his offering and killing it before the tent of meeting; and Aaron's sons shall throw its blood against the altar round about. ⁹ Then from the sacrifice of the peace offering he shall offer its fat, the fat tail entire, taking it away close by the backbone, and the fat that covers the entrails,

3.1-17: Lev 7.11-18.

and all the fat that is on the entrails, [10] and the two kidneys with the fat that is on them at the loins, and the appendage of the liver which he shall take away with the kidneys. [11] And the priest shall burn it on the altar as food offered by fire to the LORD.

12 "If his offering is a goat, then he shall offer it before the LORD, [13] and lay his hand upon its head, and kill it before the tent of meeting; and the sons of Aaron shall throw its blood against the altar round about. [14] Then he shall offer from it, as his offering for an offering by fire to the LORD, the fat covering the entrails, and all the fat that is on the entrails, [15] and the two kidneys with the fat that is on them at the loins, and the appendage of the liver which he shall take away with the kidneys. [16] And the priest shall burn them on the altar as food offered by fire for a pleasing odor. All fat is the LORD's. [17] It shall be a perpetual statute throughout your generations, in all your dwelling places, that you eat neither fat nor blood."

4 And the LORD said to Moses, [2] "Say to the people of Israel, If any one sins unwittingly in any of the things which the LORD has commanded not to be done, and does any one of them, [3] if it is the anointed priest who sins, thus bringing guilt on the people, then let him offer for the sin which he has committed a young bull without blemish to the LORD for a sin offering. [4] He shall bring the bull to the door of the tent of meeting before the LORD, and lay his hand on the head of the bull, and kill the bull before the LORD. [5] And the anointed priest shall take some of the blood of the bull and bring it to the tent of meeting; [6] and the priest shall dip his finger in the blood and sprinkle part of the blood seven times before the LORD in front of the veil of the sanctuary. [7] And the priest shall put some of the blood on the horns of the altar of fragrant incense before the LORD which is in the tent of meeting, and the rest of the blood of the bull he shall pour out at the base of the altar of burnt offering which is at the door of the tent of meeting. [8] And all the fat of the bull of the sin offering he shall take from it, the fat that covers the entrails and all the fat that is on the entrails, [9] and the two kidneys with the fat that is on them at the loins,

and the appendage of the liver which he shall take away with the kidneys [10] (just as these are taken from the ox of the sacrifice of the peace offerings), and the priest shall burn them upon the altar of burnt offering. [11] But the skin of the bull and all its flesh, with its head, its legs, its entrails, and its dung, [12] the whole bull he shall carry forth outside the camp to a clean place, where the ashes are poured out, and shall burn it on a fire of wood; where the ashes are poured out it shall be burned.

13 "If the whole congregation of Israel commits a sin unwittingly and the thing is hidden from the eyes of the assembly, and they do any one of the things which the LORD has commanded not to be done and are guilty; [14] when the sin which they have committed becomes known, the assembly shall offer a young bull for a sin offering and bring it before the tent of meeting; [15] and the elders of the congregation shall lay their hands upon the head of the bull before the LORD, and the bull shall be killed before the LORD. [16] Then the anointed priest shall bring some of the blood of the bull to the tent of meeting, [17] and the priest shall dip his finger in the blood and sprinkle it seven times before the LORD in front of the veil. [18] And he shall put some of the blood on the horns of the altar which is in the tent of meeting before the LORD; and the rest of the blood he shall pour out at the base of the altar of burnt offering which is at the door of the tent of meeting. [19] And all its fat he shall take from it and burn upon the altar. [20] Thus shall he do with the bull; as he did with the bull of the sin offering, so shall he do with this; and the priest shall make atonement for them, and they shall be forgiven. [21] And he shall carry forth the bull outside the camp, and burn it as he burned the first bull; it is the sin offering for the assembly.

22 "When a ruler sins, doing unwittingly any one of all the things which the LORD his God has commanded not to be done, and is guilty, [23] if the sin which he has committed is made known to him, he shall bring as his offering a goat, a male without blemish, [24] and shall lay his hand upon the head of the goat, and kill it in the

place where they kill the burnt offering before the LORD; it is a sin offering. 25 Then the priest shall take some of the blood of the sin offering with his finger and put it on the horns of the altar of burnt offering, and pour out the rest of its blood at the base of the altar of burnt offering. 26And all its fat he shall burn on the altar, like the fat of the sacrifice of peace offerings; so the priest shall make atonement for him for his sin, and he shall be forgiven.

27 "If any one of the common people sins unwittingly in doing any one of the things which the LORD has commanded not to be done, and is guilty, 28 when the sin which he has committed is made known to him he shall bring for his offering a goat, a female without blemish, for his sin which he has committed. 29And he shall lay his hand on the head of the sin offering, and kill the sin offering in the place of burnt offering. 30And the priest shall take some of its blood with his finger and put it on the horns of the altar of burnt offering, and pour out the rest of its blood at the base of the altar. 31And all its fat he shall remove, as the fat is removed from the peace offerings, and the priest shall burn it upon the altar for a pleasing odor to the LORD; and the priest shall make atonement for him, and he shall be forgiven.

32 "If he brings a lamb as his offering for a sin offering, he shall bring a female without blemish, 33 and lay his hand upon the head of the sin offering, and kill it for a sin offering in the place where they kill the burnt offering. 34 Then the priest shall take some of the blood of the sin offering with his finger and put it on the horns of the altar of burnt offering, and pour out the rest of its blood at the base of the altar. 35And all its fat he shall remove as the fat of the lamb is removed from the sacrifice of peace offerings, and the priest shall burn it on the altar, upon the offerings by fire to the LORD; and the priest shall make atonement for him for the sin which he has committed, and he shall be forgiven.

5 "If any one sins in that he hears a public adjuration to testify and though he is a witness, whether he has seen or come to know the matter, yet does not speak, he shall bear his iniq-

uity. 2 Or if any one touches an unclean thing, whether the carcass of an unclean beast or a carcass of unclean cattle or a carcass of unclean swarming things, and it is hidden from him, and he has become unclean, he shall be guilty. 3 Or if he touches human uncleanness, of whatever sort the uncleanness may be with which one becomes unclean, and it is hidden from him, when he comes to know it he shall be guilty. 4 Or if any one utters with his lips a rash oath to do evil or to do good, any sort of rash oath that men swear, and it is hidden from him, when he comes to know it he shall in any of these be guilty. 5 When a man is guilty in any of these, he shall confess the sin he has committed, 6 and he shall bring his guilt offering to the LORD for the sin which he has committed, a female from the flock, a lamb or a goat, for a sin offering; and the priest shall make atonement for him for his sin.

7 "But if he cannot afford a lamb, then he shall bring, as his guilt offering to the LORD for the sin which he has committed, two turtledoves or two young pigeons, one for a sin offering and the other for a burnt offering. 8He shall bring them to the priest, who shall offer first the one for the sin offering; he shall wring its head from its neck, but shall not sever it, 9 and he shall sprinkle some of the blood of the sin offering on the side of the altar, while the rest of the blood shall be drained out at the base of the altar; it is a sin offering. 10 Then he shall offer the second for a burnt offering according to the ordinance; and the priest shall make atonement for him for the sin which he has committed, and he shall be forgiven.

11 "But if he cannot afford two turtledoves or two young pigeons, then he shall bring, as his offering for the sin which he has committed, a tenth of an ephah of fine flour for a sin offering; he shall put no oil upon it, and shall put no frankincense on it, for it is a sin offering. 12And he shall bring it to the priest, and the priest shall take a handful of it as its memorial portion and burn this on the altar, upon the offerings by fire to the LORD; it is a sin offering. 13 Thus the priest shall make atonement for him for the sin which he has committed

in any one of these things, and he shall be forgiven. And the remainder shall be for the priest, as in the cereal offering."

14 The LORD said to Moses, ¹⁵"If any one commits a breach of faith and sins unwittingly in any of the holy things of the LORD, he shall bring, as his guilt offering to the LORD, a ram without blemish out of the flock, valued by you in shekels of silver, according to the shekel of the sanctuary; it is a guilt offering. ¹⁶He shall also make restitution for what he has done amiss in the holy thing, and shall add a fifth to it and give it to the priest; and the priest shall make atonement for him with the ram of the guilt offering, and he shall be forgiven.

17 "If any one sins, doing any of the things which the LORD has commanded not to be done, though he does not know it, yet he is guilty and shall bear his iniquity. ¹⁸He shall bring to the priest a ram without blemish out of the flock, valued by you at the price for a guilt offering, and the priest shall make atonement for him for the error which he committed unwittingly, and he shall be forgiven. ¹⁹It is a guilt offering; he is guilty before the LORD."

6 ᵃ The LORD said to Moses, ²"If any one sins and commits a breach of faith against the LORD by deceiving his neighbor in a matter of deposit or security, or through robbery, or if he has oppressed his neighbor ³or has found what was lost and lied about it, swearing falsely—in any of all the things which men do and sin therein, ⁴when one has sinned and become guilty, he shall restore what he took by robbery, or what he got by oppression, or the deposit which was committed to him, or the lost thing which he found, ⁵or anything about which he has sworn falsely; he shall restore it in full, and shall add a fifth to it, and give it to him to whom it belongs, on the day of his guilt offering. ⁶And he shall bring to the priest his guilt offering to the LORD, a ram without blemish out of the flock, valued by you at the price for a guilt offering; ⁷and the priest shall make atonement for him before the LORD, and he shall be forgiven for any of the things which one may do and thereby become guilty."

8ᵇ The LORD said to Moses, ⁹"Command Aaron and his sons, saying,

This is the law of the burnt offering. The burnt offering shall be on the hearth upon the altar all night until the morning, and the fire of the altar shall be kept burning on it. ¹⁰And the priest shall put on his linen garment, and put his linen breeches upon his body, and he shall take up the ashes to which the fire has consumed the burnt offering on the altar, and put them beside the altar. ¹¹Then he shall put off his garments, and put on other garments, and carry forth the ashes outside the camp to a clean place. ¹²The fire on the altar shall be kept burning on it, it shall not go out; the priest shall burn wood on it every morning, and he shall lay the burnt offering in order upon it, and shall burn on it the fat of the peace offerings. ¹³Fire shall be kept burning upon the altar continually; it shall not go out.

14 "And this is the law of the cereal offering. The sons of Aaron shall offer it before the LORD, in front of the altar. ¹⁵And one shall take from it a handful of the fine flour of the cereal offering with its oil and all the frankincense which is on the cereal offering, and burn this as its memorial portion on the altar, a pleasing odor to the LORD. ¹⁶And the rest of it Aaron and his sons shall eat; it shall be eaten unleavened in a holy place; in the court of the tent of meeting they shall eat it. ¹⁷It shall not be baked with leaven. I have given it as their portion of my offerings by fire; it is a thing most holy, like the sin offering and the guilt offering. ¹⁸Every male among the children of Aaron may eat of it, as decreed for ever throughout your generations, from the LORD's offerings by fire; whoever touches them shall become holy."

19 The LORD said to Moses, ²⁰"This is the offering which Aaron and his sons shall offer to the LORD on the day when he is anointed: a tenth of an ephah of fine flour as a regular cereal offering, half of it in the morning and half in the evening. ²¹It shall be made with oil on a griddle; you shall bring it well mixed, in bakedᶜ pieces like a cereal offering, and offer it for a pleasing odor to the LORD. ²²The priest from among Aaron's sons, who is anointed to succeed him, shall offer

ᵃCh 5.20 in Heb　ᵇCh 6.1 in Heb
ᶜMeaning of Heb is uncertain
6.1-7: Ex 22.7-15; Num 5.5-8.

it to the LORD as decreed for ever; the whole of it shall be burned. ²³ Every cereal offering of a priest shall be wholly burned; it shall not be eaten."

24 The LORD said to Moses, ²⁵ "Say to Aaron and his sons, This is the law of the sin offering. In the place where the burnt offering is killed shall the sin offering be killed before the LORD; it is most holy. ²⁶ The priest who offers it for sin shall eat it; in a holy place it shall be eaten, in the court of the tent of meeting. ²⁷ Whatever^d touches its flesh shall be holy; and when any of its blood is sprinkled on a garment, you shall wash that on which it was sprinkled in a holy place. ²⁸ And the earthen vessel in which it is boiled shall be broken; but if it is boiled in a bronze vessel, that shall be scoured, and rinsed in water. ²⁹ Every male among the priests may eat of it; it is most holy. ³⁰ But no sin offering shall be eaten from which any blood is brought into the tent of meeting to make atonement in the holy place; it shall be burned with fire.

7 "This is the law of the guilt offering. It is most holy; ² in the place where they kill the burnt offering they shall kill the guilt offering, and its blood shall be thrown on the altar round about. ³ And all its fat shall be offered, the fat tail, the fat that covers the entrails, ⁴ the two kidneys with the fat that is on them at the loins, and the appendage of the liver which he shall take away with the kidneys; ⁵ the priest shall burn them on the altar as an offering by fire to the LORD; it is a guilt offering. ⁶ Every male among the priests may eat of it; it shall be eaten in a holy place; it is most holy. ⁷ The guilt offering is like the sin offering, there is one law for them; the priest who makes atonement with it shall have it. ⁸ And the priest who offers any man's burnt offering shall have for himself the skin of the burnt offering which he has offered. ⁹ And every cereal offering baked in the oven and all that is prepared on a pan or a griddle shall belong to the priest who offers it. ¹⁰ And every cereal offering, mixed with oil or dry, shall be for all the sons of Aaron, one as well as another.

11 "And this is the law of the sacrifice of peace offerings which one may offer to the LORD. ¹² If he offers it for a thanksgiving, then he shall offer with the thank offering unleavened cakes mixed with oil, unleavened wafers spread with oil, and cakes of fine flour well mixed with oil. ¹³ With the sacrifice of his peace offerings for thanksgiving he shall bring his offering with cakes of leavened bread. ¹⁴ And of such he shall offer one cake from each offering, as an offering to the LORD; it shall belong to the priest who throws the blood of the peace offerings. ¹⁵ And the flesh of the sacrifice of his peace offerings for thanksgiving shall be eaten on the day of his offering; he shall not leave any of it until the morning. ¹⁶ But if the sacrifice of his offering is a votive offering or a freewill offering, it shall be eaten on the day that he offers his sacrifice, and on the morrow what remains of it shall be eaten, ¹⁷ but what remains of the flesh of the sacrifice on the third day shall be burned with fire. ¹⁸ If any of the flesh of the sacrifice of his peace offering is eaten on the third day, he who offers it shall not be accepted, neither shall it be credited to him; it shall be an abomination, and he who eats of it shall bear his iniquity.

19 "Flesh that touches any unclean thing shall not be eaten; it shall be burned with fire. All who are clean may eat flesh, ²⁰ but the person who eats of the flesh of the sacrifice of the LORD's peace offerings while an uncleanness is on him, that person shall be cut off from his people. ²¹ And if any one touches an unclean thing, whether the uncleanness of man or an unclean beast or any unclean abomination, and then eats of the flesh of the sacrifice of the LORD's peace offerings, that person shall be cut off from his people."

22 The LORD said to Moses, ²³ "Say to the people of Israel, You shall eat no fat, of ox, or sheep, or goat. ²⁴ The fat of an animal that dies of itself, and the fat of one that is torn by beasts, may be put to any other use, but on no account shall you eat it. ²⁵ For every person who eats of the fat of an animal of which an offering by fire is made to the LORD shall be cut off from his people. ²⁶ Moreover you shall eat no blood whatever, whether of fowl or of animal, in any of your dwellings. ²⁷ Whoever eats any blood, that person shall be cut off from his people."

^d Or *Whoever*

28 The Lord said to Moses, 29 "Say to the people of Israel, He that offers the sacrifice of his peace offerings to the Lord shall bring his offering to the Lord; from the sacrifice of his peace offerings 30 he shall bring with his own hands the offerings by fire to the Lord; he shall bring the fat with the breast, that the breast may be waved as a wave offering before the Lord. 31 The priest shall burn the fat on the altar, but the breast shall be for Aaron and his sons. 32 And the right thigh you shall give to the priest as an offering from the sacrifice of your peace offerings; 33 he among the sons of Aaron who offers the blood of the peace offerings and the fat shall have the right thigh for a portion. 34 For the breast that is waved and the thigh that is offered I have taken from the people of Israel, out of the sacrifices of their peace offerings, and have given them to Aaron the priest and to his sons, as a perpetual due from the people of Israel. 35 This is the portion of Aaron and of his sons from the offerings made by fire to the Lord, consecrated to them on the day they were presented to serve as priests of the Lord; 36 the Lord commanded this to be given them by the people of Israel, on the day that they were anointed; it is a perpetual due throughout their generations."

37 This is the law of the burnt offering, of the cereal offering, of the sin offering, of the guilt offering, of the consecration, and of the peace offerings, 38 which the Lord commanded Moses on Mount Sinai, on the day that he commanded the people of Israel to bring their offerings to the Lord, in the wilderness of Sinai.

8 The Lord said to Moses, 2 "Take Aaron and his sons with him, and the garments, and the anointing oil, and the bull of the sin offering, and the two rams, and the basket of unleavened bread; 3 and assemble all the congregation at the door of the tent of meeting." 4 And Moses did as the Lord commanded him; and the congregation was assembled at the door of the tent of meeting.

5 And Moses said to the congregation, "This is the thing which the Lord has commanded to be done." 6 And Moses brought Aaron and his sons, and washed them with water. 7 And he put on him the coat, and girded him with the girdle, and clothed him with the robe, and put the ephod upon him, and girded him with the skilfully woven band of the ephod, binding it to him therewith. 8 And he placed the breastpiece on him, and in the breastpiece he put the U´rim and the Thŭm´-mĭm. 9 And he set the turban upon his head, and on the turban, in front, he set the golden plate, the holy crown, as the Lord commanded Moses.

10 Then Moses took the anointing oil, and anointed the tabernacle and all that was in it, and consecrated them. 11 And he sprinkled some of it on the altar seven times, and anointed the altar and all its utensils, and the laver and its base, to consecrate them. 12 And he poured some of the anointing oil on Aaron's head, and anointed him, to consecrate him. 13 And Moses brought Aaron's sons, and clothed them with coats, and girded them with girdles, and bound caps on them, as the Lord commanded Moses.

14 Then he brought the bull of the sin offering; and Aaron and his sons laid their hands upon the head of bull of the sin offering. 15 And Moses killed it, and took the blood, and with his finger put it on the horns of the altar round about, and purified the altar, and poured out the blood at the base of the altar, and consecrated it, to make atonement for it. 16 And he took all the fat that was on the entrails, and the appendage of the liver, and the two kidneys with their fat, and Moses burned them on the altar. 17 But the bull, and its skin, and its flesh, and its dung, he burned with fire outside the camp, as the Lord commanded Moses.

18 Then he presented the ram of the burnt offering; and Aaron and his sons laid their hands on the head of the ram. 19 And Moses killed it, and threw the blood upon the altar round about. 20 And when the ram was cut into pieces, Moses burned the head and the pieces and the fat. 21 And when the entrails and the legs were washed with water, Moses burned the whole ram on the altar, as a burnt offering, a pleasing odor, an offering by fire to the Lord, as the Lord commanded Moses.

22 Then he presented the other ram, the ram of ordination; and Aaron and his sons laid their hands on the head

8.1-36: Ex 29.1-37.

of the ram. ²³And Moses killed it, and took some of its blood and put it on the tip of Aaron's right ear and on the thumb of his right hand and on the great toe of his right foot. ²⁴And Aaron's sons were brought, and Moses put some of the blood on the tips of their right ears and on the thumbs of their right hands and on the great toes of their right feet; and Moses threw the blood upon the altar round about. ²⁵Then he took the fat, and the fat tail, and all the fat that was on the entrails, and the appendage of the liver, and the two kidneys with their fat, and the right thigh; ²⁶and out of the basket of unleavened bread which was before the LORD he took one unleavened cake, and one cake of bread with oil, and one wafer, and placed them on the fat and on the right thigh; ²⁷and he put all these in the hands of Aaron and in the hands of his sons, and waved them as a wave offering before the LORD. ²⁸Then Moses took them from their hands, and burned them on the altar with the burnt offering, as an ordination offering, a pleasing odor, an offering by fire to the LORD. ²⁹And Moses took the breast, and waved it for a wave offering before the LORD; it was Moses' portion of the ram of ordination, as the LORD commanded Moses.

30 Then Moses took some of the anointing oil and of the blood which was on the altar, and sprinkled it upon Aaron and his garments, and also upon his sons and his sons' garments; so he consecrated Aaron and his garments, and his sons and his sons' garments with him.

31 And Moses said to Aaron and his sons, "Boil the flesh at the door of the tent of meeting, and there eat it and the bread that is in the basket of ordination offerings, as I commanded, saying, 'Aaron and his sons shall eat it'; ³²and what remains of the flesh and the bread you shall burn with fire. ³³And you shall not go out from the door of the tent of meeting for seven days, until the days of your ordination are completed, for it will take seven days to ordain you. ³⁴As has been done today, the LORD has commanded to be done to make atonement for you. ³⁵At the door of the tent of meeting you shall remain day and night for seven days, performing what the LORD has

charged, lest you die; for so I am commanded." ³⁶And Aaron and his sons did all the things which the LORD commanded by Moses.

9 On the eighth day Moses called Aaron and his sons and the elders of Israel; ²and he said to Aaron, "Take a bull calf for a sin offering, and a ram for a burnt offering, both without blemish, and offer them before the LORD. ³And say to the people of Israel, 'Take a male goat for a sin offering, and a calf and a lamb, both a year old without blemish, for a burnt offering, ⁴and an ox and a ram for peace offerings, to sacrifice before the LORD, and a cereal offering mixed with 'oil; for today the LORD will appear to you.'" ⁵And they brought what Moses commanded before the tent of meeting; and all the congregation drew near and stood before the LORD. ⁶And Moses said, "This is the thing which the LORD commanded you to do; and the glory of the LORD will appear to you." ⁷Then Moses said to Aaron, "Draw near to the altar, and offer your sin offering and your burnt offering, and make atonement for yourself and for the people; and bring the offering of the people, and make atonement for them; as the LORD has commanded."

8 So Aaron drew near to the altar, and killed the calf of the sin offering, which was for himself. ⁹And the sons of Aaron presented the blood to him, and he dipped his finger in the blood and put it on the horns of the altar, and poured out the blood at the base of the altar; ¹⁰but the fat and the kidneys and the appendage of the liver from the sin offering he burned upon the altar, as the LORD commanded Moses. ¹¹The flesh and the skin he burned with fire outside the camp.

12 And he killed the burnt offering; and Aaron's sons delivered to him the blood, and he threw it on the altar round about. ¹³And they delivered the burnt offering to him, piece by piece, and the head; and he burned them upon the altar. ¹⁴And he washed the entrails and the legs, and burned them with the burnt offering on the altar.

15 Then he presented the people's offering, and took the goat of the sin offering which was for the people, and killed it, and offered it for sin, like the first sin offering. ¹⁶And he presented the burnt offering, and offered it ac-

cording to the ordinance. ¹⁷And he presented the cereal offering, and filled his hand from it, and burned it upon the altar, besides the burnt offering of the morning.

18 He killed the ox also and the ram, the sacrifice of peace offerings for the people; and Aaron's sons delivered to him the blood, which he threw upon the altar round about, ¹⁹and the fat of the ox and of the ram, the fat tail, and that which covers the entrails, and the kidneys, and the appendage of the liver; ²⁰and they put the fat upon the breasts, and he burned the fat upon the altar, ²¹but the breasts and the right thigh Aaron waved for a wave offering before the LORD; as Moses commanded.

22 Then Aaron lifted up his hands toward the people and blessed them; and he came down from offering the sin offering and the burnt offering and the peace offerings. ²³And Moses and Aaron went into the tent of meeting; and when they came out they blessed the people, and the glory of the LORD appeared to all the people. ²⁴And fire came forth from before the LORD and consumed the burnt offering and the fat upon the altar; and when all the people saw it, they shouted, and fell on their faces.

10 Now Nā′dăb and A·bī′hū, the sons of Aaron, each took his censer, and put fire in it, and laid incense on it, and offered unholy fire before the LORD, such as he had not commanded them. ²And fire came forth from the presence of the LORD and devoured them, and they died before the LORD. ³Then Moses said to Aaron, "This is what the LORD has said, 'I will show myself holy among those who are near me, and before all the people I will be glorified.'" And Aaron held his peace.

4 And Moses called Mīsh′a·ĕl and Ĕl′za·phăn, the sons of Ŭz′zĭ·ĕl the uncle of Aaron, and said to them, "Draw near, carry your brethren from before the sanctuary out of the camp." ⁵So they drew near, and carried them in their coats out of the camp, as Moses had said. ⁶And Moses said to Aaron and to Ĕl·ē·ā′zar and Ĭth′a·mär, his sons, "Do not let the hair of your heads hang loose, and do not rend your clothes, lest you die, and lest wrath come upon all the congregation; but

your brethren, the whole house of Israel, may bewail the burning which the LORD has kindled. ⁷And do not go out from the door of the tent of meeting, lest you die; for the anointing oil of the LORD is upon you." And they did according to the word of Moses.

8 And the LORD spoke to Aaron, saying, ⁹"Drink no wine nor strong drink, you nor your sons with you, when you go into the tent of meeting, lest you die; it shall be a statute for ever throughout your generations. ¹⁰You are to distinguish between the holy and the common, and between the unclean and the clean; ¹¹and you are to teach the people of Israel all the statutes which the LORD has spoken to them by Moses."

12 And Moses said to Aaron and to Ĕl·ē·ā′zar and Ĭth′a·mär, his sons who were left, "Take the cereal offering that remains of the offerings by fire to the LORD, and eat it unleavened beside the altar, for it is most holy; ¹³you shall eat it in a holy place, because it is your due and your sons' due, from the offerings by fire to the LORD; for so I am commanded. ¹⁴But the breast that is waved and the thigh that is offered you shall eat in any clean place, you and your sons and your daughters with you; for they are given as your due and your sons' due, from the sacrifices of the peace offering of the people of Israel. ¹⁵The thigh that is offered and the breast that is waved they shall bring with the offerings by fire of the fat, to wave for a wave offering before the LORD, and it shall be yours, and your sons' with you, as a due for ever; as the LORD has commanded."

16 Now Moses diligently inquired about the goat of the sin offering, and behold, it was burned! And he was angry with Ĕl·ē·ā′zar and Ĭth′-a·mär, the sons of Aaron who were left, saying, ¹⁷"Why have you not eaten the sin offering in the place of the sanctuary, since it is a thing most holy and has been given to you that you may bear the iniquity of the congregation, to make atonement for them before the LORD? ¹⁸Behold, its blood was not brought into the inner part of the sanctuary. You certainly ought to have eaten it in the sanctuary, as I

commanded." ¹⁹And Aaron said to Moses, "Behold, today they have offered their sin offering and their burnt offering before the Lord; and yet such things as these have befallen me! If I had eaten the sin offering today, would it have been acceptable in the sight of the Lord?" ²⁰And when Moses heard that, he was content.

11 And the Lord said to Moses and Aaron, ²"Say to the people of Israel, These are the living things which you may eat among all the beasts that are on the earth. ³Whatever parts the hoof and is cloven-footed and chews the cud, among the animals, you may eat. ⁴Nevertheless among those that chew the cud or part the hoof, you shall not eat these: The camel, because it chews the cud but does not part the hoof, is unclean to you. ⁵And the rock badger, because it chews the cud but does not part the hoof, is unclean to you. ⁶And the hare, because it chews the cud but does not part the hoof, is unclean to you. ⁷And the swine, because it parts the hoof and is cloven-footed but does not chew the cud, is unclean to you. ⁸Of their flesh you shall not eat, and their carcasses you shall not touch; they are unclean to you.

9 "These you may eat, of all that are in the waters. Everything in the waters that has fins and scales, whether in the seas or in the rivers, you may eat. ¹⁰But anything in the seas or the rivers that has not fins and scales, of the swarming creatures in the waters and of the living creatures that are in the waters, is an abomination to you. ¹¹They shall remain an abomination to you; of their flesh you shall not eat, and their carcasses you shall have in abomination. ¹²Everything in the waters that has not fins and scales is an abomination to you.

13 "And these you shall have in abomination among the birds, they shall not be eaten, they are an abomination: the eagle, the vulture, the osprey, ¹⁴the kite, the falcon according to its kind, ¹⁵every raven according to its kind, ¹⁶the ostrich, the nighthawk, the sea gull, the hawk according to its kind, ¹⁷the owl, the cormorant, the ibis, ¹⁸the water hen, the pelican, the carrion vulture, ¹⁹the stork, the heron according to its kind, the hoopoe, and the bat.

20 "All winged insects that go upon all fours are an abomination to you. ²¹Yet among the winged insects that go on all fours you may eat those which have legs above their feet, with which to leap on the earth. ²²Of them you may eat: the locust according to its kind, the bald locust according to its kind, the cricket according to its kind, and the grasshopper according to its kind. ²³But all other winged insects which have four feet are an abomination to you.

24 "And by these you shall become unclean; whoever touches their carcass shall be unclean until the evening, ²⁵and whoever carries any part of their carcass shall wash his clothes and be unclean until the evening. ²⁶Every animal which parts the hoof but is not cloven-footed or does not chew the cud is unclean to you; every one who touches them shall be unclean. ²⁷And all that go on their paws, among the animals that go on all fours, are unclean to you; whoever touches their carcass shall be unclean until the evening, ²⁸and he who carries their carcass shall wash his clothes and be unclean until the evening; they are unclean to you.

29 "And these are unclean to you among the swarming things that swarm upon the earth: the weasel, the mouse, the great lizard according to its kind, ³⁰the gecko, the land crocodile, the lizard, the sand lizard, and the chameleon. ³¹These are unclean to you among all that swarm; whoever touches them when they are dead shall be unclean until the evening. ³²And anything upon which any of them falls when they are dead shall be unclean, whether it is an article of wood or a garment or a skin or a sack, any vessel that is used for any purpose; it must be put into water, and it shall be unclean until the evening; then it shall be clean. ³³And if any of them falls into any earthen vessel, all that is in it shall be unclean, and you shall break it. ³⁴Any food in it which may be eaten, upon which water may come, shall be unclean; and all drink which may be drunk from every such vessel shall be unclean. ³⁵And everything upon which any part of their carcass falls shall be unclean; whether oven or stove, it shall be broken in pieces;

11.2-47: Deut 14.3-21.

they are unclean, and shall be unclean to you. ³⁶Nevertheless a spring or a cistern holding water shall be clean; but whatever touches their carcass shall be unclean. ³⁷And if any part of their carcass falls upon any seed for sowing that is to be sown, it is clean; ³⁸but if water is put on the seed and any part of their carcass falls on it, it is unclean to you.

39 "And if any animal of which you may eat dies, he who touches its carcass shall be unclean until the evening, ⁴⁰and he who eats of its carcass shall wash his clothes and be unclean until the evening; he also who carries the carcass shall wash his clothes and be unclean until the evening.

41 "Every swarming thing that swarms upon the earth is an abomination; it shall not be eaten. ⁴²Whatever goes on its belly, and whatever goes on all fours, or whatever has many feet, all the swarming things that swarm upon the earth, you shall not eat; for they are an abomination. ⁴³You shall not make yourselves abominable with any swarming thing that swarms; and you shall not defile yourselves with them, lest you become unclean. ⁴⁴For I am the LORD your God; consecrate yourselves therefore, and be holy, for I am holy. You shall not defile yourselves with any swarming thing that crawls upon the earth. ⁴⁵For I am the LORD who brought you up out of the land of Egypt, to be your God; you shall therefore be holy, for I am holy."

46 This is the law pertaining to beast and bird and every living creature that moves through the waters and every creature that swarms upon the earth, ⁴⁷to make a distinction between the unclean and the clean and between the living creature that may be eaten and the living creature that may not be eaten.

12 The LORD said to Moses, ²"Say to the people of Israel, If a woman conceives, and bears a male child, then she shall be unclean seven days; as at the time of her menstruation, she shall be unclean. ³And on the eighth day the flesh of his foreskin shall be circumcised. ⁴Then she shall continue for thirty-three days in the blood of her purifying; she shall not touch any hallowed thing, nor come into the sanctuary, until the days of

her purifying are completed. ⁵But if she bears a female child, then she shall be unclean two weeks, as in her menstruation; and she shall continue in the blood of her purifying for sixty-six days.

6 "And when the days of her purifying are completed, whether for a son or for a daughter, she shall bring to the priest at the door of the tent of meeting a lamb a year old for a burnt offering, and a young pigeon or a turtledove for a sin offering, ⁷and he shall offer it before the LORD, and make atonement for her; then she shall be clean from the flow of her blood. This is the law for her who bears a child, either male or female. ⁸And if she cannot afford a lamb, then she shall take two turtledoves or two young pigeons, one for a burnt offering and the other for a sin offering; and the priest shall make atonement for her, and she shall be clean."

13 The LORD said to Moses and Aaron, ²"When a man has on the skin of his body a swelling or an eruption or a spot, and it turns into a leprous disease on the skin of his body, then he shall be brought to Aaron the priest or to one of his sons the priests, ³and the priest shall examine the diseased spot on the skin of his body; and if the hair in the diseased spot has turned white and the disease appears to be deeper than the skin of his body, it is a leprous disease; when the priest has examined him he shall pronounce him unclean. ⁴But if the spot is white in the skin of his body, and appears no deeper than the skin, and the hair in it has not turned white, the priest shall shut up the diseased person for seven days; ⁵and the priest shall examine him on the seventh day, and if in his eyes the disease is checked and the disease has not spread in the skin, then the priest shall shut him up seven days more; ⁶and the priest shall examine him again on the seventh day, and if the diseased spot is dim and the disease has not spread in the skin, then the priest shall pronounce him clean; it is only an eruption; and he shall wash his clothes, and be clean. ⁷But if the eruption spreads in the skin, after he has shown himself to the priest for his cleansing, he shall

11.44-45: Lev 19.2; 20.7, 26; 1 Pet 1.16.
11.46: Num 5.2, 3.   12.1-8: Lk 2.22-24.

appear again before the priest; [8] and the priest shall make an examination, and if the eruption has spread in the skin, then the priest shall pronounce him unclean; it is leprosy.

9 "When a man is afflicted with leprosy, he shall be brought to the priest; [10] and the priest shall make an examination, and if there is a white swelling in the skin, which has turned the hair white, and there is quick raw flesh in the swelling, [11] it is a chronic leprosy in the skin of his body, and the priest shall pronounce him unclean; he shall not shut him up, for he is unclean. [12] And if the leprosy breaks out in the skin, so that the leprosy covers all the skin of the diseased person from head to foot, so far as the priest can see, [13] then the priest shall make an examination, and if the leprosy has covered all his body, he shall pronounce him clean of the disease; it has all turned white, and he is clean. [14] But when raw flesh appears on him, he shall be unclean. [15] And the priest shall examine the raw flesh, and pronounce him unclean; raw flesh is unclean, for it is leprosy. [16] But if the raw flesh turns again and is changed to white, then he shall come to the priest, [17] and the priest shall examine him, and if the disease has turned white, then the priest shall pronounce the diseased person clean; he is clean.

18 "And when there is in the skin of one's body a boil that has healed, [19] and in the place of the boil there comes a white swelling or a reddish-white spot, then it shall be shown to the priest; [20] and the priest shall make an examination, and if it appears deeper than the skin and its hair has turned white, then the priest shall pronounce him unclean; it is the disease of leprosy, it has broken out in the boil. [21] But if the priest examines it, and the hair on it is not white and it is not deeper than the skin, but is dim, then the priest shall shut him up seven days; [22] and if it spreads in the skin, then the priest shall pronounce him unclean; it is diseased. [23] But if the spot remains in one place and does not spread, it is the scar of the boil; and the priest shall pronounce him clean.

24 "Or, when the body has a burn on its skin and the raw flesh of the burn becomes a spot, reddish-white or white, [25] the priest shall examine it, and if the hair in the spot has turned white and it appears deeper than the skin, then it is leprosy; it has broken out in the burn, and the priest shall pronounce him unclean; it is a leprous disease. [26] But if the priest examines it, and the hair in the spot is not white and it is no deeper than the skin, but is dim, the priest shall shut him up seven days, [27] and the priest shall examine him the seventh day; if it is spreading in the skin, then the priest shall pronounce him unclean; it is a leprous disease. [28] But if the spot remains in one place and does not spread in the skin, but is dim, it is a swelling from the burn, and the priest shall pronounce him clean; for it is the scar of the burn.

29 "When a man or woman has a disease on the head or the beard, [30] the priest shall examine the disease; and if it appears deeper than the skin, and the hair in it is yellow and thin, then the priest shall pronounce him unclean; it is an itch, a leprosy of the head or the beard. [31] And if the priest examines the itching disease, and it appears no deeper than the skin and there is no black hair in it, then the priest shall shut up the person with the itching disease for seven days, [32] and on the seventh day the priest shall examine the disease; and if the itch has not spread, and there is in it no yellow hair, and the itch appears to be no deeper than the skin, [33] then he shall shave himself, but the itch he shall not shave; and the priest shall shut up the person with the itching disease for seven days more; [34] and on the seventh day the priest shall examine the itch, and if the itch has not spread in the skin and it appears to be no deeper than the skin, then the priest shall pronounce him clean; and he shall wash his clothes, and be clean. [35] But if the itch spreads in the skin after his cleansing, [36] then the priest shall examine him, and if the itch has spread in the skin, the priest need not seek for the yellow hair; he is unclean. [37] But if in his eyes the itch is checked, and black hair has grown in it, the itch is healed, he is clean; and the priest shall pronounce him clean.

38 "When a man or a woman has spots on the skin of the body, white spots, [39] the priest shall make an ex-

amination, and if the spots on the skin of the body are of a dull white, it is tetter that has broken out in the skin; he is clean.

40 "If a man's hair has fallen from his head, he is bald but he is clean. ⁴¹And if a man's hair has fallen from his forehead and temples, he has baldness of the forehead but he is clean. ⁴² But if there is on the bald head or the bald forehead a reddish-white diseased spot, it is leprosy breaking out on his bald head or his bald forehead. ⁴³Then the priest shall examine him, and if the diseased swelling is reddish-white on his bald head or on his bald forehead, like the appearance of leprosy in the skin of the body, ⁴⁴he is a leprous man, he is unclean; the priest must pronounce him unclean; his disease is on his head.

45 "The leper who has the disease shall wear torn clothes and let the hair of his head hang loose, and he shall cover his upper lip and cry, 'Unclean, unclean.' ⁴⁶He shall remain unclean as long as he has the disease; he is unclean; he shall dwell alone in a habitation outside the camp.

47 "When there is a leprous disease in a garment, whether a woolen or a linen garment, ⁴⁸in warp or woof of linen or wool, or in a skin or in anything made of skin, ⁴⁹if the disease shows greenish or reddish in the garment, whether in warp or woof or in skin or in anything made of skin, it is a leprous disease and shall be shown to the priest. ⁵⁰And the priest shall examine the disease, and shut up that which has the disease for seven days; ⁵¹then he shall examine the disease on the seventh day. If the disease has spread in the garment, in warp or woof, or in the skin, whatever be the use of the skin, the disease is a malignant leprosy; it is unclean. ⁵²And he shall burn the garment, whether diseased in warp or woof, woolen or linen, or anything of skin, for it is a malignant leprosy; it shall be burned in the fire.

53 "And if the priest examines, and the disease has not spread in the garment in warp or woof or in anything of skin, ⁵⁴then the priest shall command that they wash the thing in which is the disease, and he shall shut it up seven days more; ⁵⁵and the priest shall examine the diseased thing after it has been washed. And if the dis-

eased spot has not changed color, though the disease has not spread, it is unclean; you shall burn it in the fire, whether the leprous spot is on the back or on the front.

56 "But if the priest examines, and the disease is dim after it is washed, he shall tear the spot out of the garment or the skin or the warp or woof; ⁵⁷then if it appears again in the garment, in warp or woof, or in anything of skin, it is spreading; you shall burn with fire that in which is the disease. ⁵⁸But the garment, warp or woof, or anything of skin from which the disease departs when you have washed it, shall then be washed a second time, and be clean."

59 This is the law for a leprous disease in a garment of wool or linen, either in warp or woof, or in anything of skin, to decide whether it is clean or unclean.

14 The LORD said to Moses, ² "This shall be the law of the leper for the day of his cleansing. He shall be brought to the priest; ³ and the priest shall go out of the camp, and the priest shall make an examination. Then, if the leprous disease is healed in the leper, ⁴the priest shall command them to take for him who is to be cleansed two living clean birds and cedarwood and scarlet stuff and hyssop; ⁵ and the priest shall command them to kill one of the birds in an earthen vessel over running water. ⁶He shall take the living bird with the cedarwood and the scarlet stuff and the hyssop, and dip them and the living bird in the blood of the bird that was killed over the running water; ⁷ and he shall sprinkle it seven times upon him who is to be cleansed of leprosy; then he shall pronounce him clean, and shall let the living bird go into the open field. ⁸And he who is to be cleansed shall wash his clothes, and shave off all his hair, and bathe himself in water, and he shall be clean; and after that he shall come into the camp, but shall dwell outside his tent seven days. ⁹And on the seventh day he shall shave all his hair off his head; he shall shave off his beard and his eyebrows, all his hair. Then he shall wash his clothes, and bathe his body in water, and he shall be clean.

10 "And on the eighth day he shall

take two male lambs without blemish, and one ewe lamb a year old without blemish, and a cereal offering of three tenths of an ephah of fine flour mixed with oil, and one log of oil. ¹¹And the priest who cleanses him shall set the man who is to be cleansed and these things before the LORD, at the door of the tent of meeting. ¹²And the priest shall take one of the male lambs, and offer it for a guilt offering, along with the log of oil, and wave them for a wave offering before the LORD; ¹³and he shall kill the lamb in the place where they kill the sin offering and the burnt offering, in the holy place; for the guilt offering, like the sin offering, belongs to the priest; it is most holy. ¹⁴The priest shall take some of the blood of the guilt offering, and the priest shall put it on the tip of the right ear of him who is to be cleansed, and on the thumb of his right hand, and on the great toe of his right foot. ¹⁵Then the priest shall take some of the log of oil, and pour it into the palm of his own left hand, ¹⁶and dip his right finger in the oil that is in his left hand, and sprinkle some oil with his finger seven times before the LORD. ¹⁷And some of the oil that remains in his hand the priest shall put on the tip of the right ear of him who is to be cleansed, and on the thumb of his right hand, and on the great toe of his right foot, upon the blood of the guilt offering; ¹⁸and the rest of the oil that is in the priest's hand he shall put on the head of him who is to be cleansed. Then the priest shall make atonement for him before the LORD. ¹⁹The priest shall offer the sin offering, to make atonement for him who is to be cleansed from his uncleanness. And afterward he shall kill the burnt offering; ²⁰and the priest shall offer the burnt offering and the cereal offering on the altar. Thus the priest shall make atonement for him, and he shall be clean.

21 "But if he is poor and cannot afford so much, then he shall take one male lamb for a guilt offering to be waved, to make atonement for him, and a tenth of an ephah of fine flour mixed with oil for a cereal offering, and a log of oil; ²²also two turtledoves or two young pigeons, such as he can afford; the one shall be a sin offering and the other a burnt offering. ²³And on the eighth day he shall bring them for his cleansing to the priest, to the door of the tent of meeting, before the LORD; ²⁴and the priest shall take the lamb of the guilt offering, and the log of oil, and the priest shall wave them for a wave offering before the LORD. ²⁵And he shall kill the lamb of the guilt offering; and the priest shall take some of the blood of the guilt offering, and put it on the tip of the right ear of him who is to be cleansed, and on the thumb of his right hand, and on the great toe of his right foot. ²⁶And the priest shall pour some of the oil into the palm of his own left hand; ²⁷and shall sprinkle with his right finger some of the oil that is in his left hand seven times before the LORD; ²⁸and the priest shall put some of the oil that is in his hand on the tip of the right ear of him who is to be cleansed, and on the thumb of his right hand, and on the great toe of his right foot, in the place where the blood of the guilt offering was put; ²⁹and the rest of the oil that is in the priest's hand he shall put on the head of him who is to be cleansed, to make atonement for him before the LORD. ³⁰And he shall offer, of the turtledoves or young pigeons such as he can afford, ³¹one^x for a sin offering and the other for a burnt offering, along with a cereal offering; and the priest shall make atonement before the LORD for him who is being cleansed. ³²This is the law for him in whom is a leprous disease, who cannot afford the offerings for his cleansing."

33 The LORD said to Moses and Aaron, ³⁴"When you come into the land of Canaan, which I give you for a possession, and I put a leprous disease in a house in the land of your possession, ³⁵then he who owns the house shall come and tell the priest, 'There seems to me to be some sort of disease in my house.' ³⁶Then the priest shall command that they empty the house before the priest goes to examine the disease, lest all that is in the house be declared unclean; and afterward the priest shall go in to see the house. ³⁷And he shall examine the disease; and if the disease is in the walls of the house with greenish or reddish spots, and if it appears to be deeper than the surface, ³⁸then the priest shall go out of the house to the door of the house, and shut up the

^{x}Gk Syr: Heb *afford*, ³¹*such as he can afford, one*

house seven days. ³⁹And the priest shall come again on the seventh day, and look; and if the disease has spread in the walls of the house, ⁴⁰then the priest shall command that they take out the stones in which is the disease and throw them into an unclean place outside the city; ⁴¹and he shall cause the inside of the house to be scraped round about, and the plaster that they scrape off they shall pour into an unclean place outside the city; ⁴²then they shall take other stones and put them in the place of those stones, and he shall take other plaster and plaster the house.

43 "If the disease breaks out again in the house, after he has taken out the stones and scraped the house and plastered it, ⁴⁴then the priest shall go and look; and if the disease has spread in the house, it is a malignant leprosy in the house; it is unclean. ⁴⁵And he shall break down the house, its stones and timber and all the plaster of the house; and he shall carry them forth out of the city to an unclean place. ⁴⁶Moreover he who enters the house while it is shut up shall be unclean until the evening; ⁴⁷and he who lies down in the house shall wash his clothes; and he who eats in the house shall wash his clothes.

48 "But if the priest comes and makes an examination, and the disease has not spread in the house after the house was plastered, then the priest shall pronounce the house clean, for the disease is healed. ⁴⁹And for the cleansing of the house he shall take two small birds, with cedarwood and scarlet stuff and hyssop, ⁵⁰and shall kill one of the birds in an earthen vessel over running water, ⁵¹and shall take the cedarwood and the hyssop and the scarlet stuff, along with the living bird, and dip them in the blood of the bird that was killed and in the running water, and sprinkle the house seven times. ⁵²Thus he shall cleanse the house with the blood of the bird, and with the running water, and with the living bird, and with the cedarwood and hyssop and scarlet stuff; ⁵³and he shall let the living bird go out of the city into the open field; so he shall make atonement for the house, and it shall be clean."

54 This is the law for any leprous disease: for an itch, ⁵⁵for leprosy in a garment or in a house, ⁵⁶and for a swelling or an eruption or a spot, ⁵⁷to show when it is unclean and when it is clean. This is the law for leprosy.

15 The LORD said to Moses and Aaron, ²"Say to the people of Israel, When any man has a discharge from his body, his discharge is unclean. ³And this is the law of his uncleanness for a discharge: whether his body runs with his discharge, or his body is stopped from discharge, it is uncleanness in him. ⁴Every bed on which he who has the discharge lies shall be unclean; and everything on which he sits shall be unclean. ⁵And any one who touches his bed shall wash his clothes, and bathe himself in water, and be unclean until the evening. ⁶And whoever sits on anything on which he who has the discharge has sat shall wash his clothes, and bathe himself in water, and be unclean until the evening. ⁷And whoever touches the body of him who has the discharge shall wash his clothes, and bathe himself in water, and be unclean until the evening. ⁸And if he who has the discharge spits on one who is clean, then he shall wash his clothes, and bathe himself in water, and be unclean until the evening. ⁹And any saddle on which he who has the discharge rides shall be unclean. ¹⁰And whoever touches anything that was under him shall be unclean until the evening; and he who carries such a thing shall wash his clothes, and bathe himself in water, and be unclean until the evening. ¹¹Any one whom he that has the discharge touches without having rinsed his hands in water shall wash his clothes, and bathe himself in water, and be unclean until the evening. ¹²And the earthen vessel which he who has the discharge touches shall be broken; and every vessel of wood shall be rinsed in water.

13 "And when he who has a discharge is cleansed of his discharge, then he shall count for himself seven days for his cleansing, and wash his clothes; and he shall bathe his body in running water, and shall be clean. ¹⁴And on the eighth day he shall take two turtledoves or two young pigeons, and come before the LORD to the door of the tent of meeting, and give them to the priest; ¹⁵and the priest shall

offer them, one for a sin offering and the other for a burnt offering; and the priest shall make atonement for him before the LORD for his discharge.

16 "And if a man has an emission of semen, he shall bathe his whole body in water, and be unclean until the evening. [17]And every garment and every skin on which the semen comes shall be washed with water, and be unclean until the evening. [18]If a man lies with a woman and has an emission of semen, both of them shall bathe themselves in water, and be unclean until the evening.

19 "When a woman has a discharge of blood which is her regular discharge from her body, she shall be in her impurity for seven days, and whoever touches her shall be unclean until the evening. [20]And everything upon which she lies during her impurity shall be unclean; everything also upon which she sits shall be unclean. [21]And whoever touches her bed shall wash his clothes, and bathe himself in water, and be unclean until the evening. [22]And whoever touches anything upon which she sits shall wash his clothes, and bathe himself in water, and be unclean until the evening; [23]whether it is the bed or anything upon which she sits, when he touches it he shall be unclean until the evening. [24]And if any man lies with her, and her impurity is on him, he shall be unclean seven days; and every bed on which he lies shall be unclean.

25 "If a woman has a discharge of blood for many days, not at the time of her impurity, or if she has a discharge beyond the time of her impurity, all the days of the discharge she shall continue in uncleanness; as in the days of her impurity, she shall be unclean. [26]Every bed on which she lies, all the days of her discharge, shall be to her as the bed of her impurity; and everything on which she sits shall be unclean, as in the uncleanness of her impurity. [27]And whoever touches these things shall be unclean, and shall wash his clothes, and bathe himself in water, and be unclean until the evening. [28]But if she is cleansed of her discharge, she shall count for herself seven days, and after that she shall be clean. [29]And on the eighth day she shall take two turtledoves or two young pigeons, and bring them to the priest, to the door of the tent of meeting. [30]And the priest shall offer one for a sin offering and the other for a burnt offering; and the priest shall make atonement for her before the LORD for her unclean discharge.

31 "Thus you shall keep the people of Israel separate from their uncleanness, lest they die in their uncleanness by defiling my tabernacle that is in their midst."

32 This is the law for him who has a discharge and for him who has an emission of semen, becoming unclean thereby; [33]also for her who is sick with her impurity; that is, for any one, male or female, who has a discharge, and for the man who lies with a woman who is unclean.

16 The LORD spoke to Moses, after the death of the two sons of Aaron, when they drew near before the LORD and died; [2]and the LORD said to Moses, "Tell Aaron your brother not to come at all times into the holy place within the veil, before the mercy seat which is upon the ark, lest he die; for I will appear in the cloud upon the mercy seat. [3]But thus shall Aaron come into the holy place: with a young bull for a sin offering and a ram for a burnt offering. [4]He shall put on the holy linen coat, and shall have the linen breeches on his body, be girded with the linen girdle, and wear the linen turban; these are the holy garments. He shall bathe his body in water, and then put them on. [5]And he shall take from the congregation of the people of Israel two male goats for a sin offering, and one ram for a burnt offering.

6 "And Aaron shall offer the bull as a sin offering for himself, and shall make atonement for himself and for his house. [7]Then he shall take the two goats, and set them before the LORD at the door of the tent of meeting; [8]and Aaron shall cast lots upon the two goats, one lot for the LORD and the other lot for A-zā'zĕl. [9]And Aaron shall present the goat on which the lot fell for the LORD, and offer it as a sin offering; [10]but the goat on which the lot fell for A-zā'zĕl shall be presented alive before the LORD to make atonement over it, that it may be sent away into the wilderness to Azazel.

11 "Aaron shall present the bull as

15.24: Lev 18.19; 20.18. **16.2, 12:** Heb 6.19; 9.7, 25.

a sin offering for himself, and shall make atonement for himself and for his house; he shall kill the bull as a sin offering for himself. [12]And he shall take a censer full of coals of fire from the altar before the LORD, and two handfuls of sweet incense beaten small; and he shall bring it within the veil [13]and put the incense on the fire before the LORD, that the cloud of the incense may cover the mercy seat which is upon the testimony, lest he die; [14]and he shall take some of the blood of the bull, and sprinkle it with his finger on the front of the mercy seat, and before the mercy seat he shall sprinkle the blood with his finger seven times.

15 "Then he shall kill the goat of the sin offering which is for the people, and bring its blood within the veil, and do with its blood as he did with the blood of the bull, sprinkling it upon the mercy seat and before the mercy seat; [16]thus he shall make atonement for the holy place, because of the uncleannesses of the people of Israel, and because of their transgressions, all their sins; and so he shall do for the tent of meeting, which abides with them in the midst of their uncleannesses. [17]There shall be no man in the tent of meeting when he enters to make atonement in the holy place until he comes out and has made atonement for himself and for his house and for all the assembly of Israel. [18]Then he shall go out to the altar which is before the LORD and make atonement for it, and shall take some of the blood of the bull and of the blood of the goat, and put it on the horns of the altar round about. [19]And he shall sprinkle some of the blood upon it with his finger seven times, and cleanse it and hallow it from the uncleannesses of the people of Israel.

20 "And when he has made an end of atoning for the holy place and the tent of meeting and the altar, he shall present the live goat; [21]and Aaron shall lay both his hands upon the head of the live goat, and confess over him all the iniquities of the people of Israel, and all their transgressions, all their sins; and he shall put them upon the head of the goat, and send him away into the wilderness by the hand of a man who is in readiness. [22]The goat shall bear all their iniquities upon him to a solitary land; and he shall let the goat go in the wilderness.

23 "Then Aaron shall come into the tent of meeting, and shall put off the linen garments which he put on when he went into the holy place, and shall leave them there; [24]and he shall bathe his body in water in a holy place, and put on his garments, and come forth, and offer his burnt offering and the burnt offering of the people, and make atonement for himself and for the people. [25]And the fat of the sin offering he shall burn upon the altar. [26]And he who lets the goat go to A·zā′zĕl shall wash his clothes and bathe his body in water, and afterward he may come into the camp. [27]And the bull for the sin offering and the goat for the sin offering, whose blood was brought in to make atonement in the holy place, shall be carried forth outside the camp; their skin and their flesh and their dung shall be burned with fire. [28]And he who burns them shall wash his clothes and bathe his body in water, and afterward he may come into the camp.

29 "And it shall be a statute to you for ever that in the seventh month, on the tenth day of the month, you shall afflict yourselves, and shall do no work, either the native or the stranger who sojourns among you; [30]for on this day shall atonement be made for you, to cleanse you; from all your sins you shall be clean before the LORD. [31]It is a sabbath of solemn rest to you, and you shall afflict yourselves; it is a statute for ever. [32]And the priest who is anointed and consecrated as priest in his father's place shall make atonement, wearing the holy linen garments; [33]he shall make atonement for the sanctuary, and he shall make atonement for the tent of meeting and for the altar, and he shall make atonement for the priests and for all the people of the assembly. [34]And this shall be an everlasting statute for you, that atonement may be made for the people of Israel once in the year because of all their sins." And Moses did as the LORD commanded him.

17 And the LORD said to Moses, [2]"Say to Aaron and his sons, and to all the people of Israel, This is the thing which the LORD has commanded. [3]If any man of the house of

Israel kills an ox or a lamb or a goat in the camp, or kills it outside the camp, ⁴and does not bring it to the door of the tent of meeting, to offer it as a gift to the Lᴏʀᴅ before the tabernacle of the Lᴏʀᴅ, bloodguilt shall be imputed to that man; he has shed blood; and that man shall be cut off from among his people. ⁵This is to the end that the people of Israel may bring their sacrifices which they slay in the open field, that they may bring them to the Lᴏʀᴅ, to the priest at the door of the tent of meeting, and slay them as sacrifices of peace offerings to the Lᴏʀᴅ; ⁶and the priest shall sprinkle the blood on the altar of the Lᴏʀᴅ at the door of the tent of meeting, and burn the fat for a pleasing odor to the Lᴏʀᴅ. ⁷So they shall no more slay their sacrifices for satyrs, after whom they play the harlot. This shall be a statute for ever to them throughout their generations.

8 "And you shall say to them, Any man of the house of Israel, or of the strangers that sojourn among them, who offers a burnt offering or sacrifice, ⁹and does not bring it to the door of the tent of meeting, to sacrifice it to the Lᴏʀᴅ; that man shall be cut off from his people.

10 "If any man of the house of Israel or of the strangers that sojourn among them eats any blood, I will set my face against that person who eats blood, and will cut him off from among his people. ¹¹For the life of the flesh is in the blood; and I have given it for you upon the altar to make atonement for your souls; for it is the blood that makes atonement, by reason of the life. ¹²Therefore I have said to the people of Israel, No person among you shall eat blood, neither shall any stranger who sojourns among you eat blood. ¹³Any man also of the people of Israel, or of the strangers that sojourn among them, who takes in hunting any beast or bird that may be eaten shall pour out its blood and cover it with dust.

14 "For the life of every creature is the blood of it;*ᵉ* therefore I have said to the people of Israel, You shall not eat the blood of any creature, for the life of every creature is its blood; whoever eats it shall be cut off. ¹⁵And every person that eats what dies of itself or what is torn by beasts, whether

he is a native or a sojourner, shall wash his clothes, and bathe himself in water, and be unclean until the evening; then he shall be clean. ¹⁶But if he does not wash them or bathe his flesh, he shall bear his iniquity."

18 And the Lᴏʀᴅ said to Moses, ²"Say to the people of Israel, I am the Lᴏʀᴅ your God. ³You shall not do as they do in the land of Egypt, where you dwelt, and you shall not do as they do in the land of Canaan, to which I am bringing you. You shall not walk in their statutes. ⁴You shall do my ordinances and keep my statutes and walk in them. I am the Lᴏʀᴅ your God. ⁵You shall therefore keep my statutes and my ordinances, by doing which a man shall live: I am the Lᴏʀᴅ.

6 "None of you shall approach any one near of kin to him to uncover nakedness. I am the Lᴏʀᴅ. ⁷You shall not uncover the nakedness of your father, which is the nakedness of your mother; she is your mother, you shall not uncover her nakedness. ⁸You shall not uncover the nakedness of your father's wife; it is your father's nakedness. ⁹You shall not uncover the nakedness of your sister, the daughter of your father or the daughter of your mother, whether born at home or born abroad. ¹⁰You shall not uncover the nakedness of your son's daughter or of your daughter's daughter, for their nakedness is your own nakedness. ¹¹You shall not uncover the nakedness of your father's wife's daughter, begotten by your father, since she is your sister. ¹²You shall not uncover the nakedness of your father's sister; she is your father's near kinswoman. ¹³You shall not uncover the nakedness of your mother's sister, for she is your mother's near kinswoman. ¹⁴You shall not uncover the nakedness of your father's brother, that is, you shall not approach his wife; she is your aunt. ¹⁵You shall not uncover the nakedness of your daughter-in-law; she is your son's wife, you shall not uncover her nakedness. ¹⁶You shall not uncover the nakedness of your brother's wife; she is your brother's nakedness. ¹⁷You

*ᵉ*Gk Syr Compare Vg: Heb *for the life of all flesh, its blood is in its life*
17.10-16: Lev 3.17; 7.26, 27; 19.26; Deut 12.16, 23-25.
18.5: Lk 10.28; Rom 10.5; Gal 3.12.
18.7: Lev 20.11.   18.9, 11: Lev 20.17; Deut 27.22.
18.12: Lev 20.19.   18.14: Lev 20.20.   18.15: Lev 20.12.
18.16: Lev 20.21.   18.17: Lev 20.14.

shall not uncover the nakedness of a woman and of her daughter, and you shall not take her son's daughter or her daughter's daughter to uncover her nakedness; they are your[f] near kinswomen; it is wickedness. [18]And you shall not take a woman as a rival wife to her sister, uncovering her nakedness while her sister is yet alive.

19 "You shall not approach a woman to uncover her nakedness while she is in her menstrual uncleanness. [20]And you shall not lie carnally with your neighbor's wife, and defile yourself with her. [21]You shall not give any of your children to devote them by fire to Mō'lĕch, and so profane the name of your God: I am the LORD. [22]You shall not lie with a male as with a woman; it is an abomination. [23]And you shall not lie with any beast and defile yourself with it, neither shall any woman give herself to a beast to lie with it: it is perversion.

24 "Do not defile yourselves by any of these things, for by all these the nations I am casting out before you defiled themselves; [25]and the land became defiled, so that I punished its iniquity, and the land vomited out its inhabitants. [26]But you shall keep my statutes and my ordinances and do none of these abominations, either the native or the stranger who sojourns among you [27](for all of these abominations the men of the land did, who were before you, so that the land became defiled); [28]lest the land vomit you out, when you defile it, as it vomited out the nation that was before you. [29]For whoever shall do any of these abominations, the persons that do them shall be cut off from among their people. [30]So keep my charge never to practice any of these abominable customs which were practiced before you, and never to defile yourselves by them: I am the LORD your God."

19 And the LORD said to Moses, [2]"Say to all the congregation of the people of Israel, You shall be holy; for I the LORD your God am holy. [3]Every one of you shall revere his mother and his father, and you shall keep my sabbaths: I am the LORD your God. [4]Do not turn to idols or make for yourselves molten gods: I am the LORD your God.

5 "When you offer a sacrifice of peace offerings to the LORD, you shall offer it so that you may be accepted. [6]It shall be eaten the same day you offer it, or on the morrow; and anything left over until the third day shall be burned with fire. [7]If it is eaten at all on the third day, it is an abomination; it will not be accepted, [8]and every one who eats it shall bear his iniquity, because he has profaned a holy thing of the LORD; and that person shall be cut off from his people.

9 "When you reap the harvest of your land, you shall not reap your field to its very border, neither shall you gather the gleanings after your harvest. [10]And you shall not strip your vineyard bare, neither shall you gather the fallen grapes of your vineyard; you shall leave them for the poor and for the sojourner: I am the LORD your God.

11 "You shall not steal, nor deal falsely, nor lie to one another. [12]And you shall not swear by my name falsely, and so profane the name of your God: I am the LORD.

13 "You shall not oppress your neighbor or rob him. The wages of a hired servant shall not remain with you all night until the morning. [14]You shall not curse the deaf or put a stumbling block before the blind, but you shall fear your God: I am the LORD.

15 "You shall do no injustice in judgment; you shall not be partial to the poor or defer to the great, but in righteousness shall you judge your neighbor. [16]You shall not go up and down as a slanderer among your people, and you shall not stand forth against the life[g] of your neighbor: I am the LORD.

17 "You shall not hate your brother in your heart, but you shall reason with your neighbor, lest you bear sin because of him. [18]You shall not take vengeance or bear any grudge against the sons of your own people, but you

[f]Gk: Heb lacks *your* [g]Heb *blood*
18.19: Lev 15.24; 20.18. **18.21:** Lev 20.2-5.
18.22: Lev 20.13; Deut 23.18.
18.23: Ex 22.19; Lev 20.15, 16; Deut 27.21.
19.2: Lev 11.44, 45; 20.7, 26; 1 Pet 1.16.
19.3, 30: Ex 20.12; Deut 5.16; Ex 20.8; 23.12; 34.21; 35.23; Deut 5.12-15.
19.4: Ex 20.4; Lev 26.1; Deut 4.15-19; 27.15.
19.9, 10: Lev 23.22; Deut 24.20, 21.
19.11: Ex 20.15, 16; Deut 5.19.
19.12: Ex 20.7; Deut 5.11; Mt 5.33.
19.13: Deut 24.15; Jas 5.4. **19.14:** Deut 27.18.
19.15: Ex 23.6; Deut 1.17.
19.18: Mt 5.43; 19.19; 22.39; Mk 12.31; Lk 10.27; Rom 13.9; Gal 5.14; Jas 2.8.

shall love your neighbor as yourself: I am the LORD.

19 "You shall keep my statutes. You shall not let your cattle breed with a different kind; you shall not sow your field with two kinds of seed; nor shall there come upon you a garment of cloth made of two kinds of stuff.

20 "If a man lies carnally with a woman who is a slave, betrothed to another man and not yet ransomed or given her freedom, an inquiry shall be held. They shall not be put to death, because she was not free; ²¹but he shall bring a guilt offering for himself to the LORD, to the door of the tent of meeting, a ram for a guilt offering. ²²And the priest shall make atonement for him with the ram of the guilt offering before the LORD for his sin which he has committed; and the sin which he has committed shall be forgiven him.

23 "When you come into the land and plant all kinds of trees for food, then you shall count their fruit as forbidden;ʰ three years it shall be forbidden to you, it must not be eaten. ²⁴And in the fourth year all their fruit shall be holy, an offering of praise to the LORD. ²⁵But in the fifth year you may eat of their fruit, that they may yield more richly for you: I am the LORD your God.

26 "You shall not eat any flesh with the blood in it. You shall not practice augury or witchcraft. ²⁷You shall not round off the hair on your temples or mar the edges of your beard. ²⁸You shall not make any cuttings in your flesh on account of the dead or tattoo any marks upon you: I am the LORD.

29 "Do not profane your daughter by making her a harlot, lest the land fall into harlotry and the land become full of wickedness. ³⁰You shall keep my sabbaths and reverence my sanctuary: I am the LORD.

31 "Do not turn to mediums or wizards; do not seek them out, to be defiled by them: I am the LORD your God.

32 "You shall rise up before the hoary head, and honor the face of an old man, and you shall fear your God: I am the LORD.

33 "When a stranger sojourns with you in your land, you shall not do him wrong. ³⁴The stranger who sojourns with you shall be to you as the native among you, and you shall love him as yourself; for you were strangers in the land of Egypt: I am the LORD your God.

35 "You shall do no wrong in judgment, in measures of length or weight or quantity. ³⁶You shall have just balances, just weights, a just ephah, and a just hin: I am the LORD your God, who brought you out of the land of Egypt. ³⁷And you shall observe all my statutes and all my ordinances, and do them: I am the LORD."

20 The LORD said to Moses, ²"Say to the people of Israel, Any man of the people of Israel, or of the strangers that sojourn in Israel, who gives any of his children to Mō′lĕch shall be put to death; the people of the land shall stone him with stones. ³I myself will set my face against that man, and will cut him off from among his people, because he has given one of his children to Mō′lĕch, defiling my sanctuary and profaning my holy name. ⁴And if the people of the land do at all hide their eyes from that man, when he gives one of his children to Mō′lĕch, and do not put him to death, ⁵then I will set my face against that man and against his family, and will cut them off from among their people, him and all who follow him in playing the harlot after Mō′lĕch.

6 "If a person turns to mediums and wizards, playing the harlot after them, I will set my face against that person, and will cut him off from among his people. ⁷Consecrate yourselves therefore, and be holy; for I am the LORD your God. ⁸Keep my statutes, and do them; I am the LORD who sanctify you. ⁹For every one who curses his father or his mother shall be put to death; he has cursed his father or his mother, his blood is upon him.

10 "If a man commits adultery with the wife ofⁱ his neighbor, both the adulterer and the adulteress shall be put to death. ¹¹The man who lies with

---

ʰHeb *their uncircumcision*
ⁱHeb repeats *if a man commits adultery with the wife of*
19.19: Deut 22.9, 11.
19.26: Lev 3.17; 7.26, 27; 17.10-16; Deut 12.16, 23-25; 18.10. **19.27:** Lev 21.5; Deut 14.1.
19.29: Deut 23.17, 18.
19.30: Ex 20.8-11; 23.12; 34.21; 35.2, 3; Lev 19.3; 26.2; Deut 5.12-15. **19.31:** Lev 20.6, 27. **19.33:** Ex 22.21.
20.2-5: Lev 18.21. **20.6:** Lev 19.31.
20.7: Lev 11.44, 45; 19.2; 20.26; 1 Pet 1.16.
20.9: Ex 21.17; Deut 27.16.
20.10: Ex 20.14; Lev 18.20; Deut 5.18. **20.11:** Lev 18.7, 8.

his father's wife has uncovered his father's nakedness; both of them shall be put to death, their blood is upon them. ¹²If a man lies with his daughter-in-law, both of them shall be put to death; they have committed incest, their blood is upon them. ¹³If a man lies with a male as with a woman, both of them have committed an abomination; they shall be put to death, their blood is upon them. ¹⁴If a man takes a wife and her mother also, it is wickedness; they shall be burned with fire, both he and they, that there may be no wickedness among you. ¹⁵If a man lies with a beast, he shall be put to death; and you shall kill the beast. ¹⁶If a woman approaches any beast and lies with it, you shall kill the woman and the beast; they shall be put to death, their blood is upon them.

17 "If a man takes his sister, a daughter of his father or a daughter of his mother, and sees her nakedness, and she sees his nakedness, it is a shameful thing, and they shall be cut off in the sight of the children of their people; he has uncovered his sister's nakedness, he shall bear his iniquity. ¹⁸If a man lies with a woman having her sickness, and uncovers her nakedness, he has made naked her fountain, and she has uncovered the fountain of her blood; both of them shall be cut off from among their people. ¹⁹You shall not uncover the nakedness of your mother's sister or of your father's sister, for that is to make naked one's near kin; they shall bear their iniquity. ²⁰If a man lies with his uncle's wife, he has uncovered his uncle's nakedness; they shall bear their sin, they shall die childless. ²¹If a man takes his brother's wife, it is impurity; he has uncovered his brother's nakedness, they shall be childless.

22 "You shall therefore keep all my statutes and all my ordinances, and do them; that the land where I am bringing you to dwell may not vomit you out. ²³And you shall not walk in the customs of the nation which I am casting out before you; for they did all these things, and therefore I abhorred them. ²⁴But I have said to you, 'You shall inherit their land, and I will give it to you to possess, a land flowing with milk and honey.' I am the LORD your God, who have separated you from the

peoples. ²⁵You shall therefore make a distinction between the clean beast and the unclean, and between the unclean bird and the clean; you shall not make yourselves abominable by beast or by bird or by anything with which the ground teems, which I have set apart for you to hold unclean. ²⁶You shall be holy to me; for I the LORD am holy, and have separated you from the peoples, that you should be mine. 27 "A man or a woman who is a medium or a wizard shall be put to death; they shall be stoned with stones, their blood shall be upon them."

21 And the LORD said to Moses, "Speak to the priests, the sons of Aaron, and say to them that none of them shall defile himself for the dead among his people, ²except for his nearest of kin, his mother, his father, his son, his daughter, his brother, ³or his virgin sister (who is near to him because she has had no husband; for her he may defile himself). ⁴He shall not defile himself as a husband among his people and so profane himself. ⁵They shall not make tonsures upon their heads, nor shave off the edges of their beards, nor make any cuttings in their flesh. ⁶They shall be holy to their God, and not profane the name of their God; for they offer the offerings by fire to the LORD, the bread of their God; therefore they shall be holy. ⁷They shall not marry a harlot or a woman who has been defiled; neither shall they marry a woman divorced from her husband; for the priest is holy to his God. ⁸You shall consecrate him, for he offers the bread of your God; he shall be holy to you; for I the LORD, who sanctify you, am holy. ⁹And the daughter of any priest, if she profanes herself by playing the harlot, profanes her father; she shall be burned with fire.

10 "The priest who is chief among his brethren, upon whose head the anointing oil is poured, and who has been consecrated to wear the garments, shall not let the hair of his head hang loose, nor rend his clothes; ¹¹he shall not go in to any dead body,

20.12: Lev 18.15.   20.13: Lev 18.22.
20.14: Lev 18.17; Deut 27.23.   20.15, 16: Lev 18.23.
20.17: Lev 18.9.   20.18: Lev 15.24; 18.19.
20.19: Lev 18.12, 13.   20.20: Lev 18.14.
20.21: Lev 18.16.   20.26: Lev 20.7.
20.27: Lev 19.31; 20.6.   21.1-3: Ezek 44.25.
21.5: Lev 19.27; Deut 14.1.

nor defile himself, even for his father or for his mother; [12] neither shall he go out of the sanctuary, nor profane the sanctuary of his God; for the consecration of the anointing oil of his God is upon him: I am the LORD. [13] And he shall take a wife in her virginity. [14] A widow, or one divorced, or a woman who has been defiled, or a harlot, these he shall not marry; but he shall take to wife a virgin of his own people, [15] that he may not profane his children among his people; for I am the LORD who sanctify him."

16 And the LORD said to Moses, [17] "Say to Aaron, None of your descendants throughout their generations who has a blemish may approach to offer the bread of his God. [18] For no one who has a blemish shall draw near, a man blind or lame, or one who has a mutilated face or a limb too long, [19] or a man who has an injured foot or an injured hand, [20] or a hunchback, or a dwarf, or a man with a defect in his sight or an itching disease or scabs or crushed testicles; [21] no man of the descendants of Aaron the priest who has a blemish shall come near to offer the LORD's offerings by fire; since he has a blemish, he shall not come near to offer the bread of his God. [22] He may eat the bread of his God, both of the most holy and of the holy things, [23] but he shall not come near the veil or approach the altar, because he has a blemish, that he may not profane my sanctuaries; for I am the LORD who sanctify them." [24] So Moses spoke to Aaron and to his sons and to all the people of Israel.

22 And the LORD said to Moses, [2] "Tell Aaron and his sons to keep away from the holy things of the people of Israel, which they dedicate to me, so that they may not profane my holy name: I am the LORD. [3] Say to them, 'If any one of all your descendants throughout your generations approaches the holy things, which the people of Israel dedicate to the LORD, while he has an uncleanness, that person shall be cut off from my presence: I am the LORD. [4] None of the line of Aaron who is a leper or suffers a discharge may eat of the holy things until he is clean. Whoever touches anything that is unclean through contact with the dead or a man who has had an emission of semen, [5] and whoever touches a creeping thing by which he may be made unclean or a man from whom he may take uncleanness, whatever his uncleanness may be— [6] the person who touches any such shall be unclean until the evening and shall not eat of the holy things unless he has bathed his body in water. [7] When the sun is down he shall be clean; and afterward he may eat of the holy things, because such are his food. [8] That which dies of itself or is torn by beasts he shall not eat, defiling himself by it: I am the LORD.' [9] They shall therefore keep my charge, lest they bear sin for it and die thereby when they profane it: I am the LORD who sanctify them.

10 "An outsider shall not eat of a holy thing. A sojourner of the priest's or a hired servant shall not eat of a holy thing; [11] but if a priest buys a slave as his property for money, the slave may eat of it; and those that are born in his house may eat of his food. [12] If a priest's daughter is married to an outsider she shall not eat of the offering of the holy things. [13] But if a priest's daughter is a widow or divorced, and has no child, and returns to her father's house, as in her youth, she may eat of her father's food; yet no outsider shall eat of it. [14] And if a man eats of a holy thing unwittingly, he shall add the fifth of its value to it, and give the holy thing to the priest. [15] The priests shall not profane the holy things of the people of Israel, which they offer to the LORD, [16] and so cause them to bear iniquity and guilt, by eating their holy things: for I am the LORD who sanctify them."

17 And the LORD said to Moses, [18] "Say to Aaron and his sons and all the people of Israel, When any one of the house of Israel or of the sojourners in Israel presents his offering, whether in payment of a vow or as a freewill offering which is offered to the LORD as a burnt offering, [19] to be accepted you shall offer a male without blemish, of the bulls or the sheep or the goats. [20] You shall not offer anything that has a blemish, for it will not be acceptable for you. [21] And when any one offers a sacrifice of peace offerings to the LORD, to fulfil a vow or as a freewill offering, from the herd or from the flock, to be accepted it must be perfect;

22.12: Lev 7.31-36.

there shall be no blemish in it. ²²Animals blind or disabled or mutilated or having a discharge or an itch or scabs, you shall not offer to the LORD or make of them an offering by fire upon the altar to the LORD. ²³A bull or a lamb which has a part too long or too short you may present for a freewill offering; but for a votive offering it cannot be accepted. ²⁴Any animal which has its testicles bruised or crushed or torn or cut, you shall not offer to the LORD or sacrifice within your land; ²⁵neither shall you offer as the bread of your God any such animals gotten from a foreigner. Since there is a blemish in them, because of their mutilation, they will not be accepted for you."

26 And the LORD said to Moses, ²⁷"When a bull or sheep or goat is born, it shall remain seven days with its mother; and from the eighth day on it shall be acceptable as an offering by fire to the LORD. ²⁸And whether the mother is a cow or a ewe, you shall not kill both her and her young in one day. ²⁹And when you sacrifice a sacrifice of thanksgiving to the LORD, you shall sacrifice it so that you may be accepted. ³⁰It shall be eaten on the same day, you shall leave none of it until morning: I am the LORD.

31 "So you shall keep my commandments and do them: I am the LORD. ³²And you shall not profane my holy name, but I will be hallowed among the people of Israel; I am the LORD who sanctify you, ³³who brought you out of the land of Egypt to be your God: I am the LORD."

23 The LORD said to Moses, ²"Say to the people of Israel, The appointed feasts of the LORD which you shall proclaim as holy convocations, my appointed feasts, are these. ³Six days shall work be done; but on the seventh day is a sabbath of solemn rest, a holy convocation; you shall do no work; it is a sabbath to the LORD in all your dwellings.

4 "These are the appointed feasts of the LORD, the holy convocations, which you shall proclaim at the time appointed for them. ⁵In the first month, on the fourteenth day of the month in the evening,ʲ is the LORD's passover. ⁶And on the fifteenth day of the same month is the feast of unleavened bread to the LORD; seven days you shall eat unleavened bread. ⁷On the first day

you shall have a holy convocation; you shall do no laborious work. ⁸But you shall present an offering by fire to the LORD seven days; on the seventh day is a holy convocation; you shall do no laborious work."

9 And the LORD said to Moses, ¹⁰"Say to the people of Israel, When you come into the land which I give you and reap its harvest, you shall bring the sheaf of the first fruits of your harvest to the priest; ¹¹and he shall wave the sheaf before the LORD, that you may find acceptance; on the morrow after the sabbath the priest shall wave it. ¹²And on the day when you wave the sheaf, you shall offer a male lamb a year old without blemish as a burnt offering to the LORD. ¹³And the cereal offering with it shall be two tenths of an ephah of fine flour mixed with oil, to be offered by fire to the LORD, a pleasing odor; and the drink offering with it shall be of wine, a fourth of a hin. ¹⁴And you shall eat neither bread nor grain parched or fresh until this same day, until you have brought the offering of your God: it is a statute for ever throughout your generations in all your dwellings.

15 "And you shall count from the morrow after the sabbath, from the day that you brought the sheaf of the wave offering; seven full weeks shall they be, ¹⁶counting fifty days to the morrow after the seventh sabbath; then you shall present a cereal offering of new grain to the LORD. ¹⁷You shall bring from your dwellings two loaves of bread to be waved, made of two tenths of an ephah; they shall be of fine flour, they shall be baked with leaven, as first fruits to the LORD. ¹⁸And you shall present with the bread seven lambs a year old without blemish, and one young bull, and two rams; they shall be a burnt offering to the LORD, with their cereal offering and their drink offerings, an offering by fire, a pleasing odor to the LORD. ¹⁹And you shall offer one male goat for a sin offering, and two male lambs a year old as a sacrifice of peace offerings. ²⁰And the priest shall wave them with the bread of the first fruits as a wave offering before the LORD, with the two lambs; they shall be holy to the LORD for the priest. ²¹And you shall make proclama-

tion on the same day; you shall hold a holy convocation; you shall do no laborious work: it is a statute for ever in all your dwellings throughout your generations.

22 "And when you reap the harvest of your land, you shall not reap your field to its very border, nor shall you gather the gleanings after your harvest; you shall leave them for the poor and for the stranger: I am the Lord your God."

23 And the Lord said to Moses, ²⁴ "Say to the people of Israel, In the seventh month, on the first day of the month, you shall observe a day of solemn rest, a memorial proclaimed with blast of trumpets, a holy convocation. ²⁵ You shall do no laborious work; and you shall present an offering by fire to the Lord."

26 And the Lord said to Moses, ²⁷ "On the tenth day of this seventh month is the day of atonement; it shall be for you a time of holy convocation, and you shall afflict yourselves and present an offering by fire to the Lord. ²⁸ And you shall do no work on this same day; for it is a day of atonement, to make atonement for you before the Lord your God. ²⁹ For whoever is not afflicted on this same day shall be cut off from his people. ³⁰ And whoever does any work on this same day, that person I will destroy from among his people. ³¹ You shall do no work: it is a statute for ever throughout your generations in all your dwellings. ³² It shall be to you a sabbath of solemn rest, and you shall afflict yourselves; on the ninth day of the month beginning at evening, from evening to evening shall you keep your sabbath."

33 And the Lord said to Moses, ³⁴ "Say to the people of Israel, On the fifteenth day of this seventh month and for seven days is the feast of booths*ᵏ* to the Lord. ³⁵ On the first day shall be a holy convocation; you shall do no laborious work. ³⁶ Seven days you shall present offerings by fire to the Lord; on the eighth day you shall hold a holy convocation and present an offering by fire to the Lord; it is a solemn assembly; you shall do no laborious work.

37 "These are the appointed feasts of the Lord, which you shall proclaim as times of holy convocation, for pre-

senting to the Lord offerings by fire, burnt offerings and cereal offerings, sacrifices and drink offerings, each on its proper day; ³⁸ besides the sabbaths of the Lord, and besides your gifts, and besides all your votive offerings, and besides all your freewill offerings, which you give to the Lord.

39 "On the fifteenth day of the seventh month, when you have gathered in the produce of the land, you shall keep the feast of the Lord seven days; on the first day shall be a solemn rest, and on the eighth day shall be a solemn rest. ⁴⁰ And you shall take on the first day the fruit of goodly trees, branches of palm trees, and boughs of leafy trees, and willows of the brook; and you shall rejoice before the Lord your God seven days. ⁴¹ You shall keep it as a feast to the Lord seven days in the year; it is a statute for ever throughout your generations; you shall keep it in the seventh month. ⁴² You shall dwell in booths for seven days; all that are native in Israel shall dwell in booths, ⁴³ that your generations may know that I made the people of Israel dwell in booths when I brought them out of the land of Egypt: I am the Lord your God."

44 Thus Moses declared to the people of Israel the appointed feasts of the Lord.

24 The Lord said to Moses, ² "Command the people of Israel to bring you pure oil from beaten olives for the lamp, that a light may be kept burning continually. ³ Outside the veil of the testimony, in the tent of meeting, Aaron shall keep it in order from evening to morning before the Lord continually; it shall be a statute for ever throughout your generations. ⁴ He shall keep the lamps in order upon the lampstand of pure gold before the Lord continually.

5 "And you shall take fine flour, and bake twelve cakes of it; two tenths of an ephah shall be in each cake. ⁶ And you shall set them in two rows, six in a row, upon the table of pure gold. ⁷ And you shall put pure frankincense with each row, that it may go with the bread as a memorial portion to be offered by fire to the Lord. ⁸ Every

ᵏ Or tabernacles
23.22: Lev 19.9, 10; Deut 24.20, 21.
24.1-4: Ex 27.20, 21.
24.5-9: Ex 25.30; 39.36; 40.23; Mt 12.4; Mk 2.26; Lk 6.4.

sabbath day Aaron shall set it in order before the LORD continually on behalf of the people of Israel as a covenant for ever. ⁹And it shall be for Aaron and his sons, and they shall eat it in a holy place, since it is for him a most holy portion out of the offerings by fire to the LORD, a perpetual due."

10 Now an Israelite woman's son, whose father was an Egyptian, went out among the people of Israel; and the Israelite woman's son and a man of Israel quarreled in the camp, ¹¹and the Israelite woman's son blasphemed the Name, and cursed. And they brought him to Moses. His mother's name was Shĕ·lō′mǐth, the daughter of Dǐb′rī, of the tribe of Dan. ¹²And they put him in custody, till the will of the LORD should be declared to them.

13 And the LORD said to Moses, ¹⁴"Bring out of the camp him who cursed; and let all who heard him lay their hands upon his head, and let all the congregation stone him. ¹⁵And say to the people of Israel, Whoever curses his God shall bear his sin. ¹⁶He who blasphemes the name of the LORD shall be put to death; all the congregation shall stone him; the sojourner as well as the native, when he blasphemes the Name, shall be put to death. ¹⁷He who kills a man shall be put to death. ¹⁸He who kills a beast shall make it good, life for life. ¹⁹When a man causes a disfigurement in his neighbor, as he has done it shall be done to him, ²⁰fracture for fracture, eye for eye, tooth for tooth; as he has disfigured a man, he shall be disfigured. ²¹He who kills a beast shall make it good; and he who kills a man shall be put to death. ²²You shall have one law for the sojourner and for the native; for I am the LORD your God." ²³So Moses spoke to the people of Israel; and they brought him who had cursed out of the camp, and stoned him with stones. Thus the people of Israel did as the LORD commanded Moses.

25 The LORD said to Moses on Mount Sinai, ²"Say to the people of Israel, When you come into the land which I give you, the land shall keep a sabbath to the LORD. ³Six years you shall sow your field, and six years you shall prune your vineyard, and gather in its fruits; ⁴but in the seventh year there shall be a sabbath of solemn rest for the land, a sabbath to the LORD;

you shall not sow your field or prune your vineyard. ⁵What grows of itself in your harvest you shall not reap, and the grapes of your undressed vine you shall not gather; it shall be a year of solemn rest for the land. ⁶The sabbath of the land shall provide food for you, for yourself and for your male and female slaves and for your hired servant and for the sojourner who lives with you; ⁷for your cattle also and for the beasts that are in your land all its yield shall be for food.

8 "And you shall count seven weeks*ˡ* of years, seven times seven years, so that the time of the seven weeks of years shall be to you forty-nine years. ⁹Then you shall send abroad the loud trumpet on the tenth day of the seventh month; on the day of atonement you shall send abroad the trumpet throughout all your land. ¹⁰And you shall hallow the fiftieth year, and proclaim liberty throughout the land to all its inhabitants; it shall be a jubilee for you, when each of you shall return to his property and each of you shall return to his family. ¹¹A jubilee shall that fiftieth year be to you; in it you shall neither sow, nor reap what grows of itself, nor gather the grapes from the undressed vines. ¹²For it is a jubilee; it shall be holy to you; you shall eat what it yields out of the field.

13 "In this year of jubilee each of you shall return to his property. ¹⁴And if you sell to your neighbor or buy from your neighbor, you shall not wrong one another. ¹⁵According to the number of years after the jubilee, you shall buy from your neighbor, and according to the number of years for crops he shall sell to you. ¹⁶If the years are many you shall increase the price, and if the years are few you shall diminish the price, for it is the number of the crops that he is selling to you. ¹⁷You shall not wrong one another, but you shall fear your God; for I am the LORD your God.

18 "Therefore you shall do my statutes, and keep my ordinances and perform them; so you will dwell in the land securely. ¹⁹The land will yield its fruit, and you will eat your fill, and dwell in it securely. ²⁰And if

ˡOr sabbaths
24.19, 20: Ex 21.23-25; Deut 19.21; Mt 5.38.
24.22: Ex 12.49; Num 9.14; 15.15, 16, 29.
25.2-7: Ex 23.10, 11.

you say, 'What shall we eat in the seventh year, if we may not sow or gather in our crop?' ²¹I will command my blessing upon you in the sixth year, so that it will bring forth fruit for three years. ²²When you sow in the eighth year, you will be eating old produce; until the ninth year, when its produce comes in, you shall eat the old. ²³The land shall not be sold in perpetuity, for the land is mine; for you are strangers and sojourners with me. ²⁴And in all the country you possess, you shall grant a redemption of the land.

25 "If your brother becomes poor, and sells part of his property, then his next of kin shall come and redeem what his brother has sold. ²⁶If a man has no one to redeem it, and then himself becomes prosperous and finds sufficient means to redeem it, ²⁷let him reckon the years since he sold it and pay back the overpayment to the man to whom he sold it; and he shall return to his property. ²⁸But if he has not sufficient means to get it back for himself, then what he sold shall remain in the hand of him who bought it until the year of jubilee; in the jubilee it shall be released, and he shall return to his property.

29 "If a man sells a dwelling house in a walled city, he may redeem it within a whole year after its sale; for a full year he shall have the right of redemption. ³⁰If it is not redeemed within a full year, then the house that is in the walled city shall be made sure in perpetuity to him who bought it, throughout his generations; it shall not be released in the jubilee. ³¹But the houses of the villages which have no wall around them shall be reckoned with the fields of the country; they may be redeemed, and they shall be released in the jubilee. ³²Nevertheless the cities of the Lē′vītes, the houses in the cities of their possession, the Levites may redeem at any time. ³³And if one of the Lē′vītes does not exercise*ᵐ* his right of redemption, then the house that was sold in a city of their possession shall be released in the jubilee; for the houses in the cities of the Levites are their possession among the people of Israel. ³⁴But the fields of common land belonging to their cities may not be sold; for that is their perpetual possession.

35 "And if your brother becomes poor, and cannot maintain himself with you, you shall maintain him; as a stranger and a sojourner he shall live with you. ³⁶Take no interest from him or increase, but fear your God; that your brother may live beside you. ³⁷You shall not lend him your money at interest, nor give him your food for profit. ³⁸I am the LORD your God, who brought you forth out of the land of Egypt to give you the land of Canaan, and to be your God.

39 "And if your brother becomes poor beside you, and sells himself to you, you shall not make him serve as a slave: ⁴⁰he shall be with you as a hired servant and as a sojourner. He shall serve with you until the year of the jubilee; ⁴¹then he shall go out from you, he and his children with him, and go back to his own family, and return to the possession of his fathers. ⁴²For they are my servants, whom I brought forth out of the land of Egypt; they shall not be sold as slaves. ⁴³You shall not rule over him with harshness, but shall fear your God. ⁴⁴As for your male and female slaves whom you may have: you may buy male and female slaves from among the nations that are round about you. ⁴⁵You may also buy from among the strangers who sojourn with you and their families that are with you, who have been born in your land; and they may be your property. ⁴⁶You may bequeath them to your sons after you, to inherit as a possession for ever; you may make slaves of them, but over your brethren the people of Israel you shall not rule, one over another, with harshness.

47 "If a stranger or sojourner with you becomes rich, and your brother beside him becomes poor and sells himself to the stranger or sojourner with you, or to a member of the stranger's family, ⁴⁸then after he is sold he may be redeemed; one of his brothers may redeem him, ⁴⁹or his uncle, or his cousin may redeem him, or a near kinsman belonging to his family may redeem him; or if he grows rich he may redeem himself. ⁵⁰He shall reckon with him who bought him from the year when he sold himself to him until the year of jubilee, and the price of his release shall be according to the

ᵐ Compare Vg: Heb *exercises*
25.35: Deut 15.7-11.   25.36: Ex 22.25; Deut 23.19, 20.
25.39-43: Ex 21.2-6; Deut 15.12-18.

number of years; the time he was with his owner shall be rated as the time of a hired servant. ⁵¹If there are still many years, according to them he shall refund out of the price paid for him the price for his redemption. ⁵²If there remain but a few years until the year of jubilee, he shall make a reckoning with him; according to the years of service due from him he shall refund the money for his redemption. ⁵³As a servant hired year by year shall he be with him; he shall not rule with harshness over him in your sight. ⁵⁴And if he is not redeemed by these means, then he shall be released in the year of jubilee, he and his children with him. ⁵⁵For to me the people of Israel are servants, they are my servants whom I brought forth out of the land of Egypt: I am the LORD your God.

26 "You shall make for yourselves no idols and erect no graven image or pillar, and you shall not set up a figured stone in your land, to bow down to them; for I am the LORD your God. ²You shall keep my sabbaths and reverence my sanctuary: I am the LORD.

3 "If you walk in my statutes and observe my commandments and do them, ⁴then I will give you your rains in their season, and the land shall yield its increase, and the trees of the the field shall yield their fruit. ⁵And your threshing shall last to the time of vintage, and the vintage shall last to the time for sowing; and you shall eat your bread to the full, and dwell in your land securely. ⁶And I will give peace in the land, and you shall lie down, and none shall make you afraid; and I will remove evil beasts from the land, and the sword shall not go through your land. ⁷And you shall chase your enemies, and they shall fall before you by the sword. ⁸Five of you shall chase a hundred, and a hundred of you shall chase ten thousand; and your enemies shall fall before you by the sword. ⁹And I will have regard for you and make you fruitful and multiply you, and will confirm my covenant with you. ¹⁰And you shall eat old store long kept, and you shall clear out the old to make way for the new. ¹¹And I will make my abode among you, and my soul shall not abhor you. ¹²And I will walk among you, and will be your God, and you shall be my people. ¹³I

am the LORD your God, who brought you forth out of the land of Egypt, that you should not be their slaves; and I have broken the bars of your yoke and made you walk erect.

14 "But if you will not hearken to me, and will not do all these commandments, ¹⁵if you spurn my statutes, and if your soul abhors my ordinances, so that you will not do all my commandments, but break my covenant, ¹⁶I will do this to you: I will appoint over you sudden terror, consumption, and fever that waste the eyes and cause life to pine away. And you shall sow your seed in vain, for your enemies shall eat it; ¹⁷I will set my face against you, and you shall be smitten before your enemies; those who hate you shall rule over you, and you shall flee when none pursues you. ¹⁸And if in spite of this you will not hearken to me, then I will chastise you again sevenfold for your sins, ¹⁹and I will break the pride of your power, and I will make your heavens like iron and your earth like brass; ²⁰and your strength shall be spent in vain, for your land shall not yield its increase, and the trees of the land shall not yield their fruit.

21 "Then if you walk contrary to me, and will not hearken to me, I will bring more plagues upon you, sevenfold as many as your sins. ²²And I will let loose the wild beasts among you, which shall rob you of your children, and destroy your cattle, and make you few in number, so that your ways shall become desolate.

23 "And if by this discipline you are not turned to me, but walk contrary to me, ²⁴then I also will walk contrary to you, and I myself will smite you sevenfold for your sins. ²⁵And I will bring a sword upon you, that shall execute vengeance for the covenant; and if you gather within your cities I will send pestilence among you, and you shall be delivered into the hand of the enemy. ²⁶When I break your staff of bread, ten women shall bake your bread in one oven, and shall deliver your bread again by weight; and you shall eat, and not be satisfied.

27 "And if in spite of this you will not hearken to me, but walk contrary

26.1: Lev 19.4; Ex 20.4, 23; Deut 4.15-18; 27.15.
26.2: Ex 20.8; 23.12; 34.21; 35.2, 3; Lev 19.3, 30; Deut 5.12-15. 26.3-13: Deut 7.12-26; 28.1-14.
26.11, 12: 2 Cor 6.16. 26.14-45: Deut 28.16-68.

to me, [28] then I will walk contrary to you in fury, and chastise you myself sevenfold for your sins. [29] You shall eat the flesh of your sons, and you shall eat the flesh of your daughters. [30] And I will destroy your high places, and cut down your incense altars, and cast your dead bodies upon the dead bodies of your idols; and my soul will abhor you. [31] And I will lay your cities waste, and will make your sanctuaries desolate, and I will not smell your pleasing odors. [32] And I will devastate the land, so that your enemies who settle in it shall be astonished at it. [33] And I will scatter you among the nations, and I will unsheathe the sword after you; and your land shall be desolation, and your cities shall be a waste.

34 "Then the land shall enjoy[n] its sabbaths as long as it lies desolate, while you are in your enemies' land; then the land shall rest, and enjoy[n] its sabbaths. [35] As long as it lies desolate it shall have rest, the rest which it had not in your sabbaths when you dwelt upon it. [36] And as for those of you that are left, I will send faintness into their hearts in the lands of their enemies; the sound of a driven leaf shall put them to flight, and they shall flee as one flees from the sword, and they shall fall when none pursues. [37] They shall stumble over one another, as if to escape a sword, though none pursues; and you shall have no power to stand before your enemies. [38] And you shall perish among the nations, and the land of your enemies shall eat you up. [39] And those of you that are left shall pine away in your enemies' lands because of their iniquity; and also because of the iniquities of their fathers they shall pine away like them.

40 "But if they confess their iniquity and the iniquity of their fathers in their treachery which they committed against me, and also in walking contrary to me, [41] so that I walked contrary to them and brought them into the land of their enemies; if then their uncircumcised heart is humbled and they make amends for their iniquity; [42] then I will remember my covenant with Jacob, and I will remember my covenant with Isaac and my covenant with Abraham, and I will remember the land. [43] But the land shall be left by them, and enjoy[n] its sabbaths while it lies desolate without them; and they

shall make amends for their iniquity, because they spurned my ordinances, and their soul abhorred my statutes. [44] Yet for all that, when they are in the land of their enemies, I will not spurn them, neither will I abhor them so as to destroy them utterly and break my covenant with them; for I am the LORD their God; [45] but I will for their sake remember the covenant with their forefathers, whom I brought forth out of the land of Egypt in the sight of the nations, that I might be their God: I am the LORD."

46 These are the statutes and ordinances and laws which the LORD made between him and the people of Israel on Mount Sinai by Moses.

27 The LORD said to Moses, [2] "Say to the people of Israel, When a man makes a special vow of persons to the LORD at your valuation, [3] then your valuation of a male from twenty years old up to sixty years old shall be fifty shekels of silver, according to the shekel of the sanctuary. [4] If the person is a female, your valuation shall be thirty shekels. [5] If the person is from five years old up to twenty years old, your valuation shall be for a male twenty shekels, and for a female ten shekels. [6] If the person is from a month old up to five years old, your valuation shall be for a male five shekels of silver, and for a female your valuation shall be three shekels of silver. [7] And if the person is sixty years old and upward, then your valuation for a male shall be fifteen shekels, and for a female ten shekels. [8] And if a man is too poor to pay your valuation, then he shall bring the person before the priest, and the priest shall value him; according to the ability of him who vowed the priest shall value him.

9 "If it is an animal such as men offer as an offering to the LORD, all of such that any man gives to the LORD is holy. [10] He shall not substitute anything for it or exchange it, a good for a bad, or a bad for a good; and if he makes any exchange of beast for beast, then both it and that for which it is exchanged shall be holy. [11] And if it is an unclean animal such as is not offered as an offering to the LORD, then the man shall bring the animal before the priest, [12] and the priest shall

[n] Or *pay for*
26.40, 41: Acts 7.51.

value it as either good or bad; as you, the priest, value it, so it shall be. [13] But if he wishes to redeem it, he shall add a fifth to the valuation.

14 "When a man dedicates his house to be holy to the LORD, the priest shall value it as either good or bad; as the priest values it, so it shall stand. [15] And if he who dedicates it wishes to redeem his house, he shall add a fifth of the valuation in money to it, and it shall be his.

16 "If a man dedicates to the LORD part of the land which is his by inheritance, then your valuation shall be according to the seed for it; a sowing of a homer of barley shall be valued at fifty shekels of silver. [17] If he dedicates his field from the year of jubilee, it shall stand at your full valuation; [18] but if he dedicates his field after the jubilee, then the priest shall compute the money-value for it according to the years that remain until the year of jubilee, and a deduction shall be made from your valuation. [19] And if he who dedicates the field wishes to redeem it, then he shall add a fifth of the valuation in money to it, and it shall remain his. [20] But if he does not wish to redeem the field, or if he has sold the field to another man, it shall not be redeemed any more; [21] but the field, when it is released in the jubilee, shall be holy to the LORD, as a field that has been devoted; the priest shall be in possession of it. [22] If he dedicates to the LORD a field which he has bought, which is not a part of his possession by inheritance, [23] then the priest shall compute the valuation for it up to the year of jubilee, and the man shall give the amount of the valuation on that day as a holy thing to the LORD. [24] In the year of jubilee the field shall return to him from whom it was bought, to whom the land belongs as a possession by inheritance. [25] Every valuation shall be according to the shekel of the sanctuary: twenty gerahs shall make a shekel.

26 "But a firstling of animals, which as a firstling belongs to the LORD, no man may dedicate; whether ox or sheep, it is the LORD's. [27] And if it is an unclean animal, then he shall buy it back at your valuation, and add a fifth to it; or, if it is not redeemed, it shall be sold at your valuation.

28 "But no devoted thing that a man devotes to the LORD, of anything that he has, whether of man or beast, or of his inherited field, shall be sold or redeemed; every devoted thing is most holy to the LORD. [29] No one devoted, who is to be utterly destroyed from among men, shall be ransomed; he shall be put to death.

30 "All the tithe of the land, whether of the seed of the land or of the fruit of the trees, is the LORD's; it is holy to the LORD. [31] If a man wishes to redeem any of his tithe, he shall add a fifth to it. [32] And all the tithe of herds and flocks, every tenth animal of all that pass under the herdsman's staff, shall be holy to the LORD. [33] A man shall not inquire whether it is good or bad, neither shall he exchange it; and if he exchanges it, then both it and that for which it is exchanged shall be holy; it shall not be redeemed."

34 These are the commandments which the LORD commanded Moses for the people of Israel on Mount Sinai.

The Fourth Book of Moses
Commonly Called
Numbers

1 The LORD spoke to Moses in the wilderness of Sinai, in the tent of meeting, on the first day of the second month, in the second year after they had come out of the land of Egypt, saying, [2] "Take a census of all the congregation of the people of Israel, by families, by fathers' houses, according to the number of names, every male,

27.28: Num 18.14. 1.1-46: Num 26.1-51.

head by head; ³from twenty years old and upward, all in Israel who are able to go forth to war, you and Aaron shall number them, company by company. ⁴And there shall be with you a man from each tribe, each man being the head of the house of his fathers. ⁵And these are the names of the men who shall attend you. From Reuben, Ĕ·lī'-zŭr the son of Shĕd'ē·ur; ⁶from Sĭm'-ē·ọn, Shĕ·lü'mĭ–ĕl the son of Zü·rī-shăd'daī; ⁷from Judah, Näh'shọn the son of Ăm·mĭn'a·dăb; ⁸from Ĭs'sa-chär, Nĕ·thăn'ĕl the son of Zü'ạr; ⁹from Zĕb'ū·lụn, Ĕ·lī'ăb the son of Hē'lŏn; ¹⁰from the sons of Joseph, from Ē'phra·ĭm, Ĕ·lĭsh'a·ma the son of Ăm·mĭ'hụd, and from Ma·năs'sẹh, Ga·mā'lĭ·ẹl the son of Pẹ·däh'zụr; ¹¹from Benjamin, A·bī'dạn the son of Gĭd·ē·ō'nī; ¹²from Dan, Ă·hī·ē'zer the son of Ăm·mĭ·shăd'daī; ¹³from Ăsh'ẹr, Pā'gĭ·ĕl the son of Ōch'rạn; ¹⁴from Găd, Ĕ·lī'a·săph the son of Deü'ĕl; ¹⁵from Năph'ta·lī, A·hī'ra the son of Ē'năn." ¹⁶These were the ones chosen from the congregation, the leaders of their ancestral tribes, the heads of the clans of Israel.

17 Moses and Aaron took these men who have been named, ¹⁸and on the first day of the second month, they assembled the whole congregation together, who registered themselves by families, by fathers' houses, according to the number of names from twenty years old and upward, head by head, ¹⁹as the LORD commanded Moses. So he numbered them in the wilderness of Sinai.

20 The people of Reuben, Israel's first-born, their generations, by their families, by their fathers' houses, according to the number of names, head by head, every male from twenty years old and upward, all who were able to go forth to war: ²¹the number of the tribe of Reuben was forty-six thousand five hundred.

22 Of the people of Sĭm'ē·ọn, their generations, by their families, by their fathers' houses, those of them that were numbered, according to the number of names, head by head, every male from twenty years old and upward, all who were able to go forth to war: ²³the number of the tribe of Sĭm'ē·ọn was fifty-nine thousand three hundred.

24 Of the people of Găd, their generations, by their families, by their

fathers' houses, according to the number of the names, from twenty years old and upward, all who were able to go forth to war: ²⁵the number of the tribe of Găd was forty-five thousand six hundred and fifty.

26 Of the people of Judah, their generations, by their families, by their fathers' houses, according to the number of names, from twenty years old and upward, every man able to go forth to war: ²⁷the number of the tribe of Judah was seventy-four thousand six hundred.

28 Of the people of Ĭs'sa·chär, their generations, by their families, by their fathers' houses, according to the number of names, from twenty years old and upward, every man able to go forth to war: ²⁹the number of the tribe of Ĭs'sa·chär was fifty-four thousand four hundred.

30 Of the people of Zĕb'ū·lụn, their generations, by their families, by their fathers' houses, according to the number of names, from twenty years old and upward, every man able to go forth to war: ³¹the number of the tribe of Zĕb'ū·lụn was fifty-seven thousand four hundred.

32 Of the people of Joseph, namely, of the people of Ē'phra·ĭm, their generations, by their families, by their fathers' houses, according to the number of names, from twenty years old and upward, every man able to go forth to war: ³³the number of the tribe of Ē'phra·ĭm was forty thousand five hundred.

34 Of the people of Ma·năs'sẹh, their generations, by their families, by their fathers' houses, according to the number of names, from twenty years old and upward, every man able to go forth to war: ³⁵the number of the tribe of Ma·năs'sẹh was thirty-two thousand two hundred.

36 Of the people of Benjamin, their generations, by their families, by their fathers' houses, according to the number of names, from twenty years old and upward, every man able to go forth to war: ³⁷the number of the tribe of Benjamin was thirty-five thousand four hundred.

38 Of the people of Dan, their generations, by their families, by their fathers' houses, according to the number of names, from twenty years old and upward, every man able to go forth

to war: [39] the number of the tribe of Dan was sixty-two thousand seven hundred.

40 Of the people of Ăsh'ẹr, their generations, by their families, by their fathers' houses, according to the number of names, from twenty years old and upward, every man able to go forth to war: [41] the number of the tribe of Ăsh'ẹr was forty-one thousand five hundred.

42 Of the people of Năph'tạ.lī, their generations, by their families, by their fathers' houses, according to the number of names, from twenty years old and upward, every man able to go forth to war: [43] the number of the tribe of Năph'tạ.lī was fifty-three thousand four hundred.

44 These are those who were numbered, whom Moses and Aaron numbered with the help of the leaders of Israel, twelve men, each representing his fathers' house. [45] So the whole number of the people of Israel, by their fathers' houses, from twenty years old and upward, every man able to go forth to war in Israel — [46] their whole number was six hundred and three thousand five hundred and fifty.

47 But the Lē'vītes were not numbered by their ancestral tribe along with them. [48] For the Lord said to Moses, [49] "Only the tribe of Lē'vī you shall not number, and you shall not take a census of them among the people of Israel; [50] but appoint the Lē'vītes over the tabernacle of the testimony, and over all its furnishings, and over all that belongs to it; they are to carry the tabernacle and all its furnishings, and they shall tend it, and shall encamp around the tabernacle. [51] When the tabernacle is to set out, the Lē'vītes shall take it down; and when the tabernacle is to be pitched, the Levites shall set it up. And if any one else comes near, he shall be put to death. [52] The people of Israel shall pitch their tents by their companies, every man by his own camp and every man by his own standard; [53] but the Lē'vītes shall encamp around the tabernacle of the testimony, that there may be no wrath upon the congregation of the people of Israel; and the Levites shall keep charge of the tabernacle of the testimony." [54] Thus did the people of Israel; they did according to all that the Lord commanded Moses.

2 The Lord said to Moses and Aaron, [2] "The people of Israel shall encamp each by his own standard, with the ensigns of their fathers' houses; they shall encamp facing the tent of meeting on every side. [3] Those to encamp on the east side toward the sunrise shall be of the standard of the camp of Judah by their companies, the leader of the people of Judah being Näh'shọn the son of Ăm·mĭn'ạ·dăb, [4] his host as numbered being seventy-four thousand six hundred. [5] Those to encamp next to him shall be the tribe of Ĭs'sạ·chär, the leader of the people of Issachar being Nẹ·thăn'ĕl the son of Zü'ạr, [6] his host as numbered being fifty-four thousand four hundred. [7] Then the tribe of Zĕb'ū·lụn, the leader of the people of Zebulun being Ĕ·lī'ăb the son of Hē'lŏn, [8] his host as numbered being fifty-seven thousand four hundred. [9] The whole number of the camp of Judah, by their companies, is a hundred and eighty-six thousand four hundred. They shall set out first on the march.

10 "On the south side shall be the standard of the camp of Reuben by their companies, the leader of the people of Reuben being Ĕ·lī'zür the son of Shĕd'ē·ụr, [11] his host as numbered being forty-six thousand five hundred. [12] And those to encamp next to him shall be the tribe of Sĭm'ē·ọn, the leader of the people of Simeon being Shĕ·lü'mĭ–ĕl the son of Zü·rĭ·shăd'daī, [13] his host as numbered being fifty-nine thousand three hundred. [14] Then the tribe of Găd, the leader of the people of Găd being Ĕ·lī'ạ·săph the son of Reü'ĕl, [15] his host as numbered being forty-five thousand six hundred and fifty. [16] The whole number of the camp of Reuben, by their companies, is a hundred and fifty-one thousand four hundred and fifty. They shall set out second.

17 "Then the tent of meeting shall set out, with the camp of the Lē'vītes in the midst of the camps; as they encamp, so shall they set out, each in position, standard by standard.

18 "On the west side shall be the standard of the camp of Ē'phrạ·ĭm by their companies, the leader of the people of Ephraim being Ĕ·lĭsh'ạ·mạ the son of Ăm·mī'hụd, [19] his host as

1.47: Num 2.33.
1.50-53: Num 3.5-8, 21-37; 4.1-33; 8.19; 18.3, 4, 23.

numbered being forty thousand five hundred. ²⁰And next to him shall be the tribe of Mạ·năs′seh, the leader of the people of Manasseh being Gạ·mā′lĭ·ẹl the son of Pẹ·däh′zụr, ²¹his host as numbered being thirty-two thousand two hundred. ²²Then the tribe of Benjamin, the leader of the people of Benjamin being Ạ·bī′dạn the son of Gĭd·ē·ō′nĭ, ²³his host as numbered being thirty-five thousand four hundred. ²⁴The whole number of the camp of Ē′phrạ·ĭm, by their companies, is a hundred and eight thousand one hundred. They shall set out third on the march.

25 "On the north side shall be the standard of the camp of Dan by their companies, the leader of the people of Dan being Ā·hī·ē′zer the son of Ăm·mĭ·shăd′daī, ²⁶his host as numbered being sixty-two thousand seven hundred. ²⁷And those to encamp next to him shall be the tribe of Ăsh′ẹr, the leader of the people of Asher being Pā′gĭ·ĕl the son of Ŏch′rạn, ²⁸his host as numbered being forty-one thousand five hundred. ²⁹Then the tribe of Năph′tạ·lī, the leader of the people of Naphtali being Ạ·hī′rạ the son of Ē′năn, ³⁰his host as numbered being fifty-three thousand four hundred. ³¹The whole number of the camp of Dan is a hundred and fifty-seven thousand six hundred. They shall set out last, standard by standard."

32 These are the people of Israel as numbered by their fathers' houses; all in the camps who were numbered by their companies were six hundred and three thousand five hundred and fifty. ³³But the Lē′vītes were not numbered among the people of Israel, as the LORD commanded Moses.

34 Thus did the people of Israel. According to all that the LORD commanded Moses, so they encamped by their standards, and so they set out, every one in his family, according to his fathers' house.

3 These are the generations of Aaron and Moses at the time when the LORD spoke with Moses on Mount Sinai. ²These are the names of the sons of Aaron: Nā′dăb the first-born, and Ạ·bī′hū, Ĕl·ē·ā′zạr, and Ĭth′ạ·mär; ³these are the names of the sons of Aaron, the anointed priests, whom he ordained to minister in the priest's office. ⁴But Nā′dăb and Ạ·bī′hū died

before the LORD when they offered unholy fire before the LORD in the wilderness of Sinai; and they had no children. So Ĕl·ē·ā′zạr and Ĭth′ạ·mär served as priests in the lifetime of Aaron their father.

5 And the LORD said to Moses, ⁶"Bring the tribe of Lē′vī near, and set them before Aaron the priest, that they may minister to him. ⁷They shall perform duties for him and for the whole congregation before the tent of meeting, as they minister at the tabernacle; ⁸they shall have charge of all the furnishings of the tent of meeting, and attend to the duties for the people of Israel as they minister at the tabernacle. ⁹And you shall give the Lē′vītes to Aaron and his sons; they are wholly given to him from among the people of Israel. ¹⁰And you shall appoint Aaron and his sons, and they shall attend to their priesthood; but if any one else comes near, he shall be put to death."

11 And the LORD said to Moses, ¹²"Behold, I have taken the Lē′vītes from among the people of Israel instead of every first-born that opens the womb among the people of Israel. The Levites shall be mine, ¹³for all the first-born are mine; on the day that I slew all the first-born in the land of Egypt, I consecrated for my own all the first-born in Israel, both of man and of beast; they shall be mine: I am the LORD."

14 And the LORD said to Moses in the wilderness of Sinai, ¹⁵"Number the sons of Lē′vī, by fathers' houses and by families; every male from a month old and upward you shall number." ¹⁶So Moses numbered them according to the word of the LORD, as he was commanded. ¹⁷And these were the sons of Lē′vī by their names: Gēr′shọn and Kō′hăth and Mẹ·rär′ī. ¹⁸And these are the names of the sons of Gēr′shọn by their families: Lĭb′nī and Shĭm′ē·ī. ¹⁹And the sons of Kō′hăth by their families: Ăm′răm, Ĭz′här, Hē′brọn, and Ŭz′zĭ·ĕl. ²⁰And the sons of Mẹ·rär′ī by their families: Mäh′lī and Mū′shī. These are the families of the Lē′vītes, by their fathers' houses. 21 Of Gēr′shọn were the family of

3.2: Num 26.60. 3.5-13: Num 8.6-26.
3.5-8: Num 1.50-53; 3.21-37; 4.1-33; 8.19.
3.11-13: Num 3.45; 8.18. 3.15-34: Num 4.34-49.
3.17-20: Ex 6.16, 22.

the Lĭb′nītes and the family of the Shĭm′ē·ītes; these were the families of the Gẽr′shŏ·nītes. ²²Their number according to the number of all the males from a month old and upward was*^a* seven thousand five hundred. ²³The families of the Gẽr′shŏ·nītes were to encamp behind the tabernacle on the west, ²⁴with Ē·lī′ạ·săph, the son of Lā′ẹl as head of the fathers′ house of the Gẽr′shŏ·nītes. ²⁵And the charge of the sons of Gẽr′shŏn in the tent of meeting was to be the tabernacle, the tent with its covering, the screen for the door of the tent of meeting, ²⁶the hangings of the court, the screen for the door of the court which is around the tabernacle and the altar, and its cords; all the service pertaining to these.

27 Of Kō′hăth were the family of the Ăm′rạ·mītes, and the family of the Ĭz′hạ·rītes, and the family of the Hē′brŏ·nītes, and the family of the Ŭz′zĭ·ẹ·lītes; these are the families of the Kō′hạ·thītes. ²⁸According to the number of all the males, from a month old and upward, there were eight thousand six hundred, attending to the duties of the sanctuary. ²⁹The families of the sons of Kō′hăth were to encamp on the south side of the tabernacle, ³⁰with Ē·lī·zā′phăn the son of Ŭz′zĭ·ĕl as head of the fathers′ house of the families of the Kō′hạ·thītes. ³¹And their charge was to be the ark, the table, the lampstand, the altars, the vessels of the sanctuary with which the priests minister, and the screen; all the service pertaining to these. ³²And Ĕl·ē·ā′zar the son of Aaron the priest was to be chief over the leaders of the Lē′vītes, and to have oversight of those who had charge of the sanctuary.

33 Of Mẹ·rār′ī were the family of the Măh′lītes and the family of the Mū′shītes: these are the families of Merari. ³⁴Their number according to the number of all the males from a month old and upward was six thousand two hundred. ³⁵And the head of the fathers′ house of the families of Mẹ·rār′ī was Zū′rī·ĕl the son of Ăb·ĭ·hā′ĭl; they were to encamp on the north side of the tabernacle. ³⁶And the appointed charge of the sons of Mẹ·rār′ī was to be the frames of the tabernacle, the bars, the pillars, the bases, and all their accessories; all the service per-

taining to these; ³⁷also the pillars of the court round about, with their bases and pegs and cords.

38 And those to encamp before the tabernacle on the east, before the tent of meeting toward the sunrise, were Moses and Aaron and his sons, having charge of the rites within the sanctuary, whatever had to be done for the people of Israel; and any one else who came near was to be put to death. ³⁹All who were numbered of the Lē′vītes, whom Moses and Aaron numbered at the commandment of the LORD, by families, all the males from a month old and upward, were twenty-two thousand.

40 And the LORD said to Moses, "Number all the first-born males of the people of Israel, from a month old and upward, taking their number by names. ⁴¹And you shall take the Lē′vītes for me—I am the LORD—instead of all the first-born among the people of Israel, and the cattle of the Levites instead of all the firstlings among the cattle of the people of Israel." ⁴²So Moses numbered all the first-born among the people of Israel, as the LORD commanded him. ⁴³And all the first-born males, according to the number of names, from a month old and upward as numbered were twenty-two thousand two hundred and seventy-three.

44 And the LORD said to Moses, ⁴⁵"Take the Lē′vītes instead of all the first-born among the people of Israel, and the cattle of the Levites instead of their cattle; and the Levites shall be mine: I am the LORD. ⁴⁶And for the redemption of the two hundred and seventy-three of the first-born of the people of Israel, over and above the number of the male Lē′vītes, ⁴⁷you shall take five shekels apiece; reckoning by the shekel of the sanctuary, the shekel of twenty gerahs, you shall take them, ⁴⁸and give the money by which the excess number of them is redeemed to Aaron and his sons." ⁴⁹So Moses took the redemption money from those who were over and above those redeemed by the Lē′vītes; ⁵⁰from the first-born of the people of Israel he took the money, one thousand three hundred and sixty-five shekels, reckoned by the shekel of the sanctuary;

^aHeb *their number was*
3.45: Num 3.11-13; 8.18.

⁵¹ and Moses gave the redemption money to Aaron and his sons, according to the word of the LORD, as the LORD commanded Moses.

4 The LORD said to Moses and Aaron, ²"Take a census of the sons of Kō'hăth from among the sons of Lē'vī, by their families and their fathers' houses, ³from thirty years old up to fifty years old, all who can enter the service, to do the work in the tent of meeting. ⁴This is the service of the sons of Kō'hăth in the tent of meeting: the most holy things. ⁵When the camp is to set out, Aaron and his sons shall go in and take down the veil of the screen, and cover the ark of the testimony with it; ⁶then they shall put on it a covering of goatskin, and spread over that a cloth all of blue, and shall put in its poles. ⁷And over the table of the bread of the Presence they shall spread a cloth of blue, and put upon it the plates, the dishes for incense, the bowls, and the flagons for the drink offering; the continual bread also shall be on it; ⁸then they shall spread over them a cloth of scarlet, and cover the same with a covering of goatskin, and shall put in its poles. ⁹And they shall take a cloth of blue, and cover the lampstand for the light, with its lamps, its snuffers, its trays, and all the vessels for oil with which it is supplied: ¹⁰and they shall put it with all its utensils in a covering of goatskin and put it upon the carrying frame. ¹¹And over the golden altar they shall spread a cloth of blue, and cover it with a covering of goatskin, and shall put in its poles; ¹²and they shall take all the vessels of the service which are used in the sanctuary, and put them in a cloth of blue, and cover them with a covering of goatskin, and put them on the carrying frame. ¹³And they shall take away the ashes from the altar, and spread a purple cloth over it; ¹⁴and they shall put on it all the utensils of the altar, which are used for the service there, the firepans, the forks, the shovels, and the basins, all the utensils of the altar; and they shall spread upon it a covering of goatskin, and shall put in its poles. ¹⁵And when Aaron and his sons have finished covering the sanctuary and all the furnishings of the sanctuary, as the camp sets out, after that the sons of Kō'hăth shall come to carry these, but they must not touch the holy things, lest they die. These are the things of the tent of meeting which the sons of Kohath are to carry.

16 "And Ĕl·ē·ā'zạr the son of Aaron the priest shall have charge of the oil for the light, the fragrant incense, the continual cereal offering, and the anointing oil, with the oversight of all the tabernacle and all that is in it, of the sanctuary and its vessels."

17 The LORD said to Moses and Aaron, ¹⁸"Let not the tribe of the families of the Kō'hạ·thītes be destroyed from among the Lē'vītes; ¹⁹but deal thus with them, that they may live and not die when they come near to the most holy things: Aaron and his sons shall go in and appoint them each to his task and to his burden, ²⁰but they shall not go in to look upon the holy things even for a moment, lest they die."

21 The LORD said to Moses, ²²"Take a census of the sons of Gēr'shọn also, by their families and their fathers' houses; ²³from thirty years old up to fifty years old, you shall number them, all who can enter for service, to do the work in the tent of meeting. ²⁴This is the service of the families of the Gēr'shọ·nītes, in serving and bearing burdens: ²⁵they shall carry the curtains of the tabernacle, and the tent of meeting with its covering, and the covering of goatskin that is on top of it, and the screen for the door of the tent of meeting, ²⁶and the hangings of the court, and the screen for the entrance of the gate of the court which is around the tabernacle and the altar, and their cords, and all the equipment for their service; and they shall do all that needs to be done with regard to them. ²⁷All the service of the sons of the Gēr'shọ·nītes shall be at the command of Aaron and his sons, in all that they are to carry, and in all that they have to do; and you shall assign to their charge all that they are to carry. ²⁸This is the service of the families of the sons of the Gēr'shọ·nītes in the tent of meeting, and their work is to be under the oversight of Ĭth'ạ·mär the son of Aaron the priest.

29 "As for the sons of Mẹ·rär'ī, you shall number them by their families and their fathers' houses; ³⁰from thirty years old up to fifty years old,

you shall number them, every one that can enter the service, to do the work of the tent of meeting. ³¹And this is what they are charged to carry, as the whole of their service in the tent of meeting: the frames of the tabernacle, with its bars, pillars, and bases, ³²and the pillars of the court round about with their bases, pegs, and cords, with all their equipment and all their accessories; and you shall assign by name the objects which they are required to carry. ³³This is the service of the families of the sons of Me·râr′ī, the whole of their service in the tent of meeting, under the hand of Ĭth′a·mǎr the son of Aaron the priest."

34 And Moses and Aaron and the leaders of the congregation numbered the sons of the Kō′ha·thītes, by their families and their fathers' houses, ³⁵from thirty years old up to fifty years old, every one that could enter the service, for work in the tent of meeting; ³⁶and their number by families was two thousand seven hundred and fifty. ³⁷This was the number of the families of the Kō′ha·thītes, all who served in the tent of meeting, whom Moses and Aaron numbered according to the commandment of the LORD by Moses.

38 The number of the sons of Gēr′shon, by their families and their fathers' houses, ³⁹from thirty years old up to fifty years old, every one that could enter the service for work in the tent of meeting—⁴⁰their number by their families and their fathers' houses was two thousand six hundred and thirty. ⁴¹This was the number of the families of the sons of Gēr′shon, all who served in the tent of meeting, whom Moses and Aaron numbered according to the commandment of the LORD.

42 The number of the families of the sons of Me·râr′ī, by their families and their fathers' houses, ⁴³from thirty years old up to fifty years old, every one that could enter the service, for work in the tent of meeting—⁴⁴their number by families was three thousand two hundred. ⁴⁵These are those who were numbered of the families of the sons of Me·râr′ī, whom Moses and Aaron numbered according to the commandment of the LORD by Moses.

46 All those who were numbered of the Lē′vītes, whom Moses and Aaron

and the leaders of Israel numbered, by their families and their fathers' houses, ⁴⁷from thirty years old up to fifty years old, every one that could enter to do the work of service and the work of bearing burdens in the tent of meeting, ⁴⁸those who were numbered of them were eight thousand five hundred and eighty. ⁴⁹According to the commandment of the LORD through Moses they were appointed, each to his task of serving or carrying; thus they were numbered by him, as the LORD commanded Moses.

5 The LORD said to Moses, ²"Command the people of Israel that they put out of the camp every leper, and every one having a discharge, and every one that is unclean through contact with the dead; ³you shall put out both male and female, putting them outside the camp, that they may not defile their camp, in the midst of which I dwell." ⁴And the people of Israel did so, and drove them outside the camp; as the LORD said to Moses, so the people of Israel did.

5 And the LORD said to Moses, ⁶"Say to the people of Israel, When a man or woman commits any of the sins that men commit by breaking faith with the LORD, and that person is guilty, ⁷he shall confess his sin which he has committed; and he shall make full restitution for his wrong, adding a fifth to it, and giving it to him to whom he did the wrong. ⁸But if the man has no kinsman to whom restitution may be made for the wrong, the restitution for wrong shall go the LORD for the priest, in addition to the ram of atonement with which atonement is made for him. ⁹And every offering, all the holy things of the people of Israel, which they bring to the priest, shall be his; ¹⁰and every man's holy things shall be his; whatever any man gives to the priest shall be his."

11 And the LORD said to Moses, ¹²"Say to the people of Israel, If any man's wife goes astray and acts unfaithfully against him, ¹³if a man lies with her carnally, and it is hidden from the eyes of her husband, and she is undetected though she has defiled herself, and there is no witness against her, since she was not taken in the act; ¹⁴and if the spirit of jealousy comes

4.34-49: Num 3.15-34.   5.2, 3: Num 12.14, 15. 5.5-8: Ex 22.7-15; Lev 6.1-7.

upon him, and he is jealous of his wife who has defiled herself; or if the spirit of jealousy comes upon him, and he is jealous of his wife, though she has not defiled herself; ¹⁵then the man shall bring his wife to the priest, and bring the offering required of her, a tenth of an ephah of barley meal; he shall pour no oil upon it and put no frankincense on it, for it is a cereal offering of jealousy, a cereal offering of remembrance, bringing iniquity to remembrance.

16 "And the priest shall bring her near, and set her before the Lord; ¹⁷and the priest shall take holy water in an earthen vessel, and take some of the dust that is on the floor of the tabernacle and put it into the water. ¹⁸And the priest shall set the woman before the Lord, and unbind the hair of the woman's head, and place in her hands the cereal offering of remembrance, which is the cereal offering of jealousy. And in his hand the priest shall have the water of bitterness that brings the curse. ¹⁹Then the priest shall make her take an oath, saying, 'If no man has lain with you, and if you have not turned aside to uncleanness, while you were under your husband's authority, be free from this water of bitterness that brings the curse. ²⁰But if you have gone astray, though you are under your husband's authority, and if you have defiled yourself, and some man other than your husband has lain with you, ²¹then' (let the priest make the woman take the oath of the curse, and say to the woman) 'the Lord make you an execration and an oath among your people, when the Lord makes your thigh fall away and your body swell; ²²may this water that brings the curse pass into your bowels and make your body swell and your thigh fall away.' And the woman shall say, 'Amen, Amen.'

23 "Then the priest shall write these curses in a book, and wash them off into the water of bitterness; ²⁴and he shall make the woman drink the water of bitterness that brings the curse, and the water that brings the curse shall enter into her and cause bitter pain. ²⁵And the priest shall take the cereal offering of jealousy out of the woman's hand, and shall wave the cereal offering before the Lord and bring it to the altar; ²⁶and the priest

shall take a handful of the cereal offering, as its memorial portion, and burn it upon the altar, and afterward shall make the woman drink the water. ²⁷And when he has made her drink the water, then, if she has defiled herself and has acted unfaithfully against her husband, the water that brings the curse shall enter into her and cause bitter pain, and her body shall swell, and her thigh shall fall away, and the woman shall become an execration among her people. ²⁸But if the woman has not defiled herself and is clean, then she shall be free and shall conceive children.

29 "This is the law in cases of jealousy, when a wife, though under her husband's authority, goes astray and defiles herself, ³⁰or when the spirit of jealousy comes upon a man and he is jealous of his wife; then he shall set the woman before the Lord, and the priest shall execute upon her all this law. ³¹The man shall be free from iniquity, but the woman shall bear her iniquity."

6 And the Lord said to Moses, ²"Say to the people of Israel, When either a man or a woman makes a special vow, the vow of a Năz′ĭ·rīte,ᵇ to separate himself to the Lord, ³he shall separate himself from wine and strong drink; he shall drink no vinegar made from wine or strong drink, and shall not drink any juice of grapes or eat grapes, fresh or dried. ⁴All the days of his separationᶜ he shall eat nothing that is produced by the grapevine, not even the seeds or the skins.

5 "All the days of his vow of separation no razor shall come upon his head; until the time is completed for which he separates himself to the Lord, he shall be holy; he shall let the locks of hair of his head grow long.

6 "All the days that he separates himself to the Lord he shall not go near a dead body. ⁷Neither for his father nor for his mother, nor for brother or sister, if they die, shall he make himself unclean; because his separation to God is upon his head. ⁸All the days of his separation he is holy to the Lord.

9 "And if any man dies very suddenly beside him, and he defiles his consecrated head, then he shall shave

ᵇThat is *one separated* or *one consecrated*
ᶜOr *Naziriteship* **6.3:** Lk 1.15.

his head on the day of his cleansing; on the seventh day he shall shave it. [10] On the eighth day he shall bring two turtledoves or two young pigeons to the priest to the door of the tent of meeting, [11] and the priest shall offer one for a sin offering and the other for a burnt offering, and make atonement for him, because he sinned by reason of the dead body. And he shall consecrate his head that same day, [12] and separate himself to the LORD for the days of his separation, and bring a male lamb a year old for a guilt offering; but the former time shall be void, because his separation was defiled.

13 "And this is the law for the Năz'ĭ·rīte, when the time of his separation has been completed: he shall be brought to the door of the tent of meeting, [14] and he shall offer his gift to the LORD, one male lamb a year old without blemish for a burnt offering, and one ewe lamb a year old without blemish as a sin offering, and one ram without blemish as a peace offering, [15] and a basket of unleavened bread, cakes of fine flour mixed with oil, and unleavened wafers spread with oil, and their cereal offering and their drink offerings. [16] And the priest shall present them before the LORD and offer his sin offering and his burnt offering, [17] and he shall offer the ram as a sacrifice of peace offering to the LORD, with the basket of unleavened bread; the priest shall offer also its cereal offering and its drink offering. [18] And the Năz'ĭ·rīte shall shave his consecrated head at the door of the tent of meeting, and shall take the hair from his consecrated head and put it on the fire which is under the sacrifice of the peace offering. [19] And the priest shall take the shoulder of the ram, when it is boiled, and one unleavened cake out of the basket, and one unleavened wafer, and shall put them upon the hands of the Năz'ĭ·rīte, after he has shaven the hair of his consecration, [20] and the priest shall wave them for a wave offering before the LORD; they are a holy portion for the priest, together with the breast that is waved and the thigh that is offered; and after that the Năz'ĭ·rīte may drink wine.

21 "This is the law for the Năz'ĭ·rīte who takes a vow. His offering to the

LORD shall be according to his vow as a Nazirite, apart from what else he can afford; in accordance with the vow which he takes, so shall he do according to the law for his separation as a Nazirite."

22 The LORD said to Moses, [23] "Say to Aaron and his sons, Thus you shall bless the people of Israel: you shall say to them,
[24] The LORD bless you and keep you:
[25] The LORD make his face to shine upon you, and be gracious to you:
[26] The LORD lift up his countenance upon you, and give you peace.
27 "So shall they put my name upon the people of Israel, and I will bless them."

7 On the day when Moses had finished setting up the tabernacle, and had anointed and consecrated it with all its furnishings, and had anointed and consecrated the altar with all its utensils, [2] the leaders of Israel, heads of their fathers' houses, the leaders of the tribes, who were over those who were numbered, [3] offered and brought their offerings before the LORD, six covered wagons and twelve oxen, a wagon for every two of the leaders, and for each one an ox; they offered them before the tabernacle. [4] Then the LORD said to Moses, [5] "Accept these from them, that they may be used in doing the service of the tent of meeting, and give them to the Lē'vītes, to each man according to his service." [6] So Moses took the wagons and the oxen, and gave them to the Lē'vītes. [7] Two wagons and four oxen he gave to the sons of Gēr'shon, according to their service; [8] and four wagons and eight oxen he gave to the sons of Me·râr'ī, according to their service, under the direction of Ĭth'·a·mär the son of Aaron the priest. [9] But to the sons of Kō'hăth he gave none, because they were charged with the care of the holy things which had to be carried on the shoulder. [10] And the leaders offered offerings for the dedication of the altar on the day it was anointed; and the leaders offered their offering before the altar. [11] And the LORD said to Moses, "They shall offer their offerings, one leader each day, for the dedication of the altar."

12 He who offered his offering the first day was Näh'shon the son of

6.13-21: Acts 21.24, 26.

Ăm·mĭn′a·dăb, of the tribe of Judah; [13] and his offering was one silver plate whose weight was a hundred and thirty shekels, one silver basin of seventy shekels, according to the shekel of the sanctuary, both of them full of fine flour mixed with oil for a cereal offering; [14] one golden dish of ten shekels, full of incense; [15] one young bull, one ram, one male lamb a year old, for a burnt offering; [16] one male goat for a sin offering; [17] and for the sacrifice of peace offerings, two oxen, five rams, five male goats, and five male lambs a year old. This was the offering of Näh′shọn the son of Ăm·mĭn′a·dăb.

18 On the second day Nẹ·thăn′ĕl the son of Zü′ar, the leader of Ĭs′-sa·chär, made an offering; [19] he offered for his offering one silver plate, whose weight was a hundred and thirty shekels, one silver basin of seventy shekels, according to the shekel of the sanctuary, both of them full of fine flour mixed with oil for a cereal offering; [20] one golden dish of ten shekels, full of incense; [21] one young bull, one ram, one male lamb a year old, for a burnt offering; [22] one male goat for a sin offering; [23] and for the sacrifice of peace offerings, two oxen, five rams, five male goats, and five male lambs a year old. This was the offering of Nẹ·thăn′ĕl the son of Zü′ar.

24 On the third day Ĕ·lī′ăb the son of Hē′lŏn, the leader of the men of Zĕb′ū·lụn: [25] his offering was one silver plate, whose weight was a hundred and thirty shekels, one silver basin of seventy shekels, according to the shekel of the sanctuary, both of them full of fine flour mixed with oil for a cereal offering; [26] one golden dish of ten shekels, full of incense; [27] one young bull, one ram, one male lamb a year old, for a burnt offering; [28] one male goat for a sin offering; [29] and for the sacrifice of peace offerings, two oxen, five rams, five male goats, and five male lambs a year old. This was the offering of Ĕ·lī′ăb the son of Hē′lŏn.

30 On the fourth day Ĕ·lī′zŭr the son of Shĕd′ē·ụr, the leader of the men of Reuben: [31] his offering was one silver plate whose weight was a hundred and thirty shekels, one silver basin of seventy shekels, according to the

shekel of the sanctuary, both of them full of fine flour mixed with oil for a cereal offering; [32] one golden dish of ten shekels, full of incense; [33] one young bull, one ram, one male lamb a year old, for a burnt offering; [34] one male goat for a sin offering; [35] and for the sacrifice of peace offerings, two oxen, five rams, five male goats, and five male lambs a year old. This was the offering of Ĕ·lī′zŭr the son of Shĕd′ē·ụr.

36 On the fifth day Shĕ·lü′mĭ–ĕl the son of Zü·rī·shăd′daī, the leader of the men of Sĭm′ē·ọn: [37] his offering was one silver plate, whose weight was a hundred and thirty shekels, one silver basin of seventy shekels, according to the shekel of the sanctuary, both of them full of fine flour mixed with oil for a cereal offering; [38] one golden dish of ten shekels, full of incense; [39] one young bull, one ram, one male lamb a year old, for a burnt offering; [40] one male goat for a sin offering; [41] and for the sacrifice of peace offerings, two oxen, five rams, five male goats, and five male lambs a year old. This was the offering of Shĕ·lü′mĭ–ĕl the son of Zü·rī·shăd′daī.

42 On the sixth day Ĕ·lī′a·săph the son of Deü′ĕl, the leader of the men of Gåd: [43] his offering was one silver plate, whose weight was a hundred and thirty shekels, one silver basin of seventy shekels, according to the shekel of the sanctuary, both of them full of fine flour mixed with oil for a cereal offering; [44] one golden dish of ten shekels, full of incense; [45] one young bull, one ram, one male lamb a year old, for a burnt offering; [46] one male goat for a sin offering; [47] and for the sacrifice of peace offerings, two oxen, five rams, five male goats, and five male lambs a year old. This was the offering of Ĕ·lī′a·săph the son of Deü′ĕl.

48 On the seventh day Ĕ·lĭsh′a·ma the son of Ăm·mī′hụd, the leader of the men of Ē′phra·ĭm: [49] his offering was one silver plate, whose weight was a hundred and thirty shekels, one silver basin of seventy shekels, according to the shekel of the sanctuary, both of them full of fine flour mixed with oil for a cereal offering; [50] one golden dish of ten shekels, full of incense; [51] one young bull, one ram, one male lamb a year old, for a burnt offering;

⁵²one male goat for a sin offering; ⁵³and for the sacrifice of peace offerings, two oxen, five rams, five male goats, and five male lambs a year old. This was the offering of Ĕ·lī́sh′ȧ·mȧ the son of Ăm·mī́′hŭd.

54 On the eighth day Gȧ·mā′lĭ·ĕl the son of Pĕ·däh′zŭr, the leader of the men of Mȧ·näs′seh: ⁵⁵his offering was one silver plate, whose weight was a hundred and thirty shekels, one silver basin of seventy shekels, according to the shekel of the sanctuary, both of them full of fine flour mixed with oil for a cereal offering; ⁵⁶one golden dish of ten shekels, full of incense; ⁵⁷one young bull, one ram, one male lamb a year old, for a burnt offering; ⁵⁸one male goat for a sin offering; ⁵⁹and for the sacrifice of peace offerings, two oxen, five rams, five male goats, and five male lambs a year old. This was the offering of Gȧ·mā′lĭ·ĕl the son of Pĕ·däh′zŭr.

60 On the ninth day Ȧ·bī′dȧn the son of Gĭd·ē·ō′nī, the leader of the men of Benjamin: ⁶¹his offering was one silver plate, whose weight was a hundred and thirty shekels, one silver basin of seventy shekels, according to the shekel of the sanctuary, both of them full of fine flour mixed with oil for a cereal offering; ⁶²one golden dish of ten shekels, full of incense; ⁶³one young bull, one ram, one male lamb a year old, for a burnt offering; ⁶⁴one male goat for a sin offering; ⁶⁵and for the sacrifice of peace offerings, two oxen, five rams, five male goats, and five male lambs a year old. This was the offering of Ȧ·bī′dȧn the son of Gĭd·ē·ō′nī.

66 On the tenth day Ā·hī·ē′zẽr the son of Ăm·mĭ·shăd′daī, the leader of the men of Dan: ⁶⁷his offering was one silver plate, whose weight was a hundred and thirty shekels, one silver basin of seventy shekels, according to the shekel of the sanctuary, both of them full of fine flour mixed with oil for a cereal offering; ⁶⁸one golden dish of ten shekels, full of incense; ⁶⁹one young bull, one ram, one male lamb a year old, for a burnt offering; ⁷⁰one male goat for a sin offering; ⁷¹and for the sacrifice of peace offerings, two oxen, five rams, five male goats, and five male lambs a year old. This was the offering of Ā·hī·ē′zẽr the son of Ăm·mĭ·shăd′daī.

72 On the eleventh day Pā′gĭ·ĕl the son of Ŏch′rȧn, the leader of the men of Ăsh′ẽr: ⁷³his offering was one silver plate, whose weight was a hundred and thirty shekels, one silver basin of seventy shekels, according to the shekel of the sanctuary, both of them full of fine flour mixed with oil for a cereal offering; ⁷⁴one golden dish of ten shekels, full of incense; ⁷⁵one young bull, one ram, one male lamb a year old, for a burnt offering; ⁷⁶one male goat for a sin offering; ⁷⁷and for the sacrifice of peace offerings, two oxen, five rams, five male goats, and five male lambs a year old. This was the offering of Pā′gĭ·ĕl the son of Ŏch′rȧn.

78 On the twelfth day Ȧ·hī′rȧ the son of Ē′năn, the leader of the men of Năph′tȧ·lī: ⁷⁹his offering was one silver plate, whose weight was a hundred and thirty shekels, one silver basin of seventy shekels, according to the shekel of the sanctuary, both of them full of fine flour mixed with oil for a cereal offering; ⁸⁰one golden dish of ten shekels, full of incense; ⁸¹one young bull, one ram, one male lamb a year old, for a burnt offering; ⁸²one male goat for a sin offering; ⁸³and for the sacrifice of peace offerings, two oxen, five rams, five male goats, and five male lambs a year old. This was the offering of Ȧ·hī′rȧ the son of Ē′năn.

84 This was the dedication offering for the altar, on the day when it was anointed, from the leaders of Israel: twelve silver plates, twelve silver basins, twelve golden dishes, ⁸⁵each silver plate weighing a hundred and thirty shekels and each basin seventy, all the silver of the vessels two thousand four hundred shekels according to the shekel of the sanctuary, ⁸⁶the twelve golden dishes, full of incense, weighing ten shekels apiece according to the shekel of the sanctuary, all the gold of the dishes being a hundred and twenty shekels; ⁸⁷all the cattle for the burnt offering twelve bulls, twelve rams, twelve male lambs a year old, with their cereal offering; and twelve male goats for a sin offering; ⁸⁸and all the cattle for the sacrifice of peace offerings twenty-four bulls, the rams sixty, the male goats sixty, the male lambs a year old sixty. This was the dedication offering for the altar, after it was anointed.

89 And when Moses went into the tent of meeting to speak with the Lord, he heard the voice speaking to him from above the mercy seat that was upon the ark of the testimony, from between the two cherubim; and it spoke to him.

8 Now the Lord said to Moses, 2 "Say to Aaron, When you set up the lamps, the seven lamps shall give light in front of the lampstand." ³And Aaron did so; he set up its lamps to give light in front of the lampstand, as the Lord commanded Moses. ⁴And this was the workmanship of the lampstand, hammered work of gold; from its base to its flowers, it was hammered work; according to the pattern which the Lord had shown Moses, so he made the lampstand.

5 And the Lord said to Moses, 6 "Take the Lē'vītes from among the people of Israel, and cleanse them. ⁷And thus you shall do to them, to cleanse them: sprinkle the water of expiation upon them, and let them go with a razor over all their body, and wash their clothes and cleanse themselves. ⁸Then let them take a young bull and its cereal offering of fine flour mixed with oil, and you shall take another young bull for a sin offering. ⁹And you shall present the Lē'vītes before the tent of meeting, and assemble the whole congregation of the people of Israel. ¹⁰When you present the Lē'-vītes before the Lord, the people of Israel shall lay their hands upon the Levites, ¹¹and Aaron shall offer the Lē'vītes before the Lord as a wave offering from the people of Israel, that it may be theirs to do the service of the Lord. ¹²Then the Lē'vītes shall lay their hands upon the heads of the bulls; and you shall offer the one for a sin offering and the other for a burnt offering to the Lord, to make atonement for the Levites. ¹³And you shall cause the Lē'vītes to attend Aaron and his sons, and shall offer them as a wave offering to the Lord.

14 "Thus you shall scparate the Lē'vītes from among the people of Israel, and the Levites shall be mine. ¹⁵And after that the Lē'vītes shall go in to do service at the tent of meeting, when you have cleansed them and offered them as a wave offering. ¹⁶For they are wholly given to me from among the people of Israel; instead of all that open the womb, the first-born of all the people of Israel, I have taken them for myself. ¹⁷For all the first-born among the people of Israel are mine, both of man and of beast; on the day that I slew all the first-born in the land of Egypt I consecrated them for myself, ¹⁸and I have taken the Lē'vītes instead of all the first-born among the people of Israel. ¹⁹And I have given the Lē'vītes as a gift to Aaron and his sons from among the people of Israel, to do the service for the people of Israel at the tent of meeting, and to make atonement for the people of Israel, that there may be no plague among the people of Israel in case the people of Israel should come near the sanctuary."

20 Thus did Moses and Aaron and all the congregation of the people of Israel to the Lē'vītes; according to all that the Lord commanded Moses concerning the Levites, the people of Israel did to them. ²¹And the Lē'vītes purified themselves from sin, and washed their clothes; and Aaron offered them as a wave offering before the Lord, and Aaron made atonement for them to cleanse them. ²²And after that the Lē'vītes went in to do their service in the tent of meeting in attendance upon Aaron and his sons; as the Lord had commanded Moses concerning the Levites, so they did to them.

23 And the Lord said to Moses, 24 "This is what pertains to the Lē'vītes: from twenty-five years old and upward they shall go in to perform the work in the service of the tent of meeting; ²⁵and from the age of fifty years they shall withdraw from the work of the service and serve no more, ²⁶but minister to their brethren in the tent of meeting, to keep the charge, and they shall do no service. Thus shall you do to the Lē'vītes in assigning their duties."

9 And the Lord spoke to Moses in the wilderness of Sinai, in the first month of the second year after they had come out of the land of Egypt, saying, 2 "Let the people of Israel keep the passover at its appointed time. ³On the fourteenth day of this month, in the evening, you shall keep it at its appointed time; according to all its

8.6-26: Num 3.5-13.   8.18: Num 3.11-13, 45.
9.1-5: Ex 12.1-14, 21-28.

statutes and all its ordinances you shall keep it." [4]So Moses told the people of Israel that they should keep the passover. [5]And they kept the passover in the first month, on the fourteenth day of the month, in the evening, in the wilderness of Sinai; according to all that the LORD commanded Moses, so the people of Israel did. [6]And there were certain men who were unclean through touching the dead body of a man, so that they could not keep the passover on that day; and they came before Moses and Aaron on that day; [7]and those men said to him, "We are unclean through touching the dead body of a man; why are we kept from offering the LORD's offering at its appointed time among the people of Israel?" [8]And Moses said to them, "Wait, that I may hear what the LORD will command concerning you."

9 The LORD said to Moses, [10]"Say to the people of Israel, If any man of you or of your descendants is unclean through touching a dead body, or is afar off on a journey, he shall still keep the passover to the LORD. [11]In the second month on the fourteenth day in the evening they shall keep it; they shall eat it with unleavened bread and bitter herbs. [12]They shall leave none of it until the morning, nor break a bone of it; according to all the statute for the passover they shall keep it. [13]But the man who is clean and is not on a journey, yet refrains from keeping the passover, that person shall be cut off from his people, because he did not offer the LORD's offering at its appointed time; that man shall bear his sin. [14]And if a stranger sojourns among you, and will keep the passover to the LORD, according to the statute of the passover and according to its ordinance, so shall he do; you shall have one statute, both for the sojourner and for the native."

15 On the day that the tabernacle was set up, the cloud covered the tabernacle, the tent of the testimony; and at evening it was over the tabernacle like the appearance of fire until morning. [16]So it was continually; the cloud covered it by day,[d] and the appearance of fire by night. [17]And whenever the cloud was taken up from over the tent, after that the people of Israel set out; and in the place where the cloud settled down, there the people

of Israel encamped. [18]At the command of the LORD the people of Israel set out, and at the command of the LORD they encamped; as long as the cloud rested over the tabernacle, they remained in camp. [19]Even when the cloud continued over the tabernacle many days, the people of Israel kept the charge of the LORD, and did not set out. [20]Sometimes the cloud was a few days over the tabernacle, and according to the command of the LORD they remained in camp; then according to the command of the LORD they set out. [21]And sometimes the cloud remained from evening until morning; and when the cloud was taken up in the morning, they set out, or if it continued for a day and a night, when the cloud was taken up they set out. [22]Whether it was two days, or a month, or a longer time, that the cloud continued over the tabernacle, abiding there, the people of Israel remained in camp and did not set out; but when it was taken up they set out. [23]At the command of the LORD they encamped, and at the command of the LORD they set out; they kept the charge of the LORD, at the command of the LORD by Moses.

10 The LORD said to Moses, [2]"Make two silver trumpets; of hammered work you shall make them; and you shall use them for summoning the congregation, and for breaking camp. [3]And when both are blown, all the congregation shall gather themselves to you at the entrance of the tent of meeting. [4]But if they blow only one, then the leaders, the heads of the tribes of Israel, shall gather themselves to you. [5]When you blow an alarm, the camps that are on the east side shall set out. [6]And when you blow an alarm the second time, the camps that are on the south side shall set out. An alarm is to be blown whenever they are to set out. [7]But when the assembly is to be gathered together, you shall blow, but you shall not sound an alarm. [8]And the sons of Aaron, the priests, shall blow the trumpets. The trumpets shall be to you for a perpetual statute throughout your generations. [9]And when you go to war in your land against the adversary who oppresses you, then you shall sound an alarm with the trumpets, that you may be

[d]Gk Syr Vg: Heb lacks *by day*
9.12: Ex 12.46; Jn 19.36.   9.15-23: Ex 40.36-38.

remembered before the LORD your God, and you shall be saved from your enemies. ¹⁰ On the day of your gladness also, and at your appointed feasts, and at the beginnings of your months, you shall blow the trumpets over your burnt offerings and over the sacrifices of your peace offerings; they shall serve you for remembrance before your God; I am the LORD your God."

11 In the second year, in the second month, on the twentieth day of the month, the cloud was taken up from over the tabernacle of the testimony, ¹² and the people of Israel set out by stages from the wilderness of Sinai; and the cloud settled down in the wilderness of Pär'ăn. ¹³ They set out for the first time at the command of the LORD by Moses. ¹⁴ The standard of the camp of the men of Judah set out first by their companies; and over their host was Näh'shọn the son of Ăm-mĭn'ạ·dăb. ¹⁵ And over the host of the tribe of the men of Ĭs'sạ·chär was Nẹ·thăn'ĕl the son of Zü'ạr. ¹⁶ And over the host of the tribe of the men of Zĕb'-ū·lụn was Ē·lī'ăb the son of Hē'lŏn.

17 And when the tabernacle was taken down, the sons of Gẽr'shọn and the sons of Mẹ·râr'ī, who carried the tabernacle, set out. ¹⁸ And the standard of the camp of Reuben set out by their companies; and over their host was Ē·lī'zŭr the son of Shĕd'ē·ụr. ¹⁹ And over the host of the tribe of the men of Sĭm'ē·ọn was Shē·lü'mĭ–ĕl the son of Zü·rĭ·shăd'daī. ²⁰ And over the host of the tribe of the men of Gàd was Ē·lī'-ạ·sàph the son of Deü'ĕl.

21 Then the Kō'hạ·thītes set out, carrying the holy things, and the tabernacle was set up before their arrival. ²² And the standard of the camp of the men of Ē'phrạ·ĭm set out by their companies; and over their host was Ē·lĭsh'ạ·mạ the son of Ăm·mī'hụd. ²³ And over the host of the tribe of the men of Mạ·năs'sẹh was Gạ·mā'lĭ·ĕl the son of Pẹ·däh'zụr. ²⁴ And over the host of the tribe of the men of Benjamin was Ạ·bī'dạn the son of Gĭd·ē·ō'nī.

25 Then the standard of the camp of the men of Dan, acting as the rear guard of all the camps, set out by their companies; and over their host was Ā·hī·ē'zẹr the son of Ăm·mĭ·shăd'daī. ²⁶ And over the host of the tribe of the men of Ăsh'ẹr was Pā'gĭ·ĕl the son of Ōch'rạn. ²⁷ And over the host of the

tribe of the men of Năph'tạ·lī was Ạ·hī'rạ the son of Ē'năn. ²⁸ This was the order of march of the people of Israel according to their hosts, when they set out.

29 And Moses said to Hō'băb the son of Reü'ĕl the Mĭd'ĭ·ạ·nīte, Moses' father-in-law, "We are setting out for the place of which the LORD said, 'I will give it to you'; come with us, and we will do you good; for the LORD has promised good to Israel." ³⁰ But he said to him, "I will not go; I will depart to my own land and to my kindred." ³¹ And he said, "Do not leave us, I pray you, for you know how we are to encamp in the wilderness, and you will serve as eyes for us. ³² And if you go with us, whatever good the LORD will do to us, the same will we do to you."

33 So they set out from the mount of the LORD three days' journey; and the ark of the covenant of the LORD went before them three days' journey, to seek out a resting place for them. ³⁴ And the cloud of the LORD was over them by day, whenever they set out from the camp.

35 And whenever the ark set out, Moses said, "Arise, O LORD, and let thy enemies be scattered; and let them that hate thee flee before thee." ³⁶ And when it rested, he said, "Return, O LORD, to the ten thousand thousands of Israel."

11 And the people complained in the hearing of the LORD about their misfortunes; and when the LORD heard it, his anger was kindled, and the fire of the LORD burned among them, and consumed some outlying parts of the camp. ² Then the people cried to Moses; and Moses prayed to the LORD, and the fire abated. ³ So the name of that place was called Tăb'ẹ·rạh,ᵉ because the fire of the LORD burned among them.

4 Now the rabble that was among them had a strong craving; and the people of Israel also wept again, and said, "O that we had meat to eat! ⁵ We remember the fish we ate in Egypt for nothing, the cucumbers, the melons, the leeks, the onions, and the garlic; ⁶ but now our strength is dried up, and there is nothing at all but this manna to look at."

7 Now the manna was like coriander seed, and its appearance like that

ᵉ That is *Burning* **10.35:** Ps 68.1, 2. **11.4:** 1 Cor 10.6.

of bdellium. ⁸The people went about and gathered it, and ground it in mills or beat it in mortars, and boiled it in pots, and made cakes of it; and the taste of it was like the taste of cakes baked with oil. ⁹When the dew fell upon the camp in the night, the manna fell with it.

10 Moses heard the people weeping throughout their families, every man at the door of his tent; and the anger of the LORD blazed hotly, and Moses was displeased. ¹¹Moses said to the LORD, "Why hast thou dealt ill with thy servant? And why have I not found favor in thy sight, that thou dost lay the burden of all this people upon me? ¹²Did I conceive all this people? Did I bring them forth, that thou shouldst say to me, 'Carry them in your bosom,' as a nurse carries the sucking child, to the land which thou didst swear to give their fathers? ¹³Where am I to get meat to give to all this people? For they weep before me and say, 'Give us meat, that we may eat.' ¹⁴I am not able to carry all this people alone, the burden is too heavy for me. ¹⁵If thou wilt deal thus with me, kill me at once, if I find favor in thy sight, that I may not see my wretchedness."

16 And the LORD said to Moses, "Gather for me seventy men of the elders of Israel, whom you know to be the elders of the people and officers over them; and bring them to the tent of meeting, and let them take their stand there with you. ¹⁷And I will come down and talk with you there; and I will take some of the spirit which is upon you and put it upon them; and they shall bear the burden of the people with you, that you may not bear it yourself alone. ¹⁸And say to the people, 'Consecrate yourselves for tomorrow, and you shall eat meat; for you have wept in the hearing of the LORD, saying, "Who will give us meat to eat?" For it was well with us in Egypt." Therefore the LORD will give you meat, and you shall eat. ¹⁹You shall not eat one day, or two days, or five days, or ten days, or twenty days, ²⁰but a whole month, until it comes out at your nostrils and becomes loathsome to you, because you have rejected the LORD who is among you, and have wept before him, saying, "Why did we come forth out of Egypt?" ' " ²¹But Moses said, "The people among whom I am number six hundred thousand on foot; and thou hast said, 'I will give them meat, that they may eat a whole month!' ²²Shall flocks and herds be slaughtered for them, to suffice them? Or shall all the fish of the sea be gathered together for them, to suffice them?" ²³And the LORD said to Moses, "Is the LORD's hand shortened? Now you shall see whether my word will come true for you or not."

24 So Moses went out and told the people the words of the LORD; and he gathered seventy men of the elders of the people, and placed them round about the tent. ²⁵Then the LORD came down in the cloud and spoke to him, and took some of the spirit that was upon him and put it upon the seventy elders; and when the spirit rested upon them, they prophesied. But they did so no more.

26 Now two men remained in the camp, one named Ĕl′dăd, and the other named Mē′dăd, and the spirit rested upon them; they were among those registered, but they had not gone out to the tent, and so they prophesied in the camp. ²⁷And a young man ran and told Moses, "Ĕl′dăd and Mē′dăd are prophesying in the camp." ²⁸And Joshua the son of Nŭn, the minister of Moses, one of his chosen men, said, "My lord Moses, forbid them." ²⁹But Moses said to him, "Are you jealous for my sake? Would that all the LORD's people were prophets, that the LORD would put his spirit upon them!" ³⁰And Moses and the elders of Israel returned to the camp.

31 And there went forth a wind from the LORD, and it brought quails from the sea, and let them fall beside the camp, about a day's journey on this side and a day's journey on the other side, round about the camp, and about two cubits above the face of the earth. ³²And the people rose all that day, and all night, and all the next day, and gathered the quails; he who gathered least gathered ten homers; and they spread them out for themselves all around the camp. ³³While the meat was yet between their teeth, before it was consumed, the anger of the LORD was kindled against the people, and the LORD smote the people with a very great plague. ³⁴Therefore the name of that place was called Kĭb′rŏth–hăt-

11.34: 1 Cor 10.6.

tā′a·vah,ʃ because there they buried the people who had the craving. [35] From Kĭb′rŏth–hăt·tā′a·vah the people journeyed to Hă·zē′rŏth; and they remained at Hazeroth.

12 Miriam and Aaron spoke against Moses because of the Cü′shīte woman whom he had married, for he had married a Cushite woman; [2] and they said, "Has the LORD indeed spoken only through Moses? Has he not spoken through us also?" And the LORD heard it. [3] Now the man Moses was very meek, more than all men that were on the face of the earth. [4] And suddenly the LORD said to Moses and to Aaron and Miriam, "Come out, you three, to the tent of meeting." And the three of them came out. [5] And the LORD came down in a pillar of cloud, and stood at the door of the tent, and called Aaron and Miriam; and they both came forward. [6] And he said, "Hear my words: If there is a prophet among you, I the LORD make myself known to him in a vision, I speak with him in a dream. [7] Not so with my servant Moses; he is entrusted with all my house. [8] With him I speak mouth to mouth, clearly, and not in dark speech; and he beholds the form of the LORD. Why then were you not afraid to speak against my servant Moses?"

9 And the anger of the LORD was kindled against them, and he departed; [10] and when the cloud removed from over the tent, behold, Miriam was leprous, as white as snow. And Aaron turned towards Miriam, and behold, she was leprous. [11] And Aaron said to Moses, "Oh, my lord, do not[g] punish us because we have done foolishly and have sinned. [12] Let her not be as one dead, of whom the flesh is half consumed when he comes out of his mother's womb." [13] And Moses cried to the LORD, "Heal her, O God, I beseech thee." [14] But the LORD said to Moses, "If her father had but spit in her face, should she not be shamed seven days? Let her be shut up outside the camp seven days, and after that she may be brought in again." [15] So Miriam was shut up outside the camp seven days; and the people did not set out on the march till Miriam was brought in again. [16] After that the people set out from Hă·zē′rŏth, and encamped in the wilderness of Pâr′ăn.

13 The LORD said to Moses, [2] "Send men to spy out the land of Canaan, which I give to the people of Israel; from each tribe of their fathers shall you send a man, every one a leader among them." [3] So Moses sent them from the wilderness of Pâr′ăn, according to the command of the LORD, all of them men who were heads of the people of Israel. [4] And these were their names: From the tribe of Reuben, Shăm′mū–a the son of Zăc′cür; [5] from the tribe of Sĭm′-ē·on, Shā′phat the son of Hō′rī; [6] from the tribe of Judah, Caleb the son of Je·phün′neh; [7] from the tribe of Ĭs′-sa·chär, Ī′găl the son of Joseph; [8] from the tribe of Ē′phra·ĭm, Hō·shē′a the son of Nŭn; [9] from the tribe of Benjamin, Păl′tī the son of Rā′phū; [10] from the tribe of Zĕb′ū·lun, Găd′dĭ·ĕl the son of Sō′dī; [11] from the tribe of Joseph (that is from the tribe of Ma·năs′seh), Găd′dī the son of Sü′sī; [12] from the tribe of Dan, Ăm′mĭ–ĕl the son of Ge·măl′lī; [13] from the tribe of Ăsh′er, Sĕth′ur the son of Michael; [14] from the tribe of Năph′ta·lī, Năh′bī the son of Vŏph′sī; [15] from the tribe of Găd, Ge·ū′ĕl the son of Mā′chī. [16] These were the names of the men whom Moses sent to spy out the land. And Moses called Hō′shē·a the son of Nŭn Joshua.

17 Moses sent them to spy out the land of Canaan, and said to them, "Go up into the Nĕg′ĕb yonder, and go up into the hill country, [18] and see what the land is, and whether the people who dwell in it are strong or weak, whether they are few or many, [19] and whether the land that they dwell in is good or bad, and whether the cities that they dwell in are camps or strongholds, [20] and whether the land is rich or poor, and whether there is wood in it or not. Be of good courage, and bring some of the fruit of the land." Now the time was the season of the first ripe grapes.

21 So they went up and spied out the land from the wilderness of Zĭn to Rĕ′hŏb, near the entrance of Hă′-măth. [22] They went up into the Nĕg′ĕb, and came to Hē′bron; and A·hī′man, Shē′shaī, and Tăl′maī, the descendants of Ā′năk, were there. (Hebron was built seven years before Zō′an in Egypt.) [23] And they came to the

Valley of Ĕsh'cọl, and cut down from there a branch with a single cluster of grapes, and they carried it on a pole between two of them; they brought also some pomegranates and figs. 24 That place was called the Valley of Ĕsh'cọl,ʰ because of the cluster which the men of Israel cut down from there.

25 At the end of forty days they returned from spying out the land. 26 And they came to Moses and Aaron and to all the congregation of the people of Israel in the wilderness of Pār'ăn, at Kā'dĕsh; they brought back word to them and to all the congregation, and showed them the fruit of the land. 27 And they told him, "We came to the land to which you sent us; it flows with milk and honey, and this is its fruit. 28 Yet the people who dwell in the land are strong, and the cities are fortified and very large; and besides, we saw the descendants of Ā'năk there. 29 The A·măl'ẹ·kītes dwell in the land of the Nĕg'ĕb; the Hīt'tītes, the Jĕb'ū·sītes, and the Ăm'ọ·rītes dwell in the hill country; and the Canaanites dwell by the sea, and along the Jordan."

30 But Caleb quieted the people before Moses, and said, "Let us go up at once, and occupy it; for we are well able to overcome it." 31 Then the men who had gone up with him said, "We are not able to go up against the people; for they are stronger than we." 32 So they brought to the people of Israel an evil report of the land which they had spied out, saying, "The land, through which we have gone, to spy it out, is a land that devours its inhabitants; and all the people that we saw in it are men of great stature. 33 And there we saw the Nĕph'ĭ·lĭm (the sons of Ā'năk, who come from the Nephilim); and we seemed to ourselves like grasshoppers, and so we seemed to them."

14 Then all the congregation raised a loud cry; and the people wept that night. 2 And all the people of Israel murmured against Moses and Aaron; the whole congregation said to them, "Would that we had died in the land of Egypt! Or would that we had died in this wilderness! 3 Why does the LORD bring us into this land, to fall by the sword? Our wives and our little ones will become a prey; would it not be better for us to go back to Egypt?" 4 And they said to one another, "Let

us choose a captain, and go back to Egypt." 5 Then Moses and Aaron fell on their faces before all the assembly of the congregation of the people of Israel. 6 And Joshua the son of Nŭn and Caleb the son of Jẹ·phün'nẹh, who were among those who had spied out the land, rent their clothes, 7 and said to all the congregation of the people of Israel, "The land, which we passed through to spy it out, is an exceedingly good land. 8 If the LORD delights in us, he will bring us into this land and give it to us, a land which flows with milk and honey. 9 Only, do not rebel against the LORD; and do not fear the people of the land, for they are bread for us; their protection is removed from them, and the LORD is with us; do not fear them." 10 But all the congregation said to stone them with stones.

Then the glory of the LORD appeared at the tent of meeting to all the people of Israel. 11 And the LORD said to Moses, "How long will this people despise me? And how long will they not believe in me, in spite of all the signs which I have wrought among them? 12 I will strike them with the pestilence and disinherit them, and I will make of you a nation greater and mightier than they."

13 But Moses said to the LORD, "Then the Egyptians will hear of it, for thou didst bring up this people in thy might from among them, 14 and they will tell the inhabitants of this land. They have heard that thou, O LORD, art in the midst of this people; for thou, O LORD, art seen face to face, and thy cloud stands over them and thou goest before them, in a pillar of cloud by day and in a pillar of fire by night. 15 Now if thou dost kill this people as one man, then the nations who have heard thy fame will say, 16 'Because the LORD was not able to bring this people into the land which he swore to give to them, therefore he has slain them in the wilderness.' 17 And now, I pray thee, let the power of the LORD be great as thou hast promised, saying, 18 'The LORD is slow to anger, and abounding in steadfast love, forgiving iniquity and transgression, but he will by no means clear the guilty, visiting the

ʰThat is *Cluster*
13.33: Gen 6.4. 14.3: Acts 7.39.
14.11-25: Ex 32.9-14, 31-35.

iniquity of fathers upon children, upon the third and upon the fourth generation.' ¹⁹Pardon the iniquity of this people, I pray thee, according to the greatness of thy steadfast love, and according as thou hast forgiven this people, from Egypt even until now."

20 Then the LORD said, "I have pardoned, according to your word; ²¹but truly, as I live, and as all the earth shall be filled with the glory of the LORD, ²²none of the men who have seen my glory and my signs which I wrought in Egypt and in the wilderness, and yet have put me to the proof these ten times and have not hearkened to my voice, ²³shall see the land which I swore to give to their fathers; and none of those who despised me shall see it. ²⁴But my servant Caleb, because he has a different spirit and has followed me fully, I will bring into the land into which he went, and his descendants shall possess it. ²⁵Now, since the A·măl′e·kītes and the Canaanites dwell in the valleys, turn tomorrow and set out for the wilderness by the way to the Red Sea."

26 And the LORD said to Moses and to Aaron, ²⁷"How long shall this wicked congregation murmur against me? I have heard the murmurings of the people of Israel, which they murmur against me. ²⁸Say to them, 'As I live,' says the LORD, 'what you have said in my hearing I will do to you: ²⁹your dead bodies shall fall in this wilderness; and of all your number, numbered from twenty years old and upward, who have murmured against me, ³⁰not one shall come into the land where I swore that I would make you dwell, except Caleb the son of Je·phŭn′neh and Joshua the son of Nŭn. ³¹But your little ones, who you said would become a prey, I will bring in, and they shall know the land which you have despised. ³²But as for you, your dead bodies shall fall in this wilderness. ³³And your children shall be shepherds in the wilderness forty years, and shall suffer for your faithlessness, until the last of your dead bodies lies in the wilderness. ³⁴According to the number of the days in which you spied out the land, forty days, for every day a year, you shall bear your iniquity, forty years, and you shall know my displeasure.' ³⁵I, the LORD,

have spoken; surely this will I do to all this wicked congregation that are gathered together against me: in this wilderness they shall come to a full end, and there they shall die."

36 And the men whom Moses sent to spy out the land, and who returned and made all the congregation to murmur against him by bringing up an evil report against the land, ³⁷the men who brought up an evil report of the land, died by plague before the LORD. ³⁸But Joshua the son of Nŭn and Caleb the son of Je·phŭn′neh remained alive, of those men who went to spy out the land.

39 And Moses told these words to all the people of Israel, and the people mourned greatly. ⁴⁰And they rose early in the morning, and went up to the heights of the hill country, saying, "See, we are here, we will go up to the place which the LORD has promised; for we have sinned." ⁴¹But Moses said, "Why now are you transgressing the command of the LORD, for that will not succeed? ⁴²Do not go up lest you be struck down before your enemies, for the LORD is not among you. ⁴³For there the A·măl′e·kītes and the Canaanites are before you, and you shall fall by the sword; because you have turned back from following the LORD, the LORD will not be with you." ⁴⁴But they presumed to go up to the heights of the hill country, although neither the ark of the covenant of the LORD, nor Moses, departed out of the camp. ⁴⁵Then the A·măl′e·kītes and the Canaanites who dwelt in that hill country came down, and defeated them and pursued them, even to Hôr′măh.

15 The LORD said to Moses, ²"Say to the people of Israel, When you come into the land you are to inhabit, which I give you, ³and you offer to the LORD from the herd or from the flock an offering by fire or a burnt offering or a sacrifice, to fulfil a vow or as a freewill offering or at your appointed feasts, to make a pleasing odor to the LORD, ⁴then he who brings his offering shall offer to the LORD a cereal offering of a tenth of an ephah of fine flour, mixed with a fourth of a hin of oil; ⁵and wine for the drink offering, a fourth of a hin, you shall prepare with the burnt offering, or for the sacrifice,

14.22, 23: Heb 3.18. 14.29: Heb 3.17.
14.33: Acts 7.36.

for each lamb. ⁶Or for a ram, you shall prepare for a cereal offering two tenths of an ephah of fine flour mixed with a third of a hin of oil; ⁷and for the drink offering you shall offer a third of a hin of wine, a pleasing odor to the LORD. ⁸And when you prepare a bull for a burnt offering, or for a sacrifice, to fulfil a vow, or for peace offerings to the LORD, ⁹then one shall offer with the bull a cereal offering of three tenths of an ephah of fine flour, mixed with half a hin of oil, ¹⁰and you shall offer for the drink offering half a hin of wine, as an offering by fire, a pleasing odor to the LORD.

11 "Thus it shall be done for each bull or ram, or for each of the male lambs or the kids. ¹²According to the number that you prepare, so shall you do with every one according to their number. ¹³All who are native shall do these things in this way, in offering an offering by fire, a pleasing odor to the LORD. ¹⁴And if a stranger is sojourning with you, or any one is among you throughout your generations, and he wishes to offer an offering by fire, a pleasing odor to the LORD, he shall do as you do. ¹⁵For the assembly, there shall be one statute for you and for the stranger who sojourns with you, a perpetual statute throughout your generations; as you are, so shall the sojourner be before the LORD. ¹⁶One law and one ordinance shall be for you and for the stranger who sojourns with you."

17 The LORD said to Moses, ¹⁸"Say to the people of Israel, When you come into the land to which I bring you ¹⁹and when you eat of the food of the land, you shall present an offering to the LORD. ²⁰Of the first of your coarse meal you shall present a cake as an offering; as an offering from the threshing floor, so shall you present it. ²¹Of the first of your coarse meal you shall give to the LORD an offering throughout your generations.

22 "But if you err, and do not observe all these commandments which the LORD has spoken to Moses, ²³all that the LORD has commanded you by Moses, from the day that the LORD gave commandment, and onward throughout your generations, ²⁴then if it was done unwittingly without the knowledge of the congregation, all the congregation shall offer one young bull

for a burnt offering, a pleasing odor to the LORD, with its cereal offering and its drink offering, according to the ordinance, and one male goat for a sin offering. ²⁵And the priest shall make atonement for all the congregation of the people of Israel, and they shall be forgiven; because it was an error, and they have brought their offering, an offering by fire to the LORD, and their sin offering before the LORD, for their error. ²⁶And all the congregation of the people of Israel shall be forgiven, and the stranger who sojourns among them, because the whole population was involved in the error.

27 "If one person sins unwittingly, he shall offer a female goat a year old for a sin offering. ²⁸And the priest shall make atonement before the LORD for the person who commits an error, when he sins unwittingly, to make atonement for him; and he shall be forgiven. ²⁹You shall have one law for him who does anything unwittingly, for him who is native among the people of Israel, and for the stranger who sojourns among them. ³⁰But the person who does anything with a high hand, whether he is native or a sojourner, reviles the LORD, and that person shall be cut off from among his people. ³¹Because he has despised the word of the LORD, and has broken his commandment, that person shall be utterly cut off; his iniquity shall be upon him."

32 While the people of Israel were in the wilderness, they found a man gathering sticks on the sabbath day. ³³And those who found him gathering sticks brought him to Moses and Aaron, and to all the congregation. ³⁴They put him in custody, because it had not been made plain what should be done to him. ³⁵And the LORD said to Moses, "The man shall be put to death; all the congregation shall stone him with stones outside the camp." ³⁶And all the congregation brought him outside the camp, and stoned him to death with stones, as the LORD commanded Moses.

37 The LORD said to Moses, ³⁸"Speak to the people of Israel, and bid them to make tassels on the corners of their garments throughout their genera-

15.14: Ex 12.49; Lev 24.22; Num 15.15, 16, 29.
15.17-21: Ex 34.26; Lev 23.14. 15.22-26: Lev 4.13-21.
15.27-29: Lev 4.2-12. 15.38-40: Deut 22.12.

tions, and to put upon the tassel of each corner a cord of blue; ³⁹ and it shall be to you a tassel to look upon and remember all the commandments of the LORD, to do them, not to follow after your own heart and your own eyes, which you are inclined to go after wantonly. ⁴⁰ So you shall remember and do all my commandments, and be holy to your God. ⁴¹ I am the LORD your God, who brought you out of the land of Egypt, to be your God: I am the LORD your God."

16 Now Kō′rah the son of Iz′hăr, son of Kō′hăth, son of Lē′vī, and Dā′than and A·bī′ram the sons of Ě·lī′ăb, and Ŏn the son of Pē′lĕth, sons of Reuben, ² took men; and they rose up before Moses, with a number of the people of Israel, two hundred and fifty leaders of the congregation, chosen from the assembly, well-known men; ³ and they assembled themselves together against Moses and against Aaron, and said to them, "You have gone too far! For all the congregation are holy, every one of them, and the LORD is among them; why then do you exalt yourselves above the assembly of the LORD?" ⁴ When Moses heard it, he fell on his face; ⁵ and he said to Kō′rah and all his company, "In the morning the LORD will show who is his, and who is holy, and will cause him to come near to him; him whom he will choose he will cause to come near to him. ⁶ Do this: take censers, Kō′rah and all his company; ⁷ put fire in them and put incense upon them before the LORD tomorrow, and the man whom the LORD chooses shall be the holy one. You have gone too far, sons of Lē′vī!" ⁸ And Moses said to Kō′rah, "Hear now, you sons of Lē′vī: ⁹ is it too small a thing for you that the God of Israel has separated you from the congregation of Israel, to bring you near to himself, to do service in the tabernacle of the LORD, and to stand before the congregation to minister to them; ¹⁰ and that he has brought you near him, and all your brethren the sons of Lē′vī with you? And would you seek the priesthood also? ¹¹ Therefore it is against the LORD that you and all your company have gathered together; what is Aaron that you murmur against him?"

¹² And Moses sent to call Dā′than and A·bī′ram the sons of Ě·lī′ăb; and

they said, "We will not come up. ¹³ Is it a small thing that you have brought us up out of a land flowing with milk and honey, to kill us in the wilderness, that you must also make yourself a prince over us? ¹⁴ Moreover you have not brought us into a land flowing with milk and honey, nor given us inheritance of fields and vineyards. Will you put out the eyes of these men? We will not come up."

¹⁵ And Moses was very angry, and said to the LORD, "Do not respect their offering. I have not taken one ass from them, and I have not harmed one of them." ¹⁶ And Moses said to Kō′rah, "Be present, you and all your company, before the LORD, you and they, and Aaron, tomorrow; ¹⁷ and let every one of you take his censer, and put incense upon it, and every one of you bring before the LORD his censer, two hundred and fifty censers; you also, and Aaron, each his censer." ¹⁸ So every man took his censer, and they put fire in them and laid incense upon them, and they stood at the entrance of the tent of meeting with Moses and Aaron. ¹⁹ Then Kō′rah assembled all the congregation against them at the entrance of the tent of meeting. And the glory of the LORD appeared to all the congregation.

20 And the LORD said to Moses and to Aaron, ²¹ "Separate yourselves from among this congregation, that I may consume them in a moment." ²² And they fell on their faces, and said, "O God, the God of the spirits of all flesh, shall one man sin, and wilt thou be angry with all the congregation?" ²³ And the LORD said to Moses, ²⁴ "Say to the congregation, Get away from about the dwelling of Kō′rah, Dā′than, and A·bī′ram."

25 Then Moses rose and went to Dā′than and A·bī′ram; and the elders of Israel followed him. ²⁶ And he said to the congregation, "Depart, I pray you, from the tents of these wicked men, and touch nothing of theirs, lest you be swept away with all their sins." ²⁷ So they got away from about the dwelling of Kō′rah, Dā′than, and A·bī′ram; and Dathan and Abiram came out and stood at the door of their tents, together with their wives, their sons, and their little ones. ²⁸ And Moses said, "Hereby you shall know

16.5: 2 Tim 2.19.

that the LORD has sent me to do all these works, and that it has not been of my own accord. ²⁹If these men die the common death of all men, or if they are visited by the fate of all men, then the LORD has not sent me. ³⁰But if the LORD creates something new, and the ground opens its mouth, and swallows them up, with all that belongs to them, and they go down alive into She'ōl, then you shall know that these men have despised the LORD."

31 And as he finished speaking all these words, the ground under them split asunder; ³²and the earth opened its mouth and swallowed them up, with their households and all the men that belonged to Kō'rah and all their goods. ³³So they and all that belonged to them went down alive into She'ōl; and the earth closed over them, and they perished from the midst of the assembly. ³⁴And all Israel that were round about them fled at their cry; for they said, "Lest the earth swallow us up!" ³⁵And fire came forth from the LORD, and consumed the two hundred and fifty men offering the incense.

36ⁱ Then the LORD said to Moses, ³⁷"Tell Ĕl·ē·ā'zar the son of Aaron the priest to take up the censers out of the blaze; then scatter the fire far and wide. For they are holy, ³⁸the censers of these men who have sinned at the cost of their lives; so let them be made into hammered plates as a covering for the altar, for they offered them before the LORD; therefore they are holy. Thus they shall be a sign to the people of Israel." ³⁹So Ĕl·ē·ā'zar the priest took the bronze censers, which those who were burned had offered; and they were hammered out as a covering for the altar, ⁴⁰to be a reminder to the people of Israel, so that no one who is not a priest, who is not of the descendants of Aaron, should draw near to burn incense before the LORD, lest he become as Kō'-rah and as his company—as the LORD said to Ĕl·ē·ā'zar through Moses.

41 But on the morrow all the congregation of the people of Israel murmured against Moses and against Aaron, saying, "You have killed the people of the LORD." ⁴²And when the congregation had assembled against Moses and against Aaron, they turned toward the tent of meeting; and be-

hold, the cloud covered it, and the glory of the LORD appeared. ⁴³And Moses and Aaron came to the front of the tent of meeting, ⁴⁴and the LORD said to Moses, ⁴⁵"Get away from the midst of this congregation, that I may consume them in a moment." And they fell on their faces. ⁴⁶And Moses said to Aaron, "Take your censer, and put fire therein from off the altar, and lay incense on it, and carry it quickly to the congregation, and make atonement for them; for wrath has gone forth from the LORD, the plague has begun." ⁴⁷So Aaron took it as Moses said, and ran into the midst of the assembly; and behold, the plague had already begun among the people; and he put on the incense, and made atonement for the people. ⁴⁸And he stood between the dead and the living; and the plague was stopped. ⁴⁹Now those who died by the plague were fourteen thousand seven hundred, besides those who died in the affair of Kō'rah. ⁵⁰And Aaron returned to Moses at the entrance of the tent of meeting, when the plague was stopped.

17 ^j The LORD said to Moses, ²"Speak to the people of Israel, and get from them rods, one for each fathers' house, from all their leaders according to their fathers' houses, twelve rods. Write each man's name upon his rod, ³and write Aaron's name upon the rod of Lē'vī. For there shall be one rod for the head of each fathers' house. ⁴Then you shall deposit them in the tent of meeting before the testimony, where I meet with you. ⁵And the rod of the man whom I choose shall sprout; thus I will make to cease from me the murmurings of the people of Israel, which they murmur against you." ⁶Moses spoke to the people of Israel; and all their leaders gave him rods, one for each leader, according to their fathers' houses, twelve rods; and the rod of Aaron was among their rods. ⁷And Moses deposited the rods before the LORD in the tent of the testimony.

8 And on the morrow Moses went into the tent of the testimony; and behold, the rod of Aaron for the house of Lē'vī had sprouted and put forth buds, and produced blossoms, and it bore ripe almonds. ⁹Then Moses brought out all the rods from before

ⁱCh 17.1 in Heb   ^jCh 17.16 in Heb

the Lord to all the people of Israel; and they looked, and each man took his rod. [10] And the Lord said to Moses, "Put back the rod of Aaron before the testimony, to be kept as a sign for the rebels, that you may make an end of their murmurings against me, lest they die." [11] Thus did Moses; as the Lord commanded him, so he did.

12 And the people of Israel said to Moses, "Behold, we perish, we are undone, we are all undone. [13] Every one who comes near, who comes near to the tabernacle of the Lord, shall die. Are we all to perish?"

18 So the Lord said to Aaron, "You and your sons and your fathers' house with you shall bear iniquity in connection with the sanctuary; and you and your sons with you shall bear iniquity in connection with your priesthood. [2] And with you bring your brethren also, the tribe of Lē'vī, the tribe of your father, that they may join you, and minister to you while you and your sons with you are before the tent of the testimony. [3] They shall attend you and attend to all duties of the tent; but shall not come near to the vessels of the sanctuary or to the altar, lest they, and you, die. [4] They shall join you, and attend to the tent of meeting, for all the service of the tent; and no one else shall come near you. [5] And you shall attend to the duties of the sanctuary and the duties of the altar, that there be wrath no more upon the people of Israel. [6] And behold, I have taken your brethren the Lē'vītes from among the people of Israel; they are a gift to you, given to the Lord, to do the service of the tent of meeting. [7] And you and your sons with you shall attend to your priesthood for all that concerns the altar and that is within the veil; and you shall serve. I give your priesthood as a gift,[k] and any one else who comes near shall be put to death."

8 Then the Lord said to Aaron, "And behold, I have given you whatever is kept of the offerings made to me, all the consecrated things of the people of Israel; I have given them to you as a portion, and to your sons as a perpetual due. [9] This shall be yours of the most holy things, reserved from the fire; every offering of theirs, every cereal offering of theirs and every sin offering of theirs and every guilt of-

fering of theirs, which they render to me, shall be most holy to you and to your sons. [10] In a most holy place shall you eat of it; every male may eat of it; it is holy to you. [11] This also is yours, the offering of their gift, all the wave offerings of the people of Israel; I have given them to you, and to your sons and daughters with you, as a perpetual due; every one who is clean in your house may eat of it. [12] All the best of the oil, and all the best of the wine and of the grain, the first fruits of what they give to the Lord, I give to you. [13] The first ripe fruits of all that is in their land, which they bring to the Lord, shall be yours; every one who is clean in your house may eat of it. [14] Every devoted thing in Israel shall be yours. [15] Everything that opens the womb of all flesh, whether man or beast, which they offer to the Lord, shall be yours; nevertheless the firstborn of man you shall redeem, and the firstling of unclean beasts you shall redeem. [16] And their redemption price (at a month old you shall redeem them) you shall fix at five shekels in silver, according to the shekel of the sanctuary, which is twenty gerahs. [17] But the firstling of a cow, or the firstling of a sheep, or the firstling of a goat, you shall not redeem; they are holy. You shall sprinkle their blood upon the altar, and shall burn their fat as an offering by fire, a pleasing odor to the Lord; [18] but their flesh shall be yours, as the breast that is waved and as the right thigh are yours. [19] All the holy offerings which the people of Israel present to the Lord I give to you, and to your sons and daughters with you, as a perpetual due; it is a covenant of salt for ever before the Lord for you and for your offspring with you." [20] And the Lord said to Aaron, "You shall have no inheritance in their land, neither shall you have any portion among them; I am your portion and your inheritance among the people of Israel.

21 "To the Lē'vītes I have given every tithe in Israel for an inheritance, in return for their service which they serve, their service in the tent of meeting. [22] And henceforth the people of Israel shall not come near the tent

of meeting, lest they bear sin and die.
23 But the Lē'vītes shall do the service
of the tent of meeting, and they shall
bear their iniquity; it shall be a perpetual statute throughout your generations; and among the people of
Israel they shall have no inheritance.
24 For the tithe of the people of Israel,
which they present as an offering to the
LORD, I have given to the Lē'vītes for
an inheritance; therefore I have said
of them that they shall have no inheritance among the people of Israel."

25 And the LORD said to Moses,
26 "Moreover you shall say to the
Lē'vītes, 'When you take from the people of Israel the tithe which I have
given you from them for your inheritance, then you shall present an offering from it to the LORD, a tithe of the
tithe. 27 And your offering shall be reckoned to you as though it were the grain
of the threshing floor, and as the fulness of the wine press. 28 So shall you
also present an offering to the LORD
from all your tithes, which you receive from the people of Israel; and
from it you shall give the LORD's offering to Aaron the priest. 29 Out of all
the gifts to you, you shall present every
offering due to the LORD, from all the
best of them, giving the hallowed part
from them.' 30 Therefore you shall say
to them, 'When you have offered from
it the best of it, then the rest shall be
reckoned to the Lē'vītes as produce of
the threshing floor, and as produce of
the wine press; 31 and you may eat it in
any place, you and your households;
for it is your reward in return for your
service in the tent of meeting. 32 And
you shall bear no sin by reason of it,
when you have offered the best of it.
And you shall not profane the holy
things of the people of Israel, lest
you die.' "

19 Now the LORD said to Moses
and to Aaron, 2 "This is the
statute of the law which the LORD has
commanded: Tell the people of Israel to bring you a red heifer without
defect, in which there is no blemish,
and upon which a yoke has never
come. 3 And you shall give her to
Ĕl-ē-à'zạr the priest, and she shall
be taken outside the camp and slaughtered before him; 4 and Ĕl-ē-à'zạr the
priest shall take some of her blood with
his finger, and sprinkle some of her
blood toward the front of the tent of

meeting seven times. 5 And the heifer
shall be burned in his sight; her skin,
her flesh, and her blood, with all her
dung, shall be burned; 6 and the priest
shall take cedarwood and hyssop and
scarlet stuff, and cast them into the
midst of the burning of the heifer.
7 Then the priest shall wash his clothes
and bathe his body in water, and afterwards he shall come into the camp;
and the priest shall be unclean until
evening. 8 He who burns the heifer
shall wash his clothes in water and
bathe his body in water, and shall be
unclean until evening. 9 And a man
who is clean shall gather up the ashes
of the heifer, and deposit them outside the camp in a clean place; and
they shall be kept for the congregation
of the people of Israel for the water
for impurity, for the removal of sin.
10 And he who gathers the ashes of
the heifer shall wash his clothes, and
be unclean until evening. And this
shall be to the people of Israel, and to
the stranger who sojourns among
them, a perpetual statute.

11 "He who touches the dead body
of any person shall be unclean seven
days; 12 he shall cleanse himself with
the water on the third day and on the
seventh day, and so be clean; but if
he does not cleanse himself on the
third day and on the seventh day, he
will not become clean. 13 Whoever
touches a dead person, the body of any
man who has died, and does not
cleanse himself, defiles the tabernacle
of the LORD, and that person shall be
cut off from Israel; because the water
for impurity was not thrown upon him,
he shall be unclean; his uncleanness
is still on him.

14 "This is the law when a man dies
in a tent: every one who comes into
the tent, and every one who is in the
tent, shall be unclean seven days.
15 And every open vessel, which has
no cover fastened upon it, is unclean.
16 Whoever in the open field touches one
who is slain with a sword, or a dead
body, or a bone of a man, or a grave,
shall be unclean seven days. 17 For the
unclean they shall take some ashes of
the burnt sin offering, and running
water shall be added in a vessel; 18 then
a clean person shall take hyssop, and
dip it in the water, and sprinkle it upon
the tent, and upon all the furnishings, and upon the persons who were

there, and upon him who touched the bone, or the slain, or the dead, or the grave; ¹⁹ and the clean person shall sprinkle upon the unclean on the third day and on the seventh day; thus on the seventh day he shall cleanse him, and he shall wash his clothes and bathe himself in water, and at evening he shall be clean.

20 "But the man who is unclean and does not cleanse himself, that person shall be cut off from the midst of the assembly, since he has defiled the sanctuary of the LORD; because the water for impurity has not been thrown upon him, he is unclean. ²¹ And it shall be a perpetual statute for them. He who sprinkles the water for impurity shall wash his clothes; and he who touches the water for impurity shall be unclean until evening. ²² And whatever the unclean person touches shall be unclean; and any one who touches it shall be unclean until evening."

20 And the people of Israel, the whole congregation, came into the wilderness of Zĭn in the first month, and the people stayed in Kā'dĕsh; and Miriam died there, and was buried there.

2 Now there was no water for the congregation; and they assembled themselves together against Moses and against Aaron. ³ And the people contended with Moses, and said, "Would that we had died when our brethren died before the LORD! ⁴ Why have you brought the assembly of the LORD into this wilderness, that we should die here, both we and our cattle? ⁵ And why have you made us come up out of Egypt, to bring us to this evil place? It is no place for grain, or figs, or vines, or pomegranates; and there is no water to drink." ⁶ Then Moses and Aaron went from the presence of the assembly to the door of the tent of meeting, and fell on their faces. And the glory of the LORD appeared to them, ⁷ and the LORD said to Moses, ⁸ "Take the rod, and assemble the congregation, you and Aaron your brother, and tell the rock before their eyes to yield its water; so you shall bring water out of the rock for them; so you shall give drink to the congregation and their cattle." ⁹ And Moses took the rod from before the LORD, as he commanded him.

10 And Moses and Aaron gathered the assembly together before the rock, and he said to them, "Hear now, you rebels; shall we bring forth water for you out of this rock?" ¹¹ And Moses lifted up his hand and struck the rock with his rod twice; and water came forth abundantly, and the congregation drank, and their cattle. ¹² And the LORD said to Moses and Aaron, "Because you did not believe in me, to sanctify me in the eyes of the people of Israel, therefore you shall not bring this assembly into the land which I have given them." ¹³ These are the waters of Mĕr'ĭ·bah,ᴵ where the people of Israel contended with the LORD, and he showed himself holy among them.

14 Moses sent messengers from Kā'dĕsh to the king of Ē'dom, "Thus says your brother Israel: You know all the adversity that has befallen us: ¹⁵ how our fathers went down to Egypt, and we dwelt in Egypt a long time; and the Egyptians dealt harshly with us and our fathers; ¹⁶ and when we cried to the LORD, he heard our voice, and sent an angel and brought us forth out of Egypt; and here we are in Kā'dĕsh, a city on the edge of your territory. ¹⁷ Now let us pass through your land. We will not pass through field or vineyard, neither will we drink water from a well; we will go along the King's Highway, we will not turn aside to the right hand or to the left, until we have passed through your territory." ¹⁸ But Ē'dom said to him, "You shall not pass through, lest I come out with the sword against you." ¹⁹ And the people of Israel said to him, "We will go up by the highway; and if we drink of your water, I and my cattle, then I will pay for it; let me only pass through on foot, nothing more." ²⁰ But he said, "You shall not pass through." And Ē'dom came out against them with many men, and with a strong force. ²¹ Thus Ē'dom refused to give Israel passage through his territory; so Israel turned away from him.

22 And they journeyed from Kā'dĕsh, and the people of Israel, the whole congregation, came to Mount Hôr. ²³ And the LORD said to Moses and Aaron at Mount Hôr, on the border of the land of Ē'dom, ²⁴ "Aaron shall be gathered to his people; for he shall not

ᴵ That is *Contention*   20.2-13: Ex 17.2-7.

enter the land which I have given to the people of Israel, because you rebelled against my command at the waters of Mĕr'ĭ·băh. ²⁵ Take Aaron and Ĕl·ē·ā'zạr his son, and bring them up to Mount Hôr; ²⁶ and strip Aaron of his garments, and put them upon Ĕl·ē·ā'zạr his son; and Aaron shall be gathered to his people, and shall die there." ²⁷ Moses did as the LORD commanded; and they went up Mount Hôr in the sight of the congregation. ²⁸ And Moses stripped Aaron of his garments, and put them upon Ĕl·ē·ā'zạr his son; and Aaron died there on the top of the mountain. Then Moses and Eleazar came down from the mountain. ²⁹ And when all the congregation saw that Aaron was dead, all the house of Israel wept for Aaron thirty days.

21 When the Canaanite, the king of Ăr'ad, who dwelt in the Nĕg'ĕb, heard that Israel was coming by the way of Ăth'ạ·rĭm, he fought against Israel, and took some of them captive. ² And Israel vowed a vow to the LORD, and said, "If thou wilt indeed give this people into my hand, then I will utterly destroy their cities." ³ And the LORD hearkened to the voice of Israel, and gave over the Canaanites; and they utterly destroyed them and their cities; so the name of the place was called Hôr'mah.^m

4 From Mount Hôr they set out by the way to the Red Sea, to go around the land of Ē'dọm; and the people became impatient on the way. ⁵ And the people spoke against God and against Moses, "Why have you brought us up out of Egypt to die in the wilderness? For there is no food and no water, and we loathe this worthless food." ⁶ Then the LORD sent fiery serpents among the people, and they bit the people, so that many people of Israel died. ⁷ And the people came to Moses, and said, "We have sinned, for we have spoken against the LORD and against you; pray to the LORD, that he take away the serpents from us." So Moses prayed for the people. ⁸ And the LORD said to Moses, "Make a fiery serpent, and set it on a pole; and every one who is bitten, when he sees it, shall live." ⁹ So Moses made a bronze serpent, and set it on a pole; and if a serpent bit any man, he would look at the bronze serpent and live.

10 And the people of Israel set out,

and encamped in Ō'bŏth. ¹¹ And they set out from Ō'bŏth, and encamped at Ĭ'yĕ-ăb'ạ·rĭm, in the wilderness which is opposite Mō'ăb, toward the sunrise. ¹² From there they set out, and encamped in the Valley of Zē'rĕd. ¹³ From there they set out, and encamped on the other side of the Ăr'nŏn, which is in the wilderness, that extends from the boundary of the Ăm'ọ·rītes; for the Arnon is the boundary of Mō'ăb, between Moab and the Amorites. ¹⁴ Wherefore it is said in the Book of the Wars of the LORD,

Wă'hĕb in Sü'phạh,
and the valleys of the Ăr'nŏn,
¹⁵ and the slope of the valleys
that extends to the seat of Ăr,
and leans to the border of Mō'ăb."

16 And from there they continued to Bē'ẹr;ⁿ that is the well of which the LORD said to Moses, "Gather the people together, and I will give them water." ¹⁷ Then Israel sang this song:

"Spring up, O well! – Sing to it! –
¹⁸ the well which the princes dug,
which the nobles of the people delved,
with the scepter and with their staves."

And from the wilderness they went on to Măt'tạ·nah, ¹⁹ and from Măt'tạ·nah to Nạ·hăl'ĭ·ĕl, and from Nahaliel to Bā'mŏth, ²⁰ and from Bā'mŏth to the valley lying in the region of Mō'ăb by the top of Pĭṣ'gạh which looks down upon the desert.^o

21 Then Israel sent messengers to Sī'họn king of the Ăm'ọ·rītes, saying, ²² "Let me pass through your land; we will not turn aside into field or vineyard; we will not drink the water of a well; we will go by the King's Highway, until we have passed through your territory." ²³ But Sī'họn would not allow Israel to pass through his territory. He gathered all his men together, and went out against Israel to the wilderness, and came to Jā'hăz, and fought against Israel. ²⁴ And Israel slew him with the edge of the sword, and took possession of his land from the Ăr'nŏn to the Jăb'bọk, as far as to the Ăm·mo'nītes; for Jā'zẹr was the boundary of the Ammonites.^p ²⁵ And Israel took all these cities, and Israel

ᵐHeb *Destruction*   ⁿThat is *Well*   ᵒOr *Jeshimon*
ᵖGk: Heb *the boundary of the Ammonites was strong*
20.25-29: Num 33.38, 39.   **21.1:** Num 33.40.
21.21-30: Deut 2.26-37.

settled in all the cities of the Ăm'ọ-rītes, in Hĕsh'bọn, and in all its villages. ²⁶For Hĕsh'bọn was the city of Sī'họn the king of the Ăm'ọ·rītes, who had fought against the former king of Mō'ăb and taken all his land out of his hand, as far as the Ăr'nŏn. ²⁷Therefore the ballad singers say,

"Come to Hĕsh'bọn, let it be built,
    let the city of Sī'họn be established.
²⁸For fire went forth from Hĕsh'bọn,
    flame from the city of Sī'họn.
It devoured Ăr of Mō'ăb,
    the lords of the heights of the
        Ăr'nŏn.
²⁹Woe to you, O Mō'ăb!
You are undone, O people of
    Chĕ'mŏsh!
He has made his sons fugitives,
    and his daughters captives,
    to an Ăm'ọ·rīte king, Sī'họn.
³⁰So their posterity perished from
    Hĕsh'bọn,^q as far as Dī'bŏn,
and we laid waste until fire spread
    to Mĕd'ẹ·ba."^r

31 Thus Israel dwelt in the land of the Ăm'ọ·rītes. ³²And Moses sent to spy out Jā'zẹr; and they took its villages, and dispossessed the Ăm'ọ·rītes that were there. ³³Then they turned and went up by the way to Bā'shạn; and Ŏg the king of Bashan came out against them, he and all his people, to battle at Ĕd'rē-ī. ³⁴But the LORD said to Moses, "Do not fear him; for I have given him into your hand, and all his people, and his land; and you shall do to him as you did to Sī'họn king of the Ăm'ọ·rītes, who dwelt at Hĕsh'bọn." ³⁵So they slew him, and his sons, and all his people, until there was not one survivor left to him; and they possessed his land.

22 Then the people of Israel set out, and encamped in the plains of Mō'ăb beyond the Jordan at Jericho. ²And Bā'lăk the son of Zĭp'pôr saw all that Israel had done to the Ăm'ọ·rītes. ³And Mō'ăb was in great dread of the people, because they were many; Moab was overcome with fear of the people of Israel. ⁴And Mō'ăb said to the elders of Mĭd'ĭ·an, "This horde will now lick up all that is round about us, as the ox licks up the grass of the field." So Bā'lăk the son of Zĭp'pôr, who was king of Moab at that time, ⁵sent messengers to Bā'lăăm the son of Bē'ôr at Pē'thôr, which is near the River, in the land of Ăm'aw to call

him, saying, "Behold, a people has come out of Egypt; they cover the face of the earth, and they are dwelling opposite me. ⁶Come now, curse this people for me, since they are too mighty for me; perhaps I shall be able to defeat them and drive them from the land; for I know that he whom you bless is blessed, and he whom you curse is cursed."

7 So the elders of Mō'ăb and the elders of Mĭd'ĭ·an departed with the fees for divination in their hand; and they came to Bā'lăăm, and gave him Bā'lăk's message. ⁸And he said to them, "Lodge here this night, and I will bring back word to you, as the LORD speaks to me"; so the princes of Mō'ăb stayed with Bā'lăăm. ⁹And God came to Bā'lăăm and said, "Who are these men with you?" ¹⁰And Bā'lăăm said to God, "Bā'lăk the son of Zĭp'pôr, king of Mō'ăb, has sent to me, saying, ¹¹'Behold, a people has come out of Egypt, and it covers the face of the earth; now come, curse them for me; perhaps I shall be able to fight against them and drive them out.'" ¹²God said to Bā'lăăm, "You shall not go with them; you shall not curse the people, for they are blessed." ¹³So Bā'lăăm rose in the morning, and said to the princes of Bā'lăk, "Go to your own land; for the LORD has refused to let me go with you." ¹⁴So the princes of Mō'ăb rose and went to Bā'lăk, and said, "Bā'lăăm refuses to come with us."

15 Once again Bā'lăk sent princes, more in number and more honorable than they. ¹⁶And they came to Bā'lăăm and said to him, "Thus says Bā'lăk the son of Zĭp'pôr: 'Let nothing hinder you from coming to me; ¹⁷for I will surely do you great honor, and whatever you say to me I will do; come, curse this people for me.'" ¹⁸But Bā'lăăm answered and said to the servants of Bā'lăk, "Though Balak were to give me his house full of silver and gold, I could not go beyond the command of the LORD my God, to do less or more. ¹⁹Pray, now, tarry here this night also, that I may know what more the LORD will say to me." ²⁰And God came to Bā'lăăm at night and

^qGk: Heb *we have shot at them. Heshbon has perished*
^rCompare Sam and Gk: Heb *we have laid waste to Nophah which to Medeba*
21.33-35: Deut 3.1-7. **22.1:** Num 33.48.

said to him, "If the men have come to call you, rise, go with them; but only what I bid you, that shall you do."

21 So Bā'laăm rose in the morning, and saddled his ass, and went with the princes of Mō'ăb. ²²But God's anger was kindled because he went; and the angel of the LORD took his stand in the way as his adversary. Now he was riding on the ass, and his two servants were with him. ²³And the ass saw the angel of the LORD standing in the road, with a drawn sword in his hand; and the ass turned aside out of the road, and went into the field; and Bā'laăm struck the ass, to turn her into the road. ²⁴Then the angel of the LORD stood in a narrow path between the vineyards, with a wall on either side. ²⁵And when the ass saw the angel of the LORD, she pushed against the wall, and pressed Bā'laăm's foot against the wall; so he struck her again. ²⁶Then the angel of the LORD went ahead, and stood in a narrow place, where there was no way to turn either to the right or to the left. ²⁷When the ass saw the angel of the LORD, she lay down under Bā'laăm; and Balaam's anger was kindled, and he struck the ass with his staff. ²⁸Then the LORD opened the mouth of the ass, and she said to Bā'laăm, "What have I done to you, that you have struck me these three times?" ²⁹And Bā'laăm said to the ass, "Because you have made sport of me. I wish I had a sword in my hand, for then I would kill you." ³⁰And the ass said to Bā'laăm, "Am I not your ass, upon which you have ridden all your life long to this day? Was I ever accustomed to do so to you?" And he said, "No."

31 Then the LORD opened the eyes of Bā'laăm, and he saw the angel of the LORD standing in the way, with his drawn sword in his hand; and he bowed his head, and fell on his face. ³²And the angel of the LORD said to him, "Why have you struck your ass these three times? Behold, I have come forth to withstand you, because your way is perverse before me; ³³and the ass saw me, and turned aside before me these three times. If she had not turned aside from me, surely just now I would have slain you and let her live." ³⁴Then Bā'laăm said to the angel of the LORD, "I have sinned, for I did not know that thou didst stand in the road against me. Now therefore, if it is evil in thy sight, I will go back again." ³⁵And the angel of the LORD said to Bā'laăm, "Go with the men; but only the word which I bid you, that shall you speak." So Balaam went on with the princes of Bā'lăk.

36 When Bā'lăk heard that Bā'laăm had come, he went out to meet him at the city of Mō'ăb, on the boundary formed by the Är'nŏn, at the extremity of the boundary. ³⁷And Bā'lăk said to Bā'laăm, "Did I not send to you to call you? Why did you not come to me? Am I not able to honor you?" ³⁸Bā'laăm said to Bā'lăk, "Lo, I have come to you! Have I now any power at all to speak anything? The word that God puts in my mouth, that must I speak." ³⁹Then Bā'laăm went with Bā'lăk, and they came to Kīr'ĭ-ăth-hū'zŏth. ⁴⁰And Bā'lăk sacrificed oxen and sheep, and sent to Bā'laăm and to the princes who were with him.

41 And on the morrow Bā'lăk took Bā'laăm and brought him up to Bā'-mŏth-bā'ạl; and from there he saw the

23 nearest of the people. ¹And Bā'laăm said to Bā'lăk, "Build for me here seven altars, and provide for me here seven bulls and seven rams." ²Bā'lăk did as Bā'laăm had said; and Balak and Balaam offered on each altar a bull and a ram. ³And Bā'laăm said to Bā'lăk, "Stand beside your burnt offering, and I will go; perhaps the LORD will come to meet me; and whatever he shows me I will tell you." And he went to a bare height. ⁴And God met Bā'laăm; and Balaam said to him, "I have prepared the seven altars, and I have offered upon each altar a bull and a ram." ⁵And the LORD put a word in Bā'laăm's mouth, and said, "Return to Bā'lăk, and thus you shall speak." ⁶And he returned to him, and lo, he and all the princes of Mō'ăb were standing beside his burnt offering. ⁷And Bā'laăm took up his discourse, and said,

"From Är'ạm Bā'lăk has brought me,
    the king of Mō'ăb from the eastern
    mountains:
'Come, curse Jacob for me,
    and come, denounce Israel!'
⁸How can I curse whom God has not
    cursed?
How can I denounce whom the
    LORD has not denounced?
⁹For from the top of the mountains I
    see him,

from the hills I behold him;
lo, a people dwelling alone,
and not reckoning itself among the
nations!
¹⁰Who can count the dust of Jacob,
or number the fourth part⁹ of Israel?
Let me die the death of the righteous,
and let my end be like his!"
11 And Bā′lăk said to Bā′laăm,
"What have you done to me? I took you
to curse my enemies, and behold, you
have done nothing but bless them."
¹²And he answered, "Must I not take
heed to speak what the LORD puts in
my mouth?"
13 And Bā′lăk said to him, "Come
with me to another place, from which
you may see them; you shall see only
the nearest of them, and shall not see
them all; then curse them for me from
there." ¹⁴And he took him to the field
of Zō′phĭm, to the top of Pĭṣ′gah, and
built seven altars, and offered a bull
and a ram on each altar. ¹⁵Bā′laăm
said to Bā′lăk, "Stand here beside your
burnt offering, while I meet the LORD
yonder." ¹⁶And the LORD met Bā′laăm,
and put a word in his mouth, and said,
"Return to Bā′lăk, and thus shall you
speak." ¹⁷And he came to him, and, lo,
he was standing beside his burnt offering, and the princes of Mō′ăb with
him. And Bā′lăk said to him, "What
has the LORD spoken?" ¹⁸And Bā′laăm
took up his discourse, and said,
"Rise, Bā′lăk, and hear;
hearken to me, O son of Zĭp′pôr:
¹⁹God is not man, that he should lie,
or a son of man, that he should
repent.
Has he said, and will he not do it?
Or has he spoken, and will he not
fulfil it?
²⁰Behold, I received a command to
bless:
he has blessed, and I cannot revoke it.
²¹He has not beheld misfortune in
Jacob;
nor has he seen trouble in Israel.
The LORD their God is with them,
and the shout of a king is among
them.
²²God brings them out of Egypt;
they have as it were the horns of
the wild ox.
²³For there is no enchantment against
Jacob,
no divination against Israel;

now it shall be said of Jacob and
Israel,
'What has God wrought!'
²⁴Behold, a people! As a lioness it
rises up
and as a lion it lifts itself;
it does not lie down till it devours
the prey,
and drinks the blood of the slain."
25 And Bā′lăk said to Bā′laăm,
"Neither curse them at all, nor bless
them at all." ²⁶But Bā′laăm answered
Bā′lăk, "Did I not tell you, 'All that the
LORD says, that I must do'?" ²⁷And
Bā′lăk said to Bā′laăm, "Come now,
I will take you to another place; perhaps it will please God that you may
curse them for me from there." ²⁸So
Bā′lăk took Bā′laăm to the top of
Pē′ôr, that overlooks the desert.ᶠ ²⁹And
Bā′laăm said to Bā′lăk, "Build for me
here seven altars, and provide for me
here seven bulls and seven rams."
³⁰And Bā′lăk did as Bā′laăm had said,
and offered a bull and a ram on each
altar.

24 When Bā′laăm saw that it
pleased the LORD to bless Israel,
he did not go, as at other times, to look
for omens, but set his face toward the
wilderness. ²And Bā′laăm lifted up his
eyes, and saw Israel encamping tribe
by tribe. And the Spirit of God came
upon him, ³and he took up his discourse, and said,
"The oracle of Bā′laăm the son of
Bē′ôr,
the oracle of the man whose eye
is opened,ᵘ
⁴the oracle of him who hears the
words of God,
who sees the vision of the Almighty,
falling down, but having his eyes
uncovered:
⁵how fair are your tents, O Jacob,
your encampments, O Israel!
⁶Like valleys that stretch afar,
like gardens beside a river,
like aloes that the LORD has planted,
like cedar trees beside the waters.
⁷Water shall flow from his buckets,
and his seed shall be in many
waters,
his king shall be higher than Ā′găg,
and his kingdom shall be exalted.
⁸God brings him out of Egypt;
he has as it were the horns of the
wild ox,

ˢOr *dust clouds* ᶠOr *Jeshimon* ᵘOr *closed* or *perfect*

he shall eat up the nations his adversaries,
and shall break their bones in pieces,
and pierce them through with his arrows.
⁹He couched, he lay down like a lion,
and like a lioness; who will rouse him up?
Blessed be every one who blesses you,
and cursed be every one who curses you."
10 And Bā'lăk's anger was kindled against Bā'laăm, and he struck his hands together; and Balak said to Balaam, "I called you to curse my enemies, and behold, you have blessed them these three times. ¹¹Therefore now flee to your place; I said, 'I will certainly honor you,' but the LORD has held you back from honor." ¹²And Bā'laăm said to Bā'lăk, "Did I not tell your messengers whom you sent to me, ¹³'If Bā'lăk should give me his house full of silver and gold, I would not be able to go beyond the word of the LORD, to do either good or bad of my own will; what the LORD speaks, that will I speak'? ¹⁴And now, behold, I am going to my people; come, I will let you know what this people will do to your people in the latter days." ¹⁵And he took up his discourse, and said,
"The oracle of Bā'laăm the son of Bē'ôr,
the oracle of the man whose eye is opened,ᵛ
¹⁶the oracle of him who hears the words of God,
and knows the knowledge of the Most High,
who sees the vision of the Almighty, falling down, but having his eyes uncovered:
¹⁷I see him, but not now;
I behold him, but not nigh:
a star shall come forth out of Jacob,
and a scepter shall rise out of Israel;
it shall crush the foreheadʷ of Mō'ăb,
and break down all the sons of Shēth.
¹⁸E'dom shall be dispossessed,
Sē'ir also, his enemies, shall be dispossessed,
while Israel does valiantly.
¹⁹By Jacob shall dominion be exercised,

and the survivors of cities be destroyed!"
20 Then he looked on Ăm'ạ·lĕk, and took up his discourse, and said,
"Amalek was the first of the nations, but in the end he shall come to destruction."
21 And he looked on the Kĕn'īte, and took up his discourse, and said,
"Enduring is your dwelling place, and your nest is set in the rock;
²²nevertheless Kāin shall be wasted.
How long shall Ăş'shŭr take you away captive?"
23 And he took up his discourse, and said,
"Alas, who shall live when God does this?
²⁴But ships shall come from Kĭt'tĭm and shall afflict Ăş'shŭr and Ē'ber;
and he also shall come to destruction."
25 Then Bā'laăm rose, and went back to his place; and Bā'lăk also went his way.

25 While Israel dwelt in Shĭt'tĭm the people began to play the harlot with the daughters of Mō'ăb. ²These invited the people to the sacrifices of their gods, and the people ate, and bowed down to their gods. ³So Israel yoked himself to Bā'al of Pē'ôr. And the anger of the LORD was kindled against Israel; ⁴and the LORD said to Moses, "Take all the chiefs of the people, and hang them in the sun before the LORD, that the fierce anger of the LORD may turn away from Israel." ⁵And Moses said to the judges of Israel, "Every one of you slay his men who have yoked themselves to Bā'al of Pē'ôr."
6 And behold, one of the people of Israel came and brought a Mĭd'ĭ·ạ-nīte woman to his family, in the sight of Moses and in the sight of the whole congregation of the people of Israel, while they were weeping at the door of the tent of meeting. ⁷When Phĭn'-e·hạs the son of Ĕl·ē·ā'zạr, son of Aaron the priest, saw it, he rose and left the congregation, and took a spear in his hand ⁸and went after the man of Israel into the inner room, and pierced both of them, the man of Israel and the woman, through her body. Thus the plague was stayed from the people of Israel. ⁹Nevertheless those that died

ᵛOr *closed* or *perfect* ʷHeb *corners* (of the head)
24.9: Gen 49.9.

by the plague were twenty-four thousand.

10 And the LORD said to Moses, ¹¹"Phĭn′e·hạs the son of Ĕl·ē·ā′zạr, son of Aaron the priest, has turned back my wrath from the people of Israel, in that he was jealous with my jealousy among them, so that I did not consume the people of Israel in my jealousy. ¹²Therefore say, 'Behold, I give to him my covenant of peace; ¹³and it shall be to him, and to his descendants after him, the covenant of a perpetual priesthood, because he was jealous for his God, and made atonement for the people of Israel.' "

14 The name of the slain man of Israel, who was slain with the Mĭd′-ĭ·ạ·nīte woman, was Zĭm′rī the son of Sā′lü, head of a fathers' house belonging to the Sĭm′ē·o·nītes. ¹⁵And the name of the Mĭd′ĭ·ạ·nīte woman who was slain was Cŏz′bī the daughter of Zŭr, who was the head of the people of a father's house in Mĭd′ĭ·ạn.

16 And the LORD said to Moses, ¹⁷"Harass the Mĭd′ĭ·ạ·nītes, and smite them; ¹⁸for they have harassed you with their wiles, with which they beguiled you in the matter of Pē′ôr, and in the matter of Cŏz′bī, the daughter of the prince of Mĭd′ĭ·ạn, their sister, who was slain on the day of the plague on account of Peor."

26 After the plague the LORD said to Moses and to Ĕl·ē·ā′zạr the son of Aaron, the priest, ²"Take a census of all the congregation of the people of Israel, from twenty years old and upward, by their fathers' houses, all in Israel who are able to go forth to war." ³And Moses and Ĕl·ē·ā′zạr the priest spoke with them in the plains of Mō′ăb by the Jordan at Jericho, saying, ⁴"Take a census of the people,ˣ from twenty years old and upward," as the LORD commanded Moses. The people of Israel, who came forth out of the land of Egypt, were:

5 Reuben, the first-born of Israel; the sons of Reuben: of Hā′nọch, the family of the Hā′nọ·chītes; of Păl′lü, the family of the Păl′lü·ītes; ⁶of Hĕz′-rọn, the family of the Hĕz′rọ·nītes; of Cär′mī, the family of the Cär′mītes. ⁷These are the families of the Reubenites; and their number was forty-three thousand seven hundred and thirty. ⁸And the sons of Păl′lü: Ĕ′lī·ăb. ⁹The sons of Ĕ′lī·ăb: Nĕm′ū–ĕl, Dā′thạn,

and Ạ·bī′rạm. These are the Dathan and Abiram, chosen from the congregation, who contended against Moses and Aaron in the company of Kō′rạh, when they contended against the LORD, ¹⁰and the earth opened its mouth and swallowed them up together with Kō′rạh, when that company died, when the fire devoured two hundred and fifty men; and they became a warning. ¹¹Notwithstanding, the sons of Kō′rạh did not die.

12 The sons of Sĭm′ē·ọn according to their families: of Nĕm′ū–ĕl, the family of the Nĕm′ū–e·lītes; of Jā′-mĭn, the family of the Jā′mĭ·nītes; of Jā′chĭn, the family of the Jā′chĭ·nītes; ¹³of Zē′rạh, the family of the Zē′-rạ·hītes: of Shā′ül, the family of the Shā′ụ·lītes. ¹⁴These are the families of the Sĭm′ē·ọ·nītes, twenty-two thousand two hundred.

15 The sons of Gȧd according to their families: of Zē′phŏn, the family of the Zē′phọ·nītes; of Hăg′gī, the family of the Hăg′gītes; of Shü′nī, the family of the Shü′nītes; ¹⁶of Ŏz′nī, the family of the Ŏz·nītes; of Ē′rī, the family of the Ē′rītes; ¹⁷of Är′ọd, the family of the Är′ọ·dītes; of Ạ·rē′lī, the family of the Ạ·rē′lītes. ¹⁸These are the families of the sons of Gȧd according to their number, forty thousand five hundred.

19 The sons of Judah were Ēr and Ō′nan; and Er and Onan died in the land of Canaan. ²⁰And the sons of Judah according to their families were: of Shē′lạh, the family of the Shē′lạ·nītes; of Pĕr′ĕz, the family of the Pĕr′-ĕ·zītes; of Zē′rạh, the family of the Zē′rạ·hītes. ²¹And the sons of Pĕr′ĕz were: of Hĕz′rọn, the family of the Hĕz′rọ·nītes; of Hā′mụl, the family of the Hā′mụ·lītes. ²²These are the families of Judah according to their number, seventy-six thousand five hundred.

23 The sons of Ĭs′sạ·chär according to their families: of Tō′lạ, the family of the Tō′lạ·ītes; of Pū′vạh, the family of the Pū′nītes; ²⁴of Jăsh′ụb, the family of the Jăsh′ụ·bītes; of Shĭm′rọn, the family of the Shĭm′rọ·nītes. ²⁵These are the families of Ĭs′sạ·chär according to their number, sixty-four thousand three hundred.

26 The sons of Zĕb′ū·lụn, according

ˣSupplying *take a census of the people* Compare verse 2
26.5-51: Num 1.22-46.

to their families: of Sē′red, the family of the Sē′re·dītes; of Ē′lŏn, the family of the Ē′lo·nītes; of Jäh′lē·el, the family of the Jäh′lē·e·lītes. ²⁷These are the families of the Zĕb′ū·lu·nītes according to their number, sixty thousand five hundred.

28 The sons of Joseph according to their families: Ma·năs′seh and Ē′phra·ĭm. ²⁹The sons of Ma·năs′seh: of Mā′chĭr, the family of the Mā′chĭ·rītes; and Machir was the father of Gilead; of Gilead, the family of the Gileadites. ³⁰These are the sons of Gilead: of Ī·ēz′er, the family of the Ī·ēz′e·rītes; of Hē′lĕk, the family of the Hē′le·kītes; ³¹and of Ăs′rĭ·ĕl, the family of the Ăs′rĭ·e·lītes; and of Shē′chĕm, the family of the Shē′che·mītes; ³²and of Shĕ·mī′da, the family of the Shĕ·mī′da·ītes; and of Hē′pher, the family of the Hē′phe·rītes. ³³Now Zĕ·lŏph′e·hăd the son of Hē′pher had no sons, but daughters: and the names of the daughters of Zelophehad were Mäh′lah, Noah, Hŏg′lah, Mĭl′cah, and Tĭr′zah. ³⁴These are the families of Ma·năs′seh; and their number was fifty-two thousand seven hundred.

35 These are the sons of Ē′phra·ĭm according to their families: of Shü′-the·lah, the family of the Shü″-the·lā′hītes; of Bē′cher, the family of the Bē′che·rītes; of Tā′hăn, the family of the Tā′ha·nītes. ³⁶And these are the sons of Shü′the·lah: of Ē′ran, the family of the Ē′ra·nītes. ³⁷These are the families of the sons of Ē′phra·ĭm according to their number, thirty-two thousand five hundred. These are the sons of Joseph according to their families.

38 The sons of Benjamin according to their families: of Bē′la, the family of the Bē′la·ītes; of Ăsh′bĕl, the family of the Ăsh′be·lītes; of A·hī′ram, the family of the A·hī′ra·mītes; ³⁹of Shĕ·phü′pham, the family of the Shĕ·phü′pha·mītes; of Hü′phăm, the family of the Hü′pha·mītes. ⁴⁰And the sons of Bē′la were Ärd and Nā′a·man: of Ard, the family of the Ärd′ītes; of Naaman, the family of the Nā′a·mītes. ⁴¹These are the sons of Benjamin according to their families; and their number was forty-five thousand six hundred.

42 These are the sons of Dan according to their families: of Shü′ham, the family of the Shü′ha·mītes. These are the families of Dan according to

their families. ⁴³All the families of the Shü′ha·mītes, according to their number, were sixty-four thousand four hundred.

44 The sons of Ăsh′er according to their families: of Ĭm′nah, the family of the Ĭm′nītes; of Ĭsh′vī, the family of the Ĭsh′vītes; of Bē·rī′ah, the family of the Bē·rī′ītes. ⁴⁵Of the sons of Bē·rī′ah: of Hē′ber, the family of the Hē′be·rītes; of Măl′chĭ–ĕl, the family of the Măl′chĭ–e·lītes. ⁴⁶And the name of the daughter of Ăsh′er was Sē′rah. ⁴⁷These are the families of the sons of Ăsh′er according to their number, fifty-three thousand four hundred.

48 The sons of Năph′ta·lī according to their families: of Jäh′zē·el, the family of the Jäh′zē·e·lītes; of Gü′nī, the family of the Gü′nītes; ⁴⁹of Jē′zer, the family of the Jē′ze·rītes; of Shĭl′lĕm, the family of the Shĭl′le·mītes. ⁵⁰These are the families of Năph′ta·lī according to their families; and their number was forty-five thousand four hundred.

51 This was the number of the people of Israel, six hundred and one thousand seven hundred and thirty.

52 The LORD said to Moses: ⁵³"To these the land shall be divided for inheritance according to the number of names. ⁵⁴To a large tribe you shall give a large inheritance, and to a small tribe you shall give a small inheritance; every tribe shall be given its inheritance according to its numbers. ⁵⁵But the land shall be divided by lot; according to the names of the tribes of their fathers they shall inherit. ⁵⁶Their inheritance shall be divided according to lot between the larger and the smaller."

57 These are the Lē′vītes as numbered according to their families: of Gēr′shon, the family of the Gēr′sho·nītes; of Kō′hăth, the family of the Kō′ha·thītes; of Me·râr′ī, the family of the Me·râr′ītes. ⁵⁸These are the families of Lē′vī: the family of the Lĭb′nītes, the family of the Hē′bro·nītes, the family of the Mäh′lītes, the family of the Mū′shītes, the family of the Kō′ra·hītes. And Kō′hăth was the father of Ăm′răm. ⁵⁹The name of Ăm′răm's wife was Jŏch′e·bĕd the daughter of Lē′vī, who was born to Levi in Egypt; and she bore to Amram Aaron and Moses and Miriam their sister. ⁶⁰And to Aaron were born

26.57-62: Num 1.47-49.

Nā'dăb, Ạ·bī'hū, Ĕl·ē·ā'zạr and Ĭth'-ạ·mär. ⁶¹But Nā'dăb and Ạ·bī'hū died when they offered unholy fire before the LORD. ⁶²And those numbered of them were twenty-three thousand, every male from a month old and upward; for they were not numbered among the people of Israel, because there was no inheritance given to them among the people of Israel.

63 These were those numbered by Moses and Ĕl·ē·ā'zạr the priest, who numbered the people of Israel in the plains of Mō'ăb by the Jordan at Jericho. ⁶⁴But among these there was not a man of those numbered by Moses and Aaron the priest, who had numbered the people of Israel in the wilderness of Sinai. ⁶⁵For the LORD had said of them, "They shall die in the wilderness." There was not left a man of them, except Caleb the son of Jẹ·phün'nẹh and Joshua the son of Nŭn.

27 Then drew near the daughters of Zĕ·lŏph'ẹ·hăd the son of Hē'-phẹr, son of Gilead, son of Mā'chĭr, son of Mạ·năs'sẹh, from the families of Manasseh the son of Joseph. The names of his daughters were: Mäh'lạh, Noah, Hŏg'lạh, Mĭl'cạh, and Tĭr'zạh. ²And they stood before Moses, and before Ĕl·ē·ā'zạr the priest, and before the leaders and all the congregation, at the door of the tent of meeting, saying, ³"Our father died in the wilderness; he was not among the company of those who gathered themselves together against the LORD in the company of Kō'rạh, but died for his own sin; and he had no sons. ⁴Why should the name of our father be taken away from his family, because he had no son? Give to us a possession among our father's brethren."

5 Moses brought their case before the LORD. ⁶And the LORD said to Moses, ⁷"The daughters of Zĕ·lŏph'ẹ·hăd are right; you shall give them possession of an inheritance among their father's brethren and cause the inheritance of their father to pass to them. ⁸And you shall say to the people of Israel, 'If a man dies, and has no son, then you shall cause his inheritance to pass to his daughter. ⁹And if he has no daughter, then you shall give his inheritance to his brothers. ¹⁰And if he has no brothers, then you shall give his inheritance to his father's brothers.

¹¹And if his father has no brothers, then you shall give his inheritance to his kinsman that is next to him of his family, and he shall possess it. And it shall be to the people of Israel a statute and ordinance, as the LORD commanded Moses.' "

12 The LORD said to Moses, "Go up into this mountain of Ăb'ạ·rĭm, and see the land which I have given to the people of Israel. ¹³And when you have seen it, you also shall be gathered to your people, as your brother Aaron was gathered, ¹⁴because you rebelled against my word in the wilderness of Zin during the strife of the congregation, to sanctify me at the waters before their eyes." (These are the waters of Mĕr'ĭ·bạh of Kā'dĕsh in the wilderness of Zĭn.) ¹⁵Moses said to the LORD, ¹⁶"Let the LORD, the God of the spirits of all flesh, appoint a man over the congregation, ¹⁷who shall go out before them and come in before them, who shall lead them out and bring them in; that the congregation of the LORD may not be as sheep which have no shepherd." ¹⁸And the LORD said to Moses, "Take Joshua the son of Nŭn, a man in whom is the spirit, and lay your hand upon him; ¹⁹cause him to stand before Ĕl·ē·ā'zạr the priest and all the congregation, and you shall commission him in their sight. ²⁰You shall invest him with some of your authority, that all the congregation of the people of Israel may obey. ²¹And he shall stand before Ĕl·ē·ā'zạr the priest, who shall inquire for him by the judgment of the Ū'rĭm before the LORD; at his word they shall go out, and at his word they shall come in, both he and all the people of Israel with him, the whole congregation." ²²And Moses did as the LORD commanded him; he took Joshua and caused him to stand before Ĕl·ē·ā'zạr the priest and the whole congregation, ²³and he laid his hands upon him, and commissioned him as the LORD directed through Moses.

28 The LORD said to Moses, ²"Command the people of Israel, and say to them, 'My offering, my food for my offerings by fire, my pleasing odor, you shall take heed to offer to me in its due season.' ³And you shall say to

them, This is the offering by fire which you shall offer to the LORD: two male lambs a year old without blemish, day by day, as a continual offering. ⁴The one lamb you shall offer in the morning, and the other lamb you shall offer in the evening; ⁵also a tenth of an ephah of fine flour for a cereal offering, mixed with a fourth of a hin of beaten oil. ⁶It is a continual burnt offering, which was ordained at Mount Sinai for a pleasing odor, an offering by fire to the LORD. ⁷Its drink offering shall be a fourth of a hin for each lamb; in the holy place you shall pour out a drink offering of strong drink to the LORD. ⁸The other lamb you shall offer in the evening; like the cereal offering of the morning, and like its drink offering, you shall offer it as an offering by fire, a pleasing odor to the LORD.

9 "On the sabbath day two male lambs a year old without blemish, and two tenths of an ephah of fine flour for a cereal offering, mixed with oil, and its drink offering: ¹⁰this is the burnt offering of every sabbath, besides the continual burnt offering and its drink offering.

11 "At the beginnings of your months you shall offer a burnt offering to the LORD: two young bulls, one ram, seven male lambs a year old without blemish; ¹²also three tenths of an ephah of fine flour for a cereal offering, mixed with oil, for each bull; and two tenths of fine flour for a cereal offering, mixed with oil, for the one ram; ¹³and a tenth of fine flour mixed with oil as a cereal offering for every lamb; for a burnt offering of pleasing odor, an offering by fire to the LORD. ¹⁴Their drink offerings shall be half a hin of wine for a bull, a third of a hin for a ram, and a fourth of a hin for a lamb; this is the burnt offering of each month throughout the months of the year. ¹⁵Also one male goat for a sin offering to the LORD; it shall be offered besides the continual burnt offering and its drink offering.

16 "On the fourteenth day of the first month is the LORD's passover. ¹⁷And on the fifteenth day of this month is a feast; seven days shall unleavened bread be eaten. ¹⁸On the first day there shall be a holy convocation: you shall do no laborious work, ¹⁹but offer an offering by fire, a burnt

offering to the LORD: two young bulls, one ram, and seven male lambs a year old; see that they are without blemish; ²⁰also their cereal offering of fine flour mixed with oil; three tenths of an ephah shall you offer for a bull, and two tenths for a ram; ²¹a tenth shall you offer for each of the seven lambs; ²²also one male goat for a sin offering, to make atonement for you. ²³You shall offer these besides the burnt offering of the morning, which is for a continual burnt offering. ²⁴In the same way you shall offer daily, for seven days, the food of an offering by fire, a pleasing odor to the LORD; it shall be offered besides the continual burnt offering and its drink offering. ²⁵And on the seventh day you shall have a holy convocation; you shall do no laborious work.

26 "On the day of the first fruits, when you offer a cereal offering of new grain to the LORD at your feast of weeks, you shall have a holy convocation; you shall do no laborious work, ²⁷but offer a burnt offering, a pleasing odor to the LORD: two young bulls, one ram, seven male lambs a year old; ²⁸also their cereal offering of fine flour mixed with oil, three tenths of an ephah for each bull, two tenths for one ram, ²⁹a tenth for each of the seven lambs; ³⁰with one male goat, to make atonement for you. ³¹Besides the continual burnt offering and its cereal offering, you shall offer them and their drink offering. See that they are without blemish.

29 "On the first day of the seventh month you shall have a holy convocation; you shall do no laborious work. It is a day for you to blow the trumpets, ²and you shall offer a burnt offering, a pleasing odor to the LORD: one young bull, one ram, seven male lambs a year old without blemish; ³also their cereal offering of fine flour mixed with oil, three tenths of an ephah for the bull, two tenths for the ram, ⁴and one tenth for each of the seven lambs; ⁵with one male goat for a sin offering, to make atonement for you; ⁶besides the burnt offering of the new moon, and its cereal offering, and the continual burnt offering and

28.16: Ex 12.1-14, 21-27; Lev 23.5; Deut 16.1, 2, 5-7.
28.17-25: Ex 12.15-20; Lev 23.6-8; Deut 16.3, 4, 8.
28.26-31: Ex 23.16; 34.22; Lev 23.15-21; Deut 16.9-12.
29.1-6: Ex 23.16; 34.22; Lev 23.23-25.

its cereal offering, and their drink offering, according to the ordinance for them, a pleasing odor, an offering by fire to the LORD.

7 "On the tenth day of this seventh month you shall have a holy convocation, and afflict yourselves; you shall do no work, ⁸but you shall offer a burnt offering to the LORD, a pleasing odor: one young bull, one ram, seven male lambs a year old; they shall be to you without blemish; ⁹and their cereal offering of fine flour mixed with oil, three tenths of an ephah for the bull, two tenths for the one ram, ¹⁰a tenth for each of the seven lambs: ¹¹also one male goat for a sin offering, besides the sin offering of atonement, and the continual burnt offering and its cereal offering, and their drink offerings.

12 "On the fifteenth day of the seventh month you shall have a holy convocation; you shall do no laborious work, and you shall keep a feast to the LORD seven days; ¹³and you shall offer a burnt offering, an offering by fire, a pleasing odor to the LORD, thirteen young bulls, two rams, fourteen male lambs a year old; they shall be without blemish; ¹⁴and their cereal offering of fine flour mixed with oil, three tenths of an ephah for each of the thirteen bulls, two tenths for each of the two rams, ¹⁵and a tenth for each of the fourteen lambs; ¹⁶also one male goat for a sin offering, besides the continual burnt offering, its cereal offering and its drink offering.

17 "On the second day twelve young bulls, two rams, fourteen male lambs a year old without blemish, ¹⁸with the cereal offering and the drink offerings for the bulls, for the rams, and for the lambs, by number, according to the ordinance; ¹⁹also one male goat for a sin offering, besides the continual burnt offering and its cereal offering, and their drink offerings.

20 "On the third day eleven bulls, two rams, fourteen male lambs a year old without blemish, ²¹with the cereal offering and the drink offerings for the bulls, for the rams, and for the lambs, by number, according to the ordinance; ²²also one male goat for a sin offering, besides the continual burnt offering and its cereal offering and its drink offering.

23 "On the fourth day ten bulls, two rams, fourteen male lambs a year old without blemish, ²⁴with the cereal offering and the drink offerings for the bulls, for the rams, and for the lambs, by number, according to the ordinance; ²⁵also one male goat for a sin offering, besides the continual burnt offering, its cereal offering and its drink offering.

26 "On the fifth day nine bulls, two rams, fourteen male lambs a year old without blemish, ²⁷with the cereal offering and the drink offerings for the bulls, for the rams, and for the lambs, by number, according to the ordinance; ²⁸also one male goat for a sin offering; besides the continual burnt offerings and its cereal offering and its drink offering.

29 "On the sixth day eight bulls, two rams, fourteen male lambs a year old without blemish, ³⁰with the cereal offering and the drink offerings for the bulls, for the rams, and for the lambs, by number, according to the ordinance; ³¹also one male goat for a sin offering; besides the continual burnt offering, its cereal offering, and its drink offerings.

32 "On the seventh day seven bulls, two rams, fourteen male lambs a year old without blemish, ³³with the cereal offering and the drink offerings for the bulls, for the rams, and for the lambs, by number, according to the ordinance; ³⁴also one male goat for a sin offering; besides the continual burnt offering, its cereal offering, and its drink offering.

35 "On the eighth day you shall have a solemn assembly: you shall do no laborious work, ³⁶but you shall offer a burnt offering, an offering by fire, a pleasing odor to the LORD: one bull, one ram, seven male lambs a year old without blemish, ³⁷and the cereal offering and the drink offerings for the bull, for the ram, and for the lambs, by number, according to the ordinance; ³⁸also one male goat for a sin offering; besides the continual burnt offering and its cereal offering and its drink offering.

39 "These you shall offer to the LORD at your appointed feasts, in addition to your votive offerings and your freewill offerings, for your burnt offerings, and for your cereal offerings,

29.7-11: Lev 16.29-34; 23.26-32.
29.12-34: Lev 23.33-35.
29.35-38: Lev 23.36.

and for your drink offerings, and for your peace offerings."

40ᵛ And Moses told the people of Israel everything just as the LORD had commanded Moses.

30 Moses said to the heads of the tribes of the people of Israel, "This is what the LORD has commanded. ²When a man vows a vow to the LORD, or swears an oath to bind himself by a pledge, he shall not break his word; he shall do according to all that proceeds out of his mouth. ³Or when a woman vows a vow to the LORD, and binds herself by a pledge, while within her father's house, in her youth, ⁴and her father hears of her vow and of her pledge by which she has bound herself, and says nothing to her; then all her vows shall stand, and her every pledge by which she has bound herself shall stand. ⁵But if her father expresses disapproval to her on the day that he hears of it, no vow of hers, no pledge by which she has bound herself, shall stand; and the LORD will forgive her, because her father opposed her. ⁶And if she is married to a husband, while under her vows or any thoughtless utterance of her lips by which she has bound herself, ⁷and her husband hears of it, and says nothing to her on the day that he hears; then her vows shall stand, and her pledges by which she has bound herself shall stand. ⁸But if, on the day that her husband comes to hear of it, he expresses disapproval, then he shall make void her vow which was on her, and the thoughtless utterance of her lips, by which she bound herself; and the LORD will forgive her. ⁹But any vow of a widow or of a divorced woman, anything by which she has bound herself, shall stand against her. ¹⁰And if she vowed in her husband's house, or bound herself by a pledge with an oath, ¹¹and her husband heard of it, and said nothing to her, and did not oppose her; then all her vows shall stand, and every pledge by which she bound herself shall stand. ¹²But if her husband makes them null and void on the day that he hears them, then whatever proceeds out of her lips concerning her vows, or concerning her pledge of herself, shall not stand: her husband has made them void, and the LORD will forgive her. ¹³Any vow and any binding oath

to afflict herself, her husband may establish, or her husband may make void. ¹⁴But if her husband says nothing to her from day to day, then he establishes all her vows, or all her pledges, that are upon her; he has established them, because he said nothing to her on the day that he heard of them. ¹⁵But if he makes them null and void after he has heard of them, then he shall bear her iniquity."

16 These are the statutes which the LORD commanded Moses, as between a man and his wife, and between a father and his daughter, while in her youth, within her father's house.

31 The LORD said to Moses, ²"Avenge the people of Israel on the Mĭd'ĭ·a·nītes; afterward you shall be gathered to your people." ³And Moses said to the people, "Arm men from among you for the war, that they may go against Mĭd'ĭ·an, to execute the LORD's vengeance on Midian. ⁴You shall send a thousand from each of the tribes of Israel to the war." ⁵So there were provided, out of the thousands of Israel, a thousand from each tribe, twelve thousand armed for war. ⁶And Moses sent them to the war, a thousand from each tribe, together with Phĭn'e·has the son of Ĕl·ē·ā'zạr the priest, with the vessels of the sanctuary and the trumpets for the alarm in his hand. ⁷They warred against Mĭd'ĭ·an, as the LORD commanded Moses, and slew every male. ⁸They slew the kings of Mĭd'ĭ·an with the rest of their slain, Ē'vī, Rē'kĕm, Zūr, Hūr, and Rē'ba, the five kings of Midian; and they also slew Bā'laăm the son of Bē'ôr with the sword. ⁹And the people of Israel took captive the women of Mĭd'ĭ·an and their little ones; and they took as booty all their cattle, their flocks, and all their goods. ¹⁰All their cities in the places where they dwelt, and all their encampments, they burned with fire, ¹¹and took all the spoil and all the booty, both of man and of beast. ¹²Then they brought the captives and the booty and the spoil to Moses, and to Ĕl·ē·ā'zạr the priest, and to the congregation of the people of Israel, at the camp on the plains of Mō'ăb by the Jordan at Jericho.

13 Moses, and Ĕl·ē·ā'zạr the priest, and all the leaders of the congrega-

tion, went forth to meet them outside the camp. [14]And Moses was angry with the officers of the army, the commanders of thousands and the commanders of hundreds, who had come from service in the war. [15]Moses said to them, "Have you let all the women live? [16]Behold, these caused the people of Israel, by the counsel of Bā′laăm, to act treacherously against the LORD in the matter of Pē′ôr, and so the plague came among the congregation of the LORD. [17]Now therefore, kill every male among the little ones, and kill every woman who has known man by lying with him. [18]But all the young girls who have not known man by lying with him, keep alive for yourselves. [19]Encamp outside the camp seven days; whoever of you has killed any person, and whoever has touched any slain, purify yourselves and your captives on the third day and on the seventh day. [20]You shall purify every garment, every article of skin, all work of goats' hair, and every article of wood."

21 And Ĕl·ē·ā′zạr the priest said to the men of war who had gone to battle: "This is the statute of the law which the LORD has commanded Moses: [22]only the gold, the silver, the bronze, the iron, the tin, and the lead, [23]everything that can stand the fire, you shall pass through the fire, and it shall be clean. Nevertheless it shall also be purified with the water of impurity; and whatever cannot stand the fire, you shall pass through the water. [24]You must wash your clothes on the seventh day, and you shall be clean; and afterward you shall come into the camp."

25 The LORD said to Moses, [26]"Take the count of the booty that was taken, both of man and of beast, you and Ĕl·ē·ā′zạr the priest and the heads of the fathers' houses of the congregation; [27]and divide the booty into two parts, between the warriors who went out to battle and all the congregation. [28]And levy for the LORD a tribute from the men of war who went out to battle, one out of five hundred, of the persons and of the oxen and of the asses and of the flocks; [29]take it from their half, and give it to Ĕl·ē·ā′zạr the priest as an offering to the LORD. [30]And from the people of Israel's half you shall take one drawn out of every fifty, of the per-

sons, of the oxen, of the asses, and of the flocks, of all the cattle, and give them to the Lē′vītes who have charge of the tabernacle of the LORD." [31]And Moses and Ĕl·ē·ā′zạr the priest did as the LORD commanded Moses.

32 Now the booty remaining of the spoil that the men of war took was: six hundred and seventy-five thousand sheep, [33]seventy-two thousand cattle, [34]sixty-one thousand asses, [35]and thirty-two thousand persons in all, women who had not known man by lying with him. [36]And the half, the portion of those who had gone out to war, was in number three hundred and thirty-seven thousand five hundred sheep, [37]and the LORD's tribute of sheep was six hundred and seventy-five. [38]The cattle were thirty-six thousand, of which the LORD's tribute was seventy-two. [39]The asses were thirty thousand five hundred, of which the LORD's tribute was sixty-one. [40]The persons were sixteen thousand, of which the LORD's tribute was thirty-two persons. [41]And Moses gave the tribute, which was the offering for the LORD, to Ĕl·ē·ā′zạr the priest, as the LORD commanded Moses.

42 From the people of Israel's half, which Moses separated from that of the men who had gone to war— [43]now the congregation's half was three hundred and thirty-seven thousand five hundred sheep, [44]thirty-six thousand cattle, [45]and thirty thousand five hundred asses, [46]and sixteen thousand persons— [47]from the people of Israel's half Moses took one of every fifty, both of persons and of beasts, and gave them to the Lē′vītes who had charge of the tabernacle of the LORD; as the LORD commanded Moses.

48 Then the officers who were over the thousands of the army, the captains of thousands and the captains of hundreds, came near to Moses, [49]and said to Moses, "Your servants have counted the men of war who are under our command, and there is not a man missing from us. [50]And we have brought the LORD's offering, what each man found, articles of gold, armlets and bracelets, signet rings, earrings, and beads, to make atonement for ourselves before the LORD." [51]And Moses and Ĕl·ē·ā′zạr the priest received from them the gold, all wrought

31.16: Rev 2.14.

articles. ⁵²And all the gold of the offering that they offered to the Lord, from the commanders of thousands and the commanders of hundreds, was sixteen thousand seven hundred and fifty shekels. ⁵³(The men of war had taken booty, every man for himself.) ⁵⁴And Moses and Ĕl·ē·ā'zạr the priest received the gold from the commanders of thousands and of hundreds, and brought it into the tent of meeting, as a memorial for the people of Israel before the Lord.

32 Now the sons of Reuben and the sons of Găd had a very great multitude of cattle; and they saw the land of Jā'zẹr and the land of Gilead, and behold, the place was a place for cattle. ²So the sons of Găd and the sons of Reuben came and said to Moses and to Ĕl·ē·ā'zạr the priest and to the leaders of the congregation, ³"Ăt'ạ·rŏth, Dī'bŏn, Jā'zẹr, Nĭm'rạh, Hĕsh'bọn, Ē''lĕ·ā'lẹh, Sē'băm, Nē'bō, and Bē'ŏn, ⁴the land which the Lord smote before the congregation of Israel, is a land for cattle; and your servants have cattle." ⁵And they said, "If we have found favor in your sight, let this land be given to your servants for a possession; do not take us across the Jordan."

6 But Moses said to the sons of Găd and to the sons of Reuben, "Shall your brethren go to the war while you sit here? ⁷Why will you discourage the heart of the people of Israel from going over into the land which the Lord has given them? ⁸Thus did your fathers, when I sent them from Kā'dĕsh–bār'nē·ạ to see the land. ⁹For when they went up to the Valley of Ĕsh'cọl, and saw the land, they discouraged the heart of the people of Israel from going into the land which the Lord had given them. ¹⁰And the Lord's anger was kindled on that day, and he swore, saying, ¹¹"Surely none of the men who came up out of Egypt, from twenty years old and upward, shall see the land which I swore to give to Abraham, to Isaac, and to Jacob, because they have not wholly followed me; ¹²none except Caleb the son of Jẹ·phün'nẹh the Kĕn'ĭz·zīte and Joshua the son of Nŭn, for they have wholly followed the Lord.' ¹³And the Lord's anger was kindled against Israel, and he made them wander in the wilderness forty years, until all the generation that had done evil in the sight of the Lord was consumed. ¹⁴And behold, you have risen in your fathers' stead, a brood of sinful men, to increase still more the fierce anger of the Lord against Israel! ¹⁵For if you turn away from following him, he will again abandon them in the wilderness; and you will destroy all this people."

16 Then they came near to him, and said, "We will build sheepfolds here for our flocks, and cities for our little ones, ¹⁷but we will take up arms, ready to go before the people of Israel, until we have brought them to their place; and our little ones shall live in the fortified cities because of the inhabitants of the land. ¹⁸We will not return to our homes until the people of Israel have inherited each his inheritance. ¹⁹For we will not inherit with them on the other side of the Jordan and beyond; because our inheritance has come to us on this side of the Jordan to the east." ²⁰So Moses said to them, "If you will do this, if you will take up arms to go before the Lord for the war, ²¹and every armed man of you will pass over the Jordan before the Lord, until he has driven out his enemies from before him ²²and the land is subdued before the Lord; then after that you shall return and be free of obligation to the Lord and to Israel; and this land shall be your possession before the Lord. ²³But if you will not do so, behold, you have sinned against the Lord; and be sure your sin will find you out. ²⁴Build cities for your little ones, and folds for your sheep; and do what you have promised." ²⁵And the sons of Găd and the sons of Reuben said to Moses, "Your servants will do as my lord commands. ²⁶Our little ones, our wives, our flocks, and all our cattle, shall remain there in the cities of Gilead; ²⁷but your servants will pass over, every man who is armed for war, before the Lord to battle, as my lord orders."

28 So Moses gave command concerning them to Ĕl·ē·ā'zạr the priest, and to Joshua the son of Nŭn, and to the heads of the fathers' houses of the tribes of the people of Israel. ²⁹And Moses said to them, "If the sons of Găd and the sons of Reuben, every man who is armed to battle before the Lord, will pass with you over the Jor-

dan and the land shall be subdued before you, then you shall give them the land of Gilead for a possession; ³⁰but if they will not pass over with you armed, they shall have possessions among you in the land of Canaan." ³¹And the sons of Gȧd and the sons of Reuben answered, "As the LORD has said to your servants, so we will do. ³²We will pass over armed before the LORD into the land of Canaan, and the possession of our inheritance shall remain with us beyond the Jordan."

33 And Moses gave to them, to the sons of Gȧd and to the sons of Reuben and to the half-tribe of Mạ·năs′sẹh the son of Joseph, the kingdom of Sī′họn king of the Ăm′ọ·rītes and the kingdom of Ŏg king of Bā′shạn, the land and its cities with their territories, the cities of the land throughout the country. ³⁴And the sons of Gȧd built Dī′bŏn, Ăt′ạ·rŏth, Ạ·rō′ẹr, ³⁵Ăt′rŏth-shō′phạn, Jă′zẹr, Jŏg′bĕ·hăh, ³⁶Bĕth-nĭm′rạh and Bĕth-hăr′ạn, fortified cities, and folds for sheep. ³⁷And the sons of Reuben built Hĕsh′bọn, Ē″lẹ-ā′lẹh, Kĭr″ĭ·ạ·thā′ĭm, ³⁸Nē′bō, and Bā′ạl-mē′ọn (their names to be changed), and Sĭb′mạh; and they gave other names to the cities which they built. ³⁹And the sons of Mā′chĭr the son of Mạ·năs′sẹh went to Gilead and took it, and dispossessed the Ăm′ọ-rītes who were in it. ⁴⁰And Moses gave Gilead to Mā′chĭr the son of Mạ·năs′-sẹh, and he settled in it. ⁴¹And Jā′ĭr the son of Mạ·năs′sẹh went and took their villages, and called them Hăv′vọth-jā′ĭr.ᶻ ⁴²And Nō′bạh went and took Kē′năth and its villages, and called it Nobah, after his own name.

33 These are the stages of the people of Israel, when they went forth out of the land of Egypt by their hosts under the leadership of Moses and Aaron. ²Moses wrote down their starting places, stage by stage, by command of the LORD; and these are their stages according to their starting places. ³They set out from Răm′ĕ·sĕş in the first month, on the fifteenth day of the first month; on the day after the passover the people of Israel went out triumphantly in the sight of all the Egyptians, ⁴while the Egyptians were burying all their first-born, whom the LORD had struck down among them; upon their gods also the LORD executed judgments.

5 So the people of Israel set out from Răm′ĕ·sĕş, and encamped at Sŭc′-cŏth. ⁶And they set out from Sŭc′cŏth, and encamped at Ē′thạm, which is on the edge of the wilderness. ⁷And they set out from Ē′thạm, and turned back to Pī–hạ·hī′rŏth, which is east of Bā′ạl–zē′phŏn; and they encamped before Mĭg′dōl. ⁸And they set out from before Hạ·hī′rŏth, and passed through the midst of the sea into the wilderness, and they went a three days' journey in the wilderness of Ē′thạm, and encamped at Mâr′ạh. ⁹And they set out from Mâr′ạh, and came to Ē′lĭm; at Elim there were twelve springs of water and seventy palm trees, and they encamped there. ¹⁰And they set out from Ē′lĭm, and encamped by the Red Sea. ¹¹And they set out from the Red Sea, and encamped in the wilderness of Sĭn. ¹²And they set out from the wilderness of Sĭn, and encamped at Dŏph′kạh. ¹³And they set out from Dŏph′kạh, and encamped at Ā′lụsh. ¹⁴And they set out from Ā′lụsh, and encamped at Rĕph′ĭ·dĭm, where there was no water for the people to drink. ¹⁵And they set out from Rĕph′ĭ·dĭm, and encamped in the wilderness of Sinai. ¹⁶And they set out from the wilderness of Sinai, and encamped at Kĭb′rŏth–hăt·tā′ạ·vạh. ¹⁷And they set out from Kĭb′rŏth–hăt·tā′ạ·vạh, and encamped at Hạ·zē′rŏth. ¹⁸And they set out from Hạ·zē′rŏth, and encamped at Rĭth′mạh. ¹⁹And they set out from Rĭth′mạh, and encamped at Rĭm′mŏn–pĕr′ĕz. ²⁰And they set out from Rĭm′-mŏn–pĕr′ĕz, and encamped at Lĭb′nạh. ²¹And they set out from Lĭb′nạh, and encamped at Rĭs′sạh. ²²And they set out from Rĭs′sạh, and encamped at Kē·hẹ·lā′thạh. ²³And they set out from Kē·hẹ·lā′thạh, and encamped at Mount Shē′phẹr. ²⁴And they set out from Mount Shē′phẹr, and encamped at Hạ·rā′dạh. ²⁵And they set out from Hạ·rā′dạh, and encamped at Măk·hē′-lŏth. ²⁶And they set out from Măk-hē′lŏth, and encamped at Tā′hăth. ²⁷And they set out from Tā′hăth, and encamped at Tĕ′rạh. ²⁸And they set out from Tĕ′rạh, and encamped at Mĭth′-kạh. ²⁹And they set out from Mĭth′kạh, and encamped at Hăsh·mō′nạh. ³⁰And they set out from Hăsh·mō′nạh, and encamped at Mō·sē′rŏth. ³¹And they set out from Mō·sē′rŏth, and encamped at

ᶻThat is *the villages of Jair*

Bē'nĕ–jā'ạ·kạn. ³²And they set out from Bē'nĕ–jā'ạ·kạn, and encamped at Hôr–hạg·gĭd'găd. ³³And they set out from Hôr–hạg·gĭd'găd, and encamped at Jŏt'bạ·thạh. ³⁴And they set out from Jŏt'bạ·thạh, and encamped at Ạ·brō'nah. ³⁵And they set out from Ạ·brō'nah, and encamped at Ē'zĭ·ŏn–gē'bẹr. ³⁶And they set out from Ē'zĭ·ŏn–gē'bẹr, and encamped in the wilderness of Zĭn (that is, Kā'dĕsh). ³⁷And they set out from Kā'dĕsh, and encamped at Mount Hôr, on the edge of the land of Ē'dọm.

38 And Aaron the priest went up Mount Hôr at the command of the LORD, and died there, in the fortieth year after the people of Israel had come out of the land of Egypt, on the first day of the fifth month. ³⁹And Aaron was a hundred and twenty-three years old when he died on Mount Hôr.

40 And the Canaanite, the king of Är'ạd, who dwelt in the Nĕg'ĕb in the land of Canaan, heard of the coming of the people of Israel.

41 And they set out from Mount Hôr, and encamped at Zăl·mō'nạh. ⁴²And they set out from Zăl·mō'nạh, and encamped at Pū'nŏn. ⁴³And they set out from Pū'nŏn, and encamped at Ō'bŏth. ⁴⁴And they set out from Ō'bŏth, and encamped at Ī'yĕ–ăb'ạ·rĭm, in the territory of Mō'ăb. ⁴⁵And they set out from Ī'yĭm, and encamped at Dī'bŏn·găd. ⁴⁶And they set out from Dī'bŏn·găd, and encamped at Äl'mọn–dĭb·lạ·thā'ĭm. ⁴⁷And they set out from Äl'mọn–dĭb·lạ·thā'ĭm, and encamped in the mountains of Äb'ạ·rĭm, before Nē'bō. ⁴⁸And they set out from the mountains of Äb'ạ·rĭm, and encamped in the plains of Mō'ăb by the Jordan at Jericho; ⁴⁹they encamped by the Jordan from Bĕth–jĕsh'ĭ·mŏth as far as Ā'bĕl–shĭt'tim in the plains of Mō'ăb.

50 And the LORD said to Moses in the plains of Mō'ăb by the Jordan at Jericho, ⁵¹"Say to the people of Israel, When you pass over the Jordan into the land of Canaan, ⁵²then you shall drive out all the inhabitants of the land from before you, and destroy all their figured stones, and destroy all their molten images, and demolish all their high places; ⁵³and you shall take possession of the land and settle in it, for I have given the land to you to possess it. ⁵⁴You shall inherit the land by lot according to your families; to a large tribe you shall give a large inheritance, and to a small tribe you shall give a small inheritance; wherever the lot falls to any man, that shall be his; according to the tribes of your fathers you shall inherit. ⁵⁵But if you do not drive out the inhabitants of the land from before you, then those of them whom you let remain shall be as pricks in your eyes and thorns in your sides, and they shall trouble you in the land where you dwell. ⁵⁶And I will do to you as I thought to do to them."

34 The LORD said to Moses, ²"Command the people of Israel, and say to them, When you enter the land of Canaan (this is the land that shall fall to you for an inheritance, the land of Canaan in its full extent), ³your south side shall be from the wilderness of Zĭn along the side of Ē'dọm, and your southern boundary shall be from the end of the Salt Sea on the east; ⁴and your boundary shall turn south of the ascent of Äk·răb'bĭm, and cross to Zĭn, and its end shall be south of Kā'dĕsh–bär'nē·ạ; then it shall go on to Hā'zär–ăd'dạr, and pass along to Äz'mọn; ⁵and the boundary shall turn from Äz'mọn to the Brook of Egypt, and its termination shall be at the sea.

6 "For the western boundary, you shall have the Great Sea and its*ᵃ* coast; this shall be your western boundary.

7 "This shall be your northern boundary: from the Great Sea you shall mark out your line to Mount Hôr; ⁸from Mount Hôr you shall mark it out to the entrance of Hā'măth, and the end of the boundary shall be at Zē'dăd; ⁹then the boundary shall extend to Zĭph'rọn, and its end shall be at Hā'zär–ē'nạn; this shall be your northern boundary.

10 "You shall mark out your eastern boundary from Hā'zär–ē'nạn to Shē'phạm; ¹¹and the boundary shall go down from Shē'phạm to Rĭb'lạh on the east side of Ā'ĭn; and the boundary shall go down, and reach to the shoulder of the sea of Chĭn'nẹ·rĕth on the

---

*Syr: Heb lacks *its*
33.38, 39: Num 20.23-29; Deut 10.6.
33.52: Ex 23.24; Deut 7.5; 12.3.
34.3-5: Josh 15.1-4.

east; ¹²and the boundary shall go down to the Jordan, and its end shall be at the Salt Sea. This shall be your land with its boundaries all round."

13 Moses commanded the people of Israel, saying, "This is the land which you shall inherit by lot, which the LORD has commanded to give to the nine tribes and to the half-tribe; ¹⁴for the tribe of the sons of Reuben by fathers' houses and the tribe of the sons of Gad by their fathers' houses have received their inheritance, and also the half-tribe of Ma·năs'seh; ¹⁵the two tribes and the half-tribe have received their inheritance beyond the Jordan at Jericho eastward, toward the sunrise."

16 The LORD said to Moses, ¹⁷"These are the names of the men who shall divide the land to you for inheritance: Ĕl·ē·ā'zar the priest and Joshua the son of Nŭn. ¹⁸You shall take one leader of every tribe, to divide the land for inheritance. ¹⁹These are the names of the men: Of the tribe of Judah, Caleb the son of Jĕ·phŭn'neh. ²⁰Of the tribe of the sons of Sĭm'ē·on, Shĕ·mū'ĕl the son of Ăm·mī'hud. ²¹Of the tribe of Benjamin, Ē·lī'dăd the son of Chĭs'lon. ²²Of the tribe of the sons of Dan a leader, Bŭk'kī the son of Jŏg'lī. ²³Of the sons of Joseph: of the tribe of the sons of Ma·năs'seh a leader, Hăn'-nĭ·ĕl the son of Ē'phŏd. ²⁴And of the tribe of the sons of Ē'phra·ĭm a leader, Kĕ'mū·ĕl the son of Shĭph'tan. ²⁵Of the tribe of the sons of Zĕb'ū·lun a leader, Ē·lī·zā'phan the son of Pār'nach. ²⁶Of the tribe of the sons of Ĭs'sa·chär a leader, Păl'tĭ–ĕl the son of Ăz'zan. ²⁷And of the tribe of the sons of Ăsh'er a leader, A·hī'hud the son of She·lō'mī. ²⁸Of the tribe of the sons of Năph'-ta·lī a leader, Pĕ·dăh'ĕl the son of Ăm·mī'hud. ²⁹These are the men whom the LORD commanded to divide the inheritance for the people of Israel in the land of Canaan."

35 The LORD said to Moses in the plains of Mō'ăb by the Jordan at Jericho, ²"Command the people of Israel, that they give to the Lē'vītes, from the inheritance of their possession, cities to dwell in; and you shall give to the Levites pasture lands round about the cities. ³The cities shall be theirs to dwell in, and their pasture lands shall be for their cattle and for their livestock and for all their beasts.

⁴The pasture lands of the cities, which you shall give to the Lē'vītes, shall reach from the wall of the city outward a thousand cubits all round. ⁵And you shall measure, outside the city, for the east side two thousand cubits, and for the south side two thousand cubits, and for the west side two thousand cubits, and for the north side two thousand cubits, the city being in the middle; this shall belong to them as pasture land for their cities. ⁶The cities which you give to the Lē'vītes shall be the six cities of refuge, where you shall permit the manslayer to flee, and in addition to them you shall give forty-two cities. ⁷All the cities which you give to the Lē'vītes shall be forty-eight, with their pasture lands. ⁸And as for the cities which you shall give from the possession of the people of Israel, from the larger tribes you shall take many, and from the smaller tribes you shall take few; each, in proportion to the inheritance which it inherits, shall give of its cities to the Lē'vītes."

9 And the LORD said to Moses, ¹⁰"Say to the people of Israel, When you cross the Jordan into the land of Canaan, ¹¹then you shall select cities to be cities of refuge for you, that the manslayer who kills any person without intent may flee there. ¹²The cities shall be for you a refuge from the avenger, that the manslayer may not die until he stands before the congregation for judgment. ¹³And the cities which you give shall be your six cities of refuge. ¹⁴You shall give three cities beyond the Jordan, and three cities in the land of Canaan, to be cities of refuge. ¹⁵These six cities shall be for refuge for the people of Israel, and for the stranger and for the sojourner among them, that any one who kills any person without intent may flee there.

16 "But if he struck him down with an instrument of iron, so that he died, he is a murderer; the murderer shall be put to death. ¹⁷And if he struck him down with a stone in the hand, by which a man may die, and he died, he is a murderer; the murderer shall be put to death. ¹⁸Or if he struck him down with a weapon of wood in the hand, by which a man may die, and he

34.13-15: Josh 14.1-5.
35.1-8: Lev 25.32-34; Josh 21.1-42.
35.6, 9-34: Deut 19.1-13.

died, he is a murderer; the murderer shall be put to death. ¹⁹The avenger of blood shall himself put the murderer to death; when he meets him, he shall put him to death. ²⁰And if he stabbed him from hatred, or hurled at him, lying in wait, so that he died, ²¹or in enmity struck him down with his hand, so that he died, then he who struck the blow shall be put to death; he is a murderer; the avenger of blood shall put the murderer to death, when he meets him.

22 "But if he stabbed him suddenly without enmity, or hurled anything on him without lying in wait, ²³or used a stone, by which a man may die, and without seeing him cast it upon him, so that he died, though he was not his enemy, and did not seek his harm; ²⁴then the congregation shall judge between the manslayer and the avenger of blood, in accordance with these ordinances; ²⁵and the congregation shall rescue the manslayer from the hand of the avenger of blood, and the congregation shall restore him to his city of refuge, to which he had fled, and he shall live in it until the death of the high priest who was anointed with the holy oil. ²⁶But if the manslayer shall at any time go beyond the bounds of his city of refuge to which he had fled, ²⁷and the avenger of blood finds him outside the bounds of his city of refuge, and the avenger of blood slays the manslayer, he shall not be guilty of blood. ²⁸For the man must remain in his city of refuge until the death of the high priest; but after the death of the high priest the manslayer may return to the land of his possession.

29 "And these things shall be for a statute and ordinance to you throughout your generations in all your dwellings. ³⁰If any one kills a person, the murderer shall be put to death on the evidence of witnesses; but no person shall be put to death on the testimony of one witness. ³¹Moreover you shall accept no ransom for the life of a murderer, who is guilty of death; but he shall be put to death. ³²And you shall accept no ransom for him who has fled to his city of refuge, that he may return to dwell in the land before the death of the high priest. ³³You shall not thus pollute the land in which you live; for blood pollutes the land, and no

expiation can be made for the land, for the blood that is shed in it, except by the blood of him who shed it. ³⁴You shall not defile the land in which you live, in the midst of which I dwell; for I the LORD dwell in the midst of the people of Israel."

36 The heads of the fathers' houses of the families of the sons of Gilead the son of Mā′chir, son of Ma·nās′seh, of the fathers' houses of the sons of Joseph, came near and spoke before Moses and before the leaders, the heads of the fathers' houses of the people of Israel; ²they said, "The LORD commanded my lord to give the land for inheritance by lot to the people of Israel; and my lord was commanded by the LORD to give the inheritance of Zĕ·lŏph′e·hăd our brother to his daughters. ³But if they are married to any of the sons of the other tribes of the people of Israel then their inheritance will be taken from the inheritance of our fathers, and added to the inheritance of the tribe to which they belong; so it will be taken away from the lot of our inheritance. ⁴And when the jubilee of the people of Israel comes, then their inheritance will be added to the inheritance of the tribe to which they belong; and their inheritance will be taken from the inheritance of the tribe of our fathers."

5 And Moses commanded the people of Israel according to the word of the LORD, saying, "The tribe of the sons of Joseph is right. ⁶This is what the LORD commands concerning the daughters of Zĕ·lŏph′e·hăd, 'Let them marry whom they think best; only, they shall marry within the family of the tribe of their father. ⁷The inheritance of the people of Israel shall not be transferred from one tribe to another; for every one of the people of Israel shall cleave to the inheritance of the tribe of his fathers. ⁸And every daughter who possesses an inheritance in any tribe of the people of Israel shall be wife to one of the family of the tribe of her father, so that every one of the people of Israel may possess the inheritance of his fathers. ⁹So no inheritance shall be transferred from one tribe to another; for each of the tribes of the people of Israel shall cleave to its own inheritance.' "

10 The daughters of Zĕ·lŏph′e·hăd

did as the LORD commanded Moses; ¹¹for Mäh′lah, Tĭr′zah, Hŏg′lah, Mĭl′- cah, and Noah, the daughters of Zĕ- lŏph′e·hăd, were married to sons of their father's brothers. ¹²They were married into the families of the sons of Ma·năs′seh the son of Joseph, and their inheritance remained in the tribe of the family of their father.

13 These are the commandments and the ordinances which the LORD commanded by Moses to the people of Israel in the plains of Mō′ăb by the Jordan at Jericho.

The Fifth Book of Moses
Commonly Called
Deuteronomy

1 These are the words that Moses spoke to all Israel beyond the Jordan in the wilderness, in the Ăr′- a·bah over against Süph, between Păr′ăn and Tō′phĕl, Lā′ban, Hă- zē′rŏth, and Dĭ′za·hăb. ²It is eleven days' journey from Hō′rĕb by the way of Mount Sē′ĭr to Kā′dĕsh–băr′nē·a. ³And in the fortieth year, on the first day of the eleventh month, Moses spoke to the people of Israel according to all that the LORD had given him in commandment to them, ⁴after he had defeated Sī′hon the king of the Ăm′o- rītes, who lived in Hĕsh′bon, and Ŏg the king of Bā′shan, who lived in Ăsh′ta·rŏth and in Ĕd′rē–ī. ⁵Beyond the Jordan, in the land of Mō′ăb, Moses undertook to explain this law, saying, ⁶"The LORD our God said to us in Hō′rĕb, 'You have stayed long enough at this mountain; ⁷turn and take your journey, and go to the hill country of the Ăm′o·rītes, and to all their neigh- bors in the Ăr′a·bah, in the hill country and in the lowland, and in the Nĕg′eb, and by the seacoast, the land of the Canaanites, and Lebanon, as far as the great river, the river Euphrates. ⁸Behold, I have set the land before you; go in and take possession of the land which the LORD swore to your fathers, to Abraham, to Isaac, and to Jacob, to give to them and to their descend- ants after them.'

9 "At that time I said to you, 'I am not able alone to bear you; ¹⁰the LORD your God has multiplied you, and be- hold, you are this day as the stars of heaven for multitude. ¹¹May the LORD, the God of your fathers, make you a thousand times as many as you are, and bless you, as he has promised you! ¹²How can I bear alone the weight and burden of you and your strife? ¹³Choose wise, understanding, and experienced men, according to your tribes, and I will appoint them as your heads.' ¹⁴And you answered me, 'The thing that you have spoken is good for us to do.' ¹⁵So I took the heads of your tribes, wise and experienced men, and set them as heads over you, commanders of thou- sands, commanders of hundreds, com- manders of fifties, commanders of tens, and officers, throughout your tribes. ¹⁶And I charged your judges at that time, 'Hear the cases between your brethren, and judge righteously between a man and his brother or the alien that is with him. ¹⁷You shall not be partial in judgment; you shall hear the small and the great alike; you shall not be afraid of the face of man, for the judgment is God's; and the case that is too hard for you, you shall bring to me, and I will hear it.' ¹⁸And I commanded you at that time all the things that you should do.

19 "And we set out from Hō′rĕb, and went through all that great and terrible wilderness which you saw, on the way to the hill country of the Ăm′- o·rītes, as the LORD our God com- manded us; and we came to Kā′dĕsh–

1.9-15: Num 11.10-25.   1.16-18: Ex 18.25, 26.

bär'nē·ạ. [20]And I said to you, 'You have come to the hill country of the Ăm'-ọ·rītes, which the LORD our God gives us. [21]Behold, the LORD your God has set the land before you; go up, take possession, as the LORD, the God of your fathers, has told you; do not fear or be dismayed.' [22]Then all of you came near me, and said, 'Let us send men before us, that they may explore the land for us, and bring us word again of the way by which we must go up and the cities into which we shall come.' [23]The thing seemed good to me, and I took twelve men of you, one man for each tribe; [24]and they turned and went up into the hill country, and came to the Valley of Ĕsh'cọl and spied it out. [25]And they took in their hands some of the fruit of the land and brought it down to us, and brought us word again, and said, 'It is a good land which the LORD our God gives us.'

26 "Yet you would not go up, but rebelled against the command of the LORD your God; [27]and you murmured in your tents, and said, 'Because the LORD hated us he has brought us forth out of the land of Egypt, to give us into the hand of the Ăm'ọ·rītes, to destroy us. [28]Whither are we going up? Our brethren have made our hearts melt, saying, "The people are greater and taller than we; the cities are great and fortified up to heaven; and moreover we have seen the sons of the Ăn'a·kĭm there."' [29]Then I said to you, 'Do not be in dread or afraid of them. [30]The LORD your God who goes before you will himself fight for you, just as he did for you in Egypt before your eyes, [31]and in the wilderness, where you have seen how the LORD your God bore you, as a man bears his son, in all the way that you went until you came to this place.' [32]Yet in spite of this word you did not believe the LORD your God, [33]who went before you in the way to seek you out a place to pitch your tents, in fire by night, to show you by what way you should go, and in the cloud by day.

34 "And the LORD heard your words, and was angered, and he swore, [35]'Not one of these men of this evil generation shall see the good land which I swore to give to your fathers, [36]except Caleb the son of Jẹ·phŭn'-neh; he shall see it, and to him and to his children I will give the land upon

which he has trodden, because he has wholly followed the LORD!' [37]The LORD was angry with me also on your account, and said, 'You also shall not go in there; [38]Joshua the son of Nŭn, who stands before you, he shall enter; encourage him, for he shall cause Israel to inherit it. [39]Moreover your little ones, who you said would become a prey, and your children, who this day have no knowledge of good or evil, shall go in there, and to them I will give it, and they shall possess it. [40]But as for you, turn, and journey into the wilderness in the direction of the Red Sea.'

41 "Then you answered me, 'We have sinned against the LORD; we will go up and fight, just as the LORD our God commanded us.' And every man of you girded on his weapons of war, and thought it easy to go up into the hill country. [42]And the LORD said to me, 'Say to them, Do not go up or fight, for I am not in the midst of you; lest you be defeated before your enemies.' [43]So I spoke to you, and you would not hearken; but you rebelled against the command of the LORD, and were presumptuous and went up into the hill country. [44]Then the Ăm'ọ·rītes who lived in that hill country came out against you and chased you as bees do and beat you down in Sē'ĭr as far as Hôr'mạh. [45]And you returned and wept before the LORD; but the LORD did not hearken to your voice or give ear to you. [46]So you remained at Kā'-dĕsh many days, the days that you remained there.

2 "Then we turned, and journeyed into the wilderness in the direction of the Red Sea, as the LORD told me; and for many days we went about Mount Sē'ĭr. [2]Then the LORD said to me, [3]'You have been going about this mountain country long enough; turn northward. [4]And command the people, You are about to pass through the territory of your brethren the sons of Esau, who live in Sē'ĭr; and they will be afraid of you. So take good heed; [5]do not contend with them; for I will not give you any of their land, no, not so much as for the sole of the foot to tread on, because I have given Mount Sē'ĭr to Esau as a possession. [6]You shall purchase food from them

1.22-46: Num 13.1-14.45; 32.8-13.   1.31: Acts 13.18.
2.1-8: Num 21.4-20.

for money, that you may eat; and you shall also buy water of them for money, that you may drink. ⁷For the LORD your God has blessed you in all the work of your hands; he knows your going through this great wilderness; these forty years the LORD your God has been with you; you have lacked nothing.' ⁸So we went on, away from our brethren the sons of Esau who live in Sē´ĭr, away from the Ăr´a·bah road from Ē´lăth and Ē´zĭ·ŏn–gē´ber.

"And we turned and went in the direction of the wilderness of Mō´ăb. ⁹And the LORD said to me, 'Do not harass Mō´ăb or contend with them in battle, for I will not give you any of their land for a possession, because I have given Ăr to the sons of Lot for a possession.' ¹⁰(The Ē´mĭm formerly lived there, a people great and many, and tall as the Ăn´a·kĭm; ¹¹like the Ăn´a·kĭm they are also known as Rĕph´a·ĭm, but the Mō´ab·ītes call them Ē´mĭm. ¹²The Hôr´ītes also lived in Sē´ĭr formerly, but the sons of Esau dispossessed them, and destroyed them from before them, and settled in their stead; as Israel did to the land of their possesssion, which the LORD gave to them.) ¹³'Now rise up, and go over the brook Zē´rĕd.' So we went over the brook Zered. ¹⁴And the time from our leaving Kā´dĕsh–bär´nē·a until we crossed the brook Zē´rĕd was thirty-eight years, until the entire generation, that is, the men of war, had perished from the camp, as the LORD had sworn to them. ¹⁵For indeed the hand of the LORD was against them, to destroy them from the camp, until they had perished.

16 "So when all the men of war had perished and were dead from among the people, ¹⁷the LORD said to me, ¹⁸'This day you are to pass over the boundary of Mō´ăb at Ăr; ¹⁹and when you approach the frontier of the sons of Ăm´mon, do not harass them or contend with them, for I will not give you any of the land of the sons of Ammon as a possession, bccause I have given it to the sons of Lot for a possession.' ²⁰(That also is known as a land of Rĕph´a·ĭm; Rephaim formerly lived there, but the Ăm´mo·nītes call them Zăm·zŭm´mĭm, ²¹a people great and many, and tall as the Ăn´a·kĭm; but the LORD destroyed them before them; and they dispossessed them, and

settled in their stead; ²²as he did for the sons of Esau, who live in Sē´ĭr, when he destroyed the Hôr´ītes before them, and they dispossessed them, and settled in their stead even to this day. ²³As for the Ăv´vĭm, who lived in villages as far as Gā´za, the Căph´to·rĭm, who came from Căph´tôr, destroyed them and settled in their stead.) ²⁴'Rise up, take your journey, and go over the valley of the Ăr´nŏn; behold, I have given into your hand Sī´hon the Ăm´o·rīte, king of Hĕsh´bon, and his land; begin to take possession, and contend with him in battle. ²⁵This day I will begin to put the dread and fear of you upon the peoples that are under the whole heaven, who shall hear the report of you and shall tremble and be in anguish because of you.'

26 "So I sent messengers from the wilderness of Kĕd´e·mŏth to Sī´hon the king of Hĕsh´bon, with words of peace, saying, ²⁷'Let me pass through your land; I will go only by the road, I will turn aside neither to the right nor to the left. ²⁸You shall sell me food for money, that I may eat, and give me water for money, that I may drink; only let me pass through on foot, ²⁹as the sons of Esau who live in Sē´ĭr and the Mō´ab·ītes who live in Ăr did for me, until I go over the Jordan into the land which the LORD our God gives to us.' ³⁰But Sī´hon the king of Hĕsh´bon would not let us pass by him; for the LORD your God hardened his spirit and made his heart obstinate, that he might give him into your hand, as at this day. ³¹And the LORD said to me, 'Behold, I have begun to give Sī´hon and his land over to you; begin to take possession, that you may occupy his land.' ³²Then Sī´hon came out against us, he and all his people, to battle at Jā´hăz. ³³And the LORD our God gave him over to us; and we defeated him and his sons and all his people. ³⁴And we captured all his cities at that time and utterly destroyed every city, men, women, and children; we left none remaining; ³⁵only the cattle we took as spoil for ourselves, with the booty of the cities which we captured. ³⁶From A·rō´er, which is on the edge of the valley of the Ăr´nŏn, and from the city that is in the valley, as far as Gilead, there was not a city too high for us; the LORD our God gave all into

2.26–37: Num 21.21-32.

our hands. [37] Only to the land of the sons of Ăm'mon you did not draw near, that is, to all the banks of the river Jăb'bŏk and the cities of the hill country, and wherever the LORD our God forbade us.

3 "Then we turned and went up the way to Bā'shạn; and Ŏg the king of Bashan came out against us, he and all his people, to battle at Ĕd'-re-ī. [2] But the LORD said to me, 'Do not fear him; for I have given him and all his people and his land into your hand; and you shall do to him as you did to Sī'hon the king of the Ăm'o·rītes, who dwelt at Hĕsh'bon.' [3] So the LORD our God gave into our hand Ŏg also, the king of Bā'shạn, and all his people; and we smote him until no survivor was left to him. [4] And we took all his cities at that time—there was not a city which we did not take from them—sixty cities, the whole region of Ăr'gŏb, the kingdom of Ŏg in Bā'shạn. [5] All these were cities fortified with high walls, gates, and bars, besides very many unwalled villages. [6] And we utterly destroyed them, as we did to Sī'hon the king of Hĕsh'bon, destroying every city, men, women, and children. [7] But all the cattle and the spoil of the cities we took as our booty. [8] So we took the land at that time out of the hand of the two kings of the Ăm'-o·rītes who were beyond the Jordan, from the valley of the Ăr'nŏn to Mount Hermon [9] (the Sī·dō'nĭ·ạns call Hermon Sīr'ĭ·on, while the Ăm'o·rītes call it Sē'nĭr), [10] all the cities of the table-land and all Gilead and all Bā'shạn, as far as Săl'ẹ·cạh and Ĕd're-ī, cities of the kingdom of Ŏg in Bā'shạn. [11] (For only Ŏg the king of Bā'shạn was left of the remnant of the Rĕph'a·ĭm; behold, his bedstead was a bedstead of iron; is it not in Răb'bạh of the Ăm'mo·nītes? Nine cubits was its length, and four cubits its breadth, according to the common cubit.[a])

12 "When we took possession of this land at that time, I gave to the Reubenites and the Găd'ītes the territory beginning at Ạ·rō'ẹr, which is on the edge of the valley of the Ăr'nŏn, and half the hill country of Gilead with its cities; [13] the rest of Gilead, and all Bā'shạn, the kingdom of Ŏg, that is, all the region of Ăr'gŏb, I gave to the half-tribe of Mạ·năs'seh. (The whole of that Bā'shạn is called the land of

Rĕph'a·ĭm. [14] Jā'ĭr the Mạ·năs'sīte took all the region of Ăr'gŏb, that is, Bā'shạn, as far as the border of the Gĕsh'ū·rītes and the Mā–ăc'a·thītes, and called the villages after his own name, Hăv'voth-jā'ĭr, as it is to this day.) [15] To Mā'chīr I gave Gilead, [16] and to the Reubenites and the Găd'ītes I gave the territory from Gilead as far as the valley of the Ăr'nŏn, with the middle of the valley as a boundary, as far over as the river Jăb'bŏk, the boundary of the Ăm'mo·nītes; [17] the Ăr'a·bạh also, with the Jordan as the boundary, from Chĭn'nẹ·rĕth as far as the sea of the Arabah, the Salt Sea, under the slopes of Pĭş'gạh on the east.

18 "And I commanded you at that time, saying. 'The LORD your God has given you this land to possess; all your men of valor shall pass over armed before your brethren the people of Israel. [19] But your wives, your little ones, and your cattle (I know that you have many cattle) shall remain in the cities which I have given you, [20] until the LORD gives rest to your brethren, as to you, and they also occupy the land which the LORD your God gives them beyond the Jordan; then you shall return every man to his possession which I have given you.' [21] And I commanded Joshua at that time, 'Your eyes have seen all that the LORD your God has done to these two kings; so will the LORD do to all the kingdoms into which you are going over. [22] You shall not fear them; for it is the LORD your God who fights for you.'

23 "And I besought the LORD at that time, saying, [24] 'O Lord GOD, thou hast only begun to show thy servant thy greatness and thy mighty hand; for what god is there in heaven or on earth who can do such works and mighty acts as thine? [25] Let me go over, I pray, and see the good land beyond the Jordan, that goodly hill country, and Lebanon.' [26] But the LORD was angry with me on your account, and would not hearken to me; and the LORD said to me, 'Let it suffice you; speak no more to me of this matter. [27] Go up to the top of Pĭş'gạh, and lift up your eyes westward and northward and southward and eastward, and behold it with your eyes; for you shall not go over this

[a]Heb *cubit of a man*
3.1-11: Num 21.33-35.   3.12-20: Num 32.
3.23-27: Num 27.12-14; Deut 32.48-52.

Jordan. ²⁸But charge Joshua, and encourage and strengthen him; for he shall go over at the head of this people, and he shall put them in possession of the land which you shall see.' ²⁹So we remained in the valley opposite Bĕth–pē′ôr.

4 "And now, O Israel, give heed to the statutes and the ordinances which I teach you, and do them; that you may live, and go in and take possession of the land which the Lᴏʀᴅ, the God of your fathers, gives you. ²You shall not add to the word which I command you, nor take from it; that you may keep the commandments of the Lᴏʀᴅ your God which I command you. ³Your eyes have seen what the Lᴏʀᴅ did at Bā′al–pē′ôr; for the Lᴏʀᴅ your God destroyed from among you all the men who followed the Bā′al of Pē′ôr; ⁴but you who held fast to the Lᴏʀᴅ your God are all alive this day. ⁵Behold, I have taught you statutes and ordinances, as the Lᴏʀᴅ my God commanded me, that you should do them in the land which you are entering to take possession of it. ⁶Keep them and do them; for that will be your wisdom and your understanding in the sight of the peoples, who, when they hear all these statutes, will say, 'Surely this great nation is a wise and understanding people.' ⁷For what great nation is there that has a god so near to it as the Lᴏʀᴅ our God is to us, whenever we call upon him? ⁸And what great nation is there, that has statutes and ordinances so righteous as all this law which I set before you this day?

9 "Only take heed, and keep your soul diligently, lest you forget the things which your eyes have seen, and lest they depart from your heart all the days of your life; make them known to your children and your children's children—¹⁰how on the day that you stood before the Lᴏʀᴅ your God at Hō′rĕb, the Lᴏʀᴅ said to me, 'Gather the people to me, that I may let them hear my words, so that they may learn to fear me all the days that they live upon the earth, and that they may teach their children so.' ¹¹And you came near and stood at the foot of the mountain, while the mountain burned with fire to the heart of heaven, wrapped in darkness, cloud, and gloom. ¹²Then the Lᴏʀᴅ spoke to you out of the midst

of the fire; you heard the sound of words, but saw no form; there was only a voice. ¹³And he declared to you his covenant, which he commanded you to perform, that is, the ten commandments;ᵇ and he wrote them upon two tables of stone. ¹⁴And the Lᴏʀᴅ commanded me at that time to teach you statutes and ordinances, that you might do them in the land which you are going over to possess.

15 "Therefore take good heed to yourselves. Since you saw no form on the day that the Lᴏʀᴅ spoke to you at Hō′rĕb out of the midst of the fire, ¹⁶beware lest you act corruptly by making a graven image for yourselves, in the form of any figure, the likeness of male or female, ¹⁷the likeness of any beast that is on the earth, the likeness of any winged bird that flies in the air, ¹⁸the likeness of anything that creeps on the ground, the likeness of any fish that is in the water under the earth. ¹⁹And beware lest you lift up your eyes to heaven, and when you see the sun and the moon and the stars, all the host of heaven, you be drawn away and worship them and serve them, things which the Lᴏʀᴅ your God has allotted to all the peoples under the whole heaven. ²⁰But the Lᴏʀᴅ has taken you, and brought you forth out of the iron furnace, out of Egypt, to be a people of his own possession, as at this day. ²¹Furthermore the Lᴏʀᴅ was angry with me on your account, and he swore that I should not cross the Jordan, and that I should not enter the good land which the Lᴏʀᴅ your God gives you for an inheritance. ²²For I must die in this land, I must not go over the Jordan; but you shall go over and take possession of that good land. ²³Take heed to yourselves, lest you forget the convenant of the Lᴏʀᴅ your God, which he made with you, and make a graven image in the form of anything which the Lᴏʀᴅ your God has forbidden you. ²⁴For the Lᴏʀᴅ your God is a devouring fire, a jealous God.

25 "When you beget children and children's children, and have grown old in the land, if you act corruptly by making a graven image in the form of anything, and by doing what is evil in the sight of the Lᴏʀᴅ your God, so

ᵇHeb *words*
4.2: Rev 22.18, 19.   4.9–14: Ex 19.1-20, 21.
4.24: Heb 12.29.

as to provoke him to anger, ²⁶I call heaven and earth to witness against you this day, that you will soon utterly perish from the land which you are going over the Jordan to possess; you will not live long upon it, but will be utterly destroyed. ²⁷And the LORD will scatter you among the peoples, and you will be left few in number among the nations where the LORD will drive you. ²⁸And there you will serve gods of wood and stone, the work of men's hands, that neither see, nor hear, nor eat, nor smell. ²⁹But from there you will seek the LORD your God, and you will find him, if you search after him with all your heart and with all your soul. ³⁰When you are in tribulation, and all these things come upon you in the latter days, you will return to the LORD your God and obey his voice, ³¹for the LORD your God is a merciful God; he will not fail you or destroy you or forget the covenant with your fathers which he swore to them.

32 "For ask now of the days that are past, which were before you, since the day that God created man upon the earth, and ask from one end of heaven to the other, whether such a great thing as this has ever happened or was ever heard of. ³³Did any people ever hear the voice of a god speaking out of the midst of the fire, as you have heard, and still live? ³⁴Or has any god ever attempted to go and take a nation for himself from the midst of another nation, by trials, by signs, by wonders, and by war, by a mighty hand and an outstretched arm, and by great terrors, according to all that the LORD your God did for you in Egypt before your eyes? ³⁵To you it was shown, that you might know that the LORD is God; there is no other besides him. ³⁶Out of heaven he let you hear his voice, that he might discipline you; and on earth he let you see his great fire, and you heard his words out of the midst of the fire. ³⁷And because he loved your fathers and chose their descendants after them, and brought you out of Egypt with his own presence, by his great power, ³⁸driving out before you nations greater and mightier than yourselves, to bring you in, to give you their land for an inheritance, as at this day; ³⁹know therefore this day, and lay it to your heart, that the LORD is God in heaven above

and on the earth beneath; there is no other. ⁴⁰Therefore you shall keep his statutes and his commandments, which I command you this day, that it may go well with you, and with your children after you, and that you may prolong your days in the land which the LORD your God gives you for ever."

41 Then Moses set apart three cities in the east beyond the Jordan, ⁴²that the manslayer might flee there, who kills his neighbor unintentionally, without being at enmity with him in time past, and that by fleeing to one of these cities he might save his life: ⁴³Bē′zer in the wilderness on the tableland for the Reubenites, and Rā′mŏth in Gilead for the Gad′ites, and Gō′lăn in Bā′shan for the Ma·năs′sītes.

44 This is the law which Moses set before the children of Israel; ⁴⁵these are the testimonies, the statutes, and the ordinances, which Moses spoke to the children of Israel when they came out of Egypt, ⁴⁶beyond the Jordan in the valley opposite Bĕth–pē′ôr, in the land of Sī′hon the king of the Ăm′o·rītes, who lived at Hĕsh′bon, whom Moses and the children of Israel defeated when they came out of Egypt. ⁴⁷And they took possession of his land and the land of Ŏg the king of Bā′shan, the two kings of the Ăm′o·rītes, who lived to the east beyond the Jordan; ⁴⁸from A·rō′er, which is on the edge of the valley of the Ăr′nŏn, as far as Mount Sīr′i·on^c (that is, Hermon), ⁴⁹together with all the Ăr′a·bah on the east side of the Jordan as far as Sea of the Arabah, under the slopes of Pisʹgah.

5 And Moses summoned all Israel, and said to them, "Hear, O Israel, the statutes and the ordinances which I speak in your hearing this day, and you shall learn them and be careful to do them. ²The LORD our God made a covenant with us in Hō′rĕb. ³Not with our fathers did the LORD make this covenant, but with us, who are all of us here alive this day. ⁴The LORD spoke with you face to face at the mountain, out of the midst of the fire, ⁵while I stood between the LORD and you at that time, to declare to you the word of the LORD; for you were afraid because of the fire, and you did not go up into the mountain. He said:

---

^cSyr: Heb *Sion* **4.35:** Mk 12.32.
4.41-43: Num 35.6, 9-34; Deut 19.2-13; Josh 20.7-9.

6 " 'I am the LORD your God, who brought you out of the land of Egypt, out of the house of bondage.

7 " 'You shall have no other gods before[d] me.

8 " 'You shall not make for yourself a graven image, or any likeness of anything that is in heaven above, or that is on the earth beneath, or that is in the water under the earth; [9]you shall not bow down to them or serve them; for I the LORD your God am a jealous God, visiting the iniquity of the fathers upon the children to the third and fourth generation of those who hate me, [10]but showing steadfast love to thousands of those who love me and keep my commandments.

11 " 'You shall not take the name of the LORD your God in vain: for the LORD will not hold him guiltless who takes his name in vain.

12 " 'Observe the sabbath day, to keep it holy, as the LORD your God commanded you. [13]Six days you shall labor, and do all your work; [14]but the seventh day is a sabbath to the LORD your God; in it you shall not do any work, you, or your son, or your daughter, or your manservant, or your maidservant, or your ox, or your ass, or any of your cattle, or the sojourner who is within your gates, that your manservant and your maidservant may rest as well as you. [15]You shall remember that you were a servant in the land of Egypt, and the LORD your God brought you out thence with a mighty hand and an outstretched arm; therefore the LORD your God commanded you to keep the sabbath day.

16 " 'Honor your father and your mother, as the LORD your God commanded you; that your days may be prolonged, and that it may go well with you, in the land which the LORD your God gives you.

17 " 'You shall not kill.

18 " 'Neither shall you commit adultery.

19 " 'Neither shall you steal.

20 " 'Neither shall you bear false witness against your neighbor.

21 " 'Neither shall you covet your neighbor's wife; and you shall not desire your neighbor's house, his field, or his manservant, or his maidservant, his ox, or his ass, or anything that is your neighbor's.'

22 "These words the LORD spoke to all your assembly at the mountain out of the midst of the fire, the cloud, and the thick darkness, with a loud voice; and he added no more. And he wrote them upon two tables of stone, and gave them to me. [23]And when you heard the voice out of the midst of the darkness, while the mountain was burning with fire, you came near to me, all the heads of your tribes, and your elders; [24]and you said, 'Behold, the LORD our God has shown us his glory and greatness, and we have heard his voice out of the midst of the fire; we have this day seen God speak with man and man still live. [25]Now therefore why should we die? For this great fire will consume us; if we hear the voice of the LORD our God any more, we shall die. [26]For who is there of all flesh, that has heard the voice of the living God speaking out of the midst of fire, as we have, and has still lived? [27]Go near, and hear all that the LORD our God will say; and speak to us all that the LORD our God will speak to you; and we will hear and do it.'

28 "And the LORD heard your words, when you spoke to me; and the LORD said to me, 'I have heard the words of this people, which they have spoken to you; they have rightly said all that they have spoken. [29]Oh that they had such a mind as this always, to fear me and to keep all my commandments, that it might go well with them and with their children for ever! [30]Go and say to them, "Return to your tents." [31]But you, stand here by me, and I will tell you all the commandment and the statutes and the ordinances which you shall teach them, that they may do them in the land which I give them to possess.' [32]You shall be careful to do therefore as the LORD your God has commanded you; you shall not turn aside to the right hand or to the left. [33]You shall walk in all the way which the LORD your God has commanded you, that you may live, and that it may go well with you, and that you may live long in the land which you shall possess.

6 "Now this is the commandment, the statutes and the ordinances

---

[d]Or *besides*

5.6-21: Ex 20.2-17. **5.14:** Ex 20.8-11; 23.12.
5.16-20: Mt 19.18, 19; Mk 10.19; Lk 18.20.
5.16: Mt 15.4; Mk 7.10; Eph 6.3. **5.17, 18:** Jas 2.11.
5.17-21: Rom 13.9. **5.18:** Mt 5.27; Rom 7.7.
5.21: Rom 7.7. **5.22-27:** Ex 20.18-21.

which the LORD your God commanded me to teach you, that you may do them in the land to which you are going over, to possess it; ²that you may fear the LORD your God, you and your son and your son's son, by keeping all his statutes and his commandments, which I command you, all the days of your life; and that your days may be prolonged. ³Hear therefore, O Israel, and be careful to do them; that it may go well with you, and that you may multiply greatly, as the LORD, the God of your fathers, has promised you, in a land flowing with milk and honey.

4 "Hear, O Israel: The LORD our God is one LORD;*ᵉ* ⁵and you shall love the LORD your God with all your heart, and with all your soul, and with all your might. ⁶And these words which I command you this day shall be upon your heart; ⁷and you shall teach them diligently to your children, and shall talk of them when you sit in your house, and when you walk by the way, and when you lie down, and when you rise. ⁸And you shall bind them as a sign upon your hand, and they shall be as frontlets between your eyes. ⁹And you shall write them on the doorposts of your house and on your gates.

10 "And when the LORD your God brings you into the land which he swore to your fathers, to Abraham, to Isaac, and to Jacob, to give you, with great and goodly cities, which you did not build, ¹¹and houses full of all good things, which you did not fill, and cisterns hewn out, which you did not hew, and vineyards and olive trees, which you did not plant, and when you eat and are full, ¹²then take heed lest you forget the LORD, who brought you out of the land of Egypt, out of the house of bondage. ¹³You shall fear the LORD your God; you shall serve him, and swear by his name. ¹⁴You shall not go after other gods, of the gods of the peoples who are round about you; ¹⁵for the LORD your God in the midst of you is a jealous God; lest the anger of the LORD your God be kindled against you, and he destroy you from off the face of the earth.

16 "You shall not put the LORD your God to the test, as you tested him at Mǎs′sah. ¹⁷You shall diligently keep the commandments of the LORD your God, and his testimonies, and his statutes, which he has commanded you.

¹⁸And you shall do what is right and good in the sight of the LORD, that it may go well with you, and that you may go in and take possession of the good land which the LORD swore to give to your fathers ¹⁹by thrusting out all your enemies from before you, as the LORD has promised.

20 "When your son asks you in time to come, 'What is the meaning of the testimonies and the statutes and the ordinances which the LORD our God has commanded you?' ²¹then you shall say to your son, 'We were Pharaoh's slaves in Egypt; and the LORD brought us out of Egypt with a mighty hand; ²²and the LORD showed signs and wonders, great and grievous, against Egypt and against Pharaoh and all his household, before our eyes; ²³and he brought us out from there, that he might bring us in and give us the land which he swore to give to our fathers. ²⁴And the LORD commanded us to do all these statutes, to fear the LORD our God, for our good always, that he might preserve us alive, as at this day. ²⁵And it will be righteousness for us, if we are careful to do all this commandment before the LORD our God, as he has commanded us.'

7 "When the LORD your God brings you into the land which you are entering to take possession of it, and clears away many nations before you, the Hīt′tītes, the Gīr′gạ·shītes, the Ăm′ọ·rītes, the Canaanites, the Pěr′ĭz·zītes, the Hī′vītes, and the Jěb′ū·sītes, seven nations greater and mightier than yourselves, ²and when the LORD your God gives them over to you, and you defeat them; then you must utterly destroy them; you shall make no covenant with them, and show no mercy to them. ³You shall not make marriages with them, giving your daughters to their sons or taking their daughters for your sons. ⁴For they would turn away your sons from following me, to serve other gods; then the anger of the LORD would be kindled against you, and he would destroy you quickly. ⁵But thus shall you deal with

ᵉOr *the* LORD *our God, the* LORD *is one*
  Or *the* LORD *is our God, the* LORD *is one*
  Or *the* LORD *is our God, the* LORD *alone*
6.4, 5: Mt 22.37; Mk 12.29, 30; Lk 10.27.
6.6-9: Deut 6.20-25; 11.18-20.
6.8: Ex 13.9, 16; Deut 11.18.   **6.13:** Mt 4.10; Lk 4.8.
6.16: Mt 4.7; Lk 4.12.   **7.1:** Acts 13.19.
7.2-4: Ex 23.32, 33; 34.12, 15, 16.   **7.3:** Ex 34.15, 16.
7.5: Ex 23.24; 34.13; Num 33.52; Deut 12.3.

them: you shall break down their altars, and dash in pieces their pillars, and hew down their A·shē′rim, and burn their graven images with fire.

6 "For you are a people holy to the LORD your God; the LORD your God has chosen you to be a people for his own possession, out of all the peoples that are on the face of the earth. ⁷It was not because you were more in number than any other people that the LORD set his love upon you and chose you, for you were the fewest of all peoples; ⁸but it is because the LORD loves you, and is keeping the oath which he swore to your fathers, that the LORD has brought you out with a mighty hand, and redeemed you from the house of bondage, from the hand of Pharaoh king of Egypt. ⁹Know therefore that the LORD your God is God, the faithful God who keeps covenant and steadfast love with those who love him and keep his commandments, to a thousand generations, ¹⁰and requites to their face those who hate him, by destroying them; he will not be slack with him who hates him, he will requite him to his face. ¹¹You shall therefore be careful to do the commandment, and the statutes, and the ordinances, which I command you this day.

12 "And because you hearken to these ordinances, and keep and do them, the LORD your God will keep with you the covenant and the steadfast love which he swore to your fathers to keep; ¹³he will love you, bless you, and multiply you; he will also bless the fruit of your body and the fruit of your ground, your grain and your wine and your oil, the increase of your cattle and the young of your flock, in the land which he swore to your fathers to give you. ¹⁴You shall be blessed above all peoples; there shall not be male or female barren among you, or among your cattle. ¹⁵And the LORD will take away from you all sickness; and none of the evil diseases of Egypt, which you knew, will he inflict upon you, but he will lay them upon all who hate you. ¹⁶And you shall destroy all the peoples that the LORD your God will give over to you, your eye shall not pity them; neither shall you serve their gods, for that would be a snare to you.

17 "If you say in your heart, 'These nations are greater than I; how can I dispossess them?' ¹⁸you shall not be afraid of them, but you shall remember what the LORD your God did to Pharaoh and to all Egypt, ¹⁹the great trials which your eyes saw, the signs, the wonders, the mighty hand, and the outstretched arm, by which the LORD your God brought you out; so will the LORD your God do to all the peoples of whom you are afraid. ²⁰Moreover the LORD your God will send hornets among them, until those who are left and hide themselves from you are destroyed. ²¹You shall not be in dread of them; for the LORD your God is in the midst of you, a great and terrible God. ²²The LORD your God will clear away these nations before you little by little; you may not make an end of them at once,ᶠ lest the wild beasts grow too numerous for you. ²³But the LORD your God will give them over to you, and throw them into great confusion, until they are destroyed. ²⁴And he will give their kings into your hand, and you shall make their name perish from under heaven; not a man shall be able to stand against you, until you have destroyed them. ²⁵The graven images of their gods you shall burn with fire; you shall not covet the silver or the gold that is on them, or take it for yourselves, lest you be ensnared by it; for it is an abomination to the LORD your God. ²⁶And you shall not bring an abominable thing into your house, and become accursed like it; you shall utterly detest and abhor it; for it is an accursed thing.

8 "All the commandment which I command you this day you shall be careful to do, that you may live and multiply, and go in and possess the land which the LORD swore to give to your fathers. ²And you shall remember all the way which the LORD your God has led you these forty years in the wilderness, that he might humble you, testing you to know what was in your heart, whether you would keep his commandments, or not. ³And he humbled you and let you hunger and fed you with manna, which you did not know, nor did your fathers know; that he might make you know that man does not live by bread alone, but that man lives by everything that pro-

/Or quickly
7.6: Ex 19.5; 22.3; Lev 11.44, 45; 19.2; 20.7, 26; Num 15.40; Deut 14.2, 21; 26.19; 28.9. **8.3:** Mt 4.4; Lk 4.4.

ceeds out of the mouth of the LORD.
⁴ Your clothing did not wear out upon
you, and your foot did not swell, these
forty years. ⁵ Know then in your heart
that, as a man disciplines his son, the
LORD your God disciplines you. ⁶ So
you shall keep the commandments of
the LORD your God, by walking in his
ways and by fearing him. ⁷ For the
LORD your God is bringing you into a
good land, a land of brooks of water,
of fountains and springs, flowing forth
in valleys and hills, ⁸ a land of wheat
and barley, of vines and fig trees and
pomegranates, a land of olive trees and
honey, ⁹ a land in which you will eat
bread without scarcity, in which you
will lack nothing, a land whose stones
are iron, and out of whose hills you can
dig copper. ¹⁰ And you shall eat and be
full, and you shall bless the LORD your
God for the good land he has given you.

11 "Take heed lest you forget the
LORD your God, by not keeping his commandments and his ordinances and
his statutes, which I command you
this day: ¹² lest, when you have eaten
and are full, and have built goodly
houses and live in them, ¹³ and when
your herds and flocks multiply, and
your silver and gold is multiplied, and
all that you have is multiplied, ¹⁴ then
your heart be lifted up, and you forget
the LORD your God, who brought you
out of the land of Egypt, out of the
house of bondage, ¹⁵ who led you
through the great and terrible wilderness, with its fiery serpents and
scorpions and thirsty ground where
there was no water, who brought you
water out of the flinty rock, ¹⁶ who fed
you in the wilderness with manna
which your fathers did not know, that
he might humble you and test you, to
do you good in the end. ¹⁷ Beware lest
you say in your heart, 'My power and
the might of my hand have gotten me
this wealth.' ¹⁸ You shall remember
the LORD your God, for it is he who
gives you power to get wealth; that he
may confirm his covenant which he
swore to your fathers, as at this day.
¹⁹ And if you forget the LORD your God
and go after other gods and serve them
and worship them, I solemnly warn
you this day that you shall surely perish. ²⁰ Like the nations that the LORD
makes to perish before you, so shall
you perish, because you would not
obey the voice of the LORD your God.

9 "Hear, O Israel; you are to pass
over the Jordan this day, to go in to
dispossess nations greater and mightier than yourselves, cities great and
fortified up to heaven, ² a people great
and tall, the sons of the Ăn´a̧·kim,
whom you know, and of whom you
have heard it said, 'Who can stand before the sons of Ā´năk? ³ Know therefore this day that he who goes over
before you as a devouring fire is the
LORD your God; he will destroy them
and subdue them before you; so you
shall drive them out, and make them
perish quickly, as the LORD has promised you.

4 "Do not say in your heart, after
the LORD your God has thrust them
out before you, 'It is because of my
righteousness that the LORD has
brought me in to possess this land';
whereas it is because of the wickedness of these nations that the LORD is
driving them out before you. ⁵ Not
because of your righteousness or the
uprightness of your heart are you going
in to possess their land; but because
of the wickedness of these nations the
LORD your God is driving them out
from before you, and that he may confirm the word which the LORD swore
to your fathers, to Abraham, to Isaac,
and to Jacob.

6 "Know therefore, that the LORD
your God is not giving you this good
land to possess because of your righteousness; for you are a stubborn people. ⁷ Remember and do not forget
how you provoked the LORD your God
to wrath in the wilderness; from the
day you came out of the land of Egypt
until you came to this place, you have
been rebellious against the LORD.
⁸ Even at Hō´rĕb you provoked the LORD
to wrath, and the LORD was so angry
with you that he was ready to destroy
you. ⁹ When I went up the mountain to
receive the tables of stone, the tables
of the covenant which the LORD made
with you, I remained on the mountain
forty days and forty nights; I neither
ate bread nor drank water. ¹⁰ And the
LORD gave me the two tables of stone
written with the finger of God; and on
them were all the words which the
LORD had spoken with you on the
mountain out of the midst of the fire
on the day of the assembly. ¹¹ And at
the end of forty days and forty nights,

9.3: Heb 12.29.   **9.8-21**: Ex 32.7-20.

the LORD gave me the two tables of stone, the tables of the covenant. [12]Then the LORD said to me, 'Arise, go down quickly from here; for your people whom you have brought from Egypt have acted corruptly; they have turned aside quickly out of the way which I commanded them; they have made themselves a molten image.'

13 "Furthermore the LORD said to me, 'I have seen this people, and behold, it is a stubborn people; [14]let me alone, that I may destroy them and blot out their name from under heaven; and I will make of you a nation mightier and greater than they.' [15]So I turned and came down from the mountain, and the mountain was burning with fire; and the two tables of the covenant were in my two hands. [16]And I looked, and behold, you had sinned against the LORD your God; you had made yourselves a molten calf; you had turned aside quickly from the way which the LORD had commanded you. [17]So I took hold of the two tables, and cast them out of my two hands, and broke them before your eyes. [18]Then I lay prostrate before the LORD as before, forty days and forty nights; I neither ate bread nor drank water, because of all the sin which you had committed, in doing what was evil in the sight of the LORD, to provoke him to anger. [19]For I was afraid of the anger and hot displeasure which the LORD bore against you, so that he was ready to destroy you. But the LORD hearkened to me that time also. [20]And the LORD was so angry with Aaron that he was ready to destroy him; and I prayed for Aaron also at the same time. [21]Then I took the sinful thing, the calf which you had made, and burned it with fire and crushed it, grinding it very small, until it was as fine as dust; and I threw the dust of it into the brook that descended out of the mountain.

22 "At Tăb′e·rạh also, and at Măs′sạh, and at Kĭb′rŏth-hăt·tā′ạ·vạh, you provoked the LORD to wrath. [23]And when the LORD sent you from Kā′dĕsh-bār′nē·ạ, saying, 'Go up and take possession of the land which I have given you,' then you rebelled against the commandment of the LORD your God, and did not believe him or obey his voice. [24]You have been rebellious against the LORD from the day that I knew you.

25 "So I lay prostrate before the LORD for these forty days and forty nights, because the LORD had said he would destroy you. [26]And I prayed to the LORD, 'O Lord GOD, destroy not thy people and thy heritage, whom thou hast redeemed through thy greatness, whom thou hast brought out of Egypt with a mighty hand. [27]Remember thy servants, Abraham, Isaac, and Jacob; do not regard the stubbornness of this people, or their wickedness, or their sin, [28]lest the land from which thou didst bring us say, "Because the LORD was not able to bring them into the land which he promised them, and because he hated them, he has brought them out to slay them in the wilderness." [29]For they are thy people and thy heritage, whom thou didst bring out by thy great power and by thy outstretched arm.'

10 "At that time the LORD said to me, 'Hew two tables of stone like the first, and come up to me on the mountain, and make an ark of wood. [2]And I will write on the tables the words that were on the first tables which you broke, and you shall put them in the ark.' [3]So I made an ark of acacia wood, and hewed two tables of stone like the first, and went up the mountain with the two tables in my hand. [4]And he wrote on the tables, as at the first writing, the ten commandments[g] which the LORD had spoken to you on the mountain out of the midst of the fire on the day of the assembly; and the LORD gave them to me. [5]Then I turned and came down from the mountain, and put the tables in the ark which I had made; and there they are, as the LORD commanded me.

6 (The people of Israel journeyed from Be̅-ẽr′oth Be̅′nĕ-jā′ạ·kan[h] to Mō·sē′rạh. There Aaron died, and there he was buried; and his son Ĕl·ē·ā′zạr ministered as priest in his stead. [7]From there they journeyed to Gŭd′gō·dạh, and from Gudgodah to Jŏt′bạ·thạh, a land with brooks of water. [8]At that time the LORD set apart the tribe of Lē′vī to carry the ark of the covenant of the LORD, to stand before the LORD to minister to him and to bless in his name, to this day. [9]Therefore Lē′vī has no portion or inheritance with his brothers; the LORD is his

[g]Heb *words* [h]Or *the wells of the Bene-jaakan*
9.25-29: Ex 32.11-14.

inheritance, as the LORD your God said to him.)

10 "I stayed on the mountain, as at the first time, forty days and forty nights, and the LORD hearkened to me that time also; the LORD was unwilling to destroy you. [11] And the LORD said to me, 'Arise, go on your journey at the head of the people, that they may go in and possess the land, which I swore to their fathers to give them.'

12 "And now, Israel, what does the LORD your God require of you, but to fear the LORD your God, to walk in all his ways, to love him, to serve the LORD your God with all your heart and with all your soul, [13] and to keep the commandments and statutes of the LORD, which I command you this day for your good? [14] Behold, to the LORD your God belong heaven and the heaven of heavens, the earth with all that is in it; [15] yet the LORD set his heart in love upon your fathers and chose their descendants after them, you above all peoples, as at this day. [16] Circumcise therefore the foreskin of your heart, and be no longer stubborn. [17] For the LORD your God is God of gods and Lord of lords, the great, the mighty, and the terrible God, who is not partial and takes no bribe. [18] He executes justice for the fatherless and the widow, and loves the sojourner, giving him food and clothing. [19] Love the sojourner therefore; for you were sojourners in the land of Egypt. [20] You shall fear the LORD your God; you shall serve him and cleave to him, and by his name you shall swear. [21] He is your praise; he is your God, who has done for you these great and terrible things which your eyes have seen. [22] Your fathers went down to Egypt seventy persons; and now the LORD your God has made you as the stars of heaven for multitude.

11 "You shall therefore love the LORD your God, and keep his charge, his statutes, his ordinances, and his commandments always. [2] And consider this day (since I am not speaking to your children who have not known or seen it), consider the discipline[i] of the LORD your God, his greatness, his mighty hand and his outstretched arm, [3] his signs and his deeds which he did in Egypt to Pharaoh the king of Egypt and to all his land; [4] and what he did to the army of Egypt, to their horses and to their chariots; how he made the water of the Red Sea overflow them as they pursued after you, and how the LORD has destroyed them to this day; [5] and what he did to you in the wilderness, until you came to this place; [6] and what he did to Dā′thạn and Ạ·bī′rạm the sons of Ē·lī′ạb, son of Reuben; how the earth opened its mouth and swallowed them up, with their households, their tents, and every living thing that followed them, in the midst of all Israel; [7] for your eyes have seen all the great work of the LORD which he did.

8 "You shall therefore keep all the commandment which I command you this day, that you may be strong, and go in and take possession of the land which you are going over to possess, [9] and that you may live long in the land which·the LORD swore to your fathers to give to them and to their descendants, a land flowing with milk and honey. [10] For the land which you are entering to take possession of it is not like the land of Egypt, from which you have come, where you sowed your seed and watered it with your feet, like a garden of vegetables; [11] but the land which you are going over to possess is a land of hills and valleys, which drinks water by the rain from heaven, [12] a land which the LORD your God cares for; the eyes of the LORD your God are always upon it, from the beginning of the year to the end of the year.

13 "And if you will obey my commandments which I command you this day, to love the LORD your God, and to serve him with all your heart and with all your soul, [14] he[j] will give the rain for your land in its season, the early rain and the later rain, that you may gather in your grain and your wine and your oil. [15] And he[j] will give grass in your fields for your cattle, and you shall eat and be full. [16] Take heed lest your heart be deceived, and you turn aside and serve other gods and worship them, [17] and the anger of the LORD be kindled against you, and he shut up the heavens, so that there be no rain, and the land yield no fruit, and you perish quickly off the good land which the LORD gives you.

[i] *Or instruction* [j] Sam Gk Vg: Heb I
10.17: Acts 10.34; Gal 2.6; Rev 17.14; 19.16.
10.19: Ex 22.21; 23.9; Lev 19.34. **10.22:** Acts 7.14.

18 "You shall therefore lay up these words of mine in your heart and in your soul; and you shall bind them as a sign upon your hand, and they shall be as frontlets between your eyes. ¹⁹And you shall teach them to your children, talking of them when you are sitting in your house, and when you are walking by the way, and when you lie down, and when you rise. ²⁰And you shall write them upon the doorposts of your house and upon your gates, ²¹that your days and the days of your children may be multiplied in the land which the LORD swore to your fathers to give them, as long as the heavens are above the earth. ²²For if you will be careful to do all this commandment which I command you to do, loving the LORD your God, walking in all his ways, and cleaving to him, ²³then the LORD will drive out all these nations before you, and you will dispossess nations greater and mightier than yourselves. ²⁴Every place on which the sole of your foot treads shall be yours; your territory shall be from the wilderness and Lebanon and from the River, the river Euphrates, to the western sea. ²⁵No man shall be able to stand against you; the LORD your God will lay the fear of you and the dread of you upon all the land that you shall tread, as he promised you.

26 "Behold, I set before you this day a blessing and a curse: ²⁷the blessing, if you obey the commandments of the LORD your God, which I command you this day, ²⁸and the curse, if you do not obey the commandments of the LORD your God, but turn aside from the way which I command you this day, to go after other gods which you have not known. ²⁹And when the LORD your God brings you into the land which you are entering to take possession of it, you shall set the blessing on Mount Gĕr'ĭ-zĭm and the curse on Mount Ē'bal. ³⁰Are they not beyond the Jordan, west of the road, toward the going down of the sun, in the land of the Canaanites who live in the Är'a·bah, over against Gĭl'gal, beside the oakᵏ of Mō'rĕh? ³¹For you are to pass over the Jordan to go in to take possession of the land which the LORD your God gives you; and when you possess it and live in it, ³²you shall be careful to do all the statutes and the ordinances which I set before you this day.

12 "These are the statutes and ordinances which you shall be careful to do in the land which the LORD, the God of your fathers, has given you to possess, all the days that you live upon the earth. ²You shall surely destroy all the places where the nations whom you shall dispossess served their gods, upon the high mountains and upon the hills and under every green tree; ³you shall tear down their altars, and dash in pieces their pillars, and burn their A·shē'rĭm with fire; you shall hew down the graven images of their gods, and destroy their name out of that place. ⁴You shall not do so to the LORD your God. ⁵But you shall seek the place which the LORD your God will choose out of all your tribes to put his name and make his habitation there; thither you shall go, ⁶and thither you shall bring your burnt offerings and your sacrifices, your tithes and the offering that you present, your votive offerings, your freewill offerings, and the firstlings of your herd and of your flock; ⁷and there you shall eat before the LORD your God, and you shall rejoice, you and your households, in all that you undertake, in which the LORD your God has blessed you. ⁸You shall not do according to all that we are doing here this day, every man doing whatever is right in his own eyes; ⁹for you have not as yet come to the rest and to the inheritance which the LORD your God gives you. ¹⁰But when you go over the Jordan, and live in the land which the LORD your God gives you to inherit, and when he gives you rest from all your enemies round about, so that you live in safety, ¹¹then to the place which the LORD your God will choose, to make his name dwell there, thither you shall bring all that I command you: your burnt offerings and your sacrifices, your tithes and the offering that you present, and all your votive offerings which you vow to the LORD. ¹²And you shall rejoice before the LORD your God, you and your sons and your daughters, your menservants and your maidservants, and the Lē'vīte that is within your towns, since he has no portion or inheritance with you. ¹³Take heed that you do not offer your burnt offerings at every place that you see; ¹⁴but at the place which the LORD

ᵏGk Syr: See Gen 12.6. Heb *oaks* or *terebinths*
12.1-28: Ex 20.24.

will choose in one of your tribes, there you shall offer your burnt offerings, and there you shall do all that I am commanding you.

15 "However, you may slaughter and eat flesh within any of your towns, as much as you desire, according to the blessing of the LORD your God which he has given you; the unclean and the clean may eat of it, as of the gazelle and as of the hart. [16] Only you shall not eat the blood; you shall pour it out upon the earth like water. [17] You may not eat within your towns the tithe of your grain or of your wine or of your oil, or the firstlings of your herd or of your flock, or any of your votive offerings which you vow, or your freewill offerings, or the offering that you present; [18] but you shall eat them before the LORD your God in the place which the LORD your God will choose, you and your son and your daughter, your manservant and your maidservant, and the Lē′vīte who is within your towns; and you shall rejoice before the LORD your God in all that you undertake. [19] Take heed that you do not forsake the Lē′vīte as long as you live in your land.

20 "When the LORD your God enlarges your territory, as he has promised you, and you say, 'I will eat flesh,' because you crave flesh, you may eat as much flesh as you desire. [21] If the place which the LORD your God will choose to put his name there is too far from you, then you may kill any of your herd or your flock, which the LORD has given you, as I have commanded you; and you may eat within your towns as much as you desire. [22] Just as the gazelle or the hart is eaten, so you may eat of it; the unclean and the clean alike may eat of it. [23] Only be sure that you do not eat the blood; for the blood is the life, and you shall not eat the life with the flesh. [24] You shall not eat it; you shall pour it out upon the earth like water. [25] You shall not eat it; that all may go well with you and with your children after you, when you do what is right in the sight of the LORD. [26] But the holy things which are due from you, and your votive offerings, you shall take, and you shall go to the place which the LORD will choose, [27] and offer your burnt offerings, the flesh and the blood, on the altar of the LORD your God; the blood of your sacrifices shall be poured out on the altar of the

LORD your God, but the flesh you may eat. [28] Be careful to heed all these words which I command you, that it may go well with you and with your children after you for ever, when you do what is good and right in the sight of the LORD your God.

29 "When the LORD your God cuts off before you the nations whom you go in to dispossess, and you dispossess them and dwell in their land, [30] take heed that you be not ensnared to follow them, after they have been destroyed before you, and that you do not inquire about their gods, saying, 'How did these nations serve their gods? — that I also may do likewise.' [31] You shall not do so to the LORD your God; for every abominable thing which the LORD hates they have done for their gods; for they even burn their sons and their daughters in the fire to their gods.

32[l] "Everything that I command you you shall be careful to do; you shall not add to it or take from it.

13 "If a prophet arises among you, or a dreamer of dreams, and gives you a sign or a wonder, [2] and the sign or wonder which he tells you comes to pass, and if he says, 'Let us go after other gods,' which you have not known, 'and let us serve them,' [3] you shall not listen to the words of that prophet or to that dreamer of dreams; for the LORD your God is testing you, to know whether you love the LORD your God with all your heart and with all your soul. [4] You shall walk after the LORD your God and fear him, and keep his commandments and obey his voice, and you shall serve him and cleave to him. [5] But that prophet or that dreamer of dreams shall be put to death, because he has taught rebellion against the LORD your God, who brought you out of the land of Egypt and redeemed you out of the house of bondage, to make you leave the way in which the LORD your God commanded you to walk. So you shall purge the evil from the midst of you.

6 "If your brother, the son of your mother, or your son, or your daughter, or the wife of your bosom, or your friend who is as your own soul, entices you secretly, saying, 'Let us go and serve other gods,' which neither you

[l] Ch 13.1 in Heb
12.16,23: Lev 17.10-14; 19.26.
12.29-32: Ex 23.24; 34.12-14; Num 33.52.

nor your fathers have known, [7] some of the gods of the peoples that are round about you, whether near you or far off from you, from the one end of the earth to the other, [8] you shall not yield to him or listen to him, nor shall your eye pity him, nor shall you spare him, nor shall you conceal him; [9] but you shall kill him; your hand shall be first against him to put him to death, and afterwards the hand of all the people. [10] You shall stone him to death with stones, because he sought to draw you away from the LORD your God, who brought you out of the land of Egypt, out of the house of bondage. [11] And all Israel shall hear, and fear, and never again do any such wickedness as this among you.

12 "If you hear in one of your cities, which the LORD your God gives you to dwell there, [13] that certain base fellows have gone out among you and have drawn away the inhabitants of the city, saying, 'Let us go and serve other gods,' which you have not known, [14] then you shall inquire and make search and ask diligently; and behold, if it be true and certain that such an abominable thing has been done among you, [15] you shall surely put the inhabitants of that city to the sword, destroying it utterly, all who are in it and its cattle, with the edge of the sword. [16] You shall gather all its spoil into the midst of its open square, and burn the city and all its spoil with fire, as a whole burnt offering to the LORD your God; it shall be a heap for ever, it shall not be built again. [17] None of the devoted things shall cleave to your hand; that the LORD may turn from the fierceness of his anger, and show you mercy, and have compassion on you, and multiply you, as he swore to your fathers, [18] if you obey the voice of the LORD your God, keeping all his commandments which I command you this day, and doing what is right in the sight of the LORD your God.

14 "You are the sons of the LORD your God; you shall not cut yourselves or make any baldness on your foreheads for the dead. [2] For you are a people holy to the LORD your God, and the LORD has chosen you to be a people for his own possession, out of all the peoples that are on the face of the earth.

3 "You shall not eat any abominable thing. [4] These are the animals you may eat: the ox, the sheep, the goat, [5] the hart, the gazelle, the roebuck, the wild goat, the ibex, the antelope, and the mountain-sheep. [6] Every animal that parts the hoof and has the hoof cloven in two, and chews the cud, among the animals, you may eat. [7] Yet of those that chew the cud or have the hoof cloven you shall not eat these: the camel, the hare, and the rock badger, because they chew the cud but do not part the hoof, are unclean for you. [8] And the swine, because it parts the hoof but does not chew the cud, is unclean for you. Their flesh you shall not eat, and their carcasses you shall not touch.

9 "Of all that are in the waters you may eat these: whatever has fins and scales you may eat. [10] And whatever does not have fins and scales you shall not eat; it is unclean for you.

11 "You may eat all clean birds. [12] But these are the ones which you shall not eat: the eagle, the vulture, the osprey, [13] the buzzard, the kite, after their kinds; [14] every raven after its kind; [15] the ostrich, the nighthawk, the sea gull, the hawk, after their kinds; [16] the little owl and the great owl, the water hen [17] and the pelican, the carrion vulture and the cormorant, [18] the stork, the heron, after their kinds; the hoopoe and the bat. [19] And all winged insects are unclean for you; they shall not be eaten. [20] All clean winged things you may eat.

21 "You shall not eat anything that dies of itself; you may give it to the alien who is within your towns, that he may eat it, or you may sell it to a foreigner; for you are a people holy to the LORD your God.

"You shall not boil a kid in its mother's milk.

22 "You shall tithe all the yield of your seed, which comes forth from the field year by year. [23] And before the LORD your God, in the place which he will choose, to make his name dwell there, you shall eat the tithe of your grain, of your wine, and of your oil, and the firstlings of your herd and flock; that you may learn to fear the LORD your God always. [24] And if the way is too long for you, so that you are

14.1: Lev 19.28.
14.2: Ex 19.5, 6; Deut 26.19; Tit 2.14; 1 Pet 2.9; Rev 1.6; 5.10. **14.3-20:** Lev 11.2-23.
14.21: Lev 11.39, 40; 17.15; Ex 23.19; 34.26.
14.22-29: Lev 27.30-33; Num 18.21-32.

not able to bring the tithe, when the LORD your God blesses you, because the place is too far from you, which the the LORD your God chooses, to set his name there, ²⁵ then you shall turn it into money, and bind up the money in your hand, and go to the place which the LORD your God chooses, ²⁶ and spend the money for whatever you desire, oxen, or sheep, or wine or strong drink, whatever your appetite craves; and you shall eat there before the LORD your God and rejoice, you and your household. ²⁷ And you shall not forsake the Lē′vīte who is within your towns, for he has no portion or inheritance with you.

28 "At the end of every three years you shall bring forth all the tithe of your produce in the same year, and lay it up within your towns; ²⁹ and the Lē′vīte, because he has no portion or inheritance with you, and the sojourner, the fatherless, and the widow, who are within your towns, shall come and eat and be filled; that the LORD your God may bless you in all the work of your hands that you do.

15 "At the end of every seven years you shall grant a release. ² And this is the manner of the release: every creditor shall release what he has lent to his neighbor; he shall not exact it of his neighbor, his brother, because the LORD's release has been proclaimed. ³ Of a foreigner you may exact it; but whatever of yours is with your brother your hand shall release. ⁴ But there will be no poor among you (for the LORD will bless you in the land which the LORD your God gives you for an inheritance to possess), ⁵ if only you will obey the voice of the LORD your God, being careful to do all this commandment which I command you this day. ⁶ For the LORD your God will bless you, as he promised you, and you shall lend to many nations, but you shall not borrow; and you shall rule over many nations, but they shall not rule over you.

7 "If there is among you a poor man, one of your brethren, in any of your towns within your land which the LORD your God gives you, you shall not harden your heart or shut your hand against your poor brother, ⁸ but you shall open your hand to him, and lend him sufficient for his need, whatever it may be. ⁹ Take heed lest there

be a base thought in your heart, and you say, 'The seventh year, the year of release is near,' and your eye be hostile to your poor brother, and you give him nothing, and he cry to the LORD against you, and it be sin in you. ¹⁰ You shall give to him freely, and your heart shall not be grudging when you give to him; because for this the LORD your God will bless you in all your work and in all that you undertake. ¹¹ For the poor will never cease out of the land; therefore I command you, You shall open wide your hand to your brother, to the needy and to the poor, in the land.

12 "If your brother, a Hebrew man, or a Hebrew woman, is sold to you, he shall serve you six years, and in the seventh year you shall let him go free from you. ¹³ And when you let him go free from you, you shall not let him go empty-handed; ¹⁴ you shall furnish him liberally out of your flock, out of your threshing floor, and out of your wine press; as the LORD your God has blessed you, you shall give to him. ¹⁵ You shall remember that you were a slave in the land of Egypt, and the LORD your God redeemed you; therefore I command you this today. ¹⁶ But if he says to you, 'I will not go out from you,' because he loves you and your household, since he fares well with you, ¹⁷ then you shall take an awl, and thrust it through his ear into the door, and he shall be your bondman for ever. And to your bondwoman you shall do likewise. ¹⁸ It shall not seem hard to you, when you let him go free from you; for at half the cost of a hired servant he has served you six years. So the LORD your God will bless you in all that you do.

19 "All the firstling males that are born of your herd and flock you shall consecrate to the LORD your God; you shall do no work with the firstling of your herd, nor shear the firstling of your flock. ²⁰ You shall eat it, you and your household, before the LORD your God year by year at the place which the LORD will choose. ²¹ But if it has any blemish, if it is lame or blind, or has any serious blemish whatever, you shall not sacrifice it to the LORD your God. ²² You shall eat it within your towns; the unclean and the clean alike may eat it, as though it were a

15.12-18: Ex 21.2-11; Lev 25.39-46.
15.19-23: Ex 13.11, 12; 22.30; 34.19; Num 18.17, 18.

gazelle or a hart. ²³Only you shall not eat its blood; you shall pour it out on the ground like water.

16 "Observe the month of Ā′bĭb, and keep the passover to the LORD your God; for in the month of Abib the LORD your God brought you out of Egypt by night. ²And you shall offer the passover sacrifice to the LORD your God, from the flock or the herd, at the place which the LORD will choose, to make his name dwell there. ³You shall eat no leavened bread with it; seven days you shall eat it with unleavened bread, the bread of affliction —for you came out of the land of Egypt in hurried flight—that all the days of your life you may remember the day when you came out of the land of Egypt. ⁴No leaven shall be seen with you in all your territory for seven days; nor shall any of the flesh which you sacrifice on the evening of the first day remain all night until morning. ⁵You may not offer the passover sacrifice within any of your towns which the LORD your God gives you; ⁶but at the place which the LORD your God will choose, to make his name dwell in it, there you shall offer the passover sacrifice, in the evening at the going down of the sun, at the time you came out of Egypt. ⁷And you shall boil it and eat it at the place which the LORD your God will choose; and in the morning you shall turn and go to your tents. ⁸For six days you shall eat unleavened bread; and on the seventh day there shall be a solemn assembly to the LORD your God; you shall do no work on it.

9 "You shall count seven weeks; begin to count the seven weeks from the time you first put the sickle to the standing grain. ¹⁰Then you shall keep the feast of weeks to the LORD your God with the tribute of a freewill offering from your hand, which you shall give as the LORD your God blesses you; ¹¹and you shall rejoice before the LORD your God, you and your son and your daughter, your manservant and your maidservant, the Lē′vīte who is within your towns, the sojourner, the fatherless, and the widow who are among you, at the place which the LORD your God will choose, to make his name dwell there. ¹²You shall remember that you were a slave in Egypt; and you shall be careful to observe these statutes.

13 "You shall keep the feast of booths seven days, when you make your ingathering from your threshing floor and your wine press; ¹⁴you shall rejoice in your feast, you and your son and your daughter, your manservant and your maidservant, the Lē′vīte, the sojourner, the fatherless, and the widow who are within your towns. ¹⁵For seven days you shall keep the feast to the LORD your God at the place which the LORD will choose; because the LORD your God will bless you in all your produce and in all the work of your hands, so that you will be altogether joyful.

16 "Three times a year all your males shall appear before the LORD your God at the place which he will choose: at the feast of unleavened bread, at the feast of weeks, and at the feast of booths. They shall not appear before the LORD empty-handed; ¹⁷every man shall give as he is able, according to the blessing of the LORD your God which he has given you.

18 "You shall appoint judges and officers in all your towns which the LORD your God gives you, according to your tribes; and they shall judge the people with righteous judgment. ¹⁹You shall not pervert justice; you shall not show partiality; and you shall not take a bribe, for a bribe blinds the eyes of the wise and subverts the cause of the righteous. ²⁰Justice, and only justice, you shall follow, that you may live and inherit the land which the LORD your God gives you.

21 "You shall not plant any tree as an A̲·shē′ra̲h beside the altar of the LORD your God which you shall make. ²²And you shall not set up a pillar, which the LORD your God hates.

17 "You shall not sacrifice to the LORD your God an ox or a sheep in which is a blemish, any defect whatever; for that is an abomination to the LORD your God.

2 "If there is found among you, within any of your towns which the LORD your God gives you, a man or woman who does what is evil in the sight of the LORD your God, in transgressing his covenant, ³and has gone and served other gods and worshiped them, or the sun or the moon or any of

16.1-17: Ex 23.14-17; Lev 23; Num 28-29.
16.19: Ex 23.6-9; Lev 19.15. **16.21, 22:** Lev 26.1.
17.1: Lev 22.17-24. **17.2-7:** Ex 22.20.

the host of heaven, which I have forbidden, ⁴ and it is told you and you hear of it; then you shall inquire diligently, and if it is true and certain that such an abominable thing has been done in Israel, ⁵ then you shall bring forth to your gates that man or woman who has done this evil thing, and you shall stone that man or woman to death with stones. ⁶ On the evidence of two witnesses or of three witnesses he that is to die shall be put to death; a person shall not be put to death on the evidence of one witness. ⁷ The hand of the witnesses shall be first against him to put him to death, and afterward the hand of all the people. So you shall purge the evil from the midst of you.

8 "If any case arises requiring decision between one kind of homicide and another, one kind of legal right and another, or one kind of assault and another, any case within your towns which is too difficult for you, then you shall arise and go up to the place which the LORD your God will choose, ⁹ and coming to the Levitical priests, and to the judge who is in office in those days, you shall consult them, and they shall declare to you the decision. ¹⁰ Then you shall do according to what they declare to you from that place which the LORD will choose; and you shall be careful to do according to all that they direct you; ¹¹ according to the instructions which they give you, and according to the decision which they pronounce to you, you shall do; you shall not turn aside from the verdict which they declare to you, either to the right hand or to the left. ¹² The man who acts presumptuously, by not obeying the priest who stands to minister there before the LORD your God, or the judge, that man shall die; so you shall purge the evil from Israel. ¹³ And all the people shall hear, and fear, and not act presumptuously again.

14 "When you come to the land which the LORD your God gives you, and you possess it and dwell in it, and then say, 'I will set a king over me, like all the nations that are round about me'; ¹⁵ you may indeed set as king over you him whom the LORD your God will choose. One from among your brethren you shall set as king over you; you may not put a foreigner over you, who is not your brother. ¹⁶ Only he must not multiply horses

for himself, or cause the people to return to Egypt in order to multiply horses, since the LORD has said to you, 'You shall never return that way again.' ¹⁷ And he shall not multiply wives for himself, lest his heart turn away; nor shall he greatly multiply for himself silver and gold.

18 "And when he sits on the throne of his kingdom, he shall write for himself in a book a copy of this law, from that which is in charge of the Levitical priests, ¹⁹ and it shall be with him, and he shall read in it all the days of his life, that he may learn to fear the LORD his God, by keeping all the words of this law and these statutes, and doing them; ²⁰ that his heart may not be lifted up above his brethren, and that he may not turn aside from the commandment, either to the right hand or to the left; so that he may continue long in his kingdom, he and his children, in Israel.

18 "The Levitical priests, that is, all the tribe of Lē′vī, shall have no portion or inheritance with Israel; they shall eat the offerings by fire to the LORD, and his rightful dues. ² They shall have no inheritance among their brethren; the LORD is their inheritance, as he promised them. ³ And this shall be the priests' due from the people, from those offering a sacrifice, whether it be ox or sheep: they shall give to the priest the shoulder and the two cheeks and the stomach. ⁴ The first fruits of your grain, of your wine and of your oil, and the first of the fleece of your sheep, you shall give him. ⁵ For the LORD your God has chosen him out of all your tribes, to stand and minister in the name of the LORD, him and his sons for ever.

6 "And if a Lē′vīte comes from any of your towns out of all Israel, where he lives — and he may come when he desires — to the place which the LORD will choose, ⁷ then he may minister in the name of the LORD his God, like all his fellow-Levites who stand to minister there before the LORD. ⁸ They shall have equal portions to eat, besides what he receives from the sale of his patrimony.ᵐ

9 "When you come into the land

which the LORD your God gives you, you shall not learn to follow the abominable practices of those nations. [10]There shall not be found among you any one who burns his son or his daughter as an offering,[n] any one who practices divination, a soothsayer, or an augur, or a sorcerer, [11]or a charmer, or a medium, or a wizard, or a necromancer. [12]For whoever does these things is an abomination to the LORD; and because of these abominable practices the LORD your God is driving them out before you. [13]You shall be blameless before the LORD your God. [14]For these nations, which you are about to dispossess, give heed to soothsayers and to diviners; but as for you, the LORD your God has not allowed you so to do.

15 "The LORD your God will raise up for you a prophet like me from among you, from your brethren – him you shall heed – [16]just as you desired of the LORD your God at Hō′rĕb on the day of the assembly, when you said, 'Let me not hear again the voice of the LORD my God, or see this great fire any more, lest I die.' [17]And the LORD said to me, They have rightly said all that they have spoken. [18]I will raise up for them a prophet like you from among their brethren; and I will put my words in his mouth, and he shall speak to them all that I command him. [19]And whoever will not give heed to my words which he shall speak in my name, I myself will require it of him. [20]But the prophet who presumes to speak a word in my name which I have not commanded him to speak, or who speaks in the name of other gods, that same prophet shall die.' [21]And if you say in your heart, 'How may we know the word which the LORD has not spoken?' – [22]when a prophet speaks in the name of the LORD, if the word does not come to pass or come true, that is a word which the LORD has not spoken; the prophet has spoken it presumptuously, you need not be afraid of him.

19 "When the LORD your God cuts off the nations whose land the LORD your God gives you, and you dispossess them and dwell in their cities and in their houses, [2]you shall set apart three cities for you in the land which the LORD your God gives you to possess. You shall prepare the roads, and divide into three parts the area of the land which the LORD your God gives

you as a possession, so that any manslayer can flee to them.

4 "This is the provision for the manslayer, who by fleeing there may save his life. If any one kills his neighbor unintentionally without having been at enmity with him in time past – [5]as when a man goes into the forest with his neighbor to cut wood, and his hand swings the axe to cut down a tree, and the head slips from the handle and strikes his neighbor so that he dies – he may flee to one of these cities and save his life; [6]lest the avenger of blood in hot anger pursue the manslayer and overtake him, because the way is long, and wound him mortally, though the man did not deserve to die, since he was not at enmity with his neighbor in time past. [7]Therefore I command you, You shall set apart three cities. [8]And if the LORD your God enlarges your border, as he has sworn to your fathers, and gives you all the land which he promised to give to your fathers – [9]provided you are careful to keep all this commandment, which I command you this day, by loving the LORD your God and by walking ever in his ways – then you shall add three other cities to these three, [10]lest innocent blood be shed in your land which the LORD your God gives you for an inheritance, and so the guilt of bloodshed be upon you.

11 "But if any man hates his neighbor, and lies in wait for him, and attacks him, and wounds him mortally so that he dies, and the man flees into one of these cities, [12]then the elders of his city shall send and fetch him from there, and hand him over to the avenger of blood, so that he may die. [13]Your eye shall not pity him, but you shall purge the guilt of innocent blood[o] from Israel, so that it may be well with you.

14 "In the inheritance which you will hold in the land that the LORD your God gives you to possess, you shall not remove your neighbor's landmark, which the men of old have set.

15 "A single witness shall not prevail against a man for any crime or

---

[n]Heb *makes his son or his daughter pass through the fire*
[o]Or *the blood of the innocent*
18.10, 11: Ex 22.18; Lev 19.26, 31; 20.6, 27.
18.13: Mt 5.48.   18.15-19: Acts 3.22, 23; 7.37.
19.1-13: Ex 21.12-14; Num 35.
19.15: Num 35.30; Deut 17.6; Mt 18.16; 2 Cor 13.1; 1 Tim 5.19; Heb 10.28.

for any wrong in connection with any offense that he has committed; only on the evidence of two witnesses, or of three witnesses, shall a charge be sustained. [16] If a malicious witness rises against any man to accuse him of wrongdoing, [17] then both parties to the dispute shall appear before the LORD, before the priests and the judges who are in office in those days; [18] the judges shall inquire diligently, and if the witness is a false witness and has accused his brother falsely, [19] then you shall do to him as he had meant to do to his brother; so you shall purge the evil from the midst of you. [20] And the rest shall hear, and fear, and shall never again commit any such evil among you. [21] Your eye shall not pity; it shall be life for life, eye for eye, tooth for tooth, hand for hand, foot for foot.

20 "When you go forth to war against your enemies, and see horses and chariots and an army larger than your own, you shall not be afraid of them; for the LORD your God is with you, who brought you up out of the land of Egypt. [2] And when you draw near to the battle, the priest shall come forward and speak to the people, [3] and shall say to them, 'Hear, O Israel, you draw near this day to battle against your enemies: let not your heart faint; do not fear, or tremble, or be in dread of them; [4] for the LORD your God is he that goes with you, to fight for you against your enemies, to give you the victory.' [5] Then the officers shall speak to the people, saying, 'What man is there that has built a new house and has not dedicated it? Let him go back to his house, lest he die in the battle and another man dedicate it. [6] And what man is there that has planted a vineyard and has not enjoyed its fruit? Let him go back to his house, lest he die in the battle and another man enjoy its fruit. [7] And what man is there that has betrothed a wife and has not taken her? Let him go back to his house, lest he die in the battle and another man take her.' [8] And the officers shall speak further to the people, and say, 'What man is there that is fearful and fainthearted? Let him go back to his house, lest the heart of his fellows melt as his heart.' [9] And when the officers have made an end of speaking to the people, then commanders shall be appointed at the head of the people.

[10] "When you draw near to a city to fight against it, offer terms of peace to it. [11] And if its answer to you is peace and it opens to you, then all the people who are found in it shall do forced labor for you and shall serve you. [12] But if it makes no peace with you, but makes war against you, then you shall besiege it; [13] and when the LORD your God gives it into your hand you shall put all its males to the sword, [14] but the women and the little ones, the cattle, and everything else in the city, all its spoil, you shall take as booty for yourselves; and you shall enjoy the spoil of your enemies, which the LORD your God has given you. [15] Thus you shall do to all the cities which are very far from you, which are not cities of the nations here. [16] But in the cities of these peoples that the LORD your God gives you for an inheritance, you shall save alive nothing that breathes, [17] but you shall utterly destroy them, the Hit'tites and the Am'o·rites, the Canaanites and the Per'iz·zites, the Hi'vites and the Jeb'u·sites, as the LORD your God has commanded; [18] that they may not teach you to do according to all their abominable practices which they have done in the service of their gods and so to sin against the LORD your God.

19 "When you besiege a city for a long time, making war against it in order to take it, you shall not destroy its trees by wielding an axe against them; for you may eat of them, but you shall not cut them down. Are the trees in the field men that they should be besieged by you? [20] Only the trees which you know are not trees for food you may destroy and cut down that you may build siegeworks against the city that makes war with you, until it falls.

21 "If in the land which the LORD your God gives you to possess any one is found slain, lying in the open country, and it is not known who killed him, [2] then your elders and your judges shall come forth, and they shall measure the distance to the cities which are around him that is slain; [3] and the elders of the city which is nearest to the slain man shall take a heifer which has never been worked and which has not pulled in the yoke

19.16-20: Ex 20.16; 23.1; Lev 19.16; Deut 5.20.
19.19: 1 Cor 5.13.   19.21: Ex 21.23-26; Lev 24.20; Mt 5.38

⁴And the elders of that city shall bring the heifer down to a valley with running water, which is neither plowed nor sown, and shall break the heifer's neck there in the valley. ⁵And the priests the sons of Lē′vī shall come forward, for the LORD your God has chosen them to minister to him and to bless in the name of the LORD, and by their word every dispute and every assault shall be settled. ⁶And all the elders of that city nearest to the slain man shall wash their hands over the heifer whose neck was broken in the valley; ⁷and they shall testify, 'Our hands did not shed this blood, neither did our eyes see it shed. ⁸Forgive, O LORD, thy people Israel, whom thou hast redeemed, and set not the guilt of innocent blood in the midst of thy people Israel; but let the guilt of blood be forgiven them.' ⁹So you shall purge the guilt of innocent blood from your midst, when you do what is right in the sight of the LORD.

10 "When you go forth to war against your enemies, and the LORD your God gives them into your hands, and you take them captive, ¹¹and see among the captives a beautiful woman, and you have desire for her and would take her for yourself as wife, ¹²then you shall bring her home to your house, and she shall shave her head and pare her nails. ¹³And she shall put off her captive's garb, and shall remain in your house and bewail her father and her mother a full month; after that you may go in to her, and be her husband, and she shall be your wife. ¹⁴Then, if you have no delight in her, you shall let her go where she will; but you shall not sell her for money, you shall not treat her as a slave, since you have humiliated her.

15 "If a man has two wives, the one loved and the other disliked, and they have borne him children, both the loved and the disliked, and if the first-born son is hers that is disliked, ¹⁶then on the day when he assigns his possessions as an inheritance to his sons, he may not treat the son of the loved as the first-born in preference to the son of the disliked, who is the first-born, ¹⁷but he shall acknowledge the first-born, the son of the disliked, by giving him a double portion of all that he has, for he is the first issue of his strength; the right of the first-born is his.

18 "If a man has a stubborn and rebellious son, who will not obey the voice of his father or the voice of his mother, and, though they chastise him, will not give heed to them, ¹⁹then his father and his mother shall take hold of him and bring him out to the elders of his city at the gate of the place where he lives, ²⁰and they shall say to the elders of his city, 'This our son is stubborn and rebellious, he will not obey our voice; he is a glutton and a drunkard.' ²¹Then all the men of the city shall stone him to death with stones; so you shall purge the evil from your midst; and all Israel shall hear, and fear.

22 "And if a man has committed a crime punishable by death and he is put to death, and you hang him on a tree, ²³his body shall not remain all night upon the tree, but you shall bury him the same day, for a hanged man is accursed by God; you shall not defile your land which the LORD your God gives you for an inheritance.

22 "You shall not see your brother's ox or his sheep go astray, and withhold your helpᵖ from them; you shall take them back to your brother. ²And if he is not near you, or if you do not know him, you shall bring it home to your house, and it shall be with you until your brother seeks it; then you shall restore it to him. ³And so you shall do with his ass; so you shall do with his garment; so you shall do with any lost thing of your brother's, which he loses and you find; you may not withhold your help. ⁴You shall not see your brother's ass or his ox fallen down by the way, and withhold your helpᵖ from them; you shall help him to lift them up again.

5 "A woman shall not wear anything that pertains to a man, nor shall a man put on a woman's garment; for whoever does these things is an abomination to the LORD your God.

6 "If you chance to come upon a bird's nest, in any tree or on the ground, with young ones or eggs and the mother sitting upon the young or upon the eggs, you shall not take the mother with the young; ⁷you shall let the mother go, but the young you may

take to yourself; that it may go well with you, and that you may live long.

8 "When you build a new house, you shall make a parapet for your roof, that you may not bring the guilt of blood upon your house, if any one fall from it.

9 "You shall not sow your vineyard with two kinds of seed, lest the whole yield be forfeited to the sanctuary,*q* the crop which you have sown and the yield of the vineyard. ¹⁰ You shall not plow with an ox and an ass together. ¹¹ You shall not wear a mingled stuff, wool and linen together.

12 "You shall make yourself tassels on the four corners of your cloak with which you cover yourself.

13 "If any man takes a wife, and goes in to her, and then spurns her, ¹⁴ and charges her with shameful conduct, and brings an evil name upon her, saying, 'I took this woman, and when I came near her, I did not find in her the tokens of virginity,' ¹⁵ then the father of the young woman and her mother shall take and bring out the tokens of her virginity to the elders of the city in the gate; ¹⁶ and the father of the young woman shall say to the elders, 'I gave my daughter to this man to wife, and he spurns her; ¹⁷ and lo, he has made shameful charges against her, saying, "I did not find in your daughter the tokens of virginity." And yet these are the tokens of my daughter's virginity.' And they shall spread the garment before the elders of the city. ¹⁸ Then the elders of that city shall take the man and whip him; ¹⁹ and they shall fine him a hundred shekels of silver, and give them to the father of the young woman, because he has brought an evil name upon a virgin of Israel; and she shall be his wife; he may not put her away all his days. ²⁰ But if the thing is true, that the tokens of virginity were not found in the young woman, ²¹ then they shall bring out the young woman to the door of her father's house, and the men of her city shall stone her to death with stones, because she has wrought folly in Israel by playing the harlot in her father's house; so you shall purge the evil from the midst of you.

22 "If a man is found lying with the wife of another man, both of them shall die, the man who lay with the woman, and the woman; so you shall purge the evil from Israel.

23 "If there is a betrothed virgin, and a man meets her in the city and lies with her, ²⁴ then you shall bring them both out to the gate of that city, and you shall stone them to death with stones, the young woman because she did not cry for help though she was in the city, and the man because he violated his neighbor's wife; so you shall purge the evil from the midst of you.

25 "But if in the open country a man meets a young woman who is betrothed, and the man seizes her and lies with her, then only the man who lay with her shall die. ²⁶ But to the young woman you shall do nothing; in the young woman there is no offense punishable by death, for this case is like that of a man attacking and murdering his neighbor; ²⁷ because he came upon her in the open country, and though the betrothed young woman cried for help there was no one to rescue her.

28 "If a man meets a virgin who is not betrothed, and seizes her and lies with her, and they are found, ²⁹ then the man who lay with her shall give to the father of the young woman fifty shekels of silver, and she shall be his wife, because he has violated her; he may not put her away all his days.

30*r* "A man shall not take his father's wife, nor shall he uncover her who is his father's.*s*

23 "He whose testicles are crushed or whose male member is cut off shall not enter the assembly of the LORD.

2 "No bastard shall enter the assembly of the LORD; even to the tenth generation none of his descendants shall enter the assembly of the LORD.

3 "No Ăm′mo·nīte or Mō′ăb·īte shall enter the assembly of the LORD; even to the tenth generation none belonging to them shall enter the assembly of the LORD for ever; ⁴ because they did not meet you with bread and with water on the way, when you came forth out of Egypt, and because they hired against you Bā′laăm the son of

q Heb *become holy*
r Ch 23.1 in Heb   *s* Heb *uncover his father's skirt*
22.9-11: Lev 19.19.   **22.12:** Num 15.37-41.
22.21: 1 Cor 5.13.
22.22-27: Ex 20.14; Lev 18.20; 20.10; Deut 5.18.
22.24: 1 Cor 5.13.   **22.28, 29:** Ex 22.16, 17.

Bē′ôr from Pē′thôr of Mĕs·o̱·po̱·tā′mĭ·a̱, to curse you. ⁵Nevertheless the LORD your God would not hearken to Bā′-laăm; but the LORD your God turned the curse into a blessing for you, because the LORD your God loved you. ⁶You shall not seek their peace or their prosperity all your days for ever.

7 "You shall not abhor an Ē′dom·īte, for he is your brother; you shall not abhor an Egyptian, because you were a sojourner in his land. ⁸The children of the third generation that are born to them may enter the assembly of the LORD.

9 "When you go forth against your enemies and are in camp, then you shall keep yourself from every evil thing.

10 "If there is among you any man who is not clean by reason of what chances to him by night, then he shall go outside the camp, he shall not come within the camp; ¹¹but when evening comes on, he shall bathe himself in water, and when the sun is down, he may come within the camp.

12 "You shall have a place outside the camp and you shall go out to it; ¹³and you shall have a stick with your weapons; and when you sit down outside, you shall dig a hole with it, and turn back and cover up your excrement. ¹⁴Because the LORD your God walks in the midst of your camp, to save you and to give up your enemies before you, therefore your camp must be holy, that he may not see anything indecent among you, and turn away from you.

15 "You shall not give up to his master a slave who has escaped from his master to you; ¹⁶he shall dwell with you, in your midst, in the place which he shall choose within one of your towns, where it pleases him best; you shall not oppress him.

17 "There shall be no cult prostitute of the daughters of Israel, neither shall there be a cult prostitute of the sons of Israel. ¹⁸You shall not bring the hire of a harlot, or the wages of a dog,ᶠ into the house of the LORD your God in payment for any vow; for both of these are an abomination to the LORD your God.

19 "You shall not lend upon interest to your brother, interest on money, interest on victuals, interest on anything that is lent for interest. ²⁰To a foreigner you may lend upon interest, but to your brother you shall not lend upon interest; that the LORD your God may bless you in all that you undertake in the land which you are entering to take possession of it.

21 "When you make a vow to the LORD your God, you shall not be slack to pay it; for the LORD your God will surely require it of you, and it would be sin in you. ²²But if you refrain from vowing, it shall be no sin in you. ²³You shall be careful to perform what has passed your lips, for you have voluntarily vowed to the LORD your God what you have promised with your mouth.

24 "When you go into your neighbor's vineyard, you may eat your fill of grapes, as many as you wish, but you shall not put any in your vessel. ²⁵When you go into your neighbor's standing grain, you may pluck the ears with your hand, but you shall not put a sickle to your neighbor's standing grain.

24 "When a man takes a wife and marries her, if then she finds no favor in his eyes because he has found some indecency in her, and he writes her a bill of divorce and puts it in her hand and sends her out of his house, ²and she departs out of his house, and if she goes and becomes another man's wife, ³and the latter husband dislikes her and writes her a bill of divorce and puts it in her hand and sends her out of his house, or if the latter husband dies, who took her to be his wife, ⁴then her former husband, who sent her away, may not take her again to be his wife, after she has been defiled; for that is an abomination before the LORD, and you shall not bring guilt upon the land which the LORD your God gives you for an inheritance.

5 "When a man is newly married, he shall not go out with the army or be charged with any business; he shall be free at home one year, to be happy with his wife whom he has taken.

6 "No man shall take a mill or an upper millstone in pledge; for he would be taking a life in pledge.

7 "If a man is found stealing one of his brethren, the people of Israel, and if he treats him as a slave or sells him,

ᶠOr *sodomite*

23.19: Ex 22.26; Lev 25.35-37. 23.21-23: Num 30.2-16.
24.1: Mt 5.31; 19.7; Mk 10.4. 24.6, 10-13: Ex 22.26, 27.
24.7: Ex 21.16; 1 Cor 5.13.

then that thief shall die; so you shall purge the evil from the midst of you.

8 "Take heed, in an attack of leprosy, to be very careful to do according to all that the Levitical priests shall direct you; as I commanded them, so you shall be careful to do. ⁹Remember what the LORD your God did to Miriam on the way as you came forth out of Egypt.

10 "When you make your neighbor a loan of any sort, you shall not go into his house to fetch his pledge. ¹¹You shall stand outside, and the man to whom you make the loan shall bring the pledge out to you. ¹²And if he is a poor man, you shall not sleep in his pledge; ¹³when the sun goes down, you shall restore to him the pledge that he may sleep in his cloak and bless you; and it shall be righteousness to you before the LORD your God.

14 "You shall not oppress a hired servant who is poor and needy, whether he is one of your brethren or one of the sojourners who are in your land within your towns; ¹⁵you shall give him his hire on the day he earns it, before the sun goes down (for he is poor, and sets his heart upon it); lest he cry against you to the LORD, and it be sin in you. 16 "The fathers shall not be put to death for the children, nor shall the children be put to death for the fathers; every man shall be put to death for his own sin.

17 "You shall not pervert the justice due to the sojourner or to the fatherless, or take a widow's garment in pledge; ¹⁸but you shall remember that you were a slave in Egypt and the LORD your God redeemed you from there; therefore I command you to do this.

19 "When you reap your harvest in your field, and have forgotten a sheaf in the field, you shall not go back to get it; it shall be for the sojourner, the fatherless, and the widow; that the LORD your God may bless you in all the work of your hands. ²⁰When you beat your olive trees, you shall not go over the boughs again; it shall be for the sojourner, the fatherless, and the widow. ²¹When you gather the grapes of your vineyard, you shall not glean it afterward; it shall be for the sojourner, the fatherless, and the widow. ²²You shall remember that you were a slave in the land of Egypt; therefore I command you to do this.

25 "If there is a dispute between men, and they come into court, and the judges decide between them, acquitting the innocent and condemning the guilty, ²then if the guilty man deserves to be beaten, the judge shall cause him to lie down and be beaten in his presence with a number of stripes in proportion to his offense. ³Forty stripes may be given him, but not more; lest, if one should go on to beat him with more stripes than these, your brother be degraded in your sight.

4 "You shall not muzzle an ox when it treads out the grain.

5 "If brothers dwell together, and one of them dies and has no son, the wife of the dead shall not be married outside the family to a stranger; her husband's brother shall go in to her, and take her as his wife, and perform the duty of a husband's brother to her. ⁶And the first son whom she bears shall succeed to the name of his brother who is dead, that his name may not be blotted out of Israel. ⁷And if the man does not wish to take his brother's wife, then his brother's wife shall go up to the gate to the elders, and say, 'My husband's brother refuses to perpetuate his brother's name in Israel; he will not perform the duty of a husband's brother to me.' ⁸Then the elders of his city shall call him, and speak to him: and if he persists, saying, 'I do not wish to take her,' ⁹then his brother's wife shall go up to him in the presence of the elders, and pull his sandal off his foot, and spit in his face; and she shall answer and say, 'So shall it be done to the man who does not build up his brother's house.' ¹⁰And the name of his houseᵘ shall be called in Israel, The house of him that had his sandal pulled off.

11 "When men fight with one another, and the wife of the one draws near to rescue her husband from the hand of him who is beating him, and puts out her hand and seizes him by the private parts, ¹²then you shall cut off her hand; your eye shall have no pity.

13 "You shall not have in your bag

ᵘHeb *its name*
24.8, 9: Lev 13-14.   24.14, 15: Lev 19.13; Jas 5.4.
24.17, 18: Ex 22.21-24; 23.9; Lev 19.33, 34.
24.19-22: Lev 19.9, 10; 23.22.   25.4: 1 Cor 9.9; 1 Tim 5.18.
25.5, 6: Mt 22.24; Mk 12.19; Lk 20.28.
25.13-16: Lev 19.35, 36.

two kinds of weights, a large and a small. ¹⁴You shall not have in your house two kinds of measures, a large and a small. ¹⁵A full and just weight you shall have, a full and just measure you shall have; that your days may be prolonged in the land which the LORD your God gives you. ¹⁶For all who do such things, all who act dishonestly, are an abomination to the LORD your God.

17 "Remember what Ăm′a·lĕk did to you on the way as you came out of Egypt, ¹⁸how he attacked you on the way, when you were faint and weary, and cut off at your rear all who lagged behind you; and he did not fear God. ¹⁹Therefore when the LORD your God has given you rest from all your enemies round about, in the land which the LORD your God gives you for an inheritance to possess, you shall blot out the remembrance of Ăm′a·lĕk from under heaven; you shall not forget.

26 "When you come into the land which the LORD your God gives you for an inheritance, and have taken possession of it, and live in it, ²you shall take some of the first of all the fruit of the ground, which you harvest from your land that the LORD your God gives you, and you shall put it in a basket, and you shall go to the place which the LORD your God will choose, to make his name to dwell there. ³And you shall go to the priest who is in office at that time, and say to him, 'I declare this day to the LORD your God that I have come into the land which the LORD swore to our fathers to give us.' ⁴Then the priest shall take the basket from your hand, and set it down before the altar of the LORD your God.

5 "And you shall make response before the LORD your God, 'A wandering Är·a·mē′an was my father; and he went down into Egypt and sojourned there, few in number; and there he became a nation, great, mighty, and populous. ⁶And the Egyptians treated us harshly, and afflicted us, and laid upon us hard bondage. ⁷Then we cried to the LORD the God of our fathers, and the LORD heard our voice, and saw our affliction, our toil, and our oppression; ⁸and the LORD brought us out of Egypt with a mighty hand and an outstretched arm, with great terror, with signs and wonders; ⁹and he brought us into this place and gave us this land, a land flowing with milk and honey. ¹⁰And behold, now I bring the first of the fruit of the ground, which thou, O LORD, hast given me.' And you shall set it down before the LORD your God, and worship before the LORD your God; ¹¹and you shall rejoice in all the good which the LORD your God has given to you and to your house, you, and the Lē′vīte, and the sojourner who is among you.

12 "When you have finished paying all the tithe of your produce in the third year, which is the year of tithing, giving it to the Lē′vīte, the sojourner, the fatherless, and the widow, that they may eat within your towns and be filled, ¹³then you shall say before the LORD your God, 'I have removed the sacred portion out of my house, and moreover I have given it to the Lē′vīte, the sojourner, the fatherless, and the widow, according to all thy commandment which thou hast commanded me; I have not transgressed any of thy commandments, neither have I forgotten them; ¹⁴I have not eaten of the tithe while I was mourning, or removed any of it while I was unclean, or offered any of it to the dead; I have obeyed the voice of the LORD my God, I have done according to all that thou hast commanded me. ¹⁵Look down from thy holy habitation, from heaven, and bless thy people Israel and the ground which thou hast given us, as thou didst swear to our fathers, a land flowing with milk and honey.'

16 "This day the LORD your God commands you to do these statutes and ordinances; you shall therefore be careful to do them with all your heart and with all your soul. ¹⁷You have declared this day concerning the LORD that he is your God, and that you will walk in his ways, and keep his statutes and his commandments and his ordinances, and will obey his voice; ¹⁸and the LORD has declared this day concerning you that you are a people for his own possession, as he has promised you, and that you are to keep all his commandments, ¹⁹that he will set you high above all nations that he has made, in praise and in fame and in honor, and that you shall be a people holy to the LORD your God, as he has spoken."

25.17-19: Ex 17.14; 1 Sam 15.
26.1-11: Ex 22.29; 23.19; 34.26; Num 18.12, 13.

27 Now Moses and the elders of Israel commanded the people, saying, "Keep all the commandment which I command you this day. ² And on the day you pass over the Jordan to the land which the LORD your God gives you, you shall set up large stones, and plaster them with plaster; ³ and you shall write upon them all the words of this law, when you pass over to enter the land which the LORD your God gives you, a land flowing with milk and honey, as the LORD, the God of your fathers, has promised you. ⁴ And when you have passed over the Jordan, you shall set up these stones, concerning which I command you this day, on Mount Eʹbal, and you shall plaster them with plaster. ⁵ And there you shall build an altar to the LORD your God, an altar of stones; you shall lift up no iron tool upon them. ⁶ You shall build an altar to the LORD your God of unhewnᵖ stones; and you shall offer burnt offerings on it to the LORD your God; ⁷ and you shall sacrifice peace offerings, and shall eat there; and you shall rejoice before the LORD your God. ⁸ And you shall write upon the stones all the words of this law very plainly."

9 And Moses and the Levitical priests said to all Israel, "Keep silence and hear, O Israel: this day you have become the people of the LORD your God. ¹⁰ You shall therefore obey the voice of the LORD your God, keeping his commandments and his statutes, which I command you this day."

11 And Moses charged the people the same day, saying, ¹² "When you have passed over the Jordan, these shall stand upon Mount Gerʹi·zim to bless the people: Simʹe·on, Leʹvi, Judah, Isʹsa·char, Joseph, and Benjamin. ¹³ And these shall stand upon Mount Eʹbal for the curse: Reuben, Gad, Ashʹer, Zebʹu·lun, Dan, and Naphʹta·li. ¹⁴ And the Leʹvites shall declare to all the men of Israel with a loud voice:

15 "'Cursed be the man who makes a graven or molten image, an abomination to the LORD, a thing made by the hands of a craftsman, and sets it up in secret.' And all the people shall answer and say, 'Amen.'

16 "'Cursed be he who dishonors his father or his mother.' And all the people shall say, 'Amen.'

17 "'Cursed be he who removes his neighbor's landmark.' And all the people shall say, 'Amen.'

18 "'Cursed be he who misleads a blind man on the road.' And all the people shall say, 'Amen.'

19 "'Cursed be he who perverts the justice due to the sojourner, the fatherless, and the widow.' And all the people shall say, 'Amen.'

20 "'Cursed be he who lies with his father's wife, because he has uncovered her who is his father's.'ʷ And all the people shall say, 'Amen.'

21 "'Cursed be he who lies with any kind of beast.' And all the people shall say, 'Amen.'

22 "'Cursed be he who lies with his sister, whether the daughter of his father or the daughter of his mother.' And all the people shall say, 'Amen.'

23 "'Cursed be he who lies with his mother-in-law.' And all the people shall say, 'Amen.'

24 "'Cursed be he who slays his neighbor in secret.' And all the people shall say, 'Amen.'

25 "'Cursed be he who takes a bribe to slay an innocent person.' And all the people shall say, 'Amen.'

26 "'Cursed be he who does not confirm the words of this law by doing them.' And all the people shall say, 'Amen.'

28 "And if you obey the voice of the LORD your God, being careful to do all his commandments which I command you this day, the LORD your God will set you high above all the nations of the earth. ² And all these blessings shall come upon you and overtake you, if you obey the voice of the LORD your God. ³ Blessed shall you be in the city, and blessed shall you be in the field. ⁴ Blessed shall be the fruit of your body, and the fruit of your ground, and the fruit of your beasts, the increase of your cattle, and the young of your flock. ⁵ Blessed shall be your basket and your kneading-trough. ⁶ Blessed shall you be when you come in, and blessed shall you be when you go out.

7 "The LORD will cause your enemies

ᵖHeb *whole*　ʷHeb *uncovered his father's skirt*
27.15: Ex 20.4, 23; 34.17; Lev 19.4; 26.1; Deut 4.16, 23, 25; 5.8; 7.25.
27.16: Ex 20.12; 21.15, 17; Lev 20.9; Deut 5.16; 21.18-21.
27.18: Lev 19.14.
27.19: Ex 22.21-24; 23.9; Lev 19.33, 34; Deut 24.17, 18.
27.20: Lev 18.8; 20.11; Deut 22.30.
27.21: Ex 22.19; Lev 18.23; 20.15.　**27.22:** Lev 18.9; 20.17.
27.23: Lev 18.17; 20.14.　**27.26:** Gal 3.10.
28: Lev 26.3-45.

who rise against you to be defeated before you; they shall come out against you one way, and flee before you seven ways. ⁸The LORD will command the blessing upon you in your barns, and in all that you undertake; and he will bless you in the land which the LORD your God gives you. ⁹The LORD will establish you as a people holy to himself, as he has sworn to you, if you keep the commandments of the LORD your God, and walk in his ways. ¹⁰And all the peoples of the earth shall see that you are called by the name of the LORD; and they shall be afraid of you. ¹¹And the LORD will make you abound in prosperity, in the fruit of your body, and in the fruit of your cattle, and in the fruit of your ground, within the land which the LORD swore to your fathers to give you. ¹²The LORD will open to you his good treasury the heavens, to give the rain of your land in its season and to bless all the work of your hands; and you shall lend to many nations, but you shall not borrow. ¹³And the LORD will make you the head, and not the tail; and you shall tend upward only, and not downward; if you obey the commandments of the LORD your God, which I command you this day, being careful to do them, ¹⁴and if you do not turn aside from any of the words which I command you this day, to the right hand or to the left, to go after other gods to serve them.

15 "But if you will not obey the voice of the LORD your God or be careful to do all his commandments and his statutes which I command you this day, then all these curses shall come upon you and overtake you. ¹⁶Cursed shall you be in the city, and cursed shall you be in the field. ¹⁷Cursed shall be your basket and your kneading-trough. ¹⁸Cursed shall be the fruit of your body, and the fruit of your ground, the increase of your cattle, and the young of your flock. ¹⁹Cursed shall you be when you come in, and cursed shall you be when you go out.

20 "The LORD will send upon you curses, confusion, and frustration, in all that you undertake to do, until you are destroyed and perish quickly, on account of the evil of your doings, because you have forsaken me. ²¹The LORD will make the pestilence cleave to you until he has consumed you off

the land which you are entering to take possession of it. ²²The LORD will smite you with consumption, and with fever, inflammation, and fiery heat, and with drought,ˣ and with blasting, and with mildew; they shall pursue you until you perish. ²³And the heavens over your head shall be brass, and the earth under you shall be iron. ²⁴The LORD will make the rain of your land powder and dust; from heaven it shall come down upon you until you are destroyed.

25 "The LORD will cause you to be defeated before your enemies; you shall go out one way against them, and flee seven ways before them; and you shall be a horror to all the kingdoms of the earth. ²⁶And your dead body shall be food for all birds of the air, and for the beasts of the earth; and there shall be no one to frighten them away. ²⁷The LORD will smite you with the boils of Egypt, and with the ulcers and the scurvy and the itch, of which you cannot be healed. ²⁸The LORD will smite you with madness and blindness and confusion of mind; ²⁹and you shall grope at noonday, as the blind grope in darkness, and you shall not prosper in your ways; and you shall be only oppressed and robbed continually, and there shall be no one to help you. ³⁰You shall betroth a wife, and another man shall lie with her; you shall build a house, and you shall not dwell in it; you shall plant a vineyard, and you shall not use the fruit of it. ³¹Your ox shall be slain before your eyes, and you shall not eat of it; your ass shall be violently taken away before your face, and shall not be restored to you; your sheep shall be given to your enemies, and there shall be no one to help you. ³²Your sons and your daughters shall be given to another people, while your eyes look on and fail with longing for them all the day; and it shall not be in the power of your hand to prevent it. ³³A nation which you have not known shall eat up the fruit of your ground and of all your labors; and you shall be only oppressed and crushed continually; ³⁴so that you shall be driven mad by the sight which your eyes shall see. ³⁵The LORD will smite you on the knees and on the legs with grievous boils of which you cannot be healed, from the sole of your foot to the crown of your head.

ˣAnother reading is *sword*

36 "The LORD will bring you, and your king whom you set over you, to a nation that neither you nor your fathers have known; and there you shall serve other gods, of wood and stone. ³⁷And you shall become a horror, a proverb, and a byword, among all the peoples where the LORD will lead you away. ³⁸You shall carry much seed into the field, and shall gather little in; for the locust shall consume it. ³⁹You shall plant vineyards and dress them, but you shall neither drink of the wine nor gather the grapes; for the worm shall eat them. ⁴⁰You shall have olive trees throughout all your territory, but you shall not anoint yourself with the oil; for your olives shall drop off. ⁴¹You shall beget sons and daughters, but they shall not be yours; for they shall go into captivity. ⁴²All your trees and the fruit of your ground the locust shall possess. ⁴³The sojourner who is among you shall mount above you higher and higher; and you shall come down lower and lower. ⁴⁴He shall lend to you, and you shall not lend to him; he shall be the head, and you shall be the tail. ⁴⁵All these curses shall come upon you and pursue you and overtake you, till you are destroyed, because you did not obey the voice of the LORD your God, to keep his commandments and his statutes which he commanded you. ⁴⁶They shall be upon you as a sign and a wonder, and upon your descendants for ever.

47 "Because you did not serve the LORD your God with joyfulness and gladness of heart, by reason of the abundance of all things, ⁴⁸therefore you shall serve your enemies whom the LORD will send against you, in hunger and thirst, in nakedness, and in want of all things; and he will put a yoke of iron upon your neck, until he has destroyed you. ⁴⁹The LORD will bring a nation against you from afar, from the end of the earth, as swift as the eagle flies, a nation whose language you do not understand, ⁵⁰a nation of stern countenance, who shall not regard the person of the old or show favor to the young, ⁵¹and shall eat the offspring of your cattle and the fruit of your ground, until you are destroyed; who also shall not leave you grain, wine, or oil, the increase of your cattle or the young of your flock, until they have caused you to perish. ⁵²They shall

besiege you in all your towns, until your high and fortified walls, in which you trusted, come down throughout all your land; and they shall besiege you in all your towns throughout all your land, which the LORD your God has given you. ⁵³And you shall eat the offspring of your own body, the flesh of your sons and daughters, whom the LORD your God has given you, in the siege and in the distress with which your enemies shall distress you. ⁵⁴The man who is the most tender and delicately bred among you will grudge food to his brother, to the wife of his bosom, and to the last of the children who remain to him; ⁵⁵so that he will not give to any of them any of the flesh of his children whom he is eating, because he has nothing left him, in the siege and in the distress with which your enemy shall distress you in all your towns. ⁵⁶The most tender and delicately bred woman among you, who would not venture to set the sole of her foot upon the ground because she is so delicate and tender, will grudge to the husband of her bosom, to her son and to her daughter, ⁵⁷her afterbirth that comes out from between her feet and her children whom she bears, because she will eat them secretly, for want of all things, in the siege and in the distress with which your enemy shall distress you in your towns.

58 "If you are not careful to do all the words of this law which are written in this book, that you may fear this glorious and awful name, the LORD your God, ⁵⁹then the LORD will bring on you and your offspring extraordinary afflictions, afflictions severe and lasting, and sicknesses grievous and lasting. ⁶⁰And he will bring upon you again all the diseases of Egypt, which you were afraid of; and they shall cleave to you. ⁶¹Every sickness also, and every affliction which is not recorded in the book of this law, the LORD will bring upon you, until you are destroyed. ⁶²Whereas you were as the stars of heaven for multitude, you shall be left few in number; because you did not obey the voice of the LORD your God. ⁶³And as the LORD took delight in doing you good and multiplying you, so the LORD will take delight in bringing ruin upon you and destroying you;

28.49: 1 Cor 14.21.

and you shall be plucked off the land which you are entering to take possession of it. [64] And the LORD will scatter you among all peoples, from one end of the earth to the other; and there you shall serve other gods, of wood and stone, which neither you nor your fathers have known. [65] And among these nations you shall find no ease, and there shall be no rest for the sole of your foot; but the LORD will give you there a trembling heart, and failing eyes, and a languishing soul; [66] your life shall hang in doubt before you; night and day you shall be in dread, and have no assurance of your life. [67] In the morning you shall say, 'Would it were evening!' and at evening you shall say, 'Would it were morning!' because of the dread which your heart shall fear, and the sights which your eyes shall see. [68] And the LORD will bring you back in ships to Egypt, a journey which I promised that you should never make again; and there you shall offer yourselves for sale to your enemies as male and female slaves, but no man will buy you."

29 [y] These are the words of the covenant which the LORD commanded Moses to make with the people of Israel in the land of Mō′ăb, besides the covenant which he had made with them at Hō′rĕb.

2 [z] And Moses summoned all Israel and said to them: "You have seen all that the LORD did before your eyes in the land of Egypt, to Pharaoh and to all his servants and to all his land, [3] the great trials which your eyes saw, the signs, and those great wonders; [4] but to this day the LORD has not given you a mind to understand, or eyes to see, or ears to hear. [5] I have led you forty years in the wilderness; your clothes have not worn out upon you, and your sandals have not worn off your feet; [6] you have not eaten bread, and you have not drunk wine or strong drink; that you may know that I am the LORD your God. [7] And when you came to this place, Sī′hon the king of Hĕsh′bon and Ŏg the king of Bā′shan came out against us to battle, but we defeated them; [8] we took their land, and gave it for an inheritance to the Reubenites, the Găd′ītes, and the half-tribe of the Mạ-năs′sītes. [9] Therefore be careful to do the words of this covenant, that you may prosper [a] in all that you do.

10 "You stand this day all of you before the LORD your God; the heads of your tribes, [b] your elders, and your officers, all the men of Israel, [11] your little ones, your wives, and the sojourner who is in your camp, both he who hews your wood and he who draws your water, [12] that you may enter into the sworn covenant of the LORD your God, which the LORD your God makes with you this day; [13] that he may establish you this day as his people, and that he may be your God, as he promised you, and as he swore to your fathers, to Abraham, to Isaac, and to Jacob. [14] Nor is it with you only that I make this sworn covenant, [15] but with him who is not here with us this day as well as with him who stands here with us this day before the LORD our God.

16 "You know how we dwelt in the land of Egypt, and how we came through the midst of the nations through which you passed; [17] and you have seen their detestable things, their idols of wood and stone, of silver and gold, which were among them. [18] Beware lest there be among you a man or woman or family or tribe, whose heart turns away this day from the LORD our God to go and serve the gods of those nations; lest there be among you a root bearing poisonous and bitter fruit, [19] one who, when he hears the words of this sworn covenant, blesses himself in his heart, saying, 'I shall be safe, though I walk in the stubbornness of my heart.' This would lead to the sweeping away of moist and dry alike. [20] The LORD would not pardon him, but rather the anger of the LORD and his jealousy would smoke against that man, and the curses written in this book would settle upon him, and the LORD would blot out his name from under heaven. [21] And the LORD would single him out from all the tribes of Israel for calamity, in accordance with all the curses of the covenant written in this book of the law. [22] And the generation to come, your children who rise up after you, and the foreigner who comes from a far land, would say, when they see the afflictions of that land and the sicknesses with which the LORD has made it sick— [23] the whole land brimstone

[y] Ch 28.69 in Heb [z] Ch 29.1 in Heb [a] Or *deal wisely*
[b] Gk Syr: Heb *your heads, your tribes*
29.4: Rom 11.8. **29.18:** Acts 8.23; Heb 12.15.

and salt, and a burnt-out waste, unsown, and growing nothing, where no grass can sprout, an overthrow like that of Sŏd'om and Go-môr'rah, Ād'mah and Zĕ-boi'ĭm, which the LORD overthrew in his anger and wrath— [24]yea, all the nations would say, 'Why has the LORD done thus to this land? What means the heat of this great anger?' [25]Then men would say, 'It is because they forsook the covenant of the LORD, the God of their fathers, which he made with them when he brought them out of the land of Egypt, [26]and went and served other gods and worshiped them, gods whom they had not known and whom he had not allotted to them; [27]therefore the anger of the LORD was kindled against this land, bringing upon it all the curses written in this book; [28]and the LORD uprooted them from their land in anger and fury and great wrath, and cast them into another land, as at this day.'

29 "The secret things belong to the LORD our God; but the things that are revealed belong to us and to our children for ever, that we may do all the words of this law.

30 "And when all these things come upon you, the blessing and the curse, which I have set before you, and you call them to mind among all the nations where the LORD your God has driven you, [2]and return to the LORD your God, you and your children, and obey his voice in all that I command you this day, with all your heart and with all your soul; [3]then the LORD your God will restore your fortunes, and have compassion upon you, and he will gather you again from all the peoples where the LORD your God has scattered you. [4]If your outcasts are in the uttermost parts of heaven, from there the LORD your God will gather you, and from there he will fetch you; [5]and the LORD your God will bring you into the land which your fathers possessed, that you may possess it; and he will make you more prosperous and numerous than your fathers. [6]And the LORD your God will circumcise your heart and the heart of your offspring, so that you will love the LORD your God with all your heart and with all your soul, that you may live. [7]And the LORD your God will put all these curses upon your foes and enemies who persecuted you. [8]And you shall again obey the

voice of the LORD, and keep all his commandments which I command you this day. [9]The LORD your God will make you abundantly prosperous in all the work of your hand, in the fruit of your body, and in the fruit of your cattle, and in the fruit of your ground; for the LORD will again take delight in prospering you, as he took delight in your fathers, [10]if you obey the voice of the LORD your God, to keep his commandments and his statutes which are written in this book of the law, if you turn to the LORD your God with all your heart and with all your soul.

11 "For this commandment which I command you this day is not too hard for you, neither is it far off. [12]It is not in heaven, that you should say, 'Who will go up for us to heaven, and bring it to us, that we may hear it and do it?' [13]Neither is it beyond the sea, that you should say, 'Who will go over the sea for us, and bring it to us, that we may hear it and do it?' [14]But the word is very near you; it is in your mouth and in your heart, so that you can do it.

15 "See, I have set before you this day life and good, death and evil. [16]If you obey the commandments of the LORD your God[c] which I command you this day, by loving the LORD your God, by walking in his ways, and by keeping his commandments and his statutes and his ordinances, then you shall live and multiply, and the LORD your God will bless you in the land which you are entering to take possession of it. [17]But if your heart turns away, and you will not hear, but are drawn away to worship other gods and serve them, [18]I declare to you this day, that you shall perish; you shall not live long in the land which you are going over the Jordan to enter and possess. [19]I call heaven and earth to witness against you this day, that I have set before you life and death, blessing and curse; therefore choose life, that you and your descendants may live, [20]loving the LORD your God, obeying his voice, and cleaving to him; for that means life to you and length of days, that you may dwell in the land which the LORD swore to your fathers, to Abraham, to Isaac, and to Jacob, to give them."

[c]Gk: Heb lacks *If you obey the commandments of the* LORD *your God*
30.4: Mt 24.31; Mk 13.27.   **30.12, 13:** Rom 10.6, 7.
30.14: Rom 10.8.

31 So Moses continued to speak these words to all Israel. ²And he said to them, "I am a hundred and twenty years old this day; I am no longer able to go out and come in. The LORD has said to me, 'You shall not go over this Jordan.' ³The LORD your God himself will go over before you; he will destroy these nations before you, so that you shall dispossess them; and Joshua will go over at your head, as the LORD has spoken. ⁴And the LORD will do to them as he did to Sī'họn and Ŏg, the kings of the Ăm'ọ-rītes, and to their land, when he destroyed them. ⁵And the LORD will give them over to you, and you shall do to them according to all the commandment which I have commanded you. ⁶Be strong and of good courage, do not fear or be in dread of them: for it is the LORD your God who goes with you; he will not fail you or forsake you."

7 Then Moses summoned Joshua, and said to him in the sight of all Israel, "Be strong and of good courage; for you shall go with this people into the land which the LORD has sworn to their fathers to give them; and you shall put them in possession of it. ⁸It is the LORD who goes before you; he will be with you, he will not fail you or forsake you; do not fear or be dismayed."

9 And Moses wrote this law, and gave it to the priests the sons of Lē'vī, who carried the ark of the covenant of the LORD, and to all the elders of Israel. ¹⁰And Moses commanded them, "At the end of every seven years, at the set time of the year of release, at the feast of booths, ¹¹when all Israel comes to appear before the LORD your God at the place which he will choose, you shall read this law before all Israel in their hearing. ¹²Assemble the people, men, women, and little ones, and the sojourner within your towns, that they may hear and learn to fear the LORD your God, and be careful to do all the words of this law, ¹³and that their children, who have not known it, may hear and learn to fear the LORD your God, as long as you live in the land which you are going over the Jordan to possess."

14 And the LORD said to Moses, "Behold, the days approach when you must die; call Joshua, and present yourselves in the tent of meeting, that I may commission him." And Moses and Joshua went and presented themselves in the tent of meeting. ¹⁵And the LORD appeared in the tent in a pillar of cloud; and the pillar of cloud stood by the door of the tent.

16 And the LORD said to Moses, "Behold, you are about to sleep with your fathers; then this people will rise and play the harlot after the strange gods of the land, where they go to be among them, and they will forsake me and break my covenant which I have made with them. ¹⁷Then my anger will be kindled against them in that day, and I will forsake them and hide my face from them, and they will be devoured; and many evils and troubles will come upon them, so that they will say in that day, 'Have not these evils come upon us because our God is not among us?' ¹⁸And I will surely hide my face in that day on account of all the evil which they have done, because they have turned to other gods. ¹⁹Now therefore write this song, and teach it to the people of Israel; put it in their mouths, that this song may be a witness for me against the people of Israel. ²⁰For when I have brought them into the land flowing with milk and honey, which I swore to give to their fathers, and they have eaten and are full and grown fat, they will turn to other gods and serve them, and despise me and break my covenant. ²¹And when many evils and troubles have come upon them, this song shall confront them as a witness (for it will live unforgotten in the mouths of their descendants); for I know the purposes which they are already forming, before I have brought them into the land that I swore to give." ²²So Moses wrote this song the same day, and taught it to the people of Israel.

23 And the LORD commissioned Joshua the son of Nŭn and said, "Be strong and of good courage; for you shall bring the children of Israel into the land which I swore to give them: I will be with you."

24 When Moses had finished writing the words of this law in a book, to the very end, ²⁵Moses commanded the Lē'vītes who carried the ark of the covenant of the LORD, ²⁶"Take this book of the law, and put it by the side of the ark of the covenant of the LORD your God, that it may be there for a witness against you. ²⁷For I know how rebellious and stubborn you are; behold,

31.6, 8: Heb 13.5.

while I am yet alive with you, today you have been rebellious against the LORD; how much more after my death! ²⁸ Assemble to me all the elders of your tribes, and your officers, that I may speak these words in their ears and call heaven and earth to witness against them. ²⁹ For I know that after my death you will surely act corruptly, and turn aside from the way which I have commanded you; and in the days to come evil will befall you, because you will do what is evil in the sight of the LORD, provoking him to anger through the work of your hands."

30 Then Moses spoke the words of this song until they were finished, in the ears of all the assembly of Israel:

32 "Give ear, O heavens, and I will speak;
and let the earth hear the words of my mouth.
² May my teaching drop as the rain, my speech distil as the dew,
as the gentle rain upon the tender grass,
and as the showers upon the herb.
³ For I will proclaim the name of the LORD.
Ascribe greatness to our God!

⁴ "The Rock, his work is perfect;
for all his ways are justice.
A God of faithfulness and without iniquity,
just and right is he.
⁵ They have dealt corruptly with him, they are no longer his children because of their blemish;
they are a perverse and crooked generation.
⁶ Do you thus requite the LORD, you foolish and senseless people?
Is not he your father, who created you,
who made you and established you?
⁷ Remember the days of old, consider the years of many generations;
ask your father, and he will show you;
your elders, and they will tell you.
⁸ When the Most High gave to the nations their inheritance,
when he separated the sons of men,
he fixed the bounds of the peoples according to the number of the sons of God.^d

⁹ For the LORD's portion is his people, Jacob his allotted heritage.

¹⁰ "He found him in a desert land, and in the howling waste of the wilderness;
he encircled him, he cared for him, he kept him as the apple of his eye.
¹¹ Like an eagle that stirs up its nest, that flutters over its young,
spreading out its wings, catching them,
bearing them on its pinions,
¹² the LORD alone did lead him, and there was no foreign god with him.
¹³ He made him ride on the high places of the earth,
and he ate the produce of the field;
and he made him suck honey out of the rock,
and oil out of the flinty rock.
¹⁴ Curds from the herd, and milk from the flock,
with fat of lambs and rams,
herds of Bā'shan and goats,
with the finest of the wheat—
and of the blood of the grape you drank wine.

¹⁵ "But Jĕsh'ū·run waxed fat, and kicked;
you waxed fat, you grew thick, you became sleek;
then he forsook God who made him, and scoffed at the Rock of his salvation.
¹⁶ They stirred him to jealousy with strange gods;
with abominable practices they provoked him to anger.
¹⁷ They sacrificed to demons which were no gods,
to gods they had never known,
to new gods that had come in of late, whom your fathers had never dreaded.
¹⁸ You were unmindful of the Rock that begot^e you,
and you forgot the God who gave you birth.

¹⁹ "The LORD saw it, and spurned them, because of the provocation of his sons and his daughters.
²⁰ And he said, 'I will hide my face from them,
I will see what their end will be,

^dCompare Gk: Heb *Israel*   ^eOr *bore*
32.5: Phil 2.15. **32.17:** 1 Cor 10.20.

for they are a perverse generation,
children in whom is no faithfulness.
²¹ They have stirred me to jealousy with
what is no god;
they have provoked me with their
idols.
So I will stir them to jealousy with
those who are no people;
I will provoke them with a foolish
nation.
²² For a fire is kindled by my anger,
and it burns to the depths of Shē′ōl,
devours the earth and its increase,
and sets on fire the foundations of
the mountains.

²³ " 'And I will heap evils upon them;
I will spend my arrows upon them;
²⁴ they shall be wasted with hunger,
and devoured with burning heat
and poisonous pestilence;
and I will send the teeth of beasts
against them,
with venom of crawling things of
the dust.
²⁵ In the open the sword shall bereave,
and in the chambers shall be
terror,
destroying both young man and
virgin,
the sucking child with the man of
gray hairs.
²⁶ I would have said, "I will scatter
them afar,
I will make the remembrance of
them cease from among men,"
²⁷ had I not feared provocation by the
enemy,
lest their adversaries should judge
amiss,
lest they should say, "Our hand is
triumphant,
the LORD has not wrought all
this." '

²⁸ "For they are a nation void of counsel,
and there is no understanding in
them.
²⁹ If they were wise, they would understand this,
they would discern their latter end!
³⁰ How should one chase a thousand,
and two put ten thousand to flight,
unless their Rock had sold them,
and the LORD had given them up?
³¹ For their rock is not as our Rock,
even our enemies themselves being judges.
³² For their vine comes from the vine
of Sŏd′om,

and from the fields of Gọ·môr′rạh;
their grapes are grapes of poison,
their clusters are bitter;
³³ their wine is the poison of serpents,
and the cruel venom of asps.

³⁴ "Is not this laid up in store with me,
sealed up in my treasuries?
³⁵ Vengeance is mine, and recompense,
for the time when their foot shall
slip;
for the day of their calamity is at
hand,
and their doom comes swiftly.
³⁶ For the LORD will vindicate his
people
and have compassion on his servants,
when he sees that their power is
gone,
and there is none remaining, bond
or free.
³⁷ Then he will say, 'Where are their
gods,
the rock in which they took refuge,
³⁸ who ate the fat of their sacrifices,
and drank the wine of their drink
offering?
Let them rise up and help you,
let them be your protection!

³⁹ " 'See now that I, even I, am he,
and there is no god beside me;
I kill and I make alive;
I wound and I heal;
and there is none that can deliver
out of my hand.
⁴⁰ For I lift up my hand to heaven,
and swear, As I live for ever,
⁴¹ if I whet my glittering sword,ʲ
and my hand takes hold on judgment,
I will take vengeance on my adversaries,
and will requite those who hate
me.
⁴² I will make my arrows drunk with
blood,
and my sword shall devour flesh —
with the blood of the slain and the
captives,
from the long-haired heads of the
enemy.'

⁴³ "Praise his people, O you nations;
for he avenges the blood of his
servants,

ʲ Heb *the lightning of my sword*
32.21: Rom 10.19; 11.11; 1 Cor 10.22.
32.35: Rom 12.19; Heb 10.30.
32.43: Rom 15.10; Heb 1.6 (Septuagint); Rev 6.10; 19.2.

and takes vengeance on his adversaries,
and makes expiation for the land
of his people."*g*

44 Moses came and recited all the words of this song in the hearing of the people, he and Joshua*h* the son of Nŭn. 45 And when Moses had finished speaking all these words to all Israel, 46 he said to them, "Lay to heart all the words which I enjoin upon you this day, that you may command them to your children, that they may be careful to do all the words of this law. 47 For it is no trifle for you, but it is your life, and thereby you shall live long in the land which you are going over the Jordan to possess."

48 And the LORD said to Moses that very day, 49 "Ascend this mountain of the Ăb'a·rǐm, Mount Nē'bō, which is in the land of Mō'ăb, opposite Jericho; and view the land of Canaan, which I give to the people of Israel for a possession; 50 and die on the mountain which you ascend, and be gathered to your people, as Aaron your brother died in Mount Hôr and was gathered to his people; 51 because you broke faith with me in the midst of the people of Israel at the waters of Mĕr'ĭ·băth-kā'dĕsh, in the wilderness of Zĭn; because you did not revere me as holy in the midst of the people of Israel. 52 For you shall see the land before you; but you shall not go there, into the land which I give to the people of Israel."

33 This is the blessing with which Moses the man of God blessed the children of Israel before his death. 2 He said,
"The LORD came from Sinai,
and dawned from Sē'ĭr upon us;*i*
he shone forth from Mount Păr'ăn,
he came from the ten thousands of holy ones,
with flaming fire*j* at his right hand.
3 Yea, he loved his people;*k*
all those consecrated to him were in his*x* hand;
so they followed*j* in thy steps,
receiving direction from thee,
4 when Moses commanded us a law,
as a possession for the assembly of Jacob.
5 Thus the LORD became king in Jĕsh'ū·rŭn,
when the heads of the people were gathered,
all the tribes of Israel together.

6 "Let Reuben live, and not die,
nor let his men be few."

7 And this he said of Judah:
"Hear, O LORD, the voice of Judah,
and bring him in to his people.
With thy hands contend*l* for him,
and be a help against his adversaries."

8 And of Lē'vī he said,
"Give to Levi*m* thy Thŭm'mĭm,
and thy Ū'rĭm to thy godly one,
whom thou didst test at Măs'săh,
with whom thou didst strive at the waters of Mĕr'ĭ·băh;
9 who said of his father and mother,
'I regard them not';
he disowned his brothers,
and ignored his children.
For they observed thy word,
and kept thy covenant.
10 They shall teach Jacob thy ordinances,
and Israel thy law;
they shall put incense before thee,
and whole burnt offering upon thy altar.
11 Bless, O LORD, his substance,
and accept the work of his hands;
crush the loins of his adversaries,
of those that hate him, that they rise not again."

12 Of Benjamin he said,
"The beloved of the LORD,
he dwells in safety by him;
he encompasses him all the day long,
and makes his dwelling between his shoulders."

13 And of Joseph he said,
"Blessed by the LORD be his land,
with the choicest gifts of heaven above,*n*
and of the deep that couches beneath,
14 with the choicest fruits of the sun,
and the rich yield of the months,
15 with the finest produce of the ancient mountains,
and the abundance of the everlasting hills,
16 with the best gifts of the earth and its fulness,

---

g Gk Vg: Heb *his land his people*   *h* Gk Syr Vg: Heb *Hoshea*
i Gk Syr Vg: Heb *them*
j The meaning of the Hebrew word is uncertain
k Gk: Heb *peoples*   *x* Heb *thy*
l Cn: Heb *with his hands he contended*
m Gk: Heb lacks *Give to Levi*
x Two Heb Mss and Tg: Heb *with the dew*

and the favor of him that dwelt in the bush.
Let these come upon the head of Joseph,
and upon the crown of the head of him that is prince among his brothers.
17 His firstling bull has majesty,
and his horns are the horns of a wild ox;
with them he shall push the peoples, all of them, to the ends of the earth;
such are the ten thousands of Ē'phra̧-ĭm,
and such are the thousands of Ma̧·năs'sȩh."

18 And of Zĕb'ū·lu̧n he said,
"Rejoice, Zebulun, in your going out;
and Ĭs'sa̧·chär, in your tents.
19 They shall call peoples to their mountain;
there they offer right sacrifices;
for they suck the affluence of the seas and the hidden treasures of the sand."

20 And of Gȧd he said,
"Blessed be he who enlarges Gad!
Gad couches like a lion,
he tears the arm, and the crown of the head.
21 He chose the best of the land for himself,
for there a commander's portion was reserved;
and he came to the heads of the people,
with Israel he executed the commands
and just decrees of the LORD."

22 And of Dan he said,
"Dan is a lion's whelp,
that leaps forth from Bā'sha̧n."

23 And of Năph'ta̧·lī he said,
"O Naphtali, satisfied with favor,
and full of the blessing of the LORD,
possess the lake and the south."

24 And of Ăsh'ȩr he said,
"Blessed above sons be Asher;
let him be the favorite of his brothers,
and let him dip his foot in oil.
25 Your bars shall be iron and bronze;

and as your days, so shall your strength be.

26 "There is none like God, O Jĕsh'ū·ru̧n,
who rides through the heavens to your help,
and in his majesty through the skies.
27 The eternal God is your dwelling place,
and underneath are the everlasting arms.
And he thrust out the enemy before you,
and said, Destroy.
28 So Israel dwelt in safety,
the fountain of Jacob alone,
in a land of grain and wine;
yea, his heavens drop down dew.
29 Happy are you, O Israel! Who is like you,
a people saved by the LORD,
the shield of your help,
and the sword of your triumph!
Your enemies shall come fawning to you;
and you shall tread upon their high places."

34 And Moses went up from the plains of Mō'ăb to Mount Nē'bō, to the top of Pĭs'ga̧h, which is opposite Jericho. And the LORD showed him all the land, Gilead as far as Dan, 2 all Năph'ta̧·lī, the land of Ē'phra̧·ĭm and Ma̧·năs'sȩh, all the land of Judah as far as the Western Sea, 3 the Nĕg'ĕb, and the Plain, that is, the valley of Jericho the city of palm trees, as far as Zō'ar. 4 And the LORD said to him, "This is the land of which I swore to Abraham, to Isaac, and to Jacob, 'I will give it to your descendants.' I have let you see it with your eyes, but you shall not go over there." 5 So Moses the servant of the LORD died there in the land of Mō'ăb, according to the word of the LORD, 6 and he buried him in the valley in the land of Mō'ăb opposite Bĕth-pē'ôr; but no man knows the place of his burial to this day. 7 Moses was a hundred and twenty years old when he died; his eye was not dim, nor his natural force abated. 8 And the people of Israel wept for Moses in the plains of Mō'ăb thirty days; then the days of weeping and mourning for Moses were ended.
9 And Joshua the son of Nŭn was full of the spirit of wisdom, for Moses had laid his hands upon him; so the

people of Israel obeyed him, and did as the LORD had commanded Moses. [10] And there has not arisen a prophet since in Israel like Moses, whom the LORD knew face to face, [11] none like him for all the signs and the wonders which the LORD sent him to do in the land of Egypt, to Pharaoh and to all his servants and to all his land, [12] and for all the mighty power and all the great and terrible deeds which Moses wrought in the sight of all Israel.

The Book of

Joshua

1 After the death of Moses the servant of the LORD, the LORD said to Joshua the son of Nŭn, Moses' minister, [2] "Moses my servant is dead; now therefore arise, go over this Jordan, you and all this people, into the land which I am giving to them, to the people of Israel. [3] Every place that the sole of your foot will tread upon I have given to you, as I promised to Moses. [4] From the wilderness and this Lebanon as far as the great river, the river Euphrates, all the land of the Hĭt'tītes to the Great Sea toward the going down of the sun shall be your territory. [5] No man shall be able to stand before you all the days of your life; as I was with Moses, so I will be with you; I will not fail you or forsake you. [6] Be strong and of good courage; for you shall cause this people to inherit the land which I swore to their fathers to give them. [7] Only be strong and very courageous, being careful to do according to all the law which Moses my servant commanded you; turn not from it to the right hand or to the left, that you may have good success wherever you go. [8] This book of the law shall not depart out of your mouth, but you shall meditate on it day and night, that you may be careful to do according to all that is written in it; for then you shall make your way prosperous, and then you shall have good success. [9] Have I not commanded you? Be strong and of good courage; be not frightened, neither be dismayed; for the LORD your God is with you wherever you go."

[10] Then Joshua commanded the officers of the people, [11] "Pass through the camp, and command the people, 'Prepare your provisions; for within three days you are to pass over this Jordan, to go in to take possession of the land which the LORD your God gives you to possess.' "

[12] And to the Reubenites, the Găd'-ītes, and the half-tribe of Mạ-năs'sẹh Joshua said, [13] "Remember the word which Moses the servant of the LORD commanded you, saying, 'The LORD your God is providing you a place of rest, and will give you this land.' [14] Your wives, your little ones, and your cattle shall remain in the land which Moses gave you beyond the Jordan; but all the men of valor among you shall pass over armed before your brethren and shall help them, [15] until the LORD gives rest to your brethren as well as to you, and they also take possession of the land which the LORD your God is giving them; then you shall return to the land of your possession, and shall possess it, the land which Moses the servant of the LORD gave you beyond the Jordan toward the sunrise." [16] And they answered Joshua, "All that you have commanded us we will do, and wherever you send us we will go. [17] Just as we obeyed Moses in all things, so we will obey you; only may the LORD your God be with you, as he was with Moses! [18] Whoever rebels against your commandment and disobeys your words, whatever you command him, shall be put to death. Only be strong and of good courage."

2 And Joshua the son of Nŭn sent two men secretly from Shĭt'tĭm as spies, saying, "Go, view the land, especially Jericho." And they went, and

34.10: Num 12.6-8.
1.5: Heb 13.5. 1.12-18: 22.1-34; Num 32.20-22.

came into the house of a harlot whose name was Rā'hăb, and lodged there. ²And it was told the king of Jericho, "Behold, certain men of Israel have come here tonight to search out the land." ³Then the king of Jericho sent to Rā'hăb, saying, "Bring forth the men that have come to you, who entered your house; for they have come to search out all the land." ⁴But the woman had taken the two men and hidden them; and she said, "True, men came to me, but I did not know where they came from; ⁵and when the gate was to be closed, at dark, the men went out; where the men went I do not know; pursue them quickly, for you will overtake them." ⁶But she had brought them up to the roof, and hid them with the stalks of flax which she had laid in order on the roof. ⁷So the men pursued after them on the way to the Jordan as far as the fords; and as soon as the pursuers had gone out, the gate was shut.

8 Before they lay down, she came up to them on the roof, ⁹and said to the men, "I know that the LORD has given you the land, and that the fear of you has fallen upon us, and that all the inhabitants of the land melt away before you. ¹⁰For we have heard how the LORD dried up the water of the Red Sea before you when you came out of Egypt, and what you did to the two kings of the Ăm'ọ‑rītes that were beyond the Jordan, to Sī'hǫn and Ŏg, whom you utterly destroyed. ¹¹And as soon as we heard it, our hearts melted, and there was no courage left in any man, because of you; for the LORD your God is he who is God in heaven above and on earth beneath. ¹²Now then, swear to me by the LORD that as I have dealt kindly with you, you also will deal kindly with my father's house, and give me a sure sign, ¹³and save alive my father and mother, my brothers and sisters, and all who belong to them, and deliver our lives from death." ¹⁴And the men said to her, "Our life for yours! If you do not tell this business of ours, then we will deal kindly and faithfully with you when the LORD gives us the land."

15 Then she let them down by a rope through the window, for her house was built into the city wall, so that she dwelt in the wall. ¹⁶And she said to them, "Go into the hills, lest the pur-

suers meet you; and hide yourselves there three days, until the pursuers have returned; then afterward you may go your way." ¹⁷The men said to her, "We will be guiltless with respect to this oath of yours which you have made us swear. ¹⁸Behold, when we come into the land, you shall bind this scarlet cord in the window through which you let us down; and you shall gather into your house your father and mother, your brothers, and all your father's household. ¹⁹If any one goes out of the doors of your house into the street, his blood shall be upon his head, and we shall be guiltless; but if a hand is laid upon any one who is with you in the house, his blood shall be on our head. ²⁰But if you tell this business of ours, then we shall be guiltless with respect to your oath which you have made us swear." ²¹And she said, "According to your words, so be it." Then she sent them away, and they departed; and she bound the scarlet cord in the window.

22 They departed, and went into the hills, and remained there three days, until the pursuers returned; for the pursuers had made search all along the way and found nothing. ²³Then the two men came down again from the hills, and passed over and came to Joshua the son of Nŭn; and they told him all that had befallen them. ²⁴And they said to Joshua, "Truly the LORD has given all the land into our hands; and moreover all the inhabitants of the land are fainthearted because of us."

3 Early in the morning Joshua rose and set out from Shit'tim, with all the people of Israel; and they came to the Jordan, and lodged there before they passed over. ²At the end of three days the officers went through the camp ³and commanded the people, "When you see the ark of the covenant of the LORD your God being carried by the Levitical priests, then you shall set out from your place and follow it, ⁴that you may know the way you shall go, for you have not passed this way before. Yet there shall be a space between you and it, a distance of about two thousand cubits; do not come near it." ⁵And Joshua said to the people, "Sanctify yourselves; for tomorrow the LORD will do wonders among you." ⁶And Joshua said to the priests, "Take

up the ark of the covenant, and pass on before the people." And they took up the ark of the covenant, and went before the people.

7 And the LORD said to Joshua, "This day I will begin to exalt you in the sight of all Israel, that they may know that, as I was with Moses, so I will be with you. ⁸And you shall command the priests who bear the ark of the covenant, 'When you come to the brink of the waters of the Jordan, you shall stand still in the Jordan.'" ⁹And Joshua said to the people of Israel, "Come hither, and hear the words of the LORD your God." ¹⁰And Joshua said, "Hereby you shall know that the living God is among you, and that he will without fail drive out from before you the Canaanites, the Hĭt′tītes, the Hī′-vītes, the Pĕr′ĭz·zītes, the Gĭr′ga·shītes, the Ăm′o·rītes, and the Jĕb′ū·sītes. ¹¹Behold, the ark of the covenant of the Lord of all the earth is to pass over before you into the Jordan. ¹²Now therefore take twelve men from the tribes of Israel, from each tribe a man. ¹³And when the soles of the feet of the priests who bear the ark of the LORD, the Lord of all the earth, shall rest in the waters of the Jordan, the waters of the Jordan shall be stopped from flowing, and the waters coming down from above shall stand in one heap."

14 So, when the people set out from their tents, to pass over the Jordan with the priests bearing the ark of the covenant before the people, ¹⁵and when those who bore the ark had come to the Jordan, and the feet of the priests bearing the ark were dipped in the brink of the water (the Jordan overflows all its banks throughout the time of harvest), ¹⁶the waters coming down from above stood and rose up in a heap far off, at Adam, the city that is beside Zâr′e·thăn, and those flowing down toward the sea of the Ăr′a·bah, the Salt Sea, were wholly cut off; and the people passed over opposite Jericho. ¹⁷And while all Israel were passing over on dry ground, the priests who bore the ark of the covenant of the LORD stood on dry ground in the midst of the Jordan, until all the nation finished passing over the Jordan.

4 When all the nation had finished passing over the Jordan, the LORD said to Joshua, ²"Take twelve men from the people, from each tribe a

man, ³and command them, 'Take twelve stones from here out of the midst of the Jordan, from the very place where the priests' feet stood, and carry them over with you, and lay them down in the place where you lodge tonight.'" ⁴Then Joshua called the twelve men from the people of Israel, whom he had appointed, a man from each tribe; ⁵and Joshua said to them, "Pass on before the ark of the LORD your God into the midst of the Jordan, and take up each of you a stone upon his shoulder, according to the number of the tribes of the people of Israel, ⁶that this may be a sign among you, when your children ask in time to come, 'What do those stones mean to you?' ⁷Then you shall tell them that the waters of the Jordan were cut off before the ark of the covenant of the LORD; when it passed over the Jordan, the waters of the Jordan were cut off. So these stones shall be to the people of Israel a memorial for ever."

8 And the men of Israel did as Joshua commanded, and took up twelve stones out of the midst of the Jordan, according to the number of the tribes of the people of Israel, as the LORD told Joshua; and they carried them over with them to the place where they lodged, and laid them down there. ⁹And Joshua set up twelve stones in the midst of the Jordan, in the place where the feet of the priests bearing the ark of the covenant had stood; and they are there to this day. ¹⁰For the priests who bore the ark stood in the midst of the Jordan, until everything was finished that the LORD commanded Joshua to tell the people, according to all that Moses had commanded Joshua.

The people passed over in haste; ¹¹and when all the people had finished passing over, the ark of the LORD and the priests passed over before the people. ¹²The sons of Reuben and the sons of Găd and the half-tribe of Ma·năs′-seh passed over armed before the people of Israel, as Moses had bidden them; ¹³about forty thousand ready armed for war passed over before the LORD for battle, to the plains of Jericho. ¹⁴On that day the LORD exalted Joshua in the sight of all Israel; and they stood in awe of him, as they had stood in awe of Moses, all the days of his life.

15 And the Lord said to Joshua, 16 "Command the priests who bear the ark of the testimony to come up out of the Jordan." 17 Joshua therefore commanded the priests, "Come up out of the Jordan." 18 And when the priests bearing the ark of the covenant of the Lord came up from the midst of the Jordan, and the soles of the priests' feet were lifted up on dry ground, the waters of the Jordan returned to their place and overflowed all its banks, as before.

19 The people came up out of the Jordan on the tenth day of the first month, and they encamped in Gĭl'gal on the east border of Jericho. 20 And those twelve stones, which they took out of the Jordan, Joshua set up in Gĭl'gal. 21 And he said to the people of Israel, "When your children ask their fathers in time to come, 'What do these stones mean?' 22 then you shall let your children know, 'Israel passed over this Jordan on dry ground.' 23 For the Lord your God dried up the waters of the Jordan for you until you passed over, as the Lord your God did to the Red Sea, which he dried up for us until we passed over, 24 so that all the peoples of the earth may know that the hand of the Lord is mighty; that you may fear the Lord your God for ever."

5 When all the kings of the Ăm'-ọ·rītes that were beyond the Jordan to the west, and all the kings of the Canaanites that were by the sea, heard that the Lord had dried up the waters of the Jordan for the people of Israel until they had crossed over, their heart melted, and there was no longer any spirit in them, because of the people of Israel.

2 At that time the Lord said to Joshua, "Make flint knives and circumcise the people of Israel again the second time." 3 So Joshua made flint knives, and circumcised the people of Israel at Gĭb'ē·ạth-hạ·ăr'a·lŏth.*a* 4 And this is the reason why Joshua circumcised them: all the males of the people who came out of Egypt, all the men of war, had died on the way in the wilderness after they had come out of Egypt. 5 Though all the people who came out had been circumcised, yet all the people that were born on the way in the wilderness after they had come out of Egypt had not been circumcised. 6 For the people of Israel walked forty years in the wilderness, till all the nation, the men of war that came forth out of Egypt, perished, because they did not hearken to the voice of the Lord; to them the Lord swore that he would not let them see the land which the Lord had sworn to their fathers to give us, a land flowing with milk and honey. 7 So it was their children, whom he raised up in their stead, that Joshua circumcised; for they were uncircumcised, because they had not been circumcised on the way.

8 When the circumcising of all the nation was done, they remained in their places in the camp till they were healed. 9 And the Lord said to Joshua, "This day I have rolled away the reproach of Egypt from you." And so the name of that place is called Gĭl'gal*b* to this day.

10 While the people of Israel were encamped in Gĭl'gal they kept the passover on the fourteenth day of the month at evening in the plains of Jericho. 11 And on the morrow after the passover, on that very day, they ate of the produce of the land, unleavened cakes and parched grain. 12 And the manna ceased on the morrow, when they ate of the produce of the land; and the people of Israel had manna no more, but ate of the fruit of the land of Canaan that year.

13 When Joshua was by Jericho, he lifted up his eyes and looked, and behold, a man stood before him with his drawn sword in his hand; and Joshua went to him and said to him, "Are you for us, or for our adversaries?" 14 And he said, "No; but as commander of the army of the Lord I have now come." And Joshua fell on his face to the earth, and worshiped, and said to him, "What does my lord bid his servant?" 15 And the commander of the Lord's army said to Joshua, "Put off your shoes from your feet; for the place where you stand is holy." And Joshua did so.

6 Now Jericho was shut up from within and from without because of the people of Israel; none went out, and none came in. 2 And the Lord said to Joshua, "See, I have given into your hand Jericho, with its king and mighty men of valor. 3 You shall march

a That is *the hill of the foreskins*
b From Heb *galal* to roll

around the city, all the men of war going around the city once. Thus shall you do for six days. ⁴And seven priests shall bear seven trumpets of rams' horns before the ark; and on the seventh day you shall march around the city seven times, the priests blowing the trumpets. ⁵And when they make a long blast with the ram's horn, as soon as you hear the sound of the trumpet, then all the people shall shout with a great shout; and the wall of the city will fall down flat, and the people shall go up every man straight before him." ⁶So Joshua the son of Nŭn called the priests and said to them, "Take up the ark of the covenant, and let seven priests bear seven trumpets of rams' horns before the ark of the LORD." ⁷And he said to the people, "Go forward; march around the city, and let the armed men pass on before the ark of the LORD."

8 And as Joshua had commanded the people, the seven priests bearing the seven trumpets of rams' horns before the LORD went forward, blowing the trumpets, with the ark of the covenant of the LORD following them. ⁹And the armed men went before the priests who blew the trumpets, and the rear guard came after the ark, while the trumpets blew continually. ¹⁰But Joshua commanded the people, "You shall not shout or let your voice be heard, neither shall any word go out of your mouth, until the day I bid you shout; then you shall shout." ¹¹So he caused the ark of the LORD to compass the city, going about it once; and they came into the camp, and spent the night in the camp.

12 Then Joshua rose early in the morning, and the priests took up the ark of the LORD. ¹³And the seven priests bearing the seven trumpets of rams' horns before the ark of the LORD passed on, blowing the trumpets continually; and the armed men went before them, and the rear guard came after the ark of the LORD, while the trumpets blew continually. ¹⁴And the second day they marched around the city once, and returned into the camp. So they did for six days.

15 On the seventh day they rose early at the dawn of day, and marched around the city in the same manner seven times: it was only on that day that they marched around the city seven times. ¹⁶And at the seventh time, when the priests had blown the trumpets, Joshua said to the people, "Shout; for the LORD has given you the city. ¹⁷And the city and all that is within it shall be devoted to the LORD for destruction; only Rā′hăb the harlot and all who are with her in her house shall live, because she hid the messengers that we sent. ¹⁸But you, keep yourselves from the things devoted to destruction, lest when you have devoted them you take any of the devoted things and make the camp of Israel a thing for destruction, and bring trouble upon it. ¹⁹But all silver and gold, and vessels of bronze and iron, are sacred to the LORD; they shall go into the treasury of the LORD." ²⁰So the people shouted, and the trumpets were blown. As soon as the people heard the sound of the trumpet, the people raised a great shout, and the wall fell down flat, so that the people went up into the city, every man straight before him, and they took the city. ²¹Then they utterly destroyed all in the city, both men and women, young and old, oxen, sheep, and asses, with the edge of the sword.

22 And Joshua said to the two men who had spied out the land, "Go into the harlot's house, and bring out from it the woman, and all who belong to her, as you swore to her." ²³So the young men who had been spies went in, and brought out Rā′hăb, and her father and mother and brothers and all who belonged to her; and they brought all her kindred, and set them outside the camp of Israel. ²⁴And they burned the city with fire, and all within it; only the silver and gold, and the vessels of bronze and of iron, they put into the treasury of the house of the LORD. ²⁵But Rā′hăb the harlot, and her father's household, and all who belonged to her, Joshua saved alive; and she dwelt in Israel to this day, because she hid the messengers whom Joshua sent to spy out Jericho.

26 Joshua laid an oath upon them at that time, saying, "Cursed before the LORD be the man that rises up and rebuilds this city, Jericho.

At the cost of his first-born shall he lay its foundation,
and at the cost of his youngest son shall he set up its gates."

6.26: 1 Kings 16.34.

27 So the Lord was with Joshua; and his fame was in all the land.

7 But the people of Israel broke faith in regard to the devoted things; for Ā′chạn the son of Cär′mī, son of Zăb′dī, son of Zē′rạh, of the tribe of Judah, took some of the devoted things; and the anger of the Lord burned against the people of Israel.

2 Joshua sent men from Jericho to Aī, which is near Bĕth-ā′vẹn, east of Bĕth′ẹl, and said to them, "Go up and spy out the land." And the men went up and spied out Aī. ³And they returned to Joshua, and said to him, "Let not all the people go up, but let about two or three thousand men go up and attack Aī; do not make the whole people toil up there, for they are but few." ⁴So about three thousand went up there from the people; and they fled before the men of Aī, ⁵and the men of Aī killed about thirty-six men of them, and chased them before the gate as far as Shĕb′ạ-rĭm, and slew them at the descent. And the hearts of the people melted, and became as water.

6 Then Joshua rent his clothes, and fell to the earth upon his face before the ark of the Lord until the evening, he and the elders of Israel; and they put dust upon their heads. ⁷And Joshua said, "Alas, O Lord God, why hast thou brought this people over the Jordan at all, to give us into the hands of the Ăm′ọ-rītes, to destroy us? Would that we had been content to dwell beyond the Jordan! ⁸O Lord, what can I say, when Israel has turned their backs before their enemies! ⁹For the Canaanites and all the inhabitants of the land will hear of it, and will surround us, and cut off our name from the earth; and what wilt thou do for thy great name?"

10 The Lord said to Joshua, "Arise, why have you thus fallen upon your face? ¹¹Israel has sinned; they have transgressed my covenant which I commanded them; they have taken some of the devoted things; they have stolen, and lied, and put them among their own stuff. ¹²Therefore the people of Israel cannot stand before their enemies; they turn their backs before their enemies, because they have become a thing for destruction. I will be with you no more, unless you destroy the devoted things from among you.

¹³Up, sanctify the people, and say, 'Sanctify yourselves for tomorrow; for thus says the Lord, God of Israel, "There are devoted things in the midst of you, O Israel; you cannot stand before your enemies, until you take away the devoted things from among you." ¹⁴In the morning therefore you shall be brought near by your tribes; and the tribe which the Lord takes shall come near by families; and the family which the Lord takes shall come near by households; and the household which the Lord takes shall come near man by man. ¹⁵And he who is taken with the devoted things shall be burned with fire, he and all that he has, because he has transgressed the covenant of the Lord, and because he has done a shameful thing in Israel.' "

16 So Joshua rose early in the morning, and brought Israel near tribe by tribe, and the tribe of Judah was taken; ¹⁷and he brought near the families of Judah, and the family of the Zē′rạhītes was taken; and he brought near the family of the Zerahites man by man, and Zăb′dī was taken; ¹⁸and he brought near his household man by man, and Ā′chạn the son of Cär′mī, son of Zăb′dī, son of Zē′rạh of the tribe of Judah, was taken. ¹⁹Then Joshua said to Ā′chạn, "My son, give glory to the Lord God of Israel, and render praise to him; and tell me now what you have done; do not hide it from me." ²⁰And Ā′chạn answered Joshua, "Of a truth I have sinned against the Lord God of Israel, and this is what I did: ²¹when I saw among the spoil a beautiful mantle from Shī′när, and two hundred shekels of silver, and a bar of gold weighing fifty shekels, then I coveted them, and took them; and behold, they are hidden in the earth inside my tent, with the silver underneath."

22 So Joshua sent messengers, and they ran to the tent; and behold, it was hidden in his tent with the silver underneath. ²³And they took them out of the tent and brought them to Joshua and all the people of Israel; and they laid them down before the Lord. ²⁴And Joshua and all Israel with him took Ā′chạn the son of Zē′rạh, and the silver and the mantle and the bar of gold, and his sons and daughters, and his oxen and asses and sheep, and his tent, and all that he had; and they

brought them up to the Valley of Aʹchôr. ²⁵And Joshua said, "Why did you bring trouble on us? The LORD brings trouble on you today." And all Israel stoned him with stones; they burned them with fire, and stoned them with stones. ²⁶And they raised over him a great heap of stones that remains to this day; then the LORD turned from his burning anger. Therefore to this day the name of that place is called the Valley of Aʹchôr.ᶜ

8 And the LORD said to Joshua, "Do not fear or be dismayed; take all the fighting men with you, and arise, go up to Aī; see, I have given into your hand the king of Ai, and his people, his city, and his land; ²and you shall do to Aī and its king as you did to Jericho and its king; only its spoil and its cattle you shall take as booty for yourselves; lay an ambush against the city, behind it."

3 So Joshua arose, and all the fighting men, to go up to Aī; and Joshua chose thirty thousand mighty men of valor, and sent them forth by night. ⁴And he commanded them, "Behold, you shall lie in ambush against the city, behind it; do not go very far from the city, but hold yourselves all in readiness; ⁵and I, and all the people who are with with me, will approach the city. And when they come out against us, as before, we shall flee before them; ⁶and they will come out after us, till we have drawn them away from the city; for they will say, 'They are fleeing from us, as before.' So we will flee from them; ⁷then you shall rise up from the ambush, and seize the city; for the LORD your God will give it into your hand. ⁸And when you have taken the city, you shall set the city on fire, doing as the LORD has bidden; see, I have commanded you." ⁹So Joshua sent them forth; and they went to the place of ambush, and lay between Bĕthʹel and Aī, to the west of Ai; but Joshua spent that night among the people.

10 And Joshua arose early in the morning and mustered the people, and went up, with the elders of Israel, before the people to Aī. ¹¹And all the fighting men who were with him went up, and drew near before the city, and encamped on the north side of Aī, with a ravine between them and Ai. ¹²And he took about five thousand men,

and set them in ambush between Bĕthʹel and Aī, to the west of the city. ¹³So they stationed the forces, the main encampment which was north of the city and its rear guard west of the city. But Joshua spent that night in the valley. ¹⁴And when the king of Aī saw this he and all his people, the men of the city, made haste and went out early to the descentᵈ toward the Arʹaˑbah to meet Israel in battle; but he did not know that there was an ambush against him behind the city. ¹⁵And Joshua and all Israel made a pretense of being beaten before them, and fled in the direction of the wilderness. ¹⁶So all the people who were in the city were called together to pursue them, and as they pursued Joshua they were drawn away from the city. ¹⁷There was not a man left in Aī or Bĕthʹel, who did not go out after Israel; they left the city open, and pursued Israel.

18 Then the LORD said to Joshua, "Stretch out the javelin that is in your hand toward Aī; for I will give it into your hand." And Joshua stretched out the javelin that was in his hand toward the city. ¹⁹And the ambush rose quickly out of their place, and as soon as he had stretched out his hand, they ran and entered the city and took it; and they made haste to set the city on fire. ²⁰So when the men of Aī looked back, behold, the smoke of the city went up to heaven; and they had no power to flee this way or that, for the people that fled to the wilderness turned back upon the pursuers. ²¹And when Joshua and all Israel saw that the ambush had taken the city, and that the smoke of the city went up, then they turned back and smote the men of Aī. ²²And the others came forth from the city against them; so they were in the midst of Israel, some on this side, and some on that side; and Israel smote them, until there was left none that survived or escaped. ²³But the king of Aī they took alive, and brought him to Joshua.

24 When Israel had finished slaughtering all the inhabitants of Aī in the open wilderness where they pursued them and all of them to the very last had fallen by the edge of the sword, all Israel returned to Ai, and smote it with the edge of the sword. ²⁵And all who fell that day, both men and

ᶜThat is *Trouble* ᵈCn: Heb *appointed time*

women, were twelve thousand, all the people of Aī. ²⁶For Joshua did not draw back his hand, with which he stretched out the javelin, until he had utterly destroyed all the inhabitants of Aī. ²⁷Only the cattle and the spoil of that city Israel took as their booty, according to the word of the LORD which he commanded Joshua. ²⁸So Joshua burned Aī, and made it for ever a heap of ruins, as it is to this day. ²⁹And he hanged the king of Aī on a tree until evening; and at the going down of the sun Joshua commanded, and they took his body down from the tree, and cast it at the entrance of the gate of the city, and raised over it a great heap of stones, which stands there to this day.

30 Then Joshua built an altar in Mount Ē′bạl to the LORD, the God of Israel, ³¹as Moses the servant of the LORD had commanded the people of Israel, as it is written in the book of the law of Moses, "an altar of unhewn stones, upon which no man has lifted an iron tool"; and they offered on it burnt offerings to the LORD, and sacrificed peace offerings. ³²And there, in the presence of the people of Israel, he wrote upon the stones a copy of the law of Moses, which he had written. ³³And all Israel, sojourner as well as homeborn, with their elders and officers and their judges, stood on opposite sides of the ark before the Levitical priests who carried the ark of the covenant of the LORD, half of them in front of Mount Gēr′ĭ-zĭm and half of them in front of Mount Ē′bạl, as Moses the servant of the LORD had commanded at the first, that they should bless the people of Israel. ³⁴And afterward he read all the words of the law, the blessing and the curse, according to all that is written in the book of the law. ³⁵There was not a word of all that Moses commanded which Joshua did not read before all the assembly of Israel, and the women, and the little ones, and the sojourners who lived among them.

9 When all the kings who were beyond the Jordan in the hill country and in the lowland all along the coast of the Great Sea toward Lebanon, the Hĭt′tītes, the Ăm′ọ-rītes, the Canaanites, the Pĕr′ĭz-zītes, the Hī′vītes, and the Jĕb′ū-sītes, heard of this, ²they gathered together with one accord to fight Joshua and Israel.

3 But when the inhabitants of Gĭb′ē-on heard what Joshua had done to Jericho and to Aī, ⁴they on their part acted with cunning, and went and made ready provisions, and took worn-out sacks upon their asses, and wineskins, worn-out and torn and mended, ⁵with worn-out, patched sandals on their feet, and worn-out clothes; and all their provisions were dry and moldy. ⁶And they went to Joshua in the camp at Gĭl′gal, and said to him and to the men of Israel, "We have come from a far country; so now make a covenant with us." ⁷But the men of Israel said to the Hī′vītes, "Perhaps you live among us; then how can we make a covenant with you?" ⁸They said to Joshua, "We are your servants." And Joshua said to them, "Who are you? And where do you come from?" ⁹They said to him, "From a very far country your servants have come, because of the name of the LORD your God; for we have heard a report of him, and all that he did in Egypt, ¹⁰and all that he did to the two kings of the Ăm′ọ-rītes who were beyond the Jordan, Sī′họn the king of Hĕsh′bọn, and Ŏg king of Bā′shạn, who dwelt in Ăsh′tạ-rŏth. ¹¹And our elders and all the inhabitants of our country said to us, 'Take provisions in your hand for the journey, and go to meet them, and say to them, "We are your servants; come now, make a covenant with us."' ¹²Here is our bread; it was still warm when we took it from our houses as our food for the journey, on the day we set forth to come to you, but now, behold, it is dry and moldy; ¹³these wineskins were new when we filled them, and behold, they are burst; and these garments and shoes of ours are worn out from the very long journey." ¹⁴So the men partook of their provisions, and did not ask direction from the LORD. ¹⁵And Joshua made peace with them, and made a covenant with them, to let them live; and the leaders of the congregation swore to them.

16 At the end of three days after they had made a covenant with them, they heard that they were their neighbors, and that they dwelt among them. ¹⁷And the people of Israel set out and reached their cities on the third day. Now their cities were Gĭb′ē-on, Chē-phī′rạh, Bē-ēr′ọth, and Kĭr′ĭ-ăth-

8.30-35: Deut 27.2-8.

jĕ´a·rĭm. ¹⁸But the people of Israel did not kill them, because the leaders of the congregation had sworn to them by the LORD, the God of Israel. Then all the congregation murmured against the leaders. ¹⁹But all the leaders said to all the congregation, "We have sworn to them by the LORD, the God of Israel, and now we may not touch them. ²⁰This we will do to them, and let them live, lest wrath be upon us, because of the oath which we swore to them." ²¹And the leaders said to them, "Let them live." So they became hewers of wood and drawers of water for all the congregation, as the leaders had said of them.

22 Joshua summoned them, and he said to them, "Why did you deceive us, saying, 'We are very far from you,' when you dwell among us? ²³Now therefore you are cursed, and some of you shall always be slaves, hewers of wood and drawers of water for the house of my God." ²⁴They answered Joshua, "Because it was told to your servants for a certainty that the LORD your God had commanded his servant Moses to give you all the land, and to destroy all the inhabitants of the land from before you; so we feared greatly for our lives because of you, and did this thing. ²⁵And now, behold, we are in your hand: do as it seems good and right in your sight to do to us." ²⁶So he did to them, and delivered them out of the hand of the people of Israel; and they did not kill them. ²⁷But Joshua made them that day hewers of wood and drawers of water for the congregation and for the altar of the LORD, to continue to this day, in the place which he should choose.

10 When A·dō´nĭ-zē´dĕk king of Jerusalem heard how Joshua had taken Ai, and had utterly destroyed it, doing to Ai and its king as he had done to Jericho and its king, and how the inhabitants of Gĭb´ē·on had made peace with Israel and were among them, ²heˣ feared greatly, because Gĭb´ē·on was a great city, like one of the royal cities, and because it was greater than Ai, and all its men were mighty. ³So A·dō´nĭ-zē´dĕk king of Jerusalem sent to Hō´hăm king of Hē´bron, to Pī´ram king of Jär´mŭth, to Ja·phī´a king of Lā´chĭsh, and to Dē´bir king of Ĕg´lŏn, saying, ⁴"Come up to me, and help me, and let us smite

Gĭb´ē·on; for it has made peace with Joshua and with the people of Israel." ⁵Then the five kings of the Ăm´o·rītes, the king of Jerusalem, the king of Hē´bron, the king of Jär´mŭth, the king of Lā´chĭsh, and the king of Ĕg´lŏn, gathered their forces, and went up with all their armies and encamped against Gĭb´ē·on, and made war against it.

6 And the men of Gĭb´ē·on sent to Joshua at the camp in Gĭl´gal, saying, "Do not relax your hand from your servants; come up to us quickly, and save us, and help us; for all the kings of the Ăm´o·rītes that dwell in the hill country are gathered against us." ⁷So Joshua went up from Gĭl´gal, he and all the people of war with him, and all the mighty men of valor. ⁸And the LORD said to Joshua, "Do not fear them, for I have given them into your hands; there shall not a man of them stand before you." ⁹So Joshua came upon them suddenly, having marched up all night from Gĭl´gal. ¹⁰And the LORD threw them into a panic before Israel, who slew them with a great slaughter at Gĭb´ē·on, and chased them by the way of the ascent of Bĕth-hō´rŏn, and smote them as far as A·zē´kah and Măk·kē´-dah. ¹¹And as they fled before Israel, while they were going down the ascent of Bĕth-hō´rŏn, the LORD threw down great stones from heaven upon them as far as A·zē´kah, and they died; there were more who died because of the hailstones than the men of Israel killed with the sword.

12 Then spoke Joshua to the LORD in the day when the LORD gave the Ăm´o·rītes over to the men of Israel; and he said in the sight of Israel,

"Sun, stand thou still at Gĭb´ē·on,
and thou Moon in the valley of
Aī´ja·lŏn."
¹³And the sun stood still, and the
moon stayed,
until the nation took vengeance on
their enemies.

Is this not written in the Book of Jăsh´ar? The sun stayed in the midst of heaven, and did not hasten to go down for about a whole day. ¹⁴There has been no day like it before or since, when the LORD hearkened to the voice of a man; for the LORD fought for Israel.

15 Then Joshua returned, and all Israel with him, to the camp at Gĭl´gal.

ˣHeb *they*

16 These five kings fled, and hid themselves in the cave at Măk·kē′dah. ¹⁷And it was told Joshua, "The five kings have been found, hidden in the cave at Măk·kē′dah." ¹⁸And Joshua said, "Roll great stones against the mouth of the cave, and set men by it to guard them; ¹⁹but do not stay there yourselves, pursue your enemies, fall upon their rear, do not let them enter their cities; for the LORD your God has given them into your hand." ²⁰When Joshua and the men of Israel had finished slaying them with a very great slaughter, until they were wiped out, and when the remnant which remained of them had entered into the fortified cities, ²¹all the people returned safe to Joshua in the camp at Măk·kē′dah; not a man moved his tongue against any of the people of Israel. 22 Then Joshua said, "Open the mouth of the cave, and bring those five kings out to me from the cave." ²³And they did so, and brought those five kings out to him from the cave, the king of Jerusalem, the king of Hē′bron, the king of Jăr′muth, the king of Lā′-chĭsh, and the king of Ĕg′lŏn. ²⁴And when they brought those kings out to Joshua, Joshua summoned all the men of Israel, and said to the chiefs of the men of war who had gone with him, "Come near, put your feet upon the necks of these kings." Then they came near, and put their feet on their necks. ²⁵And Joshua said to them, "Do not be afraid or dismayed; be strong and of good courage; for thus the LORD will do to all your enemies against whom you fight." ²⁶And afterward Joshua smote them and put them to death, and he hung them on five trees. And they hung upon the trees until evening; ²⁷but at the time of the going down of the sun, Joshua commanded, and they took them down from the trees, and threw them into the cave where they had hidden themselves, and they set great stones against the mouth of the cave, which remain to this very day. 28 And Joshua took Măk·kē′dah on that day, and smote it and its king with the edge of the sword; he utterly destroyed every person in it, he left none remaining; and he did to the king of Makkedah as he had done to the king of Jericho. 29 Then Joshua passed on from Măk·kē′dah, and all Israel with him,

to Lĭb′nah, and fought against Libnah; ³⁰and the LORD gave it also and its king into the hand of Israel; and he smote it with the edge of the sword, and every person in it; he left none remaining in it; and he did to its king as he had done to the king of Jericho. 31 And Joshua passed on from Lĭb′-nah, and all Israel with him, to Lā′-chĭsh, and laid siege to it, and assaulted it: ³²and the LORD gave Lā′chĭsh into the hand of Israel, and he took it on the second day, and smote it with the edge of the sword, and every person in it, as he had done to Lĭb′nah. 33 Then Hō′răm king of Gē′zer came up to help Lā′chĭsh; and Joshua smote him and his people, until he left none remaining. 34 And Joshua passed on with all Israel from Lā′chĭsh to Ĕg′lŏn; and they laid siege to it, and assaulted it; ³⁵and they took it on that day, and smote it with the edge of the sword; and every person in it he utterly destroyed that day, as he had done to Lā′chĭsh. 36 Then Joshua went up with all Israel from Ĕg′lŏn to Hē′bron; and they assaulted it, ³⁷and took it, and smote it with the edge of the sword, and its king and its towns, and every person in it; he left none remaining, as he had done to Ĕg′lŏn, and utterly destroyed it with every person in it. 38 Then Joshua, with all Israel, turned back to Dē′bĭr and assaulted it, ³⁹and he took it with its king and all its towns; and they smote them with the edge of the sword, and utterly destroyed every person in it; he left none remaining; as he had done to Hē′bron and to Lĭb′nah and its king, so he did to Dē′bĭr and to its king. 40 So Joshua defeated the whole land, the hill country and the Nĕg′ĕb and the lowland and the slopes, and all their kings; he left none remaining, but utterly destroyed all that breathed, as the LORD God of Israel commanded. ⁴¹And Joshua defeated them from Kā′dĕsh–băr′nē·a to Gā′za, and all the country of Gō′shen, as far as Gĭb′ē·on. ⁴²And Joshua took all these kings and their land at one time, because the LORD God of Israel fought for Israel. ⁴³Then Joshua returned, and all Israel with him, to the camp at Gĭl′gal.

11 When Jā'bĭn king of Hā'zôr heard of this, he sent to Jō'băb king of Mā'dŏn, and to the king of Shĭm'rŏn, and to the king of Ăch'shăph, ²and to the kings who were in the northern hill country, and in the Ăr'a·bah south of Chĭn'ne·rŏth, and in the lowland, and in Nā'phŏth–dôr on the west, ³to the Canaanites in the east and the west, the Ăm'o·rītes, the Hĭt'tītes, the Pĕr'ĭz·zītes, and the Jĕb'u·sītes in the hill country, and the Hī'vītes under Hermon in the land of Mĭz'pah. ⁴And they came out, with all their troops, a great host, in number like the sand that is upon the seashore, with very many horses and chariots. ⁵And all these kings joined their forces, and came and encamped together at the waters of Mē'rŏm, to fight with Israel.

6 And the LORD said to Joshua, "Do not be afraid of them, for tomorrow at this time I will give over all of them, slain, to Israel; you shall hamstring their horses, and burn their chariots with fire." ⁷So Joshua came suddenly upon them with all his people of war, by the waters of Mē'rŏm, and fell upon them. ⁸And the LORD gave them into the hand of Israel, who smote them and chased them as far as Great Sī'dŏn and Mĭs're·phŏth–mā'ĭm, and eastward as far as the valley of Mĭz'pĕh; and they smote them, until they left none remaining. ⁹And Joshua did to them as the LORD bade him; he hamstrung their horses, and burned their chariots with fire.

10 And Joshua turned back at that time, and took Hā'zôr, and smote its king with the sword; for Hazor formerly was the head of all those kingdoms. ¹¹And they put to the sword all who were in it, utterly destroying them; there was none left that breathed, and he burned Hā'zôr with fire. ¹²And all the cities of those kings, and all their kings, Joshua took, and smote them with the edge of the sword, utterly destroying them, as Moses the servant of the LORD had commanded. ¹³But none of the cities that stood on mounds did Israel burn, except Hā'zôr only; that Joshua burned. ¹⁴And all the spoil of these cities and the cattle, the people of Israel took for their booty; but every man they smote with the edge of the sword, until they had destroyed them, and they did not leave

any that breathed. ¹⁵As the LORD had commanded Moses his servant, so Moses commanded Joshua, and so Joshua did; he left nothing undone of all that the LORD had commanded Moses.

16 So Joshua took all that land, the hill country and all the Nĕg'ĕb and all the land of Gō'shen and the lowland and the Ăr'a·bah and the hill country of Israel and its lowland ¹⁷from Mount Hā'lăk, that rises toward Sē'ĭr, as far as Bā'al–găd in the valley of Lebanon below Mount Hermon. And he took all their kings, and smote them, and put them to death. ¹⁸Joshua made war a long time with all those kings. ¹⁹There was not a city that made peace with the people of Israel, except the Hī'vītes, the inhabitants of Gĭb'e·on; they took all in battle. ²⁰For it was the LORD'S doing to harden their hearts that they should come against Israel in battle, in order that they should be utterly destroyed, and should receive no mercy but be exterminated, as the LORD commanded Moses.

21 And Joshua came at that time, and wiped out the Ăn'a·kĭm from the hill country, from Hē'bron, from Dē'bĭr, from Ā'năb, and from all the hill country of Judah, and from all the hill country of Israel; Joshua utterly destroyed them with their cities. ²²There was none of the Ăn'a·kĭm left in the land of the people of Israel; only in Gā'za, in Găth, and in Ăsh'dŏd, did some remain. ²³So Joshua took the whole land, according to all that the LORD had spoken to Moses; and Joshua gave it for an inheritance to Israel according to their tribal allotments. And the land had rest from war.

12 Now these are the kings of the land, whom the people of Israel defeated, and took possession of their land beyond the Jordan toward the sunrising, from the valley of the Ăr'non to Mount Hermon, with all the Ăr'a·bah eastward: ²Sī'hon king of the Ăm'o·rītes who dwelt at Hĕsh'bon, and ruled from A·rō'er, which is on the edge of the valley of the Ăr'non, and from the middle of the valley as far as the river Jăb'bok, the boundary of the Ăm'mo·nītes, that is, half of Gilead, ³and the Ăr'a·bah to the Sea of Chĭn'ne·rŏth eastward, and in the direction of Bĕth–jĕsh'ĭ·mŏth, to the sea of the Arabah, the Salt Sea, southward to the foot of the slopes of Pĭṣ'-gah; ⁴and Ŏg⁰ king of Bā'shạn, one of the remnant of the Rĕph'ạ·ĭm, who dwelt at Ăsh'tạ·rŏth and at Ĕd'rē-ī ⁵and ruled over Mount Hermon and Săl'ẹ·cạh and all Bā'shạn to the boundary of the Gĕsh'ū·rītes and the Mā-ăc'ạ·thītes, and over half of Gilead to the boundary of Sī'họn king of Hĕsh'-bọn. ⁶Moses, the servant of the Lord, and the people of Israel defeated them; and Moses the servant of the Lord gave their land for a possession to the Reubenites and the Găd'ītes and the half-tribe of Mạ·năs'sẹh.

7 And these are the kings of the land whom Joshua and the people of Israel defeated on the west side of the Jordan, from Bā'ạl-găd in the valley of Lebanon to Mount Hā'lăk, that rises toward Sē'ĭr (and Joshua gave their land to the tribes of Israel as a possession according to their allotments, ⁸in the hill country, in the lowland, in the Ăr'ạ·bạh, in the slopes, in the wilderness, and in the Nĕg'ĕb, the land of the Hĭt'tītes, the Ăm'ọ·rītes, the Canaanites, the Pĕr'ĭz·zītes, the Hī'vītes, and the Jĕb'ū·sītes): ⁹the king of Jericho, one; the king of Aī, which is beside Bĕth'el, one; ¹⁰the king of Jerusalem, one; the king of Hē'brọn, one; ¹¹the king of Jăr'mŭth, one; the king of Lā'chĭsh, one; ¹²the king of Ĕg'lŏn, one; the king of Gē'zẹr, one; ¹³the king of Dē'bĭr, one; the king of Gē'dẹr, one; ¹⁴the king of Hôr'mạh, one; the king of Ăr'ạd, one; ¹⁵the king of Lĭb'nạh, one; the king of Ạ·dŭl'lạm, one; ¹⁶the king of Măk·kē'dạh, one; the king of Bĕth'el, one; ¹⁷the king of Tăp'pū-ah, one; the king of Hē'phẹr, one; ¹⁸the king of Ā'phĕk, one; the king of Lạ·shăr'ŏn, one; ¹⁹the king of Mā'dŏn, one; the king of Hā'zôr, one; ²⁰the king of Shĭm'rŏn-mē'rŏn, one; the king of Ăch'shăph, one; ²¹the king of Tā'ạ-năch, one; the king of Mẹ·gĭd'dō, one; ²²the king of Kē'dĕsh, one; the king of Jŏk'nē-ăm in Căr'mẹl, one; ²³the king of Dôrin Nā'phăth-dôr, one; the king of Goi'ĭm in Galilee,ᶠ one; ²⁴the king of Tīr'zạh; one: in all, thirty-one kings.

13 Now Joshua was old and advanced in years; and the Lord said to him, "You are old and advanced in years, and there remains yet very much land to be possessed. ²This is the land that yet remains: all the regions of the Phĭ·lĭs'tĭnes, and all those of the Gĕsh'ū·rītes ³(from the Shī'hôr, which is east of Egypt, northward to the boundary of Ĕk'rŏn, it is reckoned as Canaanite; there are five rulers of the Phĭ·lĭs'tĭnes, those of Gā'zạ, Ăsh'dŏd, Ăsh'kẹ·lŏn, Găth, and Ekron, and those of the Ăv'vĭm, ⁴in the south, all the land of the Canaanites, and Mĕ-ăr'ạh which belongs to the Sī·dō'nĭ-ạnṣ, to Ā'phĕk, to the boundary of the Ăm'ọ·rītes, ⁵and the land of the Gĕb'ạ-lītes, and all Lebanon, toward the sunrising, from Bā'ạl-găd below Mount Hermon to the entrance of Hā'măth, ⁶all the inhabitants of the hill country from Lebanon to Mĭs'rē-phŏth-mā'ĭm, even all the Sī-dō'nĭ-ạnṣ. I will myself drive them out from before the people of Israel; only allot the land to Israel for an inheritance, as I have commanded you. ⁷Now therefore divide this land for an inheritance to the nine tribes and half the tribe of Mạ·năs'sẹh."

8 With the other half of the tribe of Mạ·năs'sẹhᵍ the Reubenites and the Găd'ītes received their inheritance, which Moses gave them, beyond the Jordan eastward, as Moses the servant of the Lord gave them: ⁹from Ạ·rō'ẹr, which is on the edge of the valley of the Ăr'nŏn, and the city that is in the middle of the valley, and all the tableland of Mĕd'ẹ·bạ as far as Dī'bŏn; ¹⁰and all the cities of Sī'họn king of the Ăm'ọ·rītes, who reigned in Hĕsh'-bọn, as far as the boundary of the Ăm'-mọ·nītes; ¹¹and Gilead, and the region of the Gĕsh'ū·rītes and Mā-ăc'ạ·thītes, and all Mount Hermon, and all Bā'-shạn to Săl'ẹ·cạh; ¹²all the kingdom of Ŏg in Bā'shạn, who reigned in Ăsh'tạ-rŏth and in Ĕd'rē-ī (he alone was left of the remnant of the Rĕph'ạ·ĭm); these Moses had defeated and driven out. ¹³Yet the people of Israel did not drive out the Gĕsh'ū·rītes or the Mā-ăc'ạ·thītes; but Gē'shŭr and Mā'ạ-cǎth dwell in the midst of Israel to this day.

14 To the tribe of Lē'vī alone Moses gave no inheritance; the offerings by fire to the Lord God of Israel are their inheritance, as he said to him.

15 And Moses gave an inheritance to the tribe of the Reubenites according to their families. ¹⁶So their territory was from Ạ·rō'ẹr, which is on the edge of the valley of the Ăr'nŏn, and the city that is in the middle of the valley, and

ᵉGk: Heb *the boundary of Og* ᶠGk: Heb *Gilgal* ᵍCn: Heb *With it* all the tableland by Mĕd′ĕ·ba; ¹⁷with Hĕsh′bŏn, and all its cities that are in the tableland; Dī′bŏn, and Bā′moth-bā′al, and Bĕth–bā′al–mē′ŏn, ¹⁸and Jā′hăz, and Kĕd′ĕ·mŏth, and Mĕph′a-ăth, ¹⁹and Kīr″ĭ·a·thā′ĭm, and Sĭb′mah, and Zē′rĕth–shā′har on the hill of the valley, ²⁰and Bĕth–pē′ôr, and the slopes of Pĭş′gah, and Bĕth–jĕsh′ĭ·mŏth, ²¹that is, all the cities of the tableland, and all the kingdom of Sī′hon king of the Ăm′o·rītes, who reigned in Hĕsh′-bon, whom Moses defeated with the leaders of Mĭd′ĭ·an, Ē′vī and Rē′kĕm and Zūr and Hūr and Rē′ba, the princes of Sihon, who dwelt in the land. ²²Bā′laăm also, the son of Bē′ôr, the soothsayer, the people of Israel killed with the sword among the rest of their slain. ²³And the border of the people of Reuben was the Jordan as a boundary. This was the inheritance of the Reubenites, according to their families with their cities and villages.

24 And Moses gave an inheritance also to the tribe of the Găd′ītes, according to their families. ²⁵Their territory was Jā′zẽr, and all the cities of Gilead, and half the land of the Ăm′mo·nītes, to A·rō′ẽr, which is east of Răb′bah, ²⁶and from Hĕsh′bon to Rā′math-mĭz′pĕh and Bĕt′ō·nĭm, and from Mā″-ha·nā′ĭm to the territory of Dē′bĭr,ʰ ²⁷and in the valley Bĕth–hā′răm, Bĕth–nĭm′rah, Sŭc′cŏth, and Zā′phŏn, the rest of the kingdom of Sī′hon king of Hĕsh′bon, having the Jordan as a boundary, to the lower end of the Sea of Chĭn′ne·rĕth, eastward beyond the Jordan. ²⁸This is the inheritance of the Găd′ītes according to their families, with their cities and villages.

29 And Moses gave an inheritance to the half-tribe of Ma·năs′seh; it was allotted to the half-tribe of the Ma·năs′sītes according to their families. ³⁰Their region extended from Mā″-ha·nā′ĭm, through all Bā′shan, the whole kingdom of Ŏg king of Bashan, and all the towns of Jā′ĭr, which are in Bashan, sixty cities, ³¹and half Gilead, and Ăsh′ta·rŏth, and Ĕd′rē–ī, the cities of the kingdom of Ŏg in Bā′-shan; these were allotted to the people of Mā′chĭr the son of Ma·năs′seh for the half of the Mā′chĭ·rītes according to their families.

32 These are the inheritances which Moses distributed in the plains of Mō′ăb, beyond the Jordan east of Jer-

icho. ³³But to the tribe of Lē′vī Moses gave no inheritance; the Lᴏʀᴅ God of Israel is their inheritance, as he said to them.

14 And these are the inheritances which the people of Israel received in the land of Canaan, which Ĕl·ē·ā′zar the priest, and Joshua the son of Nŭn, and the heads of the fathers' houses of the tribes of the people of Israel distributed to them. ²Their inheritance was by lot, as the Lᴏʀᴅ had commanded Moses for the nine and one-half tribes. ³For Moses had given an inheritance to the two and one-half tribes beyond the Jordan; but to the Lē′vītes he gave no inheritance among them. ⁴For the people of Joseph were two tribes, Ma·năs′seh and Ē′phra·ĭm; and no portion was given to the Lē′vītes in the land, but only cities to dwell in, with their pasture lands for their cattle and their substance. ⁵The people of Israel did as the Lᴏʀᴅ commanded Moses; they allotted the land.

6 Then the people of Judah came to Joshua at Gĭl′gal; and Caleb the son of Je·phŭn′neh the Kĕn′ĭz·zīte said to him, "You know what the Lᴏʀᴅ said to Moses the man of God in Kā′dĕsh-bār′nē·a concerning you and me. ⁷I was forty years old when Moses the servant of the Lᴏʀᴅ sent me from Kā′-dĕsh–bār′nē·a to spy out the land; and I brought him word again as it was in my heart. ⁸But my brethren who went up with me made the heart of the people melt; yet I wholly followed the Lᴏʀᴅ my God. ⁹And Moses swore on that day, saying, 'Surely the land on which your foot has trodden shall be an inheritance for you and your children for ever, because you have wholly followed the Lᴏʀᴅ my God.' ¹⁰And now, behold, the Lᴏʀᴅ has kept me alive, as he said, these forty-five years since the time that the Lᴏʀᴅ spoke this word to Moses, while Israel walked in the wilderness; and now, lo, I am this day eighty-five years old. ¹¹I am still as strong to this day as I was in the day that Moses sent me; my strength now is as my strength was then, for war, and for going and coming. ¹²So now give me this hill country of which the Lᴏʀᴅ spoke on that day; for you heard on that day how the Ăn′a·kĭm were

ʰGk Syr Vg: Heb *Lidebir*
14.6-15: Num 13.6, 30; 14.6, 24, 30.

there, with great fortified cities: it may be that the LORD will be with me, and I shall drive them out as the LORD said."

13 Then Joshua blessed him; and he gave Hē′bron to Caleb the son of Jẹ-phün′nẹh for an inheritance. ¹⁴So Hē′bron became the inheritance of Caleb the son of Jẹ·phün′nẹh the Kĕn′-ĭz·zīte to this day, because he wholly followed the LORD, the God of Israel. ¹⁵Now the name of Hē′bron formerly was Kĭr′ĭ·ăth–är′bạ;ⁱ this Är′bạ was the greatest man among the Ăn′ạ·kĭm. And the land had rest from war.

15 The lot for the tribe of the people of Judah according to their families reached southward to the boundary of Ē′dom, to the wilderness of Zĭn at the farthest south. ²And their south boundary ran from the end of the Salt Sea, from the bay that faces southward; ³it goes out southward of the ascent of Ăk·răb′bĭm, passes along to Zĭn, and goes up south of Kā′dĕsh-bär′nē·ạ, along by Hĕz′ron, up to Ăd′-där, turns about to Kär′kạ, ⁴passes along to Ăz′mon, goes out by the Brook of Egypt, and comes to its end at the sea. This shall be your south boundary. ⁵And the east boundary is the Salt Sea, to the mouth of the Jordan. And the boundary on the north side runs from the bay of the sea at the mouth of the Jordan; ⁶and the boundary goes up to Bĕth–hŏg′lạh, and passes along north of Bĕth–är′ạ·bạh; and the boundary goes up to the stone of Bō′hặn the son of Reuben; ⁷and the boundary goes up to Dē′bĭr from the Valley of A′chôr, and so northward, turning toward Gĭl′gạl, which is opposite the ascent of Ạ·dŭm′mĭm, which is on the south side of the valley; and the boundary passes along to the waters of Ĕn-shē′mĕsh, and ends at Ĕn-rō′gĕl; ⁸then the boundary goes up by the valley of the son of Hĭn′nom at the southern shoulder of the Jĕb′ū·sīte (that is, Jerusalem); and the boundary goes up to the top of the mountain that lies over against the valley of Hin-nom, on the west, at the northern end of the valley of Rĕph′ạ·ĭm; ⁹then the boundary extends from the top of the mountain to the spring of the Waters of Nĕph·tō′ah, and from there to the cities of Mount Ē′phron; then the boundary bends round to Bā′ạ·lạh (that is, Kĭr′ĭ·ăth–jē′ạ·rĭm); ¹⁰and the

boundary circles west of Bā′ạ·lạh to Mount Sē″ĭr, passes along to the north-ern shoulder of Mount Jē′ạ·rĭm (that is, Chĕs′ạ·lŏn), and goes down to Bĕth-shē′mĕsh, and passes along by Tĭm′-nạh; ¹¹the boundary goes out to the shoulder of the hill north of Ĕk′ron, then the boundary bends round to Shĭk′kẹ·ron, and passes along to Mount Bā′ạ·lạh, and goes out to Jăb′nē·ẹl; then the boundary comes to an end at the sea. ¹²And the west boundary was the Great Sea with its coast-line. This is the boundary round about the people of Judah according to their families.

13 According to the commandment of the LORD to Joshua, he gave to Caleb the son of Jẹ·phün′nẹh a portion among the people of Judah, Kĭr′ĭ·ăth-är′bạ, that is, Hē′bron (Är′bạ was the father of Ā′nặk). ¹⁴And Caleb drove out from there the three sons of Ā′nặk, Shē′shaī and Ạ·hī′mạn and Tăl′maī, the descendants of Anak. ¹⁵And he went up from there against the in-habitants of Dē′bĭr; now the name of Debir formerly was Kĭr′ĭ·ăth-sē′phẹr. ¹⁶And Caleb said, "Whoever smites Kĭr′ĭ·ăth-sē′phẹr, and takes it, to him will I give Ăch′sạh my daughter as wife." ¹⁷And Ŏth′nĭ–ĕl the son of Kē′-nặz, the brother of Caleb, took it; and he gave him Ăch′sạh his daughter as wife. ¹⁸When she came to him, she urged him to ask her father for a field; and she alighted from her ass, and Caleb said to her, "What do you wish?" ¹⁹She said to him, "Give me a present; since you have set me in the land of the Nĕg′ĕb, give me also springs of water." And Caleb gave her the upper springs and the lower springs.

20 This is the inheritance of the tribe of the people of Judah according to their families. ²¹The cities belonging to the tribe of the people of Judah in the extreme South, toward the bound-ary of Ē′dom, were Kăb′zē·ẹl, Ē′dẹr, Jā′gūr, ²²Kī′nạh, Dĭ·mō′nạh, Ạ·dā′dạh, ²³Kē′dĕsh, Hā′zôr, Ĭth′nặn, ²⁴Zĭph, Tē′lĕm, Bĕ–ā′lŏth, ²⁵Hā′zôr–hạ·dăt′-tạh, Kĕr′ĭ–ŏth–hĕz′ron (that is, Hā′zôr), ²⁶Ā′mặm, Shē′mạ, Mō′lạ·dạh, ²⁷Hā′-zär–găd′dạh, Hĕsh′mon, Bĕth–pĕl′ẹt, ²⁸Hā′zär–shŭ′al, Bē′ẹr–shē′bạ, Bĭz-ĭ·ọ·thī′ah, ²⁹Bā′ạ·lạh, Ī′ĭm, Ē′zĕm, ³⁰Ĕl·tō′lăd, Chē′sĭl, Hôr′mạh, ³¹Zĭk′-lăg, Măd·măn′nạh, Săn·săn′nạh, ³²Lẹ-

ⁱThat is *The city of Arba*
15.14-19: Judg 1.10-15, 20.

bā'ŏth, Shĭl'hĭm, Ā'ĭn, and Rĭm'mŏn: in all, twenty-nine cities, with their villages.

33 And in the lowland, Ĕsh'tā-ŏl, Zō'rah, Ăsh'nah, ³⁴Za-nō'ah, Ĕn-găn'-nĭm, Tăp'pū-ah, Ē'năm, ³⁵Jār'mŭth, A-dŭl'lam, Sō'cŏh, A-zē'kah, ³⁶Shā'-a-rā'ĭm, Ăd-ĭ-thā'ĭm, Gĕ-dē'răh, Gĕ-dē'rŏth-ă"ĭm: fourteen cities with their villages.

37 Zē'nan, Hȧ-dăsh'ah, Mĭg'dȧl-găd, ³⁸Dĭ'lē-an, Mĭz'pĕh, Jŏk'thē-ĕl, ³⁹Lā'-chĭsh, Bŏz'kăth, Ĕg'lŏn, ⁴⁰Căb'bŏn, Lăh'mam, Chĭt'lĭsh, ⁴¹Gĕ-dē'rŏth, Bĕth-dā'gŏn, Nā'a-mah, and Măk-kē'-dah: sixteen cities with their villages.

42 Lĭb'nah, Ē'ther, Ā'shan, ⁴³Ĭph'-tah, Ăsh'nah, Nē'zĭb, ⁴⁴Kē-ĭ'lah, Ăch'-zĭb, and Ma-rē'shah: nine cities with their villages.

45 Ĕk'rŏn, with its towns and its villages; ⁴⁶from Ĕk'rŏn to the sea, all that were by the side of Ăsh'dŏd, with their villages.

47 Ăsh'dŏd, its towns and its villages; Gā'za, its towns and its villages; to the Brook of Egypt, and the Great Sea with its coast-line.

48 And in the hill country, Shā'mĭr, Jăt'tĭr, Sō'cŏh, ⁴⁹Dăn'nah, Kĭr'ĭ-ăth-săn'nah (that is, Dē'bĭr), ⁵⁰Ā'năb, Ĕsh'-tē-mōh, Ā'nĭm, ⁵¹Gō'shen, Hō'lŏn, and Gĭ'lōh: eleven cities with their villages.

52 Ā'rab, Dü'mah, Ē'shăn, ⁵³Jā'nĭm, Bĕth-tăp'pū-ah, A-phē'kah, ⁵⁴Hŭm'-tah, Kĭr'ĭ-ăth-är'ba (that is, Hē'brŏn), and Zī'ôr: nine cities with their villages.

55 Mā'ŏn, Cär'mel, Zĭph, Jŭt'tah, ⁵⁶Jĕz'rē-el, Jŏk'dē-ăm, Za-nō'ah, ⁵⁷Kāin, Gĭb'ē-ah, and Tĭm'nah: ten cities with their villages.

58 Hăl'hŭl, Bĕth-zūr, Gē'dôr, ⁵⁹Mā'-a-răth, Bĕth-ā'nŏth, and Ĕl'tē-kŏn: six cities with their villages.

60 Kĭr'ĭ-ăth-bā'al (that is, Kĭr'ĭ-ăth-jē'a-rĭm), and Răb'bah: two cities with their villages.

61 In the wilderness, Bĕth-är'a-bah, Mĭd'dĭn, Se-cā'cah, ⁶²Nĭb'shăn, the City of Salt, and Ĕn-gē'dī: six cities with their villages.

63 But the Jĕb'ū-sītes, the inhabitants of Jerusalem, the people of Judah could not drive out; so the Jebusites dwell with the people of Judah at Jerusalem to this day.

16 The allotment of the descendants of Joseph went from the Jordan by Jericho, east of the waters

of Jericho, into the wilderness, going up from Jericho into the hill country to Bĕth'el; ²then going from Bĕth'el to Lŭz, it passes along to Ăt'a-rŏth, the territory of the Är'chītes; ³then it goes down westward to the territory of the Jăph'le-tītes, as far as the territory of Lower Bĕth-hō'rŏn, then to Gē'zer, and it ends at the sea.

4 The people of Joseph, Ma-năs'seh and Ē'phra-im, received their inheritance.

5 The territory of the Ē'phra-im-ītes by their families was as follows: the boundary of their inheritance on the east was Ăt'a-rŏth-ăd'där as far as Upper Bĕth-hō'rŏn, ⁶and the boundary goes thence to the sea; on the north is Mĭch-mē'thăth; then on the east the boundary turns round toward Tā'a-năth-shī'lōh, and passes along beyond it on the east to Ja-nō'ah, ⁷then it goes down from Ja-nō'ah to Ăt'a-rŏth and to Nā'a-rah, and touches Jericho, ending at the Jordan. ⁸From Tăp'-pū-ah the boundary goes westward to the brook Kā'nah, and ends at the sea. Such is the inheritance of the tribe of the Ē'phra-im-ītes by their families, ⁹together with the towns which were set apart for the Ē'phra-im-ītes within the inheritance of the Ma-năs'sītes, all those towns with their villages. ¹⁰However they did not drive out the Canaanites that dwelt in Gē'zer: so the Canaanites have dwelt in the midst of Ē'phra-im to this day but have become slaves to do forced labor.

17 Then allotment was made to the tribe of Ma-năs'seh, for he was the first-born of Joseph. To Mā'chĭr the first-born of Manasseh, the father of Gilead, were allotted Gilead and Bā'shan, because he was a man of war. ²And allotments were made to the rest of the tribe of Ma-năs'seh, by their families, Ā-bĭ-ē'zer, Hē'lĕk, Ăs'-rĭ-ĕl, Shē'chĕm, Hē'pher, and Shē-mĭ'da; these were the male descendants of Manasseh the son of Joseph, by their families.

3 Now Zĕ-lŏph'e-hăd the son of Hē'pher, son of Gilead, son of Mā'chĭr, son of Ma-năs'seh, had no sons, but only daughters; and these are the names of his daughters: Măh'lah, Noah, Hŏg'lah, Mĭl'cah, and Tĭr'zah. ⁴They came before Ĕl-ē-ā'zar the priest

15.63: Judg 1.21; 2 Sam 5.6.
16.10: Judg 1.29. 17.3, 4: Num 26.33; 27.1-7.

and Joshua the son of Nŭn and the leaders, and said, "The LORD commanded Moses to give us an inheritance along with our brethren." So according to the commandment of the LORD he gave them an inheritance among the brethren of their father. ⁵Thus there fell to Mạ·năs′sẹh ten portions, besides the land of Gilead and Bā′shạn, which is on the other side of the Jordan; ⁶because the daughters of Mạ·năs′sẹh received an inheritance along with his sons. The land of Gilead was allotted to the rest of the Mạ·năs′sītes.

7 The territory of Mạ·năs′sẹh reached from Ăsh′ẹr to Mīch·mē′thăth, which is east of Shē′chĕm; then the boundary goes along southward to the inhabitants of Ĕn–tăp′pū–ăh. ⁸The land of Tăp′pū–ạh belonged to Mạ·năs′sẹh, but the town of Tappu–ah on the boundary of Manasseh belonged to the sons of Ē′phrạ·ĭm. ⁹Then the boundary went down to the brook Kā′nạh. The cities here, to the south of the brook, among the cities of Mạ·năs′sẹh, belong to Ē′phrạ·ĭm. Then the boundary of Manasseh goes on the north side of the brook and ends at the sea; ¹⁰the land to the south being Ē′phrạ·ĭm's and that to the north being Mạ·năs′sẹh's, with the sea forming its boundary; on the north Ăsh′ẹr is reached, and on the east Ĭs′sạ·chăr. ¹¹Also in Ĭs′sạ·chăr and in Ăsh′ẹr Mạ·năs′sẹh had Bĕth–shē′ạn and its villages, and Ĭb′lē·ạm and its villages, and the inhabitants of Dôr and its villages, and the inhabitants of Ĕn–dôr and its villages, and the inhabitants of Tā′ạ·năch and its villages, and the inhabitants of Mẹ·gĭd′dō and its villages; the third is Nā′phăth.ʲ ¹²Yet the sons of Mạ·năs′sẹh could not take possession of those cities; but the Canaanites persisted in dwelling in that land. ¹³But when the people of Israel grew strong, they put the Canaanites to forced labor, and did not utterly drive them out.

14 And the tribe of Joseph spoke to Joshua, saying, "Why have you given me but one lot and one portion as an inheritance, although I am a numerous people, since hitherto the LORD has blessed me?" ¹⁵And Joshua said to them, "If you are a numerous people, go up to the forest, and there clear ground for yourselves in the land of the Pĕr′ĭz·zītes and the Rĕph′ạ·ĭm, since the hill country of Ē′phrạ·ĭm is too narrow for you." ¹⁶The tribe of Joseph said, "The hill country is not enough for us; yet all the Canaanites who dwell in the plain have chariots of iron, both those in Bĕth–shē′an and its villages and those in the Valley of Jĕz′rē·ẹl." ¹⁷Then Joshua said to the house of Joseph, to Ē′phrạ·ĭm and Mạ·năs′sẹh, "You are a numerous people, and have great power; you shall not have one lot only, ¹⁸but the hill country shall be yours, for though it is a forest, you shall clear it and possess it to its farthest borders; for you ,shall drive out the Canaanites, though they have chariots of iron, and though they are strong."

18 Then the whole congregation of the people of Israel assembled at Shī′lōh, and set up the tent of meeting there; the land lay subdued before them.

2 There remained among the people of Israel seven tribes whose inheritance had not yet been apportioned. ³So Joshua said to the people of Israel, "How long will you be slack to go in and take possession of the land, which the LORD, the God of your fathers, has given you? ⁴Provide three men from each tribe, and I will send them out that they may set out and go up and down the land, writing a description of it with a view to their inheritances, and then come to me. ⁵They shall divide it into seven portions, Judah continuing in his territory on the south, and the house of Joseph in their territory on the north. ⁶And you shall describe the land in seven divisions and bring the description here to me; and I will cast lots for you here before the LORD our God. ⁷The Lē′vītes have no portion among you, for the priesthood of the LORD is their heritage; and Găd and Reuben and half the tribe of Mạ·năs′sẹh have received their inheritance beyong the Jordan eastward, which Moses the servant of the LORD gave them."

8 So the men started on their way; and Joshua charged those who went to write the description of the land, saying, "Go up and down and write a description of the land, and come again to me; and I will cast lots for you here

ʲHeb obscure
17.11-13: Judg 1.27-28.

before the LORD in Shī'lōh." ⁹So the men went and passed up and down in the land and set down in a book a description of it by towns in seven divisions; then they came to Joshua in the camp at Shī'lōh, ¹⁰and Joshua cast lots for them in Shī'lōh before the LORD; and there Joshua apportioned the land to the people of Israel, to each his portion.

11 The lot of the tribe of Benjamin according to its families came up, and the territory allotted to it fell between the tribe of Judah and the tribe of Joseph. ¹²On the north side their boundary began at the Jordan; then the boundary goes up to the shoulder north of Jericho, then up through the hill country westward; and it ends at the wilderness of Bĕth-ā'ven. ¹³From there the boundary passes along southward in the direction of Lūz, to the shoulder of Luz (the same is Bĕth'ĕl), then the boundary goes down to Ăt'a·rŏth-ăd'dăr, upon the mountain that lies south of Lower Bĕth-hō'rŏn. ¹⁴Then the boundary goes in another direction, turning on the western side southward from the mountain that lies to the south, opposite Bĕth-hō'rŏn, and it ends at Kīr'ī·ăth-bā'al (that is, Kīr'ī·ăth-jē'a·rĭm), a city belonging to the tribe of Judah. This forms the western side. ¹⁵And the southern side begins at the outskirts of Kīr'ī·ăth-jē'a·rĭm; and the boundary goes from there to Ē'phrŏn,ᵏ to the spring of the Waters of Nĕph·tō'ah; ¹⁶then the boundary goes down to the border of the mountain that overlooks the valley of the son of Hĭn'nŏm, which is at the north end of the valley of Rĕph'a·ĭm; and it then goes down the valley of Hinnom, south of the shoulder of the Jĕb'ū·sītes, and downward to Ĕn-rō'gĕl; ¹⁷then it bends in a northerly direction going on to Ĕn-shē'mĕsh, and thence goes to Gĕ·lī'lŏth, which is opposite the ascent of A·dŭm'mĭm; then it goes down to the Stone of Bō'hăn the son of Reuben; ¹⁸and passing on to the north of the shoulder of Bĕth-är·a·bahⁱ it goes down to the Är'a·bah; ¹⁹then the boundary passes on to the north of the shoulder of Bĕth-hŏg'lah; and the boundary ends at the northern bay of the Salt Sea, at the south end of the Jordan: this is the southern border. ²⁰The Jordan forms its boundary on the eastern side. This is the inheritance of the

tribe of Benjamin, according to its families, boundary by boundary round about.

21 Now the cities of the tribe of Benjamin according to their families were Jericho, Bĕth-hŏg'lah, Ē'mĕk-kē'zĭz, ²²Bĕth-är·a·bah, Zĕm·a·rā'ĭm, Bĕth'ĕl, ²³Äv'vĭm, Pär'ah, Ŏph'rah, ²⁴Chē'phâr-ăm'mo·nī, Ŏph'nī, Gē'ba—twelve cities with their villages. ²⁵Gĭb'ē·on, Rā'mah, Be-ēr'oth, ²⁶Mĭz'pĕh, Chē·phī'rah, Mō'zah, ²⁷Rē'kĕm, Ĭr'pē·el, Tär'a·lah, Zē'la, Hä-ē'lĕph, Jē'būsᵐ (that is, Jerusalem), Gĭb'ē·ahⁿ and Kĭr'ī·ăth-jē'a·rĭmᵒ—fourteen cities with their villages. This is the inheritance of the tribe of Benjamin according to its families.

19 The second lot came out for Sĭm'ē·on, for the tribe of Simeon, according to its families; and its inheritance was in the midst of the inheritance of the tribe of Judah. ²And it had for its inheritance Bē'er-shē'ba, Shē'ba, Mō'la·dah, ³Hā'zar-shü'al, Bā'lah, Ē'zĕm, ⁴Ĕl·tō'lăd, Bē'thŭl, Hôr'mah, ⁵Zĭk'lăg, Bĕth-mär'ca·bŏth, Hā'zar-sü'sah, ⁶Bĕth-le·bā'ŏth, and Sha·rü'hĕn—thirteen cities with their villages; ⁷Ĕn-rĭm'mŏn, Ē'ther, and Ā'shan—four cities with their villages; ⁸together with all the villages round about these cities as far as Bā'a·lăth-bē'er, Rā'mah of the Nĕg'ĕb. This was the inheritance of the tribe of Sĭm'ē·on according to its families. ⁹The inheritance of the tribe of Sĭm'ē·on formed part of the territory of Judah; because the portion of the tribe of Judah was too large for them, the tribe of Simeon obtained an inheritance in the midst of their inheritance.

10 The third lot came up for the tribe of Zĕb'ū·lun, according to its families. And the territory of its inheritance reached as far as Sā'rĭd; ¹¹then its boundary goes up westward, and on to Mär'ē·al, and touches Dăb'be·shĕth, then the brook which is east of Jŏk'nē-ăm; ¹²from Sā'rĭd it goes in the other direction eastward toward the sunrise to the boundary of Chĭs'lŏth-tā'bôr; thence it goes to Dăb'e·răth, then up to Ja·phī'a; ¹³from there it passes along on the east toward the sunrise to Găth-hē'pher, to Ĕth-kā'zĭn, and going

ᵏCn See 15.9. Heb *westward*
ⁱGk: Heb *to the shoulder over against the Arabah*
ᵐGk Syr Vg: Heb *the Jebusite*
ⁿHeb *Gibeath*   ᵒGk: Heb *Kiriath*

on to Rĭm′mŏn it bends toward Nē′ah; [14]then on the north the boundary turns about to Hăn·na′thŏn, and it ends at the valley of Ĭph′tah·ĕl; [15]and Kăt′-tath, Na·hăl′al, Shĭm′rŏn, Ĭ′da·lah, and Bethlehem—twelve cities with their villages. [16]This is the inheritance of the tribe of Zĕb′ū·lun, according to its families—these cities with their villages.

17 The fourth lot came out for Ĭs′sa·chär, for the tribe Issachar, according to its families. [18]Its territory included Jĕz′rē·el, Chē·sŭl′lŏth, Shü′-nĕm, [19]Hăph′a·rā-ĭm, Shĭ′ŏn, A·nā′-ha·răth, [20]Răb′bĭth, Kĭsh′ĭ-ŏn, Ē′bĕz, [21]Rē′mĕth, Ĕn-găn′nĭm, Ĕn-hăd′dah, Bĕth-păz′zĕz; [22]the boundary also touches Tā′bôr, Sha·hă·zü′mah, and Bĕth-shē′mĕsh, and its boundary ends at the Jordan—sixteen cities with their villages. [23]This is the inheritance of the tribe of Ĭs′sa·chär, according to its families—the cities with their villages.

24 The fifth lot came out for the tribe of Ăsh′er according to its families. [25]Its territory included Hĕl′kăth, Hā′lī, Bē′tĕn, Ăch′shăph, [26]Al·lăm′me-lĕch, Ā′măd, and Mĭ′shal; on the west it touches Cär′mel and Shĭ·hŏr·lĭb′-năth, [27]then it turns eastward, it goes to Bĕth-dā′gŏn, and touches Zĕb′ū·lun and the valley of Ĭph′tah·ĕl northward to Bĕth-ē′mĕk and Nē·ĭ′ĕl; then it continues in the north to Cā′bŭl, [28]Ē′brŏn, Rē′hŏb, Hăm′mŏn, Kā′nah, as far as Sī′dŏn the Great; [29]then the boundary turns to Rā′mah, reaching to the fortified city of Tȳre; then the boundary turns to Hō′sah, and it ends at the sea; Ma·hā′lab,[p] Ăch′zĭb, [30]Ŭm′mah, Ā′phĕk and Rē′hŏb—twenty-two cities with their villages. [31]This is the inheritance of the tribe of Ăsh′er according to its families—these cities with their villages.

32 The sixth lot came out for the tribe of Năph′ta·lī, for the tribe of Naphtali, according to its families. [33]And its boundary ran from Hē′lĕph, from the oak in Zā-a·năn′nĭm, and Ăd′a·mī–nĕk′ĕb, and Jăb′nē·el, as far as Lăk′kum; and it ended at the Jordan; [34]then the boundary turns westward to Ăz′nŏth-tā′bôr, and goes from there to Hŭk′kŏk, touching Zĕb′ū·lun at the south, and Ăsh′er on the west, and Judah on the east at the Jordan. [35]The fortified cities are Zĭd′dĭm, Zēr,

Hăm′măth, Răk′kăth, Chĭn′ne·rĕth, [36]Ăd′a·mah, Rā′mah, Hā′zôr, [37]Kē′-dĕsh, Ĕd′rē-ī, Ĕn-hā′zôr, [38]Yĭ′rŏn, Mĭg′dal–ĕl, Hō′rĕm, Bĕth-ā′năth, and Bĕth-shē′mĕsh—nineteen cities with their villages. [39]This is the inheritance of the tribe of Năph′ta·lī according to its families—the cities with their villages.

40 The seventh lot came out for the tribe of Dan, according to its families. [41]And the territory of its inheritance included Zō′rah, Ĕsh′ta–ŏl, Ĭr·shē′-mĕsh, [42]Shā-a·lăb′bĭn, Aī′ja·lŏn, Ĭth′-lah, [43]Ē′lŏn, Tĭm′nah, Ĕk′rŏn, [44]Ĕl′-te·keh, Gĭb′be·thŏn, Bā′a·lăth, [45]Jē′hŭd, Bĕn′ē–bē′răk, Găth-rĭm′mŏn, [46]and Mē–jär′kŏn and Răk′kŏn with the territory over against Jŏp′pa. [47]When the territory of the Dă′nītes was lost to them, the Danites went up and fought against Lē′shĕm, and after capturing it and putting it to the sword they took possession of it and settled in it, calling Leshem, Dan, after the name of Dan their ancestor. [48]This is the inheritance of the tribe of Dan, according to their families—these cities with their villages.

49 When they had finished distributing the several territories of the land as inheritances, the people of Israel gave an inheritance among them to Joshua the son of Nŭn. [50]By command of the LORD they gave him the city which he asked, Tĭm′năth–sē′rah in the hill country of Ē′phra·ĭm; and he rebuilt the city, and settled in it.

51 These are the inheritances which Ĕl·e·ā′zar the priest and Joshua the son of Nŭn and the heads of the fathers' houses of the tribes of the people of Israel distributed by lot at Shī′lŏh before the LORD, at the door of the tent of meeting. So they finished dividing the land.

20   Then the LORD said to Joshua, [2]"Say to the people of Israel, 'Appoint the cities of refuge, of which I spoke to you through Moses, [3]that the manslayer who kills any person without intent or unwittingly may flee there; they shall be for you a refuge from the avenger of blood. [4]He shall flee to one of these cities and shall stand at the entrance of the gate of the city, and explain his case to the elders

[p]Cn Compare Gk: Heb *Mehebel*
19.47: Judg 18.27-31.
20.2-9: Num 35.6-34; Deut 4.41-43; 19.1-13.

of that city; then they shall take him into the city, and give him a place, and he shall remain with them. ⁵ And if the avenger of blood pursues him, they shall not give up the slayer into his hand; because he killed his neighbor unwittingly, having had no enmity against him in times past. ⁶ And he shall remain in that city until he has stood before the congregation for judgment, until the death of him who is high priest at the time: then the slayer may go again to his own town and his own home, to the town from which he fled.' "

7 So they set apart Kē'dĕsh in Galilee in the hill country of Năph'tạ·lī, and Shē'chĕm in the hill country of Ē'phrạ·ĭm, and Kĭr'ĭ·ăth–är'bạ (that is, Hē'brọn) in the hill country of Judah. ⁸ And beyond the Jordan east of Jericho, they appointed Bē'zẹr in the wilderness on the tableland, from the tribe of Reuben, and Rā'mŏth in Gilead, from the tribe of Gâd, and Gō'lăn in Bā'shạn, from the tribe of Mạ·năs'sẹh. ⁹ These were the cities designated for all the people of Israel, and for the stranger sojourning among them, that any one who killed a person without intent could flee there, so that he might not die by the hand of the avenger of blood, till he stood before the congregation.

21 Then the heads of the fathers' houses of the Lē'vītes came to Ĕl·ē·ā'zạr the priest and to Joshua the son of Nŭn and to the heads of the fathers' houses of the tribes of the people of Israel; ² and they said to them at Shī'lōh in the land of Canaan, "The LORD commanded through Moses that we be given cities to dwell in, along with their pasture lands for our cattle." ³ So by command of the LORD the people of Israel gave to the Lē'vītes the following cities and pasture lands out of their inheritance.

4 The lot came out for the families of the Kō'hạ·thītes. So those Lē'vītes who were descendants of Aaron the priest received by lot from the tribes of Judah, Sĭm'ē·ọn, and Benjamin, thirteen cities.

5 And the rest of the Kō'hạ·thītes received by lot from the families of the tribe of Ē'phrạ·ĭm, from the tribe of Dan and the half-tribe of Mạ·năs'sẹh, ten cities.

6 The Gēr'shọ·nītes received by lot

from the families of the tribe of Ĭs'sạ·chär, from the tribe of Ăsh'ẹr, from the tribe of Năph'tạ·lī, and from the half-tribe of Mạ·năs'sẹh in Bā'shạn, thirteen cities.

7 The Mẹ·râr'ītes according to their families received from the tribe of Reuben, the tribe of Gâd, and the tribe of Zĕb'ū·lụn, twelve cities.

8 These cities and their pasture lands the people of Israel gave by lot to the Lē'vītes, as the LORD had commanded through Moses.

9 Out of the tribe of Judah and the tribe of Sĭm'ē·ọn they gave the following cities mentioned by name, ¹⁰ which went to the descendants of Aaron, one of the families of the Kō'hạ·thītes who belonged to the Lē'vītes; since the lot fell to them first. ¹¹ They gave them Kĭr'ĭ·ăth–är'bạ (Är'ba being the father of Ā'năk), that is Hē'brọn, in the hill country of Judah, along with the pasture lands round about it. ¹² But the fields of the city and its villages had been given to Caleb the son of Jẹphün'nẹh as his possession.

13 And to the descendants of Aaron the priest they gave Hē'brọn, the city of refuge for the slayer, with its pasture lands, Lĭb'nạh with its pasture lands, ¹⁴ Jăt'tīr with its pasture lands, Ĕsh·tẹ·mō'ạ with its pasture lands, ¹⁵ Hō'lŏn with its pasture lands, Dē'bīr with its pasture lands, ¹⁶ Ā'ĭn with its pasture lands, Jŭt'tạh with its pasture lands, Bĕth–shē'mĕsh with its pasture lands – nine cities out of these two tribes; ¹⁷ then out of the tribe of Benjamin, Gĭb'ē·ọn with its pasture lands, Gē'bạ with its pasture lands, ¹⁸ Ăn'ạ·thŏth with its pasture lands, and Ăl'mŏn with its pasture lands – four cities. ¹⁹ The cities of the descendants of Aaron, the priests, were in all thirteen cities with their pasture lands.

20 As to the rest of the Kō'hạ·thītes belonging to the Kohathite families of the Lē'vītes, the cities allotted to them were out of the tribe of Ē'phrạ·ĭm. ²¹ To them were given Shē'chĕm, the city of refuge for the slayer, with its pasture lands in the hill country of Ē'phrạ·ĭm, Gē'zẹr with its pasture lands, ²² Kĭb'zạ–ĭm with its pasture lands, Bĕth–hō'rŏn with its pasture lands – four cities; ²³ and out of the tribe of Dan, Ĕl'tẹ·kẹ with its pasture lands, Gĭb'bẹ·thŏn with its pas-

21.1-42: Num 35.1-8; 1 Chron 6.54-81.

ture lands, ²⁴Aï'ja·lŏn with its pasture lands, Găth–rĭm'mŏn with its pasture lands—four cities; ²⁵and out of the half-tribe of Ma·năs'sĕh, Tā'a·năch with its pasture lands, and Găth–rĭm'mŏn with its pasture lands—two cities. ²⁶The cities of the families of the rest of the Kō'ha·thītes were ten in all with their pasture lands.

27 And to the Gēr'sho·nītes, one of the families of the Lē'vītes, were given out of the half-tribe of Ma·năs'sĕh, Gō'lăn in Bā'shan with its pasture lands, the city of refuge for the slayer, and Bĕ–ĕsh·tē'rah with its pasture lands—two cities; ²⁸and out of the tribe of Ĭs'sa·chär, Kĭsh'ĭ·ŏn with its pasture lands, Dăb'e·răth with its pasture lands, ²⁹Jăr'mŭth with its pasture lands, Ĕn–găn'nĭm with its pasture lands—four cities; ³⁰and out of the tribe of Ăsh'er, Mĭ'shal with its pasture lands, Ăb'dŏn with its pasture lands, ³¹Hĕl'kăth with its pasture lands, and Rē'hŏb with its pasture lands—four cities; ³²and out of the tribe of Năph'-ta·lī, Kē'dĕsh in Galilee with its pasture lands, the city of refuge for the slayer, Hăm'mŏth–dôr with its pasture lands, and Kăr'tan with its pasture lands—three cities. ³³The cities of the several families of the Gēr'sho·nītes were in all thirteen cities with their pasture lands.

34 And to the rest of the Lē'vītes, the Me·râr'īte families, were given out of the tribe of Zĕb'ū'lun, Jŏk'nē–ăm with its pasture lands, Kăr'tah with its pasture lands, ³⁵Dĭm'nah with its pasture lands, Na·hăl'al with its pasture lands—four cities; ³⁶and out of the tribe of Reuben, Bē'zer with its pasture lands, Jā'hăz with its pasture lands, ³⁷Kĕd'-e·mŏth with its pasture lands, and Mĕph'a–ăth with its pasture lands—four cities; ³⁸and out of the tribe of Găd, Rā'mŏth in Gilead with its pasture lands, the city of refuge for the slayer, Mā"ha·nā'ĭm with its pasture lands, ³⁹Hĕsh'bon with its pasture lands, Jā'zer with its pasture lands—four cities in all. ⁴⁰As for the cities of the several Me·râr'īte families, that is, the remainder of the families of the Lē'vītes, those allotted to them were in all twelve cities.

41 The cities of the Lē'vītes in the midst of the possession of the people of Israel were in all forty-eight cities with their pasture lands. ⁴²These

cities had each its pasture lands round about it; so it was with all these cities.

43 Thus the LORD gave to Israel all the land which he swore to give to their fathers; and having taken possession of it, they settled there. ⁴⁴And the LORD gave them rest on every side just as he had sworn to their fathers; not one of all their enemies had withstood them, for the LORD had given all their enemies into their hands. ⁴⁵Not one of all the good promises which the LORD had made to the house of Israel had failed; all came to pass.

22 Then Joshua summoned the Reubenites, and the Găd'ītes, and the half-tribe of Ma·năs'sĕh, ²and said to them, "You have kept all that Moses the servant of the LORD commanded you, and have obeyed my voice in all that I have commanded you; ³you have not forsaken your brethen these many days, down to this day, but have been careful to keep the charge of the LORD your God. ⁴And now the LORD your God has given rest to your brethren, as he promised them; therefore turn and go to your home in the land where your possession lies, which Moses the servant of the LORD gave you on the other side of the Jordan. ⁵Take good care to observe the commandment and the law which Moses the servant of the LORD commanded you, to love the LORD your God, and to walk in all his ways, and to keep his commandments, and to cleave to him, and to serve him with all your heart and with all your soul." ⁶So Joshua blessed them, and sent them away; and they went to their homes.

7 Now to the one half of the tribe of Ma·năs'sĕh Moses had given a possession in Bā'shan; but to the other half Joshua had given a possession beside their brethren in the land west of the Jordan. And when Joshua sent them away to their homes and blessed them, ⁸he said to them, "Go back to your homes with much wealth, and with very many cattle, with silver, gold, bronze, and iron, and with much clothing; divide the spoil of your enemies with your brethen." ⁹So the Reubenites and the Găd'ītes and the half-tribe of Ma·năs'sĕh returned home, parting from the people of Israel at Shi'lŏh, which is in the land of

22.1–34: 1.12-18; Num 32.20-22.

Canaan, to go to the land of Gilead, their own land of which they had possessed themselves by command of the LORD through Moses.

10 And when they came to the region about the Jordan, that lies in the land of Canaan, the Reubenites and the Gåd'ītes and the half-tribe of Mạ·nặs'-sẹh built there an altar by the Jordan, an altar of great size. ¹¹ And the people of Israel heard say, "Behold, the Reubenites and the Gåd'ītes and the half-tribe of Mạ·nặs'sẹh have built an altar at the frontier of the land of Canaan, in the region about the Jordan, on the side that belongs to the people of Israel." ¹² And when the people of Israel heard of it, the whole assembly of the people of Israel gathered at Shī'lōh, to make war against them.

13 Then the people of Israel sent to the Reubenites and the Gåd'ītes and the half-tribe of Mạ·nặs'sẹh, in the land of Gilead, Phĭn'ẹ·hạs the son of Ĕl·ē·ā'zạr the priest, ¹⁴ and with him ten chiefs, one from each of the tribal families of Israel, every one of them the head of a family among the clans of Israel. ¹⁵ And they came to the Reubenites, the Gåd'ītes, and the half-tribe of Mạ·nặs'sẹh, in the land of Gilead, and they said to them, ¹⁶ "Thus says the whole congregation of the LORD, 'What is this treachery which you have committed against the God of Israel in turning away this day from following the LORD, by building yourselves an altar this day in rebellion against the LORD? ¹⁷ Have we not had enough of the sin at Pē'ôr from which even yet we have not cleansed ourselves, and for which there came a plague upon the congregation of the LORD, ¹⁸ that you must turn away this day from following the LORD? And if you rebel against the LORD today he will be angry with the whole congregation of Israel tomorrow. ¹⁹ But now, if your land is unclean, pass over into the LORD's land where the LORD's tabernacle stands, and take for yourselves a possession among us; only do not rebel against the LORD, or make us as rebels by building yourselves an altar other than the altar of the LORD our God. ²⁰ Did not Ā'chạn the son of Zē'rah break faith in the matter of the devoted things, and wrath fell upon all the congregation of Israel? And he did not perish alone for his iniquity.'"

21 Then the Reubenites, the Gåd'-ītes, and the half-tribe of Mạ·nặs'sẹh said in answer to the heads of the families of Israel, ²² "The Mighty One, God, the LORD! The Mighty One, God, the LORD! He knows; and let Israel itself know! If it was in rebellion or in breach of faith toward the LORD, spare us not today ²³ for building an altar to turn away from following the LORD; or if we did so to offer burnt offerings or cereal offerings or peace offerings on it, may the LORD himself take vengeance. ²⁴ Nay, but we did it from fear that in time to come your children might say to our children, 'What have you to do with the LORD, the God of Israel? ²⁵ For the LORD has made the Jordan a boundary between us and you, you Reubenites and Gåd'ītes; you have no portion in the LORD.' So your children might make our children cease to worship the LORD. ²⁶ Therefore we said, 'Let us now build an altar, not for burnt offering, nor for sacrifice, ²⁷ but to be a witness between us and you, and between the generations after us, that we do perform the service of the LORD in his presence with our burnt offerings and sacrifices and peace offerings; lest your children say to our children in time to come, "You have no portion in the LORD."' ²⁸ And we thought, If this should be said to us or to our descendants in time to come, we should say, 'Behold the copy of the altar of the LORD, which our fathers made, not for burnt offerings, nor for sacrifice, but to be a witness between us and you.' ²⁹ Far be it from us that we should rebel against the LORD, and turn away this day from following the LORD by building an altar for burnt offering, cereal offering, or sacrifice, other than the altar of the LORD our God that stands before his tabernacle!"

30 When Phĭn'ẹ·hạs the priest and the chiefs of the congregation, the heads of the families of Israel who were with him, heard the words that the Reubenites and the Gåd'ītes and the Mạ·nặs'sītes spoke, it pleased them well. ³¹ And Phĭn'ẹ·hạs the son of Ĕl·ē·ā'zạr the priest said to the Reubenites and the Gåd'ītes and the Mạ·nặs'sītes, "Today we know that the LORD is in the midst of us, because you have not committed this treachery against the LORD; now you have saved

the people of Israel from the hand of the LORD."

32 Then Phĭn'ẹ·hạs the son of Ĕl-ē-ā'zạr the priest, and the chiefs, returned from the Reubenites and the Gȧd'ītes in the land of Gilead to the land of Canaan, to the people of Israel, and brought back word to them. ³³And the report pleased the people of Israel; and the people of Israel blessed God and spoke no more of making war against them, to destroy the land where the Reubenites and the Gȧd'ītes were settled. ³⁴The Reubenites and the Gȧd'ītes called the altar Witness; "For," said they, "it is a witness between us that the LORD is God."

23 A long time afterward, when the LORD had given rest to Israel from all their enemies round about, and Joshua was old and well advanced in years, ²Joshua summoned all Israel, their elders and heads, their judges and officers, and said to them, "I am now old and well advanced in years; ³and you have seen all that the LORD your God has done to all these nations for your sake, for it is the LORD your God who has fought for you. ⁴Behold, I have allotted to you as an inheritance for your tribes those nations that remain, along with all the nations that I have already cut off, from the Jordan to the Great Sea in the west. ⁵The LORD your God will push them back before you, and drive them out of your sight; and you shall possess their land, as the LORD your God promised you. ⁶Therefore be very steadfast to keep and do all that is written in the book of the law of Moses, turning aside from it neither to the right hand nor to the left, ⁷that you may not be mixed with these nations left here among you, or make mention of the names of their gods, or swear by them, or serve them, or bow down yourselves to them, ⁸but cleave to the LORD your God as you have done to this day. ⁹For the LORD has driven out before you great and strong nations; and as for you, no man has been able to withstand you to this day. ¹⁰One man of you puts to flight a thousand, since it is the LORD your God who fights for you, as he promised you. ¹¹Take good heed to yourselves, therefore, to love the LORD your God. ¹²For if you turn back, and join the remnant of these nations left here among you, and make marriages with them, so that you marry their women and they yours, ¹³know assuredly that the LORD your God will not continue to drive out these nations before you; but they shall be a snare and a trap for you, a scourge on your sides, and thorns in your eyes, till you perish from off this good land which the LORD your God has given you.

14 "And now I am about to go the way of all the earth, and you know in your hearts and souls, all of you, that not one thing has failed of all the good things which the LORD your God promised concerning you; all have come to pass for you, not one of them has failed. ¹⁵But just as all the good things which the LORD your God promised concerning you have been fulfilled for you, so the LORD will bring upon you all the evil things, until he have destroyed you from off this good land which the LORD your God has given you, ¹⁶if you transgress the covenant of the LORD your God, which he commanded you, and go and serve other gods and bow down to them. Then the anger of the LORD will be kindled against you, and you shall perish quickly from off the good land which he has given to you."

24 Then Joshua gathered all the tribes of Israel to Shē'chĕm, and summoned the elders, the heads, the judges, and the officers of Israel; and they presented themselves before God. ²And Joshua said to all the people, "Thus says the LORD, the God of Israel, 'Your fathers lived of old beyond the Euphrates, Tē'rah, the father of Abraham and of Nā'hôr; and they served other gods. ³Then I took your father Abraham from beyond the River and led him through all the land of Canaan, and made his offspring many. I gave him Isaac; ⁴and to Isaac I gave Jacob and Esau. And I gave Esau the hill country of Sē'ĭr to possess, but Jacob and his children went down to Egypt. ⁵And I sent Moses and Aaron, and I plagued Egypt with what I did in the midst of it; and afterwards I brought you out. ⁶Then I brought your fathers out of Egypt, and you came to the sea; and the Egyptians pursued your fathers with chariots and horsemen to the Red Sea. ⁷And when they cried to the LORD, he put darkness between you and the Egyptians, and made the sea come upon them and

cover them; and your eyes saw what I did to Egypt; and you lived in the wilderness a long time. ⁸Then I brought you to the land of the Ăm′o·rītes, who lived on the other side of the Jordan; they fought with you, and I gave them into your hand, and you took possession of their land, and I destroyed them before you. ⁹Then Bā′lăk the son of Zĭp′pôr, king of Mō′ăb, arose and fought against Israel; and he sent and invited Bā′laăm the son of Bē′ôr to curse you, ¹⁰but I would not listen to Bā′laăm; therefore he blessed you; so I delivered you out of his hand. ¹¹And you went over the Jordan and came to Jericho, and the men of Jericho fought against you, and also the Ăm′o·rītes, the Pĕr′ĭz·zītes, the Canaanites, the Hīt′tītes, the Gīr′gashītes, the Hī′vītes, and the Jĕb′u·sītes; and I gave them into your hand. ¹²And I sent the hornet before you, which drove them out before you, the two kings of the Ăm′o·rītes; it was not by your sword or by your bow. ¹³I gave you a land on which you had not labored, and cities which you had not built, and you dwell therein; you eat the fruit of vineyards and oliveyards which you did not plant.'

14 "Now therefore fear the Lord, and serve him in sincerity and in faithfulness; put away the gods which your fathers served beyond the River, and in Egypt, and serve the Lord. ¹⁵And if you be unwilling to serve the Lord, choose this day whom you will serve, whether the gods your fathers served in the region beyond the River, or the gods of the Ăm′o·rītes in whose land you dwell; but as for me and my house, we will serve the Lord."

16 Then the people answered, "Far be it from us that we should forsake the Lord, to serve other gods; ¹⁷for it is the Lord our God who brought us and our fathers up from the land of Egypt, out of the house of bondage, and who did those great signs in our sight, and preserved us in all the way that we went, and among all the peoples through whom we passed; ¹⁸and the Lord drove out before us all the peoples, the Ăm′o·rītes who lived in the land; therefore we also will serve the Lord, for he is our God."

19 But Joshua said to the people, "You cannot serve the Lord; for he is a holy God; he is a jealous God; he will

not forgive your transgressions or your sins. ²⁰If you forsake the Lord and serve foreign gods, then he will turn and do you harm, and consume you, after having done you good." ²¹And the people said to Joshua, "Nay; but we will serve the Lord." ²²Then Joshua said to the people, "You are witnesses against yourselves that you have chosen the Lord, to serve him." And they said, "We are witnesses." ²³He said, "Then put away the foreign gods which are among you, and incline your heart to the Lord, the God of Israel." ²⁴And the people said to Joshua, "The Lord our God we will serve, and his voice we will obey." ²⁵So Joshua made a covenant with the people that day, and made statutes and ordinances for them at Shē′chĕm. ²⁶And Joshua wrote these words in the book of the law of God; and he took a great stone, and set it up there under the oak in the sanctuary of the Lord. ²⁷And Joshua said to all the people, "Behold, this stone shall be a witness against us; for it has heard all the words of the Lord which he spoke to us; therefore it shall be a witness against you, lest you deal falsely with your God." ²⁸So Joshua sent the people away, every man to his inheritance.

29 After these things Joshua the son of Nŭn, the servant of the Lord, died, being a hundred and ten years old. ³⁰And they buried him in his own inheritance at Tĭm′năth-sē′rah, which is in the hill country of Ē′phra·ĭm, north of the mountain of Gā′ăsh.

31 And Israel served the Lord all the days of Joshua, and all the days of the elders who outlived Joshua and had known all the work which the Lord did for Israel.

32 The bones of Joseph which the people of Israel brought up from Egypt were buried at Shē′chĕm, in the portion of ground which Jacob bought from the sons of Hā′môr the father of Shē′chĕm for a hundred pieces of money;*q* it became an inheritance of the descendants of Joseph.

33 And Ĕl·ē·ā′zar the son of Aaron died; and they buried him at Gĭb′ē·ah, the town of Phĭn′e·has his son, which had been given him in the hill country of Ē′phra·ĭm.

*q*Heb *qesitah*
24.32: Gen 50.24, 25; Ex 13.19; Acts 7.16.

The Book of
Judges

1 After the death of Joshua the people of Israel inquired of the LORD, "Who shall go up first for us against the Canaanites, to fight against them?" ²The LORD said, "Judah shall go up; behold, I have given the land into his hand." ³And Judah said to Sĭm'ē·ọn his brother, "Come up with me into the territory allotted to me, that we may fight against the Canaanites; and I likewise will go with you into the territory allotted to you." So Simeon went with him. ⁴Then Judah went up and the LORD gave the Canaanites and the Pĕr'ĭz·zītes into their hand; and they defeated ten thousand of them at Bē'zĕk. ⁵They came upon A·dō'nī–bē'zĕk at Bē'zĕk, and fought against him, and defeated the Canaanites and the Pĕr'ĭz·zītes. ⁶A·dō'nī–bē'zĕk fled; but they pursued him, and caught him, and cut off his thumbs and his great toes. ⁷And A·dō'nī–bē'zĕk said, "Seventy kings with their thumbs and their great toes cut off used to pick up scraps under my table; as I have done, so God has requited me." And they brought him to Jerusalem, and he died there.

8 And the men of Judah fought against Jerusalem, and took it, and smote it with the edge of the sword, and set the city on fire. ⁹And afterward the men of Judah went down to fight against the Canaanites who dwelt in the hill country, in the Nĕg'ĕb, and in the lowland. ¹⁰And Judah went against the Canaanites who dwelt in Hē'brọn (now the name of Hebron was formerly Kĭr'ĭ·ăth–är'ba); and they defeated Shē'shaī and A·hī'man and Tăl'maī.

11 From there they went against the inhabitants of Dē'bĭr. The name of Debir was formerly Kĭr'ĭ·ăth-sē'-phẹr. ¹²And Caleb said, "He who attacks Kĭr'ĭ·ăth-sē'phẹr and takes it, I will give him Ăch'sạh my daughter as wife." ¹³And Ŏth'nĭ–ĕl the son of Kē'năz, Caleb's younger brother, took it; and he gave him Ăch'sạh his daughter as wife. ¹⁴When she came to him, she urged him to ask her father for a field; and she alighted from her ass, and Caleb said to her, "What do you wish?" ¹⁵She said to him, "Give me a present; since you have set me in the land of the Nĕg'ĕb, give me also springs of water." And Caleb gave her the upper springs and the lower springs.

16 And the descendants of the Kēn'-īte, Moses' father-in-law, went up with the people of Judah from the city of palms into the wilderness of Judah, which lies in the Nĕg'ĕb near Är'ạd; and they went and settled with the people. ¹⁷And Judah went with Sĭm'-ē·ọn his brother, and they defeated the Canaanites who inhabited Zē'-phăth, and utterly destroyed it. So the name of the city was called Hôr'mạh. ¹⁸Judah also took Gā'zạ with its territory, and Ăsh'kẹ·lŏn with its territory, and Ĕk'rọn with its territory. ¹⁹And the LORD was with Judah, and he took possession of the hill country, but he could not drive out the inhabitants of the plain, because they had chariots of iron. ²⁰And Hē'brọn was given to Caleb, as Moses had said; and he drove out from it the three sons of Ā'năk. ²¹But the people of Benjamin did not drive out the Jĕb'ū·sītes who dwelt in Jerusalem; so the Jebusites have dwelt with the people of Benjamin in Jerusalem to this day.

22 The house of Joseph also went up against Bĕth'el; and the LORD was with them. ²³And the house of Joseph sent to spy out Bĕth'el. (Now the name of the city was formerly Lŭz.) ²⁴And the spies saw a man coming out of the city, and they said to him, "Pray, show us the way into the city, and we will deal kindly with you." ²⁵And he showed them the way into the city; and they smote the city with the edge of the sword, but they let the man and all his family go. ²⁶And the man went to the land of the Hĭt'tītes and built a city, and called its name Lŭz; that is its name to this day.

27 Mạ·năs'sẹh did not drive out the

1.10: Josh 15.13-19.   1.10-15: Josh 15.14-19.
1.20: Josh 15.14.   1.21: Josh 15.63.
1.27, 28: Josh 17.11-13.

inhabitants of Bĕth–shē′ạn and its villages, or Tā′ạ·năch and its villages, or the inhabitants of Dôr and its villages, or the inhabitants of Ĭb′lē·ăm and its villages, or the inhabitants of Mẹ·gĭd′dō and its villages, but the Canaanites persisted in dwelling in that land. 28 When Israel grew strong, they put the Canaanites to forced labor, but did not utterly drive them out.

29 And Ē′phrạ·ĭm did not drive out the Canaanites who dwelt in Gē′zẹr; but the Canaanites dwelt in Gezer among them.

30 Zĕb′ū·lụn did not drive out the inhabitants of Kĭt′rŏn, or the inhabitants of Nạ·hăl′ŏl; but the Canaanites dwelt among them, and became subject to forced labor.

31 Ăsh′ẹr did not drive out the inhabitants of Ăc′cō, or the inhabitants of Sī′dŏn, or of Ăh′lăb, or of Ăch′zĭb, or of Hĕl′bạh, or of Ā′phĭk, or of Rē′hōb; 32 but the Ăsh′ẹ·rītes dwelt among the Canaanites, the inhabitants of the land; for they did not drive them out.

33 Năph′tạ·lī did not drive out the inhabitants of Bĕth–shē′mĕsh, or the inhabitants of Bĕth–ā′năth, but dwelt among the Canaanites, the inhabitants of the land; nevertheless the inhabitants of Beth–shemesh and of Beth–anath became subject to forced labor for them.

34 The Ăm′ọ·rītes pressed the Dă′nītes back into the hill country, for they did not allow them to come down to the plain; 35 the Ăm′ọ·rītes persisted in dwelling in Hăr–hē′rĕs, in Aī′jạ·lŏn, and in Shā–ăl′bĭm, but the hand of the house of Joseph rested heavily upon them, and they became subject to forced labor. 36 And the border of the Ăm′ọ·rītes ran from the ascent of Ăk·răb′bĭm, from Sē′lạ and upward.

2 Now the angel of the LORD went up from Gĭl′gạl to Bō′chĭm. And he said, "I brought you up from Egypt, and brought you into the land which I swore to give to your fathers. I said, 'I will never break my covenant with you, 2 and you shall make no covenant with the inhabitants of this land; you shall break down their altars.' But you have not obeyed my command. What is this you have done? 3 So now I say, I will not drive them out before you; but they shall become adversaries[a] to you, and their gods shall be a snare to you."

4 When the angel of the LORD spoke these words to all the people of Israel, the people lifted up their voices and wept. 5 And they called the name of that place Bō′chĭm;[b] and they sacrificed there to the LORD.

6 When Joshua dismissed the people, the people of Israel went each to his inheritance to take possession of the land. 7 And the people served the LORD all the days of Joshua, and all the days of the elders who outlived Joshua, who had seen all the great work which the LORD had done for Israel. 8 And Joshua the son of Nŭn, the servant of the LORD, died at the age of one hundred and ten years. 9 And they buried him within the bounds of his inheritance in Tĭm′năth–hē′rĕṣ, in the hill country of Ē′phrạ·ĭm, north of the mountain of Gā′ăsh. 10 And all that generation also were gathered to their fathers; and there arose another generation after them, who did not know the LORD or the work which he had done for Israel.

11 And the people of Israel did what was evil in the sight of the LORD and served the Bā′ạlṣ; 12 and they forsook the LORD, the God of their fathers, who had brought them out of the land of Egypt; they went after other gods, from among the gods of the peoples who were round about them, and bowed down to them; and they provoked the LORD to anger. 13 They forsook the LORD, and served the Bā′ạls and the Ăsh′tạ·rŏth. 14 So the anger of the LORD was kindled against Israel, and he gave them over to plunderers, who plundered them; and he sold them into the power of their enemies round about, so that they could no longer withstand their enemies. 15 Whenever they marched out, the hand of the LORD was against them for evil, as the LORD had warned, and as the LORD had sworn to them; and they were in sore straits.

16 Then the LORD raised up judges, who saved them out of the power of those who plundered them. 17 And yet they did not listen to their judges; for they played the harlot after other gods and bowed down to them; they soon turned aside from the way in which their fathers had walked, who had

obeyed the commandments of the
LORD, and they did not do so. [18]Whenever
the LORD raised up judges for
them, the LORD was with the judge,
and he saved them from the hand of
their enemies all the days of the judge;
for the LORD was moved to pity by their
groaning because of those who afflicted
and oppressed them. [19]But
whenever the judge died, they turned
back and behaved worse than their
fathers, going after other gods, serving
them and bowing down to them;
they did not drop any of their practices
or their stubborn ways. [20]So the anger
of the LORD was kindled against Israel;
and he said, "Because this people
have transgressed my covenant
which I commanded their fathers, and
have not obeyed my voice, [21]I will
not henceforth drive out before them
any of the nations that Joshua left
when he died, [22]that by them I may
test Israel, whether they will take
care to walk in the way of the LORD as
their fathers did, or not." [23]So the LORD
left those nations, not driving them out
at once, and he did not give them into
the power of Joshua.

3 Now these are the nations which
the LORD left, to test Israel by them,
that is, all in Israel who had no experience
of any war in Canaan; [2]it was
only that the generations of the people
of Israel might know war, that he
might teach war to such at least as
had not known it before. [3]These are
the nations: the five lords of the Phi-
lis'tines, and all the Canaanites, and
the Si-dō'ni-ans, and the Hi'vites who
dwelt on Mount Lebanon, from Mount
Bā'al–hēr'mon as far as the entrance
of Hā'māth. [4]They were for the testing
of Israel, to know whether Israel
would obey the commandments of the
LORD, which he commanded their
fathers by Moses. [5]So the people of Israel dwelt among the Canaanites, the
Hit'tites, the Am'o-rites, the Pĕr'-
iz-zites, the Hi'vites, and the Jĕb'ū-
sites; [6]and they took their daughters
to themselves for wives, and their own
daughters they gave to their sons; and
they served their gods.

7 And the people of Israel did what
was evil in the sight of the LORD, forgetting
the LORD their God, and serving
the Bā'als and the A-shē'roth.
[8]Therefore the anger of the LORD was
kindled against Israel, and he sold

them into the hand of Cū'shăn–
rĭsh-ạ-thā'ĭm king of Mĕs-o-pọ-tā'mĭ-ạ;
and the people of Israel served Cu-
shan–rishathaim eight years. [9]But
when the people of Israel cried to the
LORD, the LORD raised up a deliverer
for the people of Israel, who delivered
them, Ŏth'nĭ–ĕl the son of Kē'năz,
Caleb's younger brother. [10]The Spirit
of the LORD came upon him, and he
judged Israel; he went out to war, and
the LORD gave Cū'shăn–rĭsh-ạ-thā'ĭm
king of Mĕs-o-pọ-tā'mĭ-ạ into his hand;
and his hand prevailed over Cushan-
rishathaim. [11]So the land had rest
forty years. Then Ŏth'nĭ–ĕl the son of
Kē'năz died.

12 And the people of Israel again
did what was evil in the sight of the
LORD; and the LORD strengthened
Ĕg'lŏn the king of Mō'ăb against Israel, because they had done what was
evil in the sight of the LORD. [13]He
gathered to himself the Ăm'mo-nītes
and the A-măl'ẹ-kītes, and went and
defeated Israel; and they took possession of the city of palms. [14]And the
people of Israel served Ĕg'lŏn the king
of Mō'ăb eighteen years.

15 But when the people of Israel
cried to the LORD, the LORD raised
up for them a deliverer, Ē'hŭd, the son
of Gē'rạ, the Benjaminite, a left-
handed man. The people of Israel sent
tribute by him to Ĕg'lŏn the king of
Mō'ăb. [16]And Ē'hŭd made for himself
a sword with two edges, a cubit in
length; and he girded it on his right
thigh under his clothes. [17]And he presented the tribute to Ĕg'lŏn king of
Mō'ăb. Now Ĕg'lŏn was a very fat
man. [18]And when Ē'hŭd had finished
presenting the tribute, he sent away
the people that carried the tribute.
[19]But he himself turned back at the
sculptured stones near Gĭl'gạl, and
said, "I have a secret message for you,
O king." And he commanded, "Silence." And all his attendants went
out from his presence. [20]And Ē'hŭd
came to him, as he was sitting alone
in his cool roof chamber. And Ehud
said, "I have a message from God for
you." And he arose from his seat. [21]And
Ē'hŭd reached with his left hand,
took the sword from his right thigh,
and thrust it into his belly; [22]and the
hilt also went in after the blade, and
the fat closed over the blade, for he
did not draw the sword out of his belly;

and the dirt came out. ²³Then Ē′hŭd went out into the vestibule,ᶜ and closed the doors of the roof chamber upon him, and locked them.

24 When he had gone, the servants came; and when they saw that the doors of the roof chamber were locked, they thought, "He is only relieving himself in the closet of the cool chamber." ²⁵And they waited till they were utterly at a loss; but when he still did not open the doors of the roof chamber, they took the key and opened them; and there lay their lord dead on the floor.

26 Ē′hŭd escaped while they delayed, and passed beyond the sculptured stones, and escaped to Sē-ī′rah. ²⁷When he arrived, he sounded the trumpet in the hill country of Ē′phra·ĭm; and the people of Israel went down with him from the hill country, having him at their head. ²⁸And he said to them, "Follow after me; for the LORD has given your enemies the Mō′ab·ītes into your hand." So they went down after him, and seized the fords of the Jordan against the Moabites, and allowed not a man to pass over. ²⁹And they killed at that time about ten thousand of the Mō′ab-ītes, all strong, able-bodied men; not a man escaped. ³⁰So Mō′ăb was subdued that day under the hand of Israel. And the land had rest for eighty years.

31 After him was Shăm′găr the son of Ā′năth, who killed six hundred of the Phi′lĭs′tīnes with an oxgoad; and he too delivered Israel.

4 And the people of Israel again did what was evil in the sight of the LORD, after Ē′hŭd died. ²And the LORD sold them into the hand of Jā′bĭn king of Canaan, who reigned in Hā′zôr; the commander of his army was Sĭs′-e·ra, who dwelt in Ha·rō′shĕth-ha-goi′ĭm. ³Then the people of Israel cried to the LORD for help; for he had nine hundred chariots of iron, and oppressed the people of Israel cruelly for twenty years.

4 Now Dĕb′o·rah, a prophetess, the wife of Lăp′pĭ·dŏth, was judging Israel at that time. ⁵She used to sit under the palm of Dĕb′o·rah between Rā′mah and Bĕth′el in the hill country of Ē′phra·ĭm; and the people of Israel came up to her for judgment. ⁶She sent and summoned Bār′ak the son of

A·bĭn′ō-ăm from Kē′dĕsh in Năph′-ta·lī, and said to him, "The LORD, the God of Israel, commands you, 'Go, gather your men at Mount Tā′bôr, taking ten thousand from the tribe of Naphtali and the tribe of Zĕb′ū·lun. ⁷And I will draw out Sĭs′e·ra, the general of Jā′bĭn′s army, to meet you by the river Kī′shŏn with his chariots and his troops; and I will give him into your hand.' " ⁸Bār′ak said to her, "If you will go with me, I will go; but if you will not go with me, I will not go." ⁹And she said, "I will surely go with you; nevertheless, the road on which you are going will not lead to your glory, for the LORD will sell Sĭs′e·ra into the hand of a woman." Then Dĕb′o·rah arose, and went with Bār′ak to Kē′dĕsh. ¹⁰And Bār′ak summoned Zĕb′ū·lun and Năph′ta·lī to Kē′dĕsh; and ten thousand men went up at his heels; and Dĕb′o·rah went up with him.

11 Now Hē′ber the Kĕn′īte had separated from the Kĕn′ītes, the descendants of Hō′băb the father-in-law of Moses, and had pitched his tent as far away as the oak in Zā–a·năn′nĭm, which is near Kē′dĕsh.

12 When Sĭs′e·ra was told that Bār′ak the son of A·bĭn′ō-ăm had gone up to Mount Tā′bôr, ¹³Sĭs′e·ra called out all his chariots, nine hundred chariots of iron, and all the men who were with him, from Ha·rō′shĕth-ha-goi′ĭm to the river Kī′shŏn. ¹⁴And Dĕb′o·rah said to Bār′ak, "Up! For this is the day in which the LORD has given Sĭs′e·ra into your hand. Does not the LORD go out before you?" So Barak went down from Mount Tā′bôr with ten thousand men following him. ¹⁵And the LORD routed Sĭs′e·ra and all his chariots and all his army before Bār′ak at the edge of the sword; and Sisera alighted from his chariot and fled away on foot. ¹⁶And Bār′ak pursued the chariots and the army to Ha·rō′shĕth-ha-goi′ĭm, and all the army of Sĭs′e·ra fell by the edge of the sword; not a man was left.

17 But Sĭs′e·ra fled away on foot to the tent of Jā′ĕl, the wife of Hē′ber the Kĕn′īte; for there was peace between Jā′bĭn the king of Hā′zôr and the house of Heber the Kenite. ¹⁸And Jā′ĕl came out to meet Sĭs′e·ra, and said to him, "Turn aside, my lord, turn aside to me;

ᶜThe meaning of the Hebrew word is unknown

have no fear." So he turned aside to her into the tent, and she covered him with a rug. ¹⁹And he said to her, "Pray, give me a little water to drink; for I am thirsty." So she opened a skin of milk and gave him a drink and covered him. ²⁰And he said to her, "Stand at the door of the tent, and if any man comes and asks you, 'Is any one here?' say, No." ²¹But Jā'ĕl the wife of Hē'-bĕr took a tent peg, and took a hammer in her hand, and went softly to him and drove the peg into his temple, till it went down into the ground, as he was lying fast asleep from weariness. So he died. ²²And behold, as Bār'ak pursued Sĭs'e·ra, Jā'ĕl went out to meet him, and said to him, "Come, and I will show you the man whom you are seeking." So he went in to her tent; and there lay Sisera dead, with the tent peg in his temple.

23 So on that day God subdued Jā'bĭn the king of Canaan before the people of Israel. ²⁴And the hand of the people of Israel bore harder and harder on Jā'bĭn the king of Canaan, until they destroyed Jabin king of Canaan.

5 Then sang Dĕb'o·rah and Bār'ak the son of A·bĭn'ō–ăm on that day:
² "That the leaders took the lead in Israel,
    that the people offered themselves willingly,
    bless*ᵈ* the Lord!

³ "Hear, O kings; give ear, O princes;
    to the Lord I will sing,
    I will make melody to the Lord,
    the God of Israel.

⁴ "Lord, when thou didst go forth from Sē'ĭr,
    when thou didst march from the region of E'dom,
    the earth trembled,
    and the heavens dropped,
    yea, the clouds dropped water.
⁵The mountains quaked before the Lord,
    yon Sinai before the Lord, the God of Israel.

⁶ "In the days of Shăm'găr, son of A'năth,
    in the days of Jā'ĕl, caravans ceased
    and travelers kept to the byways.
⁷The peasantry ceased in Israel, they ceased

until you arose, Dĕb'o·rah,
    arose as a mother in Israel.
⁸When new gods were chosen,
    then war was in the gates.
Was shield or spear to be seen
    among forty thousand in Israel?
⁹My heart goes out to the command-ers of Israel
    who offered themselves willingly among the people.
Bless the Lord.

¹⁰ "Tell of it, you who ride on tawny asses,
    you who sit on rich carpets*ᵉ*
    and you who walk by the way.
¹¹To the sound of musicians*ᵉ* at the watering places,
    there they repeat the triumphs of the Lord,
    the triumphs of his peasantry in Israel.

"Then down to the gates marched the people of the Lord.

¹² "Awake, awake, Dĕb'o·rah!
    Awake, awake, utter a song!
Arise, Bār'ak, lead away your cap-tives,
    O son of A·bĭn'ō–ăm.
¹³Then down marched the remnant of the noble;
    the people of the Lord marched down for him*ᶠ* against the mighty.
¹⁴From E'phra·ĭm they set out thither*ˣ*
    into the valley,*ᵍ*
    following you, Benjamin, with your kinsmen;
    from Mā'chĭr marched down the commanders,
    and from Zĕb'ū·lun those who bear the marshal's staff;
¹⁵the princes of Ĭs'sa·chăr came with Dĕb'o·rah,
    and Issachar faithful to Bār'ak;
    into the valley they rushed forth at his heels.
Among the clans of Reuben
    there were great searchings of heart.
¹⁶Why did you tarry among the sheep-folds,
    to hear the piping for the flocks?
Among the clans of Reuben

ᵈOr You who offered yourselves willingly among the people, bless
ᵉThe meaning of the Hebrew word is uncertain
ᶠGk: Heb me   *ˣCn: Heb From Ephraim their root*
ᵍGk: Heb in Amalek

there were great searchings of
heart.
¹⁷ Gilead stayed beyond the Jordan;
and Dan, why did he abide with the
ships?
Āsh′ẹr sat still at the coast of the sea,
settling down by his landings.
¹⁸ Zĕb′ū·lụn is a people that jeoparded
their lives to the death;
Năph′tạ·lī too, on the heights of
the field.

¹⁹ "The kings came, they fought;
then fought the kings of Canaan,
at Tā′a·năch, by the waters of Mẹ·
gĭd′dō;
they got no spoils of silver.
²⁰ From heaven fought the stars,
from their courses they fought
against Sĭs′ẹ·rạ.
²¹ The torrent Kī′shŏn swept them
away,
the onrushing torrent, the torrent
Kishon.
March on, my soul, with might!

²² "Then loud beat the horses' hoofs
with the galloping, galloping of his
steeds.

²³ "Curse Mē′rŏz, says the angel of the
LORD,
curse bitterly its inhabitants,
because they came not to the help of
the LORD,
to the help of the LORD against the
mighty.

²⁴ "Most blessed of women be Jā′ĕl,
the wife of Hē′bẹr the Kĕn′īte,
of tent-dwelling women most
blessed.
²⁵ He asked water and she gave him
milk,
she brought him curds in a lordly
bowl.
²⁶ She put her hand to the tent peg
and her right hand to the workmen's mallet;
she struck Sĭs′ẹ·rạ a blow,
she crushed his head,
she shattered and pierced his
temple.
²⁷ He sank, he fell,
he lay still at her feet;
at her feet he sank, he fell;
where he sank, there he fell dead.

²⁸ "Out of the window she peered,
the mother of Sĭs′ẹ·rạ gazed*ʰ*
through the lattice:

'Why is his chariot so long in coming?
Why tarry the hoofbeats of his
chariots?'
²⁹ Her wisest ladies make answer,
nay, she gives answer to herself,
³⁰ 'Are they not finding and dividing the
spoil? —
A maiden or two for every man;
spoil of dyed stuffs for Sĭs′ẹ·rạ,
spoil of dyed stuffs embroidered,
two pieces of dyed work embroidered for my neck as spoil?'

³¹ "So perish all thine enemies,
O LORD!
But thy friends be like the sun as
he rises in his might."

And the land had rest for forty years.

6   The people of Israel did what
was evil in the sight of the LORD;
and the LORD gave them into the hand
of Mĭd′ĭ·ạn seven years. ² And the hand
of Mĭd′ĭ·ạn prevailed over Israel; and
because of Midian the people of Israel
made for themselves the dens which
are in the mountains, and the caves
and the strongholds. ³ For whenever
the Israelites put in seed the Mĭd′-
ĭ·ạ·nītes and the A·măl′ẹ·kītes and the
people of the East would come up and
attack them; ⁴ they would encamp
against them and destroy the produce
of the land, as far as the neighborhood
of Gā′zạ, and leave no sustenance in
Israel, and no sheep or ox or ass. ⁵ For
they would come up with their cattle
and their tents, coming like locusts for
number; both they and their camels
could not be counted; so that they
wasted the land as they came in. ⁶ And
Israel was brought very low because of
Mĭd′ĭ·ạn; and the people of Israel cried
for help to the LORD.
7 When the people of Israel cried to
the LORD on account of the Mĭd′ĭ·ạ-
nītes, ⁸ the LORD sent a prophet to the
people of Israel; and he said to them,
"Thus says the LORD, the God of Israel: I led you up from Egypt, and
brought you out of the house of bondage; ⁹ and I delivered you from the
hand of the Egyptians, and from the
hand of all who oppressed you, and
drove them out before you, and gave
you their land; ¹⁰ and I said to you,
'I am the LORD your God; you shall
not pay reverence to the gods of

---

*ʰ*Gk Compare Tg: Heb *exclaimed*
5.31: Rev 1.16.

the Ăm′o·rītes, in whose land you dwell.' But you have not given heed to my voice."

11 Now the angel of the Lord came and sat under the oak at Ŏph′rah, which belonged to Jō′ăsh the Ā·bĭ·ĕz′-rīte, as his son Gideon was beating out wheat in the wine press, to hide it from the Mĭd′ĭ·a·nītes. ¹²And the angel of the Lord appeared to him and said to him, "The Lord is with you, you mighty man of valor." ¹³And Gideon said to him, "Pray, sir, if the Lord is with us, why then has all this befallen us? And where are all his wonderful deeds which our fathers recounted to us, saying, 'Did not the Lord bring us up from Egypt?' But now the Lord has cast us off, and given us into the hand of Mĭd′ĭ·an." ¹⁴And the Lord turned to him and said, "Go in this might of yours and deliver Israel from the hand of Mĭd′ĭ·an; do not I send you?" ¹⁵And he said to him, "Pray, Lord, how can I deliver Israel? Behold, my clan is the weakest in Ma·năs′seh, and I am the least in my family." ¹⁶And the Lord said to him, "But I will be with you, and you shall smite the Mĭd′ĭ·a·nītes as one man." ¹⁷And he said to him, "If now I have found favor with thee, then show me a sign that it is thou who speakest with me. ¹⁸Do not depart from here, I pray thee, until I come to thee, and bring out my present, and set it before thee." And he said, "I will stay till you return."

19 So Gideon went into his house and prepared a kid, and unleavened cakes from an ephah of flour; the meat he put in a basket, and the broth he put in a pot, and brought them to him under the oak and presented them. ²⁰And the angel of God said to him, "Take the meat and the unleavened cakes, and put them on this rock, and pour the broth over them." And he did so. ²¹Then the angel of the Lord reached out the tip of the staff that was in his hand, and touched the meat and the unleavened cakes; and there sprang up fire from the rock and consumed the flesh and the unleavened cakes; and the angel of the Lord vanished from his sight. ²²Then Gideon perceived that he was the angel of the Lord; and Gideon said, "Alas, O Lord God! For now I have seen the angel of the Lord face to face." ²³But the Lord said to him, "Peace be to you; do not

fear, you shall not die." ²⁴Then Gideon built an altar there to the Lord, and called it, The Lord is peace. To this day it still stands at Ŏph′rah, which belongs to the Ā·bĭ·ĕz′rītes.

25 That night the Lord said to him, "Take your father's bull, the second bull seven years old, and pull down the altar of Bā′al which your father has, and cut down the A·shē′rah that is beside it; ²⁶and build an altar to the Lord your God on the top of the stronghold here, with stones laid in due order; then take the second bull, and offer it as a burnt offering with the wood of the A·shē′rah which you shall cut down." ²⁷So Gideon took ten men of his servants, and did as the Lord had told him; but because he was too afraid of his family and the men of the town to do it by day, he did it by night.

28 When the men of the town rose early in the morning, behold, the altar of Bā′al was broken down, and the A·shē′rah beside it was cut down, and the second bull was offered upon the altar which had been built. ²⁹And they said to one another, "Who has done this thing?" And after they had made search and inquired, they said, "Gideon the son of Jō′ăsh has done this thing." ³⁰Then the men of the town said to Jō′ăsh, "Bring out your son, that he may die, for he has pulled down the altar of Bā′al and cut down the A·shē′-rah beside it." ³¹But Jō′ăsh said to all who were arrayed against him, "Will you contend for Bā′al? Or will you defend his cause? Whoever contends for him shall be put to death by morning. If he is a god, let him contend for himself, because his altar has been pulled down." ³²Therefore on that day he was called Jĕr·ŭb·bā′al, that is to say, "Let Bā′al contend against him," because he pulled down his altar.

33 Then all the Mĭd′ĭ·a·nītes and the A·măl′e·kītes and the people of the East came together, and crossing the Jordan they encamped in the Valley of Jĕz′rē·el. ³⁴But the Spirit of the Lord took possession of Gideon; and he sounded the trumpet, and the Ā·bĭ·ĕz′-rītes were called out to follow him. ³⁵And he sent messengers throughout all Ma·năs′seh; and they too were called out to follow him. And he sent messengers to Ăsh′er, Zĕb′u·lun, and Năph′ta·lī; and they went up to meet them.

36 Then Gideon said to God, "If thou wilt deliver Israel by my hand, as thou hast said, ³⁷ behold, I am laying a fleece of wool on the threshing floor; if there is dew on the fleece alone, and it is dry on all the ground, then I shall know that thou wilt deliver Israel by my hand, as thou hast said." ³⁸ And it was so. When he rose early next morning and squeezed the fleece, he wrung enough dew from the fleece to fill a bowl with water. ³⁹ Then Gideon said to God, "Let not thy anger burn against me, let me speak but this once; pray, let me make trial only this once with the fleece; pray, let it be dry only on the fleece, and on all the ground let there be dew." ⁴⁰ And God did so that night; for it was dry on the fleece only, and on all the ground there was dew.

7 Then Jĕr·ŭb·bā′al (that is, Gideon) and all the people who were with him rose early and encamped beside the spring of Hăr′ŏd; and the camp of Mĭd′ĭ·an was north of them, by the hill of Mō′rĕh, in the valley.

2 The LORD said to Gideon, "The people with you are too many for me to give the Mĭd′ĭ·a·nītes into their hand, lest Israel vaunt themselves against me, saying, 'My own hand has delivered me.' ³ Now therefore proclaim in the ears of the people, saying, 'Whoever is fearful and trembling, let him return home.' " And Gideon tested them;ⁱ twenty-two thousand returned, and ten thousand remained.

4 And the LORD said to Gideon, "The people are still too many; take them down to the water and I will test them for you there; and he of whom I say to you, 'This man shall go with you,' shall go with you; and any of whom I say to you, 'This man shall not go with you,' shall not go." ⁵ So he brought the people down to the water; and the LORD said to Gideon, "Every one that laps the water with his tongue, as a dog laps, you shall set by himself; likewise every one that kneels down to drink." ⁶ And the number of those that lapped, putting their hands to their mouths, was three hundred men; but all the rest of the people knelt down to drink water. ⁷ And the LORD said to Gideon, "With the three hundred men that lapped I will deliver you and give the Mĭd′ĭ·a·nītes into your hand; and let all the others go every man to his home." ʲ So he took the jars of the people from their

hands,ʲ and their trumpets; and he sent all the rest of Israel every man to his tent, but retained the three hundred men; and the camp of Mĭd′ĭ·an was below him in the valley.

9 That same night the LORD said to him, "Arise, go down against the camp; for I have given it into your hand. ¹⁰ But if you fear to go down, go down to the camp with Pū′rah your servant; ¹¹ and you shall hear what they say, and afterward your hands shall be strengthened to go down against the camp." Then he went down with Pū′rah his servant to the outposts of the armed men that were in the camp. ¹² And the Mĭd′ĭ·a·nītes and the A·māl′e·kītes and all the people of the East lay along the valley like locusts for multitude; and their camels were without number, as the sand which is upon the seashore for multitude. ¹³ When Gideon came, behold, a man was telling a dream to his comrade; and he said, "Behold, I dreamed a dream; and lo, a cake of barley bread tumbled into the camp of Mĭd′ĭ·an, and came to the tent, and struck it so that it fell, and turned it upside down, so that the tent lay flat." ¹⁴ And his comrade answered, "This is no other than the sword of Gideon the son of Jō′ăsh, a man of Israel; into his hand God has given Mĭd′ĭ·an and all the host."

15 When Gideon heard the telling of the dream and its interpretation, he worshiped; and he returned to the camp of Israel, and said, "Arise; for the LORD has given the host of Mĭd′ĭ·an into your hand." ¹⁶ And he divided the three hundred men into three companies, and put trumpets into the hands of all of them and empty jars, with torches inside the jars. ¹⁷ And he said to them, "Look at me, and do likewise; when I come to the outskirts of the camp, do as I do. ¹⁸ When I blow the trumpet, I and all who are with me, then blow the trumpets also on every side of all the camp, and shout, 'For the LORD and for Gideon.' "

19 So Gideon and the hundred men who were with him came to the outskirts of the camp at the beginning of the middle watch, when they had just set the watch; and they blew the trumpets and smashed the jars that were in their hands. ²⁰ And the three companies

---

ⁱCn: Heb *and depart from Mount Gilead*
ʲCn: Heb *the people took provisions in their hands*

blew the trumpets and broke the jars, holding in their left hands the torches, and in their right hands the trumpets to blow; and they cried, "A sword for the LORD and for Gideon!" ²¹They stood every man in his place round about the camp, and all the army ran; they cried out and fled. ²²When they blew the three hundred trumpets, the LORD set every man's sword against his fellow and against all the army; and the army fled as far as Bĕth-shĭt'-tah toward Zēr'ĕ-rah,ᵏ as far as the border of Ā-bĕl-mĕ-hō'lah, by Tăb'băth. ²³And the men of Israel were called out from Năph'ta-lī and from Ăsh'ĕr and from all Ma-năs'seh, and they pursued after Mĭd'ī-an.

24 And Gideon sent messengers throughout all the hill country of Ē'phra-ĭm, saying, "Come down against the Mĭd'ī-a-nītes and seize the waters against them, as far as Bĕth-bār'ah, and also the Jordan." So all the men of Ephraim were called out, and they seized the waters as far as Beth-barah, and also the Jordan. ²⁵And they took the two princes of Mĭd'ī-an, Ŏr'ĕb and Zē'ĕb; they killed Oreb at the rock of Oreb, and Zeeb they killed at the wine press of Zeeb, as they pursued Midian; and they brought the heads of Oreb and Zeeb to Gideon beyond the Jordan.

8 And the men of Ē'phra-ĭm said to him, "What is this that you have done to us, not to call us when you went to fight with Mĭd'ī-an?" And they upbraided him violently. ²And he said to them, "What have I done now in comparison with you? Is not the gleaning of the grapes of Ē'phra-ĭm better than the vintage of Ā'bĭ-ē'zer? ³God has given into your hands the princes of Mĭd'ī-an, Ŏr'ĕb and Zē'ĕb; what have I been able to do in comparison with you?" Then their anger against him was abated, when he had said this.

4 And Gideon came to the Jordan and passed over, he and the three hundred men who were with him, faint yet pursuing. ⁵So he said to the men of Sŭc'cŏth, "Pray, give loaves of bread to the people who follow me; for they are faint, and I am pursuing after Zē'-bah and Zăl-mŭn'na, the kings of Mĭd'ī-an." ⁶And the officials of Sŭc'-cŏth said, "Are Zē'bah and Zăl-mŭn'na already in your hand, that we should give bread to your army?" ⁷And Gideon

said, "Well then, when the LORD has given Zē'bah and Zăl-mŭn'na into my hand, I will flail your flesh with the thorns of the wilderness and with briers." ⁸And from there he went up to Pĕ-nū'ĕl, and spoke to them in the same way; and the men of Penuel answered him as the men of Sŭc'cŏth had answered. ⁹And he said to the men of Pĕ-nū'ĕl, "When I come again in peace, I will break down this tower."

10 Now Zē'bah and Zăl-mŭn'na were in Kăr'kôr with their army, about fifteen thousand men, all who were left of all the army of the people of the East; for there had fallen a hundred and twenty thousand men who drew the sword. ¹¹And Gideon went up by the caravan route east of Nō'bah and Jŏg'bĕ-hah, and attacked the army; for the army was off its guard. ¹²And Zē'bah and Zăl-mŭn'na fled; and he pursued them and took the two kings of Mĭd'ī-an, Zebah and Zalmunna, and he threw all the army into a panic.

13 Then Gideon the son of Jō'ăsh returned from the battle by the ascent of Hē'rēṣ. ¹⁴And he caught a young man of Sŭc'cŏth, and questioned him; and he wrote down for him the officials and elders of Succoth, seventy-seven men. ¹⁵And he came to the men of Sŭc'cŏth, and said, "Behold Zē'bah and Zăl-mŭn'na, about whom you taunted me, saying, 'Are Zebah and Zalmunna already in your hand, that we should give bread to your men who are faint?' " ¹⁶And he took the elders of the city and he took thorns of the wilderness and briers and with them taught the men of Sŭc'cŏth. ¹⁷And he broke down the tower of Pĕ-nū'ĕl, and slew the men of the city.

18 Then he said to Zē'bah and Zăl-mŭn'na, "Where are the men whom you slew at Tā'bôr?" They answered, "As you are, so were they, every one of them; they resembled the sons of a king." ¹⁹And he said, "They were my brothers, the sons of my mother; as the LORD lives, if you had saved them alive, I would not slay you." ²⁰And he said to Jē'ther his first-born, "Rise, and slay them." But the youth did not draw his sword; for he was afraid, because he was still a youth. ²¹Then Zē'bah and Zăl-mŭn'na said, "Rise yourself, and fall upon us; for as the man is, so is his strength." And Gideon arose and slew

ᵏAnother reading is *Zeredah*

Zebah and Zalmunna; and he took the crescents that were on the necks of their camels.

22 Then the men of Israel said to Gideon, "Rule over us, you and your son and your grandson also; for you have delivered us out of the hand of Mĭd'ĭ-an." 23 Gideon said to them, "I will not rule over you, and my son will not rule over you; the LORD will rule over you." 24 And Gideon said to them, "Let me make a request of you; give me every man of you the earrings of his spoil." (For they had golden earrings, because they were Ĭsh'ma-ĕl-ītes.) 25 And they answered, "We will willingly give them." And they spread a garment, and every man cast in it the earrings of his spoil. 26 And the weight of the golden earrings that he requested was one thousand seven hundred shekels of gold; besides the crescents and the pendants and the purple garments worn by the kings of Mĭd'ĭ-an, and besides the collars that were about the necks of their camels. 27 And Gideon made an ephod of it and put it in his city, in Ŏph'rah; and all Israel played the harlot after it there, and it became a snare to Gideon and to his family. 28 So Mĭd'ĭ-an was subdued before the people of Israel, and they lifted up their heads no more. And the land had rest forty years in the days of Gideon.

29 Jĕr-ŭb-bā'al the son of Jō'ash went and dwelt in his own house. 30 Now Gideon had seventy sons, his own offspring, for he had many wives. 31 And his concubine who was in Shē'chĕm also bore him a son, and he called his name A-bĭm'e-lĕch. 32 And Gideon the son of Jō'ash died in a good old age, and was buried in the tomb of Jō'ash his father, at Ŏph'rah of the A-bĭ-ĕz'rītes.

33 As soon as Gideon died, the people of Israel turned again and played the harlot after the Bā'als, and made Bā'al-bē'rĭth their god. 34 And the people of Israel did not remember the LORD their God, who had rescued them from the hand of all their enemies on every side; 35 and they did not show kindness to the family of Jĕr-ŭb-bā'al (that is, Gideon) in return for all the good that he had done to Israel.

9 Now A-bĭm'e-lĕch the son of Jĕr-ŭb-bā'al went to Shē'chĕm to his mother's kinsmen and said to them and to the whole clan of his mother's family, 2 "Say in the ears of all the citizens of Shē'chĕm, 'Which is better for you, that all seventy of the sons of Jĕr-ŭb-bā'al rule over you, or that one rule over you?' Remember also that I am your bone and your flesh." 3 And his mother's kinsmen spoke all these words on his behalf in the ears of all the men of Shē'chĕm; and their hearts inclined to follow A-bĭm'e-lĕch, for they said, "He is our brother." 4 And they gave him seventy pieces of silver out of the house of Bā'al-bē'rĭth with which A-bĭm'e-lĕch hired worthless and reckless fellows, who followed him. 5 And he went to his father's house at Ŏph'rah, and slew his brothers the sons of Jĕr-ŭb-bā'al, seventy men, upon one stone; but Jō'-tham the youngest son of Jerubbaal was left, for he hid himself. 6 And all the citizens of Shē'chĕm came together, and all Bĕth-mĭl'lō, and they went and made A-bĭm'e-lĕch king, by the oak of the pillar at Shechem.

7 When it was told to Jō'tham, he went and stood on the top of Mount Gĕr'ĭ-zĭm, and cried aloud and said to them, "Listen to me, you men of Shē'-chĕm, that God may listen to you. 8 The trees once went forth to anoint a king over them; and they said to the olive tree, 'Reign over us.' 9 But the olive tree said to them, 'Shall I leave my fatness, by which gods and men are honored, and go to sway over the trees?' 10 And the trees said to the fig tree, 'Come you, and reign over us.' 11 But the fig tree said to them, 'Shall I leave my sweetness and my good fruit, and go to sway over the trees?' 12 And the trees said to the vine, 'Come you, and reign over us.' 13 But the vine said to them, 'Shall I leave my wine which cheers gods and men, and go to sway over the trees?' 14 Then all the trees said to the bramble, 'Come you, and reign over us.' 15 And the bramble said to the trees, 'If in good faith you are anointing me king over you, then come and take refuge in my shade; but if not, let fire come out of the bramble and devour the cedars of Lebanon.'

16 "Now therefore, if you acted in good faith and honor when you made A-bĭm'e-lĕch king, and if you have dealt well with Jĕr-ŭb-bā'al and his house, and have done to him as his deeds deserved — 17 for my father

fought for you, and risked his life, and rescued you from the hand of Mĭd'ĭ·an; [18] and you have risen up against my father's house this day, and have slain his sons, seventy men on one stone, and have made A·bĭm'e·lĕch, the son of his maidservant, king over the citizens of Shē'chĕm, because he is your kinsman — [19] if you then have acted in good faith and honor with Jĕr·ŭb·bā'al and with his house this day, then rejoice in A·bĭm'e·lĕch, and let him also rejoice in you; [20] but if not, let fire come out from A·bĭm'e·lĕch, and devour the citizens of Shē'chĕm, and Bĕth–mĭl'lō; and let fire come out from the citizens of Shechem, and from Beth–millo, and devour Abimelech." [21] And Jō'tham ran away and fled, and went to Bē'er and dwelt there, for fear of A·bĭm'e·lĕch his brother.

22 A·bĭm'e·lĕch ruled over Israel three years. [23] And God sent an evil spirit between A·bĭm'e·lĕch and the men of Shē'chĕm; and the men of Shechem dealt treacherously with Abimelech; [24] that the violence done to the seventy sons of Jĕr·ŭb·bā'al might come and their blood be laid upon A·bĭm'e·lĕch their brother, who slew them, and upon the men of Shē'chĕm, who strengthened his hands to slay his brothers. [25] And the men of Shē'chĕm put men in ambush against him on the mountain tops, and they robbed all who passed by them along that way; and it was told A·bĭm'e·lĕch.

26 And Gā'al the son of Ē'bĕd moved into Shē'chĕm with his kinsmen; and the men of Shechem put confidence in him. [27] And they went out into the field, and gathered the grapes from their vineyards and trod them, and held festival, and went into the house of their god, and ate and drank and reviled A·bĭm'e·lĕch. [28] And Gā'al the son of Ē'bĕd said, "Who is A·bĭm'e·lĕch, and who are we of Shē'chĕm, that we should serve him? Did not the son of Jĕr·ŭb·bā'al and Zē'bŭl his officer serve the men of Hā'môr the father of Shechem? Why then should we serve him? [29] Would that this people were under my hand! then I would remove A·bĭm'e·lĕch. I would say[l] to Abimelech, 'Increase your army, and come out.'"

30 When Zē'bŭl the ruler of the city heard the words of Gā'al the son of Ē'bĕd, his anger was kindled. [31] And he sent messengers to A·bĭm'e·lĕch at A·rü'mah,[m] saying, "Behold, Gā'al the son of Ē'bĕd and his kinsmen have come to Shē'chĕm, and they are stirring up[n] the city against you. [32] Now therefore, go by night, you and the men that are with you, and lie in wait in the fields. [33] Then in the morning, as soon as the sun is up, rise early and rush upon the city; and when he and the men that are with him come out against you, you may do to them as occasion offers."

34 And A·bĭm'e·lĕch and all the men that were with him rose up by night, and laid wait against Shē'chĕm in four companies. [35] And Gā'al the son of Ē'bĕd went out and stood in the entrance of the gate of the city; and A·bĭm'e·lĕch and the men that were with him rose from the ambush. [36] And when Gā'al saw the men, he said to Zē'bŭl, "Look, men are coming down from the mountain tops!" And Zebul said to him, "You see the shadow of the mountains as if they were men." [37] Gā'al spoke again and said, "Look, men are coming down from the center of the land, and one company is coming from the direction of the Diviners' Oak." [38] Then Zē'bŭl said to him, "Where is your mouth now, you who said, 'Who is A·bĭm'e·lĕch, that we should serve him?' Are not these the men whom you despised? Go out now and fight with them." [39] And Gā'al went out at the head of the men of Shē'chĕm, and fought with A·bĭm'e·lĕch. [40] And A·bĭm'e·lĕch chased him, and he fled before him; and many fell wounded, up to the entrance of the gate. [41] And A·bĭm'e·lĕch dwelt at A·rü'mah; and Zē'bŭl drove out Gā'al and his kinsmen, so that they could not live on at Shē'chĕm.

42 On the following day the men went out into the fields. And A·bĭm'e·lĕch was told. [43] He took his men and divided them into three companies, and laid wait in the fields; and he looked and saw the men coming out of the city, and he rose against them and slew them. [44] A·bĭm'e·lĕch and the company[o] that was with him rushed forward and stood at the entrance of the gate of the city, while the two companies rushed upon all who were in

[l] Gk: Heb *and he said* [m] Cn See 9.41. Heb *Tormah*
[n] Cn: Heb *besieging*
[o] Vg and some Mss of Gk: Heb *companies*

the fields and slew them. ⁴⁵ And A·bĭm'-ḝ·lĕch fought against the city all that day; he took the city, and killed the people that were in it; and he razed the city and sowed it with salt.

46 When all the people of the Tower of Shē'chĕm heard of it, they entered the stronghold of the house of Ēl-bē'rĭth. ⁴⁷ A·bĭm'ḝ·lĕch was told that all the people of the Tower of Shē'chĕm were gathered together. ⁴⁸ And A·bĭm'-ḝ·lĕch went up to Mount Zăl'mŏn, he and all the men that were with him; and Abimelech took an axe in his hand, and cut down a bundle of brushwood, and took it up and laid it on his shoulder. And he said to the men that were with him, "What you have seen me do, make haste to do, as I have done." ⁴⁹ So every one of the people cut down his bundle and following A·bĭm'ḝ·lĕch put it against the stronghold, and they set the stronghold on fire over them, so that all the people of the Tower of Shē'chĕm also died, about a thousand men and women.

50 Then A·bĭm'ḝ·lĕch went to Thē'-bĕz, and encamped against Thebez, and took it. ⁵¹ But there was a strong tower within the city, and all the people of the city fled to it, all the men and women, and shut themselves in; and they went to the roof of the tower. ⁵² And A·bĭm'ḝ·lĕch came to the tower, and fought against it, and drew near to the door of the tower to burn it with fire. ⁵³ And a certain woman threw an upper millstone upon A·bĭm'ḝ·lĕch's head, and crushed his skull. ⁵⁴ Then he called hastily to the young man his armor-bearer, and said to him, "Draw your sword and kill me, lest men say of me, 'A woman killed him.'" And his young man thrust him through, and he died. ⁵⁵ And when the men of Israel saw that A·bĭm'ḝ·lĕch was dead, they departed every man to his home. ⁵⁶ Thus God requited the crime of A·bĭm'ḝ·lĕch, which he committed against his father in killing his seventy brothers; ⁵⁷ and God also made all the wickedness of the men of Shē'chĕm fall back upon their heads, and upon them came the curse of Jō'thạm the son of Jĕr·ŭb·bā'ạl.

10 After A·bĭm'ḝ·lĕch there arose to deliver Israel Tō'lạ the son of Pü'ạh, son of Dō'dō, a man of Ĭs'-sạ·chär; and he lived at Shā'mĭr in the hill country of Ē'phrạ·ĭm. ² And he judged Israel twenty-three years. Then he died, and was buried at Shā'mĭr.

3 After him arose Jā'ĭr the Gileadite, who judged Israel twenty-two years. ⁴ And he had thirty sons who rode on thirty asses; and they had thirty cities, called Hăv'vŏth–jā'ĭr to this day, which are in the land of Gilead. ⁵ And Jā'ĭr died, and was buried in Kā'mŏn.

6 And the people of Israel again did what was evil in the sight of the LORD, and served the Bā'ạlṣ and the Ăsh'-tạ·rŏth, the gods of Syria, the gods of Sī'dŏn, the gods of Mō'ăb, the gods of the Ăm'mọ·nītes, and the gods of the Phĭ·lĭs'tĭnes; and they forsook the LORD, and did not serve him. ⁷ And the anger of the LORD was kindled against Israel, and he sold them into the hand of the Phĭ·lĭs'tĭnes and into the hand of the Ăm'mọ·nītes, ⁸ and they crushed and oppressed the children of Israel that year. For eighteen years they oppressed all the people of Israel that were beyond the Jordan in the land of the Ăm'ọ·rītes, which is in Gilead. ⁹ And the Ăm'mọ·nītes crossed the Jordan to fight also against Judah and against Benjamin and against the house of Ē'phrạ·ĭm; so that Israel was sorely distressed.

10 And the people of Israel cried to the LORD, saying, "We have sinned against thee, because we have forsaken our God and have served the Bā'ạlṣ." ¹¹ And the LORD said to the people of Israel, "Did I not deliver you from the Egyptians and from the Ăm'-ọ·rītes, from the Ăm'mọ·nītes and from the Phĭ·lĭs'tĭnes? ¹² The Sī·dō'nĭ·ạnṣ also, and the A·mäl'ḝ·kītes, and the Mā'ọ·nītes, oppressed you; and you cried to me, and I delivered you out of their hand. ¹³ Yet you have forsaken me and served other gods; therefore I will deliver you no more. ¹⁴ Go and cry to the gods whom you have chosen; let them deliver you in the time of your distress." ¹⁵ And the people of Israel said to the LORD, "We have sinned; do to us whatever seems good to thee; only deliver us, we pray thee, this day." ¹⁶ So they put away the foreign gods from among them and served the LORD; and he became indignant over the misery of Israel.

17 Then the Ăm'mọ·nītes were called to arms, and they encamped in Gilead; and the people of Israel came together, and they encamped at Mĭz'-

pah. [18] And the people, the leaders of Gilead, said one to another, "Who is the man that will begin to fight against the Ăm'mọ·nītes? He shall be head over all the inhabitants of Gilead."

11 Now Jĕph'thạh the Gileadite was a mighty warrior, but he was the son of a harlot. Gilead was the father of Jephthah. [2] And Gilead's wife also bore him sons; and when his wife's sons grew up, they thrust Jĕph'thạh out, and said to him, "You shall not inherit in our father's house; for you are the son of another woman." [3] Then Jĕph'thạh fled from his brothers, and dwelt in the land of Tŏb; and worthless fellows collected round Jephthah, and went raiding with him.

4 After a time the Ăm'mọ·nītes made war against Israel. [5] And when the Ăm'mọ·nītes made war against Israel, the elders of Gilead went to bring Jĕph'thạh from the land of Tŏb; [6] and they said to Jĕph'thạh, "Come and be our leader, that we may fight with the Ăm'mọ·nītes." [7] But Jĕph'thạh said to the elders of Gilead, "Did you not hate me, and drive me out of my father's house? Why have you come to me now when you are in trouble?" [8] And the elders of Gilead said to Jĕph'thạh, "That is why we have turned to you now, that you may go with us and fight with the Ăm'mọ·nītes, and be our head over all the inhabitants of Gilead." [9] Jĕph'thạh said to the elders of Gilead, "If you bring me home again to fight with the Ăm'mọ·nītes, and the LORD gives them over to me, I will be your head." [10] And the elders of Gilead said to Jĕph'thạh, "The LORD will be witness between us; we will surely do as you say." [11] So Jĕph'thạh went with the elders of Gilead, and the people made him head and leader over them; and Jephthah spoke all his words before the LORD at Mĭz'pạh.

12 Then Jĕph'thạh sent messengers to the king of the Ăm'mọ·nītes and said, "What have you against me, that you have come to me to fight against my land?" [13] And the king of the Ăm'mọ·nītes answered the messengers of Jĕph'thạh, "Because Israel on coming from Egypt took away my land, from the Är'nŏn to the Jăb'bọk and to the Jordan; now therefore restore it peaceably." [14] And Jĕph'thạh sent messengers again to the king of the Ăm'mọ·nītes [15] and said to him, "Thus says Jĕph'thạh: Israel did not take away the land of Mō'äb or the land of the Ăm'mọ·nītes, [16] but when they came up from Egypt, Israel went through the wilderness to the Red Sea and came to Kā'dĕsh. [17] Israel then sent messengers to the king of Ē'dọm, saying, 'Let us pass, we pray, through your land'; but the king of Edom would not listen. And they sent also to the king of Mō'äb, but he would not consent. So Israel remained at Kā'dĕsh. [18] Then they journeyed through the wilderness, and went around the land of Ē'dọm and the land of Mō'äb, and arrived on the east side of the land of Moab, and camped on the other side of the Är'nŏn; but they did not enter the territory of Moab, for the Arnon was the boundary of Moab. [19] Israel then sent messengers to Sī'hon king of the Ăm'ọ·rītes, king of Hĕsh'bọn; and Israel said to him, 'Let us pass, we pray, through your land to our country.' [20] But Sī'hon did not trust Israel to pass through his territory; so Sihon gathered all his people together, and encamped at Jā'hăz, and fought with Israel. [21] And the LORD, the God of Israel, gave Sī'hon and all his people into the hand of Israel, and they defeated them; so Israel took possession of all the land of the Ăm'ọ·rītes, who inhabited that country. [22] And they took possession of all the territory of the Ăm'ọ·rītes from the Är'nŏn to the Jăb'bọk and from the wilderness to the Jordan. [23] So then the LORD, the God of Israel, dispossessed the Ăm'ọ·rītes from before his people Israel; and are you to take possession of them? [24] Will you not possess what Chē'mŏsh your god gives you to possess? And all that the LORD our God has dispossessed before us, we will possess. [25] Now are you any better than Bā'lăk the son of Zĭp'pôr, king of Mō'äb? Did he ever strive against Israel, or did he ever go to war with them? [26] While Israel dwelt in Hĕsh'bọn and its villages, and in Ä·rō'er and its villages, and in all the cities that are on the banks of the Är'nŏn, three hundred years, why did you not recover them within that time? [27] I therefore have not sinned against you, and you do me wrong by making war on me; the LORD, the Judge, decide this day between the people of Israel and the people of Ăm'mọn." [28] But the

king of the Ăm′mo·nītes did not heed the message of Jĕph′thạh which he sent to him.

29 Then the Spirit of the LORD came upon Jĕph′thạh, and he passed through Gilead and Mạ·năs′sẹh, and passed on to Mīz′pạh of Gilead, and from Mizpah of Gilead he passed on to the Ăm′mo·nītes. ³⁰And Jĕph′thạh made a vow to the LORD, and said, "If thou wilt give the Ăm′mo·nītes into my hand, ³¹then whoever comes forth from the doors of my house to meet me, when I return victorious from the Ăm′mo·nītes, shall be the LORD's, and I will offer him up for a burnt offering." ³²So Jĕph′thạh crossed over to the Ăm′mo·nītes to fight against them; and the LORD gave them into his hand. ³³And he smote them from Ạ·rō′ẹr to the neighborhood of Mĭn′nĭth, twenty cities, and as far as Ā′bẹl-kēr′ạ·mĭm, with a very great slaughter. So the Ăm′mo·nītes were subdued before the people of Israel.

34 Then Jĕph′thạh came to his home at Mīz′pạh; and behold, his daughter came out to meet him with timbrels and with dances; she was his only child; beside her he had neither son nor daughter. ³⁵And when he saw her, he rent his clothes, and said, "Alas, my daughter! you have brought me very low, and you have become the cause of great trouble to me; for I have opened my mouth to the LORD, and I cannot take back my vow." ³⁶And she said to him, "My father, if you have opened your mouth to the LORD, do to me according to what has gone forth from your mouth, now that the LORD has avenged you on your enemies, on the Ăm′mo·nītes." ³⁷And she said to her father, "Let this thing be done for me; let me alone two months, that I may go and wanderᵖ on the mountains, and bewail my virginity, I and my companions." ³⁸And he said, "Go." And he sent her away for two months; and she departed, she and her companions, and bewailed her virginity upon the mountains. ³⁹And at the end of two months, she returned to her father, who did with her according to his vow which he had made. She had never known a man. And it became a custom in Israel ⁴⁰that the daughters of Israel went year by year to lament the daughter of Jĕph′thạh the Gileadite four days in the year.

12 The men of Ē′phrạ·ĭm were called to arms, and they crossed to Zā′phŏn and said to Jĕph′thạh, "Why did you cross over to fight against the Ăm′mo·nītes, and did not call us to go with you? We will burn your house over you with fire." ²And Jĕph′thạh said to them, "I and my people had a great feud with the Ăm′mo·nītes; and when I called you, you did not deliver me from their hand. ³And when I saw that you would not deliver me, I took my life in my hand, and crossed over against the Ăm′mo·nītes, and the LORD gave them into my hand; why then have you come up to me this day, to fight against me?" ⁴Then Jĕph′thạh gathered all the men of Gilead and fought with Ē′phrạ·ĭm; and the men of Gilead smote Ephraim, because they said, "You are fugitives of Ephraim, you Gileadites, in the midst of Ephraim and Mạ·năs′sẹh." ⁵And the Gileadites took the fords of the Jordan against the Ē′phrạ·ĭm·ītes. And when any of the fugitives of Ē′phrạ·ĭm said, "Let me go over," the men of Gilead said to him, "Are you an Ephraimite?" When he said, "No," ⁶they said to him, "Then say Shĭb′bo·lẹth," and he said, "Sĭb′bo·lĕth," for he could not pronounce it right; then they seized him and slew him at the fords of the Jordan. And there fell at that time forty-two thousand of the Ē′phrạ·ĭm·ītes.

7 Jĕph′thạh judged Israel six years. Then Jephthah the Gileadite died, and was buried in his city in Gileadᑫ.

8 After him Ĭb′zăn of Bethlehem judged Israel. ⁹He had thirty sons; and thirty daughters he gave in marriage outside his clan, and thirty daughters he brought in from outside for his sons. And he judged Israel seven years. ¹⁰Then Ĭb′zăn died, and was buried at Bethlehem.

11 After him Ē′lŏn the Zĕb′ū·lu·nīte judged Israel; and he judged Israel ten years. ¹²Then Ē′lŏn the Zĕb′ū·lu·nīte died, and was buried at Aī′jạ·lŏn in the land of Zĕb′ū·lụn.

13 After him Ăb′dŏn the son of Hĭl′lĕl the Pīr′ạ·tho·nīte judged Israel. ¹⁴He had forty sons and thirty grandsons, who rode on seventy asses; and he judged Israel eight years. ¹⁵Then Ăb′dŏn the son of Hĭl′lĕl the Pīr′ạ·tho·nīte died, and was buried at

ᵖCn: Heb *go down*
ᑫGk: Heb *in the cities of Gilead*

Pĭr′a·thŏn in the land of Ē′phra̧·ĭm, in the hill country of the A̧·măl′ȩ·kītes.

13 And the people of Israel again did what was evil in the sight of the LORD; and the LORD gave them into the hand of the Phĭ·lĭs′tĭnes for forty years.

2 And there was a certain man of Zō′ra̧h, of the tribe of the Dä′nītes, whose name was Ma̧·nō′ăh; and his wife was barren and had no children. ³And the angel of the LORD appeared to the woman and said to her, "Behold, you are barren and have no children; but you shall conceive and bear a son. ⁴Therefore beware, and drink no wine or strong drink, and eat nothing unclean, ⁵for lo, you shall conceive and bear a son. No razor shall come upon his head, for the boy shall be a Năz′-ĭ·rīte to God from birth; and he shall begin to deliver Israel from the hand the Phĭ·lĭs′tĭnes." ⁶Then the woman came and told her husband, "A man of God came to me, and his countenance was like the countenance of the angel of God, very terrible; I did not ask him whence he was, and he did not tell me his name; ⁷but he said to me, 'Behold, you shall conceive and bear a son; so then drink no wine or strong drink, and eat nothing unclean, for the boy shall be a Năz′ĭ·rīte to God from birth to the day of his death.'"

8 Then Ma̧·nō′ăh entreated the LORD, and said, "O, LORD, I pray thee, let the man of God whom thou didst send come again to us, and teach us what we are to do with the boy that will be born." ⁹And God listened to the voice of Ma̧·nō′ăh, and the angel of God came again to the woman as she sat in the field; but Manoah her husband was not with her. ¹⁰And the woman ran in haste and told her husband, "Behold, the man who came to me the other day has appeared to me." ¹¹And Ma̧·nō′ăh arose and went after his wife, and came to the man and said to him, "Are you the man who spoke to this woman?" And he said, "I am." ¹²And Ma̧·nō′ăh said, "Now when your words come true, what is to be the boy's manner of life, and what is he to do?" ¹³And the angel of the LORD said to Ma̧·nō′ăh, "Of all that I said to the woman let her beware. ¹⁴She may not eat of anything that comes from the vine, neither let her drink wine or strong drink, or eat any unclean thing;

all that I commanded her let her observe."

15 Ma̧·nō′ăh said to the angel of the LORD, "Pray, let us detain you, and prepare a kid for you." ¹⁶And the angel of the LORD said to Ma̧·nō′ăh, "If you detain me, I will not eat of your food; but if you make ready a burnt offering, then offer it to the LORD." (For Manoah did not know that he was the angel of the LORD.) ¹⁷And Ma̧·nō′ăh said to the angel of the LORD, "What is your name, so that, when your words come true, we may honor you?" ¹⁸And the angel of the LORD said to him, "Why do you ask my name, seeing it is wonderful?" ¹⁹So Ma̧·nō′ăh took the kid with the cereal offering, and offered it upon the rock to the LORD, to him who works^r wonders.^s ²⁰And when the flame went up toward heaven from the altar, the angel of the LORD ascended in the flame of the altar while Ma̧·nō′ăh and his wife looked on; and they fell on their faces to the ground.

21 The angel of the LORD appeared no more to Ma̧·nō′ăh and to his wife. Then Manoah knew that he was the angel of the LORD. ²²And Ma̧·nō′ăh said to his wife, "We shall surely die, for we have seen God." ²³But his wife said to him, "If the LORD had meant to kill us, he would not have accepted a burnt offering and a cereal offering at our hands, or shown us all these things, or now announced to us such things as these." ²⁴And the woman bore a son, and called his name Samson; and the boy grew, and the LORD blessed him. ²⁵And the Spirit of the LORD began to stir him in Mā′ha̧·neh-dăn, between Zō′ra̧h and Ĕsh′tā-ŏl.

14 Samson went down to Tĭm′nah, and at Timnah he saw one of the daughters of the Phĭ·lĭs′tĭnes. ²Then he came up, and told his father and mother, "I saw one of the daughters of the Phĭ·lĭs′tĭnes at Tĭm′nah; now get her for me as my wife." ³But his father and mother said to him, "Is there not a woman among the daughters of your kinsmen, or among all our people, that you must go to take a wife from the uncircumcised Phĭ·lĭs′tĭnes?" But Samson said to his father, "Get her for me; for she pleases me well."

^rGk Vg: Heb *and working*
^sHeb *wonders, while Manoah and his wife looked on*
13.4, 5: Lk 1.15.   **13.24:** Lk 2.40.

4 His father and mother did not know that it was from the LORD; for he was seeking an occasion against the Phĭ·lĭs'tĭnes. At that time the Philistines had dominion over Israel.

5 Then Samson went down with his father and mother to Tĭm'nah, and he came to the vineyards of Timnah. And behold, a young lion roared against him; 6 and the Spirit of the LORD came mightily upon him, and he tore the lion asunder as one tears a kid; and he had nothing in his hand. But he did not tell his father or his mother what he had done. 7 Then he went down and talked with the woman; and she pleased Samson well. 8 And after a while he returned to take her; and he turned aside to see the carcass of the lion, and behold, there was a swarm of bees in the body of the lion, and honey. 9 He scraped it out into his hands, and went on, eating as he went; and he came to his father and mother, and gave some to them, and they ate. But he did not tell them that he had taken the honey from the carcass of the lion.

10 And his father went down to the woman, and Samson made a feast there; for so the young men used to do. 11 And when the people saw him, they brought thirty companions to be with him. 12 And Samson said to them, "Let me now put a riddle to you; if you can tell me what it is, within the seven days of the feast, and find it out, then I will give you thirty linen garments and thirty festal garments; 13 but if you cannot tell me what it is, then you shall give me thirty linen garments and thirty festal garments." And they said to him, "Put your riddle, that we may hear it." 14 And he said to them,

"Out of the eater came something to eat.
Out of the strong came something sweet."

And they could not in three days tell what the riddle was.

15 On the fourth[f] day they said to Samson's wife, "Entice your husband to tell us what the riddle is, lest we burn you and your father's house with fire. Have you invited us here to impoverish us?" 16 And Samson's wife wept before him, and said, "You only hate me, you do not love me; you have put a riddle to my countrymen, and you

have not told me what it is." And he said to her, "Behold, I have not told my father nor my mother, and shall I tell you?" 17 She wept before him the seven days that their feast lasted; and on the seventh day he told her, because she pressed him hard. Then she told the riddle to her countrymen. 18 And the men of the city said to him on the seventh day before the sun went down,

"What is sweeter than honey?
What is stronger than a lion?"

And he said to them,

"If you had not plowed with my heifer,
you would not have found out my riddle."

19 And the Spirit of the LORD came mightily upon him, and he went down to Ash'ke·lŏn and killed thirty men of the town, and took their spoil and gave the festal garments to those who had told the riddle. In hot anger he went back to his father's house. 20 And Samson's wife was given to his companion, who had been his best man.

15 After a while, at the time of wheat harvest, Samson went to visit his wife with a kid; and he said, "I will go in to my wife in the chamber." But her father would not allow him to go in. 2 And her father said, "I really thought that you utterly hated her; so I gave her to your companion. Is not her younger sister fairer than she? Pray take her instead." 3 And Samson said to them, "This time I shall be blameless in regard to the Phĭ·lĭs'tĭnes, when I do them mischief." 4 So Samson went and caught three hundred foxes, and took torches; and he turned them tail to tail, and put a torch between each pair of tails. 5 And when he had set fire to the torches, he let the foxes go into the standing grain of the Phĭ·lĭs'tĭnes, and burned up the shocks and the standing grain, as well as the olive orchards. 6 Then the Phĭ·lĭs'tĭnes said, "Who has done this?" And they said, "Samson, the son-in-law of the Tĭm'nĭte, because he has taken his wife and given her to his companion." And the Philistines came up, and burned her and her father with fire. 7 And Samson said to them, "If this is what you do, I swear I will be avenged upon you, and after that I will quit." 8 And he smote them hip and thigh with great

f Gk Syr: Heb *seventh*

slaughter; and he went down and stayed in the cleft of the rock of Ē'tăm.

9 Then the Phĭ·lĭs'tĭnes came up and encamped in Judah, and made a raid on Lē'hī. ¹⁰And the men of Judah said, "Why have you come up against us?" They said, "We have come up to bind Samson, to do to him as he did to us." ¹¹Then three thousand men of Judah went down to the cleft of the rock of Ē'tăm, and said to Samson, "Do you not know that the Phĭ·lĭs'tĭnes are rulers over us? What then is this that you have done to us?" And he said to them, "As they did to me, so have I done to them." ¹²And they said to him, "We have come down to bind you, that we may give you into the hands of the Phĭ·lĭs'tĭnes." And Samson said to them, "Swear to me that you will not fall upon me yourselves." ¹³They said to him, "No; we will only bind you and give you into their hands; we will not kill you." So they bound him with two new ropes, and brought him up from the rock.

14 When he came to Lē'hī, the Phĭ·lĭs'tĭnes came shouting to meet him; and the Spirit of the LORD came mightily upon him, and the ropes which were on his arms became as flax that has caught fire, and his bonds melted off his hands. ¹⁵And he found a fresh jawbone of an ass, and put out his hand and seized it, and with it he slew a thousand men. ¹⁶And Samson said,
"With the jawbone of an ass,
  heaps upon heaps,
  with the jawbone of an ass
  have I slain a thousand men."
¹⁷When he had finished speaking, he threw away the jawbone out of his hand; and that place was called Rā'-măth-lē'hī.ᵘ

18 And he was very thirsty, and he called on the LORD and said, "Thou hast granted this great deliverance by the hand of thy servant; and shall I now die of thirst, and fall into the hands of the uncircumcised?" ¹⁹And God split open the hollow place that is at Lē'hī, and there came water from it; and when he drank, his spirit returned, and he revived. Therefore the name of it was called Ĕn-hăk·kôr'ē;ᵛ it is at Lehi to this day. ²⁰And he judged Israel in the days of the Phĭ·lĭs'tĭnes twenty years.

16 Samson went to Gā'za, and there he saw a harlot, and he went in to her. ²The Gā'zītes were told, "Samson has come here," and they surrounded the place and lay in wait for him all night at the gate of the city. They kept quiet all night, saying, "Let us wait till the light of the morning; then we will kill him." ³But Samson lay till midnight, and at midnight he arose and took hold of the doors of the gate of the city and the two posts, and pulled them up, bar and all, and put them on his shoulders and carried them to the top of the hill that is before Hē'brŏn.

4 After this he loved a woman in the valley of Sō'rĕk, whose name was Dē·lī'lah. ⁵And the lords of the Phĭ·lĭs'-tĭnes came to her and said to her, "Entice him, and see wherein his great strength lies, and by what means we may overpower him, that we may bind him to subdue him; and we will each give you eleven hundred pieces of silver." ⁶And Dē·lī'lah said to Samson, "Please tell me wherein your great strength lies, and how you might be bound, that one could subdue you." ⁷And Samson said to her, "If they bind me with seven fresh bowstrings which have not been dried, then I shall become weak, and be like any other man." ⁸Then the lords of the Phĭ·lĭs'-tĭnes brought her seven fresh bowstrings which had not been dried, and she bound him with them. ⁹Now she had men lying in wait in an inner chamber. And she said to him, "The Phĭ·lĭs'tĭnes are upon you, Samson!" But he snapped the bowstrings, as a string of tow snaps when it touches the fire. So the secret of his strength was not known.

10 And Dē·lī'lah said to Samson, "Behold, you have mocked me, and told me lies; please tell me how you might be bound." ¹¹And he said to her, "If they bind me with new ropes that have not been used, then I shall become weak, and be like any other man." ¹²So Dē·lī'lah took new ropes and bound him with them, and said to him, "The Phĭ'lĭs'tĭnes are upon you, Samson!" And the men lying in wait were in an inner chamber. But he snapped the ropes off his arms like a thread.

ᵘ That is *The hill of the jawbone*
ᵛ That is *The spring of him who called*

13 And Dē·lī′lạh said to Samson, "Until now you have mocked me, and told me lies; tell me how you might be bound." And he said to her, "If you weave the seven locks of my head with the web and make it tight with the pin, then I shall become weak, and be like any other man." [14] So while he slept, Dē·lī′lạh took the seven locks of his head and wove them into the web.[w] And she made them tight with the pin, and said to him, "The Phĭ·lĭs′tĭnes are upon you, Samson!" But he awoke from his sleep, and pulled away the pin, the loom, and the web.

15 And she said to him, "How can you say, 'I love you,' when your heart is not with me? You have mocked me these three times, and you have not told me wherein your great strength lies." [16] And when she pressed him hard with her words day after day, and urged him, his soul was vexed to death. [17] And he told her all his mind, and said to her, "A razor has never come upon my head; for I have been a Năz′ị·rīte to God from my mother's womb. If I be shaved, then my strength will leave me, and I shall become weak, and be like any other man."

18 When Dē·lī′lạh saw that he had told her all his mind, she sent and called the lords of the Phĭ·lĭs′tĭnes, saying, "Come up this once, for he has told me all his mind." Then the lords of the Phĭ·lĭs′tĭnes came up to her, and brought the money in their hands. [19] She made him sleep upon her knees; and she called a man, and had him shave off the seven locks of his head. Then she began to torment him, and his strength left him. [20] And she said, "The Phĭ·lĭs·tĭnes are upon you, Samson!" And he awoke from his sleep, and said, "I will go out as at other times, and shake myself free." And he did not know that the LORD had left him. [21] And the Phĭ·lĭs′tĭnes seized him and gouged out his eyes, and brought him down to Gā′zạ, and bound him with bronze fetters; and he ground at the mill in the prison. [22] But the hair of his head began to grow again after it had been shaved.

23 Now the lords of the Phĭ·lĭs′tĭnes gathered to offer a great sacrifice to Dā′gŏn their god, and to rejoice; for they said, "Our god has given Samson our enemy into our hand." [24] And when the people saw him, they praised their god; for they said, "Our god has given our enemy into our hand, the ravager of our country, who has slain many of us." [25] And when their hearts were merry, they said, "Call Samson, that he may make sport for us." So they called Samson out of the prison, and he made sport before them. They made him stand between the pillars; [26] and Samson said to the lad who held him by the hand, "Let me feel the pillars on which the house rests, that I may lean against them." [27] Now the house was full of men and women; all the lords of the Phĭ·lĭs′tĭnes were there, and on the roof there were about three thousand men and women, who looked on while Samson made sport.

28 Then Samson called to the LORD and said, "O Lord GOD, remember me, I pray thee, and strengthen me, I pray thee, only this once, O God, that I may be avenged upon the Phĭ·lĭs′tĭnes for one of my two eyes." [29] And Samson grasped the two middle pillars upon which the house rested, and he leaned his weight upon them, his right hand on the one and his left hand on the other. [30] And Samson said, "Let me die with the Phĭ·lĭs′tĭnes." Then he bowed with all his might; and the house fell upon the lords and upon all the people that were in it. So the dead whom he slew at his death were more than those whom he had slain during his life. [31] Then his brothers and all his family came down and took him and brought him up and buried him between Zō′rạh and Ĕsh′tā–ŏl in the tomb of Mạ·nō′ăh his father. He had judged Israel twenty years.

17 There was a man of the hill country of Ē′phrạ·ĭm, whose name was Mī′cạh. [2] And he said to his mother, "The eleven hundred pieces of silver which were taken from you, about which you uttered a curse, and also spoke it in my ears, behold, the silver is with me; I took it." And his mother said, "Blessed be my son by the LORD." [3] And he restored the eleven hundred pieces of silver to his mother; and his mother said, "I consecrate the silver to the LORD from my hand for my son, to make a graven image and a molten image; now therefore I will restore it to you." [4] So when he restored the money to his mother, his mother

[w] Compare Gk: Heb lacks *and make it tight . . . into the* web

took two hundred pieces of silver, and gave it to the silversmith, who made it into a graven image and a molten image; and it was in the house of Mī′cah. ⁵And the man Mī′cah had a shrine, and he made an ephod and teraphim, and installed one of his sons, who became his priest. ⁶In those days there was no king in Israel; every man did what was right in his own eyes.

7 Now there was a young man of Bethlehem in Judah, of the family of Judah, who was a Lē′vīte; and he sojourned there. ⁸And the man departed from the town of Bethlehem in Judah, to live where he could find a place; and as he journeyed, he came to the hill country of Ē′phra·ĭm to the house of Mī′cah. ⁹And Mī′cah said to him, "From where do you come?" And he said to him, "I am a Lē′vīte of Bethlehem in Judah, and I am going to sojourn where I may find a place." ¹⁰And Mī′cah said to him, "Stay with me, and be to me a father and a priest, and I will give you ten pieces of silver a year, and a suit of apparel, and your living."ʷ ¹¹And the Lē′vīte was content to dwell with the man; and the young man became to him like one of his sons. ¹²And Mī′cah installed the Lē′-vīte, and the young man became his priest, and was in the house of Mī′cah. ¹³Then Mī′cah said, "Now I know that the LORD will prosper me, because I have a Lē′vīte as priest."

18 In those days there was no king in Israel. And in those days the tribe of the Dǎ′nītes was seeking for itself an inheritance to dwell in; for until then no inheritance among the tribes of Israel had fallen to them. ²So the Dǎ′nītes sent five able men from the whole number of their tribe, from Zō′rah and from Ĕsh′tā-ŏl, to spy out the land and to explore it; and they said to them, "Go and explore the land." And they came to the hill country of Ē′phra·ĭm, to the house of Mī′cah, and lodged there. ³When they were by the house of Mī′cah, they recognized the voice of the young Lē′vīte; and they turned aside and said to him, "Who brought you here? What are you doing in this place? What is your business here?" ⁴And he said to them, "Thus and thus has Mī′cah dealt with me: he has hired me, and I have become his priest." ⁵And they said to him, "Inquire of God, we pray

thee, that we may know whether the journey on which we are setting out will succeed." ⁶And the priest said to them, "Go in peace. The journey on which you go is under the eye of the LORD."

7 Then the five men departed, and came to La′ĭsh, and saw the people who were there, how they dwelt in security, after the manner of the Sī-dō′nĭ·ạns, quiet and unsuspecting, lackingˣ nothing that is in the earth, and possessing wealth, and how they were far from the Sidonians and had no dealings with any one. ⁸And when they came to their brethren at Zō′rah and Ĕsh′tā-ŏl, their brethren said to them, "What do you report?" ⁹They said, "Arise, and let us go up against them; for we have seen the land, and behold, it is very fertile. And will you do nothing? Do not be slow to go, and enter in and possess the land. ¹⁰When you go, you will come to an unsuspecting people. The land is broad; yea, God has given it into your hands, a place where there is no lack of anything that is in the earth."

11 And six hundred men of the tribe of Dan, armed with weapons of war, set forth from Zō′rah and Ĕsh′tā-ŏl, ¹²and went up and encamped at Kir′ĭ-ăth-je′a·rĭm in Judah. On this account that place is called Mā′ha·neh-dănʸ to this day; behold, it is west of Kiriath-jearim. ¹³And they passed on from there to the hill country of Ē′phra·ĭm, and came to the house of Mī′cah.

14 Then the five men who had gone to spy out the country of La′ĭsh said to their brethren, "Do you know that in these houses there are an ephod, teraphim, a graven image, and a molten image? Now therefore consider what you will do." ¹⁵And they turned aside thither, and came to the house of the young Lē′vīte, at the home of Mī′cah, and asked him of his welfare. ¹⁶Now the six hundred men of the Dǎ′nītes, armed with their weapons of war, stood by the entrance of the gate; ¹⁷and the five men who had gone to spy out the land went up, and entered and took the graven image, the ephod, the teraphim, and the molten image, while the priest stood by the entrance of the

---

ʷHeb *living, and the Levite went*
ˣCn Compare 18.10. The Hebrew text is uncertain
ʸThat is *Camp of Dan*
18.7: Judg 18.27, 28.

gate with the six hundred men armed with weapons of war. ¹⁸And when these went into Mī′cah's house and took the graven image, the ephod, the teraphim, and the molten image, the priest said to them, "What are you doing?" ¹⁹And they said to him, "Keep quiet, put your hand upon your mouth, and come with us, and be to us a father and a priest. Is it better for you to be priest to the house of one man, or to be priest to a tribe and family in Israel?" ²⁰And the priest's heart was glad; he took the ephod, and the teraphim, and the graven image, and went in the midst of the people.

21 So they turned and departed, putting the little ones and the cattle and the goods in front of them. ²²When they were a good way from the home of Mī′cah, the men who were in the houses near Micah's house were called out, and they overtook the Dă′nītes. ²³And they shouted to the Dă′nītes, who turned round and said to Mī′cah, "What ails you that you come with such a company?" ²⁴And he said, "You take my gods which I made, and the priest, and go away, and what have I left? How then do you ask me, 'What ails you?'" ²⁵And the Dă′nītes said to him, "Do not let your voice be heard among us, lest angry fellows fall upon you, and you lose your life with the lives of your household." ²⁶Then the Dă′nītes went their way; and when Mī′cah saw that they were too strong for him, he turned and went back to his home.

27 And taking what Mī′cah had made, and the priest who belonged to him, the Dă′nītes came to Lā′ish, to a people quiet and unsuspecting, and smote them with the edge of the sword, and burned the city with fire. ²⁸And there was no deliverer because it was far from Sī′dŏn, and they had no dealings with any one. It was in the valley which belongs to Bĕth–rē′hŏb. And they rebuilt the city, and dwelt in it. ²⁹And they named the city Dan, after the name of Dan their ancestor, who was born to Israel; but the name of the city was Lā′ish at the first. ³⁰And the Dă′nītes set up the graven image for themselves; and Jonathan the son of Gēr′shom, son of Moses,ᶻ and his sons were priests to the tribe of the Dă′nītes until the day of the captivity of the land. ³¹So they set up Mī′cah's

graven image which he made, as long as the house of God was at Shī′lōh.

19 In those days, when there was no king in Israel, a certain Lē′vīte was sojourning in the remote parts of the hill country of Ē′phra·ĭm, who took to himself a concubine from Bethlehem in Judah. ²And his concubine became angry withᵃ him, and she went away from him to her father's house at Bethlehem in Judah, and was there some four months. ³Then her husband arose and went after her, to speak kindly to her and bring her back. He had with him his servant and a couple of asses. And he cameᵇ to her father's house; and when the girl's father saw him, he came with joy to meet him. ⁴And his father-in-law, the girl's father, made him stay, and he remained with him three days; so they ate and drank, and lodged there. ⁵And on the fourth day they arose early in the morning, and he prepared to go; but the girl's father said to his son-in-law, "Strengthen your heart with a morsel of bread, and after that you may go." ⁶So the two men sat and ate and drank together; and the girl's father said to the man, "Be pleased to spend the night, and let your heart be merry." ⁷And when the man rose up to go, his father-in-law urged him, till he lodged there again. ⁸And on the fifth day he arose early in the morning to depart; and the girl's father said, "Strengthen your heart, and tarry until the day declines." So they ate, both of them. ⁹And when the man and his concubine and his servant rose up to depart, his father-in-law, the girl's father, said to him, "Behold, now the day has waned toward evening; pray tarry all night. Behold, the day draws to its close; lodge here and let your heart be merry; and tomorrow you shall arise early in the morning for your journey, and go home."

10 But the man would not spend the night; he rose up and departed, and arrived opposite Jē′bŭs (that is, Jerusalem). He had with him a couple of saddled asses, and his concubine was with him. ¹¹When they were near Jē′bŭs, the day was far spent, and the servant said to his master, "Come now, let us turn aside to this city of the

ᶻAnother reading is *Manasseh*
ᵃGk Old Latin: Heb *played the harlot against*
ᵇGk: Heb *she brought him*

Jĕb′ū·sītes, and spend the night in it." ¹²And his master said to him, "We will not turn aside into the city of foreigners, who do not belong to the people of Israel; but we will pass on to Gĭb′-ē-ah." ¹³And he said to his servant, "Come and let us draw near to one of these places, and spend the night at Gĭb′ē-ah or at Rā′mah." ¹⁴So they passed on and went their way; and the sun went down on them near Gĭb′-ē-ah, which belongs to Benjamin, ¹⁵and they turned aside there, to go in and spend the night at Gĭb′ē-ah. And he went in and sat down in the open square of the city; for no man took them into his house to spend the night.

16 And behold, an old man was coming from his work in the field at evening; the man was from the hill country of Ē′phra·ĭm, and he was sojourning in Gĭb′ē-ah; the men of the place were Benjaminites. ¹⁷And he lifted up his eyes, and saw the wayfarer in the open square of the city; and the old man said, "Where are you going? and whence do you come?" ¹⁸And he said to him, "We are passing from Bethlehem in Judah to the remote parts of the hill country of Ē′phra·ĭm, from which I come. I went to Bethlehem in Judah; and I am going to my home;ᶜ and nobody takes me into his house. ¹⁹We have straw and provender for our asses, with bread and wine for me and your maidservant and the young man with your servants; there is no lack of anything." ²⁰And the old man said, "Peace be to you; I will care for all your wants; only, do not spend the night in the square." ²¹So he brought him into his house, and gave the asses provender; and they washed their feet, and ate and drank.

22 As they were making their hearts merry, behold, the men of the city, base fellows, beset the house round about, beating on the door; and they said to the old man, the master of the house, "Bring out the man who came into your house, that we may know him." ²³And the man, the master of the house, went out to them and said to them, "No, my brethren, do not act so wickedly; seeing that this man has come into my house, do not do this vile thing. ²⁴Behold, here are my virgin daughter and his concubine; let me bring them out now. Ravish them and do with them what seems good to you; but against this man do not do so vile a thing." ²⁵But the men would not listen to him. So the man seized his concubine, and put her out to them; and they knew her, and abused her all night until the morning. And as the dawn began to break, they let her go. ²⁶And as morning appeared, the woman came and fell down at the door of the man's house where her master was, till it was light.

27 And her master rose up in the morning, and when he opened the doors of the house and went out to go on his way, behold, there was his concubine lying at the door of the house, with her hands on the threshold. ²⁸He said to her, "Get up, let us be going." But there was no answer. Then he put her upon the ass; and the man rose up and went away to his home. ²⁹And when he entered his house, he took a knife, and laying hold of his concubine he divided her, limb by limb, into twelve pieces, and sent her throughout all the territory of Israel. ³⁰And all who saw it said, "Such a thing has never happened or been seen from the day that the people of Israel came up out of the land of Egypt until this day; consider it, take counsel, and speak."

20 Then all the people of Israel came out, from Dan to Bē′er-shē′ba, including the land of Gilead, and the congregation assembled as one man to the LORD at Mĭz′pah. ²And the chiefs of all the people, of all the tribes of Israel, presented themselves in the assembly of the people of God, four hundred thousand men on foot that drew the sword. ³(Now the Benjaminites heard that the people of Israel had gone up to Mĭz′pah.) And the people of Israel said, "Tell us, how was this wickedness brought to pass?" ⁴And the Lē′vīte, the husband of the woman who was murdered, answered and said, "I came to Gĭb′ē-ah that belongs to Benjamin, I and my concubine, to spend the night. ⁵And the men of Gĭb′ē-ah rose against me, and beset the house round about me by night; they meant to kill me, and they ravished my concubine, and she is dead. ⁶And I took my concubine and cut her in pieces, and sent her throughout all the country of the inheritance of Israel; for they have committed abomination and wantonness in Israel. ⁷Be-

ᶜGk Compare 19.29. Heb *to the house of the* LORD

hold, you people of Israel, all of you, give your advice and counsel here."

8 And all the people arose as one man, saying, "We will not any of us go to his tent, and none of us will return to his house. ⁹But now this is what we will do to Gĭb'ē-ah: we will go up against it by lot, ¹⁰ and we will take ten men of a hundred throughout all the tribes of Israel, and a hundred of a thousand, and a thousand of ten thousand, to bring provisions for the people, that when they come they may requite Gĭb'ē-ah of Benjamin, for all the wanton crime which they have committed in Israel." ¹¹So all the men of Israel gathered against the city, united as one man.

12 And the tribes of Israel sent men through all the tribe of Benjamin, saying, "What wickedness is this that has taken place among you? ¹³Now therefore give up the men, the base fellows in Gĭb'ē-ah, that we may put them to death, and put away evil from Israel." But the Benjaminites would not listen to the voice of their brethren, the people of Israel. ¹⁴And the Benjaminites came together out of the cities to Gĭb'-ē-ah, to go out to battle against the people of Israel. ¹⁵And the Benjaminites mustered out of their cities on that day twenty-six thousand men that drew the sword, besides the inhabitants of Gĭb'ē-ah, who mustered seven hundred picked men. ¹⁶Among all these were seven hundred picked men who were left-handed; every one could sling a stone at a hair, and not miss. ¹⁷And the men of Israel, apart from Benjamin, mustered four hundred thousand men that drew sword; all these were men of war.

18 The people of Israel arose and went up to Bĕth'el, and inquired of God, "Which of us shall go up first to battle against the Benjaminites?" And the LORD said, "Judah shall go up first."

19 Then the people of Israel rose in the morning, and encamped against Gĭb'ē-ah. ²⁰And the men of Israel went out to battle against Benjamin; and the men of Israel drew up the battle line against them at Gĭb'ē-ah. ²¹The Benjaminites came out of Gĭb'-ē-ah, and felled to the ground on that day twenty-two thousand men of the Israelites. ²²But the people, the men of Israel, took courage, and again formed the battle line in the same place where they had formed it on the first day. ²³And the people of Israel went up and wept before the LORD until the evening; and they inquired of the LORD, "Shall we again draw near to battle against our brethren the Benjaminites?" And the LORD said, "Go up against them."

24 So the people of Israel came near against the Benjaminites the second day. ²⁵And Benjamin went against them out of Gĭb'ē-ah the second day, and felled to the ground eighteen thousand men of the people of Israel; all these were men who drew the sword. ²⁶Then all the people of Israel, the whole army, went up and came to Bĕth'el and wept; they sat there before the LORD, and fasted that day until evening, and offered burnt offerings and peace offerings before the LORD. ²⁷And the people of Israel inquired of the LORD (for the ark of the covenant of God was there in those days, ²⁸and Phĭn'e·has the son of Ĕl-ē-ā'zar, son of Aaron, ministered before it in those days), saying, "Shall we yet again go out to battle against our brethren the Benjaminites, or shall we cease?" And the LORD said, "Go up; for tomorrow I will give them into your hand."

29 So Israel set men in ambush round about Gĭb'ē-ah. ³⁰And the people of Israel went up against the Benjaminites on the third day, and set themselves in array against Gĭb'ē-ah, as at other times. ³¹And the Benjaminites went out against the people, and were drawn away from the city; and as at other times they began to smite and kill some of the people, in the highways, one of which goes up to Bĕth'el and the other to Gĭb'ē-ah, and in the open country, about thirty men of Israel. ³²And the Benjaminites said, "They are routed before us, as at the first." But the men of Israel said, "Let us flee, and draw them away from the city to the highways." ³³And all the men of Israel rose up out of their place, and set themselves in array at Bā'al-tā'mār; and the men of Israel who were in ambush rushed out of their place westᵈ of Gē'ba. ³⁴And there came against Gĭb'ē-ah ten thousand picked men out of all Israel, and the battle was hard; but the Benjaminites did

ᵈGk Vg: Heb *in the plain*

not know that disaster was close upon them. ³⁵And the LORD defeated Benjamin before Israel; and the men of Israel destroyed twenty-five thousand one hundred men of Benjamin that day; all these were men who drew the sword. ³⁶So the Benjaminites saw that they were defeated.

The men of Israel gave ground to Benjamin, because they trusted to the men in ambush whom they had set against Gĭb′ē-ah. ³⁷And the men in ambush made haste and rushed upon Gĭb′ē-ah; the men in ambush moved out and smote all the city with the edge of the sword. ³⁸Now the appointed signal between the men of Israel and the men in ambush was that when they made a great cloud of smoke rise up out of the city ³⁹the men of Israel should turn in battle. Now Benjamin had begun to smite and kill about thirty men of Israel; they said, "Surely they are smitten down before us, as in the first battle." ⁴⁰But when the signal began to rise out of the city in a column of smoke, the Benjaminites looked behind them; and behold, the whole of the city went up in smoke to heaven. ⁴¹Then the men of Israel turned, and the men of Benjamin were dismayed, for they saw that disaster was close upon them. ⁴²Therefore they turned their backs before the men of Israel in the direction of the wilderness; but the battle overtook them, and those who came out of the cities destroyed them in the midst of them. ⁴³Cutting down* the Benjaminites, they pursued them and trod them down from Nō′hah* as far as opposite Gĭb′ē-ah on the east. ⁴⁴Eighteen thousand men of Benjamin fell, all of them men of valor. ⁴⁵And they turned and fled toward the wilderness to the rock of Rĭm′mŏn; five thousand men of them were cut down in the highways, and they were pursued hard to Gī′-dŏm, and two thousand men of them were slain. ⁴⁶So all who fell that day of Benjamin were twenty-five thousand men that drew the sword, all of them men of valor. ⁴⁷But six hundred men turned and fled toward the wilderness to the rock of Rĭm′mŏn, and abode at the rock of Rimmon four months. ⁴⁸And the men of Israel turned back against the Benjaminites, and smote them with the edge of the sword, men and beasts and all that they found. And all the towns which they found they set on fire.

21 Now the men of Israel had sworn at Mĭz′pah, "No one of us shall give his daughter in marriage to Benjamin." ²And the people came to Bĕth′el, and sat there till evening before God, and they lifted up their voices and wept bitterly. ³And they said, "O LORD, the God of Israel, why has this come to pass in Israel, that there should be today one tribe lacking in Israel?" ⁴And on the morrow the people rose early, and built there an altar, and offered burnt offerings and peace offerings. ⁵And the people of Israel said, "Which of all the tribes of Israel did not come up in the assembly to the LORD?" For they had taken a great oath concerning him who did not come up to the LORD to Mĭz′pah, saying, "He shall be put to death." ⁶And the people of Israel had compassion for Benjamin their brother, and said, "One tribe is cut off from Israel this day. ⁷What shall we do for wives for those who are left, since we have sworn by the LORD that we will not give them any of our daughters for wives?"

8 And they said, "What one is there of the tribes of Israel that did not come up to the LORD to Mĭz′pah?" And behold, no one had come to the camp from Jā′bĕsh-gĭl′ē-ad, to the assembly. ⁹For when the people were mustered, behold, not one of the inhabitants of Jā′bĕsh-gĭl′ē-ad was there. ¹⁰So the congregation sent thither twelve thousand of their bravest men, and commanded them, "Go and smite the inhabitants of Jā′bĕsh-gĭl′ē-ad with the edge of the sword; also the women and the little ones. ¹¹This is what you shall do; every male and every woman that has lain with a male you shall utterly destroy." ¹²And they found among the inhabitants of Jā′bĕsh-gĭl′ē-ad four hundred young virgins who had not known man by lying with him; and they brought them to the camp at Shī′lōh, which is in the land of Canaan.

13 Then the whole congregation sent word to the Benjaminites who were at the rock of Rĭm′mŏn, and proclaimed peace to them. ¹⁴And Benjamin returned at that time; and they

*Gk: Heb *surrounding*
ʲGk: Heb (at their) *resting place*

gave them the women whom they had saved alive of the women of Jā'bĕsh–gĭl'ē·ạd; but they did not suffice for them. [15] And the people had compassion on Benjamin because the LORD had made a breach in the tribes of Israel.

16 Then the elders of the congregation said, "What shall we do for wives for those who are left, since the women are destroyed out of Benjamin?" [17] And they said, "There must be an inheritance for the survivors of Benjamin, that a tribe be not blotted out from Israel. [18] Yet we cannot give them wives of our daughters." For the people of Israel had sworn, "Cursed be he who gives a wife to Benjamin." [19] So they said, "Behold, there is the yearly feast of the LORD at Shī'lōh, which is north of Bĕth'ĕl, on the east of the highway that goes up from Bethel to Shē'chĕm, and south of Lẹ·bō'nạh." [20] And they commanded the Benjaminites, saying, "Go and lie in wait in the vineyards, [21] and watch; if the daughters of Shī'lōh come out to dance in the dances, then come out of the vineyards and seize each man his wife from the daughters of Shiloh, and go to the land of Benjamin. [22] And when their fathers or their brothers come to complain to us, we will say to them, 'Grant them graciously to us; because we did not take for each man of them his wife in battle, neither did you give them to them, else you would now be guilty.'" [23] And the Benjaminites did so, and took their wives, according to their number, from the dancers whom they carried off; then they went and returned to their inheritance, and rebuilt the towns, and dwelt in them. [24] And the people of Israel departed from there at that time, every man to his tribe and family, and they went out from there every man to his inheritance.

25 In those days there was no king in Israel; every man did what was right in his own eyes.

The Book of
Ruth

1 In the days when the judges ruled there was a famine in the land, and a certain man of Bethlehem in Judah went to sojourn in the country of Mō'ăb, he and his wife and his two sons. [2] The name of the man was Ē·lĭm'ẹ·lĕch and the name of his wife Nā'ọ·mī, and the names of his two sons were Mäh'lŏn and Chĭl'ĭ·ọn; they were Ĕph'rạ·thītes from Bethlehem in Judah. They went into the country of Mo'ăb and remained there. [3] But Ē·lĭm'ẹ·lĕch, the husband of Nā'ọ·mī, died, and she was left with her two sons. [4] These took Mō'ạb·īte wives; the name of the one was Ôr'pạh and the name of the other Ruth. They lived there about ten years; [5] and both Mäh'lŏn and Chĭl'ĭ·ọn died, so that the woman was bereft of her two sons and her husband.

6 Then she started with her daughters-in-law to return from the country of Mō'ăb, for she had heard in the country of Moab that the LORD had visited his people and given them food. [7] So she set out from the place where she was, with her two daughters-in-law, and they went on the way to return to the land of Judah. [8] But Nā'ọ·mī said to her two daughters-in-law, "Go, return each of you to her mother's house. May the LORD deal kindly with you, as you have dealt with the dead and with me. [9] The LORD grant that you may find a home, each of you in the house of her husband!" Then she kissed them, and they lifted up their voices and wept. [10] And they said to her, "No, we will return with you to your people." [11] But Nā'ọ·mī said, "Turn back, my daughters, why will you go with me? Have I yet sons in my womb that they may become your husbands? [12] Turn back, my daughters, go your way, for I am too old to have a husband. If I should say I have hope, even if I should have a husband this

night and should bear sons, [13] would you therefore wait till they were grown? Would you therefore refrain from marrying? No, my daughters, for it is exceedingly bitter to me for your sake that the hand of the LORD has gone forth against me." [14] Then they lifted up their voices and wept again; and Ōr'pah kissed her mother-in-law, but Ruth clung to her.

15 And she said, "See, your sister-in-law has gone back to her people and to her gods; return after your sister-in-law." [16] But Ruth said, "Entreat me not to leave you or to return from following you; for where you go I will go, and where you lodge I will lodge; your people shall be my people, and your God my God; [17] where you die I will die, and there will I be buried. May the LORD do so to me and more also if even death parts me from you." [18] And when Nā'o·mī saw that she was determined to go with her, she said no more.

19 So the two of them went on until they came to Bethlehem. And when they came to Bethlehem, the whole town was stirred because of them; and the women said, "Is this Nā'o·mī?" [20] She said to them, "Do not call me Nā'o·mī,[a] call me Mār'a,[b] for the Almighty has dealt very bitterly with me. [21] I went away full, and the LORD has brought me back empty. Why call me Nā'o·mī, when the LORD has afflicted[c] me and the Almighty has brought calamity upon me?"

22 So Nā'o·mī returned, and Ruth the Mō'ab·īt·ess her daughter-in-law with her, who returned from the country of Mō'āb. And they came to Bethlehem at the beginning of barley harvest.

2 Now Nā'o·mī had a kinsman of her husband's, a man of wealth, of the family of Ē·lĭm'e·lĕch, whose name was Bō'ăz. [2] And Ruth the Mō'ab·īt·ess said to Nā'o·mī, "Let me go to the field, and glean among the ears of grain after him in whose sight I shall find favor." And she said to her, "Go, my daughter." [3] So she set forth and went and gleaned in the field after the reapers; and she happened to come to the part of the field belonging to Bō'ăz, who was of the family of Ē·lĭm'e·lĕch. [4] And behold, Bō'ăz came from Bethlehem; and he said to the reapers, "The LORD be with you!" And they an-

swered, "The LORD bless you." [5] Then Bō'ăz said to his servant who was in charge of the reapers, "Whose maiden is this?" [6] And the servant who was in charge of the reapers answered, "It is the Mō'ab·īte maiden, who came back with Nā'o·mī from the country of Mō'āb. [7] She said, 'Pray, let me glean and gather among the sheaves after the reapers.' So she came, and she has continued from early morning until now, without resting even for a moment."[d]

8 Then Bō'ăz said to Ruth, "Now, listen, my daughter, do not go to glean in another field or leave this one, but keep close to my maidens. [9] Let your eyes be upon the field which they are reaping, and go after them. Have I not charged the young men not to molest you? And when you are thirsty, go to the vessels and drink what the young men have drawn." [10] Then she fell on her face, bowing to the ground, and said to him, "Why have I found favor in your eyes, that you should take notice of me, when I am a foreigner?" [11] But Bō'ăz answered her, "All that you have done for your mother-in-law since the death of your husband has been fully told me, and how you left your father and mother and your native land and came to a people that you did not know before. [12] The LORD recompense you for what you have done, and a full reward be given you by the LORD, the God of Israel, under whose wings you have come to take refuge!" [13] Then she said, "You are most gracious to me, my lord, for you have comforted me and spoken kindly to your maidservant, though I am not one of your maidservants."

14 And at mealtime Bō'ăz said to her, "Come here, and eat some bread, and dip your morsel in the wine." So she sat beside the reapers, and he passed to her parched grain; and she ate until she was satisfied, and she had some left over. [15] When she rose to glean, Bō'ăz instructed his young men, saying, "Let her glean even among the sheaves, and do not reproach her. [16] And also pull out some from the bundles for her, and leave it for her to glean, and do not rebuke her."

17 So she gleaned in the field until

[a] That is *Pleasant*   [b] That is *Bitter*
[c] Gk Syr Vg: Heb *testified against*
[d] Compare Gk Vg: the meaning of the Hebrew text is uncertain

evening; then she beat out what she had gleaned, and it was about an ephah of barley. ¹⁸And she took it up and went into the city; she showed her mother-in-law what she had gleaned, and she also brought out and gave her what food she had left over after being satisfied. ¹⁹And her mother-in-law said to her, "Where did you glean today? And where have you worked? Blessed be the man who took notice of you." So she told her mother-in-law with whom she had worked, and said, "The man's name with whom I worked today is Bō′ăz." ²⁰And Nā′ọ·mī said to her daughter-in-law, "Blessed be he by the LORD, whose kindness has not forsaken the living or the dead!" Naomi also said to her, "The man is a relative of ours, one of our nearest kin." ²¹And Ruth the Mō′ạb·īt·ẹss said, "Besides, he said to me, 'You shall keep close by my servants, till they have finished all my harvest.'" ²²And Nā′ọ·mī said to Ruth, her daugher-in-law, "It is well, my daughter, that you go out with his maidens, lest in another field you be molested." ²³So she kept close to the maidens of Bō′ăz, gleaning until the end of the barley and wheat harvests; and she lived with her mother-in-law.

3 Then Nā′ọ·mī her mother-in-law said to her, "My daughter, should I not seek a home for you, that it may be well with you? ²Now is not Bō′ăz our kinsman, with whose maidens you were? See, he is winnowing barley tonight at the threshing floor. ³Wash therefore and anoint yourself, and put on your best clothes and go down to the threshing floor; but do not make yourself known to the man until he has finished eating and drinking. ⁴But when he lies down, observe the place where he lies; then, go and uncover his feet and lie down; and he will tell you what to do." ⁵And she replied, "All that you say I will do."

6 So she went down to the threshing floor and did just as her mother-in-law had told her. ⁷And when Bō′ăz had eaten and drunk, and his heart was merry, he went to lie down at the end of the heap of grain. Then she came softly, and uncovered his feet, and lay down. ⁸At midnight the man was startled, and turned over, and behold, a woman lay at his feet! ⁹He said, "Who are you?" And she answered,

"I am Ruth, your maidservant; spread your skirt over your maidservant, for you are next of kin." ¹⁰And he said, "May you be blessed by the LORD, my daughter; you have made this last kindness greater than the first, in that you have not gone after young men, whether poor or rich. ¹¹And now, my daughter, do not fear, I will do for you all that you ask, for all my fellow townsmen know that you are a woman of worth. ¹²And now it is true that I am a near kinsman, yet there is a kinsman nearer than I. ¹³Remain this night, and in the morning, if he will do the part of the next of kin for you, well; let him do it; but if he is not willing to do the part of the next of kin for you, then, as the LORD lives, I will do the part of the next of kin for you. Lie down until the morning."

14 So she lay at his feet until the morning, but arose before one could recognize another; and he said, "Let it not be known that the woman came to the threshing floor." ¹⁵And he said, "Bring the mantle you are wearing and hold it out." So she held it, and he measured out six measures of barley, and laid it upon her; then she went into the city. ¹⁶And when she came to her mother-in-law, she said, "How did you fare, my daughter?" Then she told her all that the man had done for her, ¹⁷saying, "These six measures of barley he gave to me, for he said, 'You must not go back empty-handed to your mother-in-law.'" ¹⁸She replied, "Wait, my daughter, until you learn how the matter turns out, for the man will not rest, but will settle the matter today."

4 And Bō′ăz went up to the gate and sat down there; and behold, the next of kin, of whom Boaz had spoken, came by. So Boaz said, "Turn aside, friend; sit down here"; and he turned aside and sat down. ²And he took ten men of the elders of the city, and said, "Sit down here"; so they sat down. ³Then he said to the next of kin, "Nā′ọ·mī, who has come back from the country of Mō′ăb, is selling the parcel of land which belonged to our kinsman Ē′lĭm′ẹ·lĕch. ⁴So I thought I would tell you of it, and say, Buy it in the presence of those sitting here, and in the presence of the elders of my people. If you will redeem it, redeem it; but if you will not, tell me,

that I may know, for there is no one besides you to redeem it, and I come after you." And he said, "I will redeem it." ⁵Then Bō'ăz said, "The day you buy the field from the hand of Nā'ọ·mī, you are also buying Ruth^e the Mō'ạb-īt-ẹss, the widow of the dead, in order to restore the name of the dead to his inheritance." ⁶Then the next of kin said, "I cannot redeem it for myself, lest I impair my own inheritance. Take my right of redemption yourself, for I cannot redeem it."

7 Now this was the custom in former times in Israel concerning redeeming and exchanging: to confirm a transaction, the one drew off his sandal and gave it to the other, and this was the manner of attesting in Israel. ⁸So when the next of kin said to Bō'ăz, "Buy it for yourself," he drew off his sandal. ⁹Then Bō'ăz said to the elders and all the people, "You are witnesses this day that I have bought from the hand of Nā'ọ·mī all that belonged to Ē'līm'-ẹ·lĕch and all that belonged to Chīl'-i·ọn and to Mäh'lŏn. ¹⁰Also Ruth the Mō'ạb-īt-ẹss, the widow of Mäh'lŏn, I have bought to be my wife, to perpetuate the name of the dead in his inheritance, that the name of the dead may not be cut off from among his brethren and from the gate of his native place; you are witnesses this day." ¹¹Then all the people who were at the gate, and the elders, said, "We are witnesses. May the LORD make the woman, who is coming into your house, like Rachel and Lē'ạh, who together built up the house of Israel. May you prosper in Ĕph'rạ·thạh and be renowned in Bethlehem; ¹²and may your house be like the house of Pĕr'ĕz, whom Tā'mär bore to Judah, because of the children that the LORD will give you by this young woman."

13 So Bō'ăz took Ruth and she became his wife; and he went in to her, and the LORD gave her conception, and she bore a son. ¹⁴Then the women said to Nā'ọ·mī, "Blessed be the LORD, who has not left you this day without next of kin; and may his name be renowned in Israel! ¹⁵He shall be to you a restorer of life and a nourisher of your old age; for your daughter-in-law who loves you, who is more to you than seven sons, has borne him." ¹⁶Then Nā'ọ·mī took the child and laid him in her bosom, and became his nurse. ¹⁷And the women of the neighborhood gave him a name, saying, "A son has been born to Nā'ọ·mī." They named him Ō'bĕd; he was the father of Jesse, the father of David.

18 Now these are the descendants of Pĕr'ĕz: Perez was the father of Hĕz'-rọn, ¹⁹Hĕz'rọn of Räm, Ram of Ăm-mĭn'ạ·dăb, ²⁰Ăm·mĭn'ạ·dăb of Näh'-shọn, Nahshon of Săl'mọn, ²¹Săl'mọn of Bō'ăz, Boaz of Ō'bĕd, ²²Ō'bĕd of Jesse, and Jesse of David.

The First Book of
Samuel

1 There was a certain man of Rā-mạ·thā'ĭm–zō'phĭm of the hill country of Ē'phrạ·ĭm, whose name was Ĕl·kā'nạh the son of Jĕ·rō'hăm, son of Ĕ·lī'hū, son of Tō'hū, son of Zŭph, an Ē'phrạ·ĭm-īte. ²He had two wives; the name of the one was Hannah, and the name of the other Pẹ·nĭn'nạh. And Peninnah had children, but Hannah had no children.

3 Now this man used to go up year by year from his city to worship and to sacrifice to the LORD of hosts at Shī'lōh, where the two sons of Eli, Hŏph'nī and Phĭn'ẹ·has, were priests of the LORD. ⁴On the day when Ĕl·kā'-nạh sacrificed, he would give portions to Pẹ·nĭn'nạh his wife and to all her sons and daughters; ⁵and, although^a he loved Hannah, he would give Hannah only one portion, because the LORD had closed her womb. ⁶And her rival used to provoke her sorely, to ir-

^eOld Latin Vg: Heb of Naomi and from Ruth
4.7: Deut 25.8-10.
^aGk: Heb obscure

ritate her, because the LORD had closed her womb. [7]So it went on year by year; as often as she went up to the house of the LORD, she used to provoke her. Therefore Hannah wept and would not eat. [8]And Ĕl·kā′nạh, her husband, said to her, "Hannah, why do you weep? And why do you not eat? And why is your heart sad? Am I not more to you than ten sons?"

9 After they had eaten and drunk in Shī′lōh, Hannah rose. Now Eli the priest was sitting on the seat beside the doorpost of the temple of the LORD. [10]She was deeply distressed and prayed to the LORD, and wept bitterly. [11]And she vowed a vow and said, "O LORD of hosts, if thou wilt indeed look on the affliction of thy maidservant, and remember me, and not forget thy maidservant, but wilt give to thy maidservant a son, then I will give him to the LORD all the days of his life, and no razor shall touch his head."

12 As she continued praying before the LORD, Eli observed her mouth. [13]Hannah was speaking in her heart; only her lips moved, and her voice was not heard; therefore Eli took her to be a drunken woman. [14]And Eli said to her, "How long will you be drunken? Put away your wine from you." [15]But Hannah answered, "No, my lord, I am a woman sorely troubled; I have drunk neither wine nor strong drink, but I have been pouring out my soul before the LORD. [16]Do not regard your maidservant as a base woman, for all along I have been speaking out of my great anxiety and vexation." [17]Then Eli answered, "Go in peace, and the God of Israel grant your petition which you have made to him." [18]And she said, "Let your maidservant find favor in your eyes." Then the woman went her way and ate, and her countenance was no longer sad.

19 They rose early in the morning and worshiped before the LORD; then they went back to their house at Rā′mạh. And Ĕl·kā′nạh knew Hannah his wife, and the LORD remembered her; [20]and in due time Hannah conceived and bore a son, and she called his name Samuel, for she said, "I have asked him of the LORD."

21 And the man Ĕl·kā′nạh and all his house went up to offer to the LORD the yearly sacrifice, and to pay his vow. [22]But Hannah did not go up, for she said to her husband, "As soon as the child is weaned, I will bring him, that he may appear in the presence of the LORD, and abide there for ever." [23]Ĕl·kā′nạh her husband said to her, "Do what seems best to you, wait until you have weaned him; only, may the LORD establish his word." So the woman remained and nursed her son, until she weaned him. [24]And when she had weaned him, she took him up with her, along with a three-year-old bull,[b] an ephah of flour, and a skin of wine; and she brought him to the house of the LORD at Shī′lōh; and the child was young. [25]Then they slew the bull, and they brought the child to Eli. [26]And she said, "Oh, my lord! As you live, my lord, I am the woman who was standing here in your presence, praying to the LORD. [27]For this child I prayed; and the LORD has granted me my petition which I made to him. [28]Therefore I have lent him to the LORD; as long as he lives, he is lent to the LORD." And they[x] worshiped the LORD there.

2 Hannah also prayed and said, "My heart exults in the LORD; my strength is exalted in the LORD. My mouth derides my enemies, because I rejoice in thy salvation.

[2]"There is none holy like the LORD, there is none besides thee; there is no rock like our God.
[3]Talk no more so very proudly, let not arrogance come from your mouth;
for the LORD is a God of knowledge, and by him actions are weighed.
[4]The bows of the mighty are broken, but the feeble gird on strength.
[5]Those who were full have hired themselves out for bread, but those who were hungry have ceased to hunger.
The barren has borne seven, but she who has many children is forlorn.
[6]The LORD kills and brings to life; he brings down to Shĕ′ōl and raises up.
[7]The LORD makes poor and makes rich; he brings low, he also exalts.
[8]He raises up the poor from the dust; he lifts the needy from the ash heap,

[b]Gk Syr: Heb *three bulls* [x]Heb *he*
2.1-10: Lk 1.46-55.

to make them sit with princes
and inherit a seat of honor.
For the pillars of the earth are the
LORD'S,
and on them he has set the world.

9 "He will guard the feet of his faithful ones;
but the wicked shall be cut off in darkness;
for not by might shall a man prevail.
10 The adversaries of the LORD shall be broken to pieces;
against them he will thunder in heaven.
The LORD will judge the ends of the earth;
he will give strength to his king,
and exalt the power of his anointed."

11 Then Ĕl·kā′năh went home to Rā′măh. And the boy ministered to the LORD, in the presence of Eli the priest.

12 Now the sons of Eli were worthless men; they had no regard for the LORD. 13 The custom of the priests with the people was that when any man offered sacrifice, the priest's servant would come, while the meat was boiling, with a three-pronged fork in his hand, 14 and he would thrust it into the pan, or kettle, or caldron, or pot; all that the fork brought up the priest would take for himself.c So they did at Shī′lōh to all the Israelites who came there. 15 Moreover, before the fat was burned, the priest's servant would come and say to the man who was sacrificing, "Give meat for the priest to roast; for he will not accept boiled meat from you, but raw." 16 And if the man said to him, "Let them burn the fat first, and then take as much as you wish," he would say, "No, you must give it now; and if not, I will take it by force." 17 Thus the sin of the young men was very great in the sight of the LORD; for the men treated the offering of the LORD with contempt.

18 Samuel was ministering before the LORD, a boy girded with a linen ephod. 19 And his mother used to make for him a little robe and take it to him each year, when she went up with her husband to offer the yearly sacrifice. 20 Then Eli would bless Ĕl·kā′năh and his wife, and say, "The LORD give you children by this woman for the loan

which she lent tod the LORD"; so then they would return to their home.

21 And the LORD visited Hannah, and she conceived and bore three sons and two daughters. And the boy Samuel grew in the presence of the LORD.

22 Now Eli was very old, and he heard all that his sons were doing to all Israel, and how they lay with the women who served at the entrance to the tent of meeting. 23 And he said to them, "Why do you do such things? For I hear of your evil dealings from all the people. 24 No, my sons; it is no good report that I hear the people of the LORD spreading abroad. 25 If a man sins against a man, God will mediate for him; but if a man sins against the LORD, who can intercede for him?" But they would not listen to the voice of their father; for it was the will of the LORD to slay them.

26 Now the boy Samuel continued to grow both in stature and in favor with the LORD and with men.

27 And there came a man of God to Eli, and said to him, "Thus the LORD has said, 'I revealede myself to the house of your father when they were in Egypt subject to the house of Pharaoh. 28 And I chose him out of all the tribes of Israel to be my priest, to go up to my altar, to burn incense, to wear an ephod before me; and I gave to the house of your father all my offerings by fire from the people of Israel. 29 Why then look with greedy eye atf my sacrifices and my offerings which I commanded, and honor your sons above me by fattening yourselves upon the choicest parts of every offering of my people Israel?' 30 Therefore the LORD the God of Israel declares: 'I promised that your house and the house of your father should go in and out before me for ever'; but now the LORD declares: 'Far be it from me; for those who honor me I will honor, and those who despise me shall be lightly esteemed. 31 Behold, the days are coming, when I will cut off your strength and the strength of your father's house, so that there will not be an old man in your house. 32 Then in distress you will look with envious eye on all the prosperity which shall be bestowed upon Israel;

c Gk Syr Vg: Heb *with it*
d Or *for the petition which she asked of*
e Gk Tg: Heb *Did I reveal*
f Or *treat with* e*corn* Gk· Heb *kick at*
2.26: Lk 2.52.

and there shall not be an old man in your house for ever. [33] The man of you whom I shall not cut off from my altar shall be spared to weep out his[g] eyes and grieve his[g] heart; and all the increase of your house shall die by the sword of men.[h] [34] And this which shall befall your two sons, Hŏph′nī and Phĭn′ė·has, shall be the sign to you: both of them shall die on the same day. [35] And I will raise up for myself a faithful priest, who shall do according to what is in my heart and in my mind; and I will build him a sure house, and he shall go in and out before my anointed for ever. [36] And every one who is left in your house shall come to implore him for a piece of silver or a loaf of bread, and shall say, "Put me, I pray you, in one of the priest's places, that I may eat a morsel of bread." ' "

3 Now the boy Samuel was ministering to the LORD under Eli. And the word of the LORD was rare in those days; there was no frequent vision. [2] At that time Eli, whose eyesight had begun to grow dim, so that he could not see, was lying down in his own place; [3] the lamp of God had not yet gone out, and Samuel was lying down within the temple of the LORD, where the ark of God was. [4] Then the LORD called, "Samuel!"[i] and he said, "Here I am!" [5] and ran to Eli, and said, "Here I am, for you called me." But he said, "I did not call; lie down again." So he went and lay down. [6] And the LORD called again, "Samuel!" And Samuel arose and went to Eli, and said, "Here I am, for you called me." But he said, "I did not call, my son; lie down again." [7] Now Samuel did not yet know the LORD, and the word of the LORD had not yet been revealed to him. [8] And the LORD called Samuel again the third time. And he arose and went to Eli, and said, "Here I am, for you called me." Then Eli perceived that the LORD was calling the boy. [9] Therefore Eli said to Samuel, "Go, lie down; and if he calls you, you shall say, 'Speak, LORD, for thy servant hears.'" So Samuel went and lay down in his place.

[10] And the LORD came and stood forth, calling as at other times, "Samuel! Samuel!" And Samuel said, "Speak, for thy servant hears." [11] Then the LORD said to Samuel, "Behold, I am about to do a thing in Israel, at which the two ears of every one that hears it will tingle. [12] On that day I will fulfil against Eli all that I have spoken concerning his house, from beginning to end. [13] And I tell him that I am about to punish his house for ever, for the iniquity which he knew, because his sons were blaspheming God,[j] and he did not restrain them. [14] Therefore I swear to the house of Eli that the iniquity of Eli's house shall not be expiated by sacrifice or offering for ever."

15 Samuel lay until morning; then he opened the doors of the house of the LORD. And Samuel was afraid to tell the vision to Eli. [16] But Eli called Samuel and said, "Samuel, my son." And he said, "Here I am." [17] And Eli said, "What was it that he told you? Do not hide it from me. May God do so to you and more also, if you hide anything from me of all that he told you." [18] So Samuel told him everything and hid nothing from him. And he said, "It is the LORD; let him do what seems good to him."

19 And Samuel grew, and the LORD was with him and let none of his words fall to the ground. [20] And all Israel from Dan to Bē′er-shē′ba knew that Samuel was established as a prophet of the LORD. [21] And the LORD appeared again at Shī′lōh, for the LORD revealed himself to Samuel at Shiloh by the

4 word of the LORD. [1] And the word of Samuel came to all Israel.

Now Israel went out to battle against the Phĭ·lĭs′tĭnes; they encamped at Ebenezer, and the Philistines encamped at Ā′phĕk. [2] The Phĭ·lĭs′tĭnes drew up in line against Israel, and when the battle spread, Israel was defeated by the Philistines, who slew about four thousand men on the field of battle. [3] And when the troops came to the camp, the elders of Israel said, "Why has the LORD put us to rout today before the Phĭ·lĭs′tĭnes? Let us bring the ark of the covenant of the LORD here from Shī′lōh, that he may come among us and save us from the power of our enemies." [4] So the people sent to Shī′lōh, and brought from there the ark of the covenant of the LORD of hosts, who is enthroned on the cherubim; and the two sons of Eli, Hŏph′nī and Phĭn′ė·has, were there with the ark of the covenant of God.

[g] Gk: Heb *your*   [h] Gk: Heb *die as men*
[i] Gk See 3.10: Heb *the* LORD *called Samuel*
[j] Another reading is *for themselves*

5 When the ark of the covenant of the LORD came into the camp, all Israel gave a mighty shout, so that the earth resounded. ⁶And when the Phĭ-lĭs′tĭnes heard the noise of the shouting, they said, "What does this great shouting in the camp of the Hebrews mean?" And when they learned that the ark of the LORD had come to the camp, ⁷the Phĭ-lĭs′tĭnes were afraid; for they said, "A god has come into the camp." And they said, "Woe to us! For nothing like this has happened before. ⁸Woe to us! Who can deliver us from the power of these mighty gods? These are the gods who smote the Egyptians with every sort of plague in the wilderness. ⁹Take courage, and acquit yourselves like men, O Phĭ-lĭs′-tĭnes, lest you become slaves to the Hebrews as they have been to you; acquit yourselves like men and fight."

10 So the Phĭ-lĭs′tĭnes fought, and Israel was defeated, and they fled, every man to his home; and there was a very great slaughter, for there fell of Israel thirty thousand foot soldiers. ¹¹And the ark of God was captured; and the two sons of Eli, Hŏph′nĭ and Phĭn′e̯-hạs, were slain.

12 A man of Benjamin ran from the battle line, and came to Shī′lōh the same day, with his clothes rent and with earth upon his head. ¹³When he arrived, Eli was sitting upon his seat by the road watching, for his heart trembled for the ark of God. And when the man came into the city and told the news, all the city cried out. ¹⁴When Eli heard the sound of the outcry, he said, "What is this uproar?" Then the man hastened and came and told Eli. ¹⁵Now Eli was ninety-eight years old and his eyes were set, so that he could not see. ¹⁶And the man said to Eli, "I am he who has come from the battle; I fled from the battle today." And he said, "How did it go, my son?" ¹⁷He who brought the tidings answered and said, "Israel has fled before the Phĭ-lĭs′tĭnes, and there has also been a great slaughter among the people; your two sons also, Hŏph′nĭ and Phĭn′e̯-hạs, are dead, and the ark of God has been captured." ¹⁸When he mentioned the ark of God, Eli fell over backward from his seat by the side of the gate; and his neck was broken and he died, for he was an old man, and heavy. He had judged Israel forty years.

19 Now his daughter-in-law, the wife of Phĭn′e̯-hạs, was with child, about to give birth. And when she heard the tidings that the ark of God was captured, and that her father-in-law and her husband were dead, she bowed and gave birth; for her pains came upon her. ²⁰And about the time of her death the women attending her said to her, "Fear not, for you have borne a son." But she did not answer or give heed. ²¹And she named the child Ich′a̯-bŏd, saying, "The glory has departed from Israel!" because the ark of God had been captured and because of her father-in-law and her husband. ²²And she said, "The glory has departed from Israel, for the ark of God has been captured."

5 When the Phĭ-lĭs′tĭnes captured the ark of God, they carried it from Ebenezer to Ăsh′dŏd; ²then the Phĭ-lĭs′tĭnes took the ark of God and brought it into the house of Dā′gŏn and set it up beside Dagon. ³And when the people of Ăsh′dŏd rose early the next day, behold, Dā′gŏn had fallen face downward on the ground before the ark of the LORD. So they took Dagon and put him back in his place. ⁴But when they rose early on the next morning, behold, Dā′gŏn had fallen face downward on the ground before the ark of the LORD, and the head of Dagon and both his hands were lying cut off upon the threshold; only the trunk of Dagon was left to him. ⁵This is why the priests of Dā′gŏn and all who enter the house of Dagon do not tread on the threshold of Dagon in Ăsh′dŏd to this day.

6 The hand of the LORD was heavy upon the people of Ăsh′dŏd, and he terrified and afflicted them with tumors, both Ashdod and its territory. ⁷And when the men of Ăsh′dŏd saw how things were, they said, "The ark of the God of Israel must not remain with us; for his hand is heavy upon us and upon Dā′gŏn our god." ⁸So they sent and gathered together all the lords of the Phĭ-lĭs′tĭnes, and said, "What shall we do with the ark of the God of Israel?" They answered, "Let the ark of the God of Israel be brought around to Găth." So they brought the ark of the God of Israel there. ⁹But after they had brought it around, the hand of the LORD was against the city, causing a very great panic, and he

afflicted the men of the city, both young and old, so that tumors broke out upon them. ¹⁰ So they sent the ark of God to Ĕk′rọn. But when the ark of God came to Ekron, the people of Ekron cried out, "They have brought around to us the ark of the God of Israel to slay us and our people." ¹¹ They sent therefore and gathered together all the lords of the Phĭ·lĭs′tĭnes, and said, "Send away the ark of the God of Israel, and let it return to its own place, that it may not slay us and our people." For there was a deathly panic throughout the whole city. The hand of God was very heavy there; ¹² the men who did not die were stricken with tumors, and the cry of the city went up to heaven.

6 The ark of the LORD was in the country of the Phĭ·lĭs′tĭnes seven months. ² And the Phĭ·lĭs′tĭnes called for the priests and the diviners and said, "What shall we do with the ark of the LORD? Tell us with what we shall send it to its place." ³ They said, "If you send away the ark of the God of Israel, do not send it empty, but by all means return him a guilt offering. Then you will be healed, and it will be known to you why his hand does not turn away from you." ⁴ And they said, "What is the guilt offering that we shall return to him?" They answered, "Five golden tumors and five golden mice, according to the number of the lords of the Phĭ·lĭs′tĭnes; for the same plague was upon all of you and upon your lords. ⁵ So you must make images of your tumors and images of your mice that ravage the land, and give glory to the God of Israel; perhaps he will lighten his hand from off you and your gods and your land. ⁶ Why should you harden your hearts as the Egyptians and Pharaoh hardened their hearts? After he had made sport of them, did not they let the people go, and they departed? ⁷ Now then, take and prepare a new cart and two milch cows upon which there has never come a yoke, and yoke the cows to the cart, but take their calves home, away from them. ⁸ And take the ark of the LORD and place it on the cart, and put in a box at its side the figures of gold, which you are returning to him as a guilt offering. Then send it off, and let it go its way. ⁹ And watch; if it goes up on the way to its own land, to Bĕth-shē′-mĕsh, then it is he who has done us

this great harm; but if not, then we shall know that it is not his hand that struck us, it happened to us by chance."

10 The men did so, and took two milch cows and yoked them to the cart, and shut up their calves at home. ¹¹ And they put the ark of the LORD on the cart, and the box with the golden mice and the images of their tumors. ¹² And the cows went straight in the direction of Bĕth-shē′mĕsh along one highway, lowing as they went; they turned neither to the right nor to the left, and the lords of the Phĭ·lĭs′tĭnes went after them as far as the border of Beth-shemesh. ¹³ Now the people of Bĕth-shē′mĕsh were reaping their wheat harvest in the valley; and when they lifted up their eyes and saw the ark, they rejoiced to see it. ¹⁴ The cart came into the field of Joshua of Bĕth-shē′mĕsh, and stopped there. A great stone was there; and they split up the wood of the cart and offered the cows as a burnt offering to the LORD. ¹⁵ And the Lē′vītes took down the ark of the LORD and the box that was beside it, in which were the golden figures, and set them upon the great stone; and the men of Bĕth-shē′mĕsh offered burnt offerings and sacrificed sacrifices on that day to the LORD. ¹⁶ And when the five lords of the Phĭ·lĭs′tĭnes saw it, they returned that day to Ĕk′rọn.

17 These are the golden tumors, which the Phĭ·lĭs′tĭnes returned as a guilt offering to the LORD: one for Ash′dŏd, one for Gā′zạ, one for Ăsh′-kẹ·lŏn, one for Găth, one for Ĕk′rọn; ¹⁸ also the golden mice, according to the number of all the cities of the Phĭ·lĭs′tĭnes belonging to the five lords, both fortified cities and unwalled villages. The great stone, beside which they set down the ark of the LORD, is a witness to this day in the field of Joshua of Bĕth-shē′mĕsh.

19 And he slew some of the men of Bĕth-shē′mĕsh, because they looked into the ark of the LORD; he slew seventy men of them,ᵏ and the people mourned because the LORD had made a great slaughter among the people. ²⁰ Then the men of Bĕth-shē′mĕsh said, "Who is able to stand before the LORD, this holy God? And to whom shall he go up away from us?" ²¹ So they sent messengers to the inhabitants of Kĭr′-

ᵏ Cn: Heb *of the people seventy men, fifty thousand men*

ĭ·ăth–jē'ạ·rĭm, saying, "The Phĭ·lĭs'-tĭnes have returned the ark of the LORD. Come down and take it up to you." ¹And the men of Kĭr'ĭ·ăth-jē'ạ·rĭm came and took up the ark of the LORD, and brought it to the house of Ą·bĭn'ạ·dăb on the hill; and they consecrated his son, Ĕl·ē·ā'zạr, to have charge of the ark of the LORD. ²From the day that the ark was lodged at Kĭr'ĭ·ăth–jē'ạ·rĭm, a long time passed, some twenty years, and all the house of Israel lamented after the LORD.

3 Then Samuel said to all the house of Israel, "If you are returning to the LORD with all your heart, then put away the foreign gods and the Ăsh'-tạ·rŏth from among you, and direct your heart to the LORD, and serve him only, and he will deliver you out of the hand of the Phĭ·lĭs'tĭnes." ⁴So Israel put away the Bā'ạls and the Ăsh'tạ·rŏth, and they served the LORD only.

5 Then Samuel said, "Gather all Israel at Mĭz'pạh, and I will pray to the LORD for you." ⁶So they gathered at Mĭz'pạh, and drew water and poured it out before the LORD, and fasted on that day, and said there, "We have sinned against the LORD." And Samuel judged the people of Israel at Mizpah. ⁷Now when the Phĭ·lĭs'tĭnes heard that the people of Israel had gathered at Mĭz'pạh, the lords of the Philistines went up against Israel. And when the people of Israel heard of it they were afraid of the Philistines. ⁸And the people of Israel said to Samuel, "Do not cease to cry to the LORD our God for us, that he may save us from the hand of the Phĭ·lĭs'tĭnes." ⁹So Samuel took a suckling lamb and offered it as a whole burnt offering to the LORD; and Samuel cried to the LORD for Israel, and the LORD answered him. ¹⁰As Samuel was offering up the burnt offering, the Phĭ·lĭs'tĭnes drew near to attack Israel; but the LORD thundered with a mighty voice that day against the Philistines and threw them into confusion; and they were routed before Israel. ¹¹And the men of Israel went out of Mĭz'pạh and pursued the Phĭ·lĭs'tĭnes, and smote them, as far as below Bĕth–cār.

12 Then Samuel took a stone and set it up between Mĭz'pạh and Jĕ·shā'-nạh,[l] and called its name Ebenezer;[m] for he said, "Hitherto the LORD has helped us." ¹³So the Phĭ·lĭs'tĭnes were subdued and did not again enter the territory of Israel. And the hand of the LORD was against the Philistines all the days of Samuel. ¹⁴The cities which the Phĭ·lĭs'tĭnes had taken from Israel were restored to Israel, from Ĕk'rọn to Găth; and Israel rescued their territory from the hand of the Philistines. There was peace also between Israel and the Ăm'ọ·rītes.

15 Samuel judged Israel all the days of his life. ¹⁶And he went on a circuit year by year to Bĕth'ẹl, Gĭl'gạl, and Mĭz'pạh; and he judged Israel in all these places. ¹⁷Then he would come back to Rā'mạh, for his home was there, and there also he administered justice to Israel. And he built there an altar to the LORD.

8 When Samuel became old, he made his sons judges over Israel. ²The name of his first-born son was Jō'ẹl, and the name of his second, Ą·bĭ'jạh; they were judges in Bē'ẹr-shē'bạ. ³Yet his sons did not walk in his ways, but turned aside after gain; they took bribes and perverted justice.

4 Then all the elders of Israel gathered together and came to Samuel at Rā'mạh, ⁵and said to him, "Behold, you are old and your sons do not walk in your ways; now appoint for us a king to govern us like all the nations." ⁶But the thing displeased Samuel when they said, "Give us a king to govern us." And Samuel prayed to the LORD. ⁷And the LORD said to Samuel, "Hearken to the voice of the people in all that they say to you; for they have not rejected you, but they have rejected me from being king over them. ⁸According to all the deeds which they have done to me,[n] from the day I brought them up out of Egypt even to this day, forsaking me and serving other gods, so they are also doing to you. ⁹Now then, hearken to their voice; only, you shall solemnly warn them, and show them the ways of the king who shall reign over them."

10 So Samuel told all the words of the LORD to the people who were asking a king from him. ¹¹He said, "These will be the ways of the king who will reign over you: he will take your sons and appoint them to his chariots and to be his horsemen, and to run before

[l]Gk Syr: Heb *Shen*   [m]That is *Stone of help*
[n]Gk: Heb lacks *to me*

his chariots; ¹² and he will appoint for himself commanders of thousands and commanders of fifties, and some to plow his ground and to reap his harvest, and to make his implements of war and the equipment of his chariots. ¹³ He will take your daughters to be perfumers and cooks and bakers. ¹⁴ He will take the best of your fields and vineyards and olive orchards and give them to his servants. ¹⁵ He will take the tenth of your grain and of your vineyards and give it to his officers and to his servants. ¹⁶ He will take your menservants and maidservants, and the best of your cattle^o and your asses, and put them to his work. ¹⁷ He will take the tenth of your flocks, and you shall be his slaves. ¹⁸ And in that day you will cry out because of your king, whom you have chosen for yourselves; but the LORD will not answer you in that day."

19 But the people refused to listen to the voice of Samuel; and they said, "No! but we will have a king over us, ²⁰ that we also may be like all the nations, and that our king may govern us and go out before us and fight our battles." ²¹ And when Samuel had heard all the words of the people, he repeated them in the ears of the LORD. ²² And the LORD said to Samuel, "Hearken to their voice, and make them a king." Samuel then said to the men of Israel, "Go every man to his city."

9 There was a man of Benjamin whose name was Kĭsh, the son of A·bī′el, son of Zē′rôr, son of Bĕ·cō′răth, son of A·phī′ah, a Benjaminite, a man of wealth; ² and he had a son whose name was Saul, a handsome young man. There was not a man among the people of Israel more handsome than he; from his shoulders upward he was taller than any of the people.

3 Now the asses of Kĭsh, Saul's father, were lost. So Kish said to Saul his son, "Take one of the servants with you, and arise, go and look for the asses." ⁴ And they^p passed through the hill country of E′phra·im and passed through the land of Shăl′ĭ·shah, but they did not find them. And they passed through the land of Shā′a·lĭm, but they were not there. Then they passed through the land of Benjamin, but did not find them.

5 When they came to the land of Zŭph, Saul said to his servant who was with him, "Come, let us go back, lest my father cease to care about the asses and become anxious about us." ⁶ But he said to him, "Behold, there is a man of God in this city, and he is a man that is held in honor; all that he says comes true. Let us go there; perhaps he can tell us about the journey on which we have set out." ⁷ Then Saul said to his servant, "But if we go, what can we bring the man? For the bread in our sacks is gone, and there is no present to bring to the man of God. What have we?" ⁸ The servant answered Saul again, "Here, I have with me the fourth part of a shekel of silver, and I will give it to the man of God, to tell us our way." ⁹ (Formerly in Israel, when a man went to inquire of God, he said, "Come, let us go to the seer"; for he who is now called a prophet was formerly called a seer.) ¹⁰ And Saul said to his servant, "Well said; come, let us go." So they went to the city where the man of God was.

11 As they went up the hill to the city, they met young maidens coming out to draw water, and said to them, "Is the seer here?" ¹² They answered, "He is; behold, he is just ahead of you. Make haste; he has come just now to the city, because the people have a sacrifice today on the high place. ¹³ As soon as you enter the city, you will find him, before he goes up to the high place to eat; for the people will not eat till he comes, since he must bless the sacrifice; afterward those eat who are invited. Now go up, for you will meet him immediately." ¹⁴ So they went up to the city. As they were entering the city, they saw Samuel coming out toward them on his way up to the high place.

15 Now the day before Saul came, the LORD had revealed to Samuel: ¹⁶ "Tomorrow about this time I will send to you a man from the land of Benjamin, and you shall anoint him to be prince over my people Israel. He shall save my people from the hand of the Phĭ·lĭs′tines; for I have seen the affliction of^q my people, because their cry has come to me." ¹⁷ When Samuel saw Saul, the LORD told him, "Here is the man of whom I spoke to you!

^oGk: Heb *young men*
^pGk Vg: Heb *he*   ^qGk: Heb lacks *the affliction of*

He it is who shall rule over my people." ¹⁸Then Saul approached Samuel in the gate, and said, "Tell me where is the house of the seer?" ¹⁹Samuel answered Saul, "I am the seer; go up before me to the high place, for today you shall eat with me, and in the morning I will let you go and will tell you all that is on your mind. ²⁰As for your asses that were lost three days ago, do not set your mind on them, for they have been found. And for whom is all that is desirable in Israel? Is it not for you and for all your father's house?" ²¹Saul answered, "Am I not a Benjaminite, from the least of the tribes of Israel? And is not my family the humblest of all the families of the tribe of Benjamin? Why then have you spoken to me in this way?"

22 Then Samuel took Saul and his servant and brought them into the hall and gave them a place at the head of those who had been invited, who were about thirty persons. ²³And Samuel said to the cook, "Bring the portion I gave you, of which I said to you, 'Put it aside.'" ²⁴So the cook took up the leg and the upper portion*ʳ* and set them before Saul; and Samuel said, "See, what was kept is set before you. Eat; because it was kept for you until the hour appointed, that you might eat with the guests."*ˢ*

So Saul ate with Samuel that day. ²⁵And when they came down from the high place into the city, a bed was spread for Saul*ᵗ* upon the roof, and he lay down to sleep. ²⁶Then at the break of dawn*ᵘ* Samuel called to Saul upon the roof, "Up, that I may send you on your way." So Saul arose, and both he and Samuel went out into the street.

27 As they were going down to the outskirts of the city, Samuel said to Saul, "Tell the servant to pass on before us, and when he has passed on stop here yourself for a while, that I may make known to you the word of God."

10 Then Samuel took a vial of oil and poured it on his head, and kissed him and said, "Has not the LORD anointed you to be prince over his people Israel? And you shall reign over the people of the LORD and you will save them from the hand of their enemies round about. And this shall be the sign to you that the LORD has anointed you to be prince*ᵛ* over his

heritage. ²When you depart from me today you will meet two men by Rachel's tomb in the territory of Benjamin at Zĕl′zạh, and they will say to you, 'The asses which you went to seek are found, and now your father has ceased to care about the asses and is anxious about you, saying, "What shall I do about my son?"' ³Then you shall go on from there further and come to the oak of Tā′bôr; three men going up to God at Bĕth′el will meet you there, one carrying three kids, another carrying three loaves of bread, and another carrying a skin of wine. ⁴And they will greet you and give you two loaves of bread, which you shall accept from their hand. ⁵After that you shall come to Gĭb′ĕ·ăth-ĕ·lō′hĭm,*ˣ* where there is a garrison of the Phĭlĭs′tĭnes; and there, as you come to the city, you will meet a band of prophets coming down from the high place with harp, tambourine, flute, and lyre before them, prophesying. ⁶Then the spirit of the LORD will come mightily upon you, and you shall prophesy with them and be turned into another man. ⁷Now when these signs meet you, do whatever your hand finds to do, for God is with you. ⁸And you shall go down before me to Gĭl′gạl; and behold, I am coming to you to offer burnt offerings and to sacrifice peace offerings. Seven days you shall wait, until I come to you and show you what you shall do."

9 When he turned his back to leave Samuel, God gave him another heart; and all these signs came to pass that day. ¹⁰When they came to Gĭb′ĕ·ah,*ᶻ* behold, a band of prophets met him; and the spirit of God came mightily upon him, and he prophesied among them. ¹¹And when all who knew him before saw how he prophesied with the prophets, the people said to one another, "What has come over the son of Kĭsh? Is Saul also among the prophets?" ¹²And a man of the place answered, "And who is their father?" Therefore it became a proverb, "Is Saul also among the prophets?" ¹³When he had finished prophesying, he came to the high place.

14 Saul's uncle said to him and to

*ᵖHeb obscure *ʳCn: Heb *saying, I have invited the people* *ˢGk: Heb *and he spoke with Saul* *ᵗGk: Heb *and they arose early and at break of dawn* *ᵘGk: Heb lacks *over his people Israel? And you shall . . . to be prince* *ˣOr *the hill of God* *ᶻOr *the hill* 10.11-12: 19.23, 24.

his servant, "Where did you go?" And he said, "To seek the asses; and when we saw they were not to be found, we went to Samuel." [15]And Saul's uncle said, "Pray, tell me what Samuel said to you." [16]And Saul said to his uncle, "He told us plainly that the asses had been found." But about the matter of the kingdom, of which Samuel had spoken, he did not tell him anything.

17 Now Samuel called the people together to the LORD at Mĭz'pah; [18]and he said to the people of Israel, "Thus says the LORD, the God of Israel, 'I brought up Israel out of Egypt, and I delivered you from the hand of the Egyptians and from the hand of all the kingdoms that were oppressing you.' [19]But you have this day rejected your God, who saves you from all your calamities and your distresses; and you have said, 'No! but set a king over us.' Now therefore present yourselves before the LORD by your tribes and by your thousands."

20 Then Samuel brought all the tribes of Israel near, and the tribe of Benjamin was taken by lot. [21]He brought the tribe of Benjamin near by its families, and the family of the Mā'trītes was taken by lot; finally he brought the family of the Matrites near man by man,[a] and Saul the son of Kĭsh was taken by lot. But when they sought him, he could not be found. [22]So they inquired again of the LORD, "Did the man come hither?"[b] and the LORD said, "Behold, he has hidden himself among the baggage." [23]Then they ran and fetched him from there; and when he stood among the people, he was taller than any of the people from his shoulders upward. [24]And Samuel said to all the people, "Do you see him whom the LORD has chosen? There is none like him among all the people." And all the people shouted, "Long live the king!"

25 Then Samuel told the people the rights and duties of the kingship; and he wrote them in a book and laid it up before the LORD. Then Samuel sent all the people away, each one to his home. [26]Saul also went to his home at Gĭb'ē-ạh, and with him went men of valor whose hearts God had touched. [27]But some worthless fellows said, "How can this man save us?" And they despised him, and brought him no present. But he held his peace.

11 Then Nā'hăsh the Ăm'mọ·nīte went up and besieged Jā'bĕsh-gĭl'ē·ạd; and all the men of Jā'bĕsh said to Nahash, "Make a treaty with us, and we will serve you." [2]But Nā'hăsh the Ăm'mọ·nīte said to them, "On this condition I will make a treaty with you, that I gouge out all your right eyes, and thus put disgrace upon all Israel." [3]The elders of Jā'bĕsh said to him, "Give us seven days respite that we may send messengers through all the territory of Israel. Then, if there is no one to save us, we will give ourselves up to you." [4]When the messengers came to Gĭb'ē-ạh of Saul, they reported the matter in the ears of the people; and all the people wept aloud.

5 Now Saul was coming from the field behind the oxen; and Saul said, "What ails the people, that they are weeping?" So they told him the tidings of the men of Jā'bĕsh. [6]And the spirit of God came mightily upon Saul when he heard these words, and his anger was greatly kindled. [7]He took a yoke of oxen, and cut them in pieces and sent them throughout all the territory of Israel by the hand of messengers, saying, "Whoever does not come out after Saul and Samuel, so shall it be done to his oxen!" Then the dread of the LORD fell upon the people, and they came out as one man. [8]When he mustered them at Bē'zĕk, the men of Israel were three hundred thousand, and the men of Judah thirty thousand. [9]And they said to the messengers who had come, "Thus shall you say to the men of Jā'bĕsh-gĭl'ē·ạd: 'Tomorrow, by the time the sun is hot, you shall have deliverance.'" When the messengers came and told the men of Jā'bĕsh, they were glad. [10]Therefore the men of Jā'bĕsh said, "Tomorrow we will give ourselves up to you, and you may do to us whatever seems good to you." [11]And on the morrow Saul put the people in three companies; and they came into the midst of the camp in the morning watch, and cut down the Ăm'mọ·nītes until the heat of the day; and those who survived were scattered, so that no two of them were left together.

12 Then the people said to Samuel, "Who is it that said, 'Shall Saul reign over us?' Bring the men, that we may

[a]Gk: Heb lacks *finally . . . man by man*
[b]Gk: Heb *Is there yet a man to come hither?*

put them to death." [13]But Saul said, "Not a man shall be put to death this day, for today the LORD has wrought deliverance in Israel." [14]Then Samuel said to the people, "Come, let us go to Gĭl'gal and there renew the kingdom." [15]So all the people went to Gĭl'gal, and there they made Saul king before the LORD in Gilgal. There they sacrificed peace offerings before the LORD, and there Saul and all the men of Israel rejoiced greatly.

12 And Samuel said to all Israel, "Behold, I have hearkened to your voice in all that you have said to me, and have made a king over you. [2]And now, behold, the king walks before you; and I am old and gray, and behold, my sons are with you; and I have walked before you from my youth until this day. [3]Here I am; testify against me before the LORD and before his anointed. Whose ox have I taken? Or whose ass have I taken? Or whom have I defrauded? Whom have I oppressed? Or from whose hand have I taken a bribe to blind my eyes with it? Testify against me[c] and I will restore it to you." [4]They said, "You have not defrauded us or oppressed us or taken anything from any man's hand." [5]And he said to them, "The LORD is witness against you, and his anointed is witness this day, that you have not found anything in my hand." And they said, "He is witness."

6 And Samuel said to the people, "The LORD is witness,[d] who appointed Moses and Aaron and brought your fathers up out of the land of Egypt. [7]Now therefore stand still, that I may plead with you before the LORD concerning all the saving deeds of the LORD which he performed for you and for your fathers. [8]When Jacob went into Egypt and the Egyptians oppressed them,[e] then your fathers cried to the LORD and the LORD sent Moses and Aaron, who brought forth your fathers out of Egypt, and made them dwell in this place. [9]But they forgot the LORD their God; and he sold them into the hand of Sĭs'e·ra, commander of the army of Jā'bĭn king of[f] Hā'zôr, and into the hand of the Phĭ·lĭs'tĭnes, and into the hand of the king of Mō'ǎb; and they fought against them. [10]And they cried to the LORD, and said, 'We have sinned, because we have forsaken the LORD, and have served the

Bā'als and the Ăsh'ta·rŏth; but now deliver us out of the hand of our enemies, and we will serve thee.' [11]And the LORD sent Jĕr·ŭb·bā'al and Bār'ak,[g] and Jĕph'thah, and Samuel, and delivered you out of the hand of your enemies on every side; and you dwelt in safety. [12]And when you saw that Nā'hǎsh the king of the Ăm'mo·nītes came against you, you said to me, 'No, but a king shall reign over us,' when the LORD your God was your king. [13]And now behold the king whom you have chosen, for whom you have asked; behold, the LORD has set a king over you. [14]If you will fear the LORD and serve him and hearken to his voice and not rebel against the commandment of the LORD, and if both you and the king who reigns over you will follow the LORD your God, it will be well; [15]but if you will not hearken to the voice of the LORD, but rebel against the commandment of the LORD, then the hand of the LORD will be against you and your king.[h] [16]Now therefore stand still and see this great thing, which the LORD will do before your eyes. [17]Is it not wheat harvest today? I will call upon the LORD, that he may send thunder and rain; and you shall know and see that your wickedness is great, which you have done in the sight of the LORD, in asking for yourselves a king." [18]So Samuel called upon the LORD, and the LORD sent thunder and rain that day; and all the people greatly feared the LORD and Samuel.

19 And all the people said to Samuel, "Pray for your servants to the LORD your God, that we may not die; for we have added to all our sins this evil, to ask for ourselves a king." [20]And Samuel said to the people, "Fear not; you have done all this evil, yet do not turn aside from following the LORD, but serve the LORD with all your heart; [21]and do not turn aside after[i] vain things which cannot profit or save, for they are vain. [22]For the LORD will not cast away his people, for his great name's sake, because it has pleased the LORD to make you a people for himself. [23]Moreover as for me, far be it from me that I should sin against the LORD by ceasing to pray for you;

[c]Gk: Heb lacks *Testify against me*
[d]Gk: Heb lacks *is witness*
[e]Gk: Heb lacks *and the Egyptians oppressed them*
[f]Gk: Heb lacks *Jabin king of* [g]Gk Syr: Heb *Bedan*
[h]Gk: Heb *fathers* [i]Gk Syr Tg Vg: Heb *because after*

and I will instruct you in the good and the right way. [24] Only fear the LORD, and serve him faithfully with all your heart; for consider what great things he has done for you. [25] But if you still do wickedly, you shall be swept away, both you and your king."

13 Saul was . . .[j] years old when he began to reign; and he reigned . . . and two[k] years over Israel.

2 Saul chose three thousand men of Israel; two thousand were with Saul in Mĭch'măsh and the hill country of Bĕth'el, and a thousand were with Jonathan in Gĭb'ē-ah of Benjamin; the rest of the people he sent home, every man to his tent. [3] Jonathan defeated the garrison of the Phĭ-lĭs'tĭnes which was at Gē'ba; and the Philistines heard of it. And Saul blew the trumpet throughout all the land, saying, "Let the Hebrews hear." [4] And all Israel heard it said that Saul had defeated the garrison of the Phĭ-lĭs'-tĭnes, and also that Israel had become odious to the Philistines. And the people were called out to join Saul at Gĭl'gal.

5 And the Phĭ-lĭs'tĭnes mustered to fight with Israel, thirty thousand chariots, and six thousand horsemen, and troops like the sand on the seashore in multitude; they came up and encamped in Mĭch'măsh, to the east of Bĕth-ā'ven. [6] When the men of Israel saw that they were in straits (for the people were hard pressed), the people hid themselves in caves and in holes and in rocks and in tombs and in cisterns, [7] or crossed the fords of the Jordan[l] to the land of Gad and Gilead. Saul was still at Gĭl'gal, and all the people followed him trembling.

8 He waited seven days, the time appointed by Samuel; but Samuel did not come to Gĭl'gal, and the people were scattering from him. [9] So Saul said, "Bring the burnt offering here to me, and the peace offerings." And he offered the burnt offering. [10] As soon as he had finished offering the burnt offering, behold, Samuel came; and Saul went out to meet him and salute him. [11] Samuel said, "What have you done?" And Saul said, "When I saw that the people were scattering from me, and that you did not come within the days appointed, and that the Phĭ-lĭs'tĭnes had mustered at Mĭch'măsh, [12] I said, 'Now the Phĭ-lĭs'tĭnes will

come down upon me at Gĭl'gal and I have not entreated the favor of the LORD'; so I forced myself, and offered the burnt offering." [13] And Samuel said to Saul, "You have done foolishly; you have not kept the commandment of the LORD your God, which he commanded you; for now the LORD would have established your kingdom over Israel for ever. [14] But now your kingdom shall not continue; the LORD has sought out a man after his own heart; and the LORD has appointed him to be prince over his people, because you have not kept what the LORD commanded you." [15] And Samuel arose, and went up from Gĭl'gal to Gĭb'ē-ah of Benjamin.

And Saul numbered the people who were present with him, about six hundred men. [16] And Saul, and Jonathan his son, and the people who were present with them, stayed in Gē'ba of Benjamin; but the Phĭ-lĭs'-tĭnes encamped in Mĭch'măsh. [17] And raiders came out of the camp of the Phĭ-lĭs'tĭnes in three companies; one company turned toward Ŏph'rah, to the land of Shū'al, [18] another company turned toward Bĕth-hō'rŏn, and another company turned toward the border that looks down upon the valley of Zĕ-bō'ĭm toward the wilderness.

19 Now there was no smith to be found throughout all the land of Israel; for the Phĭ-lĭs'tĭnes said, "Lest the Hebrews make themselves swords or spears"; [20] but every one of the Israelites went down to the Phĭ-lĭs'tĭnes to sharpen his plowshare, his mattock, his axe, or his sickle;[m] [21] and the charge was a pim for the plowshares and for the mattocks, and a third of a shekel for sharpening the axes and for setting the goads.[n] [22] So on the day of the battle there was neither sword nor spear found in the hand of any of the people with Saul and Jonathan; but Saul and Jonathan his son had them. [23] And the garrison of the Phĭ-lĭs'tĭnes went out to the pass of Mĭch'măsh.

14 One day Jonathan the son of Saul said to the young man who bore his armor, "Come, let us go over to the Phĭ-lĭs'tĭne garrison on yonder side." But he did not tell his father.

[j] The number is lacking in Heb
[k] *Two* is not the entire number. Something has dropped out.
[l] Cn: Heb *Hebrews crossed the Jordan*
[m] Gk: Heb *plowshare* [n] The Heb of this verse is obscure
13.14: Acts 13.22.

² Saul was staying in the outskirts of Gĭb′ē–ah under the pomegranate tree which is at Mĭg′rŏn; the people who were with him were about six hundred men, ³ and A·hī′jah the son of A·hī′tŭb, Ĭch′a·bŏd′s̱ brother, son of Phĭn′e·has, son of Eli, the priest of the LORD in Shī′lōh, wearing an ephod. And the people did not know that Jonathan had gone. ⁴ In the pass,° by which Jonathan sought to go over to the Phĭ·lĭs′tĭne garrison, there was a rocky crag on the one side and a rocky crag on the other side; the name of the one was Bō′zĕz, and the name of the other Sē′nĕh. ⁵ The one crag rose on the north in front of Mĭch′măsh, and the other on the south in front of Gē′ba.

6 And Jonathan said to the young man who bore his armor, "Come, let us go over to the garrison of these uncircumcised; it may be that the LORD will work for us; for nothing can hinder the LORD from saving by many or by few." ⁷ And his armor-bearer said to him, "Do all that your mind inclines to;ᵖ behold, I am with you, as is your mind so is mine."�q ⁸ Then said Jonathan, "Behold, we will cross over to the men, and we will show ourselves to them. ⁹ If they say to us, 'Wait until we come to you,' then we will stand still in our place, and we will not go up to them. ¹⁰ But if they say, 'Come up to us,' then we will go up; for the LORD has given them into our hand. And this shall be the sign to us." ¹¹ So both of them showed themselves to the garrison of the Phĭ·lĭs′tĭnes; and the Philistines said, "Look, Hebrews are coming out of the holes where they have hid themselves." ¹² And the men of the garrison hailed Jonathan and his armor-bearer, and said, "Come up to us, and we will show you a thing." And Jonathan said to his armor-bearer, "Come up after me; for the LORD has given them into the hand of Israel." ¹³ Then Jonathan climbed up on his hands and feet, and his armor-bearer after him. And they fell before Jonathan, and his armor-bearer killed them after him; ¹⁴ and that first slaughter, which Jonathan and his armor-bearer made, was of about twenty men within as it were half a furrow's length in an acreʳ of land. ¹⁵ And there was a panic in the camp, in the field, and among all the people; the garrison and even the raiders trembled;

the earth quaked; and it became a very great panic.

16 And the watchmen of Saul in Gĭb′ē–ah of Benjamin looked; and behold, the multitude was surging hither and thither.ˢ ¹⁷ Then Saul said to the people who were with him, "Number and see who has gone from us." And when they had numbered, behold, Jonathan and his armor-bearer were not there. ¹⁸ And Saul said to A·hī′jah, "Bring hither the ark of God." For the ark of God went at that time with the people of Israel. ¹⁹ And while Saul was talking to the priest, the tumult in the camp of the Phĭ·lĭs′tĭnes increased more and more; and Saul said to the priest, "Withdraw your hand." ²⁰ Then Saul and all the people who were with him rallied and went into the battle; and behold, every man's sword was against his fellow, and there was very great confusion. ²¹ Now the Hebrews who had been with the Phĭ·lĭs′tĭnes before that time and who had gone up with them into the camp, even they also turned to be withᵗ the Israelites who were with Saul and Jonathan. ²² Likewise, when all the men of Israel who had hid themselves in the hill country of Ē′phra·ĭm heard that the Phĭ·lĭs′tĭnes were fleeing, they too followed hard after them in the battle. ²³ So the LORD delivered Israel that day; and the battle passed beyond Bĕth–ā′vĕn.

24 And the men of Israel were distressed that day; for Saul laid an oath on the people, saying, "Cursed be the man who eats food until it is evening and I am avenged on my enemies." So none of the people tasted food. ²⁵ And all the peopleᵘ came into the forest; and there was honey on the ground. ²⁶ And when the people entered the forest, behold, the honey was dropping, but no man put his hand to his mouth; for the people feared the oath. ²⁷ But Jonathan had not heard his father charge the people with the oath; so he put forth the tip of the staff that was in his hand, and dipped it in the honeycomb, and put his hand to his mouth; and his eyes became bright. ²⁸ Then one of the people said, "Your

°Heb *between the passes*
ᵖGk: Heb *Do all that is in your mind. Turn*
qGk: Heb *lacks so is mine*
ʳHeb *yoke* ˢGk: Heb *they went and thither*
ᵗGk Syr Vg Tg: Heb *round about, they also, to be with*
ᵘHeb *land*

father strictly charged the people with an oath, saying, 'Cursed be the man who eats food this day.'" And the people were faint. ²⁹Then Jonathan said, "My father has troubled the land; see how my eyes have become bright, because I tasted a little of this honey. ³⁰How much better if the people had eaten freely today of the spoil of their enemies which they found; for now the slaughter among the Phĭ·lĭs′tĭnes has not been great."

31 They struck down the Phĭ·lĭs′-tĭnes that day from Mĭch′măsh to Aĭ′jȧ·lŏn. And the people were very faint; ³²the people flew upon the spoil, and took sheep and oxen and calves, and slew them on the ground; and the people ate them with the blood. ³³Then they told Saul, "Behold, the people are sinning against the LORD, by eating with the blood." And he said, "You have dealt treacherously; roll a great stone to me here."ᵛ ³⁴And Saul said, "Disperse yourselves among the people, and say to them, 'Let every man bring his ox or his sheep, and slay them here, and eat; and do not sin against the LORD by eating with the blood.'" So every one of the people brought his ox with him that night, and slew them there. ³⁵And Saul built an altar to the LORD; it was the first altar that he built to the LORD.

36 Then Saul said, "Let us go down after the Phĭ·lĭs′tĭnes by night and despoil them until the morning light; let us not leave a man of them." And they said, "Do whatever seems good to you." But the priest said, "Let us draw near hither to God." ³⁷And Saul inquired of God, "Shall I go down after the Phĭ·lĭs′tĭnes? Wilt thou give them into the hand of Israel?" But he did not answer him that day. ³⁸And Saul said, "Come hither, all you leaders of the people; and know and see how this sin has arisen today. ³⁹For as the LORD lives who saves Israel, though it be in Jonathan my son, he shall surely die." But there was not a man among all the people that answered him. ⁴⁰Then he said to all Israel, "You shall be on one side, and I and Jonathan my son will be on the other side." And the people said to Saul, "Do what seems good to you." ⁴¹Therefore Saul said, "O LORD God of Israel, why hast thou not answered thy servant this day? If this guilt is in me or in Jonathan my son, O LORD,

God of Israel, give Ū′rĭm; but if this guilt is in thy people Israel,ʷ give Thŭm′mĭm." And Jonathan and Saul were taken, but the people escaped. ⁴²Then Saul said, "Cast the lot between me and my son Jonathan." And Jonathan was taken.

43 Then Saul said to Jonathan, "Tell me what you have done." And Jonathan told him, "I tasted a little honey with the tip of the staff that was in my hand; here I am, I will die." ⁴⁴And Saul said, "God do so to me and more also; you shall surely die, Jonathan." ⁴⁵Then the people said to Saul, "Shall Jonathan die, who has wrought this great victory in Israel? Far from it! As the LORD lives, there shall not one hair of his head fall to the ground; for he has wrought with God this day." So the people ransomed Jonathan, that he did not die. ⁴⁶Then Saul went up from pursuing the Phĭ·lĭs′tĭnes; and the Philistines went to their own place.

47 When Saul had taken the kingship over Israel, he fought against all his enemies on every side, against Mō′ăb, against the Ăm′mo·nītes, against Ē′dom, against the kings of Zō′băh, and against the Phĭ·lĭs′tĭnes; wherever he turned he put them to the worse. ⁴⁸And he did valiantly, and smote the Ȧ·măl′e·kītes, and delivered Israel out of the hands of those who plundered them.

49 Now the sons of Saul were Jonathan, Ĭsh′vī, and Măl″chī-shü′ȧ; and the names of his two daughters were these: the name of the firstborn was Mē′răb, and the name of the younger Mī′chal; ⁵⁰and the name of Saul's wife was Ȧ·hĭn′ō–ăm the daughter of Ȧ·hĭm′ȧ–ăz. And the name of the commander of his army was Abner the son of Nēr, Saul's uncle; ⁵¹Kīsh was the father of Saul, and Nēr the father of Abner was the son of Ȧ·bī′el.

52 There was hard fighting against the Phĭ·lĭs′tĭnes all the days of Saul; and when Saul saw any strong man, or any valiant man, he attached him to himself.

15 And Samuel said to Saul, "The LORD sent me to anoint you king over his people Israel; now therefore hearken to the words of the LORD. ²Thus says the LORD of hosts, 'I will

*Gk: Heb *this day*
ᵛVg Compare Gk: Heb *Saul said to the LORD, the God of Israel*
14.49: 31.2; 1 Chron 10.2.

punish what Ăm´ạ·lĕk did to Israel in opposing them on the way, when they came up out of Egypt. ³Now go and smite Ăm´ạ·lĕk, and utterly destroy all that they have; do not spare them, but kill both man and woman, infant and suckling, ox and sheep, camel and ass.' "

4 So Saul summoned the people, and numbered them in Tẹ·lā´ĭm, two hundred thousand men on foot, and ten thousand men of Judah. ⁵And Saul came to the city of Ăm´ạ·lĕk, and lay in wait in the valley. ⁶And Saul said to the Kĕn´ītes, "Go, depart, go down from among the Ạ·măl´ẹ·kītes, lest I destroy you with them; for you showed kindness to all the people of Israel when they came up out of Egypt." So the Kenites departed from among the Amalekites. ⁷And Saul defeated the Ạ·măl´ẹ·kītes, from Hăv´ĭ·lạh as far as Shŭr, which is east of Egypt. ⁸And he took Ā´găg the king of the Ạ·măl´ẹ·kītes alive, and utterly destroyed all the people with the edge of the sword. ⁹But Saul and the people spared Ā´găg, and the best of the sheep and of the oxen and of the fatlings, and the lambs, and all that was good, and would not utterly destroy them; all that was despised and worthless they utterly destroyed.

10 The word of the LORD came to Samuel: ¹¹"I repent that I have made Saul king; for he has turned back from following me, and has not performed my commandments." And Samuel was angry; and he cried to the LORD all night. ¹²And Samuel rose early to meet Saul in the morning; and it was told Samuel, "Saul came to Căr´mẹl, and behold, he set up a monument for himself and turned, and passed on, and went down to Gĭl´gạl." ¹³And Samuel came to Saul, and Saul said to him, "Blessed be you to the LORD; I have performed the commandment of the LORD." ¹⁴And Samuel said, "What then is this bleating of the sheep in my ears, and the lowing of the oxen which I hear?" ¹⁵Saul said, "They have brought them from the Ạ·măl´ẹ·kītes; for the people spared the best of the sheep and of the oxen, to sacrifice to the LORD your God; and the rest we have utterly destroyed." ¹⁶Then Samuel said to Saul, "Stop! I will tell you what the LORD said to me this night." And he said to him, "Say on."

17 And Samuel said, "Though you are little in your own eyes, are you not the head of the tribes of Israel? The LORD anointed you king over Israel. ¹⁸And the LORD sent you on a mission, and said, 'Go, utterly destroy the sinners, the Ạ·măl´ẹ·kītes, and fight against them until they are consumed.' ¹⁹Why then did you not obey the voice of the LORD? Why did you swoop on the spoil, and do what was evil in the sight of the LORD?" ²⁰And Saul said to Samuel, "I have obeyed the voice of the LORD, I have gone on the mission on which the LORD sent me, I have brought Ā´găg the king of Ăm´ạ·lĕk, and I have utterly destroyed the Ạ·măl´ẹ·kītes. ²¹But the people took of the spoil, sheep and oxen, the best of the things devoted to destruction, to sacrifice to the LORD your God in Gĭl´gạl." ²²And Samuel said,
"Has the LORD as great delight in
   burnt offerings and sacrifices,
as in obeying the voice of the
   LORD?
Behold, to obey is better than sacrifice,
and to hearken than the fat of
   rams.
²³For rebellion is as the sin of divination,
and stubbornness is as iniquity and
   idolatry.
Because you have rejected the word
   of the LORD,
he has also rejected you from
   being king."

24 And Saul said to Samuel, "I have sinned; for I have transgressed the commandment of the LORD and your words, because I feared the people and obeyed their voice. ²⁵Now therefore, I pray, pardon my sin, and return with me, that I may worship the LORD." ²⁶And Samuel said to Saul, "I will not return with you; for you have rejected the word of the LORD, and the LORD has rejected you from being king over Israel." ²⁷As Samuel turned to go away, Saul laid hold upon the skirt of his robe, and it tore. ²⁸And Samuel said to him, "The LORD has torn the kingdom of Israel from you this day, and has given it to a neighbor of yours, who is better than you. ²⁹And also the Glory of Israel will not lie or repent; for he is not a man, that he should repent." ³⁰Then he said, "I have sinned; yet honor me

15.22: Mk 12.33.

now before the elders of my people and before Israel, and return with me, that I may worship the LORD your God." ³¹ So Samuel turned back after Saul; and Saul worshiped the LORD.

32 Then Samuel said, "Bring here to me Ā'găg the king of the Ạ·măl'-ẹ·kītes." And Agag came to him cheerfully. Agag said, "Surely the bitterness of death is past." ³³And Samuel said, "As your sword has made women childless, so shall your mother be childless among women." And Samuel hewed Ā'găg in pieces before the LORD in Gĭl'găl.

34 Then Samuel went to Rā'măh; and Saul went up to his house in Gĭb'-ē–ạh of Saul. ³⁵And Samuel did not see Saul again until the day of his death, but Samuel grieved over Saul. And the LORD repented that he had made Saul king over Israel.

16 The LORD said to Samuel, "How long will you grieve over Saul, seeing I have rejected him from being king over Israel? Fill your horn with oil, and go; I will send you to Jesse the Bethlehemite, for I have provided for myself a king among his sons." ²And Samuel said, "How can I go? If Saul hears it, he will kill me." And the LORD said, "Take a heifer with you, and say, 'I have come to sacrifice to the LORD.' ³And invite Jesse to the sacrifice, and I will show you what you shall do; and you shall anoint for me him whom I name to you." ⁴Samuel did what the LORD commanded, and came to Bethlehem. The elders of the city came to meet him trembling, and said, "Do you come peaceably?" ⁵And he said, "Peaceably; I have come to sacrifice to the LORD; consecrate yourselves, and come with me to the sacrifice." And he consecrated Jesse and his sons, and invited them to the sacrifice.

6 When they came, he looked on Ē·lī'ăb and thought, "Surely the LORD's anointed is before him." ⁷But the LORD said to Samuel, "Do not look on his appearance or on the height of his stature, because I have rejected him; for the LORD sees not as man sees; man looks on the outward appearance, but the LORD looks on the heart." ⁸Then Jesse called Ạ·bĭn'ạ·dăb, and made him pass before Samuel. And he said, "Neither has the LORD chosen this one." ⁹Then Jesse made Shăm'-

măh pass by. And he said, "Neither has the LORD chosen this one." ¹⁰And Jesse made seven of his sons pass before Samuel. And Samuel said to Jesse, "The LORD has not chosen these." ¹¹And Samuel said to Jesse, "Are all your sons here?" And he said, "There remains yet the youngest, but behold, he is keeping the sheep." And Samuel said to Jesse, "Send and fetch him; for we will not sit down till he comes here." ¹²And he sent, and brought him in. Now he was ruddy, and had beautiful eyes, and was handsome. And the LORD said, "Arise, anoint him; for this is he." ¹³Then Samuel took the horn of oil, and anointed him in the midst of his brothers; and the Spirit of the LORD came mightily upon David from that day forward. And Samuel rose up, and went to Rā'măh.

14 Now the Spirit of the LORD departed from Saul, and an evil spirit from the LORD tormented him. ¹⁵And Saul's servants said to him, "Behold now, an evil spirit from God is tormenting you. ¹⁶Let our lord now command your servants, who are before you, to seek out a man who is skilful in playing the lyre; and when the evil spirit from God is upon you, he will play it, and you will be well." ¹⁷So Saul said to his servants, "Provide for me a man who can play well, and bring him to me." ¹⁸One of the young men answered, "Behold, I have seen a son of Jesse the Bethlehemite, who is skilful in playing, a man of valor, a man of war, prudent in speech, and a man of good presence; and the LORD is with him." ¹⁹Therefore Saul sent messengers to Jesse, and said, "Send me David your son, who is with the sheep." ²⁰And Jesse took an ass laden with bread, and a skin of wine and a kid, and sent them by David his son to Saul. ²¹And David came to Saul, and entered his service. And Saul loved him greatly, and he became his armorbearer. ²²And Saul sent to Jesse, saying, "Let David remain in my service, for he has found favor in my sight." ²³And whenever the evil spirit from God was upon Saul, David took the lyre and played it with his hand; so Saul was refreshed, and was well, and the evil spirit departed from him.

17 Now the Phĭ·lĭs'tĭnes gathered their armies for battle; and they were gathered at Sō'cōh, which be-

longs to Judah, and encamped between Socoh and A·zē′kah, in Ē′phĕṣdăm′mĭm. ²And Saul and the men of Israel were gathered, and encamped in the valley of Ē′lah, and drew up in line of battle against the Phĭ·lĭs′tĭnes. ³And the Phĭ·lĭs′tĭnes stood on the mountain on the one side, and Israel stood on the mountain on the other side, with a valley between them. ⁴And there came out from the camp of the Phĭ·lĭs′tĭnes a champion named Goliath, of Găth, whose height was six cubits and a span. ⁵He had a helmet of bronze on his head, and he was armed with a coat of mail, and the weight of the coat was five thousand shekels of bronze. ⁶And he had greaves of bronze upon his legs, and a javelin of bronze slung between his shoulders. ⁷And the shaft of his spear was like a weaver's beam, and his spear's head weighed six hundred shekels of iron; and his shield-bearer went before him. ⁸He stood and shouted to the ranks of Israel, "Why have you come out to draw up for battle? Am I not a Phĭ·lĭs′tĭne, and are you not servants of Saul? Choose a man for yourselves, and let him come down to me. ⁹If he is able to fight with me and kill me, then we will be your servants; but if I prevail against him and kill him, then you shall be our servants and serve us." ¹⁰And the Phĭ·lĭs′tĭne said, "I defy the ranks of Israel this day; give me a man, that we may fight together." ¹¹When Saul and all Israel heard these words of the Phĭ·lĭs′tĭne, they were dismayed and greatly afraid.

12 Now David was the son of an Ĕph′ra·thīte of Bethlehem in Judah, named Jesse, who had eight sons. In the days of Saul the man was already old and advanced in years.ˣ ¹³The three eldest sons of Jesse had followed Saul to the battle; and the names of his three sons who went to the battle were Ē·lī′ăb the first-born, and next to him A·bĭn′a·dăb, and the third Shăm′mah. ¹⁴David was the youngest; the three eldest followed Saul, ¹⁵but David went back and forth from Saul to feed his father's sheep at Bethlehem. ¹⁶For forty days the Phĭ·lĭs′tĭne came forward and took his stand, morning and evening.

17 And Jesse said to David his son, "Take for your brothers an ephah of this parched grain, and these ten loaves, and carry them quickly to the camp to your brothers; ¹⁸also take these ten cheeses to the commander of their thousand. See how your brothers fare, and bring some token from them."

19 Now Saul, and they, and all the men of Israel, were in the valley of Ē′lah, fighting with the Phĭ·lĭs′tĭnes. ²⁰And David rose early in the morning, and left the sheep with a keeper, and took the provisions, and went, as Jesse had commanded him; and he came to the encampment as the host was going forth to the battle line, shouting the war cry. ²¹And Israel and the Phĭ·lĭs′tĭnes drew up for battle, army against army. ²²And David left the things in charge of the keeper of the baggage, and ran to the ranks, and went and greeted his brothers. ²³As he talked with them, behold, the champion, the Phĭ·lĭs′tĭne of Găth, Goliath by name, came up out of the ranks of the Philistines, and spoke the same words as before. And David heard him.

24 All the men of Israel, when they saw the man, fled from him, and were much afraid. ²⁵And the men of Israel said, "Have you seen this man who has come up? Surely he has come up to defy Israel; and the man who kills him, the king will enrich with great riches, and will give him his daughter, and make his father's house free in Israel." ²⁶And David said to the men who stood by him, "What shall be done for the man who kills this Phĭ·lĭs′tĭne, and takes away the reproach from Israel? For who is this uncircumcised Philistine, that he should defy the armies of the living God?" ²⁷And the people answered him in the same way, "So shall it be done to the man who kills him."

28 Now Ē·lī′ăb his eldest brother heard when he spoke to the men; and Eliab's anger was kindled against David, and he said, "Why have you come down? And with whom have you left those few sheep in the wilderness? I know your presumption, and the evil of your heart; for you have come down to see the battle." ²⁹And David said, "What have I done now? Was it not but a word?" ³⁰And he turned away from him toward another, and spoke in the same way; and the people answered him again as before.

ˣGk Syr: Heb *among men*

31 When the words which David spoke were heard, they repeated them before Saul; and he sent for him. ³²And David said to Saul, "Let no man's heart fail because of him; your servant will go and fight with this Phĭ·lĭs'tĭne." ³³And Saul said to David, "You are not able to go against this Phĭ·lĭs'tĭne to fight with him; for you are but a youth, and he has been a man of war from his youth." ³⁴But David said to Saul, "Your servant used to keep sheep for his father; and when there came a lion, or a bear, and took a lamb from the flock, ³⁵I went after him and smote him and delivered it out of his mouth; and if he arose against me, I caught him by his beard, and smote him and killed him. ³⁶Your servant has killed both lions and bears; and this uncircumcised Phĭ·lĭs'tĭne shall be like one of them, seeing he has defied the armies of the living God." ³⁷And David said, "The Lord who delivered me from the paw of the lion and from the paw of the bear, will deliver me from the hand of this Phĭ·lĭs'tĭne." And Saul said to David, "Go, and the Lord be with you!" ³⁸Then Saul clothed David with his armor; he put a helmet of bronze on his head, and clothed him with a coat of mail. ³⁹And David girded his sword over his armor, and he tried in vain to go, for he was not used to them. Then David said to Saul, "I cannot go with these; for I am not used to them." And David put them off. ⁴⁰Then he took his staff in his hand, and chose five smooth stones from the brook, and put them in his shepherd's bag or wallet; his sling was in his hand, and he drew near to the Phĭ·lĭs'tĭne.

41 And the Phĭ·lĭs'tĭne came on and drew near to David, with his shield-bearer in front of him. ⁴²And when the Phĭ·lĭs'tĭne looked, and saw David, he disdained him; for he was but a youth, ruddy and comely in appearance. ⁴³And the Phĭ·lĭs'tĭne said to David, "Am I a dog, that you come to me with sticks?" And the Philistine cursed David by his gods. ⁴⁴The Phĭ·lĭs'tĭne said to David, "Come to me, and I will give your flesh to the birds of the air and to the beasts of the field." ⁴⁵Then David said to the Phĭ·lĭs'tĭne, "You come to me with a sword and with a spear and with a javelin; but I come to you in the name of the Lord of

hosts, the God of the armies of Israel, whom you have defied. ⁴⁶This day the Lord will deliver you into my hand, and I will strike you down, and cut off your head; and I will give the dead bodies of the host of the Phĭ·lĭs'tĭnes this day to the birds of the air and to the wild beasts of the earth; that all the earth may know that there is a God in Israel, ⁴⁷and that all this assembly may know that the Lord saves not with sword and spear; for the battle is the Lord's and he will give you into our hand."

48 When the Phĭ·lĭs'tĭne arose and came and drew near to meet David, David ran quickly toward the battle line to meet the Philistine. ⁴⁹And David put his hand in his bag and took out a stone, and slung it, and struck the Phĭ·lĭs'tĭne on his forehead; the stone sank into his forehead, and he fell on his face to the ground.

50 So David prevailed over the Phĭ·lĭs'tĭne with a sling and with a stone, and struck the Philistine, and killed him; there was no sword in the hand of David. ⁵¹Then David ran and stood over the Phĭ·lĭs'tĭne, and took his sword and drew it out of its sheath, and killed him, and cut off his head with it. When the Philistines saw that their champion was dead, they fled. ⁵²And the men of Israel and Judah rose with a shout and pursued the Phĭ·lĭs'tĭnes as far as Găthʸ and the gates of Ĕk'ron, so that the wounded Philistines fell on the way from Shā·a·rā'im as far as Gath and Ekron. ⁵³And the Israelites came back from chasing the Phĭ·lĭs'tĭnes, and they plundered their camp. ⁵⁴And David took the head of the Phĭ·lĭs'tĭne and brought it to Jerusalem; but he put his armor in his tent.

55 When Saul saw David go forth against the Phĭ·lĭs'tĭne, he said to Abner, the commander of the army, "Abner, whose son is this youth?" And Abner said, "As your soul lives, O king, I cannot tell." ⁵⁶And the king said, "Inquire whose son the stripling is." ⁵⁷And as David returned from the slaughter of the Phĭ·lĭs'tĭne, Abner took him, and brought him before Saul with the head of the Philistine in his hand. ⁵⁸And Saul said to him, "Whose son are you, young man?" And David answered, "I am the son

ʸGk: Heb *Gai*

of your servant Jesse the Bethlehemite."

18 When he had finished speaking to Saul, the soul of Jonathan was knit to the soul of David, and Jonathan loved him as his own soul. ²And Saul took him that day, and would not let him return to his father's house. ³Then Jonathan made a covenant with David, because he loved him as his own soul. ⁴And Jonathan stripped himself of the robe that was upon him, and gave it to David, and his armor, and even his sword and his bow and his girdle. ⁵And David went out and was successful wherever Saul sent him; so that Saul set him over the men of war. And this was good in the sight of all the people and also in the sight of Saul's servants.

6 As they were coming home, when David returned from slaying the Phĭ·lĭs'tĭne, the women came out of all the cities of Israel, singing and dancing, to meet King Saul, with timbrels, with songs of joy, and with instruments² of music. ⁷And the women sang to one another as they made merry,

"Saul has slain his thousands,
    and David his ten thousands."

⁸And Saul was very angry, and this saying displeased him; he said, "They have ascribed to David ten thousands, and to me they have ascribed thousands; and what more can he have but the kingdom?" ⁹And Saul eyed David from that day on.

10 And on the morrow an evil spirit from God rushed upon Saul, and he raved within his house, while David was playing the lyre, as he did day by day. Saul had his spear in his hand; ¹¹and Saul cast the spear, for he thought, "I will pin David to the wall." But David evaded him twice.

12 Saul was afraid of David, because the LORD was with him but had departed from Saul. ¹³So Saul removed him from his presence, and made him a commander of a thousand; and he went out and came in before the people. ¹⁴And David had success in all his undertakings; for the LORD was with him. ¹⁵And when Saul saw that he had great success, he stood in awe of him. ¹⁶But all Israel and Judah loved David; for he went out and came in before them.

17 Then Saul said to David, "Here is my elder daughter Mē'răb; I will give her to you for a wife; only be valiant for me and fight the LORD's battles." For Saul thought, "Let not my hand be upon him, but let the hand of the Phĭ·lĭs'tĭnes be upon him." ¹⁸And David said to Saul, "Who am I, and who are my kinsfolk, my father's family in Israel, that I should be son-in-law to the king?" ¹⁹But at the time when Mē'răb, Saul's daughter, should have been given to David, she was given to Ā'drĭ–ĕl the Mĕ·hō'lạ·thīte for a wife.

20 Now Saul's daughter Mī'chạl loved David; and they told Saul, and the thing pleased him. ²¹Saul thought, "Let me give her to him, that she may be a snare for him, and that the hand of the Phĭ·lĭs'tĭnes may be against him." Therefore Saul said to David a second time,ᵃ "You shall now be my son-in-law." ²²And Saul commanded his servants, "Speak to David in private and say, 'Behold, the king has delight in you, and all his servants love you; now then become the king's son-in-law.'" ²³And Saul's servants spoke those words in the ears of David. And David said, "Does it seem to you a little thing to become the king's son-in-law, seeing that I am a poor man and of no repute?" ²⁴And the servants of Saul told him, "Thus and so did David speak." ²⁵Then Saul said, "Thus shall you say to David, 'The king desires no marriage present except a hundred foreskins of the Phĭ·lĭs'tĭnes, that he may be avenged of the king's enemies.'" Now Saul thought to make David fall by the hand of the Philistines. ²⁶And when his servants told David these words, it pleased David well to be the king's son-in-law. Before the time had expired, ²⁷David arose and went, along with his men, and killed two hundred of the Phĭ·lĭs'tĭnes; and David brought their foreskins, which were given in full number to the king, that he might become the king's son-in-law. And Saul gave him his daughter Mī'chạl for a wife. ²⁸But when Saul saw and knew that the LORD was with David, and that all Israelᵇ loved him, ²⁹Saul was still more afraid of David. So Saul was David's enemy continually.

30 Then the princes of the Phĭ·lĭs'-

ᶻOr triangles, or three-stringed instruments
ᵃHeb by two ᵇGk: Heb Michal, Saul's daughter
18.7: 21.11; 29.5.

tĭnes came out to battle, and as often as they came out David had more success than all the servants of Saul; so that his name was highly esteemed.

19 And Saul spoke to Jonathan his son and to all his servants, that they should kill David. But Jonathan, Saul's son, delighted much in David. ²And Jonathan told David, "Saul my father seeks to kill you; therefore take heed to yourself in the morning, stay in a secret place and hide yourself; ³and I will go out and stand beside my father in the field where you are, and I will speak to my father about you; and if I learn anything I will tell you." ⁴And Jonathan spoke well of David to Saul his father, and said to him, "Let not the king sin against his servant David; because he has not sinned against you, and because his deeds have been of good service to you; ⁵for he took his life in his hand and he slew the Phĭ·lĭs'tĭne, and the LORD wrought a great victory for all Israel. You saw it, and rejoiced; why then will you sin against innocent blood by killing David without cause?" ⁶And Saul hearkened to the voice of Jonathan; Saul swore, "As the LORD lives, he shall not be put to death." ⁷And Jonathan called David, and Jonathan showed him all these things. And Jonathan brought David to Saul, and he was in his presence as before.

8 And there was war again; and David went out and fought with the Phĭ·lĭs'tĭnes, and made a great slaughter among them, so that they fled before him. ⁹Then an evil spirit from the LORD came upon Saul, as he sat in his house with his spear in his hand; and David was playing the lyre. ¹⁰And Saul sought to pin David to the wall with the spear; but he eluded Saul, so that he struck the spear into the wall. And David fled, and escaped.

11 That night Saulˣ sent messengers to David's house to watch him, that he might kill him in the morning. But Mī'chạl, David's wife, told him, "If you do not save your life tonight, tomorrow you will be killed." ¹²So Mī'chạl let David down through the window; and he fled away and escaped. ¹³Mī'chạl took an imageᶜ and laid it on the bed and put a pillowᵈ of goats' hair at its head, and covered it with the clothes. ¹⁴And when Saul sent messengers to

take David, she said, "He is sick." ¹⁵Then Saul sent the messengers to see David, saying, "Bring him up to me in the bed, that I may kill him." ¹⁶And when the messengers came in, behold, the imageᶜ was in the bed, with the pillowᵈ of goats' hair at its head. ¹⁷Saul said to Mī'chạl, "Why have you deceived me thus, and let my enemy go, so that he has escaped?" And Michal answered Saul, "He said to me, 'Let me go; why should I kill you?'"

18 Now David fled and escaped, and he came to Samuel at Rā'mạh, and told him all that Saul had done to him. And he and Samuel went and dwelt at Naī'ōth. ¹⁹And it was told Saul, "Behold, David is at Naī'ōth in Rā'mạh." ²⁰Then Saul sent messengers to take David; and when they saw the company of the prophets prophesying, and Samuel standing as head over them, the Spirit of God came upon the messengers of Saul, and they also prophesied. ²¹When it was told Saul, he sent other messengers, and they also prophesied. And Saul sent messengers again the third time, and they also prophesied. ²²Then he himself went to Rā'mạh, and came to the great well that is in Sē'cū; and he asked, "Where are Samuel and David?" And one said, "Behold, they are at Naī'ōth in Rā'mạh." ²³And he went fromᶠ there to Naī'ōth in Rā'mạh; and the Spirit of God came upon him also, and as he went he prophesied, until he came to Naioth in Ramah. ²⁴And he too stripped off his clothes, and he too prophesied before Samuel, and lay naked all that day and all that night. Hence it is said, "Is Saul also among the prophets?"

20 Then David fled from Naī'ōth in Rā'mạh, and came and said before Jonathan, "What have I done? What is my guilt? And what is my sin before your father, that he seeks my life?" ²And he said to him, "Far from it! You shall not die. Behold, my father does nothing either great or small without disclosing it to me; and why should my father hide this from me? It is not so." ³But David replied,ᵍ "Your father knows well that I have found favor in your eyes; and he thinks, 'Let not Jonathan know this, lest he be grieved.'

ˣGk Old Latin: Heb *escaped that night.* ¹¹*And Saul*
ᶜHeb *teraphim*
ᵈThe meaning of the Hebrew word is uncertain
ᶠGk: Heb lacks *from* ᵍGk: Heb *swore again*
19.23, 24: 10, 11, 12.

But truly, as the LORD lives and as your soul lives, there is but a step between me and death." ⁴Then said Jonathan to David, "Whatever you say, I will do for you." ⁵David said to Jonathan, "Behold, tomorrow is the new moon, and I should not fail to sit at table with the king; but let me go, that I may hide myself in the field till the third day at evening. ⁶If your father misses me at all, then say, 'David earnestly asked leave of me to run to Bethlehem his city; for there is a yearly sacrifice there for all the family.' ⁷If he says, 'Good!' it will be well with your servant; but if he is angry, then know that evil is determined by him. ⁸Therefore deal kindly with your servant, for you have brought your servant into a sacred covenant* with you. But if there is guilt in me, slay me yourself; for why should you bring me to your father?" ⁹And Jonathan said, "Far be it from you! If I knew that it was determined by my father that evil should come upon you, would I not tell you?" ¹⁰Then said David to Jonathan, "Who will tell me if your father answers you roughly?" ¹¹And Jonathan said to David, "Come, let us go out into the field." So they both went out into the field.

12 And Jonathan said to David, "The LORD, the God of Israel, be witness!ⁱ When I have sounded my father, about this time tomorrow, or the third day, behold, if he is well disposed toward David, shall I not then send and disclose it to you? ¹³But should it please my father to do you harm, the LORD do so to Jonathan, and more also, if I do not disclose it to you, and send you away, that you may go in safety. May the LORD be with you, as he has been with my father. ¹⁴If I am still alive, show me the loyal love of the LORD, that I may not die;ʲ ¹⁵and do not cut off your loyalty from my house for ever. When the LORD cuts off every one of the enemies of David from the face of the earth, ¹⁶let not the name of Jonathan be cut off from the house of David.ᵏ And may the LORD take vengeance on David's enemies." ¹⁷And Jonathan made David swear again by his love for him; for he loved him as he loved his own soul.

18 Then Jonathan said to him, "Tomorrow is the new moon; and you will be missed, because your seat will be empty. ¹⁹And on the third day you will be greatly missed;ˡ then go to the place where you hid yourself when the matter was in hand, and remain beside yonder stone heap.ᵐ ²⁰And I will shoot three arrows to the side of it, as though I shot at a mark. ²¹And behold, I will send the lad, saying, 'Go, find the arrows.' If I say to the lad, 'Look, the arrows are on this side of you, take them,' then you are to come, for, as the LORD lives, it is safe for you and there is no danger. ²²But if I say to the youth, 'Look, the arrows are beyond you,' then go; for the LORD has sent you away. ²³And as for the matter of which you and I have spoken, behold, the LORD is between you and me for ever."

24 So David hid himself in the field; and when the new moon came, the king sat down to eat food. ²⁵The king sat upon his seat, as at other times, upon the seat by the wall; Jonathan sat opposite,ⁿ and Abner sat by Saul's side, but David's place was empty. 26 Yet Saul did not say anything that day; for he thought, "Something has befallen him; he is not clean, surely he is not clean." ²⁷But on the second day, the morrow after the new moon, David's place was empty. And Saul said to Jonathan his son, "Why has not the son of Jesse come to the meal, either yesterday or today?" ²⁸Jonathan answered Saul, "David earnestly asked leave of me to go to Bethlehem; ²⁹he said, 'Let me go; for our family holds a sacrifice in the city, and my brother has commanded me to be there. So now, if I have found favor in your eyes, let me get away, and see my brothers.' For this reason he has not come to the king's table."

30 Then Saul's anger was kindled against Jonathan, and he said to him, "You son of a perverse, rebellious woman, do I not know that you have chosen the son of Jesse to your own shame, and to the shame of your mother's nakedness? ³¹For as long as the son of Jesse lives upon the earth, neither you nor your kingdom shall be established. Therefore send and fetch him to me, for he shall surely die." ³²Then Jonathan answered Saul his

ᵃHeb *a covenant of the* LORD
ⁱHeb lacks *be witness*   ʲHeb uncertain
ᵏGk: Heb *earth, and Jonathan made a covenant with the house of David*   ˡGk: Heb *go down quickly*
ᵐGk: Heb *the stone Ezel*
ⁿCn See Gk: Heb *stood up*

father, "Why should he be put to death? What has he done?" ³³But Saul cast his spear at him to smite him; so Jonathan knew that his father was determined to put David to death. ³⁴And Jonathan rose from the table in fierce anger and ate no food the second day of the month, for he was grieved for David, because his father had disgraced him.

35 In the morning Jonathan went out into the field to the appointment with David, and with him a little lad. ³⁶And he said to his lad, "Run and find the arrows which I shoot." As the lad ran, he shot an arrow beyond him. ³⁷And when the lad came to the place of the arrow which Jonathan had shot, Jonathan called after the lad and said, "Is not the arrow beyond you?" ³⁸And Jonathan called after the lad, "Hurry, make haste, stay not." So Jonathan's lad gathered up the arrows, and came to his master. ³⁹But the lad knew nothing; only Jonathan and David knew the matter. ⁴⁰And Jonathan gave his weapons to his lad, and said to him, "Go and carry them to the city." ⁴¹And as soon as the lad had gone, David rose from beside the stone heapᵒ and fell on his face to the ground, and bowed three times; and they kissed one another, and wept with one another, until David recovered himself.ᵖ ⁴²Then Jonathan said to David, "Go in peace, forasmuch as we have sworn both of us in the name of the LORD, saying, 'The LORD shall be between me and you, and between my descendants and your descendants, for ever.'" And he rose and departed; and Jonathan went into the city.�q

21 ʳ Then came David to Nŏb to A·hĭm'e·lĕch the priest; and Ahimelech came to meet David trembling, and said to him, "Why are you alone, and no one with you?" ²And David said to A·hĭm'e·lĕch the priest, "The king has charged me with a matter, and said to me, 'Let no one know anything of the matter about which I send you, and with which I have charged you.' I have made an appointment with the young men for such and such a place. ³Now then, what have you at hand? Give me five loaves of bread, or whatever is here." ⁴And the priest answered David, "I have no common bread at hand, but there is holy bread; if only the young men have

kept themselves from women." ⁵And David answered the priest, "Of a truth women have been kept from us as always when I go on an expedition; the vessels of the young men are holy, even when it is a common journey; how much more today will their vessels be holy?" ⁶So the priest gave him the holy bread; for there was no bread there but the bread of the Presence, which is removed from before the LORD, to be replaced by hot bread on the day it is taken away.

7 Now a certain man of the servants of Saul was there that day, detained before the LORD; his name was Dō'ĕg the Ē'dǫm·īte, the chief of Saul's herdsmen.

8 And David said to A·hĭm'e·lĕch, "And have you not here a spear or a sword at hand? For I have brought neither my sword nor my weapons with me, because the king's business required haste." ⁹And the priest said, "The sword of Goliath the Phĭ·lĭs'tīne, whom you killed in the valley of Ē'lah, behold, it is here wrapped in a cloth behind the ephod; if you will take that, take it, for there is none but that here." And David said, "There is none like that; give it to me."

10 And David rose and fled that day from Saul, and went to Ā'chĭsh the king of Găth. ¹¹And the servants of Ā'chĭsh said to him, "Is not this David the king of the land? Did they not sing to one another of him in dances,

'Saul has slain his thousands,
    and David his ten thousands'?"

¹²And David took these words to heart, and was much afraid of Ā'chĭsh the king of Găth. ¹³So he changed his behavior before them, and feigned himself mad in their hands, and made marks on the doors of the gate, and let his spittle run down his beard. ¹⁴Then said Ā'chĭsh to his servants, "Lo, you see the man is mad; why then have you brought him to me? ¹⁵Do I lack madmen, that you have brought this fellow to play the madman in my presence? Shall this fellow come into my house?"

22 David departed from there and escaped to the cave of A·dŭl'-lam; and when his brothers and all his father's house heard it, they went down there to him. ²And every one who

ᵒGk: Heb *from beside the south* ᵖOr *exceeded*
qThis sentence is 21.1 in Heb ʳCh 21.2 in Heb
21.11: 18.7; 29.5.

was in distress, and every one who was in debt, and every one who was discontented, gathered to him; and he became captain over them. And there were with him about four hundred men.

3 And David went from there to Mĭz′pĕh of Mō′ăb; and he said to the king of Moab, "Pray let my father and my mother stay⁸ with you, till I know what God will do for me." ⁴And he left them with the king of Mō′ăb, and they stayed with him all the time that David was in the stronghold. ⁵Then the prophet Găd said to David, "Do not remain in the stronghold; depart, and go into the land of Judah." So David departed, and went into the forest of Hĕ′rĕth.

6 Now Saul heard that David was discovered, and the men who were with him. Saul was sitting at Gĭb′ē–ah, under the tamarisk tree on the height, with his spear in his hand, and all his servants were standing about him. ⁷And Saul said to his servants who stood about him, "Hear now, you Benjaminites; will the son of Jesse give every one of you fields and vineyards, will he make you all commanders of thousands and commanders of hundreds, ⁸that all of you have conspired against me? No one discloses to me when my son makes a league with the son of Jesse, none of you is sorry for me or discloses to me that my son has stirred up my servant against me, to lie in wait, as at this day." ⁹Then answered Dō′ĕg the Ē′dom·īte, who stood by the servants of Saul, "I saw the son of Jesse coming to Nŏb, to Ȧ·hĭm′e̦·lĕch the son of Ȧ·hī′tŭb, ¹⁰and he inquired of the LORD for him, and gave him provisions, and gave him the sword of Goliath the Phĭ·lĭs′tĭne."

11 Then the king sent to summon Ȧ·hĭm′e̦·lĕch the priest, the son of Ȧ·hī′tŭb, and all his father's house, the priests who were at Nŏb; and all of them came to the king. ¹²And Saul said, "Hear now, son of Ȧ·hī′tŭb." And he answered, "Here I am, my lord." ¹³And Saul said to him, "Why have you conspired against me, you and the son of Jesse, in that you have given him bread and a sword, and have inquired of God for him, so that he has risen against me, to lie in wait, as at this day?" ¹⁴Then Ȧ·hĭm′e̦·lĕch answered the king, "And who among all your servants is so faithful as David, who is the king's son-in-law, and captain over⁴ your bodyguard, and honored in your house? ¹⁵Is today the first time that I have inquired of God for him? No! Let not the king impute anything to his servant or to all the house of my father; for your servant has known nothing of all this, much or little." ¹⁶And the king said, "You shall surely die, Ȧ·hĭm′-e̦·lĕch, you and all your father's house." ¹⁷And the king said to the guard who stood about him, "Turn and kill the priests of the LORD; because their hand also is with David, and they knew that he fled, and did not disclose it to me." But the servants of the king would not put forth their hand to fall upon the priests of the LORD. ¹⁸Then the king said to Dō′ĕg, "You turn and fall upon the priests." And Doeg the Ē′dom·īte turned and fell upon the priests, and he killed on that day eighty-five persons who wore the linen ephod. ¹⁹And Nŏb, the city of the priests, he put to the sword; both men and women, children and sucklings, oxen, asses and sheep, he put to the sword.

20 But one of the sons of Ȧ·hĭm′-e̦·lĕch the son of Ȧ·hī′tŭb, named Ȧ·bī′-a̦·thär, escaped and fled after David. ²¹And Ȧ·bī′a̦·thär told David that Saul had killed the priests of the LORD. ²²And David said to Ȧ·bī′a̦·thär, "I knew on that day, when Dō′ĕg the Ē′dom·īte was there, that he would surely tell Saul. I have occasioned the death of all the persons of your father's house. ²³Stay with me, fear not; for he that seeks my life seeks your life; with me you shall be in safekeeping."

23 Now they told David, "Behold the Phĭ·lĭs′tĭnes are fighting against Kē·ī′la̦h, and are robbing the threshing floors." ²Therefore David inquired of the LORD, "Shall I go and attack these Phĭ·lĭs′tĭnes?" And the LORD said to David, "Go and attack the Philistines and save Kē·ī′la̦h." ³But David's men said to him, "Behold, we are afraid here in Judah; how much more then if we go to Kē·ī′la̦h against the armies of the Phĭ·lĭs′tĭnes?" ⁴Then David inquired of the LORD again. And the LORD answered him, "Arise, go down to Kē·ī′la̦h; for I will give the Phĭ·lĭs′tĭnes into your hand." ⁵And David and his men went to Kē·ī′la̦h,

*Syr Vg: Heb *come out*
⁴Gk Tg: Heb *and has turned aside to*

and fought with the Phĭ·lĭs'tĭnes, and brought away their cattle, and made a great slaughter among them. So David delivered the inhabitants of Kē·ī'lah.

6 When A·bī'a·thär the son of A·hĭm'-e·lĕch fled to David to Kē·ī'lah, he came down with an ephod in his hand. 7 Now it was told Saul that David had come to Kē·ī'lah. And Saul said, "God has given him into my hand; for he has shut himself in by entering a town that has gates and bars." 8 And Saul summoned all the people to war, to go down to Kē·ī'lah, to besiege David and his men. 9 David knew that Saul was plotting evil against him; and he said to A·bī'-a·thär the priest, "Bring the ephod here." 10 Then said David, "O Lᴏʀᴅ, the God of Israel, thy servant has surely heard that Saul seeks to come to Kē·ī'lah, to destroy the city on my account. 11 Will the men of Kē·ī'lah surrender me into his hand? Will Saul come down, as thy servant has heard? O Lᴏʀᴅ, the God of Israel, I beseech thee, tell thy servant." And the Lᴏʀᴅ said, "He will come down." 12 Then said David, "Will the men of Kē·ī'lah surrender me and my men into the hand of Saul?" And the Lᴏʀᴅ said, "They will surrender you." 13 Then David and his men, who were about six hundred, arose and departed from Kē·ī'lah, and they went wherever they could go. When Saul was told that David had escaped from Keilah, he gave up the expedition. 14 And David remained in the strongholds in the wilderness, in the hill country of the Wilderness of Zĭph. And Saul sought him every day, but God did not give him into his hand.

15 And David was afraid because[u] Saul had come out to seek his life. David was in the Wilderness of Zĭph at Hō'rĕsh. 16 And Jonathan, Saul's son, rose, and went to David at Hō'rĕsh, and strengthened his hand in God. 17 And he said to him, "Fear not; for the hand of Saul my father shall not find you; you shall be king over Israel, and I shall be next to you; Saul my father also knows this." 18 And the two of them made a covenant before the Lᴏʀᴅ; David remained at Hō'rĕsh, and Jonathan went home.

19 Then the Zĭph'ītes went up to Saul at Gĭb'ē–ah, saying, "Does not David hide among us in the strongholds at Hō'rĕsh, on the hill of Ha·chī'-lah, which is south of Jē·shī'mŏn?

20 Now come down, O king, according to all your heart's desire to come down; and our part shall be to surrender him into the king's hand." 21 And Saul said, "May you be blessed by the Lᴏʀᴅ; for you have had compassion on me. 22 Go, make yet more sure; know and see the place where his haunt is, and who has seen him there; for it is told me that he is very cunning. 23 See therefore, and take note of all the lurking places where he hides, and come back to me with sure information. Then I will go with you; and if he is in the land, I will search him out among all the thousands of Judah." 24 And they arose, and went to Zĭph ahead of Saul.

Now David and his men were in the wilderness of Mā'ŏn, in the Är'a·bah to the south of Jē·shī'mŏn. 25 And Saul and his men went to seek him. And David was told; therefore he went down to the rock which is[v] in the wilderness of Mā'ŏn. And when Saul heard that, he pursued after David in the wilderness of Maon. 26 Saul went on one side of the mountain, and David and his men on the other side of the mountain; and David was making haste to get away from Saul, as Saul and his men were closing in upon David and his men to capture them, 27 when a messenger came to Saul, saying, "Make haste and come; for the Phĭ·lĭs'tĭnes have made a raid upon the land." 28 So Saul returned from pursuing after David, and went against the Phĭ·lĭs'-tĭnes; therefore that place was called the Rock of Escape. 29[w] And David went up from there, and dwelt in the strongholds of Ĕn–gĕ'dī.

24 When Saul returned from following the Phĭ·lĭs'tĭnes, he was told, "Behold, David is in the wilderness of Ĕn–gĕ'dī." 2 Then Saul took three thousand chosen men out of all Israel, and went to seek David and his men in front of the Wildgoats' Rocks. 3 And he came to the sheepfolds by the way, where there was a cave; and Saul went in to relieve himself. Now David and his men were sitting in the innermost parts of the cave. 4 And the men of David said to him, "Here is the day of which the Lᴏʀᴅ said to you, 'Behold, I will give your enemy into your hand, and you shall do to him as it shall seem good to you.'" Then David arose and

*Or saw that   *Gk: Heb and dwelt   *Ch 24.1 in Heb
24.1-22: 26.1-25.

stealthily cut off the skirt of Saul's robe. [5] And afterward David's heart smote him, because he had cut off Saul's skirt. [6] He said to his men, "The LORD forbid that I should do this thing to my lord, the LORD's anointed, to put forth my hand against him, seeing he is the LORD's anointed." [7] So David persuaded his men with these words, and did not permit them to attack Saul. And Saul rose up and left the cave, and went upon his way.

8 Afterward David also arose, and went out of the cave, and called after Saul, "My lord the king!" And when Saul looked behind him, David bowed with his face to the earth, and did obeisance. [9] And David said to Saul, "Why do you listen to the words of men who say, 'Behold, David seeks your hurt'? [10] Lo, this day your eyes have seen how the LORD gave you today into my hand in the cave; and some bade me kill you, but I[x] spared you. I said, 'I will not put forth my hand against my lord; for he is the LORD's anointed.' [11] See, my father, see the skirt of your robe in my hand; for by the fact that I cut off the skirt of your robe, and did not kill you, you may know and see that there is no wrong or treason in my hands. I have not sinned against you, though you hunt my life to take it. [12] May the LORD judge between me and you, may the LORD avenge me upon you; but my hand shall not be against you. [13] As the proverb of the ancients says, 'Out of the wicked comes forth wickedness'; but my hand shall not be against you. [14] After whom has the king of Israel come out? After whom do you pursue? After a dead dog! After a flea! [15] May the LORD therefore be judge, and give sentence between me and you, and see to it, and plead my cause, and deliver me from your hand."

16 When David had finished speaking these words to Saul, Saul said, "Is this your voice, my son David?" And Saul lifted up his voice and wept. [17] He said to David, "You are more righteous than I; for you have repaid me good, whereas I have repaid you evil. [18] And you have declared this day how you have dealt well with me, in that you did not kill me when the LORD put me into your hands. [19] For if a man finds his enemy, will he let him go away safe? So may the LORD reward you with good for what you have done to

me this day. [20] And now, behold, I know that you shall surely be king, and that the kingdom of Israel shall be established in your hand. [21] Swear to me therefore by the LORD that you will not cut off my descendants after me, and that you will not destroy my name out of my father's house." [22] And David swore this to Saul. Then Saul went home; but David and his men went up to the stronghold.

25 Now Samuel died; and all Israel assembled and mourned for him, and they buried him in his house at Rā′mah.

Then David rose and went down to the wilderness of Pār′ăn. [2] And there was a man in Mā′ŏn, whose business was in Cär′mel. The man was very rich; he had three thousand sheep and a thousand goats. He was shearing his sheep in Carmel. [3] Now the name of the man was Nā′băl and the name of his wife Āb′ĭ·gäil. The woman was of good understanding and beautiful, but the man was churlish and ill-behaved; he was a Cā′lĕb·īte. [4] David heard in the wilderness that Nā′băl was shearing his sheep. [5] So David sent ten young men; and David said to the young men, "Go up to Cär′mel, and go to Nā′băl, and greet him in my name.[6] And thus you shall salute him: 'Peace be to you, and peace be to your house, and peace be to all that you have. [7] I hear that you have shearers; now your shepherds have been with us, and we did them no harm, and they missed nothing, all the time they were in Cär′mel. [8] Ask your young men, and they will tell you. Therefore let my young men find favor in your eyes; for we come on a feast day. Pray, give whatever you have at hand to your servants and to your son David.'"

9 When David's young men came, they said all this to Nā′băl in the name of David; and then they waited. [10] And Nā′băl answered David's servants, "Who is David? Who is the son of Jesse? There are many servants nowadays who are breaking away from their masters. [11] Shall I take my bread and my water and my meat that I have killed for my shearers, and give it to men who come from I do not know where?" [12] So David's young men turned away, and came back and told him all this. [13] And David said to his

[x] Gk Syr Tg: Heb *you*

men, "Every man gird on his sword!" And every man of them girded on his sword; David also girded on his sword; and about four hundred men went up after David, while two hundred remained with the baggage.

14 But one of the young men told Ăb'ĭ-gāil, Nā'băl's wife, "Behold, David sent messengers out of the wilderness to salute our master; and he railed at them. ¹⁵ Yet the men were very good to us, and we suffered no harm, and we did not miss anything when we were in the fields, as long as we went with them; ¹⁶ they were a wall to us both by night and by day, all the while we were with them keeping the sheep. ¹⁷ Now therefore know this and consider what you should do; for evil is determined against our master and against all his house, and he is so ill-natured that one cannot speak to him."

18 Then Ăb'ĭ-gāil made haste, and took two hundred loaves, and two skins of wine, and five sheep ready dressed, and five measures of parched grain, and a hundred clusters of raisins, and two hundred cakes of figs, and laid them on asses. ¹⁹ And she said to her young men, "Go on before me; behold, I come after you." But she did not tell her husband Nā'băl. ²⁰ And as she rode on the ass, and came down under cover of the mountain, behold, David and his men came down toward her; and she met them. ²¹ Now David had said, "Surely in vain have I guarded all that this fellow has in the wilderness, so that nothing was missed of all that belonged to him; and he has returned me evil for good. ²² God do so to David ʸ and more also, if by morning I leave so much as one male of all who belong to him."

23 When Ăb'ĭ-gāil saw David, she made haste, and alighted from the ass, and fell before David on her face, and bowed to the ground. ²⁴ She fell at his feet and said, "Upon me alone, my lord, be the guilt; pray let your handmaid speak in your ears, and hear the words of your handmaid. ²⁵ Let not my lord regard this ill-natured fellow, Nā'băl; for as his name is, so is he; Nabal ᶻ is his name, and folly is with him; but I your handmaid did not see the young men of my lord, whom you sent. ²⁶ Now then, my lord, as the LORD lives, and as your soul lives, seeing the LORD has restrained you from bloodguilt, and

from taking vengeance with your own hand, now then let your enemies and those who seek to do evil to my lord be as Nā'băl. ²⁷ And now let this present which your servant has brought to my lord be given to the young men who follow my lord. ²⁸ Pray forgive the trespass of your handmaid; for the LORD will certainly make my lord a sure house, because my lord is fighting the battles of the LORD; and evil shall not be found in you so long as you live. ²⁹ If men rise up to pursue you and to seek your life, the life of my lord shall be bound in the bundle of the living in the care of the LORD your God; and the lives of your enemies he shall sling out as from the hollow of a sling. ³⁰ And when the LORD has done to my lord according to all the good that he has spoken concerning you, and has appointed you prince over Israel, ³¹ my lord shall have no cause of grief, or pangs of conscience, for having shed blood without cause or for my lord taking vengeance himself. And when the LORD has dealt well with my lord, then remember your handmaid."

32 And David said to Ăb'ĭ-gāil, "Blessed be the LORD, the God of Israel, who sent you this day to meet me! ³³ Blessed be your discretion, and blessed be you, who have kept me this day from bloodguilt and from avenging myself with my own hand! ³⁴ For as surely as the LORD the God of Israel lives, who has restrained me from hurting you, unless you had made haste and come to meet me, truly by morning there had not been left to Nā'băl so much as one male." ³⁵ Then David received from her hand what she had brought him; and he said to her, "Go up in peace to your house; see, I have hearkened to your voice, and I have granted your petition."

36 And Ăb'ĭ-gāil came to Nā'băl; and, lo, he was holding a feast in his house, like the feast of a king. And Nabal's heart was merry within him, for he was very drunk; so she told him nothing at all until the morning light. ³⁷ And in the morning, when the wine had gone out of Nā'băl, his wife told him these things, and his heart died within him, and he became as a stone. ³⁸ And about ten days later the LORD smote Nā'băl; and he died.

ʸ Gk Compare Syr: Heb *the enemies of David*
ᶻ That is *fool*

39 When David heard that Nā′bal was dead, he said, "Blessed be the LORD who has avenged the insult I received at the hand of Nabal, and has kept back his servant from evil; the LORD has returned the evil-doing of Nabal upon his own head." Then David sent and wooed Ăb′ĭ·gāil, to make her his wife. 40 And when the servants of David came to Ăb′ĭ·gāil at Cär′mel, they said to her, "David has sent us to you to take you to him as his wife." 41 And she rose and bowed with her face to the ground, and said, "Behold, your handmaid is a servant to wash the feet of the servants of my lord." 42 And Ăb′ĭ·gāil made haste and rose and mounted on an ass, and her five maidens attended her; she went after the messengers of David, and became his wife.

43 David also took Ă·hĭn′ō–ăm of Jĕz′rē·el; and both of them became his wives. 44 Saul had given Mī′chal his daughter, David's wife, to Păl′tī the son of Lā′ĭsh, who was of Găl′lĭm.

26 Then the Zĭph′ītes came to Saul at Gĭb′ē–ah, saying, "Is not David hiding himself on the hill of Ha·chī′lah, which is on the east of Jĕ·shī′mŏn?" 2 So Saul arose and went down to the wilderness of Zĭph, with three thousand chosen men of Israel, to seek David in the wilderness of Ziph. 3 And Saul encamped on the hill of Ha·chī′lah, which is beside the road on the east of Jĕ·shī′mŏn. But David remained in the wilderness; and when he saw that Saul came after him into the wilderness, 4 David sent out spies, and learned of a certainty that Saul had come. 5 Then David rose and came to the place where Saul had encamped; and David saw the place where Saul lay, with Abner the son of Nĕr, the commander of his army; Saul was lying within the encampment, while the army was encamped around him.

6 Then David said to Ă·hĭm′e·lĕch the Hĭt′tīte, and to Jō′ăb′ş brother Ă·bī′shaī the son of Zĕ·rü′ĭ·ah, "Who will go down with me into the camp to Saul?" And Abishai said, "I will go down with you." 7 So David and Ă·bī′shaī went to the army by night; and there lay Saul sleeping within the encampment, with his spear stuck in the ground at his head; and Abner and the army lay around him. 8 Then said Ă·bī′-

shaī to David, "God has given your enemy into your hand this day; now therefore let me pin him to the earth with one stroke of the spear, and I will not strike him twice." 9 But David said to Ă·bī′shaī, "Do not destroy him; for who can put forth his hand against the LORD's anointed, and be guiltless?" 10 And David said, "As the LORD lives, the LORD will smite him; or his day shall come to die; or he shall go down into battle and perish. 11 The LORD forbid that I should put forth my hand against the LORD's anointed; but take now the spear that is at his head, and the jar of water, and let us go." 12 So David took the spear and the jar of water from Saul's head; and they went away. No man saw it, or knew it, nor did any awake; for they were all asleep, because a deep sleep from the LORD had fallen upon them.

13 Then David went over to the other side, and stood afar off on the top of the mountain, with a great space between them; 14 and David called to the army, and to Abner the son of Nĕr, saying, "Will you not answer, Abner?" Then Abner answered, "Who are you that calls to the king?" 15 And David said to Abner, "Are you not a man? Who is like you in Israel? Why then have you not kept watch over your lord the king? For one of the people came in to destroy the king your lord. 16 This thing that you have done is not good. As the LORD lives, you deserve to die, because you have not kept watch over your lord, the LORD's anointed. And now see where the king's spear is, and the jar of water that was at his head."

17 Saul recognized David's voice, and said, "Is this your voice, my son David?" And David said, "It is my voice, my lord, O king." 18 And he said, "Why does my lord pursue after his servant? For what have I done? What guilt is on my hands? 19 Now therefore let my lord the king hear the words of his servant. If it is the LORD who has stirred you up against me, may he accept an offering; but if it is men, may they be cursed before the LORD, for they have driven me out this day that I should have no share in the heritage of the LORD, saying, 'Go, serve other gods.' 20 Now therefore, let not my blood fall to the earth away from the pres-

ence of the LORD; for the king of Israel has come out to seek my life,[a] like one who hunts a partridge in the mountains."

21 Then Saul said, "I have done wrong; return, my son David, for I will no more do you harm, because my life was precious in your eyes this day; behold, I have played the fool, and have erred exceedingly." 22 And David made answer, "Here is the spear, O king! Let one of the young men come over and fetch it. 23 The LORD rewards every man for his righteousness and his faithfulness; for the LORD gave you into my hand today, and I would not put forth my hand against the LORD's anointed. 24 Behold, as your life was precious this day in my sight, so may my life be precious in the sight of the LORD, and may he deliver me out of all tribulation." 25 Then Saul said to David, "Blessed be you, my son David! You will do many things and will succeed in them." So David went his way, and Saul returned to his place.

27 And David said in his heart, "I shall now perish one day by the hand of Saul; there is nothing better for me than that I should escape to the land of the Phĭ·lĭs'tĭnes; then Saul will despair of seeking me any longer within the borders of Israel, and I shall escape out of his hand." 2 So David arose and went over, he and the six hundred men who were with him, to Ā'chĭsh the son of Mā'ŏch, king of Găth. 3 And David dwelt with Ā'chĭsh at Găth, he and his men, every man with his household, and David with his two wives, A·hĭn'ō·ăm of Jĕz'rē·el, and Ăb'ĭ·gāil of Cār'mel, Nā'băl's widow. 4 And when it was told Saul that David had fled to Găth, he sought for him no more.

5 Then David said to Ā'chĭsh, "If I have found favor in your eyes, let a place be given me in one of the country towns, that I may dwell there; for why should your servant dwell in the royal city with you?" 6 So that day Ā'chĭsh gave him Zĭk'lăg; therefore Ziklag has belonged to the kings of Judah to this day. 7 And the number of the days that David dwelt in the country of the Phĭ·lĭs'tĭnes was a year and four months.

8 Now David and his men went up, and made raids upon the Gĕsh'ū·rītes, the Gĭr'zītes, and the A·măl'e·kītes;

for these were the inhabitants of the land from of old, as far as Shūr, to the land of Egypt. 9 And David smote the land, and left neither man nor woman alive, but took away the sheep, the oxen, the asses, the camels, and the garments, and came back to Ā'chĭsh. 10 When Ā'chĭsh asked, "Against whom[b] have you made a raid today?" David would say, "Against the Nĕg'ĕb of Judah," or "Against the Negeb of the Je·räh'mē·e·lītes," or, "Against the Negeb of the Kĕn'ītes." 11 And David saved neither man nor woman alive, to bring tidings to Găth, thinking, "Lest they should tell about us, and say, 'So David has done.'" Such was his custom all the while he dwelt in the country of the Phĭ·lĭs'tĭnes. 12 And Ā'chĭsh trusted David, thinking, "He has made himself utterly abhorred by his people Israel; therefore he shall be my servant always."

28 In those days the Phĭ·lĭs'tĭnes gathered their forces for war, to fight against Israel. And Ā'chĭsh said to David, "Understand that you and your men are to go out with me in the army." 2 David said to Ā'chĭsh, "Very well, you shall know what your servant can do." And Achish said to David, "Very well, I will make you my bodyguard for life."

3 Now Samuel had died, and all Israel had mourned for him and buried him in Rā'măh, his own city. And Saul had put the mediums and the wizards out of the land. 4 The Phĭ·lĭs'tĭnes assembled, and came and encamped at Shū'nĕm; and Saul gathered all Israel, and they encamped at Gĭl·bō'a. 5 When Saul saw the army of the Phĭ·lĭs'tĭnes, he was afraid, and his heart trembled greatly. 6 And when Saul inquired of the LORD, the LORD did not answer him, either by dreams, or by U'rĭm, or by prophets. 7 Then Saul said to his servants, "Seek out for me a woman who is a medium, that I may go to her and inquire of her." And his servants said to him, "Behold, there is a medium at Ĕn-dôr."

8 So Saul disguised himself and put on other garments, and went, he and two men with him; and they came to the woman by night. And he said, "Divine for me by a spirit, and bring up for me whomever I shall name to

---

[a] Gk: Heb *a flea* (as in 24.14)
[b] Gk Vg: Heb lacks *whom*

you." ⁹The woman said to him, "Surely you know what Saul has done, how he has cut off the mediums and the wizards from the land. Why then are you laying a snare for my life to bring about my death?" ¹⁰But Saul swore to her by the LORD, "As the LORD lives, no punishment shall come upon you for this thing." ¹¹Then the woman said, "Whom shall I bring up for you?" He said, "Bring up Samuel for me." ¹²When the woman saw Samuel, she cried out with a loud voice; and the woman said to Saul, "Why have you deceived me? You are Saul." ¹³The king said to her, "Have no fear; what do you see?" And the woman said to Saul, "I see a god coming up out of the earth." ¹⁴He said to her, "What is his appearance?" And she said, "An old man is coming up; and he is wrapped in a robe." And Saul knew that it was Samuel, and he bowed with his face to the ground, and did obeisance.

15 Then Samuel said to Saul, "Why have you disturbed me by bringing me up?" Saul answered, "I am in great distress; for the Phĭ·lĭs′tĭnes are warring against me, and God has turned away from me and answers me no more, either by prophets or by dreams; therefore I have summoned you to tell me what I shall do." ¹⁶And Samuel said, "Why then do you ask me, since the LORD has turned from you and become your enemy? ¹⁷The LORD has done to you as he spoke by me; for the LORD has torn the kingdom out of your hand, and given it to your neighbor, David. ¹⁸Because you did not obey the voice of the LORD, and did not carry out his fierce wrath against Ăm′a·lĕk, therefore the LORD has done this thing to you this day. ¹⁹Moreover the LORD will give Israel also with you into the hand of the Phĭ·lĭs′tĭnes; and tomorrow you and your sons shall be with me; the LORD will give the army of Israel also into the hand of the Philistines."

20 Then Saul fell at once full length upon the ground, filled with fear because of the words of Samuel; and there was no strength in him, for he had eaten nothing all day and all night. ²¹And the woman came to Saul, and when she saw that he was terrified, she said to him, "Behold, your handmaid has hearkened to you; I have taken my life in my hand, and have hearkened to what you have said to me. ²²Now therefore, you also hearken to your handmaid; let me set a morsel of bread before you; and eat, that you may have strength when you go on your way." ²³He refused, and said, "I will not eat." But his servants, together with the woman, urged him; and he hearkened to their words. So he arose from the earth, and sat upon the bed. ²⁴Now the woman had a fatted calf in the house, and she quickly killed it, and she took flour, and kneaded it and baked unleavened bread of it, ²⁵and she put it before Saul and his servants; and they ate. Then they rose and went away that night.

29 Now the Phĭ·lĭs′tĭnes gathered all their forces at Ā′phĕk; and the Israelites were encamped by the fountain which is in Jĕz′rē·el. ²As the lords of the Phĭ·lĭs′tĭnes were passing on by hundreds and by thousands, and David and his men were passing on in the rear with Ā′chĭsh, ³the commanders of the Phĭ·lĭs′tĭnes said, "What are these Hebrews doing here?" And Ā′chĭsh said to the commanders of the Philistines, "Is not this David, the servant of Saul, king of Israel, who has been with me now for days and years, and since he deserted to me I have found no fault in him to this day." ⁴But the commanders of the Phĭ·lĭs′tĭnes were angry with him; and the commanders of the Philistines said to him, "Send the man back, that he may return to the place to which you have assigned him; he shall not go down with us to battle, lest in the battle he become an adversary to us. For how could this fellow reconcile himself to his lord? Would it not be with the heads of the men here? ⁵Is not this David, of whom they sing to one another in dances,

'Saul has slain his thousands,
     and David his ten thousands'?"

6 Then Ā′chĭsh called David and said to him, "As the LORD lives, you have been honest, and to me it seems right that you should march out and in with me in the campaign; for I have found nothing wrong in you from the day of your coming to me to this day. Nevertheless the lords do not approve of you. ⁷So go back now; and go peaceably, that you may not dis-

29.5: 18.7; 21.11.

please the lords of the Phĭ·lĭs'tĭnes." ⁸And David said to Ā'chĭsh, "But what have I done? What have you found in your servant from the day I entered your service until now, that I may not go and fight against the enemies of my lord the king?" ⁹And Ā'chĭsh made answer to David, "I know that you are as blameless in my sight as an angel of God; nevertheless the commanders of the Phĭ·lĭs'tĭnes have said, 'He shall not go up with us to the battle.' ¹⁰Now then rise early in the morning with the servants of your lord who came with you; and start early in the morning, and depart as soon as you have light." ¹¹So David set out with his men early in the morning, to return to the land of the Phĭ·lĭs'tĭnes. But the Philistines went up to Jĕz'rē·ĕl.

30 Now when David and his men came to Zĭk'lăg on the third day, the A·mǎl'e·kītes had made a raid upon the Nĕg'ĕb and upon Ziklag. They had overcome Ziklag, and burned it with fire, ²and taken captive the women and all*ᶜ* who were in it, both small and great; they killed no one, but carried them off, and went their way. ³And when David and his men came to the city, they found it burned with fire, and their wives and sons and daughters taken captive. ⁴Then David and the people who were with him raised their voices and wept, until they had no more strength to weep. ⁵David's two wives also had been taken captive, A·hĭn'ō–ăm of Jĕz'rē·ĕl, and Ăb'ĭ·gāil the widow of Nā'băl of Cār'mĕl. ⁶And David was greatly distressed; for the people spoke of stoning him, because all the people were bitter in soul, each for his sons and daughters. But David strengthened himself in the LORD his God.

7 And David said to A·bī'a·thär the priest, the son of A·hĭm'e·lĕch, "Bring me the ephod." So Abiathar brought the ephod to David. ⁸And David inquired of the LORD, "Shall I pursue after this band? Shall I overtake them?" He answered him, "Pursue; for you shall surely overtake and shall surely rescue." ⁹So David set out, and the six hundred men who were with him, and they came to the brook Bē'sôr, where those stayed who were left behind. ¹⁰But David went on with the pursuit, he and four hundred men; two hundred stayed behind, who were too exhausted to cross the brook Bē'sôr.

11 They found an Egyptian in the open country, and brought him to David; and they gave him bread and he ate, they gave him water to drink, ¹²and they gave him a piece of a cake of figs and two clusters of raisins. And when he had eaten, his spirit revived; for he had not eaten bread or drunk water for three days and three nights. ¹³And David said to him, "To whom do you belong? And where are you from?" He said, "I am a young man of Egypt, servant to an A·mǎl'-e·kīte; and my master left me behind because I fell sick three days ago. ¹⁴We had made a raid upon the Nĕg'ĕb of the Chĕr'e·thītes and upon that which belongs to Judah and upon the Negeb of Caleb; and we burned Zĭk'-lăg with fire." ¹⁵And David said to him, "Will you take me down to this band?" And he said, "Swear to me by God, that you will not kill me, or deliver me into the hands of my master, and I will take you down to this band."

16 And when he had taken him down, behold, they were spread abroad over all the land, eating and drinking and dancing, because of all the great spoil they had taken from the land of the Phĭ·lĭs'tĭnes and from the land of Judah. ¹⁷And David smote them from twilight until the evening of the next day; and not a man of them escaped, except four hundred young men, who mounted camels and fled. ¹⁸David recovered all that the A·mǎl'-e·kītes had taken; and David rescued his two wives. ¹⁹Nothing was missing, whether small or great, sons or daughters, spoil or anything that had been taken; David brought back all. ²⁰David also captured all the flocks and herds; and the people drove those cattle before him,*ᵈ* and said, "This is David's spoil."

21 Then David came to the two hundred men, who had been too exhausted to follow David, and who had been left at the brook Bē'sôr; and they went out to meet David and to meet the people who were with him; and when David drew near to the people he saluted them. ²²Then all the wicked and base fellows among the men who had gone with David said, "Because they did

ᶜGk: Heb lacks and all
ᵈCn: Heb they drove before those cattle

not go with us, we will not give them any of the spoil which we have recovered, except that each man may lead away his wife and children, and depart." ²³But David said, "You shall not do so, my brothers, with what the LORD has given us; he has preserved us and given into our hand the band that came against us. ²⁴Who would listen to you in this matter? For as his share is who goes down into the battle, so shall his share be who stays by the baggage; they shall share alike." ²⁵And from that day forward he made it a statute and an ordinance for Israel to this day.

26 When David came to Zĭk'lăg, he sent part of the spoil to his friends, the elders of Judah, saying, "Here is a present for you from the spoil of the enemies of the LORD"; ²⁷it was for those in Bĕth'el in Rä'mŏth of the Nĕg'ĕb, in Jăt'tĭr, ²⁸in Ă·rō'er, in Sĭph'-mŏth, in Ĕsh·tĕ·mō'ạ, ²⁹in Rä'cạl, in the cities of the Jẹ·räh'mē·ẹ·lītes, in the cities of the Kĕn'ītes, ³⁰in Hôr'-mah, in Bôr·ăsh'ạn, in Ā'thăch, ³¹in Hĕ'brọn, for all the places where David and his men had roamed.

31 Now the Phĭ·lĭs'tĭnes fought against Israel; and the men of Israel fled before the Philistines, and fell slain on Mount Gĭl·bō'ạ. ²And the Phĭ·lĭs'tĭnes overtook Saul and his sons; and the Philistines slew Jonathan and Ă·bĭn'ạ·dăb and Măl"chĭ-shü'ạ, the sons of Saul. ³The battle pressed hard upon Saul, and the archers found him; and he was badly wounded by the archers. ⁴Then Saul said to his armor-bearer, "Draw your

sword, and thrust me through with it, lest these uncircumcised come and thrust me through, and make sport of me." But his armor-bearer would not; for he feared greatly. Therefore Saul took his own sword, and fell upon it. ⁵And when his armor-bearer saw that Saul was dead, he also fell upon his sword, and died with him. ⁶Thus Saul died, and his three sons, and his armor-bearer, and all his men, on the same day together. ⁷And when the men of Israel who were on the other side of the valley and those beyond the Jordan saw that the men of Israel had fled and that Saul and his sons were dead, they forsook their cities and fled; and the Phĭ·lĭs'tĭnes came and dwelt in them.

8 On the morrow, when the Phĭ-lĭs'tĭnes came to strip the slain, they found Saul and his three sons fallen on Mount Gĭl·bō'ạ. ⁹And they cut off his head, and stripped off his armor, and sent messengers throughout the land of the Phĭ·lĭs'tĭnes, to carry the good news to their idols*ᵉ* and to the people. ¹⁰They put his armor in the temple of Äsh'tạ·rŏth; and they fastened his body to the wall of Bĕth–shăn. ¹¹But when the inhabitants of Jä'bĕsh–gĭl'ē·ạd heard what the Phĭ-lĭs'tĭnes had done to Saul, ¹²all the valiant men arose, and went all night, and took the body of Saul and the bodies of his sons from the wall of Bĕth–shăn; and they came to Jä'bĕsh and burnt them there. ¹³And they took their bones and buried them under the tamarisk tree in Jä'bĕsh, and fasted seven days.

The Second Book of

Samuel

1 After the death of Saul, when David had returned from the slaughter of the Ă·măl'ẹ·kītes, David remained two days in Zĭk'lăg; ²and on the third day, behold, a man came from Saul's camp, with his clothes rent and earth upon his head. And when he came to David, he fell to the ground

and did obeisance. ³David said to him, "Where do you come from?" And he said to him, "I have escaped from the camp of Israel." ⁴And David said to him, "How did it go? Tell me." And he answered, "The people have fled from

ᵉGk Compare 1 Chron 10.9: Heb to the house of their idols **31.1-13:** 2 Sam 1.6-10; 1 Chron 10.1-12.

the battle, and many of the people also have fallen and are dead; and Saul and his son Jonathan are also dead." [5] Then David said to the young man who told him, "How do you know that Saul and his son Jonathan are dead?" [6] And the young man who told him said, "By chance I happened to be on Mount Gĭl·bō′a; and there was Saul leaning upon his spear; and lo, the chariots and the horsemen were close upon him. [7] And when he looked behind him, he saw me, and called to me. And I answered, 'Here I am.' [8] And he said to me, 'Who are you?' I answered him, 'I am an A·mắl′e·kīte.' [9] And he said to me, 'Stand beside me and slay me; for anguish has seized me, and yet my life still lingers.' [10] So I stood beside him, and slew him, because I was sure that he could not live after he had fallen; and I took the crown which was on his head and the armlet which was on his arm, and I have brought them here to my lord."

[11] Then David took hold of his clothes, and rent them; and so did all the men who were with him; [12] and they mourned and wept and fasted until evening for Saul and for Jonathan his son and for the people of the LORD and for the house of Israel, because they had fallen by the sword. [13] And David said to the young man who told him, "Where do you come from?" And he answered, "I am the son of a sojourner, an A·mắl′e·kīte." [14] David said to him, "How is it you were not afraid to put forth your hand to destroy the LORD's anointed?" [15] Then David called one of the young men and said, "Go, fall upon him." And he smote him so that he died. [16] And David said to him, "Your blood be upon your head; for your own mouth has testified against you, saying, 'I have slain the LORD's anointed.'"

[17] And David lamented with this lamentation over Saul and Jonathan his son, [18] and he said it[a] should be taught to the people of Judah; behold, it is written in the Book of Jăsh′ar.[b] He said:

[19] "Thy glory, O Israel, is slain upon thy
     high places!
How are the mighty fallen!
[20] Tell it not in Găth,
     publish it not in the streets of
     Ăsh′ke·lŏn;

lest the daughters of the Phĭ·lĭs′tĭnes
     rejoice,
lest the daughters of the uncir-
     cumcised exult.

[21] "Ye mountains of Gĭl·bō′a,
     let there be no dew or rain upon
     you,
nor upsurging of the deep![c]
For there the shield of the mighty
     was defiled,
     the shield of Saul, not anointed
     with oil.

[22] "From the blood of the slain,
     from the fat of the mighty,
the bow of Jonathan turned not back,
     and the sword of Saul returned not
     empty.

[23] "Saul and Jonathan, beloved and
     lovely!
In life and in death they were not
     divided;
they were swifter than eagles,
     they were stronger than lions.

[24] "Ye daughters of Israel, weep over
     Saul,
who clothed you daintily in scarlet,
who put ornaments of gold upon
     your apparel.

[25] "How are the mighty fallen
     in the midst of the battle!

"Jonathan lies slain upon thy high
     places.
[26]   I am distressed for you, my brother
     Jonathan;
very pleasant have you been to me;
     your love to me was wonderful,
     passing the love of women.

[27] "How are the mighty fallen,
     and the weapons of war perished!"

2   After this David inquired of the LORD, "Shall I go up into any of the cities of Judah?" And the LORD said to him, "Go up." David said, "To which shall I go up?" And he said, "To Hē′-bron." [2] So David went up there, and his two wives also, A·hĭn′ō·ăm of Jĕz′-rē·el, and Ăb′ĭ·gāil the widow of Nā′băl of Cär′mel. [3] And David brought up his men who were with him, every one with his household; and they dwelt in

[a] Gk: Heb *the Bow*   [b] Or *The upright*
[c] Cn: Heb *fields of offerings*
1.6–10: 1 Sam 31.1–13; 1 Chron 10.1–12.

the towns of Hē'brọn. ⁴And the men of Judah came, and there they anointed David king over the house of Judah.

When they told David, "It was the men of Jā'bĕsh-gĭl'ē-ạd who buried Saul," ⁵David sent messengers to the men of Jā'bĕsh-gĭl'ē-ạd, and said to them, "May you be blessed by the LORD, because you showed this loyalty to Saul your lord, and buried him! ⁶Now may the LORD show steadfast love and faithfulness to you! And I will do good to you because you have done this thing. ⁷Now therefore let your hands be strong, and be valiant; for Saul your lord is dead, and the house of Judah has anointed me king over them."

8 Now Abner the son of Nēr, commander of Saul's army, had taken Ĭsh-bō'shĕth the son of Saul, and brought him over to Mā"hạ-nā'ĭm; ⁹and he made him king over Gilead and the Āsh'ụ-rītes and Jĕz'rē-ẹl and Ē'phrạ-ĭm and Benjamin and all Israel. ¹⁰Ĭsh-bō'shĕth, Saul's son, was forty years old when he began to reign over Israel, and he reigned two years. But the house of Judah followed David. ¹¹And the time that David was king in Hē'brọn over the house of Judah was seven years and six months.

12 Abner the son of Nēr, and the servants of Ĭsh-bō'shĕth the son of Saul, went out from Mā"hạ-nā'ĭm to Gĭb'ē'ọn. ¹³And Jō'ăb the son of Zĕ-rū'-ĭ-ạh, and the servants of David, went out and met them at the pool of Gĭb'-ē-ọn; and they sat down, the one on the one side of the pool, and the other on the other side of the pool. ¹⁴And Abner said to Jō'ăb, "Let the young men arise and play before us." And Joab said, "Let them arise." ¹⁵Then they arose and passed over by number, twelve for Benjamin and Ĭsh-bō'shĕth the son of Saul, and twelve of the servants of David. ¹⁶And each caught his opponent by the head, and thrust his sword in his opponent's side; so they fell down together. Therefore that place was called Hĕl'kăth-hăz-zū'rĭm,ᵈ which is at Gĭb'ē-ọn. ¹⁷And the battle was very fierce that day; and Abner and the men of Israel were beaten before the servants of David.

18 And the three sons of Zẹ-rū'ĭ-ạh were there, Jō'ăb, Ạ-bĭ'shaī, and Ās'-ạ-hĕl. Now Asahel was as swift of foot as a wild gazelle; ¹⁹and Ās'ạ-hĕl pur-

sued Abner, and as he went he turned neither to the right hand nor to the left from following Abner. ²⁰Then Abner looked behind him and said, "Is it you, Ās'ạ-hĕl?" And he answered, "It is I." ²¹Abner said to him, "Turn aside to your right hand or to your left, and seize one of the young men, and take his spoil." But Ās'ạ-hĕl would not turn aside from following him. ²²And Abner said again to Ās'ạ-hĕl, "Turn aside from following me; why should I smite you to the ground? How then could I lift up my face to your brother Jō'ăb?" ²³But he refused to turn aside; therefore Abner smote him in the belly with the butt of his spear, so that the spear came out at his back; and he fell there, and died where he was. And all who came to the place where Ās'ạ-hĕl had fallen and died, stood still.

24 But Jō'ăb and Ạ-bĭ'shaī pursued Abner; and as the sun was going down they came to the hill of Ăm'mạh, which lies before Gī'ah on the way to the wilderness of Gĭb'ē-ọn. ²⁵And the Benjaminites gathered themselves together behind Abner, and became one band, and took their stand on the top of a hill. ²⁶Then Abner called to Jō'ăb, "Shall the sword devour for ever? Do you not know that the end will be bitter? How long will it be before you bid your people turn from the pursuit of their brethren?" ²⁷And Jō'ăb said, "As God lives, if you had not spoken, surely the men would have given up the pursuit of their brethren in the morning." ²⁸So Jō'ăb blew the trumpet; and all the men stopped, and pursued Israel no more, nor did they fight any more.

29 And Abner and his men went all that night through the Ăr'ạ-bạh; they crossed the Jordan, and marching in the whole forenoon they came to Mā"-hạ-nā'ĭm. ³⁰Jō'ăb returned from the pursuit of Abner; and when he had gathered all the people together, there were missing of David's servants nineteen men besides Ās'ạ-hĕl. ³¹But the servants of David had slain of Benjamin three hundred and sixty of Abner's men. ³²And they took up Ās'ạ-hĕl, and buried him in the tomb of his father, which was at Bethlehem. And Jō'ăb and his men marched all night, and the day broke upon them at Hē'brọn.

3 There was a long war between the house of Saul and the house of

ᵈThat is the field of sword-edges

David; and David grew stronger and stronger, while the house of Saul became weaker and weaker.

2 And sons were born to David at Hē′brọn: his first-born was Ăm′nŏn, of A̲·hĭn′ō-ăm of Jĕz′rē-ẹl; ³and his second, Chĭl′ē-ăb, of Ăb′ĭ·gāil the widow of Nā′băl of Cär′mẹl; and the third, Ăb′sa·lọm the son of Mā′a·cah the daughter of Tăl′maī king of Gĕ′shūr; ⁴and the fourth, Ăd·ọ·nī′jah the son of Hăg′gĭth; and the fifth, Shĕph·a·tī′ah the son of A·bī′tạl; ⁵and the sixth, Ĭth′-rē-ăm of Ĕg′lah, David's wife. These were born to David in Hē′brọn.

6 While there was war between the house of Saul and the house of David, Abner was making himself strong in the house of Saul. ⁷Now Saul had a concubine, whose name was Rĭz′pah, the daughter of Aī′ah; and Ĭsh-bō′-shĕth said to Abner, "Why have you gone in to my father's concubine?" ⁸Then Abner was very angry over the words of Ĭsh-bō′shĕth, and said, "Am I a dog's head of Judah? This day I keep showing loyalty to the house of Saul your father, to his brothers, and to his friends, and have not given you into the hand of David; and yet you charge me today with a fault concerning a woman. ⁹God do so to Abner, and more also, if I do not accomplish for David what the LORD has sworn to him, ¹⁰to transfer the kingdom from the house of Saul, and set up the throne of David over Israel and over Judah, from Dan to Bē′er-shē′ba." ¹¹And Ĭsh-bō′shĕth could not answer Abner another word, because he feared him.

12 And Abner sent messengers to David at Hē′brọn,ᵉ saying, "To whom does the land belong? Make your covenant with me, and behold, my hand shall be with you to bring over all Israel to you." ¹³And he said, "Good; I will make a covenant with you; but one thing I require of you; that is, you shall not see my face, unless you first bring Mī′chạl, Saul's daughter, when you come to see my face." ¹⁴Then David sent messengers to Ĭsh-bō′shĕth Saul's son, saying, "Give me my wife Mī′chạl, whom I betrothed at the price of a hundred foreskins of the Phĭ·lĭs′tĭnes." ¹⁵And Ĭsh-bō′shĕth sent, and took her from her husband Păl′-tĭ-ĕl the son of Lā′ĭsh. ¹⁶But her husband went with her, weeping after her all the way to Ba̲·hū′rĭm. Then Abner

said to him, "Go, return"; and he returned.

17 And Abner conferred with the elders of Israel, saying, "For some time past you have been seeking David as king over you. ¹⁸Now then bring it about; for the LORD has promised David, saying, 'By the hand of my servant David I will save my people Israel from the hand of the Phĭ·lĭs′tĭnes, and from the hand of all their enemies.'" ¹⁹Abner also spoke to Benjamin; and then Abner went to tell David at Hē′-brọn all that Israel and the whole house of Benjamin thought good to do.

20 When Abner came with twenty men to David at Hē′brọn, David made a feast for Abner and the men who were with him. ²¹And Abner said to David, "I will arise and go, and will gather all Israel to my lord the king, that they may make a covenant with you, and that you may reign over all that your heart desires." So David sent Abner away; and he went in peace.

22 Just then the servants of David arrived with Jō′ăb from a raid, bringing much spoil with them. But Abner was not with David at Hē′brọn, for he had sent him away, and he had gone in peace. ²³When Jō′ăb and all the army that was with him came, it was told Joab, "Abner the son of Nĕr came to the king, and he has let him go, and he has gone in peace." ²⁴Then Jō′ăb went to the king and said, "What have you done? Behold, Abner came to you; why is it that you have sent him away, so that he is gone? ²⁵You know that Abner the son of Nĕr came to deceive you, and to know your going out and your coming in, and to know all that you are doing."

26 When Jō′ăb came out from David's presence, he sent messengers after Abner, and they brought him back from the cistern of Sī′rah; but David did not know about it. ²⁷And when Abner returned to Hē′brọn, Jō′ăb took him aside into the midst of the gate to speak with him privately, and there he smote him in the belly, so that he died, for the blood of Ăs′a̲·hĕl his brother. ²⁸Afterward, when David heard of it, he said, "I and my kingdom are for ever guiltless before the LORD for the blood of Abner the son of Nĕr. ²⁹May it fall upon the head of Jō′ăb,

ᵉGk: Heb *where he was*
3.2-5: 1 Chron 3.1-4.

and upon all his father's house; and may the house of Joab never be without one who has a discharge, or who is leprous, or who holds a spindle, or who is slain by the sword, or who lacks bread!" ³⁰ So Jō'ăb and A·bĭ'shaī his brother slew Abner, because he had killed their brother Ăs'a·hĕl in the battle at Gĭb'ē·on.

31 Then David said to Jō'ăb and to all the people who were with him, "Rend your clothes, and gird on sackcloth, and mourn before Abner." And King David followed the bier. ³² They buried Abner at Hē'brŏn; and the king lifted up his voice and wept at the grave of Abner; and all the people wept. ³³ And the king lamented for Abner, saying,

"Should Abner die as a fool dies?
³⁴ Your hands were not bound,
    your feet were not fettered;
as one falls before the wicked
    you have fallen."

And all the people wept again over him. ³⁵ Then all the people came to persuade David to eat bread while it was yet day; but David swore, saying, "God do so to me and more also, if I taste bread or anything else till the sun goes down!" ³⁶ And all the people took notice of it, and it pleased them; as everything that the king did pleased all the people. ³⁷ So all the people and all Israel understood that day that it had not been the king's will to slay Abner the son of Nēr. ³⁸ And the king said to his servants, "Do you not know that a prince and a great man has fallen this day in Israel? ³⁹ And I am this day weak, though anointed king; these men the sons of Zĕ·rü'ī·ah are too hard for me. The LORD requite the evildoer according to his wickedness!"

4 When Ĭsh-bō'shĕth, Saul's son, heard that Abner had died at Hē'brŏn, his courage failed, and all Israel was dismayed. ² Now Saul's son had two men who were captains of raiding bands; the name of the one was Bā'a·nah, and the name of the other Rē'chăb, sons of Rĭm'mŏn a man of Benjamin from Bē-ēr'ŏth (for Be-eroth also is reckoned to Benjamin; ³ the Bē-ēr'ŏ·thītes fled to Gĭt·tā'ĭm, and have been sojourners there to this day).

4 Jonathan, the son of Saul, had a son who was crippled in his feet. He was five years old when the news about Saul and Jonathan came from

Jĕz'rē·ĕl; and his nurse took him up, and fled; and, as she fled in her haste, he fell, and became lame. And his name was Mĕ·phĭb'ŏ·shĕth.

5 Now the sons of Rĭm'mŏn the Bē-ēr'ŏ·thīte, Rē'chăb and Bā'a·nah, set out, and about the heat of the day they came to the house of Ĭsh-bō'shĕth, as he was taking his noonday rest. ⁶ And behold, the doorkeeper of the house had been cleaning wheat, but she grew drowsy and slept; so Rē'chăb and Bā'a·nah his brother slipped in./ ⁷ When they came into the house, as he lay on his bed in his bedchamber, they smote him, and slew him, and beheaded him. They took his head, and went by the way of the Ăr'a·bah all night, ⁸ and brought the head of Ĭsh-bō'shĕth to David at Hē'brŏn. And they said to the king, "Here is the head of Ish-bosheth, the son of Saul, your enemy, who sought your life; the LORD has avenged my lord the king this day on Saul and on his offspring." ⁹ But David answered Rē'chăb and Bā'a·nah his brother, the sons of Rĭm'mŏn the Bē-ēr'ŏ·thīte, "As the LORD lives, who has redeemed my life out of every adversity, ¹⁰ when one told me, 'Behold, Saul is dead,' and thought he was bringing good news, I seized him and slew him at Zĭk'lăg, which was the reward I gave him for his news. ¹¹ How much more, when wicked men have slain a righteous man in his own house upon his bed, shall I not now require his blood at your hand, and destroy you from the earth?" ¹² And David commanded his young men, and they killed them, and cut off their hands and feet, and hanged them beside the pool at Hē'brŏn. But they took the head of Ĭsh-bō'shĕth, and buried it in the tomb of Abner at Hebron.

5 Then all the tribes of Israel came to David at Hē'brŏn, and said, "Behold, we are your bone and flesh. ² In times past, when Saul was king over us, it was you that led out and brought in Israel; and the LORD said to you, 'You shall be shepherd of my people Israel, and you shall be prince over Israel.'" ³ So all the elders of Israel came to the king at Hē'brŏn; and King David made a covenant with them at Hebron before the LORD, and they

<hr>

*f*Gk: Heb *And hither they came into the midst of the house fetching wheat; and they smote him in the belly; and Rechab and Baanah his brother escaped*
5.1-3: 1 Chron 11.1-3.

anointed David king over Israel. ⁴David was thirty years old when he began to reign, and he reigned forty years. ⁵At Hē′brọn he reigned over Judah seven years and six months; and at Jerusalem he reigned over all Israel and Judah thirty-three years.

6 And the king and his men went to Jerusalem against the Jĕb′ū·sītes, the inhabitants of the land, who said to David, "You will not come in here, but the blind and the lame will ward you off" – thinking, "David cannot come in here." ⁷Nevertheless David took the stronghold of Zion, that is, the city of David. ⁸And David said on that day, "Whoever would smite the Jĕb′ū·sītes, let him get up the water shaft to attack the lame and the blind, who are hated by David's soul." Therefore it is said, "The blind and the lame shall not come into the house." ⁹And David dwelt in the stronghold, and called it the city of David. And David built the city round about from the Mĭl′lō inward. ¹⁰And David became greater and greater, for the LORD, the God of hosts, was with him.

11 And Hiram king of Tȳre sent messengers to David, and cedar trees, also carpenters and masons who built David a house. ¹²And David perceived that the LORD had established him king over Israel, and that he had exalted his kingdom for the sake of his people Israel.

13 And David took more concubines and wives from Jerusalem, after he came from Hē′brọn; and more sons and daughters were born to David. ¹⁴And these are the names of those who were born to him in Jerusalem: Shăm′mū–a, Shō′băb, Nathan, Solomon, ¹⁵Ib′hăr, Ē·lī′shü–a, Nē′phĕg, Jạ·phī′ạ, ¹⁶Ē·lish′ạ·mạ, Ē·lī′ạ·dạ, and Ē·lĭph′e·lĕt.

17 When the Phĭ·lĭs′tĭnes heard that David had been anointed king over Israel, all the Philistines went up in search of David; but David heard of it and went down to the stronghold. ¹⁸Now the Phĭ·lĭs′tĭnes had come and spread out in the valley of Rĕph′ạ·ĭm. ¹⁹And David inquired of the LORD, "Shall I go up against the Phĭ·lĭs′tĭnes? Wilt thou give them into my hand?" And the LORD said to David, "Go up; for I will certainly give the Philistines into your hand." ²⁰And David came to Bā′ạl–pĕ·rā′zĭm, and David defeated

them there; and he said, "The LORD has broken through*ᵍ* my enemies before me, like a bursting flood." Therefore the name of that place is called Bā′ạl–pĕ·rā′zĭm.*ʰ* ²¹And the Phĭ·lĭs′tĭnes left their idols there, and David and his men carried them away.

22 And the Phĭ·lĭs′tĭnes came up yet again, and spread out in the valley of Rĕph′ạ·ĭm. ²³And when David inquired of the LORD, he said, "You shall not go up; go around to their rear, and come upon them opposite the balsam trees. ²⁴And when you hear the sound of marching in the tops of the balsam trees, then bestir yourself; for then the LORD has gone out before you to smite the army of the Phĭ·lĭs′tĭnes." ²⁵And David did as the LORD commanded him, and smote the Phĭ·lĭs′tĭnes from Gē′bạ to Gē′zẹr.

6 David again gathered all the chosen men of Israel, thirty thousand. ²And David arose and went with all the people who were with him from Bā′ạ·lē–jü′dạh, to bring up from there the ark of God, which is called by the name of the LORD of hosts who sits enthroned on the cherubim. ³And they carried the ark of God upon a new cart, and brought it out of the house of Ạ·bĭn′ạ·dăb which was on the hill; and Ŭz′zạh and Ạ·hī′ō,*ⁱ* the sons of Abinadab, were driving the new cart*ʲ* ⁴with the ark of God; and Ạ·hī′ō*ⁱ* went before the ark. ⁵And David and all the house of Israel were making merry before the LORD with all their might, with songs*ᵏ* and lyres and harps and tambourines and castanets and cymbals.

6 And when they came to the threshing floor of Nä′cŏn, Ŭz′zạh put out his hand to the ark of God and took hold of it, for the oxen stumbled. ⁷And the anger of the LORD was kindled against Ŭz′zạh; and God smote him there because he put forth his hand to the ark;*ˡ* and he died there beside the ark of God. ⁸And David was angry because the LORD had broken forth upon Ŭz′zạh; and that place is called Pĕr′ĕz–

*ᵍ*Heb *paraz* *ʰ*That is *Lord of breaking through*
*ⁱ*Or *and his brother*
*ʲ*Compare Gk: Heb *the new cart, and brought it out of the house of Abinadab which was on the hill*
*ᵏ*Or *and his brother* *ᵏ*Gk 1 Chron 13.8: Heb *fir-trees*
*ˡ*1 Chron 13.10: Heb uncertain
5.4, 5: 1 Chron 3.4.   **5.6–10:** 1 Chron 11.4-9.
5.11–12: 1 Chron 14.1, 2.   **5.14–16:** 1 Chron 3.5-8; 14.3-7.
5.17–21: 1 Chron 14.8-12.   **5.22–25:** 1 Chron 14.13-16.
6.1–11: 1 Chron 13.1-14.

ŭz′zạh,*m* to this day. ⁹And David was afraid of the LORD that day; and he said, "How can the ark of the LORD come to me?" ¹⁰So David was not willing to take the ark of the LORD into the city of David; but David took it aside to the house of Ō′bĕd-ē′dọm the Gĭt′-tīte. ¹¹And the ark of the LORD remained in the house of Ō′bĕd-ē′dọm the Gĭt′tīte three months; and the LORD blessed Obed-edom and all his household.

12 And it was told King David, "The LORD has blessed the household of Ō′bĕd-ē′dọm and all that belongs to him, because of the ark of God." So David went and brought up the ark of God from the house of Obed-edom to the city of David with rejoicing; ¹³and when those who bore the ark of the LORD had gone six paces, he sacrificed an ox and a fatling. ¹⁴And David danced before the LORD with all his might; and David was girded with a linen ephod. ¹⁵So David and all the house of Israel brought up the ark of the LORD with shouting, and with the sound of the horn.

16 As the ark of the LORD came into the city of David, Mī′chạl the daughter of Saul looked out of the window, and saw King David leaping and dancing before the LORD; and she despised him in her heart. ¹⁷And they brought in the ark of the LORD, and set it in its place, inside the tent which David had pitched for it; and David offered burnt offerings and peace offerings before the LORD. ¹⁸And when David had finished offering the burnt offerings and the peace offerings, he blessed the people in the name of the LORD of hosts, ¹⁹and distributed among all the people, the whole multitude of Israel, both men and women, to each a cake of bread, a portion of meat,*n* and a cake of raisins. Then all the people departed, each to his house.

20 And David returned to bless his household. But Mī′chạl the daughter of Saul came out to meet David, and said, "How the king of Israel honored himself today, uncovering himself today before the eyes of his servants' maids, as one of the vulgar fellows shamelessly uncovers himself!" ²¹And David said to Mī′chạl, "It was before the LORD, who chose me above your father, and above all his house, to appoint me as prince over Israel, the people of the

LORD—and I will make merry before the LORD. ²²I will make myself yet more contemptible than this, and I will be abased in your*o* eyes; but by the maids of whom you have spoken, by them I shall be held in honor." ²³And Mī′chạl the daughter of Saul had no child to the day of her death.

7 Now when the king dwelt in his house, and the LORD had given him rest from all his enemies round about, ²the king said to Nathan the prophet, "See now, I dwell in a house of cedar, but the ark of God dwells in a tent." ³And Nathan said to the king, "Go, do all that is in your heart; for the LORD is with you."

4 But that same night the word of the LORD came to Nathan, ⁵"Go and tell my servant David, 'Thus says the LORD: Would you build me a house to dwell in? ⁶I have not dwelt in a house since the day I brought up the people of Israel from Egypt to this day, but I have been moving about in a tent for my dwelling. ⁷In all places where I have moved with all the people of Israel, did I speak a word with any of the judges*p* of Israel, whom I commanded to shepherd my people Israel, saying, "Why have you not built me a house of cedar?"' ⁸Now therefore thus you shall say to my servant David, 'Thus says the LORD of hosts, I took you from the pasture, from following the sheep, that you should be prince over my people Israel; ⁹and I have been with you wherever you went, and have cut off all your enemies from before you; and I will make for you a great name, like the name of the great ones of the earth. ¹⁰And I will appoint a place for my people Israel, and will plant them, that they may dwell in their own place, and be disturbed no more; and violent men shall afflict them no more, as formerly, ¹¹from the time that I appointed judges over my people Israel; and I will give you rest from all your enemies. Moreover the LORD declares to you that the LORD will make you a house. ¹²When your days are fulfilled and you lie down with your fathers, I will raise up your offspring after you, who shall come forth from your body, and I will establish his kingdom. ¹³He shall build a

---

*m*That is *The breaking forth upon Uzzah*
*n*Vg: Heb uncertain   *o*Gk: Heb *my*
*p*1 Chron 17.6: Heb *tribes*
6.12-19: 1 Chron 15.1-16.3.   7.1-29: 1 Chron 17.1-27.

house for my name, and I will establish the throne of his kingdom for ever. [14] I will be his father, and he shall be my son. When he commits iniquity, I will chasten him with the rod of men, with the stripes of the sons of men; [15] but I will not take[q] my steadfast love from him, as I took it from Saul, whom I put away from before you. [16] And your house and your kingdom shall be made sure for ever before me; your throne shall be established for ever.'" [17] In accordance with all these words, and in accordance with all this vision, Nathan spoke to David.

18 Then King David went in and sat before the LORD, and said, "Who am I, O Lord GOD, and what is my house, that thou hast brought me thus far? [19] And yet this was a small thing in thy eyes, O Lord GOD; thou hast spoken also of thy servant's house for a great while to come, and hast shown me future generations,[r] O Lord GOD! [20] And what more can David say to thee? For thou knowest thy servant, O Lord GOD! [21] Because of thy promise, and according to thy own heart, thou hast wrought all this greatness, to make thy servant know it. [22] Therefore thou art great, O LORD God; for there is none like thee, and there is no God besides thee, according to all that we have heard with our ears. [23] What other[s] nation on earth is like thy people Israel, whom God went to redeem to be his people, making himself a name, and doing for them[t] great and terrible things, by driving out[u] before his people a nation and its gods?[v] [24] And thou didst establish for thyself thy people Israel to be thy people for ever; and thou, O LORD, didst become their God. [25] And now, O LORD God, confirm for ever the word which thou hast spoken concerning thy servant and concerning his house, and do as thou hast spoken; [26] and thy name will be magnified for ever, saying, 'The LORD of hosts is God over Israel,' and the house of thy servant David will be established before thee. [27] For thou, O LORD of hosts, the God of Israel, hast made this revelation to thy servant, saying, 'I will build you a house'; therefore thy servant has found courage to pray this prayer to thee. [28] And now, O Lord GOD, thou art God, and thy words are true, and thou hast promised this good thing to thy servant; [29] now therefore

may it please thee to bless the house of thy servant, that it may continue for ever before thee; for thou, O Lord GOD, hast spoken, and with thy blessing shall the house of thy servant be blessed for ever."

8 After this David defeated the Phĭ·lĭs'tĭnes and subdued them, and David took Mĕth'ĕg-ăm'măh out of the hand of the Philistines. 2 And he defeated Mō'ăb, and measured them with a line, making them lie down on the ground; two lines he measured to be put to death, and one full line to be spared. And the Mō'ăb-ītes became servants to David and brought tribute.

3 David also defeated Hăd·a·dē'zer the son of Rē'hŏb, king of Zō'băh, as he went to restore his power at the river Euphrates. [4] And David took from him a thousand and seven hundred horsemen, and twenty thousand foot soldiers; and David hamstrung all the chariot horses, but left enough for a hundred chariots. [5] And when the Syrians of Damascus came to help Hăd·a·dē'zer king of Zō'băh, David slew twenty-two thousand men of the Syrians. [6] Then David put garrisons in Ăr'ăm of Damascus; and the Syrians became servants to David and brought tribute. And the LORD gave victory to David wherever he went. [7] And David took the shields of gold which were carried by the servants of Hăd·a·dē'zer, and brought them to Jerusalem. [8] And from Bē'tăh and from Bĕ·rō'thaī, cities of Hăd·a·dē'zer, King David took very much bronze.

9 When Tō'ī king of Hā'măth heard that David had defeated the whole army of Hăd·a·dē'zer, [10] Tō'ī sent his son Jō'răm to King David, to greet him, and to congratulate him because he had fought against Hăd·a·dē'zer and defeated him; for Hadadezer had often been at war with Toi. And Joram brought with him articles of silver, of gold, and of bronze; [11] these also King David dedicated to the LORD, together with the silver and gold which he dedicated from all the nations he subdued, [12] from Ē'dŏm, Mō'ăb, the Ăm'-

[q]Gk Syr Vg 1 Chron 17.13: Heb *shall not depart*
[r]Cn: Heb *this is the law for man*   [s]Gk: Heb *one*
[t]Heb *you*
[u]Gk 1 Chron 17.21: Heb *for your land*
[v]Heb *before thy people, whom thou didst redeem for thyself from Egypt, nations and its gods*
7.14: Heb 1.5.   8.1-14: 1 Chron 18.1-13.

mọ·nītes, the Phĭ·lĭs'tīnes, Ăm'ạ·lĕk, and from the spoil of Hăd·ạ·dē'zẹr the son of Rē'hŏb, king of Zō'bạh.

13 And David won a name for himself. When he returned, he slew eighteen thousand Ē'dọm·ītes*w* in the Valley of Salt. 14 And he put garrisons in Ē'dọm; throughout all Edom he put garrisons, and all the Ē'dọm·ītes became David's servants. And the LORD gave victory to David wherever he went.

15 So David reigned over all Israel; and David administered justice and equity to all his people. 16 And Jō'ăb the son of Zẹ·rü'ī·ạh was over the army; and Jĕ·hŏsh'ạ·phăt the son of Ạ·hī'lụd was recorder; 17 and Zā'dŏk the son of Ạ·hī'tụb and Ạ·hĭm'ẹ·lĕch the son of Ạ·bī'ạ·thär were priests; and Sẹ·rāi'ạh was secretary; 18 and Bẹ·nā'ī·ah the son of Jẹ·hoi'ạ·dạ was over*ꭓ* the Chēr'ẹ·thītes and the Pĕl'ẹ·thītes; and David's sons were priests.

9 And David said, "Is there still any one left of the house of Saul, that I may show him kindness for Jonathan's sake?" 2 Now there was a servant of the house of Saul whose name was Zī'bạ, and they called him to David; and the king said to him, "Are you Ziba?" And he said, "Your servant is he." 3 And the king said, "Is there not still some one of the house of Saul, that I may show the kindness of God to him?" Zī'bạ said to the king, "There is still a son of Jonathan; he is crippled in his feet." 4 The king said to him, "Where is he?" And Zī'bạ said to the king, "He is in the house of Mā'chĭr the son of Ăm'mĭ·ĕl, at Lō–dē'bär." 5 Then King David sent and brought him from the house of Mā'chĭr the son of Ăm'mĭ·ĕl, at Lō–dē'bär. 6 And Mĕ·phĭb'-ọ·shĕth the son of Jonathan, son of Saul, came to David, and fell on his face and did obeisance. And David said, "Mephibosheth!" And he answered, "Behold, your servant." 7 And David said to him, "Do not fear; for I will show you kindness for the sake of your father Jonathan, and I will restore to you all the land of Saul your father; and you shall eat at my table always." 8 And he did obeisance, and said, "What is your servant, that you should look upon a dead dog such as I?"

9 Then the king called Zī'bạ, Saul's servant, and said to him, "All that be-

longed to Saul and to all his house I have given to your master's son. 10 And you and your sons and your servants shall till the land for him, and shall bring in the produce, that your master's son may have bread to eat; but Mĕ·phĭb'ọ·shĕth your master's son shall always eat at my table." Now Zī'bạ had fifteen sons and twenty servants. 11 Then Zī'bạ said to the king, "According to all that my lord the king commands his servant, so will your servant do." So Mĕ·phĭb'ọ·shĕth ate at David's*ʸ* table, like one of the king's sons. 12 And Mĕ·phĭb'ọ·shĕth had a young son, whose name was Mī'cạ. And all who dwelt in Zī'bạ's house became Mephibosheth's servants. 13 So Mĕ·phĭb'-ọ·shĕth dwelt in Jerusalem; for he ate always at the king's table. Now he was lame in both his feet.

10 After this the king of the Ăm'-mọ·nītes died, and Hā'nụn his son reigned in his stead. 2 And David said, "I will deal loyally with Hā'nụn the son of Nā'hăsh, as his father dealt loyally with me." So David sent by his servants to console him concerning his father. And David's servants came into the land of the Ăm'mọ·nītes. 3 But the princes of the Ăm'mọ·nītes said to Hā'-nụn their lord, "Do you think, because David has sent comforters to you, that he is honoring your father? Has not David sent his servants to you to search the city, and to spy it out, and to overthrow it?" 4 So Hā'nụn took David's servants, and shaved off half the beard of each, and cut off their garments in the middle, at their hips, and sent them away. 5 When it was told David, he sent to meet them, for the men were greatly ashamed. And the king said, "Remain at Jericho until your beards have grown, and then return."

6 When the Ăm'mọ·nītes saw that they had become odious to David, the Ammonites sent and hired the Syrians of Bĕth–rē'hŏb, and the Syrians of Zō'bạh, twenty thousand foot soldiers, and the king of Mā'ạ·cạh with a thousand men, and the men of Tōb, twelve thousand men. 7 And when David heard of it, he sent Jō'ăb and all the host of

*ᵂGk: Heb *returned from smiting eighteen thousand Syrians*
*ꭓSyr Tg Vg 20.23; 1 Chron 18.17: Heb lacks *was over*
*ʸGk: Heb *my*
9.15-18: 2 Sam 20.23-26; 1 Chron 18.14-17.
10.1-19: 1 Chron 19.1-19.

the mighty men. ⁸And the Ăm′mo·nītes came out and drew up in battle array at the entrance of the gate; and the Syrians of Zō′bah and of Rē′hŏb, and the men of Tōb and Mā′a·cah, were by themselves in the open country.

9 When Jō′ăb saw that the battle was set against him both in front and in the rear, he chose some of the picked men of Israel, and arrayed them against the Syrians; ¹⁰the rest of his men he put in the charge of A·bĭ′shaī his brother, and he arrayed them against the Ăm′mo·nītes. ¹¹And he said, "If the Syrians are too strong for me, then you shall help me; but if the Ăm′mo·nītes are too strong for you, then I will come and help you. ¹²Be of good courage, and let us play the man for our people, and for the cities of our God; and may the LORD do what seems good to him." ¹³So Jō′ăb and the people who were with him drew near to battle against the Syrians; and they fled before him. ¹⁴And when the Ăm′mo·nītes saw that the Syrians fled, they likewise fled before A·bĭ′shaī, and entered the city. Then Jō′ăb returned from fighting against the Ammonites, and came to Jerusalem.

15 But when the Syrians saw that they had been defeated by Israel, they gathered themselves together. ¹⁶And Hăd·a·dē′zer sent, and brought out the Syrians who were beyond the Euphrates;ᶻ and they came to Hē′lam, with Shō′băch the commander of the army of Hadadezer at their head. ¹⁷And when it was told David, he gathered all Israel together, and crossed the Jordan, and came to Hē′lam. And the Syrians arrayed themselves against David, and fought with him. ¹⁸And the Syrians fled before Israel; and David slew of the Syrians the men of seven hundred chariots, and forty thousand horsemen, and wounded Shō′băch the commander of their army, so that he died there. ¹⁹And when all the kings who were servants of Hăd·a·dē′zer saw that they had been defeated by Israel, they made peace with Israel, and became subject to them. So the Syrians feared to help the Ăm′mo·nītes any more.

11 In the spring of the year, the time when kings go forth to battle, David sent Jō′ăb, and his servants with him, and all Israel; and they ravaged the Ăm′mo·nītes, and be-

sieged Răb′bah. But David remained at Jerusalem.

2 It happened, late one afternoon, when David arose from his couch and was walking upon the roof of the king's house, that he saw from the roof a woman bathing; and the woman was very beautiful. ³And David sent and inquired about the woman. And one said, "Is not this Băth·shē′ba, the daughter of Ē·lī′am, the wife of U·rī′ah the Hĭt′tīte?" ⁴So David sent messengers, and took her; and she came to him, and he lay with her. (Now she was purifying herself from her uncleanness.) Then she returned to her house. ⁵And the woman conceived; and she sent and told David, "I am with child."

6 So David sent word to Jō′ăb, "Send me U·rī′ah the Hĭt′tīte." And Joab sent Uriah to David. ⁷When U·rī′ah came to him, David asked how Jō′ăb was doing, and how the people fared, and how the war prospered. ⁸Then David said to U·rī′ah, "Go down to your house, and wash your feet." And Uriah went out of the king's house, and there followed him a present from the king. ⁹But U·rī′ah slept at the door of the king's house with all the servants of his lord, and did not go down to his house. ¹⁰When they told David, "U·rī′ah did not go down to his house," David said to Uriah, "Have you not come from a journey? Why did you not go down to your house?" ¹¹U·rī′ah said to David, "The ark and Israel and Judah dwell in booths; and my lord Jō′ăb and the servants of my lord are camping in the open field; shall I then go to my house, to eat and to drink, and to lie with my wife? As you live, and as your soul lives, I will not do this thing." ¹²Then David said to U·rī′ah, "Remain here today also, and tomorrow I will let you depart." So Uriah remained in Jerusalem that day, and the next. ¹³And David invited him, and he ate in his presence and drank, so that he made him drunk; and in the evening he went out to lie on his couch with the servants of his lord, but he did not go down to his house.

14 In the morning David wrote a letter to Jō′ăb, and sent it by the hand of U·rī′ah. ¹⁵In the letter he wrote, "Set U·rī′ah in the forefront of the hardest fighting, and then draw back

ᶻHeb *river* 11.1: 1 Chron 20.1.

from him, that he may be struck down, and die." ¹⁶And as Jō'ăb was besieging the city, he assigned Ū·rī'ạh to the place where he knew there were valiant men. ¹⁷And the men of the city came out and fought with Jō'ăb; and some of the servants of David among the people fell. Ū·rī'ạh the Hĭt'tīte was slain also. ¹⁸Then Jō'ăb sent and told David all the news about the fighting; ¹⁹and he instructed the messenger, "When you have finished telling all the news about the fighting to the king, ²⁰then, if the king's anger rises, and if he says to you, 'Why did you go so near the city to fight? Did you not know that they would shoot from the wall? ²¹Who killed A·bĭm'ę·lĕch the son of Jĕ·rŭb'bę·shĕth? Did not a woman cast an upper millstone upon him from the wall, so that he died at Thē'bĕz? Why did you go so near the wall?' then you shall say, 'Your servant Ū·rī'ạh the Hĭt'tīte is dead also.'"

22 So the messenger went, and came and told David all that Jō'ăb had sent him to tell. ²³The messenger said to David, "The men gained an advantage over us, and came out against us in the field; but we drove them back to the entrance of the gate. ²⁴Then the archers shot at your servants from the wall; some of the king's servants are dead; and your servant Ū·rī'ạh the Hĭt'tīte is dead also." ²⁵David said to the messenger, "Thus shall you say to Jō'ăb, 'Do not let this matter trouble you, for the sword devours now one and now another; strengthen your attack upon the city, and overthrow it.' And encourage him."

26 When the wife of Ū·rī'ạh heard that Uriah her husband was dead, she made lamentation for her husband. ²⁷And when the mourning was over, David sent and brought her to his house, and she became his wife, and bore him a son. But the thing that David had done displeased the LORD.

12 And the LORD sent Nathan to David. He came to him, and said to him, "There were two men in a certain city, the one rich and the other poor. ²The rich man had very many flocks and herds; ³but the poor man had nothing but one little ewe lamb, which he had bought. And he brought it up, and it grew up with him and with his children; it used to eat of his morsel, and drink from his cup, and lie in

his bosom, and it was like a daughter to him. ⁴Now there came a traveler to the rich man, and he was unwilling to take one of his own flock or herd to prepare for the wayfarer who had come to him, but he took the poor man's lamb, and prepared it for the man who had come to him." ⁵Then David's anger was greatly kindled against the man; and he said to Nathan, "As the LORD lives, the man who has done this deserves to die; ⁶and he shall restore the lamb fourfold, because he did this thing, and because he had no pity."

7 Nathan said to David, "You are the man. Thus says the LORD, the God of Israel, 'I anointed you king over Israel, and I delivered you out of the hand of Saul; ⁸and I gave you your master's house, and your master's wives into your bosom, and gave you the house of Israel and of Judah; and if this were too little, I would add to you as much more. ⁹Why have you despised the word of the LORD, to do what is evil in his sight? You have smitten Ū·rī'ạh the Hĭt'tīte with the sword, and have taken his wife to be your wife, and have slain him with the sword of the Ăm'mọ·nītes. ¹⁰Now therefore the sword shall never depart from your house, because you have despised me, and have taken the wife of Ū·rī'ạh the Hĭt'tīte to be your wife.' ¹¹Thus says the LORD, 'Behold, I will raise up evil against you out of your own house; and I will take your wives before your eyes, and give them to your neighbor, and he shall lie with your wives in the sight of this sun. ¹²For you did it secretly; but I will do this thing before all Israel, and before the sun.'" ¹³David said to Nathan, "I have sinned against the LORD." And Nathan said to David, "The LORD also has put away your sin; you shall not die. ¹⁴Nevertheless, because by this deed you have utterly scorned the LORD,ᵃ the child that is born to you shall die." ¹⁵Then Nathan went to his house.

And the LORD struck the child that Ū·rī'ạh's wife bore to David, and it became sick. ¹⁶David therefore besought God for the child; and David fasted, and went in and lay all night upon the ground. ¹⁷And the elders of his house stood beside him, to raise him from the ground; but he would

ᵃHeb *the enemies of the* LORD

not, nor did he eat food with them. [18] On the seventh day the child died. And the servants of David feared to tell him that the child was dead; for they said, "Behold, while the child was yet alive, we spoke to him, and he did not listen to us; how then can we say to him the child is dead? He may do himself some harm." [19] But when David saw that his servants were whispering together, David perceived that the child was dead; and David said to his servants, "Is the child dead?" They said, "He is dead." [20] Then David arose from the earth, and washed, and anointed himself, and changed his clothes; and he went into the house of the LORD, and worshiped; he then went to his own house; and when he asked, they set food before him, and he ate. [21] Then his servants said to him, "What is this thing that you have done? You fasted and wept for the child while it was alive; but when the child died, you arose and ate food." [22] He said, "While the child was still alive, I fasted and wept; for I said, 'Who knows whether the LORD will be gracious to me, that the child may live?' [23] But now he is dead; why should I fast? Can I bring him back again? I shall go to him, but he will not return to me."

24 Then David comforted his wife, Băth·shē′bạ, and went in to her, and lay with her; and she bore a son, and he called his name Solomon. And the LORD loved him, [25] and sent a message by Nathan the prophet; so he called his name Jĕd·ĭ·dī′ạh,[b] because of the LORD.

26 Now Jō′ăb fought against Răb′-bạh of the Ăm′mọ·nītes, and took the royal city. [27] And Jō′ăb sent messengers to David, and said, "I have fought against Răb′bạh; moreover, I have taken the city of waters. [28] Now, then, gather the rest of the people together, and encamp against the city, and take it; lest I take the city, and it be called by my name." [29] So David gathered all the people together and went to Răb′bạh, and fought against it and took it. [30] And he took the crown of their king[c] from his head; the weight of it was a talent of gold, and in it was a precious stone; and it was placed on David's head. And he brought forth the spoil of the city, a very great amount. [31] And he brought forth the people who were in it, and set them to labor with saws and iron picks and iron axes, and made them toil at[d] the brick-kilns; and thus he did to all the cities of the Ăm′mọ·nītes. Then David and all the people returned to Jerusalem.

13 Now Ăb′sạ·lọm, David's son, had a beautiful sister, whose name was Tā′mär; and after a time Ăm′nŏn, David's son, loved her. [2] And Ăm′nŏn was so tormented that he made himself ill because of his sister Tā′mär; for she was a virgin, and it seemed impossible to Amnon to do anything to her. [3] But Ăm′nŏn had a friend, whose name was Jŏn′ạ·dăb, the son of Shĭm′ē-ạh, David's brother; and Jonadab was a very crafty man. [4] And he said to him, "O son of the king, why are you so haggard morning after morning? Will you not tell me?" Ăm′-nŏn said to him, "I love Tā′mär, my brother Ăb′sạ·lọm′ş sister." [5] Jŏn′ạ·dăb said to him, "Lie down on your bed, and pretend to be ill; and when your father comes to see you, say to him, 'Let my sister Tā′mär come and give me bread to eat, and prepare the food in my sight, that I may see it, and eat if from her hand.'" [6] So Ăm′nŏn lay down, and pretended to be ill; and when the king came to see him, Amnon said to the king, "Pray let my sister Tā′mär come and make a couple of cakes in my sight, that I may eat from her hand."

7 Then David sent home to Tā′mär, saying, "Go to your brother Ăm′nŏn's house, and prepare food for him." [8] So Tā′mär went to her brother Ăm′-nŏn's house, where he was lying down. And she took dough, and kneaded it, and made cakes in his sight, and baked the cakes. [9] And she took the pan and emptied it out before him, but he refused to eat. And Ăm′nŏn said, "Send out every one from me." So every one went out from him. [10] Then Ăm′nŏn said to Tā′mär, "Bring the food into the chamber, that I may eat from your hand." And Tamar took the cakes she had made, and brought them into the chamber to Amnon her brother. [11] But when she brought them near him to eat, he took hold of her, and said to her, "Come, lie with me, my sister." [12] She answered him, "No, my brother, do not force me; for such a thing is not done in Israel; do not do this wanton

[b] That is *beloved of the* LORD
[c] Or *Milcom* See Zeph 1.5   [d] Cn: Heb *pass through*
12.26–31: 1 Chron 20.1–3.

folly. ¹³As for me, where could I carry my shame? And as for you, you would be as one of the wanton fools in Israel. Now therefore, I pray you, speak to the king; for he will not withhold me from you." ¹⁴But he would not listen to her; and being stronger than she, he forced her, and lay with her. 15 Then Ăm'nŏn hated her with very great hatred; so that the hatred with which he hated her was greater than the love with which he had loved her. And Amnon said to her, "Arise, be gone." ¹⁶But she said to him, "No, my brother; for this wrong in sending me away is greater than the other which you did to me."ᵉ But he would not listen to her. ¹⁷He called the young man who served him and said, "Put this woman out of my presence, and bolt the door after her." ¹⁸Now she was wearing a long robe with sleeves; for thus were the virgin daughters of the king clad of old.ᶠ So his servant put her out, and bolted the door after her. ¹⁹And Tā'mär put ashes on her head, and rent the long robe which she wore; and she laid her hand on her head, and went away, crying aloud as she went.

20 And her brother Ăb'sa·lom said to her, "Has Ăm'nŏn your brother been with you? Now hold your peace, my sister; he is your brother; do not take this to heart." So Tā'mär dwelt, a desolate woman, in her brother Absalom's house. ²¹When King David heard of all these things, he was very angry. ²²But Ăb'sa·lom spoke to Ăm'-nŏn neither good nor bad; for Absalom hated Amnon, because he had forced his sister Tā'mär.

23 After two full years Ăb'sa·lom had sheepshearers at Bā'al-hā'zôr, which is near Ē'phra·ĭm, and Absalom invited all the king's sons. ²⁴And Ăb'sa·lom came to the king, and said, "Behold, your servant has sheepshearers; pray let the king and his servants go with your servant." ²⁵But the king said to Ăb'sa·lom, "No, my son, let us not all go, lest we be burdensome to you." He pressed him, but he would not go but gave him his blessing. ²⁶Then Ăb'sa·lom said, "If not, pray let my brother Ăm'nŏn go with us." And the king said to him, "Why should he go with you?" ²⁷But Ăb'sa·lom pressed until he let Ăm'nŏn and all the king's sons go with him. ²⁸Then Ăb'-

sa·lom commanded his servants, "Mark when Ăm'nŏn's heart is merry with wine, and when I say to you, 'Strike Amnon,' then kill him. Fear not; have I not commanded you? Be courageous and be valiant." ²⁹So the servants of Ăb'sa·lom did to Ăm'nŏn as Absalom had commanded. Then all the king's sons arose, and each mounted his mule and fled.

30 While they were on the way, tidings came to David, "Ăb'sa·lom has slain all the king's sons, and not one of them is left." ³¹Then the king arose, and rent his garments, and lay on the earth; and all his servants who were standing by rent their garments. ³²But Jŏn'a·dăb the son of Shĭm'ē·ah, David's brother, said, "Let not my lord suppose that they have killed all the young men the king's sons, for Ăm'nŏn alone is dead, for by the command of Ăb'sa·lom this has been determined from the day he forced his sister Tā'-mär. ³³Now therefore let not my lord the king so take it to heart as to suppose that all the king's sons are dead; for Ăm'nŏn alone is dead."

34 But Ăb'sa·lom fled. And the young man who kept the watch lifted up his eyes, and looked, and behold, many people were coming from the Hôr·ō·nā'ĭm roadᵍ by the side of the mountain. ³⁵And Jŏn'a·dăb said to the king, "Behold, the king's sons have come; as your servant said, so it has come about." ³⁶And as soon as he had finished speaking, behold, the king's sons came, and lifted up their voice and wept; and the king also and all his servants wept very bitterly.

37 But Ăb'sa·lom fled, and went to Tăl'maī the son of Ăm·mī'hud, king of Gē'shūr. And David mourned for his son day after day. ³⁸So Ăb'sa·lom fled, and went to Gē'shūr, and was there three years. ³⁹And the spiritʰ of the king longed to go forth to Ăb'sa·lom; for he was comforted about Ăm'nŏn, seeing he was dead.

14 Now Jō'ăb the son of Zĕ·rü'-ĭ·ah perceived that the king's heart went out to Ăb'sa·lom. ²And Jō'ăb sent to Tĕ·kō'a, and fetched from there a wise woman, and said to her, "Pretend to be a mourner, and put on

ᵉCn Compare Gk Vg: Heb *No, for this great wrong in sending me away is (worse) than the other which you did to me* ᶠCn: Heb *clad in robes*
ᵍCn Compare Gk: Heb *the road behind him*
ʰGk: Heb *David*

mourning garments; do not anoint yourself with oil, but behave like a woman who has been mourning many days for the dead; ³and go to the king, and speak thus to him." So Jō′ăb put the words in her mouth.

4 When the woman of Tĕ·kō′ạ came to the king, she fell on her face to the ground, and did obeisance, and said, "Help, O king." ⁵And the king said to her, "What is your trouble?" She answered, "Alas, I am a widow; my husband is dead. ⁶And your handmaid had two sons, and they quarreled with one another in the field; there was no one to part them, and one struck the other and killed him. ⁷And now the whole family has risen against your handmaid, and they say, 'Give up the man who struck his brother, that we may kill him for the life of his brother whom he slew'; and so they would destroy the heir also. Thus they would quench my coal which is left, and leave to my husband neither name nor remnant upon the face of the earth."

8 Then the king said to the woman, "Go to your house, and I will give orders concerning you." ⁹And the woman of Tĕ′kō′ạ said to the king, "On me be the guilt, my lord the king, and on my father's house; let the king and his throne be guiltless." ¹⁰The king said, "If any one says anything to you, bring him to me, and he shall never touch you again." ¹¹Then she said, "Pray let the king invoke the LORD your God, that the avenger of blood slay no more, and my son be not destroyed." He said, "As the LORD lives, not one hair of your son shall fall to the ground."

12 Then the woman said, "Pray let your handmaid speak a word to my lord the king." He said, "Speak." ¹³And the woman said, "Why then have you planned such a thing against the people of God? For in giving this decision the king convicts himself, inasmuch as the king does not bring his banished one home again. ¹⁴We must all die, we are like water spilt on the ground, which cannot be gathered up again; but God will not take away the life of him who devises[i] means not to keep his banished one an outcast. ¹⁵Now I have come to say this to my lord the king because the people have made me afraid; and your handmaid

thought, 'I will speak to the king; it may be that the king will perform the request of his servant. ¹⁶For the king will hear, and deliver his servant from the hand of the man who would destroy me and my son together from the heritage of God.' ¹⁷And your handmaid thought, 'The word of my lord the king will set me at rest'; for my lord the king is like the angel of God to discern good and evil. The LORD your God be with you!"

18 Then the king answered the woman, "Do not hide from me anything I ask you." And the woman said, "Let my lord the king speak." ¹⁹The king said, "Is the hand of Jō′ăb with you in all this?" The woman answered and said, "As surely as you live, my lord the king, one cannot turn to the right hand or to the left from anything that my lord the king has said. It was your servant Joab who bade me; it was he who put all these words in the mouth of your handmaid. ²⁰In order to change the course of affairs your servant Jō′ăb did this. But my lord has wisdom like the wisdom of the angel of God to know all things that are on the earth."

21 Then the king said to Jō′ăb, "Behold now, I grant this; go, bring back the young man Ăb′sạ·lọm." ²²And Jō′ăb fell on his face to the ground, and did obeisance, and blessed the king; and Joab said, "Today your servant knows that I have found favor in your sight, my lord the king, in that the king has granted the request of his servant." ²³So Jō′ăb arose and went to Gĕ′shŭr, and brought Ăb′sạ·lọm to Jerusalem. ²⁴And the king said, "Let him dwell apart in his own house; but let him not come into my presence." So Ăb′sạ·lọm dwelt apart in his own house, and did not come into the king's presence.

25 Now in all Israel there was no one so much to be praised for his beauty as Ăb′sạ·lọm; from the sole of his foot to the crown of his head there was no blemish in him. ²⁶And when he cut the hair of his head (for at the end of every year he used to cut it; when it was heavy on him, he cut it), he weighed the hair of his head, two hundred shekels by the king's weight. ²⁷There were born to Ăb′sạ·lọm three sons, and one daughter whose name

ᶦCn: Heb *and he devises*

was Tā'mär; she was a beautiful woman.

28 So Ăb'să·lŏm dwelt two full years in Jerusalem, without coming into the king's presence. ²⁹ Then Ăb'să·lŏm sent for Jō'ăb, to send him to the king; but Joab would not come to him. And he sent a second time, but Joab would not come. ³⁰ Then he said to his servants, "See, Jō'ăb'ş field is next to mine, and he has barley there; go and set it on fire." So Ăb'să·lŏm's servants set the field on fire. ³¹ Then Jō'ăb arose and went to Ăb'să·lŏm at his house, and said to him, "Why have your servants set my field on fire?" ³² Ăb'să·lŏm answered Jō'ăb, "Behold, I sent word to you, 'Come here, that I may send you to the king, to ask, "Why have I come from Gē'-shŭr? It would be better for me to be there still." Now therefore let me go into the presence of the king; and if there is guilt in me, let him kill me.'" ³³ Then Jō'ăb went to the king, and told him; and he summoned Ăb'să·lŏm. So he came to the king, and bowed himself on his face to the ground before the king; and the king kissed Absalom.

15 After this Ăb'să·lŏm got himself a chariot and horses, and fifty men to run before him. ²And Ăb'să·lŏm used to rise early and stand beside the way of the gate; and when any man had a suit to come before the king for judgment, Absalom would call to him, and say, "From what city are you?" And when he said, "Your servant is of such and such a tribe in Israel," ³Ăb'să·lŏm would say to him, "See, your claims are good and right; but there is no man deputed by the king to hear you." ⁴Ăb'să·lŏm said moreover, "Oh that I were judge in the land! Then every man with a suit or cause might come to me, and I would give him justice." ⁵And whenever a man came near to do obeisance to him, he would put out his hand, and take hold of him, and kiss him. ⁶Thus Ăb'să·lŏm did to all of Israel who came to the king for judgment; so Absalom stole the hearts of the men of Israel.

7 And at the end of four^j years Ăb'să·lŏm said to the king, "Pray let me go and pay my vow, which I have vowed to the LORD, in Hē'brŏn. ⁸For your servant vowed a vow while I

dwelt at Gē'shŭr in Ăr'ăm, saying, 'If the LORD will indeed bring me back to Jerusalem, then I will offer worship to the LORD.'" ⁹The king said to him, "Go in peace." So he arose, and went to Hē'brŏn. ¹⁰But Ăb'să·lŏm sent secret messengers throughout all the tribes of Israel, saying, "As soon as you hear the sound of the trumpet, then say, 'Absalom is king at Hē'brŏn!'" ¹¹With Ăb'să·lŏm went two hundred men from Jerusalem who were invited guests, and they went in their simplicity, and knew nothing. ¹²And while Ăb'să·lŏm was offering the sacrifices, he sent for^k A·hĭth'o·phĕl the Gĭl'o·nīte, David's counselor, from his city Gī'lōh. And the conspiracy grew strong, and the people with Absalom kept increasing.

13 And a messenger came to David, saying, "The hearts of the men of Israel have gone after Ăb'să·lŏm." ¹⁴Then David said to all his servants who were with him at Jerusalem, "Arise, and let us flee; or else there will be no escape for us from Ăb'să·lŏm; go in haste, lest he overtake us quickly, and bring down evil upon us, and smite the city with the edge of the sword." ¹⁵And the king's servants said to the king, "Behold, your servants are ready to do whatever my lord the king decides." ¹⁶So the king went forth, and all his household after him. And the king left ten concubines to keep the house. ¹⁷And the king went forth, and all the people after him; and they halted at the last house. ¹⁸And all his servants passed by him; and all the Chēr'e·thītes, and all the Pĕl'e·thītes, and all the six hundred Gĭt'tītes who had followed him from Găth, passed on before the king.

19 Then the king said to Ĭt'taī the Gĭt'tīte, "Why do you also go with us? Go back, and stay with the king; for you are a foreigner, and also an exile from^l your home. ²⁰You came only yesterday, and shall I today make you wander about with us, seeing I go I know not where? Go back, and take your brethren with you; and may the LORD show^m steadfast love and faithfulness to you." ²¹But Ĭt'taī answered the king, "As the LORD lives, and as my lord the king lives, wherever my lord the king shall be, whether for

^{j}Gk Syr: Heb *forty* ^{k}Or *sent* ^{l}Gk Syr Vg: Heb *to* ^{m}Gk: Heb lacks *may the* LORD *show*

death or for life, there also will your servant be." ²²And David said to Ĭt'taī, "Go then, pass on." So Ittai the Gĭt'tīte passed on, with all his men and all the little ones who were with him. ²³And all the country wept aloud as all the people passed by, and the king crossed the brook Kĭd'rọn, and all the people passed on toward the wilderness.

24 And Ạ·bī'ạ·thär came up, and lo, Zā'dŏk came also, with all the Lē'vītes, bearing the ark of the covenant of God; and they set down the ark of God, until the people had all passed out of the city. ²⁵Then the king said to Zā'dŏk, "Carry the ark of God back into the city. If I find favor in the eyes of the LORD, he will bring me back and let me see both it and his habitation; ²⁶but if he says, 'I have no pleasure in you,' behold, here I am, let him do to me what seems good to him." ²⁷The king also said to Zā'dŏk the priest, "Look,ⁿ go back to the city in peace, you and Ạ·bī'ạ·thär,ᵒ with your two sons, Ạ·hĭm'ạ–ăz your son, and Jonathan the son of Abiathar. ²⁸See, I will wait at the fords of the wilderness, until word comes from you to inform me." ²⁹So Zā'dŏk and Ạ·bī'ạ·thär carried the ark of God back to Jerusalem; and they remained there.

30 But David went up the ascent of the Mount of Olives, weeping as he went, barefoot and with his head covered; and all the people who were with him covered their heads, and they went up, weeping as they went. ³¹And it was told David, "Ạ·hĭth'ọ·phĕl is among the conspirators with Ăb'sạ·lọm." And David said, "O LORD, I pray thee, turn the counsel of Ahithophel into foolishness."

32 When David came to the summit, where God was worshiped, behold, Hū'shaī the Är'chīte came to meet him with his coat rent and earth upon his head. ³³David said to him, "If you go on with me, you will be a burden to me. ³⁴But if you return to the city, and say to Ăb'sạ·lọm, 'I will be your servant, O king; as I have been your father's servant in time past, so now I will be your servant,' then you will defeat for me the counsel of Ạ·hĭth'-ọ·phĕl. ³⁵Are not Zā'dŏk and Ạ·bī'-ạ·thär the priests with you there? So whatever you hear from the king's house, tell it to Zadok and Abiathar the

priests. ³⁶Behold, their two sons are with them there, Ạ·hĭm'ạ–ăz, Zā'dŏk's son, and Jonathan, Ạ·bī'ạ·thär's son; and by them you shall send to me everything you hear." ³⁷So Hū'shaī, David's friend, came into the city, just as Ăb'sạ·lọm was entering Jerusalem.

16 When David had passed a little beyond the summit, Zī'bạ the servant of Mĕ·phĭb'ọ·shĕth met him, with a couple of asses saddled, bearing two hundred loaves of bread, a hundred bunches of raisins, a hundred of summer fruits, and a skin of wine. ²And the king said to Zī'bạ, "Why have you brought these?" Ziba answered, "The asses are for the king's household to ride on, the bread and summer fruit for the young men to eat, and the wine for those who faint in the wilderness to drink." ³And the king said, "And where is your master's son?" Zī'bạ said to the king, "Behold, he remains in Jerusalem; for he said, 'Today the house of Israel will give me back the kingdom of my father.'" ⁴Then the king said to Zī'bạ, "Behold, all that belonged to Mĕ·phĭb'ọ·shĕth is now yours." And Ziba said, "I do obeisance; let me ever find favor in your sight, my lord the king."

5 When King David came to Bạ·hū'-rĭm, there came out a man of the family of the house of Saul, whose name was Shĭm'ē–ī, the son of Gē'rạ; and as he came he cursed continually. ⁶And he threw stones at David, and at all the servants of King David; and all the people and all the mighty men were on his right hand and on his left. ⁷And Shĭm'ē–ī said as he cursed, "Begone, begone, you man of blood, you worthless fellow! ⁸The LORD has avenged upon you all the blood of the house of Saul, in whose place you have reigned; and the LORD has given the kingdom into the hand of your son Ăb'sạ·lọm. See, your ruin is on you; for you are a man of blood."

9 Then Ạ·bī'shaī the son of Zĕ·rü'-ĭ·ah said to the king, "Why should this dead dog curse my lord the king? Let me go over and take off his head." ¹⁰But the king said, "What have I to do with you, you sons of Zĕ·rü'ĭ·ah? If he is cursing because the LORD has said to him, 'Curse David,' who then shall say, 'Why have you done so?'"

ⁿGk: Heb *Are you a seer* or *Do you see?*
ᵒCn: Heb lacks *and Abiathar*

11And David said to A·bi'shai and to all his servants, "Behold, my own son seeks my life; how much more now may this Benjaminite! Let him alone, and let him curse; for the LORD has bidden him. 12It may be that the LORD will look upon my affliction,*p* and that the LORD will repay me with good for this cursing of me today." 13So David and his men went on the road, while Shim'ē-ī went along on the hillside opposite him and cursed as he went, and threw stones at him and flung dust. 14And the king, and all the people who were with him, arrived weary at the Jordan;*q* and there he refreshed himself.

15 Now Ăb'sa·lom and all the people, the men of Israel, came to Jerusalem, and A·hith'o·phĕl with him. 16And when Hū'shai the Ăr'chīte, David's friend, came to Ăb'sa·lom, Hushai said to Absalom, "Long live the king! Long live the king!" 17And Ăb'sa·lom said to Hū'shai, "Is this your loyalty to your friend? Why did you not go with your friend?" 18And Hū'shai said to Ăb'sa·lom, "No; for whom the LORD and this people and all the men of Israel have chosen, his I will be, and with him I will remain. 19And again, whom should I serve? Should it not be his son? As I have served your father, so I will serve you."

20 Then Ăb'sa·lom said to A·hith'-o·phĕl, "Give your counsel; what shall we do?" 21A·hith'o·phĕl said to Ăb'sa·lom, "Go in to your father's concubines, whom he has left to keep the house; and all Israel will hear that you have made yourself odious to your father, and the hands of all who are with you will be strengthened." 22So they pitched a tent for Ăb'sa·lom upon the roof; and Absalom went in to his father's concubines in the sight of all Israel. 23Now in those days the counsel which A·hith'o·phĕl gave was as if one consulted the oracle*r* of God; so was all the counsel of Ahithophel esteemed, both by David and by Ăb'sa·lom.

17 Moreover A·hith'o·phĕl said to Ăb'sa·lom, "Let me choose twelve thousand men, and I will set out and pursue David tonight. 2I will come upon him while he is weary and discouraged, and throw him into a panic; and all the people who are with him will flee. I will strike down

the king only, 3and I will bring all the people back to you as a bride comes home to her husband. You seek the life of only one man,*s* and all the people will be at peace." 4And the advice pleased Ăb'sa·lom and all the elders of Israel.

5 Then Ăb'sa·lom said, "Call Hū'-shai the Ăr'chīte also, and let us hear what he has to say." 6And when Hū'-shai came to Ăb'sa·lom, Absalom said to him, "Thus has A·hith'o·phĕl spoken; shall we do as he advises? If not, you speak." 7Then Hū'shai said to Ăb'sa·lom, "This time the counsel which A·hith'o·phĕl has given is not good." 8Hū'shai said moreover, "You know that your father and his men are mighty men, and that they are enraged, like a bear robbed of her cubs in the field. Besides, your father is expert in war; he will not spend the night with the people. 9Behold, even now he has hidden himself in one of the pits, or in some other place. And when some of the people fall*t* at the first attack, whoever hears it will say, 'There has been a slaughter among the people who follow Ăb'sa·lom.' 10Then even the valiant man, whose heart is like the heart of a lion, will utterly melt with fear; for all Israel knows that your father is a mighty man, and that those who are with him are valiant men. 11But my counsel is that all Israel be gathered to you, from Dan to Bē'er-shē'ba, as the sand by the sea for multitude, and that you go to battle in person. 12So we shall come upon him in some place where he is to be found, and we shall light upon him as the dew falls on the ground; and of him and all the men with him not one will be left. 13If he withdraws into a city, then all Israel will bring ropes to that city, and we shall drag it into the valley, until not even a pebble is to be found there." 14And Ăb'sa·lom and all the men of Israel said, "The counsel of Hū'shai the Ăr'chīte is better than the counsel of A·hith'o·phĕl." For the LORD had ordained to defeat the good counsel of Ahithophel, so that the LORD might bring evil upon Ăb'sa·lom.

15 Then Hū'shai said to Zā'dŏk and A·bī'a·thăr the priests, "Thus and so

*p*Gk Vg: Heb *iniquity*   *q*Gk: Heb lacks *at the Jordan*
*r*Heb *word*
*s*Gk: Heb *like the return of the whole (is) the man whom you seek*   *t*Or *when he falls upon them*

did A·hĭth'ọ·phĕl counsel Ăb'sạ·lọm and the elders of Israel; and thus and so have I counseled. ¹⁶Now therefore send quickly and tell David, 'Do not lodge tonight at the fords of the wilderness, but by all means pass over; lest the king and all the people who are with him be swallowed up.'" ¹⁷Now Jonathan and A·hĭm'ạ–ăz were waiting at Ēn–rō'gĕl; a maidservant used to go and tell them, and they would go and tell King David; for they must not be seen entering the city. ¹⁸But a lad saw them, and told Ăb'sạ·lọm; so both of them went away quickly, and came to the house of a man at Bạ·hū'rĭm, who had a well in his courtyard; and they went down into it. ¹⁹And the woman took and spread a covering over the well's mouth, and scattered grain upon it; and nothing was known of it. ²⁰When Ăb'sạ·lọm's servants came to the woman at the house, they said, "Where are A·hĭm'ạ–ăz and Jonathan?" And the woman said to them, "They have gone over the brook^u of water." And when they had sought and could not find them, they returned to Jerusalem.

21 After they had gone, the men came up out of the well, and went and told King David. They said to David, "Arise, and go quickly over the water; for thus and so has A·hĭth'ọ·phĕl counseled against you." ²²Then David arose, and all the people who were with him, and they crossed the Jordan; by daybreak not one was left who had not crossed the Jordan.

23 When A·hĭth'ọ·phĕl saw that his counsel was not followed, he saddled his ass, and went off home to his own city. And he set his house in order, and hanged himself; and he died, and was buried in the tomb of his father.

24 Then David came to Mā"hạ-nā'ĭm. And Ăb'sạ·lọm crossed the Jordan with all the men of Israel. ²⁵Now Ăb'sạ·lọm had set A·mā'sạ over the army instead of Jō'ăb. Amasa was the son of a man named Ĭth'rặ the Ĭsh'-mạ·ĕl·īte,^v who had married Ăb'ĭ·gāl the daughter of Nā'hăsh, sister of Zĕ·rü'ĭ·ạh, Jō'ăb'ş mother. ²⁶And Israel and Ăb'sạ·lọm encamped in the land of Gilead.

27 When David came to Mā"hạ-nā'ĭm, Shō'bī the son of Nā'hăsh from Răb'bạh of the Ăm'mọ·nītes, and Mā'-chĭr the son of Ăm'mĭ–ĕl from Lō–dē'-

bär, and Bär·zĭl'laī the Gileadite from Rō'gẹ·lĭm, ²⁸brought beds, basins, and earthen vessels, wheat, barley, meal, parched grain, beans and lentils,^w ²⁹honey and curds and sheep and cheese from the herd, for David and the people with him to eat; for they said, "The people are hungry and weary and thirsty in the wilderness."

18 Then David mustered the men who were with him, and set over them commanders of thousands and commanders of hundreds. ²And David sent forth the army, one third under the command of Jō'ăb, one third under the command of A·bĭ'shaī the son of Zĕ·rü'ĭ·ạh, Jō'ăb'ş brother, and one third under the command of Ĭt'taī the Gĭt'tīte. And the king said to the men, "I myself will also go out with you." ³But the men said, "You shall not go out. For if we flee, they will not care about us. If half of us die, they will not care about us. But you are worth ten thousand of us;^x therefore it is better that you send us help from the city." ⁴The king said to them, "Whatever seems best to you I will do." So the king stood at the side of the gate, while all the army marched out by hundreds and by thousands. ⁵And the king ordered Jō'ăb and A·bĭ'shaī and Ĭt'taī, "Deal gently for my sake with the young man Ăb'sạ·lọm." And all the people heard when the king gave orders to all the commanders about Absalom.

6 So the army went out into the field against Israel; and the battle was fought in the forest of Ē'phra'ĭm. ⁷And the men of Israel were defeated there by the servants of David, and the slaughter there was great on that day, twenty thousand men. ⁸The battle spread over the face of all the country; and the forest devoured more people that day than the sword.

9 And Ăb'sạ·lọm chanced to meet the servants of David. Absalom was riding upon his mule, and the mule went under the thick branches of a great oak, and his head caught fast in the oak, and he was left hanging^y between heaven and earth, while the mule that was under him went on. ¹⁰And a certain man saw it, and told

^uThe meaning of the Hebrew word is uncertain
^v1 Chron 2.17: Heb *Israelite*
^wHeb *lentils and parched grain*
^xGk Vg Symmachus: Heb *for now there are ten thousand such as we*   ^yGk Syr Tg: Heb *was put*

Jō'ăb, "Behold, I saw Ăb'sa·lom hanging in an oak." ¹¹Jō'ăb said to the man who told him, "What, you saw him! Why then did you not strike him there to the ground? I would have been glad to give you ten pieces of silver and a girdle." ¹²But the man said to Jō'ăb, "Even if I felt in my hand the weight of a thousand pieces of silver, I would not put forth my hand against the king's son; for in our hearing the king commanded you and A·bī'shaī and Ĭt'-taī, 'For my sake protect the young man Ăb'sa·lom.' ¹³On the other hand, if I had dealt treacherously against his life^z (and there is nothing hidden from the king), then you yourself would have stood aloof." ¹⁴Jō'ăb said, "I will not waste time like this with you." And he took three darts in his hand, and thrust them into the heart of Ăb'sa·lom, while he was still alive in the oak. ¹⁵And ten young men, Jō'ăb's armor-bearers, surrounded Ăb'sa·lom and struck him, and killed him.

16 Then Jō'ăb blew the trumpet, and the troops came back from pursuing Israel; for Joab restrained them. ¹⁷And they took Ăb'sa·lom, and threw him into a great pit in the forest, and raised over him a very great heap of stones; and all Israel fled every one to his own home. ¹⁸Now Ăb'sa·lom in his lifetime had taken and set up for himself the pillar which is in the King's Valley, for he said, "I have no son to keep my name in remembrance"; he called the pillar after his own name, and it is called Absalom's monument to this day.

19 Then said A·hĭm'a–ăz the son of Zā'dŏk, "Let me run, and carry tidings to the king that the LORD has delivered him from the power of his enemies." ²⁰And Jō'ăb said to him, "You are not to carry tidings today; you may carry tidings another day, but today you shall carry no tidings, because the king's son is dead." ²¹Then Jō'ăb said to the Cüsh'īte, "Go, tell the king what you have seen." The Cushite bowed before Joab, and ran. ²²Then A·hĭm'a–ăz the son of Zā'dŏk said again to Jō'ăb, "Come what may, let me also run after the Cüsh'īte." And Joab said, "Why will you run, my son, seeing that you will have no reward for the tidings?" ²³"Come what may," he said, "I will run." So he said to him, "Run."

Then A·hĭm'a–ăz ran by the way of the plain, and outran the Cüsh'īte. 24 Now David was sitting between the two gates; and the watchman went up to the roof of the gate by the wall, and when he lifted up his eyes and looked, he saw a man running alone. ²⁵And the watchman called out and told the king. And the king said, "If he is alone, there are tidings in his mouth." And he came apace, and drew near. ²⁶And the watchman saw another man running; and the watchman called to the gate and said, "See, another man running alone!" The king said, "He also brings tidings." ²⁷And the watchman said, "I think the running of the foremost is like the running of A·hĭm'a–ăz the son of Zā'dŏk." And the king said, "He is a good man, and comes with good tidings."

28 Then A·hĭm'a–ăz cried out to the king, "All is well." And he bowed before the king with his face to the earth, and said, "Blessed be the LORD your God, who has delivered up the men who raised their hand against my lord the king." ²⁹And the king said, "Is it well with the young man Ăb'sa·lom?" A·hĭm'a–ăz answered, "When Jō'ăb sent your servant,^b I saw a great tumult, but I do not know what it was." ³⁰And the king said, "Turn aside, and stand here." So he turned aside, and stood still.

31 And behold, the Cüsh'īte came; and the Cushite said, "Good tidings for my lord the king! For the LORD has delivered you this day from the power of all who rose up against you." ³²The king said to the Cüsh'īte, "Is it well with the young man Ăb'sa·lom?" And the Cushite answered, "May the enemies of my lord the king, and all who rise up against you for evil, be like that young man." ³³ᶜAnd the king was deeply moved, and went up to the chamber over the gate, and wept; and as he went, he said, "O my son Ăb'sa·lom, my son, my son Absalom! Would I had died instead of you, O Absalom, my son, my son!"

19 It was told Jō'ăb, "Behold, the king is weeping and mourning for Ăb'sa·lom." ²So the victory that day was turned into mourning for all the people; for the people heard that day, "The king is grieving for his son."

^zAnother reading is *at the risk of my life*
^bHeb *the king's servant, your servant* ^cCh 19.1 in Heb

³And the people stole into the city that day as people steal in who are ashamed when they flee in battle. ⁴The king covered his face, and the king cried with a loud voice, "O my son Ăb'sa·lom, O Absalom, my son, my son!" ⁵Then Jō'ăb came into the house to the king, and said, "You have today covered with shame the faces of all your servants, who have this day saved your life, and the lives of your sons and your daughters, and the lives of your wives and your concubines, ⁶because you love those who hate you and hate those who love you. For you have made it clear today that commanders and servants are nothing to you; for today I perceive that if Ăb'sa·lom were alive and all of us were dead today, then you would be pleased. ⁷Now therefore arise, go out and speak kindly to your servants; for I swear by the LORD, if you do not go, not a man will stay with you this night; and this will be worse for you than all the evil that has come upon you from your youth until now." ⁸Then the king arose, and took his seat in the gate. And the people were all told, "Behold, the king is sitting in the gate"; and all the people came before the king.

Now Israel had fled every man to his own home. ⁹And all the people were at strife throughout all the tribes of Israel, saying, "The king delivered us from the hand of our enemies, and saved us from the hand of the Phĭ·lĭs'tĭnes; and now he has fled out of the land from Ăb'sa·lom. ¹⁰But Ăb'sa·lom, whom we anointed over us, is dead in battle. Now therefore why do you say nothing about bringing the king back?"

11 And King David sent this message to Zā'dŏk and A·bī'a·thär the priests, "Say to the elders of Judah, 'Why should you be the last to bring the king back to his house, when the word of all Israel has come to the king?ᵈ ¹²You are my kinsmen, you are my bone and my flesh; why then should you be the last to bring back the king?' ¹³And say tŏ A·mā'sa, 'Are you not my bone and my flesh? God do so to me and more also, if you are not commander of my army henceforth in place of Jō'ăb.'" ¹⁴And he swayed the heart of all the men of Judah as one man; so that they sent word to the king, "Return, both you and all your servants." ¹⁵So the king came back to

the Jordan; and Judah came to Gĭl'găl to meet the king and to bring the king over the Jordan.

16 And Shĭm'ē–ī the son of Gē'ra, the Benjaminite, from Ba·hū'rĭm, made haste to come down with the men of Judah to meet King David; ¹⁷and with him were a thousand men from Benjamin. And Zī'ba the servant of the house of Saul, with his fifteen sons and his twenty servants, rushed down to the Jordan before the king, ¹⁸and they crossed the fordᵉ to bring over the king's household, and to do his pleasure. And Shĭm'ē–ī the son of Gē'ra fell down before the king, as he was about to cross the Jordan, ¹⁹and said to the king, "Let not my lord hold me guilty or remember how your servant did wrong on the day my lord the king left Jerusalem; let not the king bear it in mind. ²⁰For your servant knows that I have sinned; therefore, behold, I have come this day, the first of all the house of Joseph to come down to meet my lord the king." ²¹A·bī'shaī the son of Zĕ·rü'ī·ah answered, "Shall not Shĭm'ē–ī be put to death for this, because he cursed the LORD's anointed?" ²²But David said, "What have I to do with you, you sons of Zĕ·rü'ī·ah, that you should this day be as an adversary to me? Shall any one be put to death in Israel this day? For do I not know that I am this day king over Israel?" ²³And the king said to Shĭm'ē–ī, "You shall not die." And the king gave him his oath.

24 And Mĕ·phĭb'o·shĕth the son of Saul came down to meet the king; he had neither dressed his feet, nor trimmed his beard, nor washed his clothes, from the day the king departed until the day he came back in safety. ²⁵And when he came fromᶠ Jerusalem to meet the king, the king said to him, "Why did you not go with me, Mĕ·phĭb'o·shĕth?" ²⁶He answered, "My lord, O king, my servant deceived me; for your servant said to him, 'Saddle an ass for me,ᵍ that I may ride upon it and go with the king.' For your servant is lame. ²⁷He has slandered your servant to my lord the king. But my lord the king is like the angel of God; do therefore what seems good to you. ²⁸For all my father's house were but

---

ᵈGk: Heb *to the king, to his house*
ᵉCn: Heb *the ford crossed* ᶠHeb *to*
ᵍGk Syr Vg: Heb *said, I will saddle an ass for myself*

men doomed to death before my lord the king; but you set your servant among those who eat at your table. What further right have I, then, to cry to the king?" ²⁹ And the king said to him, "Why speak any more of your affairs? I have decided: you and Zī'ba shall divide the land." ³⁰ And Mĕ·phĭb'-o·shĕth said to the king, "Oh, let him take it all, since my lord the king has come safely home."

31 Now Bär·zĭl'laī the Gileadite had come down from Rō'ge·lĭm; and he went on with the king to the Jordan, to escort him over the Jordan. ³² Bär·zĭl'laī was a very aged man, eighty years old; and he had provided the king with food while he stayed at Mā''ha·nā'ĭm; for he was a very wealthy man. ³³ And the king said to Bär·zĭl'laī, "Come over with me, and I will provide for you with me in Jerusalem." ³⁴ But Bär·zĭl'laī said to the king, "How many years have I still to live, that I should go up with the king to Jerusalem? ³⁵ I am this day eighty years old; can I discern what is pleasant and what is not? Can your servant taste what he eats or what he drinks? Can I still listen to the voice of singing men and singing women? Why then should your servant be an added burden to my lord the king? ³⁶ Your servant will go a little way over the Jordan with the king. Why should the king recompense me with such a reward? ³⁷ Pray let your servant return, that I may die in my own city, near the grave of my father and my mother. But here is your servant Chĭm'hăm; let him go over with my lord the king; and do for him whatever seems good to you." ³⁸ And the king answered, "Chĭm'hăm shall go over with me, and I will do for him whatever seems good to you; and all that you desire of me I will do for you." ³⁹ Then all the people went over the Jordan, and the king went over; and the king kissed Bär·zĭl'laī and blessed him, and he returned to his own home. ⁴⁰ The king went on to Gĭl'gal, and Chĭm'hăm went on with him; all the people of Judah, and also half the people of Israel, brought the king on his way.

41 Then all the men of Israel came to the king, and said to the king, "Why have our brethren the men of Judah stolen you away, and brought the king and his household over the Jordan, and all David's men with him?" ⁴² All the men of Judah answered the men of Israel, "Because the king is near of kin to us. Why then are you angry over this matter? Have we eaten at all at the king's expense? Or has he given us any gift?" ⁴³ And the men of Israel answered the men of Judah, "We have ten shares in the king, and in David also we have more than you. Why then did you despise us? Were we not the first to speak of bringing back our king?" But the words of the men of Judah were fiercer than the words of the men of Israel.

20 Now there happened to be there a worthless fellow, whose name was Shē'ba, the son of Bĭch'rī, a Benjaminite; and he blew the trumpet, and said,

"We have no portion in David,
  and we have no inheritance in the son of Jesse;
every man to his tents, O Israel!"

² So all the men of Israel withdrew from David, and followed Shē'ba the son of Bĭch'rī; but the men of Judah followed their king steadfastly from the Jordan to Jerusalem.

3 And David came to his house at Jerusalem; and the king took the ten concubines whom he had left to care for the house, and put them in a house under guard, and provided for them, but did not go in to them. So they were shut up until the day of their death, living as if in widowhood.

4 Then the king said to A·mā'sa, "Call the men of Judah together to me within three days, and be here yourself." ⁵ So A·mā'sa went to summon Judah; but he delayed beyond the set time which had been appointed him. ⁶ And David said to A·bi'shaī, "Now Shē'ba the son of Bĭch'rī will do us more harm than Ăb'sa·lom; take your lord's servants and pursue him, lest he get himself fortified cities, and cause us trouble."^h ⁷ And there went out after A·bi'shaī, Jō'ăbⁱ and the Chēr'-e·thītes and the Pĕl'e·thītes, and all the mighty men; they went out from Jerusalem to pursue Shē'ba the son of Bĭch'rī. ⁸ When they were at the great stone which is in Gĭb'ē·on, A·mā'sa came to meet them. Now Jō'ăb was wearing a soldier's garment, and over it was a girdle with a sword in its

^h Tg: Heb *snatch away our eyes*
ⁱ Cn Compare Gk: Heb *after him Joab's men*

sheath fastened upon his loins, and as he went forward it fell out. ⁹ And Jō′ăb said to A·mā′să, "Is it well with you, my brother?" And Joab took Amasa by the beard with his right hand to kiss him. ¹⁰ But A·mā′să did not observe the sword which was in Jō′ăb′ş hand; so Joab struck him with it in the body, and shed his bowels to the ground, without striking a second blow; and he died.

Then Joab and A·bī′shaī his brother pursued Shē′bă the son of Bĭch′rī. ¹¹ And one of Jō′ăb′ş men took his stand by A·mā′să, and said, "Whoever favors Joab, and whoever is for David, let him follow Joab." ¹² And A·mā′să lay wallowing in his blood in the highway. And any one who came by, seeing him, stopped;ʲ and when the man saw that all the people stopped, he carried Amasa out of the highway into the field, and threw a garment over him. ¹³ When he was taken out of the highway, all the people went on after Jō′ăb to pursue Shē′bă the son of Bĭch′rī.

14 And Shē′bă passed through all the tribes of Israel to Abel of Bĕth-mā′a·cáh;ᵏ and all the Bĭch′rītesˡ assembled, and followed him in. ¹⁵ And all the men who were with Jō′ăb came and besieged him in Abel of Bĕth·mā′-a·cáh; they cast up a mound against the city, and it stood against the rampart; and they were battering the wall, to throw it down. ¹⁶ Then a wise woman called from the city, "Hear! Hear! Tell Jō′ăb, 'Come here, that I may speak to you.'" ¹⁷ And he came near her; and the woman said, "Are you Jō′ăb?" He answered, "I am." Then she said to him, "Listen to the words of your maidservant." And he answered, "I am listening." ¹⁸ Then she said, "They were wont to say in old time, 'Let them but ask counsel at Abel'; and so they settled a matter. ¹⁹ I am one of those who are peaceable and faithful in Israel; you seek to destroy a city which is a mother in Israel; why will you swallow up the heritage of the LORD?" ²⁰ Jō′ăb answered, "Far be it from me, far be it, that I should swallow up or destroy! ²¹ That is not true. But a man of the hill country of Ē′phra·ĭm, called Shē′bă the son of Bĭch′rī, has lifted up his hand against King David; give up him alone, and I will withdraw from the city." And the woman said to Jō′ăb, "Behold, his head shall be thrown to

you over the wall." ²² Then the woman went to all the people in her wisdom. And they cut off the head of Shē′bă the son of Bĭch′rī, and threw it out to Jō′ăb. So he blew the trumpet, and they dispersed from the city, every man to his home. And Joab returned to Jerusalem to the king.

23 Now Jō′ăb was in command of all the army of Israel; and Bĕ·nā′ī·ah the son of Jĕ·hoi′a·dă was in command of the Chĕr′ĕ·thītes and the Pĕl′ĕ·thītes; ²⁴ and A·dôr′ăm was in charge of the forced labor; and Jĕ·hŏsh′a·phăt the son of A·hī′lŭd was the recorder; ²⁵ and Shē′vă was secretary; and Zā′dŏk and A·bī′a·thär were priests; ²⁶ and Ira the Jā′ī·rīte was also David's priest.

21 Now there was a famine in the days of David for three years, year after year; and David sought the face of the LORD. And the LORD said, "There is bloodguilt on Saul and on his house, because he put the Gĭb′ē·ọ·nītes to death." ² So the king called the Gĭb′-ē·ọ·nītes.ᵐ Now the Gibeonites were not of the people of Israel, but of the remnant of the Ăm′ọ·rītes; although the people of Israel had sworn to spare them, Saul had sought to slay them in his zeal for the people of Israel and Judah. ³ And David said to the Gĭb′-ē·ọ·nītes, "What shall I do for you? And how shall I make expiation, that you may bless the heritage of the LORD?" ⁴ The Gĭb′ē·ọ·nītes said to him, "It is not a matter of silver or gold between us and Saul or his house; neither is it for us to put any man to death in Israel." And he said, "What do you say that I shall do for you?" ⁵ They said to the king, "The man who consumed us and planned to destroy us, so that we should have no place in all the territory of Israel, ⁶ let seven of his sons be given to us, so that we may hang them up before the LORD at Gĭb′ē·ọn on the mountain of the LORD."ⁿ And the king said, "I will give them."

7 But the king spared Mĕ·phĭb′ọ-shĕth, the son of Saul's son Jonathan, because of the oath of the LORD which was between them, between David and Jonathan the son of Saul. ⁸ The king took the two sons of Rĭz′pah the daugh-

---

ʲThis clause is transposed from the end of the verse ᵏWith 20.15: Heb *and Beth-maacah* ˡHeb *Berites* ᵐHeb *the Gibeonites and said to them* ⁿCn Compare Gk and 21.9: Heb *at Gibeah of Saul, the chosen of the* LORD
20.23-26: 8.15-18; 1 Chron 18.14-17.

ter of Aĭ'ạh, whom she bore to Saul, Är·mō'nĭ and Mĕ·phĭb'ọ·shĕth; and the five sons of Mē'răb° the daughter of Saul, whom she bore to Ā'drĭ–ĕl the son of Bär·zĭl'laī the Mẹ·hō'lạ·thīte; 9 and he gave them into the hands of the Gĭb'ē·ọ·nītes, and they hanged them on the mountain before the LORD, and the seven of them perished together. They were put to death in the first days of harvest, at the beginning of barley harvest.

10 Then Rĭz'pạh the daughter of Aĭ'ạh took sackcloth, and spread it for herself on the rock, from the beginning of harvest until rain fell upon them from the heavens; and she did not allow the birds of the air to come upon them by day, or the beasts of the field by night. 11 When David was told what Rĭz'pạh the daughter of Aĭ'ạh, the concubine of Saul, had done, 12 David went and took the bones of Saul and the bones of his son Jonathan from the men of Jā'bĕsh–gĭl'ē·ad, who had stolen them from the public square of Bĕth–shăn, where the Phĭ·lĭs'tĭnes had hanged them, on the day the Philistines killed Saul on Gĭl·bō'a; 13 and he brought up from there the bones of Saul and the bones of his son Jonathan; and they gathered the bones of those who were hanged. 14 And they buried the bones of Saul and his son Jonathan in the land of Benjamin in Zē'lạ, in the tomb of Kĭsh his father; and they did all that the king commanded. And after that God heeded supplications for the land.

15 The Phĭ·lĭs'tĭnes had war again with Israel, and David went down together with his servants, and they fought against the Philistines; and David grew weary. 16 And Ĭsh'bĭ–bē'–nŏb, one of the descendants of the giants, whose spear weighed three hundred shekels of bronze, and who was girded with a new sword, thought to kill David. 17 But Ạ·bĭ'shaī the son of Zĕ·rü'ĭ·ạh came to his aid, and attacked the Phĭ·lĭs'tĭne and killed him. Then David's men adjured him, "You shall no more go out with us to battle, lest you quench the lamp of Israel."

18 After this there was again war with the Phĭ·lĭs'tĭnes at Gŏb; then Sĭb'–bẹ·caī the Hü'shạ·thīte slew Săph, who was one of the descendants of the giants. 19 And there was again war with the Phĭ·lĭs'tĭnes at Gŏb; and Ĕl-

hā'nạn the son of Jā'ạ·rē–ôr'ẹ·gĭm, the Bethlehemite, slew Goliath the Gĭt'tīte, the shaft of whose spear was like a weaver's beam. 20 And there was again war at Găth, where there was a man of great stature, who had six fingers on each hand, and six toes on each foot, twenty-four in number; and he also was descended from the giants. 21 And when he taunted Israel, Jonathan the son of Shĭm'ē–ī, David's brother, slew him. 22 These four were descended from the giants in Găth; and they fell by the hand of David and by the hand of his servants.

22 And David spoke to the LORD the words of this song on the day when the LORD delivered him from the hand of all his enemies, and from the hand of Saul.

2 He said,
"The LORD is my rock, and my fortress, and my deliverer,
3   my^p God, my rock, in whom I take refuge,
my shield and the horn of my salvation,
my stronghold and my refuge,
my savior; thou savest me from violence.
4 I call upon the LORD, who is worthy to be praised,
and I am saved from my enemies.

5 "For the waves of death encompassed me,
the torrents of perdition assailed me;
6 the cords of Shē'ōl entangled me,
the snares of death confronted me.

7 "In my distress I called upon the LORD;
to my God I called.
From his temple he heard my voice,
and my cry came to his ears.

8 "Then the earth reeled and rocked;
the foundations of the heavens trembled
and quaked, because he was angry.
9 Smoke went up from his nostrils,
and devouring fire from his mouth;
glowing coals flamed forth from him.
10 He bowed the heavens, and came down;

° Two Hebrew Mss Gk: Heb *Michal*
^{p} Gk Ps 18.2: Heb lacks *my*
21.13–22: 1 Chron 20.4-8.   **22.2–51:** Ps 18.2-50.

thick darkness was under his feet.
11 He rode on a cherub, and flew;
    he was seen upon the wings of the
        wind.
12 He made darkness around him
    his canopy, thick clouds, a gather-
        ing of water.
13 Out of the brightness before him
    coals of fire flamed forth.
14 The LORD thundered from heaven,
    and the Most High uttered his
        voice.
15 And he sent out arrows, and scat-
        tered them;
    lightning, and routed them.
16 Then the channels of the sea were
        seen,
    the foundations of the world were
        laid bare,
    at the rebuke of the LORD,
    at the blast of the breath of his
        nostrils.

17 "He reached from on high, he took
        me,
    he drew me out of many waters.
18 He delivered me from my strong
        enemy,
    from those who hated me;
    for they were too mighty for me.
19 They came upon me in the day of my
        calamity;
    but the LORD was my stay.
20 He brought me forth into a broad
        place;
    he delivered me, because he de-
        lighted in me.

21 "The LORD rewarded me according
        to my righteousness;
    according to the cleanness of my
        hands he recompensed me.
22 For I have kept the ways of the LORD,
    and have not wickedly departed
        from my God.
23 For all his ordinances were before
        me,
    and from his statutes I did not turn
        aside.
24 I was blameless before him,
    and I kept myself from guilt.
25 Therefore the LORD has recompensed
    me according to my righteous-
        ness,
    according to my cleanness in his
        sight.

26 "With the loyal thou dost show thy-
        self loyal;

with the blameless man thou dost
    show thyself blameless;
27 with the pure thou dost show thyself
        pure,
    and with the crooked thou dost
        show thyself perverse.
28 Thou dost deliver a humble people,
    but thy eyes are upon the haughty
        to bring them down.
29 Yea, thou art my lamp, O LORD,
    and my God lightens my darkness.
30 Yea, by thee I can crush a troop,
    and by my God I can leap over a
        wall.
31 This God—his way is perfect;
    the promise of the LORD proves
        true;
    he is a shield for all those who take
        refuge in him.

32 "For who is God, but the LORD?
    And who is a rock, except our God?
33 This God is my strong refuge,
    and has made*r* my*s* way safe.
34 He made my*s* feet like hinds' feet,
    and set me secure on the heights.
35 He trains my hands for war,
    so that my arms can bend a bow
        of bronze.
36 Thou hast given me the shield of thy
        salvation,
    and thy help*t* made me great.
37 Thou didst give a wide place for my
        steps under me,
    and my feet*u* did not slip;
38 I pursued my enemies and destroyed
        them,
    and did not turn back until they
        were consumed.
39 I consumed them; I thrust them
        through, so that they did not rise;
    they fell under my feet.
40 For thou didst gird me with strength
        for the battle;
    thou didst make my assailants sink
        under me.
41 Thou didst make my enemies turn
        their backs to me,
    those who hated me, and I de-
        stroyed them.
42 They looked, but there was none to
        save;
    they cried to the LORD, but he did
        not answer them.
43 I beat them fine as the dust of the
        earth,
    I crushed them and stamped them
        down like the mire of the streets.

*r Ps 18.32: Heb set free *s Another reading is his
*t Or gentleness *u Heb ankles*

⁴⁴ "Thou didst deliver me from strife
    with the peoples;"
    thou didst keep me as the head of
    the nations;
    people whom I had not known
    served me.
⁴⁵ Foreigners came cringing to me;
    as soon as they heard of me, they
    obeyed me.
⁴⁶ Foreigners lost heart,
    and came trembling" out of their
    fastnesses.

⁴⁷ "The LORD lives; and blessed be my
    rock,
    and exalted be my God, the rock of
    my salvation,
⁴⁸ the God who gave me vengeance
    and brought down peoples under
    me,
⁴⁹ who brought me out from my
    enemies;
    thou didst exalt me above my ad-
    versaries,
    thou didst deliver me from men of
    violence.

⁵⁰ "For this I will extol thee, O LORD,
    among the nations,
    and sing praises to thy name.
⁵¹ Great triumphs he gives^x to his king,
    and shows steadfast love to his
    anointed,
    to David, and his descendants for
    ever."

23 Now these are the last words
    of David:
The oracle of David, the son of Jesse,
    the oracle of the man who was
    raised on high,
the anointed of the God of Jacob,
    the sweet psalmist of Israel:^y

² "The Spirit of the LORD speaks by
    me,
    his word is upon my tongue.
³ The God of Israel has spoken,
    the Rock of Israel has said to me:
When one rules justly over men,
    ruling in the fear of God,
⁴ he dawns on them like the morning
    light,
    like the sun shining forth upon a
    cloudless morning,
    like rain^z that makes grass to
    sprout from the earth.
⁵ Yea, does not my house stand so with
    God?

For he has made with me an ever-
    lasting covenant,
    ordered in all things and secure.
For will he not cause to prosper
    all my help and my desire?
⁶ But godless men^a are all like thorns
    that are thrown away;
    for they cannot be taken with the
    hand;
⁷ but the man who touches them
    arms himself with iron and the
    shaft of a spear,
    and they are utterly consumed
    with fire."^b

8 These are the names of the mighty
men whom David had: Jō′shĕb–băs-
shē′bĕth a Tăh–chē′mo̧-nīte; he was
chief of the three;^c he wielded his
spear^d against eight hundred whom
he slew at one time.
9 And next to him among the three
mighty men was Ĕl·ē·ā′zar the son of
Dō′dō, son of A̧·hō′hī. He was with
David when they defied the Phĭ-
lĭs′tĭnes who were gathered there for
battle, and the men of Israel withdrew.
¹⁰ He rose and struck down the Phĭ-
lĭs′tĭnes until his hand was weary,
and his hand cleaved to the sword;
and the LORD wrought a great victory
that day; and the men returned after
him only to strip the slain.
11 And next to him was Shăm′mah,
the son of A′gee the Hăr′a̧-rīte. The
Phĭ·lĭs′tĭnes gathered together at Lē′hī,
where there was a plot of ground full
of lentils; and the men fled from the
Philistines. ¹² But he took his stand in
the midst of the plot, and defended it,
and slew the Phĭ·lĭs′tĭnes; and the
LORD wrought a great victory.
13 And three of the thirty chief men
went down, and came about harvest
time to David at the cave of A̧·dŭl′lam,
when a band of Phĭ·lĭs′tĭnes was encamped in the valley of Rĕph′a̧·im.
¹⁴ David was then in the stronghold;
and the garrison of the Phĭ·lĭs′tĭnes
was then at Bethlehem. ¹⁵ And David
said longingly, "O that some one
would give me water to drink from the
well of Bethlehem which is by the
gate!" ¹⁶ Then the three mighty men
broke through the camp of the Phĭ·lĭs′-

^v Gk: Heb *from strife with my people*
^w Ps 18.45: Heb *girded themselves*
^x Another reading is *He is a tower of salvation*
^y Or *the favorite of the songs of Israel*   ^z Heb *from rain*
^a Heb *worthlessness*   ^b Heb *fire in the sitting*
^c Or *captains*   ^d 1 Chron 11.11: Heb *obscure*
22.50: Rom 15.9   **23.8-39:** 1 Chron 11.10-41.

tĭnes, and drew water out of the well of Bethlehem which was by the gate, and took and brought it to David. But he would not drink of it; he poured it out to the LORD, [17] and said, "Far be it from me, O LORD, that I should do this. Shall I drink the blood of the men who went at the risk of their lives?" Therefore he would not drink it. These things did the three mighty men.

18 Now A·bī'shaī, the brother of Jō'āb, the son of Zĕ·rū'ĭ·ah, was chief of the thirty.[e] And he wielded his spear against three hundred men and slew them, and won a name beside the three. [19] He was the most renowned of the thirty,[f] and became their commander; but he did not attain to the three.

20 And Bĕ·nā'ĭ·ah the son of Jĕ·hoi'-a·da was a valiant man[g] of Kăb'zē·ĕl, a doer of great deeds; he smote two ariels[h] of Mō'āb. He also went down and slew a lion in a pit on a day when snow had fallen. [21] And he slew an Egyptian, a handsome man. The Egyptian had a spear in his hand; but Bĕ·nā'ĭ·ah went down to him with a staff, and snatched the spear out of the Egyptian's hand, and slew him with his own spear. [22] These things did Bĕ·nā'ĭ·ah the son of Jĕ·hoi'a·da, and won a name beside the three mighty men. [23] He was renowned among the thirty, but he did not attain to the three. And David set him over his bodyguard.

24 Ăs'a·hĕl the brother of Jō'āb was one of the thirty; Ĕl·hā'nan the son of Dō'dō of Bethlehem, [25] Shăm'mah of Hăr'ŏd, Ĕ·lī'ka of Harod, [26] Hē'lĕz of Tĕ·kō'a, Ira the son of Ĭk'kĕsh of Tĕ·kō'a, [27] A·bĭ·ē'zer, of Ăn·a·thŏth, Mĕ·bŭn'naī the Hū'sha·thīte, [28] Zăl'mŏn the A·hō'hīte, Mā'ha·raī of Nĕ·tŏph'ah, [29] Hē'lĕb the son of Bā'a·nah of Nĕ·tŏph'ah, Ĭt'taī the son of Rī'baī of Gĭb'ē-ah of the Benjaminites, [30] Bĕ·nā'ĭ·ah of Pĭr'a·thŏn, Hĭd'daī of the brooks of Gā'ash, [31] Ā'bĭ–al'bon the Ăr'ba·thīte, Ăz'ma·vĕth of Ba·hū'rĭm, [32] E·lī'ah·ba of Shā–ăl'bon, the sons of Jā'shen, Jonathan, [33] Shăm'mah the Hăr'a·rīte, A·hī'am the son of Shār'ar the Hararite, [34] Ĕ·līph'e·lĕt the son of A·hăs'baī of Mā'a·cah, Ĕ·lī'am the son of A·hĭth'-o·phĕl of Gī'lō, [35] Hĕz'rō[i] of Căr'mel, Pā'a·raī the Ăr'bīte, [36] I'gal the son of Nathan of Zō'bah, Bā'nī the Găd'īte, [37] Zē'lĕk the Ăm'mo·nīte, Nā'ha·raī of Be–ēr'oth, the armor-bearer of Jō'āb

the son of Zĕ·rū'ĭ·ah, [38] Ira the Ĭth'rīte, Gā'rĕb the Ithrite, [39] Ū'rī'ah the Hĭt'-tīte: thirty-seven in all.

24 Again the anger of the LORD was kindled against Israel, and he incited David against them, saying, "Go, number Israel and Judah." [2] So the king said to Jō'āb and the commanders of the army,[j] who were with him, "Go through all the tribes of Israel, from Dan to Bē'er–shē'ba, and number the people, that I may know the number of the people." [3] But Jō'āb said to the king, "May the LORD your God add to the people a hundred times as many as they are, while the eyes of my lord the king still see it; but why does my lord the king delight in this thing?" [4] But the king's word prevailed against Jō'āb and the commanders of the army. So Joab and the commanders of the army went out from the presence of the king to number the people of Israel. [5] They crossed the Jordan, and began from A·rō'er,[k] and from the city that is in the middle of the valley, toward Gād and on to Jā'zer. [6] Then they came to Gilead, and to Kā'dĕsh in the land of the Hĭt'tītes;[l] and they came to Dan, and from Dan[m] they went around to Sī'don, [7] and came to the fortress of Tyre and to all the cities of the Hī'vītes and Canaanites; and they went out to the Nĕg'ĕb of Judah at Bē'er–shē'ba. [8] So when they had gone through all the land, they came to Jerusalem at the end of nine months and twenty days. [9] And Jō'āb gave the sum of the numbering of the people to the king: in Israel there were eight hundred thousand valiant men who drew the sword, and the men of Judah were five hundred thousand.

10 But David's heart smote him after he had numbered the people. And David said to the LORD, "I have sinned greatly in what I have done. But now, O LORD, I pray thee, take away the iniquity of thy servant; for I have done very foolishly." [11] And when David arose in the morning, the word of the LORD came to the prophet Gād, David's

---

[e] Two Hebrew Mss Syr: MT *three*
[f]1 Chron 11.25: Heb *Was he the most renowned of the three?* [g] Another reading is *the son of Ish–hai*
[h] The meaning of the word *ariel* is unknown
[i] Another reading is *Hezrai*
[j]1 Chron 21.2 Gk: Heb *to Joab the commander of the army*
[k] Gk: Heb *encamped in Aroer*
[l] Gk: Heb *to the land of Tahtim–hodshi*
[m] Cn Compare Gk: Heb *they came to Dan–jaan and*
24.1–25: 1 Chron 21.1-27.

seer, saying, [12] "Go and say to David, 'Thus says the LORD, Three things I offer[n] you; choose one of them, that I may do it to you.'" [13] So Gảd came to David and told him, and said to him, "Shall three[o] years of famine come to you in your land? Or will you flee three months before your foes while they pursue you? Or shall there be three days' pestilence in your land? Now consider, and decide what answer I shall return to him who sent me." [14] Then David said to Gảd, "I am in great distress; let us fall into the hand of the LORD, for his mercy is great; but let me not fall into the hand of man." [15] So the LORD sent a pestilence upon Israel from the morning until the appointed time; and there died of the people from Dan to Bē'er-shē'ba seventy thousand men. [16] And when the angel stretched forth his hand toward Jerusalem to destroy it, the LORD repented of the evil, and said to the angel who was working destruction among the people, "It is enough; now stay your hand." And the angel of the LORD was by the threshing floor of A·rau'nah the Jěb'ū·sīte. [17] Then David spoke to the LORD when he saw the angel who was smiting the people, and said, "Lo, I have sinned, and I have done wickedly; but these sheep, what have they done? Let thy hand, I pray thee, be against me and against my father's house."

[18] And Gảd came that day to David, and said to him, "Go up, rear an altar to the LORD on the threshing floor of A·rau'nah the Jěb'ū·sīte." [19] So David went up at Gảd's word, as the LORD commanded. [20] And when A·rau'nah looked down, he saw the king and his servants coming on toward him; and Araunah went forth, and did obeisance to the king with his face to the ground. [21] And A·rau'nah said, "Why has my lord the king come to his servant?" David said, "To buy the threshing floor of you, in order to build an altar to the LORD, that the plague may be averted from the people." [22] Then A·rau'nah said to David, "Let my lord the king take and offer up what seems good to him; here are the oxen for the burnt offering, and the threshing sledges and the yokes of the oxen for the wood. [23] All this, O king, A·rau'nah gives to the king." And Araunah said to the king, "The LORD your God accept you." [24] But the king said to A·rau'nah, "No, but I will buy it of you for a price; I will not offer burnt offerings to the LORD my God which cost me nothing." So David bought the threshing floor and the oxen for fifty shekels of silver. [25] And David built there an altar to the LORD, and offered burnt offerings and peace offerings. So the LORD heeded supplications for the land, and the plague was averted from Israel.

The First Book of the
Kings

1 Now King David was old and advanced in years; and although they covered him with clothes, he could not get warm. [2] Therefore his servants said to him, "Let a young maiden be sought for my lord the king, and let her wait upon the king, and be his nurse; let her lie in your bosom, that my lord the king may be warm." [3] So they sought for a beautiful maiden throughout all the territory of Israel, and found Ăb'-ĭ·shăg the Shū'nam·mīte, and brought her to the king. [4] The maiden was very beautiful; and she became the king's nurse and ministered to him; but the king knew her not.

[5] Now Ăd·o·nī'jah the son of Hăg'-gĭth exalted himself, saying, "I will be king"; and he prepared for himself chariots and horsemen, and fifty men to run before him. [6] His father had never at any time displeased him by asking, "Why have you done thus and so?" He was also a very handsome man; and he was born next after Ăb'sa·lom.

[n] Or *hold over* [o] 1 Chron 21.12 Gk: Heb *seven*

⁷He conferred with Jō'ăb the son of Zĕ·rü'ī·ah and with A·bī'a·thär the priest; and they followed Ăd·o·nī'jah and helped him. ⁸But Zā'dŏk the priest, and Bĕ·nā'ī·ah the son of Jĕ·hoi'a·da, and Nathan the prophet, and Shĭm'ē–ī, and Rē'ī, and David's mighty men were not with Ăd·o·nī'jah.

9 Ăd·o·nī'jah sacrificed sheep, oxen, and fatlings by the Serpent's Stone, which is beside Ĕn–rō'gĕl, and he invited all his brothers, the king's sons, and all the royal officials of Judah, ¹⁰but he did not invite Nathan the prophet or Bĕ·nā'ī·ah or the mighty men or Solomon his brother.

11 Then Nathan said to Băth·shē'ba the mother of Solomon, "Have you not heard that Ăd·o·nī'jah the son of Hăg'-gĭth has become king and David our lord does not know it? ¹²Now therefore come, let me give you counsel, that you may save your own life and the life of your son Solomon. ¹³Go in at once to King David, and say to him, 'Did you not, my lord the king, swear to your maidservant, saying, "Solomon your son shall reign after me, and he shall sit upon my throne"? Why then is Ăd·o·nī'jah king?' ¹⁴Then while you are still speaking with the king, I also will come in after you and confirm your words."

15 So Băth·shē'ba went to the king into his chamber (now the king was very old, and Ăb'ī·shăg the Shü'nam·mīte was ministering to the king). ¹⁶Băth·shē'ba bowed and did obeisance to the king, and the king said, "What do you desire?" ¹⁷She said to him, "My lord, you swore to your maidservant by the LORD your God, saying, 'Solomon your son shall reign after me, and he shall sit upon my throne.' ¹⁸And now, behold, Ăd·o·nī'jah is king, although you, my lord the king, do not know it. ¹⁹He has sacrificed oxen, fatlings, and sheep in abundance, and has invited all the sons of the king, A·bī'-a·thär the priest, and Jō'ăb the commander of the army; but Solomon your servant he has not invited. ²⁰And now, my lord the king, the eyes of all Israel are upon you, to tell them who shall sit on the throne of my lord the king after him. ²¹Otherwise it will come to pass, when my lord the king sleeps with his fathers, that I and my son Solomon will be counted offenders."

22 While she was still speaking with the king, Nathan the prophet came in. ²³And they told the king, "Here is Nathan the prophet." And when he came in before the king, he bowed before the king, with his face to the ground. ²⁴And Nathan said, "My lord the king, have you said, 'Ăd·o·nī'jah shall reign after me, and he shall sit upon my throne'? ²⁵For he has gone down this day, and has sacrificed oxen, fatlings, and sheep in abundance, and has invited all the king's sons, Jō'ăb the commander*a* of the army, and A·bī'a·thär the priest; and behold, they are eating and drinking before him, and saying, 'Long live King Ăd·o·nī'jah!' ²⁶But me, your servant, and Zā'dŏk the priest, and Bĕ·nā'ī·ah the son of Jĕ·hoi'a·da, and your servant Solomon, he has not invited. ²⁷Has this thing been brought about by my lord the king and you have not told your servants who should sit on the throne of my lord the king after him?"

28 Then King David answered, "Call Băth·shē'ba to me." So she came into the king's presence, and stood before the king. ²⁹And the king swore, saying, "As the LORD lives, who has redeemed my soul out of every adversity, ³⁰as I swore to you by the LORD, the God of Israel, saying, 'Solomon your son shall reign after me, and he shall sit upon my throne in my stead'; even so will I do this day." ³¹Then Băth·shē'ba bowed with her face to the ground, and did obeisance to the king, and said, "May my lord King David live for ever!"

32 King David said, "Call to me Zā'dŏk the priest, Nathan the prophet, and Bĕ·nā'ī·ah the son of Jĕ·hoi'a·da." So they came before the king. ³³And the king said to them, "Take with you the servants of your lord, and cause Solomon my son to ride on my own mule, and bring him down to Gī'hŏn; ³⁴and let Zā'dŏk the priest and Nathan the prophet there anoint him king over Israel; then blow the trumpet, and say, 'Long live King Solomon!' ³⁵You shall then come up after him, and he shall come and sit upon my throne; for he shall be king in my stead; and I have appointed him to be ruler over Israel and over Judah." ³⁶And Bĕ·nā'ī·ah the son of Jĕ·hoi'a·da answered the king, "Amen! May the LORD, the God of

*a*Gk: Heb *commanders*

my lord the king, say so. ³⁷As the LORD has been with my lord the king, even so may he be with Solomon, and make his throne greater than the throne of of my lord King David."

38 So Zā′dŏk the priest, Nathan the prophet, and Bĕ·nā′ī·ah the son of Jĕ·hoi′a·da, and the Chĕr′e·thītes and the Pĕl′e·thītes, went down and caused Solomon to ride on King David's mule, and brought him to Gī′hŏn. ³⁹There Zā′dŏk the priest took the horn of oil from the tent, and anointed Solomon. Then they blew the trumpet; and all the people said, "Long live King Solomon!" ⁴⁰And all the people went up after him, playing on pipes, and rejoicing with great joy, so that the earth was split by their noise.

41 Ăd·o·nī′jah and all the guests who were with him heard it as they finished feasting. And when Jō′ăb heard the sound of the trumpet, he said, "What does this uproar in the city mean?" ⁴²While he was still speaking, behold, Jonathan the son of A·bī′a·thãr the priest came; and Ăd·o·nī′jah said, "Come in, for you are a worthy man and bring good news." ⁴³Jonathan answered Ăd·o·nī′jah, "No, for our lord King David has made Solomon king; ⁴⁴and the king has sent with him Zā′dŏk the priest, Nathan the prophet, and Bĕ·nā′ī·ah the son of Jĕ·hoi′a·da, and the Chĕr′e·thītes and the Pĕl′e·thītes; and they have caused him to ride on the king's mule; ⁴⁵and Zā′dŏk the priest and Nathan the prophet have anointed him king at Gī′hŏn; and they have gone up from there rejoicing, so that the city is in an uproar. This is the noise that you have heard. ⁴⁶Solomon sits upon the royal throne. ⁴⁷Moreover the king's servants came to congratulate our lord King David, saying, 'Your God make the name of Solomon more famous than yours, and make his throne greater than your throne.' And the king bowed himself upon the bed. ⁴⁸And the king also said, 'Blessed be the LORD, the God of Israel, who has granted one of my offspring*b* to sit on my throne this day, my own eyes seeing it.' "

49 Then all the guests of Ăd·o·nī′jah trembled, and rose, and each went his own way. ⁵⁰And Ăd·o·nī′jah feared Solomon; and he arose, and went, and caught hold of the horns of the altar. ⁵¹And it was told Solomon, "Behold,

Ăd·o·nī′jah fears King Solomon; for, lo, he has laid hold of the horns of the altar, saying, 'Let King Solomon swear to me first that he will not slay his servant with the sword.' " ⁵²And Solomon said, "If he prove to be a worthy man, not one of his hairs shall fall to the earth; but if wickedness is found in him, he shall die." ⁵³So King Solomon sent, and they brought him down from the altar. And he came and did obeisance to King Solomon; and Solomon said to him, "Go to your house."

2 When David's time to die drew near, he charged Solomon his son, saying, ²"I am about to go the way of all the earth. Be strong, and show yourself a man, ³and keep the charge of the LORD your God, walking in his ways and keeping his statutes, his commandments, his ordinances, and his testimonies, as it is written in the law of Moses, that you may prosper in all that you do and wherever you turn; ⁴that the LORD may establish his word which he spoke concerning me, saying, 'If your sons take heed to their way, to walk before me in faithfulness with all their heart and with all their soul, there shall not fail you a man on the throne of Israel.'

5 "Moreover you know also what Jō′ăb the son of Zĕ·rü′ī·ah did to me, how he dealt with the two commanders of the armies of Israel, Abner the son of Nēr, and A·mā′sa the son of Jē′thẽr, whom he murdered, aveng-ing*c* in time of peace blood which had been shed in war, and putting innocent blood*d* upon the girdle about my*e* loins, and upon the sandals on my*e* feet. ⁶Act therefore according to your wisdom, but do not let his gray head go down to Shē′ōl in peace. ⁷But deal loyally with the sons of Bãr·zil′laī the Gileadite, and let them be among those who eat at your table; for with such loyalty they met me when I fled from Ăb′sa·lom your brother. ⁸And there is also with you Shĭm′ē·ī the son of Gē′ra, the Benjaminite from Ba·hū′rĭm, who cursed me with a grievous curse on the day when I went to Mā″ha·nā′ĭm; but when he came down to meet me at the Jordan, I swore to him by the LORD, saying, 'I will not put you to death with the sword.' ⁹Now therefore hold him not guiltless, for

*b*Gk: Heb *one* *c*Gk: Heb *placing*
*d*Gk: Heb *blood of war* *e*Gk: Heb *his*

you are a wise man; you will know what you ought to do to him, and you shall bring his gray head down with blood to Shē'ōl."

10 Then David slept with his fathers, and was buried in the city of David. ¹¹And the time that David reigned over Israel was forty years; he reigned seven years in Hē'brŏn, and thirty-three years in Jerusalem. ¹²So Solomon sat upon the throne of David his father; and his kingdom was firmly established.

13 Then Ăd·o·nī'jah the son of Hăg'-gĭth came to Băth·shē'ba the mother of Solomon. And she said, "Do you come peaceably?" He said, "Peaceably." ¹⁴Then he said, "I have something to say to you." She said, "Say on." ¹⁵He said, "You know that the kingdom was mine, and that all Israel fully expected me to reign; however the kingdom has turned about and become my brother's, for it was his from the LORD. ¹⁶And now I have one request to make of you; do not refuse me." She said to him, "Say on." ¹⁷And he said, "Pray ask King Solomon —he will not refuse you—to give me Ăb'ĭ·shăg the Shü'nam·mīte as my wife." ¹⁸Băth·shē'ba said, "Very well; I will speak for you to the king."

19 So Băth·shē'ba went to King Solomon, to speak to him on behalf of Ăd·o·nī'jah. And the king rose to meet her, and bowed down to her; then he sat on his throne, and had a seat brought for the king's mother; and she sat on his right. ²⁰Then she said, "I have one small request to make of you; do not refuse me." And the king said to her, "Make your request, my mother; for I will not refuse you." ²¹She said, "Let Ăb'ĭ·shăg the Shü'-nam·mīte be given to Ăd·o·nī'jah your brother as his wife." ²²King Solomon answered his mother, "And why do you ask Ăb'ĭ·shăg the Shü'nam·mīte for Ăd·o·nī'jah? Ask for him the kingdom also; for he is my elder brother, and on his side are Ạ·bī'ạ·thăr/ the priest and Jō'ăb the son of Zĕ·rü'ĭ·ah." ²³Then King Solomon swore by the LORD, saying, "God do so to me and more also if this word does not cost Ăd·o·nī'jah his life! ²⁴Now therefore as the LORD lives, who has established me, and placed me on the throne of David my father, and who has made me a house, as he promised, Ăd·o·nī'-

jah shall be put to death this day." ²⁵So King Solomon sent Bĕ·nā'ī·ah the son of Jĕ·hoi'a·da; and he struck him down, and he died.

26 And to Ạ·bī'ạ·thăr the priest the king said, "Go to Ăn'ạ·thŏth, to your estate; for you deserve death. But I will not at this time put you to death, because you bore the ark of the Lord GOD before David my father, and because you shared in all the affliction of my father." ²⁷So Solomon expelled Ạ·bī'ạ·thăr from being priest to the LORD, thus fulfilling the word of the LORD which he had spoken concerning the house of Eli in Shī'lōh.

28 When the news came to Jō'ăb —for Joab had supported Ăd·o·nī'jah although he had not supported Ăb'-sạ·lǫm—Joab fled to the tent of the LORD and caught hold of the horns of the altar. ²⁹And when it was told King Solomon, "Jō'ăb has fled to the tent of the LORD, and behold, he is beside the altar," Solomon sent Bĕ·nā'ī·ah the son of Jĕ·hoi'a·da, saying, "Go, strike him down." ³⁰So Bĕ·nā'ī·ah came to the tent of the LORD, and said to him, "The king commands, 'Come forth.'" But he said, "No, I will die here." Then Benaiah brought the king word again, saying, "Thus said Jō'ăb, and thus he answered me." ³¹The king replied to him, "Do as he has said, strike him down and bury him; and thus take away from me and from my father's house the guilt for the blood which Jō'ăb shed without cause. ³²The LORD will bring back his bloody deeds upon his own head, because, without the knowledge of my father David, he attacked and slew with the sword two men more righteous and better than himself, Abner the son of Nĕr, commander of the army of Israel, and Ạ·mā'sạ the son of Jē'thĕr, commander of the army of Judah. ³³So shall their blood come back upon the head of Jō'ăb and upon the head of his descendants for ever; but to David, and to his descendants, and to his house, and to his throne, there shall be peace from the LORD for evermore." ³⁴Then Bĕ·nā'ī·ah the son of Jĕ·hoi'-a·da went up, and struck him down and killed him; and he was buried in his own house in the wilderness. ³⁵The king put Bĕ·nā'ī·ah the son of Jĕ·hoi'-

/Gk Syr Vg: Heb *and for him and for Abiathar*
2.12: 1 Chron 29.23.

ạ·dạ over the army in place of Jō'ăb, and the king put Zā'dŏk the priest in the place of A·bī'ạ·thär.

36 Then the king sent and summoned Shĭm'ē–ī, and said to him, "Build yourself a house in Jerusalem, and dwell there, and do not go forth from there to any place whatever. ³⁷ For on the day you go forth, and cross the brook Kĭd'rọn, know for certain that you shall die; your blood shall be upon your own head." ³⁸And Shĭm'ē–ī said to the king, "What you say is good; as my lord the king has said, so will your servant do." So Shime–i dwelt in Jerusalem many days.

39 But it happened at the end of three years that two of Shĭm'ē–ī'ṣ slaves ran away to Ā'chĭsh, son of Mā'ạ·cah, king of Găth. And when it was told Shime–i, "Behold, your slaves are in Gath," ⁴⁰Shĭm'ē–ī arose and saddled an ass, and went to Găth to Ā'chĭsh, to seek his slaves; Shime–i went and brought his slaves from Gath. ⁴¹And when Solomon was told that Shĭm'ē–ī had gone from Jerusalem to Găth and returned, ⁴²the king sent and summoned Shĭm'ē–ī, and said to him, "Did I not make you swear by the LORD, and solemnly admonish you, saying, 'Know for certain that on the day you go forth and go to any place whatever, you shall die'? And you said to me, 'What you say is good; I obey.' ⁴³Why then have you not kept your oath to the LORD and the commandment with which I charged you?" ⁴⁴The king also said to Shĭm'ē–ī, "You know in your own heart all the evil that you did to David my father; so the LORD will bring back your evil upon your own head. ⁴⁵But King Solomon shall be blessed, and the throne of David shall be established before the LORD for ever." ⁴⁶Then the king commanded Bĕ·nā'ĭ·ah the son of Jĕ·hoi'ạ·dạ; and he went out and struck him down, and he died.

So the kingdom was established in the hand of Solomon.

3 Solomon made a marriage alliance with Pharaoh king of Egypt; he took Pharaoh's daughter, and brought her into the city of David, until he had finished building his own house and the house of the LORD and the wall around Jerusalem. ²The people were sacrificing at the high places, however, because no house had yet

been built for the name of the LORD. 3 Solomon loved the LORD, walking in the statutes of David his father; only, he sacrificed and burnt incense at the high places. ⁴And the king went to Gĭb'ē·ọn to sacrifice there, for that was the great high place; Solomon used to offer a thousand burnt offerings upon that altar. ⁵At Gĭb'ē·ọn the LORD appeared to Solomon in a dream by night; and God said, "Ask what I shall give you." ⁶And Solomon said, "Thou hast shown great and steadfast love to thy servant David my father, because he walked before thee in faithfulness, in righteousness, and in uprightness of heart toward thee; and thou hast kept for him this great and steadfast love, and hast given him a son to sit on his throne this day. ⁷And now, O LORD my God, thou hast made thy servant king in place of David my father, although I am but a little child; I do not know how to go out or come in. ⁸And thy servant is in the midst of thy people whom thou hast chosen, a great people, that cannot be numbered or counted for multitude. ⁹Give thy servant therefore an understanding mind to govern thy people, that I may discern between good and evil; for who is able to govern this thy great people?"

10 It pleased the LORD that Solomon had asked this. ¹¹And God said to him, "Because you have asked this, and have not asked for yourself long life or riches or the life of your enemies, but have asked for yourself understanding to discern what is right, ¹²behold, I now do according to your word. Behold, I give you a wise and discerning mind, so that none like you has been before you and none like you shall arise after you. ¹³I give you also what you have not asked, both riches and honor, so that no other king shall compare with you, all your days. ¹⁴And if you will walk in my ways, keeping my statutes and my commandments, as your father David walked, then I will lengthen your days."

15 And Solomon awoke, and behold, it was a dream. Then he came to Jerusalem, and stood before the ark of the covenant of the LORD, and offered up burnt offerings and peace offerings, and made a feast for all his servants.

3.4-15: 2 Chron 1.3-13.

16 Then two harlots came to the king, and stood before him. ¹⁷The one woman said, "Oh, my lord, this woman and I dwell in the same house; and I gave birth to a child while she was in the house. ¹⁸Then on the third day after I was delivered, this woman also gave birth; and we were alone; there was no one else with us in the house, only we two were in the house. ¹⁹And this woman's son died in the night, because she lay on it. ²⁰And she arose at midnight, and took my son from beside me, while your maidservant slept, and laid it in her bosom, and laid her dead son in my bosom. ²¹When I rose in the morning to nurse my child, behold, it was dead; but when I looked at it closely in the morning, behold, it was not the child that I had borne." ²²But the other woman said, "No, the living child is mine, and the dead child is yours." The first said, "No, the dead child is yours, and the living child is mine." Thus they spoke before the king.

23 Then the king said, "The one says, 'This is my son that is alive, and your son is dead'; and the other says, 'No; but your son is dead, and my son is the living one.'" ²⁴And the king said, "Bring me a sword." So a sword was brought before the king. ²⁵And the king said, "Divide the living child in two, and give half to the one, and half to the other." ²⁶Then the woman whose son was alive said to the king, because her heart yearned for her son, "Oh, my lord, give her the living child, and by no means slay it." But the other said, "It shall be neither mine nor yours; divide it." ²⁷Then the king answered and said, "Give the living child to the first woman, and by no means slay it; she is its mother." ²⁸And all Israel heard of the judgment which the king had rendered; and they stood in awe of the king, because they perceived that the wisdom of God was in him, to render justice.

4 King Solomon was king over all Israel, ²and these were his high officials: Ăz·a·rī′ah the son of Zā′dok was the priest; ³Ěl·ĭ·hôr′ĕph and A·hī′-jah the sons of Shī′sha were secretaries; Jĕ·hŏsh′a·phăt the son of A·hī′-lud was recorder; ⁴Bĕ·nā′ĭ·ah the son of Je·hoi′a·da was in command of the army; Zā′dok and A·bī′a·thăr were priests; ⁵Ăz·a·rī′ah the son of Nathan

was over the officers; Zā′bud the son of Nathan was priest and king's friend; ⁶A·hī′shăr was in charge of the palace; and Ăd·o·nī′ram the son of Ăb′da was in charge of the forced labor.

7 Solomon had twelve officers over all Israel, who provided food for the king and his household; each man had to make provision for one month in the year. ⁸These were their names: Bĕn–hūr, in the hill country of Ē′phra·im; ⁹Bĕn–dē′ker, in Mā′kăz, Shā–ăl′bim, Bĕth-she′mesh, and Ē′lŏn-bĕth-hā′nan; ¹⁰Bĕn-hē′sed, in A·rüb′both (to him belonged Sō′coh and all the land of Hē′pher); ¹¹Bĕn-a·bĭn′a·dab, in all Nā′phăth-dôr (he had Tā′phăth the daughter of Solomon as his wife); ¹²Bā′a·na the son of A·hī′lud, in Tā′a·năch, Me·gĭd′dō, and all Bĕth-she′an which is beside Zăr′e·thăn below Jĕz′re·el, and from Beth–shean to Ā′bel-me·hō′lah, as far as the other side of Jŏk′me·am; ¹³Bĕn-gē′ber, in Rā′mŏth-gĭl′e·ad (he had the villages of Jā′ir the son of Ma·năs′seh, which are in Gilead, and he had the region of Ăr′gob, which is in Bā′shan, sixty great cities with walls and bronze bars); ¹⁴A·hĭn′a·dab the son of Ĭd′do, in Mā″ha·nā′ĭm; ¹⁵A·hĭm′a·ăz, in Năph′ta·lī (he had taken Băs′e·măth the daughter of Solomon as his wife); ¹⁶Bā′a·na the son of Hū′shaī, in Ăsh′er and Bĕ·ā′-lŏth; ¹⁷Jĕ·hŏsh′a·phăt the son of Pa·rü′ah, in Ĭs′sa·chär; ¹⁸Shĭm′e–ī the son of Ē′la, in Benjamin; ¹⁹Gē′ber, the son of Ū′rī, in the land of Gilead, the country of Sī′hon king of the Ăm′o·rītes and of Ŏg king of Bā′shan. And there was one officer in the land of Judah.

20 Judah and Israel were as many as the sand by the sea; they ate and drank and were happy. ²¹*ᵍ*Solomon ruled over all the kingdoms from the Euphrates to the land of the Phi·lĭs′-tines and to the border of Egypt; they brought tribute and served Solomon all the days of his life.

22 Solomon's provision for one day was thirty cors of fine flour, and sixty cors of meal, ²³ten fat oxen, and twenty pasture-fed cattle, a hundred sheep, besides harts, gazelles, roebucks, and fatted fowl. ²⁴For he had dominion over all the region west of the Euphra-

*ᵍCh 5.1 in Heb

tes from Tĭph′sạh to Gā′zạ, over all the kings west of the Euphrates; and he had peace on all sides round about him. ²⁵ And Judah and Israel dwelt in safety, from Dan even to Bē′ẹr-shē′bạ, every man under his vine and under his fig tree, all the days of Solomon. ²⁶ Solomon also had forty thousand stalls of horses for his chariots, and twelve thousand horsemen. ²⁷ And those officers supplied provisions for King Solomon, and for all who came to King Solomon's table, each one in his month; they let nothing be lacking. ²⁸ Barley also and straw for the horses and swift steeds they brought to the place where it was required, each according to his charge.

29 And God gave Solomon wisdom and understanding beyond measure, and largeness of mind like the sand on the seashore, ³⁰ so that Solomon's wisdom surpassed the wisdom of all the people of the east, and all the wisdom of Egypt. ³¹ For he was wiser than all other men, wiser than Ethan the Ĕz′rạ·hīte, and Hē′man, Căl′cŏl, and Dār′dạ, the sons of Mā′hŏl; and his fame was in all the nations round about. ³² He also uttered three thousand proverbs; and his songs were a thousand and five. ³³ He spoke of trees, from the cedar that is in Lebanon to the hyssop that grows out of the wall; he spoke also of beasts, and of birds, and of reptiles, and of fish. ³⁴ And men came from all peoples to hear the wisdom of Solomon, and from all the kings of the earth, who had heard of his wisdom.

5 ʰ Now Hiram king of Tȳre sent his servants to Solomon, when he heard that they had anointed him king in place of his father; for Hiram always loved David. ²And Solomon sent word to Hiram, ³ "You know that David my father could not build a house for the name of the LORD his God because of the warfare with which his enemies surrounded him, until the LORD put them under the soles of his feet. ⁴ But now the LORD my God has given me rest on every side; there is neither adversary nor misfortune. ⁵ And so I purpose to build a house for the name of the LORD my God, as the LORD said to David my father, 'Your son, whom I will set upon your throne in your place, shall build the house for my name.' ⁶ Now therefore command that

cedars of Lebanon be cut for me; and my servants will join your servants, and I will pay you for your servants such wages as you set; for you know that there is no one among us who knows how to cut timber like the Sī-dō′nĭ·anṣ."

7 When Hiram heard the words of Solomon, he rejoiced greatly, and said, "Blessed be the LORD this day, who has given to David a wise son to be over this great people." ⁸ And Hiram sent to Solomon, saying, "I have heard the message which you have sent to me; I am ready to do all you desire in the matter of cedar and cypress timber. ⁹ My servants shall bring it down to the sea from Lebanon; and I will make it into rafts to go by sea to the place you direct, and I will have them broken up there, and you shall receive it; and you shall meet my wishes by providing food for my household." ¹⁰ So Hiram supplied Solomon with all the timber of cedar and cypress that he desired, ¹¹ while Solomon gave Hiram twenty thousand cors of wheat as food for his household, and twenty thousandⁱ cors of beaten oil. Solomon gave this to Hiram year by year. ¹² And the LORD gave Solomon wisdom, as he promised him; and there was peace between Hiram and Solomon; and the two of them made a treaty.

13 King Solomon raised a levy of forced labor out of all Israel; and the levy numbered thirty thousand men. ¹⁴ And he sent them to Lebanon, ten thousand a month in relays; they would be a month in Lebanon and two months at home; Ăd·o·nī′rạm was in charge of the levy. ¹⁵ Solomon also had seventy thousand burden-bearers and eighty thousand hewers of stone in the hill country, ¹⁶ besides Solomon's three thousand three hundred chief officers who were over the work, who had charge of the people who carried on the work. ¹⁷ At the king's command, they quarried out great, costly stones in order to lay the foundation of the house with dressed stones. ¹⁸ So Solomon's builders and Hiram's builders and the men of Gē′bạl did the hewing and prepared the timber and the stone to build the house.

ʰCh 5.15 in Heb
ⁱGk: Heb *twenty*
5.2-11: 2 Chron 2.3-16.   **5.5:** 2 Chron 2.1.
5.15, 16: 2 Chron 2.2, 18.

6 In the four hundred and eightieth year after the people of Israel came out of the land of Egypt, in the fourth year of Solomon's reign over Israel, in the month of Zīv, which is the second month, he began to build the house of the LORD. ²The house which King Solomon built for the LORD was sixty cubits long, twenty cubits wide, and thirty cubits high. ³The vestibule in front of the nave of the house was twenty cubits long, equal to the width of the house, and ten cubits deep in front of the house. ⁴And he made for the house windows with recessed frames. ⁵He also built a structure against the wall of the house, running round the walls of the house, both the nave and the inner sanctuary; and he made side chambers all around. ⁶The lowest story*ʲ* was five cubits broad, the middle one was six cubits broad, and the third was seven cubits broad; for around the outside of the house he made offsets on the wall in order that the supporting beams should not be inserted into the walls of the house.

7 When the house was built, it was with stone prepared at the quarry; so that neither hammer nor axe nor any tool of iron was heard in the temple, while it was being built.

8 The entrance for the lowest*ᵏ* story was on the south side of the house; and one went up by stairs to the middle story, and from the middle story to the third. ⁹So he built the house, and finished it; and he made the ceiling of the house of beams and planks of cedar. ¹⁰He built the structure against the whole house, each story*ˡ* five cubits high, and it was joined to the house with timbers of cedar.

11 Now the word of the LORD came to Solomon, ¹²"Concerning this house which you are building, if you will walk in my statutes and obey my ordinances and keep all my commandments and walk in them, then I will establish my word with you, which I spoke to David your father. ¹³And I will dwell among the children of Israel, and will not forsake my people Israel."

14 So Solomon built the house, and finished it. ¹⁵He lined the walls of the house on the inside with boards of cedar; from the floor of the house to the rafters*ᵐ* of the ceiling, he covered them on the inside with wood; and he covered the floor of the house with boards of cypress. ¹⁶He built twenty cubits of the rear of the house with boards of cedar from the floor to the rafters,*ᵐ* and he built this within as an inner sanctuary, as the most holy place. ¹⁷The house, that is, the nave in front of the inner sanctuary, was forty cubits long. ¹⁸The cedar within the house was carved in the form of gourds and open flowers; all was cedar, no stone was seen. ¹⁹The inner sanctuary he prepared in the innermost part of the house, to set there the ark of the covenant of the LORD. ²⁰The inner sanctuary*ⁿ* was twenty cubits long, twenty cubits wide, and twenty cubits high; and he overlaid it with pure gold. He also made*ᵒ* an altar of cedar. ²¹And Solomon overlaid the inside of the house with pure gold, and he drew chains of gold across, in front of the inner sanctuary, and overlaid it with gold. ²²And he overlaid the whole house with gold, until all the house was finished. Also the whole altar that belonged to the inner sanctuary he overlaid with gold.

23 In the inner sanctuary he made two cherubim of olivewood, each ten cubits high. ²⁴Five cubits was the length of one wing of the cherub, and five cubits the length of the other wing of the cherub; it was ten cubits from the tip of one wing to the tip of the other. ²⁵The other cherub also measured ten cubits; both cherubim had the same measure and the same form. ²⁶The height of one cherub was ten cubits, and so was that of the other cherub. ²⁷He put the cherubim in the innermost part of the house; and the wings of the cherubim were spread out so that a wing of one touched the one wall, and a wing of the other cherub touched the other wall; their other wings touched each other in the middle of the house. ²⁸And he overlaid the cherubim with gold.

\ 29 He carved all the walls of the house round about with carved figures of cherubim and palm trees and open flowers, in the inner and outer rooms. ³⁰The floor of the house he overlaid with gold in the inner and outer rooms.

*ʲ*Gk: Heb *structure*   *ᵏ*Gk Tg: Heb *middle*
*ˡ*Heb lacks *each story*   *ᵐ*Gk: Heb *walls*
*ⁿ*Vg: Heb *and before the inner sanctuary*
*ᵒ*Gk: Heb *covered*
6.1-28: 2 Chron 3.1-13; Acts 7.47.

31 For the entrance to the inner
sanctuary he made doors of olivewood;
the lintel and the doorposts formed a
pentagon.[p] 32 He covered the two doors
of olivewood with carvings of cherubim, palm trees, and open flowers;
he overlaid them with gold, and spread
gold upon the cherubim and upon the
palm trees.

33 So also he made for the entrance to the nave doorposts of olivewood, in the form of a square, 34 and
two doors of cypress wood; the two
leaves of the one door were folding,
and the two leaves of the other door
were folding. 35 On them he carved
cherubim and palm trees and open
flowers; and he overlaid them with
gold evenly applied upon the carved
work. 36 He built the inner court with
three courses of hewn stone and one
course of cedar beams.

37 In the fourth year the foundation of the house of the LORD was
laid, in the month of Zĭv. 38 And in the
eleventh year, in the month of Bŭl,
which is the eighth month, the house
was finished in all its parts, and according to all its specifications. He was
seven years in building it.

7 Solomon was building his own
house thirteen years, and he
finished his entire house.

2 He built the House of the Forest
of Lebanon; its length was a hundred
cubits, and its breadth fifty cubits,
and its height thirty cubits, and it
was built upon three[q] rows of cedar
pillars, with cedar beams upon the
pillars. 3 And it was covered with cedar
above the chambers that were upon
the forty-five pillars, fifteen in each
row. 4 There were window frames in
three rows, and window opposite window in three tiers. 5 All the doorways
and windows[r] had square frames,
and window was opposite window in
three tiers.

6 And he made the Hall of Pillars;
its length was fifty cubits, and its
breadth thirty cubits; there was a
porch in front with pillars, and a canopy before them.

7 And he made the Hall of the
Throne where he was to pronounce
judgment, even the Hall of Judgment;
it was finished with cedar from floor
to rafters.[s]

8 His own house where he was to
dwell, in the other court back of the
hall, was of like workmanship. Solomon also made a house like this hall
for Pharaoh's daughter whom he had
taken in marriage.

9 All these were made of costly
stones, hewn according to measure,
sawed with saws, back and front,
even from the foundation to the
coping, and from the court of the house
of the LORD[t] to the great court. 10 The
foundation was of costly stones, huge
stones, stones of eight and ten cubits.
11 And above were costly stones, hewn
according to measurement, and cedar.
12 The great court had three courses of
hewn stone round about, and a course
of cedar beams; so had the inner court
of the house of the LORD, and the vestibule of the house.

13 And King Solomon sent and
brought Hiram from Tȳre. 14 He was the
son of a widow of the tribe of Năph′-
tạ-lī, and his father was a man of Tȳre,
a worker in bronze; and he was full of
wisdom, understanding, and skill,
for making any work in bronze. He
came to King Solomon, and did all his
work.

15 He cast two pillars of bronze.
Eighteen cubits was the height of one
pillar, and a line of twelve cubits measured its circumference; it was hollow,
and its thickness was four fingers; the
second pillar was the same.[u] 16 He also
made two capitals of molten bronze, to
set upon the tops of the pillars; the
height of the one capital was five
cubits, and the height of the other
capital was five cubits. 17 Then he made
two[v] nets of checker work with
wreaths of chain work for the capitals
upon the tops of the pillars; a net[w]
for the one capital, and net[w] for the
other capital. 18 Likewise he made
pomegranates;[x] in two rows round
about upon the one network, to cover
the capital that was upon the top
of the pillar; and he did the same
with the other capital. 19 Now the
capitals that were upon the tops of
the pillars in the vestibule were of
lily-work, four cubits. 20 The capitals
were upon the two pillars and also
above the rounded projection which

[p] Heb obscure [q] Gk: Heb *four*
[r] Gk: Heb *posts* [s] Syr Vg: Heb *floor*
[t] With 7.12: Heb *from the outside*
[u] Tg Syr Compare Gk and Jer 52.21: Heb *and a line of twelve cubits measured the circumference of the second pillar* [v] Gk: Heb lacks *he made two* [w] Gk: Heb *seven*
[x] With 2 Mss Compare Gk: Heb *pillars*
7.15-21: 2 Chron 3.15-17.

was beside the network; there were two hundred pomegranates, in two rows round about; and so with the other capital. ²¹ He set up the pillars at the vestibule of the temple; he set up the pillar on the south and called its name Jā'chĭn; and he set up the pillar on the north and called its name Bō'ăz. ²²And upon the tops of the pillars was lily-work. Thus the work of the pillars was finished.

23 Then he made the molten sea; it was round, ten cubits from brim to brim, and five cubits high, and a line of thirty cubits measured its circumference. ²⁴ Under its brim were gourds, for thirty^y cubits, compassing the sea round about; the gourds were in two rows, cast with it when it was cast. ²⁵ It stood upon twelve oxen, three facing north, three facing west, three facing south, and three facing east; the sea was set upon them, and all their hinder parts were inward. ²⁶ Its thickness was a handbreadth; and its brim was made like the brim of a cup, like the flower of a lily; it held two thousand baths.

27 He also made the ten stands of bronze; each stand was four cubits long, four cubits wide, and three cubits high. ²⁸ This was the construction of the stands: they had panels, and the panels were set in the frames ²⁹ and on the panels that were set in the frames were lions, oxen, and cherubim. Upon the frames, both above and below the lions and oxen, there were wreaths of beveled work. ³⁰ Moreover each stand had four bronze wheels and axles of bronze; and at the four corners were supports for a laver. The supports were cast, with wreaths at the side of each. ³¹ Its opening was within a crown which projected upward one cubit; its opening was round, as a pedestal is made, a cubit and a half deep. At its opening there were carvings; and its panels were square, not round. ³²And the four wheels were underneath the panels; the axles of the wheels were of one piece with the stands; and the height of a wheel was a cubit and a half. ³³ The wheels were made like a chariot wheel; their axles, their rims, their spokes, and their hubs, were all cast. ³⁴ There were four supports at the four corners of each stand; the supports were of one piece with the stands. ³⁵And on the top of the stand there was a round band half a cubit high; and on the top of the stand its stays and its panels were of one piece with it. ³⁶And on the surfaces of its stays and on its panels, he carved cherubim, lions, and palm trees, according to the space of each, with wreaths round about. ³⁷After this manner he made the ten stands; all of them were cast alike, of the same measure and the same form.

38 And he made ten lavers of bronze; each laver held forty baths, each laver measured four cubits, and there was a laver for each of the ten stands. ³⁹And he set the stands, five on the south side of the house, and five on the north side of the house; and he set the sea at the southeast corner of the house.

40 Hiram also made the pots, the shovels, and the basins. So Hiram finished all the work that he did for King Solomon on the house of the LORD: ⁴¹ the two pillars, the two bowls of the capitals that were on the tops of the pillars, and the two networks to cover the two bowls of the capitals that were on the tops of the pillars; ⁴² and the four hundred pomegranates for the two networks, two rows of pomegranates for each network, to cover the two bowls of the capitals that were upon the pillars; ⁴³ the ten stands, and the ten lavers upon the stands; ⁴⁴ and the one sea, and the twelve oxen underneath the sea.

45 Now the pots, the shovels, and the basins, all these vessels in the house of the LORD, which Hiram made for King Solomon, were of burnished bronze. ⁴⁶ In the plain of the Jordan the king cast them, in the clay ground between Sŭc'cŏth and Zâr'e·thăn. ⁴⁷And Solomon left all the vessels unweighed, because there were so many of them; the weight of the bronze was not found out.

48 So Solomon made all the vessels that were in the house of the LORD: the golden altar, the golden table for the bread of the Presence, ⁴⁹ the lampstands of pure gold, five on the south side and five on the north, before the inner sanctuary; the flowers, the lamps, and the tongs, of gold; ⁵⁰ the cups, snuffers, basins, dishes for incense, and firepans, of pure gold; and

---

^y Heb *ten*

7.23-26: 2 Chron 4.2-5. 7.38-51: 2 Chron 4.6, 5.1.

the sockets of gold, for the doors of the innermost part of the house, the most holy place, and for the doors of the nave of the temple. 51 Thus all the work that King Solomon did on the house of the LORD was finished. And Solomon brought in the things which David his father had dedicated, the silver, the gold, and the vessels, and stored them in the treasuries of the house of the LORD.

8 Then Solomon assembled the elders of Israel and all the heads of the tribes, the leaders of the fathers' houses of the people of Israel, before King Solomon in Jerusalem, to bring up the ark of the covenant of the LORD out of the city of David, which is Zion. [2]And all the men of Israel assembled to King Solomon at the feast in the month Ĕth′a·nĭm, which is the seventh month. [3]And all the elders of Israel came, and the priests took up the ark. [4]And they brought up the ark of the LORD, the tent of meeting, and all the holy vessels that were in the tent; the priests and the Lē′vītes brought them up. [5]And King Solomon and all the congregation of Israel, who had assembled before him, were with him before the ark, sacrificing so many sheep and oxen that they could not be counted or numbered. [6]Then the priests brought the ark of the covenant of the LORD to its place, in the inner sanctuary of the house, in the most holy place, underneath the wings of the cherubim. [7]For the cherubim spread out their wings over the place of the ark, so that the cherubim made a covering above the ark and its poles. [8]And the poles were so long that the ends of the poles were seen from the holy place before the inner sanctuary; but they could not be seen from outside; and they are there to this day. [9]There was nothing in the ark except the two tables of stone which Moses put there at Hō′-reb, where the LORD made a covenant with the people of Israel, when they came out of the land of Egypt. [10]And when the priests came out of the holy place, a cloud filled the house of the LORD, [11]so that the priests could not stand to minister because of the cloud; for the glory of the LORD filled the house of the LORD.

12 Then Solomon said, "The LORD has set the sun in the heavens,

but[z] has said that he would dwell in thick darkness. [13]I have built thee an exalted house, a place for thee to dwell in for ever."

[14]Then the king faced about, and blessed all the assembly of Israel, while all the assembly of Israel stood. [15]And he said, "Blessed be the LORD, the God of Israel, who with his hand has fulfilled what he promised with his mouth to David my father, saying, [16]'Since the day that I brought my people Israel out of Egypt, I chose no city in all the tribes of Israel in which to build a house, that my name might be there; but I chose David to be over my people Israel.' [17]Now it was in the heart of David my father to build a house for the name of the LORD, the God of Israel. [18]But the LORD said to David my father, 'Whereas it was in your heart to build a house for my name, you did well that it was in your heart; [19]nevertheless you shall not build the house, but your son who shall be born to you shall build the house for my name.' [20]Now the LORD has fulfilled his promise which he made; for I have risen in the place of David my father, and sit on the throne of Israel, as the LORD promised, and I have built the house for the name of the LORD, the God of Israel. [21]And there I have provided a place for the ark, in which is the covenant of the LORD which he made with our fathers, when he brought them out of the land of Egypt."

22 Then Solomon stood before the altar of the LORD in the presence of all the assembly of Israel, and spread forth his hands toward heaven; [23]and said, "O LORD, God of Israel, there is no God like thee, in heaven above or on earth beneath, keeping covenant and showing steadfast love to thy servants who walk before thee with all their heart; [24]who hast kept with thy servant David my father what thou didst declare to him; yea, thou didst speak with thy mouth, and with thy hand hast fulfilled it this day. [25]Now therefore, O LORD, God of Israel, keep with thy servant David my father what thou hast promised him, saying, 'There shall never fail you a man be-

[z]Gk: Heb lacks *has set the sun in the heavens, but*
8.1–6: Rev 11.19. 8.10, 11: 2 Chron 5.13, 14; Rev 15.8. 8.12–50: 2 Chron 6.1-39.

fore me to sit upon the throne of Israel, if only your sons take heed to their way, to walk before me as you have walked before me.' ²⁶Now therefore, O God of Israel, let thy word be confirmed, which thou hast spoken to thy servant David my father.

27 "But will God indeed dwell on the earth? Behold, heaven and the highest heaven cannot contain thee; how much less this house which I have built! ²⁸Yet have regard to the prayer of thy servant and to his supplication, O Lord my God, hearkening to the cry and to the prayer which thy servant prays before thee this day; ²⁹that thy eyes may be open night and day toward this house, the place of which thou hast said, 'My name shall be there,' that thou mayest hearken to the prayer which thy servant offers toward this place. ³⁰And hearken thou to the supplication of thy servant and of thy people Israel, when they pray toward this place; yea, hear thou in heaven thy dwelling place; and when thou hearest, forgive.

31 "If a man sins against his neighbor and is made to take an oath, and comes and swears his oath before thine altar in this house, ³²then hear thou in heaven, and act, and judge thy servants, condemning the guilty by bringing his conduct upon his own head, and vindicating the righteous by rewarding him according to his righteousness.

33 "When thy people Israel are defeated before the enemy because they have sinned against thee, if they turn again to thee, and acknowledge thy name, and pray and make supplication to thee in this house; ³⁴then hear thou in heaven, and forgive the sin of thy people Israel, and bring them again to the land which thou gavest to their fathers.

35 "When heaven is shut up and there is no rain because they have sinned against thee, if they pray toward this place, and acknowledge thy name, and turn from their sin, when thou dost afflict them, ³⁶then hear thou in heaven, and forgive the sin of thy servants, thy people Israel, when thou dost teach them the good way in which they should walk; and grant rain upon thy land, which thou hast given to thy people as an inheritance.

37 "If there is famine in the land, if there is pestilence or blight or mildew or locust or caterpillar; if their enemy besieges them in any* of their cities; whatever plague, whatever sickness there is; ³⁸whatever prayer, whatever supplication is made by any man or by all thy people Israel, each knowing the affliction of his own heart and stretching out his hands toward this house; ³⁹then hear thou in heaven thy dwelling place, and forgive, and act, and render to each whose heart thou knowest, according to all his ways (for thou, thou only, knowest the hearts of all the children of men); ⁴⁰that they may fear thee all the days that they live in the land which thou gavest to our fathers.

41 "Likewise when a foreigner, who is not of thy people Israel, comes from a far country for thy name's sake ⁴²(for they shall hear of thy great name, and thy mighty hand, and of thy outstretched arm), when he comes and prays toward this house, ⁴³hear thou in heaven thy dwelling place, and do according to all for which the foreigner calls to thee; in order that all the peoples of the earth may know thy name and fear thee, as do thy people Israel, and that they may know that this house which I have built is called by thy name.

44 "If thy people go out to battle against their enemy, by whatever way thou shalt send them, and they pray to the Lord toward the city which thou hast chosen and the house which I have built for thy name, ⁴⁵then hear thou in heaven their prayer and their supplication, and maintain their cause.

46 "If they sin against thee—for there is no man who does not sin—and thou art angry with them, and dost give them to an enemy, so that they are carried away captive to the land of the enemy, far off or near; ⁴⁷yet if they lay it to heart in the land to which they have been carried captive, and repent, and make supplication to thee in the land of their captors, saying, 'We have sinned, and have acted perversely and wickedly'; ⁴⁸if they repent with all their mind and with all their heart in the land of their enemies, who carried them captive, and pray to thee toward their land, which thou gavest to their fathers, the

*ªGk Syr: Heb *the land*

city which thou hast chosen, and the house which I have built for thy name; [49] then hear thou in heaven thy dwelling place their prayer and their supplication, and maintain their cause [50] and forgive thy people who have sinned against thee, and all their transgressions which they have committed against thee; and grant them compassion in the sight of those who carried them captive, that they may have compassion on them [51] (for they are thy people, and thy heritage, which thou didst bring out of Egypt, from the midst of the iron furnace). [52] Let thy eyes be open to the supplication of thy servant, and to the supplication of thy people Israel, giving ear to them whenever they call to thee. [53] For thou didst separate them from among all the peoples of the earth, to be thy heritage, as thou didst declare through Moses, thy servant, when thou didst bring our fathers out of Egypt, O Lord GOD."

54 Now as Solomon finished offering all this prayer and supplication to the LORD, he arose from before the altar of the LORD, where he had knelt with hands outstretched toward heaven; [55] and he stood, and blessed all the assembly of Israel with a loud voice, saying, [56] "Blessed be the LORD who has given rest to his people Israel, according to all that he promised; not one word has failed of all his good promise, which he uttered by Moses his servant. [57] The LORD our God be with us, as he was with our fathers; may he not leave us or forsake us; [58] that he may incline our hearts to him, to walk in all his ways, and to keep his commandments, his statutes, and his ordinances, which he commanded our fathers. [59] Let these words of mine, wherewith I have made supplication before the LORD, be near to the LORD our God day and night, and may he maintain the cause of his servant, and the cause of his people Israel, as each day requires; [60] that all the peoples of the earth may know that the LORD is God; there is no other. [61] Let your heart therefore be wholly true to the LORD our God, walking in his statutes and keeping his commandments, as at this day."

62 Then the king, and all Israel with him, offered sacrifice before the LORD. [3] Solomon offered as peace offerings to the LORD twenty-two thousand oxen and a hundred and twenty thousand sheep. So the king and all the people of Israel dedicated the house of the LORD. [64] The same day the king consecrated the middle of the court that was before the house of the LORD; for there he offered the burnt offering and the cereal offering and the fat pieces of the peace offerings, because the bronze altar that was before the LORD was too small to receive the burnt offering and the cereal offering and the fat pieces of the peace offerings.

65 So Solomon held the feast at that time, and all Israel with him, a great assembly, from the entrance of Hā′măth to the Brook of Egypt, before the LORD our God, seven days.[b] [66] On the eighth day he sent the people away; and they blessed the king, and went to their homes joyful and glad of heart for all the goodness that the LORD had shown to David his servant and to Israel his people.

9 When Solomon had finished building the house of the LORD and the king's house and all that Solomon desired to build, [2] the LORD appeared to Solomon a second time, as he had appeared to him at Gĭb′ē·ŏn. [3] And the LORD said to him, "I have heard your prayer and your supplication, which you have made before me; I have consecrated this house which you have built, and put my name there for ever; my eyes and my heart will be there for all time. [4] And as for you, if you will walk before me, as David your father walked, with integrity of heart and uprightness, doing according to all that I have commanded you, and keeping my statutes and my ordinances, [5] then I will establish your royal throne over Israel for ever, as I promised David your father, saying, 'There shall not fail you a man upon the throne of Israel.' [6] But if you turn aside from following me, you or your children, and do not keep my commandments and my statutes which I have set before you, but go and serve other gods and worship them, [7] then I will cut off Israel from the land which I have given them; and the house which I have consecrated for my name I will cast out of my sight; and Israel will become a proverb and a byword among all peoples. [8] And this house will

[b] Gk: Heb *seven days and seven days, fourteen days*
8.62-66: 2 Chron 7.4-10.
9.1-9: 2 Chron 7.11-22.

become a heap of ruins;*c* every one passing by it will be astonished, and will hiss; and they will say, 'Why has the LORD done thus to this land and to this house?' ⁹Then they will say, 'Because they forsook the LORD their God who brought their fathers out of the land of Egypt, and laid hold on other gods, and worshiped them and served them; therefore the LORD has brought all this evil upon them.' "

10 At the end of twenty years, in which Solomon had built the two houses, the house of the LORD and the king's house, ¹¹and Hiram king of Tyre had supplied Solomon with cedar and cypress timber and gold, as much as he desired, King Solomon gave to Hiram twenty cities in the land of Galilee. ¹²But when Hiram came from Tyre to see the cities which Solomon had given him, they did not please him. ¹³Therefore he said, "What kind of cities are these which you have given me, my brother?" So they are called the land of Cā'bŭl to this day. ¹⁴Hiram had sent to the king one hundred and twenty talents of gold.

15 And this is the account of the forced labor which King Solomon levied to build the house of the LORD and his own house and the Mĭl'lō and the wall of Jerusalem and Hā'zôr and Mĕ·gĭd'dō and Gē'zẹr ¹⁶(Pharaoh king of Egypt had gone up and captured Gē'zẹr and burnt it with fire, and had slain the Canaanites who dwelt in the city, and had given it as dowry to his daughter, Solomon's wife; ¹⁷so Solomon rebuilt Gē'zẹr) and Lower Bĕth-hō'rŏn ¹⁸and Bā'ạ-lǎth and Tā'mär in the wilderness, in the land of Judah,*d* ¹⁹and all the store-cities that Solomon had, and the cities for his chariots, and the cities for his horsemen, and whatever Solomon desired to build in Jerusalem, in Lebanon, and in all the land of his dominion. ²⁰All the people who were left of the Ăm'ọ·rītes, the Hĭt'-tītes, the Pĕr'ĭz·zītes, the Hī'vītes, and the Jĕb'ū·sītes, who were not of the people of Israel—²¹their descendants who were left after them in the land, whom the people of Israel were unable to destroy utterly—these Solomon made a forced levy of slaves, and so they are to this day. ²²But of the people of Israel Solomon made no slaves; they were the soldiers, they were his officials, his commanders, his captains, his chariot commanders and his horsemen.

23 These were the chief officers who were over Solomon's work: five hundred and fifty, who had charge of the people who carried on the work.

24 But Pharaoh's daughter went up from the city of David to her own house which Solomon had built for her; then he built the Mĭl'lō.

25 Three times a year Solomon used to offer up burnt offerings and peace offerings upon the altar which he built to the LORD, burning incense*e* before the LORD. So he finished the house.

26 King Solomon built a fleet of ships at Ē'zĭ·on-gē'bẹr, which is near Ē'lŏth on the shore of the Red Sea, in the land of Ē'dọm. ²⁷And Hiram sent with the fleet his servants, seamen who were familiar with the sea, together with the servants of Solomon; ²⁸and they went to Ō'phĭr, and brought from there gold, to the amount of four hundred and twenty talents; and they brought it to King Solomon.

10 Now when the queen of Shē'ba heard of the fame of Solomon concerning the name of the LORD, she came to test him with hard questions. ²She came to Jerusalem with a very great retinue, with camels bearing spices, and very much gold, and precious stones; and when she came to Solomon, she told him all that was on her mind. ³And Solomon answered all her questions; there was nothing hidden from the king which he could not explain to her. ⁴And when the queen of Shē'ba had seen all the wisdom of Solomon, the house that he had built, ⁵the food of his table, the seating of his officials, and the attendance of his servants, their clothing, his cup-bearers, and his burnt offerings which he offered at the house of the LORD, there was no more spirit in her.

6 And she said to the king, "The report was true which I heard in my own land of your affairs and of your wisdom, ⁷but I did not believe the reports until I came and my own eyes had seen it; and, behold, the half was not told me; your wisdom and prosperity surpass the report which I heard. ⁸Happy are your wives!*f* Happy

c Syr Old Latin: Heb *high*   *d* Heb lacks *of Judah*
e Gk: Heb *burning incense with it which*
f Gk Syr: Heb *men*
9.10-28: 2 Chron 8.8-18.   10.1-29: 2 Chron 9.1-28.

are these your servants, who continually stand before you and hear your wisdom! ⁹Blessed be the LORD your God, who has delighted in you and set you on the throne of Israel! Because the LORD loved Israel for ever, he has made you king, that you may execute justice and righteousness." ¹⁰Then she gave the king a hundred and twenty talents of gold, and a very great quantity of spices, and precious stones; never again came such an abundance of spices as these which the queen of Shē′bạ gave to King Solomon.

11 Moreover the fleet of Hiram, which brought gold from Ō′phĭr, brought from Ophir a very great amount of almug wood and precious stones. ¹²And the king made of the almug wood supports for the house of the LORD, and for the king's house, lyres also and harps for the singers; no such almug wood has come or been seen, to this day.

13 And King Solomon gave to the queen of Shē′bạ all that she desired, whatever she asked besides what was given her by the bounty of King Solomon. So she turned and went back to her own land, with her servants.

14 Now the weight of gold that came to Solomon in one year was six hundred and sixty-six talents of gold, ¹⁵besides that which came from the traders and from the traffic of the merchants, and from all the kings of Arabia and from the governors of the land. ¹⁶King Solomon made two hundred large shields of beaten gold; six hundred shekels of gold went into each shield. ¹⁷And he made three hundred shields of beaten gold; three minas of gold went into each shield; and the king put them in the House of the Forest of Lebanon. ¹⁸The king also made a great ivory throne, and overlaid it with the finest gold. ¹⁹The throne had six steps, and at the back of the throne was a calf's head, and on each side of the seat were arm rests and two lions standing beside the arm rests, ²⁰while twelve lions stood there, one on each end of a step on the six steps. The like of it was never made in any kingdom. ²¹All King Solomon's drinking vessels were of gold, and all the vessels of the House of the Forest of Lebanon were of pure gold; none were of silver, it was not considered as anything in the days

of Solomon. ²²For the king had a fleet of ships of Tär′shĭsh at sea with the fleet of Hiram. Once every three years the fleet of ships of Tarshish used to come bringing gold, silver, ivory, apes, and peacocks.ᵍ

23 Thus King Solomon excelled all the kings of the earth in riches and in wisdom. ²⁴And the whole earth sought the presence of Solomon to hear his wisdom, which God had put into his mind. ²⁵Every one of them brought his present, articles of silver and gold, garments, myrrh, spices, horses, and mules, so much year by year.

26 And Solomon gathered together chariots and horsemen; he had fourteen hundred chariots and twelve thousand horsemen, whom he stationed in the chariot cities and with the king in Jerusalem. ²⁷And the king made silver as common in Jerusalem as stone, and he made cedar as plentiful as the sycamore of the Shē·phē′lah. ²⁸And Solomon's import of horses was from Egypt and Kü′ĕ, and the king's traders received them from Kue at a price. ²⁹A chariot could be imported from Egypt for six hundred shekels of silver, and a horse for a hundred and fifty; and so through the king's traders they were exported to all the kings of the Hĭt′tītes and the kings of Syria.

11 Now King Solomon loved many foreign women: the daughter of Pharaoh, and Mō′ạb·īte, Ăm′mọ-nīte, Ē′dọm·īte, Sī·dō′nĭ·ạn, and Hĭt′tīte women, ²from the nations concerning which the LORD had said to the people of Israel, "You shall not enter into marriage with them, neither shall they with you, for surely they will turn away your heart after their gods"; Solomon clung to these in love. ³He had seven hundred wives, princesses, and three hundred concubines; and his wives turned away his heart. ⁴For when Solomon was old his wives turned away his heart after other gods; and his heart was not wholly true to the LORD his God, as was the heart of David his father. ⁵For Solomon went after Ăsh′tō·rĕth the goddess of the Sī·dō′nĭ·ạns, and after Mĭl′cŏm the abomination of the Ăm′mọ·nītes. ⁶So Solomon did what was evil in the sight of the LORD, and did not wholly fol-

ᵍOr *baboons*

low the LORD, as David his father had done. ⁷Then Solomon built a high place for Chē′mŏsh the abomination of Mō′ăb, and for Mō′lĕch the abomination of the Ăm′mọ·nītes, on the mountain east of Jerusalem. ⁸And so he did for all his foreign wives, who burned incense and sacrificed to their gods.

9 And the LORD was angry with Solomon, because his heart had turned away from the LORD, the God of Israel, who had appeared to him twice, ¹⁰and had commanded him concerning this thing, that he should not go after other gods; but he did not keep what the LORD commanded. ¹¹Therefore the LORD said to Solomon, "Since this has been your mind and you have not kept my covenant and my statutes which I have commanded you, I will surely tear the kingdom from you and will give it to your servant. ¹²Yet for the sake of David your father I will not do it in your days, but I will tear it out of the hand of your son. ¹³However I will not tear away all the kingdom; but I will give one tribe to your son, for the sake of David my servant and for the sake of Jerusalem which I have chosen."

14 And the LORD raised up an adversary against Solomon, Hā′dăd the Ē′dọm·īte; he was of the royal house in Ē′dọm. ¹⁵For when David was in Ē′dọm, and Jō′ăb the commander of the army went up to bury the slain, he slew every male in Edom ¹⁶(for Jō′ăb and all Israel remained there six months, until he had cut off every male in Ē′dọm); ¹⁷but Hā′dăd fled to Egypt, together with certain Ē′dọm-ītes of his father's servants, Hadad being yet a little child. ¹⁸They set out from Mĭd′ĭ·an and came to Pär′ăn, and took men with them from Paran and came to Egypt, to Pharaoh king of Egypt, who gave him a house, and assigned him an allowance of food, and gave him land. ¹⁹And Hā′dăd found great favor in the sight of Pharaoh, so that he gave him in marriage the sister of his own wife, the sister of Täh′pe̩·nē̩ş the queen. ²⁰And the sister of Täh′pe̩·nē̩ş bore him Ge̩·nū′băth his son, whom Tahpenes weaned in Pharaoh's house; and Genubath was in Pharaoh's house among the sons of Pharaoh. ²¹But when Hā′dăd heard in Egypt that David slept with his fathers and that Jō′ăb the commander of the

army was dead, Hā′dăd said to Pharaoh, "Let me depart, that I may go to my own country." ²²But Pharaoh said to him, "What have you lacked with me that you are now seeking to go to your own country?" And he said to him, "Only let me go."

23 God also raised up as an adversary to him, Rē′zŏn the son of Ē·lī′a·da̩, who had fled from his master Hā′dăd–ē′zer king of Zō′ba̩h. ²⁴And he gathered men about him and became leader of a marauding band, after the slaughter by David; and they went to Damascus, and dwelt there, and made him king in Damascus. ²⁵He was an adversary of Israel all the days of Solomon, doing mischief as Hā′dăd did; and he abhorred Israel, and reigned over Syria.

26 Jĕr·ọ·bō′a̩m the son of Nē′băt, an Ē′phra̩·im·īte of Zĕr′e̩·da̩h, a servant of Solomon, whose mother's name was Ze̩·rü′a̩h, a widow, also lifted up his hand against the king. ²⁷And this was the reason why he lifted up his hand against the king. Solomon built the Mĭl′lō, and closed up the breach of the city of David his father. ²⁸The man Jĕr·ọ·bō′a̩m was very able, and when Solomon saw that the young man was industrious he gave him charge over all the forced labor of the house of Joseph. ²⁹And at that time, when Jĕr·ọ·bō′a̩m went out of Jerusalem, the prophet A̩·hī′ja̩h the Shī′lo̩·nīte found him on the road. Now Ahijah had clad himself with a new garment; and the two of them were alone in the open country. ³⁰Then A̩·hī′ja̩h laid hold of the new garment that was on him, and tore it into twelve pieces. ³¹And he said to Jĕr·ọ·bō′a̩m, "Take for yourself ten pieces; for thus says the LORD, the God of Israel, 'Behold, I am about to tear the kingdom from the hand of Solomon, and will give you ten tribes ³²(but he shall have one tribe, for the sake of my servant David and for the sake of Jerusalem, the city which I have chosen out of all the tribes of Israel), ³³because he hasʰ forsaken me, and worshiped Äsh′tō·rĕth the goddess of the Sī·dō′nĭ·a̩nș, Chē′mŏsh the god of Mō′ăb, and Mĭl′cŏm the god of the Ăm′mọ·nītes, and hasʰ not walked in my ways, doing what is right in my sight and keeping my statutes and my

ʰGk Syr Vg: Heb *they have*

ordinances, as David his father did.
³⁴Nevertheless I will not take the
whole kingdom out of his hand; but I
will make him ruler all the days of his
life, for the sake of David my servant
whom I chose, who kept my commandments and my statutes; ³⁵but I will
take the kingdom out of his son's hand,
and will give it to you, ten tribes. ³⁶Yet
to his son I will give one tribe, that
David my servant may always have a
lamp before me in Jerusalem, the city
where I have chosen to put my name.
³⁷And I will take you, and you shall
reign over all that your soul desires,
and you shall be king over Israel.
³⁸And if you will hearken to all that I
command you, and will walk in my
ways, and do what is right in my eyes
by keeping my statutes and my commandments, as David my servant did,
I will be with you, and will build you
a sure house, as I built for David, and I
will give Israel to you. ³⁹And I will for
this afflict the descendants of David,
but not for ever.' " ⁴⁰Solomon sought
therefore to kill Jĕr·o·bō'ạm; but
Jeroboam arose, and fled into Egypt,
to Shī'shăk king of Egypt, and was in
Egypt until the death of Solomon.

41 Now the rest of the acts of Solomon, and all that he did, and his wisdom, are they not written in the book
of the acts of Solomon? ⁴²And the time
that Solomon reigned in Jerusalem
over all Israel was forty years. ⁴³And
Solomon slept with his fathers, and
was buried in the city of David his
father; and Rē·ho·bō'ạm his son
reigned in his stead.

12 Rē·ho·bō'ạm went to Shē'chĕm,
for all Israel had come to Shechem to make him king. ²And when
Jĕr·o·bō'ạm the son of Nē'băt heard of
it (for he was still in Egypt, whither he
had fled from King Solomon), then
Jeroboam returned from^i Egypt. ³And
they sent and called him; and Jĕr·o·
bō'ạm and all the assembly of Israel
came and said to Rē·ho·bō'ạm, ⁴"Your
father made our yoke heavy. Now
therefore lighten the hard service of
your father and his heavy yoke upon
us, and we will serve you." ⁵He said
to them, "Depart for three days, then
come again to me." So the people went
away.

6 Then King Rē·ho·bō'ạm took counsel with the old men, who had stood
before Solomon his father while he

was yet alive, saying, "How do you advise me to answer this people?" ⁷And
they said to him, "If you will be a
servant to this people today and serve
them, and speak good words to them
when you answer them, then they will
be your servants for ever." ⁸But he
forsook the counsel which the old men
gave him, and took counsel with the
young men who had grown up with
him and stood before him. ⁹And he
said to them, "What do you advise that
we answer this people who have said
to me, 'Lighten the yoke that your
father put upon us'?" ¹⁰And the young
men who had grown up with him said
to him, "Thus shall you speak to this
people who said to you, 'Your father
made our yoke heavy, but do you
lighten it for us'; thus shall you say to
them, 'My little finger is thicker than
my father's loins. ¹¹And now, whereas
my father laid upon you a heavy yoke,
I will add to your yoke. My father chastised you with whips, but I will chastise you with scorpions.' "

12 So Jĕr·o·bō'ạm and all the people
came to Rē·ho·bō'ạm the third day, as
the king said, "Come to me again the
third day." ¹³And the king answered
the people harshly, and forsaking the
counsel which the old men had given
him, ¹⁴he spoke to them according to
the counsel of the young men, saying,
"My father made your yoke heavy,
but I will add to your yoke; my father
chastised you with whips, but I will
chastise you with scorpions." ¹⁵So the
king did not hearken to the people;
for it was a turn of affairs brought
about by the LORD that he might fulfil his word, which the LORD spoke by
A·hī'jah the Shī'lo·nīte to Jĕr·o·bō'ạm
the son of Nē'băt.

16 And when all Israel saw that the
king did not hearken to them, the people answered the king,

"What portion have we in David?
  We have no inheritance in the son
    of Jesse.
To your tents, O Israel!
  Look now to your own house,
    David."

So Israel departed to their tents.
¹⁷But Rē·ho·bō'ạm reigned over the
people of Israel who dwelt in the cities
of Judah. ¹⁸Then King Rē·ho·bō'ạm
sent A·dôr'ạm, who was taskmaster

over the forced labor, and all Israel stoned him to death with stones. And King Rehoboam made haste to mount his chariot, to flee to Jerusalem. ¹⁹So Israel has been in rebellion against the house of David to this day. ²⁰And when all Israel heard that Jĕr·o·bō'am had returned, they sent and called him to the assembly and made him king over all Israel. There was none that followed the house of David, but the tribe of Judah only.

21 When Rē·ho·bō'am came to Jerusalem, he assembled all the house of Judah, and the tribe of Benjamin, a hundred and eighty thousand chosen warriors, to fight against the house of Israel, to restore the kingdom to Rehoboam the son of Solomon. ²²But the word of God came to Shĕ·maī'ah the man of God: ²³"Say to Rē·ho·bō'am the son of Solomon, king of Judah, and to all the house of Judah and Benjamin, and to the rest of the people, ²⁴'Thus says the LORD, You shall not go up or fight against your kinsmen the people of Israel. Return every man to his home, for this thing is from me.'" So they hearkened to the word of the LORD, and went home again, according to the word of the LORD.

25 Then Jĕr·o·bō'am built Shē'chĕm in the hill country of Ē'phra·im, and dwelt there; and he went out from there and built Pĕ·nū'ĕl. ²⁶And Jĕr·o·bō'am said in his heart, "Now the kingdom will turn back to the house of David; ²⁷if this people go up to offer sacrifices in the house of the LORD at Jerusalem, then the heart of this people will turn again to their lord, to Rē·ho·bō'am king of Judah, and they will kill me and return to Rehoboam king of Judah." ²⁸So the king took counsel, and made two calves of gold. And he said to the people, "You have gone up to Jerusalem long enough. Behold your gods, O Israel, who brought you up out of the land of Egypt." ²⁹And he set one in Bĕth'ĕl, and the other he put in Dan. ³⁰And this thing became a sin, for the people went to the one at Bĕth'ĕl and to the other as far as Dan.ʲ ³¹He also made houses on high places, and appointed priests from among all the people, who were not of the Lē'vītes. ³²And Jĕr·o·bō'am appointed a feast on the fifteenth day of the eighth month like the feast that was in Judah, and he of-

fered sacrifices upon the altar; so he did in Bĕth'ĕl, sacrificing to the calves that he had made. And he placed in Bethel the priests of the high places that he had made. ³³He went up to the altar which he had made in Bĕth'ĕl on the fifteenth day in the eighth month, in the month which he had devised of his own heart; and he ordained a feast for the people of Israel, and went up to the altar to burn incense.

13 And behold, a man of God came out of Judah by the word of the LORD to Bĕth'ĕl. Jĕr·o·bō'am was standing by the altar to burn incense. ²And the man cried against the altar by the word of the LORD, and said, "O altar, altar, thus says the LORD: 'Behold, a son shall be born to the house of David, Jō·sī'ah by name; and he shall sacrifice upon you the priests of the high places who burn incense upon you, and men's bones shall be burned upon you.'" ³And he gave a sign the same day, saying, "This is the sign that the LORD has spoken: 'Behold, the altar shall be torn down, and the ashes that are upon it shall be poured out.'" ⁴And when the king heard the saying of the man of God which he cried against the altar at Bĕth'ĕl, Jĕr·o·bō'am stretched out his hand from the altar, saying, "Lay hold of him." And his hand, which he stretched out against him, dried up so that he could not draw it back to himself. ⁵The altar also was torn down and the ashes poured out from the altar, according to the sign which the man of God had given by the word of the LORD. ⁶And the king said to the man of God, "Entreat now the favor of the LORD your God, and pray for me that my hand may be restored to me." And the man of God entreated the LORD; and the king's hand was restored to him, and became as it was before. ⁷And the king said to the man of God, "Come home with me, and refresh yourself, and I will give you a reward." ⁸And the man of God said to the king, "If you give me half your house, I will not go in with you. And I will not eat bread or drink water in this place; ⁹for so was it commanded me by the word of the LORD, saying, 'You shall neither eat bread, nor drink water, nor return by the way that you

ʲGk: Heb *went to the one as far as Dan*
12.22-24: 2 Chron 11.1-4.

came.'" ¹⁰So he went another way, and did not return by the way that he came to Bĕth-ĕl.

11 Now there dwelt an old prophet in Bĕth-ĕl. And his sons*ᵏ* came and told him all that the man of God had done that day in Bethel; the words also which he had spoken to the king, they told to their father. ¹²And their father said to them, "Which way did he go?" And his sons showed him the way which the man of God who came from Judah had gone. ¹³And he said to his sons, "Saddle the ass for me." So they saddled the ass for him and he mounted it. ¹⁴And he went after the man of God, and found him sitting under an oak; and he said to him, "Are you the man of God who came from Judah?" And he said, "I am." ¹⁵Then he said to him, "Come home with me and eat bread." ¹⁶And he said, "I may not return with you, or go in with you; neither will I eat bread nor drink water with you in this place; ¹⁷for it was said to me by the word of the LORD, 'You shall neither eat bread nor drink water there, nor return by the way that you came.'" ¹⁸And he said to him, "I also am a prophet as you are, and an angel spoke to me by the word of the LORD, saying, 'Bring him back with you into your house that he may eat bread and drink water.'" But he lied to him. ¹⁹So he went back with him, and ate bread in his house, and drank water.

20 And as they sat at the table, the word of the LORD came to the prophet who had brought him back; ²¹and he cried to the man of God who came from Judah, "Thus says the LORD, 'Because you have disobeyed the word of the LORD, and have not kept the commandment which the LORD your God commanded you, ²²but have come back, and have eaten bread and drunk water in the place of which he said to you, "Eat no bread, and drink no water"; your body shall not come to the tomb of your fathers.'" ²³And after he had eaten bread and drunk, he saddled the ass for the prophet whom he had brought back. ²⁴And as he went away a lion met him on the road and killed him. And his body was thrown in the road, and the ass stood beside it; the lion also stood beside the body. ²⁵And behold, men passed by, and saw the body thrown in the road,

and the lion standing by the body. And they came and told it in the city where the old prophet dwelt.

26 And when the prophet who had brought him back from the way heard of it, he said, "It is the man of God, who disobeyed the word of the LORD; therefore the LORD has given him to the lion, which has torn him and slain him, according to the word which the LORD spoke to him." ²⁷And he said to his sons, "Saddle the ass for me." And they saddled it. ²⁸And he went and found his body thrown in the road, and the ass and the lion standing beside the body. The lion had not eaten the body or torn the ass. ²⁹And the prophet took up the body of the man of God and laid it upon the ass, and brought it back to the city,ˡ to mourn and to bury him. ³⁰And he laid the body in his own grave; and they mourned over him, saying, "Alas, my brother!" ³¹And after he had buried him, he said to his sons, "When I die, bury me in the grave in which the man of God is buried; lay my bones beside his bones. ³²For the saying which he cried by the word of the LORD against the altar in Bĕth'ĕl, and against all the houses of the high places which are in the cities of Sa-mâr'ĭ-a, shall surely come to pass."

33 After this thing Jĕr-o-bō'am did not turn from his evil way, but made priests for the high places again from among all the people; any who would, he consecrated to be priests of the high places. ³⁴And this thing became sin to the house of Jĕr-o-bō'am, so as to cut it off and to destroy it from the face of the earth.

14 At that time A-bī'jah the son of Jĕr-o-bō'am fell sick. ²And Jĕr-o-bō'am said to his wife, "Arise, and disguise yourself, that it be not known that you are the wife of Jeroboam, and go to Shī'lōh; behold, A-hī'jah the prophet is there, who said of me that I should be king over this people. ³Take with you ten loaves, some cakes, and a jar of honey, and go to him; he will tell you what shall happen to the child."

4 Jĕr-o-bō'am's wife did so; she arose, and went to Shī'lōh, and came to the house of A-hī'jah. Now Ahijah could not see, for his eyes were dim because of his age. ⁵And the LORD said

ᵏGk Syr Vg: Heb son
ˡGk: Heb he came to the city of the old prophet

to A·hī′jah, "Behold, the wife of Jĕr-o·bō′am is coming to inquire of you concerning her son; for he is sick. Thus and thus shall you say to her." When she came, she pretended to be another woman. ⁶But when A·hī′jah heard the sound of her feet, as she came in at the door, he said, "Come in, wife of Jĕr·o·bō′am; why do you pretend to be another? For I am charged with heavy tidings for you. ⁷Go, tell Jĕr·o·bō′am, 'Thus says the LORD, the God of Israel: "Because I exalted you from among the people, and made you leader over my people Israel, ⁸and tore the kingdom away from the house of David and gave it to you; and yet you have not been like my servant David, who kept my commandments, and followed me with all his heart, doing only that which was right in my eyes, ⁹but you have done evil above all that were before you and have gone and made for yourself other gods, and molten images, provoking me to anger, and have cast me behind your back; ¹⁰therefore behold, I will bring evil upon the house of Jĕr·o·bō′am, and will cut off from Jeroboam every male, both bond and free in Israel, and will utterly consume the house of Jeroboam, as a man burns up dung until it is all gone. ¹¹Any one belonging to Jĕr·o·bō′am who dies in the city the dogs shall eat; and any one who dies in the open country the birds of the air shall eat; for the LORD has spoken it." ' ¹²Arise therefore, go to your house. When your feet enter the city, the child shall die. ¹³And all Israel shall mourn for him, and bury him; for he only of Jĕr·o·bō′am shall come to the grave, because in him there is found something pleasing to the LORD, the God of Israel, in the house of Jeroboam. ¹⁴Moreover the LORD will raise up for himself a king over Israel, who shall cut off the house of Jĕr·o·bō′am today. And henceforth*ᵐ* ¹⁵the LORD will smite Israel, as a reed is shaken in the water, and root up Israel out of this good land which he gave to their fathers, and scatter them beyond the Euphrates, because they have made their A·shē′rĭm, provoking the LORD to anger. ¹⁶And he will give Israel up because of the sins of Jĕr-o·bō′am, which he sinned and which he made Israel to sin."

¹⁷Then Jĕr·o·bō′am'ş wife arose,

and departed, and came to Tĭr′zah. And as she came to the threshold of the house, the child died. ¹⁸And all Israel buried him and mourned for him, according to the word of the LORD, which he spoke by his servant A·hī′-jah the prophet. ¹⁹Now the rest of the acts of Jĕr·o·bō′am, how he warred and how he reigned, behold, they are written in the Book of the Chronicles of the Kings of Israel. ²⁰And the time that Jĕr·o·bō′am reigned was twenty-two years; and he slept with his fathers, and Nā′dăb his son reigned in his stead.

21 Now Rē·ho·bō′am the son of Solomon reigned in Judah. Rehoboam was forty-one years old when he began to reign, and he reigned seventeen years in Jerusalem, the city which the LORD had chosen out of all the tribes of Israel, to put his name there. His mother's name was Nā′a·mah the Ăm′mo·nīt·ęss. ²²And Judah did what was evil in the sight of the LORD, and they provoked him to jealousy with their sins which they committed, more than all that their fathers had done. ²³For they also built for themselves high places, and pillars, and A·shē′rĭm on every high hill and under every green tree; ²⁴and there were also male cult prostitutes in the land. They did according to all the abominations of the nations which the LORD drove out before the people of Israel.

25 In the fifth year of King Rē·ho·bō′am, Shī′shăk king of Egypt came up against Jerusalem; ²⁶he took away the treasures of the house of the LORD and the treasures of the king's house; he took away everything. He also took away all the shields of gold which Solomon had made; ²⁷and King Rē·ho·bō′am made in their stead shields of bronze, and committed them to the hands of the officers of the guard, who kept the door of the king's house. ²⁸And as often as the king went into the house of the LORD, the guard bore them and brought them back to the guard-room.

29 Now the rest of the acts of Rē·ho·bō′am, and all that he did, are they not written in the Book of the Chronicles of the Kings of Judah? ³⁰And there was war between Rē·ho·bō′am and Jĕr·o·bō′am continually. ³¹And Rē·ho·bō′am slept with his fathers and,

ᵐHeb obscure 14.25-31: 2 Chron 12.1-16.

was buried with his fathers in the city of David. His mother's name was Nā'a·mah the Ăm'mo·nīt·ess. And A·bī'jam his son reigned in his stead.

15 Now in the eighteenth year of King Jĕr·o·bō'am the son of Nē'băt, A·bī'jam began to reign over Judah. [2] He reigned for three years in Jerusalem. His mother's name was Mā'a·cah the daughter of A·bĭsh'a·lŏm. [3] And he walked in all the sins which his father did before him; and his heart was not wholly true to the LORD his God, as the heart of David his father. [4] Nevertheless for David's sake the LORD his God gave him a lamp in Jerusalem, setting up his son after him, and establishing Jerusalem; [5] because David did what was right in the eyes of the LORD, and did not turn aside from anything that he commanded him all the days of his life, except in the matter of Ū·rī'ah the Hĭt'tīte. [6] Now there was war between Rē·ho·bō'am and Jĕr·o·bō'am all the days of his life. [7] The rest of the acts of A·bī'jam, and all that he did, are they not written in the Book of the Chronicles of the Kings of Judah? And there was war between Abijam and Jĕr·o·bō'am. [8] And A·bī'jam slept with his fathers; and they buried him in the city of David. And Asa his son reigned in his stead.

9 In the twentieth year of Jĕr·o·bō'am king of Israel Asa began to reign over Judah, [10] and he reigned forty-one years in Jerusalem. His mother's name was Mā'a·cah the daughter of A·bĭsh'a·lŏm. [11] And Asa did what was right in the eyes of the LORD, as David his father had done. [12] He put away the male cult prostitutes out of the land, and removed all the idols that his fathers had made. [13] He also removed Mā'a·cah his mother from being queen mother because she had an abominable image made for A·shē'rah; and Asa cut down her image and burned it at the brook Kĭd'ron. [14] But the high places were not taken away. Nevertheless the heart of Asa was wholly true to the LORD all his days. [15] And he brought into the house of the LORD the votive gifts of his father and his own votive gifts, silver, and gold, and vessels.

16 And there was war between Asa and Bā'a·sha king of Israel all their days. [17] Bā'a·sha king of Israel went up against Judah, and built Rā'mah, that he might permit no one to go out or come in to Asa king of Judah. [18] Then Asa took all the silver and the gold that were left in the treasures of the house of the LORD and the treasures of the king's house, and gave them into the hands of his servants; and King Asa sent them to Bĕn–hā'dăd the son of Tăb·rĭm'mŏn, son of Hē'zĭ–ŏn, king of Syria, who dwelt in Damascus, saying, [19] "Let there be a league between me and you, as between my father and your father: behold, I am sending to you a present of silver and gold; go, break your league with Bā'a·sha king of Israel, that he may withdraw from me." [20] And Bĕn–hā'dăd hearkened to King Asa, and sent the commanders of his armies against the cities of Israel, and conquered Ī'jŏn, Dan, Ā'bel–bĕth–mā'a·cah, and all Chĭn'ne·rŏth, with all the land of Năph'ta·lī. [21] And when Bā'a·sha heard of it, he stopped building Rā'mah, and he dwelt in Tĭr'zah. [22] Then King Asa made a proclamation to all Judah, none was exempt, and they carried away the stones of Rā'mah and its timber, with which Bā'a·sha had been building; and with them King Asa built Gē'ba of Benjamin and Mĭz'pah. [23] Now the rest of all the acts of Asa, all his might, and all that he did, and the cities which he built, are they not written in the Book of the Chronicles of the Kings of Judah? But in his old age he was diseased in his feet. [24] And Asa slept with his fathers, and was buried with his fathers in the city of David his father; and Jĕ·hŏsh'a·phăt his son reigned in his stead.

25 Nā'dăb the son of Jĕr·o·bō'am began to reign over Israel in the second year of Asa king of Judah; and he reigned over Israel two years. [26] He did what was evil in the sight of the LORD, and walked in the way of his father, and in his sin which he made Israel to sin.

27 Bā'a·sha the son of A·hī'jah, of the house of Ĭs'sa·chār, conspired against him; and Baasha struck him down at Gĭb'be·thŏn, which belonged

to the Phĭ·lĭs'tĭnes; for Nā'dăb and all Israel were laying siege to Gibbethon. ²⁸ So Bā'ạ·shạ killed him in the third year of Asa king of Judah, and reigned in his stead. ²⁹ And as soon as he was king, he killed all the house of Jĕr-ọ·bō'ạm; he left to the house of Jeroboam not one that breathed, until he had destroyed it, according to the word of the LORD which he spoke by his servant A·hī'jạh the Shī'lọ·nīte; ³⁰ it was for the sins of Jĕr·ọ·bō'ạm which he sinned and which he made Israel to sin, and because of the anger to which he provoked the LORD, the God of Israel.

31 Now the rest of the acts of Nā'dăb, and all that he did, are they not written in the Book of the Chronicles of the Kings of Israel? ³² And there was war between Asa and Bā'ạ·shạ king of Israel all their days.

33 In the third year of Asa king of Judah, Bā'ạ·shạ the son of A·hī'jạh began to reign over all Israel at Tīr'zạh, and he reigned twenty-four years. ³⁴ He did what was evil in the sight of the LORD, and walked in the way of Jĕr·ọ·bō'ạm and in his sin which he made Israel to sin.

16 And the word of the LORD came to Jē'hū the son of Hạ·nā'nī against Bā'ạ·shạ, saying, ² "Since I exalted you out of the dust and made you leader over my people Israel, and you have walked in the way of Jĕr·ọ·bō'ạm, and have made my people Israel to sin, provoking me to anger with their sins, ³ behold, I will utterly sweep away Bā'ạ·shạ and his house, and I will make your house like the house of Jĕr·ọ·bō'ạm the son of Nē'băt. ⁴ Any one belonging to Bā'ạ·shạ who dies in the city the dogs shall eat; and any one of his who dies in the field the birds of the air shall eat."

5 Now the rest of the acts of Bā'ạ·shạ, and what he did, and his might, are they not written in the Book of the Chronicles of the Kings of Israel? ⁶ And Bā'ạ·shạ slept with his fathers, and was buried at Tīr'zạh; and Ē'lạh his son reigned in his stead. ⁷ Moreover the word of the LORD came by the prophet Jē'hū the son of Hạ·nā'nī against Bā'ạ·shạ and his house, both because of all the evil that he did in the sight of the LORD, provoking him to anger with the work of his hands, in being like the house of Jĕr·ọ·bō'ạm, and also because he destroyed it.

8 In the twenty-sixth year of Asa king of Judah, Ē'lạh the son of Bā'ạ·shạ began to reign over Israel in Tīr'zạh, and he reigned two years. ⁹ But his servant Zĭm'rī, commander of half his chariots, conspired against him. When he was at Tīr'zạh, drinking himself drunk in the house of Är'zạ, who was over the household in Tirzah, ¹⁰ Zĭm'rī came in and struck him down and killed him, in the twenty-seventh year of Asa king of Judah, and reigned in his stead.

11 When he began to reign, as soon as he had seated himself on his throne, he killed all the house of Bā'ạ·shạ; he did not leave him a single male of his kinsmen or his friends. ¹² Thus Zĭm'rī destroyed all the house of Bā'ạ·shạ, according to the word of the LORD, which he spoke against Baasha by Jē'hū the prophet, ¹³ for all the sins of Bā'ạ·shạ and the sins of Ē'lạh his son which they sinned, and which they made Israel to sin, provoking the LORD God of Israel to anger with their idols. ¹⁴ Now the rest of the acts of Ē'lạh, and all that he did, are they not written in the Book of the Chronicles of the Kings of Israel?

15 In the twenty-seventh year of Asa king of Judah, Zĭm'rī reigned seven days in Tīr'zạh. Now the troops were encamped against Gĭb'bẹ·thŏn, which belonged to the Phĭ·lĭs'tĭnes, ¹⁶ and the troops who were encamped heard it said, "Zĭm'rī has conspired, and he has killed the king"; therefore all Israel made Ŏm'rī, the commander of the army, king over Israel that day in the camp. ¹⁷ So Ŏm'rī went up from Gĭb'bẹ·thŏn, and all Israel with him, and they besieged Tīr'zạh. ¹⁸ And when Zĭm'rī saw that the city was taken, he went into the citadel of the king's house, and burned the king's house over him with fire, and died, ¹⁹ because of his sins which he committed, doing evil in the sight of the LORD, walking in the way of Jĕr·ọ·bō'ạm, and for his sin which he committed, making Israel to sin. ²⁰ Now the rest of the acts of Zĭm'rī, and the conspiracy which he made, are they not written in the Book of the Chronicles of the Kings of Israel?

21 Then the people of Israel were divided into two parts; half of the people followed Tĭb'nī the son of Gī'-

năth, to make him king, and half followed Ŏm'rĭ. ²²But the people who followed Ŏm'rĭ overcame the people who followed Tĭb'nĭ the son of Gī'-năth; so Tibni died, and Omri became king. ²³In the thirty-first year of Asa king of Judah, Ŏm'rĭ began to reign over Israel, and reigned for twelve years; six years he reigned in Tĭr'zăh. ²⁴He bought the hill of Să·mâr'ĭ·ạ from Shē'mẹr for two talents of silver; and he fortified the hill, and called the name of the city which he built, Samaria, after the name of Shemer, owner of the hill.

25 Ŏm'rĭ did what was evil in the sight of the LORD, and did more evil than all who were before him. ²⁶For he walked in all the way of Jĕr·ọ·bō'ạm the son of Nē'băt, and in the sins which he made Israel to sin, provoking the LORD, the God of Israel, to anger by their idols. ²⁷Now the rest of the acts of Ŏm'rĭ which he did, and the might that he showed, are they not written in the Book of the Chronicles of the Kings of Israel? ²⁸And Ŏm'rĭ slept with his fathers, and was buried in Să·mâr'ĭ·ạ; and Ā'hăb his son reigned in his stead.

29 In the thirty-eighth year of Asa king of Judah, Ā'hăb the son of Ŏm'rĭ began to reign over Israel, and Ahab the son of Omri reigned over Israel in Să·mâr'ĭ·ạ twenty-two years. ³⁰And Ā'hăb the son of Ŏm'rĭ did evil in the sight of the LORD more than all that were before him. ³¹And as if it had been a light thing for him to walk in the sins of Jĕr·ọ·bō'ạm the son of Nē'băt, he took for wife Jĕz'ẹ·bĕl the daughter of Ĕth·bā'ạl king of the Sī·dō'nĭ·ạnş, and went and served Bā'ạl, and worshiped him. ³²He erected an altar for Bā'ạl in the house of Baal, which he built in Să·mâr'ĭ·ạ. ³³And Ā'hăb made an A·shē'răh. Ahab did more to provoke the LORD, the God of Israel, to anger than all the kings of Israel who were before him. ³⁴In his days Hī'ẹl of Bĕth'ẹl built Jericho; he laid its foundation at the cost of A·bī'răm his firstborn, and set up its gates at the cost of his youngest son Sē'gŭb, according to the word of the LORD, which he spoke by Joshua the son of Nŭn.

17 Now Ē·lī'jạh the Tĭsh'bīte, of Tĭsh'bēⁿ in Ġilead, said to Ā'hăb, "As the LORD the God of Israel lives, before whom I stand, there shall be

neither dew nor rain these years, except by my word." ²And the word of the LORD came to him. ³"Depart from here and turn eastward, and hide yourself by the brook Chē'rĭth, that is east of the Jordan. ⁴You shall drink from the brook, and I have commanded the ravens to feed you there." So he went and did according to the word of the LORD; he went and dwelt by the brook Chē'rĭth that is east of the Jordan. ⁶And the ravens brought him bread and meat in the morning, and bread and meat in the evening; and he drank from the brook. ⁷And after a while the brook dried up, because there was no rain in the land.

8 Then the word of the LORD came to him. ⁹"Arise, go to Zăr'e·phăth, which belongs to Sī'dọn, and dwell there. Behold, I have commanded a widow there to feed you." ¹⁰So he arose and went to Zăr'ẹ·phăth; and when he came to the gate of the city, behold, a widow was there gathering sticks; and he called to her and said, "Bring me a little water in a vessel, that I may drink." ¹¹And as she was going to bring it, he called to her and said, "Bring me a morsel of bread in your hand." ¹²And she said, "As the LORD your God lives, I have nothing baked, only a handful of meal in a jar, and a little oil in a cruse; and now, I am gathering a couple of sticks, that I may go in and prepare it for myself and my son, that we may eat it, and die." ¹³And Ē·lī'jạh said to her, "Fear not; go and do as you have said; but first make me a little cake of it and bring it to me, and afterward make for yourself and your son. ¹⁴For thus says the LORD the God of Israel, 'The jar of meal shall not be spent, and the cruse of oil shall not fail, until the day that the LORD sends rain upon the earth.' " ¹⁵And she went and did as Ē·lī'jạh said; and she, and he, and her household ate for many days. ¹⁶The jar of meal was not spent, neither did the cruse of oil fail, according to the word of the LORD which he spoke by Ē·lī'jạh.

17 After this the son of the woman, the mistress of the house, became ill; and his illness was so severe that there was no breath left in him. ¹⁸And she said to Ē·lī'jạh, "What have you

ᵃGk: Heb *of the settlers*
16.34: Josh 6.26.   17.1: Rev 11.6.   17.8-16: Lk 4.25, 26.
17.18: Mt 8.29; Mk 1.24; Jn 2.4.

against me, O man of God? You have come to me to bring my sin to remembrance, and to cause the death of my son!" ¹⁹And he said to her, "Give me your son." And he took him from her bosom, and carried him up into the upper chamber, where he lodged, and laid him upon his own bed. ²⁰And he cried to the LORD, "O LORD my God, hast thou brought calamity even upon the widow with whom I sojourn, by slaying her son?" ²¹Then he stretched himself upon the child three times, and cried to the LORD, "O LORD my God, let this child's soul come into him again." ²²And the LORD hearkened to the voice of E·lī'jah; and the soul of the child came into him again, and he revived. ²³And E·lī'jah took the child, and brought him down from the upper chamber into the house, and delivered him to his mother; and Elijah said, "See, your son lives." ²⁴And the woman said to E·lī'jah, "Now I know that you are a man of God, and that the word of the LORD in your mouth is truth."

18 After many days the word of the LORD came to E·lī'jah, in the third year, saying, "Go, show yourself to A'hăb; and I will send rain upon the earth." ²So E·lī'jah went to show himself to A'hăb. Now the famine was severe in Sa·mâr'ĭ·a. ³And A'hăb called Ō·ba·dī'ah, who was over the household. (Now Obadiah revered the LORD greatly; ⁴and when Jĕz'e·bĕl cut off the prophets of the LORD, Ō·ba·dī'ah took a hundred prophets and hid them by fifties in a cave, and fed them with bread and water.) ⁵And A'hăb said to Ō·ba·dī'ah, "Go through the land to all the springs of water and to all the valleys; perhaps we may find grass and save the horses and mules alive, and not lose some of the animals." ⁶So they divided the land between them to pass through it; A'hăb went in one direction by himself, and Ō·ba·dī'ah went in another direction by himself.

7 And as Ō·ba·dī'ah was on the way, behold, E·lī'jah met him; and Obadiah recognized him, and fell on his face, and said, "Is it you, my lord Elijah?" ⁸And he answered him, "It is I. Go, tell your lord, 'Behold, E·lī'jah is here.'" ⁹And he said, "Wherein have I sinned, that you would give your servant into the hand of A'hăb, to kill me? ¹⁰As the LORD your God lives, there

is no nation or kingdom whither my lord has not sent to seek you; and when they would say, 'He is not here,' he would take an oath of the kingdom or nation, that they had not found you. ¹¹And now you say, 'Go, tell your lord, "Behold, E·lī'jah is here."' ¹²And as soon as I have gone from you, the Spirit of the LORD will carry you whither I know not; and so, when I come and tell A'hăb and he cannot find you, he will kill me, although I your servant have revered the LORD from my youth. ¹³Has it not been told my lord what I did when Jĕz'e·bĕl killed the prophets of the LORD, how I hid a hundred men of the LORD's prophets by fifties in a cave, and fed them with bread and water? ¹⁴And now you say, 'Go, tell your lord, "Behold, E·lī'jah is here"'; and he will kill me." ¹⁵And E·lī'jah said, "As the LORD of hosts lives, before whom I stand, I will surely show myself to him today." ¹⁶So Ō·ba·dī'ah went to meet A'hăb, and told him; and Ahab went to meet E·lī'jah.

17 When A'hăb saw E·lī'jah, Ahab said to him, "Is it you, you troubler of Israel?" ¹⁸And he answered, "I have not troubled Israel; but you have, and your father's house, because you have forsaken the commandments of the LORD and followed the Bā'als. ¹⁹Now therefore send and gather all Israel to me at Mount Cär'mel, and the four hundred and fifty prophets of Bā'al and the four hundred prophets of A·shē'rah, who eat at Jĕz'e·bĕl's table."

20 So A'hăb sent to all the people of Israel, and gathered the prophets together at Mount Cär'mel. ²¹And E·lī'jah came near to all the people, and said, "How long will you go limping with two different opinions? If the LORD is God, follow him; but if Bā'al, then follow him." And the people did not answer him a word. ²²Then E·lī'jah said to the people, "I, even I only, am left a prophet of the LORD; but Bā'al's prophets are four hundred and fifty men. ²³Let two bulls be given to us; and let them choose one bull for themselves, and cut it in pieces and lay it on the wood, but put no fire to it; and I will prepare the other bull and lay it on the wood, and put no fire to it. ²⁴And you call on the name of your god and I will call on the name of the LORD; and the God who answers by

fire, he is God." And all the people answered, "It is well spoken." ²⁵ Then Ē·lī′jah said to the prophets of Bā′al, "Choose for yourselves one bull and prepare it first, for you are many; and call on the name of your god, but put no fire to it." ²⁶ And they took the bull which was given them, and they prepared it, and called on the name of Bā′al from morning until noon, saying, "O Baal, answer us!" But there was no voice, and no one answered. And they limped about the altar which they had made. ²⁷ And at noon Ē·lī′jah mocked them, saying, "Cry aloud, for he is a god; either he is musing, or he has gone aside, or he is on a journey, or perhaps he is asleep and must be awakened." ²⁸ And they cried aloud, and cut themselves after their custom with swords and lances, until the blood gushed out upon them. ²⁹ And as midday passed, they raved on until the time of the offering of the oblation, but there was no voice; no one answered, no one heeded.

30 Then Ē·lī′jah said to all the people, "Come near to me"; and all the people came near to him. And he repaired the altar of the LORD that had been thrown down; ³¹ Ē·lī′jah took twelve stones, according to the number of the tribes of the sons of Jacob, to whom the word of the LORD came, saying, "Israel shall be your name"; ³² and with the stones he built an altar in the name of the LORD. And he made a trench about the altar, as great as would contain two measures of seed. ³³ And he put the wood in order, and cut the bull in pieces and laid it on the wood. And he said, "Fill four jars with water, and pour it on the burnt offering, and on the wood." ³⁴ And he said, "Do it a second time"; and they did it a second time. And he said, "Do it a third time"; and they did it a third time. ³⁵ And the water ran round about the altar, and filled the trench also with water.

36 And at the time of the offering of the oblation, Ē·lī′jah the prophet came near and said, "O LORD, God of Abraham, Isaac, and Israel, let it be known this day that thou art God in Israel, and that I am thy servant, and that I have done all these things at thy word. ³⁷ Answer me, O LORD, answer me, that this people may know that thou, O LORD, art God, and that

thou hast turned their hearts back." ³⁸ Then the fire of the LORD fell, and consumed the burnt offering, and the wood, and the stones, and the dust, and licked up the water that was in the trench. ³⁹ And when all the people saw it, they fell on their faces; and they said, "The LORD, he is God; the LORD, he is God." ⁴⁰ And Ē·lī′jah said to them, "Seize the prophets of Bā′al; let not one of them escape." And they seized them; and Elijah brought them down to the brook Kī′shŏn, and killed them there.

41 And Ē·lī′jah said to Ā′hăb, "Go up, eat and drink; for there is a sound of the rushing of rain." ⁴² So Ā′hăb went up to eat and to drink. And Ē·lī′jah went up to the top of Cär′mel; and he bowed himself down upon the earth, and put his face between his knees. ⁴³ And he said to his servant, "Go up now, look toward the sea." And he went up and looked, and said, "There is nothing." And he said, "Go again seven times." ⁴⁴ And at the seventh time he said, "Behold, a little cloud like a man's hand is rising out of the sea." And he said, "Go up, say to Ā′hăb, 'Prepare your chariot and go down, lest the rain stop you.'" ⁴⁵ And in a little while the heavens grew black with clouds and wind, and there was a great rain. And Ā′hăb rode and went to Jĕz′rē·el. ⁴⁶ And the hand of the LORD was on Ē·lī′jah; and he girded up his loins and ran before Ā′hăb to the entrance of Jĕz′rē·el.

19 Ā′hăb told Jĕz′e·bel all that Ē·lī′jah had done, and how he had slain all the prophets with the sword. ² Then Jĕz′e·bel sent a messenger to Ē·lī′jah, saying, "So may the gods do to me, and more also, if I do not make your life as the life of one of them by this time tomorrow." ³ Then he was afraid, and he arose and went for his life, and came to Bē′er-shē′ba, which belongs to Judah, and left his servant there.

4 But he himself went a day's journey into the wilderness, and came and sat down under a broom tree; and he asked that he might die, saying, "It is enough; now, O LORD, take away my life; for I am no better than my fathers." ⁵ And he lay down and slept under a broom tree; and behold, an angel touched him, and said to him, "Arise and eat." ⁶ And he looked and be-

hold, there was at his head a cake baked on hot stones and a jar of water. And he ate and drank, and lay down again. [7]And the angel of the Lord came again a second time, and touched him, and said, "Arise and eat, else the journey will be too great for you." [8]And he arose, and ate and drank, and went in the strength of that food forty days and forty nights to Hō′rĕb the mount of God.

9 And there he came to a cave, and lodged there; and behold, the word of the Lord came to him, and he said to him, "What are you doing here, Ē·lī′jah?" [10]He said, "I have been very jealous for the Lord, the God of hosts; for the people of Israel have forsaken thy covenant, thrown down thy altars, and slain thy prophets with the sword; and I, even I only, am left; and they seek my life, to take it away." [11]And he said, "Go forth, and stand upon the mount before the Lord." And behold, the Lord passed by, and a great and strong wind rent the mountains, and broke in pieces the rocks before the Lord, but the Lord was not in the wind; and after the wind an earthquake, but the Lord was not in the earthquake; [12]and after the earthquake a fire, but the Lord was not in the fire; and after the fire a still small voice. [13]And when Ē·lī′jah heard it, he wrapped his face in his mantle and went out and stood at the entrance of the cave. And behold, there came a voice to him, and said, "What are you doing here, Elijah?" [14]He said, "I have been very jealous for the Lord, the God of hosts; for the people of Israel have forsaken thy covenant, thrown down thy altars, and slain thy prophets with the sword; and I, even I only, am left; and they seek my life, to take it away." [15]And the Lord said to him, "Go, return on your way to the wilderness of Damascus; and when you arrive, you shall anoint Hăz′a·ĕl to be king over Syria; [16]and Jē′hū the son of Nĭm′shī you shall anoint to be king over Israel; and Ē·lī′sha the son of Shā′phat of Ā′bĕl-me·hō′lah you shall anoint to be prophet in your place. [17]And him who escapes from the sword of Hăz′a·ĕl shall Jē′hū slay; and him who escapes from the sword of Jehu shall Ē·lī′sha slay. [18]Yet I will leave seven thousand in Israel, all the knees that have not bowed to Bā′al,

and every mouth that has not kissed him."

19 So he departed from there, and found Ē·lī′sha the son of Shā′phat, who was plowing, with twelve yoke of oxen before him, and he was with the twelfth. Ē·lī′jah passed by him and cast his mantle upon him. [20]And he left the oxen, and ran after Ē·lī′jah, and said, "Let me kiss my father and my mother, and then I will follow you." And he said to him, "Go back again; for what have I done to you?" [21]And he returned from following him, and took the yoke of oxen, and slew them, and boiled their flesh with the yokes of the oxen, and gave it to the people, and they ate. Then he arose and went after Ē·lī′jah, and ministered to him.

20 Bĕn-hā′dăd the king of Syria gathered all his army together; thirty-two kings were with him, and horses and chariots; and he went up and besieged Sa·mâr′ĭ·a, and fought against it. [2]And he sent messengers into the city to Ā′hăb king of Israel, and said to him, "Thus says Bĕn-hā′dăd: [3]'Your silver and your gold are mine; your fairest wives and children also are mine.'" [4]And the king of Israel answered, "As you say, my lord, O king, I am yours, and all that I have." [5]The messengers came again, and said, "Thus says Bĕn-hā′dăd: 'I sent to you, saying, "Deliver to me your silver and your gold, your wives and your children"; [6]nevertheless I will send my servants to you tomorrow about this time, and they shall search your house and the houses of your servants, and lay hands on whatever pleases them,[o] and take it away.'"

7 Then the king of Israel called all the elders of the land, and said, "Mark, now, and see how this man is seeking trouble; for he sent to me for my wives and my children, and for my silver and my gold, and I did not refuse him." [8]And all the elders and all the people said to him, "Do not heed or consent." [9]So he said to the messengers of Bĕn-hā′dăd, "Tell my lord the king, 'All that you first demanded of your servant I will do; but this thing I cannot do.'" And the messengers departed and brought him word again. [10]Bĕn-hā′dăd sent to him and said, "The gods do so to me and more also, if the dust

oGk Syr Vg: Heb *you*
19.10: Rom 11.2, 3.   19.18: Rom 11.4.

of Sạ·mâr′ĭ·ạ shall suffice for handfuls for all the people who follow me." [11]And the king of Israel answered, "Tell him, 'Let not him that girds on his armor boast himself as he that puts it off.'" [12]When Bĕn-hā′dăd heard this message as he was drinking with the kings in the booths, he said to his men, "Take your positions." And they took their positions against the city.

13 And behold, a prophet came near to Ā′hăb king of Israel and said, "Thus says the LORD, Have you seen all this great multitude? Behold, I will give it into your hand this day; and you shall know that I am the LORD." [14]And Ā′hăb said, "By whom?" He said, "Thus says the LORD, By the servants of the governors of the districts." Then he said, "Who shall begin the battle?" He answered, "You." [15]Then he mustered the servants of the governors of the districts, and they were two hundred and thirty-two; and after them he mustered all the people of Israel, seven thousand.

16 And they went out at noon, while Bĕn-hā′dăd was drinking himself drunk in the booths, he and the thirty-two kings who helped him. [17]The servants of the governors of the districts went out first. And Bĕn-hā′dăd sent out scouts, and they reported to him, "Men are coming out from Sạ·mâr′ĭ·ạ." [18]He said, "If they have come out for peace, take them alive; or if they have come out for war, take them alive."

19 So these went out of the city, the servants of the governors of the districts, and the army which followed them. [20]And each killed his man; the Syrians fled and Israel pursued them, but Bĕn-hā′dăd king of Syria escaped on a horse with horsemen. [21]And the king of Israel went out, and captured[p] the horses and chariots, and killed the Syrians with a great slaughter.

22 Then the prophet came near to the king of Israel, and said to him, "Come, strengthen yourself, and consider well what you have to do; for in the spring the king of Syria will come up against you."

23 And the servants of the king of Syria said to him, "Their gods are gods of the hills, and so they were stronger than we; but let us fight against them in the plain, and surely we shall be stronger than they. [24]And

do this: remove the kings, each from his post, and put commanders in their places; [25]and muster an army like the army that you have lost, horse for horse, and chariot for chariot; then we will fight against them in the plain, and surely we shall be stronger than they." And he hearkened to their voice, and did so.

26 In the spring Bĕn-hā′dăd mustered the Syrians, and went up to Ā′phĕk, to fight against Israel. [27]And the people of Israel were mustered, and were provisioned, and went against them; the people of Israel encamped before them like two little flocks of goats, but the Syrians filled the country. [28]And a man of God came near and said to the king of Israel, "Thus says the LORD, 'Because the Syrians have said, "The LORD is a god of the hills but he is not a god of the valleys," therefore I will give all this great multitude into your hand, and you shall know that I am the LORD.'" [29]And they encamped opposite one another seven days. Then on the seventh day the battle was joined; and the people of Israel smote of the Syrians a hundred thousand foot soldiers in one day. [30]And the rest fled into the city of Ā′phĕk; and the wall fell upon twenty-seven thousand men that were left.

Bĕn-hā′dăd also fled, and entered an inner chamber in the city. [31]And his servants said to him, "Behold now, we have heard that the kings of the house of Israel are merciful kings; let us put sackcloth on our loins and ropes upon our heads, and go out to the king of Israel; perhaps he will spare your life." [32]So they girded sackcloth on their loins, and put ropes on their heads, and went to the king of Israel and said, "Your servant Bĕn-hā′dăd says, 'Pray, let me live.'" And he said, "Does he still live? He is my brother." [33]Now the men were watching for an omen, and they quickly took it up from him and said, "Yes, your brother Bĕn-hā′dăd." Then he said, "Go and bring him." Then Ben-hadad came forth to him; and he caused him to come up into the chariot. [34]And Bĕn-hā′dăd said to him, "The cities which my father took from your father I will restore; and you may establish bazaars for yourself in Damascus, as my father did in Sạ·mâr′ĭ·ạ." And Ā′hăb said, "I

ᵖGk: Heb smote

will let you go on these terms." So he made a covenant with him and let him go.

35 And a certain man of the sons of the prophets said to his fellow at the command of the LORD, "Strike me, I pray." But the man refused to strike him. ³⁶ Then he said to him, "Because you have not obeyed the voice of the LORD, behold, as soon as you have gone from me, a lion shall kill you." And as soon as he had departed from him, a lion met him and killed him. ³⁷ Then he found another man, and said, "Strike me, I pray." And the man struck him, smiting and wounding him. ³⁸ So the prophet departed, and waited for the king by the way, disguising himself with a bandage over his eyes. ³⁹ And as the king passed, he cried to the king and said, "Your servant went out into the midst of the battle; and behold, a soldier turned and brought a man to me, and said, 'Keep this man; if by any means he be missing, your life shall be for his life, or else you shall pay a talent of silver.' ⁴⁰ And as your servant was busy here and there, he was gone." The king of Israel said to him, "So shall your judgment be; you yourself have decided it." ⁴¹ Then he made haste to take the bandage away from his eyes; and the king of Israel recognized him as one of the prophets. ⁴² And he said to him, "Thus says the LORD, 'Because you have let go out of your hand the man whom I had devoted to destruction, therefore your life shall go for his life, and your people for his people.'" ⁴³ And the king of Israel went to his house resentful and sullen, and came to Sa·mâr'ĭ·a.

21 Now Nā'bŏth the Jĕz'rē·ĕ·līte had a vineyard in Jĕz'rē·ĕl, beside the palace of Ā'hăb king of Sa·mâr'ĭ·a. ² And after this Ā'hăb said to Nā'bŏth, "Give me your vineyard, that I may have it for a vegetable garden, because it is near my house; and I will give you a better vineyard for it; or, if it seems good to you, I will give you its value in money." ³ But Nā'bŏth said to Ā'hăb, "The LORD forbid that I should give you the inheritance of my fathers." ⁴ And Ā'hăb went into his house vexed and sullen because of what Nā'bŏth the Jĕz'rē·ĕ·līte had said to him; for he had said, "I will not give you the inheritance of my

fathers." And he lay down on his bed, and turned away his face, and would eat no food.

5 But Jĕz'ĕ·bĕl his wife came to him, and said to him, "Why is your spirit so vexed that you eat no food?" ⁶ And he said to her, "Because I spoke to Nā'bŏth the Jĕz'rē·ĕ·līte, and said to him, 'Give me your vineyard for money; or else, if it please you, I will give you another vineyard for it'; and he answered, 'I will not give you my vineyard.'" ⁷ And Jĕz'ĕ·bĕl his wife said to him, "Do you now govern Israel? Arise, and eat bread, and let your heart be cheerful; I will give you the vineyard of Nā'bŏth the Jĕz'rē·ĕ·līte."

8 So she wrote letters in Ā'hăb's name and sealed them with his seal, and she sent the letters to the elders and the nobles who dwelt with Nā'bŏth in his city. ⁹ And she wrote in the letters, "Proclaim a fast, and set Nā'bŏth on high among the people; ¹⁰ and set two base fellows opposite him, and let them bring a charge against him, saying, 'You have cursed God and the king.' Then take him out, and stone him to death." ¹¹ And the men of his city, the elders and the nobles who dwelt in his city, did as Jĕz'ĕ·bĕl had sent word to them. As it was written in the letters which she had sent to them, ¹² they proclaimed a fast, and set Nā'bŏth on high among the people. ¹³ And the two base fellows came in and sat opposite him; and the base fellows brought a charge against Nā'bŏth, in the presence of the people, saying, "Naboth cursed God and the king." So they took him outside the city, and stoned him to death with stones. ¹⁴ Then they sent to Jĕz'ĕ·bĕl, saying, "Nā'bŏth has been stoned; he is dead."

15 As soon as Jĕz'ĕ·bĕl heard that Nā'bŏth had been stoned and was dead, Jezebel said to Ā'hăb, "Arise, take possession of the vineyard of Naboth the Jĕz'rē·ĕ·līte, which he refused to give you for money; for Naboth is not alive, but dead." ¹⁶ And as soon as Ā'hăb heard that Nā'bŏth was dead, Ahab arose to go down to the vineyard of Naboth the Jĕz'rē·ĕ·līte, to take possession of it.

17 Then the word of the LORD came to Ē·lī'jah the Tĭsh'bīte, saying, ¹⁸ "Arise, go down to meet Ā'hăb king

of Israel, who is in Sạ·mâr'ĭ·ạ; behold, he is in the vineyard of Nā'bŏth, where he has gone to take possession. ¹⁹And you shall say to him, 'Thus says the LORD, "Have you killed, and also taken possession?"' And you shall say to him, 'Thus says the LORD: "In the place where dogs licked up the blood of Nā'bŏth shall dogs lick your own blood."'"

20 Ā'hăb said to Ē·lī'jạh, "Have you found me, O my enemy?" He answered, "I have found you, because you have sold yourself to do what is evil in the sight of the LORD. ²¹Behold, I will bring evil upon you; I will utterly sweep you away, and will cut off from Ā'hăb every male, bond or free, in Israel; ²²and I will make your house like the house of Jĕr·ọ·bō'ạm the son of Nē'băt, and like the house of Bā'ạ·shạ the son of A·hī'jạh, for the anger to which you have provoked me, and because you have made Israel to sin. ²³And of Jĕz'ẹ·bẹl the LORD also said, 'The dogs shall eat Jezebel within the bounds of Jĕz'rē·ẹl.' ²⁴Any one belonging to Ā'hăb who dies in the city the dogs shall eat; and any one of his who dies in the open country the birds of the air shall eat."

25 (There was none who sold himself to do what was evil in the sight of the LORD like Ā'hăb, whom Jĕz'ẹ·bẹl his wife incited. ²⁶He did very abominably in going after idols, as the Ăm'ọ·rītes had done, whom the LORD cast out before the people of Israel.)

27 And when Ā'hăb heard those words, he rent his clothes, and put sackcloth upon his flesh, and fasted and lay in sackcloth, and went about dejectedly. ²⁸And the word of the LORD came to Ē·lī'jạh the Tĭsh'bīte, saying, ²⁹"Have you seen how Ā'hăb has humbled himself before me? Because he has humbled himself before me, I will not bring the evil in his days; but in his son's days I will bring the evil upon his house."

22 For three years Syria and Israel continued without war. ²But in the third year Jĕ·hŏsh'ạ·phăt the king of Judah came down to the king of Israel. ³And the king of Israel said to his servants, "Do you know that Rā'mŏth–gĭl'ē·ạd belongs to us, and we keep quiet and do not take it out of the hand of the king of Syria?"

⁴And he said to Jĕ·hŏsh'ạ·phăt, "Will you go with me to battle at Rā'mŏth–gĭl'ē·ạd?" And Jehoshaphat said to the king of Israel, "I am as you are, my people as your people, my horses as your horses."

5 And Jĕ·hŏsh'ạ·phăt said to the king of Israel, "Inquire first for the word of the LORD." ⁶Then the king of Israel gathered the prophets together, about four hundred men, and said to them, "Shall I go to battle against Rā'mŏth–gĭl'ē·ạd, or shall I forbear?" And they said, "Go up; for the Lord will give it into the hand of the king." ⁷But Jĕ·hŏsh'ạ·phăt said, "Is there not here another prophet of the LORD of whom we may inquire?" ⁸And the king of Israel said to Jĕ·hŏsh'ạ·phăt, "There is yet one man by whom we may inquire of the LORD, Mī·caī'ạh the son of Ĭm'lạh; but I hate him, for he never prophesies good concerning me, but evil." And Jehoshaphat said, "Let not the king say so." ⁹Then the king of Israel summoned an officer and said, "Bring quickly Mī·caī'ạh the son of Ĭm'lạh." ¹⁰Now the king of Israel and Jĕ·hŏsh'ạ·phăt the king of Judah were sitting on their thrones, arrayed in their robes, at the threshing floor at the entrance of the gate of Sạ·mâr'ĭ·ạ; and all the prophets were prophesying before them. ¹¹And Zĕd·ẹ·kī'ạh the son of Chĕ·nā'ạ·nạh made for himself horns of iron, and said, "Thus says the LORD, 'With these you shall push the Syrians until they are destroyed.'" ¹²And all the prophets prophesied so, and said, "Go up to Rā'mŏth–gĭl'ē·ạd and triumph; the LORD will give it into the hand of the king."

13 And the messenger who went to summon Mī·caī'ạh said to him, "Behold, the words of the prophets with one accord are favorable to the king; let your word be like the word of one of them, and speak favorably." ¹⁴But Mī·caī'ạh said, "As the LORD lives, what the LORD says to me, that I will speak." ¹⁵And when he had come to the king, the king said to him, "Mī·caī'ạh, shall we go to Rā'mŏth–gĭl'ē·ad to battle, or shall we forbear?" And he answered him, "Go up and triumph; the LORD will give it into the hand of the king." ¹⁶But the king said to him, "How many

21.19: 2 Kings 9.26.   21.23: 2 Kings 9.36.
22.1-35: 2 Chron 18.1-34.

times shall I adjure you that you speak to me nothing but the truth in the name of the LORD?" ¹⁷And he said, "I saw all Israel scattered upon the mountains, as sheep that have no shepherd; and the LORD said, 'These have no master; let each return to his home in peace.' " ¹⁸And the king of Israel said to Jĕ·hŏsh'a·phăt, "Did I not tell you that he would not prophesy good concerning me, but evil?" ¹⁹And Mī·caī'ah said, "Therefore hear the word of the LORD: I saw the LORD sitting on his throne, and all the host of heaven standing beside him on his right hand and on his left; ²⁰and the LORD said, 'Who will entice A'hăb, that he may go up and fall at Rā'mŏth–gĭl'ē·ạd?' And one said one thing, and another said another. ²¹Then a spirit came forward and stood before the LORD, saying, 'I will entice him.' ²²And the LORD said to him, 'By what means?' And he said, 'I will go forth, and will be a lying spirit in the mouth of all his prophets.' And he said, 'You are to entice him, and you shall succeed; go forth and do so.' ²³Now therefore behold, the LORD has put a lying spirit in the mouth of all these your prophets; the LORD has spoken evil concerning you."

24 Then Zĕd·ę·kī'ạh the son of Chĕ·nā'a·nạh came near and struck Mī·caī'ạh on the cheek, and said, "How did the Spirit of the LORD go from me to speak to you?" ²⁵And Mī·caī'ạh said, "Behold, you shall see on that day when you go into an inner chamber to hide yourself." ²⁶And the king of Israel said, "Seize Mī·caī'ạh, and take him back to A'mŏn the governor of the city and to Jō'ăsh the king's son; ²⁷and say, 'Thus says the king, "Put this fellow in prison, and feed him with scant fare of bread and water, until I come in peace."'" ²⁸And Mī·caī'ạh said, "If you return in peace, the LORD has not spoken by me." And he said, "Hear, all you peoples!"

29 So the king of Israel and Jĕ·hŏsh'a·phăt the king of Judah went up to Rā'mŏth–gĭl'ē·ạd. ³⁰And the king of Israel said to Jĕ·hŏsh'a·phăt, "I will disguise myself and go into battle, but you wear your robes." And the king of Israel disguised himself and went into battle. ³¹Now the king of Syria had commanded the thirty-two captains of his chariots, "Fight with neither small nor great, but only with the king of Israel." ³²And when the captains of the chariots saw Jĕ·hŏsh'a·phăt, they said, "It is surely the king of Israel." So they turned to fight against him; and Jehoshaphat cried out. ³³And when the captains of the chariots saw that it was not the king of Israel, they turned back from pursuing him. ³⁴But a certain man drew his bow at a venture, and struck the king of Israel between the scale armor and the breastplate; therefore he said to the driver of his chariot, "Turn about, and carry me out of the battle, for I am wounded." ³⁵And the battle grew hot that day, and the king was propped up in his chariot facing the Syrians, until at evening he died; and the blood of the wound flowed into the bottom of the chariot. ³⁶And about sunset a cry went through the army, "Every man to his city, and every man to his country!"

37 So the king died, and was brought to Sạ·mâr'ĭ·ạ; and they buried the king in Samaria. ³⁸And they washed the chariot by the pool of Sạ·mâr'ĭ·ạ, and the dogs licked up his blood, and the harlots washed themselves in it, according to the word of the LORD which he had spoken. ³⁹Now the rest of the acts of A'hăb, and all that he did, and the ivory house which he built, and all the cities that he built, are they not written in the Book of the Chronicles of the Kings of Israel? ⁴⁰So A'hăb slept with his fathers; and A·hạ·zī'ah his son reigned in his stead.

41 Jĕ·hŏsh'a·phăt the son of Asa began to reign over Judah in the fourth year of A'hăb king of Israel. ⁴²Jĕ·hŏsh'a·phăt was thirty-five years old when he began to reign, and he reigned twenty-five years in Jerusalem. His mother's name was Ạ·zü'bah the daughter of Shĭl'hī. ⁴³He walked in all the way of Asa his father; he did not turn aside from it, doing what was right in the sight of the LORD; yet the high places were not taken away, and the people still sacrificed and burned incense on the high places. ⁴⁴Jĕ·hŏsh'a·phăt also made peace with the king of Israel.

45 Now the rest of the acts of Jĕ·hŏsh'a·phăt, and his might that he showed, and how he warred, are they not written in the Book of the Chron-

22.17: Mt 9.36. 22.41-43: 2 Chron 20.31-33.

:les of the Kings of Judah? ⁴⁶And the emnant of the male cult prostitutes vho remained in the days of his father ιsa, he exterminated from the land.

47 There was no king in Ē'dom; a eputy was king. ⁴⁸Jĕ·hōsh'a·phăt nade ships of Tär'shĭsh to go to)'phĭr for gold; but they did not go, or the ships were wrecked at Ē·zĭ·ŏn– ;ē'bĕr. ⁴⁹Then Ā·ha·zī'ah the son of ı'hăb said to Jĕ·hŏsh'a·phăt, "Let my .ervants go with your servants in the hips," but Jehoshaphat was not willng. ⁵⁰And Jĕ·hŏsh'a·phăt slept with ıis fathers, and was buried with his 'athers in the city of David his father;

and Jĕ·hō'ram his son reigned in his stead.

51 Ā·ha·zī'ah the son of Ā'hăb began to reign over Israel in Sa·mâr'ĭ·a in the seventeenth year of Jĕ·hōsh'a·phăt king of Judah, and he reigned two years over Israel. ⁵²He did what was evil in the sight of the LORD, and walked in the way of his father, and in the way of his mother, and in the way of Jĕr·o·bō'am the son of Nē'băt, who made Israel to sin. ⁵³He served Bā'al and worshiped him, and provoked the LORD, the God of Israel, to anger in every way that his father had done.

The Second Book of the
Kings

1 After the death of Ā'hăb, Mō'ăb rebelled against Israel.

2 Now Ā·ha·zī'ah fell through the attice in his upper chamber in Sa·nâr'ĭ·a, and lay sick; so he sent messengers, telling them, "Go, inquire of 3ā'al–zē'bŭb, the god of Ĕk'ron, vhether I shall recover from this sickness." ³But the angel of the LORD said to Ē·lī'jah the Tĭsh'bīte, "Arise, ɡo up to meet the messengers of the ɕing of Sa·mâr'ĭ·a, and say to them, Is it because there is no God in Israel that you are going to inquire of Bā'al–zē'bŭb, the god of Ĕk'ron?' ⁴Now therefore thus says the LORD, 'You shall not ɕome down from the bed to which you have gone, but you shall surely die.'" So Ē·lī'jah went.

5 The messengers returned to the king, and he said to them, "Why have you returned?" ⁶And they said to him, "There came a man to meet us, and said to us, 'Go back to the king who sent you, and say to him, Thus says the LORD, Is it because there is no God in Israel that you are sending to inquire of Bā'al–zē'bŭb, the god of Ĕk'ron? Therefore you shall not come down from the bed to which you have gone, but shall surely die.'" ⁷He said to them, "What kind of man was he who came to meet you and told you these things?"

⁸They answered him, "He wore a garment of haircloth, with a girdle of leather about his loins." And he said, "It is Ē·lī'jah the Tĭsh'bīte."

9 Then the king sent to him a captain of fifty men with his fifty. He went up to Ē·lī'jah, who was sitting on the top of a hill, and said to him, "O man of God, the king says, 'Come down.'" ¹⁰But Ē·lī'jah answered the captain of fifty, "If I am a man of God, let fire come down from heaven and consume you and your fifty." Then fire came down from heaven, and consumed him and his fifty.

11 Again the king sent to him another captain of fifty men with his fifty. And he went upᵃ and said to him, "O man of God, this is the king's order, 'Come down quickly!'" ¹²But Ē·lī'jah answered them, "If I am a man of God, let fire come down from heaven and consume you and your fifty." Then the fire of God came down from heaven and consumed him and his fifty.

13 Again the king sent the captain of a third fifty with his fifty. And the third captain of fifty went up, and came and fell on his knees before Ē·lī'-jah, and entreated him, "O man of God,

22.48, 49: 2 Chron 20.35-37. 22.50: 2 Chron 21.1.
ᵃGk Compare verses 9, 13: Heb *answered*
1.10-12: Lk 9.54; Rev 11.5; 20.9.

I pray you, let my life, and the life of these fifty servants of yours, be precious in your sight. ¹⁴Lo, fire came down from heaven, and consumed the two former captains of fifty men with their fifties; but now let my life be precious in your sight." ¹⁵Then the angel of the LORD said to Ė-lī'jah, "Go down with him; do not be afraid of him." So he arose and went down with him to the king, ¹⁶and said to him, "Thus says the LORD, 'Because you have sent messengers to inquire of Bā'al-zē'bŭb, the god of Ĕk'rǫn,—is it because there is no God in Israel to inquire of his word?—therefore you shall not come down from the bed to which you have gone, but you shall surely die.' "

¹⁷So he died according to the word of the LORD which Ė-lī'jah had spoken. Jė-hō'ram, his brother,*ᵇ* became king in his stead in the second year of Jehoram the son of Jė-hŏsh'a-phăt, king of Judah, because Ā-ha-zī'ah had no son. ¹⁸Now the rest of the acts of Ā-ha-zī'ah which he did, are they not written in the Book of the Chronicles of the Kings of Israel?

2 Now when the LORD was about to take Ė-lī'jah up to heaven by a whirlwind, Elijah and Ė-lī'sha were on their way from Gĭl'gal. ²And Ė-lī'jah said to Ė-lī'sha, "Tarry here, I pray you; for the LORD has sent me as far as Bĕth-ĕl." But Elisha said, "As the LORD lives, and as you yourself live, I will not leave you." So they went down to Bethel. ³And the sons of the prophets who were in Bĕth-ĕl came out to Ė-lī'sha, and said to him, "Do you know that today the LORD will take away your master from over you?" And he said, "Yes, I know it; hold your peace."

⁴Ė-lī'jah said to him, "Ė-lī'sha, tarry here, I pray you; for the LORD has sent me to Jericho." But he said, "As the LORD lives, and as you yourself live, I will not leave you." So they came to Jericho. ⁵The sons of the prophets who were at Jericho drew near to Ė-lī'sha, and said to him, "Do you know that today the LORD will take away your master from over you?" And he answered, "Yes, I know it; hold your peace."

⁶Then Ė-lī'jah said to him, "Tarry here, I pray you; for the LORD has sent me to the Jordan." But he said, "As the LORD lives, and as you your-self live, I will not leave you." So the two of them went on. ⁷Fifty men of the sons of the prophets also went, and stood at some distance from them, as they both were standing by the Jordan. ⁸Then Ė-lī'jah took his mantle, and rolled it up, and struck the water, and the water was parted to the one side and to the other, till the two of them could go over on dry ground.

9 When they had crossed, Ė-lī'jah said to Ė-lī'sha, "Ask what I shall do for you, before I am taken from you." And Elisha said, "I pray you, let me inherit a double share of your spirit." ¹⁰And he said, "You have asked a hard thing; yet, if you see me as I am being taken from you, it shall be so for you; but if you do not see me, it shall not be so." ¹¹And as they still went on and talked, behold, a chariot of fire and horses of fire separated the two of them. And Ė-lī'jah went up by a whirlwind into heaven. ¹²And Ė-lī'sha saw it and cried, "My father, my father! the chariots of Israel and its horsemen!" And he saw him no more.

Then he took hold of his own clothes and rent them in two pieces. ¹³And he took up the mantle of Ė-lī'jah that had fallen from him, and went back and stood on the bank of the Jordan. ¹⁴Then he took the mantle of Ė-lī'jah that had fallen from him, and struck the water, saying, "Where is the LORD, the God of Elijah?" And when he had struck the water, the water was parted to the one side and to the other; and Ė-lī'sha went over.

15 Now when the sons of the prophets who were at Jericho saw him over against them, they said, "The spirit of Ė-lī'jah rests on Ė-lī'sha." And they came to meet him, and bowed to the ground before him. ¹⁶And they said to him, "Behold now, there are with your servants fifty strong men; pray, let them go, and seek your master; it may be that the Spirit of the LORD has caught him up and cast him upon some mountain or into some valley." And he said, "You shall not send." ¹⁷But when they urged him till he was ashamed, he said, "Send." They sent therefore fifty men; and for three days they sought him but did not find him. ¹⁸And they came back to him, while he tarried at Jericho, and he said to them, "Did I not say to you, Do not go?"

ᵇ Gk Syr: Heb lacks his brother   **2.11: Rev 11.12.**

19 Now the men of the city said to Ĕ·lī′shạ, "Behold, the situation of this city is pleasant, as my lord sees; but the water is bad, and the land is unfruitful." ²⁰ He said, "Bring me a new bowl, and put salt in it." So they brought it to him. ²¹ Then he went to the spring of water and threw salt in it, and said, "Thus says the LORD, I have made this water wholesome; henceforth neither death nor miscarriage shall come from it." ²² So the water has been wholesome to this day, according to the word which Ĕ·lī′shạ spoke.

23 He went up from there to Bĕth′ẹl; and while he was going up on the way, some small boys came out of the city and jeered at him, saying, "Go up, you baldhead! Go up, you baldhead!" ²⁴ And he turned around, and when he saw them, he cursed them in the name of the LORD. And two she-bears came out of the woods and tore forty-two of the boys. ²⁵ From there he went on to Mount Cär′mẹl, and thence he returned to Sạ·mâr′ĭ·ạ.

3 In the eighteenth year of Jĕ·hŏsh′-ạ·phăt king of Judah, Jĕ·hō′rạm the son of Ā′hăb became king over Israel in Sạ·mâr′ĭ·ạ, and he reigned twelve years. ²He did what was evil in the sight of the LORD, though not like his father and mother, for he put away the pillar of Bā′ạl which his father had made. ³Nevertheless he clung to the sin of Jĕr·ọ·bō′am the son of Nē′băt, which he made Israel to sin; he did not depart from it.

4 Now Mē′shạ king of Mō′ăb was a sheep breeder; and he had to deliver annually𝑐 to the king of Israel a hundred thousand lambs, and the wool of a hundred thousand rams. ⁵But when Ā′hăb died, the king of Mō′ăb rebelled against the king of Israel. ⁶So King Jĕ·hō′rạm marched out of Sạ·mâr′ĭ·a at that time and mustered all Israel. ⁷And he went and sent word to Jĕ-hŏsh′ạ·phăt king of Judah, "The king of Mō′ăb has rebelled against me; will you go with me to battle against Moab?" And he said, "I will go; I am as you are, my people as your people, my horses as your horses." ⁸Then he said, "By which way shall we march?" Jĕ·hō′rạm answered, "By the way of the wilderness of Ē′dọm."

9 So the king of Israel went with the king of Judah and the king of Ē′dọm.

And when they had made a circuitous march of seven days, there was no water for the army or for the beasts which followed them. ¹⁰Then the king of Israel said, "Alas! The LORD has called these three kings to give them into the hand of Mō′ăb." ¹¹And Jĕ-hŏsh′ạ·phăt said, "Is there no prophet of the LORD here, through whom we may inquire of the LORD?" Then one of the king of Israel's servants answered, "Ĕ·lī′shạ the son of Shā′phăt is here, who poured water on the hands of Ĕ·lī′jạh." ¹²And Jĕ·hŏsh′ạ·phăt said, "The word of the LORD is with him." So the king of Israel and Jehoshaphat and the king of Ē′dọm went down to him.

13 And Ĕ·lī′shạ said to the king of Israel, "What have I to do with you? Go to the prophets of your father and the prophets of your mother." But the king of Israel said to him, "No; it is the LORD who has called these three kings to give them into the hand of Mō′ăb." ¹⁴And Ĕ·lī′shạ said, "As the LORD of hosts lives, whom I serve, were it not that I have regard for Jĕ·hŏsh′ạ·phăt the king of Judah, I would neither look at you, nor see you. ¹⁵But now bring me a minstrel." And when the minstrel played, the power of the LORD came upon him. ¹⁶And he said, "Thus says the LORD, 'I will make this dry stream-bed full of pools.' ¹⁷For thus says the LORD, 'You shall not see wind or rain, but that stream-bed shall be filled with water, so that you shall drink, you, your cattle, and your beasts.' ¹⁸This is a light thing in the sight of the LORD; he will also give the Mō′ăb·ītes into your hand, ¹⁹and you shall conquer every fortified city, and every choice city, and shall fell every good tree, and stop up all springs of water, and ruin every good piece of land with stones." ²⁰The next morning, about the time of offering the sacrifice, behold, water came from the direction of Ē′dọm, till the country was filled with water.

21 When all the Mō′ăb·ītes heard that the kings had come up to fight against them, all who were able to put on armor, from the youngest to the oldest, were called out, and were drawn up at the frontier. ²²And when they rose early in the morning, and the sun shone upon the water, the Mō′ăb·ītes saw the water opposite them as

𝑐Tg: Heb lacks *annually*

red as blood. ²³And they said, "This is blood; the kings have surely fought together, and slain one another. Now then, Mō′ăb, to the spoil!" ²⁴But when they came to the camp of Israel, the Israelites rose and attacked the Mō′ăb-ītes, till they fled before them; and they went forward, slaughtering the Moabites as they went.ᵈ ²⁵And they overthrew the cities, and on every good piece of land every man threw a stone, until it was covered; they stopped every spring of water, and felled all the good trees; till only its stones were left in Kīr-hăr′-ĕ-sĕth, and the slingers surrounded and conquered it. ²⁶When the king of Mō′ăb saw that the battle was going against him, he took with him seven hundred swordsmen to break through, opposite the king of Ē′dom; but they could not. ²⁷Then he took his eldest son who was to reign in his stead, and offered him for a burnt offering upon the wall. And there came great wrath upon Israel; and they withdrew from him and returned to their own land.

4 Now the wife of one of the sons of the prophets cried to Ĕ-lī′shạ, "Your servant my husband is dead; and you know that your servant feared the Lord, but the creditor has come to take my two children to be his slaves." ²And Ĕ-lī′shạ said to her, "What shall I do for you? Tell me; what have you in the house?" And she said, "Your maidservant has nothing in the house, except a jar of oil." ³Then he said, "Go outside, borrow vessels of all your neighbors, empty vessels and not too few. ⁴Then go in, and shut the door upon yourself and your sons, and pour into all these vessels; and when one is full, set it aside." ⁵So she went from him and shut the door upon herself and her sons; and as she poured they brought the vessels to her. ⁶When the vessels were full, she said to her son, "Bring me another vessel." And he said to her, "There is not another." Then the oil stopped flowing. ⁷She came and told the man of God, and he said, "Go, sell the oil and pay your debts, and you and your sons can live on the rest."

8 One day Ĕ-lī′shạ went on to Shü′-nĕm, where a wealthy woman lived, who urged him to eat some food. So whenever he passed that way, he would turn in there to eat food. ⁹And she said to her husband, "Behold now, I perceive that this is a holy man of God, who is continually passing our way. ¹⁰Let us make a small roof chamber with walls, and put there for him a bed, a table, a chair, and a lamp, so that whenever he comes to us, he can go in there."

11 One day he came there, and he turned into the chamber and rested there. ¹²And he said to Gĕ-hā′zī his servant, "Call this Shü′nam-mīte." When he had called her, she stood before him. ¹³And he said to him, "Say now to her, See, you have taken all this trouble for us; what is to be done for you? Would you have a word spoken on your behalf to the king or to the commander of the army?" She answered, "I dwell among my own people." ¹⁴And he said, "What then is to be done for her?" Gĕ-hā′zī answered, "Well, she has no son, and her husband is old." ¹⁵He said, "Call her." And when he had called her, she stood in the doorway. ¹⁶And he said, "At this season, when the time comes round, you shall embrace a son." And she said, "No, my lord, O man of God; do not lie to your maidservant." ¹⁷But the woman conceived, and she bore a son about that time the following spring, as Ĕ-lī′shạ had said to her.

18 When the child had grown, he went out one day to his father among the reapers. ¹⁹And he said to his father, "Oh, my head, my head!" The father said to his servant, "Carry him to his mother." ²⁰And when he had lifted him, and brought him to his mother, the child sat on her lap till noon, and then he died. ²¹And she went up and laid him on the bed of the man of God, and shut the door upon him, and went out. ²²Then she called to her husband, and said, "Send me one of the servants and one of the asses, that I may quickly go to the man of God, and come back again." ²³And he said, "Why will you go to him today? It is neither new moon nor sabbath." She said, "It will be well." ²⁴Then she saddled the ass, and she said to her servant, "Urge the beast on; do not slacken the pace for me unless I tell you." ²⁵So she set out, and came to the man of God at Mount Cär′mel.

When the man of God saw her coming, he said to Gĕ-hā′zī his servant,

ᵈGk: Heb uncertain

"Look, yonder is the Shü'nam·mīte; ²⁶run at once to meet her, and say to her, Is it well with you? Is it well with your husband? Is it well with the child?" And she answered, "It is well." ²⁷And when she came to the mountain to the man of God, she caught hold of his feet. And Ge·hā'zī came to thrust her away. But the man of God said, "Let her alone, for she is in bitter distress; and the LORD has hidden it from me, and has not told me." ²⁸Then she said, "Did I ask my lord for a son? Did I not say, Do not deceive me?" ²⁹He said to Ge·hā'zī, "Gird up your loins, and take my staff in your hand, and go. If you meet any one, do not salute him; and if any one salutes you, do not reply; and lay my staff upon the face of the child." ³⁰Then the mother of the child said, "As the LORD lives, and as you yourself live, I will not leave you." So he arose and followed her. ³¹Ge·hā'zī went on ahead and laid the staff upon the face of the child, but there was no sound or sign of life. Therefore he returned to meet him, and told him, "The child has not awaked." ³²When Ė·lī'sha came into the house, he saw the child lying dead on his bed. ³³So he went in and shut the door upon the two of them, and prayed to the LORD. ³⁴Then he went up and lay upon the child, putting his mouth upon his mouth, his eyes upon his eyes, and his hands upon his hands; and as he stretched himself upon him, the flesh of the child became warm. ³⁵Then he got up again, and walked once to and fro in the house, and went up, and stretched himself upon him; the child sneezed seven times, and the child opened his eyes. ³⁶Then he summoned Ge·hā'zī and said, "Call this Shü'-nam·mīte." So he called her. And when she came to him, he said, "Take up your son." ³⁷She came and fell at his feet, bowing to the ground; then she took up her son and went out.

³⁸And Ė·lī'sha came again to Gil'gal when there was a famine in the land. And as the sons of the prophets were sitting before him, he said to his servant, "Set on the great pot, and boil pottage for the sons of the prophets." ³⁹One of them went out into the field to gather herbs, and found a wild vine and gathered from it his lap full of wild gourds, and came and cut them up into the pot of pottage, not knowing what they were. ⁴⁰And they poured out for the men to eat. But while they were eating of the pottage, they cried out, "O man of God, there is death in the pot!" And they could not eat it. ⁴¹He said, "Then bring meal." And he threw it into the pot, and said, "Pour out for the men, that they may eat." And there was no harm in the pot.

42 A man came from Bā'al–shǎl'ī-shah, bringing the man of God bread of the first fruits, twenty loaves of barley, and fresh ears of grain in his sack. And Ė·lī'sha said, "Give to the men, that they may eat." ⁴³But his servant said, "How am I to set this before a hundred men?" So he repeated, "Give them to the men, that they may eat, for thus says the LORD, 'They shall eat and have some left.'" ⁴⁴So he set it before them. And they ate, and had some left, according to the word of the LORD.

5 Nā'a·mǎn, commander of the army of the king of Syria, was a great man with his master and in high favor, because by him the LORD had given victory to Syria. He was a mighty man of valor, but he was a leper. ²Now the Syrians on one of their raids had carried off a little maid from the land of Israel, and she waited on Nā'a·mǎn's wife. ³She said to her mistress, "Would that my lord were with the prophet who is in Sa·mâr'ĭ·a! He would cure him of his leprosy." ⁴So Nā'a·mǎn went in and told his lord, "Thus and so spoke the maiden from the land of Israel." ⁵And the king of Syria said, "Go now, and I will send a letter to the king of Israel."

So he went, taking with him ten talents of silver, six thousand shekels of gold, and ten festal garments. ⁶And he brought the letter to the king of Israel, which read, "When this letter reaches you, know that I have sent to you Nā'a·mǎn my servant, that you may cure him of his leprosy." ⁷And when the king of Israel read the letter, he rent his clothes and said, "Am I God, to kill and to make alive, that this man sends word to me to cure a man of his leprosy? Only consider, and see how he is seeking a quarrel with me."

8 But when Ė·lī'sha the man of God heard that the king of Israel had rent his clothes, he sent to the king, saying, "Why have you rent your

4.33: Mt 6.6.

clothes? Let him come now to me, that he may know that there is a prophet in Israel." ⁹So Nā′a·măn came with his horses and chariots, and halted at the door of Ē·lī′sha's house. ¹⁰And Ē·lī′sha sent a messenger to him, saying, "Go and wash in the Jordan seven times, and your flesh shall be restored, and you shall be clean." ¹¹But Nā′a·măn was angry, and went away, saying, "Behold, I thought that he would surely come out to me, and stand, and call on the name of the LORD his God, and wave his hand over the place, and cure the leper. ¹²Are not A̧·bā′na̧ᵉ and Phār′pār, the rivers of Damascus, better than all the waters of Israel? Could I not wash in them, and be clean?" So he turned and went away in a rage. ¹³But his servants came near and said to him, "My father, if the prophet had commanded you to do some great thing, would you not have done it? How much rather, then, when he says to you, 'Wash, and be clean'?" ¹⁴So he went down and dipped himself seven times in the Jordan, according to the word of the man of God; and his flesh was restored like the flesh of a little child, and he was clean.

15 Then he returned to the man of God, he and all his company, and he came and stood before him; and he said, "Behold, I know that there is no God in all the earth but in Israel; so accept now a present from your servant." ¹⁶But he said, "As the LORD lives, whom I serve, I will receive none." And he urged him to take it, but he refused. ¹⁷Then Nā′a·măn said, "If not, I pray you, let there be given to your servant two mules' burden of earth; for henceforth your servant will not offer burnt offering or sacrifice to any god but the LORD. ¹⁸In this matter may the LORD pardon your servant: when my master goes into the house of Rĭm′mŏn to worship there, leaning on my arm, and I bow myself in the house of Rimmon, when I bow myself in the house of Rimmon, the LORD pardon your servant in this matter." ¹⁹He said to him, "Go in peace."

But when Nā′a·măn had gone from him a short distance, ²⁰Gȩ·hā′zī, the servant of Ē′lī′sha the man of God, said, "See, my master has spared this Nā′a·măn the Syrian, in not accepting from his hand what he brought. As the LORD lives, I will run after him, and get something from him." ²¹So Gȩ·hā′zī followed Nā′a·măn. And when Naaman saw some one running after him, he alighted from the chariot to meet him, and said, "Is all well?" ²²And he said, "All is well. My master has sent me to say, 'There have just now come to me from the hill country of Ē′phra̧·ĭm two young men of the sons of the prophets; pray, give them a talent of silver and two festal garments.'" ²³And Nā′a·măn said, "Be pleased to accept two talents." And he urged him, and tied up two talents of silver in two bags, with two festal garments, and laid them upon two of his servants; and they carried them before Gȩ·hā′zī. ²⁴And when he came to the hill, he took them from their hand, and put them in the house; and he sent the men away, and they departed. ²⁵He went in, and stood before his master, and Ē·lī′sha said to him, "Where have you been, Gȩ·hā′zī?" And he said, "Your servant went nowhere." ²⁶But he said to him, "Did I not go with you in spirit when the man turned from his chariot to meet you? Was it a time to accept money, and garments, olive orchards and vineyards, sheep and oxen, menservants and maidservants? ²⁷Therefore the leprosy of Nā′a·măn shall cleave to you, and to your descendants for ever." So he went out from his presence a leper, as white as snow.

6 Now the sons of the prophets said to Ē′lī′sha, "See, the place where we dwell under your charge is too small for us. ²Let us go to the Jordan and each of us get there a log, and let us make a place for us to dwell there." And he answered, "Go." ³Then one of them said, "Be pleased to go with your servants." And he answered, "I will go." ⁴So he went with them. And when they came to the Jordan, they cut down trees. ⁵But as one was felling a log, his axe head fell into the water; and he cried out, "Alas, my master! It was borrowed." ⁶Then the man of God said, "Where did it fall?" When he showed him the place, he cut off a stick, and threw it in there, and made the iron float. ⁷And he said, "Take it up." So he reached out his hand and took it.

8 Once when the king of Syria was warring against Israel, he took counsel

ᶜAnother reading is *Amana*

with his servants, saying, "At such and such a place shall be my camp." ⁹But the man of God sent word to the king of Israel, "Beware that you do not pass this place, for the Syrians are going down there." ¹⁰And the king of Israel sent to the place of which the man of God told him. Thus he used to warn him, so that he saved himself there more than once or twice.

11 And the mind of the king of Syria was greatly troubled because of this thing; and he called his servants and said to them, "Will you not show me who of us is for the king of Israel?" ¹²And one of his servants said, "None, my lord, O king; but Ĕ·lī′sha, the prophet who is in Israel, tells the king of Israel the words that you speak in your bedchamber." ¹³And he said, "Go and see where he is, that I may send and seize him." It was told him, "Behold, he is in Dō′than." ¹⁴So he sent there horses and chariots and a great army; and they came by night, and surrounded the city.

15 When the servant of the man of God rose early in the morning and went out, behold, an army with horses and chariots was round about the city. And the servant said, "Alas, my master! What shall we do?" ¹⁶He said, "Fear not, for those who are with us are more than those who are with them." ¹⁷Then Ĕ·lī′sha prayed, and said, "O LORD, I pray thee, open his eyes that he may see." So the LORD opened the eyes of the young man, and he saw; and behold, the mountain was full of horses and chariots of fire round about Elisha. ¹⁸And when the Syrians came down against him, Ĕ·lī′sha prayed to the LORD, and said, "Strike this people, I pray thee, with blindness." So he struck them with blindness in accordance with the prayer of Elisha. ¹⁹And Ĕ·lī′sha said to them, "This is not the way, and this is not the city; follow me, and I will bring you to the man whom you seek." And he led them to Sa·mâr′ĭ·a.

20 As soon as they entered Sa·mâr′ĭ·a, Ĕ·lī′sha said, "O LORD, open the eyes of these men, that they may see." So the LORD opened their eyes, and they saw; and lo, they were in the midst of Samaria. ²¹When the king of Israel saw them he said to Ĕ·lī′sha, "My father, shall I slay them? Shall I slay them?" ²²He answered, "You

shall not slay them. Would you slay those whom you have taken captive with your sword and with your bow? Set bread and water before them, that they may eat and drink and go to their master." ²³So he prepared for them a great feast; and when they had eaten and drunk, he sent them away, and they went to their master. And the Syrians came no more on raids into the land of Israel.

24 Afterward Bĕn·hā′dăd king of Syria mustered his entire army, and went up, and besieged Sa·mâr′ĭ·a. ²⁵And there was a great famine in Sa·mâr′ĭ·a, as they besieged it, until an ass's head was sold for eighty shekels of silver, and the fourth part of a kab of dove's dung for five shekels of silver. ²⁶Now as the king of Israel was passing by upon the wall, a woman cried out to him, saying, "Help, my lord, O king!" ²⁷And he said, "If the LORD will not help you, whence shall I help you? From the threshing floor, or from the wine press?" ²⁸And the king asked her, "What is your trouble?" She answered, "This woman said to me, 'Give your son, that we may eat him today, and we will eat my son tomorrow.' ²⁹So we boiled my son, and ate him. And on the next day I said to her, 'Give your son, that we may eat him'; but she has hidden her son." ³⁰When the king heard the words of the woman he rent his clothes—now he was passing by upon the wall—and the people looked, and behold, he had sackcloth beneath upon his body—³¹and he said, "May God do so to me, and more also, if the head of Ĕ·lī′sha the son of Shā′phat remains on his shoulders today."

32 Ĕ·lī′sha was sitting in his house, and the elders were sitting with him. Now the king had dispatched a man from his presence; but before the messenger arrived Elisha said to the elders, "Do you see how this murderer has sent to take off my head? Look, when the messenger comes, shut the door, and hold the door fast against him. Is not the sound of his master's feet behind him?" ³³And while he was still speaking with them, the kingᶠ came down to him and said, "This trouble is from the LORD! Why should I wait for the LORD any longer?"

ᶠSee 7.2: Heb *messenger*

7 ¹But Ė·lī′shạ said, "Hear the word of the LORD: thus says the LORD, Tomorrow about this time a measure of fine meal shall be sold for a shekel, and two measures of barley for a shekel, at the gate of Sạ·mâr′ĭ·ạ." ²Then the captain on whose hand the king leaned said to the man of God, "If the LORD himself should make windows in heaven, could this thing be?" But he said, "You shall see it with your own eyes, but you shall not eat of it."

3 Now there were four men who were lepers at the entrance to the gate; and they said to one another, "Why do we sit here till we die? ⁴If we say, 'Let us enter the city,' the famine is in the city, and we shall die there; and if we sit here, we die also. So now come, let us go over to the camp of the Syrians; if they spare our lives we shall live, and if they kill us we shall but die." ⁵So they arose at twilight to go to the camp of the Syrians; but when they came to the edge of the camp of the Syrians, behold, there was no one there. ⁶For the Lord had made the army of the Syrians hear the sound of chariots, and of horses, the sound of a great army, so that they said to one another, "Behold, the king of Israel has hired against us the kings of the Hĭt′tītes and the kings of Egypt to come upon us." ⁷So they fled away in the twilight and forsook their tents, their horses, and their asses, leaving the camp as it was, and fled for their lives. ⁸And when these lepers came to the edge of the camp, they went into a tent, and ate and drank, and they carried off silver and gold and clothing, and went and hid them; then they came back, and entered another tent, and carried off things from it, and went and hid them.

9 Then they said to one another, "We are not doing right. This day is a day of good news; if we are silent and wait until the morning light, punishment will overtake us; now therefore come, let us go and tell the king's household." ¹⁰So they came and called to the gatekeepers of the city, and told them, "We came to the camp of the Syrians, and behold, there was no one to be seen or heard there, nothing but the horses tied, and the asses tied, and the tents as they were." ¹¹Then the gatekeepers called out, and it was told within in the king's household. ¹²And the king rose in the night, and said to his servants, "I will tell you what the Syrians have prepared against us. They know that we are hungry; therefore they have gone out of the camp to hide themselves in the open country, thinking, 'When they come out of the city, we shall take them alive and get into the city.'" ¹³And one of his servants said, "Let some men take five of the remaining horses, seeing that those who are left here will fare like the whole multitude of Israel that have already perished; let us send and see." ¹⁴So they took two mounted men, and the king sent them after the army of the Syrians, saying, "Go and see." ¹⁵So they went after them as far as the Jordan; and, lo, all the way was littered with garments and equipment which the Syrians had thrown away in their haste. And the messengers returned, and told the king.

16 Then the people went out, and plundered the camp of the Syrians. So a measure of fine meal was sold for a shekel, and two measures of barley for a shekel, according to the word of the LORD. ¹⁷Now the king had appointed the captain on whose hand he leaned to have charge of the gate; and the people trod upon him in the gate, so that he died, as the man of God had said when the king came down to him. ¹⁸For when the man of God had said to the king, "Two measures of barley shall be sold for a shekel, and a measure of fine meal for a shekel, about this time tomorrow in the gate of Sạ·mâr′ĭ·ạ," ¹⁹the captain had answered the man of God, "If the LORD himself should make windows in heaven, could such a thing be?" And he had said, "You shall see it with your own eyes, but you shall not eat of it." ²⁰And so it happened to him, for the people trod upon him in the gate and he died.

8 Now Ė·lī′shạ had said to the woman whose son he had restored to life, "Arise, and depart with your household, and sojourn wherever you can; for the LORD has called for a famine, and it will come upon the land for seven years." ²So the woman arose, and did according to the word of the man of God; she went with her household and sojourned in the land of the Phĭ·lĭs′tĭnes seven years. ³And at the end of the seven years, when the woman returned from the land of the

Phĭ·lĭs'tĭnes, she went forth to appeal to the king for her house and her land. ⁴Now the king was talking with Gē·hā'zī the servant of the man of God, saying, "Tell me all the great things that Ē·lī'shȧ has done." ⁵And while he was telling the king how Ē·lī'shȧ had restored the dead to life, behold, the woman whose son he had restored to life appealed to the king for her house and her land. And Gē·hā'zī said, "My lord, O king, here is the woman, and here is her son whom Elisha restored to life." ⁶And when the king asked the woman, she told him. So the king appointed an official for her, saying, "Restore all that was hers, together with all the produce of the fields from the day that she left the land until now."

7 Now Ē·lī'shȧ came to Damascus. Bĕn–hā'dăd the king of Syria was sick; and when it was told him, "The man of God has come here," ⁸the king said to Hăz'ȧ·ĕl, "Take a present with you and go to meet the man of God, and inquire of the LORD through him, saying, 'Shall I recover from this sickness?'" ⁹So Hăz'ȧ·ĕl went to meet him, and took a present with him, all kinds of goods of Damascus, forty camel loads. When he came and stood before him, he said, "Your son Bĕn–hā'dăd king of Syria has sent me to you, saying, 'Shall I recover from this sickness?'" ¹⁰And Ē·lī'shȧ said to him, "Go, say to him, 'You shall certainly recover'; but the LORD has shown me that he shall certainly die." ¹¹And he fixed his gaze and stared at him, until he was ashamed. And the man of God wept. ¹²And Hăz'ȧ·ĕl said, "Why does my lord weep?" He answered, "Because I know the evil that you will do to the people of Israel; you will set on fire their fortresses, and you will slay their young men with the sword, and dash in pieces their little ones, and rip up their women with child." ¹³And Hăz'ȧ·ĕl said, "What is your servant, who is but a dog, that he should do this great thing?" Ē·lī'shȧ answered, "The LORD has shown me that you are to be king over Syria." ¹⁴Then he departed from Ē·lī'shȧ, and came to his master, who said to him, "What did Elisha say to you?" And he answered, "He told me that you would certainly recover." ¹⁵But on the morrow he took the coverlet and dipped it in water and spread it

over his face, till he died. And Hăz'ȧ·ĕl became king in his stead.

16 In the fifth year of Jō'răm the son of Ā'hăb, king of Israel,ᵍ Jĕ·hō'răm the son of Jĕ·hŏsh'ȧ·phăt, king of Judah, began to reign. ¹⁷He was thirty-two years old when he became king, and he reigned eight years in Jerusalem. ¹⁸And he walked in the way of the kings of Israel, as the house of Ā'hăb had done, for the daughter of Ahab was his wife. And he did what was evil in the sight of the LORD. ¹⁹Yet the LORD would not destroy Judah, for the sake of David his servant, since he promised to give a lamp to him and to his sons for ever.

20 In his days Ē'dŏm revolted from the rule of Judah, and set up a king of their own. ²¹Then Jō'răm passed over to Zā'ĭr with all his chariots, and rose by night, and he and his chariot commanders smote the Ē'dŏ·mītes who had surrounded him; but his army fled home. ²²So Ē'dŏm revolted from the rule of Judah to this day. Then Lĭb'nah revolted at the same time. ²³Now the rest of the acts of Jō'răm, and all that he did, are they not written in the Book of the Chronicles of the Kings of Judah? ²⁴So Jō'răm slept with his fathers, and was buried with his fathers in the city of David; and Ā·hȧ·zī'ăh his son reigned in his stead.

25 In the twelfth year of Jō'răm the son of Ā'hăb, king of Israel, Ā·hȧ·zī'ăh the son of Jĕ·hō'răm, king of Judah, began to reign. ²⁶Ā·hȧ·zī'ăh was twenty-two years old when he began to reign, and he reigned one year in Jerusalem. His mother's name was Ăth·ȧ·lī'ăh; she was a granddaughter of Ŏm'rī king of Israel. ²⁷He also walked in the way of the house of Ā'hăb, and did what was evil in the sight of the LORD, as the house of Ahab had done, for he was son-in-law to the house of Ahab.

28 He went with Jō'răm the son of Ā'hăb to make war against Hăz'ȧ·ĕl king of Syria at Rā'mŏth–gĭl'ē·ăd, where the Syrians wounded Joram. ²⁹And King Jō'răm returned to be healed in Jĕz'rē·ĕl of the wounds which the Syrians had given him at Rā'măh, when he fought against Hăz'ȧ·ĕl king of Syria. And Ā·hȧ·zī'ăh the son of Jĕ·hō'răm king of Judah

ᵍGk Syr: Heb *Israel, Jehoshaphat being king of Judah*
8.17-24: 2 Chron 21.5-10, 20. **8.24-29:** 2 Chron 22.1-6.

went down to see Joram the son of Ā′hăb in Jezreel, because he was sick.

9 Then Ĕ·lī′sha the prophet called one of the sons of the prophets and said to him, "Gird up your loins, and take this flask of oil in your hand, and go to Rā′mŏth–gĭl′ē·ạd. ²And when you arrive, look there for Jē′hū the son of Jĕ·hŏsh′a·phăt, son of Nĭm′shī; and go in and bid him rise from among his fellows, and lead him to an inner chamber. ³Then take the flask of oil, and pour it on his head, and say, 'Thus says the Lᴏʀᴅ, I anoint you king over Israel.' Then open the door and flee; do not tarry."

4 So the young man, the prophet,ʰ went to Rā′mŏth–gĭl′ē·ạd. ⁵And when he came, behold, the commanders of the army were in council; and he said, "I have an errand to you, O commander." And Jē′hū said, "To which of us all?" And he said, "To you, O commander." ⁶So he arose, and went into the house; and the young man poured the oil on his head, saying to him, "Thus says the Lᴏʀᴅ the God of Israel, I anoint you king over the people of the Lᴏʀᴅ, over Israel. ⁷And you shall strike down the house of Ā′hăb your master, that I may avenge on Jĕz′e·bel the blood of my servants the prophets, and the blood of all the servants of the Lᴏʀᴅ. ⁸For the whole house of Ā′hăb shall perish; and I will cut off from Ahab every male, bond or free, in Israel. ⁹And I will make the house of Ā′hăb like the house of Jĕr·o·bō′ạm the son of Nē′bặt, and like the house of Bā′a·sha the son of A·hī′jạh. ¹⁰And the dogs shall eat Jĕz′e·bel in the territory of Jĕz′rē·ẹl, and none shall bury her." Then he opened the door, and fled.

11 When Jē′hū came out to the servants of his master, they said to him, "Is all well? Why did this mad fellow come to you?" And he said to them, "You know the fellow and his talk." ¹²And they said, "That is not true; tell us now." And he said, "Thus and so he spoke to me, saying, 'Thus says the Lᴏʀᴅ, I anoint you king over Israel.'" ¹³Then in haste every man of them took his garment, and put it under him on the bareⁱ steps, and they blew the trumpet, and proclaimed, "Jē′hū is king."

14 Thus Jē′hū the son of Jĕ·hŏsh′-a·phặt the son of Nĭm′shī conspired against Jō′rạm. (Now Joram with all Israel had been on guard at Rā′mŏth-gĭl′ē·ạd against Hăz′a·ĕl king of Syria; ¹⁵but King Jō′rạm had returned to be healed in Jĕz′rē·ẹl of the wounds which the Syrians had given him, when he fought with Hăz′a·ĕl king of Syria.) So Jē′hū said, "If this is your mind, then let no one slip out of the city to go and tell the news in Jezreel." ¹⁶Then Jē′hū mounted his chariot, and went to Jĕz′rē·ẹl, for Jō′rạm lay there. And Ā·hạ·zī′ạh king of Judah had come down to visit Joram.

17 Now the watchman was standing on the tower in Jĕz′rē·ẹl, and he spied the company of Jē′hū as he came, and said, "I see a company." And Jō′rạm said, "Take a horseman, and send to meet them, and let him say, 'Is it peace?'" ¹⁸So a man on horseback went to meet him, and said, "Thus says the king, 'Is it peace?'" And Jē′hū said, "What have you to do with peace? Turn round and ride behind me." And the watchman reported, saying, "The messenger reached them, but he is not coming back." ¹⁹Then he sent out a second horseman, who came to them, and said, "Thus the king has said, 'Is it peace?'" And Jē′hū answered, "What have you to do with peace? Turn round and ride behind me." ²⁰Again the watchman reported, "He reached them, but he is not coming back. And the driving is like the driving of Jē′hū the son of Nĭm′shī; for he drives furiously."

21 Jō′rạm said, "Make ready." And they made ready his chariot. Then Joram king of Israel and Ā·hạ-zī′ạh king of Judah set out, each in his chariot, and went to meet Jē′hū, and met him at the property of Nā′bŏth the Jĕz′rē·e·līte. ²²And when Jō′rạm saw Jē′hū, he said, "Is it peace, Jehu?" He answered, "What peace can there be, so long as the harlotries and the sorceries of your mother Jĕz′e·bel are so many?" ²³Then Jō′rạm reined about and fled, saying to Ā·hạ·zī′ah, "Treachery, O Ahaziah!" ²⁴And Jē′hū drew his bow with his full strength, and shot Jō′rạm between the shoulders, so that the arrow pierced his heart, and he sank in his chariot. ²⁵Jē′hū said to Bĭd′kăr his aide, "Take

---

ʰGk Syr: Heb *the young man, the young man, the prophet*
ⁱThe meaning of the Hebrew word is uncertain
9.1–10.36: 2 Chron 22.7–9.   **9.25:** 1 Kings 21.19.

him up, and cast him on the plot of ground belonging to Nā'bŏth the Jĕz'-rē-e-līte; for remember, when you and I rode side by side behind Ā'hăb his father, how the LORD uttered this oracle against him: ²⁶'As surely as I saw yesterday the blood of Nā'bŏth and the blood of his sons—says the LORD—I will requite you on this plot of ground.' Now therefore take him up and cast him on the plot of ground, in accordance with the word of the LORD."

27 When Ā·ha·zī'ah the king of Judah saw this, he fled in the direction of Bĕth–hăg'gan. And Jē'hū pursued him, and said, "Shoot him also"; and they shot himʲ in the chariot at the ascent of Gūr, which is by Ĭb'lē·am. And he fled to Me·gĭd'dō, and died there. ²⁸His servants carried him in a chariot to Jerusalem, and buried him in his tomb with his fathers in the city of David.

29 In the eleventh year of Jō'ram the son of Ā'hăb, Ā·ha·zī'ah began to reign over Judah.

30 When Jē'hū came to Jĕz'rē-el, Jĕz'e-bel heard of it; and she painted her eyes, and adorned her head, and looked out of the window. ³¹And as Jē'hū entered the gate, she said, "Is it peace, you Zĭm'rī, murderer of your master?" ³²And he lifted up his face to the window, and said, "Who is on my side? Who?" Two or three eunuchs looked out at him. ³³He said, "Throw her down." So they threw her down; and some of her blood spattered on the wall and on the horses, and they trampled on her. ³⁴Then he went in and ate and drank; and he said, "See now to this cursed woman, and bury her; for she is a king's daughter." ³⁵But when they went to bury her, they found no more of her than the skull and the feet and the palms of her hands. ³⁶When they came back and told him, he said, "This is the word of the LORD, which he spoke by his servant Ĕ·lī'-jah the Tīsh'bīte, 'In the territory of Jĕz'rē·el the dogs shall eat the flesh of Jĕz'e·bel; ³⁷and the corpse of Jĕz'-e·bel shall be as dung upon the face of the field in the territory of Jĕz'rē·el, so that no one can say, This is Jezebel.'"

10 Now Ā'hăb had seventy sons in Sa·mâr'ĭ·a. So Jē'hū wrote letters, and sent them to Samaria, to the rulers of the city,ᵏ to the elders, and to the guardians of the sons of Ahab, saying, ²"Now then, as soon as this letter comes to you, seeing your master's sons are with you, and there are with you chariots and horses, fortified cities also, and weapons, ³select the best and fittest of your master's sons and set him on his father's throne, and fight for your master's house." ⁴But they were exceedingly afraid, and said, "Behold, the two kings could not stand before him; how then can we stand?" ⁵So he who was over the palace, and he who was over the city, together with the elders and the guardians, sent to Jē'hū, saying, "We are your servants, and we will do all that you bid us. We will not make any one king; do whatever is good in your eyes." ⁶Then he wrote to them a second letter, saying, "If you are on my side, and if you are ready to obey me, take the heads of your master's sons, and come to me at Jĕz'rē·el tomorrow at this time." Now the king's sons, seventy persons, were with the great men of the city, who were bringing them up. ⁷And when the letter came to them, they took the king's sons, and slew them, seventy persons, and put their heads in baskets, and sent them to him at Jĕz'rē·el. ⁸When the messenger came and told him, "They have brought the heads of the king's sons," he said, "Lay them in two heaps at the entrance of the gate until the morning." ⁹Then in the morning, when he went out, he stood, and said to all the people, "You are innocent. It was I who conspired against my master, and slew him; but who struck down all these? ¹⁰Know then that there shall fall to the earth nothing of the word of the LORD, which the LORD spoke concerning the house of Ā'hăb; for the LORD has done what he said by his servant Ĕ·lī'jah." ¹¹So Jē'hū slew all that remained of the house of Ā'hăb in Jĕz'rē·el, all his great men, and his familiar friends, and his priests, until he left him none remaining.

12 Then he set out and went to Sa·mâr'ĭ·a. On the way, when he was at Bĕth–ĕk'ĕd of the Shepherds, ¹³Jē'hū met the kinsmen of Ā·ha·zī'ah king of Judah, and he said, "Who are

ʲSyr Vg Compare Gk: Heb lacks *and they shot him*
ᵏGk Vg: Heb *Jezreel*
9.36: 1 Kings 21.23.

you?" And they answered, "We are the kinsmen of Ahaziah, and we came down to visit the royal princes and the sons of the queen mother." [14] He said, "Take them alive." And they took them alive, and slew them at the pit of Bĕth–ĕk′ĕd, forty-two persons, and he spared none of them.

15 And when he departed from there, he met Jĕ·hŏn′a·dăb the son of Rē′chăb coming to meet him; and he greeted him, and said to him, "Is your heart true to my heart as mine is to yours?"[l] And Jehonadab answered, "It is." Jē′hū said,[m] "If it is, give me your hand." So he gave him his hand. And Jehu took him up with him into the chariot. [16] And he said, "Come with me, and see my zeal for the LORD." So he[n] had him ride in his chariot. [17] And when he came to Sa·mâr′i·a, he slew all that remained to Ā′hăb in Samaria, till he had wiped them out, according to the word of the LORD which he spoke to E·lī′jah.

18 Then Jē′hū assembled all the people, and said to them, "Ā′hăb served Bā′al a little; but Jē′hū will serve him much. [19] Now therefore call to me all the prophets of Bā′al, all his worshipers and all his priests; let none be missing, for I have a great sacrifice to offer to Baal; whoever is missing shall not live." But Jē′hū did it with cunning in order to destroy the worshipers of Baal. [20] And Jē′hū ordered, "Sanctify a solemn assembly for Bā′al." So they proclaimed it. [21] And Jē′hū sent throughout all Israel; and all the worshipers of Bā′al came, so that there was not a man left who did not come. And they entered the house of Baal, and the house of Baal was filled from one end to the other. [22] He said to him who was in charge of the wardrobe, "Bring out the vestments for all the worshipers of Bā′al." So he brought out the vestments for them. [23] Then Jē′hū went into the house of Bā′al with Jĕ·hŏn′a·dăb the son of Rē′chăb; and he said to the worshipers of Baal, "Search, and see that there is no servant of the LORD here among you, but only the worshipers of Baal." [24] Then he[o] went in to offer sacrifices and burnt offerings.

Now Jē′hū had stationed eighty men outside, and said, "The man who allows any of those whom I give into your hands to escape shall forfeit his

life." [25] So as soon as he had made an end of offering the burnt offering, Jē′hū said to the guard and to the officers, "Go in and slay them; let not a man escape." So when they put them to the sword, the guard and the officers cast them out and went into the inner room[p] of the house of Bā′al [26] and they brought out the pillar that was in the house of Bā′al, and burned it. [27] And they demolished the pillar of Bā′al, and demolished the house of Baal, and made it a latrine to this day.

28 Thus Jē′hū wiped out Bā′al from Israel. [29] But Jē′hū did not turn aside from the sins of Jĕr·o·bō′am the son of Nē′băt, which he made Israel to sin, the golden calves that were in Bĕth′el, and in Dan. [30] And the LORD said to Jē′hū, "Because you have done well in carrying out what is right in my eyes, and have done to the house of Ā′hăb according to all that was in my heart, your sons of the fourth generation shall sit on the throne of Israel." [31] But Jē′hū was not careful to walk in the law of the LORD the God of Israel with all his heart; he did not turn from the sins of Jĕr·o·bō′am, which he made Israel to sin.

32 In those days the LORD began to cut off parts of Israel. Hăz′a·ĕl defeated them throughout the territory of Israel: [33] from the Jordan eastward, all the land of Gilead, the Găd′ītes, and the Reubenites, and the Ma·năs′-sītes, from A·rō′er, which is by the valley of the Är′nŏn, that is, Gilead and Bā′shan. [34] Now the rest of the acts of Jē′hū, and all that he did, and all his might, are they not written in the Book of the Chronicles of the Kings of Israel? [35] So Jē′hū slept with his fathers, and they buried him in Sa·mâr′i·a. And Jĕ·hō′a·hăz his son reigned in his stead. [36] The time that Jē′hū reigned over Israel in Sa·mâr′i·a was twenty-eight years.

11 Now when Ăth·a·lī′ah the mother of A·ha·zī′ah saw that her son was dead, she arose and destroyed all the royal family. [2] But Jĕ·hŏsh′e·ba, the daughter of King Jō′ram, sister of A·ha·zī′ah, took Jō′ăsh the son of Ahaziah, and stole him away from among the king's sons

[l]Gk: Heb *Is it right with your heart, as my heart is with your heart?*   [m]Gk: Heb lacks *Jehu said*
[n]Gk Syr Tg: Heb *they*
[o]Gk Compare verse 25: Heb *they*   [p]Cn: Heb *city*
11.1–20: 2 Chron 22.10–23.21.

who were about to be slain, and she put[q] him and his nurse in a bedchamber. Thus she[r] hid him from Ăth·ạ·lī′ạh, so that he was not slain; [3]and he remained with her six years, hid in the house of the LORD, while Ăth·ạ·lī′ạh reigned over the land.

4 But in the seventh year Jĕ·hoi′ạ·dạ sent and brought the captains of the Căr·ĭ′tēş and of the guards, and had them come to him in the house of the LORD; and he made a covenant with them and put them under oath in the house of the LORD, and he showed them the king's son. [5]And he commanded them, "This is the thing that you shall do: one third of you, those who come off duty on the sabbath and guard the king's house [6](another third being at the gate Sūr and a third at the gate behind the guards), shall guard the palace; [7]and the two divisions of you, which come on duty in force on the sabbath and guard the house of the LORD,[s] [8]shall surround the king, each with his weapons in his hand; and whoever approaches the ranks is to be slain. Be with the king when he goes out and when he comes in."

9 The captains did according to all that Jĕ·hoi′ạ·dạ the priest commanded, and each brought his men who were to go off duty on the sabbath, with those who were to come on duty on the sabbath, and came to Jehoiada the priest. [10]And the priest delivered to the captains the spears and shields that had been King David's, which were in the house of the LORD; [11]and the guards stood, every man with his weapons in his hand, from the south side of the house to the north side of the house, around the altar and the house.[t] [12]Then he brought out the king's son, and put the crown upon him, and gave him the testimony; and they proclaimed him king, and anointed him; and they clapped their hands, and said, "Long live the king!"

13 When Ăth·ạ·lī′ạh heard the noise of the guard and of the people, she went into the house of the LORD to the people; [14]and when she looked, there was the king standing by the pillar, according to the custom, and the captains and the trumpeters beside the king, and all the people of the land rejoicing and blowing trumpets. And Ăth·ạ·lī′ạh rent her clothes, and

cried, "Treason! Treason!" [15]Then Jĕ·hoi′ạ·dạ the priest commanded the captains who were set over the army, "Bring her out between the ranks; and slay with the sword any one who follows her." For the priest said, "Let her not be slain in the house of the LORD." [16]So they laid hands on her; and she went through the horses' entrance to the king's house, and there she was slain.

17 And Jĕ·hoi′ạ·dạ made a covenant between the LORD and the king and people, that they should be the LORD's people; and also between the king and the people. [18]Then all the people of the land went to the house of Bā′ạl, and tore it down; his altars and his images they broke in pieces, and they slew Măt′tăn the priest of Baal before the altars. And the priest posted watchmen over the house of the LORD. [19]And he took the captains, the Căr·ĭ′tēş, the guards, and all the people of the land; and they brought the king down from the house of the LORD, marching through the gate of the guards to the king's house. And he took his seat on the throne of the kings. [20]So all the people of the land rejoiced; and the city was quiet after Ăth·ạ·lī′ạh had been slain with the sword at the king's house.

21[u] Jĕ·hō′ăsh was seven years old when he began to reign.

12 In the seventh year of Jĕ′hū Jĕ·hō′ăsh began to reign, and he reigned forty years in Jerusalem. His mother's name was Zĭb′ĭ·ạh of Bē′ẹr-shē′bạ. [2]And Jĕ·hō′ăsh did what was right in the eyes of the LORD all his days, because Jĕ·hoi′ạ·dạ the priest instructed him. [3]Nevertheless the high places were not taken away; the people continued to sacrifice and burn incense on the high places.

4 Jĕ·hō′ăsh said to the priests, "All the money of the holy things which is brought into the house of the LORD, the money for which each man is assessed—the money from the assessment of persons—and the money which a man's heart prompts him to bring into the house of the LORD, [5]let the priests take, each from his acquaintance; and let them repair the

^qWith 2 Chron 22.11: Heb lacks *and she put*
^rGk Syr Vg Compare 2 Chron 22.11: Heb *they*
^sHeb *the* LORD *to the king* ^tHeb *the house to the king*
^uCh 12.1 in Heb
11.21-12.14: 2 Chron 24.1-4.

house wherever any need of repairs is discovered." ⁶But by the twenty-third year of King Jĕ·hō'ăsh the priests had made no repairs on the house. ⁷Therefore King Jĕ·hō'ăsh summoned Jĕhoi'a·da the priest and the other priests and said to them, "Why are you not repairing the house? Now therefore take no more money from your acquaintances, but hand it over for the repair of the house." ⁸So the priests agreed that they should take no more money from the people, and that they should not repair the house.

9 Then Jĕ·hoi'a·da the priest took a chest, and bored a hole in the lid of it, and set it beside the altar on the right side as one entered the house of the LORD; and the priests who guarded the threshold put in it all the money that was brought into the house of the LORD. ¹⁰And whenever they saw that there was much money in the chest, the king's secretary and the high priest came up and they counted and tied up in bags the money that was found in the house of the LORD. ¹¹Then they would give the money that was weighed out into the hands of the workmen who had the oversight of the house of the LORD; and they paid it out to the carpenters and the builders who worked upon the house of the LORD, ¹²and to the masons and the stonecutters, as well as to buy timber and quarried stone for making repairs on the house of the LORD, and for any outlay upon the repairs of the house. ¹³But there were not made for the house of the LORD basins of silver, snuffers, bowls, trumpets, or any vessels of gold, or of silver, from the money that was brought into the house of the LORD, ¹⁴for that was given to the workmen who were repairing the house of the LORD with it. ¹⁵And they did not ask an accounting from the men into whose hand they delivered the money to pay out to the workmen, for they dealt honestly. ¹⁶The money from the guilt offerings and the money from the sin offerings was not brought into the house of the LORD; it belonged to the priests.

17 At that time Hăz'a·ĕl king of Syria went up and fought against Găth, and took it. But when Hazael set his face to go up against Jerusalem, ¹⁸Jĕ·hō'ăsh king of Judah took all the votive gifts that Jĕ·hŏsh'a·phăt

and Jĕ·hō'răm and Ā·ha·zī'ăh, his fathers, the kings of Judah, had dedicated, and his own votive gifts, and all the gold that was found in the treasuries of the house of the LORD and of the king's house, and sent these to Hăz'a·ĕl king of Syria. Then Hazael went away from Jerusalem.

19 Now the rest of the acts of Jō'ăsh, and all that he did, are they not written in the Book of the Chronicles of the Kings of Judah? ²⁰His servants arose and made a conspiracy, and slew Jō'ăsh in the house of Mĭl'lō, on the way that goes down to Sĭl'la. ²¹It was Jō'za·căr the son of Shĭm'ē·ăth and Jĕ·hō'za·băd the son of Shō'mer, his servants, who struck him down, so that he died. And they buried him with his fathers in the city of David, and Ăm·a·zī'ăh his son reigned in his stead.

13 In the twenty-third year of Jō'ăsh the son of Ā·ha·zī'ăh, king of Judah, Jĕ·hō'a·hăz the son of Jĕ'hū began to reign over Israel in Sa·mâr'ĭ·a, and he reigned seventeen years. ²He did what was evil in the sight of the LORD, and followed the sins of Jĕr·o·bō'am the son of Nē'băt, which he made Israel to sin; he did not depart from them. ³And the anger of the LORD was kindled against Israel, and he gave them continually into the hand of Hăz'a·ĕl king of Syria and into the hand of Bĕn–hā'dăd the son of Hazael. ⁴Then Jĕ·hō'a·hăz besought the LORD, and the LORD hearkened to him; for he saw the oppression of Israel, how the king of Syria oppressed them. ⁵(Therefore the LORD gave Israel a savior, so that they escaped from the hand of the Syrians; and the people of Israel dwelt in their homes as formerly. ⁶Nevertheless they did not depart from the sins of the house of Jĕr·o·bō'am, which he made Israel to sin, but walked*ᵛ* in them; and the A·shē'rah also remained in Sa·mâr'ĭ·a.) ⁷For there was not left to Jĕ·hō'a·hăz an army of more than fifty horsemen and ten chariots and ten thousand footmen; for the king of Syria had destroyed them and made them like the dust at threshing. ⁸Now the rest of the acts of Jĕ·hō'a·hăz and all that he did, and his might, are they not written in the Book of the Chronicles of the Kings of Israel? ⁹So Jĕ·hō'-

a·hăz slept with his fathers, and they buried him in Să·mâr′ĭ·ạ; and Jō′ăsh his son reigned in his stead.

10 In the thirty-seventh year of Jō′ăsh king of Judah Jĕ·hō′ăsh the son of Jĕ·hō′ạ·hăz began to reign over Israel in Să·mâr′ĭ·ạ, and he reigned sixteen years. ¹¹He also did what was evil in the sight of the LORD; he did not depart from all the sins of Jĕr·ọ·bō′ạm the son of Nē′băt, which he made Israel to sin, but he walked in them. ¹²Now the rest of the acts of Jō′ăsh, and all that he did, and the might with which he fought against Ăm·ạ·zī′ah king of Judah, are they not written in the Book of the Chronicles of the Kings of Israel? ¹³So Jō′ăsh slept with his fathers, and Jĕr·ọ·bō′ạm sat upon his throne; and Joash was buried in Să·mâr′ĭ·ạ with the kings of Israel.

14 Now when Ē·lī′shạ had fallen sick with the illness of which he was to die, Jō′ăsh king of Israel went down to him, and wept before him, crying, "My father, my father! The chariots of Israel and its horsemen!" ¹⁵And Ē·lī′shạ said to him, "Take a bow and arrows"; so he took a bow and arrows. ¹⁶Then he said to the king of Israel, "Draw the bow"; and he drew it. And Ē·lī′shạ laid his hands upon the king's hands. ¹⁷And he said, "Open the window eastward"; and he opened it. Then Ē·lī′shạ said, "Shoot"; and he shot. And he said, "The LORD's arrow of victory, the arrow of victory over Syria! For you shall fight the Syrians in Ā′phĕk until you have made an end of them." ¹⁸And he said, "Take the arrows"; and he took them. And he said to the king of Israel, "Strike the ground with them"; and he struck three times, and stopped. ¹⁹Then the man of God was angry with him, and said, "You should have struck five or six times; then you would have struck down Syria until you had made an end of it, but now you will strike down Syria only three times."

20 So Ē·lī′shạ died, and they buried him. Now bands of Mō′ạb·ītes used to invade the land in the spring of the year. ²¹And as a man was being buried, lo, a marauding band was seen and the man was cast into the grave of Ē·lī′shạ; and as soon as the man touched the bones of Elisha, he revived, and stood on his feet.

22 Now Hăz′ạ·ĕl king of Syria oppressed Israel all the days of Jĕ·hō′ạ·hăz. ²³But the LORD was gracious to them and had compassion on them, and he turned toward them, because of his covenant with Abraham, Isaac, and Jacob, and would not destroy them; nor has he cast them from his presence until now.

24 When Hăz′ạ·ĕl king of Syria died, Bĕn–hā′dăd his son became king in his stead. ²⁵Then Jĕ·hō′ăsh the son of Jĕ·hō′ạ·hăz took again from Bĕn–hā′dăd the son of Hăz′ạ·ĕl the cities which he had taken from Jehoahaz his father in war. Three times Jō′ăsh defeated him and recovered the cities of Israel.

14 In the second year of Jō′ăsh the son of Jō′ạ·hăz, king of Israel, Ăm·ạ·zī′ah the son of Joash, king of Judah, began to reign. ²He was twenty-five years old when he began to reign, and he reigned twenty-nine years in Jerusalem. His mother's name was Jē′hō–ăd′dĭn of Jerusalem. ³And he did what was right in the eyes of the LORD, yet not like David his father; he did in all things as Jō′ăsh his father had done. ⁴But the high places were not removed; the people still sacrificed and burned incense on the high places. ⁵And as soon as the royal power was firmly in his hand he killed his servants who had slain the king his father. ⁶But he did not put to death the children of the murderers; according to what is written in the book of the law of Moses, where the LORD commanded, "The fathers shall not be put to death for the children, or the children be put to death for the fathers; but every man shall die for his own sin."

7 He killed ten thousand Ē′dom-ītes in the Valley of Salt and took Sē′lạ by storm, and called it Jŏk′thē–ĕl, which is its name to this day.

8 Then Ăm·ạ·zī′ah sent messengers to Jĕ·hō′ăsh the son of Jĕ·hō′ạ·hăz, son of Jē′hū, king of Israel, saying, "Come, let us look one another in the face." ⁹And Jĕ·hō′ăsh king of Israel sent word to Ăm·ạ·zī′ah king of Judah, "A thistle on Lebanon sent to a cedar on Lebanon, saying, 'Give your daughter to my son for a wife'; and a wild beast of Lebanon passed by and trampled

14.2–6: 2 Chron 25.1–4.
14.7: 2 Chron 25.11. 14.8–14: 2 Chron 25.17–24.

down the thistle. ¹⁰You have indeed smitten E′dom, and your heart has lifted you up. Be content with your glory, and stay at home; for why should you provoke trouble so that you fall, you and Judah with you?" ¹¹But Ăm·a·zī′ah would not listen. So Jĕ·hō′ăsh king of Israel went up, and he and Ăm·a·zī′ah king of Judah faced one another in battle at Bĕth-shĕ′mĕsh, which belongs to Judah. ¹²And Judah was defeated by Israel, and every man fled to his home. ¹³And Jĕ·hō′ăsh king of Israel captured Ăm·a·zī′ah king of Judah, the son of Jehoash, son of Ā·ha·zī′ah, at Bĕth-shĕ′mĕsh, and came to Jerusalem, and broke down the wall of Jerusalem for four hundred cubits, from the E′phra-ĭm Gate to the Corner Gate. ¹⁴And he seized all the gold and silver, and all the vessels that were found in the house of the LORD and in the treasuries of the king's house, also hostages, and he returned to Sa·mâr′ĭ·a.

15 Now the rest of the acts of Jĕ-hō′ăsh which he did, and his might, and how he fought with Ăm·a·zī′ah king of Judah, are they not written in the Book of the Chronicles of the Kings of Israel? ¹⁶And Jĕ·hō′ăsh slept with his fathers, and was buried in Sa·mâr′-ĭ·a with the kings of Israel; and Jĕr·o-bō′am his son reigned in his stead.

17 Ăm·a·zī′ah the son of Jō′ăsh, king of Judah, lived fifteen years after the death of Jĕ·hō′ăsh son of Jĕ·hō′a·hăz, king of Israel. ¹⁸Now the rest of the deeds of Ăm·a·zī′ah, are they not written in the Book of the Chronicles of the Kings of Judah? ¹⁹And they made a conspiracy against him in Jerusalem, and he fled to Lā′chĭsh. But they sent after him to Lachish, and slew him there. ²⁰And they brought him upon horses; and he was buried in Jerusalem with his fathers in the city of David. ²¹And all the people of Judah took Ăz·a·rī′ah, who was sixteen years old, and made him king instead of his father Ăm·a·zī′ah. ²²He built E′lăth and restored it to Judah, after the king slept with his fathers.

23 In the fifteenth year of Ăm·a-zī′ah the son of Jō′ăsh, king of Judah, Jĕr·o·bō′am the son of Joash, king of Israel, began to reign in Sa·mâr′ĭ·a, and he reigned forty-one years. ²⁴And he did what was evil in the sight of the LORD; he did not depart from all the

sins of Jĕr·o·bō′am the son of Nē′băt, which he made Israel to sin. ²⁵He restored the border of Israel from the entrance of Hā′măth as far as the Sea of the Ăr′a·bah, according to the word of the LORD, the God of Israel, which he spoke by his servant Jonah the son of A·mĭt′taī, the prophet, who was from Găth-hē′phĕr. ²⁶For the LORD saw that the affliction of Israel was very bitter, for there was none left, bond or free, and there was none to help Israel. ²⁷But the LORD had not said that he would blot out the name of Israel from under heaven, so he saved them by the hand of Jĕr·o·bō′am the son of Jō′ăsh.

28 Now the rest of the acts of Jĕr-o·bō′am, and all that he did, and his might, how he fought, and how he recovered for Israel Damascus and Hā′măth, which had belonged to Judah, are they not written in the Book of the Chronicles of the Kings of Israel? ²⁹And Jĕr·o·bō′am slept with his fathers, the kings of Israel, and Zĕch·a·rī′ah his son reigned in his stead.

15 In the twenty-seventh year of Jĕr·o·bō′am king of Israel Ăz·a·rī′ah the son of Ăm·a·zī′ah, king of Judah, began to reign. ²He was sixteen years old when he began to reign, and he reigned fifty-two years in Jerusalem. His mother's name was Jĕc·o-lī′ah of Jerusalem. ³And he did what was right in the eyes of the LORD, according to all that his father Ăm·a-zī′ah had done. ⁴Nevertheless the high places were not taken away; the people still sacrificed and burned incense on the high places. ⁵And the LORD smote the king, so that he was a leper to the day of his death, and he dwelt in a separate house. And Jō′tham the king's son was over the household, governing the people of the land. ⁶Now the rest of the acts of Ăz·a·rī′ah, and all that he did, are they not written in the Book of the Chronicles of the Kings of Judah? ⁷And Ăz·a·rī′ah slept with his fathers, and they buried him with his fathers in the city of David, and Jō′tham his son reigned in his stead.

8 In the thirty-eighth year of Ăz·a-rī′ah king of Judah Zĕch·a·rī′ah the son of Jĕr·o·bō′am reigned over Israel in Sa·mâr′ĭ·a six months. ⁹And he

14.17-20: 2 Chron 25.25-28.   **14.21, 22:** 2 Chron 26.1,2.   **15.2, 3:** 2 Chron 26.3, 4.   **15.5-7:** 2 Chron 26.20-23.

did what was evil in the sight of the LORD, as his fathers had done. He did not depart from the sins of Jĕr-o-bō'ạm the son of Nē'bặt, which he made Israel to sin. ¹⁰ Shăl'lụm the son of Jā'bĕsh conspired against him, and struck him down at Ĭb'lē-ạm,ʷ and killed him, and reigned in his stead. ¹¹ Now the rest of the deeds of Zĕch-ạ-rī'ạh, behold, they are written in the Book of the Chronicles of the Kings of Israel. ¹² (This was the promise of the LORD which he gave to Jē'hū, "Your sons shall sit upon the throne of Israel to the fourth generation." And so it came to pass.)

13 Shăl'lụm the son of Jā'bĕsh began to reign in the thirty-ninth year of Ŭz-zī'ạh king of Judah, and he reigned one month in Sạ-mâr'ĭ-ạ. ¹⁴ Then Mĕn'-ạ-hĕm the son of Gā'dī came up from Tĭr'zạh and came to Sạ-mâr'ĭ-ạ, and he struck down Shăl'lụm the son of Jā'bĕsh in Samaria and slew him, and reigned in his stead. ¹⁵ Now the rest of the deeds of Shăl'lụm, and the conspiracy which he made, behold, they are written in the Book of the Chronicles of the Kings of Israel. ¹⁶ At that time Mĕn'ạ-hĕm sacked Tặp'pū-ạhˣ and all who were in it and its territory from Tĭr'zạh on; because they did not open it to him, therefore he sacked it, and he ripped up all the women in it who were with child.

17 In the thirty-ninth year of Ăz-ạ-rī'ạh king of Judah Mĕn'ạ-hĕm the son of Gā'dī began to reign over Israel, and he reigned ten years in Sạ-mâr'ĭ-ạ. ¹⁸ And he did what was evil in the sight of the LORD; he did not depart all his days from all the sins of Jĕr-o-bō'ạm the son of Nē'bặt, which he made Israel to sin. ¹⁹ Pül the king of Assyria came against the land; and Mĕn'ạ-hĕm gave Pul a thousand talents of silver, that he might help him to confirm his hold of the royal power. ²⁰ Mĕn'ạ-hĕm exacted the money from Israel, that is, from all the wealthy men, fifty shekels of silver from every man, to give to the king of Assyria. So the king of Assyria turned back, and did not stay there in the land. ²¹ Now the rest of the deeds of Mĕn'ạ-hĕm, and all that he did, are they not written in the Book of the Chronicles of the Kings of Israel? ²² And Mĕn'ạ-hĕm slept with his fathers, and Pĕk-ạ-hī'ạh his son reigned in his stead.

23 In the fiftieth year of Ăz-ạ-rī'ạh king of Judah Pĕk-ạ-hī'ạh the son of Mĕn'ạ-hĕm began to reign over Israel in Sạ-mâr'ĭ-ạ, and he reigned two years. ²⁴ And he did what was evil in the sight of the LORD; he did not turn away from the sins of Jĕr-o-bō'ạm the son of Nē'bặt, which he made Israel to sin. ²⁵ And Pē'kạh the son of Rĕm-ạ-lī'ạh, his captain, conspired against him with fifty men of the Gileadites, and slew him in Sạ-mâr'ĭ-ạ, in the citadel of the king's house;ʸ he slew him, and reigned in his stead. ²⁶ Now the rest of the deeds of Pĕk-ạ-hī'ạh, and all that he did, behold, they are written in the Book of the Chronicles of the Kings of Israel.

27 In the fifty-second year of Ăz-ạ-rī'ạh king of Judah Pē'kạh the son of Rĕm-ạ-lī'ạh began to reign over Israel in Sạ-mâr'ĭ-ạ, and reigned twenty years. ²⁸ And he did what was evil in the sight of the LORD; he did not depart from the sins of Jĕr-o-bō'ạm the son of Nē'bặt, which he made Israel to sin.

29 In the days of Pē'kạh king of Israel Tĭg'lặth–pī-lē'şer king of Assyria came and captured Ī'jŏn, Ā'bel-bĕth–mā'ạ-cạh, Jạ-nō'ạh, Kē'dĕsh, Hā'zôr, Gilead, and Galilee, all the land of Năph'tạ-lī; and he carried the people captive to Assyria. ³⁰ Then Hō-shē'ạ the son of Ē'lạh made a conspiracy against Pē'kạh the son of Rĕm-ạ-lī'ạh, and struck him down, and slew him, and reigned in his stead, in the twentieth year of Jō'thạm the son of Ŭz-zī'ạh. ³¹ Now the rest of the acts of Pē'kạh, and all that he did, behold, they are written in the Book of the Chronicles of the Kings of Israel.

32 In the second year of Pē'kạh the son of Rĕm-ạ-lī'ạh, king of Israel, Jō'thạm the son of Ŭz-zī'ạh, king of Judah, began to reign. ³³ He was twenty-five years old when he began to reign, and he reigned sixteen years in Jerusalem. His mother's name was Jĕ-rü'shạ the daughter of Zā'dŏk. ³⁴ And he did what was right in the eyes of the LORD, according to all that his father Ŭz-zī'ạh had done. ³⁵ Nevertheless the high places were not removed; the people still sacrificed and burned

ʷGk Compare 9.27: Heb *before the people*
ˣCompare Gk: Heb *Tiphsah*
ʸHeb adds *Argob and Arieh*, which probably belong to the list of places in verse 29
15.33-35: 2 Chron 27.1-3.

incense on the high places. He built the upper gate of the house of the LORD. ³⁶ Now the rest of the acts of Jō′tham, and all that he did, are they not written in the Book of the Chronicles of the Kings of Judah? ³⁷ In those days the LORD began to send Rē′zĭn the king of Syria and Pē′kah the son of Rĕm·a·lī′ah against Judah. ³⁸ Jō′tham slept with his fathers, and was buried with his fathers in the city of David his father; and Ā′hăz his son reigned in his stead.

16 In the seventeenth year of Pē′kah the son of Rĕm·a·lī′ah, Ā′hăz the son of Jō′tham, king of Judah, began to reign. ² Ā′hăz was twenty years old when he began to reign, and he reigned sixteen years in Jerusalem. And he did not do what was right in the eyes of the LORD his God, as his father David had done, ³ but he walked in the way of the kings of Israel. He even burned his son as an offering,² according to the abominable practices of the nations whom the LORD drove out before the people of Israel. ⁴ And he sacrificed and burned incense on the high places, and on the hills, and under every green tree.

5 Then Rē′zĭn king of Syria and Pē′kah the son of Rĕm·a·lī′ah, king of Israel, came up to wage war on Jerusalem, and they besieged Ā′hăz but could not conquer him. ⁶ At that timeᵃ the king of Ē′domᵇ recovered Ē′lăth for Edom,ᵇ and drove the men of Judah from Elath; and the Ē′dom-ītes came to Elath, where they dwell to this day. ⁷ So Ā′hăz sent messengers to Tĭg′lăth–pī-lē′ṣer king of Assyria, saying, "I am your servant and your son. Come up, and rescue me from the hand of the king of Syria and from the hand of the king of Israel, who are attacking me." ⁸ Ā′hăz also took the silver and gold that was found in the house of the LORD and in the treasures of the king's house, and sent a present to the king of Assyria. ⁹ And the king of Assyria hearkened to him; the king of Assyria marched up against Damascus, and took it, carrying its people captive to Kīr, and he killed Rē′zĭn.

10 When King Ā′hăz went to Damascus to meet Tĭg′lăth–pī-lē′ṣer king of Assyria, he saw the altar that was at Damascus. And King Ahaz sent to Ū·rī′ah the priest a model of the altar, and its pattern, exact in all

its details. ¹¹ And Ū·rī′ah the priest built the altar; in accordance with all that King Ā′hăz had sent from Damascus, so Uriah the priest made it, before King Ahaz arrived from Damascus. ¹² And when the king came from Damascus, the king viewed the altar. Then the king drew near to the altar, and went up on it, ¹³ and burned his burnt offering and his cereal offering, and poured his drink offering, and threw the blood of his peace offerings upon the altar. ¹⁴ And the bronze altar which was before the LORD he removed from the front of the house, from the place between his altar and the house of the LORD, and put it on the north side of his altar. ¹⁵ And King Ā′hăz commanded Ū·rī′ah the priest, saying, "Upon the great altar burn the morning burnt offering, and the evening cereal offering, and the king's burnt offering, and his cereal offering, with the burnt offering of all the people of the land, and their cereal offering, and their drink offering; and throw upon it all the blood of the burnt offering, and all the blood of the sacrifice; but the bronze altar shall be for me to inquire by." ¹⁶ Ū·rī′ah the priest did all this, as King Ā′hăz commanded.

17 And King Ā′hăz cut off the frames of the stands, and removed the laver from them, and he took down the sea from off the bronze oxen that were under it, and put it upon a pediment of stone. ¹⁸ And the covered way for the sabbath which had been built inside the palace, and the outer entrance for the king he removed fromᶜ the house of the LORD, because of the king of Assyria. ¹⁹ Now the rest of the acts of Ā′hăz which he did, are they not written in the Book of the Chronicles of the Kings of Judah? ²⁰ And Ā′hăz slept with his fathers, and was buried with his fathers in the city of David; and Hĕz·e·kī′ah his son reigned in his stead.

17 In the twelfth year of Ā′hăz king of Judah Hō·shē′a the son of Ē′lah began to reign in Sa·mâr′ĭ·a over Israel, and he reigned nine years. ² And he did what was evil in the sight of the LORD, yet not as the kings of

ᶻOr *made his son to pass through the fire*
ᵃHeb *At that time Rezin*   ᵇHeb *Aram* (Syria)
ᶜCn: Heb *turned to*
15.38: 2 Chron 27.9.   16.2-4: 2 Chron 28.1-4.
16.20: 2 Chron 28.27.

Israel who were before him. ³Against him came up Shăl·măn·ē′şẹr king of Assyria; and Hō·shē′ạ became his vassal, and paid him tribute. ⁴But the king of Assyria found treachery in Hō·shē′ạ; for he had sent messengers to So, king of Egypt, and offered no tribute to the king of Assyria, as he had done year by year; therefore the king of Assyria shut him up, and bound him in prison. ⁵Then the king of Assyria invaded all the land and came to Sạ·mâr′ĭ·a, and for three years he besieged it. ⁶In the ninth year of Hō·shē′ạ the king of Assyria captured Sạ·mâr′ĭ·a, and he carried the Israelites away to Assyria, and placed them in Hā′lạh, and on the Hā′bôr, the river of Gō′zăn, and in the cities of the Mēdẹş.

7 And this was so, because the people of Israel had sinned against the LORD their God, who had brought them up out of the land of Egypt from under the hand of Pharaoh king of Egypt, and had feared other gods ⁸and walked in the customs of the nations whom the LORD drove out before the people of Israel, and in the customs which the kings of Israel had introduced.ᵈ ⁹And the people of Israel did secretly against the LORD their God things that were not right. They built for themselves high places at all their towns, from watchtower to fortified city; ¹⁰they set up for themselves pillars and Ạ·shē′rĭm on every high hill and under every green tree; ¹¹and there they burned incense on all the high places, as the nations did whom the LORD carried away before them. And they did wicked things, provoking the LORD to anger, ¹²and they served idols, of which the LORD had said to them, "You shall not do this." ¹³Yet the LORD warned Israel and Judah by every prophet and every seer, saying, "Turn from your evil ways and keep my commandments and my statutes, in accordance with all the law which I commanded your fathers, and which I sent to you by my servants the prophets." ¹⁴But they would not listen, but were stubborn, as their fathers had been, who did not believe in the LORD their God. ¹⁵They despised his statutes, and his covenant that he made with their fathers, and the warnings which he gave them. They went after false idols, and became false, and they followed the nations that were round

about them, concerning whom the LORD had commanded them that they should not do like them. ¹⁶And they forsook all the commandments of the LORD their God, and made for themselves molten images of two calves; and they made an Ạ·shē′rạh, and worshiped all the host of heaven, and served Bā′ạl. ¹⁷And they burned their sons and their daughters as offerings,ᵉ and used divination and sorcery, and sold themselves to do evil in the sight of the LORD, provoking him to anger. ¹⁸Therefore the LORD was very angry with Israel, and removed them out of his sight; none was left but the tribe of Judah only.

19 Judah also did not keep the commandments of the LORD their God, but walked in the customs which Israel had introduced. ²⁰And the LORD rejected all the descendants of Israel, and afflicted them, and gave them into the hand of spoilers, until he had cast them out of his sight.

21 When he had torn Israel from the house of David they made Jĕr·ọ·bō′ạm the son of Nē′băt king. And Jeroboam drove Israel from following the LORD and made them commit great sin. ²²The people of Israel walked in all the sins which Jĕr·ọ·bō′ạm did; they did not depart from them, ²³until the LORD removed Israel out of his sight, as he had spoken by all his servants the prophets. So Israel was exiled from their own land to Assyria until this day.

24 And the king of Assyria brought people from Babylon, Cū′thạh, Āv′vạ, Hā′măth, and Sĕph·ăr·vā′ĭm, and placed them in the cities of Sạ·mâr′ĭ·a instead of the people of Israel; and they took possession of Samaria, and dwelt in its cities. ²⁵And at the beginning of their dwelling there, they did not fear the LORD; therefore the LORD sent lions among them, which killed some of them. ²⁶So the king of Assyria was told, "The nations which you have carried away and placed in the cities of Sạ·mâr′ĭ·a do not know the law of the god of the land; therefore he has sent lions among them, because they do not know the law of the god of the land." ²⁷Then the king of Assyria commanded,

ᵈHeb obscure
ᵉOr made their sons and their daughters pass through the fire

"Send there one of the priests whom you carried away thence; and let him/ go and dwell there, and teach them the law of the god of the land." ²⁸ So one of the priests whom they had carried away from Să·mâr'ĭ·a came and dwelt in Běth'ęl, and taught them how they should fear the LORD.

29 But every nation still made gods of its own, and put them in the shrines of the high places which the Să·mâr'ĭ·tąns had made, every nation in the cities in which they dwelt; ³⁰ the men of Babylon made Sŭc'cŏth–bē'nŏth, the men of Cŭth made Něr'găl, the men of Hā'măth made A·shī'ma, ³¹ and the Ăv'vītes made Nĭb'hăz and Tăr'tăk; and the Sě·phăr'vītes burned their children in the fire to A·drăm'mę·lěch and A·năm'mę·lěch, the gods of Sěph·ăr·vā'ĭm. ³² They also feared the LORD, and appointed from among themselves all sorts of people as priests of the high places, who sacrificed for them in the shrines of the high places. ³³ So they feared the LORD but also served their own gods, after the manner of the nations from among whom they had been carried away. ³⁴ To this day they do according to the former manner.

They do not fear the LORD, and they do not follow the statutes or the ordinances or the law or the commandment which the LORD commanded the children of Jacob, whom he named Israel. ³⁵ The LORD made a covenant with them, and commanded them, "You shall not fear other gods or bow yourselves to them or serve them or sacrifice to them; ³⁶ but you shall fear the LORD, who brought you out of the land of Egypt with great power and with an outstretched arm; you shall bow yourselves to him, and to him you shall sacrifice. ³⁷ And the statutes and the ordinances and the law and the commandment which he wrote for you, you shall always be careful to do. You shall not fear other gods, ³⁸ and you shall not forget the covenant that I have made with you. You shall not fear other gods, ³⁹ but you shall fear the LORD your God, and he will deliver you out of the hand of all your enemies." ⁴⁰ However they would not listen, but they did according to their former manner. 41 So these nations feared the LORD, and also served their graven images; their children likewise, and their children's children – as their fathers did, so they do to this day.

18 In the third year of Hō·shē'a son of Ē'lah, king of Israel, Hěz·ę·kī'ah the son of Ā·hăz, king of Judah, began to reign. ²He was twenty-five years old when he began to reign, and he reigned twenty-nine years in Jerusalem. His mother's name was Ā'bī the daughter of Zěch·ą·rī'ah. ³And he did what was right in the eyes of the LORD, according to all that David his father had done. ⁴He removed the high places, and broke the pillars, and cut down the A·shē'rah. And he broke in pieces the bronze serpent that Moses had made, for until those days the people of Israel had burned incense to it; it was called Ně·hŭsh'tan. ⁵He trusted in the LORD the God of Israel; so that there was none like him among all the kings of Judah after him, nor among those who were before him. ⁶For he held fast to the LORD; he did not depart from following him, but kept the commandments which the LORD commanded Moses. ⁷And the LORD was with him; wherever he went forth, he prospered. He rebelled against the king of Assyria, and would not serve him. ⁸He smote the Phĭ·lĭs'tĭnes as far as Gā'za and its territory, from watchtower to fortified city.

9 In the fourth year of King Hěz·ę·kī'ah, which was the seventh year of Hō·shē'a son of Ē'lah, king of Israel, Shăl·man·ē'şer king of Assyria came up against Să·mâr'ĭ·a and besieged it ¹⁰ and at the end of three years he took it. In the sixth year of Hěz·ę·kī'ah, which was the ninth year of Hō·shē'a king of Israel, Să·mâr'ĭ·a was taken. ¹¹The king of Assyria carried the Israelites away to Assyria, and put them in Hā'lah, and on the Hā'bôr, the river of Gō'zăn, and in the cities of the Mēdeş, ¹²because they did not obey the voice of the LORD their God but transgressed his covenant, even all that Moses the servant of the LORD commanded; they neither listened nor obeyed.

13 In the fourteenth year of King Hěz·ę·kī'ah Sěn·năch·ę'rĭb king of Assyria came up against all the fortified cities of Judah and took them.

/Syr Vg: Heb *them*
18.1-3: 2 Chron 29.1, 2.
18.13-19.37: 2 Chron 32.1-21; Is 36.1-37.38.

¹⁴ And Hĕz·e·kī′ah king of Judah sent to the king of Assyria at Lā′chĭsh, saying, "I have done wrong; withdraw from me; whatever you impose on me I will bear." And the king of Assyria required of Hezekiah king of Judah three hundred talents of silver and thirty talents of gold. ¹⁵ And Hĕz·e·kī′ah gave him all the silver that was found in the house of the LORD, and in the treasuries of the king's house. ¹⁶ At that time Hĕz·e·kī′ah stripped the gold from the doors of the temple of the LORD, and from the doorposts which Hezekiah king of Judah had overlaid and gave it to the king of Assyria. ¹⁷ And the king of Assyria sent the Tār′tan, the Răb′sa·rĭs, and the Răb′sha·kĕh with a great army from Lā′chĭsh to King Hĕz·e·kī′ah at Jerusalem. And they went up and came to Jerusalem. When they arrived, they came and stood by the conduit of the upper pool, which is on the highway to the Fuller's Field. ¹⁸ And when they called for the king, there came out to them Ė·lī′a·kĭm the son of Hĭl·kī′ah, who was over the household, and Shĕb′nah the secretary, and Jō′ah the son of Ā′săph, the recorder.

¹⁹ And the Răb′sha·kĕh said to them, "Say to Hĕz·e·kī′ah, 'Thus says the great king, the king of Assyria: On what do you rest this confidence of yours? ²⁰ Do you think that mere words are strategy and power for war? On whom do you now rely, that you have rebelled against me? ²¹ Behold, you are relying now on Egypt, that broken reed of a staff, which will pierce the hand of any man who leans on it. Such is Pharaoh king of Egypt to all who rely on him. ²² But if you say to me, "We rely on the LORD our God," is it not he whose high places and altars Hĕz·e·kī′ah has removed, saying to Judah and to Jerusalem, "You shall worship before this altar in Jerusalem"? ²³ Come now, make a wager with my master the king of Assyria: I will give you two thousand horses, if you are able on your part to set riders upon them. ²⁴ How then can you repulse a single captain among the least of my master's servants, when you rely on Egypt for chariots and for horsemen? ²⁵ Moreover, is it without the LORD that I have come up against this place to destroy it? The LORD said

to me, Go up against this land, and destroy it.'"

²⁶ Then Ė·lī′a·kĭm the son of Hĭl·kī′ah, and Shĕb′nah, and Jō′ah, said to the Răb′sha·kĕh, "Pray, speak to your servants in the Ăr·a·mā′ĭc language for we understand it; do not speak to us in the language of Judah within the hearing of the people who are on the wall." ²⁷ But the Răb′sha·kĕh said to them, "Has my master sent me to speak these words to your master and to you, and not to the men sitting on the wall, who are doomed with you to eat their own dung and to drink their own urine?"

²⁸ Then the Răb′sha·kĕh stood and called out in a loud voice in the language of Judah: "Hear the word of the great king, the king of Assyria! ²⁹ Thus says the king: 'Do not let Hĕz·e·kī′ah deceive you, for he will not be able to deliver you out of my hand. ³⁰ Do not let Hĕz·e·kī′ah make you to rely on the LORD by saying, The LORD will surely deliver us, and this city will not be given into the hand of the king of Assyria.' ³¹ Do not listen to Hĕz·e·kī′ah; for thus says the king of Assyria: 'Make your peace with me and come out to me; then every one of you will eat of his own vine, and every one of his own fig tree, and every one of you will drink the water of his own cistern; ³² until I come and take you away to a land like your own land, a land of grain and wine, a land of bread and vineyards, a land of olive trees and honey, that you may live, and not die. And do not listen to Hĕz·e·kī′ah when he misleads you by saying, The LORD will deliver us. ³³ Has any of the gods of the nations ever delivered his land out of the hand of the king of Assyria? ³⁴ Where are the gods of Hā′măth and Ăr′păd? Where are the gods of Sĕph·ār·vā′ĭm, Hē′na, and Ĭv′vah? Have they delivered Sa·mâr′ĭ·a out of my hand? ³⁵ Who among all the gods of the countries have delivered their countries out of my hand, that the LORD should deliver Jerusalem out of my hand?'"

³⁶ But the people were silent and answered him not a word, for the king's command was, "Do not answer him." ³⁷ Then Ė·lī′a·kĭm the son of Hĭl·kī′ah, who was over the household, and Shĕb′na the secretary, and Jō′ah the son of Ā′săph, the recorder,

came to Hĕz·e·kī′ah with their clothes rent, and told him the words of the Răb′sha·keh.

19 When King Hĕz·e·kī′ah heard it, he rent his clothes, and covered himself with sackcloth, and went into the house of the LORD. ²And he sent Ė·lī′a·kim, who was over the household, and Shĕb′na the secretary, and the senior priests, covered with sackcloth, to the prophet Ī·sāi′ah the son of Ā′mŏz. ³They said to him, "Thus says Hĕz·e·kī′ah, This day is a day of distress, of rebuke, and of disgrace; children have come to the birth, and there is no strength to bring them forth. ⁴It may be that the LORD your God heard all the words of the Răb′sha·keh, whom his master the king of Assyria has sent to mock the living God, and will rebuke the words which the LORD your God has heard; therefore lift up your prayer for the remnant that is left." ⁵When the servants of King Hĕz·e·kī′ah came to Ī·sāi′ah, ⁶Ī·sāi′ah said to them, "Say to your master, 'Thus says the LORD: Do not be afraid because of the words that you have heard, with which the servants of the king of Assyria have reviled me. ⁷Behold, I will put a spirit in him, so that he shall hear a rumor and return to his own land; and I will cause him to fall by the sword in his own land.' "

8 The Răb′sha·keh returned, and found the king of Assyria fighting against Lĭb′nah; for he heard that the king had left Lā′chĭsh. ⁹And when the king heard concerning Tĭr·hā′kah king of Ethiopia, "Behold, he has set out to fight against you," he sent messengers again to Hĕz·e·kī′ah, saying, ¹⁰"Thus shall you speak to Hĕz·e·kī′ah king of Judah: 'Do not let your God on whom you rely deceive you by promising that Jerusalem will not be given into the hand of the king of Assyria. ¹¹Behold, you have heard what the kings of Assyria have done to all lands, destroying them utterly. And shall you be delivered? ¹²Have the gods of the nations delivered them, the nations which my fathers destroyed, Gō′zăn, Hār′an, Rē′zĕph, and the people of Eden who were in Tĕl·ăs′sar? ¹³Where is the king of Hā′măth, the king of Ăr′păd, the king of the city of Sĕph·ăr·vā′im, the king of Hē′na, or the king of Ĭv′vah?' "

14 Hĕz·e·kī′ah received the letter from the hand of the messengers, and read it; and Hezekiah went up to the house of the LORD, and spread it before the LORD. ¹⁵And Hĕz·e·kī′ah prayed before the LORD, and said: "O LORD the God of Israel, who art enthroned above the cherubim, thou art the God, thou alone, of all the kingdoms of the earth; thou hast made heaven and earth. ¹⁶Incline thy ear, O LORD, and hear; open thy eyes, O LORD, and see; and hear the words of Sĕn·năch′e·rĭb, which he has sent to mock the living God. ¹⁷Of a truth, O LORD, the kings of Assyria have laid waste the nations and their lands, ¹⁸and have cast their gods into the fire; for they were no gods, but the work of men's hands, wood and stone; therefore they were destroyed. ¹⁹So now, O LORD our God, save us, I beseech thee, from his hand, that all the kingdoms of the earth may know that thou, O LORD, art God alone."

20 Then Ī·sāi′ah the son of Ā·mŏz sent to Hĕz·e·kī′ah, saying, "Thus says the LORD, the God of Israel: Your prayer to me about Sĕn·năch′e·rĭb king of Assyria I have heard. ²¹This is the word that the LORD has spoken concerning him:

"She despises you, she scorns you—
    the virgin daughter of Zion;
she wags her head behind you—
    the daughter of Jerusalem.

²²"Whom have you mocked and reviled?
    Against whom have you raised your voice
and haughtily lifted your eyes?
    Against the Holy One of Israel!
²³By your messengers you have mocked the Lord,
    and you have said, 'With my many chariots
I have gone up the heights of the mountains,
    to the far recesses of Lebanon;
I felled its tallest cedars,
    its choicest cypresses;
I entered its farthest retreat,
    its densest forest.
²⁴I dug wells
    and drank foreign waters,
and I dried up with the sole of my foot
    all the streams of Egypt.'

25 "Have you not heard
that I determined it long ago?
I planned from days of old
what now I bring to pass,
that you should turn fortified cities
into heaps of ruins,
26 while their inhabitants, shorn of
strength,
are dismayed and confounded,
and have become like plants of the
field,
and like tender grass,
like grass on the housetops;
blighted before it is grown?

27 "But I know your sitting down
and your going out and coming in,
and your raging against me.
28 Because you have raged against me
and your arrogance has come into
my ears,
I will put my hook in your nose
and my bit in your mouth,
and I will turn you back on the way
by which you came.

29 "And this shall be the sign for
you: this year you shall eat what grows
of itself, and in the second year what
springs of the same; then in the third
year sow, and reap, and plant vineyards, and eat their fruit. 30 And the surviving remnant of the house of Judah
shall again take root downward, and
bear fruit upward; 31 for out of Jerusalem shall go forth a remnant, and out
of Mount Zion a band of survivors. The
zeal of the LORD will do this.

32 "Therefore thus says the LORD
concerning the king of Assyria, He
shall not come into this city or shoot
an arrow there, or come before it
with a shield or cast up a siege mound
against it. 33 By the way that he came,
by the same he shall return, and he
shall not come into this city, says the
LORD. 34 For I will defend this city to
save it, for my own sake and for the
sake of my servant David."

35 And that night the angel of the
LORD went forth, and slew a hundred
and eighty-five thousand in the camp
of the Assyrians; and when men arose
early in the morning, behold, these
were all dead bodies. 36 Then Sĕn-
năch'ę·rĭb king of Assyria departed,
and went home, and dwelt at Nĭn'ę-
vĕh. 37 And as he was worshiping in
the house of Nĭs'rŏch his god, Ą·drăm'-
mę·lĕch and Shą·rē'zęr, his sons,

slew him with the sword, and escaped into the land of Ăr'ą·răt. And
Ē·sãr·hăd'dǫn his son reigned in his
stead.

20 In those days Hĕz·ę·kī'ąh became sick and was at the point
of death. And Ī·sāi'ąh the prophet the
son of Ā'mŏz came to him, and said to
him, "Thus says the LORD, 'Set your
house in order; for you shall die, you
shall not recover.'" 2 Then Hĕz·ę·kī'ąh
turned his face to the wall, and prayed
to the LORD, saying, 3 "Remember now,
O LORD, I beseech thee, how I have
walked before thee in faithfulness
and with a whole heart, and have
done what is good in thy sight."
And Hĕz·ę·kī'ąh wept bitterly. 4 And
before Ī·sāi'ąh had gone out of the
middle court, the word of the LORD
came to him: 5 "Turn back, and say
to Hĕz·ę·kī'ąh the prince of my people,
Thus says the LORD, the God of David
your father: I have heard your prayer,
I have seen your tears; behold, I will
heal you; on the third day you shall
go up to the house of the LORD. 6 And I
will add fifteen years to your life. I will
deliver you and this city out of the hand
of the king of Assyria, and I will defend
this city for my own sake and for my
servant David's sake." 7 And Ī·sāi'ąh
said, "Bring a cake of figs. And let them
take and lay it on the boil, that he may
recover."

8 And Hĕz·ę·kī'ąh said to Ī·sāi'ąh,
"What shall be the sign that the LORD
will heal me, and that I shall go up to
the house of the LORD on the third
day?" 9 And Ī·sāi'ąh said, "This is the
sign to you from the LORD, that the
LORD will do the thing that he has
promised: shall the shadow go forward
ten steps, or go back ten steps?" 10 And
Hĕz·ę·kī'ąh answered, "It is an easy
thing for the shadow to lengthen ten
steps; rather let the shadow go back
ten steps." 11 And Ī·sāi'ąh the prophet
cried to the LORD; and he brought
the shadow back ten steps, by which
the sun*g* had declined on the dial of
Ā'hăz.

12 At that time Mĕr'ǫ·dăch–băl'-
ą·dąn the son of Băl'ą·dąn, king of
Babylon, sent envoys with letters and a
present to Hĕz·ę·kī'ah; for he heard
that Hezekiah had been sick. 13 And
Hĕz·ę·kī'ąh welcomed them, and he

g Syr See Is 38.8 and Tg: Heb lacks *the sun*
20.1-21: 2 Chron 32.24-33; Is 38.1-39.8.

showed them all his treasure house, the silver, the gold, the spices, the precious oil, his armory, all that was found in his storehouses; there was nothing in his house or in all his realm that Hezekiah did not show them. ¹⁴Then Ī·sāi′ạh the prophet came to King Hĕz·ẹ·kī′ạh, and said to him, "What did these men say? And whence did they come to you?" And Hezekiah said, "They have come from a far country, from Babylon." ¹⁵He said, "What have they seen in your house?" And Hĕz·ẹ·kī′ạh answered, "They have seen all that is in my house; there is nothing in my storehouses that I did not show them."

16 Then Ī·sāi′ạh said to Hĕz·ẹ·kī′ạh, "Hear the word of the LORD: ¹⁷Behold, the days are coming, when all that is in your house, and that which your fathers have stored up till this day, shall be carried to Babylon; nothing shall be left, says the LORD. ¹⁸And some of your own sons, who are born to you, shall be taken away; and they shall be eunuchs in the palace of the king of Babylon." ¹⁹Then said Hĕz·ẹ·kī′ạh to Ī·sāi′ạh, "The word of the LORD which you have spoken is good." For he thought, "Why not, if there will be peace and security in my days?"

20 The rest of the deeds of Hĕz·ẹ·kī′ạh, and all his might, and how he made the pool and the conduit and brought water into the city, are they not written in the Book of the Chronicles of the Kings of Judah? ²¹And Hĕz·ẹ·kī′ạh slept with his fathers; and Mạ·nǎs′sẹh his son reigned in his stead.

21 Mạ·nǎs′sẹh was twelve years old when he began to reign, and he reigned fifty-five years in Jerusalem. His mother's name was Hĕph′zĭ·bạh. ²And he did what was evil in the sight of the LORD, according to the abominable practices of the nations whom the LORD drove out before the people of Israel. ³For he rebuilt the high places which Hĕz·ẹ·kī′ạh his father had destroyed; and he erected altars for Bā′ạl, and made an Ạ·shē′rạh, as Ā′hǎb king of Israel had done, and worshiped all the host of heaven, and served them. ⁴And he built altars in the house of the LORD, of which the LORD had said, "In Jerusalem will I put my name." ⁵And he built altars for all the host of heaven in the two courts of the house of the LORD. ⁶And he burned his son as an offering, and practiced soothsaying and augury, and dealt with mediums and with wizards. He did much evil in the sight of the LORD, provoking him to anger. ⁷And the graven image of Ạ·shē′rạh that he had made he set in the house of which the LORD said to David and to Solomon his son, "In this house, and in Jerusalem, which I have chosen out of all the tribes of Israel, I will put my name for ever; ⁸and I will not cause the feet of Israel to wander any more out of the land which I gave to their fathers, if only they will be careful to do according to all that I have commanded them, and according to all the law that my servant Moses commanded them." ⁹But they did not listen, and Mạ·nǎs′sẹh seduced them to do more evil than the nations had done whom the LORD destroyed before the people of Israel.

10 And the LORD said by his servants the prophets, ¹¹"Because Mạ·nǎs′sẹh king of Judah has committed these abominations, and has done things more wicked than all that the Ăm′ọ·rītes did, who were before him, and has made Judah also to sin with his idols; ¹²therefore thus says the LORD, the God of Israel, Behold, I am bringing upon Jerusalem and Judah such evil that the ears of every one who hears of it will tingle. ¹³And I will stretch over Jerusalem the measuring line of Sạ·mâr′i·ạ, and the plummet of the house of Ā′hǎb; and I will wipe Jerusalem as one wipes a dish, wiping it and turning it upside down. ¹⁴And I will cast off the remnant of my heritage, and give them into the hand of their enemies, and they shall become a prey and a spoil to all their enemies, ¹⁵because they have done what is evil in my sight and have provoked me to anger, since the day their fathers came out of Egypt, even to this day."

16 Moreover Mạ·nǎs′sẹh shed very much innocent blood, till he had filled Jerusalem from one end to another, besides the sin which he made Judah to sin so that they did what was evil in the sight of the LORD.

17 Now the rest of the acts of Mạ·nǎs′sẹh, and all that he did, and the sin that he committed, are they not written in the Book of the Chron-

21.1-9: 2 Chron 33.1-9.

icles of the Kings of Judah? ¹⁸And Ma·năs′seh slept with his fathers, and was buried in the garden of his house, in the garden of Ŭz′za; and Ā′mŏn his son reigned in his stead. 19 Ā′mŏn was twenty-two years old when he began to reign, and he reigned two years in Jerusalem. His mother's name was Mĕ·shŭl′lĕ·mĕth the daughter of Hā′ruz of Jŏt′bah. ²⁰And he did what was evil in the sight of the LORD, as Ma·năs′seh his father had done. ²¹He walked in all the way in which his father walked, and served the idols that his father served, and worshiped them; ²²he forsook the LORD, the God of his fathers, and did not walk in the way of the LORD. ²³And the servants of Ā′mŏn conspired against him, and killed the king in his house. ²⁴But the people of the land slew all those who had conspired against King Ā′mŏn, and the people of the land made Jŏ′sī′ah his son king in his stead. ²⁵Now the rest of the acts of Ā′mŏn which he did, are they not written in the Book of the Chronicles of the Kings of Judah? ²⁶And he was buried in his tomb in the garden of Ŭz′za; and Jŏ′sī′ah his son reigned in his stead.

22 Jŏ′sī′ah was eight years old when he began to reign, and he reigned thirty-one years in Jerusalem. His mother's name was Jĕ·dī′dah the daughter of A·dāi′ah of Bŏz′kăth. ²And he did what was right in the eyes of the LORD, and walked in all the way of David his father, and he did not turn aside to the right hand or to the left.

3 In the eighteenth year of King Jŏ′sī′ah, the king sent Shā′phan the son of Az·a·lī′ah, son of Mĕ·shŭl′lam, the secretary, to the house of the LORD, saying, ⁴"Go up to Hĭl·kī′ah the high priest, that he may reckon the amount of the money which has been brought into the house of the LORD, which the keepers of the threshold have collected from the people; ⁵and let it be given into the hand of the workmen who have the oversight of the house of the LORD; and let them give it to the workmen who are at the house of the LORD, repairing the house, ⁶that is, to the carpenters, and to the builders, and to the masons, as well as for buying timber and quarried stone to repair the house. ⁷But no accounting shall be asked from them for the

money which is delivered into their hand, for they deal honestly."

8 And Hĭl·kī′ah the high priest said to Shā′phan the secretary, "I have found the book of the law in the house of the LORD." And Hilkiah gave the book to Shaphan, and he read it. ⁹And Shā′phan the secretary came to the king, and reported to the king, "Your servants have emptied out the money that was found in the house, and have delivered it into the hand of the workmen who have the oversight of the house of the LORD." ¹⁰Then Shā′phan the secretary told the king, "Hĭl·kī′ah the priest has given me a book." And Shaphan read it before the king.

11 And when the king heard the words of the book of the law, he rent his clothes. ¹²And the king commanded Hĭl·kī′ah the priest, and A·hī′kăm the son of Shā′phan, and Ăch′bôr the son of Mī·cāi′ah, and Shaphan the secretary, and A·sāi′ah the king's servant, saying, ¹³"Go, inquire of the LORD for me, and for the people, and for all Judah, concerning the words of this book that has been found; for great is the wrath of the LORD that is kindled against us, because our fathers have not obeyed the words of this book, to do according to all that is written concerning us."

14 So Hĭl·kī′ah the priest, and A·hī′-kăm, and Ăch′bôr, and Shā′phan, and A·sāi′ah went to Hŭl′dah the prophetess, the wife of Shăl′lum the son of Tĭk′vah, son of Hār′hăs, keeper of the wardrobe (now she dwelt in Jerusalem in the Second Quarter); and they talked with her. ¹⁵And she said to them, "Thus says the LORD, the God of Israel: 'Tell the man who sent you to me, ¹⁶Thus says the LORD, Behold, I will bring evil upon this place and upon its inhabitants, all the words of the book which the king of Judah has read. ¹⁷Because they have forsaken me and have burned incense to other gods, that they might provoke me to anger with all the work of their hands, therefore my wrath will be kindled against this place, and it will not be quenched. ¹⁸But as to the king of Judah, who sent you to inquire of the LORD, thus shall you say to him, Thus says the LORD, the God of Israel: Regarding the words

21.18: 2 Chron 33.20. **21.19-24:** 2 Chron 33.21-25. **22.1, 2:** 2 Chron 34.1, 2. **22.3-7:** 2 Chron 34.8-12.

which you have heard, ¹⁹because your heart was penitent, and you humbled yourself before the LORD, when you heard how I spoke against this place, and against its inhabitants, that they should become a desolation and a curse, and you have rent your clothes and wept before me, I also have heard you, says the LORD. ²⁰Therefore, behold, I will gather you to your fathers, and you shall be gathered to your grave in peace, and your eyes shall not see all the evil which I will bring upon this place.'" And they brought back word to the king.

23 Then the king sent, and all the elders of Judah and Jerusalem were gathered to him. ²And the king went up to the house of the LORD, and with him all the men of Judah and all the inhabitants of Jerusalem, and the priests and the prophets, all the people, both small and great; and he read in their hearing all the words of the book of the covenant which had been found in the house of the LORD. ³And the king stood by the pillar and made a covenant before the LORD, to walk after the LORD and to keep his commandments and his testimonies and his statutes, with all his heart and all his soul, to perform the words of this covenant that were written in this book; and all the people joined in the covenant.

4 And the king commanded Hĭl-kī'ah, the high priest, and the priests of the second order, and the keepers of the threshold, to bring out of the temple of the LORD all the vessels made for Bā'al, for Ạ·shē'rah, and for all the host of heaven; he burned them outside Jerusalem in the fields of the Kĭd'ron, and carried their ashes to Bĕth'ĕl. ⁵And he deposed the idolatrous priests whom the kings of Judah had ordained to burn incense in the high places at the cities of Judah and round about Jerusalem; those also who burned incense to Bā'al, to the sun, and the moon, and the constellations, and all the host of the heavens. ⁶And he brought out the Ạ·shē'rah from the house of the LORD, outside Jerusalem, to the brook Kĭd'ron, and burned it at the brook Kidron, and beat it to dust and cast the dust of it upon the graves of the common people. ⁷And he broke down the houses of the male cult prostitutes which were in the house of the LORD, where the women wove

hangings for the Ạ·shē'rah. ⁸And he brought all the priests out of the cities of Judah, and defiled the high places where the priests had burned incense, from Gē'ba to Bē'ẹr-shē'ba; and he broke down the high places of the gates that were at the entrance of the gate of Joshua the governor of the city, which were on one's left at the gate of the city. ⁹However, the priests of the high places did not come up to the altar of the LORD in Jerusalem, but they ate unleavened bread among their brethren. ¹⁰And he defiled Tō'phĕth, which is in the valley of the sons of Hĭn'nom, that no one might burn his son or his daughter as an offering to Mō'lĕch. ¹¹And he removed the horses that the kings of Judah had dedicated to the sun, at the entrance to the house of the LORD, by the chamber of Nā'than–mē'lĕch the chamberlain, which was in the precincts; ʰ and he burned the chariots of the sun with fire. ¹²And the altars on the roof of the upper chamber of Ā'hăz, which the kings of Judah had made, and the altars which Mạ·nãs'sẹh had made in the two courts of the house of the LORD, he pulled down and broke in pieces,ⁱ and cast the dust of them into the brook Kĭd'-ron. ¹³And the king defiled the high places that were east of Jerusalem, to the south of the mount of corruption, which Solomon the king of Israel had built for Ăsh'tō·rĕth the abomination of the Sĭ·dō'nĭ·ạns, and for Chē'mŏsh the abomination of Mō'ăb, and for Mĭl'-cŏm the abomination of the Ăm'mo-nītes. ¹⁴And he broke in pieces the pillars, and cut down the Ạ·shē'rĭm, and filled their places with the bones of men.

15 Moreover the altar at Bĕth'ĕl, the high place erected by Jĕr·o·bō'am the son of Nē'băt, who made Israel to sin, that altar with the high place he pulled down and he broke in pieces its stones,ʲ crushing them to dust; also he burned the Ạ·shē'rah. ¹⁶And as Jō·sī'ah turned, he saw the tombs there on the mount; and he sent and took the bones out of the tombs, and burned them upon the altar, and defiled it, according to the word of the LORD which the man of God pro-

---

ʰThe meaning of the Hebrew word is uncertain
ⁱHeb *pieces from there*
ʲGk: Heb *he burned the high place*
23.4-20: 2 Chron 34.3-7.

claimed, who had predicted these things. ¹⁷Then he said, "What is yonder monument that I see?" And the men of the city told him, "It is the tomb of the man of God who came from Judah and predicted these things which you have done against the altar at Bĕth'el." ¹⁸And he said, "Let him be; let no man move his bones." So they let his bones alone, with the bones of the prophet who came out of Să·mâr'ĭ·ă. ¹⁹And all the shrines also of the high places that were in the cities of Să·mâr'ĭ·ă, which kings of Israel had made, provoking the LORD to anger, Jō·sī'ah removed; he did to them according to all that he had done at Bĕth'el. ²⁰And he slew all the priests of the high places who were there, upon the altars, and burned the bones of men upon them. Then he returned to Jerusalem.

21 And the king commanded all the people, "Keep the passover to the LORD your God, as it is written in this book of the covenant." ²²For no such passover had been kept since the days of the judges who judged Israel, or during all the days of the kings of Israel or of the kings of Judah; ²³but in the eighteenth year of King Jō·sī'ah this passover was kept to the LORD in Jerusalem.

24 Moreover Jō·sī'ah put away the mediums and the wizards and the teraphim and the idols and all the abominations that were seen in the land of Judah and in Jerusalem, that he might establish the words of the law which were written in the book that Hĭl·kī'ah the priest found in the house of the LORD. ²⁵Before him there was no king like him, who turned to the LORD with all his heart and with all his soul and with all his might, according to all the law of Moses; nor did any like him arise after him.

26 Still the LORD did not turn from the fierceness of his great wrath, by which his anger was kindled against Judah, because of all the provocations with which Mă·năs'seh had provoked him. ²⁷And the LORD said, "I will remove Judah also out of my sight, as I have removed Israel, and I will cast off this city which I have chosen, Jerusalem, and the house of which I said, My name shall be there."

28 Now the rest of the acts of Jō·sī'ah, and all that he did, are they not written in the Book of the Chronicles of the Kings of Judah? ²⁹In his days Pharaoh Nē'cō king of Egypt went up to the king of Assyria to the river Euphrates. King Jō·sī'ah went to meet him; and Pharaoh Neco slew him at Mĕ·gĭd'dō, when he saw him. ³⁰And his servants carried him dead in a chariot from Mĕ·gĭd'dō, and brought him to Jerusalem, and buried him in his own tomb. And the people of the land took Jĕ·hō'ă·hăz the son of Jō·sī'ah, and anointed him, and made him king in his father's stead.

31 Jĕ·hō'ă·hăz was twenty-three years old when he began to reign, and he reigned three months in Jerusalem. His mother's name was Hă·mü'tăl the daughter of Jĕr·e·mī'ah of Lĭb'nah. ³²And he did what was evil in the sight of the LORD, according to all that his fathers had done. ³³And Pharaoh Nē'cō put him in bonds at Rĭb'lah in the land of Hā'măth, that he might not reign in Jerusalem, and laid upon the land a tribute of a hundred talents of silver and a talent of gold. ³⁴And Pharaoh Nē'cō made Ĕ·lī'ă·kĭm the son of Jō·sī'ah king in the place of Josiah his father, and changed his name to Jĕ·hoi'ă·kĭm. But he took Jĕ·hō'ă·hăz away; and he came to Egypt, and died there. ³⁵And Jĕ·hoi'ă·kĭm gave the silver and the gold to Pharaoh, but he taxed the land to give the money according to the command of Pharaoh. He exacted the silver and the gold of the people of the land, from every one according to his assessment, to give it to Pharaoh Nē'cō.

36 Jĕ·hoi'ă·kĭm was twenty-five years old when he began to reign, and he reigned eleven years in Jerusalem. His mother's name was Zĕ·bī'dah the daughter of Pĕ·dāi'ah of Rü'mah. ³⁷And he did what was evil in the sight of the LORD, according to all that his fathers had done.

24 In his days Nĕ·bü·chăd·nĕz'zar king of Babylon came up, and Jĕ·hoi'ă·kĭm became his servant three years; then he turned and rebelled against him. ²And the LORD sent against him bands of the Chăl·dē'ans, and bands of the Syrians, and bands of the Mō'ăb·ītes, and bands of the Ăm'mo·nītes, and sent them against Judah to destroy it, according to the word of the LORD which he spoke by

23.21-23: 2 Chron 35.1-19. 23.30-34: 2 Chron 36.1-4. 23.36-24.6: 2 Chron 36.5-8.

his servants the prophets. ³Surely this came upon Judah at the command of the Lord, to remove them out of his sight, for the sins of Mạ·nǎs′sẹh, according to all that he had done, ⁴and also for the innocent blood that he had shed; for he filled Jerusalem with innocent blood, and the Lord would not pardon. ⁵Now the rest of the deeds of Jẹ·hoi′ạ·kǐm, and all that he did, are they not written in the Book of the Chronicles of the Kings of Judah? ⁶So Jẹ·hoi′ạ·kǐm slept with his fathers, and Jẹ·hoi′ạ·chǐn his son reigned in his stead. ⁷And the king of Egypt did not come again out of his land, for the king of Babylon had taken all that belonged to the king of Egypt from the brook of Egypt to the river Euphrates.

8 Jẹ·hoi′ạ·chǐn was eighteen years old when he became king, and he reigned three months in Jerusalem. His mother's name was Nẹ·hǔsh′tạ the daughter of Ěl·na′thạn of Jerusalem. ⁹And he did what was evil in the sight of the Lord, according to all that his father had done.

10 At that time the servants of Nẹ·bü·chạd·nĕz′zạr king of Babylon came up to Jerusalem, and the city was besieged. ¹¹And Nẹ·bü·chạd·nĕz′-zạr king of Babylon came to the city, while his servants were besieging it; ¹²and Jẹ·hoi′ạ·chǐn the king of Judah gave himself up to the king of Babylon, himself, and his mother, and his servants, and his princes, and his palace officials. The king of Babylon took him prisoner in the eighth year of his reign, ¹³and carried off all the treasures of the house of the Lord, and the treasures of the king's house, and cut in pieces all the vessels of gold in the temple of the Lord, which Solomon king of Israel had made, as the Lord had foretold. ¹⁴He carried away all Jerusalem, and all the princes, and all the mighty men of valor, ten thousand captives, and all the craftsmen and the smiths; none remained, except the poorest people of the land. ¹⁵And he carried away Jẹ·hoi′ạ·chǐn to Babylon; the king's mother, the king's wives, his officials, and the chief men of the land, he took into captivity from Jerusalem to Babylon. ¹⁶And the king of Babylon brought captive to Babylon all the men of valor, seven thousand, and the craftsmen and the smiths, one thousand, all of them strong and fit for war. ¹⁷And the king of Babylon made Mǎt·tạ·nī′ạh, Jẹ·hoi′-ạ·chǐn's uncle, king in his stead, and changed his name to Zĕd·ẹ·kī′ạh.

18 Zĕd·ẹ·kī′ạh was twenty-one years old when he became king, and he reigned eleven years in Jerusalem. His mother's name was Hạ·mü′tǎl the daughter of Jĕr·ẹ·mī′ạh of Lǐb′nạh. ¹⁹And he did what was evil in the sight of the Lord, according to all that Jẹ·hoi′ạ·kǐm had done. ²⁰For because of the anger of the Lord it came to the point in Jerusalem and Judah that he cast them out from his presence.

And Zĕd·ẹ·kī′ạh rebelled against **25** the king of Babylon. ¹And in the ninth year of his reign, in the tenth month, on the tenth day of the month, Nẹ·bü·chạd·nĕz′zạr king of Babylon came with all his army against Jerusalem, and laid siege to it; and they built siegeworks against it round about. ²So the city was besieged till the eleventh year of King Zĕd·ẹ·kī′ạh. ³On the ninth day of the fourth month the famine was so severe in the city that there was no food for the people of the land. ⁴Then a breach was made in the city; the king with all the men of war fled*ᵏ* by night by the way of the gate between the two walls, by the king's garden, though the Chǎl-dē′ạnṣ were around the city. And they went in the direction of the Är′ạ·bạh. ⁵But the army of the Chǎl·dē′ạnṣ pursued the king, and overtook him in the plains of Jericho; and all his army was scattered from him. ⁶Then they captured the king, and brought him up to the king of Babylon at Rǐb′lạh, who passed sentence upon him. ⁷They slew the sons of Zĕd·ẹ·kī′ạh before his eyes, and put out the eyes of Zedekiah, and bound him in fetters, and took him to Babylon.

8 In the fifth month, on the seventh day of the month – which was the nineteenth year of King Nẹ·bü·chạd·nĕz′-zạr, king of Babylon – Nẹ·bü″zạ·rǎd′ạn, the captain of the bodyguard, a servant of the king of Babylon, came to Jerusalem. ⁹And he burned the house of the Lord, and the king's house and all the houses of Jerusalem; every great house he burned down. ¹⁰And all the

---

ᵏGk Compare Jer 39.4; 52.7: Heb lacks *the king* and *fled*
24.8-17: 2 Chron 36.9-10.
24.18-25.21: 2 Chron 36.11-21; Jer 52.1-27.

army of the Chăl·dē'an̦s, who were with the captain of the guard, broke down the walls around Jerusalem. [11] And the rest of the people who were left in the city and the deserters who had deserted to the king of Babylon, together with the rest of the multitude, Ně·bü"za·răd'an the captain of the guard carried into exile. [12] But the captain of the guard left some of the poorest of the land to be vinedressers and plowmen.

13 And the pillars of bronze that were in the house of the LORD, and the stands and the bronze sea that were in the house of the LORD, the Chăl·dē'-an̦s broke in pieces, and carried the bronze to Babylon. [14] And they took away the pots, and the shovels, and the snuffers, and the dishes for incense and all the vessels of bronze used in the temple service, [15] the firepans also, and the bowls. What was of gold the captain of the guard took away as gold, and what was of silver, as silver. [16] As for the two pillars, the one sea, and the stands, which Solomon had made for the house of the LORD, the bronze of all these vessels was beyond weight. [17] The height of the one pillar was eighteen cubits, and upon it was a capital of bronze; the height of the capital was three cubits; a network and pomegranates, all of bronze, were upon the capital round about. And the second pillar had the like, with the network.

18 And the captain of the guard took Sě·rāi'ah the chief priest, and Zěph·a·nī'ah the second priest, and the three keepers of the threshold; [9] and from the city he took an officer who had been in command of the men of war, and five men of the king's council who were found in the city; and the secretary of the commander of the army who mustered the people of the land; and sixty men of the people of the land who were found in the city. [0] And Ně·bü"za·răd'an the captain of the guard took them, and brought them to the king of Babylon at Rĭb'lah. [21] And the king of Babylon smote them, and

put them to death at Rĭb'lah in the land of Hā'măth. So Judah was taken into exile out of its land.

22 And over the people who remained in the land of Judah, whom Ně·bü·chad·něz'zar king of Babylon had left, he appointed Gěd·a·lī'ah the son of A·hī'kăm, son of Shā'phan̦, governor. [23] Now when all the captains of the forces in the open country[l] and their men heard that the king of Babylon had appointed Gěd·a·lī'ah governor, they came with their men to Gedaliah at Mīz'pah, namely, Ish'-ma·ĕl the son of Něth·a·nī'ah, and Jō·hā'nan the son of Ka·rē'ah, and Se·rāi'ah the son of Tăn'hu·měth the Ně·tŏph'a·thīte, and Jā–ăz·a·nī'ah the son of the Mā–ăc'a·thīte. [24] And Gěd·a·lī'ah swore to them and their men, saying, "Do not be afraid because of the Chăl·dē'an officials; dwell in the land, and serve the king of Babylon, and it shall be well with you." [25] But in the seventh month, Ish'ma·ĕl the son of Něth·a·nī'ah, son of E·līsh'a·ma, of the royal family, came with ten men, and attacked and killed Gěd·a·lī'ah and the Jews and the Chăl·dē'-an̦s who were with him at Mīz'pah. [26] Then all the people, both small and great, and the captains of the forces arose, and went to Egypt; for they were afraid of the Chăl·dē'an̦s.

27 And in the thirty-seventh year of the exile of Jě·hoi'a·chĭn king of Judah, in the twelfth month, on the twenty-seventh day of the month, Ē'vĭl–měr'o·dăch king of Babylon, in the year that he began to reign, graciously freed Jě·hoi'a·chĭn king of Judah from prison; [28] and he spoke kindly to him, and gave him a seat above the seats of the kings who were with him in Babylon. [29] So Jě·hoi'a·chĭn put off his prison garments. And every day of his life he dined regularly at the king's table; [30] and for his allowance, a regular allowance was given him by the king, every day a portion, as long as he lived.

[l] With Jer 40.7: Heb lacks *in the open country*
25.22-26: Jer 40.7–43.7. 25.27-30: Jer 52.31-34.

The First Book of the
Chronicles

1 Adam, Seth, Ē'nŏsh; ²Kē'năn, Mă–hăl'a·lĕl, Jăr'ĕd; ³Ē'nŏch, Mĕ·thū'şe·lah, Lă'mĕch; ⁴Noah, Shĕm, Ham, and Jā'phĕth.

5 The sons of Jā'phĕth: Gō'mer, Mā'gŏg, Mā'daī, Jā'van, Tū'bal, Mē'shĕch, and Tī'ras. ⁶The sons of Gō'mer: Ăsh'ke·năz, Dī'phăth, and Tō-găr'mah. ⁷The sons of Jā'van: Ē·lī'shah, Tăr'shĭsh, Kĭt'tĭm, and Rō'da·nĭm.

8 The sons of Ham: Cŭsh, Egypt, Pŭt, and Canaan. ⁹The sons of Cŭsh: Sē'ba, Hăv'ĭ·lah, Săb'ta, Rā'a·ma, and Săb'tė·ca. The sons of Rā'a·mah: Shē'ba and Dē'dăn. ¹⁰Cŭsh was the father of Nĭm'rŏd; he began to be a mighty one in the earth.

11 Egypt was the father of Lü'dĭm, Ăn'a·mĭm, Lĕ·hā'bĭm, Năph'tü·hĭm, ¹²Păth·rü'sĭm, Căs·lü'hĭm (whence came the Phĭ·lĭs'tĭnes), and Căph'to·rĭm.

13 Canaan was the father of Sī'don his first-born, and Hĕth, ¹⁴and the Jĕb'ü·sītes, the Ăm'o·rītes, the Gĭr'ga·shītes, ¹⁵the Hī'vītes, the Ăr'kītes, the Sī'nītes, ¹⁶the Ăr'va·dītes, the Zĕm'a·rītes, and the Hā'ma·thītes.

17 The sons of Shĕm: Ē'lăm, Ăş'shŭr, Ăr·păch'shăd, Lüd, Ăr'am, Ŭz, Hŭl, Gē'ther, and Mē'shĕch. ¹⁸Ăr·păch'shăd was the father of Shē'lah; and Shelah was the father of Ē'ber. ¹⁹To Ē'ber were born two sons: the name of the one was Pē'lĕg (for in his days the earth was divided), and the name of his brother Jŏk'tăn. ²⁰Jŏk'tăn was the father of Ăl·mō'dăd, Shē'lĕph, Hā"zăr·mā'vĕth, Jē'rah, ²¹Ha·dôr'am, Ū'zal, Dĭk'lah, ²²Ē'bal, A·bĭm'a–ĕl, Shē'ba, ²³Ō'phĭr, Hăv'ĭ·lah, and Jō'băb; all these were the sons of Jŏk'tăn.

24 Shĕm, Ăr·păch'shăd, Shē'lah; ²⁵Ē'ber, Pē'lĕg, Rē'ü; ²⁶Sē'rug, Nā'hôr, Tē'rah; ²⁷Abram, that is, Abraham.

28 The sons of Abraham: Isaac and Ĭsh'ma·ĕl. ²⁹These are their genealogies: the first-born of Ĭsh'ma·ĕl, Nĕbā'ĭ·ŏth; and Kē'dăr, Ăd'bē·ĕl, Mĭb'săm, ³⁰Mĭsh'ma, Dü'mah, Măs'sa, Hā'dăd, Tē'ma, ³¹Jē'tŭr, Nā'phĭsh,

and Kĕd'e·mah. These are the sons of Ĭsh'ma·ĕl. ³²The sons of Kĕ·tū'rah, Abraham's concubine: she bore Zĭm'răn, Jŏk'shăn, Mē'dăn, Mĭd'ĭ·an, Ĭsh'băk, and Shü'ah. The sons of Jŏk'shăn: Shē'ba and Dē'dăn. ³³The sons of Mĭd'ĭ·an: Ē'phah, Ē'pher, Hā'nŏch, A·bī'da, and Ĕl·dā'ah. All these were the descendants of Kĕ·tū'rah.

34 Abraham was the father of Isaac. The sons of Isaac: Esau and Israel. ³⁵The sons of Esau: Ē·lī'phăz, Reü'ĕl, Jē'üsh, Jā'lam, and Kō'rah. ³⁶The sons of Ē·lī'phăz: Tē'man, Ō'măr, Zē'phī, Gā'tăm, Kē'năz, Tĭm'na, and Ăm'a·lĕk. ³⁷The sons of Reü'ĕl: Nā'hăth, Zē'rah, Shăm'mah, and Mīz'zah.

38 The sons of Sē'īr: Lō'tăn, Shō'bal, Zĭb'ē·on, Ăn'ah, Dī'shon, Ē'zer, and Dī'shăn. ³⁹The sons of Lō'tăn: Hō'rī and Hō'măm; and Lotan's sister was Tĭm'na. ⁴⁰The sons of Shō'bal: Ăl'ĭ·an, Măn'a·hăth, Ē'bal, Shē'phī, and Ō'nam. The sons of Zĭb'ē·on: A'ĭ·ah and Ăn'ah. ⁴¹The sons of Ăn'ah: Dī'shon. The sons of Dishon: Hăm'răn, Ĕsh'ban, Ĭth'ran, and Chē'ran. ⁴²The sons of Ē'zer: Bĭl'hăn, Zā'a·văn, and Jā'a·kăn. The sons of Dī'shăn: Ŭz and Ăr'an.

43 These are the kings who reigned in the land of Ē'dom before any king reigned over the Israelites: Bē'la the son of Bē'ôr, the name of whose city was Dĭn'ha·bah. ⁴⁴When Bē'la died, Jō'băb the son of Zē'rah of Bŏz'rah reigned in his stead. ⁴⁵When Jō'băb died, Hū'sham of the land of the Tē'ma·nītes reigned in his stead. ⁴⁶When Hū'sham died, Hā'dăd the son of Bē'dăd, who defeated Mĭd'ĭ·an in the country of Mō'ăb, reigned in his stead; and the name of his city was Ā'vĭth. ⁴⁷When Hā'dăd died, Săm'lah of Măs-rē'kah reigned in his stead. ⁴⁸When Săm'lah died, Shā'ül of Rē·hō'bŏth on the Euphrates reigned in his stead. ⁴⁹When Shā'ül died, Bā'al-hā'năn, the son of Ăch'bôr, reigned in his stead. ⁵⁰When Bā'al-hā'năn died, Hā'dăd reigned in his stead; and the name of his city was Pā'ī, and his wife's name

1.1-53: Gen 5; 10; 11; 25; 36.

Mĕ·hĕt'a·bel the daughter of Mā'trĕd, the daughter of Mē'za·hăb. ⁵¹And Hā'dăd died.

The chiefs of Ē'dom were: chiefs Tĭm'na, Ăl'ĭ·ah, Jĕ'thĕth, ⁵²Ō·hŏl·ĭ-bā'mah, Ē'lah, Pī'nŏn, ⁵³Kē'năz, Tē'man, Mĭb'zăr, ⁵⁴Măg'dĭ–ĕl, and Ī'răm; these are the chiefs of Ē'dom.

2 These are the sons of Israel: Reuben, Sĭm'ē·on, Lē'vī, Judah, Ĭs'sa·chär, Zĕb'ū·lun, ²Dan, Joseph, Benjamin, Năph'ta·lī, Gad, and Ăsh'er. ³The sons of Judah: Ēr, Ō'nan, and Shē'lah; these three Băth–shü'a the Canaanitess bore to him. Now Ēr, Judah's first-born, was wicked in the sight of the LORD, and he slew him. ⁴His daughter-in-law Tā'mär also bore him Pĕr'ĕz and Zē'rah. Judah had five sons in all.

5 The sons of Pĕr'ĕz: Hĕz'ron and Hā'mul. ⁶The sons of Zē'rah: Zĭm'rī, Ē'than, Hē'man, Căl'cŏl, and Dār'a, five in all. ⁷The sons of Cär'mī: Ā'chär, the troubler of Israel, who transgressed in the matter of the devoted thing; ⁸and Ē'than's son was Ăz·a-rī'ah.

9 The sons of Hĕz'ron, that were born to him: Je·räh'mē·el, Räm, and Che·lü'baī. ¹⁰Räm was the father of Ăm·mĭn'a·dăb, and Amminadab was the father of Năh'shon, prince of the sons of Judah. ¹¹Năh'shon was the father of Săl'ma, Salma of Bō'ăz, ¹²Bō'ăz of Ō'bĕd, Ōbed of Jesse. ¹³Jesse was the father of Ē·lī'ăb his first-born, A·bĭn'a·dăb the second, Shĭm'ē–a the third, ¹⁴Ne·thăn'ĕl the fourth, Răd'-daī the fifth, ¹⁵Ō'zĕm the sixth, David the seventh; ¹⁶and their sisters were Ze·rü'ī·ah and Ăb'ī·gäil. The sons of Zeruiah: A·bĭ'shaī, Jō'ăb, and Ăs'a-hĕl, three. ¹⁷Ăb'ī·gäil bore A·mā'sa, and the father of Amasa was Jē'ther the Ĭsh'ma-ĕl-īte.

18 Caleb the son of Hĕz'ron had children by his wife A·zü'bah, and by Jĕr'ī·ŏth; and these were her sons: Jē'shĕr, Shō'băb, and Är'dŏn. ¹⁹When A·zü'bah died, Caleb married Ĕph'răth, who bore him Hūr. ²⁰Hūr was the father of Ū'rī, and Uri was the father of Bĕz'a·lĕl.

21 Afterward Hĕz'ron went in to the daughter of Mā'chīr the father of Gilead, whom he married when he was sixty years old; and she bore him Sē'gub; ²²and Sē'gub was the father of Jā'ir, who had twenty-three cities in

the land of Gilead. ²³But Gē'shūr and Är'am took from them Hăv'vŏth-jā'ir, Kē'năth and its villages, sixty towns. All these were descendants of Mā'chīr, the father of Gilead. ²⁴After the death of Hĕz'ron, Caleb went in to Ĕph'ra·thah,ᵃ the wife of Hĕz'ron his father, and she bore him Ăsh'hūr, the father of Te'kō'a.

25 The sons of Je·räh'mē·el, the first-born of Hĕz'ron: Räm, his first-born, Bü'nah, Ō'rĕn, Ō'zĕm, and A·hī'jah. ²⁶Je·räh'mē·el also had another wife, whose name was Ăt'a·rah; she was the mother of Ō'nam. ²⁷The sons of Räm, the first-born of Je·räh'mē·el: Mā'ăz, Jā'mĭn, and Ē'ker. ²⁸The sons of Ō'nam: Shăm'maī and Jā'da. The sons of Shammai: Nā'dăb and A·bī'shūr. ²⁹The name of A·bī'shūr's wife was Ăb'ī-häil, and she bore him Ăh'băn and Mō'lid. ³⁰The sons of Nā'dăb: Sē'led and Ăp'pa–ĭm; and Seled died childless. ³¹The sons of Ăp'pa–ĭm: Ĭsh'ī. The sons of Ishi: Shē'shăn. The sons of Sheshan: Ăh'laī. ³²The sons of Jā'da, Shăm'maī's brother: Jē'ther and Jonathan; and Jether died childless. ³³The sons of Jonathan: Pē'lĕth and Zā'za. These were the descendants of Je·räh'mē·el. ³⁴Now Shē'shăn had no sons, only daughters; but Sheshan had an Egyptian slave, whose name was Jär'ha. ³⁵So Shē'shăn gave his daughter in marriage to Jär'ha his slave; and she bore him Ăt'taī. ³⁶Ăt'taī was the father of Nathan and Nathan of Zā'băd. ³⁷Zā'băd was the father of Ĕph'lăl, and Ephlal of Ō'bĕd. ³⁸Ō'bĕd was the father of Jē'hū, and Jehu of Ăz·a-rī'ah. ³⁹Ăz·a-rī'ah was the father of Hē'lĕz, and Helez of Ĕl'ē–ā'sah. ⁴⁰Ĕl'ē–ā'sah was the father of Sĭs'maī, and Sismai of Shăl'lum. ⁴¹Shăl'lum was the father of Jĕk·a·mī'ah, and Jekamiah of Ē·lĭsh'a·ma.

42 The sons of Caleb the brother of Je·räh'mē·el: Ma·rē'shahᵇ his first-born, who was the father of Zĭph. The sons of Mareshah: Hē'bron.ᶜ ⁴³The sons of Hē'bron: Kō'rah, Tăp'pū–ah, Rē'kĕm, and Shē'ma. ⁴⁴Shē'ma was the father of Rā'ham, the father of Jôr'ke–am; and Rē'kĕm was the father of Shăm'maī. ⁴⁵The son of

---

ᵃGk Vg: Heb *in Caleb Ephrathah*
ᵇGk: Heb *Mesha* ᶜHeb *the father of Hebron*
2.1-2: Gen 35.23-26.
2.3-4: Gen 38.3-7, 29-30; Num 26.19, 20.
2.5: Gen 46.12: Num 26.21. 2.6-8: Josh 7.1; 1 Kings 4.31.

Shăm'maī: Mā'ŏn; and Maon was the father of Bĕth–zūr. ⁴⁶Ē'phạh also, Caleb's concubine, bore Hār'ạn, Mō'zạ, and Gā'zĕz; and Haran was the father of Gazez. ⁴⁷The sons of Jäh'daī: Rē'gĕm, Jō'tham, Gē'shăn, Pē'lĕt, Ē'phạh, and Shā'ăph. ⁴⁸Mā'ạ-cạh, Caleb's concubine, bore Shē'bẹr and Tīr'hạ·nạh. ⁴⁹She also bore Shā'-ăph the father of Măd·măn'nạh, Shē'vạ the father of Măch·bē'nạh and the father of Gĭb'ē–ạ; and the daughter of Caleb was Ăch'sạh. ⁵⁰These were the descendants of Caleb.

The sonsᵈ of Hūr the first-born of Ĕph'rạ·thạh: Shō'bạl the father of Kīr'ĭ·ăth–jē'ạ·rīm, ⁵¹Săl'mạ, the father of Bethlehem, and Hār'ĕph the father of Bĕth–gā'dẹr. ⁵²Shō'bạl the father of Kīr'ĭ·ăth–jē'ạ·rĭm had other sons: Hạ·rō'ẹh, half of the Mĕ·nü'hŏth. ⁵³And the families of Kīr'ĭ·ăth–jē'ạ·rĭm: the Ĭth'rītes, the Pü'thītes, the Shü'-mạ·thītes, and the Mīsh'rạ·ītes; from these came the Zō'rạ·thītes and the Ĕsh'tạ·ọ·lītes. ⁵⁴The sons of Săl'mạ: Bethlehem, the Nẹ·tŏph'ạ·thītes, Ăt'rŏth–bĕth–jō'ăb, and half of the Măn"ạ·hā'thītes, the Zō'rītes. ⁵⁵The families also of the scribes that dwelt at Jā'bĕz: the Tī'rạ·thītes, the Shĭm'ē-ạ·thītes, and the Sü'cạ·thītes. These are the Kĕn'ītes who came from Hăm'-măth, the father of the house of Rē'chăb.

3 These are the sons of David that were born to him in Hē'brọn: the first-born Ăm'nŏn, by Ạ·hĭn'ō–ăm the Jĕz'rē·ẹ·līt·ẹss; the second Daniel, by Ăb'ĭ·gāil the Cār'mẹl·īt·ẹss, ²the third Ăb'sạ·lọm, whose mother was Mā'ạ-cạh, the daughter of Tăl'maī, king of Gē'shūr; the fourth Ăd·ọ·nī'jạh, whose mother was Hăg'gĭth; ³the fifth Shĕph-ạ·tī'ạh, by Ạ·bī'tạl; the sixth Ĭth'rē–ăm, by his wife Ĕg'lạh; ⁴six were born to him in Hē'brọn, where he reigned for seven years and six months. And he reigned thirty-three years in Jerusalem. ⁵These were born to him in Jerusalem: Shĭm'ē–ạ, Shō'băb, Nathan, and Solomon, four by Băth-shü'ạ, the daughter of Ăm'mĭ–ĕl; ⁶then Ĭb'hār, Ē·lĭsh'ạ·mạ, Ē·lĭph'ẹ·lĕt, ⁷Nō'gạh, Nĕ'phĕg, Jạ·phī'ạ, ⁸Ē·lĭsh'-ạ·mạ, Ē·lī'ạ·dạ, and Ē·lĭph'ẹ·lĕt, nine. ⁹All these were David's sons, besides the sons of the concubines; and Tā'mär was their sister.

10 The descendants of Solomon:

Rē·họ·bō'ạm, Ạ·bī'jạh his son, Asa his son, Jĕ·hŏsh'ạ·phăt his son, ¹¹Jō'ram his son, Ā·hạ·zī'ạh his son, Jō'ăsh his son, ¹²Ăm·ạ·zī'ạh his son, Ăz·ạ·rī'ạh his son, Jō'tham his son, ¹³Ā'hăz his son, Hĕz·ẹ·kī'ạh his son, Mạ·năs'sẹh his son, ¹⁴Ā'mŏn his son, Jō'sī·ạh his son. ¹⁵The sons of Jō'sī·ạh: Jō'hā·nạn the first-born, the second Jĕ·hoi'ạ·kĭm, the third Zĕd·ẹ·kī'ạh, the fourth Shăl'-lum. ¹⁶The descendants of Jĕ·hoi'-ạ·kĭm: Jĕc·ọ·nī'ạh his son, Zĕd·ẹ·kī'ạh his son; ¹⁷and the sons of Jĕc·ọ·nī'ạh, the captive: Shĕ–ăl'tĭ–ĕl his son, ¹⁸Măl·chī'răm, Pĕ·dāi'ạh, Shĕn·ăz'-zär, Jĕk·ạ·mī'ạh, Hŏsh'ạ·mạ, and Nĕd·ạ·bī'ạh; ¹⁹and the sons of Pĕ·dāi'ạh: Zĕ·rŭb'bạ·bĕl and Shĭm'ē–ī; and the sons of Zĕ·rŭb'bạ·bĕl: Mĕ·shŭl'lạm and Hăn·ạ·nī'ạh, and Shĕ·lō'-mĭth was their sister; ²⁰and Hă·shü'-bah, Ō'hĕl, Bĕr·ẹ·chī'ạh, Hăs·ạ·dī'ạh, and Jü'shăb–hē'sĕd, five. ²¹The sons of Hăn·ạ·nī'ạh: Pĕl·ạ·tī'ạh and Jĕ·shā'-ĭ·ạh, his sonᵉ Rĕph·āi'ạh, his sonᵉ Är'nạn, his sonᵉ Ō'bạ·dī'ạh, his sonᵉ Shĕc·ạ·nī'ạh. ²²The sons of Shĕc·ạ·nī'ạh: Shĕ·māi'ạh. And the sons of Shemaiah: Hăt'tush, Ī'găl, Bạ·rī'ạh, Nē·ạ·rī'ạh, and Shā'phăt, six. ²³The sons of Nē·ạ·rī'ạh: Ĕl'ĭ–ō–ē'naī, Hĭzkī'aj, and Ăz·rī'kăm, three. ²⁴The sons of Ĕl'ĭ–ō–ē'naī: Hŏd"ạ·vī'ah, Ē·lī'ạ-shĭb, Pĕ·lāi'ạh, Ăk'kụb, Jō·hā'nạn, Dĕ·laī'ạh, and Ạ·nā'nī, seven.

4 The sons of Judah: Pĕr'ĕz, Hĕz'-rọn, Cär'mī, Hūr, and Shō'bạl. ²Rē–āi'ạh the son of Shō'bạl was the father of Jā'hăth, and Jahath was the father of A·hü'māi and Lā'hăd. These were the families of the Zō'rạ·thītes. ³These were the sonsᶠ of Ē'tăm: Jĕz'-rē·ĕl, Ĭsh'mạ, and Ĭd'băsh; and the name of their sister was Hăz·zẹ·lĕl-pō'nī, ⁴and Pĕ·nü'ĕl was the father of Gē'dôr, and Ē'zẹr the father of Hū'-shah. These were the sons of Hūr, the first-born of Ĕph'rạ·thạh, the father of Bethlehem. ⁵Ăsh'hūr, the father of Tĕ'kō'ạ, had two wives, Hē'lạh and Nā'ạ·rạh; ⁶Nā'ạ·rạh bore him Ạ·hŭz'-zam, Hē'phẹr, Tĕ'mẹ·nī, and Hā–ạ-hăsh'tạ·rī. These were the sons of Naarah. ⁷The sons of Hē'lah: Zē'rĕth, Ĭz'hăr, and Ĕth'năn. ⁸Kŏz, and the father of Ā'nüb, Zō·bē'bah, and the

ᵈGk Vg: Heb *son*
ᵉGk Compare Syr Vg: Heb *sons of*
ᶠGk Compare Vg: Heb *father*
3.1–9: 2 Sam 3.2–5; 5.14–16; 1 Chron 14.3–6.
3.4: 2 Sam 5.4, 5.

families of Ạ·hăr′hĕl the son of Hăr′um. [9] Jā′bĕz was more honorable than his brothers; and his mother called his name Jabez, saying, "Because I bore him in pain." [10] Jā′bĕz called on the God of Israel, saying, "Oh that thou wouldst bless me and enlarge my border, and that thy hand might be with me, and that thou wouldst keep me from harm so that it might not hurt me!" And God granted what he asked. [11] Chē′lŭb, the brother of Shü′häh, was the father of Mē′hĭr, who was the father of Ĕsh′tọn. [12] Ĕsh′-tọn was the father of Bĕth-rā′phạ, Pạ·sē′ạh, and Tĕ·hĭn′nạh the father of Ir·nā′hăsh. These are the men of Rē′cạh. [13] The sons of Kē′năz: Ŏth′-nĭ–ĕl and Sĕ·rāi′ạh; and the sons of Othni–el: Hā′thăth and Mĕ·ō′nọ·thaī.[g] [14] Mĕ·ō′nọ·thaī was the father of Ŏph′-rạh; and Sĕ·rāi′ạh was the father of Jō′ăb the father of Gē–hăr′ạ·shĭm,[h] so-called because they were craftsmen. [15] The sons of Caleb the son of Jẹ·phün′nẹh: Ī′rü, Ē′lạh, and Nā′ạm; and the sons of Elah: Kē′năz. [16] The sons of Jĕ·hăl′lẹ·lĕl: Zĭph, Zī′phạh, Tīr′ĭ·ă, and Ăs′ạ·rĕl. [17] The sons of Ĕz′rạh: Jē′thẹr, Mē′rĕd, Ē′phẹr, and Jā′lọn. These are the sons of Bĭth′ĭ·ạh, the daughter of Pharaoh, whom Mered married;[i] and she conceived and bore[j] Miriam, Shăm′maī, and Ĭsh′bạh, the father of Ĕsh·tẹ·mō′ạ. [18] And his Jewish wife bore Jē′rĕd the father of Gē′dôr, Hē′bẹr the father of Sō′cō, and Jĕ·kü′thĭ·ĕl the father of Zạ·nō′ạh. [19] The sons of the wife of Hō·dī′ạh, the sister of Nā′hăm, were the fathers of Kē·ī′lạh the Găr′mīte and Ĕsh·tẹ·mō′ạ the Mā–ăc′ạ·thīte. [20] The sons of Shī′mọn: Ăm′nŏn, Rĭn′nạh, Bĕn-hā′nạn, and Tī′lŏn. The sons of Ĭsh′ī: Zō′hĕth and Bĕn–zō′hĕth. [21] The sons of Shē′lạh the son of Judah: Ēr the father of Lē′cạh, Lā′ạ·dạh the father of Mạ·rē′shạh, and the families of the house of linen workers at Bĕth–ăsh·bē′ạ; [22] and Jō′kĭm, and the men of Cō·zē′bạ, and Jō′ăsh, and Sār′ăph, who ruled in Mō′ăb and returned to Lē′hĕm[k] (now the records[l] are ancient). [23] These were the potters and inhabitants of Nĕ·tā′īm and Gĕ·dē′rạh; they dwelt there with the king for his work.

24 The sons of Sĭm′ē·on: Nĕm′ū–ĕl, Jā′mĭn, Jā′rĭb, Zē′rạh, Shā′ül; [25] Shăl′-lum was his son, Mĭb′săm his son, Mĭsh′mạ his son. [26] The sons of

Mĭsh′mạ: Hăm′mū–ĕl his son, Zăc′cūr his son, Shĭm′ē–ī his son. [27] Shĭm′ē–ī had sixteen sons and six daughters; but his brothers had not many children, nor did all their family multiply like the men of Judah. [28] They dwelt in Bē′ẹr–shē′bạ, Mō′lạ·dạh, Hā′zăr–shü′ạl, [29] Bĭl′hạh, Ē′zĕm, Tō′lăd, [30] Bĕthü′ĕl, Hôr′mạh, Zĭk′lăg, [31] Bĕth–măr′cạ·bŏth, Hā′zăr–sü′sĭm, Bĕth–bĭr′ī, and Shā–ạ·rā′īm. These were their cities until David reigned. [32] And their villages were Ē′tạm, Ā′īn, Rĭm′-mŏn, Tō′chĕn, and Ā′shạn, five cities, [33] along with all their villages which were round about these cities as far as Bā′ạl. These were their settlements, and they kept a genealogical record.

34 Mĕ·shō′băb, Jăm′lĕch, Jō′shạh the son of Ăm·ạ·zī′ạh, [35] Jō′ẹl, Jē′hü the son of Jŏsh·ĭ·bī′ạh, son of Sĕ·rāi′ạh, son of Ăs′ī–ĕl, [36] Ĕl′ī–ō–ē′naī, Jā″ạ·kō′bạh, Jĕsh·ō·hāi′ạh, A·sāi′ạh, Ăd′ī–ĕl, Jĕ·sĭm′ī–ĕl, Bĕ·nā′ĭ·ạh, [37] Zī′zạ the son of Shī′phī, son of Ăl′lŏn, son of Jĕ-daī′ạh, son of Shĭm′rī, son of Shĕ-māi′ạh — [38] these mentioned by name, were princes in their families, and their fathers' houses increased greatly. [39] They journeyed to the entrance of Gē′dôr, to the east side of the valley, to seek pasture for their flocks, [40] where they found rich, good pasture, and the land was very broad, quiet, and peaceful; for the former inhabitants there belonged to Ham. [41] These, registered by name, came in the days of Hĕz·ẹ-kī′ạh, king of Judah, and destroyed their tents and the Mĕ–ü′nĭm who were found there, and exterminated them to this day, and settled in their place, because there was pasture there for their flocks. [42] And some of them, five hundred men of the Sĭm′ē·ọ·nītes, went to Mount Sē′ĭr, having as their leaders Pĕl·ạ·tī′ạh, Nē–ạ·rī′ạh, Rĕph-āi′ạh, and Ŭz′zĭ·ĕl, the sons of Ĭsh′ī; [43] and they destroyed the remnant of the Ạ·măl′ẹ·kītes that had escaped, and they have dwelt there to this day.

5 The sons of Reuben the first-born of Israel (for he was the first-born; but because he polluted his father's couch, his birthright was

[g]Gk Vg: Heb lacks *Meonothai*
[h]That is *Valley of craftsmen*
[i]The clause: *These are . . . married* is transposed from verse 18 [j]Heb lacks *and bore*
[k]Vg Compare Gk: Heb and *Jashubi-lahem* [l]Or *matters*
4.24: Gen 46.10; Ex 6.15; Num 26.12, 13.
4.28-33: Josh 19.2-8. 5.1-26: Gen 46.9; Num 26.5, 6.

given to the sons of Joseph the son of Israel, so that he is not enrolled in the genealogy according to the birthright; [2] though Judah became strong among his brothers and a prince was from him, yet the birthright belonged to Joseph), [3] the sons of Reuben, the first-born of Israel: Hā′nŏch, Păl′lü, Hĕz′rŏn, and Cār′mī. [4] The sons of Jō′ĕl: Shĕ·māi′ah his son, Gŏg his son, Shĭm′ē-ī his son, [5] Mī′cah his son, Rē–aī′ah his son, Bā′al his son, [6] Bĕ·ēr′ah his son, whom Tĭl′găth–pĭl·nē′ṣĕr king of Assyria carried away into exile; he was a chieftain of the Reubenites. [7] And his kinsmen by their familes, when the genealogy of their generations was reckoned: the chief, Jĕ–ī′ĕl, and Zĕch·a·rī′ah, [8] and Bē′la the son of Ā′zăz, son of Shē′ma, son of Jō′ĕl, who dwelt in A·rō′er, as far as Nē′bŏ and Bā′al–mē′ŏn. [9] He also dwelt to the east as far as the entrance of the desert this side of the Euphrates, because their cattle had multiplied in the land of Gilead. [10] And in the days of Saul they made war on the Hăg′rītes, who fell by their hand; and they dwelt in their tents throughout all the region east of Gilead.

11 The sons of Gàd dwelt over against them in the land of Bā′shan as far as Săl′e·cah: [12] Jō′ĕl the chief, Shā′pham the second, Jā′naī, and Shā′phat in Bā′shan. [13] And their kinsmen according to their fathers' houses: Michael, Mĕ·shŭl′lam, Shē′ba, Jō′raī, Jā′can, Zī′a, and Ē′ber, seven. [14] These were the sons of Ăb′ī·hāil the son of Hū·rī, son of Ja·rō′ah, son of Gilead, son of Michael, son of Jĕ·shĭsh′aī, son of Jäh′dō, son of Bŭz; [15] Ā′hī the son of Ăb′dĭ–ĕl, son of Gū′nī, was chief in their fathers' houses; [16] and they dwelt in Gilead, in Bā′shan and in its towns, and in all the pasture lands of Sharon to their limits. [17] All of these were enrolled by genealogies in the days of Jō′tham king of Judah, and in the days of Jĕr·o·bō′am king of Israel.

18 The Reubenites, the Gàd′ītes, and the half-tribe of Ma·năs′seh had valiant men, who carried shield and sword, and drew the bow; expert in war, forty-four thousand seven hundred and sixty, ready for service. [19] They made war upon the Hăg′rītes, Jē′tŭr, Nā′phĭsh, and Nō′dăb; [20] and

when they received help against them, the Hăg′rītes and all who were with them were given into their hands, for they cried to God in the battle, and he granted their entreaty because they trusted in him. [21] They carried off their livestock: fifty thousand of their camels, two hundred and fifty thousand sheep, two thousand asses, and a hundred thousand men alive. [22] For many fell slain, because the war was of God. And they dwelt in their place until the exile.

23 The members of the half-tribe of Ma·năs′seh dwelt in the land; they were very numerous from Bā′shan to Bā′al–hĕr′mon, Sē′nīr, and Mount Hermon. [24] These were the heads of their fathers' houses: Ē′phĕr,[m] Ish′ī, Ē·lī′ĕl, Ăz′rī–ĕl, Jĕr·e·mī′ah, Hŏd″a–vī′ah, and Jäh′dĭ–ĕl, mighty warriors, famous men, heads of their fathers' houses. [25] But they transgressed against the God of their fathers, and played the harlot after the gods of the peoples of the land, whom God had destroyed before them. [26] So the God of Israel stirred up the spirit of Pül king of Assyria, the spirit of Tĭl′găth–pĭl·nē′ṣĕr king of Assyria, and he carried them away, namely, the Reubenites, the Gàd′ītes, and the half-tribe of Ma·năs′seh, and brought them to Hā′lah, Hā′bôr, Hâr′a, and the river Gō′zăn, to this day.

6[n] The sons of Lē′vī: Gēr′shom, Kō′hăth, and Me·râr′ī. [2] The sons of Kō′hăth: Ăm′răm, Ĭz′hār, Hē′brŏn, and Ŭz′zĭ-ĕl. [3] The children of Ăm′răm: Aaron, Moses, and Miriam. The sons of Aaron: Nā′dăb, A·bī′hū, Ĕl·ē·ā′zar, and Ĭth′a·mär. [4] Ĕl·ē·ā′zar was the father of Phĭn′e·has, Phinehas of Ăb·ĭ·shü′a, [5] Ăb·ĭ·shü′a of Bŭk′kī, Bukki of Ŭz′zī, [6] Ŭz′zī of Zĕr·a·hī′ah, Zerahiah of Mĕ·rā′ī·ŏth, [7] Mĕ·rā′ī·ŏth of Ăm·a·rī′ah, Amariah of A·hī′tub, [8] A·hī′tub of Zā′dŏk, Zadok of A·hĭm′a–ăz, [9] A·hĭm′a–ăz of Ăz·a·rī′ah, Azariah of Jō·hā′nan, [10] and Jō·hā′nan of Ăz·a·rī′ah (it was he who served as priest in the house that Solomon built in Jerusalem). [11] Ăz·a·rī′ah was the father of Ăm·a·rī′ah, Amariah of A·hī′tub, [12] A·hī′tub of Zā′dŏk, Zadok of Shăl′lum, [13] Shăl′lum of Hĭl·kī′ah, Hilkiah of Ăz·a·rī′ah, [14] Ăz·a·rī′ah of Sĕ·rāi′ah, Seraiah of Jĕ·hŏz′adăk;

m Gk Vg: Heb *and Epher*   *n* Ch 5.27 in Heb
6.1–15: Gen 46.11; Ex 6.16-20; Num 3.2.

[15]and Jĕ·hŏz′ạ·dăk went into exile
when the LORD sent Judah and Jerusalem into exile by the hand of Nĕ·bü-
chạd·nĕz′zạr.
16[o] The sons of Lē′vī: Gẽr′shọm,
Kō′hăth, and Mẹ·râr′ī. [17]And these are
the names of the sons of Gẽr′shọm:
Lĭb′nī and Shĭm′ē–ī. [18]The sons of
Kō′hăth: Ăm′răm, Ĭz′hãr, Hē′brọn,
and Ŭz′zĭ·ĕl. [19]The sons of Mẹ·râr′ī:
Mäh′lī and Mū′shī. These are the
families of the Lē′vītes according to
their fathers. [20]Of Gẽr′shọm: Lĭb′nī
his son, Jā′hăth his son, Zĭm′mạh his
son, [21]Jō′ạh his son, Ĭd′dō his son,
Zē′rạh his son, Jē–ăth′ẹ·raī his son.
[22]The sons of Kō′hăth: Ăm·mĭn′ạ·dăb
his son, Kō′rạh his son, Ăs′sĭr his son,
[23]Ĕl·kā′nạh his son, Ē·bī′ạ·săph his
son, Ăs′sĭr his son, [24]Tā′hăth his son,
Ū·rī′ẹl his son, Ŭz·zī′ạh his son, and
Shā′ül his son. [25]The sons of Ĕl·kā′-
nạh: Ạ·mā′saī and Ạ·hī′mŏth, [26]Ĕl·kā′-
nạh his son, Zō′phaī his son, Nā′hăth
his son, [27]Ē·lī′ăb his son, Jĕ·rō′hăm
his son, Ĕl·kā′nạh his son. [28]The sons of
Samuel: Jō′ẹl[p] his first-born, the
second Ạ·bī′jạh.[q] [29]The sons of Mẹ-
râr′ī: Mäh′lī, Lĭb′nī his son, Shĭm′ē–ī
his son, Ŭz′zạh his son, [30]Shĭm′ē–ạ
his son, Hăg·gī′ạh his son, and Ạ·sāi′ạh
his son.
31 These are the men whom David
put in charge of the service of song in
the house of the LORD, after the ark
rested there. [32]They ministered with
song before the tabernacle of the tent
of meeting, until Solomon had built the
house of the LORD in Jerusalem; and
they performed their service in due
order. [33]These are the men who served
and their sons. Of the sons of the
Kō′hạ·thītes: Hē′mạn the singer the
son of Jō′ẹl, son of Samuel, [34]son of
Ĕl·kā′nạh, son of Jĕ·rō′hăm, son of
Ē·lī′ĕl, son of Tō′ạh, [35]son of Zŭph, son
of Ĕl·kā′nạh, son of Mā′hăth, son of
Ạ·mā′saī, [36]son of Ĕl·kā′nạh, son of
Jō′ẹl, son of Ăz·ạ·rī′ạh, son of Zĕph·ạ-
nī′ạh, [37]son of Tā′hăth, son of Ăs′sĭr,
son of Ē·bī′ạ·săph, son of Kō′rạh, [38]son
of Ĭz′hãr, son of Kō′hăth, son of Lē′vī,
son of Israel; [39]and his brother Ā′săph,
who stood on his right hand, namely,
Asaph the son of Bĕr·ẹ·chī′ạh, son of
Shĭm′ē–ạ, [40]son of Michael, son of
Bā–ạ·sē′ī·ạh, son of Măl·chī′jạh, [41]son
of Ĕth′nī, son of Zē′rạh, son of Ạ·dāi′ạh,
[42]son of Ē′thạn, son of Zĭm′mạh, son
of Shĭm′ē–ī, [43]son of Jā′hăth, son of
Gẽr′shọm, son of Lē′vī. [44]On the left
hand were their brethren the sons of
Mẹ·râr′ī: Ē′thạn the son of Kĭsh′ī,
son of Ăb′dī, son of Măl′lụch, [45]son of
Hăsh·ạ·bī′ạh, son of Ăm·ạ·zī′ạh, son
of Hĭl·kī′ạh, [46]son of Ăm′zī, son of
Bā′nī, son of Shē′mẹr, [47]son of Mäh′lī,
son of Mū′shī, son of Mẹ·râr′ī, son of
Lē′vī; [48]and their brethren the Lē′vītes
were appointed for all the service of
the tabernacle of the house of God.
49 But Aaron and his sons made
offerings upon the altar of burnt
offering and upon the altar of incense
for all the work of the most holy place,
and to make atonement for Israel,
according to all that Moses the servant
of God had commanded. [50]These are
the sons of Aaron: Ĕl·ē·ā′zạr his son,
Phĭn′ẹ·hạs his son, Ăb·ĭ·shü′ạ his son,
[51]Bŭk′kī his son, Ŭz′zī his son, Zĕr·ạ-
hī′ạh his son, [52]Mẹ·rā′ī·ọth his son,
Ăm·ạ·rī′ạh his son, Ạ·hī′tụb his son,
[53]Zā′dŏk his son, Ạ·hĭm′ạ–ăz his son.
54 These are their dwelling places
according to their settlements within
their borders: to the sons of Aaron of
the families of Kō′hạ·thītes, for theirs
was the lot, [55]to them they gave Hē′-
brọn in the land of Judah and its
surrounding pasture lands, [56]but the
fields of the city and its villages they
gave to Caleb the son of Jẹ·phün′nẹh.
[57]To the sons of Aaron they gave the
cities of refuge: Hē′brọn, Lĭb′nạh
with its pasture lands, Jăt′tĭr, Ĕsh-
tẹ·mō′ạ with its pasture lands, [58]Hī′lĕn
with its pasture lands, Dē′bĭr with its
pasture lands, [59]Ā′shạn with its pasture lands, and Bĕth–shē′mĕsh with
its pasture lands; [60]and from the tribe
of Benjamin, Gē′bạ with its pasture
lands, Ăl′ẹ·mĕth with its pasture lands,
and Ăn′ạ·thŏth with its pasture lands.
All their cities throughout their
families were thirteen.
61 To the rest of the Kō′hạ·thītes
were given by lot out of the family of
the tribe, out of the half-tribe, the half
of Mạ·năs′sẹh, ten cities. [62]To the
Gẽr′shọ·mītes according to their families were allotted thirteen cities out of
the tribes of Ĭs′sạ·chãr, Ăsh′ẹr, Năph′-
tạ·lī, and Mạ·năs′sẹh in Bā′shạn. [63]To
the Mẹ·râr′ītes according to their
families were allotted twelve cities

[o]Ch 6.1 in Heb
[p]Gk Syr Compare verse 33 and 1 Sam 8.2: Heb lacks *Joel*
[q]Heb *and Abijah*
6.16-53: Ex 6.16-24. **6.54-81:** Josh 21.1-42.

out of the tribes of Reuben, Găd, and Zĕb'ū·lŭn. ⁶⁴So the people of Israel gave the Lē'vītes the cities with their pasture lands. ⁶⁵They also gave them by lot out of the tribes of Judah, Sĭm'-ē·ŏn, and Benjamin these cities which are mentioned by name.

66 And some of the families of the sons of Kō'hăth had cities of their territory out of the tribe of Ē'phra·ĭm. ⁶⁷They were given the cities of refuge: Shē'chĕm with its pasture lands in the hill country of Ē'phra·ĭm, Gē'zẹr with its pasture lands, ⁶⁸Jŏk'mē–am with its pasture lands, Bĕth–hō'rŏn with its pasture lands, ⁶⁹Aī'ja·lŏn with its pasture lands, Găth–rĭm'mŏn with its pasture lands, ⁷⁰and out of the half-tribe of Ma·năs'seh, Ā'nẹr with its pasture lands, and Bĭl'ē–ăm with its pasture lands, for the rest of the families of the Kō'ha·thītes.

71 To the Gẽr'sho·mītes were given out of the half-tribe of Ma·năs'seh: Gō'lan in Bā'shan with its pasture lands and Ăsh'ta·rŏth with its pasture lands; ⁷²and out of the tribe of Ĭs'sa·chär: Kē'dĕsh with its pasture lands, Dăb'e·răth with its pasture lands, ⁷³Rā'mŏth with its pasture lands, and Ā'nĕm with its pasture lands; ⁷⁴out of the tribe of Ăsh'er: Mā'shal with its pasture lands, Ăb'dŏn with its pasture lands, ⁷⁵Hū'kŏk with its pasture lands, and Rĕ'hŏb with its pasture lands; ⁷⁶and out of the tribe of Năph'ta·lī: Kē'dĕsh in Galilee with its pasture lands, Hăm'mŏn with its pasture lands, and Kīr″ĭ·a·thā'ĭm with its pasture lands. ⁷⁷To the rest of the Me·râr'ītes were allotted out of the tribe of Zĕb'ū·lun: Rĭm'mo·nō with its pasture lands, Tā'bôr with its pasture lands, ⁷⁸and beyond the Jordan at Jericho, on the east side of the Jordan, out of the tribe of Reuben: Bē'zẹr in the steppe with its pasture lands, Jăh'zah with its pasture lands, ⁷⁹Kĕd'e·mŏth with its pasture lands, and Mĕph'a–ăth with its pasture lands; ⁸⁰and out of the tribe of Găd: Rā'mŏth in Gilead with its pasture lands, Mā'ha·nā'ĭm with its pasture lands, ⁸¹Hĕsh'bon with its pasture lands, and Jā'zẹr with its pasture lands.

7 The sons^r of Ĭs'sa·chär: Tō'la, Pū'ah, Jăsh'ub, and Shĭm'ron, four. ²The sons of Tō'la: Ŭz'zī, Rĕph-āi'ah, Jē'rĭ–ĕl, Jăh'maī, Ĭb'sam, and Shĕ·mū'ĕl, heads of their fathers'

houses, namely of Tola, mighty warriors of their generations, their number in the days of David being twenty-two thousand six hundred. ³The sons of Ŭz'zī: Ĭz·ra·hī'ah. And the sons of Izrahiah: Michael, Ō'ba·dī'ah, Jō'ẹl, and Ĭs·shī'ah, five, all of them chief men; ⁴and along with them, by their generations, according to their fathers' houses, were units of the army for war, thirty-six thousand, for they had many wives and sons. ⁵Their kinsmen belonging to all the families of Ĭs'sa·chär were in all eighty-seven thousand mighty warriors, enrolled by genealogy.

6 The sons of Benjamin: Bē'la, Bē'chẹr, and Jĕ·dī'a–ĕl, three. ⁷The sons of Bē'la: Ĕz'bon, Ŭz'zī, Ŭz'zĭ–ĕl, Jẽr'ĭ·mŏth, and Ī'rī, five, heads of fathers' houses, mighty warriors; and their enrollment by genealogies was twenty-two thousand and thirty-four. ⁸The sons of Bē'chẹr: Zẹ·mī'rah, Jō'ăsh, Ē·lī–ē'zẹr, Ĕl'ĭ–ō–ē'naī, Ŏm'rī, Jẽr'e·mŏth, A·bī'jah, Ăn'a·thŏth, and Ăl'e·mĕth. All these were the sons of Becher; ⁹and their enrollment by genealogies, according to their generations, as heads of their fathers' houses, mighty warriors, was twenty thousand two hundred. ¹⁰The sons of Jĕ·dī'a–ĕl: Bĭl'hăn. And the sons of Bilhan: Jē'ŭsh, Benjamin, Ē'hŭd, Chĕ·nā'a·nah, Zē'than, Tär'shĭsh, and A·hish'a·här. ¹¹All these were the sons of Jĕ·dī'a–ĕl according to the heads of their fathers' houses, mighty warriors, seventeen thousand and two hundred, ready for service in war. ¹²And Shŭp'pĭm and Hŭp'pĭm were the sons of Īr, Hū'shĭm the sons of Ā'her.

13 The sons of Năph'ta·lī: Jäh'zĭ–ĕl, Gū'nī, Jē'zẹr, and Shăl'lum, the offspring of Bĭl'hah.

14 The sons of Ma·năs'seh: Ăs'rĭ–ĕl, whom his Är·a·mē'an concubine bore; she bore Mā'chīr the father of Gilead. ¹⁵And Mā'chīr took a wife for Hŭp'-pĭm and for Shŭp'pĭm. The name of his sister was Mā'a·cah. And the name of the second was Zĕ·lŏph'e·hăd; and Zelophehad had daughters. ¹⁶And Mā'a·cah the wife of Mā'chīr bore a son, and she called his name Pē'rĕsh; and the name of his brother was Shē'rĕsh; and his sons were Ū'lăm and Rā'kem. ¹⁷The sons of Ū'lăm: Bē'dăn. These were the sons

^r Syr Compare Vg: Heb *and to the sons*

of Gilead the son of Mā'chĭr, son of Mạ·năs'seh. [18]And his sister Hăm·mō'-lẹ·chĕth bore Īsh'hŏd, Ā·bĭ·ē'zẹr, and Măh'lạh. [19]The sons of Shĕ·mī'dạ were A·hī'ạn, Shē'chĕm, Lĭk'hī, and A·nī'ạm.

20 The sons of Ē'phrạ·ĭm: Shü-thē'lạh, and Bē'rĕd his son, Tā'hăth his son, Ĕl·ē·ā'dạh his son, Tahath his son, [21]Zā'băd his son, Shü·thē'lạh his son, and Ē'zẹr and Ē'lē·ăd, whom the men of Găth who were born in the land slew, because they came down to raid their cattle. [22]And Ē'phrạ·ĭm their father mourned many days, and his brothers came to comfort him. [23]And Ē'phrạ·ĭm went in to his wife, and she conceived and bore a son; and he called his name Bē·rī'ạh, because evil had befallen his house. [24]His daughter was Shē'ẹ·rah, who built both Lower and Upper Bĕth–hō'rŏn, and Ŭz'zẹn–shē'-ẹ·rah. [25]Rē'phạh was his son, Rē'shĕph his son, Tē'lạh his son, Tā'hăn his son, [26]Lā'dạn his son, Ăm·mī'hụd his son, Ē·līsh'ạ·mạ his son, [27]Nŭn his son, Joshua his son. [28]Their possessions and settlements were Bĕth'ĕl and its towns, and eastward Nā'ạ·răn, and west-ward Gē'zẹr and its towns, Shē'chĕm and its towns, and Āy'yạh and its towns; [29]also along the borders of the Mạ·năs'sītes, Bĕth–shē'ạn and its towns, Tā'ạ·năch and its towns, Mẹ·gĭd'dō and its towns, Dôr and its towns. In these dwelt the sons of Joseph the son of Israel.

30 The sons of Āsh'ẹr: Ĭm'nạh, Īsh'vạh, Īsh'vī, Bē·rī'ạh, and their sister Sē'rah. [31]The sons of Bē·rī'ạh: Hē'bẹr and Măl'chĭ–ĕl, who was the father of Bīr'zā·ĭth. [32]Hē'bẹr was the father of Jăph'lĕt, Shō'mẹr, Hō'thạm, and their sister Shü'ạ. [33]The sons of Jăph'lĕt: Pā'săch, Bĭm'hạl, and Āsh'-văth. These are the sons of Japhlet. [34]The sons of Shē'mẹr his brother: Rōh'gạh, Jĕ·hŭb'bạh, and Ăr'ạm. [35]The sons of Hē'lĕm his brother: Zō'phạh, Ĭm'nạ, Shē'lĕsh, and Ā'mạl. [36]The sons of Zō'phạh: Sü'ạh, Hăr'nĕ·phẹr, Shü'ạl, Bē'rī, Ĭm'rạh, [37]Bē'zẹr, Hŏd, Shăm'mạ, Shĭl'shạh, Ĭth'rạn, and Bē–ē'rạ. [38]The sons of Jē'thẹr: Jẹ·phŭn'nẹh, Pĭs'pạ, and Ăr'ạ. [39]The sons of Ŭl'lạ: Ā'rạh, Hăn'nī·ĕl, and Rĭ·zī'ạ. [40]All of these were men of Āsh'ẹr, heads of fathers' houses, approved, mighty warriors, chief of the princes. Their number enrolled

by genealogies, for service in war, was twenty-six thousand men.

8 Benjamin was the father of Bē'lạ his first-born, Āsh'bĕl the second, A'hăr·ah the third, [2]Nō'hạh the fourth, and Rā'phạ the fifth. [3]And Bē'lạ had sons: Ăd'dăr, Gē'rạ, A·bī'hụd, [4]Ăb·ĭ-shü'ạ, Nā'ạ·măn, A·hō'ạh, [5]Gē'rạ, Shĕ·phü'phạn, and Hū'rạm. [6]These are the sons of Ē'hủd (they were heads of fathers' houses of the inhabitants of Gē'bạ, and they were carried into exile to Mạ·nā'hăth): [7]Nā'ạ·măn,[s] A·hī'jạh, and Gē'rạ, that is, Hĕg'lạm,[t] who was the father of Ŭz'zạ and A·hī'hụd. [8]And Shā"hạ·rā'ĭm had sons in the country of Mō'ăb after he had sent away Hū'shĭm and Bā'ạ·rạ his wives. [9]He had sons by Hō'dĕsh his wife: Jō'băb, Zĭb'ĭ·ạ, Mē'shạ, Măl'cạm, [10]Jē'ụz, Sạ·chī'ạ, and Mīr'mạh. These were his sons, heads of fathers' houses. [11]He also had sons by Hū'shĭm: A·bī'tụb and Ĕl·pā'ạl. [12]The sons of Ĕl·pā'ạl: Ē'bẹr, Mī'shạm, and Shē'-mĕd, who built Ō'nō and Lŏd with its towns, [13]and Bē·rī'ạh and Shē'mạ (they were heads of fathers' houses of the inhabitants of Aī'jạ·lŏn, who put to flight the inhabitants of Găth); [14]and A·hī'ō, Shā'shăk, and Jĕr'ẹ·mŏth, [15]Zĕb·ạ·dī'ạh, Ăr'ạd, Ē'dẹr, [16]Michael, Ĭsh'pah, and Jō'hạ were sons of Bē·rī'ạh. [17]Zĕb·ạ·dī'ạh, Mĕ·shŭl'lạm, Hīz'kī, Hē'bẹr, [18]Ĭsh'mẹ·raī, Ĭz·lī'ạh, and Jō'băb were the sons of Ĕl·pā'ạl. [19]Jā'kĭm, Zĭch'rī, Zăb'dī, [20]Ē'lī–ē'naī, Zĭl'lẹ–thaī, Ē·lī'ĕl, [21]A·daī'ạh, Bĕ·rā'-ĭ·ah, and Shĭm'răth were the sons of Shĭm'ē–ī. [22]Ĭsh'păn, Ē'bẹr, Ē·lī'ĕl, [23]Ăb'dŏn, Zĭch'rī, Hā'nạn, [24]Hăn·ạ-nī'ah, Ē'lăm, Ăn·thọ·thī'jah, [25]Ĭph-dē'ĭ·ah, and Pĕ·nū'ĕl were the sons of Shā'shăk. [26]Shăm'shẹ·raī, Shē·hạ-rī'ah, Ăth·ạ·lī'ah, [27]Jā–ăr·ẹ·shī'ạh, Ē·lī'jạh and Zĭch'rī were the sons of Jẹ·rō'hăm. [28]These were the heads of fathers' houses, according to their generations, chief men. These dwelt in Jerusalem.

29 Jĕ–ī'ĕl[u] the father of Gĭb'ē·ọn dwelt in Gibeon, and the name of his wife was Mā'ạ·cah. [30]His first-born son: Āb'dŏn, then Zŭr, Kĭsh, Bā'ạl, Nā'dăb, [31]Gē'dôr, A·hī'ō, Zē'chẹr, [32]and Mĭk'lŏth (he was the father of Shĭm'ē–ạh). Now these also dwelt opposite their kinsmen in Jerusalem,

----

[s]Heb and Naaman [t]Or he carried them into exile
[u]Compare 9.35: Heb lacks Jeiel

with their kinsmen. ³³Nĕr was the father of Kĭsh, Kish of Saul, Saul of Jonathan, Măl″chĭ·shü′ă, Ă·bĭn′ă·dăb, and Ĕsh·bā′ăl; ³⁴and the son of Jonathan was Mĕr′ĭb–bā′ăl; and Meribbaal was the father of Mī′căh. ³⁵The sons of Mī′căh: Pī′thŏn, Mē′lĕch, Tặ·rē′ặ, and Ā′hăz. ³⁶Ā′hăz was the father of Jĕ·hō′ăd·dặh; and Jehoaddah was the father of Ăl′ĕ·mĕth, Ăz′mặ·vĕth, and Zĭm′rĭ; Zimri was the father of Mō′zặ. ³⁷Mō′zặ was the father of Bĭn′ĕ–a; Rā′phặh was his son, Ĕl–ĕ–ā′sặh his son, Ā′zĕl his son. ³⁸Ā′zĕl had six sons, and these are their names: Ăz·rĭ′kăm, Bō′chĕ·rü, Ĭsh′-mặ·ĕl, Shē·ặ·rī′ặh, Ō·bặ·dī′ặh, and Hā′nặn. All these were the sons of Azel. ³⁹The sons of Ē′shĕk his brother: Ū′lăm his first-born, Jĕ′ŭsh the second, and Ĕ·lĭph′ĕ·lĕt the third. ⁴⁰The sons of Ū′lăm were men who were mighty warriors, bowmen, having many sons and grandsons, one hundred and fifty. All these were Benjaminites.

9 So all Israel was enrolled by genealogies; and these are written in the Book of the Kings of Israel. And Judah was taken into exile in Babylon because of their unfaithfulness. ²Now the first to dwell again in their possessions in their cities were Israel, the priests, the Lē′vītes, and the temple servants. ³And some of the people of Judah, Benjamin, Ē′phrặ·ĭm, and Mặ-năs′sĕh dwelt in Jerusalem: ⁴Ū′thaī the son of Ăm·mī′hŭd, son of Ŏm′rĭ, son of Ĭm′rĭ, son of Bā′nī, from the sons of Pĕr′ĕz the son of Judah. ⁵And of the Shī′lọ·nītes: Ặ·sāi′ặh the first-born, and his sons. ⁶Of the sons of Zē′răh: Jĕ·ü′ĕl and their kinsmen, six hundred and ninety. ⁷Of the Benjaminites: Săl′lü the son of Mĕ·shŭl′lặm, son of Hŏd″ặ·vī′ặh, son of Hăs·sĕ·nü′ặh, ⁸Ĭb·nē′ĭ·ặh the son of Jĕ·rō′hăm, Ē′lặh the son of Ŭz′zī, son of Mĭch′rĭ, and Mĕ·shŭl′lặm the son of Shĕphặ·tī′ặh, son of Reü′ĕl, son of Ĭb·nī′jặh; ⁹and their kinsmen according to their generations, nine hundred and fifty-six. All these were heads of fathers' houses according to their fathers' houses.

10 Of the priests: Jĕ·daī′ặh, Jĕ·hoī′-ặ·rīb, Jā′chĭn, ¹¹and Ăz·ặ·rī′ặh the son of Hĭl′kĭ′ặh, son of Mĕ·shŭl′lặm, son of Zā′dŏk, son of Mĕ·rā′ĭ·ŏth, son of Ặ·hī′tŭb, the chief officer of the house of God; ¹²and Ặ·daī′ặh the son of

Jĕ·rō′hăm, son of Păsh′hŭr, son of Măl·chī′jặh, and Mā′ặ·saī the son of Ăd′ī–ĕl, son of Jäh″zĕ·răh, son of Mĕ·shŭl′lặm, son of Mĕ·shĭl′lĕ·mĭth, son of Ĭm′mĕr; ¹³besides their kinsmen, heads of their fathers' houses, one thousand seven hundred and sixty, very able men for the work of the service of the house of God.

14 Of the Lē′vītes: Shĕ·māi′ặh the son of Hăs′shŭb, son of Ăz·rĭ′kăm, son of Hăsh·ặ·bī′ặh, of the sons of Mĕ·râr′ī; ¹⁵and Băk·băk′kăr, Hē′rĕsh, Gā′lăl, and Măt·tặ·nī′ặh the son of Mī′cặ, son of Zĭch′rĭ, son of Ā′săph; ¹⁶and Ō′bặ·dī′ặh the son of Shĕ·māi′ặh, son of Gā′lăl, son of Jĕ·dü′thụn, and Bĕr·ặ·chī′ặh the son of Asa, son of Ĕl·kā′nặh, who dwelt in the villages of the Nặ·tŏph′ặ·thītes.

17 The gatekeepers were: Shăl′lụm, Ăk′kụb, Tăl′mọn, Ặ·hī′mặn, and their kinsmen (Shallum being the chief), ¹⁸stationed hitherto in the king's gate on the east side. These were the gatekeepers of the camp of the Lē′vītes. ¹⁹Shăl′lụm the son of Kō′rĕ, son of Ē·bī′ặ·săph, son of Kō′răh, and his kinsmen of his fathers' house, the Kō′ră·hītes, were in charge of the work of the service, keepers of the thresholds of the tent, as their fathers had been in charge of the camp of the LORD, keepers of the entrance. ²⁰And Phĭn′ĕ·hặs the son of Ĕl·ē·ā′zặr was the ruler over them in time past; the LORD was with him. ²¹Zĕch·ặ·rī′ặh the son of Mĕ·shĕl·ĕ·mī′ặh was gatekeeper at the entrance of the tent of meeting. ²²All these, who were chosen as gatekeepers at the thresholds, were two hundred and twelve. They were enrolled by genealogies in their villages. David and Samuel the seer established them in their office of trust. ²³So they and their sons were in charge of the gates of the house of the LORD, that is, the house of the tent, as guards. ²⁴The gatekeepers were on the four sides, east, west, north, and south; ²⁵and their kinsmen who were in their villages were obliged to come in every seven days, from time to time, to be with these; ²⁶for the four chief gatekeepers, who were Lē′vītes, were in charge of the chambers and the treasures of the house of God. ²⁷And they lodged round about the house of God; for upon them lay the duty of watch-

9.1, 2: Ezra 2.70; Neh 7.73; 11.3.   9.3-17: Neh 11.4-19.

ng, and they had charge of opening
every morning.

28 Some of them had charge of the
utensils of service, for they were
required to count them when they
were brought in and taken out.
⁹Others of them were appointed
over the furniture, and over all the holy
utensils, also over the fine flour, the
wine, the oil, the incense, and the
spices. ³⁰Others, of the sons of the
priests, prepared the mixing of the
spices, ³¹and Măt·tĭ·thī'ạh, one of
the Lē'vītes, the first-born of Shăl'-
um the Kō'rạ·hīte, was in charge of
making the flat cakes. ³²Also some
of their kinsmen of the Kō'hạ·thītes
had charge of the showbread, to prepare it every sabbath.

33 Now these are the singers, the
heads of fathers' houses of the Lē'-
vītes, dwelling in the chambers of the
temple free from other service, for they
were on duty day and night. ³⁴These
were heads of fathers' houses of the
Lē'vītes, according to their generations, leaders, who lived in Jerusalem.

35 In Gĭb'ē·on dwelt the father of
Gibeon, Jĕ–ī'ĕl, and the name of his
wife was Mā'ạ·cah, ³⁶and his first-
born son Ăb'dŏn, then Zŭr, Kīsh, Bā'al,
Nēr, Nā'dăb, ³⁷Gē'dôr, Ạ·hī'ō, Zĕch-
ạ·rī'ạh, and Mīk'lŏth; ³⁸and Mīk'lŏth
was the father of Shĭm'ē–ăm; and
these also dwelt opposite their kinsmen in Jerusalem, with their kinsmen. ³⁹Nēr was the father of Kīsh,
Kish of Saul, Saul of Jonathan, Măl"-
chĭ·shü'ạ, Ạ·bĭn'ạ·dăb, and Ĕsh·bā'al;
⁴⁰and the son of Jonathan was Mĕr'ĭb–
bā'al; and Merib–baal was the father
of Mī'cah. ⁴¹The sons of Mī'cah: Pī'-
hŏn, Mē'lĕch, Täh'rē–ạ, and Ā'hăz;ᵛ
²and Ā'hăz was the father of Jär'ạh,
and Jarah of Ăl'ẹ·mĕth, Ăz'mạ·vĕth,
and Zĭm'rī; and Zimri was the father
of Mō'zạ. ⁴³Mō'zạ was the father of
Bĭn'ē–ạ; and Rĕph·āi'ạh was his son,
Ĕl·ĕ–ā'sah his son, Ā'zĕl his son.
⁴Ā'zĕl had six sons and these are their
names: Ăz·rī'kăm, Bō'chĕ·rü, Ĭsh'-
na·ĕl, Shē·ạ·rī'ạh, Ō·bạ·dī'ạh, and
Hā'nạn; these were the sons of Azel.

10 Now the Phĭ·lĭs'tĭnes fought
against Israel; and the men of
Israel fled before the Philistines, and
fell slain on Mount Gĭl·bō'ạ. ²And the
Phĭ·lĭs'tĭnes overtook Saul and his
sons; and the Philistines slew Jona-
han and Ạ·bĭn'ạ·dăb and Măl"chĭ-

shü'ạ, the sons of Saul. ³The battle
pressed hard upon Saul, and the
archers found him; and he was
wounded by the archers. ⁴Then Saul
said to his armor-bearer, "Draw your
sword, and thrust me through with it,
lest these uncircumcised come and
make sport of me." But his armor-
bearer would not; for he feared greatly.
Therefore Saul took his own sword,
and fell upon it. ⁵And when his armor-
bearer saw that Saul was dead, he also
fell upon his sword, and died. ⁶Thus
Saul died; he and his three sons and all
his house died together. ⁷And when all
the men of Israel who were in the
valley saw that the armyʷ had fled
and that Saul and his sons were dead,
they forsook their cities and fled; and
the Phĭ·lĭs'tĭnes came and dwelt in
them.

8 On the morrow, when the Phĭ-
lĭs'tĭnes came to strip the slain, they
found Saul and his sons fallen on
Mount Gĭl·bō'ạ. ⁹And they stripped
him and took his head and his armor, and sent messengers throughout
the land of the Phĭ·lĭs'tĭnes, to carry
the good news to their idols and to the
people. ¹⁰And they put his armor in the
temple of their gods, and fastened his
head in the temple of Dā'gŏn. ¹¹But
when all Jā'bĕsh–gĭl'ē·ạd heard all
that the Phĭ·lĭs'tĭnes had done to Saul,
¹²all the valiant men arose, and took
away the body of Saul and the bodies
of his sons, and brought them to
Jā'bĕsh. And they buried their bones
under the oak in Jabesh, and fasted
seven days.

13 So Saul died for his unfaithfulness; he was unfaithful to the Lord
in that he did not keep the command
of the Lord, and also consulted a
medium, seeking guidance, ¹⁴and did
not seek guidance from the Lord.
Therefore the Lord slew him, and
turned the kingdom over to David the
son of Jesse.

11 Then all Israel gathered together to David at Hē'brŏn,
and said, "Behold, we are your bone
and flesh. ²In times past, even when
Saul was king, it was you that led out
and brought in Israel; and the Lord
your God said to you, 'You shall be
shepherd of my people Israel, and you
shall be prince over my people Israel.'"

³So all the elders of Israel came to the king at Hē'brŏn; and David made a covenant with them at Hebron before the LORD, and they anointed David king over Israel, according to the word of the LORD by Samuel. 4 And David and all Israel went to Jerusalem, that is Jē'bŭs, where the Jĕb'ū·sītes were, the inhabitants of the land. ⁵The inhabitants of Jē'bŭs said to David, "You will not come in here." Nevertheless David took the stronghold of Zion, that is, the city of David. ⁶David said, "Whoever shall smite the Jĕb'ū·sītes first shall be chief and commander." And Jō'ăb the son of Zĕ·rü'ĭ·ah went up first, so he became chief. ⁷And David dwelt in the stronghold; therefore it was called the city of David. ⁸And he built the city round about from the Mĭl'lō in complete circuit; and Jō'ăb repaired the rest of the city. ⁹And David became greater and greater, for the LORD of hosts was with him.

10 Now these are the chiefs of David's mighty men, who gave him strong support in his kingdom, together with all Israel, to make him king, according to the word of the LORD concerning Israel. ¹¹This is an account of David's mighty men: Ja·shō'bē–am, a Hăch'mo·nīte, was chief of the three;ˣ he wielded his spear against three hundred whom he slew at one time.

12 And next to him among the three mighty men was Ĕl·ē·ā'zar the son of Dō'dō, the A·hō'hīte. ¹³He was with David at Păs–dăm'mĭm when the Phĭ·lĭs'tĭnes were gathered there for battle. There was a plot of ground full of barley, and the men fled from the Philistines. ¹⁴But heʸ took hisʸ stand in the midst of the plot, and defended it, and slew the Phĭ·lĭs'tĭnes; and the LORD saved them by a great victory.

15 Three of the thirty chief men went down to the rock to David at the cave of A·dŭl'lam, when the army of Phĭ·lĭs'tĭnes was encamped in the valley of Rĕph'a·ĭm. ¹⁶David was then in the stronghold; and the garrison of the Phĭ·lĭs'tĭnes was then at Bethlehem. ¹⁷And David said longingly, "O that some one would give me water to drink from the well of Bethlehem which is by the gate!" ¹⁸Then the three mighty men broke through the camp of the Phĭ·lĭs'tĭnes, and drew water out

of the well of Bethlehem which was by the gate, and took and brought it to David. But David would not drink of it; he poured it out to the LORD, ¹⁹and said, "Far be it from me before my God that I should do this. Shall I drink the lifeblood of these men? For at the risk of their lives they brought it." Therefore he would not drink it. These things did the three mighty men.

20 Now A·bī'shaī, the brother of Jō'ăb, was chief of the thirty.ᶻ And he wielded his spear against three hundred men and slew them, and won a name beside the three. ²¹He was the most renownedᵃ of the thirty,ᶻ and became their commander; but he did not attain to the three.

22 And Bĕ·nā'ĭ·ah the son of Jĕhoi'a·da was a valiant manᵇ of Kăb'zē·el, a doer of great deeds; he smote two arielsᶜ of Mō'ăb. He also went down and slew a lion in a pit on a day when snow had fallen. ²³And he slew an Egyptian, a man of great stature, five cubits tall. The Egyptian had in his hand a spear like a weaver's beam; but Bĕ·nā'ĭ·ah went down to him with a staff, and snatched the spear out of the Egyptian's hand, and slew him with his own spear. ²⁴These things did Bĕ·nā'ĭ·ah the son of Jĕ·hoi'a·da, and won a name beside the three mighty men. ²⁵He was renowned among the thirty, but he did not attain to the three. And David set him over his bodyguard.

26 The mighty men of the armies were Ăs'a·hĕl the brother of Jō'ăb, Ĕl·hā'nan the son of Dō'dō of Bethlehem, ²⁷Shăm'mŏth of Hăr'ŏd,ᵈ Hē'lĕz the Pĕl'o·nīte, ²⁸Ira the son of Ĭk'kĕsh of Tĕ·kō'a, A·bī·ē'zer of Ăn'a·thŏth, ²⁹Sĭb'be·caī the Hū'sha·thīte, Ĭ'laī the A·hō'hīte, ³⁰Mā'ha·raī of Ne·tŏph'ah, Hē'lĕd the son of Bā'a·nah of Netophah, ³¹Ĭth'aī the son of Rī'baī of Gĭb'ē–ah of the Benjaminites, Bĕ·nā'ĭ·ah of Pĭr'a·thŏn, ³²Hū'raī of the brooks of Gā'ăsh, A·bī'el the Ăr'ba·thīte, ³³Ăz'ma·vĕth of Ba·hā'rum, Ĕ·lī'ah·ba of Shā–ăl'bŏn, ³⁴Hā'shĕmᵉ the Gī'zo·nīte, Jonathan the son

ˣCompare 2 Sam 23.8: Heb *thirty* or *captains*
ʸCompare 2 Sam 23.12: Heb *they ... their*
ᶻSyr: Heb *three*
ᵃCompare 2 Sam 23.19: Heb *more renowned among the two* ᵇSyr: Heb *the son of a valiant man*
ᶜThe meaning of the word *ariel* is unknown
ᵈCompare 2 Sam 23.25: Heb *the Harorite*
ᵉCompare Gk and 2 Sam 23.32: Heb *the sons of Hashem*
11.4–9: 2 Sam 5.6–10. **11.10–41:** 2 Sam 23.8–39.

of Shā'gee the Hăr'ạ·rīte, ³⁵Ạ·hī'ạm nāī eleventh. ¹⁴These Gā'dītes were
the son of Sā'chär the Hăr'ạ·rīte, officers of the army, the lesser over a
Ĕ·lī'phăl the son of Ūr, ³⁶Hē'phẹr the hundred and the greater over a thou-
Mĕ·chē'rạ·thīte, Ạ·hī'jạh the Pĕl'ọ- sand. ¹⁵These are the men who crossed
nīte, ³⁷Hĕz'rō of Căr'mẹl, Nā'hạ·raī the the Jordan in the first month, when it
son of Ĕz'baī, ³⁸Jō'ẹl the brother of was overflowing all its banks, and put
Nathan, Mĭb'här the son of Hăg'rī, to flight all those in the valleys, to the
³⁹Zē'lĕk the Ăm'mọ·nīte, Nā'ạ·raī of east and to the west.
Bẹ–ēr'ọth, the armor-bearer of Jō'äb 16 And some of the men of Ben-
the son of Zĕ·rü'ĭ·ạh, ⁴⁰Ira the Ĭth'rīte, jamin and Judah came to the strong-
Gā'rĕb the Ithrite, ⁴¹Ū·rī'ạh the Hīt'- hold to David. ¹⁷David went out to
tīte, Zā'băd the son of Äh'laī, ⁴²Ăd'ĭ·nạ meet them and said to them, "If you
the son of Shī'zạ the Reubenite, a have come to me in friendship to help
leader of the Reubenites, and thirty me, my heart will be knit to you; but
with him, ⁴³Hā'nạn the son of Mā'- if to betray me to my adversaries, al-
ạ·cạh, and Jŏsh'ạ·phăt the Mīth'nīte, though there is no wrong in my hands,
⁴⁴Ŭz·zī'ạ the Ăsh'tĕ·rạ·thīte, Shā'mạ then may the God of our fathers see
and Jĕ–ī'ĕl the sons of Hō'thạm the and rebuke you." ¹⁸Then the Spirit
Ạ·rō'ẹ·rīte, ⁴⁵Jĕ·dī'ạ–ĕl the son of came upon Ạ·mā'saī, chief of the
Shĭm'rī, and Jō'hạ his brother, the thirty, and he said,
Tī'zīte, ⁴⁶Ĕ·lī'ĕl the Mā'hạ·vīte, and
Jĕr'ĭ·baī, and Jŏsh·ạ·vī'ạh, the sons of
Ĕl'nā–ạm, and Ĭth'mạh the Mō'ạb·īte,   "We are yours, O David;
⁴⁷Ĕ·lī'ĕl, and Ō'bĕd, and Jā–ạ·sī'ĕl the   and with you, O son of Jesse!
Mĕ·zō'bạ·īte.   Peace, peace to you,
                                                and peace to your helpers!
12 Now these are the men who   For your God helps you."
      came to David at Zĭk'lăg,
while he could not move about freely Then David received them, and made
because of Saul the son of Kĭsh; and them officers of his troops.
they were among the mighty men who   19 Some of the men of Mạ·năs'sẹh
helped him in war. ²They were bow- deserted to David when he came with
men, and could shoot arrows and sling the Phĭ·lĭs'tīnes for the battle against
stones with either the right or the left Saul. (Yet he did not help them,
hand; they were Benjaminites, Saul's for the rulers of the Philistines took
kinsmen. ³The chief was Ā'hī-ē'zẹr, counsel and sent him away, saying,
then Jō'ăsh, both sons of Shĕ·mā'ạh of "At peril to our heads he will desert
Gĭb'ē–ạh; also Jē'zĭ–ĕl and Pē'lĕt the to his master Saul.") ²⁰As he went to
sons of Ăz'mạ·vĕth; Bĕr'ạ·cạh, Jē'hū Zĭk'lăg these men of Mạ·năs'sẹh de-
of Ăn'ạ·thŏth, ⁴Ĭsh·mā'ĭ·ạh of Gĭb'ē·ọn, serted to him: Ăd'nạh, Jŏz'ạ·băd,
a mighty man among the thirty and Jĕ·dī'ạ–ĕl, Michael, Jozabad, Ĕ·lī'hū,
a leader over the thirty; Jĕr·ẹ·mī'ạh,ʲ and Zĭl'lẹ·thaī, chiefs of thousands
Jạ·hā'zĭ·ĕl, Jō·hā'nạn, Jŏz'ạ·băd of in Manasseh. ²¹They helped David
Gĕ·dē'rạh, ⁵Ĕ·lü'zaī,ᵍ Jĕr'ĭ·mŏth, Bĕ- against the band of raiders;ʰ for they
ạ·lī'ạh, Shĕm·ạ·rī'ạh, Shĕph·ạ·tī'ạh the were all mighty men of valor, and were
Hăr'ụ·phīte; ⁶Ĕl·kā'nạh, Ĭs·shī'ạh, Ăz'- commanders in the army. ²²For from
ạ·rĕl, Jō–ē'zẹr, and Jạ·shō'bē–ạm, the day to day men kept coming to David
Kō'rạ·hītes; ⁷and Jō–ē'lạh and Zĕb·ạ- to help him, until there was a great
lī'ạh, the sons of Jĕ·rō'hăm of Gē'dôr. army, like an army of God.
  8 From the Gā'dītes there went   23 These are the numbers of the
over to David at the stronghold in divisions of the armed troops, who
the wilderness mighty and experi- came to David in Hē'brọn, to turn the
enced warriors, expert with shield kingdom of Saul over to him, accord-
and spear, whose faces were like the ing to the word of the LORD. ²⁴The men
faces of lions, and who were swift of Judah bearing shield and spear
as gazelles upon the mountains: were six thousand eight hundred
Ē'zẹr the chief, Ō'bạ·dī'ạh second, armed troops. ²⁵Of the Sĭm'ē·ọ·nītes,
Ĕ·lī'ăb third, ¹⁰Mīsh·măn'nạh fourth, mighty men of valor for war, seven
Jĕr·ẹ·mī'ạh fifth, ¹¹Ăt'taī sixth, Ĕ·lī'ĕl thousand and one hundred. ²⁶Of the Lē'-
seventh, ¹²Jō·hā'nạn eighth, Ĕl·zā'băd vītes four thousand six hundred.
ninth, ¹³Jĕr·ẹ·mī'ạh tenth, Măch'băn- ʲHeb verse 5 ᵍHeb verse 6 ʰOr *as officers of his troops*

²⁷The prince Jĕ·hoi′ạ·dạ, of the house of Aaron, and with him three thousand seven hundred. ²⁸Zā′dŏk, a young man mighty in valor, and twenty-two commanders from his own father's house. ²⁹Of the Benjaminites, the kinsmen of Saul, three thousand, of whom the majority had hitherto kept their allegiance to the house of Saul. ³⁰Of the Ē′phrạ·im·ites twenty thousand eight hundred, mighty men of valor, famous men in their fathers' houses. ³¹Of the half-tribe of Mạ·năs′seh eighteen thousand, who were expressly named to come and make David king. ³²Of Ĭs′sạ·chär men who had understanding of the times, to know what Israel ought to do, two hundred chiefs, and all their kinsmen under their command. ³³Of Zĕb′ū·lun fifty thousand seasoned troops, equipped for battle with all the weapons of war, to help David*ⁱ* with singleness of purpose. ³⁴Of Năph′tạ·lī a thousand commanders with whom were thirty-seven thousand men armed with shield and spear. ³⁵Of the Dă′nītes twenty-eight thousand six hundred men equipped for battle. ³⁶Of Ăsh′er forty thousand seasoned troops ready for battle. ³⁷Of the Reubenites and Găd′ītes and the half-tribe of Mạ·năs′seh from beyond the Jordan, one hundred and twenty thousand men armed with all the weapons of war.

38 All these, men of war, arrayed in battle order, came to Hē′bron with full intent to make David king over all Israel; likewise all the rest of Israel were of a single mind to make David king. ³⁹And they were there with David for three days, eating and drinking, for their brethren had made preparation for them. ⁴⁰And also their neighbors, from as far as Ĭs′sạ·chär and Zĕb′ū·lun and Năph′tạ·lī, came bringing food on asses and on camels and on mules and on oxen, abundant provisions of meal, cakes of figs, clusters of raisins, and wine and oil, oxen and sheep, for there was joy in Israel.

13 David consulted with the commanders of thousands and of hundreds, with every leader. ²And David said to all the assembly of Israel, "If it seems good to you, and if it is the will of the LORD our God, let us send abroad to our brethren who remain in all the land of Israel, and with them to the priests and Lē′vītes

in the cities that have pasture lands, that they may come together to us. ³Then let us bring again the ark of our God to us; for we neglected it in the days of Saul." ⁴All the assembly agreed to do so, for the thing was right in the eyes of all the people.

5 So David assembled all Israel from the Shī′hôr of Egypt to the entrance of Hā′măth, to bring the ark of God from Kĭr′ĭ·ăth-jē′ạ·rĭm. ⁶And David and all Israel went up to Bā′ạ·lah, that is, to Kĭr′ĭ·ăth-jē′ạ·rĭm which belongs to Judah, to bring up from there the ark of God, which is called by the name of the LORD who sits enthroned above the cherubim. ⁷And they carried the ark of God upon a new cart, from the house of Ạ·bĭn′ạ·dăb, and Ŭz′zạh and Ạ·hī′ō*ʲ* were driving the cart. ⁸And David and all Israel were making merry before God with all their might, with song and lyres and harps and tambourines and cymbals and trumpets.

9 And when they came to the threshing floor of Chī′dŏn, Ŭz′zạh put out his hand to hold the ark, for the oxen stumbled. ¹⁰And the anger of the LORD was kindled against Ŭz′zạh; and he smote him because he put forth his hand to the ark; and he died there before God. ¹¹And David was angry because the LORD had broken forth upon Ŭz′zạh; and that place is called Pĕr′ĕz-ŭz′zạ*ᵏ* to this day. ¹²And David was afraid of God that day; and he said, "How can I bring the ark of God home to me?" ¹³So David did not take the ark home into the city of David, but took it aside to the house of Ō′bĕd-ē′dom the Gĭt′tīte. ¹⁴And the ark of God remained with the household of Ō′bĕd-ē′dom in his house three months; and the LORD blessed the household of Obed–edom and all that he had.

14 And Hiram king of Tyre sent messengers to David, and cedar trees, also masons and carpenters to build a house for him. ²And David perceived that the LORD had established him king over Israel, and that his kingdom was highly exalted for the sake of his people Israel.

3 And David took more wives in

ⁱGk: Heb lacks *David*   ʲOr *and his brother*
ᵏThat is *The breaking forth upon Uzzah*
13.1–14: 2 Sam 6.1-11.   **14.1, 2:** 2 Sam 5.11, 12.
14.3–7: 3.5-8; 2 Sam 5.14-16.

Jerusalem, and David begot more sons and daughters. ⁴These are the names of the children whom he had in Jerusalem: Shăm'mū-a, Shō'băb, Nathan, Şolomon, ⁵Ĭb'hār, Ĕ·lī'shü-a, Ĕl'-ẹ·lĕt, ⁶Nō'gah, Nē'phĕg, Ja·phī'a, Ĕ·līsh'a·ma, Bē·ẹ·lī'a·da, and Ĕ·līph'-lĕt.

8 When the Phĭ·lĭs'tĭnes heard that David had been anointed king over all Israel, all the Philistines went up in search of David; and David heard of it and went out against them. ⁹Now the Phĭ·lĭs'tĭnes had come and made a raid in the valley of Rĕph'a·ĭm. ¹⁰And David inquired of God, "Shall I go up against the Phĭ·lĭs'tĭnes? Wilt thou give them into my hand?" And the LORD said to him, "Go up, and I will give them into your hand." ¹¹And he went up to Bā'al–pĕ·rā'zĭm, and David defeated them there; and David said, "God has broken through¹ my enemies by my hand, like a bursting flood." Therefore the name of that place is called Baal–perazim.ᵐ ¹²And they left their gods there, and David gave command, and they were burned.

13 And the Phĭ·lĭs'tĭnes yet again made a raid in the valley. ¹⁴And when David again inquired of God, God said to him, "You shall not go up after them; go around and come upon them opposite the balsam trees. ¹⁵And when you hear the sound of marching in the tops of the balsam trees, then go out to battle; for God has gone out before you to smite the army of the Phĭ·lĭs'tĭnes." ¹⁶And David did as God commanded him, and they smote the Phĭ·lĭs'tĭne army from Gĭb'ē·on to Gē'zer. ¹⁷And the fame of David went out into all lands, and the LORD brought the fear of him upon all nations.

15 David built houses for himself in the city of David; and he prepared a place for the ark of God, and pitched a tent for it. ²Then David said, "No one but the Lē'vītes may carry the ark of God, for the LORD chose them to carry the ark of the LORD and to minister to him for ever." ³And David assembled all Israel at Jerusalem, to bring up the ark of the LORD to its place, which he had prepared for it. ⁴And David gathered together the sons of Aaron and the Lē'-ites: ⁵of the sons of Kō'hăth, Ū·rī'ẹl the chief, with a hundred and twenty of his brethren; ⁶of the sons of Mẹ-

rār'ī, A·sāi'ah the chief, with two hundred and twenty of his brethren; ⁷of the sons of Gēr'shom, Jō'ẹl the chief, with a hundred and thirty of his brethren; ⁸of the sons of Ĕ·lī·zā'-phan, Shĕ·māi'ah the chief, with two hundred of his brethren; ⁹of the sons of Hē'bron, Ĕ·lī'ẹl the chief, with eighty of his brethren; ¹⁰of the sons of Ūz'zĭ-ĕl, Ăm·mĭn'a·dăb the chief, with a hundred and twelve of his brethren. ¹¹Then David summoned the priests Zā'dŏk and A·bī'a·thār, and the Lē'vītes Ū·rī'ẹl, A·sāi'ah, Jō'ẹl, Shĕ·māi'ah, Ĕ·lī'ẹl, and Ăm·mĭn'a·dăb, ¹²and said to them, "You are the heads of the fathers' houses of the Lē'vītes; sanctify yourselves, you and your brethren, so that you may bring up the ark of the LORD, the God of Israel, to the place that I have prepared for it. ¹³Because you did not carry it the first time,ⁿ the LORD our God broke forth upon us, because we did not care for it in the way that is ordained." ¹⁴So the priests and the Lē'vītes sanctified themselves to bring up the ark of the LORD, the God of Israel. ¹⁵And the Lē'vītes carried the ark of God upon their shoulders with the poles, as Moses had commanded according to the word of the LORD.

16 David also commanded the chiefs of the Lē'vītes to appoint their brethren as the singers who should play loudly on musical instruments, on harps and lyres and cymbals, to raise sounds of joy. ¹⁷So the Lē'vītes appointed Hē'man the son of Jō'ẹl; and of his brethren Ā'săph the son of Bĕr·ẹ·chī'ah; and of the sons of Mẹ-rār'ī, their brethren, Ē'than the son of Kū·shā'ĭ·ah; ¹⁸and with them their brethren of the second order, Zĕch-a·rī'ah, Ja–ā'zĭ·ĕl, Shĕ·mĭr'a·mŏth, Jĕ·hī'ĕl, Ŭn'nī, Ĕ·lī'ăb, Bĕ·nā'ĭ·ah, Mā'a·sēi'ah, Măt·tĭ·thī'ah, Ĕ·līph'ẹ-lĕ·hū, and Mĭk·nē'ĭ·ah, and the gatekeepers Ō'bĕd–ē'dom and Jĕ-ī'ĕl. ¹⁹The singers, Hē'man, Ā'săph, and Ē'than, were to sound bronze cymbals; ²⁰Zĕch·a·rī'ah, Ā'zĭ–ĕl, Shĕ·mĭr'a·mŏth, Jĕ·hī'ĕl, Ŭn'nī, Ĕ·lī'ăb, Mā'a·sēi'ah, and Bĕ·nā'ĭ·ah were to play harps according to Ăl'a·mŏth; ²¹but Măt·tĭ-thī'ah, Ĕ·līph'ẹ·lĕ·hū, Mĭk·nē'ĭ·ah,

¹Heb *paraz*   ᵐThat is *Lord of breaking through*
ⁿThe meaning of the Hebrew word is uncertain
14.8–12: 2 Sam 5.17-21. **14.13–16:** 2 Sam 5.22-25.
15.1–16.3: 2 Sam 6.12-19.

Ō′bĕd–ē′dǫm, Jĕ–ī′ĕl, and Ăz·a·zī′ah were to lead with lyres according to the Shĕm′ĭ·nĭth. ²²Chĕn·a·nī′ah, leader of the Lē′vītes in music, should direct the music, for he understood it. ²³Bĕr·e·chī′ah and Ĕl·kā′nah were to be gatekeepers for the ark. ²⁴Shĕb·a·nī′ah, Jŏsh′a·phăt, Ne·thăn′ĕl, A·mā′saī, Zĕch·a·rī′ah, Bĕ·nā′ī·ah, and Ĕ·lī·ē′zer, the priests, should blow the trumpets before the ark of God. Ō′bĕd–ē′dǫm and Jĕ·hī′ah also were to be gatekeepers for the ark.

25 So David and the elders of Israel, and the commanders of thousands, went to bring up the ark of the covenant of the LORD from the house of Ō′bĕd–ē′dǫm with rejoicing. ²⁶And because God helped the Lē′vītes who were carrying the ark of the covenant of the LORD, they sacrificed seven bulls and seven rams. ²⁷David was clothed with a robe of fine linen, as also were all the Lē′vītes who were carrying the ark, and the singers, and Chĕn·a·nī′ah the leader of the music of the singers; and David wore a linen ephod. ²⁸So all Israel brought up the ark of the covenant of the LORD with shouting, to the sound of the horn, trumpets, and cymbals, and made loud music on harps and lyres.

29 And as the ark of the covenant of the LORD cáme to the city of David, Mī′chal the daughter of Saul looked out of the window, and saw King David dancing and making merry; ˙and she despised him in her heart.

16 And they brought in the ark of God, and set it inside the tent which David had pitched for it; and they offered burnt offerings and peace offerings before God. ²And when David had finished offering the burnt offerings and the peace offerings, he blessed the people in the name of the LORD, ³and distributed to all Israel, both men and women, to each a loaf of bread, a portion of meat,ᵒ and a cake of raisins.

4 Moreover he appointed certain of the Lē′vītes as ministers before the ark of the LORD, to invoke, to thank, and to praise the LORD, the God of Israel. ⁵Ā′săph was the chief, and second to him were Zĕch·a·rī′ah, Jĕ–ī′ĕl, Shĕ·mǐr′a·mǒth, Jĕ·hī′ĕl, Măt·tĭ·thī′ah, Ĕ·lī′ăb, Bĕ·nā′ī·ah, Ō′bĕd–ē′dǫm, and Je–iel, who were to play harps and lyres; Asaph was to sound

the cymbals, ⁶and Bĕ·nā′ī·ah and Ja·hā′zī·ĕl the priests were to blow trumpets continually, before the ark of the covenant of God.

7 Then on that day David first appointed that thanksgiving be sung to the LORD by Ā′săph and his brethren.

⁸O give thanks to the LORD, call on his name,
make known his deeds among the peoples!
⁹Sing to him, sing praises to him,
tell of all his wonderful works!
¹⁰Glory in his holy name;
let the hearts of those who seek the LORD rejoice!
¹¹Seek the LORD and his strength,
seek his presence continually!
¹²Remember the wonderful works that he has done,
the wonders he wrought, the judgments he uttered,
¹³O offspring of Abraham his servant,
sons of Jacob, his chosen ones!

¹⁴He is the LORD our God;
his judgments are in all the earth.
¹⁵He is mindful of his covenant for ever,
of the word that he commanded for a thousand generations,
¹⁶the covenant which he made with Abraham,
his sworn promise to Isaac,
¹⁷which he confirmed as a statute to Jacob,
as an everlasting covenant to Israel,
¹⁸saying, "To you I will give the land of Canaan,
as your portion for an inheritance."

¹⁹When they were few in number,
and of little account, and sojourners in it,
²⁰wandering from nation to nation,
from one kingdom to another people,
²¹he allowed no one to oppress them;
he rebuked kings on their account,
²²saying, "Touch not my anointed ones,
do my prophets no harm!"

²³Sing to the LORD, all the earth!
Tell of his salvation from day to day.

ᵒCompare Gk Syr Vg: Heb uncertain
16.8-22: Ps 105.1-15. 16.23-33: Ps 96.1-13.

²⁴ Declare his glory among the nations,
his marvelous works among all the peoples!
²⁵ For great is the LORD, and greatly to be praised,
and he is to be held in awe above all gods.
²⁶ For all the gods of the peoples are idols;
but the LORD made the heavens.
²⁷ Honor and majesty are before him;
strength and joy are in his place.

²⁸ Ascribe to the LORD, O families of the peoples,
ascribe to the LORD glory and strength!
²⁹ Ascribe to the LORD the glory due his name;
bring an offering, and come before him!
Worship the LORD in holy array;
³⁰ tremble before him, all the earth;
yea, the world stands firm, never to be moved.
³¹ Let the heavens be glad, and let the earth rejoice,
and let them say among the nations, "The LORD reigns!"
³² Let the sea roar, and all that fills it,
let the field exult, and everything in it!
³³ Then shall the trees of the wood sing for joy
before the LORD, for he comes to judge the earth.
³⁴ O give thanks to the LORD, for he is good;
for his steadfast love endures for ever!

³⁵ Say also:
"Deliver us, O God of our salvation,
and gather and save us from among the nations,
that we may give thanks to thy holy name,
and glory in thy praise.
³⁶ Blessed be the LORD, the God of Israel,
from everlasting to everlasting!"
Then all the people said "Amen!"
and praised the LORD.

37 So David left Ā'săph and his brethren there before the ark of the covenant of the LORD to minister continually before the ark as each day required ³⁸ and also Ō'bĕd-ē'dom and his*ᵖ* sixty-eight brethren; while Obed-edom, the son of Jĕ·dü'thun, and Hō'-sah were to be gatekeepers. ³⁹ And he left Zā'dŏk .the priest and his brethren the priests before the tabernacle of the LORD in the high place that was at Gĭb'ē·ǫn, ⁴⁰ to offer burnt offerings to the LORD upon the altar of burnt offering continually morning and evening, according to all that is written in the law of the LORD which he commanded Israel. ⁴¹ With them were Hē'-mạn· and Jĕ·dü'thụn, and the rest of those chosen and expressly named to give thanks to the LORD, for his steadfast love endures for ever. ⁴² Hē'mạn and Jĕ·dü'thụn had trumpets and cymbals for the music and instruments for sacred song. The sons of Jeduthun were appointed to the gate.

43 Then all the people departed each to his house, and David went home to bless his household.

17 Now when David dwelt in his house, David said to Nathan the prophet, "Behold, I dwell in a house of cedar, but the ark of the covenant of the LORD is under a tent." ² And Nathan said to David, "Do all that is in your heart, for God is with you."

3 But that same night the word of the LORD came to Nathan, ⁴ "Go and tell my servant David, 'Thus says the LORD: You shall not build me a house to dwell in. ⁵ For I have not dwelt in a house since the day I led up Israel to this day, but I have gone from tent to tent and from dwelling to dwelling. ⁶ In all places where I have moved with all Israel, did I speak a word with any of the judges of Israel, whom I commanded to shepherd my people, saying, "Why have you not built me a house of cedar?"' ⁷ Now therefore thus shall you say to my servant David, 'Thus says the LORD of hosts, I took you from the pasture, from following the sheep, that you should be prince over my people Israel; ⁸ and I have been with you wherever you went, and have cut off all your enemies from before you; and I will make for you a name, like the name of the great ones of the earth. ⁹ And I will appoint a place for my people Israel, and will plant them, that they may dwell in their own place, and be disturbed no more; and violent men shall waste them no more, as formerly, ¹⁰ from the time that I appointed

ᵖHeb *their*
16.34: Ps 106.1. 16.35-36: Ps 106.47, 48.
17.1-27: 2 Sam 7.1-29.

judges over my people Israel; and I will subdue all your enemies. Moreover I declare to you that the LORD will build you a house. [11]When your days are fulfilled to go to be with your fathers, I will raise up your offspring after you, one of your own sons, and I will establish his kingdom. [12]He shall build a house for me, and I will establish his throne for ever. [13]I will be his father, and he shall be my son; I will not take my steadfast love from him, as I took it from him who was before you, [14]but I will confirm him in my house and in my kingdom for ever and his throne shall be established for ever.' " [15]In accordance with all these words, and in accordance with all this vision, Nathan spoke to David.

16 Then King David went in and sat before the LORD, and said, "Who am I, O LORD God, and what is my house, that thou hast brought me thus far? [17]And this was a small thing in thy eyes, O God; thou hast also spoken of thy servant's house for a great while to come, and hast shown me future generations,[q] O LORD God! [18]And what more can David say to thee for honoring thy servant? For thou knowest thy servant. [19]For thy servant's sake, O LORD, and according to thy own heart, thou hast wrought all this greatness, in making known all these great things. [20]There is none like thee, O LORD, and there is no God besides thee, according to all that we have heard with our ears. [21]What other[r] nation on earth is like thy people Israel, whom God went to redeem to be his people, making for thyself a name for great and terrible things, in driving out nations before thy people whom thou didst redeem from Egypt? [22]And thou didst make thy people Israel to be thy people for ever; and thou, O LORD, didst become their God. [23]And now, O LORD, let the word which thou hast spoken concerning thy servant and concerning his house be established for ever, and do as thou hast spoken; [24]and thy name will be established and magnified for ever, saying, 'The LORD of hosts, the God of Israel, is Israel's God,' and the house of thy servant David will be established before thee. [25]For thou, my God, hast revealed to thy servant that thou wilt build a house for him; therefore thy servant has found courage to pray before thee. [26]And now, O LORD, thou art God, and thou hast promised this good thing to thy servant; [27]now therefore may it please thee to bless the house of thy servant, that it may continue for ever before thee; for what thou, O LORD, hast blessed is blessed for ever."

18 After this David defeated the Phĭ·lĭs′tĭnes and subdued them, and he took Găth and its villages out of the hand of the Philistines.

2 And he defeated Mō′ăb, and the Mō′ab·ītes became servants to David and brought tribute.

3 David also defeated Hăd·a·dē′zer king of Zō′bah, toward Hā′măth, as he went to set up his monument[s] at the river Euphrates. [4]And David took from him a thousand chariots, seven thousand horsemen, and twenty thousand foot soldiers; and David hamstrung all the chariot horses, but left enough for a hundred chariots. [5]And when the Syrians of Damascus came to help Hăd·a·dē′zer king of Zō′bah, David slew twenty-two thousand men of the Syrians. [6]Then David put garrisons[t] in Syria of Damascus; and the Syrians became servants to David, and brought tribute. And the LORD gave victory to David wherever he went. [7]And David took the shields of gold which were carried by the servants of Hăd·a·dē′zer, and brought them to Jerusalem. [8]And from Tĭb′hăth and from Cün, cities of Hăd·a·dē′zer, David took very much bronze; with it Solomon made the bronze sea and the pillars and the vessels of bronze.

9 When Tō′u king of Hā′măth heard that David had defeated the whole army of Hăd·a·dē′zer, king of Zō′bah, [10]he sent his son Ha·dôr′am to King David, to greet him, and to congratulate him because he had fought against Hăd·a·dē′zer and defeated him; for Hadadezer had often been at war with Tō′u. And he sent all sorts of articles of gold, of silver, and of bronze; [11]these also King David dedicated to the LORD, together with the silver and gold which he had carried off from all the nations, from Ē′dom, Mō′ăb, the Ăm′mo·nītes, the Phĭ·lĭs′tĭnes, and Ăm′a·lĕk.

[q]Cn: Heb uncertain   [r]Gk Vg: Heb *one*   [s]Heb *hand*
[t]Gk Vg 2 Sam 8.6 Compare Syr: Heb lacks *garrisons*
18.1–13: 2 Sam 8.1–14.

12 And A·bĭ'shaī, the son of Zĕ·rŭ'-ĭ·ah, slew eighteen thousand Ē'dom-ītes in the Valley of Salt. ¹³And he put garrisons in Ē'dom; and all the Ē'dom-ītes became David's servants. And the LORD gave victory to David wherever he went.

14 So David reigned over all Israel; and he administered justice and equity to all his people. ¹⁵And Jō'ăb the son of Zĕ·rŭ'ī·ah was over the army; and Jĕ·hŏsh'a·phăt the son of A·hī'lud was recorder; ¹⁶and Zā'dŏk the son of A·hī'tŭb and A·hĭm'e·lĕch the son of A·bī'a·thăr were priests; and Shăv'shạ was secretary; ¹⁷and Bĕ·nā'ī·ah the son of Jĕ·hoi'a·dạ was over the Chĕr'-e·thītes and the Pĕl'e·thītes; and David's sons were the chief officials in the service of the king.

19 Now after this Nā'hăsh the king of the Ăm'mo·nītes died, and his son reigned in his stead. ²And David said, "I will deal loyally with Hā'nŭn the son of Nā'hăsh, for his father dealt loyally with me." So David sent messengers to console him concerning his father. And David's servants came to Hā'nŭn in the land of the Ăm'mo·nītes, to console him. ³But the princes of the Ăm'mo·nītes said to Hā'nŭn, "Do you think, because David has sent comforters to you, that he is honoring your father? Have not his servants come to you to search and to overthrow and to spy out the land?" ⁴So Hā'nŭn took David's servants, and shaved them, and cut off their garments in the middle, at their hips, and sent them away; ⁵and they departed. When David was told concerning the men, he sent to meet them, for the men were greatly ashamed. And the king said, "Remain at Jericho until your beards have grown, and then return."

6 When the Ăm'mo·nītes saw that they had made themselves odious to David, Hā'nŭn and the Ammonites sent a thousand talents of silver to hire chariots and horsemen from Mĕs·o·po·tā'mĭ·ạ, from Ăr'am–mā'a·cah, and from Zō'bah. ⁷They hired thirty-two thousand chariots and the king of Mā'a·cah with his army, who came and encamped before Mĕd'e·bạ. And the Ăm'mo·nītes were mustered from their cities and came to battle. ⁸When David heard of it, he sent Jō'ăb and all the army of the mighty men.

⁹And the Ăm'mo·nītes came out and drew up in battle array at the entrance of the city, and the kings who had come were by themselves in the open country.

10 When Jō'ăb saw that the battle was set against him both in front and in the rear, he chose some of the picked men of Israel, and arrayed them against the Syrians; ¹¹the rest of his men he put in the charge of A·bī'shaī his brother, and they were arrayed against the Ăm'mo·nītes. ¹²And he said, "If the Syrians are too strong for me, then you shall help me; but if the Ăm'mo·nītes are too strong for you, then I will help you. ¹³Be of good courage, and let us play the man for our people, and for the cities of our God; and may the LORD do what seems good to him." ¹⁴So Jō'ăb and the people who were with him drew near before the Syrians for battle; and they fled before him. ¹⁵And when the Ăm'mo·nītes saw that the Syrians fled, they likewise fled before A·bī'shaī, Jō'ăb's brother, and entered the city. Then Joab came to Jerusalem.

16 But when the Syrians saw that they had been defeated by Israel, they sent messengers and brought out the Syrians who were beyond the Euphrates, with Shō'phăch the commander of the army of Hăd·a·dē'zer at their head. ¹⁷And when it was told David, he gathered all Israel together, and crossed the Jordan, and came to them, and drew up his forces against them. And when David set the battle in array against the Syrians, they fought with him. ¹⁸And the Syrians fled before Israel; and David slew of the Syrians the men of seven thousand chariots, and forty thousand foot soldiers, and killed also Shō'phăch the commander of their army. ¹⁹And when the servants of Hăd·a·dē'zer saw that they had been defeated by Israel, they made peace with David, and became subject to him. So the Syrians were not willing to help the Ăm'mo·nītes any more.

20 In the spring of the year, the time when kings go forth to battle, Jō'ăb led out the army, and ravaged the country of the Ăm'mo·nītes, and came and besieged Răb'-bah. But David remained at Jeru-

18.14-17: 2 Sam 8.15-18. 19.1-19: 2 Sam 10.1-19.
20.1: 2 Sam 11.1. 20.1-3: 2 Sam 12.26-31.

salem. And Joab smote Rabbah, and overthrew it. ²And David took the crown of their king" from his head; he found that it weighed a talent of gold, and in it was a precious stone; and it was placed on David's head. And he brought forth the spoil of the city, a very great amount. ³And he brought forth the people who were in it, and set them to labor" with saws and iron picks and axes;" and thus David did to all the cities of the Ăm'-mọ·nītes. Then David and all the people returned to Jerusalem.

4 And after this there arose war with the Phĭ·lĭs'tĭnes at Gē'zẹr; then Sĭb'bẹ·caī the Hū'shạ·thīte slew Sĭp'-paī, who was one of the descendants of the giants; and the Phĭ·lĭs'tĭnes were subdued. ⁵And there was again war with the Phĭ·lĭs'tĭnes; and Ĕl·hā'-nạn the son of Jā'īr slew Läh'mī the brother of Goliath the Gĭt'tīte, the shaft of whose spear was like a weaver's beam. ⁶And there was again war at Găth, where there was a man of great stature, who had six fingers on each hand, and six toes on each foot, twenty-four in number; and he also was descended from the giants. ⁷And when he taunted Israel, Jonathan the son of Shĭm'ē–ạ, David's brother, slew him. ⁸These were descended from the giants in Găth; and they fell by the hand of David and by the hand of his servants.

21 Satan stood up against Israel, and incited David to number Israel. ²So David said to Jō'ăb and the commanders of the army, "Go, number Israel, from Bē'ẹr–shē'bạ to Dan, and bring me a report, that I may know their number." ³But Jō'ăb said, "May the LORD add to his people a hundred times as many as they are! Are they not, my lord the king, all of them my lord's servants? Why then should my lord require this? Why should he bring guilt upon Israel?" ⁴But the king's word prevailed against Jō'ăb. So Joab departed and went throughout all Israel, and came back to Jerusalem. ⁵And Jō'ăb gave the sum of the numbering of the people to David. In all Israel there were one million one hundred thousand men who drew the sword, and in Judah four hundred and seventy thousand who drew the sword. ⁶But he did not include Lē'vī and Benjamin in the

numbering, for the king's command was abhorrent to Jō'ăb.

7 But God was displeased with this thing, and he smote Israel. ⁸And David said to God, "I have sinned greatly in that I have done this thing. But now, I pray thee, take away the iniquity of thy servant; for I have done very foolishly." ⁹And the LORD spoke to Gåd, David's seer, saying, ¹⁰"Go and say to David, 'Thus says the LORD, Three things I offer you; choose one of them, that I may do it to you.'" ¹¹So Gåd came to David and said to him, "Thus says the LORD, 'Take which you will: ¹²either three years of famine; or three months of devastation by your foes, while the sword of your enemies overtakes you; or else three days of the sword of the LORD, pestilence upon the land, and the angel of the LORD destroying throughout all the territory of Israel.' Now decide what answer I shall return to him who sent me." ¹³Then David said to Gåd, "I am in great distress; let me fall into the hand of the LORD, for his mercy is very great; but let me not fall into the hand of man."

14 So the LORD sent a pestilence upon Israel; and there fell seventy thousand men of Israel. ¹⁵And God sent the angel to Jerusalem to destroy it; but when he was about to destroy it, the LORD saw, and he repented of the evil; and he said to the destroying angel, "It is enough; now stay your hand." And the angel of the LORD was standing by the threshing floor of Ôr'nạn the Jĕb'ū·sīte. ¹⁶And David lifted his eyes and saw the angel of the LORD standing between earth and heaven, and in his hand a drawn sword stretched out over Jerusalem. Then David and the elders, clothed in sackcloth, fell upon their faces. ¹⁷And David said to God, "Was it not I who gave command to number the people? It is I who have sinned and done very wickedly. But these sheep, what have they done? Let thy hand, I pray thee, O LORD my God, be against me and against my father's house; but let not the plague be upon thy people."

18 Then the angel of the LORD commanded Gåd to say to David that

---

" Or *Milcom* See 1 Kings 11.5
ᵛ Compare 2 Sam 12.31: Heb *he sawed*
ʷ Compare 2 Sam 12.31: Heb *saws*
20.4–8: 2 Sam 21.18-22.   **21.1-27:** 2 Sam 24.1-25.

David should go up and rear an altar to the LORD on the threshing floor of Ôr'năn the Jěb'ū·sīte. ¹⁹So David went up at Găd'ş word, which he had spoken in the name of the LORD. ²⁰Now Ôr'năn was threshing wheat; he turned and saw the angel, and his four sons who were with him hid themselves. ²¹As David came to Ôr'năn, Ornan looked and saw David and went forth from the threshing floor, and did obeisance to David with his face to the ground. ²²And David said to Ôr'năn, "Give me the site of the threshing floor that I may build on it an altar to the LORD—give it to me at its full price—that the plague may be averted from the people." ²³Then Ôr'năn said to David, "Take it; and let my lord the king do what seems good to him; see, I give the oxen for burnt offerings, and the threshing sledges for the wood, and the wheat for a cereal offering. I give it all." ²⁴But King David said to Ôr'năn, "No, but I will buy it for the full price; I will not take for the LORD what is yours, nor offer burnt offerings which cost me nothing." ²⁵So David paid Ôr'năn six hundred shekels of gold by weight for the site. ²⁶And David built there an altar to the LORD and presented burnt offerings and peace offerings, and called upon the LORD, and he answered him with fire from heaven upon the altar of burnt offering. ²⁷Then the LORD commanded the angel; and he put his sword back into its sheath.

28 At that time, when David saw that the LORD had answered him at the threshing floor of Ôr'năn the Jěb'ū·sīte, he made his sacrifices there. ²⁹For the tabernacle of the LORD, which Moses had made in the wilderness, and the altar of burnt offering were at that time in the high place at Gĭb'ē·on; ³⁰but David could not go before it to inquire of God, for he was afraid of the sword of the angel of the LORD. ¹Then David said, "Here 22 shall be the house of the LORD God and here the altar of burnt offering for Israel."

2 David commanded to gather together the aliens who were in the land of Israel, and he set stonecutters to prepare dressed stones for building the house of God. ³David also provided great stores of iron for nails for the doors of the gates and for clamps, as well as bronze in quantities beyond weighing, ⁴and cedar timbers without number; for the Sī·dō'nĭ·ănş and Tŷ'rĭ·ănş brought great quantities of cedar to David. ⁵For David said, "Solomon my son is young and inexperienced, and the house that is to be built for the LORD must be exceedingly magnificent, of fame and glory throughout all lands; I will therefore make preparation for it." So David provided materials in great quantity before his death.

6 Then he called for Solomon his son, and charged him to build a house for the LORD, the God of Israel. ⁷David said to Solomon, "My son, I had it in my heart to build a house to the name of the LORD my God. ⁸But the word of the LORD came to me, saying, 'You have shed much blood and have waged great wars; you shall not build a house to my name, because you have shed so much blood before me upon the earth. ⁹Behold, a son shall be born to you; he shall be a man of peace. I will give him peace from all his enemies round about; for his name shall be Solomon, and I will give peace and quiet to Israel in his days. ¹⁰He shall build a house for my name. He shall be my son, and I will be his father, and I will establish his royal throne in Israel for ever.' ¹¹Now, my son, the LORD be with you, so that you may succeed in building the house of the LORD your God, as he has spoken concerning you. ¹²Only, may the LORD grant you discretion and understanding, that when he gives you charge over Israel you may keep the law of the LORD your God. ¹³Then you will prosper if you are careful to observe the statutes and the ordinances which the LORD commanded Moses for Israel. Be strong, and of good courage. Fear not; be not dismayed. ¹⁴With great pains I have provided for the house of the LORD a hundred thousand talents of gold, a million talents of silver, and bronze and iron beyond weighing, for there is so much of it; timber and stone too I have provided. To these you must add. ¹⁵You have an abundance of workmen: stonecutters, masons, carpenters, and all kinds of craftsmen without number, skilled in working ¹⁶gold, silver, bronze, and iron. Arise and be doing! The LORD be with you!"

17 David also commanded all the leaders of Israel to help Solomon his son, saying, 18 "Is not the LORD your God with you? And has he not given you peace on every side? For he has delivered the inhabitants of the land into my hand; and the land is subdued before the LORD and his people. 19 Now set your mind and heart to seek the LORD your God. Arise and build the sanctuary of the LORD God, so that the ark of the covenant of the LORD and the holy vessels of God may be brought into a house built for the name of the LORD."

23 When David was old and full of days, he made Solomon his son king over Israel.

2 David assembled all the leaders of Israel and the priests and the Le'vites. 3 The Le'vites, thirty years old and upward, were numbered, and the total was thirty-eight thousand men. 4 "Twenty-four thousand of these," David said, "shall have charge of the work in the house of the LORD, six thousand shall be officers and judges, 5 four thousand gatekeepers, and four thousand shall offer praises to the LORD with the instruments which I have made for praise." 6 And David organized them in divisions corresponding to the sons of Le'vi: Ger'-shom, Kō'hăth, and Me·rar'ī.

7 The sons of Ger'shom* were Lā'dăn and Shĭm'ē-ī. 8 The sons of Lā'dăn: Jĕ·hī'ĕl the chief, and Zē'-thăm, and Jō'ĕl, three. 9 The sons of Shĭm'ē-ī: Shĕ·lō'mŏth, Hā'zĭ-ĕl, and Hār'ăn, three. These were the heads of the fathers' houses of Lā'dăn. 10 And the sons of Shĭm'ē-ī: Jā'hăth, Zī'nă, and Jē'ŭsh, and Bē·rī'ăh. These four were the sons of Shime-i. 11 Jā'hăth was the chief, and Zī'zăh the second; but Jē'ŭsh and Bē·rī'ăh had not many sons, therefore they became a father's house in one reckoning.

12 The sons of Kō'hăth: Ăm'răm, Ĭz'hār, Hē'brŏn, and Ŭz'zĭ-ĕl, four. 13 The sons of Ăm'răm: Aaron and Moses. Aaron was set apart to consecrate the most holy things, that he and his sons for ever should burn incense before the LORD, and minister to him and pronounce blessings in his name for ever. 14 But the sons of Moses the man of God were named among the tribe of Le'vi. 15 The sons of Moses: Ger'shŏm and Ē·lī·ē'zer. 16 The sons of Ger'shŏm: Shĕ·bū'ĕl the chief. 17 The sons of Ē·lī·ē'zer: Rĕ·hă·bī'ăh the chief; Eliezer had no other sons, but the sons of Rehabiah were very many. 18 The sons of Ĭz'hār: Shĕ·lō'mĭth the chief. 19 The sons of Hē'brŏn: Jĕ·rī'ăh the chief, Ăm·a·rī'ah the second, Ja·hā'zĭ-ĕl the third, and Jĕk·a·mē'am the fourth. 20 The sons of Ŭz'zĭ-ĕl: Mī'căh the chief and Ĭs·shī'ăh the second.

21 The sons of Me·rar'ī: Mäh'lī and Mū'shī. The sons of Mahli: Ĕl·ē·ā'zar and Kīsh. 22 Ĕl·ē·ā'zar died having no sons, but only daughters; their kinsmen, the sons of Kīsh, married them. 23 The sons of Mū'shī: Mäh'lī, Ē'der, and Jĕr'e·mŏth, three.

24 These were the sons of Le'vi by their fathers' houses, the heads of fathers' houses as they were registered according to the number of the names of the individuals from twenty years old and upward who were to do the work for the service of the house of the LORD. 25 For David said, "The LORD, the God of Israel, has given peace to his people; and he dwells in Jerusalem for ever. 26 And so the Le'vites no longer need to carry the tabernacle or any of the things for its service" — 27 for by the last words of David these were the number of the Le'vites from twenty years old and upward — 28 "but their duty shall be to assist the sons of Aaron for the service of the house of the LORD, having the care of the courts and the chambers, the cleansing of all that is holy, and any work for the service of the house of God; 29 to assist also with the showbread, the flour for the cereal offering, the wafers of unleavened bread, the baked offering, the offering mixed with oil, and all measures of quantity or size. 30 And they shall stand every morning, thanking and praising the LORD, and likewise at evening, 31 and whenever burnt offerings are offered to the LORD on sabbaths, new moons, and feast days, according to the number required of them, continually before the LORD. 32 Thus they shall keep charge of the tent of meeting and the sanctuary, and shall attend the sons of Aaron, their brethren, for the service of the house of the LORD."

*Vg Compare Gk Syr: Heb *to the Gershonite*

24 The divisions of the sons of Aaron were these. The sons of Aaron: Nā′dăb, A·bī′hū, Ĕl·ē·ā′zạr, and Ĭth′ạ·mär. ²But Nā′dăb and A·bī′hū died before their father, and had no children, so Ĕl·ē·ā′zạr and Ĭth′ạ·mär became the priests. ³With the help of Zā′dŏk of the sons of Ĕl·ē·ā′zạr, and A·hĭm′ẹ·lĕch of the sons of Ĭth′ạ·mär, David organized them according to the appointed duties in their service. ⁴Since more chief men were found among the sons of Ĕl·ē·ā′zạr than among the sons of Ĭth′ạ·mär, they organized them under sixteen heads of fathers′ houses of the sons of Eleazar, and eight of the sons of Ithamar. ⁵They organized them by lot, all alike, for there were officers of the sanctuary and officers of God among both the sons of Ĕl·ē·ā′zạr and the sons of Ĭth′ạ·mär. ⁶And the scribe Shĕ·māi′ạh the son of Nẹ·thăn′ĕl, a Lē′vīte, recorded them in the presence of the king, and the princes, and Zā′dŏk the priest, and A·hĭm′ẹ·lĕch the son of A·bī′ạ·thär, and the heads of the fathers′ houses of the priests and of the Lē′vītes; one father′s house being chosen for Ĕl·ē·ā′zạr and one chosen for Ĭth′ạ·mär.

7 The first lot fell to Jĕ·hoi′ạ·rĭb, the second to Jĕ·daī′ạh, ⁸the third to Hā′rĭm, the fourth to Sē–ō′rĭm, ⁹the fifth to Măl·chī′jạh, the sixth to Mī′jạ·mĭn, ¹⁰the seventh to Hăk′kŏz, the eighth to A·bī′jạh, ¹¹the ninth to Jĕsh′ü·ạ, the tenth to Shĕc·ạ·nī′ạh, ¹²the eleventh to Ĕ·lī′ạ·shĭb, the twelfth to Jā′kĭm, ¹³the thirteenth to Hŭp′pạh, the fourteenth to Jĕ·shĕb′ĕ–ạb, ¹⁴the fifteenth to Bĭl′gạh, the sixteenth to Ĭm′mẹr, ¹⁵the seventeenth to Hē′zīr, the eighteenth to Hăp′pĭz·zĕz, ¹⁶the nineteenth to Pĕth·ạ·hī′ạh, the twentieth to Jĕ·hĕz′kĕl, ¹⁷the twenty-first to Jā′chĭn, the twenty-second to Gā′mül, ¹⁸the twenty-third to Dĕ·laī′ạh, the twenty-fourth to Mā–ạ·zī′ạh. ¹⁹These had as their appointed duty in their service to come into the house of the LORD according to the procedure established for them by Aaron their father, as the LORD God of Israel had commanded him.

20 And of the rest of the sons of Lē′vī: of the sons of Ăm′răm, Shü′bạ–ĕl; of the sons of Shuba–el, Jĕh·dē′ī·ạh. ²¹Of Rĕ·hạ·bī′ạh: of the sons of Rehabiah, Ĭs·shī′ạh the chief. ²²Of

the Ĭz′hạ·rītes, Shĕ·lō′mŏth; of the sons of Shelomoth, Jā′hăth. ²³The sons of Hē′brọn:ᵛ Jĕ·rī′ạh the chief,ᶻ Ăm·ạ·rī′ạh the second, Jạ·hā·zī′ĕl the third, Jĕk·ạ·mē′ạm the fourth. ²⁴The sons of Ŭz′zĭ·ĕl, Mī′cạh; of the sons of Micah, Shā′mīr. ²⁵The brother of Mī′cạh, Ĭs·shī′ạh; of the sons of Isshiah, Zĕch·ạ·rī′ạh. ²⁶The sons of Mẹ·râr′ī: Mäh′lī and Mū′shī. The sons of Jā–ạ·zī′ạh: Bē′nō. ²⁷The sons of Mẹ·râr′ī: of Jā–ạ·zī′ạh, Bē′nō, Shō′hăm, Zăc′cūr, and Ĭb′rī. ²⁸Of Mäh′lī: Ĕl·ē·ā′zạr, who had no sons. ²⁹Of Kĭsh, the sons of Kish: Jẹ·räh′mē·ĕl. ³⁰The sons of Mū′shī: Mäh′lī, Ē′dẹr, and Jĕr′ī·mŏth. These were the sons of the Lē′vītes according to their fathers′ houses. ³¹These also, the head of each father′s house and his younger brother alike, cast lots, just as their brethren the sons of Aaron, in the presence of King David, Zā′dŏk, A·hĭm′ẹ·lĕch, and the heads of fathers′ houses of the priests and of the Lē′vītes.

25 David and the chiefs of the service also set apart for the service certain of the sons of A′săph, and of Hē′man, and of Jĕ·dü′thụn, who should prophesy with lyres, with harps, and with cymbals. The list of those who did the work and of their duties was: ²Of the sons of A′săph: Zăc′cūr, Joseph, Nĕth·ạ·nī′ạh, and Ăsh·ạ·rē′lạh, sons of Asaph, under the direction of Asaph, who prophesied under the direction of the king. ³Of Jĕ·dü′thụn, the sons of Jĕduthun: Gĕd·ạ·lī′ạh, Zē′rī, Jĕ·shāi′ạh, Shĭm′ē–ī,ᵃ Hăsh·ạ·bī′ạh, and Măt·tĭ·thī′ạh, six, under the direction of their father Jĕ·dü′thụn, who prophesied with the lyre in thanksgiving and praise to the LORD. ⁴Of Hē′man, the sons of Heman: Bŭk·kī′ạh, Măt·tạ·nī′ạh, Ŭz′zĭ·ĕl, Shĕ·bū′ĕl, and Jĕr′ī·mŏth, Hăn·ạ·nī′ạh, Hạ·nā′nī, Ĕ·lī′ạ·thạh, Gĭd·dăl′tī, and Rō·măm′tī–ē′zẹr, Jōsh·bĕ·kăsh′ạh, Măl·lō′thī, Hō′thīr, Mạ·hā′zĭ–ŏth. ⁵All these were the sons of Hē′man the king′s seer, according to the promise of God to exalt him; for God had given Heman fourteen sons and three daughters. ⁶They were all under the direction of their father in the music in the house of the LORD with cymbals, harps, and

---

ᵛSee 23.19: Heb lacks *Hebron*
ᶻSee 23.19: Heb lacks *the chief*
ᵃOne Ms: Gk: Heb lacks *Shimei*

lyres for the service of the house of God. Ā′săph, Jĕ·dü′thųn, and Hē′mạn were under the order of the king. ⁷The number of them along with their brethren, who were trained in singing to the LORD, all who were skilful, was two hundred and eightyeight. ⁸And they cast lots for their duties, small and great, teacher and pupil alike.

9 The first lot fell for Ā′săph to Joseph; the second to Gĕd·ạ·lī′ạh, to him and his brethren and his sons, twelve; ¹⁰the third to Zăc′cūr, his sons and his brethren, twelve; ¹¹the fourth to Ĭz′rī, his sons and his brethren, twelve; ¹²the fifth to Nĕth·ạ·nī′ạh, his sons and his brethren, twelve; ¹³the sixth to Bŭk·kī′ạh, his sons and his brethren, twelve; ¹⁴the seventh to Jĕsh·ạ·rē′lạh, his sons and his brethren, twelve; ¹⁵the eighth to Jĕ·shā′ĭ·ah, his sons and his brethren, twelve; ¹⁶the ninth to Măt·tạ·nī′ạh, his sons and his brethren, twelve; ¹⁷the tenth to Shĭm′ē–ī, his sons and his brethren, twelve; ¹⁸the eleventh to Ăz′ạ·rĕl, his sons and his brethren, twelve; ¹⁹the twelfth to Hăsh·ạ·bī′ạh, his sons and his brethren, twelve; ²⁰to the thirteenth, Shü′bạ–ĕl, his sons and his brethren, twelve; ²¹to the fourteenth, Măt·tĭ·thī′ạh, his sons and his brethren, twelve; ²²to the fifteenth, to Jĕr′ẹ·mŏth, his sons and his brethren, twelve; ²³to the sixteenth, to Hăn·ạ·nī′ạh, his sons and his brethren, twelve; ²⁴to the seventeenth, to Jŏsh·bĕ·kăsh′ạh, his sons and his brethren, twelve; ²⁵to the eighteenth, to Hạ·nā′nī, his sons and his brethren, twelve; ²⁶to the nineteenth, to Măl·lō′thī, his sons and his brethren, twelve; ²⁷to the twentieth, to Ē·lī′ạ·thạh, his sons and his brethren, twelve; ²⁸to the twentyfirst, to Hō′thĭr, his sons and his brethren, twelve; ²⁹to the twentysecond, to Gĭd·dăl′tī, his sons and his brethren, twelve; ³⁰to the twenty-third, to Mạ·hā′zī–ŏth, his sons and his brethren, twelve; ³¹to the twentyfourth, to Rō·măm′tĭ–ē′zẹr, his sons and his brethren, twelve.

26 As for the divisions of the gatekeepers: of the Kō′rạ·hītes, Mĕ·shĕl·ẹ·mī′ạh the son of Kō′rĕ, of the sons of Ā′săph. ²And Mĕ·shĕl·ẹ·mī′ạh had sons: Zĕch·ạ·rī′ạh the first-born, Jĕ·dī′ạ–ĕl the second, Zĕb·ạ·dī′ạh the third, Jăth′nī–ĕl the fourth,

³Ē′lăm the fifth, Jĕ′hō–hā′nạn the sixth, Ĕl′ĭ·ē–hō–ē′naī the seventh. ⁴And Ō′bĕd–ē′dọm had sons: Shĕmāi′ạh the first-born, Jĕ·hō′zạ·băd the second, Jō′ạh the third, Sā′chär the fourth, Nẹ·thăn′ĕl the fifth, ⁵Ăm′mĭ–ĕl the sixth, Ĭs′sạ·chär the seventh, Pĕ–ŭl′lẹ·thaī the eighth; for God blessed him. ⁶Also to his son Shĕmāi′ạh were sons born who were rulers in their fathers' houses, for they were men of great ability. ⁷The sons of Shĕ·māi′ah: Ōth′nī, Rĕph′ạ–ĕl, Ō′bĕd, and Ĕl·zā′băd, whose brethren were able men, Ē·lī′hū and Sĕm·ạ·chī′ạh. ⁸All these were of the sons of Ō′bĕd–ē′dọm with their sons and brethren, able men qualified for the service; sixty-two of Obed–edom. ⁹And Mĕ·shĕl·ẹ·mī′ạh had sons and brethren, able men, eighteen. ¹⁰And Hō′sạh, of the sons of Mẹ·râr′ī, had sons: Shĭm′rī the chief (for though he was not the first-born, his father made him chief), ¹¹Hĭl·kī′ạh the second, Tĕb·ạ·lī′ạh the third, Zĕch·ạ·rī′ạh the fourth: all the sons and brethren of Hō′sạh were thirteen.

12 These divisions of the gatekeepers, corresponding to their chief men, had duties, just as their brethren did, ministering in the house of the LORD; ¹³and they cast lots by fathers' houses, small and great alike, for their gates. ¹⁴The lot for the east fell to Shĕl·ẹ·mī′ạh. They cast lots also for his son Zĕch·ạ·rī′ạh, a shrewd counselor, and his lot came out for the north. ¹⁵Ō′bĕd–ē′dọm's came out for the south, and to his sons was allotted the storehouse. ¹⁶For Shŭp′pĭm and Hō′sạh it came out for the west, at the gate of Shăl′lẹ·chĕth on the road that goes up. Watch corresponded to watch. ¹⁷On the east there were six each day,*[b]* on the north four each day, on the south four each day, as well as two and two at the storehouse; ¹⁸and for the parbar*[c]* on the west there were four at the road and two at the parbar. ¹⁹These were the divisions of the gatekeepers among the Kō′rạ·hītes and the sons of Mẹ·râr′ī.

20 And of the Lē′vītes, Ạ·hī′jạh had charge of the treasuries of the house of God and the treasuries of the dedicated gifts. ²¹The sons of Lā′dạn, the sons of the Gĕr′shọ·nītes belonging

---

*[b]*Gk: Heb *Levites*
*[c]*The meaning of the word *parbar* is unknown

to Ladan, the heads of the fathers' houses belonging to Ladan the Gershonite: Jĕ·hī'ē·lī.[d]

22 The sons of Jĕ·hī'ē·lī, Zē'tham and Jō'ĕl his brother, were in charge of the treasuries of the house of the LORD. [23]Of the Ăm'ra·mītes, the Ĭz'ha·rītes, the Hē'brŏ·nītes, and the Ŭz'zī·ē·lītes — [24]and Shĕ·bū'ĕl the son of Gēr'shŏm, son of Moses, was chief officer in charge of the treasuries. [25]His brethren: from Ē·lī·ē'zer were his son Rē·ha·bī'ah, and his son Jĕ·shāi'ah, and his son Jō'ram, and his son Zĭch'rī, and his son Shĕ·lō'mŏth. [26]This Shĕ·lō'mŏth and his brethren were in charge of all the treasuries of the dedicated gifts which David the king, and the heads of the fathers' houses, and the officers of the thousands and the hundreds, and the commanders of the army, had dedicated. [27]From spoil won in battles they dedicated gifts for the maintenance of the house of the LORD. [28]Also all that Samuel the seer, and Saul the son of Kish, and Abner the son of Nēr, and Jō'ăb the son of Zĕ·rü'ī·ah had dedicated — all dedicated gifts were in the care of Shĕ·lō'mŏth[e] and his brethren.

29 Of the Ĭz'ha·rītes, Chĕn·a·nī'ah and his sons were appointed to outside duties for Israel, as officers and judges. [30]Of the Hē'brŏ·nītes, Hăsh·a·bī'ah and his brethren, one thousand seven hundred men of ability, had the oversight of Israel westward of the Jordan for all the work of the LORD and for the service of the king. [31]Of the Hē'brŏ·nītes, Jĕ·rī'jah was chief of the Hebronites of whatever genealogy or fathers' houses. (In the fortieth year of David's reign search was made and men of great ability among them were found at Jā'zer in Gilead.) [32]King David appointed him and his brethren, two thousand seven hundred men of ability, heads of fathers' houses, to have the oversight of the Reubenites, the Găd'ītes, and the half-tribe of the Ma·năs'sītes for everything pertaining to God and for the affairs of the king.

27 This is the list of the people of Israel, the heads of fathers' houses, the commanders of thousands and hundreds, and their officers who served the king in all matters concerning the divisions that came and went, month after month throughout the

year, each division numbering twenty-four thousand:

2 Ja·shō'bē·am the son of Zăb'dī·ĕl was in charge of the first division in the first month; in his division were twenty-four thousand. [3]He was a descendant of Pĕr'ĕz, and was chief of all the commanders of the army for the first month. [4]Dō'daī the A·hō'hīte[f] was in charge of the division of the second month; in his division were twenty-four thousand. [5]The third commander, for the third month, was Bĕ·nā'ī·ah, the son of Jĕ·hoi'a·da the priest, as chief; in his division were twenty-four thousand. [6]This is the Bĕ·nā'ī·ah who was a mighty man of the thirty and in command of the thirty; Ăm·mĭz'a·băd his son was in charge of his division.[g] [7]Ăs'a·hĕl the brother of Jō'ăb was fourth, for the fourth month, and his son Zĕb·a·dī'ah after him; in his division were twenty-four thousand. [8]The fifth commander, for the fifth month, was Shăm'hŭth, the Ĭz'ra·hīte; in his division were twenty-four thousand. [9]Sixth, for the sixth month, was Ira, the son of Ĭk'kĕsh the Tĕ·kō'īte; in his division were twenty-four thousand. [10]Seventh, for the seventh month, was Hē'lĕz the Pĕl'ō·nīte, of the sons of Ē'phra·ĭm; in his division were twenty-four thousand. [11]Eighth, for the eighth month, was Sĭb'bĕ·caī the Hū'sha·thīte, of the Zē'ra·hītes; in his division were twenty-four thousand. [12]Ninth, for the ninth month, was Ā·bī·ē'zer of Ăn'a·thŏth, a Benjaminite; in his division were twenty-four thousand. [13]Tenth, for the tenth month, was Mā'ha·raī of Ne·tŏph'ah, of the Zē'ra·hītes; in his division were twenty-four thousand. [14]Eleventh, for the eleventh month, was Bĕ·nā'ī·ah of Pĭr'a·thŏn, of the sons of Ē'phra·ĭm; in his division were twenty-four thousand. [15]Twelfth, for the twelfth month, was Hĕl'daī of Ne·tŏph'a·thīte, of Ŏth'nī–ĕl; in his division were twenty-four thousand.

16 Over the tribes of Israel, for the Reubenites Ē·lī·ē'zer the son of Zĭch'rī was chief officer; for the Sĭm'ē·o·nītes, Shĕph·a·tī'ah the son of Mā'a·cah; [17]for Lē'vī, Hăsh·a·bī'ah the son of Kĕ·mū'ĕl; for Aaron, Zā'dŏk; [18]for

[d]The Hebrew text of verse 21 is confused
[e]Heb *Shelomith*
[f]Gk: Heb *Ahohite and his division and Mikloth the chief officer* [g]Gk Vg: Heb *was his division*

Judah, Ĕ·lī′hū, one of David's brothers; for Ĭs′sa·chär, Ŏm′rī the son of Michael; ¹⁹for Zĕb′ū·lŭn, Ĭsh·mā′ī·ah the son of Ō·ba·dī′ah; for Năph′ta·lī, Jĕr′e·mŏth the son of Ăz′rī–ĕl; ²⁰for the Ē′phra·ĭm·īteṣ, Hō·shē′a the son of Ăz·a·zī′ah; for the half-tribe of Ma·năs′seh, Jō′el the son of Pĕ·dāi′ah; ²¹for the half-tribe of Ma·năs′seh in Gilead, Ĭd′dō the son of Zĕch·a·rī′ah; for Benjamin, Jā–a·sī′ĕl the son of Abner; ²²for Dan, Ăz′a·rĕl the son of Jĕ·rō′hăm. These were the leaders of the tribes of Israel. ²³David did not number those below twenty years of age, for the LORD had promised to make Israel as many as the stars of heaven. ²⁴Jō′ăb the son of Zĕ·rü′ī·ah began to number, but did not finish; yet wrath came upon Israel for this, and the number was not entered in the chronicles of King David.

25 Over the king's treasuries was Ăz′ma·vĕth the son of Ăd′ī–ĕl; and over the treasuries in the country, in the cities, in the villages and in the towers, was Jonathan the son of Ŭz·zī′ah; ²⁶and over those who did the work of the field for tilling the soil was Ēz′rī the son of Chē′lŭb; ²⁷and over the vineyards was Shĭm′e–ī the Rā′ma·thīte; and over the produce of the vineyards for the wine cellars was Zăb′dī the Shĭph′mīte. ²⁸Over the olive and sycamore trees in the Shĕphē′lah was Bā′al–hā′nan the Gĕdē′rīte; and over the stores of oil was Jō′ăsh. ²⁹Over the herds that pastured in Sharon was Shĭt′raī the Sharonite; over the herds in the valleys was Shā′phat the son of Ăd′lā·ī. ³⁰Over the camels was Ō′bĭl the Ĭsh′ma·ĕl·īte; and over the she-asses was Jĕh·dē′ī·ah the Mē·rŏn′o·thīte. Over the flocks was Jā′zĭz the Hăg′rīte. ³¹All these were stewards of King David's property.

32 Jonathan, David's uncle, was a counselor, being a man of understanding and a scribe; he and Jĕ·hī′ĕl the son of Hăch′mo·nī attended the king's sons. ³³A·hĭth′o·phĕl was the king's counselor, and Hū′shaī the Ăr′chīte was the king's friend. ³⁴A·hĭth′o·phĕl was succeeded by Jĕhoi′a·da the son of Bĕ·nā′ī·ah, and A·bī′a·thär. Jō′ăb was commander of the king's army.

28 David assembled at Jerusalem all the officials of Israel, the officials of the tribes, the officers of the divisions that served the king, the commanders of thousands, the commanders of hundreds, the stewards of all the property and cattle of the king and his sons, together with the palace officials, the mighty men, and all the seasoned warriors. ²Then King David rose to his feet and said: "Hear me, my brethren and my people. I had it in my heart to build a house of rest for the ark of the covenant of the LORD, and for the footstool of our God; and I made preparations for building. ³But God said to me, 'You may not build a house for my name, for you are a warrior and have shed blood.' ⁴Yet the LORD God of Israel chose me from all my father's house to be king over Israel for ever; for he chose Judah as leader, and in the house of Judah my father's house, and among my father's sons he took pleasure in me to make me king over all Israel. ⁵And of all my sons (for the LORD has given me many sons) he has chosen Solomon my son to sit upon the throne of the kingdom of the LORD over Israel. ⁶He said to me, 'It is Solomon your son who shall build my house and my courts, for I have chosen him to be my son, and I will be his father. ⁷I will establish his kingdom for ever if he continues resolute in keeping my commandments and my ordinances, as he is today.' ⁸Now therefore in the sight of all Israel, the assembly of the LORD, and in the hearing of our God, observe and seek out all the commandments of the LORD your God; that you may possess this good land, and leave it for an inheritance to your children after you for ever.

9 "And you, Solomon my son, know the God of your father, and serve him with a whole heart and with a willing mind; for the LORD searches all hearts, and understands every plan and thought. If you seek him, he will be found by you; but if you forsake him, he will cast you off for ever. ¹⁰Take heed now, for the LORD has chosen you to build a house for the sanctuary; be strong, and do it."

11 Then David gave Solomon his son the plan of the vestibule of the temple, and of its houses, its treasuries, its upper rooms, and its inner chambers, and of the room for the mercy seat; ¹²and the plan of all that he had in mind for the courts of the

house of the LORD, all the surrounding chambers, the treasuries of the house of God, and the treasuries for dedicated gifts; [13] for the divisions of the priests and of the Lē'vītes, and all the work of the service in the house of the LORD; for all the vessels for the service in the house of the LORD, [14] the weight of gold for all golden vessels for each service, the weight of silver vessels for each service, [15] the weight of the golden lampstands and their lamps, the weight of gold for each lampstand and its lamps, the weight of silver for a lampstand and its lamps, according to the use of each lampstand in the service, [16] the weight of gold for each table for the showbread, the silver for the silver tables, [17] and pure gold for the forks, the basins, and the cups; for the golden bowls and the weight of each; for the silver bowls and the weight of each; [18] for the altar of incense made of refined gold, and its weight; also his plan for the golden chariot of the cherubim that spread their wings and covered the ark of the covenant of the LORD. [19] All this he made clear by the writing from the hand of the LORD concerning it,[h] all the work to be done according to the plan.

20 Then David said to Solomon his son, "Be strong and of good courage, and do it. Fear not, be not dismayed; for the LORD God, even my God, is with you. He will not fail you or forsake you, until all the work for the service of the house of the LORD is finished. [21] And behold the divisions of the priests and the Lē'vītes for all the service of the house of God; and with you in all the work will be every willing man who has skill for any kind of service; also the officers and all the people will be wholly at your command."

29 And David the king said to all the assembly, "Solomon my son, whom alone God has chosen, is young and inexperienced, and the work is great; for the palace will not be for man but for the LORD God. [2] So I have provided for the house of my God, so far as I was able, the gold for the things of gold, the silver for the things of silver, and the bronze for the things of bronze, the iron for the things of iron, and wood for the things of wood, besides great quantities of onyx and

stones for setting, antimony, colored stones, all sorts of precious stones, and marble. [3] Moreover, in addition to all that I have provided for the holy house, I have a treasure of my own of gold and silver, and because of my devotion to the house of my God I give it to the house of my God: [4] three thousand talents of gold, of the gold of Ō'phir, and seven thousand talents of refined silver, for overlaying the walls of the house, [5] and for all the work to be done by craftsmen, gold for the things of gold and silver for the things of silver. Who then will offer willingly, consecrating himself today to the LORD?"

6 Then the heads of fathers' houses made their freewill offerings, as did also the leaders of the tribes, the commanders of thousands and of hundreds, and the officers over the king's work. [7] They gave for the service of the house of God five thousand talents and ten thousand darics of gold, ten thousand talents of silver, eighteen thousand talents of bronze, and a hundred thousand talents of iron. [8] And whoever had precious stones gave them to the treasury of the house of the LORD, in the care of Jĕ·hī'ĕl the Gēr'shǒ·nīte. [9] Then the people rejoiced because these had given willingly, for with a whole heart they had offered freely to the LORD; David the king also rejoiced greatly.

10 Therefore David blessed the LORD in the presence of all the assembly; and David said: "Blessed art thou, O LORD, the God of Israel our father, for ever and ever. [11] Thine, O LORD, is the greatness, and the power, and the glory, and the victory, and the majesty; for all that is in the heavens and in the earth is thine; thine is the kingdom, O LORD, and thou art exalted as head above all. [12] Both riches and honor come from thee, and thou rulest over all. In thy hand are power and might; and in thy hand it is to make great and to give strength to all. [13] And now we thank thee, our God, and praise thy glorious name.

14 "But who am I, and what is my people, that we should be able thus to offer willingly? For all things come from thee, and of thy own have we given thee. [15] For we are strangers before thee, and sojourners, as all our fathers were; our days on the earth

[h] Cn: Heb *upon me*

are like a shadow, and there is no abiding.[i] [16]O LORD our God, all this abundance that we have provided for building thee a house for thy holy name comes from thy hand and is all thy own. [17]I know, my God, that thou triest the heart, and hast pleasure in uprightness; in the uprightness of my heart I have freely offered all these things, and now I have seen thy people, who are present here, offering freely and joyously to thee. [18]O LORD, the God of Abraham, Isaac, and Israel, our fathers, keep for ever such purposes and thoughts in the hearts of thy people, and direct their hearts toward thee. [19]Grant to Solomon my son that with a whole heart he may keep thy commandments, thy testimonies, and thy statutes, performing all, and that he may build the palace for which I have made provision."

[20] Then David said to all the assembly, "Bless the LORD your God." And all the assembly blessed the LORD, the God of their fathers, and bowed their heads, and worshiped the LORD, and did obeisance to the king. [21]And they performed sacrifices to the LORD, and on the next day offered burnt offerings to the LORD, a thousand bulls, a thousand rams, and a thousand lambs, with their drink offerings, and sacrifices in abundance for all Israel;

[22]and they ate and drank before the LORD on that day with great gladness.

And they made Solomon the son of David king the second time, and they anointed him as prince for the LORD, and Zā'dŏk as priest. [23]Then Solomon sat on the throne of the LORD as king instead of David his father; and he prospered, and all Israel obeyed him. [24]All the leaders and the mighty men, and also all the sons of King David, pledged their allegiance to King Solomon. [25]And the LORD gave Solomon great repute in the sight of all Israel, and bestowed upon him such royal majesty as had not been on any king before him in Israel.

[26] Thus David the son of Jesse reigned over all Israel. [27]The time that he reigned over Israel was forty years; he reigned seven years in Hē'-bron, and thirty-three years in Jerusalem. [28]Then he died in a good old age, full of days, riches, and honor; and Solomon his son reigned in his stead. [29]Now the acts of King David, from first to last, are written in the Chronicles of Samuel the seer, and in the Chronicles of Nathan the prophet, and in the Chronicles of Gãd the seer, [30]with accounts of all his rule and his might and of the circumstances that came upon him and upon Israel, and upon all the kingdoms of the countries.

The Second Book of the
Chronicles

1 Solomon the son of David established himself in his kingdom, and the LORD his God was with him and made him exceedingly great.

2 Solomon spoke to all Israel, to the commanders of thousands and of hundreds, to the judges, and to all the leaders in all Israel, the heads of fathers' houses. [3]And Solomon, and all the assembly with him, went to the high place that was at Gĭb'ē-on; for the tent of meeting of God, which Moses the servant of the LORD had made in the wilderness, was there. [4](But David had brought up the ark of God from

Kĭr'ĭ-ăth-jē'a-rĭm to the place that David had prepared for it, for he had pitched a tent for it in Jerusalem.) [5]Moreover the bronze altar that Bĕz'-a-lĕl the son of Ū'rī, son of Hŭr, had made, was there before the tabernacle of the LORD. And Solomon and the assembly sought the LORD. [6]And Solomon went up there to the bronze altar before the LORD, which was at the tent of meeting, and offered a thousand burnt offerings upon it.

[7] In that night God appeared to

[i]Gk Vg: Heb *hope* **29.23:** 1 Kings 2.12.
1.3-13: 1 Kings 3.4-15.

Solomon, and said to him, "Ask what I shall give you." [8]And Solomon said to God, "Thou hast shown great and steadfast love to David my father, and hast made me king in his stead. [9]O LORD God, let thy promise to David my father be now fulfilled, for thou hast made me king over a people as many as the dust of the earth. [10]Give me now wisdom and knowledge to go out and come in before this people, for who can rule this thy people, that is so great?" [11]God answered Solomon, "Because this was in your heart, and you have not asked possessions, wealth, honor, or the life of those who hate you, and have not even asked long life, but have asked wisdom and knowledge for yourself that you may rule my people over whom I have made you king, [12]wisdom and knowledge are granted to you. I will also give you riches, possessions, and honor, such as none of the kings had who were before you, and none after you shall have the like." [13]So Solomon came from[a] the high place at Gĭb′ē-on, from before the tent of meeting, to Jerusalem. And he reigned over Israel.

14 Solomon gathered together chariots and horsemen; he had fourteen hundred chariots and twelve thousand horsemen, whom he stationed in the chariot cities and with the king in Jerusalem. [15]And the king made silver and gold as common in Jerusalem as stone, and he made cedar as plentiful as the sycamore of the Shē-phē′lah. [16]And Solomon's import of horses was from Egypt and Kü′ē, and the king's traders received them from Kue for a price. [17]They imported a chariot from Egypt for six hundred shekels of silver, and a horse for a hundred and fifty; likewise through them these were exported to all the kings of the Hĭt′tītes and the kings of Syria.

2[b] Now Solomon purposed to build a temple for the name of the LORD, and a royal palace for himself. [2c]And Solomon assigned seventy thousand men to bear burdens and eighty thousand to quarry in the hill country, and three thousand six hundred to oversee them. [3]And Solomon sent word to Hū′ram the king of Tyre: "As you dealt with David my father and sent him cedar to build himself a house to dwell in, so deal with me. [4]Behold, I am about to build a house for the name of the LORD my God and dedicate it to him for the burning of incense of sweet spices before him, and for the continual offering of the showbread, and for burnt offerings morning and evening, on the sabbaths and the new moons and the appointed feasts of the LORD our God, as ordained for ever for Israel. [5]The house which I am to build will be great, for our God is greater than all gods. [6]But who is able to build him a house, since heaven, even highest heaven, cannot contain him? Who am I to build a house for him, except as a place to burn incense before him? [7]So now send me a man skilled to work in gold, silver, bronze, and iron, and in purple, crimson, and blue fabrics, trained also in engraving, to be with the skilled workers who are with me in Judah and Jerusalem, whom David my father provided. [8]Send me also cedar, cypress, and algum timber from Lebanon, for I know that your servants know how to cut timber in Lebanon. And my servants will be with your servants, [9]to prepare timber for me in abundance, for the house I am to build will be great and wonderful. [10]I will give for your servants, the hewers who cut timber, twenty thousand cors of crushed wheat, twenty thousand cors of barley, twenty thousand baths of wine, and twenty thousand baths of oil."

11 Then Hū′ram the king of Tyre answered in a letter which he sent to Solomon, "Because the LORD loves his people he has made you king over them." [12]Hū′ram also said, "Blessed be the LORD God of Israel, who made heaven and earth, who has given King David a wise son, endued with discretion and understanding, who will build a temple for the LORD, and a royal palace for himself.

13 "Now I have sent a skilled man, endued with understanding, Hū′ram–ā′bī, [14]the son of a woman of the daughters of Dan, and his father was a man of Tyre. He is trained to work in gold, silver, bronze, iron, stone, and wood, and in purple, blue, and crimson fabrics and fine linen, and to do

[a]Gk Vg: Heb *to* [b]Ch 1.18 in Heb [c]Ch 2.1 in Heb
1.14–17: 1 Kings 10.26–29.
2.1: 1 Kings 5.5. **2.2:** 2.18; 1 Kings 5.15, 16.
2.3–16: 1 Kings 5.2–11.

all sorts of engraving and execute any design that may be assigned him, with your craftsmen, the craftsmen of my lord, David your father. ¹⁵ Now therefore the wheat and barley, oil and wine, of which my lord has spoken, let him send to his servants; ¹⁶ and we will cut whatever timber you need from Lebanon, and bring it to you in rafts by sea to Jŏp'pạ, so that you may take it up to Jerusalem."

17 Then Solomon took a census of all the aliens who were in the land of Israel, after the census of them which David his father had taken; and there were found a hundred and fifty-three thousand six hundred. ¹⁸ Seventy thousand of them he assigned to bear burdens, eighty thousand to quarry in the hill country, and three thousand six hundred as overseers to make the people work.

3 Then Solomon began to build the house of the LORD in Jerusalem on Mount Mō·rī'ạh, where the LORD had appeared to David his father, at the place that David had appointed, on the threshing floor of Or'nạn the Jĕb'ū·sīte. ² He began to build in the second month of the fourth year of his reign. ³ These are Solomon's measurements* for building the house of God: the length, in cubits of the old standard, was sixty cubits, and the breadth twenty cubits. ⁴ The vestibule in front of the nave of the house was twenty cubits long, equal to the width of the house;* and its height was a hundred and twenty cubits. He overlaid it on the inside with pure gold. ⁵ The nave he lined with cypress, and covered it with fine gold, and made palms and chains on it. ⁶ He adorned the house with settings of precious stones. The gold was gold of Pär·vā'ĭm. ⁷ So he lined the house with gold—its beams, its thresholds, its walls, and its doors; and he carved cherubim on the walls.

8 And he made the most holy place; its length, corresponding to the breadth of the house, was twenty cubits, and its breadth was twenty cubits; he overlaid it with six hundred talents of fine gold. ⁹ The weight of the nails was one shekel* to fifty shekels of gold. And he overlaid the upper chambers with gold.

10 In the most holy place he made two cherubim of wood* and overlaid*

them with gold. ¹¹ The wings of the cherubim together extended twenty cubits: one wing of the one, of five cubits, touched the wall of the house, and its other wing, of five cubits, touched the wing of the other cherub; ¹² and of this cherub, one wing, of five cubits, touched the wall of the house, and the other wing, also of five cubits, was joined to the wing of the first cherub. ¹³ The wings of these cherubim extended twenty cubits; the cherubim* stood on their feet, facing the nave. ¹⁴ And he made the veil of blue and purple and crimson fabrics and fine linen, and worked cherubim on it.

15 In front of the house he made two pillars thirty-five cubits high, with a capital of five cubits on the top of each. ¹⁶ He made chains like a necklace* and put them on the tops of the pillars; and he made a hundred pomegranates, and put them on the chains. ¹⁷ He set up the pillars in front of the temple, one on the south, the other on the north; that on the south he called Jā'chĭn, and that on the north Bō'ăz.

4 He made an altar of bronze, twenty cubits long, and twenty cubits wide, and ten cubits high. ² Then he made the molten sea; it was round, ten cubits from brim to brim, and five cubits high, and a line of thirty cubits measured its circumference. ³ Under it were figures of gourds,* for thirty* cubits, compassing the sea round about; the gourds* were in two rows, cast with it when it was cast. ⁴ It stood upon twelve oxen, three facing north, three facing west, three facing south, and three facing east; the sea was set upon them, and all their hinder parts were inward. ⁵ Its thickness was a handbreadth; and its brim was made like the brim of a cup, like the flower of a lily; it held over three thousand baths. ⁶ He also made ten lavers in which to wash, and set five on the south side, and five on the north side. In these they were to rinse off what was used for the burnt offering, and the sea was for the priests to wash in.

7 And he made ten golden lamp-

---

*ᵈ*Syr: Heb *foundations* *ᵉ*1 Kings 6.3: Heb uncertain
*ᶠ*Compare Gk: Heb lacks *one shekel*
*ᵍ*Gk: Heb uncertain *ʰ*Heb *they overlaid*
*ⁱ*Heb *they* *ʲ*Cn: Heb *in the inner sanctuary*
*ᵏ*1 Kings 7.24: Heb *oxen* *ˡ*Compare verse 2: Heb *ten*
3.1-13: 1 Kings 6.1-28. **3.15-17:** 1 Kings 7.15-21.
4.2-5: 1 Kings 7.23-26. **4.6-5.1:** 1 Kings 7.38-51.

stands as prescribed, and set them in the temple, five on the south side and five on the north. ⁸He also made ten tables, and placed them in the temple, five on the south side and five on the north. And he made a hundred basins of gold. ⁹He made the court of the priests, and the great court, and doors for the court, and overlaid their doors with bronze; ¹⁰and he set the sea at the southeast corner of the house. 11 Hū′ram also made the pots, the shovels, and the basins. So Huram finished the work that he did for King Solomon on the house of God: ¹²the two pillars, the bowls, and the two capitals on the top of the pillars; and the two networks to cover the two bowls of the capitals that were on the top of the pillars; ¹³and the four hundred pomegranates for the two networks, two rows of pomegranates for each network, to cover the two bowls of the capitals that were upon the pillars. ¹⁴He made the stands also, and the lavers upon the stands, ¹⁵and the one sea, and the twelve oxen underneath it. ¹⁶The pots, the shovels, the forks, and all the equipment for these Hū′ram-ā′bī made of burnished bronze for King Solomon for the house of the LORD. ¹⁷In the plain of the Jordan the king cast them, in the clay ground between Sŭc′cŏth and Zĕr′e·dạh. ¹⁸Solomon made all these things in great quantities, so that the weight of the bronze was not ascertained.

19 So Solomon made all the things that were in the house of God: the golden altar, the tables for the bread of the Presence, ²⁰the lampstands and their lamps of pure gold to burn before the inner sanctuary, as prescribed; ²¹the flowers, the lamps, and the tongs, of purest gold; ²²the snuffers, basins, dishes for incense, and firepans, of pure gold; and the sockets*ᵐ* of the temple, for the inner doors to the most holy place and for the doors of the nave of the temple were of gold.

5 Thus all the work that Solomon did for the house of the LORD was finished. And Solomon brought in the things which David his father had dedicated, and stored the silver, the gold, and all the vessels in the treasuries of the house of God.

2 Then Solomon assembled the elders of Israel and all the heads of the tribes, the leaders of the fathers'

houses of the people of Israel, in Jerusalem, to bring up the ark of the covenant of the LORD out of the city of David, which is Zion. ³And all the men of Israel assembled before the king at the feast which is in the seventh month. ⁴And all the elders of Israel came, and the Lē′vītes took up the ark. ⁵And they brought up the ark, the tent of meeting, and all the holy vessels that were in the tent; the priests and the Lē′vītes brought them up. ⁶And King Solomon and all the congregation of Israel, who had assembled before him, were before the ark, sacrificing so many sheep and oxen that they could not be counted or numbered. ⁷So the priests brought the ark of the covenant of the LORD to its place, in the inner sanctuary of the house, in the most holy place, underneath the wings of the cherubim. ⁸For the cherubim spread out their wings over the place of the ark, so that cherubim made a covering above the ark and its poles. ⁹And the poles were so long that the ends of the poles were seen from the holy place before the inner sanctuary; but they could not be seen from outside; and they are there to this day. ¹⁰There was nothing in the ark except the two tables which Moses put there at Hō′rĕb, where the LORD made a covenant with the people of Israel, when they came out of Egypt. ¹¹Now when the priests came out of the holy place (for all the priests who were present had sanctified themselves, without regard to their divisions; ¹²and all the Levitical singers, Ā′săph, Hē′man, and Jĕ·dü′thun, their sons and kinsmen, arrayed in fine linen, with cymbals, harps, and lyres, stood east of the altar with a hundred and twenty priests who were trumpeters; ¹³and it was the duty of the trumpeters and singers to make themselves heard in unison in praise and thanksgiving to the LORD), and when the song was raised, with trumpets and cymbals and other musical instruments, in praise to the LORD,

"For he is good,
for his steadfast love endures for ever,"

the house, the house of the LORD, was filled with a cloud, ¹⁴so that the priests could not stand to minister

---

*ᵐ*1 Kings 7.50: Heb *the door of the house*
5.13, 14: 1 Kings 8.10-11.

because of the cloud; for the glory of the LORD filled the house of God.

6 Then Solomon said,
"The LORD has said that he would dwell in thick darkness.
² I have built thee an exalted house, a place for thee to dwell in for ever."
³ Then the king faced about, and blessed all the assembly of Israel, while all the assembly of Israel stood. ⁴ And he said, "Blessed be the LORD, the God of Israel, who with his hand has fulfilled what he promised with his mouth to David my father, saying, ⁵ 'Since the day that I brought my people out of the land of Egypt, I chose no city in all the tribes of Israel in which to build a house, that my name might be there, and I chose no man as prince over my people Israel; ⁶ but I have chosen Jerusalem that my name may be there and I have chosen David to be over my people Israel.' ⁷ Now it was in the heart of David my father to build a house for the name of the LORD, the God of Israel. ⁸ But the LORD said to David my father, 'Whereas it was in your heart to build a house for my name, you did well that it was in your heart; ⁹ nevertheless you shall not build the house, but your son who shall be born to you shall build the house for my name.' ¹⁰ Now the LORD has fulfilled his promise which he made; for I have risen in the place of David my father, and sit on the throne of Israel, as the LORD promised, and I have built the house for the name of the LORD, the God of Israel. ¹¹ And there I have set the ark, in which is the covenant of the LORD which he made with the people of Israel."

12 Then Solomon stood before the altar of the LORD in the presence of all the assembly of Israel, and spread forth his hands. ¹³ Solomon had made a bronze platform five cubits long, five cubits wide, and three cubits high, and had set it in the court; and he stood upon it. Then he knelt upon his knees in the presence of all the assembly of Israel, and spread forth his hands toward heaven; ¹⁴ and said, "O LORD, God of Israel, there is no God like thee, in heaven or on earth, keeping covenant and showing steadfast love to thy servants who walk before thee with all their heart; ¹⁵ who hast kept with thy servant David my father

what thou didst declare to him; yea, thou didst speak with thy mouth, and with thy hand hast fulfilled it this day. ¹⁶ Now therefore, O LORD, God of Israel, keep with thy servant David my father what thou hast promised him, saying, 'There shall never fail you a man before me to sit upon the throne of Israel, if only your sons take heed to their way, to walk in my law as you have walked before me.' ¹⁷ Now therefore, O LORD, God of Israel, let thy word be confirmed, which thou hast spoken to thy servant David.

18 "But will God dwell indeed with man on the earth? Behold, heaven and the highest heaven cannot contain thee; how much less this house which I have built! ¹⁹ Yet have regard to the prayer of thy servant and to his supplication, O LORD my God, hearkening to the cry and to the prayer which thy servant prays before thee; ²⁰ that thy eyes may be open day and night toward this house, the place where thou hast promised to set thy name, that thou mayest hearken to the prayer which thy servant offers toward this place. ²¹ And hearken thou to the supplications of thy servant and of thy people Israel, when they pray toward this place; yea, hear thou from heaven thy dwelling place; and when thou hearest, forgive.

22 "If a man sins against his neighbor and is made to take an oath, and comes and swears his oath before thy altar in this house, ²³ then hear thou from heaven, and act, and judge thy servants, requiting the guilty by bringing his conduct upon his own head, and vindicating the righteous by rewarding him according to his righteousness.

24 "If thy people Israel are defeated before the enemy because they have sinned against thee, when they turn again and acknowledge thy name, and pray and make supplication to thee in this house, ²⁵ then hear thou from heaven, and forgive the sin of thy people Israel, and bring them again to the land which thou gavest to them and to their fathers.

26 "When heaven is shut up and there is no rain because they have sinned against thee, if they pray toward this place, and acknowledge thy name, and turn from their sin,

6.1-39: 1 Kings 8.12-50.

when thou dost afflict them, [27] then hear thou in heaven, and forgive the sin of thy servants, thy people Israel, when thou dost teach them the good way[n] in which they should walk; and grant rain upon thy land, which thou hast given to thy people as an inheritance.

28 "If there is famine in the land, if there is pestilence or blight or mildew or locust or caterpillar; if their enemies besiege them in any of their cities; whatever plague, whatever sickness there is; [29] whatever prayer, whatever supplication is made by any man or by all thy people Israel, each knowing his own affliction, and his own sorrow and stretching out his hands toward this house; [30] then hear thou from heaven thy dwelling place, and forgive, and render to each whose heart thou knowest, according to all his ways (for thou, thou only, knowest the hearts of the children of men); [31] that they may fear thee and walk in thy ways all the days that they live in the land which thou gavest to our fathers.

32 "Likewise when a foreigner, who is not of thy people Israel, comes from a far country for the sake of thy great name, and thy mighty hand, and thy outstretched arm, when he comes and prays toward this house, [33] hear thou from heaven thy dwelling place, and do according to all for which the foreigner calls to thee; in order that all the peoples of the earth may know thy name and fear thee, as do thy people Israel, and that they may know that this house which I have built is called by thy name.

34 "If thy people go out to battle against their enemies, by whatever way thou shalt send them, and they pray to thee toward this city which thou hast chosen and the house which I have built for thy name, [35] then hear thou from heaven their prayer and their supplication, and maintain their cause.

36 "If they sin against thee—for there is no man who does not sin—and thou art angry with them, and dost give them to an enemy, so that they are carried away captive to a land far or near; [37] yet if they lay it to heart in the land to which they have been carried captive, and repent, and make supplication to thee in the land of their captivity, saying, 'We have sinned, and have acted perversely and wickedly'; [38] if they repent with all their mind and with all their heart in the land of their captivity, to which they were carried captive, and pray toward their land, which thou gavest to their fathers, the city which thou hast chosen, and the house which I have built for thy name, [39] then hear thou from heaven thy dwelling place their prayer and their supplications, and maintain their cause and forgive thy people who have sinned against thee. [40] Now, O my God, let thy eyes be open and thy ears attentive to a prayer of this place.
[41] "And now arise, O LORD God, and go
  to thy resting place,
  thou and the ark of thy might.
Let thy priests, O LORD God, be
  clothed with salvation,
  and let thy saints rejoice in thy
  goodness.
[42] O LORD God, do not turn away the
  face of thy anointed one!
Remember thy steadfast love for
  David thy servant."[l]

7 When Solomon had ended his prayer, fire came down from heaven and consumed the burnt offering and the sacrifices, and the glory of the LORD filled the temple. [2] And the priests could not enter the house of the LORD, because the glory of the LORD filled the LORD's house. [3] When all the children of Israel saw the fire come down and the glory of the LORD upon the temple, they bowed down with their faces to the earth on the pavement, and worshiped and gave thanks to the LORD, saying,
"For he is good,
  for his steadfast love endures
  for ever."

4 Then the king and all the people offered sacrifice before the LORD. [5] King Solomon offered as a sacrifice twenty-two thousand oxen and a hundred and twenty thousand sheep. So the king and all the people dedicated the house of God. [6] The priests stood at their posts; the Lē'vītes also, with the instruments for music to the LORD which King David had made for giving thanks to the LORD—for his steadfast love endures for ever—whenever David offered praises by their

[n]Gk Syr Vg: Heb *toward the good way*
6.41-42: Ps 132.8-10. 7.4-10: 1 Kings 8.62-66.

ministry; opposite them the priests sounded trumpets; and all Israel stood.

7 And Solomon consecrated the middle of the court that was before the house of the Lord; for there he offered the burnt offering and the fat of the peace offerings, because the bronze altar Solomon had made could not hold the burnt offering and the cereal offering and the fat.

8 At that time Solomon held the feast for seven days, and all Israel with him, a very great congregation, from the entrance of Hā′măth to the Brook of Egypt. ⁹And on the eighth day they held a solemn assembly; for they had kept the dedication of the altar seven days and the feast seven days. ¹⁰On the twenty-third day of the seventh month he sent the people away to their homes, joyful and glad of heart for the goodness that the Lord had shown to David and to Solomon and to Israel his people.

11 Thus Solomon finished the house of the Lord and the king's house; all that Solomon had planned to do in the house of the Lord and in his own house he successfully accomplished. ¹²Then the Lord appeared to Solomon in the night and said to him: "I have heard your prayer, and have chosen this place for myself as a house of sacrifice. ¹³When I shut up the heavens so that there is no rain, or command the locust to devour the land, or send pestilence among my people, ¹⁴if my people who are called by my name humble themselves, and pray and seek my face, and turn from their wicked ways, then I will hear from heaven, and will forgive their sin and heal their land. ¹⁵Now my eyes will be open and my ears attentive to the prayer that is made in this place. ¹⁶For now I have chosen and consecrated this house that my name may be there for ever; my eyes and my heart will be there for all time. ¹⁷And as for you, if you walk before me, as David your father walked, doing according to all that I have commanded you and keeping my statutes and my ordinances, ¹⁸then I will establish your royal throne, as I covenanted with David your father, saying, 'There shall not fail you a man to rule Israel.'

19 "But if you*ᵒ* turn aside and forsake my statutes and my commandments which I have set before

you, and go and serve other gods and worship them, ²⁰then I will pluck you*ᵖ* up from the land which I have given you;*ᵖ* and this house, which I have consecrated for my name, I will cast out of my sight, and will make it a proverb and a byword among all peoples. ²¹And at this house, which is exalted, every one passing by will be astonished, and say, 'Why has the Lord done thus to this land and to this house?' ²²Then they will say, 'Because they forsook the Lord God of their fathers who brought them out of the land of Egypt, and laid hold on other gods, and worshiped them and served them; therefore he has brought all this evil upon them.'"

8 At the end of twenty years, in which Solomon had built the house of the Lord and his own house, ²Solomon rebuilt the cities which Hū′ram had given to him, and settled the people of Israel in them.

3 And Solomon went to Hā′măthzō′bah, and took it. ⁴He built Tăd′-môr in the wilderness and all the store-cities which he built in Hā′măth. ⁵He also built Upper Bĕth–hō′rŏn and Lower Beth–horon, fortified cities with walls, gates, and bars, ⁶and Bā′ạ·lăth, and all the store-cities that Solomon had, and all the cities for his chariots, and the cities for his horsemen, and whatever Solomon desired to build in Jerusalem, in Lebanon, and in all the land of his dominion. ⁷All the people who were left of the Hĭt′-tītes, the Ăm′ọ·rītes, the Pĕr′ĭz·zītes, the Hī′vītes, and the Jĕb′ū·sītes, who were not of Israel, ⁸from their descendants who were left after them in the land, whom the people of Israel had not destroyed—these Solomon made a forced levy and so they are to this day. ⁹But of the people of Israel Solomon made no slaves for his work; they were soldiers, and his officers, the commanders of his chariots, and his horsemen. ¹⁰And these were the chief officers of King Solomon, two hundred and fifty, who exercised authority over the people.

11 Solomon brought Pharaoh's daughter up from the city of David to the house which he had built for her, for he said, "My wife shall not live in the house of David king of

ᵒThe word *you* is plural here   ᵖHeb *them*
7.11-22: 1 Kings 9.1-9.   8.1-18: 1 Kings 9.10-28.

Israel, for the places to which the ark of the LORD has come are holy."

12 Then Solomon offered up burnt offerings to the LORD upon the altar of the LORD which he had built before the vestibule, ¹³ as the duty of each day required, offering according to the commandment of Moses for the sabbaths, the new moons, and the three annual feasts—the feast of unleavened bread, the feast of weeks, and the feast of tabernacles. ¹⁴ According to the ordinance of David his father, he appointed the divisions of the priests for their service, and the Lē´vītes for their offices of praise and ministry before the priests as the duty of each day required, and the gatekeepers in their divisions for the several gates; for so David the man of God had commanded. ¹⁵ And they did not turn aside from what the king had commanded the priests and Lē´vītes concerning any matter and concerning the treasuries.

16 Thus was accomplished all the work of Solomon from⁹ the day the foundation of the house of the LORD was laid until it was finished. So the house of the LORD was completed. 17 Then Solomon went to Ē´zĭ-ŏn-gē´ber and Ē´lŏth on the shore of the sea, in the land of Ē´dom. ¹⁸ And Hū´ram sent him by his servants ships and servants familiar with the sea, and they went to Ō´phĭr together with the servants of Solomon, and fetched from there four hundred and fifty talents of gold and brought it to King Solomon.

9 Now when the queen of Shē´ba heard of the fame of Solomon she came to Jerusalem to test him with hard questions, having a very great retinue and camels bearing spices and very much gold and precious stones. When she came to Solomon, she told him all that was on her mind. ² And Solomon answered all her questions; there was nothing hidden from Solomon which he could not explain to her. ³ And when the queen of Shē´ba had seen the wisdom of Solomon, the house that he had built, ⁴ the food of his table, the seating of his officials, and the attendance of his servants, and their clothing, his cupbearers, and their clothing, and his burnt offerings which he offered at the house of the LORD, there was no more spirit in her.

5 And she said to the king, "The report was true which I heard in my own land of your affairs and of your wisdom, ⁶ but I did not believe theʳ reports until I came and my own eyes had seen it; and behold, half the greatness of your wisdom was not told me; you surpass the report which I heard. ⁷ Happy are your wives!ˢ Happy are these your servants, who continually stand before you and hear your wisdom! ⁸ Blessed be the LORD your God, who has delighted in you and set you on his throne as king for the LORD your God! Because your God loved Israel and would establish them for ever, he has made you king over them, that you may execute justice and righteousness." ⁹ Then she gave the king a hundred and twenty talents of gold, and a very great quantity of spices, and precious stones: there were no spices such as those which the queen of Shē´ba gave to King Solomon.

10 Moreover the servants of Hū´ram and the servants of Solomon, who brought gold from Ō´phĭr, brought algum wood and precious stones. ¹¹ And the king made of the algum wood stepsᵗ for the house of the LORD and for the king's house, lyres also and harps for the singers; there never was seen the like of them before in the land of Judah.

12 And King Solomon gave to the queen of Shē´ba all that she desired, whatever she asked besides what she had brought to the king. So she turned and went back to her own land, with her servants.

13 Now the weight of gold that came to Solomon in one year was six hundred and sixty-six talents of gold, ¹⁴ besides that which the traders and merchants brought; and all the kings of Arabia and the governors of the land brought gold and silver to Solomon. ¹⁵ King Solomon made two hundred large shields of beaten gold; six hundred shekels of beaten gold went into each shield. ¹⁶ And he made three hundred shields of beaten gold; three hundred shekels of gold went into each shield; and the king put them in the House of the Forest of Lebanon. ¹⁷ The king also made a great ivory throne,

---

ᵍGk Syr Vg: Heb *to*
ʳHeb *their* ˢGk Compare 1 Kings 10.8: Heb *men*
ᵗGk Vg: The meaning of the Hebrew word is uncertain
9.1-28: 1 Kings 10.1-29.

and overlaid it with pure gold. ¹⁸The throne had six steps and a footstool of gold, which were attached to the throne, and on each side of the seat were arm rests and two lions standing beside the arm rests, ¹⁹while twelve lions stood there, one on each end of a step on the six steps. The like of it was never made in any kingdom. ²⁰All King Solomon's drinking vessels were of gold, and all the vessels of the House of the Forest of Lebanon were of pure gold; silver was not considered as anything in the days of Solomon. ²¹For the king's ships went to Tär'-shĭsh with the servants of Hū'răm; once every three years the ships of Tarshish used to come bringing gold, silver, ivory, apes, and peacocks.ˣ

22 Thus King Solomon excelled all the kings of the earth in riches and in wisdom. ²³And all the kings of the earth sought the presence of Solomon to hear his wisdom, which God had put into his mind. ²⁴Every one of them brought his present, articles of silver and of gold, garments, myrrh, spices, horses, and mules, so much year by year. ²⁵And Solomon had four thousand stalls for horses and chariots, and twelve thousand horsemen, whom he stationed in the chariot cities and with the king in Jerusalem. ²⁶And he ruled over all the kings from the Euphrates to the land of the Phĭ·lĭs'tĭnes, and to the border of Egypt. ²⁷And the king made silver as common in Jerusalem as stone, and cedar as plentiful as the sycamore of the Shĕ·phē'lah. ²⁸And horses were imported for Solomon from Egypt and from all lands.

29 Now the rest of the acts of Solomon, from first to last, are they not written in the history of Nathan the prophet, and in the prophecy of A·hī'-jah the Shī'lo·nīte, and in the visions of Ĭd'dō the seer concerning Jĕr·o-bō'ạm the son of Nē'băt? ³⁰Solomon reigned in Jerusalem over all Israel forty years. ³¹And Solomon slept with his fathers, and was buried in the city of David his father; and Rē·ho·bō'ạm his son reigned in his stead.

10 Rē·ho·bō'ạm went to Shē'chĕm, for all Israel had come to Shechem to make him king. ²And when Jĕr·o-bō'ạm the son of Nē'băt heard of it (for he was in Egypt, whither he had fled from King Solomon), then Jeroboam returned from Egypt. ³And they

sent and called him; and Jĕr·o-bō'ạm and all Israel came and said to Rē·ho-bō'ạm, ⁴"Your father made our yoke heavy. Now therefore lighten the hard service of your father and his heavy yoke upon us, and we will serve you." ⁵He said to them, "Come to me again in three days." So the people went away.

6 Then King Rē·ho·bō'ạm took counsel with the old men, who had stood before Solomon his father while he was yet alive, saying, "How do you advise me to answer this people?" ⁷And they said to him, "If you will be kind to this people and please them, and speak good words to them, then they will be your servants for ever." ⁸But he forsook the counsel which the old men gave him, and took counsel with the young men who had grown up with him and stood before him. ⁹And he said to them, "What do you advise that we answer this people who have said to me, 'Lighten the yoke that your father put upon us'?" ¹⁰And the young men who had grown up with him said to him, "Thus shall you speak to the people who said to you, 'Your father made our yoke heavy, but do you lighten it for us'; thus shall you say to them, 'My little finger is thicker than my father's loins. ¹¹And now, whereas my father laid upon you a heavy yoke, I will add to your yoke. My father chastised you with whips, but I will chastise you with scorpions.'"

12 So Jĕr·o-bō'ạm and all the people came to Rē·ho·bō'ạm the third day, as the king said, "Come to me again the third day." ¹³And the king answered them harshly, and forsaking the counsel of the old men, ¹⁴King Rē·ho·bō'ạm spoke to them according to the counsel of the young men, saying, "My father made your yoke heavy, but I will add to it; my father chastised you with whips, but I will chastise you with scorpions." ¹⁵So the king did not hearken to the people; for it was a turn of affairs brought about by God that the LORD might fulfil his word, which he spoke by A·hī'jah the Shī'lo·nīte to Jĕr·o-bō'ạm the son of Nē'băt.

16 And when all Israel saw that the king did not hearken to them, the people answered the king,

ˣ Or *baboons*

9.30, 31: 1 Kings 11.42-48. 10.1-19: 1 Kings 12.1-19.

"What portion have we in David?
We have no inheritance in the son
of Jesse.
Each of you to your tents, O Israel!
Look now to your own house, David."
So all Israel departed to their tents.
¹⁷But Rē·họ·bō′ạm reigned over the
people of Israel who dwelt in the cities
of Judah. ¹⁸Then King Rē·họ·bō′ạm
sent Hạ·dôr′ạm, who was taskmaster
over the forced labor, and the people
of Israel stoned him to death with
stones. And King Rehoboam made
haste to mount his chariot, to flee to
Jerusalem. ¹⁹So Israel has been in
rebellion against the house of David
to this day.

11 When Rē·họ·bō′ạm came to
Jerusalem, he assembled the
house of Judah, and Benjamin, a
hundred and eighty thousand chosen
warriors, to fight against Israel, to
restore the kingdom to Rehoboam.
²But the word of the LORD came to
Shě·māi′ạh the man of God: ³"Say to
Rē·họ·bō′ạm the son of Solomon king
of Judah, and to all Israel in Judah
and Benjamin, ⁴'Thus says the LORD,
You shall not go up or fight against
your brethren. Return every man to
his home, for this thing is from me.'"
So they hearkened to the word of the
LORD, and returned and did not go
against Jěr·ọ·bō′ạm.
5 Rē·họ·bō′ạm dwelt in Jerusalem,
and he built cities for defense in
Judah. ⁶He built Bethlehem, Ē′tăm,
Tě·kō′ạ, ⁷Běth–zŭr, Sō′cō, Ạ·dŭl′lạm,
⁸Găth, Mạ·rē′shạh, Zĭph, ⁹Ăd·ọ·rā′ĭm,
Lā′chĭsh, Ạ·zē′kạh, ¹⁰Zō′rạh, Aī′-
jạ·lŏn, and Hē′brọn, fortified cities
which are in Judah and in Benjamin.
¹¹He made the fortresses strong, and
put commanders in them, and stores
of food, oil, and wine. ¹²And he put
shields and spears in all the cities, and
made them very strong. So he held
Judah and Benjamin.
13 And the priests and the Lē′vītes
that were in all Israel resorted to him
from all places where they lived. ¹⁴For
the Lē′vītes left their common lands
and their holdings and came to Judah
and Jerusalem, because Jěr·ọ·bō′ạm
and his sons cast them out from serving as priests of the LORD, ¹⁵and he
appointed his own priests for the high
places, and for the satyrs, and for the
calves which he had made. ¹⁶And those

who had set their hearts to seek the
LORD God of Israel came after them
from all the tribes of Israel to Jerusalem to sacrifice to the LORD, the God
of their fathers. ¹⁷They strengthened
the kingdom of Judah, and for three
years they made Rē·họ·bō′ạm the son
of Solomon secure, for they walked
for three years in the way of David
and Solomon.
18 Rē·họ·bō′ạm took as wife Mā′-
hạ·lăth the daughter of Jěr′ĭ·mŏth the
son of David, and of Ăb′ĭ·hāil the
daughter of Ē·lī′ăb the son of Jesse;
¹⁹and she bore him sons, Jē′ŭsh,
Shěm·ạ·rī′ạh, and Zā′hăm. ²⁰After her
he took Mā′ạ·cạh the daughter of
Ăb′sạ·lọm, who bore him Ạ·bī′jạh,
Ăt′taī, Zī′zạ, and Shě·lō′mĭth. ²¹Rē·họ·
bō′ạm loved Mā′ạ·cạh the daughter of
Ăb′sạ·lọm above all his wives and concubines (he took eighteen wives and
sixty concubines, and had twenty-
eight sons and sixty daughters); ²²and
Rē·họ·bō′ạm appointed Ạ·bī′jạh the
son of Mā′ạ·cạh as chief prince among
his brothers, for he intended to make
him king. ²³And he dealt wisely, and
distributed some of his sons through
all the districts of Judah and Benjamin, in all the fortified cities; and he
gave them abundant provisions, and
procured wives for them.ᵘ

12 When the rule of Rē·họ·bō′ạm
was established and was strong,
he forsook the law of the LORD, and
all Israel with him. ²In the fifth year
of King Rē·họ·bō′ạm, because they had
been unfaithful to the LORD, Shī′-
shăk king of Egypt came up against
Jerusalem ³with twelve hundred chariots and sixty thousand horsemen. And
the people were without number who
came with him from Egypt—Libyans,
Sŭk′kĭ·ĭm, and Ethiopians. ⁴And he
took the fortified cities of Judah and
came as far as Jerusalem. ⁵Then
Shě·māi′ạh the prophet came to Rē-
họ·bō′ạm and to the princes of Judah,
who had gathered at Jerusalem because of Shī′shăk, and said to them,
"Thus says the LORD, 'You abandoned
me, so I have abandoned you to the
hand of Shishak.'" ⁶Then the princes
of Israel and the king humbled themselves and said, "The LORD is righteous." ⁷When the LORD saw that they
humbled themselves, the word of the

ᵘCn: Heb sought a multitude of wives
11.1-4: 1 Kings 12.22-24.   12.1-16: 1 Kings 14.25-31.

LORD came to Shĕ·māi′ah: "They have humbled themselves; I will not destroy them, but I will grant them some deliverance, and my wrath shall not be poured out upon Jerusalem by the hand of Shī′shăk. ⁸ Nevertheless they shall be servants to him, that they may know my service and the service of the kingdoms of the countries."

9 So Shī′shăk king of Egypt came up against Jerusalem; he took away the treasures of the house of the LORD and the treasures of the king's house; he took away everything. He also took away the shields of gold which Solomon had made; ¹⁰ and King Rē·ho·bō′am made in their stead shields of bronze, and committed them to the hands of the officers of the guard, who kept the door of the king's house. ¹¹ And as often as the king went into the house of the LORD, the guard came and bore them, and brought them back to the guardroom. ¹² And when he humbled himself the wrath of the LORD turned from him, so as not to make a complete destruction; moreover, conditions were good in Judah.

13 So King Rē·ho·bō′am established himself in Jerusalem and reigned. Rehoboam was forty-one years old when he began to reign, and he reigned seventeen years in Jerusalem, the city which the LORD had chosen out of all the tribes of Israel to put his name there. His mother's name was Nā′a·mah the Ăm′mo·nīt·ess. ¹⁴ And he did evil, for he did not set his heart to seek the LORD.

15 Now the acts of Rē·ho·bō′am, from first to last, are they not written in the chronicles of Shĕ·māi′ah the prophet and of Ĭd′dō the seer?*ᵛ* There were continual wars between Rehoboam and Jĕr·o·bō′am. ¹⁶ And Rē·ho·bō′am slept with his fathers, and was buried in the city of David; and A·bī′jah his son reigned in his stead.

13 In the eighteenth year of King Jĕr·o·bō′am A·bī′jah began to reign over Judah. ² He reigned for three years in Jerusalem. His mother's name was Mī·cāi′ah the daughter of Ū′rī·el of Gĭb′e–ah.

Now there was war between A·bī′jah and Jĕr·o·bō′am. ³ A·bī′jah went out to battle having an army of valiant men of war, four hundred thousand picked men; and Jĕr·o·bō′am drew up his line of battle against him with eight hundred thousand picked mighty warriors. ⁴ Then A·bī′jah stood up on Mount Zĕm·a·rā′ĭm which is in the hill country of Ē′phra·ĭm, and said, "Hear me, O Jĕr·o·bō′am and all Israel! ⁵ Ought you not to know that the LORD God of Israel gave the kingship over Israel for ever to David and his sons by a covenant of salt? ⁶ Yet Jĕr·o·bō′am the son of Nē′băt, a servant of Solomon the son of David, rose up and rebelled against his lord; ⁷ and certain worthless scoundrels gathered about him and defied Rē·ho·bō′am the son of Solomon, when Rehoboam was young and irresolute and could not withstand them.

8 "And now you think to withstand the kingdom of the LORD in the hand of the sons of David, because you are a great multitude and have with you the golden calves which Jĕr·o·bō′am made you for gods. ⁹ Have you not driven out the priests of the LORD, the sons of Aaron, and the Lē′vītes, and made priests for yourselves like the peoples of other lands? Whoever comes to consecrate himself with a young bull or seven rams becomes a priest of what are no gods. ¹⁰ But as for us, the LORD is our God, and we have not forsaken him. We have priests ministering to the LORD who are sons of Aaron, and Lē′vītes for their service. ¹¹ They offer to the LORD every morning and every evening burnt offerings and incense of sweet spices, set out the showbread on the table of pure gold, and care for the golden lampstand that its lamps may burn every evening; for we keep the charge of the LORD our God, but you have forsaken him. ¹² Behold, God is with us at our head, and his priests with their battle trumpets to sound the call to battle against you. O sons of Israel, do not fight against the LORD, the God of your fathers; for you cannot succeed."

13 Jĕr·o·bō′am had sent an ambush around to come on them from behind; thus his troops*ᵂ* were in front of Judah, and the ambush was behind them. ¹⁴ And when Judah looked, behold, the battle was before and behind them; and they cried to the LORD, and the priests blew the trumpets. ¹⁵ Then the men of Judah raised the battle shout. And when the men of Judah shouted, God defeated Jĕr·o·bō′am and all

Israel before A·bī′jah and Judah.
¹⁶The men of Israel fled before Judah,
and God gave them into their hand.
¹⁷A·bī′jah and his people slew them
with a great slaughter; so there fell
slain of Israel five hundred thousand
picked men. ¹⁸Thus the men of Israel
were subdued at that time, and the
men of Judah prevailed, because they
relied upon the LORD, the God of their
fathers. ¹⁹And A·bī′jah pursued Jĕr-
o·bō′am, and took cities from him,
Bĕth′el with its villages and Jĕ·shā′-
nah with its villages and Ē′phron*
with its villages. ²⁰Jĕr·o·bō′am did not
recover his power in the days of
A·bī′jah; and the LORD smote him, and
he died. ²¹But A·bī′jah grew mighty.
And he took fourteen wives, and had
twenty-two sons and sixteen daughters. ²²The rest of the acts of A·bī′jah,
his ways and his sayings, are written
in the story of the prophet Ĭd′dō.

14ʸ So A·bī′jah slept with his fathers, and they buried him in
the city of David; and Asa his son
reigned in his stead. In his days the
land had rest for ten years. ²ᶻAnd Asa
did what was good and right in the eyes
of the LORD his God. ³He took away the
foreign altars and the high places, and
broke down the pillars and hewed
down the A·shē′rĭm, ⁴and commanded
Judah to seek the LORD, the God of
their fathers, and to keep the law and
the commandment. ⁵He also took out
of all the cities of Judah the high
places and the incense altars. And the
kingdom had rest under him. ⁶He built
fortified cities in Judah, for the land
had rest. He had no war in those years,
for the LORD gave him peace. ⁷And he
said to Judah, "Let us build these
cities, and surround them with walls
and towers, gates and bars; the land
is still ours, because we have sought
the LORD our God; we have sought
him, and he has given us peace on
every side." So they built and prospered. ⁸And Asa had an army of three
hundred thousand from Judah, armed
with bucklers and spears, and two hundred and eighty thousand men from
Benjamin, that carried shields and
drew bows; all these were mighty men
of valor.

9 Zē′rah the Ethiopian came out
against them with an army of a million men and three hundred chariots,
and came as far as Ma·rē′shah. ¹⁰And

Asa went out to meet him, and they
drew up their lines of battle in the valley of Zĕph′a·thah at Ma·rē′shah.
¹¹And Asa cried to the LORD his God,
"O LORD, there is none like thee to
help, between the mighty and the weak.
Help us, O LORD our God, for we rely
on thee, and in thy name we have come
against this multitude. O LORD, thou
art our God; let not man prevail
against thee." ¹²So the LORD defeated
the Ethiopians before Asa and before
Judah, and the Ethiopians fled. ¹³Asa
and the people that were with him
pursued them as far as Gē′rar, and the
Ethiopians fell until none remained
alive; for they were broken before the
LORD and his army. The men of Ju-
dahᵃ carried away very much booty.
¹⁴And they smote all the cities round
about Gē′rar, for the fear of the LORD
was upon them. They plundered all the
cities, for there was much plunder in
them. ¹⁵And they smote the tents of
those who had cattle,ᵇ and carried
away sheep in abundance and camels.
Then they returned to Jerusalem.

15 The Spirit of God came upon
Az·a·rī′ah the son of Ō′dĕd,
²and he went out to meet Asa, and
said to him, "Hear me, Asa, and all
Judah and Benjamin: The LORD is
with you, while you are with him. If
you seek him, he will be found by you,
but if you forsake him, he will forsake
you. ³For a long time Israel was without the true God, and without a teaching priest, and without law; ⁴but when
in their distress they turned to the
LORD, the God of Israel, and sought
him, he was found by them. ⁵In those
times there was no peace to him who
went out or to him who came in, for
great disturbances afflicted all the inhabitants of the lands. ⁶They were
broken in pieces, nation against nation and city against city, for God
troubled them with every sort of distress. ⁷But you, take courage! Do not
let your hands be weak, for your work
shall be rewarded."

8 When Asa heard these words,
the prophecy of Az·a·rī′ah the son of
Ō′dĕd,ᶜ he took courage, and put
away the abominable idols from all
the land of Judah and Benjamin and

*Another reading is *Ephraim*
ʸCh 13.23 in Heb ᶻCh 14.1 in Heb
ᵃHeb *they* ᵇHeb obscure
ᶜCompare Syr Vg: Heb *the prophecy, Oded the prophet*
14.1–5: 1 Kings 15.8–12.

from the cities which he had taken in the hill country of Ē'phra·ĭm, and he repaired the altar of the LORD that was in front of the vestibule of the house of the LORD.*ᵈ* ⁹And he gathered all Judah and Benjamin, and those from Ē'phra·ĭm, Ma·năs'seh, and Sĭm'ē·ọn who were sojourning with them, for great numbers had deserted to him from Israel when they saw that the LORD his God was with him. ¹⁰They were gathered at Jerusalem in the third month of the fifteenth year of the reign of Asa. ¹¹They sacrificed to the LORD on that day, from the spoil which they had brought, seven hundred oxen and seven thousand sheep. ¹²And they entered into a covenant to seek the LORD, the God of their fathers, with all their heart and with all their soul; ¹³and that whoever would not seek the LORD, the God of Israel, should be put to death, whether young or old, man or woman. ¹⁴They took oath to the LORD with a loud voice, and with shouting, and with trumpets, and with horns. ¹⁵And all Judah rejoiced over the oath; for they had sworn with all their heart, and had sought him with their whole desire, and he was found by them, and the LORD gave them rest round about.

16 Even Mā'a·cah, his mother, King Asa removed from being queen mother because she had made an abominable image for A·shē'rah. Asa cut down her image, crushed it, and burned it at the brook Kĭd'rọn. ¹⁷But the high places were not taken out of Israel. Nevertheless the heart of Asa was blameless all his days. ¹⁸And he brought into the house of God the votive gifts of his father and his own votive gifts, silver, and gold, and vessels. ¹⁹And there was no more war until the thirty-fifth year of the reign of Asa.

16 In the thirty-sixth year of the reign of Asa, Bā'a·sha king of Israel went up against Judah, and built Rā'mah, that he might permit no one to go out or come in to Asa king of Judah. ²Then Asa took silver and gold from the treasures of the house of the LORD and the king's house, and sent them to Bĕn–hā'dăd king of Syria, who dwelt in Damascus, saying, ³"Let there be a league between me and you, as between my father and your father; behold, I am sending to you silver and

gold; go, break your league with Bā'a·sha king of Israel, that he may withdraw from me." ⁴And Bĕn–hā'dăd hearkened to King Asa, and sent the commanders of his armies against the cities of Israel, and they conquered I'jŏn, Dan, Ā'bĕl–mā'ĭm, and all the store-cities of Năph'ta·lī. ⁵And when Bā'a·sha heard of it, he stopped building Rā'mah, and let his work cease. ⁶Then King Asa took all Judah, and they carried away the stones of Rā'mah and its timber, with which Bā'a·sha had been building, and with them he built Gē'ba and Mĭz'pah.

7 At that time Ha·nā'nī the seer came to Asa king of Judah, and said to him, "Because you relied on the king of Syria, and did not rely on the LORD your God, the army of the king of Syria has escaped you. ⁸Were not the Ethiopians and the Libyans a huge army with exceedingly many chariots and horsemen? Yet because you relied on the LORD, he gave them into your hand. ⁹For the eyes of the LORD run to and fro throughout the whole earth, to show his might in behalf of those whose heart is blameless toward him. You have done foolishly in this; for from now on you will have wars." ¹⁰Then Asa was angry with the seer, and put him in the stocks, in prison, for he was in a rage with him because of this. And Asa inflicted cruelties upon some of the people at the same time.

11 The acts of Asa, from first to last, are written in the Book of the Kings of Judah and Israel. ¹²In the thirty-ninth year of his reign Asa was diseased in his feet, and his disease became severe; yet even in his disease he did not seek the LORD, but sought help from physicians. ¹³And Asa slept with his fathers, dying in the forty-first year of his reign. ¹⁴They buried him in the tomb which he had hewn out for himself in the city of David. They laid him on a bier which had been filled with various kinds of spices prepared by the perfumer's art; and they made a very great fire in his honor.

17 Jĕ·hŏsh'a·phăt his son reigned in his stead, and strengthened himself against Israel. ²He placed forces in all the fortified cities of Judah, and set garrisons in the land of

*ᵈ*Heb *the vestibule of the* LORD
15.16–16.6: 1 Kings 15.13-22.
16.12–14: 1 Kings 15.23, 24. **17.1:** 1 Kings 15.24.

Judah, and in the cities of Ē'phrạ·ĭm which Asa his father had taken. ³The LORD was with Jĕ·hŏsh'ạ·phăt, because he walked in the earlier ways of his father;ᵉ he did not seek the Bā'ạls, ⁴but sought the God of his father and walked in his commandments, and not according to the ways of Israel. ⁵Therefore the LORD established the kingdom in his hand; and all Judah brought tribute to Jĕ·hŏsh'ạ·phăt; and he had great riches and honor. ⁶His heart was courageous in the ways of the LORD; and furthermore he took the high places and the Ạ·shē'rĭm out of Judah.

7 In the third year of his reign he sent his princes, Bĕn–hā'ĭl, Ō'bạ·dī'ạh, Zĕch·ạ·rī'ạh, Nẹ·thăn'ĕl, and Mī·cāi'ạh, to teach in the cities of Judah; ⁸and with them the Lē'vītes, Shĕ·māi'ạh, Nĕth·ạ·nī'ạh, Zĕb·ạ·dī'ạh, Ās'·ạ·hĕl, Shĕ·mī'rạ·mŏth, Jĕ·hŏn'ạ·than, Ăd·o·nī'jạh, Tō·bī'jạh, and Tŏb·ăd·o·nī'jạh; and with these Levites, the priests Ĕ·lĭsh'ạ·mạ and Jĕ·hō'rạm. ⁹And they taught in Judah, having the book of the law of the LORD with them; they went about through all the cities of Judah and taught among the people.

10 And the fear of the LORD fell upon all the kingdoms of the lands that were round about Judah, and they made no war against Jĕ·hŏsh'ạ·phăt. ¹¹Some of the Phĭ·lĭs'tĭnes brought Jĕ·hŏsh'ạ·phăt presents, and silver for tribute; and the Arabs also brought him seven thousand seven hundred rams and seven thousand seven hundred he-goats. ¹²And Jĕ·hŏsh'ạ·phăt grew steadily greater. He built in Judah fortresses and store-cities, ¹³and he had great stores in the cities of Judah. He had soldiers, mighty men of valor, in Jerusalem. ¹⁴This was the muster of them by fathers' houses: Of Judah, the commanders of thousands: Ăd'nạh the commander, with three hundred thousand mighty men of valor, ¹⁵and next to him Jĕ'hō–hā'·nạn the commander, with two hundred and eighty thousand, ¹⁶and next to him Ăm·ạ·sī'ạh the son of Zĭch'rī, a volunteer for the service of the LORD, with two hundred thousand mighty men of valor. ¹⁷Of Benjamin: Ē·lī'ạ·dạ, a mighty man of valor, with two hundred thousand men armed with bow and shield, ¹⁸and next to him Jĕ·hŏ'zạ·băd with a hundred and eighty thousand armed for war. ¹⁹These were in the

service of the king, besides those whom the king had placed in the fortified cities throughout all Judah.

18 Now Jĕ·hŏsh'ạ·phăt had great riches and honor; and he made a marriage alliance with Ā'hăb. ²After some years he went down to Ā'hăb in Sạ·mâr'ĭ·ạ. And Ahab killed an abundance of sheep and oxen for him and for the people who were with him, and induced him to go up against Rā'mŏth–gĭl'ē·ạd. ³Ā'hăb king of Israel said to Jĕ·hŏsh'ạ·phăt king of Judah, "Will you go with me to Rā'mŏth–gĭl'ē·ạd?" He answered him, "I am as you are, my people as your people. We will be with you in the war."

4 And Jĕ·hŏsh'ạ·phăt said to the king of Israel, "Inquire first for the word of the LORD." ⁵Then the king of Israel gathered the prophets together, four hundred men, and said to them, "Shall we go to battle against Rā'mŏth–gĭl'ē·ạd, or shall I forbear?" And they said, "Go up; for God will give it into the hand of the king." ⁶But Jĕ·hŏsh'ạ·phăt said, "Is there not here another prophet of the LORD of whom we may inquire?" ⁷And the king of Israel said to Jĕ·hŏsh'ạ·phăt, "There is yet one man by whom we may inquire of the LORD, Mī·cāi'ạh the son of Ĭm'lạh; but I hate him, for he never prophesies good concerning me, but always evil." And Jehoshaphat said, "Let not the king say so." ⁸Then the king of Israel summoned an officer and said, "Bring quickly Mī·cāi'ạh the son of Ĭm'lah." ⁹Now the king of Israel and Jĕ·hŏsh'ạ·phăt the king of Judah were sitting on their thrones, arrayed in their robes; and they were sitting at the threshing floor at the entrance of the gate of Sạ·mâr'ĭ·ạ; and all the prophets were prophesying before them. ¹⁰And Zĕd·ẹ·kī'ạh the son of Chĕ·nā'ạ·nạh made for himself horns of iron, and said, "Thus says the LORD, 'With these you shall push the Syrians until they are destroyed.' " ¹¹And all the prophets prophesied so, and said, "Go up to Rā'mŏth–gĭl'ē·ạd and triumph; the LORD will give it into the hand of the king."

12 And the messenger who went to summon Mī·cāi'ạh said to him, "Behold, the words of the prophets with one accord are favorable to the king; let your word be like the word of one

---

ᵉAnother reading is *his father David*
18.1–34: 1 Kings 22.1–35.

of them, and speak favorably." ¹³But Mī·cāi'ah said, "As the LORD lives, what my God says, that I will speak." ¹⁴And when he had come to the king, the king said to him, "Mī·cāi'ah, shall we go to Rā'mŏth–gĭl'ē·ạd to battle, or shall I forbear?" And he answered, "Go up and triumph; they will be given into your hand." ¹⁵But the king said to him, "How many times shall I adjure you that you speak to me nothing but the truth in the name of the LORD?" ¹⁶And he said, "I saw all Israel scattered upon the mountains, as sheep that have no shepherd; and the LORD said, 'These have no master; let each return to his home in peace.'" ¹⁷And the king of Israel said to Jĕ·hŏsh'ạ·phăt, "Did I not tell you that he would not prophesy good concerning me, but evil?" ¹⁸And Mī·cāi'ah said, "Therefore hear the word of the LORD: I saw the LORD sitting on his throne, and all the host of heaven standing on his right hand and on his left; ¹⁹and the LORD said, 'Who will entice Ā'hăb the king of Israel, that he may go up and fall at Rā'mŏth–gĭl'ē·ạd?' And one said one thing, and another said another. ²⁰Then a spirit came forward and stood before the LORD, saying, 'I will entice him.' And the LORD said to him, 'By what means?' ²¹And he said, 'I will go forth, and will be a lying spirit in the mouth of all his prophets.' And he said, 'You are to entice him, and you shall succeed; go forth and do so.' ²²Now therefore behold, the LORD has put a lying spirit in the mouth of these your prophets; the LORD has spoken evil concerning you."

23 Then Zĕd·ẹ·kī'ah the son of Chĕ·nā'ạ·nah came near and struck Mī·cāi'ah on the cheek, and said, "Which way did the Spirit of the LORD go from me to speak to you?" ²⁴And Mī·cāi'ah said, "Behold, you shall see on that day when you go into an inner chamber to hide yourself." ²⁵And the king of Israel said, "Seize Mī·cāi'ah, and take him back to Ā'mŏn the governor of the city and to Jō'ăsh the king's son; ²⁶and say, 'Thus says the king, Put this fellow in prison, and feed him with scant fare of bread and water, until I return in peace.'" ²⁷And Mī·cāi'ah said, "If you return in peace, the LORD has not spoken by me." And he said, "Hear, all you peoples!"

28 So the king of Israel and Jĕ·hŏsh'ạ·phăt the king of Judah went up to Rā'mŏth–gĭl'ē·ạd. ²⁹And the king of Israel said to Jĕ·hŏsh'ạ·phăt, "I will disguise myself and go into battle, but you wear your robes." And the king of Israel disguised himself; and they went into battle. ³⁰Now the king of Syria had commanded the captains of his chariots, "Fight with neither small nor great, but only with the king of Israel." ³¹And when the captains of the chariots saw Jĕ·hŏsh'ạ·phăt, they said, "It is the king of Israel." So they turned to fight against him; and Jehoshaphat cried out, and the LORD helped him. God drew them away from him, ³²for when the captains of the chariots saw that it was not the king of Israel, they turned back from pursuing him. ³³But a certain man drew his bow at a venture, and struck the king of Israel between the scale armor and the breastplate; therefore he said to the driver of his chariot, "Turn about, and carry me out of the battle, for I am wounded." ³⁴And the battle grew hot that day, and the king of Israel propped himself up in his chariot facing the Syrians until evening; then at sunset he died.

19 Jĕ·hŏsh'ạ·phăt the king of Judah returned in safety to his house in Jerusalem. ²But Jē'hū the son of Hạ·nā'nī the seer went out to meet him, and said to king Jĕ·hŏsh'ạ·phăt, "Should you help the wicked and love those who hate the LORD? Because of this, wrath has gone out against you from the LORD. ³Nevertheless some good is found in you, for you destroyed the A·shē'rạhş out of the land, and have set your heart to seek God."

4 Jĕ·hŏsh'ạ·phăt dwelt at Jerusalem; and he went out again among the people, from Bē'ẹr–shē'bạ to the hill country of E'phrạ·ĭm, and brought them back to the LORD, the God of their fathers. ⁵He appointed judges in the land in all the fortified cities of Judah, city by city, ⁶and said to the judges, "Consider what you do, for you judge not for man but for the LORD; he is with you in giving judgment. ⁷Now then, let the fear of the LORD be upon you; take heed what you do, for there is no perversion of justice with the LORD our God, or partiality, or taking bribes."

8 Moreover in Jerusalem Jĕ·hŏsh'ạ·phăt appointed certain Lē'vītes and priests and heads of families of Israel, to give judgment for the LORD and to decide disputed cases. They had their

seat at Jerusalem. ⁹And he charged them: "Thus you shall do in the fear of the LORD, in faithfulness, and with your whole heart: ¹⁰whenever a case comes to you from your brethren who live in their cities, concerning bloodshed, law or commandment, statutes or ordinances, then you shall instruct them, that they may not incur guilt before the LORD and wrath may not come upon you and your brethren. Thus you shall do, and you will not incur guilt. ¹¹And behold, Ăm·a·rī′ah the chief priest is over you in all matters of the LORD; and Zĕb·a·dī′ah the son of Ĭsh′ma·ĕl, the governor of the house of Judah, in all the king's matters; and the Lē′vītes will serve you as officers. Deal courageously, and may the LORD be with the upright!"

20 After this the Mō′ab·ītes and Ăm′mo·nītes, and with them some of the Mē–ü′nītes,ᶠ came against Jĕ·hŏsh′a·phăt for battle. ²Some men came and told Jĕ·hŏsh′a·phăt, "A great multitude is coming against you from Ē′dom,ᵍ from beyond the sea; and, behold, they are in Hăz′a·zŏn–tā′mär" (that is, Ĕn–gē′dī). ³Then Jĕ·hŏsh′a·phăt feared, and set himself to seek the LORD, and proclaimed a fast throughout all Judah. ⁴And Judah assembled to seek help from the LORD; from all the cities of Judah they came to seek the LORD.

5 And Jĕ·hŏsh′a·phăt stood in the assembly of Judah and Jerusalem, in the house of the LORD, before the new court, ⁶and said, "O LORD, God of our fathers, art thou not God in heaven? Dost thou not rule over all the kingdoms of the nations? In thy hand are power and might, so that none is able to withstand thee. ⁷Didst thou not, O our God, drive out the inhabitants of this land before thy people Israel, and give it for ever to the descendants of Abraham thy friend? ⁸And they have dwelt in it, and have built thee in it a sanctuary for thy name, saying, ⁹'If evil comes upon us, the sword, judgment,ʰ or pestilence, or famine, we will stand before this house, and before thee, for thy name is in this house, and cry to thee in our affliction, and thou wilt hear and save.' ¹⁰And now behold, the men of Ăm′mon and Mō′ăb and Mount Sē′ïr, whom thou wouldest not let Israel invade when they came from the land of Egypt, and whom they avoided and did not destroy—¹¹behold, they reward us by coming to drive us out of thy possession, which thou hast given us to inherit. ¹²O our God, wilt thou not execute judgment upon them? For we are powerless against this great multitude that is coming against us. We do not know what to do, but our eyes are upon thee."

13 Meanwhile all the men of Judah stood before the LORD, with their little ones, their wives, and their children. ¹⁴And the Spirit of the LORD came upon Ja·hā·zī′ĕl the son of Zĕch·a·rī′ah, son of Bĕ·nā′ī·ah, son of Jĕ·ī′ĕl, son of Măt·ta·nī′ah, a Lē′vīte of the sons of Ā′săph, in the midst of the assembly. ¹⁵And he said, "Hearken, all Judah and inhabitants of Jerusalem, and King Jĕ·hŏsh′a·phăt: Thus says the LORD to you, 'Fear not, and be not dismayed at this great multitude; for the battle is not yours but God's. ¹⁶Tomorrow go down against them; behold, they will come up by the ascent of Zĭz; you will find them at the end of the valley, east of the wilderness of Jĕ·rü′ĕl. ¹⁷You will not need to fight in this battle; take your position, stand still, and see the victory of the LORD on your behalf, O Judah and Jerusalem.' Fear not, and be not dismayed; tomorrow go out against them, and the LORD will be with you."

18 Then Jĕ·hŏsh′a·phăt bowed his head with his face to the ground, and all Judah and the inhabitants of Jerusalem fell down before the LORD, worshiping the LORD. ¹⁹And the Lē′vītes, of the Kō′ha·thītes and the Kō′ra·hītes, stood up to praise the LORD, the God of Israel, with a very loud voice.

20 And they rose early in the morning and went out into the wilderness of Tĕ·kō′a; and as they went out, Jĕ·hŏsh′a·phăt stood and said, "Hear me, Judah and inhabitants of Jerusalem! Believe in the LORD your God, and you will be established; believe his prophets, and you will succeed." ²¹And when he had taken counsel with the people, he appointed those who were to sing to the LORD and praise him in holy array, as they went before the army, and say,

"Give thanks to the LORD,
    for his steadfast love endures for
    ever."

ᶠCompare 26.7: Heb *Ammonites*
ᵍOne Ms: Heb *Aram* (Syria)   ʰOr *the sword of judgment*
20.7: Jas 2.23.

²²And when they began to sing and praise, the LORD set an ambush against the men of Ăm′mŏn, Mō′ăb, and Mount Sē′ĭr, who had come against Judah, so that they were routed. ²³For the men of Ăm′mŏn and Mō′ăb rose against the inhabitants of Mount Sē′ĭr, destroying them utterly, and when they had made an end of the inhabitants of Seir, they all helped to destroy one another.

24 When Judah came to the watchtower of the wilderness, they looked toward the multitude; and behold, they were dead bodies lying on the ground; none had escaped. ²⁵When Jĕ·hŏsh′a·phăt and his people came to take the spoil from them, they found cattle[i] in great numbers, goods, clothing, and precious things, which they took for themselves until they could carry no more. They were three days in taking the spoil, it was so much. ²⁶On the fourth day they assembled in the Valley of Bĕ·rā′cah,[j] for there they blessed the LORD; therefore the name of that place has been called the Valley of Beracah to this day. ²⁷Then they returned, every man of Judah and Jerusalem, and Jĕ·hŏsh′a·phăt at their head, returning to Jerusalem with joy, for the LORD had made them rejoice over their enemies. ²⁸They came to Jerusalem, with harps and lyres and trumpets, to the house of the LORD. ²⁹And the fear of God came on all the kingdoms of the countries when they heard that the LORD had fought against the enemies of Israel. ³⁰So the realm of Jĕ·hŏsh′a·phăt was quiet, for his God gave him rest round about.

31 Thus Jĕ·hŏsh′a·phăt reigned over Judah. He was thirty-five years old when he began to reign, and he reigned twenty-five years in Jerusalem. His mother's name was A·zü′bah the daughter of Shĭl′hĭ. ³²He walked in the way of Asa his father and did not turn aside from it; he did what was right in the sight of the LORD. ³³The high places, however, were not taken away; the people had not yet set their hearts upon the God of their fathers.

34 Now the rest of the acts of Jĕ·hŏsh′a·phăt, from first to last, are written in the chronicles of Jē′hū the son of Ha·nā′nī, which are recorded in the Book of the Kings of Israel.

35 After this Jĕ·hŏsh′a·phăt king of Judah joined with A·ha·zī′ah king of Israel, who did wickedly. ³⁶He joined him in building ships to go to Tär′shĭsh, and they built the ships in Ē′zĭ·ŏn-gē′ber. ³⁷Then Ē·lī·ē′zer the son of Dō·dăv′a·hū of Ma·rē′shah prophesied against Jĕ·hŏsh′a·phăt, saying, "Because you have joined with A·ha·zī′ah, the LORD will destroy what you have made." And the ships were wrecked and were not able to go to Tär′shĭsh.

21 Jĕ·hŏsh′a·phăt slept with his fathers, and was buried with his fathers in the city of David; and Jĕ·hō′ram his son reigned in his stead. ²He had brothers, the sons of Jĕ·hŏsh′a·phăt: Ă·za·rī′ah, Jĕ·hī′ĕl, Zĕch·a·rī′ah, Azariah, Michael, and Shĕph·a·tī′ah; all these were the sons of Jehoshaphat king of Judah. ³Their father gave them great gifts, of silver, gold, and valuable possessions, together with fortified cities in Judah; but he gave the kingdom to Jĕ·hō′ram, because he was the first-born. ⁴When Jĕ·hō′ram had ascended the throne of his father and was established, he slew all his brothers with the sword, and also some of the princes of Israel. ⁵Jĕ·hō′ram was thirty-two years old when he became king, and he reigned eight years in Jerusalem. ⁶And he walked in the way of the kings of Israel, as the house of A′hăb had done; for the daughter of Ahab was his wife. And he did what was evil in the sight of the LORD. ⁷Yet the LORD would not destroy the house of David, because of the covenant which he had made with David, and since he had promised to give a lamp to him and to his sons for ever.

8 In his days Ē′dom revolted from the rule of Judah, and set up a king of their own. ⁹Then Jĕ·hō′ram passed over with his commanders and all his chariots, and he rose by night and smote the Ē′dom·ītes who had surrounded him and his chariot commanders. ¹⁰So Ē′dom revolted from the rule of Judah to this day. At that time Lĭb′nah also revolted from his rule, because he had forsaken the LORD, the God of his fathers.

11 Moreover he made high places in the hill country of Judah, and led the inhabitants of Jerusalem into unfaithfulness, and made Judah go astray. ¹²And a letter came to him from Ē·lī′-

'Gk: Heb *among them* ʲThat is *Blessing*
20.31-33: 1 Kings 22.41-43.　20.35-37: 1 Kings 22.48, 49.
21.1: 1 Kings 22.50.　21.5-10: 2 Kings 8.17-22.

jăh the prophet saying, "Thus says the Lord, the God of David your father, 'Because you have not walked in the ways of Jĕ·hŏsh'a·phăt your father, or in the ways of Asa king of Judah, ¹³but have walked in the way of the kings of Israel, and have led Judah and the inhabitants of Jerusalem into unfaithfulness, as the house of Ā'hăb led Israel into unfaithfulness, and also you have killed your brothers, of your father's house, who were better than yourself; ¹⁴behold, the Lord will bring a great plague on your people, your children, your wives, and all your possessions, ¹⁵and you yourself will have a severe sickness with a disease of your bowels, until your bowels come out because of the disease, day by day.'"

16 And the Lord stirred up against Jĕ·hŏ'răm the anger of the Phĭ·lĭs'tīnes and of the Arabs who are near the Ethiopians; ¹⁷and they came up against Judah, and invaded it, and carried away all the possessions they found that belonged to the king's house, and also his sons and his wives, so that no son was left to him except Jĕ·hŏ'a·hăz, his youngest son.

18 And after all this the Lord smote him in his bowels with an incurable disease. ¹⁹In course of time, at the end of two years, his bowels came out because of the disease, and he died in great agony. His people made no fire in his honor, like the fires made for his fathers. ²⁰He was thirty-two years old when he began to reign, and he reigned eight years in Jerusalem; and he departed with no one's regret. They buried him in the city of David, but not in the tombs of the kings.

22 And the inhabitants of Jerusalem made Ā·ha·zī'ah his youngest son king in his stead; for the band of men that came with the Arabs to the camp had slain all the older sons. So Ahaziah the son of Jĕ·hŏ'răm king of Judah reigned. ²Ā·ha·zī'ah was forty-two years old when he began to reign, and he reigned one year in Jerusalem. His mother's name was Ăth·a·lī'ah, the granddaughter of Ŏm'rī. ³He also walked in the ways of the house of Ā'hăb, for his mother was his counselor in doing wickedly. ⁴He did what was evil in the sight of the Lord, as the house of Ā'hăb had done; for after the death of his father they were his counselors, to his undoing. ⁵He even fol-

lowed their counsel, and went with Jĕ·hŏ'răm the son of Ā'hăb king of Israel to make war against Hăz'a·ĕl king of Syria at Rā'mŏth-gĭl'ē·ad. And the Syrians wounded Jō'răm, ⁶and he returned to be healed in Jĕz'rē·ĕl of the wounds which he had received at Rā'măh, when he fought against Hăz'a·ĕl king of Syria. And Ā·ha·zī'ah the son of Jĕ·hŏ'răm king of Judah went down to see Jō'răm the son of Ā'hăb in Jezreel, because he was sick.

7 But it was ordained by God that the downfall of Ā·ha·zī'ah should come about through his going to visit Jō'răm. For when he came there he went out with Jĕ·hŏ'răm to meet Jē'hū the son of Nĭm'shī, whom the Lord had anointed to destroy the house of Ā'hăb. ⁸And when Jē'hū was executing judgment upon the house of Ā'hăb, he met the princes of Judah and the sons of Ā·ha·zī'ah's brothers, who attended Ahaziah, and he killed them. ⁹He searched for Ā·ha·zī'ah, and he was captured while hiding in Sa·mâr'ĭ·a, and he was brought to Jē'hū and put to death. They buried him, for they said, "He is the grandson of Jĕ·hŏsh'a·phăt, who sought the Lord with all his heart." And the house of Ahaziah had no one able to rule the kingdom.

10 Now when Ăth·a·lī'ah the mother of Ā·ha·zī'ah saw that her son was dead, she arose and destroyed all the royal family of the house of Judah. ¹¹But Jē'hō-shăb'e-ăth, the daughter of the king, took Jō'ăsh the son of Ā·ha·zī'ah, and stole him away from among the king's sons who were about to be slain, and she put him and his nurse in a bedchamber. Thus Jeho-shabe-ath, the daughter of King Jĕ·hŏ'răm and wife of Jĕ·hoi'a·da the priest, because she was a sister of Ahaziah, hid him from Ăth·a·lī'ah, so that she did not slay him; ¹²and he remained with them six years, hid in the house of God, while Ăth·a·lī'ah reigned over the land.

23 But in the seventh year Jĕ·hoi'a·da took courage, and entered into a compact with the commanders of hundreds, Ăz·a·rī'ah the son of Jĕ·rō'hăm, Ĭsh'ma·ĕl the son of Jē'hō-hā'năn, Azariah the son of Ō'bĕd, Mā-a·sēi'ah the son of A·dāi'ah, and Ĕl·ĭ·shā'phăt the son of Zĭch'rī.

21.20: 2 Kings 8.17, 24. 22.1-6: 2 Kings 8.24-29. 22.7-9: 2 Kings 9.1-10.36. 22.10-23.21: 2 Kings 11.1-20.

²And they went about through Judah and gathered the Lē'vītes from all the cities of Judah, and the heads of fathers' houses of Israel, and they came to Jerusalem. ³And all the assembly made a covenant with the king in the house of God. And Jĕ·hoi'a·da¹ said to them, "Behold, the king's son! Let him reign, as the LORD spoke concerning the sons of David. ⁴This is the thing that you shall do: of you priests and Lē'vītes who come off duty on the sabbath, one third shall be gatekeepers, ⁵and one third shall be at the king's house and one third at the Gate of the Foundation; and all the people shall be in the courts of the house of the LORD. ⁶Let no one enter the house of the LORD except the priests and ministering Lē'vītes; they may enter, for they are holy, but all the people shall keep the charge of the LORD. ⁷The Lē'vītes shall surround the king, each with his weapons in his hand; and whoever enters the house shall be slain. Be with the king when he comes in, and when he goes out."

8 The Lē'vītes and all Judah did according to all that Jĕ·hoi'a·da the priest commanded. They each brought his men, who were to go off duty on the sabbath, with those who were to come on duty on the sabbath; for Jehoiada the priest did not dismiss the divisions. ⁹And Jĕ·hoi'a·da the priest delivered to the captains the spears and the large and small shields that had been King David's, which were in the house of God; ¹⁰and he set all the people as a guard for the king, every man with his weapon in his hand, from the south side of the house to the north side of the house, around the altar and the house. ¹¹Then he brought out the king's son, and put the crown upon him, and gave him the testimony; and they proclaimed him king, and Jĕ·hoi'a·da and his sons anointed him, and they said, "Long live the king."

12 When Āth·a·lī'ah heard the noise of the people running and praising the king, she went into the house of the LORD to the people; ¹³and when she looked, there was the king standing by his pillar at the entrance, and the captains and the trumpeters beside the king, and all the people of the land rejoicing and blowing trumpets, and the singers with their musical instruments leading in the celebration. And Āth·a·lī'ah rent her clothes, and cried, "Treason! Treason!" ¹⁴Then Jĕ·hoi'a·da the priest brought out the captains who were set over the army, saying to them, "Bring her out between the ranks; any one who follows her is to be slain with the sword." For the priest said, "Do not slay her in the house of the LORD." ¹⁵So they laid hands on her; and she went into the entrance of the horse gate of the king's house, and they slew her there.

16 And Jĕ·hoi'a·da made a covenant between himself and all the people and the king that they should be the LORD's people. ¹⁷Then all the people went to the house of Bā'al, and tore it down; his altars and his images they broke in pieces, and they slew Măt'tăn the priest of Baal before the altars. ¹⁸And Jĕ·hoi'a·da posted watchmen for the house of the LORD under the direction of the Levitical priests and the Lē'vītes whom David had organized to be in charge of the house of the LORD, to offer burnt offerings to the LORD, as it is written in the law of Moses, with rejoicing and with singing, according to the order of David. ¹⁹He stationed the gatekeepers at the gates of the house of the LORD so that no one should enter who was in any way unclean. ²⁰And he took the captains, the nobles, the governors of the people, and all the people of the land; and they brought the king down from the house of the LORD, marching through the upper gate to the king's house. And they set the king upon the royal throne. ²¹So all the people of the land rejoiced; and the city was quiet, after Āth·a·lī'ah had been slain with the sword.

24 Jō'ăsh was seven years old when he began to reign, and he reigned forty years in Jerusalem; his mother's name was Zīb'ī·ah of Bē'er·shē'ba. ²And Jō'ăsh did what was right in the eyes of the LORD all the days of Jĕ·hoi'a·da the priest. ³Jĕ·hoi'a·da got for him two wives, and he had sons and daughters.

4 After this Jō'ăsh decided to restore the house of the LORD. ⁵And he gathered the priests and the Lē'vītes, and said to them, "Go out to the cities of Judah, and gather from all Israel

¹Heb *he*
24.1-14: 2 Kings 11.21-12.14.

money to repair the house of your God from year to year; and see that you hasten the matter." But the Levites did not hasten it. ⁶So the king summoned Jĕ·hoi′a·da the chief, and said to him, "Why have you not required the Le′vītes to bring in from Judah and Jerusalem the tax levied by Moses, the servant of the LORD, on[m] the congregation of Israel for the tent of testimony?" ⁷For the sons of Äth·a·lī′ah, that wicked woman, had broken into the house of God; and had also used all the dedicated things of the house of the LORD for the Bā′als.

8 So the king commanded, and they made a chest, and set it outside the gate of the house of the LORD. ⁹And proclamation was made throughout Judah and Jerusalem, to bring in for the LORD the tax that Moses the servant of God laid upon Israel in the wilderness. ¹⁰And all the princes and all the people rejoiced and brought their tax and dropped it into the chest until they had finished. ¹¹And whenever the chest was brought to the king's officers by the Le′vītes, when they saw that there was much money in it, the king's secretary and the officer of the chief priest would come and empty the chest and take it and return it to its place. Thus they did day after day, and collected money in abundance. ¹²And the king and Jĕ·hoi′a·da gave it to those who had charge of the work of the house of the LORD, and they hired masons and carpenters to restore the house of the LORD, and also workers in iron and bronze to repair the house of the LORD. ¹³So those who were engaged in the work labored, and the repairing went forward in their hands, and they restored the house of God to its proper condition and strengthened it. ¹⁴And when they had finished, they brought the rest of the money before the king and Jĕ·hoi′a·da, and with it were made utensils for the house of the LORD, both for the service and for the burnt offerings, and dishes for incense, and vessels of gold and silver. And they offered burnt offerings in the house of the LORD continually all the days of Jehoiada.

15 But Jĕ·hoi′a·da grew old and full of days, and died; he was a hundred and thirty years old at his death. ¹⁶And they buried him in the city of David among the kings, because he had done good in Israel, and toward God and his house.

17 Now after the death of Jĕ·hoi′a·da the princes of Judah came and did obeisance to the king; then the king hearkened to them. ¹⁸And they forsook the house of the LORD, the God of their fathers, and served the A·shē′rĭm and the idols. And wrath came upon Judah and Jerusalem for this their guilt. ¹⁹Yet he sent prophets among them to bring them back to the LORD; these testified against them, but they would not give heed.

20 Then the Spirit of God took possession of[n] Zĕch·a·rī′ah the son of Jĕ·hoi′a·da the priest; and he stood above the people, and said to them, "Thus says God, 'Why do you transgress the commandments of the LORD, so that you cannot prosper? Because you have forsaken the LORD, he has forsaken you.'" ²¹But they conspired against him, and by command of the king they stoned him with stones in the court of the house of the LORD. ²²Thus Jō′ash the king did not remember the kindness which Jĕ·hoi′a·da, Zĕch·a·rī′ah's father, had shown him, but killed his son. And when he was dying, he said, "May the LORD see and avenge!"

23 At the end of the year the army of the Syrians came up against Jō′ash. They came to Judah and Jerusalem, and destroyed all the princes of the people from among the people, and sent all their spoil to the king of Damascus. ²⁴Though the army of the Syrians had come with few men, the LORD delivered into their hand a very great army, because they had forsaken the LORD, the God of their fathers. Thus they executed judgment on Jō′ash.

25 When they had departed from him, leaving him severely wounded, his servants conspired against him because of the blood of the son[o] of Jĕ·hoi′a·da the priest, and slew him on his bed. So he died; and they buried him in the city of David, but they did not bury him in the tombs of the kings. ²⁶Those who conspired against him were Zā′bǎd the son of Shĭm′e–ǎth the Ăm′mo·nīt·ess, and Jĕ·hō′za·bǎd the son of Shĭm′rĭth the Mō′ab-

---

[m] Compare Vg: Heb *and*
[n] Heb *clothed itself with*   [o] Gk Vg: Heb *sons*
24.23-26: 2 Kings 12.17, 18, 20, 21.

īt·ęss. ²⁷Accounts of his sons, and of the many oracles against him, and of the rebuilding*ᵖ* of the house of God are written in the Commentary on the Book of the Kings. And Ăm·a·zī′ah his son reigned in his stead.

25 Ăm·a·zī′ah ' was twenty-five years old when he began to reign, and he reigned twenty-nine years in Jerusalem. His mother's name was Jě′hō–ăd′dan of Jerusalem. ²And he did what was right in the eyes of the LORD, yet not with a blameless heart. ³And as soon as the royal power was firmly in his hand he killed his servants who had slain the king his father. ⁴But he did not put their children to death, according to what is written in the law, in the book of Moses, where the LORD commanded, "The fathers shall not be put to death for the children, or the children be put to death for the fathers; but every man shall die for his own sin."

5 Then Ăm·a·zī′ah assembled the men of Judah, and set them by fathers' houses under commanders of thousands and of hundreds for all Judah and Benjamin. He mustered those twenty years old and upward, and found that they were three hundred thousand picked men, fit for war, able to handle spear and shield. ⁶He hired also a hundred thousand mighty men of valor from Israel for a hundred talents of silver. ⁷But a man of God came to him and said, "O king, do not let the army of Israel go with you, for the LORD is not with Israel, with all these Ē′phra·ĭm·ītes. ⁸But if you suppose that in this way you will be strong for war,*ᵍ* God will cast you down before the enemy; for God has power to help or to cast down." ⁹And Ăm·a·zī′ah said to the man of God, "But what shall we do about the hundred talents which I have given to the army of Israel?" The man of God answered, "The LORD is able to give you much more than this." ¹⁰Then Ăm·a·zī′ah discharged the army that had come to him from Ē′phra·im, to go home again. And they became very angry with Judah, and returned home in fierce anger. ¹¹But Ăm·a·zī′ah took courage, and led out his people, and went to the Valley of Salt and smote ten thousand men of Sē′ĭr. ¹²The men of Judah captured another ten thousand alive, and took them to the top of a rock and

threw them down from the top of the rock; and they were all dashed to pieces. ¹³But the men of the army whom Ăm·a·zī′ah sent back, not letting them go with him to battle, fell upon the cities of Judah, from Sa·mâr′ĭ·a to Běth–hō′rŏn, and killed three thousand people in them, and took much spoil.

14 After Ăm·a·zī′ah came from the slaughter of the Ē′dom·ites, he brought the gods of the men of Sē′ĭr, and set them up as his gods, and worshiped them, making offerings to them. ¹⁵Therefore the LORD was angry with Ăm·a·zī′ah and sent to him a prophet, who said to him, "Why have you resorted to the gods of a people, which did not deliver their own people from your hand?" ¹⁶But as he was speaking the king said to him, "Have we made you a royal counselor? Stop! Why should you be put to death?" So the prophet stopped, but said, "I know that God has determined to destroy you, because you have done this and have not listened to my counsel."

17 Then Ăm·a·zī′ah king of Judah took counsel and sent to Jō′ăsh the son of Jě·hō′a·hăz, son of Jē′hū, king of Israel, saying, "Come, let us look one another in the face." ¹⁸And Jō′ăsh the king of Israel sent word to Ăm·a·zī′ah king of Judah, "A thistle on Lebanon sent to a cedar on Lebanon, saying, 'Give your daughter to my son for a wife'; and a wild beast of Lebanon passed by and trampled down the thistle. ¹⁹You say, 'See, I have smitten Ē′dom,' and your heart has lifted you up in boastfulness. But now stay at home; why should you provoke trouble so that you fall, you and Judah with you?"

20 But Ăm·a·zī′ah would not listen; for it was of God, in order that he might give them into the hand of their enemies, because they had sought the gods of Ē′dom. ²¹So Jō′ăsh king of Israel went up; and he and Ăm·a·zī′ah king of Judah faced one another in battle at Běth–shē′měsh, which belongs to Judah.' ²²And Judah was defeated by Israel, and every man fled to his home. ²³And Jō′ăsh king of Israel captured Ăm·a·zī′ah king of Ju-

ᵖ Heb *founding*
ᵍ Gk: Heb *But if you go, act, be strong for the battle*
25.1–4: 2 Kings 14.2-6.
25.11: 2 Kings 14.7.   25.17-20, 21-24: 2 Kings 14.8-14.

dah, the son of Joash, son of Ā·ha·zī′ah, at Bĕth–shē′mĕsh, and brought him to Jerusalem, and broke down the wall of Jerusalem for four hundred cubits, from the Ē′phra·ĭm Gate to the Corner Gate. ²⁴And he seized all the gold and silver, and all the vessels that were found in the house of God, and Ō′bĕd–ē′dom with them; he seized also the treasuries of the king's house, and hostages, and he returned to Sa·mâr′ĭ·a.

25 Ăm·a·zī′ah the son of Jō′ash king of Judah lived fifteen years after the death of Joash the son of Jē·hō′a·hăz, king of Israel. ²⁶Now the rest of the deeds of Ăm·a·zī′ah, from first to last, are they not written in the Book of the Kings of Judah and Israel? ²⁷From the time when he turned away from the LORD they made a conspiracy against him in Jerusalem, and he fled to Lā′-chĭsh. But they sent after him to Lachish, and slew him there. ²⁸And they brought him upon horses; and he was buried with his fathers in the city of David.

26 And all the people of Judah took Ŭz·zī′ah, who was sixteen years old, and made him king instead of his father Ăm·a·zī′ah. ²He built Ē′loth and restored it to Judah, after the king slept with his fathers. ³Ŭz·zī′ah was sixteen years old when he began to reign, and he reigned fifty-two years in Jerusalem. His mother's name was Jĕc·o·lī′ah of Jerusalem. ⁴And he did what was right in the eyes of the LORD, according to all that his father Ăm·a·zī′ah had done. ⁵He set himself to seek God in the days of Zĕch·a·rī′ah, who instructed him in the fear of God; and as long as he sought the LORD, God made him prosper.

6 He went out and made war against the Phĭ·lĭs′tĭnes, and broke down the wall of Găth and the wall of Jăb′neh and the wall of Ăsh′dŏd; and he built cities in the territory of Ashdod and elsewhere among the Philistines. ⁷God helped him against the Phĭ·lĭs′-tĭnes, and against the Arabs that dwelt in Gûr·bā′al, and against the Mē-ü′nītes. ⁸The Ăm′mo·nītes paid tribute to Ŭz·zī′ah, and his fame spread even to the border of Egypt, for he became very strong. ⁹Moreover Ŭz-zī′ah built towers in Jerusalem at the Corner Gate and at the Valley Gate and at the Angle, and fortified them. ¹⁰And he built towers in the wilderness, and hewed out many cisterns, for he had large herds, both in the Shĕ·phē′lah and in the plain, and he had farmers and vinedressers in the hills and in the fertile lands, for he loved the soil. ¹¹Moreover Ŭz·zī′ah had an army of soldiers, fit for war, in divisions according to the numbers in the muster made by Jĕ–ī′ĕl the secretary and Mā·a·sēi′ah the officer, under the direction of Hăn·a·nī′ah, one of the king's commanders. ¹²The whole number of the heads of fathers' houses of mighty men of valor was two thousand six hundred. ¹³Under their command was an army of three hundred and seven thousand five hundred, who could make war with mighty power, to help the king against the enemy. ¹⁴And Ŭz·zī′ah prepared for all the army shields, spears, helmets, coats of mail, bows, and stones for slinging. ¹⁵In Jerusalem he made engines, invented by skilful men, to be on the towers and the corners, to shoot arrows and great stones. And his fame spread far, for he was marvelously helped, till he was strong.

16 But when he was strong he grew proud, to his destruction. For he was false to the LORD his God, and entered the temple of the LORD to burn incense on the altar of incense. ¹⁷But Ăz·a·rī′ah the priest went in after him, with eighty priests of the LORD who were men of valor; ¹⁸and they withstood King Ŭz·zī′ah, and said to him, "It is not for you, Uzziah, to burn incense to the LORD, but for the priests the sons of Aaron, who are consecrated to burn incense. Go out of the sanctuary; for you have done wrong, and it will bring you no honor from the LORD God." ¹⁹Then Ŭz·zī′ah was angry. Now he had a censer in his hand to burn incense, and when he became angry with the priests leprosy broke out on his forehead, in the presence of the priests in the house of the LORD, by the altar of incense. ²⁰And Ăz·a·rī′ah the chief priest, and all the priests, looked at him, and behold, he was leprous in his forehead! And they thrust him out quickly, and he himself hastened to go out, because the LORD

25.25-28: 2 Kings 14.17-20.
26.1-4: 2 Kings 14.21, 22; 15.2, 3.
26.20-23: 2 Kings 15.5-7.

had smitten him. [21]And King Uz-zī'ah was a leper to the day of his death, and being a leper dwelt in a separate house, for he was excluded from the house of the LORD. And Jō'tham his son was over the king's household, governing the people of the land.

22 Now the rest of the acts of Uz-zī'ah, from first to last, Ī-sāi'ah the prophet the son of Ā'mŏz wrote. [23]And Uz-zī'ah slept with his fathers, and they buried him with his fathers in the burial field which belonged to the kings, for they said, "He is a leper." And Jō'tham his son reigned in his stead.

27 Jō'tham was twenty-five years old when he began to reign, and he reigned sixteen years in Jerusalem. His mother's name was Jĕ-rü'shah the daughter of Zā'dŏk. [2]And he did what was right in the eyes of the LORD according to all that his father Uz-zī'ah had done—only he did not invade the temple of the LORD. But the people still followed corrupt practices. [3]He built the upper gate of the house of the LORD, and did much building on the wall of Ō'phĕl. [4]Moreover he built cities in the hill country of Judah, and forts and towers on the wooded hills. [5]He fought with the king of the Ăm'mo-nītes and prevailed against them. And the Ammonites gave him that year a hundred talents of silver, and ten thousand cors of wheat and ten thousand of barley. The Ammonites paid him the same amount in the second and the third years. [6]So Jō'tham became mighty, because he ordered his ways before the LORD his God. [7]Now the rest of the acts of Jō'tham, and all his wars, and his ways, behold, they are written in the Book of the Kings of Israel and Judah. [8]He was twenty-five years old when he began to reign, and he reigned sixteen years in Jerusalem. [9]And Jō'tham slept with his fathers, and they buried him in the city of David; and Ā'hăz his son reigned in his stead.

28 Ā'hăz was twenty years old when he began to reign, and he reigned sixteen years in Jerusalem. And he did not do what was right in the eyes of the LORD, like his father David, [2]but walked in the ways of the kings of Israel. He even made molten

images for the Bā'alş; [3]and he burned incense in the valley of the son of Hĭn'nom, and burned his sons as an offering, according to the abominable practices of the nations whom the LORD drove out before the people of Israel. [4]And he sacrificed and burned incense on the high places, and on the hills, and under every green tree.

5 Therefore the LORD his God gave him into the hand of the king of Syria, who defeated him and took captive a great number of his people and brought them to Damascus. He was also given into the hand of the king of Israel, who defeated him with great slaughter. [6]For Pē'kah the son of Rĕm-a-lī'ah slew a hundred and twenty thousand in Judah in one day, all of them men of valor, because they had forsaken the LORD, the God of their fathers. [7]And Zĭch'rī, a mighty man of Ē'phra-ĭm, slew Mā-a-sēī'ah the king's son and Ăz-rī'kăm the commander of the palace and Ĕl-kā'nah the next in authority to the king.

8 The men of Israel took captive two hundred thousand of their kinsfolk, women, sons, and daughters; they also took much spoil from them and brought the spoil to Sa-mâr'ĭ-a. [9]But a prophet of the LORD was there, whose name was Ō'dĕd; and he went out to meet the army that came to Sa-mâr'ĭ-a, and said to them, "Behold, because the LORD, the God of your fathers, was angry with Judah, he gave them into your hand, but you have slain them in a rage which has reached up to heaven. [10]And now you intend to subjugate the people of Judah and Jerusalem, male and female, as your slaves. Have you not sins of your own against the LORD your God? [11]Now hear me, and send back the captives from your kinsfolk whom you have taken, for the fierce wrath of the LORD is upon you." [12]Certain chiefs also of the men of Ē'phra-ĭm, Ăz-a-rī'ah the son of Jō-hā'nan, Bĕr-e-chī'ah the son of Mĕ-shĭl'le-mŏth, Jĕ-hĭz-kī'ah the son of Shăl'lum, and A-mā'sa the son of Hăd'laī, stood up against those who were coming from the war, [13]and said to them, "You shall not bring the captives in here, for you propose to bring upon us guilt against the LORD in addi-

27.1-3: 2 Kings 15.33-35.
27.9: 2 Kings 15.38.   28.1-4: 2 Kings 16.2-4.

tion to our present sins and guilt. For our guilt is already great, and there is fierce wrath against Israel." ¹⁴ So the armed men left the captives and the spoil before the princes and all the assembly. ¹⁵ And the men who have been mentioned by name rose and took the captives, and with the spoil they clothed all that were naked among them; they clothed them, gave them sandals, provided them with food and drink, and anointed them; and carrying all the feeble among them on asses, they brought them to their kinsfolk at Jericho, the city of palm trees. Then they returned to Să·mâr'ĭ·ạ.

16 At that time King Ā'hăz sent to the king ʳ of Assyria for help. ¹⁷ For the Ē'dọm·ītes had again invaded and defeated Judah, and carried away captives. ¹⁸ And the Phĭ·lĭs'tĭnes had made raids on the cities in the Shĕphē'lạh and the Nĕg'ĕb of Judah, and had taken Bĕth–shĕ'mĕsh, Aī'jạlŏn, Gĕ·dĕ'rŏth, Sō'cō with its villages, Tĭm'nạh with its villages, and Gĭm'zō with its villages; and they settled there. ¹⁹ For the LORD brought Judah low because of Ā'hăz king of Israel, for he had dealt wantonly in Judah and had been faithless to the LORD. ²⁰ So Tĭl'găth–pĭl·nē'şer king of Assyria came against him, and afflicted him instead of strengthening him. ²¹ For Ā'hăz took from the house of the LORD and the house of the king and of the princes, and gave tribute to the king of Assyria; but it did not help him. 22 In the time of his distress he became yet more faithless to the LORD – this same King Ā'hăz. ²³ For he sacrificed to the gods of Damascus which had defeated him, and said, "Because the gods of the kings of Syria helped them, I will sacrifice to them that they may help me." But they were the ruin of him, and of all Israel. ²⁴ And Ā'hăz gathered together the vessels of the house of God and cut in pieces the vessels of the house of God, and he shut up the doors of the house of the LORD; and he made himself altars in every corner of Jerusalem. ²⁵ In every city of Judah he made high places to burn incense to other gods, provoking to anger the LORD, the God of his fathers. ²⁶ Now the rest of his acts and all his ways, from first to last, behold, they are written in the

Book of the Kings of Judah and Israel. ²⁷ And Ā'hăz slept with his fathers, and they buried him in the city, in Jerusalem, for they did not bring him into the tombs of the kings of Israel. And Hĕz·e·kī'ạh his son reigned in his stead.

29 Hĕz·e·kī'ạh began to reign when he was twenty-five years old, and he reigned twenty-nine years in Jerusalem. His mother's name was A·bī'jạh the daughter of Zĕch·ạ·rī'ạh. ² And he did what was right in the eyes of the LORD, according to all that David his father had done.

3 In the first year of his reign, in the first month, he opened the doors of the house of the LORD, and repaired them. ⁴ He brought in the priests and the Lē'vītes, and assembled them in the square on the east, ⁵ and said to them, "Hear me, Lē'vītes! Now sanctify yourselves, and sanctify the house of the LORD, the God of your fathers, and carry out the filth from the holy place. ⁶ For our fathers have been unfaithful and have done what was evil in the sight of the LORD our God; they have forsaken him, and have turned away their faces from the habitation of the LORD, and turned their backs. ⁷ They also shut the doors of the vestibule and put out the lamps, and have not burned incense or offered burnt offerings in the holy place to the God of Israel. ⁸ Therefore the wrath of the LORD came on Judah and Jerusalem, and he has made them an object of horror, of astonishment, and of hissing, as you see with your own eyes. ⁹ For lo, our fathers have fallen by the sword and our sons and our daughters and our wives are in captivity for this. ¹⁰ Now it is in my heart to make a covenant with the LORD, the God of Israel, that his fierce anger may turn away from us. ¹¹ My sons, do not now be negligent, for the LORD has chosen you to stand in his presence, to minister to him, and to be his ministers and burn incense to him."

12 Then the Lē'vītes arose, Mā'hăth the son of Ạ·mā'saī, and Jō'ĕl the son of Ăz·ạ·rī'ạh, of the sons of the Kō'hạthītes; and of the sons of Mẹ·rân'ī, Kīsh the son of Ăb'dī, and Azariah the son of Jĕ·hăl'lẹ·lĕl; and of the Gēr'shọ·nītes, Jō'ạh the son of Zĭm'-

ʳGk Syr Vg Compare 2 Kings 16.7: Heb *kings*
28.27: 2 Kings 16.20.   29.1, 2: 2 Kings 18.1-3.

măh, and Eden the son of Joah; [13] and of the sons of Ĕ·lĭ·zā′phạn, Shĭm′rī and Jĕ·ü′ĕl; and of the sons of Ā′săph, Zĕch·ạ·rī′ạh and Măt·tạ·nī′ạh; [14] and of the sons of Hē′mạn, Jĕ·hŭ′ĕl and Shĭm′ē–ī; and of the sons of Jĕ·dü′thụn, Shĕ·māi′ạh and Ŭz′zĭ·ĕl. [15] They gathered their brethren, and sanctified themselves, and went in as the king had commanded, by the words of the LORD, to cleanse the house of the LORD. [16] The priests went into the inner part of the house of the LORD to cleanse it, and they brought out all the uncleanness that they found in the temple of the LORD into the court of the house of the LORD; and the Lē′vītes took it and carried it out to the brook Kĭd′rọn. [17] They began to sanctify on the first day of the first month, and on the eighth day of the month they came to the vestibule of the LORD; then for eight days they sanctified the house of the LORD, and on the sixteenth day of the first month they finished. [18] Then they went in to Hĕz·ẹ·kī′ạh the king and said, "We have cleansed all the house of the LORD, the altar of burnt offering and all its utensils, and the table for the showbread and all its utensils. [19] All the utensils which King Ā′hăz discarded in his reign when he was faithless, we have made ready and sanctified; and behold, they are before the altar of the LORD."

20 Then Hĕz·ẹ·kī′ạh the king rose early and gathered the officials of the city, and went up to the house of the LORD. [21] And they brought seven bulls, seven rams, seven lambs, and seven he-goats for a sin offering for the kingdom and for the sanctuary and for Judah. And he commanded the priests the sons of Aaron to offer them on the altar of the LORD. [22] So they killed the bulls, and the priests received the blood and threw it against the altar; and they killed the rams and their blood was thrown against the altar; and they killed the lambs and their blood was thrown against the altar. [23] Then the he-goats for the sin offering were brought to the king and the assembly, and they laid their hands upon them, [24] and the priests killed them and made a sin offering with their blood on the altar, to make atonement for all Israel. For the king commanded that the burnt offering and the sin offering should be made for all Israel.

25 And he stationed the Lē′vītes in the house of the LORD with cymbals, harps, and lyres, according to the commandment of David and of Gȧd the king's seer and of Nathan the prophet; for the commandment was from the LORD through his prophets. [26] The Lē′vītes stood with the instruments of David, and the priests with the trumpets. [27] Then Hĕz·ẹ·kī′ạh commanded that the burnt offering be offered on the altar. And when the burnt offering began, the song to the LORD began also, and the trumpets, accompanied by the instruments of David king of Israel. [28] The whole assembly worshiped, and the singers sang, and the trumpeters sounded; all this continued until the burnt offering was finished. [29] When the offering was finished, the king and all who were present with him bowed themselves and worshiped. [30] And Hĕz·ẹ·kī′ạh the king and the princes commanded the Lē′vītes to sing praises to the LORD with the words of David and of Ā′săph the seer. And they sang praises with gladness, and they bowed down and worshiped.

31 Then Hĕz·ẹ·kī′ạh said, "You have now consecrated yourselves to the LORD; come near, bring sacrifices and thank offerings to the house of the LORD." And the assembly brought sacrifices and thank offerings; and all who were of a willing heart brought burnt offerings. [32] The number of the burnt offerings which the assembly brought was seventy bulls, a hundred rams, and two hundred lambs; all these were for a burnt offering to the LORD. [33] And the consecrated offerings were six hundred bulls and three thousand sheep. [34] But the priests were too few and could not flay all the burnt offerings, so until other priests had sanctified themselves their brethren the Lē′vītes hclped them, until the work was finished — for the Levites were more upright in heart than the priests in sanctifying themselves. [35] Besides the great number of burnt offerings there was the fat of the peace offerings, and there were the libations for the burnt offerings. Thus the service of the house of the LORD was restored. [36] And Hĕz·ẹ·kī′ạh and all the people rejoiced because of what God

had done for the people; for the thing came about suddenly.

30 Hĕz·e·kī'ah sent to all Israel and Judah, and wrote letters also to Ē'phra·ĭm and Ma·năs'seh, that they should come to the house of the LORD at Jerusalem, to keep the passover to the LORD the God of Israel. ²For the king and his princes and all the assembly in Jerusalem had taken counsel to keep the passover in the second month—³for they could not keep it in its time because the priests had not sanctified themselves in sufficient number, nor had the people assembled in Jerusalem—⁴and the plan seemed right to the king and all the assembly. ⁵So they decreed to make a proclamation throughout all Israel, from Bē'er-shē'ba to Dan, that the people should come and keep the passover to the LORD the God of Israel, at Jerusalem; for they had not kept it in great numbers as prescribed. ⁶So couriers went throughout all Israel and Judah with letters from the king and his princes, as the king had commanded, saying, "O people of Israel, return to the LORD, the God of Abraham, Isaac, and Israel, that he may turn again to the remnant of you who have escaped from the hand of the kings of Assyria. ⁷Do not be like your fathers and your brethren, who were faithless to the LORD God of their fathers, so that he made them a desolation, as you see. ⁸Do not now be stiff-necked as your fathers were, but yield yourselves to the LORD, and come to his sanctuary, which he has sanctified for ever, and serve the LORD your God, that his fierce anger may turn away from you. ⁹For if you return to the LORD, your brethren and your children will find compassion with their captors, and return to this land. For the LORD your God is gracious and merciful, and will not turn away his face from you, if you return to him."

10 So the couriers went from city to city through the country of Ē'phra·ĭm and Ma·năs'seh, and as far as Zĕb'-ū·lun; but they laughed them to scorn, and mocked them. ¹¹Only a few men of Ăsh'er, of Ma·năs'seh, and of Zĕb'ū·lun humbled themselves and came to Jerusalem. ¹²The hand of God was also upon Judah to give them one heart to do what the king and the

princes commanded by the word of the LORD.

13 And many people came together in Jerusalem to keep the feast of unleavened bread in the second month, a very great assembly. ¹⁴They set to work and removed the altars that were in Jerusalem, and all the altars for burning incense they took away and threw into the Kĭd'ron valley. ¹⁵And they killed the passover lamb on the fourteenth day of the second month. And the priests and the Lē'vītes were put to shame, so that they sanctified themselves, and brought burnt offerings into the house of the LORD. ¹⁶They took their accustomed posts according to the law of Moses the man of God; the priests sprinkled the blood which they received from the hand of the Lē'-vītes. ¹⁷For there were many in the assembly who had not sanctified themselves; therefore the Lē'vītes had to kill the passover lamb for every one who was not clean, to make it holy to the LORD. ¹⁸For a multitude of the people, many of them from Ē'phra·ĭm, Ma·năs'seh, Ĭs'sa·chär, and Zĕb'ū·lun, had not cleansed themselves, yet they ate the passover otherwise than as prescribed. For Hĕz·e·kī'ah had prayed for them, saying, "The good LORD pardon every one ¹⁹who sets his heart to seek God, the LORD the God of his fathers, even though not according to the sanctuary's rules of cleanness." ²⁰And the LORD heard Hĕz·e·kī'ah, and healed the people. ²¹And the people of Israel that were present at Jerusalem kept the feast of unleavened bread seven days with great gladness; and the Lē'vītes and the priests praised the LORD day by day, singing with all their might[*] to the LORD. ²²And Hĕz·e·kī'ah spoke encouragingly to all the Lē'vītes who showed good skill in the service of the LORD. So the people ate the food of the festival for seven days, sacrificing peace offerings and giving thanks to the LORD the God of their fathers.

23 Then the whole assembly agreed together to keep the feast for another seven days; so they kept it for another seven days with gladness. ²⁴For Hĕz·e·kī'ah king of Judah gave the assembly a thousand bulls and seven thousand sheep for offerings, and the princes gave the assembly a thousand

[*]Compare 1 Chron 13.8: Heb *with instruments of might*

bulls and ten thousand sheep. And the priests sanctified themselves in great numbers. ²⁵ The whole assembly of Judah, and the priests and the Lē′vītes, and the whole assembly that came out of Israel, and the sojourners who came out of the land of Israel, and the sojourners who dwelt in Judah, rejoiced. ²⁶ So there was great joy in Jerusalem, for since the time of Solomon the son of David king of Israel there had been nothing like this in Jerusalem. ²⁷ Then the priests and the Lē′vītes arose and blessed the people, and their voice was heard, and their prayer came to his holy habitation in heaven.

31 Now when all this was finished, all Israel who were present went out to the cities of Judah and broke in pieces the pillars and hewed down the Ạ·shē′rĭm and broke down the high places and the altars throughout all Judah and Benjamin, and in Ē′phrạ·im and Mạ·năs′seh, until they had destroyed them all. Then all the people of Israel returned to their cities, every man to his possession.

2 And Hĕz·ẹ·kī′ah appointed the divisions of the priests and of the Lē′vītes, division by division, each according to his service, the priests and the Levites, for burnt offerings and peace offerings, to minister in the gates of the camp of the LORD and to give thanks and praise. ³ The contribution of the king from his own possessions was for the burnt offerings: the burnt offerings of morning and evening, and the burnt offerings for the sabbaths, the new moons, and the appointed feasts, as it is written in the law of the LORD. ⁴ And he commanded the people who lived in Jerusalem to give the portion due to the priests and the Lē′vītes, that they might give themselves to the law of the LORD. ⁵ As soon as the command was spread abroad, the people of Israel gave in abundance the first fruits of grain, wine, oil, honey, and of all the produce of the field; and they brought in abundantly the tithe of everything. ⁶ And the people of Israel and Judah who lived in the cities of Judah also brought in the tithe of cattle and sheep, and the dedicated things[t] which had been consecrated to the LORD their God, and laid them in heaps. ⁷ In the third month they began to pile

up the heaps, and finished them in the seventh month. ⁸ When Hĕz·ẹ·kī′ah and the princes came and saw the heaps, they blessed the LORD and his people Israel. ⁹ And Hĕz·ẹ·kī′ah questioned the priests and the Lē′vītes about the heaps. ¹⁰ Ăz·ạ·rī′ah the chief priest, who was of the house of Zā′dŏk, answered him, "Since they began to bring the contributions into the house of the LORD we have eaten and had enough and have plenty left; for the LORD has blessed his people, so that we have this great store left."

11 Then Hĕz·ẹ·kī′ah commanded them to prepare chambers in the house of the LORD; and they prepared them. ¹² And they faithfully brought in the contributions, the tithes and the dedicated things. The chief officer in charge of them was Cŏn·ạ·nī′ah the Lē′vīte, with Shĭm′ē·ī his brother as second; ¹³ while Jĕ·hī′ĕl, Ăz·ạ·zī′ah, Nā′hăth, Ạ·sā′ạ·hĕl, Jĕr′ī·mŏth, Jōz′ạ·băd, Ē·lī′ĕl, Ĭs·mạ·chī′ah, Mā′hăth, and Bĕ·nā′ī·ah were overseers assisting Cŏn·ạ·nī′ah and Shĭm′ē·ī his brother, by the appointment of Hĕz·ẹ·kī′ah the king and Ăz·ạ·rī′ah the chief officer of the house of God. ¹⁴ And Kō′rĕ the son of Ĭm′nah the Lē′vīte, keeper of the east gate, was over the freewill offerings to God, to apportion the contribution reserved for the LORD and the most holy offerings. ¹⁵ Eden, Mī·nī′ạ·mĭn, Jĕsh′ü·ạ, Shĕ·māi′ah, Ăm·ạ·rī′ah, and Shĕc·ạ·nī′ah were faithfully assisting him in the cities of the priests, to distribute the portions to their brethren, old and young alike, by divisions, ¹⁶ except those enrolled by genealogy, males from three years old and upwards, all who entered the house of the LORD as the duty of each day required, for their service according to their offices, by their divisions. ¹⁷ The enrollment of the priests was according to their fathers' houses; that of the Lē′vītes from twenty years old and upwards was according to their offices, by their divisions. ¹⁸ The priests were enrolled with all their little children, their wives, their sons, and their daughters, the whole multitude; for they were faithful in keeping themselves holy. ¹⁹ And for the sons of Aaron, the priests, who were in the fields of common land belonging to their cities,

[t]*Heb the tithe of the dedicated things*

there were men in the several cities who were designated by name to distribute portions to every male among the priests and to every one among the Lē'vītes who was enrolled.

20 Thus Hĕz·e·kī'ah did throughout all Judah; and he did what was good and right and faithful before the Lord his God. ²¹And every work that he undertook in the service of the house of God and in accordance with the law and the commandments, seeking his God, he did with all his heart, and prospered.

32 After these things and these acts of faithfulness Sĕn·năch'-e·rĭb king of Assyria came and invaded Judah and encamped against the fortified cities, thinking to win them for himself. ²And when Hĕz·e·kī'ah saw that Sĕn·năch'e·rĭb had come and intended to fight against Jerusalem, ³he planned with his officers and his mighty men to stop the water of the springs that were outside the city; and they helped him. ⁴A great many people were gathered, and they stopped all the springs and the brook that flowed through the land, saying, "Why should the kings of Assyria come and find much water?" ⁵He set to work resolutely and built up all the wall that was broken down, and raised towers upon it,ᵘ and outside it he built another wall; and he strengthened the Mĭl'lō in the city of David. He also made weapons and shields in abundance. ⁶And he set combat commanders over the people, and gathered them together to him in the square at the gate of the city and spoke encouragingly to them, saying, ⁷"Be strong and of good courage. Do not be afraid or dismayed before the king of Assyria and all the horde that is with him; for there is one greater with us than with him. ⁸With him is an arm of flesh; but with us is the Lord our God, to help us and to fight our battles." And the people took confidence from the words of Hĕz·e·kī'ah king of Judah.

9 After this Sĕn·năch'e·rĭb king of Assyria, who was besieging Lā'chĭsh with all his forces, sent his servants to Jerusalem to Hĕz·e·kī'ah king of Judah and to all the people of Judah that were in Jerusalem, saying, ¹⁰"Thus says Sĕn·năch'e·rĭb king of Assyria, 'On what are you relying, that

you stand siege in Jerusalem? ¹¹Is not Hĕz·e·kī'ah misleading you, that he may give you over to die by famine and by thirst, when he tells you, "The Lord our God will deliver us from the hand of the king of Assyria"? ¹²Has not this same Hĕz·e·kī'ah taken away his high places and his altars and commanded Judah and Jerusalem, "Before one altar you shall worship, and upon it you shall burn your sacrifices"? ¹³Do you not know what I and my fathers have done to all the peoples of other lands? Were the gods of the nations of those lands at all able to deliver their lands out of my hand? ¹⁴Who among all the gods of those nations which my fathers utterly destroyed was able to deliver his people from my hand, that your God should be able to deliver you from my hand? ¹⁵Now therefore do not let Hĕz·e·kī'ah deceive you or mislead you in this fashion, and do not believe him, for no god of any nation or kingdom has been able to deliver his people from my hand or from the hand of my fathers. How much less will your God deliver you out of my hand!'"

16 And his servants said still more against the Lord God and against his servant Hĕz·e·kī'ah. ¹⁷And he wrote letters to cast contempt on the Lord the God of Israel and to speak against him, saying, "Like the gods of the nations of the lands who have not delivered their people from my hands, so the God of Hĕz·e·kī'ah will not deliver his people from my hand." ¹⁸And they shouted it with a loud voice in the language of Judah to the people of Jerusalem who were upon the wall, to frighten and terrify them, in order that they might take the city. ¹⁹And they spoke of the God of Jerusalem as they spoke of the gods of the peoples of the earth, which are the work of men's hands.

20 Then Hĕz·e·kī'ah the king and Ī·sāi'ah the prophet, the son of Ā'mŏz, prayed because of this and cried to heaven. ²¹And the Lord sent an angel, who cut off all the mighty warriors and commanders and officers in the camp of the king of Assyria. So he returned with shame of face to his own land. And when he came into the house of his god, some of his own sons

ᵘVg: Heb *and raised upon the towers*
32.1: 2 Kings 18.13.   32.9-21: 2 Kings 18.17-19.37.

struck him down there with the sword. ²² So the LORD saved Hĕz-ẹ-kī′ạh and the inhabitants of Jerusalem from the hand of Sĕn-năch′ẹ-rīb king of Assyria and from the hand of all his enemies; and he gave them rest on every side. ²³ And many brought gifts to the LORD to Jerusalem and precious things to Hĕz-ẹ-kī′ạh king of Judah, so that he was exalted in the sight of all nations from that time onward.

24 In those days Hĕz-ẹ-kī′ạh became sick and was at the point of death, and he prayed to the LORD; and he answered him and gave him a sign. ²⁵ But Hĕz-ẹ-kī′ạh did not make return according to the benefit done to him, for his heart was proud. Therefore wrath came upon him and Judah and Jerusalem. ²⁶ But Hĕz-ẹ-kī′ạh humbled himself for the pride of his heart, both he and the inhabitants of Jerusalem, so that the wrath of the LORD did not come upon them in the days of Hezekiah.

27 And Hĕz-ẹ-kī′ạh had very great riches and honor; and he made for himself treasuries for silver, for gold, for precious stones, for spices, for shields, and for all kinds of costly vessels; ²⁸ storehouses also for the yield of grain, wine, and oil; and stalls for all kinds of cattle, and sheepfolds. ²⁹ He likewise provided cities for himself, and flocks and herds in abundance; for God had given him very great possessions. ³⁰ This same Hĕz-ẹ-kī′ạh closed the upper outlet of the waters of Gī′hŏn and directed them down to the west side of the city of David. And Hezekiah prospered in all his works. ³¹ And so in the matter of the envoys of the princes of Babylon, who had been sent to him to inquire about the sign that had been done in the land, God left him to himself, in order to try him and to know all that was in his heart.

32 Now the rest of the acts of Hĕz-ẹ-kī′ạh, and his good deeds, behold, they are written in the vision of Ī-sāi′ạh the prophet the son of Ā′mŏz, in the Book of the Kings of Judah and Israel. ³³ And Hĕz-ẹ-kī′ạh slept with his fathers, and they buried him in the ascent of the tombs of the sons of David; and all Judah and the inhabitants of Jerusalem did him honor at his death. And Mạ-năs′sẹh his son reigned in his stead.

33 Mạ-năs′sẹh was twelve years old when he began to reign, and he reigned fifty-five years in Jerusalem. ² He did what was evil in the sight of the LORD, according to the abominable practices of the nations whom the LORD drove out before the people of Israel. ³ For he rebuilt the high places which his father Hĕz-ẹ-kī′ạh had broken down, and erected altars to the Bā′ạls, and made Ạ-shē′rạhs, and worshiped all the host of heaven, and served them. ⁴ And he built altars in the house of the LORD, of which the LORD had said, "In Jerusalem shall my name be for ever." ⁵ And he built altars for all the host of heaven in the two courts of the house of the LORD. ⁶ And he burned his sons as an offering in the valley of the son of Hĭn′nọm, and practiced soothsaying and augury and sorcery, and dealt with mediums and with wizards. He did much evil in the sight of the LORD, provoking him to anger. ⁷ And the image of the idol which he had made he set in the house of God, of which God said to David and to Solomon his son, "In this house, and in Jerusalem, which I have chosen out of all the tribes of Israel, I will put my name for ever; ⁸ and I will no more remove the foot of Israel from the land which I appointed for your fathers, if only they will be careful to do all that I have commanded them, all the law, the statutes, and the ordinances given through Moses." ⁹ Mạ-năs′sẹh seduced Judah and the inhabitants of Jerusalem, so that they did more evil than the nations whom the LORD destroyed before the people of Israel.

10 The LORD spoke to Mạ-năs′sẹh and to his people, but they gave no heed. ¹¹ Therefore the LORD brought upon them the commanders of the army of the king of Assyria, who took Mạ-năs′sẹh with hooks and bound him with fetters of bronze and brought him to Babylon. ¹² And when he was in distress he entreated the favor of the LORD his God and humbled himself greatly before the God of his fathers. ¹³ He prayed to him, and God received his entreaty and heard his supplication and brought him again to Jerusalem into his kingdom. Then Mạ-năs′sẹh knew that the LORD was God.

14 Afterwards he built an outer

wall for the city of David west of Gĭ'hŏn, in the valley, and for the entrance into the Fish Gate, and carried it round Ō'phĕl, and raised it to a very great height; he also put commanders of the army in all the fortified cities in Judah. ¹⁵ And he took away the foreign gods and the idol from the house of the LORD, and all the altars that he had built on the mountain of the house of the LORD and in Jerusalem, and he threw them outside of the city. ¹⁶ He also restored the altar of the LORD and offered upon it sacrifices of peace offerings and of thanksgiving; and he commanded Judah to serve the LORD the God of Israel. ¹⁷ Nevertheless the people still sacrificed at the high places, but only to the LORD their God.

18 Now the rest of the acts of Mạ·nǎs'sẹh, and his prayer to his God, and the words of the seers who spoke to him in the name of the LORD the God of Israel, behold, they are in the Chronicles of the Kings of Israel. ¹⁹ And his prayer, and how God received his entreaty, and all his sin and his faithlessness, and the sites on which he built high places and set up the Ạ·shē'rĭm and the images, before he humbled himself, behold, they are written in the Chronicles of the Seers.ᵛ ²⁰ So Mạ·nǎs'sẹh slept with his fathers, and they buried him in his house; and Ā'mŏn his son reigned in his stead.

21 Ā'mŏn was twenty-two years old when he began to reign, and he reigned two years in Jerusalem. ²² He did what was evil in the sight of the LORD, as Mạ·nǎs'sẹh his father had done. Ā'mŏn sacrificed to all the images that Manasseh his father had made, and served them. ²³ And he did not humble himself before the LORD, as Mạ·nǎs'sẹh his father had humbled himself, but this Ā'mŏn incurred guilt more and more. ²⁴ And his servants conspired against him and killed him in his house. ²⁵ But the people of the land slew all those who had conspired against King Ā'mŏn; and the people of the land made Jō·sī'ạh his son king in his stead.

34 Jō·sī'ạh was eight years old when he began to reign, and he reigned thirty-one years in Jerusalem. ² He did what was right in the eyes of the LORD, and walked in the ways of David his father; and he did not turn aside to the right or to the left. ³ For in the eighth year of his reign, while he was yet a boy, he began to seek the God of David his father; and in the twelfth year he began to purge Judah and Jerusalem of the high places, the Ạ·shē'rĭm, and the graven and the molten images. ⁴ And they broke down the altars of the Bā'ạlṣ in his presence; and he hewed down the incense altars which stood above them; and he broke in pieces the Ạ·shē'rĭm and the graven and the molten images, and he made dust of them and strewed it over the graves of those who had sacrificed to them. ⁵ He also burned the bones of the priests on their altars, and purged Judah and Jerusalem. ⁶ And in the cities of Mạ·nǎs'sẹh, Ē'phra·ĭm, and Sĭm'ē·ọn, and as far as Năph'tạ·lī, in their ruinsʷ round about, ⁷ he broke down the altars, and beat the Ạ·shē'-rĭm and the images into powder, and hewed down all the incense altars throughout all the land of Israel. Then he returned to Jerusalem.

8 Now in the eighteenth year of his reign, when he had purged the land and the house, he sent Shā'phạn the son of Ăz·ạ·lī'ạh, and Mā–ạ·sēi'ạh the governor of the city, and Jō'ạh the son of Jō'ạ·hǎz, the recorder, to repair the house of the LORD his God. ⁹ They came to Hĭl·kī'ạh the high priest and delivered the money that had been brought into the house of God, which the Lē'vītes, the keepers of the threshold, had collected from Mạ·nǎs'sẹh and Ē'phrạ·ĭm and from all the remnant of Israel and from all Judah and Benjamin and from the inhabitants of Jerusalem. ¹⁰ They delivered it to the workmen who had the oversight of the house of the LORD; and the workmen who were working in the house of the LORD gave it for repairing and restoring the house. ¹¹ They gave it to the carpenters and the builders to buy quarried stone, and timber for binders and beams for the buildings which the kings of Judah had let go to ruin. ¹² And the men did the work faithfully. Over them were set Jā'hăth and Ō·ba·dī'ạh the Lē'vītes, of the sons of Mẹ·rār'ī, and Zĕch·ạ·rī'ạh and Mĕ-

ᵛOne Ms: Gk: Heb *of Hozai* ʷHeb uncertain
33.20: 2 Kings 21.18. **33.21-25:** 2 Kings 21.19-24.
34.1, 2: 2 Kings 22.1, 2. **34.3-7:** 2 Kings 23.4-20.
34.8-12: 2 Kings 22.3-7.

shŭl'lạm, of the sons of the Kō'hạ-thītes, to have oversight. The Levites, all who were skilful with instruments of music, [13] were over the burden bearers and directed all who did work in every kind of service; and some of the Lē'vītes were scribes, and officials, and gatekeepers.

14 While they were bringing out the money that had been brought into the house of the LORD, Hĭl·kī'ạh the priest found the book of the law of the LORD given through Moses. [15] Then Hĭl·kī'ạh said to Shā'phạn the secretary, "I have found the book of the law in the house of the LORD"; and Hilkiah gave the book to Shaphan. [16] Shā'phạn brought the book to the king, and further reported to the king, "All that was committed to your servants they are doing. [17] They have emptied out the money that was found in the house of the LORD and have delivered it into the hand of the overseers and the workmen." [18] Then Shā'phạn the secretary told the king, "Hĭl·kī'ạh the priest has given me a book." And Shaphan read it before the king.

19 When the king heard the words of the law he rent his clothes. [20] And the king commanded Hĭl·kī'ạh, A·hī'kăm the son of Shā'phạn, Ăb'dŏn the son of Mī'cạh, Shaphan the secretary, and A·sāi'ạh the king's servant, saying, [21] "Go, inquire of the LORD for me and for those who are left in Israel and in Judah, concerning the words of the book that has been found; for great is the wrath of the LORD that is poured out on us, because our fathers have not kept the word of the LORD, to do according to all that is written in this book."

22 So Hĭl·kī'ạh and those whom the king had sent[x] went to Hŭl'dạh the prophetess, the wife of Shăl'lụm the son of Tŏk'hăth, son of Hăs'rạh, keeper of the wardrobe (now she dwelt in Jerusalem in the Second Quarter) and spoke to her to that effect. [23] And she said to them, "Thus says the LORD, the God of Israel: 'Tell the man who sent you to me, [24] Thus says the LORD, Behold, I will bring evil upon this place and upon its inhabitants, all the curses that are written in the book which was read before the king of Judah. [25] Because they have forsaken me and have burned incense to other gods, that they might provoke me to

anger with all the works of their hands, therefore my wrath will be poured out upon this place and will not be quenched. [26] But to the king of Judah, who sent you to inquire of the LORD, thus shall you say to him, Thus says the LORD, the God of Israel: Regarding the words which you have heard, [27] because your heart was penitent and you humbled yourself before God when you heard his words against this place and its inhabitants, and you have humbled yourself before me, and have rent your clothes and wept before me, I also have heard you, says the LORD. [28] Behold, I will gather you to your fathers, and you shall be gathered to your grave in peace, and your eyes shall not see all the evil which I will bring upon this place and its inhabitants.'" And they brought back word to the king.

29 Then the king sent and gathered together all the elders of Judah and Jerusalem. [30] And the king went up to the house of the LORD, with all the men of Judah and the inhabitants of Jerusalem and the priests and the Lē'vītes, all the people both great and small; and he read in their hearing all the words of the book of the covenant which had been found in the house of the LORD. [31] And the king stood in his place and made a covenant before the LORD, to walk after the LORD and to keep his commandments and his testimonies and his statutes, with all his heart and all his soul, to perform the words of the covenant that were written in this book. [32] Then he made all who were present in Jerusalem and in Benjamin stand to it. And the inhabitants of Jerusalem did according to the covenant of God, the God of their fathers. [33] And Jō·sī'ạh took away all the abominations from all the territory that belonged to the people of Israel, and made all who were in Israel serve the LORD their God. All his days they did not turn away from following the LORD the God of their fathers.

35 Jō·sī'ạh kept a passover to the LORD in Jerusalem; and they killed the passover lamb on the fourteenth day of the first month. [2] He appointed the priests to their offices and encouraged them in the service of the house of the LORD.

[x] Syr Vg: Heb lacks *had sent*
35.1-19: 2 Kings 23.21-23.

3 And he said to the Lē'vītes who taught all Israel and who were holy to the LORD, "Put the holy ark in the house which Solomon the son of David, king of Israel, built; you need no longer carry it upon your shoulders. Now serve the LORD your God and his people Israel. 4 Prepare yourselves according to your fathers' houses by your divisions, following the directions of David king of Israel and the directions of Solomon his son. 5 And stand in the holy place according to the groupings of the fathers' houses of your brethren the lay people, and let there be for each a part of a father's house of the Lē'-vītes.ʸ 6 And kill the passover lamb, and sanctify yourselves, and prepare for your brethren, to do according to the word of the LORD by Moses."

7 Then Jō·sī'ah contributed to the lay people, as passover offerings for all that were present, lambs and kids from the flock to the number of thirty thousand, and three thousand bulls; these were from the king's possessions. 8 And his princes contributed willingly to the people, to the priests, and to the Lē'vītes. Hĭl·kī'ah, Zĕch·a·rī'ah, and Jĕ·hī'ĕl, the chief officers of the house of God, gave to the priests for the passover offerings two thousand six hundred lambs and kids and three hundred bulls. 9 Cŏn·a·nī'ah also, and Shĕ·māi'ah and Nĕ·thăn'ĕl his brothers, and Hăsh·a·bī'ah and Jĕ–ī'ĕl and Jōz'a·băd, the chiefs of the Lē'-vītes, gave to the Levites for the passover offerings five thousand lambs and kids and five hundred bulls.

10 When the service had been prepared for, the priests stood in their place, and the Lē'vītes in their divisions according to the king's command. 11 And they killed the passover lamb, and the priests sprinkled the blood which they received from them while the Lē'vītes flayed the victims. 12 And they set aside the burnt offerings that they might distribute them according to the groupings of the fathers' houses of the lay people, to offer to the LORD, as it is written in the book of Moses. And so they did with the bulls. 13 And they roasted the passover lamb with fire according to the ordinance; and they boiled the holy offerings in pots, in caldrons, and in pans, and carried them quickly to all the lay people. 14 And afterward they prepared

for themselves and for the priests, because the priests the sons of Aaron were busied in offering the burnt offerings and the fat parts until night; so the Lē'vītes prepared for themselves and for the priests the sons of Aaron. 15 The singers, the sons of Ā'săph, were in their place according to the command of David, and Asaph, and Hē'man, and Jĕ·dü'thun the king's seer; and the gatekeepers were at each gate; they did not need to depart from their service, for their brethren the Lē'vītes prepared for them.

16 So all the service of the LORD was prepared that day, to keep the passover and to offer burnt offerings on the altar of the LORD, according to the command of King Jō·sī'ah. 17 And the people of Israel who were present kept the passover at that time, and the feast of unleavened bread seven days. 18 No passover like it had been kept in Israel since the days of Samuel the prophet; none of the kings of Israel had kept such a passover as was kept by Jō·sī'ah, and the priests and the Lē'vītes, and all Judah and Israel who were present, and the inhabitants of Jerusalem. 19 In the eighteenth year of the reign of Jō·sī'ah this passover was kept.

20 After all this, when Jō·sī'ah had prepared the temple, Nē'cō king of Egypt went up to fight at Cär'chē·mĭsh on the Euphrates and Josiah went out against him. 21 But he sent envoys to him, saying, "What have we to do with each other, king of Judah? I am not coming against you this day, but against the house with which I am at war; and God has commanded me to make haste. Cease opposing God, who is with me, lest he destroy you." 22 Nevertheless Jō·sī'ah would not turn away from him, but disguised himself in order to fight with him. He did not listen to the words of Nē'cō from the mouth of God, but joined battle in the plain of Mĕ·gĭd'dō. 23 And the archers shot King Jō·sī'ah; and the king said to his servants, "Take me away, for I am badly wounded." 24 So his servants took him out of the chariot and carried him in his second chariot and brought him to Jerusalem. And he died, and was buried in the tombs of his fathers. All Judah and Jerusalem mourned for Jō·sī'ah. 25 Jĕr·e·mī'ah also uttered

ʸHeb obscure

a lament for Jō·sī′ah; and all the singing men and singing women have spoken of Josiah in their laments to this day. They made these an ordinance in Israel; behold, they are written in the Laments. ²⁶ Now the rest of the acts of Jō·sī′ah, and his good deeds according to what is written in the law of the LORD, ²⁷ and his acts, first and last, behold, they are written in the Book of the Kings of Israel and Judah.

36 The people of the land took Jĕ·hō′a·hăz the son of Jō·sī′ah and made him king in his father's stead in Jerusalem. ² Jĕ·hō′a·hăz was twenty-three years old when he began to reign; and he reigned three months in Jerusalem. ³ Then the king of Egypt deposed him in Jerusalem and laid upon the land a tribute, of a hundred talents of silver and a talent of gold. ⁴ And the king of Egypt made Ē·lī′a·kĭm his brother king over Judah and Jerusalem, and changed his name to Jĕ·hoi′a·kĭm; but Nē′cō took Jĕ·hō′a·hăz his brother and carried him to Egypt.

5 Jĕ·hoi′a·kĭm was twenty-five years old when he began to reign, and he reigned eleven years in Jerusalem. He did what was evil in the sight of the LORD his God. ⁶ Against him came up Nĕ·bü·chăd·nĕz′zar king of Babylon, and bound him in fetters to take him to Babylon. ⁷ Nĕ·bü·chăd·nĕz′zar also carried part of the vessels of the house of the LORD to Babylon and put them in his palace in Babylon. ⁸ Now the rest of the acts of Jĕ·hoi′a·kĭm, and the abominations which he did, and what was found against him, behold, they are written in the Book of the Kings of Israel and Judah; and Jĕ·hoi′a·chĭn his son reigned in his stead.

9 Jĕ·hoi′a·chĭn was eight years old when he began to reign, and he reigned three months and ten days in Jerusalem. He did what was evil in the sight of the LORD. ¹⁰ In the spring of the year King Nĕ·bü·chăd·nĕz′zar sent and brought him to Babylon, with the precious vessels of the house of the LORD, and made his brother Zĕd·e·kī′ah king over Judah and Jerusalem.

11 Zĕd·e·kī′ah was twenty-one years old when he began to reign, and he reigned eleven years in Jerusalem. ¹² He did what was evil in the sight of the LORD his God. He did not humble himself before Jĕr·e·mī′ah the prophet, who spoke from the mouth of the LORD. ¹³ He also rebelled against King Nĕ·bü·chăd·nĕz′zar, who had made him swear by God; he stiffened his neck and hardened his heart against turning to the LORD, the God of Israel. ¹⁴ All the leading priests and the people likewise were exceedingly unfaithful, following all the abominations of the nations; and they polluted the house of the LORD which he had hallowed in Jerusalem.

15 The LORD, the God of their fathers, sent persistently to them by his messengers, because he had compassion on his people and on his dwelling place; ¹⁶ but they kept mocking the messengers of God, despising his words, and scoffing at his prophets, till the wrath of the LORD rose against his people, till there was no remedy. 17 Therefore he brought up against them the king of the Chăl·dē′ans, who slew their young men with the sword in the house of their sanctuary, and had no compassion on young man or virgin, old man or aged; he gave them all into his hand. ¹⁸ And all the vessels of the house of God, great and small, and the treasures of the house of the LORD, and the treasures of the king and of his princes, all these he brought to Babylon. ¹⁹ And they burned the house of God, and broke down the wall of Jerusalem, and burned all its palaces with fire, and destroyed all its precious vessels. ²⁰ He took into exile in Babylon those who had escaped from the sword, and they became servants to him and to his sons until the establishment of the kingdom of Persia, ²¹ to fulfil the word of the LORD by the mouth of Jĕr·e·mī′ah, until the land had enjoyed its sabbaths. All the days that it lay desolate it kept sabbath, to fulfil seventy years.

22 Now in the first year of Cyrus king of Persia, that the word of the LORD by the mouth of Jĕr·e·mī′ah might be accomplished, the LORD stirred up the spirit of Cyrus king of Persia so that he made a proclamation throughout all his kingdom and also put it in writing: ²⁸ "Thus says Cyrus king of Persia, 'The LORD, the God of

36.1-4: 2 Kings 23.30-34.   36.5-8: 2 Kings 23.36-24.6.
36.9-10: 2 Kings 24.8-17.
36.11-21: 2 Kings 24.18-25.21.   36.22, 23: Ezra 1.1-3.

heaven, has given me all the kingdoms of the earth, and he has charged me to build him a house at Jerusalem, which is in Judah. Whoever is among you of all his people, may the LORD his God be with him. Let him go up.'"

The Book of

Ezra

1 In the first year of Cyrus king of Persia, that the word of the LORD by the mouth of Jĕr·ĕ·mī'ah might be accomplished, the LORD stirred up the spirit of Cyrus king of Persia so that he made a proclamation throughout all his kingdom and also put it in writing:
2 "Thus says Cyrus king of Persia: The LORD, the God of heaven, has given me all the kingdoms of the earth, and he has charged me to build him a house at Jerusalem, which is in Judah. ³Whoever is among you of all his people, may his God be with him, and let him go up to Jerusalem, which is in Judah, and rebuild the house of the LORD, the God of Israel—he is the God who is in Jerusalem; ⁴and let each survivor, in whatever place he sojourns, be assisted by the men of his place with silver and gold, with goods and with beasts, besides freewill offerings for the house of God which is in Jerusalem."
5 Then rose up the heads of the fathers' houses of Judah and Benjamin, and the priests and the Lē'vītes, every one whose spirit God had stirred to go up to rebuild the house of the LORD which is in Jerusalem; ⁶and all who were about them aided them with vessels of silver, with gold, with goods, with beasts, and with costly wares, besides all that was freely offered. ⁷Cyrus the king also brought out the vessels of the house of the LORD which Nĕ·bü·chad·nĕz'zar had carried away from Jerusalem and placed in the house of his gods. ⁸Cyrus king of Persia brought these out in charge of Mĭth're·dăth the treasurer, who counted them out to Shĕsh–băz'zar the prince of Judah. ⁹And this was the number of them: a thousand*ᵃ* basins of gold, a thousand basins of silver,

twenty-nine censers, ¹⁰thirty bowls of gold, two thousand*ᵇ* four hundred and ten bowls of silver, and a thousand other vessels; ¹¹all the vessels of gold and of silver were five thousand four hundred and sixty-nine.*ᶜ* All these did Shĕsh–băz'zar bring up, when the exiles were brought up from Babylonia to Jerusalem.

2 Now these were the people of the province who came up out of the captivity of those exiles whom Nĕ·bü·chad·nĕz'zar the king of Babylon had carried captive to Babylonia; they returned to Jerusalem and Judah, each to his own town. ²They came with Zĕ·rŭb'ba·bĕl, Jĕsh'ü·a, Nē·he·mī'ah, Sĕ·rāi'ah, Rē–ĕl·āi'ah, Môr'dĕ·caī, Bĭl'shăn, Mĭs'par, Bĭg'vaī, Rē'hum, and Bā'a·nah.

The number of the men of the people of Israel: ³the sons of Pā'rŏsh, two thousand one hundred and seventy-two. ⁴The sons of Shĕph·a·tī'ah, three hundred and seventy-two. ⁵The sons of Ā'rah, seven hundred and seventy-five. ⁶The sons of Pā'hăth–mō'ăb, namely the sons of Jĕsh'ü·a and Jō'ăb, two thousand eight hundred and twelve. ⁷The sons of Ē'lăm, one thousand two hundred and fifty-four. ⁸The sons of Zăt'tü, nine hundred and forty-five. ⁹The sons of Zăc'caī, seven hundred and sixty. ¹⁰The sons of Bā'nī, six hundred and forty-two. ¹¹The sons of Bē'baī, six hundred and twenty-three. ¹²The sons of Āz'găd, one thousand two hundred and twenty-two. ¹³The sons of Ăd·o·nī'kam, six hundred and sixty-six. ¹⁴The sons of Bĭg'vaī, two thousand and fifty-six. ¹⁵The sons of Ā'dĭn, four hundred and

*ᵃ*1 Esdras 2.13: Heb *thirty*
*ᵇ*1 Esdras 2.13: Heb *of a second sort*
*ᶜ*1 Esdras 2.14: Heb *five thousand four hundred*
1.1-3: 5.13; 6.3; 2 Chron 36.22, 23.
2.1-70: Neh 7.6-73.

fifty-four. ¹⁶The sons of Ā′ter, namely of Hĕz·ę·kī′ah, ninety-eight. ¹⁷The sons of Bē′zaī, three hundred and twenty-three. ¹⁸The sons of Jō′rah, one hundred and twelve. ¹⁹The sons of Hā′shum, two hundred and twenty-three. ²⁰The sons of Gĭb′bar, ninety-five. ²¹The sons of Bethlehem, one hundred and twenty-three. ²²The men of Nę-tŏph′ah, fifty-six. ²³The men of Ăn′a-thŏth, one hundred and twenty-eight. ²⁴The sons of Ăz′ma·vĕth, forty-two. ²⁵The sons of Kĭr″i·āth·ar′ĭm, Chĕ-phī′rah, and Bę–ēr′ŏth, seven hundred and forty-three. ²⁶The sons of Rā′mah and Gē′ba, six hundred and twenty-one. ²⁷The men of Mĭch′măs, one hundred and twenty-two. ²⁸The men of Bĕth′ĕl and Aī, two hundred and twenty-three. ²⁹The sons of Nē′bō, fifty-two. ³⁰The sons of Măg′bĭsh, one hundred and fifty-six. ³¹The sons of the other Ē′lăm, one thousand two hundred and fifty-four. ³²The sons of Hā′rĭm, three hundred and twenty. ³³The sons of Lŏd, Hā′dĭd, and Ō′nō, seven hundred and twenty-five. ³⁴The sons of Jericho, three hundred and forty-five. ³⁵The sons of Sĕ·nā′ah, three thousand six hundred and thirty.

36 The priests: the sons of Jĕ·daī′ah, of the house of Jĕsh′ü·a, nine hundred and seventy-three. ³⁷The sons of Ĭm′mer, one thousand and fifty-two. ³⁸The sons of Pāsh′hŭr, one thousand two hundred and forty-seven. ³⁹The sons of Hā′rĭm, one thousand and seventeen.

40 The Lē′vītes: the sons of Jĕsh′ü·a and Kăd′mĭ–ĕl, of the sons of Hŏd″-a·vī′ah, seventy-four. ⁴¹The singers: the sons of Ā′săph, one hundred and twenty-eight. ⁴²The sons of the gate-keepers: the sons of Shăl′lum, the sons of Ā′ter, the sons of Tăl′mon, the sons of Ăk′kub, the sons of Ha·tī′ta, and the sons of Shō′baī, in all one hundred and thirty-nine.

43 The temple servants:*d* the sons of Zī′ha, the sons of Ha·sü′pha, the sons of Tăb·bā′ŏth, ⁴⁴the sons of Kē′rŏs, the sons of Sī′a·ha, the sons of Pā′dŏn, ⁴⁵the sons of Lĕ·bā′nah, the sons of Hăg′a·bah, the sons of Ăk′kub, ⁴⁶the sons of Hā′găb, the sons of Shăm′laī, the sons of Hā′nan, ⁴⁷the sons of Gĭd′dĕl, the sons of Gā′har, the sons of Rē–aī′ah, ⁴⁸the sons of Rē′zĭn, the sons of Nĕ·kō′da, the sons of Găz′zam, ⁴⁹the sons of Ŭz′za, the sons of Pa-

sē′ah, the sons of Bē′saī, ⁵⁰the sons of Ăs′nah, the sons of Mĕ–ü′nĭm, the sons of Nĕ·phī′sĭm, ⁵¹the sons of Băk′bŭk, the sons of Ha·kū′pha, the sons of Hăr′hŭr, ⁵²the sons of Băz′-luth, the sons of Mĕ·hī′da, the sons of Hăr′sha, ⁵³the sons of Bār′kŏs, the sons of Sĭs′e·ra, the sons of Tē′mah, ⁵⁴the sons of Nę·zī′ah, and the sons of Ha·tī′pha.

55 The sons of Solomon's servants: the sons of Sō′taī, the sons of Hăs-sō′phe·rĕth, the sons of Pĕ·rü′da, ⁵⁶the sons of Jā′a·lah, the sons of Dăr′kŏn, the sons of Gĭd′dĕl, ⁵⁷the sons of Shĕph·a·tī′ah, the sons of Hăt′tĭl, the sons of Pō′chĕ·rĕth–hăz·zę·bā′ĭm, and the sons of Ā′mī.

58 All the temple servants*d* and the sons of Solomon's servants were three hundred and ninety-two.

59 The following were those who come up from Tĕl–mē′lah, Tĕl–hār′sha, Chē′rub, Ăd′dan, and Ĭm′mer, though they could not prove their fathers' houses or their descent, whether they belonged to Israel: ⁶⁰the sons of Dĕ-laī′ah, the sons of Tō·bī′ah, and the sons of Nĕ·kō′da, six hundred and fifty-two. ⁶¹Also, of the sons of the priests: the sons of Ha·baī′ah, the sons of Hăk′kŏz, and the sons of Bār·zĭl′laī (who had taken a wife from the daughters of Barzillai the Gileadite, and was called by their name). ⁶²These sought their registration among those enrolled in the genealogies, but they were not found there, and so they were excluded from the priesthood as unclean; ⁶³the governor told them that they were not to partake of the most holy food, until there should be a priest to consult Ū′rĭm and Thŭm′mĭm.

64 The whole assembly together was forty-two thousand three hundred and sixty, ⁶⁵besides their menservants and maidservants, of whom there were seven thousand three hundred and thirty-seven; and they had two hundred male and female singers. ⁶⁶Their horses were seven hundred and thirty-six, their mules were two hundred and forty-five, ⁶⁷their camels were four hundred and thirty-five, and their asses were six thousand seven hundred and twenty.

68 Some of the heads of families, when they came to the house of the LORD which is in Jerusalem, made

*d*Heb *nethinim*

freewill offerings for the house of God, to erect it on its site; ⁶⁹according to their ability they gave to the treasury of the work sixty-one thousand darics of gold, five thousand minas of silver, and one hundred priests' garments.

70 The priests, the Lē'vītes, and some of the people lived in Jerusalem and its vicinity;^e and the singers, the gatekeepers, and the temple servants lived in their towns, and all Israel in their towns.

3 When the seventh month came, and the sons of Israel were in the towns, the people gathered as one man to Jerusalem. ²Then arose Jēsh'ü·a the son of Jō'za·dăk, with his fellow priests, and Zĕ·rŭb'ba·bĕl the son of Shĕ–ăl'tĭ–ĕl with his kinsmen, and they built the altar of the God of Israel, to offer burnt offerings upon it, as it is written in the law of Moses the man of God. ³They set the altar in its place, for fear was upon them because of the peoples of the lands, and they offered burnt offerings upon it to the LORD, burnt offerings morning and evening. ⁴And they kept the feast of booths, as it is written, and offered the daily burnt offerings by number according to the ordinance, as each day required, ⁵and after that the continual burnt offerings, the offerings at the new moon and at all the appointed feasts of the LORD, and the offerings of every one who made a freewill offering to the LORD. ⁶From the first day of the seventh month they began to offer burnt offerings to the LORD. But the foundation of the temple of the LORD was not yet laid. ⁷So they gave money to the masons and the carpenters, and food, drink, and oil to the Sī·dō'nĭ·ạns and the Tўr'ĭ·ạns to bring cedar trees from Lebanon to the sea, to Jŏp'pạ, according to the grant which they had from Cyrus king of Persia.

8 Now in the second year of their coming to the house of God at Jerusalem, in the second month, Zĕ·rŭb'ba·bĕl the son of Shĕ–ăl'tĭ–ĕl and Jēsh'ü·a the son of Jō'za·dăk made a beginning, together with the rest of their brethren, the priests and the Lē'vītes and all who had come to Jerusalem from the captivity. They appointed the Levites, from twenty years old and upward, to have the oversight of the work of the house of the

LORD. ⁹And Jēsh'ü·a with his sons and his kinsmen, and Kăd'mĭ–ĕl and his sons, the sons of Judah, together took the oversight of the workmen in the house of God, along with the sons of Hĕn'a·dăd and the Lē'vītes, their sons and kinsmen.

10 And when the builders laid the foundation of the temple of the LORD, the priests in their vestments came forward with trumpets, and the Lē'-vītes, the sons of Ā'săph, with cymbals, to praise the LORD, according to the directions of David king of Israel; ¹¹and they sang responsively, praising and giving thanks to the LORD,

"For he is good,
    for his steadfast love endures for
        ever toward Israel."

And all the people shouted with a great shout, when they praised the LORD, because the foundation of the house of the LORD was laid. ¹²But many of the priests and Lē'vītes and heads of fathers' houses, old men who had seen the first house, wept with a loud voice when they saw the foundation of this house being laid, though many shouted aloud for joy; ¹³so that the people could not distinguish the sound of the joyful shout from the sound of the people's weeping, for the people shouted with a great shout, and the sound was heard afar.

4 Now when the adversaries of Judah and Benjamin heard that the returned exiles were building a temple to the LORD, the God of Israel, ²they approached Zĕ·rŭb'ba·bĕl and the heads of fathers' houses and said to them, "Let us build with you; for we worship your God as you do, and we have been sacrificing to him ever since the days of Ē'săr–hăd'dọn king of Assyria who brought us here." ³But Zĕ·rŭb'ba·bĕl, Jēsh'ü·a, and the rest of the heads of fathers' houses in Israel said to them, "You have nothing to do with us in building a house to our God; but we alone will build to the LORD, the God of Israel, as King Cyrus the king of Persia has commanded us."

4 Then the people of the land discouraged the people of Judah, and made them afraid to build, ⁵and hired counselors against them to frustrate their purpose, all the days of Cyrus

^e1 Esdras 5.46: Heb lacks *lived in Jerusalem and its vicinity*

king of Persia, even until the reign of Da·rī′us king of Persia.

6 And in the reign of A·hăṣ′ū–ē′rus, in the beginning of his reign, they wrote an accusation against the inhabitants of Judah and Jerusalem.

7 And in the days of Är–ta–xĕrx′ēṣ, Bĭsh′lam and Mĭth′re·dăth and Tā′bē–ĕl and the rest of their associates wrote to Ar–ta–xerxes king of Persia; the letter was written in Är·a·mā′ĭc and translated.*ʃ* 8 Rē′hum the commander and Shĭm′shaī the scribe wrote a letter against Jerusalem to Är–ta–xĕrx′ēṣ the king as follows — 9 then wrote Rē′hum the commander, Shĭm′shaī the scribe, and the rest of their associates, the judges, the governors, the officials, the Persians, the men of Ē′rĕch, the Babylonians, the men of Sū′sa, that is, the Ē′lam·ītes, 10 and the rest of the nations whom the great and noble Ōs·năp′par deported and settled in the cities of Sa·mâr′ī·a and in the rest of the province Beyond the River, and now 11 this is a copy of the letter that they sent — "To Är–ta–xĕrx′ēṣ the king: Your servants, the men of the province Beyond the River, send greeting. And now 12 be it known to the king that the Jews who came up from you to us have gone to Jerusalem. They are rebuilding that rebellious and wicked city; they are finishing the walls and repairing the foundations. 13 Now be it known to the king that, if this city is rebuilt and the walls finished, they will not pay tribute, custom, or toll, and the royal revenue will be impaired. 14 Now because we eat the salt of the palace and it is not fitting for us to witness the king's dishonor, therefore we send and inform the king, 15 in order that search may be made in the book of the records of your fathers. You will find in the book of the records and learn that this city is a rebellious city, hurtful to kings and provinces, and that sedition was stirred up in it from of old. That was why this city was laid waste. 16 We make known to the king that, if this city is rebuilt and its walls finished, you will then have no possession in the province Beyond the River."

17 The king sent an answer: "To Rē′hum the commander and Shĭm′shaī the scribe and the rest of their associates who live in Sa·mâr′ī·a and in the rest of the province Beyond the River, greeting. And now 18 the letter which you sent to us has been plainly read before me. 19 And I made a decree, and search has been made, and it has been found that this city from of old has risen against kings, and that rebellion and sedition have been made in it. 20 And mighty kings have been over Jerusalem, who ruled over the whole province Beyond the River, to whom tribute, custom, and toll were paid. 21 Therefore make a decree that these men be made to cease, and that this city be not rebuilt, until a decree is made by me. 22 And take care not to be slack in this matter; why should damage grow to the hurt of the king?"

23 Then, when the copy of King Är–ta–xĕrx′ēṣ′ letter was read before Rē′hum and Shĭm′shaī the scribe and their associates, they went in haste to the Jews at Jerusalem and by force and power made them cease. 24 Then the work on the house of God which is in Jerusalem stopped; and it ceased until the second year of the reign of Da·rī′us king of Persia.

5 Now the Prophets, Hăg′gaī and Zĕch·a·rī′ah the son of Ĭd′dō, prophesied to the Jews who were in Judah and Jerusalem, in the name of the God of Israel who was over them. 2 Then Zĕ·rŭb′ba·bĕl the son of Shē–ăl′tī–ĕl and Jĕsh′ū·a the son of Jō′za·dăk arose and began to rebuild the house of God which is in Jerusaelm; and with them were the prophets of God, helping them.

3 At the same time Tăt′te·naī the governor of the province Beyond the River and Shē′thär–bŏz′e·naī and their associates came to them and spoke to them thus, "Who gave you a decree to build this house and to finish this structure?" 4 They*ᵍ* also asked them this, "What are the names of the men who are building this building?" 5 But the eye of their God was upon the elders of the Jews, and they did not stop them till a report should reach Da·rī′us and then answer be returned by letter concerning it.

6 The copy of the letter which Tăt′te·naī the governor of the province Beyond the River and Shē′thär–bŏz′e·naī and his associates the governors who were in the province

---

*ʃ*Heb adds *in Aramaic,* indicating that 4.8-6.18 is in Aramaic. Another interpretation is *The letter was written in the Aramaic script and set forth in the Aramaic language*
*ᵍ*Gk Syr: Aramaic *We* **5.1:** Hag 1.1; Zech 1.1.

Beyond the River sent to Dạ·rī'ŭs the king; ⁷they sent him a report, in which was written as follows: "To Dạ·rī'ŭs the king, all peace. ⁸Be it known to the king that we went to the province of Judah, to the house of the great God. It is being built with huge stones, and timber is laid in the walls; this work goes on diligently and prospers in their hands. ⁹Then we asked those elders and spoke to them thus, 'Who gave you a decree to build this house and to finish this structure?' ¹⁰We also asked them their names, for your information, that we might write down the names of the men at their head. ¹¹And this was their reply to us: 'We are the servants of the God of heaven and earth, and we are rebuilding the house that we built many years ago, which a great king of Israel built and finished. ¹²But because our fathers had angered the God of heaven, he gave them into the hand of Nĕ·bü·chạd·nĕz'zạr king of Babylon, the Chăl·dē'an, who destroyed this house and carried away the people to Babylonia. ¹³However in the first year of Cyrus king of Babylon, Cyrus the king made a decree that this house of God should be rebuilt. ¹⁴And the gold and silver vessels of the house of God, which Nĕ·bü·chạd·nĕz'zạr had taken out of the temple that was in Jerusalem and brought into the temple of Babylon, these Cyrus the king took out of the temple of Babylon, and they were delivered to one whose name was Shĕsh·băz'zạr, whom he had made governor; ¹⁵and he said to him, "Take these vessels, go and put them in the temple which is in Jerusalem, and let the house of God be rebuilt on its site." ¹⁶Then this Shĕsh–băz'zạr came and laid the foundations of the house of God which is in Jerusalem; and from that time until now it has been in building, and it is not yet finished.' ¹⁷Therefore, if it seem good to the king, let search be made in the royal archives there in Babylon, to see whether a decree was issued by Cyrus the king for the rebuilding of this house of God in Jerusalem. And let the king send us his pleasure in this matter."

6 Then Dạ·rī'ŭs the king made a decree, and search was made in Babylonia, in the house of the archives where the documents were stored. ²And in Ĕc·băt'ạ·nạ, the capital which is in the province of Mēd'ĭ·ạ, a scroll was found on which this was written: "A record. ³In the first year of Cyrus the king, Cyrus the king issued a decree: Concerning the house of God at Jerusalem, let the house be rebuilt, the place where sacrifices are offered and burnt offerings are brought; its height shall be sixty cubits and its breadth sixty cubits, ⁴with three courses of great stones and one course of timber; let the cost be paid from the royal treasury. ⁵And also let the gold and silver vessels of the house of God, which Nĕ·bü·chạd·nĕz'zạr took out of the temple that is in Jerusalem and brought to Babylon, be restored and brought back to the temple which is in Jerusalem, each to its place; you shall put them in the house of God."

6 "Now therefore, Tăt'tẹ·naī, governor of the province Beyond the River, Shē'thăr–bŏz'ẹ·naī, and your associates the governors who are in the province Beyond the River, keep away; ⁷let the work on this house of God alone; let the governor of the Jews and the elders of the Jews rebuild this house of God on its site. ⁸Moreover I make a decree regarding what you shall do for these elders of the Jews for the rebuilding of this house of God; the cost is to be paid to these men in full and without delay from the royal revenue, the tribute of the province from Beyond the River. ⁹And whatever is needed—young bulls, rams, or sheep for burnt offerings to the God of heaven, wheat, salt, wine, or oil, as the priests at Jerusalem require—let that be given to them day by day without fail, ¹⁰that they may offer pleasing sacrifices to the God of heaven, and pray for the life of the king and his sons. ¹¹Also I make a decree that if any one alters this edict, a beam shall be pulled out of his house, and he shall be impaled upon it, and his house shall be made a dunghill. ¹²May the God who has caused his name to dwell there overthrow any king or people that shall put forth a hand to alter this, or to destroy this house of God which is in Jerusalem. I Dạ·rī'ŭs make a decree; let it be done with all diligence."

13 Then, according to the word sent by Dạ·rī'ŭs the king, Tăt'tẹ·naī, the governor of the province Beyond the

5.13: 1.1; 6.3. 6.3: 1.1; 5.13.

River, Shē'thär-bŏz'ę-naī, and their associates did with all diligence what Darius the king had ordered. [14]And the elders of the Jews built and prospered, through the prophesying of Hăg'gaī the prophet and Zĕch·a·rī'ah the son of Ĭd'dō. They finished their building by command of the God of Israel and by decree of Cyrus and Da·rī'ŭs and Är-ta–xẽrx'ēṣ king of Persia; [15]and this house was finished on the third day of the month of A'där, in the sixth year of the reign of Da·rī'ŭs the king.

[16]And the people of Israel, the priests and the Lē'vītes, and the rest of the returned exiles, celebrated the dedication of this house of God with joy. [17]They offered at the dedication of this house of God one hundred bulls, two hundred rams, four hundred lambs, and as a sin offering for all Israel twelve he-goats, according to the number of the tribes of Israel. [18]And they set the priests in their divisions and the Lē'vītes in their courses, for the service of God at Jerusalem, as it is written in the book of Moses.

[19]On the fourteenth day of the first month the returned exiles kept the passover. [20]For the priests and the Lē'vītes had purified themselves together; all of them were clean. So they killed the passover lamb for all the returned exiles, for their fellow priests, and for themselves; [21]it was eaten by the people of Israel who had returned from exile, and also by every one who had joined them and separated himself from the pollutions of the peoples of the land to worship the LORD, the God of Israel. [22]And they kept the feast of unleavened bread seven days with joy; for the LORD had made them joyful, and had turned the heart of the king of Assyria to them, so that he aided them in the work of the house of God, the God of Israel.

7 Now after this, in the reign of Är-ta–xẽrx'ēṣ king of Persia, Ezra the son of Sĕ·rāi'ah, son of Hĭl·kī'ah, [2]son of Shăl'lum, son of Zā'dŏk, son of A·hī'tub, [3]son of Ăm·a·rī'ah, son of Ăz·a·rī'ah, son of Mĕ·rā'ĭ·ŏth, [4]son of Zĕr·a·hī'ah, son of Ŭz'zī, son of Bŭk'kī, [5]son of Ăb·ĭ·shü'a, son of Phĭn'ę·has, son of Ĕl·ē·ā'zar, son of Aaron the chief priest—[6]this Ezra went up from Babylonia. He was a scribe skilled in the law of Moses

which the LORD the God of Israel had given; and the king granted him all that he asked, for the hand of the LORD his God was upon him.

[7]And there went up also to Jerusalem, in the seventh year of Är-ta–xẽrx'ēṣ the king, some of the people of Israel, and some of the priests and Lē'vītes, the singers and gatekeepers, and the temple servants. [8]And he came to Jerusalem in the fifth month, which was in the seventh year of the king; [9]for on the first day of the first month he began[h] to go up from Babylonia, and on the first day of the fifth month he came to Jerusalem, for the good hand of his God was upon him. [10]For Ezra had set his heart to study the law of the LORD, and to do it, and to teach his statutes and ordinances to Israel.

[11]This is a copy of the letter which King Är-ta–xẽrx'ēṣ gave to Ezra the priest, the scribe, learned in matters of the commandments of the LORD and his statutes for Israel: [12]"Är-ta–xẽrx'ēṣ, king of kings, to Ezra the priest, the scribe of the law of the God of heaven.[x] And now [13]I make a decree that any one of the people of Israel or their priests or Lē'vītes in my kingdom, who freely offers to go to Jerusalem, may go with you. [14]For you are sent by the king and his seven counselors to make inquiries about Judah and Jerusalem according to the law of your God, which is in your hand, [15]and also to convey the silver and gold which the king and his counselors have freely offered to the God of Israel, whose dwelling is in Jerusalem [16]with all the silver and gold which you shall find in the whole province of Babylonia, and with the freewill offerings of the people and the priests vowed willingly for the house of their God which is in Jerusalem. [17]With this money, then, you shall with all diligence buy bulls, rams, and lambs with their cereal offerings and their drink offerings, and you shall offer them upon the altar of the house of your God which is in Jerusalem [18]Whatever seems good to you and your brethren to do with the rest of the silver and gold, you may do, according to the will of your God. [19]The vessels that have been given you for the serv

ʰ Vg See Syr: Heb *that was the foundation of the going up*
ˣ Aram adds a word of uncertain meaning

ice of the house of your God, you shall deliver before the God of Jerusalem. [20]And whatever else is required for the house of your God, which you have occasion to provide, you may provide it out of the king's treasury.

21 "And I, Ăr–tạ–xẽrx'ēş the king, make a decree to all the treasurers in the province Beyond the River: Whatever Ezra the priest, the scribe of the law of the God of heaven, requires of you, be it done with all diligence, [22]up to a hundred talents of silver, a hundred cors of wheat, a hundred baths of wine, a hundred baths of oil, and salt without prescribing how much. [23]Whatever is commanded by the God of heaven, let it be done in full for the house of the God of heaven, lest his wrath be against the realm of the king and his sons. [24]We also notify you that it shall not be lawful to impose tribute, custom, or toll upon any one of the priests, the Lē'vītes, the singers, the doorkeepers, the temple servants, or other servants of this house of God.

25 "And you, Ezra, according to the wisdom of your God which is in your hand, appoint magistrates and judges who may judge all the people in the province Beyond the River, all such as know the laws of your God; and those who do not know them, you shall teach. [26]Whoever will not obey the law of your God and the law of the king, let judgment be strictly executed upon him, whether for death or for banishment or for confiscation of his goods or for imprisonment."

27 Blessed be the LORD, the God of our fathers, who put such a thing as this into the heart of the king, to beautify the house of the LORD which is in Jerusalem, [28]and who extended to me his steadfast love before the king and his counselors, and before all the king's mighty officers. I took courage, for the hand of the LORD my God was upon me, and I gathered leading men from Israel to go up with me.

8 These are the heads of their fathers' houses, and this is the genealogy of those who went up with me from Babylonia, in the reign of Ăr–tạ–xẽrx'ēş the king: [2]Of the sons of Phĭn'ẹ·has, Gēr'shŏm. Of the sons of Ĭth'ạ·mär, Daniel. Of the sons of David, Hăt'tush, [3]of the sons of Shĕc·ạ–nī'ạh. Of the sons of Pā'rŏsh, Zĕch-

ạ·rī'ạh, with whom were registered one hundred and fifty men. [4]Of the sons of Pā'hăth–mō'ăb, Ĕl'ĭ-ē–hō–ē'naī the son of Zẽr·ạ·hī'ạh, and with him two hundred men. [5]Of the sons of Zăt'tü,[i] Shĕc·ạ·nī'ạh the son of Jạ·hā'zĭ·ĕl, and with him three hundred men. [6]Of the sons of Ā'dĭn, Ē'bĕd the son of Jonathan, and with him fifty men. [7]Of the sons of Ē'lăm, Jĕ·shāi'ạh the son of Ăth·ạ·lī'ạh, and with him seventy men. [8]Of the sons of Shĕph·ạ·tī'ạh, Zĕb·ạ·dī'ạh the son of Michael, and with him eighty men. [9]Of the sons of Jō'ăb, Ō·bạ·dī'ạh the son of Jĕ·hī'ĕl, and with him two hundred and eighteen men. [10]Of the sons of Bā'nī,[j] Shĕ·lō'mĭth the son of Jŏs·ĭ·phī'ạh, and with him a hundred and sixty men. [11]Of the sons of Bē'baī, Zĕch·ạ·rī'ạh, the son of Bebai, and with him twenty-eight men. [12]Of the sons of Ăz'găd, Jō·hā'nạn the son of Hăk'kạ·tăn, and with him a hundred and ten men. [13]Of the sons of Ăd·ọ·nī'kạm, those who came later, their names being Ĕ·lĭph'ẹ·lĕt, Jĕ·ü'ĕl, and Shĕmāi'ạh, and with them sixty men. [14]Of the sons of Bĭg'vaī, Ū'thaī and Zăc'cŭr, and with them seventy men.

15 I gathered them to the river that runs to Ạ·hā'vạ, and there we encamped three days. As I reviewed the people and the priests, I found there none of the sons of Lē'vī. [16]Then I sent for Ĕ·lĭ·ē'zẹr, Ăr'ĭ·ẹl, Shĕ·māi'ạh, Ĕl·nā'than, Jā'rĭb, Elnathan, Nathan, Zĕch·ạ·rī'ạh, and Mĕ·shŭl'lam, leading men, and for Joi'ạ·rĭb and Elnathan, who were men of insight, [17]and sent them to Ĭd'dō, the leading man at the place Căs·ĭ·phī'ạ, telling them what to say to Iddo and his brethren the temple servants[k] at the place Casiphia, namely, to send us ministers for the house of our God. [18]And by the good hand of our God upon us, they brought us a man of discretion, of the sons of Măh'lī the son of Lē'vī, son of Israel, namely Shĕr·ẹ·bī'ạh with his sons and kinsmen, eighteen; [19]also Hăsh·ạ·bī'ạh and with him Jĕ·shāi'ạh of the sons of Mẹ·rär'ī, with his kinsmen and their sons, twenty; [20]besides two hundred and twenty of the temple servants, whom David and his officials had set apart to attend the Lē'vītes. These were all mentioned by name.

21 Then I proclaimed a fast there, at the river A·hā′va, that we might humble ourselves before our God, to seek from him a straight way for ourselves, our children, and all our goods. ²² For I was ashamed to ask the king for a band of soldiers and horsemen to protect us against the enemy on our way; since we had told the king, "The hand of our God is for good upon all that seek him, and the power of his wrath is against all that forsake him." ²³ So we fasted and besought our God for this, and he listened to our entreaty.

24 Then I set apart twelve of the leading priests: Shĕr·e·bī′ah, Hăsh·a·bī′ah, and ten of their kinsmen with them. ²⁵ And I weighed out to them the silver and the gold and the vessels, the offering for the house of our God which the king and his counselors and his lords and all Israel there present had offered; ²⁶ I weighed out into their hand six hundred and fifty talents of silver, and silver vessels worth a hundred talents, and a hundred talents of gold, ²⁷ twenty bowls of gold worth a thousand darics, and two vessels of fine bright bronze as precious as gold. ²⁸ And I said to them, "You are holy to the LORD, and the vessels are holy; and the silver and the gold are a freewill offering to the LORD, the God of your fathers. ²⁹ Guard them and keep them until you weigh them before the chief priests and the Lē′vītes and the heads of fathers' houses in Israel at Jerusalem, within the chambers of the house of the LORD." ³⁰ So the priests and the Lē′vītes took over the weight of the silver and the gold and the vessels, to bring them to Jerusalem, to the house of our God.

31 Then we departed from the river A·hā′va on the twelfth day of the first month, to go to Jerusalem; the hand of our God was upon us, and he delivered us from the hand of the enemy and from ambushes by the way. ³² We came to Jerusalem, and there we remained three days. ³³ On the fourth day, within the house of our God, the silver and the gold and the vessels were weighed into the hands of Mĕr′e·mŏth the priest, son of U·rī′ah, and with him was Ĕl·ē·ā′zar the son of Phĭn′e·has, and with them were the Lē′vītes, Jŏz′a·băd the son of Jĕsh′ü·a and Nō–a·dī′ah the son of Bĭn′nü·ī. ³⁴ The whole

was counted and weighed, and the weight of everything was recorded.

35 At that time those who had come from captivity, the returned exiles, offered burnt offerings to the God of Israel, twelve bulls for all Israel, ninety-six rams, seventy-seven lambs, and as a sin offering twelve he-goats; all this was a burnt offering to the LORD. ³⁶ They also delivered the king's commissions to the king's satraps and to the governors of the province Beyond the River; and they aided the people and the house of God.

9 After these things had been done, the officials approached me and said, "The people of Israel and the priests and the Lē′vītes have not separated themselves from the peoples of the lands with their abominations, from the Canaanites, the Hĭt′tītes, the Pĕr′ĭz·zītes, the Jĕb′ü·sītes, the Ăm′mo·nītes, the Mō′ab·ītes, the Egyptians, and the Ăm′o·rītes. ² For they have taken some of their daughters to be wives for themselves and for their sons; so that the holy race has mixed itself with the peoples of the lands. And in this faithlessness the hand of the officials and chief men has been foremost." ³ When I heard this, I rent my garments and my mantle, and pulled hair from my head and beard, and sat appalled. ⁴ Then all who trembled at the words of the God of Israel, because of the faithlessness of the returned exiles, gathered round me while I sat appalled until the evening sacrifice. ⁵ And at the evening sacrifice I rose from my fasting, with my garments and my mantle rent, and fell upon my knees and spread out my hands to the LORD my God, ⁶ saying:

"O my God, I am ashamed and blush to lift my face to thee, my God, for our iniquities have risen higher than our heads, and our guilt has mounted up to the heavens. ⁷ From the days of our fathers to this day we have been in great guilt; and for our iniquities we, our kings, and our priests have been given into the hand of the kings of the lands, to the sword, to captivity, to plundering, and to utter shame, as at this day. ⁸ But now for a brief moment favor has been shown by the LORD our God, to leave us a remnant, and to give us a secure hold¹ within his holy place, that our God may brighten our

¹ Heb *nail* or *tent-pin*

eyes and grant us a little reviving in our bondage. [9] For we are bondmen; yet our God has not forsaken us in our bondage, but has extended to us his steadfast love before the kings of Persia, to grant us some reviving to set up the house of our God, to repair its ruins, and to give us protection[m] in Judea and Jerusalem.

10 "And now, O our God, what shall we say after this? For we have forsaken thy commandments, [11] which thou didst command by thy servants the prophets, saying, 'The land which you are entering, to take possession of it, is a land unclean with the pollutions of the peoples of the lands, with their abominations which have filled it from end to end with their uncleanness. [12] Therefore give not your daughters to their sons, neither take their daughters for your sons, and never seek their peace or prosperity, that you may be strong, and eat the good of the land, and leave it for an inheritance to your children for ever,' [13] And after all that has come upon us for our evil deeds and for our great guilt, seeing that thou, our God, hast punished us less than our iniquities deserved and hast given us such a remnant as this, [14] shall we break thy commandments again and intermarry with the peoples who practice these abominations? Wouldst thou not be angry with us till thou wouldst consume us, so that there should be no remnant, nor any to escape? [15] O LORD the God of Israel, thou art just, for we are left a remnant that has escaped, as at this day. Behold, we are before thee in our guilt, for none can stand before thee because of this."

10 While Ezra prayed and made confession, weeping and casting himself down before the house of God, a very great assembly of men, women, and children, gathered to him out of Israel; for the people wept bitterly. And Shĕc·a·nī′ah the son of Jĕ·hī′ĕl, of the sons of Ē′lăm, addressed Ezra: "We have broken faith with our God and have married foreign women from the peoples of the land, but even now there is hope for Israel in spite of this. Therefore let us make a covenant with our God to put away all these wives and their children, according to the counsel of my lord and of those who tremble at the commandment of

our God; and let it be done according to the law. [4] Arise, for it is your task, and we are with you; be strong and do it." [5] Then Ezra arose and made the leading priests and Lē′vītes and all Israel take oath that they would do as had been said. So they took the oath.

6 Then Ezra withdrew from before the house of God, and went to the chamber of Jē′hō–hā′nan the son of Ē·lī′a·shib, where he spent the night,[n] neither eating bread nor drinking water; for he was mourning over the faithlessness of the exiles. [7] And a proclamation was made throughout Judah and Jerusalem to all the returned exiles that they should assemble at Jerusalem, [8] and that if any one did not come within three days, by order of the officials and the elders all his property should be forfeited, and he himself banned from the congregation of the exiles.

9 Then all the men of Judah and Benjamin assembled at Jerusalem within the three days; it was the ninth month, on the twentieth day of the month. And all the people sat in the open square before the house of God, trembling because of this matter and because of the heavy rain. [10] And Ezra the priest stood up and said to them, "You have trespassed and married foreign women, and so increased the guilt of Israel. [11] Now then make confession to the LORD the God of your fathers, and do his will; separate yourselves from the peoples of the land and from the foreign wives." [12] Then all the assembly answered with a loud voice, "It is so; we must do as you have said. [13] But the people are many, and it is a time of heavy rain; we cannot stand in the open. Nor is this a work for one day or for two; for we have greatly transgressed in this matter. [14] Let our officials stand for the whole assembly; let all in our cities who have taken foreign wives come at appointed times, and with them the elders and judges of every city, till the fierce wrath of our God over this matter be averted from us." [15] Only Jonathan the son of Ăs′a·hĕl and Jäh·zēī′ah the son of Tĭk′vah opposed this, and Mĕ·shŭl′lam and Shăb′be·thaī the Lē′vīte supported them.

16 Then the returned exiles did so.

---

[m] Heb *a wall*
[n] 1 Esdras 9.2: Heb *where he went*

Ezra the priest selected men,[o] heads of fathers' houses, according to their fathers' houses, each of them designated by name. On the first day of the tenth month they sat down to examine the matter; [17] and by the first day of the first month they had come to the end of all the men who had married foreign women.

18 Of the sons of the priests who had married foreign women were found Māʾ·a·sēiʾah, Ĕ·līʹ·ēʹzẹr, Jāʹrĭb, and Gĕdʹ·a·līʹah, of the sons of Jĕshʹü·a the son of Jōʹza·dăk and his brethren. [19] They pledged themselves to put away their wives, and their guilt offering was a ram of the flock for their guilt. [20] Of the sons of Ĭmʹmẹr: Ha·nāʹnī and Zĕbʹ·a·dīʹah. [21] Of the sons of Hāʹrĭm: Māʾ·a·sēiʹah, Ĕ·līʹjah, Shĕ·māiʹah, Jĕ·hīʹĕl, and Ŭzʹ·zīʹah. [22] Of the sons of Păshʹhūr: Ĕlʹʹī·ō·ēʹnaī, Māʾ·a·sēiʹah, Ĭshʹma·ĕl, Nẹ·thănʹĕl, Jŏzʹa·băd, and Ĕl·āʹsah.

23 Of the Lēʹvītes: Jŏzʹa·băd, Shĭmʹēʹī, Kĕ·lāiʹah (that is, Kĕ·līʹta), Pĕthʹa·hīʹah, Judah, and Ĕ·līʹ·ēʹzẹr. [24] Of the singers: Ĕ·līʹa·shĭb. Of the gatekeepers: Shălʹlụm, Tēʹlĕm, and Ŭʹrī.

25 And of Israel: of the sons of Pāʹrŏsh: Ra·mīʹah, Ĭz·zīʹah, Mălʹchīʹ·jah, Mīʹja·mĭn, Ĕl·ē·āʹzar, Hăshʹa·bīʹah,[p] and Bĕ·nāʹī·ah. [26] Of the sons of

Ēʹlăm: Măt·ta·nīʹah, Zĕch·a·rīʹah, Jĕ·hīʹĕl, Ăbʹdī, Jĕrʹe·mŏth, and Ĕ·līʹjah. [27] Of the sons of Żătʹtü: Ĕlʹʹī·ō·ēʹnaī, Ĕ·līʹa·shĭb, Măt·ta·nīʹah, Jĕrʹe·mŏth, Zāʹbăd, and A·zīʹza. [28] Of the sons of Bēʹbaī were Jēʹhō·hāʹnạn, Hăn·a·nīʹah, Zăbʹbaī, and Ăthʹlaī. [29] Of the sons of Bāʹnī were Mĕ·shŭlʹlạm, Mălʹluch, A·dāiʹah, Jăshʹub, Shēʹal and Jĕrʹe·mŏth. [30] Of the sons of Pāʹhăth–mōʹăb: Ădʹna, Chēʹlăl, Bĕ·nāʹi·ah, Māʾ·a·sēiʹah, Măt·ta·nīʹah, Bĕzʹa·lĕl, Bĭnʹnü·ī, and Ma·năsʹseh. [31] Of the sons of Hāʹrĭm: Ĕ·līʹ·ēʹzẹr, Ĭs·shīʹjah, Mălʹchīʹjah, Shĕ·māiʹah, Shĭmʹē·ŏn, [32] Benjamin, Mălʹluch, and Shĕmʹ·a·rīʹah. [33] Of the sons of Hāʹshum: Măt·tēʹnaī, Măt·tạtʹtah, Zāʹbăd, Ĕ·līphʹe·lĕt, Jĕrʹe·maī, Ma·năsʹseh, and Shĭmʹē·ī. [34] Of the sons of Bāʹnī: Māʾ·a·dāʹī, Ămʹrăm, Ūʹĕl, [35] Bĕ·nāʹi·ah, Bĕ·dēiʹah, Chĕlʹü·hī, [36] Va·nīʹah, Mĕrʹe·mŏth, Ĕ·līʹa·shĭb, [37] Măt·ta·nīʹah, Măt·tēʹnaī, Jā·a·ʹsü. [38] Of the sons of Bĭnʹnü·ī:[q] Shĭmʹēʹī, [39] Shĕlʹe·mīʹah, Nathan, A·dāiʹah, [40] Măchʹnădʹe·baī Shāʹshaī, Shāʹraī, [41] Ăzʹa·rĕl, Shĕlʹe·mīʹah, Shĕmʹa·rīʹah, [42] Shălʹlụm, Ămʹ·a·rīʹah, and Joseph. [43] Of the sons of Nēʹbō: Jĕ·īʹĕl, Măt·tĭ·thīʹah, Zāʹbăd, Zĕ·bīʹna, Jădʹdaī, Jōʹĕl, and Bĕ·nāʹī·ah. [44] All these had married foreign women, and they put them away with their children.[r]

The Book of
Nehemiah

1　The words of Nē·hẹ·mīʹah the son of Hăc·a·līʹah.

Now it happened in the month of Chĭsʹlĕv, in the twentieth year, as I was in Sŭʹsa the capital, [2] that Ha·nāʹnī, one of my brethren, came with certain men out of Judah; and I asked them concerning the Jews that survived, who had escaped exile, and concerning Jerusalem. [3] And they said to me, "The survivors there in the province who escaped exile are in great trouble and shame; the wall of Jerusalem is broken down, and its gates are destroyed by fire."

4 When I heard these words I sat down and wept, and mourned for days; and I continued fasting and praying before the God of heaven. [5] And I said, "O LORD God of heaven, the great and terrible God who keeps covenant and steadfast love with those who love him and keep his commandments; [6] let thy ear be attentive, and thy eyes open, to hear the prayer of thy servant which I now pray before thee day and

[o] 1 Esdras 9.16 Syr: Heb *and there were selected Ezra, et*
[p] 1 Esdras 9.26 Gk: Heb *Malchijah*
[q] Gk: Heb *Bani, Binnui*
[r] 1 Esdras 9.36: Heb obscure

night for the people of Israel thy servants, confessing the sins of the people of Israel, which we have sinned against thee. Yea, I and my father's house have sinned. ⁷We have acted very corruptly against thee, and have not kept the commandments, the statutes, and the ordinances which thou didst command thy servant Moses. ⁸Remember the word which thou didst command thy servant Moses, saying, 'If you are unfaithful, I will scatter you among the peoples; ⁹but if you return to me and keep my commandments and do them, though your dispersed be under the farthest skies, I will gather them thence and bring them to the place which I have chosen, to make my name dwell there.' ¹⁰They are thy servants and thy people, whom thou hast redeemed by thy great power and by thy strong hand. ¹¹O LORD, let thy ear be attentive to the prayer of thy servant, and to the prayer of thy servants who delight to fear thy name; and give success to thy servant today, and grant him mercy in the sight of this man."

Now I was cupbearer to the king.

2 In the month of Nī'san, in the twentieth year of King Är-ta-xĕrx'ēṣ, when wine was before him, I took up the wine and gave it to the king. Now I had not been sad in his presence. ²And the king said to me, "Why is your face sad, seeing you are not sick? This is nothing else but sadness of the heart." Then I was very much afraid. ³I said to the king, "Let the king live for ever! Why should not my face be sad, when the city, the place of my fathers' sepulchres, lies waste, and its gates have been destroyed by fire?" ⁴Then the king said to me, "For what do you make request?" So I prayed to the God of heaven. ⁵And I said to the king, "If it pleases the king, and if your servant has found favor in your sight, that you send me to Judah, to the city of my fathers' sepulchres, that I may rebuild it." ⁶And the king said to me (the queen sitting beside him), "How long will you be gone, and when will you return?" So it pleased the king to send me; and I set him a time. ⁷And I said to the king, "If it pleases the king, let letters be given me to the governors of the province Beyond the River, that they may let me pass through until

I come to Judah; ⁸and a letter to Ā'saph, the keeper of the king's forest, that he may give me timber to make beams for the gates of the fortress of the temple, and for the wall of the city, and for the house which I shall occupy." And the king granted me what I asked, for the good hand of my God was upon me.

9 Then I came to the governors of the province Beyond the River, and gave them the king's letters. Now the king had sent with me officers of the army and horsemen. ¹⁰But when Sän-băl'lat the Hôr'ǫ-nīte and Tō-bī'ah the servant, the Ăm'mǫ-nīte, heard this, it displeased them greatly that some one had come to seek the welfare of the children of Israel.

11 So I came to Jerusalem and was there three days. ¹²Then I arose in the night, I and a few men with me; and I told no one what my God had put into my heart to do for Jerusalem. There was no beast with me but the beast on which I rode. ¹³I went out by night by the Valley Gate to the Jackal's Well and to the Dung Gate, and I inspected the walls of Jerusalem which were broken down and its gates which had been destroyed by fire. ¹⁴Then I went on to the Fountain Gate and to the King's Pool; but there was no place for the beast that was under me to pass. ¹⁵Then I went up in the night by the valley and inspected the wall; and I turned back and entered by the Valley Gate, and so returned. ¹⁶And the officials did not know where I had gone or what I was doing; and I had not yet told the Jews, the priests, the nobles, the officials, and the rest that were to do the work.

17 Then I said to them, "You see the trouble we are in, how Jerusalem lies in ruins with its gates burned. Come, let us build the wall of Jerusalem, that we may no longer suffer disgrace." ¹⁸And I told them of the hand of my God which had been upon me for good, and also of the words which the king had spoken to me. And they said, "Let us rise up and build." So they strengthened their hands for the good work. ¹⁹But when Sän·băl'lat the Hôr'ǫ-nīte and Tō-bī'ah the servant, the Ăm'mǫ-nīte, and Gē'shĕm the Arab heard of it, they derided us and despised us and said, "What is this thing that you are doing? Are you rebelling against the

king?" [20]Then I replied to them, "The God of heaven will make us prosper, and we his servants will arise and build; but you have no portion or right or memorial in Jerusalem."

3 Then Ė·lī'a·shĭb the high priest rose up with his brethren the priests and they built the Sheep Gate. They consecrated it and set its doors; they consecrated it as far as the Tower of the Hundred, as far as the Tower of Ha·nän'ĕl. [2]And next to him the men of Jericho built. And next to them[a] Zăc'cūr the son of Ĭm'rī built.

3 And the sons of Hăs·se·nä'ah built the Fish Gate; they laid its beams and set its doors, its bolts, and its bars. [4]And next to them Mĕr'e·mŏth the son of Ū·rī'ah, son of Hăk'kŏz repaired. And next to them Mĕ·shŭl'lam the son of Bĕr·e·chī'ah, son of Mĕ·shĕz'a·bĕl repaired. And next to them Zā'dŏk the son of Bā'a·na repaired. [5]And next to them the Tĕ·kō'ītes repaired; but their nobles did not put their necks to the work of their Lord.[b]

6 And Joi'a·da the son of Pa·sē'ah and Mĕ·shŭl'lam the son of Bĕs·o·dēi'ah repaired the Old Gate; they laid its beams and set its doors, its bolts, and its bars. [7]And next to them repaired Mĕ·la·tī'ah the Gĭb'ē·o·nīte and Jā'dŏn the Mē·rŏn'o·thīte, the men of Gĭb'ē·on and of Mīz'pah, who were under the jurisdiction of the governor of the province Beyond the River. [8]Next to them Ūz'zĭ·ĕl the son of Hăr·haī'ah, goldsmiths, repaired. Next to him Hăn·a·nī'ah, one of the perfumers, repaired; and they restored[c] Jerusalem as far as the Broad Wall. [9]Next to them Rĕph·aī'ah the son of Hūr, ruler of half the district of[d] Jerusalem, repaired. [10]Next to them Jĕ·daī'ah the son of Hăr·ü'măph repaired opposite his house; and next to him Hăt'tush the son of Hăsh·ăb·neī'ah repaired. [11]Măl·chī'jah the son of Hā'rĭm and Hăs'shub the son of Pā'hăth–mo'ăb repaired another section and the Tower of the Ovens. [12]Next to him Shăl'lum the son of Hăl·lō'hĕsh, ruler of half the district of[d] Jerusalem, repaired, he and his daughters.

13 Hā'nun and the inhabitants of Za·nō'ah repaired the Valley Gate; they rebuilt it and set its doors, its bolts, and its bars, and repaired a thousand cubits of the wall, as far as the Dung Gate.

14 Măl·chī'jah the son of Rē'chăb, ruler of the district of[d] Bĕth–hăc·chē'rĕm, repaired the Dung Gate; he rebuilt it and set its doors, its bolts, and its bars.

15 And Shăl'lum the son of Cŏl·hō'zĕh, ruler of the district of[d] Mīz'pah, repaired the Fountain Gate; he rebuilt it and covered it and set its doors, its bolts, and its bars; and he built the wall of the Pool of Shē'lah of the king's garden, as far as the stairs that go down from the City of David. [16]After him Nē·he·mī'ah the son of Ăz'buk, ruler of half the district of[d] Bĕth–zūr, repaired to a point opposite the sepulchres of David, to the artificial pool, and to the house of the mighty men. [17]After him the Lē'vītes repaired: Rē'hum the son of Bā'nī; next to him Hăsh·a·bī'ah, ruler of half the district of[d] Kē·ī'lah, repaired for his district. [18]After him their brethren repaired: Băv'vaī the son of Hĕn'a·dăd, ruler of half the district of[d] Kē·ī'lah; [19]next to him Ē'zer the son of Jĕsh·ü'a, ruler of Mīz'pah, repaired another section opposite the ascent to the armory at the Angle. [20]After him Bār'uch the son of Zăb'baī repaired another section from the Angle to the door of the house of Ė·lī'a·shĭb the high priest. [21]After him Mĕr'e·mŏth the son of Ū·rī'ah, son of Hăk'kŏz repaired another section from the door of the house of Ė·lī'a·shĭb to the end of the house of Eliashib. [22]After him the priests, the men of the Plain, repaired. [23]After them Benjamin and Hăs'shub repaired opposite their house. After them Ăz·a·rī'ah the son of Mā–a·sēi'ah, son of Ăn·a·nī'ah repaired beside his own house. [24]After him Bĭn'nü·ī the son of Hĕn'a·dăd repaired another section, from the house of Ăz·a·rī'ah to the Angle [25]and to the corner. Pā'lal the son of Ū'zaī repaired opposite the Angle and the tower projecting from the upper house of the king at the court of the guard. After him Pĕ·daī'ah the son of Pā'rŏsh [26]and the temple servants living[e] on Ō'phĕl repaired to a point opposite the Water Gate on the east and the projecting tower. [27]After

[a]Heb *him*   [b]Or *lords*   [c]Or *abandoned*
[d]Or *foreman of half the portion assigned to*
[e]Cn: Heb *were living*

him the Tē·kō'ītes repaired another section opposite the great projecting tower as far as the wall of Ō'phĕl.

28 Above the Horse Gate the priests repaired, each one opposite his own house. ²⁹After them Zā'dŏk the son of Ĭm'mer repaired opposite his own house. After him Shĕ·māi'ah the son of Shĕc·a·nī'ah, the keeper of the East Gate, repaired. ³⁰After him Hān·a·nī'ah the son of Shĕl·e·mī'ah and Hā'nun the sixth son of Zā'lăph repaired another section. After him Mĕ·shŭl'lam the son of Bĕr·e·chī'ah repaired opposite his chamber. ³¹After him Măl·chī'jah, one of the goldsmiths, repaired as far as the house of the temple servants and of the merchants, opposite the Muster Gate,ᶠ and to the upper chamber of the corner. ³²And between the upper chamber of the corner and the Sheep Gate the goldsmiths and the merchants repaired.

4 ⁹ Now when Săn·băl'lat heard that we were building the wall, he was angry and greatly enraged, and he ridiculed the Jews. ²And he said in the presence of his brethren and of the army of Sa·mâr'ĭ·a, "What are these feeble Jews doing? Will they restore things? Will they sacrifice? Will they finish up in a day? Will they revive the stones out of the heaps of rubbish, and burned ones at that?" ³Tō·bī'ah the Ăm'mo·nīte was by him, and he said, "Yes, what they are building—if a fox goes up on it he will break down their stone wall!" ⁴Hear, O our God, for we are despised; turn back their taunt upon their own heads, and give them up to be plundered in a land where they are captives. ⁵Do not cover their guilt, and let not their sin be blotted out from thy sight; for they have provoked thee to anger before the builders.

6 So we built the wall; and all the wall was joined together to half its height. For the people had a mind to work.

7ʰ But when Săn·băl'lat and Tō'·bī'ah and the Arabs and the Ăm'mo·nītes and the Ăsh'do·dītes heard that the repairing of the walls of Jerusalem was going forward and that the breaches were beginning to be closed, they were very angry; ⁸and they all plotted together to come and fight against Jerusalem and to cause confusion in it. ⁹And we prayed to our God,

and set a guard as a protection against them day and night.

10 But Judah said, "The strength of the burden-bearers is failing, and there is much rubbish; we are not able to work on the wall." ¹¹And our enemies said, "They will not know or see till we come into the midst of them and kill them and stop the work." ¹²When the Jews who lived by them came they said to us ten times, "From all the places where they liveⁱ they will come up against us."ʲ ¹³So in the lowest parts of the space behind the wall, in open places, I stationed the people according to their families, with their swords, their spears, and their bows. ¹⁴And I looked, and arose, and said to the nobles and to the officials and to the rest of the people, "Do not be afraid of them. Remember the Lord, who is great and terrible, and fight for your brethren, your sons, your daughters, your wives, and your homes."

15 When our enemies heard that it was known to us and that God had frustrated their plan, we all returned to the wall, each to his work. ¹⁶From that day on, half of my servants worked on construction, and half held the spears, shields, bows, and coats of mail; and the leaders stood behind all the house of Judah, ¹⁷who were building on the wall. Those who carried burdens were laden in such a way that each with one hand labored on the work and with the other held his weapon. ¹⁸And each of the builders had his sword girded at his side while he built. The man who sounded the trumpet was beside me. ¹⁹And I said to the nobles and to the officials and to the rest of the people, "The work is great and widely spread, and we are separated on the wall, far from one another. ²⁰In the place where you hear the sound of the trumpet, rally to us there. Our God will fight for us."

21 So we labored at the work, and half of them held the spears from the break of dawn till the stars came out. ²²I also said to the people at that time, "Let every man and his servant pass the night within Jerusalem, that they may be a guard for us by night and may labor by day." ²³So neither I nor my brethren nor my servants nor

ᶠOr *Hammiphkad Gate* ᵍCh 3.33 in Heb
ʰCh 4.1 in Heb ⁱCn: Heb *you return*
ʲCompare Gk Syr: Heb uncertain

the men of the guard who followed me, none of us took off our clothes; each kept his weapon in his hand.[k]

5 Now there arose a great outcry of the people and of their wives against their Jewish brethren. [2]For there were those who said, "With our sons and our daughters, we are many; let us get grain, that we may eat and keep alive." [3]There were also those who said, "We are mortgaging our fields, our vineyards, and our houses to get grain because of the famine." [4]And there were those who said, "We have borrowed money for the king's tax upon our fields and our vineyards. [5]Now our flesh is as the flesh of our brethren, our children are as their children; yet we are forcing our sons and our daughters to be slaves, and some of our daughters have already been enslaved; but it is not in our power to help it, for other men have our fields and our vineyards."

[6]I was very angry when I heard their outcry and these words. [7]I took counsel with myself, and I brought charges against the nobles and the officials. I said to them, "You are exacting interest, each from his brother." And I held a great assembly against them, [8]and said to them, "We, as far as we are able, have bought back our Jewish brethren who have been sold to the nations; but you even sell your brethren that they may be sold to us!" They were silent, and could not find a word to say. [9]So I said, "The thing that you are doing is not good. Ought you not to walk in the fear of our God to prevent the taunts of the nations our enemies? [10]Moreover I and my brethren and my servants are lending them money and grain. Let us leave off this interest. [11]Return to them this very day their fields, their vineyards, their olive orchards, and their houses, and the hundredth of money, grain, wine, and oil which you have been exacting of them." [12]Then they said, "We will restore these and require nothing from them. We will do as you say." And I called the priests, and took an oath of them to do as they had promised. [13]I also shook out my lap and said, "So may God shake out every man from his house and from his labor who does not perform this promise.

So may he be shaken out and emptied." And all the assembly said "Amen" and praised the Lord. And the people did as they had promised.

14 Moreover from the time that I was appointed to be their governor in the land of Judah, from the twentieth year to the thirty-second year of Ärta-xērx'ēṣ the king, twelve years, neither I nor my brethren ate the food allowance of the governor. [15]The former governors who were before me laid heavy burdens upon the people, and took from them food and wine, besides forty shekels of silver. Even their servants lorded it over the people. But I did not do so, because of the fear of God. [16]I also held to the work on this wall, and acquired no land; and all my servants were gathered there for the work. [17]Moreover there were at my table a hundred and fifty men, Jews and officials, besides those who came to us from the nations which were about us. [18]Now that which was prepared for one day was one ox and six choice sheep; fowls likewise were prepared for me, and every ten days skins of wine in abundance; yet with all this I did not demand the food allowance of the governor, because the servitude was heavy upon this people. [19]Remember for my good, O my God, all that I have done for this people.

6 Now when it was reported to Săn·băl'lạt and Tŏ'bī'ạh and to Gē'shĕm the Arab and to the rest of our enemies that I had built the wall, and that there was no breach left in it (although up to that time I had not set up the doors in the gates), [2]Săn·băl'lạt and Gē'shĕm sent to me, saying, "Come and let us meet together in one of the villages in the plain of Ō'nō." But they intended to do me harm. [3]And I sent messengers to them, saying, "I am doing a great work and I cannot come down. Why should the work stop while I leave it and come down to you?" [4]And they sent to me four times in this way and I answered them in the same manner. [5]In the same way Săn·băl'lạt for the fifth time sent his servant to me with an open letter in his hand. [6]In it was written, "It is reported among the nations, and Gē'shĕm[l] also says it, that you and the Jews intend to rebel; that

[k] Cn: Heb *each his weapon the water*
[l] Heb *Gashmu*

is why you are building the wall; and you wish to become their king, according to this report. ⁷And you have also set up prophets to proclaim concerning you in Jerusalem, 'There is a king in Judah.' And now it will be reported to the king according to these words. So now come, and let us take counsel together." ⁸Then I sent to him, saying, "No such things as you say have been done, for you are inventing them out of your own mind." ⁹For they all wanted to frighten us, thinking, "Their hands will drop from the work, and it will not be done." But now, O God, strengthen thou my hands.

10 Now when I went into the house of Shĕ·māi′ah the son of Dĕ·laī′ah, son of Mĕ·hĕt′a·bel, who was shut up, he said, "Let us meet together in the house of God, within the temple, and let us close the doors of the temple; for they are coming to kill you, at night they are coming to kill you." ¹¹But I said, "Should such a man as I flee? And what man such as I could go into the temple and live?ᵐ I will not go in." ²And I understood, and saw that God had not sent him, but he had pronounced the prophecy against me because Tō′bī′ah and Săn·băl′lat had hired him. ¹³For this purpose he was hired, that I should be afraid and act in this way and sin, and so they could give me an evil name, in order to taunt me. ¹⁴Remember Tō′bī′ah and Săn·băl′lat, O my God, according to these things that they did, and also the prophetess Nō–a·dī′ah and the rest of the prophets who wanted to make me afraid.

15 So the wall was finished on the twenty-fifth day of the month Ē′lul, in fifty-two days. ¹⁶And when all our enemies heard of it, all the nationsⁿ round about us were afraidⁿ and fell greatly in their own esteem; for they perceived that this work had been accomplished with the help of our God. ¹⁷Moreover in those days the nobles of Judah sent many letters to Tō·bī′ah, and Tobiah's letters came to them. ⁸For many in Judah were bound by oath to him, because he was the son-in-law of Shĕc·a·nī′ah the son of Ā′rah: and his son Jĕ′hō–hā′nan had taken the daughter of Mĕ·shŭl′lam the son of Bĕr·e·chī′ah as his wife. ¹⁹Also they spoke of his good deeds in my presence, and reported my words to him.

And Tō·bī′ah sent letters to make me afraid.

7 Now when the wall had been built and I had set up the doors, and the gatekeepers, the singers, and the Lē′vītes had been appointed, ²I gave my brother Ha·nā′nī and Hăn·a·nī′ah the governor of the castle charge over Jerusalem, for he was a more faithful and God-fearing man than many. ³And I said to them, "Let not the gates of Jerusalem be opened until the sun is hot; and while they are still standing guardᵒ let them shut and bar the doors. Appoint guards from among the inhabitants of Jerusalem, each to his station and each opposite his own house." ⁴The city was wide and large, but the people within it were few and no houses had been built.

5 Then God put it into my mind to assemble the nobles and the officials and the people to be enrolled by genealogy. And I found the book of the genealogy of those who came up at the first, and I found written in it: 6 These were the people of the province who came up out of the captivity of those exiles whom Nĕ·bü–chad·nĕz′zar the king of Babylon had carried into exile; they returned to Jerusalem and Judah, each to his town. ⁷They came with Zĕ·rŭb′ba·bel, Jĕsh′ü·a, Nē·he·mī′ah, Ăz·a·rī′ah, Rā–a·mī′ah, Nā·hăm′a·nī, Môr′dĕ·caī, Bĭl′shăn, Mĭs′pe·rĕth, Bĭg′vaī, Nē′-hum, Bā′a·nah.

The number of the men of the people of Israel: ⁸the sons of Pā′rŏsh, two thousand a hundred and seventy-two. ⁹The sons of Shĕph·a·tī′ah, three hundred and seventy-two. ¹⁰The sons of Ā′rah, six hundred and fifty-two. ¹¹The sons of Pā′hăth–mō′ăb, namely the sons of Jĕsh′ü·a and Jō′ăb, two thousand eight hundred and eighteen. ¹²The sons of Ē′lăm, a thousand two hundred and fifty-four. ¹³The sons of Zăt′tü, eight hundred and forty-five. ¹⁴The sons of Zăc′caī, seven hundred and sixty. ¹⁵The sons of Bĭn′nü·ī, six hundred and forty-eight. ¹⁶The sons of Bē′baī, six hundred and twenty-eight. ¹⁷The sons of Ăz′găd, two thousand three hundred and twenty-two. ¹⁸The sons of Ăd·o·nī′kam, six hundred and

ᵐOr *would go into the temple to save his life*
ⁿAnother reading is *saw* ᵒHeb obscure
7.6–73: Ezra 2.1–70.

sixty-seven. 19 The sons of Bĭg′vaī,
two thousand and sixty-seven. 20 The
sons of Ā′dĭn, six hundred and fifty-
five. 21 The sons of Ā′tẹr, namely of
Hĕz·ẹ·kī′ah, ninety-eight. 22 The sons
of Hā′shụm, three hundred and
twenty-eight. 23 The sons of Bē′zaī,
three hundred and twenty-four. 24 The
sons of Hā′rĭph, a hundred and twelve.
25 The sons of Gĭb′ē·ọn, ninety-five.
26 The men of Bethlehem and Nẹ-
tōph′ạh, a hundred and eighty-eight.
27 The men of Ăn′ạ·thōth, a hundred
and twenty-eight. 28 The men of Bĕth–
ăz′mạ·vĕth, forty-two. 29 The men of
Kĭr′ĭ·ăth–jē′ạ·rĭm, Chĕ·phī′rạh, and
Bẹ·ēr′ọth, seven hundred and forty-
three. 30 The men of Rā′mạh and Gē′bạ,
six hundred and twenty-one. 31 The
men of Mĭch′măs, a hundred and
twenty-two. 32 The men of Bĕth′ẹl
and Aī, a hundred and twenty-three.
33 The men of the other Nē′bō, fifty-
two. 34 The sons of the other Ē′lăm, a
thousand two hundred and fifty-
four. 35 The sons of Hā′rĭm, three
hundred and twenty. 36 The sons of
Jericho, three hundred and forty-
five. 37 The sons of Lŏd, Hā′dĭd, and
Ō′nō, seven hundred and twenty-one.
38 The sons of Sĕ·nā′ạh, three thousand
nine hundred and thirty.

39 The priests: the sons of Jĕ·daī′ạh,
namely the house of Jĕsh′ü·ạ, nine
hundred and seventy-three. 40 The sons
of Ĭm′mẹr, a thousand and fifty-two.
41 The sons of Păsh′hŭr, a thousand
two hundred and forty-seven. 42 The
sons of Hā′rĭm, a thousand and
seventeen.

43 The Lē′vītes: the sons of Jĕsh′-
ü·ạ, namely of Kăd′mĭ–ēl of the sons
of Hō′de·vạh, seventy-four. 44 The
singers: the sons of Ā′săph, a hundred
and forty-eight. 45 The gatekeepers:
the sons of Shăl′lụm, the sons of
Ā′tẹr, the sons of Tăl′mọn, the sons of
Ăk′kub, the sons of Hạ·tī′tạ, the sons
of Shō′baī, a hundred and thirty-
eight.

46 The temple servants:[p] the sons
of Zī′hạ, the sons of Hạ·sü′phạ, the
sons of Tăb·bā′ōth, 47 the sons of Kē′rŏs,
the sons of Sī′ạ, the sons of Pā′dŏn,
48 the sons of Lĕ·bā′nạ, the sons of
Hăg′ạ·bạ, the sons of Shăl′maī, 49 the
sons of Hā′nạn, the sons of Gĭd′dĕl,
the sons of Gā′hăr, 50 the sons of Rē-
aī′ạh, the sons of Rē′zĭn, the sons of
Nĕ·kō′dạ, 51 the sons of Găz′zạm, the
sons of Ŭz′zạ, the sons of Pạ·sē′ạh,
52 the sons of Bē′saī, the sons of Mĕ-
ü′nĭm, the sons of Nĕ·phüsh′ẹ·sĭm,
53 the sons of Băk′bụk, the sons of
Hạ·kū′phạ, the sons of Hăr′hŭr, 54 the
sons of Băz′lĭth, the sons of Mĕ·hī′dạ,
the sons of Hăr′shạ, 55 the sons of Băr′-
kŏs, the sons of Sĭs′ẹ·rạ, the sons of
Tē′mạh, 56 the sons of Nẹ·zī′ạh, the
sons of Hạ·tī′phạ.

57 The sons of Solomon's servants:
the sons of Sō′taī, the sons of Sō′phẹ-
rĕth, the sons of Pĕ·rī′dạ, 58 the sons of
Jā′ạ·lạ, the sons of Dăr′kŏn, the sons
of Gĭd′dĕl, 59 the sons of Shĕph·ạ·tī′ạh,
the sons of Hăt′tĭl, the sons of Pō′chẹ-
rĕth–hăz·zẹ·bā′ĭm, the sons of Ā′mŏn.

60 All the temple servants and the
sons of Solomon's servants were three
hundred and ninety-two.

61 The following were those who
came up from Tĕl–mē′lạh, Tĕl–hăr′-
shạ, Chē′rụb, Ăd′dŏn, and Ĭm′mẹr,
but they could not prove their fathers'
houses nor their descent, whether
they belonged to Israel: 62 the sons of
Dĕ·laī′ạh, the sons of Tō·bī′ạh, the sons
of Nĕ·kō′dạ, six hundred and forty-
two. 63 Also, of the priests: the sons of
Hō·baī′ạh, the sons of Hăk′kŏz, the
sons of Băr·zĭl′laī (who had taken a
wife of the daughters of Barzillai the
Gileadite and was called by their
name). 64 These sought their registration among those enrolled in the
genealogies, but it was not found there,
so they were excluded from the priesthood as unclean; 65 the governor told
them that they were not to partake
of the most holy food, until a priest
with Ū′rĭm and Thŭm′mĭm should
arise.

66 The whole assembly together was
forty-two thousand three hundred
and sixty, 67 besides their menservants
and maidservants, of whom there
were seven thousand three hundred
and thirty-seven; and they had two
hundred and forty-five singers, male
and female. 68 Their horses were seven
hundred and thirty-six, their mules two
hundred and forty-five,[q] 69 their camels
four hundred and thirty-five, and their
asses six thousand seven hundred and
twenty.

70 Now some of the heads of fathers' houses gave to the work. The

[p] Heb *nethinim*
[q] Ezra 2.66 and the margins of some Hebrew Mss: Heb lacks *their horses . . . forty-five*

overnor gave to the treasury a thou- and darics of gold, fifty basins, five undred and thirty priests' garments. And some of the heads of fathers' ouses gave into the treasury of the ⁄ork twenty thousand darics of gold nd two thousand two hundred minas f silver. ⁷²And what the rest of the eople gave was twenty thousand arics of gold, two thousand minas of ilver, and sixty-seven priests' gar- ments.

73 So the priests, the Lē′vītes, the atekeepers, the singers, some of the eople, the temple servants, and all srael, lived in their towns.

And when the seventh month had ome, the children of Israel were in } their towns. ¹And all the people } gathered as one man into the quare before the Water Gate; and they ›ld Ezra the scribe to bring the book f the law of Moses which the LORD ad given to Israel. ²And Ezra the riest brought the law before the as- ≥mbly, both men and women and all ‹ho could hear with understanding, ₁ the first day of the seventh month. ‹nd he read from it facing the square ≥fore the Water Gate from early ₁orning until midday, in the presence ⁷ the men and the women and those ‹ho could understand; and the ears of ‹l the people were attentive to the ⟩ok of the law. ⁴And Ezra the scribe ›ood on a wooden pulpit which they ›ad made for the purpose; and beside ₁m stood Măt·tĭ·thī′ah, Shē′ma, ·naī′ah, Ū·rī′ah, ′Hĭl·kī′ah, and Mā– sēi′ah on his right hand; and Pĕ– ₁ī′ah, Mīsh′a–ĕl, Măl·chī′jah, Hā′– ₁um, Hăsh–băd′da·nah, Zĕch·a·rī′ah, ₁d Mĕ·shŭl′lam on his left hand. ₁nd Ezra opened the book in the sight ⁷ all the people, for he was above all ₁e people; and when he opened it all ₁e people stood. ⁶And Ezra blessed ₁e LORD, the great God; and all the ≥ople answered, "Amen, Amen," ⁷ting up their hands; and they bowed ₁eir heads and worshiped the LORD ›ith their faces to the ground. ⁷Also ›sh′ü·a, Bā′nī, Shĕr·e·bī′ah, Jā′mĭn, ‹′kub, Shăb′be·thaī, Hō·dī′ah, Mā– sēi′ah, Kĕ·lī′ta, Ăz·a·rī′ah, Jō′za– ₁d, Hā′nan, Pĕ·lāi′ah, the Lē′vītes,ʳ ≥lped the people to understand the ›w, while the people remained in ₁eir places. ⁸And they read from the ›ok, from the law of God, clearly;ˢ

and they gave the sense, so that the people understood the reading.

9 And Nē·he·mī′ah, who was the governor, and Ezra the priest and scribe, and the Lē′vītes who taught the people said to all the people, "This day is holy to the LORD your God; do not mourn or weep." For all the people wept when they heard the words of the law. ¹⁰Then he said to them, "Go your way, eat the fat and drink sweet wine and send portions to him for whom nothing is prepared; for this day is holy to our Lord; and do not be grieved, for the joy of the LORD is your strength." ¹¹So the Lē′vītes stilled all the people, saying, "Be quiet, for this day is holy; do not be grieved." ¹²And all the people went their way to eat and drink and to send portions and to make great rejoicing, because they had understood the words that were declared to them.

13 On the second day the heads of fathers' houses of all the people, with the priests and the Lē′vītes, came to- gether to Ezra the scribe in order to study the words of the law. ¹⁴And they found it written in the law that the LORD had commanded by Moses that the people of Israel should dwell in booths during the feast of the seventh month, ¹⁵and that they should pub- lish and proclaim in all their towns and in Jerusalem, "Go out to the hills and bring branches of olive, wild olive, myrtle, palm, and other leafy trees to make booths, as it is written." ¹⁶So the people went out and brought them and made booths for themselves, each on his roof, and in their courts and in the courts of the house of God, and in the square at the Water Gate and in the square at the Gate of Ē′phra·ĭm. ¹⁷And all the assembly of those who had returned from the captivity made booths and dwelt in the booths; for from the days of Jĕsh′ü·a the son of Nŭn to that day the people of Israel had not done so. And there was very great rejoicing. ¹⁸And day by day, from the first day to the last day, he read from the book of the law of God. They kept the feast seven days; and on the eighth day there was a solemn as- sembly, according to the ordinance.

9 Now on the twenty-fourth day of this month the people of Israel

ʳ1 Esdras 9.48 Vg: Heb and the Levites
ˢOr with interpretation

were assembled with fasting and in sackcloth, and with earth upon their heads. [2] And the Israelites separated themselves from all foreigners, and stood and confessed their sins and the iniquities of their fathers. [3] And they stood up in their place and read from the book of the law of the Lord their God for a fourth of the day; for another fourth of it they made confession and worshiped the Lord their God. [4] Upon the stairs of the Lē'vītes stood Jĕsh'ü-a, Bā'nī, Kăd'mĭ–ĕl, Shĕb-a-nī'ah, Bŭn'nī, Shĕr-e-bī'ah, Bani, and Chē-nā'nī; and they cried with a loud voice to the Lord their God. [5] Then the Lē'vītes, Jĕsh'ü-a, Kăd'mĭ–ĕl, Bā'nī, Hăsh-ăb-neī'ah, Shĕr-e-bī'ah, Hō-dī'ah, Shĕb-a-nī'ah, and Pĕth-a-hī'ah said, "Stand up and bless the Lord your God from everlasting to everlasting. Blessed be thy glorious name which is exalted above all blessing and praise."

6 And Ezra said:' "Thou art the Lord, thou alone; thou hast made heaven, the heaven of heavens, with all their host, the earth and all that is on it, the seas and all that is in them; and thou preservest all of them; and the host of heaven worships thee. [7] Thou art the Lord, the God who didst choose Abram and bring him forth out of Ūr of the Chăl-dē'ạns and give him the name Abraham; [8] and thou didst find his heart faithful before thee, and didst make with him the covenant to give to his descendants the land of the Canaanite, the Hĭt'-tīte, the Ăm'ọ-rīte, the Pĕr'ĭz-zīte, the Jĕb'ū-sīte, and the Gīr'gạ-shīte; and thou hast fulfilled thy promise, for thou art righteous.

9 "And thou didst see the affliction of our fathers in Egypt and hear their cry at the Red Sea, [10] and didst perform signs and wonders against Pharaoh and all his servants and all the people of his land, for thou knewest that they acted insolently against our fathers; and thou didst get thee a name, as it is to this day. [11] And thou didst divide the sea before them, so that they went through the midst of the sea on dry land; and thou didst cast their pursuers into the depths, as a stone into mighty waters. [12] By a pillar of cloud thou didst lead them in the day, and by a pillar of fire in the night to light for them the way in which they should go. [13] Thou didst come down upon

Mount Sinai, and speak with them from heaven and give them right ordi-nances and true laws, good statute and commandments, [14] and thou dids make known to them thy holy sabbat) and command them commandment and statutes and a law by Moses th servant. [15] Thou didst give them brea from heaven for their hunger an: bring forth water for them from th rock for their thirst, and thou dids tell them to go in to possess the lan which thou hadst sworn to give them

16 "But they and our fathers acte presumptuously and stiffened thei neck and did not obey thy command ments; [17] they refused to obey, an were not mindful of the wonder which thou didst perform amon them; but they stiffened their nec. and appointed a leader to return t their bondage in Egypt. But thou ar a God ready to forgive, gracious an merciful, slow to anger and aboundin in steadfast love, and didst not forsak them. [18] Even when they had mad for themselves a molten calf and saic 'This is your God who brought you u out of Egypt,' and had committed grea blasphemies, [19] thou in thy great me cies didst not forsake them in th wilderness; the pillar of cloud whic led them in the way did not depa from them by day, nor the pillar o fire by night which lighted for them th way by which they should go. [20] Tho gavest thy good Spirit to instruct then and didst not withhold thy mann from their mouth, and gavest ther water for their thirst. [21] Forty year didst thou sustain them in the wi derness, and they lacked nothing; thei clothes did not wear out and their fee did not swell. [22] And thou didst giv them kingdoms and peoples, and did: allot to them every corner; so the took possession of the land of Sī'ho king of Hĕsh'bọn and the land of Ŏ king of Bā'shạn. [23] Thou didst mu tiply their descendants as the sta: of heaven, and thou didst bring ther into the land which thou hadst tol their fathers to enter and posses: [24] So the descendants went in and po: sessed the land, and thou didst subdu before them the inhabitants of th land, the Canaanites, and didst giv them into their hands, with their king and the peoples of the land, that the

'Gk: Heb lacks *and Ezra said*

might do with them as they would. ²⁵And they captured fortified cities and a rich land, and took possession of houses full of all good things, cisterns hewn out, vineyards, olive orchards and fruit trees in abundance; so they ate, and were filled and became fat, and delighted themselves in thy great goodness.

26 "Nevertheless they were disobedient and rebelled against thee and cast thy law behind their back and killed thy prophets, who had warned them in order to turn them back to thee, and they committed great blasphemies. ²⁷Therefore thou didst give them into the hand of their enemies, who made them suffer; and in the time of their suffering they cried to thee and thou didst hear them from heaven; and according to thy great mercies thou didst give them saviors who saved them from the hand of their enemies. ²⁸But after they had rest they did evil again before thee, and thou didst abandon them to the hand of their enemies, so that they had dominion over them; yet when they turned and cried to thee thou didst hear from heaven, and many times thou didst deliver them according to thy mercies. ²⁹And thou didst warn them in order to turn them back to thy law. Yet they acted presumptuously and did not obey thy commandments, but sinned against thy ordinances, by the observance of which a man shall live, and turned a stubborn shoulder and stiffened their neck and would not obey. ³⁰Many years thou didst bear with them, and didst warn them by thy Spirit through thy prophets; yet they would not give ear. Therefore thou didst give them into the hand of the peoples of the lands. ³¹Nevertheless in thy great mercies thou didst not make an end of them or forsake them; for thou art a gracious and merciful God.

32 "Now therefore, our God, the great and mighty and terrible God, who keepest covenant and steadfast love, let not all the hardship seem little to thee that has come upon us, upon our kings, our princes, our priests, our prophets, our fathers, and all thy people, since the time of the kings of Assyria until this day. ³³Yet thou hast been just in all that has come upon us, for thou hast dealt

faithfully and we have acted wickedly; ³⁴our kings, our princes, our priests, and our fathers have not kept thy law or heeded thy commandments and thy warnings which thou didst give them. ³⁵They did not serve thee in their kingdom, and in thy great goodness which thou gavest them, and in the large and rich land which thou didst set before them; and they did not turn from their wicked works. ³⁶Behold, we are slaves this day; in the land that thou gavest to our fathers to enjoy its fruit and its good gifts, behold, we are slaves. ³⁷And its rich yield goes to the kings whom thou hast set over us because of our sins; they have power also over our bodies and over our cattle at their pleasure, and we are in great distress."

38ᵘ Because of all this we make a firm covenant and write it, and our princes, our Lēʹvītes, and our priests set their seal to it.

10ᵛ Those who set their seal are Nēʹheˌmīʹah the governor, and Zĕdˌeˌkīʹah, ²Sēˑraiʹah, Ăzˌaˌrīʹah, Jĕrˌeˌmīʹah, ³Pǎshʹhūr, Ămˌaˌrīʹah, Mălʹchīʹjah, ⁴Hătʹtush, Shĕbˌaˌnīʹah, Mălʹluch, ⁵Hāʹrĭm, Mĕrʹeˌmŏth, Ōˌbaˌdīʹah, ⁶Daniel, Gĭnʹneˌthŏn, Bārʹuch, ⁷Mĕˑshulʹlam, Aˌbīʹjah, Mīʹjaˌmĭn, ⁸Māˌaˌzīʹah, Bĭlʹgaī, Shĕˑmāiʹah; these are the priests. ⁹And the Lēʹvītes: Jĕshʹüˑa the son of Ăzˌaˌnīʹah, Bĭnʹnüˑī of the sons of Hĕnʹaˌdǎd, Kădʹmĭˑĕl; ¹⁰and their brethren, Shĕbˌaˌnīʹah, Hōˑdīʹah, Kĕˑlīʹta, Pĕˑlāiʹah, Hāʹnan, ¹¹Mīʹca, Rēʹhŏb, Hăshˌaˑbīʹah, ¹²Zăcʹcŭr, Shĕrˌeˑbīʹah, Shĕbˌaˌnīʹah, ¹³Hōˑdīʹah, Bāʹnī, Bĕˑnīʹnü. ¹⁴The chiefs of the people: Pāʹrŏsh, Pāʹhăth-mōʹăb, Ĕʹlăm, Zătʹtü, Bāʹnī, ¹⁵Bŭnʹnī, Ăzʹgăd, Bēʹbaī, ¹⁶Ădˑoˑnīʹjah, Bĭgʹvaī, Āʹdĭn, ¹⁷Āʹter, Hĕzˌeˌkīʹah, Ăzʹzŭr, ¹⁸Hōˑdīʹah, Hāʹshum, Bēʹzaī, ¹⁹Hāʹrĭph, Ănʹaˌthŏth, Nēʹbaī, ²⁰Măgʹpĭˑăsh, Mĕˑshulʹlam, Hēʹzīr, ²¹Mĕˑshĕzʹaˑbĕl, Zāʹdŏk, Jădʹdüˑa, ²²Pĕlˌaˑtīʹah, Hāʹnan, Aˌnaiʹah, ²³Hōˑshēʹa, Hănˌaˌnīʹah, Hăsʹshub, ²⁴Hălˑlōʹhĕsh, Pĭlʹha, Shōʹbĕk, ²⁵Rēʹhum, Haˌshăbʹnah, Māˌaˑsēiʹah, ²⁶Aˌhīʹah, Hāʹnan, Āʹnăn, ²⁷Mălʹluch, Hāʹrĭm, Bāʹaˌnah.

28 The rest of the people, the priests, the Lēʹvītes, the gatekeepers, the singers, the temple servants, and all who have separated themselves from the

ᵘCh 10.1 in Heb ᵛCh 10.2 in Heb

peoples of the lands to the law of God, their wives, their sons, their daughters, all who have knowledge and understanding, [29] join with their brethren, their nobles, and enter into a curse and an oath to walk in God's law which was given by Moses the servant of God, and to observe and do all the commandments of the LORD our Lord and his ordinances and his statutes. [30] We will not give our daughters to the peoples of the land or take their daughters for our sons; [31] and if the peoples of the land bring in wares or any grain on the sabbath day to sell, we will not buy from them on the sabbath or on a holy day; and we will forego the crops of the seventh year and the exaction of every debt.

32 We also lay upon ourselves the obligation to charge ourselves yearly with the third part of a shekel for the service of the house of our God: [33] for the showbread, the continual cereal offering, the continual burnt offering, the sabbaths, the new moons, the appointed feasts, the holy things, and the sin offerings to make atonement for Israel, and for all the work of the house of our God. [34] We have likewise cast lots, the priests, the Lē'vītes, and the people, for the wood offering, to bring it into the house of our God, according to our fathers' houses, at times appointed, year by year, to burn upon the altar of the LORD our God, as it is written in the law. [35] We obligate ourselves to bring the first fruits of our ground and the first fruits of all fruit of every tree, year by year, to the house of the LORD; [36] also to bring to the house of our God, to the priests who minister in the house of our God, the first-born of our sons and of our cattle, as it is written in the law, and the firstlings of our herds and of our flocks; [37] and to bring the first of our coarse meal, and our contributions, the fruit of every tree, the wine and the oil, to the priests, to the chambers of the house of our God; and to bring to the Lē'vītes the tithes from our ground, for it is the Levites who collect the tithes in all our rural towns. [38] And the priest, the son of Aaron, shall be with the Lē'vītes when the Levites receive the tithes; and the Levites shall bring up the tithe of the tithes to the house of our God, to the chambers, to the storehouse. [39] For the people of Israel

and the sons of Lē'vī shall bring the contribution of grain, wine, and oil to the chambers, where are the vessels of the sanctuary, and the priests that minister, and the gatekeepers and the singers. We will not neglect the house of our God.

11 Now the leaders of the people lived in Jerusalem; and the rest of the people cast lots to bring one out of ten to live in Jerusalem the holy city, while nine tenths remained in the other towns. [2] And the people blessed all the men who willingly offered to live in Jerusalem.

3 These are the chiefs of the province who lived in Jerusalem; but in the towns of Judah every one lived on his property in their towns: Israel, the priests, the Lē'vītes, the temple servants, and the descendants of Solomon's servants. [4] And in Jerusalem lived certain of the sons of Judah and of the sons of Benjamin. Of the sons of Judah: Ā·thaī'ah the son of Ŭz·zī'ah, son of Zĕch·a·rī'ah, son of Ăm·a·rī'ah, son of Shĕph·a·tī'ah, son of Mă–hăl'a·lĕl, of the sons of Pĕr'ēz; [5] and Mā–a·sēī'ah the son of Bär'uch, son of Cŏl–hō'zĕh, son of Ha·zaī'ah, son of A·daī'ah, son of Joi'a·rīb, son of Zĕch·a·rī'ah, son of the Shī·lo'nīte. [6] All the sons of Pĕr'ēz who lived in Jerusalem were four hundred and sixty-eight valiant men.

7 And these are the sons of Benjamin: Săl'lü the son of Mĕ·shŭl'lam, son of Jō'ĕd, son of Pĕ·daī'ah, son of Kō'laī'ah, son of Mā–a·sēī'ah, son of Ī'thī–ĕl, son of Jĕ·shaī'ah. [8] And after him Găb·bā'ī, Săl'laī, nine hundred and twenty-eight. [9] Jō'ĕl the son of Zĭch'rī was their overseer; and Judah the son of Hăs·se·nü'ah was second over the city.

10 Of the priests: Jĕ·daī'ah the son of Joi'a·rīb, Jā'chĭn, [11] Sĕ'raī'ah the son of Hĭl'kī'ah, son of Mĕ·shŭl'lam, son of Zā'dŏk, son of Mĕ·rā'ī·ŏth, son of A·hī'tŭb, ruler of the house of God, [12] and their brethren who did the work of the house, eight hundred and twenty-two; and A·daī'ah the son of Jĕ·rō'hăm, son of Pĕl·a·lī'ah, son of Ăm'zī, son of Zĕch·a·rī'ah, son of Păsh'hūr, son of Măl·chī'jah, [13] and his brethren, heads of fathers' houses, two hundred and forty-two; and A·măsh'saī, the son Āz'a·rĕl, son of

11.3-22: 1 Chron 9.2-34.

Äh'zaī, son of Mĕ·shĭl'lĕ·mŏth, son of Ĭm'mẹr, ¹⁴and their brethren, mighty men of valor, a hundred and twenty-eight; their overseer was Zăb'dĭ·ĕl the son of Hăg·gẹ·dō'lĭm.

15 And of the Lē'vītes: Shĕ·māi'ạh the son of Hăs'shub, son of Ăz·rī'kăm, son of Hăsh·ạ·bī'ạh, son of Bŭn'nī; ¹⁶and Shăb'bẹ·thaī and Jō'zạ·băd, of the chiefs of the Lē'vītes, who were over the outside work of the house of God; ¹⁷and Măt·tạ·nī'ạh the son of Mī'cạ, son of Zăb'dī, son of Ā'săph, who was the leader to begin the thanksgiving in prayer, and Băk·bü·kī'ạh, the second among his brethren; and Ăb'dạ the son of Shăm'mū–ạ, son of Gă'lăl, son of Jĕ·dü'thụn. ¹⁸All the Lē'vītes in the holy city were two hundred and eighty-four.

19 The gatekeepers, Ăk'kụb, Tăl'mọn and their brethren, who kept watch at the gates, were a hundred and seventy-two. ²⁰And the rest of Israel, and of the priests and the Lē'vītes, were in all the towns of Judah, every one in his inheritance. ²¹But the temple servants lived on Ō'phĕl; and Zī'hạ and Gĭsh'pạ were over the temple servants.

22 The overseer of the Lē'vītes in Jerusalem was Ŭz'zī the son of Bā'nī, son of Hăsh·ạ·bī'ạh, son of Măt·tạ·nī'ạh, son of Mī'cạ, of the sons of Ā'săph, the singers, over the work of the house of God. ²³For there was a command from the king concerning them, and a settled provision for the singers, as every day required. ²⁴And Pĕth·ạ·hī'ạh the son of Mĕ·shĕz'ạ·bĕl, of the sons of Zē'rạh the son of Judah, was at the king's hand in all matters concerning the people.

25 And as for the villages, with their fields, some of the people of Judah lived in Kĭr'ī·ăth–är'bạ and its villages, and in Dī'bŏn and its villages, and in Jĕ·kăb'zē·ĕl and its villages, ²⁶and in Jĕsh'ü·ạ and in Mō'lạ·dạh and Bĕth–pĕl'ĕt, ²⁷in Hā'zär–shü'ạl, in Bē'ẹr–shē'bạ and its villages, ²⁸in Zĭk'lăg, in Mĕ·cō'nạh and its villages, ²⁹in Ĕn–rĭm'mŏn, in Zō'rạh, in Jär'mŭth, ³⁰Zạ·nō'ạh, Ạ·dŭl'lạm, and their villages, Lā'chĭsh and its fields, and Ạ·zē'kạh and its villages. So they encamped from Bē'ẹr–shē'bạ to the valley of Hĭn'nọm. ³¹The people of Benjamin also lived from Gē'bạ onward, at Mĭch'măsh, Āi'jạ, Bĕth'ĕl

and its villages, ³²Ăn'ạ·thŏth, Nŏb, Ăn·ạ·nī'ạh, ³³Hā'zŏr, Rā'mạh, Gĭt'tạ·ĭm, ³⁴Hā'dĭd, Zĕ·bō'ĭm, Nĕ·băl'lạt, ³⁵Lŏd, and Ō'nō, the valley of craftsmen. ³⁶And certain divisions of the Lē'vītes in Judah were joined to Benjamin.

12 These are the priests and the Lē'vītes who came up with Zĕ·rŭb'bạ·bĕl the son of Shĕ–ăl'tĭ·ĕl, and Jĕsh'ü·ạ: Sĕ·rāi'ạh, Jĕr·ẹ·mī'ạh, Ezra, ²Ăm·ạ·rī'ạh, Măl'lụch, Hăt'tush, ³Shĕc·ạ·nī'ạh, Rĕ'hụm, Mĕr'ẹ·mŏth, ⁴Ĭd'dō, Gĭn'nẹ·thoi, Ạ·bī'jạh, ⁵Mī'jạ·mĭn, Mā–ạ·dī'ạh, Bĭl'gạh, ⁶Shĕ·māi'ạh, Jŏi'ạ·rĭb, Jĕ·daī'ạh, ⁷Săl'lü, Ā'mŏk, Hĭl'kī'ạh, Jĕ·daī'ạh. These were the chiefs of the priests and of their brethren in the days of Jĕsh'ü·ạ.

8 And the Lē'vītes: Jĕsh'ü·ạ, Bĭn'nü·ī, Kăd'mĭ–ĕl, Shĕr·ẹ·bī'ạh, Judah, and Măt·tạ·nī'ạh, who with his brethren was in charge of the songs of thanksgiving. ⁹And Băk·bü·kī'ạh and Ŭn'nō their brethren stood opposite them in the service. ¹⁰And Jĕsh'ü·ạ was the father of Jŏi'ạ·kĭm, Joiakim the father of Ĕ·lī'ạ·shĭb, Eliashib the father of Jŏi'ạ·dạ, ¹¹Jŏi'ạ·dạ the father of Jonathan, and Jonathan the father of Jăd'dü–ạ.

12 And in the days of Jŏi'ạ·kĭm were priests, heads of fathers' houses: of Sĕ·rāi'ạh, Mĕ·raī'ạh; of Jĕr·ẹ·mī'ạh, Hăn·ạ·nī'ạh; ¹³of Ezra, Mĕ·shŭl'lạm; of Ăm·ạ·rī'ạh, Jĕ'hō–hā'nạn; ¹⁴of Măl'lu·chī, Jonathan; of Shĕb·ạ·nī'ạh, Joseph; ¹⁵of Hā'rĭm, Ăd'na; of Mĕ·rā'ĭ·ŏth, Hĕl'kaī; ¹⁶of Ĭd'dō, Zĕch·ạ·rī'ạh; of Gĭn'nẹ·thŏn, Mĕ·shŭl'lạm; ¹⁷of Ạ·bī'jạh, Zĭch'rī; of Mī·nī'ạ·mĭn, Mō·ạ·dī'ạh, Pĭl'taī; ¹⁸of Bĭl'gạh, Shăm'mū–ạ; of Shĕ·māi'ạh, Jĕ·hŏn'ạ·than; ¹⁹of Jŏi'ạ·rĭb, Măt·tẹ·naī; of Jĕ·daī'ạh, Ŭz'zī; ²⁰of Săl'laī, Kăl'laī; of Ā'mŏk, Ē'ber; ²¹of Hĭl·kī'ạh, Hăsh·ạ·bī'ạh; of Jĕ·daī'ạh, Nẹ·thăn'ĕl.

22 As for the Lē'vītes, in the days of Ĕ·lī'ạ·shĭb, Jŏi'ạ·dạ, Jō·hā'nạn, Jăd'dü–ạ, there were recorded the heads of fathers' houses; also the priests until the reign of Dạ·rī'ŭs the Persian. ²³The sons of Lē'vī, heads of fathers' houses, were written in the Book of the Chronicles until the days of Jō·hā'nạn the son of Ĕ·lī'ạ·shĭb. ²⁴And the chiefs of the Lē'vītes: Hăsh·ạ·bī'ạh, Shĕr·ẹ·bī'ạh, and Jĕsh'ü·ạ the son of Kăd'mĭ–ĕl, with their brethren over against them, to praise and to

give thanks, according to the commandment of David the man of God, watch corresponding to watch. ²⁵ Măt-ta·nī′ah, Băk·bü·kī′ah, Ō·ba·dī′ah, Mĕ·shŭl′lam, Tăl′mon, and Ăk′kub were gatekeepers standing guard at the storehouses of the gates. ²⁶ These were in the days of Joi′a·kĭm the son of Jĕsh′ü·a son of Jō′za·dăk, and in the days of Nē·he·mī′ah the governor and of Ezra the priest the scribe.

27 And at the dedication of the wall of Jerusalem they sought the Lē′vītes in all their places, to bring them to Jerusalem to celebrate the dedication with gladness, with thanksgivings and with singing, with cymbals, harps, and lyres. ²⁸ And the sons of the singers gathered together from the circuit round Jerusalem and from the villages of the Ne·tŏph′a·thītes; ²⁹ also from Bĕth–gĭl′gal and from the region of Gē′ba and Az′ma·vĕth; for the singers had built for themselves villages around Jerusalem. ³⁰ And the priests and the Lē′vītes purified themselves; and they purified the people and the gates and the wall.

31 Then I brought up the princes of Judah upon the wall, and appointed two great companies which gave thanks and went in procession. One went to the right upon the wall to the Dung Gate; ³² and after them went Hō·shaī′ah and half of the princes of Judah, ³³ and Ăz·a·rī′ah, Ezra, Mĕ·shŭl′lam, ³⁴ Judah, Benjamin, Shĕ·māi′ah, and Jĕr·e·mī′ah, ³⁵ and certain of the priests' sons with trumpets: Zĕch·a·rī′ah the son of Jonathan, son of Shĕ·māi′ah, son of Măt·ta·nī′ah, son of Mī·cāi′ah, son of Zăc′cŭr, son of Ā′săph; ³⁶ and his kinsmen, Shĕ·māi′ah, Ăz′a·rĕl, Mĭl′a·laī, Gĭl′a·laī, Mā′aī, Ne·thăn′ĕl, Judah, and Ha·nā′nī, with the musical instruments of David the man of God; and Ezra the scribe went before them. ³⁷ At the Fountain Gate they went up straight before them by the stairs of the city of David, at the ascent of the wall, above the house of David, to the Water Gate on the east.

38 The other company of those who gave thanks went to the left, and I followed them with half of the people, upon the wall, above the Tower of the Ovens, to the Broad Wall, ³⁹ and above the Gate of Ē′phra·ĭm, and by the Old Gate, and by the Fish Gate and the

Tower of Ha·năn′ĕl and the Tower of the Hundred, to the Sheep Gate; and they came to a halt at the Gate of the Guard. ⁴⁰ So both companies of those who gave thanks stood in the house of God, and I and half of the officials with me; ⁴¹ and the priests Ē·lī′a·kĭm, Mā·a·sēi′ah, Mĭ·nī′a·mĭn, Mī·cāi′ah, Ĕl′ī-ō-ē′nāi, Zĕch·a·rī′ah, and Hăn·a·nī′ah, with trumpets; ⁴² and Mā·a·sēi′ah, Shĕ·māi′ah, Ĕl·ē·ā′zar, Ŭz′zī, Jē′hō·hā′nan, Măl·chī′jah, Ē′lăm, and Ē′zer. And the singers sang with Jĕz·ra·hī′ah as their leader. ⁴³ And they offered great sacrifices that day and rejoiced, for God had made them rejoice with great joy; the women and children also rejoiced. And the joy of Jerusalem was heard afar off.

44 On that day men were appointed over the chambers for the stores, the contributions, the first fruits, and the tithes, to gather into them the portions required by the law for the priests and for the Lē′vītes according to the fields of the towns; for Judah rejoiced over the priests and the Levites who ministered. ⁴⁵ And they performed the service of their God and the service of purification, as did the singers and the gatekeepers, according to the command of David and his son Solomon. ⁴⁶ For in the days of David and Ā′săph of old there was a chief of the singers, and there were songs of praise and thanksgiving to God. ⁴⁷ And all Israel in the days of Zĕ·rŭb′ba·bĕl and in the days of Nē·he·mī′ah gave the daily portions for the singers and the gatekeepers; and they set apart that which was for the Lē′vītes; and the Levites set apart that which was for the sons of Aaron.

13 On that day they read from the book of Moses in the hearing of the people; and in it was found written that no Ăm′mo·nīte or Mō′ab·īte should ever enter the assembly of God; ² for they did not meet the children of Israel with bread and water, but hired Bā′lăam against them to curse them—yet our God turned the curse into a blessing. ³ When the people heard the law, they separated from Israel all those of foreign descent.

4 Now before this, Ē·lī′a·shĭb the priest, who was appointed over the chambers of the house of our God,

and who was connected with Tō·bī'ah, 5 prepared for Tō·bī'ah a large chamber where they had previously put the cereal offering, the frankincense, the vessels, and the tithes of grain, wine, and oil, which were given by commandment to the Lē'vītes, singers, and gatekeepers, and the contributions for the priests. 6 While this was taking place I was not in Jerusalem, for in the thirty-second year of Är-ta-xĕrx'ēṣ king of Babylon I went to the king. And after some time I asked leave of the king 7 and came to Jerusalem, and I then discovered the evil that Ė-lī'a-shīb had done for Tō·bī'ah, preparing for him a chamber in the courts of the house of God. 8 And I was very angry, and I threw all the household furniture of Tō·bī'ah out of the chamber. 9 Then I gave orders and they cleansed the chambers; and I brought back thither the vessels of the house of God, with the cereal offering and the frankincense.

10 I also found out that the portions of the Lē'vītes had not been given to them; so that the Levites and the singers, who did the work, had fled each to his field. 11 So I remonstrated with the officials and said, "Why is the house of God forsaken?" And I gathered them together and set them in their stations. 12 Then all Judah brought the tithe of the grain, wine, and oil into the storehouses. 13 And I appointed as treasurers over the storehouses Shĕl·e·mī'ah the priest, Zā'dŏk the scribe, and Pĕ·dāi'ah of the Lē'-vītes, and as their assistant Hā'nan the son of Zăc'cŭr, son of Măt·ta·nī'ah, for they were counted faithful; and their duty was to distribute to their brethren. 14 Remember me, O my God, concerning this, and wipe not out my good deeds that I have done for the house of my God and for his service.

15 In those days I saw in Judah men treading wine presses on the sabbath, and bringing in heaps of grain and loading them on asses; and also wine, grapes, figs, and all kinds of burdens, which they brought into Jerusalem on the sabbath day; and I warned them on the day when they sold food. 16 Men of Tyre also, who lived in the city, brought in fish and all kinds of wares and sold them on the sabbath to the people of Judah, and in

Jerusalem. 17 Then I remonstrated with the nobles of Judah and said to them, "What is this evil thing which you are doing, profaning the sabbath day? 18 Did not your fathers act in this way, and did not our God bring all this evil on us and on this city? Yet you bring more wrath upon Israel by profaning the sabbath."

19 When it began to be dark at the gates of Jerusalem before the sabbath, I commanded that the doors should be shut and gave orders that they should not be opened until after the sabbath. And I set some of my servants over the gates, that no burden might be brought in on the sabbath day. 20 Then the merchants and sellers of all kinds of wares lodged outside Jerusalem once or twice. 21 But I warned them and said to them, "Why do you lodge before the wall? If you do so again I will lay hands on you." From that time on they did not come on the sabbath. 22 And I commanded the Lē'vītes that they should purify themselves and come and guard the gates, to keep the sabbath day holy. Remember this also in my favor, O my God, and spare me according to the greatness of thy steadfast love.

23 In those days also I saw the Jews who had married women of Äsh'dŏd, Ăm'mon, and Mō'ăb; 24 and half of their children spoke the language of Äsh'dŏd, and they could not speak the language of Judah, but the language of each people. 25 And I contended with them and cursed them and beat some of them and pulled out their hair; and I made them take oath in the name of God, saying, "You shall not give your daughters to their sons, or take their daughters for your sons or for yourselves. 26 Did not Solomon king of Israel sin on account of such women? Among the many nations there was no king like him, and he was beloved by his God, and God made him king over all Israel; nevertheless foreign women made even him to sin. 27 Shall we then listen to you and do all this great evil and act treacherously against our God by marrying foreign women?"

28 And one of the sons of Jĕ·hoi'a·da, the son of Ė-lī'a·shīb the high priest, was the son-in-law of Săn·băl'lat the Hôr'o·nīte; therefore I chased him from me. 29 Remember them, O my

God, because they have defiled the priesthood and the covenant of the priesthood and the Lē'vītes.

30 Thus I cleansed them from everything foreign, and I established the duties of the priests and Lē'vītes, each in his work; [31] and I provided for the wood offering, at appointed times, and for the first fruits. Remember me, O my God, for good.

The Book of
Esther

1 In the days of A·hăş'ū–ē'rus, the Ahasu–erus who reigned from India to Ethiopia over one hundred and twenty-seven provinces, [2] in those days when King A·hăş'ū–ē'rus sat on his royal throne in Sū'sa the capital, [3] in the third year of his reign he gave a banquet for all his princes and servants, the army chiefs[a] of Persia and Mēd'ī·a and the nobles and governors of the provinces being before him, [4] while he showed the riches of his royal glory and the splendor and pomp of his majesty for many days, a hundred and eighty days. [5] And when these days were completed, the king gave for all the people present in Sū'sa the capital, both great and small, a banquet lasting for seven days, in the court of the garden of the king's palace. [6] There were white cotton curtains and blue hangings caught up with cords of fine linen and purple to silver rings[b] and marble pillars, and also couches of gold and silver on a mosaic pavement of porphyry, marble, mother-of-pearl and precious stones. [7] Drinks were served in golden goblets, goblets of different kinds, and the royal wine was lavished according to the bounty of the king. [8] And drinking was according to the law, no one was compelled; for the king had given orders to all the officials of his palace to do as every man desired. [9] Queen Vash'tī also gave a banquet for the women in the palace which belonged to King A·hăş'ū–ē'rus.

10 On the seventh day, when the heart of the king was merry with wine, he commanded Mĕ·hū'man, Bīz'tha, Hār·bō'na, Big'tha and A·băg'tha, Zē'thar and Căr'kăs, the seven eunuchs who served King A·hăş'ū–ē'rus as chamberlains, [11] to bring Queen Văsh'tī before the king with her royal crown, in order to show the peoples and the princes her beauty; for she was fair to behold. [12] But Queen Văsh'tī refused to come at the king's command conveyed by the eunuchs. At this the king was enraged, and his anger burned within him.

13 Then the king said to the wise men who knew the times – for this was the king's procedure toward all who were versed in law and judgment, [14] the men next to him being Cär·shē'na, Shē'thar, Ăd·mā'tha, Tār'-shīsh, Mĕ'rēş, Mār·sē'na, and Mĕmū'can, the seven princes of Persia and Mēd'ī·a, who saw the king's face, and sat first in the kingdom – : [15] "According to the law, what is to be done to Queen Văsh'tī, because she has not performed the command of King A·hăş'ū–ē'rus conveyed by the eunuchs?" [16] Then Mĕ·mū'can said in presence of the king and the princes, "Not only to the king has Queen Văsh'tī done wrong, but also to all the princes and all the peoples who are in all the provinces of King A·hăş'ū–ē'rus. [17] For this deed of the queen will be made known to all women, causing them to look with contempt upon their husbands, since they will say, 'King A·hăş'ū–ē'rus commanded Queen Văsh'tī to be brought before him, and she did not come.' [18] This very day the ladies of Persia and Mēd'ī·a who have heard of the queen's behavior will be telling it to all the king's princes, and there will be contempt and wrath in plenty. [19] If it please the king, let a royal order go forth from him, and let it be written among the laws of the

a Heb the army   b Or rods

Persians and the Mēdeş so that it may not be altered, that Vǎsh'tī is to come no more before King A·hǎş'ū-ē'rus; and let the king give her royal position to another who is better than she. ²⁰So when the decree made by the king is proclaimed throughout all his kingdom, vast as it is, all women will give honor to their husbands, high and low." ²¹This advice pleased the king and the princes, and the king did as Mě·mū'can proposed; ²²he sent letters to all the royal provinces, to every province in its own script and to every people in its own language, that every man be lord in his own house and speak according to the language of his people.

2 After these things, when the anger of King A·hǎş'ū-ē'rus had abated, he remembered Vǎsh'tī and what she had done and what had been decreed against her. ²Then the king's servants who attended him said, "Let beautiful young virgins be sought out for the king. ³And let the king appoint officers in all the provinces of his kingdom to gather all the beautiful young virgins to the harem in Sǔ'sa the capital, under custody of Hěg'aī the king's eunuch who is in charge of the women; let their ointments be given them. ⁴And let the maiden who pleases the king be queen instead of Vǎsh'tī." This pleased the king, and he did so.

5 Now there was a Jew in Sǔ'sa the capital whose name was Môr'dě-caī, the son of Jā'īr, son of Shǐm'ē-ī, son of Kǐsh, a Benjaminite, ⁶who had been carried away from Jerusalem among the captives carried away with Jěc·o·nī'ah king of Judah, whom Ně·bū·chad·něz'zar king of Babylon had carried away. ⁷He had brought up Ha·dǎs'sah, that is Esther, the daughter of his uncle, for she had neither father nor mother; the maiden was beautiful and lovely, and when her father and her mother died, Môr'dě-caī adopted her as his own daughter. ⁸So when the king's order and his edict were proclaimed, and when many maidens were gathered in Sǔ'sa the capital in custody of Hěg'aī, Esther also was taken into the king's palace and put in custody of Hegai who had charge of the women. ⁹And the maiden pleased him and won his favor; and he quickly provided her with her ointments and her portion of food, and

with seven chosen maids from the king's palace, and advanced her and her maids to the best place in the harem. ¹⁰Esther had not made known her people or kindred, for Môr'dě-caī had charged her not to make it known. ¹¹And every day Môr'dě-caī walked in front of the court of the harem, to learn how Esther was and how she fared.

12 Now when the turn came for each maiden to go in to King A·hǎş'ū-ē'rus, after being twelve months under the regulations for the women, since this was the regular period of their beautifying, six months with oil of myrrh and six months with spices and ointments for women— ¹³when the maiden went in to the king in this way she was given whatever she desired to take with her from the harem to the king's palace. ¹⁴In the evening she went, and in the morning she came back to the second harem in custody of Sha·ǎsh'gǎz the king's eunuch who was in charge of the concubines; she did not go in to the king again, unless the king delighted in her and she was summoned by name.

15 When the turn came for Esther the daughter of Ǎb'ǐ·hāil the uncle of Môr'dě-caī, who had adopted her as his own daughter, to go in to the king, she asked for nothing except what Hěg'aī the king's eunuch, who had charge of the women, advised. Now Esther found favor in the eyes of all who saw her. ¹⁶And when Esther was taken to King A·hǎş'ū-ē'rus into his royal palace in the tenth month, which is the month of Tē'běth, in the seventh year of his reign, ¹⁷the king loved Esther more than all the women, and she found grace and favor in his sight more than all the virgins, so that he set the royal crown on her head and made her queen instead of Vǎsh'tī. ¹⁸Then the king gave a great banquet to all his princes and servants; it was Esther's banquet. He also granted a remission of taxes𝒸 to the provinces, and gave gifts with royal liberality.

19 When the virgins were gathered together the second time, Môr'dě-caī was sitting at the king's gate. ²⁰Now Esther had not made known her kindred or her people, as Môr'dě-caī had charged her; for Esther obeyed Mordecai just as when she was brought up

𝒸Or *a holiday*

by him. 21And in those days, as Môr'-dĕ·caī was sitting at the king's gate, Bĭg'thăn and Tē'rĕsh, two of the king's eunuchs, who guarded the threshold, became angry and sought to lay hands on King A·hăs'ū-ē'rŭs. 22And this came to the knowledge of Môr'dĕ·caī, and he told it to Queen Esther, and Esther told the king in the name of Mordecai. 23When the affair was investigated and found to be so, the men were both hanged on the gallows. And it was recorded in the Book of the Chronicles in the presence of the king.

3 After these things King A·hăs'ū-ē'rŭs promoted Hā'man the Ag'-a·gīte, the son of Hăm·mĕ·dā'tha, and advanced him and set his seat above all the princes who were with him. 2And all the king's servants who were at the king's gate bowed down and did obeisance to Hā'man; for the king had so commanded concerning him. But Môr'dĕ·caī did not bow down or do obeisance. 3Then the king's servants who were at the king's gate said to Môr'dĕ·caī, "Why do you transgress the king's command?" 4And when they spoke to him day after day and he would not listen to them, they told Hā'man, in order to see whether Môr'dĕ·caī's words would avail; for he had told them that he was a Jew. 5And when Hā'man saw that Môr'-dĕ·caī did not bow down or do obeisance to him, Haman was filled with fury. 6But he disdained to lay hands on Môr'dĕ·caī alone. So, as they had made known to him the people of Mordecai, Hā'man sought to destroy all the Jews, the people of Mordecai, throughout the whole kingdom of A·hăs'ū-ē'rŭs.

7 In the first month, which is the month of Nī'san, in the twelfth year of King A·hăs'ū-ē'rŭs, they cast Pür, that is the lot, before Hā'man day after day; and they cast it month after month till the twelfth month, which is the month of A·där'. 8Then Hā'man said to King A·hăs'ū-ē'rŭs, "There is a certain people scattered abroad and dispersed among the peoples in all the provinces of your kingdom; their laws are different from those of every other people, and they do not keep the king's laws, so that it is not for the king's profit to tolerate them. 9If it please the king, let it be decreed that they be destroyed, and I will pay ten

thousand talents of silver into the hands of those who have charge of the king's business, that they may put it into the king's treasuries." 10So the king took his signet ring from his hand and gave it to Hā'man the Ăg'a·gīte, the son of Hăm·mĕ·dā'tha, the enemy of the Jews. 11And the king said to Hā'man, "The money is given to you, the people also, to do with them as it seems good to you."

12 Then the king's secretaries were summoned on the thirteenth day of the first month, and an edict, according to all that Hā'man commanded, was written to the king's satraps and to the governors over all the provinces and to the princes of all the peoples, to every province in its own script and every people in its own language; it was written in the name of King A·hăs'ū-ē'rŭs and sealed with the king's ring. 13Letters were sent by couriers to all the king's provinces, to destroy, to slay, and to annihilate all Jews, young and old, women and children, in one day, the thirteenth day of the twelfth month, which is the month of A·där', and to plunder their goods. 14A copy of the document was to be issued as a decree in every province by proclamation to all the peoples to be ready for that day. 15The couriers went in haste by order of the king, and the decree was issued in Sŭ'sa the capital. And the king and Hā'man sat down to drink; but the city of Susa was perplexed.

4 When Môr'dĕ·caī learned all that that had been done, Mordecai rent his clothes and put on sackcloth and ashes, and went out into the midst of the city, wailing with a loud and bitter cry; 2he went up to the entrance of the king's gate, for no one might enter the king's gate clothed with sackcloth. 3And in every province, wherever the king's command and his decree came, there was great mourning among the Jews, with fasting and weeping and lamenting, and most of them lay in sackcloth and ashes.

4 When Esther's maids and her eunuchs came and told her, the queen was deeply distressed; she sent garments to clothe Môr'dĕ·caī, so that he might take off his sackcloth, but he would not accept them. 5Then Esther called for Hā'thăch, one of the king's eunuchs, who had been appointed to

attend her, and ordered him to go to Môr′dĕ·caī to learn what this was and why it was. ⁶Hā′thăch went out to Môr′dĕ·caī in the open square of the city in front of the king's gate, ⁷and Môr′dĕ·caī told him all that had happened to him, and the exact sum of money that Hā′mặn had promised to pay into the king's treasuries for the destruction of the Jews. ⁸Môr′dĕ·caī also gave him a copy of the written decree issued in Sū′sặ for their destruction, that he might show it to Esther and explain it to her and charge her to go to the king to make supplication to him and entreat him for her people. ⁹And Hā′thăch went and told Esther what Môr′dĕ·caī had said. ¹⁰Then Esther spoke to Hā′thăch and gave him a message for Môr′dĕ·caī, saying, ¹¹"All the king's servants and the people of the king's provinces know that if any man or woman goes to the king inside the inner court without being called, there is but one law; all alike are to be put to death, except the one to whom the king holds out the golden scepter that he may live. And I have not been called to come in to the king these thirty days." ¹²And they told Môr′dĕ·caī what Esther had said. ¹³Then Môr′dĕ·caī told them to return answer to Esther, "Think not that in the king's palace you will escape any more than all the other Jews. ¹⁴For if you keep silence at such a time as this, relief and deliverance will rise for the Jews from another quarter, but you and your father's house will perish. And who knows whether you have not come to the kingdom for such a time as this?" ¹⁵Then Esther told them to reply to Môr′dĕ·caī, ¹⁶"Go, gather all the Jews to be found in Sū′sặ, and hold a fast on my behalf, and neither eat nor drink for three days, night or day. I and my maids will also fast as you do. Then I will go to the king, though it is against the law; and if I perish, I perish." ¹⁷Môr′dĕ·caī then went away and did everything as Esther had ordered him.

5 On the third day Esther put on her royal robes and stood in the inner court of the king's palace, opposite the king's hall. The king was sitting on his royal throne inside the palace opposite the entrance to the palace; ²and when the king saw Queen Esther standing in the court, she found favor in his sight and he held out to Esther the golden scepter that was in his hand. Then Esther approached and touched the top of the scepter. ³And the king said to her, "What is it, Queen Esther? What is your request? It shall be given you, even to the half of my kingdom." ⁴And Esther said, "If it please the king, let the king and Hā′-mặn come this day to a dinner that I have prepared for the king." ⁵Then said the king, "Bring Hā′mặn quickly, that we may do as Esther desires." So the king and Haman came to the dinner that Esther had prepared. ⁶And as they were drinking wine, the king said to Esther, "What is your petition? It shall be granted you. And what is your request? Even to the half of my kingdom, it shall be fulfilled." ⁷But Esther said, "My petition and my request is: ⁸If I have found favor in the sight of the king, and it if please the king to grant my petition and fulfil my request, let the king and Hā′mặn come tomorrowᵈ to the dinner which I will prepare for them, and tomorrow I will do as the king has said."

9 And Hā′mặn went out that day joyful and glad of heart. But when Haman saw Môr′dĕ·caī in the king's gate, that he neither rose nor trembled before him, he was filled with wrath against Mordecai. ¹⁰Nevertheless Hā′mặn restrained himself, and went home; and he sent and fetched his friends and his wife Zē′rĕsh. ¹¹And Hā′mặn recounted to them the splendor of his riches, the number of his sons, all the promotions with which the king had honored him, and how he had advanced him above the princes and the servants of the king. ¹²And Hā′mặn added, "Even Queen Esther let no one come with the king to the banquet she prepared but myself. And tomorrow also I am invited by her together with the king. ¹³Yet all this does me no good, so long as I see Môr′dĕ·caī the Jew sitting at the king's gate." ¹⁴Then his wife Zē′rĕsh and all his friends said to him, "Let a gallows fifty cubits high be made, and in the morning tell the king to have Môr′-dĕ·caī hanged upon it; then go merrily with the king to the dinner." This counsel pleased Hā′mặn, and he had the gallows made.

ᵈGk: Heb lacks *tomorrow*
5.3, 6: Mk 6.23.

6 On that night the king could not sleep; and he gave orders to bring the book of memorable deeds, the chronicles, and they were read before the king. ²And it was found written how Mŏr′dĕ·caī had told about Bĭg-thā′na and Tē′rĕsh, two of the king's eunuchs, who guarded the threshold, and who had sought to lay hands upon King A·hăş′ū–ē′rus. ³And the king said, "What honor or dignity has been bestowed on Mŏr′dĕ·caī for this?" The king's servants who attended him said, "Nothing has been done for him." ⁴And the king said, "Who is in the court?" Now Hā′man had just entered the outer court of the king's palace to speak to the king about having Mŏr′-dĕ·caī hanged on the gallows that he had prepared for him. ⁵So the king's servants told him, "Hā′man is there, standing in the court." And the king said, "Let him come in." ⁶So Hā′man came in, and the king said to him, "What shall be done to the man whom the king delights to honor?" And Haman said to himself, "Whom would the king delight to honor more than me?" ⁷And Hā′man said to the king, "For the man whom the king delights to honor, ⁸let royal robes be brought, which the king has worn, and the horse which the king has ridden, and on whose head a royal crown is set; ⁹and let the robes and the horse be handed over to one of the king's most noble princes; let him*ᵉ* array the man whom the king delights to honor, and let him*ᵉ* conduct the man on horseback through the open square of the city, proclaiming before him: 'Thus shall it be done to the man whom the king delights to honor.'" ¹⁰Then the king said to Hā′man, "Make haste, take the robes and the horse, as you have said, and do so to Mŏr′dĕ·caī the Jew who sits at the king's gate. Leave out nothing that you have mentioned." ¹¹So Hā′-man took the robes and the horse, and he arrayed Mŏr′dĕ·caī and made him ride through the open square of the city, proclaiming, "Thus shall it be done to the man whom the king delights to honor."

12 Then Mŏr′dĕ·caī returned to the king's gate. But Hā′man hurried to his house, mourning and with his head covered. ¹³And Hā′man told his wife Zē′rĕsh and all his friends everything that had befallen him. Then his wise men and his wife Zeresh said to him, "If Mŏr′dĕ·caī, before whom you have begun to fall, is of the Jewish people, you will not prevail against him but will surely fall before him."

14 While they were yet talking with him, the king's eunuchs arrived and brought Hā′man in haste to the banquet that Esther had prepared.

7 So the king and Hā′man went in to feast with Queen Esther. ²And on the second day, as they were drinking wine, the king again said to Esther, "What is your petition, Queen Esther? It shall be granted you. And what is your request? Even to the half of my kingdom, it shall be fulfilled." ³Then Queen Esther answered, "If I have found favor in your sight, O king, and if it please the king, let my life be given me at my petition, and my people at my request. ⁴For we are sold, I and my people, to be destroyed, to be slain, and to be annihilated. If we had been sold merely as slaves, men and women, I would have held my peace; for our affliction is not to be compared with the loss to the king." ⁵Then King A·hăş′ū–ē′rus said to Queen Esther, "Who is he, and where is he, that would presume to do this?" ⁶And Esther said, "A foe and enemy! This wicked Hā′man!" Then Haman was in terror before the king and the queen. ⁷And the king rose from the feast in wrath and went into the palace garden; but Hā′man stayed to beg his life from Queen Esther, for he saw that evil was determined against him by the king. ⁸And the king returned from the palace garden to the place where they were drinking wine, as Hā′man was falling on the couch where Esther was; and the king said, "Will he even assault the queen in my presence, in my own house?" As the words left the mouth of the king, they covered Haman's face. ⁹Then said Hăr·bō′na, one of the eunuchs in attendance on the king, "Moreover, the gallows which Hā′man has prepared for Mŏr′dĕ·caī, whose word saved the king, is standing in Haman's house, fifty cubits high." ¹⁰And the king said, "Hang him on that." So they hanged Hā′man on the gallows which he had prepared for Mŏr′dĕ·caī. Then the anger of the king abated.

ᵉHeb them   **7.2:** Mk 6.23.

8 On that day King A·hăṣ′ū–ē′rŭs gave to Queen Esther the house of Hā′man, the enemy of the Jews. And Môr′dĕ·caī came before the king, for Esther had told what he was to her; ²and the king took off his signet ring, which he had taken from Hā′-man, and gave it to Môr′dĕ·caī. And Esther set Mordecai over the house of Haman.

3 Then Esther spoke again to the king; she fell at his feet and besought him with tears to avert the evil design of Hā′man the Ăg′a·gīte and the plot which he had devised against the Jews. ⁴And the king held out the golden scepter to Esther, ⁵and Esther rose and stood before the king. And she said, "If it please the king, and if I have found favor in his sight, and if the thing seem right before the king, and I be pleasing in his eyes, let an order be written to revoke the letters devised by Hā′man the Ăg′a·gīte, the son of Hăm·mĕ·dā′tha, which he wrote to destroy the Jews who are in all the provinces of the king. ⁶For how can I endure to see the calamity that is coming to my people? Or how can I endure to see the destruction of my kindred?" ⁷Then King A·hăṣ′ū–ē′rŭs said to Queen Esther and to Môr′dĕ·caī the Jew, "Behold, I have given Esther the house of Hā′man, and they have hanged him on the gallows, because he would lay hands on the Jews. ⁸And you may write as you please with regard to the Jews, in the name of the king, and seal it with the king's ring; for an edict written in the name of the king and sealed with the king's ring cannot be revoked."

9 The king's secretaries were summoned at that time, in the third month, which is the month of Sī′van, on the twenty-third day; and an edict was written according to all that Môr′dĕ·caī commanded concerning the Jews to the satraps and the governors and the princes of the provinces from India to Ethiopia, a hundred and twenty-seven provinces, to every province in its own script and to every people in its own language, and also to the Jews in their script and their language. ¹⁰The writing was in the name of King A·hăṣ′ū–ē′rŭs and sealed with the king's ring, and letters were sent by mounted couriers riding on swift horses that were used in the king's service, bred from the royal stud. ¹¹By these the king allowed the Jews who were in every city to gather and defend their lives, to destroy, to slay, and to annihilate any armed force of any people or province that might attack them, with their children and women, and to plunder their goods, ¹²upon one day throughout all the provinces of King A·hăṣ′ū–ē′rŭs, on the thirteenth day of the twelfth month, which is the month of A·dăr′. ¹³A copy of what was written was to be issued as a decree in every province, and by proclamation to all peoples, and the Jews were to be ready on that day to avenge themselves upon their enemies. ¹⁴So the couriers, mounted on their swift horses that were used in the king's service, rode out in haste, urged by the king's command; and the decree was issued in Sŭ′sa the capital.

15 Then Môr′dĕ·caī went out from the presence of the king in royal robes of blue and white, with a great golden crown and a mantle of fine linen and purple, while the city of Sŭ′sa shouted and rejoiced. ¹⁶The Jews had light and gladness and joy and honor. ¹⁷And in every province and in every city, wherever the king's command and his edict came, there was gladness and joy among the Jews, a feast and a holiday. And many from the peoples of the country declared themselves Jews, for the fear of the Jews had fallen upon them.

9 Now in the twelfth month, which is the month of A·dăr′, on the thirteenth day of the same, when the king's command and edict were about to be executed, on the very day when the enemies of the Jews hoped to get the mastery over them, but which had been changed to a day when the Jews should get the mastery over their foes, ²the Jews gathered in their cities throughout all the provinces of King A·hăṣ′ū–ē′rŭs to lay hands on such as sought their hurt. And no one could make a stand against them, for the fear of them had fallen upon all peoples. ³All the princes of the provinces and the satraps and the governors and the royal officials also helped the Jews, for the fear of Môr′dĕ·caī had fallen upon them. ⁴For Môr′dĕ·caī was great in the king's house, and his fame spread throughout all the provinces; for the man Mordecai grew more and

more powerful. ⁵So the Jews smote all their enemies with the sword, slaughtering, and destroying them, and did as they pleased to those who hated them. ⁶In Sŭ′sa the capital itself the Jews slew and destroyed five hundred men, ⁷and also slew Pär–shan–dä′tha and Dăl′phŏn and Ăs·pä′tha ⁸and Pō·rä′tha and A·dä′lĭ·a and Ăr·ĭ·dä′tha ⁹and Păr·măsh′ta and Ăr′ĭ·saī and Ăr′ĭ·daī and Vaī·zä′tha, ¹⁰the ten sons of Hä′man the son of Hăm·me·dä′tha, the enemy of the Jews; but they laid no hand on the plunder.

11 That very day the number of those slain in Sŭ′sa the capital was reported to the king. ¹²And the king said to Queen Esther, "In Sŭ′sa the capital the Jews have slain five hundred men and also the ten sons of Hä′man. What then have they done in the rest of the king's provinces! Now what is your petition? It shall be granted you. And what further is your request? It shall be fulfilled." ¹³And Esther said, "If it please the king, let the Jews who are in Sŭ′sa be allowed tomorrow also to do according to this day's edict. And let the ten sons of Hä′man be hanged on the gallows." ¹⁴So the king commanded this to be done; a decree was issued in Sŭ′sa, and the ten sons of Hä′man were hanged. ¹⁵The Jews who were in Sŭ′sa gathered also on the fourteenth day of the month of A·där′ and they slew three hundred men in Susa; but they laid no hands on the plunder.

16 Now the other Jews who were in the king's provinces also gathered to defend their lives, and got relief from their enemies, and slew seventy-five thousand of those who hated them; but they laid no hands on the plunder. ¹⁷This was on the thirteenth day of the month of A·där′, and on the fourteenth day they rested and made that a day of feasting and gladness. ¹⁸But the Jews who were in Sŭ′sa gathered on the thirteenth day and on the fourteenth, and rested on the fifteenth day, making that a day of feasting and gladness. ¹⁹Therefore the Jews of the villages, who live in the open towns, hold the fourteenth day of the month of A·där′ as a day for gladness and feasting and holiday-making, and a day on which they send choice portions to one another.

20 And Môr′dĕ·caī recorded these things, and sent letters to all the Jews who were in all the provinces of King A·hăş′ū–ē′rus, both near and far, ²¹enjoining them that they should keep the fourteenth day of the month A·där′ and also the fifteenth day of the same, year by year, ²²as the days on which the Jews got relief from their enemies, and as the month that had been turned for them from sorrow into gladness and from mourning into a holiday; that they should make them days of feasting and gladness, days for sending choice portions to one another and gifts to the poor.

23 So the Jews undertook to do as they had begun, and as Môr′dĕ·caī had written to them. ²⁴For Hä′man the Ăg′a·gīte, the son of Hăm·me·dä′tha, the enemy of all the Jews, had plotted against the Jews to destroy them, and had cast Pür, that is the lot, to crush and destroy them; ²⁵but when Esther came before the king, he gave orders in writing that his wicked plot which he had devised against the Jews should come upon his own head, and that he and his sons should be hanged on the gallows. ²⁶Therefore they called these days Pür′ĭm, after the term Pür. And therefore, because of all that was written in this letter, and of what they had faced in this matter, and of what had befallen them, ²⁷the Jews ordained and took it upon themselves and their descendants and all who joined them, that without fail they would keep these two days according to what was written and at the time appointed every year, ²⁸that these days should be remembered and kept throughout every generation, in every family, province, and city, and that these days of Pür′ĭm should never fall into disuse among the Jews, nor should the commemoration of these days cease among their descendants.

29 Then Queen Esther, the daughter of Ăb′ĭ·hāil, and Môr′dĕ·caī the Jew gave full written authority, confirming this second letter about Pür′ĭm. ³⁰Letters were sent to all the Jews, to the hundred and twenty-seven provinces of the kingdom of A·hăş′ū–ē′rus, in words of peace and truth, ³¹that these days of Pür′ĭm should be observed at their appointed seasons, as Môr′dĕ·caī the Jew and Queen Esther enjoined upon the Jews, and as they had laid down for them-

selves and for their descendants, with regard to their fasts and their lamenting. ³²The command of Queen Esther fixed these practices of Pūr'ĭm, and it was recorded in writing.

10 King A·hăṣ'ū–ē'rŭs laid tribute on the land and on the coast-lands of the sea. ²And all the acts of his power and might, and the full account of the high honor of Môr'- dĕ·caī, to which the king advanced him, are they not written in the Book of the Chronicles of the kings of Mēd'ĭ·ạ and Persia? ³For Môr'dĕ·caī the Jew was next in rank to King A·hăṣ'ū–ē'rŭs, and he was great among the Jews and popular with the multitude of his brethren, for he sought the welfare of his people and spoke peace to all his people.

The Book of
Job

1 There was a man in the land of Ŭz, whose name was Jōb; and that man was blameless and upright, one who feared God, and turned away from evil. ²There were born to him seven sons and three daughters. ³He had seven thousand sheep, three thousand camels, five hundred yoke of oxen, and five hundred she-asses, and very many servants; so that this man was the greatest of all the people of the east. ⁴His sons used to go and hold a feast in the house of each on his day; and they would send and invite their three sisters to eat and drink with them. ⁵And when the days of the feast had run their course, Jōb would send and sanctify them, and he would rise early in the morning and offer burnt offer-ings according to the number of them all; for Job said, "It may be that my sons have sinned, and cursed God in their hearts." Thus Job did continually.

6 Now there was a day when the sons of God came to present them-selves before the LORD, and Satan*a* also came among them. ⁷The LORD said to Satan, "Whence have you come?" Satan answered the LORD, "From going to and fro on the earth, and from walking up and down on it." ⁸And the LORD said to Satan, "Have you considered my servant Jōb, that there is none like him on the earth, a blameless and upright man, who fears God and turns away from evil?" ⁹Then Satan answered the LORD, "Does Jōb fear God for nought? ¹⁰Hast thou not put a hedge about him and his house and all that he has, on every side? Thou hast blessed the work of his hands, and his possessions have increased in the land. ¹¹But put forth thy hand now, and touch all that he has, and he will curse thee to thy face." ¹²And the LORD said to Satan, "Behold, all that he has is in your power; only upon himself do not put forth your hand." So Satan went forth from the presence of the LORD.

13 Now there was a day when his sons and daughters were eating and drinking wine in their eldest brother's house; ¹⁴and there came a messenger to Jōb, and said, "The oxen were plow-ing and the asses feeding beside them; ¹⁵and the Sạ·bē'ạnṣ fell upon them and took them, and slew the servants with the edge of the sword; and I alone have escaped to tell you." ¹⁶While he was yet speaking, there came another, and said, "The fire of God fell from heaven and burned up the sheep and the servants, and consumed them; and I alone have escaped to tell you." ¹⁷While he was yet speaking, there came another, and said, "The Chăl-dē'ạnṣ formed three companies, and made a raid upon the camels and took them, and slew the servants with the edge of the sword; and I alone have escaped to tell you." ¹⁸While he was yet speaking, there came another, and said, "Your sons and daughters were eating and drinking wine in their eldest brother's house; ¹⁹and behold, a great wind came across the wilder-

a Heb *the adversary*

ness, and struck the four corners of the house, and it fell upon the young people, and they are dead; and I alone have escaped to tell you."

20 Then Jōb arose, and rent his robe, and shaved his head, and fell upon the ground, and worshiped. ²¹ And he said, "Naked I came from my mother's womb, and naked shall I return; the LORD gave, and the LORD has taken away; blessed be the name of the LORD."

22 In all this Jōb did not sin or charge God with wrong.

2 Again there was a day when the sons of God came to present themselves before the LORD, and Satan also came among them to present himself before the LORD. ² And the LORD said to Satan, "Whence have you come?" Satan answered the LORD, "From going to and fro on the earth, and from walking up and down on it." ³ And the LORD said to Satan, "Have you considered my servant Jōb, that there is none like him on the earth, a blameless and upright man, who fears God and turns away from evil? He still holds fast his integrity, although you moved me against him, to destroy him without cause." ⁴ Then Satan answered the LORD, "Skin for skin! All that a man has he will give for his life. ⁵ But put forth thy hand now, and touch his bone and his flesh, and he will curse thee to thy face." ⁶ And the LORD said to Satan, "Behold, he is in your power; only spare his life."

7 So Satan went forth from the presence of the LORD, and afflicted Jōb with loathsome sores from the sole of his foot to the crown of his head. ⁸ And he took a potsherd with which to scrape himself, and sat among the ashes.

9 Then his wife said to him, "Do you still hold fast your integrity? Curse God, and die." ¹⁰ But he said to her, "You speak as one of the foolish women would speak. Shall we receive good at the hand of God, and shall we not receive evil?" In all this Jōb did not sin with his lips.

11 Now when Jōb's three friends heard of all this evil that had come upon him, they came each from his own place, Ĕ-lī'phăz the Tē'ma-nīte, Bĭl'dăd the Shü'hīte, and Zō'phär the Nā'a-ma-thīte. They made an appointment together to come to condole

with him and comfort him. ¹² And when they saw him from afar, they did not recognize him; and they raised their voices and wept; and they rent their robes and sprinkled dust upon their heads toward heaven. ¹³ And they sat with him on the ground seven days and seven nights, and no one spoke a word to him, for they saw that his suffering was very great.

3 After this Jōb opened his mouth and cursed the day of his birth. ²And Jōb said:

³"Let the day perish wherein I was born,
  and the night which said,
  'A man-child is conceived.'
⁴Let that day be darkness!
  May God above not seek it,
  nor light shine upon it.
⁵Let gloom and deep darkness claim it.
  Let clouds dwell upon it;
  let the blackness of the day terrify it.
⁶That night—let thick darkness seize it!
  let it not rejoice among the days of the year,
  let it not come into the number of the months.
⁷Yea, let that night be barren;
  let no joyful cry be heard*ᵇ* in it.
⁸Let those curse it who curse the day,
  who are skilled to rouse up Lĕ-vī'a-thạn.
⁹Let the stars of its dawn be dark;
  let it hope for light, but have none,
  nor see the eyelids of the morning;
¹⁰because it did not shut the doors of my mother's womb,
  nor hide trouble from my eyes.

¹¹"Why did I not die at birth,
  come forth from the womb and expire?
¹²Why did the knees receive me?
  Or why the breasts, that I should suck?
¹³For then I should have lain down and been quiet;
  I should have slept; then I should have been at rest,
¹⁴with kings and counselors of the earth
  who rebuilt ruins for themselves,
¹⁵or with princes who had gold,
  who filled their houses with silver.

ᵇHeb *come*
3.3-19: Jer 20.14-18.

¹⁶ Or why was I not as a hidden untimely birth,
as infants that never see the light?
¹⁷ There the wicked cease from troubling,
and there the weary are at rest.
¹⁸ There the prisoners are at ease together;
they hear not the voice of the taskmaster.
¹⁹ The small and the great are there,
and the slave is free from his master.

²⁰ "Why is light given to him that is in misery,
and life to the bitter in soul,
²¹ who long for death, but it comes not,
and dig for it more than for hid treasures;
²² who rejoice exceedingly,
and are glad, when they find the grave?
²³ Why is light given to a man whose way is hid,
whom God has hedged in?
²⁴ For my sighing comes as*ᶜ* my bread,
and my groanings are poured out like water.
²⁵ For the thing that I fear comes upon me,
and what I dread befalls me.
²⁶ I am not at ease, nor am I quiet;
I have no rest; but trouble comes."

4 Then Ē·lĭ′phăz the Tē′mạ·nīte answered:
² "If one ventures a word with you, will you be offended?
Yet who can keep from speaking?
³ Behold, you have instructed many,
and you have strengthened the weak hands.
⁴ Your words have upheld him who was stumbling,
and you have made firm the feeble knees.
⁵ But now it has come to you, and you are impatient;
it touches you, and you are dismayed.
⁶ Is not your fear of God your confidence,
and the integrity of your ways your hope?

⁷ "Think now, who that was innocent ever perished?
Or where were the upright cut off?

⁸ As I have seen, those who plow iniquity
and sow trouble reap the same.
⁹ By the breath of God they perish,
and by the blast of his anger they are consumed.
¹⁰ The roar of the lion, the voice of the fierce lion,
the teeth of the young lions, are broken.
¹¹ The strong lion perishes for lack of prey,
and the whelps of the lioness are scattered.

¹² "Now a word was brought to me stealthily,
my ear received the whisper of it.
¹³ Amid thoughts from visions of the night,
when deep sleep falls on men,
¹⁴ dread came upon me, and trembling,
which made all my bones shake.
¹⁵ A spirit glided past my face;
the hair of my flesh stood up.
¹⁶ It stood still,
but I could not discern its appearance.
A form was before my eyes;
there was silence, then I heard a voice:
¹⁷ 'Can mortal man be righteous before*ᵈ* God?
Can a man be pure before*ᵈ* his Maker?
¹⁸ Even in his servants he puts no trust,
and his angels he charges with error;
¹⁹ how much more those who dwell in houses of clay,
whose foundation is in the dust,
who are crushed before the moth.
²⁰ Between morning and evening they are destroyed;
they perish for ever without any regarding it.
²¹ If their tent-cord is plucked up within them,
do they not die, and that without wisdom?'

5 "Call now; is there any one who will answer you?
To which of the holy ones will you turn?
² Surely vexation kills the fool,
and jealousy slays the simple.
³ I have seen the fool taking root,
but suddenly I cursed his dwelling.

ᶜHeb *before* ᵈOr *more than*

4 His sons are far from safety,
  they are crushed in the gate,
  and there is no one to deliver
    them.
5 His harvest the hungry eat,
  and he takes it even out of thorns; *e*
  and the thirsty *f* pant after his *g*
    wealth.
6 For affliction does not come from the
    dust,
  nor does trouble sprout from the
    ground;
7 but man is born to trouble
  as the sparks fly upward.

8 "As for me, I would seek God,
  and to God would I commit my
    cause;
9 who does great things and unsearch-
    able,
  marvelous things without number:
10 he gives rain upon the earth
  and sends waters upon the fields;
11 he sets on high those who are lowly,
  and those who mourn are lifted to
    safety.
12 He frustrates the devices of the
    crafty,
  so that their hands achieve no
    success.
13 He takes the wise in their own
    craftiness;
  and the schemes of the wily are
    brought to a quick end.
14 They meet with darkness in the day-
    time,
  and grope at noonday as in the
    night.
15 But he saves the fatherless from
    their mouth, *h*
  the needy from the hand of the
    mighty.
16 So the poor have hope,
  and injustice shuts her mouth.

17 "Behold, happy is the man whom
    God reproves;
  therefore despise not the chas-
    tening of the Almighty.
18 For he wounds, but he binds up;
  he smites, but his hands heal.
19 He will deliver you from six troubles;
  in seven there shall no evil touch
    you.
20 In famine he will redeem you from
    death,
  and in war from the power of the
    sword.
21 You shall be hid from the scourge of
    the tongue,

and shall not fear destruction
    when it comes.
22 At destruction and famine you shall
    laugh,
  and shall not fear the beasts of the
    earth.
23 For you shall be in league with the
    stones of the field,
  and the beasts of the field shall be
    at peace with you.
24 You shall know that your tent is safe,
  and you shall inspect your fold and
    miss nothing.
25 You shall know also that your de-
    scendants shall be many,
  and your offspring as the grass of
    the earth.
26 You shall come to your grave in ripe
    old age,
  as a shock of grain comes up to
    the threshing floor in its season.
27 Lo, this we have searched out; it is
    true.
  Hear, and know it for your good." *i*

6 Then Jōb answered:
2 "O that my vexation were
    weighed,
  and all my calamity laid in the
    balances!
3 For then it would be heavier than the
    sand of the sea;
  therefore my words have been rash.
4 For the arrows of the Almighty are
    in me;
  my spirit drinks their poison;
  the terrors of God are arrayed
    against me.
5 Does the wild ass bray when he has
    grass,
  or the ox low over his fodder?
6 Can that which is tasteless be eaten
    without salt,
  or is there any taste in the slime
    of the purslane? *j*
7 My appetite refuses to touch them;
  they are as food that is loathsome
    to me. *k*

8 "O that I might have my request,
  and that God would grant my
    desire;
9 that it would please God to crush me,
  that he would let loose his hand
    and cut me off!

---

e Heb obscure
f Aquila Symmachus Syr Vg: Heb *snare*
g Heb *their* *h* Cn: Heb uncertain
i Heb *for yourself*
j The meaning of the Hebrew word is uncertain
k Heb obscure **5.12–13:** 1 Cor 3.19.

10 This would be my consolation;
I would even exult[l] in pain un-
sparing;
for I have not denied the words of
the Holy One.
11 What is my strength, that I should
wait?
And what is my end, that I should
be patient?
12 Is my strength the strength of stones,
or is my flesh bronze?
13 In truth I have no help in me,
and any resource is driven from
me.

14 "He who withholds[m] kindness from
a friend
forsakes the fear of the Almighty.
15 My brethren are treacherous as a
torrent-bed,
as freshets that pass away,
16 which are dark with ice,
and where the snow hides itself.
17 In time of heat they disappear;
when it is hot, they vanish from
their place.
18 The caravans turn aside from their
course;
they go up into the waste, and
perish.
19 The caravans of Tē′ma look,
the travelers of Shē′ba hope.
20 They are disappointed because they
were confident;
they come thither and are confounded.
21 Such you have now become to me;[n]
you see my calamity, and are
afraid.
22 Have I said, 'Make me a gift'?
Or, 'From your wealth offer a bribe
for me'?
23 Or, 'Deliver me from the adversary's
hand'?
Or, 'Ransom me from the hand of
oppressors'?

24 "Teach me, and I will be silent;
make me understand how I have
erred.
25 How forceful are honest words!
But what does reproof from you
reprove?
26 Do you think that you can reprove
words,
when the speech of a despairing
man is wind?
27 You would even cast lots over the
fatherless,
and bargain over your friend.

28 "But now, be pleased to look at me;
for I will not lie to your face.
29 Turn, I pray, let no wrong be done.
Turn now, my vindication is at
stake.
30 Is there any wrong on my tongue?
Cannot my taste discern calamity?

7 "Has not man a hard service upon
earth,
and are not his days like the days
of a hireling?
2 Like a slave who longs for the
shadow,
and like a hireling who looks for
his wages,
3 so I am allotted months of emptiness,
and nights of misery are apportioned to me.
4 When I lie down I say, 'When shall I
arise?'
But the night is long,
and I am full of tossing till the
dawn.
5 My flesh is clothed with worms and
dirt;
my skin hardens, then breaks out
afresh.
6 My days are swifter than a weaver's
shuttle,
and come to their end without hope.

7 "Remember that my life is a breath;
my eye will never again see good.
8 The eye of him who sees me will
behold me no more;
while thy eyes are upon me, I shall
be gone.
9 As the cloud fades and vanishes,
so he who goes down to Shē′ol does
not come up;
10 he returns no more to his house,
nor does his place know him any
more.

11 "Therefore I will not restrain my
mouth;
I will speak in the anguish of my
spirit;
I will complain in the bitterness
of my soul.
12 Am I the sea, or a sea monster,
that thou settest a guard over me?
13 When I say, 'My bed will comfort me,
my couch will ease my complaint,'
14 then thou dost scare me with dreams
and terrify me with visions,

[l]The meaning of the Hebrew word is uncertain
[m]Syr Vg Compare Tg: Heb obscure
[n]Cn Compare Gk Syr: Heb obscure

¹⁵ so that I would choose strangling
and death rather than my bones.
¹⁶ I loathe my life; I would not live for
ever.
Let me alone, for my days are a
breath.
¹⁷ What is man, that thou dost make so
much of him,
and that thou dost set thy mind
upon him,
¹⁸ dost visit him every morning,
and test him every moment?
¹⁹ How long wilt thou not look away
from me,
nor let me alone till I swallow my
spittle?
²⁰ If I sin, what do I do to thee, thou
watcher of men?
Why hast thou made me thy mark?
Why have I become a burden to
thee?
²¹ Why dost thou not pardon my trans-
gression
and take away my iniquity?
For now I shall lie in the earth;
thou wilt seek me, but I shall not
be."

8 Then Bĭl'dăd the Shū'hĭte answered:
² "How long will you say these things,
and the words of your mouth be a
great wind?
³ Does God pervert justice?
Or does the Almighty pervert the
right?
⁴ If your children have sinned against
him,
he has delivered them into the
power of their transgression.
⁵ If you will seek God
and make supplication to the
Almighty,
⁶ if you are pure and upright,
surely then he will rouse himself
for you
and reward you with a rightful
habitation.
⁷ And though your beginning was
small,
your latter days will be very great.

⁸ "For inquire, I pray you, of bygone
ages,
and consider what the fathers
have found;
⁹ for we are but of yesterday, and know
nothing,
for our days on earth are a shadow.
¹⁰ Will they not teach you, and tell you,

and utter words out of their understanding?

¹¹ "Can papyrus grow where there is
no marsh?
Can reeds flourish where there is
no water?
¹² While yet in flower and not cut down,
they wither before any other plant.
¹³ Such are the paths of all who forget
God;
the hope of the godless man shall
perish.
¹⁴ His confidence breaks in sunder,
and his trust is a spider's web. ^o
¹⁵ He leans against his house, but it
does not stand;
he lays hold of it, but it does not
endure.
¹⁶ He thrives before the sun,
and his shoots spread over his
garden.
¹⁷ His roots twine about the stone-heap;
he lives among the rocks. ^p
¹⁸ If he is destroyed from his place,
then it will deny him, saying,
'I have never seen you.'
¹⁹ Behold, this is the joy of his way;
and out of the earth others will
spring.

²⁰ "Behold, God will not reject a blame-
less man,
nor take the hand of evildoers.
²¹ He will yet fill your mouth with
laughter,
and your lips with shouting.
²² Those who hate you will be clothed
with shame,
and the tent of the wicked will be
no more."

9 Then Jŏb answered:
² "Truly I know that it is so:
But how can a man be just before
God?
³ If one wished to contend with him,
one could not answer him once in
a thousand times.
⁴ He is wise in heart, and mighty in
strength
— who has hardened himself against
him, and succeeded? —
⁵ he who removes mountains, and they
know it not,
when he overturns them in his
anger;
⁶ who shakes the earth out of its place,

^oHeb *house* ^pGk Vg: Heb uncertain
7.17: Ps 8.4.

and its pillars tremble;
⁷who commands the sun, and it does
not rise;
who seals up the stars;
⁸who alone stretched out the heavens,
and trampled the waves of the sea; ��q
⁹who made the Bear and Ō·rī′ọn,
the Plēi′ạ·dēṣ and the chambers of
the south;
¹⁰who does great things beyond understanding,
and marvelous things without
number.
¹¹Lo, he passes by me, and I see him
not;
he moves on, but I do not perceive
him.
¹²Behold, he snatches away; who can
hinder him?
Who will say to him, 'What doest
thou'?

¹³"God will not turn back his anger;
beneath him bowed the helpers of
Rā′hăb.
¹⁴How then can I answer him,
choosing my words with him?
¹⁵Though I am innocent, I cannot
answer him;
I must appeal for mercy to my
accuser. ʳ
¹⁶If I summoned him and he answered
me,
I would not believe that he was
listening to my voice.
¹⁷For he crushes me with a tempest,
and multiplies my wounds without
cause;
¹⁸he will not let me get my breath,
but fills me with bitterness.
¹⁹If it is a contest of strength, behold
him!
If it is a matter of justice, who can
summon him?ˢ
²⁰Though I am innocent, my own
mouth would condemn me;
though I am blameless, he would
prove me perverse.
²¹I am blameless; I regard not myself;
I loathe my life.
²²It is all one; therefore I say,
he destroys both the blameless and
the wicked.
²³When disaster brings sudden death,
he mocks at the calamityᵗ of the
innocent.
²⁴The earth is given into the hand of
the wicked;
he covers the faces of its judges —
if it is not he, who then is it?

²⁵"My days are swifter than a runner;
they flee away, they see no good.
²⁶They go by like skiffs of reed,
like an eagle swooping on the prey.
²⁷If I say, 'I will forget my complaint,
I will put off my sad countenance,
and be of good cheer,'
²⁸I become afraid of all my suffering,
for I know thou wilt not hold me
innocent.
²⁹I shall be condemned;
why then do I labor in vain?
³⁰If I wash myself with snow,
and cleanse my hands with lye,
³¹yet thou wilt plunge me into a pit,
and my own clothes will abhor me.
³²For he is not a man, as I am, that I
might answer him,
that we should come to trial together.
³³There is noᵘ umpire between us,
who might lay his hand upon us
both.
³⁴Let him take his rod away from me,
and let not dread of him terrify me.
³⁵Then I would speak without fear of
him,
for I am not so in myself.

10 "I loathe my life;
I will give free utterance to my
complaint;
I will speak in the bitterness of my
soul.
²I will say to God, Do not condemn me;
let me know why thou dost contend
against me.
³Does it seem good to thee to oppress,
to despise the work of thy hands
and favor the designs of the
wicked?
⁴Hast thou eyes of flesh?
Dost thou see as man sees?
⁵Are thy days as the days of man,
or thy years as man's years,
⁶that thou dost seek out my iniquity
and search for my sin,
⁷although thou knowest that I am not
guilty,
and there is none to deliver out of
thy hand?
⁸Thy hands fashioned and made me;
and now thou dost turn about and
destroy me.ᵛ

�q*Or trampled the back of the sea dragon*
ʳ*Or for my right*
ˢ*Compare Gk: Heb me. The text of the verse is uncertain*
ᵗ*The meaning of the Hebrew word is uncertain*
ᵘ*Another reading is Would that there were*
ᵛ*Cn Compare Gk Syr: Heb made me together round about and thou dost destroy me*

9 Remember that thou hast made me
     of clay;*w*
and wilt thou turn me to dust
     again?
10 Didst thou not pour me out like milk
     and curdle me like cheese?
11 Thou didst clothe me with skin and
     flesh,
and knit me together with bones
     and sinews.
12 Thou hast granted me life and stead-
     fast love;
and thy care has preserved my
     spirit.
13 Yet these things thou didst hide in
     thy heart;
I know that this was thy purpose.
14 If I sin, thou dost mark me,
     and dost not acquit me of my
     iniquity.
15 If I am wicked, woe to me!
If I am righteous, I cannot lift up
     my head,
for I am filled with disgrace
and look upon my affliction.
16 And if I lift myself up,*x* thou dost
     hunt me like a lion,
and again work wonders against
     me;
17 thou dost renew thy witnesses
     against me,
and increase thy vexation toward
     me;
thou dost bring fresh hosts against
     me.*y*

18 "Why didst thou bring me forth from
     the womb?
Would that I had died before any
     eye had seen me,
19 and were as though I had not been,
carried from the womb to the
     grave.
20 Are not the days of my life few?*z*
Let me alone, that I may find a
     little comfort*a*
21 before I go whence I shall not re-
     turn,
to the land of gloom and deep dark-
     ness,
22 the land of gloom*b* and chaos,
where light is as darkness."

11   Then Zō′phăr the Nā′a·ma-
     thīte answered:
2 "Should a multitude of words go
     unanswered,
and a man full of talk be vindi-
     cated?
3 Should your babble silence men,

and when you mock, shall no one
     shame you?
4 For you say, 'My doctrine is pure,
and I am clean in God's eyes.'
5 But oh, that God would speak,
and open his lips to you,
6 and that he would tell you the secrets
     of wisdom!
For he is manifold in under-
     standing.*c*
Know then that God exacts of you
less than your guilt deserves.

7 "Can you find out the deep things of
     God?
Can you find out the limit of the
     Almighty?
8 It is higher than heaven*d*—what can
     you do?
Deeper than Shē′ōl—what can you
     know?
9 Its measure is longer than the earth,
and broader than the sea.
10 If he passes through, and imprisons,
and calls to judgment, who can
     hinder him?
11 For he knows worthless men;
when he sees iniquity, will he not
     consider it?
12 But a stupid man will get under-
     standing,
when a wild ass's colt is born a
     man.

13 "If you set your heart aright,
you will stretch out your hands
     toward him.
14 If iniquity is in your hand, put it
     far away,
and let not wickedness dwell in
     your tents.
15 Surely then you will lift up your face
     without blemish;
you will be secure, and will not
     fear.
16 You will forget your misery;
you will remember it as waters
     that have passed away.
17 And your life will be brighter than
     the noonday;
its darkness will be like the morn-
     ing.
18 And you will have confidence, be-
     cause there is hope;

---

w Gk: Heb *like clay*
x Syr: Heb *he lifts himself up*
y Cn Compare Gk: Heb *changes and a host are with me*
z Cn Compare Gk Syr: Heb *Are not my days few? Let him
cease*   *a* Heb *brighten up*
b Heb *gloom as darkness, deep darkness*
c Heb *obscure*   *d* Heb *The heights of heaven*

you will be protected *e* and take your rest in safety.
¹⁹ You will lie down, and none will make you afraid;
many will entreat your favor.
²⁰ But the eyes of the wicked will fail;
all way of escape will be lost to them,
and their hope is to breathe their last."

12 Then Jōb answered:
² "No doubt you are the people,
and wisdom will die with you.
³ But I have understanding as well as you;
I am not inferior to you.
Who does not know such things as these?
⁴ I am a laughingstock to my friends;
I, who called upon God and he answered me,
a just and blameless man, am a laughingstock.
⁵ In the thought of one who is at ease there is contempt for misfortune;
it is ready for those whose feet slip.
⁶ The tents of robbers are at peace,
and those who provoke God are secure,
who bring their god in their hand. *ᶠ*

⁷ "But ask the beasts, and they will teach you;
the birds of the air, and they will tell you;
⁸ or the plants of the earth, *ᵍ* and they will teach you;
and the fish of the sea will declare to you.
⁹ Who among all these does not know that the hand of the LORD has done this?
¹⁰ In his hand is the life of every living thing
and the breath of all mankind.
¹¹ Does not the ear try words
as the palate tastes food?
¹² Wisdom is with the aged,
and understanding in length of days.

¹³ "With God *ʰ* are wisdom and might;
he has counsel and understanding.
¹⁴ If he tears down, none can rebuild;
if he shuts a man in, none can open.
¹⁵ If he withholds the waters, they dry up;

if he sends them out, they overwhelm the land.
¹⁶ With him are strength and wisdom;
the deceived and the deceiver are his.
¹⁷ He leads counselors away stripped,
and judges he makes fools.
¹⁸ He looses the bonds of kings,
and binds a waistcloth on their loins.
¹⁹ He leads priests away stripped,
and overthrows the mighty.
²⁰ He deprives of speech those who are trusted,
and takes away the discernment of the elders.
²¹ He pours contempt on princes,
and looses the belt of the strong.
²² He uncovers the deeps out of darkness,
and brings deep darkness to light.
²³ He makes nations great, and he destroys them:
he enlarges nations, and leads them away.
²⁴ He takes away understanding from the chiefs of the people of the earth,
and makes them wander in a pathless waste.
²⁵ They grope in the dark without light;
and he makes them stagger like a drunken man.

13 "Lo, my eye has seen all this,
my ear has heard and understood it.
² What you know, I also know;
I am not inferior to you.
³ But I would speak to the Almighty,
and I desire to argue my case with God.
⁴ As for you, you whitewash with lies;
worthless physicians are you all.
⁵ Oh that you would keep silent,
and it would be your wisdom!
⁶ Hear now my reasoning,
and listen to the pleadings of my lips.
⁷ Will you speak falsely for God,
and speak deceitfully for him?
⁸ Will you show partiality toward him,
will you plead the case for God?
⁹ Will it be well with you when he searches you out?
Or can you deceive him, as one deceives a man?
¹⁰ He will surely rebuke you

e Or you will look around   f Hebrew uncertain
g Or speak to the earth   h Heb him

if in secret you show partiality.
11 Will not his majesty terrify you,
    and the dread of him fall upon you?
12 Your maxims are proverbs of ashes,
    your defenses are defenses of clay.

13 "Let me have silence, and I will
    speak,
    and let come on me what may.
14 I will take*i* my flesh in my teeth,
    and put my life in my hand.
15 Behold, he will slay me; I have no
    hope;
    yet I will defend my ways to his
    face.
16 This will be my salvation,
    that a godless man shall not come
    before him.
17 Listen carefully to my words,
    and let my declaration be in your
    ears.
18 Behold, I have prepared my case;
    I know that I shall be vindicated.
19 Who is there that will contend with
    me?
    For then I would be silent and die.
20 Only grant two things to me,
    then I will not hide myself from
    thy face:
21 withdraw thy hand far from me,
    and let not dread of thee terrify me.
22 Then call, and I will answer;
    or let me speak, and do thou reply
    to me.
23 How many are my iniquities and my
    sins?
    Make me know my transgression
    and my sin.
24 Why dost thou hide thy face,
    and count me as thy enemy?
25 Wilt thou frighten a driven leaf
    and pursue dry chaff?
26 For thou writest bitter things against
    me,
    and makest me inherit the in-
    iquities of my youth.
27 Thou puttest my feet in the stocks,
    and watchest all my paths;
    thou settest a bound to the soles of
    my feet.
28 Man*j* wastes away like a rotten
    thing,
    like a garment that is moth-eaten.

14 "Man that is born of a woman
    is of few days, and full of trouble.
2 He comes forth like a flower, and
    withers,
    he flees like a shadow, and con-
    tinues not.

3 And dost thou open thy eyes upon
    such a one
    and bring him*k* into judgment
    with thee?
4 Who can bring a clean thing out of
    an unclean?
    There is not one.
5 Since his days are determined,
    and the number of his months is
    with thee,
    and thou hast appointed his
    bounds that he cannot pass,
6 look away from him, and desist,*l*
    that he may enjoy, like a hireling,
    his day.

7 "For there is hope for a tree,
    if it be cut down, that it will
    sprout again,
    and that its shoots will not cease.
8 Though its root grow old in the earth,
    and its stump die in the ground,
9 yet at the scent of water it will bud
    and put forth branches like a
    young plant.
10 But man dies, and is laid low;
    man breathes his last, and where
    is he?
11 As waters fail from a lake,
    and a river wastes away and dries
    up,
12 so man lies down and rises not again;
    till the heavens are no more he will
    not awake,
    or be roused out of his sleep.
13 Oh that thou wouldest hide me in
    Shē′ōl,
    that thou wouldest conceal me
    until thy wrath be past,
    that thou wouldest appoint me a
    set time, and remember me!
14 If a man die, shall he live again?
    All the days of my service I would
    wait,
    till my release should come.
15 Thou wouldest call, and I would
    answer thee;
    thou wouldest long for the work of
    thy hands.
16 For then thou wouldest number my
    steps,
    thou wouldest not keep watch
    over my sin;
17 my transgression would be sealed up
    in a bag,
    and thou wouldest cover over my
    iniquity.

*i*Gk: Heb *Why should I take?*
*j*Heb *He*   *k*Gk Syr Vg: Heb *me*
*l*Cn: Heb *that he may desist*

18 "But the mountain falls and crumbles away,
and the rock is removed from its place;
19 the waters wear away the stones;
the torrents wash away the soil of the earth;
so thou destroyest the hope of man.
20 Thou prevailest for ever against him, and he passes;
thou changest his countenance, and sendest him away.
21 His sons come to honor, and he does not know it;
they are brought low, and he perceives it not.
22 He feels only the pain of his own body,
and he mourns only for himself."

15 Then Ē·lī'phăz the Tē'mạ·nīte answered:
2 "Should a wise man answer with windy knowledge,
and fill himself with the east wind?
3 Should he argue in unprofitable talk,
or in words with which he can do no good?
4 But you are doing away with the fear of God,
and hindering meditation before God.
5 For your iniquity teaches your mouth,
and you choose the tongue of the crafty.
6 Your own mouth condemns you, and not I;
your own lips testify against you.

7 "Are you the first man that was born?
Or were you brought forth before the hills?
8 Have you listened in the council of God?
And do you limit wisdom to yourself?
9 What do you know that we do not know?
What do you understand that is not clear to us?
10 Both the gray-haired and the aged are among us,
older than your father.
11 Are the consolations of God too small for you,
or the word that deals gently with you?
12 Why does your heart carry you away,

and why do your eyes flash,
13 that you turn your spirit against God,
and let such words go out of your mouth?
14 What is man, that he can be clean?
Or he that is born of a woman, that he can be righteous?
15 Behold, God puts no trust in his holy ones,
and the heavens are not clean in his sight;
16 how much less one who is abominable and corrupt,
a man who drinks iniquity like water!

17 "I will show you, hear me;
and what I have seen I will declare
18 (what wise men have told,
and their fathers have not hidden,
19 to whom alone the land was given,
and no stranger passed among them).
20 The wicked man writhes in pain all his days,
through all the years that are laid up for the ruthless.
21 Terrifying sounds are in his ears;
in prosperity the destroyer will come upon him.
22 He does not believe that he will return out of darkness,
and he is destined for the sword.
23 He wanders abroad for bread, saying, 'Where is it?'
He knows that a day of darkness is ready at his hand;
24 distress and anguish terrify him;
they prevail against him, like a king prepared for battle.
25 Because he has stretched forth his hand against God,
and bids defiance to the Almighty,
26 running stubbornly against him with a thick-bossed shield;
27 because he has covered his face with his fat,
and gathered fat upon his loins,
28 and has lived in desolate cities,
in houses which no man should inhabit,
which were destined to become heaps of ruins;
29 he will not be rich, and his wealth will not endure,
nor will he strike root in the earth; *m*
30 he will not escape from darkness;
the flame will dry up his shoots,

*m*Vg: Heb obscure

and his blossom[n] will be swept
away[o] by the wind.
31 Let him not trust in emptiness, deceiving himself;
for emptiness will be his recompense.
32 It will be paid in full before his time,
and his branch will not be green.
33 He will shake off his unripe grape,
like the vine,
and cast off his blossom, like the
olive tree.
34 For the company of the godless is
barren,
and fire consumes the tents of
bribery.
35 They conceive mischief and bring
forth evil
and their heart prepares deceit."

16   Then Jōb answered:
2 "I have heard many such
things;
miserable comforters are you all.
3 Shall windy words have an end?
Or what provokes you that you
answer?
4 I also could speak as you do,
if you were in my place;
I could join words together against
you,
and shake my head at you.
5 I could strengthen you with my
mouth,
and the solace of my lips would
assuage your pain.

6 "If I speak, my pain is not assuaged,
and if I forbear, how much of it
leaves me?
7 Surely now God has worn me out;
he has[p] made desolate all my
company.
8 And he has[p] shriveled me up,
which is a witness against me;
and my leanness has risen up against
me,
it testifies to my face.
9 He has torn me in his wrath, and
hated me;
he has gnashed his teeth at me;
my adversary sharpens his eyes
against me.
10 Men have gaped at me with their
mouth,
they have struck me insolently
upon the cheek,
they mass themselves together
against me.
11 God gives me up to the ungodly,

and casts me into the hands of
the wicked.
12 I was at ease, and he broke me
asunder;
he seized me by the neck and
dashed me to pieces;
he set me up as his target,
13   his archers surround me.
He slashes open my kidneys, and
does not spare;
he pours out my gall on the ground.
14 He breaks me with breach upon
breach;
he runs upon me like a warrior.
15 I have sewed sackcloth upon my skin,
and have laid my strength in the
dust.
16 My face is red with weeping,
and on my eyelids is deep darkness;
17 although there is no violence in my
hands,
and my prayer is pure.

18 "O earth, cover not my blood,
and let my cry find no resting
place.
19 Even now, behold, my witness is in
heaven,
and he that vouches for me is
on high.
20 My friends scorn me;
my eye pours out tears to God
21 that he would maintain the right of
a man with God,
like[q] that of a man with his
neighbor.
22 For when a few years have come
I shall go the way whence I shall
not return.

17   My spirit is broken, my days
are extinct,
the grave is ready for me.
2 Surely there are mockers about me
and my eye dwells on their provocation.

3 "Lay down a pledge for me with
thyself;
who is there that will give surety
for me?
4 Since thou hast closed their minds
to understanding,
therefore thou wilt not let them
triumph.
5 He who informs against his friends
to get a share of their property
the eyes of his children will fail

6 "He has made me a byword of the
     peoples,
     and I am one before whom men
     spit.
7 My eye has grown dim from grief,
     and all my members are like a
     shadow.
8 Upright men are appalled at this,
     and the innocent stirs himself up
     against the godless.
9 Yet the righteous holds to his way,
     and he that has clean hands grows
     stronger and stronger.
10 But you, come on again, all of you,
     and I shall not find a wise man
     among you.
11 My days are past, my plans are
     broken off,
     the desires of my heart.
12 They make night into day;
     'The light,' they say, 'is near to
     the darkness.'[r]
13 If I look for Shē'ōl as my house,
     if I spread my couch in darkness,
14 if I say to the pit, 'You are my father,'
     and to the worm, 'My mother,' or
     'My sister,'
15 where then is my hope?
     Who will see my hope?
16 Will it go down to the bars of Shē'ōl?
     Shall we descend together into the
     dust?"

18 Then Bĭl'dăd the Shü'hĭte an-
     swered:
2 "How long will you hunt for words?
     Consider, and then we will speak.
3 Why are we counted as cattle?
     Why are we stupid in your sight?
4 You who tear yourself in your anger,
     shall the earth be forsaken for you,
     or the rock be removed out of its
     place?

5 "Yea, the light of the wicked is put
     out,
     and the flame of his fire does not
     shine.
6 The light is dark in his tent,
     and his lamp above him is put out.
7 His strong steps are shortened
     and his own schemes throw him
     down.
8 For he is cast into a net by his own
     feet,
     and he walks on a pitfall.
9 A trap seizes him by the heel,
     a snare lays hold of him.
10 A rope is hid for him in the ground,
     a trap for him in the path.

11 Terrors frighten him on every side,
     and chase him at his heels.
12 His strength is hunger-bitten,
     and calamity is ready for his
     stumbling.
13 By disease his skin is consumed,[s]
     the first-born of death consumes
     his limbs.
14 He is torn from the tent in which
     he trusted,
     and is brought to the king of ter-
     rors.
15 In his tent dwells that which is none
     of his;
     brimstone is scattered upon his
     habitation.
16 His roots dry up beneath,
     and his branches wither above.
17 His memory perishes from the earth,
     and he has no name in the street.
18 He is thrust from light into darkness,
     and driven out of the world.
19 He has no offspring or descendant
     among his people,
     and no survivor where he used to
     live.
20 They of the west are appalled at his
     day,
     and horror seizes them of the east.
21 Surely such are the dwellings of the
     ungodly,
     such is the place of him who
     knows not God."

19 Then Jōb answered:
2 "How long will you torment me,
     and break me in pieces with
     words?
3 These ten times you have cast re-
     proach upon me;
     are you not ashamed to wrong me?
4 And even if it be true that I have
     erred,
     my error remains with myself.
5 If indeed you magnify yourselves
     against me,
     and make my humiliation an argu-
     ment against me,
6 know then that God has put me in
     the wrong,
     and closed his net about me.
7 Behold, I cry out, 'Violence!' but
     I am not answered;
     I call aloud, but there is no justice.
8 He has walled up my way, so that I
     cannot pass,
     and he has set darkness upon my
     paths.

[r] Heb obscure
[s] Cn: Heb *it consumes the limbs of his skin*

⁹He has stripped from me my glory,
and taken the crown from my head.
¹⁰He breaks me down on every side,
and I am gone,
and my hope has he pulled up like
a tree.
¹¹He has kindled his wrath against me,
and counts me as his adversary.
¹²His troops come on together;
they have cast up siegeworks*f*
against me,
and encamp round about my tent.

¹³"He has put my brethren far from
me,
and my acquaintances are wholly
estranged from me.
¹⁴My kinsfolk and my close friends
have failed me;
¹⁵ the guests in my house have
forgotten me;
my maidservants count me as a
stranger;
I have become an alien in their
eyes.
¹⁶I call to my servant, but he gives
me no answer;
I must beseech him with my
mouth.
¹⁷I am repulsive to my wife,
loathsome to the sons of my own
mother.
¹⁸Even young children despise me;
when I rise they talk against me.
¹⁹All my intimate friends abhor me,
and those whom I loved have
turned against me.
²⁰My bones cleave to my skin and to
my flesh,
and I have escaped by the skin of
my teeth.
²¹Have pity on me, have pity on me,
O you my friends,
for the hand of God has touched
me!
²²Why do you, like God, pursue me?
Why are you not satisfied with my
flesh?

²³"Oh that my words were written!
Oh that they were inscribed in a
book!
²⁴Oh that with an iron pen and lead
they were graven in the rock for
ever!
²⁵For I know that my Redeemer*u* lives,
and at last he will stand upon the
earth;*v*
²⁶and after my skin has been thus
destroyed,

then from*w* my flesh I shall see
God,*x*
²⁷whom I shall see on my side,*y*
and my eyes shall behold, and not
another.
My heart faints within me!
²⁸If you say, 'How we will pursue him!'
and, 'The root of the matter is
found in him';
²⁹be afraid of the sword,
for wrath brings the punishment
of the sword,
that you may know there is a
judgment."

20 Then Zō'phär the Nā'a-ma-
thīte answered:
²"Therefore my thoughts answer me,
because of my haste within me.
³I hear censure which insults me,
and out of my understanding a
spirit answers me.
⁴Do you not know this from of old,
since man was placed upon earth,
⁵that the exulting of the wicked is
short,
and the joy of the godless but for
a moment?
⁶Though his height mount up to the
heavens,
and his head reach to the clouds,
⁷he will perish for ever like his own
dung;
those who have seen him will
say, 'Where is he?'
⁸He will fly away like a dream, and
not be found;
he will be chased away like a
vision of the night.
⁹The eye which saw him will see him
no more,
nor will his place any more behold
him.
¹⁰His children will seek the favor of
the poor,
and his hands will give back his
wealth.
¹¹His bones are full of youthful vigor,
but it will lie down with him in the
dust.

¹²"Though wickedness is sweet in his
mouth,
though he hides it under his
tongue,
¹³though he is loath to let it go,
and holds it in his mouth,

---

*f*Heb *their way*   *u*Or *Vindicator*   *v*Or *dust*
*w*Or *without*   *x*The meaning of this verse is uncertain
*y*Or *for myself*

¹⁴ yet his food is turned in his stomach;
it is the gall of asps within him.
¹⁵ He swallows down riches and
vomits them up again;
God casts them out of his belly.
¹⁶ He will suck the poison of asps;
the tongue of a viper will kill him.
¹⁷ He will not look upon the rivers,
the streams flowing with honey
and curds.
¹⁸ He will give back the fruit of his
toil,
and will not swallow it down;
from the profit of his trading
he will get no enjoyment.
¹⁹ For he has crushed and abandoned
the poor,
he has seized a house which he did
not build.

²⁰ "Because his greed knew no rest,
he will not save anything in which
he delights.
²¹ There was nothing left after he had
eaten;
therefore his prosperity will not
endure.
²² In the fulness of his sufficiency he
will be in straits;
all the force of misery will come
upon him.
²³ To fill his belly to the full
God² will send his fierce anger into
him,
and rain it upon him as his food.ᵃ
²⁴ He will flee from an iron weapon;
a bronze arrow will strike him
through.
²⁵ It is drawn forth and comes out of
his body,
the glittering point comes out of
his gall;
terrors come upon him.
²⁶ Utter darkness is laid up for his
treasures;
a fire not blown upon will devour
him;
what is left in his tent will be consumed.
²⁷ The heavens will reveal his iniquity,
and the earth will rise up against
him.
²⁸ The possessions of his house will be
carried away,
dragged off in the day of God'sᵇ
wrath.
²⁹ This is the wicked man's portion
from God,
the heritage decreed for him by
God."

21 Then Jōb answered:
² "Listen carefully to my words,
and let this be your consolation.
³ Bear with me, and I will speak,
and after I have spoken, mock on.
⁴ As for me, is my complaint against
man?
Why should I not be impatient?
⁵ Look at me, and be appalled,
and lay your hand upon your
mouth.
⁶ When I think of it I am dismayed,
and shuddering seizes my flesh.
⁷ Why do the wicked live,
reach old age, and grow mighty in
power?
⁸ Their children are established in
their presence,
and their offspring before their
eyes.
⁹ Their houses are safe from fear,
and no rod of God is upon them.
¹⁰ Their bull breeds without fail;
their cow calves, and does not
cast her calf.
¹¹ They send forth their little ones like
a flock,
and their children dance.
¹² They sing to the tambourine and the
lyre,
and rejoice to the sound of the pipe.
¹³ They spend their days in prosperity,
and in peace they go down to
Shē′ōl.
¹⁴ They say to God, 'Depart from us!
We do not desire the knowledge
of thy ways.
¹⁵ What is the Almighty, that we should
serve him?
And what profit do we get if we
pray to him?'
¹⁶ Behold, is not their prosperity in
their hand?
The counsel of the wicked is far
from me.

¹⁷ "How often is it that the lamp of
the wicked is put out?
That their calamity comes upon
them?
That Godᶜ distributes pains in
his anger?
¹⁸ That they are like straw before the
wind,
and like chaff that the storm carries away?
¹⁹ You say, 'God stores up their iniquity
for their sons.'

ᶻHeb *he*   ᵃCn: Heb *in his flesh*
ᵇHeb *his*   ᶜHeb *he*

Let him recompense it to themselves, that they may know it.
²⁰ Let their own eyes see their destruction,
and let them drink of the wrath of
the Almighty.
²¹ For what do they care for their
houses after them,
when the number of their months
is cut off?
²² Will any teach God knowledge,
seeing that he judges those that
are on high?
²³ One dies in full prosperity,
being wholly at ease and secure,
²⁴ his body*ᵈ* full of fat
and the marrow of his bones moist.
²⁵ Another dies in bitterness of soul,
never having tasted of good.
²⁶ They lie down alike in the dust,
and the worms cover them.

²⁷ "Behold, I know your thoughts,
and your schemes to wrong me.
²⁸ For you say, 'Where is the house of
the prince?
Where is the tent in which the
wicked dwelt?'
²⁹ Have you not asked those who
travel the roads,
and do you not accept their testimony
³⁰ that the wicked man is spared in the
day of calamity,
that he is rescued in the day of
wrath?
³¹ Who declares his way to his face,
and who requites him for what he
has done?
³² When he is borne to the grave,
watch is kept over his tomb.
³³ The clods of the valley are sweet to
him;
all men follow after him,
and those who go before him are
innumerable.
³⁴ How then will you comfort me with
empty nothings?
There is nothing left of your
answers but falsehood."

22 Then Ė·lī′phăz the Tē′mă·nīte
answered:
² "Can a man be profitable to God?
Surely he who is wise is profitable to himself.
³ Is it any pleasure to the Almighty if
you are righteous,
or is it gain to him if you make
your ways blameless?

⁴ Is it for your fear of him that he
reproves you,
and enters into judgment with
you?
⁵ Is not your wickedness great?
There is no end to your iniquities.
⁶ For you have exacted pledges of your
brothers for nothing,
and stripped the naked of their
clothing.
⁷ You have given no water to the weary
to drink,
and you have withheld bread
from the hungry.
⁸ The man with power possessed the
land,
and the favored man dwelt in it.
⁹ You have sent widows away empty,
and the arms of the fatherless
were crushed.
¹⁰ Therefore snares are round about
you,
and sudden terror overwhelms
you;
¹¹ your light is darkened, so that*ᵉ* you
cannot see,
and a flood of water covers you.

¹² "Is not God high in the heavens?
See the highest stars, how lofty
they are!
¹³ Therefore you say, 'What does God
know?
Can he judge through the deep
darkness?
¹⁴ Thick clouds enwrap him, so that he
does not see,
and he walks on the vault of
heaven.'
¹⁵ Will you keep to the old way
which wicked men have trod?
¹⁶ They were snatched away before
their time;
their foundation was washed
away.
¹⁷ They said to God, 'Depart from us,'
and 'What can the Almighty do to
us?'*ᶠ*
¹⁸ Yet he filled their houses with good
things—
but the counsel of the wicked is
far from me.
¹⁹ The righteous see it and are glad;
the innocent laugh them to scorn,
²⁰ saying, 'Surely our adversaries are
cut off,

ᵈ The meaning of the Hebrew word is uncertain
ᵉ Cn Compare Gk: Heb or darkness
ᶠ Gk Syr: Heb them
22.2, 3: 35.6-8.

and what they left the fire has consumed.'

21 "Agree with God, and be at peace; thereby good will come to you.

22 Receive instruction from his mouth, and lay up his words in your heart.

23 If you return to the Almighty and humble yourself,*g*
if you remove unrighteousness far from your tents,

24 if you lay gold in the dust, and gold of Ō'phĭr among the stones of the torrent bed,

25 and if the Almighty is your gold, and your precious silver;

26 then you will delight yourself in the Almighty, and lift up your face to God.

27 You will make your prayer to him, and he will hear you; and you will pay your vows.

28 You will decide on a matter, and it will be established for you, and light will shine on your ways.

29 For God abases the proud,*h* but he saves the lowly.

30 He delivers the innocent man;*i* you will be delivered through the cleanness of your hands."

23 Then Jōb answered:
2 "Today also my complaint is bitter,*j* his*k* hand is heavy in spite of my groaning.

3 Oh, that I knew where I might find him, that I might come even to his seat!

4 I would lay my case before him and fill my mouth with arguments.

5 I would learn what he would answer me, and understand what he would say to me.

6 Would he contend with me in the greatness of his power? No; he would give heed to me.

7 There an upright man could reason with him, and I should be acquitted for ever by my judge.

8 "Behold, I go forward, but he is not there; and backward, but I cannot perceive him;

9 on the left hand I seek him,*l* but I cannot behold him;

I*m* turn to the right hand, but I cannot see him.

10 But he knows the way that I take; when he has tried me, I shall come forth as gold.

11 My foot has held fast to his steps; I have kept his way and have not turned aside.

12 I have not departed from the commandment of his lips; I have treasured in*n* my bosom the words of his mouth.

13 But he is unchangeable and who can turn him? What he desires, that he does.

14 For he will complete what he appoints for me; and many such things are in his mind.

15 Therefore I am terrified at his presence; when I consider, I am in dread of him.

16 God has made my heart faint; the Almighty has terrified me;

17 for I am*o* hemmed in by darkness, and thick darkness covers my face.*p*

24 "Why are not times of judgment kept by the Almighty, and why do those who know him never see his days?

2 Men remove landmarks; they seize flocks and pasture them.

3 They drive away the ass of the fatherless; they take the widow's ox for a pledge.

4 They thrust the poor off the road; the poor of the earth all hide themselves.

5 Behold, like wild asses in the desert they go forth to their toil, seeking prey in the wilderness as food*q* for their children.

6 They gather their*r* fodder in the field and they glean the vineyard of the wicked man.

7 They lie all night naked, without clothing, and have no covering in the cold.

8 They are wet with the rain of the mountains,

g Gk: Heb *you will be built up*
h Cn: Heb *when they abased you said, Proud*
i Gk Syr Vg: Heb *him that is not innocent*
j Syr Vg Tg: Heb *rebellious*   *k* Gk Syr: Heb *my*
l Compare Syr: Heb *on the left hand when he works*
m Syr Vg: Heb *he*   *n* Gk Vg: Heb *from*
o With one Ms: Heb *am not*   *p* Vg: Heb *from my face*
q Heb *food to him*   *r* Heb *his*

and cling to the rock for want of shelter.

9 (There are those who snatch the fatherless child from the breast, and take in pledge the infant of the poor.)

10 They go about naked, without clothing;

hungry, they carry the sheaves;

11 among the olive rows of the wicked' they make oil;

they tread the wine presses, but suffer thirst.

12 From out of the city the dying groan, and the soul of the wounded cries for help;

yet God pays no attention to their prayer.

13 "There are those who rebel against the light,

who are not acquainted with its ways,

and do not stay in its paths.

14 The murderer rises in the dark,'
that he may kill the poor and needy;

and in the night he is as a thief.

15 The eye of the adulterer also waits for the twilight,

saying, 'No eye will see me';

and he disguises his face.

16 In the dark they dig through houses;
by day they shut themselves up;
they do not know the light.

17 For deep darkness is morning to all of them;

for they are friends with the terrors of deep darkness.

18 "You say, 'They are swiftly carried away upon the face of the waters;

their portion is cursed in the land;
no treader turns toward their vineyards.

19 Drought and heat snatch away the snow waters;

so does She'ol those who have sinned.

20 The squares of the town*u* forget them;

their name*v* is no longer remembered;

so wickedness is broken like a tree.'

21 "They feed on the barren childless woman,

and do no good to the widow.

22 Yet God*w* prolongs the life of the mighty by his power;

they rise up when they despair of life.

23 He gives them security, and they are supported;

and his eyes are upon their ways.

24 They are exalted a little while, and then are gone;

they wither and fade like the mallow;*x*

they are cut off like the heads of grain.

25 If it is not so, who will prove me a liar,

and show that there is nothing in what I say?"

25 Then Bǐl′dǎd the Shü′hīte answered:

2 "Dominion and fear are with God;*v*
he makes peace in his high heaven.

3 Is there any number to his armies?
Upon whom does his light not arise?

4 How then can man be righteous before God?

How can he who is born of woman be clean?

5 Behold, even the moon is not bright
and the stars are not clean in his sight;

6 how much less man, who is a maggot,

and the son of man, who is a worm!"

26 Then Jōb answered:
2 "How you have helped him who has no power!

How you have saved the arm that has no strength!

3 How you have counseled him who has no wisdom,

and plentifully declared sound knowledge!

4 With whose help have you uttered words,

and whose spirit has come forth from you?

5 The shades below tremble,
the waters and their inhabitants.

6 She'ol is naked before God,
and A·bǎd′dǒn has no covering.

7 He stretches out the north over the void,

and hangs the earth upon nothing

---

*Heb *their olive rows*   'Cn: Heb *at the light*
*Cn: Heb obscure   *Cn: Heb *a worm*   *Heb *he*
*Gk: Heb *all*   *Heb *him*

⁸He binds up the waters in his thick
clouds,
and the cloud is not rent under
them.
⁹He covers the face of the moon,ᶻ
and spreads over it his cloud.
¹⁰He has described a circle upon the
face of the waters
at the boundary between light and
darkness.
¹¹The pillars of heaven tremble,
and are astounded at his rebuke.
¹²By his power he stilled the sea;
by his understanding he smote
Rā′hăb.
¹³By his wind the heavens were made
fair;
his hand pierced the fleeing serpent.
¹⁴Lo, these are but the outskirts of his
ways;
and how small a whisper do we
hear of him!
But the thunder of his power who
can understand?"

27 And Jōb again took up his discourse, and said:
²"As God lives, who has taken away
my right,
and the Almighty, who has made
my soul bitter;
³as long as my breath is in me,
and the spirit of God is in my nostrils;
⁴my lips will not speak falsehood,
and my tongue will not utter
deceit.
⁵Far be it from me to say that you are
right;
till I die I will not put away my
integrity from me.
⁶I hold fast my righteousness, and will
not let it go;
my heart does not reproach me for
any of my days.

⁷"Let my enemy be as the wicked,
and let him that rises up against
me be as the unrighteous.
⁸For what is the hope of the godless
when God cuts him off,
when God takes away his life?
⁹Will God hear his cry,
when trouble comes upon him?
¹⁰Will he take delight in the Almighty?
Will he call upon God at all times?
¹¹I will teach you concerning the hand
of God;

what is with the Almighty I will
not conceal.
¹²Behold, all of you have seen it yourselves;
why then have you become altogether vain?

¹³"This is the portion of a wicked man
with God,
and the heritage which oppressors
receive from the Almighty:
¹⁴If his children are multiplied, it is for
the sword;
and his offspring have not enough
to eat.
¹⁵Those who survive him the pestilence buries,
and their widows make no lamentation.
¹⁶Though he heap up silver like dust,
and pile up clothing like clay;
¹⁷he may pile it up, but the just will
wear it,
and the innocent will divide the
silver.
¹⁸The house which he builds is like a
spider's web,ᵃ
like a booth which a watchman
makes.
¹⁹He goes to bed rich, but will do so no
more;ᵇ
he opens his eyes, and his wealth
is gone.
²⁰Terrors overtake him like a flood;
in the night a whirlwind carries
him off.
²¹The east wind lifts him up and he is
gone;
it sweeps him out of his place.
²²Itᶜ hurls at him without pity;
he flees from itsᵈ power in headlong flight.
²³Itᶜ claps itsᵈ hands at him,
and hisses at him from itsᵈ place.

28 "Surely there is a mine for silver,
and a place for gold which they
refine.
²Iron is taken out of the earth,
and copper is smelted from the ore.
³Men put an end to darkness,
and search out to the farthest
bound
the ore in gloom and deep darkness.
⁴They open shafts in a valley away
from where men live;

ᶻOr *his throne*
ᵃCn Compare Gk Syr: Heb *He builds his house like the
moth* ᵇGk Compare Syr: Heb *shall not be gathered*
ᶜOr *he* (that is God) ᵈOr *his*

they are forgotten by travelers,
they hang afar from men, they
swing to and fro.
⁵As for the earth, out of it comes
bread;
but underneath it is turned up as
by fire.
⁶Its stones are the place of sapphires, *ᵉ*
and it has dust of gold.

⁷"That path no bird of prey knows,
and the falcon's eye has not seen it.
⁸The proud beasts have not trodden it;
the lion has not passed over it.

⁹"Man puts his hand to the flinty rock,
and overturns mountains by the
roots.
¹⁰He cuts out channels in the rocks,
and his eye sees every precious
thing.
¹¹He binds up the streams so that they
do not trickle,
and the thing that is hid he brings
forth to light.

¹²"But where shall wisdom be found?
And where is the place of understanding?
¹³Man does not know the way to it, *ᶠ*
and it is not found in the land of
the living.
¹⁴The deep says, 'It is not in me,'
and the sea says, 'It is not with me.'
¹⁵It cannot be gotten for gold,
and silver cannot be weighed as its
price.
¹⁶It cannot be valued in the gold of
O'phir,
in precious onyx or sapphire. *ᵍ*
¹⁷Gold and glass cannot equal it,
nor can it be exchanged for jewels
of fine gold.
¹⁸No mention shall be made of coral or
of crystal;
the price of wisdom is above pearls.
¹⁹The topaz of Ethiopia cannot compare with it,
nor can it be valued in pure gold.

²⁰"Whence then comes wisdom?
And where is the place of understanding?
²¹It is hid from the eyes of all living,
and concealed from the birds of
the air.
²²A·băd'don and Death say,
'We have heard a rumor of it with
our ears.'

²³"God understands the way to it,
and he knows its place.
²⁴For he looks to the ends of the earth,
and sees everything under the
heavens.
²⁵When he gave to the wind its weight,
and meted out the waters by measure;
²⁶when he made a decree for the rain,
and a way for the lightning of the
thunder;
²⁷then he saw it and declared it;
he established it, and searched it
out.
²⁸And he said to man,
'Behold, the fear of the Lord, that is
wisdom;
and to depart from evil is understanding.' "

29 And Jŏb again took up his discourse, and said:
²"Oh, that I were as in the months of
old,
as in the days when God watched
over me;
³when his lamp shone upon my head,
and by his light I walked through
darkness;
⁴as I was in my autumn days,
when the friendship of God was
upon my tent;
⁵when the Almighty was yet with me,
when my children were about me;
⁶when my steps were washed with
milk,
and the rock poured out for me
streams of oil!
⁷When I went out to the gate of the
city,
when I prepared my seat in the
square,
⁸the young men saw me and withdrew,
and the aged rose and stood;
⁹the princes refrained from talking,
and laid their hand on their mouth;
¹⁰the voice of the nobles was hushed,
and their tongue cleaved to the
roof of their mouth.
¹¹When the ear heard, it called me
blessed,
and when the eye saw, it approved;
¹²because I delivered the poor who
cried,
and the fatherless who had none
to help him.
¹³The blessing of him who was about
to perish came upon me,

ᵉ Or lapis lazuli ᶠ Gk: Heb its price ᵍ Or lapis lazuli

and I caused the widow's heart to sing for joy.
[14] I put on righteousness, and it clothed me;
my justice was like a robe and a turban.
[15] I was eyes to the blind,
and feet to the lame.
[16] I was a father to the poor,
and I searched out the cause of him whom I did not know.
[17] I broke the fangs of the unrighteous,
and made him drop his prey from his teeth.
[18] Then I thought, 'I shall die in my nest,
and I shall multiply my days as the sand,
[19] my roots spread out to the waters,
with the dew all night on my branches,
[20] my glory fresh with me,
and my bow ever new in my hand.'

[21] "Men listened to me, and waited,
and kept silence for my counsel.
[22] After I spoke they did not speak again,
and my word dropped upon them.
[23] They waited for me as for the rain;
and they opened their mouths as for the spring rain.
[24] I smiled on them when they had no confidence;
and the light of my countenance they did not cast down.
[25] I chose their way, and sat as chief,
and I dwelt like a king among his troops,
like one who comforts mourners.

30 "But now they make sport of me,
men who are younger than I,
whose fathers I would have disdained
to set with the dogs of my flock.
[2] What could I gain from the strength of their hands,
men whose vigor is gone?
[3] Through want and hard hunger
they gnaw the dry and desolate ground;[h]
[4] they pick mallow and the leaves of bushes,
and to warm themselves the roots of the broom.
[5] They are driven out from among men;
they shout after them as after a thief.

[6] In the gullies of the torrents they must dwell,
in holes of the earth and of the rocks.
[7] Among the bushes they bray;
under the nettles they huddle together.
[8] A senseless, a disreputable brood,
they have been whipped out of the land.

[9] "And now I have become their song,
I am a byword to them.
[10] They abhor me, they keep aloof from me;
they do not hesitate to spit at the sight of me.
[11] Because God has loosed my cord and humbled me,
they have cast off restraint in my presence.
[12] On my right hand the rabble rise,
they drive me[i] forth,
they cast up against me their ways of destruction.
[13] They break up my path,
they promote my calamity;
no one restrains[j] them.
[14] As through[k] a wide breach they come;
amid the crash they roll on.
[15] Terrors are turned upon me;
my honor is pursued as by the wind,
and my prosperity has passed away like a cloud.

[16] "And now my soul is poured out within me;
days of affliction have taken hold of me.
[17] The night racks my bones,
and the pain that gnaws me takes no rest.
[18] With violence it seizes my garment;[l]
it binds me about like the collar of my tunic.
[19] God has cast me into the mire,
and I have become like dust and ashes.
[20] I cry to thee and thou dost not answer me;
I stand, and thou dost not[m] heed me.

[h] Heb *ground yesterday waste*   [i] Heb *my feet*
[j] Cn: Heb *helps*   [k] Cn: Heb *like*
[l] Gk: Heb *my garment is disfigured*
[m] One Heb Ms and Vg: Heb lacks *not*

²¹ Thou hast turned cruel to me;
with the might of thy hand thou
dost persecute me.
²² Thou liftest me up on the wind, thou
makest me ride on it,
and thou tossest me about in the
roar of the storm.
²³ Yea, I know that thou wilt bring me
to death,
and to the house appointed for all
living.

²⁴ "Yet does not one in a heap of ruins
stretch out his hand,
and in his disaster cry for help?"
²⁵ Did not I weep for him whose day
was hard?
Was not my soul grieved for the
poor?
²⁶ But when I looked for good. evil
came;
and when I waited for light, darkness came.
My heart is in turmoil, and is never
still;
days of affliction come to meet
me.
²⁸ I go about blackened, but not by the
sun;
I stand up in the assembly, and cry
for help.
²⁹ I am a brother of jackals,
and a companion of ostriches.
³⁰ My skin turns black and falls from
me,
and my bones burn with heat.
³¹ My lyre is turned to mourning,
and my pipe to the voice of those
who weep.

31 "I have made a covenant with my
eyes;
how then could I look upon a
virgin?
² What would be my portion from God
above,
and my heritage from the Almighty on high?
³ Does not calamity befall the un-
righteous,
and disaster the workers of iniquity?
⁴ Does not he see my ways,
and number all my steps?

⁵ "If I have walked with falsehood,
and my foot has hastened to de-
ceit;
⁶ (Let me be weighed in a just balance,
and let God know my integrity!)

⁷ if my step has turned aside from the
way,
and my heart has gone after my
eyes,
and if any spot has cleaved to my
hands;
⁸ then let me sow, and another eat;
and let what grows for me be
rooted out.

⁹ "If my heart has been enticed to a
woman,
and I have lain in wait at my
neighbor's door;
¹⁰ then let my wife grind for another,
and let others bow down upon her.
¹¹ For that would be a heinous crime;
that would be an iniquity to be
punished by the judges;
¹² for that would be a fire which con-
sumes unto A·băd'don,
and it would burn to the root all
my increase.

¹³ "If I have rejected the cause of my
manservant or my maidservant,
when they brought a complaint
against me;
¹⁴ what then shall I do when God rises
up?
When he makes inquiry, what
shall I answer him?
¹⁵ Did not he who made me in the
womb make him?
And did not one fashion us in the
womb?

¹⁶ "If I have withheld anything that the
poor desired,
or have caused the eyes of the
widow to fail,
¹⁷ or have eaten my morsel alone,
and the fatherless has not eaten of
it
¹⁸ (for from his youth I reared him as a
father,
and from his mother's womb I
guided him^o);
¹⁹ if I have seen any one perish for lack
of clothing,
or a poor man without covering;
²⁰ if his loins have not blessed me,
and if he was not warmed with the
fleece of my sheep;
²¹ if I have raised my hand against the
fatherless,
because I saw help in the gate;

ⁿ Cn: Heb obscure
^o Cn: Heb *for from my youth he grew up to me as a father,
and from my mother's womb I guided her*

²² then let my shoulder blade fall from my shoulder,
and let my arm be broken from its socket.
²³ For I was in terror of calamity from God,
and I could not have faced his majesty.

²⁴ "If I have made gold my trust,
or called fine gold my confidence;
²⁵ if I have rejoiced because my wealth was great,
or because my hand had gotten much;
²⁶ if I have looked at the sun*ᵖ* when it shone,
or the moon moving in splendor,
²⁷ and my heart has been secretly enticed,
and my mouth has kissed my hand;
²⁸ this also would be an iniquity to be punished by the judges,
for I should have been false to God above.

²⁹ "If I have rejoiced at the ruin of him that hated me,
or exulted when evil overtook him
³⁰ (I have not let my mouth sin
by asking for his life with a curse);
³¹ if the men of my tent have not said,
'Who is there that has not been filled with his meat?'
³² (the sojourner has not lodged in the street;
I have opened my doors to the wayfarer);
³³ if I have concealed my transgressions from men,*ᵠ*
by hiding my iniquity in my bosom,
³⁴ because I stood in great fear of the multitude,
and the contempt of families terrified me,
so that I kept silence, and did not go out of doors —
³⁵ Oh, that I had one to hear me!
(Here is my signature! let the Almighty answer me!)
Oh, that I had the indictment written by my adversary!
³⁶ Surely I would carry it on my shoulder;
I would bind it on me as a crown;
³⁷ I would give him an account of all my steps;
like a prince I would approach him.

³⁸ "If my land has cried out against me,
and its furrows have wept together;
³⁹ if I have eaten its yield without payment,
and caused the death of its owners;
⁴⁰ let thorns grow instead of wheat,
and foul weeds instead of barley."

The words of Job are ended.

32 So these three men ceased to answer Job, because he was righteous in his own eyes. ²Then Ė·lī′hū the son of Bār′ạ·chĕl the Bŭz′īte, of the family of Räm, became angry. He was angry at Job because he justified himself rather than God; ³he was angry also at Job's three friends because they had found no answer, although they had declared Job to be in the wrong. ⁴Now Ė·lī′hū had waited to speak to Job because they were older than he. ⁵And when Ė·lī′hū saw that there was no answer in the mouth of these three men, he became angry.

6 And Ė·lī′hū the son of Bār′ạ·chĕl the Bŭz′īte answered:

"I am young in years,
and you are aged;
therefore I was timid and afraid
to declare my opinion to you.
⁷ I said, 'Let days speak,
and many years teach wisdom.'
⁸ But it is the spirit in a man,
the breath of the Almighty,
that makes him understand.
⁹ It is not the old*ʳ* that are wise,
nor the aged that understand what is right.
¹⁰ Therefore I say, 'Listen to me;
let me also declare my opinion.'

¹¹ "Behold, I waited for your words.
I listened for your wise sayings,
while you searched out what to say.
¹² I gave you my attention,
and, behold, there was none that confuted Job,
or that answered his words, among you.
¹³ Beware lest you say, 'We have found wisdom;
God may vanquish him, not man.'
¹⁴ He has not directed his words against me,

ᵖ Heb *the light*   *ᵠ* Cn: Heb *like men* or *like Adam*
ʳ Gk Syr Vg: Heb *many*

and I will not answer him with your speeches.

15 "They are discomfited, they answer no more;
　　they have not a word to say.
16 And shall I wait, because they do not speak,
　　because they stand there, and answer no more?
17 I also will give my answer;
　　I also will declare my opinion.
18 For I am full of words,
　　the spirit within me constrains me.
19 Behold, my heart is like wine that has no vent;
　　like new wineskins, it is ready to burst.
20 I must speak, that I may find relief;
　　I must open my lips and answer.
21 I will not show partiality to any person
　　or use flattery toward any man.
22 For I do not know how to flatter,
　　else would my Maker soon put an end to me.

33 "But now, hear my speech, O Job,
　　and listen to all my words.
2 Behold, I open my mouth;
　　the tongue in my mouth speaks.
3 My words declare the uprightness of my heart,
　　and what my lips know they speak sincerely.
4 The spirit of God has made me,
　　and the breath of the Almighty gives me life.
5 Answer me, if you can;
　　set your words in order before me;
　　take your stand.
6 Behold, I am toward God as you are;
　　I too was formed from a piece of clay.
7 Behold, no fear of me need terrify you;
　　my pressure will not be heavy upon you.

8 "Surely, you have spoken in my hearing,
　　and I have heard the sound of your words.
9 You say, 'I am clean, without transgression;
　　I am pure, and there is no iniquity in me.
10 Behold, he finds occasions against me,

he counts me as his enemy;
11 he puts my feet in the stocks,
　　and watches all my paths.'

12 "Behold, in this you are not right. I will answer you.
　　God is greater than man.
13 Why do you contend against him,
　　saying, 'He will answer none of my* words'?
14 For God speaks in one way,
　　and in two, though man does not perceive it.
15 In a dream, in a vision of the night,
　　when deep sleep falls upon men,
　　while they slumber on their beds,
16 then he opens the ears of men,
　　and terrifies them with warnings,
17 that he may turn man aside from his deed,
　　and cut off* pride from man;
18 he keeps back his soul from the Pit,
　　his life from perishing by the sword.

19 "Man is also chastened with pain upon his bed,
　　and with continual strife in his bones;
20 so that his life loathes bread,
　　and his appetite dainty food.
21 His flesh is so wasted away that it cannot be seen;
　　and his bones which were not seen stick out.
22 His soul draws near the Pit,
　　and his life to those who bring death.
23 If there be for him an angel,
　　a mediator, one of the thousand,
　　to declare to man what is right for him;
24 and he is gracious to him, and says,
　　'Deliver him from going down into the Pit,
　　I have found a ransom;
25 let his flesh become fresh with youth;
　　let him return to the days of his youthful vigor';
26 then man prays to God, and he accepts him,
　　he comes into his presence with joy.
He recounts" to men his salvation,
27　　and he sings before men, and says:
　　'I sinned, and perverted what was right,
　　and it was not requited to me.

* Compare Gk: Heb *his*
' Cn: Heb *hide*　" Cn: Heb *returns*

²⁸He has redeemed my soul from going
down into the Pit,
and my life shall see the light.'

²⁹"Behold, God does all these things,
twice, three times, with a man,
³⁰to bring back his soul from the Pit,
that he may see the light of life.ᵛ
³¹Give heed, O Jōb, listen to me;
be silent, and I will speak.
³²If you have anything to say, answer
me;
speak, for I desire to justify you.
³³If not, listen to me;
be silent, and I will teach you wisdom."

34 Then Ē·lī'hū said:
² "Hear my words, you wise men,
and give ear to me, you who know;
³for the ear tests words
as the palate tastes food.
⁴Let us choose what is right;
let us determine among ourselves
what is good.
⁵For Jōb has said, 'I am innocent,
and God has taken away my right;
⁶in spite of my right I am counted a
liar;
my wound is incurable, though I
am without transgression.'
⁷What man is like Jōb,
who drinks up scoffing like water,
⁸who goes in company with evildoers
and walks with wicked men?
⁹For he has said, 'It profits a man
nothing
that he should take delight in God.'

¹⁰"Therefore, hear me, you men of
understanding,
far be it from God that he should
do wickedness,
and from the Almighty that he
should do wrong.
¹¹For according to the work of a man
he will requite him,
and according to his ways he will
make it befall him.
¹²Of a truth, God will not do wickedly,
and the Almighty will not pervert
justice.
¹³Who gave him charge over the earth
and who laid on himʷ the whole
world?
¹⁴If he should take back his spiritˣ to
himself,
and gather to himself his breath,
¹⁵all flesh would perish together,
and man would return to dust.

¹⁶"If you have understanding, hear
this;
listen to what I say.
¹⁷Shall one who hates justice govern?
Will you condemn him who is
righteous and mighty,
¹⁸who says to a king, 'Worthless one,'
and to nobles, 'Wicked man';
¹⁹who shows no partiality to princes,
nor regards the rich more than the
poor,
for they are all the work of his
hands?
²⁰In a moment they die;
at midnight the people are shaken
and pass away,
and the mighty are taken away by
no human hand.

²¹"For his eyes are upon the ways of
a man,
and he sees all his steps.
²²There is no gloom or deep darkness
where evildoers may hide themselves.
²³For he has not appointed a timeʸ for
any man
to go before God in judgment.
²⁴He shatters the mighty without in-
vestigation,
and sets others in their place.
²⁵Thus, knowing their works,
he overturns them in the night,
and they are crushed.
²⁶He strikes them for their wickedness
in the sight of men,
²⁷because they turned aside from following him,
and had no regard for any of his
ways,
²⁸so that they caused the cry of the poor
to come to him,
and he heard the cry of the afflicted—
²⁹When he is quiet, who can condemn?
When he hides his face, who can
behold him,
whether it be a nation or a man?—
³⁰that a godless man should not reign,
that he should not ensnare the
people.

³¹"For has any one said to God,
'I have borne chastisement; I will
not offend any more;
³²teach me what I do not see;

ᵛSyr: Heb *to be lighted with the light of life*
ʷHeb lacks *on him* ˣHeb *his heart his spirit*
ʸCn: Heb *yet*

if I have done iniquity, I will do it no more'?
³³Will he then make requital to suit you, because you reject it?
For you must choose, and not I; therefore declare what you know.ᶻ
³⁴Men of understanding will say to me, and the wise man who hears me will say:
³⁵'Jōb speaks without knowledge, his words are without insight.'
³⁶Would that Jōb were tried to the end, because he answers like wicked men.
³⁷For he adds rebellion to his sin; he claps his hands among us, and multiplies his words against God."

35 And Ĕ·lī'hū said:
²"Do you think this to be just? Do you say, 'It is my right before God,'
³that you ask, 'What advantage have I?
How am I better off than if I had sinned?'
⁴I will answer you and your friends with you.
⁵Look at the heavens, and see; and behold the clouds, which are higher than you.
⁶If you have sinned, what do you accomplish against him?
And if your transgressions are multiplied, what do you do to him?
⁷If you are righteous, what do you give to him;
or what does he receive from your hand?
⁸Your wickedness concerns a man like yourself,
and your righteousness a son of man.

⁹"Because of the multitude of oppressions people cry out;
they call for help because of the arm of the mighty.
¹⁰But none says, 'Where is God my Maker,
who gives songs in the night,
¹¹who teaches us more than the beasts of the earth,
and makes us wiser than the birds of the air?'
¹²There they cry out, but he does not answer,
because of the pride of evil men.

¹³Surely God does not hear an empty cry,
nor does the Almighty regard it.
¹⁴How much less when you say that you do not see him,
that the case is before him, and you are waiting for him!
¹⁵And now, because his anger does not punish,
and he does not greatly heed transgression,ᵃ
¹⁶Jōb opens his mouth in empty talk, he multiplies words without knowledge."

36 And Ĕ·lī'hū continued, and said:
²"Bear with me a little, and I will show you,
for I have yet something to say on God's behalf.
³I will fetch my knowledge from afar,
and ascribe righteousness to my Maker.
⁴For truly my words are not false; one who is perfect in knowledge is with you.

⁵"Behold, God is mighty, and does not despise any;
he is mighty in strength of understanding.
⁶He does not keep the wicked alive, but gives the afflicted their right.
⁷He does not withdraw his eyes from the righteous,
but with kings upon the throne he sets them for ever, and they are exalted.
⁸And if they are bound in fetters and caught in the cords of affliction,
⁹then he declares to them their work and their transgressions, that they are behaving arrogantly.
¹⁰He opens their ears to instruction, and commands that they return from iniquity.
¹¹If they hearken and serve him, they complete their days in prosperity,
and their years in pleasantness.
¹²But if they do not hearken, they perish by the sword,
and die without knowledge.

ᶻThe Hebrew of verses 29-33 is obscure
ᵃTheodotion Symmachus Compare Vg: The meaning of the Hebrew word is uncertain
35.6–8: 22.2-3.

¹³ "The godless in heart cherish anger;
    they do not cry for help when he
    binds them.
¹⁴ They die in youth,
    and their life ends in shame.ᵇ
¹⁵ He delivers the afflicted by their
    affliction,
    and opens their ear by adversity.
¹⁶ He also allured you out of distress
    into a broad place where there was
    no cramping,
    and what was set on your table
    was full of fatness.

¹⁷ "But you are full of the judgment on
    the wicked;
    judgment and justice seize you.
¹⁸ Beware lest wrath entice you into
    scoffing;
    and let not the greatness of the
    ransom turn you aside.
¹⁹ Will your cry avail to keep you from
    distress,
    or all the force of your strength?
²⁰ Do not long for the night,
    when peoples are cut off in their
    place.
²¹ Take heed, do not turn to iniquity,
    for this you have chosen rather
    than affliction.
²² Behold, God is exalted in his power;
    who is a teacher like him?
²³ Who has prescribed for him his way,
    or who can say, 'Thou hast done
    wrong'?

²⁴ "Remember to extol his work,
    of which men have sung.
²⁵ All men have looked on it;
    man beholds it from afar.
²⁶ Behold, God is great, and we know
    him not;
    the number of his years is un-
    searchable.
²⁷ For he draws up the drops of water,
    heᶜ distils his mist in rain
²⁸ which the skies pour down,
    and drop upon man abundantly.
²⁹ Can any one understand the spread-
    ing of the clouds,
    the thunderings of his pavilion?
³⁰ Behold, he scatters his lightning
    about him,
    and covers the roots of the sea.
³¹ For by these he judges peoples;
    he gives food in abundance.
³² He covers his hands with the light-
    ning,
    and commands it to strike the
    mark.

³³ Its crashing declares concerning him,
    who is jealous with anger against
    iniquity.

37 "At this also my heart trembles,
    and leaps out of its place.
² Hearken to the thunder of his voice
    and the rumbling that comes from
    his mouth.
³ Under the whole heaven he lets it
    go,
    and his lightning to the corners
    of the earth.
⁴ After it his voice roars;
    he thunders with his majestic
    voice
    and he does not restrain the light-
    ningsᵈ when his voice is heard.
⁵ God thunders wondrously with his
    voice;
    he does great things which we
    cannot comprehend.
⁶ For to the snow he says, 'Fall on the
    earth';
    and to the shower and the rain,ᵉ
    'Be strong.'
⁷ He seals up the hand of every
    man,
    that all men may know his work.ᶠ
⁸ Then the beasts go into their lairs,
    and remain in their dens.
⁹ From its chamber comes the whirl-
    wind,
    and cold from the scattering winds.
¹⁰ By the breath of God ice is given,
    and the broad waters are frozen
    fast.
¹¹ He loads the thick cloud with mois-
    ture;
    the clouds scatter his lightning.
¹² They turn round and round by his
    guidance,
    to accomplish all that he com-
    mands them
    on the face of the habitable world.
¹³ Whether for correction, or for his
    land,
    or for love, he causes it to happen.

¹⁴ "Hear this, O Jōb;
    stop and consider the wondrous
    works of God.
¹⁵ Do you know how God lays his com-
    mand upon them,
    and causes the lightning of his
    cloud to shine?

ᵇ Heb *among the cult prostitutes* ᶜ Cn: Heb *they distil*
ᵈ Heb *them*
ᵉ Cn Compare Syr: Heb *shower of rain and shower of rains*
ᶠ Vg Compare Syr Tg: Heb *that all men whom he has made
may know it*

¹⁶Do you know the balancings of the clouds,
the wondrous works of him who is perfect in knowledge,
¹⁷you whose garments are hot
when the earth is still because of the south wind?
¹⁸Can you, like him, spread out the skies,
hard as a molten mirror?
¹⁹Teach us what we shall say to him;
we cannot draw up our case because of darkness.
²⁰Shall it be told him that I would speak?
Did a man ever wish that he would be swallowed up?

²¹"And now men cannot look on the light
when it is bright in the skies,
when the wind has passed and cleared them.
²²Out of the north comes golden splendor;
God is clothed with terrible majesty.
²³The Almighty—we cannot find him;
he is great in power and justice,
and abundant righteousness he will not violate.
²⁴Therefore men fear him;
he does not regard any who are wise in their own conceit."

38 Then the LORD answered Jōb out of the whirlwind:
²"Who is this that darkens counsel by words without knowledge?
³Gird up your loins like a man,
I will question you, and you shall declare to me.

⁴"Where were you when I laid the foundation of the earth?
Tell me, if you have understanding.
⁵Who determined its measurements—
surely you know!
Or who stretched the line upon it?
⁶On what were its bases sunk,
or who laid its cornerstone,
⁷when the morning stars sang together,
and all the sons of God shouted for joy?

⁸"Or who shut in the sea with doors,
when it burst forth from the womb;
⁹when I made clouds its garment,
and thick darkness its swaddling band;

¹⁰and prescribed bounds for it,
and set bars and doors,
¹¹and said, 'Thus far shall you come,
and no farther,
and here shall your proud waves be stayed'?

¹²"Have you commanded the morning since your days began,
and caused the dawn to know its place,
¹³that it might take hold of the skirts of the earth,
and the wicked be shaken out of it?
¹⁴It is changed like clay under the seal,
and it is dyed*g* like a garment.
¹⁵From the wicked their light is withheld,
and their uplifted arm is broken.

¹⁶"Have you entered into the springs of the sea,
or walked in the recesses of the deep?
¹⁷Have the gates of death been revealed to you,
or have you seen the gates of deep darkness?
¹⁸Have you comprehended the expanse of the earth?
Declare, if you know all this.

¹⁹"Where is the way to the dwelling of light,
and where is the place of darkness,
²⁰that you may take it to its territory
and that you may discern the paths to its home?
²¹You know, for you were born then,
and the number of your days is great!

²²"Have you entered the storehouses of the snow,
or have you seen the storehouses of the hail,
²³which I have reserved for the time of trouble,
for the day of battle and war?
²⁴What is the way to the place where the light is distributed,
or where the east wind is scattered upon the earth?

²⁵"Who has cleft a channel for the torrents of rain,
and a way for the thunderbolt,
²⁶to bring rain on a land where no man is,

*g*Cn: Heb *they stand forth*   **38.10:** Jer 5.22.

on the desert in which there is no
man;
27 to satisfy the waste and desolate land,
and to make the ground put forth
grass?

28 "Has the rain a father,
or who has begotten the drops of
dew?
29 From whose womb did the ice come
forth,
and who has given birth to the
hoarfrost of heaven?
30 The waters become hard like stone,
and the face of the deep is frozen.

31 "Can you bind the chains of the
Plēi'a·dēṣ,
or loose the cords of Ō·rī'ọn?
32 Can you lead forth the Măz'za·rŏth
in their season,
or can you guide the Bear with its
children?
33 Do you know the ordinances of the
heavens?
Can you establish their rule on the
earth?

34 "Can you lift up your voice to the
clouds,
that a flood of waters may cover
you?
35 Can you send forth lightnings, that
they may go
and say to you, 'Here we are'?
36 Who has put wisdom in the clouds,ʰ
or given understanding to the
mists?ʰ
37 Who can number the clouds by wisdom?
Or who can tilt the waterskins of
the heavens,
38 when the dust runs into a mass
and the clods cleave fast together?

39 "Can you hunt the prey for the lion,
or satisfy the appetite of the young
lions,
40 when they crouch in their dens,
or lie in wait in their covert?
41 Who provides for the raven its prey,
when its young ones cry to God,
and wander about for lack of food?

39 "Do you know when the mountain goats bring forth?
Do you observe the calving of the
hinds?
2 Can you number the months that
they fulfil,

and do you know the time when
they bring forth,
3 when they crouch, bring forth their
offspring,
and are delivered of their young?
4 Their young ones become strong,
they grow up in the open;
they go forth, and do not return to
them.

5 "Who has let the wild ass go free?
Who has loosed the bonds of the
swift ass,
6 to whom I have given the steppe for
his home,
and the salt land for his dwelling
place?
7 He scorns the tumult of the city;
he hears not the shouts of the
driver.
8 He ranges the mountains as his pasture,
and he searches after every green
thing.

9 "Is the wild ox willing to serve you?
Will he spend the night at your
crib?
10 Can you bind him in the furrow with
ropes,
or will he harrow the valleys after
you?
11 Will you depend on him because his
strength is great,
and will you leave to him your
labor?
12 Do you have faith in him that he will
return,
and bring your grain to your
threshing floor?ⁱ

13 "The wings of the ostrich wave
proudly;
but are they the pinions and
plumage of love?ʲ
14 For she leaves her eggs to the earth,
and lets them be warmed on the
ground,
15 forgetting that a foot may crush
them,
and that the wild beast may
trample them.
16 She deals cruelly with her young,
as if they were not hers;
though her labor be in vain, yet she
has no fear;
17 because God has made her forget
wisdom,

ʰThe meaning of the Hebrew word is uncertain
ⁱHeb your grain and your threshing floor　ʲHeb obscure

and given her no share in understanding.

18 When she rouses herself to flee,[k]
    she laughs at the horse and his
    rider.

19 "Do you give the horse his might?
    Do you clothe his neck with
    strength?[l]
20 Do you make him leap like the locust?
    His majestic snorting is terrible.
21 He paws[m] in the valley, and exults
    in his strength;
    he goes out to meet the weapons.
22 He laughs at fear, and is not dismayed;
    he does not turn back from the
    sword.
23 Upon him rattle the quiver,
    the flashing spear and the javelin.
24 With fierceness and rage he swallows
    the ground;
    he cannot stand still at the sound
    of the trumpet.
25 When the trumpet sounds, he says
    'Aha!'
    He smells the battle from afar,
    the thunder of the captains, and
    the shouting.

26 "Is it by your wisdom that the hawk
    soars,
    and spreads his wings toward the
    south?
27 Is it at your command that the eagle
    mounts up
    and makes his nest on high?
28 On the rock he dwells and makes his
    home
    in the fastness of the rocky crag.
29 Thence he spies out the prey;
    his eyes behold it afar off.
30 His young ones suck up blood;
    and where the slain are, there is
    he."

40 And the LORD said to Jōb:
2 "Shall a faultfinder contend
    with the Almighty?
He who argues with God, let him
    answer it."

3 Then Jōb answered the LORD:
4 "Behold, I am of small account;
    what shall I answer thee?
I lay my hand on my mouth.
5 I have spoken once, and I will not
    answer;
    twice, but I will proceed no further."

6 Then the LORD answered Jōb out of
    the whirlwind:
7 "Gird up your loins like a man;
    I will question you, and you declare to me.
8 Will you even put me in the wrong?
    Will you condemn me that you may
    be justified?
9 Have you an arm like God,
    and can you thunder with a voice
    like his?

10 "Deck yourself with majesty and
    dignity;
    clothe yourself with glory and
    splendor.
11 Pour forth the overflowings of your
    anger,
    and look on every one that is
    proud, and abase him.
12 Look on every one that is proud, and
    bring him low;
    and tread down the wicked where
    they stand.
13 Hide them all in the dust together;
    bind their faces in the world below.[n]
14 Then will I also acknowledge to you,
    that your own right hand can give
    you victory.

15 "Behold, Bē'he·mŏth,[o]
    which I made as I made you;
    he eats grass like an ox.
16 Behold, his strength in his loins,
    and his power in the muscles of
    his belly.
17 He makes his tail stiff like a cedar;
    the sinews of his thighs are knit
    together.
18 His bones are tubes of bronze,
    his limbs like bars of iron.

19 "He is the first of the works[p] of God;
    let him who made him bring near
    his sword!
20 For the mountains yield food for
    him
    where all the wild beasts play.
21 Under the lotus plants he lies,
    in the covert of the reeds and in
    the marsh.
22 For his shade the lotus trees cover
    him;
    the willows of the brook surround
    him.

---

[k] Heb obscure
[l] Tg: The meaning of the Hebrew word is obscure
[m] Gk Syr Vg: Heb *they dig*
[n] Heb *hidden place*   [o] Or *the hippopotamus*   [p] Heb *ways*

²³Behold, if the river is turbulent he
is not frightened;
he is confident though Jordan
rushes against his mouth.
²⁴Can one take him with hooks,*q*
or pierce his nose with a snare?

41 *r* "Can you draw out Lē·vī'ạ-
than*s* with a fishhook,
or press down his tongue with a
cord?
²Can you put a rope in his nose,
or pierce his jaw with a hook?
³Will he make many supplications to
you?
Will he speak to you soft words?
⁴Will he make a covenant with you
to take him for your servant for
ever?
⁵Will you play with him as with a
bird,
or will you put him on leash for
your maidens?
⁶Will traders bargain over him?
Will they divide him up among the
merchants?
⁷Can you fill his skin with harpoons,
or his head with fishing spears?
⁸Lay hands on him;
think of the battle; you will not do
it again!
⁹ᵗBehold, the hope of a man is disappointed;
he is laid low even at the sight of
him.
¹⁰No one is so fierce that he dares to
stir him up.
Who then is he that can stand before me?
¹¹Who has given to me,*u* that I should
repay him?
Whatever is under the whole
heaven is mine.

¹²"I will not keep silence concerning
his limbs,
or his mighty strength, or his
goodly frame.
¹³Who can strip off his outer garment?
Who can penetrate his double coat
of mail?*v*
¹⁴Who can open the doors of his
face?
Round about his teeth is terror.
¹⁵His back*w* is made of rows of shields,
shut up closely as with a seal.
¹⁶One is so near to another
that no air can come between
them.
¹⁷They are joined one to another;

they clasp each other and cannot
be separated.
¹⁸His sneezings flash forth light,
and his eyes are like the eyelids
of the dawn.
¹⁹Out of his mouth go flaming torches;
sparks of fire leap forth.
²⁰Out of his nostrils comes forth smoke,
as from a boiling pot and burning
rushes.
²¹His breath kindles coals,
and a flame comes forth from his
mouth.
²²In his neck abides strength,
and terror dances before him.
²³The folds of his flesh cleave together,
firmly cast upon him and immovable.
²⁴His heart is hard as a stone,
hard as the nether millstone.
²⁵When he raises himself up the
mighty*x* are afraid;
at the crashing they are beside
themselves.
²⁶Though the sword reaches him, it
does not avail;
nor the spear, the dart, or the
javelin.
²⁷He counts iron as straw,
and bronze as rotten wood.
²⁸The arrow cannot make him flee;
for him slingstones are turned to
stubble.
²⁹Clubs are counted as stubble;
he laughs at the rattle of javelins.
³⁰His underparts are like sharp potsherds;
he spreads himself like a threshing sledge on the mire.
³¹He makes the deep boil like a pot;
he makes the sea like a pot of ointment.
³²Behind him he leaves a shining
wake;
one would think the deep to be
hoary.
³³Upon earth there is not his like,
a creature without fear.
³⁴He beholds everything that is high;
he is king over all the sons of
pride."

42 Then Jōb answered the Lord:
²"I know that thou canst do all
things,

*q*Cn: Heb *in his eyes*   *r*Ch 40.25 in Heb   *s*Or *the crocodile*
*t*Ch 41.1 in Heb   *u*The meaning of the Hebrew is uncertain
*v*Gk: Heb *bridle*   *w*Cn Compare Gk Vg: Heb *pride*
*x*Or *gods* **41.11:** Rom 11.35.

and that no purpose of thine can be thwarted.
³'Who is this that hides counsel
without knowledge?'
Therefore I have uttered what I did
not understand,
things too wonderful for me,
which I did not know.
⁴'Hear, and I will speak;
I will question you, and you declare to me.'
⁵I had heard of thee by the hearing
of the ear,
but now my eye sees thee;
⁶therefore I despise myself,
and repent in dust and ashes."

7 After the Lord had spoken these words to Jōb, the Lord said to Ĕ·lī'phăz the Tē'ma·nīte: "My wrath is kindled against you and against your two friends; for you have not spoken of me what is right, as my servant Jōb has. ⁸Now therefore take seven bulls and seven rams, and go to my servant Jōb, and offer up for yourselves a burnt offering; and my servant Job shall pray for you, for I will accept his prayer not to deal with you according to your folly; for you have not spoken of me what is right, as my servant Job has." ⁹So Ĕ·lī'phăz the Tē'ma·nīte and Bĭl'dăd the Shü'hīte and Zō'phär the Nā'-

a·ma·thīte went and did what the Lord had told them; and the Lord accepted Jōb's prayer.

10 And the Lord restored the fortunes of Jōb, when he had prayed for his friends; and the Lord gave Job twice as much as he had before. ¹¹Then came to him all his brothers and sisters and all who had known him before, and ate bread with him in his house; and they showed him sympathy and comforted him for all the evil that the Lord had brought upon him; and each of them gave him a piece of money*ᵞ* and a ring of gold. ¹²And the Lord blessed the latter days of Jōb more than his beginning; and he had fourteen thousand sheep, six thousand camels, a thousand yoke of oxen, and a thousand she-asses. ¹³He had also seven sons and three daughters. ¹⁴And he called the name of the first Jĕ·mī'mah; and the name of the second Kĕ·zī'ah; and the name of the third Kĕr'ĕn–hăp'pŭch. ¹⁵And in all the land there were no women so fair as Jōb's daughters; and their father gave them inheritance among their brothers. ¹⁶And after this Jōb lived a hundred and forty years, and saw his sons, and his sons' sons, four generations. ¹⁷And Jōb died, an old man, and full of days.

The Psalms

BOOK I

1 Blessed is the man
who walks not in the counsel of
the wicked,
nor stands in the way of sinners,
nor sits in the seat of scoffers;
²but his delight is in the law of the
Lord,
and on his law he meditates day
and night.
³He is like a tree
planted by streams of water,
that yields its fruit in its season,
and its leaf does not wither.
In all that he does, he prospers.

⁴The wicked are not so,
but are like chaff which the wind
drives away.

⁵Therefore the wicked will not stand
in the judgment,
nor sinners in the congregation of
the righteous;
⁶for the Lord knows the way of the
righteous,
but the way of the wicked will
perish.

2 Why do the nations conspire,
and the peoples plot in vain?
²The kings of the earth set themselves,
and the rulers take counsel together,
against the Lord and his anointed,
saying,

ᵞHeb qesitah

1.1-3: Jer 17.7-8. 2.1-2: Acts 4.25-26.

³"Let us burst their bonds asunder,
    and cast their cords from us."

⁴He who sits in the heavens laughs;
    the Lord has them in derision.
⁵Then he will speak to them in his
        wrath,
    and terrify them in his fury,
        saying,
⁶"I have set my king
    on Zion, my holy hill."

⁷I will tell of the decree of the
        Lord:
He said to me, "You are my son,
    today I have begotten you.
⁸Ask of me, and I will make the na-
        tions your heritage,
    and the ends of the earth your pos-
        session.
⁹You shall break them with a rod of
        iron,
    and dash them in pieces like a
        potter's vessel."

¹⁰Now therefore, O kings, be wise;
    be warned, O rulers of the earth.
¹¹Serve the Lord with fear,
    with trembling ¹²kiss his feet,ᵃ
    lest he be angry, and you perish in
        the way;
    for his wrath is quickly kindled.

Blessed are all who take refuge in
    him.

A Psalm of David, when he fled from
    Ăb′sạ·lọm his son.

3 O Lord, how many are my foes!
    Many are rising against me;
²many are saying of me,
    there is no help for him in God.
        Selah

³But thou, O Lord, art a shield about
        me,
    my glory, and the lifter of my head.
⁴I cry aloud to the Lord,
    and he answers me from his holy
        hill.   *Selah*

⁵I lie down and sleep;
    I wake again, for the Lord sus-
        tains me.
⁶I am not afraid of ten thousands of
        people
    who have set themselves against
        me round about.

⁷Arise, O Lord!
    Deliver me, O my God!
For thou dost smite all my enemies
        on the cheek,
    thou dost break the teeth of the
        wicked.

⁸Deliverance belongs to the Lord;
    thy blessing be upon thy people!
        Selah

To the choirmaster: with stringed
    instruments. A Psalm of David

4 Answer me when I call, O God of
        my right!
    Thou hast given me room when I
        was in distress.
    Be gracious to me, and hear my
        prayer.

²O men, how long shall my honor
        suffer shame?
    How long will you love vain words,
        and seek after lies?   *Selah*
³But know that the Lord has set apart
        the godly for himself;
    the Lord hears when I call to him.

⁴Be angry, but sin not;
    commune with your own hearts
        on your beds, and be silent.
        Selah
⁵Offer right sacrifices,
    and put your trust in the Lord.

⁶There are many who say, "O that we
        might see some good!
    Lift up the light of thy counte-
        nance upon us, O Lord!"
⁷Thou hast put more joy in my heart
    than they have when their grain
        and wine abound.

⁸In peace I will both lie down and
        sleep;
    for thou alone, O Lord, makest
        me dwell in safety.

To the choirmaster: for the flutes.
    A Psalm of David.

5 Give ear to my words, O Lord;
    give heed to my groaning.
²Hearken to the sound of my cry,

ᵃCn: The Hebrew of 11b and 12a is uncertain
2.7: Mt 3.17; Acts 13.33; Heb 1.5; 5.5; 2 Pet 1.17.
2.8-9: Rev 2.26; 12.5; 19.15. 4.4: Eph 4.26.

my King and my God,
for to thee do I pray.
³O LORD, in the morning thou dost
hear my voice;
in the morning I prepare a sacrifice for thee, and watch.

⁴For thou art not a God who delights
in wickedness;
evil may not sojourn with thee.
⁵The boastful may not stand before
thy eyes;
thou hatest all evildoers.
⁶Thou destroyest those who speak lies;
the LORD abhors bloodthirsty and
deceitful men.

⁷But I through the abundance of thy
steadfast love
will enter thy house,
I will worship toward thy holy temple
in the fear of thee.
⁸Lead me, O LORD, in thy righteousness
because of my enemies;
make thy way straight before me.

⁹For there is no truth in their mouth;
their heart is destruction,
their throat is an open sepulchre,
they flatter with their tongue.
¹⁰Make them bear their guilt, O God;
let them fall by their own counsels;
because of their many transgressions cast them out,
for they have rebelled against thee.

¹¹But let all who take refuge in thee
rejoice,
let them ever sing for joy;
and do thou defend them,
that those who love thy name may
exult in thee.
¹²For thou dost bless the righteous, O
LORD;
thou dost cover him with favor as
with a shield.

To the choirmaster: with stringed
instruments; according to The
Shĕm'ĭ·nĭth. A Psalm of David.

6 O LORD, rebuke me not in thy
anger,
nor chasten me in thy wrath.
²Be gracious to me, O LORD, for I am
languishing;
O LORD, heal me, for my bones are
troubled.

³My soul also is sorely troubled.
But thou, O LORD—how long?

⁴Turn, O LORD, save my life;
deliver me for the sake of thy
steadfast love.
⁵For in death there is no remembrance
of thee;
in Shē'ōl who can give thee praise?

⁶I am weary with my moaning;
every night I flood my bed with
tears;
I drench my couch with my weeping.
⁷My eye wastes away because of grief,
it grows weak because of all my
foes.

⁸Depart from me, all you workers of
evil;
for the LORD has heard the sound
of my weeping.
⁹The LORD has heard my supplication;
the LORD accepts my prayer.
¹⁰All my enemies shall be ashamed and
sorely troubled;
they shall turn back, and be put to
shame in a moment.

A Shĭg·gā'ĭŏn of David, which he sang
to the LORD concerning Cŭsh a
Benjaminite.

7 O LORD my God, in thee do I take
refuge;
save me from all my pursuers,
and deliver me,
²lest like a lion they rend me,
dragging me away, with none to
rescue.

³O LORD my God, if I have done this,
if there is wrong in my hands,
⁴if I have requited my friend with evil
or plundered my enemy without
cause,
⁵let the enemy pursue me and overtake me,
and let him trample my life to the
ground,
and lay my soul in the dust.
　　　　　　　　　　　　　　Selah

⁶Arise, O LORD, in thy anger,
lift thyself up against the fury of
my enemies;

5.9: Rom 3.13.
6.8: Mt 7.23; Lk 13.27.

awake, O my God; [b] thou hast appointed a judgment.
[7] Let the assembly of the peoples be
gathered about thee;
and over it take thy seat[c] on high.
[8] The LORD judges the peoples;
judge me, O LORD, according to
my righteousness
and according to the integrity that
is in me.

[9] O let the evil of the wicked come to
an end,
but establish thou the righteous,
thou who triest the minds and hearts,
thou righteous God.
[10] My shield is with God,
who saves the upright in heart.
[1] God is a righteous judge,
and a God who has indignation
every day.

[2] If a man[d] does not repent, God[d] will
whet his sword;
he has bent and strung his bow;
[3] he has prepared his deadly weapons,
making his arrows fiery shafts.
[4] Behold, the wicked man conceives
evil,
and is pregnant with mischief,
and brings forth lies.
[5] He makes a pit, digging it out,
and falls into the hole which he
has made.
[6] His mischief returns upon his own
head,
and on his own pate his violence
descends.

[7] I will give to the LORD the thanks
due to his righteousness,
and I will sing praise to the name
of the LORD, the Most High.

To the choirmaster: according to The
Git'tith. A Psalm of David.

8 O LORD, our Lord,
how majestic is thy name in all the
earth!

Thou whose glory above the heavens
is chanted
by the mouth of babes and infants,
thou hast founded a bulwark because of thy foes,
to still the enemy and the avenger.

[3] When I look at thy heavens, the work
of thy fingers,

the moon and the stars which thou
hast established;
[4] what is man that thou art mindful of
him,
and the son of man that thou dost
care for him?

[5] Yet thou hast made him little less
than God,
and dost crown him with glory and
honor.
[6] Thou hast given him dominion over
the works of thy hands;
thou hast put all things under his
feet,
[7] all sheep and oxen,
and also the beasts of the field,
[8] the birds of the air, and the fish of the
sea,
whatever passes along the paths
of the sea.

[9] O LORD, our Lord,
how majestic is thy name in all the
earth!

To the choirmaster: according to
Muth'-lab'ben. A Psalm of David.

9 I will give thanks to the LORD with
my whole heart;
I will tell of all thy wonderful
deeds.
[2] I will be glad and exult in thee,
I will sing praise to thy name,
O Most High.

[3] When my enemies turned back,
they stumbled and perished before
thee.
[4] For thou hast maintained my just
cause;
thou hast sat on the throne giving
righteous judgment.

[5] Thou hast rebuked the nations, thou
hast destroyed the wicked;
thou hast blotted out their name
for ever and ever.
[6] The enemy have vanished in everlasting ruins;
their cities thou hast rooted out;
the very memory of them has
perished.

[b] Or *for me*   [c] Cn: Heb *return*   [d] Heb *he*
7.9: Rev 2.23.   **8.2:** Mt 21.16.
8.4–6: Job 7.17–18; Ps 144.3; Heb 2.6–8.
8.6: 1 Cor 15.27; Eph 1.22.

7But the LORD sits enthroned for
ever,
he has established his throne for
judgment;
8and he judges the world with righteousness,
he judges the peoples with equity.

9The LORD is a stronghold for the oppressed,
a stronghold in times of trouble.
10And those who know thy name put
their trust in thee,
for thou, O LORD, hast not forsaken
those who seek thee.

11Sing praises to the LORD, who dwells
in Zion!
Tell among the peoples his deeds!
12For he who avenges blood is mindful
of them;
he does not forget the cry of the
afflicted.

13Be gracious to me, O LORD!
Behold what I suffer from those
who hate me,
O thou who liftest me up from the
gates of death,
14that I may recount all thy praises,
that in the gates of the daughter
of Zion
I may rejoice in thy deliverance.

15The nations have sunk in the pit
which they made;
in the net which they hid has their
own foot been caught.
16The LORD has made himself known,
he has executed judgment;
the wicked are snared in the work
of their own hands.

Hig·gā'i·ŏn. Selah

17The wicked shall depart to Shē'ōl,
all the nations that forget God.

18For the needy shall not always be
forgotten,
and the hope of the poor shall not
perish for ever.

19Arise, O LORD! Let not man prevail;
let the nations be judged before
thee!
20Put them in fear, O LORD!
Let the nations know that they are
but men! *Selah*

10 Why dost thou stand afar off,
O LORD?
Why dost thou hide thyself in times
of trouble?
2In arrogance the wicked hotly pursue the poor;
let them be caught in the schemes
which they have devised.

3For the wicked boasts of the desires
of his heart,
and the man greedy for gain curses
and renounces the LORD.
4In the pride of his countenance the
wicked does not seek him;
all his thoughts are, "There is no
God."

5His ways prosper at all times;
thy judgments are on high, out of
his sight;
as for all his foes, he puffs at them.
6He thinks in his heart, "I shall not
be moved;
throughout all generations I shall
not meet adversity."

7His mouth is filled with cursing and
deceit and oppression;
under his tongue are mischief and
iniquity.
8He sits in ambush in the villages;
in hiding places he murders the
innocent.

His eyes stealthily watch for the
hapless,
9 he lurks in secret like a lion in his
covert;
he lurks that he may seize the poor,
he seizes the poor when he draws
him into his net.

10The hapless is crushed, sinks down,
and falls by his might.
11He thinks in his heart, "God has forgotten,
he has hidden his face, he will
never see it."

12Arise, O LORD; O God, lift up thy
hand;
forget not the afflicted.
13Why does the wicked renounce God,
and say in his heart, "Thou wilt not
call to account"?

14Thou dost see; yea, thou dost note
trouble and vexation,

9.8: Acts 17.31. 10.7: Rom 3.14.

that thou mayst take it into thy
hands;
the hapless commits himself to thee;
thou hast been the helper of the
fatherless.

¹⁵ Break thou the arm of the wicked and
evildoer;
seek out his wickedness till thou
find none.
¹⁶ The Lord is king for ever and ever;
the nations shall perish from his
land.

¹⁷ O Lord, thou wilt hear the desire of
the meek;
thou wilt strengthen their heart,
thou wilt incline thy ear
¹⁸ to do justice to the fatherless and the
oppressed,
so that man who is of the earth
may strike terror no more.

To the choirmaster. Of David.

11 In the Lord I take refuge;
how can you say to me,
"Flee like a bird to the mountains;ᵉ
² for lo, the wicked bend the bow,
they have fitted their arrow to the
string,
to shoot in the dark at the upright
in heart;
³ if the foundations are destroyed,
what can the righteous do"?

⁴ The Lord is in his holy temple,
the Lord's throne is in heaven;
his eyes behold, his eyelids test,
the children of men.
⁵ The Lord tests the righteous and the
wicked,
and his soul hates him that loves
violence.
⁶ On the wicked he will rain coals of
fire and brimstone;
a scorching wind shall be the portion of their cup.
⁷ For the Lord is righteous, he loves
righteous deeds;
the upright shall behold his face.

To the choirmaster: according to The
Shĕm′ĭ·nĭth. A Psalm of David.

12 Help, Lord; for there is no
longer any that is godly;
for the faithful have vanished
from among the sons of men.

² Every one utters lies to his neighbor;
with flattering lips and a double
heart they speak.

³ May the Lord cut off all flattering
lips,
the tongue that makes great boasts,
⁴ those who say, "With our tongue we
will prevail,
our lips are with us; who is our
master?"

⁵ "Because the poor are despoiled, because the needy groan,
I will now arise," says the Lord;
"I will place him in the safety for
which he longs."
⁶ The promises of the Lord are promises that are pure,
silver refined in a furnace on the
ground,
purified seven times.

⁷ Do thou, O Lord, protect us,
guard us ever from this generation.
⁸ On every side the wicked prowl,
as vileness is exalted among the
sons of men.

To the choirmaster. A Psalm of David.

13 How long, O Lord? Wilt thou
forget me for ever?
How long wilt thou hide thy face
from me?
² How long must I bear painᶠ in my
soul,
and have sorrow in my heart all
the day?
How long shall my enemy be exalted
over me?

³ Consider and answer me, O Lord my
God;
lighten my eyes, lest I sleep the
sleep of death;
⁴ lest my enemy say, "I have prevailed
over him";
lest my foes rejoice because I am
shaken.

⁵ But I have trusted in thy steadfast
love;
my heart shall rejoice in thy salvation.
⁶ I will sing to the Lord,
because he has dealt bountifully
with me.

ᵉ Gk Syr Jerome Tg: Heb *flee to your mountain, O bird*
ᶠ Syr: Heb *hold counsels*

To the choirmaster. Of David.

14 The fool says in his heart,
"There is no God."
They are corrupt, they do abominable deeds,
there is none that does good.

[2] The LORD looks down from heaven
upon the children of men,
to see if there are any that act
wisely,
that seek after God.

[3] They have all gone astray, they are
all alike corrupt;
there is none that does good,
no, not one.

[4] Have they no knowledge, all the evildoers
who eat up my people as they eat
bread,
and do not call upon the LORD?

[5] There they shall be in great terror,
for God is with the generation of
the righteous.
[6] You would confound the plans of the
poor,
but the LORD is his refuge.

[7] O that deliverance for Israel would
come out of Zion!
When the LORD restores the fortunes of his people,
Jacob shall rejoice, Israel shall be
glad.

A Psalm of David.

15 O LORD, who shall sojourn in
thy tent?
Who shall dwell on thy holy hill?

[2] He who walks blamelessly, and does
what is right,
and speaks truth from his heart;
[3] who does not slander with his tongue,
and does no evil to his friend,
nor takes up a reproach against his
neighbor;
[4] in whose eyes a reprobate is despised,
but who honors those who fear the
LORD;
who swears to his own hurt and
does not change;
[5] who does not put out his money at
interest,

and does not take a bribe against
the innocent.

He who does these things shall never
be moved.

A Mĭk′tăm of David.

16 Preserve me, O God, for in thee
I take refuge.
[2] I say to the LORD, "Thou art my
Lord;
I have no good apart from thee."[g]

[3] As for the saints in the land, they are
the noble,
in whom is all my delight.

[4] Those who choose another god multiply their sorrows;[h]
their libations of blood I will not
pour out
or take their names upon my lips.

[5] The LORD is my chosen portion and
my cup;
thou holdest my lot.
[6] The lines have fallen for me in pleasant places;
yea, I have a goodly heritage.

[7] I bless the LORD who gives me counsel;
in the night also my heart instructs
me.
[8] I keep the LORD always before me;
because he is at my right hand,
I shall not be moved.

[9] Therefore my heart is glad, and my
soul rejoices;
my body also dwells secure.
[10] For thou dost not give me up to
Shē′ōl,
or let thy godly one see the Pit.

[11] Thou dost show me the path of life;
in thy presence there is fulness of
joy,
in thy right hand are pleasures for
evermore.

A Prayer of David.

17 Hear a just cause, O LORD;
attend to my cry!

[g] Jerome Tg: The meaning of the Hebrew is uncertain
[h] Cn: The meaning of the Hebrew is uncertain
14.1-3: Rom 3.10-12. 14.1-7: Ps 53.1-6.
16.8-11: Acts 2.25-28, 31. 16.10: Acts 13.35.

Give ear to my prayer from lips
free of deceit!
2 From thee let my vindication come!
Let thy eyes see the right!

3 If thou triest my heart, if thou
visitest me by night,
if thou testest me, thou wilt find
no wickedness in me;
my mouth does not transgress.
4 With regard to the works of men,
by the word of thy lips
I have avoided the ways of the
violent.
5 My steps have held fast to thy paths,
my feet have not slipped.

6 I call upon thee, for thou wilt answer
me, O God;
incline thy ear to me, hear my
words.
7 Wondrously show thy steadfast love,
O savior of those who seek refuge
from their adversaries at thy right
hand.

8 Keep me as the apple of the eye;
hide me in the shadow of thy wings,
9 from the wicked who despoil me,
my deadly enemies who surround
me.

10 They close their hearts to pity;
with their mouths they speak arrogantly.
11 They track me down; now they surround me;
they set their eyes to cast me to the
ground.
12 They are like a lion eager to tear,
as a young lion lurking in ambush.

13 Arise, O LORD! confront them, overthrow them!
Deliver my life from the wicked by
thy sword,
14 from men by thy hand, O LORD,
from men whose portion in life is
of the world.
May their belly be filled with what
thou hast stored up for them;
may their children have more than
enough;
may they leave something over to
their babes.

15 As for me, I shall behold thy face in
righteousness;
when I awake, I shall be satisfied
with beholding thy form.

To the choirmaster. A Psalm of David
the servant of the LORD, who addressed
the words of this song to the LORD on
the day when the LORD delivered him
from the hand of all his enemies, and
from the hand of Saul. He said:

18 I love thee, O LORD, my
strength.
2 The LORD is my rock, and my fortress,
and my deliverer,
my God, my rock, in whom I take
refuge,
my shield, and the horn of my salvation, my stronghold.
3 I call upon the LORD, who is worthy
to be praised,
and I am saved from my enemies.

4 The cords of death encompassed me,
the torrents of perdition assailed
me;
5 the cords of Shē′ōl entangled me,
the snares of death confronted me.

6 In my distress I called upon the LORD;
to my God I cried for help.
From his temple he heard my voice,
and my cry to him reached his
ears.

7 Then the earth reeled and rocked;
the foundations also of the mountains trembled
and quaked, because he was angry.
8 Smoke went up from his nostrils,
and devouring fire from his mouth;
glowing coals flamed forth from
him.
9 He bowed the heavens, and came
down;
thick darkness was under his feet.
10 He rode on a cherub, and flew;
he came swiftly upon the wings
of the wind.
11 He made darkness his covering
around him,
his canopy thick clouds dark with
water.
12 Out of the brightness before him
there broke through his clouds
hailstones and coals of fire.
13 The LORD also thundered in the
heavens,
and the Most High uttered his
voice,
hailstones and coals of fire.
14 And he sent out his arrows, and
scattered them;

18.1-50: 2 Sam 22.2-51.

he flashed forth lightnings, and
   routed them.
¹⁵ Then the channels of the sea were
   seen,
   and the foundations of the world
     were laid bare,
at thy rebuke, O LORD,
   at the blast of the breath of thy
     nostrils.

¹⁶ He reached from on high, he took me,
   he drew me out of many waters.
¹⁷ He delivered me from my strong
     enemy,
   and from those who hated me;
   for they were too mighty for me.
¹⁸ They came upon me in the day of
     my calamity;
   but the LORD was my stay.
¹⁹ He brought me forth into a broad
     place;
   he delivered me, because he de-
     lighted in me.

²⁰ The LORD rewarded me according
   to my righteousness;
   according to the cleanness of my
     hands he recompensed me.
²¹ For I have kept the ways of the LORD,
   and have not wickedly departed
     from my God.
²² For all his ordinances were before me,
   and his statutes I did not put away
     from me.
²³ I was blameless before him,
   and I kept myself from guilt.
²⁴ Therefore the LORD has recompensed
   me according to my righteous-
     ness,
   according to the cleanness of my
     hands in his sight.

²⁵ With the loyal thou dost show thyself
     loyal;
   with the blameless man thou dost
     show thyself blameless;
²⁶ with the pure thou dost show thyself
     pure;
   and with the crooked thou dost
     show thyself perverse.
²⁷ For thou dost deliver a humble
     people;
   but the haughty eyes thou dost
     bring down.
²⁸ Yea, thou dost light my lamp;
   the LORD my God lightens my dark-
     ness.
²⁹ Yea, by thee I can crush a troop;
   and by my God I can leap over a
     wall.

³⁰ This God—his way is perfect;
   the promise of the LORD proves
     true;
   he is a shield for all those who take
     refuge in him.

³¹ For who is God, but the LORD?
   And who is a rock, except our
     God?—
³² the God who girded me with strength,
   and made my way safe.
³³ He made my feet like hinds' feet,
   and set me secure on the heights.
³⁴ He trains my hands for war,
   so that my arms can bend a bow
     of bronze.
³⁵ Thou hast given me the shield of thy
     salvation,
   and thy right hand supported me,
   and thy help[i] made me great.
³⁶ Thou didst give a wide place for my
     steps under me,
   and my feet did not slip.
³⁷ I pursued my enemies and overtook
     them;
   and did not turn back till they were
     consumed.
³⁸ I thrust them through, so that they
     were not able to rise;
   they fell under my feet.
³⁹ For thou didst gird me with strength
     for the battle;
   thou didst make my assailants sink
     under me.
⁴⁰ Thou didst make my enemies turn
     their backs to me,
   and those who hated me I de-
     stroyed.
⁴¹ They cried for help, but there was
     none to save,
   they cried to the LORD, but he did
     not answer them.
⁴² I beat them fine as dust before the
     wind;
   I cast them out like the mire of the
     streets.

⁴³ Thou didst deliver me from strife
     with the peoples;[j]
   thou didst make me the head of the
     nations;
   people whom I had not known
     served me.
⁴⁴ As soon as they heard of me they
     obeyed me;
   foreigners came cringing to me.
⁴⁵ Foreigners lost heart,
   and came trembling out of their
     fastnesses.

[i]Or *gentleness*   [j]Gk Tg: Heb *people*

⁴⁶The LORD lives; and blessed be my
    rock,
    and exalted be the God of my sal-
        vation,
⁴⁷the God who gave me vengeance
    and subdued peoples under me;
⁴⁸who delivered me from my enemies;
    yea, thou didst exalt me above my
        adversaries;
    thou didst deliver me from men of
        violence.

⁴⁹For this I will extol thee, O LORD,
    among the nations,
    and sing praises to thy name.
⁵⁰Great triumphs he gives to his king,
    and shows steadfast love to his
        anointed,
    to David and his descendants for
        ever.

To the choirmaster. A Psalm of David.

19   The heavens are telling the
    glory of God;
    and the firmament proclaims his
        handiwork.
²Day to day pours forth speech,
    and night to night declares knowl-
        edge.
³There is no speech, nor are there
        words;
    their voice is not heard;
⁴yet their voice*ᵏ* goes out through all
        the earth,
    and their words to the end of the
        world.

In them he has set a tent for the sun,
⁵which comes forth like a bridegroom
        leaving his chamber,
    and like a strong man runs its
        course with joy.
⁶Its rising is from the end of the
        heavens,
    and its circuit to the end of them;
    and there is nothing hid from its
        heat.

⁷The law of the LORD is perfect,
    reviving the soul;
    the testimony of the LORD is sure,
        making wise the simple;
⁸the precepts of the LORD are right,
        rejoicing the heart;
    the commandment of the LORD is
        pure,
        enlightening the eyes;
⁹the fear of the LORD is clean,

enduring for ever;
    the ordinances of the LORD are true,
        and righteous altogether.
¹⁰More to be desired are they than gold,
    even much fine gold;
    sweeter also than honey
        and drippings of the honeycomb.

¹¹Moreover by them is thy servant
        warned;
    in keeping them there is great
        reward.
¹²But who can discern his errors?
    Clear thou me from hidden faults.
¹³Keep back thy servant also from pre-
        sumptuous sins;
    let them not have dominion over
        me!
    Then I shall be blameless,
        and innocent of great transgres-
        sion.

¹⁴Let the words of my mouth and the
        meditation of my heart
    be acceptable in thy sight,
    O LORD, my rock and my redeemer.

To the choirmaster. A Psalm of David.

20   The LORD answer you in the
    day of trouble!
    The name of the God of Jacob
        protect you!
²May he send you help from the
        sanctuary,
    and give you support from Zion!
³May he remember all your offerings,
    and regard with favor your burnt
        sacrifices!   *Selah*
⁴May he grant you your heart's desire,
    and fulfil all your plans!
⁵May we shout for joy over your
        victory,
    and in the name of our God set
        up our banners!
    May the LORD fulfil all your petitions!

⁶Now I know that the LORD will help
        his anointed;
    he will answer him from his holy
        heaven
    with mighty victories by his right
        hand.
⁷Some boast of chariots, and some
        of horses;
    but we boast of the name of the
        LORD our God.

ᵏGk Jerome Compare Syr: Heb *line*
18.49: Rom 15.9. **19.4:** Rom 10.18.

⁸They will collapse and fall;
but we shall rise and stand upright.

⁹Give victory to the king, O LORD;
answer us when we call.¹

To the choirmaster. A Psalm of David.

21 In thy strength the king rejoices, O LORD;
and in thy help how greatly he
exults!
²Thou hast given him his heart's
desire,
and hast not withheld the request
of his lips.   *Selah*
³For thou dost meet him with goodly
blessings;
thou dost set a crown of fine gold
upon his head.
⁴He asked life of thee; thou gavest it to
him,
length of days for ever and ever.
⁵His glory is great through thy help;
splendor and majesty thou dost bestow upon him.
⁶Yea, thou dost make him most
blessed for ever;
thou dost make him glad with
the joy of thy presence.
⁷For the king trusts in the LORD;
and through the steadfast love of
the Most High he shall not be
moved.

⁸Your hand will find out all your
enemies;
your right hand will find out those
who hate you.
⁹You will make them as a blazing
oven
when you appear.
The LORD will swallow them up in
his wrath;
and fire will consume them.
¹⁰You will destroy their offspring from
the earth,
and their children from among the
sons of men.
¹¹If they plan evil against you,
if they devise mischief, they will
not succeed.
¹²For you will put them to flight;
you will aim at their faces with
your bows.

¹³Be exalted, O LORD, in thy strength!
We will sing and praise thy power.

To the choirmaster: according to The
Hind of the Dawn. A Psalm of David.

22 My God, my God, why hast
thou forsaken me?
Why art thou so far from helping
me, from the words of my groaning?
²O my God, I cry by day, but thou dost
not answer;
and by night, but find no rest.

³Yet thou art holy,
enthroned on the praises of Israel.
⁴In thee our fathers trusted;
they trusted, and thou didst deliver
them.
⁵To thee they cried, and were saved;
in thee they trusted, and were not
disappointed.

⁶But I am a worm, and no man;
scorned by men, and despised by
the people.
⁷All who see me mock at me,
they make mouths at me, they wag
their heads;
⁸"He committed his cause to the
LORD; let him deliver him,
let him rescue him, for he delights
in him!"

⁹Yet thou art he who took me from the
womb;
thou didst keep me safe upon my
mother's breasts.
¹⁰Upon thee was I cast from my birth,
and since my mother bore me thou
hast been my God.
¹¹Be not far from me,
for trouble is near
and there is none to help.

¹²Many bulls encompass me,
strong bulls of Bā′shan surround
me;
¹³they open wide their mouths at me,
like a ravening and roaring lion.

¹⁴I am poured out like water,
and all my bones are out of joint;
my heart is like wax,
it is melted within my breast;
¹⁵my strength is dried up like a potsherd,
and my tongue cleaves to my jaws;

¹Gk: Heb *give victory, O LORD, let the King answer us
when we call*
22.1: Mt 27.46; Mk 15.34.
22.7–8: Mt 27.39, 43; Mk 15.29; Lk 23.35.

thou dost lay me in the dust of death.

[16] Yea, dogs are round about me;
a company of evildoers encircle me;
they have pierced[m] my hands and feet—
[17] I can count all my bones—
they stare and gloat over me;
[18] they divide my garments among them,
and for my raiment they cast lots.

[19] But thou, O LORD, be not far off!
O thou my help, hasten to my aid!
[20] Deliver my soul from the sword,
my life[n] from the power of the dog!
[21] Save me from the mouth of the lion,
my afflicted soul[o] from the horns of the wild oxen!

[22] I will tell of thy name to my brethren;
in the midst of the congregation I will praise thee:
[23] You who fear the LORD, praise him!
all you sons of Jacob, glorify him,
and stand in awe of him, all you sons of Israel!
[24] For he has not despised or abhorred the affliction of the afflicted;
and he has not hid his face from him,
but has heard, when he cried to him.

[25] From thee comes my praise in the great congregation;
my vows I will pay before those who fear him.
[26] The afflicted[p] shall eat and be satisfied;
those who seek him shall praise the LORD!
May your hearts live for ever!

[27] All the ends of the earth shall remember
and turn to the LORD;
and all the families of the nations shall worship before him.[q]
[28] For dominion belongs to the LORD,
and he rules over the nations.

[29] Yea, to him[r] shall all the proud of the earth bow down;
before him shall bow all who go down to the dust,
and he who cannot keep himself alive.

[30] Posterity shall serve him;
men shall tell of the Lord to the coming generation,
[31] and proclaim his deliverance to a people yet unborn,
that he has wrought it.

A Psalm of David.

23 The LORD is my shepherd, I shall not want;
[2] he makes me lie down in green pastures.
He leads me beside still waters;[s]
[3] he restores my soul.[t]
He leads me in paths of righteousness[u]
for his name's sake.

[4] Even though I walk through the valley of the shadow of death,[v]
I fear no evil;
for thou art with me;
thy rod and thy staff,
they comfort me.

[5] Thou preparest a table before me
in the presence of my enemies;
thou anointest my head with oil,
my cup overflows.
[6] Surely[w] goodness and mercy[x] shall follow me
all the days of my life;
and I shall dwell in the house of the LORD
for ever.[y]

A Psalm of David.

24 The earth is the LORD'S and the fulness thereof,
the world and those who dwell therein;
[2] for he has founded it upon the seas,
and established it upon the rivers.

[3] Who shall ascend the hill of the LORD?
And who shall stand in his holy place?
[4] He who has clean hands and a pure heart,

[m] Gk Syr Jerome: Heb *like a lion* [n] Heb *my only one*
[o] Gk Syr: Heb *thou hast answered me*
[p] Or *poor* [q] Gk Syr Jerome: Heb *thee*
[r] Cn: Heb *they have eaten and* [s] Heb *the waters of rest*
[t] Or *life* [u] Or *right paths* [v] Or *the valley of deep darkness*
[w] Or *Only* [x] Or *kindness* [y] Or *as long as I live*
22.18: Mt 27.35; Mk 15.24; Lk 23.34; Jn 19.24.
22.22: Heb 2.12.
23.2: Rev 7.17. 24.1: 1 Cor 10.26. 24.4: Mt 5.8.

who does not lift up his soul to
what is false,
and does not swear deceitfully.
⁵He will receive blessing from the
LORD,
and vindication from the God of
his salvation.
⁶Such is the generation of those who
seek him,
who seek the face of the God of
Jacob.ᶻ   Selah

⁷Lift up your heads, O gates!
and be lifted up, O ancient doors!
that the King of glory may come
in.
⁸Who is the King of glory?
The LORD, strong and mighty,
the LORD, mighty in battle!
⁹Lift up your heads, O gates!
and be lifted up,ᵃ O ancient doors!
that the King of glory may come in.
¹⁰Who is this King of glory?
The LORD of hosts,
he is the King of glory!   Selah

A Psalm of David.

25 To thee, O LORD, I lift up my
soul.
²O my God, in thee I trust,
let me not be put to shame;
let not my enemies exult over me.
³Yea, let none that wait for thee be
put to shame;
let them be ashamed who are
wantonly treacherous.

⁴Make me to know thy ways, O LORD;
teach me thy paths.
⁵Lead me in thy truth, and teach me,
for thou art the God of my salvation;
for thee I wait all the day long.

⁶Be mindful of thy mercy, O LORD,
and of thy steadfast love,
for they have been from of old.
⁷Remember not the sins of my youth,
or my transgressions;
according to thy steadfast love remember me,
for thy goodness' sake, O LORD!

⁸Good and upright is the LORD;
therefore he instructs sinners in
the way.
⁹He leads the humble in what is right,
and teaches the humble his way.

¹⁰All the paths of the LORD are steadfast love and faithfulness,
for those who keep his covenant
and his testimonies.
¹¹For thy name's sake, O LORD,
pardon my guilt, for it is great.
¹²Who is the man that fears the LORD?
Him will he instruct in the way
that he should choose.
¹³He himself shall abide in prosperity,
and his children shall possess the
land.
¹⁴The friendship of the LORD is for
those who fear him,
and he makes known to them his
covenant.
¹⁵My eyes are ever toward the LORD,
for he will pluck my feet out of the
net.

¹⁶Turn thou to me, and be gracious to
me;
for I am lonely and afflicted.
¹⁷Relieve the troubles of my heart,
and bring meᵇ out of my distresses.
¹⁸Consider my affliction and my
trouble,
and forgive all my sins.

¹⁹Consider how many are my foes,
and with what violent hatred they
hate me.
²⁰Oh guard my life, and deliver me;
let me not be put to shame, for I
take refuge in thee.
²¹May integrity and uprightness preserve me,
for I wait for thee.

²²Redeem Israel, O God,
out of all his troubles.

A Psalm of David.

26 Vindicate me, O LORD,
for I have walked in my integrity,
and I have trusted in the LORD
without wavering.
²Prove me, O LORD, and try me;
test my heart and my mind.
³For thy steadfast love is before my
eyes,
and I walk in faithfulness to thee.ᶜ

ᶻGk Syr: Heb thy face, O Jacob
ᵃGk Syr Jerome Tg Compare verse 7: Heb lift up
ᵇOr The troubles of my heart are enlarged; bring me
ᶜOr in thy faithfulness

4I do not sit with false men,
    nor do I consort with dissemblers;
5I hate the company of evildoers,
    and I will not sit with the wicked.

6I wash my hands in innocence,
    and go about thy altar, O Lord,
7singing aloud a song of thanksgiving,
    and telling all thy wondrous deeds.

8O Lord, I love the habitation of thy house,
    and the place where thy glory dwells.
9Sweep me not away with sinners,
    nor my life with bloodthirsty men,
10men in whose hands are evil devices,
    and whose right hands are full of bribes.

11But as for me, I walk in my integrity;
    redeem me, and be gracious to me.
12My foot stands on level ground;
    in the great congregation I will bless the Lord.

A Psalm of David.

27 The Lord is my light and my salvation;
    whom shall I fear?
The Lord is the stronghold*d* of my life;
    of whom shall I be afraid?

2When evildoers assail me,
    uttering slanders against me,*e*
my adversaries and foes,
    they shall stumble and fall.

3Though a host encamp against me,
    my heart shall not fear;
though war arise against me,
    yet I will be confident.

4One thing have I asked of the Lord,
    that will I seek after;
that I may dwell in the house of the Lord
    all the days of my life,
to behold the beauty of the Lord,
    and to inquire in his temple.

5For he will hide me in his shelter
    in the day of trouble;
he will conceal me under the cover of his tent,
    he will set me high upon a rock.

6And now my head shall be lifted up
    above my enemies round about me;
and I will offer in his tent
    sacrifices with shouts of joy;
I will sing and make melody to the Lord.

7Hear, O Lord, when I cry aloud,
    be gracious to me and answer me!
8Thou hast said, "Seek ye my face."
My heart says to thee,
"Thy face, Lord, do I seek."
9   Hide not thy face from me.

Turn not thy servant away in anger,
    thou who hast been my help.
Cast me not off, forsake me not,
    O God of my salvation!
10For my father and my mother have forsaken me,
    but the Lord will take me up.

11Teach me thy way, O Lord;
    and lead me on a level path
    because of my enemies.
12Give me not up to the will of my adversaries;
    for false witnesses have risen against me,
    and they breathe out violence.

13I believe that I shall see the goodness of the Lord
    in the land of the living!
14Wait for the Lord;
    be strong, and let your heart take courage;
    yea, wait for the Lord!

A Psalm of David.

28 To thee, O Lord, I call;
    my rock, be not deaf to me,
lest, if thou be silent to me,
    I become like those who go down to the Pit.
2Hear the voice of my supplication,
    as I cry to thee for help,
as I lift up my hands
    toward thy most holy sanctuary.*f*

3Take me not off with the wicked,
    with those who are workers of evil,
who speak peace with their neighbors,
    while mischief is in their hearts.

*d*Or *refuge*   *e*Heb *to eat up my flesh*
*f*Heb *thy innermost sanctuary*

⁴Requite them according to their
 work,
 and according to the evil of their
  deeds;
requite them according to the work
 of their hands;
 render them their due reward.
⁵Because they do not regard the works
 of the LORD,
 or the work of his hands,
he will break them down and build
 them up no more.

⁶Blessed be the LORD!
 for he has heard the voice of my
  supplications.
⁷The LORD is my strength and my
 shield;
 in him my heart trusts;
so I am helped, and my heart exults,
 and with my song I give thanks to
  him.

⁸The LORD is the strength of his people,
 he is the saving refuge of his
  anointed.
⁹O save thy people, and bless thy heritage;
 be thou their shepherd, and carry
  them for ever.

A Psalm of David.

29 Ascribe to the LORD, O heavenly beings,ᵍ
 ascribe to the LORD glory and
  strength.
²Ascribe to the LORD the glory of his
 name;
 worship the LORD in holy array.

³The voice of the LORD is upon the
 waters;
 the God of glory thunders,
 the LORD, upon many waters.
⁴The voice of the LORD is powerful,
 the voice of the LORD is full of
 majesty.

⁵The voice of the LORD breaks the
 cedars,
 the LORD breaks the cedars of
 Lebanon.
⁶He makes Lebanon to skip like a calf,
 and Sir'i·on like a young wild ox.

⁷The voice of the LORD flashes forth
 flames of fire.

⁸The voice of the LORD shakes the
 wilderness,
 the LORD shakes the wilderness of
 Ka'desh.

⁹The voice of the LORD makes the oaks
 to whirl,ʰ
 and strips the forests bare;
 and in his temple all cry, "Glory!"

¹⁰The LORD sits enthroned over the
 flood;
 the LORD sits enthroned as king
 for ever.
¹¹May the LORD give strength to his
 people!
 May the LORD bless his people with
 peace!

A Psalm of David. A Song at the
dedication of the Temple.

30 I will extol thee, O LORD, for
 thou hast drawn me up,
 and hast not let my foes rejoice
 over me.
²O LORD my God, I cried to thee for
 help,
 and thou hast healed me.
³O LORD, thou hast brought up my soul
 from Shē'ōl,
 restored me to life from among
 those gone down to the Pit.ⁱ

⁴Sing praises to the LORD, O you his
 saints,
 and give thanks to his holy name.
⁵For his anger is but for a moment,
 and his favor is for a lifetime.
Weeping may tarry for the night,
 but joy comes with the morning.

⁶As for me, I said in my prosperity,
 "I shall never be moved."
⁷By thy favor, O LORD,
 thou hadst established me as a
 strong mountain;
thou didst hide thy face,
 I was dismayed.

⁸To thee, O LORD, I cried;
 and to the LORD I made supplication:
⁹"What profit is there in my death,
 if I go down to the Pit?
Will the dust praise thee?
 Will it tell of thy faithfulness?

ᵍHeb sons of gods ʰOr makes the hinds to calve
ⁱOr that I should not go down to the Pit

¹⁰ Hear, O LORD, and be gracious to me!
O LORD, be thou my helper!"

¹¹ Thou hast turned for me my mourning into dancing;
thou hast loosed my sackcloth
and girded me with gladness,
¹² that my soul[j] may praise thee and not
be silent.
O LORD my God, I will give thanks
to thee for ever.

To the choirmaster. A Psalm of David.

31 In thee, O LORD, do I seek refuge;
let me never be put to shame;
in thy righteousness deliver me!
² Incline thy ear to me,
rescue me speedily!
Be thou a rock of refuge for me,
a strong fortress to save me!

³ Yea, thou art my rock and my fortress;
for thy name's sake lead me and
guide me,
⁴ take me out of the net which is hidden for me,
for thou art my refuge.
⁵ Into thy hand I commit my spirit;
thou hast redeemed me, O LORD,
faithful God.

⁶ Thou hatest[k] those who pay regard to
vain idols;
but I trust in the LORD.
⁷ I will rejoice and be glad for thy
steadfast love,
because thou hast seen my affliction,
thou hast taken heed of my ad-
versities,
⁸ and hast not delivered me into the
hand of the enemy;
thou hast set my feet in a broad
place.

⁹ Be gracious to me, O LORD, for I am
in distress;
my eye is wasted from grief,
my soul and my body also.
¹⁰ For my life is spent with sorrow,
and my years with sighing;
my strength fails because of my
misery,[l]
and my bones waste away.

¹¹ I am the scorn of all my adversaries,
a horror[m] to my neighbors,
an object of dread to my acquaintances;
those who see me in the street flee
from me.
¹² I have passed out of mind like one
who is dead;
I have become like a broken vessel.
¹³ Yea, I hear the whispering of many—
terror on every side!—
as they scheme together against
me,
as they plot to take my life.

¹⁴ But I trust in thee, O LORD,
I say, "Thou art my God."
¹⁵ My times are in thy hand;
deliver me from the hand of my
enemies and persecutors!
¹⁶ Let thy face shine on thy servant;
save me in thy steadfast love!
¹⁷ Let me not be put to shame, O LORD,
for I call on thee;
let the wicked be put to shame,
let them go dumbfounded to
Shē′ōl.
¹⁸ Let the lying lips be dumb,
which speak insolently against the
righteous
in pride and contempt.

¹⁹ O how abundant is thy goodness,
which thou hast laid up for those
who fear thee,
and wrought for those who take
refuge in thee,
in the sight of the sons of men!
²⁰ In the covert of thy presence thou
hidest them
from the plots of men;
thou holdest them safe under thy
shelter
from the strife of tongues.

²¹ Blessed be the LORD,
for he has wondrously shown his
steadfast love to me
when I was beset as in a besieged
city.
²² I had said in my alarm,
"I am driven far[n] from thy sight."
But thou didst hear my supplications,
when I cried to thee for help.

²³ Love the LORD, all you his saints!
The LORD preserves the faithful,

---

[j]Heb *that glory*
[k]With one Heb Ms Gk Syr Jerome: Heb *I hate*
[l]Gk Syr: Heb *iniquity*   [m]Cn: Heb *exceedingly*
[n]Another reading is *cut off*
31.5: Lk 23.46.   **31.13:** Jer 6.25; 20.3, 10; 46.5; 49.29.

but abundantly requites him who
  acts haughtily.
²⁴Be strong, and let your heart take
  courage,
all you who wait for the LORD!

A Psalm of David. A Măs′kĭl.

32 Blessed is he whose transgres-
    sion is forgiven,
  whose sin is covered.
²Blessed is the man to whom the LORD
  imputes no iniquity,
  and in whose spirit there is no
  deceit.

³When I declared not my sin, my body
  wasted away
  through my groaning all day long.
⁴For day and night thy hand was
  heavy upon me;
  my strength was dried up° as by
  the heat of summer.   *Selah*

⁵I acknowledged my sin to thee,
  and I did not hide my iniquity;
I said, "I will confess my transgressions to the LORD";
  then thou didst forgive the guilt
  of my sin.   *Selah*

⁶Therefore let every one who is godly
  offer prayer to thee;
  at a time of distress,ᵖ in the rush of
  great waters,
  they shall not reach him.
⁷Thou art a hiding place for me,
  thou preservest me from trouble;
  thou dost encompass me with de-
  liverance.ᵠ   *Selah*

⁸I will instruct you and teach you
  the way you should go;
  I will counsel you with my eye
  upon you.
⁹Be not like a horse or a mule, without
  understanding,
  which must be curbed with bit
  and bridle,
  else it will not keep with you.

¹⁰Many are the pangs of the wicked;
  but steadfast love surrounds him
  who trusts in the LORD.
¹¹Be glad in the LORD, and rejoice,
  O righteous,
  and shout for joy, all you upright
  in heart!

33 Rejoice in the LORD, O you
    righteous!
  Praise befits the upright.
²Praise the LORD with the lyre,
  make melody to him with the harp
  of ten strings!
³Sing to him a new song,
  play skilfully on the strings,
  with loud shouts.

⁴For the word of the LORD is upright;
  and all his work is done in faithfulness.
⁵He loves righteousness and justice;
  the earth is full of the steadfast
  love of the LORD.

⁶By the word of the LORD the heavens
  were made,
  and all their host by the breath
  of his mouth.
⁷He gathered the waters of the sea
  as in a bottle;
  he put the deeps in storehouses.

⁸Let all the earth fear the LORD,
  let all the inhabitants of the world
  stand in awe of him!
⁹For he spoke, and it came to be;
  he commanded, and it stood forth.

¹⁰The LORD brings the counsel of the
  nations to nought;
  he frustrates the plans of the
  peoples.
¹¹The counsel of the LORD stands for
  ever,
  the thoughts of his heart to all
  generations.
¹²Blessed is the nation whose God is
  the LORD,
  the people whom he has chosen
  as his heritage!

¹³The LORD looks down from heaven
  he sees all the sons of men;
¹⁴from where he sits enthroned he
  looks forth
  on all the inhabitants of the earth
¹⁵he who fashions the hearts of them
  all,
  and observes all their deeds.
¹⁶A king is not saved by his great army
  a warrior is not delivered by his
  great strength.
¹⁷The war horse is a vain hope for
  victory,

°Heb obscure   ᵖCn: Heb *at a time of finding only*
ᵠCn: Heb *shouts of deliverance*
32.1-2: Rom 4.7-8.

and by its great might it cannot save.

[18] Behold, the eye of the LORD is on those who fear him,
on those who hope in his steadfast love,
[19] that he may deliver their soul from death,
and keep them alive in famine.

[20] Our soul waits for the LORD;
he is our help and shield.
[21] Yea, our heart is glad in him,
because we trust in his holy name.
[22] Let thy steadfast love, O LORD, be upon us,
even as we hope in thee.

A Psalm of David, when he feigned madness before A·bĭm'e·lĕch, so that he drove him out, and he went away.

34 I will bless the LORD at all times;
his praise shall continually be in my mouth.
[2] My soul makes its boast in the LORD;
let the afflicted hear and be glad.
[3] O magnify the LORD with me,
and let us exalt his name together!

[4] I sought the LORD, and he answered me,
and delivered me from all my fears.
[5] Look to him, and be radiant;
so your[r] faces shall never be ashamed.
[6] This poor man cried, and the LORD heard him,
and saved him out of all his troubles.
[7] The angel of the LORD encamps around those who fear him, and delivers them.
[8] O taste and see that the LORD is good!
Happy is the man who takes refuge in him!
[9] O fear the LORD, you his saints,
for those who fear him have no want!
[10] The young lions suffer want and hunger;
but those who seek the LORD lack no good thing.

[11] Come, O sons, listen to me,
I will teach you the fear of the LORD.

[12] What man is there who desires life,
and covets many days, that he may enjoy good?
[13] Keep your tongue from evil,
and your lips from speaking deceit.
[14] Depart from evil, and do good;
seek peace, and pursue it.

[15] The eyes of the LORD are toward the righteous,
and his ears toward their cry.
[16] The face of the LORD is against evildoers,
to cut off the remembrance of them from the earth.
[17] When the righteous cry for help, the LORD hears,
and delivers them out of all their troubles.
[18] The LORD is near to the broken-hearted,
and saves the crushed in spirit.

[19] Many are the afflictions of the righteous;
but the LORD delivers him out of them all.
[20] He keeps all his bones;
not one of them is broken.
[21] Evil shall slay the wicked;
and those who hate the righteous will be condemned.
[22] The LORD redeems the life of his servants;
none of those who take refuge in him will be condemned.

A Psalm of David.

35 Contend, O LORD, with those who contend with me;
fight against those who fight against me!
[2] Take hold of shield and buckler, and rise for my help!
[3] Draw the spear and javelin against my pursuers!
Say to my soul,
"I am your deliverance!"

[4] Let them be put to shame and dishonor
who seek after my life!
Let them be turned back and confounded
who devise evil against me!

[r] Gk Syr Jerome: Heb *their*
34.8: 1 Pet 2.3. **34.12-16:** 1 Pet 3.10-12.

⁵Let them be like chaff before the
      wind,
   with the angel of the LORD driv-
      ing them on!
⁶Let their way be dark and slippery,
   with the angel of the LORD pur-
      suing them!

⁷For without cause they hid their net
      for me;
   without cause they dug a pit*
      for my life.
⁸Let ruin come upon them unawares!
   And let the net which they hid en-
      snare them;
   let them fall therein to ruin!

⁹Then my soul shall rejoice in the
      LORD,
   exulting in his deliverance.
¹⁰All my bones shall say,
   "O LORD, who is like thee,
   thou who deliverest the weak
      from him who is too strong for
         him,
      the weak and needy from him who
         despoils him?"

¹¹Malicious witnesses rise up;
   they ask me of things that I know
      not.
¹²They requite me evil for good;
   my soul is forlorn.
¹³But I, when they were sick—
   I wore sackcloth,
   I afflicted myself with fasting.
   I prayed with head bowed* on my
      bosom,
¹⁴   as though I grieved for my friend
      or my brother;
   I went about as one who laments
      his mother,
   bowed down and in mourning.

¹⁵But at my stumbling they gathered
      in glee,
   they gathered together against me;
   cripples whom I knew not
      slandered me without ceasing;
¹⁶they impiously mocked more and
      more,*
      gnashing at me with their teeth.

¹⁷How long, O LORD, wilt thou look on?
   Rescue me from their ravages,
   my life from the lions!
¹⁸Then I will thank thee in the great
      congregation;
   in the mighty throng I will praise
      thee.

¹⁹Let not those rejoice over me
   who are wrongfully my foes,
   and let not those wink the eye
   who hate me without cause.
²⁰For they do not speak peace,
   but against those who are quiet
      in the land
   they conceive words of deceit.
²¹They open wide their mouths against
      me;
   they say, "Aha, Aha!
   our eyes have seen it!"

²²Thou hast seen, O LORD; be not
      silent!
   O Lord, be not far from me!
²³Bestir thyself, and awake for my
      right,
   for my cause, my God and my
      Lord!
²⁴Vindicate me, O LORD, my God,
   according to thy righteousness;
   and let them not rejoice over me!
²⁵Let them not say to themselves,
   "Aha, we have our heart's desire!"
   Let them not say, "We have swal-
      lowed him up."

²⁶Let them be put to shame and con-
      fusion altogether
   who rejoice at my calamity!
   Let them be clothed with shame and
      dishonor
   who magnify themselves against
      me!

²⁷Let those who desire my vindica-
      tion
   shout for joy and be glad,
   and say evermore,
   "Great is the LORD,
   who delights in the welfare of
      his servant!"
²⁸Then my tongue shall tell of thy
      righteousness
   and of thy praise all the day long.

   To the choirmaster. A Psalm of
   David, the servant of the LORD.

36   Transgression speaks to the
      wicked
   deep in his heart;
   there is no fear of God
   before his eyes.

*The word *pit* is transposed from the preceding line
*Or *My prayer turned back*
*Cn Compare Gk: Heb *like the profanest of mockers of a
cake*
35.19: Ps 69.4; Jn 15.25.   **36.1:** Rom 3.18.

² For he flatters himself in his own
eyes
that his iniquity cannot be found
out and hated.
³ The words of his mouth are mischief and deceit;
he has ceased to act wisely and do
good.
⁴ He plots mischief while on his bed;
he sets himself in a way that is
not good;
he spurns not evil.

⁵ Thy steadfast love, O LORD, extends
to the heavens,
thy faithfulness to the clouds.
⁶ Thy righteousness is like the mountains of God,
thy judgments are like the great
deep;
man and beast thou savest, O
LORD.

⁷ How precious is thy steadfast love,
O God!
The children of men take refuge
in the shadow of thy wings.
⁸ They feast on the abundance of thy
house,
and thou givest them drink from
the river of thy delights.
⁹ For with thee is the fountain of life;
in thy light do we see light.

¹⁰ O continue thy steadfast love to
those who know thee,
and thy salvation to the upright
of heart!
¹ Let not the foot of arrogance come
upon me,
nor the hand of the wicked drive
me away.
² There the evildoers lie prostrate,
they are thrust down, unable to
rise.

A Psalm of David.

37 Fret not yourself because of
the wicked,
be not envious of wrongdoers!
² For they will soon fade like the grass,
and wither like the green herb.

³ Trust in the LORD, and do good;
so you will dwell in the land, and
enjoy security.
⁴ Take delight in the LORD,

and he will give you the desires
of your heart.
⁵ Commit your way to the LORD;
trust in him, and he will act.
⁶ He will bring forth your vindication
as the light,
and your right as the noonday.

⁷ Be still before the LORD, and wait
patiently for him;
fret not yourself over him who
prospers in his way,
over the man who carries out evil
devices!

⁸ Refrain from anger, and forsake
wrath!
Fret not yourself; it tends only to
evil.
⁹ For the wicked shall be cut off;
but those who wait for the LORD
shall possess the land.

¹⁰ Yet a little while, and the wicked
will be no more;
though you look well at his place,
he will not be there.
¹¹ But the meek shall possess the land,
and delight themselves in abundant prosperity.

¹² The wicked plots against the righteous,
and gnashes his teeth at him;
¹³ but the LORD laughs at the wicked,
for he sees that his day is coming.

¹⁴ The wicked draw the sword and bend
their bows,
to bring down the poor and needy,
to slay those who walk uprightly;
¹⁵ their sword shall enter their own
heart,
and their bows shall be broken.

¹⁶ Better is a little that the righteous
has
than the abundance of many
wicked.
¹⁷ For the arms of the wicked shall be
broken;
but the LORD upholds the righteous.

¹⁸ The LORD knows the days of the
blameless,
and their heritage will abide for
ever;

37.11: Mt 5.5.

¹⁹they are not put to shame in evil
　　times,
　in the days of famine they have
　　abundance.

²⁰But the wicked perish;
　the enemies of the LORD are like
　　the glory of the pastures,
　they vanish—like smoke they
　　vanish away.

²¹The wicked borrows, and cannot
　　pay back,
　but the righteous is generous and
　　gives;
²²for those blessed by the LORD shall
　　possess the land,
　but those cursed by him shall be
　　cut off.

²³The steps of a man are from the
　　LORD,
　and he establishes him in whose
　　way he delights;
²⁴though he fall, he shall not be cast
　　headlong,
　for the LORD is the stay of his
　　hand.

²⁵I have been young, and now am old;
　yet I have not seen the righteous
　　forsaken
　or his children begging bread.
²⁶He is ever giving liberally and
　　lending,
　and his children become a bless-
　　ing.

²⁷Depart from evil, and do good;
　so shall you abide for ever.
²⁸For the LORD loves justice;
　he will not forsake his saints.

　The righteous shall be preserved for
　　ever,
　　but the children of the wicked
　　shall be cut off.
²⁹The righteous shall possess the land,
　and dwell upon it for ever.

³⁰The mouth of the righteous utters
　　wisdom,
　and his tongue speaks justice.
³¹The law of his God is in his heart;
　his steps do not slip.

³²The wicked watches the righteous,
　and seeks to slay him.
³³The LORD will not abandon him to
　　his power,

or let him be condemned when he
　is brought to trial.

³⁴Wait for the LORD, and keep to his
　　way,
　and he will exalt you to possess
　　the land;
　you will look on the destruction
　　of the wicked.

³⁵I have seen a wicked man over-
　　bearing,
　and towering like a cedar of
　　Lebanon.ᵛ
³⁶Again Iʷ passed by, and, lo, he was
　　no more;
　though I sought him, he could not
　　be found.

³⁷Mark the blameless man, and behold
　　the upright,
　for there is posterity for the man
　　of peace.
³⁸But transgressors shall be altogether
　　destroyed;
　the posterity of the wicked shall
　　be cut off.

³⁹The salvation of the righteous is
　　from the LORD;
　he is their refuge in the time of
　　trouble.
⁴⁰The LORD helps them and delivers
　　them;
　he delivers them from the wicked
　　and saves them,
　because they take refuge in him

A Psalm of David, for the memorial
　　offering.

38　O LORD, rebuke me not in
　　thy anger,
　nor chasten me in thy wrath!
²For thy arrows have sunk into me
　and thy hand has come down on
　　me.

³There is no soundness in my flesh
　　because of thy indignation;
　there is no health in my bones
　　because of my sin.
⁴For my iniquities have gone over my
　　head;
　they weigh like a burden too heavy
　　for me.

⁵My wounds grow foul and fester
　　because of my foolishness,

ᵛGk: Heb obscure　ʷGk Syr Jerome: Heb *he*

⁶I am utterly bowed down and prostrate;
   all the day I go about mourning.
⁷For my loins are filled with burning,
   and there is no soundness in my
   flesh.
⁸I am utterly spent and crushed;
   I groan because of the tumult of
   my heart.

⁹Lord, all my longing is known to thee,
   my sighing is not hidden from thee.
¹⁰My heart throbs, my strength fails
   me;
   and the light of my eyes—it also
   has gone from me.
¹¹My friends and companions stand
   aloof from my plague,
   and my kinsmen stand afar off.

¹²Those who seek my life lay their
   snares,
   those who seek my hurt speak of
   ruin,
   and meditate treachery all the day
   long.

¹³But I am like a deaf man, I do not
   hear,
   like a dumb man who does not
   open his mouth.
¹⁴Yea, I am like a man who does not
   hear,
   and in whose mouth are no rebukes.

¹⁵But for thee, O Lord, do I wait;
   it is thou, O Lord my God, who
   wilt answer.
¹⁶For I pray, "Only let them not rejoice
   over me,
   who boast against me when my
   foot slips!"

¹⁷For I am ready to fall,
   and my pain is ever with me.
¹⁸I confess my iniquity,
   I am sorry for my sin.
¹⁹Those who are my foes without
   cause*ˣ* are mighty,
   and many are those who hate me
   wrongfully.
²⁰Those who render me evil for good
   are my adversaries because I follow after good.

²¹Do not forsake me, O Lord!
   O my God, be not far from me!
²²Make haste to help me,
   O Lord, my salvation!

To the choirmaster: to Jĕ·dü′thun.
A Psalm of David.

39 I said, "I will guard my ways,
   that I may not sin with my
   tongue;
I will bridle*ʸ* my mouth,
   so long as the wicked are in my
   presence."
²I was dumb and silent,
   I held my peace to no avail;
   my distress grew worse,
³   my heart became hot within me.
As I mused, the fire burned;
   then I spoke with my tongue:

⁴"Lord, let me know my end,
   and what is the measure of my
   days;
   let me know how fleeting my life
   is!
⁵Behold, thou hast made my days
   a few handbreadths,
   and my lifetime is as nothing in
   thy sight.
Surely every man stands as a mere
   breath!   *Selah*
⁶   Surely man goes about as a
   shadow!
Surely for nought are they in turmoil;
   man heaps up, and knows not who
   will gather!

⁷"And now, Lord, for what do I wait?
   My hope is in thee.
⁸Deliver me from all my transgressions.
   Make me not the scorn of the fool!
⁹I am dumb, I do not open my mouth;
   for it is thou who hast done it.
¹⁰Remove thy stroke from me;
   I am spent by the blows*ᶻ* of thy
   hand.
¹¹When thou dost chasten man
   with rebukes for sin,
   thou dost consume like a moth what
   is dear to him;
   surely every man is a mere
   breath!   *Selah*

¹²"Hear my prayer, O Lord,
   and give ear to my cry;
   hold not thy peace at my tears!
For I am thy passing guest,
   a sojourner, like all my fathers.
¹³Look away from me, that I may know
   gladness,
   before I depart and be no more!"

*ˣ*Cn: Heb *living*   *ʸ*Heb *muzzle*   *ᶻ*Heb *hostility*

To the choirmaster. A Psalm of David.

40 I waited patiently for the Lord;
he inclined to me and heard my
cry.
[2] He drew me up from the desolate
pit,[a]
out of the miry bog,
and set my feet upon a rock,
making my steps secure.
[3] He put a new song in my mouth,
a song of praise to our God.
Many will see and fear,
and put their trust in the Lord.

[4] Blessed is the man who makes
the Lord his trust,
who does not turn to the proud,
to those who go astray after false
gods!
[5] Thou hast multiplied, O Lord my
God,
thy wondrous deeds and thy
thoughts toward us;
none can compare with thee!
Were I to proclaim and tell of
them,
they would be more than can be
numbered.

[6] Sacrifice and offering thou dost not
desire;
but thou hast given me an open
ear.[b]
Burnt offering and sin offering
thou hast not required.
[7] Then I said, "Lo, I come;
in the roll of the book it is written
of me;
[8] I delight to do thy will, O my God;
thy law is within my heart."

[9] I have told the glad news of deliverance
in the great congregation;
lo, I have not restrained my lips,
as thou knowest, O Lord.
[10] I have not hid thy saving help within
my heart,
I have spoken of thy faithfulness
and thy salvation;
I have not concealed thy steadfast
love and thy faithfulness
from the great congregation.

[11] Do not thou, O Lord, withhold
thy mercy from me,
let thy steadfast love and thy faithfulness
ever preserve me!

[12] For evils have encompassed me
without number;
my iniquities have overtaken me
till I cannot see;
they are more than the hairs of my
head;
my heart fails me.

[13] Be pleased, O Lord, to deliver me!
O Lord, make haste to help me!
[14] Let them be put to shame and confusion altogether
who seek to snatch away my life;
let them be turned back and brought
to dishonor
who desire my hurt!
[15] Let them be appalled because of
their shame
who say to me, "Aha, Aha!"

[16] But may all who seek thee
rejoice and be glad in thee;
may those who love thy salvation
say continually, "Great is the
Lord!"
[17] As for me, I am poor and needy;
but the Lord takes thought for me
Thou art my help and my deliverer
do not tarry, O my God!

To the choirmaster. A Psalm of David

41 Blessed is he who considers
the poor![c]
The Lord delivers him in the day
of trouble;
[2] the Lord protects him and keeps him
alive;
he is called blessed in the land
thou dost not give him up to the
will of his enemies.
[3] The Lord sustains him on his sick
bed;
in his illness thou healest all his
infirmities.[d]

[4] As for me, I said, "O Lord, be gracious to me;
heal me, for I have sinned against
thee!"
[5] My enemies say of me in malice
"When will he die, and his name
perish?"
[6] And when one comes to see me, he
utters empty words,
while his heart gathers mischief

---

[a] Cn: Heb *pit of tumult*   [b] Heb *ears thou hast dug for m*
[c] Or *weak*   [d] Heb *thou changest all his bed*
40.6-8: Heb 10.5-9.   **40.13-17:** Ps 70.1-5.

when he goes out, he tells it abroad.
⁷All who hate me whisper together
about me;
they imagine the worst for me.

⁸They say, "A deadly thing has
fastened upon him;
he will not rise again from where
he lies."
⁹Even my bosom friend in whom I
trusted,
who ate of my bread, has lifted
his heel against me.
¹⁰But do thou, O LORD, be gracious to
me,
and raise me up, that I may requite them!

¹¹By this I know that thou art pleased
with me,
in that my enemy has not triumphed over me.
¹²But thou hast upheld me because of
my integrity,
and set me in thy presence for
ever.

¹³Blessed be the LORD, the God of
Israel,
from everlasting to everlasting!
Amen and Amen.

BOOK II

To the choirmaster. A Măs′kĭl of
the Sons of Kō′raḥ.

42 As a hart longs
for flowing streams,
so longs my soul
for thee, O God.
²My soul thirsts for God,
for the living God.
When shall I come and behold
the face of God?
³My tears have been my food
day and night,
while men say to me continually,
"Where is your God?"

⁴These things I remember,
as I pour out my soul:
how I went with the throng,
and led them in procession to the
house of God,
with glad shouts and songs of
thanksgiving,
a multitude keeping festival.

⁵Why are you cast down, O my soul,
and why are you disquieted
within me?
Hope in God; for I shall again
praise him,
my help ⁶and my God.

My soul is cast down within me,
therefore I remember thee
from the land of Jordan and of
Hermon,
from Mount Mī′zär.
⁷Deep calls to deep
at the thunder of thy cataracts;
all thy waves and thy billows
have gone over me.
⁸By day the LORD commands his
steadfast love;
and at night his song is with me,
a prayer to the God of my life.

⁹I say to God, my rock:
"Why hast thou forgotten me?
Why go I mourning
because of the oppression of the
enemy?"
¹⁰As with a deadly wound in my body,
my adversaries taunt me,
while they say to me continually,
"Where is your God?"

¹¹Why are you cast down, O my soul,
and why are you disquieted within
me?
Hope in God; for I shall again
praise him,
my help and my God.

43 Vindicate me, O God, and defend my cause
against an ungodly people;
from deceitful and unjust men
deliver me!
²For thou art the God in whom I
take refuge;
why hast thou cast me off?
Why go I mourning
because of the oppression of the
enemy?

³Oh send out thy light and thy truth;
let them lead me,
let them bring me to thy holy hill
and to thy dwelling!
⁴Then I will go to the altar of God,
to God my exceeding joy;
and I will praise thee with the lyre,
O God, my God.

41.9: Jn 13.18.

⁵Why are you cast down, O my soul,
   and why are you disquieted within
   me?
Hope in God; for I shall again praise
   him,
   my help and my God.

To the choirmaster. A Măs'kĭl of the
   Sons of Kō'rah.

44 We have heard with our ears,
      O God,
   our fathers have told us,
what deeds thou didst perform in
   their days,
   in the days of old:
²thou with thy own hand didst drive
   out the nations,
   but them thou didst plant;
thou didst afflict the peoples,
   but them thou didst set free;
³for not by their own sword did they
   win the land,
   nor did their own arm give them
   victory;
but thy right hand, and thy arm,
   and the light of thy countenance;
   for thou didst delight in them.

⁴Thou art my King and my God,
   who ordainest*e* victories for Jacob.
⁵Through thee we push down our foes;
   through thy name we tread down
   our assailants.
⁶For not in my bow do I trust,
   nor can my sword save me.
⁷But thou hast saved us from our foes,
   and hast put to confusion those
   who hate us.
⁸In God we have boasted continually,
   and we will give thanks to thy
   name for ever.   *Selah*

⁹Yet thou hast cast us off and abased
   us,
   and hast not gone out with our
   armies.
¹⁰Thou hast made us turn back from
   the foe;
   and our enemies have gotten spoil.
¹¹Thou hast made us like sheep for
   slaughter,
   and hast scattered us among the
   nations.
¹²Thou hast sold thy people for a trifle,
   demanding no high price for them.
¹³Thou hast made us the taunt of our
   neighbors,

the derision and scorn of those
   about us.
¹⁴Thou hast made us a byword among
   the nations,
   a laughingstock*f* among the peoples.
¹⁵All day long my disgrace is before
   me,
   and shame has covered my face,
¹⁶at the words of the taunters and
   revilers,
   at the sight of the enemy and the
   avenger.

¹⁷All this has come upon us,
   though we have not forgotten thee,
   or been false to thy covenant.
¹⁸Our heart has not turned back,
   nor have our steps departed from
   thy way,
¹⁹that thou shouldst have broken us
   in the place of jackals,
   and covered us with deep darkness.

²⁰If we had forgotten the name of our
   God,
   or spread forth our hands to a
   strange god,
²¹would not God discover this?
   For he knows the secrets of the
   heart.
²²Nay, for thy sake we are slain all
   the day long,
   and accounted as sheep for the
   slaughter.

²³Rouse thyself! Why sleepest thou
   O Lord?
   Awake! Do not cast us off for ever!
²⁴Why dost thou hide thy face?
   Why dost thou forget our afflictior
   and oppression?
²⁵For our soul is bowed down to the
   dust;
   our body cleaves to the ground
²⁶Rise up, come to our help!
   Deliver us for the sake of thy
   steadfast love!

To the choirmaster: according to
   Lilies. A Măs'kĭl of the Sons
   of Kō'rah; a love song.

45 My heart overflows with a
      goodly theme;
   I address my verses to the king;

*e*Gk Syr: Heb *Thou art my King, O God; ordain*
*f*Heb *a shaking of the head*
44.22: Rom 8.36.

my tongue is like the pen of a
ready scribe.

2 You are the fairest of the sons of
men;
grace is poured upon your lips;
therefore God has blessed you
for ever.
3 Gird your sword upon your thigh,
O mighty one,
in your glory and majesty!

4 In your majesty ride forth victori-
ously
for the cause of truth and to defend[g] the right;
let your right hand teach you
dread deeds!
5 Your arrows are sharp
in the heart of the king's enemies;
the peoples fall under you.

6 Your divine throne[h] endures for ever
and ever.
Your royal scepter is a scepter of
equity;
7   you love righteousness and hate
wickedness.
Therefore God, your God, has anointed
you
with the oil of gladness above
your fellows;
8   your robes are all fragrant with
myrrh and aloes and cassia.
From ivory palaces stringed instruments make you glad;
9   daughters of kings are among your
ladies of honor;
at your right hand stands the
queen in gold of Ō'phīr.

10 Hear, O daughter, consider, and incline your ear;
forget your people and your father's house;
11 and the king will desire your
beauty.
Since he is your lord, bow to him;
12 the people[i] of Tȳre will sue your
favor with gifts,
the richest of the people 13 with
all kinds of wealth.

The princess is decked in her chamber with gold-woven robes;[j]
14 in many-colored robes she is led
to the king,
with her virgin companions, her
escort,[k] in her train.

15 With joy and gladness they are led
along
as they enter the palace of the
king.
16 Instead of your fathers shall be your
sons;
you will make them princes in all
the earth.
17 I will cause your name to be celebrated in all generations;
therefore the peoples will praise
you for ever and ever.

To the choirmaster. A Psalm of the
Sons of Kō'rah. According to
Ăl'a·mŏth. A Song.

46 God is our refuge and strength,
a very present[l] help in trouble.
2 Therefore we will not fear though
the earth should change,
though the mountains shake in
the heart of the sea;
3 though its waters roar and foam,
though the mountains tremble
with its tumult.   *Selah*

4 There is a river whose streams make
glad the city of God,
the holy habitation of the Most
High.
5 God is in the midst of her, she shall
not be moved;
God will help her right early.
6 The nations rage, the kingdoms
totter;
he utters his voice, the earth melts.
7 The LORD of hosts is with us;
the God of Jacob is our refuge.[m]
   Selah

8 Come, behold the works of the LORD,
how he has wrought desolations
in the earth.
9 He makes wars cease to the end of
the earth;
he breaks the bow, and shatters
the spear,
he burns the chariots with fire!
10 "Be still, and know that I am God.
I am exalted among the nations,
I am exalted in the earth!"

[g] Cn: Heb *and the meekness of*
[h] Or *Your throne is a throne of God*, or *Thy throne, O God*
[i] Heb *daughter*
[j] Or *people. All glorious is the princess within, gold em-
broidery is her clothing* [k] Heb *those brought to you*
[l] Or *well proved* [m] Or *fortress*
45.6-7: Heb 1.8-9.

[11] The LORD of hosts is with us;
the God of Jacob is our refuge.[m]
Selah

To the choirmaster. A Psalm of the
Sons of Kō′rah.

47 Clap your hands, all peoples!
Shout to God with loud songs of
joy!
[2] For the LORD, the Most High, is terrible,
a great king over all the earth.
[3] He subdued peoples under us,
and nations under our feet.
[4] He chose our heritage for us,
the pride of Jacob whom he loves.
Selah

[5] God has gone up with a shout,
the LORD with the sound of a
trumpet.
[6] Sing praises to God, sing praises!
Sing praises to our King, sing
praises!
[7] For God is the king of all the earth;
sing praises with a psalm![n]

[8] God reigns over the nations;
God sits on his holy throne.
[9] The princes of the peoples gather
as the people of the God of
Abraham.
For the shields of the earth belong
to God;
he is highly exalted!

A Song. A Psalm of the
Sons of Kō′rah.

48 Great is the LORD and greatly
to be praised
in the city of our God!
His holy mountain, [2] beautiful in
elevation,
is the joy of all the earth,
Mount Zion, in the far north,
the city of the great King.
[3] Within her citadels God
has shown himself a sure defense.

[4] For lo, the kings assembled,
they came on together.
[5] As soon as they saw it, they were
astounded,
they were in panic, they took to
flight;
[6] trembling took hold of them there,

anguish as of a woman in travail.
[7] By the east wind thou didst shatter
the ships of Tär′shĭsh.
[8] As we have heard, so have we seen
in the city of the LORD of hosts,
in the city of our God,
which God establishes for ever.
Selah

[9] We have thought on thy steadfast
love, O God,
in the midst of thy temple.
[10] As thy name, O God,
so thy praise reaches to the ends
of the earth.
Thy right hand is filled with victory;
[11] let Mount Zion be glad!
Let the daughters of Judah rejoice
because of thy judgments!

[12] Walk about Zion, go round about her,
number her towers,
[13] consider well her ramparts,
go through her citadels;
that you may tell the next generation
[14] that this is God,
our God for ever and ever.
He will be our guide for ever.

To the choirmaster. A Psalm of the
Sons of Kō′rah.

49 Hear this, all peoples!
Give ear, all inhabitants of the
world,
[2] both low and high,
rich and poor together!
[3] My mouth shall speak wisdom;
the meditation of my heart shall
be understanding.
[4] I will incline my ear to a proverb;
I will solve my riddle to the music
of the lyre.

[5] Why should I fear in times of trouble,
when the iniquity of my persecutors surrounds me,
[6] men who trust in their wealth
and boast of the abundance of
their riches?
[7] Truly no man can ransom himself,[o]
or give to God the price of his life,
[8] for the ransom of his[p] life is costly,
and can never suffice,

[m] Or *fortress*   [n] Heb *Maskil*
[o] Another reading is *no man can ransom his brother*
[p] Gk: Heb *their*
48.2: Mt 5.35.

9 that he should continue to live on
for ever,
and never see the Pit.

10 Yea, he shall see that even the wise
die,
the fool and the stupid alike must
perish
and leave their wealth to others.
11 Their graves[q] are their homes for
ever,
their dwelling places to all generations,
though they named lands their
own.
12 Man cannot abide in his pomp,
he is like the beasts that perish.

13 This is the fate of those who have
foolish confidence,
the end of those[r] who are pleased
with their portion. *Selah*
14 Like sheep they are appointed for
Shē'ōl;
Death shall be their shepherd;
straight to the grave they descend,[s]
and their form shall waste away;
Sheol shall be their home.[t]
15 But God will ransom my soul from
the power of Shē'ōl,
for he will receive me. *Selah*

16 Be not afraid when one becomes rich,
when the glory[u] of his house increases.
17 For when he dies he will carry
nothing away;
his glory[u] will not go down after
him.
18 Though, while he lives, he counts
himself happy,
and though a man gets praise
when he does well for himself,
19 he will go to the generation of his
fathers,
who will never more see the light.
20 Man cannot abide in his pomp,
he is like the beasts that perish.

A Psalm of Ā'săph.

50 The Mighty One, God the
LORD,
speaks and summons the earth
from the rising of the sun to its
setting.
2 Out of Zion, the perfection of beauty,
God shines forth.

3 Our God comes, he does not keep
silence,
before him is a devouring fire,
round about him a mighty tempest.
4 He calls to the heavens above
and to the earth, that he may
judge his people:
5 "Gather to me my faithful ones,
who made a covenant with me by
sacrifice!"
6 The heavens declare his righteousness,
for God himself is judge! *Selah*

7 "Hear, O my people, and I will speak,
O Israel, I will testify against you.
I am God, your God.
8 I do not reprove you for your sacrifices;
your burnt offerings are continually before me.
9 I will accept no bull from your house,
nor he-goat from your folds.
10 For every beast of the forest is
mine,
the cattle on a thousand hills.
11 I know all the birds of the air,[v]
and all that moves in the field is
mine.

12 "If I were hungry, I would not tell
you;
for the world and all that is in it
is mine.
13 Do I eat the flesh of bulls,
or drink the blood of goats?
14 Offer to God a sacrifice of thanksgiving,[w]
and pay your vows to the Most
High;
15 and call upon me in the day of
trouble;
I will deliver you, and you shall
glorify me."

16 But to the wicked God says:
"What right have you to recite
my statutes,
or take my covenant on your lips?
17 For you hate discipline,
and you cast my words behind you.
18 If you see a thief, you are a friend of
his;
and you keep company with
adulterers.

[q] Gk Syr Compare Tg: Heb *their inward* (thought)
[r] Tg: Heb *after them*
[s] Cn: Heb *the upright shall have dominion over them in the morning* [t] Heb uncertain [u] Or *wealth*
[v] Gk Syr Tg: Heb *mountains*
[w] Or *make thanksgiving your sacrifice to God*

19 "You give your mouth free rein for evil,
and your tongue frames deceit.
20 You sit and speak against your brother;
you slander your own mother's son.
21 These things you have done and I have been silent;
you thought that I was one like yourself.
But now I rebuke you, and lay the charge before you.

22 "Mark this, then, you who forget God,
lest I rend, and there be none to deliver!
23 He who brings thanksgiving as his sacrifice honors me;
to him who orders his way aright I will show the salvation of God!"

To the choirmaster. A Psalm of David, when Nathan the prophet came to him, after he had gone in to Băth·shē'bạ.

51 Have mercy on me, O God, according to thy steadfast love;
according to thy abundant mercy blot out my transgressions.
2 Wash me thoroughly from my iniquity,
and cleanse me from my sin!

3 For I know my transgressions,
and my sin is ever before me.
4 Against thee, thee only, have I sinned,
and done that which is evil in thy sight,
so that thou art justified in thy sentence
and blameless in thy judgment.
5 Behold, I was brought forth in iniquity,
and in sin did my mother conceive me.

6 Behold, thou desirest truth in the inward being;
therefore teach me wisdom in my secret heart.
7 Purge me with hyssop, and I shall be clean;
wash me, and I shall be whiter than snow.
8 Fill[x] me with joy and gladness;
let the bones which thou hast broken rejoice.

9 Hide thy face from my sins,
and blot out all my iniquities.

10 Create in me a clean heart, O God,
and put a new and right[y] spirit within me.
11 Cast me not away from thy presence,
and take not thy holy Spirit from me.
12 Restore to me the joy of thy salvation,
and uphold me with a willing spirit.

13 Then I will teach transgressors thy ways,
and sinners will return to thee.
14 Deliver me from bloodguiltiness,[z] O God,
thou God of my salvation,
and my tongue will sing aloud of thy deliverance.

15 O Lord, open thou my lips,
and my mouth shall show forth thy praise.
16 For thou hast no delight in sacrifice;
were I to give a burnt offering, thou wouldst not be pleased.
17 The sacrifice acceptable to God[a] is a broken spirit;
a broken and contrite heart, O God, thou wilt not despise.

18 Do good to Zion in thy good pleasure;
rebuild the walls of Jerusalem,
19 then wilt thou delight in right sacrifices,
in burnt offerings and whole burnt offerings;
then bulls will be offered on thy altar.

To the choirmaster. A Măs'kĭl of David, when Dō'eg, the Ē'dọm·īte, came and told Saul, "David has come to the house of Ạ·hĭm'ẹ·lĕch."

52 Why do you boast, O mighty man,
of mischief done against the godly?[b]
All the day 2 you are plotting destruction.

x Syr: Heb *Make to hear*   y Or *steadfast*   z Or *death*
a Or *My sacrifice, O God*
b Cn Compare Syr: Heb *the kindness of God*
51.4: Rom 3.4.

Your tongue is like a sharp razor,
  you worker of treachery.
[3] You love evil more than good,
  and lying more than speaking the
    truth.   *Selah*
[4] You love all words that devour,
  O deceitful tongue.

[5] But God will break you down for
    ever;
  he will snatch and tear you from
    your tent;
  he will uproot you from the land
    of the living.   *Selah*
[6] The righteous shall see, and fear,
  and shall laugh at him, saying,
[7] "See the man who would not make
    God his refuge,
  but trusted in the abundance of his
    riches,
  and sought refuge in his wealth!"[c]

[8] But I am like a green olive tree
  in the house of God.
I trust in the steadfast love of God
  for ever and ever.
[9] I will thank thee for ever,
  because thou hast done it.
I will proclaim[d] thy name, for it is
    good,
  in the presence of the godly.

To the choirmaster: according to
Mā′hä·läth. A Măs′kĭl of David.

53   The fool says in his heart,
        "There is no God."
They are corrupt, doing abomi-
    nable iniquity;
  there is none that does good.

[2] God looks down from heaven
  upon the sons of men
to see if there are any that are
    wise,
  that seek after God.

[3] They have all fallen away;
  they are all alike depraved;
there is none that does good,
  no, not one.

[4] Have those who work evil no un-
    derstanding,
  who eat up my people as they eat
    bread,
  and do not call upon God?

[5] There they are, in great terror,
  in terror such as has not been!

For God will scatter the bones of
  the ungodly;[e]
they will be put to shame,[f] for God
  has rejected them.

[6] O that deliverance for Israel would
  come from Zion!
When God restores the fortunes of
  his people,
  Jacob will rejoice and Israel be
    glad.

To the choirmaster: with stringed
instruments. A Măs′kĭl of David, when
the Zĭph′ītes went and told Saul,
"David is in hiding among us."

54   Save me, O God, by thy name,
        and vindicate me by thy might.
[2] Hear my prayer, O God;
  give ear to the words of my mouth.

[3] For insolent[g] men have risen against
    me,
  ruthless men seek my life;
  they do not set God before them.
                  Selah

[4] Behold, God is my helper;
  the Lord is the upholder[h] of my
    life.
[5] He will requite my enemies with
    evil;
  in thy faithfulness put an end to
    them.

[6] With a freewill offering I will sac-
    rifice to thee;
I will give thanks to thy name,
  O LORD, for it is good.
[7] For thou hast delivered me from
    every trouble,
  and my eye has looked in triumph
    on my enemies.

To the choirmaster: with stringed
instruments. A Măs′kĭl of David.

55   Give ear to my prayer, O God;
        and hide not thyself from my
    supplication!
[2] Attend to me, and answer me;
  I am overcome by my trouble.

[c] Syr Tg: Heb *his destruction*   [d] Cn: Heb *wait for*
[e] Cn Compare Gk Syr: Heb *him who encamps against you*
[f] Gk: Heb *you will put to shame*
[g] Another reading is *strangers*
[h] Gk Syr Jerome: Heb *of* or *with those who uphold*
53.1-3: Rom 3.10-12.   53.1-6: Ps 14.1-7.

I am distraught [3]by the noise of the
   enemy,
because of the oppression of the
   wicked.
For they bring[i] trouble upon me,
   and in anger they cherish enmity
   against me.

[4]My heart is in anguish within me,
   the terrors of death have fallen
   upon me.
[5]Fear and trembling come upon me,
   and horror overwhelms me.
[6]And I say, "O that I had wings like
   a dove!
I would fly away and be at rest;
[7]yea, I would wander afar,
I would lodge in the wilderness,
                  Selah
[8]I would haste to find me a shelter
   from the raging wind and tempest."

[9]Destroy their plans,[j] O Lord, confuse
   their tongues;
for I see violence and strife in the
   city.
[10]Day and night they go around it
   on its walls;
and mischief and trouble are within
   it,
[11] ruin is in its midst;
oppression and fraud
   do not depart from its market
   place.

[12]It is not an enemy who taunts me—
   then I could bear it;
it is not an adversary who deals
   insolently with me—
   then I could hide from him.
[13]But it is you, my equal,
   my companion, my familiar friend.
[14]We used to hold sweet converse together;
within God's house we walked in
   fellowship.
[15]Let death[k] come upon them;
let them go down to Shē'ōl alive;
let them go away in terror into
   their graves.[l]

[16]But I call upon God;
   and the Lord will save me.
[17]Evening and morning and at noon
   I utter my complaint and moan,
   and he will hear my voice.
[18]He will deliver my soul in safety
   from the battle that I wage,
   for many are arrayed against me.

[19]God will give ear, and humble them,
   he who is enthroned from of old;
because they keep no law,[m]
   and do not fear God.   *Selah*

[20]My companion stretched out his
   hand against his friends,
   he violated his covenant.
[21]His speech was smoother than butter,
   yet war was in his heart;
his words were softer than oil,
   yet they were drawn swords.

[22]Cast your burden[n] on the Lord,
   and he will sustain you;
he will never permit
   the righteous to be moved.

[23]But thou, O God, wilt cast them down
   into the lowest pit;
men of blood and treachery
   shall not live out half their days.
But I will trust in thee.

To the choirmaster: according to The
Dove on Far-off Tĕr'ĕ·bĭnths. A Mĭk'-
tăm of David, when the Phĭ·lĭs'tĭnes
   seized him in Găth.

56   Be gracious to me, O God, for
   men trample upon me;
all day long foemen oppress me;
[2]my enemies trample upon me all
   day long,
for many fight against me proudly.
[3]When I am afraid,
   I put my trust in thee.
[4]In God, whose word I praise,
   in God I trust without a fear.
What can flesh do to me?

[5]All day long they seek to injure my
   cause;
all their thoughts are against
   me for evil.
[6]They band themselves together, they
   lurk,
   they watch my steps.
As they have waited for my life,
[7] so recompense[o] them for their
   crime,
in wrath cast down the peoples,
   O God!

[i]Cn Compare Gk: Heb *they cause to totter*
[j]Tg: Heb lacks *their plans* [k]Or *desolations*
[l]Cn: Heb *evils are in their habitation, in their midst*
[m]Or *do not change*   [n]Or *what he has given you*
[o]Cn: Heb *deliver*
55.22: 1 Pet 5.7.

⁸Thou hast kept count of my tossings;
   put thou my tears in thy bottle!
   Are they not in thy book?
⁹Then my enemies will be turned
   back
   in the day when I call.
   This I know, thatᵖ God is for me.
¹⁰In God, whose word I praise,
   in the LORD, whose word I praise,
¹¹in God I trust without a fear.
   What can man do to me?

¹²My vows to thee I must perform,
   O God;
   I will render thank offerings to
   thee.
¹³For thou hast delivered my soul from
   death,
   yea, my feet from falling,
   that I may walk before God
   in the light of life.

To the choirmaster: according to Do
Not Destroy. A Mĭk'tăm of David,
when he fled from Saul, in the cave.

57   Be merciful to me, O God,
        be merciful to me,
   for in thee my soul takes refuge;
   in the shadow of thy wings I will
     take refuge,
   till the storms of destruction
     pass by.
²I cry to God Most High,
   to God who fulfils his purpose for
   me.
³He will send from heaven and
   save me,
   he will put to shame those who
    trample upon me.   *Selah*
   God will send forth his steadfast
   love and his faithfulness!

⁴I lie in the midst of lions
   that greedily devourᵍ the sons of
   men;
   their teeth are spears and arrows,
   their tongues sharp swords.

⁵Be exalted, O God, above the
   heavens!
   Let thy glory be over all the earth!

⁶They set a net for my steps;
   my soul was bowed down.
   They dug a pit in my way,
   but they have fallen into it themselves.   *Selah*

⁷My heart is steadfast, O God,
   my heart is steadfast!
   I will sing and make melody!
⁸ Awake, my soul!
   Awake, O harp and lyre!
   I will awake the dawn!
⁹I will give thanks to thee, O Lord,
   among the peoples;
   I will sing praises to thee among
   the nations.
¹⁰For thy steadfast love is great to the
   heavens,
   thy faithfulness to the clouds.
¹¹Be exalted, O God, above the
   heavens!
   Let thy glory be over all the earth!

To the choirmaster: according to Do
Not Destroy. A Mĭk'tăm of David.

58   Do you indeed decree what is
        right, you gods?ˢ
   Do you judge the sons of men
    uprightly?
²Nay, in your hearts you devise
   wrongs;
   your hands deal out violence on
   earth.

³The wicked go astray from the womb,
   they err from their birth, speaking
   lies.
⁴They have venom like the venom of
   a serpent,
   like the deaf adder that stops its
   ear,
⁵so that it does not hear the voice of
   charmers
   or of the cunning enchanter.

⁶O God, break the teeth in their
   mouths;
   tear out the fangs of the young
   lions, O LORD!
⁷Let them vanish like water that runs
   away;
   like grass let them be trodden
   down and wither.ᵗ
⁸Let them be like the snail which
   dissolves into slime,
   like the untimely birth that never
   sees the sun.
⁹Sooner than your pots can feel the
   heat of thorns,
   whether green or ablaze, may
   he sweep them away!

ᵖOr *because* ᵍCn: Heb *are aflame* ˢOr *mighty lords*
ᵗCn: Heb uncertain **57.7-11:** Ps 108.1-5.

¹⁰The righteous will rejoice when he
  sees the vengeance;
  he will bathe his feet in the blood
  of the wicked.
¹¹Men will say, "Surely there is a
  reward for the righteous;
  surely there is a God who judges
  on earth."

To the choirmaster: according to Do
Not Destroy. A Mĭk'tăm of David,
when Saul sent men to watch his
house in order to kill him.

59 Deliver me from my enemies,
     O my God,
  protect me from those who rise
  up against me,
²deliver me from those who work
  evil,
  and save me from bloodthirsty
  men.

³For, lo, they lie in wait for my life;
  fierce men band themselves
  against me.
  For no transgression or sin of mine,
  O LORD,
⁴   for no fault of mine, they run and
  make ready.

  Rouse thyself, come to my help, and
  see!
⁵   Thou, LORD God of hosts, art God
  of Israel.
  Awake to punish all the nations;
  spare none of those who treacherously plot evil.   *Selah*

⁶Each evening they come back,
  howling like dogs
  and prowling about the city.
⁷There they are, bellowing with their
  mouths,
  and snarling with" their lips—
  for "Who," they think, "will hear
  us?"

⁸But thou, O LORD, dost laugh at them;
  thou dost hold all the nations in
  derision.
⁹O my Strength, I will sing praises
  to thee;ᵛ
  for thou, O God, art my fortress.
¹⁰My God in his steadfast love will
  meet me;
  my God will let me look in triumph on my enemies.

¹¹Slay them not, lest my people forget;
  make them totter by thy power,
  and bring them down,
  O Lord, our shield!
¹²For the sin of their mouths, the
  words of their lips,
  let them be trapped in their pride.
  For the cursing and lies which they
  utter,
¹³   consume them in wrath,
  consume them till they are no
  more,
  that men may know that God rules
  over Jacob
  to the ends of the earth.   *Selah*

¹⁴Each evening they come back,
  howling like dogs
  and prowling about the city.
¹⁵They roam about for food,
  and growl if they do not get their
  fill.

¹⁶But I will sing of thy might;
  I will sing aloud of thy steadfast
  love in the morning.
  For thou hast been to me a fortress
  and a refuge in the day of my
  distress.
¹⁷O my Strength, I will sing praises
  to thee,
  for thou, O God, art my fortress,
  the God who shows me steadfast
  love.

To the choirmaster: according to
Shü'shăn Ē'dŭth. A Mĭk'tăm of David;
for instruction; when he strove with
Är'am-nā·ha'rā·ĭm and with Är'am-
zō'bah, and when Jō'ăb on his return
killed twelve thousand of Ē'dom in
the Valley of Salt.

60 O God, thou hast rejected us,
     broken our defenses;
  thou hast been angry; oh, restore
  us.
²Thou hast made the land to quake,
  thou hast rent it open;
  repair its breaches, for it totters.
³Thou hast made thy people suffer
  hard things;
  thou hast given us wine to drink
  that made us reel.

⁴Thou hast set up a banner for those
  who fear thee,

"Cn: Heb *swords in*   ᵛSyr: Heb *I will watch for thee*

to rally to it from the bow.[w] *Selah*
⁵That thy beloved may be delivered,
  give victory by thy right hand and
  answer us!

⁶God has spoken in his sanctuary:[x]
  "With exultation I will divide up
  Shē'chĕm
  and portion out the Vale of
  Sŭc'cŏth.
⁷Gilĕad is mine; Mạ·nặs'sẹh is mine;
  Ē'phrạ·im is my helmet;
  Judah is my scepter.
⁸Mō'ặb is my washbasin;
  upon Ē'dọm I cast my shoe;
  over Phĭ·lĭs'tĭ·ạ I shout in triumph."

⁹Who will bring me to the fortified
  city?
  Who will lead me to Ē'dọm?
¹⁰Hast thou not rejected us, O God?
  Thou dost not go forth, O God,
  with our armies.
¹¹O grant us help against the foe,
  for vain is the help of man!
¹²With God we shall do valiantly;
  it is he who will tread down our
  foes.

To the choirmaster: with stringed
instruments. A Psalm of David.

61 Hear my cry, O God,
     listen to my prayer;
²from the end of the earth I call to
  thee,
  when my heart is faint.

Lead thou me
  to the rock that is higher than I;
³for thou art my refuge,
  a strong tower against the enemy.

⁴Let me dwell in thy tent for ever!
  Oh to be safe under the shelter of
  thy wings!   *Selah*
⁵For thou, O God, hast heard my vows,
  thou hast given me the heritage of
  those who fear thy name.

⁶Prolong the life of the king;
  may his years endure to all generations!
⁷May he be enthroned for ever before
  God;
  bid steadfast love and faithfulness
  watch over him!

⁸So will I ever sing praises to thy name,
  as I pay my vows day after day.

To the choirmaster: according to
Jĕ·dü'thụn. A Psalm of David.

62 For God alone my soul waits in
     silence;
  from him comes my salvation.
²He only is my rock and my salvation,
  my fortress; I shall not be greatly
  moved.

³How long will you set upon a man
  to shatter him, all of you,
  like a leaning wall, a tottering
  fence?
⁴They only plan to thrust him down
  from his eminence.
  They take pleasure in falsehood.
They bless with their mouths,
  but inwardly they curse.   *Selah*

⁵For God alone my soul waits in
  silence,
  for my hope is from him.
⁶He only is my rock and my salvation,
  my fortress; I shall not be shaken.
⁷On God rests my deliverance and my
  honor;
  my mighty rock, my refuge is God.

⁸Trust in him at all times, O people;
  pour out your heart before him;
  God is a refuge for us.   *Selah*

⁹Men of low estate are but a breath,
  men of high estate are a delusion;
  in the balances they go up;
  they are together lighter than a
  breath.
¹⁰Put no confidence in extortion,
  set no vain hopes on robbery;
  if riches increase, set not your
  heart on them.

¹¹Once God has spoken;
  twice have I heard this:
  that power belongs to God;
¹² and that to thee, O Lord, belongs
  steadfast love.
For thou dost requite a man
  according to his work.

A Psalm of David, when he was in the
Wilderness of Judah.

63 O God, thou art my God, I seek
     thee,
  my soul thirsts for thee;

[w] Gk Syr Jerome: Heb *truth*   [x] Or *by his holiness*
60.5-12: Ps 108.6-13.
62.12: Jer 17.10; Rev 2.23; 22.12.

my flesh faints for thee,
  as in a dry and weary land where
    no water is.
2 So I have looked upon thee in the
  sanctuary,
  beholding thy power and glory.
3 Because thy steadfast love is better
  than life,
  my lips will praise thee.
4 So I will bless thee as long as I live;
  I will lift up my hands and call on
    thy name.

5 My soul is feasted as with marrow
  and fat,
  and my mouth praises thee with
    joyful lips,
6 when I think of thee upon my bed,
  and meditate on thee in the
    watches of the night;
7 for thou hast been my help,
  and in the shadow of thy wings I
    sing for joy.
8 My soul clings to thee;
  thy right hand upholds me.

9 But those who seek to destroy my
  life
  shall go down into the depths of
    the earth;
10 they shall be given over to the power
  of the sword,
  they shall be prey for jackals.
11 But the king shall rejoice in God;
  all who swear by him shall glory;
  for the mouths of liars will be
    stopped.

To the choirmaster. A Psalm of David.

64   Hear my voice, O God, in my
    complaint;
  preserve my life from dread of the
    enemy,
2 hide me from the secret plots of the
  wicked,
  from the scheming of evildoers,
3 who whet their tongues like swords,
  who aim bitter words like arrows,
4 shooting from ambush at the blameless,
  shooting at him suddenly and
    without fear.
5 They hold fast to their evil purpose;
  they talk of laying snares secretly,
  thinking, "Who can see us?" *y*
6   Who can search out our crimes? *z*
We have thought out a cunningly
  conceived plot."

For the inward mind and heart of a
  man are deep!

7 But God will shoot his arrow at them;
  they will be wounded suddenly.
8 Because of their tongue he will bring
  them to ruin; *a*
  all who see them will wag their
    heads.
9 Then all men will fear;
  they will tell what God has
    wrought,
  and ponder what he has done.

10 Let the righteous rejoice in the
  LORD,
  and take refuge in him!
Let all the upright in heart glory!

To the choirmaster. A Psalm of David.
A Song.

65   Praise is due to thee,
    O God, in Zion;
  and to thee shall vows be performed,
2   O thou who hearest prayer!
To thee shall all flesh come
3   on account of sins.
When our transgressions prevail
    over us, *b*
  thou dost forgive them.
4 Blessed is he whom thou dost choose
  and bring near,
  to dwell in thy courts!
We shall be satisfied with the goodness of thy house,
  thy holy temple!

5 By dread deeds thou dost answer us
  with deliverance,
  O God of our salvation,
  who art the hope of all the ends of
    the earth,
  and of the farthest seas;
6 who by thy strength hast established the mountains,
  being girded with might;
7 who dost still the roaring of the seas,
  the roaring of their waves,
  the tumult of the peoples;
8 so that those who dwell at earth's
  farthest bounds
  are afraid at thy signs;
  thou makest the outgoings of the
    morning and the evening
  to shout for joy.

y Syr: Heb *them*   *z* Cn: Heb *they search out crimes*
a Cn: Heb *They will bring him to ruin, their tongue being against them*   *b* Gk: Heb *me*

⁹Thou visitest the earth and waterest
  it,
  thou greatly enrichest it;
  the river of God is full of water;
  thou providest their grain,
  for so thou hast prepared it.
¹⁰Thou waterest its furrows abundantly,
  settling its ridges,
  softening it with showers,
  and blessing its growth.
¹¹Thou crownest the year with thy
  bounty;
  the tracks of thy chariot drip with
  fatness.
¹²The pastures of the wilderness drip,
  the hills gird themselves with
  joy,
¹³the meadows clothe themselves with
  flocks,
  the valleys deck themselves with
  grain,
  they shout and sing together for
  joy.

To the choirmaster. A Song. A Psalm.

66 Make a joyful noise to God,
  all the earth;
²   sing the glory of his name;
  give to him glorious praise!
³Say to God, "How terrible are thy
  deeds!
  So great is thy power that thy
  enemies cringe before thee.
⁴All the earth worships thee;
  they sing praises to thee,
  sing praises to thy name."

                                    Selah

⁵Come and see what God has done:
  he is terrible in his deeds among
  men.
⁶He turned the sea into dry land;
  men passed through the river on
  foot.
  There did we rejoice in him,
⁷   who rules by his might for ever,
  whose eyes keep watch on the
  nations—
  let not the rebellious exalt themselves.   *Selah*

⁸Bless our God, O peoples,
  let the sound of his praise be
  heard,
⁹who has kept us among the living,
  and has not let our feet slip.

¹⁰For thou, O God, hast tested us;
  thou hast tried us as silver is
  tried.
¹¹Thou didst bring us into the net;
  thou didst lay affliction on our
  loins;
¹²thou didst let men ride over our
  heads;
  we went through fire and through
  water;
  yet thou hast brought us forth to a
  spacious place. ᶜ

¹³I will come into thy house with burnt
  offerings;
  I will pay thee my vows,
¹⁴that which my lips uttered
  and my mouth promised when I
  was in trouble.
¹⁵I will offer to thee burnt offerings of
  fatlings,
  with the smoke of the sacrifice of
  rams;
  I will make an offering of bulls and
  goats.   *Selah*

¹⁶Come and hear, all you who fear
  God,
  and I will tell what he has done for
  me.
¹⁷I cried aloud to him,
  and he was extolled with my
  tongue.
¹⁸If I had cherished iniquity in my
  heart,
  the Lord would not have listened.
¹⁹But truly God has listened;
  he has given heed to the voice
  of my prayer.
²⁰Blessed be God,
  because he has not rejected my
  prayer
  or removed his steadfast love from
  me!

To the choirmaster: with stringed
instruments. A Psalm. A Song.

67 May God be gracious to us and
  bless us
  and make his face to shine upon us,
                                    Selah
²that thy way may be known upon
  earth,
  thy saving power among all
  nations.

ᶜCn Compare Gk Syr Jerome Tg: Heb *saturation*

³Let the peoples praise thee, O God;
   let all the peoples praise thee!

⁴Let the nations be glad and sing for
   joy,
   for thou dost judge the peoples
   with equity
   and guide the nations upon earth.
                    Selah
⁵Let the peoples praise thee, O God;
   let all the peoples praise thee!

⁶The earth has yielded its increase;
   God, our God, has blessed us.
⁷God has blessed us;
   let all the ends of the earth fear
   him!

To the choirmaster. A Psalm of David.
A Song.

68 Let God arise, let his enemies
   be scattered;
   let those who hate him flee before
   him!
²As smoke is driven away, so drive
   them away;
   as wax melts before fire,
   let the wicked perish before God!
³But let the righteous be joyful;
   let them exult before God;
   let them be jubilant with joy!

⁴Sing to God, sing praises to his name;
   lift up a song to him who rides
   upon the clouds; *d*
   his name is the LORD, exult before
   him!

⁵Father of the fatherless and pro-
   tector of widows
   is God in his holy habitation.
⁶God gives the desolate a home to
   dwell in;
   he leads out the prisoners to
   prosperity;
   but the rebellious dwell in a
   parched land.

⁷O God, when thou didst go forth
   before thy people,
   when thou didst march through
   the wilderness,   *Selah*
⁸the earth quaked, the heavens
   poured down rain,
   at the presence of God;
   yon Sinai quaked at the presence of
   God,
   the God of Israel

⁹Rain in abundance, O God, thou
   didst shed abroad;
   thou didst restore thy heritage as it
   languished;
¹⁰thy flock found a dwelling in it;
   in thy goodness, O God, thou didst
   provide for the needy.

¹¹The Lord gives the command;
   great is the host of those who bore
   the tidings:
¹² "The kings of the armies, they
   flee, they flee!"
   The women at home divide the spoil,
¹³ though they stay among the sheepfolds—
   the wings of a dove covered with
   silver,
   its pinions with green gold.
¹⁴When the Almighty scattered kings
   there,
   snow fell on Zăl'mŏn.

¹⁵O mighty mountain, mountain of
   Bā'shạn;
   O many-peaked mountain, mountain of Bashan!
¹⁶Why look you with envy, O many-
   peaked mountain,
   at the mount which God desired
   for his abode,
   yea, where the LORD will dwell
   for ever?

¹⁷With mighty chariotry, twice ten
   thousand,
   thousands upon thousands,
   the Lord came from Sinai into the
   holy place. *e*
¹⁸Thou didst ascend the high mount,
   leading captives in thy train,
   and receiving gifts among men,
   even among the rebellious, that the
   LORD God may dwell there.

¹⁹Blessed be the Lord,
   who daily bears us up;
   God is our salvation.   *Selah*
²⁰Our God is a God of salvation;
   and to GOD, the Lord, belongs
   escape from death.

²¹But God will shatter the heads of his
   enemies,
   the hairy crown of him who walks
   in his guilty ways.

*d*Or *cast up a highway for him who rides through the
deserts*
*e*Cn: Heb *The Lord among them Sinai in the holy place*
68.18: Eph 4.8.

²² The Lord said,
  "I will bring them back from
      Bā'shạn,
  I will bring them back from the
      depths of the sea,
²³ that you may bathe*ʲ* your feet in
      blood,
  that the tongues of your dogs may
      have their portion from the foe."

²⁴ Thy solemn processions are seen,*ᵍ*
      O God,
  the processions of my God, my
      King, into the sanctuary—
²⁵ the singers in front, the minstrels
      last,
  between them maidens playing
      timbrels:
²⁶ "Bless God in the great congregation,
  the LORD, O you who are of Israel's
      fountain!"
²⁷ There is Bénjamin, the least of them,
      in the lead,
  the princes of Judah in their
      throng,
  the princes of Zĕb'ū·lụn, the
      princes of Năph'tạ·lī.

²⁸ Summon thy might, O God;
  show thy strength, O God, thou
      who hast wrought for us.
²⁹ Because of thy temple at Jerusalem
      kings bear gifts to thee.
³⁰ Rebuke the beasts that dwell among
      the reeds,
  the herd of bulls with the calves of
      the peoples.
  Trample*ʰ* under foot those who lust
      after tribute;
  scatter the peoples who delight in
      war.*ⁱ*
³¹ Let bronze be brought from Egypt;
  let Ethiopia hasten to stretch out
      her hands to God.

³² Sing to God, O kingdoms of the earth;
  sing praises to the Lord,   *Selah*
³³ to him who rides in the heavens,
      the ancient heavens;
  lo, he sends forth his voice, his
      mighty voice.
³⁴ Ascribe power to God,
  whose majesty is over Israel,
  and his power is in the skies.
³⁵ Terrible is God in his*ʲ* sanctuary,
      the God of Israel,
  he gives power and strength to his
      people.

  Blessed be God!

To the choirmaster: according to
Lilies. A Psalm of David.

69 Save me, O God!
  For the waters have come up to
      my neck.
² I sink in deep mire,
  where there is no foothold;
  I have come into deep waters,
  and the flood sweeps over me.
³ I am weary with my crying;
  my throat is parched.
  My eyes grow dim
  with waiting for my God.

⁴ More in number than the hairs of
      my head
  are those who hate me without
      cause;
  mighty are those who would destroy
      me,
  those who attack me with lies.
  What I did not steal
  must I now restore?
⁵ O God, thou knowest my folly;
  the wrongs I have done are not
      hidden from thee.

⁶ Let not those who hope in thee be
      put to shame through me,
  O Lord GOD of hosts;
  let not those who seek thee be
      brought to dishonor through me,
  O God of Israel.
⁷ For it is for thy sake that I have borne
      reproach,
  that shame has covered my face.
⁸ I have become a stranger to my
      brethren,
  an alien to my mother's sons.

⁹ For zeal for thy house has consumed
      me,
  and the insults of those who insult
      thee have fallen on me.
¹⁰ When I humbled*ᵏ* my soul with
      fasting,
  it became my reproach.
¹¹ When I made sackcloth my clothing,
  I became a byword to them.
¹² I am the talk of those who sit in the
      gate,
  and the drunkards make songs
      about me.

ʲ Gk Syr Tg: Heb *shatter* *ᵍ* Or *have been seen*
ʰ Cn: Heb *trampling* *ⁱ* The Hebrew of verse 30 is obscure
ʲ Gk: Heb *from thy*
ᵏ Gk Syr: Heb *I wept with fasting my soul* or *I made my
soul mourn with fasting*
69.4: Ps 35.19; Jn 15.25.
69.9: Jn 2.17; Rom 15.3.

[13] But as for me, my prayer is to thee,
O LORD.
At an acceptable time, O God,
in the abundance of thy steadfast
love answer me.
With thy faithful help [14] rescue me
from sinking in the mire;
let me be delivered from my enemies
and from the deep waters.
[15] Let not the flood sweep over me,
or the deep swallow me up,
or the pit close its mouth over me.

[16] Answer me, O LORD, for thy steadfast love is good;
according to thy abundant mercy,
turn to me.
[17] Hide not thy face from thy servant;
for I am in distress, make haste to
answer me.
[18] Draw near to me, redeem me,
set me free because of my enemies!

[19] Thou knowest my reproach,
and my shame and my dishonor;
my foes are all known to thee.
[20] Insults have broken my heart,
so that I am in despair.
I looked for pity, but there was none;
and for comforters, but I found
none.
[21] They gave me poison for food,
and for my thirst they gave me
vinegar to drink.

[22] Let their own table before them
become a snare;
let their sacrificial feasts[l] be a
trap.
[23] Let their eyes be darkened, so that
they cannot see;
and make their loins tremble
continually.
[24] Pour out thy indignation upon them,
and let thy burning anger overtake
them.
[25] May their camp be a desolation,
let no one dwell in their tents.
[26] For they persecute him whom thou
hast smitten,
and him[m] whom thou hast
wounded, they afflict still more.[n]
[27] Add to them punishment upon
punishment;
may they have no acquittal from
thee.
[28] Let them be blotted out of the book
of the living;
let them not be enrolled among the
righteous.

[29] But I am afflicted and in pain;
let thy salvation, O God, set me on
high!

[30] I will praise the name of God with
a song;
I will magnify him with thanksgiving.
[31] This will please the LORD more than
an ox
or a bull with horns and hoofs.
[32] Let the oppressed see it and be glad;
you who seek God, let your hearts
revive.
[33] For the LORD hears the needy,
and does not despise his own that
are in bonds.

[34] Let heaven and earth praise him,
the seas and everything that moves
therein.
[35] For God will save Zion
and rebuild the cities of Judah;
and his servants shall dwell[o] there
and possess it;
[36] the children of his servants shall
inherit it,
and those who love his name shall
dwell in it.

To the choirmaster. A Psalm of David,
for the memorial offering.

70 Be pleased, O God, to deliver
me!
O LORD, make haste to help me!
[2] Let them be put to shame and
confusion
who seek my life!
Let them be turned back and brought
to dishonor
who desire my hurt!
[3] Let them be appalled because of
their shame
who say, "Aha, Aha!"

[4] May all who seek thee
rejoice and be glad in thee!
May those who love thy salvation
say evermore, "God is great!"
[5] But I am poor and needy;
hasten to me, O God!

[l]Tg: Heb *for security*
[m]One Ms Tg Compare Syr: Heb *those*
[n]Gk Syr: Heb *recount the pain of*
[o]Syr: Heb *and they shall dwell*
69.21: Mt 27.34, 48; Mk 15.36; Lk 23.36; Jn 19.29.
69.22-23: Rom 11.9-10. 69.24: Rev 16.1.
69.25: Acts 1.20.
69.28: Rev 3.5; 13.8; 17.8; 20.12, 15; 21.27.
70.1-5: Ps 40.13-17.

Thou art my help and my deliverer;
O LORD, do not tarry!

71 In thee, O LORD, do I take refuge;
let me never be put to shame!
2 In thy righteousness deliver me and rescue me;
incline thy ear to me, and save me!
3 Be thou to me a rock of refuge,
a strong fortress,[p] to save me,
for thou art my rock and my fortress.

4 Rescue me, O my God, from the hand of the wicked,
from the grasp of the unjust and cruel man.
5 For thou, O Lord, art my hope,
my trust, O LORD, from my youth.
6 Upon thee I have leaned from my birth;
thou art he who took me from my mother's womb.
My praise is continually of thee.

7 I have been as a portent to many;
but thou art my strong refuge.
8 My mouth is filled with thy praise,
and with thy glory all the day.
9 Do not cast me off in the time of old age;
forsake me not when my strength is spent.
10 For my enemies speak concerning me,
those who watch for my life consult together,
11 and say, "God has forsaken him;
pursue and seize him,
for there is none to deliver him."

12 O God, be not far from me;
O my God, make haste to help me!
13 May my accusers be put to shame and consumed;
with scorn and disgrace may they be covered
who seek my hurt.
14 But I will hope continually,
and will praise thee yet more and more.
15 My mouth will tell of thy righteous acts,
of thy deeds of salvation all the day,
for their number is past my knowledge.

16 With the mighty deeds of the Lord GOD I will come,
I will praise thy righteousness, thine alone.
17 O God, from my youth thou hast taught me,
and I still proclaim thy wondrous deeds.
18 So even to old age and gray hairs, O God, do not forsake me,
till I proclaim thy might
to all the generations to come.[q]
Thy power 19 and thy righteousness, O God,
reach the high heavens.

Thou who hast done great things, O God, who is like thee?
20 Thou who hast made me see many sore troubles
wilt revive me again;
from the depths of the earth
thou wilt bring me up again.
21 Thou wilt increase my honor,
and comfort me again.

22 I will also praise thee with the harp
for thy faithfulness, O my God;
I will sing praises to thee with the lyre,
O Holy One of Israel.
23 My lips will shout for joy,
when I sing praises to thee;
my soul also, which thou hast rescued.
24 And my tongue will talk of thy righteous help
all the day long,
for they have been put to shame and disgraced
who sought to do me hurt.

A Psalm of Solomon.

72 Give the king thy justice, O God,
and thy righteousness to the royal son!
2 May he judge thy people with righteousness,
and thy poor with justice!
3 Let the mountains bear prosperity for the people,
and the hills, in righteousness!

[p] Gk Compare 31.3: Heb *to come continually thou hast commanded*
[q] Gk Compare Syr: Heb *to a generation, to all that come*

⁴May he defend the cause of the poor
of the people,
give deliverance to the needy,
and crush the oppressor!

⁵May he live*ʳ* while the sun endures,
and as long as the moon,
throughout all generations!
⁶May he be like rain that falls on the
mown grass,
like showers that water the earth!
⁷In his days may righteousness flourish,
and peace abound, till the moon
be no more!

⁸May he have dominion from sea to
sea,
and from the River to the ends of
the earth!
⁹May his foes*ˢ* bow down before him,
and his enemies lick the dust!
¹⁰May the kings of Tär'shĭsh and of the
isles
render him tribute,
may the kings of Shē'bạ and Sē'bạ
bring gifts!
¹¹May all kings fall down before him,
all nations serve him!

¹²For he delivers the needy when he
calls,
the poor and him who has no
helper.
¹³He has pity on the weak and the
needy,
and saves the lives of the needy.
¹⁴From oppression and violence he
redeems their life;
and precious is their blood in his
sight.

¹⁵Long may he live,
may gold of Shē'bạ be given to
him!
May prayer be made for him continually,
and blessings invoked for him all
the day!
¹⁶May there be abundance of grain in
the land;
on the tops of the mountains may
it wave;
may its fruit be like Lebanon;
and may men blossom forth from the
cities
like the grass of the field!
¹⁷May his name endure for ever,
his fame continue as long as the
sun!

May men bless themselves by him,
all nations call him blessed!

¹⁸Blessed be the LORD, the God of
Israel,
who alone does wondrous things.
¹⁹Blessed be his glorious name for
ever;
may his glory fill the whole earth!
Amen and Amen!

²⁰The prayers of David, the son of
Jesse, are ended.

BOOK III

A Psalm of Ä'sặph.

73 Truly God is good to the upright,
to those who are pure in heart.*ᵗ*
²But as for me, my feet had almost
stumbled,
my steps had well nigh slipped.
³For I was envious of the arrogant,
when I saw the prosperity of the
wicked.

⁴For they have no pangs;
their bodies are sound and sleek.
⁵They are not in trouble as other men
are;
they are not stricken like other
men.
⁶Therefore pride is their necklace;
violence covers them as a garment.
⁷Their eyes swell out with fatness,
their hearts overflow with follies.
⁸They scoff and speak with malice;
loftily they threaten oppression.
⁹They set their mouths against the
heavens,
and their tongue struts through
the earth.

¹⁰Therefore the people turn and praise
them;*ᵘ*
and find no fault in them.*ᵛ*
¹¹And they say, "How can God know?
Is there knowledge in the Most
High?"
¹²Behold, these are the wicked;
always at ease, they increase in
riches.

ʳGk: Heb may they fear thee
ˢCn: Heb those who dwell in the wilderness
*ᵗOr Truly God is good to Israel, to those who are pure in
heart ᵘCn: Heb his people return hither*
ᵛCn: Heb abundant waters are drained by them

¹³ All in vain have I kept my heart clean
and washed my hands in inno-
cence.
¹⁴ For all the day long I have been
stricken,
and chastened every morning.

¹⁵ If I had said, "I will speak thus,"
I would have been untrue to the
generation of thy children.
¹⁶ But when I thought how to understand this,
it seemed to me a wearisome task,
¹⁷ until I went into the sanctuary of
God;
then I perceived their end.
¹⁸ Truly thou dost set them in slippery
places;
thou dost make them fall to ruin.
¹⁹ How they are destroyed in a moment,
swept away utterly by terrors!
²⁰ They are ʷ like a dream when one
awakes,
on awaking you despise their phan-
toms.

²¹ When my soul was embittered,
when I was pricked in heart,
²² I was stupid and ignorant,
I was like a beast toward thee.
²³ Nevertheless I am continually with
thee;
thou dost hold my right hand.
²⁴ Thou dost guide me with thy counsel,
and afterward thou wilt receive
me to glory. ˣ
²⁵ Whom have I in heaven but thee?
And there is nothing upon earth
that I desire besides thee.
²⁶ My flesh and my heart may fail,
but God is the strength ʸ of my
heart and my portion for ever.

²⁷ For lo, those who are far from thee
shall perish;
thou dost put an end to those who
are false to thee.
²⁸ But for me it is good to be near God;
I have made the Lord GOD my
refuge,
that I may tell of all thy works.

A Măs′kĭl of Ā′săph.

74 O God, why dost thou cast us
off for ever?
Why does thy anger smoke against
the sheep of thy pasture?

² Remember thy congregation, which
thou hast gotten of old,
which thou hast redeemed to be
the tribe of thy heritage!
Remember Mount Zion, where
thou hast dwelt.
³ Direct thy steps to the perpetual
ruins;
the enemy has destroyed everything in the sanctuary!

⁴ Thy foes have roared in the midst of
thy holy place;
they set up their own signs for
signs.
⁵ At the upper entrance they hacked
the wooden trellis with axes. ᶻ
⁶ And then all its carved wood
they broke down with hatchets and
hammers.
⁷ They set thy sanctuary on fire;
to the ground they desecrated the
dwelling place of thy name.
⁸ They said to themselves, "We will
utterly subdue them";
they burned all the meeting places
of God in the land.

⁹ We do not see our signs;
there is no longer any prophet,
and there is none among us who
knows how long.
¹⁰ How long, O God, is the foe to scoff?
Is the enemy to revile thy name for
ever?
¹¹ Why dost thou hold back thy hand,
why dost thou keep thy right
hand in ᵃ thy bosom?

¹² Yet God my King is from of old,
working salvation in the midst of
the earth.
¹³ Thou didst divide the sea by thy
might;
thou didst break the heads of the
dragons on the waters.
¹⁴ Thou didst crush the heads of
Lĕ·vī′a·than,
thou didst give him as food ᵇ for
the creatures of the wilderness.
¹⁵ Thou didst cleave open springs and
brooks;
thou didst dry up ever-flowing
streams.
¹⁶ Thine is the day, thine also the
night;

ʷ Cn: Heb *Lord*   ˣ Or *honor*   ʸ Heb *rock*
ᶻ Cn Compare Gk Syr: Heb uncertain
ᵃ Cn: Heb *consume thy right hand from*
ᵇ Heb *food for the people*

thou hast established the luminaries and the sun.
¹⁷Thou hast fixed all the bounds of the earth;
thou hast made summer and winter.

¹⁸Remember this, O LORD, how the enemy scoffs,
and an impious people reviles thy name.
¹⁹Do not deliver the soul of thy dove to the wild beasts;
do not forget the life of thy poor for ever.

²⁰Have regard for thy*c* covenant;
for the dark places of the land are full of the habitations of violence.
²¹Let not the downtrodden be put to shame;
let the poor and needy praise thy name.

²²Arise, O God, plead thy cause;
remember how the impious scoff at thee all the day!
²³Do not forget the clamor of thy foes,
the uproar of thy adversaries which goes up continually!

To the choirmaster: according to Do Not Destroy. A Psalm of Ā′săph. A Song.

75   We give thanks to thee, O God;
we give thanks;
we call on thy name and recount*d* thy wondrous deeds.

²At the set time which I appoint I will judge with equity.
³When the earth totters, and all its inhabitants,
it is I who keep steady its pillars.   *Selah*
⁴I say to the boastful, "Do not boast,"
and to the wicked, "Do not lift up your horn;
⁵do not lift up your horn on high, or speak with insolent neck."

⁶For not from the east or from the west
and not from the wilderness comes lifting up;
⁷but it is God who executes judgment,
putting down one and lifting up another.

⁸For in the hand of the LORD there is a cup,
with foaming wine, well mixed;
and he will pour a draught from it,
and all the wicked of the earth shall drain it down to the dregs.

⁹But I will rejoice*e* for ever,
I will sing praises to the God of Jacob.
¹⁰All the horns of the wicked he*f* will cut off,
but the horns of the righteous shall be exalted.

To the choirmaster: with stringed instruments. A Psalm of Ā′săph. A Song.

76   In Judah God is known,
his name is great in Israel.
²His abode has been established in Salem,
his dwelling place in Zion.
³There he broke the flashing arrows,
the shield, the sword, and the weapons of war.   *Selah*

⁴Glorious art thou, more majestic than the everlasting mountains.*g*
⁵The stouthearted were stripped of their spoil;
they sank into sleep;
all the men of war were unable to use their hands.
⁶At thy rebuke, O God of Jacob,
both rider and horse lay stunned.

⁷But thou, terrible art thou!
Who can stand before thee when once thy anger is roused?
⁸From the heavens thou didst utter judgment;
the earth feared and was still,
⁹when God arose to establish judgment
to save all the oppressed of the earth.   *Selah*

¹⁰Surely the wrath of men shall praise thee;
the residue of wrath thou wilt gird upon thee.
¹¹Make your vows to the LORD your God, and perform them;

c Gk Syr: Heb *the*
d Syr Compare Gk: Heb *and near is thy name. They recount* *e* Gk: Heb *declare* *f* Heb *I*
g Gk: Heb *the mountains of prey*

let all around him bring gifts
to him who is to be feared,
¹²who cuts off the spirit of princes,
who is terrible to the kings of the
earth.

To the choirmaster: according to
Jĕ·dü'thụn. A Psalm of Ā'săph.

77 I cry aloud to God,
aloud to God, that he may hear
me.
²In the day of my trouble I seek the
Lord;
in the night my hand is stretched
out without wearying;
my soul refuses to be comforted.

³I think of God, and I moan;
I meditate, and my spirit faints.
                                    Selah
⁴Thou dost hold my eyelids from
closing;
I am so troubled that I cannot
speak.
⁵I consider the days of old,
I remember the years long ago.
⁶I commune ʰ with my heart in the
night;
I meditate and search my spirit: ⁱ
⁷"Will the Lord spurn for ever,
and never again be favorable?
⁸Has his steadfast love for ever
ceased?
Are his promises at an end for all
time?
⁹Has God forgotten to be gracious?
Has he in anger shut up his
compassion?"   Selah
¹⁰And I say, "It is my grief
that the right hand of the Most
High has changed."

¹¹I will call to mind the deeds of the
LORD;
yea, I will remember thy wonders
of old.
¹²I will meditate on all thy work,
and muse on thy mighty deeds.
¹³Thy way, O God, is holy.
What god is great like our God?
¹⁴Thou art the God who workest
wonders,
who hast manifested thy might
among the peoples.
¹⁵Thou didst with thy arm redeem thy
people,
the sons of Jacob and Joseph.
                                    Selah

¹⁶When the waters saw thee, O God,
when the waters saw thee, they
were afraid,
yea, the deep trembled.
¹⁷The clouds poured out water;
the skies gave forth thunder;
thy arrows flashed on every side.
¹⁸The crash of thy thunder was in the
whirlwind;
thy lightnings lighted up the world;
the earth trembled and shook.
¹⁹Thy way was through the sea,
thy path through the great waters;
yet thy footprints were unseen.
²⁰Thou didst lead thy people like a
flock
by the hand of Moses and Aaron.

A Măs'kĭl of Ā'săph.

78 Give ear, O people, to my
teaching;
incline your ears to the words of
my mouth!
²I will open my mouth in a parable;
I will utter dark sayings from of
old,
³things that we have heard and
known,
that our fathers have told us.
⁴We will not hide them from their
children,
but tell to the coming generation
the glorious deeds of the LORD, and
his might,
and the wonders which he has
wrought.

⁵He established a testimony in Jacob,
and appointed a law in Israel,
which he commanded our fathers
to teach to their children;
⁶that the next generation might know
them,
the children yet unborn,
and arise and tell them to their
children,
⁷ so that they should set their hope
in God,
and not forget the works of God,
but keep his commandments;
⁸and that they should not be like their
fathers,
a stubborn and rebellious generation,
a generation whose heart was not
steadfast,

ʰGk Syr: Heb *my music*
ⁱSyr Jerome: Heb *my spirit searches* **78.2:** Mt 13.35.

whose spirit was not faithful to
God.

⁹The Ē′phra·ĭm·ītes, armed with ʲ
the bow,
turned back on the day of battle.
¹⁰They did not keep God's covenant,
but refused to walk according to
his law.
¹¹They forgot what he had done,
and the miracles that he had
shown them.
¹²In the sight of their fathers he
wrought marvels
in the land of Egypt, in the fields
of Zō′an.
¹³He divided the sea and let them pass
through it,
and made the waters stand like a
heap.
¹⁴In the daytime he led them with a
cloud,
and all the night with a fiery light.
¹⁵He cleft rocks in the wilderness,
and gave them drink abundantly
as from the deep.
¹⁶He made streams come out of the
rock,
and caused waters to flow down
like rivers.

¹⁷Yet they sinned still more against
him,
rebelling against the Most High in
the desert.
¹⁸They tested God in their heart
by demanding the food they
craved.
¹⁹They spoke against God, saying,
"Can God spread a table in the
wilderness?
²⁰He smote the rock so that water
gushed out
and streams overflowed.
Can he also give bread,
or provide meat for his people?"

²¹Therefore, when the LORD heard,
he was full of wrath;
a fire was kindled against Jacob,
his anger mounted against Israel;
²²because they had no faith in God,
and did not trust his saving power.
²³Yet he commanded the skies above,
and opened the doors of heaven;
²⁴and he rained down upon them
manna to eat,
and gave them the grain of heaven.
²⁵Man ate of the bread of the angels;
he sent them food in abundance.

²⁶He caused the east wind to blow in
the heavens,
and by his power he led out the
south wind;
²⁷he rained flesh upon them like dust,
winged birds like the sand of the
seas;
²⁸he let them fall in the midst of their
camp,
all around their habitations.
²⁹And they ate and were well filled,
for he gave them what they craved.
³⁰But before they had sated their craving,
while the food was still in their
mouths,
³¹the anger of God rose against them
and he slew the strongest of them,
and laid low the picked men of
Israel.

³²In spite of all this they still sinned;
despite his wonders they did not
believe.
³³So he made their days vanish like a
breath,
and their years in terror.
³⁴When he slew them, they sought for
him;
they repented and sought God
earnestly.
³⁵They remembered that God was their
rock,
the Most High God their redeemer.
³⁶But they flattered him with their
mouths;
they lied to him with their tongues.
³⁷Their heart was not steadfast toward
him;
they were not true to his covenant.
³⁸Yet he, being compassionate,
forgave their iniquity,
and did not destroy them;
he restrained his anger often,
and did not stir up all his wrath.
³⁹He remembered that they were but
flesh,
a wind that passes and comes not
again.
⁴⁰How often they rebelled against him
in the wilderness
and grieved him in the desert!
⁴¹They tested him again and again,
and provoked the Holy One of
Israel.
⁴²They did not keep in mind his power,
or the day when he redeemed them
from the foe;

ʲHeb *armed with shooting*
78.24: Jn 6.31. **78.37:** Acts 8.21.

⁴³when he wrought his signs in Egypt,
and his miracles in the fields of
Zō'an.
⁴⁴He turned their rivers to blood,
so that they could not drink of
their streams.
⁴⁵He sent among them swarms of flies,
which devoured them,
and frogs, which destroyed them.
⁴⁶He gave their crops to the caterpillar,
and the fruit of their labor to the
locust.
⁴⁷He destroyed their vines with hail,
and their sycamores with frost.
⁴⁸He gave over their cattle to the hail,
and their flocks to thunderbolts.
⁴⁹He let loose on them his fierce anger,
wrath, indignation, and distress,
a company of destroying angels.
⁵⁰He made a path for his anger;
he did not spare them from death,
but gave their lives over to the
plague.
⁵¹He smote all the first-born in Egypt,
the first issue of their strength in
the tents of Ham.
⁵²Then he led forth his people like
sheep,
and guided them in the wilderness
like a flock.
⁵³He led them in safety, so that they
were not afraid;
but the sea overwhelmed their
enemies.
⁵⁴And he brought them to his holy land,
to the mountain which his right
hand had won.
⁵⁵He drove out nations before them;
he apportioned them for a possession
and settled the tribes of Israel in
their tents.

⁵⁶Yet they tested and rebelled against
the Most High God,
and did not observe his testimonies,
⁵⁷but turned away and acted treacherously like their fathers;
they twisted like a deceitful bow.
⁵⁸For they provoked him to anger with
their high places;
they moved him to jealousy with
their graven images.
⁵⁹When God heard, he was full of
wrath,
and he utterly rejected Israel.
⁶⁰He forsook his dwelling at Shī'lōh,
the tent where he dwelt among
men,

⁶¹and delivered his power to captivity,
his glory to the hand of the foe.
⁶²He gave his people over to the sword,
and vented his wrath on his heritage.
⁶³Fire devoured their young men,
and their maidens had no marriage song.
⁶⁴Their priests fell by the sword,
and their widows made no lamentation.
⁶⁵Then the Lord awoke as from sleep,
like a strong man shouting because of wine.
⁶⁶And he put his adversaries to rout;
he put them to everlasting shame.

⁶⁷He rejected the tent of Joseph,
he did not choose the tribe of
Ē'phra·ĭm;
⁶⁸but he chose the tribe of Judah,
Mount Zion, which he loves.
⁶⁹He built his sanctuary like the high
heavens,
like the earth, which he has
founded for ever.
⁷⁰He chose David his servant,
and took him from the sheepfolds;
⁷¹from tending the ewes that had
young he brought him
to be the shepherd of Jacob his
people,
of Israel his inheritance.
⁷²With upright heart he tended them,
and guided them with skilful hand.

A Psalm of Ā'săph.

79 O God, the heathen have come
into thy inheritance;
they have defiled thy holy temple;
they have laid Jerusalem in ruins.
²They have given the bodies of thy
servants
to the birds of the air for food,
the flesh of thy saints to the beasts
of the earth.
³They have poured out their blood like
water
round about Jerusalem,
and there was none to bury them.
⁴We have become a taunt to our neighbors,
mocked and derided by those round
about us.

⁵How long, O LORD? Wilt thou be
angry for ever?
Will thy jealous wrath burn like
fire?

⁶Pour out thy anger on the nations
  that do not know thee,
and on the kingdoms
  that do not call on thy name!
⁷For they have devoured Jacob,
  and laid waste his habitation.

⁸Do not remember against us the iniquities of our forefathers;
let thy compassion come speedily
  to meet us,
for we are brought very low.
⁹Help us, O God of our salvation,
  for the glory of thy name;
deliver us, and forgive our sins,
  for thy name's sake!
¹⁰Why should the nations say,
  "Where is their God?"
Let the avenging of the outpoured
  blood of thy servants
  be known among the nations before our eyes!

¹¹Let the groans of the prisoners come
  before thee;
according to thy great power preserve those doomed to die!
¹²Return sevenfold into the bosom of
  our neighbors
the taunts with which they have
  taunted thee, O Lord!
¹³Then we thy people, the flock of thy
  pasture,
will give thanks to thee for ever;
from generation to generation we
  will recount thy praise.

To the choirmaster: according to Lilies.
A Testimony of Ā'săph. A Psalm.

80 Give ear, O Shepherd of Israel,
  thou who leadest Joseph like a
  flock!
Thou who art enthroned upon the
  cherubim, shine forth
² before Ē'phra·im and Benjamin
  and Ma·năs'seh!
Stir up thy might,
  and come to save us!

³Restore us, O God;
  let thy face shine, that we may be
  saved!

⁴O LORD God of hosts,
  how long wilt thou be angry with
  thy people's prayers?
⁵Thou hast fed them with the bread
  of tears,

and given them tears to drink in
  full measure.
⁶Thou dost make us the scorn*k* of
  our neighbors;
and our enemies laugh among
  themselves.

⁷Restore us, O God of hosts;
  let thy face shine, that we may be
  saved!

⁸Thou didst bring a vine out of Egypt;
  thou didst drive out the nations
  and plant it.
⁹Thou didst clear the ground for it;
  it took deep root and filled the land.
¹⁰The mountains were covered with
  its shade,
the mighty cedars with its
  branches;
¹¹it sent out its branches to the sea,
  and its shoots to the River.
¹²Why then hast thou broken down its
  walls,
so that all who pass along the way
  pluck its fruit?
¹³The boar from the forest ravages it,
  and all that move in the field feed
  on it.

¹⁴Turn again, O God of hosts!
  Look down from heaven, and see;
  have regard for this vine,
¹⁵ the stock which thy right hand
  planted.*l*
¹⁶They have burned it with fire, they
  have cut it down;
may they perish at the rebuke of
  thy countenance!
¹⁷But let thy hand be upon the man of
  thy right hand,
the son of man whom thou hast
  made strong for thyself!
¹⁸Then we will never turn back from
  thee;
give us life, and we will call on
  thy name!

¹⁹Restore us, O LORD God of hosts!
  let thy face shine, that we may be
  saved!

To the choirmaster: according to
The Gĭt'tĭth. A Psalm of Ā'săph.

81 Sing aloud to God our strength;
  shout for joy to the God of Jacob!

k Syr: Heb *strife*
l Heb *planted and upon the son whom thou hast reared
for thyself*

² Raise a song, sound the timbrel,
the sweet lyre with the harp.
³ Blow the trumpet at the new moon,
at the full moon, on our feast day.
⁴ For it is a statute for Israel,
an ordinance of the God of Jacob.
⁵ He made it a decree in Joseph,
when he went out over*ᵐ* the land
of Egypt.

I hear a voice I had not known:
⁶ "I relieved your*ⁿ* shoulder of the
burden;
your*ⁿ* hands were freed from the
basket.
⁷ In distress you called, and I delivered
you;
I answered you in the secret
place of thunder;
I tested you at the waters of
Mĕr′ĭ·bah. *Selah*
⁸ Hear, O my people, while I admonish
you!
O Israel, if you would but listen to
me!
⁹ There shall be no strange god among
you;
you shall not bow down to a foreign
god.
¹⁰ I am the Lord your God,
who brought you up out of the land
of Egypt.
Open your mouth wide, and I will
fill it.

¹¹ "But my people did not listen to my
voice;
Israel would have none of me.
¹² So I gave them over to their stubborn
hearts,
to follow their own counsels.
¹³ O that my people would listen to me,
that Israel would walk in my ways!
¹⁴ I would soon subdue their enemies,
and turn my hand against their
foes.
¹⁵ Those who hate the Lord would
cringe toward him,
and their fate would last for ever.
¹⁶ I would feed you*ᵒ* with the finest of
the wheat,
and with honey from the rock I
would satisfy you."

A Psalm of Ā′săph.

82 God has taken his place in the
divine council;
in the midst of the gods he holds
judgment:

² "How long will you judge unjustly
and show partiality to the wicked?
Selah
³ Give justice to the weak and the
fatherless;
maintain the right of the afflicted
and the destitute.
⁴ Rescue the weak and the needy;
deliver them from the hand of the
wicked."

⁵ They have neither knowledge nor
understanding,
they walk about in darkness;
all the foundations of the earth are
shaken.

⁶ I say, "You are gods,
sons of the Most High, all of you;
⁷ nevertheless, you shall die like men,
and fall like any prince."*ᵖ*

⁸ Arise, O God, judge the earth;
for to thee belong all the nations!

A Song. A Psalm of Ā′săph.

83 O God, do not keep silence;
do not hold thy peace or be still,
O God!
² For lo, thy enemies are in tumult;
those who hate thee have raised
their heads.
³ They lay crafty plans against thy
people;
they consult together against thy
protected ones.
⁴ They say, "Come, let us wipe them
out as a nation;
let the name of Israel be remembered no more!"
⁵ Yea, they conspire with one accord;
against thee they make a covenant—
⁶ the tents of Ē′dom and the Ish′-
ma·ĕl·ītes,
Mō′ăb and the Hăg′rītes,
⁷ Gē′bal and Ăm′mon and Ăm′a·lĕk,
Phĭ·lĭs′tĭ·a with the inhabitants of
Tyre;
⁸ Assyria also has joined them;
they are the strong arm of the
children of Lot. *Selah*

⁹ Do to them as thou didst to Mĭd′-
ĭ·an,

ᵐ Or against *ⁿ Heb his*
ᵒ Cn Compare verse 16b: Heb he would feed him
ᵖ Or fall as one man, O princes **82.6:** Jn 10.34.

as to Sĭs′ẹ·rạ and Jā′bĭn at the
river Kī′shŏn,
10 who were destroyed at Ĕn–dôr,
who became dung for the ground.
11 Make their nobles like Ôr′ĕb and
Zē′ĕb,
all their princes like Zē′bạh and
Zăl·mŭn′nạ,
12 who said, "Let us take possession for
ourselves
of the pastures of God."

13 O my God, make them like whirling
dust,[q]
like chaff before the wind.
14 As fire consumes the forest,
as the flame sets the mountains
ablaze,
15 so do thou pursue them with thy
tempest
and terrify them with thy hur-
ricane!
16 Fill their faces with shame,
that they may seek thy name,
O LORD.
17 Let them be put to shame and dismayed for ever;
let them perish in disgrace.
18 Let them know that thou alone,
whose name is the LORD,
art the Most High over all the earth.

To the choirmaster: according to The Gĭt′tĭth. A Psalm of the Sons of Kō′rạh.

84 How lovely is thy dwelling place,
O LORD of hosts!
2 My soul longs, yea, faints
for the courts of the LORD;
my heart and flesh sing for joy
to the living God.

3 Even the sparrow finds a home,
and the swallow a nest for herself,
where she may lay her young,
at thy altars, O LORD of hosts,
my King and my God.
4 Blessed are those who dwell in thy
house,
ever singing thy praise! *Selah*

5 Blessed are the men whose strength
is in thee,
in whose heart are the highways
to Zion.[r]
6 As they go through the valley of Bā′cạ
they make it a place of springs;
the early rain also covers it with
pools.
7 They go from strength to strength;
the God of gods will be seen in
Zion.

8 O LORD God of hosts, hear my prayer;
give ear, O God of Jacob! *Selah*
9 Behold our shield, O God;
look upon the face of thine
anointed!

10 For a day in thy courts is better
than a thousand elsewhere.
I would rather be a doorkeeper in the
house of my God
than dwell in the tents of wickedness.
11 For the LORD God is a sun and shield;
he bestows favor and honor.
No good thing does the LORD withhold
from those who walk uprightly.
12 O LORD of hosts,
blessed is the man who trusts in
thee!

To the choirmaster. A Psalm of the Sons of Kō′rạh.

85 LORD, thou wast favorable to
thy land;
thou didst restore the fortunes of
Jacob.
2 Thou didst forgive the iniquity of thy
people;
thou didst pardon all their sin.
Selah
3 Thou didst withdraw all thy wrath;
thou didst turn from thy hot anger.

4 Restore us again, O God of our salvation,
and put away thy indignation toward us!
5 Wilt thou be angry with us for ever?
Wilt thou prolong thy anger to all
generations?
6 Wilt thou not revive us again,
that thy people may rejoice in
thee?
7 Show us thy steadfast love, O LORD,
and grant us thy salvation.

8 Let me hear what God the LORD will
speak,
for he will speak peace to his
people,
to his saints, to those who turn to
him in their hearts.[s]

[q] Or *a tumbleweed* [r] Heb lacks *to Zion*
[s] Gk: Heb *but let them not turn back to folly*

9 Surely his salvation is at hand for
those who fear him,
that glory may dwell in our land.
10 Steadfast love and faithfulness will
meet;
righteousness and peace will kiss
each other.
11 Faithfulness will spring up from the
ground,
and righteousness will look down
from the sky.
12 Yea, the LORD will give what is good,
and our land will yield its increase.
13 Righteousness will go before him,
and make his footsteps a way.

A Prayer of David.

86 Incline thy ear, O LORD, and
answer me,
for I am poor and needy.
2 Preserve my life, for I am godly;
save thy servant who trusts in thee.
Thou art my God; 3 be gracious to me,
O Lord,
for to thee do I cry all the day.
4 Gladden the soul of thy servant,
for to thee, O Lord, do I lift up my
soul.
5 For thou, O Lord, art good and forgiving,
abounding in steadfast love to all
who call on thee.
6 Give ear, O LORD, to my prayer;
hearken to my cry of supplication.
7 In the day of my trouble I call on thee,
for thou dost answer me.

8 There is none like thee among the
gods, O Lord,
nor are there any works like thine.
9 All the nations thou hast made shall
come
and bow down before thee, O Lord,
and shall glorify thy name.
10 For thou art great and doest wondrous things,
thou alone art God.
11 Teach me thy way, O LORD,
that I may walk in thy truth;
unite my heart to fear thy name.
12 I give thanks to thee, O Lord my God,
with my whole heart,
and I will glorify thy name for
ever.
13 For great is thy steadfast love toward
me;
thou hast delivered my soul from
the depths of Shē′ōl.

14 O God, insolent men have risen up
against me;
a band of ruthless men seek my
life,
and they do not set thee before
them.
15 But thou, O Lord, art a God merciful
and gracious,
slow to anger and abounding in
steadfast love and faithfulness.
16 Turn to me and take pity on me;
give thy strength to thy servant,
and save the son of thy handmaid.
17 Show me a sign of thy favor,
that those who hate me may see
and be put to shame
because thou, LORD, hast helped
me and comforted me.

A Psalm of the Sons of Kō′raḥ.
A Song.

87 On the holy mount stands the
city he founded;
2 the LORD loves the gates of Zion
more than all the dwelling places
of Jacob.
3 Glorious things are spoken of you,
O city of God. *Selah*

4 Among those who know me I mention Rā′hăb and Babylon;
behold, Phĭ-lĭs′tĭ-ạ and Tȳre, with
Ethiopia—
"This one was born there," they
say.
5 And of Zion it shall be said,
"This one and that one were born
in her";
for the Most High himself will
establish her.
6 The LORD records as he registers
the peoples,
"This one was born there." *Selah*
7 Singers and dancers alike say,
"All my springs are in you."

A Song. A Psalm of the Sons of Kō′raḥ.
To the choirmaster: according to
Mā′hä-lath Lē′ăn-nŏth. A Măs′kĭl of
Hē′man the Ĕz′ra-hīte.

88 O LORD, my God, I call for help[f]
by day;
I cry out in the night before thee.
2 Let my prayer come before thee,
incline thy ear to my cry!

[f] Cn: Heb *O* LORD, *God of my salvation*

³For my soul is full of troubles,
   and my life draws near to She′ōl.
⁴I am reckoned among those who go
   down to the Pit;
   I am a man who has no strength,
⁵like one forsaken among the dead,
   like the slain that lie in the grave,
   like those whom thou dost remember
     no more,
   for they are cut off from thy hand.
⁶Thou hast put me in the depths of
   the Pit,
   in the regions dark and deep.
⁷Thy wrath lies heavy upon me,
   and thou dost overwhelm me with
     all thy waves.   *Selah*
⁸Thou hast caused my companions to
   shun me;
   thou hast made me a thing of
     horror to them.
   I am shut in so that I cannot escape;
⁹   my eye grows dim through sorrow.
   Every day I call upon thee, O LORD;
   I spread out my hands to thee.
¹⁰Dost thou work wonders for the
   dead?
   Do the shades rise up to praise
     thee?   *Selah*
¹¹Is thy steadfast love declared in the
   grave,
   or thy faithfulness in A·băd′don?
¹²Are thy wonders known in the darkness,
   or thy saving help in the land of
     forgetfulness?

¹³But I, O LORD, cry to thee;
   in the morning my prayer comes
     before thee.
¹⁴O LORD, why dost thou cast me off?
   Why dost thou hide thy face from
     me?
¹⁵Afflicted and close to death from my
   youth up,
   I suffer thy terrors; I am helpless.ᵘ
¹⁶Thy wrath has swept over me;
   thy dread assaults destroy me.
¹⁷They surround me like a flood all day
   long;
   they close in upon me together.
¹⁸Thou hast caused lover and friend to
   shun me;
   my companions are in darkness.

A Măs′kĭl of Ē′thạn the Ĕz′rạ·hīte.

89   I will sing of thy steadfast love,
     O LORD,ᵛ for ever;
   with my mouth I will proclaim thy
     faithfulness to all generations.

²For thy steadfast love was established for ever,
   thy faithfulness is firm as the
     heavens.
³Thou hast said, "I have made a covenant with my chosen one,
   I have sworn to David my servant:
⁴'I will establish your descendants for
   ever,
   and build your throne for all gen-
     erations.'"   *Selah*

⁵Let the heavens praise thy wonders,
   O LORD,
   thy faithfulness in the assembly of
     the holy ones!
⁶For who in the skies can be compared
   to the LORD?
   Who among the heavenly beingsʷ
     is like the LORD,
⁷a God feared in the council of the
   holy ones,
   great and terribleˣ above all that
     are round about him?
⁸O LORD God of hosts,
   who is mighty as thou art, O LORD,
   with thy faithfulness round about
     thee?
⁹Thou dost rule the raging of the sea;
   when its waves rise, thou stillest
     them.
¹⁰Thou didst crush Rā′hăb like a carcass,
   thou didst scatter thy enemies with
     thy mighty arm.
¹¹The heavens are thine, the earth also
   is thine;
   the world and all that is in it,
     thou hast founded them.
¹²The north and the south, thou hast
   created them;
   Tā′bôr and Hermon joyously praise
     thy name.
¹³Thou hast a mighty arm;
   strong is thy hand, high thy right
     hand.
¹⁴Righteousness and justice are the
   foundation of thy throne;
   steadfast love and faithfulness go
     before thee.
¹⁵Blessed are the people who know the
   festal shout,
   who walk, O LORD, in the light of
     thy countenance,
¹⁶who exult in thy name all the day,
   and extolʸ thy righteousness.

ᵘThe meaning of the Hebrew word is uncertain
ʷGk: Heb *the steadfast love of the* LORD   ˣOr *sons of gods*
ˣGk Syr: Heb *greatly terrible*   ʸCn: Heb *are exalted in*
89.3-4: Ps 132.11; Acts 2.30.

¹⁷For thou art the glory of their
strength;
by thy favor our horn is exalted.
¹⁸For our shield belongs to the LORD,
our king to the Holy One of Israel.

¹⁹Of old thou didst speak in a vision
to thy faithful one, and say:
"I have set the crown² upon one who
is mighty,
I have exalted one chosen from
the people.
²⁰I have found David, my servant;
with my holy oil I have anointed
him;
²¹so that my hand shall ever abide with
him,
my arm also shall strengthen him.
²²The enemy shall not outwit him,
the wicked shall not humble him.
²³I will crush his foes before him
and strike down those who hate
him.
²⁴My faithfulness and my steadfast
love shall be with him,
and in my name shall his horn be
exalted.
²⁵I will set his hand on the sea
and his right hand on the rivers.
²⁶He shall cry to me, 'Thou art my
Father,
my God, and the Rock of my
salvation.'
²⁷And I will make him the first-born,
the highest of the kings of the
earth.
²⁸My steadfast love I will keep for him
for ever,
and my covenant will stand firm
for him.
²⁹I will establish his line for ever
and his throne as the days of the
heavens.
³⁰If his children forsake my law
and do not walk according to my
ordinances,
³¹if they violate my statutes
and do not keep my commandments,
³²then I will punish their transgression
with the rod
and their iniquity with scourges;
³³but I will not remove from him my
steadfast love,
or be false to my faithfulness.
³⁴I will not violate my covenant,
or alter the word that went forth
from my lips.
³⁵Once for all I have sworn by my
holiness;

I will not lie to David.
³⁶His line shall endure for ever,
his throne as long as the sun before
me.
³⁷Like the moon it shall be established
for ever;
it shall stand firm while the skies
endure."ᵃ   *Selah*

³⁸But now thou hast cast off and
rejected,
thou art full of wrath against thy
anointed.
³⁹Thou hast renounced the covenant
with thy servant;
thou hast defiled his crown in the
dust.
⁴⁰Thou hast breached all his walls;
thou hast laid his strongholds in
ruins.
⁴¹All that pass by despoil him;
he has become the scorn of his
neighbors.
⁴²Thou hast exalted the right hand
of his foes;
thou hast made all his enemies
rejoice.
⁴³Yea, thou hast turned back the edge
of his sword,
and thou hast not made him stand
in battle.
⁴⁴Thou hast removed the scepter from
his hand,ᵇ
and cast his throne to the ground.
⁴⁵Thou hast cut short the days of his
youth;
thou hast covered him with shame.
Selah

⁴⁶How long, O LORD? Wilt thou hide
thyself for ever?
How long will thy wrath burn like
fire?
⁴⁷Remember, O Lord,ᶜ what the
measure of life is,
for what vanity thou hast created
all the sons of men!
⁴⁸What man can live and never see
death?
Who can deliver his soul from the
power of Shēʹōl?   *Selah*

⁴⁹Lord, where is thy steadfast love of
old,
which by thy faithfulness thou
didst swear to David?

ᶻCn: Heb *help*
ᵃCn: Heb *the witness in the skies is sure*
ᵇCn: Heb *removed his cleanness*   ᶜCn: Heb *I*
89.20: Acts 13.22.   **89.27:** Rev 1.5.
89.37: Rev 1.5; 3.14.

⁵⁰Remember, O Lord, how thy servant
is scorned;
how I bear in my bosom the
insults*ᵈ* of the peoples,
⁵¹with which thy enemies taunt, O
LORD,
with which they mock the footsteps of thy anointed.

⁵²   Blessed be the LORD for ever!
Amen and Amen.

BOOK IV

A Prayer of Moses, the man of God.

90 Lord, thou hast been our
dwelling place*ᵉ*
in all generations.
²Before the mountains were brought
forth,
or ever thou hadst formed the earth
and the world,
from everlasting to everlasting
thou art God.

³Thou turnest man back to the dust,
and sayest, "Turn back, O children
of men!"
⁴For a thousand years in thy sight
are but as yesterday when it is
past,
or as a watch in the night.

⁵Thou dost sweep men away; they are
like a dream,
like grass which is renewed in
the morning:
⁶in the morning it flourishes and is
renewed;
in the evening it fades and withers.

⁷For we are consumed by thy anger;
by thy wrath we are overwhelmed.
⁸Thou hast set our iniquities before
thee,
our secret sins in the light of thy
countenance.

⁹For all our days pass away under thy
wrath,
our years come to an end*ᶠ* like a
sigh.
¹⁰The years of our life are threescore
and ten,
or even by reason of strength four-
score;
yet their span*ᵍ* is but toil and trouble;

they are soon gone, and we fly
away.

¹¹Who considers the power of thy anger,
and thy wrath according to the
fear of thee?
¹²So teach us to number our days
that we may get a heart of wisdom.

¹³Return, O LORD! How long?
Have pity on thy servants!
¹⁴Satisfy us in the morning with thy
steadfast love,
that we may rejoice and be glad
all our days.
¹⁵Make us glad as many days as thou
hast afflicted us,
and as many years as we have
seen evil.
¹⁶Let thy work be manifest to thy
servants,
and thy glorious power to their
children.
¹⁷Let the favor of the Lord our God be
upon us,
and establish thou the work of
our hands upon us,
yea, the work of our hands establish thou it.

91 He who dwells in the shelter of
the Most High,
who abides in the shadow of the
Almighty,
²will say to the LORD, "My refuge and
my fortress;
my God, in whom I trust."
³For he will deliver you from the snare
of the fowler
and from the deadly pestilence;
⁴he will cover you with his pinions,
and under his wings you will find
refuge;
his faithfulness is a shield and
buckler.
⁵You will not fear the terror of the
night,
nor the arrow that flies by day,
⁶nor the pestilence that stalks in
darkness,
nor the destruction that wastes
at noonday.

⁷A thousand may fall at your side,
ten thousand at your right hand;
but it will not come near you.

*ᵈ*Cn: Heb *all of many*   *ᵉ*Another reading is *refuge*
*ᶠ*Syr: Heb *we bring our years to an end*
*ᵍ*Cn Compare Gk Syr Jerome Tg: Heb *pride*
90.4: 2 Pet 3.8.

8 You will only look with your eyes
and see the recompense of the
wicked.

9 Because you have made the LORD
your refuge,[h]
the Most High your habitation,
10 no evil shall befall you,
no scourge come near your tent.

11 For he will give his angels charge
of you
to guard you in all your ways.
12 On their hands they will bear you up,
lest you dash your foot against a
stone.
13 You will tread on the lion and the
adder,
the young lion and the serpent
you will trample under foot.

14 Because he cleaves to me in love,
I will deliver him;
I will protect him, because he
knows my name.
15 When he calls to me, I will answer
him;
I will be with him in trouble,
I will rescue him and honor him.
16 With long life I will satisfy him,
and show him my salvation.

A Psalm. A Song for the Sabbath.

92 It is good to give thanks to the
LORD,
to sing praises to thy name, O
Most High;
2 to declare thy steadfast love in the
morning,
and thy faithfulness by night,
3 to the music of the lute and the harp,
to the melody of the lyre.
4 For thou, O LORD, hast made me
glad by thy work;
at the works of thy hands I sing
for joy.

5 How great are thy works, O Lord!
Thy thoughts are very deep!
6 The dull man cannot know,
the stupid cannot understand this:
7 that, though the wicked sprout like
grass
and all evildoers flourish,
they are doomed to destruction for
ever,
8 but thou, O LORD, art on high for
ever.

9 For, lo, thy enemies, O LORD,
for, lo, thy enemies shall perish;
all evildoers shall be scattered.
10 But thou hast exalted my horn like
that of the wild ox;
thou hast poured over me[i] fresh
oil.
11 My eyes have seen the downfall of
my enemies,
my ears have heard the doom of
my evil assailants.

12 The righteous flourish like the palm
tree,
and grow like a cedar in Lebanon.
13 They are planted in the house of the
LORD,
they flourish in the courts of our
God.
14 They still bring forth fruit in old age,
they are ever full of sap and green,
15 to show that the LORD is upright;
he is my rock, and there is no unrighteousness in him.

93 The LORD reigns; he is robed
in majesty;
the LORD is robed, he is girded with
strength.
Yea, the world is established; it shall
never be moved;
2 thy throne is established from of
old;
thou art from everlasting.

3 The floods have lifted up, O LORD,
the floods have lifted up their
voice,
the floods lift up their roaring.
4 Mightier than the thunders of many
waters,
mightier than the waves[j] of the
sea,
the LORD on high is mighty!

5 Thy decrees are very sure;
holiness befits thy house,
O LORD, for evermore.

94 O LORD, thou God of vengeance,
thou God of vengeance, shine
forth!

[h] Cn: Heb *Because thou, LORD, art my refuge; you have
made*   [i] Syr: Heb uncertain
[j] Cn: Heb *mighty the waves*
91.11–12: Mt 4.6; Lk 4.10–11.   **91.13:** Lk 10.19.

²Rise up, O judge of the earth;
render to the proud their deserts!
³O LORD, how long shall the wicked,
how long shall the wicked exult?

⁴They pour out their arrogant words,
they boast, all the evildoers.
⁵They crush thy people, O LORD,
and afflict thy heritage.
⁶They slay the widow and the so-
journer,
and murder the fatherless;
⁷and they say, "The LORD does not
see;
the God of Jacob does not perceive."

⁸Understand, O dullest of the people!
Fools, when will you be wise?
⁹He who planted the ear, does he not
hear?
He who formed the eye, does he not
see?
¹⁰He who chastens the nations, does he
not chastise?
He who teaches men knowledge,
¹¹ the LORD, knows the thoughts of
man,
that they are but a breath.

¹²Blessed is the man whom thou dost
chasten, O LORD,
and whom thou dost teach out of
thy law
¹³to give him respite from days of
trouble,
until a pit is dug for the wicked.
¹⁴For the LORD will not forsake his
people;
he will not abandon his heritage;
¹⁵for justice will return to the right-
eous,
and all the upright in heart will
follow it.

¹⁶Who rises up for me against the
wicked?
Who stands up for me against evildoers?
¹⁷If the LORD had not been my help,
my soul would soon have dwelt
in the land of silence.
¹⁸When I thought, "My foot slips,"
thy steadfast love, O LORD, held
me up.
¹⁹When the cares of my heart are
many,
thy consolations cheer my soul.
²⁰Can wicked rulers be allied with thee,
who frame mischief by statute?

²¹They band together against the life
of the righteous,
and condemn the innocent to
death.
²²But the LORD has become my strong-
hold,
and my God the rock of my refuge.
²³He will bring back on them their
iniquity
and wipe them out for their wickedness;
the LORD our God will wipe them
out.

95

O come, let us sing to the
LORD;
let us make a joyful noise to the
rock of our salvation!
²Let us come into his presence with
thanksgiving;
let us make a joyful noise to him
with songs of praise!
³For the LORD is a great God,
and a great King above all gods.
⁴In his hand are the depths of the
earth;
the heights of the mountains are
his also.
⁵The sea is his, for he made it;
for his hands formed the dry land.

⁶O come, let us worship and bow
down,
let us kneel before the LORD, our
Maker!
⁷For he is our God,
and we are the people of his pasture,
and the sheep of his hand.

O that today you would hearken to
his voice!
⁸ Harden not your hearts, as at
Mĕr'ĭ·bah,
as on the day at Măs'sah in the
wilderness,
⁹when your fathers tested me,
and put me to the proof, though
they had seen my work.
¹⁰For forty years I loathed that genera-
tion
and said, "They are a people who
err in heart,
and they do not regard my ways."
¹¹Therefore I swore in my anger
that they should not enter my rest.

94.11: 1 Cor 3.20.
95.7-11: Heb 3.7-11; 4.3-11.

96 O sing to the Lord a new song;
sing to the Lord, all the earth!
2 Sing to the Lord, bless his name;
tell of his salvation from day to
day.
3 Declare his glory among the nations,
his marvelous works among all the
peoples!
4 For great is the Lord, and greatly to
be praised;
he is to be feared above all gods.
5 For all the gods of the peoples are
idols;
but the Lord made the heavens.
6 Honor and majesty are before him;
strength and beauty are in his
sanctuary.

7 Ascribe to the Lord, O families of
the peoples,
ascribe to the Lord glory and
strength!
8 Ascribe to the Lord the glory due his
name;
bring an offering, and come into
his courts!
9 Worship the Lord in holy array;
tremble before him, all the earth!

10 Say among the nations, "The Lord
reigns!
Yea, the world is established,
it shall never be moved;
he will judge the peoples with
equity."
11 Let the heavens be glad, and let the
earth rejoice;
let the sea roar, and all that fills it;
12 let the field exult, and everything
in it!
Then shall all the trees of the wood
sing for joy
13 before the Lord, for he comes,
for he comes to judge the earth.
He will judge the world with righteousness,
and the peoples with his truth.

97 The Lord reigns; let the earth
rejoice;
let the many coastlands be glad!
2 Clouds and thick darkness are round
about him;
righteousness and justice are the
foundation of his throne.
3 Fire goes before him,
and burns up his adversaries
round about.

4 His lightnings lighten the world;
the earth sees and trembles.
5 The mountains melt like wax before
the Lord,
before the Lord of all the earth.

6 The heavens proclaim his righteousness;
and all the peoples behold his
glory.
7 All worshipers of images are put to
shame,
who make their boast in worthless
idols;
all gods bow down before him.
8 Zion hears and is glad,
and the daughters of Judah rejoice,
because of thy judgments, O God.
9 For thou, O Lord, art most high over
all the earth;
thou art exalted far above all gods.

10 The Lord loves those who hate evil;[k]
he preserves the lives of his saints;
he delivers them from the hand of
the wicked.
11 Light dawns[l] for the righteous,
and joy for the upright in heart.
12 Rejoice in the Lord, O you righteous,
and give thanks to his holy name!

A Psalm.

98 O sing to the Lord a new song,
for he has done marvelous
things!
His right hand and his holy arm
have gotten him victory.
2 The Lord has made known his victory,
he has revealed his vindication in
the sight of the nations.
3 He has remembered his steadfast
love and faithfulness
to the house of Israel.
All the ends of the earth have seen
the victory of our God.

4 Make a joyful noise to the Lord,
all the earth;
break forth into joyous song and
sing praises!
5 Sing praises to the Lord with the
lyre,
with the lyre and the sound of
melody!

[k]Cn: Heb You *who love the* Lord *hate evil*
[l]Gk Syr Jerome: Heb *is sown*
96.1-13: 1 Chron 16.23-33.   **97.7:** Heb 1.6.

⁶With trumpets and the sound of the
horn
  make a joyful noise before the
   King, the LORD!

⁷Let the sea roar, and all that fills it;
  the world and those who dwell in
   it!
⁸Let the floods clap their hands;
  let the hills sing for joy together
⁹before the LORD, for he comes
  to judge the earth.
  He will judge the world with righteousness,
  and the peoples with equity.

99 The LORD reigns; let the peoples tremble!
  He sits enthroned upon the cherubim; let the earth quake!
²The LORD is great in Zion;
  he is exalted over all the peoples.
³Let them praise thy great and terrible name!
  Holy is he!
⁴Mighty King,ᵐ lover of justice,
  thou hast established equity;
  thou hast executed justice
  and righteousness in Jacob.
⁵Extol the LORD our God;
  worship at his footstool!
  Holy is he!

⁶Moses and Aaron were among his
priests,
  Samuel also was among those who
   called on his name.
  They cried to the LORD, and he
   answered them.
⁷He spoke to them in the pillar of
   cloud;
  they kept his testimonies,
  and the statutes that he gave
   them.

⁸O LORD our God, thou didst answer
them;
  thou wast a forgiving God to them,
  but an avenger of their wrong-
   doings.
⁹Extol the LORD our God,
  and worship at his holy mountain;
  for the LORD our God is holy!

A Psalm for the thank offering.

100 Make a joyful noise to the
LORD, all the lands!ⁿ
² Serve the LORD with gladness!

Come into his presence with singing!

³Know that the LORD is God!
  It is he that made us, and we are
   his;ᵒ
  we are his people, and the sheep
   of his pasture.

⁴Enter his gates with thanksgiving,
  and his courts with praise!
  Give thanks to him, bless his
   name!

⁵For the LORD is good;
  his steadfast love endures for ever,
  and his faithfulness to all generations.

A Psalm of David.

101 I will sing of loyalty and of
justice;
  to thee, O LORD, I will sing.
²I will give heed to the way that is
   blameless.
  Oh when wilt thou come to me?

  I will walk with integrity of heart
   within my house;
³I will not set before my eyes
  anything that is base.

  I hate the work of those who fall
   away;
  it shall not cleave to me.
⁴Perverseness of heart shall be far
   from me;
  I will know nothing of evil.

⁵Him who slanders his neighbor
   secretly
  I will destroy.
  The man of haughty looks and ar-
   rogant heart
  I will not endure.

⁶I will look with favor on the faithful
   in the land,
  that they may dwell with me;
  he who walks in the way that is
   blameless
  shall minister to me.

⁷No man who practices deceit
  shall dwell in my house;
  no man who utters lies
  shall continue in my presence.

ᵐCn: Heb *and the king's strength* ⁿHeb *land* or *earth*
ᵒAnother reading is *and not we ourselves*

⁸ Morning by morning I will destroy
all the wicked in the land,
cutting off all the evildoers
from the city of the LORD.

A prayer of one afflicted, when he is
faint and pours out his complaint
before the LORD.

102 Hear my prayer, O LORD;
let my cry come to thee!
² Do not hide thy face from me
in the day of my distress!
Incline thy ear to me;
answer me speedily in the day
when I call!

³ For my days pass away like smoke,
and my bones burn like a furnace.
⁴ My heart is smitten like grass, and
withered;
I forget to eat my bread.
⁵ Because of my loud groaning
my bones cleave to my flesh.
⁶ I am like a vulture^p of the wilderness,
like an owl of the waste places;
⁷ I lie awake,
I am like a lonely bird on the housetop.
⁸ All the day my enemies taunt me,
those who deride me use my name
for a curse.
⁹ For I eat ashes like bread,
and mingle tears with my drink,
¹⁰ because of thy indignation and anger;
for thou hast taken me up and
thrown me away.
¹¹ My days are like an evening shadow;
I wither away like grass.

¹² But thou, O LORD, art enthroned for
ever;
thy name endures to all generations.
¹³ Thou wilt arise and have pity on
Zion;
it is the time to favor her;
the appointed time has come.
¹⁴ For thy servants hold her stones dear,
and have pity on her dust.
¹⁵ The nations will fear the name of the
LORD,
and all the kings of the earth thy
glory.
¹⁶ For the LORD will build up Zion,
he will appear in his glory;
¹⁷ he will regard the prayer of the destitute,

and will not despise their supplication.

¹⁸ Let this be recorded for a generation
to come,
so that a people yet unborn may
praise the LORD:
¹⁹ that he looked down from his holy
height,
from heaven the LORD looked at
the earth,
²⁰ to hear the groans of the prisoners,
to set free those who were doomed
to die;
²¹ that men may declare in Zion the
name of the LORD,
and in Jerusalem his praise,
²² when peoples gather together,
and kingdoms, to worship the
LORD.

²³ He has broken my strength in mid-
course;
he has shortened my days.
²⁴ "O my God," I say, "take me not
hence
in the midst of my days,
thou whose years endure
throughout all generations!"

²⁵ Of old thou didst lay the foundation
of the earth,
and the heavens are the work of
thy hands.
²⁶ They will perish, but thou dost endure;
they will all wear out like a garment.
Thou changest them like raiment,
and they pass away;
²⁷ but thou art the same, and thy
years have no end.
²⁸ The children of thy servants shall
dwell secure;
their posterity shall be established
before thee.

A Psalm of David.

103 Bless the LORD, O my soul;
and all that is within me,
bless his holy name!
² Bless the LORD, O my soul,
and forget not all his benefits,
³ who forgives all your iniquity,
who heals all your diseases,
⁴ who redeems your life from the Pit,

^p The meaning of the Hebrew word is uncertain
102.25-27: Heb 1.10-12.

who crowns you with steadfast
love and mercy,
[5] who satisfies you with good as long
as you live[q]
so that your youth is renewed like
the eagle's.

[6] The LORD works vindication
and justice for all who are oppressed.
[7] He made known his ways to Moses,
his acts to the people of Israel.
[8] The LORD is merciful and gracious,
slow to anger and abounding in
steadfast love.
[9] He will not always chide,
nor will he keep his anger for ever.
[10] He does not deal with us according
to our sins,
nor requite us according to our
iniquities.
[11] For as the heavens are high above
the earth,
so great is his steadfast love toward
those who fear him;
[12] as far as the east is from the west,
so far does he remove our transgressions from us.
[13] As a father pities his children,
so the LORD pities those who fear
him.
[14] For he knows our frame;
he remembers that we are dust.

[15] As for man, his days are like grass;
he flourishes like a flower of the
field;
[16] for the wind passes over it, and it is
gone,
and its place knows it no more.
[17] But the steadfast love of the LORD is
from everlasting to everlasting
upon those who fear him,
and his righteousness to children's
children,
[18] to those who keep his covenant
and remember to do his commandments.

[19] The LORD has established his throne
in the heavens,
and his kingdom rules over all.
[20] Bless the LORD, O you his angels,
you mighty ones who do his word,
hearkening to the voice of his
word!
[21] Bless the LORD, all his hosts,
his ministers that do his will!
[22] Bless the LORD, all his works,
in all places of his dominion.
Bless the LORD, O my soul!

104

Bless the LORD, O my soul!
O LORD my God, thou art very
great!
Thou art clothed with honor and
majesty,
[2] who coverest thyself with light as
with a garment,
who hast stretched out the heavens
like a tent,
[3] who hast laid the beams of thy
chambers on the waters,
who makest the clouds thy chariot,
who ridest on the wings of the
wind,
[4] who makest the winds thy messengers,
fire and flame thy ministers.

[5] Thou didst set the earth on its foundations,
so that it should never be shaken.
[6] Thou didst cover it with the deep as
with a garment;
the waters stood above the mountains.
[7] At thy rebuke they fled;
at the sound of thy thunder they
took to flight.
[8] The mountains rose, the valleys sank
down
to the place which thou didst appoint for them.
[9] Thou didst set a bound which they
should not pass,
so that they might not again cover
the earth.

[10] Thou makest springs gush forth in
the valleys;
they flow between the hills,
[11] they give drink to every beast of the
field;
the wild asses quench their thirst.
[12] By them the birds of the air have
their habitation;
they sing among the branches.
[13] From thy lofty abode thou waterest
the mountains;
the earth is satisfied with the fruit
of thy work.

[14] Thou dost cause the grass to grow
for the cattle,
and plants for man to cultivate,[r]
that he may bring forth food from
the earth,

[q] Heb uncertain
[r] Or *fodder for the animals that serve man*
103.8: Jas 5.11.   **103.17:** Lk 1.50.   **104.4:** Heb 1.7.
104.12: Mt 13.32; Mk 4.32; Lk 13.19.

¹⁵ and wine to gladden the heart of
man,
oil to make his face shine,
and bread to strengthen man's
heart.
¹⁶ The trees of the LORD are watered
abundantly,
the cedars of Lebanon which he
planted.
¹⁷ In them the birds build their nests;
the stork has her home in the fir
trees.
¹⁸ The high mountains are for the wild
goats;
the rocks are a refuge for the
badgers.
¹⁹ Thou hast made the moon to mark
the seasons;
the sun knows its time for setting.
²⁰ Thou makest darkness, and it is
night,
when all the beasts of the forest
creep forth.
²¹ The young lions roar for their prey,
seeking their food from God.
²² When the sun rises, they get them
away
and lie down in their dens.
²³ Man goes forth to his work
and to his labor until the evening.

²⁴ O LORD, how manifold are thy works!
In wisdom hast thou made them
all;
the earth is full of thy creatures.
²⁵ Yonder is the sea, great and wide,
which teems with things innumerable,
living things both small and great.
²⁶ There go the ships,
and Le·vi′a·than which thou didst
form to sport in it.

²⁷ These all look to thee,
to give them their food in due
season.
²⁸ When thou givest to them, they
gather it up;
when thou openest thy hand, they
are filled with good things.
²⁹ When thou hidest thy face, they are
dismayed;
when thou takest away their
breath, they die
and return to their dust.
³⁰ When thou sendest forth thy Spirit,ᵉ
they are created;
and thou renewest the face of the
ground.

³¹ May the glory of the LORD endure
for ever,
may the LORD rejoice in his works,
³² who looks on the earth and it trembles,
who touches the mountains and
they smoke!
³³ I will sing to the LORD as long as I
live;
I will sing praise to my God while
I have being.
³⁴ May my meditation be pleasing to
him,
for I rejoice in the LORD.
³⁵ Let sinners be consumed from the
earth,
and let the wicked be no more!
Bless the LORD, O my soul!
Praise the LORD!

105

O give thanks to the LORD,
call on his name,
make known his deeds among the
peoples!
² Sing to him, sing praises to him,
tell of all his wonderful works!
³ Glory in his holy name;
let the hearts of those who seek the
LORD rejoice!
⁴ Seek the LORD and his strength,
seek his presence continually!
⁵ Remember the wonderful works that
he has done,
his miracles, and the judgments he
uttered,
⁶ O offspring of Abraham his servant,
sons of Jacob, his chosen ones!

⁷ He is the LORD our God;
his judgments are in all the earth.
⁸ He is mindful of his covenant for
ever,
of the word that he commanded,
for a thousand generations,
⁹ the covenant which he made with
Abraham,
his sworn promise to Isaac,
¹⁰ which he confirmed to Jacob as a
statute,
to Israel as an everlasting covenant,
¹¹ saying, "To you I will give the land
of Canaan
as your portion for an inheritance."

¹² When they were few in number,
of little account, and sojourners in
it,

ᵉOr *breath*
105.1–15: 1 Chron 16.8-22. **105.8–9:** Lk 1.72-73.

¹³ wandering from nation to nation,
from one kingdom to another people,
¹⁴ he allowed no one to oppress them;
he rebuked kings on their account;
¹⁵ saying, "Touch not my anointed ones,
do my prophets no harm!"

¹⁶ When he summoned a famine on the land,
and broke every staff of bread,
¹⁷ he had sent a man ahead of them,
Joseph, who was sold as a slave.
¹⁸ His feet were hurt with fetters,
his neck was put in a collar of iron;
¹⁹ until what he had said came to pass
the word of the LORD tested him.
²⁰ The king sent and released him,
the ruler of the peoples set him free;
²¹ he made him lord of his house,
and ruler of all his possessions,
²² to instruct[f] his princes at his pleasure,
and to teach his elders wisdom.

²³ Then Israel came to Egypt;
Jacob sojourned in the land of Ham.
²⁴ And the LORD made his people very fruitful,
and made them stronger than their foes.
²⁵ He turned their hearts to hate his people,
to deal craftily with his servants.

²⁶ He sent Moses his servant,
and Aaron whom he had chosen.
²⁷ They wrought his signs among them,
and miracles in the land of Ham.
²⁸ He sent darkness, and made the land dark;
they rebelled[u] against his words.
²⁹ He turned their waters into blood,
and caused their fish to die.
³⁰ Their land swarmed with frogs,
even in the chambers of their kings.
³¹ He spoke, and there came swarms of flies,
and gnats throughout their country.
³² He gave them hail for rain,
and lightning that flashed through their land.
³³ He smote their vines and fig trees,
and shattered the trees of their country.
³⁴ He spoke, and the locusts came,

and young locusts without number;
³⁵ which devoured all the vegetation in their land,
and ate up the fruit of their ground.
³⁶ He smote all the first-born in their land,
the first issue of all their strength.

³⁷ Then he led forth Israel with silver and gold,
and there was none among his tribes who stumbled.
³⁸ Egypt was glad when they departed,
for dread of them had fallen upon it.
³⁹ He spread a cloud for a covering,
and fire to give light by night.
⁴⁰ They asked, and he brought quails,
and gave them bread from heaven in abundance.
⁴¹ He opened the rock, and water gushed forth;
it flowed through the desert like a river.
⁴² For he remembered his holy promise,
and Abraham his servant.

⁴³ So he led forth his people with joy,
his chosen ones with singing.
⁴⁴ And he gave them the lands of the nations;
and they took possession of the fruit of the peoples' toil,
⁴⁵ to the end that they should keep his statutes,
and observe his laws.
Praise the LORD!

106 Praise the LORD!
O give thanks to the LORD, for he is good;
for his steadfast love endures for ever!
² Who can utter the mighty doings of the LORD,
or show forth all his praise?
³ Blessed are they who observe justice,
who do righteousness at all times!

⁴ Remember me, O LORD, when thou showest favor to thy people;
help me when thou deliverest them;
⁵ that I may see the prosperity of thy chosen ones,

---

[f] Gk Syr Jerome: Heb *to bind*
[u] Cn Compare Gk Syr: Heb *they did not rebel*
106.1: 1 Chron 16.34.

that I may rejoice in the gladness
of thy nation,
that I may glory with thy heritage.

⁶Both we and our fathers have sinned;
we have committed iniquity,
we have done wickedly.
⁷Our fathers, when they were in
Egypt,
did not consider thy wonderful
works;
they did not remember the abundance of thy steadfast love,
but rebelled against the Most High⁰
at the Red Sea.
⁸Yet he saved them for his name's
sake,
that he might make known his
mighty power.
⁹He rebuked the Red Sea, and it became dry;
and he led them through the deep
as through a desert.
¹⁰So he saved them from the hand of
the foe,
and delivered them from the power
of the enemy.
¹¹And the waters covered their adversaries;
not one of them was left.
¹²Then they believed his words;
they sang his praise.

¹³But they soon forgot his works;
they did not wait for his counsel.
¹⁴But they had a wanton craving in the
wilderness,
and put God to the test in the
desert;
¹⁵he gave them what they asked,
but sent a wasting disease among
them.

¹⁶When men in the camp were jealous
of Moses
and Aaron, the holy one of the
LORD,
¹⁷the earth opened and swallowed up
Dā'than,
and covered the company of
A·bī'ram.
¹⁸Fire also broke out in their company;
the flame burned up the wicked.

¹⁹They made a calf in Hō'rĕb
and worshiped a molten image.
²⁰They exchanged the glory of God
for the image of an ox that eats
grass.
²¹They forgot God, their Savior,

who had done great things in
Egypt,
²²wondrous works in the land of Ham,
and terrible things by the Red Sea.
²³Therefore he said he would destroy
them—
had not Moses, his chosen one,
stood in the breach before him,
to turn away his wrath from destroying them.

²⁴Then they despised the pleasant land,
having no faith in his promise.
²⁵They murmured in their tents,
and did not obey the voice of the
LORD.
²⁶Therefore he raised his hand and
swore to them
that he would make them fall in
the wilderness,
²⁷and would disperse⁰ their descendants among the nations,
scattering them over the lands.

²⁸Then they attached themselves to the
Bā'al of Pē'ôr,
and ate sacrifices offered to the
dead;
²⁹they provoked the LORD to anger with
their doings,
and a plague broke out among
them.
³⁰Then Phĭn'e·has stood up and interposed,
and the plague was stayed.
³¹And that has been reckoned to him
as righteousness
from generation to generation for
ever.

³²They angered him at the waters of
Mĕr'ĭ·bah,
and it went ill with Moses on their
account;
³³for they made his spirit bitter,
and he spoke words that were rash.

³⁴They did not destroy the peoples,
as the LORD commanded them,
³⁵but they mingled with the nations
and learned to do as they did.
³⁶They served their idols,
which became a snare to them.
³⁷They sacrificed their sons
and their daughters to the demons;
³⁸they poured out innocent blood,
the blood of their sons and daughters,

ᵛCn Compare 78.17, 56: Heb *at the sea*
ʷSyr Compare Ezek 20.23: Heb *cause to fall*

whom they sacrificed to the idols of
Canaan;
and the land was polluted with
blood.
³⁹Thus they became unclean by their
acts,
and played the harlot in their doings.

⁴⁰Then the anger of the Lord was
kindled against his people,
and he abhorred his heritage;
⁴¹he gave them into the hand of the na-
tions,
so that those who hated them ruled
over them.
⁴²Their enemies oppressed them,
and they were brought into subjection under their power.
⁴³Many times he delivered them,
but they were rebellious in their
purposes,
and were brought low through
their iniquity.
⁴⁴Nevertheless he regarded their dis-
tress,
when he heard their cry.
⁴⁵He remembered for their sake his
covenant,
and relented according to the
abundance of his steadfast love.
⁴⁶He caused them to be pitied
by all those who held them captive.

⁴⁷Save us, O Lord our God,
and gather us from among the nations,
that we may give thanks to thy holy
name
and glory in thy praise.

⁴⁸Blessed be the Lord, the God of Is-
rael,
from everlasting to everlasting!
And let all the people say, "Amen!"
Praise the Lord!

BOOK V

10**7**   O give thanks to the Lord,
for he is good;
for his steadfast love endures for
ever!
²Let the redeemed of the Lord say so,
whom he has redeemed from
trouble
³and gathered in from the lands,
from the east and from the west,
from the north and from the south.

⁴Some wandered in desert wastes,
finding no way to a city to dwell in;
⁵hungry and thirsty,
their soul fainted within them.
⁶Then they cried to the Lord in their
trouble,
and he delivered them from their
distress;
⁷he led them by a straight way,
till they reached a city to dwell in.
⁸Let them thank the Lord for his
steadfast love,
for his wonderful works to the sons
of men!
⁹For he satisfies him who is thirsty,
and the hungry he fills with good
things.

¹⁰Some sat in darkness and in gloom,
prisoners in affliction and in irons,
¹¹for they had rebelled against the
words of God,
and spurned the counsel of the
Most High.
¹²Their hearts were bowed down with
hard labor;
they fell down, with none to help.
¹³Then they cried to the Lord in their
trouble,
and he delivered them from their
distress;
¹⁴he brought them out of darkness and
gloom,
and broke their bonds asunder.
¹⁵Let them thank the Lord for his
steadfast love,
for his wonderful works to the sons
of men!
¹⁶For he shatters the doors of bronze,
and cuts in two the bars of iron.

¹⁷Some were sick^r through their sinful
ways,
and because of their iniquities
suffered affliction;
¹⁸they loathed any kind of food,
and they drew near to the gates of
death.
¹⁹Then they cried to the Lord in their
trouble,
and he delivered them from their
distress;
²⁰he sent forth his word, and healed
them,
and delivered them from destruction.
²¹Let them thank the Lord for his
steadfast love,

^rCn: Heb *fools*
106.47-48: 1 Chron 16.35-36.

for his wonderful works to the sons
of men!
²²And let them offer sacrifices of
thanksgiving,
and tell of his deeds in songs of joy!

²³Some went down to the sea in ships,
doing business on the great waters;
²⁴they saw the deeds of the LORD,
his wondrous works in the deep.
²⁵For he commanded, and raised the
stormy wind,
which lifted up the waves of the
sea.
²⁶They mounted up to heaven, they
went down to the depths;
their courage melted away in their
evil plight;
²⁷they reeled and staggered like
drunken men,
and were at their wits' end.
²⁸Then they cried to the LORD in their
trouble,
and he delivered them from their
distress;
²⁹he made the storm be still,
and the waves of the sea were
hushed.
³⁰Then they were glad because they
had quiet,
and he brought them to their desired haven.
³¹Let them thank the LORD for his
steadfast love,
for his wonderful works to the sons
of men!
³²Let them extol him in the congregation of the people,
and praise him in the assembly of
the elders.

³³He turns rivers into a desert,
springs of water into thirsty
ground,
³⁴a fruitful land into a salty waste,
because of the wickedness of its
inhabitants.
³⁵He turns a desert into pools of water,
a parched land into springs of
water.
³⁶And there he lets the hungry dwell,
and they establish a city to live in;
³⁷they sow fields, and plant vineyards,
and get a fruitful yield.
³⁸By his blessing they multiply greatly;
and he does not let their cattle
decrease.

³⁹When they are diminished and
brought low

through oppression, trouble, and
sorrow,
⁴⁰he pours contempt upon princes
and makes them wander in track-
less wastes;
⁴¹but he raises up the needy out of
affliction,
and makes their families like
flocks.
⁴²The upright see it and are glad;
and all wickedness stops its mouth.
⁴³Whoever is wise, let him give heed
to these things;
let men consider the steadfast
love of the LORD.

A Song. A Psalm of David.

108 My heart is steadfast, O
God, my heart is steadfast!
I will sing and make melody!
Awake, my soul!
²Awake, O harp and lyre!
I will awake the dawn!
³I will give thanks to thee, O LORD,
among the peoples,
I will sing praises to thee among
the nations.
⁴For thy steadfast love is great above
the heavens,
thy faithfulness reaches to the
clouds.

⁵Be exalted, O God, above the heavens!
Let thy glory be over all the earth!
⁶That thy beloved may be delivered,
give help by thy right hand, and
answer me!

⁷God has promised in his sanctuary:ᵛ
"With exultation I will divide up
Shē′chĕm,
and portion out the Vale of Sŭc′-
cŏth.
⁸Gilead is mine; Mă·năs′sĕh is mine;
Ē′phra·ĭm is my helmet;
Judah my scepter.
⁹Mō′ăb is my washbasin;
upon Ē′dŏm I cast my shoe;
over Phĭ·lĭs′tĭ·ạ I shout in triumph."

¹⁰Who will bring me to the fortified
city?
Who will lead me to Ē′dŏm?
¹¹Hast thou not rejected us, O God?

ᵛOr *by his holiness*
108.1-5: Ps 57.7-11. **108.6-13:** Ps 60.5-12.

Thou dost not go forth, O God, with our armies.

12 O grant us help against the foe, for vain is the help of man!

13 With God we shall do valiantly; it is he who will tread down our foes.

To the choirmaster. A Psalm of David.

109 Be not silent, O God of my praise!

2 For wicked and deceitful mouths are opened against me,
speaking against me with lying tongues.

3 They beset me with words of hate, and attack me without cause.

4 In return for my love they accuse me, even as I make prayer for them.*z*

5 So they reward me evil for good, and hatred for my love.

6 Appoint a wicked man against him; let an accuser bring him to trial.*a*

7 When he is tried, let him come forth guilty;
let his prayer be counted as sin!

8 May his days be few; may another seize his goods!

9 May his children be fatherless, and his wife a widow!

10 May his children wander about and beg;
may they be driven out of*b* the ruins they inhabit!

11 May the creditor seize all that he has;
may strangers plunder the fruits of his toil!

12 Let there be none to extend kindness to him,
nor any to pity his fatherless children!

13 May his posterity be cut off; may his name be blotted out in the second generation!

14 May the iniquity of his fathers be remembered before the LORD,
and let not the sin of his mother be blotted out!

15 Let them be before the LORD continually;
and may his*c* memory be cut off from the earth!

16 For he did not remember to show kindness,
but pursued the poor and needy

and the brokenhearted to their death.

17 He loved to curse; let curses come on him!
He did not like blessing; may it be far from him!

18 He clothed himself with cursing as his coat,
may it soak into his body like water,
like oil into his bones!

19 May it be like a garment which he wraps round him,
like a belt with which he daily girds himself!

20 May this be the reward of my accusers from the LORD,
of those who speak evil against my life!

21 But thou, O GOD my Lord,
deal on my behalf for thy name's sake;
because thy steadfast love is good, deliver me!

22 For I am poor and needy,
and my heart is stricken within me.

23 I am gone, like a shadow at evening; I am shaken off like a locust.

24 My knees are weak through fasting; my body has become gaunt.

25 I am an object of scorn to my accusers;
when they see me, they wag their heads.

26 Help me, O LORD my God!
Save me according to thy steadfast love!

27 Let them know that this is thy hand; thou, O LORD, hast done it!

28 Let them curse, but do thou bless!
Let my assailants be put to shame;*d* may thy servant be glad!

29 May my accusers be clothed with dishonor;
may they be wrapped in their own shame as in a mantle!

30 With my mouth I will give great thanks to the LORD;
I will praise him in the midst of the throng.

*z*Syr: Heb *I prayer*
*a*Heb *stand at his right hand* *b*Gk: Heb *and seek*
*c*Gk: Heb *their*
*d*Gk: Heb *they have arisen and have been put to shame*
109.8: Acts 1.20.
109.25: Mt 27.39; Mk 15.29.

³¹ For he stands at the right hand of
the needy,
  to save him from those who
condemn him to death.

A Psalm of David.

110   The LORD says to my lord:
"Sit at my right hand,
till I make your enemies
  your footstool."

² The LORD sends forth from Zion
your mighty scepter.
  Rule in the midst of your foes!
³ Your people will offer themselves
freely
  on the day you lead your host
upon the holy mountains.ᵉ
From the womb of the morning
like dew your youthᶠ will come to
you.
⁴ The LORD has sworn
and will not change his mind,
"You are a priest for ever
  after the order of Mĕl·chĭz′ę·dĕk."

⁵ The Lord is at your right hand;
he will shatter kings on the day of
  his wrath.
⁶ He will execute judgment among the
nations,
filling them with corpses;
he will shatter chiefsᵍ
  over the wide earth.
⁷ He will drink from the brook by the
way;
  therefore he will lift up his head.

111   Praise the LORD.
I will give thanks to the LORD
with my whole heart,
  in the company of the upright,
in the congregation.
² Great are the works of the LORD,
studied by all who have pleasure
  in them.
³ Full of honor and majesty is his
work,
  and his righteousness endures for
ever.
⁴ He has caused his wonderful works
to be remembered;
  the LORD is gracious and merciful.
⁵ He provides food for those who fear
him;
  he is ever mindful of his covenant.

⁶ He has shown his people the power
of his works,
  in giving them the heritage of the
nations.
⁷ The works of his hands are faithful
and just;
  all his precepts are trustworthy,
⁸ they are established for ever and
ever,
  to be performed with faithfulness
and uprightness.
⁹ He sent redemption to his people;
he has commanded his covenant
  for ever.
  Holy and terrible is his name!
¹⁰ The fear of the LORD is the beginning
of wisdom;
  a good understanding have all
those who practice it.
  His praise endures for ever!

112   Praise the LORD.
Blessed is the man who fears
the LORD,
  who greatly delights in his commandments!
² His descendants will be mighty in
the land;
  the generation of the upright
will be blessed.
³ Wealth and riches are in his house;
and his righteousness endures for
  ever.
⁴ Light rises in the darkness for the
upright;
  the LORDʰ is gracious, merciful,
and righteous.
⁵ It is well with the man who deals
generously and lends,
  who conducts his affairs with
justice.
⁶ For the righteous will never be
moved;
  he will be remembered for ever.
⁷ He is not afraid of evil tidings;
his heart is firm, trusting in the
  LORD.
⁸ His heart is steady, he will not be
afraid,
  until he sees his desire on his
adversaries.
⁹ He has distributed freely, he has
given to the poor;

ᵉ Another reading is *in holy array*
ᶠ Cn: Heb *the dew of your youth*   ᵍ Or *the head*
ʰ Gk: Heb lacks *the* LORD
110.1: Mt 22.44; 26.64; Mk 12.36; 14.62; 16.19; Lk 20.42-
43; 22.69; Acts 2.34; 1 Cor 15.25; Eph 1.20; Col 3.1; Heb
1.3, 13; 10.12-13; 12.2.
110.4: Heb 5.6, 10; 6.20; 7.11, 15, 21.   **112.9:** 2 Cor 9.9.

his righteousness endures for ever;
his horn is exalted in honor.
¹⁰ The wicked man sees it and is angry;
he gnashes his teeth and melts
away;
the desire of the wicked man
comes to nought.

113

Praise the LORD!
Praise, O servants of the LORD,
praise the name of the LORD!

² Blessed be the name of the LORD
from this time forth and for evermore!
³ From the rising of the sun to its
setting
the name of the LORD is to be
praised!
⁴ The LORD is high above all nations,
and his glory above the heavens!

⁵ Who is like the LORD our God,
who is seated on high,
⁶ who looks far down
upon the heavens and the earth?
⁷ He raises the poor from the dust,
and lifts the needy from the ash
heap,
⁸ to make them sit with princes,
with the princes of his people.
⁹ He gives the barren woman a home,
making her the joyous mother of
children.
Praise the LORD!

114

When Israel went forth
from Egypt,
the house of Jacob from a people of strange language,
² Judah became his sanctuary,
Israel his dominion.

³ The sea looked and fled,
Jordan turned back.
⁴ The mountains skipped like rams,
the hills like lambs.

⁵ What ails you, O sea, that you flee?
O Jordan, that you turn back?
⁶ O mountains, that you skip like
rams?
O hills, like lambs?

⁷ Tremble, O earth, at the presence
of the LORD,
at the presence of the God of
Jacob,

⁸ who turns the rock into a pool of
water,
the flint into a spring of water.

115

Not to us, O LORD, not to us,
but to thy name give glory,
for the sake of thy steadfast love
and thy faithfulness!
² Why should the nations say,
"Where is their God?"

³ Our God is in the heavens;
he does whatever he pleases.
⁴ Their idols are silver and gold,
the work of men's hands.
⁵ They have mouths, but do not speak;
eyes, but do not see.
⁶ They have ears, but do not hear;
noses, but do not smell.
⁷ They have hands, but do not feel;
feet, but do not walk;
and they do not make a sound in
their throat.
⁸ Those who make them are like them;
so are all who trust in them.

⁹ O Israel, trust in the LORD!
He is their help and their shield.
¹⁰ O house of Aaron, put your trust in
the LORD!
He is their help and their shield.
¹¹ You who fear the LORD, trust in the
LORD!
He is their help and their shield.

¹² The LORD has been mindful of us;
he will bless us;
he will bless the house of Israel;
he will bless the house of Aaron;
¹³ he will bless those who fear the LORD,
both small and great.

¹⁴ May the LORD give you increase,
you and your children!
¹⁵ May you be blessed by the LORD,
who made heaven and earth!

¹⁶ The heavens are the LORD's heavens,
but the earth he has given to the
sons of men.
¹⁷ The dead do not praise the LORD,
nor do any that go down into
silence.
¹⁸ But we will bless the LORD
from this time forth and for
evermore.
Praise the LORD!

115.4–8: Ps 135.15-18.   115.13: Rev 11.18; 19.5.

116 I love the Lord, because he has heard
my voice and my supplications.
2 Because he inclined his ear to me,
therefore I will call on him as long
as I live.
3 The snares of death encompassed me;
the pangs of Shē′ōl laid hold on
me;
I suffered distress and anguish.
4 Then I called on the name of the
Lord:
"O Lord, I beseech thee, save my
life!"

5 Gracious is the Lord, and righteous;
our God is merciful.
6 The Lord preserves the simple;
when I was brought low, he saved
me.
7 Return, O my soul, to your rest;
for the Lord has dealt bountifully
with you.

8 For thou hast delivered my soul from
death,
my eyes from tears,
my feet from stumbling;
9 I walk before the Lord
in the land of the living.
10 I kept my faith, even when I said,
"I am greatly afflicted";
11 I said in my consternation,
"Men are all a vain hope."

12 What shall I render to the Lord
for all his bounty to me?
13 I will lift up the cup of salvation
and call on the name of the Lord,
14 I will pay my vows to the Lord
in the presence of all his people.
15 Precious in the sight of the Lord
is the death of his saints.
16 O Lord, I am thy servant;
I am thy servant, the son of thy
handmaid.
Thou hast loosed my bonds.
17 I will offer to thee the sacrifice of
thanksgiving
and call on the name of the Lord.
18 I will pay my vows to the Lord
in the presence of all his people,
19 in the courts of the house of the
Lord,
in your midst, O Jerusalem.
Praise the Lord!

117 Praise the Lord, all nations!
Extol him, all peoples!

2 For great is his steadfast love toward us;
and the faithfulness of the Lord
endures for ever.
Praise the Lord!

118 O give thanks to the Lord,
for he is good;
his steadfast love endures for ever!

2 Let Israel say,
"His steadfast love endures for
ever."
3 Let the house of Aaron say,
"His steadfast love endures for
ever."
4 Let those who fear the Lord say,
"His steadfast love endures for
ever."

5 Out of my distress I called on the
Lord;
the Lord answered me and set
me free.
6 With the Lord on my side I do not
fear.
What can man do to me?
7 The Lord is on my side to help me;
I shall look in triumph on those
who hate me.
8 It is better to take refuge in the Lord
than to put confidence in man.
9 It is better to take refuge in the Lord
than to put confidence in princes.

10 All nations surrounded me;
in the name of the Lord I cut them
off!
11 They surrounded me, surrounded me
on every side;
in the name of the Lord I cut them
off!
12 They surrounded me like bees,
they blazed[i] like a fire of thorns;
in the name of the Lord I cut them
off!
13 I was pushed hard,[j] so that I was
falling,
but the Lord helped me.
14 The Lord is my strength and my
song;
he has become my salvation.

15 Hark, glad songs of victory
in the tents of the righteous:

iGk: Heb *were extinguished*
jGk Syr Jerome: Heb *thou didst push me hard*
116.10: 2 Cor 4.13.   **117.1:** Rom 15.11.
118.6: Heb 13.6.

"The right hand of the LORD does valiantly,
16 the right hand of the LORD is exalted,
the right hand of the LORD does valiantly!"
17 I shall not die, but I shall live,
and recount the deeds of the LORD.
18 The LORD has chastened me sorely,
but he has not given me over to death.

19 Open to me the gates of righteousness,
that I may enter through them and give thanks to the LORD.

20 This is the gate of the LORD;
the righteous shall enter through it.

21 I thank thee that thou hast answered me
and hast become my salvation.
22 The stone which the builders rejected has become the head of the corner.
23 This is the LORD's doing;
it is marvelous in our eyes.
24 This is the day which the LORD has made;
let us rejoice and be glad in it.
25 Save us, we beseech thee, O LORD!
O LORD, we beseech thee, give us success!

26 Blessed be he who enters in the name of the LORD!
We bless you from the house of the LORD.
27 The LORD is God,
and he has given us light.
Bind the festal procession with branches,
up to the horns of the altar!

28 Thou art my God, and I will give thanks to thee;
thou art my God, I will extol thee.

29 O give thanks to the LORD, for he is good;
for his steadfast love endures for ever!

119 Blessed are those whose way is blameless,
who walk in the law of the LORD!
2 Blessed are those who keep his testimonies,
who seek him with their whole heart,

3 who also do no wrong,
but walk in his ways!
4 Thou hast commanded thy precepts to be kept diligently.
5 O that my ways may be steadfast in keeping thy statutes!
6 Then I shall not be put to shame, having my eyes fixed on all thy commandments.
7 I will praise thee with an upright heart,
when I learn thy righteous ordinances.
8 I will observe thy statutes;
O forsake me not utterly!

9 How can a young man keep his way pure?
By guarding it according to thy word.
10 With my whole heart I seek thee;
let me not wander from thy commandments!
11 I have laid up thy word in my heart,
that I might not sin against thee.
12 Blessed be thou, O LORD;
teach me thy statutes!
13 With my lips I declare
all the ordinances of thy mouth.
14 In the way of thy testimonies I delight
as much as in all riches.
15 I will meditate on thy precepts,
and fix my eyes on thy ways.
16 I will delight in thy statutes;
I will not forget thy word.

17 Deal bountifully with thy servant,
that I may live and observe thy word.
18 Open my eyes, that I may behold wondrous things out of thy law.
19 I am a sojourner on earth;
hide not thy commandments from me!
20 My soul is consumed with longing for thy ordinances at all times.
21 Thou dost rebuke the insolent, accursed ones,
who wander from thy commandments;
22 take away from me their scorn and contempt,
for I have kept thy testimonies.
23 Even though princes sit plotting against me,

118.22-23: Mt 21.42; Mk 12.10-11; Lk 20.17; Acts 4.11; 1 Pet 2.7.
118.25-26: Mt 21.9; 23.39; Mk 11.9-10; Lk 13.35; 19.38; Jn 12.13.

thy servant will meditate on thy statutes.
24 Thy testimonies are my delight,
they are my counselors.

25 My soul cleaves to the dust;
revive me according to thy word!
26 When I told of my ways, thou didst answer me;
teach me thy statutes!
27 Make me understand the way of thy precepts,
and I will meditate on thy wondrous works.
28 My soul melts away for sorrow;
strengthen me according to thy word!
29 Put false ways far from me;
and graciously teach me thy law!
30 I have chosen the way of faithfulness,
I set thy ordinances before me.
31 I cleave to thy testimonies, O LORD;
let me not be put to shame!
32 I will run in the way of thy commandments
when thou enlargest my understanding!

33 Teach me, O LORD, the way of thy statutes;
and I will keep it to the end.
34 Give me understanding, that I may keep thy law
and observe it with my whole heart.
35 Lead me in the path of thy commandments,
for I delight in it.
36 Incline my heart to thy testimonies,
and not to gain!
37 Turn my eyes from looking at vanities;
and give me life in thy ways.
38 Confirm to thy servant thy promise,
which is for those who fear thee.
39 Turn away the reproach which I dread;
for thy ordinances are good.
40 Behold, I long for thy precepts;
in thy righteousness give me life!

41 Let thy steadfast love come to me, O LORD,
thy salvation according to thy promise;
42 then shall I have an answer for those who taunt me,
for I trust in thy word.

43 And take not the word of truth utterly out of my mouth,
for my hope is in thy ordinances.
44 I will keep thy law continually,
for ever and ever;
45 and I shall walk at liberty,
for I have sought thy precepts.
46 I will also speak of thy testimonies before kings,
and shall not be put to shame;
47 for I find my delight in thy commandments,
which I love.
48 I revere thy commandments, which I love,
and I will meditate on thy statutes.

49 Remember thy word to thy servant,
in which thou hast made me hope.
50 This is my comfort in my affliction
that thy promise gives me life.
51 Godless men utterly deride me,
but I do not turn away from thy law.
52 When I think of thy ordinances from of old,
I take comfort, O LORD.
53 Hot indignation seizes me because of the wicked,
who forsake thy law.
54 Thy statutes have been my songs
in the house of my pilgrimage.
55 I remember thy name in the night, O LORD,
and keep thy law.
56 This blessing has fallen to me,
that I have kept thy precepts.

57 The LORD is my portion;
I promise to keep thy words.
58 I entreat thy favor with all my heart;
be gracious to me according to thy promise.
59 When I think of thy ways,
I turn my feet to thy testimonies;
60 I hasten and do not delay
to keep thy commandments.
61 Though the cords of the wicked ensnare me,
I do not forget thy law.
62 At midnight I rise to praise thee,
because of thy righteous ordinances.
63 I am a companion of all who fear thee,
of those who keep thy precepts.
64 The earth, O LORD, is full of thy steadfast love;
teach me thy statutes!

⁶⁵ Thou hast dealt well with thy servant,
O LORD, according to thy word.
⁶⁶ Teach me good judgment and knowledge,
for I believe in thy commandments.
⁶⁷ Before I was afflicted I went astray;
but now I keep thy word.
⁶⁸ Thou art good and doest good;
teach me thy statutes.
⁶⁹ The godless besmear me with lies,
but with my whole heart I keep thy precepts;
⁷⁰ their heart is gross like fat,
but I delight in thy law.
⁷¹ It is good for me that I was afflicted,
that I might learn thy statutes.
⁷² The law of thy mouth is better to me
than thousands of gold and silver pieces.

⁷³ Thy hands have made and fashioned me;
give me understanding that I may learn thy commandments.
⁷⁴ Those who fear thee shall see me and rejoice,
because I have hoped in thy word.
⁷⁵ I know, O LORD, that thy judgments are right,
and that in faithfulness thou hast afflicted me.
⁷⁶ Let thy steadfast love be ready to comfort me
according to thy promise to thy servant.
⁷⁷ Let thy mercy come to me, that I may live;
for thy law is my delight.
⁷⁸ Let the godless be put to shame,
because they have subverted me with guile;
as for me, I will meditate on thy precepts.
⁷⁹ Let those who fear thee turn to me,
that they may know thy testimonies.
⁸⁰ May my heart be blameless in thy statutes,
that I may not be put to shame!

⁸¹ My soul languishes for thy salvation;
I hope in thy word.
⁸² My eyes fail with watching for thy promise;
I ask, "When wilt thou comfort me?"
⁸³ For I have become like a wineskin in the smoke,

yet I have not forgotten thy statutes.
⁸⁴ How long must thy servant endure?
When wilt thou judge those who persecute me?
⁸⁵ Godless men have dug pitfalls for me,
men who do not conform to thy law.
⁸⁶ All thy commandments are sure;
they persecute me with falsehood; help me!
⁸⁷ They have almost made an end of me on earth;
but I have not forsaken thy precepts.
⁸⁸ In thy steadfast love spare my life,
that I may keep the testimonies of thy mouth.

⁸⁹ For ever, O LORD, thy word
is firmly fixed in the heavens.
⁹⁰ Thy faithfulness endures to all generations;
thou hast established the earth, and it stands fast.
⁹¹ By thy appointment they stand this day;
for all things are thy servants.
⁹² If thy law had not been my delight,
I should have perished in my affliction.
⁹³ I will never forget thy precepts;
for by them thou hast given me life.
⁹⁴ I am thine, save me;
for I have sought thy precepts.
⁹⁵ The wicked lie in wait to destroy me;
but I consider thy testimonies.
⁹⁶ I have seen a limit to all perfection,
but thy commandment is exceedingly broad.

⁹⁷ Oh, how I love thy law!
It is my meditation all the day.
⁹⁸ Thy commandment makes me wiser than my enemies,
for it is ever with me.
⁹⁹ I have more understanding than all my teachers,
for thy testimonies are my meditation.
¹⁰⁰ I understand more than the aged,
for I keep thy precepts.
¹⁰¹ I hold back my feet from every evil way,
in order to keep thy word.
¹⁰² I do not turn aside from thy ordinances,
for thou hast taught me.
¹⁰³ How sweet are thy words to my taste,

sweeter than honey to my mouth!
[104] Through thy precepts I get understanding;
therefore I hate every false way.

[105] Thy word is a lamp to my feet
and a light to my path.
[106] I have sworn an oath and confirmed it,
to observe thy righteous ordinances.
[107] I am sorely afflicted;
give me life, O LORD, according to thy word!
[108] Accept my offerings of praise, O LORD,
and teach me thy ordinances.
[109] I hold my life in my hand continually,
but I do not forget thy law.
[110] The wicked have laid a snare for me,
but I do not stray from thy precepts.
[111] Thy testimonies are my heritage for ever;
yea, they are the joy of my heart.
[112] I incline my heart to perform thy statutes
for ever, to the end.

[113] I hate double-minded men,
but I love thy law.
[114] Thou art my hiding place and my shield;
I hope in thy word.
[115] Depart from me, you evildoers,
that I may keep the commandments of my God.
[116] Uphold me according to thy promise, that I may live,
and let me not be put to shame in my hope!
[117] Hold me up, that I may be safe
and have regard for thy statutes continually!
[118] Thou dost spurn all who go astray from thy statutes;
yea, their cunning is in vain.
[119] All the wicked of the earth thou dost count as dross;
therefore I love thy testimonies.
[120] My flesh trembles for fear of thee,
and I am afraid of thy judgments.

[121] I have done what is just and right;
do not leave me to my oppressors.
[122] Be surety for thy servant for good;
let not the godless oppress me.

[123] My eyes fail with watching for thy salvation,
and for the fulfilment of thy righteous promise.
[124] Deal with thy servant according to thy steadfast love,
and teach me thy statutes.
[125] I am thy servant; give me understanding,
that I may know thy testimonies!
[126] It is time for the LORD to act,
for thy law has been broken.
[127] Therefore I love thy commandments above gold, above fine gold.
[128] Therefore I direct my steps by all thy precepts;[k]
I hate every false way.

[129] Thy testimonies are wonderful;
therefore my soul keeps them.
[130] The unfolding of thy words gives light;
it imparts understanding to the simple.
[131] With open mouth I pant,
because I long for thy commandments.
[132] Turn to me and be gracious to me,
as is thy wont toward those who love thy name.
[133] Keep steady my steps according to thy promise,
and let no iniquity get dominion over me.
[134] Redeem me from man's oppression,
that I may keep thy precepts.
[135] Make thy face shine upon thy servant,
and teach me thy statutes.
[136] My eyes shed streams of tears,
because men do not keep thy law.

[137] Righteous art thou, O LORD,
and right are thy judgments.
[138] Thou hast appointed thy testimonies in righteousness
and in all faithfulness.
[139] My zeal consumes me,
because my foes forget thy words.
[140] Thy promise is well tried,
and thy servant loves it.
[141] I am small and despised,
yet I do not forget thy precepts.
[142] Thy righteousness is righteous for ever,
and thy law is true.
[143] Trouble and anguish have come upon me,

[k] Gk Jerome: Heb uncertain

but thy commandments are my delight.

¹⁴⁴Thy testimonies are righteous for ever;
give me understanding that I may live.

¹⁴⁵With my whole heart I cry; answer me, O LORD!
I will keep thy statutes.
¹⁴⁶I cry to thee; save me,
that I may observe thy testimonies.
¹⁴⁷I rise before dawn and cry for help;
I hope in thy words.
¹⁴⁸My eyes are awake before the watches of the night,
that I may meditate upon thy promise.
¹⁴⁹Hear my voice in thy steadfast love;
O LORD, in thy justice preserve my life.
¹⁵⁰They draw near who persecute me with evil purpose;
they are far from thy law.
¹⁵¹But thou art near, O LORD,
and all thy commandments are true.
¹⁵²Long have I known from thy testimonies
that thou hast founded them for ever.

¹⁵³Look on my affliction and deliver me,
for I do not forget thy law.
¹⁵⁴Plead my cause and redeem me;
give me life according to thy promise!
¹⁵⁵Salvation is far from the wicked,
for they do not seek thy statutes.
¹⁵⁶Great is thy mercy, O LORD;
give me life according to thy justice.
¹⁵⁷Many are my persecutors and my adversaries,
but I do not swerve from thy testimonies.
¹⁵⁸I look at the faithless with disgust,
because they do not keep thy commands.
¹⁵⁹Consider how I love thy precepts!
Preserve my life according to thy steadfast love.
¹⁶⁰The sum of thy word is truth;
and every one of thy righteous ordinances endures for ever.

¹⁶¹Princes persecute me without cause,
but my heart stands in awe of thy words.

¹⁶²I rejoice at thy word
like one who finds great spoil.
¹⁶³I hate and abhor falsehood,
but I love thy law.
¹⁶⁴Seven times a day I praise thee
for thy righteous ordinances.
¹⁶⁵Great peace have those who love thy law;
nothing can make them stumble.
¹⁶⁶I hope for thy salvation, O LORD,
and I do thy commandments.
¹⁶⁷My soul keeps thy testimonies;
I love them exceedingly.
¹⁶⁸I keep thy precepts and testimonies,
for all my ways are before thee.

¹⁶⁹Let my cry come before thee, O LORD;
give me understanding according to thy word!
¹⁷⁰Let my supplication come before thee;
deliver me according to thy word.
¹⁷¹My lips will pour forth praise
that thou dost teach me thy statutes.
¹⁷²My tongue will sing of thy word,
for all thy commandments are right.
¹⁷³Let thy hand be ready to help me
for I have chosen thy precepts.
¹⁷⁴I long for thy salvation, O LORD
and thy law is my delight.
¹⁷⁵Let me live, that I may praise thee
and let thy ordinances help me
¹⁷⁶I have gone astray like a lost sheep;
seek thy servant,
for I do not forget thy commandments.

A Song of Ascents.

120   In my distress I cry to the LORD,
that he may answer me:
²"Deliver me, O LORD,
from lying lips,
from a deceitful tongue."

³What shall be given to you?
And what more shall be done to you,
you deceitful tongue?
⁴A warrior's sharp arrows,
with glowing coals of the broom tree!

⁵Woe is me, that I sojourn in Me′shĕch,

that I dwell among the tents of
Kē′där!
Too long have I had my dwelling
among those who hate peace.
I am for peace;
but when I speak,
they are for war!

A Song of Ascents.

21 I lift up my eyes to the hills.
From whence does my help
come?
My help comes from the LORD,
who made heaven and earth.

He will not let your foot be moved,
he who keeps you will not slumber.
Behold, he who keeps Israel
will neither slumber nor sleep.

The LORD is your keeper;
the LORD is your shade
on your right hand.
The sun shall not smite you by day,
nor the moon by night.

The LORD will keep you from all evil;
he will keep your life.
The LORD will keep
your going out and your coming in
from this time forth and for evermore.

A Song of Ascents. Of David.

22 I was glad when they said
to me,
"Let us go to the house of the
LORD!"
Our feet have been standing
within your gates, O Jerusalem!

Jerusalem, built as a city
which is bound firmly together,
to which the tribes go up,
the tribes of the LORD,
as was decreed for Israel,
to give thanks to the name of the
LORD.
There thrones for judgment were set,
the thrones of the house of David.

Pray for the peace of Jerusalem!
"May they prosper who love you!
Peace be within your walls,
and security within your towers!"

8 For my brethren and companions'
sake
I will say, "Peace be within you!"
9 For the sake of the house of the
LORD our God,
I will seek your good.

A Song of Ascents.

123 To thee I lift up my eyes,
O thou who art enthroned in
the heavens!
2 Behold, as the eyes of servants
look to the hand of their master,
as the eyes of a maid
to the hand of her mistress,
so our eyes look to the LORD our God,
till he have mercy upon us.

3 Have mercy upon us, O LORD, have
mercy upon us,
for we have had more than enough
of contempt.
4 Too long our soul has been sated
with the scorn of those who are
at ease,
the contempt of the proud.

A Song of Ascents. Of David.

124 If it had not been the LORD
who was on our side,
let Israel now say—
2 if it had not been the LORD who
was on our side,
when men rose up against us,
3 then they would have swallowed
us up alive,
when their anger was kindled
against us;
4 then the flood would have swept us
away,
the torrent would have gone over
us;
5 then over us would have gone
the raging waters.

6 Blessed be the LORD,
who has not given us
as prey to their teeth!
7 We have escaped as a bird
from the snare of the fowlers;
the snare is broken,
and we have escaped!

8 Our help is in the name of the LORD,
who made heaven and earth.

A Song of Ascents.

125 Those who trust in the
LORD are like Mount Zion,
which cannot be moved, but
abides for ever.
[2] As the mountains are round about
Jerusalem,
so the LORD is round about his
people,
from this time forth and for
evermore.
[3] For the scepter of wickedness shall
not rest
upon the land allotted to the
righteous,
lest the righteous put forth
their hands to do wrong.
[4] Do good, O LORD, to those who are
good,
and to those who are upright in
their hearts!
[5] But those who turn aside upon their
crooked ways
the LORD will lead away with
evildoers!
Peace be in Israel!

A Song of Ascents.

126 When the LORD restored
the fortunes of Zion,[l]
we were like those who dream.
[2] Then our mouth was filled with
laughter,
and our tongue with shouts of
joy;
then they said among the nations,
"The LORD has done great things
for them."
[3] The LORD has done great things for
us;
we are glad.

[4] Restore our fortunes, O LORD,
like the watercourses in the
Nĕg′ĕb!
[5] May those who sow in tears
reap with shouts of joy!
[6] He that goes forth weeping,
bearing the seed for sowing,
shall come home with shouts of joy,
bringing his sheaves with him.

A Song of Ascents. Of Solomon.

127 Unless the LORD builds the
house,
those who build it labor in vain.

Unless the LORD watches over th
city,
the watchman stays awake in vair
[2] It is in vain that you rise up earl
and go late to rest,
eating the bread of anxious toil
for[m] he gives to his beloved sleep

[3] Lo, sons are a heritage from th
LORD,
the fruit of the womb a reward
[4] Like arrows in the hand of a warrio
are the sons of one's youth.
[5] Happy is the man who has
his quiver full of them!
He shall not be put to shame
when he speaks with his enemie
in the gate.

A Song of Ascents.

128 Blessed is every one wh
fears the LORD,
who walks in his ways!
[2] You shall eat the fruit of the labc
of your hands;
you shall be happy, and it shall b
well with you.

[3] Your wife will be like a fruitful vin
within your house;
your children will be like olive shoo
around your table.
[4] Lo, thus shall the man be blesse
who fears the LORD.

[5] The LORD bless you from Zior
May you see the prosperity of Jer
salem
all the days of your life!
[6] May you see your children's childre
Peace be upon Israel!

A Song of Ascents.

129 "Sorely have they afflicte
me from my youth,"
let Israel now say—
[2] "Sorely have they afflicted me fro
my youth,
yet they have not prevailed again
me.
[3] The plowers plowed upon my bacl
they made long their furrows
[4] The LORD is righteous;
he has cut the cords of the wicke

[l] Or *brought back those who returned to Zion*
[m] Another reading is *so*

5 May all who hate Zion
be put to shame and turned
backward!
6 Let them be like the grass on the
housetops,
which withers before it grows up,
7 with which the reaper does not fill
his hand
or the binder of sheaves his bosom,
8 while those who pass by do not say,
"The blessing of the Lord be
upon you!
We bless you in the name of the
Lord!"

A Song of Ascents.

130 Out of the depths I cry to
thee, O Lord!
2 Lord, hear my voice!
Let thy ears be attentive
to the voice of my supplications!
3 If thou, O Lord, shouldst mark
iniquities,
Lord, who could stand?
4 But there is forgiveness with thee,
that thou mayest be feared.
5 I wait for the Lord, my soul waits,
and in his word I hope;
6 my soul waits for the Lord
more than watchmen for the
morning,
more than watchmen for the
morning.
7 O Israel, hope in the Lord!
For with the Lord there is steadfast love,
and with him is plenteous redemption.
8 And he will redeem Israel
from all his iniquities.

A Song of Ascents. Of David.

131 O Lord, my heart is not
lifted up,
my eyes are not raised too high;
I do not occupy myself with things
too great and too marvelous for me.
2 But I have calmed and quieted my
soul,
like a child quieted at its mother's
breast;
like a child that is quieted is my
soul.

3 O Israel, hope in the Lord
from this time forth and for
evermore.

A Song of Ascents.

132 Remember, O Lord, in
David's favor,
all the hardships he endured;
2 how he swore to the Lord
and vowed to the Mighty One of
Jacob,
3 "I will not enter my house
or get into my bed;
4 I will not give sleep to my eyes
or slumber to my eyelids,
5 until I find a place for the Lord,
a dwelling place for the Mighty
One of Jacob."

6 Lo, we heard of it in Ĕph´ra·thạh,
we found it in the fields of Jā´ar.
7 "Let us go to his dwelling place;
let us worship at his footstool!"
8 Arise, O Lord, and go to thy resting
place,
thou and the ark of thy might.
9 Let thy priests be clothed with righteousness,
and let thy saints shout for joy.
10 For thy servant David's sake
do not turn away the face of thy
anointed one.

11 The Lord swore to David a sure oath
from which he will not turn back:
"One of the sons of your body
I will set on your throne.
12 If your sons keep my covenant
and my testimonies which I shall
teach them,
their sons also for ever
shall sit upon your throne."

13 For the Lord has chosen Zion;
he has desired it for his habitation:
14 "This is my resting place for ever;
here I will dwell, for I have desired it.
15 I will abundantly bless her provisions;
I will satisfy her poor with bread.
16 Her priests I will clothe with salvation,
and her saints will shout for joy.

130.3: Ps 143.2; Rom 3.20; Gal 2.16.
132.11: Ps 89.3-4; Acts 2.30.

17 There I will make a horn to sprout
    for David;
  I have prepared a lamp for my
    anointed.
18 His enemies I will clothe with shame,
    but upon himself his crown will
      shed its luster."

A Song of Ascents.

133 Behold, how good and pleas-
      ant it is
  when brothers dwell in unity!
2 It is like the precious oil upon the
    head,
  running down upon the beard,
upon the beard of Aaron,
  running down on the collar of his
    robes!
3 It is like the dew of Hermon,
  which falls on the mountains of
    Zion!
For there the LORD has commanded
  the blessing,
  life for evermore.

A Song of Ascents.

134 Come, bless the LORD,
      all you servants of the LORD,
  who stand by night in the house
    of the LORD!
2 Lift up your hands to the holy place,
  and bless the LORD!

3 May the LORD bless you from Zion,
  he who made heaven and earth!

135 Praise the LORD.
      Praise the name of the
      LORD,
  give praise, O servants of the
    LORD,
2 you that stand in the house of the
    LORD,
  in the courts of the house of our
    God!
3 Praise the LORD, for the LORD is
    good;
  sing to his name, for he is gra-
    cious!
4 For the LORD has chosen Jacob for
    himself,
  Israel as his own possession.

5 For I know that the LORD is great,
  and that our Lord is above all gods.

6 Whatever the LORD pleases he does,
  in heaven and on earth,
  in the seas and all deeps.
7 He it is who makes the clouds rise
    at the end of the earth,
  who makes lightnings for the rain
  and brings forth the wind from his
    storehouses.

8 He it was who smote the first-born of
    Egypt,
  both of man and of beast;
9 who in thy midst, O Egypt,
  sent signs and wonders
  against Pharaoh and all his
    servants;
10 who smote many nations
  and slew mighty kings,
11 Sï′hon, king of the Ăm′o·rïtes,
  and Ŏg, king of Bā′shạn,
  and all the kingdoms of Canaan,
12 and gave their land as a heritage,
  a heritage to his people Israel.

13 Thy name, O LORD, endures for ever,
  thy renown, O LORD, throughout
    all ages.
14 For the LORD will vindicate his
    people,
  and have compassion on his
    servants.

15 The idols of the nations are silver
    and gold,
  the work of men's hands.
16 They have mouths, but they speak
    not,
  they have eyes, but they see not,
17 they have ears, but they hear not,
  nor is there any breath in their
    mouths.
18 Like them be those who make them!—
  yea, every one who trusts in them!

19 O house of Israel, bless the LORD!
  O house of Aaron, bless the LORD!
20 O house of Lē′vï, bless the LORD!
  You that fear the LORD, bless the
    LORD!
21 Blessed be the LORD from Zion,
  he who dwells in Jerusalem!
  Praise the LORD!

136 O give thanks to the LORD,
      for he is good,
  for his steadfast love endures for
    ever.
2 O give thanks to the God of gods,
  135.14: Heb 10.30.　135.15-18: Ps 115.4-8.

for his steadfast love endures for
ever.

*O give thanks to the Lord of lords,
for his steadfast love endures for
ever;

*to him who alone does great wonders,
for his steadfast love endures for
ever;
*to him who by understanding made
the heavens,
for his steadfast love endures for
ever;
*to him who spread out the earth upon
the waters,
for his steadfast love endures for
ever;
*to him who made the great lights,
for his steadfast love endures for
ever;
*the sun to rule over the day,
for his steadfast love endures for
ever;
*the moon and stars to rule over the
night,
for his steadfast love endures for
ever;

*to him who smote the first-born of
Egypt,
for his steadfast love endures for
ever;
and brought Israel out from among
them,
for his steadfast love endures for
ever;
with a strong hand and an outstretched arm,
for his steadfast love endures for
ever;
*to him who divided the Red Sea in
sunder,
for his steadfast love endures for
ever;
*and made Israel pass through the
midst of it,
for his steadfast love endures for
ever;
but overthrew Pharaoh and his host
in the Red Sea,
for his steadfast love endures for
ever;
to him who led his people through
the wilderness,
for his steadfast love endures for
ever;
to him who smote great kings,
for his steadfast love endures for
ever;

¹⁸ and slew famous kings,
for his steadfast love endures for
ever;
¹⁹ Sī'họn, king of the Ăm'ọ-rītes,
for his steadfast love endures for
ever;
²⁰ and Ŏg, king of Bā'shạn,
for his steadfast love endures for
ever;
²¹ and gave their land as a heritage,
for his steadfast love endures for
ever;
²² a heritage to Israel his servant,
for his steadfast love endures for
ever.

²³ It is he who remembered us in our
low estate,
for his steadfast love endures for
ever;
²⁴ and rescued us from our foes,
for his steadfast love endures for
ever;
²⁵ he who gives food to all flesh,
for his steadfast love endures for
ever.

²⁶ O give thanks to the God of heaven,
for his steadfast love endures for
ever.

137 By the waters*ᵒ* of Babylon,
there we sat down and wept,
when we remembered Zion.
² On the willows*ᵖ* there
we hung up our lyres.
³ For there our captors
required of us songs,
and our tormentors, mirth, saying,
"Sing us one of the songs of
Zion!"

⁴ How shall we sing the LORD's song
in a foreign land?
⁵ If I forget you, O Jerusalem,
let my right hand wither!
⁶ Let my tongue cleave to the roof of
my mouth,
if I do not remember you,
if I do not set Jerusalem
above my highest joy!

⁷ Remember, O LORD, against the
Ē'dọm-ītes
the day of Jerusalem,
how they said, "Rase it, rase it!
Down to its foundations!"

ᵒHeb streams ᵖOr poplars

8O daughter of Babylon, you dev-
astator!*q*
Happy shall he be who requites
you
with what you have done to us!
9Happy shall he be who takes your
little ones
and dashes them against the rock!

A Psalm of David.

138   I give thee thanks, O LORD,
with my whole heart;
before the gods I sing thy praise;
2I bow down toward thy holy temple
and give thanks to thy name for
thy steadfast love and thy faithfulness;
for thou hast exalted above everything
thy name and thy word.*r*
3On the day I called, thou didst answer
me,
my strength of soul thou didst
increase.*s*

4All the kings of the earth shall
praise thee, O LORD,
for they have heard the words of
thy mouth;
5and they shall sing of the ways of the
LORD,
for great is the glory of the LORD.
6For though the LORD is high, he
regards the lowly;
but the haughty he knows from
afar.

7Though I walk in the midst of trouble,
thou dost preserve my life;
thou dost stretch out thy hand
against the wrath of my enemies,
and thy right hand delivers me.
8The LORD will fulfil his purpose for
me;
thy steadfast love, O LORD, endures
for ever.
Do not forsake the work of thy
hands.

To the choirmaster. A Psalm of David.

139   O LORD, thou hast searched
me and known me!
2Thou knowest when I sit down and
when I rise up;
thou discernest my thoughts from
afar.

3Thou searchest out my path and my
lying down,
and art acquainted with all my
ways.
4Even before a word is on my tongue,
lo, O LORD, thou knowest it altogether.
5Thou dost beset me behind and
before,
and layest thy hand upon me.
6Such knowledge is too wonderful for
me;
it is high, I cannot attain it.

7Whither shall I go from thy Spirit?
Or whither shall I flee from thy
presence?
8If I ascend to heaven, thou art there!
If I make my bed in Shē′ōl,
thou art there!
9If I take the wings of the morning
and dwell in the uttermost parts of
the sea,
10even there thy hand shall lead me
and thy right hand shall hold me.
11If I say, "Let only darkness cover me
and the light about me be night,'
12even the darkness is not dark to thee,
the night is bright as the day;
for darkness is as light with thee.

13For thou didst form my inward parts,
thou didst knit me together in my
mother's womb.
14I praise thee, for thou art fearful and
wonderful.*t*
Wonderful are thy works!
Thou knowest me right well;
15   my frame was not hidden from
thee,
when I was being made in secret,
intricately wrought in the depths
of the earth.
16Thy eyes beheld my unformed substance;
in thy book were written, every one
of them,
the days that were formed for me
when as yet there was none of
them.
17How precious to me are thy thoughts,
O God!
How vast is the sum of them!
18If I would count them, they are more
than the sand.

q Or you who are devastated
r Cn: Heb thou hast exalted thy word above all thy name
*s Syr Compare Gk Tg: Heb thou didst make me arrogant
in my soul with strength*
*t Cn Compare Gk Syr Jerome: Heb fearful things I am
wonderful*

When I awake, I am still with
   thee.[u]

[19]O that thou wouldst slay the wicked,
   O God,
   and that men of blood would de-
    part from me,
[20]men who maliciously defy thee,
   who lift themselves up against
    thee for evil![v]
[21]Do I not hate them that hate thee,
   O LORD?
   And do I not loathe them that rise
    up against thee?
[22]I hate them with perfect hatred;
   I count them my enemies.
[23]Search me, O God, and know my
   heart!
   Try me and know my thoughts!
[24]And see if there be any wicked[w]
    way in me,
   and lead me in the way ever-
    lasting![x]

To the choirmaster. A Psalm of David.

140   Deliver me, O LORD, from
        evil men;
   preserve me from violent men,
[2]who plan evil things in their heart,
   and stir up wars continually.
[3]They make their tongue sharp as a
   serpent's,
   and under their lips is the poison
    of vipers.   *Selah*

[4]Guard me, O LORD, from the hands
   of the wicked;
   preserve me from violent men,
   who have planned to trip up my
    feet.
[5]Arrogant men have hidden a trap for
   me,
   and with cords they have spread a
    net,[y]
   by the wayside they have set
    snares for me.   *Selah*

[6]I say to the LORD, Thou art my God;
   give ear to the voice of my sup-
    plications, O LORD!
[7]O LORD, my Lord, my strong deliverer,
   thou hast covered my head in the
    day of battle.
[8]Grant not, O LORD, the desires of the
   wicked;
   do not further his evil plot!
                Selah

[9]Those who surround me lift up their
   head,[z]
   let the mischief of their lips
    overwhelm them!
[10]Let burning coals fall upon them!
   Let them be cast into pits, no more
    to rise!
[11]Let not the slanderer be established
   in the land;
   let evil hunt down the violent man
    speedily!

[12]I know that the LORD maintains the
   cause of the afflicted,
   and executes justice for the needy.
[13]Surely the righteous shall give thanks
   to thy name;
   the upright shall dwell in thy
    presence.

A Psalm of David.

141   I call upon thee, O LORD;
        make haste to me!
   Give ear to my voice, when I call
    to thee!
[2]Let my prayer be counted as incense
   before thee,
   and the lifting up of my hands as
    an evening sacrifice!

[3]Set a guard over my mouth, O LORD,
   keep watch over the door of my
    lips!
[4]Incline not my heart to any evil,
   to busy myself with wicked deeds
   in company with men who work
    iniquity;
   and let me not eat of their dainties!

[5]Let a good man strike or rebuke me
   in kindness,
   but let the oil of the wicked never
    anoint my head;[a]
   for my prayer is continually[b]
    against their wicked deeds.
[6]When they are given over to those
   who shall condemn them,
   then they shall learn that the word
    of the LORD is true.
[7]As a rock which one cleaves and
   shatters on the land,

[u]Or *were I to come to the end I would still be with thee*
[v]Cn: Heb uncertain   [w]Heb *hurtful*
[x]Or *the ancient way*. Compare Jer 6.16
[y]Or *they have spread cords as a net*
[z]Cn Compare Gk: Heb *those who surround me are uplifted in head*
[a]Gk: Heb obscure
[b]Cn: Heb *for continually and my prayer*
140.3: Rom 3.13.   141.2: Rev 5.8; 8.3-4.

so shall their bones be strewn at
the mouth of Shē'ōl.*c*

8 But my eyes are toward thee, O LORD
God;
in thee I seek refuge; leave me not
defenseless!
9 Keep me from the trap which they
have laid for me,
and from the snares of evildoers!
10 Let the wicked together fall into their
own nets,
while I escape.

A Măs'kĭl of David, when he was in
the cave. A Prayer.

142 I cry with my voice to the
LORD,
with my voice I make supplication
to the LORD,
2 I pour out my complaint before him,
I tell my trouble before him.
3 When my spirit is faint,
thou knowest my way!

In the path where I walk
they have hidden a trap for me.
4 I look to the right and watch,*d*
but there is none who takes notice
of me;
no refuge remains to me,
no man cares for me.

5 I cry to thee, O LORD;
I say, Thou art my refuge,
my portion in the land of the living.
6 Give heed to my cry;
for I am brought very low!

Deliver me from my persecutors;
for they are too strong for me!
7 Bring me out of prison,
that I may give thanks to thy name!
The righteous will surround me;
for thou wilt deal bountifully
with me.

A Psalm of David.

143 Hear my prayer, O LORD;
give ear to my supplications!
In thy faithfulness answer me,
in thy righteousness!
2 Enter not into judgment with thy
servant;
for no man living is righteous
before thee.

3 For the enemy has pursued me;

he has crushed my life to the
ground;
he has made me sit in darkness
like those long dead.
4 Therefore my spirit faints within me;
my heart within me is appalled.

5 I remember the days of old,
I meditate on all that thou hast
done;
I muse on what thy hands have
wrought.
6 I stretch out my hands to thee;
my soul thirsts for thee like a
parched land.   *Selah*

7 Make haste to answer me, O LORD!
My spirit fails!
Hide not thy face from me,
lest I be like those who go down to
the Pit.
8 Let me hear in the morning of thy
steadfast love,
for in thee I put my trust.
Teach me the way I should go,
for to thee I lift up my soul.

9 Deliver me, O LORD, from my ene
mies!
I have fled to thee for refuge!
10 Teach me to do thy will,
for thou art my God!
Let thy good spirit lead me
on a level path!

11 For thy name's sake, O LORD, pre
serve my life!
In thy righteousness bring me out
of trouble!
12 And in thy steadfast love cut off
my enemies,
and destroy all my adversaries
for I am thy servant.

A Psalm of David.

144 Blessed be the LORD, my
rock,
who trains my hands for war,
and my fingers for battle;
2 my rock*f* and my fortress,
my stronghold and my deliverer
my shield and he in whom I take
refuge,
who subdues the peoples under
him.*g*

c The Hebrew of verses 5-7 is obscure
d Or *Look to the right and watch*
e One Heb Ms Gk: Heb *to thee I have hidden*
f With 18.2 2 Sam 22.2: Heb *my steadfast love*
g Another reading is *my people under me*
143.2: Ps 130.3; Rom 3.20; Gal 2.16.

3 O LORD, what is man that thou dost
    regard him,
    or the son of man that thou dost
    think of him?
4 Man is like a breath,
    his days are like a passing shadow.

5 Bow thy heavens, O LORD, and come
    down!
    Touch the mountains that they
    smoke!
6 Flash forth the lightning and scatter
    them,
    send out thy arrows and rout them!
7 Stretch forth thy hand from on high,
    rescue me and deliver me from the
    many waters,
    from the hand of aliens,
8 whose mouths speak lies,
    and whose right hand is a right
    hand of falsehood.

9 I will sing a new song to thee, O
    God;
    upon a ten-stringed harp I will
    play to thee,
10 who givest victory to kings,
    who rescuest David thy[h] servant.
11 Rescue me from the cruel sword,
    and deliver me from the hand of
    aliens,
    whose mouths speak lies,
    and whose right hand is a right
    hand of falsehood.

12 May our sons in their youth
    be like plants full grown,
    our daughters like corner pillars
    cut for the structure of a palace;
13 may our garners be full,
    providing all manner of store;
    may our sheep bring forth thousands
    and ten thousands in our fields;
14 may our cattle be heavy with young,
    suffering no mischance or failure
    in bearing;
    may there be no cry of distress in
    our streets!
15 Happy the people to whom such
    blessings fall!
    Happy the people whose God is the
    LORD!

A Song of Praise. Of David.

145 I will extol thee, my God
    and King,
    and bless thy name for ever and
    ever.

2 Every day I will bless thee,
    and praise thy name for ever and
    ever.
3 Great is the LORD, and greatly to be
    praised,
    and his greatness is unsearchable.

4 One generation shall laud thy works
    to another,
    and shall declare thy mighty acts.
5 On the glorious splendor of thy
    majesty,
    and on thy wondrous works, I will
    meditate.
6 Men shall proclaim the might of thy
    terrible acts,
    and I will declare thy greatness.
7 They shall pour forth the fame of
    thy abundant goodness,
    and shall sing aloud of thy right-
    eousness.

8 The LORD is gracious and merciful,
    slow to anger and abounding in
    steadfast love.
9 The LORD is good to all,
    and his compassion is over all that
    he has made.

10 All thy works shall give thanks to
    thee, O LORD,
    and all thy saints shall bless thee!
11 They shall speak of the glory of thy
    kingdom,
    and tell of thy power,
12 to make known to the sons of men
    thy[h] mighty deeds,
    and the glorious splendor of thy[h]
    kingdom.
13 Thy kingdom is an everlasting king-
    dom,
    and thy dominion endures through-
    out all generations.

The LORD is faithful in all his
    words,
    and gracious in all his deeds.[i]
14 The LORD upholds all who are
    falling,
    and raises up all who are bowed
    down.
15 The eyes of all look to thee,
    and thou givest them their food
    in due season.
16 Thou openest thy hand,
    thou satisfiest the desire of every
    living thing.

h Heb *his*
i These two lines are supplied by one Hebrew Ms, Gk and
Syr

¹⁷The Lord is just in all his ways,
and kind in all his doings.
¹⁸The Lord is near to all who call upon
him,
to all who call upon him in truth.
¹⁹He fulfils the desire of all who fear
him,
he also hears their cry, and saves
them.
²⁰The Lord preserves all who love him;
but all the wicked he will destroy.

²¹My mouth will speak the praise of the
Lord,
and let all flesh bless his holy
name for ever and ever.

146 Praise the Lord!
Praise the Lord, O my soul!
²I will praise the Lord as long as I
live;
I will sing praises to my God
while I have being.

³Put not your trust in princes,
in a son of man, in whom there is
no help.
⁴When his breath departs he returns
to his earth;
on that very day his plans perish.

⁵Happy is he whose help is the God
of Jacob,
whose hope is in the Lord his
God,
⁶who made heaven and earth,
the sea, and all that is in them;
who keeps faith for ever;
⁷ who executes justice for the oppressed;
who gives food to the hungry.

The Lord sets the prisoners free;
⁸ the Lord opens the eyes of the
blind.
The Lord lifts up those who are
bowed down;
the Lord loves the righteous.
⁹The Lord watches over the sojourners,
he upholds the widow and the
fatherless;
but the way of the wicked he
brings to ruin.

¹⁰The Lord will reign for ever,
thy God, O Zion, to all generations.
Praise the Lord!

147 Praise the Lord!
For it is good to sing praises
to our God;
for he is gracious, and a song of
praise is seemly.
²The Lord builds up Jerusalem;
he gathers the outcasts of Israel.
³He heals the brokenhearted,
and binds up their wounds.
⁴He determines the number of the
stars,
he gives to all of them their names.
⁵Great is our Lord, and abundant in
power;
his understanding is beyond
measure.
⁶The Lord lifts up the downtrodden,
he casts the wicked to the ground.

⁷Sing to the Lord with thanksgiving;
make melody to our God upon the
lyre!
⁸He covers the heavens with clouds,
he prepares rain for the earth,
he makes grass grow upon the
hills.
⁹He gives to the beasts their food,
and to the young ravens which
cry.
¹⁰His delight is not in the strength
of the horse,
nor his pleasure in the legs of a
man;
¹¹but the Lord takes pleasure in those
who fear him,
in those who hope in his steadfast
love.

¹²Praise the Lord, O Jerusalem!
Praise your God, O Zion!
¹³For he strengthens the bars of your
gates;
he blesses your sons within you.
¹⁴He makes peace in your borders;
he fills you with the finest of the
wheat.
¹⁵He sends forth his command to the
earth;
his word runs swiftly.
¹⁶He gives snow like wool;
he scatters hoarfrost like ashes.
¹⁷He casts forth his ice like morsels;
who can stand before his cold?
¹⁸He sends forth his word, and melts
them;
he makes his wind blow, and the
waters flow.
¹⁹He declares his word to Jacob,
his statutes and ordinances to
Israel.

He has not dealt thus with any other
    nation;
    they do not know his ordinances.
Praise the Lord!

148 Praise the Lord!
    Praise the Lord from the
    heavens,
  praise him in the heights!
Praise him, all his angels,
  praise him, all his host!

Praise him, sun and moon,
  praise him, all you shining stars!
Praise him, you highest heavens,
  and you waters above the heavens!

Let them praise the name of the
    Lord!
  For he commanded and they
    were created.
And he established them for ever
    and ever;
  he fixed their bounds which
    cannot be passed.[j]

Praise the Lord from the earth,
  you sea monsters and all deeps,
fire and hail, snow and frost,
  stormy wind fulfilling his com-
    mand!

Mountains and all hills,
  fruit trees and all cedars!
Beasts and all cattle,
  creeping things and flying birds!

Kings of the earth and all peoples,
  princes and all rulers of the earth!
Young men and maidens together,
  old men and children!

Let them praise the name of the
    Lord,
  for his name alone is exalted;
  his glory is above earth and
    heaven.
He has raised up a horn for his
    people,
  praise for all his saints,
  for the people of Israel who are
    near to him.
Praise the Lord!

149 Praise the Lord!
    Sing to the Lord a new song,
  his praise in the assembly of
    the faithful!
[2] Let Israel be glad in his Maker,
  let the sons of Zion rejoice in their
    King!
[3] Let them praise his name with
    dancing,
  making melody to him with
    timbrel and lyre!
[4] For the Lord takes pleasure in his
    people;
  he adorns the humble with vic-
    tory.
[5] Let the faithful exult in glory;
  let them sing for joy on their
    couches.
[6] Let the high praises of God be in their
    throats
  and two-edged swords in their
    hands,
[7] to wreak vengeance on the nations
  and chastisement on the peoples,
[8] to bind their kings with chains
  and their nobles with fetters of
    iron,
[9] to execute on them the judgment
    written!
  This is glory for all his faithful
    ones.
  Praise the Lord!

150 Praise the Lord!
    Praise God in his sanctuary;
  praise him in his mighty firma-
    ment!
[2] Praise him for his mighty deeds;
  praise him according to his ex-
    ceeding greatness!
[3] Praise him with trumpet sound;
  praise him with lute and harp!
[4] Praise him with timbrel and dance;
  praise him with strings and pipe!
[5] Praise him with sounding cymbals;
  praise him with loud clashing
    cymbals!
[6] Let everything that breathes praise
    the Lord!
  Praise the Lord!

[j] Or *he set a law which cannot pass away*

The Proverbs

1 The proverbs of Solomon, son of David, king of Israel:

[2] That men may know wisdom and instruction,
understand words of insight,
[3] receive instruction in wise dealing,
righteousness, justice, and equity;
[4] that prudence may be given to the simple,
knowledge and discretion to the youth—
[5] the wise man also may hear and increase in learning,
and the man of understanding acquire skill,
[6] to understand a proverb and a figure,
the words of the wise and their riddles.

[7] The fear of the LORD is the beginning of knowledge;
fools despise wisdom and instruction.

[8] Hear, my son, your father's instruction,
and reject not your mother's teaching;
[9] for they are a fair garland for your head,
and pendants for your neck.
[10] My son, if sinners entice you,
do not consent.
[11] If they say, "Come with us, let us lie in wait for blood,
let us wantonly ambush the innocent;
[12] like Shē′ōl let us swallow them alive
and whole, like those who go down to the Pit;
[13] we shall find all precious goods,
we shall fill our houses with spoil;
[14] throw in your lot among us,
we will all have one purse"—
[15] my son, do not walk in the way with them,
hold back your foot from their paths;
[16] for their feet run to evil,
and they make haste to shed blood.
[17] For in vain is a net spread
in the sight of any bird;
[18] but these men lie in wait for their own blood,
they set an ambush for their ow[n] lives.
[19] Such are the ways of all who g[et] gain by violence;
it takes away the life of its po[s]sessors.

[20] Wisdom cries aloud in the stree[t]
in the markets she raises her voic[e]
[21] on the top of the walls[a] she crie[s] out;
at the entrance of the city gate[s] she speaks:
[22] "How long, O simple ones, will yo[u] love being simple?
How long will scoffers delight i[n] their scoffing
and fools hate knowledge?
[23] Give heed[b] to my reproof;
behold, I will pour out my thought[s] to you;
I will make my words known [to] you.
[24] Because I have called and you re[fused to listen,
have stretched out my hand an[d] no one has heeded,
[25] and you have ignored all my couns[el]
and would have none of my r[e]proof,
[26] I also will laugh at your calamit[y]
I will mock when panic strike[s] you,
[27] when panic strikes you like a storm]
and your calamity comes like [a] whirlwind,
when distress and anguish com[e] upon you.
[28] Then they will call upon me, b[ut] I will not answer;
they will seek me diligently b[ut] will not find me.
[29] Because they hated knowledge
and did not choose the fear of th[e] LORD,
[30] would have none of my couns[el]
and despised all my reproof,
[31] therefore they shall eat the fruit [of] their way
and be sated with their own d[e]vices.
[32] For the simple are killed by the[ir] turning away,

a Heb uncertain *b* Heb *Turn* *c* Heb *spirit*
1.20, 21: 8.1-3.

and the complacence of fools
destroys them;
[33]but he who listens to me will dwell
secure
and will be at ease, without dread
of evil."

2 My son, if you receive my words
and treasure up my commandments with you,
[2]making your ear attentive to wisdom
and inclining your heart to understanding;
[3]yes, if you cry out for insight
and raise your voice for understanding,
[4]if you seek it like silver
and search for it as for hidden
treasures;
[5]then you will understand the fear
of the LORD
and find the knowledge of God.
[6]For the LORD gives wisdom;
from his mouth come knowledge
and understanding;
[7]he stores up sound wisdom for the
upright;
he is a shield to those who walk
in integrity,
[8]guarding the paths of justice
and preserving the way of his
saints.
[9]Then you will understand righteousness and justice
and equity, every good path;
[10]for wisdom will come into your
heart,
and knowledge will be pleasant
to your soul;
[11]discretion will watch over you;
understanding will guard you;
[12]delivering you from the way of evil,
from men of perverted speech,
[13]who forsake the paths of uprightness
to walk in the ways of darkness,
[14]who rejoice in doing evil
and delight in the perverseness of
evil;
[15]men whose paths are crooked,
and who are devious in their ways.

[16]You will be saved from the loose[d]
woman,
from the adventuress[e] with her
smooth words,
[17]who forsakes the companion of her
youth
and forgets the covenant of her
God;
[18]for her house sinks down to death,

and her paths to the shades;
[19]none who go to her come back
nor do they regain the paths of
life.

[20]So you will walk in the way of good
men
and keep to the paths of the
righteous.
[21]For the upright will inhabit the land,
and men of integrity will remain in
it;
[22]but the wicked will be cut off from
the land,
and the treacherous will be
rooted out of it.

3 My son, do not forget my teaching,
but let your heart keep my commandments;
[2]for length of days and years of life
and abundant welfare will they
give you.

[3]Let not loyalty and faithfulness
forsake you;
bind them about your neck,
write them on the tablet of your
heart.
[4]So you will find favor and good
repute[f]
in the sight of God and man.

[5]Trust in the LORD with all your heart,
and do not rely on your own insight.
[6]In all your ways acknowledge him,
and he will make straight your
paths.
[7]Be not wise in your own eyes;
fear the LORD, and turn away from
evil.
[8]It will be healing to your flesh[g]
and refreshment[h] to your bones.

[9]Honor the LORD with your substance
and with the first fruits of all your
produce;
[10]then your barns will be filled with
plenty,
and your vats will be bursting
with wine.

[11]My son, do not despise the LORD's
discipline
or be weary of his reproof,
[12]for the LORD reproves him whom
he loves,

[d]Heb *strange* [e]Heb *foreign woman*
[f]Cn: Heb *understanding* [g]Heb *navel* [h]Or *medicine*
3.4: Rom 12.17. 3.7: Rom 12.16. 3.11, 12: Heb 12.5, 6.

as a father the son in whom he delights.

13 Happy is the man who finds wisdom,
　and the man who gets understand-
　　ing,
14 for the gain from it is better than gain
　　from silver
　and its profit better than gold.
15 She is more precious than jewels,
　and nothing you desire can com-
　　pare with her.
16 Long life is in her right hand;
　in her left hand are riches and
　　honor.
17 Her ways are ways of pleasantness,
　and all her paths are peace.
18 She is a tree of life to those who lay
　　hold of her;
　those who hold her fast are called
　　happy.

19 The LORD by wisdom founded the
　　earth;
　by understanding he established
　　the heavens;
20 by his knowledge the deeps broke
　　forth,
　and the clouds drop down the dew.

21 My son, keep sound wisdom and
　　discretion;
　let them not escape from your
　　sight,^{i}
22 and they will be life for your soul
　and adornment for your neck.
23 Then you will walk on your way
　　securely
　and your foot will not stumble.
24 If you sit down,^{j} you will not be
　　afraid;
　when you lie down, your sleep will
　　be sweet.
25 Do not be afraid of sudden panic,
　or of the ruin^k of the wicked,
　　when it comes;
26 for the LORD will be your confidence
　and will keep your foot from being
　　caught.
27 Do not withhold good from those to
　　whom it^l is due,
　when it is in your power to do it.

28 Do not say to your neighbor, "Go,
　and come again,
　tomorrow I will give it" – when
　　you have it with you.
29 Do not plan evil against your
　　neighbor
　who dwells trustingly beside you.

30 Do not contend with a man for no
　　reason,
　when he has done you no harm.
31 Do not envy a man of violence
　and do not choose any of his ways;
32 for the perverse man is an abomina-
　　tion to the LORD,
　but the upright are in his con-
　　fidence.
33 The LORD's curse is on the house of
　　the wicked,
　but he blesses the abode of the
　　righteous.
34 Toward the scorners he is scornful,
　but to the humble he shows favor.
35 The wise will inherit honor,
　but fools get^m disgrace.

4 Hear, O sons, a father's instruc-
　　tion,
　and be attentive, that you may
　　gain^n insight;
2 for I give you good precepts:
　do not forsake my teaching.
3 When I was a son with my father,
　tender, the only one in the sight of
　　my mother,
4 he taught me, and said to me,
　"Let your heart hold fast my words;
　keep my commandments, and live;
5 do not forget, and do not turn away
　from the words of my mouth.
　Get wisdom; get insight.^{o}
6 Do not forsake her, and she will
　　keep you;
　love her, and she will guard you.
7 The beginning of wisdom is this:
　　Get wisdom,
　and whatever you get, get insight.
8 Prize her highly,^{p} and she will exalt
　　you;
　she will honor you if you embrace
　　her.
9 She will place on your head a fair
　　garland;
　she will bestow on you a beautiful
　　crown."

10 Hear, my son, and accept my words,
　that the years of your life may be
　　many.
11 I have taught you the way of wis-
　　dom;
　I have led you in the paths of
　　uprightness.

^{i} Reversing the order of the clauses　^{j} Gk: Heb *lie down*
^{k} Heb *storm*　^{l} Heb *Do not withhold good from its owner*
^{m} Cn: Heb *exalt*　^{n} Heb *know*
^{o} Reversing the order of the lines
^{p} The meaning of the Hebrew is uncertain
3.34 (Gk): Jas 4.6; 1 Pet 5.5.

¹²When you walk, your step will not
be hampered;
and if you run, you will not
stumble.
¹³Keep hold of instruction, do not let
go;
guard her, for she is your life.
¹⁴Do not enter the path of the wicked,
and do not walk in the way of evil
men.
¹⁵Avoid it; do not go on it;
turn away from it and pass on.
¹⁶For they cannot sleep unless they
have done wrong;
they are robbed of sleep unless
they have made some one
stumble.
¹⁷For they eat the bread of wickedness
and drink the wine of violence.
¹⁸But the path of the righteous is like
the light of dawn,
which shines brighter and brighter
until full day.
¹⁹The way of the wicked is like deep
darkness;
they do not know over what they
stumble.

²⁰My son, be attentive to my words;
incline your ear to my sayings.
²¹Let them not escape from your sight;
keep them within your heart.
²²For they are life to him who finds
them,
and healing to all his flesh.
²³Keep your heart with all vigilance;
for from it flow the springs of life.
²⁴Put away from you crooked speech,
and put devious talk far from you.
²⁵Let your eyes look directly forward,
and your gaze be straight before
you.
²⁶Take heed to⁹ the path of your feet,
then all your ways will be sure.
²⁷Do not swerve to the right or to the
left;
turn your foot away from evil.

5 My son, be attentive to my wisdom,
incline your ear to my understanding;
²that you may keep discretion,
and your lips may guard knowledge.
³For the lips of a loose woman drip
honey,
and her speechʳ is smoother than
oil;

⁴but in the end she is bitter as wormwood,
sharp as a two-edged sword.
⁵Her feet go down to death;
her steps follow the path to⁸ Shēʹōl;
⁶she does not take heed toᵗ the path
of life;
her ways wander, and she does
not know it.

⁷And now, O sons, listen to me,
and do not depart from the words
of my mouth.
⁸Keep your way far from her,
and do not go near the door of her
house;
⁹lest you give your honor to others
and your years to the merciless;
¹⁰lest strangers take their fill of your
strength,ᵘ
and your labors go to the house of
an alien;
¹¹and at the end of your life you groan,
when your flesh and body are consumed,
¹²and you say, "How I hated discipline,
and my heart despised reproof!
¹³I did not listen to the voice of my
teachers
or incline my ear to my instructors.
¹⁴I was at the point of utter ruin
in the assembled congregation."

¹⁵Drink water from your own cistern,
flowing water from your own well.
¹⁶Should your springs be scattered
abroad,
streams of water in the streets?
¹⁷Let them be for yourself alone,
and not for strangers with you.
¹⁸Let your fountain be blessed,
and rejoice in the wife of your
youth,
¹⁹ a lovely hind, a graceful doe.
Let her affection fill you at all times
with delight,
be infatuated always with her
love.
²⁰Why should you be infatuated, my
son, with a loose woman
and embrace the bosom of an
adventuress?
²¹For a man's ways are before the
eyes of the LORD,
and he watchesᵛ all his paths.

⁹The meaning of the Hebrew word is uncertain
ʳHeb *palate* ˢHeb *lay hold of*
ᵗThe meaning of the Hebrew word is uncertain
ᵘOr *wealth*
ᵛThe meaning of the Hebrew word is uncertain
4.26 (Gk): Heb 12.13.

²² The iniquities of the wicked ensnare him,
and he is caught in the toils of his sin.
²³ He dies for lack of discipline,
and because of his great folly he is lost.

6 My son, if you have become surety for your neighbor,
have given your pledge for a stranger;
² if you are snared in the utterance of your lips,[w]
caught in the words of your mouth;
³ then do this, my son, and save yourself,
for you have come into your neighbor's power:
go, hasten,[x] and importune your neighbor.
⁴ Give your eyes no sleep
and your eyelids no slumber;
⁵ save yourself like a gazelle from the hunter,[y]
like a bird from the hand of the fowler.

⁶ Go to the ant, O sluggard;
consider her ways, and be wise.
⁷ Without having any chief,
officer or ruler,
⁸ she prepares her food in summer,
and gathers her sustenance in harvest.
⁹ How long will you lie there, O sluggard?
When will you arise from your sleep?
¹⁰ A little sleep, a little slumber,
a little folding of the hands to rest,
¹¹ and poverty will come upon you like a vagabond,
and want like an armed man.

¹² A worthless person, a wicked man,
goes about with crooked speech,
¹³ winks with his eyes, scrapes[z] with his feet,
points with his finger,
¹⁴ with perverted heart devises evil,
continually sowing discord;
¹⁵ therefore calamity will come upon him suddenly;
in a moment he will be broken beyond healing.

¹⁶ There are six things which the LORD hates,
seven which are an abomination to him:
¹⁷ haughty eyes, a lying tongue,
and hands that shed innocent blood,
¹⁸ a heart that devises wicked plans,
feet that make haste to run to evil,
¹⁹ a false witness who breathes out lies,
and a man who sows discord among brothers.

²⁰ My son, keep your father's commandment,
and forsake not your mother's teaching.
²¹ Bind them upon your heart always;
tie them about your neck.
²² When you walk, they[a] will lead you;
when you lie down, they[a] will watch over you;
and when you awake, they[a] will talk with you.
²³ For the commandment is a lamp and the teaching a light,
and the reproofs of discipline are the way of life,
²⁴ to preserve you from the evil woman,
from the smooth tongue of the adventuress.
²⁵ Do not desire her beauty in your heart,
and do not let her capture you with her eyelashes;
²⁶ for a harlot may be hired for a loaf of bread,[b]
but an adulteress[c] stalks a man's very life.
²⁷ Can a man carry fire in his bosom
and his clothes not be burned?
²⁸ Or can one walk upon hot coals
and his feet not be scorched?
²⁹ So is he who goes in to his neighbor's wife;
none who touches her will go unpunished.
³⁰ Do not men despise[d] a thief if he steals
to satisfy his appetite when he is hungry?
³¹ And if he is caught, he will pay sevenfold;
he will give all the goods of his house.
³² He who commits adultery has no sense;

[w] Cn Compare Gk Syr: Heb *the words of your mouth*
[x] Or *humble yourself*   [y] Cn: Heb *hand*   [z] Or *taps*   [a] Heb *it*
[b] Cn Compare Gk Syr Vg Tg: Heb *for because of a harlot to a piece of bread*
[c] Heb *a man's wife*   [d] Or *Men do not despise*

he who does it destroys himself.
[33] Wounds and dishonor will he get,
and his disgrace will not be wiped
away.
[34] For jealousy makes a man furious,
and he will not spare when he
takes revenge.
[35] He will accept no compensation,
nor be appeased though you multiply gifts.

7 My son, keep my words
and treasure up my commandments with you;
[2] keep my commandments and live,
keep my teachings as the apple
of your eye;
[3] bind them on your fingers,
write them on the tablet of your
heart.
[4] Say to wisdom, "You are my sister,"
and call insight your intimate
friend;
[5] to preserve you from the loose
woman,
from the adventuress with her
smooth words.

[6] For at the window of my house
I have looked out through my
lattice,
[7] and I have seen among the simple,
I have perceived among the
youths,
a young man without sense,
[8] passing along the street near her
corner,
taking the road to her house
[9] in the twilight, in the evening,
at the time of night and darkness.

[10] And lo, a woman meets him,
dressed as a harlot, wily of heart.[e]
[11] She is loud and wayward,
her feet do not stay at home;
[12] now in the street, now in the market,
and at every corner she lies in
wait.
[13] She seizes him and kisses him,
and with impudent face she says to
him:
[14] "I had to offer sacrifices,
and today I have paid my vows;
[15] so now I have come out to meet
you,
to seek you eagerly, and I have
found you.
[16] I have decked my couch with coverings,
colored spreads of Egyptian linen;

[17] I have perfumed my bed with myrrh,
aloes, and cinnamon.
[18] Come, let us take our fill of love till
morning;
let us delight ourselves with love.
[19] For my husband is not at home;
he has gone on a long journey;
[20] he took a bag of money with him;
at full moon he will come home."

[21] With much seductive speech she
persuades him;
with her smooth talk she compels
him.
[22] All at once he follows her,
as an ox goes to the slaughter,
or as a stag is caught fast[f]
[23] till an arrow pierces its entrails;
as a bird rushes into a snare;
he does not know that it will cost
him his life.

[24] And now, O sons, listen to me,
and be attentive to the words of
my mouth.
[25] Let not your heart turn aside to her
ways,
do not stray into her paths;
[26] for many a victim has she laid low;
yea, all her slain are a mighty host.
[27] Her house is the way to Shē′ol,
going down to the chambers of
death.

8 Does not wisdom call,
does not understanding raise her
voice?
[2] On the heights beside the way,
in the paths she takes her stand;
[3] beside the gates in front of the town,
at the entrance of the portals she
cries aloud:
[4] "To you, O men, I call,
and my cry is to the sons of men.
[5] O simple ones, learn prudence;
O foolish men, pay attention.
[6] Hear, for I will speak noble things,
and from my lips will come what is
right;
[7] for my mouth will utter truth;
wickedness is an abomination to
my lips.
[8] All the words of my mouth are
righteous;
there is nothing twisted or crooked
in them.
[9] They are all straight to him who
understands

e The meaning of the Hebrew is uncertain
f Cn Compare Gk: Heb uncertain **8.1–3:** 1.20, 21.

and right to those who find knowledge.

¹⁰Take my instruction instead of silver,
and knowledge rather than choice gold;
¹¹for wisdom is better than jewels,
and all that you may desire cannot compare with her.
¹²I, wisdom, dwell in prudence,*g*
and I find knowledge and discretion.
¹³The fear of the Lord is hatred of evil.
Pride and arrogance and the way of evil
and perverted speech I hate.
¹⁴I have counsel and sound wisdom,
I have insight, I have strength.
¹⁵By me kings reign,
and rulers decree what is just;
¹⁶by me princes rule,
and nobles govern*h* the earth.
¹⁷I love those who love me,
and those who seek me diligently find me.
¹⁸Riches and honor are with me,
enduring wealth and prosperity.
¹⁹My fruit is better than gold, even fine gold,
and my yield than choice silver.
²⁰I walk in the way of righteousness,
in the paths of justice,
²¹endowing with wealth those who love me,
and filling their treasuries.

²²The Lord created me at the beginning of his work,*i*
the first of his acts of old.
²³Ages ago I was set up,
at the first, before the beginning of the earth.
²⁴When there were no depths I was brought forth,
when there were no springs abounding with water.
²⁵Before the mountains had been shaped,
before the hills, I was brought forth;
²⁶before he had made the earth with its fields,*j*
or the first of the dust*j* of the world.
²⁷When he established the heavens, I was there,
when he drew a circle on the face of the deep,
²⁸when he made firm the skies above,

when he established*j* the fountains of the deep,
²⁹when he assigned to the sea its limit,
so that the waters might not transgress his command,
when he marked out the foundations of the earth,
³⁰then I was beside him, like a master workman;*l*
and I was daily his*m* delight,
rejoicing before him always,
³¹rejoicing in his inhabited world
and delighting in the sons of men.

³²And now, my sons, listen to me:
happy are those who keep my ways.
³³Hear instruction and be wise,
and do not neglect it.
³⁴Happy is the man who listens to me,
watching daily at my gates,
waiting beside my doors.
³⁵For he who finds me finds life
and obtains favor from the Lord;
³⁶but he who misses me injures himself;
all who hate me love death."

9 Wisdom has built her house,
she has set up*n* her seven pillars.
²She has slaughtered her beasts,
she has mixed her wine,
she has also set her table.
³She has sent out her maids to call
from the highest places in the town,
⁴"Whoever is simple, let him turn in here!"
To him who is without sense she says,
⁵"Come, eat of my bread
and drink of the wine I have mixed.
⁶Leave simpleness,*o* and live,
and walk in the way of insight."

⁷He who corrects a scoffer gets himself abuse,
and he who reproves a wicked man incurs injury.
⁸Do not reprove a scoffer, or he will hate you;
reprove a wise man, and he will love you.
⁹Give instruction*p* to a wise man,
and he will be still wiser;

*g*Heb obscure
*h*Gk: Heb *all the governors of*   *i*Heb *way*
*j*The meaning of the Hebrew is uncertain
*l*Another reading is *little child*   *m*Gk: Heb lacks *his*
*n*Gk Syr Tg: Heb *hewn*   *o*Gk Syr Vg Tg: Heb *simple ones*
*p*Heb lacks *instruction*

teach a righteous man and he will
increase in learning.
[10] The fear of the LORD is the beginning
of wisdom,
and the knowledge of the Holy
One is insight.
[11] For by me your days will be multiplied,
and years will be added to your
life.
[12] If you are wise, you are wise for
yourself;
if you scoff, you alone will bear
it.

[13] A foolish woman is noisy;
she is wanton[q] and knows no
shame.[r]
[14] She sits at the door of her house,
she takes a seat on the high
places of the town,
[15] calling to those who pass by,
who are going straight on their
way,
[16] "Whoever is simple, let him turn in
here!"
And to him who is without sense
she says,
[17] "Stolen water is sweet,
and bread eaten in secret is pleasant."
[18] But he does not know that the dead[s]
are there,
that her guests are in the depths
of She′ōl.

10   The proverbs of Solomon.

A wise son makes a glad father,
but a foolish son is a sorrow to
his mother.
[2] Treasures gained by wickedness
do not profit,
but righteousness delivers from
death.
[3] The LORD does not let the righteous
go hungry,
but he thwarts the craving of the
wicked.
[4] A slack hand causes poverty,
but the hand of the diligent makes
rich.
[5] A son who gathers in summer is
prudent,
but a son who sleeps in harvest
brings shame.
[6] Blessings are on the head of the
righteous,
but the mouth of the wicked conceals violence.

[7] The memory of the righteous is a
blessing,
but the name of the wicked will
rot.
[8] The wise of heart will heed commandments,
but a prating fool will come to
ruin.
[9] He who walks in integrity walks
securely,
but he who perverts his ways will
be found out.
[10] He who winks the eye causes trouble,
but he who boldly reproves makes
peace.[t]
[11] The mouth of the righteous is a
fountain of life,
but the mouth of the wicked conceals violence.
[12] Hatred stirs up strife,
but love covers all offenses.
[13] On the lips of him who has understanding wisdom is found,
but a rod is for the back of him
who lacks sense.
[14] Wise men lay up knowledge,
but the babbling of a fool brings
ruin near.
[15] A rich man's wealth is his strong
city;
the poverty of the poor is their
ruin.
[16] The wage of the righteous leads to
life,
the gain of the wicked to sin.
[17] He who heeds instruction is on the
path to life,
but he who rejects reproof goes
astray.
[18] He who conceals hatred has lying
lips,
and he who utters slander is a fool.
[19] When words are many, transgression is not lacking,
but he who restrains his lips is
prudent.
[20] The tongue of the righteous is choice
silver;
the mind of the wicked is of little
worth.
[21] The lips of the righteous feed many,
but fools die for lack of sense.
[22] The blessing of the LORD makes
rich,
and he adds no sorrow with it.[u]

[q] Cn Compare Syr Vg: The meaning of the Hebrew is uncertain   [r] Gk Syr: The meaning of the Hebrew is uncertain
[s] Heb *shades*
[t] Gk: Heb *but a prating fool will come to ruin*
[u] Or *and toil adds nothing to it*
10.12: Jas 5.20; 1 Pet 4.8.

²³It is like sport to a fool to do wrong,
but wise conduct is pleasure to a man of understanding.

²⁴What the wicked dreads will come upon him,
but the desire of the righteous will be granted.

²⁵When the tempest passes, the wicked is no more,
but the righteous is established for ever.

²⁶Like vinegar to the teeth, and smoke to the eyes,
so is the sluggard to those who send him.

²⁷The fear of the LORD prolongs life,
but the years of the wicked will be short.

²⁸The hope of the righteous ends in gladness,
but the expectation of the wicked comes to nought.

²⁹The LORD is a stronghold to him whose way is upright,
but destruction to evildoers.

³⁰The righteous will never be removed,
but the wicked will not dwell in the land.

³¹The mouth of the righteous brings forth wisdom,
but the perverse tongue will be cut off.

³²The lips of the righteous know what is acceptable,
but the mouth of the wicked, what is perverse.

11 A false balance is an abomination to the LORD,
but a just weight is his delight.

²When pride comes, then comes disgrace;
but with the humble is wisdom.

³The integrity of the upright guides them,
but the crookedness of the treacherous destroys them.

⁴Riches do not profit in the day of wrath,
but righteousness delivers from death.

⁵The righteousness of the blameless keeps his way straight,
but the wicked falls by his own wickedness.

⁶The righteousness of the upright delivers them,
but the treacherous are taken captive by their lust.

⁷When the wicked dies, his hope perishes,
and the expectation of the godless comes to nought.

⁸The righteous is delivered from trouble,
and the wicked gets into it instead.

⁹With his mouth the godless man would destroy his neighbor,
but by knowledge the righteous are delivered.

¹⁰When it goes well with the righteous, the city rejoices;
and when the wicked perish there are shouts of gladness.

¹¹By the blessing of the upright a city is exalted,
but it is overthrown by the mouth of the wicked.

¹²He who belittles his neighbor lacks sense,
but a man of understanding remains silent.

¹³He who goes about as a talebearer reveals secrets,
but he who is trustworthy in spirit keeps a thing hidden.

¹⁴Where there is no guidance, a people falls;
but in an abundance of counselors there is safety.

¹⁵He who gives surety for a stranger will smart for it,
but he who hates suretyship is secure.

¹⁶A gracious woman gets honor,
and violent men get riches.

¹⁷A man who is kind benefits himself,
but a cruel man hurts himself.

¹⁸A wicked man earns deceptive wages,
but one who sows righteousness gets a sure reward.

¹⁹He who is steadfast in righteousness will live,
but he who pursues evil will die.

²⁰Men of perverse mind are an abomination to the LORD,
but those of blameless ways are his delight.

²¹Be assured, an evil man will not go unpunished,
but those who are righteous will be delivered.

²²Like a gold ring in a swine's snout is a beautiful woman without discretion.

²³The desire of the righteous ends only in good;

the expectation of the wicked in
wrath.
24 One man gives freely, yet grows all
the richer;
another withholds what he should
give, and only suffers want.
25 A liberal man will be enriched,
and one who waters will himself
be watered.
26 The people curse him who holds
back grain,
but a blessing is on the head of him
who sells it.
27 He who diligently seeks good seeks
favor,
but evil comes to him who searches
for it.
28 He who trusts in his riches will
wither, *v*
but the righteous will flourish like
a green leaf.
29 He who troubles his household will
inherit wind,
and the fool will be servant to the
wise.
30 The fruit of the righteous is a tree of
life,
but lawlessness *w* takes away lives.
31 If the righteous is requited on earth,
how much more the wicked and
the sinner!

12 Whoever loves discipline loves
knowledge,
but he who hates reproof is stupid.
2 A good man obtains favor from the
LORD,
but a man of evil devices he condemns.
3 A man is not established by wickedness,
but the root of the righteous will
never be moved.
4 A good wife is the crown of her
husband,
but she who brings shame is like
rottenness in his bones.
5 The thoughts of the righteous are
just;
the counsels of the wicked are
treacherous.
6 The words of the wicked lie in wait
for blood,
but the mouth of the upright
delivers men.
7 The wicked are overthrown and are
no more,
but the house of the righteous will
stand.
8 A man is commended according to
his good sense,

but one of perverse mind is despised.
9 Better is a man of humble standing
who works for himself
than one who plays the great man
but lacks bread.
10 A righteous man has regard for the
life of his beast,
but the mercy of the wicked is
cruel.
11 He who tills his land will have plenty
of bread,
but he who follows worthless
pursuits has no sense.
12 The strong tower of the wicked
comes to ruin,
but the root of the righteous
stands firm. *x*
13 An evil man is ensnared by the
transgression of his lips,
but the righteous escapes from
trouble.
14 From the fruit of his words a man is
satisfied with good,
and the work of a man's hand
comes back to him.
15 The way of a fool is right in his own
eyes,
but a wise man listens to advice.
16 The vexation of a fool is known at
once,
but the prudent man ignores an
insult.
17 He who speaks the truth gives honest
evidence,
but a false witness utters deceit.
18 There is one whose rash words are
like sword thrusts,
but the tongue of the wise brings
healing.
19 Truthful lips endure for ever,
but a lying tongue is but for a
moment.
20 Deceit is in the heart of those who
devise evil,
but those who plan good have joy.
21 No ill befalls the righteous,
but the wicked are filled with
trouble.
22 Lying lips are an abomination to
the LORD,
but those who act faithfully are
his delight.
23 A prudent man conceals his knowledge,
but fools *y* proclaim their folly.
24 The hand of the diligent will rule,

v Cn: Heb *fall*   *w* Cn Compare Gk Syr: Heb *a wise man*
x Cn: The Hebrew of verse 12 is obscure
y Heb *the heart of fools*   11.31 (Gk): 1 Pet 4.18.

while the slothful will be put to
forced labor.

25 Anxiety in a man's heart weighs him
down,
but a good word makes him glad.

26 A righteous man turns away from
evil,[z]
but the way of the wicked leads
them astray.

27 A slothful man will not catch his
prey,[a]
but the diligent man will get precious wealth.[b]

28 In the path of righteousness is life,
but the way of error leads to death.[c]

13 A wise son hears his father's
instruction,
but a scoffer does not listen to
rebuke.

2 From the fruit of his mouth a good
man eats good,
but the desire of the treacherous
is for violence.

3 He who guards his mouth preserves
his life;
he who opens wide his lips comes
to ruin.

4 The soul of the sluggard craves,
and gets nothing,
while the soul of the diligent is
richly supplied.

5 A righteous man hates falsehood,
but a wicked man acts shamefully
and disgracefully.

6 Righteousness guards him whose
way is upright,
but sin overthrows the wicked.

7 One man pretends to be rich, yet
has nothing;
another pretends to be poor,
yet has great wealth.

8 The ransom of a man's life is his
wealth,
but a poor man has no means of
redemption.[d]

9 The light of the righteous rejoices,
but the lamp of the wicked will be
put out.

10 By insolence the heedless make
strife,
but with those who take advice is
wisdom.

11 Wealth hastily gotten[e] will dwindle,
but he who gathers little by little
will increase it.

12 Hope deferred makes the heart sick,
but a desire fulfilled is a tree of
life.

13 He who despises the word brings
destruction on himself,

but he who respects the commandment will be rewarded.

14 The teaching of the wise is a fountain
of life,
that one may avoid the snares of
death.

15 Good sense wins favor,
but the way of the faithless is
their ruin.[f]

16 In everything a prudent man acts
with knowledge,
but a fool flaunts his folly.

17 A bad messenger plunges men into
trouble,
but a faithful envoy brings healing.

18 Poverty and disgrace come to him
who ignores instruction,
but he who heeds reproof is
honored.

19 A desire fulfilled is sweet to the soul;
but to turn away from evil is an
abomination to fools.

20 He who walks with wise men becomes wise,
but the companion of fools will
suffer harm.

21 Misfortune pursues sinners,
but prosperity rewards the righteous.

22 A good man leaves an inheritance
to his children's children,
but the sinner's wealth is laid up
for the righteous.

23 The fallow ground of the poor yields
much food,
but it is swept away through
injustice.

24 He who spares the rod hates his son,
but he who loves him is diligent
to discipline him.

25 The righteous has enough to satisfy
his appetite,
but the belly of the wicked suffers
want.

14 Wisdom[g] builds her house,
but folly with her own hands
tears it down.

2 He who walks in uprightness fears
the LORD,
but he who is devious in his ways
despises him.

3 The talk of a fool is a rod for his back,[h]
but the lips of the wise will preserve them.

z Cn: The meaning of the Hebrew is uncertain
a Cn Compare Gk Syr: The meaning of the Hebrew is uncertain   *b* Cn: The meaning of the Hebrew is uncertain
c Cn: The meaning of the Hebrew is uncertain
d Cn: Heb *does not hear rebuke*   *e* Gk Vg: Heb *from vanity*
f Cn Compare Gk Syr Vg Tg: Heb *is enduring*
g Heb *Wisdom of women*   *h* Cn: Heb *a rod of pride*

⁴Where there are no oxen, there is no[i]
    grain;
    but abundant crops come by the
    strength of the ox.
⁵A faithful witness does not lie,
    but a false witness breathes out
    lies.
⁶A scoffer seeks wisdom in vain,
    but knowledge is easy for a man
    of understanding.
⁷Leave the presence of a fool,
    for there you do not meet words
    of knowledge.
⁸The wisdom of a prudent man is to
    discern his way,
    but the folly of fools is deceiving.
⁹God scorns the wicked,[j]
    but the upright enjoy his favor.
¹⁰The heart knows its own bitterness,
    and no stranger shares its joy.
¹¹The house of the wicked will be
    destroyed,
    but the tent of the upright will
    flourish.
¹²There is a way which seems right to
    a man,
    but its end is the way to death.[k]
¹³Even in laughter the heart is sad,
    and the end of joy is grief.
¹⁴A perverse man will be filled with the
    fruit of his ways,
    and a good man with the fruit of
    his deeds.[l]
¹⁵The simple believes everything,
    but the prudent looks where he is
    going.
¹⁶A wise man is cautious and turns
    away from evil,
    but a fool throws off restraint and
    is careless.
¹⁷A man of quick temper acts fool-
    ishly,
    but a man of discretion is patient.[m]
¹⁸The simple acquire folly,
    but the prudent are crowned with
    knowledge.
¹⁹The evil bow down before the good,
    the wicked at the gates of the
    righteous.
²⁰The poor is disliked even by his
    neighbor,
    but the rich has many friends.
²¹He who despises his neighbor is a
    sinner,
    but happy is he who is kind to the
    poor.
²²Do they not err that devise evil?
    Those who devise good meet
    loyalty and faithfulness.
²³In all toil there is profit,

    but mere talk tends only to want.
²⁴The crown of the wise is their wis-
    dom,[n]
    but folly is the garland[o] of fools.
²⁵A truthful witness saves lives,
    but one who utters lies is a be-
    trayer.
²⁶In the fear of the LORD one has
    strong confidence,
    and his children will have a refuge.
²⁷The fear of the LORD is a fountain
    of life,
    that one may avoid the snares of
    death.
²⁸In a multitude of people is the glory
    of a king,
    but without people a prince is
    ruined.
²⁹He who is slow to anger has great
    understanding,
    but he who has a hasty temper
    exalts folly.
³⁰A tranquil mind gives life to the
    flesh,
    but passion makes the bones rot.
³¹He who oppresses a poor man insults
    his Maker,
    but he who is kind to the needy
    honors him.
³²The wicked is overthrown through
    his evil-doing,
    but the righteous finds refuge
    through his integrity.[p]
³³Wisdom abides in the mind of a man
    of understanding,
    but it is not[q] known in the heart of
    fools.
³⁴Righteousness exalts a nation,
    but sin is a reproach to any people.
³⁵A servant who deals wisely has the
    king's favor,
    but his wrath falls on one who acts
    shamefully.

15   A soft answer turns away wrath,
    but a harsh word stirs up anger.
²The tongue of the wise dispenses
    knowledge,[r]
    but the mouths of fools pour out
    folly.
³The eyes of the LORD are in every
    place,
    keeping watch on the evil and the
    good.
⁴A gentle tongue is a tree of life,
    but perverseness in it breaks the
    spirit.

---

[i]Cn: Heb *a manger of* [j]Ch: Heb *obscure*
[k]Heb *ways of death* [l]Ch: Heb *from upon him*
[m]Gk: Heb *is hated* [n]Cn Compare Gk: Heb *riches*
[o]Cn: Heb *folly* [p]Gk Syr: Heb *in his death*
[q]Gk Syr: Heb lacks *not* [r]Cn: Heb *makes knowledge good*

5 A fool despises his father's instruction,
but he who heeds admonition is prudent.
6 In the house of the righteous there is much treasure,
but trouble befalls the income of the wicked.
7 The lips of the wise spread knowledge;
not so the minds of fools.
8 The sacrifice of the wicked is an abomination to the Lord,
but the prayer of the upright is his delight.
9 The way of the wicked is an abomination to the Lord,
but he loves him who pursues righteousness.
10 There is severe discipline for him who forsakes the way;
he who hates reproof will die.
11 Shē'ōl and A·bǎd'don lie open before the Lord,
how much more the hearts of men!
12 A scoffer does not like to be reproved;
he will not go to the wise.
13 A glad heart makes a cheerful countenance,
but by sorrow of heart the spirit is broken.
14 The mind of him who has understanding seeks knowledge,
but the mouths of fools feed on folly.
15 All the days of the afflicted are evil,
but a cheerful heart has a continual feast.
16 Better is a little with the fear of the Lord
than great treasure and trouble with it.
17 Better is a dinner of herbs where love is
than a fatted ox and hatred with it.
18 A hot-tempered man stirs up strife,
but he who is slow to anger quiets contention.
19 The way of a sluggard is overgrown with thorns,
but the path of the upright is a level highway.
20 A wise son makes a glad father,
but a foolish man despises his mother.
21 Folly is a joy to him who has no sense,
but a man of understanding walks aright.
22 Without counsel plans go wrong,
but with many advisers they succeed.
23 To make an apt answer is a joy to a man,
and a word in season, how good it is!
24 The wise man's path leads upward to life,
that he may avoid Shē'ōl beneath.
25 The Lord tears down the house of the proud,
but maintains the widow's boundaries.
26 The thoughts of the wicked are an abomination to the Lord,
the words of the pure are pleasing to him.[s]
27 He who is greedy for unjust gain makes trouble for his household,
but he who hates bribes will live.
28 The mind of the righteous ponders how to answer,
but the mouth of the wicked pours out evil things.
29 The Lord is far from the wicked,
but he hears the prayer of the righteous.
30 The light of the eyes rejoices the heart,
and good news refreshes[t] the bones.
31 He whose ear heeds wholesome admonition
will abide among the wise.
32 He who ignores instruction despises himself,
but he who heeds admonition gains understanding.
33 The fear of the Lord is instruction in wisdom,
and humility goes before honor.

16 The plans of the mind belong to man,
but the answer of the tongue is from the Lord.
2 All the ways of a man are pure in his own eyes,
but the Lord weighs the spirit.
3 Commit your work to the Lord,
and your plans will be established.
4 The Lord has made everything for its purpose,
even the wicked for the day of trouble.
5 Every one who is arrogant is an abomination to the Lord;

^sCn Compare Gk: Heb *pleasant words are pure*
^tHeb *makes fat*

be assured, he will not go unpunished.

6 By loyalty and faithfulness iniquity
is atoned for,
and by the fear of the LORD a man
avoids evil.

7 When a man's ways please the
LORD,
he makes even his enemies to be
at peace with him.

8 Better is a little with righteousness
than great revenues with injustice.

9 A man's mind plans his way,
but the LORD directs his steps.

10 Inspired decisions are on the lips of a
king;
his mouth does not sin in judgment.

11 A just balance and scales are the
LORD's;
all the weights in the bag are his
work.

12 It is an abomination to kings to do
evil,
for the throne is established by
righteousness.

13 Righteous lips are the delight of a
king,
and he loves him who speaks what
is right.

14 A king's wrath is a messenger of
death,
and a wise man will appease it.

15 In the light of a king's face there is
life,
and his favor is like the clouds
that bring the spring rain.

16 To get wisdom is better^u than gold;
to get understanding is to be
chosen rather than silver.

17 The highway of the upright turns
aside from evil;
he who guards his way preserves
his life.

18 Pride goes before destruction,
and a haughty spirit before a fall.

19 It is better to be of a lowly spirit
with the poor
than to divide the spoil with the
proud.

20 He who gives heed to the word will
prosper,
and happy is he who trusts in the
LORD.

21 The wise of heart is called a man of
discernment,
and pleasant speech increases
persuasiveness.

22 Wisdom is a fountain of life to
him who has it,

but folly is the chastisement of
fools.

23 The mind of the wise makes his
speech judicious,
and adds persuasiveness to his
lips.

24 Pleasant words are like a honeycomb,
sweetness to the soul and health
to the body.

25 There is a way which seems right to
a man,
but its end is the way to death.^v

26 A worker's appetite works for him;
his mouth urges him on.

27 A worthless man plots evil,
and his speech is like a scorching
fire.

28 A perverse man spreads strife,
and a whisperer separates close
friends.

29 A man of violence entices his neighbor
and leads him in a way that is not
good.

30 He who winks his eyes plans^w
perverse things,
he who compresses his lips brings
evil to pass.

31 A hoary head is a crown of glory;
it is gained in a righteous life.

32 He who is slow to anger is better
than the mighty,
and he who rules his spirit than he
who takes a city.

33 The lot is cast into the lap,
but the decision is wholly from the
LORD.

17 Better is a dry morsel with quiet
than a house full of feasting
with strife.

2 A slave who deals wisely will rule
over a son who acts shamefully,
and will share the inheritance as
one of the brothers.

3 The crucible is for silver, and the
furnace is for gold,
and the LORD tries hearts.

4 An evildoer listens to wicked lips;
and a liar gives heed to a mis-
chievous tongue.

5 He who mocks the poor insults his
Maker;
he who is glad at calamity will not
go unpunished.

6 Grandchildren are the crown of the
aged,

---

^u Gk Syr Vg Tg: Heb *how much better*
^v Heb *ways of death*
^w Gk Syr Vg Tg: Heb *to plan*

and the glory of sons is their
fathers.
⁷Fine speech is not becoming to a
fool;
still less is false speech to a prince.
⁸A bribe is like a magic stone in the
eyes of him who gives it;
wherever he turns he prospers.
⁹He who forgives an offense seeks
love,
but he who repeats a matter alien-
ates a friend.
¹⁰A rebuke goes deeper into a man of
understanding
than a hundred blows into a fool.
¹¹An evil man seeks only rebellion,
and a cruel messenger will be sent
against him.
¹²Let a man meet a she-bear robbed
of her cubs,
rather than a fool in his folly.
¹³If a man returns evil for good,
evil will not depart from his house.
¹⁴The beginning of strife is like letting
out water;
so quit before the quarrel breaks
out.
¹⁵He who justifies the wicked and he
who condemns the righteous
are both alike an abomination to
the LORD.
¹⁶Why should a fool have a price in his
hand to buy wisdom,
when he has no mind?
¹⁷A friend loves at all times,
and a brother is born for adversity.
¹⁸A man without sense gives a pledge,
and becomes surety in the presence
of his neighbor.
¹⁹He who loves transgression loves
strife;
he who makes his door high seeks
destruction.
²⁰A man of crooked mind does not
prosper,
and one with a perverse tongue
falls into calamity.
²¹A stupid son is a grief to a father;
and the father of a fool has no joy.
²²A cheerful heart is a good medicine,
but a downcast spirit dries up the
bones.
²³A wicked man accepts a bribe from
the bosom
to prevert the ways of justice.
²⁴A man of understanding sets his face
toward wisdom,
but the eyes of a fool are on the
ends of the earth.
²⁵A foolish son is a grief to his father

and bitterness to her who bore him.
²⁶To impose a fine on a righteous man
is not good;
to flog noble men is wrong.
²⁷He who restrains his words has
knowledge,
and he who has a cool spirit is a
man of understanding.
²⁸Even a fool who keeps silent is considered wise;
when he closes his lips, he is
deemed intelligent.

18 He who is estranged*ˣ* seeks pre-
texts*ʸ*
to break out against all sound
judgment.
²A fool takes no pleasure in understanding,
but only in expressing his opinion.
³When wickedness comes, contempt
comes also;
and with dishonor comes disgrace.
⁴The words of a man's mouth are deep
waters;
the fountain of wisdom is a gush-
ing stream.
⁵It is not good to be partial to a wicked
man,
or to deprive a righteous man of
justice.
⁶A fool's lips bring strife,
and his mouth invites a flogging.
⁷A fool's mouth is his ruin,
and his lips are a snare to himself.
⁸The words of a whisperer are like
delicious morsels;
they go down into the inner parts
of the body.
⁹He who is slack in his work
is a brother to him who destroys.
¹⁰The name of the LORD is a strong
tower;
the righteous man runs into it and
is safe.
¹¹A rich man's wealth is his strong city,
and like a high wall protecting
him.*ᶻ*
¹²Before destruction a man's heart is
haughty,
but humility goes before honor.
¹³If one gives answer before he hears,
it is his folly and shame.
¹⁴A man's spirit will endure sickness;
but a broken spirit who can bear?
¹⁵An intelligent mind acquires knowledge,
and the ear of the wise seeks
knowledge.

*ˣHeb separated ʸGk Vg: Heb desire
ᶻOr in his imagination*

16 A man's gift makes room for him
and brings him before great men.
17 He who states his case first seems
right,
until the other comes and examines him.
18 The lot puts an end to disputes
and decides between powerful
contenders.
19 A brother helped is like a strong city,[a]
but quarreling is like the bars of a
castle.
20 From the fruit of his mouth a man is
satisfied;
he is satisfied by the yield of his
lips.
21 Death and life are in the power of the
tongue,
and those who love it will eat its
fruits.
22 He who finds a wife finds a good
thing,
and obtains favor from the LORD.
23 The poor use entreaties,
but the rich answer roughly.
24 There are[b] friends who pretend to be
friends,[c]
but there is a friend who sticks
closer than a brother.

19 Better is a poor man who walks
in his integrity
than a man who is perverse in
speech, and is a fool.
2 It is not good for a man to be without
knowledge,
and he who makes haste with his
feet misses his way.
3 When a man's folly brings his way to
ruin,
his heart rages against the LORD.
4 Wealth brings many new friends,
but a poor man is deserted by his
friend.
5 A false witness will not go unpunished,
and he who utters lies will not
escape.
6 Many seek the favor of a generous
man,
and every one is a friend to a man
who gives gifts.
7 All a poor man's brothers hate
him;
how much more do his friends go
far from him!
He pursues them with words, but
does not have them.[d]
8 He who gets wisdom loves himself;
he who keeps understanding will
prosper.

9 A false witness will not go unpunished,
and he who utters lies will perish.
10 It is not fitting for a fool to live in
luxury,
much less for a slave to rule over
princes.
11 Good sense makes a man slow to
anger,
and it is his glory to overlook an
offense.
12 A king's wrath is like the growling
of a lion,
but his favor is like dew upon the
grass.
13 A foolish son is ruin to his father,
and a wife's quarreling is a continual dripping of rain.
14 House and wealth are inherited from
fathers,
but a prudent wife is from the
LORD.
15 Slothfulness casts into a deep sleep,
and an idle person will suffer
hunger.
16 He who keeps the commandment
keeps his life;
he who despises the word[e] will die.
17 He who is kind to the poor lends to
the LORD,
and he will repay him for his deed.
18 Discipline your son while there is
hope;
do not set your heart on his destruction.
19 A man of great wrath will pay the
penalty;
for if you deliver him, you will
only have to do it again.[f]
20 Listen to advice and accept instruction,
that you may gain wisdom for the
future.
21 Many are the plans in the mind of a
man,
but it is the purpose of the LORD
that will be established.
22 What is desired in a man is loyalty,
and a poor man is better than a
liar.
23 The fear of the LORD leads to life;
and he who has it rests satisfied;
he will not be visited by harm.
24 The sluggard buries his hand in the
dish,

[a] Gk Syr Vg Tg: The meaning of the Hebrew is uncertain
[b] Syr Tg: Heb *A man of*
[c] Cn Compare Syr Vg Tg: Heb *to be broken*
[d] Heb uncertain
[e] Cn Compare 13.13: Heb *his ways*
[f] Heb obscure

and will not even bring it back to
his mouth.
25 Strike a scoffer, and the simple will
learn prudence;
reprove a man of understanding,
and he will gain knowledge.
26 He who does violence to his father
and chases away his mother
is a son who causes shame and
brings reproach.
27 Cease, my son, to hear instruction
only to stray from the words of
knowledge.
28 A worthless witness mocks at justice,
and the mouth of the wicked
devours iniquity.
29 Condemnation is ready for scoffers,
and flogging for the backs of fools.

20 Wine is a mocker, strong drink
a brawler;
and whoever is led astray by it is
not wise.
2 The dread wrath of a king is like the
growling of a lion;
he who provokes him to anger
forfeits his life.
3 It is an honor for a man to keep
aloof from strife;
but every fool will be quarreling.
4 The sluggard does not plow in the
autumn;
he will seek at harvest and have
nothing.
5 The purpose in a man's mind is like
deep water,
but a man of understanding will
draw it out.
6 Many a man proclaims his own
loyalty,
but a faithful man who can find?
7 A righteous man who walks in his
integrity—
blessed are his sons after him!
8 A king who sits on the throne of
judgment
winnows all evil with his eyes.
9 Who can say, "I have made my heart
clean;
I am pure from my sin"?
10 Diverse weights and diverse measures
are both alike an abomination to
the LORD.
11 Even a child makes himself known
by his acts,
whether what he does is pure and
right.
12 The hearing ear and the seeing eye,
the LORD has made them both.

13 Love not sleep, lest you come to
poverty;
open your eyes, and you will have
plenty of bread.
14 "It is bad, it is bad," says the buyer;
but when he goes away, then he
boasts.
15 There is gold, and abundance of
costly stones;
but the lips of knowledge are a
precious jewel.
16 Take a man's garment when he has
given surety for a stranger,
and hold him in pledge when he
gives surety for foreigners.
17 Bread gained by deceit is sweet to
a man,
but afterward his mouth will be
full of gravel.
18 Plans are established by counsel;
by wise guidance wage war.
19 He who goes about gossiping reveals
secrets;
therefore do not associate with one
who speaks foolishly.
20 If one curses his father or his
mother,
his lamp will be put out in utter
darkness.
21 An inheritance gotten hastily in the
beginning
will in the end not be blessed.
22 Do not say, "I will repay evil";
wait for the LORD, and he will
help you.
23 Diverse weights are an abomination
to the LORD,
and false scales are not good.
24 A man's steps are ordered by the
LORD;
how then can man understand his
way?
25 It is a snare for a man to say rashly,
"It is holy,"
and to reflect only after making his
vows.
26 A wise king winnows the wicked,
and drives the wheel over them.
27 The spirit of man is the lamp of the
LORD,
searching all his innermost parts.
28 Loyalty and faithfulness preserve the
king,
and his throne is upheld by righteousness. *g*
29 The glory of young men is their
strength,
but the beauty of old men is their
gray hair.

g Gk: Heb *loyalty*

30 Blows that wound cleanse away evil;
strokes make clean the innermost
parts.

21 The king's heart is a stream of
water in the hand of the LORD;
he turns it wherever he will.

2 Every way of a man is right in his
own eyes,
but the LORD weighs the heart.

3 To do righteousness and justice
is more acceptable to the LORD
than sacrifice.

4 Haughty eyes and a proud heart,
the lamp of the wicked, are sin.

5 The plans of the diligent lead surely
to abundance,
but every one who is hasty comes
only to want.

6 The getting of treasures by a lying
tongue
is a fleeting vapor and a snare of
death.

7 The violence of the wicked will sweep
them away,
because they refuse to do what is
just.

8 The way of the guilty is crooked,
but the conduct of the pure is right.

9 It is better to live in a corner of the
housetop
than in a house shared with a
contentious woman.

10 The soul of the wicked desires evil;
his neighbor finds no mercy in his
eyes.

11 When a scoffer is punished, the
simple becomes wise;
when a wise man is instructed,
he gains knowledge.

12 The righteous observes the house of
the wicked;
the wicked are cast down to ruin.

13 He who closes his ear to the cry of
the poor
will himself cry out and not be
heard.

14 A gift in secret averts anger;
and a bribe in the bosom, strong
wrath.

15 When justice is done, it is a joy to
the righteous,
but dismay to evildoers.

16 A man who wanders from the way of
understanding
will rest in the assembly of the
dead.

17 He who loves pleasure will be a poor
man;
he who loves wine and oil will not
be rich.

18 The wicked is a ransom for the
righteous,
and the faithless for the upright.

19 It is better to live in a desert land
than with a contentious and
fretful woman.

20 Precious treasure remains[h] in a
wise man's dwelling,
but a foolish man devours it.

21 He who pursues righteousness and
kindness
will find life[i] and honor.

22 A wise man scales the city of the
mighty
and brings down the stronghold in
which they trust.

23 He who keeps his mouth and his
tongue
keeps himself out of trouble.

24 "Scoffer" is the name of the proud,
haughty man
who acts with arrogant pride.

25 The desire of the sluggard kills him
for his hands refuse to labor.

26 All day long the wicked covets,[j]
but the righteous gives and does
not hold back.

27 The sacrifice of the wicked is an
abomination;
how much more when he brings it
with evil intent.

28 A false witness will perish,
but the word of a man who hears
will endure.

29 A wicked man puts on a bold face,
but an upright man considers[k]
his ways.

30 No wisdom, no understanding, no
counsel,
can avail against the LORD.

31 The horse is made ready for the day
of battle,
but the victory belongs to the
LORD.

22 A good name is to be chosen
rather than great riches,
and favor is better than silver or
gold.

2 The rich and the poor meet together;
the LORD is the maker of them all.

3 A prudent man sees danger and hides
himself;
but the simple go on, and suffer
for it.

4 The reward for humility and fear of
the LORD
is riches and honor and life.

[h] Gk: Heb *and oil* [i] Gk: Heb *life and righteousness*
[j] Gk: Heb *all day long he covets covetously*
[k] Another reading is *establishes*

⁵Thorns and snares are in the way of the perverse;
    he who guards himself will keep far from them.
⁶Train up a child in the way he should go,
    and when he is old he will not depart from it.
⁷The rich rules over the poor,
    and the borrower is the slave of the lender.
⁸He who sows injustice will reap calamity,
    and the rod of his fury will fail.
⁹He who has a bountiful eye will be blessed,
    for he shares his bread with the poor.
¹⁰Drive out a scoffer, and strife will go out,
    and quarreling and abuse will cease.
¹¹He who loves purity of heart,
    and whose speech is gracious, will have the king as his friend.
¹²The eyes of the LORD keep watch over knowledge,
    but he overthrows the words of the faithless.
¹³The sluggard says, "There is a lion outside!
    I shall be slain in the streets!"
¹⁴The mouth of a loose woman is a deep pit;
    he with whom the LORD is angry will fall into it.
¹⁵Folly is bound up in the heart of a child,
    but the rod of discipline drives it far from him.
¹⁶He who oppresses the poor to increase his own wealth,
    or gives to the rich, will only come to want.

¹⁷Incline your ear, and hear the words of the wise,
    and apply your mind to my knowledge;
¹⁸for it will be pleasant if you keep them within you,
    if all of them are ready on your lips.
¹⁹That your trust may be in the LORD,
    I have made them known to you today, even to you.

²⁰Have I not written for you thirty sayings
    of admonition and knowledge,

²¹to show you what is right and true,
    that you may give a true answer to those who sent you?

²²Do not rob the poor, because he is poor,
    or crush the afflicted at the gate;
²³for the LORD will plead their cause and despoil of life those who despoil them.
²⁴Make no friendship with a man given to anger,
    nor go with a wrathful man,
²⁵lest you learn his ways
    and entangle yourself in a snare.
²⁶Be not one of those who give pledges,
    who become surety for debts.
²⁷If you have nothing with which to pay,
    why should your bed be taken from under you?
²⁸Remove not the ancient landmark which your fathers have set.
²⁹Do you see a man skilful in his work?
    he will stand before kings;
    he will not stand before obscure men.

23 When you sit down to eat with a ruler,
    observe carefully whatᶦ is before you;
²and put a knife to your throat
    if you are a man given to appetite.
³Do not desire his delicacies,
    for they are deceptive food.
⁴Do not toil to acquire wealth;
    be wise enough to desist.
⁵When your eyes light upon it, it is gone;
    for suddenly it takes to itself wings,
    flying like an eagle toward heaven.
⁶Do not eat the bread of a man who is stingy;
    do not desire his delicacies;
⁷for he is like one who is inwardly reckoning.ᵐ
    "Eat and drink!" he says to you;
    but his heart is not with you.
⁸You will vomit up the morsels which you have eaten,
    and waste your pleasant words.
⁹Do not speak in the hearing of a fool,
    for he will despise the wisdom of your words.
¹⁰Do not remove an ancient landmark or enter the fields of the fatherless;

ᶦOr *who*   ᵐHeb obscure
22.8 (Gk): 1 Cor 9.7.

¹¹for their Redeemer is strong;
     he will plead their cause against
       you.
¹²Apply your mind to instruction
     and your ear to words of knowl-
       edge.
¹³Do not withhold discipline from a
       child;
     if you beat him with a rod, he will
       not die.
¹⁴If you beat him with the rod
     you will save his life from Shē'ōl.
¹⁵My son, if your heart is wise,
     my heart too will be glad.
¹⁶My soul will rejoice
     when your lips speak what is right.
¹⁷Let not your heart envy sinners,
     but continue in the fear of the
       LORD all the day.
¹⁸Surely there is a future,
     and your hope will not be cut off.

¹⁹Hear, my son, and be wise,
     and direct your mind in the way.
²⁰Be not among winebibbers,
     or among gluttonous eaters of
       meat;
²¹for the drunkard and the glutton will
       come to poverty,
     and drowsiness will clothe a man
       with rags.

²Hearken to your father who begot
       you,
     and do not despise your mother
       when she is old.
³Buy truth, and do not sell it;
     buy wisdom, instruction, and
       understanding.
⁴The father of the righteous will
       greatly rejoice;
     he who begets a wise son will be
       glad in him.
⁵Let your father and mother be glad,
     let her who bore you rejoice.

⁶My son, give me your heart,
     and let your eyes observe[n] my
       ways.
⁷For a harlot is a deep pit;
     an adventuress is a narrow well.
⁸She lies in wait like a robber
     and increases the faithless among
       men.

⁹Who has woe? Who has sorrow?
     Who has strife? Who has com-
       plaining?
Who has wounds without cause?
     Who has redness of eyes?

³⁰Those who tarry long over wine,
     those who go to try mixed wine.
³¹Do not look at wine when it is red,
     when it sparkles in the cup
     and goes down smoothly.
³²At the last it bites like a serpent,
     and stings like an adder.
³³Your eyes will see strange things,
     and your mind utter perverse
       things.
³⁴You will be like one who lies down
       in the midst of the sea,
     like one who lies on the top of a
       mast.[o]
³⁵"They struck me," you will say,[p]
     "but I was not hurt;
     they beat me, but I did not feel it.
When shall I awake?
     I will seek another drink."

24 Be not envious of evil men,
       nor desire to be with them;
²for their minds devise violence,
     and their lips talk of mischief.

³By wisdom a house is built,
     and by understanding it is es-
       tablished;
⁴by knowledge the rooms are filled
     with all precious and pleasant
       riches.
⁵A wise man is mightier than a strong
       man,[q]
     and a man of knowledge than he
       who has strength;
⁶for by wise guidance you can wage
       your war,
     and in abundance of counselors
       there is victory.
⁷Wisdom is too high for a fool;
     in the gate he does not open his
       mouth.

⁸He who plans to do evil
     will be called a mischief-maker.
⁹The devising of folly is sin,
     and the scoffer is an abomination
       to men.

¹⁰If you faint in the day of adversity,
     your strength is small.
¹¹Rescue those who are being taken
       away to death;
     hold back those who are stumbling
       to the slaughter.
¹²If you say, "Behold, we did not know
       this,"

---

[n]Another reading is *delight in*
[o]Heb obscure
[p]Gk Syr Vg Tg: Heb lacks *you will say*
[q]Gk Compare Syr Tg: Heb *is in strength*

does not he who weighs the heart
perceive it?
Does not he who keeps watch over
your soul know it,
and will he not requite man according to his work?

[13] My son, eat honey, for it is good,
and the drippings of the honeycomb are sweet to your taste.
[14] Know that wisdom is such to your
soul;
if you find it, there will be a future,
and your hope will not be cut off.

[15] Lie not in wait as a wicked man
against the dwelling of the
righteous;
do not violence to his home;
[16] for a righteous man falls seven times,
and rises again;
but the wicked are overthrown by
calamity.

[17] Do not rejoice when your enemy
falls,
and let not your heart be glad when
he stumbles;
[18] lest the LORD see it, and be displeased,
and turn away his anger from
him.

[19] Fret not yourself because of evildoers,
and be not envious of the wicked;
[20] for the evil man has no future;
the lamp of the wicked will be put
out.

[21] My son, fear the LORD and the
king,
and do not disobey either of them;[r]
[22] for disaster from them will rise
suddenly,
and who knows the ruin that will
come from them both?

[23]   These also are sayings of the wise.

Partiality in judging is not good.
[24] He who says to the wicked, "You
are innocent,"
will be cursed by peoples, abhorred
by nations;
[25] but those who rebuke the wicked will
have delight,
and a good blessing will be upon
them.
[26] He who gives a right answer
kisses the lips.

[27] Prepare your work outside,
get everything ready for you in the
field;
and after that build your house.

[28] Be not a witness against your neighbor without cause,
and do not deceive with your lips.
[29] Do not say, "I will do to him as he has
done to me;
I will pay the man back for what
he has done."

[30] I passed by the field of a sluggard,
by the vineyard of a man without
sense;
[31] and lo, it was all overgrown with
thorns;
the ground was covered with
nettles,
and its stone wall was broken
down.
[32] Then I saw and considered it;
I looked and received instruction.
[33] A little sleep, a little slumber,
a little folding of the hands to rest,
[34] and poverty will come upon you like
a robber,
and want like an armed man.

25   These also are proverbs of Solomon which the men of Hĕz-e-
kī'ah king of Judah copied.

[2] It is the glory of God to conceal
things,
but the glory of kings is to search
things out.
[3] As the heavens for height, and the
earth for depth,
so the mind of kings is unsearchable.
[4] Take away the dross from the silver,
and the smith has material for a
vessel;
[5] take away the wicked from the
presence of the king,
and his throne will be established
in righteousness.
[6] Do not put yourself forward in the
king's presence
or stand in the place of the great;
[7] for it is better to be told, "Come up
here,"
than to be put lower in the presence of the prince.

What your eyes have seen
[8]   do not hastily bring into court;

[r] Gk: Heb *do not associate with those who change*

for[s] what will you do in the end,
when your neighbor puts you to
shame?
[9]Argue your case with your neighbor
himself,
and do not disclose another's
secret;
[10]lest he who hears you bring shame
upon you,
and your ill repute have no end.

[1]A word fitly spoken
is like apples of gold in a setting
of silver.
[2]Like a gold ring or an ornament of
gold
is a wise reprover to a listening
ear.
[3]Like the cold of snow in the time of
harvest
is a faithful messenger to those
who send him,
he refreshes the spirit of his
masters.
[4]Like clouds and wind without rain
is a man who boasts of a gift he
does not give.

[5]With patience a ruler may be persuaded,
and a soft tongue will break a
bone.
[3]If you have found honey, eat only
enough for you,
lest you be sated with it and vomit
it.
[7]Let your foot be seldom in your
neighbor's house,
lest he become weary of you and
hate you.
[3]A man who bears false witness
against his neighbor
is like a war club, or a sword,
or a sharp arrow.
[9]Trust in a faithless man in time of
trouble
is like a bad tooth or a foot that
slips.
[ ]He who sings songs to a heavy heart
is like one who takes off a garment
on a cold day,
and like vinegar on a wound.[t]
[ ]If your enemy is hungry, give him
bread to eat;
and if he is thirsty, give him water
to drink;
[2]for you will heap coals of fire on his
head,
and the LORD will reward you.
[3]The north wind brings forth rain;

and a backbiting tongue, angry
looks.
[24]It is better to live in a corner of the
housetop
than in a house shared with a
contentious woman.
[25]Like cold water to a thirsty soul,
so is good news from a far country.
[26]Like a muddied spring or a polluted
fountain
is a righteous man who gives way
before the wicked.
[27]It is not good to eat much honey,
so be sparing of complimentary
words.[u]
[28]A man without self-control
is like a city broken into and left
without walls.

26 Like snow in summer or rain in
harvest,
so honor is not fitting for a fool.
[2]Like a sparrow in its flitting, like a
swallow in its flying,
a curse that is causeless does not
alight.
[3]A whip for the horse, a bridle for
the ass,
and a rod for the back of fools.
[4]Answer not a fool according to his
folly,
lest you be like him yourself.
[5]Answer a fool according to his folly,
lest he be wise in his own eyes.
[6]He who sends a message by the hand
of a fool
cuts off his own feet and drinks
violence.
[7]Like a lame man's legs, which hang
useless,
is a proverb in the mouth of fools.
[8]Like one who binds the stone in the
sling
is he who gives honor to a fool.
[9]Like a thorn that goes up into the
hand of a drunkard
is a proverb in the mouth of fools.
[10]Like an archer who wounds every-
body
is he who hires a passing fool
or drunkard.[v]
[11]Like a dog that returns to his vomit
is a fool that repeats his folly.
[12]Do you see a man who is wise in his
own eyes?
There is more hope for a fool than
for him.

[s]Cn: Heb *lest* [t]Gk: Heb *lye*
[u]Cn Compare Gk Syr Tg: Heb *searching out their glory
is glory* [v]The Hebrew text of this verse is uncertain
25.21, 22: Rom 12.20. **26.11:** 2 Pet 2.22.

¹³The sluggard says, "There is a lion
in the road!
There is a lion in the streets!"
¹⁴As a door turns on its hinges,
so does a sluggard on his bed.
¹⁵The sluggard buries his hand in the
dish;
it wears him out to bring it back to
his mouth.
¹⁶The sluggard is wiser in his own eyes
than seven men who can answer
discreetly.
¹⁷He who meddles in a quarrel not his
own
is like one who takes a passing
dog by the ears.
¹⁸Like a madman who throws firebrands,
arrows, and death,
¹⁹is the man who deceives his neighbor
and says, "I am only joking!"
²⁰For lack of wood the fire goes out;
and where there is no whisperer, quarreling ceases.
²¹As charcoal to hot embers and wood
to fire,
so is a quarrelsome man for kin-
dling strife.
²²The words of a whisperer are like
delicious morsels;
they go down into the inner parts
of the body.
²³Like the glaze*ʷ* covering an earthen
vessel
are smooth*ˣ* lips with an evil
heart.
²⁴He who hates, dissembles with his
lips
and harbors deceit in his heart;
²⁵when he speaks graciously, believe
him not,
for there are seven abominations
in his heart;
²⁶though his hatred be covered with
guile,
his wickedness will be exposed
in the assembly.
²⁷He who digs a pit will fall into it,
and a stone will come back upon
him who starts it rolling.
²⁸A lying tongue hates its victims,
and a flattering mouth works ruin.

27 Do not boast about tomorrow,
for you do not know what a day
may bring forth.
²Let another praise you, and not your
own mouth;
a stranger, and not your own
lips.

³A stone is heavy, and sand is weighty,
but a fool's provocation is heavier
than both.
⁴Wrath is cruel, anger is overwhelming;
but who can stand before jealousy?
⁵Better is open rebuke
than hidden love.
⁶Faithful are the wounds of a friend;
profuse are the kisses of an
enemy.
⁷He who is sated loathes honey,
but to one who is hungry everything bitter is sweet.
⁸Like a bird that strays from its nest,
is a man who strays from his
home.
⁹Oil and perfume make the heart
glad,
but the soul is torn by trouble.*ʸ*
¹⁰Your friend, and your father's friend
do not forsake;
and do not go to your brother's
house in the day of your calamity.
Better is a neighbor who is near
than a brother who is far away
¹¹Be wise, my son, and make my heart
glad,
that I may answer him who reproaches me.
¹²A prudent man sees danger and
hides himself;
but the simple go on, and suffer
for it.
¹³Take a man's garment when he has
given surety for a stranger,
and hold him in pledge when he
gives surety for foreigners.
¹⁴He who blesses his neighbor with a
loud voice,
rising early in the morning,
will be counted as cursing.
¹⁵A continual dripping on a rainy day
and a contentious woman are
alike;
¹⁶to restrain her is to restrain the
wind*ᵃ*
or to grasp oil in his right hand
¹⁷Iron sharpens iron,
and one man sharpens another
¹⁸He who tends a fig tree will eat its
fruit,
and he who guards his master will
be honored.
¹⁹As in water face answers to face

*ʷ*Cn: Heb *silver of dross*
*ˣ*Gk: Heb *burning*
*ʸ*Gk: Heb *the sweetness of his friend from hearty counsel*
*ᶻ*Vg and 20.16: Heb *a foreign woman*
*ᵃ*Heb obscure

so the mind of man reflects the man.

20 Shē'ōl and A·băd'dọn are never satisfied,
   and never satisfied are the eyes of man.

21 The crucible is for silver, and the furnace is for gold,
   and a man is judged by his praise.

22 Crush a fool in a mortar with a pestle along with crushed grain,
   yet his folly will not depart from him.

23 Know well the condition of your flocks,
   and give attention to your herds;

24 for riches do not last for ever;
   and does a crown endure to all generations?

25 When the grass is gone, and the new growth appears,
   and the herbage of the mountains is gathered,

26 the lambs will provide your clothing,
   and the goats the price of a field;

27 there will be enough goats' milk for your food,
   for the food of your household
   and maintenance for your maidens.

28 The wicked flee when no one pursues,
   but the righteous are bold as a lion.

2 When a land transgresses
   it has many rulers;
   but with men of understanding and knowledge
   its stability will long continue.

3 A poor man who oppresses the poor
   is a beating rain that leaves no food.

4 Those who forsake the law praise the wicked,
   but those who keep the law strive against them.

5 Evil men do not understand justice,
   but those who seek the LORD understand it completely.

6 Better is a poor man who walks in his integrity
   than a rich man who is perverse in his ways.

7 He who keeps the law is a wise son,
   but a companion of gluttons shames his father.

8 He who augments his wealth by interest and increase

gathers it for him who is kind to the poor.

9 If one turns away his ear from hearing the law,
   even his prayer is an abomination.

10 He who misleads the upright into an evil way
   will fall into his own pit;
   but the blameless will have a goodly inheritance.

11 A rich man is wise in his own eyes,
   but a poor man who has understanding will find him out.

12 When the righteous triumph, there is great glory;
   but when the wicked rise, men hide themselves.

13 He who conceals his transgressions will not prosper,
   but he who confesses and forsakes them will obtain mercy.

14 Blessed is the man who fears the LORD always;
   but he who hardens his heart will fall into calamity.

15 Like a roaring lion or a charging bear
   is a wicked ruler over a poor people.

16 A ruler who lacks understanding is a cruel oppressor;
   but he who hates unjust gain will prolong his days.

17 If a man is burdened with the blood of another,
   let him be a fugitive until death;
   let no one help him.

18 He who walks in integrity will be delivered,
   but he who is perverse in his ways will fall into a pit.[b]

19 He who tills his land will have plenty of bread,
   but he who follows worthless pursuits will have plenty of poverty.

20 A faithful man will abound with blessings,
   but he who hastens to be rich will not go unpunished.

21 To show partiality is not good;
   but for a piece of bread a man will do wrong.

22 A miserly man hastens after wealth,
   and does not know that want will come upon him.

23 He who rebukes a man will afterward find more favor

[b] Syr: Heb *in one*

than he who flatters with his tongue.

24 He who robs his father or his mother
and says, "That is no transgression,"
is the companion of a man who destroys.

25 A greedy man stirs up strife,
but he who trusts in the LORD will be enriched.

26 He who trusts in his own mind is a fool;
but he who walks in wisdom will be delivered.

27 He who gives to the poor will not want,
but he who hides his eyes will get many a curse.

28 When the wicked rise, men hide themselves,
but when they perish, the righteous increase.

29 He who is often reproved, yet stiffens his neck
will suddenly be broken beyond healing.

2 When the righteous are in authority, the people rejoice;
but when the wicked rule, the people groan.

3 He who loves wisdom makes his father glad,
but one who keeps company with harlots squanders his substance.

4 By justice a king gives stability to the land,
but one who exacts gifts ruins it.

5 A man who flatters his neighbor spreads a net for his feet.

6 An evil man is ensnared in his transgression,
but a righteous man sings and rejoices.

7 A righteous man knows the rights of the poor;
a wicked man does not understand such knowledge.

8 Scoffers set a city aflame,
but wise men turn away wrath.

9 If a wise man has an argument with a fool,
the fool only rages and laughs, and there is no quiet.

10 Bloodthirsty men hate one who is blameless,
and the wicked[c] seek his life.

11 A fool gives full vent to his anger,
but a wise man quietly holds it back.

12 If a ruler listens to falsehood,
all his officials will be wicked.

13 The poor man and the oppressor meet together;
the LORD gives light to the eyes of both.

14 If a king judges the poor with equity
his throne will be established for ever.

15 The rod and reproof give wisdom,
but a child left to himself brings shame to his mother.

16 When the wicked are in authority, transgression increases;
but the righteous will look upon their downfall.

17 Discipline your son, and he will give you rest;
he will give delight to your heart.

18 Where there is no prophecy the people cast off restraint,
but blessed is he who keeps the law.

19 By mere words a servant is not disciplined,
for though he understands, he will not give heed.

20 Do you see a man who is hasty in his words?
There is more hope for a fool than for him.

21 He who pampers his servant from childhood,
will in the end find him his heir.[d]

22 A man of wrath stirs up strife,
and a man given to anger causes much transgression.

23 A man's pride will bring him low,
but he who is lowly in spirit will obtain honor.

24 The partner of a thief hates his own life;
he hears the curse, but discloses nothing.

25 The fear of man lays a snare,
but he who trusts in the LORD is safe.

26 Many seek the favor of a ruler,
but from the LORD a man gets justice.

27 An unjust man is an abomination to the righteous,
but he whose way is straight is an abomination to the wicked.

30 The words of Ā′gŭr son of Jā′keh of Măs′sạ.[e]

[c] Cn: Heb *upright*
[d] The meaning of the Hebrew word is uncertain
[e] Or *the oracle*

The man says to Ĭth′ĭ-ĕl,
to Ithiel and Ū′c̣al:ʲ
²Surely I am too stupid to be a man.
I have not the understanding of
a man.
³I have not learned wisdom,
nor have I knowledge of the
Holy One.
⁴Who has ascended to heaven and
come down?
Who has gathered the wind in his
fists?
Who has wrapped up the waters in
a garment?
Who has established all the ends
of the earth?
What is his name, and what is his
son's name?
Surely you know!
⁵Every word of God proves true;
he is a shield to those who take
refuge in him.
⁶Do not add to his words,
lest he rebuke you, and you be
found a liar.
⁷Two things I ask of thee;
deny them not to me before I die:
⁸Remove far from me falsehood and
lying;
give me neither poverty nor riches;
feed me with the food that is needful for me,
⁹lest I be full, and deny thee,
and say, "Who is the LORD?"
or lest I be poor, and steal,
and profane the name of my God.

¹⁰Do not slander a servant to his master,
lest he curse you, and you be held
guilty.
¹¹There are those who curse their
fathers
and do not bless their mothers.
¹²There are those who are pure in their
own eyes
but are not cleansed of their filth.
¹³There are those—how lofty are their
eyes,
how high their eyelids lift!
¹⁴There are those whose teeth are
swords,
whose teeth are knives,
to devour the poor from off the earth,
the needy from among men.

¹⁵The leechᵍ has two daughters;
"Give, give," they cry.
Three things are never satisfied;
four never say, "Enough":
¹⁶Shĕ′ŏl, the barren womb,
the earth ever thirsty for water,
and the fire which never says,
"Enough."ʰ

¹⁷The eye that mocks a father
and scorns to obey a mother
will be picked out by the ravens
of the valley
and eaten by the vultures.

¹⁸Three things are too wonderful for
me;
four I do not understand:
¹⁹the way of an eagle in the sky,
the way of a serpent on a rock,
the way of a ship on the high seas,
and the way of a man with a
maiden.

²⁰This is the way of an adulteress:
she eats, and wipes her mouth,
and says, "I have done no wrong."

²¹Under three things the earth trembles;
under four it cannot bear up:
²²a slave when he becomes king,
and a fool when he is filled with
food;
²³an unloved woman when she gets
a husband,
and a maid when she succeeds
her mistress.

²⁴Four things on earth are small,
but they are exceedingly wise:
²⁵the ants are a people not strong,
yet they provide their food in the
summer;
²⁶the badgers are a people not mighty,
yet they make their homes in the
rocks;
²⁷the locusts have no king,
yet all of them march in rank;
²⁸the lizard you can take in your hands,
yet it is in kings' palaces.

²⁹Three things are stately in their
tread;
four are stately in their stride:
³⁰the lion, which is mightiest among
beasts
and does not turn back before any;
³¹the strutting cock,ⁱ the he-goat,

ʲThe Hebrew of this verse is obscure
ᵍThe meaning of the Hebrew word is uncertain
ʰHeb obscure ⁱGk Syr Tg Compare Vg: Heb obscure

and a king striding before[j] his people.

32 If you have been foolish, exalting
    yourself,
    or if you have been devising
    evil,
    put your hand on your mouth.
33 For pressing milk produces curds,
    pressing the nose produces blood,
    and pressing anger produces strife.

31 The words of Lĕm′ū·ĕl, king of
    Măs′sạ,[k] which his mother
taught him:

2 What, my son? What, son of my
    womb?
    What, son of my vows?
3 Give not your strength to women,
    your ways to those who destroy
    kings.
4 It is not for kings, O Lĕm′ū·ĕl,
    it is not for kings to drink wine,
    or for rulers to desire[l] strong drink;
5 lest they drink and forget what has
    been decreed,
    and pervert the rights of all the
    afflicted.
6 Give strong drink to him who is
    perishing,
    and wine to those in bitter dis-
    tress;
7 let them drink and forget their pov-
    erty,
    and remember their misery no
    more.
8 Open your mouth for the dumb,
    for the rights of all who are left
    desolate.[m]
9 Open your mouth, judge righteously,
    maintain the rights of the poor and
    needy.

10 A good wife who can find?
    She is far more precious than
    jewels.
11 The heart of her husband trusts in
    her,
    and he will have no lack of gain.
12 She does him good, and not harm,
    all the days of her life.
13 She seeks wool and flax,
    and works with willing hands.
14 She is like the ships of the merchant,
    she brings her food from afar.

15 She rises while it is yet night
    and provides food for her house-
    hold
    and tasks for her maidens.
16 She considers a field and buys it;
    with the fruit of her hands she
    plants a vineyard.
17 She girds her loins with strength
    and makes her arms strong.
18 She perceives that her merchandise
    is profitable.
    Her lamp does not go out at night.
19 She puts her hands to the distaff,
    and her hands hold the spindle.
20 She opens her hand to the poor,
    and reaches out her hands to the
    needy.
21 She is not afraid of snow for her
    household,
    for all her household are clothed
    in scarlet.
22 She makes herself coverings;
    her clothing is fine linen and
    purple.
23 Her husband is known in the gates,
    when he sits among the elders of
    the land.
24 She makes linen garments and sells
    them;
    she delivers girdles to the mer-
    chant.
25 Strength and dignity are her clothing,
    and she laughs at the time to come.
26 She opens her mouth with wisdom,
    and the teaching of kindness is on
    her tongue.
27 She looks well to the ways of her
    household,
    and does not eat the bread of
    idleness.
28 Her children rise up and call her
    blessed;
    her husband also, and he praises
    her:
29 "Many women have done excellently,
    but you surpass them all."
30 Charm is deceitful, and beauty is
    vain,
    but a woman who fears the LORD
    is to be praised.
31 Give her of the fruit of her hands,
    and let her works praise her in the
    gates.

[j] The meaning of the Hebrew is uncertain
[k] Or *King Lemuel, the oracle* [l] Cn: Heb *where*
[m] Heb *are sons of passing away*

Ecclesiastes
or the Preacher

1 The words of the Preacher,[a] the son of David, king in Jerusalem.
[2] Vanity of vanities, says the Preacher, vanity of vanities! All is vanity.
[3] What does man gain by all the toil at which he toils under the sun?
[4] A generation goes, and a generation comes,
but the earth remains for ever.
[5] The sun rises and the sun goes down, and hastens to the place where it rises.
[6] The wind blows to the south, and goes round to the north;
round and round goes the wind, and on its circuits the wind returns.
[7] All streams run to the sea, but the sea is not full;
to the place where the streams flow,
there they flow again.
[8] All things are full of weariness; a man cannot utter it;
the eye is not satisfied with seeing, nor the ear filled with hearing.
[9] What has been is what will be, and what has been done is what will be done;
and there is nothing new under the sun.
[10] Is there a thing of which it is said, "See, this is new"?
It has been already, in the ages before us.
[11] There is no remembrance of former things,
nor will there be any remembrance of later things yet to happen
among those who come after.

[12] I the Preacher have been king over Israel in Jerusalem. [13] And I applied my mind to seek and to search out by wisdom all that is done under heaven; it is an unhappy business that God has given to the sons of men to be busy with. [14] I have seen everything that is done under the sun; and behold, all is vanity and a striving after wind.[b]

[15] What is crooked cannot be made straight,
and what is lacking cannot be numbered.

[16] I said to myself, "I have acquired great wisdom, surpassing all who were over Jerusalem before me; and my mind has had great experience of wisdom and knowledge." [17] And I applied my mind to know wisdom and to know madness and folly. I perceived that this also is but a striving after wind.
[18] For in much wisdom is much vexation,
and he who increases knowledge increases sorrow.

2 I said to myself, "Come now, I will make a test of pleasure; enjoy yourself." But behold, this also was vanity. [2] I said of laughter, "It is mad," and of pleasure, "What use is it?" [3] I searched with my mind how to cheer my body with wine—my mind still guiding me with wisdom—and how to lay hold on folly, till I might see what was good for the sons of men to do under heaven during the few days of their life. [4] I made great works; I built houses and planted vineyards for myself; [5] I made myself gardens and parks, and planted in them all kinds of fruit trees. [6] I made myself pools from which to water the forest of growing trees. [7] I bought male and female slaves, and had slaves who were born in my house; I had also great possessions of herds and flocks, more than any who had been before me in Jerusalem. [8] I also gathered for myself silver and gold and the treasure of kings and provinces; I got singers, both men and women, and many concubines,[c] man's delight.

[9] So I became great and surpassed all who were before me in Jerusalem; also my wisdom remained with me.

[a] Heb *Koheleth*   [b] Or *a feeding on wind.* See Hos 12.1
[c] The meaning of the Hebrew word is uncertain

¹⁰And whatever my eyes desired I did not keep from them; I kept my heart from no pleasure, for my heart found pleasure in all my toil, and this was my reward for all my toil. ¹¹Then I considered all that my hands had done and the toil I had spent in doing it, and behold, all was vanity and a striving after wind, and there was nothing to be gained under the sun.

12 So I turned to consider wisdom and madness and folly; for what can the man do who comes after the king? Only what he has already done. ¹³Then I saw that wisdom excels folly as light excels darkness. ¹⁴The wise man has his eyes in his head, but the fool walks in darkness; and yet I perceived that one fate comes to all of them. ¹⁵Then I said to myself, "What befalls the fool will befall me also; why then have I been so very wise?" And I said to myself that this also is vanity. ¹⁶For of the wise man as of the fool there is no enduring remembrance, seeing that in the days to come all will have been long forgotten. How the wise man dies just like the fool! ¹⁷So I hated life, because what is done under the sun was grievous to me; for all is vanity and a striving after wind.

18 I hated all my toil in which I had toiled under the sun, seeing that I must leave it to the man who will come after me; ¹⁹and who knows whether he will be a wise man or a fool? Yet he will be master of all for which I toiled and used my wisdom under the sun. This also is vanity. ²⁰So I turned about and gave my heart up to despair over all the toil of my labors under the sun, ²¹because sometimes a man who has toiled with wisdom and knowledge and skill must leave all to be enjoyed by a man who did not toil for it. This also is vanity and a great evil. ²²What has a man from all the toil and strain with which he toils beneath the sun? ²³For all his days are full of pain, and his work is a vexation; even in the night his mind does not rest. This also is vanity.

24 There is nothing better for a man than that he should eat and drink, and find enjoyment in his toil. This also, I saw, is from the hand of God; ²⁵for apart from him*d* who can eat or who can have enjoyment? ²⁶For to the man who pleases him God gives wisdom and knowledge and joy; but to the sin-

ner he gives the work of gathering and heaping, only to give to one who pleases God. This also is vanity and a striving after wind.

3 For everything there is a season, and a time for every matter under heaven:
²a time to be born, and a time to die;
a time to plant, and a time to pluck up what is planted;
³a time to kill, and a time to heal;
a time to break down, and a time to build up;
⁴a time to weep, and a time to laugh;
a time to mourn, and a time to dance;
⁵a time to cast away stones, and a time to gather stones together;
a time to embrace, and a time to refrain from embracing;
⁶a time to seek, and a time to lose;
a time to keep, and a time to cast away;
⁷a time to rend, and a time to sew;
a time to keep silence, and a time to speak;
⁸a time to love, and a time to hate;
a time for war, and a time for peace.
⁹What gain has the worker from his toil?

10 I have seen the business that God has given to the sons of men to be busy with. ¹¹He has made everything beautiful in its time; also he has put eternity into man's mind, yet so that he cannot find out what God has done from the beginning to the end. ¹²I know that there is nothing better for them than to be happy and enjoy themselves as long as they live; ¹³also that it is God's gift to man that every one should eat and drink and take pleasure in all his toil. ¹⁴I know that whatever God does endures for ever; nothing can be added to it, nor anything taken from it; God has made it so, in order that men should fear before him. ¹⁵That which is, already has been; that which is to be, already has been; and God seeks what has been driven away.

16 Moreover I saw under the sun that in the place of justice, even there was wickedness, and in the place of righteousness, even there was wickedness. ¹⁷I said in my heart, God will judge the righteous and the wicked, for he has appointed a time for every matter, and for every work. ¹⁸I said in my heart with regard to the sons of men that God is testing

*d*Gk Syr: Heb *apart from me*

them to show them that they are but beasts. ¹⁹For the fate of the sons of men and the fate of beasts is the same; as one dies, so dies the other. They all have the same breath, and man has no advantage over the beasts; for all is vanity. ²⁰All go to one place; all are from the dust, and all turn to dust again. ²¹Who knows whether the spirit of man goes upward and the spirit of the beast goes down to the earth? ²²So I saw that there is nothing better than that a man should enjoy his work, for that is his lot; who can bring him to see what will be after him?

4 Again I saw all the oppressions that are practiced under the sun. And behold, the tears of the oppressed, and they had no one to comfort them! On the side of their oppressors there was power, and there was no one to comfort them. ²And I thought the dead who are already dead more fortunate than the living who are still alive; ³but better than both is he who has not yet been, and has not seen the evil deeds that are done under the sun.

4 Then I saw that all toil and all skill in work come from a man's envy of his neighbor. This also is vanity and a striving after wind.

5 The fool folds his hands, and eats his own flesh.

6 Better is a handful of quietness than two hands full of toil and a striving after wind.

7 Again, I saw vanity under the sun: ⁸a person who has no one, either son or brother, yet there is no end to all his toil, and his eyes are never satisfied with riches, so that he never asks, "For whom am I toiling and depriving myself of pleasure?" This also is vanity and an unhappy business.

9 Two are better than one, because they have a good reward for their toil. ¹⁰For if they fall, one will lift up his fellow; but woe to him who is alone when he falls and has not another to lift him up. ¹¹Again, if two lie together, they are warm; but how can one be warm alone? ¹²And though a man might prevail against one who is alone, two will withstand him. A threefold cord is not quickly broken.

13 Better is a poor and wise youth than an old and foolish king, who will no longer take advice, ¹⁴even though he had gone from prison to the throne or in his own kingdom had been

born poor. ¹⁵I saw all the living who move about under the sun, as well as that*ᶠ* youth, who was to stand in his place; ¹⁶there was no end of all the people; he was over all of them. Yet those who come later will not rejoice in him. Surely this also is vanity and a striving after wind.

5*ᵍ* Guard your steps when you go to the house of God; to draw near to listen is better than to offer the sacrifice of fools; for they do not know that they are doing evil. ²ʰBe not rash with your mouth, nor let your heart be hasty to utter a word before God, for God is in heaven, and you upon earth; therefore let your words be few.

3 For a dream comes with much business, and a fool's voice with many words.

4 When you vow a vow to God, do not delay paying it; for he has no pleasure in fools. Pay what you vow. ⁵It is better that you should not vow than that you should vow and not pay. ⁶Let not your mouth lead you into sin, and do not say before the messenger*ⁱ* that it was a mistake; why should God be angry at your voice, and destroy the work of your hands?

7 For when dreams increase, empty words grow many:*ʲ* but do you fear God.

8 If you see in a province the poor oppressed and justice and right violently taken away, do not be amazed at the matter; for the high official is watched by a higher, and there are yet higher ones over them. ⁹But in all, a king is an advantage to a land with cultivated fields.*ᵏ*

10 He who loves money will not be satisfied with money; nor he who loves wealth, with gain: this also is vanity.

11 When goods increase, they increase who eat them; and what gain has their owner but to see them with his eyes?

12 Sweet is the sleep of a laborer, whether he eats little or much; but the surfeit of the rich will not let him sleep.

13 There is a grievous evil which I have seen under the sun: riches were kept by their owner to his hurt,

---

ᶠHeb the second
ᵍCh 4.17 in Heb ʰCh 5.1 in Heb ⁱOr angel
ʲOr For in a multitude of dreams there is futility, and ruin in a flood of words
ᵏOr The profit of the land is among all of them; a cultivated field has a king

[14] and those riches were lost in a bad venture; and he is father of a son, but he has nothing in his hand. [15] As he came from his mother's womb he shall go again, naked as he came, and shall take nothing for his toil, which he may carry away in his hand. [16] This also is a grievous evil: just as he came, so shall he go; and what gain has he that he toiled for the wind, [17] and spent all his days in darkness and grief,[1] in much vexation and sickness and resentment?

[18] Behold, what I have seen to be good and to be fitting is to eat and drink and find enjoyment in all the toil with which one toils under the sun the few days of his life which God has given him, for this is his lot. [19] Every man also to whom God has given wealth and possessions and power to enjoy them, and to accept his lot and find enjoyment in his toil—this is the gift of God. [20] For he will not much remember the days of his life because God keeps him occupied with joy in his heart.

6 There is an evil which I have seen under the sun, and it lies heavy upon men: [2] a man to whom God gives wealth, possessions, and honor, so that he lacks nothing of all that he desires, yet God does not give him power to enjoy them, but a stranger enjoys them; this is vanity; it is a sore affliction. [3] If a man begets a hundred children, and lives many years, so that the days of his years are many, but he does not enjoy life's good things, and also has no burial, I say that an untimely birth is better off than he. [4] For it comes into vanity and goes into darkness, and in darkness its name is covered; [5] moreover it has not seen the sun or known anything; yet it finds rest rather than he. [6] Even though he should live a thousand years twice told, yet enjoy no good—do not all go to the one place?

[7] All the toil of man is for his mouth, yet his appetite is not satisfied. [8] For what advantage has the wise man over the fool? And what does the poor man have who knows how to conduct himself before the living? [9] Better is the sight of the eyes than the wandering of desire; this also is vanity and a striving after wind.

[10] Whatever has come to be has already been named, and it is known

what man is, and that he is not able to dispute with one stronger than he. [11] The more words, the more vanity, and what is man the better? [12] For who knows what is good for man while he lives the few days of his vain life, which he passes like a shadow? For who can tell man what will be after him under the sun?

7 A good name is better than precious ointment;
   and the day of death, than the day of birth.
[2] It is better to go to the house of mourning
   than to go to the house of feasting;
for this is the end of all men,
   and the living will lay it to heart.
[3] Sorrow is better than laughter,
   for by sadness of countenance the heart is made glad.
[4] The heart of the wise is in the house of mourning;
   but the heart of fools is in the house of mirth.
[5] It is better for a man to hear the rebuke of the wise
   than to hear the song of fools.
[6] For as the crackling of thorns under a pot,
   so is the laughter of the fools;
this also is vanity.
[7] Surely oppression makes the wise man foolish,
   and a bribe corrupts the mind.
[8] Better is the end of a thing than its beginning;
   and the patient in spirit is better than the proud in spirit.
[9] Be not quick to anger,
   for anger lodges in the bosom of fools.
[10] Say not, "Why were the former days better than these?"
   For it is not from wisdom that you ask this.
[11] Wisdom is good with an inheritance,
   an advantage to those who see the sun.
[12] For the protection of wisdom is like the protection of money;
   and the advantage of knowledge is that wisdom preserves the life of him who has it.
[13] Consider the work of God;
   who can make straight what he has made crooked?
[14] In the day of prosperity be joyful, and in the day of adversity consider;

[1] Gk: Heb *all his days also he eats in darkness*

God has made the one as well as the other, so that man may not find out anything that will be after him.

15 In my vain life I have seen everything; there is a righteous man who perishes in his righteousness, and there is a wicked man who prolongs his life in his evil-doing. 16 Be not righteous overmuch, and do not make yourself overwise; why should you destroy yourself? 17 Be not wicked overmuch, neither be a fool; why should you die before your time? 18 It is good that you should take hold of this, and from that withhold not your hand; for he who fears God shall come forth from them all.

19 Wisdom gives strength to the wise man more than ten rulers that are in a city.

20 Surely there is not a righteous man on earth who does good and never sins.

21 Do not give heed to all the things that men say, lest you hear your servant cursing you; 22 your heart knows that many times you have yourself cursed others.

23 All this I have tested by wisdom; I said, "I will be wise"; but it was far from me. 24 That which is, is far off, and deep, very deep; who can find it out? 25 I turned my mind to know and to search out and to seek wisdom and the sum of things, and to know the wickedness of folly and the foolishness which is madness. 26 And I found more bitter than death the woman whose heart is snares and nets, and whose hands are fetters; he who pleases God escapes her, but the sinner is taken by her. 27 Behold, this is what I found, says the Preacher, adding one thing to another to find the sum, 28 which my mind has sought repeatedly, but I have not found. One man among a thousand I found, but a woman among all these I have not found. 29 Behold, this alone I found, that God made man upright, but they have sought out many devices.

3 Who is like the wise man?
And who knows the interpretation of a thing?
A man's wisdom makes his face shine,
and the hardness of his countenance is changed.

2 Keep*m* the king's command, and because of your sacred oath be not dismayed; 3 go from his presence, do not delay when the matter is unpleasant, for he does whatever he pleases. 4 For the word of the king is supreme, and who may say to him, "What are you doing?" 5 He who obeys a command will meet no harm, and the mind of a wise man will know the time and way. 6 For every matter has its time and way, although man's trouble lies heavy upon him. 7 For he does not know what is to be, for who can tell him how it will be? 8 No man has power to retain the spirit, or authority over the day of death; there is no discharge from war, nor will wickedness deliver those who are given to it. 9 All this I observed while applying my mind to all that is done under the sun, while man lords it over man to his hurt.

10 Then I saw the wicked buried; they used to go in and out of the holy place, and were praised in the city where they had done such things. This also is vanity. 11 Because sentence against an evil deed is not executed speedily, the heart of the sons of men is fully set to do evil. 12 Though a sinner does evil a hundred times and prolongs his life, yet I know that it will be well with those who fear God, because they fear before him; 13 but it will not be well with the wicked, neither will he prolong his days like a shadow, because he does not fear before God.

14 There is a vanity which takes place on earth, that there are righteous men to whom it happens according to the deeds of the wicked, and there are wicked men to whom it happens according to the deeds of the righteous. I said that this also is vanity. 15 And I commend enjoyment, for man has no good thing under the sun but to eat, and drink, and enjoy himself, for this will go with him in his toil through the days of life which God gives him under the sun.

16 When I applied my mind to know wisdom, and to see the business that is done on earth, how neither day nor night one's eyes see sleep; 17 then I saw all the work of God, that man cannot find out the work that is done under the sun. However much man may toil in seeking, he will not find it out; even

m Heb inserts an *I*

though a wise man claims to know, he cannot find it out.

9 But all this I laid to heart, examining it all, how the righteous and the wise and their deeds are in the hand of God; whether it is love or hate man does not know. Everything before them is vanity,[n] [2] since one fate comes to all, to the righteous and the wicked, to the good and the evil,[o] to the clean and the unclean, to him who sacrifices and him who does not sacrifice. As is the good man, so is the sinner; and he who swears is as he who shuns an oath. [3] This is an evil in all that is done under the sun, that one fate comes to all; also the hearts of men are full of evil, and madness is in their hearts while they live, and after that they go to the dead. [4] But he who is joined with all the living has hope, for a living dog is better than a dead lion. [5] For the living know that they will die, but the dead know nothing, and they have no more reward; but the memory of them is lost. [6] Their love and their hate and their envy have already perished, and they have no more for ever any share in all that is done under the sun.

7 Go, eat your bread with enjoyment, and drink your wine with a merry heart; for God has already approved what you do.

8 Let your garments be always white; let not oil be lacking on your head.

9 Enjoy life with the wife whom you love, all the days of your vain life which he has given you under the sun, because that is your portion in life and in your toil at which you toil under the sun. [10] Whatever your hand finds to do, do it with your might; for there is no work or thought or knowledge or wisdom in Shē′ōl, to which you are going.

11 Again I saw that under the sun the race is not to the swift, nor the battle to the strong, nor bread to the wise, nor riches to the intelligent, nor favor to the men of skill; but time and chance happen to them all. [12] For man does not know his time. Like fish which are taken in an evil net, and like birds which are caught in a snare, so the sons of men are snared at an evil time, when it suddenly falls upon them.

13 I have also seen this example of wisdom under the sun, and it seemed

great to me. [14] There was a little city with few men in it; and a great king came against it and besieged it, building great siegeworks against it. [15] But there was found in it a poor wise man, and he by his wisdom delivered the city. Yet no one remembered that poor man. [16] But I say that wisdom is better than might, though the poor man's wisdom is despised, and his words are not heeded.

17 The words of the wise heard in quiet are better than the shouting of a ruler among fools. [18] Wisdom is better than weapons of war, but one sinner destroys much good.

10 Dead flies make the perfumer's
　　ointment give off an evil odor;
　　so a little folly outweighs wisdom
　　　and honor.
[2] A wise man's heart inclines him
　　toward the right,
　　but a fool's heart toward the left.
[3] Even when the fool walks on the
　　road, he lacks sense,
　　and he says to every one that he
　　is a fool.
[4] If the anger of the ruler rises against
　　you, do not leave your place,
　　for deference will make amends
　　for great offenses.

5 There is an evil which I have seen under the sun, as it were an error proceeding from the ruler: [6] folly is set in many high places, and the rich sit in a low place. [7] I have seen slaves on horses, and princes walking on foot like slaves.
[8] He who digs a pit will fall into it;
　　and a serpent will bite him who
　　breaks through a wall.
[9] He who quarries stones is hurt by
　　them;
　　and he who splits logs is en-
　　dangered by them.
[10] If the iron is blunt, and one does not
　　whet the edge,
　　he must put forth more strength;
　　but wisdom helps one to succeed.
[11] If the serpent bites before it is
　　charmed,
　　there is no advantage in a charmer.

[12] The words of a wise man's mouth
　　win him favor,
　　but the lips of a fool consume him.
[13] The beginning of the words of his
　　mouth is foolishness,

[n] Syr Compare Gk: Heb *Everything before them is everything*　[o] Gk Syr Vg: Heb lacks *and the evil*

and the end of his talk is wicked madness.

14 A fool multiplies words,
though no man knows what is to be,
and who can tell him what will be after him?

15 The toil of a fool wearies him,
so that he does not know the way to the city.

16 Woe to you, O land, when your king is a child,
and your princes feast in the morning!

17 Happy are you, O land, when your king is the son of free men,
and your princes feast at the proper time,
for strength, and not for drunkenness!

18 Through sloth the roof sinks in,
and through indolence the house leaks.

19 Bread is made for laughter,
and wine gladdens life,
and money answers everything.

20 Even in your thought, do not curse the king,
nor in your bedchamber curse the rich;
for a bird of the air will carry your voice,
or some winged creature tell the matter.

11 Cast your bread upon the waters, for you will find it after many days.

2 Give a portion to seven, or even to eight,
for you know not what evil may happen on earth.

3 If the clouds are full of rain,
they empty themselves on the earth;
and if a tree falls to the south or to the north,
in the place where the tree falls, there it will lie.

4 He who observes the wind will not sow;
and he who regards the clouds will not reap.

5 As you do not know how the spirit comes to the bones in the womb[p] of a woman with child, so you do not know the work of God who makes everything.

6 In the morning sow your seed, and at evening withhold not your hand; for you do not know which will prosper, this or that, or whether both alike will be good.

7 Light is sweet, and it is pleasant for the eyes to behold the sun.

8 For if a man lives many years, let him rejoice in them all; but let him remember that the days of darkness will be many. All that comes is vanity.

9 Rejoice, O young man, in your youth, and let your heart cheer you in the days of your youth; walk in the ways of your heart and the sight of your eyes. But know that for all these things God will bring you into judgment.

10 Remove vexation from your mind, and put away pain from your body; for youth and the dawn of life are vanity.

12 Remember also your Creator in the days of your youth, before the evil days come, and the years draw nigh, when you will say, "I have no pleasure in them"; 2 before the sun and the light and the moon and the stars are darkened and the clouds return after the rain; 3 in the day when the keepers of the house tremble, and the strong men are bent, and the grinders cease because they are few, and those that look through the windows are dimmed, 4 and the doors on the street are shut; when the sound of the grinding is low, and one rises up at the voice of a bird, and all the daughters of song are brought low; 5 they are afraid also of what is high, and terrors are in the way; the almond tree blossoms, the grasshopper drags itself along[q] and desire fails; because man goes to his eternal home, and the mourners go about the streets; 6 before the silver cord is snapped,[r] or the golden bowl is broken, or the pitcher is broken at the fountain, or the wheel broken at the cistern, 7 and the dust returns to the earth as it was, and the spirit returns to God who gave it. 8 Vanity of vanities, says the Preacher; all is vanity.

9 Besides being wise, the Preacher also taught the people knowledge, weighing and studying and arranging proverbs with great care. 10 The Preacher sought to find pleasing words,

[p] Or As you do not know the way of the wind, or how the bones grow in the womb
[q] Or is a burden [r] Syr Vg Compare Gk: Heb is removed

and uprightly he wrote words of truth.
11 The sayings of the wise are like
goads, and like nails firmly fixed are
the collected sayings which are given
by one Shepherd. ¹²My son, beware of
anything beyond these. Of making
many books there is no end, and much
study is a weariness of the flesh.
13 The end of the matter; all has
been heard. Fear God, and keep his
commandments; for this is the whole
duty of man.ˢ ¹⁴For God will bring
every deed into judgment, withᵗ every
secret thing, whether good or evil.

The Song of Solomon

1 The Song of Songs, which is
Solomon's.

²O that youᵃ would kiss me with the
    kisses of yourᵇ mouth!
For your love is better than wine,
³ your anointing oils are fragrant,
    your name is oil poured out;
    therefore the maidens love you.
⁴Draw me after you, let us make haste.
    The king has brought me into his
    chambers.
We will exult and rejoice in you;
    we will extol your love more than
    wine;
    rightly do they love you.

⁵I am very dark, but comely,
    O daughters of Jerusalem,
like the tents of Kē'dăr,
    like the curtains of Solomon.
⁶Do not gaze at me because I am
    swarthy,
    because the sun has scorched me.
My mother's sons were angry with
    me,
    they made me keeper of the vine-
    yards;
    but, my own vineyard I have not
    kept!
⁷Tell me, you whom my soul loves,
    where you pasture your flock,
    where you make it lie down at
    noon;
    for why should I be like one who
    wandersᶜ
    beside the flocks of your com-
    panions?

⁸If you do not know,
    O fairest among women,
follow in the tracks of the flock,
    and pasture your kids
    beside the shepherds' tents.

⁹I compare you, my love,
    to a mare of Pharaoh's chariots.
¹⁰Your cheeks are comely with orna-
    ments,
    your neck with strings of jewels.
¹¹We will make you ornaments of
    gold,
    studded with silver.

¹²While the king was on his couch,
    my nard gave forth its fragrance.
¹³My beloved is to me a bag of myrrh,
    that lies between my breasts.
¹⁴My beloved is to me a cluster of
    henna blossoms
    in the vineyards of Ĕn-gĕ'dī.

¹⁵Behold, you are beautiful, my love;
    behold, you are beautiful;
    your eyes are doves.
¹⁶Behold, you are beautiful, my be-
    loved,
    truly lovely.
    Our couch is green;
¹⁷   the beams of our house are cedar,
    our raftersᵈ are pine.

2 I am a roseᵉ of Sharon,
    a lily of the valleys.

²As a lily among brambles,
    so is my love among maidens.

³As an apply tree among the trees of
    the wood,
    so is my beloved among young
    men.
With great delight I sat in his shadow,
    and his fruit was sweet to my
    taste.

ˢOr *the duty of all men* ᵗOr *into the judgment on*

ᵃHeb *he* ᵇHeb *his* ᶜGk Syr Vg: Heb *is veiled*
ᵈThe meaning of the Hebrew word is uncertain
ᵉHeb *crocus*

⁴He brought me to the banqueting house,
and his banner over me was love.
⁵Sustain me with raisins,
refresh me with apples;
for I am sick with love.
⁶O that his left hand were under my head,
and that his right hand embraced me!
⁷I adjure you, O daughters of Jerusalem,
by the gazelles or the hinds of the field,
that you stir not up nor awaken love until it please.

⁸The voice of my beloved!
Behold, he comes,
leaping upon the mountains,
bounding over the hills.
⁹My beloved is like a gazelle,
or a young stag.
Behold, there he stands
behind our wall,
gazing in at the windows,
looking through the lattice.
¹⁰My beloved speaks and says to me:
"Arise, my love, my fair one,
and come away;
¹¹for lo, the winter is past,
the rain is over and gone.
¹²The flowers appear on the earth,
the time of singing has come,
and the voice of the turtledove
is heard in our land.
¹³The fig tree puts forth its figs,
and the vines are in blossom;
they give forth fragrance.
Arise, my love, my fair one,
and come away.
¹⁴O my dove, in the clefts of the rock,
in the covert of the cliff,
let me see your face,
let me hear your voice,
for your voice is sweet,
and your face is comely.
¹⁵Catch us the foxes,
the little foxes,
that spoil the vineyards,
for our vineyards are in blossom."

⁶My beloved is mine and I am his,
he pastures his flock among the lilies.
⁷Until the day breathes
and the shadows flee,
turn, my beloved, be like a gazelle,
or a young stag upon rugged*f*
mountains.

3 Upon my bed by night
I sought him whom my soul loves;
I sought him, but found him not;
I called him, but he gave no answer.*g*
²"I will rise now and go about the city,
in the streets and in the squares;
I will seek him whom my soul loves."
I sought him, but found him not.
³The watchmen found me,
as they went about in the city.
"Have you seen him whom my soul loves?"
⁴Scarcely had I passed them,
when I found him whom my soul loves.
I held him, and would not let him go
until I had brought him into my mother's house,
and into the chamber of her that conceived me.
⁵I adjure you, O daughters of Jerusalem,
by the gazelles or the hinds of the field,
that you stir not up nor awaken love until it please.

⁶What is that coming up from the wilderness,
like a column of smoke,
perfumed with myrrh and frankincense,
with all the fragrant powders of the merchant?
⁷Behold, it is the litter of Solomon!
About it are sixty mighty men
of the mighty men of Israel,
⁸all girt with swords
and expert in war,
each with his sword at his thigh,
against alarms by night.
⁹King Solomon made himself a palanquin
from the wood of Lebanon.
¹⁰He made its posts of silver,
its back of gold, its seat of purple;
it was lovingly wrought within*h*
by the daughters of Jerusalem.
¹¹Go forth, O daughters of Zion,
and behold King Solomon,
with the crown with which his mother crowned him
on the day of his wedding,
on the day of the gladness of his heart.

f The meaning of the Hebrew word is unknown
g Gk: Heb lacks this line
h The meaning of the Hebrew is uncertain

4 Behold, you are beautiful, my love,
   behold, you are beautiful!
Your eyes are doves
   behind your veil.
Your hair is like a flock of goats,
   moving down the slopes of Gilead.
² Your teeth are like a flock of shorn
      ewes
   that have come up from the wash-
      ing,
all of which bear twins,
   and not one among them is be-
      reaved.
³ Your lips are like a scarlet thread,
   and your mouth is lovely.
Your cheeks are like halves of a
      pomegranate
   behind your veil.
⁴ Your neck is like the tower of David,
   built for an arsenal,ⁱ
   whereon hang a thousand bucklers,
   all of them shields of warriors.
⁵ Your two breasts are like two fawns,
   twins of a gazelle,
   that feed among the lilies.
⁶ Until the day breathes
   and the shadows flee,
I will hie me to the mountain of
      myrrh
   and the hill of frankincense.
⁷ You are all fair, my love;
   there is no flaw in you.
⁸ Come with me from Lebanon, my
      bride;
   come with me from Lebanon.
Departʲ from the peak of Ä·mä′nä,
   from the peak of Sē′nĭr and
      Hermon,
from the dens of lions,
   from the mountains of leopards.

⁹ You have ravished my heart, my
      sister, my bride,
   you have ravished my heart with
      a glance of your eyes,
   with one jewel of your necklace.
¹⁰ How sweet is your love, my sister,
      my bride!
   how much better is your love than
      wine,
   and the fragrance of your oils
      than any spice!
¹¹ Your lips distil nectar, my bride;
   honey and milk are under your
      tongue;
   the scent of your garments is like
      the scent of Lebanon.
¹² A garden locked is my sister, my
      bride,
   a garden locked, a fountain sealed.

¹³ Your shoots are an orchard of pome-
      granates
   with all choicest fruits,
   henna with nard,
¹⁴ nard and saffron, calamus and cinna-
      mon,
   with all trees of frankincense,
   myrrh and aloes,
   with all chief spices —
¹⁵ a garden fountain, a well of living
      water,
   and flowing streams from Leb-
      anon.

¹⁶ Awake, O north wind,
   and come, O south wind!
Blow upon my garden,
   let its fragrance be wafted abroad.
Let my beloved come to his garden,
   and eat its choicest fruits.

5 I come to my garden, my sister,
   my bride,
I gather my myrrh with my spice,
I eat my honeycomb with my
      honey,
I drink my wine with my milk.

Eat, O friends, and drink:
   drink deeply, O lovers!
² I slept, but my heart was awake.
Hark! my beloved is knocking.
"Open to me, my sister, my love,
   my dove, my perfect one;
for my head is wet with dew,
   my locks with the drops of the
      night."
³ I had put off my garment,
   how could I put it on?
I had bathed my feet,
   how could I soil them?
⁴ My beloved put his hand to the latch,
   and my heart was thrilled within
      me.
⁵ I arose to open to my beloved,
   and my hands dripped with myrrh,
my fingers with liquid myrrh,
   upon the handles of the bolt.
⁶ I opened to my beloved,
   but my beloved had turned and
      gone.
My soul failed me when he spoke.
I sought him, but found him not;
   I called him, but he gave no
      answer.
⁷ The watchmen found me,
   as they went about in the city;
they beat me, they wounded me,

ⁱThe meaning of the Hebrew word is uncertain
ʲOr *Look*

they took away my mantle,
those watchmen of the walls.
⁸I adjure you, O daughters of Jerusalem,
if you find my beloved,
that you tell him
I am sick with love.

⁹What is your beloved more than
another beloved,
O fairest among women?
What is your beloved more than
another beloved,
that you thus adjure us?

¹⁰My beloved is all radiant and ruddy,
distinguished among ten thousand.
¹¹His head is the finest gold;
his locks are wavy,
black as a raven.
¹²His eyes are like doves
beside springs of water,
bathed in milk,
fitly set.ᵏ
¹³His cheeks are like beds of spices,
yielding fragrance.
His lips are lilies,
distilling liquid myrrh.
¹⁴His arms are rounded gold,
set with jewels.
His body is ivory work,ˡ
encrusted with sapphires.ᵐ
¹⁵His legs are alabaster columns,
set upon bases of gold.
His appearance is like Lebanon,
choice as the cedars.
¹⁶His speech is most sweet,
and he is altogether desirable.
This is my beloved and this is my
friend,
O daughters of Jerusalem.

6 Whither has your beloved gone,
O fairest among women?
Whither has your beloved turned,
that we may seek him with you?

²My beloved has gone down to his
garden,
to the beds of spices,
to pasture his flock in the gardens,
and to gather lilies.
³I am my beloved's and my beloved is
mine;
he pastures his flock among the
lilies.

⁴You are beautiful as Tir′zah, my love,
comely as Jerusalem,

terrible as an army with banners.
⁵Turn away your eyes from me,
for they disturb me—
Your hair is like a flock of goats,
moving down the slopes of Gilead.
⁶Your teeth are like a flock of ewes,
that have come up from the washing,
all of them bear twins,
not one among them is bereaved.
⁷Your cheeks are like halves of a
pomegranate
behind your veil.
⁸There are sixty queens and eighty
concubines,
and maidens without number.
⁹My dove, my perfect one, is only
one,
the darling of her mother,
flawless to her that bore her.
The maidens saw her and called her
happy;
the queens and concubines also,
and they praised her.
¹⁰"Who is this that looks forth like the
dawn,
fair as the moon, bright as the sun,
terrible as an army with banners?"

¹¹I went down to the nut orchard,
to look at the blossoms of the
valley,
to see whether the vines had budded,
whether the pomegranates were
in bloom.
¹²Before I was aware, my fancy set
me
in a chariot beside my prince.ⁿ

¹³ᵒReturn, return, O Shū′lam·mīte,
return, return, that we may look
upon you.

Why should you look upon the
Shulammite,
as upon a dance before two
armies?ᵖ

7 How graceful are your feet in
sandals,
O queenly maiden!
Your rounded thighs are like jewels,
the work of a master hand.
²Your navel is a rounded bowl
that never lacks mixed wine.
Your belly is a heap of wheat,

ᵏThe meaning of the Hebrew is uncertain
ˡThe meaning of the Hebrew word is uncertain
ᵐHeb *lapis lazuli*
ⁿCn: The meaning of the Hebrew is uncertain
ᵒCh 7.1 in Heb ᵖOr *dance of Mahanaim*

encircled with lilies.
³Your two breasts are like two fawns,
  twins of a gazelle.
⁴Your neck is like an ivory tower.
  Your eyes are pools in Hĕsh′bọn,
  by the gate of Băth–răb′bĭm.
  Your nose is like a tower of Lebanon,
  overlooking Damascus.
⁵Your head crowns you like Cär′mẹl,
  and your flowing locks are like
  purple;
  a king is held captive in the
  tresses.*q*

⁶How fair and pleasant you are,
  O loved one, delectable maiden!*r*
⁷You are stately*s* as a palm tree,
  and your breasts are like its
  clusters.
⁸I say I will climb the palm tree
  and lay hold of its branches.
  Oh, may your breasts be like clusters of the vine,
  and the scent of your breath like
  apples,
⁹and your kisses*t* like the best wine
  that goes down*u* smoothly,
  gliding over lips and teeth.*v*

¹⁰I am my beloved's,
  and his desire is for me.
¹¹Come, my beloved,
  let us go forth into the fields,
  and lodge in the villages;
¹²let us go out early to the vineyards,
  and see whether the vines have
  budded,
  whether the grape blossoms have
  opened
  and the pomegranates are in
  bloom.
  There I will give you my love.
¹³The mandrakes give forth fragrance,
  and over our doors are all choice
  fruits,
  new as well as old,
  which I have laid up for you, O
  my beloved.
8 O that you were like a brother to
  me,
  that nursed at my mother's breast!
  If I met you outside, I would kiss
  you,
  and none would despise me.
²I would lead you and bring you
  into the house of my mother,
  and into the chamber of her that
  conceived me.*w*

I would give you spiced wine to
  drink,
  the juice of my pomegranates.
³O that his left hand were under
  my head,
  and that his right hand embraced
  me!
⁴I adjure you, O daughters of Jerusalem,
  that you stir not up nor awaken
  love
  until it please.

⁵Who is that coming up from the
  wilderness,
  leaning upon her beloved?

Under the apple tree I awakened
  you.
There your mother was in travail
  with you,
  there she who bore you was in
  travail.

⁶Set me as a seal upon your heart,
  as a seal upon your arm;
  for love is strong as death,
  jealousy is cruel as the grave.
  Its flashes are flashes of fire,
  a most vehement flame.
⁷Many waters cannot quench love,
  neither can floods drown it.
  If a man offered for love
  all the wealth of his house,
  it would be utterly scorned.

⁸We have a little sister,
  and she has no breasts.
  What shall we do for our sister,
  on the day when she is spoken
  for?
⁹If she is a wall,
  we will build upon her a battle-
  ment of silver;
  but if she is a door,
  we will enclose her with boards of
  cedar.
¹⁰I was a wall,
  and my breasts were like towers;
  then I was in his eyes
  as one who brings*x* peace.

¹¹Solomon had a vineyard at Bā′ạl-
  hā′mŏn;

---

*q*The meaning of the Hebrew word is uncertain
*r*Syr: Heb *in delights*
*s*Heb *This your stature is*
*t*Heb *palate*   *u*Heb *down for my lover*
*v*Gk Syr Vg: Heb *lips of sleepers*
*w*Gk Syr: Heb *mother; she* (or *you*) *will teach me*
*x*Or *finds*

he let out the vineyard to keepers;
each one was to bring for its fruit
a thousand pieces of silver.
¹²My vineyard, my very own, is for
myself;
you, O Solomon, may have the
thousand,
and the keepers of the fruit two
hundred.

¹³O you who dwell in the gardens,
my companions are listening for
your voice;
let me hear it.

¹⁴Make haste, my beloved,
and be like a gazelle
or a young stag
upon the mountains of spices.

The Book of
Isaiah

1 The vision of I·sāi′ah the son of
Ā′mŏz, which he saw concerning
Judah and Jerusalem in the days of
Ŭz·zī′ah, Jō′tham, Ā′hăz, and Hĕz·e-
kī′ah, kings of Judah.
²Hear, O heavens, and give ear, O
earth;
for the LORD has spoken:
"Sons have I reared and brought up,
but they have rebelled against me.
³The ox knows its owner,
and the ass its master's crib;
but Israel does not know,
my people does not understand."

⁴Ah, sinful nation,
a people laden with iniquity,
offspring of evildoers,
sons who deal corruptly!
They have forsaken the LORD,
they have despised the Holy One
of Israel,
they are utterly estranged.

⁵Why will you still be smitten,
that you continue to rebel?
The whole head is sick,
and the whole heart faint.
⁶From the sole of the foot even to
the head,
there is no soundness in it,
but bruises and sores
and bleeding wounds;
they are not pressed out, or bound up,
or softened with oil.

⁷Your country lies desolate,
your cities are burned with fire;
in your very presence
aliens devour your land;

it is desolate, as overthrown by
aliens.
⁸And the daughter of Zion is left
like a booth in a vineyard,
like a lodge in a cucumber field,
like a besieged city.

⁹If the LORD of hosts
had not left us a few survivors,
we should have been like Sŏd′om,
and become like Go·môr′rah.

¹⁰Hear the word of the LORD,
you rulers of Sŏd′om!
Give ear to the teaching of our God,
you people of Go·môr′rah!
¹¹"What to me is the multitude of
your sacrifices?
says the LORD;
I have had enough of burnt offerings
of rams
and the fat of fed beasts;
I do not delight in the blood of bulls,
or of lambs, or of he-goats.

¹²"When you come to appear before me,
who requires of you
this trampling of my courts?
¹³Bring no more vain offerings;
incense is an abomination to me.
New moon and sabbath and the calling of assemblies—
I cannot endure iniquity and
solemn assembly.
¹⁴Your new moons and your appointed
feasts
my soul hates;
they have become a burden to me,
I am weary of bearing them.

1.9: Rom 9.29.

¹⁵ When you spread forth your hands,
  I will hide my eyes from you;
even though you make many prayers,
  I will not listen;
  your hands are full of blood.
¹⁶ Wash yourselves; make yourselves
    clean;
  remove the evil of your doings
    from before my eyes;
  cease to do evil,
¹⁷   learn to do good;
  seek justice,
    correct oppression;
  defend the fatherless,
    plead for the widow.

¹⁸ "Come now, let us reason together,
    says the Lord:
  though your sins are like scarlet,
    they shall be as white as snow;
  though they are red like crimson,
    they shall become like wool.
¹⁹ If you are willing and obedient,
    you shall eat the good of the
    land;
²⁰ But if you refuse and rebel,
    you shall be devoured by the
    sword;
  for the mouth of the Lord has
    spoken."

²¹ How the faithful city
    has become a harlot,
  she that was full of justice!
  Righteousness lodged in her,
    but now murderers.
²² Your silver has become dross,
    your wine mixed with water.
²³ Your princes are rebels
    and companions of thieves.
  Every one loves a bribe
    and runs after gifts.
  They do not defend the fatherless,
    and the widow's cause does not
    come to them.

²⁴ Therefore the Lord says,
    the Lord of hosts,
    the Mighty One of Israel:
  "Ah, I will vent my wrath on my
    enemies,
    and avenge myself on my foes.
²⁵ I will turn my hand against you
    and will smelt away your dross as
    with lye
    and remove all your alloy.
²⁶ And I will restore your judges as at
    the first,
    and your counselors as at the
    beginning.

Afterward you shall be called the
    city of righteousness,
  the faithful city."

²⁷ Zion shall be redeemed by justice,
    and those in her who repent, by
    righteousness.
²⁸ But rebels and sinners shall be de-
    stroyed together,
    and those who forsake the Lord
    shall be consumed.
²⁹ For you shall be ashamed of the
    oaks
    in which you delighted;
    and you shall blush for the gardens
    which you have chosen.
³⁰ For you shall be like an oak
    whose leaf withers,
    and like a garden without water.
³¹ And the strong shall become tow,
    and his work a spark,
    and both of them shall burn to-
    gether,
    with none to quench them.

2 The word which I·sāi'ah the son
  of Ā'mŏz saw concerning Judah
and Jerusalem.
² It shall come to pass in the latter
    days
  that the mountain of the house of
    the Lord
  shall be established as the highest
    of the mountains,
    and shall be raised above the
    hills;
  and all the nations shall flow to it,
³   and many peoples shall come, and
    say:
  "Come, let us go up to the mountain
    of the Lord,
    to the house of the God of Jacob;
  that he may teach us his ways
    and that we may walk in his
    paths."
  For out of Zion shall go forth the
    law,
    and the word of the Lord from
    Jerusalem.
⁴ He shall judge between the nations,
    and shall decide for many peoples;
  and they shall beat their swords into
    plowshares,
    and their spears into pruning
    hooks;
  nation shall not lift up sword against
    nation,
    neither shall they learn war any
    more.
2.2–4: Mic 4.1-3.

⁵O house of Jacob,
   come, let us walk
   in the light of the LORD.

⁶For thou hast rejected thy people,
   the house of Jacob,
because they are full of diviners*ᵃ*
   from the east
   and of soothsayers like the
      Phĭ·lĭs′tĭnes,
   and they strike hands with for-
      eigners.
⁷Their land is filled with silver and
   gold,
   and there is no end to their treas-
      ures;
   their land is filled with horses,
   and there is no end to their
      chariots.
⁸Their land is filled with idols;
   they bow down to the work of their
      hands,
   to what their own fingers have
      made.
⁹So man is humbled,
   and men are brought low—
      forgive them not!
¹⁰Enter into the rock,
   and hide in the dust
from before the terror of the LORD,
   and from the glory of his majesty.
¹¹The haughty looks of man shall be
   brought low,
   and the pride of men shall be
      humbled;
and the LORD alone will be exalted
   in that day.

¹²For the LORD of hosts has a day
   against all that is proud and lofty,
   against all that is lifted up and
      high;*ᵇ*
¹³against all the cedars of Lebanon,
   lofty and lifted up;
   and against all the oaks of
      Bā′shan;
¹⁴against all the high mountains,
   and against all the lofty hills;
¹⁵against every high tower,
   and against every fortified wall;
¹⁶against all the ships of Tär′shĭsh,
   and against all the beautiful
      craft.
¹⁷And the haughtiness of man shall be
   humbled,
   and the pride of men shall be
      brought low;
and the LORD alone will be exalted
   in that day.
¹⁸And the idols shall utterly pass away.

¹⁹And men shall enter the caves of the
   rocks
   and the holes of the ground,
from before the terror of the LORD,
   and from the glory of his majesty,
   when he rises to terrify the earth.

²⁰In that day men will cast forth
   their idols of silver and their idols
      of gold,
   which they made for themselves to
      worship,
   to the moles and to the bats,
²¹to enter the caverns of the rocks
   and the clefts of the cliffs,
from before the terror of the LORD,
   and from the glory of his majesty,
   when he rises to terrify the earth.
²²Turn away from man
   in whose nostrils is breath,
   for of what account is he?

3 For, behold, the Lord, the LORD
      of hosts,
   is taking away from Jerusalem
      and from Judah
stay and staff,
   the whole stay of bread,
   and the whole stay of water;
²the mighty man and the soldier,
   the judge and the prophet,
   the diviner and the elder,
³the captain of fifty
   and the man of rank,
   the counselor and the skilful ma-
      gician
   and the expert in charms.
⁴And I will make boys their princes,
   and babes shall rule over them.
⁵And the people will oppress one
   another,
   every man his fellow
   and every man his neighbor;
the youth will be insolent to the elder,
   and the base fellow to the hon-
      orable.

⁶When a man takes hold of his brother
   in the house of his father, saying:
"You have a mantle;
   you shall be our leader,
and this heap of ruins
   shall be under your rule";
⁷in that day he will speak out, saying:
"I will not be a healer;
   in my house there is neither bread
      nor mantle;
you shall not make me
   leader of the people."

ᵃCn: Heb lacks of diviners ᵇCn Compare Gk: Heb low

⁸For Jerusalem has stumbled,
and Judah has fallen;
because their speech and their
deeds are against the LORD,
defying his glorious presence.

⁹Their partiality witnesses against
them;
they proclaim their sin like Sŏd'ǫm,
they do not hide it.
Woe to them!
For they have brought evil upon
themselves.
¹⁰Tell the righteous that it shall be
well with them,
for they shall eat the fruit of their
deeds.
¹¹Woe to the wicked! It shall be ill
with him,
for what his hands have done shall
be done to him.
¹²My people—children are their oppressors,
and women rule over them.
O my people, your leaders mislead
you,
and confuse the course of your
paths.

¹³The LORD has taken his place to contend,
he stands to judge his people.ᵈ
¹⁴The LORD enters into judgment
with the elders and princes of his
people.
"It is you who have devoured the
vineyard,
the spoil of the poor is in your
houses.
¹⁵What do you mean by crushing my
people,
by grinding the face of the poor?"
says the Lord GOD of hosts.

¹⁶The LORD said:
Because the daughters of Zion are
haughty
and walk with outstretched necks,
glancing wantonly with their eyes,
mincing along as they go,
tinkling with their feet;
¹⁷the Lord will smite with a scab
the heads of the daughters of Zion,
and the LORD will lay bare their
secret parts.

18 In that day the Lord will take
away the finery of the anklets, the
headbands, and the crescents; ¹⁹the
pendants, the bracelets, and the

scarfs; ²⁰the headdresses, the armlets,
the sashes, the perfume boxes, and the
amulets; ²¹the signet rings and nose
rings; ²²the festal robes, the mantles,
the cloaks, and the handbags; ²³the
garments of gauze, the linen garments, the turbans, and the veils.
²⁴Instead of perfume there will be
rottenness;
and instead of a girdle, a rope;
and instead of well-set hair, baldness;
and instead of a rich robe, a
girding of sackcloth;
instead of beauty, shame.ᵉ
²⁵Your men shall fall by the sword
and your mighty men in battle.
²⁶And her gates shall lament and
mourn;
ravaged, she shall sit upon the
ground.

4 And seven women shall take
hold of one man in that day, saying, "We will eat our own bread
and wear our own clothes, only let
us be called by your name; take
away our reproach."

2 In that day the branch of the LORD
shall be beautiful and glorious, and
the fruit of the land shall be the pride
and glory of the survivors of Israel.
³And he who is left in Zion and remains
in Jerusalem will be called holy, every
one who has been recorded for life in
Jerusalem, ⁴when the Lord shall
have washed away the filth of the
daughters of Zion and cleansed the
bloodstains of Jerusalem from its
midst by a spirit of judgment and by a
spirit of burning. ⁵Then the LORD will
create over the whole site of Mount
Zion and over her assemblies a cloud
by day, and smoke and the shining of a
flaming fire by night; for over all the
glory there will be a canopy and a
pavilion. ⁶It will be for a shade by day
from the heat, and for a refuge and a
shelter from the storm and rain.

5 Let me sing for my beloved
a love song concerning his vineyard:
My beloved had a vineyard
on a very fertile hill.
²He digged it and cleared it of stones,

ᵈGk Syr: Heb *judge peoples*
ᵉOne ancient Ms: Heb lacks *shame*
4.2: Jer 23.5; 33.15; Zech 3.8; 6.12.
5.1-7: Mt 21.33-46; Mk 12.1-12; Lk 20.9-19.

and planted it with choice vines;
he built a watchtower in the midst
of it,
and hewed out a wine vat in it;
and he looked for it to yield grapes,
but it yielded wild grapes.

³And now, O inhabitants of Jerusalem
and men of Judah,
judge, I pray you, between me
and my vineyard.
⁴What more was there to do for my
vineyard,
that I have not done in it?
When I looked for it to yield grapes,
why did it yield wild grapes?

⁵And now I will tell you
what I will do to my vineyard.
I will remove its hedge,
and it shall be devoured;
I will break down its wall,
and it shall be trampled down.
⁶I will make it a waste;
it shall not be pruned or hoed,
and briers and thorns shall grow
up;
I will also command the clouds
that they rain no rain upon it.

⁷For the vineyard of the LORD of
hosts
is the house of Israel,
and the men of Judah
are his pleasant planting;.
and he looked for justice,
but behold, bloodshed;
for righteousness,
but behold, a cry!

⁸Woe to those who join house to house,
who add field to field,
until there is no more room,
and you are made to dwell alone
in the midst of the land.
⁹The LORD of hosts has sworn in my
hearing:
"Surely many houses shall be desolate,
large and beautiful houses, without inhabitant.
¹⁰For ten acres of vineyard shall yield
but one bath,
and a homer of seed shall yield
but an ephah."

¹¹Woe to those who rise early in the
morning,
that they may run after strong
drink,

who tarry late into the evening
till wine inflames them!
¹²They have lyre and harp,
timbrel and flute and wine at their
feasts;
but they do not regard the deeds of
the LORD,
or see the work of his hands.

¹³Therefore my people go into exile for
want of knowledge;
their honored men are dying of
hunger,
and their multitide is parched
with thirst.
¹⁴Therefore Shē'ōl has enlarged its
appetite
and opened its mouth beyond
measure,
and the nobility of Jerusalemʲ and
her multitude go down,
her throng and he who exults in
her.
¹⁵Man is bowed down, and men are
brought low,
and the eyes of the haughty are
humbled.
¹⁶But the LORD of hosts is exalted in
justice,
and the Holy God shows himself
holy in righteousness.
¹⁷Then shall the lambs graze as in
their pasture,
fatlings and kidsᵍ shall feed among
the ruins.

¹⁸Woe to those who draw iniquity with
cords of falsehood,
who draw sin as with cart ropes,
¹⁹who say: "Let him make haste,
let him speed his work
that we may see it;
let the purpose of the Holy One of
Israel draw near,
and let it come, that we may know
it!"
²⁰Woe to those who call evil good and
good evil,
who put darkness for light
and light for darkness,
who put bitter for sweet
and sweet for bitter!
²¹Woe to those who are wise in their
own eyes,
and shrewd in their own sight!
²²Woe to those who are heroes at drinking wine,
and valiant men in mixing strong
drink,

ʲHeb *her nobility*   ᵍCn Compare Gk: Heb *aliens*

²³who acquit the guilty for a bribe,
   and deprive the innocent of his
   right!

²⁴Therefore, as the tongue of fire
   devours the stubble,
   and as dry grass sinks down in the
     flame,
so their root will be as rottenness,
   and their blossom go up like dust;
for they have rejected the law of the
     LORD of hosts,
   and have despised the word of the
     Holy One of Israel.
²⁵Therefore the anger of the LORD
   was kindled against his people,
   and he stretched out his hand
     against them and smote them,
   and the mountains quaked;
and their corpses were as refuse in
   the midst of the streets.
For all this his anger is not turned
     away
   and his hand is stretched out still.

²⁶He will raise a signal for a nation
     afar off,
   and whistle for it from the ends of
     the earth;
and lo, swiftly, speedily it comes!
²⁷None is weary, none stumbles,
   none slumbers or sleeps,
   not a waistcloth is loose,
   not a sandal-thong broken;
²⁸their arrows are sharp,
   all their bows bent,
   their horses' hoofs seem like flint,
     and their wheels like the whirl-
     wind.
²⁹Their roaring is like a lion,
   like young lions they roar;
they growl and seize their prey,
   they carry it off, and none can
     rescue.
³⁰They will growl over it on that day,
   like the roaring of the sea.
And if one look to the land,
   behold, darkness and distress;
and the light is darkened by its
     clouds.

6 In the year that King Ŭz·zī′ạh
died I saw the Lord sitting upon
a throne, high and lifted up; and his
train filled the temple. ²Above him
stood the seraphim; each had six
wings: with two he covered his face,
and with two he covered his feet,
and with two he flew. ³And one called
to another and said:

"Holy, holy, holy is the LORD of
     hosts;
the whole earth is full of his glory."
⁴And the foundations of the thresholds shook at the voice of him who
called, and the house was filled with
smoke. ⁵And I said: "Woe is me! For
I am lost; for I am a man of unclean
lips, and I dwell in the midst of a
people of unclean lips; for my eyes
have seen the King, the LORD of hosts!"
6 Then flew one of the seraphim
to me, having in his hand a burning
coal which he had taken with tongs
from the altar. ⁷And he touched my
mouth, and said: "Behold, this has
touched your lips; your guilt is taken
away, and your sin forgiven." ⁸And I
heard the voice of the Lord saying,
"Whom shall I send, and who will
go for us?" Then I said, "Here am I!
Send me." ⁹And he said, "Go, and say
to this people:
'Hear and hear, but do not under-
     stand;
  see and see, but do not perceive.'
¹⁰Make the heart of this people fat,
   and their ears heavy,
   and shut their eyes;
lest they see with their eyes,
   and hear with their ears,
   and understand with their hearts,
   and turn and be healed."
¹¹Then I said, "How long, O Lord?"
And he said:
"Until cities lie waste
   without inhabitant,
   and houses without men,
   and the land is utterly desolate,
¹²and the LORD removes men far away,
   and the forsaken places are many
     in the midst of the land.
¹³And though a tenth remain in it,
   it will be burned again,
like a terebinth or an oak,
   whose stump remains standing
     when it is felled."
The holy seed is its stump.

7 In the days of Ā′hăz the son of
Jō′thạm, son of Ŭz·zī′ạh, king of
Judah, Rē′zĭn the king of Syria and
Pē′kạh the son of Rĕm·ạ·lī′ạh the king
of Israel came up to Jerusalem to
wage war against it, but they could
not conquer it. ²When the house of
David was told, "Syria is in league

6.3: Rev 4.8.   6.4: Rev 15.8.
6.9-10: Mt 13.14-15; Mk 4.12; Lk 8.10; Jn 12.39-41; Acts
28.26-27.

with Ē′phrạ·ĭm," his heart and the heart of his people shook as the trees of the forest shake before the wind.

3 And the LORD said to Ī·sāi′ạh, "Go forth to meet Ā′hăz, you and Shē′är·jăsh″ŭbʰ your son, at the end of the conduit of the upper pool on the highway to the Fuller's Field, ⁴and say to him, 'Take heed, be quiet, do not fear, and do not let your heart be faint because of these two smolder- ing stumps of firebrands, at the fierce anger of Rē′zĭn and Syria and the son of Rĕm·ạ·lī′ạh. ⁵Because Syria, with Ē′phrạ·ĭm and the son of Rĕm·ạ·lī′ạh, has devised evil against you, say- ing, ⁶"Let us go up against Judah and terrify it, and let us conquer it for ourselves, and set up the son of Tā′bē- ĕl″ as king in the midst of it," ⁷thus says the Lord GOD:
It shall not stand,
  and it shall not come to pass.
⁸For the head of Syria is Damascus,
  and the head of Damascus is Rē′zĭn.
(Within sixty-five years Ē′phrạ·ĭm will be broken to pieces so that it will no longer be a people.)
⁹And the head of Ē′phrạ·ĭm is Sạ- mâr′ĭ·ạ,
  and the head of Samaria is the son of Rĕm·ạ·lī′ạh.
If you will not believe,
  surely you shall not be estab- lished.' "

10 Again the LORD spoke to Ā′hăz, ¹¹"Ask a sign of the LORD your God; let it be deep as Shē′ōl or high as heaven." ¹²But Ā′hăz said, "I will not ask, and I will not put the LORD to the test." ¹³And he said, "Hear then, O house of David! Is it too little for you to weary men, that you weary my God also? ¹⁴Therefore the Lord himself will give you a sign. Behold, a young womanⁱ shall conceive and bearʲ a son, and shall call his name Ĭm·măn′ū–ĕl.ᵏ ¹⁵He shall eat curds and honey when he knows how to refuse the evil and choose the good. ¹⁶For before the child knows how to refuse the evil and choose the good, the land before whose two kings you are in dread will be deserted. ¹⁷The LORD will bring upon you and upon your people and upon your father's house such days as have not come since the day

that Ē′phrạ·ĭm departed from Judah— the king of Assyria."

18 In that day the LORD will whistle for the fly which is at the sources of the streams of Egypt, and for the bee which is in the land of Assyria. ¹⁹And they will all come and settle in the steep ravines, and in the clefts of the rocks, and on all the thornbushes, and on all the pastures.

20 In that day the Lord will shave with a razor which is hired beyond the River—with the king of Assyria—the head and the hair of the feet, and it will sweep away the beard also.

21 In that day a man will keep alive a young cow and two sheep; ²²and because of the abundance of milk which they give, he will eat curds; for every one that is left in the land will eat curds and honey.

23 In that day every place where there used to be a thousand vines, worth a thousand shekels of silver, will become briers and thorns. ²⁴With bow and arrows men will come there, for all the land will be briers and thorns; ²⁵and as for all the hills which used to be hoed with a hoe, you will not come there for fear of briers and thorns; but they will become a place where cattle are let loose and where sheep tread.

8 Then the LORD said to me, "Take a large tablet and write upon it in common characters, 'Belonging to Mā′hĕr–shăl′ăl–hăsh″–băz.' "ˡ ²And I got reliable witnesses, Ū·rī′ạh the priest and Zĕch·ạ·rī′ạh the son of Jĕ·bĕr·ẹ·chī′ạh, to attest for me. ³And I went to the prophetess, and she con- ceived and bore a son. Then the LORD said to me, "Call his name Mā′hĕr- shăl′ăl–hăsh″–băz; ⁴for before the child knows how to cry 'My father' or 'My mother,' the wealth of Damascus and the spoil of Sạ·mâr′ĭ·ạ will be carried away before the king of Assyria."

5 The LORD spoke to me again: ⁶"Because this people have refused the waters of Shī·lō′ạh that flow gently, and melt in fear beforeᵐ Rē′zĭn and son of Rĕm·ạ·lī′ạh; ⁷therefore, behold, the Lord is bringing up against them the waters of the River, mighty and

ʰThat is A remnant shall return ⁱOr virgin
ʲOr is with child and shall bear ᵏThat is God is with us
ˡThat is The spoil speeds, the prey hastes
ᵐCn: Heb rejoices in 7.14: Mt 1.23.

many, the king of Assyria and all his glory; and it will rise over all its channels and go over all its banks; ⁸and it will sweep on into Judah, it will overflow and pass on, reaching even to the neck; and its outspread wings will fill the breadth of your land, O Ĭm·măn′ū–ĕl.''

⁹Be broken, you peoples, and be dismayed;
give ear, all you far countries;
gird yourselves and be dismayed;
gird yourselves and be dismayed.
¹⁰Take counsel together, but it will come to nought;
speak a word, but it will not stand,
for God is with us.ˣ
11 For the LORD spoke thus to me with his strong hand upon me, and warned me not to walk in the way of this people, saying: ¹²''Do not call conspiracy all that this people call conspiracy, and do not fear what they fear, nor be in dread. ¹³But the LORD of hosts, him you shall regard as holy; let him be your fear, and let him be your dread. ¹⁴And he will become a sanctuary, and a stone of offense, and a rock of stumbling to both houses of Israel, a trap and a snare to the inhabitants of Jerusalem. ¹⁵And many shall stumble thereon; they shall fall and be broken; they shall be snared and taken.''

16 Bind up the testimony, seal the teaching among my disciples. ¹⁷I will wait for the LORD, who is hiding his face from the house of Jacob, and I will hope in him. ¹⁸Behold, I and the children whom the LORD has given me are signs and portents in Israel from the LORD of hosts, who dwells on Mount Zion. ¹⁹And when they say to you, ''Consult the mediums and the wizards who chirp and mutter,'' should not a people consult their God? Should they consult the dead on behalf of the living? ²⁰To the teaching and to the testimony! Surely for this word which they speak there is no dawn. ²¹They will pass through the land,ⁿ greatly distressed and hungry; and when they are hungry, they will be enraged and will curseᵒ their king and their God, and turn their faces upward; ²²and they will look to the earth, but behold, distress and darkness, the gloom of

anguish; and they will be thrust into thick darkness.

9 ᵖ But there will be no gloom for her that was in anguish. In the former time he brought into contempt the land of Zĕb′ū·lun and the land of Năph′ta·lī, but in the latter time he will make glorious the way of the sea, the land beyond the Jordan, Galilee of the nations.
²ᑫThe people who walked in darkness
have seen a great light;
those who dwelt in a land of deep darkness,
on them has light shined.
³Thou hast multiplied the nation,
thou hast increased its joy;
they rejoice before thee
as with joy at the harvest,
as men rejoice when they divide the spoil.
⁴For the yoke of his burden,
and the staff for his shoulder,
the rod of his oppressor,
thou hast broken as on the day of Mĭd′ĭ·an.
⁵For every boot of the tramping warrior in battle tumult
and every garment rolled in blood
will be burned as fuel for the fire.
⁶For to us a child is born,
to us a son is given;
and the government will be upon his shoulder,
and his name will be called
''Wonderful Counselor, Mighty God, Everlasting Father, Prince of Peace.''
⁷Of the increase of his government and of peace
there will be no end,
upon the throne of David, and over his kingdom,
to establish it, and to uphold it
with justice and with righteousness
from this time forth and for evermore.
The zeal of the LORD of hosts will do this.

⁸The Lord has sent a word against Jacob,
and it will light upon Israel;
⁹and all the people will know,
Ē′phra·im and the inhabitants of Sa·mâr′ĭ·a,

ˣHeb *immanu el* ⁿHeb *it*
ᵒOr *curse by* ᵖCh 8.23 in Heb ᑫCh 9.1 in Heb
8.12-13: 1 Pet 3.14-15. **8.14:** Rom 9.32-33; 1 Pet 2.8.
8.17-18: Heb 2.13. **9.1-2:** Mt 4.15-16; Lk 1.79.

who say in pride and in arrogance
of heart:
10 "The bricks have fallen,
but we will build with dressed
stones;
the sycamores have been cut down,
but we will put cedars in their
place."
11 So the LORD raises adversaries[r]
against them,
and stirs up their enemies.
12 The Syrians on the east and the
Phĭ·lĭs'tĭnes on the west
devour Israel with open mouth.
For all this his anger is not turned
away
and his hand is stretched out still.

13 The people did not turn to him who
smote them,
nor seek the LORD of hosts.
14 So the LORD cut off from Israel head
and tail,
palm branch and reed in one day—
15 the elder and honored man is the
head,
and the prophet who teaches lies
is the tail;
16 for those who lead this people lead
them astray,
and those who are led by them
are swallowed up.
17 Therefore the Lord does not rejoice
over their young men,
and has no compassion on their
fatherless and widows;
for every one is godless and an evildoer,
and every mouth speaks folly.
For all this his anger is not turned
away
and his hand is stretched out still.

18 For wickedness burns like a fire,
it consumes briers and thorns;
it kindles the thickets of the forest,
and they roll upward in a column
of smoke.
19 Through the wrath of the LORD of
hosts
the land is burned,
and the people are like fuel for the
fire;
no man spares his brother.
20 They snatch on the right, but are still
hungry,
and they devour on the left, but
are not satisfied;
each devours his neighbor's[s] flesh,

21 Mạ·năs'seh Ē'phrạ·ĭm, and Ephraim Manasseh,
and together they are against
Judah.
For all this his anger is not turned
away
and his hand is stretched out still.

10 Woe to those who decree iniqui-
tous decrees,
and the writers who keep writing oppression,
2 to turn aside the needy from justice
and to rob the poor of my people
of their right,
that widows may be their spoil,
and that they may make the
fatherless their prey!
3 What will you do on the day of
punishment,
in the storm which will come from
afar?
To whom will you flee for help,
and where will you leave your
wealth?
4 Nothing remains but to crouch
among the prisoners
or fall among the slain.
For all this his anger is not turned
away
and his hand is stretched out still.

5 Ah, Assyria, the rod of my anger,
the staff of my fury![t]
6 Against a godless nation I send him,
and against the people of my wrath
I command him,
to take spoil and seize plunder,
and to tread them down like the
mire of the streets.
7 But he does not so intend,
and his mind does not so think;
but it is in his mind to destroy,
and to cut off nations not a few;
8 for he says:
"Are not my commanders all kings?
9 Is not Căl'nō like Cär'che·mĭsh?
Is not Hä'măth like Är'păd?
Is not Sạ·mâr'ĭ·ạ like Damascus?
10 As my hand has reached to the kingdoms of the idols
whose graven images were greater
than those of Jerusalem and
Sạ·mâr'ĭ·ạ,
11 shall I not do to Jerusalem and her
idols

[r] Cn: Heb *the adversaries of Rezin*
[s] Tg Compare Gk: Heb *the flesh of his arm*
[t] Heb *a staff it is in their hand my fury*
10.5-34: Nahum; Zeph 2.13-15.

as I have done to Sạ·mâr'ĭ·ạ and her images?"

12 When the Lord has finished all his work on Mount Zion and on Jerusalem he*ᵘ* will punish the arrogant boasting of the king of Assyria and his haughty pride. ¹³ For he says:
"By the strength of my hand I have done it,
and by my wisdom, for I have understanding;
I have removed the boundaries of peoples,
and have plundered their treasures;
like a bull I have brought down those who sat on thrones.
¹⁴ My hand has found like a nest the wealth of the peoples;
and as men gather eggs that have been forsaken
so I have gathered all the earth;
and there was none that moved a wing,
or opened the mouth, or chirped."

¹⁵ Shall the axe vaunt itself over him who hews with it,
or the saw magnify itself against him who wields it?
As if a rod should wield him who lifts it,
or as if a staff should lift him who is not wood!
¹⁶ Therefore the Lord, the LORD of hosts,
will send wasting sickness among his stout warriors,
and under his glory a burning will be kindled,
like the burning of fire.
¹⁷ The light of Israel will become a fire,
and his Holy One a flame;
and it will burn and devour his thorns and briers in one day.
¹⁸ The glory of his forest and of his fruitful land
the LORD will destroy, both soul and body,
and it will be as when a sick man wastes away.
¹⁹ The remnant of the trees of his forest will be so few
that a child can write them down.

20 In that day the remnant of Israel and the survivors of the house of Jacob will no more lean upon him that

smote them, but will lean upon the LORD, the Holy One of Israel, in truth. ²¹ A remnant will return, the remnant of Jacob, to the mighty God. ²² For though your people Israel be as the sand of the sea, only a remnant of them will return. Destruction is decreed, overflowing with righteousness. ²³ For the Lord, the LORD of hosts, will make a full end, as decreed, in the midst of all the earth.

24 Therefore thus says the Lord, the LORD of hosts: "O my people, who dwell in Zion, be not afraid of the Assyrians when they smite with the rod and lift up their staff against you as the Egyptians did. ²⁵ For in a very little while my indignation will come to an end, and my anger will be directed to their destruction. ²⁶ And the LORD of hosts will wield against them a scourge, as when he smote Mĭd'ĭ·an at the rock of Or'ĕb; and his rod will be over the sea, and he will lift it as he did in Egypt. ²⁷ And in that day his burden will depart from your shoulder, and his yoke will be destroyed from your neck."

He has gone up from Rĭm'mŏn,*ᵛ*
28   he has come to Aĭ'äth;
he has passed through Mĭg'rŏn,
at Mĭch'măsh he stores his baggage;
²⁹ they have crossed over the pass,
at Gē'bạ they lodge for the night;
Rā'mạh trembles,
Gĭb'ē·ạh of Saul has fled.
³⁰ Cry aloud, O daughter of Găl'lĭm!
Hearken, O Lā'ĭ·shạh!
Answer her, O Ăn'ạ·thŏth!
³¹ Măd·mē'nạh is in flight,
the inhabitants of Gē'bĭm flee for safety.
³² This very day he will halt at Nŏb,
he will shake his fist
at the mount of the daughter of Zion,
the hill of Jerusalem.

³³ Behold, the Lord, the LORD of hosts will lop the boughs with terrifying power;
the great in height will be hewn down,
and the lofty will be brought low.

ᵘ Heb I
ᵛ Cn: Heb and his yoke from your neck, and a yoke will be destroyed because of fatness
10.22-23: Rom 9.27-28.

³⁴ He will cut down the thickets of
the forest with an axe,
and Lebanon with its majestic
trees[w] will fall.

11 There shall come forth a shoot
from the stump of Jesse,
and a branch shall grow out of his
roots.
² And the Spirit of the LORD shall
rest upon him,
the spirit of wisdom and understanding,
the spirit of counsel and might,
the spirit of knowledge and the
fear of the LORD.
³ And his delight shall be in the fear
of the LORD.

He shall not judge by what his eyes
see,
or decide by what his ears hear;
⁴ but with righteousness he shall
judge the poor,
and decide with equity for the
meek of the earth;
and he shall smite the earth with
the rod of his mouth,
and with the breath of his lips
he shall slay the wicked.
⁵ Righteousness shall be the girdle
of his waist,
and faithfulness the girdle of his
loins.

⁶ The wolf shall dwell with the lamb,
and the leopard shall lie down with
the kid,
and the calf and the lion and the
fatling together,
and a little child shall lead them.
⁷ The cow and the bear shall feed;
their young shall lie down together;
and the lion shall eat straw like
the ox.
⁸ The sucking child shall play over the
hole of the asp,
and the weaned child shall put
his hand on the adder's den.
⁹ They shall not hurt or destroy
in all my holy mountain;
for the earth shall be full of the
knowledge of the LORD
as the waters cover the sea.

10 In that day the root of Jesse shall
stand as an ensign to the peoples; him
shall the nations seek, and his dwellings shall be glorious.

11 In that day the Lord will extend
his hand yet a second time to recover
the remnant which is left of his people,
from Assyria, from Egypt, from Păth'-
rŏs, from Ethiopia, from Ē'lăm, from
Shī'när, from Hā'măth, and from the
coastlands of the sea.
¹² He will raise an ensign for the
nations,
and will assemble the outcasts of
Israel,
and gather the dispersed of Judah
from the four corners of the
earth.
¹³ The jealousy of Ē'phrạ·ĭm shall depart,
and those who harass Judah shall
be cut off;
Ephraim shall not be jealous of
Judah,
and Judah shall not harass
Ephraim.
¹⁴ But they shall swoop down upon the
shoulder of the Phĭ·lĭs'tĭnes in
the west,
and together they shall plunder the
people of the east.
They shall put forth their hand
against Ē'dọm and Mō'ăb,
and the Ăm'mọ·nītes shall obey
them.
¹⁵ And the LORD will utterly destroy
the tongue of the sea of Egypt;
and will wave his hand over the
River
with his scorching wind,
and smite it into seven channels
that men may cross dryshod.
¹⁶ And there will be a highway from
Assyria
for the remnant which is left of
his people,
as there was for Israel
when they came up from the land
of Egypt.

12 You will say in that day:
"I will give thanks to thee, O
LORD,
for though thou wast angry with
me,
thy anger turned away,
and thou didst comfort me.

² "Behold, God is my salvation;
I will trust, and will not be afraid;

---

[w] Cn Compare Gk Vg: Heb *with a majestic one*
11.1: Is 11.10; Rom 15.12. **11.2:** 1 Pet 4.14.
11.5: Eph 6.14. **11.6-9:** Is 65.25; Hab 2.14.
11.10: Is 11.1; Rom 15.12.

for the LORD GOD is my strength
and my song,
and he has become my salvation."

3 With joy you will draw water from
the wells of salvation. ⁴And you will
say in that day:
"Give thanks to the LORD,
call upon his name;
make known his deeds among the
nations,
proclaim that his name is exalted.

⁵ "Sing praises to the LORD, for he
has done gloriously;
let this be known˟ in all the earth.
⁶ Shout, and sing for joy, O inhabitant of Zion,
for great in your midst is the Holy
One of Israel."

13 The oracle concerning Babylon which Ī·sāi´ạh the son of
Ā´mŏz saw.
² On a bare hill raise a signal,
cry aloud to them;
wave the hand for them to enter
the gates of the nobles.
³ I myself have commanded my consecrated ones,
have summoned my mighty men
to execute my anger,
my proudly exulting ones.

⁴ Hark, a tumult on the mountains
as of a great multitude!
Hark, an uproar of kingdoms,
of nations gathering together!
The LORD of hosts is mustering
a host for battle.
⁵ They come from a distant land,
from the end of the heavens,
the LORD and the weapons of his
indignation,
to destroy the whole earth.

⁶ Wail, for the day of the LORD is near;
as destruction from the Almighty
it will come!
⁷ Therefore all hands will be feeble,
and every man's heart will melt,
⁸   and they will be dismayed.
Pangs and agony will seize them;
they will be in anguish like a
woman in travail.
They will look aghast at one another;
their faces will be aflame.

⁹ Behold, the day of the LORD comes,
cruel, with wrath and fierce anger,

to make the earth a desolation
and to destroy its sinners from it.
¹⁰ For the stars of the heavens and
their constellations
will not give their light;
the sun will be dark at its rising
and the moon will not shed its
light.
¹¹ I will punish the world for its evil,
and the wicked for their iniquity;
I will put an end to the pride of the
arrogant,
and lay low the haughtiness of the
ruthless.
¹² I will make men more rare than fine
gold,
and mankind than the gold of
Ō´phīr.
¹³ Therefore I will make the heavens
tremble,
and the earth will be shaken out
of its place,
at the wrath of the LORD of hosts
in the day of his fierce anger.
¹⁴ And like a hunted gazelle,
or like sheep with none to gather
them,
every man will turn to his own
people,
and every man will flee to his own
land.
¹⁵ Whoever is found will be thrust
through,
and whoever is caught will fall
by the sword.
¹⁶ Their infants will be dashed in pieces
before their eyes;
their houses will be plundered
and their wives ravished.

¹⁷ Behold, I am stirring up the Mēdes
against them,
who have no regard for silver
and do not delight in gold.
¹⁸ Their bows will slaughter the young
men;
they will have no mercy on the
fruit of the womb;
their eyes will not pity children.
¹⁹ And Babylon, the glory of kingdoms,
the splendor and pride of the
Chăl·dē´ạns,
will be like Sŏ´dọm and Gọ·môr´-
rạh
when God overthrew them.
²⁰ It will never be inhabited
or dwelt in for all generations;

˟ Or *this is made known*
13.1-14.23: Is 47; Jer 50-51; Hab 1-2.
13.10: Mt 24.29; Mk 13.24; Rev 6.12; 8.12.

no Arab will pitch his tent there,
no shepherds will make their flocks
lie down there.
²¹ But wild beasts will lie down there,
and its houses will be full of howling creatures;
there ostriches will dwell,
and there satyrs will dance.
²² Hyenas will cry in its towers,
and jackals in the pleasant palaces;
its time is close at hand
and its days will not be prolonged.

14 The LORD will have compassion on Jacob and will again
choose Israel, and will set them in their
own land, and aliens will join them and
will cleave to the house of Jacob. ²And
the peoples will take them and bring
them to their place, and the house of
Israel will possess them in the LORD's
land as male and female slaves; they
will take captive those who were their
captors, and rule over those who oppressed them.

3 When the LORD has given you rest
from your pain and turmoil and the
hard service with which you were
made to serve, ⁴you will take up this
taunt against the king of Babylon:
"How the oppressor has ceased,
the insolent fury ᵛ ceased!
⁵ The LORD has broken the staff of
the wicked,
the scepter of rulers,
⁶ that smote the peoples in wrath
with unceasing blows,
that ruled the nations in anger
with unrelenting persecution.
⁷ The whole earth is at rest and quiet;
they break forth into singing.
The cypresses rejoice at you,
the cedars of Lebanon, saying,
'Since you were laid low,
no hewer comes up against us.'
⁸ She'ōl beneath is stirred up
to meet you when you come,
it rouses the shades to greet you,
all who were leaders of the earth;
it raises from their thrones
all who were kings of the nations.
¹⁰ All of them will speak
and say to you:
'You too have become as weak as we!
You have become like us!'
¹¹ Your pomp is brought down to She'ōl,
the sound of your harps;
maggots are the bed beneath you,
and worms are your covering.

¹² "How you are fallen from heaven,
O Day Star, son of Dawn!
How you are cut down to the ground,
you who laid the nations low!
¹³ You said in your heart,
'I will ascend to heaven;
above the stars of God
I will set my throne on high;
I will sit on the mount of assembly
in the far north;
¹⁴ I will ascend above the heights of the
clouds,
I will make myself like the Most
High.'
¹⁵ But you are brought down to She'ōl,
to the depths of the Pit.
¹⁶ Those who see you will stare at you,
and ponder over you:
'Is this the man who made the earth
tremble,
who shook kingdoms,
¹⁷ who made the world like a desert
and overthrew its cities,
who did not let his prisoners go
home?'
¹⁸ All the kings of the nations lie in
glory,
each in his own tomb;
¹⁹ but you are cast out, away from your
sepulchre,
like a loathed untimely birth,ᶻ
clothed with the slain, those pierced
by the sword,
who go down to the stones of the
Pit,
like a dead body trodden under
foot.
²⁰ You will not be joined with them in
burial,
because you have destroyed your
land,
you have slain your people.

"May the descendants of evildoers
nevermore be named!
²¹ Prepare slaughter for his sons
because of the guilt of their
fathers,
lest they rise and possess the earth,
and fill the face of the world with
cities."

22 "I will rise up against them,"
says the LORD of hosts, "and will cut
off from Babylon name and remnant,
offspring and posterity, says the LORD.

ᵛ One ancient Ms Compare Gk Syr Vg: The meaning of the
Hebrew word is uncertain
ᶻ Cn Compare Tg Symmachus: Heb *a loathed branch*
13.21: Rev 18.2.

²³And I will make it a possession of the hedgehog, and pools of water, and I will sweep it with the broom of destruction, says the LORD of hosts."

²⁴The LORD of hosts has sworn:
"As I have planned,
    so shall it be,
and as I have purposed,
    so shall it stand,
²⁵that I will break the Assyrian in my land,
    and upon my mountains trample him under foot;
and his yoke shall depart from them,
    and his burden from their shoulder."
²⁶This is the purpose that is purposed concerning the whole earth;
    and this is the hand that is stretched out
    over all the nations.
²⁷For the LORD of hosts has purposed, and who will annul it?
His hand is stretched out,
    and who will turn it back?

²⁸In the year that King Ā′hăz died came this oracle:
²⁹"Rejoice not, O Phĭ·lĭs′tĭ·ạ, all of you, that the rod which smote you is broken,
for from the serpent's root will come forth an adder,
    and its fruit will be a flying serpent.
³⁰And the first-born of the poor will feed,
    and the needy lie down in safety;
but I will kill your root with famine,
    and your remnant Iᵃ will slay.
³¹Wail, O gate; cry, O city;
    melt in fear, O Phĭ·lĭs′tĭ·ạ, all of you!
For smoke comes out of the north,
    and there is no straggler in his ranks."

³²What will one answer the messengers of the nation?
"The LORD has founded Zion,
    and in her the afflicted of his people find refuge."

15 An oracle concerning Mō′ăb.
    Because Ȁr is laid waste in a night
    Moab is undone;
because Kīr is laid waste in a night
    Moab is undone.
²The daughter of Dī′bŏnᵇ has gone up

to the high places to weep;
over Nē′bō and over Mĕd′ẹ·bạ
    Mō′ăb wails.
On every head is baldness,
    every beard is shorn;
³in the streets they gird on sackcloth;
    on the housetops and in the squares
    every one wails and melts in tears.
⁴Hĕsh′bọn and Ē″lĕ·ā′lẹh cry out,
    their voice is heard as far as Jā′hăz;
therefore the armed men of Mō′ăb cry aloud;
    his soul trembles.
⁵My heart cries out for Mō′ăb;
    his fugitives flee to Zō′ăr,
    to Ĕg′lạth–shĕ·lĭsh′ĭ·yạh.
For at the ascent of Lū′hĭth
    they go up weeping;
on the road to Hôr·ō·nā′ịm
    they raise a cry of destruction;
⁶the waters of Nĭm′rĭm
    are a desolation;
the grass is withered, the new growth fails,
    the verdure is no more.
⁷Therefore the abundance they have gained
    and what they have laid up
they carry away
    over the Brook of the Willows.
⁸For a cry has gone
    round the land of Mō′ăb;
the wailing reaches to Ĕg·lā′ĭm,
    the wailing reaches to Bē′ĕr–ē′lĭm
⁹For the waters of Dī′bŏnᶜ are full of blood;
    yet I will bring upon Dibonᶜ ever more,
a lion for those of Mō′ăb who escape
    for the remnant of the land.

16 They have sent lambs
    to the ruler of the land,
from Sē′lạ, by way of the desert,
    to the mount of the daughter of Zion.
²Like fluttering birds,
    like scattered nestlings,
so are the daughters of Mō′ăb
    at the fords of the Är′nŏn.
³"Give counsel,
    grant justice;

ᵃOne ancient Ms Vg: Heb *he*
ᵇCn: Heb *the house and Dibon*
ᶜOne ancient Ms Vg Compare Syr: Heb *Dimon*
14.29-31: Jer 47; Ezek 25.15-17; Joel 3.4-8; Amos 1.6-8;
Zeph 2.4-7; Zech 9.5-7.
15-16: Is 25.10-12; Jer 48; Ezek 25.8-11; Amos 2.1-3;
Zeph 2.8-11.

make your shade like night
  at the height of noon;
hide the outcasts,
  betray not the fugitive;
⁴let the outcasts of Mō′ăb
  sojourn among you;
be a refuge to them
  from the destroyer.
When the oppressor is no more,
  and destruction has ceased,
and he who tramples under foot
  has vanished from the land,
⁵then a throne will be established in
  steadfast love
and on it will sit in faithfulness
  in the tent of David
one who judges and seeks justice
  and is swift to do righteousness."

⁶We have heard of the pride of Mō′ăb,
  how proud he was;
of his arrogance, his pride, and his
  insolence—
  his boasts are false.
⁷Therefore let Mō′ăb wail,
  let every one wail for Moab.
Mourn, utterly stricken,
  for the raisin-cakes of Kīr′-hăr′-
  ĕ·sĕth.

For the fields of Hĕsh′bŏn languish,
  and the vine of Sĭb′măh;
the lords of the nations
  have struck down its branches,
which reached to Jā′zēr
  and strayed to the desert;
its shoots spread abroad
  and passed over the sea.
Therefore I weep with the weeping
  of Jā′zēr
for the vine of Sĭb′măh;
I drench you with my tears,
  O Hĕsh′bŏn and Ē″lĕ·ā′lĕh;
for upon your fruit and your harvest
  the battle shout has fallen.
And joy and gladness are taken away
  from the fruitful field;
and in the vineyards no songs are
  sung,
  no shouts are raised;
no treader treads out wine in the
  presses;
  the vintage shout is hushed.ᵈ
Therefore my soul moans like a lyre
  for Mō′ăb,
  and my heart for Kīr·hē′rĕs.
12 And when Mō′ăb presents himself, when he wearies himself upon
the high place, when he comes to his
sanctuary to pray, he will not prevail.

13 This is the word which the LORD
spoke concerning Mō′ăb in the past.
¹⁴But now the LORD says, "In three
years, like the years of a hireling, the
glory of Mō′ăb will be brought into contempt, in spite of all his great multitude, and those who survive will be
very few and feeble."

17 An oracle concerning Damascus.
Behold, Damascus will cease to be
  a city,
  and will become a heap of ruins.
²Her cities will be deserted for ever;ᵉ
  they will be for flocks,
which will lie down, and none
  will make them afraid.
³The fortress will disappear from
  Ē′phrạ·ĭm,
and the kingdom from Damascus;
and the remnant of Syria will be
like the glory of the children of
  Israel, says the LORD of hosts.

⁴And in that day
  the glory of Jacob will be brought
  low,
and the fat of his flesh will grow
  lean.
⁵And it shall be as when the reaper
  gathers standing grain
  and his arm harvests the ears,
and as when one gleans the ears of
  grain
  in the Valley of Rĕph′ạ·ĭm.
⁶Gleanings will be left in it,
  as when an olive tree is beaten—
two or three berries
  in the top of the highest bough,
four or five
  on the branches of a fruit tree,
  says the LORD God of Israel.

7 In that day men will regard their
Maker, and their eyes will look to the
Holy One of Israel; ⁸they will not have
regard for the altars, the work of their
hands, and they will not look to what
their own fingers have made, either the
A·shē′rĭm or the altars of incense.
9 In that day their strong cities will
be like the deserted places of the
Hī′vītes and the Ăm′ọ·rītes,ᶠ which
they deserted because of the children
of Israel, and there will be desolation.

ᵈGk: Heb *I have hushed*
ᵉCn Compare Gk: Heb *the cities of Aroer are deserted*
ᶠCn Compare Gk: Heb *the wood and the highest bough*
17.1-3: Jer 49.23-27; Amos 1.3-5; Zech 9.1.

¹⁰For you have forgotten the God of
    your salvation,
    and have not remembered the
    Rock of your refuge;
therefore, though you plant pleasant
    plants
    and set out slips of an alien god,
¹¹though you make them grow on the
    day that you plant them,
    and make them blossom in the
    morning that you sow;
yet the harvest will flee away
    in a day of grief and incurable
    pain.

¹²Ah, the thunder of many peoples,
    they thunder like the thundering
    of the sea!
Ah, the roar of nations,
    they roar like the roaring of mighty
    waters!
¹³The nations roar like the roaring of
    many waters,
    but he will rebuke them, and
    they will flee far away,
chased like chaff on the mountains
    before the wind
    and whirling dust before the
    storm.
¹⁴At evening time, behold, terror!
    Before morning, they are no more!
This is the portion of those who
    despoil us,
    and the lot of those who plunder
    us.

18 Ah, land of whirring wings
    which is beyond the rivers of
    Ethiopia;
²which sends ambassadors by the
    Nile,
    in vessels of papyrus upon the
    waters!
Go, you swift messengers,
    to a nation, tall and smooth,
to a people feared near and far,
    a nation mighty and conquering,
    whose land the rivers divide.

³All you inhabitants of the world,
    you who dwell on the earth,
when a signal is raised on the moun-
    tains, look!
When a trumpet is blown, hear!
⁴For thus the LORD said to me:
"I will quietly look from my dwell-
    ing
    like clear heat in sunshine,
    like a cloud of dew in the heat of
    harvest."

⁵For before the harvest, when the
    blossom is over,
    and the flower becomes a ripening
    grape,
he will cut off the shoots with prun-
    ing hooks,
    and the spreading branches he
    will hew away.
⁶They shall all of them be left
    to the birds of prey of the moun-
    tains
    and to the beasts of the earth.
And the birds of prey will summer
    upon them,
    and all the beasts of the earth
    will winter upon them.

7 At that time gifts will be brought
to the LORD of hosts
    from a people tall and smooth,
    from a people feared near and far,
    a nation mighty and conquering,
    whose land the rivers divide,
to Mount Zion, the place of the name
of the LORD of hosts.

19 An oracle concerning Egypt.
    Behold, the LORD is riding on a
    swift cloud
    and comes to Egypt;
and the idols of Egypt will tremble
    at his presence,
    and the heart of the Egyptians
    will melt within them.
²And I will stir up Egyptians against
    Egyptians,
    and they will fight, every man
    against his brother
    and every man against his neigh-
    bor,
    city against city, kingdom against
    kingdom;
³and the spirit of the Egyptians within
    them will be emptied out,
    and I will confound their plans;
    and they will consult the idols and
    the sorcerers,
    and the mediums and the wizards;
⁴and I will give over the Egyptians
    into the hand of a hard master;
and a fierce king will rule over them,
    says the Lord, the LORD of hosts.

⁵And the waters of the Nile will be
    dried up,
    and the river will be parched and
    dry;
⁶and its canals will become foul,

18: Zeph 2.12.
19: Jer 46; Ezek 29-32; Zech 14.18-19.

and the branches of Egypt's Nile
will diminish and dry up,
reeds and rushes will rot away.
⁷There will be bare places by the Nile,
on the brink of the Nile,
and all that is sown by the Nile
will dry up,
be driven away, and be no more.
⁸The fishermen will mourn and
lament,
all who cast hook in the Nile;
and they will languish
who spread nets upon the water.
⁹The workers in combed flax will be
in despair,
and the weavers of white cotton.
¹⁰Those who are the pillars of the land
will be crushed,
and all who work for hire will be
grieved.

¹The princes of Zō'an are utterly
foolish;
the wise counselors of Pharaoh
give stupid counsel.
How can you say to Pharaoh,
"I am a son of the wise,
a son of ancient kings"?
²Where then are your wise men?
Let them tell you and make known
what the LORD of hosts has purposed against Egypt.
³The princes of Zō'an have become
fools,
and the princes of Memphis are
deluded;
those who are the cornerstones of her
tribes
have led Egypt astray.
⁴The LORD has mingled within her
a spirit of confusion;
and they have made Egypt stagger
in all her doings
as a drunken man staggers in his
vomit.
And there will be nothing for Egypt
which head or tail, palm branch or
reed, may do.

16 In that day the Egyptians will
be like women, and tremble with fear
before the hand which the LORD of
hosts shakes over them. ¹⁷And the land
of Judah will become a terror to the
Egyptians; every one to whom it is
mentioned will fear because of the purpose which the LORD of hosts has
purposed against them.
18 In that day there will be five
cities in the land of Egypt which speak

the language of Canaan and swear
allegiance to the LORD of hosts. One
of these will be called the City of the
Sun.
19 In that day there will be an altar
to the LORD in the midst of the land of
Egypt, and a pillar to the LORD at its
border. ²⁰It will be a sign and a witness
to the LORD of hosts in the land of
Egypt; when they cry to the LORD because of oppressors he will send them
a savior, and will defend and deliver
them. ²¹And the LORD will make himself known to the Egyptians; and the
Egyptians will know the LORD in that
day and worship with sacrifice and
burnt offering, and they will make
vows to the LORD and perform them.
²²And the LORD will smite Egypt, smiting and healing, and they will return
to the LORD, and he will heed their
supplications and heal them.
23 In that day there will be a highway from Egypt to Assyria, and the
Assyrian will come into Egypt, and the
Egyptian into Assyria, and the Egyptians will worship with the Assyrians.
24 In that day Israel will be the third
with Egypt and Assyria, a blessing in
the midst of the earth, ²⁵whom the
LORD of hosts has blessed, saying,
"Blessed be Egypt my people, and Assyria the work of my hands, and Israel
my heritage."

20 In the year that the commander
in chief, who was sent by Sär'-
gŏn the king of Assyria, came to
Ash'dŏd and fought against it and took
it,—²at that time the LORD had spoken
by Ī-sāi'ah the son of Ā'mŏz, saying,
"Go, and loose the sackcloth from your
loins and take off your shoes from your
feet," and he had done so, walking
naked and barefoot—³the LORD said,
"As my servant Ī-sāi'ah has walked
naked and barefoot for three years as
a sign and a portent against Egypt
and Ethiopia, ⁴so shall the king of
Assyria lead away the Egyptians captives and the Ethiopians exiles, both the
young and old, naked and barefoot,
with buttocks uncovered, to the shame
of Egypt. ⁵Then they shall be dismayed
and confounded because of Ethiopia
their hope and of Egypt their boast.
⁶And the inhabitants of this coastland will say in that day, 'Behold, this
is what has happened to those in whom
we hoped and to whom we fled for help

to be delivered from the king of Assyria! And we, how shall we escape?'"

21 The oracle concerning the wilderness of the sea.
As whirlwinds in the Nĕg′ĕb sweep on,
it comes from the desert,
from a terrible land.
² A stern vision is told to me;
the plunderer plunders,
and the destroyer destroys.
Go up, O Ē′lăm,
lay siege, O Mēd′ī·ạ;
all the sighing she has caused
·I bring to an end.
³ Therefore my loins are filled with anguish;
pangs have seized me,
like the pangs of a woman in travail;
I am bowed down so that I cannot hear,
I am dismayed so that I cannot see.
⁴ My mind reels, horror has appalled me;
the twilight I longed for
has been turned for me into trembling.
⁵ They prepare the table,
they spread the rugs,
they eat, they drink.
Arise, O princes,
oil the shield!
⁶ For thus the Lord said to me:
"Go, set a watchman,
let him announce what he sees.
⁷ When he sees riders, horsemen in pairs,
riders on asses, riders on camels,
let him listen diligently,
very diligently."
⁸ Then he who sawᵍ cried:
"Upon a watchtower I stand, O Lord,
continually by day,
and at my post I am stationed
whole nights.
⁹ And, behold, here come riders,
horsemen in pairs!"
And he answered,
"Fallen, fallen is Babylon;
and all the images of her gods
he has shattered to the ground."
¹⁰ O my threshed and winnowed one,
what I have heard from the Lord of hosts,
the God of Israel, I announce to you.

¹¹ The oracle concerning Dü′mah.
One is calling to me from Sē′ĭr,
"Watchman, what of the night?
Watchman, what of the night?"
¹² The watchman says:
"Morning comes, and also the night.
If you will inquire, inquire;
come back again."

¹³ The oracle concerning Arabia.
In the thickets in Arabia you will lodge,
O caravans of Dē′dạ·nītes.
¹⁴ To the thirsty bring water,
meet the fugitive with bread,
O inhabitants of the land of Tē′mạ.
¹⁵ For they have fled from the swords,
from the drawn sword,
from the bent bow,
and from the press of battle.
16 For thus the Lord said to me,
"Within a year, according to the years of a hireling, all the glory of Kē′dăr will come to an end; ¹⁷ and the remainder of the archers of the mighty men of the sons of Kē′dăr will be few; for the Lord, the God of Israel, has spoken."

22 The oracle concerning the valley of vision.
What do you mean that you have gone up,
all of you, to the housetops,
² you who are full of shoutings,
tumultuous city, exultant town?
Your slain are not slain with the sword
or dead in battle.
³ All your rulers have fled together
without the bow they were captured.
All of you who were found were captured,
though they had fled far away.
⁴ Therefore I said:
"Look away from me,
let me weep bitter tears;
do not labor to comfort me
for the destruction of the daughter
of my people."

⁵ For the Lord God of hosts has a day
of tumult and trampling and confusion
in the valley of vision,
a battering down of walls
and a shouting to the mountains

ᵍOne ancient Ms: Heb *a lion*
ʰGk Syr Vg: Heb *from far away*

⁶And Ē'lăm bore the quiver
  with chariots and horsemen,ⁱ
  and Kīr uncovered the shield.
⁷Your choicest valleys were full of
  chariots,
  and the horsemen took their stand
  at the gates.
⁸He has taken away the covering of
  Judah.

In that day you looked to the weapons of the House of the Forest, ⁹and
you saw that the breaches of the city
of David were many, and you collected
the waters of the lower pool, ¹⁰and
you counted the houses of Jerusalem,
and you broke down the houses to
fortify the wall. ¹¹You made a reservoir
between the two walls for the water
of the old pool. But you did not look to
him who did it, or have regard for him
who planned it long ago.

¹²In that day the Lord God of hosts
  called to weeping and mourning,
  to baldness and girding with
  sackcloth;
¹³and behold, joy and gladness,
  slaying oxen and killing sheep,
  eating flesh and drinking wine.
  "Let us eat and drink,
  for tomorrow we die."
¹⁴The Lord of hosts has revealed
  himself in my ears:
  "Surely this iniquity will not be
  forgiven you
  till you die,"
  says the Lord God of hosts.

15 Thus says the Lord God of hosts,
"Come, go to this steward, to Shĕb'na,
who is over the household, and say to
him: ¹⁶What have you to do here and
whom have you here, that you have
hewn here a tomb for yourself, you
who hew a tomb on the height, and
carve a habitation for yourself in the
rock? ¹⁷Behold, the Lord will hurl you
away violently, O you strong man. He
will seize firm hold on you, ¹⁸and whirl
you round and round, and throw you
like a ball into a wide land; there you
shall die, and there shall be your
splendid chariots, you shame of your
master's house. ¹⁹I will thrust you from
your office, and you will be cast down
from your station. ²⁰In that day I will
call my servant Ē-lī'a-kĭm the son of
Ĭl-kī'ah, ²¹and I will clothe him with
your robe, and will bind your girdle on

him, and will commit your authority
to his hand; and he shall be a father
to the inhabitants of Jerusalem and
to the house of Judah. ²²And I will
place on his shoulder the key of the
house of David; he shall open, and
none shall shut; and he shall shut, and
none shall open. ²³And I will fasten
him like a peg in a sure place, and he
will become a throne of honor to his
father's house. ²⁴And they will hang on
him the whole weight of his father's
house, the offspring and issue, every
small vessel, from the cups to all the
flagons. ²⁵In that day, says the Lord
of hosts, the peg that was fastened in
a sure place will give way; and it will
be cut down and fall, and the burden
that was upon it will be cut off, for the
Lord has spoken."

23 The oracle concerning Tyre.
    Wail, O ships of Tär'shĭsh,
    for Tyre is laid waste, without
    house or haven!
  From the land of Cyprus
    it is revealed to them.
²Be still, O inhabitants of the coast,
  O merchants of Sī'dŏn;
  your messengers passed over the seaʲ
³   and were on many waters;
  your revenue was the grain of
  Shī'hôr,
    the harvest of the Nile;
    you were the merchant of the
    nations.
⁴Be ashamed, O Sī'dŏn, for the sea
  has spoken,
    the stronghold of the sea, saying:
  "I have neither travailed nor given
  birth,
    I have neither reared young men
    nor brought up virgins."
⁵When the report comes to Egypt,
  they will be in anguish over the
  report about Tyre.
⁶Pass over to Tär'shĭsh,
  wail, O inhabitants of the coast!
⁷Is this your exultant city
  whose origin is from days of old,
  whose feet carried her
  to settle afar?
⁸Who has purposed this
  against Tyre, the bestower of
  crowns,
  whose merchants were princes,

ⁱThe Hebrew of this line is obscure
ʲOne ancient Ms: Heb *who passed over the sea, they replenished you*
22.22: Rev 3.7.
23: Ezek 26.1-28.19; Joel 3.4-8; Amos 1.9-10; Zech 9.3-4.

whose traders were the honored of the earth?

9 The Lord of hosts has purposed it,
to defile the pride of all glory,
to dishonor all the honored of the earth.

10 Overflow your land like the Nile,
O daugher of Tär'shĭsh;
there is no restraint any more.

11 He has stretched out his hand over the sea,
he has shaken the kingdoms;
the Lord has given command concerning Canaan
to destroy its strongholds.

12 And he said:
"You will no more exult,
O oppressed virgin daughter of Sī'dŏn;
arise, pass over to Cyprus,
even there you will have no rest."

13 Behold the land of the Chăl·dē'-anṣ! This is the people; it was not Assyria. They destined Tyre for wild beasts. They erected their siege towers, they razed her palaces, they made her a ruin.*

14 Wail, O ships of Tär'shĭsh,
for your stronghold is laid waste.

15 In that day Tyre will be forgotten for seventy years, like the days of one king. At the end of seventy years, it will happen to Tyre as in the song of the harlot:

16 "Take a harp,
go about the city,
O forgotten harlot!
Make sweet melody,
sing many songs,
that you may be remembered."

17 At the end of seventy years, the Lord will visit Tyre, and she will return to her hire, and will play the harlot with all the kingdoms of the world upon the face of the earth.

18 Her merchandise and her hire will be dedicated to the Lord; it will not be stored or hoarded, but her merchandise will supply abundant food and fine clothing for those who dwell before the Lord.

24 Behold, the Lord will lay waste the earth and make it desolate, and he will twist its surface and scatter its inhabitants.

2 And it shall be, as with the people, so with the priest;

as with the slave, so with his master;
as with the maid, so with her mistress;
as with the buyer, so with the seller;
as with the lender, so with the borrower;
as with the creditor, so with the debtor.

3 The earth shall be utterly laid waste
and utterly despoiled;
for the Lord has spoken this word.

4 The earth mourns and withers,
the world languishes and withers;
the heavens languish together with the earth.

5 The earth lies polluted
under its inhabitants;
for they have transgressed the laws,
violated the statutes,
broken the everlasting covenant.

6 Therefore a curse devours the earth,
and its inhabitants suffer for their guilt;
therefore the inhabitants of the earth
are scorched,
and few men are left.

7 The wine mourns,
the vine languishes,
all the merry-hearted sigh.

8 The mirth of the timbrels is stilled,
the noise of the jubilant has ceased,
the mirth of the lyre is stilled.

9 No more do they drink wine with singing;
strong drink is bitter to those who drink it.

10 The city of chaos is broken down,
every house is shut up so that none can enter.

11 There is an outcry in the streets for lack of wine;
all joy has reached its eventide
the gladness of the earth is banished.

12 Desolation is left in the city,
the gates are battered into ruins

13 For thus it shall be in the midst of the earth
among the nations,
as when an olive tree is beaten,
as at the gleaning when the vintage is done.

14 They lift up their voices, they sing for joy;

*The Hebrew of this verse is obscure
23.17: Rev 17.2. **24.8:** Rev 18.22.

over the majesty of the LORD
they shout from the west.
15 Therefore in the east give glory to
the LORD;
in the coastlands of the sea, to the
name of the LORD, the God of
Israel.
16 From the ends of the earth we hear
songs of praise,
of glory to the Righteous One.
But I say, "I pine away,
I pine away. Woe is me!
For the treacherous deal treacherously,
the treacherous deal very treacherously."

17 Terror, and the pit, and the snare
are upon you, O inhabitant of
the earth!
18 He who flees at the sound of the
terror
shall fall into the pit;
and he who climbs out of the pit
shall be caught in the snare.
For the windows of heaven are
opened,
and the foundations of the earth
tremble.
19 The earth is utterly broken,
the earth is rent asunder,
the earth is violently shaken.
20 The earth staggers like a drunken
man,
it sways like a hut;
its transgression lies heavy upon it,
and it falls, and will not rise again.

21 On that day the LORD will punish
the host of heaven, in heaven,
and the kings of the earth, on the
earth.
22 They will be gathered together
as prisoners in a pit;
they will be shut up in a prison,
and after many days they will be
punished.
23 Then the moon will be confounded,
and the sun ashamed;
for the LORD of hosts will reign
on Mount Zion and in Jerusalem
and before his elders he will manifest his glory.

25 O LORD, thou art my God;
I will exalt thee, I will praise thy
name;
for thou hast done wonderful things,
plans formed of old, faithful and
sure.

2 For thou hast made the city a heap,
the fortified city a ruin;
the palace of aliens is a city no
more,
it will never be rebuilt.
3 Therefore strong peoples will glorify
thee;
cities of ruthless nations will fear
thee.
4 For thou hast been a stronghold to
the poor,
a stronghold to the needy in his
distress,
a shelter from the storm and a
shade from the heat;
for the blast of the ruthless is like
a storm against a wall,
5 like heat in a dry place.
Thou dost subdue the noise of the
aliens;
as heat by the shade of a cloud,
so the song of the ruthless is stilled.

6 On this mountain the LORD of
hosts will make for all peoples a feast
of fat things, a feast of wine on the
lees, of fat things full of marrow, of
wine on the lees well refined. 7 And he
will destroy on this mountain the covering that is cast over all peoples,
the veil that is spread over all nations.
8 He will swallow up death for ever, and
the Lord GOD will wipe away tears
from all faces, and the reproach of his
people he will take away from all the
earth, for the LORD has spoken.
9 It will be said on that day, "Lo,
this is our God; we have waited for
him, that he might save us. This is the
LORD; we have waited for him; let
us be glad and rejoice in his salvation."
10 For the hand of the LORD will
rest on this mountain, and Mō′ăb shall
be trodden down in his place, as straw
is trodden down in a dung-pit. 11 And he
will spread out his hands in the midst
of it as a swimmer spreads his hands
out to swim; but the LORD will lay low
his pride together with the skill*l* of
his hands. 12 And the high fortifications
of his walls he will bring down, lay
low, and cast to the ground, even to
the dust.

26 In that day this song will be
sung in the land of Judah:

l The meaning of the Hebrew word is uncertain
25.8: 1 Cor 15.54; Rev 7.17; 21.4.
25.10-12: Is 15-16; Jer 48; Ezek 25.8-11; Amos 2.1-3;
Zeph 2.8-11.

"We have a strong city;
he sets up salvation
as walls and bulwarks.
2 Open the gates,
that the righteous nation which
keeps faith
may enter in.
3 Thou dost keep him in perfect
peace,
whose mind is stayed on thee,
because he trusts in thee.
4 Trust in the LORD for ever,
for the LORD GOD
is an everlasting rock.
5 For he has brought low
the inhabitants of the height,
the lofty city.
He lays it low, lays it low to the
ground,
casts it to the dust.
6 The foot tramples it,
the feet of the poor,
the steps of the needy."

7 The way of the righteous is level;
thou[m] dost make smooth the path
of the righteous.
8 In the path of thy judgments,
O LORD, we wait for thee;
thy memorial name
is the desire of our soul.
9 My soul yearns for thee in the night,
my spirit within me earnestly
seeks thee.
For when thy judgments are in the
earth,
the inhabitants of the world learn
righteousness.
10 If favor is shown to the wicked,
he does not learn righteousness;
in the land of uprightness he deals
perversely
and does not see the majesty of
the LORD.
11 O LORD, thy hand is lifted up,
but they see it not.
Let them see thy zeal for thy people,
and be ashamed.
Let the fire for thy adversaries
consume them.
12 O LORD, thou wilt ordain peace for us,
thou hast wrought for us all our
works.
13 O LORD our God,
other lords besides thee have ruled
over us,
but thy name alone we acknowledge.
14 They are dead, they will not live;
they are shades, they will not arise;

to that end thou hast visited them
with destruction
and wiped out all remembrance of
them.
15 But thou hast increased the nation,
O LORD,
thou hast increased the nation;
thou art glorified;
thou hast enlarged all the borders
of the land.

16 O LORD, in distress they sought thee,
they poured out a prayer[n]
when thy chastening was upon
them.
17 Like a woman with child,
who writhes and cries out in her
pangs,
when she is near her time,
so were we because of thee, O LORD;
18 we were with child, we writhed,
we have as it were brought forth
wind.
We have wrought no deliverance in
the earth,
and the inhabitants of the world
have not fallen.
19 Thy dead shall live, their bodies[o]
shall rise.
O dwellers in the dust, awake and
sing for joy!
For thy dew is a dew of light,
and on the land of the shades thou
wilt let it fall.

20 Come, my people, enter your chambers,
and shut your doors behind you;
hide yourselves for a little while
until the wrath is past.
21 For behold, the LORD is coming forth
out of his place
to punish the inhabitants of the
earth for their iniquity,
and the earth will disclose the blood
shed upon her,
and will no more cover her slain.

27 In that day the LORD with his
hard and great and strong sword
will punish Lĕ·vī'a·thạn the fleeing
serpent, Leviathan the twisting serpent, and he will slay the dragon that
is in the sea.

2 In that day:
"A pleasant vineyard, sing of it!
3 I, the LORD, am its keeper;

---

m Cn Compare Gk: Heb *thou (that art) upright*
n Heb uncertain   *o* Cn Compare Syr Tg: Heb *my body*

every moment I water it.
Lest any one harm it,
I guard it night and day;
4 I have no wrath.
Would that I had thorns and briers
    to battle!
I would set out against them,
I would burn them up together.
5 Or let them lay hold of my protection,
    let them make peace with me,
    let them make peace with me."

6 In days to come*q* Jacob shall take
    root,
Israel shall blossom and put forth
    shoots,
and fill the whole world with fruit.

7 Has he smitten them as he smote
    those who smote them?
Or have they been slain as their
    slayers were slain?
8 Measure by measure,*r* by exile thou
    didst contend with them;
he removed them with his fierce
    blast in the day of the east wind.
9 Therefore by this the guilt of Jacob
    will be expiated,
and this will be the full fruit of
    the removal of his sin:
when he makes all the stones of the
    altars
like chalkstones crushed to pieces,
no A·shē'rĭm or incense altars will
    remain standing.
10 For the fortified city is solitary,
    a habitation deserted and for-
    saken, like the wilderness;
there the calf grazes,
    there he lies down, and strips
    its branches.
11 When its boughs are dry, they are
    broken;
women come and make a fire of
    them.
For this is a people without dis-
    cernment;
therefore he who made them will
    not have compassion on them,
he that formed them will show
    them no favor.

12 In that day from the river Euphrates to the Brook of Egypt the
Lord will thresh out the grain, and
you will be gathered one by one, O
people of Israel. 13 And in that day
a great trumpet will be blown, and
those who were lost in the land of
Assyria and those who were driven out

to the land of Egypt will come and worship the Lord on the holy mountain
at Jerusalem.

28 Woe to the proud crown of the
    drunkards of Ē'phra·ĭm,
and to the fading flower of its
    glorious beauty,
which is on the head of the rich
    valley of those overcome with
    wine!
2 Behold, the Lord has one who is
    mighty and strong;
like a storm of hail, a destroying
    tempest,
like a storm of mighty, overflowing
    waters,
he will cast down to the earth with
    violence.
3 The proud crown of the drunkards
    of Ē'phra·ĭm
will be trodden under foot;
4 and the fading flower of its glorious
    beauty,
which is on the head of the rich
    valley,
will be like a first-ripe fig before the
    summer:
when a man sees it, he eats it up
    as soon as it is in his hand.

5 In that day the Lord of hosts will be
    a crown of glory,
and a diadem of beauty, to the
    remnant of his people;
6 and a spirit of justice to him who sits
    in judgment,
and strength to those who turn
    back the battle at the gate.

7 These also reel with wine
    and stagger with strong drink;
the priest and the prophet reel with
    strong drink,
they are confused with wine,
    they stagger with strong drink;
they err in vision,
    they stumble in giving judgment.
8 For all tables are full of vomit,
    no place is without filthiness.

9 "Whom will he teach knowledge,
    and to whom will he explain the
    message?
Those who are weaned from the milk,
    those taken from the breast?

*q*Heb *Those to come*
*r*Compare Syr Vg Tg: The meaning of the Hebrew word
is unknown
27.13: Mt 24.31; 1 Cor 15.52; 1 Thess 4.16.

¹⁰For it is precept upon precept, precept upon precept,
line upon line, line upon line,
here a little, there a little."

¹¹Nay, but by men of strange lips
and with an alien tongue
the LORD will speak to this people,
¹²   to whom he has said,
"This is rest;
give rest to the weary;
and this is repose";
yet they would not hear.
¹³Therefore the word of the LORD will be to them
precept upon precept, precept upon precept,
line upon line, line upon line,
here a little, there a little;
that they may go, and fall backward,
and be broken, and snared, and taken.

¹⁴Therefore hear the word of the LORD, you scoffers,
who rule this people in Jerusalem!
¹⁵Because you have said, "We have made a covenant with death,
and with Shē'ōl we have an agreement;
when the overwhelming scourge passes through
it will not come to us;
for we have made lies our refuge,
and in falsehood we have taken shelter";
¹⁶therefore thus says the Lord GOD,
"Behold, I am laying in Zion for a foundation
a stone, a tested stone,
a precious cornerstone, of a sure foundation:
'He who believes will not be in haste.'
¹⁷And I will make justice the line,
and righteousness the plummet;
and hail will sweep away the refuge of lies,
and waters will overwhelm the shelter."
¹⁸Then your covenant with death will be annulled,
and your agreement with Shē'ōl will not stand;
when the overwhelming scourge passes through
you will be beaten down by it.
¹⁹As often as it passes through it will take you;

for morning by morning it will pass through,
by day and by night;
and it will be sheer terror to understand the message.
²⁰For the bed is too short to stretch oneself on it,
and the covering too narrow to wrap oneself in it.
²¹For the LORD will rise up as on Mount Pĕ·rā'zĭm,
he will be wroth as in the valley of Gĭb'ē·ọn;
to do his deed—strange is his deed!
and to work his work—alien is his work!
²²Now therefore do not scoff,
lest your bonds be made strong;
for I have heard a decree of destruction
from the Lord GOD of hosts upon the whole land.

²³Give ear, and hear my voice;
hearken, and hear my speech.
²⁴Does he who plows for sowing plow continually?
does he continually open and harrow his ground?
²⁵When he has leveled its surface,
does he not scatter dill, sow cummin,
and put in wheat in rows
and barley in its proper place,
and spelt as the border?
²⁶For he is instructed aright;
his God teaches him.

²⁷Dill is not threshed with a threshing sledge,
nor is a cart wheel rolled over cummin;
but dill is beaten out with a stick,
and cummin with a rod.
²⁸Does one crush bread grain?
No, he does not thresh it for ever;
when he drives his cart wheel over it
with his horses, he does not crush it.
²⁹This also comes from the LORD of hosts;
he is wonderful in counsel,
and excellent in wisdom.

29 Ho Är'ĭ·ẹl, Ariel,
the city where David encamped!
Add year to year;
let the feasts run their round.

28.11-12: 1 Cor 14.21.   28.12: Mt 11.29.
28.16: Rom 9.33; 10.11; 1 Pet 2.4-6.

²Yet I will distress Ăr'ĭ·ĕl,
　and there shall be moaning and
　　lamentation,
　and she shall be to me like an
　　Ariel.
³And I will encamp against you round
　about,
　and will besiege you with towers
　and I will raise siegeworks against
　　you.
⁴Then deep from the earth you shall
　speak,
　from low in the dust your words
　　shall come;
 your voice shall come from the
　ground like the voice of a ghost,
　and your speech shall whisper out
　　of the dust.

⁵But the multitude of your foes*
　shall be like small dust,
　and the multitude of the ruthless
　　like passing chaff.
And in an instant, suddenly,
⁶ you will be visited by the LORD
　of hosts
with thunder and with earthquake
　and great noise,
　with whirlwind and tempest,
　and the flame of a devouring fire.
⁷And the multitude of all the nations
　that fight against Ăr'ĭ·ĕl,
　all that fight against her and her
　　stronghold and distress her,
　shall be like a dream, a vision of
　　the night.
⁸As when a hungry man dreams he is
　eating
　and awakes with his hunger not
　　satisfied,
　or as when a thirsty man dreams he
　　is drinking
　and awakes faint, with his thirst
　　not quenched,
　so shall the multitude of all the na-
　　tions be
　that fight against Mount Zion.

⁹Stupefy yourselves and be in a
　stupor,
　blind yourselves and be blind!
Be drunk, but not with wine;
　stagger, but not with strong
　　drink!
¹⁰For the LORD has poured out upon
　you
　a spirit of deep sleep,
　and has closed your eyes, the proph-
　　ets,
　and covered your heads, the seers.

11 And the vision of all this has
become to you like the words of a book
that is sealed. When men give it to
one who can read, saying, "Read this,"
he says, "I cannot, for it is sealed."
¹²And when they give the book to one
who cannot read, saying, "Read this,"
he says, "I cannot read."

¹³And the Lord said:
"Because this people draw near with
　their mouth
　and honor me with their lips,
　while their hearts are far from me,
　and their fear of me is a command-
　　ment of men learned by rote;
¹⁴therefore, behold, I will again
　do marvelous things with this
　　people,
　wonderful and marvelous;
　and the wisdom of their wise men
　　shall perish,
　and the discernment of their dis-
　　cerning men shall be hid."

¹⁵Woe to those who hide deep from
　the LORD their counsel,
　whose deeds are in the dark,
　and who say, "Who sees us? Who
　　knows us?"
¹⁶You turn things upside down!
　Shall the potter be regarded as the
　　clay;
　that the thing made should say of
　　its maker,
　"He did not make me";
　or the thing formed say of him who
　　formed it,
　"He has no understanding"?

¹⁷Is it not yet a very little while
　until Lebanon shall be turned into
　　a fruitful field,
　and the fruitful field shall be re-
　　garded as a forest?
¹⁸In that day the deaf shall hear the
　words of a book,
　and out of their gloom and darkness
　the eyes of the blind shall see.
¹⁹The meek shall obtain fresh joy in
　the LORD,
　and the poor among men shall
　exult in the Holy One of Israel.
²⁰For the ruthless shall come to
　nought and the scoffer cease,
　and all who watch to do evil shall
　be cut off,

*Cn: Heb *strangers*
29.13: Mt 15.8-9; Mk 7.6-7.　**29.14:** 1 Cor 1.19.
29.16: Is 45.9; Rom 9.20.　**29.18-19:** Mt 11.5.

²¹who by a word make a man out to
be an offender,
and lay a snare for him who reproves in the gate,
and with an empty plea turn aside
him who is in the right.

22 Therefore thus says the LORD,
who redeemed Abraham, concerning
the house of Jacob:
"Jacob shall no more be ashamed,
no more shall his face grow
pale.
²³For when he sees his children,
the work of my hands, in his midst,
they will sanctify my name;
they will sanctify the Holy One of
Jacob,
and will stand in awe of the God
of Israel.
²⁴And those who err in spirit will
come to understanding,
and those who murmur will accept
instruction."

30 "Woe to the rebellious children,"
says the LORD,
"who carry out a plan, but not
mine;
and who make a league, but not of
my spirit,
that they may add sin to sin;
²who set out to go down to Egypt,
without asking for my counsel,
to take refuge in the protection of
Pharaoh,
and to seek shelter in the shadow
of Egypt!
³Therefore shall the protection of
Pharaoh turn to your shame,
and the shelter in the shadow of
Egypt to your humiliation.
⁴For though his officials are at Zō′ạn
and his envoys reach Hā′nēṣ,
⁵every one comes to shame
through a people that cannot profit
them,
that brings neither help nor profit,
but shame and disgrace."

⁶An oracle on the beasts of the Nĕg′ĕb.
Through a land of trouble and
anguish,
from where come the lioness and
the lion,
the viper and the flying serpent,
they carry their riches on the backs
of asses,
and their treasures on the humps
of camels,

to a people that cannot profit
them.
⁷For Egypt's help is worthless and
empty,
therefore I have called her
"Rā′hăb who sits still."

⁸And now, go, write it before them on
a tablet,
and inscribe it in a book,
that it may be for the time to come
as a witness for ever.
⁹For they are a rebellious people,
lying sons,
sons who will not hear
the instruction of the LORD;
¹⁰who say to the seers, "See not",
and to the prophets, "Prophesy no
to us what is right;
speak to us smooth things,
prophesy illusions,
¹¹leave the way, turn aside from the
path,
let us hear no more of the Holy
One of Israel."
¹²Therefore thus says the Holy One
of Israel,
"Because you despise this word
and trust in oppression and per
verseness,
and rely on them;
¹³therefore this iniquity shall be to
you
like a break in a high wall, bulg
ing out, and about to collapse
whose crash comes suddenly, in
an instant;
¹⁴and its breaking is like that of a
potter's vessel
which is smashed so ruthlessly
that among its fragments not a sherd
is found
with which to take fire from the
hearth,
or to dip up water out of the
cistern."

¹⁵For thus said the Lord GOD, the
Holy One of Israel,
"In returning and rest you shall
be saved;
in quietness and in trust shall be
your strength."
And you would not, ¹⁶but you
said,
"No! We will speed upon horses,"
therefore you shall speed away
and, "We will ride upon swift steeds,"
therefore your pursuers shall be
swift.

¹⁷A thousand shall flee at the threat of
one,
at the threat of five you shall flee,
till you are left
like a flagstaff on the top of a
mountain,
like a signal on a hill.

¹⁸Therefore the LORD waits to be
gracious to you;
therefore he exalts himself to
show mercy to you.
For the LORD is a God of justice;
blessed are all those who wait
for him.
19 Yea, O people in Zion who dwell
at Jerusalem; you shall weep no more.
He will surely be gracious to you at
the sound of your cry; when he hears it,
he will answer you. ²⁰And though the
Lord give you the bread of adversity
and the water of affliction, yet your
Teacher will not hide himself any
more, but your eyes shall see your
Teacher. ²¹And your ears shall hear a
word behind you, saying, "This is the
way, walk in it," when you turn to the
right or when you turn to the left.
²²Then you will defile your silver-
covered graven images and your gold-
plated molten images. You will scatter
them as unclean things; you will say
to them, "Begone!"
23 And he will give rain for the seed
with which you sow the ground, and
grain, the produce of the ground,
which will be rich and plenteous. In
that day your cattle will graze in large
pastures; ²⁴and the oxen and the asses
that till the ground will eat salted
provender, which has been winnowed
with shovel and fork. ²⁵And upon every
lofty mountain and every high hill
there will be brooks running with
water, in the day of the great slaughter, when the towers fall. ²⁶Moreover
the light of the moon will be as the
light of the sun, and the light of the
sun will be sevenfold, as the light of
seven days, in the day when the LORD
binds up the hurt of his people, and
heals the wounds inflicted by his blow.

²⁷Behold, the name of the LORD comes
from far,
burning with his anger, and in
thick rising smoke;
his lips are full of indignation,
and his tongue is like a devouring
fire;

²⁸his breath is like an overflowing
stream
that reaches up to the neck;
to sift the nations with the sieve of
destruction,
and to place on the jaws of the
peoples a bridle that leads astray.

29 You shall have a song as in the
night when a holy feast is kept; and
gladness of heart, as when one sets
out to the sound of the flute to go to
the mountain of the LORD, to the Rock
of Israel. ³⁰And the LORD will cause
his majestic voice to be heard and the
descending blow of his arm to be seen,
in furious anger and a flame of devouring fire, with a cloudburst and
tempest and hailstones. ³¹The Assyrians will be terror-stricken at the
voice of the LORD, when he smites
with his rod. ³²And every stroke of the
staff of punishment which the LORD
lays upon them will be to the sound of
timbrels and lyres; battling with bran-
dished arm he will fight with them.
³³For a burning place[t] has long been
prepared; yea, for the king[u] it is made
ready, its pyre made deep and wide,
with fire and wood in abundance; the
breath of the LORD, like a stream of
brimstone, kindles it.

31 Woe to those who go down to
Egypt for help
and rely on horses,
who trust in chariots because they
are many
and in horsemen because they are
very strong,
but do not look to the Holy One of
Israel
or consult the LORD!
²And yet he is wise and brings disaster,
he does not call back his words,
but will arise against the house of
the evildoers,
and against the helpers of those
who work iniquity.
³The Egyptians are men, and not
God;
and their horses are flesh, and not
spirit.
When the LORD stretches out his
hand,
the helper will stumble, and he
who is helped will fall,
and they will all perish together.

ᵗOr *Topheth* ᵘOr *Molech*

⁴For thus the LORD said to me,
As a lion or a young lion growls
  over his prey,
and when a band of shepherds is
  called forth against him
is not terrified by their shouting
  or daunted at their noise,
so the LORD of hosts will come down
to fight upon Mount Zion and upon
  its hill.
⁵Like birds hovering, so the LORD of
  hosts
will protect Jerusalem;
he will protect and deliver it,
  he will spare and rescue it.

6 Turn to him from whom you[r]
have deeply revolted, O people of Israel. ⁷For in that day every one shall
cast away his idols of silver and his
idols of gold, which your hands have
sinfully made for you.
⁸"And the Assyrian shall fall by a
  sword, not of man;
and a sword, not of man, shall
  devour him;
and he shall flee from the sword,
  and his young men shall be put
  to forced labor.
⁹His rock shall pass away in terror,
  and his officers desert the standard in panic,"
says the LORD, whose fire is in Zion,
and whose furnace is in Jerusalem.

32 Behold, a king will reign in righteousness,
  and princes will rule in justice.
²Each will be like a hiding place from
  the wind,
  a covert from the tempest,
like streams of water in a dry place,
  like the shade of a great rock in
  a weary land.
³Then the eyes of those who see will
  not be closed,
  and the ears of those who hear
  will hearken.
⁴The mind of the rash will have good
  judgment,
  and the tongue of the stammerers
  will speak readily and distinctly.
⁵The fool will no more be called noble,
  nor the knave said to be honorable.
⁶For the fool speaks folly,
  and his mind plots iniquity:
to practice ungodliness,
  to utter error concerning the LORD,
to leave the craving of the hungry
  unsatisfied,

and to deprive the thirsty of
  drink.
⁷The knaveries of the knave are evil;
  he devises wicked devices
to ruin the poor with lying words,
  even when the plea of the needy
  is right.
⁸But he who is noble devises noble
  things,
  and by noble things he stands.

⁹Rise up, you women who are at ease,
  hear my voice;
you complacent daughters,
  give ear to my speech.
¹⁰In little more than a year
you will shudder, you complacent
  women;
for the vintage will fail,
  the fruit harvest will not come.
¹¹Tremble, you women who are at ease,
  shudder, you complacent ones;
strip, and make yourselves bare,
  and gird sackcloth upon your loins.
¹²Beat upon your breasts for the
  pleasant fields,
  for the fruitful vine,
¹³for the soil of my people
  growing up in thorns and briers;
yea, for all the joyous houses
  in the joyful city.
¹⁴For the palace will be forsaken,
  the populous city deserted;
the hill and the watchtower
  will become dens for ever,
a joy of wild asses,
  a pasture of flocks;
¹⁵until the Spirit is poured upon us
  from on high,
  and the wilderness becomes a
  fruitful field,
and the fruitful field is deemed a
  forest.
¹⁶Then justice will dwell in the wilderness,
  and righteousness abide in the
  fruitful field.
¹⁷And the effect of righteousness will
  be peace,
  and the result of righteousness,
  quietness and trust for ever.
¹⁸My people will abide in a peaceful
  habitation,
  in secure dwellings, and in quiet
  resting places.
¹⁹And the forest will utterly go down,[w]
  and the city will be utterly laid
  low.

ᵖHeb *they*
ʷCn: Heb *And it will hail when the forest comes down*

²⁰Happy are you who sow beside all
waters,
who let the feet of the ox and the
ass range free.

33 Woe to you, destroyer,
who yourself have not been
destroyed;
you treacherous one,
with whom none has dealt treacherously!
When you have ceased to destroy,
you will be destroyed;
and when you have made an end of
dealing treacherously,
you will be dealt with treacherously.

²O Lord, be gracious to us; we wait
for thee.
Be our arm every morning,
our salvation in the time of
trouble.
³At the thunderous noise peoples flee,
at the lifting up of thyself nations
are scattered;
⁴and spoil is gathered as the cater-
pillar gathers;
as locusts leap, men leap upon it.

⁵The Lord is exalted, for he dwells
on high;
he will fill Zion with justice and
righteousness;
⁶and he will be the stability of your
times,
abundance of salvation, wisdom,
and knowledge;
the fear of the Lord is his treasure.

⁷Behold, the valiant ones^y cry with-
out;
the envoys of peace weep bitterly.
⁸The highways lie waste,
the wayfaring man ceases.
Covenants are broken,
witnesses^z are despised,
there is no regard for man.
⁹The land mourns and languishes;
Lebanon is confounded and with-
ers away;
Sharon is like a desert;
and Bā'shạn and Cãr'mẹl shake
off their leaves.

¹⁰"Now I will arise," says the Lord,
"now I will lift myself up;
now I will be exalted.
¹¹You conceive chaff, you bring forth
stubble;

your breath is a fire that will consume you.
¹²And the peoples will be as if burned
to lime,
like thorns cut down, that are
burned in the fire."

¹³Hear, you who are far off, what I
have done;
and you who are near, acknowledge my might.
¹⁴The sinners in Zion are afraid;
trembling has seized the god-
less:
"Who among us can dwell with the
devouring fire?
Who among us can dwell with
everlasting burnings?"
¹⁵He who walks righteously and speaks
uprightly,
who despises the gain of oppressions,
who shakes his hands, lest they hold
a bribe,
who stops his ears from hearing
of bloodshed
and shuts his eyes from looking
upon evil,
¹⁶he will dwell on the heights;
his place of defense will be the
fortresses of rocks;
his bread will be given him, his
water will be sure.

¹⁷Your eyes will see the king in his
beauty;
they will behold a land that
stretches afar.
¹⁸Your mind will muse on the terror:
"Where is he who counted,
where is he who weighed the
tribute?
Where is he who counted the
towers?"
¹⁹You will see no more the insolent
people,
the people of an obscure speech
which you cannot comprehend,
stammering in a tongue which you
cannot understand.
²⁰Look upon Zion, the city of our ap-
pointed feasts!
Your eyes will see Jerusalem,
a quiet habitation, an immovable
tent,
whose stakes will never be plucked
up,
nor will any of its cords be broken.

^yThe meaning of the Hebrew word is uncertain
^zOne ancient Ms: Heb *cities*

²¹ But there the LORD in majesty will
be for us
　a place of broad rivers and
　　streams,
　where no galley with oars can go,
　　nor stately ship can pass.
²² For the LORD is our judge, the LORD
is our ruler,
　the LORD is our king; he will save
　　us.

²³ Your tackle hangs loose;
　it cannot hold the mast firm in its
　　place,
　or keep the sail spread out.

Then prey and spoil in abundance
will be divided;
　even the lame will take the prey.
²⁴ And no inhabitant will say, "I am
sick";
　the people who dwell there will
　　be forgiven their iniquity.

34 Draw near, O nations, to hear,
　　and hearken, O peoples!
Let the earth listen, and all that fills
it;
　the world, and all that comes from
　　it.
² For the LORD is enraged against all
the nations,
　and furious against all their host,
　he has doomed them, has given
　　them over for slaughter.
³ Their slain shall be cast out,
　and the stench of their corpses
　　shall rise;
　the mountains shall flow with their
　　blood.
⁴ All the host of heaven shall rot away,
　and the skies roll up like a scroll.
All their host shall fall,
　as leaves fall from the vine,
　like leaves falling from the fig tree.

⁵ For my sword has drunk its fill in
the heavens;
　behold, it descends for judgment
　　upon E'dom,
　upon the people I have doomed.
⁶ The LORD has a sword; it is sated
with blood,
　it is gorged with fat,
　with the blood of lambs and goats,
　with the fat of the kidneys of rams.
For the LORD has a sacrifice in
Bŏz'rah,
　a great slaughter in the land of
　　E'dom.

⁷ Wild oxen shall fall with them,
　and young steers with the mighty
　　bulls.
Their land shall be soaked with blood,
　and their soil made rich with fat.

⁸ For the LORD has a day of vengeance,
　a year of recompense for the cause
　　of Zion.
⁹ And the streams of E'dom*ᵃ* shall be
turned into pitch,
　and her soil into brimstone;
　her land shall become burning
　　pitch.
¹⁰ Night and day it shall not be
quenched;
　its smoke shall go up for ever.
From generation to generation it
　shall lie waste;
　none shall pass through it for
　　ever and ever.
¹¹ But the hawk and the porcupine shall
possess it,
　the owl and the raven shall dwell
　　in it.
He shall stretch the line of confusion
over it,
　and the plummet of chaos over*ᵇ*
　　its nobles.
¹² They shall name it No Kingdom
There,
　and all its princes shall be nothing.

¹³ Thorns shall grow over its strongholds,
　nettles and thistles in its for-
　　tresses.
It shall be the haunt of jackals,
　an abode for ostriches.
¹⁴ And wild beasts shall meet with
hyenas,
　the satyr shall cry to his fellow;
　yea, there shall the night hag alight,
　　and find for herself a resting place.

¹⁵ There shall the owl nest and lay
　and hatch and gather her young in
　　her shadow;
　yea, there shall the kites be gath-
　　ered,
　each one with her mate.
¹⁶ Seek and read from the book of the
LORD:
　Not one of these shall be missing;
　none shall be without her mate.

ᵃ Heb *her streams*　*ᵇ* Heb lacks *over*
34: Is 63.1-6; Jer 49.7-22; Ezek 25.12-14; 35; Amos 1.11-
12; Obad; Mal 1.2-5.
34.4: Rev 6.13-14.
34.9-10: Rev 19.3.

For the mouth of the LORD has commanded,
and his Spirit has gathered them.
[17]He has cast the lot for them,
his hand has portioned it out to
them with the line;
they shall possess it for ever,
from generation to generation they
shall dwell in it.

35 The wilderness and the dry land
shall be glad,
the desert shall rejoice and blossom;
like the crocus [2]it shall blossom
abundantly,
and rejoice with joy and singing.
The glory of Lebanon shall be given
to it,
the majesty of Cãr'mẹl and
Sharon.
They shall see the glory of the LORD,
the majesty of our God.

[3]Strengthen the weak hands,
and make firm the feeble knees.
[4]Say to those who are of a fearful
heart,
"Be strong, fear not!
Behold, your God
will come with vengeance,
with the recompense of God.
He will come and save you."

[5]Then the eyes of the blind shall be
opened,
and the ears of the deaf unstopped;
[6]then shall the lame man leap like a
hart,
and the tongue of the dumb sing
for joy.
For waters shall break forth in the
wilderness,
and streams in the desert;
[7]the burning sand shall become a pool,
and the thirsty ground springs of
water;
the haunt of jackals shall become a
swamp,[c]
the grass shall become reeds and
rushes.

[8]And a highway shall be there,
and it shall be called the Holy Way;
the unclean shall not pass over it,[d]
and fools shall not err therein.
[9]No lion shall be there,
nor shall any ravenous beast come
up on it;
they shall not be found there,

but the redeemed shall walk there.
[10]And the ransomed of the LORD shall
return,
and come to Zion with singing;
everlasting joy shall be upon their
heads;
they shall obtain joy and gladness,
and sorrow and sighing shall flee
away.

36 In the fourteenth year of King
Hẽz·ẹ·kī'ạh, Sẽn·nãch'ẹ·rĩb king
of Assyria came up against all the
fortified cities of Judah and took them.
[2]And the king of Assyria sent the
Rãb'shạ·keh from Lã'chĩsh to King
Hẽz·ẹ·kī'ạh at Jerusalem, with a great
army. And he stood by the conduit of
the upper pool on the highway to the
Fuller's Field. [3]And there came out to
him E·lī'ạkĩm the son of Hĩl·kī'ạh,
who was over the household, and
Shẽb'nạ the secretary, and Jō'ạh the
son of Ã'sãph, the recorder.
4 And the Rãb'shạ·keh said to them,
"Say to Hẽz·ẹ·kī'ạh, 'Thus says the
great king, the king of Assyria: On
what do you rest this confidence of
yours? [5]Do you think that mere words
are strategy and power for war? On
whom do you now rely, that you have
rebelled against me? [6]Behold, you are
relying on Egypt, that broken reed of a
staff, which will pierce the hand of any
man who leans on it. Such is Pharaoh
king of Egypt to all who rely on him.
[7]But if you say to me, "We rely on the
LORD our God," is it not he whose
high places and altars Hẽz·ẹ·kī'ạh
has removed, saying to Judah and to
Jerusalem, "You shall worship before this altar"? [8]Come now, make a
wager with my master the king of
Assyria: I will give you two thousand
horses, if you are able on your part
to set riders upon them. [9]How then can
you repulse a single captain among
the least of my master's servants,
when you rely on Egypt for chariots
and for horsemen? [10]Moreover, is it
without the LORD that I have come up
against this land to destroy it? The
LORD said to me, Go up against this
land, and destroy it.'"
11 Then E·lī'ạ·kĩm, Shẽb'nạ, and
Jō'ạh said to the Rãb'shạ·keh, "Pray,

[c]Cn: Heb *in the haunt of jackals is her resting place*
[d]Heb *it and he is for them a wayfarer*
35.3: Heb 12.12.   **35.5-6:** Mt 11.5; Lk 7.22.
36.1-38.8, 21-22: 2 Kings 18.13-20.11; 2 Chron 32.1-24.

speak to your servants in Ăr·ạ·mā′ĭc, for we understand it; do not speak to us in the language of Judah within the hearing of the people who are on the wall." ¹²But the Răb′shạ·kẹh said, "Has my master sent me to speak these words to your master and to you, and not to the men sitting on the wall, who are doomed with you to eat their own dung and drink their own urine?"

13 Then the Răb′shạ·kẹh stood and called out in a loud voice in the language of Judah: "Hear the words of the great king, the king of Assyria! ¹⁴Thus says the king: 'Do not let Hĕz·ẹ·kī′ạh deceive you, for he will not be able to deliver you. ¹⁵Do not let Hĕz·ẹ·kī′ạh make you rely on the LORD by saying, "The LORD will surely deliver us; this city will not be given into the hand of the king of Assyria." ¹⁶Do not listen to Hĕz·ẹ·kī′ạh; for thus says the king of Assyria: Make your peace with me and come out to me; then every one of you will eat of his own vine, and every one of his own fig tree, and every one of you will drink the water of his own cistern; ¹⁷until I come and take you away to a land like your own land, a land of grain and wine, a land of bread and vineyards. ¹⁸Beware lest Hĕz·ẹ·kī′ạh mislead you by saying, "The LORD will deliver us." Has any of the gods of the nations delivered his land out of the hand of the king of Assyria? ¹⁹Where are the gods of Hā′măth and Ăr′păd? Where are the gods of Sĕph·ar·vā′ĭm? Have they delivered Sạ·mâr′ĭ·ạ out of my hand? ²⁰Who among all the gods of these countries have delivered their countries out of my hand, that the LORD should deliver Jerusalem out of my hand?'"

21 But they were silent and answered him not a word, for the king's command was, "Do not answer him." ²²Then Ĕ·lī′ạ·kĭm the son of Hĭl·kī′ạh, who was over the household, and Shĕb′nạ the secretary, and Jō′ạh the son of Ā′săph, the recorder, came to Hĕz·ẹ·kī′ạh with their clothes rent, and told him the words of the Răb′shạ·kẹh.

37 When King Hĕz·ẹ·kī′ạh heard it, he rent his clothes, and covered himself with sackcloth, and went into the house of the LORD. ²And he sent Ĕ·lī′ạ·kĭm, who was over the household, and Shĕb′nạ the secretary, and the senior priests, clothed with sackcloth, to the prophet Ī·sāi′ạh the son of Ā′mŏz. ³They said to him, "Thus says Hĕz·ẹ·kī′ạh, 'This day is a day of distress, of rebuke, and of disgrace; children have come to the birth, and there is no strength to bring them forth. ⁴It may be that the LORD your God heard the words of the Răb′shạ·keh, whom his master the king of Assyria has sent to mock the living God, and will rebuke the words which the LORD your God has heard; therefore lift up your prayer for the remnant that is left.'"

5 When the servants of King Hĕz·ẹ·kī′ạh came to Ī·sāi′ạh, ⁶Ī·sāi′ạh said to them, "Say to your master, 'Thus says the LORD: Do not be afraid because of the words that you have heard, with which the servants of the king of Assyria have reviled me. ⁷Behold, I will put a spirit in him, so that he shall hear a rumor, and return to his own land; and I will make him fall by the sword in his own land.'"

8 The Răb′shạ·keh returned, and found the king of Assyria fighting against Lĭb′nạh; for he had heard that the king had left Lā′chĭsh. ⁹Now the king heard concerning Tīr·hā′kạh king of Ethiopia, "He has set out to fight against you." And when he heard it, he sent messengers to Hĕz·ẹ·kī′ạh, saying, ¹⁰"Thus shall you speak to Hĕz·ẹ·kī′ạh king of Judah: 'Do not let your God on whom you rely deceive you by promising that Jerusalem will not be given into the hand of the king of Assyria. ¹¹Behold, you have heard what the kings of Assyria have done to all lands, destroying them utterly. And shall you be delivered? ¹²Have the gods of the nations delivered them, the nations which my fathers destroyed, Gō′zạn, Hâr′ạn, Rē′zĕph, and the people of Eden who were in Tĕ·lăs′sạr? ¹³Where is the king of Hā′măth, the king of Ăr′păd, the king of the city of Sĕph·ar·vā′ĭm, the king of Hē′nạ, or the king of Īv′vạh?' "

14 Hĕz·ẹ·kī′ạh received the letter from the hand of the messengers, and read it; and Hezekiah went up to the house of the LORD, and spread it before the LORD. ¹⁵And Hĕz·ẹ·kī′ạh prayed to the LORD: ¹⁶"O LORD of hosts, God of Israel, who art enthroned above the cherubim, thou art the God, thou alone, of all the kingdoms of the earth; thou hast made heaven and earth. ¹⁷Incline

thy ear, O Lord, and hear; open thy eyes, O Lord, and see; and hear all the words of Sĕn·năch'e·rĭb, which he has sent to mock the living God. ¹⁸ Of a truth, O Lord, the kings of Assyria have laid waste all the nations and their lands, ¹⁹ and have cast their gods into the fire; for they were no gods, but the work of men's hands, wood and stone; therefore they were destroyed. ²⁰ So now, O Lord our God, save us from his hand, that all the kingdoms of the earth may know that thou alone art the Lord."

21 Then Ī·sāi'ah the son of Ā'mŏz sent to Hĕz·e·kī'ah, saying, "Thus says the Lord, the God of Israel: Because you have prayed to me concerning Sĕn·năch'e·rĭb king of Assyria, ²² this is the word that the Lord has spoken concerning him:

'She despises you, she scorns you—
    the virgin daughter of Zion;
she wags her head behind you—
    the daughter of Jerusalem.

²³ 'Whom have you mocked and reviled?
Against whom have you raised your voice
and haughtily lifted your eyes?
Against the Holy One of Israel!
²⁴ By your servants you have mocked the Lord,
    and you have said, With my many chariots
I have gone up the heights of the mountains,
    to the far recesses of Lebanon;
I felled its tallest cedars,
    its choicest cypresses;
I came to its remotest height,
    its densest forest.
²⁵ I dug wells
    and drank waters,
and I dried up with the sole of my foot
    all the streams of Egypt.

²⁶ 'Have you not heard
    that I determined it long ago?
I planned from days of old
    what now I bring to pass,
that you should make fortified cities
    crash into heaps of ruins,
²⁷ while their inhabitants, shorn of strength,
are dismayed and confounded,
and have become like plants of the field
    and like tender grass,

like grass on the housetops,
    blighted*ᵉ* before it is grown.

²⁸ 'I know your sitting down
    and your going out and coming in,
    and your raging against me.
²⁹ Because you have raged against me
    and your arrogance has come to my ears,
I will put my hook in your nose
    and my bit in your mouth,
and I will turn you back on the way
    by which you came.'

30 "And this shall be the sign for you: this year eat what grows of itself, and in the second year what springs of the same; then in the third year sow and reap, and plant vineyards, and eat their fruit. ³¹ And the surviving remnant of the house of Judah shall again take root downward, and bear fruit upward; ³² for out of Jerusalem shall go forth a remnant, and out of Mount Zion a band of survivors. The zeal of the Lord of hosts will accomplish this. 33 "Therefore thus says the Lord concerning the king of Assyria: He shall not come into this city, or shoot an arrow there, or come before it with a shield, or cast up a siege mound against it. ³⁴ By the way that he came, by the same he shall return, and he shall not come into this city, says the Lord. ³⁵ For I will defend this city to save it, for my own sake and for the sake of my servant David."

36 And the angel of the Lord went forth, and slew a hundred and eighty-five thousand in the camp of the Assyrians; and when men arose early in the morning, behold, these were all dead bodies. ³⁷ Then Sĕn·năch'e·rĭb king of Assyria departed, and went home and dwelt at Nĭn'e·vĕh. ³⁸ And as he was worshiping in the house of Nĭs'rŏch his god, A·drăm'me·lĕch and Shă·rē'zer, his sons, slew him with the sword, and escaped into the land of Ăr'a·răt. And Ē'săr-hăd'don his son reigned in his stead.

38 In those days Hĕz·e·kī'ah became sick and was at the point of death. And Ī·sāi'ah the prophet the son of Ā'mŏz came to him, and said to him, "Thus says the Lord: Set your house in order; for you shall die, you shall not recover." ² Then

ᵉ With 2 Kings 19.26: Heb *field*

Hĕz·ḝ·kī′ạh turned his face to the wall, and prayed to the LORD, ³and said, "Remember now, O LORD, I beseech thee, how I have walked before thee in faithfulness and with a whole heart, and have done what is good in thy sight." And Hĕz·ḝ·kī′ạh wept bitterly. ⁴Then the word of the LORD came to Ī·sāi′ạh: ⁵"Go and say to Hĕz·ḝ·kī′ạh, Thus says the LORD, the God of David your father: I have heard your prayer, I have seen your tears; behold, I will add fifteen years to your life. ⁶I will deliver you and this city out of the hand of the king of Assyria, and defend this city.

7 "This is the sign to you from the LORD, that the LORD will do this thing that he has promised: ⁸Behold, I will make the shadow cast by the declining sun on the dial of Ā′hăz turn back ten steps." So the sun turned back on the dial the ten steps by which it had declined.ᶠ

9 A writing of Hĕz·ḝ·kī′ạh king of Judah, after he had been sick and had recovered from his sickness:
¹⁰I said, In the noontide of my days
    I must depart;
I am consigned to the gates of Shē′ōl
    for the rest of my years.
¹¹I said, I shall not see the LORD
    in the land of the living;
I shall look upon man no more
    among the inhabitants of the
      world.
¹²My dwelling is plucked up and removed from me
    like a shepherd's tent;
like a weaver I have rolled up my life;
    he cuts me off from the loom;
from day to night thou dost bring me
    to an end;ᵍ
¹³   I cry for helpʰ until morning;
like a lion he breaks all my bones;
    from day to night thou dost bring
    me to an end.ᵍ

¹⁴Like a swallow or a craneⁱ I clamor,
    I moan like a dove.
My eyes are weary with looking upward.
    O Lord, I am oppressed; be thou
      my security!
¹⁵But what can I say? For he has spoken to me,
    and he himself has done it.
All my sleep has fledʲ

because of the bitterness of my soul.

¹⁶O Lord, by these things men live,
    and in all these is the life of my
      spirit.ᵏ
Oh, restore me to health and make
    me live!
¹⁷Lo, it was for my welfare
    that I had great bitterness;
but thou hast held backˡ my life
    from the pit of destruction,
for thou hast cast all my sins
    behind thy back.
¹⁸For Shē′ōl cannot thank thee,
    death cannot praise thee;
those who go down to the pit cannot
    hope
for thy faithfulness.
¹⁹The living, the living, he thanks thee,
    as I do this day;
the father makes known to the
    children
thy faithfulness.

²⁰The LORD will save me,
    and we will sing to stringed instrumentsᵐ
all the days of our life,
    at the house of the LORD.

21 Now Ī·sāi′ah had said, "Let them take a cake of figs, and apply it to the boil, that he may recover." ²²Hĕz·ḝ·kī′ah also had said, "What is the sign that I shall go up to the house of the LORD?"

39 At that time Mĕr′o·dăch-băl′a·dăn the son of Băl′a·dăn, king of Babylon, sent envoys with letters and a present to Hĕz·ḝ·kī′ah, for he heard that he had been sick and had recovered. ²And Hĕz·ḝ·kī′ah welcomed them; and he showed them his treasure house, the silver, the gold, the spices, the precious oil, his whole armory, all that was found in his storehouses. There was nothing in his house or in all his realm that Hezekiah did not show them. ³Then Ī·sāi′ah the prophet came to King Hĕz·ḝ·kī′ah, and said to him, "What did these men say? And whence did they come to you?" Hezekiah said, "They have come to me from a far country, from Babylon."

ᶠThe Hebrew of this verse is obscure   ᵍHeb uncertain
ʰCn: Heb obscure   ⁱHeb uncertain
ʲCn Compare Syr: Heb *I will walk slowly all my years*
ᵏHeb uncertain   ˡCn Compare Gk Vg: Heb *loved*
ᵐHeb *my stringed instruments*
39.1-8: 2 Kings 20.12-19; 2 Chron 32.31.

4 He said, "What have they seen in your house?" Hĕz·e̜·kī'ah answered, "They have seen all that is in my house; there is nothing in my storehouses that I did not show them."

5 Then Ī·sāi'ah said to Hĕz·e̜·kī'ah, "Hear the word of the LORD of hosts: 6 Behold, the days are coming, when all that is in your house, and that which your fathers have stored up till this day, shall be carried to Babylon; nothing shall be left, says the LORD. 7 And some of your own sons, who are born to you, shall be taken away; and they shall be eunuchs in the palace of the king of Babylon." 8 Then said Hĕz·e̜·kī'ah to Ī·sāi'ah, "The word of the LORD which you have spoken is good." For he thought, "There will be peace and security in my days."

40 Comfort, comfort my people, says your God.
2 Speak tenderly to Jerusalem,
   and cry to her
   that her warfare[n] is ended,
     that her iniquity is pardoned,
   that she has received from the
    LORD's hand
    double for all her sins.

3 A voice cries:
"In the wilderness prepare the way of
   the LORD,
   make straight in the desert a
    highway for our God.
4 Every valley shall be lifted up,
   and every mountain and hill be
    made low;
the uneven ground shall become
   level,
   and the rough places a plain.
5 And the glory of the LORD shall be
   revealed,
   and all flesh shall see it together,
for the mouth of the LORD has
   spoken."

6 A voice says, "Cry!"
   And I said, "What shall I cry?"
All flesh is grass,
   and all its beauty is like the
    flower of the field.
7 The grass withers, the flower fades,
   when the breath of the LORD blows
    upon it;
   surely the people is grass.
8 The grass withers, the flower fades;
   but the word of our God will stand
    for ever.

9 Get you up to a high mountain,
   O Zion, herald of good tidings;[o]
lift up your voice with strength,
   O Jerusalem, herald of good
    tidings,[p]
lift it up, fear not;
   say to the cities of Judah,
    "Behold your God!"
10 Behold, the Lord GOD comes with
   might,
   and his arm rules for him;
behold, his reward is with him,
   and his recompense before him.
11 He will feed his flock like a shepherd,
   he will gather the lambs in his
    arms,
he will carry them in his bosom,
   and gently lead those that are
    with young.

12 Who has measured the waters in
   the hollow of his hand
and marked off the heavens with
   a span,
enclosed the dust of the earth in a
   measure
and weighed the mountains in
   scales
   and the hills in a balance?
13 Who has directed the Spirit of the
   LORD,
   or as his counselor has instructed
    him?
14 Whom did he consult for his enlightenment,
   and who taught him the path of
    justice,
and taught him knowledge,
   and showed him the way of understanding?
15 Behold, the nations are like a drop
   from a bucket,
   and are accounted as the dust
    on the scales;
behold, he takes up the isles like
   fine dust.
16 Lebanon would not suffice for fuel,
   nor are its beasts enough for a
    burnt offering.
17 All the nations are as nothing before
   him,
   they are accounted by him as less
    than nothing and emptiness.

ⁿ Or *time of service*
ᵒ Or *O herald of good tidings to Zion*
ᵖ Or *O herald of good tidings to Jerusalem*
40.3: Mt 3.3; Mk 1.3; Lk 3.4; Jn 1.23.
40.4-5: Lk 3.5-6.
40.6-8: 1 Pet 1.24-25.
40.9: Is 52.7; Nah 1.15; Acts 10.36; Rom 10.15.
40.10: Rev 22.7, 12.
40.13: Rom 11.34; 1 Cor 2.16.

¹⁸To whom then will you liken God,
    or what likeness compare with
    him?
¹⁹The idol! a workman casts it,
    and a goldsmith overlays it with
    gold,
    and casts for it silver chains.
²⁰He who is impoverished*q* chooses for
    an offering
    wood that will not rot;
he seeks out a skilful craftsman
    to set up an image that will not
    move.

²¹Have you not known? Have you not
    heard?
    Has it not been told you from the
    beginning?
    Have you not understood from
    the foundations of the earth?
²²It is he who sits above the circle
    of the earth,
    and its inhabitants are like grass-
    hoppers;
who stretches out the heavens like
    a curtain,
    and spreads them like a tent to
    dwell in;
²³who brings princes to nought,
    and makes the rulers of the earth
    as nothing.

²⁴Scarcely are they planted, scarcely
    sown,
    scarcely has their stem taken
    root in the earth,
when he blows upon them, and they
    wither,
    and the tempest carries them off
    like stubble.

²⁵To whom then will you compare me,
    that I should be like him?
    says the Holy One.
²⁶Lift up your eyes on high and see:
    who created these?
He who brings out their host by
    number,
    calling them all by name;
by the greatness of his might,
    and because he is strong in power
    not one is missing.

²⁷Why do you say, O Jacob,
    and speak, O Israel,
"My way is hid from the Lord,
    and my right is disregarded by
    my God"?
²⁸Have you not known? Have you not
    heard?

The Lord is the everlasting God,
    the Creator of the ends of the
    earth.
He does not faint or grow weary,
    his understanding is unsearch-
    able.
²⁹He gives power to the faint,
    and to him who has no might he
    increases strength.
³⁰Even youths shall faint and be weary,
    and young men shall fall ex-
    hausted;
³¹but they who wait for the Lord shall
    renew their strength,
    they shall mount up with wings
    like eagles,
    they shall run and not be weary,
    they shall walk and not faint.

41 Listen to me in silence, O coast-
    lands;
    let the peoples renew their
    strength;
    let them approach, then let them
    speak;
    let us together draw near for
    judgment.

²Who stirred up one from the east
    whom victory meets at every step?
He gives up nations before him,
    so that he tramples kings under
    foot;
he makes them like dust with his
    sword,
    like driven stubble with his bow.
³He pursues them and passes on
    safely,
    by paths his feet have not trod.
⁴Who has performed and done this,
    calling the generations from the
    beginning?
I, the Lord, the first,
    and with the last; I am He.

⁵The coastlands have seen and are
    afraid,
    the ends of the earth tremble;
    they have drawn near and come.
⁶Every one helps his neighbor,
    and says to his brother, "Take
    courage!"
⁷The craftsman encourages the gold-
    smith,
    and he who smooths with the ham-
    mer him who strikes the anvil,
saying of the soldering, "It is good";
    and they fasten it with nails so that
    it cannot be moved.

q Heb uncertain

⁸But you, Israel, my servant,
  Jacob, whom I have chosen,
  the offspring of Abraham, my
    friend;
⁹you whom I took from the ends of
    the earth,
  and called from its farthest cor-
    ners,
  saying to you, "You are my servant,
    I have chosen you and not cast
    you off";
¹⁰fear not, for I am with you,
  be not dismayed, for I am your
    God;
  I will strengthen you, I will help
    you,
  I will uphold you with my victori-
    ous right hand.

¹¹Behold, all who are incensed against
    you
  shall be put to shame and con-
    founded;
  those who strive against you
  shall be as nothing and shall
    perish.
¹²You shall seek those who contend
    with you,
  but you shall not find them;
  those who war against you
  shall be as nothing at all.
¹³For I, the LORD your God,
  hold your right hand;
  it is I who say to you, "Fear not,
  I will help you."

¹⁴Fear not, you worm Jacob,
  you men of Israel!
  I will help you, says the LORD;
  your Redeemer is the Holy One of
    Israel.
¹⁵Behold, I will make of you a thresh-
    ing sledge,
  new, sharp, and having teeth;
  you shall thresh the mountains and
    crush them,
  and you shall make the hills like
    chaff;
¹⁶you shall winnow them and the wind
    shall carry them away,
  and the tempest shall scatter them.
And you shall rejoice in the LORD;
  in the Holy One of Israel you shall
    glory.

¹⁷When the poor and needy seek water,
  and there is none,
  and their tongue is parched with
    thirst,
  I the LORD will answer them,

I the God of Israel will not for-
    sake them.
¹⁸I will open rivers on the bare heights,
  and fountains in the midst of the
    valleys;
  I will make the wilderness a pool of
    water,
  and the dry land springs of water.
¹⁹I will put in the wilderness the
    cedar,
  the acacia, the myrtle, and the
    olive;
  I will set in the desert the cypress,
  the plane and the pine together;
²⁰that men may see and know,
  may consider and understand
    together,
  that the hand of the LORD has done
    this,
  the Holy One of Israel has cre-
    ated it.

²¹Set forth your case, says the LORD;
  bring your proofs, says the King of
    Jacob.
²²Let them bring them, and tell us
  what is to happen.
Tell us the former things, what they
    are,
  that we may consider them,
  that we may know their outcome;
  or declare to us the things to come.
²³Tell us what is to come hereafter,
  that we may know that you are
    gods;
  do good, or do harm,
  that we may be dismayed and ter-
    rified.
²⁴Behold, you are nothing,
  and your work is nought;
  an abomination is he who chooses
    you.

²⁵I stirred up one from the north,
  and he has come,
  from the rising of the sun, and he
  shall call on my name;
  he shall trample[r] on rulers as on
    mortar,
  as the potter treads clay.
²⁶Who declared it from the beginning,
  that we might know,
  and beforetime, that we might say,
  "He is right"?
There was none who declared it,
  none who proclaimed,
  none who heard your words.

[r]Cn: Heb *come*
41.8: Jas 2.23. **41.8-9:** Lk 1.54; Heb 2.16.
41.10: Acts 18.10.

²⁷I first have declared it to Zion,ˢ
and I give to Jerusalem a herald
of good tidings.
²⁸But when I look there is no one;
among these there is no counselor
who, when I ask, gives an answer.
²⁹Behold, they are all a delusion;
their works are nothing;
their molten images are empty
wind.

42 Behold my servant, whom I
uphold,
my chosen, in whom my soul delights;
I have put my Spirit upon him,
he will bring forth justice to the
nations.
²He will not cry or lift up his voice,
or make it heard in the street;
³a bruised reed he will not break,
and a dimly burning wick he will
not quench;
he will faithfully bring forth
justice.
⁴He will not failᵗ or be discouragedᵘ
till he has established justice in
the earth;
and the coastlands wait for his
law.

⁵Thus says God, the LORD,
who created the heavens and
stretched them out,
who spread forth the earth and
what comes from it,
who gives breath to the people upon
it
and spirit to those who walk in
it:
⁶"I am the LORD, I have called you
in righteousness,
I have taken you by the hand and
kept you;
I have given you as a covenant to
the people,
a light to the nations,
⁷   to open the eyes that are blind,
to bring out the prisoners from the
dungeon,
from the prison those who sit in
darkness.
⁸I am the LORD, that is my name;
my glory I give to no other,
nor my praise to graven images.
⁹Behold, the former things have
come to pass,
and new things I now declare;
before they spring forth
I tell you of them."

¹⁰Sing to the LORD a new song,
his praise from the end of the
earth!
Let the sea roarᵛ and all that fills it,
the coastlands and their inhabitants.
¹¹Let the desert and its cities lift up
their voice,
the villages that Kē'dãr inhabits;
let the inhabitants of Sē'la sing for
joy,
let them shout from the top of
the mountains.
¹²Let them give glory to the LORD,
and declare his praise in the coastlands.
¹³The LORD goes forth like a mighty
man,
like a man of war he stirs up his
fury;
he cries out, he shouts aloud,
he shows himself mighty against
his foes.

¹⁴For a long time I have held my peace,
I have kept still and restrained
myself;
now I will cry out like a woman in
travail,
I will gasp and pant.
¹⁵I will lay waste mountains and
hills,
and dry up all their herbage;
I will turn the rivers into islands,
and dry up the pools.
¹⁶And I will lead the blind
in a way that they know not,
in paths that they have not known
I will guide them.
I will turn the darkness before them
into light,
the rough places into level ground.
These are the things I will do,
and I will not forsake them.
¹⁷They shall be turned back and
utterly put to shame,
who trust in graven images,
who say to molten images,
"You are our gods."

¹⁸Hear, you deaf;
and look, you blind, that you may
see!
¹⁹Who is blind but my servant,

ˢCn: Heb *first to Zion, Behold, behold them*
ᵗOr *burn dimly*   ᵘOr *bruised*
ᵛCn Compare Ps 96.11; 98.7: Heb *Those who go down to
the sea*
42.1-4: Mt 12.18-21.   **42.5:** Acts 17.24-25.
42.6: Is 49.6; Lk 2.32; Acts 13.47; 26.23.
42.7, 16: Acts 26.18.

or deaf as my messenger whom
I send?
Who is blind as my dedicated one,
or blind as the servant of the
Lord?
20 He sees*w* many things, but does
not observe them;
his ears are open, but he does not
hear.
21 The Lord was pleased, for his
righteousness' sake,
to magnify his law and make it
glorious.
22 But this is a people robbed and
plundered,
they are all of them trapped in
holes
and hidden in prisons;
they have become a prey with none
to rescue,
a spoil with none to say, "Restore!"
23 Who among you will give ear to this,
will attend and listen for the time
to come?
24 Who gave up Jacob to the spoiler,
and Israel to the robbers?
Was it not the Lord, against whom
we have sinned,
in whose ways they would not
walk,
and whose law they would not
obey?
25 So he poured upon him the heat of
his anger
and the might of battle;
it set him on fire round about, but
he did not understand;
it burned him, but he did not take
it to heart.

43 But now thus says the Lord, he
who created you, O Jacob,
he who formed you, O Israel:
"Fear not, for I have redeemed you;
I have called you by name, you are
mine.
2 When you pass through the waters
I will be with you;
and through the rivers, they
shall not overwhelm you;
when you walk through fire you shall
not be burned,
and the flame shall not consume
you.
3 For I am the Lord your God,
the Holy One of Israel, your
Savior.
I give Egypt as your ransom,
Ethiopia and Sē′ba in exchange for
you.

4 Because you are precious in my eyes,
and honored, and I love you,
I give men in return for you,
peoples in exchange for your life.
5 Fear not, for I am with you;
I will bring your offspring from the
east,
and from the west I will gather
you;
6 I will say to the north, Give up,
and to the south, Do not withhold;
bring my sons from afar
and my daughters from the end
of the earth,
7 every one who is called by my name,
whom I created for my glory,
whom I formed and made."

8 Bring forth the people who are blind,
yet have eyes,
who are deaf, yet have ears!
9 Let all the nations gather together,
and let the peoples assemble.
Who among them can declare this,
and show us the former things?
Let them bring their witnesses to
justify them,
and let them hear and say, It is
true.
10 "You are my witnesses," says the
Lord,
"and my servant whom I have
chosen,
that you may know and believe me
and understand that I am He.
Before me no god was formed,
nor shall there be any after me.
11 I, I am the Lord,
and besides me there is no savior.
12 I declared and saved and proclaimed,
when there was no strange god
among you;
and you are my witnesses," says
the Lord.
13 "I am God, and also henceforth I
am He;
there is none who can deliver
from my hand;
I work and who can hinder it?"

14 Thus says the Lord,
your Redeemer, the Holy One of
Israel:
"For your sake I will send to Babylon
and break down all the bars,
and the shouting of the Chăl·dē′-
ans will be turned to lamentations.*x*

w Heb *you see*   *x* Heb obscure   **43.5:** Acts 18.10.

¹⁵I am the LORD, your Holy One,
　the Creator of Israel, your King."
¹⁶Thus says the LORD,
　who makes a way in the sea,
　a path in the mighty waters,
¹⁷who brings forth chariot and horse,
　army and warrior;
　they lie down, they cannot rise,
　they are extinguished, quenched
　　like a wick:
¹⁸"Remember not the former things,
　nor consider the things of old.
¹⁹Behold, I am doing a new thing;
　now it springs forth, do you not
　　perceive it?
I will make a way in the wilderness
　and rivers in the desert.
²⁰The wild beasts will honor me,
　the jackals and the ostriches;
for I give water in the wilderness,
　rivers in the desert,
to give drink to my chosen people,
²¹　the people whom I formed for
　　myself
that they might declare my praise.

²²"Yet you did not call upon me, O
　　Jacob;
but you have been weary of me,
　O Israel!
²³You have not brought me your sheep
　for burnt offerings,
　or honored me with your sacri-
　　fices.
I have not burdened you with offer-
　　ings,
　or wearied you with frankincense.
²⁴You have not bought me sweet cane
　with money,
　or satisfied me with the fat of
　your sacrifices.
But you have burdened me with
　your sins,
　you have wearied me with your
　iniquities.

²⁵"I, I am He
　who blots out your transgressions
　for my own sake,
　and I will not remember your
　sins.
²⁶Put me in remembrance, let us argue
　together;
　set forth your case, that you may
　be proved right.
²⁷Your first father sinned,
　and your mediators transgressed
　against me.
²⁸Therefore I profaned the princes of
　the sanctuary,

I delivered Jacob to utter destruc-
　tion
and Israel to reviling.

44 "But now hear, O Jacob my
　　servant,
Israel whom I have chosen!
²Thus says the LORD who made you,
　who formed you from the womb
　and will help you:
Fear not, O Jacob my servant,
　Jĕsh′ū·run whom I have chosen.
³For I will pour water on the thirsty
　land,
　and streams on the dry ground;
I will pour my Spirit upon your
　descendants,
　and my blessing on your offspring.
⁴They shall spring up like grass amid
　waters,^y
　like willows by flowing streams;
⁵This one will say, 'I am the LORD's,'
　another will call himself by the
　name of Jacob,
and another will write on his hand,
　'The LORD's,'
　and surname himself by the
　name of Israel."

⁶Thus says the LORD, the King of
　Israel
　and his Redeemer, the LORD of
　hosts:
"I am the first and I am the last;
　besides me there is no god.
⁷Who is like me? Let him proclaim it,
　let him declare and set it forth
　before me.
Who has announced from of old the
　things to come?^z
　Let them tell us^a what is yet to
　be.
⁸Fear not, nor be afraid;
　have I not told you from of old
　and declared it?
And you are my witnesses!
Is there a God besides me?
There is no Rock; I know not any."

9 All who make idols are nothing,
and the things they delight in do not
profit; their witnesses neither see nor
know, that they may be put to shame.
¹⁰Who fashions a god or casts an image,
that is profitable for nothing? ¹¹Behold,
all his fellows shall be put to shame,

^yGk Compare Tg: Heb *They shall spring up in among
grass*
^zCn: Heb *from my placing an eternal people and things
to come*　^aTg: Heb *them*
44.6: Is 48.12; Rev 1.17; 2.8; 22.13.

and the craftsmen are but men; let them all assemble, let them stand forth, they shall be terrified, they shall be put to shame together.

12 The ironsmith fashions it[b] and works it over the coals; he shapes it with hammers, and forges it with his strong arm; he becomes hungry and his strength fails, he drinks no water and is faint. [13]The carpenter stretches a line, he marks it out with a pencil; he fashions it with planes, and marks it with a compass; he shapes it into the figure of a man, with the beauty of a man, to dwell in a house. [14]He cuts down cedars; or he chooses a holm tree or an oak and lets it grow strong among the trees of the forest; he plants a cedar and the rain nourishes it. [15]Then it becomes fuel for a man; he takes a part of it and warms himself, he kindles a fire and bakes bread; also he makes a god and worships it, he makes it a graven image and falls down before it. [16]Half of it he burns in the fire; over the half he eats flesh, he roasts meat and is satisfied; also he warms himself and says, "Aha, I am warm, I have seen the fire!" [17]And the rest of it he makes into a god, his idol; and falls down to it and worships it; he prays to it and says, "Deliver me, for thou art my god!"

18 They know not, nor do they discern; for he has shut their eyes, so that they cannot see, and their minds, so that they cannot understand. [19]No one considers, nor is there knowledge or discernment to say, "Half of it I burned in the fire, I also baked bread on its coals, I roasted flesh and have eaten; and shall I make the residue of it an abomination? Shall I fall down before a block of wood?" [20]He feeds on ashes; a deluded mind has led him astray, and he cannot deliver himself or say, "Is there not a lie in my right hand?"

[21]Remember these things, O Jacob,
    and Israel, for you are my servant;
I formed you, you are my servant;
    O Israel, you will not be forgotten by me.
[22]I have swept away your transgressions like a cloud,
    and your sins like mist;
return to me, for I have redeemed you.

[23]Sing, O heavens, for the LORD has done it;
    shout, O depths of the earth;
break forth into singing, O mountains,
    O forest, and every tree in it!
For the LORD has redeemed Jacob,
    and will be glorified in Israel.

[24]Thus says the LORD, your Redeemer,
    who formed you from the womb:
"I am the LORD, who made all things,
    who stretched out the heavens alone,
    who spread out the earth—
    Who was with me?[c]—
[25]who frustrates the omens of liars,
    and makes fools of diviners;
who turns wise men back,
    and makes their knowledge foolish;
[26]who confirms the word of his servant,
    and performs the counsel of his messengers;
who says of Jerusalem, 'She shall be inhabited,'
    and of the cities of Judah, 'They shall be built,
    and I will raise up their ruins';
[27]who says to the deep, 'Be dry,
    I will dry up your rivers';
[28]who says of Cyrus, 'He is my shepherd,
    and he shall fulfil all my purpose';
saying of Jerusalem, 'She shall be built,'
    and of the temple, 'Your foundation shall be laid.'"

45 Thus says the LORD to his anointed, to Cyrus,
    whose right hand I have grasped,
to subdue nations before him
    and ungird the loins of kings,
to open doors before him
    that gates may not be closed:
[2]"I will go before you
    and level the mountains,[d]
I will break in pieces the doors of bronze
    and cut asunder the bars of iron,
[3]I will give you the treasures of darkness
    and the hoards in secret places,
that you may know that it is I, the LORD,

[b]Cn: Heb *an axe*
[c]Another reading is *who spread out the earth by myself*
[d]One ancient Ms Gk: Heb *the swellings*
44.23: Jer 51.48; Rev 12.12; 18.20. **44.25:** 1 Cor 1.20.

the God of Israel, who call you by
your name.
⁴For the sake of my servant Jacob,
and Israel my chosen,
I call you by your name,
I surname you, though you do not
know me.
⁵I am the LORD, and there is no other,
besides me there is no God;
I gird you, though you do not know
me,
⁶that men may know, from the rising
of the sun
and from the west, that there is
none besides me;
I am the LORD, and there is no
other.
⁷I form light and create darkness,
I make weal and create woe,
I am the LORD, who do all these
things.

⁸"Shower, O heavens, from above,
and let the skies rain down righteousness;
let the earth open, that salvation may
sprout forth,ᵉ
and let it cause righteousness to
spring up also;
I the LORD have created it.

⁹"Woe to him who strives with his
Maker,
an earthen vessel with the potter!ᶠ
Does the clay say to him who fashions
it, 'What are you making'?
or 'Your work has no handles'?
¹⁰Woe to him who says to a father,
'What are you begetting?'
or to a woman, 'With what are you
in travail?'"
¹¹Thus says the LORD,
the Holy One of Israel, and his
Maker:
"Will you question meᵍ about my
children,
or command me concerning the
work of my hands?
¹²I made the earth,
and created man upon it;
it was my hands that stretched out
the heavens,
and I commanded all their host.
¹³I have aroused him in righteousness,
and I will make straight all his
ways;
he shall build my city
and set my exiles free,
not for price or reward,"
says the LORD of hosts.

¹⁴Thus says the LORD:
"The wealth of Egypt and the merchandise of Ethiopia,
and the Sạ·bē'ạnṣ, men of stature,
shall come over to you and be yours,
they shall follow you;
they shall come over in chains and
bow down to you.
They will make supplication to you,
saying:
'God is with you only, and there is
no other,
no god besides him.'"
¹⁵Truly, thou art a God who hidest
thyself,
O God of Israel, the Savior.
¹⁶All of them are put to shame and
confounded,
the makers of idols go in confusion
together.
¹⁷But Israel is saved by the LORD
with everlasting salvation;
you shall not be put to shame or confounded
to all eternity.

¹⁸For thus says the LORD,
who created the heavens
(he is God!),
who formed the earth and made it
(he established it;
he did not create it a chaos,
he formed it to be inhabited!):
"I am the LORD, and there is no other.
¹⁹I did not speak in secret,
in a land of darkness;
I did not say to the offspring of Jacob,
'Seek me in chaos.'
I the LORD speak the truth,
I declare what is right.

²⁰"Assemble yourselves and come,
draw near together,
you survivors of the nations!
They have no knowledge
who carry about their wooden
idols,
and keep on praying to a god
that cannot save.
²¹Declare and present your case;
let them take counsel together!
Who told this long ago?
Who declared it of old?
Was it not I, the LORD?
And there is no other god besides
me,

ᵉOne ancient Ms: Heb *that they may bring forth salvation*
ᶠCn: Heb *potsherds* or *potters*
ᵍCn: Heb *Ask me of things to come*
45.9: Is 29.16; Rom 9.20.   **45.14**: 1 Cor 14.25.
45.17: Heb 5.9.   **45.21**: Acts 15.18.

a righteous God and a Savior;
there is none besides me.

22 "Turn to me and be saved,
all the ends of the earth!
For I am God, and there is no other.
23 By myself I have sworn,
from my mouth has gone forth
in righteousness
a word that shall not return:
'To me every knee shall bow,
every tongue shall swear.'

24 "Only in the LORD, it shall be said of
me,
are righteousness and strength;
to him shall come and be ashamed,
all who were incensed against him.
25 In the LORD all the offspring of Israel
shall triumph and glory."

46 Bĕl bows down, Nē'bō stoops,
their idols are on beasts and
cattle;
these things you carry are loaded
as burdens on weary beasts.
2 They stoop, they bow down together,
they cannot save the burden,
but themselves go into captivity.

3 "Hearken to me, O house of Jacob,
all the remnant of the house of
Israel,
who have been borne by me from
your birth,
carried from the womb;
4 even to your old age I am He,
and to gray hairs I will carry you.
I have made, and I will bear;
I will carry and will save.

5 "To whom will you liken me and
make me equal,
and compare me, that we may be
alike?
6 Those who lavish gold from the purse,
and weigh out silver in the scales,
hire a goldsmith, and he makes it
into a god;
then they fall down and worship!
7 They lift it upon their shoulders,
they carry it,
they set it in its place, and it stands
there;
it cannot move from its place.
If one cries to it, it does not answer
or save him from his trouble.

8 "Remember this and consider,
recall it to mind, you transgressors,

9 remember the former things of
old;
for I am God, and there is no other;
I am God, and there is none like
me,
10 declaring the end from the beginning
and from ancient times things not
yet done,
saying, 'My counsel shall stand,
and I will accomplish all my
purpose,'
11 calling a bird of prey from the east,
the man of my counsel from a far
country.
I have spoken, and I will bring it to
pass;
I have purposed, and I will do it.

12 "Hearken to me, you stubborn of
heart,
you who are far from deliverance:
13 I bring near my deliverance, it is not
far off,
and my salvation will not tarry;
I will put salvation in Zion,
for Israel my glory."

47 Come down and sit in the dust,
O virgin daughter of Babylon;
sit on the ground without a throne,
O daughter of the Chăl·dē'ạnş!
For you shall no more be called
tender and delicate.
2 Take the millstones and grind meal,
put off your veil,
strip off your robe, uncover your legs,
pass through the rivers.
3 Your nakedness shall be uncovered,
and your shame shall be seen.
I will take vengeance,
and I will spare no man.
4 Our Redeemer — the LORD of hosts
is his name —
is the Holy One of Israel.

5 Sit in silence, and go into darkness,
O daughter of the Chăl·dē'ạnş;
for you shall no more be called
the mistress of kingdoms.
6 I was angry with my people,
I profaned my heritage;
I gave them into your hand,
you showed them no mercy;
on the aged you made your yoke
exceedingly heavy.
7 You said, "I shall be mistress for
ever,"

45.23: Rom 14.11; Phil 2.10-11.
47: Is 13.1-14.23; Jer 50-51; Hab 1-2.

so that you did not lay these things
　　to heart
　　or remember their end.

⁸Now therefore hear this, you lover
　　of pleasures,
　　who sit securely,
who say in your heart,
　　"I am, and there is no one besides
　　　me;
　I shall not sit as a widow
　　or know the loss of children":
⁹These two things shall come to you
　　in a moment, in one day;
the loss of children and widowhood
　shall come upon you in full meas-
　　ure,
in spite of your many sorceries
　and the great power of your
　　enchantments.

¹⁰You felt secure in your wickedness,
　you said, "No one sees me";
your wisdom and your knowledge
　led you astray,
and you said in your heart,
　"I am, and there is no one besides
　　me."
¹¹But evil shall come upon you,
　for which you cannot atone;
disaster shall fall upon you,
　which you will not be able to
　　expiate;
and ruin shall come on you suddenly,
　of which you know nothing.

¹²Stand fast in your enchantments
　and your many sorceries,
　with which you have labored from
　　your youth;
perhaps you may be able to succeed,
　perhaps you may inspire terror.
¹³You are wearied with your many
　counsels;
　let them stand forth and save you,
those who divide the heavens,
　who gaze at the stars,
who at the new moons predict
　whatʰ shall befall you.

¹⁴Behold, they are like stubble,
　the fire consumes them;
they cannot deliver themselves
　from the power of the flame.
No coal for warming oneself is this,
　no fire to sit before!
¹⁵Such to you are those with whom
　you have labored,
who have trafficked with you from
　your youth;

they wander about each in his own
　direction;
there is no one to save you.

48 Hear this, O house of Jacob,
　who are called by the name of
　　Israel,
and who came forth from the loinsⁱ
　of Judah;
who swear by the name of the LORD,
　and confess the God of Israel,
　but not in truth or right.
²For they call themselves after the
　holy city,
and stay themselves on the God
　of Israel;
　the LORD of hosts is his name.

³"The former things I declared of old,
　they went forth from my mouth
　and I made them known;
　then suddenly I did them and
　they came to pass.
⁴Because I know that you are ob-
　stinate,
　and your neck is an iron sinew
　and your forehead brass,
⁵I declared them to you from of old,
　before they came to pass I an-
　　nounced them to you,
lest you should say, 'My idol did
　them,
　my graven image and my molten
　image commanded them.'

⁶"You have heard; now see all this;
　and will you not declare it?
From this time forth I make you hear
　new things,
　hidden things which you have not
　known.
⁷They are created now, not long ago;
　before today you have never heard
　of them,
　lest you should say, 'Behold, I
　knew them.'
⁸You have never heard, you have
　never known,
　from of old your ear has not been
　opened.
For I knew that you would deal very
　treacherously,
　and that from birth you were called
　a rebel.

⁹"For my name's sake I defer my
　anger,
　for the sake of my praise I restrain
　it for you,

ʰGk Syr Compare Vg: Heb *from what*　ⁱCn: Heb *waters*
47.8: Rev 18.7.　**47.9:** Rev 18.8.

that I may not cut you off.
[10] Behold, I have refined you, but not
   like[j] silver;
   I have tried you in the furnace of
     affliction.
[11] For my own sake, for my own sake, I
   do it,
   for how should my name[k] be
     profaned?
My glory I will not give to another.

[12] "Hearken to me, O Jacob,
   and Israel, whom I called!
I am He, I am the first,
   and I am the last.
[13] My hand laid the foundation of the
     earth,
   and my right hand spread out the
     heavens;
when I call to them,
   they stand forth together.

[14] "Assemble, all of you, and hear!
   Who among them has declared
     these things?
The LORD loves him;
   he shall perform his purpose on
     Babylon,
   and his arm shall be against the
     Chăl·dē'ạns.
[15] I, even I, have spoken and called
   him,
   I have brought him, and he will
     prosper in his way.
[16] Draw near to me, hear this:
   from the beginning I have not
     spoken in secret,
   from the time it came to be I have
     been there."
And now the Lord GOD has sent me
   and his Spirit.

[17] Thus says the LORD,
   your Redeemer, the Holy One of
     Israel:
"I am the LORD your God,
   who teaches you to profit,
   who leads you in the way you
     should go.
[18] O that you had hearkened to my
     commandments!
Then your peace would have been
     like a river,
   and your righteousness like the
     waves of the sea;
[19] your offspring would have been like
     the sand,
   and your descendants like its
     grains;

their name would never be cut off
   or destroyed from before me."

[20] Go forth from Babylon, flee from
     Chăl·dē'ă,
   declare this with a shout of joy,
     proclaim it,
send it forth to the end of the earth;
   say, "The LORD has redeemed his
     servant Jacob!"
[21] They thirsted not when he led them
     through the deserts;
   he made water flow for them from
     the rock;
   he cleft the rock and the water
     gushed out.
[22] "There is no peace," says the LORD,
   "for the wicked."

49 Listen to me, O coastlands,
   and hearken, you peoples from
     afar.
The LORD called me from the womb,
   from the body of my mother he
     named my name.
[2] He made my mouth like a sharp
     sword,
   in the shadow of his hand he hid
     me;
he made me a polished arrow,
   in his quiver he hid me away.
[3] And he said to me, "You are my
     servant,
   Israel, in whom I will be glorified."
[4] But I said, "I have labored in vain,
   I have spent my strength for noth-
     ing and vanity;
yet surely my right is with the LORD,
   and my recompense with my God."

[5] And now the LORD says,
   who formed me from the womb
     to be his servant,
to bring Jacob back to him,
   and that Israel might be gathered
     to him,
for I am honored in the eyes of the
     LORD,
   and my God has become my
     strength—
[6] he says:
"It is too light a thing that you
     should be my servant
   to raise up the tribes of Jacob
   and to restore the preserved of
     Israel;

[j] Cn: Heb *with*   [k] Gk Old Latin: Heb lacks *my name*
48.12: Is 44.6; Rev 1.17; 2.8; 22.13.
49.1: Jer 1.5; Gal 1.15.   **49.4:** Phil 2.16.
49.6: Is 42.6; Lk 2.32; Acts 13.47; 26.23.

I will give you as a light to the nations,
that my salvation may reach to
the end of the earth."

⁷Thus says the LORD,
the Redeemer of Israel and his
Holy One,
to one deeply despised, abhorred by
the nations,
the servant of rulers:
"Kings shall see and arise;
princes, and they shall prostrate
themselves;
because of the LORD, who is faithful,
the Holy One of Israel, who has
chosen you."

⁸Thus says the LORD:
"In a time of favor I have answered
you,
in a day of salvation I have helped
you;
I have kept you and given you
as a covenant to the people,
to establish the land,
to apportion the desolate heritages;
⁹saying to the prisoners, 'Come forth,'
to those who are in darkness,
'Appear.'
They shall feed along the ways,
on all bare heights shall be their
pasture;
¹⁰they shall not hunger or thirst,
neither scorching wind nor sun
shall smite them,
for he who has pity on them will
lead them,
and by springs of water will guide
them.
¹¹And I will make all my mountains
a way,
and my highways shall be raised
up.
¹²Lo, these shall come from afar,
and lo, these from the north and
from the west,
and these from the land of
Sȳ·ē′nē."ˡ
¹³Sing for joy, O heavens, and exult,
O earth;
break forth, O mountains, into
singing!
For the LORD has comforted his
people,
and will have compassion on his
afflicted.

¹⁴But Zion said, "The LORD has forsaken me,
my Lord has forgotten me."

¹⁵"Can a woman forget her sucking
child,
that she should have no compassion on the son of her womb?"
Even these may forget,
yet I will not forget you.
¹⁶Behold, I have graven you on the
palms of my hands;
your walls are continually before
me.
¹⁷Your builders outstrip your destroyers,
and those who laid you waste go
forth from you.
¹⁸Lift up your eyes round about and
see;
they all gather, they come to you.
As I live, says the LORD,
you shall put them all on as an
ornament,
you shall bind them on as a bride
does.

¹⁹"Surely your waste and your desolate
places
and your devastated land—
surely now you will be too narrow
for your inhabitants,
and those who swallowed you up
will be far away.
²⁰The children born in the time of your
bereavement
will yet say in your ears:
'The place is too narrow for me;
make room for me to dwell in.'
²¹Then you will say in your heart:
'Who has borne me these?
I was bereaved and barren,
exiled and put away,
but who has brought up these?
Behold, I was left alone;
whence then have these come?' "

²²Thus says the Lord GOD:
"Behold, I will lift up my hand to the
nations,
and raise my signal to the peoples;
and they shall bring your sons in
their bosom,
and your daughters shall be carried
on their shoulders.
²³Kings shall be your foster fathers
and their queens your nursing
mothers.
With their faces to the ground they
shall bow down to you,
and lick the dust of your feet.

ˡCn: Heb *Sinim*
49.8: 2 Cor 6.2. **49.10:** Rev 7.16.
49.13: Is 44.23; Jer 51.48; Rev 12.12; 18.20.

Then you will know that I am the
LORD;
those who wait for me shall not be
put to shame."

24 Can the prey be taken from the
mighty,
or the captives of a tyrant *m* be
rescued?
25 Surely, thus says the LORD:
"Even the captives of the mighty
shall be taken,
and the prey of the tyrant be
rescued,
for I will contend with those who contend with you,
and I will save your children.
26 I will make your oppressors eat their
own flesh,
and they shall be drunk with their
own blood as with wine.
Then all flesh shall know
that I am the LORD your Savior,
and your Redeemer, the Mighty
One of Jacob."

50 Thus says the LORD:
"Where is your mother's bill of
divorce,
with which I put her away?
Or which of my creditors is it
to whom I have sold you?
Behold, for your iniquities you were
sold,
and for your transgressions your
mother was put away.
Why, when I came, was there no
man?
When I called, was there no one
to answer?
Is my hand shortened, that it cannot
redeem?
Or have I no power to deliver?
Behold, by my rebuke I dry up the
sea,
I make the rivers a desert;
their fish stink for lack of water,
and die of thirst.
I clothe the heavens with blackness,
and make sackcloth their covering."

The Lord GOD has given me
the tongue of those who are taught,
that I may know how to sustain with
a word
him that is weary.
Morning by morning he wakens,
he wakens my ear
to hear as those who are taught.

5 The Lord GOD has opened my ear,
and I was not rebellious,
I turned not backward.
6 I gave my back to the smiters,
and my cheeks to those who
pulled out the beard;
I hid not my face
from shame and spitting.

7 For the Lord GOD helps me;
therefore I have not been confounded;
therefore I have set my face like a
flint,
and I know that I shall not be put
to shame;
8 he who vindicates me is near.
Who will contend with me?
Let us stand up together.
Who is my adversary?
Let him come near to me.
9 Behold, the Lord GOD helps me;
who will declare me guilty?
Behold, all of them will wear out like
a garment;
the moth will eat them up.

10 Who among you fears the LORD
and obeys the voice of his servant,
who walks in darkness
and has no light,
yet trusts in the name of the LORD
and relies upon his God?
11 Behold, all you who kindle a fire,
who set brands alight.*n*
Walk by the light of your fire,
and by the brands which you have
kindled!
This shall you have from my hand:
you shall lie down in torment.

51 "Hearken to me, you who pursue
deliverance,
you who seek the LORD;
look to the rock from which you were
hewn,
and to the quarry from which you
were digged.
2 Look to Abraham your father
and to Sarah who bore you;
for when he was but one I called
him,
and I blessed him and made him
many.
3 For the LORD will comfort Zion:
he will comfort all her waste
places,

---

m One ancient Ms Syr Vg: Heb *righteous man*
n Syr: Heb *gird yourselves with brands*
50.8-9: Rom 8.33; Heb 1.11.

and will make her wilderness like
Eden,
her desert like the garden of the
Lord;
joy and gladness will be found in her,
thanksgiving and the voice of song.

4 "Listen to me, my people,
and give ear to me, my nation;
for a law will go forth from me,
and my justice for a light to the
peoples.
5 My deliverance draws near speedily,
my salvation has gone forth,
and my arms will rule the peoples;
the coastlands wait for me,
and for my arm they hope.
6 Lift up your eyes to the heavens,
and look at the earth beneath;
for the heavens will vanish like
smoke,
the earth will wear out like a
garment,
and they who dwell in it will die
like gnats; º
but my salvation will be for ever,
and my deliverance will never be
ended.

7 "Hearken to me, you who know righteousness,
the people in whose heart is my
law;
fear not the reproach of men,
and be not dismayed at their
revilings.
8 For the moth will eat them up like
a garment,
and the worm will eat them like
wool;
but my deliverance will be for ever,
and my salvation to all generations."

9 Awake, awake, put on strength,
O arm of the Lord;
awake, as in days of old,
the generations of long ago.
Was it not thou that didst cut Rā′hăb
in pieces,
that didst pierce the dragon?
10 Was it not thou that didst dry up the
sea,
the waters of the great deep;
that didst make the depths of the sea
a way
for the redeemed to pass over?
11 And the ransomed of the Lord shall
return,
and come to Zion with singing;

everlasting joy shall be upon their
heads;
they shall obtain joy and gladness,
and sorrow and sighing shall flee
away.

12 "I, I am he that comforts you;
who are you that you are afraid of
man who dies,
of the son of man who is made like
grass,
13 and have forgotten the Lord, your
Maker,
who stretched out the heavens
and laid the foundations of the
earth,
and fear continually all the day
because of the fury of the oppressor,
when he sets himself to destroy?
And where is the fury of the oppressor?
14 He who is bowed down shall speedily
be released;
he shall not die and go down to the
Pit,
neither shall his bread fail.
15 For I am the Lord your God,
who stirs up the sea so that its
waves roar—
the Lord of hosts is his name.
16 And I have put my words in your
mouth,
and hid you in the shadow of my
hand,
stretching out ᵖ the heavens
and laying the foundations of the
earth,
and saying to Zion, 'You are my
people.' "

17 Rouse yourself, rouse yourself,
stand up, O Jerusalem,
you who have drunk at the hand of
the Lord
the cup of his wrath,
who have drunk to the dregs
the bowl of staggering.
18 There is none to guide her
among all the sons she has borne;
there is none to take her by the
hand
among all the sons she has brought
up.
19 These two things have befallen you—
who will condole with you?—
devastation and destruction, famine
and sword;

º Or *in like manner*   ᵖ Syr: Heb *plant*
51.6: Heb 1.11.

who will comfort you?*q*

²⁰Your sons have fainted,
   they lie at the head of every street
   like an antelope in a net;
they are full of the wrath of the
   LORD,
   the rebuke of your God.

²¹Therefore hear this, you who are afflicted,
   who are drunk, but not with wine:
²²Thus says your Lord, the LORD,
   your God who pleads the cause of
   his people:
"Behold, I have taken from your
   hand
   the cup of staggering;
the bowl of my wrath
   you shall drink no more;
²³and I will put it into the hand of your
   tormentors,
   who have said to you,
'Bow down, that we may pass
   over';
and you have made your back like
   the ground
   and like the street for them to pass
   over."

52 Awake, awake,
   put on your strength, O Zion;
put on your beautiful garments,
   O Jerusalem, the holy city;
for there shall no more come into you
   the uncircumcised and the unclean.
²Shake yourself from the dust, arise,
   O captive*r* Jerusalem;
loose the bonds from your neck,
   O captive daughter of Zion.

3 For thus says the LORD: "You
were sold for nothing, and you shall
be redeemed without money. ⁴For
thus says the Lord GOD: My people
went down at the first into Egypt to
sojourn there, and the Assyrian oppressed them for nothing. ⁵Now
therefore what have I here, says the
LORD, seeing that my people are taken
away for nothing? Their rulers wail,
says the LORD, and continually all the
day my name is despised. ⁶Therefore
my people shall know my name; therefore in that day they shall know that it
is I who speak; here am I."

⁷How beautiful upon the mountains
   are the feet of him who brings good
   tidings,

who publishes peace, who brings
   good tidings of good,
who publishes salvation,
   who says to Zion, "Your God
   reigns."
⁸Hark, your watchmen lift up their
   voice,
   together they sing for joy;
for eye to eye they see
   the return of the LORD to Zion.
⁹Break forth together into singing,
   you waste places of Jerusalem;
for the LORD has comforted his
   people,
   he has redeemed Jerusalem.
¹⁰The LORD has bared his holy arm
   before the eyes of all the nations;
and all the ends of the earth shall see
   the salvation of our God.

¹¹Depart, depart, go out thence,
   touch no unclean thing;
go out from the midst of her, purify
   yourselves,
you who bear the vessels of the
   LORD.
¹²For you shall not go out in haste,
   and you shall not go in flight,
for the LORD will go before you,
   and the God of Israel will be your
   rear guard.

¹³Behold, my servant shall prosper,
   he shall be exalted and lifted up,
   and shall be very high.
¹⁴As many were astonished at him*ˢ*—
   his appearance was so marred,
   beyond human semblance,
and his form beyond that of the
   sons of men—
¹⁵so shall he startle*t* many nations;
   kings shall shut their mouths because of him;
for that which has not been told
   them they shall see,
and that which they have not
   heard they shall understand.

53 Who has believed what we have
   heard?
And to whom has the arm of the
   LORD been revealed?
²For he grew up before him like a
   young plant,

*q*One ancient Ms Gk Syr Vg: Heb *how may I comfort you*
*r*Cn: Heb *sit* *ˢ*Syr Tg: Heb *you*
*t*The meaning of the Hebrew word is uncertain
52.1: Rev 21.27.
52.5: Rom 2.24.   **52.7:** Acts 10.36; Rom 10.15; Eph 6.15.
52.10: Lk 2.30; 3.6.   **52.11:** 2 Cor 6.17.
52.15: Rom 15.21.   **53.1:** Jn 12.38; Rom 10.16.

and like a root out of dry ground;
he had no form or comeliness that we
should look at him,
and no beauty that we should
desire him.
3 He was despised and rejected[u] by
men;
a man of sorrows,[v] and acquainted
with grief;[w]
and as one from whom men hide
their faces
he was despised, and we esteemed
him not.

4 Surely he has borne our griefs[x]
and carried our sorrows;[y]
yet we esteemed him stricken,
smitten by God, and afflicted.
5 But he was wounded for our transgressions,
he was bruised for our iniquities;
upon him was the chastisement that
made us whole,
and with his stripes we are healed.
6 All we like sheep have gone astray;
we have turned every one to his
own way;
and the LORD has laid on him
the iniquity of us all.

7 He was oppressed, and he was
afflicted,
yet he opened not his mouth;
like a lamb that is led to the slaughter,
and like a sheep that before its
shearers is dumb,
so he opened not his mouth.
8 By oppression and judgment he was
taken away;
and as for his generation, who
considered
that he was cut off out of the land of
the living,
stricken for the transgression of
my people?
9 And they made his grave with the
wicked
and with a rich man in his death,
although he had done no violence,
and there was no deceit in his
mouth.

10 Yet it was the will of the LORD to
bruise him;
he has put him to grief;[z]
when he makes himself[a] an offering
for sin,
he shall see his offspring, he shall
prolong his days;

the will of the LORD shall prosper
in his hand;
11 he shall see the fruit of the travail
of his soul and be satisfied;
by his knowledge shall the righteous one, my servant,
make many to be accounted righteous;
and he shall bear their iniquities.
12 Therefore I will divide him a portion
with the great,
and he shall divide the spoil with
the strong;
because he poured out his soul to
death,
and was numbered with the transgressors;
yet he bore the sin of many,
and made intercession for the
transgressors.

54 "Sing, O barren one, who did not
bear;
break forth into singing and cry
aloud,
you who have not been in travail!
For the children of the desolate one
will be more
than the children of her that is
married, says the LORD.
2 Enlarge the place of your tent,
and let the curtains of your habitations be stretched out;
hold not back, lengthen your cords
and strengthen your stakes.
3 For you will spread abroad to the
right and to the left,
and your descendants will possess
the nations
and will people the desolate cities.

4 "Fear not, for you will not be
ashamed;
be not confounded, for you will not
be put to shame;
for you will forget the shame of your
youth,
and the reproach of your widowhood you will remember no more.
5 For your Maker is your husband,
the LORD of hosts is his name;
and the Holy One of Israel is your
Redeemer,
the God of the whole earth he is
called.

[u]Or *forsaken*   [v]Or *pains*   [w]Or *sickness*   [x]Or *sickness*
[y]Or *pains*   [z]Heb *made him sick*
[a]Vg: Heb *thou makest his soul*
53.4: Mt 8.17.   53.5-6: 1 Pet 2.24-25.
53.7-8: Acts 8.32-33.   53.9: 1 Pet 2.22.   53.12: Lk 22.37.
54.1: Gal 4.27.

⁶For the LORD has called you
  like a wife forsaken and grieved in
    spirit,
  like a wife of youth when she is cast
    off,
  says your God.
⁷For a brief moment I forsook you,
  but with great compassion I will
    gather you.
⁸In overflowing wrath for a moment
    I hid my face from you,
  but with everlasting love I will have
    compassion on you,
  says the LORD, your Redeemer.

⁹"For this is like the days of Noah
    to me:
  as I swore that the waters of Noah
    should no more go over the earth,
  so I have sworn that I will not be
    angry with you
    and will not rebuke you.
¹⁰For the mountains may depart
    and the hills be removed,
  but my steadfast love shall not depart
    from you,
    and my covenant of peace shall
    not be removed,
  says the LORD, who has compassion
    on you.

¹¹"O afflicted one, storm-tossed, and
    not comforted,
  behold, I will set your stones in
    antimony,
    and lay your foundations with
    sapphires.ᵇ
¹²I will make your pinnacles of agate,
    your gates of carbuncles,
    and all your wall of precious stones.
¹³All your sons shall be taught by the
    LORD,
    and great shall be the prosperity
    of your sons.
⁴In righteousness you shall be estab-
    lished;
  you shall be far from oppression,
    for you shall not fear;
    and from terror, for it shall not
    come near you.
⁵If any one stirs up strife,
    it is not from me;
  whoever stirs up strife with you
    shall fall because of you.
⁶Behold, I have created the smith
    who blows the fire of coals,
    and produces a weapon for its
    purpose.
I have also created the ravager to
    destroy;

¹⁷ no weapon that is fashioned
    against you shall prosper,
  and you shall confute every
    tongue that rises against you in
    judgment.
This is the heritage of the servants of
    the LORD
  and their vindication from me,
  says the LORD."

55 "Ho, every one who thirsts,
    come to the waters;
  and he who has no money,
    come, buy and eat!
  Come, buy wine and milk
    without money and without price.
²Why do you spend your money for
    that which is not bread,
    and your labor for that which does
    not satisfy?
  Hearken diligently to me, and eat
    what is good,
    and delight yourselves in fat-
    ness.
³Incline your ear, and come to me;
    hear, that your soul may live;
  and I will make with you an ever-
    lasting covenant,
    my steadfast, sure love for David.
⁴Behold, I made him a witness to the
    peoples,
    a leader and commander for the
    peoples.
⁵Behold, you shall call nations that
    you know not,
  and nations that knew you not shall
    run to you,
  because of the LORD your God,
    and of the Holy One of Israel,
    for he has glorified you.

⁶"Seek the LORD while he may be
    found,
    call upon him while he is near;
⁷let the wicked forsake his way,
    and the unrighteous man his
    thoughts;
  let him return to the LORD, that he
    may have mercy on him.
    and to our God, for he will abun-
    dantly pardon.
⁸For my thoughts are not your
    thoughts,
    neither are your ways my ways,
    says the LORD.
⁹For as the heavens are higher than
    the earth,

ᵇOr *lapis lazuli*
54.11-12: Rev 21.19. **54.13:** Jn 6.45.
55.1: Rev 21.6; 22.17. **55.3:** Acts 13.34; Heb 13.20.

so are my ways higher than your
ways
and my thoughts than your
thoughts.

10 "For as the rain and the snow come
down from heaven,
and return not thither but water
the earth,
making it bring forth and sprout,
giving seed to the sower and bread
to the eater,
11 so shall my word be that goes forth
from my mouth;
it shall not return to me empty,
but it shall accomplish that which
I purpose,
and prosper in the thing for which
I sent it.

12 "For you shall go out in joy,
and be led forth in peace;
the mountains and the hills before
you
shall break forth into singing,
and all the trees of the field shall
clap their hands.
13 Instead of the thorn shall come up
the cypress;
instead of the brier shall come up
the myrtle;
and it shall be to the LORD for a
memorial,
for an everlasting sign which shall
not be cut off."

56 Thus says the LORD:
"Keep justice, and do righteousness,
for soon my salvation will come,
and my deliverance be revealed.
2 Blessed is the man who does this,
and the son of man who holds it
fast,
who keeps the sabbath, not profaning it,
and keeps his hand from doing any
evil."

3 Let not the foreigner who has joined
himself to the LORD say,
"The LORD will surely separate me
from his people";
and let not the eunuch say,
"Behold, I am a dry tree."
4 For thus says the LORD:
"To the eunuchs who keep my sabbaths,
who choose the things that please me
and hold fast my covenant,

5 I will give in my house and within
my walls
a monument and a name
better than sons and daughters;
I will give them an everlasting name
which shall not be cut off.

6 "And the foreigners who join themselves to the LORD,
to minister to him, to love the
name of the LORD,
and to be his servants,
every one who keeps the sabbath,
and does not profane it,
and holds fast my covenant—
7 these I will bring to my holy mountain,
and make them joyful in my house
of prayer;
their burnt offerings and their
sacrifices
will be accepted on my altar;
for my house shall be called a house
of prayer
for all peoples.
8 Thus says the Lord GOD,
who gathers the outcasts of Israel,
I will gather yet others to him
besides those already gathered."[c]

9 All you beasts of the field, come to
devour—
all you beasts in the forest.
10 His watchmen are blind,
they are all without knowledge;
they are all dumb dogs,
they cannot bark;
dreaming, lying down,
loving to slumber.
11 The dogs have a mighty appetite;
they never have enough.
The shepherds also have no understanding;
they have all turned to their own
way,
each to his own gain, one and all.
12 "Come," they say, "let us[d] get wine,
let us fill ourselves with strong
drink;
and tomorrow will be like this day,
great beyond measure."

57 The righteous man perishes,
and no one lays it to heart;
devout men are taken away,
while no one understands.

cHeb *his gathered ones*
dOne ancient Ms Syr Vg Tg: Heb *me*
55.10: 2 Cor 9.10. **56.7:** Mt 21.13; Mk 11.17; Lk 19.46.

For the righteous man is taken away
from calamity,
2 he enters into peace;
they rest in their beds
who walk in their uprightness.
3 But you, draw near hither,
sons of the sorceress,
offspring of the adulterer and the
harlot.
4 Of whom are you making sport?
Against whom do you open your
mouth wide
and put out your tongue?
Are you not children of transgression,
the offspring of deceit,
5 you who burn with lust among the
oaks,
under every green tree;
who slay your children in the valleys,
under the clefts of the rocks?
6 Among the smooth stones of the
valley is your portion;
they, they, are your lot;
to them you have poured out a drink
offering,
you have brought a cereal offering.
Shall I be appeased for these
things?
7 Upon a high and lofty mountain
you have set your bed,
and thither you went up to offer
sacrifice.
8 Behind the door and the doorpost
you have set up your symbol;
for, deserting me, you have uncovered your bed,
you have gone up to it,
you have made it wide;
and you have made a bargain for
yourself with them,
you have loved their bed,
you have looked on nakedness.*e*
9 You journeyed to Mō′lĕch*f* with oil
and multiplied your perfumes;
you sent your envoys far off,
and sent down even to Shē′ōl.
10 You were wearied with the length
of your way,
but you did not say, "It is hopeless";
you found new life for your strength,
and so you were not faint.

11 Whom did you dread and fear,
so that you lied,
and did not remember me,
did not give me a thought?
Have I not held my peace, even for a
long time,
and so you do not fear me?

12 I will tell of your righteousness
and your doings,
but they will not help you.
13 When you cry out, let your collection
of idols deliver you!
The wind will carry them off,
a breath will take them away.
But he who takes refuge in me shall
possess the land,
and shall inherit my holy mountain.

14 And it shall be said,
"Build up, build up, prepare the way,
remove every obstruction from my
people's way."
15 For thus says the high and lofty One
who inhabits eternity, whose
name is Holy:
"I dwell in the high and holy place,
and also with him who is of a
contrite and humble spirit,
to revive the spirit of the humble,
and to revive the heart of the
contrite.
16 For I will not contend for ever,
nor will I always be angry;
for from me proceeds the spirit,
and I have made the breath of life.
17 Because of the iniquity of his covetousness I was angry,
I smote him, I hid my face and was
angry;
but he went on backsliding in the
way of his own heart.
18 I have seen his ways, but I will heal
him;
I will lead him and requite him
with comfort,
creating for his mourners the fruit
of the lips.
19 Peace, peace, to the far and to the
near, says the LORD;
and I will heal him.
20 But the wicked are like the tossing
sea;
for it cannot rest,
and its waters toss up mire and dirt.
21 There is no peace, says my God,
for the wicked."

58 "Cry aloud, spare not,
lift up your voice like a trumpet;
declare to my people their transgression,
to the house of Jacob their sins.
2 Yet they seek me daily,
and delight to know my ways,

e The meaning of the Hebrew is uncertain f Or the king
57.15: Mt 5.3.
57.19: Acts 2.39; Eph 2.13, 17.

as if they were a nation that did
righteousness
and did not forsake the ordinance
of their God;
they ask of me righteous judgments,
they delight to draw near to God.
3 'Why have we fasted, and thou
seest it not?
Why have we humbled ourselves,
and thou takest no knowledge
of it?'
Behold, in the day of your fast you
seek your own pleasure,⁹
and oppress all your workers.
4 Behold, you fast only to quarrel and
to fight
and to hit with wicked fist.
Fasting like yours this day
will not make your voice to be
heard on high.
5 Is such the fast that I choose,
a day for a man to humble himself?
Is it to bow down his head like a
rush,
and to spread sackcloth and ashes
under him?
Will you call this a fast,
and a day acceptable to the Lord?

6 "Is not this the fast that I choose:
to loose the bonds of wickedness,
to undo the thongs of the yoke,
to let the oppressed go free,
and to break every yoke?
7 Is it not to share your bread with the
hungry,
and bring the homeless poor into
your house;
when you see the naked, to cover him,
and not to hide yourself from your
own flesh?
8 Then shall your light break forth
like the dawn,
and your healing shall spring up
speedily;
your righteousness shall go before
you,
the glory of the Lord shall be your
rear guard.
9 Then you shall call, and the Lord
will answer;
you shall cry, and he will say,
Here I am.

"If you take away from the midst
of you the yoke,
the pointing of the finger, and
speaking wickedness,
10 if you pour yourself out for the
hungry

and satisfy the desire of the afflicted,
then shall your light rise in the
darkness
and your gloom be as the noonday.
11 And the Lord will guide you continually,
and satisfy your desire with good
things,ʰ
and make your bones strong;
and you shall be like a watered
garden,
like a spring of water,
whose waters fail not.
12 And your ancient ruins shall be
rebuilt;
you shall raise up the foundations
of many generations;
you shall be called the repairer of the
breach,
the restorer of streets to dwell in.

13 "If you turn back your foot from the
sabbath,
from doing your pleasureⁱ on my
holy day,
and call the sabbath a delight
and the holy day of the Lord
honorable;
if you honor it, not going your own
ways,
or seeking your own pleasure,ʲ
or talking idly;
14 then you shall take delight in the
Lord,
and I will make you ride upon the
heights of the earth;
I will feed you with the heritage of
Jacob your father,
for the mouth of the Lord has
spoken."

59 Behold, the Lord's hand is not
shortened, that it cannot save,
or his ear dull, that it cannot hear;
2 but your iniquities have made a
separation
between you and your God,
and your sins have hid his face from
you
so that he does not hear.
3 For your hands are defiled with blood
and your fingers with iniquity;
your lips have spoken lies,
your tongue mutters wickedness.
4 No one enters suit justly,

⁹ Or *pursue your own business*
ʰ The meaning of the Hebrew word is uncertain
ⁱ Or *business* ʲ Or *pursuing your own business*
58.6: Acts 8.23.

no one goes to law honestly;
they rely on empty pleas, they speak
lies,
they conceive mischief and bring
forth iniquity.
⁵They hatch adders' eggs,
they weave the spider's web;
he who eats their eggs dies,
and from one which is crushed
a viper is hatched.
⁶Their webs will not serve as clothing;
men will not cover themselves
with what they make.
Their works are works of iniquity,
and deeds of violence are in their
hands.
⁷Their feet run to evil,
and they make haste to shed innocent blood;
their thoughts are thoughts of iniquity,
desolation and destruction are in
their highways.
⁸The way of peace they know not,
and there is no justice in their
paths;
they have made their roads crooked,
no one who goes in them knows
peace.

⁹Therefore justice is far from us,
and righteousness does not overtake us;
we look for light, and behold, darkness,
and for brightness, but we walk
in gloom.
¹⁰We grope for the wall like the blind,
we grope like those who have no
eyes;
we stumble at noon as in the twilight,
among those in full vigor we are
like dead men.
¹¹We all growl like bears,
we moan and moan like doves;
we look for justice, but there is none;
for salvation, but it is far from us.
¹²For our transgressions are multiplied before thee,
and our sins testify against us;
for our transgressions are with us,
and we know our iniquities:
¹³transgressing, and denying the LORD,
and turning away from following
our God,
speaking oppression and revolt,
conceiving and uttering from the
heart lying words.
¹⁴Justice is turned back,
and righteousness stands afar off;

for truth has fallen in the public
squares,
and uprightness cannot enter.
¹⁵Truth is lacking,
and he who departs from evil
makes himself a prey.

The LORD saw it, and it displeased
him
that there was no justice.
¹⁶He saw that there was no man,
and wondered that there was no
one to intervene;
then his own arm brought him
victory,
and his righteousness upheld him.
¹⁷He put on righteousness as a breastplate,
and a helmet of salvation upon
his head;
he put on garments of vengeance for
clothing,
and wrapped himself in fury as a
mantle.
¹⁸According to their deeds, so will
he repay,
wrath to his adversaries, requital
to his enemies;
to the coastlands he will render
requital.
¹⁹So they shall fear the name of the
LORD from the west,
and his glory from the rising of the
sun;
for he will come like a rushing
stream,
which the wind of the LORD
drives.

²⁰"And he will come to Zion as Redeemer,
to those in Jacob who turn from
transgression, says the LORD.
²¹"And as for me, this is my covenant with them, says the LORD: my
spirit which is upon you, and my words
which I have put in your mouth, shall
not depart out of your mouth, or out of
the mouth of your children, or out of
the mouth of your children's children,
says the LORD, from this time forth and
for evermore."

60 Arise, shine; for your light has
come,
and the glory of the LORD has risen
upon you.

59.7-8: Rom 3.15-17.
59.17: Eph 6.14, 17; 1 Thess 5.8.
59.19: Mt 8.11; Lk 13.29.   59.20-21: Rom 11.26-27.

²For behold, darkness shall cover the
earth,
and thick darkness the peoples;
but the LORD will arise upon you,
and his glory will be seen upon
you.
³And nations shall come to your light,
and kings to the brightness of your
rising.

⁴Lift up your eyes round about, and
see;
they all gather together, they come
to you;
your sons shall come from far,
and your daughters shall be carried in the arms.
⁵Then you shall see and be radiant,
your heart shall thrill and rejoice;ᵏ
because the abundance of the sea
shall be turned to you,
the wealth of the nations shall
come to you.
⁶A multitude of camels shall cover
you,
the young camels of Mĭd′ĭ·an and
Ē′phah;
all those from Shē′ba shall come.
They shall bring gold and frankincense,
and shall proclaim the praise of
the LORD.
⁷All the flocks of Kē′dār shall be
gathered to you,
the rams of Ně·bāi′ŏth shall
minister to you;
they shall come up with acceptance
on my altar,
and I will glorify my glorious
house.

⁸Who are these that fly like a cloud,
and like doves to their windows?
⁹For the coastlands shall wait for me,
the ships of Tār′shĭsh first,
to bring your sons from far,
their silver and gold with them,
for the name of the LORD your God,
and for the Holy One of Israel,
because he has glorified you.

¹⁰Foreigners shall build up your walls,
and their kings shall minister to
you;
for in my wrath I smote you,
but in my favor I have had mercy
on you.
¹¹Your gates shall be open continually;
day and night they shall not be
shut;

that men may bring to you the wealth
of the nations,
with their kings led in procession.
¹²For the nation and kingdom
that will not serve you shall perish;
those nations shall be utterly laid
waste.
¹³The glory of Lebanon shall come to
you,
the cypress, the plane, and the
pine,
to beautify the place of my sanctuary;
and I will make the place of my
feet glorious.
¹⁴The sons of those who oppressed you
shall come bending low to you;
and all who despised you
shall bow down at your feet;
they shall call you the City of the
LORD,
the Zion of the Holy One of Israel.

¹⁵Whereas you have been forsaken and
hated,
with no one passing through,
I will make you majestic for ever,
a joy from age to age.
¹⁶You shall suck the milk of nations,
you shall suck the breast of kings;
and you shall know that I, the LORD,
am your Savior
and your Redeemer, the Mighty
One of Jacob.

¹⁷Instead of bronze I will bring gold,
and instead of iron I will bring
silver;
instead of wood, bronze,
instead of stones, iron.
I will make your overseers peace
and your taskmasters righteousness.
¹⁸Violence shall no more be heard in
your land,
devastation or destruction within
your borders;
you shall call your walls Salvation,
and your gates Praise.

¹⁹The sun shall be no more
your light by day,
nor for brightness shall the moon
give light to you by night;ˡ
but the LORD will be your everlasting
light,

ᵏHeb *be enlarged*
ˡOne ancient Ms Gk Old Latin Tg: Heb lacks *by night*
60.6: Mt 2.11. **60.11:** Rev 21.25-26. **60.14:** Rev 3.9.
60.19: Rev 21.23; 22.5.

and your God will be your glory.
²⁰Your sun shall no more go down,
nor your moon withdraw itself;
for the LORD will be your everlasting
light,
and your days of mourning shall be
ended.
²¹Your people shall all be righteous;
they shall possess the land for
ever,
the shoot of my planting, the work
of my hands,
that I might be glorified.
²²The least one shall become a clan,
and the smallest one a mighty
nation;
I am the LORD;
in its time I will hasten it.

61 The Spirit of the Lord GOD is
upon me,
because the LORD has anointed
me
to bring good tidings to the afflicted;ᵐ
he has sent me to bind up the
brokenhearted,
to proclaim liberty to the captives,
and the opening of the prisonⁿ
to those who are bound;
²to proclaim the year of the LORD's
favor,
and the day of vengeance of our
God;
to comfort all who mourn;
³to grant to those who mourn in Zion—
to give them a garland instead of
ashes,
the oil of gladness instead of mourning,
the mantle of praise instead of a
faint spirit;
that they may be called oaks of righteousness,
the planting of the LORD, that he
may be glorified.
⁴They shall build up the ancient ruins,
they shall raise up the former
devastations;
they shall repair the ruined cities,
the devastations of many generations.

⁵Aliens shall stand and feed your
flocks,
foreigners shall be your plowmen
and vinedressers;
⁶but you shall be called the priests of
the LORD,
men shall speak of you as the ministers of our God;

you shall eat the wealth of the nations,
and in their riches you shall glory.
⁷Instead of your shame you shall
have a double portion,
instead of dishonor youᵒ shall
rejoice in yourᵖ lot;
therefore in yourᵖ land youᵒ shall
possess a double portion;
yoursᑫ shall be everlasting joy.

⁸For I the LORD love justice,
I hate robbery and wrong;ʳ
I will faithfully give them their
recompense,
and I will make an everlasting
covenant with them.
⁹Their descendants shall be known
among the nations,
and their offspring in the midst
of the peoples;
all who see them shall acknowledge
them,
that they are a people whom
the LORD has blessed.

¹⁰I will greatly rejoice in the LORD,
my soul shall exult in my God;
for he has clothed me with the
garments of salvation,
he has covered me with the robe
of righteousness,
as a bridegroom decks himself with a
garland,
and as a bride adorns herself with
her jewels.
¹¹For as the earth brings forth its
shoots,
and as a garden causes what is
sown in it to spring up,
so the Lord GOD will cause righteousness and praise
to spring forth before all the nations.

62 For Zion's sake I will not keep
silent,
and for Jerusalem's sake I will not
rest,
until her vindication goes forth as
brightness,
and her salvation as a burning
torch.
²The nations shall see your vindication,

ᵐOr *poor* ⁿOr *the opening of the eyes:* Heb *the opening*
ᵒHeb *they* ᵖHeb *their* ᑫHeb *theirs*
ʳOr *robbery with a burnt offering*
61.1-2: Mt 11.5; Lk 4.18-19; 7.22.
61.6: Ex 19.6; 1 Pet 2.5; Rev 1.6; 5.10; 20.6.
62.2: Rev 2.17.

and all the kings your glory;
and you shall be called by a new
name
which the mouth of the LORD will
give.
³You shall be a crown of beauty in
the hand of the LORD,
and a royal diadem in the hand of
your God.
⁴You shall no more be termed Forsaken,ˢ
and your land shall no more be
termed Desolate;ᵗ
but you shall be called My delight is
in her,ᵘ
and your land Married;ᵛ
for the LORD delights in you,
and your land shall be married.
⁵For as a young man marries a virgin,
so shall your sons marry you,
and as the bridegroom rejoices over
the bride,
so shall your God rejoice over you.

⁶Upon your walls, O Jerusalem,
I have set watchmen;
all the day and all the night
they shall never be silent.
You who put the LORD in remembrance,
take no rest,
⁷and give him no rest
until he establishes Jerusalem
and makes it a praise in the earth.
⁸The LORD has sworn by his right
hand
and by his mighty arm:
"I will not again give your grain
to be food for your enemies,
and foreigners shall not drink your
wine
for which you have labored;
⁹but those who garner it shall eat it
and praise the LORD,
and those who gather it shall drink
it
in the courts of my sanctuary."

¹⁰Go through, go through the gates,
prepare the way for the people;
build up, build up the highway,
clear it of stones,
lift up an ensign over the peoples.
¹¹Behold, the LORD has proclaimed
to the end of the earth:
Say to the daughter of Zion,
"Behold, your salvation comes;
behold, his reward is with him,
and his recompense before him."

¹²And they shall be called The holy
people,
The redeemed of the LORD;
and you shall be called Sought out,
a city not forsaken.

63 Who is this that comes from
Ē'dom,
in crimsoned garments from
Bŏz'rah,
he that is glorious in his apparel,
marching in the greatness of his
strength?

"It is I, announcing vindication,
mighty to save."

²Why is thy apparel red,
and thy garments like his that
treads in the wine press?

³"I have trodden the wine press alone,
and from the peoples no one was
with me;
I trod them in my anger
and trampled them in my wrath;
their lifeblood is sprinkled upon my
garments,
and I have stained all my raiment.
⁴For the day of vengeance was in my
heart,
and my year of redemptionʷ has
come.
⁵I looked, but there was no one to
help;
I was appalled, but there was no
one to uphold;
so my own arm brought me victory,
and my wrath upheld me.
⁶I trod down the peoples in my anger,
I made them drunk in my wrath,
and I poured out their lifeblood
on the earth."

⁷I will recount the steadfast love of
the LORD,
the praises of the LORD,
according to all that the LORD has
granted us,
and the great goodness to the
house of Israel
which he has granted them according to his mercy,
according to the abundance of his
steadfast love.

ˢHeb *Azubah*   ᵗHeb *Shemamah*   ᵘHeb *Hephzibah*
ᵛHeb *Beulah*
ʷOr *the year of my redeemed*
63.1-6: Is 34; Jer 49.7-22; Ezek 25.12-14; 35; Amos 1.11-
12; Obad; Mal 1.2-5.
63.3: Rev 19.15.

⁸For he said, Surely they are my
people,
sons who will not deal falsely;
and he became their Savior.
⁹In all their affliction he was afflicted,ˣ
and the angel of his presence
saved them;
in his love and in his pity he redeemed them;
he lifted them up and carried them
all the days of old.

¹⁰But they rebelled
and grieved his holy Spirit;
therefore he turned to be their
enemy,
and himself fought against them.
¹¹Then he remembered the days of old,
of Moses his servant.
Where is he who brought up out of
the sea
the shepherds of his flock?
Where is he who put in the midst
of them
his holy Spirit,
¹²who caused his glorious arm
to go at the right hand of Moses,
who divided the waters before them
to make for himself an everlasting
name,
¹³   who led them through the depths?
Like a horse in the desert,
they did not stumble.
¹⁴Like cattle that go down into the
valley,
the Spirit of the LORD gave them
rest.
So thou didst lead thy people,
to make for thyself a glorious
name.

¹⁵Look down from heaven and see,
from thy holy and glorious habitation.
Where are thy zeal and thy might?
The yearning of thy heart and thy
compassion
are withheld from me.
¹⁶For thou art our Father,
though Abraham does not know us
and Israel does not acknowledge
us;
thou, O LORD, art our Father,
our Redeemer from of old is thy
name.
¹⁷O LORD, why dost thou make us err
from thy ways
and harden our heart, so that we
fear thee not?
Return for the sake of thy servants,

the tribes of thy heritage.
¹⁸Thy holy people possessed thy sanctuary a little while;
our adversaries have trodden it
down.
¹⁹We have become like those over
whom thou hast never ruled,
like those who are not called by
thy name.

64 O that thou wouldst rend the
heavens and come down,
that the mountains might quake
at thy presence—
²ʸas when fire kindles brushwood
and the fire causes water to boil—
to make thy name known to thy
adversaries,
and that the nations might tremble
at thy presence!
³When thou didst terrible things
which we looked not for,
thou camest down, the mountains
quaked at thy presence.
⁴From of old no one has heard
or perceived by the ear,
no eye has seen a God besides thee,
who works for those who wait for
him.
⁵Thou meetest him that joyfully works
righteousness,
those that remember thee in thy
ways.
Behold, thou wast angry, and we
sinned;
in our sins we have been a long
time, and shall we be saved?ᶻ
⁶We have all become like one who is
unclean,
and all our righteous deeds are
like a polluted garment.
We all fade like a leaf,
and our iniquities, like the wind,
take us away.
⁷There is no one that calls upon thy
name,
that bestirs himself to take hold of
thee;
for thou hast hid thy face from us,
and hast deliveredᵃ us into the
hand of our iniquities.

⁸Yet, O LORD, thou art our Father;
we are the clay, and thou art our
potter;
we are all the work of thy hand.

ˣ Another reading is *he did not afflict*
ʸCh 64.1 in Heb   ᶻHebrew obscure
ᵃGk Syr Old Latin Tg: Heb *melted*
63.11: Heb 13.20.   **64.4:** 1 Cor 2.9.

⁹Be not exceedingly angry, O Lᴏʀᴅ,
  and remember not iniquity for
    ever.
Behold, consider, we are all thy
  people.
¹⁰Thy holy cities have become a wilderness,
Zion has become a wilderness,
Jerusalem a desolation.
¹¹Our holy and beautiful house,
  where our fathers praised thee,
has been burned by fire,
  and all our pleasant places have
  become ruins.
¹²Wilt thou restrain thyself at these
  things, O Lᴏʀᴅ?
Wilt thou keep silent, and afflict
  us sorely?

65 I was ready to be sought by those
  who did not ask for me;
I was ready to be found by those
  who did not seek me.
I said, "Here am I, here am I,"
  to a nation that did not call on my
  name.
²I spread out my hands all the day
  to a rebellious people,
who walk in a way that is not good,
  following their own devices;
³a people who provoke me
  to my face continually,
sacrificing in gardens
  and burning incense upon bricks;
⁴who sit in tombs,
  and spend the night in secret
  places;
who eat swine's flesh,
  and broth of abominable things is
  in their vessels;
⁵who say, "Keep to yourself,
  do not come near me, for I am set
  apart from you."
These are a smoke in my nostrils,
  a fire that burns all the day.
⁶Behold, it is written before me:
  "I will not keep silent, but I will
  repay,
yea, I will repay into their bosom
⁷ their*ᵇ* iniquities and their*ᵇ* fathers'
  iniquities together,
        says the Lᴏʀᴅ;
because they burned incense upon
  the mountains
  and reviled me upon the hills,
I will measure into their bosom
  payment for their former doings."

⁸Thus says the Lᴏʀᴅ:
"As the wine is found in the cluster,

and they say, 'Do not destroy it,
  for there is a blessing in it,'
so I will do for my servants' sake,
  and not destroy them all.
⁹I will bring forth descendants from
  Jacob,
and from Judah inheritors of my
  mountains;
my chosen shall inherit it,
  and my servants shall dwell there.
¹⁰Sharon shall become a pasture for
  flocks,
and the Valley of Āʹchôr a place for
  herds to lie down,
for my people who have sought
  me.
¹¹But you who forsake the Lᴏʀᴅ,
  who forget my holy mountain,
who set a table for Fortune
  and fill cups of mixed wine for
  Destiny;
¹²I will destine you to the sword,
  and all of you shall bow down to
  the slaughter;
because, when I called, you did not
  answer,
when I spoke, you did not listen,
  but you did what was evil in my
  eyes,
and chose what I did not delight
  in."

¹³Therefore thus says the Lord Gᴏᴅ:
  "Behold, my servants shall eat,
  but you shall be hungry;
behold, my servants shall drink,
  but you shall be thirsty;
behold, my servants shall rejoice,
  but you shall be put to shame;
¹⁴behold, my servants shall sing for
  gladness of heart,
but you shall cry out for pain of
  heart,
  and shall wail for anguish of spirit.
¹⁵You shall leave your name to my
  chosen for a curse,
and the Lord Gᴏᴅ will slay you;
  but his servants he will call by a
  different name.
¹⁶So that he who blesses himself in
  the land
shall bless himself by the God of
  truth,
and he who takes an oath in the land
  shall swear by the God of truth;
because the former troubles are
  forgotten
  and are hid from my eyes.

ᵇGk Syr: Heb your
65.1-2: Rom 10.20-21.

¹⁷"For behold, I create new heavens
    and a new earth;
and the former things shall not be
    remembered
    or come into mind.
¹⁸But be glad and rejoice for ever
    in that which I create;
for behold, I create Jerusalem a
    rejoicing,
    and her people a joy.
¹⁹I will rejoice in Jerusalem,
    and be glad in my people;
no more shall be heard in it the sound
    of weeping
    and the cry of distress.
²⁰No more shall there be in it
    an infant that lives but a few
    days,
    or an old man who does not fill
    out his days,
for the child shall die a hundred years
    old,
    and the sinner a hundred years old
    shall be accursed.
²¹They shall build houses and inhabit
    them;
    they shall plant vineyards and eat
    their fruit.
²²They shall not build and another
    inhabit;
    they shall not plant and another
    eat;
for like the days of a tree shall the
    days of my people be,
    and my chosen shall long enjoy
    the work of their hands.
²³They shall not labor in vain,
    or bear children for calamity;ᶜ
for they shall be the offspring of
    the blessed of the LORD,
    and their children with them.
²⁴Before they call I will answer,
    while they are yet speaking I will
    hear.
²⁵The wolf and the lamb shall feed
    together,
    the lion shall eat straw like the ox;
    and dust shall be the serpent's
    food.
They shall not hurt or destroy
    in all my holy mountain,
              says the LORD."

66   Thus says the LORD:
    "Heaven is my throne
  and the earth is my footstool;
what is the house which you would
    build for me,
    and what is the place of my rest?
²All these things my hand has made,

and so all these things are mine,ᵈ
           says the LORD.
But this is the man to whom I will
    look,
    he that is humble and contrite in
    spirit,
    and trembles at my word.

³"He who slaughters an ox is like him
    who kills a man;
    he who sacrifices a lamb, like him
    who breaks a dog's neck;
he who presents a cereal offering,
    like him who offers swine's
    blood;
    he who makes a memorial offer-
    ing of frankincense, like him
    who blesses an idol.
These have chosen their own ways,
    and their soul delights in their
    abominations;
⁴I also will choose affliction for them,
    and bring their fears upon them;
because, when I called, no one
    answered,
    when I spoke they did not listen;
but they did what was evil in my eyes,
    and chose that in which I did not
    delight."

⁵Hear the word of the LORD,
    you who tremble at his word:
"Your brethren who hate you
    and cast you out for my name's
    sake
have said, 'Let the LORD be glori-
    fied,
    that we may see your joy';
    but it is they who shall be put to
    shame.

⁶"Hark, an uproar from the city!
    A voice from the temple!
The voice of the LORD,
    rendering recompense to his
    enemies!

⁷"Before she was in labor
    she gave birth;
before her pain came upon her
    she was delivered of a son.
⁸Who has heard such a thing?
    Who has seen such things?
Shall a land be born in one day?
    Shall a nation be brought forth in
    one moment?

ᶜOr *sudden terror* ᵈGk Syr: Heb *came to be*
65.17: Is 66.22; 2 Pet 3.13; Rev 21.1.
65.25: Is 11.6-9.
66.1-2: Mt 5.34; Acts 7.49-50.   **66.6:** Rev 16.1, 17.
66.7: Rev 12.5.

For as soon as Zion was in labor
    she brought forth her sons.
⁹ Shall I bring to the birth and not
    cause to bring forth?
says the LORD;
shall I, who cause to bring forth,
    shut the womb?
says your God.

¹⁰ "Rejoice with Jerusalem, and be
    glad for her,
all you who love her;
rejoice with her in joy,
all you who mourn over her;
¹¹ that you may suck and be satisfied
    with her consoling breasts;
that you may drink deeply with de-
    light
from the abundance of her glory."

¹² For thus says the LORD:
"Behold, I will extend prosperity to
    her like a river,
and the wealth of the nations
    like an overflowing stream;
and you shall suck, you shall be
    carried upon her hip,
and dandled upon her knees.
¹³ As one whom his mother comforts,
    so I will comfort you;
you shall be comforted in Jeru-
    salem.
¹⁴ You shall see, and your heart shall
    rejoice;
your bones shall flourish like
    the grass;
and it shall be known that the hand
    of the LORD is with his serv-
    ants,
and his indignation is against his
    enemies.

¹⁵ "For behold, the LORD will come in
    fire,
and his chariots like the storm-
    wind,
to render his anger in fury,
and his rebuke with flames of
    fire.
¹⁶ For by fire will the LORD execute
    judgment,
and by his sword, upon all flesh;
and those slain by the LORD shall
    be many.

17 "Those who sanctify and purify themselves to go into the gardens, following one in the midst, eating swine's flesh and the abomination and mice, shall come to an end together, says the LORD.

18 "For I know[e] their works and their thoughts, and I am[f] coming to gather all nations and tongues; and they shall come and shall see my glory, ¹⁹ and I will set a sign among them. And from them I will send survivors to the nations, to Tär′shĭsh, Pŭt,[g] and Lüd, who draw the bow, to Tü′bal and Jā′van, to the coastlands afar off, that have not heard my fame or seen my glory; and they shall declare my glory among the nations. ²⁰ And they shall bring all your brethren from all the nations as an offering to the LORD, upon horses, and in chariots, and in litters, and upon mules, and upon dromedaries, to my holy mountain Jerusalem, says the LORD, just as the Israelites bring their cereal offering in a clean vessel to the house of the LORD. ²¹ And some of them also I will take for priests and for Lē′vītes, says the LORD.

22 "For as the new heavens and the new
    earth
    which I will make
shall remain before me, says the
    LORD;
    so shall your descendants and
    your name remain.
²³ From new moon to new moon,
    and from sabbath to sabbath,
all flesh shall come to worship before
    me,
says the LORD.

24 "And they shall go forth and look on the dead bodies of the men that have rebelled against me; for their worm shall not die, their fire shall not be quenched, and they shall be an abhorrence to all flesh."

ᵉ Gk Syr: Heb lacks *know*   ᶠ Gk Syr Vg Tg: Heb *it is*
ᵍ Gk: Heb *Pul*
66.22: Is 65.17; 2 Pet 3.13; Rev 21.1.   **66.24:** Mk 9.48.

The Book of
Jeremiah

1 The words of Jĕr·ẹ·mī′ah, the son of Hĭl·kī′ah, of the priests who were in Ăn′ạ·thŏth in the land of Benjamin, [2] to whom the word of the LORD came in the days of Jō·sī′ah the son of Ā′mŏn, king of Judah, in the thirteenth year of his reign. [3] It came also in the days of Jĕ·hoi′ạ·kim the son of Jō·sī′ah, king of Judah, and until the end of the eleventh year of Zĕd·ẹ·kī′ah, the son of Jō·sī′ah, king of Judah, until the captivity of Jerusalem in the fifth month.

4 Now the word of the LORD came to me saying,
[5] "Before I formed you in the womb
    I knew you,
and before you were born I conse-
    crated you;
I appointed you a prophet to the
    nations."
[6] Then I said, "Ah, Lord GOD! Behold, I do not know how to speak, for I am only a youth." [7] But the LORD said to me,
"Do not say, 'I am only a youth';
for to all to whom I send you you shall
    go,
and whatever I command you you
    shall speak.
[8] Be not afraid of them,
    for I am with you to deliver you,
                    says the LORD."
[9] Then the LORD put forth his hand and touched my mouth; and the LORD said to me,
"Behold, I have put my words in your
    mouth.
[10] See, I have set you this day over na-
    tions and over kingdoms,
to pluck up and to break down,
to destroy and to overthrow,
to build and to plant."
11 And the word of the LORD came to me, saying, "Jĕr·ẹ·mī′ah, what do you see?" And I said, "I see a rod of al-mond."[a] [12] Then the LORD said to me, "You have seen well, for I am watch-ing[b] over my word to perform it."
13 The word of the LORD came to me a second time, saying, "What do you see?" And I said, "I see a boiling pot, facing away from the north." [14] Then the LORD said to me, "Out of the north evil shall break forth upon all the inhabitants of the land. [15] For, lo, I am calling all the tribes of the kingdoms of the north, says the LORD; and they shall come and every one shall set his throne at the entrance of the gates of Jerusalem, against all its walls round about, and against all the cities of Judah. [16] And I will utter my judgments against them, for all their wickedness in forsaking me; they have burned incense to other gods, and worshiped the works of their own hands. [17] But you, gird up your loins; arise, and say to them everything that I command you. Do not be dismayed by them, lest I dismay you before them. [18] And I, behold, I make you this day a fortified city, an iron pillar, and bronze walls, against the whole land, against the kings of Judah, its princes, its priests, and the people of the land. [19] They will fight against you; but they shall not prevail against you, for I am with you, says the LORD, to deliver you."

2 The word of the LORD came to me, saying, [2] "Go and proclaim in the hearing of Jerusalem, Thus says the LORD,
I remember the devotion of your
    youth,
    your love as a bride,
how you followed me in the wil-
    derness,
    in a land not sown.
[3] Israel was holy to the LORD,
    the first fruits of his harvest.
All who ate of it became guilty;
    evil came upon them,
                    says the LORD."

4 Hear the word of the LORD, O house of Jacob, and all the families of the house of Israel. [5] Thus says the LORD:
"What wrong did your fathers find
    in me
    that they went far from me,
and went after worthlessness, and
    became worthless?

[a]Heb *shaqed* [b]Heb *shoqed*
1.5: Is 49.1; Gal 1.15. 1.8: Is 43.5; Acts 18.9-10.
1.10: Rev 10.11.

⁶They did not say, 'Where is the LORD
  who brought us up from the land
  of Egypt,
who led us in the wilderness,
  in a land of deserts and pits,
  in a land of drought and deep darkness,
  in a land that none passes through,
  where no man dwells?'
⁷And I brought you into a plentiful
  land
  to enjoy its fruits and its good
  things.
But when you came in you defiled
  my land,
  and made my heritage an abomination.
⁸The priests did not say, 'Where is the
  LORD?'
  Those who handle the law did not
  know me;
  the rulers^c transgressed against me;
  the prophets prophesied by Bā'al,
  and went after things that do not
  profit.

⁹"Therefore I still contend with you,
  says the LORD,
  and with your children's children
  I will contend.
¹⁰For cross to the coasts of Cyprus
  and see,
  or send to Kē'dār and examine
  with care;
  see if there has been such a thing.
¹¹Has a nation changed its gods,
  even though they are no gods?
But my people have changed their
  glory
  for that which does not profit.
¹²Be appalled, O heavens, at this,
  be shocked, be utterly desolate,
  says the LORD,
¹³for my people have committed two
  evils:
  they have forsaken me,
  the fountain of living waters,
  and hewed out cisterns for themselves,
  broken cisterns,
  that can hold no water.

¹⁴"Is Israel a slave? Is he a homeborn servant?
  Why then has he become a prey?
¹⁵The lions have roared against him,
  they have roared loudly.
They have made his land a waste;
  his cities are in ruins, without
  inhabitant.

¹⁶Moreover, the men of Memphis and
  Täh'păn·hēş
  have broken the crown of your
  head.
¹⁷Have you not brought this upon yourself
  by forsaking the LORD your God,
  when he led you in the way?
¹⁸And now what do you gain by going
  to Egypt,
  to drink the waters of the Nile?
Or what do you gain by going to
  Assyria,
  to drink the waters of the Euphrates?
¹⁹Your wickedness will chasten you,
  and your apostasy will reprove you.
Know and see that it is evil and bitter
  for you to forsake the LORD your
  God;
  the fear of me is not in you,
  says the Lord GOD of hosts.

²⁰"For long ago you broke your yoke
  and burst your bonds;
  and you said, 'I will not serve.'
Yea, upon every high hill
  and under every green tree
  you bowed down as a harlot.
²¹Yet I planted you a choice vine,
  wholly of pure seed.
How then have you turned degen-
  erate
  and become a wild vine?
²²Though you wash yourself with lye
  and use much soap,
  the stain of your guilt is still
  before me,
  says the Lord GOD.
²³How can you say, 'I am not defiled,
  I have not gone after the Bā'alş'?
Look at your way in the valley;
  know what you have done—
  a restive young camel interlacing
  her tracks,
²⁴ a wild ass used to the wilderness,
  in her heat sniffing the wind!
Who can restrain her lust?
None who seek her need weary
  themselves;
  in her month they will find her.
²⁵Keep your feet from going unshod
  and your throat from thirst.
But you said, 'It is hopeless,
  for I have loved strangers,
  and after them I will go.'

²⁶"As a thief is shamed when caught,
^cHeb *shepherds*

so the house of Israel shall be
  shamed:
they, their kings, their princes,
  their priests, and their prophets,
²⁷ who say to a tree, 'You are my father,'
  and to a stone, 'You gave me birth.'
For they have turned their back to
  me,
  and not their face.
But in the time of their trouble they
  say,
  'Arise and save us!'
²⁸ But where are your gods
  that you made for yourself?
Let them arise, if they can save you,
  in your time of trouble;
for as many as your cities
  are your gods, O Judah.

²⁹ "Why do you complain against me?
  You have all rebelled against me,
           says the LORD.
³⁰ In vain have I smitten your children,
  they took no correction;
your own sword devoured your
  prophets
  like a ravening lion.
³¹ And you, O generation, heed the word
  of the LORD.
Have I been a wilderness to Israel,
  or a land of thick darkness?
Why then do my people say, 'We are
  free,
  we will come no more to thee'?
³² Can a maiden forget her ornaments,
  or a bride her attire?
Yet my people have forgotten me
  days without number.

³³ "How well you direct your course
  to seek lovers!
So that even to wicked women
  you have taught your ways.
³⁴ Also on your skirts is found
  the lifeblood of guiltless poor;
you did not find them breaking
  in.
Yet in spite of all these things
³⁵ you say, 'I am innocent;
  surely his anger has turned from
  me.'
Behold, I will bring you to judgment
  for saying, 'I have not sinned.'
³⁶ How lightly you gad about,
  changing your way!
You shall be put to shame by Egypt
  as you were put to shame by Assyria.
³⁷ From it too you will come away
  with your hands upon your head,

for the LORD has rejected those in
  whom you trust,
  and you will not prosper by them.

3 "If*ᵈ* a man divorces his wife
  and she goes from him
and becomes another man's wife,
  will he return to her?
Would not that land be greatly
  polluted?
You have played the harlot with
  many lovers;
  and would you return to me?
           says the LORD.
² Lift up your eyes to the bare heights,
  and see!
Where have you not been lain
  with?
By the waysides you have sat await-
  ing lovers
  like an Arab in the wilderness.
You have polluted the land
  with your vile harlotry.
³ Therefore the showers have been
  withheld,
  and the spring rain has not come;
yet you have a harlot's brow,
  you refuse to be ashamed.
⁴ Have you not just now called to
  me,
  'My father, thou art the friend of
  my youth—
⁵ will he be angry for ever,
  will he be indignant to the end?'
Behold, you have spoken,
  but you have done all the evil
  that you could."

6 The LORD said to me in the days
of King Jō·sī'ah: "Have you seen
what she did, that faithless one, Israel, how she went up on every high
hill and under every green tree, and
there played the harlot? ⁷ And I thought,
'After she has done all this she will
return to me'; but she did not return,
and her false sister Judah saw it. ⁸ She
saw that for all the adulteries of that
faithless one, Israel, I had sent her
away with a decree of divorce; yet her
false sister Judah did not fear, but she
too went and played the harlot. ⁹ Because harlotry was so light to her, she
polluted the land, committing adultery
with stone and tree. ¹⁰ Yet for all this
her false sister Judah did not return
to me with her whole heart, but in pretense, says the LORD."

11 And the LORD said to me, "Faith-

  ᵈGk Syr: Heb *Saying, If*

less Israel has shown herself less
guilty than false Judah. ¹²Go, and proclaim these words toward the north,
and say,
'Return, faithless Israel,
               says the LORD.
I will not look on you in anger,
    for I am merciful,
               says the LORD;
I will not be angry for ever.
¹³Only acknowledge your guilt,
    that you rebelled against the LORD
      your God
and scattered your favors among
    strangers under every green
    tree,
    and that you have not obeyed my
    voice,
               says the LORD.
¹⁴Return, O faithless children,
               says the LORD;
    for I am your master;
I will take you, one from a city and
    two from a family,
    and I will bring you to Zion.
15 " 'And I will give you shepherds
after my own heart, who will feed you
with knowledge and understanding.
¹⁶And when you have multiplied and
increased in the land, in those days,
says the LORD, they shall no more
say, "The ark of the covenant of the
LORD." It shall not come to mind, or
be remembered, or missed; it shall not
be made again. ¹⁷At that time Jerusalem shall be called the throne of the
LORD, and all nations shall gather to
it, to the presence of the LORD in Jerusalem, and they shall no more stubbornly follow their own evil heart.
¹⁸In those days the house of Judah
shall join the house of Israel, and together they shall come from the land
of the north to the land that I gave your
fathers for a heritage.
¹⁹ " 'I thought
    how I would set you among my
      sons,
and give you a pleasant land,
    a heritage most beauteous of all
      nations.
And I thought you would call me,
    My Father,
    and would not turn from follow-
      ing me.
²⁰Surely, as a faithless wife leaves her
    husband,
so have you been faithless to me,
    O house of Israel,
             says the LORD.' "

²¹A voice on the bare heights is heard,
    the weeping and pleading of Is-
      rael's sons,
because they have perverted their
    way,
    they have forgotten the LORD
      their God.
²² "Return, O faithless sons,
    I will heal your faithlessness."
"Behold, we come to thee;
    for thou art the LORD our God.
²³Truly the hills are a delusion,
    the orgies on the mountains.
Truly in the LORD our God
    is the salvation of Israel.
24 "But from our youth the shameful thing has devoured all for which
our fathers labored, their flocks and
their herds, their sons and their
daughters. ²⁵Let us lie down in our
shame, and let our dishonor cover us;
for we have sinned against the LORD
our God, we and our fathers, from our
youth even to this day; and we have
not obeyed the voice of the LORD our
God."

4 "If you return, O Israel,
               says the LORD,
    to me you should return.
If you remove your abominations
    from my presence,
    and do not waver,
²and if you swear, 'As the LORD lives,'
    in truth, in justice, and in up-
      rightness,
then nations shall bless themselves
    in him,
    and in him shall they glory."
3 For thus says the LORD to the men
of Judah and to the inhabitants of
Jerusalem:
"Break up your fallow ground,
    and sow not among thorns.
⁴Circumcise yourselves to the LORD,
    remove the foreskin of your hearts,
    O men of Judah and inhabitants
      of Jerusalem;
lest my wrath go forth like fire,
    and burn with none to quench it
    because of the evil of your doings.'

5 Declare in Judah, and proclaim in
Jerusalem, and say,
"Blow the trumpet through the land;
    cry aloud and say,
'Assemble, and let us go
    into the fortified cities!'
⁶Raise a standard toward Zion,
    flee for safety, stay not,

for I bring evil from the north,
  and great destruction.
⁷A lion has gone up from his thicket,
  a destroyer of nations has set out;
  he has gone forth from his place
to make your land a waste;
  your cities will be ruins
  without inhabitant.
⁸For this gird you with sackcloth,
  lament and wail;
for the fierce anger of the LORD
  has not turned back from us."

⁹"In that day, says the LORD, courage shall fail both king and princes; the priests shall be appalled and the prophets astounded." ¹⁰Then I said, "Ah, Lord GOD, surely thou hast utterly deceived this people and Jerusalem, saying, 'It shall be well with you'; whereas the sword has reached their very life."

11 At that time it will be said to this people and to Jerusalem, "A hot wind from the bare heights in the desert toward the daughter of my people, not to winnow or cleanse, ¹²a wind too full for this comes for me. Now it is I who speak in judgment upon them." ¹³Behold, he comes up like clouds,
  his chariots like the whirlwind;
his horses are swifter than eagles—
  woe to us, for we are ruined!
¹⁴O Jerusalem, wash your heart from
  wickedness,
  that you may be saved.
How long shall your evil thoughts
  lodge within you?
¹⁵For a voice declares from Dan
  and proclaims evil from Mount
  E′phra·im.
¹⁶Warn the nations that he is coming;
  announce to Jerusalem,
"Besiegers come from a distant land;
  they shout against the cities of
  Judah.
¹⁷Like keepers of a field are they
  against her round about,
  because she·has rebelled against
  me,
            says the LORD.
¹⁸Your ways and your doings
  have brought this upon you.
This is your doom, and it is bitter;
  it has reached your very heart."

¹⁹My anguish, my anguish! I writhe
  in pain!
Oh, the walls of my heart!

My heart is beating wildly;
  I cannot keep silent;
for I hear the sound of the trumpet,
  the alarm of war.
²⁰Disaster follows hard on disaster,
  the whole land is laid waste.
Suddenly my tents are destroyed,
  my curtains in a moment.
²¹How long must I see the standard,
  and hear the sound of the trumpet?
²²"For my people are foolish,
  they know me not;
they are stupid children,
  they have no understanding.
They are skilled in doing evil,
  but how to do good they know not."

²³I looked on the earth, and lo, it was
  waste and void;
  and to the heavens, and they had
  no light.
²⁴I looked on the mountains, and lo,
  they were quaking,
  and all the hills moved to and fro.
²⁵I looked, and lo, there was no man,
  and all the birds of the air had fled.
²⁶I looked, and lo, the fruitful land was
  a desert,
  and all its cities were laid in ruins
  before the LORD, before his fierce
  anger.
27 For thus says the LORD, "The whole land shall be a desolation; yet I will not make a full end.
²⁸For this the earth shall mourn,
  and the heavens above be black,
for I have spoken, I have purposed;
  I have not relented nor will I turn
  back."

²⁹At the noise of horseman and archer
  every city takes to flight;
they enter thickets; they climb
  among rocks;
all the cities are forsaken,
  and no man dwells in them.
³⁰And you, O desolate one,
  what do you mean that you dress in
  scarlet,
  that you deck yourself with ornaments of gold,
  that you enlarge your eyes with
  paint?
In vain you beautify yourself.
  Your lovers despise you;
  they seek your life.
³¹For I heard a cry as of a woman
  in travail,
anguish as of one bringing forth
  her first child,

the cry of the daughter of Zion
  gasping for breath,
  stretching out her hands,
"Woe is me! I am fainting before
  murderers."

5 Run to and fro through the streets
     of Jerusalem,
  look and take note!
Search her squares to see
  if you can find a man,
one who does justice
  and seeks truth;
that I may pardon her.
²Though they say, "As the LORD
  lives,"
  yet they swear falsely.
³O LORD, do not thy eyes look for
  truth?
Thou hast smitten them,
  but they felt no anguish;
thou hast consumed them,
  but they refused to take correction.
They have made their faces harder
  than rock;
  they have refused to repent.

⁴Then I said, "These are only the
  poor,
  they have no sense;
for they do not know the way of the
  LORD,
  the law of their God.
⁵I will go to the great,
  and will speak to them;
for they know the way of the LORD,
  the law of their God."
But they all alike had broken the
  yoke,
  they had burst the bonds.

⁶Therefore a lion from the forest
  shall slay them,
  a wolf from the desert shall destroy them.
A leopard is watching against their
  cities,
  every one who goes out of them
  shall be torn in pieces;
because their transgressions are
  many,
  their apostasies are great.

⁷"How can I pardon you?
  Your children have forsaken me,
  and have sworn by those who are
  no gods.
When I fed them to the full,
  they committed adultery

and trooped to the houses of
  harlots.
⁸They were well-fed lusty stallions,
  each neighing for his neighbor's wife.
⁹Shall I not punish them for these
  things?
                     says the LORD;
and shall I not avenge myself
  on a nation such as this?

¹⁰"Go up through her vine-rows and
  destroy,
  but make not a full end;
strip away her branches,
  for they are not the LORD's.
¹¹For the house of Israel and the house
  of Judah
  have been utterly faithless to me,
                     says the LORD.
¹²They have spoken falsely of the
  LORD,
  and have said, 'He will do nothing;
no evil will come upon us,
  nor shall we see sword or famine.
¹³The prophets will become wind;
  the word is not in them.
Thus shall it be done to them!'"

¹⁴Therefore thus says the LORD, the
  God of hosts:
"Because they*ᵉ* have spoken this
  word,
behold, I am making my words in
  your mouth a fire,
  and this people wood, and the fire
  shall devour them.
¹⁵Behold, I am bringing upon you
  a nation from afar, O house of
  Israel,   says the LORD.
It is an enduring nation,
  it is an ancient nation,
a nation whose language you do not
  know,
  nor can you understand what
  they say.
¹⁶Their quiver is like an open tomb,
  they are all mighty men.
¹⁷They shall eat up your harvest and
  your food;
  they shall eat up your sons and
  your daughters;
they shall eat up your flocks and
  your herds;
  they shall eat up your vines and
  your fig trees;
your fortified cities in which you
  trust
  they shall destroy with the sword."
ᵉHeb you

18 "But even in those days, says the LORD, I will not make a full end of you. ¹⁹And when your people say, 'Why has the LORD our God done all these things to us?' you shall say to them, 'As you have forsaken me and served foreign gods in your land, so you shall serve strangers in a land that is not yours.' "

²⁰Declare this in the house of Jacob,
proclaim it in Judah:
²¹"Hear this, O foolish and senseless people,
who have eyes, but see not,
who have ears, but hear not.
²²Do you not fear me? says the LORD;
Do you not tremble before me?
I placed the sand as the bound for the sea,
a perpetual barrier which it cannot pass;
though the waves toss, they cannot prevail,
though they roar, they cannot pass over it.
²³But this people has a stubborn and rebellious heart;
they have turned aside and gone away.
²⁴They do not say in their hearts,
'Let us fear the LORD our God,
who gives the rain in its season,
the autumn rain and the spring rain,
and keeps for us
the weeks appointed for the harvest.'
²⁵Your iniquities have turned these away,
and your sins have kept good from you.
²⁶For wicked men are found among my people;
they lurk like fowlers lying in wait.ᶠ
They set a trap;
they catch men.
²⁷Like a basket full of birds,
their houses are full of treachery;
therefore they have become great and rich,
²⁸ they have grown fat and sleek.
They know no bounds in deeds of wickedness;
they judge not with justice
the cause of the fatherless, to make it prosper,
and they do not defend the rights of the needy.

²⁹Shall I not punish them for these things?
says the LORD,
and shall I not avenge myself
on a nation such as this?"

³⁰An appalling and horrible thing
has happened in the land:
³¹the prophets prophesy falsely,
and the priests rule at their direction;
my people love to have it so,
but what will you do when the end comes?

6 Flee for safety, O people of Benjamin,
from the midst of Jerusalem!
Blow the trumpet in Tĕ·kō´a,
and raise a signal on Bĕth″-hăc·chē´rĕm;
for evil looms out of the north,
and great destruction.
²The comely and delicately bred I will destroy,
the daughter of Zion.
³Shepherds with their flocks shall come against her;
they shall pitch their tents around her,
they shall pasture, each in his place.
⁴"Prepare war against her;
up, and let us attack at noon!"
"Woe to us, for the day declines,
for the shadows of evening lengthen!"
⁵"Up, and let us attack by night,
and destroy her palaces!"

⁶For thus says the LORD of hosts:
"Hew down her trees;
cast up a siege mound against Jerusalem.
This is the city which must be punished;
there is nothing but oppression within her.
⁷As a well keeps it water fresh,
so she keeps fresh her wickedness;
violence and destruction are heard within her;
sickness and wounds are ever before me.
⁸Be warned, O Jerusalem,
lest I be alienated from you;
lest I make you a desolation,
an uninhabited land."

ᶠHeb uncertain 5.21: Is 6.9-10; Mt 13,10-15; Mk 8.17-18.

⁹Thus says the LORD of hosts:
"Glean*ᵍ* thoroughly as a vine
 the remnant of Israel;
like a grape-gatherer pass your hand
 again
 over its branches."
¹⁰To whom shall I speak and give
 warning,
 that they may hear?
Behold, their ears are closed,*ʰ*
 they cannot listen;
behold, the word of the LORD is to
 them an object of scorn,
 they take no pleasure in it.
¹¹Therefore I am full of the wrath of
 the LORD;
 I am weary of holding it in.
"Pour it out upon the children in
 the street,
and upon the gatherings of young
 men, also;
both husband and wife shall be
 taken,
 the old folk and the very aged.
¹²Their houses shall be turned over to
 others,
 their fields and wives together;
for I will stretch out my hand
 against the inhabitants of the
 land,"
     says the LORD.
¹³"For from the least to the greatest
 of them,
 every one is greedy for unjust gain;
and from prophet to priest,
 every one deals falsely.
¹⁴They have healed the wound of my
 people lightly,
saying, 'Peace, peace,'
 when there is no peace.
¹⁵Were they ashamed when they committed abomination?
No, they were not at all ashamed;
 they did not know how to blush.
Therefore they shall fall among
 those who fall;
at the time that I punish them,
 they shall be overthrown,"
     says the LORD.

¹⁶Thus says the LORD:
"Stand by the roads, and look,
 and ask for the ancient paths,
where the good way is; and walk in it,
 and find rest for your souls.
But they said, 'We will not walk in
 it.'
¹⁷I set watchmen over you, saying,
'Give heed to the sound of the
 trumpet!'

But they said, 'We will not give heed.'
¹⁸Therefore hear, O nations,
 and know, O congregation,
 what will happen to them.
¹⁹Hear, O earth; behold, I am bringing
 evil upon this people,
 the fruit of their devices,
because they have not given heed
 to my words;
and as for my law, they have
 rejected it.
²⁰To what purpose does frankincense
 come to me from She´ba,
 or sweet cane from a distant land?
Your burnt offerings are not acceptable,
 nor your sacrifices pleasing to me.
²¹Therefore thus says the LORD:
'Behold, I will lay before this people
 stumbling blocks against which
 they shall stumble;
fathers and sons together,
 neighbor and friend shall perish.' "

²²Thus says the LORD:
"Behold, a people is coming from
 the north country,
 a great nation is stirring from the
 farthest parts of the earth.
²³They lay hold on bow and spear,
 they are cruel and have no mercy,
the sound of them is like the roaring sea;
they ride upon horses,
 set in array as a man for battle,
 against you, O daughter of Zion!"
²⁴We have heard the report of it,
 out hands fall helpless;
anguish has taken hold of us,
 pain as of a woman in travail.
²⁵Go not forth into the field,
 nor walk on the road;
for the enemy has a sword,
 terror is on every side.
²⁶O daughter of my people, gird on
 sackcloth,
 and roll in ashes;
make mourning as for an only son,
 most bitter lamentation;
for suddenly the destroyer
 will come upon us.

²⁷"I have made you an assayer and
 tester among my people,
 that you may know and assay their
 ways.
²⁸They are all stubbornly rebellious,
 going about with slanders;

*ᵍ*Cn: Heb *they shall glean* *ʰ*Heb *uncircumcised*
6.16: Mt 11.29. **6.25:** Jer 20.3, 10; 46.5; 49.29; Ps 31.13.

they are bronze and iron,
all of them act corruptly.
²⁹The bellows blow fiercely,
the lead is consumed by the fire;
in vain the refining goes on,
for the wicked are not removed.
³⁰Refuse silver they are called,
for the LORD has rejected them."

7 The word that came to Jĕr·e·mī'ạh from the LORD: ²"Stand in the gate of the LORD's house, and proclaim there this word, and say, Hear the word of the LORD, all you men of Judah who enter these gates to worship the LORD. ³Thus says the LORD of hosts, the God of Israel, Amend your ways and your doings, and I will let you dwell in this place. ⁴Do not trust in these deceptive words: 'This is the temple of the LORD, the temple of the LORD, the temple of the LORD.'
5 "For if you truly amend your ways and your doings, if you truly execute justice one with another, ⁶if you do not oppress the alien, the fatherless or the widow, or shed innocent blood in this place, and if you do not go after other gods to your own hurt, ⁷then I will let you dwell in this place, in the land that I gave of old to your fathers for ever.
8 "Behold, you trust in deceptive words to no avail. ⁹Will you steal, murder, commit adultery, swear falsely, burn incense to Bā'al, and go after other gods that you have not known, ¹⁰and then come and stand before me in this house, which is called by my name, and say, 'We are delivered!'—only to go on doing all these abominations? ¹¹Has this house, which is called by my name, become a den of robbers in your eyes? Behold, I myself have seen it, says the LORD. ¹²Go now to my place that was in Shī'lōh, where I made my name dwell at first, and see what I did to it for the wickedness of my people Israel. ¹³And now, because you have done all these things, says the LORD, and when I spoke to you persistently you did not listen, and when I called you, you did not answer, ¹⁴therefore I will do to the house which is called by my name, and in which you trust, and to the place which I gave to you and to your fathers, as I did to Shī'lōh. ¹⁵And I will cast you out of my sight, as I cast out all your kinsmen, all the offspring of Ē'phrạ·im.
16 "As for you, do not pray for this people, or lift up cry or prayer for them, and do not intercede with me, for I do not hear you. ¹⁷Do you not see what they are doing in the cities of Judah and in the streets of Jerusalem? ¹⁸The children gather wood, the fathers kindle fire, and the women knead dough, to make cakes for the queen of heaven; and they pour out drink offerings to other gods, to provoke me to anger. ¹⁹Is it I whom they provoke? says the LORD. Is it not themselves, to their own confusion? ²⁰Therefore thus says the Lord GOD: Behold, my anger and my wrath will be poured out on this place, upon man and beast, upon the trees of the field and the fruit of the ground; it will burn and not be quenched."
21 Thus says the LORD of hosts, the God of Israel: "Add your burnt offerings to your sacrifices, and eat the flesh. ²²For in the day that I brought them out of the land of Egypt, I did not speak to your fathers or command them concerning burnt offerings and sacrifices. ²³But this command I gave them, 'Obey my voice, and I will be your God, and you shall be my people; and walk in all the way that I command you, that it may be well with you.' ²⁴But they did not obey or incline their ear, but walked in their own counsels and the stubbornness of their evil hearts, and went backward and not forward. ²⁵From the day that your fathers came out of the land of Egypt to this day, I have persistently sent all my servants the prophets to them, day after day; ²⁶yet they did not listen to me, or incline their ear, but stiffened their neck. They did worse than their fathers.
27 "So you shall speak all these words to them, but they will not listen to you. You shall call to them, but they will not answer you. ²⁸And you shall say to them, 'This is the nation that did not obey the voice of the LORD their God, and did not accept discipline; truth has perished; it is cut off from their lips.
²⁹Cut off your hair and cast it away;
raise a lamentation on the bare heights,
for the LORD has rejected and forsaken
the generation of his wrath.'
30 "For the sons of Judah have

7.11: Mt 21.13; Mk 11.17; Lk 19.46.

done evil in my sight, says the LORD; they have set their abominations in the house which is called by my name, to defile it. [31]And they have built the high place[i] of Tō′phĕth, which is in the valley of the son of Hĭn′nŏm, to burn their sons and their daughters in the fire; which I did not command, nor did it come into my mind. [32]Therefore, behold, the days are coming, says the LORD, when it will no more be called Tō′phĕth, or the valley of the son of Hĭn′nŏm, but the valley of Slaughter: for they will bury in Topheth, because there is no room elsewhere. [33]And the dead bodies of this people will be food for the birds of the air, and for the beasts of the earth; and none will frighten them away. [34]And I will make to cease from the cities of Judah and from the streets of Jerusalem the voice of mirth and the voice of gladness, the voice of the bridegroom and the voice of the bride; for the land shall become a waste.

8 "At that time, says the LORD, the bones of the kings of Judah, the bones of its princes, the bones of the priests, the bones of the prophets, and the bones of the inhabitants of Jerusalem shall be brought out of their tombs; [2]and they shall be spread before the sun and the moon and all the host of heaven, which they have loved and served, which they have gone after, and which they have sought and worshiped; and they shall not be gathered or buried; they shall be as dung on the surface of the ground. [3]Death shall be preferred to life by all the remnant that remains of this evil family in all the places where I have driven them, says the LORD of hosts.

[4]"You shall say to them, Thus says the LORD:
When men fall, do they not rise again?
If one turns away, does he not return?
[5]Why then has this people turned away
in perpetual backsliding?
They hold fast to deceit,
they refuse to return.
[6]I have given heed and listened,
but they have not spoken aright;
no man repents of his wickedness,
saying, 'What have I done?'
Every one turns to his own course,

like a horse plunging headlong into battle.
[7]Even the stork in the heavens
knows her times;
and the turtledove, swallow, and crane[j]
keep the time of their coming;
but my people know not
the ordinance of the LORD.

[8]"How can you say, 'We are wise,
and the law of the LORD is with us'?
But, behold, the false pen of the scribes
has made it into a lie.
[9]The wise men shall be put to shame,
they shall be dismayed and taken;
lo, they have rejected the word of the LORD,
and what wisdom is in them?
[10]Therefore I will give their wives to others
and their fields to conquerors,
because from the least to the greatest
every one is greedy for unjust gain;
from prophet to priest
every one deals falsely.
[11]They have healed the wound of my people lightly,
saying, 'Peace, peace,'
when there is no peace.
[12]Were they ashamed when they committed abomination?
No, they were not at all ashamed;
they did not know how to blush.
Therefore they shall fall among the fallen;
when I punish them, they shall be overthrown,
       says the LORD.
[13]When I would gather them, says the LORD,
there are no grapes on the vine,
nor figs on the fig tree;
even the leaves are withered,
and what I gave them has passed away from them."[k]

[14]Why do we sit still?
Gather together, let us go into the fortified cities
and perish there;
for the LORD our God has doomed us to perish,

[i]Gk Tg: Heb *high places*
[j]The meaning of the Hebrew word is uncertain
[k]Heb uncertain **7.34:** Rev 18.23.

and has given us poisoned water
to drink,
because we have sinned against
the LORD.
15 We looked for peace, but no good
came,
for a time of healing, but behold,
terror.

16 "The snorting of their horses is
heard from Dan;
at the sound of the neighing of
their stallions
the whole land quakes.
They come and devour the land and
all that fills it,
the city and those who dwell in
it.
17 For behold, I am sending among you
serpents,
adders which cannot be charmed,
and they shall bite you,"
says the LORD.

18 My grief is beyond healing,[l]
my heart is sick within me.
19 Hark, the cry of the daughter of my
people
from the length and breadth of the
land:
"Is the LORD not in Zion?
Is her King not in her?"
"Why have they provoked me to
anger with their graven images,
and with their foreign idols?"
20 "The harvest is past, the summer
is ended,
and we are not saved."
21 For the wound of the daughter of my
people is my heart wounded,
I mourn, and dismay has taken
hold on me.

22 Is there no balm in Gilead?
Is there no physician there?
Why then has the health of the
daughter of my people
not been restored?

9[m] O that my head were waters,
and my eyes a fountain of tears,
that I might weep day and night
for the slain of the daughter of my
people!
2[n] O that I had in the desert
a wayfarers' lodging place,
that I might leave my people
and go away from them!
For they are all adulterers,
a company of treacherous men.
3 They bend their tongue like a bow;
falsehood and not truth has
grown strong[o] in the land;
for they proceed from evil to evil,
and they do not know me, says
the LORD.

4 Let every one beware of his neighbor,
and put no trust in any brother;
for every brother is a supplanter,
and every neighbor goes about as
a slanderer.
5 Every one deceives his neighbor,
and no one speaks the truth;
they have taught their tongue to
speak lies;
they commit iniquity and are too
weary to repent.[p]
6 Heaping oppression upon oppression, and deceit upon deceit,
they refuse to know me, says the
LORD.

7 Therefore thus says the LORD of
hosts:
"Behold, I will refine them and test
them,
for what else can I do, because of
my people?
8 Their tongue is a deadly arrow;
it speaks deceitfully;
with his mouth each speaks peaceably to his neighbor,
but in his heart he plans an
ambush for him.
9 Shall I not punish them for these
things? says the LORD;
and shall I not avenge myself
on a nation such as this?

10 "Take up[q] weeping and wailing for
the mountains,
and a lamentation for the pastures
of the wilderness,
because they are laid waste so that
no one passes through,
and the lowing of cattle is not
heard;
both the birds of the air and the
beasts
have fled and are gone.
11 I will make Jerusalem a heap of
ruins,
a lair of jackals;
and I will make the cities of Judah
a desolation,
without inhabitant."

[l] Cn Compare Gk: Heb uncertain
[m] Ch 8.23 in Heb [n] Ch 9.1 in Heb
[o] Gk: Heb *and not for truth they have grown strong*
[p] Cn Compare Gk: Heb *your dwelling*
[q] Gk Syr: Heb *I will take up*

12 Who is the man so wise that he can understand this? To whom has the mouth of the LORD spoken, that he may declare it? Why is the land ruined and laid waste like a wilderness, so that no one passes through? ¹³And the LORD says: "Because they have forsaken my law which I set before them, and have not obeyed my voice, or walked in accord with it, ¹⁴but have stubbornly followed their own hearts and have gone after the Bā′aḷṣ, as their fathers taught them. ¹⁵Therefore thus says the LORD of hosts, the God of Israel: Behold, I will feed this people with wormwood, and give them poisonous water to drink. ¹⁶I will scatter them among the nations whom neither they nor their fathers have known; and I will send the sword after them, until I have consumed them."

¹⁷Thus says the LORD of hosts:
"Consider, and call for the mourning women to come;
send for the skilful women to come;
¹⁸let them make haste and raise a wailing over us,
that our eyes may run down with tears,
and our eyelids gush with water.
¹⁹For a sound of wailing is heard from Zion:
'How we are ruined!
We are utterly shamed,
because we have left the land,
because they have cast down our dwellings.'"

²⁰Hear, O women, the word of the LORD,
and let your ear receive the word of his mouth;
teach to your daughters a lament,
and each to her neighbor a dirge.
²¹For death has come up into our windows,
it has entered our palaces,
cutting off the children from the streets
and the young men from the squares.
²²Speak, "Thus says the LORD:
'The dead bodies of men shall fall like dung upon the open field,
like sheaves after the reaper,
and none shall gather them.'"

23 Thus says the LORD: "Let not the wise man glory in his wisdom,

let not the mighty man glory in his might, let not the rich man glory in his riches; ²⁴but let him who glories glory in this, that he understands and knows me, that I am the LORD who practice steadfast love, justice, and righteousness in the earth; for in these things I delight, says the LORD."

25 "Behold, the days are coming, says the LORD, when I will punish all those who are circumcised but yet uncircumcised—²⁶Egypt, Judah, E′dom, the sons of Ăm′mon, Mō′ăb, and all who dwell in the desert that cut the corners of their hair; for all these nations are uncircumcised, and all the house of Israel is uncircumcised in heart."

10 Hear the word which the LORD speaks to you, O house of Israel. ²Thus says the LORD:
"Learn not the way of the nations,
nor be dismayed at the signs of the heavens
because the nations are dismayed at them,
³for the customs of the peoples are false.
A tree from the forest is cut down,
and worked with an axe by the hands of a craftsman.
⁴Men deck it with silver and gold;
they fasten it with hammer and nails
so that it cannot move.
⁵Their idolsʳ are like scarecrows in a cucumber field,
and they cannot speak;
they have to be carried,
for they cannot walk.
Be not afraid of them,
for they cannot do evil,
neither is it in them to do good."

⁶There is none like thee, O LORD;
thou art great, and thy name is great in might.
⁷Who would not fear thee, O King of the nations?
For this is thy due;
for among all the wise ones of the nations
and in all their kingdoms
there is none like thee.
⁸They are both stupid and foolish;
the instruction of idols is but wood!

ʳHeb *They*
9.24: 1 Cor 1.31; 2 Cor 10.17.   9.26: Acts 7.51.

⁹Beaten silver is brought from Tär′-
  shĭsh,
  and gold from Ū′phăz.
They are the work of the craftsman
  and of the hands of the goldsmith;
  their clothing is violet and purple;
  they are all the work of skilled
  men.
¹⁰But the LORD is the true God;
  he is the living God and the everlasting King.
At his wrath the earth quakes,
  and the nations cannot endure
  his indignation.

11 Thus shall you say to them:
"The gods who did not make the
heavens and the earth shall perish
from the earth and from under the
heavens."ˢ

¹²It is he who made the earth by his
  power,
who established the world by his
  wisdom,
and by his understanding
  stretched out the heavens.
¹³When he utters his voice there is a
  tumult of waters in the heavens,
and he makes the mist rise from
  the ends of the earth.
He makes lightnings for the rain,
  and he brings forth the wind from
  his storehouses.
¹⁴Every man is stupid and without
  knowledge;
  every goldsmith is put to shame
  by his idols;
for his images are false,
  and there is no breath in them.
¹⁵They are worthless, a work of delusion;
  at the time of their punishment
  they shall perish.
¹⁶Not like these is he who is the portion of Jacob,
  for he is the one who formed all
  things,
and Israel is the tribe of his inheritance;
  the LORD of hosts is his name.

¹⁷Gather up your bundle from the
  ground,
  O you who dwell under siege!
¹⁸For thus says the LORD:
"Behold, I am slinging out the inhabitants of the land
  at this time,

and I will bring distress on them,
  that they may feel it."

¹⁹Woe is me because of my hurt!
  My wound is grievous.
But I said, "Truly this is an affliction,
  and I must bear it."
²⁰My tent is destroyed,
  and all my cords are broken;
my children have gone from me,
  and they are not;
there is no one to spread my tent
  again,
  and to set up my curtains.
²¹For the shepherds are stupid,
  and do not inquire of the LORD;
therefore they have not prospered,
  and all their flock is scattered.

²²Hark, a rumor! Behold, it comes!—
  a great commotion out of the north
  country
to make the cities of Judah a desolation,
  a lair of jackals.

²³I know, O LORD, that the way of man
  is not in himself,
that it is not in man who walks to
  direct his steps.
²⁴Correct me, O LORD, but in just
  measure;
  not in thy anger, lest thou bring
  me to nothing.

²⁵Pour out thy wrath upon the nations that know thee not,
  and upon the peoples that call not
  on thy name;
for they have devoured Jacob;
  they have devoured him and consumed him,
  and have laid waste his habitation.

11 The word that came to Jĕr-ẹ-
mī′ạh from the LORD: ² "Hear the
words of this covenant, and speak to
the men of Judah and the inhabitants
of Jerusalem. ³ You shall say to them,
Thus says the LORD, the God of Israel:
Cursed be the man who does not heed
the words of this covenant ⁴ which I
commanded your fathers when I
brought them out of the land of Egypt,
from the iron furnace, saying, Listen
to my voice, and do all that I command
you. So shall you be my people, and I
will be your God, ⁵ that I may perform

ˢThis verse is in Aramaic
10.25: 1 Thess 4.5; Rev 16.1.

the oath which I swore to your fathers, to give them a land flowing with milk and honey, as at this day." Then I answered, "So be it, LORD."

6 And the LORD said to me, "Proclaim all these words in the cities of Judah, and in the streets of Jerusalem: Hear the words of this covenant and do them. ⁷For I solemnly warned your fathers when I brought them up out of the land of Egypt, warning them persistently, even to this day, saying, Obey my voice. ⁸Yet they did not obey or incline their ear, but every one walked in the stubbornness of his evil heart. Therefore I brought upon them all the words of this covenant, which I commanded them to do, but they did not."

9 Again the LORD said to me, "There is revolt among the men of Judah and the inhabitants of Jerusalem. ¹⁰They have turned back to the iniquities of their forefathers, who refused to hear my words; they have gone after other gods to serve them; the house of Israel and the house of Judah have broken my covenant which I made with their fathers. ¹¹Therefore, thus says the LORD, Behold, I am bringing evil upon them which they cannot escape; though they cry to me, I will not listen to them. ¹²Then the cities of Judah and the inhabitants of Jerusalem will go and cry to the gods to whom they burn incense, but they cannot save them in the time of their trouble. ¹³For your gods have become as many as your cities, O Judah; and as many as the streets of Jerusalem are the altars you have set up to shame, altars to burn incense to Bā′al.

14 "Therefore do not pray for this people, or lift up a cry or prayer on their behalf, for I will not listen when they call to me in the time of their trouble. ¹⁵What right has my beloved in my house, when she has done vile deeds? Can vows* and sacrificial flesh avert your doom? Can you then exult? ¹⁶The LORD once called you, 'A green olive tree, fair with goodly fruit'; but with the roar of a great tempest he will set fire to it, and its branches will be consumed. ¹⁷The LORD of hosts, who planted you, has pronounced evil against you, because of the evil which the house of Israel and the house of Judah have done, provoking me to anger by burning incense to Bā′al."

¹⁸The LORD made it known to me and I knew;
 then thou didst show me their evil deeds.
¹⁹But I was like a gentle lamb
 led to the slaughter.
I did not know it was against me
 they devised schemes, saying,
"Let us destroy the tree with its fruit,
 let us cut him off from the land of the living,
 that his name be remembered no more."
²⁰But, O LORD of hosts, who judgest righteously,
 who triest the heart and the mind,
let me see thy vengeance upon them,
 for to thee have I committed my cause.

21 Therefore thus says the LORD concerning the men of An′a·thŏth, who seek your life, and say, "Do not prophesy in the name of the LORD, or you will die by our hand"—²²therefore thus says the LORD of hosts: "Behold, I will punish them; the young men shall die by the sword; their sons and their daughters shall die by famine; ²³and none of them shall be left. For I will bring evil upon the men of An′a·thŏth, the year of their punishment."

12 Righteous art thou, O LORD,
 when I complain to thee;
yet I would plead my case before thee.
Why does the way of the wicked prosper?
Why do all who are treacherous thrive?
²Thou plantest them, and they take root;
 they grow and bring forth fruit;
thou art near in their mouth
 and far from their heart.
³But thou, O LORD, knowest me;
 thou seest me, and triest my mind toward thee.
Pull them out like sheep for the slaughter,
 and set them apart for the day of slaughter.
⁴How long will the land mourn,
 and the grass of every field wither?
For the wickedness of those who dwell in it

*Gk: Heb *many*

the beasts and the birds are swept
away,
because men said, "He will not
see our latter end."

⁵ "If you have raced with men on foot,
and they have wearied you,
how will you compete with horses?
And if in a safe land you fall down,
how will you do in the jungle of
the Jordan?
⁶ For even your brothers and the house
of your father,
even they have dealt treacherously with you;
they are in full cry after you;
believe them not,
though they speak fair words to
you."

⁷ "I have forsaken my house,
I have abandoned my heritage;
I have given the beloved of my soul
into the hands of her enemies.
⁸ My heritage has become to me
like a lion in the forest,
she has lifted up her voice against
me;
therefore I hate her.
⁹ Is my heritage to me like a speckled
bird of prey?
Are the birds of prey against her
round about?
Go, assemble all the wild beasts;
bring them to devour.
¹⁰ Many shepherds have destroyed
my vineyard,
they have trampled down my
portion,
they have made my pleasant portion
a desolate wilderness.
¹¹ They have made it a desolation;
desolate, it mourns to me.
The whole land is made desolate,
but no man lays it to heart.
² Upon all the bare heights in the
desert
destroyers have come;
for the sword of the LORD devours
from one end of the land to the
other;
no flesh has peace.
³ They have sown wheat and have
reaped thorns,
they have tired themselves out
but profit nothing.
They shall be ashamed of their*
harvests
because of the fierce anger of the
LORD."

14 Thus says the LORD concerning
all my evil neighbors who touch the
heritage which I have given my people
Israel to inherit: "Behold, I will pluck
them up from their land, and I will
pluck up the house of Judah from
among them. ¹⁵ And after I have
plucked them up, I will again have
compassion on them, and I will bring
them again each to his heritage and
each to his land. ¹⁶ And it shall come to
pass, if they will diligently learn the
ways of my people, to swear by my
name, 'As the LORD lives,' even as they
taught my people to swear by Bā′al,
then they shall be built up in the
midst of my people. ¹⁷ But if any nation
will not listen, then I will utterly
pluck it up and destroy it, says. the
LORD."

13 Thus said the LORD to me,
"Go and buy a linen waistcloth,
and put it on your loins, and do not dip
it in water." ² So I bought a waistcloth
according to the word of the LORD, and
put it on my loins. ³ And the word of
the LORD came to me a second time,
⁴ "Take the waistcloth which you have
bought, which is upon your loins, and
arise, go to the Euphrates, and hide it
there in a cleft of the rock." ⁵ So I went,
and hid it by the Euphrates, as the
LORD commanded me. ⁶ And after
many days the LORD said to me, "Arise,
go to the Euphrates, and take from
there the waistcloth which I commanded you to hide there." ⁷ Then I
went to the Euphrates, and dug, and I
took the waistcloth from the place
where I had hidden it. And behold,
the waistcloth was spoiled, it was good
for nothing.
8 Then the word of the LORD came
to me: ⁹ "Thus says the LORD: Even so
will I spoil the pride of Judah and the
great pride of Jerusalem. ¹⁰ This evil
people, who refuse to hear my words,
who stubbornly follow their own heart
and have gone after other gods to serve
them and worship them, shall be like
this waistcloth, which is good for
nothing. ¹¹ For as the waistcloth clings
to the loins of a man, so I made the
whole house of Israel and the whole
house of Judah cling to me, says the
LORD, that they might be for me a
people, a name, a praise, and a glory,
but they would not listen.

ᵘHeb *your*

12 "You shall speak to them this word: 'Thus says the LORD, the God of Israel, "Every jar shall be filled with wine."' And they will say to you, 'Do we not indeed know that every jar will be filled with wine?' 13 Then you shall say to them, 'Thus says the LORD: Behold, I will fill with drunkenness all the inhabitants of this land: the kings who sit on David's throne, the priests, the prophets, and all the inhabitants of Jerusalem. 14 And I will dash them one against another, fathers and sons together, says the LORD. I will not pity or spare or have compassion, that I should not destroy them.'"

15 Hear and give ear; be not proud,
   for the LORD has spoken.
16 Give glory to the LORD your God
   before he brings darkness,
   before your feet stumble
     on the twilight mountains,
   and while you look for light
    he turns it into gloom
    and makes it deep darkness.
17 But if you will not listen,
   my soul will weep in secret for
    your pride;
   my eyes will weep bitterly and run
    down with tears,
   because the LORD's flock has been
    taken captive.

18 Say to the king and the queen mother:
   "Take a lowly seat,
   for your beautiful crown
    has come down from your
    head."*v*
19 The cities of the Nĕg'ĕb are shut up,
   with none to open them;
   all Judah is taken into exile,
   wholly taken into exile.

20 "Lift up your eyes and see
   those who come from the north.
   Where is the flock that was given you,
   your beautiful flock?
21 What will you say when they set as
   head over you
    those whom you yourself have
    taught
    to be friends to you?
   Will not pangs take hold of you,
    like those of a woman in travail?
22 And if you say in your heart,
   'Why have these things come upon
    me?'
   it is for the greatness of your iniquity
    that your skirts are lifted up,

   and you suffer violence.
23 Can the Ethiopian change his skin
   or the leopard his spots?
   Then also you can do good
   who are accustomed to do evil.
24 I will scatter you*w* like chaff
   driven by the wind from the desert.
25 This is your lot,
   the portion I have measured
    out to you, says the LORD,
   because you have forgotten me
    and trusted in lies.
26 I myself will lift up your skirts over
   your face,
   and your shame will be seen.
27 I have seen your abominations,
   your adulteries and neighings,
   your lewd harlotries,
   on the hills in the field.
   Woe to you, O Jerusalem!
   How long will it be
   before you are made clean?"

14 The word of the LORD which came to Jĕr·ę·mī'ạh concerning the drought:

2 "Judah mourns
   and her gates languish;
   her people lament on the ground,
   and the cry of Jerusalem goes up.
3 Her nobles send their servants for
   water;
   they come to the cisterns,
   they find no water,
   they return with their vessels
    empty;
   they are ashamed and confounded
    and cover their heads.
4 Because of the ground which is
   dismayed,
   since there is no rain on the land
   the farmers are ashamed,
   they cover their heads.
5 Even the hind in the field forsakes
   her newborn calf
   because there is no grass.
6 The wild asses stand on the bare
   heights,
   they pant for air like jackals;
   their eyes fail
   because there is no herbage.

7 "Though our iniquities testify against
   us,
   act, O LORD, for thy name's sake;
   for our backslidings are many,
   we have sinned against thee.
8 O thou hope of Israel,
   its savior in time of trouble,

*v*Gk Syr Vg: Heb obscure   *w*Heb *them*

why shouldst thou be like a stranger
in the land,
like a wayfarer who turns aside
to tarry for a night?
⁹Why shouldst thou be like a man
confused?
like a mighty man who cannot
save?
Yet thou, O LORD, art in the midst
of us,
and we are called by thy name;
leave us not."

¹⁰Thus says the LORD concerning
this people:
"They have loved to wander thus,
they have not restrained their feet;
therefore the LORD does not accept
them,
now he will remember their iniquity
and punish their sins."

11 The LORD said to me: "Do not
pray for the welfare of this people.
¹²Though they fast, I will not hear
their cry, and though they offer burnt
offering and cereal offering, I will not
accept them; but I will consume them
by the sword, by famine, and by
pestilence."
13 Then I said: "Ah, Lord GOD,
behold, the prophets say to them,
'You shall not see the sword, nor
shall you have famine, but I will give
you assured peace in this place.'"
¹⁴And the LORD said to me: "The
prophets are prophesying lies in my
name; I did not send them, nor did I
command them or speak to them. They
are prophesying to you a lying vision,
worthless divination, and the deceit of
their own minds. ¹⁵Therefore thus says
the LORD concerning the prophets who
prophesy in my name although I did
not send them, and who say, 'Sword
and famine shall not come on this
land': By sword and famine those
prophets shall be consumed. ¹⁶And
the people to whom they prophesy
shall be cast out in the streets of
Jerusalem, victims of famine and
sword, with none to bury them—them,
their wives, their sons, and their
daughters. For I will pour out their
wickedness upon them.

⁷"You shall say to them this word:
'Let my eyes run down with tears
night and day,

and let them not cease,
for the virgin daughter of my people
is smitten with a great wound,
with a very grievous blow.
¹⁸If I go out into the field,
behold, those slain by the sword!
And if I enter the city,
behold, the diseases of famine!
For both prophet and priest ply
their trade through the land,
and have no knowledge.'"

¹⁹Hast thou utterly rejected Judah?
Does thy soul loathe Zion?
Why hast thou smitten us
so that there is no healing for us?
We looked for peace, but no good
came;
for a time of healing, but behold,
terror.
²⁰We acknowledge our wickedness,
O LORD,
and the iniquity of our fathers,
for we have sinned against thee.
²¹Do not spurn us, for thy name's sake;
do not dishonor thy glorious throne;
remember and do not break thy
covenant with us.
²²Are there any among the false gods
of the nations that can bring rain?
Or can the heavens give showers?
Art thou not he, O LORD our God?
We set our hope on thee,
for thou doest all these things.

15 Then the LORD said to me,
"Though Moses and Samuel
stood before me, yet my heart would
not turn toward this people. Send
them out of my sight, and let them go!
²And when they ask you, 'Where shall
we go?' you shall say to them, 'Thus
says the LORD:
"Those who are for pestilence, to
pestilence,
and those who are for the sword,
to the sword;
those who are for famine, to famine,
and those who are for captivity,
to captivity."'
³"I will appoint over them four kinds
of destroyers, says the LORD: the
sword to slay, the dogs to tear, and the
birds of the air and the beasts of the
earth to devour and destroy. ⁴And I will
make them a horror to all the kingdoms
of the earth because of what Ma·nas'-
seh the son of Hĕz·e·kī'ah, king of
Judah, did in Jerusalem.

14.12: Rev 6.8.
15.2: Rev 13.10.

5 "Who will have pity on you, O Jerusalem,
or who will bemoan you?
Who will turn aside
to ask about your welfare?
6 You have rejected me, says the LORD,
you keep going backward;
so I have stretched out my hand
against you and destroyed you; —
I am weary of relenting.
7 I have winnowed them with a winnowing fork
in the gates of the land;
I have bereaved them, I have destroyed my people;
they did not turn from their ways.
8 I have made their widows more in number
than the sand of the seas;
I have brought against the mothers
of young men
a destroyer at noonday;
I have made anguish and terror
fall upon them suddenly.
9 She who bore seven has languished;
she has swooned away;
her sun went down while it was yet day;
she has been shamed and disgraced.
And the rest of them I will give to the sword
before their enemies,
                says the LORD."

10 Woe is me, my mother, that you bore me, a man of strife and contention to the whole land! I have not lent, nor have I borrowed, yet all of them curse me. 11 So let it be, O LORD,*x* if I have not entreated*y* thee for their good, if I have not pleaded with thee on behalf of the enemy in the time of trouble and in the time of distress! 12 Can one break iron, iron from the north, and bronze?

13 "Your wealth and your treasures I will give as spoil, without price, for all your sins, throughout all your territory. 14 I will make you serve your enemies in a land which you do not know, for in my anger a fire is kindled which shall burn for ever."

15 O LORD, thou knowest;
remember me and visit me,
and take vengeance for me on my persecutors.
In thy forbearance take me not away;
know that for thy sake I bear reproach.

16 Thy words were found, and I ate them,
and thy words became to me a joy
and the delight of my heart;
for I am called by thy name,
O LORD, God of hosts.
17 I did not sit in the company of merrymakers,
nor did I rejoice;
I sat alone, because thy hand was upon me,
for thou hadst filled me with indignation.
18 Why is my pain unceasing,
my wound incurable,
refusing to be healed?
Wilt thou be to me like a deceitful brook,
like waters that fail?

19 Therefore thus says the LORD:
"If you return, I will restore you,
and you shall stand before me.
If you utter what is precious, and not what is worthless,
you shall be as my mouth.
They shall turn to you,
but you shall not turn to them.
20 And I will make you to this people
a fortified wall of bronze;
they will fight against you,
but they shall not prevail over you,
for I am with you
to save you and deliver you,
                says the LORD.
21 I will deliver you out of the hand of the wicked,
and redeem you from the grasp of the ruthless."

16 The word of the LORD came to me: 2 "You shall not take a wife, nor shall you have sons or daughters in this place. 3 For thus says the LORD concerning the sons and daughters who are born in this place, and concerning the mothers who bore them and the fathers who begot them in this land: 4 They shall die of deadly diseases. They shall not be lamented, nor shall they be buried; they shall be as dung on the surface of the ground. They shall perish by the sword and by famine and their dead bodies shall be food for the birds of the air and for the beasts of the earth.

5 "For thus says the LORD: Do not enter the house of mourning, or go to

*x*Gk Old Latin: Heb *the* LORD *said*   *y*Cn: Heb obscure

lament, or bemoan them; for I have taken away my peace from this people, says the LORD, my steadfast love and mercy. 6 Both great and small shall die in this land; they shall not be buried, and no one shall lament for them or cut himself or make himself bald for them. 7 No one shall break bread for the mourner, to comfort him for the dead; nor shall any one give him the cup of consolation to drink for his father or his mother. 8 You shall not go into the house of feasting to sit with them, to eat and drink. 9 For thus says the LORD of hosts, the God of Israel: Behold, I will make to cease from this place, before your eyes and in your days, the voice of mirth and the voice of gladness, the voice of the bridegroom and the voice of the bride.

10 "And when you tell this people all these words, and they say to you, 'Why has the LORD pronounced all this great evil against us? What is our iniquity? What is the sin that we have committed against the LORD our God?' 11 then you shall say to them: 'Because your fathers have forsaken me, says the LORD, and have gone after other gods and have served and worshiped them, and have forsaken me and have not kept my law, 12 and because you have done worse than your fathers, for behold, every one of you follows his stubborn evil will, refusing to listen to me; 13 therefore I will hurl you out of this land into a land which neither you nor your fathers have known, and there you shall serve other gods day and night, for I will show you no favor.'

14 "Therefore, behold, the days are coming, says the LORD, when it shall no longer be said, 'As the LORD lives who brought up the people of Israel out of the land of Egypt,' 15 but 'As the LORD lives who brought up the people of Israel out of the north country and out of all the countries where he had driven them.' For I will bring them back to their own land which I gave to their fathers.

16 "Behold, I am sending for many fishers, says the LORD, and they shall catch them; and afterwards I will send for many hunters, and they shall hunt them from every mountain and every hill, and out of the clefts of the rocks. 17 For my eyes are upon all

their ways; they are not hid from me, nor is their iniquity concealed from my eyes. 18 And ^{z} I will doubly recompense their iniquity and their sin, because they have polluted my land with the carcasses of their detestable idols, and have filled my inheritance with their abominations."

19 O LORD, my strength and my stronghold,
    my refuge in the day of trouble,
to thee shall the nations come
    from the ends of the earth and say:
"Our fathers have inherited nought
    but lies,
worthless things in which there is
    no profit.
20 Can man make for himself gods?
    Such are no gods!"

21 "Therefore, behold, I will make them know, this once I will make them know my power and my might, and they shall know that my name is the LORD."

17 "The sin of Judah is written with a pen of iron; with a point of diamond it is engraved on the tablet of their heart, and on the horns of their altars, 2 while their children remember their altars and their A·shē'rǐm, beside every green tree, and on the high hills, 3 on the mountains in the open country. Your wealth and all your treasures I will give for spoil as the price of your sin^a throughout all your territory. 4 You shall loosen your hand^b from your heritage which I gave to you, and I will make you serve your enemies in a land which you do not know, for in my anger a fire is kindled which shall burn for ever."

5 Thus says the LORD:
"Cursed is the man who trusts in
    man
    and makes flesh his arm,
    whose heart turns away from the
       LORD.
6 He is like a shrub in the desert,
    and shall not see any good
       come.
He shall dwell in the parched places
    of the wilderness,
    in an uninhabited salt land.

^{z}Gk: Heb *And first.* ^{a}Cn: Heb *your high places for sin*
^{b}Cn: Heb *and in you*
16.9: Jer 7.34; 25.10; Rev 18.23.

7 "Blessed is the man who trusts in
the LORD,
whose trust is the LORD.
8 He is like a tree planted by water,
that sends out its roots by the
stream,
and does not fear when heat comes,
for its leaves remain green,
and is not anxious in the year of
drought,
for it does not cease to bear fruit."

9 The heart is deceitful above all
things,
and desperately corrupt;
who can understand it?
10 "I the LORD search the mind
and try the heart,
to give to every man according to his
ways,
according to the fruit of his
doings."

11 Like the partridge that gathers a
brood which she did not hatch,
so is he who gets riches but not by
right;
in the midst of his days they will
leave him,
and at his end he will be a fool.

12 A glorious throne set on high from
the beginning
is the place of our sanctuary.
13 O LORD, the hope of Israel,
all who forsake thee shall be put
to shame;
those who turn away from thee *c*
shall be written in the earth,
for they have forsaken the LORD,
the fountain of living water.

14 Heal me, O LORD, and I shall be
healed;
save me, and I shall be saved;
for thou art my praise.
15 Behold, they say to me,
"Where is the word of the LORD?
Let it come!"
16 I have not pressed thee to send evil,
nor have I desired the day of
disaster,
thou knowest;
that which came out of my lips
was before thy face.
17 Be not a terror to me;
thou art my refuge in the day of
evil.
18 Let those be put to shame who persecute me,

but let me not be put to shame;
let them be dismayed,
but let me not be dismayed;
bring upon them the day of evil,
destroy them with double destruction!

19 Thus said the LORD to me: "Go
and stand in the Benjamin *d* Gate,
by which the kings of Judah enter and
by which they go out, and in all the
gates of Jerusalem, 20 and say: 'Hear
the word of the LORD, you kings of
Judah, and all Judah, and all the
inhabitants of Jerusalem, who enter by
these gates. 21 Thus says the LORD:
Take heed for the sake of your lives,
and do not bear a burden on the
sabbath day or bring it in by the gates
of Jerusalem. 22 And do not carry a
burden out of your houses on the sabbath or do any work, but keep the sabbath day holy, as I commanded your
fathers. 23 Yet they did not listen or
incline their ear, but stiffened their
neck, that they might not hear and
receive instruction.

24 "'But if you listen to me, says
the LORD, and bring in no burden by
the gates of this city on the sabbath
day, but keep the sabbath day holy and
do no work on it, 25 then there shall
enter by the gates of this city kings *e*
who sit on the throne of David, riding
in chariots and on horses, they and
their princes, the men of Judah and
the inhabitants of Jerusalem; and
this city shall be inhabited for ever.
26 And people shall come from the cities
of Judah and the places round about
Jerusalem, from the land of Benjamin,
from the Shĕ·phē'lah, from the hill
country, and from the Nĕg'ĕb, bringing burnt offerings and sacrifices,
cereal offerings and frankincense,
and bringing thank offerings to the
house of the LORD. 27 But if you do not
listen to me, to keep the sabbath day
holy, and not to bear a burden and
enter by the gates of Jerusalem on the
sabbath day, then I will kindle a fire
in its gates, and it shall devour the
palaces of Jerusalem and shall not
be quenched.'"

18 The word that came to Jĕr·e-
mī'ah from the LORD: 2 "Arise,

---

c Heb *me*   *d* Cn: Heb *sons of people*
e Cn: Heb *kings and princes*
17.7-8: Ps 1.1-3.   17.10: Ps 62.12; Rev 2.23; 22.12.

and go down to the potter's house, and there I will let you hear my words." ³ So I went down to the potter's house, and there he was working at his wheel. ⁴ And the vessel he was making of clay was spoiled in the potter's hand, and he reworked it into another vessel, as it seemed good to the potter to do.

5 Then the word of the LORD came to me: ⁶ "O house of Israel, can I not do with you as this potter has done? says the LORD. Behold, like the clay in the potter's hand, so are you in my hand, O house of Israel. ⁷ If at any time I declare concerning a nation or a kingdom, that I will pluck up and break down and destroy it, ⁸ and if that nation, concerning which I have spoken, turns from its evil, I will repent of the evil that I intended to do to it. ⁹ And if at any time I declare concerning a nation or a kingdom that I will build and plant it, ¹⁰ and if it does evil in my sight, not listening to my voice, then I will repent of the good which I had intended to do to it. ¹¹ Now, therefore, say to the men of Judah and the inhabitants of Jerusalem: 'Thus says the LORD, Behold, I am shaping evil against you and devising a plan against you. Return, every one from his evil way, and amend your ways and your doings.' 12 "But they say, 'That is in vain! We will follow our own plans, and will every one act according to the stubbornness of his evil heart.'

¹³ "Therefore thus says the LORD:
Ask among the nations,
  who has heard the like of this?
The virgin Israel
  has done a very horrible thing.
¹⁴ Does the snow of Lebanon leave
  the crags of Sīr′ī·on?ᶠ
Do the mountainᵍ waters run dry,ʰ
  the cold flowing streams?
¹⁵ But my people have forgotten me,
  they burn incense to false gods;
they have stumbledⁱ in their ways,
  in the ancient roads,
and have gone into bypaths,
  not the highway,
¹⁶ making their land a horror,
  a thing to be hissed at for ever.
Every one who passes by it is horrified
  and shakes his head.
¹⁷ Like the east wind I will scatter them
  before the enemy.

I will show them my back, not my face,
  in the day of their calamity."

18 Then they said, "Come, let us make plots against Jĕr·ĕ·mī′ah, for the law shall not perish from the priest, nor counsel from the wise, nor the word from the prophet. Come, let us smite him with the tongue, and let us not heed any of his words."

¹⁹ Give heed to me, O LORD,
  and hearken to my plea.ʲ
²⁰ Is evil a recompense for good?
  Yet they have dug a pit for my life.
Remember how I stood before thee
  to speak good for them,
  to turn away thy wrath from them.
²¹ Therefore deliver up their children
  to famine;
give them over to the power of
  the sword,
let their wives become childless and
  widowed.
May their men meet death by
  pestilence,
  their youths be slain by the sword
  in battle.
²² May a cry be heard from their houses,
  when thou bringest the marauder
  suddenly upon them!
For they have dug a pit to take me,
  and laid snares for my feet.
²³ Yet, thou, O LORD, knowest
  all their plotting to slay me.
Forgive not their iniquity,
  nor blot out their sin from thy sight.
Let them be overthrown before thee;
  deal with them in the time of thine
  anger.

19 Thus said the LORD, "Go, buy a potter's earthen flask, and take some of the elders of the people and some of the senior priests, ² and go out to the valley of the son of Hĭn′nom at the entry of the Potsherd Gate, and proclaim there the words that I tell you. ³ You shall say, 'Hear the word of the LORD, O kings of Judah and inhabitants of Jerusalem. Thus says the LORD of hosts, the God of Israel, Behold, I am bringing such evil upon this place that the ears of every one who hears of it will tingle.

ᶠ Cn: Heb *the field*   ᵍ Cn: Heb *foreign*
ʰ Cn: Heb *Are ... plucked up?*
ⁱ Gk Syr Vg: Heb *they made them stumble*
ʲ Gk Compare Syr Tg: Heb *my adversaries*
18.6: Rom 9.21.

⁴Because the people have forsaken me, and have profaned this place by burning incense in it to other gods whom neither they nor their fathers nor the kings of Judah have known; and because they have filled this place with the blood of innocents, ⁵and have built the high places of Bā'al to burn their sons in the fire as burnt offerings to Baal, which I did not command or decree, nor did it come into my mind; ⁶therefore, behold, days are coming, says the LORD, when this place shall no more be called Tō'phĕth, or the valley of the son of Hĭn'nom, but the valley of Slaughter. ⁷And in this place I will make void the plans of Judah and Jerusalem, and will cause their people to fall by the sword before their enemies, and by the hand of those who seek their life. I will give their dead bodies for food to the birds of the air and to the beasts of the earth. ⁸And I will make this city a horror, a thing to be hissed at; every one who passes by it will be horrified and will hiss because of all its disasters. ⁹And I will make them eat the flesh of their sons and their daughters, and every one shall eat the flesh of his neighbor in the siege and in the distress, with which their enemies and those who seek their life afflict them.'

10 "Then you shall break the flask in the sight of the men who go with you, ¹¹and shall say to them, 'Thus says the LORD of hosts: So will I break this people and this city, as one breaks a potter's vessel, so that it can never be mended. Men shall bury in Tō'phĕth because there will be no place else to bury. ¹²Thus will I do to this place, says the LORD, and to its inhabitants, making this city like Tō'phĕth. ¹³The houses of Jerusalem and the houses of the kings of Judah—all the houses upon whose roofs incense has been burned to all the host of heaven, and drink offerings have been poured out to other gods—shall be defiled like the place of Tō'phĕth.' "

14 Then Jĕr-e-mī'ah came from Tō'phĕth, where the LORD had sent him to prophesy, and he stood in the court of the LORD's house, and said to all the people: ¹⁵"Thus says the LORD of hosts, the God of Israel, Behold, I am bringing upon this city and upon all its towns all the evil that I have pronounced against it, because they have

stiffened their neck, refusing to hear my words."

20 Now Păsh'hŭr the priest, the son of Ĭm'mer, who was chief officer in the house of the LORD, heard Jĕr-e-mī'ah prophesying these things. ²Then Păsh'hŭr beat Jĕr-e-mī'ah the prophet, and put him in the stocks that were in the upper Benjamin Gate of the house of the LORD. ³On the morrow, when Păsh'hŭr released Jĕr-e-mī'ah from the stocks, Jeremiah said to him, "The LORD does not call your name Pashhur, but Terror on every side. ⁴For thus says the LORD: Behold, I will make you a terror to yourself and to all your friends. They shall fall by the sword of their enemies while you look on. And I will give all Judah into the hand of the king of Babylon; he shall carry them captive to Babylon, and shall slay them with the sword. ⁵Moreover, I will give all the wealth of the city, all its gains, all its prized belongings, and all the treasures of the kings of Judah into the hand of their enemies, who shall plunder them, and seize them, and carry them to Babylon. ⁶And you, Păsh'hŭr, and all who dwell in your house, shall go into captivity; to Babylon you shall go; and there you shall die, and there you shall be buried, you and all your friends, to whom you have prophesied falsely."

⁷O LORD, thou hast deceived me,
    and I was deceived;
thou art stronger than I,
    and thou hast prevailed.
I have become a laughingstock all
    the day;
    every one mocks me.
⁸For whenever I speak, I cry out,
    I shout, "Violence and destruction!"
For the word of the LORD has become
    for me
    a reproach and derision all day
    long.
⁹If I say, "I will not mention him,
    or speak any more in his name,'
there is in my heart as it were a
    burning fire
shut up in my bones,
    and I am weary with holding it in,
    and I cannot.
¹⁰For I hear many whispering.
    Terror is on every side!

19.13: Acts 7.42.
20.3, 10: Jer 6.25; 46.5; 49.29; Ps 31.13.

"Denounce him! Let us denounce
  him!"
say all my familiar friends,
  watching for my fall.
"Perhaps he will be deceived,
  then we can overcome him,
  and take our revenge on him."
[11] But the LORD is with me as a dread
    warrior;
  therefore my persecutors will
    stumble,
  they will not overcome me.
They will be greatly shamed,
  for they will not succeed.
Their eternal dishonor
  will never be forgotten.
[12] O LORD of hosts, who triest the
    righteous,
  who seest the heart and the mind,
let me see thy vengeance upon them,
  for to thee have I committed my
    cause.

[13] Sing to the LORD;
  praise the LORD!
For he has delivered the life of the
    needy
  from the hand of evildoers.

[14] Cursed be the day
  on which I was born!
The day when my mother bore me,
  let it not be blessed!
[15] Cursed be the man
  who brought the news to my
    father,
"A son is born to you,"
  making him very glad.
[16] Let that man be like the cities
  which the LORD overthrew without
    pity;
let him hear a cry in the morning
  and an alarm at noon,
[17] because he did not kill me in the
    womb;
  so my mother would have been
    my grave,
  and her womb for ever great.
[18] Why did I come forth from the womb
  to see toil and sorrow,
  and spend my days in shame?

21 This is the word which came to
    Jeremiah from the LORD, when
King Zĕd·ḛ·kī′aḥ sent to him Păsh′-
hŭr the son of Măl·chī′aḥ and Zĕph-
a·nī′ah the priest, the son of Mā–a-
sēi′ah, saying, [2] "Inquire of the LORD
for us, for Nĕ·bü·chạd·rĕz′zạr king of
Babylon is making war against us;
perhaps the LORD will deal with us ac-

cording to all his wonderful deeds, and
will make him withdraw from us."
[3] Then Jĕr·ḛ·mī′aḥ said to them:
[4] "Thus you shall say to Zĕd·ḛ·kī′aḥ,
'Thus says the LORD, the God of Israel:
Behold, I will turn back the weapons of
war which are in your hands and with
which you are fighting against the king
of Babylon and against the Chăl-
dē′aṇṣ who are besieging you outside
the walls; and I will bring them together into the midst of this city.
[5] I myself will fight against you with
outstretched hand and strong arm, in
anger, and in fury, and in great wrath.
[6] And I will smite the inhabitants of
this city, both man and beast; they
shall die of a great pestilence. [7] Afterward, says the LORD, I will give Zĕd-
ḛ·kī′aḥ king of Judah, and his servants,
and the people in this city who survive the pestilence, sword, and famine,
into the hand of Nĕ·bü·chạd·rĕz′zạr
king of Babylon and into the hand of
their enemies, into the hand of those
who seek their lives. He shall smite
them with the edge of the sword; he
shall not pity them, or spare them, or
have compassion.'

8 "And to this people you shall say:
'Thus says the LORD: Behold, I set before you the way of life and the way of
death. [9] He who stays in this city shall
die by the sword, by famine, and by
pestilence; but he who goes out and
surrenders to the Chăl·dē′aṇṣ who are
besieging you shall live and shall have
his life as a prize of war. [10] For I have
set my face against this city for evil
and not for good, says the LORD: it
shall be given into the hand of the king
of Babylon, and he shall burn it with
fire.'

11 "And to the house of the king of
Judah say, 'Hear the word of the LORD,
[12] O house of David! Thus says the
LORD:
" 'Execute justice in the morning,
  and deliver from the hand of the
    oppressor
  him who has been robbed,
lest my wrath go forth like fire,
  and burn with none to quench it,
  because of your evil doings.' "

[13] "Behold, I am against you, O inhabit-
    ant of the valley,
  O rock of the plain,
        says the LORD;

20.14–18: Job 3.3–13.

you who say, 'Who shall come down
against us,
or who shall enter our habitations?'
¹⁴I will punish you according to the
fruit of your doings,
says the LORD;
I will kindle a fire in her forest,
and it shall devour all that is round
about her.''

22 Thus says the LORD: "Go down
to the house of the king of
Judah, and speak there this word,
²and say, 'Hear the word of the LORD,
O King of Judah, who sit on the throne
of David, you, and your servants, and
your people who enter these gates.
³Thus says the LORD: Do justice and
righteousness, and deliver from the
hand of the oppressor him who has
been robbed. And do no wrong or violence to the alien, the fatherless, and
the widow, nor shed innocent blood
in this place. ⁴For if you will indeed
obey this word, then there shall enter
the gates of this house kings who sit
on the throne of David, riding in chariots and on horses, they, and their
servants, and their people. ⁵But if
you will not heed these words, I swear
by myself, says the LORD, that this
house shall become a desolation. ⁶For
thus says the LORD concerning the
house of the king of Judah:
" 'You are as Gilead to me,
as the summit of Lebanon,
yet surely I will make you a desert,
an uninhabited city.ᵏ
⁷I will prepare destroyers against
you,
each with his weapons;
and they shall cut down your choicest
cedars,
and cast them into the fire.
8 " 'And many nations will pass by
this city, and every man will say to his
neighbor, "Why has the LORD dealt
thus with this great city?" ⁹And they
will answer, "Because they forsook
the covenant of the LORD their God,
and worshiped other gods and served
them." ' "

¹⁰Weep not for him who is dead,
nor bemoan him;
but weep bitterly for him who goes
away,
for he shall return no more
to see his native land.

11 For thus says the LORD concerning Shăl'lum the son of Jō·sī'-
ah, king of Judah, who reigned instead
of Josiah his father, and who went
away from this place: "He shall return
here no more, ¹²but in the place where
they have carried him captive, there
shall he die, and he shall never see
this land again.''

¹³"Woe to him who builds his house
by unrighteousness,
and his upper rooms by injustice;
who makes his neighbor serve him
for nothing,
and does not give him his wages;
¹⁴who says, 'I will build myself a great
house
with spacious upper rooms,'
and cuts out windows for it,
paneling it with cedar,
and painting it with vermilion.
¹⁵Do you think you are a king
because you compete in cedar?
Did not your father eat and drink
and do justice and righteousness?
Then it was well with him.
¹⁶He judged the cause of the poor
and needy;
then it was well.
Is not this to know me?
says the LORD.
¹⁷But you have eyes and heart
only for your dishonest gain,
for shedding innocent blood,
and for practicing oppression and
violence.''
18 Therefore thus says the LORD
concerning Jĕ·hoi'a·kim the son of
Jō·sī'ah, king of Judah:
"They shall not lament for him,
saying,
'Ah my brother!' or 'Ah sister!'
They shall not lament for him,
saying,
'Ah lord!' or 'Ah his majesty!'
¹⁹With the burial of an ass he shall be
buried,
dragged and cast forth beyond the
gates of Jerusalem.''

²⁰"Go up to Lebanon, and cry out,
and lift up your voice in Bā'shan;
cry from Ăb'a·rĭm,
for all your lovers are destroyed.
²¹I spoke to you in your prosperity,
but you said, 'I will not listen.'
This has been your way from your
youth,

ᵏCn: Heb *cities* **22.5:** Mt 23.38; Lk 13.35.

that you have not obeyed my voice.
²²The wind shall shepherd all your shepherds,
and your lovers shall go into captivity;
then you will be ashamed and confounded
because of all your wickedness.
²³O inhabitant of Lebanon,
nested among the cedars,
how you will groan*ˡ* when pangs come upon you,
pain as of a woman in travail!"

24 "As I live, says the LORD, though Cō·nī'ạh the son of Jĕ·hoi'ạ·kịm, king of Judah, were the signet ring on my right hand, yet I would tear you off ²⁵and give you into the hand of those who seek your life, into the hand of those of whom you are afraid, even into the hand of Nĕ·bü·chạd·rĕz'zạr king of Babylon and into the hand of the Chăl·dē'ạnṣ. ²⁶I will hurl you and the mother who bore you into another country, where you were not born, and there you shall die. ²⁷But to the land to which they will long to return, there they shall not return."
²⁸Is this man Cō·nī'ạh a despised, broken pot,
a vessel no one cares for?
Why are he and his children hurled and cast
into a land which they do not know?
²⁹O land, land, land,
hear the word of the LORD!
³⁰Thus says the LORD:
"Write this man down as childless,
a man who shall not succeed in his days;
for none of his offspring shall succeed
in sitting on the throne of David,
and ruling again in Judah."

23 "Woe to the shepherds who destroy and scatter the sheep of my pasture!" says the LORD. ²Therefore thus says the LORD, the God of Israel, concerning the shepherds who care for my people: "You have scattered my flock, and have driven them away, and you have not attended to them. Behold, I will attend to you for your evil doings, says the LORD. ³Then I will gather the remnant of my flock out of all the countries where I have

driven them, and I will bring them back to their fold, and they shall be fruitful and multiply. ⁴I will set shepherds over them who will care for them, and they shall fear no more, nor be dismayed, neither shall any be missing, says the LORD.
5 "Behold, the days are coming, says the LORD, when I will raise up for David a righteous Branch, and he shall reign as king and deal wisely, and shall execute justice and righteousness in the land. ⁶In his days Judah will be saved, and Israel will dwell securely. And this is the name by which he will be called: 'The LORD is our righteousness.'
7 "Therefore, behold, the days are coming, says the LORD, when men shall no longer say, 'As the LORD lives who brought up the people of Israel out of the land of Egypt,' ⁸but 'As the LORD lives who brought up and led the descendants of the house of Israel out of the north country and out of all the countries where he*ᵐ* had driven them.' Then they shall dwell in their own land."

9 Concerning the prophets:
My heart is broken within me,
all my bones shake;
I am like a drunken man,
like a man overcome by wine,
because of the LORD
and because of his holy words.
¹⁰For the land is full of adulterers;
because of the curse the land mourns,
and the pastures of the wilderness are dried up.
Their course is evil,
and their might is not right.
¹¹"Both prophet and priest are ungodly;
even in my house I have found their wickedness,
says the LORD.
¹²Therefore their way shall be to them like slippery paths in the darkness,
into which they shall be driven and fall;
for I will bring evil upon them
in the year of their punishment,
says the LORD.
¹³In the prophets of Sạ·mâr'ĭ·ạ
I saw an unsavory thing:

---

*ˡ*Gk Vg Syr: Heb *be pitied*   *ᵐ*Gk: Heb *I*
23.5: Jer 33.15; Is 4.2; Zech 3.8; 6.12.

they prophesied by Bā'al
and led my people Israel astray.
¹⁴But in the prophets of Jerusalem
I have seen a horrible thing:
they commit adultery and walk in
lies;
they strengthen the hands of
evildoers,
so that no one turns from his
wickedness;
all of them have become like Sŏd'ǫm
to me,
and its inhabitants like Gǫ·môr'-
rah."
¹⁵Therefore thus says the LORD of
hosts concerning the prophets:
"Behold, I will feed them with wormwood,
and give them poisoned water to
drink;
for from the prophets of Jerusalem
ungodliness has gone forth into
all the land."

16 Thus says the LORD of hosts:
"Do not listen to the words of the
prophets who prophesy to you, filling
you with vain hopes; they speak visions of their own minds, not from the
mouth of the LORD. ¹⁷They say continually to those who despise the word of
the LORD, 'It shall be well with you';
and to every one who stubbornly follows his own heart, they say, 'No evil
shall come upon you.'"

¹⁸For who among them has stood in
the council of the LORD
to perceive and to hear his word,
or who has given heed to his word
and listened?
¹⁹Behold, the storm of the LORD!
Wrath has gone forth,
a whirling tempest;
it will burst upon the head of the
wicked.
²⁰The anger of the LORD will not turn
back
until he has executed and accomplished
the intents of his mind.
In the latter days you will understand
it clearly.

²¹"I did not send the prophets,
yet they ran;
I did not speak to them,
yet they prophesied.
²²But if they had stood in my coun-
cil,

then they would have proclaimed
my words to my people,
and they would have turned them
from their evil way,
and from the evil of their doings.

23 "Am I a God at hand, says the
LORD, and not a God afar off? ²⁴Can
a man hide himself in secret places so
that I cannot see him? says the LORD.
Do I not fill heaven and earth? says the
LORD. ²⁵I have heard what the prophets
have said who prophesy lies in my
name, saying, 'I have dreamed, I have
dreamed!' ²⁶How long shall there be
lies[n] in the heart of the prophets who
prophesy lies, and who prophesy the
deceit of their own heart, ²⁷who think
to make my people forget my name
by their dreams which they tell one
another, even as their fathers forgot
my name for Bā'al? ²⁸Let the prophet
who has a dream tell the dream, but
let him who has my word speak my
word faithfully. What has straw in
common with wheat? says the LORD.
²⁹Is not my word like fire, says the
LORD, and like a hammer which breaks
the rock in pieces? ³⁰Therefore, behold, I am against the prophets, says
the LORD, who steal my words from one
another. ³¹Behold, I am against the
prophets, says the LORD, who use their
tongues and say, 'Says the LORD.'
³²Behold, I am against those who
prophesy lying dreams, says the LORD,
and who tell them and lead my people
astray by their lies and their reckless-
ness, when I did not send them or
charge them; so they do not profit this
people at all, says the LORD.

33 "When one of this people, or
a prophet, or a priest asks you, 'What
is the burden of the LORD?' you shall
say to them, 'You are the burden,[o]
and I will cast you off, says the LORD.'
³⁴And as for the prophet, priest, or one
of the people who says, 'The burden of
the LORD,' I will punish that man and
his household. ³⁵Thus shall you say,
every one to his neighbor and every
one to his brother, 'What has the LORD
answered?' or 'What has the LORD
spoken?' ³⁶But 'the burden of the LORD'
you shall mention no more, for the
burden is every man's own word,
and you pervert the words of the living
God, the LORD of hosts, our God. ³⁷Thus

ⁿCn Compare Syr: Heb obscure
^oGk Vg: Heb *What burden*

you shall say to the prophet, 'What has
the LORD answered you?' or 'What has
the LORD spoken?' 38 But if you say,
'The burden of the LORD,' thus says the
LORD, 'Because you have said these
words, "The burden of the LORD,"
when I sent to you, saying, "You shall
not say, 'The burden of the LORD,'"
39 therefore, behold, I will surely lift
you up and cast you away from my
presence, you and the city which I
gave to you and your fathers. 40 And I
will bring upon you everlasting reproach and perpetual shame, which
shall not be forgotten.'"

24 After Nĕ·bü·chạd·rĕz′zạr king
of Babylon had taken into exile
from Jerusalem Jĕc·ọ·nī′ạh the son of
Jĕ·hoi′ạ·kịm, king of Judah, together
with the princes of Judah, the craftsmen, and the smiths, and had brought
them to Babylon, the LORD showed me
this vision: Behold, two baskets of figs
placed before the temple of the LORD.
2 One basket had very good figs, like
first-ripe figs, but the other basket had
very bad figs, so bad that they could not
be eaten. 3 And the LORD said to me,
"What do you see, Jĕr·ẹ·mī′ạh?" I said,
"Figs, the good figs very good, and the
bad figs very bad, so bad that they cannot be eaten."
4 Then the word of the LORD came
to me: 5 "Thus says the LORD, the God
of Israel: Like these good figs, so I will
regard as good the exiles from Judah,
whom I have sent away from this place
to the land of the Chăl·dē′ạnș. 6 I will
set my eyes upon them for good, and
I will bring them back to this land. I
will build them up, and not tear them
down; I will plant them, and not uproot them. 7 I will give them a heart to
know that I am the LORD; and they
shall be my people and I will be their
God, for they shall return to me with
their whole heart.
8 "But thus says the LORD: Like the
bad figs which are so bad they cannot
be eaten, so will I treat Zĕd·ẹ·kī′ạh
the king of Judah, his princes, the remnant of Jerusalem who remain in this
land, and those who dwell in the
land of Egypt. 9 I will make them a horror[p] to all the kingdoms of the earth,
to be a reproach, a byword, a taunt, and
a curse in all the places where I shall
drive them. 10 And I will send sword,
famine, and pestilence upon them,
until they shall be utterly destroyed
from the land which I gave to them
and their fathers."

25 The word that came to Jĕr·ẹ-
mī′ạh concerning all the people
of Judah, in the fourth year of Jĕ-
hoi′ạ·kịm the son of Jō·sī′ạh, king of
Judah (that was the first year of Nĕ-
bü·chạd·rĕz′zạr king of Babylon),
2 which Jĕr·ẹ·mī′ạh the prophet spoke to
all the people of Judah and all the inhabitants of Jerusalem: 3 "For twenty-
three years, from the thirteenth year
of Jō·sī′ạh the son of Ā′mŏn, king of
Judah, to this day, the word of the
LORD has come to me, and I have
spoken persistently to you, but you
have not listened. 4 You have neither
listened nor inclined your ears to hear,
although the LORD persistently sent to
you all his servants the prophets, 5 saying, 'Turn now, every one of you, from
his evil way and wrong doings, and
dwell upon the land which the LORD
has given to you and your fathers from
of old and for ever; 6 do not go after
other gods to serve and worship
them, or provoke me to anger with
the work of your hands. Then I will
do you no harm.' 7 Yet you have not
listened to me, says the LORD, that
you might provoke me to anger with
the work of your hands to your own
harm.
8 "Therefore thus says the LORD of
hosts: Because you have not obeyed
my words, 9 behold, I will send for all
the tribes of the north, says the LORD,
and for Nĕ·bü·chạd·rĕz′zạr the king
of Babylon, my servant, and I will
bring them against this land and its
inhabitants, and against all these
nations round about; I will utterly
destroy them, and make them a horror,
a hissing, and an everlasting reproach.[q] 10 Moreover, I will banish from
them the voice of mirth and the voice
of gladness, the voice of the bridegroom and the voice of the bride, the
grinding of the millstones and the light
of the lamp. 11 This whole land shall
become a ruin and a waste, and these
nations shall serve the king of Babylon
seventy years. 12 Then after seventy
years are completed, I will punish the
king of Babylon and that nation, the

[p] Compare Gk: Heb *horror for evil*
[q] Gk Compare Syr: Heb *desolations*
25.10: Jer 7.34; 16.9; Rev 18.23.

land of the Chăl·dē′ąns̩, for their
iniquity, says the LORD, making the
land an everlasting waste. ¹³I will
bring upon that land all the words
which I have uttered against it, everything written in this book which Jĕr·ẹ-
mī′ah prophesied against all the nations. ¹⁴For many nations and great
kings shall make slaves even of them;
and I will recompense them according
to their deeds and the work of their
hands."

15 Thus the LORD, the God of Israel, said to me: "Take from my hand
this cup of the wine of wrath, and
make all the nations to whom I send
you drink it. ¹⁶They shall drink and
stagger and be crazed because of the
sword which I am sending among
them."

17 So I took the cup from the LORD's
hand, and made all the nations to
whom the LORD sent me drink it:
¹⁸Jerusalem and the cities of Judah,
its kings and princes, to make them a
desolation and a waste, a hissing and
a curse, as at this day; ¹⁹Pharaoh king
of Egypt, his servants, his princes, all
his people, ²⁰and all the foreign folk
among them; all the kings of the land
of Ŭz and all the kings of the land of
the Phĭ·lĭs′tĭnes (Ăsh′kẹ·lŏn, Gā′za,
Ĕk′rọn, and the remnant of Ăsh′dŏd);
²¹Ē′dọm, Mō′ăb, and the sons of
Ăm′mọn; ²²all the kings of Tȳre, all
the kings of Sī′dŏn, and the kings of
the coastland across the sea; ²³Dē′dăn,
Tē′mạ, Bŭz, and all who cut the
corners of their hair; ²⁴all the kings of
Arabia and all the kings of the mixed
tribes that dwell in the desert; ²⁵all
the kings of Zĭm′rī, all the kings of
Ē′lăm, and all the kings of Mēd′ī·ạ;
²⁶all the kings of the north, far and
near, one after another, and all the
kingdoms of the world which are on
the face of the earth. And after them
the king of Babylon* shall drink.

27 "Then you shall say to them,
'Thus says the LORD of hosts, the God
of Israel: Drink, be drunk and vomit,
fall and rise no more, because of
the sword which I am sending among
you.'

28 "And if they refuse to accept the
cup from your hand to drink, then you
shall say to them, 'Thus says the LORD
of hosts: You must drink! ²⁹For behold,
I begin to work evil at the city which
is called by my name, and shall you

go unpunished? You shall not go
unpunished, for I am summoning a
sword against all the inhabitants of
the earth, says the LORD of hosts.'

30 "You, therefore, shall prophesy
against them all these words, and say
to them:
'The LORD will roar from on high,
   and from his holy habitation utter
    his voice;
he will roar mightily against his fold,
   and shout, like those who tread
    grapes,
against all the inhabitants of the
   earth.
³¹The clamor will resound to the ends
   of the earth,
for the LORD has an indictment
   against the nations;
he is entering into judgment with
   all flesh,
   and the wicked he will put to the
    sword,
           says the LORD.'

³²"Thus says the LORD of hosts:
Behold, evil is going forth
   from nation to nation,
and a great tempest is stirring
   from the farthest parts of the
    earth!

33 "And those slain by the LORD
on that day shall extend from one end
of the earth to the other. They shall
not be lamented, or gathered, or
buried; they shall be dung on the
surface of the ground.
³⁴"Wail, you shepherds, and cry,
   and roll in ashes, you lords of the
    flock,
for the days of your slaughter and
   dispersion have come,
   and you shall fall like choice
    rams.*
³⁵No refuge will remain for the shepherds,
   nor escape for the lords of the
    flock.
³⁶Hark, the cry of the shepherds,
   and the wail of the lords of the
    flock!
For the LORD is despoiling their
   pasture,
³⁷ and the peaceful folds are devastated,
   because of the fierce anger of the
    LORD.

ʳHeb *Sheshach*, a cipher for Babylon
ˢGk: Heb *a choice vessel*
25.15: Jer 51.7; Rev 14.8, 10; 16.19; 17.4; 18.3.

³⁸ Like a lion he has left his covert,
for their land has become a waste
because of the sword of the oppressor,
and because of his fierce anger."

26 In the beginning of the reign of Jĕ·hoi′a·kim the son of Jō-sī′ah, king of Judah, this word came from the LORD, ² "Thus says the LORD: Stand in the court of the LORD's house, and speak to all the cities of Judah which come to worship in the house of the LORD all the words that I command you to speak to them; do not hold back a word. ³ It may be they will listen, and every one turn from his evil way, that I may repent of the evil which I intend to do to them because of their evil doings. ⁴ You shall say to them, 'Thus says the LORD: If you will not listen to me, to walk in my law which I have set before you, ⁵ and to heed the words of my servants the prophets whom I send to you urgently, though you have not heeded, ⁶ then I will make this house like Shī′lōh, and I will make this city a curse for all the nations of the earth.' "

7 The priests and the prophets and all the people heard Jĕr·e·mī′ah speaking these words in the house of the LORD. ⁸ And when Jĕr·e·mī′ah had finished speaking all that the LORD had commanded him to speak to all the people, then the priests and the prophets and all the people laid hold of him, saying, "You shall die! ⁹ Why have you prophesied in the name of the LORD, saying, 'This house shall be like Shī′-ōh, and this city shall be desolate, without inhabitant'?" And all the people gathered about Jĕr·e·mī′ah in the house of the LORD.

10 When the princes of Judah heard these things, they came up from the king's house to the house of the LORD and took their seat in the entry of the New Gate of the house of the LORD. ¹¹ Then the priests and the prophets said to the princes and to all the people, "This man deserves the sentence of death, because he has prophesied against this city, as you have heard with your own ears."

12 Then Jĕr·e·mī′ah spoke to all the princes and all the people, saying, "The LORD sent me to prophesy against this house and this city all the words you have heard. ¹³ Now therefore amend your ways and your doings, and obey the voice of the LORD your God, and the LORD will repent of the evil which he has pronounced against you. ¹⁴ But as for me, behold, I am in your hands. Do with me as seems good and right to you. ¹⁵ Only know for certain that if you put me to death, you will bring innocent blood upon yourselves and upon this city and its inhabitants, for in truth the LORD sent me to you to speak all these words in your ears."

16 Then the princes and all the people said to the priests and the prophets, "This man does not deserve the sentence of death, for he has spoken to us in the name of the LORD our God." ¹⁷ And certain of the elders of the land arose and spoke to all the assembled people, saying, ¹⁸ "Mī′cah of Mō′re·shĕth prophesied in the days of Hĕz·e·kī′ah king of Judah, and said to all the people of Judah: 'Thus says the LORD of hosts,

Zion shall be plowed as a field;
Jerusalem shall become a heap of
ruins,
and the mountain of the house a
wooded height.'

¹⁹ Did Hĕz·e·kī′ah king of Judah and all Judah put him to death? Did he not fear the LORD and entreat the favor of the LORD, and did not the LORD repent of the evil which he had pronounced against them? But we are about to bring great evil upon ourselves."

20 There was another man who prophesied in the name of the LORD, Ū·rī′ah the son of Shĕ·māi′ah from Kīr′i·ăth–jē′a·rĭm. He prophesied against this city and against this land in words like those of Jĕr·e·mī′ah. ²¹ And when King Jĕ·hoi′a·kim, with all his warriors and all the princes, heard his words, the king sought to put him to death; but when Ū·rī′ah heard of it, he was afraid and fled and escaped to Egypt. ²² Then King Jĕ·hoi′a·kim sent to Egypt certain men, Ēl·nā′than the son of Ăch′bôr and others with him, ²³ and they fetched Ū·rī′ah from Egypt and brought him to King Jĕ·hoi′a·kim, who slew him with the sword and cast his dead body into the burial place of the common people.

24 But the hand of A·hī′kăm the son of Shā′phan was with Jĕr·e·mī′ah so that he was not given over to the people to be put to death.

27 In the beginning of the reign of Zĕd·e·kī′ah[u] the son of Jō′-sī′ah, king of Judah, this word came to Jĕr·e·mī′ah from the LORD. ²Thus the LORD said to me: "Make yourself thongs and yoke-bars, and put them on your neck. ³Send word[v] to the king of E′dom, the king of Mō′ăb, the king of the sons of Ăm′mon, the king of Tyre, and the king of Sī′dŏn by the hand of the envoys who have come to Jerusalem to Zĕd·e·kī′ah king of Judah. ⁴Give them this charge for their masters: 'Thus says the LORD of hosts, the God of Israel: This is what you shall say to your masters: ⁵ "It is I who by my great power and my out-stretched arm have made the earth, with the men and animals that are on the earth, and I give it to whom-ever it seems right to me. ⁶Now I have given all these lands into the hand of Nĕ·bü·chad·nĕz′zar, the king of Babylon, my servant, and I have given him also the beasts of the field to serve him. ⁷All the nations shall serve him and his son and his grand-son, until the time of his own land comes; then many nations and great kings shall make him their slave.

8 " ' "But if any nation or kingdom will not serve this Nĕ·bü·chad·nĕz′-zar king of Babylon, and put its neck under the yoke of the king of Babylon, I will punish that nation with the sword, with famine, and with pesti-lence, says the LORD, until I have con-sumed it by his hand. ⁹So do not listen to your prophets, your diviners, your dreamers,[w] your soothsayers, or your sorcerers, who are saying to you, 'You shall not serve the king of Babylon.' ¹⁰For it is a lie which they are proph-esying to you, with the result that you will be removed far from your land, and I will drive you out, and you will perish. ¹¹But any nation which will bring its neck under the yoke of the king of Babylon and serve him, I will leave on its own land, to till it and dwell there, says the LORD." ' "

12 To Zĕd·e·kī′ah king of Judah I spoke in like manner: "Bring your necks under the yoke of the king of Babylon, and serve him and his people, and live. ¹³Why will you and your people die by the sword, by famine, and by pestilence, as the LORD has spoken concerning any nation which will not serve the king of Babylon?

¹⁴Do not listen to the words of the prophets who are saying to you, 'You shall not serve the king of Babylon,' for it is a lie which they are proph-esying to you. ¹⁵I have not sent them, says the LORD, but they are proph-esying falsely in my name, with the result that I will drive you out and you will perish, you and the prophets who are prophesying to you."

16 Then I spoke to the priests and to all this people, saying, "Thus says the LORD: Do not listen to the words of your prophets who are prophesying to you, saying, 'Behold, the vessels of the LORD's house will now shortly be brought back from Babylon,' for it is a lie which they are prophesying to you. ¹⁷Do not listen to them; serve the king of Babylon and live. Why should this city become a desolation? ¹⁸If they are prophets, and if the word of the LORD is with them, then let them intercede with the LORD of hosts, that the vessels which are left in the house of the LORD, in the house of the king of Judah, and in Jerusalem may no go to Babylon. ¹⁹For thus says the LORD of hosts concerning the pillars, the sea the stands, and the rest of the vessel which are left in this city, ²⁰which Nĕ·bü·chad·nĕz′zar king of Babylon did not take away, when he took int exile from Jerusalem to Babylon Jĕc·o·nī′ah the son of Jĕ·hoi′a·kim king of Judah, and all the nobles o Judah and Jerusalem—²¹thus says th LORD of hosts, the God of Israel, con cerning the vessels which are left i the house of the LORD, in the house o the king of Judah, and in Jerusalem ²²They shall be carried to Babylon an remain there until the day when I giv attention to them, says the LORD. The I will bring them back and restor them to this place."

28 In that same year, at the be ginning of the reign of Zĕd·e ki′ah king of Judah, in the fifth mont of the fourth year, Hăn·a·nī′ah the so of Ăz′zūr, the prophet from Gĭb′e·on spoke to me in the house of the LORD in the presence of the priests and a the people, saying, ² "Thus says th LORD of hosts, the God of Israel: I hav broken the yoke of the king of Babylo ³Within two years I will bring bac to this place all the vessels of th

---

[u] Another reading is *Jehoiakim*   [v] Cn: Heb *send them*
[w] Gk Syr Vg: Heb *dreams*

LORD's house, which Nĕ·bü·chȧd-nĕz'zȧr king of Babylon took away from this place and carried to Babylon. [4]I will also bring back to this place Jĕc·o·nī'ah the son of Jĕ·hoi'ȧ·kim, king of Judah, and all the exiles from Judah who went to Babylon, says the LORD, for I will break the yoke of the king of Babylon."

5 Then the prophet Jĕr·ȩ·mī'ah spoke to Hȧn·ȧ·nī'ah the prophet in the presence of the priests and all the people who were standing in the house of the LORD; [6]and the prophet Jĕr·ȩ·mī'ah said, "Amen! May the LORD do so; may the LORD make the words which you have prophesied come true, and bring back to this place from Baby-lon the vessels of the house of the LORD, and all the exiles. [7]Yet hear now this word which I speak in your hear-ing and in the hearing of all the people. [8]The prophets who preceded you and me from ancient times prophesied war, famine, and pestilence against many countries and great kingdoms. [9]As for the prophet who prophesies peace, when the word of that prophet comes to pass, then it will be known that the LORD has truly sent the prophet."

10 Then the prophet Hȧn·ȧ·nī'ah took the yoke-bars from the neck of Jĕr·ȩ·mī'ah the prophet, and broke them. [11]And Hȧn·ȧ·nī'ah spoke in the presence of all the people, saying, "Thus says the LORD: Even so will I break the yoke of Nĕ·bü·chȧd·nĕz'zȧr king of Babylon from the neck of all the nations within two years." But Jĕr·ȩ·mī'ah the prophet went his way.

12 Sometime after the prophet Hȧn·ȧ·nī'ah had broken the yoke-bars from off the neck of Jĕr·ȩ·mī'ah the prophet, the word of the LORD came to Jeremiah: [13]"Go, tell Hȧn·ȧ·nī'ah, 'Thus says the LORD: You have broken wooden bars, but I[x] will make in their place bars of iron. [14]For thus says the LORD of hosts, the God of Israel: I have put upon the neck of all these nations an iron yoke of servitude to Nĕ·bü·chȧd·nĕz'zȧr king of Babylon, and they shall serve him, for I have given to him even the beasts of the field.'" [15]And Jĕr·ȩ·mī'ah the prophet said to the prophet Hȧn·ȧ·nī'ah, "Lis-ten, Hananiah, the LORD has not sent you, and you have made this people trust in a lie. [16]Therefore thus says the

LORD: 'Behold, I will remove you from the face of the earth. This very year you shall die, because you have ut-tered rebellion against the LORD.'"

17 In that same year, in the seventh month, the prophet Hȧn·ȧ·nī'ah died.

29 These are the words of the let-ter which Jĕr·ȩ·mī'ah the prophet sent from Jerusalem to the elders[v] of the exiles, and to the priests, the prophets, and all the people, whom Nĕ·bü·chȧd·nĕz'zȧr had taken into exile from Jerusalem to Babylon. [2]This was after King Jĕc·o·nī'ah, and the queen mother, the eunuchs, the princes of Judah and Jerusalem, the craftsmen, and the smiths had de-parted from Jerusalem. [3]The letter was sent by the hand of Ĕl·ā'sah the son of Shā'phȧn and Gĕm·a·rī'ah the son of Hĭl·kī'ah, whom Zĕd·ȩ·kī'ah king of Judah sent to Babylon to Nĕ·bü-chȧd·nĕz'zȧr king of Babylon. It said: [4]"Thus says the LORD of hosts, the God of Israel, to all the exiles whom I have sent into exile from Jerusalem to Baby-lon: [5]Build houses and live in them; plant gardens and eat their produce. [6]Take wives and have sons and daughters; take wives for your sons, and give your daughters in marriage, that they may bear sons and daugh-ters; multiply there, and do not de-crease. [7]But seek the welfare of the city where I have sent you into exile, and pray to the LORD on its behalf, for in its welfare you will find your welfare. [8]For thus says the LORD of hosts, the God of Israel: Do not let your prophets and your diviners who are among you deceive you, and do not listen to the dreams which they dream,[z] [9]for it is a lie which they are prophesying to you in my name; I did not send them, says the LORD.

10 "For thus says the LORD: When seventy years are completed for Baby-lon, I will visit you, and I will fulfil to you my promise and bring you back to this place. [11]For I know the plans I have for you, says the LORD, plans for welfare and not for evil, to give you a future and a hope. [12]Then you will call upon me and come and pray to me, and I will hear you. [13]You will seek me and find me; when you seek me with all your heart, [14]I will be found by you, says the LORD, and I will restore your

[x]Gk: Heb *you* [v]Gk: Heb *the rest of the elders*
[z]Cn: Heb *your dreams which you cause to dream*

fortunes and gather you from all the nations and all the places where I have driven you, says the LORD, and I will bring you back to the place from which I sent you into exile.

15 "Because you have said, 'The LORD has raised up prophets for us in Babylon,' — [16]Thus says the LORD concerning the king who sits on the throne of David, and concerning all the people who dwell in this city, your kinsmen who did not go out with you into exile: [17]'Thus says the LORD of hosts, Behold, I am sending on them sword, famine, and pestilence, and I will make them like vile figs which are so bad they cannot be eaten. [18]I will pursue them with sword, famine, and pestilence, and will make them a horror to all the kingdoms of the earth, to be a curse, a terror, a hissing, and a reproach among all the nations where I have driven them, [19]because they did not heed my words, says the LORD, which I persistently sent to you by my servants the prophets, but you would not listen, says the LORD.' — [20]Hear the word of the LORD, all you exiles whom I sent away from Jerusalem to Babylon: [21]'Thus says the LORD of hosts, the God of Israel, concerning Ā'hăb the son of Kō·laī'ah and Zĕd·ę·kī'ah the son of Mā–ą·sēi'ah, who are prophesying a lie to you in my name: Behold, I will deliver them into the hand of Nĕ·bü·chad·rĕz'zar king of Babylon, and he shall slay them before your eyes. [22]Because of them this curse shall be used by all the exiles from Judah in Babylon: "The LORD make you like Zĕd·ę·kī'ah and Ā'hăb, whom the king of Babylon roasted in the fire," [23]because they have committed folly in Israel, they have committed adultery with their neighbors' wives, and they have spoken in my name lying words which I did not command them. I am the one who knows, and I am witness, says the LORD.' "

24 To Shĕ·māi'ah of Nĕ·hĕl'am you shall say: [25]"Thus says the LORD of hosts, the God of Israel: You have sent letters in your name to all the people who are in Jerusalem, and to Zĕph·ą·nī'ah the son of Mā–ą·sēi'ah the priest, and to all the priests, saying, [26]'The LORD has made you priest instead of Jĕ·hoi'ą·dą the priest, to have charge in the house of the LORD over every madman who prophesies, to put him in the stocks and collar. [27]Now why have you not rebuked Jĕr·ę·mī'ah of Ān'ą·thŏth who is prophesying to you? [28]For he has sent to us in Babylon, saying, "Your exile will be long; build houses and live in them, and plant gardens and eat their produce." ' "

29 Zĕph·ą·nī'ah the priest read this letter in the hearing of Jĕr·ę·mī'ah the prophet. [30]Then the word of the LORD came to Jĕr·ę·mī'ah: [31]"Send to all the exiles, saying, 'Thus says the LORD concerning Shĕ·maī'ah of Nĕ·hĕl'am: Because Shemaiah has prophesied to you when I did not send him, and has made you trust in a lie, [32]therefore thus says the LORD: Behold, I will punish Shĕ·maī'ah of Nĕ·hĕl'am and his descendants; he shall not have any one living among this people to see[a] the good that I will do to my people, says the LORD, for he has talked rebellion against the LORD.' "

30   The word that came to Jĕr·ę·mī'ah from the LORD: [2]"Thus says the LORD, the God of Israel: Write in a book all the words that I have spoken to you. [3]For behold, days are coming, says the LORD, when I will restore the fortunes of my people, Israel and Judah, says the LORD, and I will bring them back to the land which I gave to their fathers, and they shall take possession of it."

4 These are the words which the LORD spoke concerning Israel and Judah:
[5]"Thus says the LORD:
We have heard a cry of panic,
    of terror, and no peace.
[6]Ask now, and see,
    can a man bear a child?
Why then do I see every man
    with his hands on his loins like a
    woman in labor?
Why has every face turned pale?
[7]Alas! that day is so great
    there is none like it;
it is a time of distress for Jacob;
    yet he shall be saved out of it.
8 "And it shall come to pass in that day, says the LORD of hosts, that I will break the yoke from off their[b] neck, and I will burst their[b] bonds, and strangers shall no more make servants of them.[c] [9]But they shall serve the

[a]Gk: Heb *and he shall not see*
[b]Gk Old Latin: Heb *your*
[c]Heb *make a servant of him*

LORD their God and David their king, whom I will raise up for them.

[10] "Then fear not, O Jacob my servant,
     says the LORD,
     nor be dismayed, O Israel;
for lo, I will save you from afar,
     and your offspring from the land
     of their captivity.
Jacob shall return and have quiet
     and ease,
     and none shall make him afraid.
[11] For I am with you to save you,
           says the LORD;
I will make a full end of all the na-
     tions
     among whom I scattered you,
but of you I will not make a full
     end.
I will chasten you in just measure,
     and I will by no means leave you
     unpunished.

[12] "For thus says the LORD:
Your hurt is incurable,
     and your wound is grievous.
[13] There is none to uphold your cause,
     no medicine for your wound,
     no healing for you.
[14] All your lovers have forgotten you;
     they care nothing for you;
for I have dealt you the blow of an
     enemy,
     the punishment of a merciless foe,
because your guilt is great,
     because your sins are flagrant.
[15] Why do you cry out over your hurt?
     Your pain is incurable.
Because your guilt is great,
     because your sins are flagrant,
     I have done these things to you.
[16] Therefore all who devour you shall
     be devoured,
     and all your foes, every one of
     them, shall go into captivity;
those who despoil you shall become a
     spoil,
and all who prey on you I will make
     a prey.
[17] For I will restore health to you,
     and your wounds I will heal,
           says the LORD,
because they have called you an out-
     cast:
'It is Zion, for whom no one
     cares!'

[18] "Thus says the LORD:
Behold, I will restore the fortunes of
     the tents of Jacob,

and have compassion on his dwell-
     ings;
the city shall be rebuilt upon its
     mound,
     and the palace shall stand where
     it used to be.
[19] Out of them shall come songs of
     thanksgiving,
     and the voices of those who make
     merry.
I will multiply them, and they shall
     not be few;
I will make them honored, and
     they shall not be small.
[20] Their children shall be as they were
     of old,
     and their congregation shall be
     established before me;
and I will punish all who oppress
     them.
[21] Their prince shall be one of them-
     selves,
     their ruler shall come forth from
     their midst;
I will make him draw near, and he
     shall approach me,
for who would dare of himself to
     approach me?
           says the LORD.
[22] And you shall be my people,
     and I will be your God."

[23] Behold the storm of the LORD!
     Wrath has gone forth,
     a whirling tempest;
     it will burst upon the head of the
     wicked.
[24] The fierce anger of the LORD will
     not turn back
     until he has executed and ac-
     complished
     the intents of his mind.
In the latter days you will under-
     stand this.

31 "At that time, says the LORD, I will be the God of all the families of Israel, and they shall be my people."
[2] Thus says the LORD:
"The people who survived the
     sword
     found grace in the wilderness;
when Israel sought for rest,
[3]   the LORD appeared to him[d] from
     afar.
I have loved you with an everlasting
     love;
     therefore I have continued my
     faithfulness to you.

[d] Gk: Heb *me*

⁴Again I will build you, and you shall
be built,
O virgin Israel!
Again you shall adorn yourself with
timbrels,
and shall go forth in the dance of
the merrymakers.
⁵Again you shall plant vineyards
upon the mountains of Sa·mâr'ĭ·a;
the planters shall plant,
and shall enjoy the fruit.
⁶For there shall be a day when watchmen will call
in the hill country of Ē'phra·ĭm:
'Arise, and let us go up to Zion,
to the LORD our God.'"

⁷For thus says the LORD:
"Sing aloud with gladness for Jacob,
and raise shouts for the chief of
the nations;
proclaim, give praise, and say,
'The LORD has saved his people,
the remnant of Israel.'
⁸Behold, I will bring them from the
north country,
and gather them from the farthest
parts of the earth,
among them the blind and the
lame,
the woman with child and her who
is in travail, together;
a great company, they shall return here.
⁹With weeping they shall come,
and with consolations*ᵉ* I will lead
them back,
I will make them walk by brooks
of water,
in a straight path in which they
shall not stumble;
for I am a father to Israel,
and Ē'phra·ĭm is my first-born.

¹⁰"Hear the word of the LORD, O
nations,
and declare it in the coastlands
afar off;
say, 'He who scattered Israel will
gather him,
and will keep him as a shepherd
keeps his flock.'
¹¹For the LORD has ransomed Jacob,
and has redeemed him from hands
too strong for him.
¹²They shall come and sing aloud on
the height of Zion,
and they shall be radiant over the
goodness of the LORD,
over the grain, the wine, and the oil,

and over the young of the flock and
the herd;
their life shall be like a watered
garden,
and they shall languish no more.
¹³Then shall the maidens rejoice in
the dance,
and the young men and the old
shall be merry.
I will turn their mourning into joy,
I will comfort them, and give them
gladness for sorrow.
¹⁴I will feast the soul of the priests
with abundance,
and my people shall be satisfied
with my goodness,
says the LORD."

¹⁵Thus says the LORD:
"A voice is heard in Rā'mah,
lamentation and bitter weeping.
Rachel is weeping for her children;
she refuses to be comforted for her
children,
because they are not."

¹⁶Thus says the LORD:
"Keep your voice from weeping,
and your eyes from tears;
for your work shall be rewarded,
says the LORD,
and they shall come back from the
land of the enemy.
¹⁷There is hope for your future,
says the LORD,
and your children shall come back
to their own country.
¹⁸I have heard Ē'phra·ĭm bemoan-
ing,
'Thou hast chastened me, and I was
chastened,
like an untrained calf;
bring me back that I may be restored,
for thou art the LORD my God.
¹⁹For after I had turned away I repented;
and after I was instructed, I
smote upon my thigh;
I was ashamed, and I was confounded,
because I bore the disgrace of my
youth.'
²⁰Is Ē'phra·ĭm my dear son?
Is he my darling child?
For as often as I speak against him,
I do remember him still.
Therefore my heart yearns for him;
I will surely have mercy on him,
says the LORD.

ᵉGk Compare Vg Tg: Heb *supplications*　**31.15:** Mt 2.18.

²¹ "Set up waymarks for yourself,
　make yourself guideposts;
　consider well the highway,
　the road by which you went.
Return, O virgin Israel,
　return to these your cities.
²² How long will you waver,
　O faithless daughter?
For the LORD has created a new
　thing on the earth:
　a woman protects a man."

23 Thus says the LORD of hosts,
the God of Israel: "Once more they
shall use these words in the land of
Judah and in its cities, when I restore
their fortunes:
　'The LORD bless you, O habitation of
　righteousness,
　O holy hill!'
²⁴ And Judah and all its cities shall
dwell there together, and the farmers and those who wander/ with their
flocks. ²⁵ For I will satisfy the weary
soul, and every languishing soul I
will replenish."
26 Thereupon I awoke and looked,
and my sleep was pleasant to me.
27 "Behold, the days are coming,
says the LORD, when I will sow the
house of Israel and the house of Judah
with the seed of man and the seed of
beast. ²⁸ And it shall come to pass that
as I have watched over them to pluck
up and break down, to overthrow,
destroy, and bring evil, so I will watch
over them to build and to plant, says
the LORD. ²⁹ In those days they shall
no longer say:
　'The fathers have eaten sour grapes,
　and the children's teeth are set on
　edge.'
³⁰ But every one shall die for his own
sin; each man who eats sour grapes,
his teeth shall be set on edge.
31 "Behold, the days are coming,
says the LORD, when I will make a new
covenant with the house of Israel and
the house of Judah, ³² not like the covenant which I made with their fathers
when I took them by the hand to bring
them out of the land of Egypt, my covenant which they broke, though I was
their husband, says the LORD. ³³ But
this is the covenant which I will make
with the house of Israel after those
days, says the LORD: I will put my
law within them, and I will write it
upon their hearts; and I will be their
God, and they shall be my people. ³⁴ And

no longer shall each man teach his
neighbor and each his brother, saying,
'Know the LORD,' for they shall all
know me, from the least of them to
the greatest, says the LORD; for I will
forgive their iniquity, and I will remember their sin no more."

³⁵ Thus says the LORD,
　who gives the sun for light by day
　and the fixed order of the moon
　and the stars for light by night,
　who stirs up the sea so that its waves
　roar—
　the LORD of hosts is his name:
³⁶ "If this fixed order departs
　from before me, says the LORD,
　then shall the descendants of Israel
　cease
　from being a nation before me for
　ever."

³⁷ Thus says the LORD:
"If the heavens above can be meas-
　ured,
　and the foundations of the earth
　below can be explored,
　then I will cast off all the descend-
　ants of Israel
　for all that they have done,
　　　　　　　　　says the LORD."

38 "Behold, the days are coming,
says the LORD, when the city shall be
rebuilt for the LORD from the tower of
Ha·năn'ĕl to the Corner Gate. ³⁹ And the
measuring line shall go out farther,
straight to the hill Gā'rĕb, and shall
then turn to Gō'ah. ⁴⁰ The whole valley
of the dead bodies and the ashes, and
all the fields as far as the brook Kĭd'-
ron, to the corner of the Horse Gate
toward the east, shall be sacred to the
LORD. It shall not be uprooted or overthrown any more for ever."

32 The word that came to Jĕr·e-
　mī'ah from the LORD in the
tenth year of Zĕd·e·kī'ah king of Judah, which was the eighteenth year
of Nĕ·bü·chad·rĕz'zar. ² At that time
the army of the king of Babylon was
besieging Jerusalem, and Jĕr·e·mī'ah
the prophet was shut up in the court
of the guard which was in the palace
of the king of Judah. ³ For Zĕd·e·kī'ah
king of Judah had imprisoned him,
saying, "Why do you prophesy and say,

/Cn Compare Syr Vg Tg: Heb *and they shall wander*
31.31: Lk 22.20; 1 Cor 11.25.
31.31–34: Jer 32.38–40; Heb 8.8–12; 10.16–17.

'Thus says the LORD: Behold, I am giving this city into the hand of the king of Babylon, and he shall take it; ⁴Zĕd·ẹ·kī'ạh king of Judah shall not escape out of the hand of the Chăl·dē'ạnṣ, but shall surely be given into the hand of the king of Babylon, and shall speak with him face to face and see him eye to eye; ⁵and he shall take Zĕd·ẹ·kī'ạh to Babylon, and there he shall remain until I visit him, says the LORD; though you fight against the Chăl·dē'ạnṣ, you shall not succeed'?''

6 Jĕr·ẹ·mī'ạh said, "The word of the LORD came to me: ⁷Behold, Hăn'ạ·mĕl the son of Shăl'lụm your uncle will come to you and say, 'Buy my field which is at Ăn'ạ·thŏth, for the right of redemption by purchase is yours.' ⁸Then Hăn'ạ·mĕl my cousin came to me in the court of the guard, in accordance with the word of the LORD, and said to me, 'Buy my field which is at Ăn'ạ·thŏth in the land of Benjamin, for the right of possession and redemption is yours; buy it for yourself.' Then I knew that this was the word of the LORD.

9 "And I bought the field at Ăn'ạ·thŏth from Hăn'ạ·mĕl my cousin, and weighed out the money to him, seventeen shekels of silver. ¹⁰I signed the deed, sealed it, got witnesses, and weighed the money on scales. ¹¹Then I took the sealed deed of purchase, containing the terms and conditions, and the open copy; ¹²and I gave the deed of purchase to Bär'ụch the son of Nĕ·rī'ạh son of Măh'sēi·ạh, in the presence of Hăn'ạ·mĕl my cousin, in the presence of the witnesses who signed the deed of purchase, and in the presence of all the Jews who were sitting in the court of the guard. ¹³I charged Bär'ụch in their presence, saying, ¹⁴'Thus says the LORD of hosts, the God of Israel: Take these deeds, both this sealed deed of purchase and this open deed, and put them in an earthenware vessel, that they may last for a long time. ¹⁵For thus says the LORD of hosts, the God of Israel: Houses and fields and vineyards shall again be bought in this land.'

16 "After I had given the deed of purchase to Bär'ụch the son of Nĕ·rī'ạh, I prayed to the LORD, saying: ¹⁷'Ah Lord GOD! It is thou who hast made the heavens and the earth by thy great power and by thy outstretched arm! Nothing is too hard for thee, ¹⁸who showest steadfast love to thousands, but dost requite the guilt of fathers to their children after them, O great and mighty God whose name is the LORD of hosts, ¹⁹great in counsel and mighty in deed; whose eyes are open to all the ways of men, rewarding every man according to his ways and according to the fruit of his doings; ²⁰who hast shown signs and wonders in the land of Egypt, and to this day in Israel and among all mankind, and hast made thee a name, as at this day. ²¹Thou didst bring thy people Israel out of the land of Egypt with signs and wonders, with a strong hand and outstretched arm, and with great terror; ²²and thou gavest them this land, which thou didst swear to their fathers to give them, a land flowing with milk and honey; ²³and they entered and took possession of it. But they did not obey thy voice or walk in thy law; they did nothing of all thou didst command them to do. Therefore thou hast made all this evil come upon them. ²⁴Behold, the siege mounds have come up to the city to take it, and because of sword and famine and pestilence the city is given into the hands of the Chăl·dē'ạnṣ who are fighting against it. What thou didst speak has come to pass, and behold, thou seest it. ²⁵Yet thou, O Lord GOD, hast said to me, "Buy the field for money and get witnesses" – though the city is given into the hands of the Chăl·dē'ạnṣ.''

26 The word of the LORD came to Jĕr·ẹ·mī'ạh: ²⁷"Behold, I am the LORD, the God of all flesh; is anything too hard for me? ²⁸Therefore, thus says the LORD: Behold, I am giving this city into the hands of the Chăl·dē'ạnṣ and into the hand of Nĕ·bü·chạd·rĕz'zạr king of Babylon, and he shall take it. ²⁹The Chăl·dē'ạnṣ who are fighting against this city shall come and set this city on fire, and burn it, with the houses on whose roofs incense has been offered to Bā'al and drink offerings have been poured out to other gods, to provoke me to anger. ³⁰For the sons of Israel and the sons of Judah have done nothing but evil in my sight from their youth; the sons of Israel have done nothing but provoke me to anger by the work of their hands, says the LORD. ³¹This city has aroused my anger

and wrath, from the day it was built to this day, so that I will remove it from my sight [32] because of all the evil of the sons of Israel and the sons of Judah which they did to provoke me to anger—their kings and their princes, their priests and their prophets, the men of Judah and the inhabitants of Jerusalem. [33] They have turned to me their back and not their face; and though I have taught them persistently they have not listened to receive instruction. [34] They set up their abominations in the house which is called by my name, to defile it. [35] They built the high places of Bā′al in the valley of the son of Hĭn′nŏm, to offer up their sons and daughters to Mō′lĕch, though I did not command them, nor did it enter into my mind, that they should do this abomination, to cause Judah to sin.

36 "Now therefore thus says the LORD, the God of Israel, concerning this city of which you say, 'It is given into the hand of the king of Babylon by sword, by famine, and by pestilence': [37] Behold, I will gather them from all the countries to which I drove them in my anger and my wrath and in great indignation; I will bring them back to this place, and I will make them dwell in safety. [38] And they shall be my people, and I will be their God. [39] I will give them one heart and one way, that they may fear me for ever, for their own good and the good of their children after them. [40] I will make with them an everlasting covenant, that I will not turn away from doing good to them; and I will put the fear of me in their hearts, that they may not turn from me. [41] I will rejoice in doing them good, and I will plant them in this land in faithfulness, with all my heart and all my soul.

42 "For thus says the LORD: Just as I have brought all this great evil upon this people, so I will bring upon them all the good that I promise them. [43] Fields shall be bought in this land of which you are saying, It is a desolation, without man or beast; it is given into the hands of the Chăl′dē′anș. [44] Fields shall be bought for money, and deeds shall be signed and sealed and witnessed, in the land of Benjamin, in the places about Jerusalem, and in the cities of Judah, in the cities of the hill country, in the cities of the Shĕ·phē′-

lah, and in the cities of the Nĕg′ĕb; for I will restore their fortunes, says the LORD."

33 The word of the LORD came to Jĕr·ę·mī′ah a second time, while he was still shut up in the court of the guard: [2] "Thus says the LORD who made the earth,*g* the LORD who formed it to establish it—the LORD is his name: [3] Call to me and I will answer you, and will tell you great and hidden things which you have not known. [4] For thus says the LORD, the God of Israel, concerning the houses of this city and the houses of the kings of Judah which were torn down to make a defense against the siege mounds and before the sword:*h* [5] The Chăl·dē′anș are coming in to fight*i* and to fill them with the dead bodies of men whom I shall smite in my anger and my wrath, for I have hidden my face from this city because of all their wickedness. [6] Behold, I will bring to it health and healing, and I will heal them and reveal to them abundance*j* of prosperity and security. [7] I will restore the fortunes of Judah and the fortunes of Israel, and rebuild them as they were at first. [8] I will cleanse them from all the guilt of their sin against me, and I will forgive all the guilt of their sin and rebellion against me. [9] And this city*k* shall be to me a name of joy, a praise and a glory before all the nations of the earth who shall hear of all the good that I do for them; they shall fear and tremble because of all the good and all the prosperity I provide for it.

10 "Thus says the LORD: In this place of which you say, 'It is a waste without man or beast,' in the cities of Judah and the streets of Jerusalem that are desolate, without man or inhabitant or beast, there shall be heard again [11] the voice of mirth and the voice of gladness, the voice of the bridegroom and the voice of the bride, the voices of those who sing, as they bring thank offerings to the house of the LORD:

'Give thanks to the LORD of hosts,
    for the LORD is good,
    for his steadfast love endures
      for ever!'

*g*Gk: Heb *it*   *h*Heb obscure
*i*Cn: Heb *They are coming in to fight against the Chaldeans*   *j*Heb uncertain   *k*Heb *and it*
32.38-40: Jer 31.31-34.

For I will restore the fortunes of the land as at first, says the LORD.

12 "Thus says the LORD of hosts: In this place which is waste, without man or beast, and in all of its cities, there shall again be habitations of shepherds resting their flocks. ¹³ In the cities of the hill country, in the cities of the Shĕ·phē'lah, and in the cities of the Nĕg'ĕb, in the land of Benjamin, the places about Jerusalem, and in the cities of Judah, flocks shall again pass under the hands of the one who counts them, says the LORD.

14 "Behold, the days are coming, says the LORD, when I will fulfil the promise I made to the house of Israel and the house of Judah. ¹⁵ In those days and at that time I will cause a righteous Branch to spring forth for David; and he shall execute justice and righteousness in the land. ¹⁶ In those days Judah will be saved and Jerusalem will dwell securely. And this is the name by which it will be called: 'The LORD is our righteousness.'

17 "For thus says the LORD: David shall never lack a man to sit on the throne of the house of Israel, ¹⁸ and the Levitical priests shall never lack a man in my presence to offer burnt offerings, to burn cereal offerings, and to make sacrifices for ever."

19 The word of the LORD came to Jĕr·e·mī'ah: ²⁰ "Thus says the LORD: If you can break my covenant with the day and my covenant with the night, so that day and night will not come at their appointed time, ²¹ then also my covenant with David my servant may be broken, so that he shall not have a son to reign on his throne, and my covenant with the Levitical priests my ministers. ²² As the host of heaven cannot be numbered and the sands of the sea cannot be measured, so I will multiply the descendants of David my servant, and the Levitical priests who minister to me."

23 The word of the LORD came to Jĕr·e·mī'ah: ²⁴ "Have you not observed what these people are saying, 'The LORD has rejected the two families which he chose'? Thus they have despised my people so that they are no longer a nation in their sight. ²⁵ Thus says the LORD: If I have not established my covenant with day and night and the ordinances of heaven and earth, ²⁶ then I will reject the descendants of

Jacob and David my servant and will not choose one of his descendants to rule over the seed of Abraham, Isaac, and Jacob. For I will restore their fortunes, and will have mercy upon them."

34 The word which came to Jĕr·e·mī'ah from the LORD, when Nĕ·bü·chad·rĕz'zar king of Babylon and all his army and all the kingdoms of the earth under his dominion and all the peoples were fighting against Jerusalem and all of its cities: ² "Thus says the LORD, the God Israel: Go and speak to Zĕd·e·kī'ah king of Judah and say to him, 'Thus says the LORD: Behold, I am giving this city into the hand of the king of Babylon, and he shall burn it with fire. ³ You shall not escape from his hand, but shall surely be captured and delivered into his hand; you shall see the king of Babylon eye to eye and speak with him face to face; and you shall go to Babylon.' ⁴ Yet hear the word of the LORD, O Zĕd·e·kī'ah king of Judah! Thus says the LORD concerning you: 'You shall not die by the sword. ⁵ You shall die in peace. And as spices were burned for your fathers, the former kings who were before you, so men shall burn spices for you and lament for you, saying, "Alas, lord!"' For I have spoken the word, says the LORD."

6 Then Jĕr·e·mī'ah the prophet spoke all these words to Zĕd·e·kī'ah king of Judah, in Jerusalem, ⁷ when the army of the king of Babylon was fighting against Jerusalem and against all the cities of Judah that were left, Lā'chĭsh and A·zē'kah; for these were the only fortified cities of Judah that remained.

8 The word which came to Jĕr·e·mī'ah from the LORD, after King Zĕd·e·kī'ah had made a covenant with all the people in Jerusalem to make a proclamation of liberty to them, ⁹ that every one should set free his Hebrew slaves, male and female, so that no one should enslave a Jew, his brother. ¹⁰ And they obeyed, all the princes and all the people who had entered into the covenant that every one would set free his slave, male or female, so that they would not be enslaved again; they obeyed and set them free. ¹¹ But afterward they turned around and took

33.15: Jer 23.5; Is 4.2; Zech 3.8; 6.12.

back the male and female slaves they had set free, and brought them into subjection as slaves. ¹²The word of the LORD came to Jĕr·e·mī'ah from the LORD: ¹³"Thus says the LORD, the God of Israel: I made a covenant with your fathers when I brought them out of the land of Egypt, out of the house of bondage, saying, ¹⁴'At the end of six¹ years each of you must set free the fellow Hebrew who has been sold to you and has served you six years; you must set him free from your service.' But your fathers did not listen to me or incline their ears to me. ¹⁵You recently repented and did what was right in my eyes by proclaiming liberty, each to his neighbor, and you made a covenant before me in the house which is called by my name; ¹⁶but then you turned around and profaned my name when each of you took back his male and female slaves, whom you had set free according to their desire, and you brought them into subjection to be your slaves. ¹⁷Therefore, thus says the LORD: You have not obeyed me by proclaiming liberty, every one to his brother and to his neighbor; behold, I proclaim to you liberty to the sword, to pestilence, and to famine, says the LORD. I will make you a horror to all the kingdoms of the earth. ¹⁸And the men who transgressed my covenant and did not keep the terms of the covenant which they made before me, I will make like*ᵐ* the calf which they cut in two and passed between its parts – ¹⁹the princes of Judah, the princes of Jerusalem, the eunuchs, the priests, and all the people of the land who passed between the parts of the calf; ²⁰and I will give them into the hand of their enemies and into the hand of those who seek their lives. Their dead bodies shall be food for the birds of the air and the beasts of the earth. ²¹And Zĕd·e·kī'ah king of Judah, and his princes I will give into the hand of their enemies and into the hand of those who seek their lives, into the hand of the army of the king of Babylon which has withdrawn from you. ²²Behold, I will command, says the LORD, and will bring them back to this city; and they will fight against it, and take it, and burn it with fire. I will make the cities of Judah a desolation without inhabitant."

35 The word which came to Jĕr·e·mī'ah from the LORD in the days of Jĕ·hoi'a·kĭm the son of Jō·sī'ah, king of Judah: ²"Go to the house of the Rē'cha·bītes, and speak with them, and bring them to the house of the LORD, into one of the chambers; then offer them wine to drink." ³So I took Jā'–ăz·a·nī'ah the son of Jĕr·e·mī'ah, son of Ha̱"băz·zĭ·nī'ah, and his brothers, and all his sons, and the whole house of the Rē'cha·bītes. ⁴I brought them to the house of the LORD into the chamber of the sons of Hā'nan the son of Ĭg·da·lī'ah, the man of God, which was near the chamber of the princes, above the chamber of Mā–a·sēi'ah the son of Shăl'lum, keeper of the threshold. ⁵Then I set before the Rē'cha·bītes pitchers full of wine, and cups; and I said to them, "Drink wine." ⁶But they answered, "We will drink no wine, for Jŏn'a·dăb the son of Rē'chăb, our father, commanded us, 'You shall not drink wine, neither you nor your sons for ever; ⁷you shall not build a house; you shall not sow seed; you shall not plant or have a vineyard; but you shall live in tents all your days, that you may live many days in the land where you sojourn.' ⁸We have obeyed the voice of Jŏn'a·dăb the son of Rē'chăb, our father, in all that he commanded us, to drink no wine all our days, ourselves, our wives, our sons, or our daughters, ⁹and not to build houses to dwell in. We have no vineyard or field or seed; ¹⁰but we have lived in tents, and have obeyed and done all that Jŏn'a·dăb our father commanded us. ¹¹But when Nĕ·bu·chad·rĕz'zar king of Babylon came up against the land, we said, 'Come, and let us go to Jerusalem for fear of the army of the Chăl·dē'ans and army of the Syrians.' So we are living in Jerusalem."

12 Then the word of the LORD came to Jĕr·e·mī'ah: ¹³"Thus says the LORD of hosts, the God of Israel: Go and say to the men of Judah and the inhabitants of Jerusalem, Will you not receive instruction and listen to my words? says the LORD. ¹⁴The command which Jŏn'a·dăb the son of Rē'chăb gave to his sons, to drink no wine, has been kept; and they drink none to this day, for they have obeyed their father's command. I have spoken to you per-

¹Gk: Heb *seven*   *ᵐCn: Heb lacks *like*

sistently, but you have not listened to me. ¹⁵I have sent to you all my servants the prophets, sending them persistently, saying, 'Turn now every one of you from his evil way, and amend your doings, and do not go after other gods to serve them, and then you shall dwell in the land which I gave to you and your fathers.' But you did not incline your ear or listen to me. ¹⁶The sons of Jŏn′a·dăb the son of Rē′chăb have kept the command which their father gave them, but this people has not obeyed me. ¹⁷Therefore, thus says the LORD, the God of hosts, the God of Israel: Behold, I am bringing on Judah and all the inhabitants of Jerusalem all the evil that I have pronounced against them; because I have spoken to them and they have not listened, I have called to them and they have not answered."

18 But to the house of the Rē′chạ-bītes Jĕr·ẹ·mī′ạh said, "Thus says the LORD of hosts, the God of Israel: Because you have obeyed the command of Jŏn′a·dăb your father, and kept all his precepts, and done all that he commanded you, ¹⁹therefore thus says the LORD of hosts, the God of Israel: Jŏn′a·dăb the son of Rē′chăb shall never lack a man to stand before me."

36 In the fourth year of Jĕ′hoi′-a·kim the son of Jō·sī′ah, king of Judah, this word came to Jĕr·ẹ·mī′ạh from the LORD: ²"Take a scroll and write on it all the words that I have spoken to you against Israel and Judah and all the nations, from the day I spoke to you, from the days of Jō·sī′ạh until today. ³It may be that the house of Judah will hear all the evil which I intend to do to them, so that every one may turn from his evil way, and that I may forgive their iniquity and their sin."

4 Then Jĕr·ẹ·mī′ạh called Bär′ụch the son of Nē·rī′ạh, and Baruch wrote upon a scroll at the dictation of Jeremiah all the words of the LORD which he had spoken to him. ⁵And Jĕr·ẹ·mī′ạh ordered Bär′ụch, saying, "I am debarred from going to the house of the LORD; ⁶so you are to go, and on a fast day in the hearing of all the people in the LORD's house you shall read the words of the LORD from the scroll which you have written at my dictation.

You shall read them also in the hearing of all the men of Judah who come out of their cities. ⁷It may be that their supplication will come before the LORD, and that every one will turn from his evil way, for great is the anger and wrath that the LORD has pronounced against this people." ⁸And Bär′ụch the son of Nē·rī′ạh did all that Jĕr·ẹ·mī′ạh the prophet ordered him about reading from the scroll the words of the LORD in the LORD's house.

9 In the fifth year of Jĕ·hoi′a·kim the son of Jō·sī′ạh, king of Judah, in the ninth month, all the people in Jerusalem and all the people who came from the cities of Judah to Jerusalem proclaimed a fast before the LORD. ¹⁰Then, in the hearing of all the people, Bär′ụch read the words of Jĕr·ẹ·mī′ạh from the scroll, in the house of the LORD, in the chamber of Gĕm·a·rī′ạh the son of Shā′phạn the secretary, which was in the upper court, at the entry of the New Gate of the LORD's house.

11 When Mĭ·cāi′ạh the son of Gĕm·a·rī′ạh, son of Shā′phạn, heard all the words of the LORD from the scroll, ¹²he went down to the king's house, into the secretary's chamber; and all the princes were sitting there: Ė·līsh′ạ·mạ the secretary, Dĕ·laī′ạh the son of Shĕ·māi′ạh, Ėl·nā′thạn the son of Ăch′bŏr, Gĕm·a·rī′ạh the son of Shā′phạn, Zĕd·e·kī′ạh the son of Hăn·a·nī′ạh, and all the princes. ¹³And Mĭ·cāi′ạh told them all the words that he had heard, when Bär′ụch read the scroll in the hearing of the people. ¹⁴Then all the princes sent Jĕ·hū′dī the son of Nĕth·a·nī′ạh, son of Shĕl-ẹ·mī′ạh, son of Cü′shī, to say to Bär′-ụch, "Take in your hand the scroll that you read in the hearing of the people, and come." So Baruch the son of Nē·rī′ạh took the scroll in his hand and came to them. ¹⁵And they said to him, "Sit down and read it." So Bär′-ụch read it to them. ¹⁶When they heard all the words, they turned one to another in fear; and they said to Bär′ụch, "We must report all these words to the king." ¹⁷Then they asked Bär′ụch, "Tell us, how did you write all these words? Was it at his dictation?" ¹⁸Bär′ụch answered them, "He dictated all these words to me, while I wrote them with ink on the scroll." ¹⁹Then the princes said to Bär′ụch,

"Go and hide, you and Jĕr·e·mī′ah, and let no one know where you are."

20 So they went into the court to the king, having put the scroll in the chamber of Ē·lĭsh′a·ma the secretary; and they reported all the words to the king. ²¹Then the king sent Jĕ·hū′dī to get the scroll, and he took it from the chamber of Ē·lĭsh′a·ma the secretary; and Jehudi read it to the king and all the princes who stood beside the king. ²²It was the ninth month, and the king was sitting in the winter house and there was a fire burning in the brazier before him. ²³As Jĕ·hū′dī read three or four columns, the king would cut them off with a penknife and throw them into the fire in the brazier, until the entire scroll was consumed in the fire that was in the brazier. ²⁴Yet neither the king, nor any of his servants who heard all these words, was afraid, nor did they rend their garments. ²⁵Even when Ĕl·nā′than and Dĕ·laī′ah and Gĕm·a·rī′ah urged the king not to burn the scroll, he would not listen to them. ²⁶And the king commanded Jĕ·räh′mē·ĕl the king's son and Sĕ·rāi′ah the son of Ăz′rĭ–ĕl and Shĕl·e·mī′ah the son of Ăb·dē′ĕl to seize Bär′uch the secretary and Jĕr·e·mī′ah the prophet, but the LORD hid them.

27 Now, after the king had burned the scroll with the words which Bär′uch wrote at Jĕr·e·mī′ah's dictation, the word of the LORD came to Jeremiah: ²⁸"Take another scroll and write on it all the former words that were in the first scroll, which Jĕ·hoi′a·kim the king of Judah has burned. ²⁹And concerning Jĕ·hoi′a·kim king of Judah you shall say, 'Thus says the LORD, You have burned this scroll, saying, "Why have you written in it that the king of Babylon will certainly come and destroy this land, and will cut off from it man and beast?" ³⁰Therefore thus says the LORD concerning Jĕ·hoi′a·kim king of Judah, He shall have none to sit upon the throne of David, and his dead body shall be cast out to the heat by day and the frost by night. ³¹And I will punish him and his offspring and his servants for their iniquity; I will bring upon them, and upon the inhabitants of Jerusalem, and upon the men of Judah, all the evil that I have pronounced against them, but they would not hear.'"

32 Then Jĕr·e·mī′ah took another scroll and give it to Bär′uch the scribe, the son of Nē·rī′ah, who wrote on it at the dictation of Jeremiah all the words of the scroll which Jĕ·hoi′a·kim king of Judah had burned in the fire; and many similar words were added to them.

37 Zĕd·e·kī′ah the son of Jō·sī′ah, whom Nĕ·bü·chad·rĕz′zar king of Babylon made king in the land of Judah, reigned instead of Cō·nī′ah the son of Jĕ·hoi′a·kim. ²But neither he nor his servants nor the people of the land listened to the words of the LORD which he spoke through Jĕr·e·mī′ah the prophet.

3 King Zĕd·e·kī′ah sent Jĕ·hū′căl the son of Shĕl·e·mī′ah, and Zĕph·a·nī′ah the priest, the son of Mā–a·sēi′ah, to Jĕr·e·mī′ah the prophet, saying, "Pray for us to the LORD our God." ⁴Now Jĕr·e·mī′ah was still going in and out among the people, for he had not yet been put in prison. ⁵The army of Pharaoh had come out of Egypt; and when the Chăl·dē′ans who were besieging Jerusalem heard news of them, they withdrew from Jerusalem.

6 Then the word of the LORD came to Jĕr·e·mī′ah the prophet: ⁷"Thus says the LORD, God of Israel: Thus shall you say to the king of Judah who sent you to me to inquire of me, 'Behold, Pharaoh's army which came to help you is about to return to Egypt, to its own land. ⁸And the Chăl·dē′ans shall come back and fight against this city; they shall take it and burn it with fire. ⁹Thus says the LORD, Do not deceive yourselves, saying, "The Chăl·dē′ans will surely stay away from us," for they will not stay away. ¹⁰For even if you should defeat the whole army of Chăl·dē′ans who are fighting against you, and there remained of them only wounded men, every man in his tent, they would rise up and burn this city with fire.'"

11 Now when the Chăl·dē′an army had withdrawn from Jerusalem at the approach of Pharaoh's army, ¹²Jĕr·e·mī′ah set out from Jerusalem to go to the land of Benjamin to receive his portion[n] there among the people. ¹³When he was at the Benjamin Gate, a sentry there named Ĭ·rī′jah the son of Shĕl·e·mī′ah, son of Hăn·a·nī′ah, seized Jĕr·e·mī′ah the prophet, saying,

ⁿHeb obscure

"You are deserting to the Chăl·dē'-anṣ." ¹⁴And Jĕr·ę·mī'ạh said, "It is false; I am not deserting to the Chăl·dē'anṣ." But Ĭ·rī'jah would not listen to him, and seized Jeremiah and brought him to the princes. ¹⁵And the princes were enraged at Jĕr·ę·mī'ạh, and they beat him and imprisoned him in the house of Jonathan the secretary, for it had been made a prison.

16 When Jĕr·ę·mī'ạh had come to the dungeon cells, and remained there many days, ¹⁷King Zĕd·ę·kī'ạh sent for him, and received him. The king questioned him secretly in his house, and said, "Is there any word from the LORD?" Jĕr·ę·mī'ạh said, "There is." Then he said, "You shall be delivered into the hand of the king of Babylon." ¹⁸Jĕr·ę·mī'ạh also said to King Zĕd·ę·kī'ạh, "What wrong have I done to you or your servants or this people, that you have put me in prison? ¹⁹Where are your prophets who prophesied to you, saying, 'The king of Babylon will not come against you and against this land'? ²⁰Now hear, I pray you, O my lord the king: let my humble plea come before you, and do not send me back to the house of Jonathan the secretary, lest I die there." ²¹So King Zĕd·ę·kī'ạh gave orders, and they committed Jĕr·ę·mī'ạh to the court of the guard; and a loaf of bread was given him daily from the bakers' street, until all the bread of the city was gone. So Jeremiah remained in the court of the guard.

38 Now Shĕph·a·tī'ạh the son of Măt'tăn, Gĕd·ạ·lī'ạh the son of Păsh'hŭr, Jū'cạl the son of Shĕl·ę·mī'ạh, and Pashhur the son of Măl·chī'ạh heard the words that Jĕr·ę·mī'ạh was saying to all the people, ²"Thus says the LORD, He who stays in this city shall die by the sword, by famine, and by pestilence; but he who goes out to the Chăl·dē'anṣ shall live; he shall have his life as a prize of war, and live. ³Thus says the LORD, This city shall surely be given into the hand of the army of the king of Babylon and be taken." ⁴Then the princes said to the king, "Let this man be put to death, for he is weakening the hands of the soldiers who are left in this city, and the hands of all the people, by speaking such words to them. For this man is not seeking the welfare of this people, but their harm." ⁵King Zĕd·ę·kī'ạh said, "Behold, he is in your hands; for

the king can do nothing against you." ⁶So they took Jĕr·ę·mī'ạh and cast him into the cistern of Măl·chī'ạh, the king's son, which was in the court of the guard, letting Jeremiah down by ropes. And there was no water in the cistern, but only mire, and Jeremiah sank in the mire.

7 When Ē'bĕd–mĕl'ĕch the Ethiopian, a eunuch, who was in the king's house, heard that they had put Jĕr·ę·mī'ạh into the cistern—the king was sitting in the Benjamin Gate—⁸Ē'bĕd–mĕl'ĕch went from the king's house and said to the king, ⁹"My lord the king, these men have done evil in all that they did to Jĕr·ę·mī'ạh the prophet by casting him into the cistern; and he will die there of hunger, for there is no bread left in the city." ¹⁰Then the king commanded Ē'bĕd–mĕl'ĕch, the Ethiopian, "Take three men with you from here, and lift Jĕr·ę·mī'ạh the prophet out of the cistern before he dies." ¹¹So Ē'bĕd–mĕl'ĕch took the men with him and went to the house of the king, to a wardrobe of ᵍ the storehouse, and took from there old rags and worn-out clothes, which he let down to Jĕr·ę·mī'ạh in the cistern by ropes. ¹²Then Ē'bĕd–mĕl'ĕch the Ethiopian said to Jĕr·ę·mī'ạh, "Put the rags and clothes between your armpits and the ropes." Jeremiah did so. ¹³Then they drew Jĕr·ę·mī'ạh up with ropes and lifted him out of the cistern. And Jeremiah remained in the court of the guard.

14 King Zĕd·ę·kī'ạh sent for Jĕr·ę·mī'ạh the prophet and received him at the third entrance of the temple of the LORD. The king said to Jeremiah "I will ask you a question; hide nothing from me." ¹⁵Jĕr·ę·mī'ạh said to Zĕd·ę·kī'ạh, "If I tell you, will you not be sure to put me to death? And if I give you counsel, you will not listen to me." ¹⁶Then King Zĕd·ę·kī'ạh swore secretly to Jĕr·ę·mī'ạh, "As the LORD lives, who made our souls, I will not put you to death or deliver you into the hand of these men who seek your life."

17 Then Jĕr·ę·mī'ạh said to Zĕd·ę· kī'ạh, "Thus says the LORD, the God of hosts, the God of Israel, If you will surrender to the princes of the king of Babylon, then your life shall be spared and this city shall not be burned with fire, and you and your house shall live

ᵍCn: Heb *to under*

[18]But if you do not surrender to the princes of the king of Babylon, then this city shall be given into the hand of the Chăl-dē'aņs, and they shall burn it with fire, and you shall not escape from their hand." [19]King Zĕd-e-kī'ah said to Jĕr-e-mī'ah, "I am afraid of the Jews who have deserted to the Chăl-dē'aņs, lest I be handed over to them and they abuse me." [20]Jĕr-e-mī'ah said, "You shall not be given to them. Obey now the voice of the LORD in what I say to you, and it shall be well with you, and your life shall be spared. [21]But if you refuse to surrender, this is the vision which the LORD has shown to me: [22]Behold, all the women left in the house of the king of Judah were being led out to the princes of the king of Babylon and were saying,

'Your trusted friends have deceived you
and prevailed against you;
now that your feet are sunk in the mire,
they turn away from you.'

[23]All your wives and your sons shall be led out to the Chăl-dē'aņs, and you yourself shall not escape from their hand, but shall be seized by the king of Babylon; and this city shall be burned with fire."

24 Then Zĕd-e-kī'ah said to Jĕr-e-mī'ah, "Let no one know of these words and you shall not die. [25]If the princes hear that I have spoken with you and come to you and say to you, 'Tell us what you said to the king and what the king said to you; hide nothing from us and we will not put you to death,' [26]then you shall say to them, 'I made a humble plea to the king that he would not send me back to the house of Jonathan to die there.'" [27]Then all the princes came to Jĕr-e-mī'ah and asked him, and he answered them as the king had instructed them. So they left off speaking with him, for the conversation had not been overheard. [28]And Jĕr-e-mī'ah remained in the court of the guard until the day that Jerusalem was taken.

39 In the ninth year of Zĕd-e-kī'ah king of Judah, in the tenth month, Nĕ-bü-chad-rĕz'zar king of Babylon and all his army came against Jerusalem and besieged it; [2]in the eleventh year of Zĕd-e-kī'ah, in the fourth month, on the ninth day of the month, a breach was made in the city. [3]When Jerusalem was taken,ᵖ all the

princes of the king of Babylon came and sat in the middle gate: Nēr'gäl-shä-rē'zer, Săm'gär-nē'bō, Sär'sĕchĭm the Răb'sa-rĭs, Nergal-sharezer the Răb'măg, with all the rest of the officers of the king of Babylon. [4]When Zĕd-e-kī'ah king of Judah and all the soldiers saw them, they fled, going out of the city at night by way of the king's garden through the gate between the two walls; and they went toward the Är'a-bah. [5]But the army of the Chăl-dē'aņs pursued them, and overtook Zĕd-e-kī'ah in the plains of Jericho; and when they had taken him, they brought him up to Nĕ-bü-chad-rĕz'zar king of Babylon, at Rĭb'lah, in the land of Hā'măth; and he passed sentence upon him. [6]The king of Babylon slew the sons of Zĕd-e-kī'ah at Rĭb'lah before his eyes; and the king of Babylon slew all the nobles of Judah. [7]He put out the eyes of Zĕd-e-kī'ah, and bound him in fetters to take him to Babylon. [8]The Chăl-dē'aņs burned the king's house and the house of the people, and broke down the walls of Jerusalem. [9]Then Nĕ-bū'za-răd'an, the captain of the guard, carried into exile to Babylon the rest of the people who were left in the city, those who had deserted to him, and the people who remained. [10]Nĕ-bū'za-răd'an, the captain of the guard, left in the land of Judah some of the poor people who owned nothing, and gave them vineyards and fields at the same time.

11 Nĕ-bü-chad-rĕz'zar king of Babylon gave command concerning Jĕr-e-mī'ah through Nĕ-bū'za-răd'an, the captain of the guard, saying, [12]"Take him, look after him well and do him no harm, but deal with him as he tells you." [13]So Nĕ-bū'za-răd'an the captain of the guard, Nĕ-bu-shăz'băn the Răb'sa-rĭs, Nēr'găl-shä-rē'zer the Răb'măg, and all the chief officers of the king of Babylon [14]sent and took Jĕr-e-mī'ah from the court of the guard. They entrusted him to Gĕd-a-lī'ah the son of A-hī'kăm, son of Shā'phan, that he should take him home. So he dwelt among the people.

15 The word of the LORD came to Jĕr-e-mī'ah while he was shut up in the court of the guard: [16]"Go, and say to Ē'bĕd-mĕl'ĕch the Ethiopian, 'Thus says the LORD of hosts, the God of

ᵖThis clause has been transposed from the end of Chapter 38

Israel: Behold, I will fulfil my words
against this city for evil and not for
good, and they shall be accomplished
before you on that day. 17 But I will
deliver you on that day, says the LORD,
and you shall not be given into the
hand of the men of whom you are
afraid. 18 For I will surely save you,
and you shall not fall by the sword; but
you shall have your life as a prize of
war, because you have put your trust in
me, says the LORD.'"

40 The word that came to Jĕr·ẹ-
mī'ạh from the LORD after
Nĕ·bū'zạ·răd'ạn the captain of the
guard had let him go from Rā'mạh,
when he took him bound in chains
along with all the captives of Jerusalem and Judah who were being
exiled to Babylon. 2 The captain of
the guard took Jĕr·ẹ·mī'ạh and said to
him, "The LORD your God pronounced
this evil against this place; 3 the LORD
has brought it about, and has done as
he said. Because you sinned against
the LORD, and did not obey his voice,
this thing has come upon you. 4 Now,
behold, I release you today from the
chains on your hands. If it seems good
to you to come with me to Babylon,
come, and I will look after you well;
but if it seems wrong to you to come
with me to Babylon, do not come. See,
the whole land is before you; go
wherever you think it good and right
to go. 5 If you remain,[q] then return to
Gĕd·ạ·lī'ạh the son of Ạ·hī'kăm, son
of Shā'phạn, whom the king of Babylon appointed governor of the cities
of Judah, and dwell with him among
the people; or go wherever you think
it right to go." So the captain of the
guard gave him an allowance of food
and a present, and let him go. 6 Then
Jĕr·ẹ·mī'ạh went to Gĕd·ạ·lī'ạh the son
of Ạ·hī'kăm, at Mĭz'pạh, and dwelt
with him among the people who were
left in the land.

7 When all the captains of the forces
in the open country and their men
heard that the king of Babylon had appointed Gĕd·ạ·lī'ạh the son of Ạ·hī'-
kăm governor in the land, and had
committed to him men, women, and
children, those of the poorest of the
land who had not been taken into exile
to Babylon, 8 they went to Gĕd·ạ·lī'ạh at
Mĭz'pạh—Ĭsh'mạ·ĕl the son of Nĕth·ạ-
nī'ạh, Jō·hā'nạn the son of Kạ·rē'ạh,
Sĕ·rāi'ạh the son of Tăn'hū·mĕth, the
sons of Ē'phaī the Nẹ·tōph'ạ·thīte,
Jĕz·ạ·nī'ạh the son of the Mā–ăc'ạ-
thīte, they and their men. 9 Gĕd·ạ·lī'ạh
the son of Ạ·hī'kăm, son of Shā'phạn,
swore to them and their men, saying,
"Do not be afraid to serve the Chăl-
dē'ạnş. Dwell in the land, and serve
the king of Babylon, and it shall be
well with you. 10 As for me, I will dwell
at Mĭz'pạh, to stand for you before the
Chăl·dē'ạnş who will come to us; but
as for you, gather wine and summer
fruits and oil, and store them in your
vessels, and dwell in your cities that
you have taken." 11 Likewise, when all
the Jews who were in Mō'ăb and
among the Ăm'mọ·nītes and in Ē'dọm
and in other lands heard that the king
of Babylon had left a remnant in Judah
and had appointed Gĕd·ạ·lī'ạh the son
of Ạ·hī'kăm, son of Shā'phạn, as governor over them, 12 then all the Jews
returned from all the places to which
they had been driven and came to
the land of Judah, to Gĕd·ạ·lī'ạh at
Mĭz'pạh; and they gathered wine and
summer fruits in great abundance.

13 Now Jō·hā'nạn the son of Kạ-
rē'ạh and all the leaders of the forces
in the open country came to Gĕd·ạ-
lī'ạh at Mĭz'pạh 14 and said to him,
"Do you know that Bā'ạ·lĭs the king of
the Ăm'mọ·nītes has sent Ĭsh'mạ·ĕl
the son of Nĕth·ạ·nī'ạh to take your
life?" But Gĕd·ạ·lī'ạh the son of Ạ·hī'-
kăm would not believe them. 15 Then
Jō·hā'nạn the son of Kạ·rē'ạh spoke
secretly to Gĕd·ạ·lī'ạh at Mĭz'pạh,
"Let me go and slay Ĭsh'mạ·ĕl the son
of Nĕth·ạ·nī'ạh, and no one will know
it. Why should he take your life, so
that all the Jews who are gathered
about you would be scattered, and the
remnant of Judah would perish?"
16 But Gĕd·ạ·lī'ạh the son of Ạ·hī'kăm
said to Jō·hā'nạn the son of Kạ·rē'ạh,
"You shall not do this thing, for you
are speaking falsely of Ĭsh'mạ·ĕl."

41 In the seventh month, Ĭsh'-
mạ·ĕl the son of Nĕth·ạ·nī'ạh,
son of Ē·lĭsh'ạ·mạ, of the royal family,
one of the chief officers of the king,
came with ten men to Gĕd·ạ·lī'ạh
the son of Ạ·hī'kăm, at Mĭz'pạh. As
they ate bread together there at
Mizpah, 2 Ĭsh'mạ·ĕl the son of Nĕth-
ạ·nī'ạh and the ten men with him rose
up and struck down Gĕd·ạ·lī'ạh the

[q] Syr: Heb obscure

son of A·hī'kăm, son of Shā'phạn, with the sword, and killed him, whom the king of Babylon had appointed governor in the land. [3] Ĭsh'mạ·ĕl also slew all the Jews who were with Gĕd·ạ·lī'ạh at Mĭz'pạh, and the Chăl·dē'ạn soldiers who happened to be there.

4 On the day after the murdẹr of Gĕd·ạ·lī'ạh, before any one knew of it, [5] eighty men arrived from Shē'chĕm and Shī'lōh and Sạ·mâr'ĭ·ạ, with their beards shaved and their clothes torn, and their bodies gashed, bringing cereal offerings and incense to present at the temple of the LORD. [6] And Ĭsh'mạ·ĕl the son of Nĕth·ạ·nī'ạh came out from Mĭz'pạh to meet them, weeping as he came. As he met them, he said to them, "Come in to Gĕd·ạ·lī'ạh the son of A·hī'kăm." [7] When they came into the city, Ĭsh'mạ·ĕl the son of Nĕth·ạ·nī'ạh and the men with him slew them, and cast them into a cistern. [8] But there were ten men among them who said to Ĭsh'mạ·ĕl, "Do not kill us, for we have stores of wheat, barley, oil, and honey hidden in the fields." So he refrained and did not kill them with their companions.

9 Now the cistern into which Ĭsh'mạ·ĕl cast all the bodies of the men whom he had slain was the large cistern[r] which King Asa had made for defense against Bā'ạ·shạ king of Israel; Ishmael the son of Nĕth·ạ·nī'ạh filled it with the slain. [10] Then Ĭsh'mạ·ĕl took captive all the rest of the people who were in Mĭz'pạh, the king's daughters and all the people who were left at Mizpah whom Nĕ·bū'zạ·răd'ạn, the captain of the guard, had committed to Gĕd·ạ·lī'ạh the son of A·hī'kăm. Ĭsh'mạ·ĕl the son of Nĕth·ạ·nī'ạh took them captive and set out to cross over to the Ăm'mọ·nītes.

11 But when Jō·hā'nạn the son of Kạ·rē'ạh and all the leaders of the forces with him heard of all the evil which Ĭsh'mạ·ĕl the son of Nĕth·ạ·nī'ạh had done, [12] they took all their men and went to fight against Ĭsh'mạ·ĕl the son of Nĕth·ạ·nī'ạh. They came upon him at the great pool which is in Gĭb'ē·ọn. [13] And when all the people who were with Ĭsh'mạ·ĕl saw Jō·hā'nạn the son of Kạ·rē'ạh and all the leaders of the forces with him, they rejoiced. [14] So all the people whom Ĭsh'mạ·ĕl had carried away captive

from Mĭz'pạh turned about and came back, and went to Jō·hā'nạn the son of Kạ·rē'ạh. [15] But Ĭsh'mạ·ĕl the son of Nĕth·ạ·nī'ạh escaped from Jō·hā'nạn with eight men, and went to the Ăm'mọ·nītes. [16] Then Jō·hā'nạn the son of Kạ·rē'ạh and all the leaders of the forces with him took all the rest of the people whom Ĭsh'mạ·ĕl the son of Nĕth·ạ·nī'ạh had carried away captive[s] from Mĭz'pạh after he had slain Gĕd·ạ·lī'ạh the son of A·hī'kăm—soldiers, women, children, and eunuchs, whom Jō·hā'nạn brought back from Gĭb'ē·ọn. [17] And they went and stayed at Gē'rüth Chĭm'hạm near Bethlehem, intending to go to Egypt [18] because of the Chăl·dē'ạns; for they were afraid of them, because Ĭsh'mạ·ĕl the son of Nĕth·ạ·nī'ạh had slain Gĕd·ạ·lī'ạh the son of A·hī'kăm, whom the king of Babylon had made governor over the land.

42 Then all the commanders of the forces, and Jō·hā'nạn the son of Kạ·rē'ạh and Ăz·ạ·rī'ạh[t] the son of Hō·shaī'ạh, and all the people from the least to the greatest, came near [2] and said to Jĕr·ẹ·mī'ạh the prophet, "Let our supplication come before you, and pray to the LORD your God for us, for all this remnant (for we are left but a few of many, as your eyes see us), [3] that the LORD your God may show us the way we should go, and the thing that we should do." [4] Jĕr·ẹ·mī'ạh the prophet said to them, "I have heard you; behold, I will pray to the LORD your God according to your request, and whatever the LORD answers you I will tell you; I will keep nothing back from you." [5] Then they said to Jĕr·ẹ·mī'ạh, "May the LORD be a true and faithful witness against us if we do not act according to all the word with which the LORD your God sends you to us. [6] Whether it is good or evil, we will obey the voice of the LORD our God to whom we are sending you, that it may be well with us when we obey the voice of the LORD our God."

7 At the end of ten days the word of the LORD came to Jĕr·ẹ·mī'ạh. [8] Then he summoned Jō·hā'nạn the son of Kạ·rē'ạh and all the commanders of the forces who were with him, and all the people from the least to the great-

[r]Gk: Heb *he had slain by the hand of Gedaliah*
[s]Cn: Heb *whom he recovered from Ishmael*
[t]Gk: Heb *Jezaniah*

est, ⁹and said to them, "Thus says the LORD, the God of Israel, to whom you sent me to present your supplication before him: ¹⁰If you will remain in this land, then I will build you up and not pull you down; I will plant you, and not pluck you up; for I repent of the evil which I did to you. ¹¹Do not fear the king of Babylon, of whom you are afraid; do not fear him, says the LORD, for I am with you, to save you and to deliver you from his hand. ¹²I will grant you mercy, that he may have mercy on you and let you remain in your own land. ¹³But if you say, 'We will not remain in this land,' disobeying the voice of the LORD your God ¹⁴and saying, 'No, we will go to the land of Egypt, where we shall not see war, or hear the sound of the trumpet, or be hungry for bread, and we will dwell there,' ¹⁵then hear the word of the LORD, O remnant of Judah. Thus says the LORD of hosts, the God of Israel: If you set your faces to enter Egypt and go to live there, ¹⁶then the sword which you fear shall overtake you there in the land of Egypt; and the famine of which you are afraid shall follow hard after you to Egypt; and there you shall die. ¹⁷All the men who set their faces to go to Egypt to live there shall die by the sword, by famine, and by pestilence; they shall have no remnant or survivor from the evil which I will bring upon them.

18 "For thus says the LORD of hosts, the God of Israel: As my anger and my wrath were poured out on the inhabitants of Jerusalem, so my wrath will be poured out on you when you go to Egypt. You shall become an execration, a horror, a curse, and a taunt. You shall see this place no more. ¹⁹The LORD has said to you, O remnant of Judah, 'Do not go to Egypt.' Know for a certainty that I have warned you this day ²⁰that you have gone astray at the cost of your lives. For you sent me to the LORD your God, saying, 'Pray for us to the LORD our God, and whatever the LORD our God says declare to us and we will do it.' ²¹And I have this day declared it to you, but you have not obeyed the voice of the LORD your God in anything that he sent me to tell you. ²²Now therefore know for a certainty that you shall die by the sword, by famine, and by pestilence

in the place where you desire to go to live."

43 When Jĕr· e·mī′ah finished speaking to all the people all these words of the LORD their God, with which the LORD their God had sent him to them, ²Ăz·a·rī′ah the son of Hō·shaī′ah and Jō·hā′nan the son of Ka·rē′ah and all the insolent men said to Jĕr·e·mī′ah, "You are telling a lie. The LORD our God did not send you to say, 'Do not go to Egypt to live there'; ³but Bär′uch the son of Nĕ·rī′ah has set you against us, to deliver us into the hand of the Chăl·dē′ans, that they may kill us or take us into exile in Babylon." ⁴So Jō·hā′nan the son of Ka·rē′ah and all the commanders of the forces and all the people did not obey the voice of the LORD, to remain in the land of Judah. ⁵But Jō·hā′nan the son of Ka·rē′ah and all the commanders of the forces took all the remnant of Judah who had returned to live in the land of Judah from all the nations to which they had been driven —⁶the men, the women, the children, the princesses, and every person whom Nĕ·bū′za·răd′an the captain of the guard had left with Gĕd·a·lī′ah the son A·hī′kăm, son of Shā′phan; also Jĕr·e·mī′ah the prophet and Bär′uch the son of Nĕ·rī′ah. ⁷And they came into the land of Egypt, for they did not obey the voice of the LORD. And they arrived at Täh′pan·hĕş.

8 Then the word of the LORD came to Jĕr·e·mī′ah in Täh′pan·hĕş: ⁹"Take in your hands large stones, and hide them in the mortar in the pavement which is at the entrance to Pharaoh's palace in Täh′pan·hĕş, in the sight of the men of Judah, ¹⁰and say to them, 'Thus says the LORD of hosts, the God of Israel: Behold, I will send and take Nĕ·bū·chad·rĕz′zar the king of Babylon, my servant, and heᵘ will set his throne above these stones which I have hid, and he will spread his royal canopy over them. ¹¹He shall come and smite the land of Egypt, giving to the pestilence those who are doomed to the pestilence, to captivity those who are doomed to captivity, and to the sword those who are doomed to the sword. ¹²Heᵛ shall kindle a fire in the temples of the gods of Egypt; and he shall burn them and carry them away captive; and he shall clean the land of

ᵘGk Syr: Heb *I*   ᵛGk Syr Vg: Heb *I*

Egypt, as a shepherd cleans his cloak of vermin; and he shall go away from there in peace. [13]He shall break the obelisks of Hē″lĭ-ŏp′ọ·lĭs which is in the land of Egypt; and the temples of the gods of Egypt he shall burn with fire.' "

44 The word that came to Jĕr·ẹ-mī′ạh concerning all the Jews that dwelt in the land of Egypt, at Mĭg′dōl, at Täh′pạn·hĕṣ, at Memphis, and in the land of Păth′rŏs, [2]"Thus says the LORD of hosts, the God of Israel: You have seen all the evil that I brought upon Jerusalem and upon all the cities of Judah. Behold, this day they are a desolation, and no one dwells in them, [3]because of the wickedness which they committed, provoking me to anger, in that they went to burn incense and serve other gods that they knew not, neither they, nor you, nor your fathers. [4]Yet I persistently sent to you all my servants the prophets, saying, 'Oh, do not do this abominable thing that I hate!' [5]But they did not listen or incline their ear, to turn from their wickedness and burn no incense to other gods. [6]Therefore my wrath and my anger were poured forth and kindled in the cities of Judah and in the streets of Jerusalem; and they became a waste and a desolation, as at this day. [7]And now thus says the LORD God of hosts, the God of Israel: Why do you commit this great evil against yourselves, to cut off from you man and woman, infant and child, from the midst of Judah, leaving you no remnant? [8]Why do you provoke me to anger with the works of your hands, burning incense to other gods in the land of Egypt where you have come to live, that you may be cut off and become a curse and a taunt among all the nations of the earth? [9]Have you forgotten the wickedness of your fathers, the wickedness of the kings of Judah, the wickedness of their[w] wives, your own wickedness, and the wickedness of your wives, which they committed in the land of Judah and in the streets of Jerusalem? [10]They have not humbled themselves even to this day, nor have they feared, nor walked in my law and my statutes which I set before you and before your fathers.

[11] "Therefore thus says the LORD of hosts, the God of Israel: Behold, I will set my face against you for evil, to cut off all Judah. [12]I will take the remnant of Judah who have set their faces to come to the land of Egypt to live, and they shall all be consumed; in the land of Egypt they shall fall; by the sword and by famine they shall be consumed; from the least to the greatest, they shall die by the sword and by famine; and they shall become an execration, a horror, a curse, and a taunt. [13]I will punish those who dwell in the land of Egypt, as I have punished Jerusalem, with the sword, with famine, and with pestilence, [14]so that none of the remnant of Judah who have come to live in the land of Egypt shall escape or survive or return to the land of Judah, to which they desire to return to dwell there; for they shall not return, except some fugitives."

15 Then all the men who knew that their wives had offered incense to other gods, and all the women who stood by, a great assembly, all the people who dwelt in Păth′rŏs in the land of Egypt, answered Jĕr·ẹ·mī′ạh: [16]"As for the word which you have spoken to us in the name of the LORD, we will not listen to you. [17]But we will do everything that we have vowed, burn incense to the queen of heaven and pour out libations to her, as we did, both we and our fathers, our kings and our princes, in the cities of Judah and in the streets of Jerusalem; for then we had plenty of food, and prospered, and saw no evil. [18]But since we left off burning incense to the queen of heaven and pouring out libations to her, we have lacked everything and have been consumed by the sword and by famine." [19]And the women said,[x] "When we burned incense to the queen of heaven and poured out libations to her, was it without our husbands' approval that we made cakes for her bearing her image and poured out libations to her?"

20 Then Jĕr·ẹ·mī′ạh said to all the people, men and women, all the people who had given him this answer: [21]"As for the incense that you burned in the cities of Judah and in the streets of Jerusalem, you and your fathers, your kings and your princes, and the people of the land, did not the

---

[w]Heb *his*
[x]Compare Syr: Heb lacks *And the women said*

LORD remember it?ʸ Did it not come
into his mind? ²²The LORD could no
longer bear your evil doings and the
abominations which you committed;
therefore your land has become a
desolation and a waste and a curse,
without inhabitant, as it is this day.
²³It is because you burned incense,
and because you sinned against the
LORD and did not obey the voice of
the LORD or walk in his law and in
his statutes and in his testimonies,
that this evil has befallen you, as at
this day."

24 Jĕr·e·mī'ah said to all the people
and all the women, "Hear the word
of the LORD, all you of Judah who are
in the land of Egypt, ²⁵Thus says the
LORD of hosts, the God of Israel: You
and your wives have declared with
your mouths, and have fulfilled it
with your hands, saying, 'We will
surely perform our vows that we have
made, to burn incense to the queen
of heaven and to pour out libations to
her.' Then confirm your vows and perform your vows! ²⁶Therefore hear the
word of the LORD, all you of Judah
who dwell in the land of Egypt: Behold,
I have sworn by my great name, says
the LORD, that my name shall no more
be invoked by the mouth of any man
of Judah in all the land of Egypt, saying, 'As the Lord GOD lives.' ²⁷Behold,
I am watching over them for evil and
not for good; all the men of Judah who
are in the land of Egypt shall be consumed by the sword and by famine,
until there is an end of them. ²⁸And
those who escape the sword shall return from the land of Egypt to the land
of Judah, few in number; and all the
remnant of Judah, who came to the
land of Egypt to live, shall know whose
word will stand, mine or theirs. ²⁹This
shall be the sign to you, says the LORD,
that I will punish you in this place,
in order that you may know that my
words will surely stand against you for
evil: ³⁰Thus says the LORD, Behold, I
will give Pharaoh Hŏph'ra king of
Egypt into the hand of his enemies and
into the hand of those who seek his
life, as I gave Zĕd·e·kī'ah king of Judah
into the hand of Nĕ·bū·chad·rĕz'zar
king of Babylon, who was his enemy
and sought his life."

45   The word that Jĕr·e·mī'ah the
prophet spoke to Bär'uch the

son of Nĕ·rī'ah, when he wrote these
words in a book at the dictation of
Jeremiah, in the fourth year of Jĕ-
hoi'a·kim the son of Jō·sī'ah, king of
Judah: ²"Thus says the LORD, the God
of Israel, to you, O Bär'uch: ³You said,
'Woe is me! for the LORD has added
sorrow to my pain; I am weary with my
groaning, and I find no rest.' ⁴Thus
shall you say to him, Thus says the
LORD: Behold, what I have built I am
breaking down, and what I have
planted I am plucking up—that is, the
whole land. ⁵And do you seek great
things for yourself? Seek them not; for,
behold, I am bringing evil upon all
flesh, says the LORD; but I will give
you your life as a prize of war in all
places to which you may go."

46   The word of the LORD which
came to Jĕr·e·mī'ah the prophet
concerning the nations.

2 About Egypt. Concerning the army
of Pharaoh Nē'cō, king of Egypt,
which was by the river Euphrates at
Cär'che·mĭsh and which Nĕ·bū·chad-
rĕz'zar king of Babylon defeated in
the fourth year of Jĕ·hoi'a·kim the
son of Jō·sī'ah, king of Judah:
³"Prepare buckler and shield,
  and advance for battle!
⁴Harness the horses;
  mount, O horsemen!
Take your stations with your helmets,
  polish your spears,
  put on your coats of mail!
⁵Why have I seen it?
They are dismayed
  and have turned backward.
Their warriors are beaten down,
  and have fled in haste;
they look not back—
  terror on every side!
          says the LORD.
⁶The swift cannot flee away,
  nor the warrior escape;
in the north by the river Euphrates
  they have stumbled and fallen.

⁷"Who is this, rising like the Nile,
  like rivers whose waters surge?
⁸Egypt rises like the Nile,
  like rivers whose waters surge.
He said, I will rise, I will cover the
  earth,
  I will destroy cities and their inhabitants.

ʸSyr: Heb *them*   46: Is 19; Ezek 29-32; Zech 14.18-19.
46.5: Jer 6.25; 20.3, 10; 49.29; Ps 31.13.

⁹Advance, O horses,
　and rage, O chariots!
Let the warriors go forth:
　men of Ethiopia and Püt who
　　handle the shield,
　men of Lüd, skilled in handling
　　the bow.
¹⁰That day is the day of the Lord GOD
　of hosts,
　a day of vengeance,
　to avenge himself on his foes.
The sword shall devour and be
　sated,
　and drink its fill of their blood.
For the Lord GOD of hosts holds a
　sacrifice
　in the north country by the river
　Euphrates.
¹¹Go up to Gilead, and take balm,
　O virgin daughter of Egypt!
In vain you have used many medi-
　cines;
　there is no healing for you.
¹²The nations have heard of your
　shame,
　and the earth is full of your cry;
for warrior has stumbled against
　warrior;
　they have both fallen together."

13 The word which the LORD spoke
to Jĕr·e·mī′ah the prophet about the
coming of Nĕ·bü·chạd·rĕz′zạr king of
Babylon to smite the land of Egypt:
¹⁴"Declare in Egypt, and proclaim in
　Mĭg′dŏl;
　proclaim in Memphis and Täh′-
　　pan·hĕṣ;
Say, 'Stand ready and be prepared,
　for the sword shall devour round
　about you.'
¹⁵Why has Ā′pĭs fled?ᶻ
　Why did not your bull stand?
　Because the LORD thrust him
　down.
¹⁶Your multitude stumbledᵃ and fell,
　and they said one to another,
'Arise, and let us go back to our own
　people
　and to the land of our birth,
　because of the sword of the op-
　pressor.'
¹⁷Call the name of Pharaoh, king of
　Egypt,
　'Noisy one who lets the hour go
　by.'

¹⁸"As I live, says the King,
　whose name is the LORD of hosts,
like Tä′bôr among the mountains,

and like Cär′mẹl by the sea, shall
　one come.
¹⁹Prepare yourselves baggage for exile,
　O inhabitants of Egypt!
For Memphis shall become a waste,
　a ruin, without inhabitant.

²⁰"A beautiful heifer is Egypt,
　but a gadfly from the north has
　come upon her.
²¹Even her hired soldiers in her midst
　are like fatted calves;
yea, they have turned and fled to-
　gether,
　they did not stand;
for the day of their calamity has
　come upon them,
　the time of their punishment.

²²"She makes a sound like a serpent
　gliding away;
for her enemies march in force,
　and come against her with axes,
　like those who fell trees.
²³They shall cut down her forest,
　　　　　　　says the LORD,
　though it is impenetrable,
because they are more numerous
　than locusts;
　they are without number.
²⁴The daughter of Egypt shall be put
　to shame,
　she shall be delivered into the
　hand of a people from the north."

25 The LORD of hosts, the God of
Israel, said: "Behold, I am bringing
punishment upon Ā′mŏn of Thebes,
and Pharaoh, and Egypt and her
gods and her kings, upon Pharaoh
and those who trust in him. ²⁶I will deliver them into the hand of those who
seek their life, into the hand of Nĕ-
bü·chạd·rĕz′zạr king of Babylon and
his officers. Afterward Egypt shall be
inhabited as in the days of old, says
the LORD.

²⁷"But fear not, O Jacob my servant,
　nor be dismayed, O Israel;
for lo, I will save you from afar,
　and your offspring from the land
　of their captivity.
Jacob shall return and have quiet
　and ease,
　and none shall make him afraid.
²⁸Fear not, O Jacob my servant,
　　　　　　　says the LORD,

ᶻGk: Heb *Why was it swept away*
ᵃGk: Heb *He made many stumble*

for I am with you.
I will make a full end of all the nations
to which I have driven you,
but of you I will not make a full end.
I will chasten you in just measure,
and I will by no means leave you unpunished."

47 The word of the LORD that came to Jĕr·e·mī'ah the prophet concerning the Phĭ·lĭs'tĭnes, before Pharaoh smote Gā'zạ.
2 "Thus says the LORD:
Behold, waters are rising out of the north,
and shall become an overflowing torrent;
they shall overflow the land and all that fills it,
the city and those who dwell in it.
Men shall cry out,
and every inhabitant of the land shall wail.
3 At the noise of the stamping of the hoofs of his stallions,
at the rushing of his chariots, at the rumbling of their wheels,
the fathers look not back to their children,
so feeble are their hands,
4 because of the day that is coming to destroy
all the Phĭ·lĭs'tĭnes,
to cut off from Tȳre and Sī'dŏn every helper that remains.
For the LORD is destroying the Philistines,
the remnant of the coastland of Căph'tôr.
5 Baldness has come upon Gā'zạ,
Ăsh'ke·lŏn has perished.
O remnant of the Ăn'ạ·kĭm,[b]
how long will you gash yourselves?
6 Ah, sword of the LORD!
How long till you are quiet?
Put yourself into your scabbard,
rest and be still!
7 How can it[c] be quiet,
when the LORD has given it a charge?
Against Ăsh'ke'lŏn and against the seashore
he has appointed it."

48 Concerning Mō'ăb.
Thus says the LORD of hosts, the God of Israel:
"Woe to Nē'bō, for it is laid waste!

Kīr"ĭ·a·thā'ĭm is put to shame, it is taken;
the fortress is put to shame and broken down;
2 the renown of Mō'ăb is no more.
In Hĕsh'bon they planned evil against her:
'Come, let us cut her off from being a nation!'
You also, O Madmen, shall be brought to silence;
the sword shall pursue you.

3 "Hark! a cry from Hôr·ō·nā'ĭm,
'Desolation and great destruction!'
4 Mō'ăb is destroyed;
a cry is heard as far as Zō'ăr.[d]
5 For at the ascent of Lū'hĭth
they go up weeping;[e]
for at the descent of Hôr·ō·nā'ĭm
they have heard the cry[f] of destruction.
6 Flee! Save yourselves!
Be like a wild ass[g] in the desert!
7 For, because you trusted in your strongholds[h] and your treasures,
you also shall be taken;
and Chē'mŏsh shall go forth into exile,
with his priests and his princes.
8 The destroyer shall come upon every city,
and no city shall escape;
the valley shall perish,
and the plain shall be destroyed,
as the LORD has spoken.

9 "Give wings to Mō'ăb,
for she would fly away;
her cities shall become a desolation,
with no inhabitant in them.

10 "Cursed is he who does the work of the LORD with slackness; and cursed is he who keeps back his sword from bloodshed.

11 "Mō'ăb has been at ease from his youth
and has settled on his lees;
he has not been emptied from vessel to vessel,
nor has he gone into exile;

---

b Gk: Heb *their valley*   *c* Gk Vg: Heb *you*
d Gk: Heb *her little ones*
e Cn: Heb *weeping goes up with weeping*
f Gk Compare Is 15.5: Heb *the distress of the cry*
g Gk Aquila: Heb *like Aroer*   *h* Gk: Heb *works*
47: Is 14.29-31; Ezek 25.15-17; Amos 1.6-8; Zeph 2.4-7; Zech 9.5-7.
48: Is 15-16; 25.10-12; Ezek 25.8-11; Amos 2.1-3; Zeph 2.8-11.

so his taste remains in him,
and his scent is not changed.
12 "Therefore, behold, the days are
coming, says the LORD, when I shall
send to him tilters who will tilt him,
and empty his vessels, and break his[i]
jars in pieces. 13 Then Mō'ăb shall be
ashamed of Chē'mŏsh, as the house of
Israel was ashamed of Bĕth'el, their
confidence.

14 "How do you say, 'We are heroes
and mighty men of war'?
15 The destroyer of Mō'ăb and his cities
has come up,
and the choicest of his young men
have gone down to slaughter,
says the King, whose name is the
LORD of hosts.
16 The calamity of Mō'ăb is near at
hand
and his affliction hastens apace.
17 Bemoan him, all you who are round
about him,
and all who know his name;
say, 'How the mighty scepter is
broken,
the glorious staff.'

18 "Come down from your glory,
and sit on the parched ground,
O inhabitant of Dī'bŏn!
For the destroyer of Mō'ăb has come
up against you;
he has destroyed your strongholds.
19 Stand by the way and watch,
O inhabitant of A·rō'er!
Ask him who flees and her who escapes;
say, 'What has happened?'
20 Mō'ăb is put to shame, for it is
broken;
wail and cry!
Tell it by the Är·nŏn,
that Moab is laid waste.

21 "Judgment has come upon the
tableland, upon Hō'lŏn, and Jäh'zah,
and Mĕph'a·ăth, 22 and Dī'bŏn, and
Nē'bō, and Bĕth"–dĭb·la·thā'ĭm, 23 and
Kīr"ĭ·a·thā'ĭm, and Bĕth–gā'mŭl, and
Bĕth–mē'ŏn, 24 and Kĕr'ĭ·ŏth, and
Bŏz'rah, and all the cities of the land
of Mō'ăb, far and near. 25 The horn of
Mō'ăb is cut off, and his arm is broken,
says the LORD.
26 "Make him drunk, because he
magnified himself against the LORD;
so that Mō'ăb shall wallow in his
vomit, and he too shall be held in de-

rision. 27 Was not Israel a derision to
you? Was he found among thieves,
that whenever you spoke of him you
wagged your head?

28 "Leave the cities, and dwell in the
rock,
O inhabitants of Mō'ăb!
Be like the dove that nests
in the sides of the mouth of a
gorge.
29 We have heard of the pride of Mō'ăb—
he is very proud—
of his loftiness, his pride, and his
arrogance,
and the haughtiness of his heart.
30 I know his insolence, says the LORD;
his boasts are false,
his deeds are false.
31 Therefore I wail for Mō'ăb;
I cry out for all Moab;
for the men of Kīr–hē'rĕs I mourn.
32 More than for Jā'zēr I weep for you,
O vine of Sīb'măh!
Your branches passed over the sea,
reached as far as Jazer,[j]
upon your summer fruits and your
vintage
the destroyer has fallen.
33 Gladness and joy have been taken
away
from the fruitful land of Mō'ăb;
I have made the wine cease from the
wine presses;
no one treads them with shouts of
joy;
the shouting is not the shout of
joy.

34 "Hĕsh'bon and Ē"lĕ·ā'lĕh cry out;[k]
as far as Jā'hăz they utter their voice,
from Zō'ăr to Hôr·ō·nā'ĭm and Ĕg'-
lath–shĕ·lĭsh'ĭ·yah. For the waters of
Nĭm'rĭm also have become desolate.
35 And I will bring to an end in Mō'ăb,
says the LORD, him who offers sacrifice in the high place and burns incense to his god. 36 Therefore my heart
moans for Mō'ăb like a flute, and my
heart moans like a flute for the men
of Kīr–hē'rĕs; therefore the riches they
gained have perished.
37 "For every head is shaved and
every beard cut off; upon all the hands
are gashes, and on the loins is sackcloth. 38 On all the housetops of Mō'ăb
and in the squares there is nothing but

[i]Gk Aquila: Heb *their*
[j]Cn: Heb *the sea of Jazer*
[k]Cn: Heb *From the cry of Heshbon to Elealeh*

lamentation; for I have broken Moab
like a vessel for which no one cares,
says the LORD. ³⁹How it is broken!
How they wail! How Mō'ăb has turned
his back in shame! So Moab has become a derision and a horror to all that
are round about him."
⁴⁰For thus says the LORD:
"Behold, one shall fly swiftly like
an eagle,
and spread his wings against
Mō'ăb;
⁴¹the cities shall be taken
and the strongholds seized.
The heart of the warriors of Mō'ăb
shall be in that day
like the heart of a woman in her
pangs;
⁴²Mō'ăb shall be destroyed and be no
longer a people,
because he magnified himself
against the LORD.
⁴³Terror, pit, and snare
are before you, O inhabitant of
Mō'ăb!
          says the LORD.
⁴⁴He who flees from the terror
shall fall into the pit,
and he who climbs out of the pit
shall be caught in the snare.
For I will bring these things^l upon
Mō'ăb
in the year of their punishment,
        says the LORD.

⁴⁵"In the shadow of Hĕsh'bon
fugitives stop without strength;
for a fire has gone forth from Heshbon,
a flame from the house of Sī'hon:
it has destroyed the forehead of
Mō'ăb,
the crown of the sons of tumult.
⁴⁶Woe to you, O Mō'ăb!
The people of Chē'mŏsh is undone;
for your sons have been taken captive,
and your daughters into captivity.
⁴⁷Yet I will restore the fortunes of
Mō'ăb
in the latter days, says the LORD."
Thus far is the judgment on Moab.

49 Concerning the Ăm'mo·nītes.
Thus says the LORD:
"Has Israel no sons?
Has he no heir?
Why then has Mīl'cŏm dispossessed
Găd,
and his people settled in its cities?

²Therefore, behold, the days are
coming,
    says the LORD,
when I will cause the battle cry to
be heard
against Răb'bah of the Ăm'mo-
nītes;
it shall become a desolate mound,
and its villages shall be burned
with fire;
then Israel shall dispossess those
who dispossessed him,
    says the LORD.

³"Wail, O Hĕsh'bon, for Aī is laid
waste!
Cry, O daughters of Răb'bah!
Gird yourselves with sackcloth,
lament, and run to and fro among
the hedges!
For Mīl'cŏm shall go into exile,
with his priests and his princes.
⁴Why do you boast of your valleys,^m
O faithless daughter,
who trusted in her treasures, saying,
'Who will come against me?'
⁵Behold, I will bring terror upon you,
    says the Lord GOD of hosts,
from all who are round about you,
and you shall be driven out, every
man straight before him,
with none to gather the fugitives.
⁶But afterward I will restore the
fortunes of the Ăm'mo·nītes, says the
LORD."

⁷Concerning Ē'dom.
Thus says the LORD of hosts:
"Is wisdom no more in Tē'man?
Has counsel perished from the
prudent?
Has their wisdom vanished?
⁸Flee, turn back, dwell in the depths,
O inhabitants of Dē'dăn!
For I will bring the calamity of Esau
upon him,
the time when I punish him.
⁹If grape-gatherers came to you,
would they not leave gleanings?
If thieves came by night,
would they not destroy only
enough for themselves?
¹⁰But I have stripped Esau bare,
I have uncovered his hiding places,
and he is not able to conceal himself.

^lGk Syr: Heb *to her*   ^mHeb *valleys, your valley flows*
49.1-6: Ezek 21.28-32; 25.1-7; Amos 1.13-15; Zeph 2.8-11.
49.7-22: Is 34; 63.1-6; Ezek 25.12-14; 35; Amos 1.11-12;
Obad; Mal 1.2-5.

His children are destroyed, and his brothers,
and his neighbors; and he is no more.
[11] Leave your fatherless children, I will keep them alive;
and let your widows trust in me."
12 For thus says the LORD: "If those who did not deserve to drink the cup must drink it, will you go unpunished? You shall not go unpunished, but you must drink. [13] For I have sworn by myself, says the LORD, that Bŏz′rah shall become a horror, a taunt, a waste, and a curse; and all her cities shall be perpetual wastes."
[14] I have heard tidings from the LORD, and a messenger has been sent among the nations:
"Gather yourselves together and come against her,
and rise up for battle!"
[15] For behold, I will make you small among the nations,
despised among men.
[16] The horror you inspire has deceived you,
and the pride of your heart,
you who live in the clefts of the rock,[n]
who hold the height of the hill.
Though you make your nest as high as the eagle's,
I will bring you down from there, says the LORD.
17 "Ē′dom shall become a horror; every one who passes by it will be horrified and will hiss because of all its disasters. [18] As when Sŏd′ọm and Gọ·môr′rah and their neighbor cities were overthrown, says the LORD, no man shall dwell there, no man shall sojourn in her. [19] Behold, like a lion coming up from the jungle of the Jordan against a strong sheepfold, I will suddenly make them[o] run away from her; and I will appoint over her whomever I choose. For who is like me? Who will summon me? What shepherd can stand before me?
[20] Therefore hear the plan which the LORD has made against Ē′dom and the purposes which he has formed against the inhabitants of Tē′man: Even the little ones of the flock shall be dragged away; surely their fold shall be appalled at their fate. [21] At the sound of their fall the earth shall tremble; the sound of their cry shall be heard at the Red Sea. [22] Behold, one shall mount up and fly swiftly like an eagle, and spread his wings against Bŏz′rah,
and the heart of the warriors of Ē′dom shall be in that day like the heart of a woman in her pangs."

23 Concerning Damascus.
"Hā′măth and Är′păd are confounded,
for they have heard evil tidings;
they melt in fear, they are troubled like the sea[p]
which cannot be quiet.
24 Damascus has become feeble, she turned to flee,
and panic seized her;
anguish and sorrows have taken hold of her,
as of a woman in travail.
25 How the famous city is forsaken,[q] the joyful city![r]
26 Therefore her young men shall fall in her squares,
and all her soldiers shall be destroyed in that day,
says the LORD of hosts.
27 And I will kindle a fire in the wall of Damascus,
and it shall devour the strongholds of Bĕn·hā′dăd."

28 Concerning Kē′där and the kingdoms of Hā′zôr which Nĕ·bü·chăd·rĕz′zar king of Babylon smote.
Thus says the LORD:
"Rise up, advance against Kedar!
Destroy the people of the east!
29 Their tents and their flocks shall be taken,
their curtains and all their goods;
their camels shall be borne away from them,
and men shall cry to them:
'Terror on every side!'
30 Flee, wander far away, dwell in the depths,
O inhabitants of Hā′zôr!
says the LORD.
For Nĕ·bü·chăd·rĕz′zar king of Babylon
has made a plan against you,
and formed a purpose against you.

31 "Rise up, advance against a nation at ease,

Or Sela   *[o] Gk Syr: Heb him*
[p] Cn: Heb there is trouble in the sea
[q] Vg: Heb not forsaken   *[r] Syr Vg Tg: Heb city of my joy*
49.23-27: Is 17.1-3; Amos 1.3-5; Zech 9.1.
49.29: Jer 6.25; 20.3, 10; 46.5; Ps 31.13.

that dwells securely,
    says the LORD,
that has no gates or bars,
that dwells alone.
³²Their camels shall become booty,
their herds of cattle a spoil.
I will scatter to every wind
those who cut the corners of their
    hair,
and I will bring their calamity
from every side of them,
    says the LORD.
³³Hā′zôr shall become a haunt of
    jackals,
an everlasting waste;
no man shall dwell there,
no man shall sojourn in her."

34 The word of the LORD that came
to Jĕr·e·mī′ah the prophet concerning
Ē′lăm, in the beginning of the reign
of Zĕd·e·kī′ah king of Judah.
35 Thus says the LORD of hosts:
"Behold, I will break the bow of Ē′lăm,
the mainstay of their might; ³⁶and I
will bring upon Ē′lăm the four winds
from the four quarters of heaven; and
I will scatter them to all those winds,
and there shall be no nation to which
those driven out of Elam shall not
come. ³⁷I will terrify Ē′lăm before
their enemies, and before those who
seek their life; I will bring evil upon
them, my fierce anger, says the LORD.
I will send the sword after them, until
I have consumed them; ³⁸and I will
set my throne in Ē′lăm, and destroy
their king and princes, says the LORD.
39 "But in the latter days I will
restore the fortunes of Ē′lăm, says the
LORD."

50 The word which the LORD
    spoke concerning Babylon,
concerning the land of the Chăl·dē′-
ans, by Jĕr·e·mī′ah the prophet:
²"Declare among the nations and pro-
    claim,
set up a banner and proclaim,
conceal it not, and say:
'Babylon is taken,
Bĕl is put to shame,
Mĕr′o·dăch is dismayed.
Her images are put to shame,
her idols are dismayed.'
3 "For out of the north a nation
has come up against her, which shall
make her land a desolation, and none
shall dwell in it; both man and beast
shall flee away.

4 "In those days and in that time,
says the LORD, the people of Israel
and the people of Judah shall come
together, weeping as they come; and
they shall seek the LORD their God.
⁵They shall ask the way to Zion,
with faces turned toward it, saying,
'Come, let us join ourselves to the
LORD in an everlasting covenant which
will never be forgotten.'

6 "My people have been lost sheep;
their shepherds have led them astray,
turning them away on the mountains;
from mountain to hill they have gone,
they have forgotten their fold. ⁷All who
found them have devoured them, and
their enemies have said, 'We are not
guilty, for they have sinned against
the LORD, their true habitation, the
LORD, the hope of their fathers.'

8 "Flee from the midst of Babylon,
and go out of the land of the Chăl-
dē′ans, and be as he-goats before the
flock. ⁹For behold, I am stirring up
and bringing against Babylon a company of great nations, from the north
country; and they shall array themselves against her; from there she
shall be taken. Their arrows are like
a skilled warrior who does not return
empty-handed. ¹⁰Chăl·dē′ā shall be
plundered; all who plunder her shall
be sated, says the LORD.

¹¹"Though you rejoice, though you
    exult,
O plunderers of my heritage,
though you are wanton as a heifer
    at grass,
and neigh like stallions,
¹²your mother shall be utterly shamed,
and she who bore you shall be dis-
    graced.
Lo, she shall be the last of the na-
    tions,
a wilderness dry and desert.
¹³Because of the wrath of the LORD
she shall not be inhabited,
but shall be an utter desolation;
every one who passes by Babylon
shall be appalled,
and hiss because of all her wounds.
¹⁴Set yourselves in array against
    Babylon round about,
all you that bend the bow;
shoot at her, spare no arrows,

50-51: Is 13.1-14.23; 47; Hab 1-2.
50.8: Jer 51.6, 9, 45; 2 Cor 6.17; Rev 18.4.

for she has sinned against the
LORD.
15 Raise a shout against her round
   about,
  she has surrendered;
her bulwarks have fallen,
  her walls are thrown down.
For this is the vengeance of the
  LORD:
take vengeance on her,
  do to her as she has done.
16 Cut off from Babylon the sower,
  and the one who handles the
   sickle in time of harvest;
because of the sword of the oppressor,
  every one shall turn to his own
   people,
and every one shall flee to his own
  land.

17 "Israel is a hunted sheep driven
away by lions. First the king of Assyria
devoured him, and now at last Nĕ·bü-
chạd·rĕz′zạr king of Babylon has
gnawed his bones. 18 Therefore, thus
says the LORD of hosts, the God of
Israel: Behold, I am bringing punishment on the king of Babylon and his
land, as I punished the king of Assyria.
19 I will restore Israel to his pasture,
and he shall feed on Cär′mĕl and in
Bä′shạn, and his desire shall be
satisfied on the hills of Ē′phra·ïm and
in Gilead. 20 In those days and in that
time, says the LORD, iniquity shall be
sought in Israel, and there shall be
none; and sin in Judah, and none
shall be found; for I will pardon those
whom I leave as a remnant.

21 "Go up against the land of Mĕr·ạ-
thā′ïm,ˢ
  and against the inhabitants of
   Pē′kŏd.ᵗ
Slay, and utterly destroy after them,
         says the LORD,
  and do all that I have commanded
   you.
22 The noise of battle is in the land,
  and great destruction!
23 How the hammer of the whole earth
  is cut down and broken!
How Babylon has become
  a horror among the nations!
24 I set a snare for you and you were
  taken, O Babylon,
  and you did not know it;
you were found and caught,
  because you strove against the
   LORD.

25 The LORD has opened his armory,
and brought out the weapons of
  his wrath,
for the Lord GOD of hosts has a work
  to do
in the land of the Chăl·dē′ạns.
26 Come against her from every quarter;
  open her granaries;
pile her up like heaps of grain, and
  destroy her utterly;
  let nothing be left of her.
27 Slay all her bulls,
  let them go down to the slaughter.
Woe to them, for their day has come,
  the time of their punishment.

28 "Hark! they flee and escape
from the land of Babylon, to declare
in Zion the vengeance of the LORD
our God, vengeance for his temple.

29 "Summon archers against Babylon, all those who bend the bow. Encamp round about her; let no one
escape. Requite her according to her
deeds, do to her according to all that
she has done; for she has proudly
defied the LORD, the Holy One of
Israel. 30 Therefore her young men shall
fall in her squares, and all her soldiers
shall be destroyed on that day, says
the LORD.

31 "Behold, I am against you, O proud
  one,
  says the Lord GOD of hosts;
for your day has come,
  the time when I will punish you.
32 The proud one shall stumble and fall,
  with none to raise him up,
and I will kindle a fire in his cities,
  and it will devour all that is round
  about him.

33 "Thus says the LORD of hosts:
The people of Israel are oppressed,
and the people of Judah with them;
all who took them captive have held
them fast, they refuse to let them go.
34 Their Redeemer is strong; the LORD
of hosts is his name. He will surely
plead their cause, that he may give
rest to the earth, but unrest to the
inhabitants of Babylon.

35 "A sword upon the Chăl·dē′ạns, says
  the LORD,
  and upon the inhabitants of
   Babylon,

ˢOr *Double Rebellion*   ᵗOr *Punishment*

and upon her princes and her wise men!
36 A sword upon the diviners,
    that they may become fools!
A sword upon her warriors,
    that they may be destroyed!
37 A sword upon her horses and upon her chariots,
    and upon all the foreign troops in her midst,
    that they may become women!
A sword upon all her treasures,
    that they may be plundered!
38 A drought upon her waters,
    that they may be dried up!
For it is a land of images,
    and they are mad over idols.

39 "Therefore wild beasts shall dwell with hyenas in Babylon, and ostriches shall dwell in her; she shall be peopled no more for ever, nor inhabited for all generations. 40 As when God overthrew Sŏd'ọm and Gọ·môr'rạh and their neighbor cities, says the Lord, so no man shall dwell there, and no son of man shall sojourn in her.

41 "Behold, a people comes from the north;
    a mighty nation and many kings
    are stirring from the farthest parts of the earth.
42 They lay hold of bow and spear;
    they are cruel, and have no mercy.
The sound of them is like the roaring of the sea;
    they ride upon horses,
arrayed as a man for battle
    against you, O daughter of Babylon!

43 "The king of Babylon heard the report of them,
    and his hands fell helpless;
anguish seized him,
    pain as of a woman in travail.

44 "Behold, like a lion coming up from the jungle of the Jordan against a strong sheepfold, I will suddenly make them run away from her; and I will appoint over her whomever I choose. For who is like me? Who will summon me? What shepherd can stand before me? 45 Therefore hear the plan which the Lord has made against Babylon, and the purposes which he has formed against the land of the Chăl·dē'ạns: Surely the little ones of their flock shall be dragged away;

surely their fold shall be appalled at their fate. 46 At the sound of the capture of Babylon the earth shall tremble, and her cry shall be heard among the nations."

51   Thus says the Lord:
       "Behold, I will stir up the spirit of a destroyer
    against Babylon,
    against the inhabitants of Chăl·dē'ạ;ᵘ
2 and I will send to Babylon winnowers,
    and they shall winnow her,
    and they shall empty her land,
    when they come against her from every side
    on the day of trouble.
3 Let not the archer bend his bow,
    and let him not stand up in his coat of mail.
Spare not her young men;
    utterly destroy all her host.
4 They shall fall down slain in the land of the Chăl·dē'ạns,
    and wounded in her streets.
5 For Israel and Judah have not been forsaken
    by their God, the Lord of hosts;
but the land of the Chăl·dē'ạnsᵛ is full of guilt
    against the Holy One of Israel.

6 "Flee from the midst of Babylon,
    let every man save his life!
Be not cut off in her punishment,
    for this is the time of the Lord's vengeance,
    the requital he is rendering her.
7 Babylon was a golden cup in the Lord's hand,
    making all the earth drunken;
the nations drank of her wine,
    therefore the nations went mad.
8 Suddenly Babylon has fallen and been broken;
    wail for her!
Take balm for her pain;
    perhaps she may be healed.
9 We would have healed Babylon,
    but she was not healed.
Forsake her, and let us go
    each to his own country;
for her judgment has reached up to heaven
    and has been lifted up even to the skies.

ᵘHeb *Leb-qamai*, a cipher for Chaldea   ᵛHeb *their land*
51.6, 9, 45: Jer 50.8; 2 Cor 6.17; Rev 18.4.
51.7-8: Jer 25.15; Rev 14.8, 10; 16.19; 17.4; 18.3.

¹⁰The LORD has brought forth our
    vindication;
    come, let us declare in Zion
    the work of the LORD our God.

¹¹ "Sharpen the arrows!
    Take up the shields!
The LORD has stirred up the spirit of
the kings of the Mēdes, because his
purpose concerning Babylon is to
destroy it, for that is the vengeance
of the LORD, the vengeance for his
temple.
¹²Set up a standard against the walls
    of Babylon;
    make the watch strong;
set up watchmen;
    prepare the ambushes;
for the LORD has both planned and
    done
what he spoke concerning the
    inhabitants of Babylon.
¹³O you who dwell by many waters,
    rich in treasures,
your end has come,
    the thread of your life is cut.
¹⁴The LORD of hosts has sworn by him-
    self:
Surely I will fill you with men, as
    many as locusts,
    and they shall raise the shout of
    victory over you.

¹⁵ "It is he who made the earth by his
    power,
    who established the world by his
    wisdom,
and by his understanding
    stretched out the heavens.
¹⁶When he utters his voice there is a
    tumult of waters in the heavens,
    and he makes the mist rise from
    the ends of the earth.
He makes lightnings for the rain,
    and he brings forth the wind from
    his storehouses.
¹⁷Every man is stupid and without
    knowledge;
    every goldsmith is put to shame by
    his idols;
for his images are false,
    and there is no breath in them.
¹⁸They are worthless, a work of de-
    lusion;
    at the time of their punishment
    they shall perish.
¹⁹Not like these is he who is the portion
    of Jacob,
    for he is the one who formed all
    things,

and Israel is the tribe of his in-
    heritance;
    the LORD of hosts is his name.

²⁰ "You are my hammer and weapon
    of war:
with you I break nations in pieces;
    with you I destroy kingdoms;
²¹with you I break in pieces the horse
    and his rider;
with you I break in pieces the
    chariot and the charioteer;
²²with you I break in pieces man and
    woman;
with you I break in pieces the old
    man and the youth;
with you I break in pieces the young
    man and the maiden;
²³   with you I break in pieces the
    shepherd and his flock;
with you I break in pieces the farmer
    and his team;
with you I break in pieces gov-
    ernors and commanders.

24 "I will requite Babylon and all
the inhabitants of Chăl-dē′ă before
your very eyes for all the evil that
they have done in Zion, says the
LORD.

²⁵ "Behold, I am against you, O de-
    stroying mountain,
           says the LORD,
    which destroys the whole earth;
I will stretch out my hand against
    you,
    and roll you down from the
    crags,
    and make you a burnt mountain.
²⁶No stone shall be taken from you
    for a corner
    and no stone for a foundation,
but you shall be a perpetual waste,
    says the LORD.

²⁷ "Set up a standard on the earth,
    blow the trumpet among the
    nations;
prepare the nations for war against
    her,
    summon against her the king-
    doms,
    Ăr′ą·răt, Mĭn′nī, and Ăsh′kę·năz;
appoint a marshal against her,
    bring up horses like bristling
    locusts.
²⁸Prepare the nations for war against
    her,

51.13: Rev 17.1.

the kings of the Mēdeṣ, with
their governors and deputies,
and every land under their dominion.
²⁹The land trembles and writhes in
pain,
for the LORD's purposes against
Babylon stand,
to make the land of Babylon a
desolation,
without inhabitant.
³⁰The warriors of Babylon have ceased
fighting,
they remain in their strongholds;
their strength has failed,
they have become women;
her dwellings are on fire,
her bars are broken.
³¹One runner runs to meet another,
and one messenger to meet an-
other,
to tell the king of Babylon
that his city is taken on every side;
³²the fords have been seized,
the bulwarks are burned with fire,
and the soldiers are in panic.
³³For thus says the LORD of hosts,
the God of Israel:
The daughter of Babylon is like a
threshing floor
at the time when it is trodden;
yet a little while
and the time of her harvest will
come."

³⁴"Nĕ·bü·chạd·rĕz'zar the king of
Babylon has devoured me,
he has crushed me;
he has made me an empty vessel,
he has swallowed me like a
monster;
he has filled his belly with my
delicacies,
he has rinsed me out.
³⁵The violence done to me and to
my kinsmen be upon Babylon,"
let the inhabitant of Zion say.
"My blood be upon the inhabitants
of Chăl·dē'ă,"
let Jerusalem say.
³⁶Therefore thus says the LORD:
"Behold, I will plead your cause
and take vengeance for you.
I will dry up her sea
and make her fountain dry;
³⁷and Babylon shall become a heap of
ruins,
the haunt of jackals,
a horror and a hissing,
without inhabitant.

³⁸"They shall roar together like lions;
they shall growl like lions' whelps.
³⁹While they are inflamed I will prepare
them a feast
and make them drunk, till they
swoon away^w
and sleep a perpetual sleep
and not wake, says the LORD.
⁴⁰I will bring them down like lambs
to the slaughter,
like rams and he-goats.

⁴¹"How Babylon^x is taken,
the praise of the whole earth
seized!
How Babylon has become
a horror among the nations!
⁴²The sea has come up on Babylon;
she is covered with its tumultuous
waves.
⁴³Her cities have become a horror,
a land of drought and a desert,
a land in which no one dwells,
and through which no son of man
passes.
⁴⁴And I will punish Bĕl in Babylon,
and take out of his mouth what he
has swallowed.
The nations shall no longer flow to
him;
the wall of Babylon has fallen.

⁴⁵"Go out of the midst of her, my
people!
Let every man save his life
from the fierce anger of the
LORD!
⁴⁶Let not your heart faint, and be not
fearful
at the report heard in the land,
when a report comes in one year
and afterward a report in another
year,
and violence is in the land,
and ruler is against ruler.

⁴⁷"Therefore, behold, the days are
coming
when I will punish the images of
Babylon;
her whole land shall be put to
shame,
and all her slain shall fall in the
midst of her.
⁴⁸Then the heavens and the earth,
and all that is in them,
shall sing for joy over Babylon;

*w*Gk Vg: Heb *rejoice*
*x*Heb *Sheshach*, a cipher for Babylon
51.48: Is 44.23; Rev 12.12; 18.20.

for the destroyers shall come
against them out of the north,
       says the LORD.
49 Babylon must fall for the slain of
Israel,
as for Babylon have fallen the
slain of all the earth.

50 "You that have escaped from the
sword,
go, stand not still!
Remember the LORD from afar,
and let Jerusalem come into your
mind:
51 'We are put to shame, for we have
heard reproach;
dishonor has covered our face,
for aliens have come
into the holy places of the LORD's
house.'

52 "Therefore, behold, the days are
coming, says the LORD,
when I will execute judgment
upon her images,
and through all her land
the wounded shall groan.
53 Though Babylon should mount up
to heaven,
and though she should fortify her
strong height,
yet destroyers would come from me
upon her,
says the LORD.

54 "Hark! a cry from Babylon!
The noise of great destruction
from the land of the Chăl·dē′ạns!
55 For the LORD is laying Babylon waste,
and stilling her mighty voice.
Their waves roar like many waters,
the noise of their voice is raised;
56 for a destroyer has come upon her,
upon Babylon;
her warriors are taken,
their bows are broken in pieces;
for the LORD is a God of recompense,
he will surely requite.
57 I will make drunk her princes and her
wise men,
her governors, her commanders,
and her warriors;
they shall sleep a perpetual sleep
and not wake,
says the King, whose name is the
LORD of hosts.

58 "Thus says the LORD of hosts:
The broad wall of Babylon
shall be leveled to the ground

and her high gates
shall be burned with fire.
The peoples labor for nought,
and the nations weary themselves
only for fire."

59 The word which Jĕr·ẹ·mī′ạh the
prophet commanded Sē·rāi′ah the son
of Nē·rī′ạh, son of Mäh·sēi′ạh, when
he went with Zĕd·ẹ·kī′ạh king of
Judah to Babylon, in the fourth year
of his reign. Seraiah was the quarter-
master. 60 Jĕr·ẹ·mī′ạh wrote in a book
all the evil that should come upon
Babylon, all these words that are written concerning Babylon. 61 And Jĕr·ẹ-
mī′ạh said to Sē·rāi′ah: "When you
come to Babylon, see that you read all
these words, 62 and say, 'O LORD, thou
hast said concerning this place that
thou wilt cut it off, so that nothing shall
dwell in it, neither man nor beast,
and it shall be desolate for ever.'
63 When you finish reading this book,
bind a stone to it, and cast it into the
midst of the Euphrates, 64 and say,
'Thus shall Babylon sink, to rise no
more, because of the evil that I am
bringing upon her.'" *y*
Thus far are the words of Jĕr·ẹ-
mī′ạh.

52   Zĕd·ẹ·kī′ạh was twenty-one
years old when he became king;
and he reigned eleven years in Jerusalem. His mother's name was Ha-
mü′tăl the daughter of Jĕr·ẹ·mī′ạh of
Lĭb′nạh. 2 And he did what was evil in
the sight of the LORD, according to all
that Jĕ·hoi′ạ·kim had done. 3 Surely
because of the anger of the LORD
things came to such a pass in Jerusalem and Judah that he cast them out
from his presence.

And Zĕd·ẹ·kī′ạh rebelled against the
king of Babylon. 4 And in the ninth
year of his reign, in the tenth month,
on the tenth day of the month, Nē-
bü·chạd·rĕz′zạr king of Babylon came
with all his army against Jerusalem,
and they laid siege to it and built siegeworks against it round about. 5 So the
city was besieged till the eleventh year
of King Zĕd·ẹ·kī′ạh. 6 On the ninth day
of the fourth month the famine was
so severe in the city, that there was no
food for the people of the land. 7 Then

a breach was made in the city; and all the men of war fled and went out from the city by night by the way of a gate between the two walls, by the king's garden, while the Chăl·dē'ạnş were round about the city. And they went in the direction of the Ăr'ạ·bạh. ⁸But the army of the Chăl·dē'ạnş pursued the king, and overtook Zĕd·ẹ·kī'ah in the plains of Jericho; and all his army was scattered from him. ⁹Then they captured the king, and brought him up to the king of Babylon at Rĭb'lạh in the land of Hā'măth, and he passed sentence upon him. ¹⁰The king of Babylon slew the sons of Zĕd·ẹ·kī'ah before his eyes, and also slew all the princes of Judah at Rĭb'lạh. ¹¹He put out the eyes of Zĕd·ẹ·kī'ah, and bound him in fetters, and the king of Babylon took him to Babylon, and put him in prison till the day of his death.

12 In the fifth month, on the tenth day of the month—which was the nineteenth year of King Nĕ·bü·chạd·rĕz'-zạr, king of Babylon—Nĕ·bū'zạ·răd'ạn the captain of the bodyguard who served the king of Babylon, entered Jerusalem. ¹³And he burned the house of the LORD, and the king's house and all the houses of Jerusalem; every great house he burned down. ¹⁴And all the army of the Chăl·dē'ạnş, who were with the captain of the guard, broke down all the walls round about Jerusalem. ¹⁵And Nĕ·bū'zạ·răd'ạn the captain of the guard carried away captive some of the poorest of the people and the rest of the people who were left in the city and the deserters who had deserted to the king of Babylon, together with the rest of the artisans. ¹⁶But Nĕ·bū'zạ·răd'ạn the captain of the guard left some of the poorest of the land to be vinedressers and plowmen.

17 And the pillars of bronze that were in the house of the LORD, and the stands and the bronze sea that were in the house of the LORD, the Chăl·dē'ạnş broke in pieces, and carried all the bronze to Babylon. ¹⁸And they took away the pots, and the shovels, and the snuffers, and the basins, and the dishes for incense, and all the vessels of bronze used in the temple service; ¹⁹also the small bowls, and the firepans, and the basins, and the pots, and the lampstands, and the dishes for incense, and the bowls

for libation. What was of gold the captain of the guard took away as gold, and what was of silver, as silver. ²⁰As for the two pillars, the one sea, and twelve bronze bulls which were under the sea,ᶻ and the stands, which Solomon the king had made for the house of the LORD, the bronze of all these things was beyond weight. ²¹As for the pillars, the height of the one pillar was eighteen cubits, its circumference was twelve cubits, and its thickness was four fingers, and it was hollow. ²²Upon it was a capital of bronze; the height of the one capital was five cubits; a network and pomegranates, all of bronze, were upon the capital round about. And the second pillar had the like, with pomegranates. ²³There were ninety-six pomegranates on the sides; all the pomegranates were a hundred upon the network round about.

24 And the captain of the guard took Sĕ·rāi'ah the chief priest, and Zĕph·ạ·nī'ah the second priest, and the three keepers of the threshold; ²⁵who had been in command of the men of war, and seven men of the king's council, who were found in the city; and the secretary of the commander of the army who mustered the people of the land; and sixty men of the people of the land, who were found in the midst of the city. ²⁶And Nĕ·bū'zạ·răd'ạn the captain of the guard took them, and brought them to the king of Babylon at Rĭb'lạh. ²⁷And the king of Babylon smote them, and put them to death at Rĭb'lạh in the land of Hā'măth. So Judah was carried captive out of its land.

28 This is the number of the people whom Nĕ·bü·chạd·rĕz'zạr carried away captive: in the seventh year, three thousand and twenty-three Jews; ²⁹in the eighteenth year of Nĕ·bü·chạd·rĕz'zạr he carried away captive from Jerusalem eight hundred and thirty-two persons; ³⁰in the twenty-third year of Nĕ·bü·chạd·rĕz'zạr, Nĕ·bū'zạ·răd'ạn the captain of the guard carried away captive of the Jews seven hundred and forty-five persons; all the persons were four thousand and six hundred.

31 And in the thirty-seventh year of the captivity of Jĕ·hoi'ạ·chĭn king

ᶻHeb lacks *the sea*

of Judah, in the twelfth month, on the twenty-fifth day of the month, E'vil-mĕr'o·dăch king of Babylon, in the year that he became king, lifted up the head of Jehoiachin king of Judah and brought him out of prison; ³²and he spoke kindly to him, and gave him a seat above the seats of the kings who were with him in Babylon. ³³So Jĕ-hoi'a·chĭn put off his prison garments. And every day of his life he dined regularly at the king's table; ³⁴as for his allowance, a regular allowance was given him by the king according to his daily need, until the day of his death as long as he lived.

The Lamentations
of Jeremiah

1 How lonely sits the city
    that was full of people!
How like a widow has she become,
    she that was great among the
        nations!
She that was a princess among the
        cities
    has become a vassal.

²She weeps bitterly in the night,
    tears on her cheeks;
among all her lovers
    she has none to comfort her;
all her friends have dealt treacher-
        ously with her,
    they have become her enemies.

³Judah has gone into exile because of
        affliction
    and hard servitude;
she dwells now among the nations,
    but finds no resting place;
her pursuers have all overtaken her
    in the midst of her distress.

⁴The roads to Zion mourn,
    for none come to the appointed
        feasts;
all her gates are desolate,
    her priests groan;
her maidens have been dragged
        away,ᵃ
    and she herself suffers bitterly.

⁵Her foes have become the head,
    her enemies prosper,
because the LORD has made her
        suffer
    for the multitude of her transgres-
        sions;

her children have gone away,
    captives before the foe.

⁶From the daughter of Zion has de-
        parted
    all her majesty.
Her princes have become like harts
    that find no pasture;
they fled without strength
    before the pursuer.

⁷Jerusalem remembers
    in the days of her affliction and
        bitternessᵇ
all the precious things
    that were hers from days of old.
When her people fell into the hand
        of the foe,
    and there was none to help her,
the foe gloated over her,
    mocking at her downfall.

⁸Jerusalem sinned grievously,
    therefore she became filthy;
all who honored her despise her,
    for they have seen her nakedness;
yea, she herself groans,
    and turns her face away.

⁹Her uncleanness was in her skirts;
    she took no thought of her doom;
therefore her fall is terrible,
    she has no comforter.
"O LORD, behold my affliction,
    for the enemy has triumphed!"

¹⁰The enemy has stretched out his
        hands
    over all her precious things;

ᵃGk Old Latin: Heb *afflicted*   ᵇCn: Heb *wandering*

yea, she has seen the nations
    invade her sanctuary,
those whom thou didst forbid
    to enter thy congregation.

[11] All her people groan
    as they search for bread;
they trade their treasures for food
    to revive their strength.
"Look, O Lord, and behold,
    for I am despised."

[12] "Is it nothing to you,[c] all you who
    pass by?
Look and see
if there is any sorrow like my sor-
    row
which was brought upon me,
which the Lord inflicted
    on the day of his fierce anger.

[13] "From on high he sent fire;
    into my bones[d] he made it descend;
he spread a net for my feet;
    he turned me back;
he has left me stunned,
    faint all the day long.

[14] "My transgressions were bound[e]
    into a yoke;
by his hand they were fastened
    together;
they were set upon my neck;
    he caused my strength to fail;
the Lord gave me into the hands
    of those whom I cannot withstand.

[15] "The Lord flouted all my mighty
    men
    in the midst of me;
he summoned an assembly against
    me
    to crush my young men;
the Lord has trodden as in a wine
    press
    the virgin daughter of Judah.

[16] "For these things I weep;
    my eyes flow with tears;
for a comforter is far from me,
    one to revive my courage;
my children are desolate,
    for the enemy has prevailed."

[17] Zion stretches out her hands,
    but there is none to comfort her;
the Lord has commanded against
    Jacob
    that his neighbors should be his
    foes;

Jerusalem has become
    a filthy thing among them.

[18] "The Lord is in the right,
    for I have rebelled against his
    word;
but hear, all you peoples,
    and behold my suffering;
my maidens and my young men
    have gone into captivity.

[19] "I called to my lovers
    but they deceived me;
my priests and elders
    perished in the city,
while they sought food
    to revive their strength.

[20] "Behold, O Lord, for I am in distress,
    my soul is in tumult,
my heart is wrung within me,
    because I have been very rebel-
    lious.
In the street the sword bereaves;
    in the house it is like death.

[21] "Hear[f] how I groan;
    there is none to comfort me.
All my enemies have heard of my
    trouble;
    they are glad that thou hast done
    it.
Bring thou[g] the day thou hast an-
    nounced,
    and let them be as I am.

[22] "Let all their evil-doing come before
    thee;
    and deal with them
as thou hast dealt with me
    because of all my transgressions;
for my groans are many
    and my heart is faint."

2 How the Lord in his anger
    has set the daughter of Zion under
    a cloud!
He has cast down from heaven to
    earth
    the splendor of Israel;
he has not remembered his footstool
    in the day of his anger.

[2] The Lord has destroyed without
    mercy
    all the habitations of Jacob;
in his wrath he has broken down

[c] Heb uncertain   [d] Gk: Heb *bones and*
[e] Cn: Heb uncertain   [f] Gk Syr: Heb *they heard*
[g] Syr: Heb *thou hast brought*

the strongholds of the daughter of
Judah;
he has brought down to the ground
in dishonor
the kingdom and its rulers.

³He has cut down in fierce anger
all the might of Israel;
he has withdrawn from them his
right hand
in the face of the enemy;
he has burned like a flaming fire in
Jacob,
consuming all around.

⁴He has bent his bow like an enemy,
with his right hand set like a foe;
and he has slain all the pride of our
eyes
in the tent of the daughter of
Zion;
he has poured out his fury like fire.

⁵The Lord has become like an enemy,
he has destroyed Israel;
he has destroyed all its palaces,
laid in ruins its strongholds;
and he has multiplied in the daughter
of Judah
mourning and lamentation.

⁶He has broken down his booth like
that of a garden,
laid in ruins the place of his appointed feasts;
the LORD has brought to an end in
Zion
appointed feast and sabbath,
and in his fierce indignation has
spurned
king and priest.

⁷The Lord has scorned his altar,
disowned his sanctuary;
he has delivered into the hand of the
enemy
the walls of her palaces;
a clamor was raised in the house of
the LORD
as on the day of an appointed feast.

⁸The LORD determined to lay in
ruins
the wall of the daughter of Zion;
he marked it off by the line;
he restrained not his hand from
destroying;
he caused rampart and wall to lament,
they languish together.

⁹Her gates have sunk into the ground;
he has ruined and broken her bars;
her king and princes are among the
nations;
the law is no more,
and her prophets obtain
no vision from the LORD.

¹⁰The elders of the daughter of Zion
sit on the ground in silence;
they have cast dust on their heads
and put on sackcloth;
the maidens of Jerusalem
have bowed their heads to the
ground.

¹¹My eyes are spent with weeping;
my soul is in tumult;
my heart is poured out in grief*
because of the destruction of the
daughter of my people,
because infants and babes faint
in the streets of the city.

¹²They cry to their mothers,
"Where is bread and wine?"
as they faint like wounded men
in the streets of the city,
as their life is poured out
on their mothers' bosom.

¹³What can I say for you, to what
compare you,
O daughter of Jerusalem?
What can I liken to you, that I may
comfort you,
O virgin daughter of Zion?
For vast as the sea is your ruin;
who can restore you?

¹⁴Your prophets have seen for you
false and deceptive visions;
they have not exposed your iniquity
to restore your fortunes,
but have seen for you oracles
false and misleading.

¹⁵All who pass along the way
clap their hands at you;
they hiss and wag their heads
at the daughter of Jerusalem;
"Is this the city which was called
the perfection of beauty,
the joy of all the earth?"

¹⁶All your enemies
rail against you;
they hiss, they gnash their teeth,
they cry: "We have destroyed her!

*Heb *to the ground*

Ah, this is the day we longed for;
    now we have it; we see it!"

17 The LORD has done what he purposed,
    has carried out his threat,
    as he ordained long ago,
he has demolished without pity;
he has made the enemy rejoice over
    you,
    and exalted the might of your foes.

18 Cry aloud[i] to the Lord!
    O[j] daughter of Zion!
Let tears stream down like a torrent
    day and night!
Give yourself no rest,
    your eyes no respite!

19 Arise, cry out in the night,
    at the beginning of the watches!
Pour out your heart like water
    before the presence of the Lord!
Lift your hands to him
    for the lives of your children,
who faint for hunger
    at the head of every street.

20 Look, O LORD, and see!
    With whom hast thou dealt thus?
Should women eat their offspring,
    the children of their tender care?
Should priest and prophet be slain
    in the sanctuary of the Lord?

21 In the dust of the streets
    lie the young and the old;
my maidens and my young men
    have fallen by the sword;
in the day of thy anger thou hast
    slain them,
    slaughtering without mercy.

22 Thou didst invite as to the day of
    an appointed feast
my terrors on every side;
and on the day of the anger of the
    LORD
none escaped or survived;
those whom I dandled and reared
    my enemy destroyed.

3 I am the man who has seen af-
    fliction
    under the rod of his wrath;
2 he has driven and brought me
    into darkness without any light;
3 surely against me he turns his
    hand
    again and again the whole day
    long.

4 He has made my flesh and my skin
    waste away,
    and broken my bones;
5 he has besieged and enveloped me
    with bitterness and tribulation;
6 he has made me dwell in darkness
    like the dead of long ago.

7 He has walled me about so that I
    cannot escape;
    he has put heavy chains on me;
8 though I call and cry for help,
    he shuts out my prayer,
9 he has blocked my ways with hewn
    stones,
    he has made my paths crooked.

10 He is to me like a bear lying in wait,
    like a lion in hiding;
11 he led me off my way and tore me to
    pieces;
    he has made me desolate;
12 he bent his bow and set me
    as a mark for his arrow.

13 He drove into my heart
    the arrows of his quiver;
14 I have become the laughingstock of
    all peoples,
    the burden of their songs all day
    long.
15 He has filled me with bitterness,
    he has sated me with wormwood.

16 He has made my teeth grind on
    gravel,
    and made me cower in ashes;
17 my soul is bereft of peace,
    I have forgotten what happiness
    is;
18 so I say, "Gone is my glory,
    and my expectation from the
    LORD."

19 Remember my affliction and my
    bitterness,[k]
    the wormwood and the gall!
20 My soul continually thinks of it
    and is bowed down within me.
21 But this I call to mind,
    and therefore I have hope:

22 The steadfast love of the LORD
    never ceases,[l]
    his mercies never come to an end;
23 they are new every morning;
    great is thy faithfulness.

[i]Cn: Heb *Their heart cried*   [j]Cn: Heb *O wall of*
[k]Cn: Heb *wandering*
[l]Syr Tg: Heb *we are not cut off*

²⁴ "The Lᴏʀᴅ is my portion," says my
    soul,
    "therefore I will hope in him."

²⁵ The Lᴏʀᴅ is good to those who wait
    for him,
    to the soul that seeks him.
²⁶ It is good that one should wait quietly
    for the salvation of the Lᴏʀᴅ.
²⁷ It is good for a man that he bear
    the yoke in his youth.

²⁸ Let him sit alone in silence
    when he has laid it on him;
²⁹ let him put his mouth in the dust—
    there may yet be hope;
³⁰ let him give his cheek to the smiter,
    and be filled with insults.

³¹ For the Lord will not
    cast off for ever,
³² but, though he cause grief, he will
    have compassion
    according to the abundance of
    his steadfast love;
³³ for he does not willingly afflict
    or grieve the sons of men.

³⁴ To crush under foot
    all the prisoners of the earth,
³⁵ to turn aside the right of a man
    in the presence of the Most High,
³⁶ to subvert a man in his cause,
    the Lord does not approve.

³⁷ Who has commanded and it came to
    pass,
    unless the Lord has ordained it?
³⁸ Is it not from the mouth of the Most
    High
    that good and evil come?
³⁹ Why should a living man complain,
    a man, about the punishment of
    his sins?

⁴⁰ Let us test and examine our ways,
    and return to the Lᴏʀᴅ!
⁴¹ Let us lift up our hearts and hands
    to God in heaven:
⁴² "We have transgressed and rebelled,
    and thou hast not forgiven.

⁴³ "Thou hast wrapped thyself with
    anger and pursued us,
    slaying without pity;
⁴⁴ thou hast wrapped thyself with a
    cloud
    so that no prayer can pass through.
⁴⁵ Thou hast made us offscouring and
    refuse
    among the peoples.

⁴⁶ "All our enemies
    rail against us;
⁴⁷ panic and pitfall have come upon us,
    devastation and destruction;
⁴⁸ my eyes flow with rivers of tears
    because of the destruction of the
    daughter of my people.

⁴⁹ "My eyes will flow without ceasing,
    without respite,
⁵⁰ until the Lᴏʀᴅ from heaven
    looks down and sees;
⁵¹ my eyes cause me grief
    at the fate of all the maidens of
    my city.

⁵² "I have been hunted like a bird
    by those who were my enemies
    without cause;
⁵³ they flung me alive into the pit
    and cast stones on me;
⁵⁴ water closed over my head;
    I said, 'I am lost.'

⁵⁵ "I called on thy name, O Lᴏʀᴅ,
    from the depths of the pit;
⁵⁶ thou didst hear my plea, 'Do not close
    thine ear to my cry for help!'ᵐ
⁵⁷ Thou didst come near when I called
    on thee;
    thou didst say, 'Do not fear!'

⁵⁸ "Thou hast taken up my cause, O
    Lord,
    thou hast redeemed my life.
⁵⁹ Thou hast seen the wrong done to
    me, O Lᴏʀᴅ;
    judge thou my cause.
⁶⁰ Thou hast seen all their vengeance,
    all their devices against me.

⁶¹ "Thou hast heard their taunts, O
    Lᴏʀᴅ,
    all their devices against me.
⁶² The lips and thoughts of my as-
    sailants
    are against me all the day long.
⁶³ Behold their sitting and their rising;
    I am the burden of their songs.

⁶⁴ "Thou wilt requite them, O Lᴏʀᴅ,
    according to the work of their
    hands.
⁶⁵ Thou wilt give them dullness of heart;
    thy curse will be on them.
⁶⁶ Thou wilt pursue them in anger
    and destroy them
    from under thy heavens, O Lᴏʀᴅ."ⁿ

ᵐ Heb uncertain
ⁿ Syr Compare Gk Vg: Heb *the heavens of the* Lᴏʀᴅ

4 How the gold has grown dim,
   how the pure gold is changed!
The holy stones lie scattered
   at the head of every street.

2 The precious sons of Zion,
   worth their weight in fine gold,
how they are reckoned as earthen
   pots,
   the work of a potter's hands!

3 Even the jackals give the breast
   and suckle their young,
but the daughter of my people has
   become cruel,
   like the ostriches in the wilderness.

4 The tongue of the nursling cleaves
   to the roof of its mouth for thirst;
the children beg for food,
   but no one gives to them.

5 Those who feasted on dainties
   perish in the streets;
those who were brought up in purple
   lie on ash heaps.

6 For the chastisement[o] of the daughter
   of my people has been greater
   than the punishment[p] of Sŏd′ŏm,
which was overthrown in a moment,
   no hand being laid on it.[q]

7 Her princes were purer than snow,
   whiter than milk;
their bodies were more ruddy than
   coral,
   the beauty of their form[r] was like
   sapphire.[s]

8 Now their visage is blacker than
   soot,
   they are not recognized in the
   streets;
their skin has shriveled upon their
   bones,
   it has become as dry as wood.

9 Happier were the victims of the
   sword
   than the victims of hunger,
who pined away, stricken
   by want of the fruits of the field.

10 The hands of compassionate women
   have boiled their own children;
they became their food
   in the destruction of the daughter
   of my people.

11 The LORD gave full vent to his
   wrath,
   he poured out his hot anger;
and he kindled a fire in Zion,
   which consumed its foundations.

12 The kings of the earth did not believe,
   or any of the inhabitants of the
   world,
that foe or enemy could enter
   the gates of Jerusalem.

13 This was for the sins of her prophets
   and the iniquities of her priests,
   who shed in the midst of her
   the blood of the righteous.

14 They wandered, blind, through the
   streets,
   so defiled with blood
that none could touch
   their garments.

15 "Away! Unclean!" men cried at
   them;
   "Away! Away! Touch not!"
So they became fugitives and wanderers;
   men said among the nations,
   "They shall stay with us no longer."

16 The LORD himself has scattered
   them,
   he will regard them no more;
no honor was shown to the priests,
   no favor to the elders.

17 Our eyes failed, ever watching
   vainly for help;
in our watching[t] we watched
   for a nation which could not
   save.

18 Men dogged our steps
   so that we could not walk in our
   streets;
our end drew near; our days were
   numbered;
   for our end had come.

19 Our pursuers were swifter
   than the vultures in the heavens;
they chased us on the mountains,
   they lay in wait for us in the
   wilderness.

[o] Or iniquity   [p] Or sin   [q] Heb uncertain
[r] Heb uncertain   [s] Heb lapis lazuli   [t] Heb uncertain

²⁰The breath of our nostrils, the
Lord's anointed,
was taken in their pits,
he of whom we said, "Under his
shadow
we shall live among the nations."

²¹Rejoice and be glad, O daughter
of Ē'dom,
dweller in the land of Ŭz;
but to you also the cup shall pass;
you shall become drunk and strip
yourself bare.

²²The punishment of your iniquity,
O daughter of Zion, is accomplished,
he will keep you in exile no longer;
but your iniquity, O daughter of
Ē'dom, he will punish,
he will uncover your sins.

5 Remember, O Lord, what has
befallen us;
behold, and see our disgrace!
²Our inheritance has been turned
over to strangers,
our homes to aliens.
³We have become orphans, fatherless;
our mothers are like widows.
⁴We must pay for the water we drink,
the wood we get must be bought.
⁵With a yoke*ᵘ* on our necks we are
hard driven;
we are weary, we are given no rest.
⁶We have given the hand to Egypt,
and to Assyria, to get bread enough.
⁷Our fathers sinned, and are no more;
and we bear their iniquities.
⁸Slaves rule over us;

there is none to deliver us from
their hand.
⁹We get our bread at the peril of our
lives,
because of the sword in the wilderness.
¹⁰Our skin is hot as an oven
with the burning heat of famine.
¹¹Women are ravished in Zion,
virgins in the towns of Judah.
¹²Princes are hung up by their hands;
no respect is shown to the elders.
¹³Young men are compelled to grind
at the mill;
and boys stagger under loads of
wood.
¹⁴The old men have quit the city gate,
the young men their music.
¹⁵The joy of our hearts has ceased;
our dancing has been turned to
mourning.
¹⁶The crown has fallen from our head;
woe to us, for we have sinned!
¹⁷For this our heart has become sick,
for these things our eyes have
grown dim,
¹⁸for Mount Zion which lies desolate;
jackals prowl over it.

¹⁹But thou, O Lord, dost reign for ever;
thy throne endures to all generations.
²⁰Why dost thou forget us for ever,
why dost thou so long forsake us?
²¹Restore us to thyself, O Lord, that
we may be restored!
Renew our days as of old!
²²Or hast thou utterly rejected us?
Art thou exceedingly angry with
us?

The Book of

Ezekiel

1 In the thirtieth year, in the fourth
month, on the fifth day of the
month, as I was among the exiles by
the river Chē'bär, the heavens were
opened, and I saw visions of God. ²On
the fifth day of the month (it was the
fifth year of the exile of King Jĕ-
hoi'ạ·chĭn), ³the word of the Lord
came to Ē·zēk'ĭ·ẹl the priest, the son
of Bü'zī, in the land of the Chăl-
dē'ạnṣ by the river Chē'bär; and the
hand of the Lord was upon him there.
4 As I looked, behold, a stormy
wind came out of the north, and a great
cloud, with brightness round about it,
and fire flashing forth continually,

*Symmachus: Heb lacks *with a yoke*
1.1: Rev 19.11.

and in the midst of the fire, as it were gleaming bronze. ⁵And from the midst of it came the likeness of four living creatures. And this was their appearance: they had the form of men, ⁶but each had four faces, and each of them had four wings. ⁷Their legs were straight, and the soles of their feet were like the sole of a calf's foot; and they sparkled like burnished bronze. ⁸Under their wings on their four sides they had human hands. And the four had their faces and their wings thus: ⁹their wings touched one another; they went every one straight forward, without turning as they went. ¹⁰As for the likeness of their faces, each had the face of a man in front;ᵃ the four had the face of a lion on the right side, the four had the face of an ox on the left side, and the four had the face of an eagle at the back.ᵇ ¹¹Such were their faces. And their wings were spread out above; each creature had two wings, each of which touched the wing of another, while two covered their bodies. ¹²And each went straight forward; wherever the spirit would go, they went, without turning as they went. ¹³In the midst ofᶜ the living creatures there was something that looked like burning coals of fire, like torches moving to and fro among the living creatures; and the fire was bright, and out of the fire went forth lightning. ¹⁴And the living creatures darted to and fro, like a flash of lightning.

15 Now as I looked at the living creatures, I saw a wheel upon the earth beside the living creatures, one for each of the four of them.ᵈ ¹⁶As for the appearance of the wheels and their construction: their appearance was like the gleaming of a chrysolite; and the four had the same likeness, their construction being as it were a wheel within a wheel. ¹⁷When they went, they went in any of their four directionsᵉ without turning as they went. ¹⁸The four wheels had rims and they had spokes;ᶠ and their rims were full of eyes round about. ¹⁹And when the living creatures went, the wheels went beside them; and when the living creatures rose from the earth, the wheels rose. ²⁰Wherever the spirit would go, they went, and the wheels rose along with them; for the spirit of the living creatures was in the

wheels. ²¹When those went, these went; and when those stood, these stood; and when those rose from the earth, the wheels rose along with them; for the spirit of the living creatures was in the wheels.

22 Over the heads of the living creatures there was the likeness of a firmament, shining like crystal,ᵍ spread out above their heads. ²³And under the firmament their wings were stretched out straight, one toward another; and each creature had two wings covering its body. ²⁴And when they went, I heard the sound of their wings like the sound of many waters, like the thunder of the Almighty, a sound of tumult like the sound of a host; when they stood still, they let down their wings. ²⁵And there came a voice from above the firmament over their heads; when they stood still, they let down their wings.

26 And above the firmament over their heads there was the likeness of a throne, in appearance like sapphire;ʰ and seated above the likeness of a throne was a likeness as it were of a human form. ²⁷And upward from what had the appearance of his loins I saw as it were gleaming bronze, like the appearance of fire enclosed round about; and downward from what had the appearance of his loins I saw as it were the appearance of fire, and there was brightness round about him.ⁱ ²⁸Like the appearance of the bow that is in the cloud on the day of rain, so was the appearance of the brightness round about.

Such was the appearance of the likeness of the glory of the LORD. And when I saw it, I fell upon my face, and I heard the voice of one speaking.

2 And he said to me, "Son of man, stand upon your feet, and I will speak with you." ²And when he spoke to me, the Spirit entered into me and set me upon my feet; and I heard him speaking to me. ³And he said to me, "Son of man, I send you to the people of Israel, to a nationʲ of rebels, who have rebelled against me; they and

ᵃCn: Heb lacks *in front* ᵇCn: Heb lacks *at the back*
ᶜGk Old Latin: Heb *And the likeness of*
ᵈHeb *of their faces* ᵉHeb *on their four sides*
ᶠCn: Heb uncertain ᵍGk: Heb *awesome crystal*
ʰHeb *lapis lazuli* ⁱOr *it* ʲSyr: Heb *nations*
1.5, 18: Rev 4.6. **1.10:** Rev 4.7.
1.13: Rev 4.5. **1.18:** Ezek 10.12; Rev 4.8.
1.24: Ezek 43.2; Rev 1.15; 14.2; 19.6.
1.26: Rev 1.13; 4.2.

their fathers have transgressed against me to this very day. [4]The people also are impudent and stubborn: I send you to them; and you shall say to them, 'Thus says the Lord God.' [5]And whether they hear or refuse to hear (for they are a rebellious house) they will know that there has been a prophet among them. [6]And you, son of man, be not afraid of them, nor be afraid of their words, though briers and thorns are with you and you sit upon scorpions; be not afraid of their words, nor be dismayed at their looks, for they are a rebellious house. [7]And you shall speak my words to them, whether they hear or refuse to hear; for they are a rebellious house.

8 "But you, son of man, hear what I say to you; be not rebellious like that rebellious house; open your mouth, and eat what I give you." [9]And when I looked, behold, a hand was stretched out to me, and, lo, a written scroll was in it; [10]and he spread it before me; and it had writing on the front and on the back, and there were written on it words of lamentation and mourning and woe. [1]And he said to me, "Son of man, eat what is offered to you; eat this scroll, and go, speak to the house of Israel." [2]So I opened my mouth, and he gave me the scroll to eat. [3]And he said to me, "Son of man, eat this scroll that I give you and fill your stomach with it." Then I ate it; and it was in my mouth as sweet as honey.

4 And he said to me, "Son of man, go, get you to the house of Israel, and speak with my words to them. [5]For you are not sent to a people of foreign speech and a hard language, but to the house of Israel— [6]not to many peoples of foreign speech and a hard language, whose words you cannot understand. Surely, if I sent you to such, they would listen to you. [7]But the house of Israel will not listen to you; for they are not willing to listen to me; because all the house of Israel are of a hard forehead and of a stubborn heart. [8]Behold, I have made your face hard against their faces, and your forehead hard against their foreheads. [9]Like adamant harder than flint have I made your forehead; fear them not, nor be dismayed at their looks, for they are a rebellious house." [10]Moreover he said to me, "Son of man, all my words

that I shall speak to you receive in your heart, and hear with your ears. [11]And go, get you to the exiles, to your people, and say to them, 'Thus says the Lord God'; whether they hear or refuse to hear."

12 Then the Spirit lifted me up, and as the glory of the Lord arose[k] from its place, I heard behind me the sound of a great earthquake; [13]it was the sound of the wings of the living creatures as they touched one another, and the sound of the wheels beside them, that sounded like a great earthquake. [14]The Spirit lifted me up and took me away, and I went in bitterness in the heat of my spirit, the hand of the Lord being strong upon me; [15]and I came to the exiles at Tĕ·lā′bĭb, who dwelt by the river Chē′bär.[l] And I sat there overwhelmed among them seven days.

16 And at the end of seven days, the word of the Lord came to me: [17]"Son of man, I have made you a watchman for the house of Israel; whenever you hear a word from my mouth, you shall give them warning from me. [18]If I say to the wicked, 'You shall surely die,' and you give him no warning, nor speak to warn the wicked from his wicked way, in order to save his life, that wicked man shall die in his iniquity; but his blood I will require at your hand. [19]But if you warn the wicked, and he does not turn from his wickedness, or from his wicked way, he shall die in his iniquity; but you will have saved your life. [20]Again, if a righteous man turns from his righteousness and commits iniquity, and I lay a stumbling block before him, he shall die; because you have not warned him, he shall die for his sin, and his righteous deeds which he has done shall not be remembered; but his blood I will require at your hand. [21]Nevertheless if you warn the righteous man not to sin, and he does not sin, he shall surely live, because he took warning; and you will have saved your life."

22 And the hand of the Lord was there upon me; and he said to me, "Arise, go forth into the plain,[m] and there I will speak with you." [23]So I arose and went forth into the plain;[m]

---

[k]Cn: Heb *blessed be the glory of the* Lord
[l]Heb *Chebar, and to where they dwelt.* Another reading is *Chebar, and I sat where they sat* [m]Or *valley*
2.8-3.3: Rev 5.1; 10.8-10. 3.16-21: Ezek 33.1-9.

and, lo, the glory of the LORD stood there, like the glory which I had seen by the river Chē′bär; and I fell on my face. ²⁴But the Spirit entered into me, and set me upon my feet; and he spoke with me and said to me, "Go, shut yourself within your house. ²⁵And you, O son of man, behold, cords will be placed upon you, and you shall be bound with them, so that you cannot go out among the people; ²⁶and I will make your tongue cleave to the roof of your mouth, so that you shall be dumb and unable to reprove them; for they are a rebellious house. ²⁷But when I speak with you, I will open your mouth, and you shall say to them, 'Thus says the Lord GOD'; he that will hear, let him hear; and he that will refuse to hear, let him refuse; for they are a rebellious house.

4 "And you, O son of man, take a brick and lay it before you, and portray upon it a city, even Jerusalem; ²and put siegeworks against it, and build a siege wall against it, and cast up a mound against it; set camps also against it, and plant battering rams against it round about. ³And take an iron plate, and place it as an iron wall between you and the city; and set your face toward it, and let it be in a state of siege, and press the siege against it. This is a sign for the house of Israel.

4 "Then lie upon your left side, and I will lay the punishment of the house of Israel upon you;ⁿ for the number of the days that you lie upon it, you shall bear their punishment. ⁵For I assign to you a number of days, three hundred and ninety days, equal to the number of the years of their punishment; so long shall you bear the punishment of the house of Israel. ⁶And when you have completed these, you shall lie down a second time, but on your right side, and bear the punishment of the house of Judah; forty days I assign you, a day for each year. ⁷And you shall set your face toward the siege of Jerusalem, with your arm bared; and you shall prophesy against the city. ⁸And, behold, I will put cords upon you, so that you cannot turn from one side to the other, till you have completed the days of your siege.

9 "And you, take wheat and barley, beans and lentils, millet and spelt, and put them into a single vessel, and make bread of them. During the number of days that you lie upon your side, three hundred and ninety days, you shall eat it. ¹⁰And the food which you eat shall be by weight, twenty shekels a day; once a day you shall eat it. ¹¹And water you shall drink by measure, the sixth part of a hin; once a day you shall drink. ¹²And you shall eat it as a barley cake, baking it in their sight on human dung." ¹³And the LORD said, "Thus shall the people of Israel eat their bread unclean, among the nations whither I will drive them." ¹⁴Then I said, "Ah Lord GOD! behold, I have never defiled myself; from my youth up till now I have never eaten what died of itself or was torn by beasts, nor has foul flesh come into my mouth." ¹⁵Then he said to me, "See, I will let you have cow's dung instead of human dung, on which you may prepare your bread." ¹⁶Moreover he said to me, "Son of man, behold, I will break the staff of bread in Jerusalem; they shall eat bread by weight and with fearfulness; and they shall drink water by measure and in dismay. ¹⁷I will do this that they may lack bread and water, and look at one another in dismay, and waste away under their punishment.

5 "And you, O son of man, take a sharp sword; use it as a barber's razor and pass it over your head and your beard; then take balances for weighing, and divide the hair. ²A third part you shall burn in the fire in the midst of the city, when the days of the siege are completed; and a third part you shall take and strike with the sword round about the city; and a third part you shall scatter to the wind, and I will unsheathe the sword after them. ³And you shall take from these a small number, and bind them in the skirts of your robe. ⁴And of these again you shall take some, and cast them into the fire, and burn them in the fire; from there a fire will come forth into all the house of Israel. ⁵Thus says the Lord GOD: This is Jerusalem; I have set her in the center of the nations, with countries round about her. ⁶And she has wickedly rebelled against my ordinancesᵒ more than the nations, and against my statutes more than the countries round about her, by

rejecting my ordinances and not walking in my statutes. [7]Therefore thus says the Lord God: Because you are more turbulent than the nations that are round about you, and have not walked in my statutes or kept my ordinances, but have acted[p] according to the ordinances of the nations that are round about you; [8]therefore thus says the Lord God: Behold, I, even I, am against you; and I will execute judgments in the midst of you in the sight of the nations. [9]And because of all your abominations I will do with you what I have never yet done, and the like of which I will never do again. [10]Therefore fathers shall eat their sons in the midst of you, and sons shall eat their fathers; and I will execute judgments on you, and any of you who survive I will scatter to all the winds. [11]Wherefore, as I live, says the Lord God, surely, because you have defiled my sanctuary with all your detestable things and with all your abominations, therefore I will cut you down;[q] my eye will not spare, and I will have no pity. [12]A third part of you shall die of pestilence and be consumed with famine in the midst of you; a third part shall fall by the sword round about you; and a third part I will scatter to all the winds and will unsheathe the sword after them.

13 "Thus shall my anger spend itself, and I will vent my fury upon them and satisfy myself; and they shall know that I, the Lord, have spoken in my jealousy, when I spend my fury upon them. [14]Moreover I will make you a desolation and an object of reproach among the nations round about you and in the sight of all that pass by. [15]You shall be[r] a reproach and a taunt, a warning and a horror, to the nations round about you, when I execute judgments on you in anger and fury, and with furious chastisements—I, the Lord, have spoken—[16]when I loose against you[s] my deadly arrows of famine, arrows for destruction, which I will loose to destroy you, and when I bring more and more famine upon you, and break your staff of bread. [17]I will send famine and wild beasts against you, and they will rob you of your children; pestilence and blood shall pass through you; and I will bring the sword upon you. I, the Lord, have spoken."

6 The word of the Lord came to me: [2]"Son of man, set your face toward the mountains of Israel, and prophesy against them, [3]and say, You mountains of Israel, hear the word of the Lord God! Thus says the Lord God to the mountains and the hills, to the ravines and the valleys: Behold, I, even I, will bring a sword upon you, and I will destroy your high places. [4]Your altars shall become desolate, and your incense altars shall be broken; and I will cast down your slain before your idols. [5]And I will lay the dead bodies of the people of Israel before their idols; and I will scatter your bones round about your altars. [6]Wherever you dwell your cities shall be waste and your high places ruined, so that your altars will be waste and ruined,[t] your idols broken and destroyed, your incense altars cut down, and your works wiped out. [7]And the slain shall fall in the midst of you, and you shall know that I am the Lord.

8 "Yet I will leave some of you alive. When you have among the nations some who escape the sword, and when you are scattered through the countries, [9]then those of you who escape will remember me among the nations where they are carried captive, when I have broken[u] their wanton heart which has departed from me, and blinded their eyes which turn wantonly after their idols; and they will be loathsome in their own sight for the evils which they have committed, for all their abominations. [10]And they shall know that I am the Lord; I have not said in vain that I would do this evil to them."

11 Thus says the Lord God: "Clap your hands, and stamp your foot, and say, Alas! because of all the evil abominations of the house of Israel; for they shall fall by the sword, by famine, and by pestilence. [12]He that is far off shall die of pestilence; and he that is near shall fall by the sword; and he that is left and is preserved shall die of famine. Thus I will spend my fury upon them. [13]And you shall know that I am the Lord, when their slain lie among their idols round about

[p]Another reading is *and have not acted*
[q]Another reading is *I will withdraw*
[r]Gk Syr Vg Tg: Heb *And it shall be* [s]Heb *them*
[t]Syr Vg Tg: Heb *and be made guilty*
[u]Syr Vg Tg: Heb *I have been broken*
6.9: Ezek 20.43; 36.31.

their altars, upon every high hill, on all the mountain tops, under every green tree, and under every leafy oak, wherever they offered pleasing odor to all their idols. [14] And I will stretch out my hand against them, and make the land desolate and waste, throughout all their habitations, from the wilderness to Rib′lah.[v] Then they will know that I am the LORD."

7 The word of the LORD came to me: [2] "And you, O son of man, thus says the Lord GOD to the land of Israel: An end! The end has come upon the four corners of the land. [3] Now the end is upon you, and I will let loose my anger upon you, and will judge you according to your ways; and I will punish you for all your abominations. [4] And my eye will not spare you, nor will I have pity; but I will punish you for your ways, while your abominations are in your midst. Then you will know that I am the LORD.

5 "Thus says the Lord GOD: Disaster after disaster! Behold, it comes. [6] An end has come, the end has come; it has awakened against you. Behold, it comes. [7] Your doom[w] has come to you, O inhabitant of the land; the time has come, the day is near, a day of tumult, and not of joyful shouting upon the mountains. [8] Now I will soon pour out my wrath upon you, and spend my anger against you, and judge you according to your ways; and I will punish you for all your abominations. [9] And my eye will not spare, nor will I have pity; I will punish you according to your ways, while your abominations are in your midst. Then you will know that I am the LORD, who smite.

10 "Behold, the day! Behold, it comes! Your doom[w] has come, injustice[x] has blossomed, pride has budded. [11] Violence has grown up into a rod of wickedness; none of them shall remain, nor their abundance, nor their wealth; neither shall there be preeminence among them.[y] [12] The time has come, the day draws near. Let not the buyer rejoice, nor the seller mourn, for wrath is upon all their multitude. [13] For the seller shall not return to what he has sold, while they live. For wrath[z] is upon all their multitude; it shall not turn back; and because of his iniquity, none can maintain his life.[a]

14 "They have blown the trumpet and made all ready; but none goes to battle, for my wrath is upon all their multitude. [15] The sword is without, pestilence and famine are within; he that is in the field dies by the sword; and him that is in the city famine and pestilence devour. [16] And if any survivors escape, they will be on the mountains, like doves of the valleys, all of them moaning, every one over his iniquity. [17] All hands are feeble, and all knees weak as water. [18] They gird themselves with sackcloth, and horror covers them; shame is upon all faces, and baldness on all their heads. [19] They cast their silver into the streets, and their gold is like an unclean thing; their silver and gold are not able to deliver them in the day of the wrath of the LORD; they cannot satisfy their hunger or fill their stomachs with it. For it was the stumbling block of their iniquity. [20] Their[b] beautiful ornament they used for vainglory, and they made their abominable images and their detestable things of it; therefore I will make it an unclean thing to them. [21] And I will give it into the hands of foreigners for a prey, and to the wicked of the earth for a spoil; and they shall profane it. [22] I will turn my face from them, that they may profane my precious[c] place; robbers shall enter and profane it, [23] and make a desolation.[d]

"Because the land is full of bloody crimes, and the city is full of violence, [24] I will bring the worst of the nations to take possession of their houses; I will put an end to their proud might, and their holy places shall be profaned. [25] When anguish comes, they will seek peace, but there shall be none. [26] Disaster comes upon disaster, rumor follows rumor; they seek a vision from the prophet, but the law perishes from the priest, and counsel from the elders. [27] The king mourns, and the prince is wrapped in despair, and the hands of the people of the land are palsied by terror. According to their way I will do to them, and according to their own judgments I will judge them; and they shall know that I am the LORD."

*Another reading is *Diblah*
[v]The meaning of the Hebrew word is uncertain
[x]Or *the rod* [y]The Hebrew of verse 11 is uncertain
[z]Cn: Heb *vision* [a]Heb obscure
[b]Syr Symmachus: Heb *Its*
[c]Or *secret* [d]Cn: Heb *make the chain*
7.2: Rev 7.1; 20.8.

8 In the sixth year, in the sixth month, on the fifth day of the month, as I sat in my house, with the elders of Judah sitting before me, the hand of the Lord GOD fell there upon me. ²Then I beheld, and, lo, a form that had the appearance of a man; *e* below what appeared to be his loins it was fire, and above his loins it was like the appearance of brightness, like gleaming bronze. ³He put forth the form of a hand, and took me by a lock of my head; and the Spirit lifted me up between earth and heaven, and brought me in visions of God to Jerusalem, to the entrance of the gateway of the inner court that faces north, where was the seat of the image of jealousy, which provokes to jealousy. ⁴And behold, the glory of the God of Israel was there, like the vision that I saw in the plain.

5 Then he said to me, "Son of man, lift up your eyes now in the direction of the north." So I lifted up my eyes toward the north, and behold, north of the altar gate, in the entrance, was this image of jealousy. ⁶And he said to me, "Son of man, do you see what they are doing, the great abominations that the house of Israel are committing here, to drive me far from my sanctuary? But you will see still greater abominations."

7 And he brought me to the door of the court; and when I looked, behold, there was a hole in the wall. ⁸Then said he to me, "Son of man, dig in the wall"; and when I dug in the wall, lo, there was a door. ⁹And he said to me, "Go in, and see the vile abominations that they are committing here." ¹⁰So I went in and saw; and there, portrayed upon the wall round about, were all kinds of creeping things, and loathsome beasts, and all the idols of the house of Israel. ¹¹And before them stood seventy men of the elders of the house of Israel, with Jā′-ăz·a·nī′ah the son of Shā′phan standing among them. Each had his censer in his hand, and the smoke of the cloud of incense went up. ¹²Then he said to me, "Son of man, have you seen what the elders of the house of Israel are doing in the dark, every man in his room*ƒ* of pictures? For they say, 'The LORD does not see us, the LORD has forsaken the land.'" ¹³He said also to me, "You will see still greater abominations which they commit."

14 Then he brought me to the entrance of the north gate of the house of the LORD; and behold, there sat women weeping for Täm′müz. ¹⁵Then he said to me, "Have you seen this, O son of man? You will see still greater abominations than these."

16 And he brought me into the inner court of the house of the LORD; and behold, at the door of the temple of the LORD, between the porch and the altar, were about twenty-five men, with their backs to the temple of the LORD, and their faces toward the east, worshiping the sun toward the east. ¹⁷Then he said to me, "Have you seen this, O son of man? Is it too slight a thing for the house of Judah to commit the abominations which they commit here, that they should fill the land with violence, and provoke me further to anger? Lo, they put the branch to their nose. ¹⁸Therefore I will deal in wrath; my eye will not spare, nor will I have pity; and though they cry in my ears with a loud voice, I will not hear them."

9 Then he cried in my ears with a loud voice, saying, "Draw near, you executioners of the city, each with his destroying weapon in his hand." ²And lo, six men came from the direction of the upper gate, which faces north, every man with his weapon for slaughter in his hand, and with them was a man clothed in linen, with a writing case at his side. And they went in and stood beside the bronze altar.

3 Now the glory of the God of Israel had gone up from the cherubim on which it rested to the threshold of the house; and he called to the man clothed in linen, who had the writing case at his side. ⁴And the LORD said to him, "Go through the city, through Jerusalem, and put a mark upon the foreheads of the men who sigh and groan over all the abominations that are committed in it." ⁵And to the others he said in my hearing, "Pass through the city after him, and smite; your eye shall not spare, and you shall show no pity; ⁶slay old men outright, young men and maidens, little children and women, but touch no one upon whom is the mark. And begin at my sanctuary." So they began with the elders who were before the house.

*e*Gk: Heb *fire ƒ*Gk Syr Vg Tg: Heb *rooms*
9.4, 6: 1 Pet 4.17; Rev 7.3; 9.4; 14.1.

7 Then he said to them, "Defile the house, and fill the courts with the slain. Go forth." So they went forth, and smote in the city. 8 And while they were smiting, and I was left alone, I fell upon my face, and cried, "Ah Lord GOD! wilt thou destroy all that remains of Israel in the outpouring of thy wrath upon Jerusalem?"

9 Then he said to me, "The guilt of the house of Israel and Judah is exceedingly great; the land is full of blood, and the city full of injustice; for they say, 'The LORD has forsaken the land, and the LORD does not see.' 10 As for me, my eye will not spare, nor will I have pity, but I will requite their deeds upon their heads."

11 And lo, the man clothed in linen, with the writing case at his side, brought back word, saying, "I have done as thou didst command me."

10 Then I looked, and behold, on the firmament that was over the heads of the cherubim there appeared above them something like a sapphire, in form resembling a throne. 2 And he said to the man clothed in linen, "Go in among the whirling wheels underneath the cherubim; fill your hands with burning coals from between the cherubim, and scatter them over the city."

And he went in before my eyes. 3 Now the cherubim were standing on the south side of the house, when the man went in; and a cloud filled the inner court. 4 And the glory of the LORD went up from the cherubim to the threshold of the house; and the house was filled with the cloud, and the court was full of the brightness of the glory of the LORD. 5 And the sound of the wings of the cherubim was heard as far as the outer court, like the voice of God Almighty when he speaks.

6 And when he commanded the man clothed in linen, "Take fire from between the whirling wheels, from between the cherubim," he went in and stood beside a wheel. 7 And a cherub stretched forth his hand from between the cherubim to the fire that was between the cherubim, and took some of it, and put it into the hands of the man clothed in linen, who took it and went out. 8 The cherubim appeared to have the form of a human hand under their wings.

9 And I looked, and behold, there were four wheels beside the cherubim, one beside each cherub; and the appearance of the wheels was like sparkling chrysolite. 10 And as for their appearance, the four had the same likeness, as if a wheel were within a wheel. 11 When they went, they went in any of their four directions*g* without turning as they went, but in whatever direction the front wheel faced the others followed without turning as they went. 12 And*h* their rims, and their spokes,*i* and the wheels were full of eyes round about—the wheels that the four of them had. 13 As for the wheels, they were called in my hearing the whirling wheels. 14 And every one had four faces: the first face was the face of the cherub, and the second face was the face of a man, and the third the face of a lion, and the fourth the face of an eagle.

15 And the cherubim mounted up. These were the living creatures that I saw by the river Chē′bär. 16 And when the cherubim went, the wheels went beside them; and when the cherubim lifted up their wings to mount up from the earth, the wheels did not turn from beside them. 17 When they stood still, these stood still, and when they mounted up, these mounted up with them; for the spirit of the living creatures*j* was in them.

18 Then the glory of the LORD went forth from the threshold of the house, and stood over the cherubim. 19 And the cherubim lifted up their wings and mounted up from the earth in my sight as they went forth, with the wheels beside them; and they stood at the door of the east gate of the house of the LORD; and the glory of the God of Israel was over them.

20 These were the living creatures that I saw underneath the God of Israel by the river Chē′bär; and I knew that they were cherubim. 21 Each had four faces, and each four wings, and underneath their wings the semblance of human hands. 22 And as for the likeness of their faces, they were the very faces whose appearance I had seen by the river Chē′bär. They went every one straight forward.

g Heb on their four sides
h Gk: Heb And their whole body and
i Heb spokes and their wings   *j* Or of life
10.1: Rev 4.2.   10.2: Rev 8.5.
10.12: Ezek 1.18; Rev 4.8.   10.14: Ezek 1.10; Rev 4.7.

11 The Spirit lifted me up, and brought me to the east gate of the house of the LORD, which faces east. And behold, at the door of the gateway there were twenty-five men; and I saw among them Jā'–āz·a·nī'ah the son of Āz'zūr, and Pĕl·a·tī'ah the son of Bĕ·nā'ī·ah, princes of the people. ²And he said to me, "Son of man, these are the men who devise iniquity and who give wicked counsel in this city; ³who say, 'The time is not near[k] to build houses; this city is the caldron, and we are the flesh.' ⁴Therefore prophesy against them, prophesy, O son of man."

5 And the Spirit of the LORD fell upon me, and he said to me, "Say, Thus says the LORD: So you think, O house of Israel; for I know the things that come into your mind. ⁶You have multiplied your slain in this city, and have filled its streets with the slain. ⁷Therefore thus says the Lord GOD: Your slain whom you have laid in the midst of it, they are the flesh, and this city is the caldron; but you shall be brought forth out of the midst of it. ⁸You have feared the sword; and I will bring the sword upon you, says the Lord GOD. ⁹And I will bring you forth out of the midst of it, and give you into the hands of foreigners, and execute judgments upon you. ¹⁰You shall fall by the sword; I will judge you at the border of Israel; and you shall know that I am the LORD. ¹¹This city shall not be your caldron, nor shall you be the flesh in the midst of it; I will judge you at the border of Israel; ¹²and you shall know that I am the LORD; for you have not walked in my statutes, nor executed my ordinances, but have acted according to the ordinances of the nations that are round about you."

13 And it came to pass, while I was prophesying, that Pĕl·a·tī'ah the son of Bĕ·nā'ī·ah died. Then I fell down upon my face, and cried with a loud voice, and said, "Ah Lord GOD! wilt thou make a full end of the remnant of Israel?"

14 And the word of the LORD came to me: ¹⁵"Son of man, your brethren, even your brethren, your fellow exiles,[l] the whole house of Israel, all of them, are those of whom the inhabitants of Jerusalem have said, 'They have gone far from the LORD; to us this land is given for a possession.' ¹⁶Therefore

say, 'Thus says the Lord GOD: Though I removed them far off among the nations, and though I scattered them among the countries, yet I have been a sanctuary to them for a while[m] in the countries where they have gone.' ¹⁷Therefore say, 'Thus says the Lord GOD: I will gather you from the peoples, and assemble you out of the countries where you have been scattered, and I will give you the land of Israel.' ¹⁸And when they come there, they will remove from it all its detestable things and all its abominations. ¹⁹And I will give them one[n] heart, and put a new spirit within them; I will take the stony heart out of their flesh and give them a heart of flesh, ²⁰that they may walk in my statutes and keep my ordinances and obey them; and they shall be my people, and I will be their God. ²¹But as for those[o] whose heart goes after their detestable things and their abominations, I will requite their deeds upon their own heads, says the Lord GOD."

22 Then the cherubim lifted up their wings, with the wheels beside them; and the glory of the God of Israel was over them. ²³And the glory of the LORD went up from the midst of the city, and stood upon the mountain which is on the east side of the city. ²⁴And the Spirit lifted me up and brought me in the vision by the Spirit of God into Chăl·dē'ă, to the exiles. Then the vision that I had seen went up from me. ²⁵And I told the exiles all the things that the LORD had showed me.

12 The word of the LORD came to me: ²"Son of man, you dwell in the midst of a rebellious house, who have eyes to see, but see not, who have ears to hear, but hear not; ³for they are a rebellious house. Therefore, son of man, prepare for yourself an exile's baggage, and go into exile by day in their sight; you shall go like an exile from your place to another place in their sight. Perhaps they will understand, though[p] they are a rebellious house. ⁴You shall bring out your baggage by day in their sight, as

---

[k]Or *Is not the time near . . .?*
[l]Gk Syr: Heb *men of your kindred*   [m]Or *in small measure*
[n]Another reading is *a new*
[o]Cn: Heb *To the heart of their detestable things and their abominations their heart goes*   [p]Or *will see that*
11.19: Ezek 18.31; 36.26; 2 Cor 3.3.   **12.2:** Mk 8.18.

baggage for exile; and you shall go forth yourself at evening in their sight, as men do who must go into exile. 5 Dig through the wall in their sight, and go[q] out through it. 6 In their sight you shall lift the baggage upon your shoulder, and carry it out in the dark; you shall cover your face, that you may not see the land; for I have made you a sign for the house of Israel."

7 And I did as I was commanded. I brought out my baggage by day, as baggage for exile, and in the evening I dug through the wall with my own hands; I went forth in the dark, carrying my outfit upon my shoulder in their sight.

8 In the morning the word of the LORD came to me: 9 "Son of man, has not the house of Israel, the rebellious house, said to you, 'What are you doing?' 10 Say to them, 'Thus says the Lord GOD: This oracle concerns the prince in Jerusalem and all the house of Israel who are in it.'[r] 11 Say, 'I am a sign for you: as I have done, so shall it be done to them; they shall go into exile, into captivity.' 12 And the prince who is among them shall lift his baggage upon his shoulder in the dark, and shall go forth; he[s] shall dig through the wall and go[t] out through it; he shall cover his face, that he may not see the land with his eyes. 13 And I will spread my net over him, and he shall be taken in my snare; and I will bring him to Babylon in the land of the Chăl·dē′ans̹, yet he shall not see it; and he shall die there. 14 And I will scatter toward every wind all who are round about him, his helpers[u] and all his troops; and I will unsheathe the sword after them. 15 And they shall know that I am the LORD, when I disperse them among the nations and scatter them through the countries. 16 But I will let a few of them escape from the sword, from famine and pestilence, that they may confess all their abominations among the nations where they go, and may know that I am the LORD."

17 Moreover the word of the LORD came to me: 18 "Son of man, eat your bread with quaking, and drink water with trembling and with fearfulness; 19 and say of the people of the land, Thus says the Lord GOD concerning the inhabitants of Jerusalem in the land of Israel: They shall eat their bread with fearfulness, and drink water in dismay, because their land will be stripped of all it contains, on account of the violence of all those who dwell in it. 20 And the inhabited cities shall be laid waste, and the land shall become a desolation; and you shall know that I am the LORD."

21 And the word of the LORD came to me: 22 "Son of man, what is this proverb that you have about the land of Israel, saying, 'The days grow long, and every vision comes to nought'? 23 Tell them therefore, 'Thus says the Lord GOD: I will put an end to this proverb, and they shall no more use it as a proverb in Israel.' But say to them, The days are at hand, and the fulfilment[v] of every vision. 24 For there shall be no more any false vision or flattering divination within the house of Israel. 25 But I the LORD will speak the word which I will speak, and it will be performed. It will no longer be delayed, but in your days, O rebellious house, I will speak the word and perform it, says the Lord GOD."

26 Again the word of the LORD came to me: 27 "Son of man, behold, they of the house of Israel say, 'The vision that he sees is for many days hence, and he prophesies of times far off.' 28 Therefore say to them, Thus says the Lord GOD: None of my words will be delayed any longer, but the word which I speak will be performed, says the Lord GOD."

13 The word of the LORD came to me: 2 "Son of man, prophesy against the prophets of Israel, prophesy[w] and say to those who prophesy out of their own minds: 'Hear the word of the LORD!' 3 Thus says the Lord GOD, Woe to the foolish prophets who follow their own spirit, and have seen nothing! 4 Your prophets have been like foxes among ruins, O Israel. 5 You have not gone up into the breaches, or built up a wall for the house of Israel, that it might stand in battle in the day of the LORD. 6 They have spoken falsehood and divined a lie; they say, 'Says the LORD,' when the LORD has not sent them, and yet they expect him to fulfil their word. 7 Have you not seen a delusive vision, and uttered a lying divina-

[q] Gk Syr Vg Tg: Heb *bring*
[r] Heb *in the midst of them* [s] Gk Syr: Heb *they*
[t] Gk Syr Tg: Heb *bring*
[u] Gk Syr Tg: Heb *his help* [v] Heb *word*
[w] Gk: Heb *who prophesy*

tion, whenever you have said, 'Says the LORD,' although I have not spoken?"

8 Therefore thus says the Lord GOD: "Because you have uttered delusions and seen lies, therefore behold, I am against you, says the Lord GOD. ⁹My hand will be against the prophets who see delusive visions and who give lying divinations; they shall not be in the council of my people, nor be enrolled in the register of the house of Israel, nor shall they enter the land of Israel; and you shall know that I am the Lord GOD. ¹⁰Because, yea, because they have misled my people, saying, 'Peace,' when there is no peace; and because, when the people build a wall, these prophets daub it with whitewash; ¹¹say to those who daub it with whitewash that it shall fall! There will be a deluge of rain,ˣ great hailstones will fall, and a stormy wind break out; ¹²and when the wall falls, will it not be said to you, 'Where is the daubing with which you daubed it?' ¹³Therefore thus says the Lord GOD: I will make a stormy wind break out in my wrath; and there shall be a deluge of rain in my anger, and great hailstones in wrath to destroy it. ¹⁴And I will break down the wall that you have daubed with whitewash, and bring it down to the ground, so that its foundation will be laid bare; when it falls, you shall perish in the midst of it; and you shall know that I am the LORD. ¹⁵Thus will I spend my wrath upon the wall, and upon those who have daubed it with whitewash; and I will say to you, The wall is no more, nor those who daubed it, ¹⁶the prophets of Israel who prophesied concerning Jerusalem and saw visions of peace for her, when there was no peace, says the Lord GOD.

17 "And you, son of man, set your face against the daughters of your people, who prophesy out of their own minds; prophesy against them ¹⁸and say, Thus says the Lord GOD: Woe to the women who sew magic bands upon all wrists, and make veils for the heads of persons of every stature, in the hunt for souls! Will you hunt down souls belonging to my people, and keep other souls alive for your profit? ¹⁹You have profaned me among my people for handfuls of barley and for pieces of bread, putting to death persons who should not die and keeping alive per-

sons who should not live, by your lies to my people, who listen to lies.

20 "Wherefore thus says the Lord GOD: Behold, I am against your magic bands with which you hunt the souls,ʸ and I will tear them from your arms; and I will let the souls that you hunt go free² like birds. ²¹Your veils also I will tear off, and deliver my people out of your hand, and they shall be no more in your hand as prey; and you shall know that I am the LORD. ²²Because you have disheartened the righteous falsely, although I have not disheartened him, and you have encouraged the wicked, that he should not turn from his wicked way to save his life; ²³therefore you shall no more see delusive visions nor practice divination; I will deliver my people out of your hand. Then you will know that I am the LORD."

14 Then came certain of the elders of Israel to me, and sat before me. ²And the word of the LORD came to me: ³"Son of man, these men have taken their idols into their hearts, and set the stumbling block of their iniquity before their faces; should I let myself be inquired of at all by them? ⁴Therefore speak to them, and say to them, Thus says the Lord GOD: Any man of the house of Israel who takes his idols into his heart and sets the stumbling block of his iniquity before his face, and yet comes to the prophet, I the LORD will answer him myselfᵃ because of the multitude of his idols, ⁵that I may lay hold of the hearts of the house of Israel, who are all estranged from me through their idols.

6 "Therefore say to the house of Israel, Thus says the Lord GOD: Repent and turn away from your idols; and turn away your faces from all your abominations. ⁷For any one of the house of Israel, or of the strangers that sojourn in Israel, who separates himself from me, taking his idols into his heart and putting the stumbling block of his iniquity before his face, and yet comes to a prophet to inquire for himself of me, I the LORD will answer him myself; ⁸and I will set my face against that man, I will make him a sign and a byword and cut him

ˣ Heb *rain and you*   ʸ Gk Syr: Heb *souls for birds*
² Cn: Heb *the souls*
ᵃ Cn Compare Tg: Heb uncertain

off from the midst of my people; and you shall know that I am the LORD. ⁹And if the prophet be deceived and speak a word, I, the LORD, have deceived that prophet, and I will stretch out my hand against him, and will destroy him from the midst of my people Israel. ¹⁰And they shall bear their punishment – the punishment of the prophet and the punishment of the inquirer shall be alike – ¹¹that the house of Israel may go no more astray from me, nor defile themselves any more with all their transgressions, but that they may be my people and I may be their God, says the Lord GOD."

12 And the word of the LORD came to me: ¹³"Son of man, when a land sins against me by acting faithlessly, and I stretch out my hand against it, and break its staff of bread and send famine upon it, and cut off from it man and beast, ¹⁴even if these three men, Noah, Daniel, and Jōb, were in it, they would deliver but their own lives by their righteousness, says the Lord GOD. ¹⁵If I cause wild beasts to pass through the land, and they ravage it, and it be made desolate, so that no man may pass through because of the beasts; ¹⁶even if these three men were in it, as I live, says the Lord GOD, they would deliver neither sons nor daughters; they alone would be delivered, but the land would be desolate. ¹⁷Or if I bring a sword upon that land, and say, Let a sword go through the land; and I cut off from it man and beast; ¹⁸though these three men were in it, as I live, says the Lord GOD, they would deliver neither sons nor daughters, but they alone would be delivered. ¹⁹Or if I send a pestilence into that land, and pour out my wrath upon it with blood, to cut off from it man and beast; ²⁰even if Noah, Daniel, and Jōb were in it, as I live, says the Lord GOD, they would deliver neither son nor daughter; they would deliver but their own lives by their righteousness.

21 "For thus says the Lord GOD: How much more when I send upon Jerusalem my four sore acts of judgment, sword, famine, evil beasts, and pestilence, to cut off from it man and beast! ²²Yet, if there should be left in it any survivors to lead out sons and daughters, when they come forth to you, and you see their ways and their doings, you will be consoled for the evil

that I have brought upon Jerusalem, for all that I have brought upon it. ²³They will console you, when you see their ways and their doings; and you shall know that I have not done without cause all that I have done in it, says the Lord GOD."

15 And the word of the LORD came to me: ²"Son of man, how does the wood of the vine surpass any wood, the vine branch which is among the trees of the forest? ³Is wood taken from it to make anything? Do men take a peg from it to hang any vessel on? ⁴Lo, it is given to the fire for fuel; when the fire has consumed both ends of it, and the middle of it is charred, is it useful for anything? ⁵Behold, when it was whole, it was used for nothing; how much less, when the fire has consumed it and it is charred, can it ever be used for anything! ⁶Therefore thus says the Lord GOD: Like the wood of the vine among the trees of the forest, which I have given to the fire for fuel, so will I give up the inhabitants of Jerusalem. ⁷And I will set my face against them; though they escape from the fire, the fire shall yet consume them; and you will know that I am the LORD, when I set my face against them. ⁸And I will make the land desolate, because they have acted faithlessly, says the Lord GOD."

16 Again the word of the LORD came to me: ²"Son of man, make known to Jerusalem her abominations, ³and say, Thus says the Lord GOD to Jerusalem: Your origin and your birth are of the land of the Canaanites; your father was an Ām'o-rīte, and your mother a Hīt'tīte. ⁴And as for your birth, on the day you were born your navel string was not cut, nor were you washed with water to cleanse you, nor rubbed with salt, nor swathed with bands. ⁵No eye pitied you, to do any of these things to you out of compassion for you; but you were cast out on the open field, for you were abhorred, on the day that you were born.

6 "And when I passed by you, and saw you weltering in your blood, I said to you in your blood, 'Live, ⁷and grow up*ᵇ* like a plant of the field.' And you grew up and became tall and

ᵇGk Syr: Heb *I made you a myriad*
14.21: Rev 6.8. 16.3: Ezek 16.45.

arrived at full maidenhood;*c* your breasts were formed, and your hair had grown; yet you were naked and bare.

8 "When I passed by you again and looked upon you, behold, you were at the age for love; and I spread my skirt over you, and covered your nakedness: yea, I plighted my troth to you and entered into a covenant with you, says the Lord GOD, and you became mine. Then I bathed you with water and washed off your blood from you, and anointed you with oil. ¹⁰I clothed you also with embroidered cloth and shod you with leather, I swathed you in fine linen and covered you with silk. And I decked you with ornaments, and put bracelets on your arms, and a chain on your neck. ¹²And I put a ring in your nose, and earrings in your ears, and a beautiful crown upon your head. Thus you were decked with gold and silver; and your raiment was of fine linen, and silk, and embroidered cloth; you ate fine flour and honey and oil. You grew exceedingly beautiful, and came to regal estate. ¹⁴And your renown went forth among the nations because of your beauty, for it was perfect through the splendor which I had bestowed upon you, says the Lord GOD.

15 "But you trusted in your beauty, and played the harlot because of your renown, and lavished your harlotries on any passer-by. ¹⁶You took some of your garments, and made for yourself gaily decked shrines, and on them played the harlot; the like has never been, nor ever shall be. ¹⁷You also took your fair jewels of my gold and of my silver, which I had given you, and made for yourself images of men, and with them played the harlot; and you took your embroidered garments to cover them, and set my oil and my incense before them. ¹⁹Also my bread which I gave you—I fed you with fine flour and oil and honey—you set before them for a pleasing odor, says the Lord GOD.*d* ²⁰And you took your sons and your daughters, whom you had borne to me, and these you sacrificed to them to be devoured. Were your harlotries so small a matter ²¹that you slaughtered my children and delivered them up as an offering by fire to them? ²²And in all your abominations and your harlotries you did not remember the days of your youth, when you were naked and bare, weltering in your blood.

23 "And after all your wickedness (woe, woe to you! says the Lord GOD), ²⁴you built yourself a vaulted chamber, and made yourself a lofty place in every square; ²⁵at the head of every street you built your lofty place and prostituted your beauty, offering yourself to any passer-by, and multiplying your harlotry. ²⁶You also played the harlot with the Egyptians, your lustful neighbors, multiplying your harlotry, to provoke me to anger. ²⁷Behold, therefore, I stretched out my hand against you, and diminished your allotted portion, and delivered you to the greed of your enemies, the daughters of the Phi·lis′tines, who were ashamed of your lewd behavior. ²⁸You played the harlot also with the Assyrians, because you were insatiable; yea, you played the harlot with them, and still you were not satisfied. ²⁹You multiplied your harlotry also with the trading land of Chăl·dē′ă, and even with this you were not satisfied.

30 "How lovesick is your heart, says the Lord GOD, seeing you did all these things, the deeds of a brazen harlot; ³¹building your vaulted chamber at the head of every street, and making your lofty place in every square. Yet you were not like a harlot, because you scorned hire. ³²Adulterous wife, who receives strangers instead of her husband! ³³Men give gifts to all harlots; but you gave your gifts to all your lovers, bribing them to come to you from every side for your harlotries. ³⁴So you were different from other women in your harlotries: none solicited you to play the harlot; and you gave hire, while no hire was given to you; therefore you were different.

35 "Wherefore, O harlot, hear the word of the LORD: ³⁶Thus says the Lord GOD, Because your shame was laid bare and your nakedness uncovered in your harlotries with your lovers, and because of all your idols, and because of the blood of your children that you gave to them, ³⁷therefore, behold, I will gather all your lovers, with whom you took pleasure, all those you loved and all those you loathed; I will gather them against you from every side, and

*c*Cn: Heb *ornament of ornaments*
*d*Syr: Heb *and it was, says the Lord* GOD

will uncover your nakedness to them, that they may see all your nakedness. [38]And I will judge you as women who break wedlock and shed blood are judged, and bring upon you the blood of wrath and jealousy. [39]And I will give you into the hand of your lovers, and they shall throw down your vaulted chamber and break down your lofty places; they shall strip you of your clothes and take your fair jewels, and leave you naked and bare. [40]They shall bring up a host against you, and they shall stone you and cut you to pieces with their swords. [41]And they shall burn your houses and execute judgments upon you in the sight of many women; I will make you stop playing the harlot, and you shall also give hire no more. [42]So will I satisfy my fury on you, and my jealousy shall depart from you; I will be calm, and will no more be angry. [43]Because you have not remembered the days of your youth, but have enraged me with all these things; therefore, behold, I will requite your deeds upon your head, says the Lord God.

"Have you not committed lewdness in addition to all your abominations? [44]Behold, every one who uses proverbs will use this proverb about you, 'Like mother, like daughter.' [45]You are the daughter of your mother, who loathed her husband and her children; and you are the sister of your sisters, who loathed their husbands and their children. Your mother was a Hĭt′tīte and your father an Ăm′o·rīte. [46]And your elder sister is Sa·mâr′ĭ·a, who lived with her daughters to the north of you; and your younger sister, who lived to the south of you, is Sŏd′om with her daughters. [47]Yet you were not content to walk in their ways, or do according to their abominations; within a very little time you were more corrupt than they in all your ways. [48]As I live, says the Lord God, your sister Sŏd′om and her daughters have not done as you and your daughters have done. [49]Behold, this was the guilt of your sister Sŏd′om: she and her daughters had pride, surfeit of food, and prosperous ease, but did not aid the poor and needy. [50]They were haughty, and did abominable things before me; therefore I removed them, when I saw it. [51]Sa·mâr′ĭ·a has not committed half your sins; you have

committed more abominations than they, and have made your sisters appear righteous by all the abominations which you have committed. [52]Bear your disgrace, you also, for you have made judgment favorable to your sisters; because of your sins in which you acted more abominably than they they are more in the right than you. So be ashamed, you also, and bear your disgrace, for you have made your sisters appear righteous.

53 "I will restore their fortunes both the fortunes of Sŏd′om and he daughters, and the fortunes of Sa mâr′ĭ·a and her daughters, and will restore your own fortunes in the midst of them, [54]that you may bear your disgrace and be ashamed of al that you have done, becoming a con solation to them. [55]As for your sisters Sŏd′om and her daughters shall re turn to their former estate, and Sa mâr′ĭ·a and her daughters shall re turn to their former estate; and yo and your daughters shall return t your former estate. [56]Was not you sister Sŏd′om a byword in your mout in the day of your pride, [57]before you wickedness was uncovered? Now yo have become like her[e] an object of re proach for the daughters of Ē′don and all her neighbors, and for th daughters of the Phĭ·lĭs′tĭnes, thos round about who despise you. [58]Yo bear the penalty of your lewdness an your abominations, says the Lord.

59 "Yea, thus says the Lord God: will deal with you as you have don who have despised the oath in breal ing the covenant, [60]yet I will remembe my covenant with you in the days o your youth, and I will establish wit you an everlasting covenant. [61]The you will remember your ways, and b ashamed when I[g] take your sister both your elder and your younger, an give them to you as daughters, but n on account of the covenant with yo [62]I will establish my covenant wit you, and you shall know that I am th Lord, [63]that you may remember ar be confounded, and never open yo mouth again because of your sham when I forgive you all that you ha done, says the Lord God."

17 The word of the Lord can to me: [2]"Son of man, propou

[e] Cn: Heb uncertain   [f] Another reading is *Aram*
[g] Syr: Heb *you*   **16.45:** Ezek 16.3.

a riddle, and speak an allegory to the house of Israel; ³say, Thus says the Lord GOD: A great eagle with great wings and long pinions, rich in plumage of many colors, came to Lebanon and took the top of the cedar; ⁴he broke off the topmost of its young twigs and carried it to a land of trade, and set it in a city of merchants. ⁵Then he took of the seed of the land and planted it in fertile soil; he placed it beside abundant waters. He set it like a willow twig, ⁶and it sprouted and became a low spreading vine, and its branches turned toward him, and its roots remained where it stood. So it became a vine, and brought forth branches and put forth foliage.

7 "But there was another great eagle with great wings and much plumage; and behold, this vine bent its roots toward him, and shot forth its branches toward him that he might water it. From the bed where it was planted ⁸he transplanted it*ʰ* to good soil by abundant waters, that it might bring forth branches, and bear fruit, and become a noble vine. ⁹Say, Thus says the Lord GOD: Will it thrive? Will he not pull up its roots and cut off its branches,*ⁱ* so that all its fresh sprouting leaves wither? It will not take a strong arm or many people to pull it from its roots. ¹⁰Behold, when it is transplanted, will it thrive? Will it not utterly wither when the east wind strikes it—wither away on the bed where it grew?"

11 Then the word of the LORD came to me: ¹²"Say now to the rebellious house. Do you not know what these things mean? Tell them, Behold, the king of Babylon came to Jerusalem, and took her king and her princes and brought them to him to Babylon. ¹³And he took one of the seed royal and made a covenant with him, putting him under oath. (The chief men of the land he had taken away, ¹⁴that the kingdom might be humble and not lift itself up, and that by keeping his covenant it might stand.) ¹⁵But he rebelled against him by sending ambassadors to Egypt, that they might give him horses and a large army. Will he succeed? Can a man escape who does such things? Can he break the covenant and yet escape? ¹⁶As I live, says the Lord GOD, surely in the place where the king dwells who made him king, whose oath

he despised, and whose covenant with him he broke, in Babylon he shall die. ¹⁷Pharaoh with his mighty army and great company will not help him in war, when mounds are cast up and siege walls built to cut off many lives. ¹⁸Because he despised the oath and broke the covenant, because he gave his hand and yet did all these things, he shall not escape. ¹⁹Therefore thus says the Lord GOD: As I live, surely my oath which he despised, and my covenant which he broke, I will requite upon his head. ²⁰I will spread my net over him, and he shall be taken in my snare, and I will bring him to Babylon and enter into judgment with him there for the treason he has committed against me. ²¹And all the pick*ʲ* of his troops shall fall by the sword, and the survivors shall be scattered to every wind; and you shall know that I, the LORD, have spoken."

22 Thus says the Lord GOD: "I myself will take a sprig from the lofty top of the cedar, and will set it out; I will break off from the topmost of its young twigs a tender one, and I myself will plant it upon a high and lofty mountain; ²³on the mountain height of Israel will I plant it, that it may bring forth boughs and bear fruit, and become a noble cedar; and under it will dwell all kinds of beasts;*ᵏ* in the shade of its branches birds of every sort will nest. ²⁴And all the trees of the field shall know that I the LORD bring low the high tree, and make high the low tree, dry up the green tree, and make the dry tree flourish. I the LORD have spoken, and I will do it."

18 The word of the LORD came to me again: ²"What do you mean by repeating this proverb concerning the land of Israel, 'The fathers have eaten sour grapes, and the children's teeth are set on edge'? ³As I live, says the Lord GOD, this proverb shall no more be used by you in Israel. ⁴Behold, all souls are mine; the soul of the father as well as the soul of the son is mine: the soul that sins shall die.

5 "If a man is righteous and does what is lawful and right— ⁶if he does not eat upon the mountains or lift up his eyes to the idols of the house of Is-

ʰCn: Heb *it was transplanted* ⁱCn: Heb *fruit*
ʲAnother reading is *fugitives*
ᵏGk: Heb lacks *all kinds of beasts*
17.23: Ezek 31.6; Mt 13.32; Mk 4.32; Lk 13.19.
18.2: Jer 31.29. **18.4:** Ezek 18.20.

rael, does not defile his neighbor's wife or approach a woman in her time of impurity, [7]does not oppress any one, but restores to the debtor his pledge, commits no robbery, gives his bread to the hungry and covers the naked with a garment, [8]does not lend at interest or take any increase, withholds his hand from iniquity, executes true justice between man and man, [9]walks in my statutes, and is careful to observe my ordinances[i]—he is righteous, he shall surely live, says the Lord God.

10 "If he begets a son who is a robber, a shedder of blood,[m] [11]who does none of these duties, but eats upon the mountains, defiles his neighbor's wife, [12]oppresses the poor and needy, commits robbery, does not restore the pledge, lifts up his eyes to the idols, commits abomination, [13]lends at interest, and takes increase; shall he then live? He shall not live. He has done all these abominable things; he shall surely die; his blood shall be upon himself.

14 "But if this man begets a son who sees all the sins which his father has done, and fears, and does not do likewise, [15]who does not eat upon the mountains or lift up his eyes to the idols of the house of Israel, does not defile his neighbor's wife, [16]does not wrong any one, exacts no pledge, commits no robbery, but gives his bread to the hungry and covers the naked with a garment, [17]withholds his hand from iniquity,[n] takes no interest or increase, observes my ordinances, and walks in my statutes; he shall not die for his father's iniquity; he shall surely live. [18]As for his father, because he practiced extortion, robbed his brother, and did what is not good among his people, behold, he shall die for his iniquity.

19 "Yet you say, 'Why should not the son suffer for the iniquity of the father?' When the son has done what is lawful and right, and has been careful to observe all my statutes, he shall surely live. [20]The soul that sins shall die. The son shall not suffer for the iniquity of the father, nor the father suffer for the iniquity of the son; the righteousness of the righteous shall be upon himself, and the wickedness of the wicked shall be upon himself.

21 "But if a wicked man turns away from all his sins which he has committed and keeps all my statutes and does what is lawful and right, he shall surely live; he shall not die. [22]None of the transgressions which he has committed shall be remembered against him; for the righteousness which he has done he shall live. [23]Have I any pleasure in the death of the wicked, says the Lord God, and not rather that he should turn from his way and live? [24]But when a righteous man turns away from his righteousness and commits iniquity and does the same abominable things that the wicked man does, shall he live? None of the righteous deeds which he has done shall be remembered; for the treachery of which he is guilty and the sin he has committed, he shall die.

25 "Yet you say, 'The way of the Lord is not just.' Hear now, O house of Israel: Is my way not just? Is it not your ways that are not just? [26]When a righteous man turns away from his righteousness and commits iniquity he shall die for it; for the iniquity which he has committed he shall die. [27]Again, when a wicked man turns away from the wickedness he has committed and does what is lawful and right, he shall save his life. [28]Because he considered and turned away from all the transgressions which he had committed, he shall surely live, he shall not die. [29]Yet the house of Israel says, 'The way of the Lord is not just.' O house of Israel, are my ways not just? Is it not your ways that are not just?

30 "Therefore I will judge you, O house of Israel, every one according to his ways, says the Lord God. Repent and turn from all your transgressions, lest iniquity be your ruin. [31]Cast away from you all the transgressions which you have committed against me, and get yourselves a new heart and a new spirit! Why will you die, O house of Israel? [32]For I have no pleasure in the death of any one, says the Lord God; so turn, and live."

19 And you, take up a lamentation for the princes of Israel

[i]Gk: Heb *has kept my ordinances, to deal truly*
[m]Heb *blood, and he does any one of these things*
[n]Gk: Heb *the poor*
[o]Or *so that they shall not be a stumbling block of iniquity to you*
18.20: Ezek 18.4.   **18.23:** Ezek 18.32; 33.11.
18.31: Ezek 11.19; 36.26.   **18.32:** Ezek 18.23; 33.11.

²and say:
What a lioness was your mother
  among lions!
She couched in the midst of young
  lions,
  rearing her whelps.
³And she brought up one of her
  whelps;
  he became a young lion,
and he learned to catch prey;
  he devoured men.
⁴The nations sounded an alarm
  against him;
  he was taken in their pit;
and they brought him with hooks
  to the land of Egypt.
⁵When she saw that she was baffled,ᵖ
  that her hope was lost,
she took another of her whelps
  and made him a young lion.
⁶He prowled among the lions;
  he became a young lion,
and he learned to catch prey;
  he devoured men.
⁷And he ravaged their strongholds,�q
  and laid waste their cities;
and the land was appalled and all
  who were in it
  at the sound of his roaring.
⁸Then the nations set against him
  snaresʳ on every side;
they spread their net over him;
  he was taken in their pit.
⁹With hooks they put him in a cage,
  and brought him to the king of
    Babylon;
they brought him into custody,
that his voice should no more be
  heard
  upon the mountains of Israel.

¹⁰Your mother was like a vine in a
  vineyardˢ
  transplanted by the water,
fruitful and full of branches
  by reason of abundant water.
Its strongest stem became
  a ruler's scepter;
it towered aloft
  among the thick boughs;
it was seen in its height
  with the mass of its branches.
But the vine was plucked up in fury,
  cast down to the ground;
the east wind dried it up;
  its fruit was stripped off,
its strong stem was withered;
  the fire consumed it.
Now it is transplanted in the wilderness,

in a dry and thirsty land.
¹⁴And fire has gone out from its stem,
  has consumed its branches and
  fruit,
so that there remains in it no strong
  stem,
  no scepter for a ruler.

This is a lamentation, and has become a lamentation.

20 In the seventh year, in the fifth month, on the tenth day of the month, certain of the elders of Israel came to inquire of the LORD, and sat before me. ²And the word of the LORD came to me: ³"Son of man, speak to the elders of Israel, and say to them, Thus says the Lord GOD, Is it to inquire of me that you come? As I live, says the Lord GOD, I will not be inquired of by you. ⁴Will you judge them, son of man, will you judge them? Then let them know the abominations of their fathers, ⁵and say to them, Thus says the Lord GOD: On the day when I chose Israel, I swore to the seed of the house of Jacob, making myself known to them in the land of Egypt, I swore to them, saying, I am the LORD your God. ⁶On that day I swore to them that I would bring them out of the land of Egypt into a land that I had searched out for them, a land flowing with milk and honey, the most glorious of all lands. ⁷And I said to them, Cast away the detestable things your eyes feast on, every one of you, and do not defile yourselves with the idols of Egypt; I am the LORD your God. ⁸But they rebelled against me and would not listen to me; they did not every man cast away the detestable things their eyes feasted on, nor did they forsake the idols of Egypt.

"Then I thought I would pour out my wrath upon them and spend my anger against them in the midst of the land of Egypt. ⁹But I acted for the sake of my name, that it should not be profaned in the sight of the nations among whom they dwelt, in whose sight I made myself known to them in bringing them out of the land of Egypt. ¹⁰So I led them out of the land of Egypt and brought them into the wilderness. ¹¹I gave them my statutes

ᵖHeb *had waited*
qTg Compare Theodotion: Heb *knew his widows*
ʳCn: Heb *from the provinces* ˢCn: Heb *in your blood*

and showed them my ordinances, by whose observance man shall live. ¹²Moreover I gave them my sabbaths, as a sign between me and them, that they might know that I the LORD sanctify them. ¹³But the house of Israel rebelled against me in the wilderness; they did not walk in my statutes but rejected my ordinances, by whose observance man shall live; and my sabbaths they greatly profaned.

"Then I thought I would pour out my wrath upon them in the wilderness, to make a full end of them. ¹⁴But I acted for the sake of my name, that it should not be profaned in the sight of the nations, in whose sight I had brought them out. ¹⁵Moreover I swore to them in the wilderness that I would not bring them into the land which I had given them, a land flowing with milk and honey, the most glorious of all lands, ¹⁶because they rejected my ordinances and did not walk in my statutes, and profaned my sabbaths; for their heart went after their idols. ¹⁷Nevertheless my eye spared them, and I did not destroy them or make a full end of them in the wilderness.

18 "And I said to their children in the wilderness, Do not walk in the statutes of your fathers, nor observe their ordinances, nor defile yourselves with their idols. ¹⁹I the LORD am your God; walk in my statutes, and be careful to observe my ordinances, ²⁰and hallow my sabbaths that they may be a sign between me and you, that you may know that I the LORD am your God. ²¹But the children rebelled against me; they did not walk in my statutes, and were not careful to observe my ordinances, by whose observance man shall live; they profaned my sabbaths.

"Then I thought I would pour out my wrath upon them and spend my anger against them in the wilderness. ²²But I withheld my hand, and acted for the sake of my name, that it should not be profaned in the sight of the nations, in whose sight I had brought them out. ²³Moreover I swore to them in the wilderness that I would scatter them among the nations and disperse them through the countries, ²⁴because they had not executed my ordinances, but had rejected my statutes and profaned my sabbaths, and their eyes were set on their fathers' idols. ²⁵More-

over I gave them statutes that were not good and ordinances by which they could not have life; ²⁶and I defiled them through their very gifts in making them offer by fire all their first born, that I might horrify them; I did it that they might know that I am the LORD.

27 "Therefore, son of man, speak to the house of Israel and say to them Thus says the Lord GOD: In this again your fathers blasphemed me, by dealing treacherously with me. ²⁸For when I had brought them into the land which I swore to give them, then whereve they saw any high hill or any leaf tree, there they offered their sacrifice and presented the provocation of thei offering; there they sent up their sooth ing odors, and there they poured ou their drink offerings. ²⁹(I said to them What is the high place to which yo go? So its name is called Bā'mal to this day.) ³⁰Wherefore say to th house of Israel, Thus says the Lor GOD: Will you defile yourselves afte the manner of your fathers and g astray after their detestable things ³¹When you offer your gifts and sa rifice your sons by fire, you defile you selves with all your idols to this da And shall I be inquired of by you, house of Israel? As I live, says the Lor GOD, I will not be inquired of by yo

32 "What is in your mind shall nev happen—the thought, 'Let us be li the nations, like the tribes of th countries, and worship wood an stone.'

33 "As I live, says the Lord Go surely with a mighty hand and an ou stretched arm, and with wrath poure out, I will be king over you. ³⁴I w bring you out from the peoples ar gather you out of the countries whe you are scattered, with a mighty har and an outstretched arm, and wit wrath poured out; ³⁵and I will brir you into the wilderness of the people and there I will enter into judgme with you face to face. ³⁶As I enter into judgment with your fathers in t wilderness of the land of Egypt, so will enter into judgment with you, sa the Lord GOD. ³⁷I will make you pa under the rod, and I will let you go by number.ᵘ ³⁸I will purge out th rebels from among you, and tho

ᵗThat is *High Place*
ᵘGk: Heb *bring you into the bond of the covenant*

who transgress against me; I will bring them out of the land where they sojourn, but they shall not enter the land of Israel. Then you will know that I am the LORD.

39 "As for you, O house of Israel, thus says the Lord GOD: Go serve every one of you his idols, now and hereafter, if you will not listen to me; but my holy name you shall no more profane with your gifts and your idols.

40 "For on my holy mountain, the mountain height of Israel, says the Lord GOD, there all the house of Israel, all of them, shall serve me in the land; there I will accept them, and there I will require your contributions and the choicest of your gifts, with all your sacred offerings. ⁴¹As a pleasing odor I will accept you, when I bring you out from the peoples, and gather you out of the countries where you have been scattered; and I will manifest my holiness among you in the sight of the nations. ⁴²And you shall know that I am the LORD, when I bring you into the land of Israel, the country which I swore to give to your fathers. ⁴³And there you shall remember your ways and all the doings with which you have polluted yourselves; and you shall loathe yourselves for all the evils that you have committed. And you shall know that I am the LORD, when I deal with you for my name's sake, not according to your evil ways, nor according to your corrupt doings, O house of Israel, says the Lord GOD."

45ᵛ And the word of the LORD came to me: ⁴⁶"Son of man, set your face toward the south, preach against the south, and prophesy against the forest land in the Něg'ěb; ⁴⁷say to the forest of the Něg'ěb, Hear the word of the LORD: Thus says the Lord GOD, Behold, I will kindle a fire in you, and it shall devour every green tree in you and every dry tree; the blazing flame shall not be quenched, and all faces from south to north shall be scorched by it. ⁴⁸All flesh shall see that I the LORD have kindled it; it shall not be quenched." ⁴⁹Then I said, "Ah Lord GOD! they are saying of me, 'Is he not a maker of allegories?' "

21ʷ The word of the LORD came to me: ²"Son of man, set your face toward Jerusalem and preach against the sanctuaries; prophesy

against the land of Israel ³and say to the land of Israel, Thus says the LORD: Behold, I am against you, and will draw forth my sword out of its sheath, and will cut off from you both righteous and wicked. ⁴Because I will cut off from you both righteous and wicked, therefore my sword shall go out of its sheath against all flesh from south to north; ⁵and all flesh shall know that I the LORD have drawn my sword out of its sheath; it shall not be sheathed again. ⁶Sigh therefore, son of man; sigh with breaking heart and bitter grief before their eyes. ⁷And when they say to you, 'Why do you sigh?' you shall say, 'Because of the tidings. When it comes, every heart will melt and all hands will be feeble, every spirit will faint and all knees will be weak as water. Behold, it comes and it will be fulfilled,' " says the Lord GOD.

8 And the word of the LORD came to me: ⁹"Son of man, prophesy and say, Thus says the Lord, Say:

A sword, a sword is sharpened
    and also polished,
¹⁰sharpened for slaughter,
    polished to flash like lightning!

Or do we make mirth? You have despised the rod, my son, with everything of wood. ¹¹So the sword is given to be polished, that it may be handled; it is sharpened and polished to be given into the hand of the slayer. ¹²Cry and wail, son of man, for it is against my people; it is against all the princes of Israel; they are delivered over to the sword with my people. Smite therefore upon your thigh. ¹³For it will not be a testing—what could it do if you despise the rod?" says the Lord GOD.

14 "Prophesy therefore, son of man; clap your hands and let the sword come down twice, yea thrice, the sword for those to be slain; it is the sword for the great slaughter, which encompasses them, ¹⁵that their hearts may melt, and many fall at all their gates. I have given the glittering sword; ah! it is made like lightning, it is polishedˣ for slaughter. ¹⁶Cut sharply to rightʸ and left where your edge is directed. ¹⁷I also will clap my hands, and I will satisfy my fury; I the LORD have spoken."

ᵛCh 21.1 in Heb   ʷCh 21.6 in Heb
ˣTg: Heb *wrapped up* ʸGk Syr Vg: Heb *right, set*
20.41: Eph 5.2; Phil 4.18.   **20.43**: Ezek 6.9; 36.31.

18 The word of the LORD came to me again: ¹⁹ "Son of man, mark two ways for the sword of the king of Babylon to come; both of them shall come forth from the same land. And make a signpost, make it at the head of the way to a city; ²⁰ mark a way for the sword to come to Răb′bah of the Ăm′mo·nītes and to Judah and toᶻ Jerusalem the fortified. ²¹ For the king of Babylon stands at the parting of the way, at the head of the two ways, to use divination; he shakes the arrows, he consults the teraphim, he looks at the liver. ²² Into his right hand comes the lot for Jerusalem,ᵃ to open the mouth with a cry,ᵇ to lift up the voice with shouting, to set battering rams against the gates, to cast up mounds, to build siege towers. ²³ But to them it will seem like a false divination; they have sworn solemn oaths; but he brings their guilt to remembrance, that they may be captured.

24 "Therefore thus says the Lord GOD: Because you have made your guilt to be remembered, in that your transgressions are uncovered, so that in all your doings your sins appear— because you have come to remembrance, you shall be taken in them.ᶜ ²⁵ And you, O unhallowed wicked one, prince of Israel, whose day has come, the time of your final punishment, ²⁶ thus says the Lord GOD: Remove the turban, and take off the crown; things shall not remain as they are; exalt that which is low, and abase that which is high. ²⁷ A ruin, ruin, ruin I will make it; there shall not be even a traceᵈ of it until he comes whose right it is; and to him I will give it.

28 "And you, son of man, prophesy, and say, Thus says the Lord GOD concerning the Ăm′mo·nītes, and concerning their reproach; say, A sword, a sword is drawn for the slaughter, it is polished to glitterᵉ and to flash like lightning—²⁹ while they see for you false visions, while they divine lies for you—to be laid on the necks of the unhallowed wicked, whose day has come, the time of their final punishment. ³⁰ Return it to its sheath. In the place where you were created, in the land of your origin, I will judge you. ³¹ And I will pour out my indignation upon you; I will blow upon you with the fire of my wrath; and I will deliver you into the hands of brutal men, skil-

ful to destroy. ³² You shall be fuel for the fire; your blood shall be in the midst of the land; you shall be no more remembered; for I the LORD have spoken."

22 Moreover the word of the LORD came to me, saying, ² "And you, son of man, will you judge, will you judge the bloody city? Then declare to her all her abominable deeds. ³ You shall say, Thus says the Lord GOD: A city that sheds blood in the midst of her, that her time may come, and that makes idols to defile herself! ⁴ You have become guilty by the blood which you have shed, and defiled by the idols which you have made; and you have brought your day near, the appointed timeᶠ of your years has come. Therefore I have made you a reproach to the nations, and a mocking to all the countries. ⁵ Those who are near and those who are far from you will mock you, you infamous one, full of tumult.

6 "Behold, the princes of Israel in you, every one according to his power have been bent on shedding blood. ⁷ Father and mother are treated with contempt in you; the sojourner suffers extortion in your midst; the fatherless and the widow are wronged in you. ⁸ You have despised my holy things, and profaned my sabbaths. ⁹ There are men in you who slander to shed blood, and men in you who eat upon the mountains; men commit lewdness in your midst. ¹⁰ In you men uncover their fathers' nakedness; in you they humble women who are unclean in their impurity. ¹¹ One commits abomination with his neighbor's wife; another lewdly defiles his daughter-in-law another in you defiles his sister, his father's daughter. ¹² In you men take bribes to shed blood; you take interest and increase and make gain of your neighbors by extortion; and you have forgotten me, says the Lord GOD.

13 "Behold, therefore, I strike my hands together at the dishonest gain which you have made, and at the blood which has been in the midst of you. ¹⁴ Can your courage endure, or can your hands be strong, in the days that

ᶻ Gk Syr: Heb *in*   ᵃ Heb *Jerusalem, to set battering ram*
ᵇ Gk: Heb *with slaughter*
ᶜ Gk: Heb *with the hand*   ᵈ Cn: Heb *not even this*
ᵉ Cn: Heb *to contain*   ᶠ Two Mss Gk Syr Vg Tg: Heb *un*
21.28-32: Ezek 25.1-7; Jer 49.1-6; Amos 1.13-15; Zep 2.8-11.

shall deal with you? I the LORD have spoken, and I will do it. ¹⁵I will scatter you among the nations and disperse you through the countries, and I will consume your filthiness out of you. ¹⁶And I⁹ shall be profaned through you in the sight of the nations; and you shall know that I am the LORD."

17 And the word of the LORD came to me: ¹⁸"Son of man, the house of Israel has become dross to me; all of them, silverʰ and bronze and tin and iron and lead in the furnace, have become dross. ¹⁹Therefore thus says the Lord GOD: Because you have all become dross, therefore, behold, I will gather you into the midst of Jerusalem. ²⁰As men gather silver and bronze and iron and lead and tin into a furnace, to blow the fire upon it in order to melt it; so I will gather you in my anger and in my wrath, and I will put you in and melt you. ²¹I will gather you and blow upon you with the fire of my wrath, and you shall be melted in the midst of it. ²²As silver is melted in a furnace, so you shall be melted in the midst of it; and you shall know that I the LORD have poured out my wrath upon you."

23 And the word of the LORD came to me: ²⁴"Son of man, say to her, You are a land that is not cleansed, or rained upon in the day of indignation. ²⁵Her princesⁱ in the midst of her are like a roaring lion tearing the prey; they have devoured human lives; they have taken treasure and precious things; they have made many widows in the midst of her. ²⁶Her priests have done violence to my law and have profaned my holy things; they have made no distinction between the holy and the common, neither have they taught the difference between the unclean and the clean, and they have disregarded my sabbaths, so that I am profaned among them. ²⁷Her princes in the midst of her are like wolves tearing the prey, shedding blood, destroying lives to get dishonest gain. ²⁸And her prophets have daubed for them with whitewash, seeing false visions and divining lies for them, saying, 'Thus says the Lord GOD,' when the LORD has not spoken. ²⁹The people of the land have practiced extortion and committed robbery; they have oppressed the poor and needy, and have extorted from the sojourner

without redress. ³⁰And I sought for a man among them who should build up the wall and stand in the breach before me for the land, that I should not destroy it; but I found none. ³¹Therefore I have poured out my indignation upon them; I have consumed them with the fire of my wrath; their way have I requited upon their heads, says the Lord GOD."

23 The word of the LORD came to me: ²"Son of man, there were two women, the daughters of one mother; ³they played the harlot in Egypt; they played the harlot in their youth; there their breasts were pressed and their virgin bosoms handled. ⁴Ō·hō'ḷah was the name of the elder and Ō·hŏl'ĭ·bah the name of her sister. They became mine, and they bore sons and daughters. As for their names, Ō·hō'ḷah is Sạ·mâr'ĭ·ạ, and Ō·hŏl'ĭ·bah is Jerusalem.

5 "Ō·hō'ḷah played the harlot while she was mine; and she doted on her lovers the Assyrians, ⁶warriors clothed in purple, governors and commanders, all of them desirable young men, horsemen riding on horses. ⁷She bestowed her harlotries upon them, the choicest men of Assyria all of them; and she defiled herself with all the idols of every one on whom she doted. ⁸She did not give up her harlotry which she had practiced since her days in Egypt; for in her youth men had lain with her and handled her virgin bosom and poured out their lust upon her. ⁹Therefore I delivered her into the hands of her lovers, into the hands of the Assyrians, upon whom she doted. ¹⁰These uncovered her nakedness; they seized her sons and her daughters; and her they slew with the sword; and she became a byword among women, when judgment had been executed upon her.

11 "Her sister Ō·hŏl'ĭ·bah saw this, yet she was more corrupt than she in her doting and in her harlotry, which was worse than that of her sister. ¹²She doted upon the Assyrians, governors and commanders, warriors clothed in full armor, horsemen riding on horses, all of them desirable young men. ¹³And I saw that she was defiled; they both took the same way. ¹⁴But she

⁹Gk Syr Vg: Heb *you*
ʰTransposed from the end of the verse. Compare verse 20
ⁱGk: Heb *a conspiracy of her prophets*

carried her harlotry further; she saw men portrayed upon the wall, the images of the Chăl·dē′anṣ portrayed in vermilion, [15]girded with belts on their loins, with flowing turbans on their heads, all of them looking like officers, a picture of Babylonians whose native land was Chăl·dē′ă. [16]When she saw them she doted upon them, and sent messengers to them in Chăl·dē′ă. [17]And the Babylonians came to her into the bed of love, and they defiled her with their lust; and after she was polluted by them, she turned from them in disgust. [18]When she carried on her harlotry so openly and flaunted her nakedness, I turned in disgust from her, as I had turned from her sister. [19]Yet she increased her harlotry, remembering the days of her youth, when she played the harlot in the land of Egypt [20]and doted upon her paramours there, whose members were like those of asses, and whose issue was like that of horses. [21]Thus you longed for the lewdness of your youth, when the Egyptians[j] handled your bosom and pressed[k] your young breasts."

22 Therefore, O Ō·hŏl′ĭ·bah, thus says the Lord God: "Behold, I will rouse against you your lovers from whom you turned in disgust, and I will bring them against you from every side: [23]the Babylonians and all the Chăl·dē′anṣ, Pē′kŏd and Shō′a and Kō′a, and all the Assyrians with them, desirable young men, governors and commanders all of them, officers and warriors,[l] all of them riding on horses. [24]And they shall come against you from the north[m] with chariots and wagons and a host of peoples; they shall set themselves against you on every side with buckler, shield, and helmet, and I will commit the judgment to them, and they shall judge you according to their judgments. [25]And I will direct my indignation against you, that they may deal with you in fury. They shall cut off your nose and your ears, and your survivors shall fall by the sword. They shall seize your sons and your daughters, and your survivors shall be devoured by fire. [26]They shall also strip you of your clothes and take away your fine jewels. [27]Thus I will put an end to your lewdness and your harlotry brought from the land of Egypt; so that you shall not lift up your eyes

to the Egyptians or remember them any more. [28]For thus says the Lord God: Behold, I will deliver you into the hands of those whom you hate, into the hands of those from whom you turned in disgust; [29]and they shall deal with you in hatred, and take away all the fruit of your labor, and leave you naked and bare, and the nakedness of your harlotry shall be uncovered. Your lewdness and your harlotry [30]have brought this upon you, because you played the harlot with the nations, and polluted yourself with their idols. [31]You have gone the way of your sister; therefore I will give her cup into your hand. [32]Thus says the Lord God:

"You shall drink your sister's cup
    which is deep and large;
you shall be laughed at and held in
    derision,
    for it contains much;
[33]you will be filled with drunkenness
    and sorrow.
A cup of horror and desolation,
    is the cup of your sister Sạ·mâr′ĭ·ạ
[34]you shall drink it and drain it out
    and pluck out your hair,[n]
    and tear your breasts;
for I have spoken, says the Lord God
[35]Therefore thus says the Lord God
Because you have forgotten me and
cast me behind your back, therefore
bear the consequences of your lewd
ness and harlotry."

36 The Lord said to me: "Son o
man, will you judge Ō·hō′lah an
Ō·hŏl′ĭ·bah? Then declare to them thei
abominable deeds. [37]For they hav
committed adultery, and blood is upo
their hands; with their idols they hav
committed adultery; and they hav
even offered up to them for food th
sons whom they had borne to me
[38]Moreover this they have done to me
they have defiled my sanctuary on th
same day and profaned my sabbaths
[39]For when they had slaughtered thei
children in sacrifice to their idols, o
the same day they came into my sanc
tuary to profane it. And lo, this is wha
they did in my house. [40]They even sen
for men to come from far, to whom
messenger was sent, and lo, the
came. For them you bathed yoursel
painted your eyes, and decked you

[j]Two Mss: Heb *from Egypt*   [k]Cn: Heb *for the sake of*
[l]Compare verses 6 and 12: Heb *called*
[m]Gk: The meaning of the Hebrew word is unknown
[n]Compare Syr: Heb *gnaw its sherds*

self with ornaments; [41] you sat upon a stately couch, with a table spread before it on which you had placed my incense and my oil. [42] The sound of a carefree multitude was with her; and with men of the common sort drunkards° were brought from the wilderness; and they put bracelets upon the hands of the women, and beautiful crowns upon their heads.

43 "Then I said, Do not men now commit adultery[p] when they practice harlotry with her? [44] For they have gone in to her, as men go in to a harlot. Thus they went in to Ō·hō′lah and to Ō·hŏl′i·bah to commit lewdness.[q] [45] But righteous men shall pass judgment on them with the sentence of adulteresses, and with the sentence of women that shed blood; because they are adulteresses, and blood is upon their hands."

46 For thus says the Lord GOD: 'Bring up a host against them, and make them an object of terror and a spoil. [47] And the host shall stone them and dispatch them with their swords; they shall slay their sons and their daughters, and burn up their houses. [48] Thus will I put an end to lewdness in the land, that all women may take warning and not commit lewdness as you have done. [49] And your lewdness shall be requited upon you, and you shall bear the penalty for your sinful idolatry; and you shall know that I am the Lord GOD."

24 In the ninth year, in the tenth month, on the tenth day of the month, the word of the LORD came to me: [2] "Son of man, write down the name of this day, this very day. The king of Babylon has laid siege to Jerusalem this very day. [3] And utter an allegory to the rebellious house and say to them, Thus says the Lord GOD:
Set on the pot, set it on,
  pour in water also;
put in it the pieces of flesh,
  all the good pieces, the thigh and
    the shoulder;
  fill it with choice bones.
Take the choicest one of the flock,
  pile the logs[r] under it;
boil its pieces,[s]
  seethe[t] also its bones in it.
6 "Therefore thus says the Lord GOD: Woe to the bloody city, to the pot whose rust is in it, and whose rust has not gone out of it! Take out of it

piece after piece, without making any choice.[u] [7] For the blood she has shed is still in the midst of her; she put it on the bare rock, she did not pour it upon the ground to cover it with dust. [8] To rouse my wrath, to take vengeance, I have set on the bare rock the blood she has shed, that it may not be covered. [9] Therefore thus says the Lord GOD: Woe to the bloody city! I also will make the pile great. [10] Heap on the logs, kindle the fire, boil well the flesh, and empty out the broth,[v] and let the bones be burned up. [11] Then set it empty upon the coals, that it may become hot, and its copper may burn, that its filthiness may be melted in it, its rust consumed. [12] In vain I have wearied myself;[w] its thick rust does not go out of it by fire. [13] Its rust is your filthy lewdness. Because I would have cleansed you and you were not cleansed from your filthiness, you shall not be cleansed any more till I have satisfied my fury upon you. [14] I the LORD have spoken; it shall come to pass, I will do it; I will not go back, I will not spare, I will not repent; according to your ways and your doings I will judge you, says the Lord GOD."

15 Also the word of the LORD came to me: [16] "Son of man, behold, I am about to take the delight of your eyes away from you at a stroke; yet you shall not mourn or weep nor shall your tears run down. [17] Sigh, but not aloud; make no mourning for the dead. Bind on your turban, and put your shoes on your feet; do not cover your lips, nor eat the bread of mourners."[x] [18] So I spoke to the people in the morning, and at evening my wife died. And on the next morning I did as I was commanded.

19 And the people said to me, "Will you not tell us what these things mean for us, that you are acting thus?" [20] Then I said to them, "The word of the LORD came to me: [21] 'Say to the house of Israel, Thus says the Lord GOD: Behold, I will profane my sanctuary, the pride of your power, the delight of your eyes, and the desire of your soul; and your sons and your

---

°Heb uncertain   [p]Compare Gk: Heb obscure
[q]Gk: Heb *a woman of lewdness*
[r]Compare verse 10: Heb *the bones*
[s]Two Mss: Heb *its boilings*   [t]Cn: Heb *its bones seethe*
[u]Heb *no lot has fallen upon it*
[v]Compare Gk: Heb *mix the spices*   [w]Cn: Heb uncertain
[x]Vg Tg: Heb *men*

daughters whom you left behind shall fall by the sword. ²²And you shall do as I have done; you shall not cover your lips, nor eat the bread of mourners.ˣ ²³Your turbans shall be on your heads and your shoes on your feet; you shall not mourn or weep, but you shall pine away in your iniquities and groan to one another. ²⁴Thus shall E·zĕk′ĭ·el be to you a sign; according to all that he has done you shall do. When this comes, then you will know that I am the Lord God.'

25 "And you, son of man, on the day when I take from them their stronghold, their joy and glory, the delight of their eyes and their heart's desire, and also their sons and daughters, ²⁶on that day a fugitive will come to you to report to you the news. ²⁷On that day your mouth will be opened to the fugitive, and you shall speak and be no longer dumb. So you will be a sign to them; and they will know that I am the Lord."

25 The word of the Lord came to me: ²"Son of man, set your face toward the Ăm′mọ·nītes, and prophesy against them. ³Say to the Ăm′mọ·nītes, Hear the word of the Lord God: Thus says the Lord God, Because you said, 'Aha!' over my sanctuary when it was profaned, and over the land of Israel when it was made desolate, and over the house of Judah when it went into exile; ⁴therefore I am handing you over to the people of the East for a possession, and they shall set their encampments among you and make their dwellings in your midst; they shall eat your fruit, and they shall drink your milk. ⁵I will make Răb′bạh a pasture for camels and the cities of the Ăm′mọ-nītesʸ a fold for flocks. Then you will know that I am the Lord. ⁶For thus says the Lord God: Because you have clapped your hands and stamped your feet and rejoiced with all the malice within you against the land of Israel, ⁷therefore, behold, I have stretched out my hand against you, and will hand you over as spoil to the nations; and I will cut you off from the peoples and will make you perish out of the countries; I will destroy you. Then you will know that I am the Lord.

8 "Thus says the Lord God: Because Mō′ăbᶻ said, Behold, the house of Judah is like all the other nations, ⁹therefore I will lay open the flank of Mō′ăb from the citiesᵃ on its frontier, the glory of the country, Bĕth–jĕsh′-ĭ·mŏth, Bā′al–mē′ọn, and Kĭr″ĭ·ạ-thā′ĭm. ¹⁰I will give it along with the Ăm′mọ·nītes to the people of the East as a possession, that itᵇ may be remembered no more among the nations, ¹¹and I will execute judgments upon Mō′ăb. Then they will know that I am the Lord.

12 "Thus says the Lord God: Because E′dọm acted revengefully against the house of Judah and has grievously offended in taking vengeance upon them, ¹³therefore thus says the Lord God, I will stretch out my hand against E′dọm, and cut off from it man and beast; and I will make it desolate; from Tē′man even to Dē′dan they shall fall by the sword. ¹⁴And I will lay my vengeance upon E′dọm by the hand of my people Israel; and they shall do in Edom according to my anger and according to my wrath; and they shall know my vengeance, says the Lord God.

15 "Thus says the Lord God: Because the Phĭ·lĭs′tĭnes acted revengefully and took vengeance with malice of heart to destroy in never-ending enmity; ¹⁶therefore thus says the Lord God, Behold, I will stretch out my hand against the Phĭ·lĭs′tĭnes, and I will cut off the Chĕr′ẹ·thītes, and destroy the rest of the seacoast. ¹⁷I will execute great vengeance upon them with wrathful chastisements. Then they will know that I am the Lord, when I lay my vengeance upon them."

26 In the eleventh year, on the first day of the month, the word of the Lord came to me: ²"Son of man, because Tȳre said concerning Jerusalem, 'Aha, the gate of the peoples is broken, it has swung open to me; I shall be replenished, now that she is laid waste,' ³therefore thus say

ˣVg Tg: Heb *men*   ʸCn: Heb lacks *the cities of*
ᶻGk Old Latin: Heb *Moab and Seir*
ᵃHeb *cities from its cities*
ᵇCn: Heb *the Ammonites*

25.1-7: Ezek 21.28-32; Jer 49.1-6; Amos 1.13-15; Zeph 2.8-11.
25.8-11: Is 15-16; 25.10-12; Jer 48; Amos 2.1-3; Zeph 2.8-11.
25.12-14: Ezek 35; Is 34; 63.1-6; Jer 49.7-22; Amos 1.11-12; Obad; Mal 1.2-5.
25.15-17: Is 14.29-31; Jer 47; Amos 1.6-8; Zeph 2.4-7; Zech 9.5-7.
26.1-28.19: Is 23; Joel 3.4-8; Amos 1.9-10; Zech 9.3-4.

the Lord God: Behold, I am against you, O Tyre, and will bring up many nations against you, as the sea brings up its waves. ⁴They shall destroy the walls of Tyre, and break down her towers; and I will scrape her soil from her, and make her a bare rock. ⁵She shall be in the midst of the sea a place for the spreading of nets; for I have spoken, says the Lord God; and she shall become a spoil to the nations; ⁶and her daughters on the mainland shall be slain by the sword. Then they will know that I am the Lord.

7 "For thus says the Lord God: Behold, I will bring upon Tyre from the north Nĕ·bü·chad·rĕz′zạr king of Babylon, king of kings, with horses and chariots, and with horsemen and a host of many soldiers. ⁸He will slay with the sword your daughters on the mainland; he will set up a siege wall against you, and throw up a mound against you, and raise a roof of shields against you. ⁹He will direct the shock of his battering rams against your walls, and with his axes he will break down your towers. ¹⁰His horses will be so many that their dust will cover you; your walls will shake at the noise of the horsemen and wagons and chariots, when he enters your gates as one enters a city which has been breached. ¹¹With the hoofs of his horses he will trample all your streets; he will slay your people with the sword; and your mighty pillars will fall to the ground. ¹²They will make a spoil of your riches and a prey of your merchandise; they will break down your walls and destroy your pleasant houses; your stones and timber and soil they will cast into the midst of the waters. ¹³And I will stop the music of your songs, and the sound of your lyres shall be heard no more. ¹⁴I will make you a bare rock; you shall be a place for the spreading of nets; you shall never be rebuilt; for I the Lord have spoken, says the Lord God.

15 "Thus says the Lord God to Tyre: Will not the coastlands shake at the sound of your fall, when the wounded groan, when slaughter is made in the midst of you? ¹⁶Then all the princes of the sea will step down from their thrones, and remove their robes, and strip off their embroidered garments;

they will clothe themselves with trembling; they will sit upon the ground and tremble every moment, and be appalled at you. ¹⁷And they will raise a lamentation over you, and say to you,

'How you have vanished[c] from the seas,
  O city renowned,
that was mighty on the sea,
  you and your inhabitants,
who imposed your terror
  on all the mainland![d]
¹⁸Now the isles tremble
  on the day of your fall;
yea, the isles that are in the sea
  are dismayed at your passing.'

19 "For thus says the Lord God: When I make you a city laid waste, like the cities that are not inhabited, when I bring up the deep over you, and the great waters cover you, ²⁰then I will thrust you down with those who descend into the Pit, to the people of old, and I will make you to dwell in the nether world, among primeval ruins, with those who go down to the Pit, so that you will not be inhabited or have a place[e] in the land of the living. ²¹I will bring you to a dreadful end, and you shall be no more; though you be sought for, you will never be found again, says the Lord God."

27 The word of the Lord came to me: ²"Now you, son of man, raise a lamentation over Tyre, ³and say to Tyre, who dwells at the entrance to the sea, merchant of the peoples on many coastlands, thus says the Lord God:

"O Tyre, you have said,
  'I am perfect in beauty.'
⁴Your borders are in the heart of the seas;
  your builders made perfect your beauty.
⁵They made all your planks
  of fir trees from Sē′nĭr;
they took a cedar from Lebanon
  to make a mast for you.
⁶Of oaks of Bā′shạn
  they made your oars;
they made your deck of pines
  from the coasts of Cyprus,
  inlaid with ivory.

[c]Gk Old Latin Aquila: Heb *vanished, O inhabited one,*
[d]Cn: Heb *her inhabitants*
[e]Gk: Heb *I will give beauty*
26.13: Rev 18.22.   26.16-17: Rev 18.9-10.

⁷Of fine embroidered linen from
Egypt
was your sail,
serving as your ensign;
blue and purple from the coasts of
Ĕ·lī′shăh
was your awning.
⁸The inhabitants of Sī′dŏn and
Är′văd
were your rowers;
skilled men of Zē′mer*f* were in you,
they were your pilots.
⁹The elders of Gē′băl and her skilled
men were in you,
caulking your seams;
all the ships of the sea with their
mariners were in you,
to barter for your wares.
10 "Persia and Lüd and Püt were in
your army as your men of war; they
hung the shield and helmet in you;
they gave you splendor. ¹¹The men of
Är′văd and Hē′lĕch*g* were upon your
walls round about, and men of Gä′măd
were in your towers; they hung their
shields upon your walls round about;
they made perfect your beauty.
12 "Tär′shĭsh trafficked with you
because of your great wealth of every
kind; silver, iron, tin, and lead they
exchanged for your wares. ¹³Jä′văn,
Tü′băl, and Mē′shĕch traded with
you; they exchanged the persons of
men and vessels of bronze for your
merchandise. ¹⁴Bĕth″–tō·gär′măh exchanged for your wares horses, war
horses, and mules. ¹⁵The men of
Rhodes*h* traded with you; many
coastlands were your own special
markets, they brought you in payment
ivory tusks and ebony. ¹⁶Ĕ′dŏm*i*
trafficked with you because of your
abundant goods; they exchanged for
your wares emeralds, purple, embroidered work, fine linen, coral, and agate.
¹⁷Judah and the land of Israel traded
with you; they exchanged for your
merchandise wheat, olives, and early
figs,*j* honey, oil, and balm. ¹⁸Damascus
trafficked with you for your abundant
goods, because of your great wealth
of every kind; wine of Hĕl′bŏn, and
white wool, ¹⁹and wine*k* from Ū′zăl
they exchanged for your wares;
wrought iron, cassia, and calamus
were bartered for your merchandise.
²⁰Dē′dăn traded with you in saddle-
cloths for riding. ²¹Arabia and all the
princes of Kē′där were your favored
dealers in lambs, rams, and goats; in

these they trafficked with you. ²²The
traders of Shē′bă and Rā′ă·măh
traded with you; they exchanged for
your wares the best of all kinds of
spices, and all precious stones, and
gold. ²³Hâr′an, Căn′nĕh, Éden,*
Ăṣ′shŭr, and Chĭl′măd traded with
you. ²⁴These traded with you in choice
garments, in clothes of blue and
embroidered work, in carpets of
colored stuff, bound with cords and
made secure; in these they traded
with you.*m* ²⁵The ships of Tär′shĭsh
traveled for you with your merchandise.*n*
"So you were filled and heavily
laden
in the heart of the seas.
²⁶Your rowers have brought you ou
into the high seas.
The east wind has wrecked you
in the heart of the seas.
²⁷Your riches, your wares, your mer
chandise,
your mariners and your pilots
your caulkers, your dealers in mer
chandise,
and all your men of war who ar
in you,
with all your company
that is in your midst,
sink into the heart of the seas
on the day of your ruin.
²⁸At the sound of the cry of you
pilots
the countryside shakes,
²⁹and down from their ships
come all that handle the oar.
The mariners and all the pilots c
the sea
stand on the shore
³⁰and wail aloud over you,
and cry bitterly.
They cast dust on their heads
and wallow in ashes;
³¹they make themselves bald for yo
and gird themselves with sac
cloth,
and they weep over you in bitterne
of soul,
with bitter mourning.
³²In their wailing they raise a lan
entation for you,

*f*Compare Gen 10.18: Heb *your skilled men, O Tyre*
*g*Or *and your army*
*h*Gk: Heb *Dedan* *i*Another reading is *Aram*
*j*Cn: Heb *wheat of minnith and pannag*
*k*Gk: Heb *Vedan and Javan*
*l*Cn: Heb *Eden the traders of Sheba*
*m*Cn: Heb *in your market*
*n*Cn: Heb *your travelers your merchandise*
27.13: Rev 18.13. **27.27-36:** Rev 18.9-19.

and lament over you:
'Who was ever destroyed[o] like
    Tyre
in the midst of the sea?
[33] When your wares came from the
    seas,
you satisfied many peoples;
with your abundant wealth and
    merchandise
you enriched the kings of the earth.
[34] Now you are wrecked by the seas,
    in the depths of the waters;
your merchandise and all your crew
    have sunk with you.
[35] All the inhabitants of the coastlands
    are appalled at you;
and their kings are horribly afraid,
    their faces are convulsed.
[36] The merchants among the peoples
    hiss at you;
you have come to a dreadful end
    and shall be no more for ever.'"

28 The word of the LORD came to
me: [2] "Son of man, say to the
prince of Tyre, Thus says the Lord
GOD:
"Because your heart is proud,
    and you have said, 'I am a god,
I sit in the seat of the gods,
    in the heart of the seas,'
yet you are but a man, and no god,
    though you consider yourself as
        wise as a god—
[3] you are indeed wiser than Daniel;
    no secret is hidden from you;
[4] by your wisdom and your under-
    standing
you have gotten wealth for your-
    self,
and have gathered gold and silver
    into your treasuries;
[5] by your great wisdom in trade
you have increased your wealth,
    and your heart has become proud
     in your wealth—
[6] therefore thus says the Lord GOD:
"Because you consider yourself
    as wise as a god,
[7] therefore, behold, I will bring stran-
    gers upon you,
    the most terrible of the nations;
and they shall draw their swords
    against the beauty of your wis-
    dom
    and defile your splendor.
[8] They shall thrust you down into the
    Pit,
and you shall die the death of the
    slain
in the heart of the seas.

[9] Will you still say, 'I am a god,'
    in the presence of those who slay
    you,
though you are but a man, and no
    god,
in the hands of those who wound
    you?
[10] You shall die the death of the un-
    circumcised
by the hand of foreigners;
for I have spoken, says the Lord
    GOD."

11 Moreover the word of the LORD
came to me: [12] "Son of man, raise a
lamentation over the king of Tyre,
and say to him, Thus says the Lord
GOD:
"You were the signet of perfection,[p]
    full of wisdom
    and perfect in beauty.
[13] You were in Eden, the garden of God;
    every precious stone was your
     covering,
carnelian, topaz, and jasper,
    chrysolite, beryl, and onyx,
sapphire,[q] carbuncle, and emerald;
    and wrought in gold were your
     settings
    and your engravings.[r]
On the day that you were created
    they were prepared.
[14] With an anointed guardian cherub
    I placed you;[s]
you were on the holy mountain
    of God;
in the midst of the stones of fire
    you walked.
[15] You were blameless in your ways
    from the day you were created,
    till iniquity was found in you.
[16] In the abundance of your trade
you were filled with violence,
    and you sinned;
so I cast you as a profane thing from
    the mountain of God,
and the guardian cherub drove
    you out
from the midst of the stones of fire.
[17] Your heart was proud because of
    your beauty;
you corrupted your wisdom for
    the sake of your splendor.
I cast you to the ground;
    I exposed you before kings,
    to feast their eyes on you.
[18] By the multitude of your iniquities,

[o] Tg Vg: Heb *like silence*
[p] Heb obscure   [q] Or *lapis lazuli*   [r] Heb uncertain
[s] Heb uncertain
28.2: Dan 11.36; 2 Thess 2.4; Rev 13.5.

in the unrighteousness of your
trade
you profaned your sanctuaries;
so I brought forth fire from the midst
of you;
it consumed you,
and I turned you to ashes upon the
earth
in the sight of all who saw you.
[19] All who know you among the peoples
are appalled at you;
you have come to a dreadful end
and shall be no more for ever."
20 The word of the LORD came to
me: [21] "Son of man, set your face
toward Sī′dŏn, and prophesy against
her [22] and say, Thus says the Lord
GOD:
"Behold, I am against you, O Sī′dŏn,
and I will manifest my glory in
the midst of you.
And they shall know that I am the
LORD
when I execute judgments in
her,
and manifest my holiness in her;
[23] for I will send pestilence into her,
and blood into her streets;
and the slain shall fall in the midst
of her,
by the sword that is against her
on every side.
Then they will know that I am the
LORD.
24 "And for the house of Israel there
shall be no more a brier to prick or
a thorn to hurt them among all their
neighbors who have treated them with
contempt. Then they will know that I
am the Lord GOD.
25 "Thus says the Lord GOD: When I
gather the house of Israel from the
peoples among whom they are scattered, and manifest my holiness in
them in the sight of the nations, then
they shall dwell in their own land
which I gave to my servant Jacob.
[26] And they shall dwell securely in it,
and they shall build houses and plant
vineyards. They shall dwell securely,
when I execute judgments upon all
their neighbors who have treated them
with contempt. Then they will know
that I am the LORD their God."

29 In the tenth year, in the tenth
month, on the twelfth day of the
month, the word of the LORD came to
me: [2] "Son of man, set your face
against Pharaoh king of Egypt, and
prophesy against him and against all
Egypt; [3] speak, and say, Thus says the
Lord GOD:
"Behold, I am against you,
Pharaoh king of Egypt,
the great dragon that lies
in the midst of his streams,
that says, 'My Nile is my own;
I made it.' [i]
[4] I will put hooks in your jaws,
and make the fish of your streams
stick to your scales;
and I will draw you up out of the
midst of your streams,
with all the fish of your streams
which stick to your scales.
[5] And I will cast you forth into the
wilderness,
you and all the fish of your
streams;
you shall fall upon the open field,
and not be gathered and buried.
To the beasts of the earth and to
the birds of the air
I have given you as food.
6 "Then all the inhabitants of Egypt
shall know that I am the LORD. Because you [u] have been a staff of reed
to the house of Israel; [7] when they
grasped you with the hand, you broke,
and tore all their shoulders; and when
they leaned upon you, you broke, and
made all their loins to shake; [v] [8] therefore thus says the Lord GOD: Behold, ∶
will bring a sword upon you, and wil
cut off from you man and beast; [9] and
the land of Egypt shall be a desola
tion and a waste. Then they will knov
that I am the LORD.
"Because you [10] said, 'The Nile i∶
mine, and I made it,' [10] therefore, be
hold, I am against you, and agains
your streams, and I will make the
land of Egypt an utter waste and
desolation; from Mĭg′dŏl to Sÿ·ē′nē
as far as the border of Ethiopia. [11] No
foot of man shall pass through it, and
no foot of beast shall pass through it
it shall be uninhabited forty years
[12] And I will make the land of Egypt ∶
desolation in the midst of desolate
countries; and her cities shall be ∶
desolation forty years among citie
that are laid waste. I will scatter th
Egyptians among the nations, an
disperse them among the countries
13 "For thus says the Lord GOD

[i] Syr Compare Gk: Heb *I have made myself*
[u] Gk Syr Vg: Heb *they*
[v] Syr: Heb *stand* [u] Gk Syr Vg: Heb *he*
28.20-26: Joel 3.4-8; Zech 9.2.
29-32: Is 19; Jer 46; Zech 14.18-19.

At the end of forty years I will gather the Egyptians from the peoples among whom they were scattered; [14] and I will restore the fortunes of Egypt, and bring them back to the land of Păth'rŏs, the land of their origin; and there they shall be a lowly kingdom. [15] It shall be the most lowly of the kingdoms, and never again exalt itself above the nations; and I will make them so small that they will never again rule over the nations. [16] And it shall never again be the reliance of the house of Israel, recalling their iniquity, when they turn to them for aid. Then they will know that I am the Lord God."

17 In the twenty-seventh year, in the first month, on the first day of the month, the word of the Lord came to me: [18] "Son of man, Nĕ·bü·chad·rĕz'ẓar king of Babylon made his army labor hard against Tȳre; every head was made bald and every shoulder was rubbed bare; yet neither he nor his army got anything from Tyre to pay for the labor that he had performed against it. [19] Therefore thus says the Lord God: Behold, I will give the land of Egypt to Nĕ·bü·chad·rĕz'-ẓar king of Babylon; and he shall carry off its wealth [x] and despoil it and plunder it; and it shall be the wages for his army. [20] I have given him the land of Egypt as his recompense for which he labored, because they worked for me, says the Lord God.

21 "On that day I will cause a horn to spring forth to the house of Israel, and I will open your lips among them. Then they will know that I am the Lord."

30 The word of the Lord came to me: [2] "Son of man, prophesy, and say, Thus says the Lord God:
"Wail, 'Alas for the day!'
[3] For the day is near,
the day of the Lord is near;
it will be a day of clouds,
a time of doom for the nations.
[4] A sword shall come upon Egypt,
and anguish shall be in Ethiopia,
when the slain fall in Egypt,
and her wealth is carried away,
and her foundations are torn down.
[5] Ethiopia, and Püt, and Lüd, and all Arabia, and Lĭb'yạ,[y] and the people of the land that is in league, shall fall with them by the sword.

[6] "Thus says the Lord:
Those who support Egypt shall fall,
and her proud might shall come down;
from Mĭg'dŏl to Sȳ·ē'nē
they shall fall within her by the sword,
says the Lord God.
[7] And she[z] shall be desolated in the midst of desolated countries
and her cities shall be in the midst of cities that are laid waste.
[8] Then they will know that I am the Lord,
when I have set fire to Egypt,
and all her helpers are broken.
9 "On that day swift[a] messengers shall go forth from me to terrify the unsuspecting Ethiopians; and anguish shall come upon them on the day of Egypt's doom; for, lo, it comes!

10 "Thus says the Lord God:
I will put an end to the wealth[b] of Egypt,
by the hand of Nĕ·bü·chad·rĕz'ẓar king of Babylon.
[11] He and his people with him, the most terrible of the nations,
shall be brought in to destroy the land;
and they shall draw their swords against Egypt,
and fill the land with the slain.
[12] And I will dry up the Nile,
and will sell the land into the hand of evil men;
I will bring desolation upon the land and everything in it,
by the hand of foreigners;
I, the Lord, have spoken.

13 "Thus says the Lord God:
I will destroy the idols,
and put an end to the images, in Memphis;
there shall no longer be a prince in the land of Egypt;
so I will put fear in the land of Egypt.
[14] I will make Păth'rŏs a desolation,
and will set fire to Zō'ạn,
and will execute acts of judgment upon Thebes.
[15] And I will pour my wrath upon Pĕ·lü'sĭ·ụm,
the stronghold of Egypt,

---

[x] Or *multitude*
[y] Gk Compare Syr Vg: Heb *Cub*
[z] Gk: Heb *they*   [a] Gk Syr: Heb *in ships*   [b] Or *multitude*

and cut off the multitude of Thebes.
16 And I will set fire to Egypt;
Pĕ·lü′sĭ·ụm shall be in great agony;
Thebes shall be breached,
and its walls broken down.*c*
17 The young men of Ŏn and of Pī-bē′sĕth shall fall by the sword;
and the women shall go into captivity.
18 At Tĕ·hăph′nẹ·hēṣ the day shall be dark,
when I break there the dominion of Egypt,
and her proud might shall come to an end;
she shall be covered by a cloud,
and her daughters shall go into captivity.
19 Thus I will execute acts of judgment upon Egypt.
Then they will know that I am the LORD."

20 In the eleventh year, in the first month, on the seventh day of the month, the word of the LORD came to me: 21 "Son of man, I have broken the arm of Pharaoh king of Egypt; and lo, it has not been bound up, to heal it by binding it with a bandage, so that it may become strong to wield the sword. 22 Therefore thus says the Lord GOD: Behold, I am against Pharaoh king of Egypt, and will break his arms, both the strong arm and the one that was broken; and I will make the sword fall from his hand. 23 I will scatter the Egyptians among the nations, and disperse them throughout the lands. 24 And I will strengthen the arms of the king of Babylon, and put my sword in his hand; but I will break the arms of Pharaoh, and he will groan before him like a man mortally wounded. 25 I will strengthen the arms of the king of Babylon, but the arms of Pharaoh shall fall; and they shall know that I am the LORD. When I put my sword into the hand of the king of Babylon, he shall stretch it out against the land of Egypt; 26 and I will scatter the Egyptians among the nations and disperse them throughout the countries. Then they will know that I am the LORD."

31 In the eleventh year, in the third month, on the first day of the month, the word of the LORD came to me: 2 "Son of man, say to Pharaoh king of Egypt and to his multitude:
"Whom are you like in your greatness?
3 Behold, I will liken you to*d* a cedar in Lebanon,
with fair branches and forest shade,
and of great height,
its top among the clouds.*e*
4 The waters nourished it,
the deep made it grow tall,
making its rivers flow*f*
round the place of its planting,
sending forth its streams
to all the trees of the forest.
5 So it towered high
above all the trees of the forest;
its boughs grew large
and its branches long,
from abundant water in its shoots.
6 All the birds of the air
made their nests in its boughs;
under its branches all the beasts of the field
brought forth their young;
and under its shadow
dwelt all great nations.
7 It was beautiful in its greatness,
in the length of its branches;
for its roots went down
to abundant waters.
8 The cedars in the garden of God
could not rival it,
nor the fir trees equal its boughs;
the plane trees were as nothing
compared with its branches;
no tree in the garden of God
was like it in beauty.
9 I made it beautiful
in the mass of its branches,
and all the trees of Eden envied it,
that were in the garden of God.

10 "Therefore thus says the Lord GOD: Because it*g* towered high and set its top among the clouds,*h* and its heart was proud of its height, 11 I will give it into the hand of a mighty one of the nations; he shall surely deal with it as its wickedness deserves. I have cast it out. 12 Foreigners, the most terrible of the nations, will cut it down and leave it. On the mountains and in all the valleys its branches will fall, and its boughs will lie broken in all the watercourses of the land; and all the

c Cn: Heb *and Memphis, distresses by day*
d Cn: Heb *Behold, Assyria* *e* Gk: Heb *thick boughs*
f Gk: Heb *going* *g* Syr Vg: Heb *you*
h Gk: Heb *thick boughs*
31.6: Ezek 17.23; Dan 4.12-21; Mt 13.32; Mk 4.32; Lk 13.19. **31.8 (Gk):** Rev 2.7.

peoples of the earth will go from its shadow and leave it. ¹³Upon its ruin will dwell all the birds of the air, and upon its branches will be all the beasts of the field. ¹⁴All this is in order that no trees by the waters may grow to lofty height or set their tops among the clouds,ʰ and that no trees that drink water may reach up to them in height; for they are all given over to death, to the nether world among mortal men, with those who go down to the Pit.

15 "Thus says the Lord GOD: When it goes down to Shē′ōl I will make the deep mourn forⁱ it, and restrain its rivers, and many waters shall be stopped; I will clothe Lebanon in gloom for it, and all the trees of the field shall faint because of it. ¹⁶I will make the nations quake at the sound of its fall, when I cast it down to Shē′ōl with those who go down to the Pit; and all the trees of Eden, the choice and best of Lebanon, all that drink water, will be comforted in the nether world. ¹⁷They also shall go down to Shē′ōl with it, to those who are slain by the sword; yea, those who dwelt under its shadow among the nations shall perish.ʲ ¹⁸Whom are you thus like in glory and in greatness among the trees of Eden? You shall be brought down with the trees of Eden to the nether world; you shall lie among the uncircumcised, with those who are slain by the sword.

"This is Pharaoh and all his multitude, says the Lord GOD."

32 In the twelfth year, in the twelfth month, on the first day of the month, the word of the LORD came to me: ²"Son of man, raise a lamentation over Pharaoh king of Egypt, and say to him:
"You consider yourself a lion among the nations,
  but you are like a dragon in the seas;
you burst forth in your rivers,
  trouble the waters with your feet,
  and foul their rivers.
³Thus says the Lord GOD:
  I will throw my net over you
  with a host of many peoples;
  and Iᵏ will haul you up in my dragnet.
⁴And I will cast you on the ground, on the open field I will fling you,

and will cause all the birds of the air
  to settle on you,
  and I will gorge the beasts of the whole earth with you.
⁵I will strew your flesh upon the mountains,
  and fill the valleys with your carcass.ˡ
⁶I will drench the land even to the mountains
  with your flowing blood;
  and the watercourses will be full of you.
⁷When I blot you out, I will cover the heavens,
  and make their stars dark;
I will cover the sun with a cloud,
  and the moon shall not give its light.
⁸All the bright lights of heaven
  will I make dark over you,
  and put darkness upon your land,
    says the Lord GOD.

9 "I will trouble the hearts of many peoples, when I carry you captiveᵐ among the nations, into the countries which you have not known. ¹⁰I will make many peoples appalled at you, and their kings shall shudder because of you, when I brandish my sword before them; they shall tremble every moment, every one for his own life, on the day of your downfall. ¹¹For thus says the Lord GOD: The sword of the king of Babylon shall come upon you. ¹²I will cause your multitude to fall by the swords of mighty ones, all of them most terrible among the nations.
"They shall bring to nought the pride of Egypt,
  and all its multitude shall perish.
¹³I will destroy all its beasts
  from beside many waters;
  and no foot of man shall trouble them any more,
  nor shall the hoofs of beasts trouble them.
¹⁴Then I will make their waters clear,
  and cause their rivers to run like oil, says the Lord GOD.
¹⁵When I make the land of Egypt desolate
  and when the land is stripped of all that fills it,
  when I smite all who dwell in it,

ʰGk: Heb *thick boughs*
ⁱGk: Heb *mourn for, I have covered*
ʲCompare Gk: Heb *obscure*
ᵏGk Vg: Heb *they* ˡSymmachus Syr Vg: Heb *your height*
ᵐGk: Heb *bring your destruction*

then they will know that I am the LORD.

16 This is a lamentation which shall be chanted; the daughters of the nations shall chant it; over Egypt, and over all her multitude, shall they chant it, says the Lord GOD."

17 In the twelfth year, in the first month,[n] on the fifteenth day of the month, the word of the LORD came to me: 18 "Son of man, wail over the multitude of Egypt, and send them down, her and the daughters of majestic nations, to the nether world, to those who have gone down to the Pit:

19 'Whom do you surpass in beauty? Go down, and be laid with the uncircumcised.'

20 They shall fall amid those who are slain by the sword,[o] and with her shall lie all her multitudes.[p] 21 The mighty chiefs shall speak of them, with their helpers, out of the midst of She′ōl: 'They have come down, they lie still, the uncircumcised, slain by the sword.'

22 "Assyria is there, and all her company, their graves round about her, all of them slain, fallen by the sword; 23 whose graves are set in the uttermost parts of the Pit, and her company is round about her grave; all of them slain, fallen by the sword, who spread terror in the land of the living.

24 "E′lăm is there, and all her multitude about her grave; all of them slain, fallen by the sword, who went down uncircumcised into the nether world, who spread terror in the land of the living, and they bear their shame with those who go down to the Pit. 25 They have made her a bed among the slain with all her multitude, their graves round about her, all of them uncircumcised, slain by the sword; for terror of them was spread in the land of the living, and they bear their shame with those who go down to the Pit; they are placed among the slain.

26 "Me′shĕch and Tü′băl are there, and all their multitude, their graves round about them, all of them uncircumcised, slain by the sword; for they spread terror in the land of the living. 27 And they do not lie with the fallen mighty men of old[q] who went down to She′ōl with their weapons of war, whose swords were laid under their heads, and whose shields[r] are

upon their bones; for the terror of the mighty men was in the land of the living. 28 So you shall be broken and lie among the uncircumcised, with those who are slain by the sword.

29 "E′dǫm is there, her kings and all her princes, who for all their might are laid with those who are slain by the sword; they lie with the uncircumcised, with those who go down to the Pit.

30 "The princes of the north are there, all of them, and all the Sī·dō′ni·anş, who have gone down in shame with the slain, for all the terror which they caused by their might; they lie uncircumcised with those who are slain by the sword, and bear their shame with those who go down to the Pit.

31 "When Pharaoh sees them, he will comfort himself for all his multitude, Pharaoh and all his army, slain by the sword, says the Lord GOD. 32 For he[s] spread terror in the land of the living; therefore he shall be laid among the uncircumcised, with those who are slain by the sword, Pharaoh and all his multitude, says the Lord GOD."

33 The word of the LORD came to me: 2 "Son of man, speak to your people and say to them, If I bring the sword upon a land, and the people of the land take a man from among them, and make him their watchman; 3 and if he sees the sword coming upon the land and blows the trumpet and warns the people; 4 then if any one who hears the sound of the trumpet does not take warning, and the sword comes and takes him away, his blood shall be upon his own head. 5 He heard the sound of the trumpet, and did not take warning; his blood shall be upon himself. But if he had taken warning, he would have saved his life. 6 But if the watchman sees the sword coming and does not blow the trumpet, so that the people are not warned, and the sword comes, and takes any one of them; that man is taken away in his iniquity, but his blood I will require at the watchman's hand.

7 "So you, son of man, I have made

*n Gk: Heb lacks in the first month
o Gk Syr: Heb sword, the sword is delivered
p Gk: Heb they have drawn her away and all her multitudes q Gk Old Latin: Heb of the uncircumcised
r Cn: Heb iniquities s Cn: Heb I
33.1–9: Ezek 3.16-21.

a watchman for the house of Israel; whenever you hear a word from my mouth, you shall give them warning from me. [8]If I say to the wicked, O wicked man, you shall surely die, and you do not speak to warn the wicked to turn from his way, that wicked man shall die in his iniquity, but his blood I will require at your hand. [9]But if you warn the wicked to turn from his way, and he does not turn from his way; he shall die in his iniquity, but you will have saved your life.

10 "And you, son of man, say to the house of Israel, Thus have you said: 'Our transgressions and our sins are upon us, and we waste away because of them; how then can we live?' [11]Say to them, As I live, says the Lord GOD, I have no pleasure in the death of the wicked, but that the wicked turn from his way and live; turn back, turn back from your evil ways; for why will you die, O house of Israel? [12]And you, son of man, say to your people, The righteousness of the righteous shall not deliver him when he transgresses; and as for the wickedness of the wicked, he shall not fall by it when he turns from his wickedness; and the righteous shall not be able to live by his righteousness when he sins. [13]Though I say to the righteous that he shall surely live, yet if he trusts in his righteousness and commits iniquity, none of his righteous deeds shall be remembered; but in the iniquity that he has committed he shall die. [14]Again, though I say to the wicked, 'You shall surely die,' yet if he turns from his sin and does what is lawful and right, [15]if the wicked restores the pledge, gives back what he has taken by robbery, and walks in the statutes of life, committing no iniquity; he shall surely live, he shall not die. [16]None of the sins that he has committed shall be remembered against him; he has done what is lawful and right, he shall surely live.

17 "Yet your people say, 'The way of the Lord is not just'; when it is their own way that is not just. [18]When the righteous turns from his righteousness, and commits iniquity, he shall die for it. [19]And when the wicked turns from his wickedness, and does what is lawful and right, he shall live by it. [20]Yet you say, 'The way of the Lord is not just.' O house of Israel, I will judge

each of you according to his ways."

21 In the twelfth year of our exile, in the tenth month, on the fifth day of the month, a man who had escaped from Jerusalem came to me and said, "The city has fallen." [22]Now the hand of the LORD had been upon me the evening before the fugitive came; and he had opened my mouth by the time the man came to me in the morning; so my mouth was opened, and I was no longer dumb.

23 The word of the LORD came to me: [24]"Son of man, the inhabitants of these waste places in the land of Israel keep saying, 'Abraham was only one man, yet he got possession of the land; but we are many; the land is surely given us to possess.' [25]Therefore say to them, Thus says the Lord GOD: You eat flesh with the blood, and lift up your eyes to your idols, and shed blood; shall you then possess the land? [26]You resort to the sword, you commit abominations and each of you defiles his neighbor's wife; shall you then possess the land? [27]Say this to them, Thus says the Lord GOD: As I live, surely those who are in the waste places shall fall by the sword; and him that is in the open field I will give to the beasts to be devoured; and those who are in strongholds and in caves shall die by pestilence. [28]And I will make the land a desolation and a waste; and her proud might shall come to an end; and the mountains of Israel shall be so desolate that none will pass through. [29]Then they will know that I am the LORD, when I have made the land a desolation and a waste because of all their abominations which they have committed.

30 "As for you, son of man, your people who talk together about you by the walls and at the doors of the houses, say to one another, each to his brother, 'Come, and hear what the word is that comes forth from the LORD.' [31]And they come to you as people come, and they sit before you as my people, and they hear what you say but they will not do it; for with their lips they show much love, but their heart is set on their gain. [32]And, lo, you are to them like one who sings love songs[u] with a beautiful voice and plays well on an instrument, for they hear

[t]Heb *by it* [u]Cn: Heb *like a love song*
33.11: Ezek 18.23, 32.

what you say, but they will not do it. [33]When this comes – and come it will! – then they will know that a prophet has been among them."

34 The word of the LORD came to me: [2]"Son of man, prophesy against the shepherds of Israel, prophesy, and say to them, even to the shepherds, Thus says the Lord GOD: Ho, shepherds of Israel who have been feeding yourselves! Should not shepherds feed the sheep? [3]You eat the fat, you clothe yourselves with the wool, you slaughter the fatlings; but you do not feed the sheep. [4]The weak you have not strengthened, the sick you have not healed, the crippled you have not bound up, the strayed you have not brought back, the lost you have not sought, and with force and harshness you have ruled them. [5]So they were scattered, because there was no shepherd; and they became food for all the wild beasts. [6]My sheep were scattered, they wandered over all the mountains and on every high hill; my sheep were scattered over all the face of the earth, with none to search or seek for them.

[7]"Therefore, you shepherds, hear the word of the LORD: [8]As I live, says the Lord GOD, because my sheep have become a prey, and my sheep have become food for all the wild beasts, since there was no shepherd; and because my shepherds have not searched for my sheep, but the shepherds have fed themselves, and have not fed my sheep; [9]therefore, you shepherds, hear the word of the LORD: [10]Thus says the Lord GOD, Behold, I am against the shepherds; and I will require my sheep at their hand, and put a stop to their feeding the sheep; no longer shall the shepherds feed themselves. I will rescue my sheep from their mouths, that they may not be food for them.

[11]"For thus says the Lord GOD: Behold, I, I myself will search for my sheep, and will seek them out. [12]As a shepherd seeks out his flock when some of his sheep[v] have been scattered abroad, so will I seek out my sheep; and I will rescue them from all places where they have been scattered on a day of clouds and thick darkness. [13]And I will bring them out from the peoples, and gather them from the countries, and will bring them into their own land; and I will feed them on the mountains of Israel, by the fountains, and in all the inhabited places of the country. [14]I will feed them with good pasture, and upon the mountain heights of Israel shall be their pasture; there they shall lie down in good grazing land, and on fat pasture they shall feed on the mountains of Israel. [15]I myself will be the shepherd of my sheep, and I will make them lie down, says the Lord GOD. [16]I will seek the lost, and I will bring back the strayed, and I will bind up the crippled, and I will strengthen the weak, and the fat and the strong I will watch over;[w] I will feed them in justice.

[17]"As for you, my flock, thus says the Lord GOD: Behold, I judge between sheep and sheep, rams and he-goats. [18]Is it not enough for you to feed on the good pasture, that you must tread down with your feet the rest of your pasture; and to drink of clear water, that you must foul the rest with your feet? [19]And must my sheep eat what you have trodden with your feet, and drink what you have fouled with your feet?

[20]"Therefore, thus says the Lord GOD to them: Behold, I, I myself will judge between the fat sheep and the lean sheep. [21]Because you push with side and shoulder, and thrust at all the weak with your horns, till you have scattered them abroad, [22]I will save my flock, they shall no longer be a prey; and I will judge between sheep and sheep. [23]And I will set up over them one shepherd, my servant David, and he shall feed them: he shall feed them and be their shepherd. [24]And I, the LORD, will be their God, and my servant David shall be prince among them; I, the LORD, have spoken.

[25]"I will make with them a covenant of peace and banish wild beasts from the land, so that they may dwell securely in the wilderness and sleep in the woods. [26]And I will make them and the places round about my hill a blessing; and I will send down the showers in their season; they shall be showers of blessing. [27]And the trees of the field shall yield their fruit, and the earth shall yield its increase, and they

[v]Cn: Heb *when he is among his sheep*
[w]Gk Syr Vg: Heb *destroy*
34.5: Mt 9.36; Mk 6.34.
34.16: Lk 19.10.   34.23: Ezek 37.24.

shall be secure in their land; and they shall know that I am the LORD, when I break the bars of their yoke, and deliver them from the hand of those who enslaved them. [28] They shall no more be a prey to the nations, nor shall the beasts of the land devour them; they shall dwell securely, and none shall make them afraid. [29] And I will provide for them prosperous* plantations so that they shall no more be consumed with hunger in the land, and no longer suffer the reproach of the nations. [30] And they shall know that I, the LORD their God, am with them, and that they, the house of Israel, are my people, says the Lord GOD. [31] And you are my sheep, the sheep of my pasture,[y] and I am your God, says the Lord GOD.

35 The word of the LORD came to me: [2] "Son of man, set your face against Mount Sē′ĭr, and prophesy against it, [3] and say to it, Thus says the Lord GOD: Behold, I am against you, Mount Sē′ĭr, and I will stretch out my hand against you, and I will make you a desolation and a waste. [4] I will lay your cities waste, and you shall become a desolation; and you shall know that I am the LORD. [5] Because you cherished perpetual enmity, and gave over the people of Israel to the power of the sword at the time of their calamity, at the time of their final punishment; [6] therefore, as I live, says the Lord GOD, I will prepare you for blood, and blood shall pursue you; because you are guilty of blood,[z] therefore blood shall pursue you. [7] I will make Mount Sē′ĭr a waste and a desolation; and I will cut off from it all who come and go. [8] And I will fill your mountains with the slain; on your hills and in your valleys and in all your ravines those slain with the sword shall fall. [9] I will make you a perpetual desolation, and your cities shall not be inhabited. Then you will know that I am the LORD.

10 "Because you said, 'These two nations and these two countries shall be mine, and we will take possession of them,' — although the LORD was there — [11] therefore, as I live, says the Lord GOD, I will deal with you according to the anger and envy which you showed because of your hatred against them; and I will make myself known among you,[a] when I judge you. [12] And you shall know that I, the LORD, have

heard all the revilings which you uttered against the mountains of Israel, saying, 'They are laid desolate, they are given us to devour.' [13] And you magnified yourselves against me with your mouth, and multiplied your words against me; I heard it. [14] Thus says the Lord GOD: For the rejoicing of the whole earth I will make you desolate. [15] As you rejoiced over the inheritance of the house of Israel, because it was desolate, so I will deal with you; you shall be desolate, Mount Sē′ĭr, and all E′dŏm, all of it. Then they will know that I am the LORD.

36 "And you, son of man, prophesy to the mountains of Israel, and say, O mountains of Israel, hear the word of the LORD. [2] Thus says the Lord GOD: Because the enemy said of you, 'Aha!' and, 'The ancient heights have become our possession,' [3] therefore prophesy, and say, Thus says the Lord GOD: Because, yea, because they made you desolate, and crushed you from all sides, so that you became the possession of the rest of the nations, and you became the talk and evil gossip of the people; [4] therefore, O mountains of Israel, hear the word of the Lord GOD: Thus says the Lord GOD to the mountains and the hills, the ravines and the valleys, the desolate wastes and the deserted cities, which have become a prey and derision to the rest of the nations round about; [5] therefore thus says the Lord GOD: I speak in my hot jealousy against the rest of the nations, and against all E′dŏm, who gave my land to themselves as a possession with wholehearted joy and utter contempt, that they might possess[b] it and plunder it. [6] Therefore prophesy concerning the land of Israel, and say to the mountains and hills, to the ravines and valleys, Thus says the Lord GOD: Behold, I speak in my jealous wrath, because you have suffered the reproach of the nations; [7] therefore thus says the Lord GOD: I swear that the nations that are round about you shall themselves suffer reproach.

8 "But you, O mountains of Israel, shall shoot forth your branches, and

*Gk Syr Old Latin: Heb *for renown*
[y]Gk Old Latin: Heb *pasture you are men*
[z]Gk: Heb *you have hated blood* *Gk: Heb *them*
[b]One Ms: Heb *drive out*

yield your fruit to my people Israel; for they will soon come home. [9] For, behold, I am for you, and I will turn to you, and you shall be tilled and sown; [10] and I will multiply men upon you, the whole house of Israel, all of it; the cities shall be inhabited and the waste places rebuilt; [11] and I will multiply upon you man and beast; and they shall increase and be fruitful; and I will cause you to be inhabited as in your former times, and will do more good to you than ever before. Then you will know that I am the LORD. [12] Yea, I will let men walk upon you, even my people Israel; and they shall possess you, and you shall be their inheritance, and you shall no longer bereave them of children. [13] Thus says the Lord GOD: Because men say to you, 'You devour men, and you bereave your nation of children,' [14] therefore you shall no longer devour men and no longer bereave your nation of children, says the Lord GOD; [15] and I will not let you hear any more the reproach of the nations, and you shall no longer bear the disgrace of the peoples and no longer cause your nation to stumble, says the Lord GOD."

16 The word of the LORD came to me: [17] "Son of man, when the house of Israel dwelt in their own land, they defiled it by their ways and their doings; their conduct before me was like the uncleanness of a woman in her impurity. [18] So I poured out my wrath upon them for the blood which they had shed in the land, for the idols with which they had defiled it. [19] I scattered them among the nations, and they were dispersed through the countries; in accordance with their conduct and their deeds I judged them. [20] But when they came to the nations, wherever they came, they profaned my holy name, in that men said of them, 'These are the people of the LORD, and yet they had to go out of his land.' [21] But I had concern for my holy name, which the house of Israel caused to be profaned among the nations to which they came.

22 "Therefore say to the house of Israel, Thus says the Lord GOD: It is not for your sake, O house of Israel, that I am about to act, but for the sake of my holy name, which you have profaned among the nations to which you came. [23] And I will vindicate

the holiness of my great name, which has been profaned among the nations, and which you have profaned among them; and the nations will know that I am the LORD, says the Lord GOD, when through you I vindicate my holiness before their eyes. [24] For I will take you from the nations, and gather you from all the countries, and bring you into your own land. [25] I will sprinkle clean water upon you, and you shall be clean from all your uncleannesses, and from all your idols I will cleanse you. [26] A new heart I will give you, and a new spirit I will put within you; and I will take out of your flesh the heart of stone and give you a heart of flesh. [27] And I will put my spirit within you, and cause you to walk in my statutes and be careful to observe my ordinances. [28] You shall dwell in the land which I gave to your fathers; and you shall be my people, and I will be your God. [29] And I will deliver you from all your uncleannesses; and I will summon the grain and make it abundant and lay no famine upon you. [30] I will make the fruit of the tree and the increase of the field abundant, that you may never again suffer the disgrace of famine among the nations. [31] Then you will remember your evil ways, and your deeds that were not good; and you will loathe yourselves for your iniquities and your abominable deeds. [32] It is not for your sake that I will act, says the Lord GOD; let that be known to you. Be ashamed and confounded for your ways, O house of Israel.

33 "Thus says the Lord GOD: On the day that I cleanse you from all your iniquities, I will cause the cities to be inhabited, and the waste places shall be rebuilt. [34] And the land that was desolate shall be tilled, instead of being the desolation that it was in the sight of all who passed by. [35] And they will say, 'This land that was desolate has become like the garden of Eden; and the waste and desolate and ruined cities are now inhabited and fortified.' [36] Then the nations that are left round about you shall know that I, the LORD, have rebuilt the ruined places, and replanted that which was desolate; I, the LORD, have spoken, and I will do it.

37 "Thus says the Lord GOD: This

36.26: Ezek 11.19; 18.31; 2 Cor 3.3.
36.27: Ezek 37.14; 1 Thess 4.8.   36.31: Ezek 6.9; 20.43.

also I will let the house of Israel ask me to do for them: to increase their men like a flock. ³⁸Like the flock for sacrifices,ᶜ like the flock at Jerusalem during her appointed feasts, so shall the waste cities be filled with flocks of men. Then they will know that I am the LORD."

37 The hand of the LORD was upon me, and he brought me out by the Spirit of the LORD, and set me down in the midst of the valley;ᵈ it was full of bones. ²And he led me round among them; and behold, there were very many upon the valley;ᵈ and lo, they were very dry. ³And he said to me, "Son of man, can these bones live?" And I answered, "O Lord GOD, thou knowest." ⁴Again he said to me, "Prophesy to these bones, and say to them, O dry bones, hear the word of the LORD. ⁵Thus says the Lord GOD to these bones: Behold, I will cause breathᵉ to enter you, and you shall live. ⁶And I will lay sinews upon you, and will cause flesh to come upon you, and cover you with skin, and put breathᵉ in you, and you shall live; and you shall know that I am the LORD."

7 So I prophesied as I was commanded; and as I prophesied, there was a noise, and behold, a rattling; and the bones came together, bone to its bone. ⁸And as I looked, there were sinews on them, and flesh had come upon them, and skin had covered them; but there was no breath in them. ⁹Then he said to me, "Prophesy to the breath, prophesy, son of man, and say to the breath,ᶠ Thus says the Lord GOD: Come from the four winds, O breath,ᶠ and breathe upon these slain, that they may live." ¹⁰So I prophesied as he commanded me, and the breath came into them, and they lived, and stood upon their feet, an exceedingly great host.

11 Then he said to me, "Son of man, these bones are the whole house of Israel. Behold, they say, 'Our bones are dried up, and our hope is lost; we are clean cut off.' ¹²Therefore prophesy, and say to them, Thus says the Lord GOD: Behold, I will open your graves, and raise you from your graves, O my people; and I will bring you home into the land of Israel. ¹³And you shall know that I am the LORD, when I open your graves, and

raise you from your graves, O my people. ¹⁴And I will put my Spirit within you, and you shall live, and I will place you in your own land; then you shall know that I, the LORD, have spoken, and I have done it, says the LORD."

15 The word of the LORD came to me: ¹⁶"Son of· man, take a stick and write on it, 'For Judah, and the children of Israel associated with him'; then take another stick and write upon it, 'For Joseph (the stick of E′phra·im) and all the house of Israel associated with him'; ¹⁷and join them together into one stick, that they may become one in your hand. ¹⁸And when your people say to you, 'Will you not show us what you mean by these?' ¹⁹say to them, Thus says the Lord GOD: Behold, I am about to take the stick of Joseph (which is in the hand of E′phra·im) and the tribes of Israel associated with him; and I will joinᵍ with it the stick of Judah, and make them one stick, that they may be one in my hand. ²⁰When the sticks on which you write are in your hand before their eyes, ²¹then say to them, Thus says the Lord GOD: Behold, I will take the people of Israel from the nations among which they have gone, and will gather them from all sides, and bring them to their own land; ²²and I will make them one nation in the land, upon the mountains of Israel; and one king shall be king over them all; and they shall be no longer two nations, and no longer divided into two kingdoms. ²³They shall not defile themselves any more with their idols and their detestable things, or with any of their transgressions; but I will save them from all the backslidings in which they have sinned, and will cleanse them; and they shall be my people, and I will be their God.

24 "My servant David shall be king over them; and they shall all have one shepherd. They shall follow my ordinances and be careful to observe my statutes. ²⁵They shall dwell in the land where your fathers dwelt that I gave to my servant Jacob; they and their children and their children's children shall dwell there for ever; and David my servant shall be their prince

ᶜHeb *flock of holy things* ᵈOr *plain* ᵉOr *spirit*
ᶠOr *wind* or *spirit* ᵍHeb *join them*
37.5, 10: Rev 11.11. **37.14:** Ezek 36.27; 1 Thess 4.8.

for ever. ²⁶I will make a covenant of peace with them; it shall be an everlasting covenant with them; and I will bless^{*h*} them and multiply them, and will set my sanctuary in the midst of them for evermore. ²⁷My dwelling place shall be with them; and I will be their God, and they shall be my people. ²⁸Then the nations will know that I the Lord sanctify Israel, when my sanctuary is in the midst of them for evermore."

38 The word of the Lord came to me: ²"Son of man, set your face toward Gŏg, of the land of Mā'gŏg, the chief prince of Mē'shĕch and Tü'bạl, and prophesy against him ³and say, Thus says the Lord God: Behold, I am against you, O Gŏg, chief prince of Mē'shĕch and Tü'bạl; ⁴and I will turn you about, and put hooks into your jaws, and I will bring you forth, and all your army, horses and horsemen, all of them clothed in full armor, a great company, all of them with buckler and shield, wielding swords; ⁵Persia, Cŭsh, and Püt are with them, all of them with shield and helmet; ⁶Gō'-mẹr and all his hordes; Bĕth"-tō-gār'mạh from the uttermost parts of the north with all his hordes—many peoples are with you.

7 "Be ready and keep ready, you and all the hosts that are assembled about you, and be a guard for them. ⁸After many days you will be mustered; in the latter years you will go against the land that is restored from war, the land where people were gathered from many nations upon the mountains of Israel, which had been a continual waste; its people were brought out from the nations and now dwell securely, all of them. ⁹You will advance, coming on like a storm, you will be like a cloud covering the land, you and all your hordes, and many peoples with you.

10 "Thus says the Lord God: On that day thoughts will come into your mind, and you will devise an evil scheme ¹¹and say, 'I will go up against the land of unwalled villages; I will fall upon the quiet people who dwell securely, all of them dwelling without walls, and having no bars or gates'; ¹²to seize spoil and carry off plunder; to assail the waste places which are now inhabited, and the people who were gathered from the nations, who have

gotten cattle and goods, who dwell at the center of the earth. ¹³Shē'bạ and Dē'dạn and the merchants of Tār'-shĭsh and all its villages will say to you, 'Have you come to seize spoil? Have you assembled your hosts to carry off plunder, to carry away silver and gold, to take away cattle and goods, to seize great spoil?'

14 "Therefore, son of man, prophesy, and say to Gŏg, Thus says the Lord God: On that day when my people Israel are dwelling securely, you will bestir yourself^{*i*} ¹⁵and come from your place out of the uttermost parts of the north, you and many peoples with you, all of them riding on horses, a great host, a mighty army; ¹⁶you will come up against my people Israel, like a cloud covering the land. In the latter days I will bring you against my land, that the nations may know me, when through you, O Gŏg, I vindicate my holiness before their eyes.

17 "Thus says the Lord God: Are you he of whom I spoke in former days by my servants the prophets of Israel, who in those days prophesied for years that I would bring you against them? ¹⁸But on that day, when Gŏg shall come against the land of Israel, says the Lord God, my wrath will be roused. ¹⁹For in my jealousy and in my blazing wrath I declare, On that day there shall be a great shaking in the land of Israel; ²⁰the fish of the sea, and the birds of the air, and the beasts of the field, and all creeping things that creep on the ground, and all the men that are upon the face of the earth, shall quake at my presence, and the mountains shall be thrown down, and the cliffs shall fall, and every wall shall tumble to the ground. ²¹I will summon every kind of terror^{*j*} against Gŏg,^{*k*} says the Lord God; every man's sword will be against his brother. ²²With pestilence and bloodshed I will enter into judgment with him; and I will rain upon him and his hordes and the many peoples that are with him, torrential rains and hailstones, fire and brimstone. ²³So I will show my greatness and my holiness and make myself known in the eyes of many nations.

^{*h*}Tg: Heb *give*   ^{*i*}Gk: Heb *will you not know?*
^{*j*}Gk: Heb *a sword to all my mountains*   ^{*k*}Heb *him*
37.26: Heb 13.20.
37.27: Ex 25.8; 29.45; Lev 26.12; Jer 31.1; 2 Cor 6.16;
Rev 21.3.   **38.2, 9, 15:** Rev 20.8.
38.22: Rev 8.7; 14.10.

Then they will know that I am the LORD.

39 "And you, son of man, prophesy against Gŏg, and say, Thus says the Lord GOD: Behold, I am against you, O Gog, chief prince of Mē'shĕch and Tü'bạl; ²and I will turn you about and drive you forward, and bring you up from the uttermost parts of the north, and lead you against the mountains of Israel; ³then I will strike your bow from your left hand, and will make your arrows drop out of your right hand. ⁴You shall fall upon the mountains of Israel, you and all your hordes and the peoples that are with you; I will give you to birds of prey of every sort and to the wild beasts to be devoured. ⁵You shall fall in the open field; for I have spoken, says the Lord GOD. ⁶I will send fire on Mā'gŏg and on those who dwell securely in the coastlands; and they shall know that I am the LORD.

7 "And my holy name I will make known in the midst of my people Israel; and I will not let my holy name be profaned any more; and the nations shall know that I am the LORD, the Holy One in Israel. ⁸Behold, it is coming and it will be brought about, says the Lord GOD. That is the day of which I have spoken.

9 "Then those who dwell in the cities of Israel will go forth and make fires of the weapons and burn them, shields and bucklers, bows and arrows, handpikes and spears, and they will make fires of them for seven years; ¹⁰so that they will not need to take wood out of the field or cut down any out of the forests, for they will make their fires of the weapons; they will despoil those who despoiled them, and plunder those who plundered them, says the Lord GOD.

11 "On that day I will give to Gŏg a place for burial in Israel, the Valley of the Travelers[l] east of the sea; it will block the travelers, for there Gog and all his multitude will be buried; it will be called the Valley of Hā'mŏn-gŏg.[m] ¹²For seven months the house of Israel will be burying them, in order to cleanse the land. ¹³All the people of the land will bury them; and it will redound to their honor on the day that I show my glory, says the Lord GOD. ¹⁴They will set apart men to pass through the land continually and bury[n]

those remaining upon the face of the land, so as to cleanse it; at the end of seven months they will make their search. ¹⁵And when these pass through the land and any one sees a man's bone, then he shall set up a sign by it, till the buriers have buried it in the Valley of Hā'mŏn-gŏg. ¹⁶(A city Hạmō'nạh[o] is there also.) Thus shall they cleanse the land.

17 "As for you, son of man, thus says the Lord GOD: Speak to the birds of every sort and to all beasts of the field, 'Assemble and come, gather from all sides to the sacrificial feast which I am preparing for you, a great sacrificial feast upon the mountains of Israel, and you shall eat flesh and drink blood. ¹⁸You shall eat the flesh of the mighty, and drink the blood of the princes of the earth – of rams, of lambs, and of goats, of bulls, all of them fatlings of Bā'shạn. ¹⁹And you shall eat fat till you are filled, and drink blood till you are drunk, at the sacrificial feast which I am preparing for you. ²⁰And you shall be filled at my table with horses and riders, with mighty men and all kinds of warriors,' says the Lord GOD.

21 "And I will set my glory among the nations; and all the nations shall see my judgment which I have executed, and my hand which I have laid on them. ²²The house of Israel shall know that I am the LORD their God, from that day forward. ²³And the nations shall know that the house of Israel went into captivity for their iniquity, because they dealt so treacherously with me that I hid my face from them and gave them into the hand of their adversaries, and they all fell by the sword. ²⁴I dealt with them according to their uncleanness and their transgressions, and hid my face from them.

25 "Therefore thus says the Lord GOD: Now I will restore the fortunes of Jacob, and have mercy upon the whole house of Israel; and I will be jealous for my holy name. ²⁶They shall forget their shame, and all the treachery they have practiced against me, when they dwell securely in their land with none to make them afraid, ²⁷when I have brought them back from

---

[l]Or *Abarim* [m]That is *the multitude of Gog*
[n]Gk Syr: Heb *bury the travelers* [o]That is *Multitude*
39.4, 17-20: Rev 19.17, 18, 21.

the peoples and gathered them from
their enemies' lands, and through
them have vindicated my holiness in
the sight of many nations. 28 Then they
shall know that I am the LORD their
God because I sent them into exile
among the nations, and then gathered them into their own land. I will
leave none of them remaining among
the nations any more; 29 and I will
not hide my face any more from them,
when I pour out my Spirit upon the
house of Israel, says the Lord GOD."

40 In the twenty-fifth year of
our exile, at the beginning of the
year, on the tenth day of the month,
in the fourteenth year after the city
was conquered, on that very day, the
hand of the LORD was upon me, 2 and
brought me in the visions of God into
the land of Israel, and set me down
upon a very high mountain, on which
was a structure like a city opposite
me.[p] 3 When he brought me there, behold, there was a man, whose appearance was like bronze, with a line of
flax and a measuring reed in his hand;
and he was standing in the gateway.
4 And the man said to me, "Son of man,
look with your eyes, and hear with
your ears, and set your mind upon all
that I shall show you, for you were
brought here in order that I might
show it to you; declare all that you see
to the house of Israel."

5 And behold, there was a wall all
around the outside of the temple
area, and the length of the measuring reed in the man's hand was six
long cubits, each being a cubit and a
handbreadth in length; so he measured the thickness of the wall, one
reed; and the height, one reed. 6 Then
he went into the gateway facing east,
going up its steps, and measured the
threshold of the gate, one reed deep;[q]
7 and the side rooms, one reed long,
and one reed broad; and the space between the side rooms, five cubits;
and the threshold of the gate by the
vestibule of the gate at the inner
end, one reed. 8 Then he measured the
vestibule of the gateway, eight cubits;
9 and its jambs, two cubits; and the
vestibule of the gate was at the inner
end. 10 And there were three side rooms
on either side of the east gate; the
three were of the same size; and the
jambs on either side were of the same
size. 11 Then he measured the breadth
of the opening of the gateway, ten
cubits; and the breadth of the gateway,
thirteen cubits. 12 There was a barrier
before the side rooms, one cubit on
either side; and the side rooms were
six cubits on either side. 13 Then he
measured the gate from the back[r] of
the one side room to the back[r] of the
other, a breadth of five and twenty
cubits, from door to door. 14 He measured also the vestibule, twenty cubits;
and round about the vestibule of the
gateway was the court.[s] 15 From the
front of the gate at the entrance to the
end of the inner vestibule of the gate
was fifty cubits. 16 And the gateway had
windows round about, narrowing in-
wards into their jambs in the side
rooms, and likewise the vestibule
had windows round about inside, and
on the jambs were palm trees.

17 Then he brought me into the
outer court; and behold, there were
chambers and a pavement, round
about the court; thirty chambers
fronted on the pavement. 18 And the
pavement ran along the side of the
gates, corresponding to the length
of the gates; this was the lower pavement. 19 Then he measured the distance from the inner front of[t] the lower
gate to the outer front of the inner
court, a hundred cubits.

Then he went before me to the
north, 20 and behold, there was a gate[u]
which faced toward the north, belonging to the outer court. He measured its length and its breadth. 21 Its
side rooms, three on either side, and its
jambs and its vestibule were of the
same size as those of the first gate;
its length was fifty cubits, and its
breadth twenty-five cubits. 22 And its
windows, its vestibule, and its palm
trees were of the same size as those of
the gate which faced toward the east;
and seven steps led up to it; and its
vestibule was on the inside. 23 And opposite the gate on the north, as on the
east, was a gate to the inner court;
and he measured from gate to gate,
a hundred cubits.

[p] Gk: Heb *on the south*
[q] Heb *deep, and one threshold, one reed deep*
[r] Compare Gk: Heb *roof*
[s] Compare Gk: Heb *and he made the jambs sixty cubits, and to the jamb of the court was the gateway round about*
[t] Compare Gk: Heb *from before*
[u] Gk: Heb *a hundred cubits on the east and on the north.* 20 *And the gate*

40.1-43.17: 1 Kings 6-7; 2 Chron 3-4. **40.2:** Rev 21.10. **40.3, 5:** Rev 21.15.

24 And he led me toward the south, and behold, there was a gate on the south; and he measured its jambs and its vestibule; they had the same size as the others. 25And there were windows round about in it and in its vestibule, like the windows of the others; its length was fifty cubits, and its breadth twenty-five cubits. 26And there were seven steps leading up to it, and its vestibule was on the inside; and it had palm trees on its jambs, one on either side. 27And there was a gate on the south of the inner court; and he measured from gate to gate toward the south, a hundred cubits.

28 Then he brought me to the inner court by the south gate, and he measured the south gate; it was of the same size as the others. 29Its side rooms, its jambs, and its vestibule were of the same size as the others; and there were windows round about in it and in its vestibule; its length was fifty cubits, and its breadth twenty-five cubits. 30And there were vestibules round about, twenty-five cubits long and five cubits broad. 31Its vestibule faced the outer court, and palm trees were on its jambs, and its stairway had eight steps.

32 Then he brought me to the inner court on the east side, and he measured the gate; it was of the same size as the others. 33Its side rooms, its jambs, and its vestibule were of the same size as the others; and there were windows round about in it and in its vestibule; its length was fifty cubits, and its breadth twenty-five cubits. 34Its vestibule faced the outer court, and it had palm trees on its jambs, one on either side; and its stairway had eight steps.

35 Then he brought me to the north gate, and he measured it; it had the same size as the others. 36Its side rooms, its jambs, and its vestibule were of the same size as the others;*v* and it had windows round about; its length was fifty cubits, and its breadth twenty-five cubits. 37Its vestibule*w* faced the outer court, and it had palm trees on its jambs, one on either side; and its stairway had eight steps.

38 There was a chamber with its door in the vestibule of the gate,*x* where the burnt offering was to be washed. 39And in the vestibule of the gate were two tables on either side, on which the burnt offering and the sin offering and the guilt offering were to be slaughtered. 40And on the outside of the vestibule*y* at the entrance of the north gate were two tables; and on the other side of the vestibule of the gate were two tables. 41Four tables were on the inside, and four tables on the outside of the side of the gate, eight tables, on which the sacrifices were to be slaughtered. 42And there were also four tables of hewn stone for the burnt offering, a cubit and a half long, and a cubit and a half broad, and one cubit high, on which the instruments were to be laid with which the burnt offerings and the sacrifices were slaughtered. 43And hooks, a handbreadth long, were fastened round about within. And on the tables the flesh of the offering was to be laid.

44 Then he brought me from without into the inner court, and behold, there were two chambers*z* in the inner court, one*a* at the side of the north gate facing south, the other at the side of the south*b* gate facing north. 45And he said to me, This chamber which faces south is for the priests who have charge of the temple, 46and the chamber which faces north is for the priests who have charge of the altar; these are the sons of Zā′dŏk, who alone among the sons of Lē′vī may come near to the LORD to minister to him. 47And he measured the court, a hundred cubits long, and a hundred cubits broad, foursquare; and the altar was in front of the temple.

48 Then he brought me to the vestibule of the temple and measured the jambs of the vestibule, five cubits on either side; and the breadth of the gate was fourteen cubits; and the sidewalls of the gate were three cubits*c* on either side. 49The length of the vestibule was twenty cubits, and the breadth twelve*d* cubits; and ten steps led up*e* to it; and there were pillars beside the jambs on either side.

41 Then he brought me to the nave, and measured the jambs;

on each side six cubits was the breadth of the jambs.*f* *2*And the breadth of the entrance was ten cubits; and the sidewalls of the entrance were five cubits on either side; and he measured the length of the nave forty cubits, and its breadth, twenty cubits. *3*Then he went into the inner room and measured the jambs of the entrance, two cubits; and the breadth of the entrance, six cubits; and the sidewalls*g* of the entrance, seven cubits. *4*And he measured the length of the room, twenty cubits, and its breadth, twenty cubits, beyond the nave. And he said to me, This is the most holy place.

5 Then he measured the wall of the temple, six cubits thick; and the breadth of the side chambers, four cubits, round about the temple. *6*And the side chambers were in three stories, one over another, thirty in each story. There were offsets*h* all around the wall of the temple to serve as supports for the side chambers, so that they should not be supported by the wall of the temple. *7*And the side chambers became broader as they rose*i* from story to story, corresponding to the enlargement of the offset*j* from story to story round about the temple; on the side of the temple a stairway led upward, and thus one went up from the lowest story to the top story through the middle story. *8*I saw also that the temple had a raised platform round about; the foundations of the side chambers measured a full reed of six long cubits. *9*The thickness of the outer wall of the side chambers was five cubits; and the part of the platform which was left free was five cubits.*k* Between the platform*l* of the temple and the *10*chambers of the court was a breadth of twenty cubits round about the temple on every side. *11*And the doors of the side chambers opened on the part of the platform that was left free, one door toward the north, and another door toward the south; and the breadth of the part that was left free was five cubits round about.

12 The building that was facing the temple yard on the west side was seventy cubits broad; and the wall of the building was five cubits thick round about, and its length ninety cubits.

13 Then he measured the temple, a hundred cubits long; and the yard and the building with its walls, a hundred cubits long; *14*also the breadth of the east front of the temple and the yard, a hundred cubits.

15 Then he measured the length of the building facing the yard which was at the west and its walls*m* on either side, a hundred cubits.

The nave of the temple and the inner room and the outer*n* vestibule *16*were paneled*o* and round about all three had windows with recessed*p* frames. Over against the threshold the temple was paneled with wood round about, from the floor up to the windows (now the windows were covered), *17*to the space above the door, even to the inner room, and on the outside. And on all the walls round about in the inner room and the nave were carved likenesses*q* *18*of cherubim and palm trees, a palm tree between cherub and cherub. Every cherub had two faces: *19*the face of a man toward the palm tree on the one side, and the face of a young lion toward the palm tree on the other side. They were carved on the whole temple round about; *20*from the floor to above the door cherubim and palm trees were carved on the wall.*r*

21 The doorposts of the nave were squared; and in front of the holy place was something resembling *22*an altar of wood, three cubits high, two cubits long, and two cubits broad;*s* its corners, its base,*t* and its walls were of wood. He said to me, "This is the table which is before the LORD." *23*The nave and the holy place had each a double door. *24*The doors had two leaves apiece, two swinging leaves for each door. *25*And on the doors of the nave were carved cherubim and palm trees, such as were carved on the walls; and there was a canopy of wood in front of the vestibule outside. *26*And there were recessed windows and palm trees on either side, on the sidewalls of the vestibule.*u*

f Compare Gk: Heb *tent*   *g* Gk: Heb *breadth*
h Gk Compare 1 Kings 6.6: Heb *they entered*
i Cn: Heb *it was surrounded*
j Gk: Heb *for the encompassing of the temple.*
k Syr: Heb lacks *five cubits*
l Cn: Heb *house of the side chambers*
m Cn: The meaning of the Hebrew term is unknown
n Gk: Heb *of the court*   *o* Gk: Heb *the thresholds*
p Cn Compare Gk 1 Kings 6.4: The meaning of the Hebrew term is unknown   *q* Cn: Heb *measures and carved*
r Cn Compare verse 25: Heb *and the wall*
s Gk: Heb lacks *two cubits broad*   *t* Gk: Heb *length*
u Cn: Heb *vestibule. And the side chambers of the temple and the canopies*

42 Then he led me out into the inner[v] court, toward the north, and he brought me to the chambers which were opposite the temple yard and opposite the building on the north. [2] The length of the building which was on the north side[w] was[x] a hundred cubits, and the breadth fifty cubits. [3] Adjoining the twenty cubits which belonged to the inner court, and facing the pavement which belonged to the outer court, was gallery[y] against gallery[y] in three stories. [4] And before the chambers was a passage inward, ten cubits wide and a hundred cubits long,[z] and their doors were on the north. [5] Now the upper chambers were narrower, for the galleries[y] took more away from them than from the lower and middle chambers in the building. [6] For they were in three stories, and they had no pillars like the pillars of the outer[a] court; hence the upper chambers were set back from the ground more than the lower and the middle ones. [7] And there was a wall outside parallel to the chambers, toward the outer court, opposite the chambers, fifty cubits long. [8] For the chambers on the outer court were fifty cubits long, while those opposite the temple were a hundred cubits long. [9] Below these chambers was an entrance on the east side, as one enters them from the outer court, [10] where the outside wall begins.[b]

On the south[c] also, opposite the yard and opposite the building, there were chambers [11] with a passage in front of them; they were similar to the chambers on the north, of the same length and breadth, with the same exits[d] and arrangements and doors. [12] And below the south chambers was an entrance on the east side, where one enters the passage, and opposite them was a dividing wall.[e]

13 Then he said to me, "The north chambers and the south chambers opposite the yard are the holy chambers, where the priests who approach the LORD shall eat the most holy offerings; there they shall put the most holy offerings — the cereal offering, the sin offering, and the guilt offering, for the place is holy. [14] When the priests enter the holy place, they shall not go out of it into the outer court without laying there the garments in which they minister, for these are holy; they shall put on other garments before

they go near to that which is for the people."

15 Now when he had finished measuring the interior of the temple area, he led me out by the gate which faced east, and measured the temple area round about. [16] He measured the east side with the measuring reed, five hundred cubits by the measuring reed. [17] Then he turned and measured[f] the north side, five hundred cubits by the measuring reed. [18] Then he turned and measured[f] the south side, five hundred cubits by the measuring reed. [19] Then he turned to the west side and measured, five hundred cubits by the measuring reed. [20] He measured it on the four sides. It had a wall around it, five hundred cubits long and five hundred cubits broad, to make a separation between the holy and the common.

43 Afterward he brought me to the gate, the gate facing east. [2] And behold, the glory of the God of Israel came from the east; and the sound of his coming was like the sound of many waters; and the earth shone with his glory. [3] And[g] the vision I saw was like the vision which I had seen when he came to destroy the city, and[h] like the vision which I had seen by the river Chē'bär; and I fell upon my face. [4] As the glory of the LORD entered the temple by the gate facing east, [5] the Spirit lifted me up, and brought me into the inner court; and behold, the glory of the LORD filled the temple.

6 While the man was standing beside me, I heard one speaking to me out of the temple; [7] and he said to me, "Son of man, this is the place of my throne and the place of the soles of my feet, where I will dwell in the midst of the people of Israel for ever. And the house of Israel shall no more defile my holy name, neither they, nor their kings, by their harlotry, and by the dead bodies[i] of their kings, [8] by setting their threshold by my threshold and their doorposts beside my doorposts,

[v]Gk: Heb *outer*
[w]Gk: Heb *door* [x]Gk: Heb *before the length*
[y]The meaning of the Hebrew word is unknown
[z]Gk Syr: Heb *a way of one cubit* [a]Gk: Heb lacks *outer*
[b]Cn Compare Gk: Heb *in the breadth of the wall of the court* [c]Gk: Heb *east* [d]Heb *and all their exits*
[e]Cn: Heb *And according to the entrances of the chambers that were toward the south was an entrance at the head of the way, the way before the dividing wall toward the east as one enters them*
[f]Gk: Heb *measuring reed round about. He measured*
[g]Gk: Heb *And like the vision* [h]Syr: Heb *and the visions*
[i]Or *the monuments* **43.2:** Ezek 1.24; Rev 1.15; 14.2; 19.6.

with only a wall between me and them. They have defiled my holy name by their abominations which they have committed, so I have consumed them in my anger. [9]Now let them put away their idolatry and the dead bodies[i] of their kings far from me, and I will dwell in their midst for ever.

10 "And you, son of man, describe to the house of Israel the temple and its appearance and plan,[j] that they may be ashamed of their iniquities. [11]And if they are ashamed of all that they have done, portray[k] the temple, its arrangement, its exits and its entrances, and its whole form; and make known to them all its ordinances and all its laws; and write it down in their sight, so that they may observe and perform all its laws[l] and all its ordinances. [12]This is the law of the temple: the whole territory round about upon the top of the mountain shall be most holy. Behold, this is the law of the temple.

13 "These are the dimensions of the altar by cubits (the cubit being a cubit and a handbreadth): its base shall be one cubit high,[m] and one cubit broad, with a rim of one span around its edge. And this shall be the height[x] of the altar: [14]from the base on the ground to the lower ledge, two cubits, with a breadth of one cubit; and from the smaller ledge to the larger ledge, four cubits, with a breadth of one cubit; [15]and the altar hearth, four cubits; and from the altar hearth projecting upward, four horns, one cubit high.[n] [16]The altar hearth shall be square, twelve cubits long by twelve broad. [17]The ledge also shall be square, fourteen cubits long by fourteen broad, with a rim around it half a cubit broad, and its base one cubit round about. The steps of the altar shall face east."

18 And he said to me, "Son of man, thus says the Lord GOD: These are the ordinances for the altar: On the day when it is erected for offering burnt offerings upon it and for throwing blood against it, [19]you shall give to the Levitical priests of the family of Zā'-dŏk, who draw near to me to minister to me, says the Lord GOD, a bull for a sin offering. [20]And you shall take some of its blood, and put it on the four horns of the altar, and on the four corners of the ledge, and upon the rim round about; thus you shall cleanse the altar

and make atonement for it. [21]You shall also take the bull of the sin offering, and it shall be burnt in the appointed place belonging to the temple, outside the sacred area. [22]And on the second day you shall offer a he-goat without blemish for a sin offering; and the altar shall be cleansed, as it was cleansed with the bull. [23]When you have finished cleansing it, you shall offer a bull without blemish and a ram from the flock without blemish. [24]You shall present them before the LORD, and the priests shall sprinkle salt upon them and offer them up as a burnt offering to the LORD. [25]For seven days you shall provide daily a goat for a sin offering; also a bull and a ram from the flock, without blemish, shall be provided. [26]Seven days shall they make atonement for the altar and purify it, and so consecrate it. [27]And when they have completed these days, then from the eighth day onward the priests shall offer upon the altar your burnt offerings and your peace offerings; and I will accept you, says the Lord GOD."

44 Then he brought me back to the outer gate of the sanctuary, which faces east; and it was shut. [2]And he[o] said to me, "This gate shall remain shut; it shall not be opened, and no one shall enter by it; for the LORD, the God of Israel, has entered by it; therefore it shall remain shut. [3]Only the prince may sit in it to eat bread before the LORD; he shall enter by way of the vestibule of the gate, and shall go out by the same way."

4 Then he brought me by way of the north gate to the front of the temple; and I looked, and behold, the glory of the LORD filled the temple of the LORD; and I fell upon my face. [5]And the LORD said to me, "Son of man, mark well, see with your eyes, and hear with your ears all that I shall tell you concerning all the ordinances of the temple of the LORD and all its laws; and mark well those who may be admitted to[p] temple and all those who are to be excluded from the sanctuary. [6]And say to the rebellious house,[q] to the house of Israel, Thus says the Lord GOD:

[i]Or *the monuments*
[j]Gk: Heb *the temple that they may measure the pattern*
[k]Gk: Heb *the form of*   [l]Compare Gk: Heb *its whole form*
[m]Gk: Heb lacks *high*   [x]Gk: Heb *back*
[n]Gk: Heb lacks *one cubit high*
[o]Cn: Heb *the LORD*   [p]Cn: Heb *the entrance of*
[q]Gk: Heb lacks *house*   **44.4:** Rev 15.8.

O house of Israel, let there be an end to all your abominations, [7]in admitting foreigners, uncircumcised in heart and flesh, to be in my sanctuary, profaning it,[r] when you offer to me my food, the fat and the blood. You[s] have broken my covenant, in addition to all your abominations. [8]And you have not kept charge of my holy things; but you have set foreigners to keep my charge in my sanctuary.

9 "Therefore[t] thus says the Lord GOD: No foreigner, uncircumcised in heart and flesh, of all the foreigners who are among the people of Israel, shall enter my sanctuary. [10]But the Lē′vītes who went far from me, going astray from me after their idols when Israel went astray, shall bear their punishment. [11]They shall be ministers in my sanctuary, having oversight at the gates of the temple, and serving in the temple; they shall slay the burnt offering and the sacrifice for the people, and they shall attend on the people, to serve them. [12]Because they ministered to them before their idols and became a stumbling block of iniquity to the house of Israel, therefore I have sworn concerning them, says the Lord GOD, that they shall bear their punishment. [13]They shall not come near to me, to serve me as priest, nor come near any of my sacred things and the things that are most sacred; but they shall bear their shame, because of the abominations which they have committed. [14]Yet I will appoint them to keep charge of the temple, to do all its service and all that is to be done in it.

15 "But the Levitical priests, the sons of Zā′dŏk, who kept the charge of my sanctuary when the people of Israel went astray from me, shall come near to me to minister to me; and they shall attend on me to offer me the fat and the blood, says the Lord GOD; [16]they shall enter my sanctuary, and they shall approach my table, to minister to me, and they shall keep my charge. [17]When they enter the gates of the inner court, they shall wear linen garments; they shall have nothing of wool on them, while they minister at the gates of the inner court, and within. [18]They shall have linen turbans upon their heads, and linen breeches upon their loins; they shall not gird themselves with anything that causes sweat. [19]And when they go out

into the outer court to the people, they shall put off the garments in which they have been ministering, and lay them in the holy chambers; and they shall put on other garments, lest they communicate holiness to the people with their garments. [20]They shall not shave their heads or let their locks grow long; they shall only trim the hair of their heads. [21]No priest shall drink wine, when he enters the inner court. [22]They shall not marry a widow, or a divorced woman, but only a virgin of the stock of the house of Israel, or a widow who is the widow of a priest. [23]They shall teach my people the difference between the holy and the common, and show them how to distinguish between the unclean and the clean. [24]In a controversy they shall act as judges, and they shall judge it according to my judgments. They shall keep my laws and my statutes in all my appointed feasts, and they shall keep my sabbaths holy. [25]They shall not defile themselves by going near to a dead person; however, for father or mother, for son or daughter, for brother or unmarried sister they may defile themselves. [26]After he is defiled,[u] he shall count for himself seven days, and then he shall be clean.[v] [27]And on the day that he goes into the holy place, into the inner court, to minister in the holy place, he shall offer his sin offering, says the Lord GOD.

28 "They shall have no[w] inheritance; I am their inheritance: and you shall give them no possession in Israel; I am their possession. [29]They shall eat the cereal offering, the sin offering, and the guilt offering; and every devoted thing in Israel shall be theirs. [30]And the first of all the first fruits of all kinds, and every offering of all kinds from all your offerings, shall belong to the priests; you shall also give to the priests the first of your coarse meal, that a blessing may rest on your house. [31]The priests shall not eat of anything, whether bird or beast, that has died of itself or is torn.

45 "When you allot the land as a possession, you shall set apart for the LORD a portion of the land as a holy district, twenty-five thousand

[r]Gk: Heb *it my temple*   [s]Gk Syr Vg: Heb *they*
[t]Gk: Heb *for you*   [u]Syr: Heb *cleansed*
[s]Syr: Heb lacks *and then he shall be clean*
[w]Vg: Heb *as an*

cubits long and twenty^x thousand cubits broad; it shall be holy throughout its whole extent. ²Of this a square plot of five hundred by five hundred cubits shall be for the sanctuary, with fifty cubits for an open space around it. ³And in the holy district you shall measure off a section twenty-five thousand cubits long and ten thousand broad, in which shall be the sanctuary, the most holy place. ⁴It shall be the holy portion of the land; it shall be for the priests, who minister in the sanctuary and approach the LORD to minister to him; and it shall be a place for their houses and a holy place for the sanctuary. ⁵Another section, twenty-five thousand cubits long and ten thousand cubits broad, shall be for the Lē′vītes who minister at the temple, as their possession for cities to live in.*

6 "Alongside the portion set apart as the holy district you shall assign for the possession of the city an area five thousand cubits broad, and twenty-five thousand cubits long; it shall belong to the whole house of Israel.

7 "And to the prince shall belong the land on both sides of the holy district and the property of the city, alongside the holy district and the property of the city, on the west and on the east, corresponding in length to one of the tribal portions, and extending from the western to the eastern boundary of the land. ⁸It is to be his property in Israel. And my princes shall no more oppress my people; but they shall let the house of Israel have the land according to their tribes.

9 "Thus says the Lord GOD: Enough, O princes of Israel! Put away violence and oppression, and execute justice and righteousness; cease your evictions of my people, says the Lord GOD.

10 "You shall have just balances, a just ephah, and a just bath. ¹¹The ephah and the bath shall be of the same measure, the bath containing one tenth of a homer, and the ephah one tenth of a homer; the homer shall be the standard measure. ¹²The shekel shall be twenty gerahs; five shekels shall be five shekels, and ten shekels shall be ten shekels, and your mina shall be fifty shekels.*

13 "This is the offering which you shall make: one sixth of an ephah from each homer of wheat, and one sixth of an ephah from each homer of barley, ¹⁴and as the fixed portion of oil,* one tenth of a bath from each cor (the cor,* like the homer, contains ten baths); ¹⁵and one sheep from every flock of two hundred, from the families* of Israel. This is the offering for cereal offerings, burnt offerings, and peace offerings, to make atonement for them, says the Lord GOD. ¹⁶All the people of the land shall give* this offering to the prince in Israel. ¹⁷It shall be the prince's duty to furnish the burnt offerings, cereal offerings, and drink offerings, at the feasts, the new moons, and the sabbaths, all the appointed feasts of the house of Israel: he shall provide the sin offerings, cereal offerings, burnt offerings, and peace offerings, to make atonement for the house of Israel.

18 "Thus says the Lord GOD: In the first month, on the first day of the month, you shall take a young bull without blemish, and cleanse the sanctuary. ¹⁹The priest shall take some of the blood of the sin offering and put it on the doorposts of the temple, the four corners of the ledge of the altar, and the posts of the gate of the inner court. ²⁰You shall do the same on the seventh day of the month for any one who has sinned through error or ignorance; so you shall make atonement for the temple.

21 "In the first month, on the fourteenth day of the month, you shall celebrate the feast of the passover, and for seven days unleavened bread shall be eaten. ²²On that day the prince shall provide for himself and all the people of the land a young bull for a sin offering. ²³And on the seven days of the festival he shall provide as a burnt offering to the LORD seven young bulls and seven rams without blemish, on each of the seven days; and a he-goat daily for a sin offering. ²⁴And he shall provide as a cereal offering an ephah for each bull, an ephah for each ram, and a hin of oil to each ephah. ²⁵In the seventh month, on the fifteenth day of the month and for the seven days of the feast, he shall make the same pro-

---

^xGk: Heb ten ^yGk: Heb *twenty chambers*
^zGk: Heb *twenty shekels, twenty-five shekels, fifteen shekels shall be your mina*
^aCn: Heb *oil, the bath the oil*
^bVg: Heb *homer* ^cGk: Heb *watering places*
^dGk Compare Syr: Heb *shall be to*

vision for sin offerings, burnt offerings, and cereal offerings, and for the oil.

46 "Thus says the Lord GOD: The gate of the inner court that faces east shall be shut on the six working days; but on the sabbath day it shall be opened and on the day of the new moon it shall be opened. ²The prince shall enter by the vestibule of the gate from without, and shall take his stand by the post of the gate. The priests shall offer his burnt offering and his peace offerings, and he shall worship at the threshold of the gate. Then he shall go out, but the gate shall not be shut until evening. ³The people of the land shall worship at the entrance of that gate before the LORD on the sabbaths and on the new moons. ⁴The burnt offering that the prince offers to the LORD on the sabbath day shall be six lambs without blemish and a ram without blemish; ⁵and the cereal offering with the ram shall be an ephah, and the cereal offering with the lambs shall be as much as he is able, together with a hin of oil to each ephah. ⁶On the day of the new moon he shall offer a young bull without blemish, and six lambs and a ram, which shall be without blemish; ⁷as a cereal offering he shall provide an ephah with the bull and an ephah with the ram, and with the lambs as much as he is able, together with a hin of oil to each ephah. ⁸When the prince enters, he shall go in by the vestibule of the gate, and he shall go out by the same way.

9 "When the people of the land come before the LORD at the appointed feasts, he who enters by the north gate to worship shall go out by the south gate; and he who enters by the south gate shall go out by the north gate: no one shall return by way of the gate by which he entered, but each shall go out straight ahead. ¹⁰When they go in, the prince shall go in with them; and when they go out, he shall go out.

11 "At the feasts and the appointed seasons the cereal offering with a young bull shall be an ephah, and with a ram an ephah, and with the lambs as much as one is able to give, together with a hin of oil to an ephah. ¹²When the prince provides a freewill offering, either a burnt offering or peace offerings as a freewill offering to the LORD,

the gate facing east shall be opened for him; and he shall offer his burnt offering or his peace offerings as he does on the sabbath day. Then he shall go out, and after he has gone out the gate shall be shut.

13 "He shall provide a lamb a year old without blemish for a burnt offering to the LORD daily; morning by morning he shall provide it. ¹⁴And he shall provide a cereal offering with it morning by morning, one sixth of an ephah, and one third of a hin of oil to moisten the flour, as a cereal offering to the LORD; this is the ordinance for the continual burnt offering.ᵉ ¹⁵Thus the lamb and the meal offering and the oil shall be provided, morning by morning, for a continual burnt offering.

16 "Thus says the Lord GOD: If the prince makes a gift to any of his sons out ofᶠ his inheritance, it shall belong to his sons, it is their property by inheritance. ¹⁷But if he makes a gift out of his inheritance to one of his servants, it shall be his to the year of liberty; then it shall revert to the prince; only his sons may keep a gift from his inheritance. ¹⁸The prince shall not take any of the inheritance of the people, thrusting them out of their property; he shall give his sons their inheritance out of his own property, so that none of my people shall be dispossessed of his property."

19 Then he brought me through the entrance, which was at the side of the gate, to the north row of the holy chambers for the priests; and there I saw a place at the extreme western end of them. ²⁰And he said to me, "This is the place where the priests shall boil the guilt offering and the sin offering, and where they shall bake the cereal offering, in order not to bring them out into the outer court and so communicate holiness to the people."

21 Then he brought me forth to the outer court, and led me to the four corners of the court; and in each corner of the court there was a court— ²²in the four corners of the court were smallᵍ courts, forty cubits long and thirty broad; the four were of the same size. ²³On the inside, around each of the four courts was a row of masonry, with hearths made at the bottom of

ᵉ Cn: Heb *perpetual ordinances continually*
ᶠ Gk: Heb *it is his inheritance*
ᵍ Gk Syr Vg: The meaning of the Hebrew word is uncertain

the rows round about. ²⁴Then he said to me, "These are the kitchens where those who minister at the temple shall boil the sacrifices of the people."

47 Then he brought me back to the door of the temple; and behold, water was issuing from below the threshold of the temple toward the east (for the temple faced east); and the water was flowing down from below the south end of the threshold of the temple, south of the altar. ²Then he brought me out by way of the north gate, and led me round on the outside to the outer gate, that faces toward the east;[h] and the water was coming out on the south side.

3 Going on eastward with a line in his hand, the man measured a thousand cubits, and then led me through the water; and it was ankle-deep. ⁴Again he measured a thousand, and led me through the water; and it was knee-deep. Again he measured a thousand, and led me through the water; and it was up to the loins. ⁵Again he measured a thousand, and it was a river that I could not pass through, for the water had risen; it was deep enough to swim in, a river that could not be passed through. ⁶And he said to me, "Son of man, have you seen this?"

Then he led me back along the bank of the river. ⁷As I went back, I saw upon the bank of the river very many trees on the one side and on the other. ⁸And he said to me, "This water flows toward the eastern region and goes down into the Ar′a·bah; and when it enters the stagnant waters of the sea,[i] the water will become fresh. ⁹And wherever the river[j] goes every living creature which swarms will live, and there will be very many fish; for this water goes there, that the waters of the sea[k] may become fresh; so everything will live where the river goes. ¹⁰Fishermen will stand beside the sea; from Ĕn-gĕ′dī to Ĕn-ĕg′lā·im it will be a place for the spreading of nets; its fish will be of very many kinds, like the fish of the Great Sea. ¹¹But its swamps and marshes will not become fresh; they are to be left for salt. ¹²And on the banks, on both sides of the river, there will grow all kinds of trees for food. Their leaves will not wither nor their fruit fail, but they will bear fresh fruit every month, because the water for them flows from the

sanctuary. Their fruit will be for food, and their leaves will be for healing."

13 Thus says the Lord GOD: "These are the boundaries by which you shall divide the land for inheritance among the twelve tribes of Israel. Joseph shall have two portions. ¹⁴And you shall divide it equally; I swore to give it to your fathers, and this land shall fall to you as your inheritance.

15 "This shall be the boundary of the land: On the north side, from the Great Sea by way of Hĕth′lŏn to the entrance of Hā′măth, and on to Zē′-dăd,[l] ¹⁶Bĕ·rō′thah, Sib′rā·im (which lies on the border between Damascus and Hā′măth), as far as Hă·zĕr·hăt′-tĭ·cŏn, which is on the border of Hau′-rän. ¹⁷So the boundary shall run from the sea to Hā′zăr-ē′nŏn, which is on the northern border of Damascus, with the border of Hā′măth to the north.[m] This shall be the north side.

18 "On the east side, the boundary shall run from Hā′zăr-ē′nŏn[n] between Hau′rän and Damascus;[m] along the Jordan between Gilead and the land of Israel; to the eastern sea and as far as Tā′măr.[o] This shall be the east side.

19 "On the south side, it shall run from Tā′măr as far as the waters of Mĕr·ĭ·bath′-kā′dĕsh, thence along the Brook of Egypt to the Great Sea. This shall be the south side.

20 "On the west side, the Great Sea shall be the boundary to a point opposite the entrance of Hā′măth. This shall be the west side.

21 "So you shall divide this land among you according to the tribes of Israel. ²²You shall allot it as an inheritance for yourselves and for the aliens who reside among you and have begotten children among you. They shall be to you as native-born sons of Israel; with you they shall be allotted an inheritance among the tribes of Israel. ²³In whatever tribe the alien resides, there you shall assign him his inheritance, says the Lord GOD.

48 "These are the names of the tribes: Beginning at the north-

[h] Heb obscure
[i] Compare Syr: Heb *into the sea to the sea those that were made to issue forth*
[j] Gk Syr Vg Tg: Heb *two rivers*
[k] Compare Syr: Heb lacks *the waters of the sea*
[l] Gk: Heb *the entrance of Zedad, Hamath*   [m] Heb obscure
[n] Cn: Heb lacks *Hazar-enon*
[o] Compare Syr: Heb *you shall measure*
47.1-2: Zech 14.8; Rev 22.1-2.

ern border, from the sea by way[p] of Hĕth'lŏn to the entrance of Hā'măth, as far as Hā'zăr–ē'nŏn (which is on the northern border of Damascus over against Hamath), and[q] extending from the east side to the west,[r] Dan, one portion. [2]Adjoining the territory of Dan, from the east side to the west, Ăsh'ẹr, one portion. [3]Adjoining the territory of Ăsh'ẹr, from the east side to the west, Năph'tạ·lī, one portion. [4]Adjoining the territory of Năph'tạ·lī, from the east side to the west, Mạnăs'sẹh, one portion. [5]Adjoining the territory of Mạ·năs'sẹh, from the east side to the west, Ē'phrạ·ĭm, one portion. [6]Adjoining the territory of Ē'phrạ·ĭm, from the east side to the west, Reuben, one portion. [7]Adjoining the territory of Reuben, from the east side to the west, Judah, one portion.

8 "Adjoining the territory of Judah, from the east side to the west, shall be the portion which you shall set apart, twenty-five thousand cubits in breadth, and in length equal to one of the tribal portions, from the east side to the west, with the sanctuary in the midst of it. [9]The portion which you shall set apart for the LORD shall be twenty-five thousand cubits in length, and twenty[s] thousand in breadth. [10]These shall be the allotments of the holy portion: the priests shall have an allotment measuring twenty-five thousand cubits on the northern side, ten thousand cubits in breadth on the western side, ten thousand in breadth on the eastern side, and twenty-five thousand in length on the southern side, with the sanctuary of the LORD in the midst of it. [11]This shall be for the consecrated priests, the sons' of Zā'dŏk, who kept my charge, who did not go astray when the people of Israel went astray, as the Lē'vītes did. [12]And it shall belong to them as a special portion from the holy portion of the land, a most holy place, adjoining the territory of the Lē'vītes. [13]And alongside the territory of the priests, the Lē'vītes shall have an allotment twenty-five thousand cubits in length and ten thousand in breadth. The whole length shall be twenty-five thousand cubits and the breadth twenty[u] thousand. [14]They shall not sell or exchange any of it; they shall not alienate this choice portion of the land, for it is holy to the LORD.

15 "The remainder, five thousand cubits in breadth and twenty-five thousand in length, shall be for ordinary use for the city, for dwellings and for open country. In the midst of it shall be the city; [16]and these shall be its dimensions: the north side four thousand five hundred cubits, the south side four thousand five hundred, the east side four thousand five hundred, and the west side four thousand five hundred. [17]And the city shall have open land: on the north two hundred and fifty cubits, on the south two hundred and fifty, on the east two hundred and fifty, and on the west two hundred and fifty. [18]The remainder of the length alongside the holy portion shall be ten thousand cubits to the east, and ten thousand to the west, and it shall be alongside the holy portion. Its produce shall be food for the workers of the city. [19]And the workers of the city, from all the tribes of Israel, shall till it. [20]The whole portion which you shall set apart shall be twenty-five thousand cubits square, that is, the holy portion together with the property of the city.

21 "What remains on both sides of the holy portion and of the property of the city shall belong to the prince. Extending from the twenty-five thousand cubits of the holy portion to the east border, and westward from the twenty-five thousand cubits to the west border, parallel to the tribal portions, it shall belong to the prince. The holy portion with the sanctuary of the temple in its midst, [22]and the property of the Lē'vītes and the property of the city,[v] shall be in the midst of that which belongs to the prince. The portion of the prince shall lie between the territory of Judah and the territory of Benjamin.

23 "As for the rest of the tribes: from the east side to the west, Benjamin, one portion. [24]Adjoining the territory of Benjamin, from the east side to the west, Sĭm'ē·ọn, one portion. [25]Adjoining the territory of Sĭm'ē·ọn, from the east side to the west, Ĭs'sạ·chär, one portion. [26]Adjoining the

[p]Compare 47.15: Heb *by the side of the way*
[q]Cn: Heb *and they shall be his*
[r]Gk Compare verses 2-8: Heb *the east side the west*
[s]Compare 45.1: Heb *ten*   [t]One Ms Gk: Heb *of the sons*
[u]Gk: Heb *ten*
[v]Cn: Heb *and from the property of the Levites and from the property of the city*
48.16: Rev 21.16.

territory of Ĭs′sạ·chär, from the east side to the west, Zĕb′ū·lụn, one portion. ²⁷Adjoining the territory of Zĕb′ū·lụn, from the east side to the west, Gȧd, one portion. ²⁸And adjoining the territory of Gȧd to the south, the boundary shall run from Tā′mär to the waters of Mĕr·ĭ·bath′–kā′dĕsh, thence along the Brook of Egypt to the Great Sea. ²⁹This is the land which you shall allot as an inheritance among the tribes of Israel, and these are their several portions, says the Lord GOD.

30 "These shall be the exits of the city: On the north side, which is to be four thousand five hundred cubits by measure, ³¹three gates, the gate of Reuben, the gate of Judah, and the gate of Levi, the gates of the city being named after the tribes of Israel. ³²On the east side, which is to be four thousand five hundred cubits, three gates, the gate of Joseph, the gate of Benjamin, and the gate of Dan. ³³On the south side, which is to be four thousand five hundred cubits by measure, three gates, the gate of Sĭm′ē·ọn, the gate of Ĭs′sạ·chär, and the gate of Zĕb′ū·lụn. ³⁴On the west side, which is to be four thousand five hundred cubits, three gates,ʷ the gate of Gȧd, the gate of Ȧsh′ẹr, and the gate of Năph′tạ·lī. ³⁵The circumference of the city shall be eighteen thousand cubits. And the name of the city henceforth shall be, The LORD is there."

The Book of
Daniel

1 In the third year of the reign of Jĕ·hoi′ạ·kịm king of Judah, Nĕ·bü·chạd·nĕz′zạr king of Babylon came to Jerusalem and besieged it. ²And the Lord gave Jĕ·hoi′ạ·kịm king of Judah into his hand, with some of the vessels of the house of God; and he brought them to the land of Shī′när, to the house of his god, and placed the vessels in the treasury of his god. ³Then the king commanded Ȧsh′·pẹ·năz, his chief eunuch, to bring some of the people of Israel, both of the royal family and of the nobility, ⁴youths without blemish, handsome and skilful in all wisdom, endowed with knowledge, understanding learning, and competent to serve in the king's palace, and to teach them the letters and language of the Chăl·dē′ạns. ⁵The king assigned them a daily portion of the rich food which the king ate, and of the wine which he drank. They were to be educated for three years, and at the end of that time they were to stand before the king. ⁶Among these were Daniel, Hăn·ạ·nī′ạh, Mĭsh′ạ·ĕl, and Ȧz·ạ·rī′ạh of the tribe of Judah. ⁷And the chief of the eunuchs gave them names: Daniel he called Bĕl·tĕ·shăz′zạr, Hăn·ạ·nī′ạh he called Shăd′răch, Mĭsh′ạ–ĕl he called Mē′shăch, and Ȧz·ạ·rī′ạh he called Ạ·bĕd′nĕ·gō.

8 But Daniel resolved that he would not defile himself with the king's rich food, or with the wine which he drank; therefore he asked the chief of the eunuchs to allow him not to defile himself. ⁹And God gave Daniel favor and compassion in the sight of the chief of the eunuchs; ¹⁰and the chief of the eunuchs said to Daniel, "I fear lest my lord the king, who appointed your food and your drink, should see that you were in poorer condition than the youths who are of your own age. So you would endanger my head with the king." ¹¹Then Daniel said to the steward whom the chief of the eunuchs had appointed over Daniel, Hăn·ạ·nī′ạh, Mĭsh′ạ–ĕl, and Ȧz·ạ·rī′ạh; ¹²"Test your servants for ten days; let us be given vegetables to eat and water to drink ¹³Then let our appearance and the appearance of the youths who eat the king's rich food be observed by you

ʷOne Ms Gk Syr: Heb *their gates three*
48.31-35: Rev 21.12-13.

and according to what you see deal with your servants." [14]So he hearkened to them in this matter, and tested them for ten days. [15]At the end of ten days it was seen that they were better in appearance and fatter in flesh than all the youths who ate the king's rich food. [16]So the steward took away their rich food and the wine they were to drink, and gave them vegetables.

17 As for these four youths, God gave them learning and skill in all letters and wisdom; and Daniel had understanding in all visions and dreams. [18]At the end of the time, when the king had commanded that they should be brought in, the chief of the eunuchs brought them in before Nĕ·bü·chad·nĕz′zar. [19]And the king spoke with them, and among them all none was found like Daniel, Hăn-a·nī′ah, Mĭsh′a-ĕl, and Ăz·a·rī′ah; therefore they stood before the king. [20]And in every matter of wisdom and understanding concerning which the king inquired of them, he found them ten times better than all the magicians and enchanters that were in all his kingdom. [21]And Daniel continued until the first year of King Cyrus.

2 In the second year of the reign of Nĕ·bü·chad·nĕz′zar, Nebuchadnezzar had dreams; and his spirit was troubled, and his sleep left him. [2]Then the king commanded that the magicians, the enchanters, the sorcerers, and the Chăl·dē′ans be summoned, to tell the king his dreams. So they came in and stood before the king. [3]And the king said to them, "I had a dream, and my spirit is troubled to know the dream." [4]Then the Chăl-dē′ans said to the king,[a] "O king, live for ever! Tell your servants the dream, and we will show the interpretation." [5]The king answered the Chăl·dē′ans, "The word from me is sure: if you do not make known to me the dream and its interpretation, you shall be torn limb from limb, and your houses shall be laid in ruins. [6]But if you show the dream and its interpretation, you shall receive from me gifts and rewards and great honor. Therefore show me the dream and its interpretation." [7]They answered a second time, "Let the king tell his servants the dream, and we will show its interpretation." [8]The king answered, "I know with certainty that

you are trying to gain time, because you see that the word from me is sure [9]that if you do not make the dream known to me, there is but one sentence for you. You have agreed to speak lying and corrupt words before me till the times change. Therefore tell me the dream, and I shall know that you can show me its interpretation." [10]The Chăl·dē′ans answered the king, "There is not a man on earth who can meet the king's demand; for no great and powerful king has asked such a thing of any magician or enchanter or Chăl·dē′an. [11]The thing that the king asks is difficult, and none can show it to the king except the gods, whose dwelling is not with flesh."

12 Because of this the king was angry and very furious, and commanded that all the wise men of Babylon be destroyed. [13]So the decree went forth that the wise men were to be slain, and they sought Daniel and his companions, to slay them. [14]Then Daniel replied with prudence and discretion to Är′ĭ·ŏch, the captain of the king's guard, who had gone out to slay the wise men of Babylon; [15]he said to Är′ĭ·ŏch, the king's captain, "Why is the decree of the king so severe?" Then Arioch made the matter known to Daniel. [16]And Daniel went in and besought the king to appoint him a time, that he might show to the king the interpretation.

17 Then Daniel went to his house and made the matter known to Hăn-a·nī′ah, Mĭsh′a-ĕl, and Ăz·a·rī′ah, his companions, [18]and told them to seek mercy of the God of heaven concerning this mystery, so that Daniel and his companions might not perish with the rest of the wise men of Babylon. [19]Then the mystery was revealed to Daniel in a vision of the night. Then Daniel blessed the God of heaven. [20]Daniel said:

"Blessed be the name of God for ever
    and ever,
  to whom belong wisdom and
    might.
[21]He changes times and seasons;
  he removes kings and sets up
    kings;
he gives wisdom to the wise
  and knowledge to those who have
    understanding;

---

[a]Heb adds *in Aramaic*, indicating that the text from this point to the end of chapter 7 is in Aramaic

²²he reveals deep and mysterious things;
he knows what is in the darkness,
and the light dwells with him.
²³To thee, O God of my fathers,
I give thanks and praise,
for thou hast given me wisdom and strength,
and hast now made known to me what we asked of thee,
for thou hast made known to us the king's matter."

24 Therefore Daniel went in to Är′ĭ-ŏch, whom the king had appointed to destroy the wise men of Babylon; he went and said thus to him, "Do not destroy the wise men of Babylon; bring me in before the king, and I will show the king the interpretation." 25 Then Är′ĭ-ŏch brought in Daniel before the king in haste, and said thus to him: "I have found among the exiles from Judah a man who can make known to the king the interpretation." ²⁶The king said to Daniel, whose name was Běl-tĕ-shăz′zạr, "Are you able to make known to me the dream that I have seen and its interpretation?" ²⁷Daniel answered the king, "No wise men, enchanters, magicians, or astrologers can show to the king the mystery which the king has asked, ²⁸but there is a God in heaven who reveals mysteries, and he has made known to King Nĕ-bụ-chạd-nĕz′zạr what will be in the latter days. Your dream and the visions of your head as you lay in bed are these: ²⁹To you, O king, as you lay in bed came thoughts of what would be hereafter, and he who reveals mysteries made known to you what is to be. ³⁰But as for me, not because of any wisdom that I have more than all the living has this mystery been revealed to me, but in order that the interpretation may be made known to the king, and that you may know the thoughts of your mind.

31 "You saw, O king, and behold, a great image. This image, mighty and of exceeding brightness, stood before you, and its appearance was frightening. ³²The head of this image was of fine gold, its breast and arms of silver, its belly and thighs of bronze, ³³its legs of iron, its feet partly of iron and partly of clay. ³⁴As you looked, a stone was cut out by no human hand, and it smote the image on its feet of

iron and clay, and broke them in pieces; ³⁵then the iron, the clay, the bronze, the silver, and the gold, all together were broken in pieces, and became like the chaff of the summer threshing floors; and the wind carried them away, so that not a trace of them could be found. But the stone that struck the image became a great mountain and filled the whole earth. 36 "This was the dream; now we will tell the king its interpretation. ³⁷You, O king, the king of kings, to whom the God of heaven has given the kingdom, the power, and the might, and the glory, ³⁸and into whose hand he has given, wherever they dwell, the sons of men, the beasts of the field, and the birds of the air, making you rule over them all—you are the head of gold. ³⁹After you shall arise another kingdom inferior to you, and yet a third kingdom of bronze, which shall rule over all the earth. ⁴⁰And there shall be a fourth kingdom, strong as iron, because iron breaks to pieces and shatters all things; and like iron which crushes, it shall break and crush all these. ⁴¹And as you saw the feet and toes partly of potter's clay and partly of iron, it shall be a divided kingdom; but some of the firmness of iron shall be in it, just as you saw iron mixed with the miry clay. ⁴²And as the toes of the feet were partly iron and partly clay, so the kingdom shall be partly strong and partly brittle. ⁴³As you saw the iron mixed with miry clay, so they will mix with one another in marriage,ᵇ but they will not hold together, just as iron does not mix with clay. ⁴⁴And in the days of those kings the God of heaven will set up a kingdom which shall never be destroyed, nor shall its sovereignty be left to another people. It shall break in pieces all these kingdoms and bring them to an end, and it shall stand for ever; ⁴⁵just as you saw that a stone was cut from a mountain by no human hand, and that it broke in pieces the iron, the bronze, the clay, the silver, and the gold. A great God has made known to the king what shall be hereafter. The dream is certain, and its interpretation sure."

46 Then King Nĕ-bụ-chạd-nĕz′zạr fell upon his face, and did homage to

ᵇAram *by the seed of men*
2.44: Rev 11.15.

Daniel, and commanded that an offering and incense be offered up to him. [47] The king said to Daniel, "Truly, your God is God of gods and Lord of kings, and a revealer of mysteries, for you have been able to reveal this mystery." [48] Then the king gave Daniel high honors and many great gifts, and made him ruler over the whole province of Babylon, and chief prefect over all the wise men of Babylon. [49] Daniel made request of the king, and he appointed Shăd′răch, Mē′shăch, and Ạ·bĕd′nĕ·gō over the affairs of the province of Babylon; but Daniel remained at the king's court.

3 King Nĕ·bü·chạd·nĕz′zạr made an image of gold, whose height was sixty cubits and its breadth six cubits. He set it up on the plain of Dura, in the province of Babylon. [2] Then King Nĕ·bü·chạd·nĕz′zạr sent to assemble the satraps, the prefects, and the governors, the counselors, the treasurers, the justices, the magistrates, and all the officials of the provinces to come to the dedication of the image which King Nebuchadnezzar had set up. [3] Then the satraps, the prefects, and the governors, the counselors, the treasurers, the justices, the magistrates, and all the officials of the provinces, were assembled for the dedication of the image that King Nĕ·bü·chạd·nĕz′zạr had set up; and they stood before the image that Nebuchadnezzar had set up. [4] And the herald proclaimed aloud, "You are commanded, O peoples, nations, and languages, [5] that when you hear the sound of the horn, pipe, lyre, trigon, harp, bagpipe, and every kind of music, you are to fall down and worship the golden image that King Nĕ·bü·chạd·nĕz′zạr has set up; [6] and whoever does not fall down and worship shall immediately be cast into a burning fiery furnace." [7] Therefore, as soon as all the peoples heard the sound of the horn, pipe, lyre, trigon, harp, bagpipe, and every kind of music, all the peoples, nations, and languages fell down and worshiped the golden image which King Nĕ·bü·chạd·nĕz′zạr had set up.

8 Therefore at that time certain Chăl·dē′ạnş came forward and maliciously accused the Jews. [9] They said to King Nĕ·bü·chạd·nĕz′zạr, "O king, live for ever! [10] You, O king, have made a decree, that every man who hears the sound of the horn, pipe, lyre, trigon, harp, bagpipe, and every kind of music, shall fall down and worship the golden image; [11] and whoever does not fall down and worship shall be cast into a burning fiery furnace. [12] There are certain Jews whom you have appointed over the affairs of the province of Babylon: Shăd′răch, Mē′shăch, and Ạ·bĕd′nĕ·gō. These men, O king, pay no heed to you; they do not serve your gods or worship the golden image which you have set up."

13 Then Nĕ·bü·chạd·nĕz′zạr in furious rage commanded that Shăd′răch, Mē′shăch, and Ạ·bĕd′nĕ·gō be brought. Then they brought these men before the king. [14] Nĕ·bü·chạd·nĕz′zạr said to them, "Is it true, O Shăd′răch, Mē′shăch, and Ạ·bĕd′nĕ·gō, that you do not serve my gods or worship the golden image which I have set up? [15] Now if you are ready when you hear the sound of the horn, pipe, lyre, trigon, harp, bagpipe, and every kind of music, to fall down and worship the image which I have made, well and good; but if you do not worship, you shall immediately be cast into a burning fiery furnace; and who is the god that will deliver you out of my hands?"

16 Shăd′răch, Mē′shăch, and Ạ·bĕd′nĕ·gō answered the king, "O Nĕ·bü·chạd·nĕz′zạr, we have no need to answer you in this matter. [17] If it be so, our God whom we serve is able to deliver us from the burning fiery furnace; and he will deliver us out of your hand, O king. *c* [18] But if not, be it known to you, O king, that we will not serve your gods or worship the golden image which you have set up."

19 Then Nĕ·bü·chạd·nĕz′zạr was full of fury, and the expression of his face was changed against Shăd′răch, Mē′shăch, and Ạ·bĕd′nĕ·gō. He ordered the furnace heated seven times more than it was wont to be heated. [20] And he ordered certain mighty men of his army to bind Shăd′răch, Mē′shăch, and Ạ·bĕd′nĕ·gō, and to cast them into the burning fiery furnace. [21] Then these men were bound in their mantles, *d* their tunics, *d* their hats, and their other garments, and they were cast into the

c Or *Behold, our God . . . king.* Or *If our God is able to deliver us, he will deliver us from the burning fiery furnace and out of your hand, O king.*
d The meaning of the Aramaic word is uncertain
3.5, 6: Rev 13.15.

burning fiery furnace. 22 Because the king's order was strict and the furnace very hot, the flame of the fire slew those men who took up Shăd'răch, Mē'shăch, and Ạ·bĕd'nē·gō. 23 And these three men, Shăd'răch, Mē'-shăch, and Ạ·bĕd'nē·gō, fell bound into the burning fiery furnace.

24 Then King Nĕ·bü·chạd·nĕz'zạr was astonished and rose up in haste. He said to his counselors, "Did we not cast three men bound into the fire?" They answered the king, "True, O king." 25 He answered, "But I see four men loose, walking in the midst of the fire, and they are not hurt; and the appearance of the fourth is like a son of the gods."

26 Then Nĕ·bü·chạd·nĕz'zạr came near to the door of the burning fiery furnace and said, "Shăd'răch, Mē'-shăch, and Ạ·bĕd'nē·gō, servants of the Most High God, come forth, and come here!" Then Shadrach, Meshach, and Abednego came out from the fire. 27 And the satraps, the prefects, the governors, and the king's counselors gathered together and saw that the fire had not had any power over the bodies of those men; the hair of their heads was not singed, their mantles *d* were not harmed, and no smell of fire had come upon them. 28 Nĕ·bü·chạd·nĕz'zạr said, "Blessed be the God of Shăd'răch, Mē'shăch, and Ạ·bĕd'nē·gō, who has sent his angel and delivered his servants, who trusted in him, and set at nought the king's command, and yielded up their bodies rather than serve and worship any god except their own God. 29 Therefore I make a decree: Any people, nation, or language that speaks anything against the God of Shăd'răch, Mē'shăch, and Ạ·bĕd'nē·gō shall be torn limb from limb, and their houses laid in ruins; for there is no other god who is able to deliver in this way." 30 Then the king promoted Shăd'răch, Mē'shăch, and Ạ·bĕd'nē·gō in the province of Babylon.

4 *e* King Nĕ·bü·chạd·nĕz'zạr to all peoples, nations, and languages, that dwell in all the earth: Peace be multiplied to you! 2 It has seemed good to me to show the signs and wonders that the Most High God has wrought toward me.
3 How great are his signs,
how mighty his wonders!

His kingdom is an everlasting kingdom,
and his dominion is from generation to generation.

4 *f* I, Nĕ·bü·chạd·nĕz'zạr, was at ease in my house and prospering in my palace. 5 I had a dream which made me afraid; as I lay in bed the fancies and the visions of my head alarmed me. 6 Therefore I made a decree that all the wise men of Babylon should be brought before me, that they might make known to me the interpretation of the dream. 7 Then the magicians, the enchanters, the Chăl·dē'ạns, and the astrologers came in; and I told them the dream, but they could not make known to me its interpretation. 8 At last Daniel came in before me—he who was named Bĕl·te·shăz'zạr after the name of my god, and in whom is the spirit of the holy gods *g*—and I told him the dream, saying, 9 "O Bĕl·te·shăz'zạr, chief of the magicians, because I know that the spirit of the holy gods *g* is in you and that no mystery is difficult for you, here is *h* the dream which I saw; tell me its interpretation. 10 The visions of my head as I lay in bed were these: I saw, and behold, a tree in the midst of the earth; and its height was great. 11 The tree grew and became strong, and its top reached to heaven, and it was visible to the end of the whole earth. 12 Its leaves were fair and its fruit abundant, and in it was food for all. The beasts of the field found shade under it, and the birds of the air dwelt in its branches, and all flesh was fed from it.

13 "I saw in the visions of my head as I lay in bed, and behold, a watcher, a holy one, came down from heaven. 14 He cried aloud and said thus, 'Hew down the tree and cut off its branches, strip off its leaves and scatter its fruit; let the beasts flee from under it and the birds from its branches. 15 But leave the stump of its roots in the earth, bound with a band of iron and bronze, amid the tender grass of the field. Let him be wet with the dew of heaven; let his lot be with the beasts in the grass of the earth; 16 let his mind be changed from a man's, and let a beast's mind be given to him; and let seven times

d The meaning of the Aramaic word is uncertain
e Ch 3.31 in Aram   *f* Ch 4.1 in Aram
g Or Spirit of the holy God
h Cn: Aram *visions of*
4.12, 21: Ezek 17.23; 31.6; Mt 13.32; Mk 4.32; Lk 13.19.

pass over him. [17] The sentence is by the decree of the watchers, the decision by the word of the holy ones, to the end that the living may know that the Most High rules the kingdom of men, and gives it to whom he will, and sets over it the lowliest of men.' [18] This dream I, King Nĕ·bü·chad·nĕz'zar, saw. And you, O Bĕl·te·shăz'zar, declare the interpretation, because all the wise men of my kingdom are not able to make known to me the interpretation, but you are able, for the spirit of the holy gods' is in you."

19 Then Daniel, whose name was Bĕl·te·shăz'zar, was dismayed for a moment, and his thoughts alarmed him. The king said, "Belteshazzar, let not the dream or the interpretation alarm you." Belteshazzar answered, "My lord, may the dream be for those who hate you and its interpretation for your enemies! [20] The tree you saw, which grew and became strong, so that its top reached to heaven, and it was visible to the end of the whole earth; [21] whose leaves were fair and its fruit abundant, and in which was food for all; under which beasts of the field found shade, and in whose branches the birds of the air dwelt — [22] it is you, O king, who have grown and become strong. Your greatness has grown and reaches to heaven, and your dominion to the ends of the earth. [23] And whereas the king saw a watcher, a holy one, coming down from heaven and saying, 'Hew down the tree and destroy it, but leave the stump of its roots in the earth, bound with a band of iron and bronze, in the tender grass of the field; and let him be wet with the dew of heaven; and let his lot be with the beasts of the field, till seven times pass over him'; [24] this is the interpretation, O king: It is a decree of the Most High, which has come upon my lord the king, [25] that you shall be driven from among men, and your dwelling shall be with the beasts of the field; you shall be made to eat grass like an ox, and you shall be wet with the dew of heaven, and seven times shall pass over you, till you know that the Most High rules the kingdom of men, and gives it to whom he will. [26] And as it was commanded to leave the stump of the roots of the tree, your kingdom shall be sure for you from the time that you know that Heaven rules. [27] Therefore, O king,

let my counsel be acceptable to you; break off your sins by practicing righteousness, and your iniquities by showing mercy to the oppressed, that there may perhaps be a lengthening of your tranquillity."

28 All this came upon King Nĕ·bü·chad·nĕz'zar. [29] At the end of twelve months he was walking on the roof of the royal palace of Babylon, [30] and the king said, "Is not this great Babylon, which I have built by my mighty power as a royal residence and for the glory of my majesty?" [31] While the words were still in the king's mouth, there fell a voice from heaven, "O King Nĕ·bü·chad·nĕz'zar, to you it is spoken: The kingdom has departed from you, [32] and you shall be driven from among men, and your dwelling shall be with the beasts of the field; and you shall be made to eat grass like an ox; and seven times shall pass over you, until you have learned that the Most High rules the kingdom of men and gives it to whom he will." [33] Immediately the word was fulfilled upon Nĕ·bü·chad·nĕz'zar. He was driven from among men, and ate grass like an ox, and his body was wet with the dew of heaven till his hair grew as long as eagles' feathers, and his nails were like birds' claws.

34 At the end of the days I, Nĕ·bü·chad·nĕz'zar, lifted my eyes to heaven, and my reason returned to me, and I blessed the Most High, and praised and honored him who lives for ever;

for his dominion is an everlasting dominion,
  and his kingdom endures from generation to generation;
[35] all the inhabitants of the earth are accounted as nothing;
  and he does according to his will in the host of heaven
  and among the inhabitants of the earth;
and none can stay his hand
  or say to him, "What doest thou?"
[36] At the same time my reason returned to me; and for the glory of my kingdom, my majesty and splendor returned to me. My counselors and my lords sought me, and I was established in my kingdom, and still more greatness was added to me. [37] Now I, Nĕ·bü·chad·nĕz'zar, praise and extol and honor the King of heaven; for all his

'Or *Spirit of the holy God*

works are right and his ways are just; and those who walk in pride he is able to abase.

5 King Běl·shăz'zạr made a great feast for a thousand of his lords, and drank wine in front of the thousand.

2 Běl·shăz'zạr, when he tasted the wine, commanded that the vessels of gold and of silver which Ně·bü·chạd·něz'zạr his father had taken out of the temple in Jerusalem be brought, that the king and his lords, his wives, and his concubines might drink from them. [3] Then they brought in the golden and silver vessels[j] which had been taken out of the temple, the house of God in Jerusalem; and the king and his lords, his wives, and his concubines drank from them. [4] They drank wine, and praised the gods of gold and silver, bronze, iron, wood, and stone.

5 Immediately the fingers of a man's hand appeared and wrote on the plaster of the wall of the king's palace, opposite the lampstand; and the king saw the hand as it wrote. [6] Then the king's color changed, and his thoughts alarmed him; his limbs gave way, and his knees knocked together. [7] The king cried aloud to bring in the enchanters, the Chăl'dē'ạns, and the astrologers. The king said to the wise men of Babylon, "Whoever reads this writing, and shows me its interpretation, shall be clothed with purple, and have a chain of gold about his neck, and shall be the third ruler in the kingdom." [8] Then all the king's wise men came in, but they could not read the writing or make known to the king the interpretation. [9] Then King Běl·shăz'zạr was greatly alarmed, and his color changed; and his lords were perplexed.

10 The queen, because of the words of the king and his lords, came into the banqueting hall; and the queen said, "O king, live for ever! Let not your thoughts alarm you or your color change. [11] There is in your kingdom a man in whom is the spirit of the holy gods.[k] In the days of your father light and understanding and wisdom, like the wisdom of the gods, were found in him, and King Ně·bü·chạd·něz'zạr, your father, made him chief of the magicians, enchanters, Chăl·dē'ạns, and astrologers,[l] [12] because an excellent spirit, knowledge, and understanding

to interpret dreams, explain riddles, and solve problems were found in this Daniel, whom the king named Běl·tẹ·shăz'zạr. Now let Daniel be called, and he will show the interpretation."

13 Then Daniel was brought in before the king. The king said to Daniel, "You are that Daniel, one of the exiles of Judah, whom the king my father brought from Judah. [14] I have heard of you that the spirit of the holy gods[k] is in you, and that light and understanding and excellent wisdom are found in you. [15] Now the wise men, the enchanters, have been brought in before me to read this writing and make known to me its interpretation; but they could not show the interpretation of the matter. [16] But I have heard that you can give interpretations and solve problems. Now if you can read the writing and make known to me its interpretation, you shall be clothed with purple, and have a chain of gold about your neck, and shall be the third ruler in the kingdom."

17 Then Daniel answered before the king, "Let your gifts be for yourself, and give your rewards to another; nevertheless I will read the writing to the king and make known to him the interpretation. [18] O king, the Most High God gave Ně·bụ·chạd·něz'zạr your father kingship and greatness and glory and majesty; [19] and because of the greatness that he gave him, all peoples, nations, and languages trembled and feared before him; whom he would he slew, and whom he would he kept alive; whom he would he raised up, and whom he would he put down. [20] But when his heart was lifted up and his spirit was hardened so that he dealt proudly, he was deposed from his kingly throne, and his glory was taken from him; [21] he was driven from among men, and his mind was made like that of a beast, and his dwelling was with the wild asses; he was fed grass like an ox, and his body was wet with the dew of heaven, until he knew that the Most High God rules the kingdom of men, and sets over it whom he will. [22] And you his son, Běl·shăz'-zạr, have not humbled your heart, though you knew all this, [23] but you

[j] Theodotion Vg: Aramaic *golden vessels*
[k] Or *Spirit of the holy God*
[l] Aramaic repeats *the king your father*

have lifted up yourself against the
Lord of heaven; and the vessels of
his house have been brought in before
you, and you and your lords, your
wives, and your concubines have
drunk wine from them; and you have
praised the gods of silver and gold, of
bronze, iron, wood, and stone, which
do not see or hear or know, but the God
in whose hand is your breath, and
whose are all your ways, you have not
honored.

24 "Then from his presence the
hand was sent, and this writing was
inscribed. ²⁵And this is the writing
that was inscribed: MENE, MENE,
TEKEL, and PARSIN. ²⁶This is the
interpretation of the matter: MENE,
God has numbered the days of your
kingdom and brought it to an end;
²⁷TEKEL, you have been weighed in
the balances and found wanting;
²⁸PERES, your kingdom is divided
and given to the Mēdeş and Persians."

29 Then Bĕl·shăz′zạr commanded,
and Daniel was clothed with purple,
a chain of gold was put about his neck,
and proclamation was made concerning him, that he should be the third
ruler in the kingdom.

30 That very night Bĕl·shăz′zạr the
Chăl·dē′ạn king was slain. ³¹And
Dạ·rī′ŭs the Mēde received the king-
dom, being about sixty-two years old.

6 It pleased Dạ·rī′ŭs to set over the
kingdom a hundred and twenty
satraps, to be throughout the whole
kingdom; ²and over them three presidents, of whom Daniel was one, to
whom these satraps should give
account, so that the king might suffer
no loss. ³Then this Daniel became
distinguished above all the other
presidents and satraps, because an
excellent spirit was in him; and the
king planned to set him over the whole
kingdom. ⁴Then the presidents and the
satraps sought to find a ground for
complaint against Daniel with regard
to the kingdom; but they could find no
ground for complaint or any fault,
because he was faithful, and no error
or fault was found in him. ⁵Then these
men said, "We shall not find any
ground for complaint against this
Daniel unless we find it in connection
with the law of his God."

6 Then these presidents and satraps
came by agreement ᵐ to the king and
said to him, "O King Dạ·rī′ŭs, live for

ever! ⁷All the presidents of the kingdom, the prefects and the satraps, the
counselors and the governors are
agreed that the king should establish
an ordinance and enforce an interdict,
that whoever makes petition to any
god or man for thirty days, except to
you, O king, shall be cast into the den
of lions. ⁸Now, O king, establish the
interdict and sign the document, so
that it cannot be changed, according
to the law of the Mēdeş and the Persians, which cannot be revoked."
⁹Therefore King Dạ·rī′ŭs signed the
document and interdict.

10 When Daniel knew that the
document had been signed, he went to
his house where he had windows in
his upper chamber open toward Jerusalem; and he got down upon his knees
three times a day and prayed and gave
thanks before his God, as he had done
previously. ¹¹Then these men came by
agreement ᵐ and found Daniel making
petition and supplication before his
God. ¹²Then they came near and said
before the king, concerning the interdict, "O king! Did you not sign an interdict, that any man who makes petition
to any god or man within thirty days
except to you, O king, shall be cast into
the den of lions?" The king answered,
"The thing stands fast, according to
the law of the Mēdeş and Persians,
which cannot be revoked." ¹³Then they
answered before the king, "That
Daniel, who is one of the exiles from
Judah, pays no heed to you, O king,
or the interdict you have signed, but
makes his petition three times a
day."

14 Then the king, when he heard
these words, was much distressed,
and set his mind to deliver Daniel;
and he labored till the sun went down
to rescue him. ¹⁵Then these men came
by agreement ᵐ to the king, and said
to the king, "Know, O king, that it is a
law of the Mēdeş and Persians that no
interdict or ordinance which the king
establishes can be changed."

16 Then the king commanded, and
Daniel was brought and cast into the
den of lions. The king said to Daniel,
"May your God, whom you serve continually, deliver you!" ¹⁷And a stone
was brought and laid upon the mouth
of the den, and the king sealed it with
his own signet and with the signet of

ᵐOr thronging

his lords, that nothing might be changed concerning Daniel. [18]Then the king went to his palace, and spent the night fasting; no diversions were brought to him, and sleep fled from him.

19 Then, at break of day, the king arose and went in haste to the den of lions. [20]When he came near to the den where Daniel was, he cried out in a tone of anguish and said to Daniel, "O Daniel, servant of the living God, has your God, whom you serve continually, been able to deliver you from the lions?" [21]Then Daniel said to the king, "O king, live for ever! [22]My God sent his angel and shut the lions' mouths, and they have not hurt me, because I was found blameless before him; and also before you, O king, I have done no wrong." [23]Then the king was exceedingly glad, and commanded that Daniel be taken up out of the den. So Daniel was taken up out of the den, and no kind of hurt was found upon him, because he had trusted in his God. [24]And the king commanded, and those men who had accused Daniel were brought and cast into the den of lions—they, their children, and their wives; and before they reached the bottom of the den the lions overpowered them and broke all their bones in pieces.

25 Then King Da·rī′us wrote to all the peoples, nations, and languages that dwell in all the earth: "Peace be multiplied to you. [26]I make a decree, that in all my royal dominion men tremble and fear before the God of Daniel,

for he is the living God,
    enduring for ever;
his kingdom shall never be destroyed,
    and his dominion shall be to the end.
[27]He delivers and rescues,
    he works signs and wonders
    in heaven and on earth,
he who has saved Daniel
    from the power of the lions."

28 So this Daniel prospered during the reign of Da·rī′us and the reign of Cyrus the Persian.

7 In the first year of Bĕl·shăz′zar king of Babylon, Daniel had a dream and visions of his head as he lay in his bed. Then he wrote down the dream, and told the sum of the mat-

ter. [2]Daniel said, "I saw in my vision by night, and behold, the four winds of heaven were stirring up the great sea. [3]And four great beasts came up out of the sea, different from one another. [4]The first was like a lion and had eagles' wings. Then as I looked its wings were plucked off, and it was lifted up from the ground and made to stand upon two feet like a man; and the mind of a man was given to it. [5]And behold, another beast, a second one, like a bear. It was raised up on one side; it had three ribs in its mouth between its teeth; and it was told, 'Arise, devour much flesh.' [6]After this I looked, and lo, another, like a leopard, with four wings of a bird on its back; and the beast had four heads; and dominion was given to it. [7]After this I saw in the night visions, and behold, a fourth beast, terrible and dreadful and exceedingly strong; and it had great iron teeth; it devoured and broke in pieces, and stamped the residue with its feet. It was different from all the beasts that were before it; and it had ten horns. [8]I considered the horns, and behold, there came up among them another horn, a little one, before which three of the first horns were plucked up by the roots; and behold, in this horn were eyes like the eyes of a man, and a mouth speaking great things. [9]As I looked,

thrones were placed
    and one that was ancient of days took his seat;
his raiment was white as snow,
    and the hair of his head like pure wool;
his throne was fiery flames,
    its wheels were burning fire.
[10]A stream of fire issued
    and came forth from before him;
a thousand thousands served him,
    and ten thousand times ten thousand stood before him;
the court sat in judgment,
    and the books were opened.

[11]I looked then because of the sound of the great words which the horn was speaking. And as I looked, the beast was slain, and its body destroyed and given over to be burned with fire. [12]As for the rest of the beasts, their do-

6.22: 2 Tim 4.17.
7.3: Rev 13.1.   7.3, 7, 21: Rev 11.7.   7.4-6: Rev 13.2.
7.7: Rev 12.3; 13.1; 17.3.   7.8, 11: Rev 13.5.
7.9: Rev 1.14; 20.4, 11.   7.10: Rev 5.11; 20.12.

minion was taken away, but their lives were prolonged for a season and a time. [13]I saw in the night visions, and behold, with the clouds of heaven there came one like a son of man, and he came to the Ancient of Days and was presented before him. [14]And to him was given dominion and glory and kingdom, that all peoples, nations, and languages should serve him; his dominion is an everlasting dominion, which shall not pass away, and his kingdom one that shall not be destroyed.

15 "As for me, Daniel, my spirit within me was anxious and the visions of my head alarmed me. [16]I approached one of those who stood there and asked him the truth concerning all this. So he told me, and made known to me the interpretation of the things. [17]'These four great beasts are four kings who shall arise out of the earth. [18]But the saints of the Most High shall receive the kingdom, and possess the kingdom for ever, for ever and ever.'

19 "Then I desired to know the truth concerning the fourth beast, which was different from all the rest, exceedingly terrible, with its teeth of iron and claws of bronze; and which devoured and broke in pieces, and stamped the residue with its feet; [20]and concerning the ten horns that were on its head, and the other horn which came up and before which three of them fell, the horn which had eyes and a mouth that spoke great things, and which seemed greater than its fellows. [21]As I looked, this horn made war with the saints, and prevailed over them, [22]until the Ancient of Days came, and judgment was given for the saints of the Most High, and the time came when the saints received the kingdom.

23 "Thus he said: 'As for the fourth beast, there shall be a fourth kingdom on earth, which shall be different from all the kingdoms, and it shall devour the whole earth, and trample it down, and break it to pieces. [24]As for the ten horns,

out of this kingdom ten kings shall arise, and another shall arise after them; he shall be different from the former ones, and shall put down three kings. [25]He shall speak words against the Most High, and shall wear out the saints of the Most High, and shall think to change the times and the law; and they shall be given into his hand for a time, two times, and half a time. [26]But the court shall sit in judgment, and his dominion shall be taken away, to be consumed and destroyed to the end. [27]And the kingdom and the dominion and the greatness of the kingdoms under the whole heaven shall be given to the people of the saints of the Most High; their kingdom shall be an everlasting kingdom, and all dominions shall serve and obey them.'

28 "Here is the end of the matter. As for me, Daniel, my thoughts greatly alarmed me, and my color changed; but I kept the matter in my mind."

8 In the third year of the reign of King Bĕl·shăz'zạr a vision appeared to me, Daniel, after that which appeared to me at the first. [2]And I saw in the vision; and when I saw, I was in Sŭ'sạ the capital, which is in the province of Ē'lăm; and I saw in the vision, and I was at the river Ū'laī. [3]I raised my eyes and saw, and behold, a ram standing on the bank of the river. It had two horns; and both horns were high, but one was higher than the other, and the higher one came up last. [4]I saw the ram charging westward and northward and southward; no beast could stand before him, and there was no one who could rescue from his power; he did as he pleased and magnified himself.

5 As I was considering, behold, a he-goat came from the west across the face of the whole earth, without touching the ground; and the goat

7.13-14: Mt 24.30; 26.64; Mk 13.26; 14.62; Lk 21.27; 22.69; Rev 1.7, 13; 14.14.
7.14, 18, 22, 27: Rev 11.15. 7.20, 24: Rev 17.12.
7.21: Rev 13.7. 7.25: Rev 12.14.

had a conspicuous horn between his eyes. [6]He came to the ram with the two horns, which I had seen standing on the bank of the river, and he ran at him in his mighty wrath. [7]I saw him come close to the ram, and he was enraged against him and struck the ram and broke his two horns; and the ram had no power to stand before him, but he cast him down to the ground and trampled upon him; and there was no one who could rescue the ram from his power. [8]Then the he-goat magnified himself exceedingly; but when he was strong, the great horn was broken, and instead of it there came up four conspicuous horns toward the four winds of heaven.

9 Out of one of them came forth a little horn, which grew exceedingly great toward the south, toward the east, and toward the glorious land. [10]It grew great, even to the host of heaven; and some of the host of the stars it cast down to the ground, and trampled upon them. [11]It magnified itself, even up to the Prince of the host; and the continual burnt offering was taken away from him, and the place of his sanctuary was overthrown. [12]And the host was given over to it together with the continual burnt offering through transgression;[n] and truth was cast down to the ground, and the horn acted and prospered. [13]Then I heard a holy one speaking; and another holy one said to the one that spoke, "For how long is the vision concerning the continual burnt offering, the transgression that makes desolate, and the giving over of the sanctuary and host to be trampled under foot?"[o] [14]And he said to him,[p] "For two thousand and three hundred evenings and mornings; then the sanctuary shall be restored to its rightful state."

15 When I, Daniel, had seen the vision, I sought to understand it; and behold, there stood before me one having the appearance of a man. [16]And I heard a man's voice between the banks of the Ū'laī, and it called, "Gabriel, make this man understand the vision." [17]So he came near where I stood; and when he came, I was frightened and fell upon my face. But he said to me, "Understand, O son of man, that the vision is for the time of the end."

18 As he was speaking to me, I fell into a deep sleep with my face to the ground; but he touched me and set me on my feet. [19]He said, "Behold, I will make known to you what shall be at the latter end of the indignation; for it pertains to the appointed time of the end. [20]As for the ram which you saw with the two horns, these are the kings of Mē'dǐ·a̧ and Persia. [21]And the he-goat[q] is the king of Greece; and the great horn between his eyes is the first king. [22]As for the horn that was broken, in place of which four others arose, four kingdoms shall arise from his[r] nation, but not with his power. [23]And at the latter end of their rule, when the transgressors have reached their full measure, a king of bold countenance, one who understands riddles, shall arise. [24]His power shall be great,[s] and he shall cause fearful destruction, and shall succeed in what he does, and destroy mighty men and the people of the saints. [25]By his cunning he shall make deceit prosper under his hand, and in his own mind he shall magnify himself. Without warning he shall destroy many; and he shall even rise up against the Prince of princes; but, by no human hand, he shall be broken. [26]The vision of the evenings and the mornings which has been told is true; but seal up the vision, for it pertains to many days hence."

27 And I, Daniel, was overcome and lay sick for some days; then I rose and went about the king's business; but I was appalled by the vision and did not understand it.

9 In the first year of Da̧·rī'ŭs the son of A̧·hǎṣ'ū·ē·rŭs, by birth a Mēde, who became king over the realm of the Chǎl-dē'anṣ—[2]in the first year of his reign, I, Daniel, perceived in the books the number of years which, according to the word of the LORD to Jĕr·ḗ·mī'a̧h the prophet, must pass before the end of the desolations of Jerusalem, namely, seventy years.

3 Then I turned my face to the Lord God, seeking him by prayer and supplications with fasting and sackcloth and ashes. [4]I prayed to the LORD my God and made confession, saying, "O Lord, the great and terrible God, who keepest covenant and steadfast love

---

[n] Heb obscure   [o] Heb obscure
[p] Theodotion Gk Syr Vg: Heb *me*   [q] Or *shaggy he-goat*
[r] Theodotion Gk Vg: Heb *the*
[s] Theodotion and Beatty papyrus of Gk: Heb repeats *but not with his power* from verse 22
8.10: Rev 12.4.   8.13: Lk 21.24.

with those who love him and keep his commandments, ⁵ we have sinned and done wrong and acted wickedly and rebelled, turning aside from thy commandments and ordinances; ⁶ we have not listened to thy servants the prophets, who spoke in thy name to our kings, our princes, and our fathers, and to all the people of the land. ⁷ To thee, O Lord, belongs righteousness, but to us confusion of face, as at this day, to the men of Judah, to the inhabitants of Jerusalem, and to all Israel, those that are near and those that are far away, in all the lands to which thou hast driven them, because of the treachery which they have committed against thee. ⁸ To us, O Lord, belongs confusion of face, to our kings, to our princes, and to our fathers, because we have sinned against thee. ⁹ To the Lord our God belong mercy and forgiveness; because we have rebelled against him, ¹⁰ and have not obeyed the voice of the LORD our God by following his laws, which he set before us by his servants the prophets. ¹¹ All Israel has transgressed thy law and turned aside, refusing to obey thy voice. And the curse and oath which are written in the law of Moses the servant of God have been poured out upon us, because we have sinned against him. ¹² He has confirmed his words, which he spoke against us and against our rulers who ruled us, by bringing upon us a great calamity; for under the whole heaven there has not been done the like of what has been done against Jerusalem. ¹³ As it is written in the law of Moses, all this calamity has come upon us, yet we have not entreated the favor of the LORD our God, turning from our iniquities and giving heed to thy truth. ¹⁴ Therefore the LORD has kept ready the calamity and has brought it upon us; for the LORD our God is righteous in all the works which he has done, and we have not obeyed his voice. ¹⁵ And now, O Lord our God, who didst bring thy people out of the land of Egypt with a mighty hand, and hast made thee a name, as at this day, we have sinned, we have done wickedly. ¹⁶ O Lord, according to all thy righteous acts, let thy anger and thy wrath turn away from thy city Jerusalem, thy holy hill; because for our sins, and for the iniquities of our fathers, Jerusalem and thy people have become a byword among all who are round about us. ¹⁷ Now therefore, O our God, hearken to the prayer of thy servant and to his supplications, and for thy own sake, O Lord,ᶠ cause thy face to shine upon thy sanctuary, which is desolate. ¹⁸ O my God, incline thy ear and hear; open thy eyes and behold our desolations, and the city which is called by thy name; for we do not present our supplications before thee on the ground of our righteousness, but on the ground of thy great mercy. ¹⁹ O LORD, hear; O LORD, forgive; O LORD, give heed and act; delay not, for thy own sake, O my God, because thy city and thy people are called by thy name."

20 While I was speaking and praying, confessing my sin and the sin of my people Israel, and presenting my supplication before the LORD my God for the holy hill of my God; ²¹ while I was speaking in prayer, the man Gabriel, whom I had seen in the vision at the first, came to me in swift flight at the time of the evening sacrifice. ²² He cameᵘ and he said to me, "O Daniel, I have now come out to give you wisdom and understanding. ²³ At the beginning of your supplications a word went forth, and I have come to tell it to you, for you are greatly beloved; therefore consider the word and understand the vision.

24 "Seventy weeks of years are decreed concerning your people and your holy city, to finish the transgression, to put an end to sin, and to atone for iniquity, to bring in everlasting righteousness, to seal both vision and prophet, and to anoint a most holy place.ᵛ ²⁵ Know therefore and understand that from the going forth of the word to restore and build Jerusalem to the coming of an anointed one, a prince, there shall be seven weeks. Then for sixty-two weeks it shall be built again with squares and moat, but in a troubled time. ²⁶ And after the sixty-two weeks, an anointed one shall be cut off, and shall have nothing; and the people of the prince who is to come shall destroy the city and the sanctuary. Itsʷ end shall come with a flood, and to the end there shall be war; desolations are decreed. ²⁷ And he shall

ᶠ Theodotion Vg Compare Syr: Heb *for the Lord's sake*
ᵘ Gk Syr: Heb *made to understand* ᵛ Or *thing* or *one*
ʷ Or *his*   **9.27:** Dan 11.31; 12.11; Mt 24.15; Mk 13.14.

make a strong covenant with many for one week; and for half of the week he shall cause sacrifice and offering to cease; and upon the wing of abominations shall come one who makes desolate, until the decreed end is poured out on the desolator."

10 In the third year of Cyrus king of Persia a word was revealed to Daniel, who was named Bĕl·tĕ·shăz'-zar. And the word was true, and it was a great conflict. And he understood the word and had understanding of the vision.

2 In those days I, Daniel, was mourning for three weeks. ³I ate no delicacies, no meat or wine entered my mouth, nor did I anoint myself at all, for the full three weeks. ⁴On the twenty-fourth day of the first month, as I was standing on the bank of the great river, that is, the Tigris, ⁵I lifted up my eyes and looked, and behold, a man clothed in linen, whose loins were girded with gold of Ū'phăz. ⁶His body was like beryl, his face like the appearance of lightning, his eyes like flaming torches, his arms and legs like the gleam of burnished bronze, and the sound of his words like the noise of a multitude. ⁷And I, Daniel, alone saw the vision, for the men who were with me did not see the vision, but a great trembling fell upon them, and they fled to hide themselves. ⁸So I was left alone and saw this great vision, and no strength was left in me; my radiant appearance was fearfully changed, and I retained no strength. ⁹Then I heard the sound of his words; and when I heard the sound of his words, I fell on my face in a deep sleep with my face to the ground.

10 And behold, a hand touched me and set me trembling on my hands and knees. ¹¹And he said to me, "O Daniel, man greatly beloved, give heed to the words that I speak to you, and stand upright, for now I have been sent to you." While he was speaking this word to me, I stood up trembling. ¹²Then he said to me, "Fear not, Daniel, for from the first day that you set your mind to understand and humbled yourself before your God, your words have been heard, and I have come because of your words. ¹³The prince of the kingdom of Persia withstood me twenty-one days; but Michael, one of the chief princes, came to help me, so I left him

there with the prince of the kingdom of Persia*ˣ* ¹⁴and came to make you understand what is to befall your people in the latter days. For the vision is for days yet to come."

15 When he had spoken to me according to these words, I turned my face toward the ground and was dumb. ¹⁶And behold, one in the likeness of the sons of men touched my lips; then I opened my mouth and spoke. I said to him who stood before me, "O my lord, by reason of the vision pains have come upon me, and I retain no strength. ¹⁷How can my lord's servant talk with my lord? For now no strength remains in me, and no breath is left in me."

18 Again one having the appearance of a man touched me and strengthened me. ¹⁹And he said, "O man greatly beloved, fear not, peace be with you; be strong and of good courage." And when he spoke to me, I was strengthened and said, "Let my lord speak, for you have strengthened me." ²⁰Then he said, "Do you know why I have come to you? But now I will return to fight against the prince of Persia; and when I am through with him, lo, the prince of Greece will come. ²¹But I will tell you what is inscribed in the book of truth: there is none who contends by my side against these except

11 Michael, your prince. ¹And as for me, in the first year of Da-rī'ŭs the Mēde, I stood up to confirm and strengthen him.

2 "And now I will show you the truth. Behold, three more kings shall arise in Persia; and a fourth shall be far richer than all of them; and when he has become strong through his riches, he shall stir up all against the kingdom of Greece. ³Then a mighty king shall arise, who shall rule with great dominion and do according to his will. ⁴And when he has arisen, his kingdom shall be broken and divided toward the four winds of heaven, but not to his posterity, nor according to the dominion with which he ruled; for his kingdom shall be plucked up and go to others besides these.

5 "Then the king of the south shall be strong, but one of his princes shall be stronger than he and his dominion

shall be a great dominion. [6]After some years they shall make an alliance, and the daughter of the king of the south shall come to the king of the north to make peace; but she shall not retain the strength of her arm, and he and his offspring shall not endure; but she shall be given up, and her attendants, her child, and he who got possession of[y] her.

7 "In those times a branch[z] from her roots shall arise in his place; he shall come against the army and enter the fortress of the king of the north, and he shall deal with them and shall prevail. [8]He shall also carry off to Egypt their gods with their molten images and with their precious vessels of silver and of gold; and for some years he shall refrain from attacking the king of the north. [9]Then the latter shall come into the realm of the king of the south but shall return into his own land.

10 "His sons shall wage war and assemble a multitude of great forces, which shall come on and overflow and pass through, and again shall carry the war as far as his fortress. [11]Then the king of the south, moved with anger, shall come out and fight with the king of the north; and he shall raise a great multitude, but it shall be given into his hand. [12]And when the multitude is taken, his heart shall be exalted, and he shall cast down tens of thousands, but he shall not prevail. [13]For the king of the north shall again raise a multitude, greater than the former; and after some years[a] he shall come on with a great army and abundant supplies.

14 "In those times many shall rise against the king of the south; and the men of violence among your own people shall lift themselves up in order to fulfil the vision; but they shall fail. [15]Then the king of the north shall come and throw up siegeworks, and take a well-fortified city. And the forces of the south shall not stand, or even his picked troops, for there shall be no strength to stand. [16]But he who comes against him shall do according to his own will, and none shall stand before him; and he shall stand in the glorious land, and all of it shall be in his power. [17]He shall set his face to come with the strength of his whole kingdom, and he shall bring terms of peace[b]

and perform them. He shall give him the daughter of women to destroy the kingdom;[c] but it shall not stand or be to his advantage. [18]Afterward he shall turn his face to the coastlands, and shall take many of them; but a commander shall put an end to his insolence; indeed[d] he shall turn his insolence back upon him. [19]Then he shall turn his face back toward the fortresses of his own land; but he shall stumble and fall, and shall not be found.

20 "Then shall arise in his place one who shall send an exactor of tribute through the glory of the kingdom; but within a few days he shall be broken, neither in anger nor in battle. [21]In his place shall arise a contemptible person to whom royal majesty has not been given; he shall come in without warning and obtain the kingdom by flatteries. [22]Armies shall be utterly swept away before him and broken, and the prince of the covenant also. [23]And from the time that an alliance is made with him he shall act deceitfully; and he shall become strong with a small people. [24]Without warning he shall come into the richest parts[e] of the province; and he shall do what neither his fathers nor his fathers' fathers have done, scattering among them plunder, spoil, and goods. He shall devise plans against strongholds, but only for a time. [25]And he shall stir up his power and his courage against the king of the south with a great army; and the king of the south shall wage war with an exceedingly great and mighty army; but he shall not stand, for plots shall be devised against him. [26]Even those who eat his rich food shall be his undoing; his army shall be swept away, and many shall fall down slain. [27]And as for the two kings, their minds shall be bent on mischief; they shall speak lies at the same table, but to no avail; for the end is yet to be at the time appointed. [28]And he shall return to his land with great substance, but his heart shall be set against the holy covenant. And he shall work his will, and return to his own land.

29 "At the time appointed he shall

[y]Or supported   [z]Gk: Heb *from a branch*
[a]Heb *at the end of the times years*
[b]Gk: Heb *upright ones*   [c]Heb *her* or *it*
[d]Heb obscure   [e]Or *among the richest men*

return and come into the south; but it shall not be this time as it was before. ³⁰ For ships of Kit'tim shall come against him, and he shall be afraid and withdraw, and shall turn back and be enraged and take action against the holy covenant. He shall turn back and give heed to those who forsake the holy covenant. ³¹ Forces from him shall appear and profane the temple and fortress, and shall take away the continual burnt offering. And they shall set up the abomination that makes desolate. ³² He shall seduce with flattery those who violate the covenant; but the people who know their God shall stand firm and take action. ³³ And those among the people who are wise shall make many understand, though they shall fall by sword and flame, by captivity and plunder, for some days. ³⁴ When they fall, they shall receive a little help. And many shall join themselves to them with flattery; ³⁵ and some of those who are wise shall fall, to refine and to cleanse them' and to make them white, until the time of the end, for it is yet for the time appointed.

36 "And the king shall do according to his will; he shall exalt himself and magnify himself above every god, and shall speak astonishing things against the God of gods. He shall prosper till the indignation is accomplished; for what is determined shall be done. ³⁷ He shall give no heed to the gods of his fathers, or to the one beloved by women; he shall not give heed to any other god, for he shall magnify himself above all. ³⁸ He shall honor the god of fortresses instead of these; a god whom his fathers did not know he shall honor with gold and silver, with precious stones and costly gifts. ³⁹ He shall deal with the strongest fortresses by the help of a foreign god; those who acknowledge him he shall magnify with honor. He shall make them rulers over many and shall divide the land for a price.

40 "At the time of the end the king of the south shall attack⁹ him; but the king of the north shall rush upon him like a whirlwind, with chariots and horsemen, and with many ships; and he shall come into countries and shall overflow and pass through. ⁴¹ He shall come into the glorious land. And tens of thousands shall fall, but these shall be delivered out of his hand: E'dom and Mō'ăb and the main part of the Ăm'mo·nītes. ⁴² He shall stretch out his hand against the countries, and the land of Egypt shall not escape. ⁴³ He shall become ruler of the treasures of gold and of silver, and all the precious things of Egypt; and the Libyans and the Ethiopians shall follow in his train. ⁴⁴ But tidings from the east and the north shall alarm him, and he shall go forth with great fury to exterminate and utterly destroy many. ⁴⁵ And he shall pitch his palatial tents between the sea and the glorious holy mountain; yet he shall come to his end, with none to help him.

12 "At that time shall arise Michael, the great prince who has charge of your people. And there shall be a time of trouble, such as never has been since there was a nation till that time; but at that time your people shall be delivered, every one whose name shall be found written in the book. ² And many of those who sleep in the dust of the earth shall awake, some to everlasting life, and some to shame and everlasting contempt. ³ And those who are wise shall shine like the brightness of the firmament; and those who turn many to righteousness, like the stars for ever and ever. ⁴ But you, Daniel, shut up the words, and seal the book, until the time of the end. Many shall run to and fro, and knowledge shall increase."

5 Then I Daniel looked, and behold, two others stood, one on this bank of the stream and one on that bank of the stream. ⁶ And Iʰ said to the man clothed in linen, who was above the waters of the stream, "How long shall it be till the end of these wonders?" ⁷ The man clothed in linen, who was above the waters of the stream, raised his right hand and his left hand toward heaven; and I heard him swear by him who lives for ever that it would be for a time, two times, and half a time and that when the shattering of the power of the holy people comes to an end all these things would be accomplished. ⁸ I heard, but I did not under

ᶠGk: Heb among them ᵍHeb thrust at
ʰGk Vg: Heb he
11.31: Dan 9.27; 12.11; Mt 24.15; Mk 13.14.
11.36: Ezek 28.2; 2 Thess 2.4; Rev 13.5.
12.1: Mt 24.21; Mk 13.19; Rev 12.7; 16.18.   12.2: Mt 25.46
12.3: Mt 13.43.   12.4: Rev 22.10.
12.7: Rev 4.9; 10.5; 12.14.

stand. Then I said, "O my lord, what shall be the issue of these things?" [9]He said, "Go your way, Daniel, for the words are shut up and sealed until the time of the end. [10]Many shall purify themselves, and make themselves white, and be refined; but the wicked shall do wickedly; and none of the wicked shall understand; but those who are wise shall understand. [11]And from the time that the continual burnt offering is taken away, and the abomination that makes desolate is set up, there shall be a thousand two hundred and ninety days. [12]Blessed is he who waits and comes to the thousand three hundred and thirty-five days. [13]But go your way till the end; and you shall rest, and shall stand in your allotted place at the end of the days."

The Book of
Hosea

1 The word of the LORD that came to Hō·sē'a the son of Bě·ē'rī, in the days of Ŭz·zī'ah, Jō'tham, Ā'hăz, and Hěz·ę·kī'ah, kings of Judah, and in the days of Jěr·ǫ·bō'ǎm the son of Jō'ǎsh, king of Israel.

2 When the LORD first spoke through Hō·sē'a, the LORD said to Hosea, "Go, take to yourself a wife of harlotry and have children of harlotry, for the land commits great harlotry by forsaking the LORD." [3]So he went and took Gō'mẹr the daughter of Dĭb·lā'ĭm, and she conceived and bore him a son.

4 And the LORD said to him, "Call his name Jěz·rē'ẹl; for yet a little while, and I will punish the house of Jē'hū for the blood of Jezreel, and I will put an end to the kingdom of the house of Israel. [5]And on that day, I will break the bow of Israel in the valley of Jěz·rē'ẹl."

6 She conceived again and bore a daughter. And the LORD said to him, "Call her name Not pitied, for I will no more have pity on the house of Israel, to forgive them at all. [7]But I will have pity on the house of Judah, and I will deliver them by the LORD their God; I will not deliver them by bow, nor by sword, nor by war, nor by horses, nor by horsemen."

8 When she had weaned Not pitied, she conceived and bore a son. [9]And the LORD said, "Call his name Not my people, for you are not my people and I am not your God."[a]

10[b] Yet the number of the people of Israel shall be like the sand of the sea, which can be neither measured nor numbered; and in the place where it was said to them, "You are not my people," it shall be said to them, "Sons of the living God." [11]And the people of Judah and the people of Israel shall be gathered together, and they shall appoint for themselves one head; and they shall go up from the land, for great shall be the day of Jěz·rē'ẹl.

2[c] Say to your brother,[d] "My people," and to your sister,[e] "She has obtained pity."

[2] "Plead with your mother, plead—
for she is not my wife,
    and I am not her husband—
that she put away her harlotry from her face,
    and her adultery from between her breasts;
[3] lest I strip her naked
    and make her as in the day she was born,
and make her like a wilderness,
    and set her like a parched land,
    and slay her with thirst.
[4] Upon her children also I will have no pity,
    because they are children of harlotry.
[5] For their mother has played the harlot;

12.11: Dan 9.27; 11.31; Mt 24.15; Mk 13.14.
[a]Heb *I am not yours* [b]Ch 2.1 in Heb [c]Ch 2.3 in Heb
[d]Gk: Heb *brothers* [e]Gk Vg: Heb *sisters*
1.6, 9: Hos 2.23; 1 Pet 2.10.
1.10: Rom 9.26. 2.1, 23: Rom 9.25; 1 Pet 2.10.

she that conceived them has
acted shamefully.
For she said, 'I will go after my lovers,
who give me my bread and my
water,
my wool and my flax, my oil and
my drink.'
⁶Therefore I will hedge up herᶠ way
with thorns;
and I will build a wall against her,
so that she cannot find her paths.
⁷She shall pursue her lovers,
but not overtake them;
and she shall seek them,
but shall not find them.
Then she shall say, 'I will go
and return to my first husband,
for it was better with me then
than now.'
⁸And she did not know
that it was I who gave her
the grain, the wine, and the oil,
and who lavished upon her silver
and gold which they used for Bā'al.
⁹Therefore I will take back
my grain in its time,
and my wine in its season;
and I will take away my wool and my
flax,
which were to cover her nakedness.
¹⁰Now I will uncover her lewdness
in the sight of her lovers,
and no one shall rescue her out of
my hand.
¹¹And I will put an end to all her mirth,
her feasts, her new moons, her sabbaths,
and all her appointed feasts.
¹²And I will lay waste her vines and
her fig trees,
of which she said,
'These are my hire,
which my lovers have given me.'
I will make them a forest,
and the beasts of the field shall
devour them.
¹³And I will punish her for the feast
days of the Bā'als
when she burned incense to them
and decked herself with her ring
and jewelry,
and went after her lovers,
and forgot me, says the LORD.

¹⁴"Therefore, behold, I will allure her,
and bring her into the wilderness,
and speak tenderly to her.
¹⁵And there I will give her her vineyards,

and make the Valley of Ā'chôr
a door of hope.
And there she shall answer as in
the days of her youth,
as at the time when she came
out of the land of Egypt.
¹⁶"And in that day, says the LORD,
you will call me, 'My husband,' and no
longer will you call me, 'My Bā'al.'
¹⁷For I will remove the names of the
Bā'als from her mouth, and they shall
be mentioned by name no more. ¹⁸And
I will make for youᵍ a covenant on that
day with the beasts of the field, the
birds of the air, and the creeping things
of the ground; and I will abolishʰ the
bow, the sword, and war from the land;
and I will make you lie down in safety.
¹⁹And I will betroth you to me for
ever; I will betroth you to me in righteousness and in justice, in steadfast
love, and in mercy. ²⁰I will betroth you
to me in faithfulness; and you shall
know the LORD.
²¹"And in that day, says the LORD,
I will answer the heavens
and they shall answer the earth;
²²and the earth shall answer the grain,
the wine, and the oil,
and they shall answer Jĕz·rē'el,ⁱ
²³ and I will sow himʲ for myself in
the land.
And I will have pity on Not pitied,
and I will say to Not my people,
'You are my people';
and he shall say, 'Thou art my
God.'"

3 And the LORD said to me, "Go
again, love a woman who is beloved of a paramour and is an adulteress; even as the LORD loves the
people of Israel, though they turn to
other gods and love cakes of raisins."
²So I bought her for fifteen shekels of
silver and a homer and a lethech of
barley. ³And I said to her, "You must
dwell as mine for many days; you shall
not play the harlot, or belong to
another man; so will I also be to you."
⁴For the children of Israel shall dwell
many days without king or prince,
without sacrifice or pillar, without
ephod or teraphim. ⁵Afterward the
children of Israel shall return and seek
the LORD their God, and David their
king; and they shall come in fear to the
LORD and to his goodness in the latter
days.

ᶠGk Syr: Heb *your*   ᵍHeb *them*   ʰHeb *break*
ⁱThat is *God sows*   ʲCn: Heb *her*

4 Hear the word of the Lord, O
    people of Israel;
  for the Lord has a controversy
    with the inhabitants of the land.
There is no faithfulness or kindness,
  and no knowledge of God in the
    land;
² there is swearing, lying, killing,
  stealing, and committing adul-
    tery;
  they break all bounds and murder
    follows murder.
³ Therefore the land mourns,
  and all who dwell in it languish,
and also the beasts of the field,
  and the birds of the air;
  and even the fish of the sea are
    taken away.

⁴ Yet let no one contend,
  and let none accuse,
  for with you is my contention, O
    priest.[k]
⁵ You shall stumble by day,
  the prophet also shall stumble with
    you by night;
  and I will destroy your mother.
⁶ My people are destroyed for lack
  of knowledge;
  because you have rejected knowl-
    edge,
  I reject you from being a priest
    to me.
And since you have forgotten the
  law of your God,
  I also will forget your children.

⁷ The more they increased,
  the more they sinned against me;
  I will change their glory into
    shame.
⁸ They feed on the sin of my people;
  they are greedy for their iniquity.
⁹ And it shall be like people, like
  priest;
  I will punish them for their ways,
  and requite them for their deeds.
¹⁰ They shall eat, but not be satisfied;
  they shall play the harlot, but not
    multiply;
because they have forsaken the Lord
  to cherish harlotry.

¹ Wine and new wine
  take away the understanding.
² My people inquire of a thing of
  wood,
  and their staff gives them oracles.
For a spirit of harlotry has led them
  astray,

and they have left their God to play
  the harlot.
¹³ They sacrifice on the tops of the
  mountains,
  and make offerings upon the hills,
under oak, poplar, and terebinth,
  because their shade is good.

Therefore your daughters play the
  harlot,
  and your brides commit adultery.
¹⁴ I will not punish your daughters
  when they play the harlot,
  nor your brides when they commit
    adultery;
for the men themselves go aside with
  harlots,
  and sacrifice with cult prostitutes,
and a people without understanding
  shall come to ruin.

¹⁵ Though you play the harlot, O Israel,
  let not Judah become guilty.
Enter not into Gil'gal,
  nor go up to Bĕth-ā'vĕn,
  and swear not, "As the Lord
    lives."
¹⁶ Like a stubborn heifer,
  Israel is stubborn;
  can the Lord now feed them
  like a lamb in a broad pasture?

¹⁷ Ē'phra·ĭm is joined to idols,
  let him alone.
¹⁸ A band[l] of drunkards, they give
  themselves to harlotry;
  they love shame more than their
    glory.[m]
¹⁹ A wind has wrapped them[n] in its
  wings,
  and they shall be ashamed be-
    cause of their altars.[o]

5 Hear this, O priests!
    Give heed, O house of Israel!
Hearken, O house of the king!
For the judgment pertains to you;
for you have been a snare at Mĭz'pah,
  and a net spread upon Tā'bôr.
² And they have made deep the pit of
  Shĭt'tĭm;[p]
  but I will chastise all of them.

³ I know Ē'phra·ĭm,
  and Israel is not hid from me;
  for now, O Ephraim, you have played
    the harlot,

---

[k]Cn: Heb uncertain   [l]Cn: Heb uncertain
[m]Cn Compare Gk: Heb of this line uncertain
[n]Heb *her*   [o]Gk Syr: Heb *sacrifices*   [p]Cn: Heb uncertain

Israel is defiled.

⁴Their deeds do not permit them
   to return to their God.
For the spirit of harlotry is within
   them,
   and they know not the LORD.

⁵The pride of Israel testifies to his
   face;
   Ē′phra·ĭm*ᵍ* shall stumble in his
   guilt;
   Judah also shall stumble with
   them.
⁶With their flocks and herds they shall
   go
   to seek the LORD,
but they will not find him;
   he has withdrawn from them.
⁷They have dealt faithlessly with the
   LORD;
   for they have borne alien children.
   Now the new moon shall devour
   them with their fields.

⁸Blow the horn in Gĭb′ē–ah,
   the trumpet in Rā′mah.
Sound the alarm at Bĕth–ā′vĕn;
   tremble,ʳ O Benjamin!
⁹Ē′phra·ĭm shall become a desolation
   in the day of punishment;
   among the tribes of Israel
   I declare what is sure.
¹⁰The princes of Judah have become
   like those who remove the landmark;
upon them I will pour out
   my wrath like water.
¹¹Ē′phra·ĭm is oppressed, crushed in
   judgment,
   because he was determined to go
   after vanity.ˢ
¹²Therefore I am like a moth to
   Ē′phra·ĭm,
   and like dry rot to the house of
   Judah.

¹³When Ē′phra·ĭm saw his sickness,
   and Judah his wound,
then Ephraim went to Assyria,
   and sent to the great king.ᵗ
But he is not able to cure you
   or heal your wound.
¹⁴For I will be like a lion to Ē′phra·ĭm,
   and like a young lion to the house
   of Judah.
I, even I, will rend and go away,
   I will carry off, and none shall
   rescue.

¹⁵I will return again to my place,
   until they acknowledge their guilt
   and seek my face,
   and in their distress they seek me,
   saying,

6 "Come, let us return to the LORD;
   for he has torn, that he may heal
   us;
   he has stricken and he will bind
   us up.
²After two days he will revive us;
   on the third day he will raise us
   up,
   that we may live before him.
³Let us know, let us press on to know
   the LORD;
   his going forth is sure as the dawn;
he will come to us as the showers,
   as the spring rains that water the
   earth."

⁴What shall I do with you, O
   Ē′phra·ĭm?
   What shall I do with you, O Judah?
Your love is like a morning cloud,
   like the dew that goes early away.
⁵Therefore I have hewn them by the
   prophets,
   I have slain them by the words of
   my mouth,
   and my judgment goes forth as
   the light.ᵘ
⁶For I desire steadfast love and not
   sacrifice,
   the knowledge of God, rather than
   burnt offerings.

⁷But atᵛ Adam they transgressed the
   covenant;
   there they dealt faithlessly with
   me.
⁸Gilead is a city of evildoers,
   tracked with blood.
⁹As robbers lie in waitʷ for a man,
   so the priests are banded together;ˣ
they murder on the way to Shē′chĕm,
   yea, they commit villainy.
¹⁰In the house of Israel I have seen a
   horrible thing;
   Ē′phra·ĭm's harlotry is there, Israel
   is defiled.

¹¹For you also, O Judah, a harvest is
   appointed.

ᵍHeb *Israel and Ephraim*
ʳCn Compare Gk: Heb *after you*   ˢGk: Heb *a command*
ᵗCn: Heb *a king that will contend*
ᵘGk Syr: Heb *thy judgment goes forth*   ᵛCn: Heb *like*
ʷCn: Heb uncertain   ˣSyr: Heb *a company*
6.6: Mt 9.13; 12.7.

When I would restore the fortunes
  of my people,

7 ¹when I would heal Israel,
  the corruption of Ē′phra·ĭm is revealed,
    and the wicked deeds of Sạ-
    mâr′ĭ·ạ;
  for they deal falsely,
    the thief breaks in,
    and the bandits raid without.
²But they do not consider
    that I remember all their evil
    works.
Now their deeds encompass them,
  they are before my face.
³By their wickedness they make the
    king glad,
  and the princes by their treachery.
⁴They are all adulterers;
  they are like a heated oven,
whose baker ceases to stir the fire,
    from the kneading of the dough
    until it is leavened.
⁵On the day of our king the princes
    became sick with the heat of
    wine;
    he stretched out his hand with
    mockers.
⁶For like an oven their hearts burnʸ
    with intrigue;
    all night their anger smolders;
    in the morning it blazes like a
    flaming fire.
⁷All of them are hot as an oven,
  and they devour their rulers.
All their kings have fallen;
  and none of them calls upon me.

⁸Ē′phra·ĭm mixes himself with the
    peoples;
  Ephraim is a cake not turned.
⁹Aliens devour his strength,
  and he knows it not;
gray hairs are sprinkled upon him,
  and he knows it not.
¹⁰The pride of Israel witnesses against
    him;
    yet they do not return to the
    LORD their God,
    nor seek him, for all this.

¹¹Ē′phra·ĭm is like a dove,
  silly and without sense,
  calling to Egypt, going to Assyria.
¹²As they go, I will spread over them
    my net;
    I will bring them down like birds
    of the air;
    I will chastise them for their
    wicked deeds. ᶻ

¹³Woe to them, for they have strayed
  from me!
Destruction to them, for they have
    rebelled against me!
I would redeem them,
  but they speak lies against me.

¹⁴They do not cry to me from the heart,
  but they wail upon their beds;
  for grain and wine they gash them-
    selves,
  they rebel against me.
¹⁵Although I trained and strengthened
    their arms,
  yet they devise evil against me.
¹⁶They turn to Bā′al;ᵃ
  they are like a treacherous bow,
their princes shall fall by the sword
    because of the insolence of their
    tongue.
This shall be their derision in the
    land of Egypt.

8 Set the trumpet to your lips,
  forᵇ a vulture is over the house of
    the LORD,
because they have broken my
    covenant,
  and transgressed my law.
²To me they cry,
  My God, we Israel know thee.
³Israel has spurned the good;
  the enemy shall pursue him.

⁴They made kings, but not through
    me.
    They set up princes, but without
    my knowledge.
With their silver and gold they made
    idols
  for their own destruction.
⁵I haveᶜ spurned your calf, O Sạ-
    mâr′ĭ·ạ.
  My anger burns against them.
How long will it be
  till they are pure ⁶in Israel?ᵈ

A workman made it;
  it is not God.
The calf of Sạ·mâr′ĭ·ạ
  shall be broken to pieces. ᵉ

⁷For they sow the wind,
  and they shall reap the whirlwind.
The standing grain has no heads,
  it shall yield no meal;

ʸGk Syr: Heb **brought near**
ᶻCn: Heb **according to the report to their congregation**
ᵃCn: Heb uncertain ᵇCn: Heb **as** ᶜHeb **He has**
ᵈGk: Heb **for from Israel** ᵉOr **shall go up in flames**

if it were to yield,
    aliens would devour it.
8 Israel is swallowed up;
    already they are among the nations
    as a useless vessel.
9 For they have gone up to Assyria,
    a wild ass wandering alone;
    E'phra·im has hired lovers.
10 Though they hire allies among the
    nations,
I will soon gather them up.
And they shall cease*f* for a little while
    from anointing*g* king and princes.

11 Because E'phra·im has multiplied
    altars for sinning,
    they have become to him altars
    for sinning.
12 Were I to write for him my laws by
    ten thousands,
    they would be regarded as a
    strange thing.
13 They love sacrifice;*h*
    they sacrifice flesh and eat it;
    but the LORD has no delight in
    them.
Now he will remember their iniquity,
    and punish their sins;
    they shall return to Egypt.
14 For Israel has forgotten his Maker,
    and built palaces;
and Judah has multiplied fortified
    cities;
    but I will send a fire upon his
    cities,
    and it shall devour his strongholds.

9   Rejoice not, O Israel!
    Exult not*i* like the peoples;
for you have played the harlot,
    forsaking your God.
You have loved a harlot's hire
    upon all threshing floors.
2 Threshing floor and winevat shall
    not feed them,
    and the new wine shall fail them.
3 They shall not remain in the land of
    the LORD;
    but E'phra'im shall return to
    Egypt,
    and they shall eat unclean food
    in Assyria.

4 They shall not pour libations of wine
    to the LORD;
    and they shall not please him with
    their sacrifices.
Their bread*j* shall be like mourners'
    bread;
    all who eat of it shall be defiled;

for their bread shall be for their
    hunger only;
it shall not come to the house of the
    LORD.

5 What will you do on the day of ap-
    pointed festival,
    and on the day of the feast of the
    LORD?
6 For behold, they are going to Assyria;*k*
    Egypt shall gather them,
    Memphis shall bury them.
Nettles shall possess their precious
    things of silver;
    thorns shall be in their tents.

7 The days of punishment have come,
    the days of recompense have
    come;
    Israel shall know it.
The prophet is a fool,
    the man of the spirit is mad,
because of your great iniquity
    and great hatred.
8 The prophet is the watchman of
    E'phra'im,
    the people of my God,
yet a fowler's snare is on all his ways,
    and hatred in the house of his God.
9 They have deeply corrupted them-
    selves
    as in the days of Gĭb'ē–ah:
he will remember their iniquity,
    he will punish their sins.

10 Like grapes in the wilderness,
    I found Israel.
Like the first fruit on the fig tree,
    in its first season,
    I saw your fathers.
But they came to Bā'al–pē'ôr,
    and consecrated themselves to
    Bā'al,*l*
    and became detestable like the
    thing they loved.
11 E'phra'im's glory shall fly away
    like a bird—
    no birth, no pregnancy, no con-
    ception!
12 Even if they bring up children,
    I will bereave them till none is
    left.
Woe to them
    when I depart from them!
13 E'phra'im's sons, as I have seen,
    are destined for a prey;*m*

f Gk: Heb *begin*   *g* Gk: Heb *burden*   *h* Cn: Heb uncertain
i Gk: Heb *to exultation*   *j* Cn: Heb *to them*
k Cn: Heb *from destruction*   *l* Heb *shame*
m Cn Compare Gk: Heb uncertain
8.14: Amos 1.4, 7, 10, 12, 14; 2.2, 5.   **9.7:** Lk 21.22.

Ephraim must lead forth his sons
to slaughter.
¹⁴ Give them, O LORD —
what wilt thou give?
Give them a miscarrying womb
and dry breasts.

¹⁵ Every evil of theirs is in Gĭl′gạl;
there I began to hate them.
Because of the wickedness of their
deeds
I will drive them out of my house.
I will love them no more;
all their princes are rebels.

¹⁶ Ē′phrạ·ĭm is stricken,
their root is dried up,
they shall bear no fruit.
Even though they bring forth,
I will slay their beloved children.
¹⁷ My God will cast them off,
because they have not hearkened
to him;
they shall be wanderers among the
nations.

10 Israel is a luxuriant vine
that yields its fruit.
The more his fruit increased
the more altars he built;
as his country improved
he improved his pillars.
² Their heart is false;
now they must bear their guilt.
The LORD[n] will break down their
altars,
and destroy their pillars.

³ For now they will say:
"We have no king,
for we fear not the LORD,
and a king, what could he do for
us?"
⁴ They utter mere words;
with empty oaths they make covenants;
so judgment springs up like poisonous weeds
in the furrows of the field.
⁵ The inhabitants of Sạ·mâr′ĭ·ạ tremble
for the calf[o] of Bĕth-ā′vẹn.
Its people shall mourn for it,
and its idolatrous priests shall
wail[p] over it,
over its glory which has departed
from it.
⁶ Yea, the thing itself shall be carried
to Assyria,
as tribute to the great king.[q]

Ē′phrạ·ĭm shall be put to shame,
and Israel shall be ashamed of his
idol.[r]

⁷ Sạ·mâr′ĭ·ạ's king shall perish,
like a chip on the face of the
waters.
⁸ The high places of Ā′vẹn, the sin of
Israel,
shall be destroyed.
Thorn and thistle shall grow up
on their altars;
and they shall say to the mountains,
Cover us,
and to the hills, Fall upon us.

⁹ From the days of Gĭb′ē–ạh, you have
sinned, O Israel;
there they have continued.
Shall not war overtake them in
Gibe–ah?
¹⁰ I will come[s] against the wayward
people to chastise them;
and nations shall be gathered
against them
when they are chastised[t] for their
double iniquity.

¹¹ Ē′phrạ·ĭm was a trained heifer
that loved to thresh,
and I spared her fair neck;
but I will put Ephraim to the yoke,
Judah must plow,
Jacob must harrow for himself.
¹² Sow for yourselves righteousness,
reap the fruit[u] of steadfast love;
break up your fallow ground,
for it is the time to seek the LORD,
that he may come and rain salvation upon you.

¹³ You have plowed iniquity,
you have reaped injustice,
you have eaten the fruit of lies.
Because you have trusted in your
chariots[v]
and in the multitude of your warriors,   )
¹⁴ therefore the tumult of war shall
arise among your people,
and all your fortresses shall be
destroyed,
as Shăl′man destroyed Bĕth-âr′-
bel on the day of battle;
mothers were dashed in pieces
with their children.

ⁿHeb *he* ᵒGk Syr: Heb *calves* ᵖCn: Heb *exult*
ᵠCn: Heb *a king that will contend* ʳCn: Heb *counsel*
ˢCn Compare Gk: Heb *in my desire* ᵗGk: Heb *bound*
ᵘGk: Heb *according to* ᵛGk: Heb *way*
10.8: Lk 23.30; Rev 6.16. **10.12:** 2 Cor 9.10.

¹⁵ Thus it shall be done to you, O house
of Israel,*ʷ*
because of your great wickedness.
In the storm*ˣ* the king of Israel
shall be utterly cut off.

11 When Israel was a child, I loved
him,
and out of Egypt I called my son.
² The more I*ʸ* called them,
the more they went from me;*ᶻ*
they kept sacrificing to the Bā′alṣ,
and burning incense to idols.

³ Yet it was I who taught Ē′phrạ·ĭm
to walk,
I took them up in my*ᵃ* arms;
but they did not know that I healed
them.
⁴ I led them with cords of compassion,*ᵇ*
with the bands of love,
and I became to them as one
who eases the yoke on their jaws,
and I bent down to them and fed
them.

⁵ They shall return to the land of
Egypt,
and Assyria shall be their king,
because they have refused to return to me.
⁶ The sword shall rage against their
cities,
consume the bars of their gates,
and devour them in their fortresses.*ᶜ*
⁷ My people are bent on turning away
from me;*ᵈ*
so they are appointed to the yoke,
and none shall remove it.

⁸ How can I give you up, O Ē′phrạ·ĭm!
How can I hand you over, O Israel!
How can I make you like Ăd′mạh!
How can I treat you like Zē·boi′-
ĭm!
My heart recoils within me,
my compassion grows warm and
tender.
⁹ I will not execute my fierce anger,
I will not again destroy Ē′phrạ·ĭm;
for I am God and not man,
the Holy One in your midst,
and I will not come to destroy.*ᵉ*

¹⁰ They shall go after the LORD,
he will roar like a lion;
yea, he will roar,
and his sons shall come trembling
from the west;

¹¹ they shall come trembling like birds
from Egypt,
and like doves from the land of
Assyria;
and I will return them to their
homes, says the LORD.
¹²ʲ Ē′phrạ·ĭm has encompassed me with
lies,
and the house of Israel with deceit;
but Judah is still known by*ᵍ* God,
and is faithful to the Holy One.

12 Ē′phrạ·ĭm herds the wind,
and pursues the east wind all
day long;
they multiply falsehood and violence;
they make a bargain with Assyria,
and oil is carried to Egypt.

² The LORD has an indictment against
Judah,
and will punish Jacob according
to his ways,
and requite him according to his
deeds.
³ In the womb he took his brother by
the heel,
and in his manhood he strove with
God.
⁴ He strove with the angel and prevailed,
he wept and sought his favor.
He met God at Bĕth′el,
⁵ the LORD the God of hosts,
the LORD is his name:
⁶ "So you, by the help of your God,
return,
hold fast to love and justice,
and wait continually for your God."

⁷ A trader, in whose hands are false
balances,
he loves to oppress.
⁸ Ē′phrạ·ĭm has said, "Ah, but I am
rich,
I have gained wealth for myself ";
but all his riches can never offset*ⁱ*
the guilt he has incurred.
⁹ I am the LORD your God
from the land of Egypt;
I will again make you dwell in tents,
as in the days of the appointed
feast.

*ʷ*Gk: Heb O *Bethel* *ˣ*Cn: Heb *dawn* *ʸ*Gk: Heb *they*
*ᶻ*Gk: Heb *them* *ᵃ*Gk Syr Vg: Heb *his* *ᵇ*Heb *man*
*ᶜ*Cn: Heb *counsels*
*ᵈ*The meaning of the Hebrew is uncertain
*ᵉ*Cn: Heb *into the city* *ᶠ*Ch 12.1 in Heb
*ᵍ*Cn Compare Gk: Heb *roams with*
*ʰ*Gk Syr: Heb *us* *ⁱ*Cn Compare Gk: Heb obscure
11.1: Mt 2.15. **12.8:** Rev 3.17.

10 I spoke to the prophets;
   it was I who multiplied visions,
   and through the prophets gave
      parables.
11 If there is iniquity in Gilead
   they shall surely come to nought;
   if in Gĭl'gal they sacrifice bulls,
   their altars also shall be like stone
      heaps
   on the furrows of the field.
12 (Jacob fled to the land of Är'am,
   there Israel did service for a wife,
   and for a wife he herded sheep.)
13 By a prophet the LORD brought
      Israel up from Egypt,
   and by a prophet he was preserved.
14 Ē'phra·ĭm has given bitter provoca-
      tion;
   so his LORD will leave his blood-
      guilt upon him,
   and will turn back upon him his
      reproaches.

13 When Ē'phra·ĭm spoke, men
      trembled;
   he was exalted in Israel;
   but he incurred guilt through
      Bā'al and died.
2 And now they sin more and more,
   and make for themselves molten
      images,
   idols skilfully made of their silver,
   all of them the work of crafts-
      men.
   Sacrifice to these, they say.[j]
   Men kiss calves!
3 Therefore they shall be like the
      morning mist
   or like the dew that goes early
      away,
   like the chaff that swirls from the
      threshing floor
   or like smoke from a window.

4 I am the LORD your God
   from the land of Egypt;
   you know no God but me,
   and besides me there is no savior.
5 It was I who knew you in the wil-
      derness,
   in the land of drought;
6 but when they had fed[k] to the full,
   they were filled, and their heart
      was lifted up;
   therefore they forgot me.
7 So I will be to them like a lion,
   like a leopard I will lurk beside
      the way.
8 I will fall upon them like a bear
   robbed of her cubs,

I will tear open their breast,
   and there I will devour them like a
      lion,
   as a wild beast would rend them.

9 I will destroy you, O Israel;
   who[l] can help you?
10 Where[m] now is your king, to save you;
   where are all[n] your princes,[o]
      to defend you[p] —
   those of whom you said,
   "Give me a king and princes"?
11 I have given you kings in my anger,
   and I have taken them away in
      my wrath.

12 The iniquity of Ē'phra·ĭm is bound
      up,
   his sin is kept in store.
13 The pangs of childbirth come for
      him,
   but he is an unwise son;
   for now he does not present himself
      at the mouth of the womb.

14 Shall I ransom them from the power
      of Shē'ōl?
   Shall I redeem them from Death?
   O Death, where[q] are your plagues?
   O Sheol, where[q] is your destruc-
      tion?
   Compassion is hid from my eyes.

15 Though he may flourish as the reed
      plant,[r]
   the east wind, the wind of the
      LORD, shall come,
   rising from the wilderness;
   and his fountain shall dry up,
   his spring shall be parched;
   it shall strip his treasury
   of every precious thing.
16s Sa·mâr'ĭ·a shall bear her guilt,
   because she has rebelled against
      her God;
   they shall fall by the sword,
   their little ones shall be dashed
      in pieces,
   and their pregnant women ripped
      open.

14 Return, O Israel, to the LORD
      your God,
   for you have stumbled because
      of your iniquity.

[j] Gk: Heb *to these they say sacrifices of*
[k] Cn: Heb *according to their pasture*
[l] Gk Syr: Heb *for in me*   [m] Gk Syr Vg: Heb *I will be*
[n] Cn: Heb *in all*   [o] Cn: Heb *cities*
[p] Cn Compare Gk: Heb *and your judges*
[q] Gk Syr: Heb *I will be*   [r] Cn: Heb *among brothers*
[s] Ch 14.1 in Heb   **13.14:** 1 Cor 15.55.

² Take with you words
  and return to the LORD;
say to him,
  "Take away all iniquity;
accept that which is good
  and we will render
  the fruit[t] of our lips.
³ Assyria shall not save us,
  we will not ride upon horses;
and we will say no more, 'Our God,'
  to the work of our hands.
In thee the orphan finds mercy."

⁴ I will heal their faithlessness;
  I will love them freely,
  for my anger has turned from
  them.
⁵ I will be as the dew to Israel;
  he shall blossom as the lily,
  he shall strike root as the poplar,[u]
⁶ his shoots shall spread out;
  his beauty shall be like the olive,
and his fragrance like Lebanon.
⁷ They shall return and dwell beneath
  my[v] shadow,
  they shall flourish as a garden;[w]
they shall blossom as the vine,
  their fragrance shall be like the
  wine of Lebanon.

⁸ O Ē′phra·im, what have I to do with
  idols?
  It is I who answer and look after
  you.[x]
I am like an evergreen cypress,
  from me comes your fruit.

⁹ Whoever is wise, let him understand
  these things;
  whoever is discerning, let him
  know them;
for the ways of the LORD are right,
  and the upright walk in them,
  but transgressors stumble in them.

The Book of
Joel

1 The word of the LORD that came
   to Jō·el, the son of Pĕ·thū′ĕl:

² Hear this, you aged men,
  give ear, all inhabitants of the
  land!
Has such a thing happened in your
  days,
  or in the days of your fathers?
³ Tell your children of it,
  and let your children tell their
  children,
  and their children another generation.

⁴ What the cutting locust left,
  the swarming locust has eaten.
What the swarming locust left,
  the hopping locust has eaten,
and what the hopping locust left,
  the destroying locust has eaten.

⁵ Awake, you drunkards, and weep;
  and wail, all you drinkers of wine,
because of the sweet wine,
  for it is cut off from your mouth.

⁶ For a nation has come up against my
  land,
  powerful and without number;
its teeth are lions' teeth,
  and it has the fangs of a lioness.
⁷ It has laid waste my vines,
  and splintered my fig trees;
it has stripped off their bark and
  thrown it down;
  their branches are made white.

⁸ Lament like a virgin girded with
  sackcloth
  for the bridegroom of her youth.
⁹ The cereal offering and the drink
  offering are cut off
  from the house of the LORD.
The priests mourn,
  the ministers of the LORD.
¹⁰ The fields are laid waste,
  the ground mourns;
  because the grain is destroyed,

[t] Gk Syr: Heb *bulls* [u] Cn: Heb *Lebanon*
[v] Heb *his* [w] Cn: Heb *they shall grow grain* [x] Heb *him*
14.2: Heb 13.15. **14.9:** Acts 13.10.
1.6: Rev 9.8.

the wine fails,
the oil languishes.

¹¹Be confounded, O tillers of the soil,
wail, O vinedressers,
for the wheat and the barley;
because the harvest of the field
has perished.
¹²The vine withers,
the fig tree languishes.
Pomegranate, palm, and apple,
all the trees of the field are withered;
and gladness fails
from the sons of men.

¹³Gird on sackcloth and lament, O
priests,
wail, O ministers of the altar.
Go in, pass the night in sackcloth,
O ministers of my God!
Because cereal offering and drink
offering
are withheld from the house of
your God.

¹⁴Sanctify a fast,
call a solemn assembly.
Gather the elders
and all the inhabitants of the land
to the house of the LORD your God;
and cry to the LORD.

¹⁵Alas for the day!
For the day of the LORD is near,
and as destruction from the Almighty it comes.
¹⁶Is not the food cut off
before our eyes,
joy and gladness
from the house of our God?

¹⁷The seed shrivels under the clods,ᵃ
the storehouses are desolate;
the granaries are ruined
because the grain has failed.
¹⁸How the beasts groan!
The herds of cattle are perplexed
because there is no pasture for them;
even the flocks of sheep are dismayed.

¹⁹Unto thee, O LORD, I cry.
For fire has devoured
the pastures of the wilderness,
and flame has burned
all the trees of the field.
²⁰Even the wild beasts cry to thee
because the water brooks are dried
up,

and fire has devoured
the pastures of the wilderness.

2 Blow the trumpet in Zion;
sound the alarm on my holy
mountain!
Let all the inhabitants of the land
tremble,
for the day of the LORD is coming,
it is near,
²a day of darkness and gloom,
a day of clouds and thick darkness!
Like blackness there is spread upon
the mountains
a great and powerful people;
their like has never been from of old,
nor will be again after them
through the years of all generations.

³Fire devours before them,
and behind them a flame burns.
The land is like the garden of Eden
before them,
but after them a desolate wilderness,
and nothing escapes them.

⁴Their appearance is like the appearance of horses,
and like war horses they run.
⁵As with the rumbling of chariots,
they leap on the tops of the mountains,
like the crackling of a flame of fire
devouring the stubble,
like a powerful army
drawn up for battle.

⁶Before them peoples are in anguish,
all faces grow pale.
⁷Like warriors they charge,
like soldiers they scale the wall.
They march each on his way,
they do not swerveᵇ from their
paths.
⁸They do not jostle one another,
each marches in his path;
they burst through the weapons
and are not halted.
⁹They leap upon the city,
they run upon the walls;
they climb up into the houses,
they enter through the windows
like a thief.

¹⁰The earth quakes before them,
the heavens tremble.

ᵃHeb uncertain ᵇGk Syr Vg: Heb *take a pledge*
2.4-5: Rev 9.7, 9. **2.10:** Rev 9.2.

The sun and the moon are darkened,
    and the stars withdraw their shin-
        ing.
11 The LORD utters his voice
    before his army,
for his host is exceedingly great;
    he that executes his word is power-
        ful.
For the day of the LORD is great and
    very terrible;
    who can endure it?

12 "Yet even now," says the LORD,
    "return to me with all your heart,
with fasting, with weeping, and with
    mourning;
13   and rend your hearts and not your
        garments."
Return to the LORD, your God,
    for he is gracious and merciful,
slow to anger, and abounding in
    steadfast love,
    and repents of evil.
14 Who knows whether he will not turn
    and repent,
    and leave a blessing behind him,
a cereal offering and a drink offer-
    ing
    for the LORD, your God?

15 Blow the trumpet in Zion;
    sanctify a fast;
call a solemn assembly;
16   gather the people.
Sanctify the congregation;
    assemble the elders;
gather the children,
    even nursing infants.
Let the bridegroom leave his room,
    and the bride her chamber.

17 Between the vestibule and the altar
    let the priests, the ministers of the
        LORD, weep
and say, "Spare thy people, O LORD,
    and make not thy heritage a re-
        proach,
    a byword among the nations.
Why should they say among the
    peoples,
    'Where is their God?'"

18 Then the LORD became jealous for
    his land,
    and had pity on his people.
19 The LORD answered and said to his
    people,
"Behold, I am sending to you
    grain, wine, and oil,
    and you will be satisfied;

and I will no more make you
    a reproach among the nations.

20 "I will remove the northerner far
    from you,
    and drive him into a parched
        and desolate land,
his front into the eastern sea,
    and his rear into the western
        sea;
the stench and foul smell of him will
    rise,
    for he has done great things.

21 "Fear not, O land;
    be glad and rejoice,
    for the LORD has done great things!
22 Fear not, you beasts of the field,
    for the pastures of the wilderness
        are green;
the tree bears its fruit,
    the fig tree and vine give their full
        yield.

23 "Be glad, O sons of Zion,
    and rejoice in the LORD, your God;
for he has given the early rain for
    your vindication,
he has poured down for you
    abundant rain,
    the early and the latter rain, as
        before.

24 "The threshing floors shall be full of
    grain,
    the vats shall overflow with wine
        and oil.
25 I will restore to you the years
    which the swarming locust has
        eaten,
the hopper, the destroyer, and the
    cutter,
    my great army, which I sent
        among you.

26 "You shall eat in plenty and be
    satisfied,
    and praise the name of the LORD
        your God,
who has dealt wondrously with
    you.
And my people shall never again be
    put to shame.
27 You shall know that I am in the
    midst of Israel,
    and that I, the LORD, am your
        God and there is none else.
And my people shall never again be
    put to shame.

2.11: Rev 6.17.

²⁸ᶜ"And it shall come to pass afterward,
that I will pour out my spirit on
all flesh;
your sons and your daughters shall
prophesy,
your old men shall dream dreams,
and your young men shall see
visions.
²⁹ Even upon the menservants and
maidservants
in those days, I will pour out my
spirit.

30 "And I will give portents in the
heavens and on the earth, blood and
fire and columns of smoke. ³¹ The sun
shall be turned to darkness, and the
moon to blood, before the great and
terrible day of the LORD comes. ³² And
it shall come to pass that all who call
upon the name of the LORD shall be
delivered; for in Mount Zion and in
Jerusalem there shall be those who
escape, as the LORD has said, and
among the survivors shall be those
whom the LORD calls.
3ᵈ "For behold, in those days and
at that time, when I restore the
fortunes of Judah and Jerusalem, ²I
will gather all the nations and bring
them down to the valley of Jĕ·hŏsh'a-
phăt, and I will enter into judgment
with them there, on account of my
people and my heritage Israel, because
they have scattered them among the
nations, and have divided up my land,
and have cast lots for my people, and
have given a boy for a harlot, and have
sold a girl for wine, and have drunk it.
4 "What are you to me, O Tyre and
Sī'dŏn, and all the regions of Phĭ·lĭs'-
ĭ·a? Are you paying me back for something? If you are paying me back, I
will requite your deed upon your own
head swiftly and speedily. ⁵ For you
have taken my silver and my gold, and
have carried my rich treasures into
your temples.ᵉ ⁶ You have sold the
people of Judah and Jerusalem to
the Greeks, removing them far from
their own border. ⁷ But now I will stir
them up from the place to which you
have sold them, and I will requite
your deed upon your own head. ⁸ I will
sell your sons and your daughters into
the hand of the sons of Judah, and
they will sell them to the Să·bē'ans,
to a nation far off; for the LORD has
spoken."

⁹ Proclaim this among the nations:
Prepare war,
stir up the mighty men.
Let all the men of war draw near,
let them come up.
¹⁰ Beat your plowshares into swords,
and your pruning hooks into
spears;
let the weak say, "I am a warrior."
¹¹ Hasten and come,
all you nations round about,
gather yourselves there.
Bring down thy warriors, O LORD.
¹² Let the nations bestir themselves,
and come up to the valley of
Jĕ·hŏsh'a·phăt;
for there I will sit to judge
all the nations round about.
¹³ Put in the sickle,
for the harvest is ripe.
Go in, tread,
for the wine press is full.
The vats overflow,
for their wickedness is great.
¹⁴ Multitudes, multitudes,
in the valley of decision!
For the day of the LORD is near
in the valley of decision.
¹⁵ The sun and the moon are darkened,
and the stars withdraw their
shining.
¹⁶ And the LORD roars from Zion,
and utters his voice from Jerusalem,
and the heavens and the earth
shake.
But the LORD is a refuge to his
people,
a stronghold to the people of
Israel.
¹⁷ "So you shall know that I am the
LORD your God,
who dwell in Zion, my holy mountain.
And Jerusalem shall be holy
and strangers shall never again
pass through it.

ᶜCh 3.1 in Heb ᵈCh 4.1 in Heb ᵉOr *palaces*
2.28-32: Acts 2.17-21.
2.31: Rev 6.12. 2.32: Rom 10.13.
3.4-8: Is 23; Ezek 26.1-28.19; Amos 1.9-10; Zech 9.3-4;
Ezek 28.20-26; Zech 9.2; Is 14.29-31; Jer 47; Ezek 25.15-
17; Amos 1.6-8; Zeph 2.4-7; Zech 9.5-7.
3.10: Is 2.4; Mic 4.3.
3.13: Mk 4.29; Rev 14.15, 18, 19.
3.16: Amos 1.2.

18 "And in that day
the mountains shall drip sweet wine,
and the hills shall flow with milk,
and all the stream beds of Judah
shall flow with water;
and a fountain shall come forth
from the house of the LORD
and water the valley of Shĭt'tĭm.

19 "Egypt shall become a desolation
and Ē'dŏm a desolate wilderness,

for the violence done to the people
of Judah,
because they have shed innocent
blood in their land.
20 But Judah shall be inhabited for
ever,
and Jerusalem to all generations.
21 I will avenge their blood, and I will
not clear the guilty,[g]
for the LORD dwells in Zion."

The Book of
Amos

1 The words of Ā'mŏs, who was
among the shepherds of Tĕ·kō'ă,
which he saw concerning Israel in
the days of Ŭz·zī'ăh king of Judah
and in the days of Jĕr·ọ·bō'ăm the
son of Jō'ăsh, king of Israel, two
years[a] before the earthquake. 2 And
he said:
"The LORD roars from Zion,
and utters his voice from Jerusalem;
the pastures of the shepherds mourn,
and the top of Cär'mĕl withers."

3 Thus says the LORD:
"For three transgressions of Damascus,
and for four, I will not revoke the
punishment;[b]
because they have threshed Gilead
with threshing sledges of iron.
4 So I will send a fire upon the house
of Hăz'ạ·ĕl,
and it shall devour the strongholds of Bĕn–hā'dăd.
5 I will break the bar of Damascus,
and cut off the inhabitants from
the Valley of Ā'vĕn,[c]
and him that holds the scepter
from Bĕth–ē'dĕn;
and the people of Syria shall go
into exile to Kir,"
            says the LORD.

6 Thus says the LORD:
"For three transgressions of Gā'zạ,
and for four, I will not revoke the
punishment;[b]
because they carried into exile a
whole people

to deliver them up to Ē'dọm.
7 So I will send a fire upon the wall of
Gā'zạ,
and it shall devour her strongholds.
8 I will cut off the inhabitants from
Ăsh'dŏd,
and him that holds the scepter
from Ăsh'kẹ·lŏn;
I will turn my hand against Ĕk'rọn;
and the remnant of the Phĭ·lĭs'-
tĭnes shall perish,"
            says the Lord GOD.

9 Thus says the LORD:
"For three transgressions of Tȳre,
and for four, I will not revoke the
punishment;[b]
because they delivered up a whole
people to Ē'dọm,
and did not remember the covenant of brotherhood.
10 So I will send a fire upon the wall
of Tȳre,
and it shall devour her strongholds."

11 Thus says the LORD:
"For three transgressions of Ē'dọm
and for four, I will not revoke the
punishment;[b]

[g] Gk Syr: Heb *I will hold innocent their blood which I have
not held innocent*
3.18: Ezek 47.1-12; Amos 9.13; Zech 14.8; Rev 22.1.

[a] Or *during two years*
[b] Heb *cause it to return*   [c] Or *On*
1.2: Joel 3.16.   1.3-5: Is 17.1-3; Jer 49.23-27; Zech 9.1.
1.6-8: Is 14.29-31; Jer 47; Ezek 25.15-17; Joel 3.4-8;
Zeph 2.4-7; Zech 9.5-7.
1.9-10: Is 23; Ezek 26.1-28.19; Joel 3.4-8; Zech 9.3-4.
1.11-12: Is 34; 63.1-6; Jer 49.7-22; Ezek 25.12-14; 35;
Obad; Mal 1.2-5.

because he pursued his brother with
the sword,
and cast off all pity,
and his anger tore perpetually,
and he kept his wrath[d] for ever.
[12] So I will send a fire upon Tē'man,
and it shall devour the strongholds of Bŏz'rạh."

[13] Thus says the LORD:
"For three transgressions of the
Ăm'mo·nītes,
and for four, I will not revoke the
punishment;[b]
because they have ripped up women
with child in Gilead,
that they might enlarge their
border.
[14] So I will kindle a fire in the wall of
Răb'bạh,
and it shall devour her strongholds,
with shouting in the day of battle,
with a tempest in the day of the
whirlwind;
[15] and their king shall go into exile,
he and his princes together,"
says the LORD.

2 Thus says the LORD:
"For three transgressions of Mō'ăb,
and for four, I will not revoke the
punishment;[e]
because he burned to lime
the bones of the king of Ē'dom.
[2] So I will send a fire upon Mō'ăb,
and it shall devour the strongholds of Kĕr'ĭ·ŏth,
and Moab shall die amid uproar,
amid shouting and the sound of
the trumpet;
[3] I will cut off the ruler from its midst,
and will slay all its princes with
him,"
says the LORD.

[4] Thus says the LORD:
"For three transgressions of Judah,
and for four, I will not revoke the
punishment;[e]
because they have rejected the law
of the LORD,
and have not kept his statutes,
but their lies have led them astray,
after which their fathers walked.
[5] So I will send a fire upon Judah,
and it shall devour the strongholds of Jerusalem."

[6] Thus says the LORD:

"For three transgressions of Israel,
and for four, I will not revoke
the punishment;[e]
because they sell the righteous for
silver,
and the needy for a pair of shoes –
[7] they that trample the head of the
poor into the dust of the earth,
and turn aside the way of the
afflicted;
a man and his father go in to the
same maiden,
so that my holy name is profaned;
[8] they lay themselves down beside
every altar
upon garments taken in pledge;
and in the house of their God they
drink
the wine of those who have been
fined.

[9] "Yet I destroyed the Ăm'o·rīte before them,
whose height was like the height
of the cedars,
and who was as strong as the oaks;
I destroyed his fruit above,
and his roots beneath.
[10] Also I brought you up out of the land
of Egypt,
and led you forty years in the
wilderness,
to possess the land of the Ăm'o-
rīte.
[11] And I raised up some of your sons
for prophets,
and some of your young men for
Năz'ĭ·rītes.
Is it not indeed so, O people of
Israel?"
says the LORD.

[12] "But you made the Năz'ĭ·rītes drink
wine,
and commanded the prophets,
saying, 'You shall not prophesy.'

[13] "Behold, I will press you down in
your place,
as a cart full of sheaves presses
down.
[14] Flight shall perish from the swift,
and the strong shall not retain his
strength,
nor shall the mighty save his life;

[b] Heb *cause it to return*
[d] Gk Syr Vg: Heb *his wrath kept*
[e] Heb *cause it to return*
1.13-15: Jer 49.1-6; Ezek 21.28-32; 25.1-7; Zeph 2.8-11.
2.1-3: Is 15–16; 25.10-12; Jer 48; Ezek 25.8-11; Zeph
2.8-11.

¹⁵he who handles the bow shall not
stand,
and he who is swift of foot shall
not save himself,
nor shall he who rides the horse
save his life;
¹⁶and he who is stout of heart among
the mighty
shall flee away naked in that day,"
says the LORD.

3 Hear this word that the LORD
has spoken against you, O people
of Israel, against the whole family
which I brought up out of the land of
Egypt:
² "You only have I known
of all the families of the earth;
therefore I will punish you
for all your iniquities.

³ "Do two walk together,
unless they have made an appointment?
⁴Does a lion roar in the forest,
when he has no prey?
Does a young lion cry out from his
den,
if he has taken nothing?
⁵Does a bird fall in a snare on the
earth,
when there is no trap for it?
Does a snare spring up from the
ground,
when it has taken nothing?
⁶Is a trumpet blown in a city,
and the people are not afraid?
Does evil befall a city,
unless the LORD has done it?
⁷Surely the Lord GOD does nothing,
without revealing his secret
to his servants the prophets.
⁸The lion has roared;
who will not fear?
The Lord GOD has spoken;
who can but prophesy?"

⁹Proclaim to the strongholds in Assyria,ᶠ
and to the strongholds in the land
of Egypt,
and say, "Assemble yourselves upon
the mountains of Sa·mâr'ĭ·a,
and see the great tumults within
her,
and the oppressions in her midst."
¹⁰"They do not know how to do right,"
says the LORD,
"those who store up violence and
robbery in their strongholds."

¹¹Therefore thus says the Lord GOD:
"An adversary shall surround the
land,
and bring down your defenses
from you,
and your strongholds shall be
plundered."

12 Thus says the LORD: "As the
shepherd rescues from the mouth of
the lion two legs, or a piece of an ear,
so shall the people of Israel who dwell
in Sa·mâr'ĭ·a be rescued, with the
corner of a couch and partᵍ of a bed."

¹³"Hear, and testify against the house
of Jacob,"
says the Lord GOD, the God of
hosts,
¹⁴"that on the day I punish Israel for
his transgressions,
I will punish the altars of Bĕth'el,
and the horns of the altar shall be
cut off
and fall to the ground.
¹⁵I will smite the winter house with
the summer house;
and the houses of ivory shall perish,
and the great housesʰ shall come
to an end,"
says the LORD.

4 "Hear this word, you cows of
Bā'shan,
who are in the mountain of
Sa·mâr'ĭ·a,
who oppress the poor, who crush the
needy,
who say to their husbands, 'Bring,
that we may drink!'
²The Lord GOD has sworn by his
holiness
that, behold, the days are coming
upon you,
when they shall take you away with
hooks,
even the last of you with fish-
hooks.
³And you shall go out through the
breaches,
every one straight before her;
and you shall be cast forth into
Hār'mon,"
says the LORD.

⁴"Come to Bĕth'el, and transgress;

ᶠGk: Heb *Ashdod*
ᵍThe meaning of the Hebrew word is uncertain
ʰOr *many houses* 3.7: Rev 10.7.

to Gĭl'gạl, and multiply transgression;
bring your sacrifices every morning,
   your tithes every three days;
⁵offer a sacrifice of thanksgiving of
   that which is leavened,
and proclaim freewill offerings,
   publish them;
for so you love to do, O people
   of Israel!"
              says the Lord God.

⁶"I gave you cleanness of teeth in all
   your cities,
and lack of bread in all your places,
yet you did not return to me,"
              says the Lord.

⁷"And I also withheld the rain from
   you
   when there were yet three months
    to the harvest;
I would send rain upon one city,
   and send no rain upon another
    city;
one field would be rained upon,
   and the field on which it did not
    rain withered;
⁸so two or three cities wandered to
   one city
   to drink water, and were not
    satisfied;
yet you did not return to me,"
              says the Lord.

⁹"I smote you with blight and mildew;
I laid waste[i] your gardens and
   your vineyards;
   your fig trees and your olive
    trees the locust devoured;
yet you did not return to me,"
              says the Lord.

¹⁰"I sent among you a pestilence
   after the manner of Egypt;
I slew your young men with the
   sword;
I carried away your horses;[j]
   and I made the stench of your
    camp go up into your nostrils;
yet you did not return to me,"
              says the Lord.

¹¹"I overthrew some of you,
   as when God overthrew Sŏd'ọm
    and Gọ·môr'ạh,
and you were as a brand plucked
   out of the burning;
yet you did not return to me,"
              says the Lord.

¹²"Therefore thus I will do to you,
   O Israel;
because I will do this to you,
prepare to meet your God, O
   Israel!"

¹³For lo, he who forms the mountains,
   and creates the wind,
and declares to man what is his
   thought;
who makes the morning darkness,
   and treads on the heights of the
   earth—
the Lord, the God of hosts, is his
   name!

5 Hear this word which I take up
   over you in lamentation, O house
of Israel:
²"Fallen, no more to rise,
   is the virgin Israel;
forsaken on her land,
   with none to raise her up."

³For thus says the Lord God:
"The city that went forth a thousand
   shall have a hundred left,
and that which went forth a hundred
   shall have ten left
to the house of Israel."

⁴For thus says the Lord to the house
   of Israel:
"Seek me and live;
⁵ but do not seek Bĕth'ĕl,
and do not enter into Gĭl'gạl
   or cross over to Bē'ẹr-shē'bạ;
for Gilgal shall surely go into exile,
   and Bethel shall come to nought."

⁶Seek the Lord and live,
   lest he break out like fire in the
   house of Joseph,
and it devour, with none to quench
   it for Bĕth'ĕl,
⁷O you who turn justice to wormwood,
and cast down righteousness to
   the earth!

⁸He who made the Pleiades and
   Orion,
and turns deep darkness into the
   morning,
and darkens the day into night,
who calls for the waters of the sea,

ⁱCn: Heb *the multitude of*
ʲHeb *with the captivity of your horses*

and pours them out upon the
surface of the earth,
the LORD is his name,
⁹who makes destruction flash forth
against the strong,
so that destruction comes upon
the fortress.

¹⁰They hate him who reproves in the
gate,
and they abhor him who speaks
the truth.
¹¹Therefore because you trample
upon the poor
and take from him exactions of
wheat,
you have built houses of hewn stone,
but you shall not dwell in them;
you have planted pleasant vineyards,
but you shall not drink their wine.
¹²For I know how many are your
transgressions,
and how great are your sins—
you who afflict the righteous, who
take a bribe,
and turn aside the needy in the
gate.
¹³Therefore he who is prudent will
keep silent in such a time;
for it is an evil time.

¹⁴Seek good, and not evil,
that you may live;
and so the LORD, the God of hosts,
will be with you,
as you have said.
¹⁵Hate evil, and love good,
and establish justice in the gate;
it may be that the LORD, the God of
hosts,
will be gracious to the remnant
of Joseph.

¹⁶Therefore thus says the LORD, the
God of hosts, the Lord:
"In all the squares there shall be
wailing;
and in all the streets they shall
say, 'Alas! alas!'
They shall call the farmers to mourning
and to wailing those who are
skilled in lamentation,
¹⁷and in all vineyards there shall be
wailing,
for I will pass through the midst
of you,"
says the LORD.

¹⁸Woe to you who desire the day of the
LORD!

Why would you have the day of
the LORD?
It is darkness, and not light;
¹⁹ as if a man fled from a lion,
and a bear met him;
or went into the house and leaned
with his hand against the wall,
and a serpent bit him.
²⁰Is not the day of the LORD darkness,
and not light,
and gloom with no brightness in it?

²¹"I hate, I despise your feasts,
and I take no delight in your
solemn assemblies.
²²Even though you offer me your
burnt offerings and cereal offerings,
I will not accept them,
and the peace offerings of your
fatted beasts
I will not look upon.
²³Take away from me the noise of
your songs;
to the melody of your harps I will
not listen.
²⁴But let justice roll down like waters,
and righteousness like an ever-
flowing stream.

25 "Did you bring to me sacrifices
and offerings the forty years in the
wilderness, O house of Israel? ²⁶You
shall take up Săk′kuth your king, and
Kaī′wän your star-god, your images,ᵏ
which you made for yourselves;
²⁷therefore I will take you into exile
beyond Damascus," says the LORD,
whose name is the God of hosts.

6 "Woe to those who are at ease in
Zion,
and to those who feel secure on
the mountain of Sa·mâr′ĭ·a,
the notable men of the first of the
nations,
to whom the house of Israel
come!
²Pass over to Căl′něh, and see;
and thence go to Hā′măth the
great;
then go down to Găth of the
Phĭ·lĭs′tĭnes.
Are they better than these kingdoms?
Or is their territory greater than
your territory,
³O you who put far away the evil day

ᵏHeb *your images, your star-god*
5.25-27: Acts 7.42-43.

and bring near the seat of violence?

4 "Woe to those who lie upon beds of ivory,
and stretch themselves upon their couches,
and eat lambs from the flock,
and calves from the midst of the stall;
5 who sing idle songs to the sound of the harp,
and like David invent for themselves instruments of music;
6 who drink wine in bowls,
and anoint themselves with the finest oils,
but are not grieved over the ruin of Joseph!
7 Therefore they shall now be the first of those to go into exile,
and the revelry of those who stretch themselves shall pass away."

8 The Lord GOD has sworn by himself (says the LORD, the God of hosts):
"I abhor the pride of Jacob,
and hate his strongholds;
and I will deliver up the city and all that is in it."

9 And if ten men remain in one house, they shall die. 10 And when a man's kinsman, he who burns him,[l] shall take him up to bring the bones out of the house, and shall say to him who is in the innermost parts of the house, "Is there still any one with you?" he shall say, "No"; and he shall say, "Hush! We must not mention the name of the LORD."

11 For behold, the LORD commands, and the great house shall be smitten into fragments,
and the little house into bits.
12 Do horses run upon rocks?
Does one plow the sea with oxen?
But you have turned justice into poison
and the fruit of righteousness into wormwood—
13 you who rejoice in Lō–dē'bär,[n]
who say, "Have we not by our own strength
taken Kär·nā'ĭm[o] for ourselves?"
14 "For behold, I will raise up against you a nation,

O house of Israel," says the LORD, the God of hosts;
"and they shall oppress you from the entrance of Hā'măth
to the Brook of the Ăr'a·bah."

7 Thus the Lord GOD showed me: behold, he was forming locusts in the beginning of the shooting up of the latter growth; and lo, it was the latter growth after the king's mowings. 2 When they had finished eating the grass of the land, I said,
"O Lord GOD, forgive, I beseech thee!
How can Jacob stand?
He is so small!"
3 The LORD repented concerning this;
"It shall not be," said the LORD.

4 Thus the Lord GOD showed me: behold, the Lord GOD was calling for a judgment by fire, and it devoured the great deep and was eating up the land. 5 Then I said,
"O Lord GOD, cease, I beseech thee!
How can Jacob stand?
He is so small!"
6 The LORD repented concerning this;
"This also shall not be," said the Lord GOD.

7 He showed me: behold, the Lord was standing beside a wall built with a plumb line, with a plumb line in his hand. 8 And the LORD said to me, "Ā'mŏs, what do you see?" And I said, "A plumb line." Then the Lord said, "Behold, I am setting a plumb line in the midst of my people Israel;
I will never again pass by them;
9 the high places of Isaac shall be made desolate,
and the sanctuaries of Israel shall be laid waste,
and I will rise against the house of Jĕr·o·bō'am with the sword."

10 Then Ăm·a·zī'ah the priest of Bĕth'el sent to Jĕr·o·bō'am king of Israel, saying, "Ā'mŏs has conspired against you in the midst of the house of Israel; the land is not able to bear all his words. 11 For thus Ā'mŏs has said, 'Jĕr·o·bō'am shall die by the sword, and Israel must go into exile away from his land.'" 12 And Ăm·a·zī'ah said to Ā'mŏs, "O seer, go, flee away to the land of Judah,

[l] Or *who makes a burning for him*
[n] Or *a thing of nought* [o] Or *horns*

and eat bread there, and prophesy there; [13] but never again prophesy at Bĕth′ĕl, for it is the king's sanctuary, and it is a temple of the kingdom."

[14] Then Ā′mŏs answered Ăm·a·zī′ah, "I am no prophet, nor a prophet's son;[p] but I am a herdsman, and a dresser of sycamore trees, [15] and the LORD took me from following the flock, and the LORD said to me, 'Go, prophesy to my people Israel.'

[16] "Now therefore hear the word of the LORD.
You say, 'Do not prophesy against Israel,
   and do not preach against the house of Isaac.'

[17] Therefore thus says the LORD:
'Your wife shall be a harlot in the city,
   and your sons and your daughters shall fall by the sword,
   and your land shall be parceled out by line;
you yourself shall die in an unclean land,
   and Israel shall surely go into exile away from its land.'"

8 Thus the Lord GOD showed me: behold, a basket of summer fruit.[q] [2] And he said, "Ā′mŏs, what do you see?" And I said, "A basket of summer fruit."[q] Then the LORD said to me, "The end[r] has come upon my people Israel;
I will never again pass by them.
[3] The songs of the temple[s] shall become wailings in that day,"
            says the Lord GOD;
"the dead bodies shall be many;
in every place they shall be cast out in silence."[t]

[4] Hear this, you who trample upon the needy,
   and bring the poor of the land to an end,
[5] saying, "When will the new moon be over,
   that we may sell grain?
And the sabbath,
   that we may offer wheat for sale,
that we may make the ephah small and the shekel great,
   and deal deceitfully with false balances,
[6] that we may buy the poor for silver and the needy for a pair of sandals, and sell the refuse of the wheat?"

[7] The LORD has sworn by the pride of Jacob:
"Surely I will never forget any of their deeds.
[8] Shall not the land tremble on this account,
   and every one mourn who dwells in it,
and all of it rise like the Nile,
   and be tossed about and sink again, like the Nile of Egypt?"

[9] "And on that day," says the Lord GOD,
"I will make the sun go down at noon,
   and darken the earth in broad daylight.
[10] I will turn your feasts into mourning,
   and all your songs into lamentation;
I will bring sackcloth upon all loins,
   and baldness on every head;
I will make it like the mourning for an only son,
   and the end of it like a bitter day.

[11] "Behold, the days are coming," says the Lord GOD,
"when I will send a famine on the land;
not a famine of bread, nor a thirst for water,
   but of hearing the words of the LORD.
[12] They shall wander from sea to sea,
   and from north to east;
they shall run to and fro, to seek the word of the LORD,
   but they shall not find it.

[13] "In that day the fair virgins and the young men
   shall faint for thirst.
[14] Those who swear by Ăsh′ĭ·mah of Sa·mâr′ĭ·a,
and say, 'As thy god lives, O Dan,'
and, 'As the way of Bē′er-shē′ba lives,'
   they shall fall, and never rise again."

9 I saw the LORD standing beside[u] the altar, and he said:
"Smite the capitals until the thresholds shake,

p Or *one of the sons of the prophets*
q Heb *qayits*   *r* Heb *quets*   *s* Or *palace*   *t* Or *be silent!*
u Or *upon*

and shatter them on the heads of
   all the people;^v
and what are left of them I will slay
   with the sword;
   not one of them shall flee away,
   not one of them shall escape.

2 "Though they dig into Shē′ōl,
   from there shall my hand take
   them;
though they climb up to heaven,
   from there I will bring them
   down.
3 Though they hide themselves on the
   top of Cär′mẹl,
   from there I will search out and
   take them;
and though they hide from my sight
   at the bottom of the sea,
   there I will command the serpent,
   and it shall bite them.
4 And though they go into captivity
   before their enemies,
   there I will command the sword,
   and it shall slay them;
and I will set my eyes upon them
   for evil and not for good."

5 The Lord, God of hosts,
he who touches the earth and it
   melts,
   and all who dwell in it mourn,
and all of it rises like the Nile,
   and sinks again, like the Nile of
   Egypt;
6 who builds his upper chambers in
   the heavens,
   and founds his vault upon the
   earth;
who calls for the waters of the sea,
   and pours them out upon the
   surface of the earth—
the Lord is his name.

7 "Are you not like the Ethiopians to
   me,
   O people of Israel?" says the Lord.
"Did I not bring up Israel from the
   land of Egypt,
   and the Phĭ·lĭs′tĭnes from Căph′-
   tôr and the Syrians from Kĭr?
8 Behold, the eyes of the Lord God
   are upon the sinful kingdom,

and I will destroy it from the surface of the ground;
except that I will not utterly destroy the house of Jacob,"
               says the Lord.

9 "For lo, I will command,
   and shake the house of Israel
   among all the nations
as one shakes with a sieve,
   but no pebble shall fall upon the
   earth.
10 All the sinners of my people shall
   die by the sword,
   who say, 'Evil shall not overtake
   or meet us.'

11 "In that day I will raise up
   the booth of David that is fallen
and repair its breaches,
   and raise up its ruins,
   and rebuild it as in the days of old;
12 that they may possess the remnant
   of Ē′dọm
   and all the nations who are called
   by my name,"
says the Lord who does this.

13 "Behold, the days are coming," says
   the Lord,
   "when the plowman shall overtake the reaper
   and the treader of grapes him who
   sows the seed;
the mountains shall drip sweet
   wine,
   and all the hills shall flow with it.
14 I will restore the fortunes of my people Israel,
   and they shall rebuild the ruined
   cities and inhabit them;
they shall plant vineyards and drink
   their wine,
   and they shall make gardens and
   eat their fruit.
15 I will plant them upon their land,
   and they shall never again be
   plucked up
out of the land which I have
   given them,"
        says the Lord your God.

^vHeb *all of them*
9.11-12: Acts 15.16-17.   **9.13:** Joel 3.18.

The Book of
Obadiah

¹The vision of Ō·ba·dī′ah.

Thus says the Lord GOD concerning
E′dom:
We have heard tidings from the LORD,
and a messenger has been sent
among the nations:
"Rise up! let us rise against her for
battle!"
²Behold, I will make you small among
the nations,
you shall be utterly despised.
³The pride of your heart has deceived
you,
you who live in the clefts of the
rock,ᵃ
whose dwelling is high,
who say in your heart,
"Who will bring me down to the
ground?"
⁴Though you soar aloft like the eagle,
though your nest is set among the
stars,
thence I will bring you down,
says the LORD.

⁵If thieves came to you,
if plunderers by night—
how you have been destroyed!—
would they not steal only enough
for themselves?
If grape gatherers came to you,
would they not leave gleanings?
⁶How Esau has been pillaged,
his treasures sought out!
⁷All your allies have deceived you,
they have driven you to the border;
your confederates have prevailed
against you;
your trusted friends have set a
trap under you—
there is no understanding of it.
⁸Will I not on that day, says the LORD,
destroy the wise men out of E′dom,
and understanding out of Mount
Esau?
⁹And your mighty men shall be dismayed, O Tē′man,
so that every man from Mount
Esau will be cut off by slaughter.
¹⁰For the violence done to your
brother Jacob,
shame shall cover you,

and you shall be cut off for ever.
¹¹On the day that you stood aloof,
on the day that strangers carried
off his wealth,
and foreigners entered his gates
and cast lots for Jerusalem,
you were like one of them.
¹²But you should not have gloated
over the day of your brother
in the day of his misfortune;
you should not have rejoiced over the
people of Judah
in the day of their ruin;
you should not have boasted
in the day of distress.
¹³You should not have entered the gate
of my people
in the day of his calamity;
you should not have gloated over his
disaster
in the day of his calamity;
you should not have looted his goods
in the day of his calamity.
¹⁴You should not have stood at the
parting of the ways
to cut off his fugitives;
you should not have delivered up
his survivors
in the day of distress.

¹⁵For the day of the LORD is near
upon all the nations.
As you have done, it shall be done to
you,
your deeds shall return on your
own head.
¹⁶For as you have drunk upon my holy
mountain,
all the nations round about shall
drink;
they shall drink, and stagger,ᵇ
and shall be as though they had
not been.
¹⁷But in Mount Zion there shall be
those that escape,
and it shall be holy;
and the house of Jacob shall possess
their own possessions.
¹⁸The house of Jacob shall be a fire,

ᵃOr *Sela*
ᵇCn: Heb *swallow*
1-21: Is 34; 63.1-6; Jer 49.7-22; Ezek 25.12-14; 35; Amos
1.11-12; Mal 1.2-5.

and the house of Joseph a flame,
and the house of Esau stubble;
they shall burn them and consume
them,
and there shall be no survivor to
the house of Esau;
for the LORD has spoken.
¹⁹ Those of the Nĕg′ĕb shall possess
Mount Esau,
and those of the Shĕ·phē′lạh the
land of the Phĭ·lĭs′tĭnes;
they shall possess the land of
Ē′phrạ·ĭm and the land of Sạ-
mâr′ĭ·ạ

and Benjamin shall possess Gilead.
²⁰ The exiles in Hā′lạhᶜ who are of the
people of Israel
shall possessᵈ Phoẹ·nĭ′çĭ·ạ as far as
Zăr′ẹ·phăth;
and the exiles of Jerusalem who are
in Sĕ·phär′ăd
shall possess the cities of the
Nĕg′ĕb.
²¹ Saviors shall go up to Mount Zion
to rule Mount Esau;
and the kingdom shall be the
LORD'S.

The Book of
Jonah

1 Now the word of the LORD came
to Jonah the son of Ạ·mĭt′taī, saying, ²"Arise, go to Nĭn′ĕ·vẹh, that great
city, and cry against it; for their
wickedness has come up before me."
³But Jonah rose to flee to Tär′shĭsh
from the presence of the LORD. He
went down to Jŏp′pạ and found a ship
going to Tarshish; so he paid the fare,
and went on board, to go with them to
Tarshish, away from the presence of
the LORD.

4 But the LORD hurled a great wind
upon the sea, and there was a mighty
tempest on the sea, so that the ship
threatened to break up. ⁵Then the mariners were afraid, and each cried to
his god; and they threw the wares that
were in the ship into the sea, to lighten
it for them. But Jonah had gone down
into the inner part of the ship and had
lain down, and was fast asleep. ⁶So
the captain came and said to him,
"What do you mean, you sleeper?
Arise, call upon your god! Perhaps the
god will give a thought to us, that we
do not perish."

7 And they said to one another,
"Come, let us cast lots, that we may
know on whose account this evil has
come upon us." So they cast lots,
and the lot fell upon Jonah. ⁸Then they
said to him, "Tell us, on whose account this evil has come upon us?
What is your occupation? And whence

do you come? What is your country?
And of what people are you?" ⁹And he
said to them, "I am a Hebrew; and I
fear the LORD, the God of heaven, who
made the sea and the dry land."
¹⁰Then the men were exceedingly
afraid, and said to him, "What is this
that you have done!" For the men
knew that he was fleeing from the
presence of the LORD, because he had
told them.

11 Then they said to him, "What
shall we do to you, that the sea may
quiet down for us?" For the sea grew
more and more tempestuous. ¹²He said
to them, "Take me up and throw me
into the sea; then the sea will quiet
down for you; for I know it is because
of me that this great tempest has come
upon you." ¹³Nevertheless the men
rowed hard to bring the ship back to
land, but they could not, for the sea
grew more and more tempestuous
against them. ¹⁴Therefore they cried
to the LORD, "We beseech thee, O LORD,
let us not perish for this man's life,
and lay not on us innocent blood; for
thou, O LORD, hast done as it pleased
thee." ¹⁵So they took up Jonah and
threw him into the sea; and the sea
ceased from its raging. ¹⁶Then the men
feared the LORD exceedingly, and they
offered a sacrifice to the LORD and
made vows.

ᶜCn: Heb *this army*   ᵈCn: Heb *which*

17ᵃ And the LORD appointed a great fish to swallow up Jonah; and Jonah was in the belly of the fish three days and three nights.

2 Then Jonah prayed to the LORD his God from the belly of the fish, ²saying,
"I called to the LORD, out of my distress,
  and he answered me;
out of the belly of Shē′ōl I cried,
  and thou didst hear my voice.
³For thou didst cast me into the deep,
  into the heart of the seas,
  and the flood was round about me;
all thy waves and thy billows
  passed over me.
⁴Then I said, 'I am cast out
  from thy presence;
how shall I again look
  upon thy holy temple?'
⁵The waters closed in over me,
  the deep was round about me;
weeds were wrapped about my head
⁶ at the roots of the mountains.
I went down to the land
  whose bars closed upon me for ever;
yet thou didst bring up my life from the Pit,
  O LORD my God.
⁷When my soul fainted within me,
  I remembered the LORD;
and my prayer came to thee,
  into thy holy temple.
⁸Those who pay regard to vain idols
  forsake their true loyalty.
⁹But I with the voice of thanksgiving
  will sacrifice to thee;
what I have vowed I will pay.
  Deliverance belongs to the LORD!"
¹⁰And the LORD spoke to the fish, and it vomited out Jonah upon the dry land.

3 Then the word of the LORD came to Jonah the second time, saying, ²"Arise, go to Nĭn′ĕ·vĕh, that great city, and proclaim to it the message that I tell you." ³So Jonah arose and went to Nĭn′ĕ·vĕh, according to the word of the LORD. Now Nineveh was an exceedingly great city, three days' journey in breadth. ⁴Jonah began to go into the city, going a day's journey. And he cried, "Yet forty days, and Nĭn′ĕ·vĕh shall be overthrown!" ⁵And the people of Nĭn′ĕ·vĕh believed God; they proclaimed a fast, and put on sackcloth, from the greatest of them to the least of them.

6 Then tidings reached the king of Nĭn′ĕ·vĕh, and he arose from his throne, removed his robe, and covered himself with sackcloth, and sat in ashes. ⁷And he made proclamation and published through Nĭn′ĕ·vĕh, "By the decree of the king and his nobles: Let neither man nor beast, herd nor flock, taste anything; let them not feed, or drink water, ⁸but let man and beast be covered with sackcloth, and let them cry mightily to God; yea, let every one turn from his evil way and from the violence which is in his hands. ⁹Who knows, God may yet repent and turn from his fierce anger, so that we perish not?"

10 When God saw what they did, how they turned from their evil way, God repented of the evil which he had said he would do to them; and he did not do it.

4 But it displeased Jonah exceedingly, and he was angry. ²And he prayed to the LORD and said, "I pray thee, LORD, is not this what I said when I was yet in my country? That is why I made haste to flee to Tär′shĭsh; for I knew that thou art a gracious God and merciful, slow to anger, and abounding in steadfast love, and repentest of evil. ³Therefore now, O LORD, take my life from me, I beseech thee, for it is better for me to die than to live." ⁴And the LORD said, "Do you do well to be angry?" ⁵Then Jonah went out of the city and sat to the east of the city, and made a booth for himself there. He sat under it in the shade, till he should see what would become of the city.

6 And the LORD God appointed a plant,ᵇ and made it come up over Jonah, that it might be a shade over his head, to save him from his discomfort. So Jonah was exceedingly glad because of the plant.ᵇ ⁷But when dawn came up the next day, God appointed a worm which attacked the plant,ᵇ so that it withered. ⁸When the sun rose, God appointed a sultry east wind, and the sun beat upon the head of Jonah so that he was faint; and he asked that he might die, and said, "It is better for me to die than to live." ⁹But God said to Jonah, "Do you do well

ᵃCh 2.1 in Heb
ᵇHeb *qiqayon*, probably *the castor oil plant*
1.17: Mt 12.40.
3.9: Joel 2.14.   4.2: Ex 34.6.

to be angry for the plant?"*b* And he said, "I do well to be angry, angry enough to die." ¹⁰And the LORD said, "You pity the plant,*b* for which you did not labor, nor did you make it grow, which came into being in a night, and perished in a night. ¹¹And should not I pity Nĭn'ĕ·veh, that great city, in which there are more than a hundred and twenty thousand persons who do not know their right hand from their left, and also much cattle?"

The Book of
Micah

1 The word of the LORD that came to Mī'cah of Mō're·shĕth in the days of Jō'tham, Ā'hăz, and Hĕz·e·kī'ah, kings of Judah, which he saw concerning Sa·mâr'ĭ·a and Jerusalem.

² Hear, you peoples, all of you;
    hearken, O earth, and all that is in it;
and let the Lord GOD be a witness against you,
    the Lord from his holy temple.
³ For behold, the LORD is coming forth out of his place,
    and will come down and tread upon the high places of the earth.
⁴ And the mountains will melt under him
    and the valleys will be cleft,
like wax before the fire,
    like waters poured down a steep place.
⁵ All this is for the transgression of Jacob
    and for the sins of the house of Israel.
What is the transgression of Jacob?
    Is it not Sa·mâr'ĭ·a?
And what is the sin of the house*a* of Judah?
    Is it not Jerusalem?
⁶ Therefore I will make Sa·mâr'ĭ·a a heap in the open country,
    a place for planting vineyards;
and I will pour down her stones into the valley,
    and uncover her foundations.
⁷ All her images shall be beaten to pieces,
    all her hires shall be burned with fire,
    and all her idols I will lay waste;

for from the hire of a harlot she gathered them,
    and to the hire of a harlot they shall return.

⁸ For this I will lament and wail;
    I will go stripped and naked;
I will make lamentation like the jackals,
    and mourning like the ostriches.
⁹ For her wound*b* is incurable;
    and it has come to Judah,
it has reached to the gate of my people,
    to Jerusalem.
¹⁰ Tell it not in Găth,
    weep not at all;
in Bĕth"–lĕ–ăph'rah
    roll yourselves in the dust.
¹¹ Pass on your way,
    inhabitants of Shā'phĭr,
    in nakedness and shame;
the inhabitants of Zā'a·năn
    do not come forth;
the wailing of Bĕth–ē'zĕl
    shall take away from you its standing place.
¹² For the inhabitants of Mā'rŏth
    wait anxiously for good,
because evil has come down from the LORD
    to the gate of Jerusalem.
¹³ Harness the steeds to the chariots,
    inhabitants of Lā'chĭsh;
you were*c* the beginning of sin
    to the daughter of Zion,
    for in you were found

---

b Heb *qiqayon*, probably *the castor oil plant*
a Gk Tg Compare Syr: Heb *what are the high places*
b Gk Syr Vg: Heb *wounds*   *c* Cn: Heb *it was*
1.2: 1 Kings 22.28.

the transgressions of Israel.

¹⁴Therefore you shall give parting
gifts
to Mō′rĕ·shĕth–gădh;
the houses of Ăch′zĭb shall be a deceitful thing
to the kings of Israel.

¹⁵I will again bring a conqueror upon
you,
inhabitants of Mạ·rē′shạh;
the glory of Israel
shall come to Ạ·dŭl′lạm.

¹⁶Make yourselves bald and cut off
your hair,
for the children of your delight;
make yourselves as bald as the eagle,
for they shall go from you into
exile.

2 Woe to those who devise wickedness
and work evil upon their beds!
When the morning dawns, they perform it,
because it is in the power of their
hand.

²They covet fields, and seize them;
and houses, and take them away;
they oppress a man and his house,
a man and his inheritance.

³Therefore thus says the LORD:
Behold, against this family I am devising evil,
from which you cannot remove
your necks;
and you shall not walk haughtily,
for it will be an evil time.

⁴In that day they shall take up a taunt
song against you,
and wail with bitter lamentation,
and say, "We are utterly ruined;
he changes the portion of my people;
how he removes it from me!
Among our captors*d* he divides our
fields."

⁵Therefore you will have none to cast
the line by lot
in the assembly of the LORD.

⁶"Do not preach" – thus they preach –
"one should not preach of such
things;
disgrace will not overtake us."

⁷Should this be said, O house of
Jacob?
Is the Spirit of the LORD impatient?
Are these his doings?
Do not my words do good
to him who walks uprightly?

⁸But you rise against my people*e* as
an enemy;
you strip the robe from the peaceful,*f*
from those who pass by trustingly
with no thought of war.

⁹The women of my people you drive
out
from their pleasant houses;
from their young children you take
away
my glory for ever.

¹⁰Arise and go,
for this is no place to rest;
because of uncleanness that destroys
with a grievous destruction.

¹¹If a man should go about and utter
wind and lies,
saying, "I will preach to you of
wine and strong drink,"
he would be the preacher for this
people!

¹²I will surely gather all of you, O
Jacob,
I will gather the remnant of Israel;
I will set them together
like sheep in a fold,
like a flock in its pasture,
a noisy multitude of men.

¹³He who opens the breach will go
up before them;
they will break through and pass
the gate,
going out by it.
Their king will pass on before them,
the LORD at their head.

3 And I said:
Hear, you heads of Jacob
and rulers of the house of Israel!
Is it not for you to know justice? –

² you who hate the good and love
the evil,
who tear the skin from off my people,
and their flesh from off their
bones;

³who eat the flesh of my people,
and flay their skin from off them,
and break their bones in pieces,
and chop them up like meat*g* in a
kettle,
like flesh in a caldron.

⁴Then they will cry to the LORD,
but he will not answer them;

d Cn: Heb *the rebellious*
e Cn: Heb *yesterday my people rose*
f Cn: Heb *from before a garment*   *g* Gk: Heb *as*

he will hide his face from them at
   that time,
   because they have made their
     deeds evil.

⁵ Thus says the LORD concerning the
   prophets
who lead my people astray,
who cry "Peace"
   when they have something to eat,
but declare war against him
   who puts nothing into their
     mouths.
⁶ Therefore it shall be night to you,
   without vision,
   and darkness to you, without divi-
     nation.
The sun shall go down upon the
   prophets,
   and the day shall be black over
     them;
⁷ the seers shall be disgraced,
   and the diviners put to shame;
they shall all cover their lips,
   for there is no answer from God.
⁸ But as for me, I am filled with power,
   with the Spirit of the LORD,
   and with justice and might,
to declare to Jacob his transgression
   and to Israel his sin.

⁹ Hear this, you heads of the house of
   Jacob
   and rulers of the house of Israel,
who abhor justice
   and pervert all equity,
¹⁰ who build Zion with blood
   and Jerusalem with wrong.
¹¹ Its heads give judgment for a bribe,
   its priests teach for hire,
   its prophets divine for money;
yet they lean upon the LORD and say,
   "Is not the LORD in the midst of
     us?
   No evil shall come upon us."
¹² Therefore because of you
   Zion shall be plowed as a field;
Jerusalem shall become a heap of
   ruins,
   and the mountain of the house a
     wooded height.

4 It shall come to pass in the latter
   days
   that the mountain of the house of
    the LORD
shall be established as the highest
   of the mountains,
and shall be raised up above the
   hills;

and peoples shall flow to it,
² and many nations shall come, and
   say:
"Come, let us go up to the mountain of the LORD,
to the house of the God of Jacob;
that he may teach us his ways
   and we may walk in his paths."
For out of Zion shall go forth the law,
   and the word of the LORD from
    Jerusalem.
³ He shall judge between many peoples,
   and shall decide for strong nations
    afar off;
and they shall beat their swords into
   plowshares,
   and their spears into pruning
    hooks;
nation shall not lift up sword against
   nation,
   neither shall they learn war any
    more;
⁴ but they shall sit every man under
   his vine and under his fig tree,
   and none shall make them afraid;
for the mouth of the LORD of hosts
   has spoken.

⁵ For all the peoples walk
   each in the name of its god,
but we will walk in the name of the
   LORD our God
   for ever and ever.

⁶ In that day, says the LORD,
   I will assemble the lame
and gather those who have been
   driven away,
   and those whom I have afflicted;
⁷ and the lame I will make the remnant;
   and those who were cast off, a
    strong nation;
and the LORD will reign over them in
   Mount Zion
   from this time forth and for ever-
    more.

⁸ And you, O tower of the flock,
   hill of the daughter of Zion,
to you shall it come,
   the former dominion shall come,
   the kingdom of the daughter of
    Jerusalem.

⁹ Now why do you cry aloud?
   Is there no king in you?
Has your counselor perished,

4.1-3: Is 2.2-4.   4.4: Zech 3.10.

that pangs have seized you like a
woman in travail?
[10] Writhe and groan,[h] O daughter of
Zion,
like a woman in travail;
for now you shall go forth from the
city
and dwell in the open country;
you shall go to Babylon.
There you shall be rescued,
there the LORD will redeem you
from the hand of your enemies.

[11] Now many nations
are assembled against you,
saying, "Let her be profaned,
and let our eyes gaze upon Zion."
[12] But they do not know
the thoughts of the LORD,
they do not understand his plan,
that he has gathered them as
sheaves to the threshing floor.
[13] Arise and thresh,
O daughter of Zion,
for I will make your horn iron
and your hoofs bronze;
you shall beat in pieces many peoples,
and shall[i] devote their gain to the
LORD,
their wealth to the Lord of the
whole earth.

5 [j] Now you are walled about with
a wall;[k]
siege is laid against us;
with a rod they strike upon the cheek
the ruler of Israel.

[2][l] But you, O Bethlehem Ĕph′ra·thah,
who are little to be among the
clans of Judah,
from you shall come forth for me
one who is to be ruler in Israel,
whose origin is from of old,
from ancient days.
[3] Therefore he shall give them up
until the time
when she who is in travail has
brought forth;
then the rest of his brethren shall
return
to the people of Israel.
[4] And he shall stand and feed his
flock in the strength of the LORD,
in the majesty of the name of the
LORD his God.
And they shall dwell secure, for now
he shall be great
to the ends of the earth.

[5] And this shall be peace,
when the Assyrian comes into our
land
and treads upon our soil,[m]
that we will raise against him seven
shepherds
and eight princes of men;
[6] they shall rule the land of Assyria
with the sword,
and the land of Nĭm′rŏd with the
drawn sword;[n]
and they[o] shall deliver us from the
Assyrian
when he comes into our land
and treads within our border.

[7] Then the remnant of Jacob shall be
in the midst of many peoples
like dew from the LORD,
like showers upon the grass,
which tarry not for men
nor wait for the sons of men.
[8] And the remnant of Jacob shall be
among the nations,
in the midst of many peoples,
like a lion among the beasts of the
forest,
like a young lion among the flocks
of sheep,
which, when it goes through, treads
down
and tears in pieces, and there is
none to deliver.
[9] Your hand shall be lifted up over
your adversaries,
and all your enemies shall be cut
off.

[10] And in that day, says the LORD,
I will cut off your horses from
among you
and will destroy your chariots;
[11] and I will cut off the cities of your
land
and throw down all your strongholds;
[12] and I will cut off sorceries from your
hand,
and you shall have no more soothsayers;
[13] and I will cut off your images
and your pillars from among you,
and you shall bow down no more
to the work of your hands;

[h] Heb uncertain   [i] Gk Syr Tg: Heb *I will*
[j] Ch 4.14 in Heb   [k] Cn Compare Gk: Heb obscure
[l] Ch 5.1 in Heb
[m] Gk: Heb *in our palaces*
[n] Cn: Heb *in its entrances*
[o] Heb *he*
5.2: Mt 2.6; Jn 7.42.

14 and I will root out your Ạ·shē′rĭm
from among you
and destroy your cities.
15 And in anger and wrath I will execute
vengeance
upon the nations that did not obey.

6 Hear what the LORD says:
Arise, plead your case before the
mountains,
and let the hills hear your voice.
2 Hear, you mountains, the controversy
of the LORD,
and you enduring foundations
of the earth;
for the LORD has a controversy with
his people,
and he will contend with Israel.

3 "O my people, what have I done to
you?
In what have I wearied you?
Answer me!
4 For I brought you up from the land
of Egypt,
and redeemed you from the house
of bondage;
and I sent before you Moses,
Aaron, and Miriam.
5 O my people, remember what Bā′-
lăk king of Mō′ăb devised,
and what Bā′laăm the son of
Bē′ôr answered him.
and what happened from Shĭt′tĭm
to Gĭl′gạl,
that you may know the saving acts
of the LORD."

6 "With what shall I come before the
LORD,
and bow myself before God on
high?
Shall I come before him with burnt
offerings,
with calves a year old?
7 Will the LORD be pleased with thousands of rams,
with ten thousands of rivers of oil?
Shall I give my first-born for my
transgression,
the fruit of my body for the sin of
my soul?"
8 He has showed you, O man, what is
good;
and what does the LORD require
of you
but to do justice, and to love kindness,[p]
and to walk humbly with your
God?

9 The voice of the LORD cries to the
city—
and it is sound wisdom to fear thy
name:
"Hear, O tribe and assembly of the
city![q]
10 Can I forget[r] the treasures of
wickedness in the house of the
wicked,
and the scant measure that is
accursed?
11 Shall I acquit the man with wicked
scales
and with a bag of deceitful
weights?
12 Your[s] rich men are full of violence;
your[s] inhabitants speak lies,
and their tongue is deceitful in
their mouth.
13 Therefore I have begun[t] to smite
you,
making you desolate because of
your sins.
14 You shall eat, but not be satisfied,
and there shall be hunger in your
inward parts;
you shall put away, but not save,
and what you save I will give to
the sword.
15 You shall sow, but not reap;
you shall tread olives, but not
anoint yourselves with oil;
you shall tread grapes, but not
drink wine.
16 For you have kept the statutes of
Ŏm′rī,[u]
and all the works of the house of
Ā′hăb;
and you have walked in their counsels;
that I may make you a desolation,
and your[v] inhabitants a hissing;
so you shall bear the scorn of the
peoples."[w]

7 Woe is me! For I have become
as when the summer fruit has been
gathered,
as when the vintage has been
gleaned:
there is no cluster to eat,
no first-ripe fig which my soul
desires.
2 The godly man has perished from the
earth,

[p] Or *steadfast love*
[q] Cn Compare Gk: Heb *and who has appointed it yet*
[r] Cn: Heb uncertain [s] Heb *whose*
[t] Gk Syr Vg: Heb *have made sick*
[u] Gk Syr Vg Tg: Heb *the statutes of Omri are kept*
[v] Heb *its* [w] Gk: Heb *my people*

and there is none upright among
men;
they all lie in wait for blood,
and each hunts his brother with a
net.
³Their hands are upon what is evil,
to do it diligently;
the prince and the judge ask for a
bribe,
and the great man utters the evil
desire of his soul;
thus they weave it together.
⁴The best of them is like a brier,
the most upright of them a thorn
hedge.
The day of their*ˣ* watchmen, of their*ˣ*
punishment, has come;
now their confusion is at hand.
⁵Put no trust in a neighbor,
have no confidence in a friend;
guard the doors of your mouth
from her who lies in your bosom;
⁶for the son treats the father with
contempt,
the daughter rises up against her
mother,
the daughter-in-law against her
mother-in-law;
a man's enemies are the men of
his own house.
⁷But as for me, I will look to the LORD,
I will wait for the God of my sal-
vation;
my God will hear me.

⁸Rejoice not over me, O my enemy;
when I fall, I shall rise;
when I sit in darkness,
the LORD will be a light to me.
⁹I will bear the indignation of the
LORD
because I have sinned against
him,
until he pleads my cause
and executes judgment for me.
He will bring me forth to the light;
I shall behold his deliverance.
¹⁰Then my enemy will see,
and shame will cover her who said
to me,
"Where is the LORD your God?"
My eyes will gloat over her;
now she will be trodden down
like the mire of the streets.

¹¹A day for the building of your walls!
In that day the boundary shall be
far extended.

¹²In that day they will come to you,
from Assyria to*ʸ* Egypt,
and from Egypt to the River,
from sea to sea and from mountain to mountain.
¹³But the earth will be desolate
because of its inhabitants,
for the fruit of their doings.

¹⁴Shepherd thy people with thy staff,
the flock of thy inheritance,
who dwell alone in a forest
in the midst of a garden land;
let them feed in Bā′shạn and Gilead
as in the days of old.

¹⁵As in the days when you came out
of the land of Egypt
I will show them*ᶻ* marvelous
things.

¹⁶The nations shall see and be ashamed
of all their might;
they shall lay their hands on their
mouths;
their ears shall be deaf;
¹⁷they shall lick the dust like a serpent,
like the crawling things of the
earth;
they shall come trembling out of
their strongholds,
they shall turn in dread to the
LORD our God,
and they shall fear because of
thee.

¹⁸Who is a God like thee, pardoning
iniquity
and passing over transgression
for the remnant of his inheritance?
He does not retain his anger for ever
because he delights in steadfast
love.
¹⁹He will again have compassion upon
us,
he will tread our iniquities under
foot.
Thou wilt cast all our*ᵃ* sins
into the depths of the sea.
²⁰Thou wilt show faithfulness to
Jacob
and steadfast love to Abraham,
as thou hast sworn to our fathers
from the days of old.

*ᶻ*Heb *your*   *ʸ*Cn: Heb *and cities of*   *ᵃ*Heb *him*
*ᶻ*Gk Syr Vg Tg: Heb *their*
7.6: Mt 10.21, 35, 36; Mk 13.12; Lk 12.53.
7.20: Lk 1.55.

The Book of

Nahum

1 An oracle concerning Nĭn′ĕ·vĕh.
The book of the vision of Nā′hŭm
of Ĕl′kŏsh.

[2] The LORD is a jealous God and avenging,
the LORD is avenging and wrathful;
the LORD takes vengeance on his adversaries
and keeps wrath for his enemies.
[3] The LORD is slow to anger and of
great might,
and the LORD will by no means
clear the guilty.

His way is in whirlwind and storm,
and the clouds are the dust of his
feet.
[4] He rebukes the sea and makes it
dry,
he dries up all the rivers;
Bā′shăn and Cär′mĕl wither,
the bloom of Lebanon fades.
[5] The mountains quake before him,
the hills melt;
the earth is laid waste before him,
the world and all that dwell therein.

[6] Who can stand before his indignation?
Who can endure the heat of his
anger?
His wrath is poured out like fire,
and the rocks are broken asunder
by him.
[7] The LORD is good,
a stronghold in the day of trouble;
he knows those who take refuge
in him.
[8] But with an overflowing flood
he will make a full end of his
adversaries,[a]
and will pursue his enemies into
darkness.
[9] What do you plot against the LORD?
He will make a full end;
he will not take vengeance[b] twice
on his foes.[c]
[10] Like entangled thorns they are consumed,[d]
like dry stubble.
[11] Did one not[e] come out from you,

who plotted evil against the LORD,
and counseled villainy?

[12] Thus says the LORD,
"Though they be strong and many,[f]
they will be cut off and pass away.
Though I have afflicted you,
I will afflict you no more.
[13] And now I will break his yoke from
off you
and will burst your bonds asunder."

[14] The LORD has given commandment
about you:
"No more shall your name be perpetuated;
from the house of your gods I will
cut off
the graven image and the molten
image.
I will make your grave, for you are
vile."

[15][g] Behold, on the mountains the feet
of him
who brings good tidings,
who proclaims peace!
Keep your feasts, O Judah,
fulfil your vows,
for never again shall the wicked
come against you,
he is utterly cut off.

2 The shatterer has come up against
you.
Man the ramparts;
watch the road;
gird your loins;
collect all your strength.

[2] (For the LORD is restoring the majesty of Jacob
as the majesty of Israel,
for plunderers have stripped them
and ruined their branches.)

[3] The shield of his mighty men is red,
his soldiers are clothed in scarlet.

[a] Gk: Heb *her place*   [b] Gk: Heb *rise up*
[c] Cn: Heb *distress*
[d] Heb *are consumed, drunken as with their drink*
[e] Cn: Heb *fully*   [f] Heb uncertain   [g] Ch 2.1 in Heb
1-3: Is 10.5-34; Zeph 2.12-15.
1.15: Is 40.9; 52.7; Acts 10.36; Rom 10.15.

The chariots flash like flame[h]
when mustered in array;
the chargers[i] prance.
4 The chariots rage in the streets,
they rush to and fro through the
squares;
they gleam like torches,
they dart like lightning.
5 The officers are summoned,
they stumble as they go,
they hasten to the wall,
the mantelet is set up.
6 The river gates are opened,
the palace is in dismay;
7 its mistress[j] is stripped, she is carried off,
her maidens lamenting,
moaning like doves,
and beating their breasts.
8 Nin′ĕ·veh is like a pool
whose waters[k] run away.
"Halt! Halt!" they cry;
but none turns back.
9 Plunder the silver,
plunder the gold!
There is no end of treasure,
or wealth of every precious thing.

10 Desolate! Desolation and ruin!
Hearts faint and knees tremble,
anguish is on all loins,
all faces grow pale!
11 Where is the lions' den,
the cave[l] of the young lions,
where the lion brought his prey,
where his cubs were, with none to
disturb?
12 The lion tore enough for his whelps
and strangled prey for his lion-
esses;
he filled his caves with prey
and his dens with torn flesh.

13 Behold, I am against you, says
the LORD of hosts, and I will burn your[m]
chariots in smoke, and the sword shall
devour your young lions; I will cut off
your prey from the earth, and the voice
of your messengers shall no more be
heard.
3 Woe to the bloody city,
all full of lies and booty—
no end to the plunder!
2 The crack of whip, and rumble of
wheel,
galloping horse and bounding
chariot!
3 Horsemen charging,
flashing sword and glittering
spear,

hosts of slain,
heaps of corpses,
dead bodies without end—
they stumble over the bodies!
4 And all for the countless harlotries
of the harlot,
graceful and of deadly charms,
who betrays nations with her harlotries,
and peoples with her charms.

5 Behold, I am against you,
says the LORD of hosts,
and will lift up your skirts over
your face;
and I will let nations look on your
nakedness
and kingdoms on your shame.
6 I will throw filth at you
and treat you with contempt,
and make you a gazingstock.
7 And all who look on you will shrink
from you and say,
Wasted is Nin′ĕ·veh; who will bemoan her?
whence shall I seek comforters
for her?[n]

8 Are you better than Thebes[o]
that sat by the Nile,
with water around her,
her rampart a sea,
and water her wall?
9 Ethiopia was her strength,
Egypt too, and that without limit;
Put and the Lib′yans were her[p]
helpers.

10 Yet she was carried away,
she went into captivity;
her little ones were dashed in pieces
at the head of every street;
for her honored men lots were cast,
and all her great men were bound
in chains.
11 You also will be drunken,
you will be dazed;
you will seek
a refuge from the enemy.
12 All your fortresses are like fig trees
with first-ripe figs—
if shaken they fall
into the mouth of the eater.
13 Behold, your troops
are women in your midst.

h Cn: The meaning of the Hebrew word is uncertain
i Cn Compare Gk Syr: Heb *cypresses*
j The meaning of the Hebrew is uncertain
k Cn Compare Gk: Heb *from the days that she has become,*
and they l Cn: Heb *pasture* m Heb *her*
n Gk: Heb *you* o Heb *No-amon* p Gk: Heb *your*

The gates of your land
are wide open to your foes;
fire has devoured your bars.

¹⁴Draw water for the siege,
strengthen your forts;
go into the clay,
tread the mortar,
take hold of the brick mold!
¹⁵There will the fire devour you,
the sword will cut you off.
It will devour you like the locust.

Multiply yourselves like the locust,
multiply like the grasshopper!
¹⁶You increased your merchants
more than the stars of the heavens.
The locust spreads its wings and
flies away.

¹⁷Your princes are like grasshoppers,
your scribes*q* like clouds of locusts
settling on the fences
in a day of cold—
when the sun rises, they fly away;
no one knows where they are.

¹⁸Your shepherds are asleep,
O king of Assyria;
your nobles slumber.
Your people are scattered on the
mountains
with none to gather them.
¹⁹There is no assuaging your hurt,
your wound is grievous.
All who hear the news of you
clap their hands over you.
For upon whom has not come
your unceasing evil?

The Book of
Habakkuk

1 The oracle of God which Hạ·băk'-
kụk the prophet saw.
²O LORD, how long shall I cry for help,
and thou wilt not hear?
Or cry to thee "Violence!"
and thou wilt not save?
³Why dost thou make me see wrongs
and look upon trouble?
Destruction and violence are before
me;
strife and contention arise.
⁴So the law is slacked
and justice never goes forth.
For the wicked surround the righteous,
so justice goes forth perverted.

⁵Look among the nations, and see;
wonder and be astounded.
For I am doing a work in your days
that you would not believe if told.
⁶For lo, I am rousing the Chăl·dē'-
ạns,
that bitter and hasty nation,
who march through the breadth of
the earth,
to seize habitations not their own.
⁷Dread and terrible are they;
their justice and dignity proceed
from themselves.
⁸Their horses are swifter than leopards,

more fierce than the evening
wolves;
their horsemen press proudly on.
Yea, their horsemen come from afar;
they fly like an eagle swift to devour.
⁹They all come for violence;
terror*a* of them goes before them.
They gather captives like sand.
¹⁰At kings they scoff,
and of rulers they make sport.
They laugh at every fortress,
for they heap up earth and take it.
¹¹Then they sweep by like the wind
and go on,
guilty men, whose own might is
their god!

¹²Art thou not from everlasting,
O LORD my God, my Holy One?
We shall not die.
O LORD, thou hast ordained them as
a judgment;
and thou, O Rock, hast established
them for chastisement.
¹³Thou who art of purer eyes than to
behold evil
and canst not look on wrong,
why dost thou look on faithless men,

q Or marshals
a Cn: Heb uncertain
1.2: Is 13.1-14.23; 47; Jer 50-51.   1.5: Acts 13.41.
1.6: Rev 20.9.   2.1: Is 21.8.

and art silent when the wicked
swallows up
the man more righteous than he?
14 For thou makest men like the fish
of the sea,
like crawling things that have no
ruler.
15 He brings all of them up with a hook,
he drags them out with his net,
he gathers them in his seine;
so he rejoices and exults.
16 Therefore he sacrifices to his net
and burns incense to his seine;
for by them he lives in luxury,[b]
and his food is rich.
17 Is he then to keep on emptying his
net,
and mercilessly slaying nations for
ever?

2 I will take my stand to watch,
and station myself on the tower,
and look forth to see what he will say
to me,
and what I will answer concerning
my complaint.
2 And the Lord answered me:
"Write the vision;
make it plain upon tablets,
so he may run who reads it.
3 For still the vision awaits its time;
it hastens to the end—it will not
lie.
If it seem slow, wait for it;
it will surely come, it will not delay.
4 Behold, he whose soul is not upright
in him shall fail,[c]
but the righteous shall live by his
faith.[d]
5 Moreover, wine is treacherous;
the arrogant man shall not abide.[e]
His greed is as wide as Shē′ōl;
like death he has never enough.
He gathers for himself all nations,
and collects as his own all peoples."

6 Shall not all these take up their taunt
against him, in scoffing derision of
him, and say,
"Woe to him who heaps up what is
not his own—
for how long?—
and loads himself with pledges!"
7 Will not your debtors suddenly arise,
and those awake who will make
you tremble?
Then you will be booty for them.
8 Because you have plundered many
nations,

all the remnant of the peoples
shall plunder you,
for the blood of men and violence to
the earth,
to cities and all who dwell therein.

9 Woe to him who gets evil gain for
his house,
to set his nest on high,
to be safe from the reach of harm!
10 You have devised shame to your
house
by cutting off many peoples;
you have forfeited your life.
11 For the stone will cry out from the
wall,
and the beam from the wood-
work respond.

12 Woe to him who builds a town with
blood,
and founds a city on iniquity!
13 Behold, is it not from the Lord of
hosts
that peoples labor only for fire,
and nations weary themselves
for nought?
14 For the earth will be filled
with the knowledge of the glory
of the Lord,
as the waters cover the sea.

15 Woe to him who makes his neighbors drink
of the cup of his wrath,[f] and makes
them drunk,
to gaze on their shame!
16 You will be sated with contempt
instead of glory.
Drink, yourself, and stagger![g]
The cup in the Lord's right hand
will come around to you,
and shame will come upon your
glory!
17 The violence done to Lebanon will
overwhelm you;
the destruction of the beasts will
terrify you,[h]
for the blood of men and violence
to the earth,
to cities and all who dwell therein.

18 What profit is an idol
when its maker has shaped it,

a metal image, a teacher of lies?
For the workman trusts in his own
creation
when he makes dumb idols!
19 Woe to him who says to a wooden
thing, Awake;
to a dumb stone, Arise!
Can this give revelation?
Behold, it is overlaid with gold and
silver,
and there is no breath at all in it.

20 But the LORD is in his holy temple;
let all the earth keep silence before him.

3 A prayer of Hạ·băk′kŭk the
prophet, according to Shĭg·ĭ-
ōn′ŏth.
2 O LORD, I have heard the report of
thee,
and thy work, O LORD, do I fear.
In the midst of the years renew it;
in the midst of the years make it
known;
in wrath remember mercy.
3 God came from Tē′mạn,
and the Holy One from Mount
Pār′ăn.
His glory covered the heavens,
and the earth was full of his
praise.   *Selah*
4 His brightness was like the light,
rays flashed from his hand;
and there he veiled his power.
5 Before him went pestilence,
and plague followed close behind.
6 He stood and measured the earth;
he looked and shook the nations;
then the eternal mountains were
scattered,
the everlasting hills sank low.
His ways were as of old.
7 I saw the tents of Cüsh′ăn in affliction;
the curtains of the land of Mĭd′-
ĭ·ạn did tremble.
8 Was thy wrath against the rivers,
O LORD?
Was thy anger against the rivers,
or thy indignation against the
sea,
when thou didst ride upon thy horses,
upon thy chariot of victory?
9 Thou didst strip the sheath from thy
bow,
and put the arrows to the string. *i*
Selah
Thou didst cleave the earth with
rivers.

10 The mountains saw thee, and
writhed;
the raging waters swept on;
the deep gave forth its voice,
it lifted its hands on high.
11 The sun and moon stood still in
their habitation *j*
at the light of thine arrows as they
sped,
at the flash of thy glittering spear.
12 Thou didst bestride the earth in fury,
thou didst trample the nations in
anger.
13 Thou wentest forth for the salvation of thy people,
for the salvation of thy anointed.
Thou didst crush the head of the
wicked, *k*
laying him bare from thigh to
neck. *l*   *Selah*
14 Thou didst pierce with thy *m* shafts
the head of his warriors, *n*
who came like a whirlwind to
scatter me,
rejoicing as if to devour the poor
in secret.
15 Thou didst trample the sea with thy
horses,
the surging of mighty waters.

16 I hear, and my body trembles,
my lips quiver at the sound;
rottenness enters into my bones,
my steps totter *o* beneath me.
I will quietly wait for the day of
trouble
to come upon people who invade
us.

17 Though the fig tree do not blossom,
nor fruit be on the vines,
the produce of the olive fail
and the fields yield no food,
the flock be cut off from the fold
and there be no herd in the stalls,
18 yet I will rejoice in the LORD,
I will joy in the God of my salvation.
19 GOD, the Lord, is my strength;
he makes my feet like hinds′
feet,
he makes me tread upon my high
places.

To the choirmaster: with stringed *p*
instruments.

i Cn: Heb obscure *j* Heb uncertain
k Cn: Heb *head from the house of the wicked*
l Heb obscure *m* Heb *his*
n Vg Compare Gk Syr: Heb uncertain
o Cn Compare Gk: Heb *I tremble because*
p Heb *my stringed* **2.20:** Zeph 1.7; Zech 2.13.

The Book of
Zephaniah

1 The word of the LORD which
came to Zĕph·a·nī′ah the son of
Cü′shī, son of Gĕd·a·lī′ah, son of
Ăm·a·rī′ah, son of Hĕz·e·kī′ah, in the
days of Jō·sī′ah the son of Ā′mŏn,
king of Judah.

2 "I will utterly sweep away everything
from the face of the earth,"
says the LORD.
3 "I will sweep away man and beast;
I will sweep away the birds of the
air
and the fish of the sea.
I will overthrow[a] the wicked;
I will cut off mankind
from the face of the earth,"
says the LORD.
4 "I will stretch out my hand against
Judah,
and against all the inhabitants
of Jerusalem;
and I will cut off from this place the
remnant of Bā′al
and the name of the idolatrous
priests;[b]
5 those who bow down on the roofs
to the host of the heavens;
those who bow down and swear to
the LORD
and yet swear by Mīl′cŏm;
6 those who have turned back from
following the LORD,
who do not seek the LORD or
inquire of him."

7 Be silent before the Lord GOD!
For the day of the LORD is at
hand;
the LORD has prepared a sacrifice
and consecrated his guests.
8 And on the day of the LORD's
sacrifice—
"I will punish the officials and the
king's sons
and all who array themselves
in foreign attire.
9 On that day I will punish
every one who leaps over the
threshold,
and those who fill their master's
house
with violence and fraud."

10 "On that day," says the LORD,
"a cry will be heard from the
Fish Gate,
a wail from the Second Quarter,
a loud crash from the hills.
11 Wail, O inhabitants of the Mortar!
For all the traders are no more;
all who weigh out silver are cut
off.
12 At that time I will search Jerusalem
with lamps,
and I will punish the men
who are thickening upon their lees,
those who say in their hearts,
'The LORD will not do good,
nor will he do ill.'
13 Their goods shall be plundered,
and their houses laid waste.
Though they build houses,
they shall not inhabit them;
though they plant vineyards,
they shall not drink wine from
them."

14 The great day of the LORD is near,
near and hastening fast;
the sound of the day of the LORD
is bitter,
the mighty man cries aloud there.
15 A day of wrath is that day,
a day of distress and anguish,
a day of ruin and devastation,
a day of darkness and gloom,
a day of clouds and thick darkness,
16 a day of trumpet blast and battle
cry
against the fortified cities
and against the lofty battlements.

17 I will bring distress on men,
so that they shall walk like the
blind,
because they have sinned against
the LORD;
their blood shall be poured out like
dust,
and their flesh like dung.
18 Neither their silver nor their gold
shall be able to deliver them
on the day of the wrath of the
LORD.

[a] Cn: Heb *the stumbling blocks*
[b] Compare Gk: Heb *idolatrous priests with the priests*
1.7: Hab 2.20; Zech 2.13.

In the fire of his jealous wrath,
all the earth shall be consumed;
for a full, yea, sudden end
he will make of all the inhabitants
of the earth.

2 Come together and hold assembly,
O shameless nation,
2 before you are driven away
like the drifting chaff,[c]
before there comes upon you
the fierce anger of the LORD,
before there comes upon you
the day of the wrath of the LORD.
3 Seek the LORD, all you humble of
the land,
who do his commands;
seek righteousness, seek humility;
perhaps you may be hidden
on the day of the wrath of the
LORD.
4 For Gā′za shall be deserted,
and Ăsh′kĕ·lŏn shall become a
desolation;
Ăsh′dŏd′ş people shall be driven
out at noon,
and Ĕk′rŏn shall be uprooted.

5 Woe to you inhabitants of the seacoast,
you nation of the Chĕr′e·thītes!
The word of the LORD is against you,
O Canaan, land of the Phĭ·lĭs′-
tĭnes;
and I will destroy you till no
inhabitant is left.
6 And you, O seacoast, shall be pastures,
meadows for shepherds
and folds for flocks.
7 The seacoast shall become the possession
of the remnant of the house of
Judah,
on which they shall pasture,
and in the houses of Ăsh′kĕ·lŏn
they shall lie down at evening.
For the LORD their God will be mindful of them
and restore their fortunes.

8 "I have heard the taunts of Mō′ăb
and the revilings of the Ăm′mo-
nĭtes,
how they have taunted my people
and made boasts against their
territory.
9 Therefore, as I live," says the LORD
of hosts,
the God of Israel,

"Mō′ăb shall become like Sŏd′om,
and the Ăm′mo·nĭtes like Go·môr′-
rah,
a land possessed by nettles and salt
pits,
and a waste for ever.
The remnant of my people shall
plunder them,
and the survivors of my nation
shall possess them."
10 This shall be their lot in return for
their pride,
because they scoffed and boasted
against the people of the LORD
of hosts.
11 The LORD will be terrible against
them;
yea, he will famish all the gods of
the earth,
and to him shall bow down,
each in its place,
all the lands of the nations.

12 You also, O Ethiopians,
shall be slain by my sword.

13 And he will stretch out his hand
against the north,
and destroy Assyria;
and he will make Nĭn′e·vĕh a desolation,
a dry waste like the desert.
14 Herds shall lie down in the midst of
her,
all the beasts of the field;[d]
the vulture[e] and the hedgehog
shall lodge in her capitals;
the owl[f] shall hoot in the window,
the raven[g] croak on the threshold;
for her cedar work will be laid bare.
15 This is the exultant city
that dwelt secure,
that said to herself,
"I am and there is none else."
What a desolation she has become,
a lair for wild beasts!
Every one who passes by her
hisses and shakes his fist.

3 Woe to her that is rebellious and
defiled,
the oppressing city!

[c] Cn Compare Gk Syr: Heb *before a decree is born; like chaff a day has passed away*
[d] Tg Compare Gk: Heb *nation*
[e] The meaning of the Hebrew word is uncertain
[f] Cn: Heb *a voice* [g] Gk Vg: Heb *desolation*
2.4-7: Is 14.29-31; Jer 47; Ezek 25.15-17; Joel 3.4-8; Amos 1.6-8; Zech 9.5-7.
2.8-11: Is 15-16; 25.10-12; Jer 48; Ezek 25.8-11; Amos 2.1-3. **2.12:** Is 18.
2.13-15: Is 10.5-34; Nahum.

2 She listens to no voice,
    she accepts no correction.
She does not trust in the LORD,
    she does not draw near to her
        God.

3 Her officials within her
    are roaring lions;
her judges are evening wolves
    that leave nothing till the morn-
        ing.
4 Her prophets are wanton,
    faithless men;
her priests profane what is sacred,
    they do violence to the law.
5 The LORD within her is righteous,
    he does no wrong;
every morning he shows forth his
      justice,
    each dawn he does not fail;
but the unjust knows no shame.

6 "I have cut off nations;
    their battlements are in ruins;
I have laid waste their streets
    so that none walks in them;
their cities have been made desolate,
    without a man, without an inhab-
      itant.
7 I said, 'Surely she will fear me,
    she will accept correction;
she will not lose sight[h]
    of all that I have enjoined upon
      her.'
But all the more they were eager
    to make all their deeds corrupt."

8 "Therefore wait for me," says the
      LORD,
    "for the day when I arise as a
      witness.
For my decision is to gather nations,
    to assemble kingdoms,
to pour out upon them my indig-
      nation,
    all the heat of my anger;
for in the fire of my jealous wrath
    all the earth shall be consumed.

9 "Yea, at that time I will change
    the speech of the peoples
    to a pure speech,
that all of them may call on the
    name of the LORD
and serve him with one accord.
10 From beyond the rivers of Ethiopia
    my suppliants, the daughter of
    my dispersed ones,
    shall bring my offering.

11 "On that day you shall not be put
    to shame
    because of the deeds by which
    you have rebelled against me;
for then I will remove from your
      midst
    your proudly exultant ones,
and you shall no longer be haughty
    in my holy mountain.
12 For I will leave in the midst of
      you
    a people humble and lowly.
They shall seek refuge in the name of
    the LORD,
13   those who are left in Israel;
they shall do no wrong
    and utter no lies,
nor shall there be found in their
      mouth
    a deceitful tongue.
For they shall pasture and lie down,
    and none shall make them afraid."

14 Sing aloud, O daughter of Zion;
    shout, O Israel!
Rejoice and exult with all your heart,
    O daughter of Jerusalem!
15 The LORD has taken away the judg-
      ments against you,
    he has cast out your enemies.
The King of Israel, the LORD, is in
    your midst;
    you shall fear evil no more.
16 On that day it shall be said to Jeru-
      salem:
"Do not fear, O Zion;
    let not your hands grow weak.
17 The LORD, your God, is in your midst,
    a warrior who gives victory;
he will rejoice over you with glad-
      ness,
    he will renew you[i] in his love;
he will exult over you with loud sing-
      ing
18   as on a day of festival.[j]
"I will remove disaster[k] from you,
    so that you will not bear reproach
      for it.
19 Behold, at that time I will deal
    with all your oppressors.
And I will save the lame
    and gather the outcast,
and I will change their shame into
      praise
    and renown in all the earth.
20 At that time I will bring you home,

ʰGk Syr: Heb *and her dwelling will not be cut off*
ⁱGk Syr: Heb *he will be silent*   ʲGk Syr: Heb obscure
ᵏCn: Heb *they were*
3.13: Rev 14.5.

at the time when I gather you together;
yea, I will make you renowned and praised

among all the peoples of the earth,
when I restore your fortunes before your eyes," says the LORD.

The Book of

Haggai

1 In the second year of Dạ·rī'ŭs the king, in the sixth month, on the first day of the month, the word of the LORD came by Hăg'gaī the prophet to Zẹ·rŭb'bạ·bĕl the son of Shĕ–ăl'tĭ–ĕl, governor of Judah, and to Joshua the son of Jĕ·hŏz'ạ·dăk, the high priest, 2 "Thus says the LORD of hosts: This people say the time has not yet come to rebuild the house of the LORD." 3 Then the word of the LORD came by Hăg'gaī the prophet, 4 "Is it a time for you yourselves to dwell in your paneled houses, while this house lies in ruins? 5 Now therefore thus says the LORD of hosts: Consider how you have fared. 6 You have sown much, and harvested little; you eat, but you never have enough; you drink, but you never have your fill; you clothe yourselves, but no one is warm; and he who earns wages earns wages to put them into a bag with holes.
7 "Thus says the LORD of hosts: Consider how you have fared. 8 Go up to the hills and bring wood and build the house, that I may take pleasure in it and that I may appear in my glory, says the LORD. 9 You have looked for much, and, lo, it came to little; and when you brought it home, I blew it away. Why? says the LORD of hosts. Because of my house that lies in ruins, while you busy yourselves each with his own house. 10 Therefore the heavens above you have withheld the dew, and the earth has withheld its produce. 11 And I have called for a drought upon the land and the hills, upon the grain, the new wine, the oil, upon what the ground brings forth, upon men and cattle, and upon all their labors."
12 Then Zẹ·rŭb'bạ·bĕl the son of Shĕ–ăl'tĭ–ĕl, and Joshua the son of

Jĕ·hŏz'ạ·dăk, the high priest, with all the remnant of the people, obeyed the voice of the LORD their God, and the words of Hăg'gaī the prophet, as the LORD their God had sent him; and the people feared before the LORD. 13 Then Hăg'gaī, the messenger of the LORD, spoke to the people with the LORD's message, "I am with you, says the LORD." 14 And the LORD stirred up the spirit of Zẹ·rŭb'bạ·bĕl the son of Shĕ–ăl'tĭ–ĕl, governor of Judah, and the spirit of Joshua the son of Jĕ·hŏz'ạ·dak, the high priest, and the spirit of all the remnant of the people; and they came and worked on the house of the LORD of hosts, their God, 15 on the twenty-fourth day of the month, in the sixth month.

2 In the second year of Dạ·rī'ŭs the king, 1 in the seventh month, on the twenty-first day of the month, the word of the LORD came by Hăg'gaī the prophet, 2 "Speak now to Zẹ·rŭb'bạ·bĕl the son of Shĕ–ăl'tĭ–ĕl, governor of Judah, and to Joshua the son of Jĕ·hŏz'ạ·dăk, the high priest, and to all the remnant of the people, and say, 3 'Who is left among you that saw this house in its former glory? How do you see it now? Is it not in your sight as nothing? 4 Yet now take courage, O Zẹ·rŭb'bạ·bĕl, says the LORD; take courage, O Joshua, son of Jĕ·hŏz'ạ·dăk, the high priest; take courage, all you people of the land, says the LORD; work, for I am with you, says the LORD of hosts, 5 according to the promise that I made you when you came out of Egypt. My Spirit abides among you; fear not. 6 For thus says the LORD of hosts: Once again, in a little while, I will shake the heavens and the earth and the sea and the dry land; 7 and I

2.6: Heb 12.26.

will shake all nations, so that the treasures of all nations shall come in, and I will fill this house with splendor, says the LORD of hosts. ⁸The silver is mine, and the gold is mine, says the LORD of hosts. ⁹The latter splendor of this house shall be greater than the former, says the LORD of hosts; and in this place I will give prosperity, says the LORD of hosts.'"

10 On the twenty-fourth day of the ninth month, in the second year of Da·rī'ŭs, the word of the LORD came by Hăg'gaī the prophet, ¹¹"Thus says the LORD of hosts: Ask the priests to decide this question, ¹²'If one carries holy flesh in the skirt of his garment, and touches with his skirt bread, or pottage, or wine, or oil, or any kind of food, does it become holy?'" The priests answered, "No." ¹³Then said Hăg'gaī, "If one who is unclean by contact with a dead body touches any of these, does it become unclean?" The priests answered, "It does become unclean." ¹⁴Then Hăg'gaī said, "So is it with this people, and with this nation before me, says the LORD; and so with every work of their hands; and what they offer there is unclean. ¹⁵Pray now, consider what will come to pass from this day onward. Before a stone was placed upon a stone in the temple of the LORD, ¹⁶how did you fare?ᵃ When

one came to a heap of twenty measures, there were but ten; when one came to the winevat to draw fifty measures, there were but twenty. ¹⁷I smote you and all the products of your toil with blight and mildew and hail; yet you did not return to me, says the LORD. ¹⁸Consider from this day onward, from the twenty-fourth day of the ninth month. Since the day that the foundation of the LORD's temple was laid, consider: ¹⁹Is the seed yet in the barn? Do the vine, the fig tree, the pomegranate, and the olive tree still yield nothing? From this day on I will bless you."

20 The word of the LORD came a second time to Hăg'gaī on the twenty-fourth day of the month, ²¹"Speak to Ze·rŭb'ba·bĕl, governor of Judah, saying, I am about to shake the heavens and the earth, ²²and to overthrow the throne of kingdoms; I am about to destroy the strength of the kingdoms of the nations, and overthrow the chariots and their riders; and the horses and their riders shall go down, every one by the sword of his fellow. ²³On that day, says the LORD of hosts, I will take you, O Ze·rŭb'ba·bĕl my servant, the son of Shĕ-ăl'tĭ-ĕl, says the LORD, and make you like a signet ring; for I have chosen you, says the LORD of hosts."

The Book of
Zechariah

1 In the eighth month, in the second year of Da·rī'ŭs, the word of the LORD came to Zĕch·a·rī'ah the son of Bĕr·e·chī'ah, son of Ĭd'dō, the prophet, saying, ²"The LORD was very angry with your fathers. ³Therefore say to them, Thus says the LORD of hosts: Return to me, says the LORD of hosts, and I will return to you, says the LORD of hosts. ⁴Be not like your fathers, to whom the former prophets cried out, 'Thus says the LORD of hosts, Return from your evil ways and from your evil deeds.' But they did not hear or heed me, says the

LORD. ⁵Your fathers, where are they? And the prophets, do they live for ever? ⁶But my words and my statutes, which I commanded my servants the prophets, did they not overtake your fathers? So they repented and said, As the LORD of hosts purposed to deal with us for our ways and deeds, so has he dealt with us."

7 On the twenty-fourth day of the eleventh month which is the month of She·băt', in the second year of Da·rī'ŭs, the word of the LORD came to Zĕch·a·rī'ah the son of Bĕr·e·chī'ah,

ᵃGk: Heb *since they were*

son of Ĭd′dō, the prophet; and Zĕch·a̧·rī′ah said, [8] "I saw in the night, and behold, a man riding upon a red horse! He was standing among the myrtle trees in the glen; and behind him were red, sorrel, and white horses. [9] Then I said, 'What are these, my lord?' The angel who talked with me said to me, 'I will show you what they are.' [10] So the man who was standing among the myrtle trees answered, 'These are they whom the LORD has sent to patrol the earth.' [11] And they answered the angel of the LORD who was standing among the myrtle trees, 'We have patrolled the earth, and behold, all the earth remains at rest.' [12] Then the angel of the LORD said, 'O LORD of hosts, how long wilt thou have no mercy on Jerusalem and the cities of Judah, against which thou hast had indignation these seventy years?' [13] And the LORD answered gracious and comforting words to the angel who talked with me. [14] So the angel who talked with me said to me, 'Cry out, Thus says the LORD of hosts: I am exceedingly jealous for Jerusalem and for Zion. [15] And I am very angry with the nations that are at ease; for while I was angry but a little they furthered the disaster. [16] Therefore, thus says the LORD, I have returned to Jerusalem with compassion; my house shall be built in it, says the LORD of hosts, and the measuring line shall be stretched out over Jerusalem. [17] Cry again, Thus says the LORD of hosts: My cities shall again overflow with prosperity, and the LORD will again comfort Zion and again choose Jerusalem.'"

[18][a] And I lifted my eyes and saw, and behold, four horns! [19] And I said to the angel who talked with me, "What are these?" And he answered me, "These are the horns which have scattered Judah, Israel, and Jerusalem." [20] Then the LORD showed me four smiths. [21] And I said, "What are these coming to do?" He answered, "These are the horns which scattered Judah, so that no man raised his head; and these have come to terrify them, to cast down the horns of the nations who lifted up their horns against the land of Judah to scatter it."

[2][b] And I lifted my eyes and saw, and behold, a man with a measuring line in his hand! [2] Then I said, "Where are you going?" And he said to me, "To measure Jerusalem, to see what is its breadth and what is its length." [3] And behold, the angel who talked with me came forward, and another angel came forward to meet him, [4] and said to him, "Run, say to that young man, 'Jerusalem shall be inhabited as villages without walls, because of the multitude of men and cattle in it. [5] For I will be to her a wall of fire round about, says the LORD, and I will be the glory within her.'"

6 Ho! ho! Flee from the land of the north, says the LORD; for I have spread you abroad as the four winds of the heavens, says the LORD. [7] Ho! Escape to Zion, you who dwell with the daughter of Babylon. [8] For thus said the LORD of hosts, after his glory sent me to the nations who plundered you, for he who touches you touches the apple of his eye: [9] "Behold, I will shake my hand over them, and they shall become plunder for those who served them. Then you will know that the LORD of hosts has sent me. [10] Sing and rejoice, O daughter of Zion; for lo, I come and I will dwell in the midst of you, says the LORD. [11] And many nations shall join themselves to the LORD in that day, and shall be my people; and I will dwell in the midst of you, and you shall know that the LORD of hosts has sent me to you. [12] And the LORD will inherit Judah as his portion in the holy land, and will again choose Jerusalem."

13 Be silent, all flesh, before the LORD; for he has roused himself from his holy dwelling.

3   Then he showed me Joshua the high priest standing before the angel of the LORD, and Satan standing at his right hand to accuse him. [2] And the LORD said to Satan, "The LORD rebuke you, O Satan! The LORD who has chosen Jerusalem rebuke you! Is not this a brand plucked from the fire?" [3] Now Joshua was standing before the angel, clothed with filthy garments. [4] And the angel said to those who were standing before him, "Remove the filthy garments from him." And to him he said, "Behold, I have taken your iniquity away from you, and I will clothe you with rich apparel." [5] And I said, "Let them

[a] Ch 2.1 in Heb   [b] Ch 2.5 in Heb
2.13: Hab 2.20; Zeph·1.7. 3.2: Jude 9.

put a clean turban on his head." So they put a clean turban on his head and clothed him with garments; and the angel of the LORD was standing by.

6 And the angel of the LORD enjoined Joshua, 7 "Thus says the LORD of hosts: If you will walk in my ways and keep my charge, then you shall rule my house and have charge of my courts, and I will give you the right of access among those who are standing here. 8 Hear now, O Joshua the high priest, you and your friends who sit before you, for they are men of good omen: behold, I will bring my servant the Branch. 9 For behold, upon the stone which I have set before Joshua, upon a single stone with seven facets, I will engrave its inscription, says the LORD of hosts, and I will remove the guilt of this land in a single day. 10 In that day, says the LORD of hosts, every one of you will invite his neighbor under his vine and under his fig tree."

4 And the angel who talked with me came again, and waked me, like a man that is wakened out of his sleep. 2 And he said to me, "What do you see?" I said, "I see, and behold, a lampstand all of gold, with a bowl on the top of it, and seven lamps on it, with seven lips on each of the lamps which are on the top of it. 3 And there are two olive trees by it, one on the right of the bowl and the other on its left." 4 And I said to the angel who talked with me, "What are these, my lord?" 5 Then the angel who talked with me answered me, "Do you not know what these are?" I said, "No, my lord." 6 Then he said to me, "This is the word of the LORD to Ze·rŭb′ba·bĕl: Not by might, nor by power, but by my Spirit, says the LORD of hosts. 7 What are you, O great mountain? Before Ze·rŭb′ba·bĕl you shall become a plain; and he shall bring forward the top stone amid shouts of 'Grace, grace to it!'" 8 Moreover the word of the LORD came to me, saying, 9 "The hands of Ze·rŭb′ba·bĕl have laid the foundation of this house; his hands shall also complete it. Then you will know that the LORD of hosts has sent me to you. 10 For whoever has despised the day of small things shall rejoice, and shall see the plummet in the hand of Ze·rŭb′ba·bĕl.

"These seven are the eyes of the LORD, which range through the whole earth." 11 Then I said to him, "What are these two olive trees on the right and the left of the lampstand?" 12 And a second time I said to him, "What are these two branches of the olive trees, which are beside the two golden pipes from which the oil*c* is poured out?" 13 He said to me, "Do you not know what these are?" I said, "No, my lord." 14 Then he said, "These are the two anointed who stand by the Lord of the whole earth."

5 Again I lifted my eyes and saw, and behold, a flying scroll! 2 And he said to me, "What do you see?" I answered, "I see a flying scroll; its length is twenty cubits, and its breadth ten cubits." 3 Then he said to me, "This is the curse that goes out over the face of the whole land; for every one who steals shall be cut off henceforth according to it, and every one who swears falsely shall be cut off henceforth according to it. 4 I will send it forth, says the LORD of hosts, and it shall enter the house of the thief, and the house of him who swears falsely by my name; and it shall abide in his house and consume it, both timber and stones."

5 Then the angel who talked with me came forward and said to me, "Lift your eyes, and see what this is that goes forth." 6 And I said, "What is it?" He said, "This is the ephah that goes forth." And he said, "This is their iniquity*d* in all the land." 7 And behold, the leaden cover was lifted, and there was a woman sitting in the ephah! 8 And he said, "This is Wickedness." And he thrust her back into the ephah, and thrust down the leaden weight upon its mouth. 9 Then I lifted my eyes and saw, and behold, two women coming forward! The wind was in their wings; they had wings like the wings of a stork, and they lifted up the ephah between earth and heaven. 10 Then I said to the angel who talked with me, "Where are they taking the ephah?" 11 He said to me, "To the land of Shī′nār, to build a house for it; and when this is prepared, they will set the ephah down there on its base."

6 And again I lifted my eyes and saw, and behold, four chariots came out from between two moun-

*c*Cn: Heb *gold*   *d*Gk Compare Syr: Heb *eye*
3.8: Is 4.2; Jer 23.5; 33.15; Zech 6.12.   **3.10**: Mic 4.4.
4.3, 11-14: Rev 11.4.   **4.10**: Rev 5.6.   **6.1-3**: Rev 6.2-8.

tains; and the mountains were mountains of bronze. ² The first chariot had red horses, the second black horses, ³ the third white horses, and the fourth chariot dappled gray*ᵉ* horses. ⁴ Then I said to the angel who talked with me, "What are these, my lord?" ⁵ And the angel answered me, "These are going forth to the four winds of heaven, after presenting themselves before the LORD of all the earth. ⁶ The chariot with the black horses goes toward the north country, the white ones go toward the west country,*ᶠ* and the dappled ones go toward the south country." ⁷ When the steeds came out, they were impatient to get off and patrol the earth. And he said, "Go, patrol the earth." So they patrolled the earth. ⁸ Then he cried to me, "Behold, those who go toward the north country have set my Spirit at rest in the north country."

9 And the word of the LORD came to me: ¹⁰ "Take from the exiles Hĕl'daī, Tō·bī'jah, and Jĕ·daī'ah, who have arrived from Babylon; and go the same day to the house of Jō·sī'ah, the son of Zĕph·a·nī'ah. ¹¹ Take from them silver and gold, and make a crown,*ᵍ* and set it upon the head of Joshua, the son of Jĕ·hŏz'a·dăk, the high priest; ¹² and say to him, 'Thus says the LORD of hosts, "Behold, the man whose name is the Branch: for he shall grow up in his place, and he shall build the temple of the LORD. ¹³ It is he who shall build the temple of the LORD, and shall bear royal honor, and shall sit and rule upon his throne. And there shall be a priest by his throne, and peaceful understanding shall be between them both."' ¹⁴ And the crown*ʰ* shall be in the temple of the LORD as a reminder to Hĕl'daī,*ⁱ* Tō·bī'jah, Jĕ·daī'ah, and Jō·sī'ah*ʲ* the son of Zĕph·a·nī'ah.

15 "And those who are far off shall come and help to build the temple of the LORD; and you shall know that the LORD of hosts has sent me to you. And this shall come to pass, if you will diligently obey the voice of the LORD your God."

7 In the fourth year of King Da·rī'ŭs, the word of the LORD came to Zĕch·a·rī'ah in the fourth day of the ninth month, which is Chĭs'lĕv. ² Now the people of Bĕth'el had sent Sha·re'zer and Rĕg'ĕm–mĕl'ĕch and their men, to entreat the favor of the LORD,

³ and to ask the priests of the house of the LORD of hosts and the prophets, "Should I mourn and fast in the fifth month, as I have done for so many years?" ⁴ Then the word of the LORD of hosts came to me; ⁵ "Say to all the people of the land and the priests, When you fasted and mourned in the fifth month and in the seventh, for these seventy years, was it for me that you fasted? ⁶ And when you eat and when you drink, do you not eat for yourselves and drink for yourselves? ⁷ When Jerusalem was inhabited and in prosperity, with her cities round about her, and the South and the lowland were inhabited, were not these the words which the LORD proclaimed by the former prophets?"

8 And the word of the LORD came to Zĕch·a·rī'ah, saying, ⁹ "Thus says the LORD of hosts, Render true judgments, show kindness and mercy each to his brother, ¹⁰ do not oppress the widow, the fatherless, the sojourner, or the poor; and let none of you devise evil against his brother in your heart." ¹¹ But they refused to hearken, and turned a stubborn shoulder, and stopped their ears that they might not hear. ¹² They made their hearts like adamant lest they should hear the law and the words which the LORD of hosts had sent by his Spirit through the former prophets. Therefore great wrath came from the LORD of hosts. ¹³ "As I called, and they would not hear, so they called, and I would not hear," says the LORD of hosts, ¹⁴ "and I scattered them with a whirlwind among all the nations which they had not known. Thus the land they left was desolate, so that no one went to and fro, and the pleasant land was made desolate."

8 And the word of the LORD of hosts came to me, saying, ² "Thus says the LORD of hosts: I am jealous for Zion with great jealousy, and I am jealous for her with great wrath. ³ Thus says the LORD: I will return to Zion, and will dwell in the midst of Jerusalem, and Jerusalem shall be called the faithful city, and the mountain of the LORD of hosts, the holy mountain. ⁴ Thus says the LORD of hosts: Old men and old women shall

ᵉ Compare Gk: The meaning of the Hebrew word is uncertain   *ʲ* Cn: Heb *after them*
ᵍ Gk Mss: Heb *crowns*   *ʰ* Gk: Heb *crowns*
ⁱ With verse 10: Heb *Helem*   *ʲ* With verse 10: Heb *Hen*
6.5: Rev 7.1.   **6.12:** Zech 3.8; Is 4.2; Jer 23.5; 33.15.

again sit in the streets of Jerusalem, each with staff in hand for very age. [5]And the streets of the city shall be full of boys and girls playing in its streets. [6]Thus says the LORD of hosts: If it is marvelous in the sight of the remnant of this people in these days, should it also be marvelous in my sight, says the LORD of hosts? [7]Thus says the LORD of hosts: Behold, I will save my people from the east country and from the west country; [8]and I will bring them to dwell in the midst of Jerusalem; and they shall be my people and I will be their God, in faithfulness and in righteousness."

9 Thus says the LORD of hosts: "Let your hands be strong, you who in these days have been hearing these words from the mouth of the prophets, since the day that the foundation of the house of the LORD of hosts was laid, that the temple might be built. [10]For before those days there was no wage for man or any wage for beast, neither was there any safety from the foe for him who went out or came in; for I set every man against his fellow. [11]But now I will not deal with the remnant of this people as in the former days, says the LORD of hosts. [12]For there shall be a sowing of peace; the vine shall yield its fruit, and the ground shall give its increase, and the heavens shall give their dew; and I will cause the remnant of this people to possess all these things. [13]And as you have been a byword of cursing among the nations, O house of Judah and house of Israel, so will I save you and you shall be a blessing. Fear not, but let your hands be strong."

14 For thus says the LORD of hosts: "As I purposed to do evil to you, when your fathers provoked me to wrath, and I did not relent, says the LORD of hosts, [15]so again have I purposed in these days to do good to Jerusalem and to the house of Judah; fear not. [16]These are the things that you shall do: Speak the truth to one another, render in your gates judgments that are true and make for peace, [17]do not devise evil in your hearts against one another, and love no false oath, for all these things I hate, says the LORD."

18 And the word of the LORD of hosts came to me, saying, [19]"Thus says the LORD of hosts: The fast of the fourth month, and the fast of the fifth, and the fast of the seventh, and the fast of the tenth, shall be to the house of Judah seasons of joy and gladness, and cheerful feasts; therefore love truth and peace.

20 "Thus says the LORD of hosts: Peoples shall yet come, even the inhabitants of many cities; [21]the inhabitants of one city shall go to another, saying, 'Let us go at once to entreat the favor of the LORD, and to seek the LORD of hosts; I am going.' [22]Many peoples and strong nations shall come to seek the LORD of hosts in Jerusalem, and to entreat the favor of the LORD. [23]Thus says the LORD of hosts: In those days ten men from the nations of every tongue shall take hold of the robe of a Jew, saying, 'Let us go with you, for we have heard that God is with you.'"

9   An Oracle

The word of the LORD is against the
    land of Hăd′răch
and will rest upon Damascus.
For to the LORD belong the cities of
    Ăr′ạm, [k]
even as all the tribes of Israel;
[2]Hā·măth also, which borders thereon,
    Tўre and Sī′dọn, though they are
    very wise.
[3]Tўre has built herself a rampart,
    and heaped up silver like dust,
    and gold like the mud of the streets.
[4]But lo, the Lord will strip her of her
    possessions
and hurl her wealth into the sea,
    and she shall be devoured by fire.

[5]Ăsh′kĕ·lŏn shall see it, and be afraid;
    Gā′zạ too, and shall writhe in
    anguish;
Ĕk′rọn also, because its hopes are
    confounded.
The king shall perish from Gaza;
    Ashkelon shall be uninhabited;
[6]a mongrel people shall dwell in Ăsh-
    dŏd;
and I will make an end of the pride
    of Phĭ·lĭs′tĭ·ạ.
[7]I will take away its blood from its
    mouth,
and its abominations from be-
    tween its teeth;
it too shall be a remnant for our God;
    it shall be like a clan in Judah,
and Ĕk′rọn shall be like the Jĕb′-
    ū·sītes.

[k]Cn: Heb *the eye of Adam* (or *man*)   8.16: Eph 4.25.

⁸Then I will encamp at my house as
    a guard,
    so that none shall march to and
      fro;
no oppressor shall again overrun
    them,
    for now I see with my own eyes.

⁹Rejoice greatly, O daughter of Zion!
    Shout aloud, O daughter of Jeru-
      salem!
Lo, your king comes to you;
    triumphant and victorious is he,
humble and riding on an ass,
    on a colt the foal of an ass.
¹⁰I will cut off the chariot from
    Ē′phra·ĭm
    and the war horse from Jerusalem;
and the battle bow shall be cut off,
    and he shall command peace to
      the nations;
his dominion shall be from sea to
    sea,
    and from the River to the ends of
      the earth.

¹¹As for you also, because of the blood
    of my covenant with you,
    I will set your captives free from
      the waterless pit.
¹²Return to your stronghold, O pris-
    oners of hope;
    today I declare that I will restore
      to you double.
¹³For I have bent Judah as my bow;
    I have made Ē′phra·ĭm its ar-
      row.
I will brandish your sons, O Zion,
    over your sons, O Greece,
    and wield you like a warrior's
      sword.
¹⁴Then the Lord will appear over
    them,
    and his arrow go forth like light-
      ning;
the Lord God will sound the trumpet,
    and march forth in the whirlwinds
      of the south.
¹⁵The Lord of hosts will protect them,
    and they shall devour and tread
      down the slingers;[*l*]
and they shall drink their blood[*m*]
    like wine,
    and be full like a bowl,
    drenched like the corners of the
      altar.

¹⁶On that day the Lord their God will
    save them
    for they are the flock of his people;

for like the jewels of a crown
    they shall shine on his land.
¹⁷Yea, how good and how fair it shall
    be!
Grain shall make the young men
    flourish,
    and new wine the maidens.

10   Ask rain from the Lord
      in the season of the spring rain,
from the Lord who makes the storm
    clouds,
who gives men showers of rain,
    to every one the vegetation in the
      field.
²For the teraphim utter nonsense,
    and the diviners see lies;
the dreamers tell false dreams,
    and give empty consolation.
Therefore the people wander like
    sheep;
    they are afflicted for want of a
      shepherd.

³"My anger is hot against the shep-
    herds,
    and I will punish the leaders;[*n*]
for the Lord of hosts cares for his
    flock, the house of Judah,
    and will make them like his proud
      steed in battle.
⁴Out of them shall come the corner-
    stone,
    out of them the tent peg,
out of them the battle bow,
    out of them every ruler.
⁵Together they shall be like mighty
    men in battle,
    trampling the foe in the mud of
      the streets;
they shall fight because the Lord is
    with them,
    and they shall confound the riders
      on horses.

⁶"I will strengthen the house of Judah,
    and I will save the house of Joseph.
I will bring them back because I
    have compassion on them,
    and they shall be as though I
      had not rejected them;
for I am the Lord their God and I
    will answer them.
⁷Then Ē′phra·ĭm shall become like
    a mighty warrior,
    and their hearts shall be glad as
      with wine.

*l*Cn: Heb *the slingstones*   *m*Gk: Heb *be turbulent*
*n*Or *he-goats*
9.9: Mt 21.5; Jn 12.15.

Their children shall see it and rejoice,
their hearts shall exult in the LORD.

8 "I will signal for them and gather them in,
for I have redeemed them,
and they shall be as many as of old.
9 Though I scattered them among the nations,
yet in far countries they shall remember me,
and with their children they shall live and return.
10 I will bring them home from the land of Egypt,
and gather them from Assyria;
and I will bring them to the land of Gilead and to Lebanon,
till there is no room for them.
11 They shall pass through the sea of Egypt,*o*
and the waves of the sea shall be smitten,
and all the depths of the Nile dried up.
The pride of Assyria shall be laid low,
and the scepter of Egypt shall depart.
12 I will make them strong in the LORD
and they shall glory*p* in his name,"
says the LORD.

11 Open your doors, O Lebanon,
that the fire may devour your cedars!
2 Wail, O cypress, for the cedar has fallen,
for the glorious trees are ruined!
Wail, oaks of Bā'shan,
for the thick forest has been felled!
3 Hark, the wail of the shepherds,
for their glory is despoiled!
Hark, the roar of the lions,
for the jungle of the Jordan is laid waste!

4 Thus said the LORD my God: "Become shepherd of the flock doomed to slaughter. 5 Those who buy them slay them and go unpunished; and those who sell them say, 'Blessed be the LORD, I have become rich'; and their own shepherds have no pity on them. 6 For I will no longer have pity on the inhabitants of this land, says the LORD. Lo, I will cause men to fall each into the hand of his shepherd, and each into the hand of his king; and

they shall crush the earth, and I will deliver none from their hand."

7 So I became the shepherd of the flock doomed to be slain for those who trafficked in the sheep. And I took two staffs; one I named Grace, the other I named Union. And I tended the sheep. 8 In one month I destroyed the three shepherds. But I became impatient with them, and they also detested me. 9 So I said, "I will not be your shepherd. What is to die, let it die; what is to be destroyed, let it be destroyed; and let those that are left devour the flesh of one another." 10 And I took my staff Grace, and I broke it, annulling the covenant which I had made with all the peoples. 11 So it was annulled on that day, and the traffickers in the sheep, who were watching me, knew that it was the word of the LORD. 12 Then I said to them, "If it seems right to you, give me my wages; but if not, keep them." And they weighed out as my wages thirty shekels of silver. 13 Then the LORD said to me, "Cast it into the treasury"*q* – the lordly price at which I was paid off by them. So I took the thirty shekels of silver and cast them into the treasury*q* in the house of the LORD. 14 Then I broke my second staff Union, annulling the brotherhood between Judah and Israel.

15 Then the LORD said to me, "Take once more the implements of a worthless shepherd. 16 For lo, I am raising up in the land a shepherd who does not care for the perishing, or seek the wandering,*r* or heal the maimed, or nourish the sound, but devours the flesh of the fat ones, tearing off even their hoofs.

17 Woe to my worthless shepherd,
who deserts the flock!
May the sword smite his arm
and his right eye!
Let his arm be wholly withered,
his right eye utterly blinded!"

12 An Oracle

The word of the LORD concerning Israel: Thus says the LORD, who stretched out the heavens and founded the earth and formed the spirit of man

o Cn: Heb *distress* *p* Gk: Heb *walk*
q Syr: Heb *to the potter*
r Syr Compare Gk Vg: Heb *the youth*
11.12-13: Mt 26.15; 27.9.

within him: ²"Lo, I am about to make Jerusalem a cup of reeling to all the peoples round about; it will be against Judah also in the siege against Jerusalem. ³On that day I will make Jerusalem a heavy stone for all the peoples; all who lift it shall grievously hurt themselves. And all the nations of the earth will come together against it. ⁴On that day, says the LORD, I will strike every horse with panic, and its rider with madness. But upon the house of Judah I will open my eyes, when I strike every horse of the peoples with blindness. ⁵Then the clans of Judah shall say to themselves, 'The inhabitants of Jerusalem have strength through the LORD of hosts, their God.'

6 "On that day I will make the clans of Judah like a blazing pot in the midst of wood, like a flaming torch among sheaves; and they shall devour to the right and to the left all the peoples round about, while Jerusalem shall still be inhabited in its place, in Jerusalem.

7 "And the LORD will give victory to the tents of Judah first, that the glory of the house of David and the glory of the inhabitants of Jerusalem may not be exalted over that of Judah. ⁸On that day the LORD will put a shield about the inhabitants of Jerusalem so that the feeblest among them on that day shall be like David, and the house of David shall be like God, like the angel of the LORD, at their head. ⁹And on that day I will seek to destroy all the nations that come against Jerusalem.

10 "And I will pour out on the house of David and the inhabitants of Jerusalem a spirit of compassion and supplication, so that, when they look on him whom they have pierced, they shall mourn for him, as one mourns for an only child, and weep bitterly over him, as one weeps over a first-born. ¹¹On that day the mourning in Jerusalem will be as great as the mourning for Hā′dăd–rĭm′mŏn in the plain of Me·gĭd′dō. ¹²The land shall mourn, each family by itself; the family of the house of David by itself, and their wives by themselves; the family of the house of Nathan by itself, and their wives by themselves; ¹³the family of the house of Lē′vī by itself, and their wives by themselves; the family of the Shĭm·ē′ītes by itself,

and their wives by themselves; ¹⁴and all the families that are left, each by itself, and their wives by themselves.

13 "On that day there shall be a fountain opened for the house of David and the inhabitants of Jerusalem to cleanse them from sin and uncleanness.

2 "And on that day, says the LORD of hosts, I will cut off the names of the idols from the land, so that they shall be remembered no more; and also I will remove from the land the prophets and the unclean spirit. ³And if any one again appears as a prophet, his father and mother who bore him will say to him, 'You shall not live, for you speak lies in the name of the LORD'; and his father and mother who bore him shall pierce him through when he prophesies. ⁴On that day every prophet will be ashamed of his vision when he prophesies; he will not put on a hairy mantle in order to deceive, ⁵but he will say, 'I am no prophet, I am a tiller of the soil; for the land has been my possessionᶠ since my youth.' ⁶And if one asks him, 'What are these wounds on your back?' he will say, 'The wounds I received in the house of my friends.' "

7 "Awake, O sword, against my shepherd,
    against the man who stands next to me,"
                    says the LORD of hosts.
"Strike the shepherd, that the sheep may be scattered;
    I will turn my hand against the little ones.
⁸In the whole land, says the LORD,
    two thirds shall be cut off and perish,
    and one third shall be left alive.
⁹And I will put this third into the fire,
    and refine them as one refines silver,
    and test them as gold is tested.
They will call on my name,
    and I will answer them.
I will say, 'They are my people';
    and they will say, 'The LORD is my God.' "

14 Behold, a day of the LORD is coming, when the spoil taken from you will be divided in the midst

ᶠCn: Heb *for man has caused me to possess*
12.10: Jn 19.37. 13.7: Mt 26.31; Mk 14.27.

of you. ²For I will gather all the nations against Jerusalem to battle, and the city shall be taken and the houses plundered and the women ravished; half of the city shall go into exile, but the rest of the people shall not be cut off from the city. ³Then the LORD will go forth and fight against those nations as when he fights on a day of battle. ⁴On that day his feet shall stand on the Mount of Olives which lies before Jerusalem on the east; and the Mount of Olives shall be split in two from east to west by a very wide valley; so that one half of the Mount shall withdraw northward, and the other half southward. ⁵And the valley of my mountains shall be stopped up, for the valley of the mountains shall touch the side of it; and you shall flee as you fled from the earthquake in the days of Ūz·zī′ah king of Judah. Then the LORD your" God will come, and all the holy ones with him.ᵛ

6 On that day there shall be neither cold nor frost.ʷ ⁷And there shall be continuous day (it is known to the LORD), not day and not night, for at evening time there shall be light.

8 On that day living waters shall flow out from Jerusalem, half of them to the eastern sea and half of them to the western sea; it shall continue in summer as in winter.

9 And the LORD will become king over all the earth; on that day the LORD will be one and his name one.

10 The whole land shall be turned into a plain from Gē′ba to Rĭm′mōn south of Jerusalem. But Jerusalem shall remain aloft upon its site from the Gate of Benjamin to the place of the former gate, to the Corner Gate, and from the Tower of Ha·nän′ĕl to the king's wine presses. ¹¹And it shall be inhabited, for there shall be no more curse;ˣ Jerusalem shall dwell in security.

12 And this shall be the plague with which the LORD will smite all the peoples that wage war against Jeru-

salem: their flesh shall rot while they are still on their feet, their eyes shall rot in their sockets, and their tongues shall rot in their mouths. ¹³And on that day a great panic from the LORD shall fall on them, so that each will lay hold on the hand of his fellow, and the hand of the one will be raised against the hand of the other; ¹⁴even Judah will fight against Jerusalem. And the wealth of all the nations round about shall be collected, gold, silver, and garments in great abundance. ¹⁵And a plague like this plague shall fall on the horses, the mules, the camels, the asses, and whatever beasts may be in those camps.

16 Then every one that survives of all the nations that have come against Jerusalem shall go up year after year to worship the King, the LORD of hosts, and to keep the feast of booths. ¹⁷And if any of the families of the earth do not go up to Jerusalem to worship the King, the LORD of hosts, there will be no rain upon them. ¹⁸And if the family of Egypt do not go up and present themselves, then upon them shallʸ come the plague with which the LORD afflicts the nations that do not go up to keep the feast of booths. ¹⁹This shall be the punishment to Egypt and the punishment to all the nations that do not go up to keep the feast of booths.

20 And on that day there shall be inscribed on the bells of the horses, "Holy to the LORD." And the pots in the house of the LORD shall be as the bowls before the altar; ²¹and every pot in Jerusalem and Judah shall be sacred to the LORD of hosts, so that all who sacrifice may come and take of them and boil the flesh of the sacrifice in them. And there shall no longer be a trader in the house of the LORD of hosts on that day.

ᵘHeb *my*   ᵛGk Syr Vg Tg: Heb *you*
ʷCompare Gk Syr Vg Tg: Heb uncertain
ˣOr *ban of utter destruction*   ʸGk Syr: Heb *shall not*
14.8: Ezek 47.1-12; Rev 22.1-2.
14.11: Rev 22.3.   14.18-19: Is 19; Jer 46; Ezek 29-32.

The Book of

Malachi

1 The oracle of the word of the LORD to Israel by Măl′a·chī.[a]

2 "I have loved you," says the LORD. But you say, "How hast thou loved us?" "Is not Esau Jacob's brother?" says the LORD. "Yet I have loved Jacob ³but I have hated Esau; I have laid waste his hill country and left his heritage to jackals of the desert." ⁴If Ē′dǫm says, "We are shattered but we will rebuild the ruins," the LORD of hosts says, "They may build, but I will tear down, till they are called the wicked country, the people with whom the LORD is angry for ever." ⁵Your own eyes shall see this, and you shall say, "Great is the LORD, beyond the border of Israel!"

6 "A son honors his father, and a servant his master. If then I am a father, where is my honor? And if I am a master, where is my fear? says the LORD of hosts to you, O priests, who despise my name. You say, 'How have we despised thy name?' ⁷By offering polluted food upon my altar. And you say, 'How have we polluted it?'[b] By thinking that the LORD's table may be despised. ⁸When you offer blind animals in sacrifice, is that no evil? And when you offer those that are lame or sick, is that no evil? Present that to your governor; will he be pleased with you or show you favor? says the LORD of hosts. ⁹And now entreat the favor of God, that he may be gracious to us. With such a gift from your hand, will he show favor to any of you? says the LORD of hosts. ¹⁰Oh, that there were one among you who would shut the doors, that you might not kindle fire upon my altar in vain! I have no pleasure in you, says the LORD of hosts, and I will not accept an offering from your hand. ¹¹For from the rising of the sun to its setting my name is great among the nations, and in every place incense is offered to my name, and a pure offering; for my name is great among the nations, says the LORD of hosts. ¹²But you profane it when you say that the LORD's table is polluted,

and the food for it[c] may be despised. ¹³'What a weariness this is,' you say, and you sniff at me,[d] says the LORD of hosts. You bring what has been taken by violence or is lame or sick, and this you bring as your offering! Shall I accept that from your hand? says the LORD. ¹⁴Cursed be the cheat who has a male in his flock, and vows it, and yet sacrifices to the Lord what is blemished; for I am a great King, says the LORD of hosts, and my name is feared among the nations.

2 "And now, O priests, this command is for you. ²If you will not listen, if you will not lay it to heart to give glory to my name, says the LORD of hosts, then I will send the curse upon you and I will curse your blessings; indeed I have already cursed them, because you do not lay it to heart. ³Behold, I will rebuke your offspring, and spread dung upon your faces, the dung of your offerings, and I will put you out of my presence.[e] ⁴So shall you know that I have sent this command to you, that my covenant with Lē′vī may hold, says the LORD of hosts. ⁵My covenant with him was a covenant of life and peace, and I gave them to him, that he might fear; and he feared me, he stood in awe of my name. ⁶True instruction[f] was in his mouth, and no wrong was found on his lips. He walked with me in peace and uprightness, and he turned many from iniquity. ⁷For the lips of a priest should guard knowledge, and men should seek instruction[f] from his mouth, for he is the messenger of the LORD of hosts. ⁸But you have turned aside from the way; you have caused many to stumble by your instruction;[f] you have corrupted the covenant of Lē′vī, says the LORD of hosts, ⁹and so I make you despised and

ᵃOr *my messenger*   ᵇGk: Heb *thee*
ᶜHeb *its fruit, its food*   ᵈAnother reading is *it*
ᵉCn Compare Gk Syr: Heb *and he shall bear you to it*
ᶠOr *law*
1.2-3: Rom 9.13.
1.2-5: Is 34; 63.1-6; Jer 49.7-22; Ezek 25.12-14; 35; Amos 1.11-12; Obad.

abased before all the people, inasmuch as you have not kept my ways but have shown partiality in your instruction."*f*

10 Have we not all one father? Has not one God created us? Why then are we faithless to one another, profaning the covenant of our fathers? ¹¹ Judah has been faithless, and abomination has been committed in Israel and in Jerusalem; for Judah has profaned the sanctuary of the LORD, which he loves, and has married the daughter of a foreign god. ¹² May the LORD cut off from the tents of Jacob, for the man who does this, any to witness*g* or answer, or to bring an offering to the LORD of hosts!

13 And this again you do. You cover the LORD's altar with tears, with weeping and groaning because he no longer regards the offering or accepts it with favor at your hand. ¹⁴ You ask, "Why does he not?" Because the LORD was witness to the covenant between you and the wife of your youth, to whom you have been faithless, though she is your companion and your wife by covenant. ¹⁵ Has not the one God made*h* and sustained for us the spirit of life?*i* And what does he desire? Godly offspring. So take heed to yourselves, and let none be faithless to the wife of his youth. ¹⁶ "For I hate*j* divorce, says the LORD the God of Israel, and covering one's garment with violence, says the LORD of hosts. So take heed to yourselves and do not be faithless."

17 You have wearied the LORD with your words. Yet you say, "How have we wearied him?" By saying, "Every one who does evil is good in the sight of the LORD, and he delights in them." Or by asking, "Where is the God of justice?"

3 "Behold, I send my messenger to prepare the way before me, and the Lord whom you seek will suddenly come to his temple; the messenger of the covenant in whom you delight, behold, he is coming, says the LORD of hosts. ² But who can endure the day of his coming, and who can stand when he appears?

"For he is like a refiner's fire and like fullers' soap; ³ he will sit as a refiner and purifier of silver, and he will purify the sons of Le͞'vi and refine them like gold and silver, till they present right offerings to the LORD. ⁴ Then the offering of Judah and Jerusalem will

be pleasing to the LORD as in the days of old and as in former years.

5 "Then I will draw near to you for judgment; I will be a swift witness against the sorcerers, against the adulterers, against those who swear falsely, against those who oppress the hireling in his wages, the widow and the orphan, against those who thrust aside the sojourner, and do not fear me, says the LORD of hosts.

6 "For I the LORD do not change; therefore you, O sons of Jacob, are not consumed. ⁷ From the days of your fathers you have turned aside from my statutes and have not kept them. Return to me, and I will return to you, says the LORD of hosts. But you say, 'How shall we return?' ⁸ Will man rob God? Yet you are robbing me. But you say, 'How are we robbing thee?' In your tithes and offerings. ⁹ You are cursed with a curse, for you are robbing me; the whole nation of you. ¹⁰ Bring the full tithes into the storehouse, that there may be food in my house; and thereby put me to the test, says the LORD of hosts, if I will not open the windows of heaven for you and pour down for you an overflowing blessing. ¹¹ I will rebuke the devourer*k* for you, so that it will not destroy the fruits of your soil; and your vine in the field shall not fail to bear, says the LORD of hosts. ¹² Then all nations will call you blessed, for you will be a land of delight, says the LORD of hosts.

13 "Your words have been stout against me, says the LORD. Yet you say, 'How have we spoken against thee?' ¹⁴ You have said, 'It is vain to serve God. What is the good of our keeping his charge or of walking as in mourning before the LORD of hosts? ¹⁵ Henceforth we deem the arrogant blessed; evildoers not only prosper but when they put God to the test they escape.' "

16 Then those who feared the LORD spoke with one another; the LORD heeded and heard them; and a book of remembrance was written before him of those who feared the LORD and thought on his name. ¹⁷ "They shall be mine, says the LORD of hosts, my special possession on the day when I

---

f Or *law*
g Cn Compare Gk: Heb *arouse*
h Or *has he not made one?*
i Cn: Heb *and a remnant of spirit was his*
j Cn: Heb *he hates*
k Or *devouring locust*
3.1: Mt 11.10; Mk 1.2; Lk 1.17, 76; 7.27. **3.2:** Rev 6.17.

act, and I will spare them as a man spares his son who serves him. [18] Then once more you shall distinguish between the righteous and the wicked, between one who serves God and one who does not serve him.

4 [1] "For behold, the day comes, burning like an oven, when all the arrogant and all evildoers will be stubble; the day that comes shall burn them up, says the LORD of hosts, so that it will leave them neither root nor branch. [2] But for you who fear my name the sun of righteousness shall rise, with healing in its wings. You shall go forth leaping like calves from the stall. [3] And you shall tread down the wicked, for they will be ashes under the soles of your feet, on the day when I act, says the LORD of hosts.

4 "Remember the law of my servant Moses, the statutes and ordinances that I commanded him at Hō'rĕb for all Israel.

5 "Behold, I will send you Ē·lī'jah the prophet before the great and terrible day of the LORD comes. [6] And he will turn the hearts of fathers to their children and the hearts of children to their fathers, lest I come and smite the land with a curse."[m]

[l]Ch 4.1-6 are Ch 3.19-24 in the Hebrew
[m]Or *ban of utter destruction*
4.5: Mt 17.11; Mk 9.12.   4.6: Lk 1.17.

THE NEW COVENANT

COMMONLY CALLED

The New Testament

OF OUR LORD AND SAVIOR

JESUS CHRIST

REVISED STANDARD VERSION

TRANSLATED FROM THE GREEK
BEING THE VERSION SET FORTH A.D. 1611
REVISED A.D. 1881 AND A.D. 1901
COMPARED WITH THE MOST ANCIENT AUTHORITIES
AND REVISED A.D. 1946
SECOND EDITION 1971

The Names and Order of the

BOOKS OF THE NEW TESTAMENT

Abbreviations

In the notes to the books of the Old Testament, the following abbreviations are used: Ms for manuscript; Mss for manuscripts; Heb denotes the Hebrew of the consonantal Masoretic Text of the Old Testament; and MT denotes the Hebrew of the pointed Masoretic Text of the Old Testament.

The ancient versions of the Old Testament are indicated by:

Gk	Septuagint, Greek Version of Old Testament
Sam	Samaritan Hebrew text of Old Testament
Syr	Syriac Version of Old Testament
Tg	Targum
Vg	Vulgate, Latin Version of Old Testament

Cn indicates a correction made where the text has suffered in transmission and the versions provide no satisfactory restoration but the Committee agrees with the judgment of competent scholars as to the most probable reconstruction of the original text. The reader is referred to the Preface for a statement of policy concerning text and notes.

Abbreviations

References to quoted and parallel passages are given following the notes on pages where these are relevant. The following abbreviations are used for the books of the Bible:

THE OLD TESTAMENT

Gen	Genesis	Eccles	Ecclesiastes
Ex	Exodus	Song	Song of Solomon
Lev	Leviticus	Is	Isaiah
Num	Numbers	Jer	Jeremiah
Deut	Deuteronomy	Lam	Lamentations
Josh	Joshua	Ezek	Ezekiel
Judg	Judges	Dan	Daniel
Ruth	Ruth	Hos	Hosea
1 Sam	1 Samuel	Joel	Joel
2 Sam	2 Samuel	Amos	Amos
1 Kings	1 Kings	Obad	Obadiah
2 Kings	2 Kings	Jon	Jonah
1 Chron	1 Chronicles	Mic	Micah
2 Chron	2 Chronicles	Nahum	Nahum
Ezra	Ezra	Hab	Habakkuk
Neh	Nehemiah	Zeph	Zephaniah
Esther	Esther	Hag	Haggai
Job	Job	Zech	Zechariah
Ps	Psalms	Mal	Malachi
Prov	Proverbs		

THE NEW TESTAMENT

Mt	Matthew	1 Tim	1 Timothy
Mk	Mark	2 Tim	2 Timothy
Lk	Luke	Tit	Titus
Jn	John	Philem	Philemon
Acts	Acts of the Apostles	Heb	Hebrews
Rom	Romans	Jas	James
1 Cor	1 Corinthians	1 Pet	1 Peter
2 Cor	2 Corinthians	2 Pet	2 Peter
Gal	Galatians	1 Jn	1 John
Eph	Ephesians	2 Jn	2 John
Phil	Philippians	3 Jn	3 John
Col	Colossians	Jude	Jude
1 Thess	1 Thessalonians	Rev	Revelation
2 Thess	2 Thessalonians		

Key to Pronunciation of Proper Names

The reader will find that the pronunciation scheme presented in this edition of the Revised Standard Version of the Holy Bible is a practical help in reading and pronouncing the more unfamiliar personal and geographic names. Retaining the text spelling, an easily used system of diacritical marks indicates to the reader the pronunciation, the syllabic division, and the word stress of all except a small number of such names. This latter group includes personal and place names which have become familiar through everyday modern English usage. Such personal names as Adam, Daniel, and Martha, and place names as Bethlehem, Euphrates, and Nile, are typical examples of such anglicized words and are to be pronounced as they are used in current English speech. The key to the symbols used:

VOWELS AND DIPHTHONGS

ȧ	as in	watch	ē	as in	herd	ŏ	as in	odd
ä	" "	calm	ĕ	" "	get	ô	" "	order
ā	" "	dart	ē	" "	key	ō	" "	cope
ă	" "	sat	ę	" "	sicken	ǫ	" "	melon
â	" "	dare	ēi	" "	receive	oi	" "	toil
ā	" "	gate	ī	" "	ice	ŭ	" "	fuss
ą	" "	above	ī	" "	third	ū	" "	curd
aă	" "	ram	ĭ	" "	hit	ü	" "	rule
āi	" "	pail	į	" "	charity	ū	" "	use
aī	" "	aisle	iă	" "	yam	ȳ	" "	type
au	" "	author	iŏ	" "	yonder	ў	" "	lynch

CONSONANTS

c	as in	clean
ç	" "	ceiling
g	" "	game
ġ	" "	gentle
s	" "	sail
ş	" "	rose (z)
x	" "	x-ray (eks)
x̣	" "	xylophone (z)

The following letters are unmarked and are to be pronounced with their normal English sounds:

b, d, f, h, j, k, l, m, n, p, r, t, v, w, z.

ch as in ache (k)
ph " " phone (f)
th " " thick

For some widely used names, as the reader undoubtedly is aware, more than one acceptable pronunciation may be heard; however, in this edition of the Holy Bible but one such standard pronunciation is recorded.

It can also be noted that certain Biblical names have become generic terms in English with a secondary or derived meaning which becomes reflected in its pronunciation. Philistine is a good example; Phĭ·lĭs′tīnes, Phĭ′lĭs·tīnes, Phĭ′lĭs·tīnes, phĭ′lĭs·tĭ(ĭ=ē)nes; the first, the name of the ancient people of Philistia; the second, a widely used variant; the third, originally British in origin; and the last the generic modern term.

It will also be observed that the letter sounds represented by ạ, ẹ, ị, ọ, and ụ are the unstressed vowels of normal English speech. When these same sounds are influenced by a following letter "r" they are marked as ā, ē, ī, ō, and ū, as shown in the familiar illustrative key words.

The word accent or stress in English follows a pattern different from that of other languages both classical and modern. By noting the stressed syllable, indicated by (′) for primary stress and (″) for secondary stress, most of the names are pronounced without any difficulty in reading running text.

When pronunciation for proper names is indicated in the text, the first time a given word is used in a verse the pronunciation is shown, but on its subsequent appearance in the same verse, the pronunciation is not repeated.

The New Testament

The Gospel According to
Matthew

1 The book of the genealogy of Jesus Christ, the son of David, the son of Abraham.
2 Abraham was the father of Isaac, and Isaac the father of Jacob, and Jacob the father of Judah and his brothers, ³ and Judah the father of Pĕr′ĕz and Zē′rạh by Tā′mār, and Perez the father of Hĕz′rọn, and Hezron the father of Rām,ᵃ ⁴ and Rāmᵃ the father of Ăm·mĭn′ạ·dăb, and Amminadab the father of Năh′-shọn, and Nahshon the father of Săl′mọn, ⁵ and Săl′mọn the father of Bō′ăz by Rā′hăb, and Boaz the father of Ō′bĕd by Ruth, and Obed the father of Jesse, ⁶ and Jesse the father of David the king.

And David was the father of Solomon by the wife of Ū·rī′ạh, ⁷ and Solomon the father of Rē·ho·bō′ạm, and Rehoboam the father of Ạ·bī′jạh, and Abijah the father of Asa,ᵇ ⁸ and Asaᵇ the father of Jĕ·hŏsh′ạ·phăt, and Jehoshaphat the father of Jō′rạm, and Joram the father of Ŭz·zī′ạh, ⁹ and Ŭz-zī′ạh the father of Jō′thạm, and Jotham the father of Ā′hăz, and Ahaz the father of Hĕz·ẹ·kī′ạh, ¹⁰ and Hĕz·ẹ·kī′ạh the father of Mạ·năs′sẹh, and Manasseh the father of Ā′mŏs,ᶜ and Amosᶜ the father of Jō·sī′ạh, ¹¹ and Jō·sī′ạh the father of Jĕch·o·nī′ạh and his brothers, at the time of the deportation to Babylon.

12 And after the deportation to Babylon: Jĕch·o·nī′ạh was the father of Shĕ–ăl′tĭ–ĕl,ᵈ and She–alti–elᵈ the father of Zĕ·rŭb′bạ·bĕl, ¹³ and Zĕ-rŭb′bạ·bĕl the father of Ạ·bī′ud, and Abiud the father of Ē·lī′ạ·kĭm, and Eliakim the father of Ā′zôr, ¹⁴ and Ā′zôr the father of Zā′dŏk, and Zadok the father of Ā′chĭm, and Achim the father of Ē·lī′ud, ¹⁵ and Ē·lī′ud the father of Ĕl·ẹ·ā′zạr, and Eleazar the father of Măt′thạn, and Matthan the father of Jacob, ¹⁶ and Jacob the father of Joseph the husband of Mary, of whom Jesus was born, who is called Christ.

17 So all the generations from Abraham to David were fourteen generations, and from David to the deportation to Babylon fourteen generations, and from the deportation to Babylon to the Christ fourteen generations.

18 Now the birth of Jesus Christ ᶠ took place in this way. When his mother Mary had been betrothed to Joseph, before they came together she was found to be with child of the Holy Spirit; ¹⁹ and her husband Joseph, being a just man and unwilling to put her to shame, resolved to divorce her quietly. ²⁰ But as he considered this, behold, an angel of the Lord appeared to him in a dream, saying, "Joseph, son of David, do not fear to take Mary your wife, for that which is conceived in her is of the Holy Spirit; ²¹ she will bear a son, and you shall call his name Jesus, for he will save his people from their sins." ²² All this took place to fulfil what the Lord had spoken by the prophet:
²³ "Behold, a virgin shall conceive and
    bear a son,
and his name shall be called
    Ĕm·măn′ū–ĕl"
(which means, God with us). ²⁴ When Joseph woke from sleep, he did as the angel of the Lord commanded him; he took his wife, ²⁵ but knew her not until she had borne a son; and he called his name Jesus.

2 Now when Jesus was born in Bethlehem of Jü·dē′ạ in the days of Hĕr′ọd the king, behold, wise men from the East came to Jerusalem, saying, ² "Where is he who has been born king of the Jews? For we have seen his star in the East, and have come to worship him." ³ When Hĕr′ọd the king heard this, he was troubled, and all Jerusalem with him; ⁴ and assembling all the chief priests and scribes of the people, he inquired of them where the Christ was to be born. ⁵ They told

ᵃGreek *Aram* ᵇGreek *Asaph*
ᶜOther authorities read *Amon* ᵈGreek *Salathiel*
ᶠOther ancient authorities read *of the Christ*
1.1-17: Lk 3.23-38. **1.3-6:** Ruth 4.18-22; 1 Chron 2.1-15.
1.11: 2 Kings 24.14; Jer 27.20. **1.18:** Lk 1.26-38.
1.21: Lk 2.21; Jn 1.29; Acts 13.23. **1.23:** Is 7.14.
2.1: Lk 2.4-7; 1.5.
2.2: Jer 23.5; Zech 9.9; Mk 15.2; Jn 1.49; Num 24.17.
2.5: Jn 7.42.

him, "In Bethlehem of Jü·dē'ạ; for so it is written by the prophet:

⁶'And you, O Bethlehem, in the land of Judah,
are by no means least among the rulers of Judah;
for from you shall come a ruler who will govern my people Israel.'"

7 Then Hĕr'ọd summoned the wise men secretly and ascertained from them what time the star appeared; ⁸and he sent them to Bethlehem, saying, "Go and search diligently for the child, and when you have found him bring me word, that I too may come and worship him." ⁹When they had heard the king they went their way; and lo, the star which they had seen in the East went before them, till it came to rest over the place where the child was. ¹⁰When they saw the star, they rejoiced exceedingly with great joy; ¹¹and going into the house they saw the child with Mary his mother, and they fell down and worshiped him. Then, opening their treasures, they offered him gifts, gold and frankincense and myrrh. ¹²And being warned in a dream not to return to Hĕr'ọd, they departed to their own country by another way.

13 Now when they had departed, behold, an angel of the Lord appeared to Joseph in a dream and said, "Rise, take the child and his mother, and flee to Egypt, and remain there till I tell you; for Hĕr'ọd is about to search for the child, to destroy him." ¹⁴And he rose and took the child and his mother by night, and departed to Egypt, ¹⁵and remained there until the death of Hĕr'ọd. This was to fulfil what the Lord had spoken by the prophet, "Out of Egypt have I called my son."

16 Then Hĕr'ọd, when he saw that he had been tricked by the wise men, was in a furious rage, and he sent and killed all the male children in Bethlehem and in all that region who were two years old or under, according to the time which he had ascertained from the wise men. ¹⁷Then was fulfilled what was spoken by the prophet Jĕr·ẹ·mī'ạh:

¹⁸"A voice was heard in Rā'mạh,
wailing and loud lamentation,
Rachel weeping for her children;
she refused to be consoled,
because they were no more."

19 But when Hĕr'ọd died, behold, an angel of the Lord appeared in a dream to Joseph in Egypt, saying, ²⁰"Rise, take the child and his mother, and go to the land of Israel, for those who sought the child's life are dead." ²¹And he rose and took the child and his mother, and went to the land of Israel. ²²But when he heard that Är·chẹ·lā'ụs reigned over Jü·dē'ạ in place of his father Hĕr'ọd, he was afraid to go there, and being warned in a dream he withdrew to the district of Galilee. ²³And he went and dwelt in a city called Nazareth, that what was spoken by the prophets might be fulfilled. "He shall be called a Nazarene."

3 In those days came John the Baptist, preaching in the wilderness of Jü·dē'ạ, ²"Repent, for the kingdom of heaven is at hand." ³For this is he who was spoken of by the prophet Ī·sāi'ạh when he said,
"The voice of one crying in the wilderness:
Prepare the way of the Lord,
make his paths straight."

⁴Now John wore a garment of camel's hair, and a leather girdle around his waist; and his food was locusts and wild honey. ⁵Then went out to him Jerusalem and all Jü·dē'ạ and all the region about the Jordan, ⁶and they were baptized by him in the river Jordan, confessing their sins.

7 But when he saw many of the Phăr'ị·seẹṣ and Săd'dū·çeeṣ coming for baptism, he said to them, "You brood of vipers! Who warned you to flee from the wrath to come? ⁸Bear fruit that befits repentance, ⁹and do not presume to say to yourselves, 'We have Abraham as our father'; for I tell you, God is able from these stones to raise up children to Abraham. ¹⁰Even now the axe is laid to the root of the trees; every tree therefore that does not bear good fruit is cut down and thrown into the fire.

11 "I baptize you with water for repentance, but he who is coming after me is mightier than I, whose sandals I am not worthy to carry; he

2.6: Mic 5.2.   **2.11:** Mt 1.18; 12.46.
2.12: Mt 2.22; Acts 10.22; Heb 11.7.
2.15: Hos 11.1; Ex 4.22.   **2.18:** Jer 31.15.
2.19: Mt 1.20; 2.13.   **2.23:** Lk 1.26; Is 11.1; Mk 1.24.
3.1-12: Mk 1.3-8; Lk 3.2-17; Jn 1.6-8, 19-28.
3.2: Mt 4.17; Dan 2.44; 4.17; Mt 10.7.   **3.3:** Is 40.3.
3.4: 2 Kings 1.8; Zech 13.4; Lev 11.22.
3.7: Mt 12.34; 23.33; 1 Thess 1.10.
3.9: Jn 8.33; Rom 4.16.   **3.10:** Mt 7.19.

will baptize you with the Holy Spirit and with fire. [12] His winnowing fork is in his hand, and he will clear his threshing floor and gather his wheat into the granary, but the chaff he will burn with unquenchable fire."

13 Then Jesus came from Galilee to the Jordan to John, to be baptized by him. [14] John would have prevented him, saying, "I need to be baptized by you, and do you come to me?" [15] But Jesus answered him, "Let it be so now; for thus it is fitting for us to fulfil all righteousness." Then he consented. [16] And when Jesus was baptized, he went up immediately from the water, and behold, the heavens were opened[g] and he saw the Spirit of God descending like a dove, and alighting on him; [17] and lo, a voice from heaven, saying, "This is my beloved Son,[h] with whom I am well pleased."

4 Then Jesus was led up by the Spirit into the wilderness to be tempted by the devil. [2] And he fasted forty days and forty nights, and afterward he was hungry. [3] And the tempter came and said to him, "If you are the Son of God, command these stones to become loaves of bread." [4] But he answered, "It is written,

'Man shall not live by bread alone,
but by every word that proceeds from
    the mouth of God.'"

[5] Then the devil took him to the holy city, and set him on the pinnacle of the temple, [6] and said to him, "If you are the Son of God, throw yourself down; for it is written,

'He will give his angels charge of
    you,'
and
'On their hands they will bear you
    up,
lest you strike your foot against
    a stone.'"

[7] Jesus said to him, "Again it is written, 'You shall not tempt the Lord your God.'" [8] Again, the devil took him to a very high mountain, and showed him all the kingdoms of the world and the glory of them; [9] and he said to him, "All these I will give you, if you will fall down and worship me." [10] Then Jesus said to him, "Begone, Satan! for it is written,

'You shall worship the Lord your
    God
and him only shall you serve.'"

[11] Then the devil left him, and behold, angels came and ministered to him.

12 Now when he heard that John had been arrested, he withdrew into Galilee; [13] and leaving Nazareth he went and dwelt in Ca̱·pēr'na̱–u̱m by the sea, in the territory of Zĕb'ū·lu̱n and Năph'tā·lī, [14] that what was spoken by the prophet Ī·sāi'a̱h might be fulfilled:

[15] "The land of Zĕb'ū·lu̱n and the land
        of Năph'ta̱·lī,
toward the sea, across the Jordan,
    Galilee of the Gentiles—
[16] the people who sat in darkness
have seen a great light,
and for those who sat in the region
    and shadow of death
light has dawned."

[17] From that time Jesus began to preach, saying, "Repent, for the kingdom of heaven is at hand."

18 As he walked by the Sea of Galilee, he saw two brothers, Simon who is called Peter and Andrew his brother, casting a net into the sea; for they were fishermen. [19] And he said to them, "Follow me, and I will make you fishers of men." [20] Immediately they left their nets and followed him. [21] And going on from there he saw two other brothers, James the son of Zĕb'e̱·dee and John his brother, in the boat with Zebedee their father, mending their nets, and he called them. [22] Immediately they left the boat and their father, and followed him.

23 And he went about all Galilee, teaching in their synagogues and preaching the gospel of the kingdom and healing every disease and every infirmity among the people. [24] So his fame spread throughout all Syria, and they brought him all the sick, those afflicted with various diseases and pains, demoniacs, epileptics, and paralytics, and he healed them. [25] And

[g] Other ancient authorities add *to him*
[h] Or *my Son, my* (or *the*) *Beloved*
3.12: Mt 13.30.
3.13–17: Mk 1.9-11; Lk 3.21-22; Jn 1.31-34.
3.17: Mt 12.18; 17.5; Mk 9.7; Lk 9.35; Ps 2.7; Is 42.1.
4.1–11: Mk 1.12-13; Lk 4.1-13; Heb 2.18; 4.15.
4.2: Ex 34.28; 1 Kings 19.8.   4.4: Deut 8.3.
4.5: Mt 27.53; Neh 11.1; Dan 9.24; Rev 21.10.
4.6: Ps 91.11-12.   4.7: Deut 6.16.
4.10: Deut 6.13; Mk 8.33.
4.11: Mt 26.53; Lk 22.43.
4.12: Mk 1.14; Lk 4.14; Mt 14.3; Jn 1.43.
4.13: Jn 2.12; Mk 1.21; Lk 4.23.   4.15: Is 9.1-2.
4.17: Mk 1.15; Mt 3.2; 10.7.
4.18–22: Mk 1.16-20; Lk 5.1-11; Jn 1.35-42.
4.23–25: Mk 1.39; Lk 4.15, 44; Mt 9.35; Mk 3.7-8; Lk 6.17.

great crowds followed him from Galilee and the Dĕ·căp′o·lĭs and Jerusalem and Jü·dĕ′ạ and from beyond the Jordan.

5 Seeing the crowds, he went up on the mountain, and when he sat down his disciples came to him. ² And he opened his mouth and taught them, saying:

3 "Blessed are the poor in spirit, for theirs is the kingdom of heaven.

4 "Blessed are those who mourn, for they shall be comforted.

5 "Blessed are the meek, for they shall inherit the earth.

6 "Blessed are those who hunger and thirst for righteousness, for they shall be satisfied.

7 "Blessed are the merciful, for they shall obtain mercy.

8 "Blessed are the pure in heart, for they shall see God.

9 "Blessed are the peacemakers, for they shall be called sons of God.

10 "Blessed are those who are persecuted for righteousness' sake, for theirs is the kingdom of heaven.

11 "Blessed are you when men revile you and persecute you and utter all kinds of evil against you falsely on my account. ¹² Rejoice and be glad, for your reward is great in heaven, for so men persecuted the prophets who were before you.

13 "You are the salt of the earth; but if salt has lost its taste, how shall its saltness be restored? It is no longer good for anything except to be thrown out and trodden under foot by men.

14 "You are the light of the world. A city set on a hill cannot be hid. ¹⁵ Nor do men light a lamp and put it under a bushel, but on a stand, and it gives light to all in the house. ¹⁶ Let your light so shine before men, that they may see your good works and give glory to your Father who is in heaven.

17 "Think not that I have come to abolish the law and the prophets; I have come not to abolish them but to fulfil them. ¹⁸ For truly, I say to you, till heaven and earth pass away, not an iota, not a dot, will pass from the law until all is accomplished. ¹⁹ Whoever then relaxes one of the least of these commandments and teaches men so, shall be called least in the kingdom of heaven; but he who does them and teaches them shall be called great in the kingdom of heaven. ²⁰ For I tell you,

unless your righteousness exceeds that of the scribes and Phăr′ị·seeṣ, you will never enter the kingdom of heaven.

21 "You have heard that it was said to the men of old, 'You shall not kill; and whoever kills shall be liable to judgment.' ²² But I say to you that every one who is angry with his brotherⁱ shall be liable to judgment; whoever insultsʲ his brother shall be liable to the council, and whoever says, 'You fool!' shall be liable to the hellᵏ of fire. ²³ So if you are offering your gift at the altar, and there remember that your brother has something against you, ²⁴ leave your gift there before the altar and go; first be reconciled to your brother, and then come and offer your gift. ²⁵ Make friends quickly with your accuser, while you are going with him to court, lest your accuser hand you over to the judge, and the judge to the guard, and you be put in prison; ²⁶ truly, I say to you, you will never get out till you have paid the last penny.

27 "You have heard that it was said, 'You shall not commit adultery.' ²⁸ But I say to you that every one who looks at a woman lustfully has already committed adultery with her in his heart. ²⁹ If your right eye causes you to sin, pluck it out and throw it away; it is better that you lose one of your members than that your whole body be thrown into hell.ᵏ ³⁰ And if your right hand causes you to sin, cut it off and throw it away; it is better that you lose one of your members than that your whole body go into hell.ᵏ

31 "It was also said, 'Whoever divorces his wife, let him give her a certificate of divorce.' ³² But I say to you that every one who divorces his wife, except on the ground of unchastity, makes her an adulteress; and whoever marries a divorced woman commits adultery.

ⁱOther ancient authorities insert *without cause*
ʲGreek *says Raca to* (an obscure term of abuse)
ᵏGreek *Gehenna*

5.1-12: Lk 6.17, 20-23; Mk 3.13; Jn 6.3.
5.3: Mk 10.14; Lk 22.29.   **5.4:** Is 61.2; Jn 16.20; Rev 7.17.
5.5: Ps 37.11.   **5.6:** Is 55.1-2; Jn 4.14; 6.48-51.
5.8: Ps 24.4; Heb 12.14; 1 Jn 3.2; Rev 22.4.
5.10: 1 Pet 3.14; 4.14.
5.12: 2 Chron 36.16; Mt 23.37; Acts 7.52; 1 Thess 2.15; Jas 5.10.   **5.13:** Mk 9.49-50; Lk 14.34-35.
5.14: Eph 5.8; Phil 2.15; Jn 8.12.
5.15-16: Lk 11.33; Mk 4.21; 1 Pet 2.12.
5.18: Lk 16.17; Mk 13.31.   **5.19:** Jas 2.10.
5.21: Ex 20.13; Deut 5.17; 16.18.   **5.25-26:** Lk 12.57-59.
5.27: Ex 20.14; Deut 5.18.   **5.29-30:** Mk 9.43-48; Mt 18.8-9.
5.31-32: Lk 16.18; Mk 10.11-12; Mt 19.9; 1 Cor 7.10-11; Deut 24.1-4.

33 "Again you have heard that it was said to the men of old, 'You shall not swear falsely, but shall perform to the Lord what you have sworn.' ³⁴ But I say to you, Do not swear at all, either by heaven, for it is the throne of God, ³⁵ or by the earth, for it is his footstool, or by Jerusalem, for it is the city of the great King. ³⁶ And do not swear by your head, for you cannot make one hair white or black. ³⁷ Let what you say be simply 'Yes' or 'No'; anything more than this comes from evil.*

38 "You have heard that it was said, 'An eye for an eye and a tooth for a tooth.' ³⁹ But I say to you, Do not resist one who is evil. But if any one strikes you on the right cheek, turn to him the other also; ⁴⁰ and if any one would sue you and take your coat, let him have your cloak as well; ⁴¹ and if any one forces you to go one mile, go with him two miles. ⁴² Give to him who begs from you, and do not refuse him who would borrow from you.

43 "You have heard that it was said, 'You shall love your neighbor and hate your enemy.' ⁴⁴ But I say to you, Love your enemies and pray for those who persecute you, ⁴⁵ so that you may be sons of your Father who is in heaven; for he makes his sun rise on the evil and on the good, and sends rain on the just and on the unjust. ⁴⁶ For if you love those who love you, what reward have you? Do not even the tax collectors do the same? ⁴⁷ And if you salute only your brethren, what more are you doing than others? Do not even the Gentiles do the same? ⁴⁸ You, therefore, must be perfect, as your heavenly Father is perfect.

6 "Beware of practicing your piety before men in order to be seen by them; for then you will have no reward from your Father who is in heaven.

2 "Thus, when you give alms, sound no trumpet before you, as the hypocrites do in the synagogues and in the streets, that they may be praised by men. Truly, I say to you, they have received their reward. ³ But when you give alms, do not let your left hand know what your right hand is doing, ⁴ so that your alms may be in secret; and your Father who sees in secret will reward you.

5 "And when you pray, you must not be like the hypocrites; for they love to stand and pray in the syna-

gogues and at the street corners, that they may be seen by men. Truly, I say to you, they have received their reward. ⁶ But when you pray, go into your room and shut the door and pray to your Father who is in secret; and your Father who sees in secret will reward you.

7 "And in praying do not heap up empty phrases as the Gentiles do; for they think that they will be heard for their many words. ⁸ Do not be like them, for your Father knows what you need before you ask him. ⁹ Pray then like this:
Our Father who art in heaven,
Hallowed be thy name.
¹⁰ Thy kingdom come,
Thy will be done,
On earth as it is in heaven.
¹¹ Give us this day our daily bread; *ᵐ*
¹² And forgive us our debts,
As we also have forgiven our debtors;
¹³ And lead us not into temptation,
But deliver us from evil.*ⁿ*
¹⁴ For if you forgive men their trespasses, your heavenly Father also will forgive you; ¹⁵ but if you do not forgive men their trespasses, neither will your Father forgive your trespasses.

16 "And when you fast, do not look dismal, like the hypocrites, for they disfigure their faces that their fasting may be seen by men. Truly, I say to you, they have received their reward. ¹⁷ But when you fast, anoint your head and wash your face, ¹⁸ that your fasting may not be seen by men but by your Father who is in secret; and your Father who sees in secret will reward you.

19 "Do not lay up for yourselves treasures on earth, where moth and rust*ᵒ* consume and where thieves break in and steal, ²⁰ but lay up for yourselves treasures in heaven, where neither moth nor rust*ᵒ* consumes and

ˡ Or the evil one   ᵐ Or our bread for the morrow
ⁿ Or the evil one. Other authorities, some ancient, add, in some form, For thine is the kingdom and the power and the glory, for ever. Amen.   ᵒ Or worm
5.33-37: Mt 23.16-22; Jas 5.12; Lev 19.12; Num 30.2; Deut 23.21.   **5.35:** Is 66.1; Acts 7.49; Ps 48.2.
5.38: Ex 21.24; Lev 24.20; Deut 19.21.
5.39-42: Lk 6.29-30; 1 Cor 6.7; Rom 12.17; 1 Pet 2.19; 3.9; Prov 24.29.
5.43-48: Lk 6.27-28, 32-36; Lev 19.18; Prov 25.21-22.
5.48: Lev 19.2.   **6.1:** Mt 23.5.   **6.4:** Col 3.23-24.
6.5: Mk 11.25; Lk 18.10-14.   **6.7:** 1 Kings 18.25-29.
6.8: Mt 6.32; Lk 12.30.   **6.9-13:** Lk 11.2-4.
6.13: 2 Thess 3.3; Jn 17.15; Jas 1.13.
6.14-15: Mt 18.35; Mk 11.25; Eph 4.32; Col 3.13.
6.16: Is 58.5.   **6.18:** Mt 6.4, 6.
6.19-21: Lk 12.33-34; Mk 10.21; 1 Tim 6.17-19; Jas 5.1-3.

where thieves do not break in and steal.
21 For where your treasure is, there will
your heart be also.
22 "The eye is the lamp of the
body. So, if your eye is sound, your
whole body will be full of light; 23 but
if your eye is not sound, your whole
body will be full of darkness. If then
the light in you is darkness, how great
is the darkness!
24 "No one can serve two masters;
for either he will hate the one and love
the other, or he will be devoted to the
one and despise the other. You cannot
serve God and mammon.[x]
25 "Therefore I tell you, do not be
anxious about your life, what you shall
eat or what you shall drink, nor about
your body, what you shall put on. Is
not life more than food, and the body
more than clothing? 26 Look at the birds
of the air: they neither sow nor reap
nor gather into barns, and yet your
heavenly Father feeds them. Are you
not of more value than they? 27 And
which of you by being anxious can add
one cubit to his span of life?[p] 28 And
why are you anxious about clothing?
Consider the lilies of the field, how they
grow; they neither toil nor spin; 29 yet
I tell you, even Solomon in all his glory
was not arrayed like one of these. 30 But
if God so clothes the grass of the field,
which today is alive and tomorrow is
thrown into the oven, will he not much
more clothe you, O men of little faith?
31 Therefore do not be anxious, saying,
'What shall we eat?' or 'What shall we
drink?' or 'What shall we wear?' 32 For
the Gentiles seek all these things; and
your heavenly Father knows that you
need them all. 33 But seek first his kingdom and his righteousness, and all
these things shall be yours as well.
34 "Therefore do not be anxious
about tomorrow, for tomorrow will be
anxious for itself. Let the day's own
trouble be sufficient for the day.
7 "Judge not, that you be not
judged. 2 For with the judgment
you pronounce you will be judged,
and the measure you give will be the
measure you get. 3 Why do you see the
speck that is in your brother's eye, but
do not notice the log that is in your own
eye? 4 Or how can you say to your
brother, 'Let me take the speck out of
your eye,' when there is the log in your
own eye? 5 You hypocrite, first take the
log out of your own eye, and then you
will see clearly to take the speck out
of your brother's eye.
6 "Do not give dogs what is holy;
and do not throw your pearls before
swine, lest they trample them under
foot and turn to attack you.
7 "Ask, and it will be given you;
seek, and you will find; knock, and it
will be opened to you. 8 For every one
who asks receives, and he who seeks
finds, and to him who knocks it will be
opened. 9 Or what man of you, if his son
asks him for bread, will give him a
stone? 10 Or if he asks for a fish, will
give him a serpent? 11 If you then, who
are evil, know how to give good gifts
to your children, how much more will
your Father who is in heaven give
good things to those who ask him!
12 So whatever you wish that men
would do to you, do so to them; for this
is the law and the prophets.
13 "Enter by the narrow gate; for
the gate is wide and the way is easy,[q]
that leads to destruction, and those
who enter by it are many. 14 For the
gate is narrow and the way is hard,
that leads to life, and those who find
it are few.
15 "Beware of false prophets, who
come to you in sheep's clothing but
inwardly are ravenous wolves. 16 You
will know them by their fruits. Are
grapes gathered from thorns, or figs
from thistles? 17 So, every sound tree
bears good fruit, but the bad tree bears
evil fruit. 18 A sound tree cannot bear
evil fruit, nor can a bad tree bear good
fruit. 19 Every tree that does not bear
good fruit is cut down and thrown into
the fire. 20 Thus you will know them by
their fruits.
21 "Not every one who says to me,
'Lord, Lord,' shall enter the kingdom of
heaven, but he who does the will of my
Father who is in heaven. 22 On that day
many will say to me, 'Lord, Lord, did

[x] *Mammon* is a Semitic word for money or riches
[p] Or *to his stature*
[q] Other ancient authorities read *for the way is wide and easy* **6.22-23:** Lk 11.34-36; Mt 20.15; Mk 7.22.
6.24: Lk 16.13.
6.25-33: Lk 12.22-31; 10.41; 12.11; Phil 4.6; 1 Pet 5.7.
6.26: Mt 10.29. **6.27:** Ps 39.5. **6.29:** 1 Kings 10.4-7.
6.30: Mt 8.26; 14.31; 16.8.
6.33: Mt 19.28; Mk 10.29-30; Lk 18.29-30.
7.1-2: Lk 6.37-38; Mk 4.24; Rom 2.1; 14.10.
7.3-5: Lk 6.41-42.
7.7-11: Lk 11.9-13; Mk 11.24; Jn 15.7; 16.23-24; Jas 4.3; 1 Jn 3.22; 5.14. **7.12:** Lk 6.31.
7.13-14: Lk 13.23-24; Jer 21.8; Deut 30.19; Jn 14.6; 10.7.
7.15: Mt 24.11, 24; Ezek 22.27; 1 Jn 4.1; Jn 10.12.
7.16-20: Lk 6.43-44; Mt 12.33-35; Mt 3.10; Jas 3.12; Lk 13.7. **7.21:** Lk 6.46.
7.22-23: Lk 13.26-27; Mt 25.12; Ps 6.8.

we not prophesy in your name, and cast out demons in your name, and do many mighty works in your name?' ²³And then will I declare to them, 'I never knew you; depart from me, you evildoers.'

24 "Every one then who hears these words of mine and does them will be like a wise man who built his house upon the rock; ²⁵and the rain fell, and the floods came, and the winds blew and beat upon that house, but it did not fall, because it had been founded on the rock. ²⁶And every one who hears these words of mine and does not do them will be like a foolish man who built his house upon the sand; ²⁷and the rain fell, and the floods came, and the winds blew and beat against that house, and it fell; and great was the fall of it."

28 And when Jesus finished these sayings, the crowds were astonished at his teaching, ²⁹for he taught them as one who had authority, and not as their scribes.

8 When he came down from the mountain, great crowds followed him; ²and behold, a leper came to him and knelt before him, saying, "Lord, if you will, you can make me clean." ³And he stretched out his hand and touched him, saying, "I will; be clean." And immediately his leprosy was cleansed. ⁴And Jesus said to him, "See that you say nothing to any one; but go, show yourself to the priest, and offer the gift that Moses commanded, for a proof to the people."^r

5 As he entered Ca·pēr′na·um, a centurion came forward to him, beseeching him ⁶and saying, "Lord, my servant is lying paralyzed at home, in terrible distress." ⁷And he said to him, "I will come and heal him." ⁸But the centurion answered him, "Lord, I am not worthy to have you come under my roof; but only say the word, and my servant will be healed. ⁹For I am a man under authority, with soldiers under me; and I say to one, 'Go,' and he goes, and to another, 'Come,' and he comes, and to my slave, 'Do this,' and he does it." ¹⁰When Jesus heard him, he marveled, and said to those who followed him, "Truly, I say to you, not even^s in Israel have I found such faith. ¹¹I tell you, many will come from east and west and sit at table

with Abraham, Isaac, and Jacob in the kingdom of heaven, ¹²while the sons of the kingdom will be thrown into the outer darkness; there men will weep and gnash their teeth." ¹³And to the centurion Jesus said, "Go; be it done for you as you have believed." And the servant was healed at that very moment.

14 And when Jesus entered Peter's house, he saw his mother-in-law lying sick with a fever; ¹⁵he touched her hand, and the fever left her, and she rose and served him. ¹⁶That evening they brought to him many who were possessed with demons; and he cast out the spirits with a word, and healed all who were sick. ¹⁷This was to fulfil what was spoken by the prophet I·sāi′ah, "He took our infirmities and bore our diseases."

18 Now when Jesus saw great crowds around him, he gave orders to go over to the other side. ¹⁹And a scribe came up and said to him, "Teacher, I will follow you wherever you go." ²⁰And Jesus said to him, "Foxes have holes, and birds of the air have nests; but the Son of man has nowhere to lay his head." ²¹Another of the disciples said to him, "Lord, let me first go and bury my father." ²²But Jesus said to him, "Follow me, and leave the dead to bury their own dead."

23 And when he got into the boat, his disciples followed him. ²⁴And behold, there arose a great storm on the sea, so that the boat was being swamped by the waves; but he was asleep. ²⁵And they went and woke him, saying, "Save, Lord; we are perishing." ²⁶And he said to them, "Why are you afraid, O men of little faith?" Then he rose and rebuked the winds and the sea; and there was a great calm. ²⁷And the men marveled, saying, "What sort of man is this, that even winds and sea obey him?"

Greek *to them*
^sOther ancient authorities read *with no one*

7.24-27: Lk 6.47-49; Jas 1.22-25.
7.28-29: Mk 1.22; Lk 4.32; Mt 11.1; 13.53; 19.1; 26.1.
8.2-4: Mk 1.40-44; Lk 5.12-14.
8.2: Mt 9.18; 15.25; 18.26; 20.20; Jn 9.38.
8.4: Mk 3.12; 5.43; 7.36; 8.30; 9.9; Lev 14.2.
8.5-13: Lk 7.1-10; Jn 4.46-53.
8.11-12: Lk 13.28-29; Is 49.12; 59.19; Mal 1.11; Ps 107.3.
8.12: Mt 13.42, 50; 22.13; 24.51; 25.30; Lk 13.28.
8.14-16: Mk 1.29-34; Lk 4.38-41; Mt 4.23-24.
8.17: Is 53.4. **8.18-22:** Lk 9.57-60; Mk 4.35; Lk 8.22.
8.22: Mt 9.9; Jn 1.43; 21.19.
8.23-27: Mk 4.36-41; Lk 8.22-25.
8.26: Mt 6.30; 14.31; 16.8.

28 And when he came to the other side, to the country of the Găd´ạ·rēneș,[f] two demoniacs met him, coming out of the tombs, so fierce that no one could pass that way. [29] And behold, they cried out, "What have you to do with us, O Son of God? Have you come here to torment us before the time?" [30] Now a herd of many swine was feeding at some distance from them. [31] And the demons begged him, "If you cast us out, send us away into the herd of swine." [32] And he said to them, "Go." So they came out and went into the swine; and behold, the whole herd rushed down the steep bank into the sea, and perished in the waters. [33] The herdsmen fled, and going into the city they told everything, and what had happened to the demoniacs. [34] And behold, all the city came out to meet Jesus; and when they saw him, they begged him to leave their neighborhood.

9 And getting into a boat he crossed over and came to his own city. [2] And behold, they brought to him a paralytic, lying on his bed; and when Jesus saw their faith he said to the paralytic, "Take heart, my son; your sins are forgiven." [3] And behold, some of the scribes said to themselves, "This man is blaspheming." [4] But Jesus, knowing[u] their thoughts, said, "Why do you think evil in your hearts? [5] For which is easier, to say, 'Your sins are forgiven,' or to say, 'Rise and walk'? [6] But that you may know that the Son of man has authority on earth to forgive sins"—he then said to the paralytic—"Rise, take up your bed and go home." [7] And he rose and went home. [8] When the crowds saw it, they were afraid, and they glorified God, who had given such authority to men.

9 As Jesus passed on from there, he saw a man called Matthew sitting at the tax office; and he said to him, "Follow me." And he rose and followed him.

10 And as he sat at table[v] in the house, behold, many tax collectors and sinners came and sat down with Jesus and his disciples. [11] And when the Phăr´i·seeș saw this, they said to his disciples, "Why does your teacher eat with tax collectors and sinners?" [12] But when he heard it, he said, "Those who are well have no need of a physician, but those who are sick. [13] Go and learn

what this means, 'I desire mercy, and not sacrifice.' For I came not to call the righteous, but sinners."

14 Then the disciples of John came to him, saying, "Why do we and the Phăr´i·seeș fast,[w] but your disciples do not fast?" [15] And Jesus said to them, "Can the wedding guests mourn as long as the bridegroom is with them? The days will come, when the bridegroom is taken away from them, and then they will fast. [16] And no one puts a piece of unshrunk cloth on an old garment, for the patch tears away from the garment, and a worse tear is made. [17] Neither is new wine put into old wineskins; if it is, the skins burst, and the wine is spilled, and the skins are destroyed; but new wine is put into fresh wineskins, and so both are preserved."

18 While he was thus speaking to them, behold, a ruler came in and knelt before him, saying, "My daughter has just died; but come and lay your hand on her, and she will live." [19] And Jesus rose and followed him, with his disciples. [20] And behold, a woman who had suffered from a hemorrhage for twelve years came up behind him and touched the fringe of his garment; [21] for she said to herself, "If I only touch his garment, I shall be made well." [22] Jesus turned, and seeing her he said, "Take heart, daughter; your faith has made you well." And instantly the woman was made well. [23] And when Jesus came to the ruler's house, and saw the flute players, and the crowd making a tumult, [24] he said, "Depart; for the girl is not dead but sleeping." And they laughed at him. [25] But when the crowd had been put outside, he went in and took her by the hand, and the girl arose. [26] And the report of this went through all that district.

27 And as Jesus passed on from there, two blind men followed him,

---

[f] Other ancient authorities read *Gergesenes*; some, *Gerasenes*   [u] Other ancient authorities read *seeing*
[v] Greek *reclined*
[w] Other ancient authorities add *much* or *often*
8.28-34: Mk 5.1-17; Lk 8.26-37.
8.29: Judg 11.12; 2 Sam 16.10; Mk 1.24; Jn 2.4.
9.1-8: Mk 2.1-12; Lk 5.17-26.
9.2: Mt 9.22; Mk 6.50; 10.49; Jn 16.33; Acts 23.11; Lk 7.48.
9.9-13: Mk 2.13-17; Lk 5.27-32; 15.1-2; 7.34.
9.13: Hos 6.6; Mt 12.7; 1 Tim 1.15.
9.14-17: Mk 2.18-22; Lk 5.33-39; 18.12.
9.18-26: Mk 5.21-43; Lk 8.40-56.
9.18: Mt 8.2; 15.25; 18.26; 20.20; Jn 9.38.
9.20: Num 15.38; Deut 22.12; Mt 14.36; Mk 3.10.
9.22: Mk 10.52; Lk 7.50; 17.19; Mt 15.28; 9.29.
9.27-31: Mt 20.29-34.

crying aloud, "Have mercy on us, Son of David." [28] When he entered the house, the blind men came to him; and Jesus said to them, "Do you believe that I am able to do this?" They said to him, "Yes, Lord." [29] Then he touched their eyes, saying, "According to your faith be it done to you." [30] And their eyes were opened. And Jesus sternly charged them, "See that no one knows it." [31] But they went away and spread his fame through all that district.

[32] As they were going away, behold, a dumb demoniac was brought to him. [33] And when the demon had been cast out, the dumb man spoke; and the crowds marveled, saying, "Never was anything like this seen in Israel." [34] But the Phăr'ĭ-seeṣ said, "He casts out demons by the prince of demons."[a]

[35] And Jesus went about all the cities and villages, teaching in their synagogues and preaching the gospel of the kingdom, and healing every disease and every infirmity. [36] When he saw the crowds, he had compassion for them, because they were harassed and helpless, like sheep without a shepherd. [37] Then he said to his disciples, "The harvest is plentiful, but the laborers are few; [38] pray therefore the Lord of the harvest to send out laborers into his harvest."

10 And he called to him his twelve disciples and gave them authority over unclean spirits, to cast them out, and to heal every disease and every infirmity. [2] The names of the twelve apostles are these: first, Simon, who is called Peter, and Andrew his brother; James the son of Zĕb'e-dee, and John his brother; [3] Philip and Bartholomew; Thomas and Matthew the tax collector; James the son of Ăl'phae'us, and Thad-dae'us;[x] [4] Simon the Cā-na-nae'ạn, and Judas Ĭs-cǎr'ĭ-ọt, who betrayed him.

[5] These twelve Jesus sent out, charging them, "Go nowhere among the Gentiles, and enter no town of the Sạ-mâr'ĭ-tạnṣ, [6] but go rather to the lost sheep of the house of Israel. [7] And preach as you go, saying, 'The kingdom of heaven is at hand.' [8] Heal the sick, raise the dead, cleanse lepers, cast out demons. You received without paying, give without pay. [9] Take no gold, nor silver, nor copper in your belts, [10] no bag for your journey, nor

two tunics, nor sandals, nor a staff; for the laborer deserves his food. [11] And whatever town or village you enter, find out who is worthy in it, and stay with him until you depart. [12] As you enter the house, salute it. [13] And if the house is worthy, let your peace come upon it; but if it is not worthy, let your peace return to you. [14] And if any one will not receive you or listen to your words, shake off the dust from your feet as you leave that house or town. [15] Truly, I say to you, it shall be more tolerable on the day of judgment for the land of Sŏd'ọm and Gọ-môr'rạh than for that town.

[16] "Behold, I send you out as sheep in the midst of wolves; so be wise as serpents and innocent as doves. [17] Beware of men; for they will deliver you up to councils, and flog you in their synagogues, [18] and you will be dragged before governors and kings for my sake, to bear testimony before them and the Gentiles. [19] When they deliver you up, do not be anxious how you are to speak or what you are to say; for what you are to say will be given to you in that hour; [20] for it is not you who speak, but the Spirit of your Father speaking through you. [21] Brother will deliver up brother to death, and the father his child, and children will rise against parents and have them put to death; [22] and you will be hated by all for my name's sake. But he who endures to the end will be saved. [23] When they persecute you in one town, flee to the next; for truly, I say to you, you will not have gone through all the towns of Israel, before the Son of man comes.

[24] "A disciple is not above his teacher, nor a servant[y] above his master; [25] it is enough for the disciple to be like his teacher, and the servant[y]

[a] Other ancient authorities omit this verse
[x] Other ancient authorities read *Lebbaeus* or *Labbaeus called Thaddaeus* [y] Or *slave*
9.32-34: Lk 11.14-15; Mt 12.22-24; Mk 3.22; Jn 7.20.
9.35: Mt 4.23; Mk 6.6.
9.36: Mk 6.34; Mt 14.14; 15.32; Num 27.17; Zech 10.2.
9.37-38: Lk 10.2; Jn 4.35.
10.1-4: Mk 6.7; 3.16-19; Lk 9.1; 6.14-16; Acts 1.13.
10.5: Lk 9.52; Jn 4.9; Acts 8.5, 25. **10.6:** Mt 15.24; 10.23.
10.7-8: Lk 9.2; 10.9-11; Mt 4.17.
10.9-14: Mk 6.8-11; Lk 9.3-5; 10.4-12; 22.35-36.
10.10: 1 Cor 9.14; 1 Tim 5.18. **10.14:** Acts 13.51.
10.15: Mt 11.24; Lk 10.12; Jude 7; 2 Pet 2.6.
10.16: Lk 10.3; Gen 3.1; Rom 16.19.
10.17-22: Mk 13.9-13; Lk 12.11-12; 21.12-19; Jn 16.2.
10.18: Acts 25.24-26. **10.20:** Jn 16.7-11.
10.21: Mt 10.35-36; Lk 12.52-53. **10.22:** Jn 15.18; Mt 24.9.
10.23: Mt 16.27; 1 Thess 4.17.
10.24: Lk 6.40; Jn 13.16; 15.20.
10.25: Mt 9.34; 12.24; Mk 3.22; Lk 11.15; 2 Kings 1.2.

like his master. If they have called the master of the house Bē–ĕl′ze·bŭl, how much more will they malign those of his household.

26 "So have no fear of them; for nothing is covered that will not be revealed, or hidden that will not be known. ²⁷What I tell you in the dark, utter in the light; and what you hear whispered, proclaim upon the housetops. ²⁸And do not fear those who kill the body but cannot kill the soul; rather fear him who can destroy both soul and body in hell.ᶻ ²⁹Are not two sparrows sold for a penny? And not one of them will fall to the ground without your Father's will. ³⁰But even the hairs of your head are all numbered. ³¹Fear not, therefore; you are of more value than many sparrows. ³²So every one who acknowledges me before men, I also will acknowledge before my Father who is in heaven; ³³but whoever denies me before men, I also will deny before my Father who is in heaven.

34 "Do not think that I have come to bring peace on earth; I have not come to bring peace, but a sword. ³⁵For I have come to set a man against his father, and a daughter against her mother, and a daughter-in-law against her mother-in-law; ³⁶and a man's foes will be those of his own household. ³⁷He who loves father or mother more than me is not worthy of me; and he who loves son or daughter more than me is not worthy of me; ³⁸and he who does not take his cross and follow me is not worthy of me. ³⁹He who finds his life will lose it, and he who loses his life for my sake will find it.

40 "He who receives you receives me, and he who receives me receives him who sent me. ⁴¹He who receives a prophet because he is a prophet shall receive a prophet's reward, and he who receives a righteous man because he is a righteous man shall receive a righteous man's reward. ⁴²And whoever gives to one of these little ones even a cup of cold water because he is a disciple, truly, I say to you, he shall not lose his reward."

11 And when Jesus had finished instructing his twelve disciples, he went on from there to teach and preach in their cities.

2 Now when John heard in prison

about the deeds of the Christ, he sent word by his disciples ³and said to him, "Are you he who is to come, or shall we look for another?" ⁴And Jesus answered them, "Go and tell John what you hear and see: ⁵the blind receive their sight and the lame walk, lepers are cleansed and the deaf hear, and the dead are raised up, and the poor have good news preached to them. ⁶And blessed is he who takes no offense at me."

7 As they went away, Jesus began to speak to the crowds concerning John: "What did you go out into the wilderness to behold? A reed shaken by the wind? ⁸Why then did you go out? To see a manᵃ clothed in soft raiment? Behold, those who wear soft raiment are in kings' houses. ⁹Why then did you go out? To see a prophet?ᵇ Yes, I tell you, and more than a prophet. ¹⁰This is he of whom it is written,

'Behold, I send my messenger before thy face,
who shall prepare thy way before thee.'

¹¹Truly, I say to you, among those born of women there has risen no one greater than John the Baptist; yet he who is least in the kingdom of heaven is greater than he. ¹²From the days of John the Baptist until now the kingdom of heaven has suffered violence,ᶜ and men of violence take it by force. ¹³For all the prophets and the law prophesied until John; ¹⁴and if you are willing to accept it, he is Ē·lī′jah who is to come. ¹⁵He who has ears to hear,ᵈ let him hear.

16 "But to what shall I compare this generation? It is like children sitting in the market places and calling to their playmates,

ᶻGreek *Gehenna*
ᵃOr *What then did you go out to see? A man* ...
ᵇOther ancient authorities read *What then did you go out to see? A prophet?*
ᶜOr *has been coming violently*
ᵈOther ancient authorities omit *to hear*
10.26-33: Lk 12.2-9. **10.26:** Mk 4.22; Lk 8.17; Eph 5.13.
10.28: Heb 10.31. **10.31:** Mt 12.12.
10.32: Mk 8.38; Lk 9.26; Rev 3.5; 2 Tim 2.12.
10.34-36: Lk 12.51-53; Mt 10.21; Mk 13.12; Mic 7.6.
10.37-39: Lk 14.25-27; 17.33; 9.23-24; Mt 16.24-25; Mk 8.34-35; Jn 12.25.
10.40: Lk 10.16; Jn 13.20; Gal 4.14; Mk 9.37; Mt 18.5; Lk 9.48. **10.42:** Mk 9.41; Mt 25.40.
11.1: Mt 7.28; 13.53; 19.1; 26.1. **11.2-19:** Lk 7.18-35.
11.3: Mk 1.7-8; Hab 2.3; Jn 11.27.
11.5: Is 35.5-6; 61.1; Lk 4.18-19.
11.9: Mt 21.26; Lk 1.76. **11.10:** Mal 3.1; Mk 1.2.
11.12-13: Lk 16.16.
11.14: Mal 4.5; Mt 17.10-13; Jn 1.21; Lk 1.17.
11.15: Mt 13.9, 43; Mk 4.23; Rev 13.9; 2.7.
11.16-19: Lk 7.31-35.

17 'We piped to you, and you did not dance;
we wailed, and you did not mourn.'
18 For John came neither eating nor drinking, and they say, 'He has a demon'; 19 the Son of man came eating and drinking, and they say, 'Behold, a glutton and a drunkard, a friend of tax collectors and sinners!' Yet wisdom is justified by her deeds."*e*

20 Then he began to upbraid the cities where most of his mighty works had been done, because they did not repent. 21 "Woe to you, Chō-rā′zĭn! woe to you, Bĕth–sā′ĭ-dạ! for if the mighty works done in you had been done in Tȳre and Sī′dŏn, they would have repented long ago in sackcloth and ashes. 22 But I tell you, it shall be more tolerable on the day of judgment for Tȳre and Sī′dŏn than for you. 23 And you, Cạ-pēr′nạ–ụm, will you be exalted to heaven? You shall be brought down to Hades. For if the mighty works done in you had been done in Sŏd′ọm, it would have remained until this day. 24 But I tell you that it shall be more tolerable on the day of judgment for the land of Sŏd′ọm than for you."

25 At that time Jesus declared, "I thank thee, Father, Lord of heaven and earth, that thou hast hidden these things from the wise and understanding and revealed them to babes; 26 yea, Father, for such was thy gracious will.*f* 27 All things have been delivered to me by my Father; and no one knows the Son except the Father, and no one knows the Father except the Son and any one to whom the Son chooses to reveal him. 28 Come to me, all who labor and are heavy laden, and I will give you rest. 29 Take my yoke upon you, and learn from me; for I am gentle and lowly in heart, and you will find rest for your souls. 30 For my yoke is easy, and my burden is light."

12 At that time Jesus went through the grainfields on the sabbath; his disciples were hungry, and they began to pluck heads of grain and to eat. 2 But when the Phăr′ĭ-seeṣ saw it, they said to him, "Look, your disciples are doing what is not lawful to do on the sabbath." 3 He said to them, "Have you not read what David did, when he was hungry, and those who were with him: 4 how he entered the house of God and ate the bread of the Presence, which it was not lawful for him to eat nor for those who were with him, but only for the priests? 5 Or have you not read in the law how on the sabbath the priests in the temple profane the sabbath, and are guiltless? 6 I tell you, something greater than the temple is here. 7 And if you had known what this means, 'I desire mercy, and not sacrifice,' you would not have condemned the guiltless. 8 For the Son of man is lord of the sabbath."

9 And he went on from there, and entered their synagogue. 10 And behold, there was a man with a withered hand. And they asked him, "Is it lawful to heal on the sabbath?" so that they might accuse him. 11 He said to them, "What man of you, if he has one sheep and it falls into a pit on the sabbath, will not lay hold of it and lift it out? 12 Of how much more value is a man than a sheep! So it is lawful to do good on the sabbath." 13 Then he said to the man, "Stretch out your hand." And the man stretched it out, and it was restored, whole like the other. 14 But the Phăr′ĭ-seeṣ went out and took counsel against him, how to destroy him.

15 Jesus, aware of this, withdrew from there. And many followed him, and he healed them all, 16 and ordered them not to make him known. 17 This was to fulfil what was spoken by the prophet Ĭ-sāi′ah:

18 "Behold, my servant whom I have chosen,
my beloved with whom my soul is well pleased.
I will put my Spirit upon him,
and he shall proclaim justice to the Gentiles.
19 He will not wrangle or cry aloud,
nor will any one hear his voice in the streets;
20 he will not break a bruised reed
or quench a smoldering wick,
till he brings justice to victory;
21 and in his name will the Gentiles hope."

e Other ancient authorities read *children* (Luke 7.35)
f Or *so it was well-pleasing before thee*
11.20–24: Lk 10.13-15. **11.24:** Mt 10.15; Lk 10.12.
11.25–27: Lk 10.21-22. **11.25:** 1 Cor 1.26-29.
11.27: Jn 3.35; 5.20; 13.3; 7.29; 10.15; 17.25; Mt 28.18.
11.29: Jn 13.15; Phil 2.5; 1 Pet 2.21; Jer 6.16.
12.1–8: Mk 2.23-28; Lk 6.1-5.
12.1: Deut 23.25. **12.3:** 1 Sam 21.1-6; Lev 24.9.
12.5: Num 28.9-10. **12.6:** Mt 12.41-42; Lk 11.31-32.
12.7: Hos 6.6; Mt 9.13. **12.8:** Jn 5.1-18; 7.19-24; 9.1-41.
12.9–14: Mk 3.1-6; Lk 6.6-11. **12.11:** Lk 14.5.
12.12: Mt 10.31.
12.14: Mk 14.1; Jn 7.30; 8.59; 10.39; 11.53.
12.15–21: Mk 3.7-12; Lk 6.17-19. **12.18–21:** Is 42.1-4.

22 Then a blind and dumb demoniac was brought to him, and he healed him, so that the dumb man spoke and saw. ²³And all the people were amazed, and said, "Can this be the Son of David?" ²⁴But when the Phăr′ĭ-seeș heard it they said, "It is only by Bē-ĕl′-ze̤-bŭl, the prince of demons, that this man casts out demons." ²⁵Knowing their thoughts, he said to them, "Every kingdom divided against itself is laid waste, and no city or house divided against itself will stand; ²⁶and if Satan casts out Satan, he is divided against himself; how then will his kingdom stand? ²⁷And if I cast out demons by Bē-ĕl′ze̤-bŭl, by whom do your sons cast them out? Therefore they shall be your judges. ²⁸But if it is by the Spirit of God that I cast out demons, then the kingdom of God has come upon you. ²⁹Or how can one enter a strong man's house and plunder his goods, unless he first binds the strong man? Then indeed he may plunder his house. ³⁰He who is not with me is against me, and he who does not gather with me scatters. ³¹Therefore I tell you, every sin and blasphemy will be forgiven men, but the blasphemy against the Spirit will not be forgiven. ³²And whoever says a word against the Son of man will be forgiven; but whoever speaks against the Holy Spirit will not be forgiven, either in this age or in the age to come.

33 "Either make the tree good, and its fruit good; or make the tree bad, and its fruit bad; for the tree is known by its fruit. ³⁴You brood of vipers! how can you speak good, when you are evil? For out of the abundance of the heart the mouth speaks. ³⁵The good man out of his good treasure brings forth good, and the evil man out of his evil treasure brings forth evil. ³⁶I tell you, on the day of judgment men will render account for every careless word they utter; ³⁷for by your words you will be justified, and by your words you will be condemned."

38 Then some of the scribes and Phăr′ĭ-seeș said to him, "Teacher, we wish to see a sign from you." ³⁹But he answered them, "An evil and adulterous generation seeks for a sign; but no sign shall be given to it except the sign of the prophet Jonah. ⁴⁰For as Jonah was three days and three nights in the belly of the whale, so will the

Son of man be three days and three nights in the heart of the earth. ⁴¹The men of Nĭn′e̤-ve̤h will arise at the judgment with this generation and condemn it; for they repented at the preaching of Jonah, and behold, something greater than Jonah is here. ⁴²The queen of the South will arise at the judgment with this generation and condemn it; for she came from the ends of the earth to hear the wisdom of Solomon, and behold, something greater than Solomon is here.

43 "When the unclean spirit has gone out of a man, he passes through waterless places seeking rest, but he finds none. ⁴⁴Then he says, 'I will return to my house from which I came.' And when he comes he finds it empty, swept, and put in order. ⁴⁵Then he goes and brings with him seven other spirits more evil than himself, and they enter and dwell there; and the last state of that man becomes worse than the first. So shall it be also with this evil generation."

46 While he was still speaking to the people, behold, his mother and his brothers stood outside, asking to speak to him.ᵍ ⁴⁸But he replied to the man who told him, "Who is my mother, and who are my brothers?" ⁴⁹And stretching out his hand toward his disciples, he said, "Here are my mother and my brothers! ⁵⁰For whoever does the will of my Father in heaven is my brother, and sister, and mother."

13 That same day Jesus went out of the house and sat beside the sea. ²And great crowds gathered about him, so that he got into a boat and sat there; and the whole crowd stood on the beach. ³And he told them many things in parables, saying: "A sower went out to sow. ⁴And as he sowed, some seeds fell along the path, and the birds came and devoured them. ⁵Other seeds fell on rocky ground, where they had not much soil,

ᵍOther ancient authorities insert verse 47, *Some one told him, "Your mother and your brothers are standing outside, asking to speak to you"*

12.22-29: Mk 3.22-27; Lk 11.14-22.   12.22: Mt 9.32-33.
12.24: Mt 9.34; 10.25; Jn 7.20; 8.52; 10.20.
12.30: Lk 11.23; Mk 9.40.   12.31-32: Mk 3.28-30; Lk 12.10.
12.33-35: Lk 6.43-45; Mt 7.16-20; Jas 3.11-12; Mt 15.18.
12.38-42: Lk 11.16, 29-32; Mk 8.11-12; Mt 16.1-4; Jn 2.18; 6.30; 1 Cor 1.22.   12.40: Jon 1.17.   12.41: Jon 3.5.
12.42: 1 Kings 10.1-10; 2 Chron 9.1-12.
12.43-45: Lk 11.24-26; 2 Pet 2.20.
12.46-50: Mk 3.31-35; Lk 8.19-21.
12.46: Jn 2.1-12; 19.25-27; 7.1-10; Mk 6.3; 1 Cor 9.5.
12.50: Mt 7.21.   13.1-9: Mk 4.1-9; Lk 8.4-8; 5.1-3.

and immediately they sprang up, since they had no depth of soil, [6]but when the sun rose they were scorched; and since they had no root they withered away. [7]Other seeds fell upon thorns, and the thorns grew up and choked them. [8]Other seeds fell on good soil and brought forth grain, some a hundredfold, some sixty, some thirty. [9]He who has ears,[h] let him hear."

10 Then the disciples came and said to him, "Why do you speak to them in parables?" [11]And he answered them, "To you it has been given to know the secrets of the kingdom of heaven, but to them it has not been given. [12]For to him who has will more be given, and he will have abundance; but from him who has not, even what he has will be taken away. [13]This is why I speak to them in parables, because seeing they do not see, and hearing they do not hear, nor do they understand. [14]With their indeed is fulfilled the prophecy of I·saī′ah which says:

'You shall indeed hear but never understand,
and you shall indeed see but never perceive.
[15]For this people's heart has grown dull,
and their ears are heavy of hearing,
and their eyes they have closed,
lest they should perceive with their eyes,
and hear with their ears,
and understand with their heart,
and turn for me to heal them.'
[16]But blessed are your eyes, for they see, and your ears, for they hear. [17]Truly, I say to you, many prophets and righteous men longed to see what you see, and did not see it, and to hear what you hear, and did not hear it.

18 "Hear then the parable of the sower. [19]When any one hears the word of the kingdom and does not understand it, the evil one comes and snatches away what is sown in his heart; this is what was sown along the path. [20]As for what was sown on rocky ground, this is he who hears the word and immediately receives it with joy; [21]yet he has no root in himself, but endures for a while, and when tribulation or persecution arises on account of the word, immediately he falls away.[i] [22]As for what was sown among thorns, this is he who hears the word, but the cares of the world and the delight in riches choke the word, and it proves unfruitful. [23]As for what was sown on good soil, this is he who hears the word and understands it; he indeed bears fruit, and yields, in one case a hundredfold, in another sixty, and in another thirty."

24 Another parable he put before them, saying, "The kingdom of heaven may be compared to a man who sowed good seed in his field; [25]but while men were sleeping, his enemy came and sowed weeds among the wheat, and went away. [26]So when the plants came up and bore grain, then the weeds appeared also. [27]And the servants[j] of the householder came and said to him, 'Sir, did you not sow good seed in your field? How then has it weeds?' [28]He said to them, 'An enemy has done this.' The servants[j] said to him, 'Then do you want us to go and gather them?' [29]But he said, 'No; lest in gathering the weeds you root up the wheat along with them. [30]Let both grow together until the harvest; and at harvest time I will tell the reapers, Gather the weeds first and bind them in bundles to be burned, but gather the wheat into my barn.'"

31 Another parable he put before them, saying, "The kingdom of heaven is like a grain of mustard seed which a man took and sowed in his field; [32]it is the smallest of all seeds, but when it has grown it is the greatest of shrubs and becomes a tree, so that the birds of the air come and make nests in its branches."

33 He told them another parable. "The kingdom of heaven is like leaven which a woman took and hid in three measures of flour, till it was all leavened."

34 All this Jesus said to the crowds in parables; indeed he said nothing to them without a parable. [35]This was to fulfil what was spoken by the prophet:[k]

"I will open my mouth in parables,
I will utter what has been hidden

[h]Other ancient authorities add here and in verse 43 *to hear*
[i]Or *stumbles* [j]Or *slaves*
[k]Other ancient authorities read *the prophet Isaiah*
13.10-13: Mk 4.10-12; Lk 8.9-10.
13.12: Mk 4.25; Lk 8.18; Mt 25.29; Lk 19.26.
13.14-15: Is 6.9-10; Mk 8.18; Jn 12.39-41; Acts 28.26-27.
13.16-17: Lk 10.23-24; Jn 8.56; Heb 11.13; 1 Pet 1.10-12.
13.18-23: Mk 4.13-20; Lk 8.11-15.
13.22: Mt 19.23; 1 Tim 6.9-10, 17.   **13.24-30:** Mk 4.26-29.
13.31-32: Mk 4.30-32; Lk 13.18-19; Mt 17.20.
13.33: Lk 13.20-21; Gal 5.9; Gen 18.6.
13.34: Mk 4.33-34; Jn 10.6; 16.25.   **13.35:** Ps 78.2.

since the foundation of the world."

36 Then he left the crowds and went into the house. And his disciples came to him, saying, "Explain to us the parable of the weeds of the field." ³⁷He answered, "He who sows the good seed is the Son of man; ³⁸the field is the world, and the good seed means the sons of the kingdom; the weeds are the sons of the evil one, ³⁹and the enemy who sowed them is the devil; the harvest is the close of the age, and the reapers are angels. ⁴⁰Just as the weeds are gathered and burned with fire, so will it be at the close of the age. ⁴¹The Son of man will send his angels, and they will gather out of his kingdom all causes of sin and all evildoers, ⁴²and throw them into the furnace of fire; there men will weep and gnash their teeth. ⁴³Then the righteous will shine like the sun in the kingdom of their Father. He who has ears, let him hear.

44 "The kingdom of heaven is like treasure hidden in a field, which a man found and covered up; then in his joy he goes and sells all that he has and buys that field.

45 "Again, the kingdom of heaven is like a merchant in search of fine pearls, ⁴⁶who, on finding one pearl of great value, went and sold all that he had and bought it.

47 "Again, the kingdom of heaven is like a net which was thrown into the sea and gathered fish of every kind; ⁴⁸when it was full, men drew it ashore and sat down and sorted the good into vessels but threw away the bad. ⁴⁹So it will be at the close of the age. The angels will come out and separate the evil from the righteous, ⁵⁰and throw them into the furnace of fire; there men will weep and gnash their teeth.

51 "Have you understood all this?" They said to him, "Yes." ⁵²And he said to them, "Therefore every scribe who has been trained for the kingdom of heaven is like a householder who brings out of his treasure what is new and what is old."

53 And when Jesus had finished these parables, he went away from there, ⁵⁴and coming to his own country he taught them in their synagogue, so that they were astonished, and said, "Where did this man get this

wisdom and these mighty works? ⁵⁵Is not this the carpenter's son? Is not his mother called Mary? And are not his brothers James and Joseph and Simon and Judas? ⁵⁶And are not all his sisters with us? Where then did this man get all this?" ⁵⁷And they took offense at him. But Jesus said to them, "A prophet is not without honor except in his own country and in his own house." ⁵⁸And he did not do many mighty works there, because of their unbelief.

14 At that time Hĕr'ŏd the tetrarch heard about the fame of Jesus; ²and he said to his servants, "This is John the Baptist, he has been raised from the dead; that is why these powers are at work in him." ³For Hĕr'ŏd had seized John and bound him and put him in prison, for the sake of Hĕ-rō'dĭ–as, his brother Philip's wife;ˡ ⁴because John said to him, "It is not lawful for you to have her." ⁵And though he wanted to put him to death, he feared the people, because they held him to be a prophet. ⁶But when Hĕr'-ŏd's birthday came, the daughter of Hĕ-rō'dĭ–as danced before the company, and pleased Herod, ⁷so that he promised with an oath to give her whatever she might ask. ⁸Prompted by her mother, she said, "Give me the head of John the Baptist here on a platter." ⁹And the king was sorry; but because of his oaths and his guests he commanded it to be given; ¹⁰he sent and had John beheaded in the prison, ¹¹and his head was brought on a platter and given to the girl, and she brought it to her mother. ¹²And his disciples came and took the body and buried it; and they went and told Jesus.

13 Now when Jesus heard this, he withdrew from there in a boat to a lonely place apart. But when the crowds heard it, they followed him on foot from the towns. ¹⁴As he went ashore he saw a great throng; and he had compassion on them, and healed their sick. ¹⁵When it was evening, the disciples came to him and said, "This

ˡOther ancient authorities read *his brother's wife*
13.38: Jn 8.44; 1 Jn 3.10. **13.41:** Mt 24.31.
13.42: Mt 13.50; 8.12; 22.13; 24.51; 25.30; Lk 13.28.
13.47-50: Mt 13.40-42. **13.53:** Mt 7.28; 11.1; 19.1; 26.1.
13.54-58: Mk 6.1-6; Lk 4.16-30.
14.1-2: Mk 6.14-16; Lk 9.7-9; Mk 8.28.
14.3-4: Mk 6.17-18; Lk 3.19-20; Lev 18.16; 20.21.
14.5-12: Mk 6.19-29.
14.13-21: Mk 6.32-44; Lk 9.10-17; Jn 6.1-13; Mt 15.32-38.

is a lonely place, and the day is now over; send the crowds away to go into the villages and buy food for themselves." [16]Jesus said, "They need not go away; you give them something to eat." [17]They said to him, "We have only five loaves here and two fish." [18]And he said, "Bring them here to me." [19]Then he ordered the crowds to sit down on the grass; and taking the five loaves and the two fish he looked up to heaven, and blessed, and broke and gave the loaves to the disciples, and the disciples gave them to the crowds. [20]And they all ate and were satisfied. And they took up twelve baskets full of the broken pieces left over. [21]And those who ate were about five thousand men, besides women and children.

22 Then he made the disciples get into the boat and go before him to the other side, while he dismissed the crowds. [23]And after he had dismissed the crowds, he went up on the mountain by himself to pray. When evening came, he was there alone, [24]but the boat by this time was many furlongs distant from the land,[m] beaten by the waves; for the wind was against them. [25]And in the fourth watch of the night he came to them, walking on the sea. [26]But when the disciples saw him walking on the sea, they were terrified, saying, "It is a ghost!" And they cried out for fear. [27]But immediately he spoke to them, saying, "Take heart, it is I; have no fear."

28 And Peter answered him, "Lord, if it is you, bid me come to you on the water." [29]He said, "Come." So Peter got out of the boat and walked on the water and came to Jesus; [30]but when he saw the wind,[n] he was afraid, and beginning to sink he cried out, "Lord, save me." [31]Jesus immediately reached out his hand and caught him, saying to him, "O man of little faith, why did you doubt?" [32]And when they got into the boat, the wind ceased. [33]And those in the boat worshiped him, saying, "Truly you are the Son of God."

34 And when they had crossed over, they came to land at Gĕn·nĕs'a·rĕt. [35]And when the men of that place recognized him, they sent round to all that region and brought to him all that were sick, [36]and besought him that they might only touch the fringe of his garment; and as many as touched it were made well.

15 Then Phăr'i·seeş and scribes came to Jesus from Jerusalem and said, [2]"Why do your disciples transgress the tradition of the elders? For they do not wash their hands when they eat." [3]He answered them, "And why do you transgress the commandment of God for the sake of your tradition? [4]For God commanded, 'Honor your father and your mother,' and, 'He who speaks evil of father or mother, let him surely die.' [5]But you say, 'If any one tells his father or his mother, What you would have gained from me is given to God,[o] he need not honor his father.' [6]So for the sake of your tradition, you have made void the word[p] of God. [7]You hypocrites! Well did I·sāi'ah prophesy of you, when he said:
[8]'This people honors me with their lips,
but their heart is far from me;
[9]in vain do they worship me,
teaching as doctrines the precepts of men.'"

10 And he called the people to him and said to them, "Hear and understand: [11]not what goes into the mouth defiles a man, but what comes out of the mouth, this defiles a man." [12]Then the disciples came and said to him, "Do you know that the Phăr'i·seeş were offended when they heard this saying?" [13]He answered, "Every plant which my heavenly Father has not planted will be rooted up. [14]Let them alone; they are blind guides. And if a blind man leads a blind man, both will fall into a pit." [15]But Peter said to him, "Explain the parable to us." [16]And he said, "Are you also still without understanding? [17]Do you not see that whatever goes into the mouth passes into the stomach, and so passes on?[q] [18]But what comes out of the mouth proceeds from the heart, and this defiles a man. [19]For out of the heart

[m] Other ancient authorities read *was out on the sea*
[n] Other ancient authorities read *strong wind*
[o] *Or an offering*   [p] Other ancient authorities read *law*
[q] *Or is evacuated*
14.19: Mk 14.22; Lk 24.30.
14.22-23: Mk 6.45-46; Jn 6.15-17.
14.24-33: Mk 6.47-52; Jn 6.16-21.   **14.26:** Lk 24.37.
14.29: Jn 21.7.   **14.31:** Mt 6.30; 8.26; 16.8.
14.33: Mt 28.9, 17.   **14.34-36:** Mk 6.53-56; Jn 6.22-26.
14.36: Mk 3.10; Num 15.38; Mt 9.20.   **15.1-20:** Mk 7.1-23.
15.4: Ex 20.12; Deut 5.16; Ex 21.17; Lev 20.9.
15.8-9: Is 29.13.   **15.11:** Acts 10.14-15; 1 Tim 4.3.
15.13: Is 60.21; Jn 15.2.
15.14: Lk 6.39; Mt 23.16, 24; Rom 2.19.
15.19: Gal 5.19-21; 1 Cor 6.9-10; Rom 14.14.

come evil thoughts, murder, adultery, fornication, theft, false witness, slander. ²⁰These are what defile a man; but to eat with unwashed hands does not defile a man."

21 And Jesus went away from there and withdrew to the district of Tȳre and Sĭ′dŏn. ²²And behold, a Canaanite woman from that region came out and cried, "Have mercy on me, O Lord, Son of David; my daughter is severely possessed by a demon." ²³But he did not answer her a word. And his disciples came and begged him, saying, "Send her away, for she is crying after us." ²⁴He answered, "I was sent only to the lost sheep of the house of Israel." ²⁵But she came and knelt before him, saying, "Lord, help me." ²⁶And he answered, "It is not fair to take the children's bread and throw it to the dogs." ²⁷She said, "Yes, Lord, yet even the dogs eat the crumbs that fall from their masters' table." ²⁸Then Jesus answered her, "O woman, great is your faith! Be it done for you as you desire." And her daughter was healed instantly.

29 And Jesus went on from there and passed along the Sea of Galilee. And he went up on the mountain, and sat down there. ³⁰And great crowds came to him, bringing with them the lame, the maimed, the blind, the dumb, and many others, and they put them at his feet, and he healed them, ³¹so that the throng wondered, when they saw the dumb speaking, the maimed whole, the lame walking, and the blind seeing; and they glorified the God of Israel.

32 Then Jesus called his disciples to him and said, "I have compassion on the crowd, because they have been with me now three days, and have nothing to eat; and I am unwilling to send them away hungry, lest they faint on the way." ³³And the disciples said to him, "Where are we to get bread enough in the desert to feed so great a crowd?" ³⁴And Jesus said to them, "How many loaves have you?" They said, "Seven, and a few small fish." ³⁵And commanding the crowd to sit down on the ground, ³⁶he took the seven loaves and the fish, and having given thanks he broke them and gave them to the disciples, and the disciples gave them to the crowds. ³⁷And they all ate and were satisfied; and they took up seven baskets full of the broken pieces left over. ³⁸Those who ate were four thousand men, besides women and children. ³⁹And sending away the crowds, he got into the boat and went to the region of Măg′ạ·dăn.

16 And the Phăr′i̇·seeṣ and Săd′dū·çeeṣ came, and to test him they asked him to show them a sign from heaven. ²He answered them,ʳ "When it is evening, you say, 'It will be fair weather; for the sky is red.' ³And in the morning, 'It will be stormy today, for the sky is red and threatening.' You know how to interpret the appearance of the sky, but you cannot interpret the signs of the times. ⁴An evil and adulterous generation seeks for a sign, but no sign shall be given to it except the sign of Jonah." So he left them and departed.

5 When the disciples reached the other side, they had forgotten to bring any bread. ⁶Jesus said to them, "Take heed and beware of the leaven of the Phăr′i̇·seeṣ and Săd′dū·çeeṣ." ⁷And they discussed it among themselves, saying, "We brought no bread." ⁸But Jesus, aware of this, said, "O men of little faith, why do you discuss among yourselves the fact that you have no bread? ⁹Do you not yet perceive? Do you not remember the five loaves of the five thousand, and how many baskets you gathered? ¹⁰Or the seven loaves of the four thousand, and how many baskets you gathered? ¹¹How is it that you fail to perceive that I did not speak about bread? Beware of the leaven of the Phăr′i̇·seeṣ and Săd′dū·çeeṣ." ¹²Then they understood that he did not tell them to beware of the leaven of bread, but of the teaching of the Phăr′i̇·seeṣ and Săd′dū·çeeṣ.

13 Now when Jesus came into the district of Caĕs·a·rē′a Phĭ·lĭp′pī, he asked his disciples, "Who do men say that the Son of man is?" ¹⁴And they said, "Some say John the Baptist, others say Ē·lī′jạh, and others Jĕr-

ʳOther ancient authorities omit the following words to the end of verse 3
15.21-28: Mk 7.24-30.   15.24: Mt 10.6, 23.
15.25: Mt 8.2; 18.26; 20.20; Jn 9.38.
15.28: Mt 9.22, 28; Mk 10.52; Lk 7.50; 17.19.
15.29-31: Mk 7.31-37.   15.32-39: Mk 8.1-10; Mt 14.13-21.
15.32: Mt 9.36.
16.1-4: Mk 8.11-12; Lk 11.16, 29; 12.54-56; Mt 12.38-39; Jn 2.18; 6.30.   16.4: Jon 3.4-5.
16.5-12: Mk 8.13-21.   16.6: Lk 12.1.
16.8: Mt 6.30; 8.26; 14.31.   16.9: Mt 14.17-21.
16.10: Mt 15.34-38.   16.13-16: Mk 8.27-30; Lk 9.18-21.
16.14: Mt 14.2; Mk 6.15; Lk 9.7-8; Jn 1.21.

e·mī′ah or one of the prophets." ¹⁵He said to them, "But who do you say that I am?" ¹⁶Simon Peter replied, "You are the Christ, the Son of the living God." ¹⁷And Jesus answered him, "Blessed are you, Simon Bār–Jō′na! For flesh and blood has not revealed this to you, but my Father who is in heaven. ¹⁸And I tell you, you are Peter,ˢ and on this rockᵗ I will build my church, and the powers of deathᵘ shall not prevail against it. ¹⁹I will give you the keys of the kingdom of heaven, and whatever you bind on earth shall be bound in heaven, and whatever you loose on earth shall be loosed in heaven." ²⁰Then he strictly charged the disciples to tell no one that he was the Christ.

21 From that time Jesus began to show his disciples that he must go to Jerusalem and suffer many things from the elders and chief priests and scribes, and be killed, and on the third day be raised. ²²And Peter took him and began to rebuke him, saying, "God forbid, Lord! This shall never happen to you." ²³But he turned and said to Peter, "Get behind me, Satan! You are a hindranceᵛ to me; for you are not on the side of God, but of men."

24 Then Jesus told his disciples, "If any man would come after me, let him deny himself and take up his cross and follow me. ²⁵For whoever would save his life will lose it, and whoever loses his life for my sake will find it. ²⁶For what will it profit a man, if he gains the whole world and forfeits his life? Or what shall a man give in return for his life? ²⁷For the Son of man is to come with his angels in the glory of his Father, and then he will repay every man for what he has done. ²⁸Truly, I say to you, there are some standing here who will not taste death before they see the Son of man coming in his kingdom."

17 And after six days Jesus took with him Peter and James and John his brother, and led them up a high mountain apart. ²And he was transfigured before them, and his face shone like the sun, and his garments became white as light. ³And behold, there appeared to them Moses and E·lī′jah, talking with him. ⁴And Peter said to Jesus, "Lord, it is well that we are here; if you wish, I will make three booths here, one for you and one for

Moses and one for E·lī′jah." ⁵He was still speaking, when lo, a bright cloud overshadowed them, and a voice from the cloud said, "This is my beloved Son,ʷ with whom I am well pleased; listen to him." ⁶When the disciples heard this, they fell on their faces, and were filled with awe. ⁷But Jesus came and touched them, saying, "Rise, and have no fear." ⁸And when they lifted up their eyes, they saw no one but Jesus only.

9 And as they were coming down the mountain, Jesus commanded them, "Tell no one the vision, until the Son of man is raised from the dead." ¹⁰And the disciples asked him, "Then why do the scribes say that first E·lī′jah must come?" ¹¹He replied, "E·lī′jah does come, and he is to restore all things; ¹²but I tell you that E·lī′jah has already come, and they did not know him, but did to him whatever they pleased. So also the Son of man will suffer at their hands." ¹³Then the disciples understood that he was speaking to them of John the Baptist.

14 And when they came to the crowd, a man came up to him and kneeling before him said, ¹⁵"Lord, have mercy on my son, for he is an epileptic and he suffers terribly; for often he falls into the fire, and often into the water. ¹⁶And I brought him to your disciples, and they could not heal him." ¹⁷And Jesus answered, "O faithless and perverse generation, how long am I to be with you? How long am I to bear with you? Bring him here to me." ¹⁸And Jesus rebuked him, and the demon came out of him, and the boy was cured instantly. ¹⁹Then the disciples came to Jesus privately and said, "Why could we not cast it

ˢGreek *Petros* ᵗGreek *petra*
ᵘGreek *the gates of Hades*
ᵛGreek *stumbling block*
ʷOr *my Son, my* (or *the*) *Beloved*
16.16: Mt 1.16; Jn 11.27; 1.49.
16.17: 1 Cor 15.50; Gal 1.16; Eph 6.12; Heb 2.14.
16.18: Jn 1.40-42; 21.15-17; 1 Cor 15.5.
16.19: Is 22.22; Rev 1.18; Mt 18.18; Jn 20.23.
16.20: Mt 8.4; Mk 3.12; 5.43; 7.36; 9.9.
16.21-28: Mk 8.31-9.1; Lk 9.22-27.
16.21: Mt 17.22-23; 20.17-19; Lk 17.25; Mt 17.12; 26.2.
16.23: Mt 4.10.
16.24-26: Mt 10.38-39; Lk 14.27; 17.33; Jn 12.25.
16.27: Mt 10.33; Lk 12.9; 1 Jn 2.28; Rom 2.6; Rev 22.12.
16.28: Mt 10.23; 1 Cor 16.22; 1 Thess 4.15-18; Rev 1.7; Jas 5.7.   **17.1-9:** Mk 9.2-10; Lk 9.28-36; 2 Pet 1.17-18.
17.1: Mt 26.37; Mk 5.37; 13.3.
17.5: Mt 3.17; Is 42.1; Ps 2.7; Jn 12.28.
17.9: Mt 8.4; 16.20; Mk 3.12; 5.43; 7.36.
17.10-13: Mk 9.11-13; Mt 11.14; Mal 4.5.
17.12: Mt 16.21; 17.22; 20.17; 26.2; Lk 17.25.
17.14-18: Mk 9.14-27; Lk 9.37-43.   **17.19-21:** Mk 9.28-29.

out?" [20] He said to them, "Because of your little faith. For truly, I say to you, if you have faith as a grain of mustard seed, you will say to this mountain, 'Move from here to there,' and it will move; and nothing will be impossible to you."[x]

22 As they were gathering[y] in Galilee, Jesus said to them, "The Son of man is to be delivered into the hands of men, [23] and they will kill him, and he will be raised on the third day." And they were greatly distressed.

24 When they came to Ca·pẽr'na-um, the collectors of the half-shekel tax went up to Peter and said, "Does not your teacher pay the tax?" [25] He said, "Yes." And when he came home, Jesus spoke to him first, saying, "What do you think, Simon? From whom do kings of the earth take toll or tribute? From their sons or from others?" [26] And when he said, "From others," Jesus said to him, "Then the sons are free. [27] However, not to give offense to them, go to the sea and cast a hook, and take the first fish that comes up, and when you open its mouth you will find a shekel; take that and give it to them for me and for yourself."

18 At that time the disciples came to Jesus, saying, "Who is the greatest in the kingdom of heaven?" [2] And calling to him a child, he put him in the midst of them, [3] and said, "Truly, I say to you, unless you turn and become like children, you will never enter the kingdom of heaven. [4] Whoever humbles himself like this child, he is the greatest in the kingdom of heaven.

5 "Whoever receives one such child in my name receives me; [6] but whoever causes one of these little ones who believe in me to sin,[z] it would be better for him to have a great millstone fastened round his neck and to be drowned in the depth of the sea.

7 "Woe to the world for temptations to sin![a] For it is necessary that temptations come, but woe to the man by whom the temptation comes! [8] And if your hand or your foot causes you to sin,[z] cut if off and throw it away; it is better for you to enter life maimed or lame than with two hands or two feet to be thrown into the eternal fire. [9] And if your eye causes you to sin,[z] pluck it out and throw it away; it is better for you to enter life with one eye than with two eyes to be thrown into the hell[b] of fire.

10 "See that you do not despise one of these little ones; for I tell you that in heaven their angels always behold the face of my Father who is in heaven.[c] [12] What do you think? If a man has a hundred sheep, and one of them has gone astray, does he not leave the ninety-nine on the mountains and go in search of the one that went astray? [13] And if he finds it, truly, I say to you, he rejoices over it more than over the ninety-nine that never went astray. [14] So it is not the will of my[d] Father who is in heaven that one of these little ones should perish.

15 "If your brother sins against you, go and tell him his fault, between you and him alone. If he listens to you, you have gained your brother. [16] But if he does not listen, take one or two others along with you, that every word may be confirmed by the evidence of two or three witnesses. [17] If he refuses to listen to them, tell it to the church; and if he refuses to listen even to the church, let him be to you as a Gentile and a tax collector. [18] Truly, I say to you, whatever you bind on earth shall be bound in heaven, and whatever you loose on earth shall be loosed in heaven. [19] Again I say to you, if two of you agree on earth about anything they ask, it will be done for them by my Father in heaven. [20] For where two or three are gathered in my name, there am I in the midst of them."

21 Then Peter came up and said to him, "Lord, how often shall my brother sin against me, and I forgive him? As many as seven times?" [22] Jesus said to him, "I do not say to you seven times, but seventy times seven.[e]

[x] Other ancient authorities insert verse 21, *"But this kind never comes out except by prayer and fasting"*
[y] Other ancient authorities read *abode*
[z] Greek *causes ... to stumble* [a] Greek *stumbling blocks*
[b] Greek *Gehenna*
[c] Other ancient authorities add verse 11, *For the Son of man came to save the lost*
[d] Other ancient authorities read *your*
[e] *Or seventy-seven times*
17.20: Lk 17.6; Mt 21.21; Mk 11.22-23; 1 Cor 13.2; Mk 9.23
17.22-23: Mk 9.30-32; Lk 9.43-45; Mt 16.21; 20.17-19; 26.2
17.24: Ex 30.13; 38.26.   **17.25:** Rom 13.7; Mt 22.17-21.
17.27: Mt 5.29; 18.6-9; Jn 6.61; 1 Cor 8.13.
18.1-5: Mk 9.33-37; Lk 9.46-48.
18.3: Mk 10.15; Lk 18.17; 1 Pet 2.2.
18.5: Mt 10.40; Lk 10.16; Jn 13.20.
18.6-9: Mk 9.42-48; Lk 17.1-2.
18.8-9: Mt 5.29-30; 17.27.   **18.10:** Acts 12.11.
18.11: Lk 19.10.   **18.12-14:** Lk 15.3-7.
18.15-17: Lk 17.3; 1 Cor 6.1-6; Gal 6.1; Jas 5.19-20; Lev 19.17; Deut 19.15.   **18.18:** Mt 16.19; Jn 20.23.
18.19-20: Mt 7.7; 21.22; Jas 1.5-7; 1 Jn 5.14; Jn 14.13.
18.21-22: Lk 17.4; Gen 4.24.

23 "Therefore the kingdom of heaven may be compared to a king who wished to settle accounts with his servants. ²⁴When he began the reckoning, one was brought to him who owed him ten thousand talents;ʲ ²⁵ and as he could not pay, his lord ordered him to be sold, with his wife and children and all that he had, and payment to be made. ²⁶ So the servant fell on his knees, imploring him, 'Lord, have patience with me, and I will pay you everything.' ²⁷And out of pity for him the lord of that servant released him and forgave him the debt. ²⁸ But that same servant, as he went out, came upon one of his fellow servants who owed him a hundred denarii;ᵍ and seizing him by the throat he said, 'Pay what you owe.' ²⁹ So his fellow servant fell down and besought him, 'Have patience with me, and I will pay you.' ³⁰ He refused and went and put him in prison till he should pay the debt. ³¹ When his fellow servants saw what had taken place, they were greatly distressed, and they went and reported to their lord all that had taken place! ³² Then his lord summoned him and said to him, 'You wicked servant! I forgave you all that debt because you besought me; ³³ and should not you have had mercy on your fellow servant, as I had mercy on you?' ³⁴And in anger his lord delivered him to the jailers,ʰ till he should pay all his debt. ³⁵ So also my heavenly Father will do to every one of you, if you do not forgive your brother from your heart."

19 Now when Jesus had finished these sayings, he went away from Galilee and entered the region of Jü·dē′ạ beyond the Jordan; ²and large crowds followed him, and he healed them there.

3 And Phăr′ị·seeş came up to him and tested him by asking, "Is it lawful to divorce one's wife for any cause?" ⁴He answered, "Have you not read that he who made them from the beginning made them male and female, ⁵and said, 'For this reason a man shall leave his father and mother and be joined to his wife, and the two shall become one flesh'? ⁶So they are no longer two but one flesh. What therefore God has joined together, let not man put asunder." ⁷They said to him, "Why then did Moses command one to

give a certificate of divorce, and to put her away?" ⁸He said to them, "For your hardness of heart Moses allowed you to divorce your wives, but from the beginning it was not so. ⁹And I say to you: whoever divorces his wife, except for unchastity,ʲ and marries another, commits adultery."ᵏ

10 The disciples said to him, "If such is the case of a man with his wife, it is not expedient to marry." ¹¹But he said to them, "Not all men can receive this saying, but only those to whom it is given. ¹²For there are eunuchs who have been so from birth, and there are eunuchs who have been made eunuchs by men, and there are eunuchs who have made themselves eunuchs for the sake of the kingdom of heaven. He who is able to receive this, let him receive it."

13 Then children were brought to him that he might lay his hands on them and pray. The disciples rebuked the people; ¹⁴but Jesus said, "Let the children come to me, and do not hinder them; for to such belongs the kingdom of heaven." ¹⁵And he laid his hands on them and went away.

16 And behold, one came up to him, saying, "Teacher, what good deed must I do, to have eternal life?" ¹⁷And he said to him, "Why do you ask me about what is good? One there is who is good. If you would enter life, keep the commandments." ¹⁸He said to him, "Which?" And Jesus said, "You shall not kill, You shall not commit adultery, You shall not steal, You shall not bear false witness, ¹⁹Honor your father and mother, and, You shall love your neighbor as yourself." ²⁰The young man said to him, "All these I have observed; what do I still lack?" ²¹Jesus said to him, "If you would be

ʲThis talent was more than fifteen years' wages of a laborer
ᵍThe denarius was a day's wage for a laborer
ʰGreek *torturers*
ʲOther ancient authorities, after *unchastity*, read *makes her commit adultery*
ᵏOther ancient authorities insert *and he who marries a divorced woman commits adultery*
18.23: Mt 25.19. **18.25:** Lk 7.42. **18.26:** Mt 8.2.
18.35: Mt 6.14. **19.1:** Mt 7.28; 11.1; 13.53; 26.1.
19.1-9: Mk 10.1-12.
19.5: Gen 1.27; 2.24; Eph 5.31; 1 Cor 6.16.
19.7: Deut 24.1-4.
19.9: Mt 5.32; Lk 16.18; 1 Cor 7.10-13.
19.11: 1 Cor 7.7-9.
19.13-15: Mk 10.13-16; Lk 18.15-17; Mt 18.2-3; 1 Cor 14.20. **19.16-22:** Mk 10.17-22; Lk 18.18-23.
19.16: Lk 10.25; Lev 18.5.
19.18: Ex 20.12-16; Deut 5.16-20; Rom 13.9; Jas 2.11.
19.19: Lev 19.18; Mt 22.39.
19.21: Lk 12.33; Acts 2.45; 4.34; Mt 6.20.

perfect, go, sell what you possess and give to the poor, and you will have treasure in heaven; and come, follow me." [22] When the young man heard this he went away sorrowful; for he had great possessions.

23 And Jesus said to his disciples, "Truly, I say to you, it will be hard for a rich man to enter the kingdom of heaven. [24] Again I tell you, it is easier for a camel to go through the eye of a needle than for a rich man to enter the kingdom of God." [25] When the disciples heard this they were greatly astonished, saying, "Who then can be saved?" [26] But Jesus looked at them and said to them, "With men this is impossible, but with God all things are possible." [27] Then Peter said in reply, "Lo, we have left everything and followed you. What then shall we have?" [28] Jesus said to them, "Truly, I say to you, in the new world, when the Son of man shall sit on his glorious throne, you who have followed me will also sit on twelve thrones, judging the twelve tribes of Israel. [29] And every one who has left houses or brothers or sisters or father or mother or children or lands, for my name's sake, will receive a hundredfold,[l] and inherit eternal life. [30] But many that are first will be last, and the last first.

20 "For the kingdom of heaven is like a householder who went out early in the morning to hire laborers for his vineyard. [2] After agreeing with the laborers for a denarius[m] a day, he sent them into his vineyard. [3] And going out about the third hour he saw others standing idle in the market place; [4] and to them he said, 'You go into the vineyard too, and whatever is right I will give you.' So they went. [5] Going out again about the sixth hour and the ninth hour, he did the same. [6] And about the eleventh hour he went out and found others standing; and he said to them, 'Why do you stand here idle all day?' [7] They said to him, 'Because no one has hired us.' He said to them, 'You go into the vineyard too.' [8] And when evening came, the owner of the vineyard said to his steward, 'Call the laborers and pay them their wages, beginning with the last, up to the first.' [9] And when those hired about the eleventh hour came, each of them received a denarius. [10] Now when the first came, they thought they would receive more; but each of them also received a denarius [11] And on receiving it they grumbled at the householder, [12] saying, 'These last worked only one hour, and you have made them equal to us who have borne the burden of the day and the scorching heat.' [13] But he replied to one of them, 'Friend, I am doing you no wrong; did you not agree with me for a denarius? [14] Take what belongs to you and go; I choose to give to this last as I give to you. [15] Am I not allowed to do what I choose with what belongs to me? Or do you begrudge my generosity?'[n] [16] So the last will be first, and the first last."

17 And as Jesus was going up to Jerusalem, he took the twelve disciples aside, and on the way he said to them, [18] "Behold, we are going up to Jerusalem; and the Son of man will be delivered to the chief priests and scribes, and they will condemn him to death, [19] and deliver him to the Gentiles to be mocked and scourged and crucified, and he will be raised on the third day."

20 Then the mother of the sons of Zeb'e·dee came up to him, with her sons, and kneeling before him she asked him for something. [21] And he said to her, "What do you want?" She said to him, "Command that these two sons of mine may sit, one at your right hand and one at your left, in your kingdom." [22] But Jesus answered, "You do not know what you are asking. Are you able to drink the cup that I am to drink?" They said to him, "We are able." [23] He said to them, "You will drink my cup, but to sit at my right hand and at my left is not mine to grant, but it is for those for whom it has been prepared by my Father." [24] And when the ten heard it they were indignant at the two brothers. [25] But Jesus called them to him and

[l] Other ancient authorities read *manifold*
[m] The denarius was a day's wage for a laborer
[n] Or *is your eye evil because I am good?*
19.23-26: Mk 10.23-27; Lk 18.24-27.
19.26: Gen 18.14; Job 42.2.
19.27-30: Mk 10.28-31; Lk 18.28-30; Mt 4.18-22.
19.28: Lk 22.30; Mt 20.21; Rev 3.21.
19.30: Mt 20.16; Lk 13.30.   20.1: Mt 21.28, 33.
20.8: Lev 19.13; Deut 24.15.   20.13: Mt 22.12; 26.50.
20.15: Mt 6.23; Mk 7.22; Deut 15.9.
20.16: Lk 13.30; Mt 19.30; Mk 10.31.
20.17-19: Mk 10.32-34; Lk 18.31-34; Mt 16.21; 17.1,
22-23; 26.2.   20.20-24: Mk 10.35-41.
20.20: Mt 8.2; 9.18; 15.25; 18.26; Jn 9.38.
20.21: Mt 19.28.   20.22: Mt 26.39; Jn 18.11.
20.23: Acts 12.2; Rev 1.9; Mt 13.11.
20.25-28: Mk 10.42-45; Lk 22.25-27.

said, "You know that the rulers of the Gentiles lord it over them, and their great men exercise authority over them. ²⁶It shall not be so among you; but whoever would be great among you must be your servant, ²⁷and whoever would be first among you must be your slave; ²⁸even as the Son of man came not to be served but to serve, and to give his life as a ransom for many."

29 And as they went out of Jericho, a great crowd followed him. ³⁰And behold, two blind men sitting by the roadside, when they heard that Jesus was passing by, cried out,ᵒ "Have mercy on us, Son of David!" ³¹The crowd rebuked them, telling them to be silent; but they cried out the more, "Lord, have mercy on us, Son of David!" ³²And Jesus stopped and called them, saying, "What do you want me to do for you?" ³³They said to him, "Lord, let our eyes be opened." ³⁴And Jesus in pity touched their eyes, and immediately they received their sight and followed him.

21 And when they drew near to Jerusalem and came to Bĕth'-phạ·gē, to the Mount of Olives, then Jesus sent two disciples, ²saying to them, "Go into the village opposite you, and immediately you will find an ass tied, and a colt with her; untie them and bring them to me. ³If any one says anything to you, you shall say, 'The Lord has need of them,' and he will send them immediately." ⁴This took place to fulfil what was spoken by the prophet, saying,
⁵"Tell the daughter of Zion,
Behold, your king is coming to you,
  humble, and mounted on an ass,
  and on a colt, the foal of an ass."
⁶The disciples went and did as Jesus had directed them; ⁷they brought the ass and the colt, and put their garments on them, and he sat thereon. ⁸Most of the crowd spread their garments on the road, and others cut branches from the trees and spread them on the road. ⁹And the crowds that went before him and that followed him shouted, "Hosanna to the Son of David! Blessed is he who comes in the name of the Lord! Hosanna in the highest!" ¹⁰And when he entered Jerusalem, all the city was stirred, saying, "Who is this?" ¹¹And the crowds said, "This is the prophet Jesus from Nazareth of Galilee."

12 And Jesus entered the temple of Godᵖ and drove out all who sold and bought in the temple, and he overturned the tables of the money-changers and the seats of those who sold pigeons. ¹³He said to them, "It is written, 'My house shall be called a house of prayer'; but you make it a den of robbers."

14 And the blind and the lame came to him in the temple, and he healed them. ¹⁵But when the chief priests and the scribes saw the wonderful things that he did, and the children crying out in the temple, "Hosanna to the Son of David!" they were indignant; ¹⁶and they said to him, "Do you hear what these are saying?" And Jesus said to them, "Yes; have you never read,
'Out of the mouth of babes and sucklings
thou hast brought perfect praise'?"
¹⁷And leaving them, he went out of the city to Bĕth'ạ·nӯ and lodged there.

18 In the morning, as he was returning to the city, he was hungry. ¹⁹And seeing a fig tree by the wayside he went to it, and found nothing on it but leaves only. And he said to it, "May no fruit ever come from you again!" And the fig tree withered at once. ²⁰When the disciples saw it they marveled, saying, "How did the fig tree wither at once?" ²¹And Jesus answered them, "Truly, I say to you, if you have faith and never doubt, you will not only do what has been done to the fig tree, but even if you say to this mountain, 'Be taken up and cast into the sea,' it will be done. ²²And whatever you ask in prayer, you will receive, if you have faith."

23 And when he entered the temple, the chief priests and the elders of the people came up to him as he was teaching, and said, "By what authority are you doing these things, and who

ᵒOther ancient authorities insert *Lord*
ᵖOther ancient authorities omit *of God*
20.26: Mt 23.11; Mk 9.35; Lk 9.48.
20.28: Mt 26.28; 1 Tim 2.5-6; Jn 13.15-16; Tit 2.14; 1 Pet 1.18. **20.29-34:** Mk 10.46-52; Lk 18.35-43; Mt 9.27-31.
21.1-9: Mk 11.1-10; Lk 19.29-38; Jn 12.12-18.
21.5: Is 62.11; Zech 9.9. **21.8:** 2 Kings 9.13.
21.9: Ps 118.26; Lk 2.14; Mt 21.15; 23.39.
21.11: Jn 6.14; 7.40; Acts 3.22; Mk 6.15; Lk 13.33.
21.12-13: Mk 11.15-17; Lk 19.45-46; Jn 2.13-17; Ex 30.13; Lev 1.14. **21.13:** Is 56.7; Jer 7.11.
21.15: Lk 19.39; Mt 21.9. **21.16:** Ps 8.2.
21.17-19: Mk 11.11-14; Lk 13.6-9. **21.20-22:** Mk 11.20-24.
21.21: Mt 17.20; Lk 17.6; 1 Cor 13.2; Jas 1.6.
21.22: Jn 14.13-14; 16.23.
21.23-27: Mk 11.27-33; Lk 20.1-8; Jn 2.18-22.

gave you this authority?" 24 Jesus answered them, "I also will ask you a
question; and if you tell me the answer, then I also will tell you by what
authority I do these things. 25 The
baptism of John, whence was it? From
heaven or from men?" And they
argued with one another, "If we say,
'From heaven,' he will say to us, 'Why
then did you not believe him?' 26 But
if we say, 'From men,' we are afraid of
the multitude; for all hold that John
was a prophet." 27 So they answered
Jesus, "We do not know." And he said
to them, "Neither will I tell you by
what authority I do these things.
28 "What do you think? A man had
two sons; and he went to the first
and said, 'Son, go and work in the vineyard today.' 29 And he answered, 'I
will not'; but afterward he repented
and went. 30 And he went to the second
and said the same; and he answered,
'I go, sir,' but did not go. 31 Which of
the two did the will of his father?"
They said, "The first." Jesus said to
them, "Truly, I say to you, the tax
collectors and the harlots go into the
kingdom of God before you. 32 For John
came to you in the way of righteousness, and you did not believe him, but
the tax collectors and the harlots believed him; and even when you saw it,
you did not afterward repent and believe him.
33 "Hear another parable. There
was a householder who planted a
vineyard, and set a hedge around it,
and dug a wine press in it, and built
a tower, and let it out to tenants, and
went into another country. 34 When the
season of fruit drew near, he sent his
servants to the tenants, to get his
fruit; 35 and the tenants took his servants and beat one, killed another, and
stoned another. 36 Again he sent other
servants, more than the first; and they
did the same to them. 37 Afterward he
sent his son to them, saying, 'They
will respect my son.' 38 But when the
tenants saw the son, they said to themselves, 'This is the heir; come, let us
kill him and have his inheritance.'
39 And they took him and cast him out of
the vineyard, and killed him. 40 When
therefore the owner of the vineyard
comes, what will he do to those tenants?" 41 They said to him, "He will put
those wretches to a miserable death,
and let out the vineyard to other tenants who will give him the fruits in
their seasons."
42 Jesus said to them, "Have you
never read in the scriptures:

'The very stone which the builders
rejected
has become the head of the corner;
this was the Lord's doing,
and it is marvelous in our eyes'?

43 Therefore I tell you, the kingdom
of God will be taken away from you
and given to a nation producing the
fruits of it."[q]
45 When the chief priests and the
Phăr'i·seeş heard his parables, they
perceived that he was speaking about
them. 46 But when they tried to arrest
him, they feared the multitudes, because they held him to be a prophet.
22 And again Jesus spoke to them
in parables, saying, 2 "The kingdom of heaven may be compared to a
king who gave a marriage feast for
his son, 3 and sent his servants to call
those who were invited to the marriage
feast; but they would not come. 4 Again
he sent other servants, saying, 'Tell
those who are invited, Behold, I have
made ready my dinner, my oxen and
my fat calves are killed, and everything is ready; come to the marriage
feast.' 5 But they made light of it and
went off, one to his farm, another to
his business, 6 while the rest seized
his servants, treated them shamefully,
and killed them. 7 The king was angry,
and he sent his troops and destroyed
those murderers and burned their
city. 8 Then he said to his servants,
'The wedding is ready, but those invited were not worthy. 9 Go therefore
to the thoroughfares, and invite to the
marriage feast as many as you find.'
10 And those servants went out into the
streets and gathered all whom they
found, both bad and good; so the
wedding hall was filled with guests.
11 "But when the king came in to
look at the guests, he saw there a man
who had no wedding garment; 12 and
he said to him, 'Friend, how did you
get in here without a wedding gar-

[q] Other ancient authorities add verse 44, *"And he who falls on this stone will be broken to pieces; but when it falls on any one, it will crush him"*

21.26: Mt 11.9; 14.5; Lk 1.76.
21.28: Mt 20.1; 21.33. **21.32:** Lk 7.29-30.
21.33-46: Mk 12.1-12; Lk 20.9-19; Is 5.1-7.
21.34: Mt 22.3. **21.41:** Mt 8.11; Acts 13.46; 18.6; 28.28.
21.42: Ps 118.22-23; Acts 4.11; 1 Pet 2.7.
22.1-10: Lk 14.16-24. **22.3:** Mt 21.34. **22.10:** Mt 13.47.
22.12: Mt 20.13; 26.50.

ment?' And he was speechless. ¹³ Then the king said to the attendants, 'Bind him hand and foot, and cast him into the outer darkness; there men will weep and gnash their teeth.' ¹⁴ For many are called, but few are chosen." 15 Then the Phăr′i·seeṣ went and took counsel how to entangle him in his talk. ¹⁶ And they sent their disciples to him, along with the Hĕ·rō′di·anṣ, saying, "Teacher, we know that you are true, and teach the way of God truthfully, and care for no man; for you do not regard the position of men. ¹⁷ Tell us, then, what you think. Is it lawful to pay taxes to Caesar, or not?" ¹⁸ But Jesus, aware of their malice, said, "Why put me to the test, you hypocrites? ¹⁹ Show me the money for the tax." And they brought him a coin.ʳ ²⁰ And Jesus said to them, "Whose likeness and inscription is this?" ²¹ They said, "Caesar's." Then he said to them, "Render therefore to Caesar the things that are Caesar's, and to God the things that are God's." ²² When they heard it, they marveled; and they left him and went away.

23 The same day Săd′du·çeeṣ came to him, who say that there is no resurrection; and they asked him a question, ²⁴ saying, "Teacher, Moses said, 'If a man dies, having no children, his brother must marry the widow, and raise up children for his brother.' ²⁵ Now there were seven brothers among us; the first married, and died, and having no children left his wife to his brother. ²⁶ So too the second and third, down to the seventh. ²⁷ After them all, the woman died. ²⁸ In the resurrection, therefore, to which of the seven will she be wife? For they all had her."

29 But Jesus answered them, "You are wrong, because you know neither the scriptures nor the power of God. ³⁰ For in the resurrection they neither marry nor are given in marriage, but are like angelsˢ in heaven. ³¹ And as for the resurrection of the dead, have you not read what was said to you by God, ³² 'I am the God of Abraham, and the God of Isaac, and the God of Jacob'? He is not God of the dead, but of the living." ³³ And when the crowd heard it, they were astonished at his teaching.

34 But when the Phăr′i·seeṣ heard that he had silenced the Săd′du·çeeṣ,

they came together. ³⁵ And one of them, a lawyer, asked him a question, to test him. ³⁶ "Teacher, which is the great commandment in the law?" ³⁷ And he said to him, "You shall love the Lord your God with all your heart, and with all your soul, and with all your mind. ³⁸ This is the great and first commandment. ³⁹ And a second is like it, You shall love your neighbor as yourself. ⁴⁰ On these two commandments depend all the law and the prophets."

41 Now while the Phăr′i·seeṣ were gathered together, Jesus asked them a question, ⁴² saying, "What do you think of the Christ? Whose son is he?" They said to him, "The son of David." ⁴³ He said to them, "How is it then that David, inspired by the Spirit,ᶠ calls him Lord, saying,

⁴⁴ 'The Lord said to my Lord,

Sit at my right hand,

till I put thy enemies under thy feet'?

⁴⁵ If David thus calls him Lord, how is he his son?" ⁴⁶ And no one was able to answer him a word, nor from that day did any one dare to ask him any more questions.

23 Then said Jesus to the crowds and to his disciples, ² "The scribes and the Phăr′i·seeṣ sit on Moses' seat; ³ so practice and observe whatever they tell you, but not what they do; for they preach, but do not practice. ⁴ They bind heavy burdens, hard to bear,ᵘ and lay them on men's shoulders; but they themselves will not move them with their finger. ⁵ They do all their deeds to be seen by men; for they make their phylacteries broad and their fringes long, ⁶ and they love the place of honor at feasts and the best seats in the synagogues, ⁷ and salutations in the market places, and being called rabbi by men. ⁸ But you are not to be called rabbi, for you

ʳGreek *a denarius* ᶠOther ancient authorities add *of God*
ᶠOr *David in the Spirit*
ᵘOther ancient authorities omit *hard to bear*
22.13: Mt 8.12; 13.42, 50; 24.51; 25.30; Lk 13.28.
22.15-22: Mk 12.13-17; Lk 20.20-26.
22.15: Mk 3.6; 8.15. 22.21: Rom 13.7.
22.23-33: Mk 12.18-27; Lk 20.27-38.
22.23: Acts 4.1-2; 23.6-10. 22.24: Deut 25.5.
22.32: Ex 3.6. 22.33: Mt 7.28.
22.34-40: Mk 12.28-34; Lk 20.39-40; 10.25-28.
22.35: Lk 7.30; 11.45; 14.3. 22.37: Deut 6.5.
22.39: Lev 19.18; Mt 19.19; Gal 5.14; Rom 13.9; Jas 2.8.
22.41-46: Mk 12.35-37; Lk 20.41-44.
22.44: Ps 110.1; Acts 2.34-35; Heb 1.13; 10.13.
22.46: Mk 12.34; Lk 20.40. 23.4: Lk 11.46; Acts 15.10.
23.5: Mt 6.1, 5, 16; Ex 13.9; Deut 6.8; Mt 9.20.
23.6-7: Mk 12.38-39; Lk 20.46; 14.7-11; 11.43.
23.8: Jas 3.1.

have one teacher, and you are all brethren. [9] And call no man your father on earth, for you have one Father, who is in heaven. [10] Neither be called masters, for you have one master, the Christ. [11] He who is greatest among you shall be your servant; [12] whoever exalts himself will be humbled, and whoever humbles himself will be exalted.

13 "But woe to you, scribes and Phăr′ĭ·sees, hypocrites! because you shut the kingdom of heaven against men; for you neither enter yourselves, nor allow those who would enter to go in.[v] [15] Woe to you, scribes and Phăr′ĭ·sees, hypocrites! for you traverse sea and land to make a single proselyte, and when he becomes a proselyte, you make him twice as much a child of hell[w] as yourselves.

16 "Woe to you, blind guides, who say, 'If any one swears by the temple, it is nothing; but if any one swears by the gold of the temple, he is bound by his oath.' [17] You blind fools! For which is greater, the gold or the temple that has made the gold sacred? [18] And you say, 'If any one swears by the altar, it is nothing; but if any one swears by the gift that is on the altar, he is bound by his oath.' [19] You blind men! For which is greater, the gift or the altar that makes the gift sacred? [20] So he who swears by the altar, swears by it and by everything on it; [21] and he who swears by the temple, swears by it and by him who dwells in it; [22] and he who swears by heaven, swears by the throne of God and by him who sits upon it.

23 "Woe to you, scribes and Phăr′ĭ·sees, hypocrites! for you tithe mint and dill and cummin, and have neglected the weightier matters of the law, justice and mercy and faith; these you ought to have done, without neglecting the others. [24] You blind guides, straining out a gnat and swallowing a camel!

25 "Woe to you, scribes and Phăr′ĭ·sees, hypocrites! for you cleanse the outside of the cup and of the plate, but inside they are full of extortion and rapacity. [26] You blind Phăr′ĭ·see! first cleanse the inside of the cup and of the plate, that the outside also may be clean.

27 "Woe to you, scribes and Phăr′ĭ·sees, hypocrites! for you are like whitewashed tombs, which outwardly appear beautiful, but within they are full of dead men's bones and all uncleanness. [28] So you also outwardly appear righteous to men, but within you are full of hypocrisy and iniquity.

29 "Woe to you, scribes and Phăr′ĭ·sees, hypocrites! for you build the tombs of the prophets and adorn the monuments of the righteous, [30] saying, 'If we had lived in the days of our fathers, we would not have taken part with them in shedding the blood of the prophets.' [31] Thus you witness against yourselves, that you are sons of those who murdered the prophets. [32] Fill up, then, the measure of your fathers. [33] You serpents, you brood of vipers, how are you to escape being sentenced to hell?[w] [34] Therefore I send you prophets and wise men and scribes, some of whom you will kill and crucify, and some you will scourge in your synagogues and persecute from town to town, [35] that upon you may come all the righteous blood shed on earth, from the blood of innocent Abel to the blood of Zĕch·a·rī′ah the son of Băr·a·chī′ah, whom you murdered between the sanctuary and the altar. [36] Truly, I say to you, all this will come upon this generation.

37 "O Jerusalem, Jerusalem, killing the prophets and stoning those who are sent to you! How often would I have gathered your children together as a hen gathers her brood under her wings, and you would not! [38] Behold, your house is forsaken and desolate.[x] [39] For I tell you, you will not see me again, until you say, 'Blessed is he who comes in the name of the Lord.'"

24 Jesus left the temple and was going away, when his disciples

[v]Other authorities add here (or after verse 12) verse 14, *Woe to you, scribes and Pharisees, hypocrites! for you devour widows' houses and for a pretense you make long prayers; therefore you will receive the greater condemnation* [w]Greek *Gehenna*
[x]Other ancient authorities omit *and desolate*

23.11: Mt 20.26; Mk 9.35; 10.43; Lk 9.48; 22.26.
23.12: Lk 14.11; 18.14; Mt 18.4; 1 Pet 5.6.
23.13: Lk 11.52.
23.15: Acts 2.10; 6.5; 13.43. 23.16-22: Mt 5.33-37; 15.14.
23.17: Ex 30.29. 23.21: 1 Kings 8.13; Ps 26.8.
23.23-24: Lk 11.42; Lev 27.30; Mic 6.8.
23.25-26: Lk 11.39-41; Mk 7.4.
23.27-28: Lk 11.44; Acts 23.3; Ps 5.9.
23.29-32: Lk 11.47-48; Acts 7.51-53.
23.33: Mt 3.7; Lk 3.7.
23.34: Mt 10.17, 23.
23.34-36: Lk 11.49-51; 2 Chron 36.15-16.
23.35: Gen 4.8; Heb 11.4; Zech 1.1; 2 Chron 24.21.
23.36: Mt 10.23; 16.28; 24.34. 23.37-39: Lk 13.34-35.
23.38: 1 Kings 9.7; Jer 22.5. 23.39: Mt 21.9; Ps 118.26.
24.1-35: Mk 13.1-31; Lk 21.1-33.

came to point out to him the buildings of the temple. ²But he answered them, "You see all these, do you not? Truly, I say to you, there will not be left here one stone upon another, that will not be thrown down."

3 As he sat on the Mount of Olives, the disciples came to him privately, saying, "Tell us, when will this be, and what will be the sign of your coming and of the close of the age?" ⁴And Jesus answered them, "Take heed that no one leads you astray. ⁵For many will come in my name, saying, 'I am the Christ,' and they will lead many astray. ⁶And you will hear of wars and rumors of wars; see that you are not alarmed; for this must take place, but the end is not yet. ⁷For nation will rise against nation, and kingdom against kingdom, and there will be famines and earthquakes in various places: ⁸all this is but the beginning of the birth-pangs.

9 "Then they will deliver you up to tribulation, and put you to death; and you will be hated by all nations for my name's sake. ¹⁰And then many will fall away,ᵞ and betray one another, and hate one another. ¹¹And many false prophets will arise and lead many astray. ¹²And because wickedness is multiplied, most men's love will grow cold. ¹³But he who endures to the end will be saved. ¹⁴And this gospel of the kingdom will be preached throughout the whole world, as a testimony to all nations; and then the end will come.

15 "So when you see the desolating sacrilege spoken of by the prophet Daniel, standing in the holy place (let the reader understand), ¹⁶then let those who are in Jü·dē′ạ flee to the mountains; ¹⁷let him who is on the housetop not go down to take what is in his house; ¹⁸and let him who is in the field not turn back to take his mantle. ¹⁹And alas for those who are with child and for those who give suck in those days! ²⁰Pray that your flight may not be in winter or on a sabbath. ²¹For then there will be great tribulation, such as has not been from the beginning of the world until now, no, and never will be. ²²And if those days had not been shortened, no human being would be saved; but for the sake of the elect those days will be shortened. ²³Then if any one says to you, 'Lo, here is the Christ!' or 'There he is!'

do not believe it. ²⁴For false Christs and false prophets will arise and show great signs and wonders, so as to lead astray, if possible, even the elect. ²⁵Lo, I have told you beforehand. ²⁶So, if they say to you, 'Lo, he is in the wilderness,' do not go out; if they say, 'Lo, he is in the inner rooms,' do not believe it. ²⁷For as the lightning comes from the east and shines as far as the west, so will be the coming of the Son of man. ²⁸Wherever the body is, there the eaglesᶻ will be gathered together.

29 "Immediately after the tribulation of those days the sun will be darkened, and the moon will not give its light, and the stars will fall from heaven, and the powers of the heavens will be shaken; ³⁰then will appear the sign of the Son of man in heaven, and then all the tribes of the earth will mourn, and they will see the Son of man coming on the clouds of heaven with power and great glory; ³¹and he will send out his angels with a loud trumpet call, and they will gather his elect from the four winds, from one end of heaven to the other.

32 "From the fig tree learn its lesson: as soon as its branch becomes tender and puts forth its leaves, you know that summer is near. ³³So also, when you see all these things, you know that he is near, at the very gates. ³⁴Truly, I say to you, this generation will not pass away till all these things take place. ³⁵Heaven and earth will pass away, but my words will not pass away.

36 "But of that day and hour no one knows, not even the angels of heaven, nor the Son,ᵃ but the Father only. ³⁷As were the days of Noah, so will be the coming of the Son of man. ³⁸For as in those days before the flood they were eating and drinking, marrying and giving in marriage, until the day

ᵞOr *stumble*
ᶻOr *vultures* ᵃOther ancient authorities omit *nor the Son*
24.2: Mt 26.61; 27.39-40; Lk 19.44; Jn 2.19.
24.3: Lk 17.20; Mt 13.39, 40, 49; 28.20; 16.27.
24.5: Mt 24.11, 23-24; 1 Jn 2.18.
24.6-7: Rev 6.3-8, 12-17; Is 19.2.
24.9: Mt 10.17-18, 22; Jn 15.18; 16.2.
24.13: Mt 10.22; Rev 2.7. 24.14: Mt 28.19; Rom 10.18.
24.15: Dan 9.27; 11.31; 12.11. 24.17-18: Lk 17.31.
24.19: Lk 23.29. 24.21: Dan 12.1; Joel 2.2.
24.26-27: Lk 17.22-24; Rev 1.7.
24.28: Lk 17.37; Job 39.30.
24.29: Rev 8.12; Is 13.10; Ezek 32.7; Joel 2.10-11; Zeph 1.15. 24.30: Mt 16.27; Dan 7.13; Rev 1.7.
24.31: 1 Cor 15.52; 1 Thess 4.16; Is 27.13; Zech 9.14.
24.34: Mt 16.28. 24.35: Mt 5.18; Lk 16.17.
24.36: Acts 1.6-7.
24.37-39: Lk 17.26-27; Gen 6.5-8; 7.6-24.

when Noah entered the ark, ³⁹ and they did not know until the flood came and swept them all away, so will be the coming of the Son of man. ⁴⁰ Then two men will be in the field; one is taken and one is left. ⁴¹ Two women will be grinding at the mill; one is taken and one is left. ⁴² Watch therefore, for you do not know on what day your Lord is coming. ⁴³ But know this, that if the householder had known in what part of the night the thief was coming, he would have watched and would not have let his house be broken into. ⁴⁴ Therefore you also must be ready; for the Son of man is coming at an hour you do not expect.

45 "Who then is the faithful and wise servant, whom his master has set over his household, to give them their food at the proper time? ⁴⁶ Blessed is that servant whom his master when he comes will find so doing. ⁴⁷ Truly, I say to you, he will set him over all his possessions. ⁴⁸ But if that wicked servant says to himself, 'My master is delayed,' ⁴⁹ and begins to beat his fellow servants, and eats and drinks with the drunken, ⁵⁰ the master of that servant will come on a day when he does not expect him and at an hour he does not know, ⁵¹ and will punish^b him, and put him with the hypocrites; there men will weep and gnash their teeth.

25 "Then the kingdom of heaven shall be compared to ten maidens who took their lamps and went to meet the bridegroom.^c ² Five of them were foolish, and five were wise. ³ For when the foolish took their lamps, they took no oil with them; ⁴ but the wise took flasks of oil with their lamps. ⁵ As the bridegroom was delayed, they all slumbered and slept. ⁶ But at midnight there was a cry, 'Behold, the bridegroom! Come out to meet him.' ⁷ Then all those maidens rose and trimmed their lamps. ⁸ And the foolish said to the wise, 'Give us some of your oil, for our lamps are going out.' ⁹ But the wise replied, 'Perhaps there will not be enough for us and for you; go rather to the dealers and buy for yourselves.' ¹⁰ And while they went to buy, the bridegroom came, and those who were ready went in with him to the marriage feast; and the door was shut. ¹¹ Afterward the other maidens came also, saying, 'Lord, lord, open to us.' ¹² But

he replied, 'Truly, I say to you, I do not know you.' ¹³ Watch therefore, for you know neither the day nor the hour.

14 "For it will be as when a man going on a journey called his servants and entrusted to them his property; ¹⁵ to one he gave five talents,^d to another two, to another one, to each according to his ability. Then he went away. ¹⁶ He who had received the five talents went at once and traded with them; and he made five talents more. ¹⁷ So also, he who had the two talents made two talents more. ¹⁸ But he who had received the one talent went and dug in the ground and hid his master's money. ¹⁹ Now after a long time the master of those servants came and settled accounts with them. ²⁰ And he who had received the five talents came forward, bringing five talents more, saying, 'Master, you delivered to me five talents; here I have made five talents more.' ²¹ His master said to him, 'Well done, good and faithful servant; you have been faithful over a little, I will set you over much; enter into the joy of your master.' ²² And he also who had the two talents came forward, saying, 'Master, you delivered to me two talents; here I have made two talents more.' ²³ His master said to him, 'Well done, good and faithful servant; you have been faithful over a little, I will set you over much; enter into the joy of your master.' ²⁴ He also who had received the one talent came forward, saying, 'Master, I knew you to be a hard man, reaping where you did not sow, and gathering where you did not winnow; ²⁵ so I was afraid, and I went and hid your talent in the ground. Here you have what is yours.' ²⁶ But his master answered him, 'You wicked and slothful servant! You knew that I reap where I have not sowed, and gather where I have not winnowed? ²⁷ Then you ought to have invested my money with the bankers, and at my coming I

^bOr *cut him in pieces*
^cOther ancient authorities add *and the bride*
^dThis talent was more than fifteen years' wages of a laborer
24.40–41: Lk 17.34-35.
24.42: Mk 13.35; Lk 12.40; Mt 25.13.
24.43-51: Lk 12.39-46.
24.43: 1 Thess 5.2; Rev 3.3; 16.15; 2 Pet 3.10.
24.45: Mt 25.21, 23. 24.49: Lk 21.34.
24.51: Mt 8.12; 13.42, 50; 22.13; 25.30; Lk 13.28.
25.1: Lk 12.35-38; Mk 13.34. 25.2: Mt 7.24-27.
25.10: Rev 19.9. 25.11-12: Lk 13.25; Mt 7.21-23.
25.13: Mt 24.42; Mk 13.35; Lk 12.40.
25.14-30: Lk 19.12-28.
25.19: Mt 18.23. 25.21: Lk 16.10; Mt 24.45.

should have received what was my own with interest. ²⁸ So take the talent from him, and give it to him who has the ten talents. ²⁹ For to every one who has will more be given, and he will have abundance; but from him who has not, even what he has will be taken away. ³⁰ And cast the worthless servant into the outer darkness; there men will weep and gnash their teeth.'

31 "When the Son of man comes in his glory, and all the angels with him, then he will sit on his glorious throne. ³² Before him will be gathered all the nations, and he will separate them one from another as a shepherd separates the sheep from the goats, ³³ and he will place the sheep at his right hand, but the goats at the left. ³⁴ Then the King will say to those at his right hand, 'Come, O blessed of my Father, inherit the kingdom prepared for you from the foundation of the world; ³⁵ for I was hungry and you gave me food, I was thirsty and you gave me drink, I was a stranger and you welcomed me, ³⁶ I was naked and you clothed me, I was sick and you visited me, I was in prison and you came to me.' ³⁷ Then the righteous will answer him, 'Lord, when did we see thee hungry and feed thee, or thirsty and give thee drink? ³⁸ And when did we see thee a stranger and welcome thee, or naked and clothe thee? ³⁹ And when did we see thee sick or in prison and visit thee?' ⁴⁰ And the King will answer them, 'Truly, I say to you, as you did it to one of the least of these my brethren, you did it to me.' ⁴¹ Then he will say to those at his left hand, 'Depart from me, you cursed, into the eternal fire prepared for the devil and his angels; ⁴² for I was hungry and you gave me no food, I was thirsty and you gave me no drink, ⁴³ I was a stranger and you did not welcome me, naked and you did not clothe me, sick and in prison and you did not visit me.' ⁴⁴ Then they also will answer, 'Lord, when did we see thee hungry or thirsty or a stranger or naked or sick or in prison, and did not minister to thee?' ⁴⁵ Then he will answer them, 'Truly, I say to you, as you did it not to one of the least of these, you did it not to me.' ⁴⁶ And they will go away into eternal punishment, but the righteous into eternal life."

26 When Jesus had finished all these sayings, he said to his disciples, ² "You know that after two days the Passover is coming, and the Son of man will be delivered up to be crucified."

3 Then the chief priests and the elders of the people gathered in the palace of the high priest, who was called Cā'ī·a·phas, ⁴ and took counsel together in order to arrest Jesus by stealth and kill him. ⁵ But they said, "Not during the feast, lest there be a tumult among the people."

6 Now when Jesus was at Bĕth'a·nў in the house of Simon the leper, ⁷ a woman came up to him with an alabaster flask of very expensive ointment, and she poured it on his head, as he sat at table. ⁸ But when the disciples saw it, they were indignant, saying, "Why this waste? ⁹ For this ointment might have been sold for a large sum, and given to the poor." ¹⁰ But Jesus, aware of this, said to them, "Why do you trouble the woman? For she has done a beautiful thing to me. ¹¹ For you always have the poor with you, but you will not always have me. ¹² In pouring this ointment on my body she has done it to prepare me for burial. ¹³ Truly, I say to you, wherever this gospel is preached in the whole world, what she has done will be told in memory of her."

14 Then one of the twelve, who was called Judas Ĭs·căr'ĭ·ọt, went to the chief priests ¹⁵ and said, "What will you give me if I deliver him to you?" And they paid him thirty pieces of silver. ¹⁶ And from that moment he sought an opportunity to betray him.

17 Now on the first day of Unleavened Bread the disciples came to Jesus, saying, "Where will you have us prepare for you to eat the passover?" ¹⁸ He said, "Go into the city to a certain one, and say to him, 'The Teacher says,

25.29: Mt 13.12; Mk 4.25; Lk 8.18.
25.30: Mt 8.12; 13.42, 50; 22.13; Lk 13.28.
25.31: Mt 16.27; 19.28. 25.32: Ezek 34.17.
25.34: Lk 12.32; Mt 5.3; Rev 13.8; 17.8.
25.35-36: Is 58.7; Jas 1.27; 2.15-16; Heb 13.2; 2 Tim 1.16.
25.40: Mt 10.42; Mk 9.41; Heb 6.10; Prov 19.17.
25.41: Mk 9.48; Lk 16.23; Rev 20.10.
25.46: Dan 12.2; Jn 5.29.
26.1: Mt 7.28; 11.1; 13.53; 19.1.
26.2-5: Mk 14.1-2; Lk 22.1-2; Jn 11.47-53.
26.6-13: Mk 14.3-9; Jn 12.1-8; Lk 7.36-38.
26.11: Deut 15.11. 26.12: Jn 19.40.
26.14-16: Mk 14.10-11; Lk 22.3-6.
26.15: Ex 21.32; Zech 11.12.
26.17-19: Mk 14.12-16; Lk 22.7-13.
26.18: Mt 26.45; Jn 7.6; 12.23; 13.1; 17.1.

My time is at hand; I will keep the passover at your house with my disciples.'" [19] And the disciples did as Jesus had directed them, and they prepared the passover.

20 When it was evening, he sat at table with the twelve disciples; [e] [21] and as they were eating, he said, "Truly, I say to you, one of you will betray me." [22] And they were very sorrowful, and began to say to him one after another, "Is it I, Lord?" [23] He answered, "He who has dipped his hand in the dish with me, will betray me. [24] The Son of man goes as it is written of him, but woe to that man by whom the Son of man is betrayed! It would have been better for that man if he had not been born." [25] Judas, who betrayed him, said, "Is it I, Master?" [f] He said to him, "You have said so."

26 Now as they were eating, Jesus took bread, and blessed, and broke it, and gave it to the disciples and said, "Take, eat; this is my body." [27] And he took a cup, and when he had given thanks he gave it to them, saying, "Drink of it, all of you; [28] for this is my blood of the [g] covenant, which is poured out for many for the forgiveness of sins. [29] I tell you I shall not drink again of this fruit of the vine until that day when I drink it new with you in my Father's kingdom."

30 And when they had sung a hymn, they went out to the Mount of Olives. [31] Then Jesus said to them, "You will all fall away because of me this night; for it is written, 'I will strike the shepherd, and the sheep of the flock will be scattered.' [32] But after I am raised up, I will go before you to Galilee." [33] Peter declared to him, "Though they all fall away because of you, I will never fall away." [34] Jesus said to him, "Truly, I say to you, this very night, before the cock crows, you will deny me three times." [35] Peter said to him, "Even if I must die with you, I will not deny you." And so said all the disciples.

36 Then Jesus went with them to a place called Gĕth·sĕm′a·nē, and he said to his disciples, "Sit here, while I go yonder and pray." [37] And taking with him Peter and the two sons of Zĕb′e·dee, he began to be sorrowful and troubled. [38] Then he said to them, "My soul is very sorrowful, even to death; remain here, and watch [h] with me." [39] And going a little farther he fell on his face and prayed, "My Father, if it be possible, let this cup pass from me; nevertheless, not as I will, but as thou wilt." [40] And he came to the disciples and found them sleeping; and he said to Peter, "So, could you not watch [h] with me one hour? [41] Watch [h] and pray that you may not enter into temptation; the spirit indeed is willing, but the flesh is weak." [42] Again, for the second time, he went away and prayed, "My Father, if this cannot pass unless I drink it, thy will be done." [43] And again he came and found them sleeping, for their eyes were heavy. [44] So, leaving them again, he went away and prayed for the third time, saying the same words. [45] Then he came to the disciples and said to them, "Are you still sleeping and taking your rest? Behold, the hour is at hand, and the Son of man is betrayed into the hands of sinners. [46] Rise, let us be going; see, my betrayer is at hand."

47 While he was still speaking, Judas came, one of the twelve, and with him a great crowd with swords and clubs, from the chief priests and the elders of the people. [48] Now the betrayer had given them a sign, saying, "The one I shall kiss is the man; seize him." [49] And he came up to Jesus at once and said, "Hail, Master!" [i] And he kissed him. [50] Jesus said to him, "Friend, why are you here?" [j] Then they came up and laid hands on Jesus and seized him. [51] And behold, one of those who were with Jesus stretched out his hand and drew his sword, and struck the slave of the high priest, and cut off his ear. [52] Then Jesus said to him, "Put your sword back into its place; for all who take the sword will perish by the sword. [53] Do you think that I cannot appeal to my

e Other authorities omit *disciples*   *f* Or *Rabbi*
g Other ancient authorities insert *new*
h Or *keep awake*   *i* Or *Rabbi*
j Or *do that for which you have come*
26.19: Mt 21.6; Deut 16.5-8.
26.20-24: Mk 14.17-21; Lk 22.14, 21-23; Jn 13.21-30.
26.24: Ps 41.9; Lk 24.25; 1 Cor 15.3; Acts 17.2-3; Mt 18.7.
26.26-29: Mk 14.22-25; Lk 22.17-19; 1 Cor 10.16; 11.23-26; Mt 14.19; 15.36.
26.28: Heb 9.20; Mt 20.28; Mk 1.4; Ex 24.6-8.
26.30-35: Mk 14.26-31; Lk 22.33-34, 39; Jn 14.31; 18.1; 13.36-38.   26.31: Zech 13.7; Jn 16.32.
26.32: Mt 28.7, 10, 16.
26.36-46: Mk 14.32-42; Lk 22.40-46.
26.38: Jn 12.27; Heb 5.7-8.   26.39: Jn 18.11; Mt 20.22.
26.41: Mt 6.13; Lk 11.4.   26.42: Jn 4.34; 5.30; 6.38.
26.45: Mt 26.18; Jn 12.23; 13.1; 17.1.
26.47-56: Mk 14.43-50; Lk 22.47-53; Jn 18.2-11.
26.50: Mt 20.13; 22.12.   26.52: Gen 9.6; Rev 13.10.

Father, and he will at once send me more than twelve legions of angels? ⁵⁴But how then should the scriptures be fulfilled, that it must be so?" ⁵⁵At that hour Jesus said to the crowds, "Have you come out as against a robber, with swords and clubs to capture me? Day after day I sat in the temple teaching, and you did not seize me. ⁵⁶But all this has taken place, that the scriptures of the prophets might be fulfilled." Then all the disciples forsook him and fled.

57 Then those who had seized Jesus led him to Cā′ĭ·a·phas the high priest, where the scribes and the elders had gathered. ⁵⁸But Peter followed him at a distance, as far as the courtyard of the high priest, and going inside he sat with the guards to see the end. ⁵⁹Now the chief priests and the whole council sought false testimony against Jesus that they might put him to death, ⁶⁰but they found none, though many false witnesses came forward. At last two came forward ⁶¹and said, "This fellow said, I am able to destroy the temple of God, and to build it in three days.'" ⁶²And the high priest stood up and said, 'Have you no answer to make? What is it that these men testify against you?" ⁶³But Jesus was silent. And the high priest said to him, "I adjure you by the living God, tell us if you are the Christ, the Son of God." ⁶⁴Jesus said to him, "You have said so. But I tell you, hereafter you will see the Son of man seated at the right hand of Power, and coming on the clouds of heaven." 'Then the high priest tore his robes, and said, "He has uttered blasphemy. Why do we still need witnesses? You have now heard his blasphemy. ⁶⁶What is your judgment?" They answered, He deserves death." ⁶⁷Then they spat in his face, and struck him; and some slapped him, ⁶⁸saying, "Prophesy to us, you Christ! Who is it that struck you?"

69 Now Peter was sitting outside in the courtyard. And a maid came up to him, and said, "You also were with Jesus the Galilean." ⁷⁰But he denied it before them all, saying, "I do not know what you mean." ⁷¹And when he went out to the porch, another maid saw him, and she said to the bystanders, "This man was with Jesus of Nazareth." ⁷²And again he denied it

with an oath, "I do not know the man." ⁷³After a little while the bystanders came up and said to Peter, "Certainly you are also one of them, for your accent betrays you." ⁷⁴Then he began to invoke a curse on himself and to swear, "I do not know the man." And immediately the cock crowed. ⁷⁵And Peter remembered the saying of Jesus, "Before the cock crows, you will deny me three times." And he went out and wept bitterly.

27 When morning came, all the chief priests and the elders of the people took counsel against Jesus to put him to death; ²and they bound him and led him away and delivered him to Pilate the governor.

3 When Judas, his betrayer, saw that he was condemned, he repented and brought back the thirty pieces of silver to the chief priests and the elders, ⁴saying, "I have sinned in betraying innocent blood." They said, "What is that to us? See to it yourself." ⁵And throwing down the pieces of silver in the temple, he departed; and he went and hanged himself. ⁶But the chief priests, taking the pieces of silver, said, "It is not lawful to put them into the treasury, since they are blood money." ⁷So they took counsel, and bought with them the potter's field, to bury strangers in. ⁸Therefore that field has been called the Field of Blood to this day. ⁹Then was fulfilled what had been spoken by the prophet Jěr·ẹ·mī′ah, saying, "And they took the thirty pieces of silver, the price of him on whom a price had been set by some of the sons of Israel, ¹⁰and they gave them for the potter's field, as the Lord directed me."

11 Now Jesus stood before the governor; and the governor asked him, "Are you the King of the Jews?" Jesus said, "You have said so." ¹²But when he was accused by the chief priests and elders, he made no answer. ¹³Then Pilate said to him, "Do you not hear how many things they testify against you?" ¹⁴But he gave him no

26.55: Lk 19.47; Jn 18.19-21.
26.57-75: Mk 14.53-72; Lk 22.54-71; Jn 18.12-27.
26.61: Mt 24.2; 27.40; Acts 6.14; Jn 2.19.
26.63: Mt 27.11; Jn 18.33.
26.64: Mt 16.28; Dan 7.13; Ps 110.1.
26.65: Num 14.6; Acts 14.14; Lev 24.16.
26.75: Mt 26.34. 27.1-2: Mk 15.1; Lk 23.1; Jn 18.28.
27.3-10: Mk 1.16-20. 27.3: Mt 26.15; Ex 21.32.
27.6: Deut 23.18. 27.9: Zech 11.12-13; Jer 32.6-15; 18.2-3.
27.11-26: Mk 15.2-15; Lk 23.3, 18-25; Jn 18.29-19.16.
27.14: Lk 23.9; Mt 26.62; Mk 14.60; 1 Tim 6.13.

answer, not even to a single charge; so that the governor wondered greatly. 15 Now at the feast the governor was accustomed to release for the crowd any one prisoner whom they wanted. [16]And they had then a notorious prisoner, called Ba·răb′bas.[k] [17]So when they had gathered, Pilate said to them, "Whom do you want me to release for you, Ba·răb′bas[k] or Jesus who is called Christ?" [18]For he knew that it was out of envy that they had delivered him up. [19]Besides, while he was sitting on the judgment seat, his wife sent word to him, "Have nothing to do with that righteous man, for I have suffered much over him today in a dream." [20]Now the chief priests and the elders persuaded the people to ask for Ba·răb′bas and destroy Jesus. [21]The governor again said to them, "Which of the two do you want me to release for you?" And they said, "Ba·răb′bas." [22]Pilate said to them, "Then what shall I do with Jesus who is called Christ?" They all said, "Let him be crucified." [23]And he said, "Why, what evil has he done?" But they shouted all the more, "Let him be crucified."

24 So when Pilate saw that he was gaining nothing, but rather that a riot was beginning, he took water and washed his hands before the crowd, saying, "I am innocent of this man's blood;[l] see to it yourselves." [25]And all the people answered, "His blood be on us and on our children!" [26]Then he released for them Ba·răb′bas, and having scourged Jesus, delivered him to be crucified.

27 Then the soldiers of the governor took Jesus into the praetorium, and they gathered the whole battalion before him. [28]And they stripped him and put a scarlet robe upon him, [29]and plaiting a crown of thorns they put it on his head, and put a reed in his right hand. And kneeling before him they mocked him, saying, "Hail, King of the Jews!" [30]And they spat upon him, and took the reed and struck him on the head. [31]And when they had mocked him, they stripped him of the robe, and put his own clothes on him, and led him away to crucify him.

32 As they went out, they came upon a man of Cy·rē′nē, Simon by name; this man they compelled to carry his cross. [33]And when they came to a place called Gŏl′go·tha

(which means the place of a skull), [34]they offered him wine to drink, mingled with gall; but when he tasted it, he would not drink it. [35]And when they had crucified him, they divided his garments among them by casting lots; [36]then they sat down and kept watch over him there. [37]And over his head they put the charge against him, which read, "This is Jesus the King of the Jews." [38]Then two robbers were crucified with him, one on the right and one on the left. [39]And those who passed by derided him, wagging their heads [40]and saying, "You who would destroy the temple and build it in three days, save yourself! If you are the Son of God, come down from the cross." [41]So also the chief priests with the scribes and elders, mocked him, saying, [42]"He saved others; he cannot save himself. He is the King of Israel; let him come down now from the cross, and we will believe in him [43]He trusts in God; let God deliver him now, if he desires him; for he said 'I am the Son of God.'" [44]And the robbers who were crucified with him also reviled him in the same way.

45 Now from the sixth hour there was darkness over all the land[m] until the ninth hour. [46]And about the ninth hour Jesus cried with a loud voice, "Ē′lī, Ē′lī, lä′ma sa·băch′-thā′nī?' that is, "My God, my God, why hast thou forsaken me?" [47]And some of the bystanders hearing it said, "This man is calling Ē·lī′jah." [48]And one of them at once ran and took a sponge, filled it with vinegar, and put it on a reed, and gave it to him to drink. [49]But the other said, "Wait, let us see whether Ē·lī′jah will come to save him."[n] [50]And Jesus cried again with a loud voice and yielded up his spirit.

51 And behold, the curtain of the temple was torn in two, from top to bottom; and the earth shook, and the

[k]Other ancient authorities read *Jesus Barabbas*
[l]Other authorities read *this righteous blood* or *this righteous man's blood*
[m]Or *earth*
[n]Other ancient authorities insert *And another took a spear and pierced his side, and out came water and blood*

27.19: Lk 23.4.   27.21: Acts 3.13-14.
27.24: Deut 21.6-9; Ps 26.6.   27.25: Acts 5.28; Josh 2.19
27.27-31: Mk 15.16-20; Lk 23.11; Jn 19.2-3.
27.32: Mk 15.21; Lk 23.26; Jn 19.17; Heb 13.12.
27.33-44: Mk 15.22-32; Lk 23.33-39; Jn 19.17-24.
27.35: Ps 22.18.   27.39: Ps 22.7-8; 109.25.
27.40: Mt 26.61; Acts 6.14; Jn 2.19.
27.45-56: Mk 15.33-41; Lk 23.44-54; Jn 19.28-30.
27.46: Ps 22.1.   27.48: Ps 69.21.
27.51: Heb 9.8; 10.19; Ex 26.31-35; Mt 28.2.

rocks were split; [52] the tombs also were opened, and many bodies of the saints who had fallen asleep were raised, [53] and coming out of the tombs after his resurrection they went into the holy city and appeared to many. [54] When the centurion and those who were with him, keeping watch over Jesus, saw the earthquake and what took place, they were filled with awe, and said, "Truly this was the Son[x] of God!"

55 There were also many women there, looking on from afar, who had followed Jesus from Galilee, ministering to him; [56] among whom were Mary Măg′dạ·lēne, and Mary the mother of James and Joseph, and the mother of the sons of Zĕb′ẹ·dee.

57 When it was evening, there came a rich man from Ăr·ĭ·ma·thē′ạ, named Joseph, who also was a disciple of Jesus. [58] He went to Pilate and asked for the body of Jesus. Then Pilate ordered it to be given to him. [59] And Joseph took the body, and wrapped it in a clean linen shroud, [60] and laid it in his own new tomb, which he had hewn in the rock; and he rolled a great stone to the door of the tomb, and departed. [61] Mary Măg′dạ·lēne and the other Mary were there, sitting opposite the sepulchre.

62 Next day, that is, after the day of Preparation, the chief priests and the Phăr′ị·seeṣ gathered before Pilate [3] and said, "Sir, we remember how that impostor said, while he was still alive, 'After three days I will rise again.' [64] Therefore order the sepulchre to be made secure until the third day, lest his disciples go and steal him away, and tell the people, 'He has risen from the dead,' and the last fraud will be worse than the first." [65] Pilate said to them, "You have a guard[o] of soldiers; go, make it as secure as you can."[p] [66] So they went and made the sepulchre secure by sealing the stone and setting a guard.

28 Now after the sabbath, toward the dawn of the first day of the week, Mary Măg′dạ·lēne and the other Mary went to see the sepulchre. [2] And behold, there was a great earthquake; for an angel of the Lord descended from heaven and came and rolled back the stone, and sat upon it. His appearance was like lightning, and his raiment white as snow. [4] And

for fear of him the guards trembled and became like dead men. [5] But the angel said to the women, "Do not be afraid; for I know that you seek Jesus who was crucified. [6] He is not here; for he has risen, as he said. Come, see the place where he[q] lay. [7] Then go quickly and tell his disciples that he has risen from the dead, and behold, he is going before you to Galilee; there you will see him. Lo, I have told you." [8] So they departed quickly from the tomb with fear and great joy, and ran to tell his disciples. [9] And behold, Jesus met them and said, "Hail!" And they came up and took hold of his feet and worshiped him. [10] Then Jesus said to them, "Do not be afraid; go and tell my brethren to go to Galilee, and there they will see me."

11 While they were going, behold, some of the guard went into the city and told the chief priests all that had taken place. [12] And when they had assembled with the elders and taken counsel, they gave a sum of money to the soldiers [13] and said, "Tell people, 'His disciples came by night and stole him away while we were asleep.' [14] And if this comes to the governor's ears, we will satisfy him and keep you out of trouble." [15] So they took the money and did as they were directed; and this story has been spread among the Jews to this day.

16 Now the eleven disciples went to Galilee, to the mountain to which Jesus had directed them. [17] And when they saw him they worshiped him; but some doubted. [18] And Jesus came and said to them, "All authority in heaven and on earth has been given to me. [19] Go therefore and make disciples of all nations, baptizing them in the name of the Father and of the Son and of the Holy Spirit, [20] teaching them to observe all that I have commanded you; and lo, I am with you always, to the close of the age."

[x] Or *a son*   [o] Or *Take a guard*   [p] Greek *know*
[q] Other ancient authorities read *the Lord*
27.54: Mt 3.17; 17.5.   **27.56:** Lk 24.10.
27.57-61: Mk 15.42-47; Lk 23.50-56; Jn 19.38-42; Acts 13.29.   **27.63:** Mt 16.21; 17.23; 20.19.
27.66: Mt 27.60; 28.11-15.
28.1-8: Mk 16.1-8; Lk 24.1-9; Jn 20.1-2.
28.1: Lk 8.2; Mt 27.56.   **28.2:** Mt 27.51, 60.
28.4: Mt 27.62-66.
28.7: Mt 26.32; 28.16; Jn 21.1-23.   **28.9:** Jn 20.14-18.
28.11: Mt 27.62-66.   **28.16-17:** 1 Cor 15.5; Jn 21.1-23.
28.18: Mt 11.27; Lk 10.22; Phil 2.9; Eph 1.20-22.
28.19: Lk 24.47; Acts 1.8.
28.20: Mt 13.39, 49; 24.3; 18.20; Acts 18.10.

The Gospel According to

Mark

1 The beginning of the gospel of Jesus Christ, the Son of God.[a]
2 As it is written in Ī'sāi'ah the prophet,[b]
"Behold, I send my messenger before thy face,
who shall prepare thy way;
3 the voice of one crying in the wilderness:
Prepare the way of the Lord,
make his paths straight—"
4 John the baptizer appeared[c] in the wilderness, preaching a baptism of repentance for the forgiveness of sins. 5 And there went out to him all the country of Jü·dē'a, and all the people of Jerusalem; and they were baptized by him in the river Jordan, confessing their sins. 6 Now John was clothed with camel's hair, and had a leather girdle around his waist, and ate locusts and wild honey. 7 And he preached, saying, "After me comes he who is mightier than I, the thong of whose sandals I am not worthy to stoop down and untie. 8 I have baptized you with water; but he will baptize you with the Holy Spirit."

9 In those days Jesus came from Nazareth of Galilee and was baptized by John in the Jordan. 10 And when he came up out of the water, immediately he saw the heavens opened and the Spirit descending upon him like a dove; 11 and a voice came from heaven, "Thou art my beloved Son;[d] with thee I am well pleased."

12 The Spirit immediately drove him out into the wilderness. 13 And he was in the wilderness forty days, tempted by Satan; and he was with the wild beasts; and the angels ministered to him.

14 Now after John was arrested, Jesus came into Galilee, preaching the gospel of God, 15 and saying, "The time is fulfilled, and the kingdom of God is at hand; repent, and believe in the gospel."

16 And passing along by the Sea of Galilee, he saw Simon and Andrew the brother of Simon casting a net in the sea; for they were fishermen. 17 And Jesus said to them, "Follow me and I will make you become fishers of men." 18 And immediately they left their nets and followed him. 19 And going on a little farther, he saw James the son of Zĕb'e·dee and John his brother, who were in their boat mending the nets. 20 And immediately he called them; and they left their father Zĕb'e·dee in the boat with the hired servants, and followed him.

21 And they went into Ca·pēr'na–um; and immediately on the sabbath he entered the synagogue and taught. 22 And they were astonished at his teaching, for he taught them as one who had authority, and not as the scribes. 23 And immediately there was in their synagogue a man with an unclean spirit; 24 and he cried out, "What have you to do with us, Jesus of Nazareth? Have you come to destroy us? I know who you are, the Holy One of God." 25 But Jesus rebuked him, saying "Be silent, and come out of him!" 26 And the unclean spirit, convulsing him and crying with a loud voice, came out of him. 27 And they were all amazed so that they questioned among themselves, saying, "What is this? A new teaching! With authority he commands even the unclean spirits, and they obey him." 28 And at once his fame spread everywhere throughout all the surrounding region of Galilee.

29 And immediately he[e] left the synagogue, and entered the house of Simon and Andrew, with James and John. 30 Now Simon's mother-in-law lay sick with a fever, and immediately they told him of her. 31 And he came and took her by the hand and lifted her up and the fever left her; and she served them.

a Other ancient authorities omit *the Son of God*
b Other ancient authorities read *in the prophets*
c Other ancient authorities read *John was baptizing*
d Or *my Son, my* (or *the*) *Beloved*
e Other ancient authorities read *they*
1.2-8: Mt 3.1-12; Lk 3.2-16; Jn 1.6, 15, 19-28.
1.2: Mal 3.1; Mt 11.10; Lk 7.27. 1.3: Is 40.3.
1.4: Acts 13.24.
1.9-11: Mt 3.13-17; Lk 3.21-22; Jn 1.29-34.
1.11: Ps 2.7; Is 42.1. 1.12-13: Mt 4.1-11; Lk 4.1-13.
1.14-15: Mt 4.12-17; Lk 4.14-15.
1.16-20: Mt 4.18-22; Lk 5.1-11; Jn 1.40-42.
1.21-22: Mt 7.28-29; Lk 4.31-32. 1.23-28: Lk 4.33-37.
1.24: Jn 6.69.
1.29-31: Mt 8.14-15; Lk 4.38-39.

32 That evening, at sundown, they brought to him all who were sick or possessed with demons. ³³And the whole city was gathered together about the door. ³⁴And he healed many who were sick with various diseases, and cast out many demons; and he would not permit the demons to speak, because they knew him.

35 And in the morning, a great while before day, he rose and went out to a lonely place, and there he prayed. ³⁶And Simon and those who were with him pursued him, ³⁷and they found him and said to him, "Every one is searching for you." ³⁸And he said to them, "Let us go on to the next towns, that I may preach there also; for that is why I came out." ³⁹And he went throughout all Galilee, preaching in their synagogues and casting out demons.

40 And a leper came to him beseeching him, and kneeling said to him, "If you will, you can make me clean." ⁴¹Moved with pity, he stretched out his hand and touched him, and said to him, "I will; be clean." ⁴²And immediately the leprosy left him, and he was made clean. ⁴³And he sternly charged him, and sent him away at once, ⁴⁴and said to him, "See that you say nothing to any one; but go, show yourself to the priest, and offer for your cleansing what Moses commanded, for a proof to the people."ᶠ ⁴⁵But he went out and began to talk freely about it, and to spread the news, so that Jesusᵍ could no longer openly enter a town, but was out in the country; and people came to him from every quarter.

2 And when he returned to Ca·pẽr'-na–um after some days, it was reported that he was at home. ²And many were gathered together, so that there was no longer room for them, not even about the door; and he was preaching the word to them. ³And they came, bringing to him a paralytic carried by four men. ⁴And when they could not get near him because of the crowd, they removed the roof above him; and when they had made an opening, they let down the pallet on which the paralytic lay. ⁵And when Jesus saw their faith, he said to the paralytic, "My son, your sins are forgiven." ⁶Now some of the scribes were sitting there, questioning in their hearts, ⁷"Why does this man speak thus? It is blasphemy! Who can forgive sins but God alone?" ⁸And immediately Jesus, perceiving in his spirit that they thus questioned within themselves, said to them, "Why do you question thus in your hearts? ⁹Which is easier, to say to the paralytic, 'Your sins are forgiven,' or to say, 'Rise, take up your pallet and walk'? ¹⁰But that you may know that the Son of man has authority on earth to forgive sins"– he said to the paralytic–¹¹"I say to you, rise, take up your pallet and go home." ¹²And he rose, and immediately took up the pallet and went out before them all; so that they were all amazed and glorified God, saying, "We never saw anything like this!"

13 He went out again beside the sea; and all the crowd gathered about him, and he taught them. ¹⁴And as he passed on, he saw Lẽ'vī the son of Äl-phaẽ'us sitting at the tax office, and he said to him, "Follow me." And he rose and followed him.

15 And as he sat at table in his house, many tax collectors and sinners were sitting with Jesus and his disciples; for there were many who followed him. ¹⁶And the scribes ofʰ the Phăr'i·seeṣ, when they saw that he was eating with sinners and tax collectors, said to his disciples, "Why does he eatⁱ with tax collectors and sinners?" ¹⁷And when Jesus heard it, he said to them, "Those who are well have no need of a physician, but those who are sick; I came not to call the righteous, but sinners."

18 Now John's disciples and the Phăr'i·seeṣ were fasting; and people came and said to him, "Why do John's disciples and the disciples of the Pharisees fast, but your disciples do not fast?" ¹⁹And Jesus said to them, "Can the wedding guests fast while the bridegroom is with them? As long as they have the bridegroom with them, they cannot fast. ²⁰The days will come, when the bridegroom is taken away from them, and then they will fast in that day. ²¹No one sews a piece of unshrunk cloth on an old gar-

ᶠGreek *to them* ᵍGreek *he*
ʰOther ancient authorities read *and*
ⁱOther ancient authorities add *and drink*
1.32–34: Mt 8.16-17; Lk 4.40-41. 1.35–38: Lk 4.42-43.
1.39: Mt 4.23-25; Lk 4.44.
1.40–45: Mt 8.2-4; Lk 5.12-16. 1.44: Lev 13.49; 14.2-32.
2.3–12: Mt 9.2-8; Lk 5.18-26. 2.12: Mt 9.33.
2.14–17: Mt 9.9-13; Lk 5.27-32. 2.16: Acts 23.9.
2.18–22: Mt 9.14-17; Lk 5.33-38. 2.20: Lk 17.22.

ment; if he does, the patch tears away from it, the new from the old, and a worse tear is made. ²²And no one puts new wine into old wineskins; if he does, the wine will burst the skins, and the wine is lost, and so are the skins; but new wine is for fresh skins."ʲ

23 One sabbath he was going through the grainfields; and as they made their way his disciples began to pluck heads of grain. ²⁴And the Phăr′i-sees said to him, "Look, why are they doing what is not lawful on the sabbath?" ²⁵And he said to them, "Have you never read what David did, when he was in need and was hungry, he and those who were with him: ²⁶how he entered the house of God, when A·bī′a·thär was high priest, and ate the bread of the Presence, which it is not lawful for any but the priests to eat, and also gave it to those who were with him?" ²⁷And he said to them, "The sabbath was made for man, not man for the sabbath; ²⁸so the Son of man is lord even of the sabbath."

3 Again he entered the synagogue, and a man was there who had a withered hand. ²And they watched him, to see whether he would heal him on the sabbath, so that they might accuse him. ³And he said to the man who had the withered hand, "Come here." ⁴And he said to them, "Is it lawful on the sabbath to do good or to do harm, to save life or to kill?" But they were silent. ⁵And he looked around at them with anger, grieved at their hardness of heart, and said to the man, "Stretch out your hand." He stretched it out, and his hand was restored. ⁶The Phăr′i·sees went out, and immediately held counsel with the Hĕ·rō′di·ans against him, how to destroy him.

7 Jesus withdrew with his disciples to the sea, and a great multitude from Galilee followed; also from Jü·dē′a ⁸and Jerusalem and Ĭd·ū·mē′a and from beyond the Jordan and from about Tȳre and Sī′dŏn a great multitude, hearing all that he did, came to him. ⁹And he told his disciples to have a boat ready for him because of the crowd, lest they should crush him; ¹⁰for he had healed many, so that all who had diseases pressed upon him to touch him. ¹¹And whenever the unclean spirits beheld him, they fell

down before him and cried out, "You are the Son of God." ¹²And he strictly ordered them not to make him known.

13 And he went up on the mountain, and called to him those whom he desired; and they came to him. ¹⁴And he appointed twelve,ᵏ to be with him, and to be sent out to preach ¹⁵and have authority to cast out demons: ¹⁶Simonˣ whom he surnamed Peter; ¹⁷James the son of Zĕb′e·dee and John the brother of James, whom he surnamed Bō-a·nĕr′ḡeş, that is, sons of thunder; ¹⁸Andrew, and Philip, and Bartholomew, and Matthew, and Thomas, and James the son of Ăl·phae′us, and Thăd·dae′us, and Simon the Cā·na-naē′an, ¹⁹and Judas Ĭs·cär′ĭ·ot, who betrayed him.

Then he went home; ²⁰and the crowd came together again, so that they could not even eat. ²¹And when his family heard it, they went out to seize him, for people were saying, "He is beside himself." ²²And the scribes who came down from Jerusalem said, "He is possessed by Bē–ĕl′ze·bŭl, and by the prince of demons he casts out the demons." ²³And he called them to him, and said to them in parables, "How can Satan cast out Satan? ²⁴If a kingdom is divided against itself, that kingdom cannot stand. ²⁵And if a house is divided against itself, that house will not be able to stand. ²⁶And if Satan has risen up against himself and is divided, he cannot stand, but is coming to an end. ²⁷But no one can enter a strong man's house and plunder his goods, unless he first binds the strong man; then indeed he may plunder his house.

28 "Truly, I say to you, all sins will be forgiven the sons of men, and whatever blasphemies they utter; ²⁹but whoever blasphemes against the Holy Spirit never has forgiveness, but is

---

ʲOther ancient authorities omit *but new wine is for fresh skins*
ᵏOther ancient authorities add *whom also he named apostles*
ˣOther authorities read *demons*. ¹⁶*So he appointed the twelve:* Simon

2.23–28: Mt 12.1-8; Lk 6.1-5. **2.23:** Deut 23.25.
2.26: 1 Sam 21.1-6; 2 Sam 8.17. **2.27:** Ex 23.12; Deut 5.14.
3.1–6: Mt 12.9-14; Lk 6.6-11. **3.2:** Lk 11.54. **3.6:** Mk 12.13.
3.7–12: Mt 4.24-25; 12.15-16; Lk 6.17-19.
3.8: Mt 11.21. **3.10:** Mk 5.29, 34; 6.56. **3.12:** Mk 1.45.
3.13: Mt 5.1; Lk 6.12. **3.14–15:** Mt 10.1.
3.16–19: Mt 10.2-4; Lk 6.14-16; Acts 1.13.
3.19: Mk 2.1; 7.17. **3.20:** Mk 6.31.
3.21: Mk 3.31-35; Jn 10.20.
3.22–27: Mt 12.24-29; Lk 11.15-22.
3.22: Mt 9.34; 10.25. **3.27:** Is 49.24-25.
3.28–30: Mt 12.31-32; Lk 12.10.

guilty of an eternal sin" — [30]for they had said, "He has an unclean spirit."

31 And his mother and his brothers came; and standing outside they sent to him and called him. [32]And a crowd was sitting about him; and they said to him, "Your mother and your brothers[l] are outside, asking for you." [33]And he replied, "Who are my mother and my brothers?" [34]And looking around on those who sat about him, he said, "Here are my mother and my brothers! [35]Whoever does the will of God is my brother, and sister, and mother."

4 Again he began to teach beside the sea. And a very large crowd gathered about him, so that he got into a boat and sat in it on the sea; and the whole crowd was beside the sea on the land. [2]And he taught them many things in parables, and in his teaching he said to them: [3]"Listen! A sower went out to sow. [4]And as he sowed, some seed fell along the path, and the birds came and devoured it. [5]Other seed fell on rocky ground, where it had not much soil, and immediately it sprang up, since it had no depth of soil; [6]and when the sun rose it was scorched, and since it had no root it withered away. [7]Other seed fell among thorns and the thorns grew up and choked it, and it yielded no grain. [8]And other seeds fell into good soil and brought forth grain, growing up and increasing and yielding thirtyfold and sixtyfold and a hundredfold." [9]And he said, "He who has ears to hear, let him hear."

10 And when he was alone, those who were about him with the twelve asked him concerning the parables. [11]And he said to them, "To you has been given the secret of the kingdom of God, but for those outside everything is in parables; [12]so that they may indeed see but not perceive, and may indeed hear but not understand; lest they should turn again, and be forgiven." [13]And he said to them, "Do you not understand this parable? How then will you understand all the parables? [14]The sower sows the word. [15]And these are the ones along the path, where the word is sown; when they hear, Satan immediately comes and takes away the word which is sown in them. [16]And these in like manner are the ones sown upon rocky ground, who, when they hear the word, immediately receive it with joy; [17]and they have no root in themselves, but endure for a while; then, when tribulation or persecution arises on account of the word, immediately they fall away.[m] [18]And others are the ones sown among thorns; they are those who hear the word, [19]but the cares of the world, and the delight in riches, and the desire for other things, enter in and choke the word, and it proves unfruitful. [20]But those that were sown upon the good soil are the ones who hear the word and accept it and bear fruit, thirtyfold and sixtyfold and a hundredfold."

21 And he said to them, "Is a lamp brought in to be put under a bushel, or under a bed, and not on a stand? [22]For there is nothing hid, except to be made manifest; nor is anything secret, except to come to light. [23]If any man has ears to hear, let him hear." [24]And he said to them, "Take heed what you hear; the measure you give will be the measure you get, and still more will be given you. [25]For to him who has will more be given; and from him who has not, even what he has will be taken away."

26 And he said, "The kingdom of God is as if a man should scatter seed upon the ground, [27]and should sleep and rise night and day, and the seed should sprout and grow, he knows not how. [28]The earth produces of itself, first the blade, then the ear, then the full grain in the ear. [29]But when the grain is ripe, at once he puts in the sickle, because the harvest has come."

30 And he said, "With what can we compare the kingdom of God, or what parable shall we use for it? [31]It is like a grain of mustard seed, which, when sown upon the ground, is the smallest of all the seeds on earth; [32]yet when it is sown it grows up and becomes the greatest of all shrubs, and puts forth large branches, so that the birds of the air can make nests in its shade."

[l]Other early authorities add *and your sisters*
[m]Or *stumble*
3.31-35: Mt 12.46-50; Lk 8.19-21.
4.1-9: Mt 13.1-9; Lk 8.4-8.
4.10-12: Mt 13.10-15; Lk 8.9-10.
4.11: 1 Cor 5.12-13; Col 4.5; 1 Thess 4.12; 1 Tim 3.7.
4.12: Is 6.9-10.   4.13-20: Mt 13.18-23; Lk 8.11-15.
4.21: Mt 5.15; Lk 8.16; 11.33.
4.22: Mt 10.26; Lk 8.17; 12.2.   4.23: Mt 11.15; Mk 4.9.
4.24: Mt 7.2; Lk 6.38.
4.25: Mt 13.12; 25.29; Lk 8.18; 19.26.
4.26-29: Mt 13.24-30.
4.30-32: Mt 13.31-32; Lk 13.18-19.

33 With many such parables he spoke the word to them, as they were able to hear it; ³⁴ he did not speak to them without a parable, but privately to his own disciples he explained everything.

35 On that day, when evening had come, he said to them, "Let us go across to the other side." ³⁶ And leaving the crowd, they took him with them in the boat, just as he was. And other boats were with him. ³⁷ And a great storm of wind arose, and the waves beat into the boat, so that the boat was already filling. ³⁸ But he was in the stern, asleep on the cushion; and they woke him and said to him, "Teacher, do you not care if we perish?" ³⁹ And he awoke and rebuked the wind, and said to the sea, "Peace! Be still!" And the wind ceased, and there was a great calm. ⁴⁰ He said to them, "Why are you afraid? Have you no faith?" ⁴¹ And they were filled with awe, and said to one another, "Who then is this, that even wind and sea obey him?"

5 They came to the other side of the sea, to the country of the Gĕr'-a·sĕneṣ.ⁿ ²And when he had come out of the boat, there met him out of the tombs a man with an unclean spirit, ³ who lived among the tombs; and no one could bind him any more, even with a chain; ⁴ for he had often been bound with fetters and chains, but the chains he wrenched apart, and the fetters he broke in pieces; and no one had the strength to subdue him. ⁵ Night and day among the tombs and on the mountains he was always crying out, and bruising himself with stones. ⁶ And when he saw Jesus from afar, he ran and worshiped him; ⁷ and crying out with a loud voice, he said, "What have you to do with me, Jesus, Son of the Most High God? I adjure you by God, do not torment me." ⁸ For he had said to him, "Come out of the man, you unclean spirit!" ⁹ And Jesusᵒ asked him, "What is your name?" He replied, "My name is Legion; for we are many." ¹⁰ And he begged him eagerly to send them out of the country. ¹¹ Now a great herd of swine was feeding there on the hillside; ¹² and they begged him, "Send us to the swine, let us enter them." ¹³ So he gave them leave. And the unclean spirits came out, and entered the swine; and the herd, numbering about two thousand, rushed down the steep bank into the sea, and were drowned in the sea.

14 The herdsmen fled, and told it in the city and in the country. And people came to see what it was that had happened. ¹⁵ And they came to Jesus, and saw the demoniac sitting there, clothed and in his right mind, the man who had had the legion; and they were afraid. ¹⁶ And those who had seen it told what had happened to the demoniac and to the swine. ¹⁷ And they began to beg Jesusᵖ to depart from their neighborhood. ¹⁸ And as he was getting into the boat, the man who had been possessed with demons begged him that he might be with him. ¹⁹ But he refused, and said to him, "Go home to your friends, and tell them how much the Lord has done for you, and how he has had mercy on you." ²⁰ And he went away and began to proclaim in the Dĕ·căp'o·lis how much Jesus had done for him; and all men marveled.

21 And when Jesus had crossed again in the boat to the other side, a great crowd gathered about him; and he was beside the sea. ²² Then came one of the rulers of the synagogue, Jā'ī·rus by name; and seeing him, he fell at his feet, ²³ and besought him, saying, "My little daughter is at the point of death. Come and lay your hands on her, so that she may be made well, and live." ²⁴ And he went with him.

And a great crowd followed him and thronged about him. ²⁵ And there was a woman who had had a flow of blood for twelve years, ²⁶ and who had suffered much under many physicians, and had spent all that she had, and was no better but rather grew worse. ²⁷ She had heard the reports about Jesus, and came up behind him in the crowd and touched his garment. ²⁸ For she said, "If I touch even his garments, I shall be made well." ²⁹ And immediately the hemorrhage ceased; and she felt in her body that she was

ⁿ Other ancient authorities read *Gergesenes,* some *Gadarenes* ᵒ Greek *he* ᵖ Greek *him*
4.34: Mt 13.34; Jn 16.25.
4.35-41: Mt 8.18, 23-27; Lk 8.22-25.
5.1-20: Mt 8.28-34; Lk 8.26-39.
5.7: Acts 16.17; Heb 7.1; Mk 1.24.   5.20: Mk 7.31.
5.21-43: Mt 9.18-26; Lk 8.40-56.
5.22: Lk 13.14; Acts 13.15; 18.8, 17.
5.23: Mk 6.5; 7.32; 8.23; Acts 9.17; 28.8.

healed of her disease. ³⁰And Jesus, perceiving in himself that power had gone forth from him, immediately turned about in the crowd, and said, "Who touched my garments?" ³¹And his disciples said to him, "You see the crowd pressing around you, and yet you say, 'Who touched me?'" ³²And he looked around to see who had done it. ³³But the woman, knowing what had been done to her, came in fear and trembling and fell down before him, and told him the whole truth. ³⁴And he said to her, "Daughter, your faith has made you well; go in peace, and be healed of your disease."

35 While he was still speaking, there came from the ruler's house some who said, "Your daughter is dead. Why trouble the Teacher any further?" ³⁶But ignoring*q* what they said, Jesus said to the ruler of the synagogue, "Do not fear, only believe." ³⁷And he allowed no one to follow him except Peter and James and John the brother of James. ³⁸When they came to the house of the ruler of the synagogue, he saw a tumult, and people weeping and wailing loudly. ³⁹And when he had entered, he said to them, "Why do you make a tumult and weep? The child is not dead but sleeping." ⁴⁰And they laughed at him. But he put them all outside, and took the child's father and mother and those who were with him, and went in where the child was. ⁴¹Taking her by the hand he said to her, "Tăl′ĭ·thạ cü′mī"; which means, "Little girl, I say to you, arise." ⁴²And immediately the girl got up and walked (she was twelve years of age), and they were immediately overcome with amazement. ⁴³And he strictly charged them that no one should know this, and told them to give her something to eat.

6 He went away from there and came to his own country; and his disciples followed him. ²And on the sabbath he began to teach in the synagogue; and many who heard him were astonished, saying, "Where did this man get all this? What is the wisdom given to him? What mighty works are wrought by his hands! ³Is not this the carpenter, the son of Mary and brother of James and Jō′sēṣ and Judas and Simon, and are not his sisters here with us?" And they took offense*r* at him. ⁴And Jesus said to them, "A

prophet is not without honor, except in his own country, and among his own kin, and in his own house." ⁵And he could do no mighty work there, except that he laid his hands upon a few sick people and healed them. ⁶And he marveled because of their unbelief.

And he went about among the villages teaching.

7 And he called to him the twelve, and began to send them out two by two, and gave them authority over the unclean spirits. ⁸He charged them to take nothing for their journey except a staff; no bread, no bag, no money in their belts; ⁹but to wear sandals and not put on two tunics. ¹⁰And he said to them, "Where you enter a house, stay there until you leave the place. ¹¹And if any place will not receive you and they refuse to hear you, when you leave, shake off the dust that is on your feet for a testimony against them." ¹²So they went out and preached that men should repent. ¹³And they cast out many demons, and anointed with oil many that were sick and healed them.

14 King Hĕr′ọd heard of it; for Jesus's name had become known. Some*t* said, "John the baptizer has been raised from the dead; that is why these powers are at work in him." ¹⁵But others said, "It is Ĕ·lī′jạh." And others said, "It is a prophet, like one of the prophets of old." ¹⁶But when Hĕr′ọd heard of it he said, "John, whom I beheaded, has been raised." ¹⁷For Hĕr′ọd had sent and seized John, and bound him in prison for the sake of Hĕ·rō′dĭ·ạs, his brother Philip's wife; because he had married her. ¹⁸For John said to Hĕr′ọd, "It is not lawful for you to have your brother's wife." ¹⁹And Hĕ·rō′dĭ·ạs had a grudge against him, and wanted to kill him. But she could not, ²⁰for Hĕr′ọd feared John, knowing that he was a righteous and holy man, and kept him safe. When he heard him, he was much perplexed; and yet he heard him gladly.

*q*Or *overhearing.* Other ancient authorities read *hearing*
*r*Or *stumbled* *s*Greek *his*
*t*Other ancient authorities read *he*
5.30: Lk 5.17.
5.34: Lk 7.50; Mk 10.52. **5.37:** Mk 9.2; 13.3.
5.41: Lk 7.14; Acts 9.40. **5.43:** Mk 1.43-44; 7.36.
6.1-6: Mt 13.53-58; Lk 4.16-30. **6.2:** Mk 1.21; Mt 7.28.
6.3: Mt 11.6. **6.5:** Mk 5.23; 7.32; 8.23.
6.6: Mk 9.35. **6.7-11:** Mt 10.1, 5, 7-11; Lk 9.1-5.
6.7: Lk 10.1. **6.11:** Mt 10.14. **6.12-13:** Mt 11.1; Lk 9.6.
6.13: Jas 5.14.
6.14-16: Mt 14.1-2; Lk 9.7-9; 9.19; Mt 21.11.
6.17-18: Mt 14.3-4; Lk 3.19-20.
6.19-29: Mt 14.5-12. **6.20:** Mt 21.26.

²¹But an opportunity came when Hĕr'ŏd on his birthday gave a banquet for his courtiers and officers and the leading men of Galilee. ²²For when Hĕ·rō'dĭ–as' daughter came in and danced, she pleased Hĕr'ŏd and his guests; and the king said to the girl, "Ask me for whatever you wish, and I will grant it." ²³And he vowed to her, "Whatever you ask me, I will give you, even half of my kingdom." ²⁴And she went out, and said to her mother, "What shall I ask?" And she said, "The head of John the baptizer." ²⁵And she came in immediately with haste to the king, and asked, saying, "I want you to give me at once the head of John the Baptist on a platter." ²⁶And the king was exceedingly sorry; but because of his oaths and his guests he did not want to break his word to her. ²⁷And immediately the king sent a soldier of the guard and gave orders to bring his head. He went and beheaded him in the prison, ²⁸and brought his head on a platter, and gave it to the girl; and the girl gave it to her mother. ²⁹When his disciples heard of it, they came and took his body, and laid it in a tomb.

30 The apostles returned to Jesus, and told him all that they had done and taught. ³¹And he said to them, "Come away by yourselves to a lonely place, and rest a while." For many were coming and going, and they had no leisure even to eat. ³²And they went away in the boat to a lonely place by themselves. ³³Now many saw them going, and knew them, and they ran there on foot from all the towns, and got there ahead of them. ³⁴As he went ashore he saw a great throng, and he had compassion on them, because they were like sheep without a shepherd; and he began to teach them many things. ³⁵And when it grew late, his disciples came to him and said, "This is a lonely place, and the hour is now late; ³⁶send them away, to go into the country and villages round about and buy themselves something to eat." ³⁷But he answered them, "You give them something to eat." And they said to him, "Shall we go and buy two hundred denariiᵘ worth of bread, and give it to them to eat? ³⁸And he said to them, "How many loaves have you? Go and see." And when they had found out, they said, "Five, and two fish."

³⁹Then he commanded them all to sit down by companies upon the green grass. ⁴⁰So they sat down in groups, by hundreds and by fifties. ⁴¹And taking the five loaves and the two fish he looked up to heaven, and blessed, and broke the loaves, and gave them to the disciples to set before the people; and he divided the two fish among them all. ⁴²And they all ate and were satisfied. ⁴³And they took up twelve baskets full of broken pieces and of the fish. ⁴⁴And those who ate the loaves were five thousand men.

45 Immediately he made his disciples get into the boat and go before him to the other side, to Bĕth–sā'ĭ·dạ, while he dismissed the crowd. ⁴⁶And after he had taken leave of them, he went up on the mountain to pray. ⁴⁷And when evening came, the boat was out on the sea, and he was alone on the land. ⁴⁸And he saw that they were making headway painfully, for the wind was against them. And about the fourth watch of the night he came to them, walking on the sea. He meant to pass by them, ⁴⁹but when they saw him walking on the sea they thought it was a ghost, and cried out; ⁵⁰for they all saw him, and were terrified. But immediately he spoke to them and said, "Take heart, it is I; have no fear." ⁵¹And he got into the boat with them and the wind ceased. And they were utterly astounded, ⁵²for they did not understand about the loaves, but their hearts were hardened.

53 And when they had crossed over, they came to land at Gĕn·nĕs'ạ·rĕt, and moored to the shore. ⁵⁴And when they got out of the boat, immediately the people recognized him, ⁵⁵and ran about the whole neighborhood and began to bring sick people on their pallets to any place where they heard he was. ⁵⁶And wherever he came, in villages, cities, or country, they laid the sick in the market places, and besought him that they might touch even the fringe of his garment; and as many as touched it were made well.

7 Now when the Phăr'ĭ·seeş gathered together to him, with some of

ᵘ The denarius was a day's wage for a laborer
6.23: Esth 5.3, 6. **6.30-31:** Lk 9.10; Mk 3.20.
6.32-44: Mt 14.13-21; Lk 9.11-17; Jn 6.5-13; Mk 8.1-10; Mt 15.32-39. **6.34:** Mt 9.36. **6.37:** 2 Kings 4.42-44.
6.41: Mk 14.22; Lk 24.30-31.
6.45-52: Mt 14.22-33; Jn 6.15-21. **6.48:** Mk 13.35.
6.50: Mt 9.2. **6.52:** Mk 8.17. **6.53-56:** Mt 14.34-36.
6.56: Mk 3.10; Mt 9.20. **7.1-15:** Mt 15.1-11; Lk 11.38.

the scribes, who had come from Jerusalem, [2] they saw that some of his disciples ate with hands defiled, that is, unwashed. [3] (For the Phăr'ĭ-seeş, and all the Jews, do not eat unless they wash their hands,[v] observing the tradition of the elders; [4] and when they come from the market place, they do not eat unless they purify[w] themselves;[a] and there are many other traditions which they observe, the washing of cups and pots and vessels of bronze.[x]) [5] And the Phăr'ĭ-seeş and the scribes asked him, "Why do your disciples not live[y] according to the tradition of the elders, but eat with hands defiled?" [6] And he said to them, "Well did I-sāi'ah prophesy of you hypocrites, as it is written,

'This people honors me with their lips,
but their heart is far from me;
[7] in vain do they worship me,
teaching as doctrines the precepts of men.'

[8] You leave the commandment of God, and hold fast the tradition of men."

9 And he said to them, "You have a fine way of rejecting the commandment of God, in order to keep your tradition! [10] For Moses said, 'Honor your father and your mother'; and 'He who speaks evil of father or mother, let him surely die'; [11] but you say, 'If a man tells his father or his mother, What you would have gained from me is Côr'ban' (that is, given to God)[z] — [12] then you no longer permit him to do anything for his father or mother, [13] thus making void the word of God through your tradition which you hand on. And many such things you do."

14 And he called the people to him again, and said to them, "Hear me, all of you, and understand: [15] there is nothing outside a man which by going into him can defile him; but the things which come out of a man are what defile him."[a] [17] And when he had entered the house, and left the people, his disciples asked him about the parable. [18] And he said to them, "Then are you also without understanding? Do you not see that whatever goes into a man from outside cannot defile him, [19] since it enters, not his heart but his stomach, and so passes on?"[b] (Thus he declared all foods clean.) [20] And he said, "What comes out of a man is what defiles

a man. [21] For from within, out of the heart of man, come evil thoughts, fornication, theft, murder, adultery, [22] coveting, wickedness, deceit, licentiousness, envy, slander, pride, foolishness. [23] All these evil things come from within, and they defile a man."

24 And from there he arose and went away to the region of Tȳre and Sī'dŏn.[c] And he entered a house, and would not have any one know it; yet he could not be hid. [25] But immediately a woman, whose little daughter was possessed by an unclean spirit, heard of him, and came and fell down at his feet. [26] Now the woman was a Greek, a Sȳ-rō-phoe-nī'çĭ-an by birth. And she begged him to cast the demon out of her daughter. [27] And he said to her, "Let the children first be fed, for it is not right to take the children's bread and throw it to the dogs." [28] But she answered him, "Yes, Lord; yet even the dogs under the table eat the children's crumbs." [29] And he said to her, "For this saying you may go your way; the demon has left your daughter." [30] And she went home, and found the child lying in bed, and the demon gone.

31 Then he returned from the region of Tȳre, and went through Sī'dŏn to the Sea of Galilee, through the region of the Dĕ-căp'ọ-lĭs. [32] And they brought to him a man who was deaf and had an impediment in his speech; and they besought him to lay his hand upon him. [33] And taking him aside from the multitude privately, he put his fingers into his ears, and he spat and touched his tongue; [34] and looking up to heaven, he sighed, and said to him, "Ĕph'pha-tha," that is, "Be opened." [35] And his ears were opened, his tongue was released, and he spoke plainly. [36] And he charged them to tell no one; but the more he charged them, the more zealously they proclaimed it. [37] And they were astonished beyond

[r] One Greek word is of uncertain meaning and is not translated   [s] Other ancient authorities read baptize
[a] Other ancient authorities read and they do not eat anything from the market unless they purify it
[x] Other ancient authorities add and beds
[v] Greek walk   [z] Or an offering
[a] Other ancient authorities add verse 16, "If any man has ears to hear, let him hear"   [b] Or is evacuated
[c] Other ancient authorities omit and Sidon
7.4: Mt 23.25; Lk 11.39.   7.5: Gal 1.14.   7.6-7: Is 29.13.
7.10: Ex 20.12; Deut 5.16; Ex 21.17; Lev 20.9.
7.17-23: Mt 15.15-20; Mk 4.10.
7.18-19: 1 Cor 10.25-27; Rom 14.14; Tit 1.15; Acts 10.15.
7.20-23: Rom 1.28-31; Gal 5.19-21.
7.22: Mt 6.23; 20.15.   7.24-30: Mt 15.21-28.
7.31-37: Mt 15.29-31.   7.32: Mk 5.23.   7.33: Mk 8.23.
7.36: Mk 1.44; 5.43.

measure, saying, "He has done all things well; he even makes the deaf hear and the dumb speak."

8 In those days, when again a great crowd had gathered, and they had nothing to eat, he called his disciples to him, and said to them, ² "I have compassion on the crowd, because they have been with me now three days, and have nothing to eat; ³ and if I send them away hungry to their homes, they will faint on the way; and some of them have come a long way." ⁴ And his disciples answered him, "How can one feed these men with bread here in the desert?" ⁵ And he asked them, "How many loaves have you?" They said, "Seven." ⁶ And he commanded the crowd to sit down on the ground; and he took the seven loaves, and having given thanks he broke them and gave them to his disciples to set before the people; and they set them before the crowd. ⁷ And they had a few small fish; and having blessed them, he commanded that these also should be set before them. ⁸ And they ate, and were satisfied; and they took up the broken pieces left over, seven baskets full. ⁹ And there were about four thousand people. ¹⁰ And he sent them away; and immediately he got into the boat with his disciples, and went to the district of Dǎl·mạ·nū'thạ.ᵈ

11 The Phǎr'i·seeş came and began to argue with him, seeking from him a sign from heaven, to test him. ¹² And he sighed deeply in his spirit, and said, "Why does this generation seek a sign? Truly, I say to you, no sign shall be given to this generation." ¹³ And he left them, and getting into the boat again he departed to the other side.

14 Now they had forgotten to bring bread; and they had only one loaf with them in the boat. ¹⁵ And he cautioned them, saying, "Take heed, beware of the leaven of the Phǎr'i·seeş and the leaven of Hěr'ǫd."ᵉ ¹⁶ And they discussed it with one another, saying, "We have no bread." ¹⁷ And being aware of it, Jesus said to them, "Why do you discuss the fact that you have no bread? Do you not yet perceive or understand? Are your hearts hardened? ¹⁸ Having eyes do you not see, and having ears do you not hear? And do you not remember? ¹⁹ When I broke the five loaves for the five thousand, how many

baskets full of broken pieces did you take up?" They said to him, "Twelve." ²⁰ "And the seven for the four thousand, how many baskets full of broken pieces did you take up?" And they said to him, "Seven." ²¹ And he said to them, "Do you not yet understand?"

22 And they came to Běth–sā'ĭ·dạ. And some people brought to him a blind man, and begged him to touch him. ²³ And he took the blind man by the hand, and led him out of the village; and when he had spit on his eyes and laid his hands upon him, he asked him, "Do you see anything?" ²⁴ And he looked up and said, "I see men; but they look like trees, walking." ²⁵ Then again he laid his hands upon his eyes; and he looked intently and was restored, and saw everything clearly. ²⁶ And he sent him away to his home, saying, "Do not even enter the village."

27 And Jesus went on with his disciples, to the villages of Çaěs·ạ·rē'a Phǐ·lǐp'pī; and on the way he asked his disciples, "Who do men say that I am?" ²⁸ And they told him, "John the Baptist; and others say, É·lī'jạh; and others one of the prophets." ²⁹ And he asked them, "But who do you say that I am?" Peter answered him, "You are the Christ." ³⁰ And he charged them to tell no one about him.

31 And he began to teach them that the Son of man must suffer many things, and be rejected by the elders and the chief priests and the scribes, and be killed, and after three days rise again. ³² And he said this plainly. And Peter took him, and began to rebuke him. ³³ But turning and seeing his disciples, he rebuked Peter, and said, "Get behind me, Satan! For you are not on the side of God, but of men."

34 And he called to him the multitude with his disciples, and said to them, "If any man would come after me, let him deny himself and take up his cross and follow me. ³⁵ For whoever would save his life will lose it;

ᵈ Other ancient authorities read *Magadan* or *Magdala*
ᵉ Other ancient authorities read *the Herodians*
8.1-10: Mt 15.32-39; Mk 6.32-44; Mt 14.13-21; Lk 9.11-17; Jn 6.5-13.   8.11-12: Mt 16.1-4; 12.38-39; Lk 11.29.
8.13-21: Mt 16.4-12.   8.15: Lk 12.1; Mk 6.14; 12.13.
8.17: Mk 6.52; Jer 5.21; Is 6.9-10; Mt 13.10-15.
8.19: Mk 6.41-44.   8.20: Mk 8.1-10.
8.22-26: Mk 10.46-52; Jn 9.1-7.   8.22: Mk 6.45; Lk 9.10.
8.23: Mk 7.33; 5.23.
8.27-30: Mt 16.13-20; Lk 9.18-21; Jn 6.66-69.
8.28: Mk 6.14.   8.30: Mk 9.9; 1.34.
8.31-9.1: Mt 16.21-28; Lk 9.22-27.   8.33: Mt 4.10.
8.34: Mt 10.38; Lk 14.27.
8.35: Mt 10.39; Lk 17.33; Jn 12.25.

and whoever loses his life for my sake and the gospel's will save it. ³⁶For what does it profit a man, to gain the whole world and forfeit his life? ³⁷For what can a man give in return for his life? ³⁸For whoever is ashamed of me and of my words in this adulterous and sinful generation, of him will the Son of man also be ashamed, when he comes in the glory of his Father with the holy angels." ¹And he said to them, "Truly, I say to you, there are some standing here who will not taste death before they see that the kingdom of God has come with power."

9

2 And after six days Jesus took with him Peter and James and John, and led them up a high mountain apart by themselves; and he was transfigured before them, ³and his garments became glistening, intensely white, as no fuller on earth could bleach them. ⁴And there appeared to them Ė·lī′jah with Moses; and they were talking to Jesus. ⁵And Peter said to Jesus, "Master,ᶠ it is well that we are here; let us make three booths, one for you and one for Moses and one for Ė·lī′jah." ⁶For he did not know what to say, for they were exceedingly afraid. ⁷And a cloud overshadowed them, and a voice came out of the cloud, "This is my beloved Son;ᵍ listen to him." ⁸And suddenly looking around they no longer saw any one with them but Jesus only.

9 And as they were coming down the mountain, he charged them to tell no one what they had seen, until the Son of man should have risen from the dead. ¹⁰So they kept the matter to themselves, questioning what the rising from the dead meant. ¹¹And they asked him, "Why do the scribes say that first Ė·lī′jah must come?" ¹²And he said to them, "Ė·lī′jah does come first to restore all things; and how is it written of the Son of man, that he should suffer many things and be treated with contempt? ¹³But I tell you that Ė·lī′jah has come, and they did to him whatever they pleased, as it is written of him."

14 And when they came to the disciples, they saw a great crowd about them, and scribes arguing with them. ¹⁵And immediately all the crowd, when they saw him, were greatly amazed, and ran up to him and greeted him. ¹⁶And he asked them, "What are you discussing with them?" ¹⁷And one of the crowd answered him, "Teacher, I brought my son to you, for he has a dumb spirit; ¹⁸and wherever it seizes him, it dashes him down; and he foams and grinds his teeth and becomes rigid; and I asked your disciples to cast it out, and they were not able." ¹⁹And he answered them, "O faithless generation, how long am I to be with you? How long am I to bear with you? Bring him to me." ²⁰And they brought the boy to him; and when the spirit saw him, immediately it convulsed the boy, and he fell on the ground and rolled about, foaming at the mouth. ²¹And Jesusʰ asked his father, "How long has he had this?" And he said, "From childhood. ²²And it has often cast him into the fire and into the water, to destroy him; but if you can do anything, have pity on us and help us." ²³And Jesus said to him, "If you can! All things are possible to him who believes." ²⁴Immediately the father of the child cried outⁱ and said, "I believe; help my unbelief!" ²⁵And when Jesus saw that a crowd came running together, he rebuked the unclean spirit, saying to it, "You dumb and deaf spirit, I command you, come out of him, and never enter him again." ²⁶And after crying out and convulsing him terribly, it came out, and the boy was like a corpse; so that most of them said, "He is dead." ²⁷But Jesus took him by the hand and lifted him up, and he arose. ²⁸And when he had entered the house, his disciples asked him privately, "Why could we not cast it out?" ²⁹And he said to them, "This kind cannot be driven out by anything but prayer."ʲ

30 They went on from there and passed through Galilee. And he would not have any one know it; ³¹for he was teaching his disciples, saying to them, "The Son of man will be delivered into the hands of men, and they will kill him; and when he is killed, after three

ᶠOr *Rabbi*   ᵍOr *my Son, my* (or *the) Beloved*   ʰGreek *he*
ⁱOther ancient authorities add *with tears*
ʲOther ancient authorities add *and fasting*
8.38: Mt 10.33; Lk 12.9.
9.1: Mk 13.30; Mt 10.23; Lk 22.18.
9.2-8: Mt 17.1-8; Lk 9.28-36.   **9.2:** Mk 5.37; 13.3.
9.3: Mt 28.3.
9.7: 2 Pet 1.17-18; Mt 3.17; Jn 12.28-29.
9.9-13: Mt 17.9-13; Lk 9.36.   **9.9:** Mk 8.30; 5.43; 7.36.
9.11: Mt 11.14.   **9.12:** Mk 8.31; 9.31; 10.33.
9.14-27: Mt 17.14-18; Lk 9.37-43.
9.23: Mt 17.20; Lk 17.6; Mk 11.22-24.
9.30-32: Mt 17.22-23; Lk 9.43-45.   **9.31:** Mk 8.31; 10.33.

days he will rise." ³²But they did not understand the saying, and they were afraid to ask him.

33 And they came to Ca·pẽr′na–ụm; and when he was in the house he asked them, "What were you discussing on the way?" ³⁴But they were silent; for on the way they had discussed with one another who was the greatest. ³⁵And he sat down and called the twelve; and he said to them, "If any one would be first, he must be last of all and servant of all." ³⁶And he took a child, and put him in the midst of them; and taking him in his arms, he said to them, ³⁷"Whoever receives one such child in my name receives me; and whoever receives me, receives not me but him who sent me."

38 John said to him, "Teacher, we saw a man casting out demons in your name,ᵏ and we forbade him, because he was not following us." ³⁹But Jesus said, "Do not forbid him; for no one who does a mighty work in my name will be able soon after to speak evil of me. ⁴⁰For he that is not against us is for us. ⁴¹For truly, I say to you, whoever gives you a cup of water to drink because you bear the name of Christ, will by no means lose his reward.

42 "Whoever causes one of these little ones who believe in me to sin,ˡ it would be better for him if a great millstone were hung round his neck and he were thrown into the sea. ⁴³And if your hand causes you to sin,ˡ cut it off; it is better for you to enter life maimed than with two hands to go to hell,ᵐ to the unquenchable fire.ⁿ ⁴⁵And if your foot causes you to sin,ˡ cut it off; it is better for you to enter life lame than with two feet to be thrown into hell.ᵐ, ⁿ ⁴⁷And if your eye causes you to sin,ˡ pluck it out; it is better for you to enter the kingdom of God with one eye than with two eyes to be thrown into hell,ᵐ ⁴⁸where their worm does not die, and the fire is not quenched. ⁴⁹For every one will be salted with fire.ᵒ ⁵⁰Salt is good; but if the salt has lost its saltness, how will you season it? Have salt in yourselves, and be at peace with one another."

10 And he left there and went to the region of Jü·dē′a and beyond the Jordan, and crowds gathered

to him again; and again, as his custom was, he taught them.

2 And Phăr′i·seeṣ came up and in order to test him asked, "Is it lawful for a man to divorce his wife?" ³He answered them, "What did Moses command you?" ⁴They said, "Moses allowed a man to write a certificate of divorce, and to put her away." ⁵But Jesus said to them, "For your hardness of heart he wrote you this commandment. ⁶But from the beginning of creation, 'God made them male and female.' ⁷'For this reason a man shall leave his father and mother and be joined to his wife,ᵖ ⁸and the two shall become one flesh.' So they are no longer two but one flesh. ⁹What therefore God has joined together, let not man put asunder."

10 And in the house the disciples asked him again about this matter. ¹¹And he said to them, "Whoever divorces his wife and marries another, commits adultery against her; ¹²and if she divorces her husband and marries another, she commits adultery."

13 And they were bringing children to him, that he might touch them; and the disciples rebuked them. ¹⁴But when Jesus saw it he was indignant, and said to them, "Let the children come to me, do not hinder them; for to such belongs the kingdom of God. ¹⁵Truly, I say to you, whoever does not receive the kingdom of God like a child shall not enter it." ¹⁶And he took them in his arms and blessed them, laying his hands upon them.

17 And as he was setting out on his journey, a man ran up and knelt before him, and asked him, "Good Teacher, what must I do to inherit eternal life?" ¹⁸And Jesus said to him,

---

ᵏOther ancient authorities add *who does not follow us*
ˡGreek *stumble*   ᵐGreek *Gehenna*
ⁿVerses 44 and 46 (which are identical with verse 48) are omitted by the best ancient authorities
ᵒOther ancient authorities add *and every sacrifice will be salted with salt*
ᵖOther ancient authorities omit *and be joined to his wife*
9.32: Jn 12.16.
9.33–37: Mt 18.1-5; Lk 9.46-48. **9.34:** Lk 22.24.
9.35: Mk 10.43-44; Mt 20.26-27; 23.11; Lk 22.26.
9.36: Mk 10.16. **9.37:** Mt 10.40; Lk 10.16; Jn 12.44; 13.20.
9.38–40: Lk 9.49-50; 11.23; Mt 12.30; Num 11.27-29.
9.41: Mt 10.42. **9.42–48:** Mt 18.6-9; 5.29-30; Lk 17.1-2.
9.48: Is 66.24. **9.49-50:** Mt 5.13; Lk 14.34-35.
9.50: Col 4.6; 1 Thess 5.13. **10.1–12:** Mt 19.1-9.
10.1: Lk 9.51; Jn 10.40; 11.7. **10.4:** Deut 24.1-4.
10.6: Gen 1.27; 5.2.
10.7–8: Gen 2.24.
10.11: Mt 5.32; Lk 16.18; 1 Cor 7.10-11; Rom 7.2-3.
10.13–16: Mt 19.13-15; 18.3; Lk 18.15-17.
10.16: Mk 9.36. **10.17–31:** Mt 19.16-30; Lk 18.18-30.

"Why do you call me good? No one is good but God alone. [19] You know the commandments: 'Do not kill, Do not commit adultery, Do not steal, Do not bear false witness, Do not defraud, Honor your father and mother.'" [20] And he said to him, "Teacher, all these I have observed from my youth." [21] And Jesus looking upon him loved him, and said to him, "You lack one thing; go, sell what you have, and give to the poor, and you will have treasure in heaven; and come, follow me." [22] At that saying his countenance fell, and he went away sorrowful; for he had great possessions.

23 And Jesus looked around and said to his disciples, "How hard it will be for those who have riches to enter the kingdom of God!" [24] And the disciples were amazed at his words. But Jesus said to them again, "Children, how hard it is[r] to enter the kingdom of God! [25] It is easier for a camel to go through the eye of a needle than for a rich man to enter the kingdom of God." [26] And they were exceedingly astonished, and said to him,[s] "Then who can be saved?" [27] Jesus looked at them and said, "With men it is impossible, but not with God; for all things are possible with God." [28] Peter began to say to him, "Lo, we have left everything and followed you." [29] Jesus said, "Truly, I say to you, there is no one who has left house or brothers or sisters or mother or father or children or lands, for my sake and for the gospel, [30] who will not receive a hundredfold now in this time, houses and brothers and sisters and mothers and children and lands, with persecutions, and in the age to come eternal life. [31] But many that are first will be last, and the last first."

32 And they were on the road, going up to Jerusalem, and Jesus was walking ahead of them; and they were amazed, and those who followed were afraid. And taking the twelve again, he began to tell them what was to happen to him, [33] saying, "Behold, we are going up to Jerusalem; and the Son of man will be delivered to the chief priests and the scribes, and they will condemn him to death, and deliver him to the Gentiles; [34] and they will mock him, and spit upon him, and scourge him, and kill him; and after three days he will arise."

35 And James and John, the sons of Zĕb′e·dee, came forward to him, and said to him, "Teacher, we want you to do for us whatever we ask of you." [36] And he said to them, "What do you want me to do for you?" [37] And they said to him, "Grant us to sit, one at your right hand and one at your left, in your glory." [38] But Jesus said to them, "You do not know what you are asking. Are you able to drink the cup that I drink, or to be baptized with the baptism with which I am baptized?" [39] And they said to him, "We are able." And Jesus said to them, "The cup that I drink you will drink; and with the baptism with which I am baptized, you will be baptized; [40] but to sit at my right hand or at my left is not mine to grant, but it is for those for whom it has been prepared." [41] And when the ten heard it, they began to be indignant at James and John. [42] And Jesus called them to him and said to them, "You know that those who are supposed to rule over the Gentiles lord it over them, and their great men exercise authority over them. [43] But it shall not be so among you; but whoever would be great among you must be your servant, [44] and whoever would be first among you must be slave of all. [45] For the Son of man also came not to be served but to serve, and to give his life as a ransom for many."

46 And they came to Jericho; and as he was leaving Jericho with his disciples and a great multitude, Băr-tĭ·mae′us, a blind begger, the son of Tĭ·mae′us, was sitting by the roadside. [47] And when he heard that it was Jesus of Nazareth, he began to cry out and say, "Jesus, Son of David, have mercy on me!" [48] And many rebuked him, telling him to be silent; but he cried out all the more, "Son of David, have mercy on me!" [49] And Jesus stopped and said, "Call him." And they called the blind man, saying

[r] Other ancient authorities add *for those who trust in riches* [s] Other ancient authorities read *to one another*
10.17: Lk 10.25; Mk 1.40.
10.19: Ex 20.12-16; Deut 5.16-20.
10.21: Mt 6.20; Lk 12.33; Acts 2.45; 4.34-35.
10.28: Mk 1.16-20. 10.30: Mt 6.33.
10.31: Mt 20.16; Lk 13.30.
10.32-34: Mt 20.17-19; Lk 18.31-34.
10.33: Mk 8.31; 9.12; 9.33. 10.34: Mk 14.65; 15.19, 26-32.
10.35-45: Mt 20.20-28. 10.37: Mt 19.28; Lk 22.30.
10.38: Lk 12.50; Jn 18.11. 10.39: Acts 12.2; Rev 1.9.
10.42-45: Lk 22.25-27. 10.43: Mk 9.35.
10.45: 1 Tim 2.5-6.
10.46-52: Mt 20.29-34; Lk 18.35-43; Mk 8.22-26.
10.47: Mt 9.27.

to him, "Take heart; rise, he is calling you." ⁵⁰And throwing off his mantle he sprang up and came to Jesus. ⁵¹And Jesus said to him, "What do you want me to do for you?" And the blind man said to him, "Master,ᶠ let me receive my sight." ⁵²And Jesus said to him, "Go your way; your faith has made you well." And immediately he received his sight and followed him on the way.

11 And when they drew near to Jerusalem, to Běth′pha·ġē and Běth′a·nў, at the Mount of Olives, he sent two of his disciples, ²and said to them, "Go into the village opposite you, and immediately as you enter it you will find a colt tied, on which no one has ever sat; untie it and bring it. ³If any one says to you, 'Why are you doing this?' say, 'The Lord has need of it and will send it back here immediately.' " ⁴And they went away, and found a colt tied at the door out in the open street; and they untied it. ⁵And those who stood there said to them, "What are you doing, untying the colt?" ⁶And they told them what Jesus had said; and they let them go. ⁷And they brought the colt to Jesus, and threw their garments on it; and he sat upon it. ⁸And many spread their garments on the road, and others spread leafy branches which they had cut from the fields. ⁹And those who went before and those who followed cried out, "Hosanna! Blessed is he who comes in the name of the Lord! ¹⁰Blessed is the kingdom of our father David that is coming! Hosanna in the highest!"

11 And he entered Jerusalem, and went into the temple; and when he had looked round at everything, as it was already late, he went out to Běth′-a·nў with the twelve.

12 On the following day, when they came from Běth′a·nў, he was hungry. ¹³And seeing in the distance a fig tree in leaf, he went to see if he could find anything on it. When he came to it, he found nothing but leaves, for it was not the season for figs. ¹⁴And he said to it, "May no one ever eat fruit from you again." And his disciples heard it.

15 And they came to Jerusalem. And he entered the temple and began to drive out those who sold and those who bought in the temple, and he overturned the tables of the money-changers and the seats of those who sold

pigeons; ¹⁶and he would not allow any one to carry anything through the temple. ¹⁷And he taught, and said to them, "Is it not written, 'My house shall be called a house of prayer for all the nations'? But you have made it a den of robbers." ¹⁸And the chief priests and the scribes heard it and sought a way to destroy him; for they feared him, because all the multitude was astonished at his teaching. ¹⁹And when evening came theyᵘ went out of the city.

20 As they passed by in the morning, they saw the fig tree withered away to its roots. ²¹And Peter remembered and said to him, "Master,ᵛ look! The fig tree which you cursed has withered." ²²And Jesus answered them, "Have faith in God. ²³Truly, I say to you, whoever says to this mountain, 'Be taken up and cast into the sea,' and does not doubt in his heart, but believes that what he says will come to pass, it will be done for him. ²⁴Therefore I tell you, whatever you ask in prayer, believe that you have receivedᵃ it, and it will be yours. ²⁵And whenever you stand praying, forgive, if you have anything against any one; so that your Father also who is in heaven may forgive you your trespasses."ʷ

27 And they came again to Jerusalem. And as he was walking in the temple, the chief priests and the scribes and the elders came to him, ²⁸and they said to him, "By what authority are you doing these things, or who gave you this authority to do them?" ²⁹Jesus said to them, "I will ask you a question; answer me, and I will tell you by what authority I do these things. ³⁰Was the baptism of John from heaven or from men? Answer me." ³¹And they argued with one another, "If we say, 'From heaven,' he will say, 'Why then did you not believe him?' ³²But shall we say, 'From men'?—they were afraid of the

ᶠOr *Rabbi* ᵘOther ancient authorities read *he* ᵛOr *Rabbi*
ᵃOther ancient authorities read *are receiving*
ʷOther ancient authorities add verse 26, *"But if you do not forgive, neither will your Father who is in heaven forgive your trespasses"*
10.52: Mt 9.22; Mk 5.34; Lk 7.50; 8.48; 17.19.
11.1-10: Mt 21.1-9; Lk 19.29-38. **11.4:** Mk 14.16.
11.7-10: Jn 12.12-15. **11.9:** Ps 118.26; Mt 21.15; 23.39.
11.11: Mt 21.10-11, 17. **11.12-14:** Mt 21.18-19; Lk 13.6-9.
11.15-18: Mt 21.12-16; Lk 19.45-48; Jn 2.13-16.
11.17: Is 56.7; Jer 7.11. **11.19:** Lk 21.37.
11.20-25: Mt 21.20-22; Mt 17.20; Lk 17.6.
11.24: Jn 14.13-14; 16.23; Mt 7.7-11.
11.25: Mt 6.14-15; 18.35.
11.27-33: Mt 21.23-27; Lk 20.1-8; Jn 2.18.

people, for all held that John was a real prophet. ³³ So they answered Jesus, "We do not know." And Jesus said to them, "Neither will I tell you by what authority I do these things."

12 And he began to speak to them in parables. "A man planted a vineyard, and set a hedge around it, and dug a pit for the wine press, and built a tower, and let it out to tenants, and went into another country. ² When the time came, he sent a servant to the tenants, to get from them some of the fruit of the vineyard. ³ And they took him and beat him, and sent him away empty-handed. ⁴ Again he sent to them another servant, and they wounded him in the head, and treated him shamefully. ⁵ And he sent another, and him they killed; and so with many others, some they beat and some they killed. ⁶ He had still one other, a beloved son; finally he sent him to them, saying, 'They will respect my son.' ⁷ But those tenants said to one another, 'This is the heir; come, let us kill him, and the inheritance will be ours.' ⁸ And they took him and killed him, and cast him out of the vineyard. ⁹ What will the owner of the vineyard do? He will come and destroy the tenants, and give the vineyard to others. ¹⁰ Have you not read this scripture:

'The very stone which the builders rejected
has become the head of the corner;
¹¹ this was the Lord's doing,
and it is marvelous in our eyes'?"

12 And they tried to arrest him, but feared the multitude, for they perceived that he had told the parable against them; so they left him and went away.

13 And they sent to him some of the Phăr'i·seeş and some of the Hĕ·rō'dĭ·anş, to entrap him in his talk. ¹⁴ And they came and said to him, "Teacher, we know that you are true, and care for no man; for you do not regard the position of men, but truly teach the way of God. Is it lawful to pay taxes to Caesar, or not? ¹⁵ Should we pay them, or should we not?" But knowing their hypocrisy, he said to them, "Why put me to the test? Bring me a coin,ˣ and let me look at it." ¹⁶ And they brought one. And he said to them, "Whose likeness and inscription is this?" They said to him, "Caesar's." ¹⁷ Jesus said to them, "Render to Caesar the things that are Caesar's, and to God the things that are God's." And they were amazed at him.

18 And Săd'dū·çeeş came to him, who say that there is no resurrection; and they asked him a question, saying, ¹⁹ "Teacher, Moses wrote for us that if a man's brother dies and leaves a wife, but leaves no child, the manʸ must take the wife, and raise up children for his brother. ²⁰ There were seven brothers; the first took a wife, and when he died left no children; ²¹ and the second took her, and died, leaving no children; and the third likewise; ²² and the seven left no children. Last of all the woman also died. ²³ In the resurrection whose wife will she be? For the seven had her as wife."

24 Jesus said to them, "Is not this why you are wrong, that you know neither the scriptures nor the power of God? ²⁵ For when they rise from the dead, they neither marry nor are given in marriage, but are like angels in heaven. ²⁶ And as for the dead being raised, have you not read in the book of Moses, in the passage about the bush, how God said to him, 'I am the God of Abraham, and the God of Isaac, and the God of Jacob'? ²⁷ He is not God of the dead, but of the living; you are quite wrong."

28 And one of the scribes came up and heard them disputing with one another, and seeing that he answered them well, asked him, "Which commandment is the first of all?" ²⁹ Jesus answered, "The first is, 'Hear, O Israel: The Lord our God, the Lord is one; ³⁰ and you shall love the Lord your God with all your heart, and with all your soul, and with all your mind, and with all your strength.' ³¹ The second is this, 'You shall love your neighbor as yourself.' There is no other commandment greater than these." ³² And the scribe said to him, "You are right, Teacher; you have truly said that he is one, and there is no other but he; ³³ and to love him with all the heart, and with

ˣGreek *a denarius*   ʸGreek *his brother*
12.1–12: Mt 21.33–46; Lk 20.9–19; Is 5.1–7.
12.10–11: Ps 118.22–23; Acts 4.11; 1 Pet 2.7.
12.12: Mk 11.18.
12.13–17: Mt 22.15–22; Lk 20.20–26.
12.13: Mk 3.6; Lk 11.54.   12.17: Rom 13.7.
12.18–27: Mt 22.23–33; Lk 20.27–38.   12.19: Deut 25.5.
12.26: Ex 3.6.
12.28–34: Mt 22.34–40; Lk 20.39–40; 10.25–28.
12.29: Deut 6.4.
12.31: Lev 19.18; Rom 13.9; Gal 5.14; Jas 2.8.
12.33: 1 Sam 15.22; Hos 6.6; Mic 6.6–8; Mt 9.13.

all the understanding, and with all the strength, and to love one's neighbor as oneself, is much more than all whole burnt offerings and sacrifices." ³⁴And when Jesus saw that he answered wisely, he said to him, "You are not far from the kingdom of God." And after that no one dared to ask him any question.

35 And as Jesus taught in the temple, he said, "How can the scribes say that the Christ is the son of David? ³⁶David himself, inspired by² the Holy Spirit, declared,

'The Lord said to my Lord,
Sit at my right hand,
till I put thy enemies under thy feet.'

³⁷David himself calls him Lord; so how is he his son?" And the great throng heard him gladly.

38 And in his teaching he said, "Beware of the scribes, who like to go about in long robes, and to have salutations in the market places ³⁹and the best seats in the synagogues and the places of honor at feasts, ⁴⁰who devour widows' houses and for a pretense make long prayers. They will receive the greater condemnation."

41 And he sat down opposite the treasury, and watched the multitude putting money into the treasury. Many rich people put in large sums. ⁴²And a poor widow came, and put in two copper coins, which make a penny. ⁴³And he called his disciples to him, and said to them, "Truly, I say to you, this poor widow has put in more than all those who are contributing to the treasury. ⁴⁴For they all contributed out of their abundance; but she out of her poverty has put in everything she had, her whole living."

13 And as he came out of the temple, one of his disciples said to him, "Look, Teacher, what wonderful stones and what wonderful buildings!" ²And Jesus said to him, "Do you see these great buildings? There will not be left here one stone upon another, that will not be thrown down."

3 And as he sat on the Mount of Olives opposite the temple, Peter and James and John and Andrew asked him privately, ⁴"Tell us, when will this be, and what will be the sign when these things are all to be accomplished?" ⁵And Jesus began to say to them, "Take heed that no one leads

you astray. ⁶Many will come in my name, saying, 'I am he!' and they will lead many astray. ⁷And when you hear of wars and rumors of wars, do not be alarmed; this must take place, but the end is not yet. ⁸For nation will rise against nation, and kingdom against kingdom; there will be earthquakes in various places, there will be famines; this is but the beginning of the birth-pangs.

9 "But take heed to yourselves; for they will deliver you up to councils; and you will be beaten in synagogues; and you will stand before governors and kings for my sake, to bear testimony before them. ¹⁰And the gospel must first be preached to all nations. ¹¹And when they bring you to trial and deliver you up, do not be anxious beforehand what you are to say; but say whatever is given you in that hour, for it is not you who speak, but the Holy Spirit. ¹²And brother will deliver up brother to death, and the father his child, and children will rise against parents and have them put to death; ¹³and you will be hated by all for my name's sake. But he who endures to the end will be saved.

14 "But when you see the desolating sacrilege set up where it ought not to be (let the reader understand), then let those who are in Jü·dē'ạ flee to the mountains; ¹⁵let him who is on the housetop not go down, nor enter his house, to take anything away; ¹⁶and let him who is in the field not turn back to take his mantle. ¹⁷And alas for those who are with child and for those who give suck in those days! ¹⁸Pray that it may not happen in winter. ¹⁹For in those days there will be such tribulation as has not been from the beginning of the creation which God created until now, and never will be. ²⁰And if the Lord had not shortened the days, no human being would be saved; but for the sake of the elect, whom he chose, he shortened the days. ²¹And then if any one says to you, 'Look, here is the Christ!' or 'Look,

²Or *himself, in*
12.35-37: Mt 22.41-46; Lk 20.41-44.
12.36: Ps 110.1; Acts 2.34-35; Heb 1.13.
12.38-40: Mt 23.5-7; Lk 20.46-47; Lk 11.43.
12.41-44: Lk 21.1-4; Jn 8.20.   **13.1-37:** Mt 24; Lk 21.5-36.
13.2: Lk 19.43-44; Mk 14.58; 15.29; Jn 2.19; Acts 6.14.
13.6: Jn 8.24; 1 Jn 2.18.   **13.9-13:** Mt 10.17-22.
13.11: Jn 14.26; 16.7-11; Lk 12.11-12.   **13.13:** Jn 15.21.
13.14: Dan 9.27; 11.31; 12.11.   **13.17:** Lk 23.29.

there he is!' do not believe it. [22]False Christs and false prophets will arise and show signs and wonders, to lead astray, if possible, the elect. [23]But take heed; I have told you all things beforehand.

24 "But in those days, after that tribulation, the sun will be darkened, and the moon will not give its light, [25]and the stars will be falling from heaven, and the powers in the heavens will be shaken. [26]And then they will see the Son of man coming in clouds with great power and glory. [27]And then he will send out the angels, and gather his elect from the four winds, from the ends of the earth to the ends of heaven.

28 "From the fig tree learn its lesson: as soon as its branch becomes tender and puts forth its leaves, you know that summer is near. [29]So also, when you see these things taking place, you know that he is near, at the very gates. [30]Truly, I say to you, this generation will not pass away before all these things take place. [31]Heaven and earth will pass away, but my words will not pass away.

32 "But of that day or that hour no one knows, not even the angels in heaven, nor the Son, but only the Father. [33]Take heed, watch;[a] for you do not know when the time will come. [34]It is like a man going on a journey, when he leaves home and puts his servants in charge, each with his work, and commands the doorkeeper to be on the watch. [35]Watch therefore—for you do not know when the master of the house will come, in the evening, or at midnight, or at cockcrow, or in the morning—[36]lest he come suddenly and find you asleep. [37]And what I say to you I say to all: Watch."

14 It was now two days before the Passover and the feast of Unleavened Bread. And the chief priests and the scribes were seeking how to arrest him by stealth, and kill him; [2]for they said, "Not during the feast, lest there be a tumult of the people."

3 And while he was at Bĕth'a·nŷ in the house of Simon the leper, as he sat at table, a woman came with an alabaster flask of ointment of pure nard, very costly, and she broke the flask and poured it over his head. [4]But there were some who said to themselves in-

dignantly, "Why was the ointment thus wasted? [5]For this ointment might have been sold for more than three hundred denarii,[b] and given to the poor." And they reproached her. [6]But Jesus said, "Let her alone; why do you trouble her? She has done a beautiful thing to me. [7]For you always have the poor with you, and whenever you will, you can do good to them; but you will not always have me. [8]She has done what she could; she has anointed my body beforehand for burying. [9]And truly, I say to you, wherever the gospel is preached in the whole world, what she has done will be told in memory of her."

10 Then Judas Ĭs·căr'ĭ·ọt, who was one of the twelve, went to the chief priests in order to betray him to them. [11]And when they heard it they were glad, and promised to give him money. And he sought an opportunity to betray him.

12 And on the first day of Unleavened Bread, when they sacrificed the passover lamb, his disciples said to him, "Where will you have us go and prepare for you to eat the passover?" [13]And he sent two of his disciples, and said to them, "Go into the city, and a man carrying a jar of water will meet you; follow him, [14]and wherever he enters, say to the householder, 'The Teacher says, Where is my guest room, where I am to eat the passover with my disciples?' [15]And he will show you a large upper room furnished and ready; there prepare for us." [16]And the disciples set out and went to the city, and found it as he had told them; and they prepared the passover.

17 And when it was evening he came with the twelve. [18]And as they were at table eating, Jesus said, "Truly, I say to you, one of you will betray me, one who is eating with me." [19]They began to be sorrowful, and to say to him one after another, "Is it I?" [20]He said to them, "It is

[a] Other ancient authorities add *and pray*
[b] The denarius was a day's wage for a laborer
13.22: Mt 7.15; Jn 4.48.
13.26: Mk 8.38; Mt 10.23; Dan 7.13.   13.30: Mk 9.1.
13.31: Mt 5.18; Lk 16.17.   13.32: Acts 1.7.
13.33: Eph 6.18; Col 4.2.   13.34: Mt 25.14.
13.35: Lk 12.35-40.
14.1-2: Mt 26.1-5; Lk 22.1-2; Jn 11.47-53.
14.3-9: Mt 26.6-13; Lk 7.36-38; Jn 12.1-8.
14.7: Deut 15.11.   14.8: Jn 19.40.
14.10-11: Mt 26.14-16; Lk 22.3-6.
14.12-16: Mt 26.17-19; Lk 22.7-13.
14.17-21: Mt 26.20-25; Lk 22.14, 21-23; Jn 13.21-30; Ps 41.9.

one of the twelve, one who is dipping bread into the dish with me. ²¹For the Son of man goes as it is written of him, but woe to that man by whom the Son of man is betrayed! It would have been better for that man if he had not been born."

22 And as they were eating, he took bread, and blessed, and broke it, and gave it to them, and said, "Take; this is my body." ²³And he took a cup, and when he had given thanks he gave it to them, and they all drank of it. ²⁴And he said to them, "This is my blood of the* covenant, which is poured out for many. ²⁵Truly, I say to you, I shall not drink again of the fruit of the vine until that day when I drink it new in the kingdom of God."

26 And when they had sung a hymn, they went out to the Mount of Olives. ²⁷And Jesus said to them, "You will all fall away; for it is written, 'I will strike the shepherd, and the sheep will be scattered.' ²⁸But after I am raised up, I will go before you to Galilee." ²⁹Peter said to him, "Even though they all fall away, I will not." ³⁰And Jesus said to him, "Truly, I say to you, this very night, before the cock crows twice, you will deny me three times." ³¹But he said vehemently, "If I must die with you, I will not deny you." And they all said the same.

32 And they went to a place which was called Gĕth·sĕm'a·nē; and he said to his disciples, "Sit here, while I pray." ³³And he took with him Peter and James and John, and began to be greatly distressed and troubled. ³⁴And he said to them, "My soul is very sorrowful, even to death; remain here, and watch."*d* ³⁵And going a little farther, he fell on the ground and prayed that, if it were possible, the hour might pass from him. ³⁶And he said, "Abba, Father, all things are possible to thee; remove this cup from me; yet not what I will, but what thou wilt." ³⁷And he came and found them sleeping, and he said to Peter, "Simon, are you asleep? Could you not watch*d* one hour? ³⁸Watch*d* and pray that you may not enter into temptation; the spirit indeed is willing, but the flesh is weak." ³⁹And again he went away and prayed, saying the same words. ⁴⁰And again he came and found them sleeping, for their eyes were very heavy; and they did not know what to answer him.

⁴¹And he came the third time, and said to them, "Are you still sleeping and taking your rest? It is enough; the hour has come; the Son of man is betrayed into the hands of sinners. ⁴²Rise, let us be going; see, my betrayer is at hand."

43 And immediately, while he was still speaking, Judas came, one of the twelve, and with him a crowd with swords and clubs, from the chief priests and the scribes and the elders. ⁴⁴Now the betrayer had given them a sign, saying, "The one I shall kiss is the man; seize him and lead him away under guard." ⁴⁵And when he came, he went up to him at once, and said, "Master!"*e* And he kissed him. ⁴⁶And they laid hands on him and seized him. ⁴⁷But one of those who stood by drew his sword, and struck the slave of the high priest and cut off his ear. ⁴⁸And Jesus said to them, "Have you come out as against a robber, with swords and clubs to capture me? ⁴⁹Day after day I was with you in the temple teaching, and you did not seize me. But let the scriptures be fulfilled." ⁵⁰And they all forsook him and fled.

51 And a young man followed him, with nothing but a linen cloth about his body; and they seized him, ⁵²but he left the linen cloth and ran away naked.

53 And they led Jesus to the high priest; and all the chief priests and the elders and the scribes were assembled. ⁵⁴And Peter had followed him at a distance, right into the courtyard of the high priest; and he was sitting with the guards, and warming himself at the fire. ⁵⁵Now the chief priests and the whole council sought testimony against Jesus to put him to death; but they found none. ⁵⁶For many bore false witness against him, and their witness did not agree. ⁵⁷And some stood up and bore false witness against him,

*c*Other ancient authorities insert *new*   *d*Or *keep awake*   *e*Or *Rabbi*

14.22-25: Mt 26.26-29; Lk 22.17-19; 1 Cor 11.23-26.
14.22: Mk 6.41; 8.6; Lk 24.30.
14.23: 1 Cor 10.16.
14.24: Ex 24.8; Heb 9.20.
14.26-31: Mt 26.30-35; Lk 22.39, 33-34.
14.27: Zech 13.7; Jn 16.32.   **14.28:** Mk 16.7.
14.30: Mk 14.66-72; Jn 13.36-38; 18.17-18, 25-27.
14.32-42: Mt 26.36-46; Lk 22.40-46; Heb 5.7-8.
14.34: Jn 12.27.
14.36: Rom 8.15; Gal 4.6; Mk 10.38; Jn 18.11.
14.38: Mt 6.13; Lk 11.4.
14.43-50: Mt 26.47-56; Lk 22.47-53; Jn 18.2-11.
14.49: Lk 19.47; Jn 18.19-21.
14.53-65: Mt 26.57-68; Lk 22.54-55, 63-71; Jn 18.12-24.

saying, [58]"We heard him say, 'I will destroy this temple that is made with hands, and in three days I will build another, not made with hands.'" [59]Yet not even so did their testimony agree. [60]And the high priest stood up in the midst, and asked Jesus, "Have you no answer to make? What is it that these men testify against you?" [61]But he was silent and made no answer. Again the high priest asked him, "Are you the Christ, the Son of the Blessed?" [62]And Jesus said, "I am; and you will see the Son of man seated at the right hand of Power, and coming with the clouds of heaven." [63]And the high priest tore his garments, and said, "Why do we still need witnesses? [64]You have heard his blasphemy. What is your decision?" And they all condemned him as deserving death. [65]And some began to spit on him, and to cover his face, and to strike him, saying to him, "Prophesy!" And the guards received him with blows.

66 And as Peter was below in the courtyard, one of the maids of the high priest came; [67]and seeing Peter warming himself, she looked at him, and said, "You also were with the Nazarene, Jesus." [68]But he denied it, saying, "I neither know nor understand what you mean." And he went out into the gateway.*f* [69]And the maid saw him, and began again to say to the bystanders, "This man is one of them." [70]But again he denied it. And after a little while again the bystanders said to Peter, "Certainly you are one of them; for you are a Galilean." [71]But he began to invoke a curse on himself and to swear, 'I do not know this man of whom you speak." [72]And immediately the cock crowed a second time. And Peter remembered how Jesus had said to him, "Before the cock crows twice, you will deny me three times." And he broke down and wept.

15 And as soon as it was morning the chief priests, with the elders and scribes, and the whole council held a consultation; and they bound Jesus and led him away and delivered him to Pilate. [2]And Pilate asked him, "Are you the King of the Jews?" And he answered him, "You have said so." [3]And the chief priests accused him of many things. [4]And Pilate again asked him, "Have you no answer to make? See how many charges they bring

against you." [5]But Jesus made no further answer, so that Pilate wondered.

6 Now at the feast he used to release for them one prisoner for whom they asked. [7]And among the rebels in prison, who had committed murder in the insurrection, there was a man called Ba·răb'bas. [8]And the crowd came up and began to ask Pilate to do as he was wont to do for them. [9]And he answered them, "Do you want me to release for you the King of the Jews?" [10]For he perceived that it was out of envy that the chief priests had delivered him up. [11]But the chief priests stirred up the crowd to have him release for them Ba·răb'bas instead. [12]And Pilate again said to them, "Then what shall I do with the man whom you call the King of the Jews?" [13]And they cried out again, "Crucify him." [14]And Pilate said to them, "Why, what evil has he done?" But they shouted all the more, "Crucify him." [15]So Pilate, wishing to satisfy the crowd, released for them Ba·răb'bas; and having scourged Jesus, he delivered him to be crucified.

16 And the soldiers led him away inside the palace (that is, the praetorium); and they called together the whole battalion. [17]And they clothed him in a purple cloak, and plaiting a crown of thorns they put it on him. [18]And they began to salute him, "Hail, King of the Jews!" [19]And they struck his head with a reed, and spat upon him, and they knelt down in homage to him. [20]And when they had mocked him, they stripped him of the purple cloak, and put his own clothes on him. And they led him out to crucify him.

21 And they compelled a passer-by, Simon of Cy·rē'nē, who was coming in from the country, the father of Alexander and Rufus, to carry his cross. [22]And they brought him to the place called Gŏl'go·tha (which means the place of a skull). [23]And they offered him wine mingled with myrrh; but he

f Or *fore-court.* Other ancient authorities add *and the cock crowed*
14.58: Mk 13.2; 15.29; Acts 6.14; Jn 2.19.
14.62: Dan 7.13; Mk 9.1; 13.26.
14.63: Acts 14.14; Num 14.6.   **14.64:** Lev 24.16.
14.66-72: Mt 26.69-75; Lk 22.56-62; Jn 18.16-18, 25-27; Mk 14.30.
15.1: Mt 27.1-2; Lk 23.1; Jn 18.28.
15.2-15: Mt 27.11-26; Lk 23.2-3, 18-25; Jn 18.29-19.16.
15.11: Acts 3.14.
15.16-20: Mt 27.27-31; Lk 23.11; Jn 19.2-3.
15.21: Mt 27.32; Lk 23.26; Rom 16.13.
15.22-32: Mt 27.33-44; Lk 23.33-39; Jn 19.17-24.

did not take it. ²⁴ And they crucified him, and divided his garments among them, casting lots for them, to decide what each should take. ²⁵ And it was the third hour, when they crucified him. ²⁶ And the inscription of the charge against him read, "The King of the Jews." ²⁷ And with him they crucified two robbers, one on his right and one on his left.ᵍ ²⁹ And those who passed by derided him, wagging their heads, and saying, "Aha! You who would destroy the temple and build it in three days, ³⁰ save yourself, and come down from the cross!" ³¹ So also the chief priests mocked him to one another with the scribes, saying, "He saved others; he cannot save himself. ³² Let the Christ, the King of Israel, come down now from the cross, that we may see and believe." Those who were crucified with him also reviled him.

33 And when the sixth hour had come, there was darkness over the whole landʰ until the ninth hour. ³⁴ And at the ninth hour Jesus cried with a loud voice, "Ē'lō-ī, Ē'lō-ī, lä'mạ sạ·băch-thā'nī?" which means, "My God, my God, why hast thou forsaken me?" ³⁵ And some of the bystanders hearing it said, "Behold, he is calling Ē·lī'jạh." ³⁶ And one ran and, filling a sponge full of vinegar, put it on a reed and gave it to him to drink, saying, "Wait, let us see whether Ē·lī'jạh will come to take him down." ³⁷ And Jesus uttered a loud cry, and breathed his last. ³⁸ And the curtain of the temple was torn in two, from top to bottom. ³⁹ And when the centurion, who stood facing him, saw that he thusⁱ breathed his last, he said, "Truly this man was the Sonˣ of God!"

40 There were also women looking on from afar, among whom were Mary Măg'dạ·lēne, and Mary the mother of James the younger and of Jō'sēş, and Sạ·lō'mē, ⁴¹ who, when he was in Galilee, followed him, and ministered to him; and also many other women who came up with him to Jerusalem.

42 And when evening had come, since it was the day of Preparation, that is, the day before the sabbath, ⁴³ Joseph of Ăr·ĭ·mạ·thē'ạ, a respected member of the council, who was also himself looking for the kingdom of God, took courage and went to Pilate, and asked for the body of Jesus. ⁴⁴ And Pilate wondered if he were already dead; and summoning the centurion, he asked him whether he was already dead.ʲ ⁴⁵ And when he learned from the centurion that he was dead, he granted the body to Joseph. ⁴⁶ And he bought a linen shroud, and taking him down, wrapped him in the linen shroud, and laid him in a tomb which had been hewn out of the rock; and he rolled a stone against the door of the tomb. ⁴⁷ Mary Măg'dạ·lēne and Mary the mother of Jō'sēş saw where he was laid.

16 And when the sabbath was past, Mary Măg'dạ·lēne, and Mary the mother of James, and Sạ·lō'mē, bought spices, so that they might go and anoint him. ² And very early on the first day of the week they went to the tomb when the sun had risen. ³ And they were saying to one another, "Who will roll away the stone for us from the door of the tomb?" ⁴ And looking up, they saw that the stone was rolled back—it was very large. ⁵ And entering the tomb, they saw a young man sitting on the right side, dressed in a white robe; and they were amazed. ⁶ And he said to them, "Do nŏt be amazed; you seek Jesus of Nazareth, who was crucified. He has risen, he is not here; see the place where they laid him. ⁷ But go, tell his disciples and Peter that he is going before you to Galilee; there you will see him, as he told you." ⁸ And they went out and fled from the tomb; for trembling and astonishment had come upon them; and they said nothing to any one, for they were afraid.

9 Now when he rose early on the first day of the week, he appeared first to Mary Magdalene, from whom he had cast out seven demons. ¹⁰ She went

ᵍ Other ancient authorities insert verse 28, *And the scripture was fulfilled which says, "He was reckoned with the transgressors"* ʰ Or *earth*
ⁱ Other ancient authorities insert *cried out and*
ˣ Or *a son*
ʲ Other ancient authorities read *whether he had been some time dead*

15.24: Ps 22.18.   15.29: Mk 13.2; 14.58; Jn 2.19.
15.31: Ps 22.7-8.
15.33-41: Mt 27.45-56; Lk 23.44-49; Jn 19.28-30.
15.34: Ps 22.1.   15.36: Ps 69.21.   15.38: Heb 10.19-20.
15.39: Mk 1.11; 9.7.   15.40: Jn 19.25.   15.41: Lk 8.1-3.
15.42-47: Mt 27.57-61; Lk 23.50-56; Jn 19.38-42; Acts 13.29.   15.42: Deut 21.22-23.
16.1-8: Mt 28.1-8; Lk 24.1-10; Jn 20.1-2.
16.1: Lk 23.56; Jn 19.39.
16.7: Mk 14.28; Jn 21.1-23; Mt 28.7.

and told those who had been with him, as they mourned and wept. ¹¹But when they heard that he was alive and had been seen by her, they would not believe it.

12 After this he appeared in another form to two of them, as they were walking into the country. ¹³And they went back and told the rest, but they did not believe them.

14 Afterward he appeared to the eleven themselves as they sat at table; and he upbraided them for their unbelief and hardness of heart, because they had not believed those who saw him after he had risen. ¹⁵And he said to them, "Go into all the world and preach the gospel to the whole creation. ¹⁶He who believes and is baptized will be saved; but he who does not believe will be condemned. ¹⁷And these signs will accompany those who believe: in my name they will cast out demons; they will speak in new tongues; ¹⁸they will pick up serpents, and if they drink any deadly thing, it will not hurt them; they will lay their hands on the sick, and they will recover."

19 So when the Lord Jesus, after he had spoken to them, was taken up into heaven, and sat down at the right hand of God. ²⁰And they went forth and preached everywhere, while the Lord worked with them and confirmed the message by the signs that attended it. Amen.*ᵏ*

The Gospel According to

Luke

1 Inasmuch as many have undertaken to compile a narrative of the things which have been accomplished among us, ²just as they were delivered to us by those who from the beginning were eyewitnesses and ministers of the word, ³it seemed good to me also, having followed all things closely*ᵃ* for some time past, to write an orderly account for you, most excellent Thē·ŏph′ĭ·lŭs, ⁴that you may know the truth concerning the things of which you have been informed.

5 In the days of Hĕr′ŏd, king of Jū·dē′a, there was a priest named Zĕch·a·rī′ah,*ᵇ* of the division of A·bī′-jah; and he had a wife of the daughters of Aaron, and her name was Elizabeth. ⁶And they were both righteous before God, walking in all the commandments and ordinances of the Lord blameless. ⁷But they had no child, because Elizabeth was barren, and both were advanced in years.

8 Now while he was serving as priest before God when his division was on duty, ⁹according to the custom of the priesthood, it fell to him by lot to enter the temple of the Lord and burn incense. ¹⁰And the whole multitude of the people were praying outside at the hour of incense. ¹¹And there appeared to him an angel of the Lord standing on the right side of the altar of incense. ¹²And Zĕch·a·rī′ah was troubled when he saw him, and fear fell upon him. ¹³But the angel said to him, "Do not be afraid, Zĕch·a·rī′ah, for your prayer is heard, and your wife Elizabeth will bear you a son, and you shall call his name John. ¹⁴And you will have joy and gladness, and many will rejoice at his birth; ¹⁵for he will be great before the Lord, and he shall drink no wine nor strong drink, and he will be filled with the Holy Spirit, even from his mother's womb. ¹⁶And he will turn many of the sons of Israel to the Lord their God,

---

*ᵏ*Some of the most ancient authorities bring the book to a close at the end of verse 8. One authority concludes the book by adding after verse 8 the following: *But they reported briefly to Peter and those with him all that they had been told. And after this, Jesus himself sent out by means of them, from east to west, the sacred and imperishable proclamation of eternal salvation.* Other authorities include the preceding passage and continue with verses 9-20. In most authorities verses 9-20 follow immediately after verse 8; a few authorities insert additional material after verse 14.

*ᵃ*Or *accurately*   *ᵇ*Greek *Zacharias*
1.2: 1 Jn 1.1; Acts 1.21; Heb 2,3.   **1.3:** Acts 1.1.
1.4: Jn 20.31.   **1.5:** Mt 2.1; 1 Chron 24.10; 2 Chron 31.2.
1.9: Ex 30.7.   **1.11:** Lk 2.9; Acts 5.19.   **1.13:** Lk 1.30, 60.
1.15: Num 6.3; Lk 7.33.

¹⁷ and he will go before him in the spirit
　and power of E·lī′jah,
　to turn the hearts of the fathers to
　　the children,
　and the disobedient to the wisdom
　　of the just,
　to make ready for the Lord a people
　　prepared."
¹⁸ And Zĕch·a·rī′ah said to the angel,
"How shall I know this? For I am an
old man, and my wife is advanced in
years." ¹⁹ And the angel answered him,
"I am Gabriel, who stand in the presence of God; and I was sent to speak
to you, and to bring you this good news.
²⁰ And behold, you will be silent and
unable to speak until the day that these
things come to pass, because you did
not believe my words, which will be
fulfilled in their time." ²¹ And the
people were waiting for Zĕch·a·rī′ah,
and they wondered at his delay in the
temple. ²² And when he came out, he
could not speak to them, and they perceived that he had seen a vision in the
temple; and he made signs to them and
remained dumb. ²³ And when his time
of service was ended, he went to his
home.

24 After these days his wife Elizabeth conceived, and for five months
she hid herself, saying, ²⁵ "Thus the
Lord has done to me in the days when
he looked on me, to take away my
reproach among men."

26 In the sixth month the angel
Gabriel was sent from God to a city of
Galilee named Nazareth, ²⁷ to a virgin
betrothed to a man whose name was
Joseph, of the house of David; and the
virgin's name was Mary. ²⁸ And he came
to her and said, "Hail, O favored one,
the Lord is with you!"ᶜ ²⁹ But she was
greatly troubled at the saying, and
considered in her mind what sort of
greeting this might be. ³⁰ And the angel
said to her, "Do not be afraid, Mary,
for you have found favor with God.
³¹ And behold, you will conceive in
your womb and bear a son, and you
shall call his name Jesus.
³² He will be great, and will be called
　the Son of the Most High;
　and the Lord God will give to him
　　the throne of his father David,
³³ and he will reign over the house of
　　Jacob for ever;
　and of his kingdom there will be no
　　end."
³⁴ And Mary said to the angel, "How

shall this be, since I have no husband?"
³⁵ And the angel said to her,
"The Holy Spirit will come upon you,
　and the power of the Most High will
　　overshadow you;
therefore the child to be bornᵈ will
　be called holy,
　the Son of God.
³⁶ And behold, your kinswoman Elizabeth in her old age has also conceived
a son; and this is the sixth month with
her who was called barren. ³⁷ For with
God nothing will be impossible." ³⁸ And
Mary said, "Behold, I am the handmaid of the Lord; let it be to me according to your word." And the angel departed from her.

39 In those days Mary arose and
went with haste into the hill country,
to a city of Judah, ⁴⁰ and she entered
the house of Zĕch·a·rī′ah and greeted
Elizabeth. ⁴¹ And when Elizabeth heard
the greeting of Mary, the babe leaped
in her womb; and Elizabeth was filled
with the Holy Spirit ⁴² and she exclaimed with a loud cry, "Blessed are
you among women, and blessed is the
fruit of your womb! ⁴³ And why is this
granted me, that the mother of my
Lord should come to me? ⁴⁴ For behold,
when the voice of your greeting came
to my ears, the babe in my womb
leaped for joy. ⁴⁵ And blessed is she who
believed that there would beᵉ a fulfil
ment of what was spoken to her from
the Lord."
⁴⁶ And Mary said,
"My soul magnifies the Lord,
⁴⁷ and my spirit rejoices in God my
　　Savior,
⁴⁸ for he has regarded the low estate
　of his handmaiden.
For behold, henceforth all gen
　erations will call me blessed
⁴⁹ for he who is mighty has done grea
　things for me,
and holy is his name.
⁵⁰ And his mercy is on those who fear
　him
from generation to generation.
⁵¹ He has shown strength with his arm
he has scattered the proud in the
　imagination of their hearts

ᶜOther ancient authorities add *"Blessed are you among
women!"* ᵈOther ancient authorities add *of you*
ᵉOr *believed, for there will be*
1.17: Mt 11.14; 17.13; Mal 4.5.　**1.18:** Lk 1.34.
1.19: Dan 8.16; 9.21; Mt 18.10.　**1.25:** Gen 30.23; Is 4.1.
1.30: Lk 1.13.　**1.31:** Lk 2.21; Mt 1.21.
1.33: Mt 28.18; Dan 2.44.　**1.34:** Lk 1.18.
1.35: Mt 1.20.　**1.37:** Gen 18.14.　**1.42:** Lk 11.27-28.
1.46-55: 1 Sam 2.1-10.　**1.47:** 1 Tim 2.3; Tit 2.10; Jude 25

52 he has put down the mighty from their thrones,
and exalted those of low degree;
53 he has filled the hungry with good things,
and the rich he has sent empty away.
54 He has helped his servant Israel,
in remembrance of his mercy,
55 as he spoke to our fathers,
to Abraham and to his posterity for ever."

56 And Mary remained with her about three months, and returned to her home.

57 Now the time came for Elizabeth to be delivered, and she gave birth to a son. 58 And her neighbors and kinsfolk heard that the Lord had shown great mercy to her, and they rejoiced with her. 59 And on the eighth day they came to circumcise the child; and they would have named him Zĕch·a·rī′ah after his father, 60 but his mother said, "Not so; he shall be called John." 61 And they said to her, "None of your kindred is called by this name." 62 And they made signs to his father, inquiring what he would have him called. 63 And he asked for a writing tablet, and wrote, "His name is John." And they all marveled. 64 And immediately his mouth was opened and his tongue loosed, and he spoke, blessing God. 65 And fear came on all their neighbors. And all these things were talked about through all the hill country of Jū·dē′a; 66 and all who heard them laid them up in their hearts, saying, "What then will this child be?" For the hand of the Lord was with him.

67 And his father Zĕch·a·rī′ah was filled with the Holy Spirit, and prophesied, saying,
68 "Blessed be the Lord God of Israel,
for he has visited and redeemed his people,
69 and has raised up a horn of salvation for us
in the house of his servant David,
70 as he spoke by the mouth of his holy prophets from of old,
71 that we should be saved from our enemies,
and from the hand of all who hate us;
72 to perform the mercy promised to our fathers,
and to remember his holy covenant,
73 the oath which he swore to our father Abraham, 74 to grant us

that we, being delivered from the hand of our enemies,
might serve him without fear,
75 in holiness and righteousness before him all the days of our life.
76 And you, child, will be called the prophet of the Most High;
for you will go before the Lord to prepare his ways,
77 to give knowledge of salvation to his people
in the forgiveness of their sins,
78 through the tender mercy of our God,
when the day shall dawn upon*ᶠ* us from on high
79 to give light to those who sit in darkness and in the shadow of death,
to guide our feet into the way of peace."

80 And the child grew and became strong in spirit, and he was in the wilderness till the day of his manifestation to Israel.

2 In those days a decree went out from Caesar Augustus that all the world should be enrolled. 2 This was the first enrollment, when Quī·rĭn′ī·us was governor of Syria. 3 And all went to be enrolled, each to his own city. 4 And Joseph also went up from Galilee, from the city of Nazareth, to Jū·dē′a, to the city of David, which is called Bethlehem, because he was of the house and lineage of David, 5 to be enrolled with Mary his betrothed, who was with child. 6 And while they were there, the time came for her to be delivered. 7 And she gave birth to her first-born son and wrapped him in swaddling cloths, and laid him in a manger, because there was no place for them in the inn.

8 And in that region there were shepherds out in the field, keeping watch over their flock by night. 9 And an angel of the Lord appeared to them, and the glory of the Lord shone around them, and they were filled with fear. 10 And the angel said to them, "Be not afraid; for behold, I bring you good news of a great joy which will come to all the people; 11 for to you is born this day in the city of David a Savior, who

ᶠOr whereby the dayspring will visit. Other ancient authorities read since the dayspring has visited
1.55: Mic 7.20; Gen 17.7; 18.18; 22.17.
1.59: Lev 12.3; Gen 17.12.
1.63: Lk 1.13. 1.76: Lk 7.26; Mal 4.5. 1.77: Mk 1.4.
1.78: Mal 4.2; Eph 5.14. 1.79: Is 9.2; Mt 4.16.
1.80: Lk 2.40; 2.52. 2.1: Lk 3.1. 2.4: Lk 1.27.
2.9: Lk 1.11; Acts 5.19.
2.11: Jn 4.42; Acts 5.31; Mt 16.16; Acts 2.36.

is Christ the Lord. [12] And this will be a sign for you: you will find a babe wrapped in swaddling cloths and lying in a manger." [13] And suddenly there was with the angel a multitude of the heavenly host praising God and saying,
[14] "Glory to God in the highest,
and on earth peace among men with whom he is pleased!"[g]

15 When the angels went away from them into heaven, the shepherds said to one another, "Let us go over to Bethlehem and see this thing that has happened, which the Lord has made known to us." [16] And they went with haste, and found Mary and Joseph, and the babe lying in a manger. [17] And when they saw it they made known the saying which had been told them concerning this child; [18] and all who heard it wondered at what the shepherds told them. [19] But Mary kept all these things, pondering them in her heart. [20] And the shepherds returned, glorifying and praising God for all they had heard and seen, as it had been told them.

21 And at the end of eight days, when he was circumcised, he was called Jesus, the name given by the angel before he was conceived in the womb.

22 And when the time came for their purification according to the law of Moses, they brought him up to Jerusalem to present him to the Lord [23] (as it is written in the law of the Lord, "Every male that opens the womb shall be called holy to the Lord") [24] and to offer a sacrifice according to what is said in the law of the Lord, "a pair of turtledoves, or two young pigeons." [25] Now there was a man in Jerusalem, whose name was Sĭm'ē·on, and this man was righteous and devout, looking for the consolation of Israel, and the Holy Spirit was upon him. [26] And it had been revealed to him by the Holy Spirit that he should not see death before he had seen the Lord's Christ. [27] And inspired by the Spirit[h] he came into the temple; and when the parents brought in the child Jesus, to do for him according to the custom of the law, [28] he took him up in his arms and blessed God and said,
[29] "Lord, now lettest thou thy servant depart in peace,
according to thy word;

[30] for mine eyes have seen thy salvation
[31] which thou hast prepared in the presence of all peoples,
[32] a light for revelation to the Gentiles, and for glory to thy people Israel."

33 And his father and his mother marveled at what was said about him; [34] and Sĭm'ē·on blessed them and said to Mary his mother,
"Behold, this child is set for the fall and rising of many in Israel,
and for a sign that is spoken against
[35] (and a sword will pierce through your own soul also),
that thoughts out of many hearts may be revealed."

36 And there was a prophetess, Anna, the daughter of Phăn'ū–ĕl, of the tribe of Ăsh'er; she was of a great age, having lived with her husband seven years from her virginity, [37] and as a widow till she was eighty-four. She did not depart from the temple, worshiping with fasting and prayer night and day. [38] And coming up at that very hour she gave thanks to God, and spoke of him to all who were looking for the redemption of Jerusalem.

39 And when they had performed everything according to the law of the Lord, they returned into Galilee, to their own city, Nazareth. [40] And the child grew and became strong, filled with wisdom; and the favor of God was upon him.

41 Now his parents went to Jerusalem every year at the feast of the Passover. [42] And when he was twelve years old, they went up according to custom; [43] and when the feast was ended, as they were returning, the boy Jesus stayed behind in Jerusalem. His parents did not know it, [44] but supposing him to be in the company they went a day's journey, and they sought him among their kinsfolk and acquaintances; [45] and when they did not find him, they returned to Jerusalem, seeking him. [46] After three days they found him in the temple, sitting

[g]Other ancient authorities read *peace, good will among men*   [h]*Or in the Spirit*
2.12: 1 Sam 2.34; 2 Kings 19.29; Is 7.14.
2.14: Lk 19.38; 3.22.   2.19: Lk 2.51.
2.21: Lk 1.59, 31; Mt 1.25.   2.22-24: Lev 12.2-8.
2.23: Ex 13.2, 12.   2.25: Lk 2.38; 23.51.
2.30: Is 52.10; Lk 3.6.
2.32: Is 42.6; 49.6; Acts 13.47; 26.23.
2.36: Acts 21.9; Josh 19.24; 1 Tim 5.9.
2.40: Judg 13.24; 1 Sam 2.26.
2.41: Deut 16.1-8; Ex 23.15.

among the teachers, listening to them and asking them questions; [47] and all who heard him were amazed at his understanding and his answers. [48] And when they saw him they were astonished; and his mother said to him, "Son, why have you treated us so? Behold, your father and I have been looking for you anxiously." [49] And he said to them, "How is it that you sought me? Did you not know that I must be in my Father's house?" [50] And they did not understand the saying which he spoke to them. [51] And he went down with them and came to Nazareth, and was obedient to them; and his mother kept all these things in her heart.

[52] And Jesus increased in wisdom and in stature,[i] and in favor with God and man.

3 In the fifteenth year of the reign of Tī·bē′rĭ·us Caesar, Pŏn′tĭ·us Pilate being governor of Jü·dē′a, and Hĕr′od being tetrarch of Galilee, and his brother Philip tetrarch of the region of Ī·tü·raē′a and Trăch·o·nī′tĭs, and Lȳ·sā′nĭ–as tetrarch of Ăb·ĭ·lē′nē, [2] in the high-priesthood of Ăn′năs and Cāi′a-phas, the word of God came to John the son of Zĕch·a·rī′ah in the wilderness; [3] and he went into all the region about the Jordan, preaching a baptism of repentance for the forgiveness of sins. [4] As it is written in the book of the words of Ī·sāi′ah the prophet,

"The voice of one crying in the wilderness:
Prepare the way of the Lord,
make his paths straight.
[5] Every valley shall be filled,
and every mountain and hill shall be brought low,
and the crooked shall be made straight,
and the rough ways shall be made smooth;
[6] and all flesh shall see the salvation of God."

[7] He said therefore to the multitudes that came out to be baptized by him, "You brood of vipers! Who warned you to flee from the wrath to come? [8] Bear fruits that befit repentance, and do not begin to say to yourselves, 'We have Abraham as our father'; for I tell you, God is able from these stones to raise up children to Abraham. [9] Even now the axe is laid to the root of the trees; every tree therefore that does not bear good fruit is cut down and thrown into the fire."

[10] And the multitudes asked him, "What then shall we do?" [11] And he answered them, "He who has two coats, let him share with him who has none; and he who has food, let him do likewise." [12] Tax collectors also came to be baptized, and said to him, "Teacher, what shall we do?" [13] And he said to them, "Collect no more than is appointed you." [14] Soldiers also asked him, "And we, what shall we do?" And he said to them, "Rob no one by violence or by false accusation, and be content with your wages."

[15] As the people were in expectation, and all men questioned in their hearts concerning John, whether perhaps he were the Christ, [16] John answered them all, "I baptize you with water; but he who is mightier than I is coming, the thong of whose sandals I am not worthy to untie; he will baptize you with the Holy Spirit and with fire. [17] His winnowing fork is in his hand, to clear his threshing floor, and to gather the wheat into his granary, but the chaff he will burn with unquenchable fire."

[18] So, with many other exhortations, he preached good news to the people. [19] But Hĕr′od the tetrarch, who had been reproved by him for Hĕ·rō′dĭ–as, his brother's wife, and for all the evil things that Herod had done, [20] added this to them all, that he shut up John in prison.

[21] Now when all the people were baptized, and when Jesus also had been baptized and was praying, the heaven was opened, [22] and the Holy Spirit descended upon him in bodily form, as a dove, and a voice came from heaven, "Thou art my beloved Son;[j] with thee I am well pleased."[k]

[23] Jesus, when he began his min-

[i] Or *years* [j] Or *my Son, my* (or *the*) *Beloved*
[k] Other ancient authorities read *today I have begotten thee*
2.48: Mk 3.31-35. **2.51:** Lk 2.19. **2.52:** Lk 1.80; 2.40.
3.1: Lk 23.1; 9.7; 13.31; 23.7.
3.2: Jn 18.13; Acts 4.6; Mt 26.3; Jn 11.49.
3.3-9: Mt 3.1-10; Mk 1.1-5; Jn 1.6, 23.
3.4-6: Is 40.3-5. **3.6:** Lk 2.30. **3.7:** Mt 12.34; 23.33.
3.8: Jn 8.33, 39. **3.9:** Mt 7.19; Heb 6.7-8.
3.11: Lk 6.29. **3.15:** Acts 13.25; Jn 1.19-22.
3.16-18: Mt 3.11-12; Mk 1.7-8; Jn 1.26-27, 33; Acts 1.5;
11.16; 19.4. **3.19-20:** Mt 14.3-4; Mk 6.17-18.
3.21-22: Mt 3.13-17; Mk 1.9-11; Jn 1.29-34.
3.21: Lk 5.16; 6.12; 9.18; 9.28; 11.1; Mk 1.35.
3.22: Ps 2.7; Is 42.1; Lk 9.35; Acts 10.38; 2 Pet 1.17.
3.23-38: Mt 1.1-17; Gen 5.3-32; 11.10-26; Ruth 4.18-22;
1 Chron 1.1-4, 24.28; 2.1-15. **3.23:** Jn 8.57; Lk 1.27.

istry, was about thirty years of age, being the son (as was supposed) of Joseph, the son of Hēʹlī, ²⁴the son of Măt′thạt, the son of Lēʹvī, the son of Mĕl′chī, the son of Jăn′nạ-ī, the son of Joseph, ²⁵the son of Măt·tạ·thīʹạs, the son of Āʹmŏs, the son of Nāʹhụm, the son of Ĕsʹlī, the son of Năgʹgạ-ī, ²⁶the son of Māʹạth, the son of Măt·tạ·thīʹạs, the son of Sĕmʹē-ĭn, the son of Jōʹsĕch, the son of Jōʹdạ, ²⁷the son of Jō-ănʹạn, the son of Rhēʹsạ, the son of Zĕ·rŭbʹbạ·bĕl, the son of Shĕ-ălʹ-tĭ-ĕl,¹ the son of Nēʹrī, ²⁸the son of Mĕlʹchī, the son of Ădʹdī, the son of Cōʹsạm, the son of Ĕl·māʹdạm, the son of Ēr, ²⁹the son of Joshua, the son of Ē·lī·ēʹzẹr, the son of Jōʹrĭm, the son of Măt′thạt, the son of Lēʹvī, ³⁰the son of Sĭmʹē·ọn, the son of Judah, the son of Joseph, the son of Jōʹnạm, the son of Ē·līʹạ·kịm, ³¹the son of Mēʹlĕ-ä, the son of Mĕnʹnạ, the son of Măt′tạ·thạ, the son of Nathan, the son of David, ³²the son of Jesse, the son of Ōʹbĕd, the son of Bōʹăz, the son of Sāʹlạ, the son of Năhʹshọn, ³³the son of Ăm·mĭnʹ-ạ·dăb, the son of Ăd·mĭn, the son of Ärʹnī, the son of Hĕzʹrọn, the son of Pĕrʹĕz, the son of Judah, ³⁴the son of Jacob, the son of Isaac, the son of Abraham, the son of Tēʹrạh, the son of Nāʹhôr, ³⁵the son of Sēʹrụg, the son of Rēʹu, the son of Pēʹlĕg, the son of Ēʹbẹr, the son of Shēʹlạh, ³⁶the son of Cā-īʹnạn, the son of Är·phāʹxăd, the son of Shĕm, the son of Noah, the son of Lāʹmĕch, ³⁷the son of Mĕ·thü·sẹʹlạh, the son of Ēʹnọch, the son of Jărʹẹd, the son of Mạ·hāʹlạ·lēʺ-ĕl, the son of Cā-īʹnạn, ³⁸the son of Ēʹnọs, the son of Seth, the son of Adam, the son of God.

4 And Jesus, full of the Holy Spirit, returned from the Jordan, and was led by the Spirit ²for forty days in the wilderness, tempted by the devil. And he ate nothing in those days; and when they were ended, he was hungry. ³The devil said to him, "If you are the Son of God, command this stone to become bread." ⁴And Jesus answered him, "It is written, 'Man shall not live by bread alone.'" ⁵And the devil took him up, and showed him all the kingdoms of the world in a moment of time, ⁶and said to him, "To you I will give all this authority and their glory; for it has been delivered to me, and I give it to whom I will. ⁷If you, then, will worship me, it shall all be yours." ⁸And Jesus answered him, "It is written,

'You shall worship the Lord your God,
and him only shall you serve.'"

⁹And he took him to Jerusalem, and set him on the pinnacle of the temple, and said to him, "If you are the Son of God, throw yourself down from here; ¹⁰for it is written,

'He will give his angels charge of you, to guard you,'

¹¹and

'On their hands they will bear you up,
lest you strike your foot against a stone.'"

¹²And Jesus answered him, "It is said, 'You shall not tempt the Lord your God.'" ¹³And when the devil had ended every temptation, he departed from him until an opportune time.

14 And Jesus returned in the power of the Spirit into Galilee, and a report concerning him went out through all the surrounding country. ¹⁵And he taught in their synagogues, being glorified by all.

16 And he came to Nazareth, where he had been brought up; and he went to the synagogue, as his custom was, on the sabbath day. And he stood up to read; ¹⁷and there was given to him the book of the prophet Ī·sāiʹạh. He opened the book and found the place where it was written,

¹⁸"The Spirit of the Lord is upon me,
because he has anointed me to
preach good news to the poor.
He has sent me to proclaim release
to the captives
and recovering of sight to the blind,
to set at liberty those who are oppressed,
¹⁹to proclaim the acceptable year of
the Lord."

²⁰And he closed the book, and gave it back to the attendant, and sat down; and the eyes of all in the synagogue were fixed on him. ²¹And he began to say to them, "Today this scripture has been fulfilled in your hearing." ²²And all spoke well of him, and wondered at the gracious words which proceeded

ʹGreek *Salathiel*
4.1–13: Mt 4.1–11; Mk 1.12–13.　　**4.2:** Deut 9.9; 1 Kings 19.8.
4.4: Deut 8.3.　**4.6:** 1 Jn 5.19.　**4.8:** Deut 6.13.
4.10–11: Ps 91.11–12.　**4.12:** Deut 6.16.　**4.13:** Lk 22.28.
4.14: Mt 4.12; Mk 1.14; Mt 9.26; Lk 4.37.
4.15: Mt 4.23; 9.35; 11.1.
4.16–30: Mt 13.53–58; Mk 6.1–6; Acts 13.14–16.
4.18–19: Is 61.1–2.　**4.22:** Jn 6.42; 7.15.

out of his mouth; and they said, "Is not this Joseph's son?" ²³And he said to them, "Doubtless you will quote to me this proverb, 'Physician, heal yourself; what we have heard you did at Cạ·pẽr'nạ–ụm, do here also in your own country.' " ²⁴And he said, "Truly, I say to you, no prophet is acceptable in his own country. ²⁵But in truth, I tell you, there were many widows in Israel in the days of Ē·lī'jạh, when the heaven was shut up three years and six months, when there came a great famine over all the land; ²⁶and Ē·lī'jạh was sent to none of them but only to Zăr'ẹ·phăth, in the land of Sī'dŏn, to a woman who was a widow. ²⁷And there were many lepers in Israel in the time of the prophet Ē·lī'shạ; and none of them was cleansed, but only Nā'ạ·măn the Syrian." ²⁸When they heard this, all in the synagogue were filled with wrath. ²⁹And they rose up and put him out of the city, and led him to the brow of the hill on which their city was built, that they might throw him down headlong. ³⁰But passing through the midst of them he went away.

31 And he went down to Cạ·pẽr'nạ–ụm, a city of Galilee. And he was teaching them on the sabbath; ³²and they were astonished at his teaching, for his word was with authority. ³³And in the synagogue there was a man who had the spirit of an unclean demon; and he cried out with a loud voice, ³⁴"Ah!ᵐ What have you to do with us, Jesus of Nazareth? Have you come to destroy us? I know who you are, the Holy One of God." ³⁵But Jesus rebuked him, saying, "Be silent, and come out of him!" And when the demon had thrown him down in the midst, he came out of him, having done him no harm. ³⁶And they were all amazed and said to one another, "What is this word? For with authority and power he commands the unclean spirits, and they come out." ³⁷And reports of him went out into every place in the surrounding region.

38 And he arose and left the synagogue, and entered Simon's house. Now Simon's mother-in-law was ill with a high fever, and they besought him for her. ³⁹And he stood over her and rebuked the fever, and it left her; and immediately she rose and served them.

40 Now when the sun was setting, all those who had any that were sick with various diseases brought them to him; and he laid his hands on every one of them and healed them. ⁴¹And demons also came out of many, crying, "You are the Son of God!" But he rebuked them, and would not allow them to speak, because they knew that he was the Christ.

42 And when it was day he departed and went into a lonely place. And the people sought him and came to him, and would have kept him from leaving them; ⁴³but he said to them, "I must preach the good news of the kingdom of God to the other cities also; for I was sent for this purpose." ⁴⁴And he was preaching in the synagogues of Jü·dē'ạ.ⁿ

5 While the people pressed upon him to hear the word of God, he was standing by the lake of Gĕn·nĕs'ạ·rĕt. ²And he saw two boats by the lake; but the fishermen had gone out of them and were washing their nets. ³Getting into one of the boats, which was Simon's, he asked him to put out a little from the land. And he sat down and taught the people from the boat. ⁴And when he had ceased speaking, he said to Simon, "Put out into the deep and let down your nets for a catch." ⁵And Simon answered, "Master, we toiled all night and took nothing! But at your word I will let down the nets." ⁶And when they had done this, they enclosed a great shoal of fish; and as their nets were breaking, ⁷they beckoned to their partners in the other boat to come and help them. And they came and filled both the boats, so that they began to sink. ⁸But when Simon Peter saw it, he fell down at Jesus' knees, saying, "Depart from me, for I am a sinful man, O Lord." ⁹For he was astonished, and all that were with him, at the catch of fish which they had taken; ¹⁰and so also were James and John, sons of Zĕb'ẹ·dee, who were partners with Simon. And Jesus said to Simon, "Do not be afraid;

ⁿOr Let us alone
ᵐOther ancient authorities read Galilee
4.23: Mk 1.21; 2.1; Jn 4.46.   4.24: Jn 4.44.
4.25: 1 Kings 17.1, 8-16; 18.1; Jas 5.17-18.
4.27: 2 Kings 5.1-14.   4.29: Acts 7.58; Num 15.35.
4.30: Jn 8.59; 10.39.   4.31-37: Mk 1.21-28.
4.32: Mt 7.28; 13.54; 22.33; Mk 11.18; Jn 7.46.
4.37: Lk 4.14; 5.15; Mt 9.26.
4.38-41: Mt 8.14-17; Mk 1.29-34.   4.42-43: Mk 1.35-38.
4.44: Mt 4.23; Mk 1.39; Mt 9.35.
5.1-11: Mt 4.18-22; Mk 1.16-20; Jn 1.40-42; 21.1-19.
5.3: Mt 13.1-2; Mk 4.1.   5.5: Lk 8.24, 45; 9.33, 49; 17.13.

henceforth you will be catching men."
11 And when they had brought their
boats to land, they left everything
and followed him.
12 While he was in one of the cities,
there came a man full of leprosy; and
when he saw Jesus, he fell on his
face and besought him, "Lord, if you
will, you can make me clean." 13 And
he stretched out his hand, and touched
him, saying, "I will; be clean." And
immediately the leprosy left him. 14 And
he charged him to tell no one; but "go
and show yourself to the priest, and
make an offering for your cleansing,
as Moses commanded, for a proof to
the people."[o] 15 But so much the more
the report went abroad concerning
him; and great multitudes gathered to
hear and to be healed of their infirmities. 16 But he withdrew to the wilderness and prayed.
17 On one of those days, as he was
teaching, there were Phăr′ị·seeş and
teachers of the law sitting by, who had
come from every village of Galilee
and Jü·dē′ạ and from Jerusalem; and
the power of the Lord was with him to
heal.[p] 18 And behold, men were bringing on a bed a man who was paralyzed,
and they sought to bring him in and
lay him before Jesus;[q] 19 but finding
no way to bring him in, because of the
crowd, they went up on the roof and
let him down with his bed through the
tiles into the midst before Jesus. 20 And
when he saw their faith he said, "Man,
your sins are forgiven you." 21 And the
scribes and the Phăr′ị·seeş began to
question, saying, "Who is this that
speaks blasphemies? Who can forgive sins but God only?" 22 When
Jesus perceived their questionings, he
answered them, "Why do you question
in your hearts? 23 Which is easier, to
say, 'Your sins are forgiven you,' or
to say, 'Rise and walk'? 24 But that you
may know that the Son of man has
authority on earth to forgive sins"—
he said to the man who was paralyzed—"I say to you, rise, take up
your bed and go home." 25 And immediately he rose before them, and took up
that on which he lay, and went home,
glorifying God. 26 And amazement
seized them all, and they glorified
God and were filled with awe, saying,
"We have seen strange things today."
27 After this he went out, and saw
a tax collector, named Lē′vī, sitting
at the tax office; and he said to him,
"Follow me." 28 And he left everything,
and rose and followed him.
29 And Lē′vī made him a great feast
in his house; and there was a large
company of tax collectors and others
sitting at table[r] with them. 30 And the
Phăr′ị·seeş and their scribes murmured against his disciples, saying,
"Why do you eat and drink with tax
collectors and sinners?" 31 And Jesus
answered them, "Those who are well
have no need of a physician, but those
who are sick; 32 I have not come to
call the righteous, but sinners to repentance."
33 And they said to him, "The disciples of John fast often and offer
prayers, and so do the disciples of the
Phăr′ị·seeş, but yours eat and drink."
34 And Jesus said to them, "Can you
make wedding guests fast while the
bridegroom is with them? 35 The days
will come, when the bridegroom is
taken away from them, and then they
will fast in those days." 36 He told them
a parable also: "No one tears a piece
from a new garment and puts it upon
an old garment; if he does, he will
tear the new, and the piece from the
new will not match the old. 37 And no
one puts new wine into old wineskins;
if he does, the new wine will burst the
skins and it will be spilled, and the
skins will be destroyed. 38 But new
wine must be put into fresh wineskins. 39 And no one after drinking old
wine desires new; for he says, 'The
old is good.'"[s]

6 On a sabbath,[t] while he was
going through the grainfields, his
disciples plucked and ate some heads of
grain, rubbing them in their hands.
2 But some of the Phăr′ị·seeş said,
"Why are you doing what is not lawful
to do on the sabbath?" 3 And Jesus
answered, "Have you not read what

[o] Greek *to them*
[p] Other ancient authorities read *was present to heal them*
[q] Greek *him*
[r] Greek *reclining*
[s] Other ancient authorities read *better*
[t] Other ancient authorities read *On the second first sabbath* (on the second sabbath after the first)

5.12-16: Mt 8.1-4; Mk 1.40-45; Lk 17.11-19.
5.14: Lev 13.49; 14.2-32. **5.15:** Lk 4.14, 37; Mt 9.26.
5.16: Lk 3.21; 6.12; 9.18, 28; 11.1.
5.17-26: Mt 9.1-8; Mk 2.1-12; Jn 5.1-9.
5.17: Mt 15.1; Mk 5.30; Lk 6.19. **5.20:** Lk 7.48-49.
5.27-32: Mt 9.9-13; Mk 2.13-17.
5.30: Lk 15.1-2.
5.32: 1 Tim 1.15. **5.33-38:** Mt 9.14-17; Mk 2.18-22.
5.33: Lk 7.18; 11.1; Jn 3.25-26. **5.35:** Lk 9.22; 17.22.
6.1-5: Mt 12.1-8; Mk 2.23-28. **6.1:** Deut 23.25.
6.2: Ex 20.10; 23.12; Deut 5.14. **6.3:** 1 Sam 21.1-6.

David did when he was hungry, he and those who were with him: ⁴how he entered the house of God, and took and ate the bread of the Presence, which it is not lawful for any but the priests to eat, and also gave it to those with him?" ⁵And he said to them, "The Son of man is lord of the sabbath."

6 On another sabbath, when he entered the synagogue and taught, a man was there whose right hand was withered. ⁷And the scribes and the Phăr'i·seeṣ watched him, to see whether he would heal on the sabbath, so that they might find an accusation against him. ⁸But he knew their thoughts, and he said to the man who had the withered hand, "Come and stand here," And he rose and stood there. ⁹And Jesus said to them, "I ask you, is it lawful on the sabbath to do good or to do harm, to save life or to destroy it?" ¹⁰And he looked around on them all, and said to him, "Stretch out your hand." And he did so, and his hand was restored. ¹¹But they were filled with fury and discussed with one another what they might do to Jesus.

12 In these days he went out to the mountain to pray; and all night he continued in prayer to God. ¹³And when it was day, he called his disciples, and chose from them twelve, whom he named apostles; ¹⁴Simon, whom he named Peter, and Andrew his brother, and James and John, and Philip, and Bartholomew, ¹⁵and Matthew, and Thomas, and James the son of Ăl-phaē'us, and Simon who was called the Zealot, ¹⁶and Judas the son of James, and Judas Ĭs·căr'ĭ·ọt, who became a traitor.

17 And he came down with them and stood on a level place, with a great crowd of his disciples and a great multitude of people from all Jü·dē'a and Jerusalem and the seacoast of Tȳre and Sī'dŏn, who came to hear him and to be healed of their diseases; ¹⁸and those who were troubled with unclean spirits were cured. ¹⁹And all the crowd sought to touch him, for power came forth from him and healed them all.

20 And he lifted up his eyes on his disciples, and said:
"Blessed are you poor, for yours is the kingdom of God.

21 "Blessed are you that hunger now, for you shall be satisfied.
"Blessed are you that weep now, for you shall laugh.
22 "Blessed are you when men hate you, and when they exclude you and revile you, and cast out your name as evil, on account of the Son of man! ²³Rejoice in that day, and leap for joy, for behold, your reward is great in heaven; for so their fathers did to the prophets.
24 "But woe to you that are rich, for you have received your consolation.
25 "Woe to you that are full now, for you shall hunger.
"Woe to you that laugh now, for you shall mourn and weep.
26 "Woe to you, when all men speak well of you, for so their fathers did to the false prophets.
27 "But I say to you that hear, Love your enemies, do good to those who hate you, ²⁸bless those who curse you, pray for those who abuse you. ²⁹To him who strikes you on the cheek, offer the other also; and from him who takes away your coat do not withhold even your shirt. ³⁰Give to every one who begs from you; and of him who takes away your goods do not ask them again. ³¹And as you wish that men would do to you, do so to them.
32 "If you love those who love you, what credit is that to you? For even sinners love those who love them. ³³And if you do good to those who do good to you, what credit is that to you? For even sinners do the same. ³⁴And if you lend to those from whom you hope to receive, what credit is that to you? Even sinners lend to sinners, to receive as much again. ³⁵But love your enemies, and do good, and lend, expecting nothing in return;ᵘ and your reward will be great, and you will be sons of the Most High; for he is kind to the ungrateful and the selfish. ³⁶Be merciful, even as your Father is merciful.
37 "Judge not, and you will not be

ᵘOther ancient authorities read *despairing of no man*
6.4: Lev 24.9. 6.6-11: Mt 12.9-14; Mk 3.1-6.
6.12-16: Mk 3.13-19; Mt 10.2-4; Acts 1.13.
6.12: Lk 3.21; 5.16; 9.18, 28; 11.1.
6.17-19: Mt 5.1-2; 4.24-25; Mk 3.7-12.
6.19: Mk 3.10; Mt 9.21; 14.36; Lk 5.17.
6.20-23: Mt 5.3-12. 6.22: 1 Pet 4.14; Jn 9.22; 16.2.
6.24-26: Lk 10.13-15; 11.38-52; 17.1; 21.23; 22.22.
6.24: Lk 16.25; Jas 5.1-5; Mt 6.2.
6.27-30: Mt 5.39-44; Rom 12.17; 1 Cor 6.7.
6.31: Mt 7.12. 6.32-36: Mt 5.44-48. 6.35: Mt 5.9.
6.37-38: Mt 7.1-2; Rom 2.1.

judged; condemn not, and you will not be condemned; forgive, and you will be forgiven; [38] give, and it will be given to you; good measure, pressed down, shaken together, running over, will be put into your lap. For the measure you give will be the measure you get back."

39 He also told them a parable: "Can a blind man lead a blind man? Will they not both fall into a pit? [40] A disciple is not above his teacher, but every one when he is fully taught will be like his teacher. [41] Why do you see the speck that is in your brother's eye, but do not notice the log that is in your own eye? [42] Or how can you say to your brother, 'Brother, let me take out the speck that is in your eye,' when you yourself do not see the log that is in your own eye? You hypocrite, first take the log out of your own eye, and then you will see clearly to take out the speck that is in your brother's eye.

43 "For no good tree bears bad fruit, nor again does a bad tree bear good fruit; [44] for each tree is known by its own fruit. For figs are not gathered from thorns, nor are grapes picked from a bramble bush. [45] The good man out of the good treasure of his heart produces good, and the evil man out of his evil treasure produces evil; for out of the abundance of the heart his mouth speaks.

46 "Why do you call me 'Lord, Lord,' and not do what I tell you? [47] Every one who comes to me and hears my words and does them, I will show you what he is like: [48] he is like a man building a house, who dug deep, and laid the foundation upon rock; and when a flood arose, the stream broke against that house, and could not shake it, because it had been well built.[w] [49] But he who hears and does not do them is like a man who built a house on the ground without a foundation; against which the stream broke, and immediately it fell, and the ruin of that house was great."

7 After he had ended all his sayings in the hearing of the people he entered Ca·pēr′na–um. [2] Now a centurion had a slave who was dear[x] to him, who was sick and at the point of death. [3] When he heard of Jesus, he sent to him elders of the Jews, asking

him to come and heal his slave. [4] And when they came to Jesus, they besought him earnestly, saying, "He is worthy to have you do this for him, [5] for he loves our nation, and he built us our synagogue." [6] And Jesus went with them. When he was not far from the house, the centurion sent friends to him, saying to him, "Lord, do not trouble yourself, for I am not worthy to have you come under my roof; [7] therefore I did not presume to come to you. But say the word, and let my servant be healed. [8] For I am a man set under authority, with soldiers under me: and I say to one, 'Go,' and he goes; and to another, 'Come,' and he comes; and to my slave, 'Do this,' and he does it." [9] When Jesus heard this he marveled at him, and turned and said to the multitude that followed him, "I tell you, not even in Israel have I found such faith." [10] And when those who had been sent returned to the house, they found the slave well.

11 Soon afterward[y] he went to a city called Nā′in, and his disciples and a great crowd went with him. [12] As he drew near to the gate of the city, behold, a man who had died was being carried out, the only son of his mother, and she was a widow; and a large crowd from the city was with her. [13] And when the Lord saw her, he had compassion on her and said to her, "Do not weep." [14] And he came and touched the bier, and the bearers stood still. And he said, "Young man, I say to you, arise." [15] And the dead man sat up, and began to speak. And he gave him to his mother. [16] Fear seized them all; and they glorified God, saying, "A great prophet has arisen among us!" and "God has visited his people!" [17] And this report concerning him spread through the whole of Jü·dē′a and all the surrounding country.

18 The disciples of John told him of all these things. [19] And John, calling to him two of his disciples, sent them to the Lord, saying, "Are you he who

[w] Other ancient authorities read *founded upon the rock*
[x] Or *valuable*   [y] Other ancient authorities read *Next day*
6.38: Mk 4.24; Acts 20.35.   **6.39:** Mt 15.14.
6.40: Mt 10.24-25; Jn 13.16; 15.20.   **6.41-42:** Mt 7.3-5.
6.43-45: Mt 7.18-19; 12.33-35; Jas 3.11-12.
6.45: Mk 7.20.   **6.46:** Mt 7.21.
6.47-49: Mt 7.24-27; Jas 1.22-25.
7.1-10: Mt 8.5-10, 13; Jn 4.46-53.   **7.5:** Acts 10.2.
7.11-17: Mk 5.21-24, 35-43; Jn 11.1-44; 1 Kings 17.17-24;
2 Kings 4.32-37.
7.13: Lk 7.19; 10.1; 11.39; 12.42; 13.15; 17.5-6; 18.6;
19.8; 22.61; 24.3.   **7.16:** Lk 7.39; 24.19; Mt 21.11; Jn 6.14.
7.18-35: Mt 11.2-19.

is to come, or shall we look for another?" [20]And when the men had come to him, they said, "John the Baptist has sent us to you, saying, 'Are you he who is to come, or shall we look for another?'" [21]In that hour he cured many of diseases and plagues and evil spirits, and on many that were blind he bestowed sight. [22]And he answered them, "Go and tell John what you have seen and heard: the blind receive their sight, the lame walk, lepers are cleansed, and the deaf hear, the dead are raised up, the poor have good news preached to them. [23]And blessed is he who takes no offense at me."

24 When the messengers of John had gone, he began to speak to the crowds concerning John: "What did you go out into the wilderness to behold? A reed shaken by the wind? [25]What then did you go out to see? A man clothed in soft clothing? Behold, those who are gorgeously appareled and live in luxury are in kings' courts. [26]What then did you go out to see? A prophet? Yes, I tell you, and more than a prophet. [27]This is he of whom it is written,

'Behold, I send my messenger before thy face,
who shall prepare thy way before thee.'

[28]I tell you, among those born of women none is greater than John; yet he who is least in the kingdom of God is greater than he." [29](When they heard this all the people and the tax collectors justified God, having been baptized with the baptism of John; [30]but the Phăr′ĭ-seeş and the lawyers rejected the purpose of God for themselves, not having been baptized by him.)

31 "To what then shall I compare the men of this generation, and what are they like? [32]They are like children sitting in the market place and calling to one another,

'We piped to you, and you did not dance;
we wailed, and you did not weep.'

[33]For John the Baptist has come eating no bread and drinking no wine; and you say, 'He has a demon.' [34]The Son of man has come eating and drinking; and you say, 'Behold, a glutton and a drunkard, a friend of tax collectors and sinners!' [35]Yet wisdom is justified by all her children."

36 One of the Phăr′ĭ-seeş asked him to eat with him, and he went into the Pharisee's house, and took his place at table. [37]And behold, a woman of the city, who was a sinner, when she learned that he was at table in the Phăr′ĭ-see′ş house, brought an alabaster flask of ointment, [38]and standing behind him at his feet, weeping, she began to wet his feet with her tears, and wiped them with the hair of her head, and kissed his feet, and anointed them with the ointment. [39]Now when the Phăr′ĭ-see who had invited him saw it, he said to himself, "If this man were a prophet, he would have known who and what sort of woman this is who is touching him, for she is a sinner." [40]And Jesus answering said to him, "Simon, I have something to say to you." And he answered, "What is it, Teacher?" [41]"A certain creditor had two debtors; one owed five hundred denarii, and the other fifty. [42]When they could not pay, he forgave them both. Now which of them will love him more?" [43]Simon answered, "The one, I suppose, to whom he forgave more." And he said to him, "You have judged rightly." [44]Then turning toward the woman he said to Simon, "Do you see this woman? I entered your house, you gave me no water for my feet, but she has wet my feet with her tears and wiped them with her hair. [45]You gave me no kiss, but from the time I came in she has not ceased to kiss my feet. [46]You did not anoint my head with oil, but she has anointed my feet with ointment. [47]Therefore I tell you, her sins, which are many, are forgiven, for she loved much; but he who is forgiven little, loves little." [48]And he said to her, "Your sins are forgiven." [49]Then those who were at table with him began to say among themselves, "Who is this, who even forgives sins?" [50]And he said to the woman, "Your faith has saved you; go in peace."

8 Soon afterward he went on through cities and villages, preaching and bringing the good news of the

7.21: Mt 4.23; Mk 3.10.
7.22: Is 29.18-19; 35.5-6; 61.1; Lk 4.18-19.
7.27: Mal 3.1; Mk 1.2.   7.29-30: Mt 21.32; Lk 3.12.
7.33: Lk 1.15.   7.34: Lk 5.29; 15.1-2; 7.36-50.
7.36-50: Mt 26.6-13; Mk 14.3-9; Jn 12.1-8.
7.36: Lk 11.37; 14.1.
7.39: Lk 7.16; 24.19; Mt 21.11; Jn 6.14.
7.42: Mt 18.25.   7.43: Lk 10.28.
7.48: Mt 9.2; Mk 2.5; Lk 5.20.
7.50: Mt 9.22; Mk 5.34; Lk 8.48.
8.1-3: Lk 4.15; Mk 15.40-41; Mt 27.55-56; Lk 23.49.

kingdom of God. And the twelve were with him, ²and also some women who had been healed of evil spirits and infirmities: Mary, called Măg′dạ·lēne, from whom seven demons had gone out, ³and Jō-ăn′nạ, the wife of Chü′zạ, Hĕr′ọd's steward, and Susanna, and many others, who provided for them² out of their means.

4 And when a great crowd came together and people from town after town came to him, he said in a parable: ⁵"A sower went out to sow his seed; and as he sowed, some fell along the path, and was trodden under foot, and the birds of the air devoured it. ⁶And some fell on the rock; and as it grew up, it withered away, because it had no moisture. ⁷And some fell among thorns; and the thorns grew with it and choked it. ⁸And some fell into good soil and grew, and yielded a hundredfold." As he said this, he called out, "He who has ears to hear, let him hear."

9 And when his disciples asked him what this parable meant, ¹⁰he said, "To you it has been given to know the secrets of the kingdom of God; but for others they are in parables, so that seeing they may not see, and hearing they may not understand. ¹¹Now the parable is this: The seed is the word of God. ¹²The ones along the path are those who have heard; then the devil comes and takes away the word from their hearts, that they may not believe and be saved. ¹³And the ones on the rock are those who, when they hear the word, receive it with joy; but these have no root, they believe for a while and in time of temptation fall away. ¹⁴And as for what fell among the thorns, they are those who hear, but as they go on their way they are choked by the cares and riches and pleasures of life, and their fruit does not mature. ¹⁵And as for that in the good soil, they are those who, hearing the word, hold it fast in an honest and good heart, and bring forth fruit with patience.

16 "No one after lighting a lamp covers it with a vessel, or puts it under a bed, but puts it on a stand, that those who enter may see the light. ¹⁷For nothing is hid that shall not be made manifest, nor anything secret that shall not be known and come to light. ¹⁸Take heed then how you hear;

for to him who has will more be given, and from him who has not, even what he thinks that he has will be taken away."

19 Then his mother and his brothers came to him, but they could not reach him for the crowd. ²⁰And he was told, "Your mother and your brothers are standing outside, desiring to see you." ²¹But he said to them, "My mother and my brothers are those who hear the word of God and do it."

22 One day he got into a boat with his disciples, and he said to them, "Let us go across to the other side of the lake." So they set out, ²³and as they sailed he fell asleep. And a storm of wind came down on the lake, and they were filling with water, and were in danger. ²⁴And they went and woke him saying, "Master, Master, we are perishing!" And he awoke and rebuked the wind and the raging waves; and they ceased, and there was a calm. ²⁵He said to them, "Where is your faith?" And they were afraid, and they marveled, saying to one another, "Who then is this, that he commands even wind and water, and they obey him?"

26 Then they arrived at the country of the Gĕr′ạ·sēneṣ,ᵃ which is opposite Galilee. ²⁷And as he stepped out on land, there met him a man from the city who had demons; for a long time he had worn no clothes, and he lived not in a house but among the tombs. ²⁸When he saw Jesus, he cried out and fell down before him, and said with a loud voice, "What have you to do with me, Jesus, Son of the Most High God? I beseech you, do not torment me." ²⁹For he had commanded the unclean spirit to come out of the man. (For many a time it had seized him; he was kept under guard, and bound with chains and fetters, but he broke the bonds and was driven by the demon into the desert.) ³⁰Jesus then asked him, "What is your name?" And he

ᶻOther ancient authorities read *him*
ᵃOther ancient authorities read *Gadarenes*, others *Gergesenes*

8.4-8: Mt 13.1-9; Mk 4.1-9.   8.8: Mt 11.15.
8.9-10: Mt 13.10-13; Mk 4.10-12; Is 6.9-10; Jer 5.21; Ezek 12.2.   8.11-15: Mt 13.18-23; Mk 4.13-20.
8.11: 1 Thess 2.13; 1 Pet 1.23.
8.16: Mt 4.21; Mk 5.15; Lk 11.33.
8.17: Mk 4.22-23; Mt 10.26-27; Lk 12.2-3; Eph 5.13.
8.18: Mk 4.24-25; Mk 13.12; 25.29; Lk 19.26.
8.19-21: Mt 12.46-50; Mk 3.31-35.
8.21: Lk 11.28; Jn 15.14.
8.22-25: Mt 8.23-27; Mk 4.35-41; 6.47-52; Jn 6.16-21.
8.24: Lk 5.5; 8.45; 9.33, 49; 17.13.
8.26-39: Mt 8.28-34; Mk 5.1-20.   8.28: Mk 1.24; Jn 2.4.

said, "Legion"; for many demons had entered him. ³¹And they begged him not to command them to depart into the abyss. ³²Now a large herd of swine was feeding there on the hillside; and they begged him to let them enter these. So he gave them leave. ³³Then the demons came out of the man and entered the swine, and the herd rushed down the steep bank into the lake and were drowned.

34 When the herdsmen saw what had happened, they fled, and told it in the city and in the country. ³⁵Then people went out to see what had happened, and they came to Jesus, and found the man from whom the demons had gone, sitting at the feet of Jesus, clothed and in his right mind; and they were afraid. ³⁶And those who had seen it told them how he who had been possessed with demons was healed. ³⁷Then all the people of the surrounding country of the Gĕr′a·sēnes*ᵃ* asked him to depart from them; for they were seized with great fear; so he got into the boat and returned. ³⁸The man from whom the demons had gone begged that he might be with him; but he sent him away, saying, ³⁹"Return to your home, and declare how much God has done for you." And he went away, proclaiming throughout the whole city how much Jesus had done for him.

40 Now when Jesus returned, the crowd welcomed him, for they were all waiting for him. ⁴¹And there came a man named Jā′ĭ·rŭs, who was a ruler of the synagogue; and falling at Jesus' feet he besought him to come to his house, ⁴²for he had an only daughter, about twelve years of age, and she was dying.

As he went, the people pressed round him. ⁴³And a woman who had had a flow of blood for twelve years*ᵇ* and could not be healed by any one, ⁴⁴came up behind him, and touched the fringe of his garment; and immediately her flow of blood ceased. ⁴⁵And Jesus said, "Who was it that touched me?" When all denied it, Peter*ᶜ* said, "Master, the multitudes surround you and press upon you!" ⁴⁶But Jesus said, "Some one touched me; for I perceive that power has gone forth from me." ⁴⁷And when the woman saw that she was not hidden, she came trembling, and falling

down before him declared in the presence of all the people why she had touched him, and how she had been immediately healed. ⁴⁸And he said to her, "Daughter, your faith has made you well; go in peace."

49 While he was still speaking, a man from the ruler's house came and said, "Your daughter is dead; do not trouble the Teacher any more." ⁵⁰But Jesus on hearing this answered him, "Do not fear; only believe, and she shall be well." ⁵¹And when he came to the house, he permitted no one to enter with him, except Peter and John and James, and the father and mother of the child. ⁵²And all were weeping and bewailing her; but he said, "Do not weep; for she is not dead but sleeping." ⁵³And they laughed at him, knowing that she was dead. ⁵⁴But taking her by the hand he called, saying, "Child, arise." ⁵⁵And her spirit returned, and she got up at once; and he directed that something should be given her to eat. ⁵⁶And her parents were amazed; but he charged them to tell no one what had happened.

9 And he called the twelve together and gave them power and authority over all demons and to cure diseases, ²and he sent them out to preach the kingdom of God and to heal. ³And he said to them, "Take nothing for your journey, no staff, nor bag, nor bread, nor money; and do not have two tunics. ⁴And whatever house you enter, stay there, and from there depart. ⁵And wherever they do not receive you, when you leave that town shake off the dust from your feet as a testimony against them." ⁶And they departed and went through the villages, preaching the gospel and healing everywhere.

7 Now Hĕr′od the tetrarch heard of all that was done, and he was perplexed, because it was said by some that John had been raised from the dead, ⁸by some that E·lī′jah had appeared, and by others that one of the old prophets had risen. ⁹Hĕr′od said,

ᵃOther ancient authorities read Gadarenes, others Gergesenes
ᵇOther ancient authorities add and had spent all her living upon physicians
ᶜOther ancient authorities add and those who were with him **8.40-56:** Mt 9.18-26; Mk 5.21-43. **8.45:** Lk 8.24.
8.46: Lk 5.17; 6.19. **8.48:** Mt 9.22; Lk 7.50; 17.19; 18.42.
8.56: Mt 8.4; Mk 3.12; 7.36; Lk 9.21.
9.1-6: Mt 10.1, 5, 7-11, 14; Mk 6.7-12; Lk 10.4-11.
9.5: Acts 13.51. **9.7-9:** Mt 14.1-2; Mk 6.14-16; Lk 9.19.
9.9: Lk 23.8.

"John I beheaded; but who is this about whom I hear such things?" And he sought to see him.

10 On their return the apostles told him what they had done. And he took them and withdrew apart to a city called Bĕth-sā'ĭ·dạ. ¹¹When the crowds learned it, they followed him; and he welcomed them and spoke to them of the kingdom of God, and cured those who had need of healing. ¹²Now the day began to wear away; and the twelve came and said to him, "Send the crowd away, to go into the villages and country round about, to lodge and get provisions; for we are here in a lonely place." ¹³But he said to them, "You give them something to eat." They said, "We have no more than five loaves and two fish—unless we are to go and buy food for all these people." ¹⁴For there were about five thousand men. And he said to his disciples, "Make them sit down in companies, about fifty each." ¹⁵And they did so, and made them all sit down. ¹⁶And taking the five loaves and the two fish he looked up to heaven, and blessed and broke them, and gave them to the disciples to set before the crowd. ¹⁷And all ate and were satisfied. And they took up what was left over, twelve baskets of broken pieces.

18 Now it happened that as he was praying alone the disciples were with him; and he asked them, "Who do the people say that I am?" ¹⁹And they answered, "John the Baptist; but others say, Ė·lī'jạh; and others, that one of the old prophets has risen." ²⁰And he said to them, "But who do you say that I am?" And Peter answered, "The Christ of God." ²¹But he charged and commanded them to tell this to no one, ²²saying, "The Son of man must suffer many things, and be rejected by the elders and chief priests and scribes, and be killed, and on the third day be raised."

23 And he said to all, "If any man would come after me, let him deny himself and take up his cross daily and follow me. ²⁴For whoever would save his life will lose it; and whoever loses his life for my sake, he will save it. ²⁵For what does it profit a man if he gains the whole world and loses or forfeits himself? ²⁶For whoever is ashamed of me and of my words, of him will the Son of man be ashamed

when he comes in his glory and the glory of the Father and of the holy angels. ²⁷But I tell you truly, there are some standing here who will not taste death before they see the kingdom of God."

28 Now about eight days after these sayings he took with him Peter and John and James, and went up on the mountain to pray. ²⁹And as he was praying, the appearance of his countenance was altered, and his raiment became dazzling white. ³⁰And behold, two men talked with him, Moses and Ė·lī'jạh, ³¹who appeared in glory and spoke of his departure, which he was to accomplish at Jerusalem. ³²Now Peter and those who were with him were heavy with sleep, and when they wakened they saw his glory and the two men who stood with him. ³³And as the men were parting from him, Peter said to Jesus, "Master, it is well that we are here; let us make three booths, one for you and one for Moses and one for Ė·lī'jạh"—not knowing what he said. ³⁴As he said this, a cloud came and overshadowed them; and they were afraid as they entered the cloud. ³⁵And a voice came out of the cloud, saying, "This is my Son, my Chosen;ᵈ listen to him!" ³⁶And when the voice had spoken, Jesus was found alone. And they kept silence and told no one in those days anything of what they had seen.

37 On the next day, when they had come down from the mountain, a great crowd met him. ³⁸And behold, a man from the crowd cried, "Teacher, I beg you to look upon my son, for he is my only child; ³⁹and behold, a spirit seizes him, and he suddenly cries out; it convulses him till he foams, and shatters him, and will hardly leave him. ⁴⁰And I begged your disciples

---

ᵈ Other ancient authorities read *my Beloved*
9.10: Mk 6.30-31; Lk 10.17; Jn 1.44.
9.11-17: Mt 14.13-21; Mk 6.32-44; Jn 6.1-14, Mk 8.4-10.
9.13: 2 Kings 4.42-44.
9.16: Lk 22.19; 24.30-31; Acts 2.42; 20.11; 27.35.
9.18-21: Mt 16.13-20; Mk 8.27-30; Jn 1.49; 11.27; 6.66-69.
9.18: Lk 3.21; 5.16; 6.12; 9.28; 11.1.
9.19: Lk 9.9; Mk 9.11-13.
9.22: Mt 16.21; Mk 8.31; Lk 9.43-45; 18.31-34; 17.25.
9.23-27: Mt 16.24-28; Mk 8.34-9.1.
9.24-25: Mt 10.38-39; Lk 14.27; 17.33; Jn 12.25.
9.26: Mt 10.33; Lk 12.9; 1 Jn 2.28.
9.27: Lk 22.18; Mt 10.23; 1 Thess 4.15-18; Jn 21.22.
9.28-36: Mt 17.1-8; Mk 9.2-8; 2 Pet 1.17-18.
9.28: Lk 8.51; 3.21; 5.16; 6.12; 9.18; 11.1.
9.30: Acts 1.9-11.
9.32: Jn 1.14. **9.33:** Lk 5.5; 8.24, 45; 9.49; 17.13.
9.35: Lk 3.22; Jn 12.28-30. **9.36:** Mt 17.9; Mk 9.9-10.
9.37-43: Mt 17.14-18; Mk 9.14-27.

to cast it out, but they could not." [41] Jesus answered, "O faithless and perverse generation, how long am I to be with you and bear with you? Bring your son here." [42] While he was coming, the demon tore him and convulsed him. But Jesus rebuked the unclean spirit, and healed the boy, and gave him back to his father. [43] And all were astonished at the majesty of God.

But while they were all marveling at everything he did, he said to his disciples, [44] "Let these words sink into your ears; for the Son of man is to be delivered into the hands of men." [45] But they did not understand this saying, and it was concealed from them, that they should not perceive it; and they were afraid to ask him about this saying.

46 And an argument arose among them as to which of them was the greatest. [47] But when Jesus perceived the thought of their hearts, he took a child and put him by his side, [48] and said to them, "Whoever receives this child in my name receives me, and whoever receives me receives him who sent me; for he who is least among you all is the one who is great."

49 John answered, "Master, we saw a man casting out demons in your name, and we forbade him, because he does not follow with us." [50] But Jesus said to him, "Do not forbid him; for he that is not against you is for you."

51 When the days drew near for him to be received up, he set his face to go to Jerusalem. [52] And he sent messengers ahead of him, who went and entered a village of the Sa̱·mârʹi·tan̦s, to make ready for him; [53] but the people would not receive him, because his face was set toward Jerusalem. [54] And when his disciples James and John saw it, they said, "Lord, do you want us to bid fire come down from heaven and consume them?"[e] [55] But he turned and rebuked them.[f] [56] And they went on to another village.

57 As they were going along the road, a man said to him, "I will follow you wherever you go." [58] And Jesus said to him, "Foxes have holes, and birds of the air have nests; but the Son of man has nowhere to lay his head." [59] To another he said, "Follow me." But he said, "Lord, let me first go and bury my father." [60] But he said to him, "Leave the dead to bury their own dead; but as for you, go and proclaim the kingdom of God." [61] Another said, "I will follow you, Lord; but let me first say farewell to those at my home." [62] Jesus said to him, "No one who puts his hand to the plow and looks back is fit for the kingdom of God."

10 After this the Lord appointed seventy[g] others, and sent them on ahead of him, two by two, into every town and place where he himself was about to come. [2] And he said to them, "The harvest is plentiful, but the laborers are few; pray therefore the Lord of the harvest to send out laborers into his harvest. [3] Go your way; behold, I send you out as lambs in the midst of wolves. [4] Carry no purse, no bag, no sandals; and salute no one on the road. [5] Whatever house you enter, first say, 'Peace be to this house!' [6] And if a son of peace is there, your peace shall rest upon him; but if not, it shall return to you. [7] And remain in the same house, eating and drinking what they provide, for the laborer deserves his wages; do not go from house to house. [8] Whenever you enter a town and they receive you, eat what is set before you; [9] heal the sick in it and say to them, 'The kingdom of God has come near to you.' [10] But whenever you enter a town and they do not receive you, go into its streets and say, [11] 'Even the dust of your town that clings to our feet, we wipe off against you; nevertheless know this, that the kingdom of God has come near.' [12] I tell you, it shall be more tolerable on that day for Sŏd'om than for that town.

13 "Woe to you, Chō·rā'zĭn! woe to you, Bĕth–sā'i·dạ! for if the mighty works done in you had been done in Tyre and Si'dŏn, they would have repented long ago, sitting in sackcloth and ashes. [14] But it shall be more tol-

[e] Other ancient authorities add *as Elijah did*
[f] Other ancient authorities add *and he said, "You do not know what manner of spirit you are of; for the Son of man came not to destroy men's lives but to save them"*
9.43-45: Mt 17.22-23; Mk 9.30-32; Lk 9.22; 18.31-34; 17.25.
9.46-48: Mt 18.1-5; Mk 9.33-37. **9.48:** Lk 10.16; Mt 10.40.
9.49-50: Mk 9.38-40; Lk 11.23.
9.49: Lk 5.5; 8.24, 45; 9.33; 17.13.
9.51-56: Mk 10.1; Lk 17.11; Jn 4.40-42.
9.52: Mt 10.5; Jn 4.4. **9.54:** Mk 3.17; 2 Kings 1.9-16.
9.57-60: Mt 8.19-22. **9.61:** 1 Kings 19.20; Phil 3.13.
10.1: Lk 9.1-2, 51-52; 7.13. **10.2:** Mt 9.37-38; Jn 4.35.
10.3-12: Mt 10.7-16; Mk 6.8-11; Lk 9.2-5; 22.35-36.
10.5: 1 Sam 25.6.
10.7: 1 Cor 10.27; 9.14; 1 Tim 5.18; Deut 24.15.
10.11: Acts 13.51. **10.12:** Mt 11.24; Gen 19.24-28; Jude 7.
10.13-15: Mt 11.21-23; Lk 6.24-26.

erable in the judgment for Tÿre and Sī'dŏn than for you. [15]And you, Cạpẽr'nạ-ụm, will you be exalted to heaven? You shall be brought down to Hades.

16 "He who hears you hears me, and he who rejects you rejects me, and he who rejects me rejects him who sent me."

17 The seventy[g] returned with joy, saying, "Lord, even the demons are subject to us in your name!" [18]And he said to them, "I saw Satan fall like lightning from heaven. [19]Behold, I have given you authority to tread upon serpents and scorpions, and over all the power of the enemy; and nothing shall hurt you. [20]Nevertheless do not rejoice in this, that the spirits are subject to you; but rejoice that your names are written in heaven."

21 In that same hour he rejoiced in the Holy Spirit and said, "I thank thee, Father, Lord of heaven and earth, that thou hast hidden these things from the wise and understanding and revealed them to babes; yea, Father, for such was thy gracious will.[h] [22]All things have been delivered to me by my Father; and no one knows who the Son is except the Father, or who the Father is except the Son and any one to whom the Son chooses to reveal him."

23 Then turning to the disciples he said privately, "Blessed are the eyes which see what you see! [24]For I tell you that many prophets and kings desired to see what you see, and did not see it, and to hear what you hear, and did not hear it."

25 And behold, a lawyer stood up to put him to the test, saying, "Teacher, what shall I do to inherit eternal life?" [26]He said to him, "What is written in the law? How do you read?" [27]And he answered, "You shall love the Lord your God with all your heart, and with all your soul, and with all your strength, and with all your mind; and your neighbor as yourself." [28]And he said to him, "You have answered right; do this, and you will live."

29 But he, desiring to justify himself, said to Jesus, "And who is my neighbor?" [30]Jesus replied, "A man was going down from Jerusalem to Jericho, and he fell among robbers, who stripped him and beat him, and departed, leaving him half dead.

[31]Now by chance a priest was going down that road; and when he saw him he passed by on the other side. [32]So likewise a Lē'vīte, when he came to the place and saw him, passed by on the other side. [33]But a Sạ·mâr'ĭ·tạn, as he journeyed, came to where he was; and when he saw him, he had compassion, [34]and went to him and bound up his wounds, pouring on oil and wine; then he set him on his own beast and brought him to an inn, and took care of him. [35]And the next day he took out two denarii[i] and gave them to the innkeeper, saying, 'Take care of him; and whatever more you spend, I will repay you when I come back.' [36]Which of these three, do you think, proved neighbor to the man who fell among the robbers?" [37]He said, "The one who showed mercy on him." And Jesus said to him, "Go and do likewise."

38 Now as they went on their way, he entered a village; and a woman named Martha received him into her house. [39]And she had a sister called Mary, who sat at the Lord's feet and listened to his teaching. [40]But Martha was distracted with much serving; and she went to him and said, "Lord, do you not care that my sister has left me to serve alone? Tell her then to help me." [41]But the Lord answered her, "Martha, Martha, you are anxious and troubled about many things; [42]one thing is needful.[j] Mary has chosen the good portion, which shall not be taken away from her."

11 He was praying in a certain place, and when he ceased, one of his disciples said to him, "Lord, teach us to pray, as John taught his disciples." [2]And he said to them, "When you pray, say:
"Father, hallowed be thy name.

[g] Other ancient authorities read *seventy-two*
[h] Or *so it was well-pleasing before thee*
[i] The denarius was a day's wage for a laborer
[j] Other ancient authorities read *few things are needful, or only one*

10.16: Mt 10.40; 18.5; Mk 9.37; Lk 9.48; Jn 13.20; 12.48.
10.18: Rev 12.9; Jn 12.31.
10.20: Ex 32.32; Ps 69.28; Dan 12.1; Phil 4.3; Heb 12.23; Rev 3.5; 13.8; 21.27.
10.21-22: Mt 11.25-27. 10.21: 1 Cor 1.26-29.
10.22: Mt 28.18; Jn 3.35; 13.3; 10.15; 17.25.
10.23-24: Mt 13.16-17; Jn 8.56; Heb 11.13; 1 Pet 1.10-12.
10.25-28: Mt 22.34-39; Mk 12.28-31.
10.25: Mk 10.17; Mt 19.16; Lk 18.18.
10.27: Deut 6.5; Lev 19.18; Rom 13.9; Gal 5.14; Jas 2.8.
10.28: Lk 20.39; Lev 18.5.
10.33: Lk 9.51-56; 17.11-19; Jn 4.4-42.
10.38-42: Jn 12.1-3; 11.1-45. 10.41: Lk 7.13.
11.1: Mk 1.35; Lk 3.21; 5.16; 6.12; 9.18, 28; 5.33; 7.18.
11.2-4: Mt 6.9-13.

Thy kingdom come. [3] Give us each day our daily bread; [k] [4] and forgive us our sins, for we ourselves forgive every one who is indebted to us; and lead us not into temptation."

5 And he said to them, "Which of you who has a friend will go to him at midnight and say to him, 'Friend, lend me three loaves; [6] for a friend of mine has arrived on a journey, and I have nothing to set before him'; [7] and he will answer from within, 'Do not bother me; the door is now shut, and my children are with me in bed; I cannot get up and give you anything'? [8] I tell you, though he will not get up and give him anything because he is his friend, yet because of his importunity he will rise and give him whatever he needs. [9] And I tell you, Ask, and it will be given you; seek, and you will find; knock, and it will be opened to you. [10] For every one who asks receives, and he who seeks finds, and to him who knocks it will be opened. [11] What father among you, if his son asks for [l] a fish, will instead of a fish give him a serpent; [12] or if he asks for an egg, will give him a scorpion? [13] If you then, who are evil, know how to give good gifts to your children, how much more will the heavenly Father give the Holy Spirit to those who ask him!"

14 Now he was casting out a demon that was dumb; when the demon had gone out, the dumb man spoke, and the people marveled. [15] But some of them said, "He casts out demons by Bē-ĕl′-zĕ·bŭl, the prince of demons"; [16] while others, to test him, sought from him a sign from heaven. [17] But he, knowing their thoughts, said to them, "Every kingdom divided against itself is laid waste, and a divided household falls. [18] And if Satan also is divided against himself, how will his kingdom stand? For you say that I cast out demons by Bē-ĕl′-zĕ·bŭl. [19] And if I cast out demons by Bē-ĕl′zĕ·bŭl, by whom do your sons cast them out? Therefore they shall be your judges. [20] But if it is by the finger of God that I cast out demons, then the kingdom of God has come upon you. [21] When a strong man, fully armed, guards his own palace, his goods are in peace; [22] but when one stronger than he assails him and overcomes him, he takes away his armor in which he trusted, and divides his spoil. [23] He who

is not with me is against me, and he who does not gather with me scatters.

24 "When the unclean spirit has gone out of a man, he passes through waterless places seeking rest; and finding none he says, 'I will return to my house from which I came.' [25] And when he comes he finds it swept and put in order. [26] Then he goes and brings seven other spirits more evil than himself, and they enter and dwell there; and the last state of that man becomes worse than the first."

27 As he said this, a woman in the crowd raised her voice and said to him, "Blessed is the womb that bore you, and the breasts that you sucked!" [28] But he said, "Blessed rather are those who hear the word of God and keep it!"

29 When the crowds were increasing, he began to say, "This generation is an evil generation; it seeks a sign, but no sign shall be given to it except the sign of Jonah. [30] For as Jonah became a sign to the men of Nĭn′ĕ·vĕh, so will the Son of man be to this generation. [31] The queen of the South will arise at the judgment with the men of this generation and condemn them; for she came from the ends of the earth to hear the wisdom of Solomon, and behold, something greater than Solomon is here. [32] The men of Nĭn′ĕ·vĕh will arise at the judgment with this generation and condemn it; for they repented at the preaching of Jonah, and behold, something greater than Jonah is here.

33 "No one after lighting a lamp puts it in a cellar or under a bushel, but on a stand, that those who enter may see the light. [34] Your eye is the lamp of your body; when your eye is sound, your whole body is full of light; but when it is not sound, your body is full of darkness. [35] Therefore be careful lest the light in you be darkness.

[k] *Or our bread for the morrow*
[l] Other ancient authorities insert *bread, will give him a stone; or if he asks for*
11.4: Mk 11.25; Mt 18.35.
11.5-8: Lk 18.1-8.   **11.9-13:** Mt 7.7-11.
11.9: Mt 18.19; 21.22; Mk 11.24; Jas 1.5-8; 1 Jn 5.14-15; Jn 15.7; 16.23-24.
11.14-23: Mt 12.22-30; 10.25; Mk 3.23-27.
11.14-15: Mt 9.32-34.
11.16: Mt 12.38; 16.1; Mk 8.11; Jn 2.18; 6.30.
11.23: Lk 9.50.
11.24-26: Mt 12.43-45.   **11.27:** Lk 1.42; 23.29.
11.28: Lk 8.21; Jn 15.14.   **11.29-32:** Mt 12.39-42.
11.29: Mt 16.4; Mk 8.12; Lk 11.16; Jon 3.4-5.
11.31: 1 Kings 10.1-10; 2 Chron 9.1-12.   **11.32:** Mt 12.6.
11.33: Mt 5.15; Mk 4.21; Lk 8.16.
11.34-35: Mt 6.22-23.

³⁶If then your whole body is full of light, having no part dark, it will be wholly bright, as when a lamp with its rays gives you light."

37 While he was speaking, a Phăr'-i·see asked him to dine with him; so he went in and sat at table. ³⁸The Phăr'i·see was astonished to see that he did not first wash before dinner. ³⁹And the Lord said to him, "Now you Phăr'i·seeş cleanse the outside of the cup and of the dish, but inside you are full of extortion and wickedness. ⁴⁰You fools! Did not he who made the outside make the inside also? ⁴¹But give for alms those things which are within; and behold, everything is clean for you.

42 "But woe to you Phăr'i·seeş! for you tithe mint and rue and every herb, and neglect justice and the love of God; these you ought to have done, without neglecting the others. ⁴³Woe to you Phăr'i·seeş! for you love the best seat in the synagogues and salutations in the market places. ⁴⁴Woe to you; for you are like graves which are not seen, and men walk over them without knowing it."

45 One of the lawyers answered him, "Teacher, in saying this you reproach us also." ⁴⁶And he said, "Woe to you lawyers also! for you load men with burdens hard to bear, and you yourselves do not touch the burdens with one of your fingers. ⁴⁷Woe to you! for you build the tombs of the prophets whom your fathers killed. ⁴⁸So you are witnesses and consent to the deeds of your fathers; for they killed them, and you build their tombs. ⁴⁹Therefore also the Wisdom of God said, 'I will send them prophets and apostles, some of whom they will kill and persecute,' ⁵⁰that the blood of all the prophets, shed from the foundation of the world, may be required of this generation, ⁵¹from the blood of Abel to the blood of Zĕch·a·rī'ah, who perished between the altar and the sanctuary. Yes, I tell you, it shall be required of this generation. ⁵²Woe to you lawyers! for you have taken away the key of knowledge; you did not enter yourselves, and you hindered those who were entering."

53 As he went away from there, the scribes and the Phăr'i·seeş began to press him hard, and to provoke him to speak of many things, ⁵⁴lying in wait for him, to catch at something he might say.

12 In the meantime, when so many thousands of the multitude had gathered together that they trod upon one another, he began to say to his disciples first, "Beware of the leaven of the Phăr'i·seeş, which is hypocrisy. ²Nothing is covered up that will not be revealed, or hidden that will not be known. ³Therefore whatever you have said in the dark shall be heard in the light, and what you have whispered in private rooms shall be proclaimed upon the housetops.

4 "I tell you, my friends, do not fear those who kill the body, and after that have no more that they can do. ⁵But I will warn you whom to fear: fear him who, after he has killed, has power to cast into hell;^m yes, I tell you, fear him! ⁶Are not five sparrows sold for two pennies? And not one of them is forgotten before God. ⁷Why, even the hairs of your head are all numbered. Fear not; you are of more value than many sparrows.

8 "And I tell you, every one who acknowledges me before men, the Son of man also will acknowledge before the angels of God; ⁹but he who denies me before men will be denied before the angels of God. ¹⁰And every one who speaks a word against the Son of man will be forgiven; but he who blasphemes against the Holy Spirit will not be forgiven. ¹¹And when they bring you before the synagogues and the rulers and the authorities, do not be anxious how or what you are to answer or what you are to say; ¹²for the Holy Spirit will teach you in that very hour what you ought to say."

13 One of the multitude said to him, "Teacher, bid my brother divide the inheritance with me." ¹⁴But he said to him, "Man, who made me a judge or

^mGreek *Gehenna*
11.37: Lk 7.36; 14.1.   11.38: Mk 7.1-5.
11.39-41: Mt 23.25-26.   11.39: Lk 7.13.
11.41: Tit 1.15; Mk 7.19.
11.42: Mt 23.23-24; Lev 27.30; Mic 6.8.
11.43: Mt 23.6-7; Mk 12.38-39; Lk 20.46.
11.44: Mt 23.27.   11.46: Mt 23.4.
11.47-48: Mt 23.29-32; Acts 7.51-53.
11.49-51: Mt 23.34-36.   11.49: 1 Cor 1.24; Col 2.3.
11.51: Gen 4.8; 2 Chron 24.20-21; Zech 1.1.
11.52: Mt 23.13.   11.53-54: Mk 12.13.
12.1: Mt 16.6; Mk 8.15.
12.2-3: Mt 10.26-27; Mk 4.22; Lk 8.17; Eph 5.13.
12.4: Jn 15.14-15.   12.4-9: Mt 10.28-33.
12.5: Heb 10.31.   12.7: Lk 21.18; Acts 27.34; Mt 12.12.
12.9: Mk 8.38; Lk 9.26; 2 Tim 2.12.
12.10: Mt 12.31-32; Mk 3.28-29.
12.11-12: Mt 10.19-20; Mk 13.11; Lk 21.14-15.

divider over you?" [15]And he said to them, "Take heed, and beware of all covetousness; for a man's life does not consist in the abundance of his possessions." [16]And he told them a parable, saying, "The land of a rich man brought forth plentifully; [17]and he thought to himself, 'What shall I do, for I have nowhere to store my crops?' [18]And he said, 'I will do this: I will pull down my barns, and build larger ones; and there I will store all my grain and my goods. [19]And I will say to my soul, Soul, you have ample goods laid up for many years; take your ease, eat, drink, be merry.' [20]But God said to him, 'Fool! This night your soul is required of you; and the things you have prepared, whose will they be?' [21]So is he who lays up treasure for himself, and is not rich toward God."

22 And he said to his disciples, "Therefore I tell you, do not be anxious about your life, what you shall eat, nor about your body, what you shall put on. [23]For life is more than food, and the body more than clothing. [24]Consider the ravens: they neither sow nor reap, they have neither storehouse nor barn, and yet God feeds them. Of how much more value are you than the birds! [25]And which of you by being anxious can add a cubit to his span of life?[n] [26]If then you are not able to do as small a thing as that, why are you anxious about the rest? [27]Consider the lilies, how they grow; they neither toil nor spin;[o] yet I tell you, even Solomon in all his glory was not arrayed like one of these. [28]But if God so clothes the grass which is alive in the field today and tomorrow is thrown into the oven, how much more will he clothe you, O men of little faith! [29]And do not seek what you are to eat and what you are to drink, nor be of anxious mind. [30]For all the nations of the world seek these things; and your Father knows that you need them. [31]Instead, seek his[p] kingdom, and these things shall be yours as well.

32 "Fear not, little flock, for it is your Father's good pleasure to give you the kingdom. [33]Sell your possessions, and give alms; provide yourselves with purses that do not grow old, with a treasure in the heavens that does not fail, where no thief approaches and no moth destroys. [34]For where your treasure is, there will your heart be also.

35 "Let your loins be girded and your lamps burning, [36]and be like men who are waiting for their master to come home from the marriage feast, so that they may open to him at once when he comes and knocks. [37]Blessed are those servants whom the master finds awake when he comes; truly, I say to you, he will gird himself and have them sit at table, and he will come and serve them. [38]If he comes in the second watch, or in the third, and finds them so, blessed are those servants! [39]But know this, that if the householder had known at what hour the thief was coming, he[q] would not have left his house to be broken into. [40]You also must be ready; for the Son of man is coming at an unexpected hour."

41 Peter said, "Lord, are you telling this parable for us or for all?" [42]And the Lord said, "Who then is the faithful and wise steward, whom his master will set over his household, to give them their portion of food at the proper time? [43]Blessed is that servant whom his master when he comes will find so doing. [44]Truly, I say to you, he will set him over all his possessions. [45]But if that servant says to himself, 'My master is delayed in coming,' and begins to beat the menservants and the maidservants, and to eat and drink and get drunk, [46]the master of that servant will come on a day when he does not expect him and at an hour he does not know, and will punish[r] him, and put him with the unfaithful. [47]And that servant who knew his master's will, but did not make ready or act according to his will, shall receive a severe beating. [48]But he who did not know, and did what deserved a beating, shall receive a light beating. Every one to whom much is given, of him will much be required; and of him to whom men commit much they will demand the more.

[n]Or *to his stature*
[o]Other ancient authorities read *Consider the lilies; they neither spin nor weave*
[p]Other ancient authorities read *God's*
[q]Other ancient authorities add *would have watched and*
[r]Or *cut him in pieces*
12.15: 1 Tim 6.6-10.
12.20: Jer 17.11; Job 27.8; Ps 39.6; Lk 12.33-34.
12.22-31: Mt 6.25-33.
12.24: Lk 12.6-7.   12.27: 1 Kings 10.1-10.   12.30: Mt 6.8.
12.32: Jn 21.15-17.   12.33-34: Mt 6.19-21; Lk 18.22.
12.35: Eph 6.14; Mt 25.1-13; Mk 13.33-37.
12.37: Jn 13.3-5; Mt 24.42; Lk 21.36.
12.39-40: Mt 24.43-44; 1 Thess 5.2; Rev 3.3; 16.15; 2 Pet 3.10.   12.42-46: Mt 24.45-51.   12.42: Lk 7.13.
12.47-48: Deut 25.2-3; Num 15.29-30; Lk 8.18; 19.26.

49 "I came to cast fire upon the earth; and would that it were already kindled! ⁵⁰I have a baptism to be baptized with; and how I am constrained until it is accomplished! ⁵¹Do you think that I have come to give peace on earth? No, I tell you, but rather division; ⁵²for henceforth in one house there will be five divided, three against two and two against three; ⁵³they will be divided, father against son and son against father, mother against daughter and daughter against her mother, mother-in-law against her daughter-in-law and daughter-in-law against her mother-in-law."

54 He also said to the multitudes, "When you see a cloud rising in the west, you say at once, 'A shower is coming'; and so it happens. ⁵⁵And when you see the south wind blowing, you say, 'There will be scorching heat'; and it happens. ⁵⁶You hypocrites! You know how to interpret the appearance of earth and sky; but why do you not know how to interpret the present time?

57 "And why do you not judge for yourselves what is right? ⁵⁸As you go with your accuser before the magistrate, make an effort to settle with him on the way, lest he drag you to the judge, and the judge hand you over to the officer, and the officer put you in prison. ⁵⁹I tell you, you will never get out till you have paid the very last copper."

13 There were some present at that very time who told him of the Galileans whose blood Pilate had mingled with their sacrifices. ²And he answered them, "Do you think that these Galileans were worse sinners than all the other Galileans, because they suffered thus? ³I tell you, No; but unless you repent you will all likewise perish. ⁴Or those eighteen upon whom the tower in Sī·lō′ạm fell and killed them, do you think that they were worse offenders than all the others who dwelt in Jerusalem? ⁵I tell you, No; but unless you repent you will all likewise perish."

6 And he told this parable: "A man had a fig tree planted in his vineyard; and he came seeking fruit on it and found none. ⁷And he said to the vinedresser, 'Lo, these three years I have come seeking fruit on this fig tree, and

I find none. Cut it down; why should it use up the ground?' ⁸And he answered him, 'Let it alone, sir, this year also, till I dig about it and put on manure. ⁹And if it bears fruit next year, well and good; but if not, you can cut it down.'"

10 Now he was teaching in one of the synagogues on the sabbath. ¹¹And there was a woman who had had a spirit of infirmity for eighteen years; she was bent over and could not fully straighten herself. ¹²And when Jesus saw her, he called her and said to her, "Woman, you are freed from your infirmity." ¹³And he laid his hands upon her, and immediately she was made straight, and she praised God. ¹⁴But the ruler of the synagogue, indignant because Jesus had healed on the sabbath, said to the people, "There are six days on which work ought to be done; come on those days and be healed and not on the sabbath day." ¹⁵Then the Lord answered him, "You hypocrites! Does not each of you on the sabbath untie his ox or his ass from the manger, and lead it away to water it? ¹⁶And ought not this woman, a daughter of Abraham whom Satan bound for eighteen years, be loosed from this bond on the sabbath day?" ¹⁷As he said this, all his adversaries were put to shame; and all the people rejoiced at all the glorious things that were done by him.

18 He said therefore, "What is the kingdom of God like? And to what shall I compare it? ¹⁹It is like a grain of mustard seed which a man took and sowed in his garden; and it grew and became a tree, and the birds of the air made nests in its branches."

20 And again he said, "To what shall I compare the kingdom of God? ²¹It is like leaven which a woman took and hid in three measures of flour, till it was all leavened."

22 He went on his way through towns and villages, teaching, and journeying toward Jerusalem. ²³And some one said to him, "Lord, will those who are saved be few?" And he

12.49: Lk 22.15. 12.50: Mk 10.38-39; Jn 12.27.
12.51-53: Mt 10.34-36; Lk 21.16; Mic 7.6.
12.54-56: Mt 16.2-3. 12.57-59: Mt 5.25-26.
13.2: Jn 9.1-3. 13.6-9: Mt 21.18-20; Mk 11.12-14, 20-21.
13.7: Mt 3.10; 7.19; Lk 3.9.
13.14: Ex 20.9-10; Lk 6.6-11; 14.1-6; Jn 5.1-18.
13.15: Lk 7.13; 14.5; Mt 12.11. 13.16: Lk 19.9.
13.18-19: Mt 13.31-32; Mk 4.30-32. 13.20-21: Mt 13.33.
13.22: Lk 9.51; 17.11; 18.31; 19.11.
13.23-24: Mt 7.13-14; Jn 10.7.

said to them, ²⁴"Strive to enter by the narrow door; for many, I tell you, will seek to enter and will not be able. ²⁵When once the householder has risen up and shut the door, you will begin to stand outside and to knock at the door, saying, 'Lord, open to us.' He will answer you, 'I do not know where you come from.' ²⁶Then you will begin to say, 'We ate and drank in your presence, and you taught in our streets.' ²⁷But he will say, 'I tell you, I do not know where you come from; depart from me, all you workers of iniquity!' ²⁸There you will weep and gnash your teeth, when you see Abraham and Isaac and Jacob and all the prophets in the kingdom of God and you yourselves thrust out. ²⁹And men will come from east and west, and from north and south, and sit at table in the kingdom of God. ³⁰And behold, some are last who will be first, and some are first who will be last."

31 At that very hour some Phăr'-ĭ·seeṣ came, and said to him, "Get away from here, for Hĕr'ọd wants to kill you." ³²And he said to them, "Go and tell that fox, 'Behold, I cast out demons and perform cures today and tomorrow, and the third day I finish my course. ³³Nevertheless I must go on my way today and tomorrow and the day following; for it cannot be that a prophet should perish away from Jerusalem.' ³⁴O Jerusalem, Jerusalem, killing the prophets and stoning those who are sent to you! How often would I have gathered your children together as a hen gathers her brood under her wings, and you would not! ³⁵Behold, your house is forsaken. And I tell you, you will not see me until you say, 'Blessed is he who comes in the name of the Lord!'"

14 One sabbath when he went to dine at the house of a ruler who belonged to the Phăr'ĭ·seeṣ, they were watching him. ²And behold, there was a man before him who had dropsy. ³And Jesus spoke to the lawyers and Phăr'ĭ·seeṣ, saying, "Is it lawful to heal on the sabbath, or not?" ⁴But they were silent. Then he took him and healed him, and let him go. ⁵And he said to them, "Which of you, having a son⁵ or an ox that has fallen into a well, will not immediately pull him out on a sabbath day?" ⁶And they could not reply to this.

7 Now he told a parable to those who were invited, when he marked how they chose the places of honor, saying to them, ⁸"When you are invited by any one to a marriage feast, do not sit down in a place of honor, lest a more eminent man than you be invited by him; ⁹and he who invited you both will come and say to you, 'Give place to this man,' and then you will begin with shame to take the lowest place. ¹⁰But when you are invited, go and sit in the lowest place, so that when your host comes he may say to you, 'Friend, go up higher'; then you will be honored in the presence of all who sit at table with you. ¹¹For every one who exalts himself will be humbled, and he who humbles himself will be exalted."

12 He said also to the man who had invited him, "When you give a dinner or a banquet, do not invite your friends or your brothers or your kinsmen or rich neighbors, lest they also invite you in return, and you be repaid. ¹³But when you give a feast, invite the poor, the maimed, the lame, the blind, ¹⁴and you will be blessed, because they cannot repay you. You will be repaid at the resurrection of the just."

15 When one of those who sat at table with him heard this, he said to him, "Blessed is he who shall eat bread in the kingdom of God!" ¹⁶But he said to him, "A man once gave a great banquet, and invited many; ¹⁷and at the time for the banquet he sent his servant to say to those who had been invited, 'Come; for all is now ready.' ¹⁸But they all alike began to make excuses. The first said to him, 'I have bought a field, and I must go out and see it; I pray you, have me excused.' ¹⁹And another said, 'I have bought five yoke of oxen, and I go to examine them; I pray you, have me excused.' ²⁰And another said, 'I have married a wife, and therefore I cannot come.' ²¹So the servant came and reported this to his master. Then

ʳOther ancient authorities read *an ass*
13.25: Mt 25.10-12. **13.26-27:** Mt 7.21-23; 25.41; Lk 6.46.
13.28-29: Mt 8.11-12. **13.30:** Mt 19.30; Mk 10.31.
13.32: Heb 2.10; 7.28 **13.34-35:** Mt 23.37-39; Lk 19.41.
13.35: Jer 22.5; Ps 118.26; Lk 19.38.
14.1: Lk 7.36; 11.37; Mk 3.2.
14.3: Mt 12.10; Mk 3.4; Lk 6.9. **14.5:** Mt 12.11; Lk 13.15.
14.8: Prov 25.6-7; Lk 11.43; 20.46.
14.11: Mt 23.12; Lk 18.14; Mt 18.4; 1 Pet 5.6.
14.12: Jas 2.2-4. **14.13:** Lk 14.21. **14.15:** Rev 19.9.
14.16-24: Mt 22.1-10. **14.20:** Deut 24.5; 1 Cor 7.33.
14.21: Lk 14.13.

the householder in anger said to his servant, 'Go out quickly to the streets and lanes of the city, and bring in the poor and maimed and blind and lame.' ²² And the servant said, 'Sir, what you commanded has been done, and still there is room.' ²³ And the master said to the servant, 'Go out to the highways and hedges, and compel people to come in, that my house may be filled ²⁴ For I tell you,^a none of those men who were invited shall taste my banquet.'"

25 Now great multitudes accompanied him; and he turned and said to them, ²⁶ "If any one comes to me and does not hate his own father and mother and wife and children and brothers and sisters, yes, and even his own life, he cannot be my disciple. ²⁷ Whoever does not bear his own cross and come after me, cannot be my disciple. ²⁸ For which of you, desiring to build a tower, does not first sit down and count the cost, whether he has enough to complete it? ²⁹ Otherwise, when he has laid a foundation, and is not able to finish, all who see it begin to mock him, ³⁰ saying, 'This man began to build, and was not able to finish.' ³¹ Or what king, going to encounter another king in war, will not sit down first and take counsel whether he is able with ten thousand to meet him who comes against him with twenty thousand? ³² And if not, while the other is yet a great way off, he sends an embassy and asks terms of peace. ³³ So therefore, whoever of you does not renounce all that he has cannot be my disciple.

34 "Salt is good; but if salt has lost its taste, how shall its saltness be restored? ³⁵ It is fit neither for the land nor for the dunghill; men throw it away. He who has ears to hear, let him hear."

15 Now the tax collectors and sinners were all drawing near to hear him. ² And the Phăr'i·seeş and the scribes murmured, saying, "This man receives sinners and eats with them."

3 So he told them this parable: ⁴ "What man of you, having a hundred sheep, if he has lost one of them, does not leave the ninety-nine in the wilderness, and go after the one which is lost, until he finds it? ⁵ And when he has found it, he lays it on his shoulders, rejoicing. ⁶ And when he comes home, he calls together his friends and his neighbors, saying to them, 'Rejoice with me, for I have found my sheep which was lost.' ⁷ Just so, I tell you, there will be more joy in heaven over one sinner who repents than over ninety-nine righteous persons who need no repentance.

8 "Or what woman, having ten silver coins,^t if she loses one coin, does not light a lamp and sweep the house and seek diligently until she finds it? ⁹ And when she has found it, she calls together her friends and neighbors, saying, 'Rejoice with me, for I have found the coin which I had lost.' ¹⁰ Just so, I tell you, there is joy before the angels of God over one sinner who repents."

11 And he said, "There was a man who had two sons; ¹² and the younger of them said to his father, 'Father, give me the share of property that falls to me.' And he divided his living between them. ¹³ Not many days later, the younger son gathered all he had and took his journey into a far country, and there he squandered his property in loose living. ¹⁴ And when he had spent everything, a great famine arose in that country, and he began to be in want. ¹⁵ So he went and joined himself to one of the citizens of that country, who sent him into his fields to feed swine. ¹⁶ And he would gladly have fed on^u the pods that the swine ate; and no one gave him anything. ¹⁷ But when he came to himself he said, 'How many of my father's hired servants have bread enough and to spare, but I perish here with hunger! ¹⁸ I will arise and go to my father, and I will say to him, "Father, I have sinned against heaven and before you; ¹⁹ I am no longer worthy to be called your son; treat me as one of your hired servants."' ²⁰ And he arose and came to his father. But while he was yet at a distance, his father saw him and had compassion, and ran and embraced him and

^a The Greek word for *you* here is plural
^t The drachma, rendered here by *silver coin*, was about a day's wage for a laborer
^u Other ancient authorities read *filled his belly with*
14.26-27: Mt 10.37-38.   14.27: Mt 16.24; Mk 8.34; Lk 9.23.
14.33: Lk 18.29-30; Phil 3.7.
14.34-35: Mt 5.13; Mk 9.49-50; Mt 11.15.
15.1-2: Lk 5.29-30; 19.7.   15.4-7: Mt 18.10-14.
15.7: Jas 5.20; Lk 19.10; 15.10.   15.11: Mt 21.28.
15.12: Deut 21.15-17.

kissed him. ²¹And the son said to him, 'Father, I have sinned against heaven and before you; I am no longer worthy to be called your son.'*v* ²²But the father said to his servants, 'Bring quickly the best robe, and put it on him; and put a ring on his hand, and shoes on his feet; ²³and bring the fatted calf and kill it, and let us eat and make merry; ²⁴for this my son was dead, and is alive again; he was lost, and is found.' And they began to make merry.

25 "Now his elder son was in the field; and as he came and drew near to the house, he heard music and dancing. ²⁶And he called one of the servants and asked what this meant. ²⁷And he said to him, 'Your brother has come, and your father has killed the fatted calf, because he has received him safe and sound.' ²⁸But he was angry and refused to go in. His father came out and entreated him, ²⁹but he answered his father, 'Lo, these many years I have served you, and I never disobeyed your command; yet you never gave me a kid, that I might make merry with my friends. ³⁰But when this son of yours came, who has devoured your living with harlots, you killed for him the fatted calf!' ³¹And he said to him, 'Son, you are always with me, and all that is mine is yours. ³²It was fitting to make merry and be glad, for this your brother was dead, and is alive; he was lost, and is found.'"

16 He also said to the disciples, "There was a rich man who had a steward, and charges were brought to him that this man was wasting his goods. ²And he called him and said to him, 'What is this that I hear about you? Turn in the account of your stewardship, for you can no longer be steward.' ³And the steward said to himself, 'What shall I do, since my master is taking the stewardship away from me? I am not strong enough to dig, and I am ashamed to beg. ⁴I have decided what to do, so that people may receive me into their houses when I am put out of the stewardship.' ⁵So, summoning his master's debtors one by one, he said to the first, 'How much do you owe my master?' ⁶He said, 'A hundred measures of oil.' And he said to him, 'Take your bill, and sit down quickly and write fifty.' ⁷Then he said to another, 'And how much do you owe?' He said, 'A hundred measures of wheat.' He said to him, 'Take your bill, and write eighty.' ⁸The master commended the dishonest steward for his shrewdness; for the sons of this world*w* are more shrewd in dealing with their own generation than the sons of light. ⁹And I tell you, make friends for yourselves by means of unrighteous mammon,*a* so that when it fails they may receive you into the eternal habitations.

10 "He who is faithful in a very little is faithful also in much; and he who is dishonest in a very little is dishonest also in much. ¹¹If then you have not been faithful in the unrighteous mammon,*a* who will entrust to you the true riches? ¹²And if you have not been faithful in that which is another's, who will give you that which is your own? ¹³No servant can serve two masters; for either he will hate the one and love the other, or he will be devoted to the one and despise the other. You cannot serve God and mammon."*a*

14 The Phăr′ĭ·seeṣ, who were lovers of money, heard all this, and they scoffed at him. ¹⁵But he said to them, "You are those who justify yourselves before men, but God knows your hearts; for what is exalted among men is an abomination in the sight of God.

16 "The law and the prophets were until John; since then the good news of the kingdom of God is preached, and every one enters it violently. ¹⁷But it is easier for heaven and earth to pass away, than for one dot of the law to become void.

18 "Every one who divorces his wife and marries another commits adultery, and he who marries a woman divorced from her husband commits adultery.

19 "There was a rich man, who was clothed in purple and fine linen and who feasted sumptuously every day. ²⁰And at his gate lay a poor man named

v Other ancient authorities add *treat me as one of your hired servants*
w Greek *age*
a *Mammon* is a Semitic word for money or riches
15.22: Gen 41.42; Zech 3.4.
15.24: 1 Tim 5.6; Eph 2.1; Lk 9.60.
16.8: 1 Thess 5.5; Eph 5.8; Lk 20.34; Jn 12.36.
16.9: Lk 12.33; 18.22. 16.10: Mt 25.21; Lk 19.17.
16.13: Mt 6.24.
16.15: 1 Sam 16.7; Prov 21.2; Acts 1.24; Lk 10.29.
16.16: Mt 11.12-13. 16.17: Mt 5.17-18; Lk 21.33.
16.18: Mt 5.31-32; 19.9; Mk 10.11-12; 1 Cor 7.10-11.
16.20: Jn 11.1-44; 12.1, 9.

Lăz'a·rŭs, full of sores, ²¹who desired to be fed with what fell from the rich man's table; moreover the dogs came and licked his sores. ²²The poor man died and was carried by the angels to Abraham's bosom. The rich man also died and was buried; ²³and in Hades, being in torment, he lifted up his eyes, and saw Abraham far off and Lăz'a·rŭs in his bosom. ²⁴And he called out, 'Father Abraham, have mercy upon me, and send Lăz'a·rŭs to dip the end of his finger in water and cool my tongue; for I am in anguish in this flame.' ²⁵But Abraham said, 'Son, remember that you in your lifetime received your good things, and Lăz'a·rŭs in like manner evil things; but now he is comforted here, and you are in anguish. ²⁶And besides all this, between us and you a great chasm has been fixed, in order that those who would pass from here to you may not be able, and none may cross from there to us.' ²⁷And he said, 'Then I beg you, father, to send him to my father's house, ²⁸for I have five brothers, so that he may warn them, lest they also come into this place of torment.' ²⁹But Abraham said, 'They have Moses and the prophets; let them hear them.' ³⁰And he said, 'No, father Abraham; but if some one goes to them from the dead, they will repent.' ³¹He said to him, 'If they do not hear Moses and the prophets, neither will they be convinced if some one should rise from the dead.'"

17 And he said to his disciples, "Temptations to sin* are sure to come; but woe to him by whom they come! ²It would be better for him if a millstone were hung round his neck and he were cast into the sea, than that he should cause one of these little ones to sin.ʸ ³Take heed to yourselves; if your brother sins, rebuke him, and if he repents, forgive him; ⁴and if he sins against you seven times in the day, and turns to you seven times, and says, 'I repent,' you must forgive him."

5 The apostles said to the Lord, "Increase our faith!" ⁶And the Lord said, "If you had faith as a grain of mustard seed, you could say to this sycamine tree, 'Be rooted up, and be planted in the sea,' and it would obey you.

7 "Will any one of you, who has a servant plowing or keeping sheep,

say to him when he has come in from the field, 'Come at once and sit down at table'? ⁸Will he not rather say to him, 'Prepare supper for me, and gird yourself and serve me, till I eat and drink; and afterward you shall eat and drink'? ⁹Does he thank the servant because he did what was commanded? ¹⁰So you also, when you have done all that is commanded you, say, 'We are unworthy servants; we have only done what was our duty.'"

11 On the way to Jerusalem he was passing along between Sa·mâr'ĭ·a and Galilee. ¹²And as he entered a village, he was met by ten lepers, who stood at a distance ¹³and lifted up their voices and said, "Jesus, Master, have mercy on us." ¹⁴When he saw them he said to them, "Go and show yourselves to the priests." And as they went they were cleansed. ¹⁵Then one of them, when he saw that he was healed, turned back, praising God with a loud voice; ¹⁶and he fell on his face at Jesus' feet, giving him thanks. Now he was a Sa·mâr'ĭ·tan. ¹⁷Then said Jesus, "Were not ten cleansed? Where are the nine? ¹⁸Was no one found to return and give praise to God except this foreigner?" ¹⁹And he said to him, "Rise and go your way; your faith has made you well."

20 Being asked by the Phăr'ĭ·seeṣ when the kingdom of God was coming, he answered them, "The kingdom of God is not coming with signs to be observed; ²¹nor will they say, 'Lo, here it is!' or 'There!' for behold, the kingdom of God is in the midst of you."ᶻ

22 And he said to the disciples, "The days are coming when you will desire to see one of the days of the Son of man, and you will not see it. ²³And they will say to you, 'Lo, there!' or 'Lo, here!' Do not go, do not follow them. ²⁴For as the lightning flashes and lights up the sky from one side to the other, so will the Son of man be

*Greek *stumbling blocks* ʸGreek *stumble*
ᶻOr *within you*

16.22: Jn 13.23.   16.25: Lk 6.24.
16.29: Jn 5.45-47; Acts 15.21; Lk 4.17.   16.30: Lk 3.8; 19.9.
17.1-2: Mt 18.6-7; Mk 9.42; 1 Cor 8.12.
17.3-4: Mt 18.15, 21-22.
17.5-6: Mt 17.20; 21.21; Mk 11.22-23.   17.5: Lk 7.13.
17.8: Lk 12.37; Jn 13.3-5.
17.11: Lk 9.51; 13.22; 19.11.   17.12: Lev 13.45-46.
17.13: Lk 5.5; 8.24, 45; 9.33, 49.
17.14: Lk 5.14; Mt 8.4; Mk 1.44; Lev 14.2-32.
17.19: Mt 9.22; Mk 5.34; Lk 8.48; 18.42.
17.20: Lk 19.11; 21.7; Acts 1.6.
17.22: Mt 9.15; Mk 2.20; Lk 5.35.
17.23: Mt 24.23; Mk 13.21.   17.24: Mt 24.27; Rev 1.7.

in his day.*ᵃ* ²⁵But first he must suffer many things and be rejected by this generation. ²⁶As it was in the days of Noah, so will it be in the days of the Son of man. ²⁷They ate, they drank, they married, they were given in marriage, until the day when Noah entered the ark, and the flood came and destroyed them all. ²⁸Likewise as it was in the days of Lot—they ate, they drank, they bought, they sold, they planted, they built, ²⁹but on the day when Lot went out from Sŏd′om fire and sulphur rained from heaven and destroyed them all—³⁰so will it be on the day when the Son of man is revealed. ³¹On that day, let him who is on the housetop, with his goods in the house, not come down to take them away; and likewise let him who is in the field not turn back. ³²Remember Lot's wife. ³³Whoever seeks to gain his life will lose it, but whoever loses his life will preserve it. ³⁴I tell you, in that night there will be two in one bed; one will be taken and the other left. ³⁵There will be two women grinding together; one will be taken and the other left."*ᵇ* ³⁷And they said to him, "Where, Lord?" He said to them, "Where the body is, there the eagles*ᶜ* will be gathered together."

18 And he told them a parable, to the effect that they ought always to pray and not lose heart. ²He said, "In a certain city there was a judge who neither feared God nor regarded man; ³and there was a widow in that city who kept coming to him and saying, 'Vindicate me against my adversary.' ⁴For a while he refused; but afterward he said to himself, 'Though I neither fear God nor regard man, ⁵yet because this widow bothers me, I will vindicate her, or she will wear me out by her continual coming.'" ³And the Lord said, "Hear what the unrighteous judge says. ⁷And will not God vindicate his elect, who cry to him day and night? Will he delay long over them? ⁸I tell you, he will vindicate them speedily. Nevertheless, when the Son of man comes, will he find faith on earth?"

9 He also told this parable to some who trusted in themselves that they were righteous and despised others: ¹⁰"Two men went up into the temple to pray, one a Phăr′ĭ·see and the other a tax collector. ¹¹The Phăr′ĭ·see stood and prayed thus with himself, 'God, I thank thee that I am not like other men, extortioners, unjust, adulterers, or even like this tax collector. ¹²I fast twice a week, I give tithes of all that I get.' ¹³But the tax collector, standing far off, would not even lift up his eyes to heaven, but beat his breast, saying, 'God, be merciful to me a sinner!' ¹⁴I tell you, this man went down to his house justified rather than the other; for every one who exalts himself will be humbled, but he who humbles himself will be exalted."

15 Now they were bringing even infants to him that he might touch them; and when the disciples saw it, they rebuked them. ¹⁶But Jesus called them to him, saying, "Let the children come to me, and do not hinder them; for to such belongs the kingdom of God. ¹⁷Truly, I say to you, whoever does not receive the kingdom of God like a child shall not enter it."

18 And a ruler asked him, "Good Teacher, what shall I do to inherit eternal life?" ¹⁹And Jesus said to him, "Why do you call me good? No one is good but God alone. ²⁰You know the commandments: 'Do not commit adultery, Do not kill, Do not steal, Do not bear false witness, Honor your father and mother.'" ²¹And he said, "All these I have observed from my youth." ²²And when Jesus heard it, he said to him, "One thing you still lack. Sell all that you have and distribute to the poor, and you will have treasure in heaven; and come, follow me." ²³But when he heard this he became sad, for he was very rich. ²⁴Jesus looking at him said, "How hard it is for those who have riches to enter the kingdom of God! ²⁵For it is easier for a camel to go through the eye of a needle than for a rich man to enter the kingdom of God." ²⁶Those

ᵃOther ancient authorities omit in his day
ᵇOther ancient authorities add verse 36, "Two men will be in the field; one will be taken and the other left"
ᶜOr vultures
17.25: Lk 9.22.   **17.26-27:** Mt 24.37-39; Gen 6.5-8; 7.6-24.
17.28-30: Gen 18.20-33; 19.24-25.
17.31: Mt 24.17-18; Mk 13.15-16; Lk 21.21.
17.32: Gen 19.26.
17.33: Mt 10.39; 16.25; Mk 8.35; Lk 9.24; Jn 12.25.
17.34-35: Mt 24.40-41.   **17.37:** Mt 24.28.
18.1-8: Lk 11.5-8.   **18.6:** Lk 7.13.
18.7: Rev 6.10; Mt 24.22; Rom 8.33; Col 3.12; 2 Tim 2.10.
18.11: Mt 6.5; Mk 11.25.   **18.12:** Lk 5.33; 11.42.
18.14: Mt 18.4; 23.12; Lk 14.11; 1 Pet 5.6.
18.15-17: Mt 19.13-15; 18.3; Mk 10.13-16.
18.18-23: Mt 19.16-22; Mk 10.17-22.   **18.18:** Lk 10.25.
18.20: Ex 20.12-16; Deut 5.16-20; Rom 13.9; Jas 2.11.
18.22: Lk 12.33; Acts 2.45; 4.32.
18.24-27: Mt 19.23-26; Mk 10.23-27.

who heard it said, "Then who can be saved?" ²⁷ But he said, "What is impossible with men is possible with God." ²⁸ And Peter said, "Lo, we have left our homes and followed you." ²⁹ And he said to them, "Truly, I say to you, there is no man who has left house or wife or brothers or parents or children, for the sake of the kingdom of God, ³⁰ who will not receive manifold more in this time, and in the age to come eternal life."

31 And taking the twelve, he said to them, "Behold, we are going up to Jerusalem, and everything that is written of the Son of man by the prophets will be accomplished. ³² For he will be delivered to the Gentiles, and will be mocked and shamefully treated and spit upon, ³³ they will scourge him and kill him, and on the third day he will rise." ³⁴ But they understood none of these things; this saying was hid from them, and they did not grasp what was said.

35 As he drew near to Jericho, a blind man was sitting by the roadside begging; ³⁶ and hearing a multitude going by, he inquired what this meant. ³⁷ They told him, "Jesus of Nazareth is passing by." ³⁸ And he cried, "Jesus, Son of David, have mercy on me!" ³⁹ And those who were in front rebuked him, telling him to be silent; but he cried out all the more, "Son of David, have mercy on me!" ⁴⁰ And Jesus stopped, and commanded him to be brought to him; and when he came near, he asked him, ⁴¹ "What do you want me to do for you?" He said, "Lord, let me receive my sight." ⁴² And Jesus said to him, "Receive your sight; your faith has made you well." ⁴³ And immediately he received his sight and followed him, glorifying God; and all the people, when they saw it, gave praise to God.

19 He entered Jericho and was passing through. ² And there was a man named Zác·chae´us; he was a chief tax collector, and rich. ³ And he sought to see who Jesus was, but could not, on account of the crowd, because he was small of stature. ⁴ So he ran on ahead and climbed up into a sycamore tree to see him, for he was to pass that way. ⁵ And when Jesus came to the place, he looked up and said to him, "Zác·chae´us, make haste and come down;

for I must stay at your house today." ⁶ So he made haste and came down, and received him joyfully. ⁷ And when they saw it they all murmured, "He has gone in to be the guest of a man who is a sinner." ⁸ And Zác·chae´us stood and said to the Lord, "Behold, Lord, the half of my goods I give to the poor; and if I have defrauded any one of anything, I restore it fourfold." ⁹ And Jesus said to him, "Today salvation has come to this house, since he also is a son of Abraham. ¹⁰ For the Son of man came to seek and to save the lost."

11 As they heard these things, he proceeded to tell a parable, because he was near to Jerusalem, and because they supposed that the kingdom of God was to appear immediately. ¹² He said therefore, "A nobleman went into a far country to receive a kingdom and then return. ¹³ Calling ten of his servants, he gave them ten pounds,ᵉ and said to them, 'Trade with these till I come.' ¹⁴ But his citizens hated him and sent an embassy after him, saying, 'We do not want this man to reign over us.' ¹⁵ When he returned, having received the kingdom, he commanded these servants, to whom he had given the money, to be called to him, that he might know what they had gained by trading. ¹⁶ The first came before him, saying, 'Lord, your pound has made ten pounds more.' ¹⁷ And he said to him, 'Well done, good servant! Because you have been faithful in a very little, you shall have authority over ten cities.' ¹⁸ And the second came, saying, 'Lord, your pound has made five pounds.' ¹⁹ And he said to him, 'And you are to be over five cities.' ²⁰ Then another came, saying, 'Lord, here is your pound, which I kept laid away in a napkin; ²¹ for I was afraid of you, because you are a severe man; you take up what you did not lay down, and reap what you did not sow.' ²² He said to him, 'I will condemn you out of your own mouth, you wicked servant!

ᵉThe mina, rendered here by *pound*, was about three months' wages for a laborer

18.27: Gen 18.14; Job 42.2; Jer 32.17; Lk 1.37.
18.28-30: Mt 19.27-30; Mk 10.28-31; Lk 5.1-11.
18.31-34: Mt 20.17-19; Mk 10.32-34; Lk 9.22, 44-45; 17.25.
18.35-43: Mt 20.29-34; Mk 10.46-52; Mt 9.27-31; Mk 8.22; Jn 9.1-7.
18.42: Mt 9.22; Mk 5.34; 10.52; Lk 7.50; 8.48; 17.19.
19.1: Mk 1.3.   19.7: Lk 5.29-30; 15.1-2.
19.8: Lk 7.13; 3.14; Ex 22.1; Lev 6.5; Num 5.6-7.
19.9: Lk 3.8; 13.16; Rom 4.16.
19.11: Lk 9.51; 13.22; 17.11; 18.31; 9.27.
19.12-28: Mt 25.14-30.   19.12: Mk 13.34   19.17: Lk 16.10.

You knew that I was a severe man, taking up what I did not lay down and reaping what I did not sow?' ²³Why then did you not put my money into the bank, and at my coming I should have collected it with interest?' ²⁴And he said to those who stood by, 'Take the pound from him, and give it to him who has the ten pounds.' ²⁵(And they said to him, 'Lord, he has ten pounds.') ²⁶'I tell you, that to every one who has will more be given; but from him who has not, even what he has will be taken away. ²⁷But as for these enemies of mine, who did not want me to reign over them, bring them here and slay them before me.'"

28 And when he had said this, he went on ahead, going up to Jerusalem. ²⁹When he drew near to Bĕth'-phạ·gē and Bĕth'ạ·nў, at the mount that is called Ŏl'ĭ·vĕt, he sent two of the disciples, ³⁰saying, "Go into the village opposite, where on entering you will find a colt tied, on which no one has ever yet sat; untie it and bring it here. ³¹If any one asks you, 'Why are you untying it?' you shall say this, 'The Lord has need of it.'" ³²So those who were sent went away and found it as he had told them. ³³And as they were untying the colt, its owners said to them, "Why are you untying the colt?" ³⁴And they said, "The Lord has need of it." ³⁵And they brought it to Jesus, and throwing their garments on the colt they set Jesus upon it. ³⁶And as he rode along, they spread their garments on the road. ³⁷As he was now drawing near, at the descent of the Mount of Olives, the whole multitude of the disciples began to rejoice and praise God with a loud voice for all the mighty works that they had seen, ³⁸saying, 'Blessed is the King who comes in the name of the Lord! Peace in heaven and glory in the highest!" ³⁹And some of the Phăr'ĭ·sees̨ in the multitude said to him, "Teacher, rebuke your disciples." ⁴⁰He answered, "I tell you, if these were silent, the very stones would cry out."

41 And when he drew near and saw the city he wept over it, ⁴²saying, 'Would that even today you knew the things that make for peace! But now they are hid from your eyes. ⁴³For the days shall come upon you, when your enemies will cast up a bank about you and surround you, and hem you in on every side, ⁴⁴and dash you to the ground, you and your children within you, and they will not leave one stone upon another in you; because you did not know the time of your visitation."

45 And he entered the temple and began to drive out those who sold, ⁴⁶saying to them, "It is written, 'My house shall be a house of prayer'; but you have made it a den of robbers."

47 And he was teaching daily in the temple. The chief priests and the scribes and the principal men of the people sought to destroy him; ⁴⁸but they did not find anything they could do, for all the people hung upon his words.

20 One day, as he was teaching the people in the temple and preaching the gospel, the chief priests and the scribes with the elders came up ²and said to him, "Tell us by what authority you do these things, or who it is that gave you this authority." ³He answered them, "I also will ask you a question; now tell me, ⁴Was the baptism of John from heaven or from men?" ⁵And they discussed it with one another, saying, "If we say, 'From heaven,' he will say, 'Why did you not believe him?' ⁶But if we say, 'From men,' all the people will stone us; for they are convinced that John was a prophet." ⁷So they answered that they did not know whence it was. ⁸And Jesus said to them, "Neither will I tell you by what authority I do these things."

9 And he began to tell the people this parable: "A man planted a vineyard, and let it out to tenants, and went into another country for a long while. ¹⁰When the time came, he sent a servant to the tenants, that they should give him some of the fruit of the vineyard; but the tenants beat him, and sent him away empty-handed. ¹¹And he sent another servant; him also they beat and treated shamefully, and sent him away empty-handed. ¹²And he sent yet a third;

19.26: Mt 13.12; Mk 4.25; Lk 8.18. **19.28:** Mk 10.32.
19.29-38: Mt 21.1-9; Mk 11.1-10; Jn 12.12-18.
19.32: Lk 22.13. **19.34:** Lk 7.13. **19.36:** 2 Kings 9.13.
19.38: Ps 118.26; Lk 13.35; 2.14.
19.39-40: Mt 21.15-16; Hab 2.11. **19.41:** Lk 13.33-34.
19.43: Lk 21.21-24; 21.6; Is 29.3; Jer 6.6; Ezek 4.2.
19.44: 1 Pet 2.12.
19.45-46: Mt 21.12-13; Mk 11.15-17; Jn 2.13-17.
19.47-48: Mk 11.18; Lk 21.37; 22.53.
20.1-8: Mt 21.23-27; Mk 11.27-33. **20.2:** Jn 2.18.
20.6: Mt 14.5; Lk 7.29. **20.9-19:** Mt 21.33-46; Mk 12.1-12.
20.9: Is 5.1-7; Mt 25.14.

this one they wounded and cast out. [13] Then the owner of the vineyard said, 'What shall I do? I will send my beloved son; it may be they will respect him.' [14] But when the tenants saw him, they said to themselves, 'This is the heir; let us kill him, that the inheritance may be ours.' [15] And they cast him out of the vineyard and killed him. What then will the owner of the vineyard do to them? [16] He will come and destroy those tenants, and give the vineyard to others." When they heard this, they said, "God forbid!" [17] But he looked at them and said, "What then is this that is written:

'The very stone which the builders rejected
has become the head of the corner'?

[18] Every one who falls on that stone will be broken to pieces; but when it falls on any one it will crush him."

19 The scribes and the chief priests tried to lay hands on him at that very hour, but they feared the people; for they perceived that he had told this parable against them. [20] So they watched him, and sent spies, who pretended to be sincere, that they might take hold of what he said, so as to deliver him up to the authority and jurisdiction of the governor. [21] They asked him, "Teacher, we know that you speak and teach rightly, and show no partiality, but truly teach the way of God. [22] Is it lawful for us to give tribute to Caesar, or not?" [23] But he perceived their craftiness, and said to them, [24] "Show me a coin.*f* Whose likeness and inscription has it?" They said, "Caesar's." [25] He said to them, "Then render to Caesar the things that are Caesar's, and to God the things that are God's." [26] And they were not able in the presence of the people to catch him by what he said; but marveling at his answer they were silent.

27 There came to him some Săd'-dū·çeeṣ, those who say that there is no resurrection, [28] and they asked him a question, saying, "Teacher, Moses wrote for us that if a man's brother dies, having a wife but no children, the man*g* must take the wife and raise up children for his brother. [29] Now there were seven brothers; the first took a wife, and died without children; [30] and the second [31] and the third took her, and likewise all seven left no children and died. [32] Afterward the woman also died. [33] In the resurrection, therefore, whose wife will the woman be? For the seven had her as wife."

34 And Jesus said to them, "The sons of this age marry and are given in marriage; [35] but those who are accounted worthy to attain to that age and to the resurrection from the dead neither marry nor are given in marriage, [36] for they cannot die any more, because they are equal to angels and are sons of God, being sons of the resurrection. [37] But that the dead are raised, even Moses showed, in the passage about the bush, where he calls the Lord the God of Abraham and the God of Isaac and the God of Jacob. [38] Now he is not God of the dead, but of the living; for all live to him." [39] And some of the scribes answered, "Teacher, you have spoken well." [40] For they no longer dared to ask him any question.

41 But he said to them, "How can they say that the Christ is David's son? [42] For David himself says in the Book of Psalms,

'The Lord said to my Lord,
Sit at my right hand,
[43] till I make thy enemies a stool for thy feet.'

[44] David thus calls him Lord; so how is he his son?"

45 And in the hearing of all the people he said to his disciples, [46] "Beware of the scribes, who like to go about in long robes, and love salutations in the market places and the best seats in the synagogues and the places of honor at feasts, [47] who devour widows' houses and for a pretense make long prayers. They will receive the greater condemnation."

21 He looked up and saw the rich putting their gifts into the treasury; [2] and he saw a poor widow put in two copper coins. [3] And he said, "Truly I tell you, this poor widow has put in more than all of them; [4] for they all contributed out of their abun

---

*f*Greek *denarius* *g*Greek *his brother*
20.16: Acts 13.46; 18.6; 28.28.
20.17: Ps 118.22-23; Acts 4.11; 1 Pet 2.6-7.
20.18: Is 8.14-15. **20.19:** Lk 19.47.
20.20-26: Mt 22.15-22; Mk 12.13-17. **20.21:** Jn 3.2.
20.25: Rom 13.7; Lk 23.2.
20.27-38: Mt 22.23-33; Mk 12.18-27.
20.27: Acts 4.1-2; 23.6-10. **20.28:** Deut 25.5.
20.37: Ex 3.6. **20.39:** Mk 12.28.
20.40: Mk 12.34; Mt 22.46.
20.41-44: Mt 22.41-45; Mk 12.35-37; Ps 110.1.
20.45-47: Mk 12.38-40; Mt 23.6-7; Lk 11.43; 14.7-11.
21.1-4: Mk 12.41-44. **21.5-23:** Mt 24.1-19; Mk 13.1-17.

dance, but she out of her poverty put in all the living that she had."

5 And as some spoke of the temple, how it was adorned with noble stones and offerings, he said, ⁶"As for these things which you see, the days will come when there shall not be left here one stone upon another that will not be thrown down." ⁷ And they asked him, "Teacher, when will this be, and what will be the sign when this is about to take place?" ⁸ And he said, "Take heed that you are not led astray; for many will come in my name, saying, 'I am he!' and, 'The time is at hand!' Do not go after them. ⁹ And when you hear of wars and tumults, do not be terrified; for this must first take place, but the end will not be at once."

10 Then he said to them, "Nation will rise against nation, and kingdom against kingdom; ¹¹ there will be great earthquakes, and in various places famines and pestilences; and there will be terrors and great signs from heaven. ¹² But before all this they will lay their hands on you and persecute you, delivering you up to the synagogues and prisons, and you will be brought before kings and governors for my name's sake. ¹³ This will be a time for you to bear testimony. ¹⁴ Settle it therefore in your minds, not to meditate beforehand how to answer; ¹⁵ for I will give you a mouth and wisdom, which none of your adversaries will be able to withstand or contradict. ¹⁶ You will be delivered up even by parents and brothers and kinsmen and friends, and some of you they will put to death; ¹⁷ you will be hated by all for my name's sake. ¹⁸ But not a hair of your head will perish. ¹⁹ By your endurance you will gain your lives.

20 "But when you see Jerusalem surrounded by armies, then know that its desolation has come near. ²¹ Then let those who are in Jü·dē´a flee to the mountains, and let those who are inside the city depart, and let not those who are out in the country enter it; ²² for these are days of vengeance, to fulfil all that is written. ²³ Alas for those who are with child and for those who give suck in those days! For great distress shall be upon the earth and wrath upon this people; ²⁴ they will fall by the edge of

the sword, and be led captive among all nations; and Jerusalem will be trodden down by the Gentiles, until the times of the Gentiles are fulfilled.

25 "And there will be signs in sun and moon and stars, and upon the earth distress of nations in perplexity at the roaring of the sea and the waves, ²⁶ men fainting with fear and with foreboding of what is coming on the world; for the powers of the heavens will be shaken. ²⁷ And then they will see the Son of man coming in a cloud with power and great glory. ²⁸ Now when these things begin to take place, look up and raise your heads, because your redemption is drawing near."

29 And he told them a parable: "Look at the fig tree, and all the trees; ³⁰ as soon as they come out in leaf, you see for yourselves and know that the summer is already near. ³¹ So also, when you see these things taking place, you know that the kingdom of God is near. ³² Truly, I say to you, this generation will not pass away till all has taken place. ³³ Heaven and earth will pass away, but my words will not pass away.

34 "But take heed to yourselves lest your hearts be weighed down with dissipation and drunkenness and cares of this life, and that day come upon you suddenly like a snare; ³⁵ for it will come upon all who dwell upon the face of the whole earth. ³⁶ But watch at all times, praying that you may have strength to escape all these things that will take place, and to stand before the Son of man."

37 And every day he was teaching in the temple, but at night he went out and lodged on the mount called Ŏl´ĭ·vĕt. ³⁸ And early in the morning all the people came to him in the temple to hear him.

21.6: Lk 19.43-44; Mk 14.58; 15.29; Acts 6.14.
21.7: Lk 17.20; Acts 1.6.
21.8: Lk 17.23; Mk 13.21; 1 Jn 2.18.
21.10: 2 Chron 15.6; Is 19.2. 21.12-17: Mt 10.17-21.
21.12: Acts 25.24; Jn 16.2. 21.13: Phil 1.12.
21.14-15: Lk 12.11-12. 21.16: Lk 12.52-53.
21.17: Mt 10.22; Jn 15.18-25.
21.18: Lk 12.7; Mt 10.30; Acts 27.34; 1 Sam 14.45.
21.19: Mt 10.22; Rev 2.7.
21.20-22: Lk 19.41-44; 23.28-31; 17.31. 21.23: Lk 23.29.
21.24: Rom 11.25; Is 63.18; Dan 8.13; Rev 11.2.
21.25-27: Mt 24.29-30; Mk 13.24-26.
21.25: Rev 6.12-13; Is 13.10; Joel 2.10; Zeph 1.15.
21.27: Lk 9.27; Dan 7.13-14.
21.28: Lk 18.7-8. 21.29-33: Mt 24.32-35; Mk 13.28-31.
21.32: Lk 9.27. 21.33: Lk 16.17.
21.34: Lk 12.45; Mk 4.19; 1 Thess 5.6-7.
21.36: Mk 13.33. 21.37: Lk 19.47; Mk 11.19.

22 Now the feast of Unleavened Bread drew near, which is called the Passover. ²And the chief priests and the scribes were seeking how to put him to death; for they feared the people.

3 Then Satan entered into Judas called Is·căr′ĭ·ọt, who was of the number of the twelve; ⁴he went away and conferred with the chief priests and officers how he might betray him to them. ⁵And they were glad, and engaged to give him money. ⁶So he agreed, and sought an opportunity to betray him to them in the absence of the multitude.

7 Then came the day of Unleavened Bread, on which the passover lamb had to be sacrificed. ⁸So Jesus[h] sent Peter and John, saying, "Go and prepare the passover for us, that we may eat it." ⁹They said to him, "Where will you have us prepare it?" ¹⁰He said to them, "Behold, when you have entered the city, a man carrying a jar of water will meet you; follow him into the house which he enters, ¹¹and tell the householder, 'The Teacher says to you, Where is the guest room, where I am to eat the passover with my disciples?' ¹²And he will show you a large upper room furnished; there make ready." ¹³And they went, and found it as he had told them; and they prepared the passover.

14 And when the hour came, he sat at table, and the apostles with him. ¹⁵And he said to them, "I have earnestly desired to eat this passover with you before I suffer; ¹⁶for I tell you I shall not eat it[i] until it is fulfilled in the kingdom of God." ¹⁷And he took a cup, and when he had given thanks he said, "Take this, and divide it among yourselves; ¹⁸for I tell you that from now on I shall not drink of the fruit of the vine until the kingdom of God comes." ¹⁹And he took bread, and when he had given thanks he broke it and gave it to them, saying, "This is my body which is given for you. Do this in remembrance of me." ²⁰And likewise the cup after supper, saying, "This cup which is poured out for you is the new covenant in my blood.[i] ²¹But behold, the hand of him who betrays me is with me on the table. ²²For the Son of man goes as it has been determined; but woe to that man by whom he is betrayed!" ²³And they began to question one another, which of them it was that would do this.

24 A dispute also arose among them, which of them was to be regarded as the greatest. ²⁵And he said to them, "The kings of the Gentiles exercise lordship over them; and those in authority over them are called benefactors. ²⁶But not so with you; rather let the greatest among you become as the youngest, and the leader as one who serves. ²⁷For which is the greater, one who sits at table, or one who serves? Is it not the one who sits at table? But I am among you as one who serves.

28 "You are those who have continued with me in my trials; ²⁹and I assign to you, as my Father assigned to me, a kingdom, ³⁰that you may eat and drink at my table in my kingdom, and sit on thrones judging the twelve tribes of Israel.

31 "Simon, Simon, behold, Satan demanded to have you,[k] that he might sift you[k] like wheat, ³²but I have prayed for you that your faith may not fail; and when you have turned again, strengthen your brethren." ³³And he said to him, "Lord, I am ready to go with you to prison and to death." ³⁴He said, "I tell you, Peter, the cock will not crow this day, until you three times deny that you know me."

35 And he said to them, "When I sent you out with no purse or bag or sandals, did you lack anything?" They said, "Nothing." ³⁶He said to them, "But now, let him who has a purse take it, and likewise a bag. And let him who has no sword sell his mantle and buy one. ³⁷For I tell you that this scripture must be fulfilled in me, 'And he was reckoned with transgressors'; for what is written

[h] Greek *he*
[i] Other ancient authorities read *never eat it again*
[j] Other authorities omit, in whole or in part, verses 19b-20 (*which is given . . . in my blood*)
[k] The Greek word for *you* here is plural; in verse 32 it is singular   22.1-2: Mt 26.2-5; Mk 16.1-2; Jn 11.47-53.
22.3-6: Mt 26.14-16; Mk 14.10-11; Jn 13.2.
22.7-13: Mt 26.17-19; Mk 14.12-16.
22.7: Ex 12.18-20; Deut 16.5-8.   22.8: Acts 3.1; Lk 19.29.
22.14: Mt 26.20; Mk 14.17; Jn 13.17.
22.15: Lk 12.49-50.   22.16: Lk 14.15.
22.17: Mt 26.27; Mk 14.23; 1 Cor 10.16.
22.18: Mt 26.29; Mk 14.25.
22.19: Mt 26.26; Mk 14.22; 1 Cor 10.16; 11.23-26; Lk 9.16.
22.21-23: Mt 26.21-24; Mk 14.18-21; Ps 41.9; Jn 13.21-30.
22.24: Lk 9.46; Mk 9.34.
22.25-27: Mt 20.25-28; Mk 10.42-45; Jn 13.3-16.
22.26: Lk 9.48.   22.28-30: Mt 19.28.
22.28: Lk 4.13; Heb 2.18; 4.15.   22.29: Mk 14.24; Heb 9.20.
22.30: Mk 10.37; Rev 3.21; 20.4.
22.31: Job 1.6-12; Amos 9.9.   22.32: Jn 17.15; 21.15-17.
22.33-34: Mt 26.33-35; Mk 14.29-31; Jn 13.37-38.
22.35: Lk 10.4; Mt 10.9.   22.36: Lk 22.49-50.
22.37: Is 53.12.

about me has its fulfilment." ³⁸ And they said, "Look, Lord, here are two swords." And he said to them, "It is enough."

39 And he came out, and went, as was his custom, to the Mount of Olives; and the disciples followed him. ⁴⁰ And when he came to the place he said to them, "Pray that you may not enter into temptation." ⁴¹ And he withdrew from them about a stone's throw, and knelt down and prayed, ⁴² "Father, if thou art willing, remove this cup from me; nevertheless not my will, but thine, be done."ⁱ ⁴⁵ And when he rose from prayer, he came to the disciples and found them sleeping for sorrow, ⁴⁶ and he said to them, "Why do you sleep? Rise and pray that you may not enter into temptation."

47 While he was still speaking, there came a crowd, and the man called Judas, one of the twelve, was leading them. He drew near to Jesus to kiss him; ⁴⁸ but Jesus said to him, "Judas, would you betray the Son of man with a kiss?" ⁴⁹ And when those who were about him saw what would follow, they said, "Lord, shall we strike with the sword?" ⁵⁰ And one of them struck the slave of the high priest and cut off his right ear. ⁵¹ But Jesus said, "No more of this!" And he touched his ear and healed him. ⁵² Then Jesus said to the chief priests and officers of the temple and elders, who had come out against him, "Have you come out as against a robber, with swords and clubs? ⁵³ When I was with you day after day in the temple, you did not lay hands on me. But this is your hour, and the power of darkness."

54 Then they seized him and led him away, bringing him into the high priest's house. Peter followed at a distance; ⁵⁵ and when they had kindled a fire in the middle of the courtyard and sat down together, Peter sat among them. ⁵⁶ Then a maid, seeing him as he sat in the light and gazing at him, said, "This man also was with him." ⁵⁷ But he denied it, saying, "Woman, I do not know him." ⁵⁸ And a little later some one else saw him and said, "You also are one of them." But Peter said, "Man, I am not." ⁵⁹ And after an interval of about an hour still another insisted, saying, "Certainly this man also was with him; for he is a Galilean." ⁶⁰ But Peter said, "Man, I

do not know what you are saying." And immediately, while he was still speaking, the cock crowed. ⁶¹ And the Lord turned and looked at Peter. And Peter remembered the word of the Lord, how he had said to him, "Before the cock crows today, you will deny me three times." ⁶² And he went out and wept bitterly.

63 Now the men who were holding Jesus mocked him and beat him; ⁶⁴ they also blindfolded him and asked him, "Prophesy! Who is it that struck you?" ⁶⁵ And they spoke many other words against him, reviling him.

66 When day came, the assembly of the elders of the people gathered together, both chief priests and scribes; and they led him away to their council, and they said, ⁶⁷ "If you are the Christ, tell us." But he said to them, "If I tell you, you will not believe; ⁶⁸ and if I ask you, you will not answer. ⁶⁹ But from now on the Son of man shall be seated at the right hand of the power of God." ⁷⁰ And they all said, "Are you the Son of God, then?" And he said to them, "You say that I am." ⁷¹ And they said, "What further testimony do we need? We have heard it ourselves from his own lips."

23 Then the whole company of them arose, and brought him before Pilate. ² And they began to accuse him, saying, "We found this man perverting our nation, and forbidding us to give tribute to Caesar, and saying that he himself is Christ a king." ³ And Pilate asked him, "Are you the King of the Jews?" And he answered him, "You have said so." ⁴ And Pilate said to the chief priests and the multitudes, "I find no crime in this man." ⁵ But they were urgent, saying, "He stirs up the people, teaching

---

ⁱOther ancient authorities add verses 43 and 44: ⁴³And there appeared to him an angel from heaven, strengthening him. ⁴⁴And being in an agony he prayed more earnestly; and his sweat became like great drops of blood falling down upon the ground.

22.39: Mt 26.30; Mk 14.26; Jn 18.1.
22.40–46: Mt 26.36-46; Mk 14.32-42; Heb 5.7-8.
22.40: Lk 11.4.   **22.42:** Mk 10.38; Jn 18.11; 5.30.
22.47-53: Mt 26.47-56; Mk 14.43-49; Jn 18.3-11.
22.49: Lk 22.38.   **22.53:** Lk 19.47.
22.54-55: Mt 26.57-58; Mk 14.53-54; Jn 18.12-16.
22.56-62: Mt 26.69-75; Mk 14.66-72; Jn 18.16-18, 25-27.
22.61: Lk 7.13; 22.34.
22.63-65: Mt 26.67-68; Mk 14.65; Jn 18.22-24.
22.66: Mt 26.57; Mk 14.53; Lk 22.54.
22.67-71: Mt 26.63-66; Mk 14.61-64; Jn 18.19-21.
22.70: Lk 23.3; Mt 27.11.
23.1: Mt 27.1-2; Mk 15.1; Lk 20.25.
23.2: Lk 20.25.
23.3: Mt 27.11-12; Mk 15.2-3; Jn 18.29-38; Lk 22.70.
23.4: Lk 23.14, 22, 41; Mt 27.24; Jn 19.4, 6; Acts 13.28.

throughout all Jū·dē′ạ, from Galilee even to this place."

6 When Pilate heard this, he asked whether the man was a Galilean. [7]And when he learned that he belonged to Hĕr′ọd's jurisdiction, he sent him over to Herod, who was himself in Jerusalem at that time. [8]When Hĕr′ọd saw Jesus, he was very glad, for he had long desired to see him, because he had heard about him, and he was hoping to see some sign done by him. [9]So he questioned him at some length; but he made no answer. [10]The chief priests and the scribes stood by, vehemently accusing him. [11]And Hĕr′ọd with his soldiers treated him with contempt and mocked him; then, arraying him in gorgeous apparel, he sent him back to Pilate. [12]And Hĕr′ọd and Pilate became friends with each other that very day, for before this they had been at enmity with each other.

13 Pilate then called together the chief priests and the rulers and the people, [14]and said to them, "You brought me this man as one who was perverting the people; and after examining him before you, behold, I did not find this man guilty of any of your charges against him; [15]neither did Hĕr′ọd, for he sent him back to us. Behold, nothing deserving death has been done by him; [16]I will therefore chastise him and release him."[m]

18 But they all cried out together, "Away with this man, and release to us Bạ·răb′bạs"—[19]a man who had been thrown into prison for an insurrection started in the city, and for murder. [20]Pilate addressed them once more, desiring to release Jesus; [21]but they shouted out, "Crucify, crucify him!" [22]A third time he said to them, "Why, what evil has he done? I have found in him no crime deserving death; I will therefore chastise him and release him." [23]But they were urgent, demanding with loud cries that he should be crucified. And their voices prevailed. [24]So Pilate gave sentence that their demand should be granted. [25]He released the man who had been thrown into prison for insurrection and murder, whom they asked for; but Jesus he delivered up to their will.

26 And as they led him away, they seized one Simon of Cỹ·rē′nē, who was coming in from the country, and laid on him the cross, to carry it behind Jesus. [27]And there followed him a great multitude of the people, and of women who bewailed and lamented him. [28]But Jesus turning to them said, "Daughters of Jerusalem, do not weep for me, but weep for yourselves and for your children. [29]For behold, the days are coming when they will say, 'Blessed are the barren, and the wombs that never bore, and the breasts that never gave suck!' [30]Then they will begin to say to the mountains, 'Fall on us'; and to the hills, 'Cover us.' [31]For if they do this when the wood is green, what will happen when it is dry?"

32 Two others also, who were criminals, were led away to be put to death with him. [33]And when they came to the place which is called The Skull, there they crucified him, and the criminals, one on the right and one on the left. [34]And Jesus said, "Father, forgive them; for they know not what they do."[n] And they cast lots to divide his garments. [35]And the people stood by, watching; but the rulers scoffed at him, saying, "He saved others; let him save himself, if he is the Christ of God, his Chosen One!" [36]The soldiers also mocked him, coming up and offering him vinegar, [37]and saying, "If you are the King of the Jews, save yourself!" [38]There was also an inscription over him,[o] "This is the King of the Jews."

39 One of the criminals who were hanged railed at him, saying, "Are you not the Christ? Save yourself and us!" [40]But the other rebuked him, saying, "Do you not fear God, since you are under the same sentence of condemnation? [41]And we indeed justly; for we are receiving the due reward of our deeds; but this man has done nothing wrong." [42]And he said, "Jesus, remember me when you come into[p] your kingdom." [43]And he said to him, "Truly,

[m]Here, or after verse 19, other ancient authorities add verse 17, *Now he was obliged to release one man to them at the festival*

[o]Other ancient authorities omit the sentence *And Jesus … what they do*

[o]Other ancient authorities add *in letters of Greek and Latin and Hebrew* [p]Other ancient authorities read *in*

23.8: Lk 9.9; Acts 4.27-28. 23.9: Mk 15.5.
23.11: Mk 15.17-19; Jn 19.2-3.
23.14: Lk 23.4, 22, 41. 23.16: Lk 23.22; Jn 19.12-14.
23.18: Mt 27.20-23; Mk 15.11-14; Acts 3.13-14; Jn 18.38-40; 19.14-15. 23.23-25: Mt 27.26; Mk 15.15.
23.26: Mt 27.32; Mk 15.21; Jn 19.17.
23.28-31: Lk 21.23-24; 19.41-44.
23.33-39: Mt 27.33-44; Mk 15.22-32; Jn 19.17-24.
23.34: Acts 7.60; Ps 22.18. 23.35: Lk 4.23.
23.36: Mk 15.23; Ps 69.21.
23.41: Lk 23.4, 14, 22. 23.43: 2 Cor 12.3; Rev 2.7.

I say to you, today you will be with me in Paradise."

44 It was now about the sixth hour, and there was darkness over the whole land *q* until the ninth hour, *45* while the sun's light failed; *r* and the curtain of the temple was torn in two. *46* Then Jesus, crying with a loud voice, said, "Father, into thy hands I commit my spirit!" And having said this he breathed his last. *47* Now when the centurion saw what had taken place, he praised God, and said, "Certainly this man was innocent!" *48* And all the multitudes who assembled to see the sight, when they saw what had taken place, returned home beating their breasts. *49* And all his acquaintances and the women who had followed him from Galilee stood at a distance and saw these things.

50 Now there was a man named Joseph from the Jewish town of Ăr·ĭ·ma·thē'a̤. He was a member of the council, a good and righteous man, *51* who had not consented to their purpose and deed, and he was looking for the kingdom of God. *52* This man went to Pilate and asked for the body of Jesus. *53* Then he took it down and wrapped it in a linen shroud, and laid him in a rock-hewn tomb, where no one had ever yet been laid. *54* It was the day of Preparation, and the sabbath was beginning. *s 55* The women who had come with him from Galilee followed, and saw the tomb, and how his body was laid; *56* then they returned, and prepared spices and ointments.

On the sabbath they rested according to the commandment.

24 But on the first day of the week, at early dawn, they went to the tomb, taking the spices which they had prepared. *2* And they found the stone rolled away from the tomb, *3* but when they went in they did not find the body. *t* *4* While they were perplexed about this, behold, two men stood by them in dazzling apparel; *5* and as they were frightened and bowed their faces to the ground, the men said to them, "Why do you seek the living among the dead? *u* *6* Remember how he told you, while he was still in Galilee, *7* that the Son of man must be delivered into the hands of sinful men, and be crucified, and on the the third day rise." *8* And they remembered his words, *9* and returning from the tomb they told

all this to the eleven and to all the rest. *10* Now it was Mary Măg'da̤·lēne and Jō–ăn'na̤ and Mary the mother of James and the other women with them who told this to the apostles; *11* but these words seemed to them an idle tale, and they did not believe them. *v*

13 That very day two of them were going to a village named Ĕm·mā'ṳs, about seven miles *w* from Jerusalem, *14* and talking with each other about all these things that had happened. *15* While they were talking and discussing together, Jesus himself drew near and went with them. *16* But their eyes were kept from recognizing him. *17* And he said to them, "What is this conversation which you are holding with each other as you walk?" And they stood still, looking sad. *18* Then one of them, named Clē'o̤·pas, answered him, "Are you the only visitor to Jerusalem who does not know the things that have happened there in these days?" *19* And he said to them, "What things?" And they said to him, "Concerning Jesus of Nazareth, who was a prophet mighty in deed and word before God and all the people, *20* and how our chief priests and rulers delivered him up to be condemned to death, and crucified him. *21* But we had hoped that he was the one to redeem Israel. Yes, and besides all this, it is now the third day since this happened. *22* Moreover, some women of our company amazed us. They were at the tomb early in the morning *23* and did not find his body; and they came back saying that they had even seen a vision of angels, who said that he was alive. *24* Some of those who were with us went to the tomb, and found

---

q Or *earth*
r Or *the sun was eclipsed*. Other ancient authorities read *the sun was darkened*
s Greek *was dawning*
t Other ancient authorities add *of the Lord Jesus*
u Other ancient authorities add *He is not here, but has risen*
v Other ancient authorities add verse 12, *But Peter rose and ran to the tomb; stooping and looking in, he saw the linen cloths by themselves; and he went home wondering at what had happened*
w Greek *sixty stadia*; some ancient authorities read *a hundred and sixty stadia*

23.44–49: Mt 27.45-56; Mk 15.33-41; Jn 19.25-30.
23.45: Ex 26.31-35; Heb 9.8; 10.19. **23.46:** Ps 31.5.
23.49: Lk 8.1-3; 23.55-56; 24.10.
23.50–56: Mt 27.57-61; Mk 15.42-47; Jn 19.38-42; Acts 13.29. **23.56:** Mk 16.1; Ex 12.16; 20.10.
24.1–9: Mt 28.1-8; Mk 16.1-7; Jn 20.1, 11-13.
24.6: Lk 9.22; 13.32-33.
24.10: Mk 16.1; Lk 8.1-3; Jn 20.2.
24.16: Jn 20.14; 21.4.
24.19: Mt 21.11; Lk 7.16; 13.33; Acts 3.22.
24.24: Jn 20.3-10.

it just as the women had said; but him they did not see." [25] And he said to them, "O foolish men, and slow of heart to believe all that the prophets have spoken! [26] Was it not necessary that the Christ should suffer these things and enter into his glory?" [27] And beginning with Moses and all the prophets, he interpreted to them in all the scriptures the things concerning himself.

28 So they drew near to the village to which they were going. He appeared to be going further, [29] but they constrained him, saying, "Stay with us, for it is toward evening and the day is now far spent." So he went in to stay with them. [30] When he was at table with them, he took the bread and blessed, and broke it, and gave it to them. [31] And their eyes were opened and they recognized him; and he vanished out of their sight. [32] They said to each other, "Did not our hearts burn within us[c] while he talked to us on the road, while he opened to us the scriptures?" [33] And they rose that same hour and returned to Jerusalem; and they found the eleven gathered together and those who were with them, [34] who said, "The Lord has risen indeed, and has appeared to Simon!" [35] Then they told what had happened on the road, and how he was known to them in the breaking of the bread.

36 As they were saying this, Jesus himself stood among them.[x] [37] But they were startled and frightened, and supposed that they saw a spirit. [38] And he said to them, "Why are you troubled, and why do questionings rise in your hearts? [39] See my hands and my feet, that it is I myself; handle me, and see; for a spirit has not flesh and bones as you see that I have."[y] [41] And while they still disbelieved for joy, and wondered, he said to them, "Have you anything here to eat?" [42] They gave him a piece of broiled fish, [43] and he took it and ate before them.

44 Then he said to them, "These are my words which I spoke to you, while I was still with you, that everything written about me in the law of Moses and the prophets and the psalms must be fulfilled." [45] Then he opened their minds to understand the scriptures, [46] and said to them, "Thus it is written, that the Christ should suffer and on the third day rise from the dead, [47] and that repentance and forgiveness of sins should be preached in his name to all nations,[z] beginning from Jerusalem. [48] You are witnesses of these things. [49] And behold, I send the promise of my Father upon you; but stay in the city, until you are clothed with power from on high."

50 Then he led them out as far as Bĕth′a·nȳ, and lifting up his hands he blessed them. [51] While he blessed them, he parted from them, and was carried up into heaven.[a] [52] And they[b] returned to Jerusalem with great joy, [53] and were continually in the temple blessing God.

The Gospel According to

John

1 In the beginning was the Word, and the Word was with God, and the Word was God. [2] He was in the beginning with God; [3] all things were made through him, and without him was not anything made that was made. [4] In him was life,[a] and the life was the light of men. [5] The light shines in the

[c] Other ancient authorities omit *within us*
[x] Other ancient authorities add *and said to them, "Peace to you!"*
[y] Other ancient authorities add verse 40, *And when he had said this, he showed them his hands and his feet*
[z] Or *nations. Beginning from Jerusalem you are witnesses*

[a] Other ancient authorities omit *and was carried up into heaven*
[b] Other ancient authorities add *worshiped him, and*
24.27: Lk 24.44-45; Acts 28.23; 1 Pet 1.11.
24.28: Mk 6.48.
24.30: Lk 9.16; 22.19.   **24.34:** 1 Cor 15.5.
24.36-43: Jn 20.19-20, 27; Jn 21.5, 9-13; 1 Cor 15.5; Acts 10.40-41.   **24.39:** 1 Jn 1.1.
24.44: Lk 24.26-27; Acts 28.23.
24.46: Hos 6.2; 1 Cor 15.3-4.
24.47: Acts 1.4-8; Mt 28.19.
24.49: Acts 2.1-4; Jn 14.26; 20.21-23.
24.51: Acts 1.9-11.   **24.52-53:** Acts 1.12-14.

[a] Or *was not anything made. That which has been made was life in him*
1.1: Gen 1.1; 1 Jn 1.1; Rev 19.13; Jn 17.5.
1.3: Col 1.16; 1 Cor 8.6; Heb 1.2.   **1.4:** Jn 5.26; 11.25; 14.6.
1.5: Jn 9.5; 12.46.

darkness, and the darkness has not overcome it.

6 There was a man sent from God, whose name was John. [7] He came for testimony, to bear witness to the light, that all might believe through him. [8] He was not the light, but came to bear witness to the light.

9 The true light that enlightens every man was coming into the world. [10] He was in the world, and the world was made through him, yet the world knew him not. [11] He came to his own home, and his own people received him not. [12] But to all who received him, who believed in his name, he gave power to become children of God; [13] who were born, not of blood nor of the will of the flesh nor of the will of man, but of God.

14 And the Word became flesh and dwelt among us, full of grace and truth; we have beheld his glory, glory as of the only Son from the Father. [15] (John bore witness to him, and cried, "This was he of whom I said, 'He who comes after me ranks before me, for he was before me.'") [16] And from his fulness have we all received, grace upon grace. [17] For the law was given through Moses; grace and truth came through Jesus Christ. [18] No one has ever seen God; the only Son,[b] who is in the bosom of the Father, he has made him known.

19 And this is the testimony of John, when the Jews sent priests and Lē'-vītes from Jerusalem to ask him, "Who are you?" [20] He confessed, he did not deny, but confessed, "I am not the Christ." [21] And they asked him, "What then? Are you Ē·lī'jah?" He said, "I am not." "Are you the prophet?" And he answered, "No." [22] They said to him then, "Who are you? Let us have an answer for those who sent us. What do you say about yourself?" [23] He said, "I am the voice of one crying in the wilderness, 'Make straight the way of the Lord,' as the prophet Ī·sāi'ah said."

24 Now they had been sent from the Phăr'ĭ·seeş. [25] They asked him, "Then why are you baptizing, if you are neither the Christ, nor Ē·lī'jah, nor the prophet?" [26] John answered them, "I baptize with water; but among you stands one whom you do not know, [27] even he who comes after me, the thong of whose sandal I am not worthy to untie." [28] This took place in Bĕth'-

ạ·nỹ beyond the Jordan, where John was baptizing.

29 The next day he saw Jesus coming toward him, and said, "Behold, the Lamb of God, who takes away the sin of the world! [30] This is he of whom I said, 'After me comes a man who ranks before me, for he was before me.' [31] I myself did not know him; but for this I came baptizing with water, that he might be revealed to Israel." [32] And John bore witness, "I saw the Spirit descend as a dove from heaven, and it remained on him. [33] I myself did not know him; but he who sent me to baptize with water said to me, 'He on whom you see the Spirit descend and remain, this is he who baptizes with the Holy Spirit.' [34] And I have seen and have borne witness that this is the Son of God."

35 The next day again John was standing with two of his disciples; [36] and he looked at Jesus as he walked, and said, "Behold, the Lamb of God!" [37] The two disciples heard him say this, and they followed Jesus. [38] Jesus turned, and saw them following, and said to them, "What do you seek?" And they said to him, "Rabbi" (which means Teacher), "where are you staying?" [39] He said to them, "Come and see." They came and saw where he was staying; and they stayed with him that day, for it was about the tenth hour. [40] One of the two who heard John speak, and followed him, was Andrew, Simon Peter's brother. [41] He first found his brother Simon, and said to him, "We have found the Messiah" (which means Christ). [42] He brought him to Jesus. Jesus looked at him, and said, "So you are Simon the son of John? You shall be called Çē'phạş" (which means Peter[c]).

43 The next day Jesus decided to go

[b] Other ancient authorities read God
[c] From the word for *rock* in Aramaic and Greek, respectively

1.6: Mk 1.4; Mt 3.1; Lk 3.3; Jn 1.19-23. 1.9: 1 Jn 2.8.
1.12: Gal 3.26; Jn 3.18; 1 Jn 5.13.
1.13: Jn 3.5; 1 Pet 1.23; Jas 1.18; 1 Jn 3.9.
1.14: Rom 1.3; Gal 4.4; Phil 2.7; 1 Tim 3.16; Heb 2.14; 1 Jn 4.2. 1.15: Jn 1.30.
1.16: Col 1.19; 2.9; Eph 1.23; Rom 5.21. 1.17: Jn 7.19.
1.18: Ex 33.20; Jn 6.26; 1 Jn 4.12; Jn 3.11. 1.19: Jn 1.6.
1.20: Jn 3.28.
1.21: Mt 11.14; 16.14; Mk 9.13; Mt 17.13; Deut 18.15, 18.
1.23: Is 40.3; Mt 3.3; Lk 3.4.
1.26-27: Mk 1.7-8; Mt 3.11; Lk 3.16. 1.28: Jn 3.26; 10.40.
1.29: Jn 1.36; Is 53.7; Acts 8.32; 1 Pet 1.19; Rev 5.6; 1 Jn 3.5. 1.30: Jn 1.15.
1.32: Mk 1.10; Mt 3.16; Lk 3.22. 1.35: Lk 7.18.
1.40-42: Mt 4.18-22; Mk 1.16-20; Lk 5.2-11.
1.41: Dan 9.25; Jn 4.25.
1.42: Jn 21.15-17; 1 Cor 15.5; Mt 16.18.
1.43: Mt 10.3; Jn 6.5; 12.21; 14.8.

to Galilee. And he found Philip and said to him, "Follow me." [44] Now Philip was from Bĕth-să′ĭ-dạ, the city of Andrew and Peter. [45] Philip found Nạ-thăn′ạ-ĕl, and said to him, "We have found him of whom Moses in the law and also the prophets wrote, Jesus of Nazareth, the son of Joseph." [46] Nạ-thăn′ạ-ĕl said to him, "Can anything good come out of Nazareth?" Philip said to him, "Come and see." [47] Jesus saw Nạ-thăn′ạ-ĕl coming to him, and said of him, "Behold, an Israelite indeed, in whom is no guile!" [48] Nạ-thăn′ạ-ĕl said to him, "How do you know me?" Jesus answered him, "Before Philip called you, when you were under the fig tree, I saw you." [49] Nạ-thăn′ạ-ĕl answered him, "Rabbi, you are the Son of God! You are the King of Israel!" [50] Jesus answered him, "Because I said to you, I saw you under the fig tree, do you believe? You shall see greater things than these." [51] And he said to him, "Truly, truly, I say to you, you will see heaven opened, and the angels of God ascending and descending upon the Son of man."

2 On the third day there was a marriage at Cā′nạ in Galilee, and the mother of Jesus was there; [2] Jesus also was invited to the marriage, with his disciples. [3] When the wine gave out, the mother of Jesus said to him, "They have no wine." [4] And Jesus said to her, "O woman, what have you to do with me? My hour has not yet come." [5] His mother said to the servants, "Do whatever he tells you." [6] Now six stone jars were standing there, for the Jewish rites of purification, each holding twenty or thirty gallons. [7] Jesus said to them, "Fill the jars with water." And they filled them up to the brim. [8] He said to them, "Now draw some out, and take it to the steward of the feast." So they took it. [9] When the steward of the feast tasted the water now become wine, and did not know where it came from (though the servants who had drawn the water knew), the steward of the feast called the bridegroom [10] and said to him, "Every man serves the good wine first; and when men have drunk freely, then the poor wine; but you have kept the good wine until now." [11] This, the first of his signs, Jesus did at Cā′nạ in Galilee, and manifested his glory; and his disciples believed in him.

[12] After this he went down to Cạ-pĕr′nạ-ụm, with his mother and his brothers and his disciples; and there they stayed for a few days.

[13] The Passover of the Jews was at hand, and Jesus went up to Jerusalem. [14] In the temple he found those who were selling oxen and sheep and pigeons, and the money-changers at their business. [15] And making a whip of cords, he drove them all, with the sheep and oxen, out of the temple; and he poured out the coins of the money-changers and overturned their tables. [16] And he told those who sold the pigeons, "Take these things away; you shall not make my Father's house a house of trade." [17] His disciples remembered that it was written, "Zeal for thy house will consume me." [18] The Jews then said to him, "What sign have you to show us for doing this?" [19] Jesus answered them, "Destroy this temple, and in three days I will raise it up." [20] The Jews then said, "It has taken forty-six years to build this temple, and will you raise it up in three days?" [21] But he spoke of the temple of his body. [22] When therefore he was raised from the dead, his disciples remembered that he had said this; and they believed the scripture and the word which Jesus had spoken.

[23] Now when he was in Jerusalem at the Passover feast, many believed in his name when they saw the signs which he did; [24] but Jesus did not trust himself to them, [25] because he knew all men and needed no one to bear witness of man; for he himself knew what was in man.

3 Now there was a man of the Phăr′ĭ-seeṣ, named Nĭc-ọ-dē′mụs, a ruler of the Jews. [2] This man came to Jesus[d] by night and said to him, "Rabbi, we know that you are a teacher come from God; for no one can do these signs that you do, unless God is with him." [3] Jesus answered him, "Truly,

[d] Greek *him*

1.45: Lk 24.27.   1.46: Jn 7.41; Mk 6.2.
1.49: Ps 2.7; Mk 15.32; Jn 12.13.   1.51: Lk 3.21; Gen 28.12.
2.1: Jn 4.46; 21.2.   2.3: Jn 19.26; Mk 3.31.
2.4: Mk 1.24; 5.7; Jn 7.6, 30; 8.20.
2.6: Mk 7.3; Jn 3.25.   2.11: Jn 2.23; 3.2; 4.54; 6.2.
2.12: Mt 4.13; Jn 7.3; Mk 3.31.
2.13: Jn 6.4; 11.55; Deut 16.1-6; Lk 2.41.
2.14-16: Mt 21.12-13; Mk 11.15-17; Lk 19.45-46.
2.16: Lk 2.49.   2.17: Ps 69.9.
2.18: Mk 11.28; Mt 21.23; Lk 20.2.
2.19: Mk 14.58; Acts 6.14.   2.21: 1 Cor 6.19; Jn 8.57.
2.22: Jn 12.16; 14.26.   2.25: Jn 1.47; 6.61; 13.11; Mk 2.8.
3.1: Jn 7.50; 19.39; Lk 23.13; Jn 7.26.
3.2: Jn 2.11; 7.31; 9.16; Acts 10.38.
3.3: Jn 1.13; 1 Pet 1.23; Jas 1.18; 1 Jn 3.9.

truly, I say to you, unless one is born anew,[e] he cannot see the kingdom of God." [4] Nĭc·o·dē'mŭs said to him, "How can a man be born when he is old? Can he enter a second time into his mother's womb and be born?" [5] Jesus answered, "Truly, truly, I say to you, unless one is born of water and the Spirit, he cannot enter the kingdom of God. [6] That which is born of the flesh is flesh, and that which is born of the Spirit is spirit.[f] [7] Do not marvel that I said to you, 'You must be born anew.'[e] [8] The wind[f] blows where it wills, and you hear the sound of it, but you do not know whence it comes or whither it goes; so it is with every one who is born of the Spirit." [9] Nĭc·o·dē'mŭs said to him, "How can this be?" [10] Jesus answered him, "Are you a teacher of Israel, and yet you do not understand this? [11] Truly, truly, I say to you, we speak of what we know, and bear witness to what we have seen; but you do not receive our testimony. [12] If I have told you earthly things and you do not believe, how can you believe if I tell you heavenly things? [13] No one has ascended into heaven but he who descended from heaven, the Son of man.[g] [14] And as Moses lifted up the serpent in the wilderness, so must the Son of man be lifted up, [15] that whoever believes in him may have eternal life."[h]

[16] For God so loved the world that he gave his only Son, that whoever believes in him should not perish but have eternal life. [17] For God sent the Son into the world, not to condemn the world, but that the world might be saved through him. [18] He who believes in him is not condemned; he who does not believe is condemned already, because he has not believed in the name of the only Son of God. [19] And this is the judgment, that the light has come into the world, and men loved darkness rather than light, because their deeds were evil. [20] For every one who does evil hates the light, and does not come to the light, lest his deeds should be exposed. [21] But he who does what is true comes to the light, that it may be clearly seen that his deeds have been wrought in God.

[22] After this Jesus and his disciples went into the land of Jü·dē'a; there he remained with them and baptized. [23] John also was baptizing at Ae'nŏn near Sā'lĭm, because there was much water there; and people came and were baptized. [24] For John had not yet been put in prison.

[25] Now a discussion arose between John's disciples and a Jew over purifying. [26] And they came to John, and said to him, "Rabbi, he who was with you beyond the Jordan, to whom you bore witness, here he is, baptizing, and all are going to him." [27] John answered, "No one can receive anything except what is given him from heaven. [28] You yourselves bear me witness, that I said, I am not the Christ, but I have been sent before him. [29] He who has the bride is the bridegroom; the friend of the bridegroom, who stands and hears him, rejoices greatly at the bridegroom's voice; therefore this joy of mine is now full. [30] He must increase, but I must decrease."[i]

[31] He who comes from above is above all; he who is of the earth belongs to the earth, and of the earth he speaks; he who comes from heaven is above all. [32] He bears witness to what he has seen and heard, yet no one receives his testimony; [33] he who receives his testimony sets his seal to this, that God is true. [34] For he whom God has sent utters the words of God, for it is not by measure that he gives the Spirit; [35] the Father loves the Son, and has given all things into his hand. [36] He who believes in the Son has eternal life; he who does not obey the Son shall not see life, but the wrath of God rests upon him.

4 Now when the Lord knew that the Phăr'ĭ·seeṣ had heard that Jesus was making and baptizing more disciples than John [2] (although Jesus himself did not baptize, but only his disciples), [3] he left Jü·dē'a and departed again to Galilee. [4] He had to pass

*Or *from above*
/The same Greek word means both *wind* and *spirit*
*Other ancient authorities add *who is in heaven*
*Some interpreters hold that the quotation continues through verse 21
*Some interpreters hold that the quotation continues through verse 36
3.5: Ezek 36.25-27; Eph 5.26; Tit 3.5.   **3.6:** 1 Cor 15.50.
3.8: Ezek 37.9.   **3.11:** Jn 8.26; 1.18; 3.32.
3.13: Rom 10.6; Eph 4.9.   **3.14:** Num 21.9; Jn 8.28; 12.34.
3.16: Rom 5.8; 8.32; Eph 2.4; 1 Jn 4.9-10.
3.17: Jn 8.15; 12.47; Lk 19.10; 1 Jn 4.14.
3.19: Jn 1.4; 8.12; Eph 5.11, 13.   **3.21:** 1 Jn 1.6.
3.22: Jn 4.2.   **3.24:** Mk 1.14; 6.17-18.   **3.26:** Jn 1.7, 28.
3.27: 1 Cor 4.7.   **3.28:** Jn 1.20, 23.
3.29: Mk 2.19-20; Mt 25.1; Jn 15.11.
3.31: Jn 3.13; 8.23; 1 Jn 4.5.   **3.32:** Jn 3.11.
3.36: Jn 3.16; 5.24.   **4.1:** Jn 3.22.   **4.4:** Lk 9.52; 17.11.

through Sa·mâr′ĭ·ạ. ⁵So he came to a city of Sạ·mâr′ĭ·ạ, called Sȳ′chăr, near the field that Jacob gave to his son Joseph. ⁶Jacob's well was there, and so Jesus, wearied as he was with his journey, sat down beside the well. It was about the sixth hour.

7 There came a woman of Sạ·mâr′ĭ·ạ to draw water. Jesus said to her, "Give me a drink." ⁸For his disciples had gone away into the city to buy food. ⁹The Sạ·mâr′ĭ·tạn woman said to him, "How is it that you, a Jew, ask a drink of me, a woman of Sạ·mâr′ĭ·ạ?" For Jews have no dealings with Sạ·mâr′- ĭ·tạnş. ¹⁰Jesus answered her, "If you knew the gift of God, and who it is that is saying to you, 'Give me a drink,' you would have asked him and he would have given you living water." ¹¹The woman said to him, "Sir, you have nothing to draw with, and the well is deep; where do you get that living water? ¹²Are you greater than our father Jacob, who gave us the well, and drank from it himself, and his sons, and his cattle?" ¹³Jesus said to her, "Every one who drinks of this water will thirst again, ¹⁴but whoever drinks of the water that I shall give him will never thirst; the water that I shall give him will become in him a spring of water welling up to eternal life." ¹⁵The woman said to him, "Sir, give me this water, that I may not thirst, nor come here to draw."

16 Jesus said to her, "Go, call your husband, and come here." ¹⁷The woman answered him, "I have no husband." Jesus said to her, "You are right in saying, 'I have no husband'; ¹⁸for you have had five husbands, and he whom you now have is not your husband; this you said truly." ¹⁹The woman said to him, "Sir, I perceive that you are a prophet. ²⁰Our fathers worshiped on this mountain; and you say that in Jerusalem is the place where men ought to worship." ²¹Jesus said to her, "Woman, believe me, the hour is coming when neither on this mountain nor in Jerusalem will you worship the Father. ²²You worship what you do not know; we worship what we know, for salvation is from the Jews. ²³But the hour is coming, and now is, when the true worshipers will worship the Father in spirit and truth, for such the Father seeks to worship him. ²⁴God is spirit, and

those who worship him must worship in spirit and truth." ²⁵The woman said to him, "I know that Messiah is coming (he who is called Christ); when he comes, he will show us all things." ²⁶Jesus said to her, "I who speak to you am he."

27 Just then his disciples came. They marveled that he was talking with a woman, but none said, "What do you wish?" or, "Why are you talking with her?" ²⁸So the woman left her water jar, and went away into the city, and said to the people, ²⁹"Come, see a man who told me all that I ever did. Can this be the Christ?" ³⁰They went out of the city and were coming to him.

31 Meanwhile the disciples besought him, saying, "Rabbi, eat." ³²But he said to them, "I have food to eat of which you do not know." ³³So the disciples said to one another, "Has any one brought him food?" ³⁴Jesus said to them, "My food is to do the will of him who sent me, and to accomplish his work. ³⁵Do you not say, 'There are yet four months, then comes the harvest'? I tell you, lift up your eyes, and see how the fields are already white for harvest. ³⁶He who reaps receives wages, and gathers fruit for eternal life, so that sower and reaper may rejoice together. ³⁷For here the saying holds true, 'One sows and another reaps.' ³⁸I sent you to reap that for which you did not labor; others have labored, and you have entered into their labor."

39 Many Sạ·mâr′ĭ·tạnş from that city believed in him because of the woman's testimony, "He told me all that I ever did." ⁴⁰So when the Sạ·mâr′- ĭ·tạnş came to him, they asked him to stay with them; and he stayed there two days. ⁴¹And many more believed because of his word. ⁴²They said to the woman, "It is no longer because of your words that we believe, for we have heard for ourselves, and we know that this is indeed the Savior of the world."

43 After the two days he departed

4.5: Gen 33.19; 48.22; Josh 24.32.
4.9: Mt 10.5; Jn 8.48; Ezra 4.3-6.
4.10: Jn 7.37; Rev 21.6; 22.17.   **4.14:** Jn 6.35; 7.38.
4.15: Jn 6.34.   **4.18:** 2 Kings 17.24; Hos 2.7.
4.20: Deut 11.29; Josh 8.33; Lk 9.53.
4.21: Jn 5.25; 16.2, 32; Mal 1.11.
4.22: 2 Kings 17.28-41; Is 2.3; Rom 9.4.   **4.24:** Phil 3.3.
4.26: Jn 8.24.   **4.29:** Jn 7.26; Mt 12.23.   **4.32:** Mt 4.4.
4.34: Jn 5.30; 6.38; 17.4.   **4.35:** Lk 10.2; Mt 9.37.
4.37: Job 31.8; Mic 6.15.   **4.42:** 1 Jn 4.14; 2 Tim 1.10.

to Galilee. ⁴⁴For Jesus himself testified that a prophet has no honor in his own country. ⁴⁵So when he came to Galilee, the Galileans welcomed him, having seen all that he had done in Jerusalem at the feast, for they too had gone to the feast.

46 So he came again to Cā′na in Galilee, where he had made the water wine. And at Ca.pēr′na–um there was an official whose son was ill. ⁴⁷When he heard that Jesus had come from Jü·dē′a to Galilee, he went and begged him to come down and heal his son, for he was at the point of death. ⁴⁸Jesus therefore said to him, "Unless you see signs and wonders you will not believe." ⁴⁹The official said to him, "Sir, come down before my child dies." ⁵⁰Jesus said to him, "Go; your son will live." The man believed the word that Jesus spoke to him and went his way. ⁵¹As he was going down, his servants met him and told him that his son was living. ⁵²So he asked them the hour when he began to mend, and they said to him, "Yesterday at the seventh hour the fever left him." ⁵³The father knew that was the hour when Jesus had said to him, "Your son will live"; and he himself believed, and all his household. ⁵⁴This was now the second sign that Jesus did when he had come from Jü·dē′a to Galilee.

5 After this there was a feast of the Jews, and Jesus went up to Jerusalem.

2 Now there is in Jerusalem by the Sheep Gate a pool, in Hebrew called Bĕth–zā′tha,ʲ which has five porticoes. ³In these lay a multitude of invalids, blind, lame, paralyzed.ᵏ ⁵One man was there, who had been ill for thirty-eight years. ⁶When Jesus saw him and knew that he had been lying there a long time, he said to him, "Do you want to be healed?" ⁷The sick man answered him, "Sir, I have no man to put me into the pool when the water is troubled, and while I am going another steps down before me." ⁸Jesus said to him, "Rise, take up your pallet, and walk." ⁹And at once the man was healed, and he took up his pallet and walked.

Now that day was the sabbath. ¹⁰So the Jews said to the man who was cured, "It is the sabbath, it is not lawful for you to carry your pallet." ¹¹But he answered them, "The man who

healed me said to me, 'Take up your pallet, and walk.' " ¹²They asked him, "Who is the man who said to you, 'Take up your pallet, and walk'?" ¹³Now the man who had been healed did not know who it was, for Jesus had withdrawn, as there was a crowd in the place. ¹⁴Afterward, Jesus found him in the temple, and said to him, "See, you are well! Sin no more, that nothing worse befall you." ¹⁵The man went away and told the Jews that it was Jesus who had healed him. ¹⁶And this was why the Jews persecuted Jesus, because he did this on the sabbath. ¹⁷But Jesus answered them, "My Father is working still, and I am working." ¹⁸This was why the Jews sought all the more to kill him, because he not only broke the sabbath but also called God his own Father, making himself equal with God.

19 Jesus said to them, "Truly, truly, I say to you, the Son can do nothing of his own accord, but only what he sees the Father doing; for whatever he does, that the Son does likewise. ²⁰For the Father loves the Son, and shows him all that he himself is doing; and greater works than these will he show him, that you may marvel. ²¹For as the Father raises the dead and gives them life, so also the Son gives life to whom he will. ²²The Father judges no one, but has given all judgment to the Son, ²³that all may honor the Son, even as they honor the Father. He who does not honor the Son does not honor the Father who sent him. ²⁴Truly, truly, I say to you, he who hears my word and believes him who sent me, has eternal life; he does not come into judgment, but has passed from death to life. 25 "Truly, truly, I say to you, the hour is coming, and now is, when the dead will hear the voice of the Son of God, and those who hear will live. ²⁶For as the Father has life in himself,

ʲOther ancient authorities read *Bethesda*, others *Bethsaida*
ᵏOther ancient authorities insert, wholly or in part, *waiting for the moving of the water; ʲfor an angel of the Lord went down at certain seasons into the pool, and troubled the water; whoever stepped in first after the troubling of the water was healed of whatever disease he had*

4.44: Mk 6.4; Mt 13.57.
4.46: Jn 2.1-11; Mt 8.5-10; Lk 7.2-10.
4.48: Dan 4.2; Mk 13.22; Acts 2.19; 4.30; Rom 15.19; Heb 2.4. **4.53:** Acts 11.14. **4.54:** Jn 2.11.
5.2: Neh 3.1; 12.39. **5.8:** Mk 2.11; Mt 9.6; Lk 5.24.
5.10: Neh 13.19; Jer 17.21; Jn 7.23; 9.16; Mk 2.24.
5.14: Mk 2.5. **5.17:** Gen 2.3. **5.18:** Jn 7.1; 10.33.
5.19: Jn 5.30; 8.28; 14.10. **5.20:** Jn 14.12.
5.21: Rom 4.17; 8.11; Jn 11.25. **5.23:** Lk 10.16; 1 Jn 2.23.
5.24: Jn 3.18. **5.25:** Jn 4.21; 16.2, 32.

so he has granted the Son also to have life in himself, ²⁷ and has given him authority to execute judgment, because he is the Son of man. ²⁸ Do not marvel at this; for the hour is coming when all who are in the tombs will hear his voice ²⁹ and come forth, those who have done good, to the resurrection of life, and those who have done evil, to the resurrection of judgment.

30 "I can do nothing on my own authority; as I hear, I judge; and my judgment is just, because I seek not my own will but the will of him who sent me. ³¹ If I bear witness to myself, my testimony is not true; ³² there is another who bears witness to me, and I know that the testimony which he bears to me is true. ³³ You sent to John, and he has borne witness to the truth. ³⁴ Not that the testimony which I receive is from man; but I say this that you may be saved. ³⁵ He was a burning and shining lamp, and you were willing to rejoice for a while in his light. ³⁶ But the testimony which I have is greater than that of John; for the works which the Father has granted me to accomplish, these very works which I am doing, bear me witness that the Father has sent me. ³⁷ And the Father who sent me has himself borne witness to me. His voice you have never heard, his form you have never seen; ³⁸ and you do not have his word abiding in you, for you do not believe him whom he has sent. ³⁹ You search the scriptures, because you think that in them you have eternal life; and it is they that bear witness to me; ⁴⁰ yet you refuse to come to me that you may have life. ⁴¹ I do not receive glory from men. ⁴² But I know that you have not the love of God within you. ⁴³ I have come in my Father's name, and you do not receive me; if another comes in his own name, him you will receive. ⁴⁴ How can you believe, who receive glory from one another and do not seek the glory that comes from the only God? ⁴⁵ Do not think that I shall accuse you to the Father; it is Moses who accuses you, on whom you set your hope. ⁴⁶ If you believed Moses, you would believe me, for he wrote of me. ⁴⁷ But if you do not believe his writings, how will you believe my words?"

6 After this Jesus went to the other side of the Sea of Galilee,

which is the Sea of Tĭ·bē'rĭ·as. ² And a multitude followed him, because they saw the signs which he did on those who were diseased. ³ Jesus went up on the mountain, and there sat down with his disciples. ⁴ Now the Passover, the feast of the Jews, was at hand. ⁵ Lifting up his eyes, then, and seeing that a multitude was coming to him, Jesus said to Philip, "How are we to buy bread, so that these people may eat?" ⁶ This he said to test him, for he himself knew what he would do. ⁷ Philip answered him, "Two hundred denarii*ˡ* would not buy enough bread for each of them to get a little." ⁸ One of his disciples, Andrew, Simon Peter's brother, said to him, ⁹ "There is a lad here who has five barley loaves and two fish; but what are they among so many?" ¹⁰ Jesus said, "Make the people sit down." Now there was much grass in the place; so the men sat down, in number about five thousand. ¹¹ Jesus then took the loaves, and when he had given thanks, he distributed them to those who were seated; so also the fish, as much as they wanted. ¹² And when they had eaten their fill, he told his disciples, "Gather up the fragments left over, that nothing may be lost." ¹³ So they gathered them up and filled twelve baskets with fragments from the five barley loaves, left by those who had eaten. ¹⁴ When the people saw the sign which he had done, they said, "This is indeed the prophet who is to come into the world!"

15 Perceiving then that they were about to come and take him by force to make him king, Jesus withdrew again to the mountain by himself.

16 When evening came, his disciples went down to the sea, ¹⁷ got into a boat, and started across the sea to Ca·pēr'na-um. It was now dark, and Jesus had not yet come to them. ¹⁸ The sea rose because a strong wind was blowing. ¹⁹ When they had rowed about three or four miles,*ᵐ* they saw Jesus

---

ˡThe denarius was a day's wage for a laborer
ᵐGreek *twenty-five or thirty stadia*

5.29: Dan 12.2; Acts 24.15; Jn 11.24; Mt 25.46; 1 Cor 15.52.
5.30: Jn 5.19; 8.16; 6.38.
5.31-37: Jn 8.14-18. 5.33: Jn 1.7, 19. 5.34: 1 Jn 5.9.
5.36: Jn 10.25; 14.11; 15.24; Mt 11.4.
5.39: Lk 24.27; Acts 13.27. 5.43: Mt 24.5.
5.45: Jn 9.28; Rom 2.17. 5.47: Jn 16.29, 31.
6.1-13: Mt 14.13-21; Mk 6.32-44; Lk 9.10-17.
6.5: Jn 1.43; 12.21. 6.8: Jn 1.40; 12.22. 6.9: Jn 21.9-13.
6.14: Mt 21.11. 6.15: Jn 6.3; 18.36.
6.16-21: Mt 14.22-27; Mk 6.45-51.

walking on the sea and drawing near to the boat. They were frightened, [20] and he said to them, "It is I; do not be afraid." [21] Then they were glad to take him into the boat, and immediately the boat was at the land to which they were going.

22 On the next day the people who remained on the other side of the sea saw that there had been only one boat there, and that Jesus had not entered the boat with his disciples, but that his disciples had gone away alone. [23] However, boats from Tī·bē′rĭ-as came near the place where they ate the bread after the Lord had given thanks. [24] So when the people saw that Jesus was not there, nor his disciples, they themselves got into the boats and went to Ca·pĕr′na̠-um, seeking Jesus.

25 When they found him on the other side of the sea, they said to him, "Rabbi, when did you come here?" [26] Jesus answered them, "Truly, truly, I say to you, you seek me, not because you saw signs, but because you ate your fill of the loaves. [27] Do not labor for the food which perishes, but for the food which endures to eternal life, which the Son of man will give to you; for on him has God the Father set his seal." [28] Then they said to him, "What must we do, to be doing the works of God?" [29] Jesus answered them, "This is the work of God, that you believe in him whom he has sent." [30] So they said to him, "Then what sign do you do, that we may see, and believe you? What work do you perform? [31] Our fathers ate the manna in the wilderness; as it is written, 'He gave them bread from heaven to eat.'" [32] Jesus then said to them, "Truly, truly, I say to you, it was not Moses who gave you the bread from heaven; my Father gives you the true bread from heaven. [33] For the bread of God is that which comes down from heaven, and gives life to the world." [34] They said to him, "Lord, give us this bread always."

35 Jesus said to them, "I am the bread of life; he who comes to me shall not hunger, and he who believes in me shall never thirst. [36] But I said to you that you have seen me and yet do not believe. [37] All that the Father gives me will come to me; and him who comes to me I will not cast out. [38] For I have come down from heaven, not to do my own will, but the will of him who

sent me; [39] and this is the will of him who sent me, that I should lose nothing of all that he has given me, but raise it up at the last day. [40] For this is the will of my Father, that every one who sees the Son and believes in him should have eternal life; and I will raise him up at the last day."

41 The Jews then murmured at him, because he said, "I am the bread which came down from heaven." [42] They said, "Is not this Jesus, the son of Joseph, whose father and mother we know? How does he now say, 'I have come down from heaven'?" [43] Jesus answered them, "Do not murmur among yourselves. [44] No one can come to me unless the Father who sent me draws him; and I will raise him up at the last day. [45] It is written in the prophets, 'And they shall all be taught by God.' Every one who has heard and learned from the Father comes to me. [46] Not that any one has seen the Father except him who is from God; he has seen the Father. [47] Truly, truly, I say to you, he who believes has eternal life. [48] I am the bread of life. [49] Your fathers ate the manna in the wilderness, and they died. [50] This is the bread which comes down from heaven, that a man may eat of it and not die. [51] I am the living bread which came down from heaven; if any one eats of this bread, he will live for ever; and the bread which I shall give for the life of the world is my flesh."

52 The Jews then disputed among themselves, saying, "How can this man give us his flesh to eat?" [53] So Jesus said to them, "Truly, truly, I say to you, unless you eat the flesh of the Son of man and drink his blood, you have no life in you; [54] he who eats my flesh and drinks my blood has eternal life, and I will raise him up at the last day. [55] For my flesh is food indeed, and my blood is drink indeed. [56] He who eats my flesh and drinks my blood abides in me, and I in him. [57] As the living Father sent me, and I live because of the Father, so he who eats me

6.27: Is 55.2.
6.29: 1 Thess 1.3; 1 Jn 3.23. **6.30:** Mt 12.38; Mk 8.11.
6.31: Ex 16.4, 15; Num 11.8; Neh 9.15; Ps 78.24; 105.40.
6.34: Jn 4.15; Mt 6.11. **6.35:** Jn 6.48-50; 4.14.
6.37: Jn 17.2. **6.38:** Jn 4.34; 5.30. **6.39:** Jn 17.12; 18.9.
6.40: Jn 5.29; 11.24; 6.54. **6.42:** Lk 4.22; Jn 7.27.
6.44: Jer 31.3; Hos 11.4; Jn 12.32; 6.65.
6.45: 1 Thess 4.9; 1 Jn 2.27; Is 54.13. **6.46:** Jn 1.18.
6.52: Jn 3.4; 4.9. **6.56:** Jn 15.4; 1 Jn 3.24; 4.15.

will live because of me. [58] This is the bread which came down from heaven, not such as the fathers ate and died; he who eats this bread will live for ever." [59] This he said in the synagogue, as he taught at Ca·pẽr'na–um.

60 Many of his disciples, when they heard it, said, "This is a hard saying; who can listen to it?" [61] But Jesus, knowing in himself that his disciples murmured at it, said to them, "Do you take offense at this? [62] Then what if you were to see the Son of man ascending where he was before? [63] It is the spirit that gives life, the flesh is of no avail; the words that I have spoken to you are spirit and life. [64] But there are some of you that do not believe." For Jesus knew from the first who those were that did not believe, and who it was that would betray him. [65] And he said, "This is why I told you that no one can come to me unless it is granted him by the Father."

66 After this many of his disciples drew back and no longer went about with him. [67] Jesus said to the twelve, "Do you also wish to go away?" [68] Simon Peter answered him, "Lord, to whom shall we go? You have the words of eternal life; [69] and we have believed, and have come to know, that you are the Holy One of God." [70] Jesus answered them, "Did I not choose you, the twelve, and one of you is a devil?" [71] He spoke of Judas the son of Simon Is·cär'i·ot, for he, one of the twelve, was to betray him.

7 After this Jesus went about in Galilee; he would not go about in Jü·dē'a, because the Jews[n] sought to kill him. [2] Now the Jews' feast of Tabernacles was at hand. [3] So his brothers said to him, "Leave here and go to Jü·dē'a, that your disciples may see the works you are doing. [4] For no man works in secret if he seeks to be known openly. If you do these things, show yourself to the world." [5] For even his brothers did not believe in him. [6] Jesus said to them, "My time has not yet come, but your time is always here. [7] The world cannot hate you, but it hates me because I testify of it that its works are evil. [8] Go to the feast yourselves; I am not[o] going up to this feast, for my time has not yet fully come." [9] So saying, he remained in Galilee.

10 But after his brothers had gone up to the feast, then he also went up, not publicly but in private. [11] The Jews were looking for him at the feast, and saying, "Where is he?" [12] And there was much muttering about him among the people. While some said, "He is a good man," others said, "No, he is leading the people astray." [13] Yet for fear of the Jews no one spoke openly of him.

14 About the middle of the feast Jesus went up into the temple and taught. [15] The Jews marveled at it, saying, "How is it that this man has learning,[p] when he has never studied?" [16] So Jesus answered them, "My teaching is not mine, but his who sent me; [17] if any man's will is to do his will, he shall know whether the teaching is from God or whether I am speaking on my own authority. [18] He who speaks on his own authority seeks his own glory; but he who seeks the glory of him who sent him is true, and in him there is no falsehood. [19] Did not Moses give you the law? Yet none of you keeps the law. Why do you seek to kill me?" [20] The people answered, "You have a demon! Who is seeking to kill you?" [21] Jesus answered them, "I did one deed, and you all marvel at it. [22] Moses gave you circumcision (not that it is from Moses, but from the fathers), and you circumcise a man upon the sabbath. [23] If on the sabbath a man receives circumcision, so that the law of Moses may not be broken, are you angry with me because on the sabbath I made a man's whole body well? [24] Do not judge by appearances, but judge with right judgment."

25 Some of the people of Jerusalem therefore said, "Is not this the man whom they seek to kill? [26] And here he is, speaking openly, and they say nothing to him! Can it be that the authorities really know that this is the Christ? [27] Yet we know where this man comes from; and when the Christ appears, no one will know where he

Or Judeans *Other ancient authorities add* yet
[p] *Or this man knows his letters*
6.58: Jn 6.41, 51. **6.59:** Jn 6.25. **6.61:** Mt 11.6.
6.62: Jn 3.13; 17.5. **6.63:** 2 Cor 3.6; Jn 6.68.
6.64: Jn 2.25. **6.65:** Jn 6.44; 3.27.
6.68–69: Mk 8.27-30. **6.70:** Jn 15.16, 19.
6.71: Jn 13.2, 27; 17.12. **7.2:** Lev 23.34; Deut 16.16.
7.3: Mk 3.21, 31; Mt 12.46. **7.6:** Mt 26.18; Jn 2.4; 7.30.
7.7: Jn 15.18-21. **7.12:** Jn 7.40-43. **7.13:** Jn 19.38; 20.19.
7.19: Jn 1.17. **7.20:** Jn 8.48; 10.20; Mt 11.18; Mk 3.22.
7.21: Jn 5.9. **7.22:** Lev 12.3; Gen 17.10; 21.4.
7.23: Mk 3.5; Lk 13.12; 14.4.
7.24: Jn 8.15; Is 11.3; Zech 7.9. **7.27:** Jn 6.42; 7.41; 9.29.

comes from." ²⁸ So Jesus proclaimed, as he taught in the temple, "You know me, and you know where I come from? But I have not come of my own accord; he who sent me is true, and him you do not know. ²⁹ I know him, for I come from him, and he sent me." ³⁰ So they sought to arrest him; but no one laid hands on him, because his hour had not yet come. ³¹ Yet many of the people believed in him; they said, "When the Christ appears, will he do more signs than this man has done?"

32 The Phăr′i·seeṣ heard the crowd thus muttering about him, and the chief priests and Pharisees sent officers to arrest him. ³³ Jesus then said, "I shall be with you a little longer, and then I go to him who sent me; ³⁴ you will seek me and you will not find me; where I am you cannot come." ³⁵ The Jews said to one another, "Where does this man intend to go that we shall not find him? Does he intend to go to the Dispersion among the Greeks and teach the Greeks? ³⁶ What does he mean by saying, 'You will seek me and you will not find me,' and, 'Where I am you cannot come'?"

37 On the last day of the feast, the great day, Jesus stood up and proclaimed, "If any one thirst, let him come to me and drink. ³⁸ He who believes in me, as⁹ the scripture has said, 'Out of his heart shall flow rivers of living water.'" ³⁹ Now this he said about the Spirit, which those who believed in him were to receive; for as yet the Spirit had not been given, because Jesus was not yet glorified.

40 When they heard these words, some of the people said, "This is really the prophet." ⁴¹ Others said, "This is the Christ." But some said, "Is the Christ to come from Galilee? ⁴² Has not the scripture said that the Christ is descended from David, and comes from Bethlehem, the village where David was? ⁴³ So there was a division among the people over him. ⁴⁴ Some of them wanted to arrest him, but no one laid hands on him.

45 The officers then went back to the chief priests and Phăr′i·seeṣ, who said to them, "Why did you not bring him?" ⁴⁶ The officers answered, "No man ever spoke like this man!" ⁴⁷ The Phăr′i·seeṣ answered them, "Are you led astray, you also? ⁴⁸ Have any of the authorities or of the Phăr′i·seeṣ believed in him? ⁴⁹ But this crowd, who do not know the law, are accursed." ⁵⁰ Nĭc·o·dē′mus, who had gone to him before, and who was one of them, said to them, ⁵¹ "Does our law judge a man without first giving him a hearing and learning what he does?" ⁵² They replied, "Are you from Galilee too? Search and you will see that no prophet is to rise from Galilee."

53 They went each to his own house, 8 ¹ but Jesus went to the Mount of Olives. ² Early in the morning he came again to the temple; all the people came to him, and he sat down and taught them. ³ The scribes and the Pharisees brought a woman who had been caught in adultery, and placing her in the midst ⁴ they said to him, "Teacher, this woman has been caught in the act of adultery. ⁵ Now in the law Moses cammanded us to stone such. What do you say about her?" ⁶ This they said to test him, that they might have some charge to bring against him. Jesus bent down and wrote with his finger on the ground. ⁷ And as they continued to ask him, he stood up and said to them, "Let him who is without sin among you be the first to throw a stone at her." ⁸ And once more he bent down and wrote with his finger on the ground. ⁹ But when they heard it, they went away, one by one, beginning with the eldest, and Jesus was left alone with the woman standing before him. ¹⁰ Jesus looked up and said to her, "Woman, where are they? Has no one condemned you?" ¹¹ She said, "No one, Lord." And Jesus said, "Neither do I condemn you; go, and do not sin again."ʳ

12 Again Jesus spoke to them, saying, "I am the light of the world; he who follows me will not walk in darkness, but will have the light

---

⁹ Or *let him come to me, and let him who believes in me drink. As*
ʳ The most ancient authorities omit 7.53-8.11; other authorities add the passage here or after 7.36 or after 21.25 or after Luke 21.38, with variations of text
7.28: Jn 8.42. **7.29:** Jn 8.55; 17.25; Mt 11.27.
7.30: Jn 7.44; 10.39; Mk 12.12; Jn 8.20.
7.31: Jn 8.30; 10.42; 11.45.
7.33: Jn 8.21; 12.35; 13.33; 14.19; 16.16-19.
7.35: Jas 1.1; 1 Pet 1.1; Jn 12.20; Acts 11.20.
7.37: Lev 23.36; Jn 4.10, 14. **7.38:** Is 44.3; 55.1; 58.11.
7.39: Jn 20.22; 12.23. **7.40:** Jn 1.21; Mt 21.11.
7.42: Mic 5.2; Mt 1.1; Lk 2.4. **7.44:** Jn 7.30; 10.39.
7.46: Mt 7.28. **7.50:** Jn 3.1; 19.39.
7.51: Deut 17.6; Ex 23.1. **7.52:** 2 Kings 14.25.
8.12: Jn 9.5; 12.35; 1.4.

of life." [13]The Phăr'ị·sees then said to him, "You are bearing witness to yourself; your testimony is not true." [14]Jesus answered, "Even if I do bear witness to myself, my testimony is true, for I know whence I have come and whither I am going, but you do not know whence I come or whither I am going. [15]You judge according to the flesh, I judge no one. [16]Yet even if I do judge, my judgment is true, for it is not I alone that judge, but I and he[s] who sent me. [17]In your law it is written that the testimony of two men is true; [18]I bear witness to myself, and the Father who sent me bears witness to me." [19]They said to him therefore, "Where is your Father?" Jesus answered, "You know neither me nor my Father; if you knew me, you would know my Father also." [20]These words he spoke in the treasury, as he taught in the temple; but no one arrested him, because his hour had not yet come.

[21]Again he said to them, "I go away, and you will seek me and die in your sin; where I am going, you cannot come." [22]Then said the Jews, "Will he kill himself, since he says, 'Where I am going, you cannot come'?" [23]He said to them, "You are from below, I am from above; you are of this world, I am not of this world. [24]I told you that you would die in your sins, for you will die in your sins unless you believe that I am he." [25]They said to him, "Who are you?" Jesus said to them, "Even what I have told you from the beginning.[t] [26]I have much to say about you and much to judge; but he who sent me is true, and I declare to the world what I have heard from him." [27]They did not understand that he spoke to them of the Father. [28]So Jesus said, "When you have lifted up the Son of man, then you will know that I am he, and that I do nothing on my own authority but speak thus as the Father taught me. [29]And he who sent me is with me; he has not left me alone, for I always do what is pleasing to him." [30]As he spoke thus, many believed in him.

[31]Jesus then said to the Jews who had believed in him, "If you continue in my word, you are truly my disciples, [32]and you will know the truth, and the truth will make you free." [33]They answered him, "We are descendants of Abraham, and have never been in bondage to any one. How is it that you say, 'You will be made free'?"

[34]Jesus answered them, "Truly, truly, I say to you, every one who commits sin is a slave to sin. [35]The slave does not continue in the house for ever; the son continues for ever. [36]So if the Son makes you free, you will be free indeed. [37]I know that you are descendants of Abraham; yet you seek to kill me, because my word finds no place in you. [38]I speak of what I have seen with my Father, and you do what you have heard from your father."

[39]They answered him, "Abraham is our father." Jesus said to them, "If you were Abraham's children, you would do what Abraham did, [40]but now you seek to kill me, a man who has told you the truth which I heard from God; this is not what Abraham did. [41]You do what your father did." They said to him, "We were not born of fornication; we have one Father, even God." [42]Jesus said to them, "If God were your Father, you would love me, for I proceeded and came forth from God; I came not of my own accord, but he sent me. [43]Why do you not understand what I say? It is because you cannot bear to hear my word. [44]You are of your father the devil, and your will is to do your father's desires. He was a murderer from the beginning, and has nothing to do with the truth, because there is no truth in him. When he lies, he speaks according to his own nature, for he is a liar and the father of lies. [45]But, because I tell the truth, you do not believe me. [46]Which of you convicts me of sin? If I tell the truth, why do you not believe me? [47]He who is of God hears the words of God; the reason why you do not hear them is that you are not of God."

[48]The Jews answered him, "Are we not right in saying that you are a Sạmâr'ị·tạn and have a demon?" [49]Jesus answered, "I have not a demon; but I honor my Father, and you dishonor me.

[s] Other ancient authorities read the Father
[t] Or Why do I talk to you at all?

8.13-18: Jn 5.31-39.　8.15: Jn 7.24; 3.17.　8.16: Jn 5.30.
8.17: Deut 19.15; Mt 18.16.　8.19: Jn 14.7.
8.20: Mk 12.41; Jn 7.30.　8.21-22: Jn 7.33-36.
8.23: Jn 3.31; 17.14; 1 Jn 4.5.
8.24: Jn 8.28; 4.26; 13.19; Mk 13.6.　8.28: Jn 3.14; 12.32.
8.30: Jn 7.31; 10.42; 11.45.　8.31: Jn 15.7; 2 Jn 9.
8.32: 2 Cor 3.17; Gal 5.1.　8.33: Mt 3.9; Gal 3.7.
8.34: Rom 6.16; 2 Pet 2.19.　8.35: Gen 21.10; Gal 4.30.
8.41: Deut 32.6; Is 63.16; 64.8.　8.42: Jn 13.3; 16.28.
8.44: 1 Jn 3.8, 15; Gen 3.4; 1 Jn 2.4; Mt 12.34.
8.46: 1 Jn 3.5; Jn 18.37.　8.48: Jn 7.20; 10.20; 4.9.

[50] Yet I do not seek my own glory; there is One who seeks it and he will be the judge. [51] Truly, truly, I say to you, if any one keeps my word, he will never see death." [52] The Jews said to him, "Now we know that you have a demon. Abraham died, as did the prophets; and you say, 'If any one keeps my word, he will never taste death.' [53] Are you greater than our father Abraham, who died? And the prophets died! Who do you claim to be?" [54] Jesus answered, "If I glorify myself, my glory is nothing; it is my Father who glorifies me, of whom you say that he is your God. [55] But you have not known him; I know him. If I said, I do not know him, I should be a liar like you; but I do know him and I keep his word. [56] Your father Abraham rejoiced that he was to see my day; he saw it and was glad." [57] The Jews then said to him, "You are not yet fifty years old, and have you seen Abraham?"[u] [58] Jesus said to them, "Truly, truly, I say to you, before Abraham was, I am." [59] So they took up stones to throw at him; but Jesus hid himself, and went out of the temple.

9 As he passed by, he saw a man blind from his birth. [2] And his disciples asked him, "Rabbi, who sinned, this man or his parents, that he was born blind?" [3] Jesus answered, "It was not that this man sinned, or his parents, but that the works of God might be made manifest in him. [4] We must work the works of him who sent me, while it is day; night comes, when no one can work. [5] As long as I am in the world, I am the light of the world." [6] As he said this, he spat on the ground and made clay of the spittle and anointed the man's eyes with the clay, [7] saying to him, "Go, wash in the pool of Sī·lō′am" (which means Sent). So he went and washed and came back seeing. [8] The neighbors and those who had seen him before as a beggar, said, "Is not this the man who used to sit and beg?" [9] Some said, "It is he"; others said, "No, but he is like him." He said, "I am the man." [10] They said to him, "Then how were your eyes opened?" [11] He answered, "The man called Jesus made clay and anointed my eyes and said to me, 'Go to Sī·lō′am and wash'; so I went and washed and received my sight." [12] They said to him, "Where is he?" He said, "I do not know."

[13] They brought to the Phăr′i·seeş the man who had formerly been blind. [14] Now it was a sabbath day when Jesus made the clay and opened his eyes. [15] The Phăr′i·seeş again asked him how he had received his sight. And he said to them, "He put clay on my eyes, and I washed, and I see." [16] Some of the Phăr′i·seeş said, "This man is not from God, for he does not keep the sabbath." But others said, "How can a man who is a sinner do such signs?" There was a division among them. [17] So they again said to the blind man, "What do you say about him, since he has opened your eyes?" He said, "He is a prophet."

[18] The Jews did not believe that he had been blind and had received his sight, until they called the parents of the man who had received his sight, [19] and asked them, "Is this your son, who you say was born blind? How then does he now see?" [20] His parents answered, "We know that this is our son, and that he was born blind; [21] but how he now sees we do not know, nor do we know who opened his eyes. Ask him; he is of age, he will speak for himself." [22] His parents said this because they feared the Jews, for the Jews had already agreed that if any one should confess him to be Christ, he was to be put out of the synagogue. [23] Therefore his parents said, "He is of age, ask him."

[24] So for the second time they called the man who had been blind, and said to him, "Give God the praise; we know that this man is a sinner." [25] He answered, "Whether he is a sinner, I do not know; one thing I know, that though I was blind, now I see." [26] They said to him, "What did he do to you? How did he open your eyes?" [27] He answered them, "I have told you already, and you would not listen. Why do you want to hear it again? Do you too want to become his disciples?" [28] And they reviled him, saying, "You are his disciple, but we are disciples of Moses. [29] We know that God has spoken to Moses, but as for this man, we do

[u] Other ancient authorities read *has Abraham seen you?*
8.53: Jn 4.12.   8.56: Mt 13.17; Heb 11.13.
8.57: Jn 2.20.   8.58: Jn 1.1; 17.5, 24.
8.59: Jn 10.31; 11.8.
9.2: Lk 13.2; Acts 28.4; Ezek 18.20; Ex 20.5.
9.3: Jn 11.4.   9.4: Jn 11.9; 12.35.
9.5: Jn 1.4; 8.12; 12.46.   9.6: Mk 7.33; 8.23.
9.7: Lk 13.4.   9.16: Mt 12.2; Jn 5.9; 7.43; 10.19.
9.22: Jn 7.13; 12.42; Lk 6.22.   9.28: Jn 5.45.

not know where he comes from." ³⁰The man answered, "Why, this is a marvel! You do not know where he comes from, and yet he opened my eyes. ³¹We know that God does not listen to sinners, but if any one is a worshiper of God and does his will, God listens to him. ³²Never since the world began has it been heard that any one opened the eyes of a man born blind. ³³If this man were not from God, he could do nothing." ³⁴They answered him, "You were born in utter sin, and would you teach us?" And they cast him out.

35 Jesus heard that they had cast him out, and having found him he said, "Do you believe in the Son of man?"ᵛ ³⁶He answered, "And who is he, sir, that I may believe in him?" ³⁷Jesus said to him, "You have seen him, and it is he who speaks to you." ³⁸He said, "Lord, I believe"; and he worshiped him. ³⁹Jesus said, "For judgment I came into this world, that those who do not see may see, and that those who see may become blind." ⁴⁰Some of the Phăr′i·seeş near him heard this, and they said to him, "Are we also blind?" ⁴¹Jesus said to them, "If you were blind, you would have no guilt; but now that you say, 'We see,' your guilt remains.

10 "Truly, truly, I say to you, he who does not enter the sheepfold by the door but climbs in by another way, that man is a thief and a robber; ²but he who enters by the door is the shepherd of the sheep. ³To him the gatekeeper opens; the sheep hear his voice, and he calls his own sheep by name and leads them out. ⁴When he has brought out all his own, he goes before them, and the sheep follow him, for they know his voice. ⁵A stranger they will not follow, but they will flee from him, for they do not know the voice of strangers." ⁶This figure Jesus used with them, but they did not understand what he was saying to them.

7 So Jesus again said to them, "Truly, truly, I say to you, I am the door of the sheep. ⁸All who came before me are thieves and robbers; but the sheep did not heed them. ⁹I am the door; if any one enters by me, he will be saved, and will go in and out and find pasture. ¹⁰The thief comes only to steal and kill and destroy; I

came that they may have life, and have it abundantly. ¹¹I am the good shepherd. The good shepherd lays down his life for the sheep. ¹²He who is a hireling and not a shepherd, whose own the sheep are not, sees the wolf coming and leaves the sheep and flees; and the wolf snatches them and scatters them. ¹³He flees because he is a hireling and cares nothing for the sheep. ¹⁴I am the good shepherd; I know my own and my own know me, ¹⁵as the Father knows me and I know the Father; and I lay down my life for the sheep. ¹⁶And I have other sheep, that are not of this fold; I must bring them also, and they will heed my voice. So there shall be one flock, one shepherd. ¹⁷For this reason the Father loves me, because I lay down my life, that I may take it again. ¹⁸No one takes it from me, but I lay it down of my own accord. I have power to lay it down, and I have power to take it again; this charge I have received from my Father."

19 There was again a division among the Jews because of these words. ²⁰Many of them said, "He has a demon, and he is mad; why listen to him?" ²¹Others said, "These are not the sayings of one who has a demon. Can a demon open the eyes of the blind?"

22 It was the feast of the Dedication at Jerusalem; ²³it was winter, and Jesus was walking in the temple, in the portico of Solomon. ²⁴So the Jews gathered round him and said to him, "How long will you keep us in suspense? If you are the Christ, tell us plainly." ²⁵Jesus answered them, "I told you, and you do not believe. The works that I do in my Father's name, they bear witness to me; ²⁶but you do not believe, because you do not belong to my sheep. ²⁷My sheep hear my voice, and I know them, and they follow me; ²⁸and I give them eternal life, and they shall never perish, and no one shall snatch them out of my hand. ²⁹My

ᵛOther ancient authorities read *the Son of God*
9.38: Mt 28.9. 9.39: Jn 5.27; 3.19; Mt 15.14.
9.41: Jn 15.22. 10.2: Mk 6.34. 10.6: Jn 16.25.
10.8: Jer 23.1; Ezek 34.2.
10.11: Is 40.11; Ezek 34.11-16; Heb 13.20; 1 Pet 5.4; Rev 7.17; 1 Jn 3.16; Jn 15.13. 10.15: Mt 11.27.
10.16: Is 56.8; Jn 11.52; 17.20; Eph 2.13-18; 1 Pet 2.25.
10.18: Jn 14.31; 15.10; Phil 2.8; Heb 5.8.
10.19: Jn 7.43; 9.16. 10.20: Jn 7.20; 8.48; Mt 11.18.
10.21: Jn 9.32; Ex 4.11. 10.23: Acts 3.11; 5.12.
10.25: Jn 5.36; 10.38. 10.26: Jn 8.47.
10.28: Jn 17.2; 1 Jn 2.25.

Father, who has given them to me,[w] is greater than all, and no one is able to snatch them out of the Father's hand. [30] I and the Father are one."

31 The Jews took up stones again to stone him. [32] Jesus answered them, "I have shown you many good works from the Father; for which of these do you stone me?" [33] The Jews answered him, "It is not for a good work that we stone you but for blasphemy; because you, being a man, make yourself God." [34] Jesus answered them, "Is it not written in your law, 'I said, you are gods'? [35] If he called them gods to whom the word of God came (and scripture cannot be broken), [36] do you say of him whom the Father consecrated and sent into the world, 'You are blaspheming,' because I said, 'I am the Son of God'? [37] If I am not doing the works of my Father, then do not believe me; [38] but if I do them, even though you do not believe me, believe the works, that you may know and understand that the Father is in me and I am in the Father." [39] Again they tried to arrest him, but he escaped from their hands.

40 He went away again across the Jordan to the place where John at first baptized, and there he remained. [41] And many came to him; and they said, "John did no sign, but everything that John said about this man was true." [42] And many believed in him there.

11 Now a certain man was ill, Lăz′a·rŭs of Bĕth′a·nў, the village of Mary and her sister Martha. [2] It was Mary who anointed the Lord with ointment and wiped his feet with her hair, whose brother Lăz′a·rŭs was ill. [3] So the sisters sent to him, saying, "Lord, he whom you love is ill." [4] But when Jesus heard it he said, "This illness is not unto death; it is for the glory of God, so that the Son of God may be glorified by means of it."

5 Now Jesus loved Martha and her sister and Lăz′a·rŭs. [6] So when he heard that he was ill, he stayed two days longer in the place where he was. [7] Then after this he said to the disciples, "Let us go into Jū·dē′a again." [8] The disciples said to him, "Rabbi, the Jews were but now seeking to stone you, and are you going there again?" [9] Jesus answered, "Are there not twelve hours in the day? If any one walks in the day, he does not stumble, because he sees

the light of this world. [10] But if any one walks in the night, he stumbles, because the light is not in him." [11] Thus he spoke, and then he said to them, "Our friend Lăz′a·rŭs has fallen asleep, but I go to awake him out of sleep." [12] The disciples said to him, "Lord, if he has fallen asleep, he will recover." [13] Now Jesus had spoken of his death, but they thought that he meant taking rest in sleep. [14] Then Jesus told them plainly, "Lăz′a·rŭs is dead; [15] and for your sake I am glad that I was not there, so that you may believe. But let us go to him." [16] Thomas, called the Twin, said to his fellow disciples, "Let us also go, that we may die with him."

17 Now when Jesus came, he found that Lăz′a·rŭs[x] had already been in the tomb four days. [18] Bĕth′a·nў was near Jerusalem, about two miles[y] off, [19] and many of the Jews had come to Martha and Mary to console them concerning their brother. [20] When Martha heard that Jesus was coming, she went and met him, while Mary sat in the house. [21] Martha said to Jesus, "Lord, if you had been here, my brother would not have died. [22] And even now I know that whatever you ask from God, God will give you." [23] Jesus said to her, "Your brother will rise again." [24] Martha said to him, "I know that he will rise again in the resurrection at the last day." [25] Jesus said to her, "I am the resurrection and the life;[z] he who believes in me, though he die, yet shall he live, [26] and whoever lives and believes in me shall never die. Do you believe this?" [27] She said to him, "Yes, Lord; I believe that you are the Christ, the Son of God, he who is coming into the world."

28 When she had said this, she went and called her sister Mary, saying quietly, "The Teacher is here and is calling for you." [29] And when she heard it, she rose quickly and went to him. [30] Now Jesus had not

[w] Other ancient authorities read *When my Father has given to me*
[x] Greek *he* [y] Greek *fifteen stadia*
[z] Other ancient authorities omit *and the life*
10.30: Jn 17.21. **10.31:** Jn 8.59; 11.8. **10.33:** Lev 24.16; 14.64. **10.34:** Jn 8.17; Ps 82.6.
10.39: Jn 7.30; 8.59; Lk 4.30. **10.40:** Jn 1.28.
10.42: Jn 7.31; 11.45. **11.1:** Mk 11.1; Lk 10.38.
11.2: Jn 12.3; Lk 7.38; Mk 14.3. **11.4:** Jn 9.3.
11.8: Jn 8.59; 10.31. **11.9:** Jn 9.4; 12.35; Lk 13.33.
11.11: Mk 5.39; Acts 7.60. **11.16:** Mt 10.3; Jn 20.24-28.
11.19: Job 2.11. **11.24:** Dan 12.2; Jn 5.28; Acts 24.15.
11.25: Jn 1.4; 5.26; Rev 1.18. **11.26:** Jn 6.47; 8.51.
11.27: Mt 16.16.

yet come to the village, but was still in the place where Martha had met him. [31] When the Jews who were with her in the house, consoling her, saw Mary rise quickly and go out, they followed her, supposing that she was going to the tomb to weep there. [32] Then Mary, when she came where Jesus was and saw him, fell at his feet, saying to him, "Lord, if you had been here, my brother would not have died." [33] When Jesus saw her weeping, and the Jews who came with her also weeping, he was deeply moved in spirit and troubled; [34] and he said, "Where have you laid him?" They said to him, "Lord, come and see." [35] Jesus wept. [36] So the Jews said, "See how he loved him!" [37] But some of them said, "Could not he who opened the eyes of the blind man have kept this man from dying?"

38 Then Jesus, deeply moved again, came to the tomb; it was a cave, and a stone lay upon it. [39] Jesus said, "Take away the stone." Martha, the sister of the dead man, said to him, "Lord, by this time there will be an odor, for he has been dead four days." [40] Jesus said to her, "Did I not tell you that if you would believe you would see the glory of God?" [41] So they took away the stone. And Jesus lifted up his eyes and said, "Father, I thank thee that thou hast heard me. [42] I knew that thou hearest me always, but I have said this on account of the people standing by, that they may believe that thou didst send me." [43] When he had said this, he cried with a loud voice, "Lăz'-a-rŭs, come out." [44] The dead man came out, his hands and feet bound with bandages, and his face wrapped with a cloth. Jesus said to them, "Unbind him, and let him go."

45 Many of the Jews therefore, who had come with Mary and had seen what he did, believed in him; [46] but some of them went to the Phăr'ĭ-seeş and told them what Jesus had done. [47] So the chief priests and the Phăr'-ĭ-seeş gathered the council, and said, "What are we to do? For this man performs many signs. [48] If we let him go on thus, every one will believe in him, and the Romans will come and destroy both our holy place*a* and our nation." [49] But one of them, Cāi'a-phăs, who was high priest that year, said to them, "You know nothing at all; [50] you do not understand that it is

expedient for you that one man should die for the people, and that the whole nation should not perish." [51] He did not say this of his own accord, but being high priest that year he prophesied that Jesus should die for the nation, [52] and not for the nation only, but to gather into one the children of God who are scattered abroad. [53] So from that day on they took counsel how to put him to death.

54 Jesus therefore no longer went about openly among the Jews, but went from there to the country near the wilderness, to a town called Ē'phra-ĭm; and there he stayed with the disciples.

55 Now the Passover of the Jews was at hand, and many went up from the country to Jerusalem before the Passover, to purify themselves. [56] They were looking for Jesus and saying to one another as they stood in the temple, "What do you think? That he will not come to the feast?" [57] Now the chief priests and the Phăr'ĭ-seeş had given orders that if any one knew where he was, he should let them know, so that they might arrest him.

12 Six days before the Passover, Jesus came to Bĕth'a-nў, where Lăz'a-rŭs was, whom Jesus had raised from the dead. [2] There they made him a supper; Martha served, and Lăz'-a-rŭs was one of those at table with him. [3] Mary took a pound of costly ointment of pure nard and anointed the feet of Jesus and wiped his feet with her hair; and the house was filled with the fragrance of the ointment. [4] But Judas Ĭs-căr'ĭ-ŏt, one of his disciples (he who was to betray him), said, [5] "Why was this ointment not sold for three hundred denarii*b* and given to the poor?" [6] This he said, not that he cared for the poor but because he was a thief, and as he had the money box he used to take what was put into it. [7] Jesus said, "Let her alone, let her keep it for the day of my burial. [8] The poor you always have with you, but you do not always have me."

*a*Greek *our place*
*b*The denarius was a day's wage for a laborer
11.32: Jn 11.22.   11.35: Lk 19.41.   11.37: Jn 9.7.
11.38: Mt 27.60; Mk 15.46; Lk 24.2; Jn 20.1.
11.41: Jn 17.1; Mt 11.25.   11.42: Jn 12.30.
11.44: Jn 19.40; 20.7.   11.49: Mt 26.3.
11.52: Jn 10.16; 17.21.
11.55: Mt 26.1; Mk 14.1; Lk 22.1; Jn 13.1.
11.56: Jn 7.11.   12.1-8: Mt 26.6-13; Mk 14.3-9; Lk 7.37-38.
12.4: Jn 6.71; 13.26.   12.6: Lk 8.3.
12.7: Jn 19.40.

9 When the great crowd of the Jews learned that he was there, they came, not only on account of Jesus but also to see Lăz′a·rus, whom he had raised from the dead. [10] So the chief priests planned to put Lăz′a·rus also to death, [11] because on account of him many of the Jews were going away and believing in Jesus.

12 The next day a great crowd who had come to the feast heard that Jesus was coming to Jerusalem. [13] So they took branches of palm trees and went out to meet him, crying, "Hosanna! Blessed is he who comes in the name of the Lord, even the King of Israel!" [14] And Jesus found a young ass and sat upon it; as it is written, [15] "Fear not, daughter of Zion;

behold, your king is coming,
sitting on an ass's colt!"

[16] His disciples did not understand this at first; but when Jesus was glorified, then they remembered that this had been written of him and had been done to him. [17] The crowd that had been with him when he called Lăz′a·rus out of the tomb and raised him from the dead bore witness. [18] The reason why the crowd went to meet him was that they heard he had done this sign. [19] The Phăr′i·seeş then said to one another, "You see that you can do nothing; look, the world has gone after him."

20 Now among those who went up to worship at the feast were some Greeks. [21] So these came to Philip, who was from Bĕth-sā′ĭ·da in Galilee, and said to him, "Sir, we wish to see Jesus." [22] Philip went and told Andrew; Andrew went with Philip and they told Jesus. [23] And Jesus answered them, "The hour has come for the Son of man to be glorified. [24] Truly, truly, I say to you, unless a grain of wheat falls into the earth and dies, it remains alone; but if it dies, it bears much fruit. [25] He who loves his life loses it, and he who hates his life in this world will keep it for eternal life. [26] If any one serves me, he must follow me; and where I am, there shall my servant be also; if any one serves me, the Father will honor him.

27 "Now is my soul troubled. And what shall I say? 'Father, save me from this hour'? No, for this purpose I have come to this hour. [28] Father, glorify thy name." Then a voice came from heaven, "I have glorified it, and I will glorify it again." [29] The crowd standing by heard it and said that it had thundered. Others said, "An angel has spoken to him." [30] Jesus answered, "This voice has come for your sake, not for mine. [31] Now is the judgment of this world, now shall the ruler of this world be cast out; [32] and I, when I am lifted up from the earth, will draw all men to myself." [33] He said this to show by what death he was to die. [34] The crowd answered him, "We have heard from the law that the Christ remains for ever. How can you say that the Son of man must be lifted up? Who is this Son of man?" [35] Jesus said to them, "The light is with you for a little longer. Walk while you have the light, lest the darkness overtake you; he who walks in the darkness does not know where he goes. [36] While you have the light, believe in the light, that you may become sons of light."

When Jesus had said this, he departed and hid himself from them. [37] Though he had done so many signs before them, yet they did not believe in him; [38] it was that the word spoken by the prophet Ī·sāi′ah might be fulfilled:

"Lord, who has believed our report,
and to whom has the arm of the Lord
been revealed?"

[39] Therefore they could not believe. For Ī·sāi′ah again said,

[40] "He has blinded their eyes and
hardened their heart,
lest they should see with their eyes
and perceive with their heart,
and turn for me to heal them."

[41] Ī·sāi′ah said this because he saw his glory and spoke of him. [42] Nevertheless many even of the authorities believed in him, but for fear of the Phăr′i·seeş they did not confess it, lest they should be put out of the synagogue: [43] for they loved the praise of men more than the praise of God.

44 And Jesus cried out and said,

12.10: Mk 14.1.
12.12-15: Mt 21.4-9; Mk 11.7-10; Lk 19.35-38.
12.13: Ps 118.25; Jn 1.49. **12.15:** Zech 9.9.
12.16: Mk 9.32; Jn 2.22. **12.20:** Jn 7.35; Acts 11.20.
12.21: Jn 1.44; 6.5. **12.23:** Jn 13.1; 17.1; Mk 14.35, 41.
12.24: 1 Cor 15.36.
12.25: Mt 10.39; Mk 8.35; Lk 9.24; 14.26.
12.27: Jn 11.33; Mt 26.38; Mk 14.34. **12.28:** Mk 1.11; 9.7.
12.31: Jn 16.11; 2 Cor 4.4; Eph 2.2. **12.32:** Jn 3.14; 8.28.
12.34: Ps 110.4; Is 9.7; Ezek 37.25; Dan 7.14.
12.35: Jn 7.33; 9.4; Eph 5.8; 1 Jn 2.11.
12.36: Lk 16.8; Jn 8.59. **12.38:** Is 53.1; Rom 10.16.
12.40: Is 6.10; Mt 13.14. **12.41:** Is 6.1; Lk 24.27.
12.42: Jn 9.22; Lk 6.22. **12.44:** Mt 10.40; Jn 5.24.

"He who believes in me, believes not in me but in him who sent me. [45] And he who sees me sees him who sent me. [46] I have come as light into the world, that whoever believes in me may not remain in darkness. [47] If any one hears my sayings and does not keep them, I do not judge him; for I did not come to judge the world but to save the world. [48] He who rejects me and does not receive my sayings has a judge; the word that I have spoken will be his judge on the last day. [49] For I have not spoken on my own authority; the Father who sent me has himself given me commandment what to say and what to speak. [50] And I know that his commandment is eternal life. What I say, therefore, I say as the Father has bidden me."

13 Now before the feast of the Passover, when Jesus knew that his hour had come to depart out of this world to the Father, having loved his own who were in the world, he loved them to the end. [2] And during supper, when the devil had already put it into the heart of Judas Is′ca·ri·ot, Simon's son, to betray him, [3] Jesus, knowing that the Father had given all things into his hands, and that he had come from God and was going to God, [4] rose from supper, laid aside his garments, and girded himself with a towel. [5] Then he poured water into a basin, and began to wash the disciples' feet, and to wipe them with the towel with which he was girded. [6] He came to Simon Peter; and Peter said to him, "Lord, do you wash my feet?" [7] Jesus answered him, "What I am doing you do not know now, but afterward you will understand." [8] Peter said to him, "You shall never wash my feet." Jesus answered him, "If I do not wash you, you have no part in me." [9] Simon Peter said to him, "Lord, not my feet only but also my hands and my head!" [10] Jesus said to him, "He who has bathed does not need to wash, except for his feet,[c] but he is clean all over; and you[x] are clean, but not every one of you." [11] For he knew who was to betray him; that was why he said, "You are not all clean."

12 When he had washed their feet, and taken his garments, and resumed his place, he said to them, "Do you know what I have done to you? [13] You call me Teacher and Lord; and you are right, for so I am. [14] If I then, your Lord and Teacher, have washed your feet, you also ought to wash one another's feet. [15] For I have given you an example, that you also should do as I have done to you. [16] Truly, truly, I say to you, a servant[d] is not greater than his master; nor is he who is sent greater than he who sent him. [17] If you know these things, blessed are you if you do them. [18] I am not speaking of you all; I know whom I have chosen; it is that the scripture may be fulfilled, 'He who ate my bread has lifted his heel against me.' [19] I tell you this now, before it takes place, that when it does take place you may believe that I am he. [20] Truly, truly, I say to you, he who receives any one whom I send receives me; and he who receives me receives him who sent me."

21 When Jesus had thus spoken, he was troubled in spirit, and testified, "Truly, truly, I say to you, one of you will betray me." [22] The disciples looked at one another, uncertain of whom he spoke. [23] One of his disciples, whom Jesus loved, was lying close to the breast of Jesus; [24] so Simon Peter beckoned to him and said, "Tell us who it is of whom he speaks." [25] So lying thus, close to the breast of Jesus, he said to him, "Lord, who is it?" [26] Jesus answered, "It is he to whom I shall give this morsel when I have dipped it." So when he had dipped the morsel, he gave it to Judas, the son of Simon Is′ca·ri·ot. [27] Then after the morsel, Satan entered into him. Jesus said to him, "What you are going to do, do quickly." [28] Now no one at the table knew why he said this to him. [29] Some thought that, because Judas had the money box, Jesus was telling him, "Buy what we need for the feast"; or, that he should give something to the poor. [30] So, after receiving the morsel, he immediately went out; and it was night.

[c] Other ancient authorities omit *except for his feet*
[x] The Greek word for *you* here is plural
[d] Or *slave*　12.45: Jn 14.9.
12.46: Jn 1.4; 8.12; 9.5.　12.47: Jn 3.17.
12.48: Mt 10.14-15.　13.1: Jn 11.55; 12.23; 16.28.
13.2: Jn 6.71; Mk 14.10.　13.5: Lk 7.44; 22.27.
13.8: Deut 12.12; Jn 3.5; 9.7.　13.11: Jn 13.2.
13.15: 1 Pet 2.21.　13.16: Mt 10.24; Lk 6.40.
13.17: Lk 11.28; Jas 1.25.　13.18: Ps 41.9.
13.19: Jn 14.29; 8.28.　13.20: Mt 10.40; Lk 10.16.
13.21-26: Mt 26.21-25; Mk 14.18-21; Lk 22.21-23.
13.23: Jn 19.26; 20.2; 21.7, 20.　13.26: Jn 6.71.
13.29: Jn 12.6.　13.30: Lk 22.53.

31 When he had gone out, Jesus said, "Now is the Son of man glorified, and in him God is glorified; [32] if God is glorified in him, God will also glorify him in himself, and glorify him at once. [33] Little children, yet a little while I am with you. You will seek me; and as I said to the Jews so now I say to you, 'Where I am going you cannot come.' [34] A new commandment I give to you, that you love one another; even as I have loved you, that you also love one another. [35] By this all men will know that you are my disciples, if you have love for one another."

36 Simon Peter said to him, "Lord, where are you going?" Jesus answered, "Where I am going you cannot follow me now; but you shall follow afterward." [37] Peter said to him, "Lord, why cannot I follow you now? I will lay down my life for you." [38] Jesus answered, "Will you lay down your life for me? Truly, truly, I say to you, the cock will not crow, till you have denied me three times.

14 "Let not your hearts be troubled; believe[e] in God, believe also in me. [2] In my Father's house are many rooms; if it were not so, would I have told you that I go to prepare a place for you? [3] And when I go and prepare a place for you, I will come again and will take you to myself, that where I am you may be also. [4] And you know the way where I am going."[f] [5] Thomas said to him, "Lord, we do not know where you are going; how can we know the way?" [6] Jesus said to him, "I am the way, and the truth, and the life; no one comes to the Father, but by me. [7] If you had known me, you would have known my Father also; henceforth you know him and have seen him."

8 Philip said to him, "Lord, show us the Father, and we shall be satisfied." [9] Jesus said to him, "Have I been with you so long, and yet you do not know me, Philip? He who has seen me has seen the Father; how can you say, 'Show us the Father'? [10] Do you not believe that I am in the Father and the Father in me? The words that I say to you I do not speak on my own authority; but the Father who dwells in me does his works. [11] Believe me that I am in the Father and the Father in me; or else believe me for the sake of the works themselves.

12 "Truly, truly, I say to you, he who believes in me will also do the works that I do; and greater works than these will he do, because I go to the Father. [13] Whatever you ask in my name, I will do it, that the Father may be glorified in the Son; [14] if you ask[g] anything in my name, I will do it.

15 "If you love me, you will keep my commandments. [16] And I will pray the Father, and he will give you another Counselor, to be with you for ever, [17] even the Spirit of truth, whom the world cannot receive, because it neither sees him nor knows him; you know him, for he dwells with you, and will be in you.

18 "I will not leave you desolate; I will come to you. [19] Yet a little while, and the world will see me no more, but you will see me; because I live, you will live also. [20] In that day you will know that I am in my Father, and you in me, and I in you. [21] He who has my commandments and keeps them, he it is who loves me; and he who loves me will be loved by my Father, and I will love him and manifest myself to him." [22] Judas (not Is·căr'ĭ·ot) said to him, "Lord, how is it that you will manifest yourself to us, and not to the world?" [23] Jesus answered him, "If a man loves me, he will keep my word, and my Father will love him, and we will come to him and make our home with him. [24] He who does not love me does not keep my words; and the word which you hear is not mine but the Father's who sent me.

25 "These things I have spoken to you, while I am still with you. [26] But the Counselor, the Holy Spirit, whom the Father will send in my name, he will teach you all things, and bring to your remembrance all that I have said to you. [27] Peace I leave with you; my peace I give to you; not as the world gives do I give to you. Let not your

---

Or you believe
Other ancient authorities read where I am going you know, and the way you know
Other ancient authorities add me
13.31-32: Jn 17.1.   13.33: 1 Jn 2.1; Jn 7.33.
13.34: Jn 15.12, 17; 1 Jn 3.23; 2 Jn 5; Lev 19.18; 1 Thess 4.9; 1 Pet 1.22; Heb 13.1; Eph 5.2; 1 Jn 4.10.
13.36: Jn 21.18; 2 Pet 1.14.
13.37-38: Mt 26.33-35; Mk 14.29-31; Lk 22.33-34.
14.2: Jn 13.33.   14.5: Jn 11.16.   14.6: Jn 10.9; 1.4, 14.
14.9: Jn 12.45.   14.11: Jn 10.38.
14.13: Mt 7.7; Jn 15.7, 16; 16.23; Jas 1.5.
14.15: Jn 15.10; 1 Jn 5.3; 2 Jn 6.
14.16: Jn 14.26; 15.26; 16.7; 1 Jn 2.1.   14.19: Jn 7.33.
14.22: Acts 1.13; 10.40-41.   14.23: 1 Jn 2.24; Rev 21.3.
14.27: Jn 16.33; Phil 4.7; Col 3.15; Jn 20.19.

hearts be troubled, neither let them be afraid. [28] You heard me say to you, 'I go away, and I will come to you.' If you loved me, you would have rejoiced, because I go to the Father; for the Father is greater than I. [29] And now I have told you before it takes place, so that when it does take place, you may believe. [30] I will no longer talk much with you, for the ruler of this world is coming. He has no power over me; [31] but I do as the Father has commanded me, so that the world may know that I love the Father. Rise, let us go hence.

15 "I am the true vine, and my Father is the vinedresser. [2] Every branch of mine that bears no fruit, he takes away, and every branch that does bear fruit he prunes, that it may bear more fruit. [3] You are already made clean by the word which I have spoken to you. [4] Abide in me, and I in you. As the branch cannot bear fruit by itself, unless it abides in the vine, neither can you, unless you abide in me. [5] I am the vine, you are the branches. He who abides in me, and I in him, he it is that bears much fruit, for apart from me you can do nothing. [6] If a man does not abide in me, he is cast forth as a branch and withers; and the branches are gathered, thrown into the fire and burned. [7] If you abide in me, and my words abide in you, ask whatever you will, and it shall be done for you. [8] By this my Father is glorified, that you bear much fruit, and so prove to be my disciples. [9] As the Father has loved me, so have I loved you; abide in my love. [10] If you keep my commandments, you will abide in my love, just as I have kept my Father's commandments and abide in his love. [11] These things I have spoken to you, that my joy may be in you, and that your joy may be full.

12 "This is my commandment, that you love one another as I have loved you. [13] Greater love has no man than this, that a man lay down his life for his friends. [14] You are my friends if you do what I command you. [15] No longer do I call you servants,[h] for the servant[i] does not know what his master is doing; but I have called you friends, for all that I have heard from my Father I have made known to you. [16] You did not choose me, but I chose you and appointed you that you should

go and bear fruit and that your fruit should abide; so that whatever you ask the Father in my name, he may give it to you. [17] This I command you, to love one another.

18 "If the world hates you, know that it has hated me before it hated you. [19] If you were of the world, the world would love its own; but because you are not of the world, but I chose you out of the world, therefore the world hates you. [20] Remember the word that I said to you, 'A servant[i] is not greater than his master.' If they persecuted me, they will persecute you; if they kept my word, they will keep yours also. [21] But all this they will do to you on my account, because they do not know him who sent me. [22] If I had not come and spoken to them, they would not have sin; but now they have no excuse for their sin. [23] He who hates me hates my Father also. [24] If I had not done among them the works which no one else did, they would not have sin; but now they have seen and hated both me and my Father. [25] It is to fulfil the word that is written in their law, 'They hated me without a cause.' [26] But when the Counselor comes, whom I shall send to you from the Father, even the Spirit of truth, who proceeds from the Father, he will bear witness to me; [27] and you also are witnesses, because you have been with me from the beginning.

16 "I have said all this to you to keep you from falling away. [2] They will put you out of the synagogues; indeed, the hour is coming when whoever kills you will think he is offering service to God. [3] And they will do this because they have not known the Father, nor me. [4] But I have said these things to you, that when their hour comes you may remember that I told you of them.

"I did not say these things to you from the beginning, because I was

[h]Or *slaves*   [i]Or *slave*
14.29: Jn 13.19.   14.30: Jn 12.31.
14.31: Mk 14.42; Jn 18.1.
15.1: Is 5.1-7; Ezek 19.10; Mk 12.1-9; Mt 15.13; Rom 11.17.
15.3: Jn 13.10.   15.4: Jn 6.56; 1 Jn 2.6.
15.7: Jn 14.13; 16.23; Mt 7.7; Jas 1.5.   15.8: Mt 5.16.
15.10: Jn 14.15; 1 Jn 5.3.   15.12: Jn 13.34.
15.13: Rom 5.7; Jn 10.11.   15.14: Lk 12.4.
15.16: Jn 6.70; 13.18; 14.13; 16.23.
15.18: Jn 7.7; 1 Jn 3.13; Mt 10.22; 24.9.
15.20: Jn 13.16; Mt 10.24; 1 Cor 4.12; Acts 4.17; 1 Pet 4.14; Rev 2.3.   15.22: Jn 9.41.   15.25: Ps 35.19; 69.4.
15.26: Jn 14.16, 26; 16.7; 1 Jn 2.1; 5.7.
15.27: Jn 19.35; 21.24; 1 Jn 4.14.
16.2: Jn 9.22; Acts 26.9-11; Is 66.5.

with you. [5] But now I am going to him who sent me; yet none of you asks me, 'Where are you going?' [6] But because I have said these things to you, sorrow has filled your hearts. [7] Nevertheless I tell you the truth: it is to your advantage that I go away, for if I do not go away, the Counselor will not come to you; but if I go, I will send him to you. [8] And when he comes, he will convince[x] the world concerning sin and righteousness and judgment: [9] concerning sin, because they do not believe in me; [10] concerning righteousness, because I go to the Father, and you will see me no more; [11] concerning judgment, because the ruler of this world is judged.

12 "I have yet many things to say to you, but you cannot bear them now. [13] When the Spirit of truth comes, he will guide you into all the truth; for he will not speak on his own authority, but whatever he hears he will speak, and he will declare to you the things that are to come. [14] He will glorify me, for he will take what is mine and declare it to you. [15] All that the Father has is mine; therefore I said that he will take what is mine and declare it to you.

16 "A little while, and you will see me no more; again a little while, and you will see me." [17] Some of his disciples said to one another, "What is this that he says to us, 'A little while, and you will not see me, and again a little while, and you will see me'; and, 'because I go to the Father'? [18] They said, "What does he mean by 'a little while'? We do not know what he means." [19] Jesus knew that they wanted to ask him; so he said to them, "Is this what you are asking yourselves, what I meant by saying, 'A little while, and you will not see me, and again a little while, and you will see me'? [20] Truly, truly, I say to you, you will weep and lament, but the world will rejoice; you will be sorrowful, but your sorrow will turn into joy. [21] When a woman is in travail she has sorrow, because her hour has come; but when she is delivered of the child, she no longer remembers the anguish, for joy that a child[j] is born into the world. [22] So you have sorrow now, but I will see you again and your hearts will rejoice, and no one will take your joy from you. [23] In that day you will ask nothing of me. Truly, truly, I say to you, if you ask any-

thing of the Father, he will give it to you in my name. [24] Hitherto you have asked nothing in my name; ask, and you will receive, that your joy may be full.

25 "I have said this to you in figures; the hour is coming when I shall no longer speak to you in figures but tell you plainly of the Father. [26] In that day you will ask in my name; and I do not say to you that I shall pray the Father for you; [27] for the Father himself loves you, because you have loved me and have believed that I came from the Father. [28] I came from the Father and have come into the world; again, I am leaving the world and going to the Father."

29 His disciples said, "Ah, now you are speaking plainly, not in any figure! [30] Now we know that you know all things, and need none to question you; by this we believe that you came from God." [31] Jesus answered them, "Do you now believe? [32] The hour is coming, indeed it has come, when you will be scattered, every man to his home, and will leave me alone; yet I am not alone, for the Father is with me. [33] I have said this to you, that in me you may have peace. In the world you have tribulation; but be of good cheer, I have overcome the world."

17 When Jesus had spoken these words, he lifted up his eyes to heaven and said, "Father, the hour has come; glorify thy Son that the Son may glorify thee, [2] since thou hast given him power over all flesh, to give eternal life to all whom thou hast given him. [3] And this is eternal life, that they know thee the only true God, and Jesus Christ whom thou hast sent. [4] I glorified thee on earth, having accomplished the work which thou gavest me to do; [5] and now, Father, glorify thou me in thy own presence with the glory which I had with thee before the world was made.

6 "I have manifested thy name to the men whom thou gavest me out of the world; thine they were, and thou

*x*Or *convict* *j*Greek *a human being*
16.5: Jn 7.33; 14.5. **16.7:** Jn 14.16, 26; 15.26.
16.9: Jn 15.22. **16.10:** Acts 3.14; 7.52; 1 Pet 3.18.
16.11: Jn 12.31. **16.14:** Jn 7.39.
16.16-24: Jn 14.18-24. **16.20:** Jn 20.20.
16.21: Is 13.8; Hos 13.13; Mic 4.9; 1 Thess 5.3.
16.24: Jn 14.14; 15.11. **16.25:** Jn 10.6; Mt 13.34.
16.32: Jn 4.23; Mk 14.27; Zech 13.7.
16.33: Jn 14.27; 15.18; Rom 8.37; 2 Cor 2.14; Rev 3.21.
17.1: Jn 11.41; 13.31.
17.5: Jn 1.1; 8.58; Phil 2.6.

gavest them to me, and they have kept thy word. ⁷Now they know that everything that thou hast given me is from thee; ⁸for I have given them the words which thou gavest me, and they have received them and know in truth that I came from thee; and they have believed that thou didst send me. ⁹I am praying for them; I am not praying for the world but for those whom thou hast given me, for they are thine; ¹⁰all mine are thine, and thine are mine, and I am glorified in them. ¹¹And now I am no more in the world, but they are in the world, and I am coming to thee. Holy Father, keep them in thy name, which thou hast given me, that they may be one, even as we are one. ¹²While I was with them, I kept them in thy name, which thou hast given me; I have guarded them, and none of them is lost but the son of perdition, that the scripture might be fulfilled. ¹³But now I am coming to thee; and these things I speak in the world, that they may have my joy fulfilled in themselves. ¹⁴I have given them thy word; and the world has hated them because they are not of the world, even as I am not of the world. ¹⁵I do not pray that thou shouldst take them out of the world, but that thou shouldst keep them from the evil one.ᵏ ¹⁶They are not of the world, even as I am not of the world. ¹⁷Sanctify them in the truth; thy word is truth. ¹⁸As thou didst send me into the world, so I have sent them into the world. ¹⁹And for their sake I consecrate myself, that they also may be consecrated in truth.

20 "I do not pray for these only, but also for those who believe in me through their word, ²¹that they may all be one; even as thou, Father, art in me, and I in thee, that they also may be in us, so that the world may believe that thou hast sent me. ²²The glory which thou hast given me I have given to them, that they may be one even as we are one, ²³I in them and thou in me, that they may become perfectly one, so that the world may know that thou hast sent me and hast loved them even as thou hast loved me. ²⁴Father, I desire that they also, whom thou hast given me, may be with me where I am, to behold my glory which thou hast given me in thy love for me before the foundation of the world. ²⁵O righteous Father, the world has not known thee,

but I have known thee; and these know that thou hast sent me. ²⁶I made known to them thy name, and I will make it known, that the love with which thou hast loved me may be in them, and I in them."

18 When Jesus had spoken these words, he went forth with his disciples across the Kĭd′rŏn valley, where there was a garden, which he and his disciples entered. ²Now Judas, who betrayed him, also knew the place; for Jesus often met there with his disciples. ³So Judas, procuring a band of soldiers and some officers from the chief priests and the Phăr′ĭ·seęs, went there with lanterns and torches and weapons. ⁴Then Jesus, knowing all that was to befall him, came forward and said to them, "Whom do you seek?" ⁵They answered him, "Jesus of Nazareth." Jesus said to them, "I am he." Judas, who betrayed him, was standing with them. ⁶When he said to them, "I am he," they drew back and fell to the ground. ⁷Again he asked them, "Whom do you seek?" And they said, "Jesus of Nazareth." ⁸Jesus answered, "I told you that I am he; so, if you seek me, let these men go." ⁹This was to fulfil the word which he had spoken, "Of those whom thou gavest me I lost not one." ¹⁰Then Simon Peter, having a sword, drew it and struck the high priest's slave and cut off his right ear. The slave's name was Măl′chŭs. ¹¹Jesus said to Peter, "Put your sword into its sheath; shall I not drink the cup which the Father has given me?"

12 So the band of soldiers and their captain and the officers of the Jews seized Jesus and bound him. ¹³First they led him to Ăn′năs; for he was the father-in-law of Cāi′a·phas, who was high priest that year. ¹⁴It was Cāi′a·phas who had given counsel to the Jews that it was expedient that one man should die for the people.

15 Simon Peter followed Jesus,

ᵏOr *from evil*
17.9: Lk 22.32; Jn 14.16.
17.11: Phil 2.9; Rev 19.12; Rom 12.5; Gal 3.28; Jn 17.21.
17.12: Ps 41.9; Jn 6.70; 18.9.   17.14: Jn 15.19; 8.23.
17.21: Jn 10.38; 17.11.   17.24: Jn 1.14; 17.5; Mt 25.34.
18.1: Mt 26.30, 36; Mk 14.26, 32; Lk 22.39; 2 Sam 15.23.
18.3-11: Mt 26.47-56; Mk 14.43-50; Lk 22.47-53.
18.4: Jn 6.64; 13.1.
18.9: Jn 17.12; 6.39.   18.11: Mk 10.38; 14.36.
18.12-13: Mt 26.57; Mk 14.53; Lk 22.54; 3.2.
18.14: Jn 11.49-51.
18.15-16: Mt 26.58; Mk 14.54; Lk 22.54.

and so did another disciple. As this disciple was known to the high priest, he entered the court of the high priest along with Jesus, [16] while Peter stood outside at the door. So the other disciple, who was known to the high priest, went out and spoke to the maid who kept the door, and brought Peter in. [17] The maid who kept the door said to Peter, "Are not you also one of this man's disciples?" He said, "I am not." [18] Now the servants[*l*] and officers had made a charcoal fire, because it was cold, and they were standing and warming themselves; Peter also was with them, standing and warming himself.

19 The high priest then questioned Jesus about his disciples and his teaching. [20] Jesus answered him, "I have spoken openly to the world; I have always taught in synagogues and in the temple, where all Jews come together; I have said nothing secretly. [21] Why do you ask me? Ask those who have heard me, what I said to them; they know what I said." [22] When he had said this, one of the officers standing by struck Jesus with his hand, saying, "Is that how you answer the high priest?" [23] Jesus answered him, "If I have spoken wrongly, bear witness to the wrong; but if I have spoken rightly, why do you strike me?" [24] Ān′nǎs then sent him bound to Cāi′a·phǎs the high priest.

25 Now Simon Peter was standing and warming himself. They said to him, "Are not you also one of his disciples?" He denied it and said, "I am not." [26] One of the servants[*l*] of the high priest, a kinsman of the man whose ear Peter had cut off, asked, "Did I not see you in the garden with him?" [27] Peter again denied it; and at once the cock crowed.

28 Then they led Jesus from the house of Cāi′a·phǎs to the praetorium. It was early. They themselves did not enter the praetorium, so that they might not be defiled, but might eat the passover. [29] So Pilate went out to them and said, "What accusation do you bring against this man?" [30] They answered him, "If this man were not an evildoer, we would not have handed him over." [31] Pilate said to them, "Take him yourselves and judge him by your own law." The Jews said to him, "It is not lawful for us to put any

man to death." [32] This was to fulfil the word which Jesus had spoken to show by what death he was to die.

33 Pilate entered the praetorium again and called Jesus, and said to him, "Are you the King of the Jews?" [34] Jesus answered, "Do you say this of your own accord, or did others say it to you about me?" [35] Pilate answered, "Am I a Jew? Your own nation and the chief priests have handed you over to me; what have you done?" [36] Jesus answered, "My kingship is not of this world; if my kingship were of this world, my servants would fight, that I might not be handed over to the Jews; but my kingship is not from the world." [37] Pilate said to him, "So you are a king?" Jesus answered, "You say that I am a king. For this I was born, and for this I have come into the world, to bear witness to the truth. Every one who is of the truth hears my voice." [38] Pilate said to him, "What is truth?"

After he had said this, he went out to the Jews again, and told them, "I find no crime in him. [39] But you have a custom that I should release one man for you at the Passover; will you have me release for you the King of the Jews?" [40] They cried out again, "Not this man, but Ba·rǎb′bas!" Now Barabbas was a robber.

19 Then Pilate took Jesus and scourged him. [2] And the soldiers plaited a crown of thorns, and put it on his head, and arrayed him in a purple robe; [3] they came up to him, saying, "Hail, King of the Jews!" and struck him with their hands. [4] Pilate went out again, and said to them, "See, I am bringing him out to you, that you may know that I find no crime in him." [5] So Jesus came out, wearing the crown of thorns and the purple robe. Pilate said to them, "Behold the man!" [6] When the chief priests and the officers saw him, they cried out, "Crucify him, crucify him!" Pilate said to them, "Take him yourselves and crucify him, for I find no crime in

l Or *slaves*
18.17-18: Mt 26.69-72; Mk 14.66-69; Lk 22.56-58.
18.19-23: Mt 26.59-66; Mk 14.55-64; Lk 22.67-71.
18.23: Mt 5.39; Acts 23.2-5. 18.24: Jn 18.13; Lk 3.2.
18.25-27: Mt 26.73-75; Mk 14.70-72; Lk 22.59-62.
18.28: Jn 11.55; Mt 27.1-2; Mk 15.1; Lk 23.1.
18.29-38: Mt 27.11-14; Mk 15.2-5; Lk 23.2-3.
18.32: Jn 3.14; 12.32. 18.36: Jn 6.15; Mt 26.53.
18.37: Jn 3.32; 8.14, 47; 1 Jn 4.6.
18.38-40: Mt 27.15-26; Mk 15.6-15; Lk 23.18-19; Acts 3.14.
19.2-3: Mt 27.27-31; Mk 15.16-20; Lk 22.63-65; 23.11.
19.4: Jn 18.38; 19.6; Lk 23.4.

him." [7]The Jews answered him, "We have a law, and by that law he ought to die, because he has made himself the Son of God." [8]When Pilate heard these words, he was the more afraid; [9]he entered the praetorium again and said to Jesus, "Where are you from?" But Jesus gave no answer. [10]Pilate therefore said to him, "You will not speak to me? Do you not know that I have power to release you, and power to crucify you?" [11]Jesus answered him, "You would have no power over me unless it had been given you from above; therefore he who delivered me to you has the greater sin."

12 Upon this Pilate sought to release him, but the Jews cried out, "If you release this man, you are not Caesar's friend; every one who makes himself a king sets himself against Caesar." [13]When Pilate heard these words, he brought Jesus out and sat down on the judgment seat at a place called The Pavement, and in Hebrew, Găb'ba·thą. [14]Now it was the day of Preparation of the Passover; it was about the sixth hour. He said to the Jews, "Behold your King!" [15]They cried out, "Away with him, away with him, crucify him!" Pilate said to them, "Shall I crucify your King?" The chief priests answered, "We have no king but Caesar." [16]Then he handed him over to them to be crucified.

17 So they took Jesus, and he went out, bearing his own cross, to the place called the place of a skull, which is called in Hebrew Gŏl'gŏ·thą. [18]There they crucified him, and with him two others, one on either side, and Jesus between them. [19]Pilate also wrote a title and put it on the cross; it read, "Jesus of Nazareth, the King of the Jews." [20]Many of the Jews read this title, for the place where Jesus was crucified was near the city; and it was written in Hebrew, in Latin, and in Greek. [21]The chief priests of the Jews then said to Pilate, "Do not write, 'The King of the Jews,' but, 'This man said, I am King of the Jews.'" [22]Pilate answered, "What I have written I have written."

23 When the soldiers had crucified Jesus they took his garments and made four parts, one for each soldier; also his tunic. But the tunic was without seam, woven from top to bottom; [24]so they said to one another, "Let us not tear it, but cast lots for it to see whose it shall be." This was to fulfil the scripture,
"They parted my garments among them,
and for my clothing they cast lots."
25 So the soldiers did this. But standing by the cross of Jesus were his mother, and his mother's sister, Mary the wife of Clō'pąs, and Mary Măg'dą·lēne. [26]When Jesus saw his mother, and the disciple whom he loved standing near, he said to his mother, "Woman, behold, your son!" [27]Then he said to the disciple, "Behold, your mother!" And from that hour the disciple took her to his own home.

28 After this Jesus, knowing that all was now finished, said (to fulfil the scripture), "I thirst." [29]A bowl full of vinegar stood there; so they put a sponge full of the vinegar on hyssop and held it to his mouth. [30]When Jesus had received the vinegar, he said, "It is finished"; and he bowed his head and gave up his spirit.

31 Since it was the day of Preparation, in order to prevent the bodies from remaining on the cross on the sabbath (for that sabbath was a high day), the Jews asked Pilate that their legs might be broken, and that they might be taken away. [32]So the soldiers came and broke the legs of the first, and of the other who had been crucified with him; [33]but when they came to Jesus and saw that he was already dead, they did not break his legs. [34]But one of the soldiers pierced his side with a spear, and at once there came out blood and water. [35]He who saw it has borne witness—his testimony is true, and he knows that he tells the truth—that you also may believe. [36]For these things took place that the scripture might be fulfilled, "Not a bone of him shall be broken." [37]And again another scripture says, "They shall look on him whom they have pierced."

38 After this Joseph of Ăr·ĭ·mą·thē'ą,

19.7: Lev 24.16; Mk 14.61-64; Jn 5.18; 10.33.
19.11: Rom 13.1; Jn 18.28. 19.12: Lk 23.2.
19.14: Mk 15.42; Jn 19.31, 42; Mk 15.25, 33.
19.17-24: Mt 27.33-44; Mk 15.22-32; Lk 23.33-43.
19.24: Ex 28.32; Ps 22.18.
19.25: Mt 27.55-56; Mk 15.40-41; Lk 23.49; Jn 2.3; Mk 3.31; Lk 24.18; Jn 20.1, 18. 19.26: Jn 13.23; 20.2; 21.20.
19.28-30: Ps 69.21; Mt 27.45-50; Mk 15.33-37; Lk 23.44-46; Jn 17.4. 19.31: Deut 21.23; Ex 12.16.
19.34: 1 Jn 5.6-8. 19.35: Jn 15.27; 21.24.
19.36: Ex 12.46; Num 9.12; Ps 34.20. 19.37: Zech 12.10.
19.38-42: Mt 27.57-61; Mk 15.42-47; Lk 23.50-56.

who was a disciple of Jesus, but secretly, for fear of the Jews, asked Pilate that he might take away the body of Jesus, and Pilate gave him leave. So he came and took away his body. ³⁹ Nĭc·o·dē'mus also, who had at first come to him by night, came bringing a mixture of myrrh and aloes, about a hundred pounds' weight. ⁴⁰They took the body of Jesus, and bound it in linen cloths with the spices, as is the burial custom of the Jews. ⁴¹Now in the place where he was crucified there was a garden, and in the garden a new tomb where no one had ever been laid. ⁴²So because of the Jewish day of Preparation, as the tomb was close at hand, they laid Jesus there.

20 Now on the first day of the week Mary Măg'da·lēne came to the tomb early, while it was still dark, and saw that the stone had been taken away from the tomb. ²So she ran, and went to Simon Peter and the other disciple, the one whom Jesus loved, and said to them, "They have taken the Lord out of the tomb, and we do not know where they have laid him." ³Peter then came out with the other disciple, and they went toward the tomb. ⁴They both ran, but the other disciple outran Peter and reached the tomb first; ⁵and stooping to look in, he saw the linen cloths lying there, but he did not go in. ⁶Then Simon Peter came, following him, and went into the tomb; he saw the linen cloths lying, ⁷and the napkin, which had been on his head, not lying with the linen cloths but rolled up in a place by itself. ⁸Then the other disciple, who reached the tomb first, also went in, and he saw and believed; ⁹for as yet they did not know the scripture, that he must rise from the dead. ¹⁰Then the disciples went back to their homes.

11 But Mary stood weeping outside the tomb, and as she wept she stooped to look into the tomb; ¹²and she saw two angels in white, sitting where the body of Jesus had lain, one at the head and one at the feet. ¹³They said to her, "Woman, why are you weeping?" She said to them, "Because they have taken away my Lord, and I do not know where they have laid him." ¹⁴Saying this, she turned round and saw Jesus standing, but she did not know that it was Jesus. ¹⁵Jesus said to her, "Woman,

why are you weeping? Whom do you seek?" Supposing him to be the gardener, she said to him, "Sir, if you have carried him away, tell me where you have laid him, and I will take him away." ¹⁶Jesus said to her, "Mary." She turned and said to him in Hebrew, "Rab–bō'nī!" (which means Teacher). ¹⁷Jesus said to her, "Do not hold me, for I have not yet ascended to the Father; but go to my brethren and say to them, I am ascending to my Father and your Father, to my God and your God." ¹⁸Mary Măg'da·lēne went and said to the disciples, "I have seen the Lord"; and she told them that he had said these things to her.

19 On the evening of that day, the first day of the week, the doors being shut where the disciples were, for fear of the Jews, Jesus came and stood among them and said to them, "Peace be with you." ²⁰When he had said this, he showed them his hands and his side. Then the disciples were glad when they saw the Lord. ²¹Jesus said to them again, "Peace be with you. As the Father has sent me, even so I send you." ²²And when he had said this, he breathed on them, and said to them, "Receive the Holy Spirit. ²³If you forgive the sins of any, they are forgiven; if you retain the sins of any, they are retained."

24 Now Thomas, one of the twelve, called the Twin, was not with them when Jesus came. ²⁵So the other disciples told him, "We have seen the Lord." But he said to them, "Unless I see in his hands the print of the nails, and place my finger in the mark of the nails, and place my hand in his side, I will not believe."

26 Eight days later, his disciples were again in the house, and Thomas was with them. The doors were shut, but Jesus came and stood among them, and said, "Peace be with you." ²⁷Then he said to Thomas, "Put your finger here, and see my hands; and put out your hand, and place it in my side; do not be faithless, but believing." ²⁸Thomas answered him, "My Lord and

19.39: Jn 3.1; 7.50. 19.40: Mk 16.1; 14.8.
20.1-10: Mt 28.1-8; Mk 16.1-8; Lk 24.1-10.
20.3-10: Lk 24.11-12. 20.9: Lk 24.26, 46.
20.12: Lk 24.4; Mt 28.5; Mk 16.5. 20.13: Jn 20.2.
20.14: Mt 28.9; Jn 21.4.
20.17: Jn 20.27; Mt 28.10; Jn 7.33. 20.18: Lk 24.10, 23.
20.19-20: Lk 24.36-39. 20.21: Jn 17.18; Mt 28.19.
20.22: Acts 2.4, 33. 20.23: Mt 16.19; 18.18.
20.24: Jn 11.16. 20.27: Lk 24.40.

my God!" ²⁹ Jesus said to him, "Have you believed because you have seen me? Blessed are those who have not seen and yet believe."

30 Now Jesus did many other signs in the presence of the disciples, which are not written in this book; ³¹ but these are written that you may believe that Jesus is the Christ, the Son of God, and that believing you may have life in his name.

21 After this Jesus revealed himself again to the disciples by the Sea of Tī·bē′rī-as; and he revealed himself in this way. ² Simon Peter, Thomas called the Twin, Na̱thăn′a̱–ĕl of Cā′na̱ in Galilee, the sons of Zĕb′e̱·dee, and two others of his disciples were together. ³ Simon Peter said to them, "I am going fishing." They said to him, "We will go with you." They went out and got into the boat; but that night they caught nothing.

4 Just as day was breaking, Jesus stood on the beach; yet the disciples did not know that it was Jesus. ⁵ Jesus said to them, "Children, have you any fish?" They answered him, "No." ⁶ He said to them, "Cast the net on the right side of the boat, and you will find some." So they cast it, and now they were not able to haul it in, for the quantity of fish. ⁷ That disciple whom Jesus loved said to Peter, "It is the Lord!" When Simon Peter heard that it was the Lord, he put on his clothes, for he was stripped for work, and sprang into the sea. ⁸ But the other disciples came in the boat, dragging the net full of fish, for they were not far from the land, but about a hundred yards *ᵐ* off.

9 When they got out on land, they saw a charcoal fire there, with fish lying on it, and bread. ¹⁰ Jesus said to them, "Bring some of the fish that you have just caught." ¹¹ So Simon Peter went aboard and hauled the net ashore, full of large fish, a hundred and fifty-three of them; and although there were so many, the net was not torn. ¹² Jesus said to them, "Come and have breakfast." Now none of the disciples dared ask him, "Who are you?" They knew it was the Lord. ¹³ Jesus came and took the bread and gave it to them, and so with the fish. ¹⁴ This was now the third time that Jesus was revealed to the disciples after he was raised from the dead.

15 When they had finished breakfast, Jesus said to Simon Peter, "Simon, son of John, do you love me more than these?" He said to him, "Yes, Lord; you know that I love you." He said to him, "Feed my lambs." ¹⁶ A second time he said to him, "Simon, son of John, do you love me?" He said to him, "Yes, Lord; you know that I love you." He said to him, "Tend my sheep." ¹⁷ He said to him the third time, "Simon, son of John, do you love me?" Peter was grieved because he said to him the third time, "Do you love me?" And he said to him, "Lord, you know everything; you know that I love you." Jesus said to him, "Feed my sheep. ¹⁸ Truly, truly, I say to you, when you were young, you girded yourself and walked where you would; but when you are old, you will stretch out your hands, and another will gird you and carry you where you do not wish to go." ¹⁹ (This he said to show by what death he was to glorify God.) And after this he said to him, "Follow me."

20 Peter turned and saw following them the disciple whom Jesus loved, who had lain close to his breast at the supper and had said, "Lord, who is it that is going to betray you?" ²¹ When Peter saw him, he said to Jesus, "Lord, what about this man?" ²² Jesus said to him, "If it is my will that he remain until I come, what is that to you? Follow me!" ²³ The saying spread abroad among the brethren that this disciple was not to die; yet Jesus did not say to him that he was not to die, but, "If it is my will that he remain until I come, what is that to you?"

24 This is the disciple who is bearing witness to these things, and who has written these things; and we know that his testimony is true.

25 But there are also many other things which Jesus did; were every one of them to be written, I suppose that the world itself could not contain the books that would be written.

ᵐ Greek *two hundred cubits*
20.29: 1 Pet 1.8.   **20.30:** Jn 21.25.   **20.31:** Jn 3.15.
21.2: Jn 11.16; 1.45; Lk 5.10.   **21.3–6:** Lk 5.3-7.
21.4: Jn 20.14; Lk 24.16.   **21.5:** Lk 24.41.
21.7: Jn 13.23; 19.26; 20.2; 21.20.   **21.14:** Jn 20.19, 26.
21.15: Jn 1.42; 13.37; Mk 14.29-31; Lk 12.32.
21.16: Mt 2.6; Acts 20.28; 1 Pet 5.2; Rev 7.17.
21.19: 2 Pet 1.14; Mk 1.17.   **21.20:** Jn 13.25.
21.22: 1 Cor 4.5; Jas 5.7; Rev 2.25; Mt 16.28.
21.24: Jn 15.27; 19.35.   **21.25:** Jn 20.30.

The
Acts of the Apostles

1 In the first book, O Thē-ŏph'ĭ-lŭs, I have dealt with all that Jesus began to do and teach, [2] until the day when he was taken up, after he had given commandment through the Holy Spirit to the apostles whom he had chosen. [3] To them he presented himself alive after his passion by many proofs, appearing to them during forty days, and speaking of the kingdom of God. [4] And while staying[a] with them he charged them not to depart from Jerusalem, but to wait for the promise of the Father, which, he said, "you heard from me, [5] for John baptized with water, but before many days you shall be baptized with the Holy Spirit."

6 So when they had come together, they asked him, "Lord, will you at this time restore the kingdom to Israel?" [7] He said to them, "It is not for you to know times or seasons which the Father has fixed by his own authority. [8] But you shall receive power when the Holy Spirit has come upon you; and you shall be my witnesses in Jerusalem and in all Jü-dē'ạ and Sạ-mâr'ĭ-ạ and to the end of the earth." [9] And when he had said this, as they were looking on, he was lifted up, and a cloud took him out of their sight. [10] And while they were gazing into heaven as he went, behold, two men stood by them in white robes, [11] and said, "Men of Galilee, why do you stand looking into heaven? This Jesus, who was taken up from you into heaven, will come in the same way as you saw him go into heaven."

12 Then they returned to Jerusalem from the mount called Ŏl'ĭ-vĕt, which is near Jerusalem, a sabbath day's journey away; [13] and when they had entered, they went up to the upper room, where they were staying, Peter and John and James and Andrew, Philip and Thomas, Bartholomew and Matthew, James the son of Ăl-phaē'ŭs and Simon the Zealot and Judas the son of James. [14] All these with one accord devoted themselves to prayer, together with the women and Mary the mother of Jesus, and with his brothers.

15 In those days Peter stood up among the brethren (the company of persons was in all about a hundred and twenty), and said, [16] "Brethren, the scripture had to be fulfilled, which the Holy Spirit spoke beforehand by the mouth of David, concerning Judas who was guide to those who arrested Jesus. [17] For he was numbered among us, and was allotted his share in this ministry. [18] (Now this man bought a field with the reward of his wickedness; and falling headlong[b] he burst open in the middle and all his bowels gushed out. [19] And it became known to all the inhabitants of Jerusalem, so that the field was called in their language A·kĕl'dạ·mạ, that is, Field of Blood.) [20] For it is written in the book of Psalms,

'Let his habitation become desolate,
and let there be no one to live in it';

and

'His office let another take.'

[21] So one of the men who have accompanied us during all the time that the Lord Jesus went in and out among us, [22] beginning from the baptism of John until the day when he was taken up from us—one of these men must become with us a witness to his resurrection." [23] And they put forward two, Joseph called Bär·săb'bạs, who was surnamed Justus, and Măt·thī'ạs. [24] And they prayed and said, "Lord, who knowest the hearts of all men, show which one of these two thou hast chosen [25] to take the place in this ministry and apostleship from which Judas turned aside, to go to his own place." [26] And they cast lots for them, and the lot fell on Măt·thī'ạs; and he was enrolled with the eleven apostles.

2 When the day of Pentecost had come, they were all together in one place. [2] And suddenly a sound came from heaven like the rush of a mighty wind, and it filled all the house where they were sitting. [3] And there appeared to them tongues as of fire, distributed and resting on each one of them. [4] And

[a]Or *eating* [b]Or *swelling up*
1.1: Lk 1.1-4.
1.4: Lk 24.49. **1.8**: Lk 24.48-49. **1.9-12**: Lk 24.50-53.
1.13: Mt 10.2-4; Mk 3.16-19; Lk 6.14-16.
1.16-19: Mt 27.3-10. **1.20**: Ps 69.25; 109.8.

they were all filled with the Holy Spirit and began to speak in other tongues, as the Spirit gave them utterance.

5 Now there were dwelling in Jerusalem Jews, devout men from every nation under heaven. ⁶And at this sound the multitude came together, and they were bewildered, because each one heard them speaking in his own language. ⁷And they were amazed and wondered, saying, "Are not all these who are speaking Galileans? ⁸And how is it that we hear, each of us in his own native language? ⁹Pär'-thĭ·ạnṣ and Mēdeṣ and É'lạm·ītes and residents/ of Mĕs·ọ·pọ·tā'mĭ·ạ, Jü·dē'ạ and Căp·pạ·dō'çi·ạ, Pŏn'tụs and Asia, ¹⁰Phrȳg'ĭ·a and Păm·phȳl'ĭ·ạ, Egypt and the parts of Lĭb'yạ belonging to Cȳ·rē'nē, and visitors from Rome, both Jews and proselytes, ¹¹Cretans and Arabians, we hear them telling in our own tongues the mighty works of God." ¹²And all were amazed and perplexed, saying to one another, "What does this mean?" ¹³But others mocking said, "They are filled with new wine."

14 But Peter, standing with the eleven, lifted up his voice and addressed them, "Men of Jü·dē'ạ and all who dwell in Jerusalem, let this be known to you, and give ear to my words. ¹⁵For these men are not drunk, as you suppose, since it is only the third hour of the day; ¹⁶but this is what was spoken by the prophet Jō'el:
¹⁷'And in the last days it shall be, God declares,
that I will pour out my Spirit upon all flesh,
and your sons and your daughters shall prophesy,
and your young men shall see visions, and your old men shall dream dreams;
¹⁸yea, and on my menservants and my maidservants in those days
I will pour out my Spirit; and they shall prophesy.
¹⁹And I will show wonders in the heaven above
and signs on the earth beneath,
blood, and fire, and vapor of smoke;
²⁰the sun shall be turned into darkness
and the moon into blood,
before the day of the Lord comes,
the great and manifest day.
²¹And it shall be that whoever calls on

the name of the Lord shall be saved.'

22 "Men of Israel, hear these words: Jesus of Nazareth, a man attested to you by God with mighty works and wonders and signs which God did through him in your midst, as you yourselves know—²³this Jesus, delivered up according to the definite plan and foreknowledge of God, you crucified and killed by the hands of lawless men. ²⁴But God raised him up, having loosed the pangs of death, because it was not possible for him to be held by it. ²⁵For David says concerning him,
'I saw the Lord always before me,
for he is at my right hand that I may not be shaken;
²⁶therefore my heart was glad, and my tongue rejoiced;
moreover my flesh will dwell in hope.
²⁷For thou wilt not abandon my soul to Hades,
nor let thy Holy One see corruption.
²⁸Thou hast made known to me the ways of life;
thou wilt make me full of gladness with thy presence.'

29 "Brethren, I may say to you confidently of the patriarch David that he both died and was buried, and his tomb is with us to this day. ³⁰Being therefore a prophet, and knowing that God had sworn with an oath to him that he would set one of his descendants upon his throne, ³¹he foresaw and spoke of the resurrection of the Christ, that he was not abandoned to Hades, nor did his flesh see corruption. ³²This Jesus God raised up, and of that we all are witnesses. ³³Being therefore exalted at the right hand of God, and having received from the Father the promise of the Holy Spirit, he has poured out this which you see and hear. ³⁴For David did not ascend into the heavens; but he himself says,
'The Lord said to my Lord, Sit at my right hand,
³⁵till I make thy enemies a stool for thy feet.'
³⁶Let all the house of Israel therefore know assuredly that God has made him both Lord and Christ, this Jesus whom you crucified."

37 Now when they heard this they were cut to the heart, and said to

2.17-21: Joel 2.28-32.   **2.25-28:** Ps 16.8-11.
2.30: Ps 132.11.   **2.31:** Ps 16.10.   **2.34-35:** Ps 110.1.

Peter and the rest of the apostles, "Brethren, what shall we do?" [38]And Peter said to them, "Repent, and be baptized every one of you in the name of Jesus Christ for the forgiveness of your sins; and you shall receive the gift of the Holy Spirit. [39]For the promise is to you and to your children and to all that are far off, every one whom the Lord our God calls to him." [40]And he testified with many other words and exhorted them, saying, "Save yourselves from this crooked generation." [41]So those who received his word were baptized, and there were added that day about three thousand souls. [42]And they devoted themselves to the apostles' teaching and fellowship, to the breaking of bread and the prayers.

43 And fear came upon every soul; and many wonders and signs were done through the apostles. [44]And all who believed were together and had all things in common; [45]and they sold their possessions and goods and distributed them to all, as any had need. [46]And day by day, attending the temple together and breaking bread in their homes, they partook of food with glad and generous hearts, [47]praising God and having favor with all the people. And the Lord added to their number day by day those who were being saved.

3 Now Peter and John were going up to the temple at the hour of prayer, the ninth hour. [2]And a man lame from birth was being carried, whom they laid daily at that gate of the temple which is called Beautiful to ask alms of those who entered the temple. [3]Seeing Peter and John about to go into the temple, he asked for alms. [4]And Peter directed his gaze at him, with John, and said, "Look at us." [5]And he fixed his attention upon them, expecting to receive something from them. [6]But Peter said, "I have no silver and gold, but I give you what I have; in the name of Jesus Christ of Nazareth, walk." [7]And he took him by the right hand and raised him up; and immediately his feet and ankles were made strong. [8]And leaping up he stood and walked and entered the temple with them, walking and leaping and praising God. [9]And all the people saw him walking and praising God, [10]and recognized him as the one who sat for alms at the Beautiful Gate of the tem-

ple; and they were filled with wonder and amazement at what had happened to him.

11 While he clung to Peter and John, all the people ran together to them in the portico called Solomon's, astounded. [12]And when Peter saw it he addressed the people, "Men of Israel, why do you wonder at this, or why do you stare at us, as though by our own power or piety we had made him walk? [13]The God of Abraham and of Isaac and of Jacob, the God of our fathers, glorified his servant[c] Jesus, whom you delivered up and denied in the presence of Pilate, when he had decided to release him. [14]But you denied the Holy and Righteous One, and asked for a murderer to be granted to you, [15]and killed the Author of life, whom God raised from the dead. To this we are witnesses. [16]And his name, by faith in his name, has made this man strong whom you see and know; and the faith which is through Jesus[d] has given the man this perfect health in the presence of you all.

17 "And now, brethren, I know that you acted in ignorance, as did also your rulers. [18]But what God foretold by the mouth of all the prophets, that his Christ should suffer, he thus fulfilled. [19]Repent therefore, and turn again, that your sins may be blotted out, that times of refreshing may come from the presence of the Lord, [20]and that he may send the Christ appointed for you, Jesus, [21]whom heaven must receive until the time for establishing all that God spoke by the mouth of his holy prophets from of old. [22]Moses said, 'The Lord God will raise up for you a prophet from your brethren as he raised me up. You shall listen to him in whatever he tells you. [23]And it shall be that every soul that does not listen to that prophet shall be destroyed from the people.' [24]And all the prophets who have spoken, from Samuel and those who came afterwards, also proclaimed these days. [25]You are the sons of the prophets and of the covenant which God gave to your fathers, saying to Abraham, 'And in your posterity shall all the families of the earth be blessed.' [26]God, having raised up his servant,[c] sent him to you first, to bless

[c] Or *child* [d] Greek *him*
2.39: Is 57.19; Joel 2.32. 2.44–45: Acts 4.32-35.
3.13: Ex 3.6; Is 52.13. 3.22: Deut 18.15-16.
3.23: Deut 18.19; Lev 23.29. 3.25: Gen 22.18.

you in turning every one of you from your wickedness."

4 And as they were speaking to the people, the priests and the captain of the temple and the Săd′dū·çeeş came upon them, ²annoyed because they were teaching the people and proclaiming in Jesus the resurrection from the dead. ³And they arrested them and put them in custody until the morrow, for it was already evening. ⁴But many of those who heard the word believed; and the number of the men came to about five thousand.

5 On the morrow their rulers and elders and scribes were gathered together in Jerusalem, ⁶with Ăn′năs the high priest and Cāi′a·phăş and John and Alexander, and all who were of the high-priestly family. ⁷And when they had set them in the midst, they inquired, "By what power or by what name did you do this?" ⁸Then Peter, filled with the Holy Spirit, said to them, "Rulers of the people and elders, ⁹if we are being examined today concerning a good deed done to a cripple, by what means this man has been healed, ¹⁰be it known to you all, and to all the people of Israel, that by the name of Jesus Christ of Nazareth, whom you crucified, whom God raised from the dead, by him this man is standing before you well. ¹¹This is the stone which was rejected by you builders, but which has become the head of the corner. ¹²And there is salvation in no one else, for there is no other name under heaven given among men by which we must be saved."

13 Now when they saw the boldness of Peter and John, and perceived that they were uneducated, common men, they wondered; and they recognized that they had been with Jesus. ¹⁴But seeing the man that had been healed standing beside them, they had nothing to say in opposition. ¹⁵But when they had commanded them to go aside out of the council, they conferred with one another, ¹⁶saying, "What shall we do with these men? For that a notable sign has been performed through them is manifest to all the inhabitants of Jerusalem, and we cannot deny it. ¹⁷But in order that it may spread no further among the people, let us warn them to speak no more to any one in this name." ¹⁸So they called them and charged them not to speak or teach at all in the name of Jesus. ¹⁹But Peter and John answered them, "Whether it is right in the sight of God to listen to you rather than to God, you must judge; ²⁰for we cannot but speak of what we have seen and heard." ²¹And when they had further threatened them, they let them go, finding no way to punish them, because of the people; for all men praised God for what had happened. ²²For the man on whom this sign of healing was performed was more than forty years old.

23 When they were released they went to their friends and reported what the chief priests and the elders had said to them. ²⁴And when they heard it, they lifted their voices together to God and said, "Sovereign Lord, who didst make the heaven and the earth and the sea and everything in them, ²⁵who by the mouth of our father David, thy servant,ᶜ didst say by the Holy Spirit,

'Why did the Gentiles rage,
  and the peoples imagine vain things?
²⁶The kings of the earth set themselves
  in array,
and the rulers were gathered together,
against the Lord and against his Anointed' — ᵉ

²⁷for truly in this city there were gathered together against thy holy servantᶜ Jesus, whom thou didst anoint, both Hĕr′od and Pŏn′tĭ·us Pilate, with the Gentiles and the peoples of Israel, ²⁸to do whatever thy hand and thy plan had predestined to take place. ²⁹And now, Lord, look upon their threats, and grant to thy servantsᶠ to speak thy word with all boldness, ³⁰while thou stretchest out thy hand to heal, and signs and wonders are performed through the name of thy holy servantᶜ Jesus." ³¹And when they had prayed, the place in which they were gathered together was shaken; and they were all filled with the Holy Spirit and spoke the word of God with boldness.

32 Now the company of those who believed were of one heart and soul, and no one said that any of the things which he possessed was his own, but

ᶜOr *child*   ᵉOr *Christ*   ᶠOr *slaves*
4.11: Ps 118.22.
4.24: Ex 20.11; Ps 146.6.   **4.25-26:** Ps 2.1-2.
4.27: Ps 2.2; 2.1.   **4.32-35:** Acts 2.44-45.

they had everything in common. ³³And with great power the apostles gave their testimony to the resurrection of the Lord Jesus, and great grace was upon them all. ³⁴There was not a needy person among them, for as many as were possessors of lands or houses sold them, and brought the proceeds of what was sold ³⁵and laid it at the apostles' feet; and distribution was made to each as any had need. ³⁶Thus Joseph who was surnamed by the apostles Bär′na·bas (which means, Son of encouragement), a Lē′vīte, a native of Cyprus, ³⁷sold a field which belonged to him, and brought the money and laid it at the apostles' feet.

5 But a man named Ăn·a·nī′as with his wife Săp·phī′ra sold a piece of property, ²and with his wife's knowledge he kept back some of the proceeds, and brought only a part and laid it at the apostles' feet. ³But Peter said, "Ăn·a·nī′as, why has Satan filled your heart to lie to the Holy Spirit and to keep back part of the proceeds of the land? ⁴While it remained unsold, did it not remain your own? And after it was sold, was it not at your disposal? How is it that you have contrived this deed in your heart? You have not lied to men but to God." ⁵When Ăn·a·nī′as heard these words, he fell down and died. And great fear came upon all who heard of it. ⁶The young men rose and wrapped him up and carried him out and buried him.

7 After an interval of about three hours his wife came in, not knowing what had happened. ⁸And Peter said to her, "Tell me whether you sold the land for so much." And she said, "Yes, for so much." ⁹But Peter said to her, "How is it that you have agreed together to tempt the Spirit of the Lord? Hark, the feet of those that have buried your husband are at the door, and they will carry you out." ¹⁰Immediately she fell down at his feet and died. When the young men came in they found her dead, and they carried her out and buried her beside her husband. ¹¹And great fear came upon the whole church, and upon all who heard of these things.

12 Now many signs and wonders were done among the people by the hands of the apostles. And they were all together in Solomon's Portico. ¹³None of the rest dared join them, but the people held them in high honor.

¹⁴And more than ever believers were added to the Lord, multitudes both of men and women, ¹⁵so that they even carried out the sick into the streets, and laid them on beds and pallets, that as Peter came by at least his shadow might fall on some of them. ¹⁶The people also gathered from the towns around Jerusalem, bringing the sick and those afflicted with unclean spirits, and they were all healed.

17 But the high priest rose up and all who were with him, that is, the party of the Săd′dū·çeeş, and filled with jealousy ¹⁸they arrested the apostles and put them in the common prison. ¹⁹But at night an angel of the Lord opened the prison doors and brought them out and said, ²⁰"Go and stand in the temple and speak to the people all the words of this Life." ²¹And when they heard this, they entered the temple at daybreak and taught.

Now the high priest came and those who were with him and called together the council and all the senate of Israel, and sent to the prison to have them brought. ²²But when the officers came, they did not find them in the prison, and they returned and reported, ²³"We found the prison securely locked and the sentries standing at the doors, but when we opened it we found no one inside." ²⁴Now when the captain of the temple and the chief priests heard these words, they were much perplexed about them, wondering what this would come to. ²⁵And some one came and told them, "The men whom you put in prison are standing in the temple and teaching the people." ²⁶Then the captain with the officers went and brought them, but without violence, for they were afraid of being stoned by the people.

27 And when they had brought them, they set them before the council. And the high priest questioned them, ²⁸saying, "We strictly charged you not to teach in this name, yet here you have filled Jerusalem with your teaching and you intend to bring this man's blood upon us." ²⁹But Peter and the apostles answered, "We must obey God rather than men. ³⁰The God of our fathers raised Jesus whom you killed by hanging him on a tree. ³¹God exalted him at his right hand as Leader and Savior, to give repentance to Is-

5.30: Deut 21.22-23.

rael and forgiveness of sins. ³²And we are witnesses to these things, and so is the Holy Spirit whom God has given to those who obey him."

33 When they heard this they were enraged and wanted to kill them. ³⁴But a Phăr′ĭ·see in the council named Ga̧·mā′lĭ·el, a teacher of the law, held in honor by all the people, stood up and ordered the men to be put outside for a while. ³⁵And he said to them, "Men of Israel, take care what you do with these men. ³⁶For before these days Theū′da̧s arose, giving himself out to be somebody, and a number of men, about four hundred, joined him; but he was slain and all who followed him were dispersed and came to nothing. ³⁷After him Judas the Galilean arose in the days of the census and drew away some of the people after him; he also perished, and all who followed him were scattered. ³⁸So in the present case I tell you, keep away from these men and let them alone; for if this plan or this undertaking is of men, it will fail; ³⁹but if it is of God, you will not be able to overthrow them. You might even be found opposing God!"

40 So they took his advice, and when they had called in the apostles, they beat them and charged them not to speak in the name of Jesus, and let them go. ⁴¹Then they left the presence of the council, rejoicing that they were counted worthy to suffer dishonor for the name. ⁴²And every day in the temple and at home they did not cease teaching and preaching Jesus as the Christ.

6 Now in these days when the disciples were increasing in number, the Hellenists murmured against the Hebrews because their widows were neglected in the daily distribution. ²And the twelve summoned the body of the disciples and said, "It is not right that we should give up preaching the word of God to serve tables. ³Therefore, brethren, pick out from among you seven men of good repute, full of the Spirit and of wisdom, whom we may appoint to this duty. ⁴But we will devote ourselves to prayer and to the ministry of the word." ⁵And what they said pleased the whole multitude, and they chose Stephen, a man full of faith and of the Holy Spirit, and Philip, and Prŏch′o̧·rus, and Nĭ·cā′nor, and

Tĭ′mon, and Pār′mȩ·nas, and Nĭc-o̧·lā′us, a proselyte of Ăn′tĭ·ŏch. ⁶These they set before the apostles, and they prayed and laid their hands upon them.

7 And the word of God increased; and the number of the disciples multiplied greatly in Jerusalem, and a great many of the priests were obedient to the faith.

8 And Stephen, full of grace and power, did great wonders and signs among the people. ⁹Then some of those who belonged to the synagogue of the Freedmen (as it was called), and of the Cy̧·rē′nĭ·ans, and of the Alexandrians, and of those from Çĭ·lĭ′çĭ·a and Asia, arose and disputed with Stephen. ¹⁰But they could not withstand the wisdom and the Spirit with which he spoke. ¹¹Then they secretly instigated men, who said, "We have heard him speak blasphemous words against Moses and God." ¹²And they stirred up the people and the elders and the scribes, and they came upon him and seized him and brought him before the council, ¹³and set up false witnesses who said, "This man never ceases to speak words against this holy place and the law; ¹⁴for we have heard him say that this Jesus of Nazareth will destroy this place, and will change the customs which Moses delivered to us." ¹⁵And gazing at him, all who sat in the council saw that his face was like the face of an angel.

7 And the high priest said, "Is this so?" ²And Stephen said:

"Brethren and fathers, hear me. The God of glory appeared to our father Abraham, when he was in Mĕs·o̧·po̧-tā′mĭ·a, before he lived in Hăr′an, ³and said to him, 'Depart from your land and from your kindred and go into the land which I will show you.' ⁴Then he departed from the land of the Chăl·dē′ans, and lived in Hăr′an. And after his father died, God removed him from there into this land in which you are now living; ⁵yet he gave him no inheritance in it, not even a foot's length, but promised to give it to him in possession and to his posterity after him, though he had no child. ⁶And God spoke to this effect, that his posterity would be aliens in a land belonging to others, who would enslave them and

7.2: Ps 29.3; Gen 11.31; 15.7.   7.3: Gen 12.1.
7.4: Gen 11.31; 15.7; 12.5.
7.5: Deut 2.5; Gen 12.7; 17.8.   7.6–7: Gen 15.13-14.

ill-treat them four hundred years. ⁷'But I will judge the nation which they serve,' said God, 'and after that they shall come out and worship me in this place.' ⁸And he gave him the covenant of circumcision. And so Abraham became the father of Isaac, and circumcised him on the eighth day; and Isaac became the father of Jacob, and Jacob of the twelve patriarchs.

9 "And the patriarchs, jealous of Joseph, sold him into Egypt; but God was with him, ¹⁰and rescued him out of all his afflictions, and gave him favor and wisdom before Pharaoh, king of Egypt, who made him governor over Egypt and over all his household. ¹¹Now there came a famine throughout all Egypt and Canaan, and great affliction, and our fathers could find no food. ¹²But when Jacob heard that there was grain in Egypt, he sent forth our fathers the first time. ¹³And at the second visit Joseph made himself known to his brothers, and Joseph's family become known to Pharaoh. ¹⁴And Joseph sent and called to him Jacob his father and all his kindred, seventy-five souls; ¹⁵and Jacob went down into Egypt. And he died, himself and our fathers, ¹⁶and they were carried back to Shĕ'chĕm and laid in the tomb that Abraham had bought for a sum of silver from the sons of Hā'-môr in Shechem.

17 "But as the time of the promise drew near, which God had granted to Abraham, the people grew and multiplied in Egypt ¹⁸till there arose over Egypt another king who had not known Joseph. ¹⁹He dealt craftily with our race and forced our fathers to expose their infants, that they might not be kept alive. ²⁰At this time Moses was born, and was beautiful before God. And he was brought up for three months in his father's house; ²¹and when he was exposed, Pharaoh's daughter adopted him and brought him up as her own son. ²²And Moses was instructed in all the wisdom of the Egyptians, and he was mighty in his words and deeds.

23 "When he was forty years old, it came into his heart to visit his brethren, the sons of Israel. ²⁴And seeing one of them being wronged, he defended the oppressed man and avenged him by striking the Egyptian. ²⁵He supposed that his brethren understood

that God was giving them deliverance by his hand, but they did not understand. ²⁶And on the following day he appeared to them as they were quarreling and would have reconciled them, saying, 'Men, you are brethren, why do you wrong each other?' ²⁷But the man who was wronging his neighbor thrust him aside, saying, 'Who made you a ruler and a judge over us? ²⁸Do you want to kill me as you killed the Egyptian yesterday?' ²⁹At this retort Moses fled, and became an exile in the land of Mĭd'ĭ-an, where he became the father of two sons.

30 "Now when forty years had passed, an angel appeared to him in the wilderness of Mount Sinai, in a flame of fire in a bush. ³¹When Moses saw it he wondered at the sight; and as he drew near to look, the voice of the Lord came, ³²'I am the God of your fathers, the God of Abraham and of Isaac and of Jacob.' And Moses trembled and did not dare to look. ³³And the Lord said to him, 'Take off the shoes from your feet, for the place where you are standing is holy ground. ³⁴I have surely seen the ill-treatment of my people that are in Egypt and heard their groaning, and I have come down to deliver them. And now come, I will send you to Egypt.'

35 "This Moses whom they refused, saying, 'Who made you a ruler and a judge?' God sent as both ruler and deliverer by the hand of the angel that appeared to him in the bush. ³⁶He led them out, having performed wonders and signs in Egypt and at the Red Sea, and in the wilderness for forty years. ³⁷This is the Moses who said to the Israelites, 'God will raise up for you a prophet from your brethren as he raised me up.' ³⁸This is he who was in the congregation in the wilderness with the angel who spoke to him at Mount Sinai, and with our fathers; and he received living oracles to give to us. ³⁹Our fathers refused to obey him, but thrust him aside, and in their hearts they turned to Egypt, ⁴⁰saying to

7.7: Ex 3.12.
7.8: Gen 17.10-14; 21.2-4; 25.26; 29.31-35; 30.1-24; 35.16-18; 35.23-26. **7.9:** Gen 37.11, 28; 45.4.
7.9-10: Gen 39.2-3, 21. **7.10:** Gen 41.40-46; Ps 105.21.
7.11: Gen 41.54-55; 42.5. **7.12:** Gen 42.2.
7.13: Gen 45.1-4. **7.14:** Gen 45.9-10.
7.14-15: Deut 10.22. **7.16:** Josh 24.32; Gen 50.13.
7.17-18: Ex 1.7-8. **7.19:** Ex 1.10-11; 1.15-22.
7.20: Ex 2.2. **7.21:** Ex 2.5-6, 10. **7.23-29:** Ex 2.11-15.
7.29: Ex 2.22; 18.3-4. **7.30-34:** Ex 3.1-10.
7.35: Ex 2.14. **7.36:** Ex 7.3; 14.21; Num 14.33.
7.37: Deut 18.15, 18. **7.38:** Ex 19. **7.39:** Num 14.3-4.
7.40: Ex 32.1, 23.

Aaron, 'Make for us gods to go before us; as for this Moses who led us out from the land of Egypt, we do not know what has become of him.' ⁴¹And they made a calf in those days, and offered a sacrifice to the idol and rejoiced in the works of their hands. ⁴²But God turned and gave them over to worship the host of heaven, as it is written in the book of the prophets:
'Did you offer to me slain beasts and sacrifices,
forty years in the wilderness, O house of Israel?
⁴³And you took up the tent of Mō′lŏch, and the star of the god Rē′phạn,
the figures which you made to worship;
and I will remove you beyond Babylon.'
44 "Our fathers had the tent of witness in the wilderness, even as he who spoke to Moses directed him to make it, according to the pattern that he had seen. ⁴⁵Our fathers in turn brought it in with Joshua when they dispossessed the nations which God thrust out before our fathers. So it was until the days of David, ⁴⁶who found favor in the sight of God and asked leave to find a habitation for the God of Jacob. ⁴⁷But it was Solomon who built a house for him. ⁴⁸Yet the Most High does not dwell in houses made with hands; as the prophet says,
⁴⁹'Heaven is my throne,
and earth my footstool.
What house will you build for me,
says the Lord,
or what is the place of my rest?
⁵⁰Did not my hand make all these things?'
51 "You stiff-necked people, uncircumcised in heart and ears, you always resist the Holy Spirit. As your fathers did, so do you. ⁵²Which of the prophets did not your fathers persecute? And they killed those who announced beforehand the coming of the Righteous One, whom you have now betrayed and murdered, ⁵³you who received the law as delivered by angels and did not keep it."
54 Now when they heard these things they were enraged, and they ground their teeth against him. ⁵⁵But he, full of the Holy Spirit, gazed into heaven and saw the glory of God, and Jesus standing at the right hand of God; ⁵⁶and he said, "Behold, I see the

heavens opened, and the Son of man standing at the right hand of God." ⁵⁷But they cried out with a loud voice and stopped their ears and rushed together upon him. ⁵⁸Then they cast him out of the city and stoned him; and the witnesses laid down their garments at the feet of a young man named Saul. ⁵⁹And as they were stoning Stephen, he prayed, "Lord Jesus, receive my spirit." ⁶⁰And he knelt down and cried with a loud voice, "Lord, do not hold this sin against them." And when he had said this, he
8 fell asleep. ¹And Saul was consenting to his death.
And on that day a great persecution arose against the church in Jerusalem; and they were all scattered throughout the region of Jü·dē′ạ and Sạ·mâr′ĭ·ạ, except the apostles. ²Devout men buried Stephen, and made great lamentation over him. ³But Saul was ravaging the church, and entering house after house, he dragged off men and women and committed them to prison.
4 Now those who were scattered went about preaching the word. ⁵Philip went down to a city of Sạ·mâr′ĭ·ạ, and proclaimed to them the Christ. ⁶And the multitudes with one accord gave heed to what was said by Philip, when they heard him and saw the signs which he did. ⁷For unclean spirits came out of many who were possessed, crying with a loud voice; and many who were paralyzed or lame were healed. ⁸So there was much joy in that city.
9 But there was a man named Simon who had previously practiced magic in the city and amazed the nation of Sạ·mâr′ĭ·ạ, saying that he himself was somebody great. ¹⁰They all gave heed to him, from the least to the greatest, saying, "This man is that power of God which is called Great." ¹¹And they gave heed to him, because for a long time he had amazed them with his magic. ¹²But when they believed Philip as he preached good news about the kingdom of God and the name of Jesus Christ, they were bap-

7.41: Ex 32.4, 6. **7.42:** Jer 19.13.
7.42-43: A mos 5.25-27. **7.44:** Ex 25.9, 40.
7.45: Josh 3.14-17; Deut 32.49.
7.46: 2 Sam 7.8-16; Ps 132.1-5. **7.47:** 1 Kings 6.
7.49-50: Is 66.1-2.
7.51: Ex 33.3, 5; Jer 9.26; 6.10; Num 27.14; Is 63.10.
8.1: Acts 11.19.

tized, both men and women. ¹³Even Simon himself believed, and after being baptized he continued with Philip. And seeing signs and great miracles performed, he was amazed.

14 Now when the apostles at Jerusalem heard that Sạ·mâr′ĭ·ạ had received the word of God, they sent to them Peter and John, ¹⁵who came down and prayed for them that they might receive the Holy Spirit; ¹⁶for it had not yet fallen on any of them, but they had only been baptized in the name of the Lord Jesus. ¹⁷Then they laid their hands on them and they received the Holy Spirit. ¹⁸Now when Simon saw that the Spirit was given through the laying on of the apostles' hands, he offered them money, ¹⁹saying, "Give me also this power, that any one on whom I lay my hands may receive the Holy Spirit." ²⁰But Peter said to him, "Your silver perish with you, because you thought you could obtain the gift of God with money! ²¹You have neither part nor lot in this matter, for your heart is not right before God. ²²Repent therefore of this wickedness of yours, and pray to the Lord that, if possible, the intent of your heart may be forgiven you. ²³For I see that you are in the gall of bitterness and in the bond of iniquity." ²⁴And Simon answered, "Pray for me to the Lord, that nothing of what you have said may come upon me."

25 Now when they had testified and spoken the word of the Lord, they returned to Jerusalem, preaching the gospel to many villages of the Sạ·mâr′ĭ·tạns.

26 But an angel of the Lord said to Philip, "Rise and go toward the south *g* to the road that goes down from Jerusalem to Gā′zạ." This is a desert road. ²⁷And he rose and went. And behold, an Ethiopian, a eunuch, a minister of Căn·dā′cē, queen of the Ethiopians, in charge of all her treasure, had come to Jerusalem to worship ²⁸and was returning; seated in his chariot, he was reading the prophet Ĭ·sāi′ạh. ²⁹And the Spirit said to Philip, "Go up and join this chariot." ³⁰So Philip ran to him, and heard him reading Ĭ·sāi′ạh the prophet, and asked, "Do you understand what you are reading?" ³¹And he said, "How can I, unless some one guides me?" And he invited Philip to come up and sit with him. ³²Now

the passage of the scripture which he was reading was this:
"As a sheep led to the slaughter
or a lamb before its shearer is dumb,
so he opens not his mouth.
³³In his humiliation justice was denied
 him.
Who can describe his generation?
For his life is taken up from the
 earth."
³⁴And the eunuch said to Philip, "About whom, pray, does the prophet say this, about himself or about some one else?" ³⁵Then Philip opened his mouth, and beginning with this scripture he told him the good news of Jesus. ³⁶And as they went along the road they came to some water, and the eunuch said, "See, here is water! What is to prevent my being baptized?"*h* ³⁸And he commanded the chariot to stop, and they both went down into the water, Philip and the eunuch, and he baptized him. ³⁹And when they came up out of the water, the Spirit of the Lord caught up Philip; and the eunuch saw him no more, and went on his way rejoicing. ⁴⁰But Philip was found at Ạ·zō′tụs, and passing on he preached the gospel to all the towns till he came to Çaĕs·ạ·rē′ạ.

9 But Saul, still breathing threats and murder against the disciples of the Lord, went to the high priest ²and asked him for letters to the synagogues at Damascus, so that if he found any belonging to the Way, men or women, he might bring them bound to Jerusalem. ³Now as he journeyed he approached Damascus, and suddenly a light from heaven flashed about him. ⁴And he fell to the ground and heard a voice saying to him, "Saul, Saul, why do you persecute me?" ⁵And he said, "Who are you, Lord?" And he said, "I am Jesus, whom you are persecuting; ⁶but rise and enter the city, and you will be told what you are to do." ⁷The men who were traveling with him stood speechless, hearing the voice but seeing no one. ⁸Saul arose from the ground; and when his eyes were opened, he could see nothing; so they led him by the hand and brought him into Damascus. ⁹And for three

g Or at noon
h Other ancient authorities add all or most of verse 37, And Philip said, "If you believe with all your heart, you may." And he replied, "I believe that Jesus Christ is the Son of God." 8.21: Ps 78-37. 8.23: Is 58.6. 8.32-33: Is 53.7-8. 9.1-19: Acts 22.4-16; 26.9-18.

days he was without sight, and neither ate nor drank.

10 Now there was a disciple at Damascus named Ăn·a·nī′as. The Lord said to him in a vision, "Ananias." And he said, "Here I am, Lord." ¹¹And the Lord said to him, "Rise and go to the street called Straight, and inquire in the house of Judas for a man of Tär′sus named Saul; for behold, he is praying, ¹²and he has seen a man named Ăn·a·nī′as come in and lay his hands on him so that he might regain his sight." ¹³But Ăn·a·nī′as answered, "Lord, I have heard from many about this man, how much evil he has done to thy saints at Jerusalem; ¹⁴and here he has authority from the chief priests to bind all who call upon thy name." ¹⁵But the Lord said to him, "Go, for he is a chosen instrument of mine to carry my name before the Gentiles and kings and the sons of Israel; ¹⁶for I will show him how much he must suffer for the sake of my name." ¹⁷So Ăn·a·nī′as departed and entered the house. And laying his hands on him he said, "Brother Saul, the Lord Jesus who appeared to you on the road by which you came, has sent me that you may regain your sight and be filled with the Holy Spirit." ¹⁸And immediately something like scales fell from his eyes and he regained his sight. Then he rose and was baptized, ¹⁹and took food and was strengthened.

For several days he was with the disciples at Damascus. ²⁰And in the synagogues immediately he proclaimed Jesus, saying, "He is the Son of God." ²¹And all who heard him were amazed, and said, "Is not this the man who made havoc in Jerusalem of those who called on this name? And he has come here for this purpose, to bring them bound before the chief priests." ²²But Saul increased all the more in strength, and confounded the Jews who lived in Damascus by proving that Jesus was the Christ.

23 When many days had passed, the Jews plotted to kill him, ²⁴but their plot became known to Saul. They were watching the gates day and night, to kill him; ²⁵but his disciples took him by night and let him down over the wall, lowering him in a basket.

26 And when he had come to Jerusalem he attempted to join the disciples; and they were all afraid of him, for they did not believe that he was a disciple. ²⁷But Băr′na·bas took him, and brought him to the apostles, and declared to them how on the road he had seen the Lord, who spoke to him, and how at Damascus he had preached boldly in the name of Jesus. ²⁸So he went in and out among them at Jerusalem, ²⁹preaching boldly in the name of the Lord. And he spoke and disputed against the Hellenists; but they were seeking to kill him. ³⁰And when the brethren knew it, they brought him down to Çaĕs·a·rē′a, and sent him off to Tär′sus.

31 So the church throughout all Jü·dē′a and Galilee and Sa·mâr′ĭ·a had peace and was built up; and walking in the fear of the Lord and in the comfort of the Holy Spirit it was multiplied.

32 Now as Peter went here and there among them all, he came down also to the saints that lived at Lÿd′da. ³³There he found a man named Aē·nē′as, who had been bedridden for eight years and was paralyzed. ³⁴And Peter said to him, "Aē·nē′as, Jesus Christ heals you; rise and make your bed." And immediately he rose. ³⁵And all the residents of Lÿd′da and Sharon saw him, and they turned to the Lord.

36 Now there was at Jŏp′pa a disciple named Tăb′ĭ·tha, which means Dôr′cas.ˣ She was full of good works and acts of charity. ³⁷In those days she fell sick and died; and when they had washed her, they laid her in an upper room. ³⁸Since Lÿd′da was near Jŏp′pa, the disciples, hearing that Peter was there, sent two men to him entreating him, "Please come to us without delay." ³⁹So Peter rose and went with them. And when he had come, they took him to the upper room. All the widows stood beside him weeping, and showing tunics and other garments which Dôr′cas made while she was with them. ⁴⁰But Peter put them all outside and knelt down and prayed; then turning to the body he said, "Tăb′ĭ·tha, rise." And she opened her eyes, and when she saw Peter she sat up. ⁴¹And he gave her his hand and lifted her up. Then calling the saints and widows he presented her alive. ⁴²And it became known throughout all Jŏp′pa, and many

ˣThe name Tabitha in Aramaic and the name Dorcas in Greek mean *gazelle* **9.24-25:** 2 Cor 11.32-33.

believed in the Lord. ⁴³And he stayed in Jŏp′pạ for many days with one Simon, a tanner.

10 At Çaĕs·ạ·rē′ạ there was a man named Cornelius, a centurion of what was known as the Italian Cohort, ²a devout man who feared God with all his household, gave alms liberally to the people, and prayed constantly to God. ³About the ninth hour of the day he saw clearly in a vision an angel of God coming in and saying to him, "Cornelius." ⁴And he stared at him in terror, and said, "What is it, Lord?" And he said to him, "Your prayers and your alms have ascended as a memorial before God. ⁵And now send men to Jŏp′pạ, and bring one Simon who is called Peter; ⁶he is lodging with Simon, a tanner, whose house is by the seaside." ⁷When the angel who spoke to him had departed, he called two of his servants and a devout soldier from among those that waited on him, ⁸and having related everything to them, he sent them to Jŏp′pạ.

9 The next day, as they were on their journey and coming near the city, Peter went up on the housetop to pray, about the sixth hour. ¹⁰And he became hungry and desired something to eat; but while they were preparing it, he fell into a trance ¹¹and saw the heaven opened, and something descending, like a great sheet, let down by four corners upon the earth. ¹²In it were all kinds of animals and reptiles and birds of the air. ¹³And there came a voice to him, "Rise, Peter; kill and eat." ¹⁴But Peter said, "No, Lord; for I have never eaten anything that is common or unclean." ¹⁵And the voice came to him again a second time, "What God has cleansed, you must not call common." ¹⁶This happened three times, and the thing was taken up at once to heaven.

17 Now while Peter was inwardly perplexed as to what the vision which he had seen might mean, behold, the men that were sent by Cornelius, having made inquiry for Simon's house, stood before the gate ¹⁸and called out to ask whether Simon who was called Peter was lodging there. ¹⁹And while Peter was pondering the vision, the Spirit said to him, "Behold, three men are looking for you. ²⁰Rise and go down, and accompany them without hesitation; for I have sent them." ²¹And Peter went down to the men and said, "I am the one you are looking for; what is the reason for your coming?" ²²And they said, "Cornelius, a centurion, an upright and God-fearing man, who is well spoken of by the whole Jewish nation, was directed by a holy angel to send for you to come to his house, and to hear what you have to say." ²³So he called them in to be his guests.

The next day he rose and went off with them, and some of the brethren from Jŏp′pạ accompanied him. ²⁴And on the following day they entered Çaĕs·ạ·rē′ạ. Cornelius was expecting them and had called together his kinsmen and close friends. ²⁵When Peter entered, Cornelius met him and fell down at his feet and worshiped him. ²⁶But Peter lifted him up, saying, "Stand up; I too am a man." ²⁷And as he talked with him, he went in and found many persons gathered; ²⁸and he said to them, "You yourselves know how unlawful it is for a Jew to associate with or to visit any one of another nation; but God has shown me that I should not call any man common or unclean. ²⁹So when I was sent for, I came without objection. I ask then why you sent for me."

30 And Cornelius said, "Four days ago, about this hour, I was keeping the ninth hour of prayer in my house; and behold, a man stood before me in bright apparel, ³¹saying, 'Cornelius, your prayer has been heard and your alms have been remembered before God. ³²Send therefore to Jŏp′pạ and ask for Simon who is called Peter; he is lodging in the house of Simon, a tanner, by the seaside.' ³³So I sent to you at once, and you have been kind enough to come. Now therefore we are all here present in the sight of God, to hear all that you have been commanded by the Lord."

34 And Peter opened his mouth and said: "Truly I perceive that God shows no partiality, ³⁵but in every nation any one who fears him and does what is right is acceptable to him. ³⁶You know the word which he sent to Israel, preaching good news of peace by Jesus Christ (he is Lord of all), ³⁷the word which was proclaimed throughout all Jü·dē′ạ, beginning from

10.1-48: Acts 11.4-17.

Galilee after the baptism which John preached: [38]how God anointed Jesus of Nazareth with the Holy Spirit and with power; how he went about doing good and healing all that were oppressed by the devil, for God was with him. [39]And we are witnesses to all that he did both in the country of the Jews and in Jerusalem. They put him to death by hanging him on a tree; [40]but God raised him on the third day and made him manifest; [41]not to all the people but to us who were chosen by God as witnesses, who ate and drank with him after he rose from the dead. [42]And he commanded us to preach to the people, and to testify that he is the one ordained by God to be judge of the living and the dead. [43]To him all the prophets bear witness that every one who believes in him receives forgiveness of sins through his name."

44 While Peter was still saying this, the Holy Spirit fell on all who heard the word. [45]And the believers from among the circumcised who came with Peter were amazed, because the gift of the Holy Spirit had been poured out even on the Gentiles. [46]For they heard them speaking in tongues and extolling God. Then Peter declared, [47]"Can any one forbid water for baptizing these people who have received the Holy Spirit just as we have?" [48]And he commanded them to be baptized in the name of Jesus Christ. Then they asked him to remain for some days.

11 Now the apostles and the brethren who were in Jü·dē'a heard that the Gentiles also had received the word of God. [2]So when Peter went up to Jerusalem, the circumcision party criticized him, [3]saying, "Why did you go to uncircumcised men and eat with them?" [4]But Peter began and explained to them in order: [5]"I was in the city of Jŏp'pa praying; and in a trance I saw a vision, something descending, like a great sheet, let down from heaven by four corners; and it came down to me. [6]Looking at it closely I observed animals and beasts of prey and reptiles and birds of the air. [7]And I heard a voice saying to me, 'Rise, Peter; kill and eat.' [8]But I said, 'No, Lord; for nothing common or unclean has ever entered my mouth.' [9]But the voice answered a second time from heaven,

'What God has cleansed you must not call common.' [10]This happened three times, and all was drawn up again into heaven. [11]At that very moment three men arrived at the house in which we were, sent to me from Çaĕs·a·rē'a. [12]And the Spirit told me to go with them, making no distinction. These six brethren also accompanied me, and we entered the man's house. [13]And he told us how he had seen the angel standing in his house and saying, 'Send to Jŏp'pa and bring Simon called Peter; [14]he will declare to you a message by which you will be saved, you and all your household.' [15]As I began to speak, the Holy Spirit fell on them just as on us at the beginning. [16]And I remembered the word of the Lord. how he said, 'John baptized with water, but you shall be baptized with the Holy Spirit.' [17]If then God gave the same gift to them as he gave to us when we believed in the Lord Jesus Christ, who was I that I could withstand God?" [18]When they heard this they were silenced. And they glorified God, saying, "Then to the Gentiles also God has granted repentance unto life."

19 Now those who were scattered because of the persecution that arose over Stephen traveled as far as Phoe·nī'çi·a and Cyprus and Ăn'tĭ·ŏch, speaking the word to none except Jews. [20]But there were some of them, men of Cyprus and Cȳ·rē'nē, who on coming to Ăn'tĭ·ŏch spoke to the Greeks[i] also, preaching the Lord Jesus. [21]And the hand of the Lord was with them, and a great number that believed turned to the Lord. [22]News of this came to the ears of the church in Jerusalem, and they sent Bär'na·bas to Ăn'tĭ·ŏch. [23]When he came and saw the grace of God, he was glad; and he exhorted them all to remain faithful to the Lord with steadfast purpose; [24]for he was a good man, full of the Holy Spirit and of faith. And a large company was added to the Lord. [25]So Bär'na·bas went to Tär'sus to look for Saul; [26]and when he had found him, he brought him to Ăn'tĭ·ŏch. For a whole year they met with[j] the church, and taught a large company of people; and in Antioch the disciples were

[i]Other ancient authorities read *Hellenists*
[j]Or *were guests of*
11.4-17: Acts 10.1-48. 11.16: Acts 1.5. 11.19: Acts 8.4.

for the first time called Christians. 27 Now in these days prophets came down from Jerusalem to Ăn'tĭ-ŏch. 28 And one of them named Ăg'a-bŭs stood up and foretold by the Spirit that there would be a great famine over all the world; and this took place in the days of Claudius. 29 And the disciples determined, every one according to his ability, to send relief to the brethren who lived in Jü-dē'a; 30 and they did so, sending it to the elders by the hand of Băr'na-bas and Saul.

12 About that time Hĕr'ŏd the king laid violent hands upon some who belonged to the church. 2 He killed James the brother of John with the sword; 3 and when he saw that it pleased the Jews, he proceeded to arrest Peter also. This was during the days of Unleavened Bread. 4 And when he had seized him, he put him in prison, and delivered him to four squads of soldiers to guard him, intending after the Passover to bring him out to the people. 5 So Peter was kept in prison; but earnest prayer for him was made to God by the church.

6 The very night when Hĕr'ŏd was about to bring him out, Peter was sleeping between two soldiers, bound with two chains, and sentries before the door were guarding the prison; 7 and behold, an angel of the Lord appeared, and a light shone in the cell; and he struck Peter on the side and woke him, saying, "Get up quickly." And the chains fell off his hands. 8 And the angel said to him, "Dress yourself and put on your sandals." And he did so. And he said to him, "Wrap your mantle around you and follow me." 9 And he went out and followed him; he did not know that what was done by the angel was real, but thought he was seeing a vision. 10 When they had passed the first and the second guard, they came to the iron gate leading into the city. It opened to them of its own accord, and they went out and passed on through one street; and immediately the angel left him. 11 And Peter came to himself, and said, "Now I am sure that the Lord has sent his angel and rescued me from the hand of Hĕr'ŏd and from all that the Jewish people were expecting."

12 When he realized this, he went to the house of Mary, the mother of John whose other name was Mark, where many were gathered together and were praying. 13 And when he knocked at the door of the gateway, a maid named Rhō'da came to answer. 14 Recognizing Peter's voice, in her joy she did not open the gate but ran in and told that Peter was standing at the gate. 15 They said to her, "You are mad." But she insisted that it was so. They said, "It is his angel!" 16 But Peter continued knocking; and when they opened, they saw him and were amazed. 17 But motioning to them with his hand to be silent, he described to them how the Lord had brought him out of the prison. And he said, "Tell this to James and to the brethren." Then he departed and went to another place.

18 Now when day came, there was no small stir among the soldiers over what had become of Peter. 19 And when Hĕr'ŏd had sought for him and could not find him, he examined the sentries and ordered that they should be put to death. Then he went down from Jü-dē'a to Çaĕs-a-rē'a, and remained there.

20 Now Hĕr'ŏd was angry with the people of Tyre and Sī'dŏn; and they came to him in a body, and having persuaded Blăs'tŭs, the king's chamberlain, they asked for peace, because their country depended on the king's country for food. 21 On an appointed day Hĕr'ŏd put on his royal robes, took his seat upon the throne, and made an oration to them. 22 And the people shouted, "The voice of a god, and not of man!" 23 Immediately an angel of the Lord smote him, because he did not give God the glory; and he was eaten by worms and died.

24 But the word of God grew and multiplied.

25 And Băr'na-bas and Saul returned from[k] Jerusalem when they had fulfilled their mission, bringing with them John whose other name was Mark.

13 Now in the church at Ăn'tĭ-ŏch there were prophets and teachers, Băr'na-bas, Sĭm'ē-ọn who was called Nī'gẹr, Lucius of Cy-rē'nē, Măn'a-ĕn a member of the court of Hĕr'ŏd the tetrarch, and Saul. 2 While they were worshiping the Lord and fasting, the Holy Spirit said, "Set apart for me Băr'na-bas and Saul for the work to which I have called them."

[k] Other ancient authorities read *to*

³Then after fasting and praying they laid their hands on them and sent them off.

4 So, being sent out by the Holy Spirit, they went down to Se·leü′çi·a; and from there they sailed to Cyprus. ⁵When they arrived at Săl′a·mĭs, they proclaimed the word of God in the synagogues of the Jews. And they had John to assist them. ⁶When they had gone through the whole island as far as Pā′phŏs, they came upon a certain magician, a Jewish false prophet, named Bār–Jē′sus. ⁷He was with the proconsul, Sĕr′gĭ·us Paul′us, a man of intelligence, who summoned Bār′-na·bas and Saul and sought to hear the word of God. ⁸But Ĕl′ў·mas the magician (for that is the meaning of his name) withstood them, seeking to turn away the proconsul from the faith. ⁹But Saul, who is also called Paul, filled with the Holy Spirit, looked intently at him ¹⁰and said, "You son of the devil, you enemy of all righteousness, full of all deceit and villainy, will you not stop making crooked the straight paths of the Lord? ¹¹And now, behold, the hand of the Lord is upon you, and you shall be blind and unable to see the sun for a time." Immediately mist and darkness fell upon him and he went about seeking people to lead him by the hand. ¹²Then the proconsul believed, when he saw what had occurred, for he was astonished at the teaching of the Lord.

13 Now Paul and his company set sail from Pā′phŏs, and came to Pĕr′ga in Păm·phўl′ĭ·a. And John left them and returned to Jerusalem; ¹⁴but they passed on from Pĕr′ga and came to Ăn′tĭ·ŏch of Pĭ·sĭd′ĭ·a. And on the sabbath day they went into the synagogue and sat down. ¹⁵After the reading of the law and the prophets, the rulers of the synagogue sent to them, saying, "Brethren, if you have any word of exhortation for the people, say it." ¹⁶So Paul stood up, and motioning with his hand said:

"Men of Israel, and you that fear God, listen. ¹⁷The God of this people Israel chose our fathers and made the people great during their stay in the land of Egypt, and with uplifted arm he led them out of it. ¹⁸And for about forty years he bore with ᵐ them in the wilderness. ¹⁹And when he had destroyed seven nations in the land of Canaan, he gave them their land as an inheritance, for about four hundred and fifty years. ²⁰And after that he gave them judges until Samuel the prophet. ²¹Then they asked for a king; and God gave them Saul the son of Kĭsh, a man of the tribe of Benjamin, for forty years. ²²And when he had removed him, he raised up David to be their king; of whom he testified and said, 'I have found in David the son of Jesse a man after my heart, who will do all my will.' ²³Of this man's posterity God has brought to Israel a Savior, Jesus, as he promised. ²⁴Before his coming John had preached a baptism of repentance to all the people of Israel. ²⁵And as John was finishing his course, he said, 'What do you suppose that I am? I am not he. No, but after me one is coming, the sandals of whose feet I am not worthy to untie.'

26 "Brethren, sons of the family of Abraham, and those among you that fear God, to us has been sent the message of this salvation. ²⁷For those who live in Jerusalem and their rulers, because they did not recognize him nor understand the utterances of the prophets which are read every sabbath, fulfilled these by condemning him. ²⁸Though they could charge him with nothing deserving death, yet they asked Pilate to have him killed. ²⁹And when they had fulfilled all that was written of him, they took him down from the tree, and laid him in a tomb. ³⁰But God raised him from the dead; ³¹and for many days he appeared to those who came up with him from Galilee to Jerusalem, who are now his witnesses to the people. ³²And we bring you the good news that what God promised to the fathers, ³³this he has fulfilled to us their children by raising Jesus; as also it is written in the second psalm,

'Thou art my Son,
  today I have begotten thee.'

³⁴And as for the fact that he raised him from the dead, no more to return to corruption, he spoke in this way, 'I will give you the holy and sure blessings of David.'

³⁵Therefore he says also in another

ᵐOther ancient authorities read *cared for* (Deut 1.31).
13.10: Hos 14.9.   **13.17:** Ex 6.1, 6.   **13.18:** Deut 1.31.
13.19: Deut 7.1; Josh 14.1.
13.22: Ps 89.20; 1 Sam 13.14; Is 44.28.   **13.24:** Mk 1.1-4.
13.25: Jn 1.20; Mt 3.11; Mk 1.7; Lk 3.16.
13.26: Ps 107.20.   **13.33:** Ps 2.7.   **13.34:** Is 55.3.
13.35: Ps 16.10.

psalm,

'Thou wilt not let thy Holy One see corruption.'

³⁶ For David, after he had served the counsel of God in his own generation, fell asleep, and was laid with his fathers, and saw corruption; ³⁷ but he whom God raised up saw no corruption. ³⁸ Let it be known to you therefore, brethren, that through this man forgiveness of sins is proclaimed to you, ³⁹ and by him every one that believes is freed from everything from which you could not be freed by the law of Moses. ⁴⁰ Beware, therefore, lest there come upon you what is said in the prophets: ⁴¹ 'Behold, you scoffers, and wonder, and perish;

for I do a deed in your days,

a deed you will never believe, if one declares it to you.'"

42 As they went out, the people begged that these things might be told them the next sabbath. ⁴³ And when the meeting of the synagogue broke up, many Jews and devout converts to Jū'dă'ĭsm followed Paul and Bār'nạ·bạs, who spoke to them and urged them to continue in the grace of God.

44 The next sabbath almost the whole city gathered together to hear the word of God. ⁴⁵ But when the Jews saw the multitudes, they were filled with jealousy, and contradicted what was spoken by Paul, and reviled him. ⁴⁶ And Paul and Bār'nạ·bạs spoke out boldly, saying, "It was necessary that the word of God should be spoken first to you. Since you thrust it from you, and judge yourselves unworthy of eternal life, behold, we turn to the Gentiles. ⁴⁷ For so the Lord has commanded us, saying,

'I have set you to be a light for the Gentiles,

that you may bring salvation to the uttermost parts of the earth.'"

48 And when the Gentiles heard this, they were glad and glorified the word of God; and as many as were ordained to eternal life believed. ⁴⁹ And the word of the Lord spread throughout all the region. ⁵⁰ But the Jews incited the devout women of high standing and the leading men of the city, and stirred up persecution against Paul and Bār'-nạ·bạs, and drove them out of their district. ⁵¹ But they shook off the dust from their feet against them, and went

to Ĭ·cō'nĭ·ụm. ⁵² And the disciples were filled with joy and with the Holy Spirit.

14 Now at Ĭ·cō'nĭ·ụm they entered together into the Jewish synagogue, and so spoke that a great company believed, both of Jews and of Greeks. ² But the unbelieving Jews stirred up the Gentiles and poisoned their minds against the brethren. ³ So they remained for a long time, speaking boldly for the Lord, who bore witness to the word of his grace, granting signs and wonders to be done by their hands. ⁴ But the people of the city were divided; some sided with the Jews, and some with the apostles. ⁵ When an attempt was made by both Gentiles and Jews, with their rulers, to molest them and to stone them, ⁶ they learned of it and fled to Lỹs'trạ and Dēr'bē, cities of Lỹc·ā·ō'nĭ·ạ, and to the surrounding country; ⁷ and there they preached the gospel.

8 Now at Lỹs'trạ there was a man sitting, who could not use his feet; he was a cripple from birth, who had never walked. ⁹ He listened to Paul speaking; and Paul, looking intently at him and seeing that he had faith to be made well, ¹⁰ said in a loud voice, "Stand upright on your feet." And he sprang up and walked. ¹¹ And when the crowds saw what Paul had done, they lifted up their voices, saying in Lỹc·ā·ō'nĭ·ạn, "The gods have come down to us in the likeness of men!" ¹² Bār'nạ·bạs they called Zeüs, and Paul, because he was the chief speaker, they called Hēr'mēṣ. ¹³ And the priest of Zeüs, whose temple was in front of the city, brought oxen and garlands to the gates and wanted to offer sacrifice with the people. ¹⁴ But when the apostles Bār'nạ·bạs and Paul heard of it, they tore their garments and rushed out among the multitude, crying, ¹⁵ "Men, why are you doing this? We also are men, of like nature with you, and bring you good news, that you should turn from these vain things to a living God who made the heaven and the earth and the sea and all that is in them. ¹⁶ In past generations he allowed all the nations to walk in their own ways; ¹⁷ yet he did not leave himself without witness, for he did good and gave you from heaven rains and fruitful seasons, satisfying your hearts with food and gladness." ¹⁸ With these

13.41: Hab 1.5.　13.47: Is 49.6.　14.15: Ex 20.11; Ps 146.6.

words they scarcely restrained the people from offering sacrifice to them. 19 But Jews came there from Ăn'tĭ·ŏch and Ĭ·cō'nĭ·um; and having persuaded the people, they stoned Paul and dragged him out of the city, supposing that he was dead. 20 But when the disciples gathered about him, he rose up and entered the city; and on the next day he went on with Băr'na·băs to Dĕr'bē. 21 When they had preached the gospel to that city and had made many disciples, they returned to Lўs'tra and to Ĭ·cō'nĭ·um and to Ăn'tĭ·ŏch, 22 strengthening the souls of the disciples, exhorting them to continue in the faith, and saying that through many tribulations we must enter the kingdom of God. 23 And when they had appointed elders for them in every church, with prayer and fasting, they committed them to the Lord in whom they believed.

24 Then they passed through Pĭ·sĭd'ĭ·a, and came to Păm·phўl'ĭ·a. 25 And when they had spoken the word in Pĕr'ga, they went down to Ăt·ta·lī'a; 26 and from there they sailed to Ăn'tĭ·ŏch, where they had been commended to the grace of God for the work which they had fulfilled. 27 And when they arrived, they gathered the church together and declared all that God had done with them, and how he had opened a door of faith to the Gentiles. 28 And they remained no little time with the disciples.

15 But some men came down from Jŭ·dē'a and were teaching the brethren, "Unless you are circumcised according to the custom of Moses, you cannot be saved." 2 And when Paul and Băr'na·băs had no small dissension and debate with them, Paul and Barnabas and some of the others were appointed to go up to Jerusalem to the apostles and the elders about this question. 3 So, being sent on their way by the church, they passed through both Phoe·nĭ'çĭ·a and Sa·mâr'ĭ·a, reporting the conversion of the Gentiles, and they gave great joy to all the brethren. 4 When they came to Jerusalem, they were welcomed by the church and the apostles and the elders, and they declared all that God had done with them. 5 But some believers who belonged to the party of the Phăr'ĭ·seeş rose up, and

said, "It is necessary to circumcise them, and to charge them to keep the law of Moses."

6 The apostles and the elders were gathered together to consider this matter. 7 And after there had been much debate, Peter rose and said to them, "Brethren, you know that in the early days God made choice among you, that by my mouth the Gentiles should hear the word of the gospel and believe. 8 And God who knows the heart bore witness to them, giving them the Holy Spirit just as he did to us; 9 and he made no distinction between us and them, but cleansed their hearts by faith. 10 Now therefore why do you make trial of God by putting a yoke upon the neck of the disciples which neither our fathers nor we have been able to bear? 11 But we believe that we shall be saved through the grace of the Lord Jesus, just as they will."

12 And all the assembly kept silence; and they listened to Băr'na·băs and Paul as they related what signs and wonders God had done through them among the Gentiles. 13 After they finished speaking, James replied, "Brethren, listen to me. 14 Sĭm'ē·on has related how God first visited the Gentiles, to take out of them a people for his name. 15 And with this the words of the prophets agree, as it is written,

16 'After this I will return,
and I will rebuild the dwelling of David, which has fallen;
I will rebuild its ruins,
and I will set it up,
17 that the rest of men may seek the Lord,
and all the Gentiles who are called by my name,
18 says the Lord, who has made these things known from of old.'

19 Therefore my judgment is that we should not trouble those of the Gentiles who turn to God, 20 but should write to them to abstain from the pollutions of idols and from unchastity and from what is strangled[n] and from blood. 21 For from early generations Moses has had in every city those who preach him, for he is read every sabbath in the synagogues."

22 Then it seemed good to the apostles and the elders, with the whole church, to choose men from among them and to send them to Ăn'tĭ·ŏch with Paul and Băr'nạ·bạs. They sent Judas called Băr·săb'bạs, and Silas, leading men among the brethren, 23 with the following letter: "The brethren, both the apostles and the elders, to the brethren who are of the Gentiles in Ăn'tĭ·ŏch and Syria and Çĭ·lĭ'çĭ·ạ, greeting. 24 Since we have heard that some persons from us have troubled you with words, unsettling your minds, although we gave them no instructions, 25 it has seemed good to us, having come to one accord, to choose men and send them to you with our beloved Băr'nạ·bạs and Paul, 26 men who have risked their lives for the sake of our Lord Jesus Christ. 27 We have therefore sent Judas and Silas, who themselves will tell you the same things by word of mouth. 28 For it has seemed good to the Holy Spirit and to us to lay upon you no greater burden than these necessary things: 29 that you abstain from what has been sacrificed to idols and from blood and from what is strangled[n] and from unchastity. If you keep yourselves from these, you will do well. Farewell."

30 So when they were sent off, they went down to Ăn'tĭ·ŏch; and having gathered the congregation together, they delivered the letter. 31 And when they read it, they rejoiced at the exhortation. 32 And Judas and Silas, who were themselves prophets, exhorted the brethren with many words and strengthened them. 33 And after they had spent some time, they were sent off in peace by the brethren to those who had sent them.[o] 35 But Paul and Băr'nạ·bạs remained in Ăn'tĭ·ŏch, teaching and preaching the word of the Lord, with many others also.

36 And after some days Paul said to Băr'nạ·bạs, "Come, let us return and visit the brethren in every city where we proclaimed the word of the Lord, and see how they are." 37 And Băr'-nạ·bạs wanted to take with them John called Mark. 38 But Paul thought best not to take with them one who had withdrawn from them in Păm·phўl'ĭ·ạ, and had not gone with them to the work. 39 And there arose a sharp con-

tention, so that they separated from each other; Băr'nạ·bạs took Mark with him and sailed away to Cyprus, 40 but Paul chose Silas and departed, being commended by the brethren to the grace of the Lord. 41 And he went through Syria and Çĭ·lĭ'çĭ·ạ, strengthening the churches.

16 And he came also to Dĕr'bē and to Lўs'trạ. A disciple was there, named Timothy, the son of a Jewish woman who was a believer; but his father was a Greek. 2 He was well spoken of by the brethren at Lўs'trạ and Ī·cō'nĭ·ụm. 3 Paul wanted Timothy to accompany him; and he took him and circumcised him because of the Jews that were in those places, for they all knew that his father was a Greek. 4 As they went on their way through the cities, they delivered to them for observance the decisions which had been reached by the apostles and elders who were at Jerusalem. 5 So the churches were strengthened in the faith, and they increased in numbers daily.

6 And they went through the region of Phrўg'ĭ·a and Galatia, having been forbidden by the Holy Spirit to speak the word in Asia. 7 And when they had come opposite Mў'sĭ·a, they attempted to go into Bĭ·thўn'ĭ·ạ, but the Spirit of Jesus did not allow them; 8 so, passing by Mў'sĭ·ạ, they went down to Trō'ăs. 9 And a vision appeared to Paul in the night: a man of Măç·ẹ·dō'nĭ·ạ was standing beseeching him and saying, "Come over to Macedonia and help us." 10 And when he had seen the vision, immediately we sought to go on into Măç·ẹ·dō'nĭ·ạ, concluding that God had called us to preach the gospel to them.

11 Setting sail therefore from Trō'ăs, we made a direct voyage to Săm'ọ·thrāçe, and the following day to Nē–ăp'ọ·lĭs, 12 and from there to Phĭ·lĭp'pī, which is the leading city of the district[x] of Măç·ẹ·dō'nĭ·ạ, and a Roman colony. We remained in this city some days; 13 and on the sabbath day we went outside the gate to the riverside, where we supposed there was a place of prayer; and we sat down and spoke to the women who had

---

[n] Other early authorities omit *and from what is strangled*
[o] Other ancient authorities insert verse 34, *But it seemed good to Silas to remain there*
[x] The Greek text is uncertain

come together. ¹⁴One who heard us was a woman named Lӯd′ĭ·a, from the city of Thӯ·a·tī′ra, a seller of purple goods, who was a worshiper of God. The Lord opened her heart to give heed to what was said by Paul. ¹⁵And when she was baptized, with her household, she besought us, saying, "If you have judged me to be faithful to the Lord, come to my house and stay." And she prevailed upon us.

16 As we were going to the place of prayer, we were met by a slave girl who had a spirit of divination and brought her owners much gain by soothsaying. ¹⁷She followed Paul and us, crying, "These men are servants of the Most High God, who proclaim to you the way of salvation." ¹⁸And this she did for many days. But Paul was annoyed, and turned and said to the spirit, "I charge you in the name of Jesus Christ to come out of her." And it came out that very hour.

19 But when her owners saw that their hope of gain was gone, they seized Paul and Silas and dragged them into the market place before the rulers; ²⁰and when they had brought them to the magistrates they said, "These men are Jews and they are disturbing our city. ²¹They advocate customs which it is not lawful for us Romans to accept or practice." ²²The crowd joined in attacking them; and the magistrates tore the garments off them and gave orders to beat them with rods. ²³And when they had inflicted many blows upon them, they threw them into prison, charging the jailer to keep them safely. ²⁴Having received this charge, he put them into the inner prison and fastened their feet in the stocks.

25 But about midnight Paul and Silas were praying and singing hymns to God, and the prisoners were listening to them, ²⁶and suddenly there was a great earthquake, so that the foundations of the prison were shaken; and immediately all the doors were opened and every one's fetters were unfastened. ²⁷When the jailer woke and saw that the prison doors were open, he drew his sword and was about to kill himself, supposing that the prisoners had escaped. ²⁸But Paul cried with a loud voice, "Do not harm yourself, for we are all here." ²⁹And he called for lights and rushed in, and trembling

with fear he fell down before Paul and Silas, ³⁰and brought them out and said, "Men, what must I do to be saved?" ³¹And they said, "Believe in the Lord Jesus, and you will be saved, you and your household." ³²And they spoke the word of the Lord to him and to all that were in his house. ³³And he took them the same hour of the night, and washed their wounds, and he was baptized at once, with all his family. ³⁴Then he brought them up into his house, and set food before them; and he rejoiced with all his household that he had believed in God.

35 But when it was day, the magistrates sent the police, saying, "Let those men go." ³⁶And the jailer reported the words to Paul, saying, "The magistrates have sent to let you go; now therefore come out and go in peace." ³⁷But Paul said to them, "They have beaten us publicly, uncondemned, men who are Roman citizens, and have thrown us into prison; and do they now cast us out secretly? No! let them come themselves and take us out." ³⁸The police reported these words to the magistrates, and they were afraid when they heard that they were Roman citizens; ³⁹so they came and apologized to them. And they took them out and asked them to leave the city. ⁴⁰So they went out of the prison, and visited Lӯd′ĭ·a; and when they had seen the brethren, they exhorted them and departed.

17 Now when they had passed through Ăm·phĭp′o·lĭs and Ăp·ol·lō′nĭ·a they came to Thĕs·sa·lo·nī′ca, where there was a synagogue of the Jews. ²And Paul went in, as was his custom, and for three weeksᵖ he argued with them from the scriptures, ³explaining and proving that it was necessary for the Christ to suffer and to rise from the dead, and saying, "This Jesus, whom I proclaim to you, is the Christ." ⁴And some of them were persuaded, and joined Paul and Silas; as did a great many of the devout Greeks and not a few of the leading women. ⁵But the Jews were jealous, and taking some wicked fellows of the rabble, they gathered a crowd, set the city in an uproar, and attacked the house of Jason, seeking to bring them out to the people. ⁶And when they could not

ᵖOr *sabbaths* 16.22-23: 2 Cor 11.25.

find them, they dragged Jason and some of the brethren before the city authorities, crying, "These men who have turned the world upside down have come here also, [7] and Jason has received them; and they are all acting against the decrees of Caesar, saying that there is another king, Jesus." [8] And the people and the city authorities were disturbed when they heard this. [9] And when they had taken security from Jason and the rest, they let them go.

10 The brethren immediately sent Paul and Silas away by night to Bĕ-roē′a̤; and when they arrived they went into the Jewish synagogue. [11] Now these Jews were more noble 'than those in Thĕs·sa̤·lo̤·nī′ca̤, for they received the word with all eagerness, examining the scriptures daily to see if these things were so. [12] Many of them therefore believed, with not a few Greek women of high standing as well as men. [13] But when the Jews of Thĕs-sa̤·lo̤·nī′ca̤ learned that the word of God was proclaimed by Paul at Bĕ-roē′a̤ also, they came there too, stirring up and inciting the crowds. [14] Then the brethren immediately sent Paul off on his way to the sea, but Silas and Timothy remained there. [15] Those who conducted Paul brought him as far as Athens; and receiving a command for Silas and Timothy to come to him as soon as possible, they departed.

16 Now while Paul was waiting for them at Athens, his spirit was provoked within him as he saw that the city was full of idols. [17] So he argued in the synagogue with the Jews and the devout persons, and in the market place every day with those who chanced to be there. [18] Some also of the Epicurean and Stoic philosophers met him. And some said, "What would this babbler say?" Others said, "He seems to be a preacher of foreign divinities" —because he preached Jesus and the resurrection. [19] And they took hold of him and brought him to the Ăr′ē-ŏp′a̤-gṳs, saying, "May we know what this new teaching is which you present? [20] For you bring some strange things to our ears; we wish to know therefore what these things mean." [21] Now all the Athenians and the foreigners who lived there spent their time in nothing except telling or hearing something new.

22 So Paul, standing in the middle of the Ăr′ē-ŏp′a̤-gṳs, said: "Men of Athens, I perceive that in every way you are very religious. [23] For as I passed along, and observed the objects of your worship, I found also an altar with this inscription, 'To an unknown god.' What therefore you worship as unknown, this I proclaim to you. [24] The God who made the world and everything in it, being Lord of heaven and earth, does not live in shrines made by man, [25] nor is he served by human hands, as though he needed anything, since he himself gives to all men life and breath and everything. [26] And he made from one every nation of men to live on all the face of the earth, having determined allotted periods and the boundaries of their habitation, [27] that they should seek God, in the hope that they might feel after him and find him. Yet he is not far from each one of us, [28] for

'In him we live and move and have
    our being';

as even some of your poets have said,
    'For we are indeed his offspring.'

[29] Being then God's offspring, we ought not to think that the Deity is like gold, or silver, or stone, a representation by the art and imagination of man. [30] The times of ignorance God overlooked, but now he commands all men everywhere to repent, [31] because he has fixed a day on which he will judge the world in righteousness by a man whom he has appointed, and of this he has given assurance to all men by raising him from the dead."

32 Now when they heard of the resurrection of the dead, some mocked; but others said, "We will hear you again about this." [33] So Paul went out from among them. [34] But some men joined him and believed, among them Dī·o̤·nȳs′ĭ·ṳs the Ăr′ē-ŏp′a̤-gīte and a woman named Dăm′a̤·ris and others with them.

18   After this he left Athens and went to Corinth. [2] And he found a Jew named Ă·qui′la̤, a native of Pŏn′tṳs, lately come from Italy with his wife Priscilla, because Claud′ĭ·ṳs had commanded all the Jews to leave Rome. And he went to see them; [3] and because he was of the same trade he stayed with them, and they worked,

17.24-25: Is 42.5.
17.28: Epimenides; Aratus, *Phaenomena*, 5.
17.31: Ps 9.8; 96.13; 98.9.

for by trade they were tentmakers.
⁴And he argued in the synagogue
every sabbath, and persuaded Jews
and Greeks.

5 When Silas and Timothy arrived
from Măç·ẹ·dō'nĭ·ạ, Paul was occupied
with preaching, testifying to the Jews
that the Christ was Jesus. ⁶And when
they opposed and reviled him, he shook
out his garments and said to them,
"Your blood be upon your heads! I am
innocent. From now on I will go to the
Gentiles." ⁷And he left there and went
to the house of a man named Tĭt'ĭ·ụs⁰
Jŭst'ụs, a worshiper of God; his house
was next door to the synagogue.
⁸Crĭs'pụs, the ruler of the synagogue,
believed in the Lord, together with all
his household; and many of the
Corinthians hearing Paul believed and
were baptized. ⁹And the Lord said to
Paul one night in a vision, "Do not be
afraid, but speak and do not be silent;
¹⁰for I am with you, and no man shall
attack you to harm you; for I have
many people in this city." ¹¹And he
stayed a year and six months, teaching
the word of God among them.

12 But when Găl'lĭ·ō was proconsul
of A·chā'ĭ·ạ, the Jews made a united
attack upon Paul and brought him before the tribunal, ¹³saying, "This man
is persuading men to worship God
contrary to the law." ¹⁴But when Paul
was about to open his mouth, Găl'lĭ·ō
said to the Jews, "If it were a matter of
wrongdoing or vicious crime, I should
have reason to bear with you, O Jews;
¹⁵but since it is a matter of questions
about words and names and your own
law, see to it yourselves; I refuse to
be a judge of these things." ¹⁶And he
drove them from the tribunal. ¹⁷And
they all seized Sŏs'thẹ·nĕṣ, the ruler of
the synagogue, and beat him in front of
the tribunal. But Găl'lĭ·ō paid no attention to this.

18 After this Paul stayed many days
longer, and then took leave of the
brethren and sailed for Syria, and with
him Priscilla and A·quĭ'lạ. At Çĕn'-
chrē–ae he cut his hair, for he had a
vow. ¹⁹And they came to Ĕph'ẹ·sụs,
and he left them there; but he himself
went into the synagogue and argued
with the Jews. ²⁰When they asked
him to stay for a longer period, he declined; ²¹but on taking leave of them
he said, "I will return to you if God
wills," and he set sail from Ĕph'ẹ·sụs.

22 When he had landed at Çaĕs-
ạ·rē'ạ, he went up and greeted the
church, and then went down to Ăn'-
tĭ·ŏch. ²³After spending some time
there he departed and went from place
to place through the region of Galatia and Phrўg'ĭ·ạ, strengthening all the
disciples.

24 Now a Jew named Apŏl'lŏs, a
native of Alexandria, came to Ĕph'-
ẹ·sụs. He was an eloquent man, well
versed in the scriptures. ²⁵He had been
instructed in the way of the Lord; and
being fervent in spirit, he spoke and
taught accurately the things concerning Jesus, though he knew only the
baptism of John. ²⁶He began to speak
boldly in the synagogue; but when
Priscilla and A·quĭ'lạ heard him, they
took him and expounded to him the
way of God more accurately. ²⁷And
when he wished to cross to A·chā'ĭ·ạ,
the brethren encouraged him, and
wrote to the disciples to receive him.
When he arrived, he greatly helped
those who through grace had believed,
²⁸for he powerfully confuted the Jews
in public, showing by the scriptures
that the Christ was Jesus.

19 While A·pŏl'lŏs was at Corinth,
Paul passed through the upper
country and came to Ĕph'ẹ·sụs. There
he found some disciples. ²And he said
to them, "Did you receive the Holy
Spirit when you believed?" And they
said, "No, we have never even heard
that there is a Holy Spirit." ³And he
said, "Into what then were you baptized?" They said, "Into John's baptism." ⁴And Paul said, "John baptized
with the baptism of repentance,
telling the people to believe in the one
who was to come after him, that is,
Jesus." ⁵On hearing this, they were
baptized in the name of the Lord
Jesus. ⁶And when Paul had laid his
hands upon them, the Holy Spirit
came on them; and they spoke with
tongues and prophesied. ⁷There were
about twelve of them in all.

8 And he entered the synagogue
and for three months spoke boldly,
arguing and pleading about the
kingdom of God; ⁹but when some were
stubborn and disbelieved, speaking evil
of the Way before the congregation, he
withdrew from them, taking the
disciples with him, and argued daily

⁰Other early authorities read *Titus* 18.9-10: Is 43.5; Jer 1.8.

in the hall of Tў·răn′nŭs.[r] ¹⁰This continued for two years, so that all the residents of Asia heard the word of the Lord, both Jews and Greeks.

11 And God did extraordinary miracles by the hands of Paul, ¹²so that handkerchiefs or aprons were carried away from his body to the sick, and diseases left them and the evil spirits came out of them. ¹³Then some of the itinerant Jewish exorcists undertook to pronounce the name of the Lord Jesus over those who had evil spirits, saying, "I adjure you by the Jesus whom Paul preaches." ¹⁴Seven sons of a Jewish high priest named Scẹ′vạ were doing this. ¹⁵But the evil spirit answered them, "Jesus I know, and Paul I know; but who are you?" ¹⁶And the man in whom the evil spirit was leaped on them, mastered all of them, and overpowered them, so that they fled out of that house naked and wounded. ¹⁷And this became known to all residents of Ĕph′ẹ·sŭs, both Jews and Greeks; and fear fell upon them all; and the name of the Lord Jesus was extolled. ¹⁸Many also of those who were now believers came, confessing and divulging their practices. ¹⁹And a number of those who practiced magic arts brought their books together and burned them in the sight of all; and they counted the value of them and found it came to fifty thousand pieces of silver. ²⁰So the word of the Lord grew and prevailed mightily.

21 Now after these events Paul resolved in the Spirit to pass through Măc·ẹ·dō′nĭ·ạ and A·chā′ĭ·ạ and go to Jerusalem, saying, "After I have been there, I must also see Rome." ²²And having sent into Măc·ẹ·dō′nĭ·ạ two of his helpers, Timothy and Ĕ·răs′-tŭs, he himself stayed in Asia for a while.

23 About that time there arose no little stir concerning the Way. ²⁴For a man named Dĕ·mē′trĭ·ŭs, a silversmith, who made silver shrines of Ăr′tẹ·mĭs, brought no little business to the craftsmen. ²⁵These he gathered together, with the workmen of like occupation, and said, "Men, you know that from this business we have our wealth. ²⁶And you see and hear that not only at Ĕph′ẹ·sŭs but almost throughout all Asia this Paul has persuaded and turned away a consider-

able company of people, saying that gods made with hands are not gods. ²⁷And there is danger not only that this trade of ours may come into disrepute but also that the temple of the great goddess Ăr′tẹ·mĭs may count for nothing, and that she may even be deposed from her magnificence, she whom all Asia and the world worship."

28 When they heard this they were enraged, and cried out, "Great is Ăr′tẹ·mĭs of the Ĕ·phē′ṣiạnṣ!" ²⁹So the city was filled with the confusion; and they rushed together into the theater, dragging with them Gā′ĭ·ŭs and Ăr·ĭs·tär′chŭs, Măc·ẹ·dō′nĭ·anṣ who were Paul's companions in travel. ³⁰Paul wished to go in among the crowd, but the disciples would not let him; ³¹some of the A′sĭ–ärchs also, who were friends of his, sent to him and begged him not to venture into the theater. ³²Now some cried one thing, some another; for the assembly was in confusion, and most of them did not know why they had come together. ³³Some of the crowd prompted Alexander, whom the Jews had put forward. And Alexander motioned with his hand, wishing to make a defense to the people. ³⁴But when they recognized that he was a Jew, for about two hours they all with one voice cried out, "Great is Ăr′tẹ·mĭs of the Ĕ·phē′ṣiạnṣ!" ³⁵And when the town clerk had quieted the crowd, he said, "Men of Ĕph′ẹ·sŭs, what man is there who does not know that the city of the Ĕ·phē′ṣiạnṣ is temple keeper of the great Ăr′tẹ·mĭs, and of the sacred stone that fell from the sky?[s] ³⁶Seeing then that these things cannot be contradicted, you ought to be quiet and do nothing rash. ³⁷For you have brought these men here who are neither sacrilegious nor blasphemers of our goddess. ³⁸If therefore Dĕ·mē′-trĭ·ŭs and the craftsmen with him have a complaint against any one, the courts are open, and there are proconsuls; let them bring charges against one another. ³⁹But if you seek anything further,[t] it shall be settled in the regular assembly. ⁴⁰For we are in danger of being charged with rioting today, there being no cause that we can give to justify this commotion."

[r] Other ancient authorities add *from the fifth hour to the tenth*
[s] The meaning of the Greek is uncertain
[t] Other ancient authorities read *about other matters*

⁴¹And when he had said this, he dismissed the assembly.

20 After the uproar ceased, Paul sent for the disciples and having exhorted them took leave of them and departed for Măç·e·dō'nǐ·ạ. ²When he had gone through these parts and had given them much encouragement, he came to Greece. ³There he spent three months, and when a plot was made against him by the Jews as he was about to set sail for Syria, he determined to return through Măç·e·dō'nǐ·ạ. ⁴Sŏp'ạ·tẹr of Bē·roē'ạ, the son of Pÿr'rhụs, accompanied him; and of the Thĕs·sạ·lō'nǐ·ạns, Ăr·ĭs·tăr'chụs and Sĕ·cŭn'dụs; and Gā'ī·ụs of Dĕr'bē, and Timothy; and the Asians, Tўch'-ĭ·cụs and Trŏph'ĭ·mụs. ⁵These went on and were waiting for us at Trō'ăs, ⁶but we sailed away from Phĭ·lĭp'pī after the days of Unleavened Bread, and in five days we came to them at Trō'ăs, where we stayed for seven days.

7 On the first day of the week, when we were gathered together to break bread, Paul talked with them, intending to depart on the morrow; and he prolonged his speech until midnight. ⁸There were many lights in the upper chamber where we were gathered. ⁹And a young man named Eü'tў·chụs was sitting in the window. He sank into a deep sleep as Paul talked still longer; and being overcome by sleep, he fell down from the third story and was taken up dead. ¹⁰But Paul went down and bent over him, and embracing him said, "Do not be alarmed, for his life is in him." ¹¹And when Paul had gone up and had broken bread and eaten, he conversed with them a long while, until daybreak, and so departed. ¹²And they took the lad away alive, and were not a little comforted.

13 But going ahead to the ship, we set sail for Ăs'sŏs, intending to take Paul aboard there; for so he had arranged, intending himself to go by land. ¹⁴And when he met us at Ăs'sŏs, we took him on board and came to Mĭt·ў·lē'nē. ¹⁵And sailing from there we came the following day opposite Chī'ŏs; the next day we touched at Sā'mŏs; and ᵘ the day after that we came to Mĭ·lē'tụs. ¹⁶For Paul had decided to sail past Ĕph'e·sụs, so that he might not have to spend time in Asia; for he was hastening to be at Jerusalem, if possible, on the day of Pentecost.

17 And from Mĭ·lē'tụs he sent to Ĕph'e·sụs and called to him the elders of the church. ¹⁸And when they came to him, he said to them:

"You yourselves know how I lived among you all the time from the first day that I set foot in Asia, ¹⁹serving the Lord with all humility and with tears and with trials which befell me through the plots of the Jews; ²⁰how I did not shrink from declaring to you anything that was profitable, and teaching you in public and from house to house, ²¹testifying both to Jews and to Greeks of repentance to God and of faith in our Lord Jesus Christ. ²²And now, behold, I am going to Jerusalem, bound in the Spirit, not knowing what shall befall me there; ²³except that the Holy Spirit testifies to me in every city that imprisonment and afflictions await me. ²⁴But I do not account my life of any value nor as precious to myself, if only I may accomplish my course and the ministry which I received from the Lord Jesus, to testify to the gospel of the grace of God. ²⁵And now, behold, I know that all you among whom I have gone preaching the kingdom will see my face no more. ²⁶Therefore I testify to you this day that I am innocent of the blood of all of you, ²⁷for I did not shrink from declaring to you the whole counsel of God. ²⁸Take heed to yourselves and to all the flock, in which the Holy Spirit has made you overseers, to care for the church of God*ᵛ* which he obtained with the blood of his own Son.*ʷ* ²⁹I know that after my departure fierce wolves will come in among you, not sparing the flock; ³⁰and from among your own selves will arise men speaking perverse things, to draw away the disciples after them. ³¹Therefore be alert, remembering that for three years I did not cease night or day to admonish every one with tears. ³²And now I commend you to God and to the word of his grace, which is able to build you up and to give you the inheritance among all those who are sanctified. ³³I coveted no one's silver or gold or apparel. ³⁴You yourselves know that these

*Other ancient authorities add *after remaining at Trogyl-lium* ᵛOther ancient authorities read *of the Lord* ʷGreek *with the blood of his Own* or *with his own blood*

hands ministered to my necessities, and to those who were with me. ³⁵ In all things I have shown you that by so toiling one must help the weak, remembering the words of the Lord Jesus, how he said, 'It is more blessed to give than to receive.' "

36 And when he had spoken thus, he knelt down and prayed with them all. ³⁷ And they all wept and embraced Paul and kissed him, ³⁸ sorrowing most of all because of the word he had spoken, that they should see his face no more. And they brought him to the ship.

21 And when we had parted from them and set sail, we came by a straight course to Cŏs, and the next day to Rhōdes, and from there to Păt'a·ra.ˣ ² And having found a ship crossing to Phoę·nĭ'çĭ·a, we went aboard, and set sail. ³ When we had come in sight of Cyprus, leaving it on the left we sailed to Syria, and landed at Tȳre; for there the ship was to unload its cargo. ⁴ And having sought out the disciples, we stayed there for seven days. Through the Spirit they told Paul not to go on to Jerusalem. ⁵ And when our days there were ended, we departed and went on our journey; and they all, with wives and children, brought us on our way till we were outside the city; and kneeling down on the beach we prayed and bade one another farewell. ⁶ Then we went on board the ship, and they returned home.

7 When we had finished the voyage from Tȳre, we arrived at Ptŏl·ę·mā'ĭs; and we greeted the brethren and stayed with them for one day. ⁸ On the morrow we departed and came to Çæs·a·rē'a; and we entered the house of Philip the evangelist, who was one of the seven, and stayed with him. ⁹ And he had four unmarried daughters, who prophesied. ¹⁰ While we were staying for some days, a prophet named Ăg'a·bus came down from Jü·dē'a. ¹¹ And coming to us he took Paul's girdle and bound his own feet and hands, and said, "Thus says the Holy Spirit, 'So shall the Jews at Jerusalem bind the man who owns this girdle and deliver him into the hands of the Gentiles.' " ¹² When we heard this, we and the people there begged him not to go up to Jerusalem. ¹³ Then Paul answered, "What are you doing, weeping and breaking my heart? For I am ready not only to be imprisoned but even to die at Jerusalem for the name of the Lord Jesus." ¹⁴ And when he would not be persuaded, we ceased and said, "The will of the Lord be done."

15 After these days we made ready and went up to Jerusalem. ¹⁶ And some of the disciples from Çæs·a·rē'a went with us, bringing us to the house of Mnā'son of Cyprus, an early disciple, with whom we should lodge.

17 When we had come to Jerusalem, the brethren received us gladly. ¹⁸ On the following day Paul went in with us to James; and all the elders were present. ¹⁹ After greeting them, he related one by one the things that God had done among the Gentiles through his ministry. ²⁰ And when they heard it, they glorified God. And they said to him, "You see, brother, how many thousands there are among the Jews of those who have believed; they are all zealous for the law, ²¹ and they have been told about you that you teach all the Jews who are among the Gentiles to forsake Moses, telling them not to circumcise their children or observe the customs. ²² What then is to be done? They will certainly hear that you have come. ²³ Do therefore what we tell you. We have four men who are under a vow; ²⁴ take these men and purify yourself along with them and pay their expenses, so that they may shave their heads. Thus all will know that there is nothing in what they have been told about you but that you yourself live in observance of the law. ²⁵ But as for the Gentiles who have believed, we have sent a letter with our judgment that they should abstain from what has been sacrificed to idols and from blood and from what is strangledʸ and from unchastity." ²⁶ Then Paul took the men, and the next day he purified himself with them and went into the temple, to give notice when the days of purification would be fulfilled and the offering presented for every one of them.

27 When the seven days were almost completed, the Jews from Asia, who had seen him in the temple, stirred up all the crowd, and laid hands on him, ²⁸ crying out, "Men of Israel, help! This is the man who

ˣ Other ancient authorities add *and Myra*
ʸ Other early authorities omit *and from what is strangled*

is teaching men everywhere against the people and the law and this place; moreover he also brought Greeks into the temple, and he has defiled this holy place." ²⁹For they had previously seen Trŏph'ĭ·mus the Ē·phē'şĭ·an with him in the city, and they supposed that Paul had brought him into the temple. ³⁰Then all the city was aroused, and the people ran together; they seized Paul and dragged him out of the temple, and at once the gates were shut. ³¹And as they were trying to kill him, word came to the tribune of the cohort that all Jerusalem was in confusion. ³²He at once took soldiers and centurions, and ran down to them; and when they saw the tribune and the soldiers, they stopped beating Paul. ³³Then the tribune came up and arrested him, and ordered him to be bound with two chains. He inquired who he was and what he had done. ³⁴Some in the crowd shouted one thing, some another; and as he could not learn the facts because of the uproar, he ordered him to be brought into the barracks. ³⁵And when he came to the steps, he was actually carried by the soldiers because of the violence of the crowd; ³⁶for the mob of the people followed, crying, "Away with him!"

37 As Paul was about to be brought into the barracks, he said to the tribune, "May I say something to you?" And he said, "Do you know Greek? ³⁸Are you not the Egyptian, then, who recently stirred up a revolt and led the four thousand men of the Assassins out into the wilderness?" ³⁹Paul replied, "I am a Jew, from Tär'sus in Çĭ·lĭ·çĭ'a, a citizen of no mean city; I beg you, let me speak to the people." ⁴⁰And when he had given him leave, Paul, standing on the steps, motioned with his hand to the people; and when there was a great hush, he spoke to them in the Hebrew language, saying:

22 "Brethren and fathers, hear the defense which I now make before you."

2 And when they heard that he addressed them in the Hebrew language, they were the more quiet. And he said: 3 "I am a Jew, born at Tär'sus in Çĭ·lĭ·çĭ'a, but brought up in this city at the feet of Ga·mā'lĭ·el, educated according to the strict manner of the law of our fathers, being zealous for God as you all are this day. ⁴I persecuted

this Way to the death, binding and delivering to prison both men and women, ⁵as the high priest and the whole council of elders bear me witness. From them I received letters to the brethren, and I journeyed to Damascus to take those also who were there and bring them in bonds to Jerusalem to be punished.

6 "As I made my journey and drew near to Damascus, about noon a great light from heaven suddenly shone about me. ⁷And I fell to the ground and heard a voice saying to me, 'Saul, Saul, why do you persecute me?' ⁸And I answered, 'Who are you, Lord?' And he said to me, 'I am Jesus of Nazareth whom you are persecuting.' ⁹Now those who were with me saw the light but did not hear the voice of the one who was speaking to me. ¹⁰And I said, 'What shall I do, Lord?' And the Lord said to me, 'Rise, and go into Damascus, and there you will be told all that is appointed for you to do.' ¹¹And when I could not see because of the brightness of that light, I was led by the hand by those who were with me, and came into Damascus.

12 "And one Ăn·a·nī'as, a devout man according to the law, well spoken of by all the Jews who lived there, ¹³came to me, and standing by me said to me, 'Brother Saul, receive your sight.' And in that very hour I received my sight and saw him. ¹⁴And he said, 'The God of our fathers appointed you to know his will, to see the Just One and to hear a voice from his mouth; ¹⁵for you will be a witness for him to all men of what you have seen and heard. ¹⁶And now why do you wait? Rise and be baptized, and wash away your sins, calling on his name.'

17 "When I had returned to Jerusalem and was praying in the temple, I fell into a trance ¹⁸and saw him saying to me, 'Make haste and get quickly out of Jerusalem, because they will not accept your testimony about me.' ¹⁹And I said, 'Lord, they themselves know that in every synagogue I imprisoned and beat those who believed in thee. ²⁰And when the blood of Stephen thy witness was shed, I also was standing by and approving, and keeping the garments of those who killed him.' ²¹And he said to me, 'De-

22.4-16: Acts 9.1-19; 26.9-18; Gal 1.14.

part; for I will send you far away to the Gentiles.' "

22 Up to this word they listened to him; then they lifted up their voices and said, "Away with such a fellow from the earth! For he ought not to live." ²³And as they cried out and waved their garments and threw dust into the air, ²⁴the tribune commanded him to be brought into the barracks, and ordered him to be examined by scourging, to find out why they shouted thus against him. ²⁵But when they had tied him up with the thongs, Paul said to the centurion who was standing by, "Is it lawful for you to scourge a man who is a Roman citizen, and uncondemned?" ²⁶When the centurion heard that, he went to the tribune and said to him, "What are you about to do? For this man is a Roman citizen." ²⁷So the tribune came and said to him, "Tell me, are you a Roman citizen?" And he said, "Yes." ²⁸The tribune answered, "I bought this citizenship for a large sum." Paul said, "But I was born a citizen." ²⁹So those who were about to examine him withdrew from him instantly; and the tribune also was afraid, for he realized that Paul was a Roman citizen and that he had bound him.

30 But on the morrow, desiring to know the real reason why the Jews accused him, he unbound him, and commanded the chief priests and all the council to meet, and he brought Paul down and set him before them.

23 And Paul, looking intently at the council, said, "Brethren, I have lived before God in all good conscience up to this day." ²And the high priest Ăn·a·nī'as commanded those who stood by him to strike him on the mouth. ³Then Paul said to him, "God shall strike you, you whitewashed wall! Are you sitting to judge me according to the law, and yet contrary to the law you order me to be struck?" ⁴Those who stood by said, "Would you revile God's high priest?" ⁵And Paul said, "I did not know, brethren, that he was the high priest; for it is written, 'You shall not speak evil of a ruler of your people.'"

6 But when Paul perceived that one part were Săd'du·çeeş and the other Phăr'i·seeş, he cried out in the council, "Brethren, I am a Pharisee, a son of Pharisees; with respect to the hope and the resurrection of the dead I am on trial." ⁷And when he had said this, a dissension arose between the Phăr'i·seeş and the Săd'du·çeeş; and the assembly was divided. ⁸For the Săd'du·çeeş say that there is no resurrection, nor angel, nor spirit; but the Phăr'i·seeş acknowledge them all. ⁹Then a great clamor arose; and some of the scribes of the Phăr'i·seeş' party stood up and contended, "We find nothing wrong in this man. What if a spirit or an angel spoke to him?" ¹⁰And when the dissension became violent, the tribune, afraid that Paul would be torn in pieces by them, commanded the soldiers to go down and take him by force from among them and bring him into the barracks.

11 The following night the Lord stood by him and said, "Take courage, for as you have testified about me at Jerusalem, so you must bear witness also at Rome."

12 When it was day, the Jews made a plot and bound themselves by an oath neither to eat nor drink till they had killed Paul. ¹³There were more than forty who made this conspiracy. ¹⁴And they went to the chief priests and elders, and said, "We have strictly bound ourselves by an oath to taste no food till we have killed Paul. ¹⁵You therefore, along with the council, give notice now to the tribune to bring him down to you, as though you were going to determine his case more exactly. And we are ready to kill him before he comes near."

16 Now the son of Paul's sister heard of their ambush; so he went and entered the barracks and told Paul. ¹⁷And Paul called one of the centurions and said, "Take this young man to the tribune; for he has something to tell him." ¹⁸So he took him and brought him to the tribune and said, "Paul the prisoner called me and asked me to bring this young man to you, as he has something to say to you." ¹⁹The tribune took him by the hand, and going aside asked him privately, "What is it that you have to tell me?" ²⁰And he said, "The Jews have agreed to ask you to bring Paul down to the council tomorrow, as though they were going to inquire somewhat more closely about him. ²¹But do not yield to them; for more than forty of their men lie in

23.5: Ex 22.28.

ambush for him, having bound themselves by an oath neither to eat nor drink till they have killed him; and now they are ready, waiting for the promise from you." ²²So the tribune dismissed the young man, charging him, "Tell no one that you have informed me of this."

23 Then he called two of the centurions and said, "At the third hour of the night get ready two hundred soldiers with seventy horsemen and two hundred spearmen to go as far as Çaĕs·ạ·rē'ạ. ²⁴Also provide mounts for Paul to ride, and bring him safely to Felix the governor." ²⁵And he wrote a letter to this effect:

26 "Claud'ĭ·ụs Lўs'ĭ·ạs to his Excellency the governor Felix, greeting. ²⁷This man was seized by the Jews, and was about to be killed by them, when I came upon them with the soldiers and rescued him, having learned that he was a Roman citizen. ²⁸And desiring to know the charge on which they accused him, I brought him down to their council. ²⁹I found that he was accused about questions of their law, but charged with nothing deserving death or imprisonment. ³⁰And when it was disclosed to me that there would be a plot against the man, I sent him to you at once, ordering his accusers also to state before you what they have against him."

31 So the soldiers, according to their instructions, took Paul and brought him by night to Ăn·tĭp'ạ·trĭs. ³²And on the morrow they returned to the barracks, leaving the horsemen to go on with him. ³³When they came to Çaĕs·ạ·rē'ạ and delivered the letter to the governor, they presented Paul also before him. ³⁴On reading the letter, he asked to what province he belonged. When he learned that he was from Çĭ·lĭ'çĭ·ạ ³⁵he said, "I will hear you when your accusers arrive." And he commanded him to be guarded in Hĕr'ọd's praetorium.

24 And after five days the high priest Ăn·ạ·nī'ạs came down with some elders and a spokesman, one Tĕr·tŭl'lụs. They laid before the governor their case against Paul; ²and when he was called, Tĕr·tŭl'lụs began to accuse him, saying:

"Since through you we enjoy much peace, and since by your provision, most excellent Felix, reforms are introduced on behalf of this nation, ³in every way and everywhere we accept this with all gratitude. ⁴But, to detain you no further, I beg you in your kindness to hear us briefly. ⁵For we have found this man a pestilent fellow, an agitator among all the Jews throughout the world, and a ringleader of the sect of the Năz'ạ·rēnẹs. ⁶He even tried to profane the temple, but we seized him.ᶻ ⁸By examining him yourself you will be able to learn from him about everything of which we accuse him."

9 The Jews also joined in the charge, affirming that all this was so.

10 And when the governor had motioned to him to speak, Paul replied:

"Realizing that for many years you have been judge over this nation, I cheerfully make my defense. ¹¹As you may ascertain, it is not more than twelve days since I went up to worship at Jerusalem; ¹²and they did not find me disputing with any one or stirring up a crowd, either in the temple or in the synagogues, or in the city. ¹³Neither can they prove to you what they now bring up against me. ¹⁴But this I admit to you, that according to the Way, which they call a sect, I worship the God of our fathers, believing everything laid down by the law or written in the prophets, ¹⁵having a hope in God which these themselves accept, that there will be a resurrection of both the just and the unjust. ¹⁶So I always take pains to have a clear conscience toward God and toward men. ¹⁷Now after some years I came to bring to my nation alms and offerings. ¹⁸As I was doing this, they found me purified in the temple, without any crowd or tumult. But some Jews from Asia—¹⁹they ought to be here before you and to make an accusation, if they have anything against me. ²⁰Or else let these men themselves say what wrongdoing they found when I stood before the council, ²¹except this one thing which I cried out while standing among them, 'With respect to the resurrection of the dead I am on trial before you this day.' "

22 But Felix, having a rather accurate knowledge of the Way, put them off, saying, "When Lўs'ĭ·ạs the tribune

ᶻ Other ancient authorities add *and we would have judged him according to our law.* ᵀBut *the chief captain Lysias came and with great violence took him out of our hands,* ᵉcommanding his accusers to come before you.

comes down, I will decide your case." 23 Then he gave orders to the centurion that he should be kept in custody but should have some liberty, and that none of his friends should be prevented from attending to his needs.

24 After some days Felix came with his wife Drü·sĭl′la, who was a Jewess; and he sent for Paul and heard him speak upon faith in Christ Jesus. 25 And as he argued about justice and self-control and future judgment, Felix was alarmed and said, "Go away for the present; when I have an opportunity I will summon you." 26 At the same time he hoped that money would be given him by Paul. So he sent for him often and conversed with him. 27 But when two years had elapsed, Felix was succeeded by Pôr′çĭ·us Fĕs′-tus; and desiring to do the Jews a favor, Felix left Paul in prison.

25 Now when Fĕs′tus had come into his province, after three days he went up to Jerusalem from Çaĕs·a·rē′a. 2 And the chief priests and the principal men of the Jews informed him against Paul; and they urged him, 3 asking as a favor to have the man sent to Jerusalem, planning an ambush to kill him on the way. 4 Fĕs′tus replied that Paul was being kept at Çaĕs·a·rē′a, and that he himself intended to go there shortly. 5 "So," said he, "let the men of authority among you go down with me, and if there is anything wrong about the man, let them accuse him."

6 When he had stayed among them not more than eight or ten days, he went down to Çaĕs·a·rē′a; and the next day he took his seat on the tribunal and ordered Paul to be brought. 7 And when he had come, the Jews who had gone down from Jerusalem stood about him, bringing against him many serious charges which they could not prove. 8 Paul said in his defense, "Neither against the law of the Jews, nor against the temple, nor against Caesar have I offended at all." 9 But Fĕs′tus, wishing to do the Jews a favor, said to Paul, "Do you wish to go up to Jerusalem, and there be tried on these charges before me?" 10 But Paul said, "I am standing before Caesar's tribunal, where I ought to be tried; to the Jews I have done no wrong, as you know very well. 11 If then I am a wrongdoer, and have committed any-thing for which I deserve to die, I do not seek to escape death; but if there is nothing in their charges against me, no one can give me up to them. I appeal to Caesar." 12 Then Fĕs′tus, when he had conferred with his council, answered, "You have appealed to Caesar; to Caesar you shall go."

13 Now when some days had passed, A·grĭp′pa the king and Bĕr·nī′çē arrived at Çaĕs·a·rē′a to welcome Fĕs′tus. 14 And as they stayed there many days, Fĕs′tus laid Paul's case before the king, saying, "There is a man left prisoner by Felix; 15 and when I was at Jerusalem, the chief priests and the elders of the Jews gave information about him, asking for sentence against him. 16 I answered them that it was not the custom of the Romans to give up any one before the accused met the accusers face to face, and had opportunity to make his defense concerning the charge laid against him. 17 When therefore they came together here, I made no delay, but on the next day took my seat on the tribunal and ordered the man to be brought in. 18 When the accusers stood up, they brought no charge in his case of such evils as I supposed; 19 but they had certain points of dispute with him about their own superstition and about one Jesus, who was dead, but whom Paul asserted to be alive. 20 Being at a loss how to investigate these questions, I asked whether he wished to go to Jerusalem and be tried there regarding them. 21 But when Paul had appealed to be kept in custody for the decision of the emperor, I commanded him to be held until I could send him to Caesar." 22 And A·grĭp′pa said to Fĕs′tus, "I should like to hear the man myself." "Tomorrow," said he, "you shall hear him."

23 So on the morrow A·grĭp′pa and Bĕr·nī′çē came with great pomp, and they entered the audience hall with the military tribunes and the prominent men of the city. Then by command of Fĕs′tus Paul was brought in. 24 And Fĕs′tus said, "King A·grĭp′pa and all who are present with us, you see this man about whom the whole Jewish people petitioned me, both at Jerusalem and here, shouting that he ought not to live any longer. 25 But I found that he had done nothing deserving

death; and as he himself appealed to the emperor, I decided to send him. ²⁶But I have nothing definite to write to my lord about him. Therefore I have brought him before you, and, especially before you, King Ạ·grĭp′pạ, that, after we have examined him, I may have something to write. ²⁷For it seems to me unreasonable, in sending a prisoner, not to indicate the charges against him."

26 Ạ·grĭp′pạ said to Paul, "You have permission to speak for yourself." Then Paul stretched out his hand and made his defense:

"I think myself fortunate that it is before you, King Ạ·grĭp′pạ, I am to make my defense today against all the accusations of the Jews, ³because you are especially familiar with all customs and controversies of the Jews; therefore I beg you to listen to me patiently.

4 "My manner of life from my youth, spent from the beginning among my own nation and at Jerusalem, is known by all the Jews. ⁵They have known for a long time, if they are willing to testify, that according to the strictest party of our religion I have lived as a Phăr′i·see. ⁶And now I stand here on trial for hope in the promise made by God to our fathers, ⁷to which our twelve tribes hope to attain, as they earnestly worship night and day. And for this hope I am accused by Jews, O king! ⁸Why is it thought incredible by any of you that God raises the dead?

9 "I myself was convinced that I ought to do many things in opposing the name of Jesus of Nazareth. ¹⁰And I did so in Jerusalem; I not only shut up many of the saints in prison, by authority from the chief priests, but when they were put to death I cast my vote against them. ¹¹And I punished them often in all the synagogues and tried to make them blaspheme; and in raging fury against them, I persecuted them even to foreign cities.

12 "Thus I journeyed to Damascus with the authority and commission of the chief priests. ¹³At midday, O king, I saw on the way a light from heaven, brighter than the sun, shining round me and those who journeyed with me. ¹⁴And when we had all fallen to the ground, I heard a voice saying to me in the Hebrew language, 'Saul, Saul, why do you persecute me? It

hurts you to kick against the goads.' ¹⁵And I said, 'Who are you, Lord?' And the Lord said, 'I am Jesus whom you are persecuting. ¹⁶But rise and stand upon your feet; for I have appeared to you for this purpose, to appoint you to serve and bear witness to the things in which you have seen me and to those in which I will appear to you, ¹⁷delivering you from the people and from the Gentiles—to whom I send you ¹⁸to open their eyes, that they may turn from darkness to light and from the power of Satan to God, that they may receive forgiveness of sins and a place among those who are sanctified by faith in me.'

19 "Wherefore, O King Ạ·grĭp′pạ, I was not disobedient to the heavenly vision, ²⁰but declared first to those at Damascus, then at Jerusalem and throughout all the country of Jü·dē′ạ, and also to the Gentiles, that they should repent and turn to God and perform deeds worthy of their repentance. ²¹For this reason the Jews seized me in the temple and tried to kill me. ²²To this day I have had the help that comes from God, and so I stand here testifying both to small and great, saying nothing but what the prophets and Moses said would come to pass: ²³that the Christ must suffer, and that, by being the first to rise from the dead, he would proclaim light both to the people and to the Gentiles."

24 And as he thus made his defense, Fĕs′tus said with a loud voice, "Paul, you are mad; your great learning is turning you mad." ²⁵But Paul said, "I am not mad, most excellent Fĕs′tus, but I am speaking the sober truth. ²⁶For the king knows about these things, and to him I speak freely; for I am persuaded that none of these things has escaped his notice, for this was not done in a corner. ²⁷King Ạ·grĭp′pạ, do you believe the prophets? I know that you believe." ²⁸And Ạ·grĭp′pạ said to Paul, "In a short time you think to make me a Christian!" ²⁹And Paul said, "Whether short or long, I would to God that not only you but also all who hear me this day might become such as I am—except for these chains."

30 Then the king rose, and the governor and Bẹr·nī′çē and those who

26.9-18: Acts 9.1-8; 22.4-16.
26.16-17: Ezek 2.1, 3. 26.18: Is 42.7, 16.

were sitting with them; [31] and when they had withdrawn, they said to one another, "This man is doing nothing to deserve death or imprisonment." [32] And Ạ·grĭp'pạ said to Fĕs'tŭs, "This man could have been set free if he had not appealed to Caesar."

27 And when it was decided that we should sail for Italy, they delivered Paul and some other prisoners to a centurion of the Augustan Cohort, named Julius. [2] And embarking in a ship of Ăd·rạ·mȳt'tĭ·ụm, which was about to sail to the ports along the coast of Asia, we put to sea, accompanied by Ăr·ĭs·tãr'chụs, a Maç·ẹ·dō'nĭ·ạn from Thĕs·sạ·lo·nī'cạ. [3] The next day we put in at Sī'dŏn; and Julius treated Paul kindly, and gave him leave to go to his friends and be cared for. [4] And putting to sea from there we sailed under the lee of Cyprus, because the winds were against us. [5] And when we had sailed across the sea which is off Çĭ·lĭ'çĭ·ạ and Păm·phȳl'ĭ·ạ, we came to Mȳ'rạ and Lȳ'çĭ·ạ. [6] There the centurion found a ship of Alexandria sailing for Italy, and put us on board. [7] We sailed slowly for a number of days, and arrived with difficulty off Cnī'dụs, and as the wind did not allow us to go on, we sailed under the lee of Crete off Săl·mō'nē. [8] Coasting along it with difficulty, we came to a place called Fair Havens, near which was the city of Lạ·sē'ạ.

9 As much time had been lost, and the voyage was already dangerous because the fast had already gone by, Paul advised them, [10] saying, "Sirs, I perceive that the voyage will be with injury and much loss, not only of the cargo and the ship, but also of our lives." [11] But the centurion paid more attention to the captain and to the owner of the ship than to what Paul said. [12] And because the harbor was not suitable to winter in, the majority advised to put to sea from there, on the chance that somehow they could reach Phoenix, a harbor of Crete, looking northeast and southeast,[a] and winter there.

13 And when the south wind blew gently, supposing that they had obtained their purpose, they weighed anchor and sailed along Crete, close inshore. [14] But soon a tempestuous wind, called the northeaster, struck down from the land; [15] and when the ship was caught and could not face the wind, we gave way to it and were driven. [16] And running under the lee of a small island called Cau'dạ,[b] we managed with difficulty to secure the boat; [17] after hoisting it up, they took measures[c] to undergird the ship; then, fearing that they should run on the Sȳr'tĭs, they lowered the gear, and so were driven. [18] As we were violently storm-tossed, they began next day to throw the cargo overboard; [19] and the third day they cast out with their own hands the tackle of the ship. [20] And when neither sun nor stars appeared for many a day, and no small tempest lay on us, all hope of our being saved was at last abandoned.

21 As they had been long without food, Paul then came forward among them and said, "Men, you should have listened to me, and should not have set sail from Crete and incurred this injury and loss. [22] I now bid you take heart; for there will be no loss of life among you, but only of the ship. [23] For this very night there stood by me an angel of the God to whom I belong and whom I worship, [24] and he said, 'Do not be afraid, Paul; you must stand before Caesar; and lo, God has granted you all those who sail with you.' [25] So take heart, men, for I have faith in God that it will be exactly as I have been told. [26] But we shall have to run on some island."

27 When the fourteenth night had come, as we were drifting across the sea of Ā'drĭ·ạ, about midnight the sailors suspected that they were nearing land. [28] So they sounded and found twenty fathoms; a little farther on they sounded again and found fifteen fathoms. [29] And fearing that we might run on the rocks, they let out four anchors from the stern, and prayed for day to come. [30] And as the sailors were seeking to escape from the ship, and had lowered the boat into the sea, under pretense of laying out anchors from the bow, [31] Paul said to the centurion and the soldiers, "Unless these men stay in the ship, you cannot be saved." [32] Then the soldiers cut away the ropes of the boat, and let it go.

33 As day was about to dawn, Paul urged them all to take some food, saying, "Today is the fourteenth day that

[a] Or southwest and northwest
[b] Other ancient authorities read Clauda [c] Greek helps

you have continued in suspense and without food, having taken nothing. [34] Therefore I urge you to take some food; it will give you strength, since not a hair is to perish from the head of any of you." [35] And when he had said this, he took bread, and giving thanks to God in the presence of all he broke it and began to eat. [36] Then they all were encouraged and ate some food themselves. [37] (We were in all two hundred and seventy-six[d] persons in the ship.) [38] And when they had eaten enough, they lightened the ship, throwing out the wheat into the sea.

39 Now when it was day, they did not recognize the land, but they noticed a bay with a beach, on which they planned if possible to bring the ship ashore. [40] So they cast off the anchors and left them in the sea, at the same time loosening the ropes that tied the rudders; then hoisting the foresail to the wind they made for the beach. [41] But striking a shoal[e] they ran the vessel aground; the bow stuck and remained immovable, and the stern was broken up by the surf. [42] The soldiers' plan was to kill the prisoners, lest any should swim away and escape; [43] but the centurion, wishing to save Paul, kept them from carrying out their purpose. He ordered those who could swim to throw themselves overboard first and make for the land, [44] and the rest on planks or on pieces of the ship. And so it was that all escaped to land.

28 After we had escaped, we then learned that the island was called Malta. [2] And the natives showed us unusual kindness, for they kindled a fire and welcomed us all, because it had begun to rain and was cold. [3] Paul had gathered a bundle of sticks and put them on the fire, when a viper came out because of the heat and fastened on his hand. [4] When the natives saw the creature hanging from his hand, they said to one another, "No doubt this man is a murderer. Though he has escaped from the sea, justice has not allowed him to live." [5] He, however, shook off the creature into the fire and suffered no harm. [6] They waited, expecting him to swell up or suddenly fall down dead; but when they had waited a long time and saw no misfortune come to him, they changed their minds and said that he was a god.

7 Now in the neighborhood of that place were lands belonging to the chief man of the island, named Pŭb′lĭ·ŭs, who received us and entertained us hospitably for three days. [8] It happened that the father of Pŭb′lĭ·ŭs lay sick with fever and dysentery; and Paul visited him and prayed, and putting his hands on him healed him. [9] And when this had taken place, the rest of the people on the island who had diseases also came and were cured. [10] They presented many gifts to us;[f] and when we sailed, they put on board whatever we needed.

11 After three months we set sail in a ship which had wintered in the island, a ship of Alexandria, with the Twin Brothers as figurehead. [12] Putting in at Syracuse, we stayed there for three days. [13] And from there we made a circuit and arrived at Rhē′-gĭ·ŭm; and after one day a south wind sprang up, and on the second day we came to Pū·tē′ọ·lī. [14] There we found brethren, and were invited to stay with them for seven days. And so we came to Rome. [15] And the brethren there, when they heard of us, came as far as the Forum of Ăp′pĭ·ŭs and Three Taverns to meet us. On seeing them Paul thanked God and took courage. [16] And when we came into Rome, Paul was allowed to stay by himself, with the soldier that guarded him.

17 After three days he called together the local leaders of the Jews; and when they had gathered, he said to them, "Brethren, though I had done nothing against the people or the customs of our fathers, yet I was delivered prisoner from Jerusalem into the hands of the Romans. [18] When they had examined me, they wished to set me at liberty, because there was no reason for the death penalty in my case. [19] But when the Jews objected, I was compelled to appeal to Caesar — though I had no charge to bring against my nation. [20] For this reason therefore I have asked to see you and speak with you, since it is because of the hope of Israel that I am bound with this chain." [21] And they said to him, "We have received no letters from Jū·dē′ạ

[d] Other ancient authorities read *seventy-six* or *about seventy-six*
[e] Greek *place of two seas*
[f] Or *honored us with many honors*

about you, and none of the brethren coming here has reported or spoken any evil about you. ²²But we desire to hear from you what your views are; for with regard to this sect we know that everywhere it is spoken against."

23 When they had appointed a day for him, they came to him at his lodging in great numbers. And he expounded the matter to them from morning till evening, testifying to the kingdom of God and trying to convince them about Jesus both from the law of Moses and from the prophets. ²⁴And some were convinced by what he said, while others disbelieved. ²⁵So, as they disagreed among themselves, they departed, after Paul had made one statement: "The Holy Spirit was right in saying to your fathers through Ī·sāi′ah the prophet:
²⁶'Go to this people, and say,

You shall indeed hear but never understand,
and you shall indeed see but never perceive.
²⁷For this people's heart has grown dull,
and their ears are heavy of hearing,
and their eyes they have closed;
lest they should perceive with their eyes,
and hear with their ears,
and understand with their heart,
and turn for me to heal them.'
²⁸Let it be known to you then that this salvation of God has been sent to the Gentiles; they will listen." *g*

30 And he lived there two whole years at his own expense, *h* and welcomed all who came to him, ³¹preaching the kingdom of God and teaching about the Lord Jesus Christ quite openly and unhindered.

The Letter of Paul to the

Romans

1 Paul, a servant *a* of Jesus Christ, called to be an apostle, set apart for the gospel of God ²which he promised beforehand through his prophets in the holy scriptures, ³the gospel concerning his Son, who was descended from David according to the flesh ⁴and designated Son of God in power according to the Spirit of holiness by his resurrection from the dead, Jesus Christ our Lord, ⁵through whom we have received grace and apostleship to bring about the obedience of faith for the sake of his name among all the nations, ⁶including yourselves who are called to belong to Jesus Christ;

7 To all God's beloved in Rome, who are called to be saints:

Grace to you and peace from God our Father and the Lord Jesus Christ.

8 First, I thank my God through Jesus Christ for all of you, because your faith is proclaimed in all the world. ⁹For God is my witness, whom I serve with my spirit in the gospel of his Son, that without ceasing I mention you always in my prayers, ¹⁰asking that somehow by God's will I may now at last succeed in coming to you. ¹¹For I long to see you, that I may impart to you some spiritual gift to strengthen you, ¹²that is, that we may be mutually encouraged by each other's faith, both yours and mine. ¹³I want you to know, brethren, that I have often intended to come to you (but thus far have been prevented), in order that I may reap some harvest among you as well as among the rest of the Gentiles. ¹⁴I am under obligation both to Greeks and to barbarians, both to the wise and to the foolish: ¹⁵so I am eager to preach the gospel to you also who are in Rome.

16 For I am not ashamed of the gospel: it is the power of God for salvation to every one who has faith, to the

*g*Other ancient authorities add verse 29, *And when he had said these words, the Jews departed, holding much dispute among themselves* *h*Or *in his own hired dwelling* 28.26-27: Is 6.9-10. 28.28: Ps 67.2.

*a*Or *slave*

1.1: Acts 9.15; 13.2; 1 Cor 1.1; 2 Cor 1.1; Gal 1.15.
1.5: Acts 26.16-18; Rom 15.18; Gal 2.7, 9.
1.7: 1 Cor 1.3; 2 Cor 1.2; Gal 1.3; Eph 1.2; Phil 1.2; Col 1.2; 1 Thess 1.2; 2 Thess 1.2; 1 Tim 1.2; 2 Tim 1.2; Tit 1.4; Philem 3; 2 Jn 3.   1.8: Rom 16.19.
1.10: Rom 15.23, 32; Acts 19.21.
1.13: Rom 15.22.   1.14: 1 Cor 9.16.   1.16: 1 Cor 1.18, 24.

Jew first and also to the Greek. [17] For in it the righteousness of God is revealed through faith for faith; as it is written, "He who through faith is righteous shall live."[b]

18 For the wrath of God is revealed from heaven against all ungodliness and wickedness of men who by their wickedness suppress the truth. [19] For what can be known about God is plain to them, because God has shown it to them. [20] Ever since the creation of the world his invisible nature, namely, his eternal power and deity, has been clearly perceived in the things that have been made. So they are without excuse; [21] for although they knew God they did not honor him as God or give thanks to him, but they became futile in their thinking and their senseless minds were darkened. [22] Claiming to be wise, they became fools, [23] and exchanged the glory of the immortal God for images resembling mortal man or birds or animals or reptiles.

24 Therefore God gave them up in the lusts of their hearts to impurity, to the dishonoring of their bodies among themselves, [25] because they exchanged the truth about God for a lie and worshiped and served the creature rather than the Creator, who is blessed for ever! Amen.

26 For this reason God gave them up to dishonorable passions. Their women exchanged natural relations for unnatural, [27] and the men likewise gave up natural relations with women and were consumed with passion for one another, men committing shameless acts with men and receiving in their own persons the due penalty for their error.

28 And since they did not see fit to acknowledge God, God gave them up to a base mind and to improper conduct. [29] They were filled with all manner of wickedness, evil, covetousness, malice. Full of envy, murder, strife, deceit, malignity, they are gossips, [30] slanderers, haters of God, insolent, haughty, boastful, inventors of evil, disobedient to parents, [31] foolish, faithless, heartless, ruthless. [32] Though they know God's decree that those who do such things deserve to die, they not only do them but approve those who practice them.

2 Therefore you have no excuse, O man, whoever you are, when you judge another; for in passing judgment upon him you condemn yourself, because you, the judge, are doing the very same things. [2] We know that the judgment of God rightly falls upon those who do such things. [3] Do you suppose, O man, that when you judge those who do such things and yet do them yourself, you will escape the judgment of God? [4] Or do you presume upon the riches of his kindness and forbearance and patience? Do you not know that God's kindness is meant to lead you to repentance? [5] But by your hard and impenitent heart you are storing up wrath for yourself on the day of wrath when God's righteous judgment will be revealed. [6] For he will render to every man according to his works: [7] to those who by patience in well-doing seek for glory and honor and immortality, he will give eternal life; [8] but for those who are factious and do not obey the truth, but obey wickedness, there will be wrath and fury. [9] There will be tribulation and distress for every human being who does evil, the Jew first and also the Greek, [10] but glory and honor and peace for every one who does good, the Jew first and also the Greek. [11] For God shows no partiality.

12 All who have sinned without the law will also perish without the law, and all who have sinned under the law will be judged by the law. [13] For it is not the hearers of the law who are righteous before God, but the doers of the law who will be justified. [14] When Gentiles who have not the law do by nature what the law requires, they are a law to themselves, even though they do not have the law. [15] They show that what the law requires is written on their hearts, while their conscience also bears witness and their conflicting thoughts accuse or perhaps excuse them [16] on that day when, according to my gospel, God judges the secrets of men by Christ Jesus.

17 But if you call yourself a Jew and rely upon the law and boast of your relation to God [18] and know his will and

[b]Or *The righteous shall live by faith*
1.17: Rom 3.21; Gal 3.11; Phil 3.9; Heb 10.38; Hab 2.4.
1.18: Eph 5.6; Col 3.6.   1.20: Ps 19.1-4.
1.21: Eph 4.17-18.   1.23: Acts 17.29.
2.1: Rom 14.22.   2.4: Eph 1.7; 2.7; Phil 4.19; Col 1.27.
2.6: Mt 16.27; 1 Cor 3.8; 2 Cor 5.10; Rev 22.12.
2.11: Deut 10.17; 2 Chron 19.7; Gal 2.6; Eph 6.9; Col 3.25; 1 Pet 1.17.   2.12: Rom 3.19; 1 Cor 9.21.
2.13: Jas 1.22-23, 25.
2.16: Eccles 12.14; Rom 16.25; 1 Cor 4.5.   2.18: Phil 1.10.

approve what is excellent, because you are instructed in the law, ¹⁹and if you are sure that you are a guide to the blind, a light to those who are in darkness, ²⁰a corrector of the foolish, a teacher of children, having in the law the embodiment of knowledge and truth—²¹you then who teach others, will you not teach yourself? While you preach against stealing, do you steal? ²²You who say that one must not commit adultery, do you commit adultery? You who abhor idols, do you rob temples? ²³You who boast in the law, do you dishonor God by breaking the law? ²⁴For, as it is written, "The name of God is blasphemed among the Gentiles because of you."

25 Circumcision indeed is of value if you obey the law; but if you break the law, your circumcision becomes uncircumcision. ²⁶So, if a man who is uncircumcised keeps the precepts of the law, will not his uncircumcision be regarded as circumcision? ²⁷Then those who are physically uncircumcised but keep the law will condemn you who have the written code and circumcision but break the law. ²⁸For he is not a real Jew who is one outwardly, nor is true circumcision something external and physical. ²⁹He is a Jew who is one inwardly, and real circumcision is a matter of the heart, spiritual and not literal. His praise is not from men but from God.

3 Then what advantage has the Jew? Or what is the value of circumcision? ²Much in every way. To begin with, the Jews are entrusted with the oracles of God. ³What if some were unfaithful? Does their faithlessness nullify the faithfulness of God? ⁴By no means! Let God be true though every men be false, as it is written, "That thou mayest be justified in thy words, and prevail when thou art judged." ⁵But if our wickedness serves to show the justice of God, what shall we say? That God is unjust to inflict wrath on us? (I speak in a human way.) ⁶By no means! For then how could God judge the world? ⁷But if through my falsehood God's truthfulness abounds to his glory, why am I still being condemned as a sinner? ⁸And why not do evil that good may come?—as some people slanderously charge us with saying. Their condemnation is just.

9 What then? Are we Jews any better off?ᶜ No, not at all; for I ᵈ have already charged that all men, both Jews and Greeks, are under the power of sin, ¹⁰as it is written:
"None is righteous, no, not one;
¹¹no one understands, no one seeks for God.
¹²All have turned aside, together they have gone wrong;
no one does good, not even one."
¹³"Their throat is an open grave,
they use their tongues to deceive."
"The venom of asps is under their lips."
¹⁴"Their mouth is full of curses and bitterness."
¹⁵"Their feet are swift to shed blood,
¹⁶in their paths are ruin and misery,
¹⁷and the way of peace they do not know."
¹⁸"There is no fear of God before their eyes."

19 Now we know that whatever the law says it speaks to those who are under the law, so that every mouth may be stopped, and the whole world may be held accountable to God. ²⁰For no human being will be justified in his sight by works of the law, since through the law comes knowledge of sin.

21 But now the righteousness of God has been manifested apart from law, although the law and the prophets bear witness to it, ²²the righteousness of God through faith in Jesus Christ for all who believe. For there is no distinction; ²³since all have sinned and fall short of the glory of God, ²⁴they are justified by his grace as a gift, through the redemption which is in Christ Jesus, ²⁵whom God put forward as an expiation by his blood, to be received by faith. This was to show God's righteousness, because in his divine forbearance he had passed over former sins; ²⁶it was to prove at the present

ᶜOr *at any disadvantage?* ᵈGreek *we*
2.20: Rom 6.17; 2 Tim 1.13. 2.21: Mt 23.3-4.
2.24: Is 52.5.
2.25: Jer 9.25. 2.26: 1 Cor 7.19; Acts 10.35.
2.27: Mt 12.41. 2.28: Mt 3.9; Jn 8.39; Rom 9.6-7; Gal 6.15.
2.29: 2 Cor 3.6; Phil 3.3; Col 2.11; 1 Pet 3.4.
3.2: Ps 147.19; Rom 9.4. 3.4: Ps 51.4.
3.5: Rom 5.9; 6.19; 1 Cor 9.8; Gal 3.15. 3.8: Rom 6.1, 15.
3.9: Rom 1.18-32; 2.1-29; 11.32; 3.23.
3.10-12: Ps 14.1-3; 53.1-3. 3.13: Ps 5.9; 140.3.
3.14: Ps 10.7. 3.15-17: Is 59.7-8. 3.18: Ps 36.1.
3.19: Rom 2.12.
3.20: Ps 143.2; Acts 13.39; Gal 2.16; 3.11; Rom 7.7.
3.21: Rom 1.17; Phil 3.9; 2 Pet 1.1.
3.22: Rom 4.5; 9.30; 10.12; Gal 2.16. 3.23: Rom 3.9.
3.24: Rom 4.16; 5.9; Eph 2.8; Tit 3.7; Eph 1.7; Col 1.14;
Heb 9.15. 3.26: 1 Jn 2.2; Col 1.20.

time that he himself is righteous and that he justifies him who has faith in Jesus.

27 Then what becomes of our boasting? It is excluded. On what principle? On the principle of works? No, but on the principle of faith. ²⁸For we hold that a man is justified by faith apart from works of law. ²⁹Or is God the God of Jews only? Is he not the God of Gentiles also? Yes, of Gentiles also, ³⁰since God is one; and he will justify the circumcised on the ground of their faith and the uncircumcised through their faith. ³¹Do we then overthrow the law by this faith? By no means! On the contrary, we uphold the law.

4 What then shall we say about*ᵉ* Abraham, our forefather according to the flesh? ²For if Abraham was justified by works, he has something to boast about, but not before God. ³For what does the scripture say? "Abraham believed God, and it was reckoned to him as righteousness." ⁴Now to one who works, his wages are not reckoned as a gift but as his due. ⁵And to one who does not work but trusts him who justifies the ungodly, his faith is reckoned as righteousness. ⁶So also David pronounces a blessing upon the man to whom God reckons righteousness apart from works:

⁷"Blessed are those whose iniquities are forgiven, and whose sins are covered;
⁸blessed is the man against whom the Lord will not reckon his sin."

9 Is this blessing pronounced only upon the circumcised, or also upon the uncircumcised? We say that faith was reckoned to Abraham as righteousness. ¹⁰How then was it reckoned to him? Was it before or after he had been circumcised? It was not after, but before he was circumcised. ¹¹He received circumcision as a sign or seal of the righteousness which he had by faith while he was still uncircumcised. The purpose was to make him the father of all who believe without being circumcised and who thus have righteousness reckoned to them, ¹²and likewise the father of the circumcised who are not merely circumcised but also follow the example of the faith which our father Abraham had before he was circumcised.

13 The promise to Abraham and his descendants, that they should inherit the world, did not come through the law but through the righteousness of faith. ¹⁴If it is the adherents of the law who are to be the heirs, faith is null and the promise is void. ¹⁵For the law brings wrath, but where there is no law there is no transgression.

16 That is why it depends on faith, in order that the promise may rest on grace and be guaranteed to all his descendants—not only to the adherents of the law but also to those who share the faith of Abraham, for he is the father of us all, ¹⁷as it is written, "I have made you the father of many nations"—in the presence of the God in whom he believed, who gives life to the dead and calls into existence the things that do not exist. ¹⁸In hope he believed against hope, that he should become the father of many nations; as he had been told, "So shall your descendants be." ¹⁹He did not weaken in faith when he considered his own body, which was as good as dead because he was about a hundred years old, or when he considered the barrenness of Sarah's womb. ²⁰No distrust made him waver concerning the promise of God, but he grew strong in his faith as he gave glory to God, ²¹fully convinced that God was able to do what he had promised. ²²That is why his faith was "reckoned to him as righteousness." ²³But the words, "it was reckoned to him," were written not for his sake alone, ²⁴but for ours also. It will be reckoned to us who believe in him that raised from the dead Jesus our Lord, ²⁵who was put to death for our trespasses and raised for our justification.

5 Therefore, since we are justified by faith, we*ʲ* have peace with God through our Lord Jesus Christ. ²Through him we have obtained access*ᵍ* to this grace in which we stand, and we*ʰ* rejoice in our hope of sharing the glory of God. ³More than that, we*ʰ*

*ᵉ*Other ancient authorities read *was gained by*
*ʲ*Other ancient authorities read *let us*
*ᵍ*Other ancient authorities add *by faith* *ʰ*Or *let us*

3.28: Acts 13.39; Rom 5.1; Eph 2.9.
3.29: Rom 9.24; Acts 10.34-35.   3.30: Rom 4.11-12, 16.
3.31: Rom 8.4; Mt 5.17. 4.2: 1 Cor 1.31.
4.3: Gen 15.6; Rom 4.9, 22; Gal 3.6; Jas 2.23.
4.4: Rom 11.6. 4.5: Rom 3.22. 4.7: Ps 32.1-2.
4.11: Gen 17.10; Rom 3.22, 30.
4.13: Gen 17.4-6; 22.17-18; Gal 3.29. 4.14: Gal 3.18.
4.15: Gal 3.10. 4.17: Gen 17.5; Jn 5.21. 4.18: Gen 15.5.
4.19: Heb 11.12; Gen 17.17; 18.11. 4.22: Rom 4.3.
4.23-24: Rom 15.4; 1 Cor 9.10; 10.11. 4.25: Rom 8.32.
5.1: Rom 3.28. 5.2: Eph 2.18; 3.12; Heb 10.19-20.
5.3: Rom 5.11; 2 Cor 12.10; Jas 1.3.

rejoice in our sufferings, knowing that suffering produces endurance, [4] and endurance produces character, and character produces hope, [5] and hope does not disappoint us, because God's love has been poured into our hearts through the Holy Spirit which has been given to us.

6 While we were still weak, at the right time Christ died for the ungodly. [7] Why, one will hardly die for a righteous man—though perhaps for a good man one will dare even to die. [8] But God shows his love for us in that while we were yet sinners Christ died for us. [9] Since, therefore, we are now justified by his blood, much more shall we be saved by him from the wrath of God. [10] For if while we were enemies we were reconciled to God by the death of his Son, much more, now that we are reconciled, shall we be saved by his life. [11] Not only so, but we also rejoice in God through our Lord Jesus Christ, through whom we have now received our reconciliation.

12 Therefore as sin came into the world through one man and death through sin, and so death spread to all men because all men sinned—[13] sin indeed was in the world before the law was given, but sin is not counted where there is no law. [14] Yet death reigned from Adam to Moses, even over those whose sins were not like the transgression of Adam, who was a type of the one who was to come.

15 But the free gift is not like the trespass. For if many died through one man's trespass, much more have the grace of God and the free gift in the grace of that one man Jesus Christ abounded for many. [16] And the free gift is not like the effect of that one man's sin. For the judgment following one trespass brought condemnation, but the free gift following many trespasses brings justification. [17] If, because of one man's trespass, death reigned through that one man, much more will those who receive the abundance of grace and the free gift of righteousness reign in life through the one man Jesus Christ.

18 Then as one man's trespass led to condemnation for all men, so one man's act of righteousness leads to acquittal and life for all men. [19] For as by one man's disobedience many were made sinners, so by one man's obedience many will be made righteous. [20] Law came in, to increase the trespass; but where sin increased, grace abounded all the more, [21] so that, as sin reigned in death, grace also might reign through righteousness to eternal life through Jesus Christ our Lord.

6 What shall we say then? Are we to continue in sin that grace may abound? [2] By no means! How can we who died to sin still live in it? [3] Do you not know that all of us who have been baptized into Christ Jesus were baptized into his death? [4] We were buried therefore with him by baptism into death, so that as Christ was raised from the dead by the glory of the Father, we too might walk in newness of life.

5 For if we have been united with him in a death like his, we shall certainly be united with him in a resurrection like his. [6] We know that our old self was crucified with him so that the sinful body might be destroyed, and we might no longer be enslaved to sin. [7] For he who has died is freed from sin. [8] But if we have died with Christ, we believe that we shall also live with him. [9] For we know that Christ being raised from the dead will never die again; death no longer has dominion over him. [10] The death he died he died to sin, once for all, but the life he lives he lives to God. [11] So you also must consider yourselves dead to sin and alive to God in Christ Jesus.

12 Let not sin therefore reign in your mortal bodies, to make you obey their passions. [13] Do not yield your members to sin as instruments of wickedness, but yield yourselves to God as men who have been brought from death to life, and your members to God as instruments of righteousness. [14] For sin will have no dominion over you, since you are not under law but under grace.

5.5: Ps 119.116; Acts 2.33; Phil 1.20.
5.8: Jn 15.13; Rom 8.32; 1 Pet 3.18; 1 Jn 3.16; 4.10.
5.9: Rom 3.5, 24-25; Eph 1.7; 1 Thess 1.10.
5.10: Col 1.21.   **5.11:** Rom 5.3.
5.12: 1 Cor 15.21-22; Rom 6.23; Jas 1.15.
5.14: 1 Cor 15.22, 45.   **5.15:** Acts 15.11.   **5.16:** Rom 8.1.
5.19: Phil 2.8.
5.20: Rom 7.7-8; Gal 3.19; 1 Tim 1.14.   **5.21:** Rom 6.23.
6.1: Rom 3.8; 6.15.
6.2: Rom 7.4, 6; Gal 2.19; 1 Pet 2.24.
6.3: Acts 2.38; 8.16; 19.5.   **6.4:** Col 2.12.
6.5: 2 Cor 4.10; Col 2.12.   **6.6:** Rom 7.24; Col 2.13.
6.7: 1 Pet 4.1.   **6.8:** 2 Tim 2.11.   **6.9:** Acts 2.24; Rev 1.18.
6.11: Rom 7.4, 6; Gal 2.19; 1 Pet 2.24.
6.13: Rom 6.19; 7.5; 12.1.   **6.14:** Rom 8.2.

15 What then? Are we to sin because we are not under law but under grace? By no means! [16]Do you not know that if you yield yourselves to any one as obedient slaves, you are slaves of the one whom you obey, either of sin, which leads to death, or of obedience, which leads to righteousness? [17]But thanks be to God, that you who were once slaves of sin have become obedient from the heart to the standard of teaching to which you were committed, [18]and, having been set free from sin, have become slaves of righteousness. [19]I am speaking in human terms, because of your natural limitations. For just as you once yielded your members to impurity and to greater and greater iniquity, so now yield your members to righteousness for sanctification.

20 When you were slaves of sin, you were free in regard to righteousness. [21]But then what return did you get from the things of which you are now ashamed? The end of those things is death. [22]But now that you have been set free from sin and have become slaves of God, the return you get is sanctification and its end, eternal life. [23]For the wages of sin is death, but the free gift of God is eternal life in Christ Jesus our Lord.

7 Do you not know, brethren—for I am speaking to those who know the law—that the law is binding on a person only during his life? [2]Thus a married woman is bound by law to her husband as long as he lives; but if her husband dies she is discharged from the law concerning the husband. [3]Accordingly, she will be called an adulteress if she lives with another man while her husband is alive. But if her husband dies she is free from that law, and if she marries another man she is not an adulteress.

4 Likewise, my brethren, you have died to the law through the body of Christ, so that you may belong to another, to him who has been raised from the dead in order that we may bear fruit for God. [5]While we were living in the flesh, our sinful passions, aroused by the law, were at work in our members to bear fruit for death. [6]But now we are discharged from the law, dead to that which held us captive, so that we serve not under the old written code but in the new life of the Spirit.

7 What then shall we say? That the law is sin? By no means! Yet, if it had not been for the law, I should not have known sin. I should not have known what it is to covet if the law had not said, "You shall not covet." [8]But sin, finding opportunity in the commandment, wrought in me all kinds of covetousness. Apart from the law sin lies dead. [9]I was once alive apart from the law, but when the commandment came, sin revived and I died; [10]the very commandment which promised life proved to be death to me. [11]For sin, finding opportunity in the commandment, deceived me and by it killed me. [12]So the law is holy, and the commandment is holy and just and good.

13 Did that which is good, then, bring death to me? By no means! It was sin, working death in me through what is good, in order that sin might be shown to be sin, and through the commandment might become sinful beyond measure. [14]We know that the law is spiritual; but I am carnal, sold under sin. [15]I do not understand my own actions. For I do not do what I want, but I do the very thing I hate. [16]Now if I do what I do not want, I agree that the law is good. [17]So then it is no longer I that do it, but sin which dwells within me. [18]For I know that nothing good dwells within me, that is, in my flesh. I can will what is right, but I cannot do it. [19]For I do not do the good I want, but the evil I do not want is what I do. [20]Now if I do what I do not want, it is no longer I that do it, but sin which dwells within me.

21 So I find it to be a law that when I want to do right, evil lies close at hand. [22]For I delight in the law of God, in my inmost self, [23]but I see in my members another law at war with the law of my mind and making me captive to the law of sin which dwells in my members. [24]Wretched man that I am! Who will deliver me from this body of death? [25]Thanks be to God through Jesus Christ our Lord! So then, I of my-

6.15: Rom 3.8; 6.1.   6.16: Mt 6.24; Jn 8.34; Rom 12.1.
6.18: Rom 8.2.   6.19: Rom 3.5; 6.13; 12.1.
6.20: Mt 6.24; Jn 8.34.   6.21: Rom 7.5; 8.6, 13, 21.
6.23: Rom 5.12, 21; Gal 6.7, 8.   7.2: 1 Cor 7.39.
7.4: Rom 6.2, 11; Gal 2.19; Col 1.22.
7.5: Rom 6.13, 21; 8.8; Jas 1.15.
7.7: Rom 3.20; 5.20; Ex 20.17; Deut 5.21.
7.8: 1 Cor 15.56.   7.10: Lev 18.5; Rom 10.5.
7.12: 1 Tim 1.8.   7.14: 1 Cor 3.1.   7.15: Gal 5.17.
7.22: Ps 1.2.   7.23: Gal 5.17.   7.24: Rom 6.6; Col 2.11.

self serve the law of God with my mind, but with my flesh I serve the law of sin.

8 There is therefore now no condemnation for those who are in Christ Jesus. ²For the law of the Spirit of life in Christ Jesus has set me free from the law of sin and death. ³For God has done what the law, weakened by the flesh, could not do: sending his own Son in the likeness of sinful flesh and for sin,ⁱ he condemned sin in the flesh, in order that the just requirement of the law might be fulfilled in us, who walk not according to the flesh but according to the Spirit. ⁵For those who live according to the flesh set their minds on the things of the flesh, but those who live according to the Spirit set their minds on the things of the Spirit. ⁶To set the mind on the flesh is death, but to set the mind on the Spirit is life and peace. ⁷For the mind that is set on the flesh is hostile to God; it does not submit to God's law, indeed it cannot; ⁸and those who are in the flesh cannot please God.

9 But you are not in the flesh, you are in the Spirit, if in fact the Spirit of God dwells in you. Any one who does not have the Spirit of Christ does not belong to him. ¹⁰But if Christ is in you, although your bodies are dead because of sin, your spirits are alive because of righteousness. ¹¹If the Spirit of him who raised Jesus from the dead dwells in you, he who raised Christ Jesus from the dead will give life to your mortal bodies also through his Spirit which dwells in you.

12 So then, brethren, we are debtors, not to the flesh, to live according to the flesh—¹³for if you live according to the flesh you will die, but if by the Spirit you put to death the deeds of the body you will live. ¹⁴For all who are led by the Spirit of God are sons of God. ¹⁵For you did not receive the spirit of slavery to fall back into fear, but you have received the spirit of sonship. When we cry, "Ăb′bạ! Father!" ¹⁶it is the Spirit himself bearing witness with our spirit that we are children of God, ¹⁷and if children, then heirs, heirs of God and fellow heirs with Christ, provided we suffer with him in order that we may also be glorified with him.

18 I consider that the sufferings of this present time are not worth comparing with the glory that is to be revealed to us. ¹⁹For the creation waits with eager longing for the revealing of the sons of God; ²⁰for the creation was subjected to futility, not of its own will but by the will of him who subjected it in hope; ²¹because the creation itself will be set free from its bondage to decay and obtain the glorious liberty of the children of God. ²²We know that the whole creation has been groaning in travail together until now; ²³and not only the creation, but we ourselves, who have the first fruits of the Spirit, groan inwardly as we wait for adoption as sons, the redemption of our bodies. ²⁴For in this hope we were saved. Now hope that is seen is not hope. For who hopes for what he sees? ²⁵But if we hope for what we do not see, we wait for it with patience.

26 Likewise the Spirit helps us in our weakness; for we do not know how to pray as we ought, but the Spirit himself intercedes for us with sighs too deep for words. ²⁷And he who searches the hearts of men knows what is the mind of the Spirit, becauseʲ the Spirit intercedes for the saints according to the will of God.

28 We know that in everything God works for goodᵏ with those who love him,ˡ who are called according to his purpose. ²⁹For those whom he foreknew he also predestined to be conformed to the image of his Son, in order that he might be the first-born among many brethren. ³⁰And those whom he predestined he also called; and those whom he called he also justified; and those whom he justified he also glorified.

31 What then shall we say to this? If God is for us, who is against us? ³²He who did not spare his own Son but gave him up for us all, will he not also give

ⁱOr *and as a sin offering*
ʲOr *that*
ᵏOther ancient authorities read *in everything he works for good,* or *everything works for good* ˡGreek *God*

8.1: Rom 5.16.   **8.2:** 1 Cor 15.45; Rom 6.14, 18.
8.3: Acts 13.39; Heb 7.18; 10.1-2; Phil 2.7; Heb 2.14.
8.4: Rom 3.31; Gal 5.16, 25.   **8.5:** Gal 5.19-25.
8.6: Rom 6.21; 8.13, 27; Gal 6.8.   **8.8:** Rom 7.5.
8.9: 1 Cor 3.16; 6.19; 2 Cor 6.16; 2 Tim 1.14.
8.10: Gal 2.20; Eph 3.17.   **8.11:** Jn 5.21.
8.13: Rom 8.6; Col 3.5.   **8.14:** Gal 5.18.
8.15: Rom 9.4; Gal 4.5-7; Mk 14.36.   **8.16:** Acts 5.32.
8.17: Gal 3.29; 4.7; 2 Cor 1.5, 7; 2 Tim 2.12; 1 Pet 4.13.
8.18: 2 Cor 4.17; Col 3.4; 1 Pet 5.1.
8.19: 1 Pet 1.7, 13; 1 Jn 3.2.   **8.20:** Eccles 1.2.
8.21: Acts 3.21; Rom 6.21; 2 Pet 3.13; Rev 21.1.
8.22: Jer 12.4, 11.   **8.23:** 2 Cor 1.22; 5.2, 4; Gal 5.5.
8.24: 2 Cor 5.7; Heb 11.1.
8.27: Ps 139.1-2; Lk 16.15; Rev 2.23; Rom 8.6, 34.
8.29: Rom 9.23; 11.2; 1 Pet 1.2, 20; Eph 1.5, 11.
8.31: Ps 118.6.   **8.32:** Jn 3.16; Rom 4.25; 5.8.

us all things with him? [33] Who shall bring any charge against God's elect? It is God who justifies; [34] who is to condemn? Is it Christ Jesus, who died, yes, who was raised from the dead, who is at the right hand of God, who indeed intercedes for us?[m] [35] Who shall separate us from the love of Christ? Shall tribulation, or distress, or persecution, or famine, or nakedness, or peril, or sword? [36] As it is written,

"For thy sake we are being killed all the day long;
we are regarded as sheep to be slaughtered."

[37] No, in all these things we are more than conquerors through him who loved us. [38] For I am sure that neither death, nor life, nor angels, nor principalities, nor things present, nor things to come, nor powers, [39] nor height, nor depth, nor anything else in all creation, will be able to separate us from the love of God in Christ Jesus our Lord.

9 I am speaking the truth in Christ, I am not lying; my conscience bears me witness in the Holy Spirit, [2] that I have great sorrow and unceasing anguish in my heart. [3] For I could wish that I myself were accursed and cut off from Christ for the sake of my brethren, my kinsmen by race. [4] They are Israelites, and to them belong the sonship, the glory, the covenants, the giving of the law, the worship, and the promises; [5] to them belong the patriarchs, and of their race, according to the flesh, is the Christ. God who is over all be blessed for ever.[n] Amen.

[6] But it is not as though the word of God had failed. For not all who are descended from Israel belong to Israel, [7] and not all are children of Abraham because they are his descendants; but "Through Isaac shall your descendants be named." [8] This means that it is not the children of the flesh who are the children of God, but the children of the promise are reckoned as descendants. [9] For this is what the promise said, "About this time I will return and Sarah shall have a son." [10] And not only so, but also when Rebecca had conceived children by one man, our forefather Isaac, [11] though they were not yet born and had done nothing either good or bad, in order that God's purpose of election might continue, not because of works but because of his call, [12] she was told, "The elder will serve the younger." [13] As it is written, "Jacob I loved, but Esau I hated."

[14] What shall we say then? Is there injustice on God's part? By no means! [15] For he says to Moses, "I will have mercy on whom I have mercy, and will have compassion on whom I have compassion." [16] So it depends not upon man's will or exertion, but upon God's mercy. [17] For the scripture says to Pharaoh, "I have raised you up for the very purpose of showing my power in you, so that my name may be proclaimed in all the earth." [18] So then he has mercy upon whomever he wills, and he hardens the heart of whomever he wills.

[19] You will say to me then, "Why does he still find fault? For who can resist his will?" [20] But who are you, a man, to answer back to God? Will what is molded say to its molder, "Why have you made me thus?" [21] Has the potter no right over the clay, to make out of the same lump one vessel for beauty and another for menial use? [22] What if God, desiring to show his wrath and to make known his power, has endured with much patience the vessels of wrath made for destruction, [23] in order to make known the riches of his glory for the vessels of mercy, which he has prepared beforehand for glory, [24] even us whom he has called, not from the Jews only but also from the Gentiles? [25] As indeed he says in Hō·ṣē'a,

"Those who were not my people
I will call 'my people,'
and her who was not beloved
I will call 'my beloved.'"
[26] "And in the very place where it was said to them, 'You are not my people,'
they will be called 'sons of the living God.'"

[27] And Ī·sāi'ah cries out concerning

---

[m] Or *It is Christ Jesus ... for us*
[n] Or *Christ, who is God over all, blessed for ever*
8.33: Lk 18.7; Is 50.8-9.　8.34: Rom 8.27.　8.36: Ps 44.22.
8.37: 1 Cor 15.57.　9.3: Ex 32.32.　9.4: Rom 3.2; 8.15.
9.6: Rom 2.28-29.　9.7: Gen 21.12; Heb 11.18.
9.8: Gal 3.29; 4.28.　9.9: Gen 18.10.　9.10: Gen 25.21.
9.12: Gen 25.23.　9.13: Mal 1.2-3.　9.14: 2 Chron 19.7.
9.15: Ex 33.19.　9.17: Ex 9.16.　9.18: Rom 11.7.
9.20: Is 29.16; 45.9.　9.21: 2 Tim 2.20.
9.22: Prov 16.4.　9.23: Rom 8.29.　9.24: Rom 3.29.
9.25: Hos 2.23; 1 Pet 2.10.　9.26: Hos 1.10.
9.27: Is 10.22-23; Gen 22.17; Hos 1.10; Rom 11.5; 2 Kgs 19.4; Is 11.11.

Israel: "Though the number of the sons of Israel be as the sand of the sea, only a remnant of them will be saved; ²⁸for the Lord will execute his sentence upon the earth with rigor and dispatch." ²⁹And as Ī·sāi'ah predicted,
"If the Lord of hosts had not left us children,
we would have fared like Sŏd'ọm and been made like Gọ·môr'rah."
30 What shall we say, then? That Gentiles who did not pursue righteousness have attained it, that is, righteousness through faith; ³¹but that Israel who pursued the righteousness which is based on law did not succeed in fulfilling that law. ³²Why? Because they did not pursue it through faith, but as if it were based on works. They have stumbled over the stumbling stone, ³³as it is written,
"Behold, I am laying in Zion a stone
that will make men stumble,
a rock that will make them fall;
and he who believes in him will not be put to shame."

10 Brethren, my heart's desire and prayer to God for them is that they may be saved. ²I bear them witness that they have a zeal for God, but it is not enlightened. ³For, being ignorant of the righteousness that comes from God, and seeking to establish their own, they did not submit to God's righteousness. ⁴For Christ is the end of the law, that every one who has faith may be justified.

5 Moses writes that the man who practices the righteousness which is based on the law shall live by it. ⁶But the righteousness based on faith says, Do not say in your heart, "Who will ascend into heaven?" (that is, to bring Christ down) ⁷or "Who will descend into the abyss?" (that is, to bring Christ up from the dead). ⁸But what does it say? The word is near you, on your lips and in your heart (that is, the word of faith which we preach); ⁹because, if you confess with your lips that Jesus is Lord and believe in your heart that God raised him from the dead, you will be saved. ¹⁰For man believes with his heart and so is justified, and he confesses with his lips and so is saved. ¹¹The scripture says, "No one who believes in him will be put to shame." ¹²For there is no distinction between Jew and Greek; the

same Lord is Lord of all and bestows his riches upon all who call upon him. ¹³For, "every one who calls upon the name of the Lord will be saved."

14 But how are men to call upon him in whom they have not believed? And how are they to believe in him of whom they have never heard? And how are they to hear without a preacher? ¹⁵And how can men preach unless they are sent? As it is written, "How beautiful are the feet of those who preach good news!" ¹⁶But they have not all obeyed the gospel; for Ī·sāi'ah says, "Lord, who has believed what he has heard from us?" ¹⁷So faith comes from what is heard, and what is heard comes by the preaching of Christ.

18 But I ask, have they not heard? Indeed they have; for
"Their voice has gone out to all the earth,
and their words to the ends of the world."
¹⁹Again I ask, did Israel not understand? First Moses says,
"I will make you jealous of those who are not a nation;
with a foolish nation I will make you angry."
²⁰Then Ī·sāi'ah is so bold as to say,
"I have been found by those who did not seek me;
I have shown myself to those who did not ask for me."
²¹But of Israel he says, "All day long I have held out my hands to a disobedient and contrary people."

11 I ask, then, has God rejected his people? By no means! I myself am an Israelite, a descendant of Abraham, a member of the tribe of Benjamin. ²God has not rejected his people whom he foreknew. Do you not know what the scripture says of Ē·lī'jah, how he pleads with God

9.29: Is 1.9.
9.30: Rom 3.22; 10.6, 20; Gal 2.16; 3.24; Phil 3.9; Heb 11.7.
9.31: Is 51.1; Rom 10.2-3; 11.7.   9.32: 1 Pet 2.8.
9.33: Is 28.16; Rom 10.11.   10.2-4: Rom 9.31.
10.3: Rom 1.17.   10.4: Gal 3.24; Rom 3.22; 7.1-4.
10.5: Lev 18.5; Neh 9.29; Ezek 20.11, 13, 21; Rom 7.10.
10.6: Deut 30.12-13; Rom 9.30.
10.8: Deut 30.14.
10.9: Mt 10.32; Lk 12.8; Acts 16.31.
10.11: Is 28.16; Rom 9.33.
10.13: Joel 2.32; Acts 2.21.
10.15: Is 52.7.   10.16: Is 53.1; Jn 12.38.
10.18: Ps 19.4; Col 1.6, 23.
10.19: Deut 32.21; Rom 11.11, 14.
10.20: Is 65.1; Rom 9.30.   10.21: Is 65.2.
11.1: 1 Sam 12.22; Jer 31.37; 33.24-26; 2 Cor 11.22; Phil 3.5.   11.2: Ps 94.14; 1 Kings 19.10.

against Israel? ³"Lord, they have killed thy prophets, they have demolished thy altars, and I alone am left, and they seek my life." ⁴But what is God's reply to him? "I have kept for myself seven thousand men who have not bowed the knee to Bā'al." ⁵So too at the present time there is a remnant, chosen by grace. ⁶But if it is by grace, it is no longer on the basis of works; otherwise grace would no longer be grace.

7 What then? Israel failed to obtain what it sought. The elect obtained it, but the rest were hardened, ⁸as it is written,

"God gave them a spirit of stupor,
eyes that should not see and ears
   that should not hear,
down to this very day."

⁹And David says,
"Let their table become a snare and
   a trap,
a pitfall and a retribution for them;
¹⁰let their eyes be darkened so that
   they cannot see,
and bend their backs for ever."

11 So I ask, have they stumbled so as to fall? By no means! But through their trespass salvation has come to the Gentiles, so as to make Israel jealous. ¹²Now if their trespass means riches for the world, and if their failure means riches for the Gentiles, how much more will their full inclusion mean!

13 Now I am speaking to you Gentiles. Inasmuch then as I am an apostle to the Gentiles, I magnify my ministry ¹⁴in order to make my fellow Jews jealous, and thus save some of them. ¹⁵For if their rejection means the reconciliation of the world, what will their acceptance mean but life from the dead? ¹⁶If the dough offered as first fruits is holy, so is the whole lump; and if the root is holy, so are the branches.

17 But if some of the branches were broken off, and you, a wild olive shoot, were grafted in their place to share the richness*ᵒ* of the olive tree, ¹⁸do not boast over the branches. If you do boast, remember it is not you that support the root, but the root that supports you. ¹⁹You will say, "Branches were broken off so that I might be grafted in." ²⁰That is true. They were broken off because of their unbelief, but you stand fast only through faith.

So do not become proud, but stand in awe. ²¹For if God did not spare the natural branches, neither will he spare you. ²²Note then the kindness and the severity of God: severity toward those who have fallen, but God's kindness to you, provided you continue in his kindness; otherwise you too will be cut off. ²³And even the others, if they do not persist in their unbelief, will be grafted in, for God has the power to graft them in again. ²⁴For if you have been cut from what is by nature a wild olive tree, and grafted, contrary to nature, into a cultivated olive tree, how much more will these natural branches be grafted back into their own olive tree.

25 Lest you be wise in your own conceits, I want you to understand this mystery, brethren: a hardening has come upon part of Israel, until the full number of the Gentiles come in, ²⁶and so all Israel will be saved; as it is written,

"The Deliverer will come from Zion,
he will banish ungodliness from
   Jacob";
²⁷"and this will be my covenant with
   them
when I take away their sins."
²⁸As regards the gospel they are enemies of God, for your sake; but as regards election they are beloved for the sake of their forefathers. ²⁹For the gifts and the call of God are irrevocable. ³⁰Just as you were once disobedient to God but now have received mercy because of their disobedience, ³¹so they have now been disobedient in order that by the mercy shown to you they also may*ᵖ* receive mercy. ³²For God has consigned all men to disobedience, that he may have mercy upon all.

33 O the depth of the riches and wisdom and knowledge of God! How unsearchable are his judgments and how inscrutable his ways! ³⁴"For who has known the mind of the Lord,

*ᵒ*Other ancient authorities read *rich root*
*ᵖ*Other ancient authorities add *now*   **11.4:** 1 Kings 19.18
11.5: 2 Kings 19.4; Is 11.11; Rom 9.27.   **11.6:** Rom 4.4.
11.7: Rom 9.18, 31; 11.25.
11.8: Is 29.10; Deut 29.4; Mt 13.13-14.   **11.9:** Ps 69.22-23.
11.11: Rom 10.19; 11.14.   **11.13:** Acts 9.15.
11.14: Rom 10.19; 11.11; 1 Cor 9.22.
11.15: Lk 15.24, 32.   **11.20:** 2 Cor 1.24.
11.25: 1 Cor 2.7-10; Eph 3.3-5, 9; Rom 9.18; 11.7; Lk 21.24.
11.26: Is 59.20-21.   **11.27:** Jer 31.33; Is 27.9.
11.32: Rom 3.9; Gal 3.22-29.   **11.33:** Col 2.3.
11.34: Is 40.13-14; 1 Cor 2.16.

or who has been his counselor?"
35 "Or who has given a gift to him that he might be repaid?"
36 For from him and through him and to him are all things. To him be glory for ever. Amen.

12 I appeal to you therefore, brethren, by the mercies of God, to present your bodies as a living sacrifice, holy and acceptable to God, which is your spiritual worship. 2 Do not be conformed to this world*q* but be transformed by the renewal of your mind, that you may prove what is the will of God, what is good and acceptable and perfect.*r*
3 For by the grace given to me I bid every one among you not to think of himself more highly than he ought to think, but to think with sober judgment, each according to the measure of faith which God has assigned him. 4 For as in one body we have many members, and all the members do not have the same function, 5 so we, though many, are one body in Christ, and individually members one of another. 6 Having gifts that differ according to the grace given to us, let us use them: if prophecy, in proportion to our faith; 7 if service, in our serving; he who teaches, in his teaching; 8 he who exhorts, in his exhortation; he who contributes, in liberality; he who gives aid, with zeal; he who does acts of mercy, with cheerfulness.
9 Let love be genuine; hate what is evil, hold fast to what is good; 10 love one another with brotherly affection; outdo one another in showing honor. 11 Never flag in zeal, be aglow with the Spirit, serve the Lord. 12 Rejoice in your hope, be patient in tribulation, constant in prayer. 13 Contribute to the needs of the saints, practice hospitality.
14 Bless those who persecute you; bless and do not curse them. 15 Rejoice with those who rejoice, weep with those who weep. 16 Live in harmony with one another; do not be haughty, but associate with the lowly;*s* never be conceited. 17 Repay no one evil for evil, but take thought for what is noble in the sight of all. 18 If possible, so far as it depends upon you, live peaceably with all. 19 Beloved, never avenge yourselves, but leave it*t* to the wrath of God; for it is written, "Vengeance is mine, I will repay, says the

Lord." 20 No, "if your enemy is hungry, feed him; if he is thirsty, give him drink; for by so doing you will heap burning coals upon his head." 21 Do not be overcome by evil, but overcome evil with good.

13 Let every person be subject to the governing authorities. For there is no authority except from God, and those that exist have been instituted by God. 2 Therefore he who resists the authorities resists what God has appointed, and those who resist will incur judgment. 3 For rulers are not a terror to good conduct, but to bad. Would you have no fear of him who is in authority? Then do what is good, and you will receive his approval, 4 for he is God's servant for your good. But if you do wrong, be afraid, for he does not bear the sword in vain; he is the servant of God to execute his wrath on the wrongdoer. 5 Therefore one must be subject, not only to avoid God's wrath but also for the sake of conscience. 6 For the same reason you also pay taxes, for the authorities are ministers of God, attending to this very thing. 7 Pay all of them their dues, taxes to whom taxes are due, revenue to whom revenue is due, respect to whom respect is due, honor to whom honor is due.
8 Owe no one anything, except to love one another; for he who loves his neighbor has fulfilled the law. 9 The commandments, "You shall not commit adultery, You shall not kill, You shall not steal, You shall not covet," and any other commandment, are summed up in this sentence, "You shall love your neighbor as yourself." 10 Love does no wrong to a neighbor;

q Greek *age*
r Or *what is the good and acceptable and perfect will of God* *s* Or *give yourselves to humble tasks*
t Greek *give place*   **11.35:** Job 35.7; 41.11.
11.36: 1 Cor 8.6; 11.12; Col 1.16; Heb 2.10.
12.1: Rom 6.13, 16, 19; 1 Pet 2.5.
12.2: 1 Jn 2.15; Eph 4.23; 5.10.
12.4: 1 Cor 12.12-14; Eph 4.4, 16.
12.5: 1 Cor 10.17; 12.20, 27; Eph 4.25.
12.6-8: 1 Cor 7.7; 12.4-11; 1 Pet 4.10-11.
12.12: Acts 1.14; Rom 5.2; 1 Thess 5.17.
12.14: Mt 5.44; Lk 6.28.
12.16: Rom 11.25; 15.5; 1 Cor 1.10; 2 Cor 13.11; Phil 2.2; 4.2; Prov 3.7; 26.12.
12.17: Prov 20.22; 2 Cor 8.21; 1 Thess 5.15.
12.18: Mk 9.50; Rom 14.19.
12.19: Lev 19.18; Deut 32.35; Heb 10.30.
12.20: Prov 25.21-22; Mt 5.44; Lk 6.27.
13.1: Tit 3.1; 1 Pet 2.13-14; Prov 8.15; Jn 19.11.
13.3: 1 Pet 2.14.   **13.4:** 1 Thess 4.6.
13.7: Mt 22.21; Mk 12.17; Lk 20.25.
13.8: Mt 22.39-40; Rom 13.10; Gal 5.14; Col 3.14; Jas 2.8.
13.9: Ex 20.13-14; Deut 5.17-18; Lev 19.18; Mt 19.19.
13.10: Mt 22.39-40; Rom 13.8; Gal 5.14; Jas 2.8.

therefore love is the fulfilling of the law.

11 Besides this you know what hour it is, how it is full time now for you to wake from sleep. For salvation is nearer to us now than when we first believed; ¹²the night is far gone, the day is at hand. Let us then cast off the works of darkness and put on the armor of light; ¹³let us conduct ourselves becomingly as in the day, not in reveling and drunkenness, not in debauchery and licentiousness, not in quarreling and jealousy. ¹⁴But put on the Lord Jesus Christ, and make no provision for the flesh, to gratify its desires.

14 As for the man who is weak in faith, welcome him, but not for disputes over opinions. ²One believes he may eat anything, while the weak man eats only vegetables. ³Let not him who eats despise him who abstains, and let not him who abstains pass judgment on him who eats; for God has welcomed him. ⁴Who are you to pass judgment on the servant of another? It is before his own master that he stands or falls. And he will be upheld, for the Master is able to make him stand.

5 One man esteems one day as better than another, while another man esteems all days alike. Let every one be fully convinced in his own mind. ⁶He who observes the day, observes it in honor of the Lord. He also who eats, eats in honor of the Lord, since he gives thanks to God; while he who abstains, abstains in honor of the Lord and gives thanks to God. ⁷None of us lives to himself, and none of us dies to himself. ⁸If we live, we live to the Lord, and if we die, we die to the Lord; so then, whether we live or whether we die, we are the Lord's. ⁹For to this end Christ died and lived again, that he might be Lord both of the dead and of the living.

10 Why do you pass judgment on your brother? Or you, why do you despise your brother? For we shall all stand before the judgment seat of God; ¹¹for it is written,

"As I live, says the Lord, every knee
    shall bow to me,
and every tongue shall give praise*
    to God."

¹²So each of us shall give account of himself to God.

13 Then let us no more pass judgment on one another, but rather decide never to put a stumbling block or hindrance in the way of a brother. ¹⁴I know and am persuaded in the Lord Jesus that nothing is unclean in itself; but it is unclean for any one who thinks it unclean. ¹⁵If your brother is being injured by what you eat, you are no longer walking in love. Do not let what you eat cause the ruin of one for whom Christ died. ¹⁶So do not let your good be spoken of as evil. ¹⁷For the kingdom of God is not food and drink but righteousness and peace and joy in the Holy Spirit; ¹⁸he who thus serves Christ is acceptable to God and approved by men. ¹⁹Let us then pursue what makes for peace and for mutual upbuilding. ²⁰Do not, for the sake of food, destroy the work of God. Everything is indeed clean, but it is wrong for any one to make others fall by what he eats; ²¹it is right not to eat meat or drink wine or do anything that makes your brother stumble.ᵛ ²²The faith that you have, keep between yourself and God; happy is he who has no reason to judge himself for what he approves. ²³But he who has doubts is condemned, if he eats, because he does not act from faith; for whatever does not proceed from faith is sin.ʷ

15 We who are strong ought to bear with the failings of the weak, and not to please ourselves; ²let each of us please his neighbor for his good, to edify him. ³For Christ did not please himself; but, as it is written, "The reproaches of those who reproached thee fell on me." ⁴For whatever was written in former days was written for our instruction, that by steadfastness and by the encouragement of the scriptures we might have hope. ⁵May the God of steadfastness and encouragement grant you to live

ᵘOr *confess*
ᵛOther ancient authorities add *or be upset or be weakened*
ʷOther authorities, some ancient, insert here Ch. 16.25-27
13.11: Eph 5.14; 1 Thess 5.6.
13.12: 1 Jn 2.8; Eph 5.11; 1 Thess 5.8.
13.13: 1 Thess 4.12; Gal 5.19-21. **13.14:** Gal 3.27; 5.16.
14.3: Col 2.16. **14.5:** Gal 4.10.
14.7: Gal 2.20; 2 Cor 5.15. **14.8:** Phil 1.20.
14.10: 2 Cor 5.10.
14.11: Is 45.23; Phil 2.10-11.
14.13: Mt 7.1; 1 Cor 8.13.
14.15: Rom 14.20; 1 Cor 8.11.
14.16: 1 Cor 10.30.
14.19: Mk 9.50; Rom 12.18; 1 Thess 5.11.
14.20: Rom 14.15; 1 Cor 8.9-12. **14.21:** 1 Cor 8.13.
14.22: Rom 2.1. **15.3:** Ps 69.9.
15.4: Rom 4.23-24; 1 Cor 9.10; 2 Tim 3.16.
15.5: Rom 12.16; 1 Cor 1.10; 2 Cor 13.11; Phil 2.2; 4.2.

in such harmony with one another, in accord with Christ Jesus, ⁶that together you may with one voice glorify the God and Father of our Lord Jesus Christ.

7 Welcome one another, therefore, as Christ has welcomed you, for the glory of God. ⁸For I tell you that Christ became a servant to the circumcised to show God's truthfulness, in order to confirm the promises given to the patriarchs, ⁹and in order that the Gentiles might glorify God for his mercy. As it is written,

"Therefore I will praise thee among the Gentiles,
and sing to thy name";
¹⁰and·again it is said,
"Rejoice, O Gentiles, with his people";
¹¹and again,
"Praise the Lord, all Gentiles,
and let all the peoples praise him";
¹²and further Ī·sāi'ah says,
"The root of Jesse shall come,
he who rises to rule the Gentiles;
in him shall the Gentiles hope."
¹³May the God of hope fill you with all joy and peace in believing, so that by the power of the Holy Spirit you may abound in hope.

14 I myself am satisfied about you, my brethren, that you yourselves are full of goodness, filled with all knowledge, and able to instruct one another. ¹⁵But on some points I have written to you very boldly by way of reminder, because of the grace given me by God ¹⁶to be a minister of Christ Jesus to the Gentiles in the priestly service of the gospel of God, so that the offering of the Gentiles may be acceptable, sanctified by the Holy Spirit. ¹⁷In Christ Jesus, then, I have reason to be proud of my work for God. ¹⁸For I will not venture to speak of anything except what Christ has wrought through me to win obedience from the Gentiles, by word and deed, ¹⁹by the power of signs and wonders, by the power of the Holy Spirit, so that from Jerusalem and as far round as Ĭl-lȳr'ĭ-cum I have fully preached the gospel of Christ, ²⁰thus making it my ambition to preach the gospel, not where Christ has already been named, lest I build on another man's foundation, ²¹but as it is written,

"They shall see who have never been told of him,

and they shall understand who have never heard of him."

22 This is the reason why I have so often been hindered from coming to you. ²³But now, since I no longer have any room for work in these regions, and since I have longed for many years to come to you, ²⁴I hope to see you in passing as I go to Spain, and to be sped on my journey there by you, once I have enjoyed your company for a little. ²⁵At present, however, I am going to Jerusalem with aid for the saints. ²⁶For Măç·ę·dō'nĭ·a and Ą·chā'-ĭ·ą have been pleased to make some contributions for the poor among the saints at Jerusalem; ²⁷they were pleased to do it, and indeed they are in debt to them, for if the Gentiles have come to share in their spiritual blessings, they ought also to be of service to them in material blessings. ²⁸When therefore I have completed this, and have delivered to them what has been raised,ˣ I shall go on by way of you to Spain; ²⁹and I know that when I come to you I shall come in the fulness of the blessingʸ of Christ.

30 I appeal to you, brethren, by our Lord Jesus Christ and by the love of the Spirit, to strive together with me in your prayers to God on my behalf, ³¹that I may be delivered from the unbelievers in Jü·dē'ą, and that my service for Jerusalem may be acceptable to the saints, ³²so that by God's will I may come to you with joy and be refreshed in your company. ³³The God of peace be with you all. Amen.

16 I commend to you our sister Phoē'bē, a deaconess of the church at Çĕn'chrē–ąe, ²that you may receive her in the Lord as befits the saints, and help her in whatever she may require from you, for she has been a helper of many and of myself as well.

3 Greet Prĭs'cą and Ā'quĭ·lą, my fellow workers in Christ Jesus, ⁴who risked their necks for my life, to whom

ˣGreek *sealed to them this fruit*
ʸOther ancient authorities insert *of the gospel*
15.9: Ps 18.49; 2 Sam 22.50. **15.10:** Deut 32.43.
15.11: Ps 117.1. **15.12:** Is 11.10; Mt 12.21.
15.16: Acts 9.15. **15.18:** Rom 1.5; Acts 15.12; 21.19.
15.19: Acts 19.11; 2 Cor 12.12. **15.20:** 2 Cor 10.15-16.
15.21: Is 52.15. **15.22:** Rom 1.13.
15.23: Acts 19.21; Rom 1.10-11; 15.32.
15.24: Rom 15.28. **15.25:** Acts 19.21; 24.17; 15.31.
15.26: 2 Cor 8.1-5; 9.2; 1 Thess 1.7-8. **15.27:** 1 Cor 9.11.
15.28: Rom 15.24. **15.29:** Acts 19.21.
15.31: 2 Thess 3.2; Rom 15.25-26; 2 Cor 8.4; 9.1.
15.32: Rom 1.10; Acts 19.21. **15.33:** 2 Cor 13.11; Phil 4.9.
16.3: Acts 18.2.

not only I but also all the churches of the Gentiles give thanks; ⁵greet also the church in their house. Greet my beloved Ĕ·paē'nĕ·tŭs, who was the first convert in Asia for Christ. ⁶Greet Mary, who has worked hard among you. ⁷Greet Ăn·drŏn'ĭ·cŭs and Jü'nĭ·ăs, my kinsmen and my fellow prisoners; they are men of note among the apostles, and they were in Christ before me. ⁸Greet Ăm·plĭ·ā'tŭs, my beloved in the Lord. ⁹Greet Ūr·bā'nŭs, our fellow worker in Christ, and my beloved Stā'chўs. ¹⁰Greet A·pĕl'lēṣ, who is approved in Christ. Greet those who belong to the family of Ăr·ĭs·tŏb'ū·lŭs. ¹¹Greet my kinsman Hĕ·rō'dĭ·ọn. Greet those in the Lord who belong to the family of Năr·çĭs'sŭs. ¹²Greet those workers in the Lord, Trŷ·phaē'nạ and Trŷ·phō'sạ. Greet the beloved Pĕr'sĭs, who has worked hard in the Lord. ¹³Greet Rufus, eminent in the Lord, also his mother and mine. ¹⁴Greet A·sŷn'crĭ·tŭs, Phlē'gŏn, Hĕr'mēṣ, Păt·rŏ'băs, Hĕr'mạs, and the brethren who are with them. ¹⁵Greet Phĭ·lŏl'ọ·gŭs, Julia, Nē'rẹ·ŭs and his sister, and Ō·lŷm'pạs, and all the saints who are with them. ¹⁶Greet one another with a holy kiss. All the churches of Christ greet you.

17 I appeal to you, brethren, to take note of those who create dissensions and difficulties, in opposition to the doctrine which you have been taught; avoid them. ¹⁸For such persons do not serve our Lord Christ, but their own appetites,ᶻ and by fair and flattering words they deceive the hearts of the simple-minded. ¹⁹For while your obedience is known to all, so that I rejoice over you, I would have you wise as to what is good and guileless as to what is evil; ²⁰then the God of peace will soon crush Satan under your feet. The grace of our Lord Jesus Christ be with you.ᵃ

21 Timothy, my fellow worker, greets you; so do Lucius and Jason and Sō·sĭp'ạ·tẹr, my kinsmen.

21 I Tertius, the writer of this letter, greet you in the Lord.

23 Gā'ĭ·ŭs, who is host to me and to the whole church, greets you. Ĕ·răs'tŭs, the city treasurer, and our brother Quăr'tŭs, greet you.ᵇ

25 Now to him who is able to strengthen you according to my gospel and the preaching of Jesus Christ, according to the revelation of the mystery which was kept secret for long ages ²⁶but is now disclosed and through the prophetic writings is made known to all nations, according to the command of the eternal God, to bring about the obedience of faith—²⁷to the only wise God be glory for evermore through Jesus Christ! Amen.

The First Letter of Paul to the
Corinthians

1 Paul, called by the will of God to be an apostle of Christ Jesus, and our brother Sŏs'thẹ·nēṣ,

2 To the church of God which is at Corinth, to those sanctified in Christ Jesus, called to be saints together with all those who in every place call on the name of our Lord Jesus Christ, both their Lord and ours:

3 Grace to you and peace from God our Father and the Lord Jesus Christ.

4 I give thanks to Godᵃ always for you because of the grace of God which was given you in Christ Jesus, ⁵that in every way you were enriched in him with all speech and all knowledge —⁶even as the testimony to Christ was confirmed among you—⁷so that you are not lacking in any spiritual gift, as you wait for the revealing of our

ᶻGreek their own belly (Phil 3.19)
ᵃOther ancient authorities omit this sentence
ᵇOther ancient authorities insert verse 24, The grace of our Lord Jesus Christ be with you all. Amen
16.5: 1 Cor 16.19.
16.16: 2 Cor 13.12; 1 Thess 5.26; 1 Pet 5.14.
16.17: Gal 1.8-9; 2 Thess 3.6, 14; 2 Jn 10.
16.19: Rom 1.8; 1 Cor 14.20.
16.20: 1 Cor 16.23; 2 Cor 13.14; Gal 6.18; Phil 4.23; 1 Thess 5.28; 2 Thess 3.18; Rev 22.21.　16.21: Acts 16.1.
16.23: 1 Cor 1.14.

ᵃOther ancient authorities read my God
1.1: Rom 1.1; Acts 18.17.　1.2: Acts 18.1.　1.3: Rom 1.7.
1.4: Rom 1.8.

Lord Jesus Christ; [8] who will sustain you to the end, guiltless in the day of our Lord Jesus Christ. [9] God is faithful, by whom you were called into the fellowship of his Son, Jesus Christ our Lord.

10 I appeal to you, brethren, by the name of our Lord Jesus Christ, that all of you agree and that there be no dissensions among you, but that you be united in the same mind and the same judgment. [11] For it has been reported to me by Chlō'ē's people that there is quarreling among you, my brethren. [12] What I mean is that each one of you says, "I belong to Paul," or "I belong to A·pŏl'lŏs," or "I belong to Çē'phas," or "I belong to Christ." [13] Is Christ divided? Was Paul crucified for you? Or were you baptized in the name of Paul? [14] I am thankful[b] that I baptized none of you except Crĭs'pŭs and Gā'ĭ·ŭs; [15] lest any one should say that you were baptized in my name. [16] (I did baptize also the household of Stĕph'a·nas. Beyond that, I do not know whether I baptized any one else.) [17] For Christ did not send me to baptize but to preach the gospel, and not with eloquent wisdom, lest the cross of Christ be emptied of its power.

18 For the word of the cross is folly to those who are perishing, but to us who are being saved it is the power of God. [19] For it is written,

"I will destroy the wisdom of the wise,
and the cleverness of the clever I will thwart."

[20] Where is the wise man? Where is the scribe? Where is the debater of this age? Has not God made foolish the wisdom of the world? [21] For since, in the wisdom of God, the world did not know God through wisdom, it pleased God through the folly of what we preach to save those who believe. [22] For Jews demand signs and Greeks seek wisdom, [23] but we preach Christ crucified, a stumbling block to Jews and folly to Gentiles, [24] but to those who are called, both Jews and Greeks, Christ the power of God and the wisdom of God. [25] For the foolishness of God is wiser than men, and the weakness of God is stronger than men.

26 For consider your call, brethren; not many of you were wise according to worldly standards, not many were powerful, not many were of noble birth; [27] but God chose what is foolish in the world to shame the wise, God chose what is weak in the world to shame the strong, [28] God chose what is low and despised in the world, even things that are not, to bring to nothing things that are, [29] so that no human being might boast in the presence of God. [30] He is the source of your life in Christ Jesus, whom God made our wisdom, our righteousness and sanctification and redemption; [31] therefore, as it is written, "Let him who boasts, boast of the Lord."

2 When I came to you, brethren, I did not come proclaiming to you the testimony[c] of God in lofty words or wisdom. [2] For I decided to know nothing among you except Jesus Christ and him crucified. [3] And I was with you in weakness and in much fear and trembling; [4] and my speech and my message were not in plausible words of wisdom, but in demonstration of the Spirit and of power, [5] that your faith might not rest in the wisdom of men but in the power of God.

6 Yet among the mature we do impart wisdom, although it is not a wisdom of this age or of the rulers of this age, who are doomed to pass away. [7] But we impart a secret and hidden wisdom of God, which God decreed before the ages for our glorification. [8] None of the rulers of this age understood this; for if they had, they would not have crucified the Lord of glory. [9] But, as it is written,

"What no eye has seen, nor ear heard,
nor the heart of man conceived,
what God has prepared for those who love him,"

[10] God has revealed to us through the Spirit. For the Spirit searches everything, even the depths of God. [11] For what person knows a man's thoughts

---

[b] Other ancient authorities read *I thank God*
[c] Other ancient authorities read *mystery* (or *secret*)
1.8: 1 Cor 5.5; 2 Cor 1.14. **1.9:** Rom 8.28; 1 Jn 1.3.
1.12: 1 Cor 3.4; Acts 18.24; 1 Cor 3.22; Jn 1.42; 1 Cor 9.5; 15.5. **1.13:** Mt 28.19; Acts 2.38.
1.14: Acts 18.8; Rom 16.23. **1.16:** 1 Cor 16.15.
1.17: Jn 4.2; Acts 10.48; 1 Cor 2.1; 4.13. **1.19:** Is 29.14.
1.22: Mt 12.38. **1.23:** 1 Cor 2.2; Gal 3.1; 5.11.
1.27: Jas 2.5. **1.28:** Rom 4.17. **1.29:** Eph 2.9.
1.30: 1 Cor 4.15; Rom 8.1; 2 Cor 5.21; 1 Cor 6.11; 1 Thess 5.23; Eph 1.7, 14; Col 1.14; Rom 3.24.
1.31: Jer 9.24; 2 Cor 10.17. **2.1:** 1 Cor 1.17.
2.2: Gal 6.14; 1 Cor 1.23.
2.3: Acts 18.1, 6, 12; 1 Cor 4.10; 2 Cor 11.30.
2.4: Rom 15.19; 1 Cor 4.20.
2.5: 2 Cor 4.7; 6.7; 1 Cor 12.9. **2.6:** Eph 4.13.
2.7: Rom 8.29-30. **2.8:** Acts 7.2; Jas 2.1.
2.9: Is 64.4; 65.17.
2.10: Mt 11.25; 13.11; 16.17; Eph 3.3, 5.

except the spirit of the man which is in him? So also no one comprehends the thoughts of God except the Spirit of God. [12] Now we have received not the spirit of the world, but the Spirit which is from God, that we might understand the gifts bestowed on us by God. [13] And we impart this in words not taught by human wisdom but taught by the Spirit, interpreting spiritual truths to those who possess the Spirit.[d]
14 The unspiritual[e] man does not receive the gifts of the Spirit of God, for they are folly to him, and he is not able to understand them because they are spiritually discerned. [15] The spiritual man judges all things, but is himself to be judged by no one. [16] "For who has known the mind of the Lord so as to instruct him?" But we have the mind of Christ.

3 But I, brethren, could not address you as spiritual men, but as men of the flesh, as babes in Christ. [2] I fed you with milk, not solid food; for you were not ready for it; and even yet you are not ready, [3] for you are still of the flesh. For while there is jealousy and strife among you, are you not of the flesh, and behaving like ordinary men? [4] For when one says, "I belong to Paul," and another, "I belong to A·pŏl'lŏs," are you not merely men?
5 What then is A·pŏl'lŏs? What is Paul? Servants through whom you believed, as the Lord assigned to each. [6] I planted, A·pŏl'lŏs watered, but God gave the growth. [7] So neither he who plants nor he who waters is anything, but only God who gives the growth. [8] He who plants and he who waters are equal, and each shall receive his wages according to his labor. [9] For we are God's fellow workers; you are God's field, God's building.
10 According to the grace of God given to me, like a skilled master builder I laid a foundation, and another man is building upon it. Let each man take care how he builds upon it. [11] For no other foundation can any one lay than that which is laid, which is Jesus Christ. [12] Now if any one builds on the foundation with gold, silver, precious stones, wood, hay, straw— [13] each man's work will become manifest; for the Day will disclose it, because it will be revealed with fire, and the fire will test what sort of work each one has done. [14] If the work which

any man has built on the foundation survives, he will receive a reward. [15] If any man's work is burned up, he will suffer loss, though he himself will be saved, but only as through fire.
16 Do you not know that you are God's temple and that God's Spirit dwells in you? [17] If any one destroys God's temple, God will destroy him. For God's temple is holy, and that temple you are.
18 Let no one deceive himself. If any one among you thinks that he is wise in this age, let him become a fool that he may become wise. [19] For the wisdom of this world is folly with God. For it is written, "He catches the wise in their craftiness," [20] and again, "The Lord knows that the thoughts of the wise are futile." [21] So let no one boast of men. For all things are yours, [22] whether Paul or A·pŏl'lŏs or Çē'phas or the world or life or death or the present or the future, all are yours; [23] and you are Christ's; and Christ is God's.

4 This is how one should regard us, as servants of Christ and stewards of the mysteries of God. [2] Moreover it is required of stewards that they be found trustworthy. [3] But with me it is a very small thing that I should be judged by you or by any human court. I do not even judge myself. [4] I am not aware of anything against myself, but I am not thereby acquitted. It is the Lord who judges me. [5] Therefore do not pronounce judgment before the time, before the Lord comes, who will bring to light the things now hidden in darkness and will disclose the purposes of the heart. Then every man will receive his commendation from God.
6 I have applied all this to myself and A·pŏl'lŏs for your benefit, brethren, that you may learn by us not to go beyond what is written, that none of you

[d] Or interpreting spiritual truths in spiritual language; or comparing spiritual things with spiritual [e] Or natural   2.12: Rom 8.15.   2.13: 1 Cor 1.17.
2.14: 1 Cor 1.18; Jas 3.15.
2.15: 1 Cor 3.1; 14.37; Gal 6.1.
2.16: Is 40.13; Rom 11.34.   3.1: Rom 7.14; Heb 5.13.
3.2: Heb 5.12-13; 1 Pet 2.2.   3.4: 1 Cor 1.12.
3.5: 2 Cor 6.4; Eph 3.7; Col 1.25.
3.6: Acts 18.4-11, 24-27; 1 Cor 1.12.
3.9: Is 61.3; Eph 2.20-22; 1 Pet 2.5.
3.10: Rom 12.3; 1 Cor 15.10.   3.11: Eph 2.20.
3.13: 2 Thess 1.7-10.   3.15: Job 23.10.
3.16: 1 Cor 6.19; 2 Cor 6.16.
3.18: Is 5.21; 1 Cor 8.2; Gal 6.3.
3.19: Job 5.13; 1 Cor 1.20.   3.20: Ps 94.11.
3.21: 1 Cor 4.6; Rom 8.32.   3.22: 1 Cor 1.12; Rom 8.38.
4.1: 1 Cor 9.17; Rom 11.25; 16.25.   4.4: 2 Cor 1.12.
4.5: Rom 2.16; 1 Cor 3.13; 2 Cor 10.18; Rom 2.29.
4.6: 1 Cor 1.19, 31; 3.19-20; 1.12; 3.4.

may be puffed up in favor of one against another. [7] For who sees anything different in you? What have you that you did not receive? If then you received it, why do you boast as if it were not a gift?

8 Already you are filled! Already you have become rich! Without us you have become kings! And would that you did reign, so that we might share the rule with you! [9] For I think that God has exhibited us apostles as last of all, like men sentenced to death; because we have become a spectacle to the world, to angels and to men. [10] We are fools for Christ's sake, but you are wise in Christ. We are weak, but you are strong. You are held in honor, but we in disrepute. [11] To the present hour we hunger and thirst, we are ill-clad and buffeted and homeless, [12] and we labor, working with our own hands. When reviled, we bless; when persecuted, we endure; [13] when slandered, we try to conciliate; we have become, and are now, as the refuse of the world, the offscouring of all things.

14 I do not write this to make you ashamed, but to admonish you as my beloved children. [15] For though you have countless guides in Christ, you do not have many fathers. For I became your father in Christ Jesus through the gospel. [16] I urge you, then, be imitators of me. [17] Therefore I sent[g] to you Timothy, my beloved and faithful child in the Lord, to remind you of my ways in Christ, as I teach them everywhere in every church. [18] Some are arrogant, as though I were not coming to you. [19] But I will come to you soon, if the Lord wills, and I will find out not the talk of these arrogant people but their power. [20] For the kingdom of God does not consist in talk but in power. [21] What do you wish? Shall I come to you with a rod, or with love in a spirit of gentleness?

5 It is actually reported that there is immorality among you, and of a kind that is not found even among pagans; for a man is living with his father's wife. [2] And you are arrogant! Ought you not rather to mourn? Let him who has done this be removed from among you.

3 For though absent in body I am present in spirit, and as if present, I have already pronounced judgment [4] in the name of the Lord Jesus on the man who has done such a thing. When you are assembled, and my spirit is present, with the power of our Lord Jesus, [5] you are to deliver this man to Satan for the destruction of the flesh, that his spirit may be saved in the day of the Lord Jesus.[h]

6 Your boasting is not good. Do you not know that a little leaven leavens the whole lump? [7] Cleanse out the old leaven that you may be a new lump, as you really are unleavened. For Christ, our paschal lamb, has been sacrificed. [8] Let us, therefore, celebrate the festival, not with the old leaven, the leaven of malice and evil, but with the unleavened bread of sincerity and truth.

9 I wrote to you in my letter not to associate with immoral men; [10] not at all meaning the immoral of this world, or the greedy and robbers, or idolaters, since then you would need to go out of the world. [11] But rather I wrote[i] to you not to associate with any one who bears the name of brother if he is guilty of immorality or greed, or is an idolater, reviler, drunkard, or robber —not even to eat with such a one. [12] For what have I to do with judging outsiders? Is it not those inside the church whom you are to judge? [13] God judges those outside. "Drive out the wicked person from among you."

6 When one of you has a grievance against a brother, does he dare go to law before the unrighteous instead of the saints? [2] Do you not know that the saints will judge the world? And if the world is to be judged by you, are you incompetent to try trivial cases? [3] Do you not know that we are to judge angels? How much more, matters pertaining to this life! [4] If then you have such cases, why do you lay them before those who are least esteemed by the church? [5] I say this to your shame. Can it be that there is no man among you wise enough to decide between members of the brotherhood, [6] but brother

g Or *am sending*
h Other ancient authorities omit *Jesus*   *i* Or *now I write*
4.9: 1 Cor 15.31; 2 Cor 11.23; Rom 8.36; Heb 10.33.
4.10: 1 Cor 1.18; 2 Cor 11.19; 1 Cor 3.18; 2 Cor 13.9; 1 Cor 2.3.   **4.11:** Rom 8.35; 2 Cor 11.23-27.
4.12: Acts 18.3; 1 Pet 3.9.
4.15: 1 Cor 1.30; Philem 10.
4.17: 1 Cor 16.10; Acts 16.1; 1 Cor 7.17.
4.21: 1 Cor 1.23.   **5.1:** Deut 22.30; 27.20.
5.3: Col 2.5.   **5.4:** 2 Thess 3.6.   **5.5:** Mt 4.10; 1 Cor 1.8.
5.6: Gal 5.9.   **5.8:** Ex 12.19; 13.7; Deut 16.3.
5.9: 2 Cor 6.14.   **5.10:** 1 Cor 10.27.
5.11: 2 Thess 3.6; 1 Cor 10.7, 14, 20-21.   **5.12:** Mk 4.11.
5.13: Deut 17.7; 1 Cor 5.2.   **6.1:** Mt 18.17.

goes to law against brother, and that before unbelievers?

7 To have lawsuits at all with one another is defeat for you. Why not rather suffer wrong? Why not rather be defrauded? ⁸But you yourselves wrong and defraud, and that even your own brethren.

9 Do you not know that the unrighteous will not inherit the kingdom of God? Do not be deceived; neither the immoral, nor idolaters, nor adulterers, nor sexual perverts, ¹⁰nor thieves, nor the greedy, nor drunkards, nor revilers, nor robbers will inherit the kingdom of God. ¹¹And such were some of you. But you were washed, you were sanctified, you were justified in the name of the Lord Jesus Christ and in the Spirit of our God.

12 "All things are lawful for me," but not all things are helpful. "All things are lawful for me," but I will not be enslaved by anything. ¹³"Food is meant for the stomach and the stomach for food"—and God will destroy both one and the other. The body is not meant for immorality, but for the Lord, and the Lord for the body. ¹⁴And God raised the Lord and will also raise us up by his power. ¹⁵Do you not know that your bodies are members of Christ? Shall I therefore take the members of Christ and make them members of a prostitute? Never! ¹⁶Do you not know that he who joins himself to a prostitute becomes one body with her? For, as it is written, "The two shall become one flesh." ¹⁷But he who is united to the Lord becomes one spirit with him. ¹⁸Shun immorality. Every other sin which a man commits is outside the body; but the immoral man sins against his own body. ¹⁹Do you not know that your body is a temple of the Holy Spirit within you, which you have from God? You are not your own; ²⁰you were bought with a price. So glorify God in your body.

7 Now concerning the matters about which you wrote. It is well for a man not to touch a woman. ²But because of the temptation to immorality, each man should have his own wife and each woman her own husband. ³The husband should give to his wife her conjugal rights, and likewise the wife to her husband. ⁴For the wife does not rule over her own body, but the husband does; likewise the husband does not rule over his own body, but the wife does. ⁵Do not refuse one another except perhaps by agreement for a season, that you may devote yourselves to prayer; but then come together again, lest Satan tempt you through lack of self-control. ⁶I say this by way of concession, not of command. ⁷I wish that all were as I myself am. But each has his own special gift from God, one of one kind and one of another.

8 To the unmarried and the widows I say that it is well for them to remain single as I do. ⁹But if they cannot exercise self-control, they should marry. For it is better to marry than to be aflame with passion.

10 To the married I give charge, not I but the Lord, that the wife should not separate from her husband ¹¹(but if she does, let her remain single or else be reconciled to her husband)—and that the husband should not divorce his wife.

12 To the rest I say, not the Lord, that if any brother has a wife who is an unbeliever, and she consents to live with him, he should not divorce her. ¹³If any woman has a husband who is an unbeliever, and he consents to live with her, she should not divorce him. ¹⁴For the unbelieving husband is consecrated through his wife, and the unbelieving wife is consecrated through her husband. Otherwise, your children would be unclean, but as it is they are holy. ¹⁵But if the unbelieving partner desires to separate, let it be so; in such a case the brother or sister is not bound. For God has called us¹ to peace. ¹⁶Wife, how do you know whether you will save your husband? Husband, how do you know whether you will save your wife?

17 Only, let every one lead the life which the Lord has assigned to him, and in which God has called him. This is my rule in all the churches. ¹⁸Was any one at the time of his call already

¹Other ancient authorities read *you*
6.7: Mt 5.39-40.   **6.9:** 1 Cor 15.50.
6.11: Acts 22.16; Rom 8.30.   **6.12:** 1 Cor 10.23.
6.15: Rom 12.5; 1 Cor 12.27.
6.16: Gen 2.24; Mt 19.5; Mk 10.8; Eph 5.31.
6.17: Jn 17.21-23; Rom 8.9; Gal 2.20.
6.19: 1 Cor 3.16; Jn 2.21.
6.20: 1 Cor 7.23; Acts 20.28; Rom 12.1.
7.5: Ex 19.15.   **7.7:** 1 Cor 7.8; 9.5.   **7.9:** 1 Tim 5.14.
7.12: 2 Cor 11.17.   **7.16:** 1 Pet 3.1.
7.17: Rom 12.3; 1 Cor 14.33; 2 Cor 8.18; 11.28.
7.18: 1 Maccabees 1.15; Acts 15.1-2.

circumcised? Let him not seek to remove the marks of circumcision. Was any one at the time of his call uncircumcised? Let him not seek circumcision. ¹⁹ For neither circumcision counts for anything nor uncircumcision, but keeping the commandments of God. ²⁰ Every one should remain in the state in which he was called. ²¹ Were you a slave when called? Never mind. But if you can gain your freedom, avail yourself of the opportunity.ˣ ²² For he who was called in the Lord as a slave is a freedman of the Lord. Likewise he who was free when called is a slave of Christ. ²³ You were bought with a price; do not become slaves of men. ²⁴ So, brethren, in whatever state each was called, there let him remain with God.

25 Now concerning the unmarried,ʸ I have no command of the Lord, but I give my opinion as one who by the Lord's mercy is trustworthy. ²⁶ I think that in view of the presentᵐ distress it is well for a person to remain as he is. ²⁷ Are you bound to a wife? Do not seek to be free. Are you free from a wife? Do not seek marriage. ²⁸ But if you marry, you do not sin, and if a girlᶻ marries she does not sin. Yet those who marry will have worldly troubles, and I would spare you that. ²⁹ I mean, brethren, the appointed time has grown very short; from now on, let those who have wives live as though they had none, ³⁰ and those who mourn as though they were not mourning, and those who rejoice as though they were not rejoicing, and those who buy as though they had no goods, ³¹ and those who deal with the world as though they had no dealings with it. For the form of this world is passing away.

32 I want you to be free from anxieties. The unmarried man is anxious about the affairs of the Lord, how to please the Lord; ³³ but the married man is anxious about worldly affairs, how to please his wife, ³⁴ and his interests are divided. And the unmarried woman or girlᶻ is anxious about the affairs of the Lord, how to be holy in body and spirit; but the married woman is anxious about worldly affairs, how to please her husband. ³⁵ I say this for your own benefit, not to lay any restraint upon you, but to promote good order and to secure your undivided devotion to the Lord.

36 If any one thinks that he is not behaving properly toward his betrothed,ᶻ if his passions are strong, and it has to be, let him do as he wishes: let them marry—it is no sin. ³⁷ But whoever is firmly established in his heart, being under no necessity but having his desire under control, and has determined this in his heart, to keep her as his betrothed,ᶻ he will do well. ³⁸ So that he who marries his betrothedᶻ does well; and he who refrains from marriage will do better.

39 A wife is bound to her husband as long as he lives. If the husband dies, she is free to be married to whom she wishes, only in the Lord. ⁴⁰ But in my judgment she is happier if she remains as she is. And I think that I have the Spirit of God.

8 Now concerning food offered to idols: we know that "all of us possess knowledge." "Knowledge" puffs up, but love builds up. ² If any one imagines that he knows something, he does not yet know as he ought to know. ³ But if one loves God, one is known by him.

4 Hence, as to the eating of food offered to idols, we know that "an idol has no real existence," and that "there is no God but one." ⁵ For although there may be so-called gods in heaven or on earth—as indeed there are many "gods" and many "lords"—⁶ yet for us there is one God, the Father, from whom are all things and for whom we exist, and one Lord, Jesus Christ, through whom are all things and through whom we exist.

7 However, not all possess this knowledge. But some, through being hitherto accustomed to idols, eat food as really offered to an idol; and their conscience, being weak, is defiled. ⁸ Food will not commend us to God. We are no worse off if we do not eat, and no better off if we do. ⁹ Only take care lest this liberty of yours somehow become a stumbling block to the weak. ¹⁰ For if any one sees you, a man of

ᶻ Or *make use of your present condition instead* ʸ Greek *virgins* ᵐ Or *impending* ᶻ Greek *virgin*
7.19: Gal 5.6; 6.15; Rom 2.25. **7.22:** Jn 8.32, 36.
7.23: 1 Cor 6.20. **7.29:** Rom 13.11-12; 1 Cor 7.31.
7.32: 1 Tim 5.5. **7.39:** Rom 7.2.
7.40: 1 Cor 7.25. **8.1:** Rom 15.14.
8.2: 1 Cor 3.18; 13.8, 9, 12. **8.3:** Gal 4.9; Rom 8.29.
8.4: 1 Cor 10.19; Deut 6.4.
8.6: Mal 2.10; Eph 4.6; Rom 11.36; 1 Cor 1.2; Eph 4.5;
Jn 1.3; Col 1.16. **8.7:** 1 Cor 8.4-5. **8.8:** Rom 14.17.
8.9: 1 Cor 8.10-11; Rom 14.1.

knowledge, at table in an idol's temple, might he not be encouraged, if his conscience is weak, to eat food offered to idols? ¹¹And so by your knowledge this weak man is destroyed, the brother for whom Christ died. ¹²Thus, sinning against your brethren and wounding their conscience when it is weak, you sin against Christ. ¹³Therefore, if food is a cause of my brother's falling, I will never eat meat, lest I cause my brother to fall.

9 Am I not free? Am I not an apostle? Have I not seen Jesus our Lord? Are not you my workmanship in the Lord? ²If to others I am not an apostle, at least I am to you; for you are the seal of my apostleship in the Lord.

3 This is my defense to those who would examine me. ⁴Do we not have the right to our food and drink? ⁵Do we not have the right to be accompanied by a wife,ⁿ as the other apostles and the brothers of the Lord and Çē'phas? ⁶Or is it only Bār'na·bas and I who have no right to refrain from working for a living? ⁷Who serves as a soldier at his own expense? Who plants a vineyard without eating any of its fruit? Who tends a flock without getting some of the milk?

8 Do I say this on human authority? Does not the law say the same? ⁹For it is written in the law of Moses, "You shall not muzzle an ox when it is treading out the grain." Is it for oxen that God is concerned? ¹⁰Does he not speak entirely for our sake? It was written for our sake, because the plowman should plow in hope and the thresher thresh in hope of a share in the crop. ¹¹If we have sown spiritual good among you, is it too much if we reap your material benefits? ¹²If others share this rightful claim upon you, do not we still more?

Nevertheless, we have not made use of this right, but we endure anything rather than put an obstacle in the way of the gospel of Christ. ¹³Do you not know that those who are employed in the temple service get their food from the temple, and those who serve at the altar share in the sacrificial offerings? ¹⁴In the same way, the Lord commanded that those who proclaim the gospel should get their living by the gospel.

15 But I have made no use of any of these rights, nor am I writing this to secure any such provision. For I would rather die than have any one deprive me of my ground for boasting. ¹⁶For if I preach the gospel, that gives me no ground for boasting. For necessity is laid upon me. Woe to me if I do not preach the gospel! ¹⁷For if I do this of my own will, I have a reward; but if not of my own will, I am entrusted with a commission. ¹⁸What then is my reward? Just this: that in my preaching I may make the gospel free of charge, not making full use of my right in the gospel.

19 For though I am free from all men, I have made myself a slave to all, that I might win the more. ²⁰To the Jews I became as a Jew, in order to win Jews; to those under the law I became as one under the law—though not being myself under the law—that I might win those under the law. ²¹To those outside the law I became as one outside the law—not being without law toward God but under the law of Christ—that I might win those outside the law. ²²To the weak I became weak, that I might win the weak. I have become all things to all men, that I might by all means save some. ²³I do it all for the sake of the gospel, that I may share in its blessings.

24 Do you not know that in a race all the runners compete, but only one receives the prize? So run that you may obtain it. ²⁵Every athlete exercises self-control in all things. They do it to receive a perishable wreath, but we an imperishable. ²⁶Well, I do not run aimlessly, I do not box as one beating the air; ²⁷but I pommel my body and subdue it, lest after preaching to others I myself should be disqualified.

10 I want you to know, brethren, that our fathers were all under the cloud, and all passed through the sea, ²and all were baptized into Moses in the cloud and in the sea, ³and all

ⁿGreek *a sister as wife* **8.11:** Rom 14.15, 20.
8.12: Mt 18.6; Rom 14.20. **8.13:** Rom 14.21.
9.1: 1 Cor 9.19; 2 Cor 12.12; 1 Thess 2.6; Acts 9.3, 17; 1 Cor 15.8. **9.4:** 1 Cor 9.14.
9.5: 1 Cor 7.7-8; Mt 12.46; 8.14; Jn 1.42. **9.6:** Acts 4.36.
9.9: Deut 25.4; 1 Tim 5.18.
9.10: 2 Tim 2.6. **9.11:** Rom 15.27. **9.12:** 2 Cor 6.3.
9.13: Deut 18.1. **9.14:** Mt 10.10; Lk 10.7-8.
9.15: 2 Cor 11.10. **9.17:** 1 Cor 4.1; Gal 2.7.
9.18: 2 Cor 11.7. **9.20:** Rom 11.14. **9.21:** Rom 2.12, 14.
9.22: 2 Cor 11.29; Rom 15.1; 1 Cor 10.33; Rom 11.14.
9.24: Heb 12.1. **9.25:** 2 Tim 2.5; 4.8; Jas 1.12; 1 Pet 5.4.
10.1: Rom 1.13; Ex 13.21; 14.22, 29.
10.2: Rom 6.3; Gal 3.27. **10.3:** Ex 16.4, 35.

ate the same supernatural° food ⁴and all drank the same supernatural° drink. For they drank from the supernatural° Rock which followed them, and the Rock was Christ. ⁵Nevertheless with most of them God was not pleased; for they were overthrown in the wilderness.

6 Now these things are warnings for us, not to desire evil as they did. ⁷Do not be idolaters as some of them were; as it is written, "The people sat down to eat and drink and rose up to dance." ⁸We must not indulge in immorality as some of them did, and twenty-three thousand fell in a single day. ⁹We must not put the Lord^p to the test, as some of them did and were destroyed by serpents; ¹⁰nor grumble, as some of them did and were destroyed by the Destroyer. ¹¹Now these things happened to them as a warning, but they were written down for our instruction, upon whom the end of the ages has come. ¹²Therefore let any one who thinks that he stands take heed lest he fall. ¹³No temptation has overtaken you that is not common to man. God is faithful, and he will not let you be tempted beyond your strength, but with the temptation will also provide the way of escape, that you may be able to endure it.

14 Therefore, my beloved, shun the worship of idols. ¹⁵I speak as to sensible men; judge for yourselves what I say. ¹⁶The cup of blessing which we bless, is it not a participation^q in the blood of Christ? The bread which we break, is it not a participation^q in the body of Christ? ¹⁷Because there is one bread, we who are many are one body, for we all partake of the one bread. ¹⁸Consider the people of Israel;^a are not those who eat the sacrifices partners in the altar? ¹⁹What do I imply then? That food offered to idols is anything, or that an idol is anything? ²⁰No, I imply that what pagans sacrifice they offer to demons and not to God. I do not want you to be partners with demons. ²¹You cannot drink the cup of the Lord and the cup of demons. You cannot partake of the table of the Lord and the table of demons. ²²Shall we provoke the Lord to jealousy? Are we stronger than he?

23 "All things are lawful," but not all things are helpful. "All things are lawful," but not all things build up.

²⁴Let no one seek his own good, but the good of his neighbor. ²⁵Eat whatever is sold in the meat market without raising any question on the ground of conscience. ²⁶For "the earth is the Lord's, and everything in it." ²⁷If one of the unbelievers invites you to dinner and you are disposed to go, eat whatever is set before you without raising any question on the ground of conscience. ²⁸(But if some one says to you, "This has been offered in sacrifice," then out of consideration for the man who informed you, and for conscience' sake—²⁹I mean his conscience, not yours—do not eat it.) For why should my liberty be determined by another man's scruples? ³⁰If I partake with thankfulness, why am I denounced because of that for which I give thanks?

31 So, whether you eat or drink, or whatever you do, do all to the glory of God. ³²Give no offense to Jews or to Greeks or to the church of God, ³³just as I try to please all men in everything I do, not seeking my own advantage, but that of many, that they may be saved. ¹Be imitators of me, as I am of Christ.

11

2 I commend you because you remember me in everything and maintain the traditions even as I have delivered them to you. ³But I want you to understand that the head of every man is Christ, the head of a woman is her husband, and the head of Christ is God. ⁴Any man who prays or prophesies with his head covered dishonors his head, ⁵but any woman who prays or prophesies with her head unveiled dishonors her head—it is the same as if her head were shaven. ⁶For if a woman will not veil herself, then she should cut off her hair; but if it is disgraceful for a woman to be shorn or shaven, let her wear a veil. ⁷For a man ought not to cover his head, since he is

°Greek spiritual
^pOther ancient authorities read Christ ^qOr communion
^aGreek Israel according to the flesh
10.4 Ex 17.6; Num 20.11. 10.5: Num 14.29-30.
10.6: Num 11.4, 34. 10.7: Ex 32.4, 6. 10.8: Num 25.1-18.
10.9: Num 21.5-6. 10.10: Num 16.41, 49.
10.13: 1 Cor 1.9.
10.14: 1 Jn 5.21. 10.16: Mt 26.27-28; Acts 2.42.
10.17: Rom 12.5. 10.18: Lev 7.6. 10.20: Deut 32.17.
10.21: 2 Cor 6.16. 10.22: Deut 32.21; Eccles 6.10; Is 45.9.
10.23: 1 Cor 6.12; Phil 2.21. 10.26: Ps 24.1; 50.12.
10.28: 1 Cor 8.7, 10-12. 10.32: 1 Cor 8.13.
10.33: 1 Cor 9.22; Rom 15.2; 1 Cor 13.5.
11.1: 1 Thess 2.15.
11.3: Eph 1.22; 4.15; 5.23; Col 1.8; 2.19.
11.5: Lk 2.36; Acts 21.9; 1 Cor 14.34. 11.7: Gen 1.26.

the image and glory of God; but woman is the glory of man. [8](For man was not made from woman, but woman from man. [9]Neither was man created for woman, but woman for man.) [10]That is why a woman ought to have a veil*r* on her head, because of the angels. [11](Nevertheless, in the Lord woman is not independent of man nor man of woman; [12]for as woman was made from man, so man is now born of woman. And all things are from God.) [13]Judge for yourselves; is it proper for a woman to pray to God with her head uncovered? [14]Does not nature itself teach you that for a man to wear long hair is degrading to him, [15]but if a woman has long hair, it is her pride? For her hair is given to her for a covering. [16]If any one is disposed to be contentious, we recognize no other practice, nor do the churches of God.

17 But in the following instructions I do not commend you, because when you come together it is not for the better but for the worse. [18]For, in the first place, when you assemble as a church, I hear that there are divisions among you; and I partly believe it, [19]for there must be factions among you in order that those who are genuine among you may be recognized. [20]When you meet together, it is not the Lord's supper that you eat. [21]For in eating, each one goes ahead with his own meal, and one is hungry and another is drunk. [22]What! Do you not have houses to eat and drink in? Or do you despise the church of God and humiliate those who have nothing? What shall I say to you? Shall I commend you in this? No, I will not.

23 For I received from the Lord what I also delivered to you, that the Lord Jesus on the night when he was betrayed took bread, [24]and when he had given thanks, he broke it, and said, "This is my body which is for*s* you. Do this in remembrance of me." [25]In the same way also the cup, after supper, saying, "This cup is the new covenant in my blood. Do this, as often as you drink it, in remembrance of me." [26]For as often as you eat this bread and drink the cup, you proclaim the Lord's death until he comes.

27 Whoever, therefore, eats the bread or drinks the cup of the Lord in an unworthy manner will be guilty of profaning the body and blood of the Lord. [28]Let a man examine himself, and so eat of the bread and drink of the cup. [29]For any one who eats and drinks without discerning the body eats and drinks judgment upon himself. [30]That is why many of you are weak and ill, and some have died. [31]But if we judged ourselves truly, we should not be judged. [32]But when we are judged by the Lord, we are chastened*u* so that we may not be condemned along with the world.

33 So then, my brethren, when you come together to eat, wait for one another—[34]if any one is hungry, let him eat at home—lest you come together to be condemned. About the other things I will give directions when I come.

12 Now concerning spiritual gifts,*x* brethren, I do not want you to be uninformed. [2]You know that when you were heathen, you were led astray to dumb idols, however you may have been moved. [3]Therefore I want you to understand that no one speaking by the Spirit of God ever says "Jesus be cursed!" and no one can say "Jesus is Lord" except by the Holy Spirit.

4 Now there are varieties of gifts, but the same Spirit; [5]and there are varieties of service, but the same Lord; [6]and there are varieties of working, but it is the same God who inspires them all in every one. [7]To each is given the manifestation of the Spirit for the common good. [8]To one is given through the Spirit the utterance of wisdom, and to another the utterance of knowledge according to the same Spirit, [9]to another faith by the same Spirit, to another gifts of healing by the one Spirit, [10]to another the working of miracles, to another prophecy, to another the ability to distinguish between spirits, to another various kinds of tongues, to another the interpretation of tongues. [11]All these are inspired by one and the same Spirit, who appor-

*r*Greek *authority* (the veil being a symbol of this)
*s*Other ancient authorities read *broken for*
*t*Greek *have fallen asleep* (as in 15.6, 20)
*u*Or *when we are judged we are being chastened by the Lord*   *x*Or *spiritual persons*
11.8: Gen 2.21-23.   **11.9:** Gen 2.18.
11.16: 1 Cor 7.17.   **11.18:** 1 Cor 1.10.   **11.23:** 1 Cor 15.3.
11.23-25: Mt 26.26-28; Mk 14.22-24; Lk 22.17-19; 1 Cor 10.16.   **11.25:** 2 Cor 3.6; Lk 22.20.   **11.26:** 1 Cor 4.5.
11.32: 1 Cor 1.20.   **11.34:** 1 Cor 4.19.   **12.2:** Eph 2.11-12.
12.3: Rom 10.9.   **12.10:** 1 Cor 14.26.

tions to each one individually as he wills.

12 For just as the body is one and has many members, and all the members of the body, though many, are one body, so it is with Christ. 13 For by one Spirit we were all baptized into one body—Jews or Greeks, slaves or free—and all were made to drink of one Spirit.

14 For the body does not consist of one member but of many. 15 If the foot should say, "Because I am not a hand, I do not belong to the body," that would not make it any less a part of the body. 16 And if the ear should say, "Because I am not an eye, I do not belong to the body," that would not make it any less a part of the body. 17 If the whole body were an eye, where would be the hearing? If the whole body were an ear, where would be the sense of smell? 18 But as it is, God arranged the organs in the body, each one of them, as he chose. 19 If all were a single organ, where would the body be? 20 As it is, there are many parts, yet one body. 21 The eye cannot say to the hand, "I have no need of you," nor again the head to the feet, "I have no need of you." 22 On the contrary, the parts of the body which seem to be weaker are indispensable, 23 and those parts of the body which we think less honorable we invest with the greater honor, and our unpresentable parts are treated with greater modesty, 24 which our more presentable parts do not require. But God has so composed the body, giving the greater honor to the inferior part, 25 that there may be no discord in the body, but that the members may have the same care for one another. 26 If one member suffers, all suffer together; if one member is honored, all rejoice together.

27 Now you are the body of Christ and individually members of it. 28 And God has appointed in the church first apostles, second prophets, third teachers, then workers of miracles, then healers, helpers, administrators, speakers in various kinds of tongues. 29 Are all apostles? Are all prophets? Are all teachers? Do all work miracles? 30 Do all possess gifts of healing? Do all speak with tongues? Do all interpret? 31 But earnestly desire the higher gifts.

And I will show you a still more excellent way.

13 If I speak in the tongues of men and of angels, but have not love, I am a noisy gong or a clanging cymbal. 2 And if I have prophetic powers, and understand all mysteries and all knowledge, and if I have all faith, so as to remove mountains, but have not love, I am nothing. 3 If I give away all I have, and if I deliver my body to be burned,*º but have not love, I gain nothing.

4 Love is patient and kind; love is not jealous or boastful; 5 it is not arrogant or rude. Love does not insist on its own way; it is not irritable or resentful; 6 it does not rejoice at wrong, but rejoices in the right. 7 Love bears all things, believes all things, hopes all things, endures all things.

8 Love never ends; as for prophecies, they will pass away; as for tongues, they will cease; as for knowledge, it will pass away. 9 For our knowledge is imperfect and our prophecy is imperfect; 10 but when the perfect comes, the imperfect will pass away. 11 When I was a child, I spoke like a child, I thought like a child, I reasoned like a child; when I became a man, I gave up childish ways. 12 For now we see in a mirror dimly, but then face to face. Now I know in part; then I shall understand fully, even as I have been fully understood. 13 So faith, hope, love abide, these three; but the greatest of these is love.

14 Make love your aim, and earnestly desire the spiritual gifts, especially that you may prophesy. 2 For one who speaks in a tongue speaks not to men but to God; for no one understands him, but he utters mysteries in the Spirit. 3 On the other hand, he who prophesies speaks to men for their upbuilding and encouragement and consolation. 4 He who speaks in a tongue edifies himself, but he who prophesies edifies the church. 5 Now I want you all to speak in tongues, but even more to prophesy. He who prophesies is greater than he who speaks in tongues, unless some one interprets, so that the church may be edified.

6 Now, brethren, if I come to you

ºOther ancient authorities read *body that I may glory*
12.12: Rom 12.4.
12.13: Gal 3.28; Col 3.11; Eph 2.13-18; Jn 7.37-39.
12.27: Eph 1.23; 4.12; Col 1.18, 24; Eph 5.30; Rom 12.5.
12.28: Eph 4.11; 2.20; 3.5. 13.1: Ps 150.5.
13.2: 1 Cor 14.2; Mt 17.20; 21.21. 13.5: 1 Cor 10.24.
13.7: 1 Cor 9.12.

speaking in tongues, how shall I benefit you unless I bring you some revelation or knowledge or prophecy or teaching? [7]If even lifeless instruments, such as the flute or the harp, do not give distinct notes, how will any one know what is played? [8]And if the bugle gives an indistinct sound, who will get ready for battle? [9]So with yourselves; if you in a tongue utter speech that is not intelligible, how will any one know what is said? For you will be speaking into the air. [10]There are doubtless many different languages in the world, and none is without meaning; [11]but if I do not know the meaning of the language, I shall be a foreigner to the speaker and the speaker a foreigner to me. [12]So with yourselves; since you are eager for manifestations of the Spirit, strive to excel in building up the church.

13 Therefore, he who speaks in a tongue should pray for the power to interpret. [14]For if I pray in a tongue, my spirit prays but my mind is unfruitful. [15]What am I to do? I will pray with the spirit and I will pray with the mind also; I will sing with the spirit and I will sing with the mind also. [16]Otherwise, if you bless[w] with the spirit, how can any one in the position of an outsider[x] say the "Amen" to your thanksgiving when he does not know what you are saying? [17]For you may give thanks well enough, but the other man is not edified. [18]I thank God that I speak in tongues more than you all; [19]nevertheless, in church I would rather speak five words with my mind, in order to instruct others, than ten thousand words in a tongue.

20 Brethren, do not be children in your thinking; be babes in evil, but in thinking be mature. [21]In the law it is written, "By men of strange tongues and by the lips of foreigners will I speak to this people, and even then they will not listen to me, says the Lord." [22]Thus, tongues are a sign not for believers but for unbelievers, while prophecy is not for unbelievers but for believers. [23]If, therefore, the whole church assembles and all speak in tongues, and outsiders or unbelievers enter, will they not say that you are mad? [24]But if all prophesy, and an unbeliever or outsider enters, he is convicted by all, he is called to account by all, [25]the secrets of his heart are disclosed; and so, falling on his face, he will worship God and declare that God is really among you.

26 What then, brethren? When you come together, each one has a hymn, a lesson, a revelation, a tongue, or an interpretation. Let all things be done for edification. [27]If any speak in a tongue, let there be only two or at most three, and each in turn; and let one interpret. [28]But if there is no one to interpret, let each of them keep silence in church and speak to himself and to God. [29]Let two or three prophets speak, and let the others weigh what is said. [30]If a revelation is made to another sitting by, let the first be silent. [31]For you can all prophesy one by one, so that all may learn and all be encouraged; [32]and the spirits of prophets are subject to prophets. [33]For God is not a God of confusion but of peace.

As in all the churches of the saints, [34]the women should keep silence in the churches. For they are not permitted to speak, but should be subordinate, as even the law says. [35]If there is anything they desire to know, let them ask their husbands at home. For it is shameful for a woman to speak in church. [36]What! Did the word of God originate with you, or are you the only ones it has reached?

37 If any one thinks that he is a prophet, or spiritual, he should acknowledge that what I am writing to you is a command of the Lord. [38]If any one does not recognize this, he is not recognized. [39]So, my brethren, earnestly desire to prophesy, and do not forbid speaking in tongues; [40]but all things should be done decently and in order.

15 Now I would remind you, brethren, in what terms I preached to you the gospel, which you received, in which you stand, [2]by which you are saved, if you hold it fast —unless you believed in vain.

3 For I delivered to you as of first importance what I also received, that Christ died for our sins in accordance with the scriptures, [4]that he was

[w]That is, *give thanks to God*
[x]Or *him that is without gifts*
14.15: Eph 5.19; Col 3.16.
14.16: 1 Chron 16.36; Ps 106.48; Mt 15.36.
14.20: Eph 4.14.   14.21: Is 28.11-12.   14.26: Eph 5.19.
14.34: 1 Tim 2.11-12; 1 Pet 3.1.
15.3: 1 Cor 11.23; 1 Pet 2.24; Is 53.5-12.
15.4: Mt 16.21; Ps 16.8-9.

buried, that he was raised on the third day in accordance with the scriptures, [5] and that he appeared to Çĕ′phạs, then to the twelve. [6] Then he appeared to more than five hundred brethren at one time, most of whom are still alive, though some have fallen asleep. [7] Then he appeared to James, then to all the apostles. [8] Last of all, as to one untimely born, he appeared also to me. [9] For I am the least of the apostles, unfit to be called an apostle, because I persecuted the church of God. [10] But by the grace of God I am what I am, and his grace toward me was not in vain. On the contrary, I worked harder than any of them, though it was not I, but the grace of God which is with me. [11] Whether then it was I or they, so we preach and so you believed.

12 Now if Christ is preached as raised from the dead, how can some of you say that there is no resurrection of the dead? [13] But if there is no resurrection of the dead, then Christ has not been raised; [14] if Christ has not been raised, then our preaching is in vain and your faith is in vain. [15] We are even found to be misrepresenting God, because we testified of God that he raised Christ, whom he did not raise if it is true that the dead are not raised. [16] For if the dead are not raised, then Christ has not been raised. [17] If Christ has not been raised, your faith is futile and you are still in your sins. [18] Then those also who have fallen asleep in Christ have perished. [19] If for this life only we have hoped in Christ, we are of all men most to be pitied.

20 But in fact Christ has been raised from the dead, the first fruits of those who have fallen asleep. [21] For as by a man came death, by a man has come also the resurrection of the dead. [22] For as in Adam all die, so also in Christ shall all be made alive. [23] But each in his own order: Christ the first fruits, then at his coming those who belong to Christ. [24] Then comes the end, when he delivers the kingdom to God the Father after destroying every rule and every authority and power. [25] For he must reign until he has put all his enemies under his feet. [26] The last enemy to be destroyed is death. [27] "For God[z] has put all things in subjection under his feet." But when it says, "All things are put in subjection under him," it is plain that he is excepted who put all things under

him. [28] When all things are subjected to him, then the Son himself will also be subjected to him who put all things under him, that God may be everything to every one.

29 Otherwise, what do people mean by being baptized on behalf of the dead? If the dead are not raised at all, why are people baptized on their behalf? [30] Why am I in peril every hour? [31] I protest, brethren, by my pride in you which I have in Christ Jesus our Lord, I die every day! [32] What do I gain if, humanly speaking, I fought with beasts at Ėph′ẹ·sụs? If the dead are not raised, "Let us eat and drink, for tomorrow we die." [33] Do not be deceived: "Bad company ruins good morals." [34] Come to your right mind, and sin no more. For some have no knowledge of God. I say this to your shame.

35 But some one will ask, "How are the dead raised? With what kind of body do they come?" [36] You foolish man! What you sow does not come to life unless it dies. [37] And what you sow is not the body which is to be, but a bare kernel, perhaps of wheat or of some other grain. [38] But God gives it a body as he has chosen, and to each kind of seed its own body. [39] For not all flesh is alike, but there is one kind for men, another for animals, another for birds, and another for fish. [40] There are celestial bodies and there are terrestrial bodies; but the glory of the celestial is one, and the glory of the terrestrial is another. [41] There is one glory of the sun, and another glory of the moon, and another glory of the stars; for star differs from star in glory.

42 So is it with the resurrection of the dead. What is sown is perishable, what is raised is imperishable. [43] It is sown in dishonor, it is raised in glory. It is sown in weakness, it is raised in power. [44] It is sown a physical body, it is raised a spiritual body. If there is a physical body, there is also a spiritual body. [45] Thus it is written, "The first

[z] Greek *he*　**15.5:** Lk 24.34; Mt 28.17.
15.8: 1 Cor 9.1; Gal 1.16; Acts 9.3-6.
15.9: Acts 8.3.　**15.14:** 1 Thess 4.14.　**15.18:** 1 Thess 4.16.
15.21: Rom 5.12.　**15.22:** Rom 5.14-18.
15.23: 1 Thess 2.19.
15.25: Ps 110.1.　**15.27:** Ps 8.6; Eph 1.22.
15.28: Phil 3.21.　**15.30:** 2 Esdr 7.89.　**15.31:** Rom 8.36.
15.32: 2 Cor 1.8, 9; Is 22.13.　**15.33:** Menander, *Thais*.
15.34: Rom 13.11.　**15.36:** Jn 12.24.　**15.38:** Gen 1.11.
15.42: Dan 12.3.　**15.45:** Gen 2.7.

man Adam became a living being"; the last Adam became a life-giving spirit. [46] But it is not the spiritual which is first but the physical, and then the spiritual. [47] The first man was from the earth, a man of dust; the second man is from heaven. [48] As was the man of dust, so are those who are of the dust; and as is the man of heaven, so are those who are of heaven. [49] Just as we have borne the image of the man of dust, we shall[a] also bear the image of the man of heaven. [50] I tell you this, brethren: flesh and blood cannot inherit the kingdom of God, nor does the perishable inherit the imperishable.

[51] Lo! I tell you a mystery. We shall not all sleep, but we shall all be changed, [52] in a moment, in the twinkling of an eye, at the last trumpet. For the trumpet will sound, and the dead will be raised imperishable, and we shall be changed. [53] For this perishable nature must put on the imperishable, and this mortal nature must put on immortality. [54] When the perishable puts on the imperishable, and the mortal puts on immortality, then shall come to pass the saying that is written:

"Death is swallowed up in victory."
[55] "O death, where is thy victory?
　O death, where is thy sting?"
[56] The sting of death is sin, and the power of sin is the law. [57] But thanks be to God, who gives us the victory through our Lord Jesus Christ.

[58] Therefore, my beloved brethren, be steadfast, immovable, always abounding in the work of the Lord, knowing that in the Lord your labor is not in vain.

16 Now concerning the contribution for the saints: as I directed the churches of Galatia, so you also are to do. [2] On the first day of every week, each of you is to put something aside and store it up, as he may prosper, so that contributions need not be made when I come. [3] And when I arrive, I will send those whom you accredit by letter to carry your gift to Jerusalem. [4] If it seems advisable that I should go also, they will accompany me.

[5] I will visit you after passing through Măc̣·e·dō′nĭ·a, for I intend to pass through Macedonia, [6] and per-

haps I will stay with you or even spend the winter, so that you may speed me on my journey, wherever I go. [7] For I do not want to see you now just in passing; I hope to spend some time with you, if the Lord permits. [8] But I will stay in Ĕph′e·sŭs until Pentecost, [9] for a wide door for effective work has opened to me, and there are many adversaries.

[10] When Timothy comes, see that you put him at ease among you, for he is doing the work of the Lord, as I am. [11] So let no one despise him. Speed him on his way in peace, that he may return to me; for I am expecting him with the brethren.

[12] As for our brother A·pŏl′los, I strongly urged him to visit you with the other brethren, but it was not at all his will[b] to come now. He will come when he has opportunity.

[13] Be watchful, stand firm in your faith, be courageous, be strong. [14] Let all that you do be done in love.

[15] Now, brethren, you know that the household of Stĕph′a·nas were the first converts in A·chā′ī·a, and they have devoted themselves to the service of the saints; [16] I urge you to be subject to such men and to every fellow worker and laborer. [17] I rejoice at the coming of Stĕph′a·nas and Fôr·tū·nā′tus and A·chā′ī·cus, because they have made up for your absence; [18] for they refreshed my spirit as well as yours. Give recognition to such men.

[19] The churches of Asia send greetings. A′quĭ·la and Prĭs′ca, together with the church in their house, send you hearty greetings in the Lord. [20] All the brethren send greetings. Greet one another with a holy kiss.

[21] I, Paul, write this greeting with my own hand. [22] If any one has no love for the Lord, let him be accursed. Our Lord, come![c] [23] The grace of the Lord Jesus be with you. [24] My love be with you all in Christ Jesus. Amen.

[a] Other ancient authorities read *let us*
[b] Or *God's will for him*　[c] Greek *Maranatha*
15.51-52: 1 Thess 4.15-17.　15.54: Is 25.8.
15.55: Hos 13.14.　16.1: Acts 24.17.
16.2: Acts 20.7; 2 Cor 9.4-5.　16.3: 2 Cor 8.18-19.
16.5: Rom 15.26; Acts 19.21.　16.7: Acts 18.21.
16.8: Acts 18.19.　16.9: Acts 19.9.　16.10: Acts 16.1.
16.12: Acts 18.24.　16.13: Ps 31.24; Eph 6.10.
16.19: Acts 18.2; Rom 16.5.　16.20: Rom 16.16.
16.21: Col 4.18; Gal 6.11; 2 Thess 3.17.　16.22: Rom 9.3.
16.23: Rom 16.20.

The Second Letter of Paul to the
Corinthians

1 Paul, an apostle of Christ Jesus by the will of God, and Timothy our brother.

To the church of God which is at Corinth, with all the saints who are in the whole of A·chā′ĭ·a:

2 Grace to you and peace from God our Father and the Lord Jesus Christ.

3 Blessed be the God and Father of our Lord Jesus Christ, the Father of mercies and God of all comfort, 4 who comforts us in all our affliction, so that we may be able to comfort those who are in any affliction, with the comfort with which we ourselves are comforted by God. 5 For as we share abundantly in Christ's sufferings, so through Christ we share abundantly in comfort too.[a] 6 If we are afflicted, it is for your comfort and salvation; and if we are comforted, it is for your comfort, which you experience when you patiently endure the same sufferings that we suffer. 7 Our hope for you is unshaken; for we know that as you share in our sufferings, you will also share in our comfort.

8 For we do not want you to be ignorant, brethren, of the affliction we experienced in Asia; for we were so utterly, unbearably crushed that we despaired of life itself. 9 Why, we felt that we had received the sentence of death; but that was to make us rely not on ourselves but on God who raises the dead; 10 he delivered us from so deadly a peril, and he will deliver us; on him we have set our hope that he will deliver us again. 11 You also must help us by prayer, so that many will give thanks on our behalf for the blessing granted us in answer to many prayers.

12 For our boast is this, the testimony of our conscience that we have behaved in the world, and still more toward you, with holiness and godly sincerity, not by earthly wisdom but by the grace of God. 13 For we write you nothing but what you can read and understand; I hope you will understand fully, 14 as you have understood in part, that you can be proud of

us as we can be of you, on the day of the Lord Jesus.

15 Because I was sure of this, I wanted to come to you first, so that you might have a double pleasure;[b] 16 I wanted to visit you on my way to Măç·e·dō′nĭ·a, and to come back to you from Macedonia and have you send me on my way to Jü·dē′a. 17 Was I vacillating when I wanted to do this? Do I make my plans like a worldly man, ready to say Yes and No at once? 18 As surely as God is faithful, our word to you has not been Yes and No. 19 For the Son of God, Jesus Christ, whom we preached among you, Sĭl·vā′nŭs and Timothy and I, was not Yes and No; but in him it is always Yes. 20 For all the promises of God find their Yes in him. That is why we utter the Amen through him, to the glory of God. 21 But it is God who establishes us with you in Christ, and has commissioned us; 22 he has put his seal upon us and given us his Spirit in our hearts as a guarantee.

23 But I call God to witness against me—it was to spare you that I refrained from coming to Corinth. 24 Not that we lord it over your faith; we work with you for your joy, for you stand firm in your faith. 2 For I made up my mind not to make you another painful visit. 2 For if I cause you pain, who is there to make me glad but the one whom I have pained? 3 And I wrote as I did, so that I might not suffer pain from those who should have made me rejoice, for I felt sure of all of you, that my joy would be the joy of you all. 4 For I wrote you out of much affliction and anguish of heart and with many tears, not to cause you pain but to let you know the abundant love that I have for you.

5 But if any one has caused pain, he has caused it not to me, but in some measure—not to put it too severely—

[a] Or, For as the sufferings of Christ abound for us, so also our comfort abounds through Christ
[b] Other ancient authorities read favor
1.1: Eph 1.1; Col 1.1; 2 Cor 1.19; Acts 16.1; 18.1.
1.2: Rom 1.7. 1.3: Eph 1.3; 1 Pet 1.3; Rom 15.5.
1.4: 2 Cor 7.6, 7, 13. 1.16: Acts 19.21.
1.19: 1 Thess 1.1; Acts 15.22. 1.20: 1 Cor 14.16; Rev 3.14.

to you all. ⁶For such a one this punishment by the majority is enough; ⁷so you should rather turn to forgive and comfort him, or he may be overwhelmed by excessive sorrow. ⁸So I beg you to reaffirm your love for him. ⁹For this is why I wrote, that I might test you and know whether you are obedient in everything. ¹⁰Any one whom you forgive, I also forgive. What I have forgiven, if I have forgiven anything, has been for your sake in the presence of Christ, ¹¹to keep Satan from gaining the advantage over us; for we are not ignorant of his designs.

12 When I came to Trő′ǎs to preach the gospel of Christ, a door was opened for me in the Lord; ¹³but my mind could not rest because I did not find my brother Titus there. So I took leave of them and went on to Măç·ę·dō′ni·ạ.

14 But thanks be to God, who in Christ always leads us in triumph, and through us spreads the fragrance of the knowledge of him everywhere. ¹⁵For we are the aroma of Christ to God among those who are being saved and among those who are perishing, ¹⁶to one a fragrance from death to death, to the other a fragrance from life to life. Who is sufficient for these things? ¹⁷For we are not, like so many, peddlers of God's word; but as men of sincerity, as commissioned by God, in the sight of God we speak in Christ.

3 Are we beginning to commend ourselves again? Or do we need, as some do, letters of recommendation to you, or from you? ²You yourselves are our letter of recommendation, written on your^c hearts, to be known and read by all men; ³and you show that you are a letter from Christ delivered by us, written not with ink but with the Spirit of the living God, not on tablets of stone but on tablets of human hearts.

4 Such is the confidence that we have through Christ toward God. ⁵Not that we are competent of ourselves to claim anything as coming from us; our competence is from God, ⁶who has made us competent to be ministers of a new covenant, not in a written code but in the Spirit; for the written code kills, but the Spirit gives life.

7 Now if the dispensation of death, carved in letters on stone, came with such splendor that the Israelites could not look at Moses' face because of its brightness, fading as this was, ⁸will

not the dispensation of the Spirit be attended with greater splendor? ⁹For if there was splendor in the dispensation of condemnation, the dispensation of righteousness must far exceed it in splendor. ¹⁰Indeed, in this case, what once had splendor has come to have no splendor at all, because of the splendor that surpasses it. ¹¹For if what faded away came with splendor, what is permanent must have much more splendor.

12 Since we have such a hope, we are very bold, ¹³not like Moses, who put a veil over his face so that the Israelites might not see the end of the fading splendor.¹⁴But their minds were hardened; for to this day, when they read the old covenant, that same veil remains unlifted, because only through Christ is it taken away. ¹⁵Yes, to this day whenever Moses is read a veil lies over their minds; ¹⁶but when a man turns to the Lord the veil is removed. ¹⁷Now the Lord is the Spirit, and where the Spirit of the Lord is, there is freedom. ¹⁸And we all, with unveiled face, beholding^d the glory of the Lord, are being changed into his likeness from one degree of glory to another; for this comes from the Lord who is the Spirit.

4 Therefore, having this ministry by the mercy of God,^e we do not lose heart. ²We have renounced disgraceful, underhanded ways; we refuse to practice cunning or to tamper with God's word, but by the open statement of the truth we would commend ourselves to every man's conscience in the sight of God. ³And even if our gospel is veiled, it is veiled only to those who are perishing. ⁴In their case the god of this world has blinded the minds of the unbelievers, to keep them from seeing the light of the gospel of the glory of Christ, who is the likeness of God. ⁵For what we preach is not ourselves, but Jesus Christ as Lord, with ourselves as your servants^f for Jesus' sake. ⁶For it is the God who said, "Let light shine out of darkness," who has shone in our hearts to give the light of the knowledge of the glory of God in the face of Christ.

^cOther ancient authorities read *our*   ^dOr *reflecting*
^eGreek *as we have received mercy*   ^fOr *slaves*
2.12: Acts 16.8.   3.1: Acts 18.27; Rom 16.1; 1 Cor 16.3.
3.3: Ex 24.12; 31.18; 32.15-16; Jer 31.33.   3.6: Jer 31.31.
3.7: Ex 34.29-35.
3.17: Is 61.1-2.   4.4: Jn 12.31; Col 1.15.   4.6: Gen 1.3.

7 But we have this treasure in earthen vessels, to show that the transcendent power belongs to God and not to us. ⁸We are afflicted in every way, but not crushed; perplexed, but not driven to despair; ⁹persecuted, but not forsaken; struck down, but not destroyed; ¹⁰always carrying in the body the death of Jesus, so that the life of Jesus may also be manifested in our bodies. ¹¹For while we live we are always being given up to death for Jesus' sake, so that the life of Jesus may be manifested in our mortal flesh. ¹²So death is at work in us, but life in you.

13 Since we have the same spirit of faith as he had who wrote, "I believed, and so I spoke," we too believe, and so we speak, ¹⁴knowing that he who raised the Lord Jesus will raise us also with Jesus and bring us with you into his presence. ¹⁵For it is all for your sake, so that as grace extends to more and more people it may increase thanksgiving, to the glory of God.

16 So we do not lose heart. Though our outer nature is wasting away, our inner nature is being renewed every day. ¹⁷For this slight momentary affliction is preparing for us an eternal weight of glory beyond all comparison, ¹⁸because we look not to the things that are seen but to the things that are unseen; for the things that are seen are transient, but the things that are unseen are eternal.

5 For we know that if the earthly tent we live in is destroyed, we have a building from God, a house not made with hands, eternal in the heavens. ²Here indeed we groan, and long to put on our heavenly dwelling, ³so that by putting it on we may not be found naked. ⁴For while we are still in this tent, we sigh with anxiety; not that we would be unclothed, but that we would be further clothed, so that what is mortal may be swallowed up by life. ⁵He who has prepared us for this very thing is God, who has given us the Spirit as a guarantee.

6 So we are always of good courage; we know that while we are at home in the body we are away from the Lord, ⁷for we walk by faith, not by sight. ⁸We are of good courage, and we would rather be away from the body and at home with the Lord. ⁹So whether we are at home or away, we make it our aim to please him. ¹⁰For we must all

appear before the judgment seat of Christ, so that each one may receive good or evil, according to what he has done in the body.

11 Therefore, knowing the fear of the Lord, we persuade men; but what we are is known to God, and I hope it is known also to your conscience. ¹²We are not commending ourselves to you again but giving you cause to be proud of us, so that you may be able to answer those who pride themselves on a man's position and not on his heart. ¹³For if we are beside ourselves, it is for God; if we are in our right mind, it is for you. ¹⁴For the love of Christ controls us, because we are convinced that one has died for all; therefore all have died. ¹⁵And he died for all, that those who live might live no longer for themselves but for him who for their sake died and was raised.

16 From now on, therefore, we regard no one from a human point of view; even though we once regarded Christ from a human point of view, we regard him thus no longer. ¹⁷Therefore, if any one is in Christ, he is a new creation;ᵍ the old has passed away, behold, the new has come. ¹⁸All this is from God, who through Christ reconciled us to himself and gave us the ministry of reconciliation; ¹⁹that is, in Christ God was reconcilingʰ the world to himself, not counting their trespasses against them, and entrusting to us the message of reconciliation. ²⁰So we are ambassadors for Christ, God making his appeal through us. We beseech you on behalf of Christ, be reconciled to God. ²¹For our sake he made him to be sin who knew no sin, so that in him we might become the righteousness of God.

6 Working together with him, then, we entreat you not to accept the grace of God in vain. ²For he says,

"At the acceptable time I have listened to you,
and helped you on the day of salvation."

Behold, now is the acceptable time; behold, now is the day of salvation. ³We put no obstacle in any one's way,

ᵍOr *creature*   ʰOr *God was in Christ reconciling*
4.13: Ps 116.10.   **4.14:** 1 Thess 4.14.   **5.10:** Mt 16.27.
5.12: 2 Cor 3.1.   **5.14:** Rom 5.15; 6.6-7.
5.17: Rom 16.7; Gal 6.15.
5.18: 1 Cor 11.12; Col 1.20; Rom 5.10.   **5.20:** Eph 6.20.
5.21: Heb 4.15; 7.25; 1 Pet 2.22; 1 Jn 3.5; Acts 3.14.
6.2: Is 49.8.

so that no fault may be found with our ministry, ⁴but as servants of God we commend ourselves in every way: through great endurance, in afflictions, hardships, calamities, ⁵beatings, imprisonments, tumults, labors, watching, hunger; ⁶by purity, knowledge, forbearance, kindness, the Holy Spirit, genuine love, ⁷truthful speech, and the power of God; with the weapons of righteousness for the right hand and for the left; ⁸in honor and dishonor, in ill repute and good repute. We are treated as impostors, and yet are true; ⁹as unknown, and yet well known; as dying, and behold we live; as punished, and yet not killed; ¹⁰as sorrowful, yet always rejoicing; as poor, yet making many rich; as having nothing, and yet possessing everything.

11 Our mouth is open to you, Corinthians; our heart is wide. ¹²You are not restricted by us, but you are restricted in your own affections. ¹³In return—I speak as to children—widen your hearts also.

14 Do not be mismated with unbelievers. For what partnership have righteousness and iniquity? Or what fellowship has light with darkness? ¹⁵What accord has Christ with Bē'-li·al?ⁱ Or what has a believer in common with an unbeliever? ¹⁶What agreement has the temple of God with idols? For we are the temple of the living God; as God said,
"I will live in them and move among them,
and I will be their God,
and they shall be my people.
¹⁷Therefore come out from them,
and be separate from them, says the Lord,
and touch nothing unclean;
then I will welcome you,
¹⁸and I will be a father to you,
and you shall be my sons and daughters,
says the Lord Almighty."

7 Since we have these promises, beloved, let us cleanse ourselves from every defilement of body and spirit, and make holiness perfect in the fear of God.

2 Open your hearts to us; we have wronged no one, we have corrupted no one, we have taken advantage of no one. ³I do not say this to condemn you,

for I said before that you are in our hearts, to die together and to live together. ⁴I have great confidence in you; I have great pride in you; I am filled with comfort. With all our affliction, I am overjoyed.

5 For even when we came into Măç·ẹ·dō'nĭ·ạ, our bodies had no rest but we were afflicted at every turn—fighting without and fear within. ⁶But God, who comforts the downcast, comforted us by the coming of Titus, ⁷and not only by his coming but also by the comfort with which he was comforted in you, as he told us of your longing, your mourning, your zeal for me, so that I rejoiced still more. ⁸For even if I made you sorry with my letter, I do not regret it (though I did regret it), for I see that that letter grieved you, though only for a while. ⁹As it is, I rejoice, not because you were grieved, but because you were grieved into repenting; for you felt a godly grief, so that you suffered no loss through us. ¹⁰For godly grief produces a repentance that leads to salvation and brings no regret, but worldly grief produces death. ¹¹For see what earnestness this godly grief has produced in you, what eagerness to clear yourselves, what indignation, what alarm, what longing, what zeal, what punishment! At every point you have proved yourselves guiltless in the matter. ¹²So although I wrote to you, it was not on account of the one who did the wrong, nor on account of the one who suffered the wrong, but in order that your zeal for us might be revealed to you in the sight of God. ¹³Therefore we are comforted.

And besides our own comfort we rejoiced still more at the joy of Titus, because his mind has been set at rest by you all. ¹⁴For if I have expressed to him some pride in you, I was not put to shame; but just as everything we said to you was true, so our boasting before Titus has proved true. ¹⁵And his heart goes out all the more to you, as he remembers the obedience of you all, and the fear and trembling with

ⁱGreek *Beliar*
6.4: 2 Cor 4.8-11; 11.23-27. 6.5: Acts 16.23.
6.7: 2 Cor 10.4; Rom 13.12; Eph 6.11-12. 6.9: Rom 8.36.
6.10: Rom 8.32; 1 Cor 3.21. 6.11: Ezek 33.22; Is 60.5.
6.16: 1 Cor 10.21; 3.16; Ex 25.8; 29.45; Lev 26.12; Ezek 37.27; Jer 31.1. 6.17: Is 52.11. 6.18: Hos 1.10; Is 43.6.
7.2: 2 Cor 6.12-13. 7.3: 2 Cor 6.11-12.
7.5: 2 Cor 2.13; 4.8. 7.6: 2 Cor 2.13; 7.13-14.
7.8: 2 Cor 2.2. 7.12: 2 Cor 7.8; 2.3, 9.

which you received him. [16]I rejoice, because I have perfect confidence in you.

8 We want you to know, brethren, about the grace of God which has been shown in the churches of Măçe·dō'nĭ·a, [2]for in a severe test of affliction, their abundance of joy and their extreme poverty have overflowed in a wealth of liberality on their part. [3]For they gave according to their means, as I can testify, and beyond their means, of their own free will, [4]begging us earnestly for the favor of taking part in the relief of the saints—[5]and this, not as we expected, but first they gave themselves to the Lord and to us by the will of God. [6]Accordingly we have urged Titus that as he had already made a beginning, he should also complete among you this gracious work. [7]Now as you excel in everything—in faith, in utterance, in knowledge, in all earnestness, and in your love for us—see that you excel in this gracious work also.

8 I say this not as a command, but to prove by the earnestness of others that your love also is genuine. [9]For you know the grace of our Lord Jesus Christ, that though he was rich, yet for your sake he became poor, so that by his poverty you might become rich. [10]And in this matter I give my advice: it is best for you now to complete what a year ago you began not only to do but to desire, [11]so that your readiness in desiring it may be matched by your completing it out of what you have. [12]For if the readiness is there, it is acceptable according to what a man has, not according to what he has not. [13]I do not mean that others should be eased and you burdened, [14]but that as a matter of equality your abundance at the present time should supply their want, so that their abundance may supply your want, that there may be equality. [15]As it is written, "He who gathered much had nothing over, and he who gathered little had no lack."

16 But thanks be to God who puts the same earnest care for you into the heart of Titus. [17]For he not only accepted our appeal, but being himself very earnest he is going to you of his own accord. [18]With him we are sending the brother who is famous among all the churches for his preaching of the gospel; [19]and not only that, but he has been appointed by the churches to travel with us in this gracious work which we are carrying on, for the glory of the Lord and to show our good will. [20]We intend that no one should blame us about this liberal gift which we are administering, [21]for we aim at what is honorable not only in the Lord's sight but also in the sight of men. [22]And with them we are sending our brother whom we have often tested and found earnest in many matters, but who is now more earnest than ever because of his great confidence in you. [23]As for Titus, he is my partner and fellow worker in your service; and as for our brethren, they are messengers[j] of the churches, the glory of Christ. [24]So give proof, before the churches, of your love and of our boasting about you to these men.

9 Now it is superfluous for me to write to you about the offering for the saints, [2]for I know your readiness, of which I boast about you to the people of Măç·e·dō'nĭ·a, saying that A·chā'ĭ·a has been ready since last year; and your zeal has stirred up most of them. [3]But I am sending the brethren so that our boasting about you may not prove vain in this case, so that you may be ready, as I said you would be; [4]lest if some Măç·e·dō'nĭ·ạns come with me and find that you are not ready, we be humiliated—to say nothing of you—for being so confident. [5]So I thought it necessary to urge the brethren to go on to you before me, and arrange in advance for this gift you have promised, so that it may be ready not as an exaction but as a willing gift.

6 The point is this: he who sows sparingly will also reap sparingly, and he who sows bountifully will also reap bountifully. [7]Each one must do as he has made up his mind, not reluctantly or under compulsion, for God loves a cheerful giver. [8]And God is able to provide you with every blessing in abundance, so that you may always have enough of everything and may provide in abundance for every good work. [9]As it is written,

[j]Greek *apostles*
8.3: 1 Cor 16.2.
8.4: Acts 24.17; Rom 15.31. **8.6:** 2 Cor 8.16, 23; 2.13.
8.9: 2 Cor 6.10. **8.10:** 2 Cor 9.2; 1 Cor 16.2-3.
8.15: Ex 16.18. **8.18:** 2 Cor 12.18. **8.19:** 1 Cor 16.3-4.
9.1: 2 Cor 8.4. **9.2:** Rom 15.26; 2 Cor 8.10. **9.3:** 1 Cor 16.2.
9.7: Prov 22.8 Septuagint. **9.8:** Eph 3.20. **9.9:** Ps 112.9.

"He scatters abroad, he gives to the poor;

his righteousness[k] endures for ever."
[10] He who supplies seed to the sower and bread for food will supply and multiply your resources[l] and increase the harvest of your righteousness.[k] [11] You will be enriched in every way for great generosity, which through us will produce thanksgiving to God; [12] for the rendering of this service not only supplies the wants of the saints but also overflows in many thanksgivings to God. [13] Under the test of this service, you[m] will glorify God by your obedience in acknowledging the gospel of Christ, and by the generosity of your contribution for them and for all others; [14] while they long for you and pray for you, because of the surpassing grace of God in you. [15] Thanks be to God for his inexpressible gift!

10 I, Paul, myself entreat you, by the meekness and gentleness of Christ—I who am humble when face to face with you, but bold to you when I am away!—[2] I beg of you that when I am present I may not have to show boldness with such confidence as I count on showing against some who suspect us of acting in worldly fashion. [3] For though we live in the world we are not carrying on a worldly war, [4] for the weapons of our warfare are not worldly but have divine power to destroy strongholds. [5] We destroy arguments and every proud obstacle to the knowledge of God, and take every thought captive to obey Christ, [6] being ready to punish every disobedience, when your obedience is complete.

[7] Look at what is before your eyes. If any one is confident that he is Christ's, let him remind himself that as he is Christ's, so are we. [8] For even if I boast a little too much of our authority, which the Lord gave for building you up and not for destroying you, I shall not be put to shame. [9] I would not seem to be frightening you with letters. [10] For they say, "His letters are weighty and strong, but his bodily presence is weak, and his speech of no account." [11] Let such people understand that what we say by letter when absent, we do when present. [12] Not that we venture to class or compare ourselves with some of those who commend themselves. But when they measure themselves by one another, and compare themselves with one another, they are without understanding.

[13] But we will not boast beyond limit, but will keep to the limits God has apportioned us, to reach even to you. [14] For we are not overextending ourselves, as though we did not reach you; we were the first to come all the way to you with the gospel of Christ. [15] We do not boast beyond limit, in other men's labors; but our hope is that as your faith increases, our field among you may be greatly enlarged, [16] so that we may preach the gospel in lands beyond you, without boasting of work already done in another's field. [17] "Let him who boasts, boast of the Lord." [18] For it is not the man who commends himself that is accepted, but the man whom the Lord commends.

11 I wish you would bear with me in a little foolishness. Do bear with me! [2] I feel a divine jealousy for you, for I betrothed you to Christ to present you as a pure bride to her one husband. [3] But I am afraid that as the serpent deceived Eve by his cunning, your thoughts will be led astray from a sincere and pure devotion to Christ. [4] For if some one comes and preaches another Jesus than the one we preached, or if you receive a different spirit from the one you received, or if you accept a different gospel from the one you accepted, you submit to it readily enough. [5] I think that I am not in the least inferior to these superlative apostles. [6] Even if I am unskilled in speaking, I am not in knowledge; in every way we have made this plain to you in all things.

[7] Did I commit a sin in abasing myself so that you might be exalted, because I preached God's gospel without cost to you? [8] I robbed other churches by accepting support from them in order to serve you. [9] And when I was with you and was in want, I did not burden any one, for my needs were supplied by the brethren who came from Măç·e·dō'nĭ·a. So I refrained and

[k] Or *benevolence*   [l] Greek *sowing*   [m] Or *they*
9.10: Is 55.10; Hos 10.12.   9.13: 2 Cor 8.4; Rom 15.31.
9.15: Rom 5.15-16.   10.1: 2 Cor 10.10.
10.2: 2 Cor. 13.2, 10; 1 Cor 4.21.   10.6: 2 Cor 2.9.
10.7: 1 Cor 1.12.   10.10: 1 Cor 2.3.   10.15: Rom 15.20.
10.17: Jer 9.24.   11.1: 2 Cor 11.21.
11.2: Hos. 2.19-20; Eph 5.26-27.   11.3: Gen 3.4.
11.4: Gal 1.6.   11.5: 2 Cor 12.11; Gal 2.6   11.6: 1 Cor 1.17.
11.7: 2 Cor 12.13; 1 Cor 9.18.   11.8: Phil 4.15, 18.

will refrain from burdening you in any way. [10] As the truth of Christ is in me, this boast of mine shall not be silenced in the regions of A·chā′·ǎ. [11] And why? Because I do not love you? God knows I do!

12 And what I do I will continue to do, in order to undermine the claim of those who would like to claim that in their boasted mission they work on the same terms as we do. [13] For such men are false apostles, deceitful workmen, disguising themselves as apostles of Christ. [14] And no wonder, for even Satan disguises himself as an angel of light. [15] So it is not strange if his servants also disguise themselves as servants of righteousness. Their end will correspond to their deeds.

16 I repeat, let no one think me foolish; but even if you do, accept me as a fool, so that I too may boast a little. [17] (What I am saying I say not with the Lord's authority but as a fool, in this boastful confidence; [18] since many boast of worldly things, I too will boast.) [19] For you gladly bear with fools, being wise yourselves! [20] For you bear it if a man makes slaves of you, or preys upon you, or takes advantage of you, or puts on airs, or strikes you in the face. [21] To my shame, I must say, we were too weak for that!

But whatever any one dares to boast of—I am speaking as a fool—I also dare to boast of that. [22] Are they Hebrews? So am I. Are they Israelites? So am I. Are they descendants of Abraham? So am I. [23] Are they servants of Christ? I am a better one—I am talking like a madman—with far greater labors, far more imprisonments, with countless beatings, and often near death. [24] Five times I have received at the hands of the Jews the forty lashes less one. [25] Three times I have been beaten with rods; once I was stoned. Three times I have been shipwrecked; a night and a day I have been adrift at sea; [26] on frequent journeys, in danger from rivers, danger from robbers, danger from my own people, danger from Gentiles, danger in the city, danger in the wilderness, danger at sea, danger from false brethren; [27] in toil and hardship, through many a sleepless night, in hunger and thirst, often without food, in cold and exposure. [28] And, apart from other things,

there is the daily pressure upon me of my anxiety for all the churches. [29] Who is weak, and I am not weak? Who is made to fall, and I am not indignant?

30 If I must boast, I will boast of the things that show my weakness. [31] The God and Father of the Lord Jesus, he who is blessed for ever, knows that I do not lie. [32] At Damascus, the governor under King Ăr′ę·tăs guarded the city of Damascus in order to seize me, [33] but I was let down in a basket through a window in the wall, and escaped his hands.

12 I must boast; there is nothing to be gained by it, but I will go on to visions and revelations of the Lord. [2] I know a man in Christ who fourteen years ago was caught up to the third heaven—whether in the body or out of the body I do not know, God knows. [3] And I know that this man was caught up into Paradise—whether in the body or out of the body I do not know, God knows—[4] and he heard things that cannot be told, which man may not utter. [5] On behalf of this man I will boast, but on my own behalf I will not boast, except of my weaknesses. [6] Though if I wish to boast, I shall not be a fool, for I shall be speaking the truth. But I refrain from it, so that no one may think more of me than he sees in me or hears from me. [7] And to keep me from being too elated by the abundance of revelations, a thorn was given me in the flesh, a messenger of Satan, to harass me, to keep me from being too elated. [8] Three times I besought the Lord about this, that it should leave me; [9] but he said to me, "My grace is sufficient for you, for my power is made perfect in weakness." I will all the more gladly boast of my weaknesses, that the power of Christ may rest upon me. [10] For the sake of Christ, then, I am content with weaknesses, insults, hardships, persecutions, and calamities; for when I am weak, then I am strong.

11 I have been a fool! You forced me to it, for I ought to have been commended by you. For I was not at all

11.10: 1 Cor 9.15.   11.11: 2 Cor 12.15.   11.12: 1 Cor 9.12.
11.17: 1 Cor 7.12, 25.   11.19: 1 Cor 4.10.
11.23: Acts 16.23; 2 Cor 6.5.   11.24: Deut 25.3.
11.25: Acts 16.22; 14.19.   11.26: Acts 9.23; 14.5.
11.27: 1 Cor 4.11.   11.29: 1 Cor 9.22.
11.32-33: Acts 9.24-25.
12.4: Lk 23.43.   12.7: Job 2.6.
12.10: Rom 5.3; 2 Cor 6.4-5.   12.11: 2 Cor 11.5.

inferior to these superlative apostles, even though I am nothing. [12] The signs of a true apostle were performed among you in all patience, with signs and wonders and mighty works. [13] For in what were you less favored than the rest of the churches, except that I myself did not burden you? Forgive me this wrong!

14 Here for the third time I am ready to come to you. And I will not be a burden, for I seek not what is yours but you; for children ought not to lay up for their parents, but parents for their children. [15] I will most gladly spend and be spent for your souls. If I love you the more, am I to be loved the less? [16] But granting that I myself did not burden you, I was crafty, you say, and got the better of you by guile. [17] Did I take advantage of you through any of those whom I sent to you? [18] I urged Titus to go, and sent the brother with him. Did Titus take advantage of you? Did we not act in the same spirit? Did we not take the same steps?

19 Have you been thinking all along that we have been defending ourselves before you? It is in the sight of God that we have been speaking in Christ, and all for your upbuilding, beloved. [20] For I fear that perhaps I may come and find you not what I wish, and that you may find me not what you wish; that perhaps there may be quarreling, jealousy, anger, selfishness, slander, gossip, conceit, and disorder. [21] I fear that when I come again my God may humble me before you, and I may have to mourn over many of those who sinned before and have not repented of the impurity, immorality, and licentiousness which they have practiced.

13 This is the third time I am coming to you. Any charge must be sustained by the evidence of two or three witnesses. [2] I warned those who

sinned before and all the others, and I warn them now while absent, as I did when present on my second visit, that if I come again I will not spare them — [3] since you desire proof that Christ is speaking in me. He is not weak in dealing with you, but is powerful in you. [4] For he was crucified in weakness, but lives by the power of God. For we are weak in him, but in dealing with you we shall live with him by the power of God.

5 Examine yourselves, to see whether you are holding to your faith. Test yourselves. Do you not realize that Jesus Christ is in you? — unless indeed you fail to meet the test! [6] I hope you will find out that we have not failed. [7] But we pray God that you may not do wrong — not that we may appear to have met the test, but that you may do what is right, though we may seem to have failed. [8] For we cannot do anything against the truth, but only for the truth. [9] For we are glad when we are weak and you are strong. What we pray for is your improvement. [10] I write this while I am away from you, in order that when I come I may not have to be severe in my use of the authority which the Lord has given me for building up and not for tearing down.

11 Finally, brethren, farewell. Mend your ways, heed my appeal, agree with one another, live in peace, and the God of love and peace will be with you. [12] Greet one another with a holy kiss. [13] All the saints greet you.

14 The grace of the Lord Jesus Christ and the love of God and the fellowship of[n] the Holy Spirit be with you all.

[n] Or *and participation in*

12.13: 2 Cor 11.7.   12.16: 2 Cor 11.9.
12.18: 2 Cor 2.13; 8.18.   12.20: 2 Cor 2.1-4; 1 Cor 1.11; 3.3.
13.1: 2 Cor 12.14; Deut 19.15.   13.4: Phil 2.7-8; Rom 6.8.
13.10: 2 Cor 2.3.   13.12: Rom 16.16.   13.13: Phil 4.22.
13.14: Rom 16.20.

Galatians

1 Paul an apostle—not from men nor through man, but through Jesus Christ and God the Father, who raised him from the dead— [2] and all the brethren who are with me, To the churches of Galatia:

3 Grace to you and peace from God the Father and our Lord Jesus Christ, [4] who gave himself for our sins to deliver us from the present evil age, according to the will of our God and Father; [5] to whom be the glory for ever and ever. Amen.

6 I am astonished that you are so quickly deserting him who called you in the grace of Christ and turning to a different gospel—[7] not that there is another gospel, but there are some who trouble you and want to pervert the gospel of Christ. [8] But even if we, or an angel from heaven, should preach to you a gospel contrary to that which we preached to you, let him be accursed. [9] As we have said before, so now I say again, If any one is preaching to you a gospel contrary to that which you received, let him be accursed.

10 Am I now seeking the favor of men, or of God? Or am I trying to please men? If I were still pleasing men, I should not be a servant[a] of Christ.

11 For I would have you know, brethren, that the gospel which was preached by me is not man's[b] gospel. [12] For I did not receive it from man, nor was I taught it, but it came through a revelation of Jesus Christ. [13] For you have heard of my former life in Jū·dā'ism, how I persecuted the church of God violently and tried to destroy it; [14] and I advanced in Jū·dā'ism beyond many of my own age among my people, so extremely zealous was I for the traditions of my fathers. [15] But when he who had set me apart before I was born, and had called me through his grace, [16] was pleased to reveal his Son to[c] me, in order that I might preach him among the Gentiles, I did not confer with flesh and blood, [17] nor did I go up to Jerusalem to those who were apostles before me, but I went away into Arabia; and again I returned to Damascus.

18 Then after three years I went up to Jerusalem to visit Çē'phạs, and remained with him fifteen days. [19] But I saw none of the other apostles except James the Lord's brother. [20] (In what I am writing to you, before God, I do not lie!) [21] Then I went into the regions of Syria and Çĭ·lĭ'çĭ·ạ. [22] And I was still not known by sight to the churches of Christ in Jū·dē'ạ; [23] they only heard it said, "He who once persecuted us is now preaching the faith he once tried to destroy." [24] And they glorified God because of me.

2 Then after fourteen years I went up again to Jerusalem with Bär'na·bạs, taking Titus along with me. [2] I went up by revelation; and I laid before them (but privately before those who were of repute) the gospel which I preach among the Gentiles, lest somehow I should be running or had run in vain. [3] But even Titus, who was with me, was not compelled to be circumcised, though he was a Greek. [4] But because of false brethren secretly brought in, who slipped in to spy out our freedom which we have in Christ Jesus, that they might bring us into bondage—[5] to them we did not yield submission even for a moment, that the truth of the gospel might be preserved for you. [6] And from those who were reputed to be something (what they were makes no difference to me; God shows no partiality)—those, I say, who were of repute added nothing to me; [7] but on the contrary, when they saw that I had been entrusted with the gospel to the uncircumcised, just as Peter had been entrusted with the gospel to the circumcised [8] (for he who worked through Peter for the mission to the circumcised worked through me

[a] Or *slave*   [b] Greek *according to man*   [c] Greek *in*
1.3: Rom 1.7.   **1.4:** Gal 2.20; 1 Tim 2.6.   **1.5:** Rom 16.27.
1.8: 2 Cor 11.4.   **1.10:** 1 Thess 2.4.   **1.11:** Rom 1.16-17.
1.13: Acts 8.3.   **1.14:** Acts 22.3.
1.15: Acts 9.1-19; Is 49.1; Jer 1.5.
1.18: Acts 9.26-30; 11.30.   **2.1:** Acts 15.2.
2.5: Acts 15.23-29.   **2.6:** Deut 10.17.

also for the Gentiles), ⁹ and when they perceived the grace that was given to me, James and Çē′phas and John, who were reputed to be pillars, gave to me and Bär′na·bas the right hand of fellowship, that we should go to the Gentiles and they to the circumcised; ¹⁰ only they would have us remember the poor, which very thing I was eager to do.

11 But when Çē′phas came to Ăn′-ti·öch I opposed him to his face, because he stood condemned. ¹² For before certain men came from James, he ate with the Gentiles; but when they came he drew back and separated himself, fearing the circumcision party. ¹³ And with him the rest of the Jews acted insincerely, so that even Bär′-na·bas was carried away by their insincerity. ¹⁴ But when I saw that they were not straightforward about the truth of the gospel, I said to Çē′phas before them all, "If you, though a Jew, live like a Gentile and not like a Jew, how can you compel the Gentiles to live like Jews?" ¹⁵ We ourselves, who are Jews by birth and not Gentile sinners, ¹⁶ yet who know that a man is not justified ᵈ by works of the law but through faith in Jesus Christ, even we have believed in Christ Jesus, in order to be justified by faith in Christ, and not by works of the law, because by works of the law shall no one be justified. ¹⁷ But if, in our endeavor to be justified in Christ, we ourselves were found to be sinners, is Christ then an agent of sin? Certainly not! ¹⁸ But if I build up again those things which I tore down, then I prove myself a transgressor. ¹⁹ For I through the law died to the law, that I might live to God. ²⁰ I have been crucified with Christ; it is no longer I who live, but Christ who lives in me; and the life I now live in the flesh I live by faith in the Son of God, who loved me and gave himself for me. ²¹ I do not nullify the grace of God; for if justification ᵉ were through the law, then Christ died to no purpose.

3 O foolish Galatians! Who has bewitched you, before whose eyes Jesus Christ was publicly portrayed as crucified? ² Let me ask you only this: Did you receive the Spirit by works of the law, or by hearing with faith? ³ Are you so foolish? Having

begun with the Spirit, are you now ending with the flesh? ⁴ Did you experience so many things in vain? — if it really is in vain. ⁵ Does he who supplies the Spirit to you and works miracles among you do so by works of the law, or by hearing with faith?

6 Thus Abraham "believed God, and it was reckoned to him as righteousness." ⁷ So you see that it is men of faith who are the sons of Abraham. ⁸ And the scripture, foreseeing that God would justify the Gentiles by faith, preached the gospel beforehand to Abraham, saying, "In you shall all the nations be blessed." ⁹ So then, those who are men of faith are blessed with Abraham who had faith.

10 For all who rely on works of the law are under a curse; for it is written, "Cursed be every one who does not abide by all things written in the book of the law, and do them." ¹¹ Now it is evident that no man is justified before God by the law; for "He who through faith is righteous shall live"; ᶠ ¹² but the law does not rest on faith, for "He who does them shall live by them." ¹³ Christ redeemed us from the curse of the law, having become a curse for us — for it is written, "Cursed be every one who hangs on a tree" — ¹⁴ that in Christ Jesus the blessing of Abraham might come upon the Gentiles, that we might receive the promise of the Spirit through faith.

15 To give a human example, brethren: no one annuls even a man's will, ᵍ or adds to it, once it has been ratified. ¹⁶ Now the promises were made to Abraham and to his offspring. It does not say, "And to offsprings," referring to many; but, referring to one, "And to your offspring," which is Christ. ¹⁷ This is what I mean: the law, which came four hundred and thirty years afterward, does not annul a covenant previously ratified by God, so as to make the promise void. ¹⁸ For if the inheritance is by the law, it is no longer by promise; but God gave it to Abraham by a promise.

ᵈ Or *reckoned righteous*; and so elsewhere
ᵉ Or *righteousness* ᶠ Or *the righteous shall live by faith*
ᵍ Or *covenant* (as in verse 17)
2.11: Acts 11.19-26.
2.16: Ps 143.2; Rom 3.20. 2.20: Gal 1.4.
3.6: Gen 15.6; Rom 4.3. 3.8: Gen 12.3; 18.18; Acts 3.25.
3.9: Rom 4.16. 3.10: Deut 27.26.
3.11: Hab 2.4; Rom 1.17; Heb 10.38.
3.12: Lev 18.5; Rom 10.5. 3.13: Deut 21.23.
3.16: Gen 12.7. 3.17: Ex 12.40. 3.18: Rom 11.6.

19 Why then the law? It was added because of transgressions, till the offspring should come to whom the promise had been made; and it was ordained by angels through an intermediary. ²⁰ Now an intermediary implies more than one; but God is one. 21 Is the law then against the promises of God? Certainly not; for if a law had been given which could make alive, then righteousness would indeed be by the law. ²² But the scripture consigned all things to sin, that what was promised to faith in Jesus Christ might be given to those who believe.

23 Now before faith came, we were confined under the law, kept under restraint until faith should be revealed. ²⁴ So that the law was our custodian until Christ came, that we might be justified by faith. ²⁵ But now that faith has come, we are no longer under a custodian; ²⁶ for in Christ Jesus you are all sons of God, through faith. ²⁷ For as many of you as were baptized into Christ have put on Christ. ²⁸ There is neither Jew nor Greek, there is neither slave nor free, there is neither male nor female; for you are all one in Christ Jesus. ²⁹ And if you are Christ's, then you are Abraham's offspring, heirs according to promise.

4 I mean that the heir, as long as he is a child, is no better than a slave, though he is the owner of all the estate; ² but he is under guardians and trustees until the date set by the father. ³ So with us; when we were children, we were slaves to the elemental spirits of the universe. ⁴ But when the time had fully come, God sent forth his Son, born of woman, born under the law, ⁵ to redeem those who were under the law, so that we might receive adoption as sons. ⁶ And because you are sons, God has sent the Spirit of his Son into our hearts, crying, "Ăb′ba! Father!" ⁷ So through God you are no longer a slave but a son, and if a son then an heir.

8 Formerly, when you did not know God, you were in bondage to beings that by nature are no gods; ⁹ but now that you have come to know God, or rather to be known by God, how can you turn back again to the weak and beggarly elemental spirits, whose slaves you want to be once more? ¹⁰ You observe days, and months, and seasons, and years! ¹¹ I am afraid I have labored over you in vain.

12 Brethren, I beseech you, become as I am, for I also have become as you are. You did me no wrong; ¹³ you know it was because of a bodily ailment that I preached the gospel to you at first; ¹⁴ and though my condition was a trial to you, you did not scorn or despise me, but received me as an angel of God, as Christ Jesus. ¹⁵ What has become of the satisfaction you felt? For I bear you witness that, if possible, you would have plucked out your eyes and given them to me. ¹⁶ Have I then become your enemy by telling you the truth?ʰ ¹⁷ They make much of you, but for no good purpose; they want to shut you out, that you may make much of them. ¹⁸ For a good purpose it is always good to be made much of, and not only when I am present with you. ¹⁹ My little children, with whom I am again in travail until Christ be formed in you! ²⁰ I could wish to be present with you now and to change my tone, for I am perplexed about you.

21 Tell me, you who desire to be under law, do you not hear the law? ²² For it is written that Abraham had two sons, one by a slave and one by a free woman. ²³ But the son of the slave was born according to the flesh, the son of the free woman through promise. ²⁴ Now this is an allegory: these women are two covenants. One is from Mount Sinai, bearing children for slavery; she is Hā′gar. ²⁵ Now Hā′gar is Mount Sinai in Arabia;ⁱ she corresponds to the present Jerusalem, for she is in slavery with her children. ²⁶ But the Jerusalem above is free, and she is our mother. ²⁷ For it is written,

"Rejoice, O barren one who does
    not bear;
break forth and shout, you who are
    not in travail;
for the children of the desolate
    are many more
than the children of her that is
    married."

²⁸ Now we,ʲ brethren, like Isaac, are children of promise. ²⁹ But as at that time he who was born according to

ʰ Or *by dealing truly with you*
ⁱ Other ancient authorities read *For Sinai is a mountain in Arabia.* ʲ Other ancient authorities read *you*
3.19: Rom 5.20.   **3.21:** Rom 8.2-4.
3.22: Rom 3.9-19; 11.32.   **3.28:** Rom 10.12.
4.3: Col 2.20.   **4.6:** Rom 8.15.   **4.13:** Acts 16.6.
4.19: 1 Cor 4.15.   **4.22:** Gen 16.15; 21.2, 9.
4.23: Rom 9.7-9.   **4.27:** Is 54.1.   **4.29:** Gen 21.9.

the flesh persecuted him who was born according to the Spirit, so it is now. [30] But what does the scripture say? "Cast out the slave and her son; for the son of the slave shall not inherit with the son of the free woman." [31] So, brethren, we are not children of the slave but of the free woman.

5 For freedom Christ has set us free; stand fast therefore, and do not submit again to a yoke of slavery. 2 Now I, Paul, say to you that if you receive circumcision, Christ will be of no advantage to you. [3] I testify again to every man who receives circumcision that he is bound to keep the whole law. [4] You are severed from Christ, you who would be justified by the law; you have fallen away from grace. [5] For through the Spirit, by faith, we wait for the hope of righteousness. [6] For in Christ Jesus neither circumcision nor uncircumcision is of any avail, but faith working* through love. [7] You were running well; who hindered you from obeying the truth? [8] This persuasion is not from him who calls you. [9] A little leaven leavens the whole lump. [10] I have confidence in the Lord that you will take no other view than mine; and he who is troubling you will bear his judgment, whoever he is. [11] But if I, brethren, still preach circumcision, why am I still persecuted? In that case the stumbling block of the cross has been removed. [12] I wish those who unsettle you would mutilate themselves!

13 For you were called to freedom, brethren; only do not use your freedom as an opportunity for the flesh, but through love be servants of one another. [14] For the whole law is fulfilled in one word, "You shall love your neighbor as yourself." [15] But if you bite and devour one another take heed that you are not consumed by one another. 16 But I say, walk by the Spirit, and do not gratify the desires of the flesh. [17] For the desires of the flesh are against the Spirit, and the desires of the Spirit are against the flesh; for these are opposed to each other, to prevent you from doing what you would. [18] But if you are led by the Spirit you are not under the law. [19] Now the works of the flesh are plain: fornication, impurity, licentiousness, [20] idolatry, sorcery, enmity,

strife, jealousy, anger, selfishness, dissension, party spirit, [21] envy,* drunkenness, carousing, and the like. I warn you, as I warned you before, that those who do such things shall not inherit the kingdom of God. [22] But the fruit of the Spirit is love, joy, peace, patience, kindness, goodness, faithfulness, [23] gentleness, self-control; against such there is no law. [24] And those who belong to Christ Jesus have crucified the flesh with its passions and desires.

25 If we live by the Spirit, let us also walk by the Spirit. [26] Let us have no self-conceit, no provoking of one another, no envy of one another.

6 Brethren, if a man is overtaken in any trespass, you who are spiritual should restore him in a spirit of gentleness. Look to yourself, lest you too be tempted. [2] Bear one another's burdens, and so fulfil the law of Christ. [3] For if any one thinks he is something, when he is nothing, he deceives himself. [4] But let each one test his own work, and then his reason to boast will be in himself alone and not in his neighbor. [5] For each man will have to bear his own load.

6 Let him who is taught the word share all good things with him who teaches.

7 Do not be deceived; God is not mocked, for whatever a man sows, that he will also reap. [8] For he who sows to his own flesh will from the flesh reap corruption; but he who sows to the Spirit will from the Spirit reap eternal life. [9] And let us not grow weary in well-doing, for in due season we shall reap, if we do not lose heart. [10] So then, as we have opportunity, let us do good to all men, and especially to those who are of the household of faith.

11 See with what large letters I am writing to you with my own hand. [12] It is those who want to make a good showing in the flesh that would compel you to be circumcised, and only in order that they may not be persecuted for the cross of Christ. [13] For even those who receive circumcision do not themselves keep the law, but they desire

*Or *made effective*
*k*Other ancient authorities add *murder*
4.30: Gen 21.10-12. **5.6:** 1 Cor 7.19; Gal 6.15.
5.9: 1 Cor 5.6. **5.14:** Lev 19.18; Rom 13.8-10.
5.17: Rom 7.15-23. **5.19:** Rom 1.28. **6.11:** 1 Cor 16.21.

to have you circumcised that they may glory in your flesh. [14] But far be it from me to glory except in the cross of our Lord Jesus Christ, by which[f] the world has been crucified to me, and I to the world. [15] For neither circumcision counts for anything, nor uncircumcision, but a new creation. [16] Peace and mercy be upon all who walk by this rule, upon the Israel of God.

17 Henceforth let no man trouble me; for I bear on my body the marks of Jesus.

18 The grace of our Lord Jesus Christ be with your spirit, brethren. Amen.

The Letter of Paul to the

Ephesians

1 Paul, an apostle of Christ Jesus by the will of God,

To the saints who are also faithful[a] in Christ Jesus:

2 Grace to you and peace from God our Father and the Lord Jesus Christ.

3 Blessed be the God and Father of our Lord Jesus Christ, who has blessed us in Christ with every spiritual blessing in the heavenly places, [4] even as he chose us in him before the foundation of the world, that we should be holy and blameless before him. [5] He destined us in love[b] to be his sons through Jesus Christ, according to the purpose of his will, [6] to the praise of his glorious grace which he freely bestowed on us in the Beloved. [7] In him we have redemption through his blood, the forgiveness of our trespasses, according to the riches of his grace [8] which he lavished upon us. [9] For he has made known to us in all wisdom and insight the mystery of his will, according to his purpose which he set forth in Christ [10] as a plan for the fulness of time, to unite all things in him, things in heaven and things on earth.

11 In him, according to the purpose of him who accomplishes all things according to the counsel of his will, [12] we who first hoped in Christ have been destined and appointed to live for the praise of his glory. [13] In him you also, who have heard the word of truth, the gospel of your salvation, and have believed in him, were sealed with the promised Holy Spirit, [14] which is the guarantee of our inheritance until we acquire possession of it, to the praise of his glory.

15 For this reason, because I have heard of your faith in the Lord Jesus and your love[c] toward all the saints, [16] I do not cease to give thanks for you, remembering you in my prayers, [17] that the God of our Lord Jesus Christ, the Father of glory, may give you a spirit of wisdom and of revelation in the knowledge of him, [18] having the eyes of your hearts enlightened, that you may know what is the hope to which he has called you, what are the riches of his glorious inheritance in the saints, [19] and what is the immeasurable greatness of his power in us who believe, according to the working of his great might [20] which he accomplished in Christ when he raised him from the dead and made him sit at his right hand in the heavenly places, [21] far above all rule and authority and power and dominion, and above every name that is named, not only in this age but also in that which is to come; [22] and he has put all things under his feet and has made him the head over all things for the church, [23] which is his body, the fulness of him who fills all in all.

2 And you he made alive, when you were dead through the trespasses and sins [2] in which you once walked,

---

[f] Or *through whom* **6.16:** Ps 125.5.

[a] Other ancient authorities read *who are at Ephesus and faithful* [b] Or *before him in love, having destined us*
[c] Other ancient authorities omit *your love*
1.3: 2 Cor 1.3. **1.6:** Col 1.13. **1.7:** Col 1.14. **1.10:** Gal 4.4.
1.14: 2 Cor 1.22. **1.15:** Col 1.9. **1.16:** Col 1.3.
1.18: Deut 33.3. **1.20:** Ps 110.1. **1.21:** Col 1.6; 2.10, 15.
1.22: Ps 8.6; Col 1.19. **1.23:** Rom 12.5; Col 2.17.
2.2: Col 1.13.

following the course of this world, following the prince of the power of the air, the spirit that is now at work in the sons of disobedience. ³Among these we all once lived in the passions of our flesh, following the desires of body and mind, and so we were by nature children of wrath, like the rest of mankind. ⁴But God, who is rich in mercy, out of the great love with which he loved us, ⁵even when we were dead through our trespasses, made us alive together with Christ (by grace you have been saved), ⁶and raised us up with him, and made us sit with him in the heavenly places in Christ Jesus, ⁷that in the coming ages he might show the immeasurable riches of his grace in kindness toward us in Christ Jesus. ⁸For by grace you have been saved through faith; and this is not your own doing, it is the gift of God— ⁹not because of works, lest any man should boast. ¹⁰For we are his workmanship, created in Christ Jesus for good works, which God prepared beforehand, that we should walk in them.

11 Therefore remember that at one time you Gentiles in the flesh, called the uncircumcision by what is called the circumcision, which is made in the flesh by hands—¹²remember that you were at that time separated from Christ, alienated from the commonwealth of Israel, and strangers to the covenants of promise, having no hope and without God in the world. ¹³But now in Christ Jesus you who once were far off have been brought near in the blood of Christ. ¹⁴For he is our peace, who has made us both one, and has broken down the dividing wall of hostility, ¹⁵by abolishing in his flesh the law of commandments and ordinances, that he might create in himself one new man in place of the two, so making peace, ¹⁶and might reconcile us both to God in one body through the cross, thereby bringing the hostility to an end. ¹⁷And he came and preached peace to you who were far off and peace to those who were near; ¹⁸for through him we both have access in one Spirit to the Father. ¹⁹So then you are no longer strangers and sojourners, but you are fellow citizens with the saints and members of the household of God, ²⁰built upon the foundation of the apostles and prophets, Christ Jesus himself being the cornerstone, ²¹in whom the whole structure is joined together and grows into a holy temple in the Lord; ²²in whom you also are built into it for a dwelling place of God in the Spirit.

3 For this reason I, Paul, a prisoner for Christ Jesus on behalf of you Gentiles—²assuming that you have heard of the stewardship of God's grace that was given to me for you, ³how the mystery was made known to me by revelation, as I have written briefly. ⁴When you read this you can perceive my insight into the mystery of Christ, ⁵which was not made known to the sons of men in other generations as it has now been revealed to his holy apostles and prophets by the Spirit; ⁶that is, how the Gentiles are fellow heirs, members of the same body, and partakers of the promise in Christ Jesus through the gospel.

7 Of this gospel I was made a minister according to the gift of God's grace which was given me by the working of his power. ⁸To me, though I am the very least of all the saints, this grace was given, to preach to the Gentiles the unsearchable riches of Christ, ⁹and to make all men see what is the plan of the mystery hidden for ages in ᵃ God who created all things; ¹⁰that through the church the manifold wisdom of God might now be made known to the principalities and powers in the heavenly places. ¹¹This was according to the eternal purpose which he has realized in Christ Jesus our Lord, ¹²in whom we have boldness and confidence of access through our faith in him. ¹³So I ask you not to ᵉ lose heart over what I am suffering for you, which is your glory.

14 For this reason I bow my knees before the Father, ¹⁵from whom every family in heaven and on earth is named, ¹⁶that according to the riches of his glory he may grant you to be strengthened with might through his Spirit in the inner man, ¹⁷and that Christ may dwell in your hearts through faith; that you, being rooted and grounded in love, ¹⁸may have power to comprehend with all the saints what is the breadth and length and height and depth, ¹⁹and to know the love of Christ which surpasses

ᵃOr *by* ᵉOr *I ask that I may not*
2.8: Gal 2.16.   2.12: Is 57.19.   2.17: Is 57.19.
3.2: Col 1.25.   3.6: Col 1.27.   3.9: Col 1.26.

knowledge, that you may be filled with all the fulness of God.

20 Now to him who by the power at work within us is able to do far more abundantly than all that we ask or think, 21 to him be glory in the church and in Christ Jesus to all generations, for ever and ever. Amen.

4 I therefore, a prisoner for the Lord, beg you to lead a life worthy of the calling to which you have been called, 2 with all lowliness and meekness, with patience, forbearing one another in love, 3 eager to maintain the unity of the Spirit in the bond of peace. 4 There is one body and one Spirit, just as you were called to the one hope that belongs to your call, 5 one Lord, one faith, one baptism, 6 one God and Father of us all, who is above all and through all and in all. 7 But grace was given to each of us according to the measure of Christ's gift. 8 Therefore it is said,

"When he ascended on high he led a
　　host of captives,
and he gave gifts to men."

9 (In saying, "He ascended," what does it mean but that he had also descended into the lower parts of the earth? 10 He who descended is he who also ascended far above all the heavens, that he might fill all things.) 11 And his gifts were that some should be apostles, some prophets, some evangelists, some pastors and teachers, 12 to equip the saints for the work of ministry, for building up the body of Christ, 13 until we all attain to the unity of the faith and of the knowledge of the Son of God, to mature manhood, to the measure of the stature of the fulness of Christ; 14 so that we may no longer be children, tossed to and fro and carried about with every wind of doctrine, by the cunning of men, by their craftiness in deceitful wiles. 15 Rather, speaking the truth in love, we are to grow up in every way into him who is the head, into Christ, 16 from whom the whole body, joined and knit together by every joint with which it is supplied, when each part is working properly, makes bodily growth and upbuilds itself in love.

17 Now this I affirm and testify in the Lord, that you must no longer live as the Gentiles do, in the futility of their minds; 18 they are darkened in their understanding, alienated from the life of God because of the ignorance that is in them, due to their hardness of heart; 19 they have become callous and have given themselves up to licentiousness, greedy to practice every kind of uncleanness. 20 You did not so learn Christ!— 21 assuming that you have heard about him and were taught in him, as the truth is in Jesus. 22 Put off your old nature which belongs to your former manner of life and is corrupt through deceitful lusts, 23 and be renewed in the spirit of your minds, 24 and put on the new nature, created after the likeness of God in true righteousness and holiness.

25 Therefore, putting away falsehood, let every one speak the truth with his neighbor, for we are members one of another. 26 Be angry but do not sin; do not let the sun go down on your anger, 27 and give no opportunity to the devil. 28 Let the thief no longer steal, but rather let him labor, doing honest work with his hands, so that he may be able to give to those in need. 29 Let no evil talk come out of your mouths, but only such as is good for edifying, as fits the occasion, that it may impart grace to those who hear. 30 And do not grieve the Holy Spirit of God, in whom you were sealed for the day of redemption. 31 Let all bitterness and wrath and anger and clamor and slander be put away from you, with all malice, 32 and be kind to one another, tenderhearted, forgiving one another, as God in Christ forgave you.

5 Therefore be imitators of God, as beloved children. 2 And walk in love, as Christ loved us and gave himself up for us, a fragrant offering and sacrifice to God.

3 But fornication and all impurity or covetousness must not even be named among you, as is fitting among saints. 4 Let there be no filthiness, nor silly talk, nor levity, which are not fitting; but instead let there be thanksgiving. 5 Be sure of this, that no fornicator or impure man, or one who is covetous (that is an idolater), has any inheritance in the kingdom of Christ and of God. 6 Let no one deceive you with empty words, for it is because of these things that the wrath of God

4.2: Col 3.12-13.　4.8: Ps 68.18.　4.15: Col 1.18.
4.16: Col 2.19.　4.25: Zech 8.16; Rom 12.5.
5.2: Ex 29.18; Ezek 20.41.

comes upon the sons of disobedience. [7]Therefore do not associate with them, [8]for once you were darkness, but now you are light in the Lord; walk as children of light [9](for the fruit of light is found in all that is good and right and true), [10]and try to learn what is pleasing to the Lord. [11]Take no part in the unfruitful works of darkness, but instead expose them. [12]For it is a shame even to speak of the things that they do in secret; [13]but when anything is exposed by the light it becomes visible, for anything that becomes visible is light. [14]Therefore it is said,

"Awake, O sleeper, and arise from the dead,
and Christ shall give you light."

15 Look carefully then how you walk, not as unwise men but as wise, [16]making the most of the time, because the days are evil. [17]Therefore do not be foolish, but understand what the will of the Lord is. [18]And do not get drunk with wine, for that is debauchery; but be filled with the Spirit, [19]addressing one another in psalms and hymns and spiritual songs, singing and making melody to the Lord with all your heart, [20]always and for everything giving thanks in the name of our Lord Jesus Christ to God the Father.

21 Be subject to one another out of reverence for Christ. [22]Wives, be subject to your husbands, as to the Lord. [23]For the husband is the head of the wife as Christ is the head of the church, his body, and is himself its Savior. [24]As the church is subject to Christ, so let wives also be subject in everything to their husbands. [25]Husbands, love your wives, as Christ loved the church and gave himself up for her, [26]that he might sanctify her, having cleansed her by the washing of water with the word, [27]that he might present the church to himself in splendor, without spot or wrinkle or any such thing, that she might be holy and without blemish. [28]Even so husbands should love their wives as their own bodies. He who loves his wife loves himself. [29]For no man ever hates his own flesh, but nourishes and cherishes it, as Christ does the church, [30]because we are members of his body. [31]"For this reason a man shall leave his father and mother and be joined to his wife, and the two shall become one flesh." [32]This mystery is a profound one, and I am saying that it refers to Christ and the church; [33]however, let each one of you love his wife as himself, and let the wife see that she respects her husband.

6 Children, obey your parents in the Lord, for this is right. [2]"Honor your father and mother" (this is the first commandment with a promise), [3]"that it may be well with you and that you may live long on the earth." [4]Fathers, do not provoke your children to anger, but bring them up in the discipline and instruction of the Lord.

5 Slaves, be obedient to those who are your earthly masters, with fear and trembling, in singleness of heart, as to Christ; [6]not in the way of eye-service, as men-pleasers, but as servants[f] of Christ, doing the will of God from the heart, [7]rendering service with a good will as to the Lord and not to men, [8]knowing that whatever good any one does, he will receive the same again from the Lord, whether he is a slave or free. [9]Masters, do the same to them, and forbear threatening, knowing that he who is both their Master and yours is in heaven, and that there is no partiality with him.

10 Finally, be strong in the Lord and in the strength of his might. [11]Put on the whole armor of God, that you may be able to stand against the wiles of the devil. [12]For we are not contending against flesh and blood, but against the principalities, against the powers, against the world rulers of this present darkness, against the spiritual hosts of wickedness in the heavenly places. [13]Therefore take the whole armor of God, that you may be able to withstand in the evil day, and having done all, to stand. [14]Stand therefore, having girded your loins with truth, and having put on the breastplate of righteousness, [15]and having shod your feet with the equipment of the gospel of peace; [16]besides all these, taking the shield of faith, with which you can quench all the flaming darts of the evil one. [17]And take the helmet of salvation, and the sword of the Spirit, which is the word of God. [18]Pray at all times in the Spirit, with all prayer and supplica-

---

[f]Or *slaves*　**5.16:** Col 4.5.
5.19: Col 3.16-17.　**5.22-6.9:** Col 3.18-4.1.　**5.31:** Gen 2.24.
6.2: Ex 20.12.　**6.3:** Deut 5.16.
6.14: Is 11.5; 59.17; 1 Thess 5.8.　**6.15:** Is 52.7.

tion. To that end keep alert with all perseverance, making supplication for all the saints, [19] and also for me, that utterance may be given me in opening my mouth boldly to proclaim the mystery of the gospel, [20] for which I am an ambassador in chains; that I may declare it boldly, as I ought to speak.

21 Now that you also may know how I am and what I am doing, Tўch′ĭ·cŭs

the beloved brother and faithful minister in the Lord will tell you everything. [22] I have sent him to you for this very purpose, that you may know how we are, and that he may encourage your hearts.

23 Peace be to the brethren, and love with faith, from God the Father and the Lord Jesus Christ. [24] Grace be with all who love our Lord Jesus Christ with love undying.

The Letter of Paul to the
Philippians

1 Paul and Timothy, servants[a] of Christ Jesus,
To all the saints in Christ Jesus who are at Phĭ·lĭp′pī, with the bishops[b] and deacons:

2 Grace to you and peace from God our Father and the Lord Jesus Christ.

3 I thank my God in all my remembrance of you, [4] always in every prayer of mine for you all making my prayer with joy, [5] thankful for your partnership in the gospel from the first day until now. [6] And I am sure that he who began a good work in you will bring it to completion at the day of Jesus Christ. [7] It is right for me to feel thus about you all, because I hold you in my heart, for you are all partakers with me of grace, both in my imprisonment and in the defense and confirmation of the gospel. [8] For God is my witness, how I yearn for you all with the affection of Christ Jesus. [9] And it is my prayer that your love may abound more and more, with knowledge and all discernment, [10] so that you may approve what is excellent, and may be pure and blameless for the day of Christ, [11] filled with the fruits of righteousness which come through Jesus Christ, to the glory and praise of God.

12 I want you to know, brethren, that what has happened to me has really served to advance the gospel, [13] so that it has become known throughout the whole praetorian guard[c] and to all the rest that my imprisonment is for Christ; [14] and most of the brethren

have been made confident in the Lord because of my imprisonment, and are much more bold to speak the word of God without fear.

15 Some indeed preach Christ from envy and rivalry, but others from good will. [16] The latter do it out of love, knowing that I am put here for the defense of the gospel; [17] the former proclaim Christ out of partisanship, not sincerely but thinking to afflict me in my imprisonment. [18] What then? Only that in every way, whether in pretense or in truth, Christ is proclaimed; and in that I rejoice.

19 Yes, and I shall rejoice. For I know that through your prayers and the help of the Spirit of Jesus Christ this will turn out for my deliverance [20] as it is my eager expectation and hope that I shall not be at all ashamed, but that with full courage now as always Christ will be honored in my body, whether by life or by death. [21] For to me to live is Christ, and to die is gain. [22] If it is to be life in the flesh, that means fruitful labor for me. Yet which I shall choose I cannot tell. [23] I am hard pressed between the two. My desire is to depart and be with Christ, for that is far better. [24] But to remain in the flesh is more necessary

6.21-22: Col 4.7-8.
[a] *Or slaves*   [b] *Or overseers*
[c] Greek *in the whole praetorium*
1.1: Acts 16.1, 12-40; Rom 1.1; 2 Cor 1.1; Gal 1.10; Col 1.1; 1 Thess 1.1; 2 Thess 1.1; Philem 1.   1.2: Rom 1.7.
1.6, 10: 1 Cor 1.8.   1.7: Acts 21.33; 2 Cor 7.3; Eph 6.20.
1.12: Lk 21.13.   1.13: Acts 28.30; 2 Tim 2.9.
1.19: Acts 16.7; 2 Cor 1.11.   1.20: Rom 14.8.
1.21: Gal 2.20.

on your account. ²⁵ Convinced of this, I know that I shall remain and continue with you all, for your progress and joy in the faith, ²⁶ so that in me you may have ample cause to glory in Christ Jesus, because of my coming to you again.

27 Only let your manner of life be worthy of the gospel of Christ, so that whether I come and see you or am absent, I may hear of you that you stand firm in one spirit, with one mind striving side by side for the faith of the gospel, ²⁸ and not frightened in anything by your opponents. This is a clear omen to them of their destruction, but of your salvation, and that from God. ²⁹ For it has been granted to you that for the sake of Christ you should not only believe in him but also suffer for his sake, ³⁰ engaged in the same conflict which you saw and now hear to be mine.

2 So if there is any encouragement in Christ, any incentive of love, any participation in the Spirit, any affection and sympathy, ² complete my joy by being of the same mind, having the same love, being in full accord and of one mind. ³ Do nothing from selfishness or conceit, but in humility count others better than yourselves. ⁴ Let each of you look not only to his own interests, but also to the interests of others. ⁵ Have this mind among yourselves, which is yours in Christ Jesus, ⁶ who, though he was in the form of God, did not count equality with God a thing to be grasped, ⁷ but emptied himself, taking the form of a servant,ᵈ being born in the likeness of men. ⁸ And being found in human form he humbled himself and became obedient unto death, even death on a cross. ⁹ Therefore God has highly exalted him and bestowed on him the name which is above every name, ¹⁰ that at the name of Jesus every knee should bow, in heaven and on earth and under the earth, ¹¹ and every tongue confess that Jesus Christ is Lord, to the glory of God the Father.

12 Therefore, my beloved, as you have always obeyed, so now, not only as in my presence but much more in my absence, work out your own salvation with fear and trembling; ¹³ for God is at work in you, both to will and to work for his good pleasure.

14 Do all things without grumbling or questioning, ¹⁵ that you may be blameless and innocent, children of God without blemish in the midst of a crooked and perverse generation, among whom you shine as lights in the world, ¹⁶ holding fast the word of life, so that in the day of Christ I may be proud that I did not run in vain or labor in vain. ¹⁷ Even if I am to be poured as a libation upon the sacrificial offering of your faith, I am glad and rejoice with you all. ¹⁸ Likewise you also should be glad and rejoice with me.

19 I hope in the Lord Jesus to send Timothy to you soon, so that I may be cheered by news of you. ²⁰ I have no one like him, who will be genuinely anxious for your welfare. ²¹ They all look after their own interests, not those of Jesus Christ. ²² But Timothy's worth you know, how as a son with a father he has served with me in the gospel. ²³ I hope therefore to send him just as soon as I see how it will go with me; ²⁴ and I trust in the Lord that shortly I myself shall come also.

25 I have thought it necessary to send to you Ep·aph·ro·di′tus my brother and fellow worker and fellow soldier, and your messenger and minister to my need, ²⁶ for he has been longing for you all, and has been distressed because you heard that he was ill. ²⁷ Indeed he was ill, near to death. But God had mercy on him, and not only on him but on me also, lest I should have sorrow upon sorrow. ²⁸ I am the more eager to send him, therefore, that you may rejoice at seeing him again, and that I may be less anxious. ²⁹ So receive him in the Lord with all joy; and honor such men, ³⁰ for he nearly died for the work of Christ, risking his life to complete your service to me.

3 Finally, my brethren, rejoice in the Lord. To write the same things to you is not irksome to me, and is safe for you.

2 Look out for the dogs, look out for the evil-workers, look out for those who mutilate the flesh. ³ For we are the

---

ᵈ Or *slave*
1.28: 2 Thess 1.5.
1.30: Acts 16.19-40; 1 Thess 2.2.   2.1: 2 Cor 13.14.
2.3-4: Rom 12.10; 15.1-2.
2.5-8: Mt 11.29; 20.28; Jn 1.1; 2 Cor 8.9; Heb 5.8.
2.9-11: Rom 10.9; 14.9; Eph 1.20-21.   2.13: 1 Cor 15.10.
2.15: Mt 5.45, 48.   3.3: Rom 2.28-29; Gal 6.14-15.

true circumcision, who worship God in spirit,[e] and glory in Christ Jesus, and put no confidence in the flesh. [4] Though I myself have reason for confidence in the flesh also. If any other man thinks he has reason for confidence in the flesh, I have more: [5] circumcised on the eighth day, of the people of Israel, of the tribe of Benjamin, a Hebrew born of Hebrews; as to the law a Phăr'ĭ-see, [6] as to zeal a persecutor of the church, as to righteousness under the law blameless. [7] But whatever gain I had, I counted as loss for the sake of Christ. [8] Indeed I count everything as loss because of the surpassing worth of knowing Christ Jesus my Lord. For his sake I have suffered the loss of all things, and count them as refuse, in order that I may gain Christ [9] and be found in him, not having a righteousness of my own, based on law, but that which is through faith in Christ, the righteousness from God that depends on faith; [10] that I may know him and the power of his resurrection, and may share his sufferings, becoming like him in his death, [11] that if possible I may attain the resurrection from the dead.

[12] Not that I have already obtained this or am already perfect; but I press on to make it my own, because Christ Jesus has made me his own. [13] Brethren, I do not consider that I have made it my own; but one thing I do, forgetting what lies behind and straining forward to what lies ahead, [14] I press on toward the goal for the prize of the upward call of God in Christ Jesus. [15] Let those of us who are mature be thus minded; and if in anything you are otherwise minded, God will reveal that also to you. [16] Only let us hold true to what we have attained.

[17] Brethren, join in imitating me, and mark those who so live as you have an example in us. [18] For many, of whom I have often told you and now tell you even with tears, live as enemies of the cross of Christ. [19] Their end is destruction, their god is the belly, and they glory in their shame, with minds set on earthly things. [20] But our commonwealth is in heaven, and from it we await a Savior, the Lord Jesus Christ, [21] who will change our lowly body to be like his glorious body, by the power which enables him even to subject all things to himself.

4 Therefore, my brethren, whom I love and long for, my joy and crown, stand firm thus in the Lord, my beloved.

[2] I entreat Eū-ō'dĭ-ạ and I entreat Sўn'tў-chē to agree in the Lord. [3] And I ask you also, true yokefellow, help these women, for they have labored side by side with me in the gospel together with Clement and the rest of my fellow workers, whose names are in the book of life.

[4] Rejoice in the Lord always; again I will say, Rejoice. [5] Let all men know your forbearance. The Lord is at hand. [6] Have no anxiety about anything, but in everything by prayer and supplication with thanksgiving let your requests be made known to God. [7] And the peace of God, which passes all understanding, will keep your hearts and your minds in Christ Jesus.

[8] Finally, brethren, whatever is true, whatever is honorable, whatever is just, whatever is pure, whatever is lovely, whatever is gracious, if there is any excellence, if there is anything worthy of praise, think about these things. [9] What you have learned and received and heard and seen in me, do; and the God of peace will be with you.

[10] I rejoice in the Lord greatly that now at length you have revived your concern for me; you were indeed concerned for me, but you had no opportunity. [11] Not that I complain of want; for I have learned, in whatever state I am, to be content. [12] I know how to be abased, and I know how to abound; in any and all circumstances I have learned the secret of facing plenty and hunger, abundance and want. [13] I can do all things in him who strengthens me.

[14] Yet it was kind of you to share my trouble. [15] And you Phĭ-lĭp'pĭ-anṣ yourselves know that in the beginning of the gospel, when I left Măç-ẹ-dō'nĭ-ạ, no church entered into partnership with me in giving and receiving except you only; [16] for even in Thĕs-sạ-lọ-nī'cạ you sent me help[f] once and again.

---

[e] Other ancient authorities read *worship by the Spirit of God*
[f] Other ancient authorities read *money for my needs*
3.4-7: Acts 8.3; 22.3-21; 23.6; 26.4-23; Rom 11.1; 2 Cor 11.18-31.
3.17: 1 Cor 4.15-17.
3.21: 1 Cor 15.35-58; Col 3.4.　**4.3:** Lk 10.20.
4.6: Mt 6.25-34.　**4.9:** Rom 15.33.　**4.10:** 2 Cor 11.9.
4.13: 2 Cor 12.9.　**4.16:** Acts 17.1-9; 1 Thess 2.9.

[17] Not that I seek the gift; but I seek the fruit which increases to your credit. [18] I have received full payment, and more; I am filled, having received from Ĕp·ăph·rō·dī'tus the gifts you sent, a fragrant offering, a sacrifice acceptable and pleasing to God. [19] And my God will supply every need of yours according to his riches in glory in Christ Jesus. [20] To our God and Father be glory for ever and ever. Amen.

21 Greet every saint in Christ Jesus. The brethren who are with me greet you. [22] All the saints greet you, especially those of Caesar's household.

23 The grace of the Lord Jesus Christ be with your spirit.

The Letter of Paul to the
Colossians

1 Paul, an apostle of Christ Jesus by the will of God, and Timothy our brother,

2 To the saints and faithful brethren in Christ at Cō·lŏs'saē:

Grace to you and peace from God our Father.

3 We always thank God, the Father of our Lord Jesus Christ, when we pray for you, [4] because we have heard of your faith in Christ Jesus and of the love which you have for all the saints, [5] because of the hope laid up for you in heaven. Of this you have heard before in the word of the truth, the gospel [6] which has come to you, as indeed in the whole world it is bearing fruit and growing—so among yourselves, from the day you heard and understood the grace of God in truth, [7] as you learned it from Ĕp'a·phrăs our beloved fellow servant. He is a faithful minister of Christ on our[a] behalf [8] and has made known to us your love in the Spirit.

9 And so, from the day we heard of it, we have not ceased to pray for you, asking that you may be filled with the knowledge of his will in all spiritual wisdom and understanding, [10] to lead a life worthy of the Lord, fully pleasing to him, bearing fruit in every good work and increasing in the knowledge of God. [11] May you be strengthened with all power, according to his glorious might, for all endurance and patience with joy, [12] giving thanks to the Father, who has qualified us[b] to share in the inheritance of the saints in light. [13] He has delivered us from the dominion of darkness and transferred us to the kingdom of his beloved Son, [14] in whom we have redemption, the forgiveness of sins.

15 He is the image of the invisible God, the first-born of all creation; [16] for in him all things were created, in heaven and on earth, visible and invisible, whether thrones or dominions or principalities or authorities—all things were created through him and for him. [17] He is before all things, and in him all things hold together. [18] He is the head of the body, the church; he is the beginning, the first-born from the dead, that in everything he might be pre-eminent. [19] For in him all the fulness of God was pleased to dwell, [20] and through him to reconcile to himself all things, whether on earth or in heaven, making peace by the blood of his cross.

21 And you, who once were estranged and hostile in mind, doing evil deeds, [22] he has now reconciled in his body of flesh by his death, in order to present you holy and blameless and irreproachable before him, [23] provided that you continue in the faith, stable and steadfast, not shifting from the hope of the gospel which you heard, which has been preached to every creature under heaven, and of which I, Paul, became a minister.

24 Now I rejoice in my sufferings for your sake, and in my flesh I com-

---

4.23: Gal 6.18; Philem 25.
[a] Other ancient authorities read *your*
[b] Other ancient authorities read *you*
1.2: Rom 1.7.   1.3: Eph 1.16.   1.7: Col 4.12; Philem 23. 1.9: Eph 1.15-17.   1.13: Eph 1.21; 2.2.   1.15: 2 Cor 4.4. 1.17: Prov 8.22-31.   1.18: Eph 4.15.

plete what is lacking in Christ's afflictions for the sake of his body, that is, the church, 25 of which I became a minister according to the divine office which was given to me for you, to make the word of God fully known, 26 the mystery hidden for ages and generations*c* but now made manifest to his saints. 27 To them God chose to make known how great among the Gentiles are the riches of the glory of this mystery, which is Christ in you, the hope of glory. 28 Him we proclaim, warning every man and teaching every man in all wisdom, that we may pre-sent every man mature in Christ. 29 For this I toil, striving with all the energy which he mightily inspires within me.

2 For I want you to know how greatly I strive for you, and for those at Lā–o̧-dĭ-çē'a̧, and for all who have not seen my face, 2 that their hearts may be encouraged as they are knit together in love, to have all the riches of assured understanding and the knowledge of God's mystery, of Christ, 3 in whom are hid all the treasures of wisdom and knowledge. 4 I say this in order that no one may delude you with beguiling speech. 5 For though I am absent in body, yet I am with you in spirit, rejoicing to see your good order and the firmness of your faith in Christ.

6 As therefore you received Christ Jesus the Lord, so live in him, 7 rooted and built up in him and established in the faith, just as you were taught, abounding in thanksgiving.

8 See to it that no one makes a prey of you by philosophy and empty deceit, according to human tradition, according to the elemental spirits of the universe, and not according to Christ. 9 For in him the whole fulness of deity dwells bodily, 10 and you have come to fulness of life in him, who is the head of all rule and authority. 11 In him also you were circumcised with a circumcision made without hands, by putting off the body of flesh in the circumcision of Christ; 12 and you were buried with him in baptism, in which you were also raised with him through faith in the working of God, who raised him from the dead. 13 And you, who were dead in trespasses and the uncircumcision of your flesh, God made

alive together with him, having forgiven us all our trespasses, 14 having canceled the bond which stood against us with its legal demands; this he set aside, nailing it to the cross. 15 He disarmed the principalities and powers and made a public example of them, triumphing over them in him.*d*

16 Therefore let no one pass judgment on you in questions of food and drink or with regard to a festival or a new moon or a sabbath. 17 These are only a shadow of what is to come; but the substance belongs to Christ. 18 Let no one disqualify you, insisting on self-abasement and worship of angels, taking his stand on visions, puffed up without reason by his sensuous mind, 19 and not holding fast to the Head, from whom the whole body, nourished and knit together through its joints and ligaments, grows with a growth that is from God.

20 If with Christ you died to the elemental spirits of the universe, why do you live as if you still belonged to the world? Why do you submit to regulations, 21 "Do not handle, Do not taste, Do not touch" 22 (referring to things which all perish as they are used), according to human precepts and doctrines? 23 These have indeed an appearance of wisdom in promoting rigor of devotion and self-abasement and severity to the body, but they are of no value in checking the indulgence of the flesh.*e*

3 If then you have been raised with Christ, seek the things that are above, where Christ is, seated at the right hand of God. 2 Set your minds on things that are above, not on things that are on earth. 3 For you have died, and your life is hid with Christ in God. 4 When Christ who is our life appears, then you also will appear with him in glory.

5 Put to death therefore what is earthly in you: fornication, impurity, passion, evil desire, and covetousness, which is idolatry. 6 On account of these the wrath of God is coming.*f* 7 In these you once walked, when you lived in them. 8 But now put them all away:

c Or *from angels and men*
d Or *in it* (that is, the cross)
e Or *are of no value, serving only to indulge the flesh*
f Other ancient authorities add *upon the sons of disobedience* 1.25: Eph 3.2. 1.26: Eph 3.9.
2.3: Is 45.3. 2.10: Eph 1.21-22. 2.15: Eph 1.21.
2.16: Rom 14.1-12. 2.17: Eph 1.23. 2.19: Eph 1.22; 4.16.
2.20: Gal 4.3. 2.22: Is 29.13; Mk 7.7. 3.1: Ps 110.1.

anger, wrath, malice, slander, and foul talk from your mouth. ⁹Do not lie to one another, seeing that you have put off the old nature with its practices ¹⁰and have put on the new nature, which is being renewed in knowledge after the image of its creator. ¹¹Here there cannot be Greek and Jew, circumcised and uncircumcised, barbarian, Scŷth′ĭ·ạn, slave, free man, but Christ is all, and in all.

12 Put on then, as God's chosen ones, holy and beloved, compassion, kindness, lowliness, meekness, and patience, ¹³forbearing one another and, if one has a complaint against another, forgiving each other; as the Lord has forgiven you, so you also must forgive. ¹⁴And above all these put on love, which binds everything together in perfect harmony. ¹⁵And let the peace of Christ rule in your hearts, to which indeed you were called in the one body. And be thankful. ¹⁶Let the word of Christ dwell in you richly, teach and admonish one another in all wisdom, and sing psalms and hymns and spiritual songs with thankfulness in your hearts to God. ¹⁷And whatever you do, in word or deed, do everything in the name of the Lord Jesus, giving thanks to God the Father through him.

18 Wives, be subject to your husbands, as is fitting in the Lord. ¹⁹Husbands, love your wives, and do not be harsh with them. ²⁰Children, obey your parents in everything, for this pleases the Lord. ²¹Fathers, do not provoke your children, lest they become discouraged. ²²Slaves, obey in everything those who are your earthly masters, not with eyeservice, as menpleasers, but in singleness of heart, fearing the Lord. ²³Whatever your task, work heartily, as serving the Lord and not men, ²⁴knowing that from the Lord you will receive the inheritance as your reward; you are serving the Lord Christ. ²⁵For the wrongdoer will be paid back for the wrong he has done, and there is no partiality.

4 Masters, treat your slaves justly and fairly, knowing that you also have a Master in heaven.

2 Continue steadfastly in prayer, being watchful in it with thanksgiving; ³and pray for us also, that God may open to us a door for the word, to declare the mystery of Christ, on account of which I am in prison, ⁴that I may make it clear, as I ought to speak.

5 Conduct yourselves wisely toward outsiders, making the most of the time. ⁶Let your speech always be gracious, seasoned with salt, so that you may know how you ought to answer every one.

7 Tŷch′ĭ·cụs will tell you all about my affairs; he is a beloved brother and faithful minister and fellow servant in the Lord. ⁸I have sent him to you for this very purpose, that you may know how we are and that he may encourage your hearts, ⁹and with him Ō·nĕs′ĭ·mụs, the faithful and beloved brother, who is one of yourselves. They will tell you of everything that has taken place here.

10 Ăr·ĭs·tär′chụs my fellow prisoner greets you, and Mark the cousin of Bär′nạ·bạs (concerning whom you have received instructions—if he comes to you, receive him), ¹¹and Jesus who is called Jŭs′tụs. These are the only men of the circumcision among my fellow workers for the kingdom of God, and they have been a comfort to me. ¹²Ĕp′ạ·phrăs, who is one of yourselves, a servant*ᵍ* of Christ Jesus, greets you, always remembering you earnestly in his prayers, that you may stand mature and fully assured in all the will of God. ¹³For I bear him witness that he has worked hard for you and for those in Lā·ọ·dĭ·çē′ạ and in Hī–ĕr·ăp′ọ·lĭs. ¹⁴Luke the beloved physician and Dē′mạs greet you. ¹⁵Give my greetings to the brethren at Lā·ọ·dĭ·çē′ạ, and to Nŷm′phạ and the church in her house. ¹⁶And when this letter has been read among you, have it read also in the church of the Lā·ọ·dĭ·çē′ạnṣ; and see that you read also the letter from Lā·ọ·dĭ·çē′ạ. ¹⁷And say to Ăr·chĭp′pụs, "See that you fulfil the ministry which you have received in the Lord."

18 I, Paul, write this greeting with my own hand. Remember my fetters. Grace be with you.

*ᵍ*Or *slave*

3.10: Gen 1.26. **3.12-13:** Eph 4.2. **3.16-17:** Eph 5.19. **3.18-4.1:** Eph 5.22-6.9. **3.23:** Rom 12.11. **4.1:** Lev 25.43, 53. **4.2:** Rom 12.12. **4.5:** Eph 5.16. **4.7-8:** Eph 6.21-22. **4.9:** Philem 10. **4.10-11:** Acts 19.29; 27.2; Philem 24. **4.12:** Col 1.7; Philem 23. **4.14:** 2 Tim 4.10-11; Philem 24. **4.18:** 1 Cor 16.21.

The First Letter of Paul to the
Thessalonians

1 Paul, Sĭl·vā'nŭs, and Timothy,
To the church of the Thĕs·sạ·lŏ'nĭ·ạnş in God the Father and the Lord Jesus Christ:
Grace to you and peace.

2 We give thanks to God always for you all, constantly mentioning you in our prayers, ³remembering before our God and Father your work of faith and labor of love and steadfastness of hope in our Lord Jesus Christ. ⁴For we know, brethren beloved by God, that he has chosen you; ⁵for our gospel came to you not only in word, but also in power and in the Holy Spirit and with full conviction. You know what kind of men we proved to be among you for your sake. ⁶And you became imitators of us and of the Lord, for you received the word in much affliction, with joy inspired by the Holy Spirit; ⁷so that you became an example to all the believers in Măc̣·ẹ·dō'nĭ·ạ and in A·chā'ĭ·ạ. ⁸For not only has the word of the Lord sounded forth from you in Măc̣·ẹ·dō'nĭ·ạ and A·chā'ĭ·ạ, but your faith in God has gone forth everywhere, so that we need not say anything. ⁹For they themselves report concerning us what a welcome we had among you, and how you turned to God from idols, to serve a living and true God, ¹⁰and to wait for his Son from heaven, whom he raised from the dead, Jesus who delivers us from the wrath to come.

2 For you yourselves know, brethren, that our visit to you was not in vain; ²but though we had already suffered and been shamefully treated at Phĭ·lĭp'pī, as you know, we had courage in our God to declare to you the gospel of God in the face of great opposition. ³For our appeal does not spring from error or uncleanness, nor is it made with guile; ⁴but just as we have been approved by God to be entrusted with the gospel, so we speak, not to please men, but to please God who tests our hearts. ⁵For we never used either words of flattery, as you know, or a cloak for greed, as God is

witness; ⁶nor did we seek glory from men, whether from you or from others, though we might have made demands as apostles of Christ. ⁷But we were gentle*ᵃ* among you, like a nurse taking care of her children. ⁸So, being affectionately desirous of you, we were ready to share with you not only the gospel of God but also our own selves, because you had become very dear to us.

9 For you remember our labor and toil, brethren; we worked night and day, that we might not burden any of you, while we preached to you the gospel of God. ¹⁰You are witnesses, and God also, how holy and righteous and blameless was our behavior to you believers; ¹¹for you know how, like a father with his children, we exhorted each one of you and encouraged you and charged you ¹²to lead a life worthy of God, who calls you into his own kingdom and glory.

13 And we also thank God constantly for this, that when you received the word of God which you heard from us, you accepted it not as the word of men but as what it really is, the word of God, which is at work in you believers. ¹⁴For you, brethren, became imitators of the churches of God in Christ Jesus which are in Jü·dē'ạ; for you suffered the same things from your own countrymen as they did from the Jews, ¹⁵who killed both the Lord Jesus and the prophets, and drove us out, and displease God and oppose all men ¹⁶by hindering us from speaking to the Gentiles that they may be saved—so as always to fill up the measure of their

*ᵃ*Other ancient authorities read *babes*
1.1: 2 Thess 1.1; 2 Cor 1.19; Acts 16.1; 17.1; Rom 1.7.
1.2: 2 Thess 1.3; 2.13; Rom 1.9.
1.3: 2 Thess 1.11; 1.3; Rom 8.25; 15.4; Gal 1.4.
1.4: 2 Thess 2.13; Rom 1.7; 2 Pet 1.10.
1.5: 2 Thess 2.14; Rom 15.19.
1.6: Col 2.2; 1 Thess 2.10; 1 Cor 4.16; 11.1; Acts 17.5-10; 13.52. **1.7:** Rom 15.26; Acts 18.12.
1.8: 2 Thess 3.1; Rom 1.8. **1.10:** Mt 3.7.
2.2: Acts 16.19-24; 17.1-9; Rom 1.1. **2.5:** Acts 20.33.
2.6: 1 Cor 9.1. **2.7:** 1 Thess 2.11; Gal 4.19.
2.8: 2 Cor 12.15; 1 Jn 3.16. **2.11:** 1 Cor 4.14.
2.12: 1 Pet 5.10. **2.13:** 1 Thess 1.2.
2.14: 1 Thess 1.6; 1 Cor 7.17; Gal 1.22; Acts 17.5; 2 Thess 1.4. **2.15:** Lk 24.20; Acts 2.23; 7.52.
2.16: Acts 9.23; 13.45, 50; 14.2, 5, 19; 17.5, 13; 18.12; 21.21, 27; 25. 2, 7; 1 Cor 10.33; Gen 15.16; 1 Thess 1.10.

sins. But God's wrath has come upon them at last!*ᵇ*

17 But since we were bereft of you, brethren, for a short time, in person not in heart, we endeavored the more eagerly and with great desire to see you face to face; ¹⁸ because we wanted to come to you—I, Paul, again and again—but Satan hindered us. ¹⁹ For what is our hope or joy or crown of boasting before our Lord Jesus at his coming? Is it not you? ²⁰ For you are our glory and joy.

3 Therefore when we could bear it no longer, we were willing to be left behind at Athens alone, ² and we sent Timothy, our brother and God's servant in the gospel of Christ, to establish you in your faith and to exhort you, ³ that no one be moved by these afflictions. You yourselves know that this is to be our lot. ⁴ For when we were with you, we told you beforehand that we were to suffer affliction; just as it has come to pass, and as you know. ⁵ For this reason, when I could bear it no longer, I sent that I might know your faith, for fear that somehow the tempter had tempted you and that our labor would be in vain.

6 But now that Timothy has come to us from you, and has brought us the good news of your faith and love and reported that you always remember us kindly and long to see us, as we long to see you—⁷ for this reason, brethren, in all our distress and affliction we have been comforted about you through your faith; ⁸ for now we live, if you stand fast in the Lord. ⁹ For what thanksgiving can we render to God for you, for all the joy which we feel for your sake before our God, ¹⁰ praying earnestly night and day that we may see you face to face and supply what is lacking in your faith?

11 Now may our God and Father himself, and our Lord Jesus, direct our way to you; ¹² and may the Lord make you increase and abound in love to one another and to all men, as we do to you, ¹³ so that he may establish your hearts unblamable in holiness before our God and Father, at the coming of our Lord Jesus with all his saints.

4 Finally, brethren, we beseech and exhort you in the Lord Jesus, that as you learned from us how you ought to live and to please God, just as you are doing, you do so more and more. ² For you know what instructions we gave you through the Lord Jesus. ³ For this is the will of God, your sanctification: that you abstain from unchastity; ⁴ that each one of you know how to take a wife for himself*ˣ* in holiness and honor, ⁵ not in the passion of lust like heathen who do not know God; ⁶ that no man transgress, and wrong his brother in this matter,*ᶜ* because the Lord is an avenger in all these things, as we solemnly forewarned you. ⁷ For God has not called us for uncleanness, but in holiness. ⁸ Therefore whoever disregards this, disregards not man but God, who gives his Holy Spirit to you.

9 But concerning love of the brethren you have no need to have any one write to you, for you yourselves have been taught by God to love one another; ¹⁰ and indeed you do love all the brethren throughout Măç·ȩ·dō'nĭ·ạ. But we exhort you, brethren, to do so more and more, ¹¹ to aspire to live quietly, to mind your own affairs, and to work with your hands, as we charged you; ¹² so that you may command the respect of outsiders, and be dependent on nobody.

13 But we would not have you ignorant, brethren, concerning those who are asleep, that you may not grieve as others do who have no hope. ¹⁴ For since we believe that Jesus died and rose again, even so, through Jesus, God will bring with him those who have fallen asleep. ¹⁵ For this we declare to you by the word of the Lord, that we who are alive, who are left until the coming of the Lord, shall not precede those who have fallen asleep. ¹⁶ For the Lord himself will descend from heaven with a cry of command, with the archangel's call, and with the sound of the trumpet of God. And the dead in Christ will rise first; ¹⁷ then we who are alive, who are left, shall be caught up together with them in the clouds to meet the Lord in the air; and

*ᵇ*Or *completely*, or *for ever*
*ˣ*Or *how to control his own body*
*ᶜ*Or *defraud his brother in business* **2.17:** 1 Cor 5.3.
2.19: Phil 4.1; 1 Thess 3.13; 4.15; 5.23; Mt 16.27; Mk 8.38.
2.20: 2 Cor 1.14. **3.1:** Phil 2.19; Acts 17.15.
3.2: 2 Cor 1.1; Col 1.1. **3.3:** Acts 14.22. **3.4:** 1 Thess 2.14.
3.5: Mt 4.3; Phil 2.16. **3.6:** Acts 18.5.
3.13: 1 Cor 1.8; 1 Thess 2.19; 4.17. **4.3:** 1 Cor 6.18.
4.4: 1 Cor 7.2; 1 Pet 3.7.
4.11: Eph 4.28; 2 Thess 3.10-12.
4.13: Eph 2.12. **4.14:** 2 Cor 4.14.
4.16: Mt 24.31; 1 Cor 15.23; 2 Thess 2.1.

so we shall always be with the Lord. [18]Therefore comfort one another with these words.

5 But as to the times and the seasons, brethren, you have no need to have anything written to you. [2]For you yourselves know well that the day of the Lord will come like a thief in the night. [3]When people say, "There is peace and security," then sudden destruction will come upon them as travail comes upon a woman with child, and there will be no escape. [4]But you are not in darkness, brethren, for that day to surprise you like a thief. [5]For you are all sons of light and sons of the day; we are not of the night or of darkness. [6]So then let us not sleep, as others do, but let us keep awake and be sober. [7]For those who sleep sleep at night, and those who get drunk are drunk at night. [8]But, since we belong to the day, let us be sober, and put on the breastplate of faith and love, and for a helmet the hope of salvation. [9]For God has not destined us for wrath, but to obtain salvation through our Lord Jesus Christ, [10]who died for us so that whether we wake or sleep we might live with him. [11]Therefore encourage one another and build one another up, just as you are doing.

12 But we beseech you, brethren, to respect those who labor among you and are over you in the Lord and admonish you, [13]and to esteem them very highly in love because of their work. Be at peace among yourselves. [14]And we exhort you, brethren, admonish the idlers, encourage the fainthearted, help the weak, be patient with them all. [15]See that none of you repays evil for evil, but always seek to do good to one another and to all. [16]Rejoice always, [17]pray constantly, [18]give thanks in all circumstances; for this is the will of God in Christ Jesus for you. [19]Do not quench the Spirit, [20]do not despise prophesying, [21]but test everything; hold fast what is good, [22]abstain from every form of evil.

23 May the God of peace himself sanctify you wholly; and may your spirit and soul and body be kept sound and blameless at the coming of our Lord Jesus Christ. [24]He who calls you is faithful, and he will do it.

25 Brethren, pray for us.

26 Greet all the brethren with a holy kiss.

27 I adjure you by the Lord that this letter be read to all the brethren.

28 The grace of our Lord Jesus Christ be with you.

The Second Letter of Paul to the

Thessalonians

1 Paul, Sĭl·vā'nŭs, and Timothy,
To the church of the Thĕs·sạ·lō'-nĭ·ạns in God our Father and the Lord Jesus Christ:
2 Grace to you and peace from God the Father and the Lord Jesus Christ.

3 We are bound to give thanks to God always for you, brethren, as is fitting, because your faith is growing abundantly, and the love of every one of you for one another is increasing. [4]Therefore we ourselves boast of you in the churches of God for your steadfastness and faith in all your persecutions and in the afflictions which you are enduring.

5 This is evidence of the righteous judgment of God, that you may be made worthy of the kingdom of God, for which you are suffering — [6]since indeed God deems it just to repay with affliction those who afflict you, [7]and to

5.1: Acts 1.7.
5.2: 1 Cor 1.8. **5.3:** 2 Thess 1.9. **5.4:** 1 Jn 2.8; Acts 26.18.
5.5: Lk 16.8. **5.6:** Rom 13.11; 1 Pet 1.13.
5.7: Acts 2.15; 2 Pet 2.13. **5.8:** Eph 6.14, 23, 17; Rom 8.24.
5.9: 1 Thess 1.10; 2 Thess 2.13; Rom 14.9.
5.12: 1 Cor 16.18; 1 Tim 5.17; 1 Cor 16.16; Rom 16.6, 12; 1 Cor 15.10; Heb 13.17. **5.13:** Mk 9.50.
5.14: Is 35.4; Rom 14.1; 1 Cor 8.7; 2 Thess 3.6, 7, 11.
5.15: Rom 12.17; 1 Pet 3.9. **5.16:** Phil 4.4.
5.17: Eph 6.18. **5.18:** Eph 5.20. **5.19:** Eph 4.30.
5.20: 1 Cor 14.31. **5.21:** 1 Cor 14.29; 1 Jn 4.1.
5.23: Rom 15.33. **5.26:** Rom 16.16. **5.27:** Col 4.16.
5.28: Rom 16.20; 2 Thess 3.18.
1.1: 1 Thess 1.1; 2 Cor 1.19; Acts 16.1. **1.2:** Rom 1.7.
1.3: 1 Thess 1.2.

grant rest with us to you who are afflicted, when the Lord Jesus is revealed from heaven with his mighty angels in flaming fire, [8]inflicting vengeance upon those who do not know God and upon those who do not obey the gospel of our Lord Jesus. [9]They shall suffer the punishment of eternal destruction and exclusion from the presence of the Lord and from the glory of his might, [10]when he comes on that day to be glorified in his saints, and to be marveled at in all who have believed, because our testimony to you was believed. [11]To this end we always pray for you, that our God may make you worthy of his call, and may fulfil every good resolve and work of faith by his power, [12]so that the name of our Lord Jesus may be glorified in you, and you in him, according to the grace of our God and the Lord Jesus Christ.

2 Now concerning the coming of our Lord Jesus Christ and our assembling to meet him, we beg you, brethren, [2]not to be quickly shaken in mind or excited, either by spirit or by word, or by letter purporting to be from us, to the effect that the day of the Lord has come. [3]Let no one deceive you in any way; for that day will not come, unless the rebellion comes first, and the man of lawlessness[a] is revealed, the son of perdition, [4]who opposes and exalts himself against every so-called god or object of worship, so that he takes his seat in the temple of God, proclaiming himself to be God. [5]Do you not remember that when I was still with you I told you this? [6]And you know what is restraining him now so that he may be revealed in his time. [7]For the mystery of lawlessness is already at work; only he who now restrains it will do so until he is out of the way. [8]And then the lawless one will be revealed, and the Lord Jesus will slay him with the breath of his mouth and destroy him by his appearing and his coming. [9]The coming of the lawless one by the activity of Satan will be with all power and with pretended signs and wonders, [10]and with all wicked deception for those who are to perish, because they refused to love the truth and so be saved. [11]Therefore God sends upon them a strong delusion, to make them believe what is false, [12]so that all may be condemned who did not believe the truth

but had pleasure in unrighteousness.

[13]But we are bound to give thanks to God always for you, brethren beloved by the Lord, because God chose you from the beginning[b] to be saved through sanctification by the Spirit[c] and belief in the truth. [14]To this he called you through our gospel, so that you may obtain the glory of our Lord Jesus Christ. [15]So then, brethren, stand firm and hold to the traditions which you were taught by us, either by word of mouth or by letter.

[16]Now may our Lord Jesus Christ himself, and God our Father, who loved us and gave us eternal comfort and good hope through grace, [17]comfort your hearts and establish them in every good work and word.

3 Finally, brethren, pray for us, that the word of the Lord may speed on and triumph, as it did among you, [2]and that we may be delivered from wicked and evil men; for not all have faith. [3]But the Lord is faithful; he will strengthen you and guard you from evil.[d] [4]And we have confidence in the Lord about you, that you are doing and will do the things which we command. [5]May the Lord direct your hearts to the love of God and to the steadfastness of Christ.

[6]Now we command you, brethren, in the name of our Lord Jesus Christ, that you keep away from any brother who is living in idleness and not in accord with the tradition that you received from us. [7]For you yourselves know how you ought to imitate us; we were not idle when we were with you, [8]we did not eat any one's bread without paying, but with toil and labor we worked night and day, that we might not burden any of you. [9]It was not because we have not that right, but to give you in our conduct an example to imitate. [10]For even when we were with you, we gave you this command: If

[a]Other ancient authorities read *sin*
[b]Other ancient authorities read *as the first converts*
[c]Or *of spirit*   [d]Or *the evil one*
1.8: Gal 4.8.   **1.11:** 1 Thess 1.3.
2.1: 1 Thess 4.15-17.   **2.2:** 2 Thess 3.17.
2.3: Eph 5.6-8; Dan 7.25; 8.25; 11.36; Rev 13.5; Jn 17.12.
2.4: Ezek 28.2.   **2.5:** 1 Thess 3.4.   **2.8:** Is 11.4.
2.9: Mt 24.24; Jn 4.48.   **2.11:** Rom 1.28.
2.13: 2 Thess 1.3; Eph 1.4; 1 Pet 1.2.
2.15: 1 Cor 16.13; 11.2.   **2.16:** 1 Thess 3.11; 1 Pet 1.3.
3.1: 1 Thess 5.25; 1.8.   **3.2:** Rom 15.31.
3.3: 1 Cor 1.9; 1 Thess 5.24.
3.6: 1 Cor 5.4, 5, 11; 1 Thess 5.14.   **3.7:** 1 Thess 1.6, 9.
3.8: 1 Thess 2.9; Acts 18.3; Eph 4.28.   **3.9:** 2 Thess 3.7.
3.10: 1 Thess 4.11.

any one will not work, let him not eat. [11] For we hear that some of you are living in idleness, mere busybodies, not doing any work. [12] Now such persons we command and exhort in the Lord Jesus Christ to do their work in quietness and to earn their own living. [13] Brethren, do not be weary in well-doing.

14 If any one refuses to obey what we say in this letter, note that man, and have nothing to do with him, that he may be ashamed. [15] Do not look on him as an enemy, but warn him as a brother.

16 Now may the Lord of peace himself give you peace at all times in all ways. The Lord be with you all.

17 I, Paul, write this greeting with my own hand. This is the mark in every letter of mine; it is the way I write. [18] The grace of our Lord Jesus Christ be with you all.

The First Letter of Paul to

Timothy

1 Paul, an apostle of Christ Jesus by command of God our Savior and of Christ Jesus our hope,

2 To Timothy, my true child in the faith:

Grace, mercy, and peace from God the Father and Christ Jesus our Lord.

3 As I urged you when I was going to Măç·ḝ·dō′nĭ·a, remain at Ēph′ḝ·sṳs that you may charge certain persons not to teach any different doctrine, [4] nor to occupy themselves with myths and endless genealogies which promote speculations rather than the divine training[a] that is in faith; [5] whereas the aim of our charge is love that issues from a pure heart and a good conscience and sincere faith. [6] Certain persons by swerving from these have wandered away into vain discussion, [7] desiring to be teachers of the law, without understanding either what they are saying or the things about which they make assertions.

8 Now we know that the law is good, if any one uses it lawfully, [9] understanding this, that the law is not laid down for the just but for the lawless and disobedient, for the ungodly and sinners, for the unholy and profane, for murderers of fathers and murderers of mothers, for manslayers, [10] immoral persons, sodomites, kidnapers, liars, perjurers, and whatever else is contrary to sound doctrine, [11] in accordance with the glorious gospel of the blessed God with which I have been entrusted.

12 I thank him who has given me strength for this, Christ Jesus our Lord, because he judged me faithful by appointing me to his service, [13] though I formerly blasphemed and persecuted and insulted him; but I received mercy because I had acted ignorantly in unbelief, [14] and the grace of our Lord overflowed for me with the faith and love that are in Christ Jesus. [15] The saying is sure and worthy of full acceptance, that Christ Jesus came into the world to save sinners. And I am the foremost of sinners; [16] but I received mercy for this reason, that in me, as the foremost, Jesus Christ might display his perfect patience for an example to those who were to believe in him for eternal life. [17] To the King of ages, immortal, invisible, the only God, be honor and glory for ever and ever.[b] Amen.

18 This charge I commit to you, Timothy, my son, in accordance with the prophetic utterances which pointed to you, that inspired by them you may wage the good warfare, [19] holding faith and a good conscience. By rejecting conscience, certain persons have made shipwreck of their faith, [20] among them Hȳ·mḝ·naē′ṳs

3.11: 2 Thess 3.6.
3.12: 1 Thess 4.1, 11. 3.13: Gal 6.9. 3.16: Ruth 2.4.
3.17: 1 Cor 16.21. 3.18: Rom 16.20; 1 Thess 5.28.

[a] Or *stewardship*, or *order* [b] Greek *to the ages of ages*

and Alexander, whom I have delivered to Satan that they may learn not to blaspheme.

2 First of all, then, I urge that supplications, prayers, intercessions, and thanksgivings be made for all men, ²for kings and all who are in high positions, that we may lead a quiet and peaceable life, godly and respectful in every way. ³This is good, and it is acceptable in the sight of God our Savior, ⁴who desires all men to be saved and to come to the knowledge of the truth. ⁵For there is one God, and there is one mediator between God and men, the man Christ Jesus, ⁶who gave himself as a ransom for all, the testimony to which was borne at the proper time. ⁷For this I was appointed a preacher and apostle (I am telling the truth, I am not lying), a teacher of the Gentiles in faith and truth.

8 I desire then that in every place the men should pray, lifting holy hands without anger or quarreling; ⁹also that women should adorn themselves modestly and sensibly in seemly apparel, not with braided hair or gold or pearls or costly attire ¹⁰but by good deeds, as befits women who profess religion. ¹¹Let a woman learn in silence with all submissiveness. ¹²I permit no woman to teach or to have authority over men; she is to keep silent. ¹³For Adam was formed first, then Eve; ¹⁴and Adam was not deceived, but the woman was deceived and became a transgressor. ¹⁵Yet woman will be saved through bearing children,ᶜ if she continuesᵈ in faith and love and holiness, with modesty.

3 The saying is sure: If any one aspires to the office of bishop, he desires a noble task. ²Now a bishop must be above reproach, the husband of one wife, temperate, sensible, dignified, hospitable, an apt teacher, ³no drunkard, not violent but gentle, not quarrelsome, and no lover of money. ⁴He must manage his own household well, keeping his children submissive and respectful in every way; ⁵for if a man does not know how to manage his own household, how can he care for God's church? ⁶He must not be a recent convert, or he may be puffed up with conceit and fall into the condemnation of the devil;ᶠ ⁷moreover he must be well thought of by

outsiders, or he may fall into reproach and the snare of the devil.ᶠ

8 Deacons likewise must be serious, not double-tongued, not addicted to much wine, not greedy for gain; ⁹they must hold the mystery of the faith with a clear conscience. ¹⁰And let them also be tested first; then if they prove themselves blameless let them serve as deacons. ¹¹The women likewise must be serious, no slanderers, but temperate, faithful in all things. ¹²Let deacons be the husband of one wife, and let them manage their children and their households well; ¹³for those who serve well as deacons gain a good standing for themselves and also great confidence in the faith which is in Christ Jesus.

14 I hope to come to you soon, but I am writing these instructions to you so that, ¹⁵if I am delayed, you may know how one ought to behave in the household of God, which is the church of the living God, the pillar and bulwark of the truth. ¹⁶Great indeed, we confess, is the mystery of our religion:

Heʰ was manifested in the flesh,
vindicatedⁱ in the Spirit,
  seen by angels,
preached among the nations,
believed on in the world,
  taken up in glory.

4 Now the Spirit expressly says that in later times some will depart from the faith by giving heed to deceitful spirits and doctrines of demons, ²through the pretensions of liars whose consciences are seared, ³who forbid marriage and enjoin abstinence from foods which God created to be received with thanksgiving by those who believe and know the truth. ⁴For everything created by God is good, and nothing is to be rejected if it is received with thanksgiving; ⁵for then it is consecrated by the word of God and prayer.

6 If you put these instructions before the brethren, you will be a good minister of Christ Jesus, nourished on the words of the faith and of the good doctrine which you have followed. ⁷Have nothing to do with godless and silly myths. Train yourself in godliness; ⁸for while bodily training is of

ᶜOr *by the birth of the child*   ᵈGreek *they continue*
ᶠOr *slanderer*
ʰGreek *Who*; other ancient authorities read *God*; others, *Which*   ⁱOr *justified*
2.13: Gen 2.7, 21-22.   2.14: Gen 3.1-6.

some value, godliness is of value in every way, as it holds promise for the present life and also for the life to come. ⁹The saying is sure and worthy of full acceptance. ¹⁰For to this end we toil and strive,ʲ because we have our hope set on the living God, who is the Savior of all men, especially of those who believe.

11 Command and teach these things. ¹²Let no one despise your youth, but set the believers an example in speech and conduct, in love, in faith, in purity. ¹³Till I come, attend to the public reading of scripture, to preaching, to teaching. ¹⁴Do not neglect the gift you have, which was given you by prophetic utterance when the council of elders laid their hands upon you. ¹⁵Practice these duties, devote yourself to them, so that all may see your progress. ¹⁶Take heed to yourself and to your teaching: hold to that, for by so doing you will save both yourself and your hearers.

5 Do not rebuke an older man but exhort him as you would a father; treat younger men like brothers, ²older women like mothers, younger women like sisters, in all purity.

3 Honor widows who are real widows. ⁴If a widow has children or grandchildren, let them first learn their religious duty to their own family and make some return to their parents; for this is acceptable in the sight of God. ⁵She who is a real widow, and is left all alone, has set her hope on God and continues in supplications and prayers night and day; ⁶whereas she who is self-indulgent is dead even while she lives. ⁷Command this, so that they may be without reproach. ⁸If any one does not provide for his relatives, and especially for his own family, he has disowned the faith and is worse than an unbeliever.

9 Let a widow be enrolled if she is not less than sixty years of age, having been the wife of one husband; ¹⁰and she must be well attested for her good deeds, as one who has brought up children, shown hospitality, washed the feet of the saints, relieved the afflicted, and devoted herself to doing good in every way. ¹¹But refuse to enrol younger widows; for when they grow wanton against Christ they desire to marry, ¹²and so they incur condemnation for having violated their first

pledge. ¹³Besides that, they learn to be idlers, gadding about from house to house, and not only idlers but gossips and busybodies, saying what they should not. ¹⁴So I would have younger widows marry, bear children, rule their households, and give the enemy no occasion to revile us. ¹⁵For some have already strayed after Satan. ¹⁶If any believing womanˡ has relatives who are widows, let her assist them; let the church not be burdened, so that it may assist those who are real widows.

17 Let the elders who rule well be considered worthy of double honor, especially those who labor in preaching and teaching; ¹⁸for the scripture says, "You shall not muzzle an ox when it is treading out the grain," and, "The laborer deserves his wages." ¹⁹Never admit any charge against an elder except on the evidence of two or three witnesses. ²⁰As for those who persist in sin, rebuke them in the presence of all, so that the rest may stand in fear. ²¹In the presence of God and of Christ Jesus and of the elect angels I charge you to keep these rules without favor, doing nothing from partiality. ²²Do not be hasty in the laying on of hands, nor participate in another man's sins; keep yourself pure.

23 No longer drink only water, but use a little wine for the sake of your stomach and your frequent ailments.

24 The sins of some men are conspicuous, pointing to judgment, but the sins of others appear later. ²⁵So also good deeds are conspicuous; and even when they are not, they cannot remain hidden.

6 Let all who are under the yoke of slavery regard their masters as worthy of all honor, so that the name of God and the teaching may not be defamed. ²Those who have believing masters must not be disrespectful on the ground that they are brethren; rather they must serve all the better since those who benefit by their service are believers and beloved.

Teach and urge these duties. ³If any one teaches otherwise and does not agree with the sound words of our Lord Jesus Christ and the teaching which accords with godliness, ⁴he is

---

ʲOther ancient authorities read *suffer reproach*
ˡOther ancient authorities read *man or woman;* others, simply *man*
5.18: Deut 25.4; 1 Cor 9.9;·Mt 10.10; Lk 10.7; 1 Cor 9.14.
5.19: Deut 19.15.

puffed up with conceit, he knows nothing; he has a morbid craving for controversy and for disputes about words, which produce envy, dissension, slander, base suspicions, [5] and wrangling among men who are depraved in mind and bereft of the truth, imagining that godliness is a means of gain. [6] There is great gain in godliness with contentment; [7] for we brought nothing into the world, and[m] we cannot take anything out of the world; [8] but if we have food and clothing, with these we shall be content. [9] But those who desire to be rich fall into temptation, into a snare, into many senseless and hurtful desires that plunge men into ruin and destruction. [10] For the love of money is the root of all evils; it is through this craving that some have wandered away from the faith and pierced their hearts with many pangs.

11 But as for you, man of God, shun all this; aim at righteousness, godliness, faith, love, steadfastness, gentleness. [12] Fight the good fight of the faith; take hold of the eternal life to which you were called when you made the good confession in the presence of many witnesses. [13] In the presence of God who gives life to all things, and of Christ Jesus who in his testimony before Pŏn′tĭ·us Pilate made the good confession, [14] I charge you to keep the commandment unstained and free from reproach until the appearing of our Lord Jesus Christ; [15] and this will be made manifest at the proper time by the blessed and only Sovereign, the King of kings and Lord of lords, [16] who alone has immortality and dwells in unapproachable light, whom no man has ever seen or can see. To him be honor and eternal dominion. Amen.

17 As for the rich in this world, charge them not to be haughty, nor to set their hopes on uncertain riches but on God who richly furnishes us with everything to enjoy. [18] They are to do good, to be rich in good deeds, liberal and generous, [19] thus laying up for themselves a good foundation for the future, so that they may take hold of the life which is life indeed.

20 O Timothy, guard what has been entrusted to you. Avoid the godless chatter and contradictions of what is falsely called knowledge, [21] for by professing it some have missed the mark as regards the faith.

Grace be with you.

The Second Letter of Paul to

Timothy

1 Paul, an apostle of Christ Jesus by the will of God according to the promise of the life which is in Christ Jesus,

2 To Timothy, my beloved child:

Grace, mercy, and peace from God the Father and Christ Jesus our Lord.

3 I thank God whom I serve with a clear conscience, as did my fathers, when I remember you constantly in my prayers. [4] As I remember your tears, I long night and day to see you, that I may be filled with joy. [5] I am reminded of your sincere faith, a faith that dwelt first in your grandmother Lō′ĭs and your mother Eū′nĭçe and now, I am sure, dwells in you. [6] Hence I remind you to rekindle the gift of God that is within you through the laying on of my hands; [7] for God did not give us a spirit of timidity but a spirit of power and love and self-control.

8 Do not be ashamed then of testifying to our Lord, nor of me his prisoner, but share in suffering for the gospel in the power of God, [9] who saved us and called us with a holy calling, not in virtue of our works but in virtue of his own purpose and the grace which he gave us in Christ Jesus ages ago, [10] and now has mani-

*Other ancient authorities insert *it is certain that*
6.13: Jn 18.37.
1.5: Acts 16.1.

fested through the appearing of our Savior Christ Jesus, who abolished death and brought life and immortality to light through the gospel. ¹¹For this gospel I was appointed a preacher and apostle and teacher, ¹²and therefore I suffer as I do. But I am not ashamed, for I know whom I have believed, and I am sure that he is able to guard until that Day what has been entrusted to me.ᵃ ¹³Follow the pattern of the sound words which you have heard from me, in the faith and love which are in Christ Jesus; ¹⁴guard the truth that has been entrusted to you by the Holy Spirit who dwells within us.

15 You are aware that all who are in Asia turned away from me, and among them Phȳ'gē·lŭs and Hĕr·mŏġ'e·nēṣ. ¹⁶May the Lord grant mercy to the household of Ŏn·e·sĭph'-ō·rŭs, for he often refreshed me; he was not ashamed of my chains, ¹⁷but when he arrived in Rome he searched for me eagerly and found me—¹⁸may the Lord grant him to find mercy from the Lord on that Day—and you well know all the service he rendered at Ĕph'e·sŭs.

2 You then, my son, be strong in the grace that is in Christ Jesus, ²and what you have heard from me before many witnesses entrust to faithful men who will be able to teach others also. ³Share in suffering as a good soldier of Christ Jesus. ⁴No soldier on service gets entangled in civilian pursuits, since his aim is to satisfy the one who enlisted him. ⁵An athlete is not crowned unless he competes according to the rules. ⁶It is the hardworking farmer who ought to have the first share of the crops. ⁷Think over what I say, for the Lord will grant you understanding in everything.

8 Remember Jesus Christ, risen from the dead, descended from David, as preached in my gospel, ⁹the gospel for which I am suffering and wearing fetters like a criminal. But the word of God is not fettered. ¹⁰Therefore I endure everything for the sake of the elect, that they also may obtain salvation in Christ Jesus with its eternal glory. ¹¹The saying is sure:

If we have died with him, we shall also live with him;
¹²if we endure, we shall also reign with him;

if we deny him, he also will deny us; ¹³if we are faithless, he remains faithful—for he cannot deny himself.

14 Remind them of this, and charge them before the Lordᵇ to avoid disputing about words, which does no good, but only ruins the hearers. ¹⁵Do your best to present yourself to God as one approved, a workman who has no need to be ashamed, rightly handling the word of truth. ¹⁶Avoid such godless chatter, for it will lead people into more and more ungodliness, ¹⁷and their talk will eat its way like gangrene. Among them are Hȳ·me·naē'ŭs and Phĭ·lē'tŭs, ¹⁸who have swerved from the truth by holding that the resurrection is past already. They are upsetting the faith of some. ¹⁹But God's firm foundation stands, bearing this seal: "The Lord knows those who are his," and, "Let every one who names the name of the Lord depart from iniquity."

20 In a great house there are not only vessels of gold and silver but also of wood and earthenware, and some for noble use, some for ignoble. ²¹If any one purifies himself from what is ignoble, then he will be a vessel for noble use, consecrated and useful to the master of the house, ready for any good work. ²²So shun youthful passions and aim at righteousness, faith, love, and peace, along with those who call upon the Lord from a pure heart. ²³Have nothing to do with stupid, senseless controversies; you know that they breed quarrels. ²⁴And the Lord's servant must not be quarrelsome but kindly to every one, an apt teacher, forbearing, ²⁵correcting his opponents with gentleness. God may perhaps grant that they will repent and come to know the truth, ²⁶and they may escape from the snare of the devil, after being captured by him to do his will.ᶜ

3 But understand this, that in the last days there will come times of stress. ²For men will be lovers of self, lovers of money, proud, arrogant, abusive, disobedient to their parents, ungrateful, unholy, ³inhuman, implacable, slanderers, profligates, fierce, haters of good, ⁴treacherous, reckless,

---

ᵃOr *what I have entrusted to him*
ᵇOther ancient authorities read *God*
ᶜOr *by him, to do his* (that is, God's) *will*
2.19: Num 16.5; Is 26.13.

swollen with conceit, lovers of pleasure rather than lovers of God, ⁵holding the form of religion but denying the power of it. Avoid such people. ⁶For among them are those who make their way into households and capture weak women, burdened with sins and swayed by various impulses, ⁷who will listen to anybody and can never arrive at a knowledge of the truth. ⁸As Jăn′nēṣ and Jăm′brēṣ opposed Moses, so these men also oppose the truth, men of corrupt mind and counterfeit faith; ⁹but they will not get very far, for their folly will be plain to all, as was that of those two men.

10 Now you have observed my teaching, my conduct, my aim in life, my faith, my patience, my love, my steadfastness, ¹¹my persecutions, my sufferings, what befell me at Ăn′-ti·ŏch, at Ī·cō′nĭ·ụm, and at Lỹs′trạ, what persecutions I endured; yet from them all the Lord rescued me. ¹²Indeed all who desire to live a godly life in Christ Jesus will be persecuted, ¹³while evil men and impostors will go on from bad to worse, deceivers and deceived. ¹⁴But as for you, continue in what you have learned and have firmly believed, knowing from whom you learned it ¹⁵and how from childhood you have been acquainted with the sacred writings which are able to instruct you for salvation through faith in Christ Jesus. ¹⁶All scripture is inspired by God and*ᵈ* profitable for teaching, for reproof, for correction, and for training in righteousness, ¹⁷that the man of God may be complete, equipped for every good work.

4 I charge you in the presence of God and of Christ Jesus who is to judge the living and the dead, and by his appearing and his kingdom: ²preach the word, be urgent in season and out of season, convince, rebuke, and exhort, be unfailing in patience and in teaching. ³For the time is coming when people will not endure sound teaching, but having itching ears they will accumulate for themselves teachers to suit their own likings, ⁴and will turn away from listening to the truth

and wander into myths. ⁵As for you, always be steady, endure suffering, do the work of an evangelist, fulfil your ministry.

6 For I am already on the point of being sacrificed; the time of my departure has come. ⁷I have fought the good fight, I have finished the race, I have kept the faith. ⁸Henceforth there is laid up for me the crown of righteousness, which the Lord, the righteous judge, will award to me on that Day, and not only to me but also to all who have loved his appearing.

9 Do your best to come to me soon. ¹⁰For Dē′mạs, in love with this present world, has deserted me and gone to Thĕs·ṣạ·lọ·nī′cạ; Crĕs′çĕns has gone to Galatia,*ᵉ* Titus to Dalmatia. ¹¹Luke alone is with me. Get Mark and bring him with you; for he is very useful in serving me. ¹²Tўch′ĭ·cụs I have sent to Ĕph′ẹ·sụs. ¹³When you come, bring the cloak that I left with Căr′pụs at Trō′ăs, also the books, and above all the parchments. ¹⁴Alexander the coppersmith did me great harm; the Lord will requite him for his deeds. ¹⁵Beware of him yourself, for he strongly opposed our message. ¹⁶At my first defense no one took my part; all deserted me. May it not be charged against them! ¹⁷But the Lord stood by me and gave me strength to proclaim the message fully, that all the Gentiles might hear it. So I was rescued from the lion's mouth. ¹⁸The Lord will rescue me from every evil and save me for his heavenly kingdom. To him be the glory for ever and ever. Amen.

19 Greet Prĭs′cạ and Ă′quĭ·lạ, and the household of Ŏn·ẹ·sĭph′ọ·rụs. ²⁰Ĕ·răs′tụs remained at Corinth; Trŏph′ĭ·mụs I left ill at Mī·lē′tụs. ²¹Do your best to come before winter. Eụ·bū′lụs sends greetings to you, as do Pū′dĕnṣ and Lī′nụs and Claudia and all the brethren.

22 The Lord be with your spirit. Grace be with you.

ᵈOr Every scripture inspired by God is also
ᵉOther ancient authorities read Gaul
3.8: Ex 7.11.   3.11: Acts 13.14-52; 14.1-20; 16.1-5.

Titus

1 Paul, a servant[a] of God and an apostle of Jesus Christ, to further the faith of God's elect and their knowledge of the truth which accords with godliness, [2]in hope of eternal life which God, who never lies, promised ages ago [3]and at the proper time manifested in his word through the preaching with which I have been entrusted by command of God our Savior;

4 To Titus, my true child in a common faith:

Grace and peace from God the Father and Christ Jesus our Savior.

5 This is why I left you in Crete, that you might amend what was defective, and appoint elders in every town as I directed you, [6]if any man is blameless, the husband of one wife, and his children are believers and not open to the charge of being profligate or insubordinate. [7]For a bishop, as God's steward, must be blameless; he must not be arrogant or quick-tempered or a drunkard or violent or greedy for gain, [8]but hospitable, a lover of goodness, master of himself, upright, holy, and self-controlled; [9]he must hold firm to the sure word as taught, so that he may be able to give instruction in sound doctrine and also to confute those who contradict it. [10]For there are many insubordinate men, empty talkers and deceivers, especially the circumcision party; [11]they must be silenced, since they are upsetting whole families by teaching for base gain what they have no right to teach. [12]One of themselves, a prophet of their own, said, "Cretans are always liars, evil beasts, lazy gluttons." [13]This testimony is true. Therefore rebuke them sharply, that they may be sound in the faith, [14]instead of giving heed to Jewish myths or to commands of men who reject the truth. [15]To the pure all things are pure, but to the corrupt and unbelieving nothing is pure; their very minds and consciences are corrupted. [16]They profess to know God, but they deny him by their deeds; they are detestable, disobedient, unfit for any good deed.

2 But as for you, teach what befits sound doctrine. [2]Bid the older men be temperate, serious, sensible, sound in faith, in love, and in steadfastness. [3]Bid the older women likewise to be reverent in behavior, not to be slanderers or slaves to drink; they are to teach what is good, [4]and so train the young women to love their husbands and children, [5]to be sensible, chaste, domestic, kind, and submissive to their husbands, that the word of God may not be discredited. [6]Likewise urge the younger men to control themselves. [7]Show yourself in all respects a model of good deeds, and in your teaching show integrity, gravity, [8]and sound speech that cannot be censured, so that an opponent may be put to shame, having nothing evil to say of us. [9]Bid slaves to be submissive to their masters and to give satisfaction in every respect; they are not to be refractory, [10]nor to pilfer, but to show entire and true fidelity, so that in everything they may adorn the doctrine of God our Savior.

11 For the grace of God has appeared for the salvation of all men, [12]training us to renounce irreligion and worldly passions, and to live sober, upright, and godly lives in this world, [13]awaiting our blessed hope, the appearing of the glory of our great God and Savior[c] Jesus Christ, [14]who gave himself for us to redeem us from all iniquity and to purify for himself a people of his own who are zealous for good deeds.

15 Declare these things; exhort and reprove with all authority. Let no one disregard you.

3 Remind them to be submissive to rulers and authorities, to be obedient, to be ready for any honest work, [2]to speak evil of no one, to avoid quarreling, to be gentle, and to show perfect courtesy toward all men. [3]For we ourselves were once foolish, disobedient, led astray, slaves to various passions and pleasures, passing our

[a]Or *slave*
[c]Or *of the great God and our Savior*
1.12: Epimenides. **2.14:** Ps 130.8; Ezek 37.23; Deut 14.2.

days in malice and envy, hated by men and hating one another; ⁴but when the goodness and loving kindness of God our Savior appeared, ⁵he saved us, not because of deeds done by us in righteousness, but in virtue of his own mercy, by the washing of regeneration and renewal in the Holy Spirit, ⁶which he poured out upon us richly through Jesus Christ our Savior, ⁷so that we might be justified by his grace and become heirs in hope of eternal life. ⁸The saying is sure.

I desire you to insist on these things, so that those who have believed in God may be careful to apply themselves to good deeds;*ᵈ* these are excellent and profitable to men. ⁹But avoid stupid controversies, genealogies, dissensions, and quarrels over the law,

for they are unprofitable and futile. ¹⁰As for a man who is factious, after admonishing him once or twice, have nothing more to do with him, ¹¹knowing that such a person is perverted and sinful; he is self-condemned.

12 When I send Ár′tẹ·mạs or Tých′-ĭ·cụs to you, do your best to come to me at Nĭ·cŏp′ỏ·lĭs, for I have decided to spend the winter there. ¹³Do your best to speed Zē′nạs the lawyer and A·pŏl′lŏs on their way; see that they lack nothing. ¹⁴And let our people learn to apply themselves to good deeds,*ᵈ* so as to help cases of urgent need, and not to be unfruitful.

15 All who are with me send greetings to you. Greet those who love us in the faith.

Grace be with you all.

The Letter of Paul to

Philemon

1 Paul, a prisoner for Christ Jesus, and Timothy our brother,

To Phĭ·lē′mọn our beloved fellow worker ²and Ăp′phĭ·ạ our sister and Ăr·chĭp′pụs our fellow soldier, and the church in your house:

3 Grace to you and peace from God our Father and the Lord Jesus Christ.

4 I thank my God always when I remember you in my prayers, ⁵because I hear of your love and of the faith which you have toward the Lord Jesus and all the saints, ⁶and I pray that the sharing of your faith may promote the knowledge of all the good that is ours in Christ. ⁷For I have derived much joy and comfort from your love, my brother, because the hearts of the saints have been refreshed through you.

8 Accordingly, though I am bold enough in Christ to command you to do what is required, ⁹yet for love's sake I prefer to appeal to you—I, Paul, an ambassador*ᵃ* and now a prisoner also for Christ Jesus—¹⁰I appeal to you for my child, Ō·nĕs′ĭ·mụs, whose father I have become in my imprison-

ment. ¹¹(Formerly he was useless to you, but now he is indeed useful*ᵇ* to you and to me.) ¹²I am sending him back to you, sending my very heart. ¹³I would have been glad to keep him with me, in order that he might serve me on your behalf during my imprisonment for the gospel; ¹⁴but I preferred to do nothing without your consent in order that your goodness might not be by compulsion but of your own free will.

15 Perhaps this is why he was parted from you for a while, that you might have him back for ever, ¹⁶no longer as a slave but more than a slave, as a beloved brother, especially to me but how much more to you, both in the flesh and in the Lord. ¹⁷So if you consider me your partner, receive him as you would receive me. ¹⁸If he has wronged you at all, or owes you anything, charge that to my account. ¹⁹I, Paul, write this with my own hand, I

ᵈOr enter honorable occupations

ᵃOr an old man
ᵇThe name Onesimus means useful or (compare verse 20) beneficial
3: Rom 1.7.　**4:** Rom 1.8.　**10:** Col 4.9.

will repay it—to say nothing of your owing me even your own self. ²⁰Yes, brother, I want some benefit from you in the Lord. Refresh my heart in Christ.

21 Confident of your obedience, I write to you, knowing that you will do even more than I say. ²²At the same time, prepare a guest room for me, for I am hoping through your prayers to be granted to you.

23 Ĕp′a·phrăs, my fellow prisoner in Christ Jesus, sends greetings to you, ²⁴and so do Mark, Ăr·ĭs·tăr′chus, Dē′mas, and Luke, my fellow workers.

25 The grace of the Lord Jesus Christ be with your spirit.

The Letter to the
Hebrews

1 In many and various ways God spoke of old to our fathers by the prophets; ²but in these last days he has spoken to us by a Son, whom he appointed the heir of all things, through whom also he created the world. ³He reflects the glory of God and bears the very stamp of his nature, upholding the universe by his word of power. When he had made purification for sins, he sat down at the right hand of the Majesty on high, ⁴having become as much superior to angels as the name he has obtained is more excellent than theirs.

5 For to what angel did God ever say,
"Thou art my Son,
today I have begotten thee"?
Or again,
"I will be to him a father,
and he shall be to me a son"?
⁶And again, when he brings the first-born into the world, he says,
"Let all God's angels worship him."
⁷Of the angels he says,
"Who makes his angels winds,
and his servants flames of fire."
⁸But of the Son he says,
"Thy throne, O God,ᵃ is for ever and ever,
the righteous scepter is the scepter of thyᵇ kingdom.
⁹Thou hast loved righteousness and hated lawlessness;
therefore God, thy God, has anointed thee
with the oil of gladness beyond thy comrades."
¹⁰And,
"Thou, Lord, didst found the earth in the beginning,

and the heavens are the work of thy hands;
¹¹they will perish, but thou remainest;
they will all grow old like a garment,
¹²like a mantle thou wilt roll them up,
and they will be changed.ᶜ
But thou art the same,
and thy years will never end."
¹³But to what angel has he ever said,
"Sit at my right hand,
till I make thy enemies
a stool for thy feet"?
¹⁴Are they not all ministering spirits sent forth to serve, for the sake of those who are to obtain salvation?

2 Therefore we must pay the closer attention to what we have heard, lest we drift away from it. ²For if the message declared by angels was valid and every transgression or disobedience received a just retribution, ³how shall we escape if we neglect such a great salvation? It was declared at first by the Lord, and it was attested to us by those who heard him, ⁴while God also bore witness by signs and wonders and various miracles and by gifts of the Holy Spirit distributed according to his own will.

5 For it was not to angels that God subjected the world to come, of which we are speaking. ⁶It has been testified somewhere,
"What is man that thou art mindful of him,

23: Col 1.7; 4.12. **24:** Col 4.10, 14.

ᵃOr *God is thy throne* ᵇOther ancient authorities read *his*
ᶜOther ancient authorities add *like a garment*
1.5: Ps 2.7; 2 Sam 7.14.
1.6: Deut 32.43 Septuagint; Ps 97.7. **1.7:** Ps 104.4.
1.8-9: Ps 45.6-7. **1.10-12:** Ps 102.25-27. **1.13:** Ps 110.1.
2.6-9: Ps 8.4-6.

or the son of man, that thou carest
for him?
⁷Thou didst make him for a little
ᶜwhile lower than the angels,
thou hast crowned him with glory
and honor,ᵈ
⁸putting everything in subjection
under his feet."
Now in putting everything in subjection to him, he left nothing outside his
control. As it is, we do not yet see everything in subjection to him. ⁹But we
see Jesus, who for a little while was
made lower than the angels, crowned
with glory and honor because of the
suffering of death, so that by the grace
of God he might taste death for every
one.
10 For it was fitting that he, for
whom and by whom all things exist,
in bringing many sons to glory, should
make the pioneer of their salvation
perfect through suffering. ¹¹For he
who sanctifies and those who are sanctified have all one origin. That is why
he is not ashamed to call them
brethren, ¹²saying,
"I will proclaim thy name to my
brethren,
in the midst of the congregation I
will praise thee."
¹³And again,
"I will put my trust in him."
And again,
"Here am I, and the children God has
given me."
14 Since therefore the children
share in flesh and blood, he himself
likewise partook of the same nature,
that through death he might destroy
him who has the power of death, that
is, the devil, ¹⁵and deliver all those who
through fear of death were subject
to lifelong bondage. ¹⁶For surely it is
not with angels that he is concerned
but with the descendants of Abraham.
¹⁷Therefore he had to be made like
his brethren in every respect, so that
he might become a merciful and faithful high priest in the service of God, to
make expiation for the sins of the people. ¹⁸For because he himself has
suffered and been tempted, he is able
to help those who are tempted.

3 Therefore, holy brethren, who
share in a heavenly call, consider
Jesus, the apostle and high priest of
our confession. ²He was faithful to
him who appointed him, just as Moses

also was faithful inᵉ God's house.
³Yet Jesus has been counted worthy
of as much more glory than Moses as
the builder of a house has more honor
than the house. ⁴(For every house is
built by some one, but the builder of
all things is God.) ⁵Now Moses was
faithful in all God's house as a servant, to testify to the things that were to
be spoken later, ⁶but Christ was faithful over God'sᶠ house as a son. And we
are his house if we hold fast our confidence and pride in our hope.ᵍ
7 Therefore, as the Holy Spirit says,
"Today, when you hear his voice,
⁸do not harden your hearts as in the
rebellion,
on the day of testing in the wilderness,
⁹where your fathers put me to the test
and saw my works for forty years.
¹⁰Therefore I was provoked with that
generation,
and said, 'They always go astray in
their hearts;
they have not known my ways.'
¹¹As I swore in my wrath,
'They shall never enter my rest.' "
¹²Take care, brethren, lest there be
in any of you an evil, unbelieving
heart, leading you to fall away from
the living God. ¹³But exhort one another every day, as long as it is called
"today," that none of you may be hardened by the deceitfulness of sin.
¹⁴For we share in Christ, if only we
hold our first confidence firm to the
end, ¹⁵while it is said,
"Today, when you hear his voice,
do not harden your hearts
as in the rebellion."
¹⁶Who were they that heard and yet
were rebellious? Was it not all those
who left Egypt under the leadership
of Moses? ¹⁷And with whom was he
provoked forty years? Was it not with
those who sinned, whose bodies fell
in the wilderness? ¹⁸And to whom did
he swear that they should never enter
his rest, but to those who were disobedient? ¹⁹So we see that they were
unable to enter because of unbelief.

4 Therefore, while the promise of
entering his rest remains, let us

ᵈOther ancient authorities insert *and didst set him over
the works of thy hands*
ᵉOther ancient authorities insert *all* ᶠGreek *his*
ᵍOther ancient authorities insert *firm to the end*
2.12: Ps 22.22.   2.13: Is 8.17-18.   2.16: Is 41.8-9.
3.2: Num 12.7.   3.5: Num 12.7.   3.7-11: Ps 95.7-11.
3.15: Ps 95.7-8.   3.16-19: Num 14.1-35.   3.17: Num 14.29.

fear lest any of you be judged to have failed to reach it. [2] For good news came to us just as to them; but the message which they heard did not benefit them, because it did not meet with faith in the hearers.[h] [3] For we who have believed enter that rest, as he has said,

"As I swore in my wrath,
'They shall never enter my rest,'"

although his works were finished from the foundation of the world. [4] For he has somewhere spoken of the seventh day in this way, "And God rested on the seventh day from all his works." [5] And again in this place he said,

"They shall never enter my rest."

[6] Since therefore it remains for some to enter it, and those who formerly received the good news failed to enter because of disobedience, [7] again he sets a certain day, "Today," saying through David so long afterward, in the words already quoted,

"Today, when you hear his voice,
do not harden your hearts."

[8] For if Joshua had given them rest, God[i] would not speak later of another day. [9] So then, there remains a sabbath rest for the people of God; [10] for whoever enters God's rest also ceases from his labors as God did from his.

[11] Let us therefore strive to enter that rest, that no one fall by the same sort of disobedience. [12] For the word of God is living and active, sharper than any two-edged sword, piercing to the division of soul and spirit, of joints and marrow, and discerning the thoughts and intentions of the heart. [13] And before him no creature is hidden, but all are open and laid bare to the eyes of him with whom we have to do.

[14] Since then we have a great high priest who has passed through the heavens, Jesus, the Son of God, let us hold fast our confession. [15] For we have not a high priest who is unable to sympathize with our weaknesses, but one who in every respect has been tempted as we are, yet without sin. [16] Let us then with confidence draw near to the throne of grace, that we may receive mercy and find grace to help in time of need.

5 For every high priest chosen from among men is appointed to act on behalf of men in relation to God, to offer gifts and sacrifices for sins. [2] He can deal gently with the ignorant and wayward, since he himself is beset with weakness. [3] Because of this he is bound to offer sacrifice for his own sins, as well as for those of the people. [4] And one does not take the honor upon himself, but he is called by God, just as Aaron was.

5 So also Christ did not exalt himself to be made a high priest, but was appointed by him who said to him,
"Thou art my Son,
today I have begotten thee";
[6] as he says also in another place,
"Thou art a priest for ever,
after the order of Měl·chĭz'e·děk."

7 In the days of his flesh, Jesus[j] offered up prayers and supplications, with loud cries and tears, to him who was able to save him from death, and he was heard for his godly fear. [8] Although he was a Son, he learned obedience through what he suffered; [9] and being made perfect he became the source of eternal salvation to all who obey him, [10] being designated by God a high priest after the order of Měl·chĭz'e·děk.

11 About this we have much to say which is hard to explain, since you have become dull of hearing. [12] For though by this time you ought to be teachers, you need some one to teach you again the first principles of God's word. You need milk, not solid food; [13] for every one who lives on milk is unskilled in the word of righteousness, for he is a child. [14] But solid food is for the mature, for those who have their faculties trained by practice to distinguish good from evil.

6 Therefore let us leave the elementary doctrine of Christ and go on to maturity, not laying again a foundation of repentance from dead works and of faith toward God, [2] with instruction[k] about ablutions, the laying on of hands, the resurrection of the dead, and eternal judgment. [3] And this we will do if God permits.[l] [4] For it is impossible to restore again to repentance those who have once been enlightened, who have tasted the heav-

---

[h] Other manuscripts read *they were not united in faith with the hearers* [i] Greek *he* [j] Greek *he*
[k] Other ancient manuscripts read *of instruction*
[l] Other ancient manuscripts read *let us do this if God permits*
4.3: Ps 95.11.   4.4: Gen 2.2.   4.5: Ps 95.11.
4.7: Ps 95.7-8.   4.10: Gen 2.2.   5.5: Ps 2.7.
5.6: Ps 110.4.   5.7: Mt 26.36-46; Mk 14.32-42; Lk 22.40-46.
5.9: Is 45.17.   5.10: Ps 110.4.

enly gift, and have become partakers of the Holy Spirit, [5] and have tasted the goodness of the word of God and the powers of the age to come, [6] if they then commit apostasy, since they crucify the Son of God on their own account and hold him up to contempt. [7] For land which has drunk the rain that often falls upon it, and brings forth vegetation useful to those for whose sake it is cultivated, receives a blessing from God. [8] But if it bears thorns and thistles, it is worthless and near to being cursed; its end is to be burned.

9 Though we speak thus, yet in your case, beloved, we feel sure of better things that belong to salvation. [10] For God is not so unjust as to overlook your work and the love which you showed for his sake in serving the saints, as you still do. [11] And we desire each one of you to show the same earnestness in realizing the full assurance of hope until the end, [12] so that you may not be sluggish, but imitators of those who through faith and patience inherit the promises.

13 For when God made a promise to Abraham, since he had no one greater by whom to swear, he swore by himself, [14] saying, "Surely I will bless you and multiply you." [15] And thus Abraham,[m] having patiently endured, obtained the promise. [16] Men indeed swear by a greater than themselves, and in all their disputes an oath is final for confirmation. [17] So when God desired to show more convincingly to the heirs of the promise the unchangeable character of his purpose, he interposed with an oath, [18] so that through two unchangeable things, in which it is impossible that God should prove false, we who have fled for refuge might have strong encouragement to seize the hope set before us. [19] We have this as a sure and steadfast anchor of the soul, a hope that enters into the inner shrine behind the curtain, [20] where Jesus has gone as a forerunner on our behalf, having become a high priest for ever after the order of Měl·chĭz'ę·děk.

7 For this Měl·chĭz'ę·děk, king of Salem, priest of the Most High God, met Abraham returning from the slaughter of the kings and blessed him; [2] and to him Abraham apportioned a tenth part of everything. He is first, by translation of his name, king of righteousness, and then he is also king of Salem, that is, king of peace. [3] He is without father or mother or genealogy, and has neither beginning of days nor end of life, but resembling the Son of God he continues a priest for ever.

4 See how great he is! Abraham the patriarch gave him a tithe of the spoils. [5] And those descendants of Lē'vī who receive the priestly office have a commandment in the law to take tithes from the people, that is, from their brethren, though these also are descended from Abraham. [6] But this man who has not their genealogy received tithes from Abraham and blessed him who had the promises. [7] It is beyond dispute that the inferior is blessed by the superior. [8] Here tithes are received by mortal men; there, by one of whom it is testified that he lives. [9] One might even say that Lē'vī himself, who receives tithes, paid tithes through Abraham, [10] for he was still in the loins of his ancestor when Měl·chĭz'ę·děk met him.

11 Now if perfection had been attainable through the Levitical priesthood (for under it the people received the law), what further need would there have been for another priest to arise after the order of Měl·chĭz'ę·děk, rather than one named after the order of Aaron? [12] For when there is a change in the priesthood, there is necessarily a change in the law as well. [13] For the one of whom these things are spoken belonged to another tribe, from which no one has ever served at the altar. [14] For it is evident that our Lord was descended from Judah, and in connection with that tribe Moses said nothing about priests.

15 This becomes even more evident when another priest arises in the likeness of Měl·chĭz'ę·děk, [16] who has become a priest, not according to a legal requirement concerning bodily descent but by the power of an indestructible life. [17] For it is witnessed of him,

"Thou art a priest for ever,
after the order of Měl·chĭz'ę·děk."

[18] On the one hand, a former commandment is set aside because of its weak-

*Greek *he
6.8: Gen 3.17-18.   6.13-14: Gen 22.16-17.
6.19: Lev 16.2.   6.20: Ps 110.4.   7.1-10: Gen 14.17-20.
7.11, 15, 17, 21, 28: Ps 110.4.

ness and uselessness [19](for the law made nothing perfect); on the other hand, a better hope is introduced, through which we draw near to God.

20 And it was not without an oath. [21]Those who formerly became priests took their office without an oath, but this one was addressed with an oath,

"The Lord has sworn
and will not change his mind,
'Thou art a priest for ever.'"

[22]This makes Jesus the surety of a better covenant.

23 The former priests were many in number, because they were prevented by death from continuing in office; [24]but he holds his priesthood permanently, because he continues for ever. [25]Consequently he is able for all time to save those who draw near to God through him, since he always lives to make intercession for them.

26 For it was fitting that we should have such a high priest, holy, blameless, unstained, separated from sinners, exalted above the heavens. [27]He has no need, like those high priests, to offer sacrifices daily, first for his own sins and then for those of the people; he did this once for all when he offered up himself. [28]Indeed, the law appoints men in their weakness as high priests, but the word of the oath, which came later than the law, appoints a Son who has been made perfect for ever.

8 Now the point in what we are saying is this: we have such a high priest, one who is seated at the right hand of the throne of the Majesty in heaven, [2]a minister in the sanctuary and the true tent[n] which is set up not by man but by the Lord. [3]For every high priest is appointed to offer gifts and sacrifices; hence it is necessary for this priest also to have something to offer. [4]Now if he were on earth, he would not be a priest at all, since there are priests who offer gifts according to the law. [5]They serve a copy and shadow of the heavenly sanctuary; for when Moses was about to erect the tent,[n] he was instructed by God, saying, "See that you make everything according to the pattern which was shown you on the mountain." [6]But as it is, Christ[o] has obtained a ministry which is as much more excellent than the old as the covenant he mediates is

better, since it is enacted on better promises. [7]For if that first covenant had been faultless, there would have been no occasion for a second.

8 For he finds fault with them when he says:

"The days will come, says the Lord,
when I will establish a new covenant
with the house of Israel
and with the house of Judah;
[9]not like the covenant that I made
with their fathers
on the day when I took them by the hand
to lead them out of the land of Egypt;
for they did not continue in my covenant,
and so I paid no heed to them, says the Lord.
[10]This is the covenant that I will make
with the house of Israel
after those days, says the Lord:
I will put my laws into their minds,
and write them on their hearts,
and I will be their God,
and they shall be my people.
[11]And they shall not teach every one his fellow
or every one his brother, saying, 'Know the Lord.'
for all shall know me,
from the least of them to the greatest.
[12]For I will be merciful toward their iniquities,
and I will remember their sins no more."

[13]In speaking of a new covenant he treats the first as obsolete. And what is becoming obsolete and growing old is ready to vanish away.

9 Now even the first covenant had regulations for worship and an earthly sanctuary. [2]For a tent[p] was prepared, the outer one, in which were the lampstand and the table and the bread of the Presence;[q] it is called the Holy Place. [3]Behind the second curtain stood a tent[p] called the Holy of Holies, [4]having the golden altar of incense and the ark of the covenant covered on all sides with gold, which contained a golden urn holding the manna, and Aaron's rod that budded, and the tables

[n] Or *tabernacle*   [o] Greek *he*   [p] Or *tabernacle*
[q] Greek *the presentation of the loaves*
8.1: Ps 110.1.   **8.5:** Ex 25.40.
8.8-12: Jer 31.31-34.   **9.1-10:** Ex 25.10-40.
9.2: Lev 24.5.   **9.3:** Ex 26.31-33.
9.4: Ex 30.1-5; 16.32-33; Num 17.8-10.

of the covenant; ⁵above it were the cherubim of glory overshadowing the mercy seat. Of these things we cannot now speak in detail.

6 These preparations having thus been made, the priests go continually into the outer tent,ᵖ performing their ritual duties; ⁷but into the second only the high priest goes, and he but once a year, and not without taking blood which he offers for himself and for the errors of the people. ⁸By this the Holy Spirit indicates that the way into the sanctuary is not yet opened as long as the outer tentᵖ is still standing ⁹(which is symbolic for the present age). According to this arrangement, gifts and sacrifices are offered which cannot perfect the conscience of the worshiper, ¹⁰but deal only with food and drink and various ablutions, regulations for the body imposed until the time of reformation.

11 But when Christ appeared as a high priest of the good things that have come,ʳ then through the greater and more perfect -tentᵖ (not made with hands, that is, not of this creation) ¹²he entered once for all into the Holy Place, takingˢ not the blood of goats and calves but his own blood, thus securing an eternal redemption. ¹³For if the sprinkling of defiled persons with the blood of goats and bulls and with the ashes of a heifer sanctifies for the purification of the flesh, ¹⁴how much more shall the blood of Christ, who through the eternal Spirit offered himself without blemish to God, purify yourᵗ conscience from dead works to serve the living God.

15 Therefore he is the mediator of a new covenant, so that those who are called may receive the promised eternal inheritance, since a death has occurred which redeems them from the transgressions under the first covenant.ᵘ ¹⁶For where a willᵘ is involved, the death of the one who made it must be established. ¹⁷For a willᵘ takes effect only at death, since it is not in force as long as the one who made it is alive. ¹⁸Hence even the first covenant was not ratified without blood. ¹⁹For when every commandment of the law had been declared by Moses to all the people, he took the blood of calves and goats, with water and scarlet wool and hyssop, and sprinkled both the book itself and all the people, ²⁰saying, "This is the blood of the covenant which God commanded you." ²¹And in the same way he sprinkled with the blood both the tentᵖ and all the vessels used in worship. ²²Indeed, under the law almost everything is purified with blood, and without the shedding of blood there is no forgiveness of sins.

23 Thus it was necessary for copies of the heavenly things to be purified with these rites, but the heavenly things themselves with better sacrifices than these. ²⁴For Christ has entered, not into a sanctuary made with hands, a copy of the true one, but into heaven itself, now to appear in the presence of God on our behalf. ²⁵Nor was it to offer himself repeatedly, as the high priest enters the Holy Place yearly with blood not his own; ²⁶for then he would have had to suffer repeatedly since the foundation of the world. But as it is, he has appeared once for all at the end of the age to put away sin by the sacrifice of himself. ²⁷And just as it is appointed for men to die once, and after that comes judgment, ²⁸so Christ, having been offered once to bear the sins of many, will appear a second time, not to deal with sin but to save those who are eagerly waiting for him.

10 For since the law has but a shadow of the good things to come instead of the true form of these realities, it can never, by the same sacrifices which are continually offered year after year, make perfect those who draw near. ²Otherwise, would they not have ceased to be offered? If the worshipers had once been cleansed, they would no longer have any consciousness of sin. ³But in these sacrifices there is a reminder of sin year after year. ⁴For it is impossible that the blood of bulls and goats should take away sins.

5 Consequently, when Christᵛ came into the world, he said,

"Sacrifices and offerings thou hast
    not desired,
but a body hast thou prepared for me;
⁶in burnt offerings and sin offerings
    thou hast taken no pleasure.

ᵖ Or *tabernacle*
ʳ Other manuscripts read *good things to come*
ˢ Greek *through* ᵗ Other manuscripts read *our*
ᵘ The Greek word here used means both *covenant* and *will*
ᵛ Greek *he*
9.7: Lev 16.   9.13: Lev 16.6, 16; Num 19.9, 17-18.
9.19-20: Ex 24.6-8.   10.5-9: Ps 40.6-8.

⁷Then I said, 'Lo, I have come to do thy will, O God,'
as it is written of me in the roll of the book."
⁸When he said above, "Thou hast neither desired nor taken pleasure in sacrifices and offerings and burnt offerings and sin offerings" (these are offered according to the law), ⁹then he added, "Lo, I have come to do thy will." He abolishes the first in order to establish the second. ¹⁰And by that will we have been sanctified through the offering of the body of Jesus Christ once for all.

11 And every priest stands daily at his service, offering repeatedly the same sacrifices, which can never take away sins. ¹²But when Christ*ʷ* had offered for all time a single sacrifice for sins, he sat down at the right hand of God, ¹³then to wait until his enemies should be made a stool for his feet. ¹⁴For by a single offering he has perfected for all time those who are sanctified. ¹⁵And the Holy Spirit also bears witness to us; for after saying,

¹⁶"This is the covenant that I will make with them
after those days, says the Lord:
I will put my laws on their hearts,
and write them on their minds,"
¹⁷then he adds,
"I will remember their sins and their misdeeds no more."

¹⁸Where there is forgiveness of these, there is no longer any offering for sin.

19 Therefore, brethren, since we have confidence to enter the sanctuary by the blood of Jesus, ²⁰by the new and living way which he opened for us through the curtain, that is, through his flesh, ²¹and since we have a great priest over the house of God, ²²let us draw near with a true heart in full assurance of faith, with our hearts sprinkled clean from an evil conscience and our bodies washed with pure water. ²³Let us hold fast the confession of our hope without wavering, for he who promised is faithful; ²⁴and let us consider how to stir up one another to love and good works, ²⁵not neglecting to meet together, as is the habit of some, but encouraging one another, and all the more as you see the Day drawing near.

26 For if we sin deliberately after receiving the knowledge of the truth, there no longer remains a sacrifice for sins, ²⁷but a fearful prospect of judgment, and a fury of fire which will consume the adversaries. ²⁸A man who has violated the law of Moses dies without mercy at the testimony of two or three witnesses. ²⁹How much worse punishment do you think will be deserved by the man who has spurned the Son of God, and profaned the blood of the covenant by which he was sanctified, and outraged the Spirit of grace? ³⁰For we know him who said, "Vengeance is mine, I will repay." And again, "The Lord will judge his people." ³¹It is a fearful thing to fall into the hands of the living God.

32 But recall the former days when, after you were enlightened, you endured a hard struggle with sufferings, ³³sometimes being publicly exposed to abuse and affliction, and sometimes being partners with those so treated. ³⁴For you had compassion on the prisoners, and you joyfully accepted the plundering of your property, since you knew that you yourselves had a better possession and an abiding one. ³⁵Therefore do not throw away your confidence, which has a great reward. ³⁶For you have need of endurance, so that you may do the will of God and receive what is promised.
³⁷"For yet a little while,
and the coming one shall come and shall not tarry;
³⁸but my righteous one shall live by faith,
and if he shrinks back,
my soul has no pleasure in him."
³⁹But we are not of those who shrink back and are destroyed, but of those who have faith and keep their souls.

11 Now faith is the assurance of things hoped for, the conviction of things not seen. ²For by it the men of old received divine approval. ³By faith we understand that the world was created by the word of God, so that what is seen was made out of things which do not appear.

4 By faith Abel offered to God a more acceptable sacrifice than Cain, through which he received approval as righteous, God bearing witness by

ʷGreek *this one*
10.12-13: Ps 110.1.
10.16-17: Jer 31.33-34.   10.27: Is 26.11.
10.28: Deut 17.2-6.   10.29: Ex 24.8.
10.30: Deut 32.35-36.   10.37: Is 26.20 Septuagint.
10.37-38: Hab 2.3-4.   11.4: Gen 4.3-10.

accepting his gifts; he died, but through his faith he is still speaking. ⁵ By faith Ĕ′nŏch was taken up so that he should not see death; and he was not found, because God had taken him. Now before he was taken he was attested as having pleased God. ⁶ And without faith it is impossible to please him. For whoever would draw near to God must believe that he exists and that he rewards those who seek him. ⁷ By faith Noah, being warned by God concerning events as yet unseen, took heed and constructed an ark for the saving of his household; by this he condemned the world and became an heir of the righteousness which comes by faith.

8 By faith Abraham obeyed when he was called to go out to a place which he was to receive as an inheritance; and he went out, not knowing where he was to go. ⁹ By faith he sojourned in the land of promise, as in a foreign land, living in tents with Isaac and Jacob, heirs with him of the same promise. ¹⁰ For he looked forward to the city which has foundations, whose builder and maker is God. ¹¹ By faith Sarah herself received power to conceive, even when she was past the age, since she considered him faithful who had promised. ¹² Therefore from one man, and him as good as dead, were born descendants as many as the stars of heaven and as the innumerable grains of sand by the seashore.

13 These all died in faith, not having received what was promised, but having seen it and greeted it from afar, and having acknowledged that they were strangers and exiles on the earth. ¹⁴ For people who speak thus make it clear that they are seeking a homeland. ¹⁵ If they had been thinking of that land from which they had gone out, they would have had opportunity to return. ¹⁶ But as it is, they desire a better country, that is, a heavenly one. Therefore God is not ashamed to be called their God, for he has prepared for them a city.

17 By faith Abraham, when he was tested, offered up Isaac, and he who had received the promises was ready to offer up his only son, ¹⁸ of whom it was said, "Through Isaac shall your descendants be named." ¹⁹ He considered that God was able to raise men even from the dead; hence, figuratively

speaking, he did receive him back. ²⁰ By faith Isaac invoked future blessings on Jacob and Esau. ²¹ By faith Jacob, when dying, blessed each of the sons of Joseph, bowing in worship over the head of his staff. ²² By faith Joseph, at the end of his life, made mention of the exodus of the Israelites and gave directions concerning his burial.ˣ

23 By faith Moses, when he was born, was hid for three months by his parents, because they saw that the child was beautiful; and they were not afraid of the king's edict. ²⁴ By faith Moses, when he was grown up, refused to be called the son of Pharaoh's daughter, ²⁵ choosing rather to share ill-treatment with the people of God than to enjoy the fleeting pleasures of sin. ²⁶ He considered abuse suffered for the Christ greater wealth than the treasures of Egypt, for he looked to the reward. ²⁷ By faith he left Egypt, not being afraid of the anger of the king; for he endured as seeing him who is invisible. ²⁸ By faith he kept the Passover and sprinkled the blood, so that the Destroyer of the first-born might not touch them.

29 By faith the people crossed the Red Sea as if on dry land; but the Egyptians, when they attempted to do the same, were drowned. ³⁰ By faith the walls of Jericho fell down after they had been encircled for seven days. ³¹ By faith Rā′hăb the harlot did not perish with those who were disobedient, because she had given friendly welcome to the spies.

32 And what more shall I say? For time would fail me to tell of Gideon, Bār′ak, Samson, Jĕph′thah, of David and Samuel and the prophets — ³³ who through faith conquered kingdoms, enforced justice, received promises, stopped the mouths of lions, ³⁴ quenched raging fire, escaped the edge of the sword, won strength out of weakness,

ˣ Greek *bones*
11.5: Gen 5.21-24.
11.7: Gen 6.13-22.   11.8-9: Gen 12.1-8.
11.11: Gen 17.19; 18.11-14; 21.2.
11.12: Gen 15.5-6; 22.17; 32.12.
11.13: Ps 39.12; Gen 23.4.   11.16: Ex 3.6, 15; 4.5.
11.17: Gen 22.1-10.   11.18: Gen 21.12.
11.20: Gen 27.27-29, 39-40.
11.21: Gen 48; 47.31 Septuagint.
11.22: Gen 50.24-25; Ex 13.19.   11.23: Ex 2.2; 1.22.
11.24: Ex 2.10, 11-15.   11.27: Ex 2.15.
11.28: Ex 12.21-28, 29-30.   11.29: Ex 14.21-31.
11.30: Josh 6.12-21.   11.31: Josh 2.1-21; 6.22-25.
11.32: Judg 6-8; 4-5; 13-16; 11-12; 1 Sam 16-30; 2 Sam 1-24; 1 Kings 1-2.11; 1 Sam 1-12; 15; 16.1-13.
11.33: Dan 6.   11.34: Dan 3.

became mighty in war, put foreign armies to flight. ³⁵Women received heir dead by resurrection. Some were ortured, refusing to accept release, hat they might rise again to a better ife. ³⁶Others suffered mocking and scourging, and even chains and imprisonment. ³⁷They were stoned, they vere sawn in two,ʸ they were killed vith the sword; they went about in skins of sheep and goats, destitute, afflicted, ill-treated—³⁸of whom the world was not worthy—wandering over deserts and mountains, and in dens and caves of the earth.

39 And all these, though well attested by their faith, did not receive what was promised, ⁴⁰since God had foreseen something better for us, that apart from us they should not be made perfect.

12   Therefore, since we are surrounded by so great a cloud of witnesses, let us also lay aside every weight, and sin which clings so closely, and let us run with perseverance the race that is set before us, looking to Jesus the pioneer and perfecter of our faith, who for the joy that was set before him endured the cross, despising the shame, and is seated at he right hand of the throne of God.

³Consider him who endured from sinners such hostility against himself, so that you may not grow weary or fainthearted. ⁴In your struggle against sin you have not yet resisted to the point of shedding your blood. ⁵And have you forgotten the exhortation which addresses you as sons?—

"My son, do not regard lightly the discipline of the Lord,
nor lose courage when you are punished by him.
⁶For the Lord disciplines him whom he loves,
and chastises every son whom he receives."

It is for discipline that you have to endure. God is treating you as sons; for what son is there whom his father does not discipline? ⁸If you are left without discipline, in which all have participated, then you are illegitimate children and not sons. ⁹Besides this, we have had earthly fathers to discipline us and we respected them. Shall we not much more be subject to the Father of spirits and live? ¹⁰For they disciplined us for a short time at

their pleasure, but he disciplines us for our good, that we may share his holiness. ¹¹For the moment all discipline seems painful rather than pleasant; later it yields the peaceful fruit of righteousness to those who have been trained by it.

12 Therefore lift your drooping hands and strengthen your weak knees, ¹³and make straight paths for your feet, so that what is lame may not be put out of joint but rather be healed. ¹⁴Strive for peace with all men, and for the holiness without which no one will see the Lord. ¹⁵See to it that no one fail to obtain the grace of God; that no "root of bitterness" spring up and cause trouble, and by it the many become defiled; ¹⁶that no one be immoral or irreligious like Esau, who sold his birthright for a single meal. ¹⁷For you know that afterward, when he desired to inherit the blessing, he was rejected, for he found no chance to repent, though he sought it with tears.

18 For you have not come to what may be touched, a blazing fire, and darkness, and gloom, and a tempest, ¹⁹and the sound of a trumpet, and a voice whose words made the hearers entreat that no further messages be spoken to them. ²⁰For they could not endure the order that was given, "If even a beast touches the mountain, it shall be stoned." ²¹Indeed, so terrifying was the sight that Moses said, "I tremble with fear." ²²But you have come to Mount Zion and to the city of the living God, the heavenly Jerusalem, and to innumerable angels in festal gathering, ²³and to the assemblyᶻ of the first-born who are enrolled in heaven, and to a judge who is God of all, and to the spirits of just men made perfect, ²⁴and to Jesus, the mediator of a new covenant, and to the sprinkled blood that speaks more graciously than the blood of Abel.

25 See that you do not refuse him who is speaking. For if they did not escape when they refused him who warned them on earth, much less shall

---

ʸOther manuscripts add *they were tempted*
ᶻOr *angels, and to the festal gathering and assembly*
11.35: 1 Kings 17.17-24; 2 Kings 4.25-37.   **12.2:** Ps 110.1.
12.5-8: Prov 3.11-12.   **12.12:** Is 35.3.
12.13: Prov 4.26 Septuagint.
12.15: Deut 29.18 Septuagint.   **12.16:** Gen 25.29-34.
12.17: Gen 27.30-40.
12.18-19: Ex 19.12-22; 20.18-21; Deut 4.11-12; 5.22-27.
12.20: Ex 19.12-13.   **12.21:** Deut 9.19.
12.24: Gen 4.10.   **12.25:** Ex 20.19.

we escape if we reject him who warns from heaven. [26] His voice then shook the earth; but now he has promised, "Yet once more I will shake not only the earth but also the heaven." [27] This phrase, "Yet once more," indicates the removal of what is shaken, as of what has been made, in order that what cannot be shaken may remain. [28] Therefore let us be grateful for receiving a kingdom that cannot be shaken, and thus let us offer to God acceptable worship, with reverence and awe; [29] for our God is a consuming fire.

13 Let brotherly love continue. [2] Do not neglect to show hospitality to strangers, for thereby some have entertained angels unawares. [3] Remember those who are in prison, as though in prison with them; and those who are ill-treated, since you also are in the body. [4] Let marriage be held in honor among all, and let the marriage bed be undefiled; for God will judge the immoral and adulterous. [5] Keep your life free from love of money, and be content with what you have; for he has said, "I will never fail you nor forsake you." [6] Hence we can confidently say,

"The Lord is my helper,
I will not be afraid;
what can man do to me?"

7 Remember your leaders, those who spoke to you the word of God; consider the outcome of their life, and imitate their faith. [8] Jesus Christ is the same yesterday and today and for ever. [9] Do not be led away by diverse and strange teachings; for it is well that the heart be strengthened by grace, not by foods, which have not benefited their adherents. [10] We have an altar from which those who serve the tent[a] have no right to eat. [11] For the bodies of those animals whose blood is brought into the sanctuary by the high priest as a sacrifice for sin are burned outside the camp. [12] So Jesus also suffered outside the

gate in order to sanctify the people through his own blood. [13] Therefore let us go forth to him outside the camp and bear the abuse he endured. [14] For here we have no lasting city, but we seek the city which is to come [15] Through him then let us continually offer up a sacrifice of praise to God that is, the fruit of lips that acknowledge his name. [16] Do not neglect to do good and to share what you have, for such sacrifices are pleasing to God.

17 Obey your leaders and submit to them; for they are keeping watch over your souls, as men who will have to give account. Let them do this joyfully, and not sadly, for that would be of no advantage to you.

18 Pray for us, for we are sure that we have a clear conscience, desiring to act honorably in all things. [19] I urge you the more earnestly to do this in order that I may be restored to you the sooner.

20 Now may the God of peace who brought again from the dead our Lord Jesus, the great shepherd of the sheep by the blood of the eternal covenant [21] equip you with everything good that you may do his will, working in you that which is pleasing in his sight through Jesus Christ; to whom be glory for ever and ever. Amen.

22 I appeal to you, brethren, bear with my word of exhortation, for I have written to you briefly. [23] You should understand that our brother Timothy has been released, with whom I shall see you if he comes soon. [24] Greet all your leaders and all the saints. Those who come from Italy send you greetings. [25] Grace be with all of you. Amen

[a] Or *tabernacle*
[b] Other ancient authorities read *us*
12.26: Hag 2.6.
12.29: Deut 4.24.   13.2: Gen 18.1-8; 19.1-3.
13.5: Deut 31.6, 8; Josh 1.5.   13.6: Ps 118.6.
13.11, 13: Lev 16.27.   13.15: Lev 7.12; Is 57.19; Hos 14.2.
13.20: Is 63.11; Zech 9.11; Is 55.3; Ezek 37.26.

The Letter of

James

1 James, a servant of God and of the Lord Jesus Christ,
To the twelve tribes in the Dispersion:
Greeting.

2 Count it all joy, my brethren, when you meet various trials, 3 for you know that the testing of your faith produces steadfastness. 4 And let steadfastness have its full effect, that you may be perfect and complete, lacking in nothing.

5 If any of you lacks wisdom, let him ask God, who gives to all men generously and without reproaching, and it will be given him. 6 But let him ask in faith, with no doubting, for he who doubts is like a wave of the sea that is driven and tossed by the wind. 7, 8 For that person must not suppose that a double-minded man, unstable in all his ways, will receive anything from the Lord.

9 Let the lowly brother boast in his exaltation, 10 and the rich in his humiliation, because like the flower of the grass he will pass away. 11 For the sun rises with its scorching heat and withers the grass; its flower falls, and its beauty perishes. So will the rich man fade away in the midst of his pursuits.

12 Blessed is the man who endures trial, for when he has stood the test he will receive the crown of life which God has promised to those who love him. 13 Let no one say when he is tempted, "I am tempted by God"; for God cannot be tempted with evil and he himself tempts no one; 14 but each person is tempted when he is lured and enticed by his own desire. 15 Then desire when it has conceived gives birth to sin; and sin when it is full-grown brings forth death.

16 Do not be deceived, my beloved brethren. 17 Every good endowment and every perfect gift is from above, coming down from the Father of lights with whom there is no variation or shadow due to change.*a* 18 Of his own will he brought us forth by the word

of truth that we should be a kind of first fruits of his creatures.

19 Know this, my beloved brethren. Let every man be quick to hear, slow to speak, slow to anger, 20 for the anger of man does not work the righteousness of God. 21 Therefore put away all filthiness and rank growth of wickedness and receive with meekness the implanted word, which is able to save your souls.

22 But be doers of the word, and not hearers only, deceiving yourselves. 23 For if any one is a hearer of the word and not a doer, he is like a man who observes his natural face in a mirror; 24 for he observes himself and goes away and at once forgets what he was like. 25 But he who looks into the perfect law, the law of liberty, and perseveres, being no hearer that forgets but a doer that acts, he shall be blessed in his doing.

26 If any one thinks he is religious, and does not bridle his tongue but deceives his heart, this man's religion is vain. 27 Religion that is pure and undefiled before God and the Father is this: to visit orphans and widows in their affliction, and to keep oneself unstained from the world.

2 My brethren, show no partiality as you hold the faith of our Lord Jesus Christ, the Lord of glory. 2 For if a man with gold rings and in fine clothing comes into your assembly, and a poor man in shabby clothing also comes in, 3 and you pay attention to the one who wears the fine clothing and say, "Have a seat here, please," while you say to the poor man, "Stand there," or, "Sit at my feet," 4 have you not made distinctions among yourselves, and become judges with evil thoughts? 5 Listen, my beloved brethren. Has not God chosen those who are poor in the world to be rich in faith and heirs of the kingdom which he has promised to those who love

a Other ancient authorities read *variation due to a shadow of turning*
1.10-11: Is 40.6-7.

him? ⁶But you have dishonored the poor man. Is it not the rich who oppress you, is it not they who drag you into court? ⁷Is it not they who blaspheme the honorable name which was invoked over you?

8 If you really fulfil the royal law, according to the scripture, "You shall love your neighbor as yourself," you do well. ⁹But if you show partiality, you commit sin, and are convicted by the law as transgressors. ¹⁰For whoever keeps the whole law but fails in one point has become guilty of all of it. ¹¹For he who said, "Do not commit adultery," said also, "Do not kill." If you do not commit adultery but do kill, you have become a transgressor of the law. ¹²So speak and so act as those who are to be judged under the law of liberty. ¹³For judgment is without mercy to one who has shown no mercy; yet mercy triumphs over judgment.

14 What does it profit, my brethren, if a man says he has faith but has not works? Can his faith save him? ¹⁵If a brother or sister is ill-clad and in lack of daily food, ¹⁶and one of you says to them, "Go in peace, be warmed and filled," without giving them the things needed for the body, what does it profit? ¹⁷So faith by itself, if it has no works, is dead.

18 But some one will say, "You have faith and I have works." Show me your faith apart from your works, and I by my works will show you my faith. ¹⁹You believe that God is one; you do well. Even the demons believe—and shudder. ²⁰Do you want to be shown, you shallow man, that faith apart from works is barren? ²¹Was not Abraham our father justified by works, when he offered his son Isaac upon the altar? ²²You see that faith was active along with his works, and faith was completed by works, ²³and the scripture was fulfilled which says, "Abraham believed God, and it was reckoned to him as righteousness"; and he was called the friend of God. ²⁴You see that a man is justified by works and not by faith alone. ²⁵And in the same way was not also Rā′hăb the harlot justified by works when she received the messengers and sent them out another way? ²⁶For as the body apart from the spirit is dead, so faith apart from works is dead.

3 Let not many of you become teachers, my brethren, for you know that we who teach shall be judged with greater strictness. ²For we all make many mistakes, and if any one makes no mistakes in what he says he is a perfect man, able to bridle the whole body also. ³If we put bits into the mouths of horses that they may obey us, we guide their whole bodies. ⁴Look at the ships also; though they are so great and are driven by strong winds, they are guided by a very small rudder wherever the will of the pilot directs. ⁵So the tongue is a little member and boasts of great things. How great a forest is set ablaze by a small fire!

6 And the tongue is a fire. The tongue is an unrighteous world among our members, staining the whole body, setting on fire the cycle of nature,^b and set on fire by hell.^c ⁷For every kind of beast and bird, of reptile and sea creature, can be tamed and has been tamed by humankind, ⁸but no human being can tame the tongue—a restless evil, full of deadly poison. ⁹With it we bless the Lord and Father, and with it we curse men, who are made in the likeness of God. ¹⁰From the same mouth come blessing and cursing. My brethren, this ought not to be so. ¹¹Does a spring pour forth from the same opening fresh water and brackish? ¹²Can a fig tree, my brethren, yield olives, or a grapevine figs? No more can salt water yield fresh.

13 Who is wise and understanding among you? By his good life let him show his works in the meekness of wisdom. ¹⁴But if you have bitter jealousy and selfish ambition in your hearts, do not boast and be false to the truth. ¹⁵This wisdom is not such as comes down from above, but is earthly, unspiritual, devilish. ¹⁶For where jealousy and selfish ambition exist, there will be disorder and every vile practice. ¹⁷But the wisdom from above is first pure, then peaceable, gentle, open to reason, full of mercy and good fruits, without uncertainty or insincerity. ¹⁸And the harvest of righteousness is sown in peace by those who make peace.

^bOr *wheel of birth*   ^cGreek *Gehenna*
2.8: Lev 19.18.   **2.11:** Ex 20.13-14; Deut 5.17-18.
2.21: Gen 22.1-14.   **2.23:** Gen 15.6; Is 41.8; 2 Chron 20.7.
2.25: Josh 2.1-21.

4 What causes wars, and what causes fightings among you? Is it not your passions that are at war in your members? ² You desire and do not have; so you kill. And you covet*ᵈ* and cannot obtain; so you fight and wage war. You do not have, because you do not ask. ³ You ask and do not receive, because you ask wrongly, to spend it on your passions. ⁴ Unfaithful creatures! Do you not know that friendship with the world is enmity with God? Therefore whoever wishes to be a friend of the world makes himself an enemy of God. ⁵ Or do you suppose it is in vain that the scripture says, "He yearns jealously over the spirit which he has made to dwell in us"? ⁶ But he gives more grace; therefore it says, "God opposes the proud, but gives grace to the humble." ⁷ Submit yourselves therefore to God. Resist the devil and he will flee from you. ⁸ Draw near to God and he will draw near to you. Cleanse your hands, you sinners, and purify your hearts, you men of double mind. ⁹ Be wretched and mourn and weep. Let your laughter be turned to mourning and your joy to dejection. ¹⁰ Humble yourselves before the Lord and he will exalt you.

11 Do not speak evil against one another, brethren. He that speaks evil against a brother or judges his brother, speaks evil against the law and judges the law. But if you judge the law, you are not a doer of the law but a judge. ¹² There is one lawgiver and judge, he who is able to save and to destroy. But who are you that you judge your neighbor?

13 Come now, you who say, "Today or tomorrow we will go into such and such a town and spend a year there and trade and get gain"; ¹⁴ whereas you do not know about tomorrow. What is your life? For you are a mist that appears for a little time and then vanishes. ¹⁵ Instead you ought to say, "If the Lord wills, we shall live and we shall do this or that." ¹⁶ As it is, you boast in your arrogance. All such boasting is evil. ¹⁷ Whoever knows what is right to do and fails to do it, for him it is sin.

5 Come now, you rich, weep and howl for the miseries that are coming upon you. ² Your riches have rotted and your garments are moth-eaten.

³ Your gold and silver have rusted, and their rust will be evidence against you and will eat your flesh like fire. You have laid up treasure*ᵉ* for the last days. ⁴ Behold, the wages of the laborers who mowed your fields, which you kept back by fraud, cry out; and the cries of the harvesters have reached the ears of the Lord of hosts. ⁵ You have lived on the earth in luxury and in pleasure; you have fattened your hearts in a day of slaughter. ⁶ You have condemned, you have killed the righteous man; he does not resist you.

7 Be patient, therefore, brethren, until the coming of the Lord. Behold, the farmer waits for the precious fruit of the earth, being patient over it until it receives the early and the late rain. ⁸ You also be patient. Establish your hearts, for the coming of the Lord is at hand. ⁹ Do not grumble, brethren, against one another, that you may not be judged; behold, the Judge is standing at the doors. ¹⁰ As an example of suffering and patience, brethren, take the prophets who spoke in the name of the Lord. ¹¹ Behold, we call those happy who were steadfast. You have heard of the steadfastness of Jōb, and you have seen the purpose of the Lord, how the Lord is compassionate and merciful.

12 But above all, my brethren, do not swear, either by heaven or by earth or with any other oath, but let your yes be yes and your no be no, that you may not fall under condemnation.

13 Is any one among you suffering? Let him pray. Is any cheerful? Let him sing praise. ¹⁴ Is any among you sick? Let him call for the elders of the church, and let them pray over him, anointing him with oil in the name of the Lord; ¹⁵ and the prayer of faith will save the sick man, and the Lord will raise him up; and if he has committed sins, he will be forgiven. ¹⁶ Therefore confess your sins to one another, and pray for one another, that you may be healed. The prayer of a righteous man has great power in its effects. ¹⁷ Ē·lī'jah was a man of like nature with ourselves and he prayed fervently that it might not rain, and for three years and six months it did not rain on the

ᵈ Or *you kill and you covet*
ᵉ Or *will eat your flesh, since you have stored up fire*
4.6: Prov 3.34.
5.11: Job 1.21-22; 2.10; Ps 103.8; 111.4.   **5.12:** Mt 5.37.
5.17: 1 Kings 17.1; 18.1; Luke 4.25.

earth. [18]Then he prayed again and the heaven gave rain, and the earth brought forth its fruit.

19 My brethren, if any one among you wanders from the truth and some one brings him back, [20]let him know that whoever brings back a sinner from the error of his way will save his soul from death and will cover a multitude of sins.

The First Letter of
Peter

1 Peter, an apostle of Jesus Christ, To the exiles of the Dispersion in Pŏn'tus, Galatia, Căp·pa·dō'çi·a, Asia, and Bĭ·thў̆n'ĭ·a, [2]chosen and destined by God the Father and sanctified by the Spirit for obedience to Jesus Christ and for sprinkling with his blood:

May grace and peace be multiplied to you.

3 Blessed be the God and Father of our Lord Jesus Christ! By his great mercy we have been born anew to a living hope through the resurrection of Jesus Christ from the dead, [4]and to an inheritance which is imperishable, undefiled, and unfading, kept in heaven for you, [5]who by God's power are guarded through faith for a salvation ready to be revealed in the last time. [6]In this you rejoice,[a] though now for a little while you may have to suffer various trials, [7]so that the genuineness of your faith, more precious than gold which though perishable is tested by fire, may redound to praise and glory and honor at the revelation of Jesus Christ. [8]Without having seen[b] him you[c] love him; though you do not now see him you[c] believe in him and rejoice with unutterable and exalted joy. [9]As the outcome of your faith you obtain the salvation of your souls.

10 The prophets who prophesied of the grace that was to be yours searched and inquired about this salvation; [11]they inquired what person or time was indicated by the Spirit of Christ within them when predicting the sufferings of Christ and the subsequent glory. [12]It was revealed to them that they were serving not themselves but you, in the things which have now been announced to you by those who preached the good news to you through the Holy Spirit sent from heaven, things into which angels long to look.

13 Therefore gird up your minds, be sober, set your hope fully upon the grace that is coming to you at the revelation of Jesus Christ. [14]As obedient children, do not be conformed to the passions of your former ignorance, [15]but as he who called you is holy, be holy yourselves in all your conduct; [16]since it is written, "You shall be holy, for I am holy." [17]And if you invoke as Father him who judges each one impartially according to his deeds, conduct yourselves with fear throughout the time of your exile. [18]You know that you were ransomed from the futile ways inherited from your fathers, not with perishable things such as silver or gold, [19]but with the precious blood of Christ, like that of a lamb without blemish or spot. [20]He was destined before the foundation of the world but was made manifest at the end of the times for your sake. [21]Through him you have confidence in God, who raised him from the dead and gave him glory, so that your faith and hope are in God.[d]

22 Having purified your souls by your obedience to the truth for a sincere love of the brethren, love one another earnestly from the heart. [23]You have been born anew, not of perishable seed but of imperishable, through the living and abiding word of God; [24]for

"All flesh is like grass
   and all its glory like the flower of
    grass.

5.18: 1 Kings 18.42.

[a]Or *Rejoice in this* [b]Other ancient authorities read *known* [c]Or omit *you* [d]Or *so that your faith is hope in God* 1.16: Lev 11.44-45. 1.24-25: Is 40.6-9.

The grass withers, and the flower falls,
25 but the word of the Lord abides for ever."
That word is the good news which was preached to you.

2 So put away all malice and all guile and insincerity and envy and all slander. ² Like newborn babes, long for the pure spiritual milk, that by it you may grow up to salvation; ³ for you have tasted the kindness of the Lord.

4 Come to him, to that living stone, rejected by men but in God's sight chosen and precious; ⁵ and like living stones be yourselves built into a spiritual house, to be a holy priesthood, to offer spiritual sacrifices acceptable to God through Jesus Christ. ⁶ For it stands in scripture:

"Behold, I am laying in Zion a stone,
    a cornerstone chosen and precious,
and he who believes in him will not
    be put to shame."

⁷ To you therefore who believe, he is precious, but for those who do not believe,

"The very stone which the builders rejected
has become the head of the corner,"
⁸ and
"A stone that will make men stumble,
    ble,
a rock that will make them fall";
for they stumble because they disobey the word, as they were destined to do.

9 But you are a chosen race, a royal priesthood, a holy nation, God's own people,ᵉ that you may declare the wonderful deeds of him who called you out of darkness into his marvelous light. ¹⁰ Once you were no people but now you are God's people; once you had not received mercy but now you have received mercy.

11 Beloved, I beseech you as aliens and exiles to abstain from the passions of the flesh that wage war against your soul. ¹² Maintain good conduct among the Gentiles, so that in case they speak against you as wrongdoers, they may see your good deeds and glorify God on the day of visitation.

13 Be subject for the Lord's sake to every human institution,ᶠ whether it be to the emperor as supreme, ¹⁴ or to governors as sent by him to punish those who do wrong and to praise those who do right. ¹⁵ For it is God's will that by doing right you should put to silence the ignorance of foolish men. ¹⁶ Live as free men, yet without using your freedom as a pretext for evil; but live as servants of God. ¹⁷ Honor all men. Love the brotherhood. Fear God. Honor the emperor.

18 Servants, be submissive to your masters with all respect, not only to the kind and gentle but also to the overbearing. ¹⁹ For one is approved if, mindful of God, he endures pain while suffering unjustly. ²⁰ For what credit is it, if when you do wrong and are beaten for it you take it patiently? But if when you do right and suffer for it you take it patiently, you have God's approval. ²¹ For to this you have been called, because Christ also suffered for you, leaving you an example, that you should follow in his steps. ²² He committed no sin; no guile was found on his lips. ²³ When he was reviled, he did not revile in return; when he suffered, he did not threaten; but he trusted to him who judges justly. ²⁴ He himself bore our sins in his body on the tree,ᵍ that we might die to sin and live to righteousness. By his wounds you have been healed. ²⁵ For you were straying like sheep, but have now returned to the Shepherd and Guardian of your souls.

3 Likewise you wives, be submissive to your husbands, so that some, though they do not obey the word, may be won without a word by the behavior of their wives, ² when they see your reverent and chaste behavior. ³ Let not yours be the outward adorning with braiding of hair, decoration of gold, and wearing of fine clothing, ⁴ but let it be the hidden person of the heart with the imperishable jewel of a gentle and quiet spirit, which in God's sight is very precious. ⁵ So once the holy women who hoped in God used to adorn themselves and were submissive to their husbands, ⁶ as Sarah obeyed Abraham, calling him lord. And you are now her children if you do right and let nothing terrify you.

ᵉ Greek *a people for his possession*
ᶠ Or *every institution ordained for men*
ᵍ Or *carried up . . . to the tree*
2.3: Ps 34.8.   2.4: Ps 118.22; Is 28.16.   2.6: Is 28.16.
2.7: Ps 118.22.   2.8: Is 8.14-15.   2.9: Ex 19.5-6.
2.10: Hos 2.23.   2.22: Is 53.9.   2.24: Is 53.12 Septuagint.
2.24-25: Is 53.5-6.   3.6: Gen 18.12.

7 Likewise you husbands, live considerately with your wives, bestowing honor on the woman as the weaker sex, since you are joint heirs of the grace of life, in order that your prayers may not be hindered.

8 Finally, all of you, have unity of spirit, sympathy, love of the brethren, a tender heart and a humble mind. 9 Do not return evil for evil or reviling for reviling; but on the contrary bless, for to this you have been called, that you may obtain a blessing. 10 For

"He that would love life
and see good days,
let him keep his tongue from evil
and his lips from speaking guile;
11 let him turn away from evil and do right;
let him seek peace and pursue it.
12 For the eyes of the Lord are upon the righteous,
and his ears are open to their prayer.
But the face of the Lord is against those that do evil."

13 Now who is there to harm you if you are zealous for what is right? 14 But even if you do suffer for righteousness' sake, you will be blessed. Have no fear of them, nor be troubled, 15 but in your hearts reverence Christ as Lord. Always be prepared to make a defense to any one who calls you to account for the hope that is in you, yet do it with gentleness and reverence; 16 and keep your conscience clear, so that, when you are abused, those who revile your good behavior in Christ may be put to shame. 17 For it is better to suffer for doing right, if that should be God's will, than for doing wrong. 18 For Christ also died[h] for sins once for all, the righteous for the unrighteous, that he might bring us to God, being put to death in the flesh but made alive in the spirit; 19 in which he went and preached to the spirits in prison, 20 who formerly did not obey, when God's patience waited in the days of Noah, during the building of the ark, in which a few, that is, eight persons, were saved through water. 21 Baptism, which corresponds to this, now saves you, not as a removal of dirt from the body but as an appeal to God for a clear conscience, through the resurrection of Jesus Christ, 22 who has gone into heaven and is at the right hand of God, with angels, authorities, and powers subject to him.

4 Since therefore Christ suffered in the flesh,[i] arm yourselves with the same thought, for whoever has suffered in the flesh has ceased from sin, 2 so as to live for the rest of the time in the flesh no longer by human passions but by the will of God. 3 Let the time that is past suffice for doing what the Gentiles like to do, living in licentiousness, passions, drunkenness, revels, carousing, and lawless idolatry. 4 They are surprised that you do not now join them in the same wild profligacy, and they abuse you; 5 but they will give account to him who is ready to judge the living and the dead. 6 For this is why the gospel was preached even to the dead, that though judged in the flesh like men, they might live in the spirit like God.

7 The end of all things is at hand; therefore keep sane and sober for your prayers. 8 Above all hold unfailing your love for one another, since love covers a multitude of sins. 9 Practice hospitality ungrudgingly to one another. 10 As each has received a gift, employ it for one another, as good stewards of God's varied grace: 11 whoever speaks, as one who utters oracles of God; whoever renders service, as one who renders it by the strength which God supplies; in order that in everything God may be glorified through Jesus Christ. To him belong glory and dominion for ever and ever. Amen.

12 Beloved, do not be surprised at the fiery ordeal which comes upon you to prove you, as though something strange were happening to you. 13 But rejoice in so far as you share Christ's sufferings, that you may also rejoice and be glad when his glory is revealed. 14 If you are reproached for the name of Christ, you are blessed, because the spirit of glory[j] and of God rests upon you. 15 But let none of you suffer as a murderer, or a thief, or a wrongdoer, or a mischief-maker; 16 yet if one suffers as a Christian, let him not be ashamed, but under that name let him glorify God. 17 For the time has come for judgment to begin with the household of God; and if it begins with us, what will be the end of those who do not obey the gospel of God? 18 And

h Other ancient authorities read *suffered*
i Other ancient authorities add *for us;* some *for you*
j Other ancient authorities insert *and of power*
3.10-12: Ps 34.12-16. 3.14-15: Is 8.12-13. 3.20: Gen 6-8.
4.14: Is 11.2. 4.18: Prov 11.31 Septuagint.

"If the righteous man is scarcely saved,
where will the impious and sinner appear?"

[19] Therefore let those who suffer according to God's will do right and entrust their souls to a faithful Creator.

5 So I exhort the elders among you, as a fellow elder and a witness of the sufferings of Christ as well as a partaker in the glory that is to be revealed. [2] Tend the flock of God that is your charge,[k] not by constraint but willingly,[l] not for shameful gain but eagerly, [3] not as domineering over those in your charge but being examples to the flock. [4] And when the chief Shepherd is manifested you will obtain the unfading crown of glory. [5] Likewise you that are younger be subject to the elders. Clothe yourselves, all of you, with humility toward one another, for "God opposes the proud, but gives grace to the humble."

6 Humble yourselves therefore under the mighty hand of God, that in due time he may exalt you. [7] Cast all your anxieties on him, for he cares about you. [8] Be sober, be watchful. Your adversary the devil prowls around like a roaring lion, seeking some one to devour. [9] Resist him, firm in your faith, knowing that the same experience of suffering is required of your brotherhood throughout the world. [10] And after you have suffered a little while, the God of all grace, who has called you to his eternal glory in Christ, will himself restore, establish, and strengthen[m] you. [11] To him be the dominion for ever and ever. Amen.

12 By Sĭl·vā′nŭs, a faithful brother as I regard him, I have written briefly to you, exhorting and declaring that this is the true grace of God; stand fast in it. [13] She who is at Babylon, who is likewise chosen, sends you greetings; and so does my son Mark. [14] Greet one another with the kiss of love.

Peace to all of you that are in Christ.

The Second Letter of
Peter

1 Simeon[x] Peter, a servant and apostle of Jesus Christ,

To those who have obtained a faith of equal standing with ours in the righteousness of our God and Savior Jesus Christ:[a]

2 May grace and peace be multiplied to you in the knowledge of God and of Jesus our Lord.

3 His divine power has granted to us all things that pertain to life and godliness, through the knowledge of him who called us to[b] his own glory and excellence, [4] by which he has granted to us his precious and very great promises, that through these you may escape from the corruption that is in the world because of passion, and become partakers of the divine nature. [5] For this very reason make every effort to supplement your faith with virtue, and virtue with knowledge, [6] and knowledge with self-control, and self-control with steadfastness, and steadfastness with godliness, [7] and godliness with brotherly affection, and brotherly affection with love. [8] For if these things are yours and abound, they keep you from being ineffective or unfruitful in the knowledge of our Lord Jesus Christ. [9] For whoever lacks these things is blind and shortsighted and has forgotten that he was cleansed from his old sins. [10] Therefore, brethren, be the more zealous to confirm your call and election, for if you do this you will never fall; [11] so there will be richly provided for you an entrance into the eternal kingdom of our Lord and Savior Jesus Christ.

[k] Other ancient authorities add *exercising the oversight*
[l] Other ancient authorities add *as God would have you*
[m] Other ancient authorities read *restore, establish, strengthen and settle* **5.5:** Prov 3.34. **5.7:** Ps 55.22.

[x] Other authorities read *Simon*
[a] Or *of our God and the Savior Jesus Christ* [b] Or *by*

12 Therefore I intend always to remind you of these things, though you know them and are established in the truth that you have. [13]I think it right, as long as I am in this body,[c] to arouse you by way of reminder, [14]since I know that the putting off of my body[c] will be soon, as our Lord Jesus Christ showed me. [15]And I will see to it that after my departure you may be able at any time to recall these things.

16 For we did not follow cleverly devised myths when we made known to you the power and coming of our Lord Jesus Christ, but we were eyewitnesses of his majesty. [17]For when he received honor and glory from God the Father and the voice was borne to him by the Majestic Glory, "This is my beloved Son,[d] with whom I am well pleased," [18]we heard this voice borne from heaven, for we were with him on the holy mountain. [19]And we have the prophetic word made more sure. You will do well to pay attention to this as to a lamp shining in a dark place, until the day dawns and the morning star rises in your hearts. [20]First of all you must understand this, that no prophecy of scripture is a matter of one's own interpretation, [21]because no prophecy ever came by the impulse of man, but men moved by the Holy Spirit spoke from God.[e]

2 But false prophets also arose among the people, just as there will be false teachers among you, who will secretly bring in destructive heresies, even denying the Master who bought them, bringing upon themselves swift destruction. [2]And many will follow their licentiousness, and because of them the way of truth will be reviled. [3]And in their greed they will exploit you with false words; from of old their condemnation has not been idle, and their destruction has not been asleep.

4 For if God did not spare the angels when they sinned, but cast them into hell[f] and committed them to pits of nether gloom to be kept until the judgment; [5]if he did not spare the ancient world, but preserved Noah, a herald of righteousness, with seven other persons, when he brought a flood upon the world of the ungodly; [6]if by turning the cities of Sŏd'om and Go·môr'rah to ashes he condemned them to extinction and made them an example to those who were to be ungodly;

[7]and if he rescued righteous Lot, greatly distressed by the licentiousness of the wicked [8](for by what that righteous man saw and heard as he lived among them, he was vexed in his righteous soul day after day with their lawless deeds), [9]then the Lord knows how to rescue the godly from trial, and to keep the unrighteous under punishment until the day of judgment, [10]and especially those who indulge in the lust of defiling passion and despise authority.

Bold and wilful, they are not afraid to revile the glorious ones, [11]whereas angels, though greater in might and power, do not pronounce a reviling judgment upon them before the Lord. [12]But these, like irrational animals, creatures of instinct, born to be caught and killed, reviling in matters of which they are ignorant, will be destroyed in the same destruction with them, [13]suffering wrong for their wrongdoing. They count it pleasure to revel in the daytime. They are blots and blemishes, reveling in their dissipation,[g] carousing with you. [14]They have eyes full of adultery, insatiable for sin. They entice unsteady souls. They have hearts trained in greed. Accursed children! [15]Forsaking the right way they have gone astray; they have followed the way of Bā'lăam, the son of Bē'ôr, who loved gain from wrongdoing, [16]but was rebuked for his own transgression; a dumb ass spoke with human voice and restrained the prophet's madness.

17 These are waterless springs and mists driven by a storm; for them the nether gloom of darkness has been reserved. [18]For, uttering loud boasts of folly, they entice with licentious passions of the flesh men who have barely escaped from those who live in error. [19]They promise them freedom, but they themselves are slaves of corruption; for whatever overcomes a man, to that he is enslaved. [20]For if, after they have escaped the defilements of the world through the knowledge of our Lord and Savior Jesus Christ, they are again entangled in them and overpowered,

[c]Greek tent   [d]Or *my Son, my* (or *the) Beloved*
[e]Other authorities read *moved by the Holy Spirit holy men of God spoke*   [f]Greek *Tartarus*
[g]Other ancient authorities read *love feasts*
1.17-18: Mt 17.1-8; Mk 9.2-8; Lk 9.28-36.
2.1-18: Jude 4-16.
2.5: Gen 8.18; 6.6-8.   **2.6:** Gen 19.24.   **2.7:** Gen 19.16, 29.
2.15: Num 22.5, 7.   **2.16:** Num 22.21, 23, 28, 30-31.

the last state has become worse for them than the first. ²¹ For it would have been better for them never to have known the way of righteousness than after knowing it to turn back from the holy commandment delivered to them. ²² It has happened to them according to the true proverb, The dog turns back to his own vomit, and the sow is washed only to wallow in the mire.

3 This is now the second letter that I have written to you, beloved, and in both of them I have aroused your sincere mind by way of reminder; ² that you should remember the predictions of the holy prophets and the commandment of the Lord and Savior through your apostles. ³ First of all you must understand this, that scoffers will come in the last days with scoffing, following their own passions ⁴ and saying, "Where is the promise of his coming? For ever since the fathers fell asleep, all things have continued as they were from the beginning of creation." ⁵ They deliberately ignore this fact, that by the word of God heavens existed long ago, and an earth formed out of water and by means of water, ⁶ through which the world that then existed was deluged with water and perished. ⁷ But by the same word the heavens and earth that now exist have been stored up for fire, being kept until the day of judgment and destruction of ungodly men.

8 But do not ignore this one fact, beloved, that with the Lord one day is as a thousand years, and a thousand years as one day. ⁹ The Lord is not slow about his promise as some count slowness, but is forbearing toward you,ʰ not wishing that any should perish, but that all should reach repentance. ¹⁰ But the day of the Lord will come like a thief, and then the heavens will pass away with a loud noise, and the elements will be dissolved with fire, and the earth and the works that are upon it will be burned up.

11 Since all these things are thus to be dissolved, what sort of persons ought you to be in lives of holiness and godliness, ¹² waiting for and hasteningⁱ the coming of the day of God, because of which the heavens will be kindled and dissolved, and the elements will melt with fire! ¹³ But according to his promise we wait for new heavens and a new earth in which righteousness dwells.

14 Therefore, beloved, since you wait for these, be zealous to be found by him without spot or blemish, and at peace. ¹⁵ And count the forbearance of our Lord as salvation. So also our beloved brother Paul wrote to you according to the wisdom given him, ¹⁶ speaking of this as he does in all his letters. There are some things in them hard to understand, which the ignorant and unstable twist to their own destruction, as they do the other scriptures. ¹⁷ You therefore, beloved, knowing this beforehand, beware lest you be carried away with the error of lawless men and lose your own stability. ¹⁸ But grow in the grace and knowledge of our Lord and Savior Jesus Christ. To him be the glory both now and to the day of eternity. Amen.

The First Letter of
John

1 That which was from the beginning, which we have heard, which we have seen with our eyes, which we have looked upon and touched with our hands, concerning the word of life — ² the life was made manifest, and we saw it, and testify to it, and proclaim to you the eternal life which was with the Father and was made manifest to us — ³ that which we have seen and heard we proclaim also to you, so that you may have fellowship with us; and our fellowship is with the Father

ʰ Other ancient authorities read *on your account*
ⁱ Or *earnestly desiring*
2.22: Prov 26.11. **3.5-6:** Gen 1.6-8; 7.11.
3.8: Ps 90.4. **3.12:** Is 34.4. **3.13:** Is 65.17; 66.22.

1.1-2: Lk 24.39; Jn 1.1; 4.14; 15.27; 20.20, 25; Acts 4.20;
1 Jn 2.13.

and with his Son Jesus Christ. ⁴And we are writing this that our*a* joy may be complete.

5 This is the message we have heard from him and proclaim to you, that God is light and in him is no darkness at all. ⁶If we say we have fellowship with him while we walk in darkness, we lie and do not live according to the truth; ⁷but if we walk in the light, as he is in the light, we have fellowship with one another, and the blood of Jesus his Son cleanses us from all sin. ⁸If we say we have no sin, we deceive ourselves, and the truth is not in us. ⁹If we confess our sins, he is faithful and just, and will forgive our sins and cleanse us from all unrighteousness. ¹⁰If we say we have not sinned, we make him a liar, and his word is not in us.

2 My little children, I am writing this to you so that you may not sin; but if any one does sin, we have an advocate with the Father, Jesus Christ the righteous; ²and he is the expiation for our sins, and not for ours only but also for the sins of the whole world. ³And by this we may be sure that we know him, if we keep his commandments. ⁴He who says "I know him" but disobeys his commandments is a liar, and the truth is not in him; ⁵but whoever keeps his word, in him truly love for God is perfected. By this we may be sure that we are in him: ⁶he who says he abides in him ought to walk in the same way in which he walked.

7 Beloved, I am writing you no new commandment, but an old commandment which you had from the beginning; the old commandment is the word which you have heard. ⁸Yet I am writing you a new commandment, which is true in him and in you, because*b* the darkness is passing away and the true light is already shining. ⁹He who says he is in the light and hates his brother is in the darkness still. ¹⁰He who loves his brother abides in the light, and in it*c* there is no cause for stumbling. ¹¹But he who hates his brother is in the darkness and walks in the darkness, and does not know where he is going, because the darkness has blinded his eyes.

12 I am writing to you, little children, because your sins are forgiven

for his sake. ¹³I am writing to you, fathers, because you know him who is from the beginning. I am writing to you, young men, because you have overcome the evil one. I write to you, children, because you know the Father. ¹⁴I write to you, fathers, because you know him who is from the beginning. I write to you, young men, because you are strong, and the word of God abides in you, and you have overcome the evil one.

15 Do not love the world or the things in the world. If any one loves the world, love for the Father is not in him. ¹⁶For all that is in the world, the lust of the flesh and the lust of the eyes and the pride of life, is not of the Father but is of the world. ¹⁷And the world passes away, and the lust of it; but he who does the will of God abides for ever.

18 Children, it is the last hour; and as you have heard that antichrist is coming, so now many antichrists have come; therefore we know that it is the last hour. ¹⁹They went out from us, but they were not of us; for if they had been of us, they would have continued with us; but they went out, that it might be plain that they all are not of us. ²⁰But you have been anointed by the Holy One, and you all know.*d* ²¹I write to you, not because you do not know the truth, but because you know it, and know that no lie is of the truth. ²²Who is the liar but he who denies that Jesus is the Christ? This is the antichrist, he who denies the Father and the Son. ²³No one who denies the Son has the Father. He who confesses the Son has the Father also. ²⁴Let what you heard from the beginning abide in you. If what you heard from the beginning abides in you, then you will abide in the Son and in the Father. ²⁵And this is what he has promised us,*e* eternal life.

26 I write this to you about those who would deceive you; ²⁷but the

a Other ancient authorities read *your* *b* Or *that* *c* Or *him*
d Other ancient authorities read *you know everything*
e Other ancient authorities read *you*
1.4: Jn 15.11; 2 Jn 12. 1.5: 1 Jn 3.11.
1.6-8: Jn 3.21; 1 Jn 2.4, 11. 1.7: Rev 1.5.
1.10: 1 Jn 5.10. 2.1: Jn 14.16.
2.2: Jn 1.29; 3.14-16; 11.51-52; 1 Jn 4.10.
2.3: Jn 15.10. 2.4: 1 Jn 1.6-8; 4.20.
2.5: Jn 14.21, 23; 1 Jn 5.3. 2.6: Jn 13.15.
2.7: Jn 13.34. 2.8: Jn 8.12.
2.10-11: Jn 11.9-10; 1 Jn 1.6. 2.13: Jn 1.1; 1 Jn 1.1.
2.18: 1 Jn 4.3. 2.22: 2 Jn 7. 2.23: 1 Jn 4.15; 2 Jn 9.
2.27: Jn 14.26.

anointing which you received from him abides in you, and you have no need that any one should teach you; as his anointing teaches you about everything, and is true, and is no lie, just as it has taught you, abide in him.

28 And now, little children, abide in him, so that when he appears we may have confidence and not shrink from him in shame at his coming. ²⁹If you know that he is righteous, you may be sure that every one who does right is born of him.

3 See what love the Father has given us, that we should be called children of God; and so we are. The reason why the world does not know us is that it did not know him. ²Beloved, we are God's children now; it does not yet appear what we shall be, but we know that when' he appears we shall be like him, for we shall see him as he is. ³And every one who thus hopes in him purifies himself as he is pure.

4 Every one who commits sin is guilty of lawlessness; sin is lawlessness. ⁵You know that he appeared to take away sins, and in him there is no sin. ⁶No one who abides in him sins; no one who sins has either seen him or known him. ⁷Little children, let no one deceive you. He who does right is righteous, as he is righteous. ⁸He who commits sin is of the devil; for the devil has sinned from the beginning. The reason the Son of God appeared was to destroy the works of the devil. ⁹No one born of God commits sin; for God's*ᶠ* nature abides in him, and he cannot sin because he is*ᵍ* born of God. ¹⁰By this it may be seen who are the children of God, and who are the children of the devil: whoever does not do right is not of God, nor he who does not love his brother.

11 For this is the message which you have heard from the beginning, that we should love one another, ¹²and not be like Cain who was of the evil one and murdered his brother. And why did he murder him? Because his own deeds were evil and his brother's righteous. ¹³Do not wonder, brethren, that the world hates you. ¹⁴We know that we have passed out of death into life, because we love the brethren. He who does not love abides in death. ¹⁵Any one who hates his brother is a murderer, and you know that no mur-

derer has eternal life abiding in him. ¹⁶By this we know love, that he laid down his life for us; and we ought to lay down our lives for the brethren. ¹⁷But if any one has the world's goods and sees his brother in need, yet closes his heart against him, how does God's love abide in him? ¹⁸Little children, let us not love in word or speech but in deed and in truth.

19 By this we shall know that we are of the truth, and reassure our hearts before him ²⁰whenever our hearts condemn us; for God is greater than our hearts, and he knows everything. ²¹Beloved, if our hearts do not condemn us, we have confidence before God; ²²and we receive from him whatever we ask, because we keep his commandments and do what pleases him. ²³And this is his commandment, that we should believe in the name of his Son Jesus Christ and love one another, just as he has commanded us. ²⁴All who keep his commandments abide in him, and he in them. And by this we know that he abides in us, by the Spirit which he has given us.

4 Beloved, do not believe every spirit, but test the spirits to see whether they are of God; for many false prophets have gone out into the world. ²By this you know the Spirit of God: every spirit which confesses that Jesus Christ has come in the flesh is of God, ³and every spirit which does not confess Jesus is not of God. This is the spirit of antichrist, of which you heard that it was coming, and now it is in the world already. ⁴Little children, you are of God, and have overcome them; for he who is in you is greater than he who is in the world. ⁵They are of the world, therefore what they say is of the world, and the world listens to them. ⁶We are of God. Whoever knows God listens to us, and he who is not of God does not listen to us. By this we know the spirit of truth and the spirit of error.

*ᶠ*Greek *his*
*ᵍ*Or *for the offspring of God abide in him, and they cannot sin because they are*
2.28: 1 Jn 4.17. **2.29:** 1 Jn 3.7-10; 4.7.
3.1: Jn 1.12; 16.3. **3.5:** Jn 1.29. **3.8:** Jn 8.34, 44.
3.9: 1 Jn 5.18. **3.11:** 1 Jn 1.5. **3.13:** Jn 15.18-19.
3.14: Jn 5.24. **3.15:** Jn 8.44. **3.16:** Jn 13.1; 15.13.
3.18: Jas 1.22. **3.21:** 1 Jn 5.14.
3.23: Jn 6.29; 13.34; 15.17. **3.24:** 1 Jn 4.13.
4.3: 1 Jn 2.18. **4.5:** Jn 15.19. **4.6:** Jn 8.47.

7 Beloved, let us love one another; for love is of God, and he who loves is born of God and knows God. [8]He who does not love does not know God; for God is love. [9]In this the love of God was made manifest among us, that God sent his only Son into the world, so that we might live through him. [10]In this is love, not that we loved God but that he loved us and sent his Son to be the expiation for our sins. [11]Beloved, if God so loved us, we also ought to love one another. [12]No man has ever seen God; if we love one another, God abides in us and his love is perfected in us.

13 By this we know that we abide in him and he in us, because he has given us of his own Spirit. [14]And we have seen and testify that the Father has sent his Son as the Savior of the world. [15]Whoever confesses that Jesus is the Son of God, God abides in him, and he in God. [16]So we know and believe the love God has for us. God is love, and he who abides in love abides in God, and God abides in him. [17]In this is love perfected with us, that we may have confidence for the day of judgment, because as he is so are we in this world. [18]There is no fear in love, but perfect love casts out fear. For fear has to do with punishment, and he who fears is not perfected in love. [19]We love, because he first loved us. [20]If any one says, "I love God," and hates his brother, he is a liar; for he who does not love his brother whom he has seen, cannot[h] love God whom he has not seen. [21]And this commandment we have from him, that he who loves God should love his brother also.

5 Every one who believes that Jesus is the Christ is a child of God, and every one who loves the parent loves the child. [2]By this we know that we love the children of God, when we love God and obey his commandments. [3]For this is the love of God, that we keep his commandments. And his commandments are not burdensome. [4]For whatever is born of God overcomes the world; and this is the victory that overcomes the world, our faith. [5]Who is it that overcomes the world but he who believes that Jesus is the Son of God? 6 This is he who came by water and blood, Jesus Christ, not with the water only but with the water and the blood. [7]And the Spirit is the witness, because the Spirit is the truth. [8]There are three witnesses, the Spirit, the water, and the blood; and these three agree. [9]If we receive the testimony of men, the testimony of God is greater; for this is the testimony of God that he has borne witness to his Son. [10]He who believes in the Son of God has the testimony in himself. He who does not believe God has made him a liar, because he has not believed in the testimony that God has borne to his Son. [11]And this is the testimony, that God gave us eternal life, and this life is in his Son. [12]He who has the Son has life; he who has not the Son of God has not life.

13 I write this to you who believe in the name of the Son of God, that you may know that you have eternal life. [14]And this is the confidence which we have in him, that if we ask anything according to his will he hears us. [15]And if we know that he hears us in whatever we ask, we know that we have obtained the requests made of him. [16]If any one sees his brother committing what is not a mortal sin, he will ask, and God[i] will give him life for those whose sin is not mortal. There is sin which is mortal; I do not say that one is to pray for that. [17]All wrongdoing is sin, but there is sin which is not mortal.

18 We know that any one born of God does not sin, but He who was born of God keeps him, and the evil one does not touch him.

19 We know that we are of God, and the whole world is in the power of the evil one.

20 And we know that the Son of God has come and has given us understanding, to know him who is true; and we are in him who is true, in his Son Jesus Christ. This is the true God and eternal life. [21]Little children, keep yourselves from idols.

[h]Other ancient authorities read *how can he*
[i]Greek *he*
4.7: 1 Jn 2.29.   **4.9:** Jn 3.16.
4.10: Jn 15.12; 1 Jn 4.19; 2.2.   **4.12:** Jn 1.18.
4.13: 1 Jn 3.24.   **4.14:** Jn 4.42; 3.17.   **4.17:** 1 Jn 2.28.
4.19: 1 Jn 4.10.   **4.20:** 1 Jn 2.4.
5.1: Jn 8.42.   **5.3:** Jn 14.15; 1 Jn 2.5; 2 Jn 6.
5.4: Jn 16.33.   **5.6-8:** Jn 19.34; 4.23; 15.26.
5.9: Jn 5.32, 36; 8.18.   **5.10:** 1 Jn 1.10.
5.12: Jn 3.36.   **5.13:** Jn 20.31.   **5.14:** Mt 7.7; 1 Jn 3.21.
5.18: Jn 17.15; 1 Jn 3.9.   **5.20-21:** Jn 17.3; Rev 3.7.

The Second Letter of
John

1 The elder to the elect lady and her children, whom I love in the truth, and not only I but also all who know the truth, ²because of the truth which abides in us and will be with us for ever:

3 Grace, mercy, and peace will be with us, from God the Father and from Jesus Christ the Father's Son, in truth and love.

4 I rejoiced greatly to find some of your children following the truth, just as we have been commanded by the Father. ⁵And now I beg you, lady, not as though I were writing you a new commandment, but the one we have had from the beginning, that we love one another. ⁶And this is love, that we follow his commandments; this is the commandment, as you have heard from the beginning, that you follow love. ⁷For many deceivers have gone out into the world, men who will not acknowledge the coming of Jesus Christ in the flesh; such a one is the deceiver and the antichrist. ⁸Look to yourselves, that you may not lose what you*a* have worked for, but may win a full reward. ⁹Any one who goes ahead and does not abide in the doctrine of Christ does not have God; he who abides in the doctrine has both the Father and the Son. ¹⁰If any one comes to you and does not bring this doctrine, do not receive him into the house or give him any greeting; ¹¹for he who greets him shares his wicked work.

12 Though I have much to write to you, I would rather not use paper and ink, but I hope to come to see you and talk with you face to face, so that our joy may be complete.
13 The children of your elect sister greet you.

The Third Letter of
John

1 The elder to the beloved Gā′i·ụs, whom I love in the truth.
2 Beloved, I pray that all may go well with you and that you may be in health; I know that it is well with your soul. ³For I greatly rejoiced when some of the brethren arrived and testified to the truth of your life, as indeed you do follow the truth. ⁴No greater joy can I have than this, to hear that my children follow the truth.
5 Beloved, it is a loyal thing you do when you render any service to the brethren, especially to strangers, ⁶who have testified to your love before the church. You will do well to send them on their journey as befits God's service. ⁷For they have set out for his sake and have accepted nothing from the heathen. ⁸So we ought to support such men, that we may be fellow workers in the truth.

9 I have written something to the church; but Dī·ŏt′rẹ·phēṣ, who likes to put himself first, does not acknowledge my authority. ¹⁰So if I come, I will bring up what he is doing, prating against me with evil words. And not content with that, he refuses himself to welcome the brethren, and also stops those who want to welcome them and puts them out of the church.

11 Beloved, do not imitate evil but imitate good. He who does good is of God; he who does evil has not seen God.

*Other ancient authorities read *we*
1: 3 Jn 1.   5: Jn 13.34.   6: 1 Jn 5.3.   7: 1 Jn 2.22.
12: 1 Jn 1.4; 3 Jn 13.
1: Acts 19.29; 2 Jn 1.

¹²Dĕ·mē′trĭ·ụs has testimony from every one, and from the truth itself; I testify to him too, and you know my testimony is true.

13 I had much to write to you, but I would rather not write with pen and ink; ¹⁴I hope to see you soon, and we will talk together face to face.

15 Peace be to you. The friends greet you. Greet the friends, every one of them.

The Letter of
Jude

1 Jude, a servant of Jesus Christ and brother of James,

To those who are called, beloved in God the Father and kept for Jesus Christ:

2 May mercy, peace, and love be multiplied to you.

3 Beloved, being very eager to write to you of our common salvation, I found it necessary to write appealing to you to contend for the faith which was once for all delivered to the saints. ⁴For admission has been secretly gained by some who long ago were designated for this condemnation, ungodly persons who pervert the grace of our God into licentiousness and deny our only Master and Lord, Jesus Christ.ᵃ

5 Now I desire to remind you, though you were once for all fully informed, that heᵇ who saved a people out of the land of Egypt, afterward destroyed those who did not believe. ⁶And the angels that did not keep their own position but left their proper dwelling have been kept by him in eternal chains in the nether gloom until the judgment of the great day; ⁷just as Sŏd′ọm and Gọ-môr′rạh and the surrounding cities, which likewise acted immorally and indulged in unnatural lust, serve as an example by undergoing a punishment of eternal fire.

8 Yet in like manner these men in their dreamings defile the flesh, reject authority, and revile the glorious ones.ᶜ ⁹But when the archangel Michael, contending with the devil, disputed about the body of Moses, he did not presume to pronounce a reviling judgment upon him, but said, "The Lord rebuke you." ¹⁰But these men revile whatever they do not understand, and by those things that they know by instinct as irrational animals do, they are destroyed. ¹¹Woe to them! For they walk in the way of Cain, and abandon themselves for the sake of gain to Bā′lăam′ş error, and perish in Kō′-rạh′ş rebellion. ¹²These are blemishesᵈ on your love feasts, as they boldly carouse together, looking after themselves; waterless clouds, carried along by winds; fruitless trees in late autumn, twice dead, uprooted; ¹³wild waves of the sea, casting up the foam of their own shame; wandering stars for whom the nether gloom of darkness has been reserved for ever.

14 It was of these also that Ē′nŏch in the seventh generation from Adam prophesied, saying, "Behold, the Lord came with his holy myriads, ¹⁵to execute judgment on all, and to convict all the ungodly of all their deeds of ungodliness which they have committed in such an ungodly way, and of all the harsh things which ungodly sinners have spoken against him." ¹⁶These are grumblers, malcontents, following their own passions, loudmouthed boasters, flattering people to gain advantage.

17 But you must remember, beloved, the predictions of the apostles of our Lord Jesus Christ; ¹⁸they said to you, "In the last time there will be scoffers, following their own ungodly passions." ¹⁹It is these who set up divisions, wordly people, devoid of the Spirit. ²⁰But you, beloved, build yourselves up on your most holy faith; pray in the

---

12: Jn 21.24. 13: 2 Jn 12.

ᵃOr *the only Master and our Lord Jesus Christ* ᵇAncient authorities read *Jesus* or *the Lord* or *God* ᶜGreek *glories* ᵈOr *reefs*
4-16: 2 Pet 2.1-18. 7: Gen 19. 9: Zech 3.2.
11: Gen 4.3-8; Num 22-24; 16. 14-15: Enoch 1.9.

Holy Spirit; [21] keep yourselves in the love of God; wait for the mercy of our Lord Jesus Christ unto eternal life. [22] And convince some, who doubt; [23] save some, by snatching them out of the fire; on some have mercy with fear, hating even the garment spotted by the flesh.[e]

24 Now to him who is able to keep you from falling and to present you without blemish before the presence of his glory with rejoicing, [25] to the only God, our Savior through Jesus Christ our Lord, be glory, majesty, dominion, and authority, before all time and now and for ever. Amen.

The
Revelation to John
(The Apocalypse)

1 The revelation of Jesus Christ, which God gave him to show to his servants what must soon take place; and he made it known by sending his angel to his servant John, [2] who bore witness to the word of God and to the testimony of Jesus Christ, even to all that he saw. [3] Blessed is he who reads aloud the words of the prophecy, and blessed are those who hear, and who keep what is written therein; for the time is near.

4 John to the seven churches that are in Asia:
Grace to you and peace from him who is and who was and who is to come, and from the seven spirits who are before his throne, [5] and from Jesus Christ the faithful witness, the first-born of the dead, and the ruler of kings on earth.
To him who loves us and has freed us from our sins by his blood [6] and made us a kingdom, priests to his God and Father, to him be glory and dominion for ever and ever. Amen. [7] Behold, he is coming with the clouds, and every eye will see him, every one who pierced him; and all tribes of the earth will wail on account of him. Even so. Amen.
8 "I am the Alpha and the Omega," says the Lord God, who is and who was and who is to come, the Almighty.
9 I John, your brother, who share with you in Jesus the tribulation and the kingdom and the patient endurance, was on the island called Păt'mŏs on account of the word of God and the testimony of Jesus. [10] I was in the Spirit on the Lord's day, and I

heard behind me a loud voice like a trumpet [11] saying, "Write what you see in a book and send it to the seven churches, to Ĕph'ḗ·sṵs and to Smyrna and to Pĕr'gȧ·mṵm and to Thȳ·ȧ·tī'rȧ and to Sär'dĭs and to Philadelphia and to Lā̇–o·dĭ·çē'ȧ."
12 Then I turned to see the voice that was speaking to me, and on turning I saw seven golden lampstands, [13] and in the midst of the lampstands one like a son of man, clothed with a long robe and with a golden girdle round his breast; [14] his head and his hair were white as white wool, white as snow; his eyes were like a flame of fire, [15] his feet were like burnished bronze, re-fined as in a furnace, and his voice was like the sound of many waters; [16] in his right hand he held seven stars, from his mouth issued a sharp two-edged sword, and his face was like the sun shining in full strength.
17 When I saw him, I fell at his feet as though dead. But he laid his right hand upon me, saying, "Fear not, I am the first and the last, [18] and the living one; I died, and behold I am alive for evermore, and I have the keys of Death and Hades. [19] Now write what you see, what is and what is to take place hereafter. [20] As for the mystery of the seven stars which you saw in my right hand, and the seven golden lampstands, the seven stars are the angels of the seven churches and the

[e] The Greek text in this sentence is uncertain at several points

23: Zech 3.3-4.

1.4: Ex 3.14.   1.5: Ps 89.27.   1.6: Ex 19.6; Is 61.6.
1.7: Dan 7.13; Mt 24.30; Mk 14.62; Zech 12.10.
1.8: Ex 3.14.   1.13: Dan 7.13; 10.5.   1.15: Ezek 1.24.
1.16: Ex 34.29.   1.17: Is 44.2, 6.

seven lampstands are the seven churches.

2 "To the angel of the church in Ĕph′e·sus write: 'The words of him who holds the seven stars in his right hand, who walks among the seven golden lampstands.

2 " 'I know your works, your toil and your patient endurance, and how you cannot bear evil men but have tested those who call themselves apostles but are not, and found them to be false; ³I know you are enduring patiently and bearing up for my name's sake, and you have not grown weary. ⁴But I have this against you, that you have abandoned the love you had at first. ⁵Remember then from what you have fallen, repent and do the works you did at first. If not, I will come to you and remove your lampstand from its place, unless you repent. ⁶Yet this you have, you hate the works of the Nĭc·ō·lā′ĭ·tạns, which I also hate. ⁷He who has an ear, let him hear what the Spirit says to the churches. To him who conquers I will grant to eat of the tree of life, which is in the paradise of God.'

8 "And to the angel of the church in Smyrna write: 'The words of the first and the last, who died and came to life.

9 " 'I know your tribulation and your poverty (but you are rich) and the slander of those who say that they are Jews and are not, but are a synagogue of Satan. ¹⁰Do not fear what you are about to suffer. Behold, the devil is about to throw some of you into prison, that you may be tested, and for ten days you will have tribulation. Be faithful unto death, and I will give you the crown of life. ¹¹He who has an ear, let him hear what the Spirit says to the churches. He who conquers shall not be hurt by the second death.'

12 "And to the angel of the church in Pĕr′ga·mum write: 'The words of him who has the sharp two-edged sword.

13 " 'I know where you dwell, where Satan's throne is; you hold fast my name and you did not deny my faith even in the days of Ăn′tĭ·pas my witness, my faithful one, who was killed among you, where Satan dwells. ¹⁴But I have a few things against you: you have some there who hold the teaching of Bā′lăam, who taught Bā′lăk to put

a stumbling block before the sons of Israel, that they might eat food sacrificed to idols and practice immorality. ¹⁵So you also have some who hold the teaching of the Nĭc·ō·lā′ĭ·tạns. ¹⁶Repent then. If not, I will come to you soon and war against them with the sword of my mouth. ¹⁷He who has an ear, let him hear what the Spirit says to the churches. To him who conquers I will give some of the hidden manna, and I will give him a white stone, with a new name written on the stone which no one knows except him who receives it.'

18 "And to the angel of the church in Thӯ·a·tī′ra write: 'The words of the Son of God, who has eyes like a flame of fire, and whose feet are like burnished bronze.

19 " 'I know your works, your love and faith and service and patient endurance, and that your latter works exceed the first. ²⁰But I have this against you, that you tolerate the woman Jĕz′e·bel, who calls herself a prophetess and is teaching and beguiling my servants to practice immorality and to eat food sacrificed to idols. ²¹I gave her time to repent, but she refuses to repent of her immorality. ²²Behold, I will throw her on a sickbed, and those who commit adultery with her I will throw into great tribulation, unless they repent of her doings; ²³and I will strike her children dead. And all the churches shall know that I am he who searches mind and heart, and I will give to each of you as your works deserve. ²⁴But to the rest of you in Thӯ·a·tī′ra, who do not hold this teaching, who have not learned what some call the deep things of Satan, to you I say, I do not lay upon you any other burden; ²⁵only hold fast what you have, until I come. ²⁶He who conquers and who keeps my works until the end, I will give him power over the nations, ²⁷and he shall rule them with a rod of iron, as when earthen pots are broken in pieces, even as I myself have received power from my Father; ²⁸and I will give him the morning star. ²⁹He who has an ear, let him hear what the Spirit says to the churches.'

2.7: Gen 2.9.   **2.8:** Is 44.6.   **2.10:** Dan 1.12.
2.14: Num 31.16; 25.1-2.   **2.17:** Ps 78.24; Is 62.2.
2.18: Dan 10.6.
2.20: 1 Kings 16.31; 2 Kings 9.22, 30; Num 25.1.
2.23: Jer 17.10; Ps 62.12.   **2.26:** Ps 2.8-9.

3 "And to the angel of the church in Sär'dĭs write: 'The words of him who has the seven spirits of God and the seven stars.

" 'I know your works; you have the name of being alive, and you are dead. ²Awake, and strengthen what remains and is on the point of death, for I have not found your works perfect in the sight of my God. ³Remember then what you received and heard; keep that, and repent. If you will not awake, I will come like a thief, and you will not know at what hour I will come upon you. ⁴Yet you have still a few names in Sär'dĭs, people who have not soiled their garments; and they shall walk with me in white, for they are worthy. ⁵He who conquers shall be clad thus in white garments, and I will not blot his name out of the book of life; I will confess his name before my Father and before his angels. ⁶He who has an ear, let him hear what the Spirit says to the churches.'

7 "And to the angel of the church in Philadelphia write: 'The words of the holy one, the true one, who has the key of David, who opens and no one shall shut, who shuts and no one opens.

8 " 'I know your works. Behold, I have set before you an open door, which no one is able to shut; I know that you have but little power, and yet you have kept my word and have not denied my name. ⁹Behold, I will make those of the synagogue of Satan who say that they are Jews and are not, but lie—behold, I will make them come and bow down before your feet, and learn that I have loved you. ¹⁰Because you have kept my word of patient endurance, I will keep you from the hour of trial which is coming on the whole world, to try those who dwell upon the earth. ¹¹I am coming soon; hold fast what you have, so that no one may seize your crown. ¹²He who conquers, I will make him a pillar in the temple of my God; never shall he go out of it, and I will write on him the name of my God, and the name of the city of my God, the new Jerusalem which comes down from my God out of heaven, and my own new name. ¹³He who has an ear, let him hear what the Spirit says to the churches.'

14 "And to the angel of the church in Lā-o·dĭ·çē'a write: 'The words of the Amen, the faithful and true wit-

ness, the beginning of God's creation. 15 " 'I know your works: you are neither cold nor hot. Would that you were cold or hot! ¹⁶So, because you are lukewarm, and neither cold nor hot, I will spew you out of my mouth. ¹⁷For you say, I am rich, I have prospered, and I need nothing; not knowing that you are wretched, pitiable, poor, blind, and naked. ¹⁸Therefore I counsel you to buy from me gold refined by fire, that you may be rich, and white garments to clothe you and to keep the shame of your nakedness from being seen, and salve to anoint your eyes, that you may see. ¹⁹Those whom I love, I reprove and chasten; so be zealous and repent. ²⁰Behold, I stand at the door and knock; if any one hears my voice and opens the door, I will come in to him and eat with him, and he with me. ²¹He who conquers, I will grant him to sit with me on my throne, as I myself conquered and sat down with my Father on his throne. ²²He who has an ear, let him hear what the Spirit says to the churches.' "

4 After this I looked, and lo, in heaven an open door! And the first voice, which I had heard speaking to me like a trumpet, said, "Come up hither, and I will show you what must take place after this." ²At once I was in the Spirit, and lo, a throne stood in heaven, with one seated on the throne! ³And he who sat there appeared like jasper and carnelian, and round the throne was a rainbow that looked like an emerald. ⁴Round the throne were twenty-four thrones, and seated on the thrones were twenty-four elders, clad in white garments, with golden crowns upon their heads. ⁵From the throne issue flashes of lightning, and voices and peals of thunder, and before the throne burn seven torches of fire, which are the seven spirits of God; ⁶and before the throne there is as it were a sea of glass, like crystal.

And round the throne, on each side of the throne, are four living creatures, full of eyes in front and behind: ⁷the first living creature like a lion, the

3.5: Ex 32.32; Ps 69.28; Dan 12.1; Mt 10.32.
3.7: Is 22.22. 3.9: Is 60.14; 49.23; 43.4.
3.12: Is 62.2; Ezek 48.35; Rev 21.2.
3.14: Ps 89.28; Prov 8.22; Jn 1.1-3. 3.17: Hos 12.8.
3.19: Prov 3.12. 4.1: Ex 19.16, 24. 4.2: Ezek 1.26-28.
4.5: Ex 19.16; Zech 4.2. 4.6: Ezek 1.5, 18.
4.7: Ezek 1.10.

second living creature like an ox, the third living creature with the face of a man, and the fourth living creature like a flying eagle. ⁸And the four living creatures, each of them with six wings, are full of eyes all round and within, and day and night they never cease to sing,

"Holy, holy, holy, is the Lord God Almighty,
    who was and is and is to come!"
⁹And whenever the living creatures give glory and honor and thanks to him who is seated on the throne, who lives for ever and ever, ¹⁰the twenty-four elders fall down before him who is seated on the throne and worship him who lives for ever and ever; they cast their crowns before the throne, singing,
¹¹"Worthy art thou, our Lord and God,
    to receive glory and honor and power,
    for thou didst create all things,
    and by thy will they existed and were created."

5 And I saw in the right hand of him who was seated on the throne a scroll written within and on the back, sealed with seven seals; ²and I saw a strong angel proclaiming with a loud voice, "Who is worthy to open the scroll and break its seals?" ³And no one in heaven or on earth or under the earth was able to open the scroll or to look into it, ⁴and I wept much that no one was found worthy to open the scroll or to look into it. ⁵Then one of the elders said to me, "Weep not; lo, the Lion of the tribe of Judah, the Root of David, has conquered, so that he can open the scroll and its seven seals."

6 And between the throne and the four living creatures and among the elders, I saw a Lamb standing, as though it had been slain, with seven horns and with seven eyes, which are the seven spirits of God sent out into all the earth; ⁷and he went and took the scroll from the right hand of him who was seated on the throne. ⁸And when he had taken the scroll, the four living creatures and the twenty-four elders fell down before the Lamb, each holding a harp, and with golden bowls full of incense, which are the prayers of the saints; ⁹and they sang a new song, saying,

"Worthy art thou to take the scroll
    and to open its seals,
for thou wast slain and by thy blood didst ransom men for God

from every tribe and tongue and people and nation,
¹⁰and hast made them a kingdom and priests to our God,
    and they shall reign on earth."
¹¹Then I looked, and I heard around the throne and the living creatures and the elders the voice of many angels, numbering myriads of myriads and thousands of thousands, ¹²saying with a loud voice, "Worthy is the Lamb who was slain, to receive power and wealth and wisdom and might and honor and glory and blessing!" ¹³And I heard every creature in heaven and on earth and under the earth and in the sea, and all therein, saying, "To him who sits upon the throne and to the Lamb be blessing and honor and glory and might for ever and ever!" ¹⁴And the four living creatures said, "Amen!" and the elders fell down and worshiped.

6 Now I saw when the Lamb opened one of the seven seals, and I heard one of the four living creatures say, as with a voice of thunder, "Come!" ²And I saw, and behold, a white horse, and its rider had a bow; and a crown was given to him, and he went out conquering and to conquer.

3 When he opened the second seal, I heard the second living creature say, "Come!" ⁴And out came another horse, bright red; its rider was permitted to take peace from the earth, so that men should slay one another; and he was given a great sword.

5 When he opened the third seal, I heard the third living creature say, "Come!" And I saw, and behold, a black horse, and its rider had a balance in his hand; ⁶and I heard what seemed to be a voice in the midst of the four living creatures saying, "A quart of wheat for a denarius,ᵃ and three quarts of barley for a denarius;ᵃ but do not harm oil and wine!"

7 When he opened the fourth seal, I heard the voice of the fourth living creature say, "Come!" ⁸And I saw, and behold, a pale horse, and its rider's name was Death, and Hades followed

ᵃThe denarius was a day's wage for a laborer
4.8: Is 6.2-3. **4.9:** Ps 47.8.
5.1: Ezek 2.9; Is 29.11. **5.5:** Gen 49.9.
5.6: Is 53.7; Zech 4.10. **5.8:** Ps 141.2. **5.9:** Ps 33.3.
5.10: Ex 19.6; Is 61.6. **5.11:** Dan 7.10.
6.2: Zech 1.8; 6.1-3. **6.6:** 2 Kings 6.25.
6.8: Hos 13.14; Ezek 5.12.

him; and they were given power over a fourth of the earth, to kill with sword and with famine and with pestilence and by wild beasts of the earth.

9 When he opened the fifth seal, I saw under the altar the souls of those who had been slain for the word of God and for the witness they had borne; [10] they cried out with a loud voice, "O Sovereign Lord, holy and true, how long before thou wilt judge and avenge our blood on those who dwell upon the earth?" [11] Then they were each given a white robe and told to rest a little longer, until the number of their fellow servants and their brethren should be complete, who were to be killed as they themselves had been.

12 When he opened the sixth seal, I looked, and behold, there was a great earthquake; and the sun became black as sackcloth, the full moon became like blood, [13] and the stars of the sky fell to the earth as the fig tree sheds its winter fruit when shaken by a gale; [14] the sky vanished like a scroll that is rolled up, and every mountain and island was removed from its place. [15] Then the kings of the earth and the great men and the generals and the rich and the strong, and every one, slave and free, hid in the caves and among the rocks of the mountains, [16] calling to the mountains and rocks, "Fall on us and hide us from the face of him who is seated on the throne, and from the wrath of the Lamb; [17] for the great day of their wrath has come, and who can stand before it?"

7 After this I saw four angels standing at the four corners of the earth, holding back the four winds of the earth, that no wind might blow on earth or sea or against any tree. [2] Then I saw another angel ascend from the rising of the sun, with the seal of the living God, and he called with a loud voice to the four angels who had been given power to harm earth and sea, [3] saying, "Do not harm the earth or the sea or the trees, till we have sealed the servants of our God upon their foreheads." [4] And I heard the number of the sealed, a hundred and forty-four thousand sealed, out of every tribe of the sons of Israel, [5] twelve thousand sealed out of the tribe of Judah, twelve thousand of the tribe of Reuben, twelve thousand of the tribe of Gȧd,

[6] twelve thousand of the tribe of Ăsh'er, twelve thousand of the tribe of Năph'tạ·lī, twelve thousand of the tribe of Mạ·năs'sẹh, [7] twelve thousand of the tribe of Sĭm'ē·ọn, twelve thousand of the tribe of Lē'vī, twelve thousand of the tribe of Ĭs'sạ·chär, [8] twelve thousand of the tribe of Zĕb'ū·lụn, twelve thousand of the tribe of Joseph, twelve thousand sealed out of the tribe of Benjamin.

9 After this I looked, and behold, a great multitude which no man could number, from every nation, from all tribes and peoples and tongues, standing before the throne and before the Lamb, clothed in white robes, with palm branches in their hands, [10] and crying out with a loud voice, "Salvation belongs to our God who sits upon the throne, and to the Lamb!" [11] And all the angels stood round the throne and round the elders and the four living creatures, and they fell on their faces before the throne and worshiped God, [12] saying, "Amen! Blessing and glory and wisdom and thanksgiving and honor and power and might be to our God for ever and ever! Amen."

13 Then one of the elders addressed me, saying, "Who are these, clothed in white robes, and whence have they come?" [14] I said to him, "Sir, you know." And he said to me, "These are they who have come out of the great tribulation; they have washed their robes and made them white in the blood of the Lamb.
[15] Therefore are they before the throne of God,
    and serve him day and night within his temple;
    and he who sits upon the throne will shelter them with his presence.
[16] They shall hunger no more, neither thirst any more;
    the sun shall not strike them, nor any scorching heat.
[17] For the Lamb in the midst of the throne will be their shepherd,
    and he will guide them to springs of living water;
    and God will wipe away every tear from their eyes."

6.10: Zech 1.12; Ps 79.5; Gen 4.10.
6.12: Joel 2.31; Acts 2.20. 6.13: Is 34.4.
6.15: Is 2.10. 6.16: Hos 10.8. 6.17: Joel 2.11; Mal 3.2.
7.1: Zech 6.5. 7.3: Ezek 9.4.
7.14: Dan 12.1; Gen 49.11. · 7.16: Is 49.10; Ps 121.6.
7.17: Ezek 34.23; Ps 23.2; Is 25.8.

8 When the Lamb opened the seventh seal, there was silence in heaven for about half an hour. ²Then I saw the seven angels who stand before God, and seven trumpets were given to them. ³And another angel came and stood at the altar with a golden censer; and he was given much incense to mingle with the prayers of all the saints upon the golden altar before the throne; ⁴and the smoke of the incense rose with the prayers of the saints from the hand of the angel before God. ⁵Then the angel took the censer and filled it with fire from the altar and threw it on the earth; and there were peals of thunder, voices, flashes of lightning, and an earthquake.

6 Now the seven angels who had the seven trumpets made ready to blow them.

7 The first angel blew his trumpet, and there followed hail and fire, mixed with blood, which fell on the earth; and a third of the earth was burnt up, and a third of the trees were burnt up, and all green grass was burnt up.

8 The second angel blew his trumpet, and something like a great mountain, burning with fire, was thrown into the sea; ⁹and a third of the sea became blood, a third of the living creatures in the sea died, and a third of the ships were destroyed.

10 The third angel blew his trumpet, and a great star fell from heaven, blazing like a torch, and it fell on a third of the rivers and on the fountains of water. ¹¹The name of the star is Wormwood. A third of the waters became wormwood, and many men died of the water, because it was made bitter.

12 The fourth angel blew his trumpet, and a third of the sun was struck, and a third of the moon, and a third of the stars, so that a third of their light was darkened; a third of the day was kept from shining, and likewise a third of the night.

13 Then I looked, and I heard an eagle crying with a loud voice, as it flew in midheaven, "Woe, woe, woe to those who dwell on the earth, at the blasts of the other trumpets which the three angels are about to blow!"

9 And the fifth angel blew his trumpet, and I saw a star fallen from heaven to earth, and he was given the key of the shaft of the bottomless pit; ²he opened the shaft of the bottomless pit, and from the shaft rose smoke like the smoke of a great furnace, and the sun and the air were darkened with the smoke from the shaft. ³Then from the smoke came locusts on the earth, and they were given power like the power of scorpions of the earth; ⁴they were told not to harm the grass of the earth or any green growth or any tree, but only those of mankind who have not the seal of God upon their foreheads; ⁵they were allowed to torture them for five months, but not to kill them, and their torture was like the torture of a scorpion, when it stings a man. ⁶And in those days men will seek death and will not find it; they will long to die, and death will fly from them.

7 In appearance the locusts were like horses arrayed for battle; on their heads were what looked like crowns of gold; their faces were like human faces, ⁸their hair like women's hair, and their teeth like lions' teeth; ⁹they had scales like iron breastplates, and the noise of their wings was like the noise of many chariots with horses rushing into battle. ¹⁰They have tails like scorpions, and stings, and their power of hurting men for five months lies in their tails. ¹¹They have as king over them the angel of the bottomless pit; his name in Hebrew is A·băd′don, and in Greek he is called A·pŏl′lyon.ᵇ

12 The first woe has passed; behold, two woes are still to come.

13 Then the sixth angel blew his trumpet, and I heard a voice from the four horns of the golden altar before God, ¹⁴saying to the sixth angel who had the trumpet, "Release the four angels who are bound at the great river Euphrates." ¹⁵So the four angels were released, who had been held ready for the hour, the day, the month, and the year, to kill a third of mankind. ¹⁶The number of the troops of cavalry was twice ten thousand times ten thousand; I heard their number. ¹⁷And this was how I saw the horses in

ᵇ Or *Destroyer*
8.3: Amos 9.1; Ps 141.2. 8.5: Lev 16.12; Ezek 10.2.
8.7: Ex 9.23-25. 8.8: Jer 51.25.
8.10: Is 14.12. 9.2: Gen 19.28; Ex 19.18; Joel 2.10.
9.3: Ex 10.12-15. 9.4: Ezek 9.4. 9.6: Job 3.21.
9.7: Joel 2.4. 9.8: Joel 1.6. 9.9: Joel 2.5.
9.13: Ex 30.1-3.

my vision: the riders wore breastplates the color of fire and of sapphire[c] and of sulphur, and the heads of the horses were like lions' heads, and fire and smoke and sulphur issued from their mouths. [18] By these three plagues a third of mankind was killed, by the fire and smoke and sulphur issuing from their mouths. [19] For the power of the horses is in their mouths and in their tails; their tails are like serpents, with heads, and by means of them they wound.

20 The rest of mankind, who were not killed by these plagues, did not repent of the works of their hands nor give up worshiping demons and idols of gold and silver and bronze and stone and wood, which cannot either see or hear or walk; [21] nor did they repent of their murders or their sorceries or their immorality or their thefts.

10 Then I saw another mighty angel coming down from heaven, wrapped in a cloud, with a rainbow over his head, and his face was like the sun, and his legs like pillars of fire. [2] He had a little scroll open in his hand. And he set his right foot on the sea, and his left foot on the land, [3] and called out with a loud voice, like a lion roaring; when he called out, the seven thunders sounded. [4] And when the seven thunders had sounded, I was about to write, but I heard a voice from heaven saying, "Seal up what the seven thunders have said, and do not write it down." [5] And the angel whom I saw standing on sea and land lifted up his right hand to heaven [6] and swore by him who lives for ever and ever, who created heaven and what is in it, the earth and what is in it, and the sea and what is in it, that there should be no more delay, [7] but that in the days of the trumpet call to be sounded by the seventh angel, the mystery of God, as he announced to his servants the prophets, should be fulfilled.

8 Then the voice which I had heard from heaven spoke to me again, saying, "Go, take the scroll which is open in the hand of the angel who is standing on the sea and on the land." [9] So I went to the angel and told him to give me the little scroll; and he said to me, "Take it and eat; it will be bitter to your stomach, but sweet as honey in your mouth." [10] And I took the little scroll from the hand of the angel and ate it; it was sweet as honey in my mouth, but when I had eaten it my stomach was made bitter. [11] And I was told, "You must again prophesy about many peoples and nations and tongues and kings."

11 Then I was given a measuring rod like a staff, and I was told: "Rise and measure the temple of God and the altar and those who worship there, [2] but do not measure the court outside the temple; leave that out, for it is given over to the nations, and they will trample over the holy city for forty-two months. [3] And I will grant my two witnesses power to prophesy for one thousand two hundred and sixty days, clothed in sackcloth."

4 These are the two olive trees and the two lampstands which stand before the Lord of the earth. [5] And if any one would harm them, fire pours from their mouth and consumes their foes; if any one would harm them, thus he is doomed to be killed. [6] They have power to shut the sky, that no rain may fall during the days of their prophesying, and they have power over the waters to turn them into blood, and to smite the earth with every plague, as often as they desire. [7] And when they have finished their testimony, the beast that ascends from the bottomless pit will make war upon them and conquer them and kill them, [8] and their dead bodies will lie in the street of the great city which is allegorically[d] called Sŏd'ọm and Egypt, where their Lord was crucified. [9] For three days and a half men from the peoples and tribes and tongues and nations gaze at their dead bodies and refuse to let them be placed in a tomb, [10] and those who dwell on the earth will rejoice over them and make merry and exchange presents, because these two prophets had been a torment to those who dwell on the earth. [11] But after the three and a half days a breath of life from God entered them, and they stood up on their feet, and great fear fell on those who saw them. [12] Then they heard a

[c]Greek *hyacinth* [d]Greek *spiritually*
9.20: Is 17.8; Ps 115.4-7; 135.15-17.
10.5: Deut 32.40; Dan 12.7. 10.9: Ezek 2.8; 3.1-3.
10.11: Jer 1.10. 11.1: Ezek 40.3.
11.2: Zech 12.3; Is 63.18; Lk 21.24.
11.4: Zech 4.3, 11-14. 11.5: 2 Kings 1.10; Jer 5.14.
11.6: 1 Kings 17.1; Ex 7.17, 19. 11.7: Dan 7.3, 7, 21.
11.8: Is 1.9. 11.11: Ezek 37.5, 10. 11.12: 2 Kings 2.11.

loud voice from heaven saying to them, "Come up hither!" And in the sight of their foes they went up to heaven in a cloud. ¹³And at that hour there was a great earthquake, and a tenth of the city fell; seven thousand people were killed in the earthquake, and the rest were terrified and gave glory to the God of heaven.

14 The second woe has passed; behold, the third woe is soon to come.

15 Then the seventh angel blew his trumpet, and there were loud voices in heaven, saying, "The kingdom of the world has become the kingdom of our Lord and of his Christ, and he shall reign for ever and ever." ¹⁶And the twenty-four elders who sit on their thrones before God fell on their faces and worshiped God, ¹⁷saying,

"We give thanks to thee, Lord God
  Almighty, who art and who wast,
  that thou hast taken thy great
  power and begun to reign.
¹⁸The nations raged, but thy wrath
    came,
  and the time for the dead to be
    judged,
for rewarding thy servants, the
    prophets and saints,
  and those who fear thy name, both
    small and great,
and for destroying the destroyers
    of the earth."

19 Then God's temple in heaven was opened, and the ark of his covenant was seen within his temple; and there were flashes of lightning, voices, peals of thunder, an earthquake, and heavy hail.

12 And a great portent appeared in heaven, a woman clothed with the sun, with the moon under her feet, and on her head a crown of twelve stars; ²she was with child and she cried out in her pangs of birth, in anguish for delivery. ³And another portent appeared in heaven; behold, a great red dragon, with seven heads and ten horns, and seven diadems upon his heads. ⁴His tail swept down a third of the stars of heaven, and cast them to the earth. And the dragon stood before the woman who was about to bear a child, that he might devour her child when she brought it forth; ⁵she brought forth a male child, one who is to rule all the nations with a rod of iron, but her child was caught up to

God and to his throne, ⁶and the woman fled into the wilderness, where she has a place prepared by God, in which to be nourished for one thousand two hundred and sixty days.

7 Now war arose in heaven, Michael and his angels fighting against the dragon; and the dragon and his angels fought, ⁸but they were defeated and there was no longer any place for them in heaven. ⁹And the great dragon was thrown down, that ancient serpent, who is called the Devil and Satan, the deceiver of the whole world—he was thrown down to the earth, and his angels were thrown down with him. ¹⁰And I heard a loud voice in heaven, saying, "Now the salvation and the power and the kingdom of our God and the authority of his Christ have come, for the accuser of our brethren has been thrown down, who accuses them day and night before our God. ¹¹And they have conquered him by the blood of the Lamb and by the word of their testimony, for they loved not their lives even unto death. ¹²Rejoice then, O heaven and you that dwell therein! But woe to you, O earth and sea, for the devil has come down to you in great wrath, because he knows that his time is short!"

13 And when the dragon saw that he had been thrown down to the earth, he pursued the woman who had borne the male child. ¹⁴But the woman was given the two wings of the great eagle that she might fly from the serpent into the wilderness, to the place where she is to be nourished for a time, and times, and half a time. ¹⁵The serpent poured water like a river out of his mouth after the woman, to sweep her away with the flood. ¹⁶But the earth came to the help of the woman, and the earth opened its mouth and swallowed the river which the dragon had poured from his mouth. ¹⁷Then the dragon was angry with the woman, and went off to make war on the rest of her offspring, on those who keep the commandments of God and bear testimony to Jesus. And he stood*e* on the sand of the sea.

*e*Other ancient authorities read *And I stood*, connecting the sentence with 13.1

11.15: Ps 22.28; Dan 7.14, 27. 11.18: Ps 2.1.
11.19: 1 Kings 8.1-6; 2 Maccabees 2.4-8.
12.1: Mic 4.10. 12.3: Dan 7.7. 12.4: Dan 8.10.
12.5: Is 66.7; Ps 2.9. 12.7: Dan 10.13.
12.9: Gen 3.1, 14-15; Zech 3.1. 12.10: Job 1.9-11.
12.12: Is 44.23; 49.13. 12.14: Dan 7.25; 12.7.

13 And I saw a beast rising out of the sea, with ten horns and seven heads, with ten diadems upon its horns and a blasphemous name upon its heads. ²And the beast that I saw was like a leopard, its feet were like a bear's, and its mouth was like a lion's mouth. And to it the dragon gave his power and his throne and great authority. ³One of its heads seemed to have a mortal wound, but its mortal wound was healed, and the whole earth followed the beast with wonder. ⁴Men worshiped the dragon, for he had given his authority to the beast, and they worshiped the beast, saying, "Who is like the beast, and who can fight against it?"

5 And the beast was given a mouth uttering haughty and blasphemous words, and it was allowed to exercise authority for forty-two months; ⁶it opened its mouth to utter blasphemies against God, blaspheming his name and his dwelling, that is, those who dwell in heaven. ⁷Also it was allowed to make war on the saints and to conquer them.ᶠ And authority was given it over every tribe and people and tongue and nation, ⁸and all who dwell on earth will worship it, every one whose name has not been written before the foundation of the world in the book of life of the Lamb that was slain. ⁹If any one has an ear, let him hear:

¹⁰If any one is to be taken captive,
   to captivity he goes;
 if any one slays with the sword,
   with the sword must he be slain.
Here is a call for the endurance and faith of the saints.

11 Then I saw another beast which rose out of the earth; it had two horns like a lamb and it spoke like a dragon. ¹²It exercises all the authority of the first beast in its presence, and makes the earth and its inhabitants worship the first beast, whose mortal wound was healed. ¹³It works great signs, even making fire come down from heaven to earth in the sight of men; ¹⁴and by the signs which it is allowed to work in the presence of the beast, it deceives those who dwell on earth, bidding them make an image for the beast which was wounded by the sword and yet lived; ¹⁵and it was allowed to give breath to the image of the beast so that the image of the beast should even speak, and to cause those who would not worship the image of the beast to be slain. ¹⁶Also it causes all, both small and great, both rich and poor, both free and slave, to be marked on the right hand or the forehead, ¹⁷so that no one can buy or sell unless he has the mark, that is, the name of the beast or the number of its name. ¹⁸This calls for wisdom: let him who has understanding reckon the number of the beast, for it is a human number, its number is six hundred and sixty-six.ᵍ

14 Then I looked, and lo, on Mount Zion stood the Lamb, and with him a hundred and forty-four thousand who had his name and his Father's name written on their foreheads. ²And I heard a voice from heaven like the sound of many waters and like the sound of loud thunder; the voice I heard was like the sound of harpers playing on their harps, ³and they sing a new song before the throne and before the four living creatures and before the elders. No one could learn that song except the hundred and forty-four thousand who had been redeemed from the earth. ⁴It is these who have not defiled themselves with women, for they are chaste;ʰ it is these who follow the Lamb wherever he goes; these have been redeemed from mankind as first fruits for God and the Lamb, ⁵and in their mouth no lie was found, for they are spotless.

6 Then I saw another angel flying in midheaven, with an eternal gospel to proclaim to those who dwell on earth, to every nation and tribe and tongue and people; ⁷and he said with a loud voice, "Fear God and give him glory, for the hour of his judgment has come; and worship him who made heaven and earth, the sea and the fountains of water."

8 Another angel, a second, followed, saying, "Fallen, fallen is Babylon the great, she who made all nations drink the wine of her impure passion."

9 And another angel, a third, followed them, saying with a loud voice, "If any one worships the beast and its image, and receives a mark on his fore-

ᶠOther ancient authorities omit this sentence
ᵍOther ancient authorities read *six hundred and sixteen*
ʰGreek *virgins*
13.1: Dan 7.1-6. **13.5:** Dan 7.8. **13.7:** Dan 7.21.
13.9: Mk 4.23. **13.10:** Jer 15.2. **13.14:** Deut 13.1-5.
13.15: Dan 3.5. **14.1:** Ezek 9.4.
14.8: Is 21.9.

head or on his hand, [10]he also shall drink the wine of God's wrath, poured unmixed into the cup of his anger, and he shall be tormented with fire and sulphur in the presence of the holy angels and in the presence of the Lamb. [11]And the smoke of their torment goes up for ever and ever; and they have no rest, day or night, these worshipers of the beast and its image, and whoever receives the mark of its name."

12 Here is a call for the endurance of the saints, those who keep the commandments of God and the faith of Jesus.

13 And I heard a voice from heaven saying, "Write this: Blessed are the dead who die in the Lord henceforth." "Blessed indeed," says the Spirit, "that they may rest from their labors, for their deeds follow them!"

14 Then I looked, and lo, a white cloud, and seated on the cloud one like a son of man, with a golden crown on his head, and a sharp sickle in his hand. [15]And another angel came out of the temple, calling with a loud voice to him who sat upon the cloud, "Put in your sickle, and reap, for the hour to reap has come, for the harvest of the earth is fully ripe." [16]So he who sat upon the cloud swung his sickle on the earth, and the earth was reaped.

17 And another angel came out of the temple in heaven, and he too had a sharp sickle. [18]Then another angel came out from the altar, the angel who has power over fire, and he called with a loud voice to him who had the sharp sickle, "Put in your sickle, and gather the clusters of the vine of the earth, for its grapes are ripe." [19]So the angel swung his sickle on the earth and gathered the vintage of the earth, and threw it into the great wine press of the wrath of God; [20]and the wine press was trodden outside the city, and blood flowed from the wine press, as high as a horse's bridle, for one thousand six hundred stadia.[i]

15 Then I saw another portent in heaven, great and wonderful, seven angels with seven plagues, which are the last, for with them the wrath of God is ended.

2 And I saw what appeared to be a sea of glass mingled with fire, and those who had conquered the beast and its image and the number of its name, standing beside the sea of glass with harps of God in their hands. [3]And they sing the song of Moses, the servant of God, and the song of the Lamb, saying,

"Great and wonderful are thy deeds, O Lord God the Almighty! Just and true are thy ways, O King of the ages![j]
[4]Who shall not fear and glorify thy name, O Lord? For thou alone art holy. All nations shall come and worship thee, for thy judgments have been revealed."

5 After this I looked, and the temple of the tent of witness in heaven was opened, [6]and out of the temple came the seven angels with the seven plagues, robed in pure bright linen, and their breasts girded with golden girdles. [7]And one of the four living creatures gave the seven angels seven golden bowls full of the wrath of God who lives for ever and ever; [8]and the temple was filled with smoke from the glory of God and from his power, and no one could enter the temple until the seven plagues of the seven angels were ended.

16 Then I heard a loud voice from the temple telling the seven angels, "Go and pour out on the earth the seven bowls of the wrath of God."

2 So the first angel went and poured his bowl on the earth, and foul and evil sores came upon the men who bore the mark of the beast and worshiped its image.

3 The second angel poured his bowl into the sea, and it became like the blood of a dead man, and every living thing died that was in the sea.

4 The third angel poured his bowl into the rivers and the fountains of water, and they became blood. [5]And I heard the angel of water say,

"Just art thou in these thy judgments, thou who art and wast, O Holy One.

[i] About two hundred miles
[j] Other ancient authorities read *the nations*
14.10: Jer 51.7; Gen 19.24.
14.11: Is 34.10.   **14.14:** Dan 7.13.
14.15: Joel 3.13; Mt 13.30.   **14.20:** Joel 3.13.
15.1: Lev 26.21.
15.3: Ex 15.1; Ps 145.17.   **15.4:** Jer 10.7; Ps 86.9-10.
15.5: Ex 40.34.   **15.8:** 1 Kings 8.10; Is 6.4; Ezek 44.4.
16.1: Is 66.6; Ps 69.24.   **16.2:** Ex 9.10-11; Deut 28.35.
16.3-4: Ex 7.17-21.

⁶For men have shed the blood of
saints and prophets,
and thou hast given them blood to
drink.
It is their due!"
⁷And I heard the altar cry,
"Yea, Lord God the Almighty,
true and just are thy judgments!"
8 The fourth angel poured his bowl
on the sun, and it was allowed to
scorch men with fire; ⁹men were
scorched by the fierce heat, and they
cursed the name of God who had
power over these plagues, and they did
not repent and give him glory.
10 The fifth angel poured his bowl
on the throne of the beast, and its
kingdom was in darkness; men
gnawed their tongues in anguish ¹¹ and
cursed the God of heaven for their
pain and sores, and did not repent of
their deeds.
12 The sixth angel poured his bowl
on the great river Euphrates, and its
water was dried up, to prepare the
way for the kings from the east. ¹³And
I saw, issuing from the mouth of the
dragon and from the mouth of the
beast and from the mouth of the false
prophet, three foul spirits like frogs;
¹⁴for they are demonic spirits, performing signs, who go abroad to the kings of
the whole world, to assemble them for
battle on the great day of God the Almighty. ¹⁵("Lo, I am coming like a
thief! Blessed is he who is awake,
keeping his garments that he may
not go naked and be seen exposed!")
¹⁶And they assembled them at the
place which is called in Hebrew
Är·ma·gĕd'dŏn.
17 The seventh angel poured his
bowl into the air, and a loud voice
came out of the temple, from the
throne, saying, "It is done!" ¹⁸And
there were flashes of lightning, voices,
peals of thunder, and a great earthquake such as had never been since
men were on the earth, so great was
that earthquake. ¹⁹The great city was
split into three parts, and the cities
of the nations fell, and God remembered great Babylon, to make her drain
the cup of the fury of his wrath. ²⁰And
every island fled away, and no mountains were to be found; ²¹and great
hailstones, heavy as a hundredweight,
dropped on men from heaven, till men
cursed God for the plague of the hail,
so fearful was that plague.

17 Then one of the seven angels
who had the seven bowls came
and said to me, "Come, I will show you
the judgment of the great harlot who
is seated upon many waters, ²with
whom the kings of the earth have committed fornication, and with the wine
of whose fornication the dwellers on
earth have become drunk." ³And he
carried me away in the Spirit into a
wilderness, and I saw a woman sitting on a scarlet beast which was full
of blasphemous names, and it had
seven heads and ten horns. ⁴The
woman was arrayed in purple and
scarlet, and bedecked with gold and
jewels and pearls, holding in her hand
a golden cup full of abominations and
the impurities of her fornication; ⁵and
on her forehead was written a name
of mystery: "Babylon the great, mother
of harlots and of earth's abominations." ⁶And I saw the woman, drunk
with the blood of the saints and the
blood of the martyrs of Jesus.
When I saw her I marveled greatly.
⁷But the angel said to me, "Why marvel? I will tell you the mystery of the
woman, and of the beast with seven
heads and ten horns that carries her.
⁸The beast that you saw was, and is
not, and is to ascend from the bottomless pit and go to perdition; and the
dwellers on earth whose names have
not been written in the book of life
from the foundation of the world, will
marvel to behold the beast, because it
was and is not and is to come. ⁹This
calls for a mind with wisdom: the seven
heads are seven mountains on which
the woman is seated; ¹⁰they are also
seven kings five of whom have fallen,
one is, the other has not yet come, and
when he comes he must remain only
a little while. ¹¹As for the beast that
was and is not, it is an eighth but it
belongs to the seven, and it goes to
perdition. ¹²And the ten horns that you
saw are ten kings who have not yet
received royal power, but they are to
receive authority as kings for one
hour, together with the beast. ¹³These
are of one mind and give over their
power and authority to the beast;

16.6: Ps 79.3. 16.7: Ps 119.137.
16.10: Ex 10.21. 16.12: Is 11.15-16.
16.13: 1 Kings 22.21-23; Ex 8.3. 16.15: 1 Thess 5.2.
16.16: 2 Kings 9.27. 16.17: Is 66.6.
16.18: Ex 19.16; Dan 12.1. 16.21: Ex 9.23.
17.1: Jer 51.13. 17.2: Is 23.17; Jer 25.15-16.
17.4: Jer 51.7. 17.8: Dan 7.3; Rev 3.5.
17.12: Dan 7.20-24.

¹⁴ they will make war on the Lamb, and the Lamb will conquer them, for he is Lord of lords and King of kings, and those with him are called and chosen and faithful."

15 And he said to me, "The waters that you saw, where the harlot is seated, are peoples and multitudes and nations and tongues. ¹⁶And the ten horns that you saw, they and the beast will hate the harlot; they will make her desolate and naked, and devour her flesh and burn her up with fire, ¹⁷for God has put it into their hearts to carry out his purpose by being of one mind and giving over their royal power to the beast, until the words of God shall be fulfilled. ¹⁸And the woman that you saw is the great city which has dominion over the kings of the earth."

18 After this I saw another angel coming down from heaven, having great authority; and the earth was made bright with his splendor. ²And he called out with a mighty voice,

"Fallen, fallen is Babylon the great!
It has become a dwelling place of demons,
a haunt of every foul spirit,
a haunt of every foul and hateful bird;
³for all nations have drunkᵏ the wine of her impure passion,
and the kings of the earth have committed fornication with her,
and the merchants of the earth have grown rich with the wealth of her wantonness."

⁴Then I heard another voice from heaven saying,
"Come out of her, my people,
lest you take part in her sins,
lest you share in her plagues;
⁵for her sins are heaped high as heaven,
and God has remembered her iniquities.
⁶Render to her as she herself has rendered,
and repay her double for her deeds;
mix a double draught for her in the cup she mixed.
⁷As she glorified herself and played the wanton,
so give her a like measure of torment and mourning.
Since in her heart she says, 'A queen I sit,
I am no widow, mourning I shall never see,'

⁸so shall her plagues come in a single day,
pestilence and mourning and famine,
and she shall be burned with fire;
for mighty is the Lord God who judges her."

9 And the kings of the earth, who committed fornication and were wanton with her, will weep and wail over her when they see the smoke of her burning; ¹⁰they will stand far off, in fear of her torment, and say,
"Alas! alas! thou great city,
thou mighty city, Babylon!
In one hour has thy judgment come."

11 And the merchants of the earth weep and mourn for her, since no one buys their cargo any more, ¹²cargo of gold, silver, jewels and pearls, fine linen, purple, silk and scarlet, all kinds of scented wood, all articles of ivory, all articles of costly wood, bronze, iron and marble, ¹³cinnamon, spice, incense, myrrh, frankincense, wine, oil, fine flour and wheat, cattle and sheep, horses and chariots, and slaves, that is, human souls.
¹⁴"The fruit for which thy soul longed has gone from thee,
and all thy dainties and thy splendor are lost to thee, never to be found again!"

¹⁵The merchants of these wares, who gained wealth from her, will stand far off, in fear of her torment, weeping and mourning aloud,
¹⁶"Alas, alas, for the great city
that was clothed in fine linen, in purple and scarlet,
bedecked with gold, with jewels, and with pearls!
¹⁷In one hour all this wealth has been laid waste."

And all shipmasters and seafaring men, sailors and all whose trade is on the sea, stood far off ¹⁸and cried out as they saw the smoke of her burning,
"What city was like the great city?"
¹⁹And they threw dust on their heads, as they wept and mourned, crying out,
"Alas, alas, for the great city
where all who had ships at sea grew rich by her wealth!
In one hour she has been laid waste.

ᵏ Other ancient authorities read *fallen by*
17.14: Dan 2.47.   18.2: Is 21.9; Jer 50.39.
18.3: Jer 25.15, 27.   18.4: Is 48.20; Jer 50.8.
18.5: Jer 51.9.   18.6: Ps 137.8.   18.7: Is 47.8-9.
18.9: Ezek 26.16-17.   18.11: Ezek 27.36.
18.12: Ezek 27.12-13, 22.   18.15: Ezek 27.36, 31.
18.17: Is 23.14; Ezek 27.26-30.   18.19: Ezek 27.30-34.

²⁰ Rejoice over her, O heaven,
  O saints and apostles and prophets,
  for God has given judgment for you
    against her!"
21 Then a mighty angel took up a
stone like a great millstone and threw
it into the sea, saying,
  "So shall Babylon the great city be
    thrown down with violence,
  and shall be found no more;
²² and the sound of harpers and min-
    strels, of flute players and trum-
    peters,
  shall be heard in thee no more;
  and a craftsman of any craft
    shall be found in thee no more;
  and the sound of the millstone
    shall be heard in thee no more;
²³ and the light of a lamp
    shall shine in thee no more;
  and the voice of bridegroom and
    bride
    shall be heard in thee no more;
  for thy merchants were the great
    men of the earth,
  and all nations were deceived by
    thy sorcery.
²⁴ And in her was found the blood of
    prophets and of saints,
  and of all who have been slain on
    earth."

19 After this I heard what seemed
    to be the loud voice of a great
multitude in heaven, crying,
  "Hallelujah! Salvation and glory and
    power belong to our God,
² for his judgments are true and just;
  he has judged the great harlot who
    corrupted the earth with her
    fornication,
  and he has avenged on her the blood
    of his servants."
³ Once more they cried,
  "Hallelujah! The smoke from her
    goes up for ever and ever."
⁴ And the twenty-four elders and the
four living creatures fell down and
worshiped God who is seated on the
throne, saying, "Amen. Hallelujah!"
⁵ And from the throne came a voice
crying,
  "Praise our God, all you his serv-
    ants,
  you who fear him, small and great."
⁶ Then I heard what seemed to be the
voice of a great multitude, like the
sound of many waters and like the
sound of mighty thunderpeals, crying,
  "Hallelujah! For the Lord our God
    the Almighty reigns.

⁷ Let us rejoice and exult and give
    him the glory,
  for the marriage of the Lamb has
    come,
  and his Bride has made herself
    ready;
⁸ it was granted her to be clothed
    with fine linen, bright and pure" —
for the fine linen is the righteous
deeds of the saints.
  9 And the angel said¹ to me, "Write
this: Blessed are those who are invited to the marriage supper of the
Lamb." And he said to me, "These are
true words of God." ¹⁰ Then I fell down
at his feet to worship him, but he said
to me, "You must not do that! I am a
fellow servant with you and your
brethren who hold the testimony of
Jesus. Worship God." For the testimony of Jesus is the spirit of prophecy.
  11 Then I saw heaven opened, and
behold, a white horse! He who sat
upon it is called Faithful and True,
and in righteousness he judges and
makes war. ¹² His eyes are like a flame
of fire, and on his head are many
diadems; and he has a name inscribed
which no one knows but himself. ¹³ He
is clad in a robe dipped in ᵐ blood, and
the name by which he is called is The
Word of God. ¹⁴ And the armies of
heaven, arrayed in fine linen, white
and pure, followed him on white
horses. ¹⁵ From his mouth issues a
sharp sword with which to smite the
nations, and he will rule them with
a rod of iron; he will tread the wine
press of the fury of the wrath of
God the Almighty. ¹⁶ On his robe and
on his thigh he has a name inscribed,
King of kings and Lord of lords.
  17 Then I saw an angel standing in
the sun, and with a loud voice he called
to all the birds that fly in midheaven,
"Come, gather for the great supper of
God, ¹⁸ to eat the flesh of kings, the flesh
of captains, the flesh of mighty men,
the flesh of horses and their riders, and
the flesh of all men, both free and slave,
both small and great." ¹⁹ And I saw the
beast and the kings of the earth with
their armies gathered to make war

¹Greek *he said*
ᵐOther ancient authorities read *sprinkled with*
18.20: Is 44.23; Jer 51.48.
18.21: Jer 51.63; Ezek 26.21. 18.22: Is 24.8; Ezek 26.13.
18.23: Jer 25.10. 18.24: Jer 51.49. 19.2: Deut 32.43.
19.3: Is 34.10. 19.5: Ps 115.13. 19.7: Ps 118.24.
19.11: Ezek 1.1. 19.12: Dan 10.6. 19.15: Ps 2.9.
19.16: Deut 10.17; Dan 2.47.
19.17: Ezek 39.4, 17-20.

against him who sits upon the horse and against his army. [20]And the beast was captured, and with it the false prophet who in its presence had worked the signs by which he deceived those who had received the mark of the beast and those who worshiped its image. These two were thrown alive into the lake of fire that burns with sulphur. [21]And the rest were slain by the sword of him who sits upon the horse, the sword that issues from his mouth; and all the birds were gorged with their flesh.

20 Then I saw an angel coming down from heaven, holding in his hand the key of the bottomless pit and a great chain. [2]And he seized the dragon, that ancient serpent, who is the Devil and Satan, and bound him for a thousand years, [3]and threw him into the pit, and shut it and sealed it over him, that he should deceive the nations no more, till the thousand years were ended. After that he must be loosed for a little while.

[4]Then I saw thrones, and seated on them were those to whom judgment was committed. Also I saw the souls of those who had been beheaded for their testimony to Jesus and for the word of God, and who had not worshiped the beast or its image and had not received its mark on their foreheads or their hands. They came to life, and reigned with Christ a thousand years. [5]The rest of the dead did not come to life until the thousand years were ended. This is the first resurrection. [6]Blessed and holy is he who shares in the first resurrection! Over such the second death has no power, but they shall be priests of God and of Christ, and they shall reign with him a thousand years.

[7]And when the thousand years are ended, Satan will be loosed from his prison [8]and will come out to deceive the nations which are at the four corners of the earth, that is, Gŏg and Mā'gŏg, to gather them for battle; their number is like the sand of the sea. [9]And they marched up over the broad earth and surrounded the camp of the saints and the beloved city; but fire came down from heaven[n] and consumed them, [10]and the devil who had deceived them was thrown into the lake of fire and sulphur where the beast and the false prophet were, and

they will be tormented day and night for ever and ever.

[11]Then I saw a great white throne and him who sat upon it; from his presence earth and sky fled away, and no place was found for them. [12]And I saw the dead, great and small, standing before the throne, and books were opened. Also another book was opened, which is the book of life. And the dead were judged by what was written in the books, by what they had done. [13]And the sea gave up the dead in it, Death and Hades gave up the dead in them, and all were judged by what they had done. [14]Then Death and Hades were thrown into the lake of fire. This is the second death, the lake of fire; [15]and if any one's name was not found written in the book of life, he was thrown into the lake of fire.

21 Then I saw a new heaven and a new earth; for the first heaven and the first earth had passed away, and the sea was no more. [2]And I saw the holy city, new Jerusalem, coming down out of heaven from God, prepared as a bride adorned for her husband; [3]and I heard a loud voice from the throne saying, "Behold, the dwelling of God is with men. He will dwell with them, and they shall be his people,[o] and God himself will be with them;[p] [4]he will wipe away every tear from their eyes, and death shall be no more, neither shall there be mourning nor crying nor pain any more, for the former things have passed away."

5 And he who sat upon the throne said, "Behold, I make all things new." Also he said, "Write this, for these words are trustworthy and true." [6]And he said to me, "It is done! I am the Alpha and the Omega, the beginning and the end. To the thirsty I will give from the fountain of the water of life without payment. [7]He who conquers shall have this heritage, and I will be his God and he shall be my son. [8]But as for the cowardly, the faithless, the polluted, as for murderers, fornicators,

---

[n] Other ancient authorities read *from God, out of heaven,* or *out of heaven from God*
[o] Other ancient authorities read *peoples*
[p] Other ancient authorities add *and be their God*
20.4: Dan 7.9, 22, 27.   20.8: Ezek 38.2, 9, 15.
20.9: 2 Kings 1.10-12.   20.11-12: Dan 7.9-10.
20.15: Rev 3.5.   21.1: Is 66.22.
21.2: Rev 3.12.   21.3: Ezek 37.27.   21.4: Is 25.8; 35.10.
21.5: Is 43.19.   21.6: Is 55.1.   21.7: Ps 89.27-28.
21.8: Is 30.33.

sorcerers, idolaters, and all liars, their lot shall be in the lake that burns with fire and sulphur, which is the second death."

9 Then came one of the seven angels who had the seven bowls full of the seven last plagues, and spoke to me, saying, "Come, I will show you the Bride, the wife of the Lamb." 10 And in the Spirit he carried me away to a great, high mountain, and showed me the holy city Jerusalem coming down out of heaven from God, 11 having the glory of God, its radiance like a most rare jewel, like a jasper, clear as crystal. 12 It had a great, high wall, with twelve gates, and at the gates twelve angels, and on the gates the names of the twelve tribes of the sons of Israel were inscribed; 13 on the east three gates, on the north three gates, on the south three gates, and on the west three gates. 14 And the wall of the city had twelve foundations, and on them the twelve names of the twelve apostles of the Lamb.

15 And he who talked to me had a measuring rod of gold to measure the city and its gates and walls. 16 The city lies foursquare, its length the same as its breadth; and he measured the city with his rod, twelve thousand stadia;q its length and breadth and height are equal. 17 He also measured its wall, a hundred and forty-four cubits by a man's measure, that is, an angel's. 18 The wall was built of jasper, while the city was pure gold, clear as glass. 19 The foundations of the wall of the city were adorned with every jewel; the first was jasper, the second sapphire, the third agate, the fourth emerald, 20 the fifth onyx, the sixth carnelian, the seventh chrysolite, the eighth beryl, the ninth topaz, the tenth chrysoprase, the eleventh jacinth, the twelfth amethyst. 21 And the twelve gates were twelve pearls, each of the gates made of a single pearl, and the street of the city was pure gold, transparent as glass.

22 And I saw no temple in the city, for its temple is the Lord God the Almighty and the Lamb. 23 And the city has no need of sun or moon to shine upon it, for the glory of God is its light, and its lamp is the Lamb. 24 By its light shall the nations walk; and the kings of the earth shall bring their glory into it, 25 and its gates shall never be shut

by day—and there shall be no night there; 26 they shall bring into it the glory and the honor of the nations. 27 But nothing unclean shall enter it, nor any one who practices abomination or falsehood, but only those who are written in the Lamb's book of life.

22 Then he showed me the river of the water of life, bright as crystal, flowing from the throne of God and of the Lamb 2 through the middle of the street of the city; also, on either side of the river, the tree of lifer with its twelve kinds of fruit, yielding its fruit each month; and the leaves of the tree were for the healing of the nations. 3 There shall no more be anything accursed, but the throne of God and of the Lamb shall be in it, and his servants shall worship him; 4 they shall see his face, and his name shall be on their foreheads. 5 And night shall be no more; they need no light of lamp or sun, for the Lord God will be their light, and they shall reign for ever and ever.

6 And he said to me, "These words are trustworthy and true. And the Lord, the God of the spirits of the prophets, has sent his angel to show his servants what must soon take place. 7 And behold, I am coming soon."

Blessed is he who keeps the words of the prophecy of this book.

8 I John am he who heard and saw these things. And when I heard and saw them, I fell down to worship at the feet of the angel who showed them to me; 9 but he said to me, "You must not do that! I am a fellow servant with you and your brethren the prophets, and with those who keep the words of this book. Worship God."

10 And he said to me, "Do not seal up the words of the prophecy of this book, for the time is near. 11 Let the evildoer still do evil, and the filthy still be filthy, and the righteous still do right, and the holy still be holy."

12 "Behold, I am coming soon, bringing my recompense, to repay

---

qAbout fifteen hundred miles
rOr the Lamb. *In the midst of the street of the city, and on either side of the river, was the tree of life, etc.*
21.10: Ezek 40.2.
21.12: Ezek 48.30-35; Ex 28.21.   **21.15:** Ezek 40.5.
21.19: Is 54.11-12.   **21.23:** Is 24.23; 60.1, 19.
21.25: Is 60.11.   **21.27:** Is 52.1; Rev 3.5.
22.2: Gen 2.9.   **22.3:** Zech 14.11.   **22.4:** Ps 17.15.
22.11: Dan 12.10.   **22.12:** Is 40.10; Jer 17.10.

every one for what he has done. [13] I am the Alpha and the Omega, the first and the last, the beginning and the end."

14 Blessed are those who wash their robes,[s] that they may have the right to the tree of life and that they may enter the city by the gates. [15] Outside are the dogs and sorcerers and fornicators and murderers and idolaters, and every one who loves and practices falsehood.

16 "I Jesus have sent my angel to you with this testimony for the churches. I am the root and the offspring of David, the bright morning star."

17 The Spirit and the Bride say, "Come." And let him who hears say, "Come." And let him who is thirsty come, let him who desires take the water of life without price.

18 I warn every one who hears the words of the prophecy of this book: if any one adds to them, God will add to him the plagues described in this book, [19] and if any one takes away from the words of the book of this prophecy, God will take away his share in the tree of life and in the holy city, which are described in this book.

20 He who testifies to these things says, "Surely I am coming soon." Amen. Come, Lord Jesus!

21 The grace of the Lord Jesus be with all the saints.[t] Amen.

[s]Other ancient authorities read *do his commandments*
[t]Other ancient authorities omit *all;* others omit *the saints*
22.13: Is 44.6; 48.12.　**22.14:** Gen 2.9; 3.22.
22.16: Is 11.1, 10.　**22.17:** Is 55.1.　**22.21:** 2 Thess 3.18.

BIBLE
STUDY HELPS

BIBLE STUDY HELPS

Contents

THE BIBLE AND ITS TRANSLATIONS

ORIGINAL LANGUAGES OF THE BIBLE

Nearly all the Old Testament was originally written in Hebrew; the small remaining portion was written in Aramaic, sometimes called Syriac. The Aramaic section comprises three passages (Ezra 4.8—6.18; 7.12–26; Dan. 2.4—7.28), one verse of Jeremiah (10.11), and two words in Genesis (31.47, a place name meaning "heap of witness"). Aramaic was the language spoken by the people and was the language spoken by Jesus during His public ministry. However, the New Testament was written in Greek, the language used in letters and other writings. Greek was the language understood practically everywhere throughout the Roman Empire, even in the remote provinces, and was recognized as the language of culture.

Since few persons can easily read the ancient languages of the Scriptures, many versions and translations of the Bible have been made. It has been translated, either in whole or in part, into nearly every language of the world today; but, because the spoken languages change from generation to generation, the work of translation continues.

Hebrew.—All of the Old Testament manuscripts which have been found are written in square, black letters which resemble the printed Hebrew of today. These square characters came into use some years prior to the birth of Christ.

Two facts made the translator's task difficult. First, Hebrew then was written without any spaces separating the words. For this reason, the translator sometimes was puzzled to know where one word ended and the next began. Second, the Hebrew alphabet consisted of twenty-two letters, all of them consonants. (Four of these consonants, however, were sometimes used to represent vowels.) In writing, only the consonants were put down. The reader was expected to know what vowels should be added. Evidently it was believed that the reader would be sufficiently familiar with the sacred text to be able to supply from memory the omitted vowels, or else it was thought that the context in which each word occurred would suggest the proper vowel or vowels to be inserted. If we may use English to illustrate the problem, let us suppose one came upon the consonants *m* and *n*. Could one tell with certainty what word was intended? Would it be "man" or "men" or "main" or "mean" or even "moon"?

In the sixth and seventh centuries A.D., when Hebrew as a spoken language was beginning to die out, it was observed that the rabbis were not always agreed as to the proper reading of passages in the synagogue scrolls. As a result, there was danger of confusion and misunderstanding. Accordingly, Jewish scholars of that period, who became known as the Massoretes, undertook to determine and to indicate the proper vowel or vowels for every word in the Hebrew Scriptures. They indicated these vowels by means of small marks above, within, or below the consonants. They did not regard these vowel points as a part of the sacred text, and for that reason they refrained from marking them on the synagogue scrolls. They did insert them, however, on other scrolls and in their commentaries on the Scriptures.

Furthermore, in Hebrew there are no capital letters to distinguish proper nouns from common nouns and to mark the beginning of each new sentence. Finally, Hebrew is read from right to left, rather than from left to right as in English. The lines of Hebrew follow naturally down the page, from top to bottom. In the case of a scroll or book, one begins to read at what we would consider the end or back, and continues his reading till he reaches what we would consider the beginning or front.

Greek.—The Greek in which the New Testament books were written differs somewhat from the classical Greek of a few centuries earlier. It is the *koiné*; that is to say, the everyday speech of the common people (and of the aristocrats also) in the first century A.D. Greek is like English in that it is read from left to right. The vowels are included in the Greek alphabet, and they appear in all Greek words except a few frequently used abbreviations. The oldest and most important New Testament manuscripts are written entirely in capital letters, and for this reason are called uncials. As a rule, there are no spaces separating the words. Later Greek manuscripts are written in a running hand (cursives). Both capital letters and small letters are employed. The latter frequently are joined together, much as in handwriting today. In the later manuscripts there are spaces between the words and some punctuation is employed. These manuscripts come from the ninth to the fifteenth century A.D., and they are called miniscules. The name means "rather small"; they take that name from the fact that they are written in small letters rather than in capitals.

Although much writing in Old Testament times was done on papyrus (a kind of paper), important documents were written on carefully prepared skins (vellum or parchment), because of their greater durability and permanence. In the case of a long roll, the skins were stitched together. The New Testament manuscripts doubtless were written originally on papyrus. Later, when their great value had been perceived, they were copied on vellum. It is not possible to state precisely when the change from scrolls to books took place. It did not happen all at once. It is now known that there were papyrus books much earlier than had been supposed. For several centuries both scrolls and books were in common use. Important books were made of vellum rather than the more fragile papyrus. A manuscript which is in the form of a book, rather than a roll, is called a codex. The word codex means "book."

THE HISTORY OF THE CHAPTER DIVISIONS

In the Hebrew manuscripts there were some indications of where the major divisions of the text began and ended. Because these sections sometimes were rather long, it was inevitable that someone eventually would make marks of one sort or another in the margins. Perhaps these marks at first merely indicated the point at which he had stopped reading. Later, they may have been added for the guidance of the reader in the synagogue, and were meant to show him appropriate points at which his reading might begin and end.

In the case of the New Testament, sections were marked off at an early date. These sections were shorter than the present chapter divisions, but longer than the present verse divisions.

The chapter divisions usually are attributed to Stephen Langton, Archbishop of Canterbury, in England. Langton died in 1228. Cardinal Hugo, who died in 1263, used these chapter divisions in a concordance which he prepared for use with the Latin Vulgate. Chapter divisions are found in Wyclif's version of the New Testament (1382), and in all subsequent English versions.

These chapter divisions proved so convenient when referring to passages of Scripture that Jewish scholars borrowed the idea and employed it in editions of the Hebrew Scriptures. Thus, the present-day Hebrew Old Testament has the same chapter divisions as does our English Old Testament.

THE ORIGIN OF THE VERSE DIVISIONS

The material within each chapter is further divided into verses, numbered in regular order throughout each chapter. Although these verse divisions are helpful, they should not be emphasized, for they are not properly a part of the Holy Scriptures. They should not be permitted to interrupt the connected reading of the Scriptures, especially when the passage is of a narrative or poetical character.

Most authorities hold that the verse divisions for the Old Testament were first worked out by Rabbi Nathan in 1448. A Greek New Testament, which was published in 1551 by Robert Stephanus, a printer of Paris, contains the same verse divisions and numbers which we have now in the New Testament. His Latin Vulgate, published in 1551, was the first complete Bible to contain the verse numbers with which we are familiar. The first English Bible to contain them was the Geneva Bible, published in 1560. Since then, all English Bibles have contained the verse numbers.

THE WORDS IN ITALICS

Readers of some translations of the English Bible, notably the King James Version, now and again come upon words which are printed in italics; that is to say, with slanting letters. Some have supposed, mistakenly, that these words were printed in this fashion for emphasis. This is not the case. The explanation, really, is quite simple. The words in italics are words which do not have any equivalents in the Hebrew or Greek text. They are words which have been supplied by the translators in order to make the meaning of the sentence clearer, or in order to make the passage read more smoothly in English. Numerous italicized words are found in the fifth chapter of Matthew, and they occur with almost equal frequency in other parts of the Scriptures.

The Geneva Bible, which was a pioneer version

in many different ways, was the first to use italics in this fashion.

THE MANY VERSIONS OF THE BIBLE

When scholarly research sheds new light on the meaning of the original Bible text, new versions are needed. These new translations have sometimes been made by individual scholars, sometimes by groups working together. The versions which follow are those most important in the development of the Tyndale-King James tradition. Since the beginning of this century many individual translations into modern English have been made available. Of these, the most widely used are *The Complete Bible, an American Translation* (Goodspeed, 1939); *The Bible, a New Translation* (Moffatt, 1935); and *The New English Bible, New Testament* (Oxford and Cambridge University Presses, 1961). Among the popular Roman Catholic translations from the Latin Vulgate are *The New Testament of Our Lord and Savior Jesus Christ. Translated from the Latin Vulgate. A Revision of the Challoner-Rheims Version* (Episcopal Committee of the Confraternity of Christian Doctrine, 1942) and *Translations of Holy Scripture* (Knox, 1944).

The Septuagint.—The Old Testament was translated into Greek even before there was a New Testament. In the centuries immediately preceding the Christian era, the Jews became widely scattered. A large colony of Jews was located in Alexandria, Egypt, and their native tongue, Hebrew, was little used, being superseded by the Greek. In order that the Hebrew Scriptures not be lost, a group of seventy (or seventy-two) scholars was commissioned by the high priest in Jerusalem to make a translation into Greek. This was at about the middle of the third century B.C. The name of this translation, "Septuagint," comes from the Latin word for seventy, and is commonly abbreviated by using the Roman numeral LXX.

The LXX received the endorsement of eminent rabbis, and within a short time was being widely used by the Jews and their Gentile proselytes in the Greek-speaking world. It was only natural that it became the Old Testament which was read in the early Christian churches. And, too, it was natural for the authors of the New Testament books to use the LXX when they wished to quote the Old Testament. Many copies of the LXX, dating from the third century A.D., have been of great help to scholars in determining the original Hebrew text.

The Vulgate.—Latin, the official language of the Roman Empire, gradually replaced Greek in the Roman Church, and became the language of the ritual of the Church. Various versions of the Scriptures, in what is known as Old Latin, came into use. Finally, with the approval and aid of Pope Damascus, the scholar Jerome (A.D. 340?–420) undertook the translation of the Bible into Latin. He went to Bethlehem, where he might visit the places mentioned in the Bible, and there completed the translation of the Scriptures known as The Vulgate and also founded two religious orders. This Latin translation became the official Bible of the Roman Catholic Church. The first book printed from movable type, the Gutenberg Bible, is a printing of Jerome's Latin Vulgate.

Early English Bible History.—Although the gospel was carried to what we know as Great Britain as early as the second century, it was not until the seventh century that Christianity became established there. There were few Bibles, all in Latin and handwritten, from which learned men could read the Scriptures. In order that the common people, who used Anglo-Saxon, might understand the Scriptures, translations or paraphrases were needed.

Caedmon, an unschooled servant in one of the monasteries, by a rare gift, was able to put the Bible stories into Anglo-Saxon verse, which he sang in minstrel fashion. These verses cannot be called a translation but they deserve mention as one of the earliest attempts to put the Bible narratives into the language of the people.

The first real translation was a version of the Psalms by Aldhelm, bishop of Sherborne, who died in 709. The Venerable Bede (673–735) completed a translation of the Gospel according to John just before his death. King Alfred (848–901) supported the Christian movement and either prepared himself, or had prepared under his supervision, portions of the Acts of the Apostles, Exodus, and some of the Psalms. Also to this period belongs a translation of the Heptateuch by Aelfric, abbot of Eynsham (995–1020).

In the Middle English period (1150–1500) were completed a metrical paraphrase of the Gospels called the Ormulum, the Psalter of Richard Rolle (1290?–1349), and a prose version of the Psalms attributed to William of Shoreham (1270?–1350).

John Wyclif.—The first English versions of the entire Bible were two associated with the work of John Wyclif (1320?–1384), which were translated from the Latin Vulgate. How much he did himself and how much was done by his associates is not clear. The first version was a careful literal translation of the Vulgate, following the order of the Latin words as closely as possible, and thus perpetuating some of Jerome's errors. The second version was completed (1397) after Wyclif's death by his secretary, John Purvey. Wyclif did more than translate the Scriptures; he also recruited and trained men, called Lollards, who would read the Scriptures to the people.

The Wyclif Bibles were small books, copied by hand, and very few persons could afford to purchase one. Then too, laws were passed prohibiting the ownership of or the copying of the Scriptures in English.

William Tyndale.—The martyr, William Tyndale, (1490?–1536) believed, as did Wyclif, that there should be universal reading of the Scriptures. At this time there was a renewed interest in Greek and Hebrew, and increased knowledge of these languages made possible a translation based on Hebrew and Greek manuscripts which were available. By reason of Gutenberg's invention of movable type, books could be produced in larger numbers and at much less expense than could the Wyclif Bibles.

Tyndale tried in vain to get official approval and support in Britain for his work. Finally, in 1524, when he realized there was no place in England where he could carry on his scholarly work with safety, he went to Germany. In Cologne he made arrangements for the printing but before it was complete he was forced to flee to Worms where, in 1525, three thousand copies of the New Testament were printed for him. Copies were sent into England but, because such translations had been banned by church authorities, they were seized and publicly burned. Undaunted, Tyndale continued to revise and improve his translation and to print several editions of the New Testament before his imprisonment in 1535. Tyndale's translation of the Pentateuch was published in 1530 and of the book of Jonah in 1531. In 1534 he issued a revision of his translation of Genesis and a revision of his translation of the New Testament. *The New Testament yet once again corrected by William Tyndale,* published in 1535, became the basis for all later revisions and the main source of the authorized versions of the New Testament in English.

During the sixteen months of his imprisonment in Antwerp, where he had been safe for a time, Tyndale tried to complete his translation of the Old Testament. Despite all efforts to save him, he was condemned to death and on October 6, 1536, was strangled and then his body was burned at the stake.

Miles Coverdale.—To Miles Coverdale (1488–1568) goes the distinction of being the first to prepare and publish a complete printed Bible in English (1535). This was not a firsthand translation from the original ancient languages but was based on the Latin Vulgate and upon translations by Tyndale into English, by Luther and by Zwingli and his associates into German, and by Pagninus into Latin. Although Coverdale's translation appeared in England while Tyndale was still in prison, the attitude of the church authorities in England had already become less hostile. At a Convocation of the English Church there had been discussion of the desirability of an English translation. Coverdale was not hindered in his work, and he dedicated his translation to King Henry VIII.

When Queen Mary came to the throne in 1553 translations were again forbidden and Coverdale was imprisoned. Upon his release he fled to the Continent where he remained the rest of his life. However, his translation of the Psalms was adopted for inclusion in *The Book of Common Prayer,* where, with some modernizing of spelling, it still appears. Many of Coverdale's phrases reappear in the King James Version and in the Revised Standard Version. Coverdale was responsible for removing the books of the Apocrypha from the places where they had been located in the Septuagint and, out of deference for those unwilling to discard them completely, printed them together in a separate section between the Old and the New Testaments.

Thomas Matthew.—In 1537 there appeared a translation of the Bible by Thomas Matthew. Matthew was probably a pseudonym for John Rogers, a friend of Tyndale, to whom Tyndale had left his unpublished work on the Old Testament. This new material, including many notes and New Testament revisions, was combined by Rogers with the work of Coverdale for his translation of the Bible.

A license was secured by Archbishop Cranmer for Thomas Cromwell, prime minister of Henry

VIII, to print the Thomas Matthew Bible. Thus, after a long battle, the Bible could now be published in England without fear of reprisals from either the Crown or the church.

Richard Tavener.—The next English Bible appeared in 1539 and was the work of Richard Tavener, a wealthy and distinguished man who followed the Reformation cause. Tavener apparently prepared this translation at the request of Thomas Cromwell. While the Tavener Bible is of little literary significance, as it was largely a revision of Matthew's Bible, it is important to note that this was the first Bible to be published in England; all preceding English Bibles had been printed on the Continent.

The Great Bible.—After the publication of Matthew's Bible, controversy arose among members of the Anglican Church concerning certain marginal notes in this Bible. These church leaders also thought that there was need for a large size Bible that could be placed in the churches so that members of the congregation could come and read from it. As an answer to these problems Thomas Cromwell appointed a group of scholars to prepare a new translation. This company was led, in the beginning at least, by Miles Coverdale.

This Bible appeared in 1539. Because of its large size (similar to today's "pulpit" Bibles) and the great number of scholars who worked on it, it gained the popular name of the Great Bible.

Geneva Bible.—Under the Roman Catholic Queen Mary no Bibles were printed in England and the use of the English Bible was banned. Because of the widespread persecution of English Protestants under Mary, many English citizens fled to the Continent. A group of these refugees settled at Geneva and undertook the next revision of the English Bible, which was published in 1560 and became known as the Geneva Bible. A small book, as compared to the unwieldy Great Bible, it was the first Bible to contain both chapter and verse divisions. This Bible was never authorized, nor did it have to be, as it quickly became very popular with the people. It was reprinted at least one hundred and forty times, between 1560 and 1644, and competed with the King James Version longer than any other version of the English Bible.

Bishops' Bible.—Shortly after the accession of Queen Elizabeth, an injunction was issued from the throne that a large English Bible be placed in every church. Matthew Parker, Archbishop of Canterbury, commissioned a group of eminent clergymen to produce a new translation in order to carry out the Queen's wish. Each scholar was responsible for translating one or more of the books of the Bible. The entire work was collated and edited by Archbishop Parker.

The finished version, known as the Bishops' Bible, was published in 1568. It was authorized by Convocation and replaced the Great Bible on the church lecturns.

Douai Bible.—Up to this time the only Bible used by the Roman Catholic Church was the Vulgate, the Latin version of the Scriptures based on the work of Jerome, done over a thousand years earlier. However, scholars insisted on a more accurate translation and the increased reading of the English Bible led Roman Catholic authorities to approve an English version.

The work on the Catholic version was done at a Roman Catholic college in Douai, Flanders. Chief among the English translators was Gregory Martin, formerly a Fellow of St. John's College at Oxford. During this time the college moved to Rheims, where the New Testament was published in 1582, and then back to Douai. Because of financial troubles the Old Testament was not published until 1609.

This translation, known as the Douai Version or the Rheims-Douai Bible, became the official Roman Catholic Bible in English. Until recent times this was the only English translation receiving the official sanction of the Roman Church.

King James Version.—James I came to the throne of England in 1603. Being the secular head of the Anglican Church, James was opposed to the various rivals of Anglicanism in England at that time. In January, 1604, the King called a meeting at Hampton Court to discuss religious toleration. During the conference, mention was made of the need for a new translation of the Bible. The Puritans protested against what they thought were mistranslations in the Bishops' Bible and they also preferred the Geneva Bible, thereby antagonizing the Anglicans.

Shortly after the Hampton Court conference, the King took steps to begin a new version. The work was to be done by a large number of English scholars who were free to use any of the preceding translations which they found satisfactory. When completed, their work was to be reviewed by the Bishops, the Privy Council, and finally by the king himself. The company of translators was divided into six groups; two working at Oxford, two at Cambridge, and two at Westminster. Work did not actually begin until 1607, and in 1611 the first edition of the King James Version of the Bible was printed and distributed.

American Standard Version (Revised Version).— It was not until the end of the nineteenth century that any serious thought was given to a major revision of the King James Version. However, many new Biblical manuscripts had been discovered, adding new information to the knowledge of the Bible. Also, many of the words and phrases current in King James' era had, by this time, become archaic or obsolete. Thus it was believed that an up-to-date revision would be more correct than the old King James Version.

A group of British and American scholars co-operated on this project and in 1881 the New Testament of the English Revised Version was printed, with the Old Testament appearing four years later. The American group of scholars decided, when some of its suggestions were rejected by the British group, to continue the work on its own responsibility. This American committee published the American Standard Version in 1901.

Revised Standard Version.—In 1928 the copyright of the American Standard Version was acquired by the International Council of Religious Education and thus passed into the ownership of the churches of the United States and Canada which were associated in the Council through their boards of education and publication. In 1937, after two years of study and experimental work, a revision was authorized by vote of the Council, which directed that the resulting version should

6

"embody the best results of modern scholarship as to the meaning of the Scriptures, and express this meaning in English diction which is designed for use in public and private worship and preserves those qualities which have given to the King James Version a supreme place in English Literature." Thirty-two scholars served as members of the Committee charged with making the revision.

The Revised Standard Version of the New Testament was published in 1946. In 1950 the International Council of Religious Education merged with other bodies to become the Division of Christian Education of the newly organized National Council of Churches. The Revised Standard Version of the Bible, containing the Old and New Testaments, was published in 1952, the Revised Standard Version of the Apocrypha in 1957, both having been authorized by vote of the National Council of the Churches of Christ in the United States of America.

The Revised Standard Version has taken full account of the new knowledge of the history, geography, religions, and cultures of Bible lands, and of the rich new resources for understanding the vocabulary, grammar, and idioms of the Biblical and related languages. It breaks away from the literalism and mechanical exactitude of the revisions of 1881–1901, and returns to the basic structure and more natural cadence of the Tyndale-King James tradition.

WHAT IS THE BIBLE?

The name "Bible" is derived from the Greek word *biblos*, meaning "book." This "Book," actually composed of sixty-six separate books, is a collection of ancient Hebrew and Christian writings, each complete in itself. The order of the sixty-six books in the Old Testament and New Testament is a logical one, giving, in general, a consecutive history of mankind—from the story of creation in the first chapter of Genesis to the visionary future of the book of Revelation.

The order of Old Testament books in the English Bible differs somewhat from the order of the books of Hebrew Scriptures. The sacred writings of the Jews were divided into three parts: (1) the Law, actually five books ("pentateuch") setting forth the laws which God gave through Moses; (2) the Prophets, including the four "Former Prophets," Joshua, Judges, Samuel, and Kings, and the four "Latter Prophets," Isaiah, Jeremiah, Ezekiel, and the Twelve (the Twelve consisting of twelve brief prophetical books contained in a single scroll, thus looked upon as a single book); and (3) the Writings, which are divided into four sections. See Plate I of the accompanying chart. The relative importance of the scriptural writings according to Jewish thinking is shown by this order: The Law, standing first, was considered the most important; second, the Prophets; and third, the Writings, which were truly inspired and to be treasured but were not as important as the Law and the Prophets.

In English translations of the Old Testament, the books may be regarded as falling into four categories: (1) History, the books from Genesis to Esther; (2) Poetry, the books from Job to the Song of Solomon; (3) the Major Prophets, the books of Isaiah, Jeremiah, Ezekiel, and Daniel (with Lamentations, a brief and largely poetical book, regarded as an appendix to the book of Jeremiah); and (4) the Minor Prophets, the same brief prophetical books spoken of by the Jews as "the Twelve." See Plate II of the accompanying chart.

The twenty-seven New Testament books are also divided into four categories: (1) History, including the four Gospels (i.e. books proclaiming the good news) and the book of Acts; (2) Paul's Epistles, the books of Romans through Philemon; (3) the General Epistles, the books of Hebrews through Jude; and (4) the Apocalypse, the book of Revelation. See Plate III of the chart.

THE OLD TESTAMENT

The thirty-nine books of the Old Testament are grouped into four divisions as follows: (1) Historical Books (Genesis–Esther) including the Pentateuch (Genesis–Deuteronomy); (2) Poetical Books (Job–Song of Solomon); (3) the Major Prophets (Isaiah–Daniel); and (4) the Minor Prophets (Hosea-Malachi).

The word "pentateuch," derived from the Greek, means five books, here designating the first five books of the Old Testament. This section is also called "The Law" or "The Books of Moses," following the Jewish tradition that these five books were written by Moses.

Genesis is the first book of the Old Testament and is a collection of the earliest Israelite traditions concerning the origin of things. The book has two main divisions. The first is the history of early mankind, narrating the events of the Creation, the Fall, the Flood, and the Dispersion. The second section concerns the lives of Abraham, Isaac, Jacob, and Joseph.

Exodus relates the history of the Israelites from after the death of Joseph to the erection of the Tabernacle by Moses. The book includes an account of the wanderings in the wilderness of Sinai and the giving of the law to the nation.

Leviticus can also be called "The Book of the Law of the Priests" as it contains very little historical matter, concerning itself with priestly legislation and the practice of the law among the people. In Leviticus much importance is placed upon Israel's separation from all heathen influences so that the nation may retain its religious purity.

Numbers is a continuation of Exodus, recording the stay of the Israelites in the wilderness of Sinai until their arrival at Moab. The title of the book is derived from the two numberings of the people recorded here.

Deuteronomy is a sequel to Numbers. Narrated in it are three speeches and two poems, supposedly spoken by Moses in Moab before the crossing of Jordan, in which he gives the Ten Commandments to the chosen people. A minor narrative in three of the chapters tells of the last days of Moses.

Joshua tells the story of Moses' successor. It was Joshua who led the people into the Promised Land after the death of Moses. The book is also a narrative of the conquest of Canaan and the di-

7

THE OLD TESTAMENT BOOKS
As Listed and Grouped by the Hebrews

THE LAW	THE PROPHETS		THE WRITINGS
	The Former Prophets	The Latter Prophets — The Twelve	
GENESIS, EXODUS, LEVITICUS, NUMBERS, DEUTERONOMY	JOSHUA, JUDGES, SAMUEL, KINGS	ISAIAH, JEREMIAH, EZEKIEL / HOSEA, JOEL, AMOS, OBADIAH, JONAH, MICAH, NAHUM, HABAKKUK, ZEPHANIAH, HAGGAI, ZECHARIAH, MALACHI	PSALMS, PROVERBS, JOB, SONG OF SOLOMON, RUTH, LAMENTATIONS, ECCLESIASTES, ESTHER, DANIEL, EZRA, NEHEMIAH, CHRONICLES

Plate I

THE OLD TESTAMENT BOOKS
As Listed and Grouped in the English Bible

HISTORY	POETRY	MAJOR PROPHETS	MINOR PROPHETS
GENESIS, EXODUS, LEVITICUS, NUMBERS, DEUTERONOMY, JOSHUA, JUDGES, RUTH, 1 SAMUEL, 2 SAMUEL, 1 KINGS, 2 KINGS, 1 CHRONICLES, 2 CHRONICLES, EZRA, NEHEMIAH, ESTHER	JOB, PSALMS, PROVERBS, ECCLESIASTES, SONG OF SOLOMON	ISAIAH, JEREMIAH-LAMENTATIONS, EZEKIEL, DANIEL	HOSEA, JOEL, AMOS, OBADIAH, JONAH, MICAH, NAHUM, HABAKKUK, ZEPHANIAH, HAGGAI, ZECHARIAH, MALACHI

Plate II

THE NEW TESTAMENT BOOKS
As Listed and Grouped in the English Bible

HISTORY	PAUL'S EPISTLES	GENERAL EPISTLES	APOCALYPSE
Gospels			
MATTHEW, MARK, LUKE, JOHN, ACTS	ROMANS, 1 CORINTHIANS, 2 CORINTHIANS, GALATIANS, EPHESIANS, PHILIPPIANS, COLOSSIANS, 1 THESSALONIANS, 2 THESSALONIANS, 1 TIMOTHY, 2 TIMOTHY, TITUS, PHILEMON	HEBREWS, JAMES, 1 PETER, 2 PETER, 1 JOHN, 2 JOHN, 3 JOHN, JUDE	REVELATION

Plate III

8

vision of the land among the twelve tribes of Israel.

Judges is so called because it relates of the times of various rulers, or judges, of Israel from the possession of Canaan until the time of Samuel. Also found in Judges is the recounting of the adventures of Samson.

Ruth is a beautiful pastoral idyll telling the story of Ruth, the Moabitess, and her mother-in-law Naomi. The two women return to Naomi's homeland, Judah, and there Ruth, the foreigner, marries Boaz. Ruth was the great-grandmother of David, the ancestor of Jesus.

The two *Books of Samuel* contain valuable historical material concerning the religious and moral conditions of the period. Samuel is the great prophet-judge who helps to unite the scattered tribes under one king, Saul. The history of the reigns of Saul and David is also recorded.

The two *Books of Kings* follow the monarchy to its summit under Solomon and the nation's division, decline, and fall under Jeroboam and Rehoboam. Kings also gives an outline of the double captivity of Israel under the Assyrians and Judah under the Chaldeans.

The two *Books of Chronicles* have much in common with the books of Samuel and Kings. They contain genealogical tables from Adam to the death of Saul, the reign of Solomon, the division of the kingdom, the exile, and the proclamation of Cyrus.

Ezra-Nehemiah are companion books, continuing the narration of Chronicles. Ezra details the first return of the Jews from their captivity in Babylon and the rebuilding of the Temple. Nehemiah gives an account of the rebuilding of Jerusalem and of the efforts to bring religious reform to the people.

Esther, the last of the historical books, contains an early example of pre-Christian anti-Semitism. Esther, a Jewess, was chosen as the new queen for Ahasuerus, the king of Persia. Her uncle Mordecai had incurred the enmity of Haman, the evil court favorite, and so brought the threat of death to his people. Esther, through her position was able to avert the tragedy and save her people.

Job, first of the poetical books, deals with the problem of suffering. God allows Satan to afflict Job, a prosperous and pious Jew, with many hardships in order to test his faith. Job loses his children and his worldly goods, and is afflicted by a terrible disease. Finally when God questions Job, he is forced to admit to the limits of human wisdom, and bows humbly before the will of God. With this new humility his faith is strengthened and Job finds peace.

Psalms is a collection of poems written over a long period of time by various authors. They express the heart of humanity in all generations through a variety of religious experiences. Originally the poems were chanted or sung to the accompaniment of a stringed instrument. One of the characteristics of this Hebrew poetry is parallelism; that is, the second line reiterates the idea of the first line.

Proverbs is a part of the Wisdom literature of the Old Testament. Contained in the book are short, pithy sayings of common sense and sound advice that relate to all ways of life; in short, a practical, everyday philosophy of living.

Ecclesiastes contains the writings of a wealthy Jew who suffered from the sorrows and disappointments of life and now tries to discover the true value and meaning of life through God. The author of this book calls himself "The Preacher," "The son of David," and "king in Jerusalem." But whether this was Solomon or a later "son of David" is uncertain.

The *Song of Solomon* is also called "Song of Songs" and "Canticles." This collection of love songs has long been an enigma and many interpretations have been offered for it. This love-relationship could signify the relation between God and His people, or that between Christ and the Church.

The Prophetical books follow, and complete the Old Testament. The prophets include seventeen books, the first five known as the "Major Prophets"; the other twelve as the "Minor Prophets." The period covered is over four centuries, from *ca.* 870 to 440 B.C.

Isaiah is the first collection of prophecy of the five major Hebrew prophets. Judgment to come is fundamental to Isaiah's teaching. Israel and Judah are to perish but a remnant will survive and a new Jerusalem will rise up as a city of the faithful. It is also in Isaiah that memorable prophecies of Christ's coming are found.

Jeremiah is the book of the prophet Jeremiah, who received the divine call to prophesy while very young. It was his mission to predict doom upon his nation for its many sins. For this he was hated by the priests and the people. More important than prophecies was the emphasis Jeremiah placed on personal religion.

Lamentations consists of five poems occasioned by the fall of Jerusalem and the Babylonian captivity. The first three elegies describe the terrible plight of the nation, the fourth compares the past history of Zion with her present state, and the last is a prayer for compassion and deliverance.

Ezekiel is written by the prophet of the exile. The book is divided into two sections; the first denounces the sins and abominations of Jerusalem and the second looks to the future with the hope that the city will be restored after it has been cleansed. This latter section contains passages strongly messianic in nature.

Daniel, like Ezekiel, is divided into two parts. The first six chapters tell of Daniel's faith and the greatness of his God over the idols of Babylon. The last six chapters contain the four visions of Daniel and their interpretations.

Hosea is the first book of the twelve minor prophets. Because the times were outwardly prosperous, idolatry prevailed and immorality was rampant. Hosea urges a return to God in order that he may show mercy and forgiveness.

Joel was written during a locust plague, a time of great distress for the people. The prophet sees in the devastation of the locusts an indication of the coming day of the Lord. Therefore all must repent with fasting and mourning. With repentance, however, there is a promise for relief and God's blessing for Israel.

Amos is the book of the herdsman from Tekoa, a small town in Judah. He received a direct call from God to prophecy against the unrighteousness of both Judah and Israel. Amos was the first

What Is the Bible?

prophet to proclaim that God was the ruler of the whole world.

Obadiah is the shortest book of the Old Testament containing only one chapter. In it is given a prophetic interpretation of a great calamity that has already occured in Edom and a prediction of a universal judgment.

Jonah is the story of a prophet sent by God to Nineveh. Jonah was fearful of the call and tried to flee by sea to Tarshish. During the sea voyage he was thrown overboard by his fellow passengers and swallowed by a great fish sent by God. The prophet was saved and went on to Nineveh to successfully convert the people of that city.

Micah, the prophecy of the fourth in the great quartet of eighth-century B.C. prophets, with Amos, Hosea, and Isaiah, who preached against the idolatrous and unjust nations of their generation. Micah's message was stern and uncompromising; judgment was to come soon for Judah.

Nahum consists of two poems. The prophet tells of the fall of Nineveh, the capital of the Assyrian nation. God is depicted as revengeful to those who conspire against Him. The book of Nahum also contains a classic rebuke against warfare and militarism.

Habakkuk, a book of prophecy, is concerned with the problem of unpunished evil in the world. It was revealed to Habakkuk that the Chaldean armies were to be God's means of punishing the wicked and that evil would destroy itself. The book concludes with a poem of thanksgiving and great faith.

Zephaniah reveals that only the judgment of God can cleanse Judah of the sins that she has committed. The day of the Lord is coming and the nation must prepare for its salvation. According to the genealogy at the beginning of the book, Zephaniah was active during the reign of King Josiah.

Haggai is a report on the utterances of the prophet Haggai during the second year of the reign of Darius, king of the Persian Empire, in the post-exilic period. The prophet is singularly concerned with the rebuilding of the Temple, which was essential to restoring the nation's religious purity. Haggai also believed that a great messianic age was at hand.

Zechariah is a book of prophesies of a contemporary of Haggai. Zechariah urged the people to rebuild the Temple for he too believed in the imminent coming of the messianic kingdom. Zechariah and Haggai are equally responsible for determining the narrow exclusiveness of post-exilic Judaism, since they declared that the blessings of God would be shared by Judah alone.

Malachi is the last book of the Old Testament and belongs to the period of Nehemiah. The prophet's message is to the priests and the people, charging them with indifference, doubt, and immorality. Malachi tells of the coming day of the Lord and closes the book with a prophecy of John the Baptist.

THE NEW TESTAMENT

The New Testament, which has a total of twenty-seven books, begins with the four Gospels,

which record the life and teachings of Christ from four different viewpoints. Although the Gospels are anonymous, church tradition has assigned them to the four evangelists. Because of their striking similarity of form, language, and content the Gospels according to Matthew, Mark, and Luke are called the Synoptic Gospels; the Gospel according to John is in a different tradition.

Matthew has been pre-eminently the Gospel of the church. It tells us of God's love for Israel and of the fulfillment in Christ of God's promise to the nation. It gives the complete story of Jesus' ministry, death, and resurrection. The Sermon on the Mount, and some of the most precious of Jesus' parables are contained in this Gospel.

Mark is the earliest of the Gospels and contains much of the teaching of Peter. This Gospel presents Jesus as the man of power, the strong and active Son of God; its climax is reached when Peter makes his great confession, "You are the Christ."

Luke, the third Gospel, was written by "the beloved physician," the companion of the apostle Paul. Only in Luke are found the Magnificat, the story of the birth of John the Baptist, the Christmas story of the shepherds, the parables of the good Samaritan, the lost sheep, and the prodigal son, and the great hymns—the *Gloria in Excelsis* and *Nunc Dimitis*. Jesus is presented as the compassionate Savior, healer, redeemer, and friend of the weak. From this Gospel comes a special feeling of the mercy of God as Jesus made men understand it.

John, written by "the disciple whom Jesus loved," tells us who Jesus was and what He is; what He can always mean to those who love Him. This Gospel contains more than the other Gospels about the stories of Lazarus and Nicodemus and Jesus' trial, crucifixion, and resurrection, and about the disciples Andrew, Philip, and Thomas.

The Acts of the Apostles, written by the author of the Gospel according to Luke, is the account of what Jesus' disciples did after His resurrection. It tells about the early Christian church and its missionaires, the baptism of Cornelius, the Council in Jerusalem, and about the conversion of Paul and his journeys to establish churches and to teach. Acts emphasizes that the church is guided continually by the Holy Spirit.

The Letter of Paul to the Romans was written from Corinth about 58 A.D. The purpose of the letter is to secure the active support of the church in Rome for his missionary program. Paul stresses the universality of man's sin but that God saves all men through faith in Christ. He discusses the place of Israel in God's plan of salvation and how Christians should conduct themselves.

The Letters of Paul to the Corinthians were written from Ephesus about 57 A.D. The Christians of Corinth found it hard to live as they knew they should and questioned Paul about their difficulties. In *First Corinthians* Paul answers their question, points out what they have done wrong, and encourages them with his message, "You are Christ's." *Second Corinthians* contains Paul's message of thanksgiving and love. Then he goes on to describe his tribulations as he went about preaching the gospel of Christ.

The Letter of Paul to the Galatians, written in 57 or 58 A.D., probably from Antioch, is the cornerstone of Christian freedom. In Galatians

10

Paul tells of his own conversion and of how he stood firm in his belief that Christ was the Savior of people everywhere, not just those who observed every detail of the Jewish law.

The Letter of Paul to the Ephesians, written about 62 A.D., seems to be a general letter to the churches of Asia Minor. Paul presents God's eternal purpose to save men through faith in Christ; "the dividing wall of hostility" between Jews and Gentiles has been broken down through the cross of Christ. Paul exhorts us to live as worthy, true Christians.

The Letter of Paul to the Philippians was written while Paul was a prisoner in Rome. This Letter Paul's farewell message, is filled with gratitude and affection for his Philippian friends, the church which was perhaps dearest to him.

The Letter of Paul to the Colossians was written by Paul, while he was a prisoner in Rome, to the Christians at Colossae in Asia Minor. Paul writes to encourage them with real truth—that through Christ they have the everlasting love of God.

The Letters of Paul to the Thessalonians were written by Paul from Corinth about 52 A.D. These two Letters are the earliest writings of the N.T. Paul tells these Christians what sort of persons they must be, and that they must do their duty every day and not stand idle, waiting for the Second Coming.

The Letters of Paul to Timothy, written by the apostle to his friend Timothy at Lystra, tell of the conditions in the church and describe the qualifications and duties of church officers. *Second Timothy* contains Paul's request that Timothy come to Rome to see him.

The Letter of Paul to Titus encourages Titus, Paul's "true child in a common faith," to lead the church in Crete.

The Letter of Paul to Philemon, is a personal letter in which the apostle beseeches Philemon to take back a runaway slave, Onesimus. The slave had come to Rome, where Paul was being held prisoner, and there had been converted by Paul.

The Letter to Hebrews, an anonymous book, urges the Hebrew Christian community not to fall back into Judaism and argues for Christian superiority.

The Letter of James, according to tradition written by the brother of our Lord, provides ethical instruction for all Jewish people who have become Christians. It is clear and practical in its dealing with Christian behavior.

The First Letter of Peter was probably written by the apostle Peter from Rome between 64 and 67 A.D. to Christians who had fled Asia Minor. It admonishes the pilgrims to have hope and courage and to trust in the power of God.

The Second Letter of Peter was written by an unknown Christian leader, perhaps a disciple of Peter's, in the middle of the second century. It warns of false teachers who had come into the early church and urges Christians to be brave and patient.

The Letters of John traditionally assigned to the writer of the Fourth Gospel and Revelation, testify that God is love and that love is the test of religion. *Second John* is written to "the elect lady and her children," probably a church; *Third John* is addressed to the beloved Gaius."

The Letter of Jude designates its author as "a servant of Jesus Christ and brother of James." Its message was for Christians wherever unity was threatened by heretical teaching and where Christian doctrinal and moral standards were questioned.

The Revelation to John, or *The Apocalypse*, is the only prophetic book in the N.T. Generally presumed to have been written by John, one of the apostles of Christ, the book is addressed to the seven Christian churches in Asia Minor, whose members were being persecuted by Roman officials. The images and illusions of Revelation are difficult for us to understand today, but to the persecuted members of the seven churches John's message was clearly one of hope, courage, and faith in times of trouble; and that on the Lord's day the faithful would be greatly rewarded.

THE APOCRYPHA

The Apocrypha are those books and portions of books which appear in the Latin Vulgate, either as part of the Old Testament or as an appendix, but are not included in Hebrew Scripture. With the exception of 2 Esdras these books appear in the Septuagint, but are not found in the Hebrew Canon of Holy Scripture.

Because they were included in the Latin Vulgate, the church of the medieval period considered them to be part of the Scriptures. The Council of Trent, in 1546, decreed that the apocryphal books, (with the exception of the Prayer of Manasseh and 1 and 2 Esdras) were to be part of the Canon of the Old Testament and declared anathema on anyone who rejected them.

In Luther's German translation of the Bible (1534), the Apocrypha stand between the Old and New Testaments. Coverdale's English Bible of 1535 gave them the same position. These books had a place in all English translations of the Bible in the sixteenth century and also in the King James Version of 1611. In all of the above translations, mention was made to the effect that the Apocrypha, while not accepted by Protestant and Hebrew Canons, were nonetheless "useful and good to read." However, the Puritans rejected them as not being of divine inspiration and therefore having no authority in the church. Due to this opposition by the Puritans, later editions of the King James Version in general omitted them. Nearly all modern versions of the Bible exclude the Apocrypha although some editions do include it.

The books of the Apocrypha are: 1 and 2 Esdras; Tobit; Judith; Additions to Esther; The Wisdom of Solomon; Ecclesiasticus, or the Wisdom of Jesus the Son of Sirach; Baruch; the Letter of Jeremiah; the Prayer of Azariah and the Song of the Three Young Men; Susanna; Bel and the Dragon; the Prayer of Manasseh; 1 and 2 Maccabees.

THE KINGS OF JUDAH AND ISRAEL

The chart on the following pages outlines the period of Hebrew history when the people were ruled by kings. It sets forth the essential facts about each king and his reign.

The Hebrew monarchy was founded *ca.* 1051 B.C. Saul, David, and Solomon were the first three kings and ruled over all the twelve tribes. Traditionally each king is said to have ruled for forty years.

About 931 B.C. the northern tribes, lead by Jeroboam, revolted from the harsh rule of Rehoboam, Solomon's son. From that time there were two kingdoms where there had been one: the southern kingdom called Judah and the northern kingdom called Israel. In 722 B.C. the Assyrian armies destroyed Samaria, the capital of Israel, and many people were taken as captives into Assyria. Judah with its capital, Jerusalem, was able to survive under the rule of its righteous kings until 586 B.C., when Jerusalem was destroyed by the Assyrians.

It is interesting to note that during the entire history of Judah the king was a member of the Davidic dynasty, in fulfillment of the prophecy of Nathan to David (2 Sam. 7.4–17). At one time the throne was held by Athaliah, an Israelite who married Jehoram, the son of Jehoshaphat. Athaliah usurped the throne after the death of Jehoram and held it for seven years, putting to death all of the Davidic heirs. However, the people of Judah revolted, killed her, and placed Jehoash, a son of Ahaziah who had been kept hidden, on the throne when he was seven years old. In Israel, at various times, nine different families seized the throne. This large number was due to numerous rebellions and assassinations.

The chart gives the names of the kings, with variant spellings as necessary. After the division of the kingdom each column is positioned to show contemporaries. Next is listed the father of the king. Then the length of each reign is given, the number being taken from either Kings or Chronicles. Also the designations of each reign as either "good" or "evil" are those found in the books of the Bible.

THE UNITED KINGDOM
(Established *ca.* 1051 B.C.)

1. Saul
   Son of Kish. Reigned 40 years. Died in battle.
   1 Sam. 9.1—2 Sam. 1.27
   1 Chron. 8.33—10.14

THE HOUSE OF DAVID

1. David
   Son of Jesse. Reigned 40 years.
   1 Sam. 16.1—1 Kings 2.11
   1 Chron. 11.1—29.30

2. Solomon
   Son of David. Reigned 40 years.
   1 Kings 1.11—11.43
   1 Chron. 29.20—2 Chron. 9.31

THE DIVIDED KINGDOM
(Established *ca.* 931 B.C.)

THE KINGDOM OF JUDAH	THE KINGDOM OF ISRAEL
HOUSE OF DAVID, *Cont.*	HOUSE OF JEROBOAM
3. Rehoboam	
Son of Solomon. Reigned 17 years. Evil.	*1. Jeroboam*
1 Kings 11.43—14.31	Son of Nebat. Reigned 22 years. Evil.
2 Chron. 9.31—12.16	1 Kings 12.20—14.20
	2 Chron. 10.2—13.20
4. Abijam (Abijah)	
Son of Rehoboam. Reigned 3 years. Evil.	
1 Kings 14.31—15.8	
2 Chron. 12.16—14.1	
5. Asa	
Son of Abijam. Reigned 41 years. Good.	*2. Nadab*
1 Kings 15.8—24	Son of Jeroboam. Reigned 2 years. Evil. Slain by Baasha.
2 Chron. 14.1—16.14	1 Kings 14.20—15.31

HOUSE OF BAASHA

1. Baasha
Son of Ahijah. Reigned 24 years.
Evil.
1 Kings 15.16—16.7
2 Chron. 16.1–6

2. Elah
Son of Baasha. Reigned 2 years. Evil. Slain
by Zimri.
1 Kings 16.8–14

HOUSE OF ZIMRI

1. Zimri
Captain in Elah's army. Reigned only 7 days.
Realizing his cause was lost, committed
suicide.
1 Kings 16.8–20

HOUSE OF OMRI

1. Omri
Captain in Elah's army. Reigned 12 years.
Evil.
1 Kings 16.16–28

6. Jehoshaphat
Son of Asa. Reigned 25 years.
Good.
1 Kings 15.24—22.50
2 Chron. 17.1—21.1

2. Ahab
Son of Omri. Reigned 22 years. Evil. Slain
in battle.
1 Kings 16.28—22.40
2 Chron. 18.1–34

3. Ahaziah
Son of Ahab. Reigned 2 years. Evil.
1 Kings 22.40—2 Kings 1.1
2 Chron. 20.35–37

4. Jehoram (Joram)
Son of Ahab. Reigned 12 years. Evil.
Slain by Jehu.
2 Kings 1.17—9.29
2 Chron. 22.5–7

7. Jehoram (Joram)
Son of Jehoshaphat. Reigned 8 years.
Evil.
2 Kings 8.16–24
2 Chron. 21.1–20

8. Ahaziah
Son of Jehoram. Reigned 1 year.
Evil. Slain by Jehu.
2 Kings 8.25—9.28
2 Chron. 22.1–9

HOUSE OF JEHU

1. Jehu
Son of Jehoshaphat; grandson often called
"son" of Nimshi. Reigned 28 years. Evil.
2 Kings 9.11—10.36
2 Chron. 22.7–9

Athaliah
Daughter of Ahab, king of Israel, and Jezebel; wife of Jehoram, former king of Judah,
and mother of Ahaziah. When Ahaziah was
slain by Jehu, she, as queen mother, usurped
the throne of Judah. Reigned 7 years. Evil.
Slain by the people of Judah.
2 Kings 11.1–20
2 Chron. 22.10—23.15

9. Jehoash (Joash)
Son of Ahaziah. Having escaped death at
hands of Athaliah, was put on throne at age
of 7, thereby restoring the Davidic dynasty.

Reigned 40 years. Good. Slain by his servants.
2 Kings 11.21—12.21
2 Chron. 24.1–27

2. Jehoahaz
Son of Jehu. Reigned 17 years. Evil.
2 Kings 10.35—13.9

3. Jehoash (Joash)
Son of Jehoahaz. Reigned 16 years.
Evil.
2 Kings 13.9—14.16
2 Chron. 25.17–25

10. Amaziah
Son of Jehoash. Reigned 29 years.
Good. Slain by conspirators.
2 Kings 14.1–20
2 Chron. 24.27—25.28

4. Jeroboam II
Son of Jehoash. Reigned 41 years.
Evil.
2 Kings 13.13—14.29

11. Uzziah (Azariah)
Son of Amaziah. Reigned 52 years.
Good. Became a leper.
2 Kings 14.21—15.7
2 Chron. 26.1–23

12. Jotham
Son of Uzziah. Reigned 16 years.
Good.
2 Kings 15.7–38
2 Chron. 26.23—27.9

5. Zachariah (Zechariah)
Son of Jeroboam II. Reigned 6 months.
Evil. Slain by Shallum.
2 Kings 14.29—15.12

HOUSE OF SHALLUM

1. Shallum
Son of Jabesh. Reigned 1 month.
Evil. Slain by Menahem.
2 Kings 15.10–15

HOUSE OF MENAHEM

1. Menahem
Son of Gadi. Reigned 10 years. Evil.
2 Kings 15.14–22

13. Ahaz
Son of Jotham. Reigned 16 years.
Evil.
2 Kings 15.38—16.20
2 Chron. 27.9—28.27

2. Pekahiah
Son of Menahem. Reigned 2 years.
Evil. Slain by Pekah.
2 Kings 15.22–26

HOUSE OF PEKAH

1. Pekah
Son of Remaliah. Reigned 20 years.
Evil. Slain by Hoshea.
2 Kings 15.25–31
2 Chron. 28.6

14. Hezekiah
Son of Ahaz. Reigned 29 years.
Good.
2 Kings 16.20—20.21
2 Chron. 28.27—32.33

15. Manasseh
Son of Hezekiah. Reigned 55 years.
Evil. Taken in chains to Babylon by the
Assyrians.
2 Kings 20.21—21.18
2 Chron. 32.31—33.20

16. Amon
Son of Manasseh. Reigned 2 years.
Evil. Slain by his servants.
2 Kings 21.18–26
2 Chron. 33.20–25

17. Josiah
Son of Amon. Reigned 31 years.
Good. Slain in battle.
2 Kings 21.24—23.30
2 Chron. 33.25—35.27

18. Jehoahaz (Shallum)
Son of Josiah. Reigned 3 months.
Deposed by Neco and died a prisoner in
Egypt.
2 Kings 23.30–34
2 Chron. 36.1–4

19. Jehoiakim (Eliakim)
Son of Josiah. Reigned 11 years.
Evil. Died just before Jerusalem was captured by Nebuchadnezzar.
2 Kings 23.34—24.6
2 Chron. 36.4–8

20. Jehoiachin (Jeconiah, Coniah)
Son of Johoiakim. Reigned 2 months.
Evil. Taken captive to Babylon; later
released.
2 Kings 24.6—25.30
2 Chron. 36.8–10

FIRST BABYLONIAN CAPTIVITY, 597 B.C.

21. Zedekiah (Mattaniah)
Son of Josiah. Reigned 11 years.
Evil. Blinded and taken prisoner to Babylon,
where he died.
2 Kings 24.17—25.7
2 Chron. 36.10–21

DESTRUCTION OF JERUSALEM AND SECOND DEPORTA-
TION OF CAPTIVES TO BABYLON, 586 B.C.

HOUSE OF HOSHEA

1. Hoshea
Son of Elah. Reigned 9 years. Evil.
Taken captive by Shalmaneser.
2 Kings 13.30—18.12

THE FALL OF SAMARIA AND THE ASSYRIAN CAPTIVITY,
722 B.C.

JEWISH RELIGIOUS AND POLITICAL GROUPS

The following paragraphs give a summary of the various groups of Jews, their history and tenets, in existence in New Testament times.

The *Essenes* appear as a sect soon after the Maccabaean War (*ca.* 150 B.C.). In time they became the first instance of organized monasticism in the Mediterranean area, with the main group established near the Dead Sea. They endeavored to achieve absolute purity by strict observance of the Torah and the Levitical laws of cleanliness; they rejected marriage and the holding of private property. They believed Moses to be a holy prophet, next in rank to God, and denounced the use of animals in temple sacrifices. At one point the Essenes numbered about 4,000 but by Jesus' time they appear to have had little influence on the Jews.

The *Nazirites* (*nāzar* = to separate) were persons of either sex who were consecrated to the Lord by their parents or by voluntary act. This was done under a special vow to God either for life or for a certain period of time as the individual might establish for himself. By this special vow the Nazirite was to abstain from wine and strong drink, wear the hair uncut, and avoid all contact with the dead, and unclean food. John the Baptist and James the Just appear to have been Nazirites.

The origins of the *Pharisees* (*pārūsh* = separated) are obscure but according to rabbinic tradition they were the transmitters of the oral law of Ezra. Their predecessors were the Hasidim, a group which instigated the Maccabean revolt (150 B.C.). They gradually disappeared after the siege of Jerusalem (A.D. 70) but their influence is still felt in the Jewish religion. The Pharisees believed in punishment after death and a resurrection. They were also bound to the precise fulfillment of both the oral traditions and the Torah. Because of their concern with the law, the Pharisees separated themselves from the less observant Jews.

The *Sadducees* represent the aristocratic party which claimed its descent from the sons of Zadok (Ezek. 40.46) who, in the time of Solomon, had control of the Temple. The Sadducees were primarily interested in keeping their privileged position within the Jewish society and favored the

Graeco-Roman culture as a means of maintaining their favorable status; thus scorning the other Jewish sects. They acknowledged as binding only the written law, and rejected the oral traditions observed by the Scribes and the Pharisees.

The *Samaritans* were a people of mixed blood (partly Jewish) established by Sargon in Samaria after he destroyed the kingdom of Israel (*ca.* 720 B.C.). They were taught a form of the Hebrew religion which they added to their own religious ceremonies. Enmity soon grew up between the two nations after the return of the Jews from captivity. The Samaritans tried to prevent the rebuilding of Jerusalem and were aggressive and insulting to their neighbors. Today there is a small settlement of Samaritans in the town of Nablus, near the site of ancient Shechem. The Samaritan religion asserts to be the pure and untarnished teachings of Moses, as they accept only the Pentateuch as holy scripture.

The *Scribes* (*Sopherim*) became, after the Exile, the interpreters and administrators of the Mosaic Torah, the ancient law of Israel. They were in charge of the Houses of Assembly, located throughout the country, for teaching and worship. The Scribes developed a number of functions, including those of preacher, lawyer, scholar, and teacher. Because there was such a wide variety of duties among the Scribes there arose much difference of opinion and interpretation concerning tradition and ceremony.

The *Zealots* were a sect founded by Judas of Gamala in opposition to the census of Quirinius (A.D. 6 or 7). A militant group, they were intensely nationalistic and ardent in their practice of the law. They despised the foreign domination by Rome and recognised only the authority of God. They hoped for an earthly Messiah but were willing to hasten deliverance by political revolt. During Jesus' early ministry they endeavored to persuade Him to join their sect. During the siege of Jerusalem (A.D. 70) their fanaticism made them not only opponents of the Romans but of the Jews as well.

PARABLES AND MIRACLES IN THE BIBLE

PARABLES IN THE OLD TESTAMENT

Parable	By whom and to whom spoken	Reference
The trees choosing a king	by Jotham to the Shechemites	Judg. 9.7–15
Samson's riddle	by Samson to his companions	Judg. 14.14
The poor man's ewe lamb	by Nathan to David	2 Sam. 12.1–4
The two sons and avengers	by the widow of Tekoa to David	2 Sam. 14.6–11
The escaped captive	by a man of the sons of the prophets to Ahab	1 Kings 20.35–40
Micaiah's vision	by Micaiah to Ahab	1 Kings 22.19–23
Thistle and cedar	by Jehoash to Amaziah	2 Kings 14.9; 2 Chron. 25.18
The drunkard	by Solomon to the people of Israel	Prov. 23.29–35
The sluggard and his vineyard	by Solomon to the people of Israel	Prov. 24.30–34
The unfruitful vineyard	by Isaiah to Egypt	Isa. 5.1–7
The plowman	by Isaiah to the people of Israel	Isa. 28.23–29
Eagles and the vine	by Ezekiel to the people of Israel	Ezek. 17.2–10
Lion's whelps	by Ezekiel to the people of Israel	Ezek. 19.2–9
The two harlots	by Ezekiel to the people of Israel	Ezek. 23.1–49
The boiling pot	by Ezekiel to the people of Israel	Ezek. 24.3–5
Cedar of Lebanon	by Ezekiel to Egypt	Ezek. 31.3–18
Dragon in the seas	by Ezekiel to Pharaoh	Ezek. 32.1–16
Shepherds and the flock	by Ezekiel to the people of Israel	Ezek. 34.1–31
Dry bones in the valley	by Ezekiel to the people of Israel	Ezek. 37.1–28
living waters	by Ezekiel to the people of Israel	Ezek. 47.1–23

For other parables see Amos 7.1—9.15; Zechariah 1.7—6.8; 11.3–17.

MIRACLES IN THE OLD TESTAMENT

Preceding the Exodus

	Reference
Destruction of Sodom and Gomorrah	Gen. 19.24
Lot's wife turned into a pillar of salt	Gen. 19.26
The birth of Isaac	Gen. 21.1–3
The burning bush not consumed	Ex. 3.2

In Egypt

Aaron's rod turned into a serpent	Ex. 7.10–12
The ten plagues:	
1. Water made blood	Ex. 7.20–25
2. Frogs	Ex. 8.5–14
3. Gnats	Ex. 8.16–18
4. Flies	Ex. 8.20–24
5. Death to herds and flocks	Ex. 9.3–6
6. Boils and sores	Ex. 9.8–11
7. Thunder and hail	Ex. 9.22–26
8. Locusts	Ex. 10.12–19
9. Darkness	Ex. 10.21–23
10. The first-born slain	Ex. 12.29–30
Parting of the Red Sea	Ex. 14.21–31

In the Wilderness

The sweetening of the waters of Marah	Ex. 15.23–25
Feeding with manna	Ex. 16.14–35
Water from the rock at Rephidim	Ex. 17.5–7
Death of Nadab and Abihu for offering unholy fire	Lev. 10.1–2
Burning of the camp at Taberah	Num. 11.1–3
Death of Korah, Dathan, and Abiram	Num. 16.31–35
Aaron's rod bears buds, blossoms, and almonds	Num. 17.8
Water from the rock at Meribah	Num. 20.7–11
The healing powers of the bronze serpent	Num. 21.8–9
Stopping of the river Jordan	Jos. 3.14–17

In Canaan—under Joshua

Fall of the walls of Jericho	Jos. 6.6–25
Staying of the sun and moon	Jos. 10.12–14

	Reference
Strength of Samson	Judg. 14.1— 16.30
The water flows from the hollow place at Lehi	Judg. 15.19.
Men of Bethshemesh slain for looking into the ark	1 Sam. 6.19
Thunderstorm causes panic in Philistine army	1 Sam. 7.10–12
Thunder and rain in harvest	1 Sam. 12.17–18
Sound of marching in balsam trees	2 Sam. 5.23–25

Under the Kings

Death of Uzzah for touching the ark of God	2 Sam. 6.7
Withering of Jeroboam's hand and destruction of the altar	1 Kings 13.4–5

By Elijah

Drought, fire from heaven, and rain at Elijah's prayer; Elijah wondrously fed	1 Kings 17.1—19.18
The increase of the oil and meal at Zarephath	1 Kings 17.14–16
The raising of the widow's son at Zarephath	1 Kings 17.17–24
Wall of Aphek falls upon thousands of Syrians	1 Kings 20.30
Burning of the captains and their companies	2 Kings 1.10–12
Dividing of the river Jordan	2 Kings 2.8
Elijah taken by a whirlwind into heaven	2 Kings 2.11

By Elisha

Dividing of the river Jordan	2 Kings 2.14
The waters of Jericho made wholesome	2 Kings 2.21–22
Bears destroy forty-two mocking boys at Bethel	2 Kings 2.24
Water supplied to the allied armies in Moab	2 Kings 3.16–20
Increase of the widow's oil	2 Kings 4.2–7
Raising of the Shunammite's son	2 Kings 4.32–37
The deadly pottage purified with meal	2 Kings 4.38–41
Feeding one hundred men with twenty loaves	2 Kings 4.42–44
Naaman's leprosy cured; the leprosy transferred to Gehazi	2 Kings 5.10–14, 27
An iron axe floats on the water	2 Kings 6.5–7
The Syrian army struck with blindness	2 Kings 6.18–20
Elisha's bones revive a dead man	2 Kings 13.21

Recorded by Isaiah

Destruction of Sennacherib's army	2 Kings 19.35
The shadow goes back on the sundial of Ahaz	2 Kings 20.9–11

During Captivity

Deliverance of Shadrach, Meshach, and Abednego from the furnace	Dan. 3.19–27
Daniel is saved from the den of lions	Dan. 6.16–23

Miscellaneous

Dagon falls twice before the ark of God; Philistines afflicted by tumors	1 Sam. 5.1–12
Uzziah is smitten with leprosy	2 Chron. 26.16–21
Deliverance of Jonah from the great fish	Jonah 2.1–10

PARABLES OF OUR LORD

Parable	Lesson	Matthew	Mark	Luke	John
Recorded in one gospel only					
Weeds among the wheat	Good and evil in life	13.24–30			
The hidden treasure	Value of the gospel	13.44			
The pearl of great price	Finding salvation	13.45–46			
The full net	The all-inclusive Church	13.47–48			
The unmerciful servant	Duty of forgiveness	18.23–34			
Laborers in the vineyard	The last will be first, and the first last	20.1–16			
The father and two sons	Insincerity and repentance	21.28–32			
Marriage of the king's son	Necessity for righteousness	22.1–14			
Wise and foolish maidens	Careful and heedless preparation	25.1–13			
The talents	Use of advantages	25.14–30			
The sheep and the goats	Righteousness brings eternal life	25.31–46			

18

Parable	Lesson	Matthew	Mark	Luke	John
Growth of a seed of grain	Growth in religion		4.26–29		
The watchful doorkeeper	Watchfulness		13.34–36		
The two debtors	Gratitude for forgiveness			7.41–50	
The good Samaritan	Compassion for all			10.30–37	
The friend at midnight	Perseverance in prayer			11.5–8	
The rich fool	No anxiety for worldly goods			12.16–21	
The waiting servants	Expectancy of the Second Coming			12.35–40	
Faithful and wise steward	Conscientiousness in trust			12.42–48	
The barren fig tree	Unfruitfulness under grace			13.6–9	
The great banquet	Universality of the divine call			14.16–24	
The tower; the warring king	Prudence; self-denial			14.28–33	
The lost coin	Joy over penitence			15.8–10	
The prodigal son	Father's love for a returning sinner			15.11–32	
The dishonest steward	Faithfulness to trust			16.1–8	
The rich man and Lazarus	Hopeless future to the unfaithful			16.19–31	
The farmer and his servant	Duty to God			17.7–10	
The unrighteous judge	Vindication by continuing prayer			18.1–8	
Pharisee and tax collector	Self-righteousness and humility			18.9–14	
Nobleman and the ten pounds	Diligence rewarded, sloth punished			19.12–27	
The bread of life	Eternal salvation through Christ				6.25–59
Shepherd and the sheep	God revealed through Christ				10.1–39
Vine and the branches	God's love through Christ				15.1–27

Recorded in two gospels

Parable	Lesson	Matthew	Mark	Luke	John
Houses on rock and on sand	Christ the true foundation	7.24–27		6.48–49	
The leaven	Pervading influence of religion	13.33		13.20–21	
The lost sheep	Joy over the penitent	18.12–14		15.4–7	

Recorded in three gospels

Parable	Lesson	Matthew	Mark	Luke	John
The lamp under a bushel	Dissemination of truth	5.14–16	4.21–23	8.16–18	
New cloth on old garment; new wine in old wineskins	Old forms and new faith	9.16–17	2.19–22	5.36–39	
The sower	Exercise of understanding	13.18–30	4.3–9	8.5–8	
The mustard seed	Spread of the gospel	13.31–32	4.31–32	13.18–19	
Vineyard and husbandmen	Rejection of Christ by the Jews	21.33–41	12.1–8	20.9–16	
Young leaves of the fig tree	Indications of the Second Coming	24.32	13.38	21.29–30	

Other passages sometimes designated as parables

Parable	Lesson	Matthew	Mark	Luke	John
The speck and the log	Judgment of others	7.3–5		6.41–42	
The wedding guests	Indication of the Second Coming	9.15	12.19–20	5.34–35	
Children at play	Rejections of the gospel	11.16–17		7.31–32	
Seven unclean spirits	Sloth in faith	12.43–45		11.24–26	
Old and new treasures	Combining old and new	13.52			
The rejected stones	God's love of outcasts	21.42–45	12.10–11	20.17–18	
The shut door	Aquaintances meaningless in Heaven			13.25–27	
Places of honor	Humble to be exalted			14.7–11	

MIRACLES OF OUR LORD

		Matthew	Mark	Luke	John
Narrated in one gospel only					
Two blind men cured		9.27–31			
The dumb demoniac healed		9.32–33			

	Matthew	Mark	Luke	John
The shekel in the mouth of the fish	17.24–27			
A deaf and dumb man healed		7.31–37		
A blind man cured		8.22–26		
Jesus passes unseen through the multitude			4.28–30	
The great catch of fish			5.1–11	
The widow's son is raised from the dead			7.11–15	
A woman freed from her infirmity			13.11–13	
A man with dropsy cured			14.1–4	
Ten lepers cleansed			17.11–19	
Servant's ear healed (Malchus)			22.50–51	
Water changed to wine at Cana				2.1–11
Official's son healed of fever				4.46–54
Invalid man cured at Jerusalem				5.1–9
Jesus passes through the crowd in the temple				8.59
Man born blind cured at Jerusalem				9.1–7
Lazarus raised from the dead				11.38–44
Falling to the ground of soldiers				18.5–6
The catch of 153 fish				21.1–14

Narrated in two gospels

	Matthew	Mark	Luke	John
Centurion's paralyzed servant cured	8.5–13		7.1–10	
The blind and dumb demoniac healed	12.22		11.14	
Daughter of the Syrophoenician woman healed	15.21–28	7.24–30		
The four thousand fed	15.32–38	8.1–9		
The fig tree cursed by Jesus	21.19	11.14		
A demoniac in the synagogue cured		1.23–26	4.33–35	

Narrated in three gospels

	Matthew	Mark	Luke	John
The leper cured	8.2–3	1.40–41	5.12–13	
Peter's mother-in-law cured of a fever	8.14–15	1.30–31	4.38–39	
The storm at sea stilled	8.23–26	4.35–39	8.22–24	
The devils entered into swine	8.28–32	5.1–13	8.26–33	
The paralytic cured	9.2–7	2.3–12	5.18–25	
Jairus' daughter raised to life	9.18–26	5.22–42	8.41–56	
A woman's hemorrhage cured	9.20–22	5.25–29	8.43–48	
A man's whithered hand cured	12.10–13	3.1–5	6.6–11	
Jesus walks on the sea	14.25–27	6.48–51		6.19–20
The epileptic boy cured	17.14–18	9.17–27	9.37–42	
A blind man cured	20.30–34	10.46–52	18.35–43	

Narrated in four gospels

	Matthew	Mark	Luke	John
Feeding the five thousand	14.15–21	6.35–44	9.10–17	6.1–14

MIRACLES RECORDED IN THE ACTS OF THE APOSTLES

	Reference
The disciples are filled with the Holy Spirit, with the accompanying signs	2.1–47
The gift of tongues	2.4–11; 10.44–48
Lame man at the Beautiful Gate of the temple	3.1–26
Death of Ananias and Sapphira	5.1–11
Peter healing the sick in the streets	5.12–16
Prison doors opened for the apostles by an angel	5.17–21
Stephen's vision of Christ at the right hand of God	7.55–56
Philip casts out unclean spirits	8.6–7
Christ appears to Saul on the way to Damascus	9.1–9; 22.6–11; 26.12–18
Saul's blindness healed by Ananias	9.17–19; 22.12–13
Aeneas' paralysis healed by Peter	9.33–34
Tabitha (Dorcas) raised to life by Peter	9.36–41
Vision of Cornelius	10.3–6, 30–32
Vision of Peter	10.10–16; 11.5–10
Prophecies of Agabus	11.27–28; 21.10–11
Peter's release from prison	12.6–10
Elymas blinded by Paul	13.9–11
Healing of the cripple at Lystra by Paul	14.8–10
Paul's vision of a man of Macedonia	16.9
Paul casts out spirit of divination from slave girl	16.16–18
Earthquake at Philippi	16.25–26
Extraordinary miracles done by Paul at Ephesus	19.11–12

	Reference
Evil spirit puts Sceva's sons to flight	19.13–16
Paul raises Eutychus to life	20.9–12
Appearances of Christ to Paul	22.17–21; 23.11; 27.23–24
Paul unharmed by a viper's bite	28.3–6
Paul heals Publius' father and others at Malta	28.8–9

MIRACLES REFERRED TO IN THE EPISTLES AND REVELATION

	Reference
Miracles by Paul and others	Rom. 15.18–19; 1 Cor. 12.8–10; 28–31; 14.18; Gal. 3.5; 1 Tim. 1.20
Miracle of tongues	1 Cor. 14.27–33
Appearances of Christ after His resurrection	1 Cor. 15.3–8
Visions and revelations of Paul	2 Cor. 12.1–4, 12
Powers of the age to come	Heb. 2.4; 6.5
The visions of John at Patmos	Rev. 1.10–11; 4.1—22.21

A HARMONY OF THE FOUR GOSPELS

(References in *Italics* are verses out of the order in which they appear in their respective Gospels. The publishers gratefully acknowledge the use of *Gospel Parallels, a Synopsis of the First Three Gospels*, edited by Burton H. Throckmorton, Jr., in preparing this chart of Gospel Harmony.)

	Matthew	Mark	Luke	John
I. Gospel History before Jesus' Public Ministry				
1. Prologue to the gospel	—	—	1.1–4	1.1–18
2. The promise of John the Baptist's birth	—	—	1.5–25	—
3. The salutation of Mary; Mary visits Elizabeth	—	—	1.26–56	—
4. The birth of John the Baptist	—	—	1.57–80	—
5. The birth of Jesus; the shepherds	1.18–25	—	2.1–20	—
6. Visit of the wise men	2.1–12	—	—	—
7. Circumcision of Jesus; presentation in the temple	—	—	2.21–40	—
8. Flight into Egypt; Herod slays the babies of Bethlehem; return from Egypt	2.13–23	—	—	—
9. Jesus at twelve years of age	—	—	2.41–52	—
II. Preparation for Jesus' Public Ministry				
10. Of John the Baptist and his ministry	3.1–12	1.1–8	3.1–18	1.19–34
11. John's imprisonment	—	—	3.19–20	—
12. The baptism of Jesus	3.13–17	1.9–11	3.21–22	—
13. The genealogy of Jesus	1.1–17	—	3.23–38	—
14. The temptation of Jesus	4.1–11	1.12–13	4.1–13	—
III. Jesus' Public Ministry in Galilee				
15. Jesus' first miracle (water made wine); Jesus visits Capernaum	—	—	—	2.1–12
16. Jesus cleanses the temple during the Passover	—	—	—	2.13–25
17. Nicodemus visits Jesus at night ("God so loved the world")	—	—	—	3.1–21
18. Jesus remains and baptizes, through his disciples, in Judea; John the Baptist again testifies to Jesus	—	—	—	3.22—4.3
19. Jesus converses with the woman of Samaria	—	—	—	4.4–42
20. Jesus arrives in Galilee; his first preaching there	4.12–17	1.14–15	4.14–15	4.43–45
21. Jesus' first rejection at Nazareth	—	—	4.16–30	—

	Matthew	Mark	Luke	John
22. The miraculous catch of fish; the call of the first disciples	4.18–22	1.16–20	5.1–11	*1.35–41*
23. Jesus in the synagogue at Capernaum; heals a demoniac	*7.28–29*	1.21–28	4.31–37	*7.46*
24. Jesus heals Peter's mother-in-law and others	*8.14–17*	1.29–34	4.38–41	—
25. Jesus departs from Capernaum	—	1.35–38	4.42–43	—
26. A preaching journey in Galilee	4.23–25	1.39	4.44	—

A. The Sermon on the Mount (or, the Plain)

	Matthew	Mark	Luke	John
27. Introduction	5.1–2	—	6.20	—
28. The Beatitudes	5.3–12	—	6.20–23	—
29. The Woes	—	—	6.24–26	—
30. The parables of salt and of light	5.13–16	*9.50*	*11.33–36; 14.34–35*	—
31. On the law	5.17–20	—	*16.16–17*	—
32. On murder	5.21–26	—	*12.57–59*	—
33. On adultery and lust	5.27–30	—	—	—
34. On divorce	5.31–32	—	*16.18*	—
35. On swearing; on retaliation	5.33–42	—	*6.29–30*	—
36. On love of one's enemies	5.43–48	—	*6.27–28, 32–36*	—
37. On almsgiving; on prayer	6.1–8	—	—	—
38. The Lord's Prayer	6.9–15	—	*11.1–4*	—
39. On fasting; on treasures	6.16–21	—	*12.33–34*	—
40. The sound eye	6.22–23	—	*11.34–36*	—
41. On serving two masters	6.24	—	*16.13*	—
42. On anxiety	6.25–34	—	*12.22–31*	—
43. On judging	7.1–5	—	*6.37–42*	—
44. On profaning the holy	7.6	—	—	—
45. God's answering of prayer	7.7–11	—	*11.9–13*	—
46. The Golden Rule	7.12	—	6.31	—
47. The narrow gate	7.13–14	—	*13.23–24*	—
48. The test of a good man	7.15–20	—	6.43–45	—
49. Warning against self-deception	7.21–23	—	*6.46; 13.26–27*	—
50. Hearers and doers of the Word	7.24–27	—	6.47–49	—
51. The end of the Sermon	7.28–29	—	—	*7.46*

B. Continuing Jesus' Public Ministry in Galilee

	Matthew	Mark	Luke	John
52. The healing of a leper	8.1–4	1.40–45	5.12–16	—
53. The healing of a centurion's servant	8.5–13	—	7.1–10	*4.46–54*
54. The healing of the widow's son at Nain	—	—	7.11–17	—
55. The nature of discipleship	8.18–22	—	*9.57–62*	—
56. The healing of the paralytic at Capernaum	9.1–8	2.1–12	5.17–26	*5.8–9*
57. The call of Levi (Matthew)	9.9–13	2.13–17	5.27–32	—
58. The question about fasting	9.14–17	2.18–22	5.33–39	—
59. Jesus heals the man at Bethzatha in Jerusalem; the testimony to Jesus	—	—	—	*5.1–47*
60. Two blind men healed	9.27–31	—	—	—
61. The healing of a dumb demoniac	9.32–34	*3.22–27*	*11.14–23*	—
62. The sending out of the twelve disciples	9.35—10.16	—	*10.1–16*	*1.42; 4.35*
63. The fate of the disciples	10.17–25	*13.9–13*	*21.12–17*	*13.16; 14.26; 15.20*
64. Exhortation to fearless confession	10.26–33	—	*12.2–12*	*14.26*
65. Division in households	10.34–36	—	*12.49–56*	—
66. Conditions of discipleship	10.37–39	—	*14.25–33*	*12.25*
67. End of the discourse to the disciples	10.40—11.1	—	*10.16*	*5.23; 12.44–45*
68. John's question to Jesus	11.2–6	—	7.18–23	—
69. Jesus' words about John	11.7–19	—	7.24–35	—
70. Woes on the cities of Galilee	11.20–24	—	*10.13–15*	—
71. Jesus' thanksgiving to the Father	11.25–27	—	*10.21–22*	*3.35; 7.29; 10.14–15; 17.2*
72. Comfort for the heavy laden	11.28–30	—	—	—
73. Plucking ears of grain on the sabbath	12.1–8	2.23–28	6.1–5	*5.10*
74. The healing of the man with a withered hand	12.9–14	3.1–6	6.6–11	—
75. Jesus heals the multitudes	12.15–21	3.7–12	6.17–19	—
76. The call of the twelve	*10.1–4*	3.13–19	6.12–16	*1.42*
77. The woman with the ointment	*26.6–13*	*14.3–9*	7.36–50	*12.1–8*

22

	Matthew	Mark	Luke	John
78. The ministering women	—	—	8.1–3	—
79. Accusations against Jesus; a house divided	12.22–37	3.20–30	11.14–23	7.20; 8.48, 52
80. Against seeking for signs	12.38–42	8.11–12	11.29–32	—
81. The return of the evil spirit	12.43–45	—	11.24–26	—
82. Jesus' true relatives	12.46–50	3.31–35	8.19–21	15.14
83. Jesus teaches by parables: the sower, the tares, the seed growing secretly, the mustard seed, the leaven, the hidden treasure, the pearl, the dragnet, the householder	13.1–52	4.1–34	8.4–18; 10.23–24; 13.18–21	12.40
84. The stilling of the storm	8.23–27	4.35–41	8.22–25	—
85. The Gerasene (Gadarene) demoniac	8.28–34	5.1–20	8.26–39	—
86. Jairus' daughter and a woman's faith	9.18–26	5.21–43	8.40–56	—
87. Jesus is again rejected at Nazareth	13.53–58	6.1–6	—	4.44; 6.42; 7.5, 15
88. The sending out of the twelve	9.35; 10.1–11, 14	6.6–13	9.1–6	—
89. Herod thinks Jesus is John, risen	14.1–2	6.14–16	9.7–9	—
90. The death of John	14.3–12	6.17–29	—	—
91. The return of the twelve and the feeding of the 5,000	14.13–21	6.30–44	9.10–17	6.1–14
92. Walking on the water	14.22–33	6.45–52	—	6.15–21
93. Jesus' discourse on the bread of life	—	—	—	6.22–71
94. Healings at Gennesaret	14.34–36	6.53–56	—	—
95. What defiles a man	15.1–20	7.1–23	—	—
96. The Syrophoenician woman	15.21–28	7.24–30	—	—
97. Healing of many; healing of the deaf mute	15.29–31	7.31–37	—	—
98. The feeding of the 4,000	15.32–39	8.1–10	—	—
99. The Pharisees seek a sign	16.1–4	8.11–13	11.29–32; 12.54–56	6.30
100. A discourse on leaven	16.5–12	8.14–21	12.1	—
101. The blind man at Bethsaida	—	8.22–26	—	9.1–7
102. Peter's confession at Caesarea Philippi; first prediction of the Passion	16.13–23	8.27–33	9.18–22	6.68–69; 20.21–23
103. The conditions of discipleship	16.24–28	8.34–9.1	9.23–27	12.25
104. The transfiguration	17.1–8	9.2–8	9.28–36	1.14
105. The coming of Elijah	17.9–13	9.9–13	—	—
106. The epileptic boy healed	17.14–21	9.14–29	9.37–43a	14.9
107. The second prediction of the Passion	17.22–23	9.30–32	9.43b–45	7.1
108. The temple tax	17.24–27	—	—	—
109. The dispute about greatness	18.1–5	9.33–37	9.46–48	3.3, 5; 12.44–45; 13.20
110. The strange exorcist	—	9.38–41	9.49–50	—
111. On temptations	18.6–9	9.42–48	17.1–2	—
112. Concerning salt	5.13	9.49–50	14.34–35	—
113. The lost sheep	18.10–14	—	15.1–10	—
114. On reproving one's brother	18.15–20	—	17.3	20.23
115. On reconciliation	18.21–22	—	17.3–4	—
116. The parable of the unmerciful servant	18.23–35	—	—	—
117. Jesus goes to Jerusalem at the feast of Tabernacles; His discourses there	—	—	—	7.1–53
118. A woman taken in adultery is brought before Jesus	—	—	—	8.1–11
119. Jesus declares Himself the light of the world; unbelieving Jews attempt to stone Him	—	—	—	8.12–59
120. Jesus heals a beggar blind from birth	—	—	—	9.1–41
121. The Good Shepherd	—	—	—	10.1–21

C. Luke's Special Section

	Matthew	Mark	Luke	John
122. The Samaritan villagers	—	—	9.51–56	—
123. The nature of discipleship	8.18–22	—	9.57–62	—
124. The sending out of the seventy	9.35–10.16	—	10.1–16	4.35; 5.23
125. The return of the seventy	—	—	10.17–20	12.31
126. Jesus' gratitude to the Father	11.25–27	—	10.21–24	10.15; 17.2
127. The blessedness of the disciples	13.16–17	—	10.23–24	—
128. The lawyer's question	22.34–40	12.28–31	10.25–28	—
129. The parable of the good Samaritan	—	—	10.29–37	—

23

	Matthew	Mark	Luke	John
130. Mary and Martha	—	—	10.38–42	11.1–3
131. The friend at midnight	—	—	11.5–8	—
132. The answer to prayer	7.7–11	—	11.9–13	—
133. The Beelzebul controversy	9.32–34; 12.22–30	—	11.14–23	—
134. The blessedness of Jesus' mother	—	—	11.27–28	—
135. The sign for this generation	12.38–42; 16.1–4	8.11–12	11.29–32	—
136. Concerning light	5.14–16; 6.22–23	—	11.33–36	—
137. Discourse against the Pharisees	23.1–36	12.37–40	11.37– 12.1	—
138. Exhortation to fearless confession	10.19–20, 20–33; 12.32	4.22; 8.38	12.2–12	14.26
139. The parable of the rich fool	—	—	12.13–21	—
140. Cares about earthly things	6.16–21, 25–34	—	12.22–34	—
141. Watchfulness and faithfulness	24.43–51	13.32–33	12.35–46	13.4–5
142. The servant's wages	—	—	12.47–48	—
143. Interpreting the present time	10.34–36; 16.1–4	—	12.49–56	12.27
144. Agreement with one's accuser	5.25–26	—	12.57–59	—
145. Repentance or destruction	—	—	13.1–9	—
146. Healing of the woman with a spirit of infirmity	—	—	13.10–17	—
147. Parables of the mustard seed, of the leaven	13.31–33	4.30–32	13.18–21	—
148. Exclusion from the kingdom	7.13–14; 25.10–12; 7.22–23	—	13.22–30	—
149. The departure from Galilee	—	—	13.31–33	—
150. The lament over Jerusalem	23.37–39	—	13.34–35	—
151. The healing of a man with dropsy	—	—	14.1–6	—
152. Teaching on humility	—	—	14.7–14	—
153. The parable of the great supper	22.1–14	—	14.15–24	—
154. The cost of discipleship	10.26–33, 37–39	—	14.25–35	—
155. The lost sheep and the lost coin	18.12–14	—	15.1–10	—
156. The prodigal son	—	—	15.11–32	—
157. The unjust steward	6.24	—	16.1–13	—
158. The hypocrisy of the Pharisees	—	—	16.14–15	—
159. About the law and about divorce	5.17–20, 31–32; 11.12–13	—	16.16–18	—
160. The rich man and Lazarus	—	—	16.19–31	—
161. On causing sin	18.6–9	9.42–48	17.1–2	—
162. On forgiveness	18.15, 21–22	—	17.3–4	—
163. On faith	17.20	—	17.5–6	—
164. The servant's wages	—	—	17.7–10	—
165. The healing of ten lepers	—	—	17.11–19	—
166. On the kingdom of God	24.23–25	13.21–23	17.20–21	—
167. The day of the Son of man	24.26–28, 37–41	—	17.22–37	—
168. The parable of the unjust judge	—	—	18.1–8	—
169. The parable of the Pharisee and the publican	—	—	18.9–14	—

IV. The Judean Ministry

A. The Journey to Jerusalem

	Matthew	Mark	Luke	John
170. Marriage and divorce	19.1–12	10.1–12	—	—
171. Jesus blesses the children	19.13–15	10.13–16	18.15–17	3.3, 5
172. The rich young man	19.16–30	10.17–31	18.18–30	—
173. The parable of the laborers in the vineyard	20.1–10	—	—	—
174. The third prediction of the Passion	20.17–19	10.32–34	18.31–34	—
175. Jesus and the sons of Zebedee	20.20–28	10.35–45	22.24–27	—
176. The healing of Bartimaeus	20.29–34	10.46–52	18.35–43	—
177. Zacchaeus	—	—	19.1–10	—
178. The parable of the pounds	25.14–30	—	19.11–27	—

B. The Days in Jerusalem

	Matthew	Mark	Luke	John
179. The entry into Jerusalem; prediction of the destruction of Jerusalem; Jesus in the temple	21.1–17	11.1–11	19.28–46	12.12–50; 2.13–15
180. Jesus keeps the feast of Dedication at Jerusalem	—	—	—	10.22–39

	Matthew	Mark	Luke	John
181. Jesus goes to Bethany; raises Lazarus from the dead	—	—	—	10.40—11.44
182. A meeting of the chief priests and Pharisees	—	—	—	11.45–53
183. Jesus at Ephraim; the coming of the Passover	—	—	—	11.54–57
184. The cursing of the fig tree	21.18–19	11.12–14	—	—
185. The cleansing of the temple	21.12–13	11.15–19	19.45–48	2.13–17
186. The meaning of the withered fig tree	21.20–22	11.20–26	—	14.13–14
187. The question about authority	21.23–27	11.27–33	20.1–8	2.18
188. The parable of the two sons	21.28–32	—	—	—
189. The parable of the wicked tenants	21.33–46	12.1–12	20.9–19	—
190. The parable of the marriage feast (great supper)	22.1–14	—	14.16–24	—
191. Question concerning tribute to Caesar	22.15–22	12.13–17	20.20–26	3.2
192. Question concerning the resurrection	22.23–33	12.18–27	20.27–40	—
193. The great commandment	22.34–40	12.28–34	10.25–28	—
194. About David's son	22.41–46	12.35–37	20.41–44	—
195. Woes against the Pharisees	23.1–36	12.37–40	20.45–47; 11.37–52	—
196. The lament over Jerusalem	23.37–39	—	13.34–35	—
197. The widow's gift	—	12.41–44	21.1–4	—
198. Prediction of the destruction of the temple	24.1–3	13.1–4	21.5–7	—
199. The signs of the parousia	24.4–8	13.5–8	21.8–11	—
200. The beginning of the troubles	24.9–14	13.9–13	21.12–19	14.26; 15.21; 16.2
201. The desolating sacrilege	24.15–22	13.14–20	21.20–24	—
202. The culmination of the troubles	24.23–25	13.21–23	17.20–23	—
203. The day of the Son of man	24.26–28	—	17.23–24, 37	—
204. The parousia of the Son of man	24.29–31	13.24–27	21.25–28	—
205. The parable of the fig tree	24.32–33	13.28–29	21.29–31	—
206. The time of the parousia	24.34–36	13.30–32	21.32–33	—
207. Mark's ending to the discourse	—	13.33–37	—	—
208. Luke's ending to the discourse	—	—	21.34–36	—
209. The need for watchfulness	24.37–41	—	17.26–27, 34–35	—
210. Watchfulness and faithfulness	24.42–51	—	12.39–46	—
211. The parable of the ten maidens	25.1–13	—	—	—
212. The parable of the talents	25.14–30	—	19.12–27	—
213. The last judgment	25.31–46	—	—	5.28–29
214. A summary of the days spent in Jerusalem	—	—	21.37–38	—

C. The Passion Narrative

	Matthew	Mark	Luke	John
215. The conspiracy against Jesus	26.1–5	14.1–2	22.1–2	11.47–53
216. The anointing at Bethany	26.6–13	14.3–9	7.36–50	12.1–11
217. The betrayal by Judas	26.14–16	14.10–11	22.3–6	18.2–5
218. Preparation for the Passover	26.17–19	14.12–16	22.7–13	—
219. Jesus washes the feet of his disciples	—	—	—	13.1–20
220. The traitor	26.20–25	14.17–21	22.14, 21–23	13.21–30
221. The institution of the Lord's Supper	26.26–29	14.22–25	22.15–20	—
222. Last words: the betrayal foretold; greatness in the kingdom of God; Peter's denial prophesied; the two swords	19.28; 20.25–28	10.42–45	22.21–38	13.4–5, 12–14; 36–38
223. Jesus' farewell discourse; His intercessory prayer	—	—	—	13.31—17.26
224. The way to Gethsemane; Peter's denial prophesied	26.30–35	14.26–31	22.39; 22.31–34	18.1; 13.36–38; 16.32
225. Jesus in Gethsemane	26.36–46	14.32–42	22.40–46	18.1; 12.27; 14.31 18.11
226. Jesus taken captive	26.47–56	14.43–52	22.47–53	18.2–12, 20
227. Jesus before the Sanhedrin and others; Peter's denial	26.57–75	14.53–72	22.54–71	18.13–27
228. Jesus delivered to Pilate	27.1–2	15.1	23.1	18.28–32
229. The death of Judas	27.3–10	—	—	—
230. The trial before Pilate	27.11–14	15.2–5	23.2–5	18.33–37; 19.6, 9–10
231. Jesus before Herod	—	—	23.6–16	—

	Matthew	Mark	Luke	John
232. The sentence of death	27.15–26	15.6–15	23.17–25	18.38–40; 19.4–16
233. The mocking by the soldiers	27.27–31	15.16–20	—	19.1–3
234. The road to Golgotha; the Crucifixion	27.32–44	15.21–32	23.26–43	19.17–24
235. The death on the cross; the burial of Jesus	27.45–61	15.33–47	23.44–56	19.25–42
236. The guard at the tomb	27.62–66	—	—	—

V. The Resurrection

	Matthew	Mark	Luke	John
237. The empty tomb	28.1–10	16.1–11	24.1–12	20.1–18
238. The bribing of the Roman soldiers	28.11–15	—	—	—
239. Jesus appears to the two men on the road to Emmaus	—	16.12–13	24.13–35	—
240. Jesus appears in Jerusalem	—	—	24.36–49	—
241. Jesus appears to the disciples twice	—	—	—	20.19–29
242. Jesus appears at the sea of Tiberias	—	—	—	21.1–24
243. Jesus' appearance on the mountain in Galilee	28.16–20	16.14–16	—	—
244. Signs to accompany believers	—	16.17–18	—	—
245. The Ascension	—	16.19	24.50–53	—
246. The disciples go out into the world to preach	—	16.20	—	—
247. John's conclusion to the gospel	—	—	—	20.30–31; 21.25

THE LIFE AND JOURNEYS OF THE APOSTLE PAUL

Event   *Reference*

I. Paul's Birth and Education

Born in Tarsus, in Cilicia (Asia Minor)..............(About A.D. 1) Acts 21.39; 22.3; 2 Cor. 11.22; Rom. 11.1; Phil. 3.4–5

Boyhood and early training in Tarsus (Paul's education in the Greek culture)...............................Implied in many passages

Trained as a rabbi in Jerusalem (Paul's education in the Judaic culture; i.e. in the Torah)...................Acts 22.3; 23.6; 26.4–5; Gal. 1.13–14; Phil. 3.5

Out of zeal for the Mosaic law, persecuted the Church...Acts 7.57—8.3; 22.4—5, 19; 26.9–11; Gal. 1.13–14; Phil. 3.6; 1 Tim. 1.12–13

II. Paul's Conversion and Early Experiences as a Christian

Converted on the road to Damascus.................(About A.D. 33) Acts 9.1–9; 22.5–11; 26.12–20; 1 Tim. 1.12–16

Given his commission as a Christian..................Acts 9.6, 8–16; 22.11–16; 26.16–18

His sight is restored and he is baptized...............Acts 9.17–19; 22.11–16

Bears testimony to Christ in Damascus...............Acts 9.17–22; 26.19–20

Retires to Arabia for prayer and reflection...........Gal. 1.15–18

Returns to Damascus; then flees to Jerusalem........Gal. 1.17–18; Acts 9.23–26; 2 Cor. 11.32–33

Warned in a vision to leave Jerusalem................Acts 9.26–29; 22.17–21; Gal. 1.18–20

Preaches in Tarsus...................................Acts 9.29–30; Gal. 1.21–24

Persuaded by Barnabas to come to Antioch in Syria....Acts 11.19–25

Preaches in Antioch in Syria........................Acts 11.26

Takes to Jerusalem an offering for the poor........!...Acts 11.27–30; 12.25

Commissioned by the Antioch Church to preach to the Gentiles.......................................Acts 13.1–3

III. Paul's Campaigns to Win the Gentile World to Christ
1. The First Missionary Journey (A.D. 46–48)

Acts 13.4—14.28. (For the events in each place visited, the reader is referred to the Scripture passage indicated.)

Seleucia (the port of Antioch)......................Acts 13.4

Salamis, on the island of Cyprus....................Acts 13.4–5

Paphos, on the island of Cyprus.....................Acts 13.6–12

Perga, in Pamphylia (Asia Minor)...................Acts 13.13

Antioch, in Pisidia.................................Acts 13.14–49

Iconium, in Lycaonia.........................,....Acts 13.51–52; 14.1–6

Lystra, in Lycaonia...............................Acts 14.6–20

Derbe, in Lycaonia................................Acts 14.20–21

Lystra, in Lycaonia...............................Acts 14.21–23

The Life and Journeys of the Apostle Paul

Event	Reference
Iconium, in Lycaonia	Acts 14.21–23
Antioch, in Pisidia	Acts 14.21–23
Perga, in Pamphylia	Acts 14.24–25
Attalia, in Pamphylia	Acts 14.25
Antioch, in Syria	Acts 14.25–28
At the Council in Jerusalem	Acts 15.1–35; Gal. 2.1–14

2. The Second Missionary Journey (A.D. 49–52)

Syria and *Cilicia*	Acts 15.36–41
Derbe and *Lystra*, in Lycaonia	Acts 16.1–5
Phrygia and *Galatia*	Acts 16.6
Troas, in Mysia	Acts 16.6–11
Samothrace (an island)	Acts 16.11
Neapolis, in Macedonia (Europe)	Acts 16.11
Philippi, in Macedonia	Acts 16.12–40
Amphipolis, in Macedonia	Acts 17.1
Apollonia, in Macedonia	Acts 17.1
Thessalonica, in Macedonia	Acts 17.1–9
Beroea, in Macedonia	Acts 17.10–14
Athens, in Achaia (Greece)	Acts 17.15–34
Corinth, in Achaia (Greece)	Acts 18.1–18
Cenchreae, (one of Corinth's two ports)	Acts 18.18
Ephesus, in the province of Asia (Asia Minor)	Acts 18.19–21
Caesarea	Acts 18.22
Jerusalem	Acts 18.22
Antioch, in Syria	Acts 18.22

3. The Third Missionary Journey (A.D. 53–57)

Antioch, in Syria	Acts 18.22–23
Galatia and *Phrygia*	Acts 18.23
Ephesus, in the province of Asia	Acts 19.1–20
Corinth (A brief visit is implied in 2 Cor. 12.14 and 13.1)	
Ephesus, in the province of Asia	Acts 19.22–41
Troas, in Mysia	2 Cor. 2.12–13
Philippi, in Macedonia	Acts 20.1–2
Illyricum, or Dalmatia	Rom. 15.19
Corinth, in Achaia	Acts 20.3

IV. Paul's Journey to Jerusalem with the Offering from the Gentile Churches
(Sometimes considered the return portion of the Third Missionary Journey)

Philippi, in Macedonia	Acts 20.6
Troas, in Mysia	Acts 20.6–12
Assos, in Mysia	Acts 20.13–14
Mitylene, on the island of Lesbos	Acts 20.14
Chios, an island	Acts 20.15
Samos, and island	Acts 20.15
Trogyllium, a cape	Acts 20.15
Miletus, in the province of Asia	Acts 20.15–38
Cos, an island	Acts 21.1
Rhodes, an island	Acts 21.1
Patara, in Lycia	Acts 21.1
Cyprus, an island	Acts 21.3
Tyre, in Phoenicia	Acts 21.3–6
Ptolemais, in Phoenicia	Acts 21.7
Caesarea	Acts 21.8–14
Jerusalem	Acts 21.15–16

V. Paul in Jerusalem, His Arrest and Imprisonment (A.D. 57)

Makes his report to James and the elders	Acts 21.17–19
By a vow, shows his regard for the Mosaic law	Acts 21.20–26; 24.17–18
In the Temple, is seized by the Jews, but is rescued by the captain of the Roman guard	Acts 21.27–39; 26.21
On the castle stairs, addresses the crowd	Acts 21.40—22.29
Bears testimony before the Sanhedrin	Acts 22.30—23.9; 24.20–21
Assured by the Lord that he will live to bear witness in Rome	Acts 23.10–11

Event	Reference
The Jews plot his death, but their plans are thwarted...	Acts 23.12–32
Taken to Caesarea for trial........................	Acts 23.23–35

VI. Paul's Imprisonment in Caesarea (A.D. 57–59)

His trial before Felix...............................	Acts 24.1–23
The hearing before Felix and Drusilla................	Acts 24.24–27
The trial before Festus; appeals to Caesar............	Acts 25.1–12; 28.17–19
The trial before Agrippa...........................	Acts 25.13–32

VII. Paul Taken as Prisoner to Rome (A.D. 59–60)

Caesarea..	Acts 27.1–2
Sidon, in Phoenicia...............................	Acts 27.3
Cyprus, an island.................................	Acts 27.4
Myra, in Lycia....................................	Acts 27.5–6
Cnidus, an island.................................	Acts 27.7
Crete, an island..................................	Acts 27.7
Salmone, on island of Crete........................	Acts 27.7
Fair Havens, on island of Crete.....................	Acts 27.8
Cauda (Clauda), an island...........................	Acts 27:16–17
Malta (Melita), an island...........................	Acts 27.17–44
Following the shipwreck, three months are spent on the island of Malta...............................	Acts 28.1–10
Syracuse, in Sicily................................	Acts 28.11–12
Rhegium, in Italy.................................	Acts 28.13
Puteoli, in Italy...................................	Acts 28.13–14
Forum of Apius, in Italy...........................	Acts 28.15
The Three Taverns, in Italy........................	Acts 28.15
Rome, in Italy....................................	Acts 28.16

VIII. Paul, a Prisoner in Rome (A.D. 60–62)

Meets the leading Jews of Rome.....................	Acts 28.16–22
Preaches to a larger number of Jews.................	Acts 28.23–29
For two years he is permitted to dwell in his own rented house; he preaches Christ to all who come to him....	Acts 28.30–31

NOTE: Here the account in the book of Acts ends. Some scholars hold that at the end of the two years' imprisonment Paul was executed. A larger number of scholars, however, maintain that in Paul's later letters there are numerous statements which can be understood only on the assumption that he was released from prison and permitted to resume his missionary travels. Places he possibly visited are Macedonia (1 Tim. 1.3); Ephesus (1 Tim. 3.14; 2 Tim. 4.18); Miletum (2 Tim. 4.20); Troas (2 Tim. 4.13); Corinth (2 Tim. 4.20); Crete (Titus 1.5); and Nicopolis (Titus 3.12). If Paul was able to carry out his plan to visit Spain (Rom. 15.24–28), there is no indication of it. The events mentioned in the verses listed above cannot be fitted easily into any period of missionary activity prior to Paul's first imprisonment in Rome. After possibly two years of renewed missionary labors, it appears that Paul was again arrested. It may be that he was charged with preaching a religion (Christianity) which Rome had outlawed. So, once again, Paul is a prisoner in Rome. His fair-weather friends desert him (2 Tim. 1.15; 4.10). Luke remains steadfast (2 Tim. 4.11). Paul asks Timothy to come to his relief, and to bring Mark with him (2 Tim. 4.9, 11, 13). Paul now is fully prepared for martyrdom.

Tradition tells us (and there is no sufficient reason for doubting its correctness) that this second Roman imprisonment ended with a sentence of death imposed on Paul. He was led from his dungeon along the Ostian Way to a place about three miles distant. There he was beheaded. The date, most probably, was A.D. 64, but could have been as late as A.D. 67.

CONSECUTIVE DAILY BIBLE READING

(A plan for reading the entire Bible in one year)

JANUARY

Date	MORNING	EVENING	Date	MORNING	EVENING
1	Matt. 1	Gen. 1, 2, 3	17	Matt. 12 . 1–23	Gen. 41, 42
2	Matt. 2	Gen. 4, 5, 6	18	Matt. 12 . 24–50	Gen. 43, 44, 45
3	Matt. 3	Gen. 7, 8, 9	19	Matt. 13 . 1–30	Gen. 46, 47, 48
4	Matt. 4	Gen. 10, 11, 12	20	Matt. 13 . 31–58	Gen. 49, 50
5	Matt. 5 . 1–26	Gen. 13, 14, 15	21	Matt. 14 . 1–21	Ex. 1, 2, 3
6	Matt. 5 . 27–48	Gen. 16, 17	22	Matt. 14 . 22–36	Ex. 4, 5, 6
7	Matt. 6 . 1–18	Gen. 18, 19	23	Matt. 15 . 1–20	Ex. 7, 8
8	Matt. 6 . 19–34	Gen. 20, 21, 22	24	Matt. 15 . 21–39	Ex. 9, 10, 11
9	Matt. 7	Gen. 23, 24	25	Matt. 16	Ex. 12, 13
10	Matt. 8 . 1–17	Gen. 25, 26	26	Matt. 17	Ex. 14, 15
11	Matt. 8 . 18–34	Gen. 27, 28	27	Matt. 18 . 1–20	Ex. 16, 17, 18
12	Matt. 9 . 1–17	Gen. 29, 30	28	Matt. 18 . 21–35	Ex. 19, 20
13	Matt. 9 . 18–38	Gen. 31, 32	29	Matt. 19	Ex. 21, 22
14	Matt. 10 . 1–20	Gen. 33, 34, 35	30	Matt. 20 . 1–16	Ex. 23, 24
15	Matt. 10 . 21–42	Gen. 36, 37, 38	31	Matt. 20 . 17–34	Ex. 25, 26
16	Matt. 11	Gen. 39, 40			

FEBRUARY

Date	MORNING	EVENING	Date	MORNING	EVENING
1	Matt. 21 . 1–22	Ex. 27, 28	16	Matt. 27 . 51–66	Lev. 19, 20
2	Matt. 21 . 23–46	Ex. 29, 30	17	Matt. 28	Lev. 21, 22
3	Matt. 22 . 1–22	Ex. 31, 32, 33	18	Mark 1 . 1–22	Lev. 23, 24
4	Matt. 22 . 23–46	Ex. 34, 35	19	Mark 1 . 23–45	Lev. 25
5	Matt. 23 . 1–22	Ex. 36, 37, 38	20	Mark 2	Lev. 26, 27
6	Matt. 23 . 23–39	Ex. 39, 40	21	Mark 3 . 1–19	Num. 1, 2
7	Matt. 24 . 1–28	Lev. 1, 2, 3	22	Mark 3 . 20–35	Num. 3, 4
8	Matt. 24 . 29–51	Lev. 4, 5	23	Mark 4 . 1–20	Num. 5, 6
9	Matt. 25 . 1–30	Lev. 6, 7	24	Mark 4 . 21–41	Num. 7, 8
10	Matt. 25 . 31–46	Lev. 8, 9, 10	25	Mark 5 . 1–20	Num. 9, 10, 11
11	Matt. 26 . 1–25	Lev. 11, 12	26	Mark 5 . 21–43	Num. 12, 13, 14
12	Matt. 26 . 26–50	Lev. 13	27	Mark 6 . 1–29	Num. 15, 16
13	Matt. 26 . 51–75	Lev. 14	28	Mark 6 . 30–56	Num. 17, 18, 19
14	Matt. 27 . 1–26	Lev. 15, 16	29	Mark 7 . 1–13	Num. 20, 21, 22
15	Matt. 27 . 27–50	Lev. 17, 18			

MARCH

Date	MORNING	EVENING	Date	MORNING	EVENING
1	Mark 7 . 14–37	Num. 23, 24, 25	17	Mark 15 . 1–25	Deut. 30, 31
2	Mark 8 . 1–21	Num. 26, 27	18	Mark 15 . 26–47	Deut. 32, 33, 34
3	Mark 8 . 22–38	Num. 28, 29, 30	19	Mark 16	Josh. 1, 2, 3
4	Mark 9 . 1–29	Num. 31, 32, 33	20	Luke 1 . 1–20	Josh. 4, 5, 6
5	Mark 9 . 30–50	Num. 34, 35, 36	21	Luke 1 . 21–38	Josh. 7, 8, 9
6	Mark 10 . 1–31	Deut. 1, 2	22	Luke 1 . 39–56	Josh. 10, 11, 12
7	Mark 10 . 32–52	Deut. 3, 4	23	Luke 1 . 57–80	Josh. 13, 14, 15
8	Mark 11 . 1–18	Deut. 5, 6, 7	24	Luke 2 . 1–24	Josh. 16, 17, 18
9	Mark 11 . 19–33	Deut. 8, 9, 10	25	Luke 2 . 25–52	Josh. 19, 20, 21
10	Mark 12 . 1–27	Deut. 11, 12, 13	26	Luke 3	Josh. 22, 23, 24
11	Mark 12 . 28–44	Deut. 14, 15, 16	27	Luke 4 . 1–30	Judg. 1, 2, 3
12	Mark 13 . 1–20	Deut. 17, 18, 19	28	Luke 4 . 31–44	Judg. 4, 5, 6
13	Mark 13 . 21–37	Deut. 20, 21, 22	29	Luke 5 . 1–16	Judg. 7, 8
14	Mark 14 . 1–26	Deut. 23, 24, 25	30	Luke 5 . 17–39	Judg. 9, 10
15	Mark 14 . 27–53	Deut. 26, 27	31	Luke 6 . 1–26	Judg. 11, 12
16	Mark 14 . 54–72	Deut. 28, 29			

APRIL

Date	MORNING	EVENING	Date	MORNING	EVENING
1	Luke 6 . 27–49	Judg. 13, 14, 15	16	Luke 13 . 23–35	1 Sam. 30, 31
2	Luke 7 . 1–30	Judg. 16, 17, 18	17	Luke 14 . 1–24	2 Sam. 1, 2
3	Luke 7 . 31–50	Judg. 19, 20, 21	18	Luke 14 . 25–35	2 Sam. 3, 4, 5
4	Luke 8 . 1–25	Ruth 1, 2, 3, 4	19	Luke 15 . 1–10	2 Sam. 6, 7, 8
5	Luke 8 . 26–56	1 Sam. 1, 2, 3	20	Luke 15 . 11–32	2 Sam. 9, 10, 11
6	Luke 9 . 1–17	1 Sam. 4, 5, 6	21	Luke 16	2 Sam. 12, 13
7	Luke 9 . 18–36	1 Sam. 7, 8, 9	22	Luke 17 . 1–19	2 Sam. 14, 15
8	Luke 9 . 37–62	1 Sam. 10, 11, 12	23	Luke 17 . 20–37	2 Sam. 16, 17, 18
9	Luke 10 . 1–24	1 Sam. 13, 14	24	Luke 18 . 1–23	2 Sam. 19, 20
10	Luke 10 . 25–42	1 Sam. 15, 16	25	Luke 18 . 24–43	2 Sam. 21, 22
11	Luke 11 . 1–28	1 Sam. 17, 18	26	Luke 19 . 1–27	2 Sam. 23, 24
12	Luke 11 . 29–54	1 Sam. 19, 20, 21	27	Luke 19 . 28–48	1 Ki. 1, 2
13	Luke 12 . 1–31	1 Sam. 22, 23, 24	28	Luke 20 . 1–26	1 Ki. 3, 4, 5
14	Luke 12 . 32–59	1 Sam. 25, 26	29	Luke 20 . 27–47	1 Ki. 6, 7
15	Luke 13 . 1–22	1 Sam. 27, 28, 29	30	Luke 21 . 1–19	1 Ki. 8, 9

MAY

Date	MORNING	EVENING	Date	MORNING	EVENING
1	Luke 21 . 20–38	1 Ki. 10, 11	17	John 5 . 25–47	1 Ch. 1, 2, 3
2	Luke 22 . 1–20	1 Ki. 12, 13	18	John 6 . 1–21	1 Ch. 4, 5, 6
3	Luke 22 . 21–46	1 Ki. 14, 15	19	John 6 . 22–44	1 Ch. 7, 8, 9
4	Luke 22 . 47–71	1 Ki. 16, 17, 18	20	John 6 . 45–71	1 Ch. 10, 11, 12
5	Luke 23 . 1–25	1 Ki. 19, 20	21	John 7 . 1–27	1 Ch. 13, 14, 15
6	Luke 23 . 26–56	1 Ki. 21, 22	22	John 7 . 28–52	1 Ch. 16, 17, 18
7	Luke 24 . 1–35	2 Ki. 1, 2, 3	23	John 8 . 1–27	1 Ch. 19, 20, 21
8	Luke 24 . 36–53	2 Ki. 4, 5, 6	24	John 8 . 28–59	1 Ch. 22, 23, 24
9	John 1 . 1–28	2 Ki. 7, 8, 9	25	John 9 . 1–23	1 Ch. 25, 26, 27
10	John 1 . 29–51	2 Ki. 10, 11, 12	26	John 9 . 24–41	1 Ch. 28, 29
11	John 2	2 Ki. 13, 14	27	John 10 . 1–23	2 Ch. 1, 2, 3
12	John 3 . 1–18	2 Ki. 15, 16	28	John 10 . 24–42	2 Ch. 4, 5, 6
13	John 3 . 19–36	2 Ki. 17, 18	29	John 11 . 1–29	2 Ch. 7, 8, 9
14	John 4 . 1–30	2 Ki. 19, 20, 21	30	John 11 . 30–57	2 Ch. 10, 11, 12
15	John 4 . 31–54	2 Ki. 22, 23	31	John 12 . 1–26	2 Ch. 13, 14
16	John 5 . 1–24	2 Ki. 24, 25			

JUNE

Date	MORNING	EVENING	Date	MORNING	EVENING
1	John 12 . 27–50	2 Ch. 15, 16	16	Acts 2 . 22–47	Neh. 4, 5, 6
2	John 13 . 1–20	2 Ch. 17, 18	17	Acts 3	Neh. 7, 8, 9
3	John 13 . 21–38	2 Ch. 19, 20	18	Acts 4 . 1–22	Neh. 10, 11
4	John 14	2 Ch. 21, 22	19	Acts 4 . 23–37	Neh. 12, 13
5	John 15	2 Ch. 23, 24	20	Acts 5 . 1–21	Esth. 1, 2
6	John 16	2 Ch. 25, 26, 27	21	Acts 5 . 22–42	Esth. 3, 4, 5
7	John 17	2 Ch. 28, 29	22	Acts 6	Esth. 6, 7, 8
8	John 18 . 1–18	2 Ch. 30, 31	23	Acts 7 . 1–21	Esth. 9, 10
9	John 18 . 19–40	2 Ch. 32, 33	24	Acts 7 . 22–43	Job 1, 2
10	John 19 . 1–22	2 Ch. 34, 35, 36	25	Acts 7 . 44–60	Job 3, 4
11	John 19 . 23–42	Ezra 1, 2	26	Acts 8 . 1–25	Job 5, 6, 7
12	John 20	Ezra 3, 4, 5	27	Acts 8 . 26–40	Job 8, 9, 10
13	John 21	Ezra 6, 7, 8	28	Acts 9 . 1–21	Job 11, 12, 13
14	Acts 1	Ezra 9, 10	29	Acts 9 . 22–43	Job 14, 15, 16
15	Acts 2 . 1–21	Neh. 1, 2, 3	30	Acts 10 . 1–23	Job 17, 18, 19

JULY

Date	MORNING	EVENING	Date	MORNING	EVENING
1	Acts 10 . 24–48	Job 20, 21	17	Acts 20 . 17–38	Ps. 18, 19
2	Acts 11	Job 22, 23, 24	18	Acts 21 . 1–17	Ps. 20, 21, 22
3	Acts 12	Job 25, 26, 27	19	Acts 21 . 18–40	Ps. 23, 24, 25
4	Acts 13 . 1–25	Job 28, 29	20	Acts 22	Ps. 26, 27, 28
5	Acts 13 . 26–52	Job 30, 31	21	Acts 23 . 1–15	Ps. 29, 30
6	Acts 14	Job 32, 33	22	Acts 23 . 16–35	Ps. 31, 32
7	Acts 15 . 1–21	Job 34, 35	23	Acts 24	Ps. 33, 34
8	Acts 15 . 22–41	Job 36, 37	24	Acts 25	Ps. 35, 36
9	Acts 16 . 1–21	Job 38, 39, 40	25	Acts 26	Ps. 37, 38, 39
10	Acts 16 . 22–40	Job 41, 42	26	Acts 27 . 1–26	Ps. 40, 41, 42
11	Acts 17 . 1–15	Ps. 1, 2, 3	27	Acts 27 . 27–44	Ps. 43, 44, 45
12	Acts 17 . 16–34	Ps. 4, 5, 6	28	Acts 28	Ps. 46, 47, 48
13	Acts 18	Ps. 7, 8, 9	29	Rom. 1	Ps. 49, 50
14	Acts 19 . 1–20	Ps. 10, 11, 12	30	Rom. 2	Ps. 51, 52, 53
15	Acts 19 . 21–41	Ps. 13, 14, 15	31	Rom. 3	Ps. 54, 55, 56
16	Acts 20 . 1–16	Ps. 16, 17			

AUGUST

Date	MORNING	EVENING	Date	MORNING	EVENING
1	Rom. 4	Ps. 57, 58, 59	17	Rom. 16	Ps. 97, 98, 99
2	Rom. 5	Ps. 60, 61, 62	18	1 Cor. 1	Ps. 100, 101, 102
3	Rom. 6	Ps. 63, 64, 65	19	1 Cor. 2	Ps. 103, 104
4	Rom. 7	Ps. 66, 67	20	1 Cor. 3	Ps. 105, 106
5	Rom. 8 . 1–21	Ps. 68, 69	21	1 Cor. 4	Ps. 107, 108, 109
6	Rom. 8 . 22–39	Ps. 70, 71	22	1 Cor. 5	Ps. 110, 111, 112
7	Rom. 9 . 1–15	Ps. 72, 73	23	1 Cor. 6	Ps. 113, 114, 115
8	Rom. 9 . 16–33	Ps. 74, 75, 76	24	1 Cor. 7 . 1–19	Ps. 116, 117, 118
9	Rom. 10	Ps. 77, 78	25	1 Cor. 7 . 20–40	Ps. 119 . 1–88
10	Rom. 11 . 1–18	Ps. 79, 80	26	1 Cor. 8	Ps. 119 . 89–176
11	Rom. 11 . 19–36	Ps. 81, 82, 83	27	1 Cor. 9	Ps. 120, 121, 122
12	Rom. 12	Ps. 84, 85, 86	28	1 Cor. 10 . 1–18	Ps. 123, 124, 125
13	Rom. 13	Ps. 87, 88	29	1 Cor. 10 . 19–33	Ps. 126, 127, 128
14	Rom. 14	Ps. 89, 90	30	1 Cor. 11 . 1–16	Ps. 129, 130, 131
15	Rom. 15 . 1–13	Ps. 91, 92, 93	31	1 Cor. 11 . 17–34	Ps. 132, 133, 134
16	Rom. 15 . 14–33	Ps. 94, 95, 96			

SEPTEMBER

Date	MORNING	EVENING	Date	MORNING	EVENING
1	1 Cor. 12	Ps. 135, 136	16	2 Cor. 9	Prov. 25, 26
2	1 Cor. 13	Ps. 137, 138, 139	17	2 Cor. 10	Prov. 27, 28, 29
3	1 Cor. 14 . 1–20	Ps. 140, 141, 142	18	2 Cor. 11 . 1–15	Prov. 30, 31
4	1 Cor. 14 . 21–40	Ps. 143, 144, 145	19	2 Cor. 11 . 16–33	Eccl. 1, 2, 3
5	1 Cor. 15 . 1–28	Ps. 146, 147	20	2 Cor. 12	Eccl. 4, 5, 6
6	1 Cor. 15 . 29–58	Ps. 148, 149, 150	21	2 Cor. 13	Eccl. 7, 8, 9
7	1 Cor. 16	Prov. 1, 2	22	Gal. 1	Eccl. 10, 11, 12
8	2 Cor. 1	Prov. 3, 4, 5	23	Gal. 2	Song 1, 2, 3
9	2 Cor. 2	Prov. 6, 7	24	Gal. 3	Song 4, 5
10	2 Cor. 3	Prov. 8, 9	25	Gal. 4	Song 6, 7, 8
11	2 Cor. 4	Prov. 10, 11, 12	26	Gal. 5	Isa. 1, 2
12	2 Cor. 5	Prov. 13, 14, 15	27	Gal. 6	Isa. 3, 4
13	2 Cor. 6	Prov. 16, 17, 18	28	Eph. 1	Isa. 5, 6
14	2 Cor. 7	Prov. 19, 20, 21	29	Eph. 2	Isa. 7, 8
15	2 Cor. 8	Prov. 22, 23, 24	30	Eph. 3	Isa. 9, 10

OCTOBER

Date	MORNING	EVENING	Date	MORNING	EVENING
1	Eph. 4	Isa. 11, 12, 13	17	1 Thes. 5	Isa. 50, 51, 52
2	Eph. 5 . 1–16	Isa. 14, 15, 16	18	2 Thes. 1	Isa. 53, 54, 55
3	Eph. 5 . 17–33	Isa. 17, 18, 19	19	2 Thes. 2	Isa. 56, 57, 58
4	Eph. 6	Isa. 20, 21, 22	20	2 Thes. 3	Isa. 59, 60, 61
5	Phil. 1	Isa. 23, 24, 25	21	1 Tim. 1	Isa. 62, 63, 64
6	Phil. 2	Isa. 26, 27	22	1 Tim. 2	Isa. 65, 66
7	Phil. 3	Isa. 28, 29	23	1 Tim. 3	Jer. 1, 2
8	Phil. 4	Isa. 30, 31	24	1 Tim. 4	Jer. 3, 4, 5
9	Col. 1	Isa. 32, 33	25	1 Tim. 5	Jer. 6, 7, 8
10	Col. 2	Isa. 34, 35, 36	26	1 Tim. 6	Jer. 9, 10, 11
11	Col. 3	Isa. 37, 38	27	2 Tim. 1	Jer. 12, 13, 14
12	Col. 4	Isa. 39, 40	28	2 Tim. 2	Jer. 15, 16, 17
13	1 Thes. 1	Isa. 41, 42	29	2 Tim. 3	Jer. 18, 19
14	1 Thes. 2	Isa. 43, 44	30	2 Tim. 4	Jer. 20, 21
15	1 Thes. 3	Isa. 45, 46	31	Titus 1	Jer. 22, 23
16	1 Thes. 4	Isa. 47, 48, 49			

NOVEMBER

Date	MORNING	EVENING	Date	MORNING	EVENING
1	Titus 2	Jer. 24, 25, 26	16	Heb. 11 . 20–40	Ezek. 3, 4
2	Titus 3	Jer. 27, 28, 29	17	Heb. 12	Ezek. 5, 6, 7
3	Philemon	Jer. 30, 31	18	Heb. 13	Ezek. 8, 9, 10
4	Heb. 1	Jer. 32, 33	19	Jas. 1	Ezek. 11, 12, 13
5	Heb. 2	Jer. 34, 35, 36	20	Jas. 2	Ezek. 14, 15
6	Heb. 3	Jer. 37, 38, 39	21	Jas. 3	Ezek. 16, 17
7	Heb. 4	Jer. 40, 41, 42	22	Jas. 4	Ezek. 18, 19
8	Heb. 5	Jer. 43, 44, 45	23	Jas. 5	Ezek. 20, 21
9	Heb. 6	Jer. 46, 47	24	1 Pet. 1	Ezek. 22, 23
10	Heb. 7	Jer. 48, 49	25	1 Pet. 2	Ezek. 24, 25, 26
11	Heb. 8	Jer. 50	26	1 Pet. 3	Ezek. 27, 28, 29
12	Heb. 9	Jer. 51, 52	27	1 Pet. 4	Ezek. 30, 31, 32
13	Heb. 10 . 1–18	Lam. 1, 2	28	1 Pet. 5	Ezek. 33, 34
14	Heb. 10 . 19–39	Lam. 3, 4, 5	29	2 Pet. 1	Ezek. 35, 36
15	Heb. 11 . 1–19	Ezek. 1, 2	30	2 Pet. 2	Ezek. 37, 38, 39

DECEMBER

Date	MORNING	EVENING	Date	MORNING	EVENING
1	2 Pet. 3	Ezek. 40, 41	17	Rev. 8	Amos 7, 8, 9
2	1 John 1	Ezek. 42, 43, 44	18	Rev. 9	Obadiah
3	1 John 2	Ezek. 45, 46	19	Rev. 10	Jon. 1, 2, 3, 4
4	1 John 3	Ezek. 47, 48	20	Rev. 11	Mic. 1, 2, 3
5	1 John 4	Dan. 1, 2	21	Rev. 12	Mic. 4, 5
6	1 John 5	Dan. 3, 4	22	Rev. 13	Mic. 6, 7
7	2 John	Dan. 5, 6, 7	23	Rev. 14	Nah. 1, 2, 3
8	3 John	Dan. 8, 9, 10	24	Rev. 15	Hab. 1, 2, 3
9	Jude	Dan. 11, 12	25	Rev. 16	Zeph. 1, 2, 3,
10	Rev. 1	Hos. 1, 2, 3, 4	26	Rev. 17	Hag. 1, 2
11	Rev. 2	Hos. 5, 6, 7, 8	27	Rev. 18	Zec. 1, 2, 3, 4
12	Rev. 3	Hos. 9, 10, 11	28	Rev. 19	Zec. 5, 6, 7, 8
13	Rev. 4	Hos. 12, 13, 14	29	Rev. 20	Zec. 9, 10, 11, 12
14	Rev. 5	Joel 1, 2, 3	30	Rev. 21	Zec. 13, 14
15	Rev. 6	Amos 1, 2, 3	31	Rev. 22	Mal. 1, 2, 3, 4
16	Rev. 7	Amos 4, 5, 6			